A CONCISE SANSKRIT–ENGLISH DICTIONARY

Containing an appendix on Sanskrit prosody and another on the Names of noted mythological persons, and a Map of Ancient India

By

Vidyadhar Vaman Apte

GYAN

A Concise Sanskrit-English Dictionary

First Published 1990, reprint 2013 in India by
Gyan Publishing House
23, Main Ansari Road, Daryaganj,
New Delhi - 110002
Phones : 23282060, 23261060
Fax : (011) 23285914
E-mail: books@gyanbooks.com
website: gyanbooks.com

Printed at : Sagar Color Scan, New Delhi.

A
CONCISE
SANSKRIT-ENGLISH DICTIONARY

Preface.

The dictionary now offered to the public is intended to supply to the student of classical literature in Sanskrit all the information that he is likely to require in the study of the books that he reads for his examinations.

Only the most important technical terms in Grammar, Rhetoric, Logic, Law, Mathematics, Philosophy, Music, Medicine, Astronomy &c. have been explained. It was at first my intention to define in detail and illustrate by examples the technical terms in these branches of science, but as I proceeded, it became evident that my book would far exceed the limits imposed upon me by the publishers. I, therefore, withheld much of the information that I had collected for the dictionary and contented myself with bare definitions of the technical terms in the above mentioned branches of science. It was also my intention to give Marathi equivalents for names of medical trees and plants, but as I proceeded in my work, I had to give up the plan for the same reason.

As to quotations, though I gave them copiously in the beginning, yet later on withheld them, especially such of them as were rather ornamental that useful.

Poona,
25th March, 1926.

V. V. Bhide.

A list of Abbreviations and symbols used in the Dictionary.

A. or Atm. ... ... Atmanepada.
a. ... ... Adjective.
abl. ... ... Ablative.
acc. ... ... Accusative.
adv. ... ... Adverb.
astr. ... ... Astronomy.
astrol. ... ... Astrology.
Avyayî. ... ... Avyayìbhâva.
Bah. ... ... Bahuvrîhi.
Caus. ... ... Causal
cf. ... ... Compare.
Comp. ... ... Compound.
dat. ... ... Dative.
Den. ... ... Denominative.
desid. ... ... Desiderative.
du. ... ... Dual.
e. g. ... ... *Exempli gratia*, for example.
f. ... ... Feminine.
fig. ... ... Figurative or figuratively.
gen. ... ... Genitive.
i. e. ... ... *id est*, that is.
ind. ... ... Indeclinable.
inf. ... ... Infinitive.
instr. ... ... Instrumental.
lit. ... ... Literal or literally
loc. ... ... Locative.
m. ... ... Masculine.
Mar. ... ... Marâthì.

Math. ... ... Mathematics.
Medic. ... ... Medicine.
n. ... ... Neuter.
N. ... ... Name.
Nom. ... ... Nominative.
opp. ... ... Opposite of or to.
P. ... ... Parasmaipada.
pass. ... ... Passive.
phil. ... ... Philosophy.
pl. ... ... Plural.
pot. p. ... ... Potential passive participle.
p. p. ... ... Past passive participle.
Pres. ... ... Present tense.
pres. p. ... ... Present participle.
pron. a. ... ... Pronominal adjective.
q. v. ... ... *qu d vide*, which see.
Rhet. ... ... Rhetoric.
sing. ... ... Singular.
Tat. ... ... Tatpurusha.
U. ... ... Ubhayapada (Parasmai. and Atmane.)
Voc. ... ... Vocative.
= ... ... Equal or equivalent to, same as.
+ ... ... Plus.
&c. ... ... Et cætera.

Abbreviations used to indicate the names of works from which quotations have been taken will be easily intelligible.

A CONCISE

SANSKRIT ENGLISH DICTIONARY.

अ

अ The first letter of the Sanskrit Alphabet.–अः 1 N. of Vishnu. It is the first of the three letters constituting the mystic syllable ओम्; अकारो विष्णुरुद्दिष्ट उकारस्तु महेश्वरः। मकारस्तु स्मृतो ब्रह्मा प्रणवस्तु त्रयात्मकः॥ See ओम्.—*ind.* 1 A prefix joined to nouns, adjectives, indeclinables, and sometime to verbs, and changed to अन् before vowels, except in the word अ-ऋणिन्. The meanings of अ or अन् are as follows. (*a*) सादृश्य 'likeness' or 'resemblance'; अब्राह्मणः one resembling a Brahmana but not a Brahmana. अनिक्षुः a reed appearing like इक्षु, but really not इक्षु. (*b*) अभाव 'absence', 'negation', 'want', 'privation'; अज्ञानं absence of knowledge, ignorance; अक्रोधः, अघटः, &c. (*c*) भेद 'difference' or 'distinction;' अपटः not a cloth, something different from, or other than, a cloth. (*d*) अल्पता 'smallness', 'diminution' अनुदरा haviug a slender waist. (*e*), अप्राशस्त्य 'badness,' 'unfitness,' अनाचारः wrong or improper conduct; अकार्यं not fit to be done, an improper, unworthy, bad act. (*f*) विरोध 'opposition,' 'contrariety'; अनीतिः the opposite of morality; immorality; असित not white, black; असुर not a god, a demon &c. The following verse gives succinctly these six senses. तत्सादृश्यमभावश्च तदन्यत्वं तदल्पता। अप्राशस्त्यं विरोधश्च नञर्थाः षट् प्रकीर्तिताः॥ With gerunds, infinitives, participles, it has usually the sense of 'not'; अगत्वा not having gone; अपश्यन् not seeing; so असकृत् not once, अमृषा, अकस्मात् &c. 2 An interjection of (*a*) Pity (*ah!*) अ अवद्यं (*b*) Reproach, censure (fie! shame!), अपचासि त्वं जाल्म P. VI. 3·73. (*c*) Used in addressing, or calling अ अनंत!

अऋणिन् a. (*f.*–नी) Not a debtor, free from debt; अनृणिन् also occurs in this sense.

अंश् 10 U. अंशयति–ते To divide, distribute, share among; with वि.–1 To break asunder; to break. 2 To deceive.

अंशः *m.* 1 A share, part, portion, member, division. ममैवांशो जीवलोके जीवभूतः सनातनः ॥ भगव. 15-7 भुवमंशाविव धर्मयोर्गतौ ॥ रघुवं. 8.16; अंशेन Partly.–2 A share in property, inheritance;-3 The numerator of a fraction; sometimes used for fraction itself. 4 A degree of latitude, (or longitude); 5 The shoulder (more usual form अंस, q. v.).-अंशि *adv* share by share. — अवतार:, — तरणं Descent (on earth) of parts of deities, partial incarnation; अंशावतारमिव कृतांतस्य * कादंब. -भाज्,-हर,-हारिन् *a.* An heir, a co-heir;-विवर्तिन् *a.* Slightly turned away, or turned away towards the shoulder; मुखमंशविवर्ति पक्ष्मलाक्ष्या:— * शकुंत. 3. 26.—सवर्णनं Reduction of fractions to the same denominator—स्वर: The keynote.

अंशक: *m.* (*f.* अंशिका) 1 One having a share, a coheir, a relative. 2—A share, portion, division;—कं *n.* A solar day.

अंशनं *n.* Act of dividing, sharing.

अंशयितृ (*f.* -त्री) A divider, sharer.

अंशल *a.* Having, or entitled to a share, (अंशग्राहक).

अंशिन् *a.* (*f.* अंशिनी) 1 A sharer, coheir; entitled to the same share. 2 Having parts or members.

अंशु: 1 A ray, beam of light; चंडांशु,-घर्मांशु: Hot-rayed, the sun. 2 Lustre, brilliance;- 3 A point or end.- 4 A small or minute particle, an atom. 5 End of a thread.- 6 A filament, especially of the Soma plant (Ved). 7 Garment; decoration. -Comp. -जालं A collection of rays, a blaze or halo of light —धर:,-पति:-भृत्,-बाण:, -भर्तृ,-मालिन,-स्वामी,-हस्त: The sun.-माला A garland of light, halo of light.

अंशुमत् *a.* 1 Luminous, radiant; ज्योतिषां रविरंशुमान् *भगव. 10.21.-2 Pointed. 3 Fibrous, abounding in filaments (Ved.)—*m.* (मान्) 1 The sun; बालखिल्यैरिवांशुमान् * रघुवं. 15. 10. 2 N. of the grandson of Sagara, son of Asamanjasa, and father of Dilipa. 3 N. of a mountain. अंशुमत्फला. N. of a plant, the plantain tree, कदली, Musa Sapientum or Paradisiace.-ती 1 N. of a plant सालपर्णी, (Mar. डवला, सालवण), Hedysarum Gangeticum. -2 N. of the river Yamunà.

अंशुकं 1 A cloth, garment in general;-2 A fine or white cloth; धुन्वन् कल्पद्रुमकिसलयान्यंशुकानीव वातै: * मेघदू. 62-3. An upper garment; - 4 A leaf.-5 Mild or gentle blaze of light.

अंशुल *a.* (*f.*-ला) Radiant, luminous. —ल: *m.* N. of the sage Chánakya.

अंश्य *a.* Divisible.

अंस (अंसयति, अंसापयति) See अंश्.

अंस: 1 A part, portion; See अंश.-2 The shoulder, shoulder-blade.-3 N. of a prince. (-सौ) The two angles of an altar.—Comp-कूट: A bull's hump, the protuberance between the shoulders. -त्रं 1 An armour to protect the shoulders. 2 A bow. -फलक: The upper part of the spine. —भार: (अंसे॰) A burden or yoke put upon the shoulder.—भारिक,-भारिन् *a.* (अंसे॰) Bearing a yoke or burden on the shoulder.—विवर्तिन् *a.* Turned towards the shoulders.

अंसल *a.* Strong, powerful, lusty having strong shoulders; युवा. युगव्यायतबाहुरंसल: * रघुवं. 3.34.

अंहुर *a.* Moving. (गतियुक्त); Rv. 10.5.6; distressed, straitened.

अंहूरण *a.* Ved. Distressing, troublesome; sinful; straitened.

अंहति:—ती *f.* -A gift, donation.

अंहस् *n.* Sin. Leaving one's religion or duty (स्वधर्मत्याग).-2 Trouble, anxiety, care.

अंहितीः—ती f. A gift.

अंह्रिः 1 A foot.-2 The root of a tree.-3 The number four.-Comp.-पः: 'Foot-drinker', a tree,—स्कंधः The upper part of the sole of the foot.

अक् I. P. (अकति) To go, move tortuously like a serpent.

अकं n. Absence of happiness; pain, misery; sin.

अकच a.] Bald, having no hair —चः N. of Ketu.

अकथित a. 'Not told,' (Gram.) not otherwise mentioned by way of any of the other case-relations, such as अपादान &c.; a name given to the indirect (गौण) object governed by verbs like दुह्, याच्, पच् &c.

अकनिष्ठ a. (f. ष्ठा) Not the youngest, elder, superior.—ष्ठः m. N. of Buddha Gautama.

अकन्या No virgin, a maid that is not so any longer.

अकम्पन a. Not shaking—नः N. of a Râkshasa.

अकंपित a. Unshaken, firm; resolute; not tremulous.—तः N. of a Jaina or Buddha saint, a pupil of the last Tirthamkara.

अकर a.] 1 Handless, maimed.-2 Exempt from tax or duty-3 Not doing or acting;-अकरा N. of a plant (आमलकी,) Emblic Myrobalan, Phyllanthus Emblica.

अकरणं Not doing, absence of action; अकरणात् मंदकरणं श्रेयः Slow doing is better than no doing at all.—णः: (Devoid of all organs) Epithet of the Supreme Spirit.

अकरणिः f. Failure, disappointment, non-accomplishment,(mostly used in imprecation.) ; तस्याकरणिरेवास्तु May he be disappointed, or may he experience a failure !

अकर्ण a. 1 Devoid of ears; deaf.-2 In which there is no कर्ण. अनङ्गुलमकर्णो वा जगद्ध्येति निश्चितः * महाभा. -र्णः A serpent.

अकर्तृ m. Not an agent; °त्वं-ता Inability to do (any thing). An inferior or subordinate position.

अकर्मन् I a 1 Having no work, idle; inefficient.—2 Wicked, degraded —3 (Gram) Intransitive, (usually, अकर्मक). II m. Absence of occupation; non observance or neglect of necessary rites, inaction.—2 An improper act, crime, sin.—Comp. -कृत् a. Free from action, or doing an improper act. —भोगः 1. Enjoyment of freedom from the fruits of one's acts. 2. Abandonment of self-righteousness.—शील a. Lazy, indolent.

अकर्मक a. (f.—र्मिका) Gram. Intransitive.

अकर्मण्य a. 1 Unable to work, inefficient, unfit for work.-2 Unfit to be done.

अकल I. a. Entire, whole. II. n. The Supreme Spirit. अकलित a. (f. ता.) Incomprehensible.

अकल्क a. (f. ल्का.) 1 Free from sediment, pure.-2 Sinless, honest.

अकल्का f. Moonlight.

अकल्प (f. ल्पा.) Uncontrolled, unrestrained, unfettered.—2 Weak, unable.—3. Incomparable.

अकल्पित a. (f. ता) Not artificial or invented, natural, genuine.

अकल्य a (f.—ल्या) 1 Not healthy, sick. Unwell, 2 True. Comp.-संध a

One whose promise never remains unfulfilled.

अकल्याण *a* Forboding evil, inauspicious, unlucky.-णं Inauspiciousness, ill, evil, adversity.

अकस्मात् *ind* I Accidentally, suddenly, unexpectedly, all of a sudden. 2. Without cause or ground.

अकाण्ड *a* (*f.* डा.) I Accidental, untoward, sudden, unexpected, out of season; 2 Having no stem or stock, (as a plant). comp - शूलं A sudden attack of colic.

अकांडे *adv.* Unexpectedly, all of a sudden, suddenly, conselessly; दर्भांकुरेण चरण : क्षत इत्यकांडे तन्वी स्थिता कतिचिदेव पदानि गत्वा * शकुंत. 2. 12

अकाम *a* I Free from desire, affection, love. 2 Unwilling. Comp. -हत *a* Not influenced by desire or affection.

अकामत: *adv.* Reluctantly, unwillingly, unintentionally, unconsciously.

अकामता Freedom from, or absence, of desire.

अकाय (*f.* या) Body-less, having no body. Incorporeal. 2. य: *m.* I An epithet of Rahu. 2. The supreme Spirit (without body, parts, &c.)

अकार: The letter अ. अक्षराणामकारोस्मि * भग्व. 10. 33.

अकारण I *a* Causeless, groundless, spontaneous. II —णं *n.* Absence of a cause, motive, or ground. III *adv.* Causelessly without cause or ground अकारणात्-णे Causelessly, in vain.

अकार्य *a.* (*f.* र्या) I. Improper, not fit to be done. II.-र्यं An improper, unworthy or bad act, a criminal or sinful action. Comp.-कारिन् *m.* I. An evil-doer, one who commits a misdeed. 2. One that neglects one's duty.

अकाल *a* (*f.*-ला) I Premature, untimely, inopportune unseasonable. 2 Not black, white. II *n.* —ल: Wrong, inauspicious or improper time, not the proper time. राजा—भवतु! अकाले स्वस्थवाक्यं म न्युमुत्पादयति * भास. पं. रा. Comp.—कुसुमं,-पुष्पं A flower blossoming out of season; —ज,-उत्पन्न, -जात. *a.* Produced out of season, premature ; unseasonable.—जलद: an untimely cloud.—जलदोदय:,- मेघोदय: An unseasonable gathering of clouds. 2. A mist or fog.-वेला Unseasonable or improper time.—सह *a.* I. Impatient. 2. Not able to hold out (for a long time, said of a fort under a siege).

अकिञ्चन *a.* (*f.* ना.) Not possessing any thing, quite poor, indigent. अकिंचन: सन् प्रभव: स संपदां * कुमार्सं. 5. 77.

अकिंचनता Voluntary proverty, the condition of having no money. Poverty; आकिंचनत्वं मखजं व्यनक्ति. * रघुवं. 5.16.

अकिंचिज्ज्ञ *a.* (*f.*ज्ञा) Knowing nothing, quite ignorant.

अकिंचित्कर *a.* (*f.* रा.) I. Innocent. 2. Useless.

अकीर्ति: *f.* Bad reputation, infamy, ill-repute, disgrace.

अकुण्ठ *a.* I. Not blunted, unobstructed, unchallenged, sharp, unimpeded, आस्त्रग्रहणादकुंठपरशो रस्त्यापि जेता मुने: * वेणीसं. 2. 2. 2. Vigorous, excessive, that has reached a high degree. अकुंठोत्कंठया पूर्ण * काव्यप्र. 7. 3. Firm, immovable, fixed.-धिष्ण्यं Heaven.

अंकुठित *a.* Not blunted; able to pierce, or to penetrate; able to pass onwards; शास्त्रेष्वकुंठिता बुद्धिः * रघुवं. I-19. बिभ्रतोऽस्त्रमचलेऽप्यकुंठितं * रघुवं. 11-74 (taking effect on, prevailing against even mountains.)

अकुतः *adv.* Not from any where; not from any cause (in comp. only). Comp -भय *a* Secure, not threatened from any quarter, free from danger or fear; safe.

अकुप्यं *n.* Not a base metal, gold or silver. 2 Any base metal.

अकुल *a* (*f.*-ला) Of a low or mean family.

अकुलीन *a* (*f.*-ना) 1 Low-born; of no high descent.

अकुशल *a* (*f*-ला) 1 Inauspicious, evil, unlucky, unfortunate.-2 Not clever or skilful, clumsy.—लं *n.* Evil; an untoward circumstance.

अकुहः *m.* One who does not cheat, an honest man.

अकूपारः (or अकूवारः) *m.* 1. The sea, the receptacle of waters —2 The sun.—3 A tortoise in general.—4 The tortoise sustaining the world.

अकृच्छ्र *a.* Free from difficulty.-च्छ्रं Freedom from, or absence of, difficulty, facility.

अकृत *a.* (*f.* -ता.) 1 Not done; unperformed.-2 Wrongly or differently done:—3 Imperfectly done or accomplished —4 Uncreated.-5 That has done no work—6 Unripe, immature. Comp —अर्थ *a.* Unsuccessful.—अस्त्र *a.* Unpractised in missiles.—आत्मन् *a.* 1 Ignorant, foolish, having an uncultivated mind. —2 Sinful, having a vicious mind. अकृतात्मदुरावापं ब्रह्मलोकमवाप्नुहि (difficult to be obtained by sinful people) *भास. म, ह्या. -3 Not identified with the Supreme Spirit.—ज्ञ. *a.* Ungrateful. —धी,-बुद्धि *a.* Having an unformed or uncultivated mind, ignorant.

अकृता *f.* A daughter not placed on a level with sons.

अकृत्य *a.* Not fit to be done.—त्यं *n.* An improper act.

अकृष्ट *a.* (*f.*-ष्टा.) Not tilled. Unploughed. Comp.-पच्य,-रोहिन् *a.* Growing or ripening in unploughed land, growing wild; अकृष्टपच्या इव शस्यसंपदः * किराता. I.17. बीजं च बालेयमकृष्टरोहि * रघुवं. 14. 77.

अक्का *f.* A mother.

अक्तं *n.* Oil 2 Ointment.

अक्तुः *m.* 1 Ointment.

अक्त्रं *n.* An armour.

अक्रम *a.* (*f.*-मा.) 1 Devoid of order, confused.-2 Having no power of going or moving—मः 1 Want of order, confusion.—2 Absence of motion or movement.-3 Breach of propriety or decorum. *adv.*-मं Indecently, immodestly; in disorder.

अक्रिय *a.* (*f.*-या.) 1 Inactive, dull, motionless.—2 Not performing religious rites.-3 Worthless, good for nothing. *f.* —या Inactivity, neglect of duty

अक्रूर *a m.* Not cruel—रः N. of a Yâdava, a friend and uncle of Krishna.

अक्रोध *a.* (*f.*-धा.) Free from anger. *m.*—धः Absence or suppression of anger; freedom from anger. अक्रोधस्तपसः क्षमा प्रभवितुर्धर्मस्य निर्व्याजता (विभूषणं) * भर्तृह.

अक्रोधन *a.* Free from anger. *m.*—नः N. of a prince, son of Ayutáyú.

अक्लिन्न *a.* (*f.* न्ना.) Not wet or moist.

आक्लिष्ट *a.* (*f.*-ष्टा) 1 Not troubled' Unwearied, indefatigable.-2 Not marred, unimpaired; इदमुपनतमेवं रूपमक्लिष्टकांति * शकुंत. 5.19.—3 Not laboured or elaborate.—Comp.—कर्मन्, कारिन् *a.* Unwearied in actions.-व्रत *a.*, Unwearied in observing religious vows.

अक्ष् I. 5. P. [अक्षति, अक्ष्णोति] 1 To reach.—2 To pervade, penetrate. —3 To accumulate.

अक्षः *m.* 1 An axis, axle, pivot, axle-pole.—2 The pole of a cart. —3 A cart.—4 A wheel.—5 The beam of a balance.—6 Terrestrial latitude.-7 A die for playing with cube.-8 The seed of which rosaries are made.—9 A weight equal to 16 mâshas and called कर्ष. —10 N. of the plant विभीतक. —11 A shrub producing the rosary seed. Eleocarpus Ganitrus; the seed of this plant.-12A serpent. 13 Garuda. -14 N. of a son of Râvana. -15 The soul. -16 Sacred lore -17 Law; a law suit; legal procedings. -18 A person born blind- *n.*-अक्षं 1. An organ of sense, an object of sense -2. The eye, (at the end of Comp.-(as जलजाक्ष, कमलाक्ष, &c.) -3. Sea salt.-Comp.- आवपनं A dice board.—आवापः A gambler, keeper of the dice or gambling table; also—अतिवाप: -कर्णः The hypotenuse. — कुशल,- शौंड *a.* Skilful in gambling. — कूटः The pupil of the eye.—कोविद, -ज्ञ,-विद्-वेतृ *a.* Skilled in dice. - ग्लहः Gambling, playing at dice. —जं Direct knowledge or cognition. 3. A diamond. -जः N. of Vishnu. — तत्त्वं,- विद्या The science of gambling; — दर्शकः ; - दृश् 1. A judge 2. A superintendent of gambling.,-देविन् *m.* A gambler, gamester; so अक्षधूः,-धूर्तः A gambler.- द्यूतं Dice play, gambling-द्यूतिकं Dispute at play.-धरः 1.N. of Vishnu. 2. N. of the plant (शाखोट) Trophis Aspera. 3. A wheel. 4. Any one who bears a wheel, or who holds dice. — धूः (धुर्) The yoke attached to the fore-part of the pole of a car. — धूर्तः Dice-rogue, a gamester, a gambler. — धूर्तिलः A bull or ox yoked to the pole of a cart. -पटलं 1. A court of law. 2. Depository of legal documents.—पाटकः,-पाटिक A judge -पाटः-वाटः; A gambling house. पाठकः-One who is well-versed in law.,-पातः Cast of dice.—पादः N. of the sage Gautama, founder of the Nyâya system of philosophy, or a follower of that system. — पीडा 1. Injury to the organs. N. of the plant यवातिता.— भागः (अंशः) A degree of latitude. - भारः A cart-load. - मदः Passion for gambling. — मात्रं 1. Any thing as large as dice. 2. A moment of time (निमिषः); twinkling of an eye— माला, - सूत्रं A rosary. -राजः One addicted to gambling. -वामः An unfair gambler. —वाटः 1. A gambling house; the gambling table. 2. Wrestling ground- — वृत्त *a* Engaged in, addicted to, gambling. — हृदयं Perfect skill in gambling.

अक्षवती (*f.*) Gambling, playing with dice, a game at dice.

अक्षण *a.* (*f.*- णा.) Untimely, inopportune, unseasanable.

अक्षणिक *a*. (*f*.- का.) Steady, firm, not frail or transitory. हरिवीक्षणाक्षणिकचंचुवान्यया... * शिशुपा. 13-44.

अक्षण्वत् *a*. (*f*.-ती) Having eyes.

अक्षत *a*.(*f*.-ता) Uninjured, unhurt; Unbroken, whole; not crushed, undivided; unafflicted. *m*. *pl*. Grains of rice wet with water, and used as an article of worship. साक्षतपात्रहस्ता * रघुवं. 2. 21. आर्द्राक्षतारोपणमन्वभूतां * रघुवं. 7. 28:—3. Barley (यवाः). तः, *m*. तं *n*. 4. A eunuch—ता. A virgin, a maiden not blemished or enjoyed.—Comp. —योनिः A virgin not yet blemished by enjoyment.

अक्षत्र *a*. Devoid of, or not containing, the Kashatriya caste.

अक्षम *a*. (*f*.मा.) 1. Unfit, incompetent, unable. 2. Unable to bear or endure, impatient. नामक्षमं मदनकाक्षमते: * रघुवं. 13. 16. —मा. 1. Impatience, intolerance; jealousy; आर्कान्ती सुवजवाक्षमयेव रथ्याः * शाकुंत. 1 8.2. Anger, passion.

अक्षय *a*. (*f*.-या.) Undecaying, imperishable, unfailing, inexhaustible. निवासश्च शान्तिरिवाक्षयं * रघुवं. 3, 13. One who is houseless, a hermit.—यः *m*. Supreme spirit Comp. - तृतीया The third day of the bright half of Vaisâkha —लोकः The heaven.

अक्षय्य *a*. (*f*.-य्या,) Inexhaustible, imperishable. अक्षय्यांतर्भवनमिधयः प्रत्यहं रक्तकंठैः * मेघदू. 2. 8.—नवमी The 9th day of the bright half of Asvina.

अक्षर 1. *a*. (*f*.-रा.) Imperishable, undecaying. —2. Fixed, firm, unalterable. -रः N. 1. Siva, N. Visnu, -2. A sword. -रं 1. A letter of the alphabet; a syllable; a speech; any document, letter (generally in the *pl*.) 2. Penance. 3. Sacrifice, 4 Water. 5A vowel. अक्षराणामकारोस्मि * भगव.—6. The highest deity or Godhead, the indestructible spirit, Brahma, 7. The sky 8. Final beatitude, -9. A measure of time, equal to one-fifth of a Kâshthâ—Comp.—अंगं I. A part of a syllable. 2. Alphabet. अक्षर चंचुः चणःA scribe, writer, copyist; -जीवकः -जीवी, -जीविकः One who is a professional scribe or writer.—च्युतकं A kind of puzzle or riddle in which by the omission of a letter in a sentence a different meaning can be got.-छंदस्, —वृत्तं *n*. 1. A metre regulated by the number of syllables it contains, such as मंदाक्रान्ता, शिखरिणी, स्रग्धरा, &c. -2. Of unshaken resolve, resolute an epithet of परमात्मन् .— जननी,- तूलिका A reed or pen, c (वि) न्यासः Writing, arrangement of letters; the alphabet. 3. Scripture. — भूमिका A writing-board.- मुखः A scholar, student. - मुष्टिका 'Finger speech', speaking by means of finger-signs, — वर्जित *a*. Unletterd, illiterate, not knowing how to read or write. — संस्थानं Arrangemeut of letters, writing, alphabet.

अक्षरशः *adv*. Syllable by syllable, literally.

अक्षरि The rainy season.

अक्षान्ति *f*. Malice, intolerance. non-forbearance.

अक्षार *a*. Free from artificial salt, — रः Natural salt.

अक्षि *n*. 1. The eye. 2. The number two; (- क्षिणी). Comp - कंपः Twinkling of the eye.—कूटः -टकः, —गोलः, —तारा, The eye—ball.

or the pupil to the eye. — गत *a* 1. Visible, present. 2. Hateful, disliked, rankling in the eye. — जाहः The root of the eye. — पक्ष्मन्, — लोमन् *n.* The eye-lash. — पटलं A coat of the eye. 2. A disease of the eye pertaining to this coat — भू *a.* Visible, perceptible, manifest; true, real, -विकूणितं, विकूशितं A side-look, leer, a sidelong look.

अक्षित *a* (f. ता.) Undecayed, uninjured, undecaying. —तं 1. Water. 2. 100000, million.

अक्षिति *a* Imperishable, Preventing decay. —तिः *f.* Imperishable nature.

आक्षिवं (also अक्षीवं) Sea-salt.

अक्षीव --(ब) *a.* Not intoxicated.—वं *n.* Sea-salt.

अक्षुण्ण *a.* (*f.* -ण्णा) 1. Unbroken. uncurtailed.—2. Not conquered or frustrated, successful; —3. Not trodden or beaten, unusual, strange; —4. Inexperienced, not expert.

अक्षुध्य *a.* 1. That which prevents hunger. —2. Not liable to hunger.

अक्षेत्र *a.* Destitute of fields; uncultivated.— त्रं *n.* 1. A bad field. 2. A bad pupil, unworthy recipient or receptacle (of any thing). Comp—विद्,—ज्ञ *a.* Wanting in spiritual knowledge.

अक्षोट : (also ड:) 1. N. of a tree, (Mar. डोंगरी अक्रोड). -2. The walnut tree.

अक्षोभ *a.* (*f.*- भा) Not agitated, unmoved.-भ: 1. Absence of agitation. -2. The tying post of an elephant.

अक्षोभ्य *a.*(*f.*-भ्या) That cannot be excited, imperturbable, unassailable.

अक्षौहिणी An army consisting of 21870 chariots, as many elephants, 65610 horse, and 109350 foot. किं नो व्याप्तादिशां प्रकंपितभुवामक्षौहिणीनां फलं (of what avail are our battations spreading over the quarters, and shaking the earth?) * वेणीसं. 2.16.

अखट्टिः *m. f.* Improper conduct; a childish whim.

अखण्ड *a.* (*f.*- ण्डा) Unbroken, full. whole, uninterrupted, unblemished, अखंडं पुण्यानां फलमिव * शकुंत. 2. 10. -द्वादशी The 12th day of the bright half of मार्गशीर्ष. - साम्राज्य *n.* Full sovereignity. - डं *adv.* Uninterruptedly

अखंडन *a.* (*f.*-ना)1. Unbroken, not capable of being broken or divided. -2. Full entire. - नं *n.* 1 Not breaking, leaving entire. -2. Non-refutation — न: *m.* Time.

अखंडित *a.* (*f.*- ता) 1. Unbroken, undivided, uninterrupted, perpetual, continuous. - 2. Unrefuted-3. Not obstructed शतमखं तमखंडितपौरुषं * रघुवं. 9. 13.

अखर्व *a.* (*f.* - र्वा) Not short or stunted; not small, great,

अखात *m. n.* 1. A natural lake. 2. A pool of water before a temple.

अखिन्न *a.* (*f.* - न्ना) 1. Not fatigued or wearied. —2. Not causing fatigue.

अखिल *a.* (*f.* -ला)1. Whole, entire, complete. -2. Not uncultivated or fallow, ploughed (said of land). -आत्मन् The universal spirit. (ब्रम्हन्).

अख्याति : *f.* Infamy, ill-repute -कर *a* Disgraceful, disreputable.

अग् 1 P. 1 To wind, move tortuously, or in a zigzag way -2 To go-

अग *a*. 1 Unable to walk, not going, stationary, -गः *m*. 1 A tree. -2 A mountain. -3 A snake. -4 The sun. -5 The number 'seven' (in math.) - Comp —आत्मजा The daughter of the mountain, N. of Parvati. - ओकस् *m*. A mountain-dweller. 2. A bird.(वृक्षवासी). 3 . A beast. 4 The शरभ a fabulous animal with eight legs, and stronger than a lion.

अगच्छ *a* Not going.- च्छः *m*. A tree.

अगणेय— *a*. (*f*. --या) That cannot be counted,countless. इंद्रायुधश्यानुगामिनस्तुरंगमानगणेयान् * कादंब. उ. भा.

अगण्य *a*. (*f*. --ण्या) 1 Countless, immense; 2. Worthless, immaterial.

अगतिः *f* 1 Want of resort or recourse, necessity. -2 Want of access or scope.(lit. & fig.). मनोरथानामगतिर्न विद्यते * कुमा. सं. 5. 64. अगत्या Through necessity, under compulsion.

अगति (ती) क *a*. (*f*. -का) Helpless, having no resort or resource.

अगद् *a*. (*f*. -दा) Having no disease, healthy, sound in health; free from disease, -दः *m*. 1 A medicine, *a*. medicinal drug; इति चिंताविषघ्नोयमगदः किं न पीयते * हितोप, 2 Health, freedom from disease. 3The science of antidotes.

अगंदकारः *m*. A physician.

अगमः *m*. A mountain. 2. A tree.

अगम्य *a* (*f*. म्या)1 Not fit to be approached,unappraochable, inaccessible. —2 Inconceivable, incomprehensible; 3. या: संपद्स्ता मनसोप्यगम्याः शिशुपा. 3.59. Unfit for sexual intercourse . -Comp. —गमनं Illicit intercourse. -गामिन् *a*. Practising illicit intercourse.

अगरुः *m*. रु *n*. A kind of sandal wood (also अगुरु).

अगस्तिः (or -स्त्यः) *m*. N. of a celebrated Rishi or sage. He is regarded as the pioneer of Aryan civilization south of the Vindya mountain. 2 N. of the star Canopus of which the sage अगस्त्य is regarded as the regent, and whose appearance in the sky is believed to make turbid waters clear.

अगस्त्यः *m*. See अगस्तिः above.

अगाध *a*. (*f*. --धा) Unfathomable, very deep, bottomless. (fig.) Profound, sound, very deep. -धः *m*. -धं *n*. A deep hole or chasm. —धः *m*. N. of one of the 5 fires at the स्वाहाकार. -Comp. —जलः A deep pool or pond, a deep lake.

अगारं *n*. A house ; तत्रागारं धनपतिगृहादुत्तरेणास्मदीयं —मेघदू. 2. 12 ; -दाहिन् An incendiary.

अगिरः 1 Heaven. -Comp. -ओकस् *a*. Dwelling in the heaven (as a god).

अगुण *a*. (*f*. --णा). 1 Destitute of attributes. (God). -2 Having no good qualities, worthless. -णः *m*. Want of merit, a fault, defect, demerit, vice. लोभश्चेदगुणेन किं * भर्तृह.

अगुरु *a*. (*f*. रु or र्वी) 1 Not heavy, light. -2 (In prosody) Short. -3 Having no teacher. -4 One who is not a teacher. —रु *n*., रुः *m*. The fragrant aloe wood and tree. —सार: A sort of perfume.

अगूढ *a*. (*f*. -ढा) Not hidden or concealed, manifest, clear. —भाव *a*. 1. having an open or unreserved disposition. 2. Having an obvious meaning or import.

अगृहः *m*. A houseless wanderer, a hermit (वानप्रस्थ).

अगोचर *a*. (*f*. --रा) Imperceptible by the senses, not obvious, —रं *n*. 1

Anything beyond the cognizance of the senses. 2. Brahman. अगोचरे वागिव चोपरेमे * किरात. 17. 11.

अगोह्य *a.* (*f.* --या) Not to be concealed or covered, bright.

अग्नि: 1 Fire. -2 The God of fire. -3 Sacrificial fire which is of three kinds (गार्हपत्य, आहवनीय, and दक्षिण).4. The fire of the stomach *i.e.* The digestive faculty. 5. Bile. 6. Gold. 7. The number three. -Comp. —अ (आ) गारं-रः, -आलय:, -गृहं A fire-sanctuary, house or place for keeping the sacred fire । वसंश्चतुर्थोग्निरिवाग्न्यगारे रघुवं. 5. 25.—अस्त्रं Fire missile. -आत्मक *a.* Having the nature of fire । —आधानं Consecrating or maintaining the perpetual and sacred fire । so —आहिति. —आधेय: A Brahmana who maintains the sacred fire. -आधेयं *n.* Maintenance of the sacered fire. —आहित: One who perpetually maintains the sacred fire । also आहिताग्नि. —इन्धनं Kindling the fire. —उत्पात: A fiery portent, meteor, comet. —उपस्थानं. 1. Offering prayers to the god of fire. 2 The Mantra or hymn with which Agni is worshipped. —कण:, -स्तोक: A spark. —कर्मन् *n.*, —क्रिया *f.* 1. Any religious rite performed by means of fire 2. Burning with a hot iron. 3. Action of fire. 4. Oblation to Agni, worship of Agni. (अग्निकार्य also). —कारिका 1. Kindling sacrificial fire with clarified butter. 2. The means of consecrating the sacred fire. —काष्ठं Agallochum (अगुरु). —कुक्कुट: A firebrand, lighted wisp of straw. —कुंडं An enclosed space for the consecrated fire, a fire-vessel. —कुमार:, -तनय:, -सुत: 1. N. of Kârttikeya. See कार्तिकेय. -केतु: 1. Smoke. 2. N. of two Râkshasas on the side of Râva*n*a and killed by Râma.—कोण: -दिक् The south-east corner ruled over by Agni. —क्रिया 1. Obsequies, funeral ceremonies 2. Branding. —क्रीडा Fire-works, illuminations. —गर्भ *a.* Containing fire, having fire in the interior गर्भ: 1. The sun-stone, name of a crystal supposed to contain and give out fire when touched by the rays of the sun. —गर्भा 1. N. of the *S*amî plant. 2. N. of the earth. —गृहं A place for keeping the sacred fire. —घृतं A kind of medicinal preparation of ghee used to stimulate the digestive power. —चित् *m.* A householder who has kept the sacred fire.—चित्या *f.* -चय: *m.*—चयनं *n.* Maintaining the sacred fire. —ज, -जात *a.* Produced by or from fire, born from fire. —ज:, -जात: N. of Kârttikeya, Skanda. —जिह्वा *f.* 1. A tongue or flame of fire. 2. One of the 7 tongues of Agni. -ज्वाला *f.* The flame or glow of fire. —तप् *a.* -तपस् *a.* 1. Practising very austere penance, standing in the midst of the five fires; 2 Glowing, shining or burning like fire । hot as fire. -तेजस् *a.* Having the lustre or power of fire (—स् *m.*) N. of one of the 7 *Ri*shis of the 11th Manvantara.—त्रयं The three fires. —दग्ध *a.* 1. Burnt on the funeral pile 2 Burnt with fire. —दातृ One who performs the last (funeral) ceremonies of a man। —दीपन *a.* Stimulating digestion, stomachic tonic. —दीप्ति: *f.* Vigorous digestion —देव: 1. Agni. । 2. A worshipper of Agni. —देवा *f.* The third lunar mansion the Pleiades (कृत्तिका). —धानं The place or receptacle for keeping the sacred fire. —धारणं Maintaining the sacred fire. —परिक्रि-ष्क्रि-या Care of the sacred fire, worship of fire, offering oblations; --परिच्छद: The whole sacrificial apparatus. —परीक्षा Ordeal by fire. —पर्वत: A volcano. —पुराणं One of the 18 Purânas ascribed to Vyâsa, so called because it was communicated by Agni to the sage Vasishtha for instructing him in the knowledge of Brahma. The number of its stanzas is about 14500. It is a sort of an encyclopaedia of Sanskrit literature. It gives information about ritual and mystic worship, it describes duties of kings. It has Chapters on साहित्य, छंद:शास्त्र, ब्रह्मविद्या, योग, आयुर्वेद, काव्यालंकार· &c. —प्रतिष्ठा Consecration of fire, especially the nuptial fire. —प्रवेश:m. —शनं n. Entering the fire, self-immolation of a widow on the funeral pile of her husband. —प्रस्तर: A flint, a stone producing fire. —बाहु: I. Smoke. N. of the constellation कृत्तिका. -भु. n. Water. 2. Gold. —भू a. Produced from fire. —भू: m. Fire-born, N. of Kârttikeya, or स्कंद —मणि: The sunstone. 2. The flint. -मांद्यं n. Slowness of digestion, loss of appetite, dyspepsia. —मुख: m. 1. A Deity, god. 2. A Brahmana in general 3. A bug. —मुखीf. A kitchen. 6. —रक्षणं n. 1. Consecrating or preserving the sacred (domestic) fire or अग्निहोत्र. 2. The house of an अग्निहोतृ. -रज:;-रजस् m. 1. A scarlet insect by name इंद्रगोप. 2. n. The might or power of Agni 3. Gold. —रेतस् n. The seed of Agni, (hence) gold. --रोहिणी A hard inflamatory swelling in the armpit. —लोक:m. The world of Agni -वधू: f. Svâhâ, The daughter of Daksha and wife of Agni. -वर्णा f. A strong liquor. -वर्धक a. Stimulating digestion, tonic. -क: 1. m. A tonic. 2. Regimen, diet. -वीर्यं n. 1. Power or might of Agni. 2. Gold.-शरणं n. -शाला f. -लं n. A fire-sanctuary; a house or place for keeping the sacred fire; -शिख a. Fiery, fire-crested. —शिख: m. A lamp. 2. A rocket, fiery arrow. 3 An arrow in general. 4. Safflower plant. 5. Saffron. -शिखं n. 1. Saffron. 2 Gold. —शिखा f. A Flame. —शुश्रुषा f. Careful service or worship of fire. —शेखर a. Fire-creasted -शेखरं n. Saffron. -संस्कार: m. 1. Consecration of fire. 2. Hallowing or consecrating by means of fire; burning on the funeral pile; —सख:, —सहाय: m. 1. The wind. 2. The wild pigeon (smoke-coloured) 3. Smoke. -संभव a. Sprung or produced from fire. —संभव: m.—संभवं n. Gold. -व: m. Wild safflower. 2. Lymph, result of digestion. --साक्षिक a. or adv. Keeping fire for a witness, in the presence of fire. —स्तोम: (-ष्टोम:) m. N. of a sacrificial rite extending over several days. 2. A Mantra or Kalpa with refernce to this sacrifice —होत्रं n. 1. An oblation to Agni. 2. Maintenance of the sacred fire and offering oblation to it; or the sacred fire itself; —आहुति: f. Invocation or oblation connected with अग्निहोत्र. —होत्रिन् a. 1. One who practises the Agnihotra, or consecrates and maintains the sacred fire. 2. One who has prepared the sacrificial place.

अग्नायी *f.* 1. The wife of agni 2. The Tretâ age.

अग्निध् *m.* One who consecrates the sacred fire.

अग्निमत्,-वत् *a.* 1 Having fire or enjoying it. -2 Maintaining the sacrificial fire. -3 Having a good digestion.

अग्निसात् *ind.* To the state of fire, used in comp. with कृ 'to burn', 'to consign to flames', with भू to be burnt, or consigned to flames भ्रातृशरीरमाग्निसात्कृत्वा * मालवि. 5 ; न चकार शरीरमाग्निसात् * रघुवं. 8.-72.

अग्निय (*f.* -या) *a.* Referring to fire. Situated near the fire, relating to fire, fiery

अग्नीषोम *m* (—मौ) Agni and Soma.

अग्र *a.* (*f.* --ग्रा) 1 First, foremost, chief, prominent, principal, pre-eminent ; best (as in अग्रमाहिषी), chief queen, —आसनं Chief seat, seat of honour. -2 Excessive, protruding —ग्रं *n.* 1. The foremost or topmost point, tip, point (as in जिह्वाग्रं, नासाग्रं, सूच्यग्रं &c.). 2. Top, summit, surface ; (as in पर्वताग्र &c.). Front, van ; (as in सेनाग्रं &c.). -3 The best of any kind ; (as in स्यंदनाग्रं &c. प्रासादाग्रं). -4 Superiority, excellance. -5 Goal, aim. -6 Beginning. -7 A multitude, assemblage. -8 Excess, surplus. -9 A weight = पल. -10 A certain measure of food given as alms. -11 (Astr.) Amplitude of the sun (अग्रा, अग्रका also). As standing first in a compound अग्र means the front, tip, forepart of, as in अग्रपाद the fore part of the foot. -*adv.* In front, before, ahead -Comp. —अंगुलिः *m.* The tip of the finger. —अनी (णी) कः *m.* -कं *n.* The front of an army, van guard. —आसनं *n.* The first seat, seat of honour. —उपहरणं *n.* First supply. —उपहरणीय *a.* That which is first offered or supplied. —करः *m.* 1. The forepart of the hand. 2. The right hand. —गः A leader, a guide ; taking the lead; marching foremost. —गण्य *a.* Foremost, to be ranked first. —गामिन् *a.* A leader. —ज *a.* Frst-born or produced ; (-जः) 1. The first born, an elder brother ; a Bráhmana. (-जा) An elder sister; so —जात, -आतक, —जाति, —जंघा *f.* The forepart of the calf. —जन्मन् *m.* 1. The first-born, an elder brother. 2. A Bráhmaṇa. —जिह्वा *f.* The tip of the tongue. —दुतः *m.* A. —दूती दूतिका *f.* A female harbinger —नीः (णीः) *m.* Harbinger. 1. Leader, foremost, first, chief; —पादः *m.* The fore part of the foot; toes; —पाणिः, —हस्तः *m.* The Fore part of the hand. —पूजा *f.* The highest or first mark of reverence or respect. —पेयं *n.* Precedence in drinking. —भागः *m.* 1. The forepart ; the first or best part 2. Remnant, remainder —मांसं *n.* Flesh in the heart, the heart, —यान *a.* Taking the lead, foremost. —नं *n.* An army that stops in front to defy the enemy. —यायिन् *a.* Taking the lead, leading the van ; —योधिन् The leader in a fight, the principal hero, champion. —सद्या *f.* The first place or rank. —संध्या *f.* Early dawn; —सर *a.* Taking the lead ; that which must be given first. —हस्तः *m.* करः, *m.* पाणिः *m.* The forepart of the hand or arm ; the forearm. यद्यपि मेऽस्तिसाध्वसेन वेपने अयमतिमात्रमग्रहस्तस्तथापि नास्ति तस्य.

जनस्थान्यो दुर्शनोपाय इति यथात् थाकिफ्वेनं प्रेक्षिष्ये * रत्नाव. 2. —हायन: (णः) *m.* The beginning of the year ; N. of the month मार्गशीर्ष; —हार: *m.* A grant of land given by king (to Brâhmanas) for sustenance.

अग्रत: *adv.* (with gen.) 1 Before (opp. पृष्ठत:), in front of, at the head of ; forward. -2. In the presence of. -3. First ; अग्रत:कृ To give precedence to, consider most important ; to put in front or at the head of -Comp --सर *a.* Going in front, taking the lead. -र: *m* A leader.

अग्रह:*m.* Houseless man, i. e. a Vânaprastha.

अग्रिम *a.* (*f* -मा) 1. First (in order, rank &c) ; foremost, best, excellent. -2 Prior, preceding. -3 Elder, eldest -म: *m.* An elder brother.

अग्रिय *a.* (*f.* -या) Foremost, best &c. —य: An elder brother. —यं *n.* The first fruits; the best part.

अग्रीय *a.* (*f.*-या) Foremost, best.

अग्रे *adv.* 1 In front of, at the head of -2 In the presence of, before ; further on, subsequently, in the sequel : in the beginning ; at first; first ; first, in preference to others ; -Comp. -ग: -गा,-गू, *m.* A leader, one that goes in front or before. -दिधिषु: -षू: A man (of one of the first three castes) who marries a wife married before (-षू: *f.*) A married woman whose elder sister is still unmarried; वनं (णं)*n.* Border or skirt of a forest. -सर *a.* Going in front, taking the lead, a leader, foremost, first; -सरिक: *m.* A servant (who precedes his master). 2. A leader.

अग्र्य *a.* (*f.* -ग्र्या) 1 Foremost, best, most important, highest, preeminent, first, highest in rank. -ग्र्य: *m.* An elder brother -ग्र्यं *n.* The roof of a house.

अघं *n.* 1 Sin; misdeed. -2. An evil, mishap, misfortune, accident, injury, harm ; -4. Pain, suffering, grief, distress ; -5 Passion. —घ: *m.* N. of a demon, brother of Baka and Putanâ and commander-in-chief of Kamsa. —Comp.— असुर: *m.* See अघ above. —अह: *m.* A day of impurity. Time of impurity from the death of a relative. —नाश, —नाशन *a.* Expiatory, destroying sin (such as gifts, muttering holy prayers &c.). -न: *m.* Destroyer of the demon अघ; N. of Krishna -मर्षण *a.* Expiatory, removing or destroying sin, usually applied to a prayer repeated by Brâhmanas (the 190th hymn of Rv. 10.) ; -विष: *m* . A serpent. शंस: *m.* 1. Indication or reporting of sin. 2. A wicked man, such as a thief. —शंसिन *a.* Wicked; reporting or telling one's sin or guilt.

अघ्न्या *f.* A cow.

अघर्म *a.* (*f.* -र्मा) Not hot, cold ; —अंशु, —धामन् The moon.

अघोर *a.* . (*f.* -रा), 1 Not terrific or fearful. 2. Formidable, terrible -र: *m.* 1 N. of Siva -Comp —पथ:, *m.*-मार्ग: *m.* A follower of Siva; a follower of the terrific forms of शिव and दुर्गा.

अंकू. —10. U. (अंकयति-ते, अंकयितुं) 1. To count, enumerate. 2. To mark, stamp. —3 To censure, condemn, brand, stain, stigmatize; तर्को नाम गुणो भवेत्सुगुणिनां यो दुर्जनैर्नांकित: * भर्तृह. 4. To walk, stalk, go.

अंकः *m.* 1 Mark; stain; निमज्जतींदोः किरणोष्विवांकः *कुमा. सं. 1. 3. -2 The lap (*n.* also). -3 A numerical figure; a number; the number 9. -4 A side, flank, proximity, reach -5 One of the ten kinds of a drama. -6 An act of a drama. -7 A hook or curved instrument. -8 An ornament (भूषा). -9 A sham fight, military show. -10 A line, curved line; a curve or bend generally, the bend in the arm. -Comp. —अवतारः The closing part of a dramatic act which prepares the audience for the next act as the sixth act of Sakuntalâ or second of Mâlavikâgnimitra —तंत्रं *n.* The science of numbers. —धारणं *n* -णा *f.* 1. Bearing or having marks, such as those on the body of a Vaishnava. 2. Manner of holding the person, or the body. —परिवर्तः *m.* 1. Turning on the other side. 2. Rolling or dallying in the lap. —पालिः, *f.*, —पालिका *f.* —ली *f.* 1. The extremity of the lap, a seat in the lap; hence, an embrace. 2. A nurse. —पाशः *m.* Permutations and combinations (in math.). —भाज् *a.* 1. Seated in the lap or carried on the hip, as an infant. 2. Being within easy reach, drawing near, soon to be obtained. 3. Premature, early-ripe, forced (as fruit.) —मुखं (or -आस्यं) *n.* That act, or part of an act, which furinshes a clue to the whole plot of the drama. —लोपः *m.* Subtraction of numbers. —विद्या *n.* The science of numbers, arithmetic.

-अंकति *m.* 1. Air. 2. Fire. 3. Brahman (ब्रह्मा). 4. A Brâhmana who keeps the sacred fire. —तिः -ती *f.* 1. Going; 2 One who goes. -2 अंकनं *n.* A mark, token. 2. Act of marking.-3 Means of marking, stamping, &c.

अंकिन् *m. n.* A sort of drum or tabor.

अंकी *f.* A small oblong drum.

अंकुरः *m.* -रं *n.* A sprout, shoot, blade; दुर्भांकुरेण चरणः क्षत इत्यकांडे * शाकुंत 2. 01 (fig.) Scion, offspring, progeny. -2. Water. -3 Blood. -4 A hair. -5 A tumour, swelling.

अंकुरित *a.* (*f.* -ता) Having sprouts.

अंकुशः *m.* A hook, a goad; (fig) One who checks, a corrector, governor, director; निरंकुशाः कवयः poets have license, or are unfettered. -Comp. —ग्रहः *m.* An elephant-driver; -दुर्धरः *m.* A restive elephant. —धारिन् *m.* A keeper of an elephant. —मुद्रा *f.* A mark resembling a goad in form.

अंकुशित *a* (*f.* -ता) Urged on by a hook, goaded.

अंकुशिन् *a.* Having a hook or goad; laying hold of with a hook.

अंकूरः *m.* A sprout, See अंकुर.

अंकुषः *m.* —षं *n.* An elephant-driver's hook.

अंकोटः, -ठः, -लः *m.* N. of a tree (Mar. पिस्ते) Alangium Hexapetalum.

अंकोलिका *f.* An embrace.

अंक्यः *m.* A kind of drum.

अंग् 1. P. (*pp.* अंगित) To go, walk. —10 P. 1. To walk, go round. -2 To mark.

अंग *ind.* A vocative particle meaning 'well,' 'indeed,' 'true;' used with किं in the sense of 'how much less?', or 'how much more;'? तृणेन कार्यं भवतीश्वराणां किमंग वाग्हस्तवता नरेण *पंचतं.

अंगं *n.* 1 The body. 2. A limb or member or the body. 3 Scope, space. —3. (*a.*) A division of any thing ; a part or portion. 5. A department of a science. -5 An expedient, a means. 7. A supplement. 8 That which is subordinate to another. 8. That part of a word to which the affix is attached (gram.). 9. The number six. अंगा: *m. pl.* N. of Bengal proper, or its inhabitants. 11. (Drama) One of the sub-divisions of the five joints or sandhis in dramas.

—अंगि *ind.* Jointly or reciprocally. —अंगिभाव: The relation of a limb to the body, of the subordinate to the principal. —आधिप:, -अधीश: 1. Lord of the Angas, N. of Karna. Also. --राज:, -पति:, -ईश्वर:, -अधिश्वर:. -ज:. -जात: —जनु: *m.* 1. A son. 2. Love, cupid, intoxicating passion. —जा *f.* A daughter. —जं *n.* Blood. —द्वीप: *m.* One of the six minor Dvîpas. —न्यास: *m.* The ceremony of touching the limbs of the body with the hand accompanied by appropriate Mantras. —पालि: *f.* An embrace. 2 A nurse -पालिका, -भू: 1. A son. 2 Cupid. -भंग: 1. *m.* Palsy or paralysis of limbs; —मर्द: 1. One who shampoos his master's body. 2. Act of shampooing ; so -मर्दक or -मर्दिन्, मृद् *m.* One who shampoos. —मर्ष: *m.* Rheumatism; —रक्षक: *m.* A body-guard. Personal attendant -रक्षणी *f.* A coat of mail, or a garment. -णं Protection of person. —राग: *m.* 1 . A scented cosmetic, fragrant unguent; 2. Act of anointing the body with unguents. —रुहं *n.* Hair ; —लेप: *m.* 1. A cented cosmetic. 2 Act of anointing. —विकल *a.* 1. Maimed, paralysed. 2. Fainting, swooning. —विकृति: *f.* 1. Change of bodily appearance; collapse. 2. An apoplectic fit, swooning, apoplexy, (अपस्मार). —विकार: *m.* A bodily defect. -विक्षेप: *m.* 1. Movement of the limbs; gesticulation. 2 A kind of dance. —विद्या *f.* 1. The science of grammar &c. 2. The science of foretelling good or evil by the movements of limbs; —वीर: *m.* Chief or principal hero. वैकृतं *n.* Sign, token, hint. —संस्कार:, *m.* —संस्क्रिया *f.* 1. Embellishment of person; personal decoration, doing whatever secures a fine personal appearance, —संहति: *f.* Compactness, symmetry of the body, strength of the body. -संग: *m.* Bodily contact, union;- सेवक: *m.* A personal attendant, body-guard. -हारि: 1. Gesticulation. 2. Stage ; dancing-hall -हीन *a.* Maimed, mutilated, deprived of some limb, crippled. 2. Having some defective limb.

अंगकं *m.* 1. A limb, 2. The body.

अंगिका *f.* A bodice or jacket.

अंगिन् *a.* 1 Corporeal, having limbs, embodied, incarnate. That has a body ; having subordinate parts ; chief, principal.

अंगीय *a.* (*f.*.-या) 1. Belonging to the body. -2 Referring to the Anga country.

अंग्य *a.* (*f.* - ग्या) Belonging to, or connected with, the body, corporeal.

अंगणं (-नं) A *n.* yard, a court.

अंगति: *m.* 1 A conveyance, vehicle (*f.* also). -2. Fire. -3 Brâhma -4.

A Brâhaman who maintains the sacred fire.

अंगदं *n.* An oanament, bracelet, &c. worn on the upper arm, an armlet;

अंगदा *f.* A woman who offers her person for use —दः *m.* N. of a son of Vâli, monkey-king of Kishkindhâ.

अंगना *f.* 1 A woman or female in general; 2. A woman with well-rounded limbs. -3 (Astr.) Virgo. -4 The female elephant of the north. -Comp. —जनः *m.* 1. Womankind. 2. Women.

अंगस् *m.* A bird.

अंगारः *m.* -रं *n.* 1. Charcoal (whether heated or not); -2. The planet Mars -3. A plant हितावली. -4 N. of a prince who fought with king Mândhatri. -Comp. —धानी —धानिका -पात्री, -शकटी *f.* A portable fire-pan, brazier.— वल्लरी, -वल्ली *f.* N. of various plants, करंज, भार्गी, गुंजा. —वेणुः *m.* A sort of bamboo.

अंगारकः *m.*1 Charcoal. -2 Mars. —Comp. —मणिः *m.* A coral (प्रवाल).

अंगारिः *f.* A portable fire-pan, brazier.

अंगारिका *f.* 1 A portable fire-pan. -2 The stalk of the sugar-cane. -3 The bud of the Butea Frondosa (किंशुक).

अंगारितं *n.* The early blossom of the किंशुक tree.

अंगारिता *f.* 1. A bud. 2. A creeper

अंगिका *f.* Bodice or jacket.

अंगारिणी *f.* 1 A small fire-pan. -2. The region heated by the sun, though no longer exposed to its rays. —3 A creeper in general.

अंगारीय *a* (*f.* -या) Useful in preparing coal.

अंगार्या *f.* A heap of charcoal.

अंगिर् *m.* N. of a sage who received the ब्रह्मविद्या from Atharvan and imparted it to Satyavâha.

अंगिरः, अंगिरस् *m.* N. of a celebrated sage to whom many hymns of the *Rig*veda are ascribed.

अंगीकृ 8 U. 1 To accept, to resort to, to betake oneself to, to take to -2. To undertake, promise to do, to agree or consent to. -3. To own; acknowledge, confess, admit, grant. -4. To subdue, to make one's own.

अंगीकारः *m.* -कृतिः *f.* -करणं *n.*1 Acceptance. -2. Agreement, promise, undertaking.

अंगुः *m.* A hand.

अंगु (-ली) गीयं *n.* A finger-ring.

अंगुरी (ली)यकं *n.* A finger-ring.

अंगुलः *m.* 1 A finger. -2 The thumb -3 A finger's breadth equal to 8 barley-corns, joind side by side in breadth. -4. (Astr.) A digit or 12th part,

अंगुलिः -ली, -रिः,-री, *f.* A finger; a toe (of the foot). -2 The thumb, great toe. -3 The tip of an elephant's trunk. -Comp. —तोरणं *n.* A mark on the forehead made with sandal &c. in the form of the half moon by the followers of शिव —त्रं, -त्राणं *n.* A finger-protector (a contrivance like a thimble used by archers to protect the thumb or finger from being injured by the bow-string). -पंचकं*n.* The five fingers collectively. —मुद्रा, *f.* -मुद्रिका *f.* A seal-ring. -मोटनं, -स्फोटनं Snapping or cracking the fingers (Mar. चुटका). —संज्ञा A sign made by the finger ; —स्फोटनं *n.*, —भंगः *m.* Cracking the fingers.

—संदेश: *m*. Making signs with fingers; cracking or snapping the fingers as a sign.

अंगुष्ठ: *m*. I The thumb; great toe. -2. A thumb's breadth, used as a measure. -Comp. —मात्र *a*. Of the length or size of a thumb.

अंगुष्ठ्य: *m*. The thumb-nail.

अंगूष: *m*. I An ichneumon. -2 An arrow.

अंघस् *n*. A sin.

अंघ्रि: *m*. I A foot. -2 The root of a tree. -3 A quarter of a stanza (चतुर्थपाद)—ज: *m*. A शूद्र. -Comp. —प: *m*. A tree. —पर्णी, -पर्णिका, -वल्ली, -वल्लिका *f*. N. of a plant सिंहपुच्छी (Mar. डुवला, पिठवण). —पान *a*. Sucking his foot or toes, as an infant. —स्कंध: *m*.The ankle.

अच् I U. (अचति, -अचते) I To go, move. 2. To honour, to worship. With —अप To run away. —उत् To rise, go up. -नि I. To bend down. 2. To lessen. —परा To go back. —परि To go about.

अच् *m*. A term for vowels (gram.)

अचक्षुस् *a*. Eyeless, blind. —*n*. A bad or miserable eye.

अचंड *a*. (*f*.-डा) Not hot-tempered; mild, gentle. -डी *f*. A tractable cow.

अचर *a*. Immoveable. -2 (Astr.) Epithet of the zodiacal signs वृषभ, सिंह, वृश्चिक and कुंभ.

अचरम *a*. (*f*. -मा) Not the last, middle, &c.,

अचल *a*. (*f*. —ला) Fixed, firm, steady, immovable motionless, permanent. —क: *m*. I A mountain; a rock, -2 A bolt or pin (शंकु). *n*. Brahman. -ला *f*. The earth. -Comp. -अधिप: *m*. The king of mountains, i.e. the Himalayas. -कन्यका, -सुता, -दुहिता, -तनया *f*. &c. N. of Pârvatî, daughter of the Himâlaya mountain. —कीला *f*. The earth. -जा, -जाता N. of Pârvati. —त्विष् *a*. Of fixed or permanent lustre or colour. -त्विट् *m*. The Indian cuckoo. —द्विष् *m*. The enemy of mountains, an epithet of Indra who cut off their wings. —धृति: *f*. A metre of four lines of 16 short syllables each(गीत्यार्या).-पति:-राट् *m*. Lord of mountains, N. of the Himâlayas; so —अधिप:, —श्रेष्ठ:.

अचित् *a*. Without understanding, foolish.

अचित्ति: *f*. Want of sense, infatuation, ignorance.

अचिंता *f*. Disregard, thoughtlessness.

अचिंत्य,-तनीय*a*. (*f* -त्या,—या) Inconceivable, incomprehensible, unexpected.

अचिंतित *a*. (*f*. -ता) Not thought of, unexpected, sudden.

अचिर *a*. (*f*. --रा) I Brief, transitory, of short duration; -2 Recent, late, new. In compounds अचिर may be rendered by 'recently,' 'just', 'not long ago '—रं *adv*. (अचिरेण, अचिराय, अचिरात्, अचिरस्य also). I Not long since, not long ago. -2 Recently, lately. -3 Soon, quickly, not long hence. —Comp. —अंशु,-आभा,-द्युति:,-प्रभा,-भास्,-रोचिस् *f*. Lightning.

अचेतन *a*. (*f*. -ना) Inanimate, not sentient, irrational. -2 Not conscious, insensible, senseless.

अचेष्ट *a*. (*f*. -ष्टा) I. Effortless, motionless.-2 Not requiring direct effort.

अचैतन्यं *n*. I Unconsciousness, nsensibility; ignorance in spiritual matters. -2 The material world, matter.

अच्छ *a.* (*f.* -च्छा) Clear, pellucid, transparent, pure. -च्छ: *m.* 1 A crystal. -2 A bear. -3 N. of a plant. —Comp. —उदक *a.* (i. e. अच्छोद) Having clear water. -दा *f.* N. of a river ; -दं *n* N. of a lake on the Himâlayas —भल्ल: *m.* A bear.

अच्छलं *n.* An action free from fraud *a.* (*f.* -ला) Simple, guileless

अच्छिद्र *a.* (*f.* —द्रा) Faultless. Unbroken, complete, unimpaired, without holes or weak points, without defect. —द्रं *n* A faultless action or condition, absence of defect; -द्रेण *adv* Uninterruptedly, from first to last.

अच्छिन्न (*f.* —न्ना) 1 Uninterrupted, continuous, constant, undisturbed, undivided, uninjured; inseparable

अच्छोटनं *n.* Hunting.

अच्युत *a.* (*f.*-ता) 1 Not fallen, firm, fixed; not giving way, solid. -त: *m.* N. of Vishnu.-Comp. —अग्रज: *m.* N. of Balarâma or Indra. —अंगज:, पुत्र:,-आत्मज: *m.* N. of Cupid, —आवास:, -वास: *m.* The sacred fig-tree.

अज् 1 P. (*pp.* वीत or अजित) 1 To go. -2 To drive, lead. -3 To throw, cast.

अज *a.* (*f* —जा) Unborn, existing from all eternity. —ज: *m.* 1 The 'unborn,' the Almighty Being. 2. N. of विष्णु, शिव, ब्रह्मा, and कामदेव. 3. The (individual) soul (जीव). -3 A ram, a he-goat. - 4 N. of the father of Dasaratha and grand-father of Râma ; —अविकं *n.* Goats and sheep (collectively) —आजीव: —जीविक: *m.* A goat-herd. —अश्वं *n.* Goats and horses. —एडकं *n.* Goats and rams. -गर: *m.* A huge serpent who swallows goats. -गल:*m* See अजागल below. —प:,—पाल: *m.* A Goat-herd —पति: *m.* 1. The best of goats. —बंधु: *m.* A fool —मार: *m.* 1. A butcher. —मीढ: *m* N. A surname of Yudhishthira. —मादा, -मोदिका *f.* N. of a medicinal plant, (Mar. ओंवा).

अजक (-का-) वं *n.* The bow of god शिव.

अजका, अजिका *f.* A young she-goat.

अजग (-गा-) वं *n.* The bow of god शिव.

अजघन्य *a.* (*f.* -न्या) Not the last, not the least.

अजड्धी *a.* Of a vigorous mind.

अजनि: *f.* A path, road.

अजननि: *f.* 1. Destruction ; 2 Cessation of existence, (used in imprecations e. g. तस्याजननिरेवास्तु).

अजन्य *a.* (*f.* -न्या) Not fit to be produced ; not favourable to mankind. —न्यं *n.* A portent, an omen.

अजप: *m.* A Brâhmana who does not (properly) repeat his prayers (कुपाठक) ; one who reads heretical books.

अजंभ *a.* (*f.* -भा) Toothless.-भ: *m.* 1 A frog. 2. A child (because it has no teeth) 3. The sun.

अजय *a.* (*f.* -या) Invincible, unconquerable. -य: *m.* 1 A defeat ; -2 N. of Agni, or of Vishnu. —या *f* Hemp, (Mar. भांग). -3 Mâyâ or illusion.

अजय्य *a.* (*f.* -य्या) Unconquerable, invincible.

अजर *a.* (*f.*-रा) 1 Not subject to old age or decay ; ever young, undecaying, imperishable -र: *m.* A god (since he is not subject to old age). -रं *n.* The Supreme Spirit

अजर्य *a.* (*f.* -र्या) 1 ot dige stib e. -2 Not decaying, imperishable, everlasting, perpetual. -र्यं *n.* (with संगतं expressed or implied) Friends ip.

अजस्र *a.* (*f.* -स्रा) Not ceasing, constant, pe petual, continual. -स्रं *ind.* Ever, constantly, perpetually.

अजहत *a.* (*f.* -ती) Not abandoning, not giving up.

अजहत्स्वार्था *f.* That kind of लक्षणा, in which the wo d retains its pri mary sense, and conveys something in addition. When it is said काकेभ्यो दधि रक्ष्यतां, the word काक signifies not only crows, but all he other creatures eating or spoil ng दधि

अजहल्लिंगं *n.* A noun which does not change its original gender even when used like an adjective ; *e. g.* वेदः or श्रुतः प्रमाणं, r वेदाः प्रमाणं.

अजा *f.* (Sankha ph losophy) 1 Prakiti or Mâ á -2 A she-goat. -C mp. -गलस्तनः *m.* The fleshy protubera ce or nipple hanging down from the neck of goats. (fig.) An emblem of anything worthless or useless -जीवः,-पालकः *m.* A goat-herd.

अजागर *a.* (*f* रा) Not wakeful.

अजात (*f* -ता Unborn, not yet born, produced, or fully developed ;. अजातमृतमूर्खेभ्यो मृताजातौ सुतौ वरं * हितोप —Comp. —अरि, —शत्रु *a.* Having no enemy or adversary. Not a enemy or adversary, not an enemy of any one. -अरिः, शत्रुः *m.* An epithet of Yudhishthira —ककुत-द *m.* A young bull whose hump is not yet grown. -दंत *a.* One without teeth, or a state in which one has got no teeth. —पक्ष *a.* Having undevloped or unfledged wings. —व्यंजन *a.* Having no distinctive marks or features (as a beard). —व्यवहारः *m.* A minor, a youth under sixteen (in law).

अजानिः *m.* Without a wife ; a widower.

अजानिकः *m* 1. One that has no wife. 2. A goat-herd.

अजिका *f.* A young she-goat.

अजित *a.* (*f.* -ता) 1 Invincible, unconquerable, irresistible. 2 Not conquered or won (as a country &c.); not restrained, or curbed, or controlled. —तः *m.* 1 N. of Vishnu, or of Siva, or of Buddha. -2 N. of a powerful anti lote. Comp. —आत्मन् (-त्मा)*m* One who has not subdued his mind. —इंद्रियः *m.* One who has not subdued his senses.

अजिनं *n.* 1 The (hairy) skin of a tiger, lion, especially of a black antelope (used as a seat, &c.) ; अथाजिनाषाढधरः * कुमा. सं. 5. 30. -Comp. —योनिः *m.* A deer, an antelope. —वासिन् *a.* Clad in an antelope hide.

अजिर *a.* Quick, swift. -रः *m.* 1 A sort of mouse, hairy mole. -रं *n.* 1 A court-yard, an enclosed space, arena. —2 The body. -3 Any object of sense. -4 The wind, air. -5 A frog. -रा *f.* 1 N. of a river.

अजिह्म *a.* (*f.* —ह्मा) 1 Straight, not crooked. -2 Upright, straightforward, honest. —ह्मः *m.* A frog. -Comp. —ग *a.* (*f.* —गा) Going straight on. -गः *m.* An arrow.

अजिह्वः *m,* A frog.

अजीकवं *n.* The bow of god शिव.

अजीगर्तः *m.* 1 A serpent. -2 N. of

a Brâhmana in the family of भृगु and father of शुनःशेप.

अजीत *a*. Not faded or withered, –Comp. —पुनर्वण्यं N. of a two-fold rite performed by Kshatriyas (अप्राप्तप्राप्तिकरणार्थो विधि :).

अजीर्ण *a*.(*f*. —र्णा) Undigested; undecomposed. —र्णे *n*. -र्णि: *f*. 1 Indigestion. -2 Vigour, energy, absence of decay.

अजीव *a*. (*f*. -वा) Devoid of life, lifeless. —वः *m*. 1 Non-existence, death.

अजीवन *a*. (*f*. —ना) Devoid of livelihood. —नं *n*. Non-existence, death.

अजीवनि: *f*. 1 Death, non-existence, (used as an imprecation); अजीवनिस्तव भुयात् Mayest thou cease to live!

अजुष्टि: *f*. Non enjoyment.

अजेय *a*. (*f*. -या) Not fit to be conquered.

अज्जु (ज्जू) का *f*. A courtezan, (in theatrical language).

अज्झटा *f*. N. of a plant, (Mar. भुई आंवळा).

अज्झलं *n*. 1 A shield. -2 A live-coal.

अज्ञ *a*. (*f*. -ज्ञा) 1 Not knowing, unaware, unconscious, devoid of knowledge or experience. -2 Ignorant, unwise, foolish, silly, stupid. -3 Inanimate, (अचेतन.)

अज्ञात *a*. (*f*. -ता) Unknown, unexpected, unconscious, unaware. -Comp. —चर्या, *f*. —वास: *m*. Remaining *incognito*.

अज्ञातचर्या *f*. Life passed in obscurity, or led without people knowing of it द्यूतमिषेण राजेंद्र तथा तद्भवता कृतं भायेणाज्ञातचर्यायां वयं सर्वे निपातिता: * वनप५२

अज्ञान *a*. (*f*. —ना) Ignorant, unwise. —नं *n*. Ignorance, unconsciousness; especially, spirtual ignorance (अविद्या) which makes one consider one's self as distinct from the Supreme Spirit and the material world as a reality.

अंच् 1 U. (अंचति-ते) 1 To bend, incline, curve. 2 To go move, towards. -3 To worship, honour, request, ask or call for, desire. -5 To murmur, speak indistinctly. —*caus*. or 10 U. To manifest, unfold With अप to put away, drive away; (intr.) To run away. —आ To bend —उप To draw or raise (water). —परि To cause to revolve, whirl, twist. —वि To draw or bend asunder, to extend, stretch out. —सं To crowd or drive together, to bend together.

अंचति: *f*. 1. Wind. 2. Fire. 3. One that goes.

अंचनं *n*. Bending, curving.

अंचल: *m*. —कं *n*. 1 The border or end (of a garment), skirt or hem -2 Corner or outer angle (as of the eye).

अंचित *pp*. (*f*. -ता) 1 Curved, bent. -2 Gone. -3 Honoured; graced graceful, handsome. -4 Sewn or woven, arranged. -Comp. —पत्रं *n*. A lotus with curved leaves. —भ्रू: *f*. A woman having arched or handsome eyebrows.

अंज् 7 P. 1 To anoint, smear with. -2 To make clear, show, represent. -3 To go. -4 To shine, -5 To honour, celebrate. -6 To decorate, smear with. -With अभि To fit out, equip, furnish. —आ 1. To anoint, smear. 2 To extol, to honour. —प्रति I. To smear. 2. To adorn, decorate. —वि To manifest, reveal.

अंजन: *m.* 1 A kind of lizard (Mar. घोपई सरडा). -2 N. of a tree or mountain. -3 N. of the guardian elephant of the west. —नं *n.* 1 Anointing, smearing with. -2 Collyrium or black pigment applied to the eye-lashes; वर्षतीवाजनं नभ: * मृच्छक. 1. (fig.). Impurity, as in निरंजन. -3 Paint, a cosmetic ointment. -4 Magic ointment. -5 A special kind of material of the black pigment, such as antimony (used as collyrium, lamp-black, &c.). -6 Ink. -7 Fire. -8 Night. -9 -नं *n.*,-ना *f.* (Rhet.) A suggested meaning, or the process by which such meaning is suggested. अन्यार्थधीकृद् व्यापृतिरंजनं * काव्यप्र. 1.-Comp. -आधिका *f.* A kind of lizard —अद्रि: *m.* The mountain नीलगिरि: —केशी *f.* N. of a plant, (Mar. नखला). —शलाका *f.* A stick or pencil for the application of collyrium.

अंजना *f.* N. of the female elephant of the north. -2 N. of the mother of Mâruti or Hanumat. 3. The process by which a suggested meaning is got at.

अंजनावती *f.* 1 N. of the female elephant of the north-east quarter. -2 N. of a tree (Mar. काळी कापशी)

अंजनिका *f.* 1 A species of lizard; a small mouse. -2 N. of the wife of the elephant सुप्रतीक who guards the north-east quarter.

अंजलि: *m.* 1 A cavity or hollow formed by folding and joining the open hands together, 2. A cavity-ful of anything; प्रकीर्ण: पुष्पाणां हरिचरणयोरंजलिरयं * वेणीसं. I. I. The hollow part of any thing. श्रवणांजलिपुटपेयं * वेणीसं. I. 4. -3 Hence a mark of respect or salutation used with verbs रच्, बंध्, कृ, आधा, etc. बध्यतामभययाचनांजलि: * रघुवं. 11. 78. -3 A measure of corn. -Comp. -कर्मन् *n.* Folding the hands, respectful salutation; लुब्धमर्थेन गृह्णीयात् क्रुद्धं चांजलिकर्मणा —कारिका *f.* 1. An earthen doll 2. N. of a plant, Mimosa Pudica (Mar. लाजाळू). —पुट: *m.* टं *n.* The cavity formed by joining the hands together; hollowed palms of the hand.

अंजालिका *f.* A small mouse. —क: *m.* N. of one of Arjuna's arrows.

अंजस् *n.* (-ज:) Speed, velocity, strength. 2. Ointment, -Comp -पा *m.* Drinking some offering

अंजस *a.* (*f.* -सी) Straight; honest, upright.

अंजसा *adv.* (Instr. of अंजस्) Straight on. -2 Truly, Correctly, properly, justly, साक्षाद् दृष्टोसि न पुनर्विद्मस्त्वां वयमंजसा * कुमा. सं. 6. 22. -3 Directly (साक्षात्). -4 Soon, quickly, instantly.

अंजि *a.* Unctuous, slimy; 2. Brilliant. —जि: *m.* A mark made with sandal &c. a tilaka mark; -2 A commander, pigment, leader. —जि:,-जी *f.* An ointment,

अंजिष्ठ:-ष्णु: *m.* The sun.

अंजी *f.* 1 A blessing, auspicious desire. -2 A pounding machine.

अंजीर: *m.*-रं *n.* 1. The fig-tree 2. The fruit of the tree.

अट् 1 P. (अटति, अटित). To wander or roam about (with loc.); roam over (sometimes with acc.).

अट *a.* Wandering. अटः *m.* A night-roamer.

अटनं *n.* Wandering, roaming; as in भिक्षा°. रात्र° &c.

अटल *a.* (*f.* —ला) Firm, fast. Solid.

अटनिः-नी *f.* The notched extremity of a bow; निन्यतुः स्थलनिवेशिताटनी लीलयैव धनुषी अधिज्यतां * रघुवं. II. 14

अटविः (—वी) *f.* A wood, forest.

अटविकः *m.* A wood-man, a forester; also आटविकः

अटा *f* The habit of roaming about, especially of a religious mendicant.

अट्ट् I A. I To hurt, injure. -2 To trangress, go beyond (fig also). —*Caus.* I To despise, condemn, disregard.

· अट्ट *a.* (*f.* -ट्टा) I High, lofty Dried, dry. —ट्टः *m.* —ट्टं *n.* A room at the top of a house. -2 A turret, tower. नरेंद्रमार्गाट्ट इव प्रपेदे विवर्णभावं स स भूमिपालः * रघुवं. 6. 67. -3 A market-place, market. -4 A fine linen cloth. -5 A palace, palatial building. -6 Injuring. -7 Excess, superiority. -ट्टं *n.* Food, boiled rice. -Comp. —हासः *m.* Very violent laughter. —स्थली *f.* A place or country full of palaces &c. —हासः *m.* -हसितं,*n* हास्यं*n.* A loud or boisterous laughter, a horse-laugh. -हासिन् *m.* An epithet of Siva. 2 One who laughs very loudly.

अट्टकः *m.* A room on the roof of a house. 2. A palace also.

अट्टनं *n.* A weapon shaped like a discus. 2. Disregard.

अट्टाट्टः *m.* I Overbearing conduct, contempt, disdain. -2 Excess, superiority.

अट्टालः *m.* —लकः *m.* I. An apartment on the roof of a house, an upper story. 2 A palace.

अट्टालिका *f* A lofty house; a palace. -Comp. —कारः *m.* A mason, a bricklayer —बंधः *m.* A kind of base or foundation in architecture.

अड्डं *n.* A shield.

अड्डुचः *m* A part of the plough.

अण् I P. To sound. -2 (4 A) To breathe, live (for अन्).

अणक *a.* (*f.* —का). Small, insignificant, low. As the first part of a कर्मधारय Comp it shows contempt, as अणककुलालः *a.* Bad potter.

अणिः *m.* -णी *f.* I The point of a needle. -2 A linch-pin, the pin or bolt at the end of the pole of a carriage. —3 A limit. -4 The corner of a house -Comp. —माण्डव्यः *m.* N. of a sage said to have been impaled on an अणी or linch-pin.

अणिमन् *m.* अणुता *f.* अणुत्वं *n.* I Minuteness, smallness, thinness, leanness, fineness -2 The nature of an atom. -3 The superhuman power of becoming as small as an atom, one of the 8 powers or siddhis which are as follow :-अणिमा लघिमा प्राप्तिः प्राकाम्यं महिमा तथा। ईशित्वं च वशित्वं च तथा कामावसायिता.

अणुः *m.* I An atom, a very small particle 2 The smallest perceptible quantity. -3 N. of Siva. अणु *n.* The fourth part of a Matra.-Comp. -अंतः*m.* A hair-splitting question. —भा *f.* Lightning. -मात्र *a.* Of the size of an atom. -रेणुः *m.*,-णु *n.* Atomic dust. -वादः*m.* The doctrine of atoms; atomic theory. —वीक्षणं *n.* I. Minute observation, observation of very minute parts.

2 An instrument, like the microscope, enaoling one to discern the smallest objects.

अणुक a (f. —का) 1 Very small, atomic. -2 Subtle, too fine. -3 Acute.

अणीयस्, अणिष्ठ a. Smaller, smallest, very small.

अंडः m. —डं n. 1 An egg. 2. The testicles. 3 The scrotum. 4. The world as having sprung from the primordial egg of Brahma ; (ब्रह्मांड used in the same sense). -5 The musk-bag. 6. An epithet of Siva. -Comp. —आकर्षणं n Castration —आकार, —आकृति a. Egg-shaped, oval, elliptical. —रः m., —ति: f. An ellipse. —कटाहः m. —हं n. The shell of the ब्रह्मांड or mundane egg. —कोशः,-षः, -षकः m. The scrotum. —ज a. Born from an egg. —जः m. 1. A bird, an oviparous being. 2. Any creature born from an egg, as a bird, snake. One of the four great divisions into which the animal creation is classed by Hindu philosophers. -3. A fish 4. A snake. 5. Brahmâ. —वर्धनं n. —वृद्धिः f. Swelling of the scrotum, hydrocele. —सू a. Oviparous. अंडजा f. Musk.

अंडकः m. The scrotum. —कं n. A small gg.

अंडालुः m. A fish.

अंडीरः m A full-grown man, a strong or powerful person.

अत् 1 P. (अत्त-अतित) 1 To go, walk ; wander. -2 To bind.

अतज्ज्ञ a. 1 Not knowing that (तत् i. e. Brahman). 2 One not an expert in any particular branch of knowledge.

अतट a. (f. -टा) Having no shore or beach ; precipitate, steep. —टः m. 1 A precipice. -Comp. —प्रपात m. A steep precipice; a headlong fall from a precipice.

अतथा ind. Not so. Comp. —उचित a. Not deserving that, not used to such things.

अतदर्हम् ind. Unjustly, undeservedly.

अतद्गुणः m. (Rhet.) A figure of speech in which the thing to be described does not assume the quality of another thing though in its neighbourhood. तद्रूपाननुहारश्चेदस्य तत्स्यादतद्गुणः ; e. g. धवलोसि यद्यपि सुंदर तथापि त्वया मम रंजितं हृदयम् । रागपूरितेपि हृदये सुभग निहितो न रक्तोसि ॥ * काव्य प्र. 10.

अतंत्र a. (f. —त्री) 1 Having no musical strings. (as a musical instrument). -2 Unrestrained ; not being the object of the rule under consideration.

अतंद्र-न्द्रित-द्रिन्-द्रिक a (f.-न्द्रा,-ता,-णी,-ला.) Alert, unwearied, careful, vigilant. अतंद्रिता सा स्वयमेव वृक्षकान् * कुमा. सं. 5. 14.

अतर्क a. (f. —र्का) Illogical. —र्कः m. 1 Absence of argument or reasoning, bad logic. -2 An illogical reasoner.

अतर्कित a. (f. —ता) Unthought of, unexpected. —तं adv. Unexpectedly. -Comp. —आगत, —उपनत a. Coming, occuring or befalling unexpectedly, accidental, sudden.

अतर्क्य a. (f. -र्क्या) Inconceivable, unimaginable.

अतल a. (f. -ला) Bottomless. -लं n. N. of a पाताल or lower region, one of the 7 Patalas, being the first among them. —लः m. N. of

Siva. -Comp. —स्पृश्,-स्पर्श *a* Bottomless, very deep, unfathomable.

अतस् *ind.* 1 Therefore. 2. Hence, from this place, henceforward, from this time onward. -Comp. अतः परं, अत ऊर्ध्वं Hereafter, beyond this, afterwards. -Comp. -अर्थं,-निमित्तं, On this account, hence, for this reason. —एव For this very reason.

अतसः *m* 1 Wind, air. 2. A garment made of the bark of a tree.

अतसी *f.*1 Common flax -2 Hemp. -3 Linseed.

अति *ind.* 1 A prefix used with adjectives and adverbs meaning 'very', 'too', 'excessively', 'very much,' often prefixed to verbs and verbal forms, it means 1. Beyond, over; 2. Too far, past. (As अत्येति, अतिक्रमितुं. 3. When prefixed to nouns or pronouns it means beyond, past, surpassing, superior to, eminent, respectable. Compounds with अति as first member are given below in their alphabetical order.

अतिकथा *f.* An exaggerated tale or meaningless talk. -थ *a.*(*f.*-था)1 Exaggerated, incredible. 2 Unfit to be told.-3 Past narration, or mention, dead lost.

अतिकाय *a* (*f.* -या) Of an extraordinary size, gigantic.—यः *m.* N. of a Rakshasa, son of Ravana and killed by Lakshmana.

अतिकृच्छ्र *a.* (*f.* —च्छ्रा) Very difficult. —च्छ्रं *n.* च्छ्रः *m.* Extraordinary hardship, a kind of hard penance.

अतिकृतं *n.* Overdone, done too much.

अतिकृतिः *f.* Overdoing.

अतिक्रम् 1 U., 4. P. 1 (*a*) To step or pass beyond; get across, go over, cross. To pass over, pass by. -2 To excel, surpass; exceed. -3. To transgress, violate, go beyond, overstep. -4 To exclude, neglect, set aside. -5 To go or pass away, elapse.-6 To overcome, overpower.

अतिक्रमः *m.* 1. Going over or beyond (lit. and fig.). 2. Surpassing. 3. Transgression. 4. Neglect. 5. An imposition. 6. Opposition. 7. Passing away (said of time).

अतिक्रमणं *n.* Transgression; going over; excess; fault, offence.

अतिक्रमणीय *pot. p.* (*f.* -या) To be transgressed or violated, to be disregarded, passed by, neglected or avoided.

अतिक्रान्त *pp.* (*f.* -न्ता) Surpassed, gone beyond, exceeded. —न्तं *n.* The past, a thing of the past.

अतिगम् 1 P. 1 To pass, elapse, pass away (as time). -2 To overcome, exceed, excel. -3 To pass over, neglect. To die. -5 To escape.

अतिग *a.* (*f.* —गा) (in comp.) Exceeding, going beyond, excelling, surpassing.

अतिगंध *a.* (*f.* -धा) Having an excessive or overpowering smell. —धः *m.* Sulphur.

अतिगुरु *a* Very heavy (such as mercury &c.) —रुः *m.* A very respectable person, such as father, mother, &c. (त्रयः पुरुषस्य अतिगुरवो भवन्ति पिता माता आचार्यश्च).

अतिग्रह् 9 P. 1 To overtake or surpass. 2. To take beyond the usual measure.

अतिग्रह *a.* (*f,* —हा) Difficult to be comprehended. —हः, *m* —ग्राहः *m.* 1 Object of an apprehensive organ

-2 Right knowledge. -3 Overtaking, surpassing -4 One who seizes or takes to a large extent.

अतिग्राह्य *a.* (*f.* —ह्या) To be held in check, to be controlled. —ह्यः *m.* N. of three libations made at the Jyotishtoma sacrifice.

अतिचर् 1 P. 1 To transgress, violate ; be unfaithful to. -2 To pass by, neglect, omit. -3 To overtake, overcome, surpass.

अतिचर *a.* (*f.* —रा, or —री) going over or beyond. Very changeable, transient.

अतिचरणं *n.* Excessive practice, overdoing.

अतिचारः *m.* 1 Transgression. -2 Excelling, -3 Overtaking. -4 Accelerated motion of planets; passage of a planet from one zodiacal sign to another.

अतिचारिन् *a* (*f.* णी) Transgressing, surpassing.

अतिचिरं *adv.* Very long, too long.

अतिजात *a.* (Opp. अपजात). Superior to one's parentage.

अतिजीव् 1 P. 1. To live longer than, outlive. -2 To surpass (in the mode of living).

अतिजीवनं *n.* Surviving, living longer than.

अतितरां, —अतितमां *ind.* More, in a higher degree. (abl.) -2 Exceedingly, very much. -3. Excessive.

अतितरणं *n.* Crossing, surmounting.

अतितॄ 1. P. To cross, pass or get over, surmount, overcome.

अतितृष्णा *f.* Inordinate desire. Rapacity, excessive greed or desire. —ष्ण *a.* Rapacious, very greedy.

अतिथिः *m.* 1 A guest, (fig. also). 2. N. of a son of Kusa and Kumudavati and grandson of Râma. -Comp. —क्रिया,—पूजा,—सत्कारः—सत्क्रिया,—सेवा Hospitality. Hospitable reception of guests. —देव *a.* Honouring a guest as a god. -धर्मः *m.* Title or claim to hospitality ; hospitality due to guests. —पतिः *m.* The host or entertainer.

अतिदानं *n.* Munificence, liberality ; अतिदाने बलिर्बद्धः Chân. 50.

अतिदाहः *m.* Violent inflammation.

अतिदिश् 6 P. 1 To make over, transfer. -2 To extend the application of by analogy.

अतिदेशः *m.* 1. Assignment, transfer, extension. 2. (gram.) Extended aplication of something stated before by analogy. It is thus defined:— अन्यत्रैव प्रणीतायाः कृत्स्नाया धर्मसंहतेः । अन्यत्र कार्यतः प्राप्तिरतिदेशः स उच्यते ॥

अतिदूर *a.* (*f.* —रा) Very far. -रे, -रात्, -रेण (usually with न and gen.) Not far from.

अतिद्वय *a.* Surpassing the two. Having no second or equal, incomparable, matchless.

अतिधन्वन् *m.* An unrivalled archer or warrior.

अतिधृतिः *f.* N. of a class of metres.

अतिनिद्रा *f.* Excessive sleeping. —द्र *a.* (*f.* —द्रा) 1 Given to excessive sleep. -2 Without sleep, sleepless.

अतिनिर्हारिन् *a.* Very attractive (as an attributive of smell), आमोदः सोऽतिनिर्हारी * अम.को.

अतिपत् 1 P. 1 To pass over; neglect, transgress, to cross. —*Caus.*

1 To delay, neglect ; -2 To disrespect, offend, violate. -3 To cause to fly past or by. -4 To make ineffectual. -4 To snatch away, drag away.

अतिपतनं *n*. Flying past or beyond; omission, neglect, missing, transgressing ; going beyond due bounds.

अतिपातः *m*. 1 Passing away, lapse (of time). -2 Neglect, omission, transgression ; न चेद्न्यकार्यातिपातः * शाकुंत. 1. -3 Befalling, occurrence. -4 Ill-treatment. -5 Opposition, contrariety.

अतिपातित *pp*. (*f*. —ता) 1 Postponed, delayed -2 Quite or entirely broken.

अतिपातिन् *a*. 1 Acute, running a rapid course. -2 Surpassing in speed; ततार विद्याः पवनातिपातिभिर्दिशो हरिद्भिर्हरितामिवेश्वरः * रघुवं. 3. 30. Urgent; that must be attended to at once. भटः— आर्य, अतिपाति कार्यमेतत् शीघ्रं निवेद्यतां * भास. पं. रा.

अतिपद् 4 A. To pass over. To go beyond. -2 To neglect, omit, trangress. —*Caus*. To allow to pass by.

अतिपत्तिः *f*. 1 Going beyond, passing, lapse. -2 Non-performance, failure. 3. One surpassing a foot-soldier.

अतिपन्न *pp*. (*f* —न्ना). Gone beyond, transgressed, missed, past.

अतिपरिचयः *m* Excessive familiarity or intimacy. अतिपरिचयादवज्ञा ' Familiarity breeds contempt. '

अतिपरोक्ष *a*. 1 Far out of sight, quite indiscernible. -2 Not hidden; visible.

अतिपातकं *n*. A very heinous sin,

अतिप्रबंधः *m*. Great continuity ; rapid succession —प्रहितास्त्रवृष्टिभिः * रघुवं. 3. 58.

अतिप्रगे *ind*. Very early ; in the early dawn.

अतिप्रवृद्ध *a*. 1 Overbearing, grown very much.

अतिप्रसंगः *m*. —प्रसक्तिः *f*. 1 Excessive attachment. -2 Impertinence, indiscretion or imprudence ; insult. -3 Extraordinary or unwarrantable stretch of a (grammatical) rule, or principle. -4 Too close contact. -5 Exaggeration, prolixity.

अतिप्रौढा *f*. A girl who has attained a marriageable age, a grown-up girl.

अतिबल *a*. (*f*. —ला) Very strong or powerful. —लः *m*. An eminent or matchless warrior (अतिरथ). —लं *n*. 1 Great strength or power. -2 A powerful army. —ला *f*. 1 N. of a medicinal plant. -2 N. of a powerful charm or lore taught by Visvâmitra to Rama. -3 N. of one of Daksha's daughters.

अतिबाला *f*. A cow two years old.

अतिब्रह्मचर्यं *n*. Over-continence, or abstinence. —र्यः *m*. One who has violated the student's life by cohabiting with women.

अतिभ (भा) रः *m*. 1 Excessive burden, great load ; कोऽतिभारः समर्थानं * पंचत. सा मुक्तकंठं व्यसनातिभारात् चक्रंद विग्ना कुररीव * रघुवं. 14. 68. -2 Speed.

अतिभवः *m*. Surpassing, defeating, conquering.

अतिभू 1 P. 1 To spring forth, arise. -2 To exceed, surpass, excel ; to overcome, subdue, overpower.

अतिभूमिः *f*. 1 Excess, culmination, highest pitch. -2 Boldness, violat-

oneself of to escape the notice of avoid -4 To remove (to another place) bring or carry over 5 To follow, tread (as a path)

अतिवाह *m* Carrying over

अतिवाहन *n* 1 Passing spending -2 Excessive toiling or enduring bearing too much load or too heavy burden 3 Despatching, sending away eluding search

अतिवाहित *pp* (*f* —ता) Spent passed

अतिविकर्त *n* A pardonable offence or misdemeanour (in civil law)

अतिवाद *m* 1 Very harsh abusive or insulting language reprimand -2 Exaggeration

अतिवादिन् *a* Talkative obstinately establishing one's own assertion

अतिविस्तर *m* Prolixity diffuseness

अतिवृत् 1 A 1 To pass over or by cross -2 To go beyond, exceed, (fig also) Overstep transgress violate To neglect omit, disregard slight, offend injure 3 To surpass excel To overcome subdue vanquish get over, escape 4 To pass away glide away elapse (as time) to be late -5 To go away from leave abandon (abl) —*Caus* To slight not to heed to disregard

अतिवर्तिन् *a* 1 Crossing, surpassing, excelling passing over stepping transgressing 2 Excessive 3 Foremost

अतिवृत्ति *f* 1 Surpassing violation transgression -2 Exaggeration -3 Violent effusion

अतिवर्धन *n* Excessive growth increase

अतिवृष्टि *f* Excessive or heavy rain.

अतिवेल *a* 1 Exceeding the due limits or boundary -2 Excessive, extravagant —लम् *adv* 1 Excessively, too much 2 Unseasonably

अतिव्याप्ति *f* 1 Inclusion in a definition of that which is not intended to be included in it Unwarranted extension of a definition to things not intended to be defined by it one of the three faults to which a definition is open ; अलक्ष्ये लक्षणगमनं अतिव्याप्तिः ; यथा मनुष्या ब्राह्मण इति लक्षणस्य शूद्रेऽतिव्याप्तिः मनुष्यत्वात्

अतिशक्वरी f A class of metres

अतिशय *m* 1 Excess, preeminence, excellence height of excellence perfection of art गतिमति विज्ञानातिशये विचारः R 6 11 -2 Superiority in quality rank quantity or number —*a* Superior pre-eminent, excessive very great, abundant -Comp —उक्ति *f* Exaggerated or hyperbolical language 2 The figure of speech in which the विषयिन् (i e उपमान or अप्रस्तुत) is described as swallowing (or altogether taking in) the विषय (the subject on which something else is superimposed) and there is therefore an apprehension of identity, this sort of swallowing up is called अध्यवसाय निगीर्य अध्यवसानं तु प्रकृतस्य परेण यत् विज्ञेया

3 Verbosity

अतिशयन *a* (*f* —नी) Great eminent, abundant —नम् Excess abundance superfluity —नी *f* N of a metre of four lines also called चित्रलेखा

अतिशयिन् *a* Tending to excel or surpass

अतिशयित *a pp* (*f* —ता) 1 Excelled surpassed 2 Excessive exce eding, going beyond

अतिश (–शा) –यिन्, (*f* –नी) *a* Superior, excellent, pre eminent, excelling, surpassing –2 Excessive, abundant

अतिशायन *n* Excellence, superiority

अतिशी 2 A 1 To surpass excel; पूर्वान् महाभाग तयाऽतिशेषे • रघु 5 14 –*Caus* (–शाययति) To excel

अतिशेष *m* Remainder remnant a small remainder

अतिश्रि 1 P To excel; be over

अतिसक्ति *f* Close contact or proximity; great attachment

अतिसंधा 3 U 1 To deceive, over reach, cheat –2 To wrong injure, encroach upon

अतिसंधान *n* Cheating, deception trick, fraud

अतिसंधेय *a* (*f* –या) To be cheated or deceived; कथं खलु मया न [illegible] अतिसंधेय • विक्रमो 2

अतिसंध्या *f* The time just before and after the morning and evening twilight

अतिसर *m* 1 One who goes beyond or exceeds, Leader 2 Effort or exertion

अतिसर्गः *m* 1 Granting (of a wish); giving; [illegible] • रघु 10 42 –2 Granting permission (to do what one likes [illegible]) –3 Dismissal, discharge, parting with; giving away –*a* Everlasting, permanent (नित्य); emancipated (मुक्त)

अतिसर्जन *n* 1 Giving granting; consigning; [illegible] • कुमा 4 32 consigning to the flames; [illegible] सि 14 48; [illegible] • किरात 13 5; giving back –2 Liberality munificence –3 Killing –4 Deception –5 Separation from, parting with

अतिस्पन्दन *n* Violent motion or movement of the child in the womb

अतिसर्व *a* (*f* –र्वा) Transcending, or superior to all, above all –र्वः *m* The Supreme Being

अतिसांवत्सर *a* (*f* –री) Extending over more than a year

अतिसांतपन *n* A kind of very austere penance

अति (ती) सारः *m* Dysentery, violent straining at stool

अति (ती) सारिन् (?) The disease called dysentery (अतिसार) –*a* –अतिसारकिन् Affected by, afflicted with dysentery; [illegible] अम [illegible]

अतिसृ 1 P To extend –*Caus* To extend to drive out, give out

अतिसृज् 6 P 1 To give, present, grant To give away once for all (never to be taken back) to give away for good) [illegible] • विक्रमो 1 14 [illegible] अतिसृष्टा॰ • रघु 11 46 2 Part with 3 To remit forgive (as fine &c) 4 To leave as a remnant

अतिसौरभ *a* (*f* –भा) Very fragrant –भं *n* Great fragrance –भः *m* The mango tree

[illegible] *a* (*f* –री) Not liberal niggardly

अतिस्नेह *m* Over affection; [illegible] • मृच्छ 2 (sees or finds what is to be done) –[illegible] • शकु 4 (is apt to suspect evil)

अती (अति beyond and इ to go) 2 P 1 To go beyond to cross to pass on or beyond (said of time or space) 2 To excel, surpass, outstrip to exceed, to transcend सत्यमताय ह रतो ह ta वतत वाजन * सुवन 1 3 To overcome subdue vanquish to be superior to ; अतीत्य हृ गुणान् सर्वान् स्वभावा भूरिवेतत *शिव प 4 To omit neglect disregard 5 (Intrans) To pass elapse (time) 6 To overflow, be redundant be in excess -7 To die

अतीत pp a (f —ता) 1 Gone beyond; crossed 2 Past dead —तं n The past past time

अतीन्द्रिय a Beyond the cognizance (reach) of the senses ; अतीन्द्रिये त्वदुपपत्तद्वाक् * रघुर 3 41 —य m The Soul or Purusha (in Sânkhya phil); the Supreme Soul —यं n 1 Pradhâna or Nature (in Sânkhya phil) 2 The mind (in Vedanta)

अतीव ind 1 Exceedingly, excessively very much, quite -2 Superior to (acc)

अतुच्छ a Not bulky lean lank

अतुल a (f —ला) Unparalleled unequalled unsurpassed matchless incomparable, —ल m The sesamum seed and plant (तिलकाष्ठ)

अतुल्य a Unequalled, unsurpassed, unparallele l

अतुषार a Not cold -Comp -कर m The Sun ; so अतुषारकर —रश्मि —धामन् —रुचि &c m The sun

अतृणता f A small quantity of grass

अतेजस् a 1 Not bright dim -2 Weak feeble -3 Insignificant —स् n Dimness darkness ; feebleness dullness

अतेजस्क a (f —स्का) Not bright feeble dim insignificant

अतेजोमय a (f —यी) See अतेजस्

अत्ता f 1 A mother -2 An elder sister -3 A mother in law

आत्त f See अत्ता

अत्तिका f Elder sister (in theatrical language)

अत्तृ m One who eats

अत्न n A battle fight

अत्न , अत्नु m 1 Wind -2 The sun 3 A traveller

अत्य m A courser steed

अत्यग्नि Surpassing fire

अत्यङ्कुश a (f —शा) Past the goad, uncontrollable, unmanageable

अत्यध्वन् m Long or wearisome travelling ; a long journey

अत्यन्त a (f —ता Past the proper limit, excessive, much very great 2 Endless, everlasting perpetual 3 Complete perfect, absolute ; as in अत्यन्ताभाव absolute non existence —तं ind 1 Exceedingly, excessively very much fully -2 For ever, to the end (of life), through life -3 Absolutely perfectly, completely -Comp —गत a Gone or departed for ever, gone never to return ; कथमत्यन्तगता न मां दहेः * रघु 8 56 —गामिन् a 1 Going or walking very much, going too fast or quickly 2 Excessive much —तिरोधान f Complete disappearance, absolute cessation —वासिन् m One who constantly lodges with his preceptor, as a student. —संयोग m Close proximity, uninterrupted continuity ; का [illegible] 2 Inseparable co existence

अत्यन्तिक a (f —की) 1 Going too much or too fast -2 Very near -3 Not near distant —कं n 1 Close proximity -2 Great distance

अत्यतीन *a* (*f* —ना) Going or walk ing too much going too fast

अत्यम्ल *a* (*f* –म्ला) Very acid or sour

अत्यय *m* Passing away, lapse; End, conclusion, coming to a close, disppearance 2 Death, destruction, passing a way, perish ing –3 Danger, injury, evil, jeopardy –4 Suffering, misery, distress –5 Guilt, offence –6 Attack, assault –7 Overcoming comprehending

अत्ययिक *a* (*f* —की) 1 Destruct ive disastrous; unpropitious 2 Pressing urgent, not suffering delay, emergent

अत्यायत *a* 1 Exceeded, surpassed –2 Outraged, violated

अत्ययिन् *a* (*f* —नी) Exceeding, surpassing

अत्यर्थ *a* Excessive, very great, too much, exorbitant —र्थं *ad* Very much, exceedingly, exces sively

अत्यष्टि *f* A kind of metre

अत्यह *a* Exceeding a day in duration

अत्याकार *m* 1 Contempt, blame censure –2 A very large body, or a person of a very big body

अत्याचार *a* Violating the establsh ed usages or customs र *m* Doing of acts contrary to usage or religion

अत्यादित्य *a* Surpsssing the sun in brilliance अत्यादित्य हुतवहमुख संभृत तद्धि तेजः • मेघदू 43

अत्याय *a* Transgressing —य *m* Transgression, violation excess

अत्याधु *n* Vessel used in sacrifices

अत्यारूढ *a* Grown to excess That has reached a high degree –ढि भवति कमलश्री मनाभव • रघुव 12 33 —ढ *n* —ढि *f* A very high position, great elevation or rise; अत्यारूढिर्भवति महतामप्यपभ्रंशनिष्ठा • शकुन्त 4 अत्यारूढ रिपो सोढ चन्दनवद्भागन • रघुव 10 42

अत्याहित *n* A great calamity, misfortune mishap accident विदुषक —कथ सुसगता; ससगत किंनिमित्त दयिता न खलु सागरिकाया अत्याहितं किमपि मनुत • रत्नाव 4 –2 A rash or daring deed पाडुपुत्रैन किमप्यत्याहितमाचेष्टित मवेत् • वणास

अत्युक्ता नाम *f* N of a class of metres of 4 lines each of 2 syllables

अत्युक्ति *f* Exaggeration over coloured description

अत्युग्र *a* Very fierce —ग्र *n* Asafoetida, (Mar हिंग)

अत्युपध *a* Trustworthy, tried

अत्यूह *m* 1 Close meditation or thinking; earnest reasoning –2 A gallinule, called also दात्यूह –त्यूहा *f* A plant (Mar रानाबरी)

अत्र *ind* 1 In this place here –2 In this respect in this matter or case; as to this –Comp —अन्तरे *adv* In the meanwhile meantime —द्घ *a* (घ्नी *f*) Reaching so far up; as tall as this —भवत् (*m* भवान् *f* —भवती) Worthy, revered honour able It refers to a person that is present or near the speaker, (opp तत्रभवत्) *m* His honour *f* Her honour प्रयतत्रभवानवतीह मन्मथो

अत्रत्य *a* (*f* त्या) 1 Belonging to or connected with, this place –2 Produced or found here; local

अत्रप *a* (*f* —पा) Shameless im pudent, immodest

अत्रस्न अत्रास अत्रस्नु *a* Not afraid, fearless द्वयाप्यत्रस्नुमेव • रघुव 1 21

अत्रि *m* N of a celebrated sage and author of many Vedic hymns

—Comp —[illegible] —[illegible] —[illegible] —[illegible] *m* The moon

अथ *ind* It is used as an auspicious particle [illegible] It is said that अथ does not mean auspiciousness but the very hearing of the word is auspicious अथ is a particle expressing 1 Beginning e g अथ [illegible] 2 Doubt e g [illegible] 3 Subsequent time (then afterwards) e g [illegible] 4 Interrogation e g [illegible] 5 Condition if in case when then e g अथ [illegible] 6 Totality entirety e g [illegible] (We shall explain the whole अथ) 7 Addition e g [illegible] Comp —अपि Moreover —[illegible] *ind* What else certainly yes assuredly —[illegible] *ind* What else yes exactly so quite so certainly —[illegible] And moreover likewise —[illegible] *ind* But on the contrary —[illegible] *ind* Or or perhaps

अथर *m* Same as [illegible] q v

अथर्वन् *m* 1 Siva 2 N of the Atharvaveda

अथर्वणि *m* 1 A Brâhmana versed in the [illegible] or skilled in the performance of the rites enjoined by it —2 A family priest (पुरोहित)

अथर्वन् *m* 1 A priest who has to worship fire and Soma —2 A Brâhmana —3 N of the priest who is said to have first brought down fire from the heaven offered Soma and recited prayers

अथर्वाण *n* The ritual of the अथर्ववेद [illegible] Same as अथ

अथो *ind* Used in the senses of अथ q v

अद् 2 P 1 To eat devour —2 To destroy —*Caus* To feed with cause to eat —*Desid* जिघत्सति To wish to eat

अत्तृ *n* One who eats

अद *a* (at the end of comp) Eating devouring e g मांसाद Carnivorous feeding on flesh so मत्स्याद Feeding on fish

अदत् *a* Toothless —[illegible] *m* A serpent without teeth one whose fangs have been taken out

अदक्षिण (*f* [illegible]) 1 Not right left (as hand or side —2 Not bringing in Dakshinâ to the priests i e without any gifts (as a sacrifice) —3 Simple weakminded silly —4 Clumsy unskilful awkward —5 Inauspicious unfavourable

अदक्षिणीय अदक्षिण्य *a* Not deserving Dakshinâ

अदग्ध *a* (*f* [illegible]) Not burnt i not burnt according to the rites

अदण्ड *a* Free or exempt from punishment

अदण्ड्य *a* 1 Not deserving punishment —2 Exempt or free from punishment

अदन्त *a* Toothless

अदत्त *a* (*f* —त्ता) 1 Not given —2 Unjustly or improperly given —3 Not given in marriage —त्ता *f* An unmarried girl —त्त *n* A donation which becomes null and void because it has not been given according to prescribed rules or forms —Comp —आदायिन् *a* The receiver of such a donation; one who takes what has not been given away a thief —[illegible] *f* Not affianced or betrothed before

अदत्ता *f* An unmarried girl

अदद्र्यच् *a* Going to that side.

अदत *a* (*f* —ता) 1 Toothless, whose teeth have fallen away 2 That has not yet got the teeth formed or grown —तः *m* 1 A leech 2 N of Pushan, one of the 12 Adityas, who had lost his teeth at the destruction of Daksha s sacrifice by वीरभद्र

अदन्त्य *a* (*f* —त्या) 1 Not dental 2 Not fit for the teeth; injurious to the teeth

अदभ्र *a* (*f* —भ्रा) Profuse, not scanty, plentiful copious अदभ्रदर्भाम धिशय्य स स्थलीं • किरात I 38

अदम्भ *a* (*f* —म्भा) Honest undeceitful म्भ *m* 1 Honesty, absence of deceit —2 N of Siva

अदय *a* (*f* —या) Merciless, unkind cruel —यं *ind* Mercilessly; ardently; closely (said of an embrace)

अदर्श *m* 1 Day of new moon —2 A mirror (= आदर्श)

अदर्शन *n* 1 Not seeing absence, not being seen The state of not being within sight —2 Neglect or failure to see —3 (Gram) Disappearance elision omission; अदर्शनं लोपः • पाणिनि

अदल *a* Leafless 2 Without parts or members

अदस् *pron a* (असौ *m f* अदः *n*) 1 That (referring to a person or thing not present or near the speaker) 2 Also often used with reference to objects near the speaker and means 'this here' 3 It is often used in the sense of तत् as a correlative of यत् 4 When अदः immediately follows the relative pronoun (as यासौ ये अमी &c) it conveys the sense of प्रसिद्ध well known celebrated renowned 5 Sometimes अदस् used by itself conveys this sense —*ind* There at that time, then thus

अदातृ *a* 1 Not giving miserly, not liberal —2 Not giving (a daughter) in marriage —3 Not liable to payment

अदान *a* (*f* —ना) 1 Not giving, miserly. 2 Without rut (as an elephant)

अदान्त *a* (*f* —न्ता) Untamed 2 Unsubdued

अदाय *a* (*f* —या) Not entitled to a share

अदायाद *a* (*f* —दा) 1 Not entitled to be an heir 2 Having no heirs

अदायिक *a* (की *f*) 1 That which is not claimed by an heir; destitute of heirs; अदायिकं धनं राजगामि —2 Not relating to inheritance

अदार *m* 1 One who has no wife a widower or bachelor —2 Not injuring or tearing

अदास *m* One who is not a slave a free man

आदिति *m* 1 Devourer *i e* death —2 —ति *f* 1 Inability to give, poverty —2 The earth The goddess Aditi mother of the Adityas the mother of gods 3 Freedom security 4 Boundlessness immensity of space 4 Inexhaustible abundance perfection 5 The lunar mansion called पुनर्वसु 6 Speech 7 A cow —ती (*dual*) Heaven and earth —Comp —नन्दनः *m* A god a divine being

अदीर्घ *a* Not long —Comp —सूत्र —सूत्रिन् *a* Quick prompt in action

अदुःख *a* Free from evil, propitious -Comp —नवमी The 9th day in the bright half of भाद्रपद, which is supposed to be propitious to women worshipping Devi to avert evil for the ensuing year

अदुर्ग *a* 1 Not inaccessible, not difficult of access -2 Destitute of forts —विषय *m* An unfortified country

अदूर *a* (*f* —रा) Not distant near (in time or space) त्रिंशा Not far from 30 i e nearly 30 कोप *a* Easily provoked irascible —रं *n* Proximity, vicinity अदूरे, -रात् -रेण, -रतः adv (with gen or abl) Not far from, at no great distance from not far distant very near

अदूषित *a* (*f* —ता) Not vitiated uncorrupted, unspotted irreproachable

अदृप्त *a* (*f* —प्ता) Not proud not vain

अदृश् *a* 1 Sightless, blind -2 Not seeing, not perceiving

अदृश्य *a* (*f* —श्या) 1 Invisible -2 Not capable of being seen an epithet of परमेश्वर

अदृष्ट *a* (*f* —ष्टा) 1 Invisible not observed 2 Not known or experienced, not felt -3 Unforeseen not previously thought of -4 Not permitted or sanctioned illegal —ष्टं *n* 1 The invisible one -2 Destiny fate luck, (good or bad) -3 Virtue or vice as the eventual cause of pleasure or pain -4 An unforeseen calamity or danger -Comp —अर्थ *a* (*f* —र्था) Having a deep or occult meaning i metaphysical ; having an object not evident to the senses —कर्मन् *a* One who has had no practice or experience, inexperienced -नर, -पुरुष *a* A treaty concluded by the parties themselves without a mediator —पूर्व *a* Not seen before —फल *a* That of which the consequences are not yet visible —फलं *n* The future ; the result of good or bad actions

अदृष्टि *f* An evil or malicious eye evil look-*a* Blind sightless

अदेय *a* (*f* —या) Not to be given what cannot or ought not to be given away —यं *n* That which it is not proper or necessary to give Wife sons deposits, and some other things are considered as अदेय in Hindu law -Comp —दानं *n* An unlawful gift

अदेव *a* (*f* —वा) 1 Not god like or divine, not pertaining to a god -2 Godless, impious —वः *m* One who is not a god Comp —मातृक *a* Not having the god Indra as mother i e that upon which rain does not fall said of land irrigated and fertilised by rivers canals &c वितन्वति क्षेममदेवमातृकाश्चिराय तस्मिन्कुरवश्चकासति Ki 1 17

अदेश *m* 1 A wrong place a bad or improper place 2 A bad country

अदैव *a* (*f* —वी) 1 Not predetermined (by Gods or by fate) 2 Not divine -3 Unfortunate, ill-fated

अदण्डुक *a* Not exacting, not screwing out money under sham pretexts from subjects (as a king)

अदोह *m* The time when milking is impracticable -2 Abstaining from milking

अदोष *a* (*f* —षा) 1 Free from faults demerits vices or defects &c ; innocent , जायामदोषामुत संत्यजामि * रघुव 14 34 2 Free from the faults (of compostion) —ष *m* Not a fault That which cannot be cons dered to be a fault

अद्व *m* A sacrificial oblation called पुराड श q v

अद्धा *ind* 1 Ti ily, surely un doubted y certainly, अद्धा श्रिय पालित सगराय प्र थर्प विदधत्यनघो स स घ * रघुव 13 65 –2 Manifestly, clearly ; ध्यात्वाथ च यतत परिदधुमद्धा * भामि वि 1 95 –3 In this way thus Comp —पुरुष *m* A right or true m n —वैधेषा (pl) N of a school of the ग्रुद्धपद्धर्वे

अद्भुत *a* (*f* –ता) 1 Wonderful marvellous —त *n* 1 A wonder ; a wonderful thing or occurrence a prodigy, mira le –2 Surprise astonishmen , wonder, (*m*) also —त *m* One of the 8 or 9 *Rasas* the marvellous sentiment 2 N of the Indra of the 9th Man vantara –Comp —ब्राह्मण *n* N of a portion of a Brâhmana belong ing to the Samaveda —सार *m* The wonderful resin of the खाद्र or Catechu plant ; Mimo a Catechu —स्वन *m* N of Siva

अद्मान *m* Fire

अद्मर *a* (*f* —रा) Voracious glut tonous

अद्य *a* Eatable, fit to be eaten that should be eaten द्वित च परिणामे यत्तद्य भू त मरुता * पमत 4 23 —द्य *n* Food an thing eatable —*ind* 1 To-d y this day oft in comp with दिन दिवस &c , and meaning of this day to-day s –2 Now –3 At present now a days Comp —अपि Still yet eve i now to this day down to the present time or moment —अवधि *ind* 1 From to day 2 Till to day —पूर्व *ind* Before now प्रभृति *ind* From to day this day forward henceforth —श्वीन *a* Likely to happen to day or tomorrow imminent अद्यश्वीना *f* A female near delivery (आसन्नप्रसवा) —सुत्या *f* Extraction of the same day

अद्यतन *a* (*f* —नी) 1 Pertaining or referring to extending over to day as in अद्यतनदिवस काल 2 Current now a days preva lent at present modern —न *n* The period of a current day अद्यत नभूत *m* The Aorist tense as it denotes an action d ne to-day or on the same day

अद्यतनीय (*f* —या) Referring to to day of to day 2 Modern

अद्रव *a* (*f* —वा) Not l qu d not of the nature of a liq uid व *m* Not a liqu d

अद्रव्य *n* A worthless thing any thing utterly useless नाद्रव्ये नाद्रव्ये निहिता काचित् क्रिया फलवती भवतु * हितोप Hence a worthless or bad p upil or recipi ent of instruction

अद्रि *m* 1 A mountain 2 A stone especially one for pounding S ma with 3 A thunderb lt –4 A tree –5 The sun –6 A mass of clouds a cloud –7 A kind of measure –8 The number seven –Comp —ईश *m* —पति *m* —नाथ *m* 1 The lord of mountains the Himâlayas 2 An epithet of Siva (L rd of Kailâsa) —कर्णी *f* A plant (अपराजिता) Clitoria Ternatea

Lin —कन्या f The earth —श m N of the mountain विदुम —गुहा A mountain cave mountain side —ज —जात a Produced from or found among mountains mountain born —ज n Red chalk (गैरिकधातु) —जा f A plant (सिंहली) 2 —कन्या,—तनया —सुता &c Pârvatî —तनया —नन्दिनी 1 N of Pârvatî 2 N of a metre of 4 lines each having 23 syllables —द्विष् —भिद् m Indra the enemy or splitter of mountains (or clouds personified) —द्रोणी f 1 A mountain valley 2 A river rising in a mountain —पति राज &c m The Himalaya mountain —भू a Mountain born —भू f N of a plant (आखुकर्णी or अपराजिता) —वह्नि m A forest conflagration —शय्य m N of Siva —शृङ्ग n, —सानु m —सानु n A mountain peak —सार m The essence of mountains i e iron —सार a Hard like a mountain

अद्रोह m Absence of malice or ill feeling; moderation mildness

अद्वयस् a Free Not envious

अद्वन्द्व a (f —न्द्वा) Without duality or enmity

अद्वय a (f —या) 1 Not two 2 Without a second unique, sole —य m 1 N of Buddha 2 A follower of बुद्ध —य n Non-duality unity identity especially the identity of Brahman and the universe or of spirit and matter; the highest truth Comp —आनन्द m The joy arising from a knowledge of the identity of the Supreme Spirit and the world —वादिन् m One who holds or teaches the doctrine of the identity of Brahman and the universe 2 Buddha

अद्वयु a Free from duplicity, the same internally or externally

अद्वार n Not a door; a passage or entrance which is not meant to serve as a door

अद्वितीय a (f —या) 1 Without a second matchless, peerless; अद्वितीयं रूपं तस्य ... मालविका 2 2 Without a companion alone —3 Sole unique supreme —यं n Brahman

अद्वेष a Free from hatred or malevolence —ष m Freedom from hatred

अद्वैत a (f —ता) 1 Not dual; of one or uniform nature, unchanging; —तं सुखदुःखयोः ... 1 —2 Matchless, peerless, sole, unique —तं n 1 Non-duality, identity 2 The identity of Brahman with the universe or with the soul; the identity of the soul and matter —3 The supreme or highest truth or Brahman itself —Comp —आनन्द m The joy arising from a knowledge of the identity of the universe and the Supreme Spirit —वादिन् m One who holds the doctrine of the identity of ब्रह्मन् (n) with the universe; a वेदान्तिन्

अद्वैध a Pure deep attachment

अधन a (f —ना) 1 Without wealth poor —2 Not entitled to possess independent property (in law) n Poverty

अधन्य a (f —न्या) Unhappy wretched, miserable

अधम a (f —मा) The lowest, meanest; very bad, low, or vile —म m 1 An unblushing sensu alist. -2 A sort of योग or conjunction of planets. —मा *f.* A bad mistress. -Comp.—अंग *n.* The foot (as opp. to उत्तमांग which means the head). —अधम *a.* The vilest of the vile, the meanest of the mean. -अर्ध *n.* The lower half of the body (below the navel). —आचार *a.* Of the vilest conduct. —आचार: *m.* A person of the meanest conduct. —ऋण:, -ऋणिक: *m.* A debtor, (opp. उत्तमर्ण:). —भृत:-भृतक *m.* A porter, groom, a servant of the lowest class.

अधर *a.* (*f.* —रा) 1 Lower, inferior, under, nether, downward. -2 Low, mean, vile. -3 Silenced, worsted, vanqnished (in a debate). -4 Previous, preceding. —र: *m.* The lower lip ; a lip in general. पक्वबिंबाधरोष्ठी * मेघदू. पिबासि रतिसर्वस्वमधरं * शाकुंत. 1 24. *f.* —रा *f.* The point in the sky diametrically opposite to the zenith ; the nadir. 2. Southern direction. —रं *n.* 1. The lower part (of the body). -2 Address, speech (opp. उत्तर). 3. A statement. 4. A reply.-Comp. —उत्तर *a.* 1. Higher and lower, inferior and superior, worse and better ; राज्ञ: समक्षमेवावयो: —व्यक्तिर्भविष्यति * मालवि. 1. 2. Prior and later ; sooner and later 3. Inverted in order, topsy-turvy. 4. Nearer and further. अधरोत्तरं *n.* Question and answer. —ओष्ठ: *m.* (forming अधरोष्ठ) The lower lip. —कंठ: *m.* The lower part of the neck. —काय: *m.* The lower part of the body. —पानं *n.* Kissing (drinking) the lower lip. —मधु, *n.* अमृतं *n.* The nectar of the lips. —स्वस्तिकं *n.* The nadir.

अधराचीन-राच्य *a.* Situated in the region below ; being downwards.

अधराच् *a.* Southward ; tending downwards, tending to the south. —ची *f.* The southern direction. —क् *ind.* Beneath.

अधरीण *a.* (*f.* —णा) 1 Lower. -2 Censured, reproached.

अधरेद्यु: *ind.* 1 On a previous day. -2 The day before yesterday ; the other day.

अधर्म: *m.* 1 Unrighteous conduct, irreligion, wickedness, injustice ; an unjust, guilty or wicked act ; a sin. 2. N. of a Prajâpati. —र्मा *f.* Goddess of unrighteousness. —र्मं *n.* Brahman (*n.*). -Comp. चारिन् *a.* Committing unjust or unrighteous deeds. —आत्मन् *m.* Of an irreligious spirit. —मय *a* Full of wickedness or sin.

अधर्मिन् *a.* (*f.* —र्मिणी) Impious wicked.

अधर्म्य *a.* 1 Wicked, impious. Illegal, unlawful.

अधवा *f.* A widow.

अधस्, अध: *ind.* 1 Below, down ; downwards. 2. In the lower region, to the infernal regions or hell ; in the Patâlâ Loka. As first member of compound words अध: may have an adjectival sense. अध: may govern the ablative, the locative, and the accusative.—अंशुकं *n.* The under or lower garment. -Comp. —अक्ष *a.* Situated below the axle or car, the axle. —अक्षज: *m.* A N. of Vishnu or Krishna. —अधस् *ind.* Lower and lower. *adv.* Situated below the car, under axle. -उपासनं *n* The act of sexual intercourse, —अंगं, —द्वारं, —मर्म *n.* The anus. —का: *m.* The lower part of the hand (करभ). —करणं *n.*, —क्रिया *f.* Excelling, defeating, degradation, dishonour. —खननं *n.* Undermining. —गतिः *f.*. —गमनं *n.* —पातः *m.* A downward fall or motion, descent ; going downwards, degradation, downfall, going to perdition or hell. —खनु *m.* One who digs downwards, a mouse. —गं-घं-टा *f.* A plant Achyranthes Aspera, (Mar. आघाडा). —चरः *m.* A thief. —जानु *n.* The lower part of the knee. -*ind.* Below the knee. —जिह्विका *f.* The uvula (Mar. पडजीभ). —तलं *n.* The lower part or surface. —दिश् *f.* The lower region, the nadir; the southern direction. —दृष्टि *a.* Casting a downward look ; a posture in Yoga. —पदं *n.* The place under the foot, a lower place. —पातः *m.* Degradation, sinking downwards, fall into Hell. —प्रस्तरः *m.* A seat of grass for persons in mourning to sit upon. —भक्तं *n.* A dose of water, medicine, &c. to be taken after meals. —भागः *m.* The lower part (of the body), or of any thing ; the region below. —भुवनं *n.* The nether world. —भूः *f.* The lower ground, land at the foot of a hill. —मुख,-वदन *a.* Having the face downwards. —जः *m.* N. of Vishnu. —खं *n.* A group of certain *nakshatras*, which are मूलाश्लेषा कृत्तिका च विशाखा भरणी तथा । मघा पूर्वात्रयं चैव अधोमुखगणः स्मृतः ॥ —मुखं *n.* N. of a hell. —यंत्रं *n.* An apparatus in which the liquid to be distilled is placed, the vapour being afterwards cooled down into a liquid ; a still. —रक्तपित्तं *n.* The discharge of blood from the anus and urethra. —लंबः *m.* 1. A plummet. 2. A perpendicular. -3. The lower world. —लोकः *m.* The nether world. —वायुः *m.* Breaking wind, flatulency. —शय,-श्य *a.* Sleeping on the ground. —शय्या *f.* Sleeping on the ground. —स्थ,-स्थित *a.* Situated below. —स्वस्तिकं The nadir.

अधस्तन *a.* (*f* -नी) 1 Lower, situated beneath. -2 Prior, previous.

अधस्तरा (मा) म् *ind.* Very low.

अधस्तात् *adv* or *prep.* Down; below, under, beneath, under-neath, &c. (with gen),

अधामार्गवः *m.* A plant Achyranthes Aspera, (Mar. आघाडा).

अधारणक *a.* Not profitable ; profitless.

आधिः *f.* Same as आधिः 1 Mental pain or agony. -2 A woman in her courses.

अधि —*ind.* 1 As a prefix to verbal forms अधि means above, over and above, besides. As a prefix to nominal forms अधि shows excellence, superiority, abundance. As a separable adverb or preposition, अधि means over, upon, concerning. In composition with nouns अधि often forms adverbs and has the sense of on, concerning, in, &c. -Comp. —क्ष *a.* (*f.* —क्षा) 1. Perceptible to the senses. 2. Presiding over, superintending. —क्षः *m.* A superintendent, president. —अक्षरं *n.* The syllable ओम्. —अग्नि *ind.* Near the fire, on the fire. *n.* A gift given to a woman at the time of her marriage. —अधि *ind.* On high, (with *acc.*) —अधिक्षेपः *m.* High censure —अर्ध *a.* Together with its half. e. g. अध्यर्धांशः *a.* Portion together with its whole, *i. e.* a portion and its half. —आत्म *ind.* Concerning the soul or ब्रह्म (*n*) —आत्मन् *m.* The soul. —आत्मविद्या *f.*, —आत्मशास्त्रं *n.* The science of the soul. —आत्मरतिः *f.* Delight in the contemplation of the Supreme Soul. —ईश्वरः *m.* The Supreme lord. —कर्मन् *n.* Supervision, superintendence. —कर्मकरः *m.* Supervisor. —कामः *m.* Ardent passion. —गुण *a.* Highly meritorious, possessing highly praise-worthy qnalities. —जिह्वः *m.* A tumour on the tongue. —ज्य *a.* Having the bow-string attached (to the bow). —दंतः *m.* A tooth growing over another. दिनः *m.* An intercalated day. —देवः *m.* A supreme deity. –*a* देवता *f.* The presiding deity. —दैवतं *n.* A tutelary or presiding divinity. —नाथः *m.* The supreme lord. —पतिः *m.* The master, owner, ruler, king. —पुरुषः, —पूरुषः *m.* The Supreme Spirit. —प्रज *a.* Having many children. —भूतं *n* The Supreme Spirit. —मात्र *a.* Past measure, excessive. —मासः *m.* An intercalary month. —यज्ञः *m.* The Supreme Spirit. —राज्, —राजः *m* An emperor, a supreme ruler. —राज्यं *n.* Supremacy, an empire. —लोकं *ind.* In the universe; about the universe. —वचनं *n.* I. Advocacy. 2. A name, a title. –श्री *a.* Very beautiful, very rich. —हरि *ind.* About Hari, in Hari. A Superintendent, president.

अधिक *a.* (*f.* —का) I More, additional, greater. 2. Plus, greater by; *e. g.* अष्टाधिकं शतं 100 plus8=108. 3. Inordinate, grown, increased, become greater; abounding in; full of; strong in; senior in years. 4. Superior to, better than; higher than (with abl. तपस्विभ्योऽधिको योगी *भग* 6. 46. –5 Later, subsequent, further than (of time). –6 Eminent, uncommon, special, peculiar (असाधारण); विद्या नाम नरस्य रूपमधिकं *भर्तृह*. धर्मो हि तेषामधिको विशेषः *हितोप*. Redundant, superfluous. –7. Intercalated, intercalary (as a month &c.). –9 Inferior, secondary. —कं *n.* I Surplus, excess. –2 Abundance, redundancy, superfluity. –3 A figure of speech in which the container or the contained is represented as being vaster than the contained or the container. आश्रयाश्रयिणोरेकस्याधिक्येऽधिकमुच्यते साहि. द. *e. g.* अहो विशालं भूपाल भुवनत्रितयोदरं। माति मातुमशक्योऽपि यशोराशिर्यदत्र ते। –*adv.* I More, in a greater degree. –Comp. —अंग *a.* (गी *f.*) Having a redundant limb. —गं *n.* A girdle or belt worn over the mail coat. —अधिक *a.* More and more, out doing one another. —अर्थ *a.* Exaggerated. वचनं *n.* Exaggeration, hyperbole, caricature. —ऋद्धि *a.* Abundant, prosperous. —तिथिः, *f.* -दिनं *n.* -दिवसः *m.* An intercalated day. —दंतः *m.* A tooth growing over another. —मासः *m.* An intercalary month —वाक्योक्तिः *f.* Exaggeration, hyperbole.

अधिकरणं *n.* I Placing at the head of, appointing –2 Relation, reference, connection. –3 (In gram.) Agreement, concord, apposition. –4 A receptacle or subject, substratum. –5 Location, place, the sense of the location, place, the sense of the locative case. –6 A topic, subject; section, or argument treating of one subject; the

Sutras of Vyâsa and Jaimini are divided into Adhyayas, an Adhaya into Padas and a Pâda into Adhikaranas or sections. The general Adhikarana consists of five members :—विषय the subject matter tc be explained. विशय or संशय the doubt or question arising upon that matter, पूर्वपक्ष the view taken by the opponent उत्तर or उत्तरपक्ष or सिद्धांत the rejoinder or answer or demonstrated conclusion, representing the correct ultimate view maintaned by the सिद्धांतिन्, and lastly the निर्णय the final conclusion arrived at after a weighing of the two views by arguments for and against. विषयो विशयश्चैव पूर्वपक्षस्तथोत्तरं । निर्णयश्चेति सिद्धांतः शास्त्रेऽधिकरणं स्मृतम् ॥ -7 Court of justice, court, tribunal. -8 Stuff, material, -9 A claim. -10 Supremacy. -Comp. —भोजकः *m.* A judge. —मंडपः *m.* A court or hall of justice —सिद्धांतः *m.* A syllogism or conclusion which involves others.

अधिकरणिकः *m* 1 A judge, magistrate. -2 A government official.

अधिकरण्यं *n.* Authority, power.

अधिकर्मन् *n.* 1 A higher or superior act. -2 Superintendence. -*m.* One who is charged with superintendence. - Comp. —करः,-कृत् *m.* A servant, overseer of workmen. —वृत् *m.* One appointed to superintend an institution or establishment.

अधिकाम *a.* Of vehement desires, impassioned, lustful. —मः *m* Strong desi e.

आधिकार्मिकः *m* The overseer of a market whose duty it is to recover toll or duties from the traders.

अधिकारः *m.* 1 Superintendence, watching over. -2 Duty, office, charge ; power, post of authority; authority. स्वाधिकारात् प्रमत्तः * मेघदू. 1. -3 Sovereignity, government or administration, jurisdiction, rule. -3 Position, dignity, rank. -5 Right of ownership or possession; claim, privilege, title as to a property, &c. Qualification or authority to perform certain specified duties. -6 Prerogative of a king. -7 Effort, exertion ; कर्मण्येवाधिकारस्ते मा फलेषु कदाचन * भगव. 2. 47. -8. Relation, reference. -9 Place ; location. -10 A topic, paragraph or section. -11. (In gram.) A governing rule, which exerts a governing influence over other rules. -Comp. —स्थ, —आरूढ *a.* Invested with authority, or office.

अधिकारिन्, अधिकारवत् *a.* (*f.* —णी, -ती) 1 Possessed of authority, having power. -2 Entitled to, having a right to. -3 Belonging to, owned by. -4 Fit for. —री *m.* 1 An official, officer ; superintendent, director, governor. -2 A rightful claimant, proprietor, master. -3 One qualified to sacrifice or perform sacred rites. -4 Man as the lord of creation. -5 One well versed in the Vedânta.

अधिकृ 8 U. 1 To authorize, be entitled to, have a right to. -2 To place at the head of, appoint, set. -3 To allude or refer to, make the subject of. -4 To be used as the head or governing rule. -5 To superintend, be at the head. -6 (A.) To bear, endure or over power, be superior to. -7 To feel, enjoy. -8 To refrain or desist from

अधिकृत *p. p. a.* (*f.* —ता) Authorised, appointed; possessing authority, qualification, &c. —त: *m.* An officer, official, functionary, superintendent, one in charge of any thing.

अधिकृति: *f.* Right, privilege, ownership.

अधिकृत्य *ind.* With reference to, about, regarding, concerning ; ग्रीष्मसमयमधिकृत्य गीयतां * शाकुंत. I; शाकुंतलामधिकृत्य ब्रवीमि * शाकुंत. 2.

अधिक्रम् (अधि + क्रम् I U.) To ascend, mount upon. -2 To attack, scale.

अधिक्रम:, *m.* —क्रमणं *n.* An attack, invasion.

अधिक्षित् *m.* Decay or one that causes decay.

अधिक्षिप् (अधि + क्षिप् 6. P. I To insult, abuse, asperse, censure. न मे पादरजसा तुल्य इत्यधिक्षिप्त: * मालवि. I. -2 To throw or lay upon, bespatter. -3 To superinduce (disease). -4 To surpass.

अधिक्षेप: *m.* I Comtempt, scorn, blame, abuse, insult. -2 Laying upon ; fixing; throwing. -3 Dismissal. साधिक्षेपं *ind* Scornfully.

अधिगत *pp. a.* (*f.* —ता). I Obtained, acquired. 2. Reached. 3. Accomplished. 4. Studied, known, mastered. 5. Seen, discovered, found.

अधिगंतृ *a.* One who attains or acquires.

अधिगम (अधि + गम्, गच्छ् I. P.) I. To obtain, to acquire. 2. To go to, approach, reach, to have access to. 3. To accomplish, fulfill. 4. To study, learn, understand; know, to master. 5 To meet with, find, see, discover. 6. To cohabit with; to take a husband.

अधिगम: *m.* —मनं *n.* I Acquisition, obtaining, getting, finding reaching. -2 Mastery, study, knowledge. -3 Profit ; acquiring property. -4 Acceptance. -5 Intercourse.

अधिगम्य , -गमनीय, -गंतव्य *pot p.* (*f.* —म्या, —नीया, —व्या) Attainable, obtainable, approachable, that can be seen, mastered, studied.

अधिगुण *a.* (*f.* —णा) I Possessing superior qualities, worthy, meritorious ; याच्ञा मोघा वरमधिगुणे नाधमे लब्धकामा * मेघदू. 6. -2 That has the string attached to it or well strung (as a bow). —ण: *m* A superior.

अधिचर् (अधि + चर I P.) To walk or move over or on something.

अधिचरणं *n.* Act of walking over something.

अधिजननं *n.* Birth.

अधिजिह्व: *m.* A serpent.—ह्वा-जिह्विका *f.* I The uvula. (Mar. पडजीभ). -2 A sort of swelling of the tongue or epiglottis.

अधिज्य *a.* Having the bow-string stretched, well strung (as a bow). Comp. —धन्वन्,-कार्मुक *a.* Having the bow strung; कृष्णसारे ददच्चक्षु: त्वयि चाधिज्यकार्मुके * शकुंत. I. 6.

अधिज्यता *f.* I The state of being strung ; -तां नी to string; निन्यतु: स्थलनिवेशिताटनी कीलयैव धनुषी अधिज्यतां * रघुवं. II. 14.

अधित्यका *f.* A table-land, highland ; स्थाणुं तपस्यंतमधित्यकायां * कुमा. सं. 3. 17; अधित्यकायामिवधातुमय्यां. * रघुवं. 2. 59.

अधिदंडनेतृ *m.* N. of Yama.

अधिदंत: *m.* A redundant tooth, or a tooth growing over another.

अधिदीधिति *a.* Of a superior or transcendental lustre.

अधिदेव: *m.*, अधिदेवता *f.*, अधिदैवतं *n.* 1 A presiding or tutelary deity. ता राजिरायकानिवेरधिदेवता वा * माल. मा. 1. 21. 2. The supreme or highest god, Almighty.

अधिदेवनं *n.* Gambling table, board for gambling.

अधिदैवं, दैवतं *n.* 1 The presiding god or deity. -2 The supreme deity.

अधिनाथ: *m.* The Supreme lord. Regarding creation (of the world). Concerning the production of the race.

अधिनाथ: *m.* Fragrance, odour.

अधिप: *m.* A lord, ruler, king, sovereign, head ; अथ प्रजानामधिप: प्रभाते * रघुवं. 2. 1. श्रिय: कुरूणामधिपस्य... * किराता. 1. 1.

अधिपति: *m.* A king, lord, head, sovereign, ruler. -2 A certain sensitive part of the head where the wound proves immediately fatal.

अधिपु (पू) रुष: *m.* The Supreme Being.

अधिप्रज *a.* Having many children (as a man, woman, &c.) —जं *ind.* Regarding creation of the world.

अधिबलं *n.* An angry and vehement debate, discourse.

अधिभू: *m.* A master, superior, ruler, foremost.

अधिभूतं *n.* The Supreme Spirit ; the whole inanimate creation ; अधिभुतं च किं प्रोक्तं * भगव. 8. 1; अधिभूतं क्षरो भाव: भगव. 8. 4.

अधिभोजनं *n.* 1 Excess in eating. Iudulging in costly or valuable food.

अधिमख: *m.* The regulator of a sacrifice.

अधिमंथ: *m.* 1 A disease of the eye, severe ophthalmia. 2. Production of fire by friction.

अधिमंथनं *n.* Friction exerted in producing fire. Rubing together for producing fire. *a.* Suitable for such friction (as wood).

अधिमंथित *a.* Suffering from eye-disease.

अधिमांस: *m.* A sort of disease in the white of the eye, a sort of cancer or protuberance of flesh. (Mar. राजणवाढी).

अधिमांसक: *m.* A disease of the gums. A sort of cancer in the back of the gums.

अधिमात्र *a* Beyond measure, excessive, inordinate. —त्रं *ind.* On the subject of prosody.

अधिमास: *m.* An intercalary (lunar) month.

अधिमुक्ति: *f.* Trust, confidence.

अधिमुह्य: *m.* N. of Buddha in one of his 34 former births.

अधियज्ञ *a.* Pertaining to a sacrifice —ज्ञ: *m.* Principal sacrifice ; the presiding deity of such a sacrifice. —ज्ञं *ind.* On the subject of sacrifices.

अधियांगं *n.* A belt, a girdle.

अधियोग: *m.* An auspicious conjunction of stars for departure, expedition, &c.

अधियोध: *m.* A great warrior. The foremost hero (in fighting).

अधिरज्जु *a.* Fastening, fettering.

आधिरथ *a.* That has mounted a chariot. Being on or over a car. —थ: *m.* 1 A charioteer, driver. -2 N. of a charioteer. Husband of राधा and foster-father of Karna.

अधिराज्, —जः m. A sovereign or supreme ruler, an emperor. हिमालयो नाम नगाधिराजः * कुमा. स. 1. 1.

अधिराज्य-ई n. Imperial or sovereign sway, supremacy, imperial dignity, an empire.

अधिरुक्म a. Having ornaments of gold on the body.

अधिरुह् (अधि + रुह् 1 P.) 1 To ascend, mount (a throne, hill &c.), sit in or on (acc.). -3 (Intran.) To rise or grow over or above. -*Caus.* 1 To raise, place, seat, cause to mount or ascend. -2 To restore, give back. -3 To string (as a bow). -4 To give, to grant.

अधिरुह् a. (At the end of comp.) Growing on.

अधिरूढ p. p. a. (f. —ढा) 1 Mounted, ascended. -2 Increased.

अधिरोपणं n. Act of raising, exalting or causing to mount.

अधिरोह: m. An elephant rider.

अधिरोहणं n Ascending, mounting. —हणी, or —हिणी f. A ladder, flight of steps (Mar. शिडी).

अधिरोहिन् a. Ascending, mounting, rising above —णी f. A ladder flight of steps.

अधिवक्तृ m. One who advocates a particular cause, an advocate. -2 An orator. -3 A comforter.

अधिवच् (अधि + वच् 2. P.) To speak in favour of, advocate, side with.

अधिवचनं n. 1 Advocacy, speaking in favour of -2 A title, name, epithet, appellation.

अधिवस् (अधि + वस् 1 P.) To inhabit, fix one's abode or residence in, settle, dwell or reside in (with acc. of place); नीचैराख्यं गिरिमधिवसेस्तत्र विश्रामहेतोः * मेघदू. 25; वाल्यात्परामिव दशां मदनोऽध्युवास * रघुवं. 5. 63. -2 To settle, alight or perch on. -*Caus.* 1 To cause to stay overnight. -2 To consecrate, set up (as an image). (अधि + वस् 2 A.) To put on (clothes).

अधिवास: m. 1 Abode, residence; dwelling, settlement, habitation. -2 An inhabitant, neighbour. -3 Obstinate pertinacity in making a demand. Sitting without food before a person's house till he grants a demand (Mar. धरणें धेऊन बसणें.). The act of causing a divinity to take up its abode in an image. See अधिवासनं also. -5 An upper garment, mantle, (अधीवास: also).

अधिवाक: m. Advocacy. A speech made on behalf of or in fovour of another.

अधिवास (अधि + वास् 10 U.) To scent, perfume; to fumigate.

अधिवास: m. Application of perfumes or fragrant cosmetics; scenting, perfuming; fragrance, scent, fragrant odour; अधिवासस्पृहयेव मारुतः * रघुवं 8. 34.

अधिवासनं n. Scenting with perfumes or odorous substances. -2 The act of making a divinity assume its abode in an image.

अधिवासिन् a. (f. —नी) 1 Inhabiting, dwelling or siting in. -2 Scenting, perfuming, fumigating.

अधिवासित p. p. a. (f. —ता) Taking up, carrying over, conveying.

अधिविद् (अधि + विद् 6 U.) To marry in addition to, supersede (as a wife).

अधिविन्ना f. A superseded wife, one whose husband has married again.

अधिवेतृ m. A husband who supersedes his first wife.

अधिवेद: *m*. Marrying an additional wife. -दं *adv*. Concerning the Vedas.

अधिवेदनं *n*. Marrying an additional wife.

अधिशयित *p. p. a*. (*f*. —ता) Reclining upon.

अधिशी (अधि + शी 2 A.) To lie or sleep upon, sleep in, to dwell, inhabit, (with acc. of place). —*Caus*. To cause to sleep on.

अधिश्रय: *m*. A place, a receptacle.

अधिश्रयणं-पणं *n*. Placing on fire ; warming, boiling. —णी *f*. An oven, a fire-place.

अधिश्रि (अधि + श्रि I U.) I To sleep on, ascend, mount, resort to

अधिश्री *a* Of a high rank or of exalted dignity, supreme ; very rich, sovereign lord.

अधिषवणं *n*. I A contrivance to extract and strain the Soma juice. &c. -2 Straining or extracting the Soma juice.

अधिषवण्या *f*. The wooden plank used for extracting Soma juice.

अधिष्ठा (अधि + स्था I P.) (used with acc.) I. To stand on or upon, to sit in or upon, occupy, to inhabit, reside, resort to ; to stand by or near, to stand, be. -2 To take possession of, overpower, conquer. 3. To lead, conduct as head or chief. To be at the head of, superintend. -4 To use, employ.

अधिष्ठातृ *a*. (*f*. त्री) Superintending, presiding over, guiding, governing, tutelary, guardian. *m*. -ष्ठाता *m*. *nom sing*. A superintendent, head, chief, controller.

अधिष्ठानं *n*. I. Approach. 2. A basis, site. 3. Residence, seat, occupation, abode. 4. A town. 5. Power, domination, authority, government. 6 A prescribed rule, a precedent. 7. A benediction. 8. A wheel of a cart. -Comp. —शरीरं *n* A body which forms the medium between the subtle and the gross body.

अधिष्ठित *p. p. a*. (*f*. —ता) I Standing, being. 2 Directing, presiding over. ; watched over, guarded, superintended. 3 Inhabited, occupied, possessed by. 4 Full of, seized with, smitten, affected, overpowered. 5 Led, conducted, presided over. 6 Ridden, mounted upon.

अधिस्त्रि *ind*. Concerning a woman or wife. —स्त्री *f*. A superior or distinguished woman.

अधिस्यंदं *ind*. More quickly.

अधी (अधि + इ 2 A) I To study, learn (by heart), read, to know. 2. To think of with regret. -*Caus*. To teach, instruct.

अधीकार: *m*. The same as अधिकार: *q. v*.

अधीत *p. p. a*. (*f*. —ता) Learnt, studied, read, remembered, mastered.

अधीति: *f*. I Study, perusal. -2 Remembrance, recollection.

अधीतिन् *a*. (*f*. —नी) Well-read proficient in (with loc.).

अधीन *a*. (*f*. —ना) Dependent on subservient, being in the power of. त्वदधीनं खलु देहिनां सुखं * कुमा. सं. 4. 10,

अधीमंथ: *m*. A disease of the eye.

अधीयान: *pres. p*. A student, one who recites the Vedas.

अधीर *a*. (*f*. —रा) Confused, excited, -2 Fitful, capricious. -3 Unsteady, tremulous, rolling. -4 Foolish, weak-minded. —रा *f*. I. Lightning. -2 A capricious or quarrelsome mistress, one of the नायिका s. 8. —र: *m*. A bad physician.

अधीवास: *m*. A long coat or mantle covering the whole person.

अधीश: *m*. Lord, sovereign ruler.

अधीश्वर: *m*. 1 A supreme lord or an employer.

अधीष्ट *a*. (*f*. —ष्टा) Honourary, solicited. —ष्टं *n*. Solicitation. 2. Honourary office or duty.

अधुना *ind*. Now, at this time ; असति त्वयि वारुणीमद: प्रमदानामधुना विडंबना * कुमा. सं. 4. 12.

अधुनातन *a*. (*f*. —नी) Belonging to the present times; of modern time.

अधुर् *a*. Not laden, free from the burden of cares &c. —धू: *f*. Absence of burden or cares.

अधूमक: *m*. Burning or blazing fire. Fire without smoke.

अधृत *a*. (*f*. —ता) Not held or controlled. —त: *m*. One of the 1000 names of Vishnu.

अधृति: *f*. 1 Want of firmness or control. -2 Incontinence. -3 Unhappiness.

अधृष्ट *a*. (*f*. -ष्टा) 1 Not bold, modest, shy. -2 Invincible, irresistible.

अधृष्य *a*. (*f*. —ष्या) 1 Invincible, unassailable ; unapproachable; अधृष्यश्चाभिगम्यश्च यादोरत्नैरिवार्णव: * रघुवं. 1. 16. 2 Modest, shy. -3 Proud.

अधेनु: *f*. A cow not yielding milk.

अधोऽक्ष: *a*. Lying or being under the axle.

अधोपहास: *m*. Sexual intercourse.

अध्यक्ष *a*. 1 Perceptible ot the senses, visible. Exercising supervision. —क्ष: *m*. 1 A superintendent, president, controller, lord, master, -2 An eye-witness. -3 N. of a plant (क्षीरिका) Mimusops Kauki. (Mar मोठी रूई)

अध्यक्षरं *ind*. On the subject of syllables. —रं *n*. The syllable ओम्.

अध्यग्नि *ind*. Over, by, or near the nupital fire. -*n*. A gift made to a woman at the time of her marriage.

अध्यंच् *a*. 1 Tending upwards ; superior, eminent. -2 One who obtains or acquires.

अध्यंडा *f*. N. of two plants (अजशृंगी) Carpopogon Pruriens, and भूम्यामलकी Flacourtia Cataphracta.

अध्यधि *ind*. On high (acc.).

अध्याधिक्षेप: *m*. Excessive abuse or censure, gross abuse.

अध्यधीन, *a*. a Completely subject, or dependent, as a slave.

अध्यय: *m*. Studying. Remembering.

अध्ययनं *n*. Reading, study, learning.

अध्यर्ध *a*. Having an additional half. —र्ध: *m*. 1 Wind. 2. The upper half.

अध्यर्बुदं *n*. A tumour, goitre. —द: *m*. The wind.

अध्यवसानं *n*. 1 Effort, exertion, determination. -2 (In Rhet.) The swallowing up of an obiect by another ; the expressing in words, of an obiect, with which a certain other object is identi fied, without expressing the object so identified. e. g. when we are speaking of माणवक if we only say अग्निरयं it is अध्यवसान and such an expression is called साध्यवसाना लक्षणा.

अध्यवसाय: *m*. 1. An undertaking, attempt, effort, exertion. -2 Determination; mental effort or apprehension. -3 Perseverance, energy, constancy.

अध्यवसायिन् *a.* (*f.* —नी)· Attempting ; resolute, persevering, energetic.

अध्यवसित *p. p. a.* (*f.* —ता) Attempted, mentally apprehended, determined

अध्यवसो (अधि + अव + सो 4 P.) 1 To determine, resolve. वासवदत्ता-कथं मम दु:खभागिन्यावयनादिवमध्यवसितमार्यपुत्रेण * रत्नाव. 4-2 To attempt, exert, undertake. -3. To grapple with. -4 To conceive, apprehen , think·

अध्यवहननं *n.* Pounding again what has once been pounded.

अध्यशनं *n.* Excessive eating, eating before the last meal is digested.

अध्यस् (अधि + अस् 4 P.) 1 To place upon another, add or append to. -2 (In Phil.) To attribute the nature of one thing to another.

अध्यस्त *p. p a* (*f.* —स्ता) 1 Placed upon or over. -2 Attributed, wrongly ascribed or supposed.

अध्यस्थि *n.* A bone growing over another.

अध्याक्रम् (अधि +आ + क्रम् 1 U.) 1 To fix upon, to occupy. -2 To attack.

अध्याक्रांत *a.* (*f.* —ता) Taken possession of, occupied.

अध्यात्म *a.* Belonging to self or person ; concerning self or person ; concerning an individual. —त्मं *ind.* Concerning self. —त्मं The Supreme Spirit or the relation betw en the supreme and the individiual soul -Comp. — ज्ञानं *n.* -विद्या *f.* The knowledge of the Supreme Spirit or आत्मन्. अध्यात्मज्ञ्-विद् *a.* One proficient in the knowledge of the Supreme Spirit· अध्यात्मयोग: *m* The concentrati n of the mind on the Atman, drawing it off from all objects of sense. अध्यात्मरति *a* One who delights in the contemplation of the Supreme Spirit । अध्यात्मरामायण *n.* N. of a Ramayana which treats of the relation between the supreme and the individual soul, while it narrates Rama's story.

अध्यात्मिक *a.* (*f.* की) Relating to the knowledge the Brahman (*n.*)

अध्यापक: *m.* A teacher, a preceptor

अध्यापनं *n.* Instruction, teaching

अध्याय: *m* 1. Study. 2. A lecture. 3. The time when sacred books are to be read. 4. A chapter of a book. 5. A reader. *a.* That studies.

अध्यायिन् *m.* (*f.* —नी). Studious, engaged in reading.

अध्यारुह् (अधि + आ + रुह्) 1 P. 1 To ascend, mount. (fig.). To gain ascendancy over, domineer over ; -*Caus.* 1 To cause to ascend, mount or sit in. -2 (-रोपयति) To entrust, to appoint, to cause to produce or bring about. To attribute falsely ; to exaggerate.

अध्यारूढ *p p. a* (*f.* —ढा) 1 Mounted, ascended, exalted, elevated.

अध्यारोप: *m.* 1. Act of raising, elevating -2 (In Vedânta phil.) Act of falsely or erroneously attributing the properties of one thing to another ; *e. g.* Considering a rope to be a serpent, or Brahman to be the material world. -3 Erroneous knowledge.

अध्यारोपणं *n.* 1 Raising &c. Same as अध्यारोप: -2 Sowing (seed).

अध्यारोपित *p. p. a.* (*f* —ता) Falsely attributed or supposed

अध्यावाप: *m* 1 Act of sowing or scattering (seed &c.). -2 A field in which seed &c. is sown.

अध्यावाहनिकं *n.* That part of a wife's property, which she receives when leaving her father's house for her husband's.

अध्यास् (अधि + आस् 2 A.) 1 (*a*) To lie down upon, occupy, dwell in, to inhabit, enter upon, get into. (with acc. of place). -2 To cohabit with. -3 To be directed or fixed upon. —*Caus.* To cause one to sit down upon or to occupy.

अध्यासः *m.* 1. Attributing erroneously the nature or properties of one thing to anotner (same as अध्यारोप). *2.* Residing in, presiding over. 3. Putting down upon (as in पदाध्यास).

अध्यासनं *n.* 1 Sitting down upon, occupying, presiding over. -*2* A seat, place.

अध्याहार: *m* —हरणं *n.* 1 Supplying an ellipsis. -2 Arguing; discussing; reasoning; inference or conjecture.

अध्युषित *a.* (*f.* —ता) Occupied, inhabited, dwelt in. —षितं *n.* Early morning.

अध्युष्ट *a.* Coiled up three and a half times.

अध्युष्ट्र: *m.* A Conveyance drawn or borne by camels.

अध्यूढ *a.* 1 Raised, exalted, elevated, hanging over. -2 Abundant, increased, copious. -3 Rich, affluent. —ढ: *m.* 1 Son of a wowan pregnant at the time of marriage. -2 Siva. —ढा *f* A wife whose husband has married another wife and thus superseded her (=आधिविन्ना q.v.)

अध्यूध्नी *f.* 1 A cow with full and fat udders. -2 The vessel (in the body) above the udder or above the scrotum.

अध्यूह् 1 U. 1 To overlay, place on or upon. -2 To raise above.

अध्यूहनं *n.* Raising or elevating, putting of a layer.

अध्येषणं *n.* Causing the preceptor to perform some religious rite. —णा *f.* Solicitation, entreaty.

अध्रिपुष्पिका *f.* The betelnut plant:

अध्रियमाण *a.* (*f.* —णा) 1 Not held, not to be got hold of.

अध्रुव *a.* (*f.* —वा) 1 Uncertain, doubtful. -2 Unsteady, moving, not fixed or permanent. —वं *n.* An uncertainty ; यो ध्रुवाणि परित्यज्य अध्रुवाणि निषेवते । ध्रुवाणि तस्य नश्यंति अध्रुवं नष्टमेव च * हितोप.

अध्रुष: *m.* A kind of disease attended with fever arising from the affection of blood ; quinsy.

अध्वन् *m.* 1 A way, road; passage, orbit. 2. Distance, space gone over. 3. Journey, travel, course, march. 4. A recension of the Vedas and the school upholding it. 5. Time (Kâla), time personified. 6. Air ; sky, atmosphere. -7 Place. —8. Means, resource ; method. -9 Attack. -Comp. —अति: *m.* A traveller. 2. An intelligent person. —अधिप:, —ईश: *m.* An officer in charge of the public roads. —अयनं *n* A journey, travel. —ग: 1 *m.* A traveller. way-farer. 2 A camel. 3 A mule. 4. The sun. -गा *f.* The Ganges. -जा A plant otherwise called स्वर्णपुष्पी. —पति: *m.* 1 The sun, 2. The inspector of the road. —रथ: *m.* 1. A travelling carriage. 2. A messenger. —शल्य: *m.* N. of a tree (अपामार्ग). (Mar आघाडा).

अध्वगमिन्, अध्वन्य *a.* (*f.* —ना,—न्या) Able to underake a journey, speeding on a journey. —गः-न्यः *m.* A traveller, way-farer.

अध्वरः *m* A sacrifice, a religious ceremony ; also a Soma sacrifice ; तमध्वरे विश्वजिति क्षितीशं * रघुवं. 5. 1. —रः *m.* —रं *n.* 1 Sky or air. -2 The second of the 8 Vasus. -Comp. —कल्पा *f.* An optional sacrifice (काम्येष्टि). —कांडं *n.* A part of the शतपथ. ब्राह्मण which treats of sacrifices. —ग *a.* Intended or meant for a sacrifice. —दीक्षणिया *f.* The consecration connected with an Adhvara. —मीमांसा *f.* N. of Jaimini's Purvamimânsâ. —श्रीः *f.* The glory of the Adhvara.

अध्वर्युः *m.* 1 An officiating priest, whose duty was to measure the ground, build the altar, prepare sacrificial vessels, to fetch wood and water, kindle the fire, bring the animal and immolate it, and while doing this to repeat Yajurveda. -2 The Yajurveda itself. —pl. Adherents of that Veda. -Comp. —वेदः *m.* The Yajaurveda.

अध्वातिः *m.* A traveller.

अध्वाम *a.* Dumb, mute.

अध्वांत *n.* Twilight, gloom, shade. —तः *m.* End of the journey. -Comp. —शात्रवः *m.* A plant (श्योनाक) Cassia Fistula or Bignonia Indica (blossoming in shade.).

अन् 2 P. 1 To breathe, live. 2 To move, go about.

अनः *m.* 1 Breath, respiration. 2. Each one of the five winds exhaled from the body. They are प्राण, अपान, व्यान, उदान, and समान.

अनंश *a.* 1 Not entitled to a share the inheritance. -2 Without parts, undivided, portionless ; an epithet of the sky, or the Supreme Being.

अनकदुंदुभिः *m.* Same as आनकदुंदुभि a name of वसुदेव.

अननं *n.* Act of breathing, living, &c.

अनकस्मात् *ind.* Not causelessly, not suddenly or accidentally.

अनक्ष *a.* 1 Without an axle-tree. -2 Sightless, blind.

अनक्षर *a.* (*f.* —रा) 1 Unable to speak, mute, dumb ; unlettered. -3 Unfit to be uttered. —रं *n.* Abusive language, foul or abusive words, censure. —रं *-adv.* Without the use of words, mutely, dumbly; by means of signs &c.

अनक्षि *n.* A bad eye, sore or weak eye.

अनगार *a.* Houseless. —रः *m.* An ascetic.

अनग्निः *m.* 1. That which is not fire, a substance other than fire. -2 Absence of fire. -*a.* 1 Not requiring fire, performed without the use of fire ; विद्वधे विधिमस्य नैष्ठिकं यतिभिः सार्धमनग्निमग्निचित् * रघुवं. -2 Not maintaining the sacred fire. Irreligious. -3 Dyspeptic. -4 Unmarried. -Comp. —दग्ध *a.* Not burnt according to the proper religious rites.

अनघ *a.* (*f.* —घा) 1 Sinless, innocent ; अवैमि चैनामनघेति * रघुवं. 14. 40. -2 Free from blame, faultless; handsome ; praisewarthy ; pure, spotless, free from dirt. 3. Free from danger, evil, calamity &c. ; safe, unhurt, कच्चिन्मृगीणामनघा प्रसूतिः * रघुवं 5. 7.

-4. Without grief or sorrow. —वः- *m.* 1 White mustard. -2 N. of Vishnu, also of Siva.

अनंकुश *a.* (*f.* —शा) 1 Ungovernable, unruly. -2 Taking licence(as a poet).

अनंग *a.* (*f.* —गा) 1 Bodiless; without a body; incorporeal; deprived of a body. त्वमनंगः कथमक्षता रतिः *. कुमा. सं. 4. 9. 2 Without parts or members. —गः *m.* Cupid; god of love. —गं *n.* 1 Sky, air, ther. -2 The mind. -Comp. —क्रीडा *f.* 1. Amorous sports. 2. N. of a metre of two lines, the first with 16 long, and second with 32 short, syllables. —द *a.* (*f.* —दा) Inspiring love; exciting love. —शत्रुः, —असुहृत् &c. *m.* N. of Siva. —शेखरः *m.* N. of a metre of four lines, each with 15 iambic feet.

अनच्छः *a.* (*f.* —च्छा) Not clear, dirty.

अनजका, अनजिका *f.* A miserable or small goat.

अनंजन *a.* (*f.* —ना) 1 Without collyrium, pigment, or paint. -2 Faultless, taintless. -3 Without any connection. —नं *n.* 1 The sky, the atmosphere. -2 The Supreme Spirit (परब्रह्म). 3. N. of Vishnu, or Naráyana.

अनडुत्क *a.* Having oxen.

अनडुह् *m.* (nom. अनड्वान्, –ह्वौ, –हः; instr. अनडुहा –डुद्भ्यां –डुद्भिः) (*f.* –अनडुही or –ड्वाही). 1 An ox, bull. -2 (Astr.) The sign Taurus. —ही or अनड्वाही *f.* A cow. -Comp. —जिव्हा *f.* A plant (गोजिव्हा, Mar. अंतमूळ).

अनणु *a.* Not small minute or fine; coarse. —णुः *m.* Coarse grain, peas, &c.

अनति *ind.* Not very much. अनति Stands as first member of many compound words whose meanings can easily be understood by the student.

अनतिविलंबिता *f.* The absence of delay; fluency as a speaker's qualification, one of the 35 Vâgqunas, mentioned by हेमचंद्र.

अनद्यः *m.* White mustard. (Mar. पांढरी मोहरी.).

अनद्यतन *a* (*f.* —नी) Not pertaining to this or the current day. Sanskrit grammarians use this term to denote the sense of the Imperfect or the Periphrastic future. —नः *m.* Not the current day; अतीतायाः रात्रेः पश्चार्धेन आगामिन्या रात्रेः पूर्वार्धेन सहितो दिवसोऽद्यतनः तद्भिन्नः कालः.

अनधिक *a.* (*f.* —का) Not more or excessive. -2 Boundless, perfect, vast. -3 Not capable of being enlarged or extended.

अनधिकारः *m.* Absence of authority, right, claim, &c. -Comp. —चर्चा *f.* Intermedling, officiousness.

अनधिकारिन् *a.* Not entitled to; not qualified for.

अनधिगत (*f.* —ता) Not obtained, acquired, mastered, or studied.

अनधीन *a.* (*f.* —ना) Independent. —नः,-नकः *m.* A carpenter working on his own account.

अनध्यक्ष *a.* (*f.* —क्षा) 1 Not before the eyes; unperceived; invisible. -2 Without a controller, having no superintendent.

अनध्ययनं *n.* अनध्यायः, *m.* Not studying; intermission of study; the time when there is or ought to be such intermission; a holiday.

अननं *n*. Breathing, living.

अननुभावुक *a*. (*f*. —विका) Unable to comprehend.

अनंत *a*. (*f*. —ता) Boundless (in time, space, quantity, or number). —तः *m*. 1 N. of Vishnu ; also of Vishnu's couch, the serpent *Sesha* ; of Krishna and his brother ; of Siva ; of the 14 th. Arhat ; of Vâsuki, the lord of serpents. -2 A cloud. -3 Talc, (Mar. अभ्रक). -4 The 23rd asterism श्रवण. -5 A silken cord with 14 knots tied round the right arm on the अनंतचतुर्दशी day. -6 The letter आ. —ता *f*. 1 The earth. -2 The number one. -3. N. of Parvati. -4 N. of various plants.—ती *f*. A small silken thread tied round the left arm of a woman. —तं *n*. 1 The sky, atmosphere. -2 Infinity, eternity. -3 Absolution, final beatitude. -4 The Supreme Spirit, Brahman. -Comp. —आत्मन् *m* the Supreme Spirit. —चतुर्दशी *f*. The 14th day of the bright half of Bhâdrapada when Ananta is worshipped. -जित् *m*. N. of Vâsudeva.-तीर्थकृत *m*. 1. One who visits many holy places. -तृतीया *f*. The third day of the bright half of भाद्रपद, मार्गशीर्ष, or वैशाख. —दृष्टि. *m*. N. of Siva, or of Indra. —देवः *m*. The serpent Sesha. 2. N. of Nârayana who sleeps on Sesha. —पार *a*. Of endless width ; boundless ; अनंतपारं किल शब्दशास्त्रं * पंचतं. —मूलः *m*. A medicinal plant ; (शारिवा). —राशिः *m*. An infinite quantity.-रूपः *n*. A name of Vishnu. —वातः *m*. A disease of the head. —विजयः *m*. N. of Yudhishthira's conchshell. —व्रतं *n*. The worship done on the अनंतचतुर्दशी day. —शीर्षः *m*. N. of Vishnu or the Supreme Being. —शीर्षा *f*. N. of the wife of Vâsuki.

अनंतक *a*. Boundless, endless ; eternal. —कं *n*. The Eternal or Infinite (among the Jainas).

अनंतर *a*. (*f*. —रा) 1 Having no interior. -2 Having no interval or interstice or pause (of space or time); compact, close. -3 Contiguous, neighbouring, adjoining. -4 Coming or happening immediately before or after. -5 Following, coming close upon. -6 Uninterrupted, unbroken, continuous. —रं *n*. 1 Contiguity, proximity. 2 Brahman, the Supreme Soul. —रं *ind*. Immediately after; afterwards. -Comp. —जः *m*. 1. The child of a Kshatriya or Vaisyâ mother, by a father belonging to the caste immediately above the mother's, (in religious law). 2. One born immediately before or after; a younger or elder brother. —जा *f*. A younger or elder sister.

अनंतराय *a*. (*f*. —या)Uninterrupted, without a break.

अनंतरीय *a*. (*f*. —या) Next in succession.

अनंतर्गर्भिन् *m*. N. of Kusa grass used for the पवित्रक.

अनंतवत् *a*. Endless, eternal. —*m*. One of Brahma's four feet ; earth, intermediate region, heaven, and ocean.

अनंत्य *a*. Endless, eternal, infinite. —त्यं *n*. 1 Eternity, infinity. -2 The foot of हिरण्यगर्भ.

अनंद *a.* Joyless, cheerless. —दः *m.* N. of a purgatory.

अनन्नं *n.* Not food ; that which is unfit to be eaten.

अनन्य *a.* (*f.* —न्या) 1 Not different ; identical, same, no other. -2 Sole, unique, without a second. भक्त्या लभ्यस्त्वनन्यया * भगव. 8. 22. -3 Undistracted (mind &c.) ; having no other object or person to think of ; अनन्याश्चिंतयंतो मां ये जनाः पर्युपासते * भगव. 9. 22. –Comp. —अर्थ *a.* Not subordinate ; principal. —आश्रित *a.* Independent ; not resorting to another. —आश्रितं *n.* An unencumbered estate (in law). —गतिः *f.* Sole resort or resource. —गतिक *a.* Having no other resource or help, having no other resource left. —चित्त,-चिंत, -चेतस्, -मनस्,-मानस,-हृदय *a.* Solely intent upon giving one's undivided thought or attention to. विचिंतयंती यमनन्यमानसा * शकुंत. 4. 1. —जः, जन्मन् *m.* Cupid, the god of love. —दृष्टि *a.* Gazing intently or steadfastly at. —देवः *m.* The Supreme Being. —परायण *a.* Devoted to no other (woman). -पूर्वः *m.* A husband having no other wife. -पूर्वा *f.* A wife who has had no previous husband. —भाज् *a.* Not devoted to any other person. —विषय *a.* Not applicable or belonging to any one else; exclusively applicable. —वृत्ति *a.* 1. Of the same nature. 2. Having no other means of livelihood. 3. Closely attentive. —शासन *a.* Not ruled over by any one else. -सामान्य, —साधारण *a.* Not common to any one else; applicable or belonging to one. —सदृश *a.* (*f.* —शी) Having no equal; matchless, peerless.

अनन्यादृश *a* (*f.* —शी) Not like others, singular.

अनन्वयः *m* 1 Want of connection. -2 (Rhet.) The figure of speech in which a thing is compared to itself. उपमानोपमेयत्वमेकस्यैव त्वनन्वयः * साहित्य. द. उपमानोपमेयत्वे एकस्यैवैक वाक्यगे अनन्वयः। गगनं गगनाकारं सागरः सागरोपमः। रामरावणयोर्युद्धं रामरावणयोरिव ॥.

अनन्वित *a.* 1 Unconnected. -2 Irrelevant, incoherent. -3 Not accompanied by ; devoid of.

अनप *a.* (*f.* —पा) Destitute of much water (as a pond).

अनपकरणं *n.* -कर्मन्, *n.* -क्रिया *f.* 1 Not harming or injuring. -2 Non-delivery. -3 (In law) Non-payment.

अनपकारः *m.* Harmlessness. -कार, or —कारिन् *a.* Harmless, innocent.

अनपत्य *a.* (*f.* —त्या) Without issue; childless, without heir. —ता *f.*, —त्वं *n.* Childlessness.

अनपत्रप *a.* (*f.* —पा) Impudent, shameless.

अनपभ्रंशः *m.* Not a corrupt word ; a grammatically correct form.

अनपर *a.* 1. Not otherwise engaged. 2. Having no other or second, sole.

अनपराध, -धिन् *a.* Innocent, guiltless, harmless. —धः *m.* Innocence.

अनपसर *a.* (*f.* —रा) Having no egress or passage to creep out of; unjustifiable, inexcusable. —रः *m.* An usurper.

अनपाय *a.* (*f.* —या) 1 Not liable to loss or decay. -2 Imperishable, undiminished, undecaying. —यः *m.* 1 Imperishable nature, freedom from decay, permanence. -2 N. of Siva.

अनपायिन् a. (f. —नी) Constant, steady, unfailing, durable; not transient.

अनपार्थ a. (f. —र्था) Having a reason based on good ground.

अनपुंसक n. Not the neuter, i. e. the masculine or feminine gender.

अनपेक्ष a. (f. —क्षा) 1 Regardless. -2 Careless, not heeding; indifferent. -3 Independent or irrespective (of another); not requiring any other thing; absolute. -4 Impartial. -5 Irrelevent, unconnected.

अनपेक्षा f. Disregard, indifference, carelessness. अनपेक्षं adv Without regard to, regardlessly, independently or irrespectively of; carelessly, accidentally.

अनपेक्षिन् a. (f. —क्षिणी) See अनपेक्ष above.

अनपेत a. 1 Not gone off, not past; present. -2 Not deviating from; faithful to, in harmony with, not leaving (with abl.). -3 Not devoid of; possessed of; ऐश्वर्यादनपेतमीश्वरमयं लोकोऽर्थत: सेवते * मुद्रा रा. 1. 14.

अनफा f. A particular configuration of planets.

अनभिज्ञ a. (f. —ज्ञा) Ignorant of, unacquainted with, unused to, (usually with gen.).

अनभिलक्षित: m. An impostor.

अनभीष्ट a. (f. —ष्टा) Undesirable.

अनभ्यन्तर a. (f. —रा) Ignorant, unfamiliar.

अनभ्यावृत्ति: f. Non-repetition.

अनभ्याश,—स a. (f.—शा, -सा) Not near; distant

अनम m. A Brâhmana (one who does not bow down to others, and returns salutations made to him by others with a blessing).

अनमितंपच a. (f. —चा) Miserly, niggardly.

अनमीव a. Happy; free from disease; sinless. —वं n. Good or comfortable state, happiness, prosperity.

अनंबर a. (f. —रा) Wearing no garment; naked, unclad. —र: m. A Buddhist mendicant.

अनय: 1. Misfortune, bad luck. 2. Adversity, calamity. 3 Gambling. 4. Misconduct, injustice, unfairness. 5 Fraud.

अनयंगत a. (f. —ता) Fallen into misfortune.

अनर्गल a. (f —ला) Free, unrestrained, unhampered; तुरंगमुत्सृष्टमनर्गलं * रघुवं. 3. 39. 2. Unlocked.

अनर्घ a. (f. —र्घा) Invaluable, priceless, inestimable. —र्घ: m. Wrong or improper value.

अनर्घ्य a (f. -र्घ्या) 1 Invaluable. 2. Highly respected.

अनर्थ a. 1 Useless, worthless. -2 Unfortunate, unlucky. -3 Harmful, disastrous, bad. -4 Having no meaning; nonsensical, meaningless. —र्थ: m. 1. A useless, worthless thing. 2. Misfortune, a calamity. 3. A mischievous or harmful thing. -4 Want of meaning; nonsense. -5 N. of Vishnu. -Comp. —अंतरं n. Sameness or identity. —भाव a- Envious, malicious. —संशय: m. A great evil, hazardous adventure.

अनर्थक a. अनर्थ्य, (f. -का, -र्थ्या,) 1 Useless; meaningless. -2 Nonsensical. -3 Unprofitable. -4 Unfortunate. —र्कं *n.* Nonsensical, or foolish talk.

अनर्ह *a.* (*f.* —र्हा) 1 Not deserving, not fit; unworthy (with gen. or in comp). -2 Inadequate, unsuitable. -3 Not deserving of reward or punishment

अनलः *m.* 1 Fire. -2 Agni or the god of fire. -3 Digestive power, gastric juice. -4 Wind. -5 Bile. -6 The fifth of the 8 Vasus. -7 N. of Vâsudeva. 8 (Astr.) The 50th year of Brihaspati's cycle. 9 The third lunar mansion कृत्तिका. 10 A variety of Pitridevas or manes. 11. The soul (जीव). 12 N. of Vishnu. 13 The Supreme Being. -Comp. —द *a.* 1. Removing or destroying heat or fire. —दीपन *a.* Promoting digestion, stomachic. —प्रिया *f.* N. of Agni's wife स्वाहा. -सादः *m.* Loss of appetite ; dyspepsia.

अनलस *a.* (*f.* —सा) 1 Not indolent ; active, diligent, watchful. -2 Unable, incompetent.

अनल्प *a.* (*f.* —ल्पा) 1 Numerous. -2 Not a little. i. e. much.

अनवकाश *a.* (*f.* —शा) 1 Having no scope or occasion ; uncalled for. -2 Inapplicable. -3 Having no • opportunity or space. -शः *m.* Absence of room or scope.

अनवगीत *a.* (*f.* -ता) Faultless.

अनवग्रह *a.* (*f.* —हा) Resistless. uncontrolled, सुकुमारकायमनवग्रहः स्मरः अभिहंति * माल. मा. 1 -39.

अनवच्छिन्न *a.* 1 Not separated or cut. -2 Unlimited, unbounded, excessive. -3 Undefined, undis criminated, unmodified. -4 Having no break or interruption; continuous.

अनवद्य *a.* (*f.* —द्या) Blameless, unobjectionable, faultless, irreproachable. -Comp. —अंग, -रूप (*f.* —अंगी,-रूपा) *a.* Having faultless limbs or form ; exquisitely handsome ; तत्र स्म राजते भैमी सर्वाभरणभूषिता सखीमध्येऽनवद्यांगी विद्युत्सौदामिनी यथा * नलोपा. ५३. —गी *f.* A woman with a faultless form.

अनवधान *a.* (*f.* —ना) Careless, inattentive. —नं *n.* Inadvertence; want or absence of attention.

अनवधि *a.* Unlimited, infinite.

अनवनं *n.* Not protecting.

अनवम *a.* (*f.* —मा) Not low or inferior ; high, exalted, superior ; सुधर्मानवमां सभां * रघुवं. 17. 27.

अनवरत *a.* (*f.* —ता) incessant, continuous, uninterrupted. —तं *adv.* Incessantly, continuously. व्यस्तः कपानुबंधादनवरतमुरोहंति हारोऽयमस्याः * रत्नाव. 1. सागरिका -आलिखितः खलु मयैपः किंपुनरनवरत निपतद्बाष्पसलिलेन न मे दृष्टिः प्रेक्षितुं प्रभवति * रत्नाव. 2.

अनवरार्ध्य *a.* Principal, chief, best, excellent.

अनवलंब, —बन *a.* Having no prop or support ; not dependent. —बः *m.*, —बनं *n.* Independence, absence of support.

अनवलोभनं *n.* A purificatory ceremony to be observed by a pregnant woman in the third month after conception.

अनवसर *a.* 1 Busy, having no leisure -2 Illtimed, inopportune. -3 Out of place, baseless. —रः *m.* 1 Absence of leisure. -2 Unseasonableness. कं याचे यत्र तत्र ध्रुवमन. वसरग्रस्त एवार्थिभावः * माल. मा. 9. 30.

अनवसान a. (f. —ना) Endless, having no end.

अनवसित a (f. —ता) Not ended or finished; not determined. —ता f. A kind of Trishtubh metre.

अनवस्कर a. (f. —रा) Pure, free from dirt; clear.

अनवस्थ a. (f. —स्था) Not steady; unsettled; not fixed. —स्था f. 1. Unsettled state; disorder, confusion. -2 Loose or unsteady conduct, incontinence. -3 (In phil.) An endless series of statements of causes and effects, one of the faults of reasoning; a regressus.

अनवस्थान a. (f. —ना) Unstable, fickle. —नः m. Wind. —नं n. 1 Instability, uncertainty. -2 Looseness of conduct, misconduct, incontinence.

अनवस्थित a. (f. —ता) 1 Unsteady, fickle, unsettled. -2 Changed, altered. -3 Faithless, loose in moral conduct, dissolute. -4 Unable to stay or remain. —तः m. The wind —ता f. A bad faithless woman.

अनवाच् a. (f. —ची) Not tending downwards; looking up.

अनवेक्ष a. (f. —क्षा) Regardless, careless, indifferent.

अनवेक्षणं n. 1 Carelessness, inattention. -2 Want of supervision.

अनवेक्षा f. Carelessness, want of supervision.

अनशनं n Fasting, abstinence from food. -a. (f. —ना) Without food; abstaining from food.

अनश्वर a. (f. —री) Imperishable, eternal.

अनस् n. A cart. -2 Food, boiled rice. -3 Birth. -4 A living being. -5 A kitchen. -6 A parent (father or mother).

अनसूय,-यक a. (f. -या,-का) Free from malice. -या f. 1 Absence of envy; freedom from spite or ill-will. -2 N. of a friend of Sakuntalâ. -3 N. of Atri's wife.

अनसूयु a. Free from envy or malice. इदं तु ते गुह्यतमं प्रवक्ष्याम्यनसूयवे * भग. गी. 9-1.

अनस्थ-स्थिक a. Boneless. —स्थः m. 1 A boneless limb or member. -2 That which is without parts, an epithet of प्रधान of the Sânkhyas or ईश्वरमाया.

अनहन् n. A bad or unlucky day.

अनाकार a. Formless, shapeless, an epithet of the Supreme Being.

अनाकाल: m. 1 Inopportune time. -2 Famine. -Comp. —भृत: m. A man who, in a famine, voluntarily becomes a slave of another.

अनाकाश a. (f. —शा) 1 Opaque, not transparent. -2 Having no transparent atmosphere; —शः m., —शं. n. What is not an atmosphere.

अनाकुल a. (f. —ला) Undisturbed, composed, calm, self-possessed.

अनाक्रांत a. (f. —ता) Unassailed. —ता f. Prickly nightshade, Solanum Jacquini (कंटकारिवृक्ष, Mar. रिंगणी).

अनागत a (f. —ता) 1 Not come or arrived; तावद्भयस्य भेतव्यं यावद्भयमनागतं * हितोप. -2 Not got or obtained. -3 Future, to come. -4 Not learnt or attained, unknown. —तं n. The future time, future.-Comp. —अवेक्षणं n. Looking to the future; provident thought, foresight. —आबाधः m. Future physical trouble or calamity, illness, &c. —आर्तवा f. A girl who has not yet arrived at. puberty. —विधातृ *m.* One who provides for the future; provident, prudent.

अनागम *a.* (*f.* —मा) 1 Not arrived; not present. -2 (In law) Having no title-deed or document of possession (such as purchase deed &c.); possessed without any documentary proof. -Comp. —उपभोगः *m.* Enjoyment of property without such a deed. —मः *m.* 1 Non-arrival. -2 Non-attainment.

अनाघ्रात *a.* Not smelt ; (fig.)not touched or affected.

अनागस् *a.* 1 Innocent, blameless ; free from fault or sin. आर्तत्राणाय वः शस्त्रं न प्रहर्तुमनागसि * शकुंत. 1 11.

अनागामिन् *a.* 1 Not coming, not arriving. -2 Not future, not likely to return. —*m.* The third of the Buddhist orders.

अनागामुक *a.* Not likely to return.

अनाचार *a.* (*f.* —रा) Improper in behaviour ; unprincipled ; violating proper rules of couduct. —रः *m.*, अनाचरणं *n.* Non observance of customary duties ; improper conduct ; departure from established usage or principle.

अनातप *a.* (*f.* —पा) Free from heat or the blaze of the sun ; not exposed to heat ; cool, shady. —पः *m.* Coolness, shade.

अनातुर *a.* (*f.* —रा) 1 Not eager. -2 Not fatigued, unwearied ; भेजे धर्ममनातुरः * रघु. 1. 21. -3 Not ill or diseased ; healthy, in good condition of health.

अनात्मक *a.* Unreal, transitory, an epithet of the world (in Buddhistic phil.)

अनात्मन् *a.* 1 Destitute of spirit or mind. -2 Not spiritual ; corporeal. -3 One who has not restrained his self.—त्मा *m.* Not self ; another, something different from आत्मन् (spirit or soul) *i. e.* the perishable body. -Comp. —ज्ञ, —वेदिन् *a.* 1. Not possessing spiritual knowledge or true wisdom. 2. Not knowing oneself ; foolish, silly. —वत् *a.* Having no control upon one's senses. —संपन्न *a.* Wayward, foolish ; not selfpossessed.

अनात्मनीन *a.* (*f.* —ना) Not suitable ; not fit for one's self.

अनात्म्य *a.* Impersonal ; different from the body. —त्म्यं *n.* Want of affection for one's own family.

अनाथ *a.* (*f.* —था) Without lord or master. 2 Helpless, poor, forlorn ; विदूषकः —भो वयस्य स्मर मां अनाथं देव्या बंधनाद्विपद्यमानं * रत्नाव. 3 -Comp. —सभा *f.* A poor-house.

अनादर *a.* (*f.* —रा) Showing no respect; regardless. —रः *m.* 1 Disregard, disrespect, disdain, contempt. -2 Absence of effort or exertion ; facillty.

अनादरणं *n.* Want of respect. Disrespectful conduct.

अनादि *a.* Having no beginning ; eternal, existing from eternity. -Comp. —अनंत,—अंत *a.* Having no beginning and end ; eternal. —निधन *a.* Having neither beginning nor end ; eternal. —मध्यांत *a.* Having no beginning, middle or end ; eternal.

अनादिमत् *a.* Not having a beginning.

अनादीनव *a.* Faultless ; गद्गदस्वरदेवेनादीनवमनादीनवक्षरं शिरितं * शिशुपा. 2. 22.

अनाहत *a.* (*f.* —ता) 1 Disrespected, rejected, despised. -2 Regardless of, indifferent to. —तं *n.* Disrespect, contempt.

अनाद्य *a.* Not eatable ; what ought not to be eaten.

अनाधृष्ट-ष्य *a.* (*f.* —ष्टा, -ष्या) 1 Invincible, unchecked, irresistible. -2 Perfect, entire, unimpaired.

अनानुपूर्व्य *n.* 1 Separation of the different members of compounds by the intervention of others. -2 Not coming in regular order.

अनाप्त *a.* (*f.* —प्ता) 1 Not obtained. -2 Not attaining the object aimed at. -3 Unfit ; not apt ; unskilful. —प्तः *m.* A stranger.

अनामक *a.* (*f.* —मिका) 1 Nameless. 2. Having a bad name, of ill repute.

अनामन् *a.* 1 Nameless. -2 Infamous. —*m.* 1 The intercalary month. -2 The ringfinger ; (also अनामिका). —*n.* Piles (अर्शोरोग Mar. मुळव्याध).

अनामय *a.* Free from disease, healthy, sound.-2 Free from pain or sorrow. 3. Preventing disease. -यः *m.*, —यं *n.* Good or sound health ; health, well-being, welfare. -यः *m.* N. of Vishnu or Siva.

अनामा, अनामिका *f.* The ring-finger; the finger near the little finger of the hand

अनामृत *a.* (*f.* -ता) Immortal.

अनायत *a.* (*f.* —ता) 1 Unrestrained, unchecked. -2 Having no support. -3 Of short duration. -4 Continuous, close, unseparated.

अनायत्त *a.* (*f.* —त्ता) Not dependent ; uncontrolled, independent.

अनायास *a.* (*f.* —सा) Not involving labour, trouble, or exertion; easy. —सः *m.* 1 Facility, case, absence of difficulty or exertion. -2 Idleness, neglect. -Comp. —कृतं *n.* An infusion prepared without effort or exertion *i. e.* prepared extemporaneously(Med).

अनारत *a.* (*f.* —ता) 1 Not ceasing or stopping; continual, continuous, uninterrupted. -2 Eternal. —तं *n.* 1 Continuity. -2 Absolute nonentity (अत्यंताभाव). -*adv.* Continuously, eternally.

अनारंभः *m.* Non-commenecment, not undertaking. अनारंभो हि कार्याणां प्रथमं बुद्धिलक्षणम्.

अनारंभ (—ब) ण *a.* Having no support.

अनार्जव *a.* (*f.* —वा) Crooked ; dishonest. —वं *n.* 1 Crooked ness, (moral or physical). 2 Disease.

अनार्तव *a.* (*f.* वा) Unseasonable, inopportune, premature (as a flower blossoming out of season). —वा *f.* A girl who has not attained to puberty.

अनार्य *a.* (*f.* —र्या) Ignoble ; not respectable; not polite or decent ; vulgar. —र्यः 1 One who is not an Arya. -2 A country not inhabited by the Aryas. -3 A Sudra. -4 A Mlechchha. -5 An ignoble person. -Comp. —तिक्तः *m.* N. of the plant Gentiana Cherayta Rox. (Mar. किराईत.)

अनार्ष *a.* (*f.* -र्षी) 1 Not referring or belonging to a Rishi. 2 Not Vedic; not belonging to the text of a Vedic hymn. -2 Not added to a Rishi's name (as an affix).

अनार्षेय See अनार्ष.

अनालंब *a.* (*f.*—बा) Without support or stay. —बः *m.* Want of support ; despondency. —बी *f.* Siva's lute (वीणा).

अनालंबु (भु) का *f.* A woman during menstruation.

अनावर्तिन् *a.* (*f.* —नी) Not recurring or returning.

अनाविद्ध *a.* (*f.* —द्धा) 1 Not pierced or wounded ; unperforated. -2 Unhurt, uninjured.

अनाविल *a.* (*f.* —ला) 1 Not turbid or muddy ; pure, clear. -2 Not marshy ; wholesome, salubrious, (as a country).

अनावृत्त *a.*(*f.*-त्ता) Not returning, not repeated ; being for the first time.

अनावृत्तिः *f.* 1 Non-return, absence of repetition or recurrence. -2 Nonreturn (to birth); final emancipation.

अनावृष्टिः *f.* Drought, one of the many kinds of ईति q. v.

अनाशकं *n.* Fast, abstaining from eating even to death. (प्रायोपवेशनं).

अनाशकायनं *n.* The state of unmarried or student's life, devoted to contemplation and knowledge of the soul.

अनाशिन् *a.* Imperishable, indestuctible, as the Soul or Supreme Being.

अनाश्रमिन् *m* One not belonging to any of the four आश्रमs or orders of life. अनाश्रमी न तिष्ठेत्तु क्षणमेकमपि द्विजः.

अनाश्रम-मे-वासः *m.* Not belonging to any of the four आश्रमs.

अनाश्रय *a.* (*f.* —या) Defenceless, unprotected. —यः *m.* Self-dependence, absence of support.

अनाश्रव *a.* (*f.* —वा) Not listening to advice ; obstinate.

अनास्थ *a.* (*f.* —स्था) Indifferent.

अनास्था *f.* 1. Disrespect. 2. Indifference.

अनाहत *a.* 1 Unbeaten, unwounded, intact. -2 New and unbleached (as cloth). -3 Not produced by beating (as sound). —तं *n.* A new garment.

अनाहार *a.* Abstaining from food; fasting. —रः *m.* Abstinence from food; fasting.

अनाहार्य *a.* 1 Not artificial; natural; not producible. -2 Not eatable.

अनाहुतिः *f.* Not sacrificing ; bad sacrificing ; an improper oblation.

अनाहूत *a.* (*f.* —ता) Not called, uninvited. —Comp. —उपजल्पिन् *m.* An uncalled for speaker or boaster. —उपविष्ट *a.* Seated as an uninvited guest.

अनिकेत *a.* Houseless, vagrant. —तः *m.* An ascetic.

अनिक्षुः *m.* Not a (true) sugarcane; a sort of long grass or reed producing coarse sugar.

अनिगीर्ण *a.* 1 Not swallowed up. -2 (In Rhet.) Not hidden or concealed ; present; not to be supplied.

अनिच्छा *f.* Unwillingness, indifference, reluctance.

अनित्य *a.* (*f.* —त्या) 1. Transient, not eternal or lasting. 2. Occasional, temporary, casual ; not peremptory or obligatory as a rule &c ; special. -3 Unusual, extraordinary. -4 Unsteady, fickle; not permanent. -5 Uncertain, doubtful. —त्यं *adv.* Occasionally, not permanently ; incidentally, casually. -Comp. —कर्मन् n., क्रिया f. A sacrifice or any act of worship which is volunatry and occasional. —दत्त:, -दत्तक:, -दात्रिम: m. A son given by his parents to another for temporary or preliminary adoption (in law). —प्रत्यवेक्षा f. (in Buddhistic phil.) The consciousness that every thing is perishable and is passing away. —सम: m. A sophism or fallacious reasoning which generalizes what is exceptional. —समास: m. A compound the sense of which may be equally expressed by using its component parts separately.

आनैंद्रियं n. 1 Reason. -2 Not an organ of sense ; the mind.

अनिबद्ध a. Not coherent.

अनिभृत a. (f. —ता) 1 Not private; public, open ; not hidden. -2 Immodest, bold. -3 Unsteady ; not firm ; tremulous.

अनिमक: m. 1 A frog. -2. A cuckoo. -3 A bee. -4 The filament of a lotus. -5 N. of the tree मधूक.

अनिमित्त a. (f. —त्ता) Causeless, groundless ; casual, incidental. —त्तं n. 1 Absence of an adequate cause or occasion ; causelessness, groundlessness. -2 A bad omen, an evil omen ; आ: ममापि नाम दुर्योधनस्य अनिमित्तानि हृदयक्षोभमावेदयंति (These evil omens cause alarm even to me, Duryodhan) * वेणीसं. 2. अनिमित्तं, अनिमित्ततः -adv. Causelessly, without any adequate cause. -Comp. —निराक्रिया f. Aversion of evil omens.

अनिमिष: m. 1 A god. -2 A fish. —Comp. —आचार्य: m. Brihaspati. —क्षेत्रं n. The holy place called विष्णुक्षेत्र.

अनिमेष a. Without twinkling (as eyes) —ष: m. 1 Absence of twinkling. -2 A god. 3 A fish.

अनियत a. (f. -ता) 1 Uncontrolled. -2 Indefinite, uncertain, irregular. -3 Causeless, casual, incidental, -Comp. —आत्मन् a. Not self-possessed —पुंस्का f. A woman loose in conduct, unchaste. —वृत्ति a. 1. Having no regular or fixed employment or regular income.

अनियंत्रण a. (f.—णा) Unrestrained uncontrolled, free.

अनियम: m. 1 Absence of rule control, or fixed order. -2 Irregularity, uncertainty, indefiniteness, doubt. -3 Improper conduct

अनिरुक्त a. (f. —क्ता) 1 Not indicated. 2 Not explained; not clearly spoken.-2 Not clearly stated or explained. -Comp. —गानं n. Indistinct singing or humming : a particular mode of chanting the सामवेद.

अनिरुद्ध a. (f. -द्धा) 1 Ungovernable. 2 Unrestrained. —द्ध: m. 1 A spy. -2. Son of प्रद्युम्न. 3. A N. of विष्णु, शिव, or of an अर्हत. -द्धं n. A cord for fastening cattle. -Comp. —पथ n. The sky. 2 An unobstructed path.

अनिर्देश, अनिर्दशाह (f.-शा,-हा) a. Coming or happening within the 10 days of impurity caused either by childbirth or death.

अनिर्देश्य a. Undefinable, ineffable, indescribable, inexplicable, incomparable. —श्यं n. An epithet of the Supreme Being.

अनिर्धारित *a.* (*f.* —ता) Not determined or ascertained.

अनिर्लोडित *a.* Not well considered.

अनिर्वचनीय *a.*(*f.*–या) 1 Unutterable, indescribable, undefinable, epithet of the Supreme Being. –2 Improper to be mentioned —यं *n.* (In Vedânta) 1 Mâyâ or illusion, ignorance. –2 The world.

अनिर्विण्ण *a.* Not fatigued or tired.

अनिर्वृत *a.* (*f.*–ता) 1 Unhappy. –2 Unaccomplished, unfulfilled.

अनिर्वृति: *f.* 1 Absence of happiness. –2 Poverty, destitution.

अनिर्वेद: *m* Non-depression ; self-reliance.

अनिल: *m.* 1. Wind. 2 God of wind. 3 Rheumatism. 4 One of the three humours of the body, the other two being कफ and पित्त. 5 The fifth वसु. –6 The letter य्. –7 Symbolical expression for the number 49. –8 N. of the lunar asterism स्वाति. –9 N. of Vishnu. –Comp.—आत्मज: *m.* N. of हनुमत्, also of भीम. —आशिन्, —भुज् *a.* Feeding on wind i. e. fasting. *m.* A serpent. —सख: *m.* The fire.

अनिशं *ind.* Incessantly, cease lessly.

अनिष्ट *a.* (*f.* —ष्टा) 1 Unwished, undesirable ; disagreeable. –2 Evil, forbidden. –3 Bad, unlucky, ominous. –4 Not honoured with a sacrifice. –ष्टं *n.* An evil, mishap, misfortune, calamity, a crime, wrong, an unwelcome thing. –Comp. —आपत्ति: *f.*, –आपादनं *n.* Getting what is not desired, an undesired occurrence. —आशंसिन् *a.* Indicating or boding ill. —ग्रह: *m* An evil or malignant planet.

अनिष्पत्रं *ind.* In such a manner that the arrow (the feathery portion of it) does not come out on the other side ; *i. e.* not with great force.

अनिस्तीर्ण *a.* 1 Not crossed. –2 Unanswered, unrefuted (as a charge).

अनीक: *m.*, —कं *n.* 1 Army, forces, troop, host. 2 A collection, group, mass. –3 Battle, fight, combat. –4 A row, a marching column. –5 Front ; head ; chief. –6 Edge, point. –Comp. —स्थ: *m.* A warrior, combatant. –2 A sentinel, a watch. –3 An elephant-driver, or its trainer. –4 A war-drum or trumpet. –5 A signal, mark, sign.

अनीकिनी *f.* 1 An army. 2. A certain force, viz. one tenth of an अक्षौहिणी.

अनीति: *f.* 1 Impropriety, immorality. 2 Injustice, wrong act ; indiscretion, foolish conduct.

अनीश *a.* 1 (*f.* –शा) Having no lord, or superior or controller. 2. Uncontrolled. 3 Powerless. 4 Not independent. —श: *m.* A N. of vishnu. —शा *f.* Helplessness.

अनीश्वर *a.* (*f.*–री) Having no superior, unchecked uncontrolled. –2 Unable. –3 Not relating to God. –4 Not acknowledging God, atheistical. —रं *n.* (Sankhya phil.) The world. –Comp. —वाद: *m.* Atheism. —वादिन् *m.* One who maintains the doctrine that there is no god ; an atheist.

अनीह *a.* (*f.* —हा) Indifferent, careless. —हः *m.* —हा *f.* Disregard, apathy, indifference, disinclination.

अनीहित *a.* (*f,* —ता) Undesired, disagreeable, unpleasant. —तं *n.* Displeasure.

अनु *ind.* As a prefix to nouns and verbs, अनु expresses after, along, by the side of, next, under, &c. When prefixed to nouns in adv. compounds it shows nearness, (अनुवनं near the forest); propriety, (अनुरूपं according to nature, i. e. properly); conformity, (अनुक्रमं according to order) ; along the side of (अनुगंगं by the Ganges.) As a separable preposition (with acc.) it expresses I. Subsequent time ; 2, Likeness, 3 Inferiority, 4 Proximity, 5 Couformability, 6 Participation, &c. e. g. I जप मनुप्रावर्षत् it rained after prayer ; 2 सर्वं मामनु ते everything thine resembles mine. 3 अनुहरिं सुराः Gods are inferior to हरि, 4 वृक्ष मनुविद्योतते विद्युत् the lightening flashes near the tree. 5 नदी मन्ववासिता सेना the army was encamped along the river. 6 हरिमनुलक्ष्मीः Lakshmi participates with हरि.

अनुक *a.* (*f.* —का) I. Lustful, libidinous. 2 Greedy. 3 Sloping.

अनुकथनं I *n.* Subsequent mention. -2 Relation, narration ; discourse, conversation.

अनुकनीयस् *a.* The next youngest.

अनुकंप (अनु + कंप् I A.) To take pity or compassion on ; sympathize with ; pity ; (with acc; sometimes loc.).

अनुकंपक *a.* One who pities ; kind-hearted, compassionate. —पं *n.* Compassion, pity, fellow-feeling sympathy.

अनुकंपा *f.* Compassion, fellow-feeling, pity ; (with gen. or with loc.) भक्त्या गुरौ मय्यनुकंपया च * रघुवं. 2. 63.

अनुकंपिन् *a.* (*f.* —नी) Pitying ; sympathizing with.

अनुकंप्य *pot. p. a.* (*f.* —प्या) Pitiable, worthy of sympathy ; —प्यः *m.* I A courier, a swift messenger. -2 An ascetic.

अनुकर *a.* Imitating. —रः *m.* An assistant.

अनुकरणं *n.*, —कृतिः *f.* I Imitation , copy. -2 Resemblance, similarity.

अनुकर्तृ *m.* I An imitator. -2 Actor, performer.

अनुकर्मन् *n.* I Imitation. -2 A subsequent rite.

अनुकर्षः *m.* -र्षणं *n* I Dragging along ; attraction in general. -2 Invoking (by means of mystic words or spells). -3 Grammatical attraction ; employing a word occuring in a preceding rule to a subsequent rule, &c. -4 The axle-tree or bottom of a carriage. -5 Delayed performance of a duty.

अनुकल्पः *m.* An alternative or substituted rule to be used in case of necessity when the primary one (प्रथमकल्प) is not possible.

अनुकाम *a.* (*f.* —मा) I Agreeable to, or according to one's desire. -2 Desirous, lustful. —मं *ind.* According to one's desire or wish. —मः *m.* Proper or worthy desire ; desire.

अनुकामीन *a.* (*f.* —ना) Going at will or pleasure ; acting as one pleases.

अनुकारः *m.* Imitation, resemblance

अनुकारिन् *a.* (*f* —णी) Imitating, resembling (with gen.)

अनुकार्य, –करणीय, –कर्तव्य *pot. p. a.* (*f.* —र्या, –या, –व्या) Fit to be imitated or followed. अनुकार्यं *n.* —अनुक्रिया *f.* A subsequent rite or ceremony.

अनुकाल *a.* (*f.* —ला) Opportune, timely, suited to the time. —लं *ind.* Opportunely, on a proper occasion.

अनुकीर्तनं *n.* Act of proclaiming or publishing.

अनुकूल *a.* 1 Favourable, agreeable, -2 Friendly, kind. -3 Suitable or conformable to; pleasing, agreeable or favourable to, fit for. —लः *m.* 1 A faithful or kind husband. -2 An epithet of Vishnu. —ला *f.* N. of a metre. —लं *n.* 1 Favour, kindness; -2 (Rhet.) The figure of speech in which an unfavourable thing is represented as turning out favourable. अनुकूलं प्रातिकूल्यमानुकूल्यानुबंधि चेत् *साहि. द. *e. g* कुपितासि यदा तन्वि निधाय करजक्षतम्। बधान भुजपाशाभ्यां कंठमस्य दृढं तदा ॥ .

अनुकूलता *f.*, —त्वं *n.* 1 Favour, conformity, kindness, good will. -2 Prosperity.

अनुकूलय Den. P. To conciliate, to try to please. Propitiate, act in a friendly way towards.

अनुकृ (अनु + कृ 8 U.) 1 To do after or afterwards; follow; to imitate, do in imitation of, resemble, equal, copy (with gen. or acc.) -2 To requite, recompense. -3 To try on, use, adjust, adapt.

अनुकृष् (अनु + कृष् 1 P.) To drag along, to attract (in gram.); see अनुकर्ष below. —*Caus.* To subject.

अनुक्लृप् (अनु + क्लृप् 1 A.) To follow duly. -*Caus.* To cause others to follow duly.

अनुक्त *a.* (*f.* —क्ता) 1 Unuttered unsaid. -2 Unheard of, extraordinary. -3 Not mentioned or told असावनुक्तोऽपि सहाय एव * कुमा. स. 3.21.

अनुक्रकच *a.* (*f.* —चा) Serrated dentated like a saw.

अनुक्रंद् (अनु + क्रंद् 1 P.) To cry after, or in reply to a cry.

अनुक्रंदनं *n.* A cry in reply.

अनुक्रम् (अनु + क्रम् 1 U., 4 P.) 1 To go after, follow (fig. also); to betake oneself to; -2 To count up, enumerate, state or go through in order. 3 To give a table of contents, (as of a book).

अनुक्रम *a.* Coming or happening in due order. —मः *m.* 1 Succession; order; serial arrangement; proper method, due order. -2 A table of contents, index, such as of a book.

अनुक्रमणं *n.* 1 Proceeding in order. -2 Following. —णी, –णिका *f.* A table of contents: an index showing the successive contents of a work.

अनुक्री: *f.* A kind of sacrificial rite called साद्यस्क.

अनुक्रुश् (अनु + क्रुश् 1 P.) To shout at or after. -*Caus.* To join in lamenting, condole with, show sympathy to.

अनुक्रोशः *m.* 1 Pity, compassion, tenderness (with loc.)

अनुक्षणं *ind* Every instant, perpetually, constantly, frequently.

अनुक्षत्तृ *m.* (त्ता) A door-keeper's or charioteer's attendant.

अनुक्षेत्रं *n.* The stipend given to temple servants .

अनुख्याति: *f.* 1 Descrying. -2 Reporting, revealing.

अनुख्यातृ *m.* (ता) A discoverer ; reporter.

अनुग *a.* (*f.* --गा) (In comp.) Following, going after; corresponding or tallying with ; adequate to. —गः *m.* A follower, servant, companion.

अनुगत *p. p. a.* (*f.* --ता) 1 (Used passively) Followed. (lit & fig.), attended ; full of, filled with ; acquired, obtained. -2 (Used actively). Following, obeying, observing ; corresponding, adapted or answering to, in harmony with. Adequate or suitable to, fit for ; imitating. —तं *n.* Moderate time in music. -Comp. —अर्थ *a.* (*f.* —र्था) That can be easily understood.

अनुगति: *f.* 1 Following ; going after ; imitating. -2 Consent, approval.

अनुगम् (अनु + गम्, गच्छ 1 P.) 1 To go after, follow, attend, accompany.-2 To observe, follow, practise, obey, act up to. -3 To seek, wander through. -4 To come, arrive, approach. -5 To correspond with, be suitable to ; imitate, resemble. —*Caus.* To cause to follow ; follow.

अनुगम:*m.*, -गमं *n.* 1 Following. -2 Comprehending, grasping (as the sense). 3. The post-cremation, self-immolation of a widow on her husband's funeral pile. -4 Imitating ; approaching. -5 Conformity, accordance.

अनुगर्जित *p. p.* Roared. —तं *n.* A roaring echo.

अनुगव *a.* Suiting (the length of) the oxen.

अनुगवीन: *m.* A cowherd.

अनुगामिन् *a.* (*f.* —नी) Following. --*m.* A follower.

अनुगामुक *a.* Habitually or constantly following.

अनुगिरं *ind.* By the mountain-side.

अनुगीतं *n.* Singing in response to.

अनुगीति: *f* N. of a metre.

अनुगुण *a.* (*f.* —णा) Of the same nature ; congenial with, suitable to ; conformable to, favourable or agreeable to, suitable, according to. --णः *m.* A natural peculiarity —णं *adv.* 1 Favourably, conformably to one's desires. -2 Agreeably, or conformably to. -3 Naturally.

अनुगै(अनु + गै 1 P) 1 To sing after, follow in singing. -2 To sing ; to celebrate in song.

अनुग्रह् (अनु + ग्रह् 9 P.) 1 To favour, oblige, treat with kindness. -2 To protect, maintain (as fire). -3 To receive, welcome. -4 To hold up, support, uphold. -5 To follow in robbing, seizing or depriving -6 To conform or correspond to, follow, take after. —*Caus.* To cause to favour or to favour.

अनुग्रह: *m.* —हणं *n.* 1 A favour, kindness, obligation. -2 Assistance, help, conferring benefits. -3 Facilitating by spells. -4 Acceptance. -5 Rear-guard of an army.

अनुग्रासक: *m.* A mouthful.

अनुग्राहक *a.* 1 Favouring, helping, succouring. -2 Gracious, kind.

अनुग्राह्य *pot. p. a.* (*f.* —ह्या) Fit to be favoured or obliged ; deserving to be helped.

अनुघटनं *n.* Linking together with; supplement, addition.

अनुचर् (अनु + चर् 1 P.) 1 To go after, follow, pursue; to serve, attend or wait upon -2 To go through, wander. -3 To conduct oneself, behave.

अनुचरः *m.* 1 A companion, follower, servant. —री, —रा *f.* A female attendant.

अनुचरित *p. p. a.* (*f.* —ता) Followed. —तं *n.* Walk; walk in life; conduct.

अनुचारकः *m.* A follower, servant, &c. —रिका *f.* A female servant or follower.

अनुचित *a.* (*f.* —ता) 1 Wrong, improper. -2 Unusual; unwonted.

अनुचिंत् (अनु + चिंत् 10 P.) To consider, to ponder over, think of, call to mind.

अनुचिंता *f.* —चिंतनं *n.* 1 Calling to mind, meditating, pondering upon. -2 Recalling, recollecting. -3 Anxiety.

अनुच्छादः *m.* A garment which hangs down in front from the waist to the feet.

अनुच्छित्तिः *f.*, अनुच्छेदः *m.* Non-extirpation; non-destruction; indestructibility.

अनुच्छिष्ट *a.* (*f.* —ष्टा) Not rejected; pure, holy; fresh, unused.

अनुज,-जात *p. p. a.* (*f.* —जा, -ता) Born after, younger. —जः, -जातः *m.* 1 A younger brother. 2. One born again *i. e.* one invested with the sacred thread. —जा,-जाता *f.* 1 A younger sister.

अनुजन् (अनु + जन् 4 A.) 1 To be born after, to be produced after, -2 To take after (one's parents) to be born similar to.

अनुजन्मन् *m.* A younger brother.

अनुजात See अनुज above.

अनुजीव् (अनु + जीव् 1 P.) 1 To depend upon for subsistence, live by or upon (something). 2 To live as a subordinate to. -3 To live for any one. -4 To follow or imitate in living. -5 To survive.

अनुजीविन् *a.* Dependent, living on or upon. —*m.* A dependant, servant, follower.

अनुजीव्य *a.* To be served as a master.

अनुज्ञा (अनु + ज्ञा 9 U.) 1 To permit, allow, assent, or consent to, approve, authorise, sanction. -2 To betroth, affiance. -3 To excuse, to overlook, forgive. 4. To dismiss, bid farewell. -*Caus.* (-ज्ञापयति) 1 To ask or beg for, request. -2 To take leave of, bid adieu to.

अनुज्ञा *f.*, —ज्ञानं *n.* 1 Permission, consent, sanction. -2 Permission or leave to depart. -3 Excusing, forgiving. -4 An order, command.

अनुज्ञात *p. p. a.* (*f.* —ता) Permitted, allowed, assented to, granted, authorised, dismissed.

अनुज्ञापकः *m.* One who commands or orders.

अनुज्ञापनं *n.*, -ज्ञप्तिः *f.* 1 Authorisation. -2 Issuing an order, or permission.

अनुतप् (अनु + तप् 1 P.) 1 To heat, vex, annoy (fig.). -2 (4 A. or *pass.*) To repent, grieve, be sorry for, be stung with remorse;

—*Caus.* To cause pain, to, afflict distress.

अनुतप्त *p. p. a.* (*f.* —प्ता) 1 Heated. -2 Filled with repentance.

अनुतरं *n.* Fare, freight.

अनुतर्षः *m.* 1 Thirst, desire to drink. -2 Wish, desire. -3 Drinking spirituous liquors. -4 A drinking vessel. -5 Liquor itself.

अनुतर्षणं *n.* 1. The drinking of spirituous liquors. -2 A drinking vessel (to drink spirituous liquors off).

अनुतापः *m.* 1 Repentance. -2 Heat.

अनुतापन *a.* Causing distress; regret, repentance or sorrow.

अनुतिलं *ind.* Grain after grain, very minutely.

अनुतॄ (अनु + तॄ 1 P.) 1 To go across or to the end. -2 To stretch lengthwise.

अनुत्क (*f.* —त्का) *a.* Free from regret, auxiety or eagerness.

अनुत्तम (*f.* —मा) 1 Having no better, unsurpassed, the very best. 2. (Gram.) Not used in the उत्तम or the first person. 3. Not the best. -मः *m.* N. of Siva or Vishnu.

अनुत्तर *a.* (*f.* —रा) 1 Principal, chief. -2 Best, excellent; unsurpassed. -3 Unable to answer. -4 Fixed, firm. -5 Low, inferior, base, mean. -6 Southern. —रं *n.* A reply which is evasive and therefore held to be no answer. —रा *f.* The south.

अनुत्तरंग *a.* 1 Steady, not ruffled. 2 Having no waves. अपामिवाधारमनुत्तरंगं * कुमा. सं. 3. 48.

अनुत्तालः *m.* Sweet sound.

अनुत्थानं *n.* Absence of exertion.

अनुत्पत्तिः *f.* Non-production. -*a.* Not yet produced. -Comp. —धर्मक्षांतिः *f.* The preparation for a future state, (In Boudha phil.). —समः*m.*-मा *f.* A method of arguing against a thing by attempting to prove that nothing exists from which it could spring.

अनुत्पादः *m.* Not coming into existence, not taking effect. -Comp. —क्षांतिः *f.* The preparation for a future state.

अनुत्साह *a.* Destitute of energy or determination. —हः *m.* Want of energy ; langour; indifference.

अनुत्सुक *a.* Not very eager, quiet.

अनुत्सूत्र *a.* Not deviating from the Sutra (of Pánini or of morality) ; not anomalous or irregular —पदन्यासा सद्वृत्तिः सन्निबंधना * शिशुपा 2. 112.

अनुत्सेकः *m.* Absence of haughtiness or pride ; modesty ; युक्तमेतत अनुत्सेकः खलु विक्रमालंकारः (Modesty is an ornament to heroism * विक्रमो. 1.

अनुत्सेकिन् *a.* (*f.* —नी) Not puffed up, not proud or arrogant.

अनुदक *a.* 1 Waterless. 2 Having very little water. -3 Devoid of the libations of water (a sort of श्राद्ध.)

अनुदर *a.* 1 Having a slender waist ; thin, lank.

अनुदात्त *a.* (*f.* —त्ता) 1. Not raised, not elevated. 2 Having no accent. —त्तः *m.* One of the three accents to be observed in reciting the Vedas.

अनुदर्शनं *n.* Inspection, survey; consideration, regard ; perception.

अनुदार *a.* (*f.* —रा) 1 Not generous ; niggardly ; mean. 2 Followed by a wife. 3 Having a suitable or worthy wife.

अनुदित *a.* (*f.* —ता) 1 Unsaid; not uttered. -2 Not risen ; that has not appeared yet.

अनुदिनं,-दिवसं *ind.* Daily, day after day.

अनुदृश् (अनु + दृश्, पश्य् 1 P.) To survey, behold ; to keep in view or mind. —*Caus.* To show, tell, inform.

अनुदृष्टि *a.* Having a favourable look. —ष्टिः *f* A favourable look.

अनुदेशः *m.* 1 Order, injunction 2 A rule or injunction relating to a preceding one (Gram.).

अनुद्धट *a.* (*f.* —टा) 1 Not bold ; soft, mild. -2 Not exalted or lofty.

अनुद्रु (अनु + द्रु 1 P.) 1 To run after, follow, accompany. -2 To chase, pursue.

अनुद्रुत *p. p. a.* (*f.* —ता) Followed, pursued ; (sometimes used actively). following, pursuing. —तं *n.* A time of measure in music.

अनुद्वाहः *m* Non-marriage, celibacy.

अनुधाव् (अनु + धाव् 1 P) 1 To run after ; follow -2 To run up to, approach. -3 To cleanse, wash.

अनुधावनं *n.* 1 Going or running after, following, pursuing. -2 Close pursuit of an object ; research, investigation. -3 Seeking a mistress though unattainable. -4 Cleansing, purification.

अनुध्यानं *n.* 1 Thought; meditation, religious contemplation. -2 Thinking of, remembrance. -3 Wishing well of, affectionate solicitude for.

अनुध्यै (अनु + ध्यै 1 P.) 1 To think of, muse, consider attentively. -2 To wish well of, to bless, favour

अनुनयः *m.* 1. Conciliation ; सानुनयं in a conciliatory tone ; conciliatingly. 2 Courtesy. 3. Humble supplication. 4 Regulation of conduct; discipline Comp. —आमंत्रणं *n.* A conciliatory address.

अनुनादः *m.* Sound, noise ; reverberation, echo.

अनुनादिन् *a.* Echoing, sounding, reverberating.

अनुनायिक *a.* (*f.* —का) Conciliating. —का *f.* A female character subordinate to the Náyikâ. A Nâyika of a subordinate importance.

अनुनासिक *a.* (*f.* —का) 1 Nasal, *i. e.* uttered through the nose. -2 The sign used to mark the nasalization in the case of some consonants -Comp. —आदिः *m.* A conjunct consonant beginning with a nasal

अनुनिर्देशः *m.* Description or relation in the previous order or sequence ; भूयसामुपदिष्टानां क्रियाणामथ कर्मणाम । क्रमशो योऽनुनिर्देशो यथासंख्यं तदुच्यते ॥ साहि. द.

अनुनिर्वापः *m.* Subsequent libation of ghee.

अनुनी (अनु + नी 1 P.) 1 To conciliate, persuade, supplicate, propitiate, pacify, appease. 2 To cherish love for. -3 To bring near to (with dat. of person). -4 To train, discipline. -5 To honour.

अनुनीतिः *f.* 1 Conciliation. 2 Courtesy. -3 Humble supplication.

4 Regulation of conduct. discipline.

अनुप a. (f. —पा) 1 Watery, marshy. —पं n. 1 A marsh. 2 A pond of water. 3. Bank, side. —पः m. 1. A he-buffalo. 2. The francoline partridge (Mar. तित्तिर). 3 An elephant. 4. A frog. —पाः m. pl. N. of a country in ancient India.

अनुपघातार्जित a. (f. —ता) Acquired without detriment to the paternal estate (in law).

अनुपजीवनीय a. (f. —या) Insufficient for livelihood.

अनुपत् (अनु + पत् 1 P.) 1 To fly to or towards. 2 To fly or run after, follow (fig. also) pursue, chase. 2 To fall upon, attack. —Caus. 1 To fly to. -2 To throw another down along with oneself.

अनुपतनं n. —पातः m. 1 Falling upon. -2 Following, going after, pursuit. -3 Going or proceeding in order or as a consequence. -4 (in mathe.) Proportion or the Rule of three. -5 A degree of latitude opposite to the one given.

अनुपथ a. Following the road —थः m. A road, a favourable road. —थं adv. Along the road.

अनुपद् (अनु + पद् 4. P., or A &P. in epic poetry) 1 To follow, attend. -2 To be attached to. -3 To enter, go to or into. -4 To fall down. -5 To enter upon; betake oneself to; to resort to.

अनुपदं n. A chorus, burden of a song or words sung again at regular intervals. —ind. 1 Along the feet, near the feet. -2 Step by step, at every step. 3 Word for word. -4 On the heels of, immediately after (of time or space).

अनुपदवी f. A way, road.

अनुपदिन् m. A searcher, inquirer.

अनुपदीना f. A kind of slippers or of boots.

अनुपधः m. A letter or syllable not preceded by another.

अनुपधि a. Guileless, taintless, without fraud.

अनुपन्यासः m. 1 Failure of proof or determination; doubt. 2 Non-statement.

अनुपपत्तिः f. 1 Failure, failing to be; लक्षणा शक्यसंबंधस्तात्पर्यानुपपत्तितः भाषाप. 82 (तात्पर्यानुपपत्ति is the failure of the meaning aimed at, or any connected meaning.). -2 Inapplicability, not being applicable. -3 Inconclusive reasoning; absence of reasonable grounds -4 Poverty, adversity.

अनुपपन्न a. Improper, impossible. inapplicable, not leading to the desired end, impracticable, inconclusive, irrelevant. राजा-उभयमप्यनुपपन्नं * विक्रमो. 2.

अनुपम a. (f. —मा) Incomparable, matchless, peerless, best, most excellent. —मा f. The female elephant of the south-west (wife of कुमुद).

अनुपमर्दनं n. Non-refutation of a charge.

अनुपमित,-मेय a. (f. -ता,-या) Matchless, incomparable.

अनुपलब्धिः f. 1 Non-recognition, non-perception. 2 Non-perception as one the six kinds of proof according to the मीमांसकs. -Comp. —समः m. A fallacy, trying to establish a fact (say, the eternity of sound) from the impossibility of seeing the nonperception of it.

अनुपलंभः m. Want of apprehension ; non-perception.

अनुपशयः m. Any thing or circumstance that aggravates a disease.

अनुपसंहारिन् m. A particular fallacy in logic. In this fallacy the argument being one of all comprehensiveness does not leave out anything to serve as a दृष्टांत

अनुपसर्गः m. A particle which is not, or has not the force of, an *Upasarga*, as अंतर.

अनुपस्कृत a. (f —ता) 1 Unpolished. -2 Genuine, blameless. -3 Not cooked or dressed (as food).

अनुपस्थानं n. Absence; not being present or at hand.

अनुपस्थित a. Not present, absent; not at hand or near ; not current. —तं A word that is not उपस्थित.q.v.

अनुपस्थितिः f. 1 Absence. -2 Inability to remember.

अनुपहत a. (f. —ता) 1 Not injured, unvitiated. -2 Not used, unbleached, new (as cloth) .

अनुपा (अनु + पा 1 P.) 1 To drink after (a person or thing), drink along with. -2 To follow in drinking. -3 (2 P.) See the next word.

अनुपा (अनु + पा 2 P.) To protect, preserve, defend.

अनुपाकृत a. (f. —ता) Not rendered fit for, or not consecrated for sacrificial purposes.

अनुपाख्य a. (f. —ख्या) Not clearly visible or discernible.

अनुपातं ind. Following in succession, going after successively.

अनुपातकं n. A heinous crime such as theft, murder, adultery, &c.

अनुपातिन् a. (f. —नी) Following as a result. —m. A follower.

अनुपानं n. 1 A drink taken along with or after medicine. -2 A drink close at hand.

अनुपानीय a. (f —या) Serving as a liquid vehicle of medicine —यं n. An after-drink ; what is fit to be drunk after.

अनुपार्श्व a. Lateral; being along or by the side. —र्श्वाः m. pl. N. of a people.

अनुपाल् 10 P. 1 To guard, protect, defend. -2 To conform to, obey, observe ; to execute, to carry out.

अनुपालनं n. Preserving, keeping up, obeying.

अनुपावृत्त a. (Ved.) Western.

अनुपुरुषः m. A follower.

अनुपूर्व a.(f. -र्वा) 1 Regular, regularly shaped, orderly, symmetrical. 2 Orderly, successive, coming in due order or succession. -3 The lowest.-Comp. —ज a. Descended in a regular line. —वत्सा f. A cow that calves regularly.

अनुपूर्वशः, -पूर्वेण adv. In regular order, one by one, successively.

अनुपूर्व्य a. 1 Regular, orderly, successive. 2 Proportionate.

अनुपेत a. (f. —ता) 1 Not endowed with. -2 Not invested with the sacred thread (अनुपनीत).

अनुप्त a. (f —प्ता) Not sown.

अनुप्तिम a. Growing spontaneously. Grown without being sown.

अनुप्रज्ञानं n. Tracing, tracking.

अनुप्रदानं n. 1 A gift, donation. -2 External effort in pronouncing letters.

अनुप्रपातं-दं *ind.* Going in succession.

अनुप्रयुज् (अनु + प्र + युज् 7 A.) To employ, apply, employ in addition.

अनुप्रयोगः *m.* Additional use, repetition.

अनुप्रवचनं *n.* Repetition or reproduction of what has been said by the teacher.

अनुप्राविश् (अनु + प्र + विश् 6 P.) 1 To enter into ; join. -2 To accommodate or adapt oneself to. -3 To enter after, to follow in entering ; sleep with. -4 To attack.

अनुप्रवेशः *m.* 1 Entrance into ; पुपोष वृद्धिं हरिदश्वदीधितेरनुप्रवेशादिव बालपादपः रघुवं. 3. 22. -2 Adapting oneself to the will of. -3 Imitation.

अनुप्रश्नः *m.* A question referring to what the teacher has previously explained.

अनुप्रसक्तिः *f.* 1 Very close attachment. -2 Very close logical connection.

अनुप्रसादनं *n.* Propitiation, conciliation.

अनुप्रस्थ *a.* Latitudinal ; following the breadth or latitude.

अनुप्राप् (अनु + प्र + आप् 5 P.) 1 To get, obtain. -2 To reach, go to, overtake -3 To imitate. -4 (intrans). To arrive, come -5 To get back.

अनुप्राप्त *p. p. a.* (*f.* —प्ता) Reached, got, obtained.

अनुप्राप्तिः *f.* Getting to, reaching, arriving.

अनुप्रासः *m.* Alliteration, repetition of similar letters, syllables, or sounds. The repetition of the same letters (consonants). वर्णसाम्यमनुप्रासः There are several kinds of अनुप्रासs. छेकानुप्रास takes place when a number of consonants are repeated again in the same order, e. g. कावेरीवारिपावनः पवनः 2 लाटानुप्रास occurs when the same words are repeated in the same sense but with a different construction. e. g. दिनकरकुलचंद्र चंद्रकेतो सरभसमेहि दृढं परिष्वजस्व (उत्तर रा. 6.) 3वृत्त्यनुप्रास occurs when a single consonant is repeated once or many times, or when many consonants occur once again but not in the same order, or when many consonants occur more than once and in the same order. 4 श्रुत्यनुप्रास occurs when consonants belonging to the same organs of articulation come in several times in the same or different order. अंत्यानुप्रास occurs when final letters tally.

अनुप्लवः *m.* A companion, follower, servant.

अनुप्लु (अनु + प्लु 1 A.) To run after, follow.

अनुबद्ध *p. p. a.* (*f.* —द्धा) 1 Bound, attached, tied to. -2 Coming after or as a consequence ; related to ; continued.

अनुबध् (अनु + बंध् 9 P.) 1 To bind or fasten to, tie, connect. 2 To have coming after. 3. To bring about, produce, to lead to, result in. 4. To press, to urge. 5 To follow, to pursue, to stick or cling to ; to continue 6 To entertain. 7 To bear, endure. 8 To keep together.

अनुबंधः *m* 1. Connection, attachment. (lit. & fig.). -2Uninterrupted succession, continuous flow, series. राजा–अयि प्रसीद् । न खलु क्षुधः सर्वीजन एवंविधः कोपानुबंधः * रत्नाव. -3 Descendants, posterity. -4 Consequence, result (good or bad). -5 A follower, partisan, adherent. कालो दुर्योधनं हंतुं सानुबंधमरिंदम * मकोपा. 52. 6 Intention, design, motive, cause of an action. -7 An adjunct of a thing. -8 Introductory reasons. 9 (Gram.) An indicatory syllable or letter which is annexed to a word to denote some peculiarity in the inflection, accent, &c. of the word. -10 A requisite of a book as insisted upon by ancient sanskrit writers. These अनुबंधs. are four, अधिकारिन्, विषय, संबंध, and प्रयोजन. An अधिकारिन् is one that wants to learn a subject. विषय is the subject of a book. प्रयोजन is the object or reward to be gained by reading a book. संबंध is the कार्यकारणभाव between the प्रयोजन and the विषय. -11 Offence, fault. -12 An obstacle, impediment. -12 A child or pupil who follows the example set by his parent or teacher. -13 Beginning, commencement. -14 Repeated application or devotion. -15 Course, pursuit. -16 A small bit or part, a trifle. -17 The junction of a fraction (with an integer), as भागानुबंधपूर्णांक.- -18 Base, stem (प्रकृति).

अनुबंधनं *n.* Connection, succession, association.

अनुबंधिन् *a.* (*f* —नी) 1 Following in unbroken continuity, continuous, uninterrupted 2 All pervading. -3 Mixed or blended with. -4 Followed by, accompanied with.

अनुबंध्य *a.* 1 Principal, chief. -2 To be killed (as a bull).

अनुबलं *n.* A rearguard of an army; an auxiliary force.

अनुबोधः *m.* 1 An after-thought, recollection. -2 Reviving the scent of a faded perfume.

अनुबोधनं *n.* Recollection, reminding, recollecting.

अनुब्राह्मणं *n.* A work resembling a Brâhmana .(*n*)

अनुभवः *m.* 1. Knowledge other than remembrance. 2. Understanding. 3 Impression on the mind arsing from direct perception. -4 Experience. -Comp. -सिद्ध *a.* (*f.* —द्धा) Established by experience.

अनुभावः *m* 1 Dignity, authority, splendour, might, power, अनुभावविशेषात्तु सेनापरिवृताविव * रघुवं. 1. 37; अहो महानुभावः पार्थिवो दुष्यतः * शाकुं. 3 जाने वो रक्षसाक्रांतावनुभावपराक्रमौ * रघुवं. 10. 38, -2 (In Rhet.) A symptom which indicates the feeling (भाव) produced by its appropriate causes. An effect or external manifestation of रति, हास, शोक, क्रोध, उत्साह, भय, जुगुप्सा, विस्मय, in the form of glances, perspiration, &c. अनुभावो विकारस्तु भावसंसूचनात्मकः. -3 Firm opinion, a fixed resolution.

अनुभावनं *n.* 1. Representing feelings so as to make them the characteristic of a poetical composition. 2 Indication of feelings by signs, gestures, &c.

अनुभासः *m.* A kind of crow.

अनुभुज् (अनु + भुज् 7 A.) To enjoy, experience, to bear, to undergo.

अनुभू (अनु + भू 1 P.) 1 To bear, to undergo: to experience, suffer, enjoy. 2 To understand, to notice, perceive. -3 To try, test, put to the test. -4 To comprise, include, grasp. —*Caus.* 1 To cause to enjoy, suffer, feel, experience, or bear. -2 To ponder over, to revolve in mind, reflect on, meditate, to brood upon -3 To infer, know.

अनुभू *a.* Perceiving, understanding, experiencing, feeling.

अनुभूति: *f.* 1 Perception, apprehension, experience.-2 (In Nyaya) Knowledge derived from four sources: namely direct perception, inference, comparison, and verbal knowledge. 3 Dignity, consequence.

अनुभोग: *m.* 1 Enjoyment. -2 A grant of hereditary land in return for services rendered.

अनुभ्रातृ *m.* A younger brother.

अनुमत *p.p. a.* (*f.* —ता) 1. Allowed, permitted. -2 Approved, assented to 3. Agreeable, dear, beloved. 4. Agreei g with, concurring with. —त: *m.* A lover. -तं *n.* Consent, approval, permission.

अनुमति: *f.* 1 Permission, consent, approval, assent. -2 The day on which the moon rises full less one digit. 3 The same personified as a goddess -Comp. —पत्रं *n.* A deed expressing assent.

अनुमन् (अनु + मन् 4 A.) 1 To permit, to allow; to agree or consent to, comply with, approve, sanction, grant. तत्र नाहमनुमंतुमुत्सहे मोघवृत्ति कलभस्य चेष्टितम् * रघुवं. 11. 39.

अनुमननं *n.* 1 Assent, sufferance. -2 Independence.

अनुमंत्र (अनु + मंत्र् 10 A.) To consecrate by the recital of appropriate, hymns or magical formulas. 2 To dismiss with a blessing.

अनुमंत्रणं *n.* Consecration by the recital of appropriate hymns, blessings, or prayers.

अनुमरणं *n.* 1. Following in death. 2 The cremation of a widow with the dead body of her husband.

अनुमा (अनु + मा 3 A, 2 P.) 1 To infer or conclude, guess, conjecture (as from signs, premises, &c.) -2 To reconcile, equal. —*Caus.* (-मापयति) To lead one to infer, guess, conjecture, or conclude.

अनुमा *f.* Inference, conclusion from given premises. The same as अनुमिति.

अनुमातृ *a* One who infers.

अनुमानं *n.* 1 Inferring as the cause of an अनुमिति, or conclusion from given premises (in सांख्य and न्याय phil.).-2 A guess, conjecture, sign to know. -3 Analogy, similarity. -4 (In Rhet.) An inference drawn from a poetic reason and expressed in a striking or charming manner. अनुमानं तदुक्तं यत्साध्यसाधनयोर्वचः * काव्यप्र. 10. अनुमानं तु विच्छित्त्या ज्ञानं साध्यस्य साधनात् * साहि. द. e. g. तव सुचरितमंगुलीय नूनं प्रतनु ममेव विभाव्यते फलेन ॥ अरुणनखमनोहरासु तस्याश्च्युतमसि लब्धपदं यदंगुलीषु * शकुं. 6 -Comp. —उक्ति *f.* The act of reasoning, logical inference.

अनुमापक *a.* (-पिका *f.*) Being the ground of inference. Causing an inference as an effect.

अनुमास: *m.* The following month. —सं *adv.* Every month, month after month.

अनुमितिः *f.* A conclusion from given premises; the knowledge resulting from syllogising.

अनुमुद् (अनु + मुद् 1 A. or P.) 1 To rejoice with. 2 To express approval; approve, applaud, to allow or permit.

अनुमृ (अनु + मृ 6 A.) To follow in death; त्वया कृत एव सा पुनर्भवता नानुमृतापि लभ्यते * रघुवं 8. 85 (followed in death by you); गतिविभ्रमसादनीरवा न शुचा नानुमृतेव लक्ष्यते * रघुवं 58 (used actively.).

अनुमेय *pot. p. a.* (*f.* –या) Inferable, to be inferred; फलानुमेयाः प्रारंभाः * रघुवं. 1. 20.

अनुमोदः *m.* 1 The pleasure arising from sympathy. –2 Approval, assent. –3 Compliance, acceptance. –4 Causing pleasure.

अनुमोदनं *n.* 1 Approval, assent. –2 Acceptance, compliance. –3 Causing pleasure.

अनुया (अनु + या 2 P.) 1 To follow, go after. सत्यं ब्रह्मानुयाहि साधुपदवीं * भर्तृह. 77. अनुयास्यन्मुनितनयां सहसा विनयेन वारितप्रसरः * शाकुंत. I. 29. –2 To imitate, equal; न किलानुययुस्तस्य राजानो रक्षितुर्यशः * रघुवं. I. 27. –3 To attend, accompany; to keep time with.

अनुयातृ *m.* A follower.

अनुयात्रं *n.* –त्रा *f.* Retinue, train; attendance, following. –त्रं *adv.* In or after a procession.

अनुयात्रिकः *m.* A follower, attendant.

अनुयानं *n.* Following, going after.

अनुयायिन् *a.* (*f.*–नी) 1 Following; attending, consequent. –2 Of the same nature; similar. –3 Following a course or principle prescribed or dictated or enunciated by a person. –*m.* A follower (lit. & fig.); a dependant or attendant; न्यषेधि शेषोऽप्यनुयायिवर्गः * रघुवं 2. 4.

अनुयुक्त *p. p.* (*f.* –क्ता) 1 Asked, questioned, examined, ordered. –2 Censured, reproached.

अनुयुज् (अनु + युज् 7 A) 1 To ask, question. –2 To question or examine (as an accused), put on trial. –3 To give specific instructions to. –4 To order, enjoin. –5 To select as husband.

अनुयोक्तृ *m.* An examiner, interrogator; inquirer; a teacher, especially hired or mercenary.

अनुयोगः *m.* 1 A question, inquiry, examination. 2 Solicitation. 3 Censure, reproof. –4 Exertion, effort. –5 Religious meditation. –6 Comment; explanation. –Comp. —कृत 1. An interrogator. –2 A teacher, spiritual preceptor.

अनुयोजनं *n.* A question, inquiry.

अनुयोज्य *pot. p. a.* (*f.* —ज्या) Fit to be questioned, asked. —ज्यः *m.* A servant.

अनुरक्त *p. p. a.* (*f.* —क्ता) 1 Reddened, dyed, coloured. –2 Pleased, contented; loved, beloved; liked, loyally devoted; fond of (with loc. or acc.).

अनुरक्तिः *f.* Love, attachment, devotion, affection.

अनुरंज् (अनु + रंज् 4. U.) 1 To be or to become red. –2 To be pleased स्थाने हृषीकेश तव प्रकीर्त्या जगत्प्रहृष्यत्यनुरज्यते च * भगवं. गी. 11. 36. –3 To be attached or devoted to, be fond of, to be delighted at, to love, like (with acc. or loc.). —*Caus.* 1 To make red, redden, dye, colour. –2 To attach oneself to, please, to love, gratify, conciliate.

अनुरंजक *a* Gratifying, pleasing.

अनुरंजनं *n.* Conciliating, satisfying, gratifying, pleasing, keeping contented.

अनुरंजित *p. p. a.* (*f.* —ता)Pleased, gratified ; conciliated, kept contented.

अनुरणनं *n.* 1. A continuous tinkling echo produced by the sound of a bell &c. 2 (Rhetoric) A meaning suggested by what is actually said.

अनुरक्तिः *f.* Love, attachment.

अनुरथ्या *f.* A foot-path, a by-road, the path along the side of a road ; प्रकाशीकरणार्थं च निशागमनशंकया । दीपवृक्षास्तथा चक्रुरनुरथ्यासु सर्वशः * रामाय.

अनुरसः *m.*, रसितं *n.* Echo, reverberation.

अनुरसः *m.* 1 A secondary feeling (in Rhet.). -2 A secondary flavour.

अनुरसित *a.* Echoing ; sounding.

अनुरहस *a.* (*f.* —सा) Secret, solitary, private. —सं *adv.* In secret, apart, privately.

अनुरागः *m.* 1 Redness. -2 Devotion, attachment, contentment, loyalty, love, affection, passion (with loc.)नूनं सा कामरी भविष्यति यतस्त्वा अनुरागतः सकलमपि दिनं तत्र गमयासि * पंचतं. 4. -Comp.-इंगितं *n.* A gesture or external sign expressive of love.

अनुरागवत, अनुरागिन्: *a* (*f.*-ती,-णी).1 Attached, enamoured, impassioned, inspired with love; स वृद्धस्तस्याम्सतीवानुरागवान् *हितोप 1; सा केनापि वणिक्पुत्रेण सहानुरागवती बभूव * हितोप.-2 Causing or inspiring love. —णी *f.* Personification of a musical note.

अनुरात्रं *adv.* In the night ; every night, night after night.

अनुराधा *f.* N. of the 17th of the 27 lunar mansions or asterisms consisting of four stars. -Comp. -ग्रामः, *m.* -पुरं *n.* The ancient capital of Lanka or Ceylon ; also called अनुरोधपुर.

अनुरुद् (अनु + रुद् 2 P.) To weep after or in sympathy with. शुकशोका मनुरोदितीव मां * कुमा. सं. 4. 15

अनुरुध् (अनु + रुध् 7 U.) 1 To obstruct, block up ; to surround, hem in. -2 To bind, fasten. -3 To follow closely ; observe, practise. -4 To be devoted to, attach oneself to. -5 To conform to, obey, follow, adapt oneself to, act up to ; नियति लोक इवानुरुध्यते * किराता. 2. 12 ; -6 To propitate, gratify, flatter, soothe. 7 To urge, press, entreat. -8 To permit, assent or agree to, approve ; comply with.

अनुरूप *a.* (*f.* —पा) 1 Like, resembling, corresponding to. -2 Suitable, or fit ; adapted to; harmonising with. (with gen.)—पं *n.* 1 Resemblance, likeness, conformity. 2 Suitability, fitness.

अनुरूपतः,—पशः —पेण, *adv.* In harmony with, in accordance to,. Conformably or agreeably to.

अनुरोदनं *n.* Weeping in condolence or sympathy.

अनुरोधः *m.* —धनं *n.* 1 Compliance, fulfilling one's wishes. -2 Conformity, regard, consideration. -3. Pressing, entreaty, solicitation, request. 4 The application or bearing of a rule.

अनुरोधक, -धिन्. *a.* (*f.* —का, -नी.)

Complying with, observing, having regard to.

अनुलाप: *m.* Repetition of what has been said; tautology

अनुभास:, —स्व: *m.* A peacock.

अनुलिप् (अनु + लिप् 6 P.) To anoint, besmear, smear.

अनुलेप: *m* —लेपनं *n.* 1 Unction, anointing, smearing. -2 Ointment, unguent ; any emollient or oily substance applied to the skin.

अनुलोम *a.* (*f.* —मा) 1 With the hair, *i. e.* in natural order; successive (opp. प्रातिलोम); favourable, agreeable. -2 Mixed (as a caste or tribe.). —मा *f.* A woman of a lower caste than that of the man's whom she marries. -मं *adv.* In regular or natural order. —मा: (*m.pl.*) Mixed castes. -Comp. -अर्थ *a.* Speaking in favour of. —कृष्ट *a.* Ploughed with the grain. —ज, -जन्मन् *a.* Born from a mother of an inferior caste to the father's; offspring of a mother inferior in caste to the father.

अनुलोमनं *n.* 1 Regular gradation. -2 (In medicine) Expelling by the regular channels from the body.

अनुल्बण *a.* (*f.* —णा) 1 Not excessive. -2 Not clear or manifest.

अनुवंश: *m.* 1 A genealogical table. -2 Modern race or species ; new family.

अनुवक्र *a.* (*f.* —क्रा) Very crooked ; somewhat crooked or oblique. —ग *a.* Moving somewhat obliquely or retrogressively (said of planets).

अनुवच् (अनु + वच् 2 P.) 1 To say, repeat, or speak after or for one. -2 To recite, reiterate ; शतमनूच्यमानः युक्तामस्य * ऐतरेय ब्रा. -3 Learn, study. -4 To assent to, yield. -5 To name, call. —*Caus.* To cause to recite ; to read to oneself (before reading aloud); reading to oneself. राजा—नाखयगतिर्मिनोरथानां । (गृहीत्वानुवाच्य सहर्षं) सखे प्रसन्नस्ते तर्कः * विक्रमो. 2.

अनुवचनं *n.* 1 Repetition, recitation. 2 Teaching, instruction. -3 A chapter or section of a book. -4 Repetition of Mantras or texts in a certain manner.

अनुवत्सर: *m.* 1 A year. —रं *adv.* Every year.

अनुवद् (अनु + वद् 1 P.) 1 To imitate in speaking. 2 To speak after. 3 To speak like a person to mock him. (with acc.) (P. & A.) To resound, echo. -2 To repeat or say again by way of explanation, illustration or corroboration. -3 To repeat, tell, say. -4 To abuse, rail at. -*Caus.* To cause to resound or echo.

अनुवर्तनं *n.* 1. Obliging, gratifying another 2 Compliance, obedience, conformity. 3 Consequence, result, continuance. -4 Supplying from a preceding Sutra.

अनुवर्तिन् *a.* (*f.* —नी) 1 Following, obeying, conforming to, (with acc.) -2 Obedient, faithful, compliant. -3 Suitable, worthy.

अनुवर्त्मन् *a.* Following, attending.

अनुवश *a.* (*f.* —शा) Subject to the will of another, obedient. —श: *m.* Obedience (to the will of another).

अनुवस् (अनु + वस् 1 P.) To dwell near to or along with (with acc.).

अनुवासित *a.* (*f.* —ता) 1 Dressed, clothed, wrapped up. -2 Fastened or bound to, attached to.

अनुवह *m.* One of the 7 tongues of fire.

अनुवाक *m.* 1 Recital, repeating, reading. -2 A chapter of the Vedas. -3 A collection of hymns of the Vedas.

अनुवाक्या *f.* A verse recited by the मैत्रावरुण or in his absence by the होतृ to invoke a deity to accept the offering prepared for the deity.

अनुवाच् *f.* Repetition, recitation. —*m.* A lecture, a lesson.

अनुवाचन *n.* 1 Causing to recite, teaching, instructing. -2 Reading to oneself. -3 Recitation of passages of the Rigveda by the Hotri priest in obedience to the injunction (प्रैष) of the अध्वर्यु priest.

अनुवात *m.* 1 The wind that blows from behind. -2 The windward direction; अनुवाते To windward.

अनुवाद *m.* 1 Repetition. -2 Repetition by way of explanation, illustration or corroboration. -3 Explanatory reference to what has been already mentioned, paraphrase. A reference to an injunction given before in order to illustrate it by way of comment (opp. विधि). -4 Corroboration, confirmation. -5 Slander, abuse. -6 A report, rumour. -7 Commencement of speech.

अनुवादक,-वादिन् *a.* 1 Explanatory. -2 Agreeing with, conformable to, in harmony with, like.

अनुवाद्य *pot. p. a.* (*f.* —द्या) 1 To be explained or illustrated. -2 (In gram.) Fit to be made the subject of an assertion (in a sentence). Every sentence consists of two parts, the अनुवाद्य and the विधेय. The अनुवाद्य is the subject, i. e. that about which something is affirmed or denied, and the विधेय is the predicate, i. e. that which affirms or denies something about the subject.

अनुवारम् *ind.* Often and often, repeatedly, frequently.

अनुवास् (अनु + वास् 10 P.) 1 To scent, perfume. -2 To use the oily enema.

अनुवास *m.*, **-सन** *n.* Perfuming or scenting. A syringe (Mar. पिचकारी) an oily enema or the act of administering the enema.

अनुवासित *a.* (*f.* —ता) 1 Fumigated, perfumed. -2 Treated by administering an enema.

अनुवासिन् *a.* One who dwells near, resident.

अनुवित्ति *f.* Finding, obtaining.

अनुविद् (अनु + विद् 6 U.) 1 To find, obtain. -2 To consider. -3 To marry.

अनुविद्ध *p. p. a.* (*f.* —द्धा) 1 Pierced, bored. -2 Overspread, interwoven with, surrounded, filled with, intermixed; सरसिजमनुविद्धं शैवलेन [illegible] 1.20. -4 Set, inlaid, variegated; रत्नानुविद्धार्णवमेखलाया दिशः सपत्नी भव दक्षिणस्याः ॥ रघु. 6.63.

अनुविधा (अनु + वि + धा 3 U.) 1 To lay down a rule, regulate. -2 To obey, follow in the footsteps of, conform to; [illegible] भट्टि. -3 To resemble, imitate.

अनुविधान *n.* 1 Obedience. -2 Acting in conformity to rules &c.

अनुविधायिन् *a* (*f* —नी) 1 Obedient, submissive, compliant, conforming to orders –2 Similar, like

अनुविश् *m* (अनु + विश् 6 P) To enter or go after, follow

अनुवृत् (अनु + वृत् 1 A) 1 To go after, follow, pursue; (fig) to follow, conform to act according to, obey be guided by, humour; किमत्र चित्रं यदि विशाखे शशाङ्कलेखामनुवर्तेते * शकुन्तलोककान्तां हि साधुनामर्थं वागनुवर्तते * उत्त 1 1 10 2 To imitate, resemble, equal 3 To gratify, please, to come after –4 To continue, to behave –5 (In gram) To be repeated or supplied from a preceding rule, Sutra, or assertion

अनुवृत्त *p p a* (*f* —ता) 1 Obeying –2 Continuous continued –3 Rounded off 4 To be borrowed from a preceding rule –5 Conforming to one's own disposition –त्तं *n* Obedience, conformity, compliance

अनुवृत्ति *f* 1 Pleasing another by acting conformably to his will 2 Application or bearing of a preceding rule or a part of it to the following rule 3 Compliance assent, approval, obedience, following 4 Imitating, resembling 5 Remembrance 6 Repetition (of letters, &c)

अनुवेध —व्याध *m* 1 Hurting, piercing, perforating –2 Contact, union –3 Blending mixture; fusion –4 Obstruction

अनुवेलं *ind* Ever and anon, continually, constantly; इति स्म पृच्छत्यनुवेलमादृतः * रघु 3 5

अनुवेष्टित *a* (*f* —ता) Folded up; covered up; bandaged —तं *n* Bandaging, or bandage

अनुवेश *m* —शन *n* 1 Following entering after –2 Marriage of a younger brother before that of the elder

अनुवेश्य *a* (*f* —श्या) A next door neighbour

अनुव्यञ्जन *n* A secondary mark.

अनुव्यध् (अनु + व्यध् 4 P) 1 To hit, pierce 2 To wound; 3 To blend with –4 To propel, urge on

अनुव्यवसाय *m* (In Nyaya) Consciousness of direct knowledge (in Vedānta phil) Perception of a sentiment or judgment

अनुव्याख्यान *n* Explanation of Mantras Sutras, &c

अनुव्याहरण *n*, —व्याहार *m* A curse imprecation 2 Repeating, repetition, mentioning along with something else

अनुव्रज् (अनु + व्रज् 1 P) 1 To follow, go after 2 To go after or follow a guest as a mark of honour 2 To keep (company) मृगा मूर्छन्समनुव्रजन्ति 3 To go and seek 4 To do homage to

अनुव्रजन *n*, —व्रज्या *f* 1 Following going after, especially a departing guest 2 Attendance

अनुव्रत *a* (*f* —ता) 1 Devout faithful devoted, attached 2 Observing vows or duties prescribed 3 Favourable —तः *m* 1 A devotee 2 A class of Jaina ascetics —ता *f* A wife faithful to her husband

अनुशतिक *a* (*f* —की) Followed by a hundred 2 Bought for a hundred

अनुशय *m* 1 Repentance; regret 2 Deep and intense hatred 3 Enmity 4 Close attachment 5

Sorrow. 6 The evil result of an act which makes the soul enter other bodies (Vedânta phil.). 7. Rescission of sale (in law.). —यी *f.* A disease of the foot.

अनुशयान *a.* (*f.* —ना) Repenting. —ना *f.* One of the heroines described in rhetorical literature ; a mistress who is saddened at the thought that her lover may forsake her.

अनुशयिन् *a.* (*f.* —नी) 1 Devoted, attached. 2 Penitent, regretful, sorry. 3 Bearing intense hatred. 4 Connected with past actions.

अनुशर: *m.* A sort of evil spirit, Rákshasa.

अनुशास् (अनु + शास् 2 P.) 1 To rule, to govern. 2 To advise, to teach, persuade, order, enjoin. 3 To punish, to chastise, to correct. 4 To praise. 5 To perform.

अनुशासक: *m.* One who advises, persuades, directs, instructs, governs or chastises.

अनुशासनं *n.* 1 Instruction, precept, order, command, advice. 2 Explanation, an explanatory treatise —Comp. —पर *a.* Obedient. —पर्वन् N. of the 13th book of the Mahabhârata.

अनुशासितृ *m.* He who commands, teaches, advises or punishes.

अनुशासिन् *a.* (*f.* —नी) Instructor, adviser, chastiser

अनुशिष्ट *a.* (*f.* —ष्टा) Taught, ordered, punished.

अनुशिष्टि: *f.* 1. Instruction, teaching. 2 Command.

अनुशी (अनु + शी 2 A.) 1 To lie down with, to sleep along with. 2. To repent ; to be sorry for. 3 To cling to.

अनुशीलनं *n.* 1 Constant study or application. 2 Faithful and devoted service or attachment.

अनुशीलित *a.* (*f.* —ता) 1. Repeatedly done. 2 Carefully attended to.

अनुशुच् (अनु + शुच् 1 P.) 1. To lament for, to mourn. 2. To repent, to regret.

अनुशोक: *m.* —शोचनं *n.* Sorrow, repentance, regret.

अनुश्रव: *m* Vedic or sacred tradition.

अनुश्रु (अनु + श्रु 5 P.) 1 To hear. 2. To hear as a tradition. 3 To hear repeatedly as from a sacred authority.

अनुषक्, —द् *adv.* In succession.

अनुषक्त *p. p. a.* (*f.* —क्ता) 1. Clinging to, adhering to. 2 Connected with ; related or attached to.

अनुषंग: *m* 1 Connection, association, attachment. 2. Connection of word with word (Gram.). 3 A word borrowed from a previous sentence to supply an ellipsis. 4 A necessary result. 5. Intermixture. 6 Connection of an act with a subsequent act. 7 Incidental mention or relation. -8 Yearning, eager longing. -9 Compassion, pity, tenderness. 10 (In Nyaya). Connecting the conclusion (निगमन) to the application (उपनय) by some demonstrative pronoun.

अनुषंगिन् *a.* (*f.* —णी) 1 Connected with, as a necessary result. 2 Following as a necessary consequence -3 Related or applicable to associated with. -4 Attached to fond of.

अनुषंज् (अनु + संज् 1 P.) To adhere or stick to, follow closely. -2 To be supplied from a preceding rule or statement. To connect word with word (Gram.). —*Caus*. 1 To fasten or attach (something) to. -2 To supply a word from the preceding sentence.

अनुषंजनं *n*. Concord, grammatical connection or agreement.

अनुषंजनीय *a*. (*f*. —या) To be supplied as a word from a preceding sentence.

अनुषेकः *m*. Sprinkling over again.

अनुषेचनं *n*. See अनुषेक.

अनुष्टुति: *f*. Praise.

अनुष्टुभ् *f*. 1 Following in praise ; speech. -2 A N. Sarasvatî. -3 N. of a class of metres consisting of four Pâdas of 8 syllables each, the whole stanza consisting of 32 syllables. The most general form of this metre is thus roughly defined. पंचमं लघु सर्वत्र सप्तमं द्विचतुर्थयोः । गुरु षष्ठं च पादानां शेषेष्वनियमो मतः ॥

अनुष्ठा (अनु + स्था 1 U.) 1 To do, perform, execute, bring about. -2 To perform, to celebrate, to observe as a vow, a religious rite, &c. -3 To superintend, appoint, to rule, to govern. -4 To sit on ; occupy. -5 To follow, go after. -6 To imitate, to tread in the footsteps of.

अनुष्ठातव्य,-अनुष्ठेय *pot. p. a*. (*f*. —व्या, —या) To be accomplished, practised, performed, followed, or done conformably to.

अनुष्ठातृ,-ष्ठायिन् *a*. (*f*. —त्री, —नी) Doing, practising, performing, executing; one who does, performs, practises, undertakes or begins.

अनुष्ठानं *n*. 1. Commencement or course of proceeding. 2 Undertaking. 3. Performance. Doing. 4. Religious rite. 5. Accomplishment, execution. —नी *f*. Performance, commencement, practice. -Comp. -शरीरं *n*. (Sânkhya doctrine) The intermediate body between the सूक्ष्म or subtle and the स्थूल or gross body.

अनुष्ठापक *a*. Causing to perform.

अनुष्ठापनं *n*. Causing to do an act.

अनुष्ठायिन् *a*. (*f*. —नी) Doing, performing.

अनुष्ठित *p. p*. (*f*. —ता) Done, performed, accomplished, followed, practised.

अनुष्ण *a*. (*f*. —ष्णा) 1 Not hot; cold. -2 Lazy, sluggish. 3 Indifferent —ष्णः *m*. Cold touch or sensation. —ष्णं *n*. A waterlily, blue lotus. -Comp. —गुः *m*. That has cold rays, the moon.

अनुष्यंदः *m*. A hind wheel.

अनुष्वध *a*. Accompanied by food —धं *adv*. 1 During or after food. -2 According to food. 3 After every sacrifice. -4 At will.

अनुसंहित *p. p. a*. (*f*. —ता) Inquired into, investigated ; connected with. —तं *adv*. In the Samhitâ text ; according to the संहिता or the वेद.

अनुसंचर् (अनु + सम् + चर् 1 P.) 1 To go after ; to pursue ; to go towards, to visit ; to penetrate. 2 To become assimilated.

अनुसंचरणं *n*. Following, pursuing.

अनुसंततिः *f*. Continued succession, continuity.

अनुसंधा (अनु + सम् + धा 3 U.) 1 To inquire or search into or after, look after, investigate, examine, to find out -2 To tranquilise, calm, quiet. -3 To think of, allude to, consider, deliberate, to contemplate, to aim at. -4 To arrange ; prepare, set in order. -5 To follow, go after, attend, pursue. -6 To carry on, to take up, follow, continue.

अनुसंधानं *n* 1 Inquiry, investigation ; close inspection ; examination. -2 Aiming at. -3 Planning, arranging, preparing. -4 A plan, scheme. -5 Suitable connection. -6 (In the Vais. phil.) The -4th step in a syllogism, the उपनय or application.

अनुसंधायिन्, -संधायिन् *a.* (*f.* -नी) Investigating, contemplating, arranging, looking after ; skilful in concerting plans.

अनुसमयः *m.* Regular connection which is the result of reasoning. Regular or proper connection, as of words.

अनुसमापनं *n.* Regular completion.

अनुसंबद्ध *a.* (*f.* —द्धा) Connected with.

अनुसरः *m.* A follower, companion, attendant.

अनुसरणं *n.* 1 Following, pursuing, going after. -2 Conformity to, accordance with, result of. -3 Custom, practice, usage.

अनुसर्पः *m.* A serpent-like being ; a reptile in general.

अनुसवनं *ind.* 1 After a sacrifice. -2 At every sacrifice ; after ablutions. -3 Every moment.

अनुसाम *a.* (*f.* —मा) Conciliated, friendly, favourable.

अनुसायं *ind.* Every evening.

अनुसारः *m.* 1 Going after, following, pursuit. -2 Accordance with. conformity to usage, suitability. -3 Custom, usage, practice. -4 Established authority. -5 Nature, natural condition. -6 Currency, prevalence -7 Consequence, result.

अनुसारक, -सारिन् *a.* 1 Going after, following, pursuing ; consequent upon, attendant on ; मृगानुसारिणं साक्षात्पश्यामीव पिनाकिनं *Śāk.* 1. 6. पारिमल-पवनानुसारि *Daśak.* -2 Conformable to, following -3 Seeking, looking out for, investigating, scrutinizing.

अनुसारणा *f.* Going after, pursuit.

अनुसार्यकं *n.* A fragrant substance, such as sandal, aloe, &c.

अनुसूचक *a.* (*f.* —चिका) Indicative of, pointing out to.

अनुसूचनं *n.* Indication, pointing out.

अनुसृ (अनु + सृ 1 P.) 1 To follow, attend, pursue ; to practise, observe. -2 To go over or through. -*Caus.* 1 To lead, to conduct. -3 To cause to pursue, or follow.

अनुसृतिः *f.* 1 Going after, following ; conforming to, accordance with. -2 An unchaste woman, harlot.

अनुसैन्यं *n.* The rear guard, the rear of an army

अनुस्कंदं *ind.* Having entered, having gone into in succession ; गेहं गेहमनुस्कंदं having entered house after house.

अनुस्तरणं *n.* Strewing or spreading round. —णी *f.* 1 A cover.-2 A cow, especially the cow sacrificed at the funeral ceremony, to enable the departed spirit to safely cross the river of Hell called वैतरिणी.

अनुस्मरणं *n.* 1 Recollection, remembering. -2 Repeated remembrance or recollection.

अनुस्मृ (अनु + स्मृ 1 P.) To recollect, to remember, think of, call to mind, (with acc. or gen.) —*Caus.* To remind (painfully), cause to remember with regret.

अनुस्मृतिः *f.* The same as अनुस्मरणं.

अनुस्यूत *a.* (*f.* —ता) 1 Sewn on, or woven ; fastened to ; closely linked to. 2. Uninterrupted. 3 Woven together.

अनुस्वानः *m.* 1 An after-sound ; an echo. 2 Sounding conformably to.

अनुस्वारः *m.* The nasal sound which is marked by a dot (̇) above the line and which always belongs to the preceding vowel.

अनुहरणं *n.* Imitation, resemblance, similarity.

अनुहारः *m.* Same as अनुहरणं q. v.

अनुहार्य *pot. p. a.* (*f.* —र्या) Fit to be imitated. —र्यं *n.* Monthly obsequies on the Darsa or new moon day.

अनुहुंकृ (अनु + हुं an imitative particle + कृ 8 U.) To roar in imitation of, reply to ; अनुहुंकुरुते घनध्वनिं न हि गोमायुरुतानि केसरी • शिशुपा. 16. 25.

अनुहृ (अनु + हृ 1 P.) 1 To imitate, resemble. -2 To take after.

अनूकः *m.* -कं *n.* 1 The back bone, spine. -2 A kind of sacrificial vessel. -3 Former birth or state of existence. —कं *n.* 1 Family, race. -2 Disposition, temperament ; characteristic of race.

अनूकाशः *m.* 1 Reflection (of light). -2 Example, reference, illustration.

अनूक्त *p. p. a.* (*f.* —क्ता) Repeated, recited after ; occurring in the text studied. —क्तं *n.* -क्तिः *f.* 1 Subsequent mention ; repetition by way of explanation or illustration. -2 Study of the Vedas.

अनूक्तिः *f.* See अनूक्तं.

अनूचान *a.* Learned, devoted to study. -नः *m.* One wellversed in the Vedas with their Angas so as to be able to repeat, read, and teach them. -2 Modest, humble, well-behaved.

अनूढ *a.* (*f.* —ढा) 1 Not borne or carried. -2 Unmarried. —ढा *f.* An unmarried woman. -Comp. -गमनं *n.* Fornication. —भ्रातृ *m.* 1 The brother of an unmarried woman. -2 The brother of the concubine of a king.

अनूदकं *n.* Want of water ; draught.

अनूद्देशः *m.* A figure of speech in which a reference is made in successive order to what precedes ; यथासंख्यमनूद्देश उद्दिष्टानां क्रमेण यत् • साहि.द. 10.

अनून *a.* (*f.* —ना) 1 Whole, entire, full, large, great, not inferior, not less, not wanting or lacking in. -2 Having full power.

अनूप *a.* (*f.* —पा) Situated near water, abounding in water, marshy. —पं *n.* 1 A watery place or country ; a marsh, a bog. -2 A pond or tank of water. -3 Bank of a river. —पाः *m. pl.* N. of a particular country. —पः *m.* 1 A he buffalo. -2 A frog. -3 A kind of partridge. -4 An elephant. -Comp.—जं *n.* Moist ginger. —प्राय *a.* Marshy, boggy.

अनूरु *a.* Thighless. —रु: *m.* 1 Aruna, the charioteer of the sun. 2 The dawn. -Comp. —सारथि: *m.* The sun (having अनूरु for his charioteer).

अनूर्जित *a.* (*f.* —ता) 1 Not strong; weak, powerless. -2 Free from pride.

अनूषर *a.* (*f.* —रा) 1 Saline. -2 Not saline.

अनूह *a.* (*f.* —हा) 1. Free from doubt, doubtless. 2 Thoughtless, careless.

अनृक्ष See अनृच्.

अनृच्-च *a.* 1 Not studying the Vedas. 2 Not invested with the sacred thread and hence not yet entitled to study the Vedas (as a boy).

अनृजु *a.* Not straight ; crooked. 2 Wicked, dishonest.

अनृण *a.* (*f.* —णा) Free from debt; who has paid off the debt, (lit. and fig.).

अनृणता *f*, —आनृण्यं *n.* Freedom from debt.

अनृणिन *a.* Free from debt ; that has paid off his debts.

अनृत *a.* (*f.* —ता) 1 Not true ; False. 2 Obtained by fraud. —तं *n.* 1 Falsehood, deception, fraud. -2 Agriculture. -Comp. —वदनं, —भाषणं,—आख्यानं *n.* Lying, falsehood. —वादिन,—वाच् *a.* A liar. —व्रत *a.* False to one's vows or promises.

अनृतु: *m.* 1 Unfit season, improper or premature time. -2 Time before menstruation.

अनेक *a.* 1 Not one ; more than one ; many, several, various. -2 Separated ; divided. -Comp. —अक्षर *a.* Consisting of more than one syllable.—अच् *a.* Having more than one vowel. —अंत *a.* Uncertain, doubtful, variable. —त: *m.* 1. Want of permanence. Unsettled condition. -3 An uncertainty, doubtfulness 4 Non essential part, as the several. अनुबंधs. *e. g.* अनेकांता अनुबंधा: Indicatory letters are not an essential part. अनेकांतवाद *m.* Scepticism. अनेकांतवादिन *m.* A sceptic, a Jaina. —अर्थ *a.* 1 Having more than one meaning, homonymous. -2. Having the sense of the word अनेक. -3 Having many objects or topics. —आश्रय,—आश्रित *a* (in Vais. phil.) Dwelling or abiding in more than one; dependence upon more than one. —गोत्र *a.* Belonging to two families viz, that of his own, and that of his adoptive, father. —ज *a.* Born more than once. —ज: *m.* A bird. —प: *m.* An elephant. -धा *ind.* In various ways. —मुख *a.* (—खी *f.*) *a.* 1. Having many faces, manyfaced. -2 Scattered dispersed, going in various directions, taking to various ways. —मूर्ति: *m.* of Vishnu. —रूप *a.* 1. Of various forms, multiform. -2 Of various kinds or sorts. -3 Of a varying nature. —प: *m.* Epithet of the Supreme Being. —लोचन: *m.* N. of Siva ; also of Indra. —वचन *n.* The dual and the plural. -विध *a.* Various, different. —शफ *a.* Cloven-hoofed. —शस् *ind.* In large numbers or quantities; in various manners; frequently.

अनेड: *m*. A fool. -Comp. -मूक *a*. (*f*. —का) 1 Deaf and dumb. -2. Blind. -3. Dishonest, wicked, perverse.

अनेनस् *a*. Sinless, blameless ; not liable to error.

अनेहस् *m*. (nom. sing. अनेहा) Time.

अनैकांत *a*. (*f*. —ता) See अनैकांतिक.

अनैकांतिक *a*. 1 Unsteady, uncertain ; not to the point, not very important. -2 (in Logic) Involving a fallacy (हेत्वाभास) which is of three kinds (1) साधारण if the argument is too general; (2) असाधारण if it is not general enough, and (3) अनुपसंहारिन् if it is nonconclusive.

अनैक्यं *n*. 1 Plurality. 2 Absence of union. 3 Disorder.

अनैतिह्यं *n*. Absence of traditional sanction or authority.

अनो *ind*. No, not.

अनोकशायिन् *m*. Not sleeping in a house ; a beggar.

अनोकह: *m*. A tree.

अनौचित्यं *n*. Unfitness, impropriety,

अनौजस्यं *n*. Want of vigour, energy, or strength.

अनौद्धत्यं *n*. 1 Modesty, humility. 2 Tranquility, calmness.

अनौरस: *m*. A son not one's own, but adopted.

अंत *a*. (*f*. —ता) 1 Lowest, worst. 2 Youngest. 3 Near. 4 Last, concluding. 5 Beautiful. —त: *m*. 1 End, conclusion. 2 Limit, boundary. 3. Extremity. 4. Extent, expanse. 5 Death. 6 (Gram.) The final letter of a word. 7 The last member or word of a compound. 8 The settlement of a question. 9 Neighbourhood. —तं *n*. Nature, disposition, essence of a thing. —त: *m*. or तं *n*. The concluding portion, (as in वेदांत or सिद्धांत). -Comp. —अवसायिन् or अंतवसायिन् *m*. A barber. 2 A chandâla, a low-caste. -उदात्त *a*. Having acute accent on the last syllable. —त्त: *m*. The acute accent on the last syllable. —कर, —करण, —कारिन् *a*. Causing death or destruction ; fatal, mortal, destructive. —काल: *m*. -वेला *f*. The time or hour of death. —कृत् *m*. Death. -ग *a*. Going to the end of, thoroughly conversant or familiar with. —गमनं *n*. 1 Going to the end, finishing, completing. 2 Death, perishing, dying. —दीपकं *n*. A figure of speech (in Rhetoric). —पाल: *m*. 1 A frontier-guard. -2. A doorkeeper. -लीन *a*. Hidden, concealed. —लोप: *m*. The dropping of the final of a word. —वासिन् (अंतेवासिन् also) *a*. Dwelling near the frontiers, dwelling close by. (-*m*.) 1. A pupil, a student. -2. A chandâla. —वेला *f*. The time of death. —शय्या *f*. 1 The death-bed; hence death itself. -2 The place for burial or burning. -3. A bier or funeral pile. -सत्क्रिया *f*. The funeral ceremonies, obsequies. —सद् *m*. A pupil. —स्वरित: *m*. The svarita accent on the last syllable of a word.

अंतक *a*. Causing death, destroying. —क: *m*. A 1 Death. -2 Yama, the god of death. -3 A border, boundary.

अंततः *ind* 1 From the end. -2 At last, finally ; at length, lastly. -3 In part, partly. -4 Inside, within. -5 In the lowest way. अंततः may signify any oblique case of अंत.

अंतर् *ind.* (Used adverbially) In the middle, within, inside, between. (Used as a separable prep.) Within, between. (Used with verbs) In the middle, between, under. (With nouns) In the middle of, in the interior of. -Comp. —अग्निः *m.* The fire in the body *i.e.* the digestive faculty. —अंग *a.* 1. Included, (with abl.), त्रयमंतरंगं पूर्वेभ्यः The three are included in the former. 2. Essential, indispensable. 3 Dear. —अंतरंगं *n.* Interior. —आकाशः *m.* Brahman (*n.*). —आकूतं *n.* Hidden intention. —आत्मन् *m.* 1 The soul. 2 The heart. 3 The Supreme Spirit or Soul (residing in the interior of man). —आरामः *m.* He who rejoices in himself, finding pleasure in his soul or heart. —इंद्रियं *n.* An internal organ or sense. —करणं *n.* The internal organ ; the heart, soul ; the thinking faculty, mind, conscience. —कुटिल *a.* Inwardly crooked (fig. also) ; fraudulent. —कुटिलः *m.* A conch-shell. —कृमिः, —क्रिमिः *m.* A disease of worms in the body. —गडु *a.* Useless, unprofitable ; unnecessary. —गत *a.* 1. Gone into, slipt into. 2 Included in or by ; belonging to. 3 Interior, hidden. 4 Destroyed, forgotten. —गर्भ *a.* Bearing a young one ; pregnant. —गृहं, —गेहं, —भवनं *n.* The inner apartment of a house, the interior of a house. —चर *a.* Pervading the body ; internally situated; internal, inward. —जठरं *n.* The stomach. (*-ind.*) In the stomach. —जानु *ind.* Between the knees. —ज्ञानं *n.* Inward or secret knowledge. —ताप *a.* Burning inwardly. —तापः *m.* Internal fever or heat. —दहनं *n.*, —दाहः *m.* 1. Inward heat. -2 Inflammation. —दुःख *a.* Sad or afflicted at heart. —दृष्टिः *f.* Examining one's own soul ; insight into oneself. —देशः *m.* An intermediate region of the compass. —द्वारं *n.* A private or secret door within the house. —नगरं *n.* The palace of a king. —निष्ठ *a.* Engaged in internal meditation. —पटः *m.*, —टं *n.* A screen of cloth held between two persons who are to be united (as a bride and bridegroom, or pupil and preceptor) until the actual time of union arrives. —पदं *ind.* In the interior of an inflected word. —परिधानं *n.* The innermost garment. —पातः *m.*, —पात्यः *m.* 1 The insertion of a letter (in gram.). -2. A post fixed in the middle of the sacrificial ground (used in ritual works). —पातित, —पातिन् *a.* 1. Involved in, inserted. 2. Included or comprised in ; falling within. —पालः *m.* One who watches over the inner apartments of a palace. —पुरं *n.* 1 The inner apartment of a palace (set apart for women). -2. The inmates of the female apartments. -3 The principal wife of a king. अंतःपुरचरः, —अध्यक्षः, —रक्षकः, —वर्तिन् *m.* The guardian or superintendent of the harem. —पुरिकः *m.* The chamberlain. —प्रकृतिः *f.* 1 The internal nature or constitution of a man. 2. The ministry, or body of ministers of a king. -3. The heart or soul. —बाष्प *a.* Having the tears suppressed *i. e.* prevented from falling. —भूमिः *f.* The interior of the earth. —मनस् *a.* 1. Afflicted, distracted ; disconsolate, dejected. -2. He who has concentrated and turned his mind inward ; lost in abstract meditation. —मुख *a.* (-खी *f.*) 1. Pointing or turned inward. -2 Having an inward entrance or opening. -3 An epithet of the soul. —मं *n.* A sort of surgical scissors. —मृत *a.* Stillborn. —याम: *m.* The suppression of the breath and voice. —योग: *m.* Deep meditation, abstraction. —लीन *a.* 1. Latent, hidden, concealed inside. -2. Inherent. —वंश: *m.* The female apartments of a king. —वंशिक:,-वासिक: *m.* The superintendent of the women's apartments. —वती, —वत्नी *f.* A pregnant woman. —वस्त्रं,—वासस् *n.* An undergarment. —वाणि *a.* Skilled or versed in scriptures, very learned. —वेग: *m.* Inward uneasiness or anxiety, inward fever. -वेदि:,-दी *f.* The tract of land between the rivers Gangâ and Yamunâ, -वेश्मन् *n.* The inner apartments, interior of a house. —वेश्मिक: *m.* A chamberlain. —शरीरं *n.* The internal and Spiritual part of man; the interior of the body. —संज्ञ *a.* Inwardly conscious. —सत्त्वा *f.* A pregnant woman. —सार *a.* Having inward strength and vigour ; powerful, strong, heavy or ponderous. -सार: *m.* Internal treasure or store, inner store or contents. —सैन्यं *ind.* Into the midst of armies. -स्थ: *m.* A term applied to the semivowels, य्, र्, ल्, व्, as standing between vowels and consonants (in gram.). -स्वेद: *m.* An elephant (in rut). —हास: *m.* Laughing inwardly. —हृदयं *n.* The interior of the heart.

अंतर *a.* (*f.* रा) Internal, lying in the middle. 2 Exterior, external. 3 Neighbouring, adjoining 4. Similar. 5. Related, dear. 6 Another, different. —रं *n.* 1 The interior (*lit.* and *fig.*). The pith, essence substance. 2 Intermediate space or time. A screen ; the thing that lies between two and separates them. 3. Period, term. 4. Space in general. 5 Scope, admission, entrance. A receptacle for a thing ; an abode. 6 Occasion ; अत्रांतरे At this time; on this occasion. 7 Difference. 8 The remainder (in math.). A variety, a kind. 10. A hole, breach, break, perforation. 11. Deficiency, shortcoming. 12, Supreme Soul. 13. The mind. The heart. 14. Surety. 15. Another In this sense अंतर always stands as the last member of a कर्मधारय Compound which is of neuter gender whatever may be the gender of the first member. राजांतरं *n.* Another ki... वस्त्रांतरं *n.* Another piece of cloth, देशांतरं *n.* Another country, मतांतरं *n.* Another opinion, &c. 16 Excellence. A peculiarity. A characteristic mark. 17 Garment. 18. Purpose. 19 An obstacle, an impediment. 20. A substitute. -Comp. —अपत्या *f.* A pregnant woman. -ज्ञ *a.* Knowing the interior prudent ; farseeing. —तम *a.* 1. Nearest, immediate. 2 Most similar (in gram.). —तर *a.* Nearer, more intimate. —तस् *ind.* On the inside. —द: *m.* A connoisseur. —दिशा *f.* An intermediate direction of the compass. -पुरुषः, -पूरुषः *m*. The soul that resides in the heart. —प्रभवः *m*. One of a mixed caste. -मनस् *a*. Dejected. —स्थ *a*. 1. Inward, internal. 2 Standing between.

अंतरं *ind*. In the interior, on the inside, within, in the middle.

अंतराय् *m*. 1 An obstacle, an impediment. 2 A screen. 3 What bars final absolution (Jain phil.).

अंतरयणं *n*. See अंतरय.

अंतरा *ind*. Used adverbially, अंतरा means in the way, between, in the meantime, secretly, near. अंतरांतरा means at intervals. As a prep. अंतरा with a noun in acc. means between, without. -Comp. —वेदि, —वेदी *f*. 1. A kind of open portico. An arch in the door. 2. A kind of wall. —शृंगं *ind*. Between the horns.

अंतरायः *m*. Obstacle, impediment.

अंतरालं *n*. 1. Intermediate space. 2 Intermediate time. 3. The middle (of any thing). 4 Mixed caste.

अंतरि (अंतर् + इ 2 P.) 1 To go between; to separate; to intervene. 2 To omit ; to exclude. 3 To disappear, to be concealed, covered, or screened.

अंतरि (रि) क्षं *n*. 1 The intermediate region between earth and heaven. 2 The atmosphere. Sky. -Comp. —गः, —चरः *m*. A bird. —लोकः *m*. The intermediate world.

अंतरित *a*. (*f*. —ता) 1 Separated, concealed, obscured, screened, covered, lost to sight, prevented from being seen, disappeared. 2 Reflected. 3 Obstructed, inpeded. 4 Coming between, intervening. 5 Omitted, passed over. 6 Occupied.

अंतरीपं *n*. 1. Island. 2 A promontary, a cape.

अंतरीयं *n*. An under-garment.

अंतरे *ind*. Amidst, among, between.

अंतरेण *ind*. 1 Amidst, between. 2 Without (with acc.). 3 Besides, without. अंतरेणापि कौंतेय निकृतिं पापनिश्चयां । हंता त्वमसि दुर्बुद्धे ! सानुबंधं सुयोधनं ॥ वनप. 52. 4. In respect of, with regard to. देव्या एव वचनेन मालविकार्थमाचार्यगणदासं उपदेशग्रहणे कीदृशी मालविकेति प्रष्टुं ॥ मालवि. 1.

अंतर्गत *p. p. a.* (*f*. —ता) 1 Gone in, into, or between. 2. Included, existing in. Lying or situated in, in the interior. 3 Concealed, hidden, suppressed. 4. Disappeared ; forgotten ; destroyed. -Comp. —मनस् *a*. 1 Afflicted, distracted. 2 Engaged in meditation.

अंतर्गम् (अंतर् + गम्, गच्छ् 1 P.) 1 To interpose, to go between, to intervene. 2 To be comprised or included in.

अंतर्धा (अंतर् + धा 3 U.) 1 To deposit, to place within ; to place within oneself, to admit to take in, to receive. 2 To show, indicate. 3 To conceal oneself from the sight of. 4 To hide, to suppress, to cover up -*Caus*. (—धापयति) To cause to disappear, or pass beyond observation.

अंतर्धा *f*. Concealment, covering.

अंतर्धानं *n*. Invisibility, disappearance.

अंतर्धिः *m*. Concealment.

अंतर्भव *a*. (*f*. —वा). Situated or lying in. Placed inside.

अंतर्भावः *m.* 1. Inclusion. 2. Disappearance. 3 Inherent disposition or condition.

अंतर्भावना *f.* 1 Inclusion. 2. Anxiety.

अंतर्भू (अंतर् + भू 1 P.) 1 To be contained, comprised or included in.

अंतर्भूत *a.* (*f.* —ता) 1 Included. Comprised or contained in. 2 Inward, internal.

अंतर्य *a.* (*f.* —र्या) Situated on the inside, or in the middle.

अंतर्हित *a.* (*f.* —ता) 1 Placed between. 2 Concealed, screened, made invisible, covered up. 3. Disappeared, vanished.

अंतवत् *a.* Having an end ; limited ; perishable.

अंतिः *f.* An elder sister (in theatrical language).

अंतिक *a.* (*f.* —का) Neighbouring, proximate ; being, lying, or situated near. —कं *n.* Neighbourhood, vicinity, proximity. —कं, —केन, —कात्, -के, *ind.* have an adverbial force, and with a noun in gen. or abl. case mean near.

अंतिका *f.* 1 An elder sister (in theatrical language). 2 A fireplace.

अंतिम *a.* (*f.* —मा) 1 Last, final, ultimate. 2 Immediately following. -Comp. —अंकः *m.* The digit 1. —अंगुलिः *f.* The little finger.

अंती *f.* A fire place.

अंते *ind.* (Loc. sing. of अंत used as an *adv.*) 2 In the end, at last. 2 In the interior. 3 Near. -Comp. —वासः *m.* 1 A pupil. 2 A neighbour. —वासिन् *m.* 1 A pupil. 2 A chandâla.

अंत्य *a.* (*f.* —त्या) 1 Last (in time, place, or order). 2 Immediately following. 3 Lowest, inferior. 4. Non-permanent. 5. Adjoining. —त्यः *m.* 1 The last syllable of a word. 2. A man of the lowest caste. 3 The month फाल्गुन. 4 A foreigner ; a म्लेच्छ. —त्यं *n.* The 12th sign of the zodiac. i. e. The fishes. 2 A thousand billions, the number denoted by 1 with fifteen zeros. -Comp. —अवसायिन् *a.* (*f.* —नी) Born in the lowest caste. —आश्रमिन् *m.* A संन्यासिन्. —आहुतिः *f.* A funeral sacrifice. —इष्टिः *f.* Funeral sacrifice. —ऋणं *n.* The last debt viz, begetting children. —कर्मन् *n.*, —क्रिया *f* The funeral rite. —ज, —जन्मन् *m.* 1. A शूद्र. 2 A चांडाल. —जाति, —जातीय *a.* Belonging to the lowest caste. -युगं *n.* The last or the कलि age. —योनि *a.* Of the lowest origin. —लोपः *m.* The dropping of the last letter.

अंत्यकः *m* A man of the lowest tribe.

अंत्या *f.* A woman of the lowest tribe

अंत्रं *n.* The entrails, intestines. -Comp. —वृद्धिः *f.* Rupture. 2 The swelling of the scrotum. —स्रज् *f.* Garland of entrails.

अंदुः, अंदूः *f* 1 A chain, a fetter. 2 The chain to tie an elephant's feet. 3 An ornament for the ankles.

अंदूकः *m.* See अंदु.

अंदोलनं *n.* 1 The act of swinging. 2 A swing.

अंध् 10 U. To make blind.

अंध *a.* (*f.* —धा) 1 Blind (*lit.* and *fig.*). 2 Making blind causing blindness: obstructing vision.

—धं *n.* 1 Darkness. 2 Turbid water. -Comp. —कारः *m.*, —रं *n.* Darkness (*lit.* and *fig.*). —कूपः *m.* A well the mouth of which is hidden. —तमसं, —तामसं, —तामिस्रं *n.* Total darkness; intense darkness. अंधातमसं *n.* Complete darkness. —धी *a.* Mentally blind, having a dull intellect. —पूतना *f.* A female imp causing diseases in children. अंधंभविष्णु, अंधंभावुक *a.* Becoming blind.

अंधक *a.* (*f.* —का) Blind (*lit* and *fig*). —कः *m.* N. of a Rākshasa killed by god शंकर. -Comp. —अराति: —अरिः —रिपुः, &c. *m.* God शंकर who killed अंधक.

अंधस् *n.* Food. द्विजातिशेषेण यदेतदंधसा * किराता. I. 39

अंधिका *f.* 1 Night. 2 A disease of the eye. 3 A kind of game; the blind man's buff, (mar. आंधळी कोशिंबीर).

अंधुः *m.* A well.

अंध्राः *m. pl.* The N. of a country and its people.

अंध्रः *m.* A name of a low caste. -Comp. —जातीय *a.* Belonging to the अंध्र tribe. —भृत्याः *m. pl.* Kings of a certain dynasty of अंध्र Kings.

अन्नः *m.* The sun. —न्नं *n.* Food. 2 Food as the lowest form in which the Supreme Soul is manifested (Vedant phil.). 3 Boiled rice. -Comp. —अद्यं *n.* Food in general (used in the same sense as अन्न). —आच्छादनं *n.* Food and clothing. (Another term for अन्नवस्त्रं). —कूटः *m*, —कूटं *n.* A large heap of boiled rice. —कोष्ठकः *m.* 1 A granary. 2 Vishnu. 3 The sun. —गंधि *m.* Dysentery. —जलं *n.* Food and water *i. e.* support; maintenance. —दासः *m.* A servant who works for food only. —देवता *f.* The Goddess supposed to preside over articles of food. —दोषः *m.* The fault of eating prohibited food. —द्वेषः *m.* Want of appetite. —पूर्णा *f.* A manifestation of goddess —दुर्गा. —प्राशः *m.*, —प्राशनं *n.* The ceremony of putting rice or some other article of food into a child's mouth for the first time (Mar. उष्टावण). —ब्रह्मन् *n.* Brahman (*n.*) as represented by food. —मयं *n.* Plenty of food. —मयकोशः (—षः) *m.* The material creation, being the lowest form in which Brahman (*n.*) is considered as manifesting itself in its worldly existence. —रक्षा *f.* Precaution in eating food. —वस्त्रं *n.* Food and clothing, (the bare necessaries of life). —व्यवहारः *m.* The law or custom relating to food *i. e.* to the practice of eating together or not. —संस्कारः *m.* Consecration of food by means of a sacrificial act.

अन्य *pron.* (—न्यः *m*, —न्या *f.*, —न्यत् *n.*) 1 Other (in general). 2 Other than, different from (with abl.). 3 Extraordinary, not met with in ordinary life. The neuter form अन्यत् with a following means and further, moreover. —असाधारण *a.* Not common to others; rare. —ऊढा *f.* Another's wife. —उदर्यः *m.* A son of a step mother. —क्षेत्रं *n.* 1 Another or another's field. 2 A foreign domain. 3 Another's wife. —ग, —गामिन् *a.* 1 Going, referring, or belonging to another. 2 Adulterous. —चित्त *a.* Having the mind fixed on some one else or something else. Thinking of somebody or something else. —तम *a.* One of more than two. —तर *a.* One of two. —दुर्वह *a* Difficult to be borne, or endured by others. —दैवत, —दैवत्य. *a.* Referring to, or addressed to another divinity, (as a मंत्र) —नाभि *a.* Of another family.

अन्यकः *m.* Same as अन्य.

अन्यतरतस् *ind.* On one of two sides.

अन्यतोद्युस् *ind* On either of two days ; on the one day or on the other.

अन्यतस् *ind* On the other side.

अन्यत्र *ind* 1 Elsewhere, in another place (with abl.). -2 On another occasion, at another time. -3 Except, without, other than ; यथा फलानां जातानां नान्यत्र पतनाद्भयं । एवं नरस्य जातस्य नान्यत्र मरणाद्भयं ॥ -4 Otherwise, in another way, in the other case. -Comp. —मनस्, —चित्त *a.* Whose mind is directed to something else, inattentive.

अन्यथा *ind.* 1 In another way or manner, in a different manner ; यदभावि न तद्भावि भावि चेन्न तदन्यथा * हितोप. 2. Or else, otherwise. 3. On the other hand ; on the contrary. 4. Badly, wrongly, erroneously. अन्यथा कृ, means to undo.

अन्यदा *ind* 1 At another time. On another occasion. 2. Once upon a time. At one time, once 3. Sometimes ; now and then.

अन्यदीय *a.* (*f.* —या) 1 Belonging to another. -2 Being or existing in another.

अन्यर्हि *ind.* At another time, (the same as अन्यदा).

अन्यादृश्,-दृ-क्ष *a.* 1 Of another kind, like another. -2 Changed, unusual, strange ; being different or otherwise.

अन्यायः *m.* A wrong, unjust thing or act. —यं *ind.* Unjustly, unlawfully. -Comp. —दण्डः *m.* An unjust punishment.

अन्यायिन्. *a.* (*f.* —नी) Unjust, improper.

अन्याय्य *a.* (*f.* —य्यां) 1 Not authoritative. 2 Unlawful, unjust, illegal. 3. Improper, indecorous.

अन्यून *a.* (*f.* —ना) Entire, complete, not deficient. -Comp. —अंग *a.* (*f.* —गा, or —गी) Not wanting in a limb. —अधिक *a.* Neither deficient nor excessive.

अन्येद्युः *ind* On the other or following day ; अन्येद्युरात्मानुचरस्य भावं जिज्ञासमाना * रघुवं 2. 26. -2 One day, once.

अन्योन्य *a.* (*f.* —न्या) One another, each other, mutual. —न्यं *ind.* Mutually —न्यं (In Rhet.) A figure of speech, in which two things are represented as doing the same act to each other ; अन्योन्यमुभयोरेकक्रियायाः करणं मिथः । त्वया सा शोभते तन्वी तया त्वमपि शोभसे । रजन्या शोभते चंद्रश्चंद्रेणापि निशाशिमी * साहि. द. -Comp. —अभावः *m.* Mutual non-existence or negation; one of the four kinds of अभाव —आश्रय *a.* Mutually dependent. —आश्रयः *m.* Mutual or reciprocal dependence, reciprocal relation of cause and effect (a term in Nyâya). —उक्तिः *f.* Conversation. —कलहः *m.* Quarrel with one another. —विभागः *m.* Mutual partition of an inheritance made by the sharers (without the presence of any other party). —वृत्तिः f. Mutual effect of one thing upon another. —व्यतिकरः,—संश्रयः m. Reciprocal action or influence; mutual relation of cause and effect.

अन्वक् ind. 1 Afterwards. -2 From behind; पिद्दधानमन्वगुपयान्य हस्तौ • शिशुपा.9. 76. -3 Friendly disposed, favourably. अन्वग्भूत्वा, -भावं,-आस्ते Becoming friendly disposed. -4 (with acc.) Following, going after. अन्वग्ययौ मध्यमलोकपालः • रघुवं.2.16.

अन्वग्भावं ind. Favourably, in a friendly manner.

अन्वक्ष a. Being within sight, visible, perceptible. -2 Following, coming immediately after. —क्षं ind. 1 Afterwards, after ; forthwith, directly.

अन्वंच् a. (f. —अनूची) 1 Going after, following. -2 Lying lengthwise. अनूचि loc. sing. means behind, from behind.

अन्वयं a. Following.

अन्वयः m. Connection, association. -2 Retinue, attendants. -3 Family, race, lineage. 4 The male descendants. -5 Grammatical connection of words in a sentence. -6 Logical continuance (opp. व्यतिरेक). -Comp. —ज्ञः m. A geneologist. —व्यतिरेकं n, or —कौ m. dual 1 Agreement and contrariety. -2 Rule and exception. -3 Logical continuance and discontinuance —व्याप्तिः f. An affirmative, universal.

अन्वयिन् a. (f. —नी) Connected with as a consequence.

अन्वर्थ a. Having a meaning obvious or easily to be understood from the etymology. Having the meaning clear or intelligible; true to the sense, significant ; तथैव सोऽभूदन्वर्थो राजा प्रकृतिरंजनात् • रघुवं. 4. -Comp. —ग्रहणं n. The literal acceptation of the meaning of a word (opp. to रूढ or conventional). —संज्ञा f. 1. An appropriate name, a technical term which directly conveys its own meaning. -2. A proper name the meaning of which is obvious.

अन्ववकिरणं n. Scattering about successively.

अन्ववसर्गः m. 1 Slackening, letting loose (opp. आयाम). -2 Following one's own will. Permission to do as one likes.

अन्ववसित a. (f. —ता) Connected with, bound or fastened to.

अन्ववायः m. A race, family, lineage.

अन्ववेक्षा f. Regard, consideration.

अन्वष्टका f. The 9th day of the dark half of the three months पौष, माघ and फाल्गुन.

अन्वष्टक्यं n. The Srâddha ceremony performed on the अन्वष्टका days.

अन्वहं ind. Day after day, every day.

अन्वाख्या (अनु + आ + ख्या 2 P.) To repeat in succession, enumerate.

अन्वाख्यानं n. Subsequent mention or enumeration ; an explanation referring to a subject mentioned before. -2 Section, chapter.

अन्वाचयः m. Adding an object of secondary importance to the main object. Statement of a secondary (गौण) rite or action after the mention of a primary (प्रधान) one ; as भो भिक्षो भिक्षामट गां चानय where going out to beg alms is enjoined to the beggar as his principal object, and the bringing of a cow (if he can see any , is added on to it as a secondary object. -2 Such an object itself.

अन्वाचित *a*. Secondary, inferior.

अन्वाधे *ind*. (Only used in combination with the root कृ) To support, to assist. (It is either regarded as a prefix or not).

अन्वादिश् (अनु + आ + दिश् 6 P.) To name or mention again ; to mention or refer to in a subsequent place.

अन्वादिष्ट *p. p. a*. (*f*. —ष्टा) 1 Mentioned or employed again. -2 (Hence) Inferior, of secondary importance.

अन्वादेश: *m*. Subsequent or repeated mention, referring to what has been previously mentioned ; reemployment of the same word in a subsequent part of a sentence.

अन्वाधानं *n*. Putting fuel on the sacred fires.

अन्वाधि: *m*. (In civil law) 1 A bail, deposit or security delivered to a third person to be handed over ultimately to the right owner. -2 A second deposit. -3 Remorse, repentance, regret.

अन्वाधेयं *n*. A sort of स्त्रीधन or property presented to the wife after marriage by her husband's family or by her own relatives. विवाहात्परतो यत्तु लब्धं भर्तृकुलात्स्त्रिया । अन्वाधेयं तु तद्द्रव्यं लब्धं बंधुकुलात्तथा ॥ • कात्यायन.

अन्वाधेयकं *n*. Same as अन्वाधेय.

अन्वारब्ध *p. p*. 1 Touched on the back or on any part of the body. 2 Followed.

अन्वारभ् (अनु + आ + रभ् 1 A.) To begin, commence. -2 To touch (especially to touch a person who institutes a sacrifice)

अन्वारंभ: *m*., -भणं *n*. Touching, contact, especially touching the यजमान (the performer of a sacrifice) to make him entitled to the fruits and merits of the holy rite.

अन्वारुह् (अनु + आ + रुह् 1 P.) To follow in ascending, especially the funeral pile. To ascend, climb, mount.

अन्वारोहणं *n*. A widow's ascending the funeral pile after or with the body of her husband.

अन्वास् (अनु + आस् 2 A.) 1 To be seated near or round; to wait upon, serve, attend upon ; सखीभ्यामन्वास्यत • शाकुंत. 3; to sit after one (acc. of peron). -2 To perform, as a religious ceremony.

अन्वासनं *n*. 1 Service, attendance, waiting upon, worship. -2 Taking a seat after another. -3 Regret, sorrow. -4 A place of industry, a manufactory, a work-shop, &c. -5 An oily or cooling enema.

अन्वासीन *p. p. a*. (*f*. -ना) Sitting down after, seated along side of.

अन्वाहार्य: *m* ,(also -र्यं *n*.), -र्यकं *n* . 1 A sacrificial gift or offering presented to the priests (अन्वाहरंति यज्ञसंबंधिदोषजातं परिहरत्यनेन इत्यन्वाहार्यो नाम ब्राह्मणेभ्यो देय ओदन: • सायन.) -2 The monthly Srâddha performed in honuor of the manes on the day of new moon; पितॄणां मासिकं श्राद्धमन्वाहार्यं विदुर्बुधा: • मनुस्मृ. 3, 123. -Comp. -पचन: *m*. The southern sacrificial fire used in the अन्वाहार्य sacrifice.

अन्वाहिक a. (f.-की) Daily, diurnal.

अन्वाहित Same as अन्वाधेय q. v.

अन्वि (अनु + इ 2 P.) 1 To follow, come or go after, succeed, attend, accompany. -2 (in grammar) To follow or be connected or construed with. -3 To obey, conform to, to be guided by; यास्तितमन्वेति परस्य • महात्मा.

अन्विष् (अनु + इष् 6 P.) To desire, seek, search, look out for, seek to get. (अनु + इष् 4 P.) To seek, search, look out for, to inquire, investigate. *-Caus.* To seek, search.

अन्विष्ट *p. p.* a. (f. -ष्टा) Desired, sought, searched.

अन्वीक्ष् (अनु + ईक्ष् 1 A.) 1 To look intently at, to observe closely. -2 To search, seek for, inquire into; reflect or meditate upon, think of.

अन्वीक्षणं n., -क्षा f. 1 Search, seeking for; investigation. -2 Reflection; meditation.

अन्वीत Same as अन्वित *q. v.*

अन्वृचं *ind.* Verse after verse.

अन्वेषः m. Seeking for, inquiry, watching, searching.

अन्वेषक a. Searching, seeking, inquiring.

अन्वेषणं n. See अन्वेष..

अन्वेषणा f. See अन्वेषः.

अन्वेषिन् a. See अन्वेषक.

अन्वेष्टृ a. See अन्वेषक.

अप् f. (Declined in classical language only in pl. as आपः, अपः, अद्भिः, अद्भ्यः अपां and अप्सु,) 1 Water. -Comp. —चरः m. An aquatic animal. —पतिः m. 1. Lord of waters, N. of Varuna. -2 The ocean. —पित्त n. Fire.

अप *ind.* 1 As a prefix to verbs it means away, away from, (as अपनी to take way); deterioration (as अपकरोति does wrongly or badly); opposition, negation, contradiction (as अपवद् to deny); extension of a rule direction or mention or illustration (as अपदिशति He directs, extends, &c.). -2 As first member of Tat. or Bahuvrihi comp. it has all the above senses. -3 As a separable preposition (with a noun in the abl.) it means away from; without, on the outside of; with the exception of, excepting. -Comp. —अध्वन् m. Bad road. —अनृत a. Free from falsehood. —असु a. Lifeless. —कलंकः m. An indelible or deep disgrace. —कलंक a. Free from disgrace. —चरित n. A fault, offence. —दक्षिणं *ind.* On the left side. —दश a. Not near ten. —दिशं *ind.* Between two regions of the compass. —देवता f. An evil spirit. —द्वारं n. The wrong entrance to a a house. —नस a. Noseless, having a small nose —निद्र a. Sleepless (*lit.* and *fig.*). —पाठः m. A wrong reading. —पात्र a. Of low caste. —भय a. Free from fear; undaunted. —भरणी f. The last lunar mansion (same as भरणी). —मन्यु a. Free from grief or anger. —मार्गः m. A by way, a side way. —मुख a. 1 Having a bad or ugly face. -2 Having the face averted. —मृत्युः m. 1 Accidental death. —यशस् n. Disgrace, infamy. —रूप a. (f. -पा, or -पी) Deformed, ugly. —विद्या f. Illusion (माया). —शकुनं n. A bad omen. —शब्दः m. A corrupted word. —सव्य a. 1 Not left, i. e. right. -2. Contrary, apposite. —सव्यं *ind.* To the right. —सिद्धांत: *m.* A wrong statement ; a faulty conclusion. —स्नानं *n.* Funeral bathing. —हसितं *n.* A silly laughter. —हेला *f.* Disrespect, contempt.

अपकरणं *n.* 1 Acting improperly. -2 Doing wrong. -3 Ill treating offence.

अपकर्तृ *m.* An enemy. One that does harm, injury.

अपकर्मन् *a.* Of bad actions ; corrupted, depraved. —*n.* (—र्म) 1 Discharge, paying off (of a debt). -2 An improper or unworthy act ; evil doing. -3 Wickedness, violence, oppression.

अपकर्ष: *m.* 1 Drawing off, detraction, decrease, reduction ; loss, decline, deterioration, inferiority; dishonour, degradation, infamy, sinking down, loss or destruction. देवस्य अनातक्षशरल्प्ययमीहशस्ते कोऽपकर्षइति यत्सत्यं कंपितमिव मे हृदयं • वेणीसं 1. -2 Anticipated performance of a duty, as of a Srâddha. -3 Anticipation of a word occurring later on (in gram , poetry, or Mimámsâ, &c.) -Comp. —सम: *m.* A sort of fallacy.

अपकर्षक *a.* (*f.* —र्षिका) Detracting, depreciation, lowering, diminishing. दोषास्तस्य (काव्यस्य) अपकर्षका: • साहि. द.

अपकर्षणं *n.* 1 Taking or drawing away, removing, diminishing. -2 Depreciation, detraction. -3 Superseding. -4 Denying; abolishing.

अपकार: *m.* 1 Harm, hurt, offence, misdeed, wrong deed, injury. -2 Thinking ill of, -3 Wickedness, injury, violence. -4 A mean or degraded action.

अपकारक *a.* Injuring, doing harm or wrong to, harmful, hurtful, mischievous, offending, injurious. —कृ *m.* An evil-doer, enemy,

अपकारिन् *a.* and *m.* See अपकारक *a.* and *m.*

अपकिरणं *n.* Scattering about.

अपकृ (अप + कृ 8 U.) 1 To carry or bear away, remove, drag away -2 To hurt, injure, wrong, harm.

अपकृत *p. p. a.* (*f.* —ता) 1 Injured, wronged. —तं *n.* 1 An injury, harm, offence. -2 Loss.

अपकृति: *f.*, अपकृत्यं *n.* 1 Harm, injury, hurt, damage, offence. -2 Opposition, enmity.

अपकृष् (अप + कृष् 1 P., 6 U.) 1 (*a*) To draw off or aside, drag down, drag away, take or carry off, draw out, to take or carry away, remove. -2 To diminish, decrease, omit. -3 To bend (as a bow). -4 To lower or debase, dishonour, disparage ; to lessen the excellence of. -5 To drag a word from a preceding or succeeding sentence.

अपकृष्ट *p. p* (*f* —ष्टा) 1 Drawn or taken away, removed; diminished, brought down, depressed, lowered. -3 Low, vile, base, of a low rank. —ष्ट: *m.* A crow. -Comp. —चेतस *a.* Mentally debased or corrupted, low-minded. —जाति *a.* Of a low tribe or origin.

अपकॄ (अप + कॄ 6 P.) To scatter. -2 To scrape or scratch.

अपक्वोशली *f.* News, information.

अपाक्ति: *f.* 1 Unripeness, immaturity. -2 Indigestion.

अपक्रम् (अप + क्रम् 1 P.) 1 To go away, run away, fly, escape, retreat, retire (from). 2 To glide away, pass away, (as time).

अपक्रमः *m.* 1 Going away, flight, gliding or passing away, escape, retreat. -2 The place of retreat. —*a.* (*f.* —मा) 1 Without order. -2 Irregular, in wrong order.

अपक्रमणं *n.* Retreat, retiring, flight, escape &c.

अपक्रामिन् *a.* Going forth or away ; not going fast.

अपक्रामः *m.* See अपक्रमणं.

अपक्रिया *f.* 1 Hurt, injury; wrong or faulty action ; misdeed. -2 Paying or clearing off (debts).

अपक्रोशः *m.* Abuse, reviling.

अपक्व *a.* (*f.* —क्वा) 1 Unripe, immature. 2 Undigested (as food.) 3 Not yet cooked ; imperfecty cooked, raw.

अपक्ष *a.* (*f.* —क्षा) 1 Without wings. -2 Not being on the same side. Not belonging to the same party ; adverse. -3 Having no adherents or friends, adverse. -Comp. —पातः *m.* Impartiality. —पातिन् *a* (*f.* —नी) Impartial.

अपक्षयः *m.* Decline, decay, waste.

अपक्षि (अप + क्षि 1. 5. 9. P.) To bring to an end, destroy, annihilate. —*pass.* To decline, decay, waste away ; wane (as the moon).

अपक्षिप् (अप + क्षिप् 6 P.) To throw away or down; take away, remove.

अपक्षीण *pp. a.* (*f.* —णा) Declined, wasted.

अपक्षेपः *m.* 1 Casting away or throwing down. -2 Throwing or putting down, one of the 5 kinds of कर्मन् in the Vaiseshika phil.

अपक्षेपणं *n.* See अपक्षेपः.

अपग *a.* (*f.* —गा) Going, turning away. —गा *f.* A river (wrongly for आपगा).

अपगंडः *m.* One who has attained his majority.

अपगत *p. p. a.* (*f.* —ता) 1 Gone away, departed, passed away, being remote. -2 Dead, deceased.

अपगतिः *f.* A bad fate.

अपगम् (अप + गम्, गच्छ् 1 P.) 1 To go away, depart ; pass away, elapse (as time). To vanish, disappear.

अपगमः *m.* 1 Going away or off, departure, separation., removal, disappearance. -2 Lapse, passing away. -3 Death, decease.

अपगमनं *n.* See अपगमः

अपगरः 1 Censure, blame. -2 One who reviles or says what is disagreeable, reviler.

अपगर्जित *a.* (*f.* —ता) Thunderless (as a cloud).

अपगुणः *m.* A demerit, fault, Si. 15. 32.

अपगोपुर *a.* (*f* —रा) Deprived of its gates. (as a town).

अपघनः *m.* A limb or member of the body, as a hand or foot (also used in the sense of 'the body'). —*a.* (*f.* —ना) Free from the obstruction of clouds, cloudless.

अपघातः *m.* 1 Warding off, preventing. -2 Killing. -3 A violent death ; any evil accident proving fatal.

अपघातिन् *a.* (*f.* —नी) Killing, murdering.

अपचः *m.* 1 Unable to cook, one who does not cook for himself. -2 A bad cook.

अपचय: *m.* Decrease, decline, deterioration, taking away, loss.

अपचर् (अप + चर् 1 P.) 1 To depart. -2 To go astray, transgress ; offend, act wrongly.

अपचरित *p. p. a.* (*f.* —ता) Gone away, departed ; deceased. —तं *n.* A fault ; wrong or wicked deed, misdeed.

अपचार: *m.* 1 Departure ; death. -2 A failure, a deficiency, defect, flaw. 3 A misdeed, improper conduct, crime, hurtful conduct, injury, mistake, omission (to do a thing). -6 Unwholesome or improper regimen (अपथ्य).

अपचारिन् *a.* (*f.* —णी) Offending, doing wrong ; wicked, bad.

अपचि (अप + चि 5 U.) To diminish, to loose.

अपचित *p. p. a.* (*f.* —ता) 1 Reduced, decreased, wasted, spent, emaciated, thin, lean. -2 Honoured. —तं *n.* Honouring.

अपचिति: *f.* 1 Loss, decay, decline, deterioration. -2 Expense. -3 Atonement, expiation of sin. -4 Exclusion. -5 Punishing. -6 Honouring, worship.

अपची *f.* A disease in which the glands of the neck are enlarged and swollen. (Mar. गंडमाळा).

अपच्छाय *a.* (*f.* —या) 1 Shadowless. -2 Devoid of brightness, dim. —य: *m.* One that has no shadow, i. e. a god.

अपच्छेद: *m.* 1 Cutting off or away. -2 Loss. -3 Interruption.

अपच्छेदनं *n.* See अपच्छेद:.

अपच्युत *p. p.* Fallen off ; departed, perished ; melted away.

अपजय: *m.* Defeat, overthrow

अपजात: *m.* A son inferior to his parents in qualities.

अपजि (अप + जि 1 P.) To defeat, conquer ; turn off or away, avert.

अपज्ञा (अप + ज्ञा 9 A.) To deny, disown, dissemble, conceal.

अपज्ञानं *n.* Denying, concealing.

अपंचीकृतं *n.* Each one of the five subtle elementary substances ; a simple elementary substance not made of the five (पंच) gross elements; the five subtle elements are पंचप्राणमनोबुद्धिदशेंद्रियसमन्वितं अपंचीकृतभूतोत्थं सूक्ष्मांगं भोगसाधनम् ॥ वेदां. प. (aether, air, fire, water, and earth before becoming gross.)

अपटांतर *a.* 1 Not separated (by a curtain or screen). -2 Adjoining, contiguous.

अपटी *f.* 1 A screen or wall of cloth, particularly the screen or *kanât* surrounding a tent. -2 A curtain. -Comp. —क्षेप: *m.* Tossing aside the curtain. अपटीक्षेपेण with a toss of the curtain (a stage direction when a character enters suddenly in hurry and agitation).

अपटु *a.* 1 Not clever or skilful. -2 Ineloquent. -3 Sick or diseased.

अपठ *a.* 1 Unable to read. 2 A bad reader.

अपंडित *a.* (*f.* —ता) Not learned or wise ; foolish ; विभूषणं मौनमपंडितानाम् ॥ भर्तृ. -2 Wanting in skill or taste.

अपण्य *a.* (*f.* —ण्या) Not saleable ; articles, which ought not to be sold by particular persons and on particular occasions).

अपतंत्रक: *m.* A kind of वातरोग, spasmodic contraction of the body or stomach. (Mar. वायूचे पेटके)

अपतर्पणं *n.* Fasting (as a cure in illness ; Mar. लंघन). 2 Absence of satisfaction.

अपतानकः *m.* Occasional spasmodic contraction.

अपतानकिन् *a.* (*f.* —नी) Affected with spasmodic contraction.

अपति,-तिक *a.* Without a master or husband.

अपतीर्थं *n.* A bad Tirtha or place of pilgrimage.

अपतुप् *n.* (अप + तुप् 10 P.) To cause to fast or starve.

अपत्नी *f.* She who is not yet a wife. Unmarried woman.

अपत्नीक *a.* Without a wife. -2 To be performed without the company of a wife.

अपत्यं *n.* Offspring, child, progeny, whether of animals or men, and whether male or female). The descendants of a गोत्र. -Comp. —काम *a.* Desirous of progeny. —पथः *m.* The female organ of generation. —प्रत्ययः *m.* A patronymic affix. —शत्रुः *m.* 1 A crab. -2 A serpent.

अपत्रप् (अप + त्रप् 1 A.) To be ashamed, to be bashful, (with instr. of person or thing).

अपत्रप *a.* (*f.* —पा) Shameless, impudent. —पा *f.*, -पणं *n* 1 Shame, bashfulness. -2 Embarrassment.

अपत्रपिष्णु *a* Bashful.

अपत्रस्त *p. p. a.* (*f.* —स्ता) Afraid of, deterred from.

अपथ *a*, Pathless, roadless. —थं *n.*, —थः *m.* 1 Not a way ; a bad or wrong road (lit. and fig.).-2 Heresy, heterodoxy (in opinions) —थं *ind.* By or in the wrong way; astray. -Comp. —गामिन् *a.* (*f.* —नी) Pursuing evil courses ; heretical.

—प्रपन्न *a.* (*f.* —न्ना) Taking to evil ways. 2 Misapplied, misspent (as money, &c.).

अपथ्य *a.* (*f.* —थ्या) 1 Unfit, unsuited, obnoxious. -2 (In medicine) Unwholesome, unsalutary, (as food, regimen, &c.). -3 Bad, unlucky. 4 Inconsistent.

अपद्, -पाद् *a.* (पदी *f.*) 1 Incomprehensible, unknowable. -2 Having no feet ; footless.

अपद *a.* 1 Footless. -2 Having no office or post. —दः *m.* A reptile. —दं *n.* 1 No place or abode. -2 A wrong or bad place or abode. -3 A word which is not a *pada* or an inflected word. —4 Ether. -Comp. —अंतर *a.* Adjoining, contiguous, very near. —अंतरं *n.* Proximity, contiguity. —रुहा, —रोहिणी *f.* N. of a parasitical plant.

अपदानं, —दानकं *n.* 1 Pure conduct, approved course of life. -2 A great or noble work, excellent work. -3 A work well or completely done; an accomplished work.

अपदार्थः *m.* 1 Nothing, non-entity. -2 Not the meaning of words actually used in a sentence.

अपदिश् (अप + दिश् 6 P.) 1 To point out, indicate, show ; assign, allot. -2 To declare, put forward, communicate ; announce, say, tell ; inform against, accuse. -3 To feign, pretend. -4 To refer to, have reference to.

अपदिशं *ind.* Half a point between two regions of the compass (दिशोर्मध्ये); in an intermediate region.

अपदेवता *f.* A goblin, an evil spirit.

अपदेशः *m.* 1 Statement, adducing, mentioning. -2 A pretext, pretence, plea, excuse. -3 Guise, disguise. -4 An argument; reason. -5 A butt, mark. -6 A place, quarter. -7 Refusal, rejection. -8 Fame, name, reputation. -9 Deceit. -10 A bad or wrong place.

अपध्यानं *n.* Evil thoughts.

अपध्यै (अप + ध्यै 1 P.) To think ill of, to have evil thoughts about, to curse mentally.

अपध्वंस् (अप + ध्वंस् 1 A., rarely P.) 1 To pack off, clear out. -2 To abuse, scold.

अपध्वंसः *m.* 1 Degradation, disgrace. -2 Concealment. -Comp. Progeny of a mother of a higher caste and a father of a lower caste.

अपध्वस्त *p. p. a.* (*f.* -स्ता) 1 Reviled, cursed. -2 Pounded badly or imperfectly. -त्मा *m.* A vile wretch, lost to all sense of right and virtue.

अपध्वानं *n.* A wrong or harsh sound.

अपनयः *m.* 1 Taking away, removing; refuting. -2 A bad conduct. A wrong policy, a false step from the stand point of politics; अविदितापनयो वा संचयो वा पदा वा भवतु नृप ! अतोऽत्र तत्त्वमभिज्ञातुमिच्छामि • माल. पंचमः. -3 Injury, disservice.

अपनयनं *n.* 1 Taking away, removing. -2 Healing, destroying, curing (disease &c.). -3 Discharge or acquittance of a debt or obligation. -4 Subtraction, deduction.

अपनस *a.* Without a nose.

अपनामन् *a.* Having a bad name. -*n.* (-म) A bad name.

अपनिर्वाण *a.* Not yet extinct.

अपनी(अप + नी 1 P.) 1 To lead or carry away, cause to retire. -2 To remove. -3 To extract, take or draw out (arrow, oil &c.). -4 To put off or away, (as dress, ornaments, fetters, &c.). -5 To deny. -6 To except, exclude from a rule.

अपनीत *p. p. a.* (*f.* -ता) 1 Taken away; removed, pulled off, &c. -2 Removed from, opposed to, contradictory. -3 Badly done or executed; spoiled. -4 Paid off, discharged. -तं *n.* Bad conduct.

अपनुद् (अप + नुद् 6 P.) To drive or take away, destroy. -2 To expiate, or atone for (a sin).

अपनुत्तिः *f.*, -नोदः *m.*, -नोदनं *n.* Driving away, removal, destroying, expiation, atonement (as of a sin)

अपपाठः *m.* A wrong or bad reading.

अपपात्र *a.* 1 Deprived of the use of common vessels; using separate vessels (from which no one else will eat or drink). -2 Of low caste.

अपपात्रितः *m.* One who has lost his caste through some great sin or offence, and who is, therefore, not allowed by his relatives to eat or drink from a common vessel.

अपपानं *n.* A bad drink.

अपपूत *a.* Having badly formed buttocks. -तौ *m. dual.* Badly formed lips.

अपप्रजाता *f.* A woman that has miscarried.

अपप्रदानं *n.* A bribe.

अपभरणी *f.* The last asterism.

अपभाष् (अप + भाष् 1 A.) To abuse. To speak ill of.

अपभाषणं *n.* Defamation, calumny

अपभ्रंश् (अप + भ्रंश् 1 A.) To fall away or off.

अपभ्रंशः m. 1 Falling down, downfall. -2 A corruption; an incorrect word. -3 A corrupt language or dialect used by illiterate people.

अपभ्रष्ट p. p. a. (f. —ष्टा) Fallen away, corrupted (as a dialect).

अपमः m. The ecliptic.

अपमर्दः m Sweepings. Dust, dirt.

अपमर्शः m. Scratching, touching; grazing.

अपमानः m. Disrespect, disgrace; contempt.

अपमार्गः m. 1 A by-path, a bad way. -2 Shampooing of the body.

अपमार्जनं n. 1 Cleaning, cleansing, purifying. -2 Shaving, paring. -3 Chips.

अपमृज् (अप + मृज् 2 P. 10 P.) To wipe off.

अपमृत्युः m. 1 Sudden or untimely death; accidental or unnatural death. -2 Any great danger, illness, &c. from which a person recovers, contrary to expectation.

अपमृषित a. (f —ता) 1 Unintelligible, obscure as a वाक्य or speech. -2 Unpalatable, unbearable.

अपयशस् n. (शः) Infamy.

अपया (अप + या 2 P.) To depart, go away, retire, withdraw, fall off or away, disappear; अपयातमेव हि विनाशमं ...; * उत्त. रा. 6. 4; ... * हितोप. 4. 82.

अपयानं n. Retreat, flight, escape.

अपर a. (f. —रा) (Treated as a pronoun in some senses). 1 Having nothing higher or superior; unrivalled, matchless; without a rival or second (नास्ति परो यस्मात्). -2 Posterior, later, following. -3 Western. -4 Last (in space or time). -5 Other, different. -6 Low, inferior. -7 Supreme (lit. than which nothing is higher, better, &c.). -8 Latter (of two things previously mentioned). —रं n. 1 The hind quarter of an elephant. -2 The future. —रः m. An enemy. -Comp. —अग्नि (अग्नी m. dual). 1 The दक्षिण and गार्हपत्य fires. —अंगं n. One of the 8 divisions of गुणीभूतव्यंग्य i. e. That in which the व्यंग्य (suggested sense) is subordinate to something else. —अंत a. Living at the western borders. —अंतः m. 1 The western border; the western shore. -4 Death. —ताः m. pl. The country or the inhabitants of the western borders. —अंतकाः m. pl. The same as अपरांताः. —अपराः, —रे, —राणि Several, various. —अर्धं n. The latter or second half. —अह्नः m. The latter part of the day, the afternoon, closing or last watch of the day. —इतरा f. The east. —कायः m. The hind part of the body. —कालः m. The later period. —जनः m. An inhabitant of the west, the western people. —त्र ind. In another place. —दक्षिणं ind. In the south-west. —पक्षः m. 1 The second or dark half of the month. -2. The other or opposite side; a defendant (in law). —पर a. Several, various. —पाणिनीयाः m. pl. The pupils of Panini living in the west. —प्रणेय a. (f. —या) Easily led or influenced by others, docile, tractable. —रात्रः m. The latter or closing part of night, the last watch of of night. -लोकः m. The other world, the next world, Paradise. —वक्त्रा f. —वक्त्रं n. N. of a metre. —स्वस्तिकं n. The western point in the horizon. —हैमन a. Belonging to the latter half of winter.

अपरक्त a. (f. —क्ता) 1 Dissatisfied. -2 Bloodless, pale.

अपरंज् (अप + रंज् 1, 4 U.) (Used in pass. only) To be disaffected or discontented (with abl); भयहीनादपरज्यते जनः * किरात. 2. 49.

अपरतिः f. 1 Cessation. -2 Dissatisfaction.

अपरत्र ind. In another place.

अपरथा ind. In another manner.

अपरवः m. 1 Contest, dispute (about the enjoyment of property). -2 Ill-repute.

अपरस्पर a. (f. —रा) 1 Continued, uninterrupted. -2 Not reciprocal, not mutual : असत्यमप्रतिष्ठं ते जगदाहुरनीश्वरं । अपरस्परसंभूतं किमन्यत्कामहैतुकं * भगवद्गीता 16. 8.

अपरा f. 1 The hind part of an elephant. -2 The west. -3 Suppressed menstruation (as in pregnancy).

अपराक् ind. In front of.

अपरागः m. Disaffection, discontent, dissatisfaction. -2 Antipathy, enmity.

अपराच् a. (f. -राची). Not averted; fronting, facing, in front. -ind. In front of. -Comp. —मुख a. (f. -खी) 1. With unaverted face. -2. Presenting a firm front.

अपराजित a. 1 Unconquered, unsurpassed. —ता दिक् f. The north-east direction. -तः m. A N. of Vishnu; also of Siva. -ता f. 1 A N. of Durga. -2 A kind of plant (or ओषधि) fastened round the wrist and serving as a charm or amulet. -3 A charm or spell (शिखा) calculated to protect one from harm. -4 The north-east quarter. -5 A kind of metre of 6 lines with 14 syllables in each.

अपराजिता f. 1 A N. of goddess दुर्गा. -2 The northeast quarter. -3 A kind of drug.

अपराजिष्णु a. Invincible.

अपराजेय a. (f. —या) Not possible or fit to be vanquished.

अपराद्ध p. p. (f. —द्धा) 1 Sinned, offended, committed (as an offence), guilty, criminal (used in an active sense). -2 Missed, that has not hit the mark (as an arrow). -3 Violated, transgressed. —द्धं n. An offence, crime, injury.

अपराद्धिः f. Sin; offence, fault, mistake.

अपराध् (अप + राध् 4, 5 P.) 1 To offend, wrong, commit an offence against; (with gen. or loc. of person or thing, sometimes with dat. also). -2 To annoy, disturb. -3 To prohibit.

अपराधः m. 1 Fault, offence, transgression, guilt, mistake.

अपराधिन् a. (f. —नी) Offending; that has committed an offence, sin, or mistake.

अपरिग्रह a. (f.-हा) Without possessions or belongings, servants, attendants &c; quite destitute. -हः m. 1 Non-acceptance, rejection; one of the several kinds of mental restraints stated in Yoga Sâstra by Patanjali. -2 Utter destitution or poverty.

अपरिच्छद *a.* (*f.* —दा) Poor, destitute ; having no property.

अपरिच्छिन्न (*f.* —न्ना) 1 Indiscriminated, undiscerned, undistinguished. -2 Continuous, connected, without a break.

अपरिच्छेदः *m.* 1 Want of distinction, separation, or division. -2 Absence of order or arrangement. -3 Want of judgment. -4 Continuance, connection.

अपरिणयः *m.* celibacy.

अपरिणीता *f.* An unmarried girl.

अपरिपक्व *a.* (*f.* —क्वा) Not fully ripe or mature. (*lit.* and *fig.*).

अपरिपंथिन् *a.* (*f.* —नी) Not hostile or antagonistic ; not barring the way.

अपरिसंख्यानं *n.* Innumerableness, infinity.

अपरीक्षित *a.* (*f.* —ता) 1 Not well-considered or examined. -2 Not tried or tested. -3 Not clearly established. -Comp. —कारिन् *a.* Acting foolishly.

अपरेण *ind.* In the west.

अपरेद्युः *ind.* On the following day.

अपरोक्ष *a.* (*f.* —क्षा) 1 Not invisible ; perceptible to the senses. -2 Not distant, not remote.

अपरोक्षं *ind.* In the sight (of) ; perceptibly.

अपरोधः *m.* Exclusion, prohibition.

अपर्णा *f.* A N. of दुर्गा.

अपर्याप्त *a.* (*f.* —प्ता) Insufficient or incomplete. -2 Unbounded. -3 Unable, incompetent.

अपर्याय *a.* (*f.* —या) Having no order or method. —यः *m.* Want of order or method.

अपलं *n.* A pin or bolt.

अपलप् (अप + लप् 1 P.) 1 To deny, disown, refuse. -2 To conceal, hide. -3 To detract from, slander. -*Caus.* To outwit, overreach, deceive.

अपलपनं *n.* 1 Act of concealing or hiding. -2 Concealment or denial of knowledge ; evasion, concealment of thoughts, feelings, &c. -Comp. —दंडः *m.* (in law). The fine laid on a defendant for denying the charge on which he is convicted.

अपलापः *m.* See अपलपनं.

अपलाषिका *f.* Excessive thirst or desire (अपलासिका is sometimes used in the same sense, but probably wrongly.)

अपलाषिन् *a.* (*f.* —णी) Free from thirst or desire.

अपलाषुक *a.* See अपलाषिन्.

अपल्पूलनं *n.* Not cleansing or washing.

अपवद् (अप + वद् 1 U.) 1 To abuse, censure, reproach. -2 To disown, deny (A.). -3 To argue out, refute, contradict. -*Caus.* 1 To blame, censure. -2 To oppose or contradict.

अपवनं *n.* A park or forest planted in the vicinity of a town.

अपवरकः *m.* 1 A hole, an aperture. -2 An inner apartment ; a lying-in chamber.

अपवरणं *n.* Covering, screening.

अपवर्गः *m.* 1 Completion ; complete performance. -2 Final beatitude ; absolution ; delivery of the soul from the body. -3 A donation, a gift. -4 Restriction of a general rule. -5 Abandonment.

अपवर्जनं *n*. 1. Abandonment. -2 A gift, donation. -3 Final beatitude.

अपवादः *m*. 1 Refutation (as of an erroneous imputation.). -2 An exception (*opp*. to उत्सर्ग). -3 Censure, blame, evil report. -4 An order, a command. -5 A small bell or other instrument sounded to decoy deer.

अपवारणं *n* Covering, concealment, disappearance.

अपवारित *p. p. a.* (*f*. —ता) Covered, concealed. —तं, अपवारितकं *n*. Concealed or secret manner. —तं, अपवारितकेन, अपवार्य *ind.* (In theatrical language) Aside, in such a manner that only the person addressed may understand what is meant to be expressed (*opp*. प्रकाशं). तद्भवेदपवारितं रहस्यं तु यदन्यस्य परावृत्य प्रकाश्यते। त्रिपताककरेणान्यमपवार्यान्तरा कथां * साहि. द.6.

अपवाहः *m*. Taking or carrying away, removal. -2 Deduction, subtraction (in math.) -3 N. of a metre.

अपवाहनं *n* See अपवाहः.

अपविद्ध *p. p. a.* (*f*. —द्धा) Rejected, discarded, thrown off or away, abandoned, forsaken, dismissed. -2 Abject, contemptible, mean. —द्धः, or अपविद्धपुत्रः *m*. A son that is abandoned by his parents, and adopted by a stranger ; one of the 12 kinds of sons among Hindus. -Comp. —लोक *a*. Dead ; departed from this world.

अपवृक्तिः *f*. Completion, fulfilment, accomplishment.

अपवृतिः *f*. Uncovering, opening.

अपवेधः *m*. Piercing a pearl, ruby, &c. wrongly, or in the wrong direction.

अपव्ययः *m*. Extravagant expenditure ; prodigality, lavishness.

अपव्ययिन्,-व्ययमान *a*. 1 Squandering, spending lavishly, prodigal. -2 Denying a debt.

अपशदः *m*. A low man, a wretch. (the same as अपसदः which is perhaps the more correct form of the word.)

अपशब्दः *m*. 1 A bad or ungrammatical word. -2 Vulgar speech. -3 A reproachful word, censure.

अपशुच् *a*. Without sorrow. -*m*. The Soul.

अपशोक *a*. (*f*. —का) Free from sorrow or grief. —कः *m*. The *Asoka* tree.

अपश्चिम *a*. (*f*. —मा) 1 Not the last. Having none behind or in the rear. -2 Extreme. -3 Not the last *i. e.* foremost.

अपश्रयः *m*. A bolster, pillow

अपश्वासः *m*. See अपान.

अपष्ठं *n*. The point of the hook for driving an elephant.

अपष्ठु *a*. See अपष्ठुर below

अपष्ठुर,-ल *a*. Contrary, adverse, opposite.

अपसदः *m*. 1 A low man ; an outcast ; usually at the end of comp. in the sense of 'vile,' 'wretched,' 'accursed'; आः दुरात्मन् वृथामंगलपाठक शैलूषापसद (Ah villain, wretch of an actor, thou ranter of a vain benediction) * वेणीसं. 1. 2 A child of six degrading connections, viz. of a Brâhman with a woman of any of the three lower classes ; of a Kshatriya with a woman of any of the two lower classes ; and of a Vaishya with a woman of the Shudra class.

अपसरः *m* 1 A valid reason. -2 departure, retreat, withdrawal.

अपसरणं *n.* Going away, retreat.

अपसर्जनं *n.* Abandonment. -2 A gift, a donation. -3 Final deliverance or beatitude.

अपसर्पः *m* A spy, a secret emissary.

अपसर्पणं *n.* 1 Going away, retreating. -2 Observing in the capacity of a spy.

अपसारः *m.* 1 Going out or away. -2 Retreating. -3 An egress, an outlet. -4 Escaping, running away.

अपसारणं *n.* Removing to a distance, driving away, expelling.

अपसारणा *f.* The same as अपसारणं.

अपसृतिः *f.* See अपसर्पणं.

अपस्करः *m.* 1 Any part of a carriage except the wheel. -2 The anus. -3 The female organ of generation. -4 The excrement.

अपस्पर्श *a.* (*f.* —र्शा) Insensible.

अपस्मारः *m.* 1. Forgetfulness, loss of memory. -2 Epilepsy, falling sickness.

अपस्मारिन् *a.* (*f.* —णी) Epileptic.

अपस्मृति *a.* Forgetful. —तिः *f.* See अपस्मारः.

अपह *a.* (*f.* —हा) Destroying, removing, warding off, repelling. (This word occurs only as the last part of a तत्पुरुष Comp.).

अपहृतिः *f.* Removing, destroying.

अपहननं *n.* Repelling, warding off.

अपहरणं *n.* 1 Removing ; taking or carrying away or off. -2 Stealing, robbing (in law).

अपहसितं *n.* Silly and causeless laughter.

अपहस्तित *a.* (*f.* —ता) Thrown off, cast off, given up, lost ; parted with, discarded.

अपहानं *n.* Leaving, abandoning.

अपहानिः *f.* 1 Abandonment. 2 Exception. 3 Exclusion.

अपहारः *m.* 1 See अपहरणं. 2. Concealment.

अपहीन *a.* (*f.* —ना) Left, lost, abandoned.

अपह्नवः *m.* 1 Denial; concealment of knowledge. 2. Dissimulation. 3. Affection, love.

अपह्नुतिः *f.* 1 Denial, concealment of knowledge. -2 (In Rhet.) The figure in which the real nature of a thing is denied and that of another is attributed to it. प्रकृतं प्रतिषिध्यान्यस्थापनं स्यादपह्नुतिः • साहि. द. *e. g.* नायं सुधांशुः किं तर्हि सुधांशुः प्रेयसीमुखं • कुवल.

अपह्रासः *m.* Reduction, lessening, diminution.

अपाक् *ind.* 1 Westward. 2 Southward.

अपाकरणं *n.* 1 Driving away ; carrying away ; removal. 2 Discharge of a debt (in law). 3 Rejection, refutation.

अपाकर्मन् *n.* Payment or discharge of a debt ; liquidation.

अपाकृ (अप + आ + कृ 8 U.) 1 To drive away, remove, reject, give up. 2 To discharge, to liquidate.

अपाकृत *p. p. a.* (*f.* —ता) 1 Removed, driven away, cast off, rejected. 2 Paid off, discharged, liquidated. 3. Freed from ; destitute of ; left by.

अपाकृतिः *f.* Emotion arising from fear.

अपाक्ष *a.* (*f.* —क्षा) 1 Present, perceptible. 2. Eyeless ; having bad eyes, or no eyes at all.

अपांक्त a. (f. —क्ता) One who is not allowed by his castemen to sit in the same row with them at meals ; degraded, excommunicated.

अपांक्तेय a. (f. —या) See अपांक्त.

अपांक्त्य a. (f. —क्त्या) See अपांक्त.

अपांग a. 1 Wanting or deformed in some limb of the body ; crippled, maimed. —ग: m. 1 The outer corner or angle of the eye. -2 A sectarial mark on the forehead. -3 Cupid, the god of love. -4 N. of a plant (अपामार्ग Mar. आघाडा). -Comp. —दर्शनं n., —दृष्टि: f., —विलोकितं n., -वीक्षणं n. &c. A side-glance, side-long wink.

अपांगक: m. See अपांग.

अपाच्, अपाञ्च् (f. अपाची) 1 Going or being backwards. -2 Indistinct. -3 Western. -4 Southern. —क ind. 1 Behind, backwards. -2 Westward. 3 Southward.

अपाची f. The south. The west. -Comp. —इतरा f The North.

अपाचीन a. (f. —ना) 1 Opposite. 2 Turned backwards. 3 Western. 4 Southern. 5 Not clearly visible.

अपाच्य a. (f. —च्या) Western or southern.

अपाणिनीय a. (f. —या) 1 Not taught or sanctioned by Pânini in his works. -2 One who does not (properly) study Pânini's grammar ; i. e. a superficial Sanskritist.

अपात्रं n. 1 A worthless vessel or utensil. -2 (fig.) An undeserving person, unfit receptacle or recipient, -3 One not worthy of receiving donations, or gifts. -Comp. —कृत्या f., अपात्रीकरणं n. Any action which makes a man worthless. —क्रिया f The doing of an improper act. —दायिन् a. Giving to unworthy persons. —भृत् a. Supporting the unworthy or worthless.

अपादा (अप + आ + दा 3 A.) To take off or away, to remove.

अपादानं n. 1 Taking away, removal. -2 (.In gram.) The sense of the ablative case.

अपाध्वन् m. A bad way.

अपान: m. Breathing out, respiration, (opp. प्राण), one of the five life-winds in the body which goes downwards and out at the anus. —न:, —नं The anus. -Comp. —द्वारं n. The anus. —पवन:, —वायु: m. The life-wind called अपान.

अपापकाशिन् a. (f. —नी) 1 Not ill-looking. 2 Not revealing evil.

अपां (Gen. pl. of अप् f. water). -Comp. —ज्योतिस् Lightning. —नपात् m. An epithet of अग्नि or fire.—नाथ:, -पति:, -निधि: m. The lord of waters; god Varuna.—पाथस् n. Food. —पित्तं, or अप्पित्तं n. Fire. —योनि: m The ocean.

अपामार्ग: N. of a plant Achyranthes Aspera (Mar आघाडा) largely used in medicine, washing teeth, sacrificial and other religious purposes and in incantations. -Comp. —क्षारतैलं,-तैलं N. of two medicated oils.

अपामार्जनं n. Cleansing, purifying, removing (diseases, evils, &c.).

अपाय: m. 1 Going away, departure. -2 Separation. -3 Disappearance, vanishing, absence. -4 Loss, injury. 5 Death. -6 Misfortune. calamity. 7 Destruction, annihilation. 8 The end (of a word).

अपायिन् *a.* (*f.* —नी) Departing, transient ; perishable.

अपार *a.* (*f.* —रा) 1 Shoreless. 2 Unbounded, unlimited, vast in extent. 3 Beyond reach ; not within grasp. 4 Difficult to cross. 5 Difficult to conquer or overcome. —रं *n.* 1 Not the other bank of a river (*i. e.* this bank). 2 Implied denial or refusal. 3 The other shore. 4 Satisfaction. 5 Want of satisfaction. —र: *m.* The sea. —रा *f.* The earth.

अपारक *a.* (*f.*—रिका) Incapable, incompetent ; unable.

अपारण *a.* (*f.* —णा) Distant.

अपारवार *a.* (*f.* —रा) Whose beginning and end cannot be seen.

अपार्ण *a.* (*f.* —र्णा) 1 Remote ; lying far away. 2 Neighbouring. —र्णे *ind.* Far away ; (with abl.) *e. g.* अपार्णे ग्रामात्.

अपार्थ *a.* (*f.* —र्था) 1 Profitless ; useless. 2 Having no meaning. —र्थं *n.* 1 Senseless talk. 2. Incoherent language (A fault of composition in rhetoric.) 3 Uselessness. -Comp. —करणं *n.* 1 Advancing a false plea in a law suit. 2 Unwarranted suit.

अपार्थक *a* (*f.* —का) See अपार्थ.

अपावरणं *n.* Covering, hiding, concealing.

अपावर्तनं *n.* 1 Retreat, repulse, retiring. 2 Revolving, revolution.

अपावृ (अप + आ + वृ 5 P.) 1 To open ; to lay bare, uncover, expose, reveal. 2 To cover.

अपावृत् (अप + आ + वृत् 1 A.) 1 To turn away ; to return ; to desist from. 2 To come to nothing.

अपावृत *a.* (*f.* —ता) 1 Unrestrained ; vast ; boundless. 2 Self-willed. 3 Open, free. 4 Laid bare, exposed.

अपावृति: *f.* 1 Covering concealing. 2 Laying open ; opening.

अपावृत्त *a.* (*f.* —त्ता) 1. Thrown back ; repelled. 2 Turned away from ; averted ; reversed. 3. Checked, baffled. —त्तं *n.* 1 Rolling on the ground. 2 Retreat, turning away.

अपावृत्ति: *f.* Same as अपावर्तनं.

अपाश्रय *a.* (*f.* —या) Shelterless, supportless, helpless, destitute. —य: *m.* 1 Refuge, support, recourse. 2. An awning or canopy spread over a court yard (Mar. चांदणी or छत).

अपाश्रित *a.* (*f.* —ता) (Passively used) Restored (to); fastened. 2 Inhabited (by). (Actively used) 2 Resting on or resorting to.

अपास् (अप + अस् 4 P.) 1 To throw away, to keep aside, reject, discard. 2 To abandon ; to retire or withdraw from. 3. To drive away. 4. To disregard, to forsake, to overlook.

अपासंग: *m.* A quiver, (of arrows.)

अपासनं *n.* Throwing away, quitting. 2 Killing.

अपासरणं *n.* Going away, departure, retreat, removal.

अपासु *a.* Lifeless, dead.

अपि *ind.* (Sometimes shortened into पि when prefixed to nouns and verbs as in पिधान for अपिधान) As a prefix to verbs अपि means (1) on, as in अपिधा, अपिनह् (2) near, towards, as in अपिगम्. As a separable prep.

(with the gen.) अपि means a little of, as in सर्पिषोऽपि स्यात्. There might be a small quantity of ghee. As an adverb or conjunction अपि means (1) moreover, in addition, also. (2) Even though, even if. (3) Therefore, as in राजलोकोऽपि गुणापहार्य: where अपि has the sense of अत एव. (4) Even, as in इयमधिकमनोज्ञा वल्कलेनापि तन्वी. (5) Fear, anxiety, possibility, probability, as in अपि चोरो भवेत् is it possible that there can be a thief? (6) Hope, as in अपि स्तुहियां वेदं I hope to master the Veda. (7) Contempt as in धिग्जाल्मं देवदत्तमपि सिंचेत्पलांडुं Shame upon the wretched देवदत्त, he would go and water the onion! (8) Indifference.

अपि expresses an exclamation as in अपिसिञ्चहीहि इडोपलूहलं.

अपि introduces a question as in अपि क्रियार्थं सुलभं समित्कुशं. * कुमा. सं.

अपि used with numerals shows totality, as in चतुर्णामपि वर्णानां of all the four castes.

अपि used with interrogative pronouns and adverbs shows indefiniteness, as in कोऽपि somebody, कुत्रापि somewhere.

अपि used with particles or adverbs makes them emphatic as in अपिच, एवापि.

अपि (often in conjunction with नाम) makes a rhetorical question or a question of appeal; such a question expects a reply wished by the speaker, as in अपि नाम रामभद्र: पुनरपीदं वनमलंकुर्यात्. * उत्त. रा. 2.

अपिगीर्ण a. (f. —र्णा) 1 Praised, celebrated. 2 Told, described.

अपिच्छिल a. (f. —ला) 1 Free from mud or sediment; clear. 2 Deep.

अपितृक a. (f. —का) 1. Not ancestral ; not inherited. 2 Fatherless.

अपित्र्य a. (f. —त्र्या) Not inherited ; not ancestral.

अपिधा (अपि + धा 3 P. and A.) To shut, to conceal, to cover.

अपिधानं n 1 Covering, concealing. 2 A cover, lid, covering (lit. and fig). (पिधान also).

अपिधि: m. Concealment.

अपिनद्ध a. (f. —द्धा) 1 Tied on, fastened on. 2 Accoutred (पिनद्ध also).

अपिव्रत a. Sharing in the same religious acts or other works. —त: m. One who is joint in property with others and shares in the same religious acts.

अपिहित a. (f. —ता) 1 Covered. Concealed (lit and fig.). 2. Plain, not obscured.

अपीति: f. 1 Destruction, loss. 2 Destruction of the universe.

अपीनस: m. A cold (a disease of the nose).

अपुंस्का f. Having no husband.

अपुत्रक a. (f. —त्रिका) Sonless.

अपुत्रिका f. The daughter of a sonless father who herself has no male child ; one who is not appointed by her father to beget male issue for him on failure of a son. —क: m. The father of such a daughter.

अपुनर् ind. Not again; once for all, for ever. -Comp. —आदानं n. Not taking back again. —आवृत्ति: f. Final beatitude. —भव a. Not occurring again. —भव: m. 1 Final beatitude. 2 Knowledge of the Supreme Soul. 3 A person released from metempsychosis.

अपुष्ट *a.* (*f.* —ष्टा) Not nourished or fed ; not fat, lean. -2 Not loud, not violent, soft, low 3. Irrelevant ; not assisting the meaning. (considered as an अर्थदोष in rhetoric).

अपूप: *m.* 1 A small, round cake of flour, meal &c. (Mar. वडा, घारगा, अनारसा &c) 2. Wheat. 3 Honey-comb. —प्यं *n.* Flour, meal.

अपूरणी *f.* The silk cotton tree (otherwise called शाल्मली ; mar. सावरी).

अपूर्ण *a.* (*f.* —र्णा) Not full, not complete. —र्णं *n.* Incomplete number ; a fraction. -Comp. —काल *a.* Premature.

अपूर्व *a.* (*f.* —र्वा) 1 Not existing before ; quite new. 2. Unknown ; unacquainted. -3 Unequalled unparalled, extraordinary, wonderful, singular. 4 Not the first. —र्व: *m.* The Supreme Soul. —र्वं *n.* Merit and sin as the cause of future happiness or misery. —Comp. —पति: *f.* She who has had no husband before *i. e.* a virgin. —वाद: *m.* Discussion about the Supreme Soul. —विधि: *m.* A quite new authoritative injunction or direction.

अपृक्त *a.* (*f.* —क्ता) Not united ; uncombined ; distinct, separated. —क्त: *m.* (Gram.) An affix or a word consisting of a single letter.

अपृथक् *ind.* Not separately ; collectively. -Comp. —धी *a.* Holding the doctrine of the existance of God in all things ; maintaining the doctrine of pantheism.

अपे (अप + इ 2 P.) 1 To go away, to depart, to escape. 2. To be wanting ; to be deprived of, to be free from.

अपेक्ष् (अप + ईक्ष् 1 A.) 1 To look for, to expect, to hope for. 2. To wait for. 3 To require, to need. 4 To have regard to ; to look to ; to have in view. 5 To take into account.

अपेक्षणं *n.* See अपेक्षा.

अपेक्षणीय *a.* (*f.* —या) To be regarded or considered.

अपेक्षा *f.* 1 Heedfulness, attention -2 Respect, honour, deference. -3 Consideration, regard. -4 Care. -5 Expectation. -6 Reference, relation. -7 Need, necessity, requirement. -8 Wish, hope, desire. -9 (Gram.) The presence of a word necessary to complete the sense; same as आकांक्षा. -Comp. —बुद्धि: *f.* The distinguishing perception by which we apprehend 'this is one', 'that is one' &c., and which gives rise to the notion of duality.

अपेक्षित *a.* (*f.* —ता) 1 Regarded, looked upon. -2 Considered -3 Desired, wished for, expected, hoped for.

अपेत *a.* (*f.* —ता) 1 Gone away, departed, lost (*lit.* and *fig.*). -2 Free or freed from (with abl.). -3 Contrary to.

अपेहि *Imperative sing.* of इ with अप. Standing as first member of compounds अपेहि means excluding, refusing admission to. -Comp. —द्वितीया *f.* A festival or ceremony at which followers are denied admission. —वणिजा *f.* A ceremony where merchants are excluded.

अपोगंड *a.* (*f.* —डा) 1. Having a limb too many or too few. Having a redundant limb or a deficient limb. -2 Not under sixteen years of age. -3 Being a child or infant. -4 Very timid or fearful.

अपोढ *a.* (*f.* —ढा) 1 Carried away ; removed from (with abl). -2 Not put on.

अपोहः *m.* 1 Removing, taking off; healing. -2 Removal of a doubt by the exercise of the reasoning faculty. -3 Reasoning, arguing ; the reasoning faculty. -4 Negative reasoning (*op.* to ऊह). -5 The exclusion of all things not coming under the category in question (= अतद् व्यावृत्तिः)

अपोहनं *n.* Reasoning faculty (the same as अपोहः *q. v.*).

अपोह्य *a.* (*f.* -ह्या) 1 To be removed or taken away ; to be expiated (as sin). -2 To be established by reason.

अपौरुषेय *a.* (*f.* —या) 1 Unmanly, timid. -2 Superhuman ; not made or created by man ; of divine origin. —यं *n.* 1 Timidity. -2 Superhuman power.

अप्तोर्यामः *m* The name of the last or the seventh part of the ज्योतिष्टोम Sacrifice.

अप्ययः *m.* 1 Going away ; passing away. -2 Approaching, nearing. -3 Absorption. -4 Destruction -5 Destruction of the universe.

अप्रकंप *a.* (*f.* —पा). 1 Not shaking ; firm ; steady. -2 Unanswerable (as an argument).

अप्रकरणं *n.* Incidental or irrelevant matter.

अप्रकांड *a.* (*f.*—डा)Stemless (small). -डः *m.* A bush or shrub.

अप्रकाश *a.* (*f.* —शा) 1 Not bright; dark ; wanting in brightness (*lit* and *fig.*).-2 Self-illuminated. -3 Hidden, secret, concealed. —शं, *ind.* —शे (*loc. sing.*) In secret ; privately. —शः *m.* 1 Indistinctness; secrecy. -2 A private or secret place.

अप्रकृत *a.* (*f.* —ता) 1 Not pertaining to the matter in hand ; irrelevant. -2 Occasional ; incidental ; not principal or chief. —तं *n.* (In rhetoric) The standard of comparison, (the उपमान).

अप्रकृतिः *f.* 1 Not the inherent or natural property ; accidental property or nature ; an accident (=विकृति). -2 The पुरुष of सांख्य philosophy. -3 Not the original word, such as a termination.

अप्रकृष्ट *a.* (*f.* —ष्टा) Low, vile.—ष्टः A crow.

अप्रगम *a.* (*f.* —मा) Going too fast for others to follow.

अप्रगल्भ *a.* (*f.* —ल्भा) Not bold ; modest, bashful.

अप्रगुण *a.* (*f.* —णा) Perplexed. Confounded.

अप्रग्राह *a.* (*f.* —हा) Unrestrained

अप्रचेतस् *a.* 1 Not liberal-minded. -2 Foolish, stupid.

अप्रज *a.* 1 Having no progeny. -2 Unborn. -3 Uninhabited, unpeopled. —जा *f.* Having no child ; not prolific.

अप्रजस् *a* Having no child.

अप्रजाता *f.* A woman who has not borne a child ; a barren woman.

अप्रति a. Unsurpassed. -Comp. —वीर्य a. Of irresistible prowess.

अप्रतिकर a. Trusty, confidential.

अप्रति (ती) कार a. That cannot be remedied or helped.

अप्रतिग्राह्य a. One from whom nothing must the accepted as a gift.

अप्रतिघ a. Invincible.

अप्रतिद्वन्द्व a. (f. —न्द्वा) 1 Having no adversary in battle ; irresistible. -2 Unsurpassed, unrivalled.

अप्रतिपक्ष a. (f. —क्षा) 1 Without an opponent or rival. -2 Unlike.

अप्रतिपत्तिः f 1 Non performance -2 Non-acceptance. -3 Neglect, omission, disregard. -4 Absence of ready wit ; want of determination ; perplexity. -5 Want of understanding

अप्रतिबन्ध a. (f. —न्धा) 1 Unobstructed, unimpeded. -2 Acquired by birth, without any obstruction, as दाय (in civil law).

अप्रतिबल a. (f. —ला) Possessing unequalled power ; of irresistible might.

अप्रतिभ a. (f. —भा) 1 Not possessing ready wit. -2 Modest, bashful.

अप्रतिभट a. (f. —टा) Without an equal or parallel ; incomparable, unrivalled, matchless.

अप्रतिम a. (f. —मा) Unequalled, matchless.

अप्रतियोगिन् a. 1 Without an adversary. -2 Having no opposite or counterpart.

अप्रतिरथ a. (f. —था) An unrivalled warrior; (प्रतिरथ: Means a rival warrior.)

अप्रतिरव a. (f. —वा) Free from dispute ; uncontested.

अप्रतिरूप a. (f. —पा) 1 Not corresponding with. -2 Unequalled in form. -3 Incomparable.

अप्रतिवीर्य a. (f. —र्या) Of incomparable valour.

अप्रतिशासन a. (f. —ना) Having no rival in sovereignity ; having no rival ruler; subject to one rule.

अप्रतिष्ठ a. (f. —ष्ठा) 1 Not stable ; not permanent ; fluctuating. -2 Unprofitable, useless. -3 Infamous. —ष्ठः m. N. of a hell. —ष्ठं n. Brahman (n.). —ष्ठा f. 1 Instabilitly. -2 Infamy, dishonour.

अप्रतिष्ठानं n. Want of solidity or firmness (*lit* and *fig.*).

अप्रतिष्ठित a. (f. —ता) 1 Unsettled. -2 Not celebrated ; obscure. -3 Unconsecrated, unholy. —तः m. N. of विष्णु.

अप्रतिहत a. (f. —ता) 1 Unimpaired, unaffected. -2 Unobstructed, unimpeded. -Comp. —चित्त a. Of unimpaired intellect.

अप्रतीक a. Without parts or body, an epithet of ब्रह्मन् (n.).

अप्रतीत a. (f. —ता) 1 Not perceived; not clearly understood; not clearly intelligible (in rhetoric). -2 Not pleased ; not satisfied. -3 Unapproached. -4 Unopposed.

अप्रत्त a. (f. —त्ता) Not given —त्ता f. A girl not given away in marriage.

अप्रत्यक्ष a. (f. —क्षा) 1 Not visible; invisible ; imperceptible. -2 Absent.

अप्रत्यय a. (f. —या) 1 Having no confidence ; distrusting ; diffident. बलवदपि शिक्षितानामात्मन्यप्रत्ययं चेतः । शाकुं. 1. 2. Having no knowledge.

–3 Having no affix (in gram.). —यः *m.* 1 Distrust, want of confidence; diffidence. –2 Not being understood. –3 Not an affix ; a non-affix.

अप्रदक्षिणं *ind.* From the left to the right.

अप्रधान *a.* (*f.* —ना) Subordinate, secondary, inferior, not principal. —नं *n.* 1 Subordinate or secondary state ; inferiority. –2 A secondary or subordinate act.

अप्रधृष्य *a.* (*f.* —ष्या) Invincible, unconquerable.

अप्रभु *a.* 1 Incompetent ; unable, incapable (with loc.). –2 Not powerful.

अप्रमत्त *a.* (*f.* —त्ता) Not inattentive ; not careless ; assiduous, attentive, vigilant.

अप्रमद *a.* (*f.* —दा) Joyless, sad.

अप्रमा *f.* The reverse of प्रमा ; incorrect knowledge. (प्रमा=correct knowledge).

अप्रमाण *a.* (*f.* —णा) 1 Unlimited, immeasurable , boundless. –2 Unauthorised ; having no proof. —णं *n.* 1 A rule, or instruction which cannot be accepted as authority. –2 Irrelevancy.

अप्रमेय *a* (*f.* —या) 1 Immeasurable, unbounded. –2 That which cannot be properly understood or ascertained. —यं *n.* The Supreme Soul ; the ब्रह्मन् (*n.*).

अप्रयाणि: *f.* Not going ; not progressing. (used only in venting a curse *e. g.* अप्रयाणिस्ते भूयात Mayest thou not move onward.).

अप्रयुक्त *a.* (*f.* —क्ता) 1 Not employed, not applied 2– Wrongly or incorrectly employed (as a word). –3 Not generally used ; unusual, strange (as a word in a particular sense or gender). अप्रयुक्त or अप्रयुक्तदोष is the employment of a word which though authorised by lexicons, is not used by poe' e. g. दैवत though according to lexicographers is of the masculine gender as well as of the neuter gender, is not used by poets in the neuter gender. If it is so used, there will be the अप्रयुक्तदोष.

अप्रयोग: *m.* Non-employment ; wrong or incorrect employment or application.

अप्रवर्तनं *n.* See अप्रवृत्ति:

अप्रवृत्ति: *f.* 1 Not taking place ; not proceeding, not engaging. not engaging in action. –2 Inactivity, inertness, nonexcitement. –3 (In medicine) Stoppage of the natural evacuations of the body (as constipation, ischury &c.)

अप्रसक्त *a.* 1 Not attached or addicted ; moderate, temperate. –2 Unconnected.

अप्रसक्ति: *f.* Non-attachment ; moderation.

अप्रसंग: *m.* 1 Want of attachment –2 Want of connection. –3 Improper time or occasion.

अप्रसन्न *a.* (*f.* —न्ना) 1 Not pleased. –2 Not clear ; muddy, turbid, (as water.)

अप्रसिद्ध *a.* (*f.* —द्धा) Unknown. –2 Unimportant. –3 Insignificant.

अप्रसिद्धि: *f.* Insignificance, obscurity.

अप्रस्ताविक *a.* (*f.* —का) Not referring or relating to the subject-matter ; irrelevant.

अप्रस्तुत *a.* (*f.* —ता) 1 Unsuitable to the time or subject ; irrelevant; not to the point. -2 Accidental, extraneons. -3 Absurd, foolish. -4 Not ready. -Comp. —प्रशंसा *f.* (Rhetoric) The figure of speech in which there is indirect description with reference to the matter in hand. The figure of speech in which the matter in hand is understood though the matter not in hand is described. An indirect description. अप्रस्तुतप्रशंसा या सैव प्रस्तुताश्रया * काव्यप्र. 10. See साहित्यदर्पण 10,58-59.

अप्रहत *a.* (*f.* —ता) 1 Unhurt, intact. -2 Waste, unploughed. -3 New and unbleached (as cloth).

अप्राकरणिक *a.* (की *f.*) Not belonging to the subject-matter ; अप्राकरणिकस्याभिधानेन प्राकरणिकस्याक्षेपोऽप्रस्तुतप्रशंसा * काव्यप्र. 10.

अप्राकृत *a.* 1 Not vulgar. -2 Not original. -3 Not ordinary, extraordinary. -4 Special.

अप्राग्र्य *a.* (*f.* —ग्र्या) Secondary, subordinate ; of small importance.

अप्राप्त *a.* (*f.* —प्ता) 1 Not obtained ; not got; not taken possession of. -2 Not arrived ; not come ; not reached. -3 Not authorised (as a rule). -Comp. —काल *a.* 1 Inopportune, ill-timed, out of season. अप्राप्तकालं वचनं बृहस्पतिरपि ब्रुवन् । लभते बुद्ध्यवज्ञानमपमानं च पुष्कलं * पंचतं. —यौवन *a.* Not arrived at puberty. —व्यवहार, —वयस् *a* (in law) A minor ; one not old enough to engage in public business on his own responsibility, (a boy before he reaches his 16th year). अप्राप्तव्यवहारोऽसौ यावत् षोडशवार्षिकः

अप्राप्तिः *f.* 1 Non-acquisition ; non-attainment; non obtainment. 2 The not being proved or established by a rule before. -3 Non occurrence, not taking place. -4 Not being applicable ; inapplicability.

अप्रामाणिक *a.* (की *f.*) 1 Unauthoritative, unwarranted. -2 Untrustworthy, unworthy of being trusted, unreliable.

अप्रिय *a.* 1 (*f.* —या) Disliked, disagreeable, offensive, hated, distasteful. अप्रियस्य च पथ्यस्य वक्ता श्रोता च दुर्लभः -2 Unkind, unfriendly. —यः *m.* A foe, an enemy. —या *f.* A sort of fish (शृंगीमत्स्यः). —यं *n* An unfriendly or offensive act ; -Comp. —कर, —कारिन्, —कारक *a.* Unfriendly, ill-disposed. —भागिन् *a.* Illfated. अप्रियंवद, अप्रियवादिन् *a* Speaking unkind or harsh words. माता यस्य गृहे नास्ति भार्या चाप्रियवादिनी * चाणक्य.

अप्रीतिः *f.* 1 Dislike, aversion. -2 Unfriendly feeling. -Comp. —कर (*f.* -री). 1 Unkind, unfavourable. -2 Disagreeable, disliked.

अप्रौढ *a.* (*f.* —ढा) 1 Not full grown -2 Timid, gentle, not bold. -3 Not arrogant. —ढा *f* 1 An unmarried girl. -2 A girl very recently married and not arrived at puberty or womanhood.

अप्लुत *a.* (*f.* —ता) (*in gram.*) Not protracted (as a vowel).

अप्सरस् *f.* (—राः,—रा) Certain female divinities or celestial damsels who reside in the sky and are regarded as the wives of the Gandharvas. They are very fond of bathing, can change their shapes, and are endowed with superhuman power (प्रभाव). They are described as the servants of Indra, who, when alarmed by the rigorous austerities of some mighty sage, sends down one of them to disturb his penance. They are also said to covet heroes who die on the battle-field. The word is usually said to be in pl. (स्त्रियां बहुष्वप्सरसः * अमको.) but the singular, as also the form अप्सरा, sometimes occurs. -Comp. —तीर्थं n. N. of a sacred pool in which the Apsarasas bathe. —पतिः m. The lord of the Apsarasas, an epithet of Indra

अप्सरा f. The same as अप्सरस्.

अफल a. (f —ला) 1 Unfruitful, fruitless, barren (lit. & fig.). -2 Unproductive, useless, vain. -3 Castrated ; emasculated. -4 A goat. -Comp. —आकांक्षिन्, -प्रेप्सु a. One who desires no reward (for his labours); disinterested.

अफेन a. (f. —ना) Frothless, without scum or foam. —नं n. Opium.

अबद्ध a. (f. —द्धा) 1 Not bound or restrained. -2 Unmeaning, nonsensical, absurd, contradictory. -Comp. —मुख a. Abusive, foul-mouthed, scurrilous.

अबद्धक (f. —द्धिका) The same as अबद्ध.

अबंधु a. Having no friends or companions.

अबल a. (f. —ला) 1 Weak, feeble. -2 Unprotected. —ला f. A woman (as belonging to the weaker sex). —आसः m. A woman. -लं n. Weakness, want of strength.

अबाध a. (f. धा) 1 Unrestrained, unobstructed. -2 Free from pain. —धा The segment of the base of a triangle. —धः m. 1 Non-obstruction. -2 Non-refutation.

अबांधव a. (f. —धा) Without friends or relations.

अबाल a. (f. —ला) 1 Not childish, youthful. -2 Not young, full (as the moon).

अबाह्य a. (f. -ह्या) 1 Not exterior. -2 Familiar or intimately acquainted with. -3 Without an exterior.

अबिंधनः m. The submarine fire (lit. having water for fuel.) अबिंधनं वह्निमसौ बिभर्ति * रघुवं. 13. 4.

अबुद्ध a. (f. —द्धा) Foolish, unwise ; ignorant.

अबुद्धिः f. 1 Want of intellect. -2 Ignorance, stupidity. -a. Ignorant, dull-witted, stupid. -Comp. —पूर्वं, —पूर्वकं ind. Unintentionally ; unconsciously, ignorantly.

अबुध् (nom. sing. अभुत्) a. Foolish, stupid, ignorant. —m. A fool. -f (nom. sing. अभुत्) Ignorance, want of intellect.

अबोध a. (f. —धा) 1 Ignorant, foolish, stupid. -2 Perplexed, puzzled. —धः m. 1 Ignorance, stupidity, want of understanding. निसर्गदुर्बोधमबोधविक्लवाः क्व भूपतीनां चरितं क्व जंतवः * किराता. 1. 6. -2 Not knowing. Not being aware of. -Comp. —गम्य a. Incomprehensible, inconceivable.

अब्ज a. Born in or produced from water. —ब्जः m. 1 The conch (n. also). -2 The moon. -3 Camphor. -4 Dhanvantari, physician of the gods. —ब्जं n. 1 A lotus. -2 One thousand millions.

-Comp. --कर्णिका f. The seed vessel of a lotus. --जः,--भवः, --भूः, --योनिः m. Epithets of Brahman (m.). -दृश्, -नयन, -नेत्र, -लोचन &c. a. Lotus-eyed, having large beautiful eyes. -बांधवः m. The sun. -भोगः 1. The root of a lotus. -2. A cowrie (वराटक) as large as a conch. —वाहनः m. An epithet of Siva. —वाहना f. N. of Lakshmi. —स्थितः m. The N. of Brahman (m.). —हस्तः m. The sun.

अब्जा f. A pearl-oyster.

अब्जिनी f. 1 A lotus-plant. -2 A collection of lotuses. -3 A place full of lotuses. -Comp. —पतिः m. The sun.

अब्दः m. 1 A cloud. -2 A year, (in this sense n. also). -3 N. of a grass (मुस्ता Mar. नागरमोथा). 4 N. or a mountain. -Comp. --वाहनः m. N. of Siva. —सारः m. A kind of camphor.

अब्दुर्गः m. A fortress in water. (Mar. जंजिरा); fortress.

अब्धिः m. 1 The ocean. -2 A store or reservoir of anything. -3 A pond, lake. -4 (In Math.) The number four (Sometimes 7 also). -Comp. —कफः, m. Froth, foam. —जः m. 1 The moon. 2 The conch. -जा f. Spirituous liquor (produced from the ocean). -2 The Goddess Lakshmi. —द्वीपा f. The earth. -नगरी f The N. of Dwarakâ, the capital of Krishna. -नवनीतकः m. The moon (the butter of the ocean). —मंडूकी f. The pearl oyster. --शयनः m. N. of Vishnu —सारः m. A gem.

अब्रह्मचर्य a. Unchaste. —र्यं, -र्यकं n. 1 Unchastity. -2 Sexual union.

अब्रह्मण्य a. (f. --ण्या) 1 Not fit for a Brâhmana. -2 Hostile to Brâhmanas. —ण्यं n. 1 An act not befitting a Brâhmana; an un-Brâhmanical act. -2 An exclamation of distress uttered by a Brâhmana and meaning 'help!'

अब्रह्मन् a. Devoid of Brâhmanas; having no Brâhmanas. नाब्रह्म क्षत्रमृध्नोति. -Comp. —विद् a. Not knowing the Supreme Spirit.

अब्राह्मण: m. Not a Brâhmana.

अभक्त a. 1 Not devoted. -2 Detached. -3 Not worshipping. -4 Not eaten. —क्तं n. What is not food. —छंदः, -रुच् Want of appetite.

अभक्तिः f 1 Want of attachment. -2 Incredulity.

अभक्ष्य a. (f. —क्ष्या) 1 Not fit to be eaten. -2 Prohibited from being eaten. —क्ष्यं n. A prohibited article of food.

अभग a. (f. —गा) Luckless, ill-fated.

अभंग a. Not broken or fractured. —गः m. 1 Absence of fracture or defeat. -2 (In Rhet.) A variety of श्लेष where another meaning is obtained without dividing the words.

अभद्र a. (f. —द्रा) Unpropitious inauspicious, evil, wicked. —द्रं n. 1 Sin, wickedness. -2 Sorrow.

अभय a (f. —या) Free from fear or danger; safe, secure. —यः m. 1. An epithet of the Supreme Being. -2 N. of Siva. —या f. 1 N. of a plant (हरितकी, Mar. हिरडा). -2 A form of the goddess Durgâ. —यं n. 1 Absence or removal of fear. -2 Security, protection from fear or danger -3 The root of a fragrant grass (उशीरं, Mar. वाळा). -Comp. --अभयंकर, अभयंकृत a. 1. Giving safety. —डिंडिम: *m.* 1 A military or war-drum. -2 A proclamation of reassurance. —दक्षिणा *f.*, -दानं *n.*, प्रदानं *n.* Giving a promise, assurance, or guarantee of safety or protection (from danger). —पत्रं *n* A written document or paper granting assurance of safety ; the same as modern ' safe-conduct '. –याचना *f.* Asking for protection. –वचनं *n* , —वाच् *f.* An assurance or promise of safety.

अभव: *m.* 1 Non-existence. -2 Absolution, final beatitude. -3End or destruction.

अभव्य *a.* (*f.* —व्या) 1 Inauspicious. -2 Unfortunate, luckless ; unhappy.

अभाग *a.* 1 Without a share (as in an inheritance). -2 Undivided.

अभाव: *m.* 1 Not being or existing ; non-existence. -2 Absence, want, failure. -3 Annihilation, death, destruction, non-entity. -4 Non-entitity considered as the seventh category in कणाद्'s system of philosophy. -Comp. —संपत्ति: *f.* False attribution; same as (अध्यास q. v.).

अभावना *a.* Non-perception; absence of correct understanding.

अभावितपुंस्कं *n.* A word which cannot become mas. or neuter, *i. e.* a word which is aways feminine.

अभि *ind.* 1 As a prefix to verbs and nouns अभि means ' to ' ' towards, 'in the direction of, अभिगम् go towards; ' for ',' against '; as अभिलष् to wish for ; ' on ', ' upon '; as अभिषिच् to sprinkle on ; ' over ', ' above, ', ' across '; to overpower; 'greatly'; 'excessively as अभिकंप् to shake very much.

As a separable preposition (with a noun in acc.) अभि expresses (1) towards, in the direction of, as वृक्षमभिविद्योततं विद्युत. (2) With regard to, as भक्तोहरिमाभि. (3) By, separately, as वृक्षं वृक्षं अभिसिंचति.

In composition with nouns अभि implies (1) superiority or intensity, as in अभिधर्म, अभिताम्र. (2) towards as अभिमुखं, अभिदाक्षिण्यं, अभिवातं. In this last sense अभि forms adv. comps. as अभिवृक्षं.

अभि'(भी).क *a.* (*f.* —का) 1 Lustful, libidinous, voluptuous. —क: *m.* A lover, voluptuous person.

अभिकांक्षा *f.* Wish, desire, longing

अभिकाम *a.* (*f.* —मा) Affectionate, loving, lustful, (with the object of love in acc. or in comp.). -म: *m.* 1 Affection, love. -2 Wish, desire. —मं *ind.* Longingly, with desire.

अभिक्रम: *m.* 1 Beginning, attempting, an undertaking. -2 A determined attack or onset; an assault. -3 Ascending, mounting.

अभिक्रमणं *n.* See अभिक्रम:.

अभिक्रांति: *f.* See अभिक्रम:.

अभिक्रुश (अभि + क्रुश 1 P.) 1 To cry out at, call out to. -2 To call out (to one) in a scolding manner. -3 To weep over, lament with tears, bemoan.

अभिक्रोश: *m.* 1 Calling out, crying. -2 Reviling, censure.

अभिक्रोशक: *m.* 1 A reviler, calumniator. -2 A herald.

अभिख्या (अभि + ख्या 2 P.) 1 To be gracious, to look graciously. *-Caus.* (—ख्यापयति) To tell, declare, make known, proclaim.

अभिख्या *f.* 1 A name, an appellation. -2 A word ; a synonym. -3 Fame, renown. -4 Beauty, splendour. -5 Proclamation ; declaring.

अभिख्यात *p. p. a.* (*f.* —ता) Become or made known ; celebrated.

अभिख्यानं *n.* Fame, glory.

अभिगम् (अभि + गम्, गच्छ् 1 P.) 1 To go to, approach (with acc). -2 To follow, go after. -3 To find, meet with (casually or by chance). -4 To cohabit. -5 To betake oneself to. -6 To get, to share in ; be subject to. -7 To conceive, apprehend, understand.

अभिगमः *m.*, —गमनं *n.* 1 Approaching, coming near ; visit. -2 Obtainment, acquisition, enjoying. -3 Sexual intercourse.

अभिगम्य *pot. p. a* (*f.* —म्या) 1 Accessible ; that can be approached without fear.

अभिगर्ज् (अभि + गर्ज् 1 P.) To roar or bawl at.

अभिगर्जनं, अभिगर्जितं *n.* A tumult, uproar.

अभिगामिन् *a* (*f.* —नी) Coming near, approaching ; having intercourse with.

अभिगीत *p. p. a.* (*f.* —ता) Sung, or chanted ; celebrated in song.

अभिगुप्तिः *f.* Guarding, protecting.

अभिगै (अभि + गै 1 P.) 1 To call to, sing to. -2 To make noisy with songs. -3 To sing, celebrate in song. -4 To approve, allow.

अभिग्रह् (अभि + ग्रह् 9 U.) 1 To take, seize, catch, attack. -2 To accept, take. -3 To receive, (as a guest). -4 To fold, or bring together (as the hands). -5 To bring forth (as blossom, fruit, &c.)

अभिग्रहः *m.* 1 Seizing, plundering. -2 Attack, onset. -3 Challenge. -4 Complaint. -5 Authority, power, weight.

अभिग्रहणं *n.* Robbing, or seizing.

अभिघर्षणं *n.* 1 Rubbing, friction. -2 Possession by an evil spirit.

अभिघातः *m.* 1 Striking, beating -2 Annihilation, extirpation. —तं *n.* The harsh sound produced by neglect of sandhi rules.

अभिघातक *a.* (*f.* —तिका) Warding off ; extirpating.

अभिघातिन् *m.* An enemy

अभिघारः *m.* 1 Ghee or clarified butter. -2 Dropping down ghee upon offerings at sacrifices.

अभिघारण *n.* Same as अभिघार.

अभिचक्ष् (अभि + चक्ष् 2 A.) 1 To look at, view, perceive. -2 To address. -3 To name, call.

अभिचर् (अभि + चर् 1 P.) 1 To act wrongly -2 To be faithless (as wife or husband). -2 To charm, conjure, by spells or incantations ; employ spells for magical purposes. -3 To possess, occupy.

अभिचरः *m.* A follower, servant, attendant.

अभिचरणं *n* Employment of spells for malevolent purposes.

अभिचारः *m* 1 Exorcising, enchanting ; employment of magical spells for malevolent purposes ; magic itself. -2 Killing. -Comp. —कल्पः *m.* N. of a work on incantations regarded as part of the Atharvaveda. —ज्वरः *m.* A fever caused by magical spells. —मंत्र *m.* A magical formula. —यज्ञः, -होमः *m.* A sacrifice made for magical purposes.

अभिचारक,-चारिन् *a.* (-रिका, -रिणी *f.*) Using magical spells. —कः *m.*, —री *m.* A conjurer, magician.

अभिजन् (अभि + जन् 4 A.) 1 To be born to or for (a person or thing), -2 To be born or produced from. -3 To be born or produced again. -4 To be, become, or be turned into. -5 To be born of a high family.

अभिजनः *m.* 1 A family, a race. -2 Noble descent. -3 Native country. -4 The head of a family. -5 Renown, reputation. -6 Attendants.

अभिजयः *m.* Conquest ; complete victory.

अभिजात *a.* (*f.* —ता) 1 Born, produced. -2 Of noble birth. -3 Learned, wise. -4. Having no fault ; pure. -5 Beautiful, handsome. -6 Honest.

अभिजातिः *f.* Noble descent, high birth.

अभिजि (अभि + जि 1 P.) 1 To conquer completely. -2 To acquire by conquest.

अभिजिघ्रणं *n.* Touching the head with the nose (as a sign of affection).

अभिजित् *m.* 1 N. of Vishnu. -2 N. of a sacrifice, part of the great sacrifice called गवामयन. -3 N. of a star ; N. of the twenty-second asterism. -*n.* 1 The 8th Muhurta of the day, midday (fit for a Sraddhā ceremony). -2 N. of a क्षण favourable to setting out.

अभिजुष् (अभि + जुष् 6 A.) 1 To visit.

अभिजुष्ट *p. p.* (*f.* -ष्टा) Visited, frequented.

अभिज्ञ *a.* (*f.* —ज्ञा) 1 Knowing, acquainted with, (with gen. or loc. or in comp.) -2 Skilled in, proficient, skilful. -ज्ञा *f.* 1 Recognition. -2 Remembrance, recollection. -3 A supernatural faculty or power.

अभिज्ञा (अभि + ज्ञा 9 U.) 1 To recognize. -2 To know, understand; perceive. -3 To look upon, regard as, know to be. -4 To own, acknowledge.

अभिज्ञानं *n.* 1 Recollection. -2 Recognition. -3 A token of recognition. -4 The dark portion of the moon's disc. -Comp.—पत्रं *n.* A certificate, letter of recommendation.

अभितप् (अभि + तप् 1 P.) 1 To heat, inflame. -2 To distress, afflict.

अभितप्त *p. p. a.* (*f.* —प्ता) 1 Heated, scorched, burnt. -2 Distressed.

अभितरां *ind.* Nearer to.

अभितस् *ind.* (used absolutely or with a noun in acc.) 1 Before, in the presence of. -2 Towards. -3 Near. -4 On both sides. -5 Thoroughly, throughout. 6 Quickly.

अभितापः *m.* Extreme heat ; great pain whether of body or mind. -2 Affliction, great distress.

अभिताम्र *a.* (*f.* —म्रा) Deep red, dark red.

अभितृप् (अभि + तृप् 10 P.) 1 To satiate, satisfy. -2 To refresh.

अभिदक्षिणं *ind.* To or towards the right.

अभिद्रवः *m.* An attack.

अभिद्रवणं *n.* An attack, assault.

अभिद्रु (अभि + द्रु 1 P.) 1 To run up to. -2 To invade, march against, attack, assail. -2 To overrun, infest, trouble. -4 To befall.

अभिद्रुत *p. p. a.* (*f.* —ता) Attacked, overrun.

अभिद्रुह् (अभि + द्रुह् 4 P.) To hate, seek to injure, plot against (with acc.).

अभिद्रोहः *m.* I Injuring, plotting against. -2 Cruelty, oppression. -3 Abuse ; censure.

अभिधर्षणं *n.* I Possession by evil spirits. -2 Oppressing. -3 Striking against.

अभिधा (अभि + धा 3 U.) I To say, speak, tell. -2 To express or convey directly or primarily (as sense &c.) -3 To speak, to address. -4 To name, call, designate.

अभिधा *f.* I A name, appellation. -2 A word, sound. -3 The power which a word has of directly signifying a certain sense ; the sense that is so expressed is called the वाच्यार्थ of that word. वाच्योऽर्थोऽभिधया बोध्यः • साहि. द. 2 -Comp. —मूल *a.* Founded on the literal or original meaning of a word or a sentence, (as a ध्वनि).

अभिधानं *n.* I Naming, telling, mentioning, denotation. -2 A speech, a discourse. -3 A vocabulary. -नं *n.*, -नः *m.* I A name, an appellation. -2 A word. -Comp. —माला *f.*, —कोषः *m.* A lexicon, dictionary.

अभिधायक *a.* (*f.*-यिका), अभिधायिन् *a.* (*f.* -नी) I Naming, expressing, denominating. -2 Saying, speaking, telling.

अभिधेय *pot.p.* (*f.*-या) To be named, to be expressed. -2 Nameable, as a category or predicament (in logic). —यं *n.* I Signification, meaning, sense. -2 A substance. -3 The subject-matter. -4 The primary or literal sense of a word (called अभिधा).

अभिध्या *f.* I Desire, wish. -2 Coveting another's property.-3 Desire of taking (generally).

अभिध्यानं *n.* Desiring or longing for ; coveting ; a wish or desire ; परद्रव्येष्वभिध्यानं • मनुस्मृ. 12. 5. -2 Meditation, profound thought.

अभिध्यै (अभि + ध्यै I P.) I To reflect, consider, think of. -2 To covet, to wish or desire for.

अभिनंद् (अभि + नंद् I P.) I To rejoice at or in ; to be glad or satisfied. -2 To celebrate.

अभिनंद *a.* (*f.* -दा)That which delights.-दः *m.* I Rejoicing, delighting. 2 Praising, applauding, congratulating. -3 Wish, desire. -4 Encouraging, inciting to action. -5 An epithet of परमात्मन् the Supreme Being. —दा *f.* I Delight. -2 Wish, desire.

अभिनंदनं *n.* I Rejoicing at, greeting welcoming. -2 Praising, congratulating. -3 Wish, desire.

अभिनंदनीय *pot. p. a.* (*f.* —या) I To be rejoiced at, praised, or congratulated. -2 Fit for congratulation.

अभिनंद्य *a.* (*f.* —द्या) Fit for congratulation or praise.

अभिनम्र *a.* (*f.* —म्रा) Bent, curved.

अभिनयः *m.* I Action and postures of some sentiment, passion, &c. especially when exhibited in a dramatic performance. -2 Dramatic representation ; exhibition on the stage. -Comp. —आचार्यः *m.* A dancing-master. —विद्या *f.* The science of acting or dramatic representation ; art of dancing.

अभिनव *a.* (*f.* —वा) New, fresh, young, पदपंक्तिर्दृश्यतेऽभिनवा • शकुंत. 3. 8. -Comp. -यौवन, -वयस्क *a.*Quite youthful, very young. —वैयाकरण: *m.* One who has newly begun his study of grammar.

अभिनह् (अभि + नह् 4 P.) 1 To bind up (as the eyes). -2 To bind, tie, fasten.

अभिनहनं *n.* A bandage for the eyes); a blind.

अभिनियुक्त *a.* (*f.* —क्ता) Engaged or occupied in.

अभिनियोग: *m.* Close application.

अभिनिर्मुक्त *a.* (*f.* —क्ता) 1 Left or quitted. -2 One asleep at sunset.

अभिनिर्याणं *n.* 1 A march in general. -2 Invasion, marching against an enemy.

अभिनिविश् (अभि + नि + विश् 6 A.) 1 To enter into, to occupy. -2 To take possession of, resort to, be attached to (with acc.).

अभिनिविष्ट *p. p. a.* (*f.* —ष्टा) 1 Endowed with, possessed of. -2 Determined. -3 Engrossed in, intent on. —ष्टं *n.* Perseverance.

अभिनिर्वृत्ति: *f.* Fulfilment, accomplishment, completion.

अभिनिवेश: 1 *m.* Devotion, attachment, intentness, firm adherence, strong or passionate attachment, close application (with loc. or in comp.) ; ईदृश एव तवाभिनिवेशो भवतु • विक्रमो. 2. अहो नु खलु दुर्लभाभिनिवेशी मदन: • विक्रमो. 1. -2 Earnest desire, ardent longing, wish, desire. -3 Resolution, determination of purpose, perseverance. -4 (In Yoga phil.) The instinctive clinging to worldly life and bodily enjoyments.

अभिनिवेशिन् *a.* 1 Devoted to, adhering or clinging to. -2 Fixing, directing or turning (the mind) to. -3 Determined, resolute.

अभिनिष्क्रमणं *n.* 1 Going out or forth. -2 (With Buddhists) Leaving the house to become an anchorite.

अभिनिष्पतनं *n.* Going forth, sallying, issuing.

अभिनिष्पत्ति: *f.* Completion, consummation, accomplishment, fulfilment.

अभिनिष्पद् (अभि + नि: + पद् 4 A.) 1 To go or come to. -2 To enter into, become. -3 To appear.

अभिनिह्नव: *m.* Denial, concealment.

अभिनी (अभि + नी 1 P.) 1 To bring near, conduct or lead towards, carry to. -2 To act, represent or exhibit dramatically. -3 To quote, adduce. -4 To allow to elapse.

अभिनीत *p. p. a.* (*f.* —ता) 1 Performed, represented dramatically. -2 Highly ornamented or polished, -3 Fit, proper, suitable. -4 Patient, forgiving, even-minded. -5 Angry. -6 Kind, friendly.

अभिनीति: *f.* Kindness, friendship, patience. -2 Expressive gesticulation.

अभिनेतृ *m.* An actor. —त्री *f.* An actress.

अभिनेय, -नेतव्य *pot. p. a.* (*f.* —या, —व्या) To be acted or dramatically represented.

अभिन्न *a.* (*f.* —न्ना) 1 Not broken or cut. -2 Unaffected. -3 Not changed or altered. -4 Not different from; the same as, identical (with abl.). -5 Undivided, whole, one (as number). -6 Holding together, continuous.

अभिपत् (अभि + पत् 1 P.) 1 To fly near, approach. -2 To fall upon, attack, assail. -3 To fall down, fall (as tears). -4 To pass over, traverse. -7 To withdraw, retire.

अभिपतनं *n.* 1 Approaching. –2 Falling upon, assault, attack. –3 Going forth, departure.

अभिपत्तिः *f.* 1 Approaching. –2 Completion.

अभिपद् (अभि + पद् 4 A.) 1 To go to, approach (with acc.). –2 To regard ; to know to be. –3 To help, assist. –4 To seize, overpower, attack, overcome, afflict. –5 To take, assume ; accept, receive.

अभिपन्न *p. p. a.* (*f.* —न्ना) 1 Gone or come near, approached, gone to (a state &c.). –2 Fled ; seeking refuge with. –3 Subdued, overpowered, afflicted, seized. –4 Unfortunate, fallen into difficulties &c. –5 Accepted. –6 Guilty. –7 Removed to a distance. –8 Dead.

अभिपरिप्लुत *a.* (*f.* —ता) Overflowed, inundated. (fig.) Overcome, overwhelmed, affected.

अभिपूज् (अभि + पूज् 10 P.) 1 To adorn. –2 To honour ; worship. –3 Approve, assent to.

अभिपूजनं *n.* 1 Honouring. –2 Approving.

अभिपूरणं *n.* 1 Filling. –2 Overpowering.

अभिपूर्व *ind.* Successively.

अभिप्रणयः *m.* Affection, favour, propitiation.

अभिप्रणयनं *n.* Consecrating by sacred hymns.

अभिप्रवनं *n.* Spreading or extending over, throwing over.

अभिप्रदक्षिणं *ind.* Towards the right, rightwards.

अभिप्रवर्तनं *n.* 1 Advancing up to. –2 Proceeding, acting. –3 Coming forth, (as sweat.).

अभिप्रवृत्त *p. p.* (*f.* —त्ता) 1 Advancing, going up to. –2 Occurring. –3 Engaged or occupied in (with loc.).

अभिप्राप्तिः *f.* Approach, arrival. –2 Attainment.

अभिप्रायः *m.* 1 Intention, design, aim, wish. –2 Opinion, belief, meaning. –3 Implied sense ; the bearing of a word or sentence. –4 Reference, relation. 5. A. N. of विष्णु.

अभिप्रेत *p. p. a.* (*f.* –ता) 1 Intended ; designed. –2 Wished, desired ; agreeable. –3 Approved, accepted. –4 Dear, beloved.

अभिप्रोक्षणं *n.* Sprinkling upon.

अभिप्लवः *m.* 1 Affliction, disturbance. –2 Inundation, overflowing. –3 N. of a religious ceremony performed as part of the sacrifice गवामयन.

अभिप्लु (अभि + प्लु 4 A.) 1 To go up to. –2 To overflow. –3 (fig.) To fill with, overwhelm. –4 To spring to or over, spring upon.

अभिबुद्धिः *f.* An organ of apprehension, of which there are five, viz. the eye, tongue, ear, nose and skin.

अभिभवः *m.* 1 Defeat, subjugation, overpowering. अभिभवः कुत एव सपत्नजः॰ रघुवं. 9. 4. –2 Being overpowered ; being attacked or affected. –3 Contempt, disrespect. निरभिभवसाराः परकथाः॰ भर्तृह. –4 Humiliation, mortification. अलब्धशोकाभिभवेयमाकृतिः॰ कुमा. सं. 5. 43. –5 Predominance, prevalence, rise, spread ; अधर्माभिभवात्कृष्ण प्रदुष्यन्ति कुलस्त्रियः॰ भगवद्गीता 1. 41.

अभिभवनं *n.* Overpowering, overcoming, being subjected to or overpowered by.

अभिभावनं *n.* Making victorious, overpowering; giving mastership.

अभिभाविन् *a.* (*f.* —नी) 1 Overpowering, defeating, conquering. -2 Surpassing, excelling; सर्वतेजोभिभाविना • रघुवं. 1. 14. -3 Disrespecting, humiliating.-4 Attacking.

अभिभावुक *a.* (*f.* —का) See अभिभाविन्.

अभिभाषणं *n.* Addressing.

अभिभू (अभि + भू 1 P.) 1 To overcome, subdue, conquer, (of persons or things); prevail over, (hence) excel, surpass. अभिभूय विभूतिमार्तवीं • रघुवं. 8. 36; धर्मे नष्टे कुलं कृत्स्नमधर्मोऽभिभवत्युत • भग. गीता 1. 40. -2 To attack, assail. विपदोऽभिभवन्त्यविक्रमं • किराता. 2. 14. -3 To humiliate, mortify.

अभिभूति: *f.* 1 Predominance, excessive or superior power. -2 Conquering, defeat, subjugation. अभिभूतिभयादसूनतः सुखमुज्झन्ति न धाम मानिनः •किराता. 2. 20. -3 Disrespect, disgrace, humiliation.

अभिमत *p. p. a.* (*f.* -ता) 1 Desired, wished, dear, beloved, agreeable, desirable. -2 Agreed or assented to, approved, accepted; न किल भवतां स्थानं देव्या गृहेऽभिमतं ततः • उत्त. रा. 3. 32. -तं *n.* Wish, desire. -तः *m.* A beloved person, lover.

अभिमति: *f.* 1 Desire. -2 Pride. -3 Respect, regard.

अभिमन् (अभि + मन् 4 A.) I To wish, or desire, long for. -2 To assent to, approve of, give a grant to any one, (dat.). -3 To think, consider, believe, regard.

अभिमनस् *a.* Desirous of, anxious, longing for.

अभिमंत्र् (अभि + मंत्र् 10 A. and P.) 1 To consecrate with sacred hymns. -2 To consecrate with magical formulas. -3 To speak to, to address. -4 To invite.

अभिमंत्रणं *n.* 1 Calling, addressing, inviting. -2 Consecrating by reciting mantras.

अभिमंथ: *m.* Severe ophthalmia.

अभिमन्यु: *m.* N. of a Son of अर्जुन from सुभद्रा sister of कृष्ण and बलराम.

अभिमर: *m.* 1 Killing, destruction, slaughter. -2 War, combat. -3 Treachery; danger from one's own men or party. -4 Binding; a tie or fetter. -5 One's own party or army. -6 One who desperately goes to fight with tigers, elephants, &c.

अभिमर्द: *m.* 1 Rubbing, friction, crushing. -2 Invasion, devastation of a country (by enemy). -3 War, battle. -4 Spirituous liquor.

अभिमर्दिन *a.* Crushing down, oppressing. -नं *n.* Crushing, oppression.

अभिमर्श: *m.*, -र्शनं *n.*, -मर्ष: *m.*, -र्षणं *n.* Touch, contact. -2 Assault, attack. -3 Outraging; sexual intercourse कृताभिमर्शामनुमन्यमान: • शाकुंत. 5. 20.

अभिमर्शक,-र्षक, -मर्शिन्,-र्षिन् *a.* 1 Touching. -2 Outraging, assaulting.

अभिमाद: *m.* Ebriety, intoxication.

अभिमान: *m.* 1 Pride, self-respect; honourable or worthy feeling. -2 Self-conceit, arrogance, haughtiness, high-opinion of oneself. 3 Affection. -4 Wish, desire, solicitation. -5 Misconception; conceiving objects with the notion that they refer to one's own self (in phil.). -6 Killing. -Comp. —शालिन् *a.* Respecting oneself very highly; proud. -शून्य *a.* Void of pride or arrogance, humble.

अभिमानिन् *a.* (*f.* -नी) Possessed of self-respect. -2 Proud, arrogant, conceited. -3 Regarding all objects as referring to one's own self. -4

Fancying, pretending, or regarding oneself to be.

अभिमुख a. (f. -खा or -खी) 1 With the face turned or directed towards; fronting, facing. -2 Near, approaching, ready for; पुरप्रवेशाभिमुखो बभूव* रघु. 7. 1. -3 Favourable, friendly or favourably disposed. -4 With the face turned upwards. —खं, —खे *ind.* Towards, in the direction of, facing, in front or presence of, near to; (with acc., gen., or by itself.)

अभिमुखता f. 1 Presence, proximity. -2 Favourableness.

अभिमुखीकरणं n. 1 Causing (one) to turn the face towards. -2 Speaking to, addressing (in gram.).

अभिमृद् (अभि + मृद् 1 P.) 1 To tread under foot; trample down; oppress, devastate (as a country). -2 (In astr.) To be in opposition.

अभिमृश् (अभि + मृश् 6 P.) To touch, come in contact with; strike or rub gently.

अभिमृष्ट p. p. a. (f. —ष्टा) 1 Touched rubbed or stroked gently. -2 Brought close to.

अभिम्लात,—न a. (f. —ता, —ना) Altogether faded or withered, decayed.

अभिया (अभि + या 2 P.) 1 To go up to, approach. -2 To come or draw near. -3 To march against, attack. -4 To give or resign oneself to, devote. -5 To partake or share in, get, obtain.

अभियाच् (अभि + याच् 1 A.) To beg, request, ask for, solicit.

अभियाचनं n., Asking for, request, an entreaty, solicitation.

अभियांचा f. See अभियाचनं.

अभियाति, अभियातिन्, अभियातृ, अभियायिन् m. An enemy, an assailant.

अभियानं n. 1 Approaching. -2 Marching against, attack.

अभियुक्त p. p. a. (f. -क्ता) 1 Assaulted, attacked. -2 Assiduous; studiously engaged in. -3 Versed in, skilled in. -4 Learned; illustrious. -5 (In law) Charged, prosecuted.

अभियुज् (अभि + युज् 7 A.). 1 To apply oneself to, make oneself ready for, strive or endeavour. -2 To attack, assail. -3 To accuse, charge; inform against, prosecute, claim or demand (as in a law-suit). -4 To wish or long for, request. -5 To say, speak, tell. -6 To appoint to, entrust with (with loc.). -7 To use (with instr.) -8 To be working or exerting oneself -9 To harness. -10 To hurt.

अभियोक्तव्य, —योज्य pot. p. (f. —व्या, —ज्या) 1 To be rebuked or blamed; to be accused. -2 Assailable, indictable.

अभियोक्तृ m (nom. sing.-क्ता) 1 An enemy, assailant, invader. -2 (In law) A complainant, plaintiff, prosecutor. -3 A pretender, claimant; stronger party.

अभियोगः m. 1 Application or devotion (to some thing). -2 Close application, perseverance, exertion. -3 Learning, scholarship. -4 Attack, assault; invasion. -5 Battle, war, conflict. -5 (In law) A charge, accusation, plaint.

अभियोगिन् -m. A plaintiff, complainant, a prosecutor (in law).

अभिरक्त p. p. a. (f. —क्ता) Devoted, attached.

अभिरक्ष् (अभि + रक्ष् 1 P.) 1 To protect, preserve, keep, help. -2 To rule over, govern.

अभिरक्षणं *n.* Universal or complete protection ; protection in every quarter.

अभिरक्षा *f.* See अभिरक्षणं.

अभिरक्षितृ *a.* Protecting, guarding.

अभिरंजनं *n.* Colouring.

अभिरत *p. p. a.* (*f.* –ता) 1 Glad, delighted, satisfied. –2 Engaged in, devoted to ; performing, practising. –3 Attentive to.

अभिरति: *f.* 1 Pleasure, delight, satisfaction ; attachment or devotion to. –2 Practice, occupation.

अभिरम् (अभि + रम् A., rarely P.) 1 To be pleased or delighted, take pleasure or delight in (with loc.). –*Caus.* To gratify, please.

अभिरमणं *n.* Finding pleasure in, delighting in.

अभिराम *a.* (*f.* —मा) 1 Pleasing, delightful, sweet, agreeable. –2 Beautiful, lovely, graceful. —म: *m.* An epithet of Siva. —मं *ind.* Beautifully.

अभिरुच् (अभि + रुच् 1 A.) 1 To shine, look fine. –2 To like, desire.

अभिरुचि: *f.* 1 Relish, taste, liking, delight, pleasure. –2 Desire of fame, ambition. –3 A strong desire.

अभिरुचित *p. p. a.* (*f.* –ता) Liked, beloved. —त: *m.* A lover.

अभिरुचिर *a.* (*f.* —रा) Very pleasant or agreeable; beautiful, splendid.

अभिरुतं *n.* A sound, cry, noise.

अभिरूप *a* (*f.* –पा) 1. Pleasing, agreeable, handsome, corresponding with, conformable or suitable to, congruous –3 Dear to, beloved or liked by, favourite. –4 Learned, wise, enlightend: अभिरूपभूयिष्ठा परिषदियं शाकुंत. 1. –प: *m.* 1 The moon. –2 Siva. –3 Vishnu. –4 Cupid. Comp. —पति: *m.* N. of a fast or rite performed to secure a good husband in the next world.

अभिलक्षित *a.* (*f.* —ता) Marked with signs; bearing marks.

अभिलक्ष्य *a.* (*f.* —क्ष्या) To be marked or noted.

अभिलंघ् (अभि + लंघ् 1. 10. P.) 1 To jump across or over. –2 To attack, rush upon. –3 To violate, transgress ; to offend, injure.

अभिलंघनं *n.* Jumping across or over.

अभिलष् (अभि + लष् 4. P.) 1 To desire or wish for.

अभिलषणं *n.* Desiring, longing.

अभिलाप: *m.* 1 Expression, word, speech. –2 Declaration, mention, specification. –3 Declaration of the object of a vow or religious obligation.

अभिलाव: *m.* 1 Cutting, destroying –2 Reaping, mowing.

अभिलाष: *m* A desire, wish, affection, love.

अभिलाषिक,–लाषिन्,–लाषुक. *a.* Wishing or desiring for, desirous, covetous.

अभिलाषित *p. p. a.* (*f.* –ता) Desired, wished. –तं *n.* Desire, wish, pleasure.

अभिलीन *a.* (*f.* —ना) 1 Adhering. –2 Embracing, shrouding.

अभिलुलित *a.* 1 Agitated, disturbed, inconvenienced. –2 Playful, unsteady.

अभिलूता *f.* A sort of spider.

अभिवद् (अभि + वद् 1 U.) 1 To speak to, address. –2 To speak with reference to, tell, declare, mention. –3 To name, call. –4 To salute, greet. —*Caus.* 1 To greet or salute respectfully. –2 To cause to salute (with acc. or instr. of the agent of the action). अभिवादयते देवं भक्तं भक्तेन वा.

–3 To utter, pronounce. –4 To play on an instrument.

अभिवदनं *n.* 1 Addressing, allocution. –2 Salutation.

अभिवंद् (अभि + वंद् 1 A.) To salute respectfully.

अभिवंदनं *n.* Respectful salutation.

अभिवयस् *a.* 1 Very fresh or young. –2 Possessed of food.

अभिवर्तनं *n.* Going towards, approaching, attacking.

अभिवर्षणं *n.* Raining ; rain.

अभिवहनं *n.* Carrying towards.

अभिवादः *m* 1 Respecful salutation. –2 Salutation of a superior or elder by an inferior or junior, or of a teacher by his disciple for the sake of obtaining his blessing.

अभिवादक *a.* (*f.*—दिका) Respectful, humble.

अभिवादनं *n.* See अभिवादः.

अभिवादनीय *a.* (*f.* —या) To be respectfuly saluted.

अभिवादयितृ *m.* A respectful saluter.

अभिवादिन् *a.* Saluting respectfully.

अभिवाद्य(*f.* —द्या) To be respectfully saluted.

अभिवाह्य *pot. p. a.* (*f.* —ह्या) To be carried near. –ह्यं *n.* 1 Convoyance, transmission, carrying ; offering.

अभिविधिः *m.* 1 Complete pervasion, inclusion of the point of limit.

अभिविनीत *p. p. a.* (*f.* —ता) Well-behaved, well-principled. –2 Taught, instructed. –3 Pious, pure, devout.

अभिविश्रुत *a.* (*f.* —ता) Widely known or celebrated, renowned.

अभिवीक्षणं *n.* Perceiving, beholding.

अभिवृत् (अभि + वृत् 1 A.) 1 To go towards or near ; to approach. –2 To attack, rush upon. –3 To face, encounter. –4 To extend towards. –5 To arise, begin, appear. –6 To be, to exist, chance to be.

अभिवृद्धिः *f.* Increase, growth, augmentation, prosperity.

अभिवृध् (अभि + वृध् 1 A.) 1 To grow, increase, prosper. —*Caus.* 1 To increase, augment, extend, lengthen. –2 To bring up, to rear.

अभिव्यक्त *p. p. a.* (*f.* —क्ता) 1 Manifested, revealed. –2 Distinct, clear.

अभिव्यक्तिः *f.* 1 Manifestation, declaration, revelation, exhibition. –2 Association, concomitance.

अभिव्यंज् (अभि + व्यंज् 7 P.) To manifest, reveal, exhibit, display.

अभिव्यंजक *a.* Displaying, showing, indicating.

अभिव्यंजनं *n.* Manifesting, revealing.

अभिव्याप् (अभि + वि + आप् 5 P.) 1 To extend to, include, comprehend. –2 To pervade, surround.

अभिव्यापक *a.* (*f.* —पिका) Including, comprehending, pervading.

अभिव्याप्तिः *f.* 1 Universal pervasion. –2 Comprehension, co-extension.

अभिव्याहरणं *n.*, —व्याहारः *m.* 1 Uttering, pronunciation, speaking, –2 An uttered word or speech. –3 A name, appellation.

अभिशंस् (अभि + शंस् 1 P.) 1 To blame, accuse. –2 To praise, extol.

अभिशंसनं *n.* 1 Accusation, charge. –2 Abuse, insult.

अभिशस्त *p. p. a.* (*f.* —स्ता) 1 Charged, abused, insulted. –2 Wicked, sinful, infamous. –3 Blamed, accused. –4 Ill-famed, defamed. –5 Hurt, injured.

अभिशस्तिः *f.* 1 A curse. –2 A misfortune. –3 Censure, insult. –4 Asking, begging.

अभिशंक् (अभि + शंक् 1. A.) To doubt, suspect, (with acc. or dat. of person or thing).

अभिशंका *f.* Fear, alarm; doubt, anxiety.

अभिशंकित *p. p. a.* (*f.* —ता) Doubtful, suspicious

अभिशपनं *n.* 1 A curse. -2 An accusation. -3 Slander, calumny. -4 An injury, hurt. —Comp. —ज्वर: *m.* The fever caused by the pronunciation of a curse.

अभिशब्दित *a.* (*f.* —ता) *a* Declared, announced, said, named.

अभिशाप: *m.* 1 Charge, accusation. -2 A curse -3 Calumny. -Comp. —ज्वर: *m.* The fever produced by imprecation.

अभिशापनं *n.* Pronouncing a curse.

अभिशीत *a.* Cold, chilly (as wind).

अभिशीन *a.* Congealed, coagulated.

अभिशोचनं *n.* Intense grief, excessive pain, torment.

अभिश्यान *a.* See अभिशीन.

अभिश्रवणं *n.* Repeating Vedic texts while Brahmanas are sitting down to a Sraddha.

अभिषक्त *a* (*f.* —क्ता) Defeated, humiliated.

अभिषंग: (also अभिसंग:) *m.* 1 Complete contact or union; connection. -2 Defeat, discomfiture; misfortune, calamity. -4 Possession by devils or evil spirits -5 An oath. -6 Sexual embrace. -7 A curse or imprecation, abuse. -8 A false charge or accusation, calumny -9 Contempt, disrespect. -Comp —ज्वर: *m.* The fever caused by the action of evil spirits.

अभिषंज् (अभि + संज् 1 P.) To be in contact with, touch.

अभिषंजनं Same as अभिषंग: q. v.

अभिषव: *m.* The religious act of pressing out the juice of the *soma* plant -2 The ablution preparatory to religious rites -3 Sacrifice (in general). -4 Bathing (in general). 5 Extracting liquor.

अभिषवणं *n* See अभिषव:.

अभिषिक्त *a.* (*f.* —क्ता) 1 Sprinkled over. -2 Inaugurated, solemnly invested, enthroned.

अभिषिच् (अभि + सिच् 6 U) 1 To sprinkle, shower upon (fig. also) -2 To anoint consecrate, to crown, inaugurate (with loc of the post of authority).

अभिषु (अभि + सु 5 P.) 1 To extract Soma juice or any juice -2 To apply water to or press out. -3 To moisten, to sprinkle.

अभिषेक: *m.* 1 Sprinkling, watering, wetting. -2 Anointing, consecrating by sprinkling water -3 Coronation, inauguration, installation. -4 The coronation water. -5 Bathing; holy or religious bathing. 6 The sprinkling with water (of a divinity to whom worship is offered). -Comp. -अह: *m.* The day of coronation. —शाला *f.* The coronation-hall.

अभिषेचनं *n* 1 Sprinkling. -2 Coronation, inauguration.

अभिषेणनं *n* Marching against an enemy, encountering a foe. यत्सेनयाभिगमनमरौ तदभिषेणनं ∗ अमर:.

अभिषेणय (Denom.) To march against (with an army), to attack, to face or encounter (another) with an army; क: शिशुपालमभिषेणयितुं समर्थ: ∗ वेणीसं. 2.

अभिष्टव: *m.* Praise, eulogy.

अभिष्यं (-स्यं-) द: *m.* 1 Oozing, flowing. -2 Running at the eyes. -3 Great increase or enlargement, surplus, excess

अभिष्यंद् (अभि + स्यंद् 1 A.) 1 To ooze, flow, trickle. -2 (fig.) To be melted (with pity, love &c), to overflow with.

अभिष्वंग: *m.* 1 Contact. -2 Intense attachment, love, affection.

अभिसंश्रय: *m.* R fuse, shelter.

अभिसंस्तव: *m.* High praise.

अभिसंक्षेप: *m* 1 Throwing together -2 Abridgment. -3 Concisement.

अभिसंताप: *m.* War, battle, contest.

अभिसंदेह: *m.* 1 Exchange. -2 Organ of generation (written also अभिसंदोह:).

अभिसंध:, -धक: *m.* 1 A deceiver, cheat. -2 Traducer, calumniator.

अभिसंधा (अभि + सं + धा 3 U.) 1 To hold together. -2 To recognize, own. -3 To fit or fix a missile, arrow &c. to the bow. -4 To aim at, have in view, think of, (with acc.). -5 To deceive, cheat; जन विद्वानेक: सकमभिसंधाय *माल-मा. I. 14. -6 To come to an understanding or agreement. -7 To win over, ally oneself with. -8 To declare solemnly, to promise -9 To calumniate, traduce. -10 To add -11 To prefer.

अभिसंधा *f.* 1 Speech, word, promise. -2 Deceit.

अभिसंधानं *n.* 1 Speech, word, promise -2 Cheating, deception. -3 Aim, intention, purpose. -4 Making peace. -5 Attachment

अभिसंधि: *m.* 1 Speech, deliberate declaration, promise. -2 Intention, object, purpose, aim. -3 Implied sense, the meaning intended. -4 Opinion, belief. -5 Special agreement, terms of an agreement. -6 Deception. -7 Making peace or alliance. -8 Combination.

अभिसमवाय: *m.* Union.

अभिसंपत् (अभि + सं + पत् 1 P.) 1 To fly towards, jump upon; fly along.

अभिसंपद् (अभि + सं + पद् 4 A.) 1 To become (any thing); to be changed to, to assume the state of. -2 To come or go to, arrive at. -3 To get, obtain. -*Caus.* To change into.

अभिसंपात: *m.* 1 Concourse, confluence -2 War, battle, contest. -3 A curse.

अभिसंबंध: *m.* Connection, association, relation; sexual connection

अभिसंबाध *a* (*f.* —धा) Very much contracted or confined.

अभिसंमुख *a.* (*f.* -खा or -खी) Facing, fronting; looking respectfully towards.

अभिसर: *m.* 1 A companion. -2 A servant; a follower.

अभिसरणं *n.* 1 Approaching (to attach). -2 An appointment or rendezvous of lovers.

अभिसर्ग: *m.* Creation.

अभिसर्जनं *n.* 1 A gift, a donation. -2 Killing.

अभिसर्पणं *n.* Approaching. drawing near (with hostile intention).

अभिसां (सां) त्व: *m*, -त्वनं *n* Conciliation, consolation.

अभिसायं *ind.* At sunset, about evening.

अभिसार: *m* 1 An assignation or rendezvous of lovers. -2 The place of a rendezvous. -3 An attack, assault. -4 War, battle. -5 A follower, companion. -6 Might, power. -7 An instrument. -8 A purificatory rite.

-Comp. —स्थानं *n.* A place fit for making appointments.

अभिसारणं *n.* Going to meet a lover.

अभिसारिका *f.* A woman who makes an appointment with her lover and stealthily goes to keep it at night or makes her lover approach her. तडित्प्रभादर्शितमार्गभूमयः प्रयान्ति रागादभिसारिकाः स्त्रियः * ऋतुसं. 2-10.

अभिसारिणी *f.* See अभिसारिका.

अभिसृ (अभि + सृ I P.) I To go towards. -2 To attack. -3 To go to meet at an appointed place.

अभिसृज् (अभि + सृज् 6 P.) I To pour out or forth. -2 To make, prepare. -3 To unloose, untie. -4 To give, grant. -5 To fall upon, attack.

अभिसेवनं *n.* Indulgence in, fondness of.

अभिस्नेहः *m.* Attachment, affection, love, desire.

अभिस्फुरित *a.* (*f.* —ता) Expanded, full-grown (as a blossom).

अभिहत *a.* (*f.* -ता) I Struck, hurt, injured. -2 Subdued, overcome. -3 Multiplied (in math.)-4 Obstructed.

अभिहतिः *f.* I Striking, injuring, beating, hurting. -2 (In Math.) Multiplication.

अभिहन् (अभि + हन् 2 P.) I To strike smite, beat (fig. also). -2 To hurt, injure, destroy. -3 To drive or beat off, ward off. -4 To strike or beat (as a drum &c.). -5 .To attack, overpower.

अभिहरः *m.* Carrying off, removing.

अभिहरणं *n.* I Bringing near. -2 Robbing.

अभिहवः *m.* I Invocation, calling. -2 Sacrificing.

अभिहारः *m.* I Carrying away, robbing, stealing. -2 An attack, assault. -3 Arming oneself, taking up arms -4 Mingling together, mixture. -5 An effort. -6 A drunkard.

अभिहासः *m* Laughter, merriment, sport.

अभिहित *a.* (*f.* -ता), Said, spoken, declared, named. -2 Fastened on. -Comp. —अन्वयवादः *m.* The doctrine of the Naiyayikas that the purport of a sentence arises out of the logical connection between the words and not out of the the sense of the words themselves.

अभिहोमः *m.* Making an oblation of clarified butter.

अभी (अभि + इ 2 P.) I To approach, go up to (with acc.). -2 To follow, serve.

अभी *a.* Without fear.

अभीक *a,* (*f.* -का) Lustful. -2 Libidinous, voluptuous. -3 Fearless. -4 Anxious -5 Dreadful. -कः *m.* I A lover, husband -2 A poet. -3 A master.

अभीक्ष्ण *a.* (*f.* -क्ष्णा) I Repeated, frequent. -2 Constant, perpetual. -3 Excessive. —क्ष्णं *ind.* I Frequently, repeatedly. -2 Constantly. -3 Very much, exceedingly. -4 Quickly.

अभीप्सित *a.* (*f.* -ता) Desired, wished -तं *n* A wish, desire.

अभीप्सिन्, अभीप्सु *a* Wishing for, desirous of obtaining.

अभीरः *m.* I A cowherd. -2 N. of a pastoral tribe (more usually written आभीर) *f.*,-री The language of the अभीर people. —रं N. of a metre. -Comp. -पल्ली, -पल्लिः *f.* A hamlet of cowherds.

अभीशापः *m.* The same as अभिशापः.

अभीशुः *m.* 1 A rein, bridle. -2 A ray of light. -3 An arm. -4 A finger.

अभीष् (अभि + इष् 6 P.) To wish or desire for, seek for, strive to get.

अभीषंग: The same as अभिषंग q. v.

अभीषुः *m.* See अभीशुः.

अभीष्ट *p. p. a.* (*f.* —ष्टा) 1 Wished, desired. -2 Dear, favourite, darling. -3 Optional. —ष्टः *m.* A darling. -ष्टा *f.* 1 A mistress, beloved woman. -2 Betel —ष्टं 1 An object of desire. -2 A desirable object. -Comp. —देवता *f.* The favourite deity. —लाभः, —सिद्धिः *f.* Gaining a desired object.

अभुग्न *a.* (*f.* —ग्ना) 1 Not bent or crooked, straight. -2 Well, free from disease.

अभुजिष्य *a.* (*f.* —ष्या) Not a slave or servant; independent.

अभूः *m.* ' Unborn, ' N. of Vishnu.

अभूत *a.* (*f.* —ता) Non-existent, what is not or has not been; not true or real, false. -Comp. —आहरणं *n.* ' Utterance of an unreality, ' a covert expression, a speech founded on fraud, one of the members of *garbha* * साहित्य द. —तद्भावः *m.* The becoming or being changed into, or making, that which it is not before; (a term in gram)-पूर्व *a.* (*f.* -र्वा) Unprecedented, unsurpassed. —प्रादुर्भावः *m* The becoming manifest of that which has not been before -शत्रु *a.* Having no enemy.

अभूतिः *f.* 1 Non-existence, non-entity. -2 Want of power. -3 Poverty.

अभूमिः *f.* 1 Non-earth, any thing but earth. -2 An unfit place or object, no proper object for; beyond the reach or scope of; स खलु मनोरथानामप्यभूमिर्विसर्जनावसरसत्कारः *का-दंब.* The honour at the occasion of dismissing me was indeed no object for (*i. e.* beyond) my wishes.

अभृत,-अभृत्रिम *a.* 1 Not hired or paid; not supported.

अभेद *a.* (*f.* —दा) 1 Undivided. -2 Identical, same, alike. —दः *m.* 1 Absence of difference or distinction; identity, sameness. -2 Close union.

अभेद्य, अभेद्दिक *a.* Not to be divided, broken or pierced through, impenetrable. -2 Indivisible. —द्यं *n.* A diamond.

अभोगः *m.* Non-enjoyment.

अभोज्य *a* (*f* —ज्या) 1 Not to be eaten; prohibited as food, impure, unholy -Comp.—अन्न *a.* One whose food is prohibited from being eaten by others.

अभौतिक *a.* (*f* —की) Not material. Not belonging to, or not produced by, the gross elements.

अभ्यग्र *a.* (*f.* —ग्रा) 1 Near, proximate. -2 Fresh, new. —ग्रं *n.* Proximity, vicinity.

अभ्यंगः *m* 1 Smearing the body with unctuous or oily substances. -2 Smearing in general, inunction. -3 An unguent, salve, liniment

अभ्यंजनं *n.* 1 Smearing the body with oily substances; inunction. -2 Smearing or anointing in general -3 Applying collyrium to the eye lashes. -4 An oily substance; oil, unguent.

अभ्यधिक *a* (*f.* —का) 1 More than, exceeding, beyond -2 Surpassing more than (in quality or quantity); higher, greater. -3 More than ordinary ; extraordinary, preeminent. —कं *adv.* Very much, exceedingly.

अभ्यनुज्ञा *f.* 1 Consent, permission. -2 Order, command -3 Granting leave of absence ; dismissing. -4 Admission of an argument.

अभ्यनुज्ञानं *n.* Same as अभ्यनुज्ञा.

अभ्यंतर *a.* (*f.* —रा) 1 Interior, internal, inner (opp. बाह्य). -2 Included in -3 Initiated in, skilled or proficient in, familiar or conversant with. -4 Intimate, closely or intimately related. —रं *n.* 1 The inside or interior, inner or interior part -2 Included space ; interval (of time or place). -3 The mind. —रं, -रतः *ind.* In the interior, inside, inward. -Comp. —कला *f.* The secret art ; the art of coquetry or flirtation.

अभ्यंतरकः *m.* An intimate friend.

अभ्यंतरीकरणं *n.* Initiating, introducing.

अभ्यंतरीकृ (अभ्यंतर + कृ 8 U.) 1 To initiate, familiarize with. -2 To admit or introduce to. -3 To make a near friend of a person.

अभ्यमित *p. p.* (*f.* —ता) 1 Diseased, sick. -2 Injured.

अभ्यमित्रं *n.* An attack on an enemy. —*adv.* Towards or against the enemy.

अभ्यमित्रीणः *m.* A soldier who valiantly encounters his enemy.

अभ्यमित्रीयः *m.* The same as अभ्यमित्रीणः

अभ्यमित्र्यः *m.* The same as अभ्यमित्रीणः.

अभ्ययः *m.* 1 Arrival. -2 Setting (of the sun)

अभ्यर्च् (अभि + अर्च् 1 10 P.) 1 To honour, worship. -2 To praise, celebrate in song.

अभ्यर्चनं *n.*, -र्चा *f.* Worship, adoration, reverence.

अभ्यर्ण *a.* (*f.* —र्णा) Near, proximate, adjoining, approaching, drawing near (of time). —र्णं *n.* Proximity, vicinity.

अभ्यर्थ् (अभि + अर्थ् 10 A.) 1 To request, beg, solicit, ask, entreat (with two acc.). -2. To long for, desire.

अभ्यर्थनं *n.* A request, an entreaty petition, suit.

अभ्यर्थना *f.* See अभ्यर्थनं.

अभ्यर्थिन् *a.* (*f.* -नी) One who solicites or requests.

अभ्यर्दनं *n.* Torturing, distressing.

अभ्यर्ह् (अभि + अर्ह् 10 P.) 1. To salute, honor, worship .

अभ्यर्हणा *f.* 1 Worship. -2 Respect.

अभ्यर्हित *a.* (*f.* —ता) 1 Honoured revered, venerable. -2 Fit, becoming, suitable.

अभ्यवकर्षणं *n.* Extraction, drawing out.

अभ्यवकाशः *m.* An open space.

अभ्यवस्कंदः *m.* 1 An impetuous attack. -2 Marching against an enemy. -3 Disabling an enemy by blows. -4 A blow in general. -5 Overtaking, reaching up to. -6 A fall.

अभ्यवस्कंदनं *n.* See अभ्यवस्कंदः.

अभ्यवहरणं *n.* 1 Throwing away -2 Eating, taking food.

अभ्यवहारः *m.* Taking food or drink. -2 Food.

अभ्यवहार्य *pot. p.* (*f.* -र्या) Fit to eat, eatable. —र्यं *n.* Food.

अभ्यवहृ (अभि + अव + हृ 1 P.) 1 To throw, fling, cast. -2 To collect draw in, procure, obtain. -3 To take food or drink; to eat.

अभ्यशनं *n.* Pervading, reaching to; gaining.

अभ्यसनं 1 Practice or exercise. -2 Constant study, close application (to any thing).

अभ्यसूय (-यति) Den. P. 1 To be angry with; bear malice against; envy, be jealous of (with acc.) न च मां योऽभ्यसूयति • भगव. 18, 67. -2 Not to like, detract from, calumniate. ये त्वेतदभ्यसूयन्तो नानुतिष्ठन्ति मे मतं • भगव. 3. 32.

अभ्यसूय *a.* Angry, jealous.

अभ्यसूयक *a.* (*f.* —यिका) Jealous, envious.

अभ्यसूया *f.* Envy, jealousy, disfavour, anger.

अभ्यस्त *p. p. a.* (*f.* —स्ता) Repeated, frequently practised, exercised. -2 Learnt, studied. -3 (In Math.) Multiplied. -4 (In gram.) Reduplicated. -स्तं *n.* Reduplicated base of a root.

अभ्यस्तं *ind.* Towards sunset.

अभ्यस्तमयः *m.* Setting of the sun during or with reference to some act.

अभ्यस्तमित *a.* One on whom the sun has set while asleep.

अभ्याकर्षः *m.* Striking the breast with the flat of the hand as a sign of defiance (as by wrestlers &c).

अभ्याकाङ्क्षितं *n.* 1 A false charge; groundless complaint. -2 A desire.

अभ्याख्यात *a.* (*f.* —ता) Falsely accused.

अभ्याख्यानं *n.* A false charge.

अभ्यागत *p. p. a* (*f.* —ता) 1 Come near, approached, arrived. -2 Come as a guest. सर्वस्याभ्यागतो गुरुः • हितोप. —तः *m.* A guest, visitor.

अभ्यागम् (अभि + आ + गम्, गच्छ् 1 P.) 1 To go near to, visit; to come, arrive (as time). -2 To come to, fall into, go to any state; e. g. चिन्तामभ्यागतः he fell to thinking.

अभ्यागमः *m.* 1 Arrival; a visit. -2 Neighbourhood. -3 Arriving at or enjoying a result. -4 Rising, getting, up. -5 Striking, killing. -6 Encountering, attacking. 7 War, battle. -8 Enmity.

अभ्यागमनं *n.* Arrival, visit

अभ्यागारिकः *m* One who takes care of his family.

अभ्याघातः *m.* 1 An attack, assault. -2 Persuading to steal.

अभ्यात्त *p. p. a.* (*f.* —त्ता) 1 Obtained, got. -2 Occupied or pervaded. -3 An epithet of the Supreme Being.

अभ्यात्म *a.* Directed towards oneself. —त्मं *adv.* Towards oneself.

अभ्यादा (अभि + आ + दा 3 A.) 1 To take, seize, snatch. -2 To put on, wear (garland &c.). -3 To commence speaking (after another).

अभ्यादानं *n.* 1 Beginning, commencement.

अभ्याधानं *n.* Laying on, adding (as fuel).

अभ्यान्त *a.* (*f.* —न्ता). Diseased, ill.

अभ्यापातः *m.* A calamity, misfortune, evil.

अभ्यामर्दः *m.* War, battle.

अभ्यामर्दनं *n.* See अभ्यामर्दः.

अभ्यारुह् (अभि + आ + रुह् 1 P.) 1 To ascend, go up to, reach.

अभ्यारूढ *p. p. a.* (*f.* —ढा) 1 Ascended, gone up to. -2 Surpassed, excelled.

अभ्यारोहः *m.* 1 Ascending. -2 Transition from one place or state to another. -3 Progress.

अभ्यारोहणं *n.* See अभ्यारोहः.

अभ्यावर्तः *m.* 1 Repetition. -2 A hymn the verses of which are repeated in singing.

अभ्यावृत् (अभि + आ + वृत् 1 A.) 1 To come up to, approach. -2 To be repeated.

अभ्यावृत्त *p. p.* Come near to, repeated. —त्तः *m.* The residue of sacrificial offerings.

अभ्यावृत्तिः *f.* Repetition, recurrence (so many times).

अभ्याश *a.* (*f.* —शा) Neighbouring, proximate. —शः *m.* 1 Reaching to, pervading. -2 Neighbourhood, vicinity (also written as अभ्यास) -3 Result, consequence -4 Prospect, hope of gaining.

अभ्याशं *ind.* Near (with abl. or gen.) e. g. अभ्याशं ग्रामात् or ग्रामस्य.

अभ्यासः *m.* 1 Repetition in general. -2 Repeated practice or exercise, continued practice or use. -3 The effort of the mind to remain in its unmodified condition of purity (in yoga phil.). -4 Habit, custom, practice. -5 Discipline in arms, exercise, military discipline. -6 Reciting, study, repeated reading or learning by heart. -7 Vicinity, proximity, neighbourhood (for अभ्याश). -8 (In gram.) Reduplication. -9 The first syllable of a reduplicated base; reduplicative syllable. -10 (In Math.) Multiplication. -11 (In poetry) Repetition of the last verses or lines (as of a chorus); chorus, burden of a song. -Comp. —योगः *m.* Deep meditation preceded by the effort to keep the mind in its unmodified condition. —लोपः *m.* The dropping of the reduplication-syllable. —व्यवायः *m.* The interval caused by the reduplicative syllable.

अभ्यासादनं *n.* Attacking or facing an enemy.

अभ्याहत *p. p. a.* (*f.* —ता) 1 Struck, beaten. -2 Affected, smitten. -3 Impeded, obstructed.

अभ्याहन् (अभि + आ + हन् 2) P. To strike, smite, wound, injure, kill, destroy.

अभ्याहननं *n.* 1 Striking, hurting, killing. -2 Impeding, obstructing.

अभ्याहारः *m.* 1 Bringing near or towards. -2 Robbing.

अभ्याहृ (अभि + आ + हृ 1 P). 1 To bring near; to give or hand over -2 To rob, plunder.

अभ्युक्ष् (अभि + उक्ष् 1 6. U.) To sprinkle over.

अभ्युक्षणं *n.* 1 Sprinkling over, wetting. -2 Consecration by sprinkling.

अभ्युचित (*f.* —ता) Usual, customary.

अभ्युच्चयः *m.* 1 Increase, augmentation, growth. -2 Prosperity.

अभ्युच्छ्रित *a.* (*f.* —ता) Uplifted, elevated, distinguished.

अभ्युत्क्रोशनं *n.* Loud acclamation.

अभ्युत्था (अभि + उत् + स्था 1 P.) To rise in honour of, rise to greet.

अभ्युत्थानं *n.* 1 Rising (from a seat) to do honour. -2 Starting, departure, setting out. -3 Rise (lit. and fig.), elevation, prosperity, high position -4 Sunrise.

अभ्युत्थित *p. p. a.* (*f.* —ता) 1 Risen, arisen, gone up. -2 Blazing, flaming. (as of fire). -3 Elevated, exalted.

अभ्युत्पत् (अभि + उत् + पत् 1 P.) To fly up to, leap upon.

अभ्युत्पतनं *n.* Springing or leaping against, assault.

अभ्युदय: *m.* 1 Rise (as of the sun or of the moon.) -2 Elevation, prosperity. -3 Beginning, commencement. -4 A festival.

अभ्युदाहरणं *n.* An example or illustration of a thing by its reverse.

अभ्युदि (अभि + उद् + इ 2 P.) 1 To rise (fig. also). -2 To go up (as the sun). -3 To come into existence, happen, originate. -4 To engage in combat with ; to encounter. -5 To prosper, thrive.

अभ्युदित *p. p. a.* (*f.* —ता) 1 Risen; occurred. -2 Elevated, risen to prosperity. -3 Asleep at sunrise ; over whom the sun has risen. -4 Celebrated (as a festival).—ता *f.* N. of a religious ceremony. —तं *n.* Rising ; sunrise.

अभ्युद्गत *p. p. a.* (*f.* —ता) 1 Gone forth to meet. -2 Extended, spread; elevated.

अभ्युद्गति: *f.* See अभ्युद्गम:.

अभ्युद्गम (अभि + उद् + गम् 1 P.) 1 To go forth to meet. -2 To extend, spread.

अभ्युद्गम: *m.* 1 Going forth to meet or to do honour (to a guest or to a venerable person). -2 Rising, occurring, originating.

अभ्युद्गमनं *n.* See अभ्युद्गम:.

अभ्युद्यत *p. p. a.* (*f.* —ता) 1 Raised, lifted up- -2 Prepared or ready; exerting oneself for. -3 Gone forth, risen. -4 Given or brought unsolicited.

अभ्युद्यम् (अभि + उद् + यम् 1 P) 1 To bring, offer. -2 To lift up.

अभ्युन्नत *a.* (*f.* —ता) 1 Raised, elevated ; very high.

अभ्युन्नति: *f.* Great elevation or prosperity.

अभ्युपगत *p. p. a.* (*f.* —ता) 1 Approached. -2 Agreed or assented to; granted. -3 Promised -4 Inferred, probable. -5 Similar.

अभ्युपगम् (अभि + उप + गम् 1 P.) 1 To go to or near, approach ; to come to the help of ; to have recourse to to arrive at (a point of time). -2 To obtain, get. -3 To admit, grant. -4 To assent to, undertake, promise.

अभ्युपगम: *m.* 1 Approach, arrival. -2 Granting, admitting, confession (as of guilt). -3 Undertaking, promising. 4- A contract agreement, promise. -5 Belief ; judgment, a view accepted ; supposition, inference. -6 Analogy. -Comp. —सिद्धान्त: *m.* An admitted proposition or axiom.

अभ्युपपत्ति: *f.* 1 Defence, protection. -2 Consolation. -3 Agreement, assent. -4 Impregnation of a woman (especially of a brother's widow as an act of duty).

अभ्युपपद् (अभि + उप + पद् 4 A.) 1 To protect ; to console, comfort, favour. -2 To ask for help, seek protection, submit. -3 To furnish with.

अभ्युपपादनं *n.* Protection.

अभ्युपस्थित *a* (*f.* —ता) Accompanied, assisted.

अभ्युपाकृत *a.* (*f.* —ता) Asked to take part in a ceremony.

अभ्युपाय: *m.* 1 A promise, an engagement, agreement. -2 A means, an expedient, remedy.

अभ्युपायनं *n.* A complimentary present ; an inducement, a bribe.

अभ्युपे (अभि + उप + इ 2 P.) 1 To go near, approach, enter. -2 To enter a particular state, attain to. -3 To promise, to undertake. -4 To admit, acknowledge. -5 To approve, assent to. -6 To obey, submit to.

अभ्युषः *m.* 1 A sort of cake or bread (Mar. पोळी or रोटी). -2 Half parched food (in general).

अभ्युषित *a.* (*f.* —ता) Dwelling near or with. —तः *m.* A servant who is in attendance.

अभ्यूढ *a.* (*f.* -ढा) Brought near.

अभ्यूषः *m.* A kind of bread. See अभ्युषः.

अभ्यूह् (अभि + ऊह् 1 U.) 1 To cover over, clothe. -2 (A.) To watch for; form a plot against. -3 To infer, guess. -4 To reason, argue, think over. -5 To supply an ellipsis.

अभ्यूहः *m.* 1 Arguing, reasoning, discussion.-2 Deduction, inference, conjecture. -3 Supplying an ellipsis. -4 Understanding.

अभ्येषणं *n.* 1 Desiring, wishing. -2 Going towards, to attack.

अभ्योषः *m.* A kind of bread. See अभ्युषः.

अभ्रं *n.* 1 A cloud. -2 Atmosphere, sky. -3 Mica (Mar. अभ्रक). -4 Gold -5 Camphor -6 A kind of reed ; Calamus Rotang. -7 Cyperus Rotundus (मुस्ता Mar. नागरमोथा). -8 (In arith.) A zero or cypher. -Comp. —अवकाशः *m.* 1 Clouds as the only shelter 2. Fall of rain. —अवकाशिक,-काशिन् *a.* Exposed to the rain, (and so practising penance) ; not seeking shelter from the rain. -उत्थः *m.* The thunderbolt of Indra. —कूटं *n.* A peak of a mountain-like cloud. -गंगा *f.* The heavenly river. -घनः *m.* A mass of clouds. —नागः *m.* One of the elephants supporting the globe ; N. of Airâvata. —पथः *m.* 1 The atmosphere. -2 A balloon. —पिशाचः, —पिशाचकः *m.* An epithet of Râhu. -पुष्पः *m.* N. of a cane (Mar. वेत). —पुष्पं *n.* 1. Water. -2 Anything impossible, a castle in the air. 3. A reed. -मांसी *f.* N. of a plant (जटामांसी). —मातंगः *m.* Indra's elephant, Airâvata. —माला *f.*, —वृंदं *n.* A series of clouds.

अभ्रंलिह *a.* (*f.* —हा) 'Cloudlicking', very high. —हः *m.* Wind.

अभ्रकं *n.* Mica. -Comp. —भस्मन् *n.* Calx of mica. —सत्वं *n.* Steel.

अभ्रंकष *a.* Touching the sky. —षः *m.* 1. Wind, air. -2 A mountain.

अभ्रमुः *f.* The female elephant of the east, the mate of Airâvata, Indra's elephant. -Comp. —प्रियः, —वल्लभः *m.* Airávata.

अभ्रिः *f.* 1 A sharp-pointed stick (for cleaning a boat). -2 A spade; a hoe in general.

अभ्रित *a.* (*f.* —ता) Overcast with clouds, clouded.

अभ्रिय *a.* (*f.* —या) Belonging to or produced from clouds. —यः *m.* Lightning. —यं *n.* A mass of thunder clouds.

अभ्री *f.* See अभ्रिः.

अभ्रेषः *m.* Fitness, propriety.

अभ्रुषः *m.* An ascetic who is starknaked.

अम् *ind.* 1 Quickly. -2 A little.

अम् 1 P. 1 To go to or towards. -2 To serve, honour.-3 To sound. -4 To eat. -10. P. or *Caus.* 1 To hurt. -2 To be ill or be afflicted or diseased.

अम *a.* (*f.* —मा) Unripe (as fruit). —मः *m.* 1 Going. -2 Sickness, disease. -3 This, self. —मा *f.* 1 Soul. -2 Unmeasured state.

अमंगल *a.* (*f.* —ला) 1 Inauspicious, unlucky, evil, ill. —लः *m.* The castor-oil tree (एरंड). —लं *n.* Inauspiciousness, illluck ; evil.

अमंगल्य *a.* (*f.* —ल्या) Unlucky, inauspicious.

अमंड *a.* (*f.* -डा) 1 Without decoration or ornaments. -2 Without froth or foam, (as boiled rice). —डः *m.* The castor oil tree (एरंड).

अमत *a* (*f* —ता) 1 Not felt, not perceptible by the mind, unknown.-2 Not liked, not agreed to. —तः *m.* 1 Death. -2 Time. -3 Disease. -Comp. —परार्थता *f.* 'An unaccepted second sense', one of the faults of a word (शब्ददोष).

अमति *a.* Evil-minded, wicked, depraved. —तिः *m.* A rogue, cheat. —तिः *f.* 1 Ignorance, unconsciousness, absence of intention, or fore-thought. -Comp. —पूर्व *a.* Unconscious, unintentional.

अमत्त *a.* (*f.* —त्ता) Sober, sane.

अमत्रं *n.* 1 A pot, vessel, utensil. -2 Strength, power.

अमत्सर *a* (*f.* —रा) Not jealous or envious.

अमद *a.* (*f.* —दा) 1 Free from intoxication ; grave, serious. -2 Sorrowful.

अमधुपर्क्य *a.* (*f.* —र्क्या) Not worthy of the मधुपर्क ceremony.

अमनस् *a.* 1 Without the organ of desire, thought &c. -2 Devoid of intellect (as a child). -3 Inattentive, careless. -4 Having no control over the mind. -5 Devoid of affection. -*n.* Inattention. -*m.* The Supreme Being. -Comp. —गत *a.* Unknown, unthought of. —मित, -ज्ञ *a.* Disapproved, condemned. -2 Reprobate. —योगः *m.* Absence of concentration of mind; inattention. —हर *a.* Displeasing, disagreeable.

अमनस्क *a.* (*f.* —स्का) See अमनस् *a.*

अमनस्विन् *a.* 1 Unintelligent. -2 Inhuman (as a demon).

अमनाक् *ind.* Not a little; greatly. very much.

अमनुष्य *a.* 1 Not human, not manly. -2 Not frequented by man. —ष्यः *m.* 1 Not a man. -2 A demon. fiend.

अमन्तु *a.* Guiltless, innocent.

अमंत्र,—त्रक *a.* 1 Not requiring the repetition of Vedic texts(as a ceremony &c.). -2 Not entitled to Vedic verses, such as a Súdra, a female, &c. -3 Not knowing Vedic texts. -4 Not accompanied by the use of spells or incantations, as a cure &c. -Comp. —विद् *a.* Not knowing Vedic hymns.

अमंद *a.* (*f.* —दा) 1 Not slow; active, intelligent. -2 Strong, violent (wind &c.). -3 Not a little; much, excessive, great, violent.

अमम *a.* (*f.* —मा) Having no egotism; without any selfish or wordly attachment; devoid of personal ties or desires.

अममता *f.*, —त्वं *n.* Indifference, disinterestedness.

अमर *a.* (*f.* —रा) Immortal, imperishable. -रः *m.* 1 A god, deity. -2 Quicksilver. -3 Gold. -4 A species of pine. -5 The number 33 (that being the number of

Gods). -6 A heap of bones. —रा *f.* 1 The residence of Indra (अमरावती). -2 The navel string; the umbilical cord. -3 The womb. -4 A house-post (स्थूणा). -5 N. of several plants. -री *f.* The same as अमरा. -Comp. —अंगना, —स्त्री *f.* A celestial nymph, heavenly damsel. —अद्रिः *m.* N. of the mountain Sumeru. —अधिपः, —इंद्रः, -ईशः, -ईश्वरः, -पतिः, -भर्ता, -राजः &c. *m.* 'Lordof the gods', epithets of Indra; sometimes of Siva and Vishnu also. —आचार्यः, -गुरुः, -इज्यः *m.* The preceptor of the gods, epithets of Brihaspati. -आपगा, -तटिनी, —सरित् *f.* The heavenly river, the Ganges. —आलयः *m.* The abode of the gods, heaven. —उपम *a.* Godlike. —कोशः, -षः *m.* N. of the most popular Sanskrit lexicon called after the author अमरसिंह. —तरुः,-दारुः *m.* 1 A celestial tree, a tree in the paradise of Indra. -2 The देवदारु tree.-3 The wish-yielding tree. -द्विजः *m.* A Brâhmana who lives by attending a temple or idol; or one who superintends a temple. —पुरं *n.* The residence of the gods, the paradise. —प्रख्य, —प्रभ *a.* Like an immortal. -रत्नं *n.* A crystal. —लोकः *m.* The world of the gods, heaven. —सिंहः *m.* N. of the author of *Amarakosha*, a Sanskrit lexicon.

अमरावती *f.* 1 Abode of the gods, residence of Indra. -2 N. of a modern town in Berar, Amraoti.

अमरी *f.* 1. N. of Indra's capital. -2 A female of gods.

अमर्त्य *a.* (*f.* —र्त्या) 1 Immortal, divine. -2 Imperishable. -र्त्यः *m.* A god. -Comp. —आपगा *f.* The celestial river; an epithet of the Ganges.

अमर्मवेधिन् *a.* (*f.* —नी) Not injuring the vital parts; mild, soft.

अमर्याद *a.* (*f.* —दा) 1 Transgressing every bound; disrespectful, improper. -2 Boundless, infinite.

अमर्यादा *f.* Transgression of due limits or bounds; impropriety of conduct; forwardness, disrespect, violation of due respect.

अमर्ष *a.* Not enduring or bearing. —र्षः *m.* 1 Non endurance, impatience; jealousy, jealous anger. -2 (In Rhet.) One of the 33 minor feelings or व्यभिचारिभाव. -2 Anger, passion, wrath. (सामर्षं *ind.* Angrily). -3 Impetuosity, violence. -4 Determination of purpose. -Comp. —हासः *m.* An angry laugh, sarcastic sneer.

अमर्षण *a.* (*f.* —णा) 1 Impatient, intolerant, unforgiving.-2 Angry, passionate. -3 Impetuous, determined.

अमर्षित *a.* (*f.* —ता) Angry, wrathful.

अमर्षिन् *a.* (*f.* —णी) Angry, passionate.

अमल *a.* (*f.* —ला) 1 Spotless, pure, defectless. -2 White, bright. —लं *n.* 1 Mica (Mar. अभ्रक). -2. The Supreme Spirit. -3 Purity. —ला *f.* 1 Goddess लक्ष्मी. -2 The navel cord. -3 N. of a tree (Mar. आंवळा). -Comp. —आत्मन् *a.* Of pure or undefiled mind. -पतत्रिन् *m.* (त्री) The wild goose. —रत्नं *n.*, -मणिः *m.* A crystal.

अमलिन *a* (*f.* —ना) Clean, spotless, pure (morally also).

अमसः *m.* 1 Disease. -2 Stupidity. -3 A fool. -4 Time.

अमा *a.* Measureless. *-ind.* -1 With, near, close to. -2 Together with, in conjunction or company with. *-f.* 1 The day of the new moon, the day of the conjunction of the sun and moon. -2 The sixteenth digit of the moon. -3 The fifteenth digit also. -Comp. —अंतः *m.* The end of the day of new moon. —पर्वन् *n.* The sacred time of अमा, day of new moon.

अमांस *a.* (*f.* —सा) 1 Without flesh; not containing flesh. -2 Feeble, thin, weak. —सं *n.* Not flesh; any thing but flesh. -Comp. —ओदनिक *a.* (*f.* —की) Not relating to a preparation of rice with meat.

अमात्यः *m.* 1 A companion or follower of a king; a minister.

अमात्र *a.* (*f.* —त्रा) 1 Boundless, immeasurable. -2 Not whole or entire. -3 Not elementary. —त्रः *m.* the Supreme Spirit.

अमानन *n.* (*f.*-ना) Disrespect, insult; disobedience.

अमानव *a.* 1 Not human. -2 Superhuman.

अमानस्यं *n.* Pain.

अमानिन् *a.* (*f.* —नी) Modest, humble.

अमानुष *a.* (*f.* -षी) 1 Not human; supernatural, superhuman. -2 Inhuman, monster-like. -3 Tenantless, desolate. -षः, *m.*, -षी *f.* An irrational animal.

अमानुष्य *a.* (*f.* —ष्या) Not human; superhuman.

अमाम (-मा-) सी *f.* The same as अमावास्या *q. v.*

अमाय *a.* (*f.* -या) 1 Not cunning, guileless, sincere, honest. -2 Immeasurable. —या *f.* 1 Absence of fraud or deceit. -2 (In Vedânta phil.) Absence of delusion, or error; knowledge of the supreme truth. —यं *n.* The Supreme Spirit.

अमाव (-वा-) सी *f.* See अमावस्या.

अमावस्या, —वास्या, —वसी, —वासी *f.* 1 The day of new moon, when the sun and moon dwell together or are in conjunction; the 15th day of the dark half of every lunar month. -2 A sacrifice offered at that time. -3 The sacrificial oblation.

अमित *a.* (*f.* —ता) 1 Unmeasured, boundless, great, immense. -2 Neglected, disregarded. -3 Unknown. -4 Unpolished. -Comp. -आभ *a.* Of great lustre; of unbounded splendour. —ओजस् *a.* Of unbounded energy, all-powerful; Almighty. —तेजस्, —द्युति *a.* Of unbounded lustre or glory. —विक्रम *a.* Of unbounded valour. —विक्रमः *m.* A name of Vishnu. —वीर्य *a.* Of immense strength.

अमित्रः *m.* Not a friend; an enemy, adversary, a foe, rival, opponent.

अमिथ्या *adv.* Not falsely; truly.

अमिन् *a.* (*f.* —नी) Sick, diseased.

अमिष *a.* Free from guile or deceit. —षं *n.* 1 An object of worldly enjoyment; luxury. -2 Honesty, absence of fraud or deceit. -3 Flesh.

अमीवं *n.* 1 Affliction, sickness, disease. -2 Distress, terror.

अमुक *pron. a.* (*f.* —का) Any person or thing referred to without a name.

अमुक्त *a.* (*f.* —क्ता) 1 Not loosened, not let go. -2 Not liberated from recurring birth and death; not having got final beatitude. —क्तं *n*. A weapon (knife, sword &c.). -Comp.—हस्त *a*. (*f*. -स्ता). *a*. Sparing, stingy (in a bad sense); frugal, economical, prudent, (in a good sense).

अमुक्तिः *f*. 1 Non-liberation. -2 Want of freedom or liberty.

अमुतः *ind*. 1 From there.-2 From that place, from above, *i. e*. from the other world or heaven. -3 Upon this, thereupon; henceforth.

अमुत्र *ind*. 1 There, in that place. -2 There (in what precedes or has been said); in that case. -3 There above, in the next world; in the life to come. -Comp. —स्थ *a*. Belonging to a future state or world.

अमुथा *ind*. Thus, in that manner.

अमुष्य (gen. sing. of अदस्). Of such a one (in comp. only). -Comp.-कुल *a*.(अलुक् समास) Belonging to the family of such a one. -कुलं *n*. A well-known family. -पुत्रः *m*.,-त्री *f*. The son or daughter of such a one or of a good or well-known family or origin. अमुष्यायण *a*. (*f*. -णा) Of respectable birth; of a well-known race.

अमूदृश्, -श, -क्ष *a*. (*f*.-शी, -क्षी) Like that; of such a form or kind.

अमूर्त *a*. (*f*. —र्ता) Formless, incorporeal; unembodied. —र्तः *m*. N. of Siva. -Comp. —गुणः *m*. (In Vais. phil.) A quality considered to be अमूर्त or incorporeal such as धर्म, अधर्म, &c.

अमूर्ति *a*. Formless, shapeless. -र्तिः *m*. N. of Vishnu. -र्तिः *f*. Shapelessness.

अमूल, -लक *a*. (*f*. -ला, -का) 1 Rootless (lit.); (fig.) without basis or support; baseless, groundless. -2 Without authority; not being in the original. -3 Without material cause, as the *Pradhâna* of the Sânkhyas. -4 Not fixed in the earth; moving.

अमूल्य *a*. (*f*. -ल्या) Priceless, invaluable.

अमृणालं *n*. The root of a fragrant grass (वीरण, Mar. काळा वाळा used for screens &c.).

अमृत *a*. (*f*. -ता) 1 Not dead. -2 Immortal. -3 Imperishable, indestructible. -4 Causing immortality. -5 Beautiful, agreeable, desired. -तः *m*.1 A god, an immortal, a deity. -2 N. of Dhanvantari, physician of the gods. —ता *f*. Spirituous liquor. —तं *n*. 1 Immortality, imperishable state, final beatitude, absolution. -2 The collective body of immortals. -3 The world of immortality; Paradise, Heaven. -4 Nectar of immortality, ambrosia, beverage of the gods.नाथ क्व एवंविधानि अमृतकल्पानि फलानि प्राप्नोषि • पंचतं. 4. -5 The Soma juice. -6 Antidote against poison. -7 The residue or leavings of a sacrifice. -8 Unsolicited alms. -9 Water. -10 Clarified butter. -11 Milk. -12 Food in general. 13 Boiled rice. -14 A sweetmeat. -15 Property. -16 Gold. -17 Quicksiver. -18 Poison -19 The poison called वत्सनाभ. -20 The Supreme Spirit (ब्रह्म *n*.). -21 N. of particular conjunctions of *Nakshatras* (lunar asterisms) with week-days (वारनक्षत्रयोग) or of lunar days with week days (तिथिवारयोग). -22 The number four. -23 Splendour, light. -Comp. —अंशुः, -करः, -दीधितिः, -द्युतिः, -रश्मिः, &c. The moon.-अंधस्, -अशनः, -आशिस् m. A god, an immortal. —आहरणः m. N. of Garuda who once stole Amrita. -उत्पन्ना f. A fly. —कुंडं n. A vessel containing nectar. —गर्भः m. I The individual soul. -2 The Supreme Soul. —तरंगिणि f. The moonlight. —पः m. A drinker of nectar, a god or deity. -2. N. of Vishnu. -3. One who drinks wine. —फला f. A grape (द्राक्षा). —बंधुः m. The moon. —भुज् m. A god. —मंथनं n. The churning (of the ocean) for nectar. —मालिनी f. N. of Durga. —रसः m. I. Nectar, ambrosia. —लता. —लतिका f. A nectar-giving creeping plant (गुडूची). —सूः, —सूतिः m. I The moon. -2 The mother of the gods.

अमृतमय a. (f. -यी) I Consisting of nectar; ambrosial, full of nectar. -2 Immortal.

अमृतायते Den. A. To be like nectar.

अमृतेशयः m. N. of Vishnu (sleeping in waters).

अमृत्तिः f. A drinking vessel.

अमृषा ind. Not falsely; truly.

अमेदस्क a. (f. —स्का) Fatless, lean.

अमेधस् a. Foolish, stupid, idiotic.

अमेध्य a. (f. —ध्या) I Not allowed to sacrifice. -2 Unfit for a sacrifice. -3 Unholy, filthy, dirty, impure. —ध्यं n. I Excrement; ordure. -2 An unlucky or inauspicious omen. -Comp. —लिप्त a. Smeared with ordure; foul, defiled, dirty. —लेपः m. Smearing with ordure.

अमेय a. (f. -या) I Immeasurable, boundless. -2 Unknowable. -Comp. —आत्मन् a. Magnanimous, large-minded. (m.) N. of Vishnu.

अमोघ a. (f. -घा) I Unfailing; reaching the mark. -2 Unerring, infallible. -3 Not vain or useless; fruitful, productive. —घः m. I Not failing or erring; unerringness, -2 N. of Vishnu (or of Siva). -घा f. N. of the plant पाटला (Mar- पाडळी). -Comp. —दंडः m. Unerring in punishment, N. of Siva. —दर्शिन्, —दृष्टि a. Of unerring mind or view. —बल a. Of never-failing strength or vigour. —वाच् a. One whose words are not vain. —विक्रमः m. Of neverfailing valour; N. of Siva.

अंबं n. I The eye. -2 Water. - अंब ind. A particle of affirmation; 'well,' 'well now.'

अंबकं n. I An eye (in त्र्यंबक). —कः m. A father.

अंबरं n. I Sky, atmosphere, ether. -2 A garment, apparel, dress. -3 Saffron. -4 Mica (mar. अभ्रक). -5 A kind of perfume (Ambergris). -6 Cotton. -7 Circumference, compass. -Comp. -अंतः m. I The end of a garment. -2 The horizon. -ओकस् m. Dwelling in heaven, a god. —दं n. Cotton. —मणिः m. The sun. —युगं n. The two principal garments used by men viz. upper and lower.

अंबरीषं n., or -षः m. I A frying-pan. -2 One of the hells. —षः m. I A young animal, colt. -2 The sun. -3 N. of Vishnu. -4 N. of Siva. -5 N. of a king of the solar race who was celebrated as a worshipper of Vishnu.

अंबष्ठः *m.* 1 The offspring of a man of the Bráhmana and a woman of the Vaisya tribe. -2 An elephant-driver. -ष्ठाः *m. pl.* N. of a country and its inhabitants.

अंबष्ठा *f.* 1 A sort of jasmin. -2 A woman of the अंबष्ठ caste (in this sense अंबष्ठी also).

अंबा *f.* (अंब in later Sanskrit) 1 A mother; also used as a term of respect (*Voc. Sing.* अंब). -2 N. of Durgâ, wife of Siva. -3 N. of a sister of Pându's mother, a daughter of Kásirâja.

अंबाडा (Ved. -का) *f.* A mother.

अंबालिका 1 A mother (also used as a term of respect or endearment). -2 N. of a plant (Mar. अंबाडा). -3 N. of the youngest daughter of Kâsîrâja, wife of Vichitra-Vîrya.

अंबिका *f.* 1 A mother, (also used like अंबा as a term of respect or endearment). -2 N. of Párvatì, wife of Siva. -3 N. of the middle daughter of Kâsirája and the eldest wife of Vichitra-Virya. -Comp. —पतिः, -भर्तृ *m.* N. of Siva. —पुत्रः, -सुतः *m.* N. of धृतराष्ट्र.

आंबिकेयः, -यकः *m.* N. of Ganesha, Kârttikeya or Dhritaráshtra; more correctly written आंबिकेय.

अंबु *n.* 1 Water. -2 The watery element of the blood. -Comp. —कणः *m.* A drop of water. —कंटकः *m.* An alligator. —किरातः *m.* An alligator. —कीशः, -कूर्मः *m.* A Porpoise (शिशुमार) particularly Gangetic. —क्रिया *f.* The libation of water to the Manes of the deceased. —घनः *m.* Hail. -चत्वरं *n.* A lake. -चर *a.* Aquatic. -ज *a.* Produced in water, aquatic. —जं *n.* 1 A lotus. -2. The thunderbolt of Indra. —जः *m.* 1 The moon. -2 The Sárasa bird. -3 The conch. -4 Camphor. -भूः, -आसनः *m.* Brahmâ (-*m.*) -आसना *f.* The goddess Lakshmi. -जन्मन् *n.* 1 A lotus. (-*m*) -2 The moon. -3 The conch. -4 Sârasa. —तस्करः *m.* 'Water-thief,' the sun. -दः *m.* A cloud. —धरः *m.* 1 A cloud. -2 Mica. —धिः *m.* 1 The ocean. -3 The number four (in Math.). —निधिः *m.* The ocean. —पः *m.* Varuna, the regent of waters. -प्रसादः *m.*, -प्रसादनं *n.* The clearing nut tree (कतक). —भवं *n.* A lotus. —भृत् *m.* 1. A cloud. -2. The ocean. -राजः *m.* 1 The ocean. -2 Varuna. -राशिः *m.* The receptacle or store of water, the ocean. —रुहं *n.* A lotus. —रुहः *m.* A lotus. -रोहिणी *f.* A lotus. —वाहः *m.* 1 A cloud. -2 A lake. -3 Water-bearer. -4. The number 17. -5. A sort of grass. -वाहिन् (-*m.*) 1. A cloud. -वाहिनी *f.* 1. A wooden vessel, a sort of bucket. -2 A woman fetching water. —विहारः *m.* Sporting in water. —वेतसः *m.* A kind of cane or reed growing in water. —सरणं *n.* A flow or current of water. —सर्पिणी *f.* A leech. —सेचनी *f.* A bucket.

अंबूकृत *a.* (*f.* -ता). Pronounced in shutting the lips, the sound thus remaining as it were in the mouth; uttered while emitting saliva from the mouth. —तं *n.* A growling of a bear.

अंभ् 1 A. To sound.

अंभस् *n.* 1 Water. -2 The sky. -3 The fourth sign of the zodiac.

-Comp. —ज *a.* Produced in water, aquatic. —ज: *m.* 1 The moon. -2. The (Indian) crane or Sârasa. -जं *n.* A lotus. -जन्मन् *m.*,-जनि:,-योनि:, *m.* An epithet of Brahmá. —जन्मन् *n.* A lotus. —द:, -धर: *m.* A cloud. —धि:, -निधि:, -राशि: *m.* The ocean. —रुह् *n.* (ट्), -रुहं *n.* A lotus. —सारं *n.* A pearl.—सू: *m.* Smoke; cloudiness. -स्थ *a.* Living in water; what holds or contains water.

अंभोजिनी *f.* 1 A lotus-plant or its flowers. -2 A group of lotus flowers. -3 A place abounding in lotuses.

अम्मय *a*, (*f.* -यी) Watery, formed from water.

अम्र: *m.* The mango-tree. See आम्र.

अम्ल (*f.* —म्ला) Sour, acid. —म्ल: *m.* 1 Sourness, acidity, (one of the six kinds of tastes or 'rasas.' -2 Vinegar. -3 The common citron tree. -4 Belch, eructation. —म्ली *f.* Wood-sorrel. —म्लं *n.* Sour curds, butter-milk, with a fourth part of water. -Comp. -अक्त *a.* Acidulated. -उद्गार:*m.* A sour eructation. -गंधि *a.* Having a sour smell. —गोरस: *m.* Sour butter-milk. -जंबीर:, -निंबक: *m.* The lime-tree. —पित्तं *n.* Acidity of stomach, sour bile. —फल: *m.* The tamarind tree. —फलं *n.* The tamarind fruit. —रस *a.* Having an acid taste. —रस: *m.* Sourness, acidity. —वृक्ष: *m.* The tamarind tree.

अम्लक: *m.* N. of a plant (लकुच), a sort of bread-fruit tree.

अम्ला *f.* The tamarind tree.

अम्लान *a.* (*f.* -ना) 1 Not withered or faded (flowers &c.). -2 Clean, clear, bright; pure, unclouded. —न: *m.* Globe-amaranth (Mar. आंबोळी). —नं *n.* A lotus.

अम्लानि *a.* Vigorous, not fading. —नि: *f.* 1 Vigour. -2 Freshness; verdure.

अम्लिका *f.* 1 Sour taste in the mouth. -2 The tamarind tree.

आम्लिमन् *m.* Sourness.

अम्लीका *f.* See आम्लिका.

अय् 1 A. (sometimes P. also, especially with उद्). To go. With अंतर् To intervene. अभ्युद्.- 1 To prosper. -2 To rise (as sun, moon, &c.). उद्,1 To come in sight. -2 To rise (as sun, moon, &c.). -3 To arise from, to be produced from. परा— (Changed into पला) To run away; to retreat.

अय *a.* Going, moving. —य: *m.* 1 Going, moving (mostly in comp. as in अस्तमय). -2 Good actions of former birth. -3 Good fortune, good luck. -4 A move towards the right (in chess). -5 A die or cube (to play with). -Comp. —अन्वित, अयवत् *a.* Fortunate, lucky. -शोभिन् *a.* Bright with good fortune.

अयक्ष्मं *n.* Healthiness, freedom from disease.

अयाज्ञिय *a.* (*f.* —या). 1 Not fit for sacrifice (as माष). -2 Not fit to perform a sacrifice (as a boy not invested with the sacred thread). -3 Profane, vulgar, common.

अयत्न *a.* Not requiring any effort. —त्न: *m.* Absence of effort or exertion. अयत्नेन,—त्नात्, —त्नत: have the sense of indeclinables and mean 'without effort or exertion,' 'easily,' 'readily.' -कृत, -ज *a.* Easily produced, spontaneous. —लभ्य *a.* Easily obtainable.

अयथा *ind.* Unsuitably, not as it should be or is intended to be, unfitly, improperly, wrongly. -Comp. —अर्थ *a.* 1 Not true to the sense, unmeaning, nonsensical. -2 Incongruous, unfit, incorrect, wrong. —इष्ट *a.* 1. Not as wished or desired, disliked. -2 Not enough or sufficient. —उचित *a.* Unfit, unworthy. —उचितं *ind.* Unfitly. —तथ *a.* 1. Not as it should be, unfit, unsuitable. -2 Useless, profitless. —तथं 1 *ind.* Unfitly, unsuitably. -2 In vain, uselessly. -3 Wrongly. —तथ्यं *n.* Unsuitableness, incongruity ; uselessness. —द्योतनं *n.* Intimation or occurrence of some thing or act which is not expected. —पूर्व *a.* Unprecedented, unparalleled, unusual. -शास्त्रकारिन् *a.* Not acting according to the Sâstras ; irreligious.

अयथावत् *ind.* Wrongly, erroneously, improperly.

अयन *a.* 1 Going (at the end of comp.). -2 (As a patronymic affix) Descended from ; *e. g.* शाकटायन. —नं *n.* 1 Going, moving, walking ; as in रामायणं. -2 A walk, path, way, road. -3 A place, site, abode. -4 A way of entrance, an entrance (to an array of troops or व्यूह). -5 Rotation, circulation, period. -6 The sun's passage, north and south of the equator. -7 (Hence) The period or duration of this passage, half year, the time from one solstice to another (उत्तरायण and दाक्षिणायन). -8 The equinoctial and solstitial points ; दाक्षिणं अयनं Winter solstice. उत्तरं अयनं Summer solstice. -9 Method, manner, way. -10 Final emancipation. -Comp. —अंशः, —भागः *m.* The arc between the vernal equinoctial point and the beginning of the fixed zodiac or the first point in Aries. —कालः *m.* The interval between the solstices. -संक्रमः, -संक्रांतिः, *f.* The Sun's passage through the zodiac. —वृत्तं *n.* The ecliptic.

अयंत्रित *a.* (*f.* —ता) Unrestrained, unchecked, self-willed.

अयमित *a.* (*f.* —ता) 1 Unrestrained, unchecked. -2 Untrimmed, undecorated (as nails &c.).

अयशस् *a.* Disreputable, infamous, disgraceful ; (also अयशस्क in this sense). अयशः *n.* Infamy, disgrace, ignominy, ill-repute, scandal. -Comp. —कर *a.* (*f.* —री) Disgraceful, ignominious.

अयशस्य *a.* (*f.* —स्या) Infamous, ignominious.

अयस् *n.* (-यः) 1 Iron. -2 Steel. -3 Gold. -4 A metal in general. -5 Aloe wood. -*m.* Fire. -Comp. —अग्रं, —अग्रकं *n.* A hammer, a mace or club tipped with iron ; a pestle for cleaning grain. —कोशः *m.*, or —कोशं *n.* A large quantity of iron. -2 Excellent iron. —कांतः (अयस्कांतः) *m.* 1 A magnet, load-stone. -2 A precious stone. —मणिः *m.* A loadstone. —कारः *m.* 1 An iron-smith, black-smith. —कीटं *n.* Rust of iron. —घनः *m.* An iron hammer, forge hammer. —चूर्णं *n.* Iron filings. —जालं *n.* An iron net-work. —प्रतिमा *f* (अयःप्रतिमा) An iron image. —मलं *n.* Rust of iron. —मुखः *m.* An arrow (iron-pointed). —शंकुः *m*, 1 An iron spear. -2 An iron nail, pointed iron spike. —शूलं *n.* An iron lance. —हृदय *a.* Iron-hearted, stern, cruel, unrelenting.

अयाचित *a.* (*f.* —ता) Unasked, unsolicited (as alms, food &c.). —तं *n.* Unsolicited alms. —Comp. -उपनत,-उपस्थित *a.* (*f.* —ता, —ता) Got unasked or without solicitation. —वृत्तिः *f.*, व्रतं *n.* Subsisting on alms got without begging or solicitation.

अयाज्य *a.* 1 (A person) for whom one must not perform sacrifices. -2 One who is not competent to offer sacrifices (as a Sudra &c.). -3 (Hence) Out-cast. -4 Not fit for sacrificial offerings. -Comp. —याजनं,-संयाज्यं *n.* Sacrificing for a person for whom one must not perform sacrifices.

अयाथार्थिक *a.* (*f.* -की) 1 Improper. -2 Incongruous, absurd.

अयाथार्थ्यं *n.* 1 Unfitness, incorrectness. -2 Absurdity, incongruity.

अयानं *n.* 1 Stopping, halt. -2 Natural disposition, nature.

अयि *ind.* 1 A vocative particle of simple or gentle address or of entreaty or solicitation, of encouragement, persuasion and may be rendered by ' friend ', ' oh ' 'ah,' 'please,' 'I pray,' 'kindly,' &c.

अयुक्त *a.* (*f.* —क्ता) 1 Not yoked or harnessed. -2 Not joined. -3 Not devout or pious ; inattentive, negligent.-4 Unpractised, unused, unemployed. -5 Unfit, improper, unsuitable. -6 Untrue, wrong. -7 Unmarried. -Comp. —कृत् *a.* Doing improper or wrong acts. —रूप *a.* Incongruous, unsuitable.

अयुग *a.* 1 Separate, single, -2 Odd, uneven. —Comp. —अर्चिस *m.* Fire. —नेत्रः, -नयनः, *m.* God शिव. —शरः *m.* Cupid, god of love. —सप्तिः *m.* The sun.

अयुगपद् *ind* Not all together, gradually, *seriatim.* -Comp. —ग्रहणं *n.* Apprehending gradually. —भावः *m.* Successive order, successiveness.

अयुगल *a.* See अयुग.

अयुग्म *a.* (*f.* -ग्मा) 1 Not in pairs or couples ; single, separate. -2 Odd, uneven (as a number) -Comp. —छदः, —पत्रः *m.* Having an odd (*i.e.* 7) number of leaves; the सप्तपर्ण tree (Mar. सातवीण). —नयनः, —नेत्रः, —लोचनः *m.* N of Siva. —बाणः, —शरः *m.* N. of Cupid. —वाहः, —सप्तिः *m.* The Sun.

अयुज् *a.* Not being in couples ; odd, uneven (opp. युज् even). -Comp. —इषुः, -बाणः, -शरः *m.* N. of Cupid.-छदः*m.*सप्तपर्ण tree(Mar.सातवीण). —पादयमकं *n.* A kind of alliteration having the same syllables (in a different sense) in the first and third pádas. —नेत्रः, -लोचनः, —अक्षः, *m.* N. of Siva.

अयुत *a.* (*f.* —ता) Disjoined, detached, not connected. —तं *n.* Ten thousand, a myriad. -Comp. —सिद्धिः *a.* (in Vais. phil.) Proved to be inseparable and inherent. —सिद्धः *m.* Proof that certain things or notions are inseparable and inherent. —होमः *m.* A kind of sacrifice.

अये *ind.* 1 Used as vocative particle or as a kind of gentle address. -2 An interjection of anger, fatigue, recollection, fear; surprise, grief.

अयोगः *m.* 1 Separation, disjunction, interval. -2 A widower. -3 Unfitness, unsuitableness. -4 Dislike. -5 An iron hammer.

अयोगवः *m.* The child of a शूद्र father and वैश्य mother.

अयोग्य *a.* (*f.* —ग्या) Unfit, improper, unsuitable, useless.

अयोच्छिष्टं *n.* Rust of iron.

अयोध्य *a.* Not to be warred against, unassailable, irrestible. —ध्या *f.* The capital of solar kings, born of the line of Raghu; it is situated on the river Sarayu.

अयोनि *a.* 1 Without origin or source; eternal. -2 Not born from the womb; born in a manner not approved by law or religion. —निः *f.* 1 Not the womb. —निः *m.* 1 N. of Brahmâ. -2 N. of Siva. -Comp. —ज, -जन्मन् *a.* Not born from the womb, not produced in the ordinary course of generation. —जः *m.* N. of Vishnu. —जा, —संभवा *f.* N. of Sitâ, daughter of Janaka, who was born from a furrow in a field.

अयौगपद्यं *n.* Absence of simultaneity.

अयौगिक (*f.* —की) 1 Having no regular derivation. -2 Not etymologically derived (as a word).

अरः *m.* The spoke or radius of a wheel. (—रं also). -Comp. —घट्टः, -घट्टकः *m.* 1 A wheel or machine for raising water from a well (Mar. राहाट). -2 A deep well. —घट्टघटी or —घट्टघटिका *f.* A bucket so used अथ कूपमासाद्य अरघट्टघटिकामार्गेण सर्पस्तेनान्वितः (by the passage afforded by the buckets of the water-wheel) *पंचतं. 4. स कदाचिद्वाप्यादेरघट्टोज्झितोऽरघट्टघटीमारुह्य निष्क्रांतः * पंचतं 4.

अरकः *m.* The spoke of a wheel.

अरजस्, अरजस्क *a.* 1 Dustless, clean, pure (fig. also). -2 Free from passion (रजस्). -3 Not having the monthly courses. —*f.* (—जाः) A young girl who has not reached the age of puberty; a girl before menstruation.

अरणि *m. f. dual* (अरणी) Two pieces of wood used in kindling the sacred fire. —णिः *m.* 1 The sun. -2 Fire. तद्युतारणिसंभृतं नृपवधूकेशाम्बराकर्षणैः * वेणी-सं I. 24.

अरणी *f.* A piece of wood used in kindling sacred fire by being rubbed against another.

अरण्यं *n.* (Sometimes *m.* also) A wilderness, forest, desert. -Comp. —अध्यक्षः *m.* The headman or superintendent of a forest district; forest keeper or ranger. -अयनं, -यानं *n.* Going into the forest, becoming a hermit. -ओकस् *m.* An anchorite. A Vânaprastha. -कदली *f.* A wild plantain. -काण्डं *n.* N. of the third book of the Râmâyana which narrates Râmá's exploits while journeying in the forest with Visvámitra. —गजः *m.* A wild elephant (one not tamed). —चटकः *m.* A wild sparrow. —चंद्रिका *f.* (lit.) Moonlight in a forest; (fig.) an ornament or decoration which is not appreciated or enjoyed by those for whom it is intended. —चर (-ज्येचर also), —जीव *a.* Living in woods. -द्वादशी *f.*, -व्रतं *n.* N. of a ceremony performed on the 12th day of Márga-Sirsha. -धर्मः *m.* 1 Wild or savage condition; wild nature. -2 The duties of a Vánaprastha or anchorite. -पंडितः *m.* A foolish person (who can display his learning only in a forest where no one will hear him and correct his errors). —मक्षिका *f.* A gadfly. –रक्षकः *m.* The conservator of forests, forest-keeper. –राजः *m.* King of the forest, *i. e.* the lion or tiger. –रुदितं *n.*, or अरण्येरुदितं *n.*' Weeping in a forest', (fig.) a vain or useless speech, or a cry with no one to heed it, or any thing done to no purpose. विदूषक :— भो डासिह । मता देवी । ... अरण्यरुदितं कोषि • रत्नाव. 3. —वायसः *m.* A wild crow, raven. —वासः, –समाश्रयः *m.* 1 Residence in a forest. –2. A hermitage, forest habitation. —वासिन् *m.* An anchorite. –विलपितं *n*, –विलापः *m.* (–ण्ये-) See अरण्यरुदितं. –श्वन् *m.* The wolf. –षष्ठी *f.* N. of a festival celebrated onthe 6th day of the bright half of Jyestha.

अरण्यकं *n.* A Forest.

अरण्यानिः, –नी *f.* 1 A large forest or desert, vast wilderness. –2 The presiding deity of the woods.

अरण्येतिलकः *m.* Sesamum yielding no oil ; (fig.) any thing which does not fulfil one's expectation.

अरत *a.* (*f.* –ता) 1 Dull, apathetic. –2 Not pleased with, averse to. –तं *n.* Non-copulation. –Comp. —त्रप *a.* Not ashamed of copulation. –पः *m.* A dog.

अरति *f.* 1 Absence of pleasure or amusement, regarded as arising from the longings of love. –2 Pain, distress. –3 Anxiety, uneasiness. –4 Dissatisfaction, discontent. –5 Languor, dullness. –6 A bilious disease.

अरत्निः *m.* or *f.* 1 The elbow; sometimes the fist itself. –*f.* A cubit of the middle length, from the elbow to the tip of the little finger.

अरत्निक *a.* (*f.* –का) Having the length of an अरत्नि *q. v.*

अरंधनं *n.* Absense of cooking.

अरम् *ind.* 1 Swiftly, readily.

अरमण *a.* 1 Not pleasing or gratifying.

अरमति *a.* Active, diligent. —तिः *f.* 1 Splendour. –2 Readiness to serve, obedience, devotion to God.

अररं *n.* A covering, a sheath. –रः *m.*, –रं *n.* The leaf or panel of a door. —रः *m.* An awl.

अररिः *m.*, –रि *n.* The leaf or panel of a door.

अररुः *m.* 1 An enemy. –2 A weapon. –3 N. of an Asura.

अररे *ind.* A vocative particle expressive of (1) haste ; (2) contempt.

अरविंदं *n.* 1 A lotus which opens at sunrise. (This flower is considered as one of the five arrows of the God of Love). –2 Also a red or blue lotus. —दः *m.* 1 The (Indian) crane. –2 Copper. –Comp. —अक्षः *m.* An epithet of Vishnu. –नाभिः, –नाभः *m.* N. of Vishnu, from whose navel sprang the lotus which supported Brahmâ. –सद् *m.* N. of Brahma.

अरविंदिनी *f.* 1 A lotus-plant. –2 An assemblage of lotus flowers. –3 A place abounding in lotus flowers.

अरस *a.* (*f.* -सा) 1 Sapless, tasteless, insipid. –2 Dull, flat. –3 Weak, inefficacious. –Comp. —आशः *m.* 1 Eating sapless food. –2 Maceration of the body. —आशिन् *a.* 1. Eating sapless food. –2 Macerating the body.

अरसिक *a.* (*f.* –का) 1 Devoid of taste ; sapless, insipid, flavourless (of a thing). –2 Unfeeling, inappreciative, insensible to the charms (of poetry &c).

अराग *a.* (*f.* –गा) Cool, dispâssionate.

अरागिन् *a.* (*f.* –णी) Cool, unimpassioned.

अराजक *a.* (*f.* –का) Having no king ; anarchical.

अराजन् *m.* A no-king ; one not a king. –Comp. —भोगीन *a.* Not fit for the use or enjoyment of a king. —स्थापित *a.* Not established or licensed by a king ; illegal.

अरातिः *m.* 1 An enemy, foe. –2 The number six. –Comp. —भंगः *m.* Destruction of enemies.

अराल *a.* (*f.* –ला) Curved, crooked. –कः *m.* 1 A bent or crooked arm. –2 An elephant in rut. –Comp. —केशी *f.* A woman with curled hair. —पक्ष्मन् *a.* Having curved eyelashes.

अराला *f.* A courtezan, a harlot.

अरिः *m.* 1 An enemy, foe. –2 An enemy of mankind (said of the six feelings which disturb man's mind ; *viz.* काम, क्रोध, लोभ, मोह, मद, and मत्सर.). –3 The number six (from the six enemies). –4 Any part of a carriage. –5 A wheel. –Comp. —कुलं *n.*, 1 A host of enemies. –2 An enemy. —घ्नः *m.* Destroyer of enemies. –चिंतनं *n.*, –चिंता *f.* Schemes directed against enemies; administration of foreign affairs. —मर्दन *a.* Crushing or trampling foes, destroying enemies. —सूदनः, –हन्, –हिंसकः *m.* Destroyer of enemies.

अरिक्थभाज्, अरिक्थीय *a.* Not entitled to a share in the ancestral property (as an heir incapacitated by apostacy, impotence, &c.).

अरित्रं *n.* 1 An oar. –2 A rudder, helm. –3 A ship, boat. —त्रः *m.* A Soma vessel. –Comp. —गाध *a.* 'Oardeep,' *i. e.* shallow (water).

अरिंदम *a.* Subduer of enemies, victorious, conquering.

अरिषं *n.* 1 A continuous downpour of rain. –षः *m.* –2 A sort of disease in the anus.

अरिष्ट *a.* Unhurt ; perfect, undecaying, secure, free from danger भिमसेन:— अरिष्टोऽस्तुपंथाः * भास. मध्या –ष्टः *m.* 1 A heron (कंक). –2 A raven, crow. –3 An enemy. –4 N. of a demon killed by Krishna ; a son of Bali. —ष्टा *f.* 1 A bandage. –2 N. of a daughter of Daksha and one of the wives of Kasyapa. —ष्टं *n.* 1 Bad or ill luck, evil, misfortune ; calamity. –2 A portentous phenomenon fore-boding misfortune ; unlucky omen (such as earth-quake). –3 Unfavourable symptom, especially of approaching death. –4 Good fortune or luck, happiness. –5 The lying-in-chamber. –6 Butter-milk. –7 Spirituous liquor. –Comp. —गृहं *n.* The lying-in chamber. –मथनः *m.* N. of Siva or Vishnu. —शय्या *f.* A lying-in couch. —सूदनः, –हन् *m*, The killer of Arishta, epithet of Vishnu.

अरिष्टकः *m.* The soap-berry tree.

अरुंषिका *f.* Scab on the head (Mar. खवडे).

अरुचिः *f.* 1 Aversion, dislike in general. –2 Want of appetite, disrelish, disgust. –3 Absence of a satisfactory explanation.

अरुचिर *a* (*f.* -रा) Disagreeable, disgusting.

अरुज् *a.* Free from disease, healthy.

अरुज *a.* (*f.* -जा) 1 Sound, healthy. -2 Not breaking.

अरुण *a.* (*f.* -णा, -णी) 1 Reddish brown tawny. -2 Perplexed, embarrassed. -3 Dumb. -णः *m.* 1 Red colour. -2 The dawn personified as the charioteer of the sun. -3 The sun. -4 A kind of leprosy with red spots and insensibility of the skin. -5 A little poisonous creature. -6 N. of one of the 12 Adityas, the one presiding over Mágha. —णा *f.* 1 N. of several plants. -2 N. of a river. —णं *n.* 1 Red colour. -2 Gold. -3 Saffron. -Comp. —अग्रज: *m.* N. of Garuda. —अनुजः, -अवरजः *m.* N. of Garuda, younger brother of Aruna. -अर्चिस् *m.* The sun. -आत्मजः *m.* 1. Son of Aruna, N. of Jatáyu. -2 N. of saturn, Sâvarni Manu, Karna, Sugriva, Yama and the two Asvins. -आ *f.* N. of Yamunâ and Tápti. —उदयः *m.* Break of day, dawn. —उपलः *m.* A ruby. —कमलं *n.* A red lotus. -ज्योतिस् *m.* N. of Siva. -प्रियः *m.* N. of the sun. -प्रिया *f.* 1 The sun's wife. -2 Shadow. —लोचनः *m.* A pigeon. —सारथिः *m.* The sun.

अरुणित, अरुणीकृत *a.* (*f.* -ता, -ता) Reddened, dyed red.

अरुणिमन् *m.*, अरुणता *f.* Redness, red colour.

अरुंतुद *a.* 1 Cutting or wounding the vital parts, corrosive, sharp (fig. also). Caustic. -2 Acrimonious, sour (disposition).

अरुन्धती *f.* 1 A medicinal climbing plant. -2 N. of the wife of Vasishtha. -3 The morning star personified as the wife of Vasishtha; one of the Pleiades. -Comp. -जानिः, -नाथः, -पतिः *m.* N. of Vasishtha, one of the seven Rishis or stars in the Ursa Major. -दर्शनन्यायः *m.* A method of explanation in which one starts from a false assumption, and finally indicates the true thing.

अरुष्,-ष *a.* Not angry, calm, good-tempered.

अरुष *a.* (*f.* -षा) 1 Not angry. -2 Bright, reddish. -3 Unhurt. —षः *m.* 1 The red horse of Agni; a flame. -2 The sun; the day as presided over by the sun. —षी *f.* 1 The dawn. -2 A flame. -3 N. of the wife of Bhrigu and mother of Aurva.

अरुष्कः *m.* N. of a tree (भल्लातक Mar. बिब्बा).

अरुस् *a.* Wounded, sore. अरुः -*m.* 1 The Arka tree. (Mar. रुई). -2 Red *Khadira*, (Mar. तांबडा खैर). *m.*, *n.* 1 A vital part. -2 A wound, sore. -3 An eye. -Comp. —कर *a.* Causing or inflicting wound. -करः *m.* N. of a tree, अरुष्क (Mar. बिब्याचें झाड).

अरुसिका *f.* Eruption on the scalp with acute pain.

अरुहा *f.* N. of a plant (भूम्यामलकी Mar. भुइ आंवळी).

अरूप *a.* (*f.*-पा) 1 Formless. -2 Ugly. -3 Dissimilar, unlike. -पं *n.* 1 A bad or ugly figure. -2 The Pradhána of the Sânkhyas and Brahman. (*n.*) of the Vedântins. -Comp. —हार्य *n.* *a.* Not to be attracted or won over by beauty.

अरे *ind.* An interjection o calling inferiors, of anger, of envy.

अरेरे *ind.* An interjection of calling out angrily, or of addressing inferiors, or by way of contempt.

अरोक *a.* (*f.* —का) 1 Without holes. -2 Destitute of splendour, dim.

अरोग *a.* (*f.* —गा) Free from disease, healthy. —गः *m.* Sound health.

अरोगिन् *a.* (*f.* —णी) Healthy.

अरोचक *a.* (*f.* -चिका) 1 Not shining or bright. -2 Causing loss of appetite. —कः *m.* Loss of appetite; disgust, loathing.

अरोचिष्णु *a.* 1 Not shining, dark. -2 Disagreeable, ugly.

अर्क् 10 P. 1 To heat or warm. -2 To praise.

अर्कः *m.* 1 The sun. -2 A ray. -3 Fire. -4 A crystal. -5 Copper. -6 Sunday. -7 N. of a plant calatropis Gigantea, (Mar. रुई). -8. N. of Indra. -9 N. of Vishnu. -10 The seventh day of a month. -11 The उत्तरफल्गुनी asterism. -12 The number 12. -Comp. —अंशः *m.*, —कला *f.* A. digit or 12th part of the sun's disc. —अश्मन्, —उपलः *m.* 1. The sun-stone, heliotrope, girasol. -2 A sort of crystal or ruby. —इन्दुसंगमः *m.* The time of conjunction of the sun and moon (दर्श or अमावास्या). —कान्ता, *f.* 1 Sun's wife, संज्ञा. -2 The sun's shadow. -चंदनः *m.* A kind of red sandal (रक्तचंदन). —जः *m.* An epithet of Karna, Yama, Sugriva. —जौ *m. dual* The two Aswins regarded as the physicians of Heaven. —तनयः *m.* An epithet of Karna. Yama, Manu Vaivasvata, Manu Sávarni, and Saturn. —तनया *f.* N. of the rivers Yamuná and Tâpti. —त्विष् *f.* The light of the sun. -दिनं *n.*, -वासरः *m.* Sunday. —दुग्धं *n.* The milky sap or exudation of *arka*. -नंदनः, -पुत्रः, -सुतः, -सूनुः *m.* N. of Saturn. Karna or Yama. -नामन् *m.* The red *arka* tree. —बंधुः, —बान्धवः *m.* 1 N. of Buddha Shâkyamuni. -2 A lotus (the sun-lotus). —मंडलं *n.* The disc of the sun. —विवाहः *m.* The marriage with the *arka* plant (enjoined to be performed before a man marries a *third* wife, who thus becomes his fourth).

अर्गडः *m.* See अर्गलः below.

अर्गलः *m.*, अर्गलं *n.*, अर्गला, अर्गली *f.* 1 A wooden bolt, pin, bar, latch &c. (for fastening a door or the cover of a vessel) ; used figuratively in the sense of an impediment, something intervening as an obstruction. -2 A wave or billow. -3 The leaf of a door (कपाट).

अर्गलिका *f.* A small door-pin, a small bolt.

अर्घ् 1 P. To be worth, have value, to cost.

अर्घः *m.* 1 Price, value. -2 A respectful offering or oblation of various ingredients to gods or venerable men, consisting of rice, Durva grass &c. with or without water. -Camp. —अर्ह *a.* Worthy of a respectful offering. —दानं *n.* Presentation of a respectful offering. —बलाबलं *n.* Rate of price, proper price, the cheapness or dearness of articles, fall or rise in prices.

—संस्थापनं, सस्थापनं *n.* The fixing of the prices of commodities.

अर्घीशः *m.* A N. of Siva.

अर्घ्य *a.* (*f.* —र्घ्या) 1 Valuable. -2 Venerable, deserving respectful offering. —र्घ्यं *n.* 1 A respectful offering or oblation to a god or venerable person. -2 A kind of honey.

अर्च् 1 U. 1 To worship, salute, welcome with respect, honour, decorate, adorn. —10 P. or -*Caus.* 1 To honour, adore, worship. -2 To praise. -3 To cause to shine. WITH अनु- To congratulate. प्र— 1. To praise. -2 To honour, worship.

अर्चक *a.* (*f.* —का) Worshipping, adoring. —कः *m.* A worshipper.

अर्चनं *n.*, —ना *f.* Worship, reverence or respect paid to deities and superiors.

अर्चनीय, अर्च्य *pot. p.* (*f.* —या, —र्च्या) To be adored or worshipped; respectable.

अर्चा *f.* 1 Worship, adoration. -2 An idol or image intended to be worshipped.

अर्चिः *f.* Ray, flame.

अर्चित *p. p. a.* (*f.* —ता) Worshipped, respected, honoured.

अर्चिष्मत् *a.* Flaming brilliant, bright. —*m.* 1 Fire, the god of fire. -2 The sun. -3 N. of Vishnu.

अर्चिस् *n.* (—र्चिः) 1 A ray of light, flame. -2 Light; lustre, (also *f.*). —*m.* 1 A ray of light. -2 Fire.

अर्ज् 1 P. 1 To procure, secure, gain, earn. -2 To take up. With उप— To procure, to obtain. -10. P. or -*Caus.* 1 To procure, acquire, obtain.

अर्जक *a.* (*f.* —र्जिका) Procuring, acquiring; one who acquires or gets.

अर्जनं *n.* Getting, acquisition.

अर्जुन *a.* (*f.* —ना, or —नी) 1 White, clear, bright. -2 Silvery. —नः *m.* 1 The white colour. -2 Peacock. -3 A tree having a useful rind. (Mar. अर्जुनसादडा). -5 N. of the third Pândava who was a son of Kuntī by Indra. -6 N. of Kârtavirya, slain by Parasurama. -7 The only son of his mother. -8 N. of Indra. —नी *f.* 1 A procuress, bawd. -2 A cow. —नं *n.* 1 Silver. -2 Gold. -3 Slight inflammation of the white of the eye. -4 Grass. -Comp. —छवि *a.* White; of a white colour. —ध्वजः *m.* N. of Hanumat.

अर्णः *m.* 1 The teak tree. -2 A letter (of the alphabet).

अर्णवः *m.* 1 The sea, ocean (fig. also). -Comp. —अंतः *m.* The extremity of the ocean. —उद्भवः *m.* The moon. —जं *n.* Nectar. —जा *f.* Goddess लक्ष्मी. —मंदिरः *m.* N. of Varuna regent of the waters. -2 N. of Vishnu.

अर्णस् *n.* 1 Water; a wave, flood, stream. -Comp. —दः *m.* A cloud. —भवः *m.* A conch-shell.

अर्णस्वत् *m.* The ocean.

अर्तनं *n.* Censure, reproach, abuse.

अर्तिः *f.* 1 Pain, sorrow, grief. -2 The end of a bow.

अर्तिका *f.* An elder sister (in dramas).

अर्थ् 10 A. 1 To request, beg, supplicate, ask, entreat, solicit, (with two acc.). -2 To strive to obtain, desire, wish. With अभि- To beg, to request, to supplicate. अभिप्र— To request, to desire. प्र— 1 To desire, to wish for, to request, to beg. -2 To go in search of. -3 To fall upon, to attack. प्रति— To encounter, to meet with a hostile purpose. सम्— 1 To consider, to regard. 2 To corroborate, to prove. संप्र— To beg, to request, to supplicate.

अर्थः *m.* 1 Object, purpose, end and aim; wish, desire. [Oft. used in this sense as the last member of compounds and translated by, 'by' 'for', 'meant for,' 'for the sake of', 'on account of', 'on behalf of,' and used like an adj. to qualify nouns, *e. g.* संतानार्थाय विधये *रघुवं. 1. 34; तां देवतापित्रतिथिक्रियार्थां (धेनुं) *रघुवं. 2. 16; द्विजार्था यवागूः; मशकार्थो धूमः &c. It mostly occurs in this sense as अर्थे, अर्थं or अर्थाय, and has an adverbial force; किमर्थं for what purpose, why; यदर्थं for whom or which.] -2 Cause, motive, reason, ground, means. -3 Meaning, sense, signification, import. अर्थ is of 3 kinds :— वाच्य or expressed, लक्ष्य or indicated (secondary), and व्यंग्य or suggested. -4 A thing, object, substance. अर्थो हि कन्या परकीय एव *शाकुंत. 4. 21. -5 That which can be perceived by the senses; an object of sense; these objects are रूप, रस, गंध, स्पर्श and शब्द. -6 An affair, business, matter, work, concern, job. -7 Subject-matter, contents (as of letters &c.). -8 Wealth, riches, property, money. -9 Attainment of riches or worldly prosperity. -10 Use, advantage, profit, good. -11 Use, want, need, concern, (with instr.); कोऽर्थः पुत्रेण जातेन *पंचतं. 1. -12 A request, suit. petition. -13 Action, plaint (in law). -14 The actual state, fact of the matter. -15 Manner, kind, sort. -16 Fruit, result (फलं). -16 N. of Vishnu. -Comp. —अधिकारः *m.* The charge of money, office of treasurer. -अधिकारिन् *m.* A treasurer, one charged with financial duties; finance minister. —अन्वेषणं *n.* An inquiry after a matter. —अंतरं *n.* 1. Another or different meaning. -2. Another cause or motive. -3. A new matter or circumstance, new affair. -4. An opposite or antithetical meaning, difference of meaning. अर्थांतरन्यासः *m.* (Rhet). The figure of speech in which a general proposition is brought in to support a particular instance, or a particular instance to support a general proposition. उक्तिरर्थांतरन्यासः स्यात् सामान्यविशेषयोः । हनुमानब्धिमतरद् दुष्करं किं महात्मनां ॥ गुणवद्वस्तुसंसर्गाद्याति नीचोऽपि गौरवं । पुष्पमालानुषंगेण सूत्रं शिरसि धार्यते * कुवलयानंद. —अन्वित *a.* 1 Rich, wealthy. -2 Significant. —अर्थिन् *a.* One who longs for or strives to get wealth or gain any object. —अलंकारः *m.* A figure of speech determined by and dependent on the sense, and not on sound (opp. शब्दालंकार). —आगमः 1. Acquisition of wealth, income. -2. Conveying of a sense. —आपत्तिः *f.* (Mimâmsa) A conclusion, inference, presumption, or admission, that follows or results from a fact that is known to be true, or that has been accepted. When it is said पीनो देवदत्तो दिवा न भुंक्ते, the fact that देवदत्त is fat, and that he does not eat by day is admitted, and the inference that देवदत्त must be eating by night, is drawn. This inference is called अर्थापत्ति by मीमांसकs. The term अर्थापत्ति is used both of the करण of the inference and the फलं of the inference, *i. e,* both of the means and the results. उपपाद्यज्ञानेन उपपादककल्पनं अर्थापत्तिः. –ऊष्मन् *m.* The warmth of wealth. –ओघः, –राशिः *m.* A treasure, hoard of money. —कर (*f.* –री), –कृत् *a.* 1 Yielding wealth, enriching. –2 Useful, advantageous. —काम *a.* Desirous of wealth. —कामौ *m. dual.* Wealth and (sensual) desire or pleasure. —कृच्छ्रं *n.* A difficult matter. –2 A pecuniary difficulty. —कृत्यं *n.* The doing or execution of a business. —गौरवं *n.* The depth of meaning. —घ *a.* (*f.* –घ्नी) Extravagant, wasteful, prodigal. –चिंता *f.*, –चिंतनं *n.* The charge or administration of (royal) affairs. –जात *a.* 1 Full of meaning. –2 Wealthy (जातधन). —जातं *n.* 1 A collection of things. –2 A large amount of wealth, considerable property. –ज्ञ *a.* Knowing the sense or purpose. —तत्वं *n.* 1 The real truth, the fact of the matter. –2 The real nature or cause of any thing. —द *a.* 1 Yielding wealth. –2 Advantageous, productive of good, useful. –3. Liberal, munificent. –4 Favourable, compliant. –दः *m.* N. of Kubera. —दूषणं *n.* 1 Extravagance, waste. –2 Unjust seizure of property or withholding what is due. –3 Finding fault with the meaning. –4 The spoiling of another's property. —दोषः *m.* A literary fault or blemish with regard to the sense, one of the four *doshas* or blemishes of literary composition. –निबंधन *a.* Dependent on wealth. —निश्चयः *m.* Determination, decision. —पतिः *m.* Lord of riches; a king. –2 An epithet of Kubera. —पर, –लुब्ध *a.* 1 Intent on gaining wealth, greedy of wealth, covetous. –2 Niggardly, parsimonious. —प्रकृतिः *f* The leading source or occasion of the grand object in drama; (they are five: बीज, बिंदु, पताका, प्रकरी, and कार्य). –प्रयोगः *m.* 1 Usury. –2 Administration of the affairs (of a state). —प्राप्त *a.* Derived or understood from the sense. —बंधः *m.* 1 The arrangement of words, composition, text; stanza, verse. –2 Connection (of the soul) with the objects of sense. —बुद्धि *a.* Selfish. —बोधः *m.* Indication of the (real) import. —भेदः *m.* Distinction or difference of meaning. –मात्रं *n.*, –त्रा *f.* 1 Property, wealth. –2 The whole sense or object. –युक्त *a* Significant, full of meaning. –लाभः *m.* Acquisition of wealth. —लोभः *m.* Avarice. —वादः *m.* 1 Declaration of any purpose. –2 Affirmation, declaratory assertion, an explanatory remark. –3. One of the six means of finding out the *tátparya*. –4. Praise, eulogy. —विज्ञानं *n.* Comprehending the sense, one of the six exercises of the understanding (धीगुण). –विद् *a.* Sensible, wise, sagacious. —विमर्शः *m.* Difficulty in the comprehension of the sense, —विकरणं *n.* The change of meaning. –विकल्पः *m.* 1. Deviation from truth, perversion of fact. –2. Prevarication. (also. —वैकल्पं.) —व्ययः *m.* Expenditure. —शास्त्रं *n.* 1. The science of wealth

(political economy). -2. The science of polity, political sciences, politics. —व्यवहारिन् m. One dealing with politics, a politician. -3. Science giving precepts on general conduct, the science of practical life. —शौचं n. Purity or honesty in money-matters. —संस्थानं n. 1 Accumulation of wealth. -2. treasure. —संग्रहः, -सचयः m. Accumulation or acquisition of wealth, treasure, property. -संबंधः m. Connection of the sense with the word or sentence. —साधक a. 1. Accomplishing any object. -2, Bringing any matter to a conclusion. —सिद्ध a. Understood from the very context (though not expressed in words). —सिद्धिः f. Fulfilment of a desired object, success. —हर a. Inheriting wealth. —हीन a. 1. Deprived of wealth, poor. -2. Unmeaning, nonsensical. -3. Failing.

अर्थतः ind. 1 With reference to the meaning or a particular object. -2 In fact, really, truly. -3 For the sake of money, gain or profit. -4 On account of, by reason of.

अर्थना f. Request, entreaty, suit, petition.

अर्थवत् a. 1 Wealthy, rich. -2 Significant, full of sense or meaning. -3 Serving some purpose; successful, useful. —adv. According to a purpose.

अर्थात् ind. (abl. of अर्थ) 1 As a matter of course, of course, in fact. -2 As a matter of fact. -3 That is to say, namely.

अर्थिकः m 1 A crier, watchman. -2 Especially, a minstrel whose duty it is to annouce (by song &c.) the different hours of the day, such as the hours of rising, sleeping, eating &c.

अर्थित p. p. (f. -ता) Requested, asked, desired. —तं n. Wish, desire; suplication, petition.

अर्थिता f. 1 Condition of a supplicant. -2 A request. -3 Wish, desire.

अर्थित्वं n. See अर्थिता.

अर्थिन् a. (f. -नी) One who seeks for any thing. (with instr. or in comp.) -2 Entreating or begging any one (with gen.). -3 Possessed of desires. —m. 1 One who asks, begs or solicits; a beggar, suppliant, suitor. -2 (In law) A plaintiff, complainant, prosecutor. -3 A servant, follower. -4 A master, or lord. -Comp. —भावः m. State of a suppliant; begging, request. —सात् adv. At the disposal of beggars.

अर्थीय a. (f. -या) (In comp.) 1 Destined or intended for, doomed to suffer. -2 Belonging or relating to.

अर्थ्य a. (f. —र्थ्या) 1 Fit to be asked or sought for. -2 Fit, proper, suitable. -3 Appropriate, significant. -4 Rich, wealthy. -5 wise, intelligent. —र्थ्यं n. Red chalk.

अर्द् 1 P. 1 To ask or beg. -2 To go. -3. To be hurt, to be troubled. -4 To afflict, torment; strike; hurt, kill. -5 To move, to be agitated or moved; be scattered (as dust). -WITH अति- To torment excessively, fall upon or attack. अभि— To distress, afflict, pain, oppress. प्र—

To over-work. प्रति— To oppress or press hard in return, return an attack.

अर्दनं *n.* Pain, trouble, anxiety, excitement, agitation, restlessness. —नं *n.*, —ना *f.* 1 Going, moving. -2 Asking, begging. -3 Killing, hurting, giving pain.

अर्दित *p. p.* (*f.* —ता) Tormented, afflicted; begged. —तं *n.* A disease of the jaw-bones.

अर्ध *a.* (*f.* —र्धा) Half, forming a half. —र्धः *m.*, —र्धं *n.* 1 A half, half portion. -2 A part. With numeral adjectives अर्ध may mean either 'a half of' or 'with an additional half, *e. g.* -शतं Half of 100 *i. e.* 50 or अर्धेन सहितं शतं *i. e.* 150. -Comp. —अंशः *m.* A half, the half. —अंशिन् *a.* Sharing a half. -अर्धः *m.*, -र्धं *n* 1. Half of a half, quarter. -2. Half and half. —अवशेष *a.* Having only a half left. —आसनं 1. Half a seat; अर्धासनं गोत्रभिदोऽधितष्ठौ • रघुवं. 6. 73. (It is considered a mark of very great respect to make room for a guest &c. on the same seat with oneself). -2. Greeting kindly or with great respect. -3. Exemption from censure. -इंदुः *m.* 1. The half or crescent moon. -2. Semicircular impression of a finger nail, crescent-shaped nail-print. -3. An arrow with a crescent-shaped head. -अर्धेंदुमौलिः *m.* N. of Siva. -उक्त *a.* Half said or uttered. —उक्तिः *f.* A broken speech; an interrupted speech. —उदयः *m.* 1 The rising of the half moon. -2. Partial rise. —उदित *a.* 1 Half risen. -2. Half uttered. —ऊरुक *n.* A short petticoat (Mar. परकर). —कृत *a.* Half done, incomplete. —केतुः *m.* N. of Rudra. —खारं *n.*, -री *f.* A kind of measure, half a Khâri. —गंगा *f.* N. of the river Kâveri. —गुच्छः *m.* A necklace of 24 strings. —गोलः *m.* hemisphere. —चंद्रः *m.* 1. The half moon, crescent moon. -2. The semicircular marks on a peacock's tail. -3. An arrow with a crescent-shaped head. -4. A crescent-shaped nail-print. -5. The hand bent into a semicircle, as for the purpose of seizing or clutching anything. दत्तः कदशनभोज्याबद्धयाबलबाधार्धचंद्रेण • पंचतं 4. —चंद्राकार, -चंद्राकृति *a* Half-moon-shaped. —चोलकः *m.* A short bodice. -जरतीयन्यायः *m.* A kind of न्याय. When a thing has some good and some bad points, we must accept the thing such as it is i. e, wholy and in its entirety; it is foolish to insist upon having the thing partially i. e. with its good points only. -तूरः *m.* A kind of musical instrument. —दिनं *n.*, -दिवसः *m.* 1. Half a day, mid-day. -2. A day of 12 hours. —नाराचः *m.* A crescent-shaped iron-pointed arrow. —नारायणः *m.* A form of Vishnu. —नारीशः, —नारीश्वरः *m.* A form of Siva, (half male and half female). —निशा *f.* Mid-night. —पंचाशत् *f.* Twenty-five. —पणः *m.* A measure containing half a 'pana.' —पथं *n.* Half way. —पथे *ind.* Mid-way. —प्रहरः *m.* Half a watch, one hour and a half. —भागः *m.* A half, half a share or part. —भागिक *a.* Sharing a half. —भाज् *a.* 1. Sharing a half, entitled to a half. -2. A companion, sharer. —भास्करः *m.* Mid-day. —मोदिका *f.* A kind of cake. —माणवकः, —माणवः *m.* A necklace of 12 strings (माणवक consisting of 24).

—मात्रा *f.* 1 Half a (short) syllable. -2 A term for a consonant (व्यंजनं चार्धमात्रकं). —मार्गे *ind.* Mid-way. —मास: *m.* Half a month, a fortnight. —मासिक *a.* 1. Happening every fortnight. -2. Lasting for a fortnight. —मुष्टिः *f.* A half-clenched hand. -याम: *m.* Half a watch. -रथ: *m.* A warrior who fights on a car with another (who is not so skilled as a रथी). -रात्र: *m.* 1 Mid-night-2. A night containing half a whole day of 24 hours. —विसर्ग:, -विसर्जनीय: *m.* The Visarga sound before क, ख, प and फ. —वीक्षणं *n.* A side-look, glance, leer. —वैनाशिक: *m* N. of the followers of Kanâda (arguing half perishableness). —व्यास: *m.* The radius of a circle. —शतं *n.* Fifty. —शनं *n.* Half a meal. —शब्द *a.* Having a low voice. —शेष *a.* Having only a half left. —श्याम *a.* Half clouded. —श्लोक: *m.* Half a shloka or verse. —सम *a.* Equal to a half. —मं *n.* N. of a class of metres in which the Ist and the 3rd, the 2nd and the 4th lines have the same syllables and Ganas ; such as पुष्पिताग्रा. —सीरिन् *m.* A cultivator, or ploughman who takes half the crop for his labour. —हार: *m.* A necklace of 64 strings. —ह्रस्व: *m.* Half a (short) syllable.

अर्धक *a.* Half. See अर्ध.

अर्धर्च: *m.*,-र्चं *n.* Half a verse, hemistich.

आर्धिक *a.* (*f.* की) 1 Measuring a half. -2 Entitled to half a share. —क: *m.* A half-caste man.

आर्धिन् *a.* (*f.* —नी) Sharing or entitled to a half.

अर्ध्य *a.* (*f.* -र्ध्या) Belonging to the half (of anything).

अर्पणं *n.* 1 Placing or putting in or upon. -2 Inserting, placing or putting in. -3 Giving, offering, resigning. -4 Restoration, delivery, giving back. -5 Piercing, perforating.

अर्पिस: *m.* The heart ; flesh in the heart.

अर्बु (-बु-) द: *m.*,-दं *n.* 1 A swelling, tumour. -2 One hundred millions. -3 N. of a mountain in the west of India (Abu). -4 A serpent-like demon killed by Indra. -5 A serpent. -6 A cloud.

अर्बुदि: *m.* 1 A serpent-like demon conquered by Indra. -2 All-pervading lord.

अर्भ: *m.* A child, pupil.

अर्भक *a.* 1 Small, minute, short. -2 Weak, emaciated, lean. -3 Foolish. -4 Young, childish. -5 Like, similar. —क: *m.* 1 A boy, child. -2 The young of an animal. -3 A fool, idiot.

अर्म: *m.*, —र्मं *n.* A disease of the eye.

अर्मक *a.* Narrow, thin. —कं *n.* Narrowness.

अर्मणं *n.* A measure of one drona.

अर्मन् *n.* A disease of the eye.

अर्य (*f.* -र्या) 1 Excellent, best. -2 Respectable. -3 Attached, devoted. -4 Dear, kind. —र्य: *m.* 1 A master, lord. -2 A man of the third tribe, Vaisya. See अर्या, अर्याणी and अर्यी below. Comp. —वर्य: *m.* A Vaisya of rank.

अर्यमन् *m.* 1 The sun. -2 The head of the Pitris or manes. -3 The constellation उत्तराफल्गुनी. -4 N. of the *arka* plant. -5 One of the Adityas.

अर्या *f.* 1 A mistress. -2 A woman of the वैश्य caste.

अर्याणी *f.* The same as अर्या.

अर्यी *f.* The wife of a वैश्य.

अर्वन् *a.* Mean, unworthy. *-m.* (अर्वा अर्वन्तौ, अर्वन्तः &c.) 1 A horse. -2 One of the ten horses of the moon. -3 Indra. -5 A short span (गोकर्णपरिमाण). -र्ती *f.* 1 A mare. -2 A bawd, procuress. -3 A nymph. -Comp. -वसुः *m.* One of the principal seven rays of the sun.

अर्वाक् *ind.* 1 Before; behind, (in time or place). -2 Hitherward, on this side. -3 Within, near (with loc). -Comp. —कालः *m.* Posterior time. —कालिक *a.* Belonging to proximate time; modern. —कूलं *n.* The near bank of a river.

अर्वाच् *a.* (*f.* अर्वाची) 1 Coming hitherward. -2 Coming to meet any one. -3 Being behind. -4 Following, coming on or after, subsequent.

अर्वाचीन *a.* (*f.* -ना) 1 Turned towards; favouring. -2 Being on this side, below. -3 Born afterwards, posterior. -4 Modern, recent. -5 Reverse, contrary. —नं *ind.* (with abl.) 1 On this side of. -2 Thenceforward -3 Less than. -4 Later than.

अर्शस् *n.* Piles. -Comp. —घ्न *a.* Destroying piles. —घ्नः *m.* 1 N. of the plant सूरण. -2 A mixture of one part of buttermilk with three parts of water. -घ्नी *f.* 1. N. of the plant Curculigo Archioides Lin. (Mar. देवकंदरी). -2 The marking nut-plant भल्लातक (Mar. बिब्बा). -हितः *m.* The marking nut plant.

अर्शस *a.* Afflicted with piles.

अर्शसानः *m.* Fire.

अर्शिन् *a.* Afflicted with piles.

अर्ह् 1 P. (In epic poetry A. also). 1 To deserve, merit, be worthy of (with acc. or inf.). -2 To have a right to, be entitled to, (with acc.) न स्त्री स्वातंत्र्यमर्हति *मनुस्मृति. 9. 3; (also with inf.) -3 To be obliged or required to do a thing, oft. implying duty or obligation. -4 To be fit, or deserve to be done. -5 To be equal to; be worth; न ते गात्राण्युपचारमर्हति *शाकुंतल. 3. 18. -6 To be able, as in न मे वचनमन्यथा भवितुमर्हति * शाकुंतल. विनाशमव्ययस्यास्य न कश्चित्कर्तुमर्हति * भगवद्गीता. 2 17. -7 To worship, honour. -8 (Used with inf. in the second pers. and sometimes in the third) अर्ह represents a mild form of command, advice or request; द्वित्राण्यहान्यर्हसि सोढुमर्हन् * रघुवंश. 5. 25. तं संतः श्रोतुमर्हन्ति * रघुवंश. 1. 10. —*Caus.* or 10 P. To honour, worship.

अर्ह *a.* (*f.* —र्हा) 1 Respectable, worthy of respect, deserving. -2 Worthy of, having a claim to, entitled to, with acc., inf., or in Comp. -3 Being required, obliged, or allowed. -4 Becoming, proper. —र्हः *m.* 1 N. of Indra. -2 N. of Vishnu. -3 Price (as in महार्ह). -4 Fitness, propriety. -5 Motion, course (गति).

अर्हणं *n.* Worship, adoration, honour, treating with respect or veneration.

अर्हणा *f.* See अर्हणं.

अर्हत् *a.* 1 Worthy, deserving respect, respectable. -3 —*m.* 1 A Buddha; the highest rank in Buddhist hierarchy. -2 A superior divinity with the Jainas.

अर्हत a. (f. अर्हती) Worthy, deserving. —तः m. 1 A Buddha. -2 A Buddhist mendicant. -3 N. of Siva.

अर्हा f. Worship, adoration.

अर्ह्य a. (f. —र्ह्या) 1 Worthy, respectable. -2 Fit to be praised. -3 Right, fit, proper. -4 Fit to be obtained.

अल् I U. 1 To adorn. -2 To be competent or able. -3 To prevent, ward off.

अलं n. 1 The sting in the tail of a scorpion. -2 Yellow pigment.

अलकः m., —कं n. 1 A curl ; lock of hair, hair in general. -2 Curls on the fore-head. -3 Saffron besmeared on the body.

अलका f. 1 A girl from eight to ten years of age. -2 N. of the capital of Kubera. -Comp. —अधिपः, —पतिः, —ईश्वरः m. 'The lord of Alaká', N. of Kubera. —अंतः m. The end of a curl or ringlet. —नंदा f. 1. N. of the Ganges, or a river falling into it. -2 A girl from eight to ten years of age. —प्रभा f. N. of the capital of Kubera. —प्रियः m. N. of a tree (पीतसाल Mar. आसणा).

अलक्तः, —क्तकः m. The red resin of certain trees, red lac or sap (formerly used by women to dye the soles of the feet and lips). -Comp. —रसः m. Red lac or अलक्त juice. —रागः m. The colour of *alakta*.

अलक्षण a. (f. —णा) Having no signs or marks. -2 Having no characteristic or distinguishing marks, undefined, undistinguished. -3 Having no good marks ; inauspicious, unfortunate, ill-omened. —णं n. 1 A bad or inauspicious sign. -2 That which is no definition ; a faulty definition.

अलक्ष्य a. (f. —क्ष्या) 1 Invisible, unknown, unobserved. -2 Unmarked. -3 Having no particular marks. -4 Insignificant in appearance. -5 Having no pretence, free from fraud. -6 Not लक्ष्य or secondary (as meaning). -Comp —गति a. Moving invisibly. —जन्मता f. Unknown birth, obscure origin. —लिंग a Disguised ; *incognito*.

अलगर्दः, or अलगर्धः m. A water-serpent, the black variety of the Cobra de Capello.

अलघु a. (f. घुः,-घ्वी) 1 Not light, heavy, weighty. -2 Not short ; long (in prosody). -3 Serious, solemn. -4 Intense, violent. -Comp. —उपलः m. A rock.

अलंकरणं n. 1 Decoration, ornamenting. -2 An ornament (lit. and fig.) ; सृजति तावदशेषगुणाकरं पुरुषरत्नमलंकरणं भुवः ॥ भर्तृ. -3 Preparation. a. Decorating, adorning.

अलंकरिष्णु a. 1 Fond of ornaments, or decorations. -2 Skilled in decorating. —ष्णुः m. An epithet of Siva.

अलंकर्तृ a. (f. —र्त्री) A decorator, skilled in decoration.

अलंकर्मीण a. (f. —णा) Clever, skilful.

अलंकारः m. 1 Decoration, act of decorating or ornamenting. -2 An ornament (fig. also). अलंकारः स्वर्गस्य ॥ विक्रमो. 1. अनुत्सेकः खलु विक्रमालंकारः ॥ विक्रमो. -3 A figure of speech of which there are three kinds, शब्दालंकार, अर्थालंकार, and शब्दार्थालंकार -4 The whole science of Rhetoric. -Comp. —शास्त्रं n. The science and art of rhetoric, poetics. —सुवर्णं *n.* Gold for ornaments. —हीन *a.* Unadorned.

अलंकारकः *m.* Ornament, decoration.

अलंकृ (अलं + कृ 8 U.) 1 To ornament, adorn, decorate, grace.

अलंकृतिः *f.* 1 Decoration. -2 An ornament. -3 A rhetorical ornament, a figure of speech. (See अलंकारः).

अलंक्रिया *f.* Adorning, ornamenting, decoration (fig. also).

अलंघनीय *a.* (*f* —या) Insurmountable, impassable, inaccessible.

अलंघनीयता *f.* 1 Impassableness, insurmountableness, inaccessibility. -2 Inviolability ; respectability. -3 Authoritative or absolute rule.

अलंघ्य *a.* (*f.* —घ्या) 1 Not to be transgressed or overcome. -2 Beyond reach. -3 Difficult to secure ; unattainable.

अलजः *m.* A kind of bird.

अलज्ज *a.* (*f.* —ज्जा) Shameless. —ज्जा *f.* 1 Boldness. -2 Impudence.

अलंजरः, —जुरः *m.* An earthen jar.

अलब्ध *a.* (*f.* —ब्धा) Unobtained.

अलभ्य *a.* (*f.* —भ्या) Unobtainable, unattainable.

अलम् *ind.* A particle signifying (a) enough, no more of, as in अलं महीपाल तव श्रमेण * रघुवं. 2. 34. (in this sense used with *instr.* or a gerund.). (b) no need of, no use of. (c) in a high degree, excessively. (d) sufficient for, equal to (with *dat.*) तस्यालमेषा क्षुधितस्य तृप्त्यै * रघुवं. 2. 39. दैत्येभ्योऽलं हरिः. (e) able, competent (with loc., or infinitive) as in प्रधानामपि लोकानामलमास्मि निवारणे * रामाय. As prefixed to कृ, अलं is an उपपद and means to decorate. -Comp. —कर्मीण *a.* Competent to do any act ; skilful, clever. —कृ, —कार &c. See *ad. loc.* —जीविक *a.* Sufficient for livelihood. —धन *a.* Possessing sufficient wealth, rich. —धूम *a.* Thick smoke, volume of smoke. —पुरुषीण *a.* 1 Fit for a man, becoming a man. —बल *a.* 1. Strong enough, having sufficient power. -2 An epithet of Siva. —बुद्धिः *f.* 1 Sufficient sense. -2 A false notion. —भूष्णु *a.* Able, competent.

अलंपट *a.* (*f.* —टा) Not libidinous, chaste. —टः *m.* Women's apartments.

अलंबुषः *m.* 1 Vomiting. -2 The palm of the hand with the fingers extended. -3 Prahasta, the minister of Râvana. -4 A deman killed by Ghatotkacha. -षा *f.* 1 N. of a nymph or of a class of nymphs. -2 A N. of several plants.

अलय *a.* (*f.* —या) 1 Houseless, vagrant, homeless. -2 Without destruction or loss ; imperishable. —यः *m.* 1 Nondestruction, permanance. -2 Production.

अलर्कः *m.* 1 A mad dog or one rendered furious. -2 A fabulous animal like a hog with eight legs. -3 A kind of worm. -4 N. of a plant (श्वेतार्क, Mar. पांढरी रुई).

अलले *ind.* A word of no import, occurring in the dialect of the Pishâchas (mostly used in dramas).

अलवालं *n.* A basin for water at the foot of a tree ; same as आलवाल.

अलस *a.* (*f.* —सा) 1 Idle, inactive, without energy ; lazy, indolent. -2 Tired, fatigued, languid. -4 Slow, dull (as in gait or motion). अलसं *n.* Sluggishness मदनजनितकासैः सालसैर्दृष्टिपातैः * ऋतुसं. —सः *m.* 1 A sore or ulcer between the toes (Mar. चिखली). -Comp. —ईक्षणा *f.* A woman with languishing looks.

अलसक *a.* (*f.* —का) Same as अलस.

अलातं *n.* A fire-brand, half-burnt wood.

अलाबुः,-बूः *f.* The bottle-gourd. —बु (*n.*) 1 A vessel made of gourd. -2 A fruit of the gourd which when fully dried is very light and floats in water. -Comp. —पात्रं *n.* A jar made of the bottle-gourd.

अलांबुः *f.* See अलाबुः *f.*

अलारं *n.* A door.

अलासं *n.* Inflammation and abscess at the root of the tongue.

अलिः *m.* 1 A large black bee. -2 A scorpion. -3 A crow. -4 The (Indian) cuckoo. -5 The sign of the zodiac called वृश्चिक. -6 Spirituous liquor. -Comp. —कुलं *n.* A flight or number of bees. —जिह्वा, —जिह्विका *f.* The uvula, soft palate. —प्रियः *m.* The red lotus. —प्रिया *f.* The trumpet flower. —माला *f.* A flight of bees.

अलिकं *n.* The forehead.

अलिगर्दः *m.* The same अलगर्द.

अलिंग *a.* 1 Having no characteristic marks; having no marks. -2 Having bad marks. -3 (In gram.) Having no gender. —गः *m.* An epithet of the Supreme Being. —गं *n.* Absence of marks.

अलिंगिन् *m.* An impostor, a pretended ascetic.

अलिंजरः *m.* A water-jar.

अलिन् *m.* 1 A scorpion. -2 A bee. —नी *f.* 1 A swarm of bees.

अलिंदः *m.* 1 A terrace before a house-door. -2 A place (like a square) at the door. —दाः *m. pl.* N. of a country and its inhabitants.

अलिपकः *m.* 1 The Indian cuckoo. -2 A bee. -3 A dog.

अलिमकः *m.* 1 The Indian cuckoo. -2 A bee. -3 A frog.

अलिंपकः *m.* The same as अलिमकः.

अलीक *a.* (*f.* -का) 1 Unpleasing, disagreeable. -2 Vain, untrue, not based upon reason; false, pretended. तद्भ्रूभङ्गमत्याः स्त्रीस्वभावसुलभामलीकाशंकामपनयामि * वेणी सं. 2. -3 Little, not much, few. —कं *n.* The forehead. -2 Anything displeasing, falsehood, untruth. -3 Heaven. -4 A fault. -5 Pain, sorrow.

अलीकिन् *a.* (*f.* -नी) 1 Disagreeable. -2 False.

अलीगर्दः *m.* A snake. See अलिगर्द.

अलुः *f.* A small water pot.

अलुक् समासः *m.* A compound in which the case terminations are not dropped, but retained; *e. g.* सरसिजं, परस्मैपदं, जनुषान्धः &c.

अलूक्ष *a.* Soft.

अले *ind.* Unmeaning words. in the dialect of the Pishâchas (mostly occurring in dramatic literature).

अलेपक *a.* (*f.* -पिका) Stainless. —कः *m.* An epithet of the Supreme Spirit.

अलेले *ind.* See अले.

अलेश *a.* Not little much, large. —शं *ind.* Not at all.

अलोक *a.* (*f.* -का) 1 That which cannot be seen, as in लोकालोक इवाचलः * रघुवं. 1. 68 -3 Having no people. -4 One who does not go to any other world after death (not having performed meritorious deeds). —कः *m.*, —कं *n.* 1 The nether world (पाताल). -5 —कः *m.* A *Ritvij* or any such priest.

-Comp. —सामान्य a. (f. —न्या) Extraordinary, uncommon, supernatural.

अलोकनं n. Invisibility, disappearance.

अलोक्य a. (f. -क्या) 1 Unusual. -2 Coming in the way of the acquision of heaven. -3 Dark. -4 Unholy.

अलोल a. (f. -ला) 1 Firm, steady. -2 Tranquil, unagitated. -3 Not thirsty, free from desire.

अलोलु a. Indifferent to sensual objects.

अलोलुप a. (f. -पा) 1 Free from desire. -2 Indifferent to sensual objects.

अलोहित a. Bloodless, not red. —तं n. A red lotus.

अलौकिक a. (f. -की A) 1 Uncommon, supernatural. -2 Unusual, rare. -3 Peculiar to the sacred writings; not used in classics; Vedic; (as a word or phrase). -4 Theoretical.

अल्प a. (f. -ल्पा). 1 Small, little, minute, scanty. -3 Trifling, insignificant. -3 Seldom, rare. -4 Of short existance. -5 Young. —ल्पं n. Very little. —ल्पं, —ल्पेन, —ल्पात् adv. 1 A little. -2 For a slight reason; प्रीतिरल्पेन भिद्यते -3 Easily, without much trouble or difficulty. -Comp. —अल्प a. Very little or minute. —आकांक्षिन् a. Desiring little, contented or satisfied with little. -आयुस् a. Short-lived. —अः m. 1 A young one, cub. -2. A goat. —आरंभः m. A small or gradual beginning. -आहारः, m. A light meal. Abstinence in food. -इतर a. 1. Other than small, large. -2. Other than few, many. —ऊन a. Slightly defective, not quite complete. —उपायः m. A small means. —गंध a. Having little scent or odour. —गंधं n. A red lotus. —चेष्टित a. Inert. —छद, -छाद a. Scantily clad. —ज्ञ a. Knowing little, shallow, superficial. -दृष्टि a. Narrow-minded, short-sighted. —धन a. Not affluent or rich; poor. —धी a. Weak-minded, foolish.—प्रजस् a. Having few descendants or subjects. —प्रमाण, -प्रमाणक a. 1 Of little weight or measure. -2. Of little authority, resting on little evidence. —फलः, —फलकः m. Common cucumber, (Mar. काकडी). —प्रयोग a. Of rare application or use, rarely used. —प्राणः m. (in gram.) A name given to the unaspirated letters of the alphabet. These are the vowels, semivowels, nasals and the letters क् च् ट् त् प् ग् ज् ड् द् ब्. -प्राण a. Asthmatic. —बल a. Weak, feeble, having little strength. —बुद्धि, —मति a. Weak-minded, unwise, silly, ignorant. —भाषिन् a. Speaking little, taciturn. —मध्यम a. Slender-waisted. -मात्रं n., 1. A little. -2. A short time, a few moments. —मूल्य a. Cheap. —मेधस् a. Ignorant, silly. —वयस् a. Young in age, youthful. —वादिन् a. Speaking little, taciturn. —विद्य a. Ignorant, ill-taught, uneducated. —विषय a. 1. Of limited range or capacity; क्व चाल्पविषया मतिः • रघुवं. 1. 2. -2 Engaged in trifling matters. —सरस् n. A small pond which is dry in the hot season.

अल्पक a. (f. -ल्पिका) 1 Small, little, minute. -2 Contemptible, mean. —कं n. Little.

अल्पशः ind. 1 In a low degree, slightly, a little. -2 Separately. -3 Seldom, now and then.

अल्पित *a.* (*f.* —ता) 1 Diminished. -2 Lowered in position or estimation, disparaged.

अल्पिष्ठ *a.* (*f.* -ष्ठा) Least, smallest, very small.

अल्पीकृ (अल्प + कृ 8 U.) To make small, diminish, reduce in number.

अल्पीयस् *a.* (*f.* -सी) Smaller, less; very small.

अल्ला *f.* A mother (Voc. अल्ल).

अव् 1. P. 1 To protect, defend. -2 To please, give pleasure to; do good to. -3 To like, desire, love. -4 To favour, promote, animate. —With अनु- To encourage inspire. उद्— 1. To regard, attend to. -2. To wait for. -3 To promote, impel. उप— 1 To cherish, behave friendly towards. -2. To encourage. सं— 1. To satisfy, satiate. -2. To protect, maintain.

अव *ind.* (the initial अ is sometimes dropped, as in पूर्वापरौ तोयनिधी वगाह्य * कुमा. सं. 1. 1) As a preposition अव means 'Away,' 'off,' 'away from,' 'down.' As a prefix to verbal themes अव expresses. (1) Disrespect (*e. g.* अवज्ञा); (2) Support, rest upon (*e. g.* अवलंब). (3) Purifying (*e. g.* अवदात). (4) Littleness (*e. g.* अवहस). (5) Diffusion, pervasion (*e. g,* अवकीर्ण). (6) Determination(*e. g.* अवसो, अवधृ) (7) Depression ,bending (*e. g.* अवनम्). (8) Commanding (*e. g.* अवकृप्) (9) Down (*e. g.* अवतृ, अवगाह्). As first member of Tat. compounds it means अवकृष्ट; अवकोकिलः= अवकृष्टः कोकिलया.

अवंशः *m.* A bad family, wrong family.

अवकट *a.* (*f.* -टा) 1 Downwards; backwards. -2 Opposite, contrary. —टं *n.* Contrariety, opposition.

अवकरः *m.* Dust, sweepings.

अवकर्तनं *n.* Cutting off, excision.

अवकर्षणं *n.* 1 Taking or putting out. -2 Expulsion.

अवकलित *a.* (*f.* -ता) 1 Seen. -2 Known. -3 Taken, received. -4 Wicked.

अवकाश् (अव + काश् 1. 4. A.) To be visible, to be manifest.

अवकाशः *m* 1 Occasion, opportunity. -2 Place, room, space. -3 Footing, admission, scope, access, entrance. -4 Interval, intermediate space or time. -5 An aperture, opening.

अवकीर्ण *a.* (*f.* -र्णा) 1 Scattered. -2 Occupied.-3 Pulverised.-4 Broken. -5 Destroyed.

अवकीर्णिन् *a.* A religious student who contrary to his vow has committed an act of incontinency.

अवकुंचनं *n.* 1 Bending, curving. contraction. -2 A kind of disease.

अवकुटार *a.* Very deep, downwards, backwards. —रं *n.* Deformity.

अवकुंठनं *n.* 1 Investing, surrounding. -2 Attracting, engaging.

अवकृष् (अव + कृष् 1. P.) 1 To draw off or away, pull down. -2 To extract, take out.

अवकृष्ट *p. p. a.* (*f.* -ष्टा) 1 Drawn away or pulled down. -2 Removed. -3 Expelled. -4 Inferior, low, outcast. —ष्टः *m.* A servant who performs the lowest menial duties.

अवकॄ (अव + कॄ 6. P.) 1 To bestow, pour upon, to shower upon, cover with. -2 To put out, throw out. -3 To shake off, throw away.

अवक्लृप् (अव + क्लृप् 1 A.) 1 To correspond with, to answer. -2 To be right or fit, to be possible. -3 To help to, to serve, to accomplish, result in (with dat). —*Caus.* 1 To prepare; to make ready. -2 To use or employ becomingly. -3 To consider as possible.

अवक्लृप्तिः *f.* 1 Considering as possible, possibility, probability. -2 Suitableness.

अवकेश *a.* Having the hair hanging down.

अवकेशिन् *a.* (*f.* -नी) 1 Unfruitful, barren (as a tree). -2 Having small or very few hair. —*m.* A fruitless tree.

अवकोकिल *a.* Drawn or called down to by a cuckoo. -2 Looked down upon by a cuckoo.

अवक्तव्य *a.* (*f.* -व्या) 1 Not fit to be uttered, improper. -2 Censurable (as a saying). -3 False. -4 Indescribable, inexpressible.

अवक्रंद् (अव + क्रंद् 1. U.) To cry out, roar.

अवक्रंद *a.* Crying slowly, roaring, neighing. —दः *m.* A cry.

अवक्रंदन *n.* Crying out, weeping aloud.

अवक्रम् (अव + क्रम् 1 U., 4 P.) 1 To step down, run away, escape, withdraw. -2 To tread down, overcome. -3 To descend, come cown. -*Caus.* To cause to go down.

अवक्रमः *m.* Descending, descent.

अवक्रयः *m.* 1 Price. -2 Wages, hire, farm, rent. -3 Letting out to hire, leasing. -4 A tax or tribute, duty.

अवक्रांतिः *f.* 1 Descending, descent. -2 Approach.

अवक्रिया *f.* Neglect, omission, non-performance (of prescribed acts).

अवक्री (अव + क्री 9 U.) 1 To purchase. -2 To let out, hire. -3 To bribe, buy off.

अवक्रुश् (अव + क्रुश् 1 P.) To call down to; to revile.

अवक्रुष्ट *p. p.* (*f.* -ष्टा) Reviled, censured.

अवक्रोशः *m.* 1 Discordant noise. -2 A curse. -3 Abuse, censure.

अवक्लिन्न *a.* (*f.* -न्ना) Wet, moistened.

अवक्लेदः *m.* Trickling, descent of moisture. -2 Ichor, fetid discharge.

अवक्लेदनं *n* Trickling, falling (as dew or moisture).

अवक्वाथः *m.* An imperfect digestion or decoction.

अवक्षयः *m.* 1 Destruction, decay, waste, loss. -2 A kind of malady.

अवक्षि (अव + क्षि 1, 5, 9, P.) To remove, carry off, destroy. *Pass.* To decay.

अवक्षिप् (अव + क्षिप् 6 U.) 1 To fling away, to throw off. -2 To cause to fly down or away. -3 To reprimand, revile any one, censure, slander. -4 To grant, yield. —*Caus.* To cause to fall down.

अवक्षिप्त *p. p.* (*f.* -प्ता) 1 Thrown down; badly thrown. -2 Sarcastically said, imputed, insinuated. -3 Reviled, censured, blamed.

अवक्षीण *p. p.* (*f.* -णा) Wasted, emaciated.

अवक्षेपः *m.* 1 Blaming, reviling. -2 Objection.

अवक्षेपणं *n.* 1 Throwing down, considered as one of the five kinds of *karman*, in वैशेषिक phil. -2 Contempt, despising. -3 Censure, blame. -4

Overcoming, subduing. —णी *f.* Rein, bridle.

अवखातं *n.* A deep ditch.

अवगण् (अव + गण् 10 P.) To disregard, not to heed, despise.

अवगणनं *n.* 1 Disobedience, disrespect, contempt, disregard, -2 Censure, blame. -3 Insult, mortification -4 -4 Defeat.

अवगंड: *m.* A boil or pimple upon the face or cheeks.

अवगत *p. p.* (*f.* -ता) 1 Gone away or down. -2 Known, learnt, understood (sometimes used actively). -3 Assented, promissed.

अवगति: *f.* 1 Knowledge, perception. -2 True knowledge.

अवगम् (अव + गम् 1 P.) To go down, descend -2 To visit, go near. -3 To reach, obtain. -4 To know, learn, understand, believe. -5 To consider, look upon. -6 To assure oneself, be convinced. —*Caus.* 1 To bring near. -2 To inform oneself of, find out, know. -3 To inform, cause to know, teach. -4 To point out, show

अवगम: *m* 1 Going near, descending. -2 Understanding, perception, knowledge. -3 True knowledge.

अवगमनं *n.* See अवगम:.

अवगाढ *a.* (*f* -ढा) 1 Plunged into, entered into, immersed(*lit.* and *fig.*). -2 Depressed, low, deep (lit. and fig.). -3 That in which one bathes. -4 Congealed, curdling (as blood). (This word is sometimes written वगाढ).

अवगाह् (अव + गाह् 1 A.) 1 To bathe oneself in, plunge into, dive into; with acc. or loc. -2 To go deep into, be absorbed in (fig). -3 To enter, penetrate, fully pervade. पूर्वापरौ तोयनिधी वगाह्य * कुमा सं. 1. 1. —*Caus.* To cause to bathe.

अवगाह *m.* 1 Bathing; सुभगसलिलावगाहा: * शाकुंत. 1. 3; अवगाढप्रस्थितमिव वनमहिषयूथं * कादंब. सदावगाहक्षमवारिसंचय: * ऋतुसं. 1. 1. -2 Plunging, immersing (in general). -3 (fig.) Mastering, learning, studying completely; सकलशास्त्रावगाहगंभीरबुद्धि: * कादंब. -4 A place of bathing. -5 A bucket

अवगाहनं *n.* See अवगाह:.

अवगाह्य *pot. p.* (*f.* —ह्या) 1 Fit for bathing. -2 Fit to be plunged into.

अवगीत *p. p.* (*f* -ता) 1 Sung in a discordant tone, sung badly.-2 Reproached, abused. -3 Wicked, vile. -4 Satirized in a song. —तं *n.* 1 A satire in song. -2 Reproach, blame. -3 Bad or discordant singing.

अवगुण: *m.* A fault, demerit.

अवगुंठ् (अव + गुंठ् 10 P.) 1 To cover with, shroud. -2 To draw over; conceal, veil.

अवगुंठनं *n.* 1 The act of covering the head of women; veiling. -2 A veil (for the face); (fig. also). -3 A covering mantle (in general).

अवगुंठिका *f.* 1 Veiling. -2 A veil. -3 A curtain.

अवगुंठित *a.* (*f.* -ता) 1 Veiled, covered, concealed; रजनीतिमिरावगुंठिते * कुमा. सं. 4. 11.-2 Powdered, pounded

अवगुरणं *n.* Assaulting with intent to kill, (in criminal law).

अवगुह् (अव + गुह् 1 U.) 1 To cover, to hide, -2 To put into or inside. -3 To embrace; या मर्मोद्भिन्नते नित्यं सा माम लावगूहते * पंचतं.

अवगूहनं *n.* 1 Hiding, concealing. -2 Embracing.

अवगृहीत *p. p.* (*f.* —ता) Obstructed, impeded, restrained.

अवगै (अव + गै 1 P.) 1 To sing in a discordant tone. -2 To sing deprecatingly, satirize in a song, revile, reproach.

अवगोरणं *n.* See अवगुरणं.

अवग्रह् (अव + ग्रह् 9. U.) 1 To let loose, let go (as reins). -2 To divide, separate (as words or parts of words). -3 To break off, discontinue ; to distinguish. -4 To punish, chastise. -5 To seize. choke. -6 To capture, overpower. -7 To obstruct. -8 To lay hold of (with the feet).

अवग्रह: *m.* 1 The failure or absence of rain. -2 Drought. -3 An obstacle, a hindrance. -4 A hiatus, absence of संधि (in gram.) as in विकतां च तं च मदनं च इमां च मां च * भट्टि. 5 Nature, temperament. -6 The mark (ऽ) used to mark the elision of अ after ए and ओ. -7 A herd of elephants. -8 The forehead of an elephant. -9 A wrong sort of knowledge, a false idea. -10 Punishment (opp अनुग्रह). -11 An imprecation, a term of abuse. -12 An iron hook with which elephants are driven. -13 Fighting, quarreling तौ स्थास्यतस्ते नृपती निदेशे । परस्परावग्रहानिर्विकारौ * मालवि. 4.

अवग्रहणं *n.* 1 An obstacle, impediment. -2 Disrespect, disregard. -3 -3 Knowledge.

अवग्राह: *m.* 1 Breaking, separation. -2 Impediment. -3 A curse.

अवघट्ट् (अव + घट्ट् 1. A.) 1 To push away or off. -2 To split, to break पंचबाणान् अवघट्टयंती. * दशकु. -3 To touch, feel, rub (in medicine). -4 To stir up, agitate.

अवघट्ट: *m.* 1 A hole in the ground, a cave, a cavern. -2 A stone-mill for grinding corn. -3 Stirring up, shaking.

अवघट्टनं *n.* Rubbing away or off.

अवघर्षणं *n.* 1 Rubbing into. -2 Grinding. -3 Cleaning, rubbing off.

अवघात: *m.* 1 Striking. -2 Killing, hurting. -3 A stroke, a blow. -4 Threshing corn in a mortar. -5 Unnatural or accidental death.

अवघुष् (अव + घुष् 1 P.) 1 To proclaim aloud. -2 To summon, convoke. -3 To fill with cries, make resonant.

अवघूर्ण् (अव + घूर्ण् 1 U.) To whirl round, move to and fro.

अवघूर्ण: *m.* Whirling round; a whirlpool.

अवघूर्णनं *n.* Rolling or whirling round.

अवघृष् (अव + घृष् 1 U.) To rub off, to grind to powder. —*Caus.* To rub off, scratch.

अवघोष: *m.*, —षणं *n.* Proclaiming, denouncing. —णा *f.* A proclamation.

अवघ्रा (अव + घ्रा 1 P.) 1 To smell at. -2 To kiss (as the head). —*Caus.* (—घ्रापयति) To cause to smell at.

अवघ्राणं *n.* The act of smelling at.

अवच *a.* (*f.* —चा) Lower.

अवचक्ष् (अव + चक्ष् 2 A.) 1 To perceive, observe.

अवचक्षणं *n.* Looking down upon.

अवचन *a.* (*f.* —ना) Not speaking, silent, speechless ; शकुंतला साध्वसाद-वचना तिष्ठति * शाकुंत. 1. —नं *n.* Silence, taciturnity. -2 Censure, blame, reproof. -Comp. —कर *a.* Disobedient.

अवचनीय *a.* (*f.* —या) 1 Not fit to be spoken or uttered, (as obscene or indecent language). -2 Not censurable.

अवचय: *m.* Gathering (such as flowers, fruits &c.)

अवचाय: *m.* Gathering flowers &c.

अवचार: *m.* A place of descent, road ; field of action.

अवचारणं *n.* 1 Employing, application, mode of proceeding. -2 A kind of saline preparation.

अवचि (अव + चि 3 P.) 1 To worship, honour, respect. -2 (5 U.) To gather, pick up, pluck (with two acc.) -3 To take off.

अवचित *p. p.* A (*f.* —ता) Gathered.

अवचूड: *m.* The pendent cloth on a chariot, an ornament (like a *chowri*) hanging from the top of a banner. दिवसकरवारणस्यावचूडचामरकलाप: • कादंब.

अवचूर्णनं *n.* 1 Pounding, grinding, reducing to powder. -2 Sprinkling with powder ; especially, throwing absorbent powders on wounds.

अवचूर्णित *a.* (*f.* —ता) Pounded coarsely. -2 Ground, reduced to powder.

अवचूल: *m.* Same as अवचूड:.

अवचूलक: *m.*, —कं *n.* A *chowri* or brush (formed of a cow's tail or peacock's feathers) for fanning off flies.

अवच्छद (च्छाद) द: *m.* A cover, covering.

अवच्छिद् (अव + छिद् 7 U.) 1 To cut off, separate, break asunder. -2 To discriminate, distinguish. -3 To define, limit, modify (as by time, space &c.). -4 To detach, excerpt. -5 To interrupt.

अवच्छिन्न *p. p.* (*f.* —न्ना) 1 Cut off. -2 Separated, excerpted. -3 (In Logic) Separated or excluded from all other things by the properties predicated of a thing as peculiar to itself. -4 Bounded, modified, determined ; दिक्कालाद्यनवच्छिन्न • भतृह. -5 Particularised, distinguished, characterized, as by an attributive word.

अवच्छुरित *a.* Mixed. —तं *n.* A horse-laugh.

अवच्छेद: *m.* 1 A part, portion. -2 Boundary, limit. -3 Separation. -4 Distinction, distinguishing, particularization (as by attributes). -5 Determination, decision, settlement. -6 A characteristic property. -7 Bounding, defining. -8 Pervading.

अवच्छेदक *a.* (*f.* —दिका) 1 Separating. -2 Determining, deciding. -3 Bounding, limiting. -4 Pervading. -5 Distinguishing, particularizing. -6 Peculiar, characteristic. —क: *m.* 1 That which distinguishes. -2 A predicate, characteristic property (in logic). -3 Boundary, limit.

अवच्छेदनं *n.* Cutting off, separating; determining, bounding.

अवजय: *m.* Defeat, victory. पर्येंद्रलोकावजयाय दृप्त: • रघुवं. 6. 62.

अवजि (अव + जि 1 P.) 1 To deprive by conquest, to win. -2 To recover. -3 To ward off, prevent. -4 To conquer.

अवजित *p. p.* (*f.* —ता) Conquered ; contemned, disregarded.

अवजिति: *f.* Conquest, defeat.

अवज्ञा (अव + ज्ञा 9 P.) To despise, to treat with contempt, disregard.

अवजानंति मां मूढा मानुषीं तनुमाश्रितं Bhagavadgītā. 9. 11.

अवज्ञा *f.* Disrespect, contempt; low opinion; disregard (with the obj. in loc. or gen.). आत्मन्यवज्ञां शिथिलीचकार. Raghuvaṃśa. 2. 41; ये नाम केचिदिह नः प्रथयंत्यवज्ञां Māl. Mā. 1. -Comp. —उपहत *a.* (*f* -ता) Treated with contempt, humiliated. —दुःखं *n.* The agonies of humiliation.

अवज्ञात *p. p.* (*f.* -ता) Disrespected, contemned, disregarded.

अवज्ञानं *n* Disrespect, contempt.

अवज्ञेय *pot. p.* (*f.* -या) To be treated with disrespect; contemptible.

अवटः *m.* 1 A hole, cavity. -2 A pit -3 A well. -4 Any low or depressed part of the body. -5 A juggler. -Comp. —कच्छपः *m.* A tortoise in a hole. (fig.) One who has had no experience, who has seen nothing of the world.

अवटिः, -टी *f.* 1 A hole. -2 A well. -3 Any low or depressed part of the body.

अवटीट *a.* (*f.* -टा) Having a flat nose, flat-nosed.

अवटुः *m.* 1 A hole in the ground. -2 A well. -3 The back of the neck. -4 The depressed part of the body. —टुः *f.* The raised portion of the neck. —टु *n.* A hole, a rent.

अवडीनं *n.* A particular fight of birds flying down-wards.

अवतंसः *m.*, -सं *n.* 1 A garland. -2 An ear-ing (fig. also). -3 An ornament worn on the head, crest; (fig.) anything that serves as an ornament.

अवतंसकः *m.* An ear-ornament, an ornament in general.

अवतंसयति Den. P. To use as ear-rings, make ear-rings of.

अवतत *p. p.* (*f.* —ता) 1 Overspread, covered. -2 Loosened, slackened.

अवतति: *f.* Stretching, extending.

अवतन् (अव + तन् 8 U.) 1 To stretch downwards. -2 To overspread, cover. -3 To loosen, undo (especially a bow-string).

अवतप्त *p. p.* (*f.* —प्ता) Heated, irradiated.

अवतमसं *n* 1 Slight darkness. -2 Darkness (in general). -3 Obscurity.

अवतरः *m.* Descent. See अवतरणं.

अवतरणं *n.* 1 Descending for bathing in water &c., coming down. -2 An incarnation; See अवतार. -3 Crossing. -4 Sudden disappearance. -5 Steps or stairs leading down to a river. -6 A holy bathing-place (तीर्थ). -7 Translating from one language into another. -8 Introduction. -9 An extract, a quotation.

अवतरणिका *f.* 1 A short prayer at the beginning of a work which, it is supposed, causes the divinity so addressed to descend from heaven. -2 Introduction, preface.

अवतरणी *f.* 1 Preface. -2 Succession, order, method. See अवतरणिका.

अवतर्पणं *n.* A soothing remedy.

अवताडनं *n* 1 Crushing, trampling under. -2 Striking.

अवतानः *m.* 1 Stretching. -2 The unbending of a bow. -3 A downward face. -4 The spreading of a plant. -5 A cover (in general); an awning (Mar. चांदणी).

अवतारः *m.* 1 Descent, alighting. (fig.) Accepting, resorting to. -2

Advent, coming on. -3 Form, manifestation. -3 Descent of a deity upon earth, incarnation in general. -4 An incarnation of Vishnu. (There are ten incarnations of Vishnu ; viz. मत्स्य, कूर्म, वराह, नृसिंह, वामन, परशुराम, राम, कृष्ण, बुद्ध, and कल्कि). -5 Any new appearance, growth, rise. -6 Any distinguished person (who, in the language of respect, is called an अवतार or incarnation of a deity). -7 Aiming at an object. -8 A landing-place. -9 A sacred bathing-place, -10 Translation. -11 A pond, tank. -12 Introduction, preface. -13 Crossing. —रं लभ् To gain one's object (with gen.). -Comp. —कथा *f.* An account of an अवतार. —मंत्रः *m.* The prayer causing the descent of a deity.

अवतारक *a.* (*f.* —रिका) 1 Making one's appearance. -2 Making a descent.

अवतारणं *n.* 1 Causing to descend. -2 Translation. -3 Possession by an evil spirit. -4 Adoration. -5 The border of a garment. -6 Preface or introduction (to a work).

अवतीर्ण *p. p* (*f.* —र्णा) 1 Descended, alighted, come down, entered into. -2 Bathed in ; come to. -3 Appeared as an incarnation. -4 Crossed, passed over, come within the range of. -5 Approached, come on (as the night). -6 Translated. -Comp. —ऋण *a.* Absolved from debt.

अवतॄ *n.* (अव + तॄ 1 P.) 1 To descend, alight, come down (fig. also). -2 To flow or run into, to join (as a river). -3 To enter into, to come to. -4 To begin, commence. -5 To present oneself, to come forth. -6 To descend (as a deity) into the world in the form of a mortal. -7 To get over (a difficulty, a disease, &c.). —*Caus.* 1 To cause to descend. -2 To put or set down. -3 To take off, put aside. -4 To bend down. -5 To bring downwards. -6 To introduce, make current, begin.

अवतोका *f.* A woman or a cow that has miscarried.

अवत्त *a.* (*f.* —त्ता) Cut off, severed.

अवदंशः *m.* 1 A stimulant. -2 Any pungent food which excites thirst.

अवदरणं *n.* 1 The breaking or opening of a boil. -2 Bursting, separating.

अवदाघः *m.* 1 Heat, burning down. -2 The hot season, summer.

अवदात *a.* (*f.* —ता) 1 Clean, pure, unsinful. -2 White, bright. -3 Beautiful. -4 Meritorious. -5 Yellow. —तः *m.* The white colour.

अवदातं *n.* (From अव + दै 1 P. to purify.) 1 A pure or approved occupation. -2 An accomplished act. -3 A valorous or glorious act, heroism. -4 Object of a legend. See अवदानं below.

अवदानं *n.* (From अव + दो 4 P. to cut). 1 Cutting or dividing into pieces. -2 A portion, part. -3 Transgression. -4 The root of a plant (Mar. वाळा).

अवदान्य *a.* (*f.* —न्या) Niggardly, stingy.

अवदारणं *n.* 1 Tearing, dividing, digging down, cutting into pieces. -2 A spade, hoe.

अवदाहः *m.*, —हं *n.* Burning down, heat.

अवदीर्ण *p. p.* (*f.* —र्णा) 1 Split into two, divided, broken. -2 Melted, fused, liquefied. –3 Bewildered, perplexed.

अवद्रो (अव + द्रो 4 P.) 1 To cut off, divide.

अवदोहः m. 1 Milking. –2 Milk.

अवद्य a. (f. –द्या) 1 Low, inferior. –2 Fit to be condemned, censurable; not fit to be praised. –2 Defective, faulty, blamable, disagreeable, disliked. –3 Unfit to be told. –5 Sinful. –द्यं n. 1 A fault, defect. –2 Sin, vice. –3 Blame, reproach. –4 Shame.

अवद्रंगः, or –कः m. A market.

अवधर्ष्य a. (f. –र्ष्या) To be defied; fit to be defied.

अवधा (अव + धा 3 A.) 1 To place down, deposit. –2 To apply (as the mind). –3 To be attentive. –4 To shut, close, press together.

अवधातव्य pot. p. a. (f. –व्या) To be attended to, deserving attention and care.

अवधानं n. 1 Attention, intentness, attentiveness. –2 Devotion, care, carefulness.

अवधानिन् a. (f. –नी) Attentive.

अवधानीय a. (f. –या) See अवधातव्य.

अवधारः m. 1 Accurate determination. 2 A decision. –3 Emphasis or stress upon a word. –4 Restricting the sense of a word. –5 Limitation to certain instances to the exclusin of others.

अवधारक a. 1 Determining accurately. –2 Restricting oneself to anything.

अवधारण a. 1 Restrictive, limiting. –णं n. 1 Ascertainment, determination. –2 Affirmation, emphasis. –3 Limitation (of the sense of words). –4 Restriction to a certain instance or instances to the exclusion of all others.

अवधारणा f. See अवधारणं.

अवधारणीय pot. p. a. (f. –या) To be ascertained, determined or considered.

अवधारित p. p. (f. –ता) Ascertained, known, well-marked.

अवधार्य a. (f. –र्या) See अवधारणीय.

अवधावनं n. 1 Pursuit. –2 Purifying, cleaning. –3 Seizing, or capturing by force.

अवधावित a. (f. –ता) 1 Pursued, –2 Washed, cleaned, purified.

अवधिः m. 1 Applicaticn, attention. –2 Boundary, limit exclusive or inclusive, (of time or space). –3 Furthest limit –4 A division, district, department. –5 A period of time. –6 An engagement, appointment. यदवधि... तदवधि From...till. –7 A hole, a pit.

अवधिमत् a. Limited, bounded.

अवधीर् (अव + धीर् 10 P.) To disregard, disrespect, treat with contempt, to despise, repulse.

अवधीरणं n. Treating with disrespect.

अवधीरणा f. Disrespect, despising; repulse.

अवधीरित p. p. (f. –ता) Disrespected, disregarded.

अवधू (अव + धू 5 U.) 1 To shake, move, cause to tremble. –2 To shake off or out, to put away, to check. –3 To discard, reject, treat with contempt, disregard. —*Caus.* (–धूनयति) To shake.

अवधूकः m. Having no wife.

अवधूत p. p. (f. –ता) 1 Shaken, waved. –2 Discarded, rejected, despised. -3 Insulted, humiliated. -4 Excelled, surpassed. -5 Attacked, overcome.-6 Separated from worldly attachments. —तः *m.* An ascetic who has renounced all worldly attachments and connections. -Comp. —वेश *a.* Undressed, naked.

अवधूननं *n.* 1 Shaking, waving. -2 The practice of medicine; curing. -3 Agitation, trembling. -4 Disregarding. -5 Trampling on, treading.

अवधूलनं *n.* Sprinkling absorbent powders on sores.

अवधृ (अव + धृ 10 U.) 1 To determine, fix, resolve; ascertain, make out, know, perceive, understand. -2 To regard, think, look upon. -3 To hear, listen to, to learn. -4 To consider, think. -5 To limit, restrict.

अवधृत *p. p.* (*f.* -ता.) 1 Determined, resolved, settled. -2 Heard.

अवधेय *pot p.* (*f.* -या) 1 To be placed down or deposited. -3 To be known or apprehended. -यं *n.* Attention.

अवध्य *a.* (*f.* -ध्या) 1 Not to be killed. -2 Inviolable. -3 Sacred.

अवध्वंस् (अव + ध्वंस् 1 A.) 1 To apply oneself to, set about. -2 To strew over, scatter, spread ; चूर्णैरवध्वंसते. *Caus.* 1 To cast down. -2 To strew over.

अवध्वंसः *m.* 1 Abandoning, quitting. -2 Powder, dust. -3 Disrespect, censure, blame. -4 Falling off or from. -5 Sprinkling.

अवध्वस्त *p. p.* (*f.* -स्ता) 1 Destroyed, perished. -2 Censured, disrespected. -3 Pounded coarsely. -4 Abandoned. -5 Sprinkled. -6 Scattered.

अवनं *n.* 1 Protection, defence. -2 Wish, desire. -3 Delight, gratification, pleasure, satisfaction. -4 Hurry, speed.

अवनक्षत्रं *n.* The disappearance of the stars.

अवनत *p. p.* (*f.* -ता) 1 Bent down, hung down, downcast. -2 Setting (as heavenly bodies.). -3 Humble. -Comp. —अंग *a.* Stooping. —काय *a.* Bending the body, crouching down. —मुख *a.* Having downcast countenance. —शीर्षन् *a.* Bowing the head.

अवनतिः *f.* 1 Bending, bowing down, stooping. -2 Sinking down in the west, setting. -3 Salutation, prostration. -4 Bending (as a bow). -5 Modesty, absence; of insolence, humility.

अवनद्ध *p. p.* (*f.* -द्धा) 1 Forme made. -2 Fixed, seated. -3 Covered, encircled ; bound on, tied. -द्धं *n.* A drum.

अवनम् (अव + नम् 1 P.) 1 To bow down, to bend down, stoop. -2 To bend oneself ; hang down. —*Caus.* (अवन -मा—मयति) To bend down, bend.

अवनम्र *a.* (*f.* -म्रा) Bowed, bent.

अवनयः *m.* 1 Throwing down, precipitating. -2 Causing to descend.

अवनयनं *n.* Leading down, pouring down.

अवनह् (अव + नह् 4 U.) To bind on, to tie on, to put on, to cover with.

अवनाट *a.* Flat-nosed. -टं *n.* The condition of having a flat-nose.

अवनामः *m.* 1 Bending or bowing,

falling at the feet. -2 Causing to bend down.

अवनायः *m.* Throwing down.

अवनायक *a.* Causing to descend.

अवनाहः *m.* Binding, girding, putting on.

अवनिः *f.* 1 The earth. -2 The ground. -3 The place. -4 A river. -5 Course, bed of a river. -Comp. —ईशः, -ईश्वरः, -नाथः, -पतिः, -पालः *m.* The lord of the earth, king. —चर *a.* Roving over the earth, a vagabond. —ध्रः *m.* A mountain. -मंडलं *n.* The globe. —रुहः, -रुट् *m.* A tree.

अवनिक्त *p. p.* (*f.* -क्ता) Washed, cleansed. -2 Searched.

अवनिज् (अव + निज् 3 U.) To wash, purify, cleanse, to wipe off.

अवनिश्चयः *m.* Deduction, ascertainment.

अवनी *f.* See अवनिः.

अवनी (अव + नी 1 P.) 1 To lead or bring down, to push into. -2 To cause to descend or flow. -3 To lead away. -4 To pour down or over.

अवनेजनं *n.* 1 Washing, ablution. -2 Water for washing, foot-bath. -4 Sprinkling water on the *darbha* grass at a Srâddha ceremony.

अवनेज्य *a.* (*f.* -ज्या) 1 Used for washing.

अवंतिः,-ती *f.* 1 N. of a city, the modern उज्जयिनी, one of the seven sacred cities of the Hindus. -2 N. of a river. —*m. pl.* N. of a country and its inhabitants; its capital being उज्जयिनी on the river सिप्रा. -Comp. —पुरं *n.* The city of Avanti उज्जयिनी. —सोमः *m.* Sour gruel (prepared from the fermentation of rice-water (Mar. कांजी).

अवंध्य *a.* (*f.* -ध्या) Not barren; fruitful, productive.

अवपत् (अव+पत् 1 P.) To fall down, fly down, jump down, descend, alight. —*Caus.* To cause to fall down, to throw down, fell down.

अवपतनं *n.* Alighting, descending.

अवपद् (अव + पद् 4 A.) 1 To go down, to descend, fall down. -2 To be deprived of (with abl.). -3 To fall, meet with an accident. -4 To overthrow, ruin.

अवपन्न *p. p.* (*f.* —न्ना) 1 Mixed with. -2 Cooked together with. -3 Fallen on or into. -4 Alighted, descended.

अवपाक *a.* 1 Badly or ill cooked. -2 Without a net. —कः *m.* Bad cooking.

अवपातः *m.* 1 Falling down. -2 Descent, descending. -3 A hole, pit. -4 Particularly, a hole or pit for catching elephants.

अवपातनं *n.* Felling, knocking down.

अवपात्र *a.* A 'mlechchha' whose eating in a vessel makes it useless for others.

अवपात्रित *a.* (*f.* —ता) One who has lost his caste; a person not allowed by his kindred to eat in a common vessel.

अवपादः *m.* Falling down.

अवपाशित *a.* (*f.* —ता) Caught in a snare. Having a snare laid over (on all sides).

अवपीड् (अव + पीड् 10 P.) To compress.

अवपीड *a.* Pressed on all sides. —डः *m.* 1 Pressing down, pressure. -2 A drug producing sneezing, (Mar. नाकशिंकणी). -3 A kind of medical treatment.

अवपीडनं n. 1 The act of pressing down. -2 A drug causing sneezing. —ना Damage, violation.

अवफः m. Flatulence ; wind from the bowels.

अवबधा f. Segment of the base of a triangle.

अवबंध् (अव + बंध्)9 P. 1 To bind, fasten (fig. also), to attract.

अवबंधः m. 1 Falling or palsy of the eyelids. -2 Binding on all sides.

अवबाधा f. 1 Pain, agony. -2 Resistance, restriction, opposition.

अवबाहुकः m. Spasm in the arm.

अवबुद्ध p. p. (f. —द्धा) 1 Known. -2 (Actively used) One who knows.

अवबुध् (अव + बुध् 4 A.) 1 To awake, -2 To recognise, to become sensible or aware of, feel, perceive, know, understand. *-Caus.* 1 To awaken, rouse. -2 To make one aware of, inform, to remind, put in mind of. -3 To teach, instruct.

अवबोधः m. 1 Waking, becoming awake. -2 Knowledge, perception. -3 Discrimination, judgment. -4 Teaching, informing.

अवबोधक a. Indicating, showing. —कः m. 1 The awakener, the sun. -2 A panegyrist, bard. -3 A [teacher.

अवबोधनं n. Knowledge, perception.

अवब्रवः m. Ill-report, defamation.

अवभंगः m. Humbling, overcoming, defeating.

अवभंज् (अव + भंज् 7 P.) To break off, smash.

अवभंजनं m. 1 Breaking off, tearing humbling.

अवभास् (अव + भास् 1 A.) 1 To shine. -2 To shine forth, become manifest, to appear, seem. *-Caus.* To cause to shine, to irradiate, illuminate.

अवभासः m. 1 Splendour, lustre, light. -2 Knowledge, perception. -3 Appearance, manifestation. -4 Space, reach, compass. -5 False knowledge.

अवभासक a. Luminious, irradiating. —कं n. The Supreme Spirit.

अवभासिन् a. Shining, bright. —नी f. The outer skin or cuticle.

अवभुग्न p. p. (f. —ग्ना) Contracted, bent, crooked.

अवभृथः m. 1 The end or completion of a principal sacrifice. -3 Bathing at the end of a principal sacrifice. -3 Purification by bathing of the sacrificer and the sacrificial vessels at the end of a sacrifice. -4 The water of purification. -5 A supplementary sacrifice to atone for defects in a principal and preceding one ; a sacrifice in general. -Comp. —स्नानं n. The ablution after a sacrificial ceremony.

अवभ्रः m. Abduction, carrying off.

अवभ्रट a. Flat-nosed. —टं n. The state of having a flat nose.

अवम a. (f. —मा) 1 Sinful, wicked. -2 Contemptible, mean. -3 Base, low, inferior. -4 Next, intimate. -5 Last, youngest. —मः m. 1 A protector. -2 A class of Manes. —मं n. 1 Sin. -2 A lunar day exactly coinciding with a solar one ; the difference between a Chándra month (29 days, 31 Ghatrkâs and 50 Palas) and a solar month (30 days)

अवमत *p. p* (*f.* —ता) Despised, contemned. -Comp. —अंकुशः *m.* A restive elephant, or one in rut.

अवमतः *m.* A master, an owner. —तिः *f.* 1 Disregard, disrespect. -2 Aversion, dislike.

अवमन् (अव + मन् 4 A.) 1 To despise, contemn, disregard, disrespect.-2 To undervalue, depreciate.

अवमंतव्य, अवमान्य *pot. p.* (*f.* -व्या,-न्या) 1 To be treated with disrespect, to be slighted. -2 Contemptible, mean.

अवमंथ *a.* Producing swellings. —थः *m.* A kind of disease in which swellings are caused by boils or contusions.

अवमर्दः *m.* 1 Trampling upon. -2 Pain, toils. -3 Destruction or devastation of a country. -4 Slaying, killing.

अवमर्दन *a.* Trampling down, grinding, crushing. —नं *n.* 1 Rubbing, shampooing. -2 Oppression, crushing down.

अवमर्शः *m.* Touch, contact.

अवमर्षः *m.* 1 Consideration, investigation. -2 One of the five principal parts or *Sandhis* of a play. -3 Attacking.

अवमर्षणं *n.* 1 Intolerance, impatience. -2 Effacing; banishing from recollection.

अवमानः *m.* Disrespect, contempt, disregard.

अवमाननं *n.*, -ना *f.* Despising, disrespect, contempt.

अवमानिन् *a.* Contemning, despising.

अवमार्जनं *n.* Washing off, removing, wiping away.

अवमुच् (अव + मुच् 6 P.) 1 To let loose, loosen (as a horse). -2 To take off (a garment &c.). -3 To unharness.

अवमूर्धन् *a.* With one's head hanging down. -Comp. —शय *a.* Lying with the head hanging down. -शयः *m.* He who sleeps with his head hanging down, such as man (opp. देव).

अवमृज् (अव + मृज् 2 P.) 1 To rub off, to remove, to efface.

अवमृद् (अव + मृद् 9 P.) 1 To grind or pound down, crush, trample upon. -2 To rub.

अवमृश् (अव + मृश् 6 P.) To touch. -2 To consider.

अवमोचनं *n.* Setting at liberty, loosening, letting go.

अवयजनं *n.* Purification, means of expiating.

अवयवः *m.* 1 A limb of the body. -2 A part, portion (as of a whole). -3 A member or a component part of logical argument or syllogism. (These are five:- प्रतिज्ञा, हेतु, उदाहरण, उपनय and निगमन). -4 The body. -5 A component, constituent, ingredient (in general); as of a compound &c. -6 A means (साधन, उपकरण). -Comp. —अर्थः *m.* The meaning of the component parts of a word.

अवयवशः *ind.* Part by part, severally, piece-meal.

अवयविन् *a.* Having limbs, having portions or subdivisions (as a whole). —*m.* (वी) 1 A whole any substance formed of several constituents. -2 A syllogism, or any logical argument.

अवया (अव + या 2 U.) 1 To go down, to give way. -2 To desist from, turn off or away. -3 To know, understand. 4 To remove.

अवयानं n. Going away, retreat.

अवर a. (f. -रा) 1 Low, inferior. -2 Mean, insignificant, unimportant. -3 Posterior, last. -4 Least. -5 Younger. -6 Western. -Comp. —अर्धः m 1 The minimum. -2 The latter half.—अवर a. Lowest. —ज a. Younger, junior. -जः m. A Younger brother. -2 A शूद्र. —जा f. A younger sister. —वर्ण a. Belonging to a low caste. —वर्णः m. A low tribe. —वतः m. The sun. —शैलः m. The western mountain over which the sun sets.

अवरत p. p. (f. -ता) Stopped, ceased, resting.

अवरतः ind. Afterwards, from beind ; downwards, below, from below.

अवरतिः f. 1 Cessation. -2 Repose, relaxation, rest.

अवरस्तात् ind. From behind ; below, downwards.

अवरिण a. (f. -णा) Degraded, censured, debased, despised.

अवरुद्ध p. p. (f. -द्धा) 1 Obstructed, stopped. -2 Shut up or in, enclosed. -3 Living *incognito*, disguised. -4 Protected and not seen by others. -5 Imprisoned, secluded as in the inner appartments.

अवरुद्धिः f. 1 Obstruction, restraint. -2 Besieging. -3 Gaining.

अवरुध् (अव + रुध् 7 U.) 1 To obstruct, hinder, stop, prevent, detain. -2 To shut up, besiege. -3 To suspend.

अवरुह् (अव + रुह् 1 P.) To descend, go down to come down (in general), to dismount, get down from. —*Caus.* (-रोहयति or -रोपयति) 1 To cause to descend or alight. -2 To lower, lessen. -3 To plant (as trees). -4 To depose, dethrone, dismiss, remove (as from a throne &c).

अवरूढ p. p. (f. -ढा) 1 Descended, alighted ; dismounted. -2 Uprooted.

अवरेण ind. (With acc.) Below.

अवरोचकः m. A kind of disease, loss of appetite.

अवरोहः m. (From अव + रुह्) 1 Moving down, descending. -2 A shoot sent up by the root of a plant, a slip (for planting) ; the pendent shoots of the Indian fig-tree.

अवरोधः m. (From अव + रुध) 1 Obstruction. -2 Restraint. -3 A seige, a blockade, an investment. -4 Inner appartments, or women's apartments, harem, seraglio. -5 The wives of a king taken collectivley(oft. pl.) -6 An enclosure, confinement. -7 A covering, lid. -8 A fence. -9 A watchman. -10 Depression, hollow. See अवरोहः above.

अवरोध (-धि-) क a. 1 Obstructing, hindering, impeding. -2 Besieging. —कः m. A guard. —कं n. A barrier, fence.

अवरोधनं n. 1 A siege, blockade. -2 Hindering, obstructing. -3 An obstacle. -4 A closed or private place.-5 The interior of anything. -6 The women's apartments in a royal palace. -7 An inmate of the harem; a queen; wife.

अवरोधिक *a.* Obstructing, impeding. —कः *m* A guard of the queens apartments. —का *f.* A female of the inner apartments.

अवरोधिन् *a.* 1 Obstructing, hindering. -2 Besieging.

अवरोपणं *n.* 1 Uprooting. -2 Causing to descend. -3 Taking away, depriving, diminishing. -4 Setting (as of the sun).

अवरोपित *p.p.* (*f.* -ता) 1 Uprooted. -2 Curtailed, diminished, lost.

अवरोहः *m.* 1 Descent, going or coming down. -2 A creeper encircling a tree from the bottom to the top. -3 Heaven. -4 Mounting, ascending. -5 A shoot sent out by a plant, a pendent branch, one that strikes fresh roots into the earth, as of the fig-tree (वट). -6 The growth of a plant or vine. -7 (In music) The descending scale of notes. -Comp. —शाखः, —शाखिन., —शाखिन् *m.* The Indian fig-tree.

अवरोहणं *n.* 1 Alighting, descending. -2 Ascending.

अवरोहिन् *a.* Descending. -*m.* (*nom. sing.* ही) N. of the Indian fig-tree (वट).

अवर्ग *a.* Having no class. —र्गः *m.* The vowels.

अवर्ण *a.* 1. Colourless. -2 Bad, low, destitute of good qualities. —र्णः *m.*, 1 Scandal, ill-repute.

अवर्षः *m.*, **अवर्षणं** *n.* Want of rain, drought.

अवलक्ष *a.* (Also written बलक्ष) White. —क्षः *m.* The white colour.

अवलग्न *a.* 1 Clinging or adhering to; touching; being in contact with. -2 Hanging down. —ग्नः *m.* The waist.

अवलंब् *m.*(अव + लंब् 1 A.) 1 To hang or hang down.-2 To cling to, to lean on, rest on.-3 To support, sustain, take up, to depend upon; to have recourse to, rely upon, to resort to. -4 To be slow or tardy, be late. —*Caus.* 1 To cause to hang down from. -2 To make one rest upon or catch hold of.

अवलंबः 1 Hanging down. -2 Dependence on (fig. also). -3 A prop; support (lit. and fig.). -4 Hence; a crutch or stick for support. -5 A suspender. -6 An appendage. -7 A perpendicular line.

अवलंबनं *n.* 1 A prop; support, stay.-2 Help; assistance -3 Having recourse to, resorting to; adoption. -4 Walking-stick.

अवलंबित *p. p.* (*f.* -ता) 1 Supported, protected. -2 Suspended, hung down. -3 Expeditious, prompt.

अवलंबितव्य *pot. p.* (*f.* -व्या) To be caught hold of or grasped.

अवलंबिन् *a.* (*f.* -नी) Hanging down; depending upon; resting on, holding; supporting.

अवलिप्त *p. p.* (*f.* -प्ता) 1 Proud, arrogant, haughty. -2 Plastered, smeared. -3 Sullied.

अवलिह् (अव + लिह् 2 U.) To lick, lap.

अवलीढ *p. p.* (*f.* -ढा) 1 Eaten, chewed. -2 Licked, lapped; touched (fig. also). -3 Devoured, destroyed.

अवलीन *p. p.* (*f.* -ना) Sticking to, clinging to, resting under.

अवलीला *f.* 1 Sport, play, mirth. -2 Disrespect, contempt.

अवलुंचनं *n.* 1 Cutting off, tearing or pulling out. -2 Uprooting. -3 Not tying up, allowing to hang down. -4 Taking away, pulling out.

अवलुंठनं *n.* 1 Rolling or wallowing on the ground. -2 Robbing.

अवलूंपनं *n.* Leaping on suddenly.

अवलेखः *m.* 1 Breaking, scraping or scratching off. -2 Anything scraped off.

अवलेखनं *n.* Scraping off.

अवलेखा *f.* 1 Rubbing. -2 Adorning the person.

अवलेपः *m.* 1 Pride, haughtiness. -2 Violence, attack, assault, insult, outrage. -3 Smearing, anointing.. -5 Ornament. -5 Union, association.

अवलेपनं *n.* 1 Anointing, besmearing. -2 Oil, any unctuous substance. -3 Union, association. -4 Pride, arrogance. -5 The sandal tree.

अवलेहः *m.* I Licking. -2 An extract. -3 An electuary, confection.

अवलेहनं *n.* Licking with the tongue.

अवलोक् (अव + लोक् 1 A. or 10 P). 1 To see, behold. view, observe -2 To look at or see. -3 (In astr.) To exercise influcnce upon. -4 To obserye, meditate or reflect upon.

अवलोकः *m.* 1 Seeing, beholding. -2 Sight. -3 Looking down upon with compassion.

अवलोकक *a.* Looking at, wishing to see. —कः *m.* A spy.

अवलोकनं *n.* 1 Looking at; beholding, seeing. -2 Looking over, commanding a view of. -3 Sight, eye. -4 A look, glance. -5 Looking out for ; inquiry, seeking.

अवलोकयितृ *a.* Looking upon, considering.

अवलोकित *p. p.* (*f.* -ता) Seen, observed. —तः *m.* N. of a Buddha. —तं *n.* A look, glance.

अवलोकिन् *a.* Looking at, seeing.

अवलोपः *m.* 1 Cutting off or away ; destruction. -2 Biting.

अवलोम *a.* One who is favourable, suitable.

अववदः *m.*, -वदनं *n.* Censure, an evil report or bad reputation.

अववरकः *m.* 1 An aperture. -2 Window.

अववादः *m.* 1 Censure. -2 Confidence. -3 Disregard. -4 Support. -5 Evil report. -6 A command, an order. -7 Information.

अवव्रश्चः *m.* A splinter, chip.

अवश *a.* (*f.* -शा) 1 Independent; free. -2 Not having one's own free will, dependent. -3 Disobedient, self-willed. -4 Uncontrolled, unrestrained. -5 Unavoidable. -Comp. —इंद्रियचित्त *a.* (*f.* -त्ता) Whose mind and senses are not held in subjection.

अवशक्थिका *f.* 1 A cloth girt round the legs and knees (by a person), when sitting on his hams ; also, the act of so girding this cloth, or the posture itself. -2 (Hence) A wrapper, a girth, or a band in general.

अवशंगमः *m.* Not submitting to another's will.

अवशस् *f.* 1 A wrong desire. -2 Censure, abuse.

अवशातनं *n.* 1 Destroying, cutting or lopping off. -2 Withering. -3 Emaciation.

अवशिरस् *a.* Having the head bent or hung down.

अवशिष्ट *p. p.* (*f.* —ष्टा) 1 Left, remaining. -2 The surplus. —ष्टं, -ष्टकं *n.* Rest, remainder, remnant.

अवशीनः *m.* A scorpion.

अवशेषः *m.* 1 Remnant, leavings, remainder. -2 End, termination. (*e. g.* नामावशेष Having only the name left behind. कथावशेष Having only the tale remaining behind; both these expressions are metaphorically used to signify " dead ").

अवश्य *a.* (*f.* —श्या) 1 Ungovernable, unruly. -2 Unavoidable. -3 Indispensable, necessary. -Comp. —पुत्रः *m.* A son whom it is impossible to govern or teach.

अवश्यक *a.* (*f.* —का) Necessary, inevitable, indispensable.

अवश्यकता *f.* Necessity, obligation.

अवश्यकत्वं *n.* See अवश्यकता.

अवश्यम् *ind.* 1 Necessarily, inevitably. -2 Certainly, at all events, by all means, surely, of course; certainty.

अवश्यमेव Most surely. (If compounded with pot. pass. the final nasal is dropped; *e. g.* अवश्यकार्य to be necessarily done).

अवश्यंभाविन् *a.* Destined to take place; inevitable.

अवश्या *f.* 1 Hoar-frost, a fog or mist. -2 An independent woman.

अवश्यायः *m.* 1 Frost, dew. -2 Hoar-frost, white dew. -3 Pride.

अवश्रयणं *n.* Taking anything from off the fire (opp. अधिश्रयणं).

अवष्कयणी *f.* A cow that bears a calf after a long interval.

अवष्टब्ध *p. p.* (*f.* —ब्धा) 1 Haughty, stubborn. -2 Near, contiguous. -3 Bound, tied. -4 Supported; protected; held, seized. -5 Hanging from or upon. -6 Obstructed, stopped, suspended. -7 Paralysed. -8 Wrapped up, enfolded. -8 Opposed. -9 Surpassed, overcome.

अवष्टंभ् (अव + स्तंभ् 5, 9. P.) 1 To lean or rest upon. -2 To block up. -3 To wrap, envelop, cover with, to occupy. -4 To support, prop, clasp, embrace. -5 To stop, hold or keep back.

अवष्टंभः *m.* 1 Leaning, resting upon. -2 Support, prop; (hence) having recourse to, as courage; तत्कथमहं धैर्यावष्टंभं करोमि * पंचतं. -3 Haughtiness, pride, (as in सावष्टंभं). -4 A post, pillar. -5 Gold. -6 Commencement, beginning. -7 Stopping, staying. -8 Courage, steadiness. -9 Obstruction, impediment. -10 Paralysis, stupefaction. -11 Excellence.

अवष्टंभनं *n.* Resting upon, having recourse to. -2 Supporting. -3 Stupefying. -4 A post, pillar. -5 Stopping, staying.

अवष्टंभमय *a.* (*f.* —यी) Full of boldness, breathing defiance.

अवष्वाणः *m*, Noisy eating; smacking (the lips).

अवसक्त *p. p.* (*f.* —क्ता) 1 Suspended from, placed on. -2 Bound round, touching. -3 Engaged in, intent on. —क्तं n. Contact.

अवसंज् (अव + संज् 1 P.) 1 To suspend, attach, place. -2 To entrust to, throw on.

अवसविथका p. See अवशक्थिका.

अवसंजनं, अवसञ्जनं n. Embracing, clinging.

अवसंडीनं n. The united downward flight of birds.

अवसथ: m. 1 A dwelling place, habitation. -2 A village. -3 A school, college. See आवसथ —थं n. A house.

अवसथ्य: m. A college, a school.

अवसद् (अव + सद् 1 P.) 1 To sink down; fail, give way. -2 To be neglected or interfered with. -3 To become disheartened or exhausted. -4 To perish, come to an end, be ruined.

अवसन्न p. p. (f. -न्ना) 1 Sunk down (fig. also), enervated, sinking, drooping. -2 Disheartened, sad, melancholy, unhappy ; दाविकर्णोऽवसन्नो मृते • हितोप. -3 Ended, terminated. -4 Unable to do one's duty. -5 Lost, deprived of. -6 (In law) Non-suited, defeated.

अवसर: m. 1 Occasion, opportunity, time. -2 A fit or proper opportunity, proper or opportune time. -3 Space, room, scope. -4 Leisure. -5 Advantageous position. -6 Introduction. -7 A year. -8 Raining. -9 Descent. -10 A consultation in private. -Comp. —वाक्ति: f. Extempore speech.

अवसर्ग: m. 1 Permission to do as one likes. -2 Relaxation. -3 Independence.

अवसर्जनं n. Liberation.

अवसर्प: m. A spy, a secret emissary.

अवसर्पणं n. Stepping or going down.

अवसव्य a. Not left (same as -अपसव्य).

अवसाद: m. 1 Sinking, fainting. -2 Ruin, loss, destruction, decline. -3 End, termination. -4 Want of energy, languor, fatigue. -5 (In law) Badness of a cause, defeat, losing (a cause),

अवसादनं n. 1 Decline, loss, destruction. -2 Inability to do one's duty. -3 Oppression. -4 Finishing. -5 An escharotic application. -6 Removing proud flesh (from boils) by escharotic application.

अवसानं n. 1 Stopping. -2 Conclusion; termination, cessation, end -3 Death, decease. -4 Boundary, limit. -5 (In gram.) The last part of a word or period (opp. आदि). -6 A pause. -7 The end of a verse, or the verse itself. -8 A place of dismounting from a horse. -9 A place (स्थान) ; resting place, residence.

अवसाय: m. 1 Conclusion, end, termination ; destruction. -2 Remainder. -3 Completion. -4 Determination, decision, certainty.

अवसायिन् a. Residing ; attack,

अवसारणं n. Removing, causing to move.

अवसिक्त p. p. (f. -क्ता) Sprinkled.

अवसित p. p. (f. -ता) 1 Finished, ended. -2 Known, understood. -3 Resolved, determined, ascertained. -4 Stored up, gathered (as grain). -5 Tied, fastened, bound. -6 Gone.

अवसृ (अव + सृ 1 P.) To spread, pervade.

अवसृष्ट *p. p.* (*f.* -ष्टा) Given away, left, abandoned, dismissed, let go. -*Caus.* 1 To cause to sink ; to dishearten. -2 To allay, remove, to stop.

अवसेक: *m.* 1 Sprinkling, bedewing. -2 A disease of the eye.

अवसेचनं *n.* 1 Sprinkling. -2 Water used for sprinkling. -3 (In surgery) Bleeding.

अवसेय *pot. p.* (*f.* -या) 1 To be determined, or finished. -2 Perishable.

अवसो (अव + सो 4 P.) 1 To finish, accomplish. -2 To destroy. -3 To determine, understand. -4 (Intransitive) To fail; be at an end. -5 To know. —*Caus.* 1 To cause to be completed, to finish, complete ; अथ विधिमवसाय्य शास्त्रदृष्टं • रघुवं. 5. 76. -2 To understand, comprehend ; अवसाययितुं क्षमाः सुखं • किराता. 2. 29.

अवस्कन्द् (अव+स्कंद् 1 P.) 1 To attack, storm, assault; overpower, overwhelm. -2 To spring or leap down. -3 To pour out.

अवस्कंद: *m.* 1 Attacking ; attack, assault. -2 Descending. -3 A camp.

अवस्कंदनं *n.* See अवस्कंद:.

अवस्कर: *m.* 1 Ordure, excrement. -2 The privities. -3 Dirt, sweepings (in general). -4 A dunghill. -Comp. —मंदिरं *n.* A privy, water-closet.

अवस्करक: *m.* 1 A broom. -2 A sweeper.

अवस्तरणं *n.* Spreading out.

अवस्तार: *m.* 1 A curtain. -2 A covering ; a screen or wall of cloth around a tent. -3 A mat.

अवस्तु *n.* 1 A worthless thing or matter. -2 Unreality (of matter). insubstantiality.

अवस्था (अव + स्था. तिष्ठ् 1 A.) 1 To remain, stay, abide, to abide by, conform to, obey. -2 To live. -3 To stand (still), make a halt, stop. -4 To stand, exist, chance to be. -5 To fall to, devolve on. -6 To enter ; reach, attain to. -7 To stand apart, go off, withdraw. -8 To descend ; go to. —*Caus.* (स्थापयति-ते) 1 To cause to stand or stop ; to keep, place, to fix, settle, to establish, found ; to steady, fix (as heart &c.). -5 To comfort, console. -6 To separate, divide.

अवस्था *f.* 1 State, condition, situation. -2 Posture. राजा —अहो सर्वास्ववस्थासु चारुता शोभान्तरं पुष्यति • मालवि. १. -3 Position, circumstance. -4 Period, stage (of life &c.). -5 Form, appearance. -6 Degree, proportion. -7 Satability, fixity, as in अनवस्था. -8 Appearance in a court of law. -Comp. —अंतरं *n.* Another or altered state. —चतुष्टयं *n.* The four periods or states of human life ; *i. e.* बाल्यं (childhood) ; कौमारं (youth) ; यौवनं (manhood) ; and वार्धकं (old age). —त्रयं *n.* (In वेदांत phil.) The states *i. e.* जागृति (waking), स्वप्न (dreaming), and सुषुप्ति (sound sleep). —द्वयं *n.* (In philosophy) The two states of life *i. e.* सुखं and दुःखं (happiness and misery).

अवस्थानं *n.* 1 Remaining, residing, dwelling. -2 Situation, station, position. -3 Residence, abode ; place. -4 Period of staying.

अवस्थापनं *n.* 1 Fixing, settling. -2 Residence, abode.

अवस्थायिन् *a.* (*f.* -नी) Staying, residing, dwelling.

अवस्थित *p. p* (*f.* -ता) 1 Remained, stayed. एवमवस्थिते Under these circumstances. -2 Firm of purpose, steady. -3 Engaged in prosecuting ; following ; abiding by. -4 Resting with, dependent on. -5 Settled, being a matter of course. -6 Resolved.

अवस्थितिः *f.* Tne same as अवस्थानं.

अवस्यंदनं *n.* Trickling, oozing.

अवस्रंसनं *n.* Dropping or falling down, falling off, a fall.

अवहतिः *f.* Beating, threshing.

अवहन् (अव + हन् 2 P.) 1 To strike, beat off, hit, kill. -2 To destroy, remove. 3- To thresh (as rice).

अवहननं *n.* 1 Threshing, beating off rice. -2 The lungs.

अवहस्तः *m.*, The back of the hand.

अवहानिः *f.* Loss.

अवहासः *m.* 1 Smiling, a smile. -2 A jest, joke.

अवहास्यः *pot. p.* (*f.* -स्या) To be derided, fit to be ridiculed ; ridiculous.

अवहित *p. p.* 1 Deposited, placed. -2 Attentive, careful ; शृणुत मनोभिरवहितैः V. 1. 2; शृणुमेऽवहिता वचः * रामाय. -5 Clebrated, known. अवहितता Application, attention. -Comp. —अंजलि *a.* With joined hands.

अव(व)हित्था, *f.* -त्थं *n.* 1 Dissimulation in general. -2 Dissimulation or concealment of an internal feeling regarded as one of the 33 subordinate feeilngs (in rhetoric).

अवहीन *p. p.* (*f.* -ना) Abandoned, left.

अवहेलः *m.* (*f.* -ला) Disrespect, disdain, contempt, disregard.

अवहेलनं *n.* (*f.*—ना) Disregard.

अवहेलित *a.* (*f.* —ता) Disregarded, slighted, contemned. —तं *n.* Disregard.

अवह्वर *a.* Crooked. —रः *m.* A crooked way ; (fig.) deceit.

अवाक् *ind.* 1 Downwards. -2 Southwards. -Comp. —ज्ञानं *n.* Disrespect, insult.

अवाकरः *m.* A mint.

अवाक्ष *a.* (*f.* —क्षी) A guardian, keeper.

अवाग्र *a.* (*f.* —ग्रा) Having the head bent down, stooping, bending.

अवाच् *a.* Speechless, dumb. -*n.* Brahman (*n.*) -Comp. —श्रुति *a.* Deaf and dumb.

अवाच् *a.* (*f.* —ची) 1 Turned downwards. -2 Lower than (with abl.). -3 Headlong. -4 Southern. —चः *m.* Brahman (*n.*). -Comp. -शिरस् *a.* Having the head downwards. —भव *a.* 1 Southern.

अवाची *f.* 1 The South -2 Lower region.

अवाचीन *a.* (*f.* —ना) 1 Downward, headlong. -2 Southern. -3 Descended, gone down.

अवाच्य *a.* (*f.* —च्या) 1 Not prope. to be addressed. -2 Improper to be uttered. -3 Not distinctly expressed, not expressible in words.

अवांच् See अवाच्. -ची *f.* 1 The south. -2 The lower region.

अवांचित *a.* (*f.* —ता) Bent, low.

अवात *a.* (*f.* —ता) 1 Windless.

-2 Not exposed to, or not dried up by the wind.

अवात a. Dried, dry. -तः m. Respiration.

अवान्तर (f. —रा) 1 Situated or standing between. -2 Included, involved. -3 Subordinate, secondary. -4 Not closely connected, extraneous, extra. -Comp. —दिश्, —दिशा f. An intermediate quarter (such as the आग्नेयी, ऐशानी, नैर्ऋती and वायवी). —देशः m. A place situated between (two others); an intermediate region.

अवाप् (अव + आप् 5 U.) 1 To get, obtain, secure, gain. -2 To reach, go to, enter. -3 To suffer, incur, meet with.

अवाप्त a. (f. —प्ता) Got, obtained, received.

अवाप्तव्य a. (f. —व्या) Attainable, fit to be obtained.

अवाप्तिः f. Obtaining, getting, receiving.

अवाप्य a. (f. —प्या) Attainable.

अवाम a. (f. —मा) 1 Not left; right. -2 Favourable, not adverse. -3 Inauspicious, inelegant.

अवारः m., -रं n. 1 The near bank of a river. -2 This side. -तस् ind. To this side. -Comp. —पारः m. The ocean. —पारीण a. (f. —णा) 1 Belonging to the ocean. -2 Crossing a river.

अवारयितव्य a (f. -व्या) See अवार्य.

अवारीण a. (f. —णा) Crossing a river.

अवार्य a. (f. —र्या) Not to be warded or kept off, irremediable.

अवावटः m. The son of a woman by any man (of the same caste) other than her first husband

अवावन् m. A thief.

अवासस् a. Unclothed, naked. —m. N. of Buddha.

अवास्तव a. (f. वी) 1 Unreal, unsubstantial. -2 Unfounded, irrational (as an argument).

अविः m. f. 1 A sheep. -विः m. -2 The sun. -3 N. of a tree (अर्क). -4 A goat. -5 A mountain. -6 Air, wind. -7 A woollen blanket (of the skin of mice). -8 A blanket, shawl in general, -9 A woollen strainer (for Soma juice.). -10 A master. -11 A wall, enclosure. -12 A rat. -विः f. 1 An ewe. -2 Shame. -3 A woman in her courses. -Comp. —कटः m. A flock of sheep. -कटोरणः m. A kind of tribute (consisting of sheep). —पटः m. 1 A sheep's skin, a woollen cloth. —पालः m. A shepherd. —स्थलं n. A sheep-place. -2 N. of a town.

अविकः m. A sheep. —का f. An ewe. —कं n. A diamond.

अविकत्थन a. (f. —ना) Not vaunting, modest.

अविकल a. (f. —ला) 1 Unimpaired, entire, perfect, whole, all. -2 Regular, orderly.

अविकल्प a. (f. —ल्पा) Unchangeable. —ल्पः m. 1 Absence of doubt. -2 Absence of option or alternative. -3 Positive act or precept. —ल्पं ind. Without doubt, unhesitatingly.

अविकार a. (f. —रा) Immutable, unchangeable. —रः m Immutability.

अविकृत a. (f. —ता) Unchanged.

अविकृतिः f. 1 Absence of change. -2 (In Sân. phil.) The inanimate principle called प्रकृति, regarded as the material cause of the universe ; मूलप्रकृतिरविकृतिः • सांख्यका.

अविक्रिय *a.* (*f.* —या) Unchangeable, immutable. —यं *n.* Brahman (*n.*)

अविक्षत *a.* (*f.* —ता) Uninjured unhurt, whole, entire, undiminished.

अविक्षिप्त *a.* (*f.* —प्ता) 1 Not thrown away. -2 Attentive, composed.

अविग्रह *a.* (*f.* —हा) 1 Bodiless, incorporeal -2 An epithet of the Supreme Being (who has no body). —हः *m.*(In gram.) A compound the sense of which cannot be expressed by its constituent parts separately (called also नित्यसमास).

अविघ्न *a.* (*f.* —घ्ना) Unobstructed, free from impediments. —घ्नं *n.* Freedom from obstacle or impdiment, welfare (this word is usually neuter, though विघ्न is *m.* (*cf.* मित्र a friend, अमित्रः an enemy).

अविचारः *m.* Absence of judgment ; indiscretion, error, folly.

अविचारित *a.* (*f.* —ता) Ill-judged, not well thought out or considered. -Comp. —निर्णयः *m.* A prejudice, prejudiced opinion.

अविच्छिन्न *a.* (*f.* —न्ना) 1 Not separated, undivided. -2 Continuous, uninterrupted.

अविच्छेद *a.* 1 Uninterrupted. -2 Undivided, entire, whole. —दः *m.* 1 Entirety, wholeness. -2 Connection, continuity.

अविज्ञेय *a.* (*f.* —या) Undistinguishable, not to be recognized or known, unknowable. —यः *m.* The Supreme God.

अविडीनं *n.* A direct flight of birds.

अवितथ *a.* (*f.* —था) 1 Not false, true. -2 Realised, not fruitless. —थं *n.* Truth. —थं *ind.* Not falsely, according to truth. —था N. of a metre.

अवित्यजः *m.*, —जं *n.* Quicksilver.

अविदग्ध *a.* (*f.* —ग्धा) 1 Unlearned, inexperienced, stupid. -2 Not well burnt ; undigested.

अविदित *a.* (*f.* —ता) Unknown, unperceived. —तः *m.* The Supreme God.

अविदूर *a.* (*f.* —रा) Not distant ; near, contiguous. —रं *n.* Proximity, vicinity. —रं *ind.* Near to, not far from ; so अविदूरेण, अविदूरात्, अविदूरतः, अविदूरे.

अविद्ध *a.* (*f.* —द्धा) Unpierced. unhurt ; not hit.

अविद्य *a.* (*f.* —द्या) Not educated; unlearned, foolish, unwise. —द्या *f.* 1 Ignorance. -2 Spiritual ignorance. -3(In वेदान्त phil.) Illusion, or Mâyâ (It is on account of this illusion that one perceives the universe which does not really exist, as inherent in Brahman (*n*) which alone really exists). (With Buddhists) Ignorance together with non-existence.

अविधवा *f.* Not a widow. A married woman whose husband is still living.

अविधा *ind.* An interjection meaning 'help, help' used in calling for help in danger. विदूषकः— अविधा अविधा, भोः किंतु खल्वेतत्सूर्यनिर्मोक इव संवृत्तेऽस्माकं निपतितं • विक्रमो. 2.

अविधि *a.* Not lawful ; contrary to rule. —धिः *m.* Irregularity, absence of a rule or precept.

अविनयः *m.* 1 Want of good manners or modesty. -2 Rude behaviour, rudeness, immodest or rude act, indecorum, impropriety of conduct. -3 Incivility, disrespect. -4 Offence, crime, fault. -5 Pride, arrogance, insolence.

अविनाभावः *m.* 1 Non-separation. -2 Inherent or essential character, inseparable connection. -3 Connection (in general).

अविनिगमः *m.* An illogical conclusion.

अविनीत *a.* (*f.* —ता) 1 Immodest, ill-bred. -2 Acting improperly, wicked, vile. -3 Insolent, rude. -4 Not-tamed, ill-trained. —ता *f.* An unchaste woman.

अविपन्न *a.* (*f.* -न्ना) 1 Uninjured, unhurt. -2 Not defiled or polluted; pure.

अविभक्त *a.* (*f.* -क्ता) 1 Undivided, unpartitioned, joint, (as property of a family, or co-heirs). -2 Not broken, entire. -3 Not different.

अविभाग *a.* (*f.* -गा) Unpartitioned, undivided. —गः *m.* 1 Not dividing. -2 Undivided inheritance.

अविभाज्य *a.* (*f.* -ज्या) Indivisible. —ज्यं *n.* 1 Indivisibility. -2 Not being liable to be partitioned ; (said of certain articles which are not to be divided at the time of partition) ; *e. g.* वस्त्रं पात्रमलंकारं कृतान्नमुदकं स्त्रियः । योगक्षेमं प्रचारं च न विभाज्यं प्रचक्षते * मनुस्मृ. 9. 219.

अविभावनं *n.* Non-perception, disapperance.

अविभावना *f.* See अविभावनं.

अविमृष्ट *a.* Not prominently mentioned. —विधेयांशदोषः —*m.* The fault occuring in a sentence or phrase in which the predicate (विधेय) is placed before the subject (अनुवाद्य or उद्देश्य). This दोष is also called विधेयाविमर्शः. *e. g.* सपत्रलेखानि मुखाम्बुजानि × × कुर्वंति नार्यः सुरतोत्सवाय where we ought to have मुखाम्बुजानि &c. * ऋतुसं. 4-5.

अविमृष्य *a.* (*f.* -ष्या) Undoubted, unquestionable.

अवियोग *a.* (*f.* -गा) Not separated; united; conneced. —गः *m.* 1 Non-separation, presence. -2 Conjunction, association. -Comp. —तृतीया *f.* N. of a certain festival or holiday. —व्रतं *n.* A vow to be observed by women on the third day of the first fortnight of Mârgasîrsha.

अविरत *a.* (*f.* -ता) Not desisting or ceasing from (with abl.) ; uninterrupted, continual, unbroken, perpetual. -2 Sleeping soundly. —तं *ind.* Eternally, continually.

अविरतिः *f.* 1 Continuity, uninterruptedness. -2 Incontinence.

अविराम *a.* (*f.* -मा) Uninterrupted, continuous. —मः *m.* Uninterrupted succession, continuance. —मं *ind.* Uninterruptdly.

अविरल *a.* (*f.* -ला) 1 Thick, dense. -2 Contiguous, close. -3 Coarse, gross, substantial. -4 Uninterrupted, continuous. —लं *ind.* 1 Closely. -2 Uninterruptedly, incessantly.

अविरोधः *m.* 1 Consistency, compatibility, congruity. -2 Absence of impediment. -3 Assent, concurrence.

अविलंब *a.* Prompt, not delaying, quick. —बः *m.* Absence of delay, quickness, promptitude. —बं, अविलंबेन *ind.* Without delay ; quickly

अविलंबित *a.* (*f.* —ता) Without delay; quick, expeditious, prompt. -तं *ind.* Quickly, without delay.

अविला *f.* An ewe.

अविवक्षित *a.* (*f.* —ता) 1 Not intended or aimed at. -2 Not to be said or spoken.

अविविक्त *a.* (*f.* —क्ता) 1 Uninvestigated, not properly thought out. -2 Indiscriminate, confounded. -3 Public. -4 Making no difference.

अविवेकः *m.* 1 Want of discrimination or judgment; absence of prudence; imprudence । अविवेकः परमापदां पदं * किराता. 2. 30. -2 Hastiness, rashness, recklessness. -3 Ignorance.

अविशंकित *a.* (*f.* —ता) 1 Unapprehensive, fearless. -2 Without doubt; confiding.

अविशेष *a.* (*f.* —षा) Without any difference; alike, similar, uniform. —षः *m.* 1 Absence of difference; uniformity, similarity. -2 Identity, sameness. -3 The subtle elements (in San. phil.).

अविश्वस्त *a.* (*f.* —स्ता) Not trusted; suspected.

अविश्वास *a.* Not inspiring confidence; mistrusted. —सः *m* Mistrust, suspicion. —सा *f.* A cow calving after long intervals.

अविष *a.* Not poisonous. -2 Antivenomous antidote. —षः *m.* 1 An ocean. -2 A king. -3 Sky. -षी *f.* 1 A river. -2 The earth. -3 Heaven.

अविषय *a.* (*f.* —या) 1 Unperceived, invisible, beyond the reach of the senses. -2 Insensible. -3 Disregarding objects of sense. —यः *m.* 1 Absence, disappearance. -2 Not an object of (anything); not within the reach of; beyond; transcending. -3 Disregard of the objects of sense.

अविसर्गिन् *m.* An unintermittent fever.

अवी *f.* A woman in her courses.

अवीचि *a.* Waveless. —चिः *m.* N. of a hell. अवीचिमयः *m.* A place of punishment for liars.

अवीरा *f.* A woman who has neither sons nor husband.

अवृत्ति *a.* 1 Not existing; not present; not being in. -2 Having no livelihood. —त्तिः *f.* 1 Absence of subsistence or means of livelihood inadequate support. -2 Absence of wages.

अवृथा *ind.* Not in vain; successfully.

अवृद्धिकं *n.* Original capital; principal.

अवृष्टिः *f.* Want of rain; drought, famine.

अवे (अव + इ 2. P.) 1 To know understand, learn, perceive, to be cognizant of, be aware of, look upon or consider, regard. -2 To go or move away. -3 To go to, approach (with acc.).

अवेक्ष् (अव + ईक्ष् 1 A.) 1 To perceive, observe, behold. -2 To have in view, to take into account or consideration, have regard to. -3 To take care of, guard, watch over, protect. -4 To think, consider. -5 To superintend, to attend to the welfare of; to inspect; to inquire into. -6 To expect, hope for.

अवेक्षकः *m.* An inspector, a supervisor, an overseer, a superintendent.

अवेक्षणं *n.* 1 Looking towards or at, seeing. -2 Guarding, watching over, taking care of, supervision, inspection. -3 Attention, care, observation. -4 Regarding, considering.

अवेक्षणीय *a.* (*f.* —या) To be looked upon ; to be considered.

अवेक्षा *f.* 1 Seeing, looking at. -2 Attention, care, regard. -3 Agreement, engagement.

अवेणि *a* 1 Not braided. -2 Having no braid of hair. -3 Not flowing together or commingled (as the waters of rivers).

अवेद: *f.* Absence of knowledge.

अवेद्य *a.* (*f.* —द्या) 1 Unknowable, secret. -2 Unattainable. —द्य: *m.* A calf.

अवेल *a.* (*f.* —ला) 1 Having no boundary or limit ; unlimited. -2 Untimely. —ल: *m.* Concealment of knowledge. —ला *f.* Unfavourable or unseasonable time.

अवैध *a.* (*f.* —धी) 1 Irregular, not conformable to law or rule. -2 Not sanctioned by the Sâstras.

अवोक्षणं *n.* Sprinkling with the slanting hand.

अवोद: *m.* Sprinkling, moistening.

अवोष: *m.* Hot food.

अव्यक्त *a.* (*f.* —क्ता) 1 Indistinct; not manifest or apparent. -2 Invisible, imperceptible. -3 Undetermined ; अव्यक्तोयमचिंत्योयं * भगवद्गीता 2. 25. -4 Undeveloped, uncreated. -5 (In m·th.) Unknown (as a quantity or number). —क्त: *m.* 1 N. of Vishnu. -2 N. of Siva. -3 Cupid. -4 Primary matter which has not yet entered into real existence. -5 A fool. —क्तं *n.* (In Vedânta phil.) 1 The Supreme Being or universal Spirit Brahman (*n*). -2 Spiritual ignorance. -3 The subtle body. -4 The state of sleep(सुषुप्त्यवस्था). -5 (In Sán. phil.) The primary germ of nature from which all the phenomena of the material world are developed ; महत: परमव्यक्तमव्यक्तात्पुरुष: पर: * कठोपनिषद्. -6 The soul. -7 Nature. —क्तं *ind.* Imperceptibly, indistinctly, inarticulately. -Comp. —अनुकरणं *n.* The imitating of unmeaning sounds —आदि *a.* Whose begining is inscrutable. —पद *a.* Inarticulate. —मूर्ति *a.* Having an incomprehensible form. —मूलप्रभव: *m.* The tree of worldly existence (in Sán. phil.). —राग *a.* Ruddy. —राग: *m.* The colour of the dawn. —राशि: *m.* An unknown number or quantity (in algebra). —लक्षण:, *m.* An epithet of Siva (whose qualities are not perceptible). —लिंग *a.* Whose signs are invisible (as a disease). —लिंग: *m.* An ascetic. -लिंगं *n.* The great principle (महत) (in Sân. phil.). -वर्त्मन्, —मार्ग *a.* Whose ways are mysterious or inscrutable. —वर्ण *a.* (*f.* -र्णा) Inarticulate ; indistinctly uttered. —वाच् *a.* Speaking indistinctly. —साम्यं *n.* An equation of unknown quantities.

अव्यग्र *a.* (*f.* —ग्रा) 1 Not agitated or ruffled ; steady, cool. -2 Not engaged or occupied (in business). -3 Indifferent, undisturbed. -4 Attentive, careful. —ग्रं *ind.* Quietly, coolly, leisurely.

अव्यंग *a.* (*f.* —गा) 1 Not mutilated or defective ; sound, perfect. -2

Plain ; not figurative (as a meaning). —ना *f.* A legume or pod of the awn of barley.

अव्यंजन *a.* 1 Having no distinctive or characteristic marks or singns (as of the sex). -2 Having no good marks. -3 Indistinct. -4 Not figurative. —नः *m.* An animal without horns though of an age to have them.

अव्यथ *a.* (*f.* —था) 1 Not giving or inflicting pain; merciful. -2 Free from pain. —थः *m.* A snake.

अव्यथिन् *a.* 1 Free from pain. -2 Free from fear, fearless. -3 Not giving pain.

अव्यथिषः *m.* 1 The sun. -2 The ocean. —षी *f.* 1 The earth. -2 Midnight ; night.

अव्याध *a.* (*f.* —धा) Not pierced.

अव्यभि (-भी-) चारः *m.* 1 Non-separation. -2 Constancy, steadiness, fidelity.

अव्यभिचारिन् *a.* (*f.* —णी) 1 Not opposed or adverse; favourable. -2 Not subject to exceptions ; true in all cases without any instance to the contrary. -3 Virtuous, moral. chaste. -4 Steady, permanent, faithful (as devotion) (भक्तिरव्यभिचारिणी).

अव्यय *a.* (*f.* —या) 1 Imperishable, undecaying, immutable ; वेदाविनाशिनं नित्यं य एनमजमव्ययं • भगवद्गीता. 2. 21. विनाशमव्ययस्यास्य न कश्चित्कर्तुमर्हति • भगवद्गीता 2. 17. Eternal, everlasting; अश्वत्थं प्राहुरव्ययं • भ. गी. 15. 1. -2 Unexpended, unwasted. -3 Economical. —यः *m.* 1 N. of Vishnu. -2 N. of Siva. —यं *n.* (In Vedánta phil.) Brahman (*n.*) -3 (In gram.) An indeclinable particle &c.; सदृशं त्रिषु लिंगेषु सर्वासु च विभक्तिषु। वचनेषु च सर्वेषु यन्न व्येति तदव्ययम्॥. -4 Safety, prosperity. -Comp. —आत्मन् *a.* Having an imperishable or eternal nature. *m.* (*nom. sing.* —त्मा) The soul or spirit. —वर्गः *m.* The clsss of indeclinables.

अव्ययीभावः *m.* One of the four principal kinds of compounds in Sanskrit ; an adverbial compound; *e. g.* उपकुंभं. -2 Absence of expenditure (owing to poverty). -3 Unchangeable state, imperishableness.

अव्यलीक *a.* (*f.* —का) 1 Not false ; true. -2 Agreeable, having no disagreeable element.

अव्यवधान *a.* (*f.* —ना) 1. Close, immediate, contiguous, without any intervening object. -2 Not screened or concealed ; open. -3 Not covered; bare (as ground). -4 Careless, inattentive. —नं *n.* Carelessness.

अव्यवस्थ *a.* (*f.* —स्था) 1 Not fixed; moving, unstable. -2 Unlimited. -3 Unsettled, indiscriminate, disorderly, irregular, —स्था *f.* 1 Irregularity. -2 An incorrect opinion given on a point of civil or religious law.

अव्यवस्थित *a.* (*f.* —ता) 1 Not conformable to law or practice ; unacquainted with the law or custom. -2 Ill-regulated. -3 Fickle, unstable- -3 Not in due order; unmethodical.

अव्यवहार्य *a.* (*f.* —र्या) 1 Not entitled to eat, drink, &c. with people of the same caste ; excommunicated. -2 Not to be discussed in a law—court ; not to be made the subject of litigation. -3 Impracticable.

अव्यवहित a. (f. -ता) Immediate, without any intervening thing ; direct.

अव्याकृत a. 1 Not developed, not manifest. -2 Not decomposed; elementary. —तं n. (In Vedânta phil.) 1 An elementary substance from which all things were created (considered as one with Brahman (n.) -2 (In Sán. phil.) The primary germ of nature (प्रधान).

अव्याज a. (f. -जा) Free from guile or fraud. —जः m., —जं n. 1 Absence of guile or fraud ; honesty. -2 Simplicity, artlessness.

अव्यापक a. 1 Not comprehensive. -2 Not an invariable concomitant ; special, individual, peculiar.

अव्यापार a. Having no work; unemployed. —रः m. 1 Cessation from work ; the state of being unemployed. -2 A business not practised or understood. -3 Not one's own business.

अव्याप्ति: f. 1 Inadequate extent or pervasion of a proposition. -2 (In logic) Non-inclusion or exclusion of a part of the thing defined.

अव्याप्य a. (f. -प्या) Not extending to the whole circumstances; not pervading the whole extent. -Comp. —वृत्ति: f. (In Vais. phil.) A category of limited application, partial inherence as regards time or space.

अव्याहत a. (f. —ता) Not broken or interrupted; unobstructed; obeyed. —तं n. A true or uncontradicted statement.

अव्युत्पन्न a. (f. —ना) 1 Not proficient; inexperienced; not practised ignorant. -2 Having no proper or regular derivation (as a word . —न्नः m. A person not versed in the grammar, idiom &c. of a language; a superficial linguist.

अव्रत a. (f. —ता) Not observing (the prescribed) religious rites or obligations.

अश् I. 5 A. (pp. अशित-अष्ट). 1 To pervade, fill completely, penetrate -2 To reach, go or come to, arrive at, attain to, obtain, enjoy, or suffer, experience. WITH अनु — 1 To reach, come up to. -2. To equal. उप— 1 To obtain, enjoy, acquire. -2. To become master of. -II. 9 P. (rarely A.) 1 To eat, to consume -2 To taste, to experience, enjoy the fruits of.

अशंक a. (f. -का), अशंकित a. (f. -ता) 1 Fearless, undaunted. -2 Secure, certain; having no doubt.

अशकुन: m., -नं n. An inauspicious or bad omen.

अशक्ति: f. 1 Weakness, powerlessness. -2 Inability, incapacity. -3 (In Sân. phil.) Incapacity of the intellect to produce knowledge.

अशक्य a. Impossible, impracticable.

अशनं n. 1 Pervasion, penetration -2 The act of eating, feeding. Tasting, enjoying. -4 Food.

अशना f. Desire to eat, hunger.

अशनाया f. Hunger.

अशनायित a. (f. -ता) Hungry.

अशनि: m., f. 1 Indra's thunderbolt. -2 Flash of lightning. -3 A missile. -4 The tip of a missile. —निः m. 1

Indra. -2 Fire. -3 Fire produced from lightning.

अशब्दं *n.* 1 The ' inexpressible, ' *i. e.* Brahman (*n.*) -2 (In Sân. phil.) प्रधान or primary germ of nature.

अशरण *a.* (*f.* -णा) Defenceless, helpless, forlorn, destitute of refuge.

अशरीर *a.* Bodiless, incorporeal. -रः 1 The Supreme Being; Brahman (*n.*) -2 Cupid, the god of love. -3 An ascetic who has renounced all worldly connections.

अशरीरिन् *a.* (*f.* -णी) Incorporeal, unearthly, heavenly ; usually with words like वाणी, वाक् &c.

अशासन *a.* Having no order or rule. -नं *n.* Want of government; anarchy, disorder.

अशास्त्र *a.* (*f.* -स्त्रा) Not conformable to sacred authority. -Comp. -विहित, -सिद्ध *a* Not sanctioned or enjoined by scriptures.

अशास्त्रीय *a.* (*f.* -या) 1 Unscriptural, heterodox. -2 Illegal, immoral.

अशित *a.* (*f.* -ता) 1 Eaten, enjoyed. -2 Not sharpened. -तं *n.* 1 Eating. -2 Enjoyment.

अशित्र: *m.* 1 A thief. -2 An oblation of rice.

अशिर: *m.* 1 The fire -2 The sun. -3 Wind. -4 A demon; N. of a Râkshasa. -रं *n.* A diamond.

अशिरस् *a.* Headless. -*m.* A body without head ; a trunk. -Comp. -स्नानं *n.* Bathing the whole body except the head.

अशिव *a.* (*f.* -वा) 1 Inauspicious, threatening mischief. -2 Unlucky, unfortunate. -3 Unkind, unfriendly, envious. -4 Pernicious, dangerous. -वं *n.* 1 Ill-luck, misfortune. -2 Mischief. -Comp. -आचार: *m.* Improper behaviour, rudeness of conduct. -2 Conduct not sanctioned by any recognized authority.

अशिशु: *m.* A youth ; a boy above eight years of age. -श्वी, अशिश्विका *f.* A childless female.

अशिष्ट *a.* (*f.* -ष्टा) 1 Ill-bred, ill-behaved, rude. -2 Unrefined, barbarous, not respectable. -3 Atheistical. -4 Not sanctioned by any recognized authority. -5 Not prescribed in any work of authority.

अशीत *a.* (*f.* -ता) Not cold ; hot. -Comp. -कर:, -रश्मि: &c. *m.* The sun.

अशीति: *f. num.* Eighty (used in the singular and fem. gender whatever be the number and gender of the noun it qualifies) *m., f.* The number eighty.

अशीतिक *a.* 1 An octogenerian, one eighty years of age. -2 Measuring eighty.

अशीर्षक *a.* Headless.

अशुचि *a.* 1 Not clean ; dirty; impure. -2 Black. -चि: *f.* 1 Impurity. -2 Degradation. -3 Disgrace.

अशुद्ध *a.* (*f.* -द्धा) 1 Impure. -2 Inaccurate, incorrect, wrong. -Comp. -वासक: *m.* A vagrant; a suspicious person.

अशुद्धि: *f.* Impurity, foulness.

अशुभ *a.* 1 Inauspicious. -2 Impure, dirty, (opp. शुभ). -3 Unlucky, unfortunate. -भं *n.* 1 Inauspiciousness. -2 Sin, a shameful deed. -3 Misfortune, calamity. -Comp. -उदय: *m.* An inauspicious omen.

अशून्य *a.* (*f.* -न्या) 1 Not empty or vacant. -2 Not unattended to; fulfilled, or executed. -न्यं *n.* 1 Not a void. -2 Something sent to accompany another (such as a present along with a letter).

अशृत *a.* (*f.* —ता) Uncooked, raw; unripe.

अशेष *a* (*f* —षा) Without remainder; whole, all, complete, perfect. —षः *m.* Non-remainder. —षं, अशेषेण, अशेषतः are used as *ind.* in the sense of 'wholly,' entirely.' 'completely.'

अशैक्षः *m.* An Arhat (no longer a pupil).

अशोक *a.* (*f.* —का) Without sorrow; not feeling or causing sorrow. —कः *m.* N. of a tree having red flowers (Jonesia Asoka Roxb.); (said, according to the convention of poets, to put forth flowers when it receives kicks from young ,and beautiful ladies. -2 N. of Vishnu. -3 N. of a celebrated king of the Maurya dynasty, said to have reigned from 234-198 B. C. N. of the tree बकुल. —कं *n.* 1 Quicksilver. -2 The blossom of the Asoka plant (forming one of the five arrows of Cupid). -Comp. —अरिः *m.* The कदंब tree. —अष्टमी *f.* The eighth day in the first half of *Chaitra.* —तरुः, —नगः,—वृक्षः *m.* The Asoka tree. —त्रिरात्रः *m.*, —त्रं *n.* N. of a festival or व्रत which lasts for three nights. —पूर्णिमा N. of a certain holiday, a ceremony to be observed on the 15th day of the month of Phâlguna. -रोहिणी N. of a medical plant (कटुका.) —वनिका*f.* A grove of Asoka trees.

अशोकवनिकान्यायः *m.* The maxim of the grove of Ashoka trees. Râvana kept Sitâ in his grove of Ashoka trees; we connot say why he chose this grove and chose no other. When there are several ways of doing a thing all equally good, a man has to adopt some particular way, and it is not possible to say why he adopted that one and no other.

अशोच्य *a.* (*f.* —च्या) Not to be lamented or deplored.

अशोचं *n.* 1 Uncleanliness. -2 Inaccuracy, incorrectness.

अशौचं *n.* 1 Impurity, dirtiness, foulness.-2 Defilement caused either by child-birth (called जननाशौच) or by the death of some relation (called मृताशौच).

अश्नितपिबता *f.* Invitation to eat and drink; a feast where people are called to eat and drink.

अश्मकाः *m. pl.* N. of a country in the south, (probably an old name of Travancore). -3 The inhabitants of the country.

अश्मन् *m.* 1 A stone. -2 A hard stone, rock. -3 Flint. -4 A cloud. -5 A thunderbolt. -6 A mountain. -Comp. —उत्थं *n.* Bitumen. —कदली *f.* N. of a plant, a kind of कदली (Mar. लोखंडी केळ). —कुट्टः, —कुट्टकः *m.* A partilcular class of devotees. —गर्भः, *m.*,—र्भं *n.* An emerald. —जः, *m.*, —जं *n.* 1 Red-chalk. -2 Iron. —जतु *n.*, —जतुकं *n.* Bitumen. —जातिः *f.* An emerald. —दारणः *m.* An axe or crow for breaking stones. —पुष्पं *n.* Bitumen, benzoin. —भालं *n.* A mortar of stone or iron. —सारः *m.*, —रं, *n.* 1 Iron. 2 Sapphire.

अश्मंतं *n.* 1 A fire-place. -2 A field, plain. -3 Death.

अश्मंतकः *m.*, —कं *n.* A fire-place.

अश्मर *a.* Stony, rocky.

अश्मरी *f.* (In medicine) A disease

called *stone* (in the bladder); gravel, strangury.

अश्मीरः *m.*, -रं *n.* Stone or gravel (the disease).

अश्रः *m.* A corner, (as in चतुरश्र, त्र्यश्र, &c.). -श्रं *n.* 1 A tear. -2 Blood, (usually written अस्र q. v.). -Comp. -पः *m.* A blood-drinker, a fiend, cannibal.

अश्रद्धेय *a.* (*f.* -या) Not to be believed; incredible.

अश्रमः *m.* 1 Freedom from fatigue; freshness, vigour. -2 Absence of toil; laziness.

अश्रवण *a.* (*f.* -णा) Deaf. -णः *m.* A snake.

अश्राद्धः *m.* Non-performance of a Srâddha. -Comp. -भोजिन् *a.* One who has vowed not to eat during the performance of a Srâddha ceremony.

अश्रान्त *a.* (*f.* -न्ता) 1 Unwearied, untired. -2 Incessant, continual. -न्तं *ind.* Incessantly, continually.

अश्रिः, -श्री *f.* 1 A corner, angle (of a room, house &c.) (changed to अश्र at the end of comp. with चतुर्, त्रि, षट् &c.). -2 The sharp side or edge (of a weapon &c.). -3 The sharp side of anything.

अश्रीक *a.* (*f.* -का) 1 Having no splendour; pale. -2 Unlucky; not prosperous.

अश्रील *a.* (*f.* -ला) Same as अश्रीक.

अश्रु *n.* A tear. -Comp. -उपहत *a.* (*f.* -ता) Affected by tears, covered with tears. -परिप्लुत *a.* (*f.* -ता) Suffused or filled with tears. -पातः *m.* Flow of tears, shedding tears. -पूर्ण *a.* (*f.* -र्णा) Filled with tears. -लोचन, -नेत्र *a.* Having tears in the eyes, having tearful eyes.

अश्रुत *a.* (*f.* -ता) 1 Unheard. -2 Contrary to the वेदs.

अश्रेयस् *n.* Mischief, unhappiness.

अश्रौत *a.* (*f.* -ता) Not sanctioned by the Vedas.

अश्लीक *a.* Unlucky, unpropitious.

अश्लील *a.* 1 Unpleasant, ugly. -2 Vulgar, obscene, coarse. -3 Abusive. -लं *n.* 1 Rustic or coarse language, low abuse. -2 (In Rhet.) A fault of composition; using such words as produce in the mind of the hearer a feeling of shame, disgust or inauspiciousness.

अश्लेषा *f.* 1 The 9th Nakshatra or lunar mansion containing five stars. -2 Disunion, disjunction. -Comp. -जः, -भवः, -भूः *m.* A N. of Ketu.

अश्वः *m.* 1 A horse. -2 The number 'seven'. -3 A race of men (horse-like in strength). -श्वौ *m. dual* A horse and a mare. -Comp. -अजनि *f.* A whip. -आधिक *a.* Strong in cavalry, superior in horses. -अध्यक्षः *m.* A guardian of horses; commander of cavalry. -अनीकं *n.* A troop of horsemen, cavalry. -अरिः *m.* A buffalo. -आयुर्वेदः *m.* The veterinary science. -आरूढ *a.* Mounted, sitting on horse-back. -आरोहः *m.* 1 A horseman, rider. -उरस *a.* Broad-chested like a horse. -कुटी *f.* A stable for horses. -कुशल, -कोविद *a.* Skilled in managing horses. -खरजः *m.* A kind of horse mule. -गन्धा *f.* N. of a plant Physalis Flexuosa Lin. (आसंध). -गोयुगः *m.*, -गं *n.* A pair of horses. -गोष्ठं *n.* A stable. -घासः, *m.* A pasture for horses. -चलनशाला *f.* A riding-house. -चिकित्सकः, -वैद्यः *m.* A farrier, a veterinary surgeon. —चिकित्सा *f.* Farriery, veterinary science. —जघन: *m.* A kind of centaur; a creature having his lower limbs like those of a horse. —तर: *m.* A mule. —तरी *f.* A female mule. —दूत: *m.* A riding messenger. —नाय: *m.* One who has the charge of a drove of grazing horses; a horse-herd. —निबंधिक: *m.* A groom, a horse-fastener. —प: *m.* A groom. पालः, -पालकः, -रक्षः *m.* A horse-groom. —बंध: *m.* A groom. —भा *f.* Lighnting. —महिषिका *f.* The natural enmity between a horse and a buffalo. —मुख: *m.* A horse-faced creature; a Kinnara or celestial chorister. —मुखी *f.* A Kinnar woman. —मेध: *m.* A horse-sacrifice. —मेधिक, -मेधीय *a.* Fit for a horse-sacrifice, or relating to it. —युज् *f.* I. N. of a constellation, the head of Aries. -2. The first lunar mansion. -3. The month of Asvina. -4. A chariot having horses. —यूप: *m.* The post to which the sacrificial horse was bound. —रक्ष: *m.* The keeper or rider of a horse, a groom. —रथ: *m.* A carriage drawn by horses. —रत्नं *n.*, -राज: *m.* The best or lord of horses *i. e.* उच्चैःश्रवस्. —लक्षणं *n.* A sign or mark of a horse. —लाला *f.* A kind of snake. —वक्त्र:*m.* =अश्वमुख q. v.; a Kinnara or Gandharva. —वडवं *n.* A stud of horses and mares. (-वडवौ *m.dual.* A horse and a mare.) -वडवा: *m. pl.* Horses and mares. —वह: A horseman. —वार:, वाल:, -वारक: *m.* A horseman, groom. —वाह:, —वाहक: *m.* A horseman, —विक्रयिन् *a.* A horse-dealer. —विद् *a.* I. Skilled in taming or managing horses. -2. Procuring horses. -विद् *m.* I. A jockey. -2. An epithet of Nala. —वृष: *m.* A stallion. —वैद्य: *m.* A farrier. —शंकु: *m.* A pillar to tie a horse. —शाला *f.* A stable. —शाव: *m.* A colt, a foal. —शास्त्रं *n.* A manual or text-book of veterinary science. —शृगालिका *f.* The natural enmity between a horse and jackal. —साद:, -सादिन् *m.* A horseman, a rider, a horse-soldier. —सारथ्यं *n.* Coachmanship, charioteership, management of horses and chariots. —हृदयं *n.* A kind of veterinary science. -2. Horsemanship.

अश्वक: *m.* I A small horse. -2 A hack, a bad horse. -3 A stray horse, one whose owner is not known.

अश्वकिनी *f.* The first Nakshatra or lunar mansion (also called अश्विनी).

अश्वतर: *m.* (री *f.*) I A A female mule.

अश्वत्थ: *m.* I The holy fig-tree. -2 The constellation Asvini. -3 The time indicated or presided over by Asvini. -4 The fruit of the sacred fig-tree. —त्थी *f.* A small fig-tree. -Comp. —फल: *m.* The fruit-season of the holy fig-tree

अश्वत्थक *a.* To be given or to be done when the Asvatha tree bears fruit. —क: *m.* I A debt to be given when the Asvattha tree bears fruits. -2 The Asvattha tree.

अश्वत्थामन् *m.* N. of a celebrated Brâhmana warrior and general on the side of the Kauravas, son of Drona and Kripi.

अश्वस्तन *a.* (*f.* —नी) Of today; not of tomorrow. -2 Making no provision for tomorrow.

अश्वस्तनिक *a.* (*f.* —की) Same as अश्वस्तन.

आश्विक *a.* (*f.* —की) Drawn or conveyed by horses.

अश्विन् *a.* Possessed of horses. *-m.* A cavalier, a horse-tamer. —नौ *m. dual* 1 The two physicians of the gods who are represented as the twin sons of the sun by a nymph in the form of a mare. -2 Two horses. -3 (Astr.) The twins of the zodiac.

अश्विनी *f.* 1 The first of the 27 Nakshatras or lunar mansions (consisting of three stars). -2 A nymph considered as the mother of the Asvins. -Comp. —कुमारौ, -पुत्रौ, -सुतौ *m. dual* The twin sons of Asvini, the sun's wife.

आश्विय *a.* (*f.* —या) Referring to horses.

अश्वीय *a.* (*f.* —या) 1 Belonging or selating to a horse; agreeable to horses. —यं *n.* A number of horses, cavalry.

अषडक्षीण *a.* Not seen by six eyes; known or determined by two persons only, (to the exclusion of a third). —णं *n.* A secret.

अषाढः *m.* 1 The same as आषाढ which is the more usual form of the word. -2 A stick of *palâsha* wood carried by a ब्रह्मचारिन्.

अषाढा *f.* The twentieth and the twenty-first lunar mansions.

अष्टक *a.* (*f.* —का) Consisting of 8 parts; eigth-fold. —कः *m.* One who studies or is acquainted with the eight books of Pânini's grammar. —का *f.* 1 A collection of three days (7th, 8th, and 9th) beginning from the seventh day after the full moon. -2 The 8th day of three months on which the Manes are to be propitiated. -3 A Sraddha to be performed on any of those days. -4 The 8th day of a month. —कं *n.* 1 A whole consisting of 8 parts. -2 The 8 chapters of Panini's sutras, or a study of them. -3 The study of the Sutras. -4 One of the eight divisions of the Rigveda. -5 A group of eight. -6 The number eight. -Comp. —अंगः, *m.*, —गं *n.* A kind of board or cloth for playing with dice on, ('having eight divisions).

अष्टतयं *n.* An aggregate of eight.

अष्टधा *ind.* 1 Eight times. -2 In eight ways. -3 Into eight divisions, or branches.

अष्टन् *num.* always *pl.* (nom. acc. अष्ट-ष्टौ) Eight. (In composition with other numerals and some nouns it often assumes the form of अष्टा as अष्टादशन्, अष्टाविंशतिः, अष्टापद &c.) -Comp. —अक्षर *a.* Consisting of eight letters or parts. —अंग *a.* Consisting of eight parts or members. —गं *n.* 1. The eight parts of the body with which a very low obeisance is performed. -2 The 8 parts of yoga or concentration which are यम, नियम, आसन, प्राणायाम, प्रत्याहार, धारणा, ध्यान and समाधि. -3. The eight materials of worship taken collectively. -4. The eight departments of medical science; (they are:— शल्यं, शालाक्यं, कायचिकित्सा, भूतविद्या, कौमारभृत्यं, अगदतंत्रं, रसायनतंत्रं, and वाजीकरणतंत्रं). -5. The eight parts of a court; 1 the law, 2 the judge. 3 assessors. 4 scribe. 5 astrologer. 6 gold. 7 fire, and 8 water. -6. Any whole consisting of eight parts. —अंगहृदयं *n.* N. of a medical work. —अध्यायी *f.* N. of Panini's grammatical work consisting of 8 Adhyâyas or chapters. —अस्रं *n.* An octagon. —अस्रिय *a.* Octangular. —अह *a.* Lasting for 8 days. —आदिशाब्दिकाः *m. pl.* The first eight grammarians ; they are इंद्र, चंद्र, काशकृत्स्न, आपिशलि, शाकटायन, पाणिनि, अमर, and जैनेंद्र. —कपाल: *m.* A sacrifice in which ghee is offered in eight pans. —कर्ण: *m.* An epithet of Brahman (*m.*). —कर्मन् *m.*, —गतिक: *m.* A king who has 8 duties to perform. —कृत्वस् *ind.* Eight times. —कोण: *m.* An octagon. —गवं *n. sing.* A flock of 8 cows. —गाद *m.* 1. A fabulous animal supposed to have eight legs. -2. A spider. —गुण *a.* Eight-fold. —गुणं *n. sing.* Eight qualities which a Brâhmana should posses ; दया, क्षांति, अनसूया, शौचं, अनायासः, मंगलं, अकार्पण्यं, अस्पृहा. —गुणाश्रय *a.* Endowed with the eight qualities mentioned above. —च (चा) त्वारिंशत् *a.* Forty-eight. —त्रिंशत् (-टा) *a.* Thirty-eight. —त्रिकं *n.* The number 24. -दलं *n.* 1. A lotus having eight petals. -2. An octagon. —दिश् *f.* The eight cardinal points ; पूर्वाग्नेयी दक्षिणा च नैर्ऋती पश्चिमा तथा । वायवी चोत्तरैशानी दिशा अष्टाविमाः स्मृताः॥ —करिण्य: *f. pl.* Eight female elephants living in the eight points. -दिक्पाला: *m. pl.* Eight regents of the cardinal points ; इंद्रो वह्निः पितृपतिः (यमः) नैर्ऋतो वरुणो मरुत् (वायुः) । कुबेर ईशः पतयः पूर्वादीनां दिशां क्रमात् ॥ * अमर को. -दिग्गजा: *m. pl.* The eight elephants guarding the 8 quarters ; ऐरावतः पुंडरीको वामनः कुमुदोऽजनः । पुष्पदंतः सार्वभौमः सुप्रतीकश्च दिग्गजाः ॥ * अमरको. —धातु *n. sing.* The eight metals taken collectively ; स्वर्णं रूप्यं च ताम्रं च रंगं यशदमेव च । शीसं लौहं रसश्चेति धातवोऽष्टौ प्रकीर्तिताः ॥. —पद् —द् (-ष्ट or ष्टा-) *a.* Eight-footed. —पद: (-ष्टा-) *m.* 1 A spider. -2. A fabulous animal called Sarabha. —पद: *m.*, —पदं *n.* Gold. —पदी (-ष्ट- ष्टा-) *f.* 1 A variety of metre, often used in Jayadeva's Gitagovinda. —मंगल: *m.* A horse with a white face, tail, mane, breast and hoofs. —मंगलं *n.* A collection of eight lucky things. —मासिक *a* Occurring once in 8 months. —मूर्ति: *m.* The ' eight-formed ', an epithe of Siva ; the 8 forms being the 5 elements (earth, water, fire, air, and ether), the sun and moon, and the sacrificing priest. —मूर्तिधर: *m.* ' Having 8 forms', Siva. —रत्नं *n.* The eight jewels taken collectively. —रसा: *m. pl.* The 8 sentiments in dramas &c.; शृंगारहास्यकरुणरौद्रवीरभयानकाः । बीभत्साद्भुतसंज्ञौ चेत्यष्टौ नाट्ये रसाः स्मृताः ॥ * काव्यप्र. 4. —रसाश्रय *a.* Embodying or representing the eight sentiments. —विध *a.* Eight-fold ; of eight kinds. —शतं *n.* Eight hundred. —श्रवण:, -श्रवस् N. of Brahman (*m.*).

अष्टम *a.* (*f.* मी) Eighth. —म: *m.* The eighth part —मी *f.* The eighth day in a lunar half month. -Comp. —अंश: *m.* An 8th part. —कालिक *a.* (One) who omits seven meals (*i. e.* full three days and the morning of the fourth) and partakes only of the 8th.

अष्टमक *a.* (*f.* —का) The eighth part.

अष्टमिका *f.* A weight of four Tolas.

अष्टातय *a.* Consisting of eight parts. —य: *m.* A collection of eight things.

अष्टादशन् *a.* Eighteen. -Comp. -अंगः *m.*, -गं *n.* The eighteen parts of medical science. —उपचारः *m.* The eighteen modes of showing respect or worshiping, such as giving a seat, welcoming, &c. —धान्यं *n.* The 18 kinds of corn such as rice wheet &c. —पुराणं *n.* The eighteen Puranas : ब्राह्मं पाद्मं वैष्णवं च शैवं भागवतं तथा । तथान्यन्नारदीयं च मार्कंडेयं च सप्तमं ॥ आग्नेयमष्टकं प्रोक्तं भविष्यन्नवमं तथा । दशमं ब्रह्मवैवर्तं लिंगमेकादशं तथा ॥ वाराहं द्वादशं प्रोक्तं स्कांदं चात्र त्रयोदशं । चतुर्दशं वामनं च कौर्मं पंचदशं तथा ॥ मात्स्यं च गारुडं चैव ब्रह्मांडाष्टादशं तथा ॥. —विद्या *f.* The eighteen kinds of learnings or lores. They are stated thus. अंगानि वेदाश्चत्वारो मीमांसा न्यायविस्तरः । धर्मशास्त्रं पुराणं च विद्या ह्येताश्चतुर्दश ॥ आयुर्वेदो धनुर्वेदो गांधर्वश्चेति ते त्रयः । अर्थशास्त्रं चतुर्थं तु विद्या ह्यष्टादशैव तु ॥. —स्मृतिकारिणः *m. pl.* The eighteen Smritikâras or law-givers of the Aryas.

अष्टावक्रः *m.* N. of a celebrated Brahmana, son of the great sage Kahoda.

अष्ठिः *f.* 1 A stone or kernel. -2 Seed.

अष्ट्रा *f.* A prick or goad for driving cattle ; whip.

अष्ठीला *f.* 1 A round swelling below the navel produced by wind. -2 A globular or round body (in general). -3 A round pebble or stone. -4 Kernel. -5 Seed-corn.

अष्ठीलिका 1 A kind of abscess. -2 A pebble.

अष्ठीवत् *m. n.* The knee, the knee-bone.

अस् 2 P. Defective in non-conjugational tenses, its forms being made from the root भू. 1 To be, live, (showing mere existence.) -2 To be (used as a copula being followed by a noun, or adjective, or adverb, or some other equivalent). -3 To belong to, to be in the possession of, with gen. of possessor. -4 To fall to the share of, to happen to, or befall any one (with gen.). -5 To arise, spring out, occur. -6 To become. -7 To lead or tend to, turn out or prove to be (with dat.). -8 To suffice (with dat). -9 To stay, reside, dwell, live. -10 To take place, happen. -11 To be in a particular relation towards (with loc.). अस्तु well, well let it be ; एवमस्तु, तथास्तु so be it, amen. With अति- To be over, excel, surpass. अनु— To be at hand, reach. आविस्— To arise, spring up, be visible. To be near to or in. परि— 1 To be in the way. -2 To surpass. -3 To pass or spend (time). -4 To pervade. प्र— 1 To be in front of. -2 To preponderate, surpass. प्रति— 1 To be equal to, be a match for. -2 To be a representative of, stand in place of. प्रादुस्— To appear, spring up. व्यति— (Atm. व्यतिहे, व्यतिसे ; व्यतिस्ते) To excel, surpass, be above or superior to, outweigh.

अस् 4 P. (Preceded by a preposition U.) 1 To throw, cast, hurl, discharge, (with loc. of the mark, sometimes with dat. or gen.) -2 drive away, remove. -3. To leave, give up. -With अति To surpass, overpower. —अप 1 To quit, leave, abandon. -2 To refute. —अभि 1 To practise. -2 To do repeatedly. -3 To study. —उद् 1 To throw up, to raise. -2 To turn away from. उपनि- 1 To put near. -2 To trust. -3 To propose, to suggest. -4 To prove. -5 To hint. नि- 1 To cast down, to place down. -2 To abanbon, to leave. -3 To put upon or into -4 To state. -5 To bestow upon. निस्- (निरस्) 1 To give up, drive away. -2 To send back, to ward off, defeat, destroy. -3 To put into the back ground. परा- 1 To refute. परि- 1 To spread. -2 To turn round. -3 To surround. -4 To turn away. -5 To get entangled. परिनि- To stretch. —पर्युद् To exclude, to prohibit. प्र— To throw. वि- 1 To separate, to extricate, to disentangle. -2 To put separately. विनि- To put down. -2 To consign to the care of. -3 To fix on or in. विपरि- To take wrongly. —सम् 1 To join together. -2 To unite into a compound. -3 To take collectively. संनि- 1 To relinquish all worldly concerns and become an anchorite. -2 To put down, place down. -3 To abandon, to give up. -4 To consign to the care of.

अस् 1 U. (असति-ते, असित). 1 To go. -2 To take or receive, seize. -3 To shine (?).

असंयत a. (f. —ता) 1 Unrestrained, not under control. -2 Not tied. —तः m. N. of Vishnu.

असंयमः m. Absence of control or restraint.

असंयुत a. (f. —ता) Uublended, not joined. —तः m. An epithet of Vishnu.

असंविद्वान a. Ignorant, foolish.

असंवृत a. (f. —ता) Uncovered, exposed. —तं n. N. of a hell.

असंव्यवाहित a. (f. —ता) Immediate; without any interval (of time or space).

असंशय a. Free from doubt, certain. -यं ind. Without doubt; undoubtedly, certainly, assuredly.

असंश्रव a. (f. —वा) Out of hearing ; inaudible. असंश्रवे (loc. sing.) Out of the hearing of.

असंश्रावं ind. Inaudibly (with gen. of the person spoken to).

असंश्लिष्ट a. (f. —ष्टा) Not joined or united. —ष्टः m. An epithet of Siva.

असंसृतिः f. Non-return to worldly existence ; absorption into the Supreme Spirit.

असंसृष्ट a. (f.-ष्टा) 1 Not connected. or mixed. -2 Not reunited after partition of property (as an heir).

असंस्कृत a. (f. —ता) 1 Unpolished; not refined or cleansed. -2 Not decorated or adorned. -3 One over whom no purificatory rites have been performed. —तः m. An ungrammatical from (अपशब्द).

असंस्तुत a. (f. —ता) 1 Unknown, not familiar. -2 Unusual, strange. -3 Not in harmony or agreement with.

असंस्थानं n. 1 Absence of cohesion. -2 Disorder, confusion. -3 Want, destitution.

असंस्थित a. 1 Not properly arranged ; irregular. -2 Not collected. -3 Not stationary.

असंस्थितिः f. Same as असंस्थानं.

असंहत a. (f. —ता) Not joined or united ; scattered, loose. —तः m. The Purusha or soul (in Sân.phil.). —तं n. A form of array; open order of troops.

असकृत् *ind* Oftener than once, repeatedly, often and often. Comp. —समाधिः *m.* Repeated meditation. —गर्भवासः *m.* Repeated birth.

असकौ *a.* = असौ This or that ; * शिशुपा.

असक्त (*f.* —क्ता) 1 Not attached, not feeling interested in, indifferent (to). -2 Not entangled. -3 Not united; detached. -4 Not attached to worldly feelings and connections. —क्तं *ind.* 1 Without being excessively attached or addicted to. -2 Incessantly, ceaselessly.

असक्थ *a.* (*f.* —क्था) Thighless.

असखिः *m.* An enemy, adversary.

असगोत्र *a.* (*f.* —त्रा) Not belonging to the same *Gotra* or family.

असंकसुक *a.* Not fickle; steady.

असंकुल *a.* Not crowded; open, clear, broad, (as a road &c.). —लः *m.* A broad road.

असंक्रांत *a.* Not gone over or transmitted. -Comp. —मासः *m.* An intercalary month.

असंख्य *a.* (*f.* —ख्या) Numberless, countless, innumerable.

असंख्यात *a.* (*f.* —ता) Countless, innumerable.

असंख्येय (*f.* —या) *a.* Innumerable. —यः *m.* 1 An epithet of Siva ; of Vishnu. —यं *n.* An exceedingly large number.

असंग *a.* (*f.* —गा) 1 Not attached; free from worldly ties. -2 Not obstructed. —गः *m.* 1 Non-attachment. -2 *Purusha* or soul (in San. phil.)

असंगत *a.* (*f.* —ता) 1 Not united; unaccompanied with. -2 Improbable. -3 Unequal. -4 Unesteemed. -5 Unbecoming; improper. -6 Rude, ill-mannered, unpolished.

असंगतिः *f.* 1 Incongruity, improbability. (In Rhet.) A figure of speech in which the cause and its effect are represented as having different locations. कार्यकारणयोर्भिन्नदेशताया मसंगतिः * साहित्यदर्पण 10. e. g. दशाङ्कनो हरेत्सितां बंधनं तु महोदधेः

असंगमः *m.* 1 Separation. -2 Incongruity.

असंगिन् *a.* (*f.* —नी) 1 Not united or associated. -2 Not attached to the world.

असत् *a.* (*f.* —ती) 1 Not being or existing. -2 Not really existent, unreal. -3 Bad, Wicked, vile, evil. -4 Not manifest. -5 Wrong, improper, false, untrue. —*m.* (न्) Indra. (त्) —*n.* 1 Non-existence, nonentity. -2 An evil, a harm. -3 Untruth, falsehood. —ती *f.* An unchaste woman. -Comp. —अध्येतृ *m.* A Brahmana who reads heterodox works, one who neglects his own Sâkhâ and studies another ; also called शाखारंडः. —आगमः *m.* 1 A heterodox Sastra or doctrine. -2 Acquisition of wealth by unfair or foul means.-3 A foul means itself. —आचार *a.* Following evil practices, wicked. —आचारः *m.* An evil practice. —कर्मन् *n.* A bad deed. —कल्पना *f.* 1 An untrue action, one which never took place. -2 Fabrication of falsehood. —ग्र (ग्रा) हः *m.* A bad trick. -2. A bad opinion, prejudice. -3 A childish desire. —चेष्टितं *n.* Harm, injury. —जनः *m.* A bad, wicked, or contemptible man. —पथः *m.* 1 A bad road.

-2. Evil practices or doctrines. -परि-ग्रहः m. Acceptance of a bad road. —प्रतिग्रहः m.1. Present of bad things. -2 Receiving unfit presents (such as तिल), or from improper persons. —भावः m. 1 Non-existence, absence. -2 A bad or wicked opinion. -वृत्तिः f., —व्यवहारः m. 1 A low or degrading occupation. -2. Wickedness. —हेतुः m. 1. A statement having exceptions (in न्याय). -2. A bad or fallacious *hetu*.

असतायी f. Wickedness.

असत्कारः m. Disrespect, dishonour; bad or inhospitable reception.

असत्कृ (असत + कृ 8 U.) To dishonour ; not to receive hospitably.

असत्कृत a. (f. —ता) 1 Not honoured, disrespected, -2 Done from improper motives. —तं n. A bad or wicked deed.

असत्क्रिया f. See असत्कारः.

असत्ता f. 1 Non-existence -2 Untruth. 3 Wickedness, badness.

असत्त्व a. (f. —त्वा) 1 Without energy or strength. -2 Having no goodness. —त्वं n. 1 Non-existence. -2 Unreality, untruth. -3 Wickedness, badness. -·Darkness.

असत्य a. (f. —त्या) 1 Untrue, false, unreal. —त्यः m. A liar. —त्यं n. 3. Falsehood, untruth. -Comp. —वादिन् a. Speaking falsely, liar. —संध a. Not true to one's promise; false, perfidious.

असदृश a. (f. —शी) 1 Dissimilar, unlike. -2 Unfit, improper, incongruous.

असद्यस् ind. Not immediately ; after delay.

असन् n. Blood (used only in the declension of असृज् after acc. pl.).

असनं n. Throwing, discharging, casting ; (इष्वसनं n. A bow.) —नः m. N. of a tree (पीतसाल).

असंदिग्ध a. (f. —ग्धा) Not doubtful ; distinct, certain, clear. -2 Confident, unsuspected. —ग्धं ind. Certainly, undoubtedly.

असंधि a. 1 Not joined together (as words). -2 Not bound or restrained. —धिः m. Not joining together according to the rules of *Sandhi* (in gram.).

असंनिकर्षः m. 1 Non-perception of objects ; not bringing them to the mind. -2 Remoteness.

असंनिकृष्ट a. (f. —ष्टा) 1 Unperceived. -2 Not near; remote.

असंनिधानं n. 1 Absence, distance. -2 Confidence.

असंनिधिः m. See असंनिधानं.

असंनिवृत्तिः f. Non-return.

असंनिहित a. (f. —ता) 1 Not near ; distant. -2 Placed in a wrong manner.

असपिंड a. (f. —डा) 1 Not connected by offerings of rice-balls. -2 Not connected by blood-relationship.

असभ्य a. (f. —भ्या) Unfit for an assembly ; vulgar, low, obscene, indecent.

असम a. (f. —मा) 1 Uneven, odd (as a number). -2 Mean; contemptible. -3 Unequal (in space, number, or dignity). -4 Having no equal; matchless, unsurpassed. -5 Uneven, not level (as ground). -Comp. —इषुः, —बाणः, —सायकः m. 'One having an odd number of arrows," epithets of Cupid who has five arrows. —नयन, -नेत्र, लोचन *a.* 'Having an odd number of eyes', epithets of Siva, who has three eyes. -वृत्तं *n.* A metre in which the *ganas* are not the same in all lines.

असमंजस *a.* (*f.* —सा) 1 Indistinct, unintelligible. -2 Unbecoming, improper. -3 Absurd, nonsensical, foolish.

असमर्थसमासः *m.* A compound in which the conjunction of words is not as it should be; *e. g.* in अश्राद्धभोजिन्, असूर्यपश्य, अ goes not with श्राद्ध or सूर्य but with भोजिन् or पश्य.

असमवायिन् *a.* (*f.* —नी) Not intimate or inherent ; accidental, separable. -Comp. —कारणं *n.*(In logic) An accidental cause ; not inherent and intimate relation ; गुणकर्ममात्रवृत्तिज्ञेयमथाप्यसमवायिहेतुत्वं यथा तंतुयोगः पटस्य.

असमस्त *a.*(*f.* —स्ता) 1 Incomplete, imperfect. -2 (In gram.) Not joined in a compound. -3 Uncollected. -4 Separate, detached, unconnected (opp. व्यस्त).

असमाप्त *a.* (*f.* —प्ता) 1 Not completed or finished ; left incomplete. -2 Not fully acquired.

असमावृत्तः,-त्तकः, असमावर्तकः, असमावृत्तिकः *m.* A religious student who has not completed the period of his residence with his preceptor.

असमाहारः *m.* 1 Non-recovery of anything. -2 Disunion.

असमीक्ष्य *ind.* Not having (properly) considered. -Comp. —कारिन् *a.* (*f.* —णी) Acting inconsiderately ; imprudent ; not circumspect.

असंपूर्ण *a.* (*f* 1. -र्णा)Not complete. 2 Not whole or entire. -3 Not full as the moon.

असंप्रज्ञात *a.* Not well discerned or distinguished, a kind of समाधि known as निर्विकल्पसमाधि.

असंबद्ध *a.* (*f.* —द्धा) 1 Unconnected, incoherent. -2 Nonsensical, absurd, unmeaning. -3 Improper, wrong.

असंबंधः *m.* Non-connection, absence of any relation or connection.

असंबाध *a.* (*f.* —धा) 1 Not crowded ; open, accessible. -2 Spacious. —धा *f.* N. of a metre consisting of 14 syllables.

असंभवः *m.* 1 Non-existence. -2 Improbability, impossibility.

असंभव्य, असंभाविन् *a.* (*f.* —व्या, -नी) 1 Impossible. -2 Incomprehensible. —व्यं *ind.* In an incomprehensible or extraordinary manner.

असंभावना *f.* 1 Difficulty or impossibility of comprehending. -2 Improbability.

असंभावनीय, असंभाव्य *a.* (*f.* -या,-व्या) 1 Impossible. -2 Inconceivable, incomprehensible.

असंभृत *a.* (*f.* —ता) 1 Not artificial, natural. -2 Not properly nourished.

असंभ्रम *a.* (*f.* —मा) Free from agitation ; composed, cool. —मः *m.* Calmness.

असंमत *a.* (*f*, —ता) 1 Disapproved, not consented to. -2 Disliked, averse. -3 Dissentient, differing from. -Comp. —आदायिन् *a.* (*f.* —नी) Taking without the consent of the possessor, such as a thief (in law).

असंमतिः *f.* 1 Dissent, disagreement. -2 Disapproval ; dislike aversion.

असंमानः *m.* Disrespect, disgrace.

असंमोहः *m.* 1 Absence of infatuation. -2 Steadiness, composure, coolness. -3 Real knowledge, true insight (into a thing).

असम्यंच् *a.* (*f.* —मीची) *a* Improper, incorrect. -2 Imperfect, incomplete.

असलं *n.* 1 Iron. -2 A Mantra used in discharging a missile. -3 Arms.

असवर्ण *a.* (*f.* र्णा) Of a different caste or tribe.

असह *a.* (*f.* —हा) 1 Not enduring; intolerant, impatient. -2 Unable to bear or endure ; (oft. with gen. of object). —हं *n.* The middle of the breast.

असहन: *m.* An enemy. —नं *n.* Intolerance, impatience.

असहनीय, असहितव्य, असह्य *a.* (*f.* -या, -व्या -ह्या) Unbearable, insufferable, intolerable.

असहमान *a.* (*f.* —ना) Impatient.

असहाय *a.* (*f.* —या) 1 Friendless, lonely, solitary. -2 Without companions or assistants.

असहिष्णु *a.* 1 Impatient, unenduring, envious or jealous of.-2 Quarrelsome.

असाक्षात् *ind.* 1 Invisibly, imperceptibly. -2 Indirectly. -Comp. —कार: *m.* Absence, non-perception.

असाक्षिक *a.* (-की *f.*) 1 Having no witness, unattested, unwitnessed. -2 Without a superintendent.

असाक्षिन् *a.* (*f.* —णी) 1 Not an eyewitness. -2 One whose evidence is not admisible (in law). -3 Who is disqualified to attest a legal document.

असाधनीय, असाध्य *a.* (*f.* —या,-ध्या) 1 Not to be accomplished; not proper, easy, or capable of being accomplished. -2 Not capable of being proved. -3 Incurable, irremediable (as a disease or patient).

असाधारण *a.* (*f.* —णा) 1 Not common ; peculiar, special, specific. -2 (In logic) Existing neither in सपक्ष or विपक्ष as a *hetu* ; यस्तूभयस्माद् व्यावृत्तः स त्वसाधारणो मतः. -3 Not to be claimed by any one else; exclusively belonging to one (as wealth &c.); —णं *m.* A fallacy or हेत्वाभास: in Logic. *n.* Speciality, special property.

असाधु *a.* (*f.* -धु: or -ध्वी) 1 Not good ; distasteful, unpleasant. -2 Wicked. -3 Ill-behaved (with loc.) ; -4 Corrupt, not properly formed or *Sanskrit* (as a word). —ध्वी *f.* An unchaste woman. —Comp.-वृत्ता *f.* An unchaste woman.

असाम्प्रतिक *a.* (की *f.*) Inopportune, unseasonable.

असामान्य *a.* (*f.* —न्या) 1 Not common, peculiar, exclusive. -2 Extraordinary. —न्यं *n.* A peculiar or special property.

असांप्रत *a.* (*f.* -ता) Unfit, unbecoming, improper. —तं *ind.* Improperly, unfitly ; oft. used with an adjectival force and means असांप्रत ; विषवृक्षोऽपि संवर्ध्य स्वयं छेत्तुमसांप्रतं • कुमा. सं.2.55.

असार *a.* (*f.* —रा) 1 Sapless, insipid. -2 Without essence, strength, stuff or value. -3 Vain, unprofitable. -4 Weak, feeble, infirm, fragile. -5 Poor. —र: *m.*, -रं *n.* 1 Unessential or unimportant portion.

असि: *m.* 1 A sword. -2 A knife used for killing animals. -3 Breath (श्वास). —सि *ind.* The 2nd pers. sing. of the Present of अस् to be, used as an indeclinable in the sense of 'त्वम्,' thou. -Comp. —असि *ind.* Sword against sword. —गंड: *m.* A small pillow for the cheeks. —जीविन् *m.* A soldier fighting for wages. —दंष्ट्र:, दंष्ट्रक: *m.* The marine monster *makara* or crocodile —दंत: *m.* A crocodile. —धारा *f.* The edge of a sword. —धाराव्रतं *n.* 1 The vow of standing on the edge of a sword. -2 The vow of keeping constant company with a young wife and yet steadily resisting the temptation of sexual intercourse with her. -3 (Hence fig.) Any hopelessely difficult task. —धाव:, —धावक: *m.* An armourer, furbisher. —धेनु:,-धेनुका *f.* A knife. —पत्र: *m.*, —पत्रं *n.* 1 The blade of a sword. -2 A sheath. —पत्र: *m.*, -पत्रक *m.* A sugar-cane. —पुत्रिका, -पुत्री *f.* A knife.-हत्यं *n.* Fighting with knives or swords. —हेति: *m.* A soldier armed with a sword ; a swordsman.

आसिकं *n.* The part of the face between the underlip and the chin.

असिक्निका *f.* A young woman-servant.

असिक्नी *f.* A young maid-servant of the harem.

असित *a.* (*f.* —ता) 1 Not white, dark-blue, black, dark-coloured. -त: *m.* 1 The dark or blue colour.-2 The dark fortnight of a lunar month. -3 N. of the planet Saturn. -4 A black snake. -5 N. of Krishna. -ता *f.* 1 The Indigo plant. -2 A girl attending upon the harem. -3 The river Yamunâ. -Comp. —अर्चिस् *m.* The fire. —अश्मन्, —उपल: *m.* A dark-blue stone ; *lapis lazuli.* —केशा *f.* A woman having black hair —पीत: *m.* 1 Fire. -2 A peacock. —पक्ष: *m.* The dark fortnight of the lunar month. —फलं *n.* The sweet cocoa-nut. —भ्रू *a.* Having black eye-lids. —मृग: *m.* The black antelope. -यवन: *m.* A king of Yavans, enemy of कृष्ण who managed to get him burnt by the fire of the eye of the sage मुचकुंद. असितयवन is also called कालयवन.

असिद्ध *a.* (*f.* —द्धा) 1 Not accomplished. -2 Imperfect, incomplete. -3 Unproved. -4 Unripe, raw, uncooked. -5 Not derivable by inference. —द्ध: *m*. A fallacious *hetu*, one of the five principal divisions of हेत्वाभास or fallacies. It is of three kinds. *viz.* आश्रयासिद्ध which consists in the पक्षत्व property not existing in the पक्ष ; स्वरूपासिद्ध which consists in the so called हेतु not residing in the पक्ष ; and the व्याप्यत्वासिद्ध consists in the साध्यत्व property not residing in the साध्य.

असिद्धि: *f* 1 Incomplete accomplishment; failure. -2 Want of ripeness. -3 Non-accomplishment (in Yoga phil.). -4 (In logic) Conclusion not warranted by the premises.

असु: *m.* 1 Breath, life, spiritual life. -2 Life of departed spirits. -3 Water. -4 Heat. असव: *m. pl.* The five vital breaths or life-winds in the body. असु *n.* 1 Reflection, thought. -2 Heart, mind. -3 Grief. -Comp. —धारणं *n.*, -णा *f.* Sustenance of life; life; existence. -भंग: *m.* 1 The destruction or loss of life. -2 The danger or fear about life. —भृत् *m.* A living being, a creature. -सम: *m.* 1 The husband. -2 A paramour.

असुख *a.* 1 Unhappy, miserable, sorrowful. -2 Not easy (to obtain), difficult. -खं *n.* Sorrow, pain, affliction.

असुप्त *a.* Not asleep. असुप्तदृश् *a.* Not closing the eyes in sleep.

असुर: *m.* I An evil spirit, a demon. -2 The sun. -3 An elephant. -4 The planet राहु. -5 A cloud. -Comp. —अधिप:,-राज्, -ज: *m.* I The lord of the Asuras. -2 An epithet of Bali, grandson of Pralhâda. -आचार्य:,-गुरु: *m.* I N. of the preceptor of the Asuras, Sukrâchârya. -2 The planet Venus. —आह्व *n.* Bell-metal. —द्विष् *m.* An enemy of the Asuras, *i. e.* a god. —रिपु:, —सूदन: *m.* An epithet of Vishnu. —हन् *m.* An epithet of Agni, Indra, Vishsnu &c.

असुरसा *f.* A variety of तुलसी plant.

असुलभ *a.* (*f.* —भा) Not easily attainable, difficult to secure.

असुषु: *m.* An arrow.

असुहृद् *m.* An enemy.

असू *a.* Not bringing forth, barren (as a cow).

असूक्षणं *n.* Disrespect.

असूत, असूतिक *a.* One who has not brought forth, barren.

असूति: *f.* I Non-production, barrenness. -2 Obstruction, removal.

असूय् I U. I To envy, to be jealous of. -2 To murmur, grumble at, be displeased with, scorn, to be angry (with dat. of person or thing). With अभि- To calumniate.

असूयक *a.* I Envious. -2 Discontented, displeased. —क: *m.* A detractor, an envious man.

असूयनं *n.* I Detraction, calumny. -2 Envy, jealousy.

असूया *f.* I Envy, jealousy, -2 Calumny. -3 Anger, indignation.

असूयु *a.* I Envious, jealous. -2 Displeased.

असूर्यंपश्य *a.* Not seeing even the sun; said of the wives of a king who, being shut up in the harem, have no opportunity of seeing the sun; असूर्यंपश्या राजदारा:. —श्या *f.* A chaste and loyal wife.

असृज् *n.* I Blood. -2 The planet Mars. -3 Saffron. -Comp. —दर: *m.* An irregular or excessive menstruation, mœnorrhagia. —धरा *f.* The skin. —धारा *f.* I A stream of blood. -2 The skin. -प:,-पा: *m.* A Râkshasa. —पात: *m.* The falling of blood. —वहा *f.* A blood-vessel; pulse. —विमोक्षणं *n.* Blood-letting, bleeding. —स्रा (स्रा) व: *m.* Bleeding.

असेचन, —नक *a.* Beautiful, charming, lovely.

असौष्ठव: *a.* (*f.* —वा Devoid of beauty or lovelines. -2 Ugly, deformed. —वं *n.* Worthlessness, absence of merit. -2 Deformity, ugliness.

अस्खलित *a.* (*f.* —ता) I Unshaken, permanent. -2 Unhurt, sound. -3 Undeviating, careful.

अस्त *p. p.* (*f.* —स्ता) I Thrown, given up, left. -2 Finished. -3 Despatched. -Comp. —करुण *a.* (*f.* —णा) Merciless. —कोप,-रुष् *a.* Whose anger is pacified. —धी *a.* Foolish. -व्यस्त *a.* Scattered here and there, confused, disordered. —संख्य *a.* Innumerable.

अस्त: *m.* I The setting or western mountain (behind which the sun is supposed to set). -2 Sunset. -3 Setting in general; (fig.) fall, decline. -4 Conjunction of a planet with the sun as in शुक्रास्त, बुधास्त &c. अस्तं followed by गम्, या, इ, प्राप् &c. means I To set, decline in the western horizon. -2 To cease, vanish, be removed, disappear, be at an end. -3 To die. -Comp. —अचलः, —अद्रिः,—गिरिः,—पर्वतः *m.* The setting or western mountain. —अवलंबनं *n.* The resting of a heavenly body on the western part of the horizon, being about to set. —उदयौ *m. dual* Rising and setting, rise and fall. —गमनं *n.* 1 Setting, disappearance. -2 Death, sunset of life.

अस्तकः *m.* Final beatitude, absolution (मोक्ष).

अस्तमनं *n.* Setting (of the sun). -2 The time of setting.

अस्तमयः *m.* 1 Setting (of the sun). -2 Destruction, end, decline, loss. -3 Fall, subjugation. -4 Obscuring, eclipsing. -5 Conjunction (of a planet) with the sun.

अस्ति *ind.* 1 Being, existent, present; as in अस्तिक्षीरा, अस्तिकाय. -2 Often used at the commencement of a tale or narrative in the sense of 'so it is', 'there', or merely as an expletive. -Comp. —कायः *m.* A category or predicament (with the Jainas). —क्षीर *a.* Having milk. —नास्ति *ind.* Doubtfully (Shall I or shall I not?).

आस्तिकः *m.* N. of a sage who saved the serpents from being burnt down in the sacrificial fire of Janamejaya.

अस्तित्वं *n.* Existence.

अस्तिमत् *a.* Possessed of property, wealthy.

अस्तु *ind.* 3rd. pers. sing. imperative of अस् to be, used as an *ind.* Let it be, be it so, well.

अस्तेयं *n.* Abstaining from stealing.

अस्त्यनं *n.* Reproach, blame.

अस्त्रं *n.* 1 A missile; a weapon in general. -2 An arrow; sword. -3 A bow. -Comp. —अ (आ) गारं *n.* An arsenal, armoury. —आघातः *m.* A wound, a cut (made by a weapon). —कंटकः *m.* An arrow. —कारः, —कारकः, —कारिन् *m.* A maker of weapons. —चिकित्सकः *m.* A surgeon. —चिकित्सा *f.* Surgery. —जीवः, —जीविन्, —धारिन् *m.* A soldier, professional warrior. —निवारणं *n.* The warding of a weapon. —मंत्रः *m.* A Mantra to be repeated in discharging or withdrawing a missile. —मार्जः, —शंकः *m.* A furbisher. —युद्धं *n.* Fighting with weapons. —लाघवं *n.* Dexterity in wielding or throwing missiles. —विद् *a.* Skilled in the science of arms. —विद्या *f.*, शास्त्रं *n.*, —वेदः *m.* The art or science of throwing missiles; military science, science of arms. —वृष्टिः *f.* A shower of missiles. —शस्त्रं *n. sing.* All sorts of weapons. —शिक्षा *f.* Military exercise.

अस्त्रिन् *m.* A warrior fighting with missiles.

अस्त्री *f.* 1 Not a woman. -2 (In gram.). The masculine and neuter genders.

अस्त्रीक *a.* Having no wife; without a woman.

अस्थान *a.* (*f.* —ना) Very deep. -नं *n.* 1 A bad or wrong place. -2 An improper place or object or occasion.

अस्थाने *ind.* (Loc. *sing.* of अस्थान), Unseasonably, in a wrong place or on an unworthy object.

अस्थायिन् *a.* (*f.* —नी) Not permanant; transitory, perishable.

अस्थावर *a.* (*f.* —रा) 1 Moveable, moving, not fixed. -2 (In law

Personal, (as property, money, cattle &c. as opposed to land; it is the same as जंगम).

अस्थि *n.* 1 A bone. (अस्थि is changed to अस्थ at the end of some compounds). -2 The kernel or stone of a fruit. Comp. —कृत् *n.*, —तेजस् *n.*, —संभवः, —सारः, —स्नेहः *m.* Marrow —जः *m.* 1 Marrow. -2 The thunderbolt. —तुंडः *m.* 1 A kind of bird whose mouth or beak is as hard as a bone. -2 A bird —धन्वन् *m.* N. of Siva. —पंजरः *m.* 'A cage of bones', a skeleton. —प्रक्षेपः *m.* Throwing the bones of the dead into the Ganges or any holy waters. —भक्षः, —भुक्, —भुजः *m.* 'An eater of bones', a dog. —भंगः *m.* Fracture of the bones. —माला *f.* 1 A string or wreath of bones. -2 A row of bones. —मालिन् *m.* N. of Siva. —योगः *m.* The joining of a broken limb. —शेष *a.* Very lean, reduced to a skeleton. —संचयः *m.* 1 Collecting the bones or the ashes after burning a corpse. -2 A heap of bones. —संधिः *m.* 1 A joint. -2 Uniting a broken bone. —समर्पणं *n.* Throwing the bones of the dead body into the Ganges or holy waters. —स्थूणः *m.* The body.

अस्थिति *f.* 1 Want of firmness or fixity (fig. also.). -2 Want of good manners or decorum.

अस्थिर *a.* (*f.* –रा) 1 Not stable; unsteady, fickle. -2 Uncertain.

अस्पृश्य *a.* (*f.* –श्या) 1 Not to be touched. -2 Impure, unholy.

अस्फुट *a.* (*f.* –टा) Indistinct, obscure. —टं *n.* An indistinct speech. -Comp. —फलं *n.* Indistinct fruit or result. —वाच् *a.* Lisping, speaking indistinctly.

अस्मद् *pron.* It is the base of the first personal pronoun; it is also abl. pl. of the word. -Comp. —विध *a.* Similar or like us.

अस्मदीय *a.* (*f.* –या) Our, ours.

अस्मादृश् *a.* Like us.

अस्मादृश *a.* (*f.* —शी) Like us.

अस्मार्त *a.* (*f.* –र्ता) 1 Not within memory; immemorial. -2 Illegal, not according to the Hindu institutes of Law. -3 Not belonging to the *Smârta* sect.

अस्मि *ind.* Ist pers, sing. Pres. of अस् to be; sometimes used in the sense of अहं 'I'

अस्मिता *f.* Egotism.

अस्रः *m.* 1 A corner, an angle. -2 Hair of the head. —स्रं *n.* 1 Tear. -2 Blood. -Comp. —कंठः *m.* An arrow. —पं *n.* Flesh. —पः *m.* A Rákshasa or goblin. —पा *f.* 1 A leech. -2 A Dâkini or female imp.

अस्राय् Den. A. To shed tears.

अस्रिः *f.* 1 An angle. -2 Ten millions; see अश्रि.

अस्व *a.* (*f.* –स्वा) 1 Indigent, poor. -2 Not one's own.

अस्वक, अस्वकीय, आस्विक *a.* Not one's own; belonging to another.

अस्वतंत्र *a.* 1 Dependent, subject; not one's own master. -2 Docile, humble, tractable.

अस्वप्न *a.* Sleepless, wakeful. —जः *m.* 1 A god, deity. -2 Sleeplessness.

अस्वरः *m.* 1 A low tone. -2 A consonant. -3 Absence of any accent. —रं *ind.* Not aloud; in a low tone.

अस्वर्ग्य *a.* Not securing or leading to heaven.

अस्वाध्यायः *m.* 1 A Brahman who is not invested with the sacred thread and who has not yet commenced his studies. -2 Interruption of studies

अस्वामिक *a.* Unowned, unclaimed. —कं *n.* Unclaimed treasure &c.

अस्वामिन् *a.* 1 Having no right to anything. -2 Unowned, unclaimed. -Comp. -विक्रयः *m.* A sale without ownership (in civil law).

अस्वाम्य *a.* 1 Unowned. -2 Not one's own. -म्यं *n.* Absence of right to property.

अह् 1 A. (*pp.* अंहित) To go. 10 U. (*pp.* अंहित) To shine.

अह *ind.* A particle implying praise, rejection, deviation from custom, separation, resolution &c.

अहंयु *a.* Proud, haughty, selfish. —युः *m.* A warrior.

अहतं *n.* An unwashed or new cloth.

अहन् *n.* (Nom. अहः, अह्नी-अहनी, अहानि, अह्ना, अहोभ्यां &c.) 1 A day (including day and night). -2 Day-time. -3 The sky (as traversed by the sun). -4 A.) Day and night. (At the end of comp. अहन् is changed to अहः,-ह्नं or to अह्नः At the beginning of comp. it assumes the forms अहस् or अहर् *e. g.* सप्ताहः, पञ्चाहः, अपराह्णः, पुण्याहं, अहःपतिः or अहर्पतिः &c.) -Comp. —आगमः (अहरा-) *m.* The approach of day. -आदिः *m.* The dawn. —करः (-हः or -स्करः) *m.* The sun. —गणः, (अहर्गणः) 1 A series of sacrificial days. -2 A month. —दिवं *ind.* Daily, every day, day by day. -दिवि *ind.* Day by day, every day, constantly. -निशं *n.* A day and night, a whole day. —निशं *ind.* Day and night, during the whole day, continually. -पतिः 1 The sun. -2 An epithet of Siva. —बांधवः (अहर्बान्धवः) *m.* The sun. —मणिः (अहर्मणिः) *m.* The sun: —मुखं *n.* The commencement of the day, morning, dawn. -रात्रः *m.* (-त्रं also) 1 A day and night. —शेषः, -षं (-हःशे-) 1 The evening. -2 The last day of defilement.

अहम् *pron* (Nom. Sing. of अस्मद्). I -Comp. -अग्रिका *f.* I; myself. -2 A contest for superiority, rivalry. —अहमिका *f.* Emulation, competition, assertion of superiority. -2 Egotism. -3 Military vaunting. -कारः *m.*, -कृतिः *f.* 1 Egotism, sense of self, self-love considered as an अविद्या or spiritual ignorance in Vedânta phil. -2 Pride, self-consciousness, self conceit, haughtiness. -3 (in San. phil.) One of the 25 elements of creation. -पूर्विका,-प्रथमिका *f.* 1 The running forward of soldiers with emulation; (hence) emulation, competition. -2 Vaunting. -प्रत्ययः *m.* Self-conceit. -भद्रं *n.* Self-conceit, high opinion of one's own superiority. -भावः *m.* 1 Pride, egotism; self-love considered as ignorance (in Vedânta phil.) -वादिन् *a.* Speaking only of oneself, proud, haughty. —मतिः *f.*, -मानः *m.* Same as अहंभावः.

अहल्य *a.* (*f.* -ल्या) 1 Unploughed. -2 Not arable. —ल्या *f.* N. of the wife of Gautama. -Comp. -जारः *m.* Indra. -नंदनः *m.* The sage Satânanda, son of Ahalyâ.

अहल्लिकः *m.* 1 A dead body.

अहह,-हा *ind.* A particle or interjection implying (1) sorrow or regret. (2) wonder or surprise. (3) pity. (4) calling (5) fatigue.

अहार्य *a.* (*f.* -र्या) 1 Not to be taken or stolen away. -2 Not to be shaken. -र्यः *m.* A mountain.

अहिः *m.* 1 A serpent, snake. -2 The sun. -3 The planet Râhu. -4 A traveller. -5 The demon Vritra. -6 A wicked man. -7 A cheat, rogue. -8 The Asleshâ Nakshatra. -9 Water. -10 Earth. -11 Lead. -12 The navel. -13 A cloud. -ही (du.) Heaven and earth. -Comp. —कांतः *m.* Air, wind. -कोषः *m.* The slough of a snake. -छत्रकं *n.* A mushroom. -जित् *m.* 1 N. of Krishna (the slayer of the serpent Kaliya). -2 N. of Indra. -तुंडिकः *m.* A Snake-catcher, conjurer, juggler. -द्विष्,-द्रुह्, -मार,-रिपु, -विद्विष् *m.* 1 N. of Garuda. -2 An ichneumon. -3 A peacock. -4 Indra. -5 Krishna. -नकुलं *n. sing.* Snakes and ichneumons. —नकुलिका *f.* The natural antipathy between a serpent and an ichneumon. -पतिः *m.* Vâsuki. -2 Any large serpent. -पुत्रकः *m.* A kind of boat -फेनः*m.*, —नं*n.* Opium. -भुज् *m.* 1 Garuda. -2 A peacock. -3 Ichneumon. -भृत्*m.*Siva.

अहिंसा *f.* 1 Harmlessness, abstaining from killing or giving pain to others in thought, word, or deed. -2 Security.

अहिंस्र *a. f.* Harmless, innocent.

अहिकः *m.* A blind snake not venomous.

अहित *a.* (*f.* —ता) 1 Not placed, or fixed. -2 Unfit, improper. -3 Hurtful, harmful, injurious. -4 Disadvantageous, evil. -5 Inimical, hostile. —तः *m.* An enemy, a rival. —तं *n.* 1 Damage.

अहिम *a.* (*f.* —मा) Not cold, hot. -Comp. —अंशुः, -करः, -तेजस्—द्युतिः, -रश्मिः *m.* The sun.

अहीन *a.* (*f.* —ना) 1 Unimpaired, whole, entire, all. -2 Not inferior, great. -3 Not deprived of; possessed of. -4 Not outcast or vile. —नः *m.* 1 A sacrifice lasting for several days (—नं also). -2 A large snake. -3 The lord of serpents, Vâsuki. -Comp. —वादिन् *m.* A witness unfit or incapable of giving evidence.

अहीर *m.* A cowherd.

अहु *a.* 1 Narrow. -2 Pervading.

अहुत *a.* (*f.* —ता) Not sacrificed or offered (as an oblation). —तः *m.* Religious meditation, prayer, and the study of the Vedas (one of the five great Yajnas and necessary duties.).

अहृदय *a.* (*f.* —या) 1 Heartless. -2 Absent-minded.

अहे *ind.* A particle implying reproach, regret, separation.

अहेतु *a.* Causeless, spontaneons, involuntary. —तुः *m.* Absence of cause and reason.

अहे (-है-) तुक *a.* Groundless, causeless, without any motive.

अहो *ind.* 1 A particle showing Surprise or wonder; often agreeable; painful suprise. -2 Sorrow or regret in general; ('alas,' 'ah'). -3 Praise. -4 Reproach. -5 Calling out or addressing. -6 Envy or jealousy. -7 Enjoyment, satisfaction. -8 Fatigue. -9 Doubt. अहो नु खलु भोः generally indicates surprise, often agreeable (आश्चर्य); अहो बत shows compassion, pity, regret; satisfaction or admiration (संतोष); addressing, calling; fatigue. -Comp. -पुरुषिका *f.* The same as आहोपुरुषिका.

अह्नाय *ind.* Instantly, speedily, at once.

अह्नय *a.* That can be traversed in a day.

अन्हीकः *m.* A Jaina ascetic.

आ.

आ *ind.* As a particle आ shows (1) assent, (2) compassion, (3) pain, (4) reminiscence. It is sometimes used as an expletive.

As a prefix to verbs आ means 'near', 'towards', 'from all sides', 'around'. When prefixed to roots meaning to go, to give, to carry, आ reverses the meaning, as आया to come, आदा to take, आवह् to bring.

As a prefix to nouns, adjectives. &c. आ shows smallness or diminution, as आकंप a gentle shake, आपांडु whitish.

As a separable adv. or prep. आ forms with nouns compound adverbs implying the limit inclusive or the limit exclusive; sometimes आ is used with a noun in the ablative case and means until inclusively or exclusively.

आ *ind.* An interjection showing (1) Recollection, (2) Determination, (3) Acceptance.

आः *ind.* See आ above.

आकत्थन *a.* (*f.* —ना) Boasting, swaggering.

आकंप: *m.* Shaking, trembling.

आकंपनं *n.* See आकंप:.

आकंप्र *a.* (*f.* —प्रा) Shaking, trembling, agitated.

आकर: *m.* 1 A mine. -2 A multitude. -3 The best, excellent.

आकरिक: *m.* A superintendent of a mine.

आकरिन् *a.* (*f.* —णी) 1 Produced in a mine, mineral -2 Of excellent breed.

आकर्णनं *n.* Hearing, listening.

आकर्ष: *m.* 1 Drawing towards one' self. -2 The drawing of the bow. -3 Attraction, fascination. -4 A die. -5 Playing with dice. -6 A board for playing with dice. -7 An organ of sense. -8 A touch-stone.

आकर्षक *a.* (*f.* —की) Attractive. —क: *m.* A magnet, a load-stone.

आकर्षणं *n.* 1 Pulling, attracting. -2 Seduction.

आकर्षणी *f.* A crooked stick for pulling down flowers, fruits &c.

आकर्षिक *a.* (*f.* —की) Attractive.

आकर्षिन् *a.* (*f.* —णी) Attracting.

आकलनं *n.* 1 Wish, desire. -2 Taking hold of, confinement. -3 Understanding, comprehending, grasping. -4 Reckoning, counting.

आकल्प: *m.* 1 Decoration, ornament. -2 Dress. -3 A disease.

आकल्पक: *m.* 1 Missing, remembering with regret. -2 Fainting. -3 Darkness. -4 A joint, a knot.

आकल्यं *n.* Sickness, disease.

आकष: *m.* A touch-stone.

आकषिक *a.* (*f.* —की) Testing with a touch-stone.

आकस्मिक *a.* (*f.* —की) 1 Causeless, groundless. -2 Unforeseen, unexpected, sudden, accidental.

आकांक्ष् (आ + कांक्ष् 1 U.) 1 To desire, long or wish for, expect. -2 To require, need. -4 (In gram.) To require some word or words to be supplied for the completion of the sense.

आकांक्ष *a.* 1 Desiring, wishing. -2 (In gram.) Requiring some words to complete the sense. -3 Looking at or towards. -4 Purpose, intention. -5 Inquiry. -6 The significancy of a word.

आकांक्षा *f.* 1 Wish, desire -2 (In gram.) One of the three requisites of a sentence, the other two being योग्यता, and संनिधि (or आसत्ति). आकांक्षा is the presence of a word in a sentence necessary to complete the sense of the sentence.

आकांक्षित *p. p.* (*f.* -ता) Desired, wished, inquired ; looked at, wanted, necessary.

आकांक्षिन् *a.* (*f.* —णी) 1. Desiring, wishing, expecting. -2 Asking, inquiring.

आकांक्ष्य *a.* (*f.* —क्ष्या) Desirable. —क्ष्यं *n.* Need of supplying a word or words for the completion of the sense.

आकाय: *m.* 1 The fire on the funeral pile. -2 A funeral pile. -3 Abode, residence.

आकार: *m.* 1 Form, shape, figure; द्विधा- Of two forms or sorts; -2 Aspect, appearance, mien, countenance, आकारसदृशप्रज्ञः * रघुवं 1.15. -3 (Particularly) The expression of the face, as giving a clue to one's inward thoughts or mental disposition तस्य संवृतमन्त्रस्य गूढाकारेङ्गितस्य च * रघुवं 1.20. -4 Hint, sign, token. -5 Identity, oneness. -6 Recognition of identity (in Sân. phil.). -7 The letter आ. -Comp. —गुप्तिः, —गोपनं, —गूहनं Dissimulation, suppressing all outward manifestation of the internal feelings.

आका (क)रणं *n* , -णा *f.* 1 Invitation, calling. -2 A challenge.

आकाल: *m.* The right time.

आकालिक *a.* (*f.* —की) 1 Momentary, transitory. -2 Unseasonable, premature, untimely.

आकालिकी *f.* Lightning.

आकाशः *m.*, -शं *n.* 1 Light, clearness. -2 Vacuity, free space. -3 Sky, atmosphere. -4 Eether or atmosphere considered as the fifth element. -5 Atmosphere considered as one of the nine substances (द्रव्य) by the वैशेषिक philosphers. As such it is the substratum of the quality of sound. -6 Space, place in general. -7 Brahman (*n.*) as identical with ether. -8 A hole. -9 A dot, zero (in Math.). आकाशे in the air ; direction when a character on the stage asks questions to some one not on the stage, and listens to an imaginary speech supposed to be a reply. -Comp. —ईशः *m.* 1 An epithet of Indra. -2 (in law.) Any helpless person (such as a child, a woman, a pauper) who has no other possession than the air. —कक्षा *f.* The horizon. —कल्पः *m.* Brahman. (*n.*) —गः *m.* A bird. —गा *f.* The heavenly Ganges. —गंगा *f.* The celestial Ganges. —चमसः *m.* The moon. —जननी *f.* A casement, loophole, an embrasure (left in castle-walls) ; also —जननिन् —जननिनी. —दीपः,-प्रदीपः *m.* 1 A lamp lighted in honour of Lakshmi or Vishnu and raised on a pole in the air at the Divali festival in the month of Kârtika. -2 A beacon-light. -3 A lantern on a pole. —भाषितं 1 Speaking off the stage, a supposed speech to which a reply is made as if it had been actually spoken and heard. -2 A sound or voice in the air.

—मंडलं *n.* The celestial sphere. —यानं *n.* 1 A heavenly car, a balloon. -2 Moving or travelling through the sky. —रक्षिन् *m.* A watchman on the outer battlements of a castle. —वचनं *n.* 1 See आकाशभाषितं. -2 Superhuman voice from heaven. —वर्त्मन् *n.* 1 The firmament. -2 The atmosphere, air. —वाणी. *f.* A voice from heaven; an incorporeal speech also called अशरिणी वाणी. —सलिलं *n.* Rain; dew. —स्फटिक: *m.* 1 A kind of crystal supposed to be formed in the atmosphere. -2 Hail (करका).

आकिंचनं, आकिंचन्यं *n.* Poverty, want of any possession.

आकीर्ण *a.* (*f.* —र्णा) 1 Crowded, overspread, full of. -2 Scattered.

आकुंचनं *n.* 1 Bending, contraction, compression. -2 Contraction, regarded as one of the 5 *karmans* by वैशेषिक philosophers. -3 Collecting, heaping. -4 Curving. -5 Contortion.

आकुंचित *a.* (*f.* —ता) Contracted, compressed.

आकुंठित *a.* (*f.* —ता) Confounded, rash.

आकुल *a.* (*f.* —ला) 1 Full of, filled with (in general). -2 Overcome, affected or afflicted, smit. -3 Busily or intently engaged or absorbed in. -4 Confounded, agitated, distracted, perplexed, at a loss what to do, undetermined. -5 Dishevelled, disordered (as hair). -6 Wild, dreary. -7 Incoherent, contradictory. —लं *n.* An inhabited place. —*adv.* In bewilderment.

आकुलय् Den. P. To confound, make disordered, agitate.

आकुलित (*f.* —ता) 1 Distressed, confounded, agitated. -2 Entangled. -3 Obscured, blinded, as धूमाकुलित दृष्टि. -4 Overcome or affected as in शोकाकुल, पिपासाकुल. -5 Disordered, deranged. -6 Tilled.

आकूणित *a.* (*f.* —ता) A little contracted.

आकूतं *n.* 1 Meaning, intention, purpose. -2 A feeling, emotion. साकूतं *ind.* Feelingly, meaningly (oft. occurring in plays as a stage-direction). -3 Wonder or curiosity. -4 Wish, desire.

आकूति: *f.* Intention, wish, desire.

आकृ (आ + कृ 8 U, 5 P.) To bring near or towards; to drive near or towards; to drive near or together. —*Caus.* 1 To invite, call, summon. -2 To prompt, incite, propel. -3 To call out boldly, challenge.

आकृति: *f.* 1 Form, figure, shape (of anything). -2 Bodily form, body. -3 Appearance; oft. a good or noble appearance, good form. -Comp. —गण: *m.* A list of words belonging to a certain grammatical rule which does not give every word belonging to that rule, but only specimens *e. g.* स्वरादिगण, चादिगण &c.

आकृतिमत् *a.* (*f.* —ती) 1 Embodied. -2 Self-formed.

आकृष्टि: *f.* 1 Attraction, gravitation. -2 The bending of a bow.

आकेकर *a.* (*f.* —रा) Half-shut, half-closed (eyes).

आकोकेर: *m.* The sign Capricornus (a word of Greek origin).

आक्रंद् (आ + क्रंद् 1 U.) 1 To lament, weep, cry, cry out. -2 To shout, roar. -3 To invoke, call out to.

—*Caus*. 1 To cause to weep or cry. -2 To call out to. -3 To inspire courage by the sound of a drum.

आक्रंदः *m*. 1 Weeping, crying out. -2 Calling, invoking. -3 Sound, war-cry, a cry (in general). -4 A friend, defender. -5 A brother. -6 A fierce combat, war, battle. -7 A place of crying. -8 A king who prevents an ally from aiding another; a king whose kingdom lies next but one.

आक्रंदनं *n*. 1 Lamentation, weeping, cry of lamentation. -2 Calling out.

आक्रंदिक *a*. (*f*. —की) One who runs to a place where cries (of distress) are heard.

आक्रंदितं *n*. 1 A cry, roar. -2 Lamentation, weeping.

आक्रम् (आ + क्रम् 1 U.) 1 To go towards or near, approach. -2 To step or tread upon, enter, take possession of, cover. -3 To occupy, extend over. -4 To attack, invade, seize, conquer, overcome, -5 To surpass, excel, eclipse. -6 To undertake. -7 (A.) To rise, come up (as the sun). -8 To ascend, mount, occupy (as sky, throne &c.). -9 To lie heavily upon.

आक्रमः *m*., —मणं *n*. 1 Coming near, approaching. -2 Falling upon, attacking, attack. -3 Seizing, covering, occupying. -4 Overcoming, obtaining. -5 Spreading or going over, surpassing. -6 Overloading. -7 Might, valour.

आक्रयः *m*. A dealer, petty trader, a pedlar.

आक्रांत *p. p.* (*f*. —ता) 1 Seized, takén possession of, overpowered, defeated, vanquished, overcome, occupied, covered, filled, overcome. -2 Loaded (as with a burden). -3 Surpassed, superseded. -4 Obtained, possessed of. -5 Accompanied, attended. -6 Pained, distressed.

आक्रांतिः *f*. 1 Stepping upon, occupying. -2 Going over or beyond, surpassing, overcoming, pressing upon, loading. -4 Ascending, rising. -5 Might, valour, force.

आक्रामकः *m*. An invader.

आक्री (आ + क्री 9 U.) To purchase, buy.

आक्रीडः *m*., —डं *n*. 1 Play, sport, pleasure. -2 A pleasure-grove, pleasure-garden.

आक्रुश् (आ + क्रुश् 1 P.) 1 To cry, cry out loudly. -2 To abuse, scold, to censure. -3 To curse.

आक्रुष्ट *a*. (*f*. —ष्टा) 1 Scolded, cursed, censured, abused. -2 Sounded, reverberated. —ष्टं *n*. 1 Calling out. -2 A harsh cry or sound, an abusive speech.

आक्रोशः *m*., —शनं *n*. 1 Calling or crying out, loud cry or sound. -2 Censure, blame, curse. -3 An oath

आक्लेदः *m*. Moistening, wetting, sprinkling.

आक्षद्यूतिक *a*. (*f*. —की) Effected or completed by gambling.

आक्षपणं *n*. 1 Fasting, purification by fasting, abstinence.

आक्षपाटिकः *m*. 1 A judge. -2 The superintendent of a gambling house.

आक्षपाद *a*. (*f*. —दी) Taught or propounded by Akshapâda or Gautama. —दः *m*. A follower of the

Nyaya system of philosophy, a logician. —दं *n.* The Nyāya system of philosophy.

आक्षारः *m.* A charge of adultery.

आक्षारणं *n.*, —णा *f.* See आक्षारः.

आक्षारित (*f.* —ता) 1 Calumniated. -2 Accused of adultery. -3 Guilty, criminal.

आक्षिक *a.* (*f.* —की) 1 Relating to gambling. -2 Won at dice. -3 Gambling at dice. —कः *m.* 1 One who uses loaded dice. -2 One who gains by gambling. आक्षिकं ऋणं Debt incurred in gambling. —कं *n.* 1 Money gained by gambling. -2 Gambling debt, money lost at play. -Comp. —पणः *m.* A stake, a wager.

आक्षिप् (आ + क्षिप् 6 U.) 1 To throw down, dash down. -2 To overcome, attract, win over. -3 To strike with a dart, missile &c. -4 To interrupt, cut short. -6 To draw back or withdraw ; draw away, pull off. -7 To drive out of a place. -8 To hang out, expose to view (as a banner). -9 To point to, refer to. -10 To reject, disregard. -11 To object to (as argument). -12 To insult, to blame.-13 To eclipse, obscure. -14 To infer (from circumstances). -15 To say ironically. -16 To pass (as time).

आक्षिप्त *p. p.* (*f.* —प्ता) 1 Cast, thrown down. -2 Overthrown, repulsed. -3 Seized, grasped, snatched away. -4 Drawn, attracted, overpowered ; seduced, enticed. -5. Perplexed, distracted. -6 Insulted, reviled, abused.-7 Equal or equivalent to.

आक्षिप्तिका *f.* A particular song sung by a character while approaching the stage.

आक्षीब *a.* 1 Somewhat drunk. -2 Intoxicated.

आक्षेपः *m.* 1 Reviling. censure, blame. -2 Throwing off, tossing, pulling off, snatching away, throwing away, giving up, withdrawing. -2 Reviling, censure, reproach. -3 Drawing together, attraction, diverting ; power to interest. -4 Distraction, allurement, -6 Laying on, putting in or into (as a colour). -7 Hinting at, reference to, taking to oneself or assuming (as the meaning of another word). -8 An inference. -9 A deposit. -10 An objection or doubt. -11 A deposit. -12 Sustaining, as sound. -13 (In Rhet.) A figure of speech in which there is an apparent denial or suppression of a thing desired to be spoken, with an intention of conveying some special meaning. It is two-fold as when what was meant to be spoken has been spoken or has yet to be spoken ; also called निषेधः This figure corresponds to the English figure paralepsis. वस्तुनो वक्तुमिष्टस्य विशेष प्रतिपत्तये । निषेधाभास आक्षेपो वक्ष्यमाणोक्तगो द्विधा ॥ * साहित्यद. 10. स्मरशरशतविधुराया भणामि सख्याः कृते किमपि । क्षणमिह विश्राम्य सखे निर्दयहृदयस्य किं वदाम्यहं * साहि. द. 10.

आक्षेपकः *m.* 1 A thrower. -2 A detractor, calumniator, accuser. -3 A hunter. -4 (In medic.) Convulsion, spasm.

आक्षेपणं *n.* Throwing, tossing.

आक्षोटः, —डः *m.* A walnut.

आक्षोदनं *n.* Hunting.

आखंडलः *m.* Indra.

आखः, आखनः *m.* A spade, hoe.

आखनिकः *m.* 1 A digger, ditcher, miner. -2 A mouse or rat. -3 A hog. -4 A thief. -5 A spade.

आखनिकबकः *m.* A man who behaves like a hero towards a weak person. -2 A spade, a hoe.

आखरः *m.* 1 A spade. -2 A digger, miner.

आखातः *m.*, —तं *a.* A natural pond or pool of water, bay.

आखानः *m.* 1 A spade, a digger.

आखुः *m.* 1 A mouse, rat, mole. -2 A thief. -3 A hog. -4 A spade. -5 A miser. -Comp. —उत्करः *m.* A mole-hill. —उत्थः *m.* A swarm of rats. —करीषं *n.* A mole-hill. —गः, -पत्रः, -रथः, -वाहनः *m.* Epithets of Ganesa (whose vehicle is a rat. —घातः *m.* A Sudra or a man of low caste and profession. —पाषाणः *m.* A loadstone. —भुज्, -भुजः *m.* A cat.

आखेटः *m.* Hunting, chase. -Comp. —शीर्षकं *n.* A mine, cavern.

आखेटकः *m.* A hunter. —कं *n.* Hunting.

आखेटिकः *m.* 1 A hunter -2 A hound.

आखोटः *m.* The walnut tree.

आख्या (आ + ख्या 2 P.) 1 To tell, say, inform, communicate, narrate (usually with dat. of person sometimes with gen.). -2 To declare, to call, denominate, name.

आख्या *f.* 1 A name, appellation.

आख्यात *p. p.* (*f.* —ता) 1 Said; to be declared. -2 Counted, recited. -3 Made known. -4 Inflected or conjugated. —तं *n.* A verb.

आख्यातिः *f.* 1 Publication. -2 Fame. -3 A name, appellation.

आख्यातृ *m.* 1 One who tells, communicates &c. -2 A teacher, instructor.

आख्यानं *n.* 1 Speaking, declaring, making known, relation, communication. -2 Allusion to some old tale. -3 A tale, story; especially, a legendary story, legend. -4 A legendary work such as the Mahâbhârata. -5 A reply. -6 A differentiating property (भेदकधर्म). -7 A canto of an epic poem.

आख्यानकं *n.* A tale, a short legendary story, an episode.

आख्यापकः *m.* 1 A messenger, courier -2 A herald.

आख्यायिका 1 A species of prose composition, a connected story or narrative. Some writers on Rhetoric divide prose composition into कथा and आख्यायिका and make a distinction between them; they regard Bana's हर्षचरित as an आख्यायिका and कादंबरी as a कथा. -2 Narration (of what is known).

आख्यायिन् *a.* (*f.* —नी) One who tells, informs, or communicates.

आख्येय *pot p.* (*f.* —या) Fit to be communicated or told. शब्दाख्येयं= Fit to be told in words.

आगत *p. p.* (*f.* —ता) 1 Come, arrived. -2 Occurred, happended. -3 Obtained, got. -4 Reduced to, fallen into (a particular state). -5 Living or residing in. —तं *n.* 1 Coming, arrival. -2 Occurrence, event.

आगतिः *f.* 1 Arrival, coming. -2 Obtaining, acquisition. -3 Return. -4 Origin. -5 Accident, chance.

आगंतव्य *pot. p.* Likely to come,

to be arrived ; coming as a matter of course.

आगंतु a. 1 Coming, arriving. -2 Stray. -3 Coming from the outside, external (as a cause &c.). -4 Adventitious, accidental. —तु: m. A new-comer, stranger, guest. -Comp. —ज a. Local (as a disease).

आगंतुक a. (f. —का, -की) 1 Coming of one's own accord ; arriving uninvited. -2 Stray (as an animal). -3 Incidental, accidental ; adventitious. -4 Interpolated, spurious (as a reading). —क: m. 1 An intruder, interloper. -2 A stranger, guest, new-comer. -3 Interpolated reading.

आगम् (आ + गम्, गच्छ् 1 P.) 1 To come, approach. -2 To arrive at, attain, reach. -3 To have recourse to. —Caus. (-गमयति) 1 To cause to come or draw near. -2 To lead onwards, convey. -3 To ascertain, inform oneself about. -4 To learn, acquire, study. -5 (Atm.) To wait for, have patience.

आगम: m. 1 Arrival, approach, appearance. -2 Acquisition. -3 Birth, origin, source. -4 Addition, accumulation. -5 Flow, course, current. -6 A voucher or written testimony. -7 Knowledge. -8 Income, revenue ; increase of property. -9 Lawful acquisition of anything. -10 A traditional doctrine or precept, Sâstra. -11 The study of Sâstras, sacred knowledge or learning. -12 Science, a system of philosophy. -13 The Vedas, the sacred scripture. -14 The last of the four kinds of proof, of the Naiyayiks, otherwise called शब्द or आप्तवाक्य, the Vedas being considered as such. -15 An affix or suffix. -16 The addition or insertion of a letter. -17 An augment (in gram.). -18 Theory (opp. प्रयोग). -19 The mouth of a river. -Comp. —गीत a. Studied, read, examined. —वृद्ध a. Advanced in knowledge, a very learned man. —वेदिन् a. 1 Knowing the Vedas. -2 Learned in Sâstras. —वेदिन् (nom. sing. —वेदी) An epithet of Sankaracharya's preceptor Gaudapâda. —सापेक्ष a. Supported by a voucher.

आगमनं n. 1 Coming, approaching, arrival. -2 Return, returning. -3 Acquisition, getting into. -4 Arising, birth. -5 Approaching a woman for sexual intercourse.

आगस् n. 1 Sin. -2 Fault, offence. -Comp. —आगस्कृत a. Giving offence, committing a mischief.

आगस्ती f. The South.

आगस्त्य a. 1 Southern. -2 Pertaining to Agastya.

आगाध a. (f. —धा) 1 Very deep or unfathomable (fig. also). -2 Difficult to obtain.

आगामिक a. (f. —की) 1 Relating to the future time. -2 Impeding, arriving.

आगामुक a. 1 Coming, arriving. -2 Future.

आगारं n. A house, dwelling. -Comp. —गोधिका f. A small lizard. —दाह: m. Setting a house on fire. —दाहिन् a. m. An incendiary. —धूम: m. 1. Smoke issuing from a house.

आगुर्, —आगू: f. Assent, agreement, promise

आगु (-गू-) रणं n. Recitation of the

'Agur'. -2 A concealed suggestion.

आग्निक *a.* (*f.* —की) Belonging to fire, belonging to the sacrificial fire.

आग्निध्र *n.* 1 The place where the sacrificial or sacred fire is kindled. -2 The duty of the priest who kindles the sacred fire. —ध्रा *f.* Care of the sacred fire. —ध्रः *m.* The priest who kindles the sacred fire.

आग्नेय (*f.* —यी) 1 Belonging to Agni. -2 Fire. -3 Offered or consecrated to Agni. -4 Similar to fire (as an insect). -5 Increasing the fire in the stomach ; stimulating digestion. -6 Kindling the fire (as ghee &c.). -7 Belonging to Agnáyi. —यः *m.* 1 An epithet of Skanda or Kârtikeya. -यी *f.* 1 N. of the wife of Agni. -2 The south-east quarter (presided over by Agni). —यं *n.* 1 The lunar mansion called Krittikâ. -2 Gold -3 Blood. -4 Lac, the red animal dye. -5 Ghee. -6 A missile presided over by Agni.

आग्रभोजनिकः *m.* A Brâhmana entitled to occupy the foremost seat at a dinner.

आग्रयणः *m.* The first Soma libation at the Agnishtoma sacrifice.

आग्रह् (आ + ग्रह् 9 U.) 1 To seize, catch.-2 To draw tight (as the reins). -3 To persist in.

आग्रहः *m.* 1 Seizing, taking. -2 Attack -3 Determination, strong attachment ; insisting. -4 Favour, patronage.-5 Surpassing, surmounting. -6 Moral power, courage.

आग्रहायणः *m.* N. of the month of मार्गशीर्ष.

आग्रहायण (-णि-) कः *m.* The month of मार्गशीर्ष.

आग्रहायणी *f.* The full moon day of मार्गशीर्ष. -2 N. of a constellation called also मृगशिरस्.

आग्रहारिक *a.* (*f.* —की) One who appropriates to himself an अग्रहार (which is an endowment of land conferred upon a Brâhmana).

आघट्ट् (आ + घट्ट् 10 P.) 1 To strike against, touch. -2 To move.

आघट्टना *f.* 1 Moving, shaking, striking against. -2 Friction, contact.

आघर्षः *m.*, -र्षणं *n.* Rubbing, friction, striking against. —र्षणी *f.* A brush, rubber.

आघाटः *m.* 1 Killing, striking. -2 A musical instrument. -3 A cymbal or rattle. -4 Boundary, limit

आघातः *m. m.* 1 Striking, a blow, a stroke ; a wound. -2 Killing. -3 A misfortune. -4 A slaughter-house. -5 Retention of urine. (मूत्राघात).

आघारः 1 Sprinkling (in general). -2 Sprinkling clarified butter upon the fire at certain sacrifices -3 Ghee, clarified butter.

आघुष् (आ + घुष् 1 P.) 1 To proclaim, cry aloud, declare. -2 To praise. —10 P. or —*Caus.* 1 To make a noise, to cause to sound. -2 To proclaim, announce publicly. -3 To complain continually.

आघूर्ण् (आ + घूर्ण् 1 A., 6 P.) 1 To roll, stagger, whirl, toss about. -2 To swim, roll (as eyes).

आघूर्णनं *n.* Rolling, tossing about, whirling round, swimming.

आघृणि *a.* Bright. —णिः *m.* The sun.

आघ्रा (आ + घ्रा 1 P.) 1 To smell at. -2 To kiss, touch (with the nose) as the head. -3 (Fig.) To attack, devour, seize upon; to smite, affect.

आघ्राणं *n.* 1 Smelling. -2 Satisfaction, satiety.

आघ्रात *p. p.* (*f.* —ता) 1 Smelt, scented, touched. -2 Satisfied. -3 Surpassed.

आघ्रातनं *n.* 1 Striking, killing. -2 A slaughter-house.

आंकृति *f.* A musical instrument, a tabor.

आंग *a.* (*f.* —गी) 1 Bodily, corporeal. -2 (In gram.) Relating to the base (अंग). -3 Having limbs or parts. -4 Belonging to a portion of the Vedas. —गं *n.* A delicate body.

आंगारं *n.* A multitude of fire-brands, charcoal.

आंगिक *a.* (*f.* —की) 1 Bodily, corporeal. -2 Gesticulated, expressed by bodily actions. —क: *m.* A player on a tabor or drum.

आंगिरस: *m.* 1 N. of Brihaspati, son of Angiras. -2 Descendants of Angiras (pl.).

आचक्ष् (आ + चक्ष् 2 A.) 1 To speak, announce, declare, teach, tell, say, narrate (usually with dat. of person; sometimes with acc.). -2 To name, call, say.

आचक्षुस् *m.* A learned man.

आचतुरं *ind.* Till the fourth generation.

आचम् (आ + चम् 1 P.) 1 To sip, lick, lap, drink (a small quantity). -2 To rinse the mouth. -3 To lick up, dry or drink up, absorb.

आंचम: *m.* Rinsing the mouth, sipping.

आचमनं *n.* 1 Rinsing the mouth, sipping water before religious ceremonies, before and after meals &c. -2 The water used for rinsing the mouth. -3 Gargling the throat.

आचमनकं *n.* 1 The water used for sipping. -2 A spitting pot (Mar. पिकदाणी).

आचमनीय] *pot. p.* (*f.* —या) Used for rinsing the mouth. —यं *n.* Water used for rinsing the mouth; a gargle.

आचाम: *m.* 1 Sipping water; rinsing the mouth. -2 The water or foam of boiled water (Mar पेज).

आचामक *a.* Rinsing the mouth.

आचामनकं *n.* A spitting pot.

आचय: *m.* 1 Collecting, gathering. -2 A collection, heap; plenty.

आचर् (आ + चर् 1 P.) 1 To act, practise, do, perform. -2 To act or behave towards (with loc). -3 To act, proceed, behave, intrans.). -4 To treat. -5 To observe the usual formality. -7 To wander over or about; frequent, resort to, to follow.

आचरणं *n.* 1 Practising, doing, performing, following, observing. -2 Conduct, behaviour; example (opp. precept). -3 Usage, practice. -4 A rite or rule of conduct.

आचरणीय, आचरितव्य, आचर्य *pot. p.* (*f.* —या, —व्या, —र्या) 1 To be done, performed, followed, observed. -2 Deserving, fit, right.

आचरित. *p. p.* (*f.* —ता) 1 Done, observed, performed, practised, as a rite or usage &c. -2 Usual, customary. -3 Enjoined, fixed by rule. —तं *n.* Conduct, behaviour.

आचार: *m.* 1 Conduct, behaviour,

manner of action or of conducting oneself. --2 Good conduct or behaviour. -3 A custom, usage, practice. -4 An established usage, customary law, institute or precept -5 Any customary observance or duty: form, formality. —Comp. —दीपः *m.* A lamp waved about a person as a formality and token of auspiciousness. —धूमग्रहणं *n.* Inhaling smoke as a customary rite. —भेदः *m.* Difference in the customary law. —भ्रष्ट,--पतित *a.* (*f.* —ष्टा,--ता) Fallen from established usages or rules of conduct. —लाजाः *m. pl.* Fried grain customarily showered upon a king or other important personage as a mark of respect. —वेदि *f.* Aryâvarta, the sacred region of the Aryas.

आचारवत् *a.* Well-conducted, virtuous.

आचारिक *a.* (*f.* —की) Conformable to rule or practice, authorized, —कं *n.* Rules for the preservation of health; hygiene, regimen, diet.

आचार्यः *m.* 1 A teacher or preceptor (in general). -2 A spiritual guide or preceptor, -3 One who propounds a particular doctrine. -4 Learned, venerable, used like a title e. g. शंकराचार्य, माधवाचार्य &c. --5 An adviser or preceptor at a sacrifice &c. -6 An epithet of Drona. —र्या *f.* A female preceptor, a spiritual preceptress. —Comp. —उपासनं *n.* Waiting upon or serving the spiritual preceptor. —मिश्र *a.* Venerable, honourable.

आचार्यकं *n.* 1 Instruction, tuition, teaching (lessons &c.). --2 The proficiency of a holy teacher.

आचार्यानी *f.* The wife of an आचार्य or holy preceptor.

आचि (आ + चि 5 U.) 1 To accumulate, heap up, collect. --2 To fill or cover with, spread.

आचिख्यासा *f.* The desire of communicating something.

आचित *p. p.* (*f.* —ता) 1 Filled, loaded with, covered with. --2 Tied, strung, woven; inlaid, set (as with gems). --3 Collected, accumulated, heaped. --4 Spread, diffused. —तः *m.* 1 A cart-load. --2 (*n.* also) A measure of 80,000 Tolas.

आच्छद् (आ + छद् 10 P.) 1 To cover (in general). --2 To hide. --3 To clothe, dress.

आच्छादः *m.* Cloth, clothes.

आच्छादक *a.* Covering, concealing.

आच्छादनं *n.* 1 Covering, concealing, hiding. --2 A covering, a mantle, a cloak, sheath. --3 Cloth, clothes. --4 Disappearance. --5 The wooden frame of a roof.

आच्छिद् (आ + छिद् 7 U.) 1 To cut off or away, tear, break. --2 To snatch away, remove, take away, cut off, exclude. --3 To disregard, take no notice of (as words). --4 To take out, extract, draw or pull off.

आच्छुरित *a.* (*f.* —ता) 1 Mixed, blended with. --2 Scratched. --3 Irritated. -तं *n.* 1 Making a noise with the finger-nails by rubbing them on one another. --2 A horse-laugh.

आच्छुरितकं *n.* 1 A scratch with a finger-nail. --2 A horse-laugh.

आच्छेदः *m.*, —दनं *n.* 1 Cutting off, exclusion. --2 Taking away by force, snatching away.

आच्छोटनं *n.* Cracking the fingers.

आच्छोदन *n.* Hunting, chase

आज *a.* (*f.* —जी , About, belonging to, or produced by, goats. —जः *m.* A vulture. —जं *n.* Ghee or clarified butter.

आजकं *n.* A flock of goats.

आजकार: *m.* Siva's bull.

आजगवं *n.* 1 The bow of Siva. --2 A strong bow like that of Siva.

आजननं *n.* High birth or origin; famous or well-known origin.

आजन्म,-न्मं *ind.* From or ever since birth.

आजान: *m.*, —नं *n.* Origin, original cause.

आजानदेव: *m* A god from birth.

आजानु *ind.* Up to the knees.

आजानेय *a.* (*f.* —यी) 1 Of good breed (as a horse). --2 Of noble birth; fearless, undaunted. —यः *m.* A well-bred horse.

आजि: *m.*, *f.* 1 A battle, fight, combat. -2 A match. -3 Battle-field, race-course. -4 Limit, boundary. --5 A road, way (*m.*). --6 An instant (*m.*). -7 Abuse, invective. —Comp. —अंत: *m.* The goal in a race-course.

आजिगीषु *a.* Ambitious, wishing to excel or surpass.

आजीव: *m.*, --वनं *n.* 1 Livelihood, subsistence, maintenance; means of livelihood. -2 Profession, the means of maintaining oneself. —वः *m.* A Jaina beggar.

आजीवक: *m.* A beggar.

आजीवनिक: *m.* One who serves simply to earn livelihood (without any higher ambition of securing fame or high position.

आजीविका *f.* Profession, means of subsistence.

आजीविन् *m.* A particular kind of beggar (एकदंडिन्).

आजीव्य *pot. p.* (*f.* —व्या) 1 To be practised (as a profession). --2 Fit for or affording a livelihood. —व्यं *n.* A means of subsistence.

आजुर् *f.*, -आजू: *f.* 1 Working without wages. --2 A servant working without wages.

आज्ञप्ति: *f.* An order, injunction, command.

आज्ञा (आ + ज्ञा 9 P.) To know, understand, learn, ascertain, notice, perceive. —*Caus.* (—ज्ञापयति) 1 To order, command, direct. -2 To assure.

आज्ञा *f.* 1 An order, command. -2 Permission, allowance. -Comp. —अनुग, —अनुगामिन्, --अनुयायिन्, —अनुवर्तिन्, --अनुसारिन्, --संपादक, -वह *a.* Obedient, submissive. —कर, ---कारिन् *a* Obeying or executing orders, obedient. --कर: *m.* A servant. —करणं, --पालनं *n.* Obedience, execution of commands. —पत्रं *n.* An edict, written order. —प्रतिघात:, --भंग: *m.* 1 Disobedience, insubordination. -2 Rebellion, disloyalty. —विधेय *a.* Obedient to commands; ready to execute master's commands. मुक्त्वाचापमिहैव तिष्ठतु भर्तानाज्ञाविधेया वयं • भास पं. रा.

आज्ञापनं *n.* 1 Ordering, commanding. --2 Making known.

आज्यं *n.* 1 Clarified butter, ghee. -Comp.—पात्रं *n.*, —स्थाली *f.* A vessel. or dish to hold clarified butter.—भुज् *m.* 1 An epithet of Agni. -2 A god, deity.

आंचनं *n.* Partial extraction of thorns, arrows and the like from the body.

आंछनं *n.* Setting (a bone or leg).

आंजन *a.* (*f.* —नी) Anointing or belonging to ointment. —नं *n.* 1 Ointment, especially for the eyes. -2 Fat. —नः *m.* N. of Maruti, or Hanumat.

आंजनिक्यं *n.* Materials used in preparing ointments.

आंजनी *f.* Ointment, especially for the eyes. —Comp. —कारी *f.* A woman who anoints or prepares ointments.

आंजनेयः *m.* N. of Maruti.

आंजलिकः *m.* A crescant-shaped arrow.

आंजलिक्यं *n.* Folding the hands in supplication.

आंजिनेयः *m.* A kind of insect, a kind of lizard.

आटरूषः *m.* N. of a tree, (Mar. अडुळसा).

आटविकः *m.* A forester,a wood-man-an inhabitant of a forest.

आटिः, आटी, आडिः, आडी *f.* 1 A kind of bird (शरारि). -2 A sort of fish. —Comp. —मुखः *m.*, —खं *n.* A surgical instrument used in bloodletting.

आटीकनं, आटीकंकं *n.* The leaping motion of a calf.

आटीकरः *m.* A bull.

आटोपः *m.* 1 Pride, self-conceit, arrogance. साटोपं Proudly, in a stately or majestic manner, with impatience : with hauter ; with an air of indignation or pride. -2 Swelling, spreading, expanding, puffing. -3 Flatulence (in the belly).

आडंबरः *m.* 1, Pride, arrogance. -2 Show ; means, external appendage. -3 The sounding of a trumpet as a sign of attack. -4 Commencement. -5 Fury, anger, passion. -6 The roaring of clouds or of elephants. -8 The eyelid. -9 A drum used in a battle. -10 (Hence) A charge sounded by musical instruments ; the din or uproar of the battle. —रं *n.* Rubbing and kneading the body.

आडिः *f.* See आटिः.

आढकः *m*, —कं *n.* A measure of grain. —की *f.* 1 A kind of pulse. -2 A kind of fragrant earth. (mar. गोपीचंदन).

आढकिक, आढकीन *a.* Measuring an आढक.

आढ्य *a.* (*f.* —ढ्या) 1 Rich, wealthy; Rich in, abounding in, possessing abundantly, (with instr.). -3 Abundant, copious. —Comp. —चर *a.* (*f.* -री) Formerly opulent.

आढ्यंकरणं *n.* The means of enriching ; wealth, prosperity.

आढ्यंभविष्णु,-भावुक *a.* Becoming rich or eminent.

आणक *a.* (*f.* —का) Low, inferior, vile.

आणवं *n.* Exceeding smallness or minuteness.

आणिः *m.*, *f.* 1 The pin of the axle of a cart ; the linch-pin. -2 The part of the leg just above the knee. -3 The corner of a house. -4 A boundary, limit. -5 The edge of a sword.

आंडः *m.* An epithet of Hiranyagarabha or Brahman(*m.*). —डं *n.* A multitude of eggs, brood.

आंडीर (*f.* —रा) 1 Having many eggs. -2 Grown up, full-grown (as a bull).

आतंकः *m.* 1 Disease, sickness of the body. -2 Fever. -3 Pain, affliction (of the mind). -4 Doubt, uncertainty. -5 Fear, fright, terror.

-6 The sound of a drum or tabor.

आतंचनं *n.* 1 Casting butter-milk into heated milk to turn it. -2 Curdled milk. -3 A sort of whey. -4 Gratifying, satisfying. -5 Danger, calamity.

आतत *p. p.* (*f.* ता) 1 Spread, extended. -2 Stretched (as a bow-string).

आततायिन् *a.* 1 Endeavouring to kill some one; a desperado. -2 Any one who commits a heinous crime.

आतन् (आ + तन् 8 U.) 1 To extend, stretch over, cover; pervade, penetrate. -2 To spread, diffuse. -3 To cause, produce. -4 To bring to pass, do, perform. -5 To stretch (as a bow).

आतनं *n.* 1 Spreading, expanding. -2 Sight, view.

आतपः *m.* 1 Heat (of the sun, fire, &c.), sunshine. -2 Light. —Comp. —अत्ययः *m.* Passing of the sun's heat; sunset. —अभावः *m.* Shadow. —उदकं *n.* Mirage. —त्रं, —त्रकं *n.* An umbrella. —लंघनं *n.* The sun-stroke. —वारणं *n.* An umbrella, parasol. —शुष्क *a.* Dried in the sunshine.

आतपनः *m.* N. of Siva.

आतरः, -आतारः *m.* Fare for being ferried over a river; passage-money, freight.

आतापिः *m.* N. of a demon.

आतापि (-यि-) *m.* N. of a bird, a kite.

आतिथेय *a.* (*f.* यी) 1 Hospitable (as a man). -2 Proper for, or suited to, a guest; intended for a guest. —यं *n.* Hospitality. —यी *f.* Hospitality.

आतिथ्यः *m.* A guest. —थ्यं *n.* 1 Hospitable reception; hospitality.

आतिदेशिक *a.* (*f.* —की) (In gram.) Connected with अतिदेश q. v.

आतिरे (-रै-) क्यं *n.* Superfluity, excess, abundance.

आतिवाहिक *a.* Employed to convey to the other world. —कः An epithet of the सूक्ष्मशरीर (in San. phil.)

आतिशय्यं *n.* Excess, abundance, large quantity.

आतिष्ठं *n.* Being a universal ruler (अतिष्ठ).

आतुः *m.* A raft, float.

आतुरः *a.* (*f* —रा) 1 Hurt, injured. -2 Affected by, tormented, afflicted. -3 Sick (in body or mind). -4 Eager. -5 Weak, feeble, —Comp. —शाला *f.* An hospital —संन्यासः *m.* A kind of संन्यास (taken by a person when sick and grown hopeless of life).

आतृप्यः *m.* A kind of tree, the custard apple tree. (Mar. सीताफळ). —प्यं *n.* The fruit of the tree.

आतोदिन् *a.* Striking, pushing, pricking.

आतोद्यं,-द्यकं *n.* A musical instrument. प्रवर्त्यतां आतोद्यविन्यासादिका विधयः॰ वेणी स. १ सममातोद्यशिरोनिवेशितां ॰ रघुवं. 8. 34.

आत्त *a.* (*f.* -त्ता) 1. Taken, accepted. -2 Attracted. -3 Extracted. -Comp. —गंध *a.* 1 One whose pride is humbled; one who is defeated. -2 (A flower) already smelt. —गर्व *a.* Humiliated, disgraced. —मनस्क *a.* Whose mind is transported.

आत्मकीय, आत्मीय *a.* Pertaining oneself, one's own.

आत्मन् *m.* 1 The soul. -2 Self, oneself; (used reflexively for all three persons and in the singular number, masculine gender, whatever be the genderor number of the noun to which it refers.) -3 The Supreme Soul, Brahman (*n.*) -4 Essence, nature. -5 Spirit, vitality, courage. -6 The natural temperament or disposition. -7 Mind, intellect. -9 The understanding. -10 Thinking faculty, the faculty of thought and reason. -11 Form, image. -12 Effort. -13 A son. -14 The sun. -15 Fire. -16 Wind, air. –Comp. -अधीन *a.* 1. Independent. -2 Sentient, existing. —अधीन: *m.* 1 A son. -2 A wife's brother. -3 The jester or विदूषक (in dramatic literature). —अपहार: *m.* Concealing oneself. —अपहारक: *m.* An impostor, a pretender. —आदिष्ट: *m.* A treaty dictated by the party wishing it himself. —आराम *a.* 1 Finding pleasure in self. -2 Seeking spiritual knowledge. -आशिन् *m.* A fish. —आश्रय: *m.* Self-dependence. -ईश्वर *a.* Self-possessed, master of self. —उद्भव: *m.* 1 A son. -2 Cupid. —उपजीविन् *m.* 1 One who lives by his own labour. -2 A day-labourer. -3 One who lives by his wife. -4 An actor, public performer. —काम *a.* 1. Loving oneself, proud. -2 Loving Brahman (*n.*) or the Supreme Spirit only. -गतं *ind.* Aside to oneself. It is the same as स्वगतं. (opp. प्रकाशं aloud), (a stage-direction in dramas). —गुप्ति: *f.* A cave, the hiding place of an animal, —ग्राहिन् *a.* Selfish, greedy. —घात: *m.* 1 Suicide. -2 Heresy. —घातक:,-घातिन् *m.* 1 A suicide. -2 A heretic. -घोष: *m.* 1 A Cock -2 A crow. —ज:,-जन्मन् —जात:, -प्रभव:, -संभव: *m.* 1 A son. -2 Cupid. -3 A descendant. —जा *f.* 1 A daughter. -2 The reasoning faculty, understanding. —जय: *m.* Victory over oneself; self-denial or abnegation. —ज्ञ:,-विद् *m* A sage; one who knows himself. —ज्ञानं *n.* 1 Self-knowledge. -2 Spiritual knowledge. -3 True wisdom. -तत्त्वं *n.* The true nature of the soul or the Supreme Spirit. -त्याग: *m.* 1. Self-sacrifice. -2 Suicide. —त्यागिन् *m.* 1 A suicide. -2 A heretic. —त्राणं *n.* 1 Preservation of self. -2 A body-guard. —दर्श: *m.* A mirror. —दर्शनं *n.* 1 Spiritual knowledge, true wisdom. —दानं *n.* Self-sacrifice, resigning oneself. —देवता *f.* A tutelary deity. —द्रोहिन् *m.* 1 A suicide. —नित्य *a.* Being constantly in the heart, greatly endeared to oneself. —निवेदनं *n.* Offering oneself (as a living sacrifice to the deity). —निष्ठ *a.* One who constantly seeks for spiritual knowledge. —बंधु:, -बांधव: *m.* 1 One's own kinsman; they are three *i. e.* mother's sister's son, father's sister's son, and mother's brother's son. -2 The soul, the self. —बोध: *m.* 1 Spiritual Knowledge. -2 Knowledge of self. —भू: *m.*, -योनि: 1 N. of Brahman (*m.*) -2 N. of Vishnu. -3 N. of Siva. -4 Cupid, god of love. -5 A son. —भू: *f.* A daughter. -2 Talent, understanding. —भूत: *m* A son. -2 Cupid. —भूता *f.* A daughter. -2 Talent. —मात्रा *f.* A portion of the Supreme Spirit. —याजिन् *m.* A learned man who studies his own nature and that of the soul (of others, with a view to attain final beatitude.. —योनि: *m.* 1 Brahmán (*m.*) -2 Vishnu. -3 Siva. -4 Cupid. —रक्षा *f.* Self-protection. —लाभ: Birth, production, origin. —वंचना *f.* Self-delusion; self-deception. —विद् m. 1 A wise man, sage. -2 N. of Siva. —विद्या f. Spiritual knowledge. —वीरः m. 1 A son. -2 Wife's brother. -3 A jester (in dramas). —वृत्तिः f. 1 Action as regards oneself ; one's own state or circumstance. -2 Practising one's own duties or occupation. —शक्तिः f. One's own power or ability. आत्मशक्त्या To the best of one's power. —संयमः m. Self-restraint. —संभवः, -समुद्भवः m. 1 A son. -2 Cupid. -3 An epithet of Brahmâ, Vishnu, or Siva. -4 The Supreme Being (परमात्मन्). —संभवा f. 1 A daughter. -2 Understanding, intellect. —संपन्न a. 1 Self-possessed. -2 Talented, intelligent. —हननं n., -हत्या f. Suicide.

आत्मनीन a. (f. —ना) 1 Belonging to one-self ; one's own. -2 Beneficial to oneself. -3 Existent, sentient. —नः m. 1 A son. -2 A wife's brother. -3 A jester (in dramas).

आत्मनेपदं n. 1 A voice for oneself, one of the two voices in which roots are conjugated in Sanskrit. -2 The terminations of this voice.

आत्मवत् a. 1 Self-possessed. -2 Composed, prudent, wise. -*ind.* Like oneself.

आत्मसात् *ind.* In one's own possession, one's own.

आत्यंतिक a. (f. -की) 1 Continual, uninterrupted, everlasting. -2 Excessive, abundant. -3 Supreme, absolute. -Comp. —प्रलयः m. The grand or universal destruction of the world.

आत्ययिक a. (f. -की) 1 Destructive, -2 Painful, unpropitious. -3 Pressing, urgent.

आत्रेय a. (f. -यी) Descended or sprung from Atri. —यः m. 1 A descendant of Atri. -यी f. 1 A female descendant of Atri. -2 The wife of Atri. -3 A woman in her courses (रजस्वला). -4 Any woman of the Brâhmanical order.

आत्रेयिका f. A woman in her courses.

आथर्वण a. (f. -णी) Relating to the Atharvaveda. —णः m. 1 A Brahmana knowing or studying the Atharvaveda. -2 A descendant of Atharvan. -4 The Atharvaveda itself.

आथर्वणिकः m. A Brâhmana who has studied the Atharvaveda.

आदंशः m. 1 A bite. -2 A tooth.

आदत्त, आत्त p. p. (f. —त्ता, —त्ता) 1 Taken, received, assumed, accepted. -2 Undertaken, begun. -3 Attracted, extracted. -Comp. —दंष a. 1 Having one's pride humbled, defeated. -2 Already smelt (as a flower). —गर्व a. Humiliated, insulted. —लक्ष्मी a. Deprived of wealth.

आदरः m. 1 Respect, regard, reverence. -2 Commencement. -3 Care, close application. -4 Love. -5 Effort.

आदरणं n. Respect, notice.

आदर्शः m. 1 A mirror (also used figuratively). -2 A copy of a work. -3 A gloss or commentary.

आदर्शकः m. A mirror.

आदर्शनं n. 1 Showing. -2 A mirror.

आदहनं n. 1 Burning. -2 Injuring, killing. -3 Reviling. -4 A cemetery.

आदा (आ + दा 3 A.) 1 To receive, accept, resort to. -2 To begin (to speak, utter). -3 To seize. -4 To put on (as clothes &c). -5 To perceive, comprehend. -6 To undertake, begin.

आदातृ *m.* One who takes or receives.

आदानं *n.* 1 Taking, receiving, seizing. -2 Earning, getting. -3 A symptom (of a disease). -4 A horse's trappings.

आदाय: *m.* Receiving, taking.

आदि *a.* 1 First, primary, primitive. -2 Chief, principal, pre-eminent. —दि: *m.* 1 Beginning, commencement. (As last member of compounds आदि means 'and others', 'such like'). -2 First part or portion. -3 Prime cause. -Comp.-अंतं *n.* The beginning and the end. —उदात्त *a* Having the acute accent on the first syllable. —कर:, -कर्तृ, -कृत् *m.* The creator, an epithet of Brahman(*m*). —कवि: *m.* 'The first poet', an epithet of Brahman (*m.*) and of Vâlmiki. —कांडं *n.* The first book of the Râmâyana. —कारणं *n.* The first or primary cause (of the universe). -2 Analysis. -3 Algebra. —काव्यं *n.* The first poem; *i. e.* the Râmâyana. —देव: *m.* 1 The first or Supreme God. -2 Nârâyana or Vishnu. -3 Siva. -4 The sun. -दत्य: *m.* An epithet of Hiranyakasipu. —पु (-पू-) रुष: *m.* 1 The first or primeval being, the lord of the creation. -2 Vishnu, Krishna, or Nârâyana. —बलं *n.* The generative power, first vigour. —भव:, -भूत: *m.* 1 The first-born, primeval being, an epithet of Brahman (*m.*). -2 N. of Vishnu. -3 An elder brother. —मूलं *n.* The first foundation, primeval cause. —वराह: *m.* Vishnu in his third incarnation. —शक्ति: *f.* 1 The power of माया or illusion. -2 An epithet of Durgâ. —शरीरं *n.* 1 The primitive body. -2 Ignorance -3 The subtle body. —सर्ग: *m.* The first creation.

आदितेय: *m.* 1 A son of Aditi. -2 A god, divinity in general. -3 The sun.

आदित्य: *m.* 1 A son of Aditi; a god, divinity in general. -2 The sun. -3 A name of Vishnu in his fifth or dwarf-incarnation. -4 N. of the *Arka* plant —त्यौ (dual) N. of a constellation, the seventh lunar mansion. Comp. —सूनु: *m.* 'The son of the sun', N. of Sugriva Yama, Saturn and Karna.

आदि (-दी-) नव:, -वं *n.* 1 Misfortune, distress. -2 Hinderance, want of luck (in dice). -3 Fault.

आदिम *a.* First, primitive, original.

आदिश् (आ + दिश् 6 U.) 1 To indicate, show; to specify, determine. -2 To direct, command. -3 To appoint; assign. -4 To teach, lay down, prescribe, instruct, advise; to inform.

आदिष्ट *p. p.* (*f.* —ष्टा) 1 Directed, commanded, advised. -2 Said, foretold. —ष्टं *n.* 1 Command, order. -2 Advice.

आदीनव: *m.* 1 Distress, pain. -2 Fault.

आदीपनं *n.* 1 Setting on fire, inflaming. -2 Exciting, stimulating. -3 Embellishing, whitening the walls, floors &c. on festive occasions.

आदृ (आ + दृ 6 A.) 1 To respect, honour, reverence; receive respectfully.

आदृत *p. p.* (*f* —ता) 1 Honoured, respected. -2 (Used actively) Zealous, diligent, earnest, attentive, careful, respectful.

आदेवनं *n.* 1 Gambling. -2 A die used in gambling. -3 A board for gambling. -4 A place for playing.

आदेश: *m.* 1 An order, command. -2 Advice, instruction, precept, rule. -3 Account, information, relation, pointing out, indication. -4 A prediction, prophecy. -5 (Gram.) A substitute.

आद्य *a.*(*f.* -द्या) 1 First in position, preeminent, foremost, unparalleled. -2 First in time. —द्यं *n.* 1 The beginning. -2 Grain, food. -Comp. —कवि: *m.* An epithet of Brahman (*m.*) or Vâlmiki. —बीजं *n.* The primary or material cause of the universe, which, according to the Sânkhyas, is प्रधान.

आद्यून *a.* (*f.* —ना) Voracious, gluttonous, hungry.

आद्योत: *m.* Light, brilliance.

आधमनं *n.* A deposit, pledge. -2 Fraudulent puffing up of goods at a sale.

आधमर्ण्यं *n.* (Law) The state of being indebted.

आधर्ष: *m.* 1 Contempt. -2 Injuring forcibly.

आधर्षणं *n.* 1 Conviction of crime or error ; sentence. -2 Refutation. -3 Injuring, annoying.

आधा (आ + धा 3 U.) 1 To put, place, deposit, to appoint. -2 To exert, apply, propose, direct towards. -3 To hold, possess, take, carry, bear ; to uphold, to support. -4 To excite (fear, wonder &c.); -5 To supply, give, impart (with dat., gen., or loc). -6 To consecrate (as fire). -7 To perform, practise (as a vow &c.).

आधानं *n.* 1 Doing, executing, providing, performing. -2 Infusing or putting. -3 Producing, creating, engendering. -4 A deposit, a pledge. -5 Keeping the sacred fire (same as अग्न्याधानं). -6 Assigning, attributing, employing. -7 Effort, exertion, application. -8 A place where anything is deposited, a receptacle. -9 A surety. -10 Enclosure, circuit.

आधानिक: *m.* A ceremony performed after cohabitation to cause or favour conception.

आधार: *m.* 1 Support, prop, stay. -2 A receptacle, reservoir. -3 A part, character (in dramas). -4 A basin round the foot of a tree. -5 A dam, embankment. -6 The sense of the locative case, location. -Comp. —आधेयभाव: *m.* The relation between the container and the thing contained.

आधि: *m.* 1 Mental pain or anguish, agony, anxiety, (opp. व्याधि which is bodily pain). -2 A bane, curse, misery. -3 pledge, deposit, pawn, mortgage ; (in law). -4 A place, residence. -5 Location, site. -Comp. —भोग: *m.* The use or enjoyment of a deposit (as of a horse, cow &c. when pledged). —स्तेन: *m.* One who uses a deposit without the owner's consent.

आधिकरणिक: *m.* A judge.

आधिकारिक *a.* (*f.* —की) 1 Supreme, superior. -2 Official.

आधिक्यं *n.* 1 Excess, abundance, preponderance. -2 Superiority, supremacy.

आधिदैविक *a.* (*f.* —की) 1 Relating to अधिदैव or tutelary deity (as a

Mantra). -2 Brought on by fate.

आधिपत्यं *n.* 1 Supremacy, power, sovereignty, lordship. -2 The duties of a king.

आधिभौतिक *a.* (*f.* —की) 1 Caused by animals (as pain). -2 Relating to beings. -3 Elementary, material, derived from the primitive elements.

आधिराज्यं *n.* Royalty, sovereignty, supreme sway.

आधिवेदनिकं *n.* A gift made to a first wife upon marrying a second.

आधीकरणं *n.* Pledging, a pledge.

आधुनिक *a* (*f.* —की) New, modern, of recent origin.

आधृ (आ + धृ 1, 10 P.) 1 To hold, keep, contain. -2 To support, bear, -3 To bring, supply.

आधेय *a.* (*f.* —या) 1 To be placed, pledged, or given. -2 To be received, held, or supported; to be contained.

आधोरणः *m.* The rider or driver of an elephant.

आध्मा (आ + ध्मा 1 P.) 1 To inflate, puff up, swell. -2 To blow or fill with wind, sound (as a conch &c.).

आध्मात *p. p.* (*f* —ता) 1 Puffed up, inflated, filled with (lit. and fig.), charged with. -2 Excessively affected, increased, magnified. -3 Sounded, sounding. -4 Burnt. -5 Suffering from the swelling of the belly. —तः *m.* 1 Flatulence, swelling of the abdomen. -2 War, battle.

आध्या *f.* See आध्यानं.

आध्यात्मिक *a.* (*f.* —की) 1 Relating to the Supreme Spirit.-2 Spiritual, holy. -3 Relating to self. -4 Caused by the mind (pain, sorrow &c.).

आध्मानं *n.* 1 Blowing, inflation; (fig.) growth, increase. -2 Boasting, vaunting. -3 A bellows. -4 A swelling of the belly, body &c., dropsy.

आध्यानं *n.* 1 Anxiety. -2 A sorrowful recollection.

आध्यापकः *m.* A teacher, a spiritual preceptor.

आध्यायिक *a.* (*f.* —की) Occupied or employed in reading or studying (the Vedas).

आध्यासिक *a.* (*f.* —की) Caused by *adhyâsa i. e.* by attributing the nature and properties of one thing to another (in Vedânta phil.).

आध्वनिक *a.* (*f.* —की) Being on a journey.

आध्वर्यवं *n.* 1 Service at a sacrifice. -2 The office of an Adhvaryu priest.

आनकः *m.* A large military drum. -2 The thunder-cloud. -Comp. -दुंदुभिः *m.* An epithet of Vasudeva, father of Krishna. (-भिः,-भी *f.*) A large drum, kettle-drum (beaten at one end).

आनत *a.* (*f.* —ता) Respectfully saluted or bowed to. -2 (Active) Bent down, stooping, inclined. -3 Making a bow. -4 Humble, obedient, conciliated.

आनतिः *f.* Bending, bowing, stooping. -2 Salutation. -3 Homage, reverence.

आनद्धं *n.* 1 A drum. -2 Dressing, putting on clothes or ornaments.

आननं *n.* The mouth, face.

आनंतर्यं *n.* 1 Immediate succession. -2 Immediate proximity, absence of interval (of time or space).

आनंत्यं *n.* 1 Infinity, endlessness (in time, space or number). -2

Boundlessness. -3 Immortality, eternity. -4 An upper world; heaven, future happiness.

आनंद: *m.* 1 Happiness, joy, delight, pleasure. -4 N. of Siva. -5 N. of Vishnu. -6 N. of Balarâma. -दं *n.* 1 Wine, liquor. -2 The Supreme Spirit (in वेदांत phil.). -Comp. —काननं,—वनं *n.* N. of Kâsi. —पट: *m.* The bridal garment. —प्रभव: *m.* Semen.

आनंदथु: *m.* Happiness, joy, pleasure.

आनंदन *a.* Pleasing, delighting. —नं *n.* 1 Delighting, making happy. -2 Paying respects to. -3 Courteous treatment of a friend or a guest at meeting and parting. -4 What gives or produces delight.

आनंदमय *a.* Blissful, full of joy. —य: *m.* The Supreme Spirit.-Comp. —कोष: (-श:) *m.* The innermost case of the body.

आनंदि: *m.* 1 Joy, happiness. -2 Curiosity.

आनपत्यं *n.* Childlessness.

आनम् (आ + नम् 1 P.) 1 To bend, bend down, stoop. -2 To salute (respectfully), bow down to. -3 To humble. -*Caus.* (—नमयति) To cause to bend down.

आनय: *m.* 1 Bringing. -2 Investiture with the sacred thread.

आनयनं *n.* 1 Bringing. -2 Investiture with the sacred thread.

आनर्त: *m.* 1 A stage, theatre, a dancing-hall. -2 War, battle. -3 —र्ता: *m. pl.* N. of a country or its inhabitants.

आनर्थक्यं *n.* 1 Uselessness, unprofitableness. -2 Unfitness, impropriety.

आनाय: *m.* A net.

आनायिन् *m.* A fisherman, fisher.

आनाय्य *a.* To be brought near. —य्य: *m.* Consecrated fire taken from गार्हपत्य or household fire and placed on the south side (also called दक्षिणाग्नि).

आनाह: *m.* 1 Binding. -2 Suppression of urine; constipation; epistasis. -3 Length (especially of cloth).

आनी (आ + नी 1 P.) 1 To bring, to fetch. -2 To bring on or about -3 To lead on, convey. -4 To reduce to any condition. -5 To lead away.

आनील *a.* Darkish, slightly blue. —ल: *m.* A black horse.

आनुकूल्यं *n.* 1 Favourableness, conformity, suitableness. -2 Kindness, favour.

आनुगतिक *a.* (*f.* —की) Relating to a follower.

आनुगत्यं *n.* Acquaintance.

आनुगुण्यं *n.* Favourableness, suitableness, congruity.

आनुग्रामिक *a.* (*f.* की) Rural, rustic.

आनुनासिक्यं *n.* Nasality.

आनुपातिक *a.* (की *f.*) Following, pursuing, taking.

आनुपूर्व *n.* 1 Order, succession, series. -2 (In law) The regular order of the castes. -3 (In logic) Conclusion regularly or syllogistically drawn.

आनुपूर्वी *f.* See आनुपूर्व.

आनुपूर्व्य *n.* See आनुपूर्व.

आनुमानिक *a.* (*f.* की) 1 Relating to a conclusion. -2 Derived from an inference, subject to inference, inferential. -3 Inferred. —कं *n.* The Pradhana of the Sânkhyas. आनु-

आनिकधट्येकेषामिति यत्र श्रृंगरूपकविम्यस्तगृहीते दर्शयति च * ब्रह्मसूत्र.

आनुयात्रं *n.* Retinue.

आनुयात्रिकः *m.* A follower, attendant.

आनुलोमिक *a.* (*f.* —की) 1 Regular, orderly. -2 Favourable, suitable.

आनुलोम्यं *n* 1 Natural or direct order, proper arrangement. -2 Regular series or succession -3 Favourableness, fit disposition.

आनुवेश्यः *m.* A neighbour who lives next to the next door neighbour.

आनुषंगिक *a.* (*f.* —की) 1 Connected with, concomitant. -2 Implied, inherent. -3 Necessarily following, inevitable, necessary. -4 Of secondary importance, secondary. -5 Relative, proportionate. -6 (In gram.) Elliptical.

आनूप *a.* (*f.* —पी) 1 Watery, marshy, wet. -2 Produced in a marshy place. —पः *m.* Any animal frequenting marshy or watery places (as a buffalo.)

आनृण्यं *n.* Acquittance of debt or obligation.

आनृशंसं, -स्यं *n.* 1 Mildness. -2 Kindness. -3 Compassion, pity, mercy. -4 Sinlessness.

आनेतव्य *a.* (*f.* —व्या) To be brought.

आनेय *a.* (*f.* —या) To be brought.

आनेतृ *m.* One who brings.

आनैपुणं, -ण्यं *n.* Clumsiness, stupidity.

आंत *a.* (*f.* —ता) Final, terminal. —तं *ind.* Completely, to the end.

आंतर *a.* (*f.* —रा) 1 Internal, secret, hidden. -2 Inmost, inward. —रं *n.* Inmost nature. —Comp. —ज्ञ *a.* Knowing the hidden secret (of things &c.).

आंतरि (-रि-) क्ष *a.* (*f.* —क्षी) 1 Atmospherical, heavenly, celestial. -2 Produced in the atmosphere. —क्षं *n.* The firmament, the intermediate region between the earth and sky.

आंतर्गणिक *a.* (*f.* —की) Included, comprised (as in a class, troop, &c.

आंतर्गेहिक *a.* (*f.* —की) Being or produced inside a house.

आंतर्वेश्मिक *a.* (*f.* —की) See आंतर्गेहिक.

आंतिका *f.* An elder sister.

आंत्र *a.* (*f.* —त्री) Relating to the bowels.

आंदोलः *m.* 1 Swinging; a swing. -2 Trembling.

आंदोलनं *n.* 1 Swinging; a swing. -2 Moving to and fro, shaking, rocking. -3 Trembling, oscillation.

आंधसः *m.* The scum of boiled rice.

आंधसिकः *m.* A cook.

आंध्यं *n.* Blindness.

आंध्राः *m. pl.* The Telagu country, modern Telangana.

आन्वयिक *a.* (*f.* —की) 1 Of a good family, well-born, of noble birth. -2 Orderly.

आन्वाहिक *a.* (*f.* —की) Daily occurring or to be performed every day.

आन्वीक्षिकी *f.* 1 Logic, logical philosophy. -2 Metaphysics.

आप् 5 P., rarely 1 P. (आप्नोति or आपति, आप, आपत्, आप्स्यति, आप्त, आप्तुं) 1 To obtain, attain, get, to meet with. -2 To reach, overtake, fall in with. -3 To pervade, occupy, enter into. With अनुप्र- To reach. अव— To obtain, to attain, to reach. परि— 1 To be able, to be competent. -2 To be full. -3 To defend, to save. प्र— 1 To obtain. -2 To reach. -3 To meet. वि— To pervade. सम् To complete, finish, to end.

आपकर *a.* (*f.* —री) Offensive, unfriendly, mischievous.

आपक्व *a.* Crude, raw, half-baked. —क्वं *n.* A cake, bread.

आपगा *f.* A river, stream.

आपगेयः *m.* A son of the river, an epithet of Bhishma or Krishna.

आपणः *m.* A market ; shop.

आपणिक *a.* (*f.* —की) 1 Relating to traffic, market &c., mercantile. -2 Got from the market (as duties). —कः *m.* 1 A shop-keeper, merchant, dealer. -2 A tax on market-shops. -3 Assize, market-rate.

आपत् (आ + पत् 1 P.) 1 To fall upon, attack, assail. -2 To approach, come towards. -3 To fly towards, rush upon. -4 To happen, take place, occur, come to pass, befall. -5 To occur to, cross (the mind) ; to be felt or regarded.

आपतनं *n.* 1 Approaching, arising. -2 Happening, occurence. -3 Descending, alighting. -4 Natural sequence necessarily following.

आपतिक *a.* (*f* —की) Accidental, unforeseen, sent from heaven. —कः *m.* A hawk, falcon.

आपतित *a.* (*f.* —ता) 1 Fallen to the lot of. -2 Happened, befallen, occurred, come to pass. -3 Alighted, descended.

आपत्तिः *f.* 1 Changing into. -2 Obtaining, procuring, getting. -3 Misfortune, calamity, adversity. -4 (In phil.) An undesirable conclusion or occurrence (अनिष्टप्रसंग).

आपद् (आ + पद् 4 A.) 1 To go near, approach. -2 To enter into, attain to (a place, state &c.). -3 To happen, occur. —*Caus.* 1 To bring about, bring to pass. -2 To cause, to produce, bring on. -3 To turn or change into.

आपद् *f.* A calamity, misfortune, adversity. -Comp. —कालः *m.* The days of adversity, time of distress, hour of danger. —धर्मः *m.* A practice, profession, or course of procedure, not usually proper for a caste, but allowable in times of distress.

आपदा *f.* Misfortune, calamity.

आपन्न *p. p.* (*f.* —न्ना) 1 Gained, obtained, acquired. -2 Reached, fallen into. -3 Afflicted, distressed. -Comp. —सत्त्वा *f.* Pregnant, quick or big with child ; a pregnant woman.

आपमित्यकं *n.* Property or anything obtained by barter or for a consideration.

आपराह्णिक *a.* (*f.* —की) Occurring in the afternoon.

आपस् *n.* Water. -2 Sin. -3 A religious ceremony.

आपा (आ + पा 1 P.) 1 To drink up (lit. and fig.) -2 To drink with the ears or eyes ; hear or see intently. -3 To eclipse, surpass.

आपातः *m.* 1 Rushing, falling, descending, alighting suddenly upon. -2 Throwing down. -3 The present or current moment, instant, or month.-4 (Hence) First sight or appearance. (आपाततः means 'at first sight'). -5 Happening, appearance.

आपाततः *ind.* 1 At the first sight. -2 Instantly, immediately.

आपादः *m.* 1 Reward, remuneration. -2 Attainment, obtaining.

आपादनं *n.* Tending to.

आपानं, -नकं *n.* 1 A drinking party. -2 A tavern, liquor-shop, a place for drinking in company. —भूमिः *f.* A tavern.

आपालिः *m.* A louse.

आपीड् (आ + पीड् 10 P.) 1 To press, weigh down. -2 To afflict, perplex, worry. -3 To compress.

आपीडः *m.* 1 Squeezing, compressing. -3 A chaplet, garland. -4 (Hence fig.) A crest-jewel.

आपीन *a.* (*f.* —ना) Fat, stout. —नः *m.* 1 A well. —नं *n.* An udder, teat.

आपूपिकः *m.* A baker; confectioner. —कं *n.* A multitude of cakes

आपूप्यः *m.* Flour-meal.

आपूरः *m.* 1 Flow, current, large quantity. -2 Fillng, making full.

आपूरणं *n.* Filling, making full.

आपूषं *n.* Tin.

आपृच्छा *f.* 1 Conversation. -2 Bidding farewell. -3 Curiosity.

आपृच्छ्य *pot. p. a.* (*f.* —च्छ्या) 1 To be saluted, welcomed or honoured. -2 Praise-worthy, commendable. -3 Beautiful,

आपोशा (-श-)नः *m.* N. of a kind of prayer repeated before and after eating.—नं *n.* The act of making an उपस्तरण (seat) and अपिधान (covering) for the food eaten.

आप्त *p. p.* (*f.* —प्ता) 1 Got, obtained, gained. -2 Trustworthy, reliable, credible (as news &c.); confidential, faithful (person). -3 Clever, skilful. -4 Full, complete, abundant. -5 True, exact. -6 Intimate, closely related, acquainted. -7 Appointed. -8 Accused, prosecuted. -9 Reasonable, sensible. —प्तः *m.* 1 A trustworthy, reliable, or fit person. A person who is worthy of confidence, or who can be safely relied upon. आप्तस्तु यथार्थ वक्ता * तर्कसं. आप्तस्तु यथाभूतस्यार्थस्योपदेष्टा पुरुषः * तर्कभा. -2 A relative, friend. -3 An ' Arhat.' —प्तं *n.* 1 A quotient. -2 (Math) Equation of a degree. -Comp. —काम *a.* 1 One who has obtained his desire. -2 One who has renounced all worldly desires and attachments. —कामः The Supreme Soul. —गर्भा *f.* A pregnant woman. —वाक्यं, -वचनं *n.* A true or correct sentence. —वाच् *a.* Worthy of belief, regarded as authority, one whose words are credible and authoritative. —वाच् *f.* 1 The advice of a friend or credible person. -2 The Vedas and smritis (which are considered as authoritative evidence.).—श्रुतिः *f.* 1 The Vedas. -2 Smritis &c.

आप्तिः *f.* 1 Getting, gain, acquisition. -2 Reaching, overtaking. -3 Connection. -4 Fitness, aptitude. -5 Completion, fulfilment. -6 Future time.

आप्य *a.* (*f.* —प्या) 1 Watery. -2 Obtainable. attainable —प्याः *m.* A class of gods.

आप्यान *p. p.* (*f.* —ना) 1 Fat, stout, robust, strong.—नं *n.* 1 Love. -2 Growth, increase.

आप्यायः *m.* Becoming full or fat.

आप्यायनं *n.*, —ना *f.* 1 The act of making full or fat. -2 Satisfaction satiety. -3 Advancing, promoting. -4 Corpulency, growing fat or stout. -5 Anything which causes corpulency or good condition. -6 strengthening medicine.

आप्यायित *a.* (*f.* —ता) 1 Satisfied. pleased. -2 Grown, increased. -3 Stout, tat, robust.

आप्रच्छनं *n.* 1 Bidding adieu, taking leave at the time of departure. -2 Welcoming.

आप्रपदं *n.* A dress reaching to the feet. —*ind.* To the end of the foot; reaching to the feet.

आप्रपदीन *a.* (*f.* —ना) Reaching to the feet (as dress).

आप्लवः *m.*, -प्लवनं *n.* 1 Bathing. -2 Sprinkling with water (on all sides).

आप्लावः *m.* Same as आप्लवः.

आप्लु (आ + प्लु 1 A.) 1 To jump up; dance. -2 To bathe, wash, immerse oneself (fig. also).

आप्लुत *p. p.* (*f.* —ता) 1 Bathed. -2 Wetted, sprinkled. -3 Overflowing with, filled or overcome with. —तं *n.* Bathing.

आफूकं *n.* Opium.

आबद्ध *p. p.* (*f.* —द्धा) 1 Bound, tied. -2 Fixed. -2 Formed, made. -4 Hindered. —द्धं *n.*,(द्धः *m.* also). 1 Binding. joining. -2 A yoke. -3 Ornament. -4 Affection.

आबंध् (आ + बंध् 9 P.) 1 To bind, fasten. -2 To hold fast, cling to.

आबंधः *m.* -धनं *n.* 1 A tie or bond (fig. also). -2 The tie of a yoke. -3 Ornament, decoration. -4 Affection.

आबर्हः *m.*, —र्हणं *n.* 1 Tearing or pulling out. -2 Killing.

आबाधः *m.* 1 Affliction, injury, molestation, damage. -2 Interruption. hinderance. —धा *f.* 1 Pain, distress. Mental agony or anguish. -2 Segment of the base of a triangle.

आबिल *a.* (*f.* —ला) Turbid, dirty.

आबुत्तः *m.* Sister's husband (in theatrical language).

आबोधनं *n.* 1 Knowledge, understanding. -2 Instructing, informing.

आब्द *a.* (*f.* ब्दी) Belonging to, or produced from. a cloud.

आब्दिक *a.* (*f.* —की) Annual, yearly.

आभरणं *n.* 1 Ornament, decoration. -2 Nourishing.

आभा *f.* 1 Light, splendour, lustre. -2 Colour, appearance, beauty. -3 Likeness, resemblanece. -4 A reflected image, shadow, reflection.

आभाणकः *m.* A popular saying, proverb.

आभाष् (आ + भाष् 1 A.) 1 To address, speak to. converse with. -2 To say or speak. -3 To name. -4 To short.

आभाषः *m.* 1 Addressing. -2 An introduction, preface.

आभाषणं *n.* 1 Addressing. speaking to. -2 Conversation.

आभास् *f.* Splendour. lustre, light.

आभासः *m.* 1 Splendour, light, lustre. -2 A reflection. -3 Appearance. -4 A fallacy, fallacious reasoning. -5 An intention, purpose.

आभासु (-स्व-) रः *m.* A collective name of 64 demi-gods.

आभिचरणिक, आभिचारिक *a.* (*f.* —की) 1 Magical. -2 Imprecatory, maleditory. —कं *n.* A spell or incantation, magic.

आभिजन *a.* (*f.* —नी) Relating to birth (अभिजन); patronymic (as a name). —नं *n.* Nobility or loftiness of birth.

आभिजात्यं *n.* 1 Nobility of birth. -2 Rank. -3 Learning. -4 Beauty.

आभिधा *f.* Same as अभिधा.

आभिधानिकः *m.* A lexicographer.

आभिमुख्यं *n.* 1 Direction towards; -ख्यं याति goes to meet or encounter. -2 Being in front of. -3 Favourableness.

आभिरामिक *a.* (*f.* —की) Good, agreeable.

आभिरूपकं, आभिरूप्यं *n.* Beauty.

आभिषेचनिक *a.* (*f.* —की) Relating to the inauguration of a king.

आभिहारिक *a.* (*f.* —की) 1 To be offered as a present. -2 Taken by force, or fraud. —कं *n.* 1 A present. -2 A room.

आभीक्ष्ण्यं *n.* Continued repetition.

आभीरः *m.* 1 A cowherd. —राः *m. pl.* N. of a country or its inhabitants. —री *f.* 1 A cowherd's wife. -2 A woman of the Abhira tribe. -Comp. —पल्लिः, -ल्ली:, —पल्लिका *f.* A village inhabited by cowherds.

आभीलं *n.* Physical pain, injury.

आभुग्न *a.* (*f.* —ग्ना) A little curved or bent.

आभोगः *m.* 1 Curving, winding. -2 A curve. -3 Circuit; circumference, expanse, precincts, environs. -4 Magnitude, extent. -5 Effort. -6 The expanded hood of a cobra. -7 Enjoyment. -8 A serpent.

आभ्यंतर *a.* (*f.* —री) Interior, inner.

आभ्यवहारिक *a.* (*f.* —की) Eatable.

आभ्यासिक *a.* (*f.* की) 1 Resulting from practice. -2 Being near, neighbouring, adjoining.

आभ्युदयिक *a.* (*f.* की) 1 Tending to good: granting prosperity. -2 High, exalted, important. —कं *n.* A Srâddha or offering to ancestors.

आम् *ind* See अं.

आम (*f.* मा) 1 Raw, uncooked, undressed, unbaked; unannealed. -4 Undigested. —मं *n.* 1 State of being raw. -2 Constipation. —मः *m.* 1 Disease; sickness. -2 Indigestion. -Comp. —आशयः *m.* The upper part of the belly. —कुंभः *m.* A jar of clay yet unbaked.—गंधि *a.* Smelling of raw meat or of a burning corpse. —ज्वरः *m.* A kind of fever. —त्वच् *a.* Of tender skin.—पात्रं *n.* An unbaked or unannealed vessel. —रक्तं *n.* Dysentery. —वातः *m.* Constipation. —शूलः *m.* The pain of indigestion, colic.

आमंजु *a.* Lovely, charming.

आम (-मा-) नस्यं *n.* Pain, sorrow.

आमंत्र् (आ + मंत्र 10 A.) 1 To bid farewell. -2 To speak to, call out to, address, converse with. -3 To speak. -4 To call, invite. -5 To invoke.

आमंत्रणं *n.*, —णा *f.* 1 Addressing, calling, calling out to. -2 Bidding adieu to. -3 Greeting, welcome, -4 Invitation. -5 Permission. -6 Conversation.-7 Asking; interrogation.

आमंत्रित *p. p.* (*f.* —ता) 1 Invited, culled.

आमंद्र *a.* (*f.* —द्रा)Having a slightly deep tone, rumbling. —द्रः *m.* A slightly deep tone, rumbling.

आमयः *m.* 1 Disease, sickness, distemper. -2 Damage, hurt. -3 Indigestion.

आमयाविन् *a.* (*f.* -नी) Sick, dyspeptic, affected with indigestion.

आमरणांत *a.* (*f.* —ता) Lasting till death, lasting for life.

आमरणांतिक *a.* (*f.* —की) See आमरणांत.

आमर्दः *m.* 1 Crushing. -2 Roughly handling. -3 Pressing, squeezing.

आमर्शः *m.* Advice, counsel.

आमर्शनं *n.* Counsel, advice.

आमर्षः *m.* Same as आमर्शः.

आमलकः *m.*, -की *f.* 1 The tree, Emblic Myrobalan, Emblica Officinalis Gaertn (Mar. आंवळा). —कं *n.* Fruit of the Emblic Myrobalan.

आमात्यः *m.* 1 A minister, counsellor. -2 A general.

आमानस्यं *n.* Pain, sorrow.

आमावास्यं *a.* (*f.* स्यी) 1 Belonging to the new moon or its festival. -2 Happening or born at the time of new moon or conjunction. —स्यं *n.* The new moon oblation.

आमिक्षा *f.* Curd of milk and whey.

आमिषः *m.*, *n.* 1 Flesh. -2 (Hence fig.) A prey, victim, object of enjoyment. -3 Food, bait. -4 A bribe. -5 Enjoyment.

आमीलनं *n.* Shutting or closing of the eyes.

आमुक्त *a.* (*f.* —क्ता) Loosened, liberated. -2 Put on, worn. -3 Shot, discharged.

आमुक्तिः *f.* 1 Wearing, putting on (clothes or ornaments). -2 Liberation. -3 Final beatitude.

आमुखं *n.* 1 Commencement. -2 (In dramans) A prologue, prelude.

आमुच् (आ + मुच् 6 U.) 1 To loosen, let go. -2 To wear, put on (as a garment &c.). -3 To throw, cast, discharge. -4 To take off, put aside (as garments &c.).

आमुष्मिक *a.* (*f.* की) Belonging to the next or other world.

आमुष्यायण *m.* (*f.* णी ; A son or descendant of such a one ; *i. e.* a scion of an illustrious family.

आमृश् (आ + मृश् 6 P.) 1 To touch; handle (roughly). To seize upon, -2 To attack, assail. -3 To rub, injure.

आमोचनं *n.* 1 The act of liberating, -2 Emitting, discharging. -3 Putting or tying on (as ornaments)

आमोदः *m.* 1 Joy, pleasure, delight. -2 Fragrance, perfume पुष्पासवामोदसुगंधिवक्त्रः × × शेते जनः कामशरानुविद्धः * ऋतुसं 4-11. -3 Strong smell.

आमोदन *a.* Delighting, pleasing. —नं *n.* 1 Delighting, rejoicing. -2 Making fragrant.

आमोषः *m.* Theft, robbing.

आम्ना (आ + म्ना 1 P.) 1 To hand down traditionally or in sacred texts ; lay down, to consider. -2 To learn, study, repeat. -3 To celebrate, hail.

आम्नात *p. p.* (*f.* —ता) 1 Considered, regarded, said to be. -2 Studied, repeated. -3 Remembered, kept in mind. -4 Handed down in sacred texts or traditionally.

आम्नानं *n.* 1 Recitation or study of the sacred texts or Vedas. -2 Mention ; repetition in general.

आम्नायः *m.* 1 Sacred tradition, sacred texts handed down by tradition or repetition. -2 Hence, the Veda, Vedas taken collectively. -3

Traditional usage. -4 Received doctrine. -5 Advice or instruction.

आंबिकेयः *m.* An epithet of Dhritarâshtra ; also of Kârtikeya.

आंभसिकः *m.* A fish.

आम्रः *m* The mango-tree. —म्रं *n.* The fruit of the mango-tree -Comp. —कूटः *m.* The name of a mountain. —पेशी *f.* A portion of dried mango-fruit. —वणं *n.* grove of mango trees.

आम्रातः *m* The hog-plum. —तं *n.* The fruit of this tree.

आम्रातकः *m.* 1 The hog plum. -2 Inspissated mango juice (Mar. साट.)

आम्रिमन् *m.* Acid taste.

आम्रेडितं *n.* Tautology ; repetition of words or sounds.

आम्रेडित *a.* (*f.* —ता) Reiterated, repeated (as words). —तं *n.* 1 Repetition of sound or word. -2 (In gram.) Reduplication, the second word in reduplication,

आम्लः *m.*, —म्ला *f.* The tamarind tree. —म्लं *n.* Sourness, acidity.

आम्लि (—म्ली—) का *f.* 1 The tamarind tree. -2 Acidity of stomach.

आयः *m.* 1 Arrival, approach. -2 Acquisition of money. -2 Income, revenue. receipt. -4 Gain, profit. -5 The eleventh house (in astrology). -6 The guard of the woman's apartments. -Comp. —व्ययौ (*m. dual.*) Receipt and disbursement, income and expenditure.

आयत *a.* (*f.* —ता) 1 Diffuse, prolix. -2 Long. -3 Large. big. -4 Attracted, drawn. -5 Curbed, restrained. -Comp. —अक्षी *f.* A woman with large eyes. —अपांग *a.* Having long-cornered eyes. —आयतिः *f.* Remote futurity. —च्छदा *f.* The plantain tree. —स्तूः *m.* A panegyrist.

आयतनं *n.* 1 Place, house, resting-place ; (fig. also). -2 The place of the sacred fire. -3 A sanctuary. -4 The site of a house, ground-plot. -5 The cause of disease.

आयतिः *f.* 1 Length, extension. -2 Future time. -3 Future consequence or result. -4 Majesty, dignity. -5 Stretching the hand, accepting, obtaining. -6 Work (कर्मन्). -7 Connection, junction. -8 Meeting, union. -9 Source, descent. -10 Restraint (of mind).

आयत्त *p. p.* (*f.* —त्ता) 1 Dependent. -2 Docile, humble, tractable. -3 Attempted, tried.

आयत्तिः *f.* 1 Dependence, subjection. -2 Affection. -3 Strength, might. -4 Boundary, limit. -5 An expedient, remedy. -6 Majesty, dignity. -7 Steadiness of conduct. -8 Length.

आयथातथ्यं *n.* Unfitness, unsuitableness, impropriety.

आयम् (आ + यम् 1 U.) 1 To extend, stretch out.

आयमनं *n.* 1 Length, extension, -2 Restraint, curbing. -3 Stretching (as a bow).

आयल्लकः *m.* Impatience, longing.

आयःशूलिक *a.* (*f.* —की) Active, diligent, indefatigble. —कः *m.* A man who, in order to gain an object, uses forcibile instead of gentle means.

आयस् (आ + यस् 4 P.) 1 To exert one-self. -2 To become exhausted or fatigued. —*Caus.* 1 To trouble, afflict. -2 To tire out, worry. -3 To injure, diminish. -4 To string (as a bow).

आयस *a.* (*f.* —सी) 1 Made of iron. —सी *f.* A coat of mail, an armour for the body. —सं *n.* 1 Iron. -2 Anything made of iron. -3 A weapon.

आयस्त *p. p.* (*f.* —स्ता) 1 Pained, afflicted. -2 Hurt, injured, killed. -3 Vexed, angry. -4 Thrown, cast. -5 Sharpened, violently agitated, tossed about, whetted.

आया (आ + या 2 P.) 1 To come, arrive, approach. -2 To reach, attain, (any particular state). -3 To follow, result. -4 To be possible or practicable (with inf.).

आयात *a.* (*f.* —ता) Come, approached. —तं *n.* Excess, superabundance.

आयानं *n.* Coming, arrival.

आयाम: *m.* 1 Length. -2 Expansion, extension. -3 Stretching, extending. -4 Restraint, control.

आयास: *m.* 1 Effort, exertion, difficulty, pain. -2 Fatigue, weariness. -3 Mental pain, anguish.

आयुक्त *p. p.* (*f.* —क्ता) 1 Appointed, charged. -2 United, joined. —क्त: *m.* A minister, an agent or deputy.

आयुध: *m.*, -धं *n.* 1 A weapon. -Comp. आगारं (-अ-) *n.* An armoury, arsenal. —जीविन् *a.* Living by one's weapon.(*m.*) A warrior, soldier.

आयुधिक: *m.* A soldier, warrior.

आयुधिन् *m.* A warrior.

आयुष्मत् *a.* 1 Alive,living. -2 Long-lived. (Generally used in dramas by elderly persons in addressing a nobly-born person.) A Brâhmana is also so addressed in saluting.

आयुष्य *a.* Promoting long life, preservative of life. —ष्यं *n.* Vital power, abundance of life or vigour.

आयुस् *n.* 1 Life, duration of life. -2 Vital power. -3 Food. -Comp. —काम *a.* Wishing for long life or health. —वेद: *m.* The science of health or medicine. —वेदिक. -वेदिन् *m.* A physician. —शेष: *m.* Decline of life. —स्तोम: (आयुष्टोम:) *m.* A sacrifice performed to obtain long life.

आये *ind.* An interjection of calling, expressive of affection.

आयोग: *m.* 1 Appointment, entrussting one with something. -2 Action. -3 Worship. -4 A shore or bank. -5 Connection, union. -6 Obstruction (रोध).

आयोगव: *m.* The son of a Sudra by a Vaisya wife (his business being carpentry). —वी *f.* A woman of this tribe.

आयोजनं *n.* 1 Joining. -2 Taking, seizing. -3 Collecting. -4 Effort.

आयोधनं *n.* 1 A battle, fight, war. -2 Battle-field.-3 Slaughter, killing.

आर: *m.*, -रं *n.* 1 Brass. -2 Oxide of iron. —र: *m.*1 The planet Mars. -2 The planet Saturn. -3 Extremity. —रा *f.* 1 A shoemaker's awl. -2 A knife, probe. -3 A spoke. -4 A goad, or whip. -Comp. —कूट: *m.*, -टं *n.* Brass.

आरक्ष: *m.*, —क्षा *f.* 1 Protection, preservation, guard. -2 The junction of the frontal sinuses of an elephant. -3 The part of the forehead below this junction. -4 An army.

आरक्ष (-क्षि-) क: *m.* 1 A watchman, sentinel. -2 A village or police magistrate.

आरग्वधः *m.* The tree Cassia Fistula (Mar बाहवा). —धं *n.* Its fruit.

आरटः *m.* An actor.

आराणिः *m.* An eddy, whirlpool.

आरण्य *a.* (*f.*-ण्या,-ण्यी) Wild,forest-born, relating to a forest (opp.ग्राम्य). —ण्यः *m.*, —ण्यं *n.* A forest. -Comp. —कुक्कुटः *m.* A wild cock. —पशुः *m.* A wild beast.—मुद्गा *f.* A kind of bean.

आरण्यक *a.* (*f.* —का) Relating to or produced in a forest; wild, forest-born. —कः *m* A forester, an inhabitant of the woods. —कं *n.* An Aranyaka ; it is one of a class of religious and philosophical writings (connected with the Bráhmanas) which are either composed in forests, or must be studied there.

आरत *p. p.* (*f.* —ता) 1 Stopped, ceased. -2 Quiet, gentle.

आरतिः *f.* 1 Cessation, stopping. -2 Waving lights before an image (Mar. आरती).

आरथः *m.* A carriage drawn by one horse or ox.

आरनालं *n.* Gruel made from the fermentation of boiled ric

आरब्ध *a.* (*f.* —ब्धा) Begun. —ब्धं *n.* Beginning.

आरब्धिः *f.* Beginning, commencement.

आरभ् (आ + रभ् 1 A.) 1 To begin, undertake. -2 To reach or attain to, obtain. -3 To seize, grasp. -4 To form, make.

आरभटः *m.* An enterprising or courageous man. -टः *m.*, —टी *f.* Boldness, confidence. —टी *f.* 1 A branch of the dramatic art ; machinery of the drama, representation of supernatural or horrible events on the stage. -2 A kind of literary style (वृत्ति). -3 A particular style of dancing.

आरभ्य *ind.* Beginning with, ever since, since, (with a prepositional force with abl, sometimes with acc. also).

आरम् (आ + रम् 1 P.) 1 To take pleasure in. -2 To leave off, stop. -3 To take rest.

आरमणं *n.* 1 Taking delight. -2 Cessation, pause. -3 A resting place.

आरंभः *m.* 1 Beginning, commencement. -2 An introduction. -3 work, undertaking, deed. -4 A thing begun. -5 Effort, exertion. -6 Posture, action. -7 Pride. -8 Killing, slaughter.

आरंभणं *n.* 1 Taking hold of, seizing. -2 The handle.

आरवः *m.* Sound, howling.

आरस्यं *n.* Insipidity, tastelessness.

आरा *f.* 1 A shoe-maker's awl. -2 A probe.

आरात् *ind.* 1 From, or to a distant place, remote. -2 Near, in the vicinity of ; (with abl. or by itself). -3 Far from. -4 Directly, immediately.

आरातिः *m.* An enemy.

आरातीय *a.* 1 Near, proximate. -2 Remote, distant.

आरात्रिकं *n.* Waving a light (or the vessel containing it) at night before an idol (Mar. आरती ओंवाळणें). -2 The light so waved.

आराध् (आ + राध् 5. 10. P.) 1 To propitiate, please, try to win the favour of. -2 To honour, worship.

आराधनं *n.* 1 Serving, worshipping, adoration, propitiation (as of a deity). -2 A means of pleasing. -3 Accomplishment, undertaking. -4 Pleasing, satisfying, gratifying. -5 Honouring, respecting. -6 Cooking. -7 Acquirement, attainment. —ना *f.* Service. —नी *f.* Worship, adoration, propitiation (of a deity).

आरामः *m.* 1 Delight, pleasure. -2 A garden, a grove.

आराम्य *a.* Pleasing, delightful.

आरामिकः *m.* A gardener.

आरालिकः *m.* A cook.

आरावः *m.* 1 A cry, howling. -2 Sound.

आरुः *m.* 1 A hog. -2 A crab. —रूः *f.* A pitcher.

आरुरुक्षु *a.* Wishing to ascend, mount or reach.

आरुह् (आ + रुह् 1 P.) 1 To ascend, mount, get upon (with acc., sometimes loc.). -2 To attain, gain, get to reach. —*Caus.* (-रोह -प-यति). 1 To cause to go up or ascend, raise up, elevate ; to place. -2 To cause to grow, plant (lit.). -3 To establish, install, seat, (fig.). -4 To ascribe, attribute, impute. -5 To string (as a bow).

आरूढ *p. p.* (*f.* —ढा) 1 Mounted; ascended ; seated on. -2 Raised up. -3 Arisen, produced.

आरूढिः *f.* Ascent, mounting; rise, elevation (lit. and fig.).

आरोग्यं *n.* Freedom from disease ; good health. -Comp. —शाला *f.* A hospital.

आरोपः *m.* 1 Attributing the nature or properties of one thing to another; वस्तुन्यवस्त्वारोपोऽध्यारोपः * वेदां. सा. -2 Identification, superimposition. -3 Imposing (as a burden). -4 Placing in or upon.

आरोपणं *n.* 1 Placing or fixing in or upon. -2 Causing to mount or ascend, raising (to heaven.) -3 Planting. -4 The stringing of a bow.

आरोपित *p. p.* (*f.* —ता) Raised, elevated. -2 Fixed, placed. -3 Strung (as a bow). -4 Deposited, entrusted. -5 Accidental, adventitious, ascribed.

आरोहः *m.* 1 One who mounts, a rider. -2 Ascent, ascending. -3 An elevated place, elevation, height. -4 Haughtiness, pride. -5 A mountain, a heap. -6 A woman's waist; the buttocks. -7 Length. -8 A measure. -9 A ride.

आरोहणं *n.* 1 The act of rising, ascending, mounting. -2 Riding (on a horse &c). -3 A stair-case, ladder. -4 A raised stage for dancing.

आर्किः *m.* A son of अर्क, epithet of (1) Yama, (2) the planet Saturn, (3) Karna, (4) Sugriva, (5) वैवस्वतमनु.

आर्क्ष (*f.* —क्षी) Stellar, regulated by stars or pertaining to them.

आर्गलः *m.*, —ली *f.* A bolt or bar.

आर्घा *f.* A kind of yellow bee.

आर्घ्यं *n.* Wild honey.

आर्चिक *a.* (*f.* —की) Relating to the Rigveda. —कं *n.* An epithet of the Sáma-Veda.

आर्जवं *n.* 1 Straightness. -2 Straightforwardness, uprightness, honesty, sincerity. -3 Simplicity, humility.

आर्त *a.* (*f.* —र्ता) 1 Afflicted with, suffering from. -2 Sick, diseased. -3 Distressed, afflicted, unhappy.

-4 Perishable.-Comp. —नादः,—ध्वनिः, —स्वरः *m.* A cry of distress. —बंधुः, —साधुः *m.* A friend of the distressed.

आर्तव *a.* (*f.*—वा,-वी) 1 Conforming or relating to the season. -2 Menstrual. —वः *m.* A section of the year. —वं *n.* The menstrual discharge (of women).-2 Certain days after menstrual discharge favourable to conception. -3 A flower.

आर्तवेयी *f.* A woman during her courses.

आर्तिः *f.* 1 Distress, sickness, disease, suffering, pain, injury (bodily or mental). -2 Evil, mischief. -3 The end of a bow.

आर्त्विजीन *a.* (*f.* —नी) Fit for the office of a sacrificial priest (ऋत्विज्).

आर्त्विज्यं *n.* The office of a priest or his rank.

आर्थ *a.* (*f.* —र्थी) 1 Relating to a thing or object. -2 Relating to, or dependent on sense (opp. शाब्द). -3 Material, significant.

आर्थिक *a.* (*f.* —की) 1 Significant. -2 Wise. -3 Rich. -4 Substantial, real, material.

आर्द्र *a.* (*f.* —र्द्रा) 1 Wet, moist, damp. -2 Fresh, new. -3 Soft, tender. -4 Full of feeling, warm. -5 Loose, flaccid. —र्द्रा *f.* N. of a constellation or the sixth lunar mansion.

आर्द्रकं *n.* Ginger in its undried state; wet ginger (Mar. आलें).

आर्धधातुक *a.* (*f.* —की) (In gram.) Applicable to half the root or to the shorter form of the verbal base. —कं *n.* A name given to those terminations and affixes which belong to the six non-conjugational or general tenses (opp. सार्वधातुक).

आर्धिक *a.* (*f.* —की) Sharing half, relating to a half. —कः *m.* 1 One who ploughs the land for half the crop. -2 A person born of a Vaisya woman, and brought up by a Brâhmana.

आर्य *a.* (*f.* —र्या) 1 Noble, high, respectable. -2 Venerable, worthy. —र्यः *m.* 1 N. of the Hindu and Iranian people, as distinguished from अनार्य, दस्यु and दास. -2 A man who is faithful to the religion and laws of his country. -3 N. of the first three castes (as opp. to शूद्र). -4 A respectable or honourable man, esteemed person. -5 A man of noble birth or of noble character. -6 A master, owner. -7 A preceptor. -8 A friend. -9 A Vaisya. -10 A father-in-law (as in आर्यपुत्र). -11 An honorific designation (in theatrical language) —र्या *f.* 1 N. of Pârvati. -2 A mother-in-law. -3 A respectable woman. -4 N. of a metre. -Comp. —आवर्तः *m.* N. of the tract extending from the eastern to the western ocean, and bounded on the north and south by the Himálaya and Vindhya respectively. —गृह्य *a.* 1 To be respected by the noble. -2 A friend of the noble, readily accessible to honourable men. —देशः *m.* A country inhabited by the Aryas. —पुत्रः *m.* 1 Son of an honourable man. -2 The son of a spiritual preceptor. -3 Honourific designation of the son of the elder brother ; of a husband by his wife ; or of a prince by his general &c. -4 The son of the father-in-law, *i. e.* a husband (occurring in every drama). —प्राय *a.* 1 Inhabited by the Aryas. -2 Abounding with respectable people. —मार्गः *m.* The path or course of the respectable, a respectable way. —मिश्र *a.* Respectable, worthy, distinguished. —मिश्रः *m.* A gentleman, a man of consequence; (pl.). 1 Worthy or respectable men ; an assembly of honourable men. -2 Your reverence or honour (a respectful address). —वृत्त *a.* Virtuous, good, pious. —वृत्तं *n.* The conduct of an Arya or nobleman. —सत्यं *n.* A noble or sublime truth. —हृद्य *a.* Liked by the noble.

आर्यकः *m.* (*f.* आर्यका or आर्यिका) 1 An honourable or respectable man. -2 A grand-father.

आर्यका, आर्यिका *f.* A respectable woman.

आर्वाक् *ind.* After, afterwards ; behind.

आर्ष *a.* (*f.* —र्षी) 1 Relating or belonging to a ऋषि. -2 Vedic (opp. लौकिक or classical). -3 Sacred, holy, divine, superhuman. —आर्षः *m.* One of the eight forms of marriage in which the father of the bride receives one or two pairs of cows from the bride-groom. —र्षं *n.* The holy text, the Vedas.

आर्षभ्यः *m.* A steer sufficiently full grown to be used or let loose ; one fit to be castrated.

आर्षेय *a.* (*f.*–यी) 1 Relating to a Rishi. -2 Worthy, venerable, respectable.

आर्हतः *m.* A Jaina ; a follower of Jaina doctrines. —तं *n.* The doctrines of the Jainas.

आर्हती *f.*, —त्यं *n.* Fitness.

आल *a.* Much, extensive. —लं *n.* 1 Trick, fraud. -2 Yellow arsenic, orpiment.

आलक्ष्य *a.* (*f.* —क्ष्या) 1 Visible, apparent. -2 Slightly visible.

आलर्दः *m.* A water cobra.

आलप् (आ + लप् 1 P.) To address, speak to, converse.

आलभ् (आ + लभ् 1 A.) 1 To touch. -2 To get, attain to. -3 To kill, immolate (as a victim in sacrifices). -4 To take hold of, seize. -5 To gain over.

आलभनं *n.* 1 Taking hold of, seizing. -2 Touching. -3 Killing.

आलंबः *m.* 1 Depending on or from. -2 A prop, stay. -3 Support, protection. -4 Receptacle. -5 A perpendicular.

आलंबनं *n.* 1 Depending on or from. -2 Support, prop. -3 Receptacle. -4 Reason, cause. -5 Base. -6 (In Rhet.) That on which a रस or sentiment, as it were hangs, *i. e.* the person or thing with reference to whom or which a sentiment arises.

आलंभः *m.* See आलभन.

आलर्क *a.* Relating to or caused by a mad dog.

आलवण्यं *n.* 1 Insipidity, tastelessness. -2 Ugliness.

आलवालं *n.* A basin for water round the root of a tree.

आलस *a.* (*f.* —सी) Idle, lazy, slothful.

आलस्य *a.* Idle, slothful, apathetic. —स्यं *n.* 1 Idleness, want of energy.

आलातं *n.* A fire-brand.

आलानं *n.* 1 The post to which an elephant is tied. -2 The rope that ties him. -3 A fetter, tie. -4 Tying.

आलानिक *a.* (*f.* —की) Serving as a post to which an elephant is tied.

आलाप: *m.* 1 Conversation. -2 Narration, mention. -3 The seven notes in music (Mar. सा, रि, ग, म, प, ध, नि). -4 Statement of a question in an arithmetical or algebraical sum. -5 A question.

आलापनं *n.* 1 Speaking to, conversation. -2 Congratulation (स्वस्तिवाचनं).

आलाबु: (-बू) *f.* A pumpkin gourd, same as अलाबू.

आलावर्तं *n.* A fan made of cloth.

आलास्य: *m.* A crocodile.

आलि: *m.* 1 A scorpion. -2 A bee. —लि:, —ली *f.* 1 A female companion or friend (of a woman). -2 A row, range, continuous line. -3 A line, streak. -4 A bridge. -5 A dike -6 A line, race, family.

आलिंगनं *n.* Embracing, an embrace.

आलिंग्य: *m.* A small drum.

आलिंजर: *m.* A large clay water-jar.

आलिंद:, -दक: *m.* 1 A terrace before a house. -2 A raised place for sleeping upon.

आलिंपनं *n.* Whitening the walls, floor &c. on festive occasions.

आली *f.* See आलि.

आलीढ *a.* 1 Licked, lapped, scraped. -2 Wounded, hurt. —ढं *n.* A particular attitude in shooting, the right knee being advanced and the left leg retracted.

आलीन *a.* (*f.* —ना) 1 Embraced. -2 Sticking or clinging to. -3 Melted, fused. —नं, -नकं *n.* 1 Tin. -2 Lead. -3 Contact.

आलु: *m.* 1 An owl. -2 Ebony; black ebony. —लु: *f.* A pitcher, water jar. —लु *n.* A raft, float.

आलुंचनं *n.* Rending, tearing to pieces.

आलू See आलु.

आलेख: *m.* 1 Writing. -2 A letter, document.

आलेखनी *f.* A brush, pencil. -नं *n.* 1 Writing. -2 Painting. -3 Scratching.

आलेख्यं *n.* 1 A painting, picture. -2 A writing. -Comp. —लेखा *f.* A painting. —शेष *a.* Having nothing left but a painting, *i. e.* deceased, dead.

आलेप: *m.*, -पनं *n.* 1 Anointing, smearing. -2 Liniment.

आलोक् (आ + लोक् 1 A., 10 P.) 1 To see, perceive, behold. -2 To consider, contemplate. -3 To greet.

आलोक: *m*., -कनं *n.* 1 Seeing, beholding. -2 Sight, aspect, appearance. -3 Range of sight. -4 Light, lustre. -5 A word of praise uttered by a bard (such as जय, आलोकय). -6 Section, chapter of a book.

आलोच् (आ + लोच् 1 A. 10 U.) 1 To see, perceive. -2 To consider, think, study.

आलोचनं *n.*, -ना *f.* 1 Seeing, perceiving, view. -2 Considering, reflecting.

आलोडनं *n.* 1 Stirring, shaking, agitating. -2 Mixing, blending.

आलोल *a.* (*f.* —ला) Slightly trembling, -2 Shaken, agitated.

आवनेय: *m.* A epithet of the planet Mars.

आवपनं *n.* 1 The act of sowing, throwing, scattering. -2 Sowing seed. -3 Wearing. -4 Shaving. -5 A vessel, jar, ewer.

आवरक *n.* A veil.

आवरणं *n.* 1 A shield. -2 Ignorance (in वेदांत phil.). -3 Covering, hiding. -4 A cover. -5 A cloth, a garment. -6 A wall.

आवर्जनं *n.* 1 Bending down. -2 Giving. -3 Winning over.

आवर्तः *m.* 1 Turning round, revolving. -2 A whirlpool, an eddy. -3 Deliberation (in the mind). -4 A lock of hair curling backwards, especially on a horse. -5 A crowded place (where many men live closely together). -6 A kind of jewel. -7 Melting (of metals). -8 Doubt. -9 Worldly existence (संसार).

आवर्तकः *m.* 1 N. of a form of cloud personified. -2 Depression above the eye-brows. -3 A whirlpool. -4 Revolution. -5 A curl of hair.

आवर्तनं *n.* 1 Turning round, revolution. -2 Circular motion, gyration. -3 Melting together, fusion, alligation (said of metals). -4 Mid-day, the time when shadows are cast in an opposite direction. -5 Repeating, doing over and over again. -6 Study, practising. —नी *f.* 1 A crucible. -2 A spoon, ladle.

आवर्तिन् *a.* (*f.* —नी) 1 Whirling or turning upon itself. -2 Melting, mixing. —र्ती *m.* A horse having curls of hair on various parts of the body (considered as a sign of auspiciousness). —नी *f.* A whirlpool.

आवलिः, —ली *f.* 1 A line, row, range. -2 A series. -3 A dynasty, lineage.

आवलित *a.* (*f.* —ता) Slightly turned.

आवश्यक *a.* (*f.* —की) Inevitable, necessary. —कं *n.* 1 Necessity, inevitable act or duty. -2 An inevitable conclusion.

आवसतिः *f.* 1 Night. -2 Mid-night.

आवसथः *m.*, *n.* 1 A dwelling, dwelling-place, residence. -2 A resting place, asylum. -3 A dwelling for pupils and ascetics. -4 A village.

आवसथ्यः *m.* The sacred fire kept in the house, one of the five fires used in sacrifices.—स्थः *m.*, —थ्यं *n.* A dwelling for pupils and ascetics. —थ्यं *n.* 1 Placing a sacred fire within a house. -2 A house.

आवसित *a.* 1 Finished or completed. -2 Decided, determined. -3 Stored (as grain) ; winnowed. -4 Ripe, full-grown. —तं *n.* Ripe corn (when thrashed).

आवह् (आ + वह् 1 P.) 1 To bring. -2 To bring home (as a bride). -3 To lead or tend to, produce, bring on. -4 To pay. -5 To lead forth, conduct away. -6 To flow (as blood &c.). -7 To bear, support, wear. -8 To use, employ. —*Caus.* 1 To send for, cause to be brought. -2 To invoke a deity (by means of Mantras).

आवह *a.* (as last member of comp.) Producing, leading or tending to, bringing on.

आवहनं *n.* Bringing near, producing.

आवापः *m.* 1 Sowing seed. -2 Scattering, throwing in general. -3 Mixing, inserting. -4 A basin for water round the root of a tree (आलवाल). -5 A vessel, jar for corn. -6 A bracelet. -7 Uneven ground.

आवापकः *m.* A bracelet.

आवापनं *n.* 1 A loom. -2 A reel or frame for winding thread.

आवारः *m.* Enclosing, keeping off.

आवालं *n.* A basin for water round the root of a tree.

आवासः *m.* 1 A house, abode. -2 Apartment, room. -3 A place of refuge.

आवाहः *m.* Marrying.

आवाहनं *n.* 1 Sending for, inviting, calling. -2 Invoking a deity (to be present) (opp. विसर्जन). -3 Offering oblations to fire.

आविक *a.* (*f.* —की) Relating to a sheep. —कं *n* A woollen cloth, blanket. -Comp. —सौत्रिक *a.* Made of woollen thread.

आविद् *Caus.* (आ + विद्, आवेदय्) To make known, report, declare, tell, inform. -2 To bring to, offer, give.

आविद्ध *p. p.* (*f.* —द्धा) 1 Pierced, rent, splintered, broken down. -2 Curved, crooked. -3 Cast with force. -4 Thrown, put in motion. -5 Disappointed. -6 Fallacious, false. -7 Stupid, foolish.

आविधः *m.* An awl, a drill.

आविर्भावः *m.* 1 Manifestation, presence, appearance. -2 An incarnation. -3 Nature or property of things.

आविल *a.* (*f.* —ला) 1 Turbid, foul, dirty. -2 Impure, spoiled. (fig. also). -3 Dim, obscure.

आविलय् Den. P. To sully, make turbid; stain, blot.

आविश् (आ + विश् 6 U.) 1 To enter. -2 To take possession of, possess, affect. -3 To go towards, approach. -4 To go or attain to a particular state.

आविष्करणं *n.*, —ष्कारः *m.* 1 Manifestation, making visible. -2 The means of making visible.

आविष्ट *p. p.* (*f.* —ष्टा) 1 Entered. -2 Possessed (by an evil spirit). -3 Possessed of, seized, overpowered or overcome. -4 Engrossed or occupied in, intent on.

आविस् *ind.* A particle meaning 'before the eyes', 'openly', 'evidently' (usually prefixed to the roots अस्, भू and कृ).

आवी *f.* 1 A woman in her courses. -2 A pregnant woman. -3 The pangs of child-birth.

आवीत *a.* 1 Worn, put on, held after throwing round. -2 Entered, passed, gone. —तं *n.* The sacrificial cord hanging from the right shoulder.

आवीरचूर्णः *m.* The opposite-leaved fig-tree.

आवुकः *m.* A father (in theatrical language).

आवुत्तः *m.* A sister's husband.

आवृ (आ + वृ 5. 9. 10. U) 1 To cover, hide, conceal. -2 To choose, desire. -3 To enclose, obstruct. -4 To keep off.

आवृत् (आ + वृत् 1 A.) 1 To turn round, revolve. -2 To return, come or turn back. -3 To go to or towards. -4 To be restless or uneasy. —*Caus* 1 To cause to turn or revolve, to roll, turn about or over. -2 To cause to roll down, shed (as tears &c.). -3 To attract win over -4 To repeat, recite.

आवृत् *f.* 1 Order, succession, method, mode. -2 Progress of an action, occurrence. -3 Turn of a path, course, direction. -4 A purificatory rite.

आवृत *a.* (*f.* —ता) 1 Covered. -2 Invested, blocked. -3 Enclosed. -4 Spread, overspread. -5 Filled or abounding with. —तः *m.* A man of mixed origin, the son of a Brâhmana by a woman of the उग्र caste.

आवृतिः *f.* Covering, hiding.

आवृत्त *p.p.* (*f.* —त्ता) 1 Turned round, whirled. -2 Repeated. -3 Learnt (by heart), studied. -4 Reverted, returned. -5 Averted. -6 Retreated, fled.

आवृत्तिः *f.* 1 Return, coming back. -2 Retreat, flight -3 Revolving, whirling, going round. -4 Recurrence to the same point or place (of the sun). -5 Repetition of birth and death, worldly existence. -6 Repetition in general. -7 Repeated reading, study. -8 Use, employment, application. -9 Turn of a way, course or direction. -10 Occurrence.

आवेगः *m.* 1 Hurry. -2 Flurry. -3 Agitation regarded as one of the 33 subordinate feelings (In rhetoric).

आवेदनं *n.* 1 Communicating, reporting, or addressing respectfully -2 Representation. -3 Stating a complaint (in law). -4 A plaint.

आवेशः *m.* 1 Entering into, entrance. -2 Taking possession of, influence, exercise. -3 Intentness, complete absorption in one wish or idea. -4 Pride, arrogance. -5 Flurry, agitation, passion. -6 Demoniacal possession. -7 Apoplectic or epileptic giddiness.

आवेशनं *n.* 1 Entering, entrance. -2 Demoniacal possession. -3 Passion, anger, fury. -4 A manufacttory, work-shop. -5 The disc of the sun or the moon. -6 A house, dwelling.

आवेशिक *a.* (*f.* की) 1 Peculiar, one's own. -2 Inherent. —कः *m.* A guest, visitor. —कं *n.* 1 Entering into. -2 Hospitality.

आवेष्टकः *m.* A wall, fence, an enclosure.

आवेष्टनं *n.* 1 Wrapping round, tying, binding. -2 A wrapper, an envelope. -3 A wall, fence, enclosure.

आश *a.* One who eats, eater (mostly as the last member of comp.) *e. g.* हुताश, आश्रयाश &c. —शः *m.* Eating (as in प्रातराशः, सायमाशः).

आशंस् (आ + शंस् 1 A., rarely P.) 1 To hope for, desire, wish or long for. -2 To bless, wish well to. -3 To speak, say, tell. -4 To ask for, beg. -5 To praise.

आशंसनं *n.* 1 Expecting, wishing. -2 Telling, declaring.

आशंसा *f.* 1 Desire, wish, expectation, hope. -2 Speech, declaration. -3 The desire to express. -4 Indication, expression. -5 Imagination.

आशंसु *a.* Desirous, hopeful.

आशंक् (आ + शंक् 1 A.) 1 To suspect, distrust, to be in doubt or suspense. -2 To fear, be afraid, apprehend. -3 To start a doubt or objection.

आशंका *f.* 1 Fear, apprehension. -2 Doubt, uncertainty. -3 Distrust, suspicion.

आशयः *m.* 1 The seat of feelings *i. e.* the mind, the heart. -2 Meaning, purport. -3 A seat, a place of residence. -4 A receptacle, reservoir. -5 Prosperity. -6 A barn. -7 Will or pleasure. -8 Fate, fortune.

-9 A pit made for catching animals.

आशर: *m.* 1 Fire. -2 A demon. -3 Wind.

आशवं *n.* 1 Speed, quickness. -2 Distilled spirit, more usually written आसव.

आशा *f.* 1 Hope, expectation, prospect. -2 Wish, desire. -3 False hope or expectation. -4 Space, region, quarter of the compass, direction. -Comp. —गज: *m.* A guardian elephant of a quarter or point of the compass. —तंतु: *m.* A thread of hope, slender hope. —पाल: *m.* A guardian or regent of the regions or quarters. —पिशाचिका *f.* Deceptive or illusive hope, phantom of hope. -प्राप्त *a.* Successful (=मामाश) -बंध: *m.* 1. The tie or bond of hope, confidence, trust, expectation. -2 Consolation. -3 A spider's web. —भंग: *m.* Disappointment. —वह *a.* Inspiring hope.

आशास् (आ + शास् 2 A.) 1 To bless. -2 To desire, wish, hope, expect. -3 To order, command, relate (P. also in this sense). -4 To praise.

आशित *a.* 1 Eaten. -2 Satisfied by eating. -3 Voracious, gluttonous. —तं *n.* Eating.

आशितंगवीन *a.* Formerly grazed by cattle.

आशितंभव *a.* Satiating, satisfying (as food). —वं *n.* 1 Food. -2 Satisfaction, satiety (*m.* also).

आशिर *a.* Voracious. -र: *m.* 1 Fire. -2 The sun. -3 A demon.

आशिस् *f.* A blessing, benediction. -2 Act of bestowing a blessing upon others. -3 A prayer, wish, desire -4 A serpent's fang. -Comp. —वाद: *m.* —वचनं *n.* (आशीर्वादः, आशीर्वचनं) A blessing, benediction, expression of a prayer or wish. —विष: (आशीर्विष:) *m.* Snake.

आशी *f.* 1 A serpent's fang. -2 A kind of venom. -3 A blessing, benediction -Comp. —विष: *m.* 1 A snake. -2 A particular kind of snake.

आशु *a.* Fast, swift, active, quick.

आशु: *m.* 1 Rice (ripening quickly in the rainy season). —शु *ind.* Fast, quickly, immediately, directly. --Comp. -कारिन्, —कृत् *a.* 1 Smart, active. -2 Operating quickly (as a medicine). —ग *a.* Swift, quick. —ग: *m.* 1 The wind. -2 The sun. -3 An arrow. —तोष *a.* Easily appeased or pleased. —तोष: *m.* An epithet of Siva. —व्रीहि: *m.* Rice ripening in the rainy season.

आशुशुक्षणि: *m.* 1 Wind, air. -2 Fire.

आशोकुटिन् *m.* A mountain.

आशोषणं *n.* The act of drying.

आशौचं *n.* (-च्यं) Impurity. Same as अशौचं

आश्चर्य *a.* (*f.* —र्या) Marvellous, wonderful, extraordinary. -र्यं *n.* 1 A wonder, miracle, marvel. -2 Surprise, astonishment. -3 (Used as an exclamation. Ah wonder ! How strange or curious !

आश्चो (-श्च्यो-) तनं *n.* 1 Aspersion, sprinkling. -2 Applying ghee &c. to the eyelids.

आश्म *a.* Made of stone, stony.

आश्मन *a.* (*f.* —नी) Stony, made of stones. —न: *m.* 1 Anything made of stone. -2 N. of Aruna, the charioteer of the sun.

आश्मारिक *a.* (*f.* —की) 1 Suffering from stone in the bladder. — क: *m.*

The disease, stone in the bladder.

आश्मिक *a.* (*f.* —की) 1 Made of stone. -2 Carrying stones.

आश्यान *p. p.* (*f.* —ना) 1 Congealed. -2 Partially dried, dried by fumigation (as hair).

आश्रपणं *n.* The act of cooking or boiling.

आश्रमः *m.*, —मं *n.* 1 A hermitage, hut, dwelling or abode of ascetics. —2 A period in the religious life of a Brâhmana. (These are four:- ब्रह्मचर्य the life of a student; गार्हस्थ्य the life of a house-holder; वानप्रस्थ the life of an anchorite or hermit, and संन्यास the life of a Bhikshu or beggar. -3 A college, school. -4 A wood or thicket where ascetics practise penance. -5 N. of Vishnu. --Comp. —गुरुः *m.* The head of a religious order, a preceptor, principal. —धर्मः *m.* 1 The special duties of each order or life. -2 The duties of one leading a hermit's life य इमामाश्रमधर्मे नियुंक्ते • शाकुंत. 1. -पदं, —मंडलं, —स्थानं *n.* 1 A hermitage (including the surrounding grounds), a penance forest (तपोवनं). --2 A period in the religious life of a Brâhmana. —भ्रष्ट *a.* Fallen from any religious order. —वासिन्, -आलयः *m.* An ascetic, hermit.

आश्रमिक *a.* (*f.* —की) 1 Belonging to any of the four orders or periods of religious life. --2 Belonging to a hermitage.

आश्रयः *m.* 1 Substratum, receptacle, a resting place. --2 An asylum a place of refuge. --3 A prop, a support. --4 A quiver. -5 Help, assistance. -6 Authority, sanction. -7 Dependence. --8 Supporter, master. —9 Connection, association. —10 Seeking protection (one of the six modes of foreign policy). --Comp. —आसिद्धः *m.*, --द्धिः *f.* A kind of fallacy. —आशः, -भुज् *m.* Fire. —लिंगं *n.* An adjective; a word which must agree in gender with the word which it qualifies or refers to.

आश्रयणं *n.* 1 Taking refuge with. -2 Accepting, choosing. -3 Joining. -4 Refuge, asylum.

आश्रव *a.* (*f.* —वा) Obedient. —वः *m.* 1 A promise, engagement. -2 Fault, transgression.

आश्रिः *f.* The edge of a sword.

आश्रि (आ + श्रि 1 U.) 1 To resort or betake oneself to; to have recourse to. -2 To seek refuge with, inhabit (as a place &c). -2 To experience. --3 To assist, help.

आश्रित *p. p.* (Used actively)(with an acc.) 1 Resorting to, having recourse to; dwelling in, seated or resting on. -2 Using, employing. -3 Following, practising, observing. -4 Dependent on. -5 Referring to, regarding. -6 (Passively used) Resorted to, inhabited. —तः *m.* A dependent servant, follower.

आश्रु (आ + श्रु 5 P.) 1 To hear, listen to. -2 To promise (with dat. of person). -3 To accept, undertake.

आश्रुत *p. p.* (*f.* —ता) 1 Heard. -2 Promised, accepted.

आश्लिष् (आ + श्लिष् 4 P.) 1 To embrace, clasp. -2 To cleave or stick to.

आश्लिष्ट *p. p.* (*f.* —ष्टा) 1 Embraced, clasped; used actively also. -2 Connected, interwoven, blended. -3 Joined to, being in contact with.

आश्लेषः *m.* 1 Embracing, clasping,

an embrace. -2 Contact, intimate connection ; relation. —षा *f.* (pl.) N. of the ninth Nakshatra.

आश्वं *n.* I A number of horses. -2 A chariot drawn by horses. -3 The state or action of a horse.

आश्वत्थ *a.* (*f.* —त्थी), आश्वत्थिक *a.* (*f.* की) Relating to or made of the holy fig-tree. —त्थं *n.* The fruit of the holy fig tree.

आश्वयुज *a.* (*f.* —जी) I Belonging to the month Asvina. -2 Born under the constellation अश्वयुज्. —ज: *m.* The month आश्विन. —जी *f.* The day of the full moon in Asvina.

आश्वयुजक *a.* (*f.* —की). Sown at the day of full moon in Asvina.

आश्वलक्षणिक *a.* (*f.* —की) Knowing the marks of horses. —क: *m.* A farrier, groom.

आश्वस् (आ + श्वस 2 P.) I To breathe, to breathe freely, recover breath, rest secure, be at ease. -2 To revive. —*Caus.* I To encouage, console, cheer up. -2 To refresh, gratify. -3 To conciliate.

आश्वस्त *a.* adv. Refreshed, siting at ease आश्वस्तं चैनमासीन मुपासीनो युधिष्ठिर: । अभिप्रेक्ष्य महा बाहु: कृपणं बह्वभाषत * वनप. 52.

आश्वास: *m.* I Taking or recovering breath. -2 Consolation, inspiring confidence. -3 An assurance of safety or protection. -4 Ceasation.

आश्वासनं *n.* Consoling, encouraging, eheering up.

आश्विक: *m.* A cavalier.

आश्विन: *m.* I N. of a month in the Hindu cycle. -2 (du.) The Asvins.

आश्विनेय: *m.* Each of the two Asvins (physicians of gods). —या: *m.* I N. of Nakula and Sahadeva, the last two of the five Pándava princes.

आश्वीन *a.* Made or traversed by a horse (as a journey &c.).—न: *m.*, नं *n.* The distance travelled by a horse in a day.

आश्वीयं *n.* A number of horses.

आषाढ: *m.* I N. of a Hindu month, (corresponding to June and July). -2 A staff of the Pàlâsa wood carried by an ascetic. -3 The Malaya mountain. —ढा *f.*. The 20th and the 21st lunar mansions, usually called पूर्वाषाढा and उत्तराषाढा. —ढी *f.* The day of full moon in the month of Ashádha. –Comp. —भव:, —भू: *m.* The planet Mars.

आष्टम: *m.* The 8th part.

आस्, आ: *ind.* An interjection, implying (*a*) Recollection ; (*b*) Anger ; (*c*) Pain; (*d*) Angry contradiction (*e*) Sorrow, regret.

आस् I. 2 A. (आस्ते, आमाचक्रे, आसिष्ट ; आसितुं, आसित) I To sit, lie, rest. -2 To live, dwell. -3 To sit quietly, take no hostile méasures, remain idle. -4 To be, exist. -5 To be contained in. -6 To abide, remain, continue or be doing anything. -7 To lead to, result in (with dat). -8 To cease, have an end. -9 To solemnize, celebrate. -10 To let go, lay or put aside. आस्तां तावत् let it go, to say nothing of, not to mention With अधि— To occupy (with *acc.* अनु— To sit down after. -2 To serve, to follow. —उद्— To be indifferent to, to be neglectful, to be careless. उप— I To wait upon, to be in attendance upon. -2 To pass (as time). -3 To go to. -4 To undergo. -5 To resort to. -6 To perform (as a rite). -7 To practise archery. पर्युप I To be in attendance upon, to attend respectfully. -2 To seek the protection or patronage of. -3 To surround. -4 To partake of. सम्— To sit down. समुप- To wait upon. -2 To perform.

आसः m. I A seat. -2 A bow (· सं also).

आसक्त p. p. (f. —क्ता) I Strongly attached to, intent on (usually with loc.) -2 Continuous, perpetual, eternal. -3 Trusting to, confiding in. —Comp. —चित्त, —चेतस्, —मनस् a. Having the mind fixed on any object.

आसक्ति: f. I Attachment, devotion, fondness, application.

आसंग: m. I Attachment, devotion (to any object), close application. -2 Contact, adherence, clinging. -3 Association, connection, union. -4 Fixing, fastening to.

आसंगिनी f. A whirlwind.

आसंज् (आ + संज् I P.) I To fasten, fix on, place or put on (dress, armour &c.). -2 To confer upon, conduce to.

आसंजनं n. I Fastening to, fixing, putting on the body (as dress, armour &c.). -2 Getting entangled, clinging. -3 Attachment, devotion. -4 Contact, proximity. -5 A handle, hook.

आसत्ति: f. I Meeting, junction. -2 Intimate union, nearness, close contact. -3 Gain, profit. -4 (In Logic) The relation between two or more proximate terms and the sense conveyed by them.

आसद् (आ + सद् I P.) I To sit down or near (with acc. or loc.). -2 To watch or lie in wait for. -3 To approach, reach. -4 To encounter, attack. -5 To commence, undertake. -6 To place.

आसन् n. Mouth ; (a word optionally substituted for आस्य in all cases after acc. dual).

आसनं n. I Sitting down. -2 A seat, place, stool. The seat or throne sitting on which the king hears complaints and dispenses justice ; this is also called कार्यासन, धर्मासन, व्यवहारासन &c. -3 A particular posture or mode of sitting. -4 Halting, stopping, encamping. -5 Abiding, dwelling. -6 Maintaining a post against an enemy (opp. यानं). -7 The front part of an elephant's body. —Comp. —बंधधीर a. Firm in one's seat.

आसना f. A seat, a stool.

आसनी f. I A small seat. -2 A shop.

आसंद: m. Vishnu or Vâsudeva. —दी f. I A small couch. -2 A raised seat in a hall or assembly.

आसंदिका f. A small chair.

आसन्न p. p. (f. —न्ना) I Approached, near (in time, place or number). -2 Adjacent, imminent. -Comp. —काल: m. I The hour of death. -2 One whose death is near. —परिचारक:, —चारिका Personal attendant, body-guard. —प्रसव a. About to be confined or delivered, about to bring forth or lay eggs (as a hen &c.). —मृत्यु, —शरीरपात a. One whose death has drawn near.

आसंबाध a. Blocked up, obstructed.

आसव: m. I Distillation, decoction. -2 Spirituous liquor.

आसादनं n. I Putting or laying down. -2 Attacking. -3 Overtak ing, meeting with. -4 Obtaining, accomplishing.

आसाधनं *n.* Accomplishment, attainment.

आसारः *m.* 1 A hard shower. -2 Violent gust; भीषणः समीरणासारः sweeping, violent gust of wind * वेणीसं. २ -3 Surrounding an enemy. -4 Attack, incursion. -5 The army of an ally. -6 Provision, food.

आसिकः *m.* A swordsman.

आसिधारं *n.* N. of a particular vow.

आसीन *pres. p.* (*f.* —ना) Sitting, seated.

आसुर *a.* (*f.* —री) 1 Belonging to or relating to evil spirits. -2 Infernal, demoniacal. —रः *m.* 1 A demon. -2 One of the eight forms of marriage. —री *f.* 1 Surgery, curing by cutting by instruments. -2 A female demon, demoness —रं *n.* 1 Blood. -2 Black salt.

आसूत्रित *a.* (*f.* —ता) 1 Forming or wearing a garland. -2 Interwoven.

आसेकः *m.* Wetting, watering.

आसेचनं *n.* Pouring into, wetting, sprinkling.

आसेधः *m.* Arrest, custody, legal restraint.

आसेवा *f.*, --वनं *n.*1 Zealous practice, assiduous performance of any action. -2 Frequency, repetition.

आस्कंद् (आ + स्कंद् 1 P.) 1 To invade, attack. -2 To jump, leap.

आस्कंदः *m.*, -दनं *n.* 1 An attack, assault; assailing, rape, outraging. -2 Ascending, mounting, stepping over. -3 Reproach, abuse. -4 The walk of a horse. -5 Battle, war

आस्कन्दित, -तकं *n.* The galloping at full speed (of a horse).

आस्तरः *m.* 1 A covering, coverlet. -2 A carpet, bed, mat.

आस्तरणं *n.* 1 Spreading, strewing. -2 A bed, layer. -3 A cushion, bedclothes. -4 A rug; carpet. -5 An elephant's housings. -6 A layer of Kusa grass spread out at a sacrifice.

आस्तारः *m.* Spreading, strewing, scattering.

आस्तिक *a.* (*f* —की) 1 One who believes in God and another world. -2 A believer in sacred tradition. -3 Pious, faithful, believing.

आस्तिकता, *f.* -त्वं, -आस्तिक्यं *n.* 1 Belief in God and another world. -2 Piety, faith, belief.

आस्तृ,—स्तॄ (आ + स्तृ, स्तॄ 5. 9. U.) To spread over, cover, scatter over.

आस्था (आ + स्था 1 U.) 1 To stand or remain on or by, to occupy. -2 To ascend, mount. -3 To use, resort to, practise, take, assume, follow. -4 To perform, carry out. -5 To acknowledge, own. -6 To aim at. -7 To undertake, promise. -8 To behave. —*Caus.* 1 To cause to stand. -2 To hold fast. -3 To collect, obtain. -4 To show, represent, introduce. -5 To step.

आस्था *f.* 1 Regard, respect, consideration, care for (with loc). -2 Assent, promise. -3 Prop, support, stay. -4 Hope, confidence. -5 An effort. -6 State, condition. -7 An assembly. -8 A place or means of abiding.

आस्थानं *n.* 1 A place, site. -2 Ground, base. -3 An assembly -4 Care, regard. -5A hall of audience. -6 Recreation-ground. —नी *f.* An assembly-room. -Comp. —गृहं, -निके-

वनं, -मंडप: An assembly-room.

आस्थापनं *n.* 1 Placing, fixing, causing to stay or remain. -2 A strengthening remedy. -3 An enema of oil or ghee.

आस्थायिका *f.* An audience.

आस्पदं *n.* 1 A place, site, seat. -2 (Fig.) An abode, subject, receptacle. -3 Rank, position, station, dignity. authority, office. -4 Business, affair. -5 Prop, support

आस्पंदनं *n.* Trembling.

आस्पर्धा *f* Rivalry, emulation.

आस्फाल: *m.* 1 Striking, rubbing, forcibly striking; collision; अन्योन्यास्फालभिन्नद्विपरुधिरवसामांसमस्तिष्कपंके * वेणीसं. 1. 27. -2 Flapping.-3 Particularly, the flapping motion of an elephant's ears.

आस्फालनं *n.* 1 Rubbing, stirring, flapping. -2 Pride, arrogance.

आस्फोट: *m.* 1 The Arka plant. -2 The sound made by striking on the arms (Mar. दंड ठोकणें). -3 Trembling, quivering. -4 Striking or rubbing against. blow. —टा *f.* The नवमल्लिका plant, wild variety of jasmin.

आस्फोटनं *n.* 1 Flapping, moving to and fro, shaking. -2 Blowing, expanding. -3 Slapping or clapping the arms, or the sound produced by it. -4 Disclosing, manifasting. -5 Winnowing, thrashing. —नी *f.* A gimlet.

आस्माक *a.* (*f.* —की), आस्माकीन (*f.* —ना) *a.* Our, ours.

आस्यं *n.* 1 The mouth, jaws. -2 Face. -3 A Mouth, opening; व्रणास्यं, अंकास्यं &c -Comp. —आसव: *m.* Spittle, saliva. —पत्रं *n.* A lotus. —लांगल: *m.* 1 A dog. -2 A boar. —लोमन् *n.* The beard.

आस्यंदनं *n.* Flowing, oozing.

आस्यंधय *a.* Kissing.

आस्या *f.* Sitting, abode, state of rest.

आस्रं *n.* Blood. -Comp —प: *m.* 1 A demon. -2 The 19th lunar mansion.

आस्रव: *m.* 1 Pain, affliction, distress. -2 Flowing, running. -3 Discharge, emission. -4 Fault, transgression. -5 The foam on boiling rice.

आस्राव: *m.* 1 A wound. -2 Flow, issue, discharge. -3 Spittle, saliva. -4 Pain, affliction.

आस्वाद: *m.* 1 Tasting, eating. -2 Relish, flavour, taste. -3 Enjoying, experiencing.

आस्वादनं *n.* Tasting, eating.

आस्वाद्य *pot. p.* (*f.* —द्या) To be tasted, delicious, sweet, palatable.

आह *ind.* 1 An interjection showing reproof; severity; command. -2 An irregular verbal form of the 3rd. pers. sing. Pres. of a defective verb meaning ' to say', or ' to speak ' the only forms of the root existing in the language are:— आत्थ, आहथु:, आह, आहतु:, and आहु:.).

आहत *p. p.* (*f.* —ता) 1 Struck, beaten (as a drum &c.). -2 Trodden. -3 Injured. killed. -4 Multiplied (in Math.) -5 Rolled (as dice). -6 Uttered falsely. —त: *m.* A drum. —तं *n.* 1 A new cloth or garment. -2 An old garment. -3 A nonsensical or meaningless speech an assertion of impossibility. *e. g.* एष वंध्यासुतो याति -Comp. —लक्षण *a.* Noted for good qualities cf. आहितलक्षण.

आहति: *f.* 1 Killing. -2 A blow,

hit, striking. -3 Coming (आगति). -4 Multiplication.

आहन् (आ + हन् 2 P.) 1 To strike, hit, beat. -2 To kill, slaughter.

आहननं *n.* 1 Beating. -2 A stick.

आहर *a.* (At the end of comp.) Bringing, fetching, taking, seizing. —रः *m.* 1 Taking, seizing. -2 Accomplishing, performing. -3 Offering a sacrifice. -4 Inhaling. -5 The air so inhaled. -6 Inspiration, breath inspired.

आहरणं *n.* 1 Fetching, bringing (near). -2 Seizing, taking. -3 Removing, extracting. -4 Performing, (as a sacrifice). -5 A dowry or present given to a bride (at the time of her marriage). -6 Causing, inducing.

आहर्तृ *a.* 1 One who takes or seizes. -2 Bringing, fetching. -3 Performing (as a sacrifice).

आहवः *m.* 1 A sacrifice. -2 Battle, war. -Comp. —काम्या *f.* Desire to fight.

आहवनं *n* 1 A sacrifice. -2 An oblation.

आहवनीय *a.* To be offered as an oblation. —यः *m.* One of the three sacred fires (taken from the householder's perpetual fire).

आहारः *m.* 1 Taking, fetching or bringing near. -2 Employing, using. -3 Taking food. -4 Food. —Comp. —अर्थिन् *a.* Begging or seeking for food. -पाकः *m.* 1 Cooking. -2 Digestion (of food). —विरहः *m.* Want of food, privation, starvation. —संभवः *m.* The juice of the body, chyle, lymph

आहार्य *pot. p.* (*f.* -र्या) 1 To be taken or seized. -2 To be brought near. -3 To be removed -4 To be pervaded (व्याप्य)-5 Artificial, adventitious. -6 (Rhet.) Borrowed, as knowledge in the identification of one thing with another as in a रूपक. In रूपक we identify the उपमान with the उपमेय with full consciousness that they are distinct things, and we do this because there is a great similarity between them; this knowledge is आहार्य. In भ्रांतिमान् we are not conscious that the उपमान and the उपमेय are distinct things. In भ्रांतिमान् The knowledge is अनाहार्य. -7 Effected or accomplished by decoration, or ornamentation. -8 To be eaten. -र्यं *n.* The ornamentative part of the drama, such as dress, decorations &c.

आहावः *m.* 1 A trough near a well for watering cattle. -2 War, battle. -3 Invoking, calling.

आहिकः *m.* The descending node (केतु).

आहिंडकः *m.* The son of a Nishâda father and Vaidehi mother.

आहित *p. p.* (*f.* —ता) 1 Placed, set, deposited. -2 Given, imparted. -3 Entertained, felt. -4 Comprising, containing. -5 Made, done. -Comp. —अग्नि *a.* 1 A Bráhman who keeps the sacred fire on the altar. cf. अत्याहित. -2 A Brâhmana who maintains and consecrates sacred fire in his house perpetually. —अंक *a.* Marked, spotted. —लक्षण *a.* Noted or well-known for good qualities).

आहितुंडिकः *m.* A juggler, a snake-catcher, conjurer.

आहुत *p. p.* (*f.* —ता) Offered to the gods, sacrificed. —तं *n.* 1 An offering made to men, hospitality.

आहुतिः *f.* 1 Offering an oblation to a deity, any solemn rite accompanied with oblations. -2 An oblation offered to a deity.

आहूतिः *f.* Calling, invoking, challenging.

आहूत *p. p.* (*f.* —ता) 1 Called, invoked, invited. -2 Named, called. —तं *n.* Calling.

आहूतिः *f.* Calling, invoking.

आहृ (आ + हृ 1 P.) 1 To bring, fetch. -2 To bring near, give. -3 To recover, bring back. -4 To obtain, get, receive. -5 To have, assume. -6 To cause, produce. -7 To bring near (as wife), marry. -8 To wear, put on (as armour &c.). -9 To perform (as a sacrifice). -10 To take away, attract (as mind). -11 To separate, remove, draw off from. -12 To frighten away, drive forth. -13 To use as food or drink, eat. -14 To speak, say, name, call. —*Caus.* 1 To make one fetch or bring; to cause to give or pay. -2 To eat. -3 To bring together, collect. -4 To cause, produce. -5 To show, exhibit.

आहेय *a.* Pertaining to a serpent (as poison).

आहो *ind.* An interjection expressing (*a*) Doubt or alternative (or), (*b*) Interrogation. —Comp. —पुरुषिका *f.* 1 Great self-conceit or pride. -2 Military vaunting, boasting. -3 Vaunting of one's own prowess. —स्वित् *ind.* A particle implying doubt, ' or perhaps, ' 'or it may be' &c. (Both आहो and आहोस्वित् are usually correlatives of किं whether).

आह्न *a.* (*f.* -ह्नी) Daily, performed in a day. —ह्नं *n.* A series of days, many days.

आह्निक *a.* (*f.* —की) 1 Daily, performed every day or on a day. -2 employed or occurring every day (as a teacher, servant, or fever). —कं *n.* 1 Any religious rite which is to be performed every day at a fixed hour. -2 Anything to be performed daily. -3 Daily food. -4 Daily work or occupation.

आह्लादः *m.* Delight, joy.

आह्लादनं *a.* Giving delight. —नं *n.* Gladdening, delighting.

आह्व *a.* 1 Who or what calls ; a crier. -2 Named, called. —ह्वा *f.* 1 Calling, calling out. -2 A name, appellation.

आह्वयः *m.* 1 A name, appellation (as last member of comp.). -2 A lawsuit arising from a dispute about games with animals, as cock-fighting &c.

आह्वयनं *n.* Name, appellation.

आह्वान *n.* 1 Calling, inviting. -2 A call, invitation, summons (in general). -3 A legal summons from court or govt. to appear before a tribunal). -4 Invocation of a deity. -5 A challenge. -6 A name, appellation.

आह्वानय् Den. P. (In law) To summon.

आह्वायः *m.* 1 A summons. -2 A name.

आह्वायकः *m.* A messenger, courier

आह्वे (आ + ह्वे 1 P.) 1 To call summon. -2 To invite, invoke -3.(A.) To provoke, challenge.

इ.

इ The third letter of the Devanâgari alphabet.

इ *ind.* An interjection of (1) anger; (2) calling; (3) compassion; (4) reproach; (5) wonder; (6) sorrow; (7) distress.

इ 1 P. 1 To go, go to or towards, come to or near. -2 Reach; go to or be reduced to a particular state, fall into. With —उद् To rise, to ascend. —अभ्युद् To prosper.

इ 2 P. To go, to go towards. With अति— 1 To surpass. -2 To pass (time). -3 To go away or beyond. अधि— 1 To remember, to think of (often with *gen.*). -2 A. To study, to learn. अनु— 1 To follow. -2 To imitate. -3 To succeed. अन्वा— To follow, come after. अंतर्— To intervene, to screen, to obstruct. अप— 1 To depart, to be deprived of, to be free from (with *abl*). -3 To perish. अभि— 1 To get. -2 To approach. -3 To serve अभ्या— To approach अभ्युद्- To flourish, to prosper. अभ्युप— 1 To arrive. -2 To accept. -3 To attain to, to be subject of. अभिप्र— To intend, to mean. अव— To know. आ— To come. उद्— 1 To arise, ascend. -2 To flourish. उप— To go to. निर्— To set out, to go out. परा— 1 To depart life. -2 To run away, to retreat. परि— 1 To go round. -2 To surround. -3 To change. प्र— To depart life. प्रति— 1 To trust, confide. -2 To go back to. -3 To be well-known. -4 To be pleased or satisfied. (causal प्रत्यायय् means to inspire confidence, to convince). प्रत्युद्— 1 To go to receive. वि— 1 To expend. -2 To undergo a change. -3 To go away. व्यति— 1 To pass away. -2 To go out, transgress. व्यप— 1 To go away. -2 To separate, to depart. विपरि— To change into something worse or contrary. सम्— To meet, to come together. समनु— To accompany. समव— 1 To be connected (in logic). -2 To assemble, to meet. समा— To come together, to unite. समुद्— To collect. समुप— To obtain. संप्रति— To determine, to judge.

इकट: *m.* A kind of reed or grass for mats

इक्षव: *m.* A sugar-cane.

इक्षु: *m.* Sugar-cane. -Comp. —कांड:, *m.*, —कं *n.* Two different species of sugar-cane. —कुट्टक: *m.* A gatherer of sugar-cane. —पाक: *m.* Molasses. (Mar. गूळ). —भक्षिका *f.* A meal of sugar and molasses. —मती, —मालिनी, —मालवी *f.* N. of a river. —यंत्रं *n.* A sugar-mill. —रस: *m.* 1 The juice of sugar-cane. -2 Molasses, unrefined sugar. —वणं *n.* A sugar-cane wood. —वाटिका, —वाटी *f.* A garden of sugar-canes. -विकार: *m.* 1 Sugar, molasses. -2 Any sweetmeat. -सार: *m.* Molasses, raw or unrefined sugar.

इक्षुक: *m.* Sugar-cane.

इक्षुकीया *f.* A place abounding in sugar-cane.

इक्षुर: *m.* Sugar-cane.

इक्ष्वाकु: *m.* 1 The first king of the solar dynasty in अयोध्या. -2 A descendent of इक्ष्वाकु. —कु: *f.* A kind of bitter gourd. (Mar. कडू दुध्या).

इख् 1 P. (*p. p.* एखित.) To go, to move. 1 P. (*p. p.* इंखित.) To go, to move. With प्र— To move to and fro.

इंख् P. 1 To move, shake.–2 To go.

इंग a. 1 Movable. –2 Wonderful, surprising. —गः m. 1 A hint or sign. –2 An indication of a sentiment by gesture.

इंगनं n. 1 Moving, shaking.–2 An indication of a sentiment by gesture.

इंगितं n. 1 Palpitation, shaking. –2 Intention, purpose.–3 A hint, sign, gesture. –4 The gesture or motion of the various limbs of the body indicating one's intentions; gesture suited to betray internal feelings. –Comp. —कोविद्, –ज्ञ a. Skilled in the interpretation of internal sentiments by external gestures.

इंगुदः m., –दी f., इंगुदः m. N. of a medicinal tree, (Mar. हिंगणबेट).

इच्छा f. 1 Wish, desire, will. –2 (In Math.) A question or problem. –3 (In gram.) The form of the desiderative. –Comp. —दानं n. Fulfilment of a wish. —फलं n. The solution of a question or problem. —वसु a. 'Possessing wealth according to wish', epithet of Kubera. –संपद् f. Fulfilment of one's wishes.

इज्य pot p (f. —ज्या) To be worshipped. —ज्यः m. 1 A teacher. –2 An epithet of बृहस्पति, the teacher of the gods. –3 An epithet of Vishnu. —ज्या f. 1 A sacrifice. –2 A gift, donation. –3 An image. –4 Worship, reverence. –5 A bawd or procuress. –6 A cow. –Comp. –शीलः m. A constant sacrificer.

इट्चरः m. A bull or steer allowed to go at liberty.

इडा f. 1 The earth. –2 Speech. –3 An offering, libation. –4 A cow. –5 N. of the wife of Budha and mother of Pururavas. –6 N. of Durgā. –7 A tubular vessel(नाडिभेद).

इडिका f. The earth.

इड्वरः m. An ox let loose.

इत p. p. 1 Gone to. –2 Returned. –3 Obtained. –4 Remembered. –5 Attended by. —तं n. 1 Course, mode of going. –2 A way. –3 Knowledge.

इतर pron. a. (f. –रा, n. –रत्) 1 Another, the other (of two). –2 The rest or others (pl.). –3 Other than, different from (with abl.).–4 Opposite of, as दक्षिण– left; वाम–right &c. –5 Low, mean, vulgar, ordinary. इतर–इतर the one–the other, this-that. –Comp. –इतर pron. a. Respective, reciprocal, one with another. इतरेतराश्रयः m. Mutual dependence, inter-connection. इतरेतरयोगः m. 1 Mutual connection or union. –2 A variety of the Dvandva compound (opp. समाहारद्वंद्व).

इतरतः, इतरत्र ind. Otherwise than, different from, elsewhere.

इतरथा ind 1 In another manner. –2 Perversely.–3 On the other hand.

इतरेद्युः ind. On another day, the other day.

इतस् ind. 1 Hence, from here. –2 From this person. –3 In this direction, here. –4 Hence, for this reason, on this ground. –5 From this world. –6 From this time. इतस्ततः Here and there, hither and thither, to and fro.

इति ind. 1 This particle is generally used to report the very words spoken by some one, as represented by the quotation marks in English. The speech reported may be (1) a single word used merely to express what the form of the word is, when it is used as it is (शब्दस्वरूपद्योतक) ; राम रामेति रामेति

कूजितं मधुराक्षरं (2) or a substantive, which must be put in the nominative case when its meaning is to be indicated (प्रातिपदिकार्थद्योतक); दिलीप इति राजेंदु: * रघुवं 1. 12. (3) sometimes with acc. कैवर्तमिति वं प्राहु:. (4) or a whole sentence when इति is merely used at the end of that sentence ; (वाक्यार्थद्योतक); इास्यासि कियद्‍दूरं मे रक्षाति मौर्वीकिणांक इति * शाकुंत. 1. 13.

Besides this general sense इति has the following senses. 1 Cause, purpose or motive, (because, since, that) पुराणमित्येव न साधु सर्वं In this sense it is sometimes preceded by किं and then it means 'for what purpose,' किमित्यपास्याभरणानि यौवने धृतं त्वया वार्धक शोभिवल्कलं * कुमा. सं 5. 44). -2 Manner, method (so, thus) इतिमदमदनाभ्यां रागिण: स्पष्टरागा: * शिशुपा. 10. 91. -3 Manifestation ; e g इतिहरि:. -4 Finis; e. g. इति रघुवंशे पंचम: सर्ग:. -5 Capacity, relation ; e. g. पितेतिपूज्य:. -6 Illustration (generally with आदि). e. g. गौ: शुक्लश्चलोडित्थ इत्यादौ. -7 A quotation or opinion. e. g. एकोऽपि दोषो गुणसंनिपाते निमज्जतींदोरिति यो बभाषे. -8 Reporting (as follows). e. g. रामाभिधानो हरिरित्युवाच * रघुवं. 13. 1. -Comp. —अर्थ: m. Sum and substance, meaning in short. —अर्थं ind. For this purpose, hence. —आदि a. Having such a thing or things at the beginning, and so forth, et caetera —उक्तं n. Information, report. —कथा f. A meaningless or nonsensical talk. —कर्तव्यं, करणीयं n. Duty, obligation. —मात्र a. Of such extent or quality. —वृत्त n 1 Occurrence, event. -2 A tale, story.

इतिवत् ind. In the same manner.

इतिह ind. Thus indeed ; in conformity to tradition.

इतिहास: m. 1 History. -2 Legend. -3 Tradition recognized as a proof.

इत्थं ind. Thus, so, in this manner. -Comp. —कारं ind. In this manner. —भूत a. 1 So circumstanced, being in this state, being thus. -2 True or faithful (as a story). —विध a. Of such kind, endowed with such qualities.

इत्य a. (f. —त्या) To be gone towards or approached. —त्या f. 1 Going; way. -2 A litter, palanquin.

इत्वर a. (f. —री) 1 Going, travelling. -2 Cruel, harsh. -3 Low. -4 vile, contemned. -4 Poor. —र: m. A eunuch. —री f. 1 A disloyal or unchaste woman. -2 An अभिसारिका.

इदं pron. a. 1 This here, referring to something near the speaker. -2 Present, seen. -3 What the speaker has in mind. -4 It often refers to something immediately following, while एतद् refers to what precedes. -5 It occurs connected with यत्, तत्, एतद्, अदस्, किं or a personal pronoun, either to point out anything more distinctly and emphatically, or sometimes pleonastically; सेयं, सोयं, इमास्ता:; अयमहं भो: &c.

इदानीं ind. 1 Now, at this moment, in this case, just now, even now.

इदानीतन a. (f. —नी) Present, of the present moment.

इद्धं n. 1 Sunshine. -2 Refulgence. -3 Wonder.

इध्मं n. Fuel, especially that which is used for sacred fire. -Comp. —प्रव्रश्चन: m. A hatchet, an axe.

इध्या f Kindling, lighting.

इन a. 1 Able, strong, powerful,

mighty. -2 Bold, determined. -3 Glorious —नः *m.* I A lord, master, a king. -2 The sun. -3 The lunar mansion Hasta.

इंदिदरः *m.* A large bee.

इंदिरा *f* N. of Lakshmi, wife of Vishnu. -Comp. —आलयं *n.* The blue lotus. —मंदिरः *m.* An epithet of Vishnu. —मंदिरं *n.* The blue lotus.

इंदि (-दी-) वरं *n.* The blue lotus.

इंदीवरिणी *f.* A group of blue lotuses.

इंदीवारः *m.* A blue lotus.

इंदुः *m.* I The moon. -2 The मृगशिरस् Nakshatra. -3 (In Math.) The number ' one '. -4 Camphor. -Comp. —कमलं *n.* The white lotus. —कला *f.* A digit of the moon. —कलिका *f.* I N. of a plant (केतकी). -2 A digit of the moon. —कांतः *m.* The moon-stone. —जः, -पुत्रः *m.* The planet Mercury. —जा *f.* N. of the river Revâ or Narmadâ. —जनकः *m.* I The ocean. -2 The sage अत्रि. -दलः *m.* A digit, crescent. —भा *f.* A kind of water-lily. —भृत —शेखरः, —मौलिः *m.* Epithets of Siva. —मणिः *m.* I The moon-stone. -2 A pearl. —मंडलं *n.* The orb or disc of the moon. —रत्नं *n.* Pearl. -ले (-रे-) खा *f.* I A digit of the moon. —लोकः *m.* The world of the moon. —लोहकं, -लौहं *n.* Silver. -वदना *f.* N. of a metre. -वासरः *m.* Monday.

इंदुमती *f.* I A day of full moon. -2 The wife of अज and sister of भोज.

इंदूरः *m.* A rat, mouse.

इंद्रः *m.* I The lord of gods. -2 The god of rain, rain, cloud.-3 A lord or ruler (as of men &c.), first or best (of any class of objects), as नरेंद्र &c. -4 A prince, king. -Comp. —अनुजः, —अवरजः *m.* An epithet of Vishnu and of Nârâyana. —अरिः *m.* A demon. —आयुधं *n.* Indra's weapon, the rainbow. —कीलः *m.* I N. of the mountain मंदर. -2 A rock. —कीलं *n.* The banner of Indra. —कुंजरः *m.* Indra's elephant. Airàvata. —कूटः *m.* N. of a mountain. —केतुः *m.* Indra's banner. —कोशः, —षः, -षकः *m.* I A couch, sofa. -2 A platform. —गुरुः, आचार्यः *m.* The teacher of Indra; *i. e.* बृहस्पति —गोपः, —गोपकः *m.* A kind of insect of red or white colour. —चापं, —धनुस् *n.* I A rainbow. -2 The bow of Indra. —जालं *n.* I A stratagem or trick in war. -2 Deception, cheating. -3 Conjuring, jugglery, magical tricks. —जालिक *a.* Deceptive, unreal, delusive. —जालिकः *m.* A juggler, conjurer. -जित *m.* 'Conqueror of Indra', N. of a son of Râvana who was killed by Lakshmana. —नीलः *m.* A sapphire. —नीलकः *m.* An emerald. —पत्नी *f.* Indra's wife शची. —पुरोहितः *m.* N. of बृहस्पति. -प्रस्थं *n.* N. of a city on the Yamunâ, the residence of the Pándavas (identified with the modern Delhi). —प्रहरणं *n.* Indra's weapon, the thunderbolt. —महः *m.* I A festival in honour of Indra. -2 The rainy season. — लोकः *m.* Indra's world, Svarga or Paradise. —वंशा,-वज्रा N. of two metres. -शत्रुः *m.* I An enemy or destroyer of Indra (when the accent is on the last syllable), an epithet of प्रल्हाद. -2 One whose enemy is Indra, an epithet of वृत्र (when the accent is on the first syllable). —शलभः *m.* A kind of insect. —सुतः, —सूनुः *m.* N. of Jayanta; Arjuna; Vâli, the king of monkeys. —सेनानीः *m.* The leader of Indra's armies, epithet of Kârtikeya.

इंद्रकं *n.* An assembly room, a hall.

इंद्राणी *f.* 1 The wife of Indra. -2 N. of Durgâ.

इंद्रियं *n.* 1 Power, force. -2 An organ of sense, sense or faculty of sense. -3 Bodily or virile power, power of the sense. -4 Semen. -5 Symbolical expression for the number 5. —Comp. —अर्थः *m.* 1 An object of sense ; these objects are:—रूपं शब्दो गंधरसस्पर्शाश्च विषया अमी. -2 Anything exciting these senses. —आयतनं *n.* The abode of the senses, *i. e.* the body. -2 The soul. —गोचर *a.* Perceptible to the senses. -गोचरः *m.* An object of sense. -ग्रामः, —वर्गः *m.* The assemblage or collection of organs, the five organs of sense taken collectively. —ज्ञानं *n.* Consciousness, the faculty of perception. —निग्रहः *m.* Restraint of senses. —वधः *m.* Insensibility. —विप्रतिपत्तिः *f.* Perversion of the organs. —संनिकर्षः *m.* The contact of an organ of sense (either with its object or with the mind). —स्वापः *m.* Insensibility, unconsciousness, stupor.

इंधु 7 A. (इंद्धे or इंधे, इंधांचक्रे, ऐंधिष्ट, इद्ध). To kindle, light,set on fire. With सं— To kindle.

इंधः *m.* 1 Fuel. -2 The Supreme Being.

इंधनं *n.* 1 Kindling, lighting. -2 Fuel, wood, &c.

इभः *m.* An elephant. -Comp. -अरिः *m.* A lion. —आननः *m.* N. of Ganesa. —निमीलिका *f.* 1 Shrewdness, sagacity, sharpness. —पोटा *f.* A young female elephant. —पोतः *m.* A young elephant, a cub. —भरः *m.* A collection of elephants. —युवतिः *f.* A female elephant.

इभी *f.* A female elephant.

इभ्य *a.* (*f.* —भ्या) Wealthy, opulent, rich. —भ्यः *m.* 1 A king. -2 An elephant-driver. —भ्या *f.* A female elephant.

इभ्यक *a.* (*f.* —भ्यका, -भ्यिका) Wealthy, rich.

इयत् *a.* (*f.* —ती) 1 So much, so large of this extent.

इयत्ता *f.*, इयत्वं *n.* 1 Fixed measure or quantity. -2 Limited number, limitation. -2 Limit, standard.

इरणं *n.* 1 A desert. -2 Salt or barren ground.

इरंमदः *m.* 1 A flash of lightning. -2 The submarine fire.

इरा *f.* 1 The earth. -2 Speech. -3 The goddess of speech, Sarasvati. -4 Water. -5 Food. -6 Spirituous liquor.—Comp. —क्षीरः *m.* The milk-ocean. —चरं *n.* Hail.

इरावत् *m.* (—वान्) The ocean.

इरिणं *n.* 1 A salt ground, saline soil. -2 Hence, a bare or barren soil, desert, dreary region.

इर्वारुः *m.*, *f.* A cucumber.

इर्वालुकः *m.* An animal living in caves.

इल् 6 P. To sleep. -2 To throw, send, cast.

इला *f.* 1 The earth. -2 A cow. -3 Speech. -Comp. —गोलः *m.*, —लं *n.* The earth, the globe. —धरः *m.* A mountain.

इलिका *f.* The earth.

इल्वकाः, -लाः *m.pl.* N. of the five stars in the head of Orion (मृगशिरस्).

इव *ind.* 1 Like, as (showing उपमा or comparison). -2 As if, as it were (denoting उत्प्रेक्षा). -3 A little, somewhat. -4 (Added to interrogative words), ' Possibly ', ' I should like to know ', ' indeed. -5 Nearly, almost ; *e. g.* मुहूर्तमिव. -6 इव is sometimes used for emphasis, or for elegance and may be, translated by ' just,' ' quite ', ' in deed ' &c. *e. g.* किंचिदिव Just a little bit ; so ईषदिव just a little ; नचिरादिव presently, very soon.

इष् 6. P. 1 To wish, desire, long for. -2 To choose. -3 To seek for. -4 To request, ask. -5 To assent or consent. इष् 4 P. (इष्यति, इयेष, एषिष्यति, एषितुं). 1 To move; to cause to move. इष् 9 P. (इष्णाति). 1 To cause to move quickly, animate, promote.

इष 1 U. (एषति-ते, एषितुं-एषिष्ट)To go, move.

इष: *m.* The month आश्विन.

इषि (-षी-) *f.* का 1 Reed, rush, stalk of grass. -2 An arrow. -3 A sort of sugar-cane. -4 A brush. -5 The eye-ball of an elephant. -Comp. -तूलं *n.* The point or upper part of a reed.

इषिर: *m.*,-र: *m.*Fire. -रं *ind.*Quickly.

इषु: *m.*,*f.* 1 An arrow. -2 The number five. -Comp. —असनं, -अस्त्रं *n.* The bow. —आस: *m.* 1 A bow. -2 An archer, a warrior. —पथ: *m.*, -विक्षेप:*m.* An arrow-shot, the range of an arrow.

इषुधि: *m.*, *f.* A quiver.

इष्ट *p. p.* (*f.* —ष्टा) 1 Wished, desired. -2 Beloved, agreeable, liked, dear. -3 Worshipped, reverenced. -4 Respected. -5 Approved, regarded as good. -6 Desirable. —ष्ट: *m.* 1 A lover, husband, beloved person. -2 A friend. -3 A sacrifice. —ष्टं *n.* 1 Wish, desire. -2 A sacrifice. —*ind.* Voluntarily. -Comp. —आपत्ति: *f.* Occurrence of what is desired; a statement by a debater which is favourable to his opponent also. —गंध *a.* Fragrant. —गंध: *m.* Any fragrant substance. —जन: *m.* A beloved person (whether man or woman). —देव: *m.*, -देवता *f.* A favourite god, one's tutelary deity.

इष्टका *f.* 1 A brick. -Comp. —न्यास: *m.* Laying the foundation of a house. —पथ: *m.* A road made of bricks

इष्टम *ind.* To one's contentment or satisfaction.

इष्टापूर्त *n.* Performance of pious, charitable deeds ; performing sacrifices and digging wells and doing other acts of charity.

इष्टि: *f.* 1 Wish, desire. -2 Seeking, striving to get. -3 Any desired object. -4 A desired rule or desideratum. -5 Impulse, hurry. -6 Invitation, order. -7 A sacrifice. -8 An oblation consisting of butter, food &c. -Comp. —पच: *m.* A miser. —पशु: *m.* An animal to be killed at a sacrifice.

इष्टिका *f.* A brick. See इष्टका.

इष्म: *m.* 1 Cupid; god of love. -2 The spring. -3 Course, going.

इष्य: *m.*, -ष्यं *n.* The spring.

इष्व: *m.* A spiritual teacher.

इस् *ind.* An interjection of anger pain or sorrow.

इह *ind.* 1 Here (referring to time, place or direction). -2 In this world (opp. परत्र or अमुत्र). -3 In this case ; in this instance. -4 Now, at this time. —Comp. -अमुत्र *ind.* In this world and the next world, here and there. —इह *ind*

Here and there, now and then, repeatedly. —कालः *m.* This life. —लोकः *m.* This world or life. —समये *ind.* Here, now, at such a time as this. —स्थ *a.* Standing here.

इहत्य *a.* Being here, of this place or world.

ई.

ई *ind.* An interjection of (1) dejection; (2) pain; (3) sorrow; (4) anger; (5) compassion; (6) perception or consciousness; (7) calling.

ई I. 4 A. (ईयते) To go. -II. 2 P. 1 To go. -2 To shine. -3 To pervade. -4 To desire, wish. -5 To throw. -6 To eat. -7 To beg. (A.). -8 To become pregnant.

ईक्ष् 1 A. (ईक्षते, ईक्षांचक्रे, ऐक्षिष्ट, ईक्षितुं, ईक्षित्वा, ईक्षित).1 To see, view, observe, look. -2 To regard, consider.-3 To care for. -4 To think, reflect. -5 To look to, or to investigate the good or bad luck of any one (with dat. of the person); कृष्णाय ईक्षते गर्गः गर्ग foretells the future of कृष्ण. अनु— To inquire after, to investigate. अप— 1 To expect. -2 To require. -3 To pay regard to. अव— 1 To look at. -2 To consider, to think. उत्— 1 To look up to. -2 To wait. -3 उत्प— 1 To see in prospect. -2 To conjecture, to expect. अभि— To suspect. उद्वि— To look up. उप— 1 To overlook, to neglect. -2 To let go. निर— 1 To view completely. -2 To look for. परि- To examine. प्र— To see, to look at. प्रति— To wait. प्रतिवि— To look in return. वि— To see, behold. व्यप— To mind, care for. सम् 1 To behold. -2 To think, consider. समव— 1 To inspect, to consider. समुप— To neglect.

ईक्षणं *n.* 1 Seeing, beholding. -2 A look, sight, view. -3 An eye. -4 Looking after, caring for.

ईक्षणिकः *m.* (*f.* —का) A fortune-teller.

ईक्षतिः *f.* Looking, sight.

ईक्षा *f.* 1 Sight. -2 Viewing, considering.

ईख्, ईङ्ख् 1 P. To go, move, vacillate. With प्र— To shake, to tremble.

ईड् -2 A. (ईट्टे, ईडांचक्रे, ऐडिष्ट, ईडितुं, ईडित). 1 To praise. -2 To implore, ask for (with two acc.).

ईडा *f.* Praise, commendation.

ईड्य *pot. p.* (*f.* —ड्या) To be praised or glorified, praiseworthy, laudable.

ईतिः *f.* 1 Plague, distress, a calamity of the season. The *itis* are usually said to be six :— 1 Excessive rain. -2 Drought. -3 Locusts. -4 Rats.-5 Parrots. and-6 Foreign invasions. -2 An infectious disease. - 3 Travelling in a foreign country, sojourning (प्रवास). -4 An affray.

ईदृत्ता *f.* Quality (opp. इयत्ता).

ईदृक्ष,-श, also ईदृश् *a.* (*f.* क्षी,-शी) Such, of this kind, of this aspect, endowed with such qualities. —क्षं *n.* Such a condition; such occasion.

ईप्सा *f.* 1 Desire to obtain. -2 A wish, desire.

ईप्सित *a.* (*f.* —ता) Desired, wished for, dear to. —तं *n.* Desire, wish.

ईप्सु *a.* Wishing or desiring to get.

ईर् 1 P. (*p. p.* ईरित) 1 To go. -2

To shake. With. —उद् To rise.

ईर् 2 A. (ईर्ते, ईरांचक्रे, ऐरिष्ट, ईरिढ्वे, ईर्णि) See ईर् 1 P. above.

ईर् 10 U. (ईरयति, ईरित) 1 To agitate, throw, cast, discharge, dart, hurl. -3 To cause to rise, produce. -4 To utter, proclaim. -5 To cause to go, set in motion, move, shake. -6 To bring to life, revive. -7 To elevate.

ईरण: *m.* The wind. -णं *n.* 1 Agitating. -2 Going. -3 A desert. -4 Saline soil.

ईरिण *a.* (*f.* —णा) Desert, barren. —णं *n.* A desert, barren soil.

ईरित *p.p.* 1 Sent, despatched. -2 Said, uttered.

ईर्म: *m.* The arm ; the fore-quarter of an animal. —र्मं *n.* A wound, sore (*m.* also).

ईर्या *f.* Wandering about as a religious mendicant.

ईर्वारु: *m.*, *f.* A cucumber.

ईर्ष्य, ईर्ष्यक ईर्ष्यु, *a,* Envious, jealous.

ईर्षा, ईर्ष्या *f.* Envy, jealousy.

ईर्ष्या, —र्षा Envy, jealousy, envy of another's success.

ईर्ष्या (-र्षा-) लु, ईर्ष्यु (-र्षु) *a.* Envious, impatient.

ईलि:, (-ली *f*) 1 A weapon, a cudgel or a short sword. -2 A stick shaped like a sword.

ईश् 2 A. (ईष्टे, ईशांचक्रे, ऐशिष्ट, ईशिता, ईशितुं, ईशित) 1 To rule, govern, command (with gen). -2 To be able, have power. -3 To own, possess.

ईश *a.* (*f.* —शा) 1 Owning, possessing, master or lord of. -2 Capable of (with gen.). -3 Powerful, supreme. —श: *m.* 1 A lord, master; (with gen.) A Rudra. -3 The number 11. -4 N. of Siva. —शा *f.* 1 Supremacy, power. -2 N. of Durgâ. -3 A rich lady. —Comp. —पुरी, —नगरी *f.* N. of Benares.

ईशान: *m.* 1 A ruler, master, lord. -2 N. of Siva. -3 The number 'eleven '. -4 N. of Vishnu. (*f.* —नी) N. of Durgâ -नं *n.* Light, splendour.

ईशिता *f.*, —त्वं *n.* Superiority greatness, one of the eight *Siddhis* or attributes of Siva.

ईश्वित्तृ *m.* The lord of the Universe.

ईश्वर *a.* (*f.* —रा,or—री) 1 Powerful, able. -2 Rich, wealthy. —र: *m.* 1 A lord, master. -2 A king, prince, ruler. -3 A rich or great man. -4 A husband. -5 The Supreme God. -6 N. of Siva. -7 The God of love, Cupid. -8 The Supreme Soul ; the soul. -9 The eleventh year (संवत्सर) of the Sâlivâhana era. (*f.* —रा,-री) N. of Durgâ ; of Lakshmi ; or of any other of the Saktis. —Comp.—निषेध: *m.* Denial of the existence of god, atheism. —सद्मन् *n.* A temple. —सभं *n.* A royal court or assembly.

ईष् A. (*p.p.* ईषित) 1 To go, to move. -2 To kill. -3 To see.

ईष *m.* The month आश्विन.

ईषत् *ind.* Slightly, to some extent, a little. -Comp. —कर *a.* 1 Doing little. -2 Easy to be accomplished. —पांडु *a.* Whitish. —पुरुष: *m.* A mean or contemptible person. -हास: *m.* Slight laughter, a smile.

ईषा *f.* 1 The pole or shaft of a carriage or a plough. -Comp. —दंड: *m.* The handle of a plough.

ईषिका *f.* 1 An elephant's eye-ball. -2 A painter's brush. -3 A weapon, arrow, dart. -4 A kind of missile.

ईषिर: *m.* Fire.

ईषीका *f.* 1 A painter's brush. -2 An ingot-mould. -3 An elephant's eye-ball. -4 An arrow.

ईष्मः, -ष्वः *m.* 1 God of love. -2 Spring.

ईह् 1 A.(ईहते, ईहांचक्रे, ऐहिष्ट, ईहिष्यते, ईहितुं, ईहित). 1 To wish, desire, think of. -2 To endeavour to obtain. -3 To aim at or attempt. -4 To take care of. With सम्- 1 To desire. -2 To attempt to perform.

ईहा *f.* 1 Wish, desire. -2 An undertaking, act. -3 Effort, exertion. -Comp. —मृगः *m.* 1 A wolf. -2 An artificial deer. -3 A division of the drama consisting of four acts. -वृकः *m.* A wolf.

ईहित *p. p.*(*f.* ता)1 Wished, desired. -2 Attempted, sought. —तं *n.* 1 A wish, desire. -2 Effort, exertion. -3 An undertaking, act.

उ.

उ *ind.* 1 A particle used expletively. -2 An interjection of:- (*a*) calling, (*b*) anger; (*c*) compassion; (*d*) command; (*e*) acceptance; (*f*) interrogation; or (*g*) used merely as an expletive.

उः *m.* Siva. This word forms the second part of the mystic syllable ओम्.

उक्त *a.* (*f.* —क्ता) 1 Addressed, spoken to. -2 Said, spoken. -3 Said, told, stated (opp. to inferred). —क्तं *n.* A word, a sentence, a speech. -Comp. —अनुक्त *a.* Spoken and not spoken. —उपसंहारः *m.* A peroration, recapitulation, the summing up of speech. —निर्वाहः *m.* Defending an assertion. —पुंस्क *a.* A word *fem.* or *neuter* of which a *masculine* also exists, and the meaning of which differs only by the notion of gender (in gram). —प्रत्युक्तं *n.* Speech and reply, a discourse. —वाक्यं *n.* A dictum, a decree.

उक्तिः *f.* 1 Speech, statement, expression. -2 A Sentence. -3 The power of expression; the expressive power of a word.

उक्थं *n.* 1 A saying, sentence, hymn (स्तोत्रं). -2 Eulogy, praise. -3 N. of the Sâmaveda; a variety of Sama. -4 The उक्थ sacrifice.

उक्ष् 6. U. 1. To sprinkle, wet, moisten, pour down upon. -2 To send forth. -3 To scatter, (as sparks). -4 To clean With. अभि— To sprinkle with consecrated water. परि — To sprinkle around. प्र— To consecrate by sprinkling. संप्र— To hallow by sprinkling.

उक्षणं *n.* 1 Sprinkling. -2 Consecrating as by sprinkling.

उक्षन् *a.* 1 Large. -2 Sprinkling. —*m.* (-क्षा) An ox or bull. —तरः *m.* A small bull or ox.

उक्षाल *a.* Swift, terrible, high; large, excellent. —कः *m.* A monkey.

उख्, उंख् 1 P. (ओखति, उंखति, उवोख or उंखांचकार, ओखित, उंखित). To go, move.

उखः *m.* A boiler, pot, vessel. —खा *f.* 1 A boiling vessel. -2 A fireplace at a sacrifice. -3 A part of the body.

उख्य *a.* Dressed or boiled in a pot (as flesh &c.).

उग्र *a.* 1 Fierce, cruel, ferocious. -2 Formidable, terrific, fearful. -3 Powerful, mighty. -4 Sharp, pungent, hot. -5 High, noble. -6 Angry, wrathful. -7 Industrious.-ग्र: m. 1 N. of Siva or Rudra. -2 A descendant of a Kshatriya father and Sudra mother. -3 The poetic sentiment ealled रौद्र. -4 Wind. -Comp. —गंधः m. 1 The चंपक tree. -2 Garlic. —चारिणी, —चंडा f. N. of —दुर्गा. —जाति a. Base-born. —धन्वन् m. N. of शिव; of इंद्र. —शेखरा f. The Ganges. —रेतस् m. A form of Rudra.

उग्रा f. A cruel woman.

उच् 4 P. 1 To collect, to gather together. -2 To take pleasure in.-4 To be suitable.

उचित p.p. (f. —ता) 1 Fit, proper. -2 Usual, customary. -3 Accustomed or used to. -4 Praiseworthy. -5 Acceptable (ग्राह्य).

उच्च a. (f. —च्चा) 1 High, lofty (*lit.* and *fig.*). -2 Loud, high-sounding. -3 Intense, violent, strong. -4 (In astr.) Ascendant —च्चं: m. The apex of the orbit of a planet. -Comp. -तरु: m. The cocoa-nut tree. —ताल: m. Music, dancing &c. at a tavern. —नीच a. 1 High and low. -2 Various, multiform. —संश्रय a. Occupying a high station (said of a planet).

उच्चैः ind. 1 High, being above, lofty (fig. also). -2 Pre-eminently. -3 Loud.

उच्चक्षुस् a. 1 With the eyes directed upwards. -2 With the eyes taken out; blind.

उच्चंड a. 1 Fierce, formidable. -2 Quick. -3 Loud. -4 Angry, violent. -5 Hanging down.

उच्चंद्र: m. The last watch of the night.

उच्चय: m. 1 A collection, heap, multitude. -2 Gathering, collecting (flowers &c.). -3 The knot of a woman's (wearing) garment (नीविबंध). -4 Prosperity, rise. -5 The opposite side of a triangle.

उच्चर् (उत् + चर् 1 P.) 1 To go upwards, to rise. -2 To ascend or go forth, go up. -3 To arise, rise (as a voice), to be heard. -4 To empty the body by evacuations ; void one's excrement. -5 To utter pronounce. (Used in the Atm). -1 To quit, leave.-2 To sin against, be unfaithful (to a husband or wife.). -3 To violate or transgress. —*Caus.* 1 To cause to issue. -2 To utter, pronounce. -3 To void one's excrement. -4 To emit.

उच्चरणं n. 1 Going up or out. -2 Utterance, pronunciation.

उच्चारणं n. 1 Pronunciation, utterance. -2 Declaration, announcement, enunciation.

उच्चरित p.p. (f. —ता) 1 Gone up or out. -2 Uttered, pronounced. —तं n. Excrement.

उच्चल् (उत् + चल् 1 P.) To start, set out.

उच्चलं n. Mind, understanding.

उच्चलनं n. Moving away, setting out.

उच्चाटनं n. 1 Driving away. -2 Separation. -3 Eradication, extirpation. -4 A kind of charm or magical incantation.-5 Working this charm.

उच्चार: m. 1 Utterance, pronunciation, declaration. -2 Excrement, dung, faeces. -3 Discharge (in general).-4 Passage (of heavenly bodies), to another zodiacal sign or asterism.

उच्चावच a. 1 High and low, uneven. -2 Various, multiform, of various kinds, diverse.

उच्चि (उत् + चि 5 U.) To collect, gather, accumulate.

उच्चूडः,—लः *m.* 1 The flag of a banner, or the banner itself. -2 An ornament fastened on the top of a banner.

उच्चैः *ind.* 1 Aloft, high, on high, above, upwards. --2 Loudly. --3 Powerfully, very much, greatly. -4 (Used as an adj, in comp, or by itself) High, noble, distinguished, famous. —Comp. —घुष्टं *n.* 1 Clamour, great uproar. -2 Loud proclamation. —शिरस् *a.* High-minded, one of high rank, magnanimous. —श्रवस्, —स *m.* N. of the horse of Indra.

उच्चैस्तम *a.* Highest, tallest, loudest.

उच्चैस्तमां *ind.* 1 Exceedingly high. --2 Very loudly.

उच्चैस्तर *a.* Higher, taller, louder.

उच्चैस्तरं,—रां *ind.* 1 Very loud. --2 Exceedingly high, on high.

उच्चरित *p. p.* (*f.* —ता) Pronounced, uttered.

उच्छन्न *a.* (*f.* —न्ना) 1 Destroyed, cut down. -2 Extinct (as a work).

उच्छलनं *n.* Going or moving upwards.

उच्छादनं *n.* 1 Covering. -2 Rubbing the body with perfumes.

उच्छासन *a.* (*f.* —ना) Not amenable to rule or command, ungovernable, unruly.

उच्छास्त्र *a.* (*f.* —स्त्रा) Contrary or opposed to शास्त्र (civil or religious law-books).

उच्छिख *a.* (*f.* —खा) 1 Crested, with erected crest. -2 Flaming up, blazing up (as fire). -3 Radiant, bright.

उच्छित्तिः *f.* Extirpation, destruction.

उच्छिद् (उद् + छिद् 7 U.) 1 To cut off, extirpate, destroy, dispel, chase away. -2 To interfere with, interrupt, stop.

उच्छिन्न *p. p.* (*f.* —न्ना) 1 Extirpated, destroyed. -2 Abject, vile. —न्नः *m.* Peace obtained by ceding valuable lands.

उच्छिरस् *a.* 1 With the neck raised (lit.). -2 High, lofty. -3 Noble, great, exalted.

उच्छिष्ट *p, p.* (*f.* —ष्टा) 1 Left, rejected, abandoned. -2 Stale. —ष्टं *n.* 1 Leavings, fragments, remainder (especially of food or sacrifice).

उच्छिलीन्ध्र *a.* Full of mushrooms. —न्ध्रं *n.* A mushroom.

उच्छीर्षकं *n.* A pillow.

उच्छुष्क *a.* (*f.* —ष्का) Dried up, withered.

उच्छून *a.* (*f.* —ना) 1 Swollen. -2 Fat, bulky. -3 High, lofty.

उच्छृङ्खल *a.* (*f.* —ला) 1 Unbridled, unrestrained. -2 Self-willed, perverse. -3 Irregular, desultory, unsystematic.

उच्छेदः *m.*, —दनं *n.* 1 Cutting off. -2 Extirpation, destruction.

उच्छोषण *a.* 1 Making dry, withering up. -2 Burning, parching. —णं *n.* Drying up; parching, withering.

उच्छ्र (-च्छ्रा-) यः *m.* 1 Rising (of a planet &c.). -2 Raising, erecting. --3 Height, elevation (physical or moral). -4 Growth, increase. -5 Pride. -6 The upright side of a triangle.

उच्छ्रयणं *n.* Raising, elevation.

उच्छ्रायिन् *a.* (*f.* —नी) High, raised, lofty.

उच्छ्रित *p. p.* (*f.* —ता) 1 Raised, lifted up, risen. -2 High, tall, lofty, exalted. -3 Produced, born, -4 Increasing, growing, prosperous. -5 Proud.

उच्छ्रितिः *f.* See उच्छ्रयः.

उच्छ्रेय *a.* High, lofty, tall.

उच्छ्वस् (उत्+श्वस् 2 P.) 1 To breathe, live. -2 To cheer up, revive. -3 To open, bloom (as a lotus). -4 To pant, sigh deeply. -5 To throb, heave, palpitate. -6 To be loosened or relaxed. —Caus. 1 To cause to breathe. -2 To console, cheer up. -3 To loosen, relax, disjoin.

उच्छ्वसनं *n.* 1 Breathing, sighing. -2 Taking a deep breath, heaving. -3 Loosening.

उच्छ्वसित *p. p.* (*f.* —ता) 1 Breathing. -2 Emitting or sending out vapour. -3 Full-blown, opened, expanded. -4 Enlivened, refreshed. -5 Breathing a sigh of relief. -6 Consoled. -7 Waving, dishevelled. —तं *n.* 1 Breath, the (very) life. -2 Blooming, blowing. -3 Exhalation. --4 Heaving, throbbing. --5 Becoming loose. --6 Sighing. --7 The vital airs of the body.

उच्छ्वासः *m.* 1 Breath. -2 A sigh. -3 Consolation, encouragement. -4 Expiring, dying.-5 An air-hole. -6 A division or chapter of a book, as of the Harsha-charita.

उछ् 6 P. 1 To finish. --2 To bind. --3 To abandon.

उंछ् 6 P. (*p. p.* उंछित) To glean. With. —प्र To wipe out.

उज्जय (-यि-) नी. *f.*N. of a city, the modern Oujein in Mâlva, the capital of Vikramâditya.

उज्जासनं *n.* Killing, slaughter.

उज्जीव् (उद् + जीव् 1 P.) To revive, return to life.-*Caus.*To restore life.

उज्जीवनं *n.* Revival.

उज्जृम्भ् (उत् + जृम्भ् 1 A.) 1 To gape, open. --2 To part asunder. -3 To expand, to rise. -4 To revive.

उज्जृंभ *a.* 1 Blown, expanded. -2 Gaping, open. —भः *m.* 1 Opening, expansion. -2 Gaping of the mouth. -3 Parting.

उज्जृंभणं *n.* 1 Gaping, opening the mouth, yawning. -2 Spreading, increase. -3 Agitation.

उज्जृंभा *f.* See उज्जृंभणं.

उज्जृंभित *a.* Opened, stretched, expanded, blown. —तं *n.* Gaping. -2 Effort, exertion.

उज्ज्य *a.* (*f.* —ज्या) Having the bow-string loosened.

उज्ज्वल *a.* (*f.* —ला) 1 Bright, shining. -2 Burning. -3 Clean, clear, white. -4 Lovely, beautiful. -5 Blown, expanded. —लः *m.* Love, passion. —ला *f.* 1 Splendour, brightness.-2 Clearness. —लं *n.*Gold.

उज्ज्वलनं *n.* 1 Burning, shining. -2 Splendour, brilliance. -3 Fire. -4 Gold.

उज्झ् 6 P.1 To abandon, leave. --2 To avoid, escape from. -3 To emit. give out.

उज्झकः *m.* 1 A cloud. -2 A devotee.

उज्झनं *n.* Abandoning, leaving.

उंछ् 6 P. To glean, gather.

उंछः *m.* Gleaning. —छं *n.*Gleaning. -Comp. —वृत्ति, —शील *a.* One who lives by gleaning grains, a gleaner.

उंछनं *n.* Gleaning grains of corn in market-places &c.

उटः *m.* 1 A leaf. -2 Grass. -Comp. —जः *m.*, —जं *n.* A hut, cottage, the residence of hermits, or saints, a hermitage.

उडुः *f.*, उडु *n.* 1 A lunar mansion

a star. -2 Water. -Comp. —चक्रं n. The zodiacal circle. —पः m., —पं n. A raft, boat. —पः m. The moon. —पतिः, —राज् m. 1 The moon. -2 Vuruna, regent of waters. —पथः m. The sky, the firmament.

उडुंबरः m. 1 N. of a tree. (Mar. औदुंबर). -2 The threshold of a house. -3 Eunuch. —रं n. 1 The fruit of the उडुंबर tree.

उड्डामर a. (f. -रा) 1 Agreeable, excellent -2 Formidable, terrific.

उडूपः m. Same as उडुपः q v.

उड्डयनं n. Flying up, soaring.

उड्डी (उत् + डी 1.4.A.) To fly up, soar.

उड्डीन p. p. (f. —ना) Flown up, flying up. —नं n. 1 Flying up, soaring. -2 A particular flight of birds.

उड्डीयनं n. Flying up.

उड्डीशः m. 1 N. of Siva.

उड्रः m. N. of a country ; the modern Orissa.

उंडेरकः m. A ball of flour.

उत् ind. A particle of (a) doubt ; (b) interrogation ; (c) deliberation ; (d) intensity.

उत ind. 1 A particle expressing (a) doubt, uncertainty, guess (or); (b) alternative; usually a correlative of किं (whether, or) ; (c) association, connection, 'and', 'also,' (d) interrogation; (e) deliberation; (f) intensity; (g) wishing 'would that' ; (h) sometimes used as an expletive ; or for the sake of emphasis especially at the end of a line after इति or a verb. -2 With a preceding प्रति = on the contrary, on the other hand; but. -3 With a preceding किं = how much more or how much less; उत -उत Either-or. उतवा or else, and; वा-उतवा, उताहोवा पि-वा either...or.

उत्क a. (f. —त्का) 1 Desirous of, anxiously wishing for. -2 Regretting, sad, sorrowful. -3 Absent-minded. —त्कः m. 1 Desire. -2 Opportunity.

उत्कट a. (f. —टा) 1 Large, spacious. -2 Powerful, mighty, fierce. -3 Excessive, much. -4 Conspicuous. -5 Abounding in, richly endowed with. -6 Drunk, mad, furious. -7 Superior, high. -8 Proud, haughty, -9 Uneven. -10 Difficult. —टः m. 1 A fluid (ichor) dropping from the temples of an elephant in rut. -2 An elephant in rut. -3 Pride, intoxication.

उत्कंचुक a. (f. —का) 1 Without a coat of mail. -2 Without a bodice or jacket.

उत्कणिका f. A raised particle.

उत्कंठ a. (f. —ठा) 1 Having the neck uplifted, ready. -2 (Hence) Anxious, eager.

उत्कंठ् Den. A. 1 To be anxious. -2 To yearn, be eagerly desirous of (with gen. or dat.). -Caus. (उत्कंठयति). To create anxiety or longing.

उत्कंठा f. 1 Anxiety, uneasiness. -2 Longing for a beloved person or thing. -3 Regret, sorrow.

उत्कंठित p. p. (f. —ता) 1 Anxious, uneasy. -2 Regretting, sorrowful. -3 Longing for a beloved person or thing. —ता f. A mistress longing for her absent lover or husband.

उत्कंधर a. (f. —रा) Having the neck uplifted.

उत्कंप a. Trembling. —पः m., —पनं n. Trembling, tremor, agitation.

उत्करः m. 1 Rubbish. -2 Heap,

multitude. -3 A pile, stack.

उत्कर्करः *m.* A kind of musical instrument.

उत्कर्ण *a.* (*f.* —र्णा) Having the ears erect.

उत्कर्षः *m.* 1 Pulling off or upwards. -2 Elevation, eminence, rise, prosperity. -3 Increase, abundance. -4 Excellence, glory. -5 Self conceit, boasting. -6 Joy, pleasure.

उत्कर्षणं *n.* 1 Drawing upwards. -2 Taking or pulling off.

उत्कलः *m.* 1 A fowler, bird-catcher. -2 A porter (carrying a load with him). *m. pl.* N. of a country and its inhabitants (modern Orissa).

उत्कलाप *a.* (*f.* —पा) Having the tail erect and expanded.

उत्कलिका *f.* 1 Anxiety, uneasiness; प्रजा एवान्वरुध्यत च . मन्मथोत्कलिका: *. कादंब. ह. भा. -2 Longing for, regretting. -3 Wanton sport, dalliance (हेला). -4 A bud. -5 A wave. –Comp. —प्रायं *n.* A variety of prose composition abounding in compound words and hard letters.

उत्कषणं *n.* 1 Tearing, pulling up. -2 Ploughing.

उत्कासः *m.*, -सनं *n.* उत्कासिका *f.* Hemming, clearing the throat of mucus.

उत्कीर्ण *p. p.* (*f.* —र्णा) 1 Thrown or piled up, scattered. -2 Engraven, carved, sculptured. -3 Bored, perforated.

उत्कीर्तनं *n.* 1 Crying out, proclaiming. -2 Praising, celebrating.

उत्कुटं *n.* Lying down with the face upwards.

उत्कुणः 1 A bug. -2 A louse.

उत्कुल *a.* (*f.* —ला) Fallen from the family, disgracing or dishonouring one's family.

उत्कूजः *m.* The singing (of the cuckoo).

उत्कूदः *m.* A parasol or umbrella.

उत्कूर्दनं *n.* Jumping up, springing upwards.

उत्कृष् (उद् + कृष् 1 P.) 1 To draw or pull up, raise or lift up. -2 To draw, attract. -3 To increase, enhance (opp. अपकृष्). -4 To bend (as a bow).–*Caus.* To elevate, raise.

उत्कृष्ट *p. p.* (*f.* —ष्टा) 1 Drawn up or out, raised, elevated. -2 Extracted. -3 Excellent, best, highest. -4 Much, excessive, increased. -5 Tilled ; poughed.

उत्कृत् (उद् + कृत् 10 P.) To proclaim, celebrate, praise, extol.

उत्कृ (उद् + कृ 6 U.) 1 To scatter upwards, throw up. -2 To dig up, excavate. -3 To engrave, carve.

उत्कोचः *m.* A bribe.

उत्कोचकः 1 A bribe. -2 The receiver of a bribe.

उत्क्रम् (उद् + क्रम् 1 U. 4 P.) 1 To go up, step up, ascend. -2 To step beyond. -3 To go out or away, depart. -4 To pass away, die. -5 To pass over. -6 To disregard, neglect. 7 To transgress, violate.

उत्क्रमः *m.* 1 Going up or out. -2 Progressive increase. -3 Deviation, transgression.

उत्क्रमणं *n.* 1 Going up or out, departure. -2 Ascent. -3 Surpassing, exceeding. -4 The passage of the soul (out of the body), *i. e.* death.

उत्क्रांत *p. p.* (*f.* —ता) Departed. -2 Faded, effaced (as colour). -3 Gone over, surpassed. -4 Dead.

उत्क्रांतिः *f.* 1 Going up or out, departure. -2 The flight or passage of the soul (out of the body), death.

उत्क्रामः *m.* 1 Going out or up, departure. -2 Surpassing. -3 Violation, transgression. -4 Opposition, contrariety.

उत्क्रुश् (उत् + क्रुश् 1 P.) 1 To cry out, cry aloud. -2 To call out to. -3 To proclaim.

उत्क्रुष्ट *p. p.* (*f.* —ष्टा) Crying out. -ष्टं *n.* 1 Calling, exclaiming. -2 Loud speaking or conversation.

उत्क्रोशः *m.* 1 Clamour, loud noise. -2 Proclamation. -3 An osprey (कुररी).

उत्क्लेशः *m.* 1 Excitement, disquietude. -2 Sickness, particularly, seasickness, nausea.

उत्क्लेदः *m.* Becoming wet or moist.

उत्क्षिप् (उत् + क्षिप् 6 P.) To throw up, raise, erect. -2 To throw away, reject. -3 To emit, vomit up.

उत्क्षिप्त *p. p.* (*f.* —प्ता) 1 Thrown upwards, tossed. -2 Held up, supported. -3 Distracted by, struck with. -4 Destroyed. -5 Thrown out, rejected. —प्तः *m.* The thorn apple, the Dhatura plant.

उत्क्षिप्तिका *f.* A crescent-shaped ornament worn in the upper part of the ear.

उत्क्षेपः *m.* 1 Throwing or tossing up. -2 That which is thrown or tossed up. -3 Sending, despatching. -4 Vomiting.

उत्क्षेपक *a.* 1 One who throws or tosses up. -2 Who or what elevates or raises. —कः *m* A stealer of clothes &c.

उत्क्षेपणं *n.* 1 Throwing upwards, lifting or tossing up. -2 Throwing upwards, regarded by the Vaiseshikas as one of the five *karmans.* -3 Vomiting. -4 Sending away, espatching. -5 A kind of basket for cleaning corn ; a kind of stick for threshing corn. -6 A fan. -7 A measure of sixteen Panas.

उत्खचित *a.* (*f.* —ता) Intermixed, interwoven, inlaid with.

उत्खन् (उत् + खन् 1 P.) 1 To dig up or out, excavate. -2 To draw or put out.

उत्खात *p. p.* (*f* —ता) 1 Excavated. -2 Extracted, drawn out. -3 Uprooted. -4 (fig.) Eradicated, totally destroyed. -5 Deposed, deprived of power or authority. —तं *n.* A hole, cavity, uneven ground, Comp. —केलिः *f.* Digging out earth in sport (by means of horns, tusks &c.).

उत्खातिन् *a.* (*f* —नी) 1 Uneven, having ups and downs, rugged (opp. सम). -2 Destructive.

उत्त *a.* (*f.* —त्ता) Wet, moist.

उत्तंसः *m.*, -सं *n.* 1 A crest, an ornament worn on the crown of the head. -2 An ear-ring.

उत्तंसय् Den. P. 1 To cause to serve as a crest. -2 Deck, adorn. -3 To tie or bind up (as hair).

उत्तट *a.* (*f.* —टा) Overflowing the bank.

उत्तप्तं 1 Dried flesh. -2 Great heat.

उत्तम *a.* (*f.* —मा) 1 Best, exellent. -2 Foremost, uppermost, highest. -3. Most elevated, principal. -4 Greatest, first. —मः *m.* 1 N. of Vishnu. -2 The last person (in gram. corresponding to the first person in English gram.). —मा *f.* An excellent woman. -Comp. -अंगं *n.* The head. —अधम *a.* High and low. —अर्धः *m.* 1 The best half. -2 The last half or part. —अहः *m.* The last or latest day; a fine or lucky day. —ऋणः, —ऋणिकः (उत्तमर्णः, उत्तमर्णिकः)

m. A creditor (opp. अधमर्णः).–पु(पू)रुषः *m.* 1 The last person in verbal conjugation (corresponding to the first person in English grammar). –2 The Supreme Spirit. –3 An excellent man. —श्लोक *a.* Of excellent fame; glorious, famous. —स्त्रीसंग्रहः *m.* Intriguing with another man's wife, *i. e.* speaking with her privately, looking amorously at her &c. –साहसः,–सं *n.* 1 The highest (of the fixed) pecuniary punishments.

उत्तम् (उत् + तम् 4 P.) 1 To be afflicted. –2 To be uneasy.

उत्तमीय *a.* (*f.* —या) Uppermost, highest, best, principal.

उत्तंभः *m.*, —भनं *n.* 1 Upholding, propping, supporting. –2 A prop, support. –3 Stopping, arresting.

उत्तर *a.* (*f.* —रा) 1 Northern (declined like a pronoun). –2 Upper, higher (opp. अधर). –3 Later, latter, subsequent, (opp. पूर्व); पूर्वः –उत्तरः Former-latter. –4 Future, concluding. –5 Left (opp. दक्षिण). –6 Superior, chief, excellent; powerful. –7 Exceeding, beyond. –8 More, more than (generally as the last member of a comp. with numerals). –9 Accompanied by, followed by. –10 To be crossed over. —रः *m.* 1 Future time, futurity. –2 N. of Vishnu. –3 N. of Siva. –रा *f.* 1 The north. –2 A lunar mansion. –3 N. of the daughter of Virâta and wife of Abhimanyu. —रं *n.* 1 An answer, reply. –2 (In law). Defence, a rejoinder. –3 The last part or following member of a compound. –4 (In Mim.) The fourth member of an अधिकरण, the answer. –5 The upper surface or cover. –6 Conclusion. –7 Remainder. –8 Superiority, excellence. –9 Result. –10 Excess. –11 Remainder, difference (in arith). –12 (In Rhet.). The figure of speech in which (I) a question is inferred from an answer, or (II) in which there being many questions, there are also many answers which do not ordinarily occur to one. उत्तरं प्रश्नस्योत्तरादुन्नयो यदि यच्चासकृदसंभाव्यं सत्यपि प्रश्न उत्तरं ॥ * साहि. e. *g.* वीक्षितुं न क्षमा श्वश्रूः स्वामी दूरतरं गतः । अहमेकाकिनी बाला तवेह वसतिः कुतः ॥ —रं *ind.* 1 Above. –2 Afterwards, after. –Comp. —अधर *a.* Higher and lower (fig. also). (–रौ dual.) The upper and under lips, the two lips. —अधिकारः, *m.* –रिता *f.*, –त्वं *n.* Heirship, inheritance. —अधिकारिन् *m.* An heir or claimant (subsequent to the death of the original owner). —अयनं *n.* (–यणं) 1 The progress of the sun to the North (of the equator). –2 The period or time of the summer solstice. —अर्धं *n.* 1 The upper part of the body. –2 The latter half (opp. पूर्वार्धं). –3 The further end. —अहः *m.* The following day. –आभासः *m.* A false reply, an indirect reply. —आशा *f.* The northern direction. —आषाढा *f.* The 21st lunar mansion consisting of three stars. —आसंगः *m.* An upper garment. —इतर *a.* Other than उत्तर *i. e.* southern. —इतरा *f.* The southern direction. —उत्तर *a.* 1 Successive. —उत्तरं *ind.* Higher and higher, in constant continuation, more and more. –ओष्ठः *m.* (उत्तरो.रौ-ष्ठः) The upper lip. –कायः *m.* The upper part of the body. —कालः *m.* Future time. –कुरवः (*m. pl.*) The northern Kurus. —कोसलाः (*m.*

pl.) The northern Kosalas.—कोसला *f.* The city of Ayodhyâ. —क्रिया *f.* The funeral rites,obsequies. —च्छदः *m.* A bed-covering, a covering in general. —ज *a.* Born subsequently or afterwards.-ज्योतिषाः(*m.pl.*)The northern Jyotishas. -ईशः, —पालः *m.* 1 Kubera,the regent of the north. -2 The planet बुध. —पक्षः *m.* 1 The northern wing or side. -2 The dark half of a lunar month. -3 The second part of an argument. *i. e.* a reply. -4 A demonstrated truth or conclusion. -5 The minor proposition in a syllgism. -6 (In Mim. The fifth member of an *Adhikarana*. —पटः *m.* 1 An upper garment. -2 A bed-covering. —पथः *m.* The northern way, way leading to the north. —पदं *n.* 1 The last member of a compound. -2 A word that can be compounded with another. —पश्चिमा *f.* The north-west. —पादः *m.* The second division of a legal plaint, the part which relates to the reply or defence. —पुरुषः *m.* Same as उत्तमपुरुषः —पूर्वा *f.* The north-east, —प्रच्छदः *m.* A coverlid, quilt. —प्रत्युत्तरं *n.* 1 A dispute, debate a rejoinder, retort. -2 The pleadings in a lawsuit. —फ (-फा-) ल्गुनी *f.* The twelfth lunar mansion consisting of two stars. —भाद्रपद्-दा *f.* The 26th lunar mansion. -मीमांसा *f.* The later Mimâmsâ, the Vedânta philosophy. —लक्षण *n.* The indication of an (actual) reply. —वयसं,-स *n.* Old age, the declining period of life. —वस्त्रं, -वासस् *n.* An upper garment, mantle, cloak. —वादिन् *m.* 1 A defendant, respondent. -2 One whose claims are of later date than another's. —वेदिः *f.* The northern altar made for the sacred fire. —सक्थं *n.* The left thigh. —साधकः *m.* An assistant, helper.

उत्तरंग *a.* 1 Washed by waves, inundated. -2 Trembling, tremulous. -3 With surging waves.

उत्तरणः *m.* N. of Vishnu. —णं *n.* 1 The act of landing, delivering or rescuing. -2 Conveying across.

उत्तरणं *n.* 1 Coming forth or out of (water &c.). -2 Landing, disembarking. -3 Crossing, passing over.

उत्तरतः, -तात् *ind.* 1 From the north; to the north. -2 To the left. -3 At the top, above. -4 Behind. -5 Afterwards.

उत्तरत्र *ind.* 1 Subsequently, later on, below (in a work). -2 Northward.

उत्तरीयं, -यकं *n.* An upper garment.

उत्तरेण *ind.* (With gen., acc. or at the end of a comp.) Northward, on the north side of.

उत्तरेद्युः *ind.* On a sbusequent day.

उत्तर्जनं *n.* Violent threatening.

उत्तान *a.* 1 Stretched out, expanded. -2 Lying on the back, with the face upwards, upright, erect. -3 Open. -4 Unreserved, frank, candid. -5 Elevated. -6 Shallow. -Comp. —पादः *m.* With extended legs (as children). 1 N. of a king, father of Dhruva. -2 The Supreme Spirit. —पादजः *m.* N. of Dhruva, the polar star. —शय *a.* Sleeping supinely or on the back. —शयः *m.*, —शय्या *f.* A little child, a suckling, an infant.

उत्तापः *m.* 1 Great heat. -2 Affliction,distress. -3 Excitement. -4 Anxiety, ardour.

उत्तार *a.* 1 Surpassing others, preeminent. -2 Having the eye-balls turned up (as eyes). -रः *m.* 1 Conveying. -2 Fording, crossing. -3 Landing. -4 Delivering, rescuing -5 Getting rid of. -6 Vomiting.

उत्तारकः *m.* 1 A deliverer. -2 N. of Siva

उत्ताल *a.* (*f.* —ला) 1 Great, strong. -2 Violent, loud. -3 Roaring, gusty (as wind). -4 Formidable, terrific. -5 Difficult. -6 Manifest. -7 Speedy, swift. -8 Best, excellent. -9 Elevated, lofty. —लः *m.* An ape.

उत्तीर्ण *p. p.* *f.* —र्णा) 1 Landed, crossed. -2 Rescued. -3 Released from obligation. -4 One who has finished his course of studies ; experienced, clever.

उत्तुंग *a.* (*f.* —गा) 1 Lofty, high, tall. -2 Swollen, (as a stream).

उत्तेजक *a.* (*f.* —जिका) 1 Instigating. -2 Exciting, stimulating.

उत्तेजन *n.*,-ना *f.* 1 Excitement, instigation, stirring up. -2 Urging on, driving. -3 Sending, despatching. -4 Whetting, sharpening. -5 An exciting speech. -6 An inducement, stimulant.

उत्तेजित *p. p.* (*f.* —ता) 1 Instigated. -2 Animated. -3 Sent. -4Sharpened, polished. —तं *n.* 1 An inducement. -2 One of the five paces of a horse, moderate velocity in a horse's pace.

उत्तेरितं *n.* One of the five paces of a horse.

उत्तोरण *a.* (*f.* —णा) Adorned with raised or upright arches.

उत्तोलनं *n.* Lifting up, raising.

उत्त्यागः *m.* 1 Abandonment. -2 Throwing up, tossing. -3 Renunciation of all worldly attachments.

उत्त्रासः *m.* Extreme fear.

उत्थ *a.* (*f.* —त्था) (Used only at the end of comp.) 1 Born or produced from. -2 Standing up, coming up or forth.

उत्था (उद् + स्था 1 P.) 1 To get up, stand, rise. -2 To get up from, leave, or cease from. -3 To rise, (as the sun &c.). -4 To rebound (as a ball). -5 To come forth. -6 To increase in strength or power, grow (Atm.). -7 To rise (from the dead). -8 To rise up. -9 To strive, try. -10 To excel, surpass. —*Caus.* (उत्थापयति) 1 To cause to stand up, raise, lift up. -2 To instigate, rouse to action. -3 To arouse, raise to life. -4 To support, help.

उत्थानं *n.*, 1 The act of rising or standing up. -2 Rising (as of luminaries). -3 Rise, origin. -4 Resurrection. -5 Effort, exertion, activity, energy. -6 Joy, pleasure. -7 War, battle. -8 An army. -9 Evacuating (by stool &c.). -10 A book. -11 A court-yard. -12 A shed for sacrifices. -13 A limit, boundary. -14 Business (cares &c.) of a family or a realm. -15 Reflection. -16 Proximate cause of a disease -17 Awakening. -Comp. -एकादशी *f.* The eleventh day in the light fortnight of Kârtika.

उत्थापनं *n.* 1 Causing to rise, to come up, or to get up. -2 Raising, elevating. -3 Exciting. -4 Awakening, rousing (fig. also). -5 Vomiting. -6 Finishing, completing.

उत्थित *p. p.* (*f.* —ता) 1 Risen or rising (as from a seat). -2 Raised, gone up. -3 Rescued, saved. -4 Born, sprung up, arisen. -5 Striving, active. -6 Increasing, (in strength). -7 Occurring. -8 High, lofty, eminent.-9 Extended, stretched. -Comp. —अंगुलिः m. The palm of the hand with the fingers extended.

उत्पक्ष्मन् a. With up-turned eyelashes.

उत्पटः m. Sap issuing from a tree.

उत्पत् (उत् + पत् 1 P.) 1 To fly or jump up; to rush towards. -2 To come up or out. -3 To rise, be produced. -4 To be born (as from the womb).

उत्पतः m. A bird.

उत्पतनं n. 1 Flying up, a leap. -2 Rising or going up. -3 Throwing up. -4 Birth, production.

उत्पताक a. (f. —का) With uplifted banners.

उत्पतिष्णु a. Flying up, going up.

उत्पत्तिः f. 1 Birth.-2 Production.-3 Source, origin. -4 Rising, coming into existence. -5 Profit, produce. -6 Producing as a result or effect.-7 Resurrection. -Comp. —व्यंजकः m. A type of birth (as investiture with the sacred thread); a mark of the twice-born.

उत्पथः m. A wrong road (fig. also). —थं ind. Astray, on the wrong road.

उत्पद् (उत् + पद् 4 A.) 1 To be born or produced, originate. -2 To occur, happen. —*Caus.* 1 To produce, cause, bring about. -2 To bring forward.

उत्पन्न p. p. (f. —न्ना) 1 Born, produced, arisen, gone up. -2 Acquired, gained. -3 Effected, accomplished. -4 Occurred. -5 Ascertained.

उत्पल a. (f. —ला) Fleshless, emaciated. —लं n. A blue lotus. -2 Any lotus or water-lily. -3 A plant in general. -Comp. —अक्ष, —चक्षुस् a Lotus-eyed. —पत्रं n. A nail-print, a broad-bladed knife or lancet.

उत्पलिनी f. An assemblage of lotus-flowers. -2 A lotus plant having lotuses.

उत्पवनं n. Cleaning, cleansing.

उत्पाटकः m. 1 One who roots out, -2 A disease of the ear.

उत्पाटनं n. Uprooting.

उत्पाटिका f. The outer bark of a tree.

उत्पातः m. 1 Flying up, a jump. -2 Rebounding, rising up (fig. also). -3 A portent, any unusual phenomenon boding calamity. -4 Any public calamity(as earthquake &c). -Comp. -पवनः, —वातः, m. A portentous or violent wind, whirlwind, a hurricane.

उत्पाद a. (f. —दा) With the feet up-lifted. —दः m. Birth, production, appearance. -Comp. -शयः, -शयनः m. 1 A child. -2 A kind of partridge. -3 The francoline partridge.

उत्पादक a. (f. —दिका) Productive, effective, bringing about. —कः m. A producer, generator, a father. —कं n. Origin, cause.

उत्पादन a. Producing. —नं n. Giving birh, production, generating.

उत्पादिका f. 1 N. of a certain insect, the white ant. -2 A mother.

उत्पाली f. Health.

उत्पिंजर,-ल a (f. —रा, —ला) 1 Unconfined, uncaged. -2 Excessively confused, disordered.

उत्पीड् (उत् + पीड् 10 P.) 1 To press against, strike or rub against. -2 To throw upwards; press out, propel, urge. -3 To overwhelm, overpower.

उत्पीड a. Pressing out. —डः m. 1 Pressing out. -2 Gush, gushing flow, rushing mass, overflow, excess. -3 Froth, foam.

उत्पीडनं *n.* 1 Pressing out. -2 Pressing or striking against.

उत्पुच्छ *a.* (*f.* —च्छा) With the tail erect.

उत्पुट *a.* (*f.* —टा) Blown, expanded.

उत्पुलक *a.* (*f.* —का) 1 Bristling. -2 Joyful, delighted.

उत्पवनं *n.* 1 Cleansing, purifying. -2 Straining liquids. -3 Any instrument for cleansing. -4 Sprinkling ghee &c. (on a sacred fire).

उत्प्रभ *a.* (*f.* -भा) Flashing forth or diffusing light, bright. -भः *m.* Blazing fire.

उत्प्रसवः *m.* Abortion.

उत्प्रासः *m.*, -सनं *n.* 1 Hurling, flinging away. -2 Jest, joke. -3 Violent burst of laughter. -4 Ridicule, derision, irony. -5 Excess.

उत्प्रेक्ष् (उत् + प्र + ईक्ष् 1 A.) 1 To look up to, to expect, to anticipate. -2 To perceive, behold. -3 To guess, conjecture. -4 To believe, fancy -5 To think of. -6 To illustrate.

उत्प्रेक्षणं *n.* 1 Looking into, perceiving. -2 Looking upwards. -3 Guess, conjecture. -4 Comparing.

उत्प्रेक्षा *f.* 1 Conjecture. -2 Carelessness, indifference. -3 (In Rhet.) A figure in which one thing is imagined under the character of another; भवेत्संभावनोत्प्रेक्षा प्रकृतस्य परात्मना * साहि. द. e. g. ऊरुः कुरंगकदृशश्चंचलचेलांचलो भाति । सपताकः कनकमयो विजयस्तंभः स्मरस्येव॥ रावणस्यापि रामास्तो भित्त्वा हृदयमाशुगः । विवेश भुवमाख्यातुमुरगेभ्य इव प्रियं * रघुवं. -4 A parable.

उत्प्लवः *m.* A jump, leap, bound. -वा *f.* A boat.

उत्प्लवनं *n.* 1 Jumping or leaping up, springing upon. -2 Skimming off impurities floating upon a liquid by passing a blade of Kusa grass over it.

उत्फलं *n.* An excellent fruit.

उत्फालः *m.* 1 A jump, spring. -2 The jumping attitude.

उत्फुल्ल *p. p.* (*f.* —ल्ला) 1 Opened, full blown (as flowers). -2 Widely opened, expanded (eyes). -3 Swollen, increased in bulk. -4 Sleeping supinely or on the back. -ल्लं *n.* The female organ of generation.

उत्सः *m.* 1 A spring, fountain. -2 A watery place.

उत्संगः *m.* 1 The lap. -2 Embrace, contact, union. -3 Interior, vicinity. -4 Surface, side. -5 The haunch (नितंब). -6 The upper part, top. -7 The edge of a hill. -8 The summit of a hill. -9 The roof of a house. -10 Vault, canopy (as of sky).

उत्संगित *a.* (*f.* —ता) 1 Associated, joined. -2 Taken in the lap.

उत्संजनं *n.* Throwing upwards, lifting up.

उत्सद् (उत् + सद् 1 P.) 1 To sink (fig. also), fall into ruin or decay. -2 To leave off, quit. -3 To rise up. —*Caus.* 1 To destroy, annihilate, bring to ruin. -2 To overturn, upset. -3 To anoint (as with oil, perfumes &c.).

उत्सन्न *p. p.* (*f.* —न्ना) 1 Decayed. -2 Destroyed, uprooted. -2 Extirpated. -3 Cursed, wretched. -4 Fallen into disuse (as a book). -5 Finished, completed.

उत्सर्गः *m.* 1 Abandoning, suspension. -2 Pouring out, emission. -3 A gift, donation. -4 Spending -5 Loosening, letting loose. -6 An oblation, libation. -7 Excretion. -8 Completion (as of study or a vow). -9 A general rule or precept (opp. अपवाद a particular rule or exception). -10 Offering what is promised(to Gods, Brâhmanas &c). -11 The anus.

उत्सर्जनं *n.* 1 Leaving, abandoning, letting loose. -2 A gift, donation. -3 Suspension of a Vedic study. -4 A ceremony connected with this suspension (to be performed half-yearly).

उत्सर्पः *m.*, -र्पणं *n.* 1 Going or gliding upwards. -2 Swelling.

उत्सर्पिन् *a.* (*f.* -णी) 1 Moving or gliding upwards, rising. -2 Soaring, towering.

उत्सवः *m* 1 A festival, festive occasion, jubilee. -2 Joy, merriment, pleasure.-3 Height, elevation. -4 Wrath. -5 Wish. -6 A section of a book. -7 Enterprise. -8 An undertaking.—Comp. —संकेताः (*m. pl.*) N of a people, a wild tribe of the Himâlayas.

उत्सह् (उत् + सह् 1 A.) 1 To be able, have power or energy ; (expressed by ' can ') ; dare, venture. -2 To attempt, be prompted or incited, to cheer up, not to sink or give way. -3 To feel at ease. -4 To go forward, march on. —*Caus.* To encourage, excite.

उत्सादः *m.* Destruction, decay, ruin, loss.

उत्सादक *a.* Destroying.

उत्सादनं *n.* 1 Destroying, overturning. -2 Interrupting. -3 Cleaning the person with perfumes, chafing the limbs. -4 Healing a sore. -5 Ascending, rising. 6 Elevating, raising. -7 Ploughing a field thoroughly.

उत्सारकः *m.* 1 A policeman. -2 A guard. -3 A porter, door-keeper.

उत्सारणं *n.* 1 Removing, keeping at a distance, driving out of the way. -2 Reception of a guest.

उत्साहः *m.* 1 Effort, exertion. -2 Energy. -3 Perseverance, one of the three Saktis or powers of a ruler (the other two being मंत्र and प्रभाव). -4 Determination, resolution. -5 Power, ability. -6 Firmness, fortitude, strength. -7 (In Rhet) Firmness or fortitude considered as the feeling which gives rise to the वीर or heroic sentiment. -8 Happiness. -Comp. —वर्धनः *m.* The heroic sentiment (वीररस). -वर्धनं *n.* Increase of energy, heroism. —शक्तिः *f.* Firmness, energy.

उत्साहनं *n.* 1 Effort, perseverance. -2 Encouraging, exciting.

उत्सिक्त *p. p.* (*f.* -क्ता) 1 Sprinkled. -2 Proud, haughty. -3 Flooded, overflowing. -4 Enlarged, increased. -5 Raised, elevated. -6 Fickle, disturbed (in mind). -Comp. -वीर्योत्सिक्त *a* Buoyant with the spirit of heroism.

उत्सुक *a.* 1 Anxiously desirous, striving for (any object) (with instr. or loc.). -2 Restless, uneasy, anxious, alarmed. -3 Fond of, affected with longing, attached to. -4 Regretting, repining, sorrowing for.

उत्सूत्र *a.* (*f.* -त्रा) 1 Unstrung, loose. -2 Irregular. -3 Deviating from the rule (सूत्र) of Pânini.

उत्सूरः *m.* Evening twilight.

उत्सृज् (उत् + सृज् 6 P.) 1 Pour out, send forth. -2 To leave, abandon, lay aside. -3 To let loose. -4 To discharge, throw (as arrows). -5 To sow, scatter (as seed &c.). -6 To present, give. -7 To abolish

(as a rule). -8 To send one to a place.

उत्सृष्ट *a.* (*f.* —ष्टा) 1 Left, thrown. -2 Used, employed. -3 Given, offered. -4 Poured forth. —Comp. —पशुः *m.* A bull set at liberty upon particular occasions.

उत्सृष्टिः *f.* Abandonment, leaving

उत्सेकः *m.* 1 Sprinkling, pouring. -2 Spouting out, showering. -3 Overflow, increase. -4 Pride, haughtiness.

उत्सेचनं *n.* The act of showering or spouting upwards.

उत्सेधः *m.* 1 A height, elevation; (fig. also). -2 Thickness, fatness. -3 Swelling. -4 The body. -5 Sublimity, greatness. —धं *n.* Killing, slaughter.

उत्स्मयः *m.* Smile.

उत्स्वनः *m.* A loud sound.

उद् *ind.* A prefix to verbs and nouns implying. 1 Superiority (*e. g.* उद्कुल). -2 Separation, disjunction (*e.g.* उद्गच्छति). -3 Motion upwards (*e. g.* उत्तिष्ठति). -4 Acquisition, gain (*e. g.* उत्पन्न). -5 Publicity (*e. g.* उच्चारित). -6 Wonder; anxiety (*e. g.* उत्सुक). -7 Liberation (*e. g.* उद्गत). -8 Absence (*e. g.* उत्पथ). -9 Blowing, expanding, opening (*e. g.* उत्फुल्ल). -10 Preeminence (*e. g.* उद्दिष्ट). -11 Power (*e. g.* उत्साहः). With nouns it forms adj. and adv. compounds (*e. g.* उच्छिख, उद्बाहु, उन्निद्र,).

उदक् *ind.* 1 Above. -2 Northwards (with abl.). -3 Subsequently.

उदकं *n.* Water. —Comp. —अंतः *m.* Margin of water, bank, shore. —आधारः *m.* A reservoir, a cistern, well. —उदंजनः *m.* A water-jar. —उदरं *n.* Dropsy. —कर्मन्, —कार्यं *n.*, —क्रिया *f.*, —दानं *n.* Presentation of (a libation) of water to dead ancestors or the manes. —कुंभः *m.* A water-jar. —कृच्छ्रः *m.* A kind of vow. —गाहः *m.* Entering water, bathing. —द, —दातृ, —दायिन्, —दानिक *a.* Giver of water. —दः *m.* 1 A giver of water to the manes. -2 An heir, a near kinsman. —धरः *m.* A cloud. —भारः, —वीवधः *m.* A yoke for carrying water. —वज्रः *m.* A thunder-shower. —शाकं *n.* Any aquatic herb. —शांतिः *f.* Sprinkling holy or consecrated water over a sick person to allay fever. —स्पर्शः *m.* 1 Touching different parts of the body with water. -2 Touching water preparatory to or in confirmation of an oath, gift, or promise.

उदक (-कि-) ल *a.* Watery, containing water.

उदकेचर, *m.* An aquatic animal.

उदक्त *a.* (*f.* —क्ता) Raised up (as from a well).

उदक्तात् *ind.* Towards the north, northwards.

उदक्या *f.* A woman in her courses.

उदग्र *a* (*f.* —ग्रा) 1 With elevated top. projecting. -2 Tall, lofty, high, exalted (fig. also). -3 Large, broad, big. -4 Noble, good-looking. -5 Advanced in age. -6 Conspicuous, distinguished, exalted, increased. -7 Intense, unbearable (as heat). -8 Fierce, fearful. -9 Excited, enraptured. -10 Powerful, strong.

उदङ्कः *m.* 1 A leathern vessel.

उदंच् (उत् + अंच् 1 U.) 1 To raise, lift or throw up, draw up. -2 To utter, send forth. -3 (Intrans.) To go up, to rise

उदञ्च्, उदंच् *a.* (*m.* उदङ्, *n.* उदक्, *f* उदीची) 1 Turned or going upwards -2 Upper. -3 Northern, turned to wards the north. -4 Subsequent.

-Comp. —अद्रिः *m.* The northern mountain, Himâlaya. —अयनं *n.* The sun's progress north of the equator (*i. e.* उत्तरायणं). —आवृत्तिः *f.* Return from the north. —पथः *m.* A northern country. —प्रवण *a.* 1 Inclining or sloping towards the north. -2 Proceeding well (as a sacrifice). —मुख *a.* Facing the north.

उदंचनं *n.* 1 A bucket, a pail for drawing water out of a well. -2 Throwing upwards. -3 Rising, ascending. -4 A cover or lid.

उदंजलि *a.* One who hollows the palms and raises them, folding the hands in supplication.

उदंडपालः *m.* 1 A fish. -2 A kind of snake.

उदन् *n.* Water (usually occurring in compounds either at the beginning or at the end, and as an optional substitute for उदक after the acc. dual. It has no forms for the first five inflections. In comp. it drops its न); *e. g.* उदधि, अच्छोद, क्षीरोद &c. Comp. -कुंभः *m.* A water-jar. -ज *a.* Aquatic, watery, produced in or by water. —धानः *m* 1 A water-jar. -2 A cloud. —धिः *m.* 1 The receptacle of waters, ocean. -2 A cloud. -3 A lake, any lage reservoir of water. -4 A water-jar. -5 A symbolical expression for the number 4 or 7. उद—धिकन्या,-तनया,-सुता *f.* Lakshmi, the daughter of the ocean. उदधिमेखला *f.* The earth. उदधिराजः *m.* The king of waters. *i. e.* the chief ocean. उदधिसुता *f.* 1 N. of Lakshmi. -2 Dváraka, the capital of Krishna. —पात्रं, *n*, -त्री *f.* A water-jug, vessel. —पानः *m.*, -नं *n.* A small pool or pond near a well, or the well itself. उदपान मंडूकः. *m.* (lit.) A frog in a well (fig.). One who has had no experience of the world; a man of limited ideas who knows only his own neighbourhood. —पेषं *n.* A paste. —भारः *m.* A water-carrier, *i. e.* a cloud. —मानः *m.*, -नं *n.* A fiftieth part of an आढकः. —मेघः *m.* 1 A watery cloud. -2 A shower of rain. —लावणिक *a.* Salted, prepared with brine, briny. —वज्रः *m.* A thunder-shower; water-spout. —वापः *m.* One who offers waters to the manes. —वाहः *m.* A cloud. —वाहनं *n.* A water-vessel. —शरावः *m.* A jar filled with water. —श्वित *n.* Butter-milk containing fifty per cent water. —हरणः *m.* A vessel for drawing water. —हारः *m.* A cloud(water-carrier).

उदंतः *m.* 1 News, intelligence, report, full tidings, account, history. -2 A pure and virtuous man (साधु).

उदंतकः *m.* News, intellgence.

उदंतिका: *m. f.* Satisfaction, satiety.

उदन्य *a.* 1 Thirsty. -2 Watery.

उदन्या *f.* Thirst.

उदन्यु *a.* 1 Thirsty. -2 Walking in water.

उदन्वत् *m.* The ocean.

उदय *a.* (In gram) Following, coming after or upon (as a letter, accent, &c.) —यः *m.* 1 Rise (fig. also); going upwards, rising (as of the sun, stars &c.). -2 Acquisition (of wealth &c.). -3 Becoming visible, production. -4 Rising or accomplishment of the fruit. -5 Creation (opp. प्रलय). -6 The eastern mountain (behind which the sun is supposed to rise). -7 Advancement, prosperity, rise ; (opp. व्यसनं). -8 Exaltation, growth. -9 Result, consequence. -10 Profit, advantage. -11 Income, revenue. -12 Interest, or consideration, paid for the use of money. -13 Light splendour. -14

Outlet, exit. -Comp. —अचलः, —अद्रिः, —गिरिः,—पर्वतः, —शैलः *m.* The eastern mountain behind which the sun, moon &c. are supposed to rise. —प्रस्थः *m.* The plateau of the mountain behind which the sun is supposed to rise.

उदयनं *n.* 1 Rising, ascending, going up. -2 Result. -3 End, conclusion. —नः *m.* 1 N. of Agastya.-2 N. of the king Vatsa.

उदयनीय *a.* (*f.* —या) Concluding (as a ceremony). —या *f.* A concluding sacrifice.

उदर *n.* 1 The belly. -2 The interior or inside of anything; cavity. -3 Enlargement of the abdomen from dropsy or flatulence. -4 Any morbid abdominal affection, such as liver, spleen &c. Slaughter.-Comp. —आध्मानः *m.* Flatulence of the belly. —आवर्तः *m.* The navel. —आवेष्टः *m.* The tape-worm. —त्राणं *n.* 1 A cuirass, armour covering the front of the body. -2 A belly-band. -पिशाचः *m.* A glutton. —पूरं *ind.* Till the belly is full. —पोषणं, —भरणं *n.* Feeding the belly, support of life. —शयः *m.* The foetus. —सर्वस्वः *m.* A glutton, an epicure.

उदराधिः *m.* 1 The ocean. -2 The sun.

उदरंभरि *a.* 1 Nourishing one's own belly, selfish. -2 Gluttonous, voracious.

उदरिक *a.* (*f.* —का) Having a large belly, corpulent, fat.

उदरिन् *a.* 1 Having a large belly, fat, corpul nt. -2 Abdominal. -णी *f.* A pregnant woman.

उदरिल *a.* (*f.* —ला) Fat, corpulent.

उदर्कः *m.* End, conclusion, result, consequence. -2 Future time, futurity.-5 Elevation of a building (as of a tower).

उदर्चिस् *a.* Shining or blazing upwards, radiant, glowing. —*m.* 1 Fire. -2 The god of love. -3 N. of Siva.

उदर्दः *m.* (In Medic.) Erysipelas.

उदर्धः *m.* Scarlet fever, (Mar. आग्या ताप).

उदवसान *a.* Last, final.

उदवसितं *n.* A house, dwelling.

उदश्रु *a.* One whose tears are gushing forth, weeping.

उदस् (उद् + अस् 4 P.) 1 To cast up, throw up, to lift up, elevate, erect. -2 To throw down. -3 To throw out, leave, quit. -4 To destroy, dispel. -5 To drive, propel. -6 To make efforts.

उदसनं *n.* 1 Throwing up, raising, erecting.-2 Driving out, turning out.

उदात्त *a.* (*f.* —त्ता) 1 High, elevated, lofty, exalted, noble, excellent, sublime. -2 Noble, dignified. -3 Generous, bountiful.-4 Famous, illustrious. -5 Dear, beloved. -6 Highly or acutely accented (as a Svara). —त्तः *m.* 1 The acute accent. -2 Gift, donation. -3 A kind of musical instrument, a large drum. -4 A variety of the hero in drama. -त्तं *n.* (In Rhet.) A figure of speech in which there is a description of prosperity exceeding all ordinary experience; also that in which the actions of the great become subordinate or collateral to the subject in hand. लोकातिशयसंपत्तिवर्णनोदात्तमुच्यते । यद्वापि प्रस्तुतस्याङ्गंमहतां चरितं भवेत् ॥ * साहि. द. 10

उदानः *m.* 1 Breathing upwards. -2 Breathing; breath in and out. -3 One of the five vital airs or life-winds which rises up at the throat, the other four being प्राण, अपान, समान and व्यान. -4 The navel.

–5 An eye-lash. –6 A kind of snake.

उदायुध *a.* (*f.* –धा) With uplifted weapon; upraising weapons.

उदार *a* (*f.* –रा, or री) 1 Generous, liberal. –2 Noble, exalted. –2 Lofty, great, illustrious. –3 Honest, sincere, upright. –4 Beautiful, charming. –5 Proper, right. –6 Eloquent. –7 Kind, agreeable: –8 Plentiful. –9 Extensive, splendid. —रं *ind.* 1 Loudly. –रं *n.* –2 A figure in Rhetoric in which greatness is attributed to inanimate objects. –Comp. —आत्मन्, –चेतस्, –चरित, –मनस्, –सत्त्व *a.* Noble-minded, magnanimous. —धी *a.* 1. Of sublime genius; highly intelligent. –2 Noble-minded.

उदावत्सर: *m.* A year, one of the five years forming a period.

उदावर्त: *m.* A disease of the bowels.

उदास् (उत् + आस् 2A.) To be indifferent or unconcerened, careless or apathetic; to be passive or inactive; to show no interest in

उदास *a.* (*f.* –सा) Indifferent, apathetic. —स: *m.* 1 A stoic; a philosopher. –2 Indifference, apathy.

उदासीन *pres. p.* (*f.* –ना) 1 Indiferent, unconcerned, passive. –2 (In law) Not involved in any dispute. –3 Neutral (as a king or nation). —न: *m.* 1 A stranger. –2 A neutral, an indifferent person. –3 A common acquaintance.

उदास्थित: *m.* 1 A superintendent. –2 A door-keeper. –3 A spy, an emissary –4 An ascetic who has given up his vow.

उदाहरणं *n.* 1 Relating, declaration, recital, opening a discourse. –3 A sort of panegyric beginning with words like जयति and full of alliteration. –4 An instance, example, illustration. –5 (In Nyâya) The third member of a syllogism (which has five members). –6 Beginning, commencement, introduction. –7 (In Rhet.) An illustration reckoned as a figure of speech by some rhetoricians. It resembles अर्थान्तरन्यास.

उदाहार: *m.* 1 An example or illustration –2 The beginning of a speech.

उदाहृ (उत् + आ + हृ 1 P.) 1 To relate, narrate –2 To say, speak, utter. –3 To cite as an instance or illustration, illustrate.

उदि (उत् + इ 2 P.) 1 To rise (as a star, cloud &c.) (fig. also); come up; to be seen, appear. –2 To be produced, to proceed from. –3 To go out, escape. –4 To rise up against.

उदित *p. p.* (*f.* –ता) 1 Risen, ascended. –2 High, tall, lofty. –3 Grown. –4 Born, produced. –5 Spoken, uttered. —तं *n.* 1 A kind of perfume. –2 A kind of accent. –Comp. —उदित *a.* Well-grounded in the Sástras.

उदीक्ष् (उत् + ईक्ष् 1 A.) 1 To look up to, view, behold. –2 To expect, wait for.

उदीक्षणं *n.* 1 Looking up to. –2 Seeing, beholding, seeking.

उदीची *f.* The north.

उदीचीन *a.* (*f.* –ना) Northern, turned towards the north.

उदीच्य *a.* (*f.* –च्या) Being in the north. —च्य: *m.* 1 The country to the north and west of the river सरस्वती. –2 One living in the north. —च्यं *n.* A kind of perfume

उदीप: *m.* High water, inundation, flood.

उदीर् (उत् + ईर् 2 A.) 1 To rise (as sound &c.). –2 To start. –3 To move upwards, go up. –4 To arise, originate. —*Caus.* 1 To cause to rise or move.-2 To utter, pronounce, speak. -3 To name -4 To put forth, to display, manifest, to make visible, to cause. -5 To cast, throw, as dice), discharge, drive forward. -6 To raise, throw up, to bring about, effect.-7 To excite, stimulate.

उदीरणं *n.* 1 Utterance, pronunciation, expression. -2 Speaking, saying. -3 Throwing, discharging (as a missile.).

उदीर्ण *p. p.* (*f.* —र्णा) 1 Grown, risen, produced, caused. -2 Puffed up, elated, grown haughty. -3 Excited, roused. -4 Increased, intense. -5 Generous, excellent. -6 Uttered, pronounced. -7 Ready, strung.(as bow.)-र्णः *m.*N.of Vishnu.

उदुंबरः *m.* 1 A kind of fig-tree. -2 A kind of leprosy. -3 A threshhold. -4 A eunuch. —रं *n.* Copper, brass.

उदूखलः *m.*, -लं *r* 1 A wooden mortar used for pounding rice and separating the husk. -2 A mortar in general.

उदूढा *f.* A married woman.

उद्वेजय *a.* (*f.* —या) Shaking, causing to tremble, terrifying.

उद्गत *p. p.* (*f.* —ता) 1 Gone up, risen. -2 Proceeded forth or from. -3 Gone, departed.-4 Vomited. -ता *f.*N. of a metre

उद्गतिः *f.* 1 Going up, rising, ascent. -2 Appearance. -2 Rise, origin. -4 Vomiting.

उद्गंधि *a.* 1 Fragrant. -2 Having a strong smell (good or bad).

उद्गम् (उत् + गम् 1 P.) 1 To rise or go up, ascend (as a star &c.). -2 To shoot up, appear. -3 To rise or spring up from, originate, arise ; to spread about. -4 To depart (as life &c.).

उद्गमः *m.* 1. Going up, rising (of stars); ascent. -2 Standing erect (of hair). -3 Going out, departure; (as in प्राणोत्क्रमणं). -4 Birth, production, creation, appearance, origin, parentage. -5 Projection, elevation. -6 A shoot (of a plant). -8 Vomiting.

उद्गमनं *n.* Rising, ascending, becoming visible.

उद्गमनीयं *n.* A pair of bleached or washed clothes.

उद्गाढ *a.* (*f.* —ढा) Deep, intense, violent, strong, excessive, much. —ढं *n.* Excess. —*ind* Excessively, extremely.

उद्गातृ *m* One of the four chief priests at a sacrifice ; he recites the सामवेद.

उद्गाथा *f.* A variety of the Aryâ metre, the same as Giti.

उद्गारः *m.* Spitting out, vomiting, giving out, emitting, flowing out, issuing out. -2 Repeating, narration, expression ; declaring. -3 Quantity, mass (thrown out). -4 Spittle, saliva. -5 Eructation, belching. -6 Sound, roaring, echo, hissing sound. -7 A big wave.

उद्गिरणं *n.* 1 Vomiting.-2 Ejecting anything (as saliva) from the mouth. -3 Eructation, belch. -4 Extermination.

उद्गीतिः *f.* 1 Singing aloud.-2 Chanting of the Sâmaveds. -3 A variety of the Aryâ metre.

उद्गीथः *m.* 1 Chanting of the Sâmaveda (the office of an Udgâtri). -2 The second part of the Sâmaveda. -3 Designation of ओम्, the three syllabled name of God.

उद्गीर्ण *a.* (*f.* —र्णा) 1 Vomited. -2 Let out, emitted, poured out.

उद्गूर्ण *p. p.* (*f.* —र्णा) 1 Raised, uplifted, held up. -2 Erected, excited.

उद्गॄ (उत् + गॄ 6 P.) 1 To eject, spit out, vomit. -2 To put forth, pour out, discharge, belch out.-3 To send out of the mouth, speak, utter (as words). -3 To breathe out.

उद्गै (उत् + गै 1 P.) 1 To sing aloud, to sing (in general). -2 To begin to sing. -3 To sing or chant the Sámaveda. -4 To celebrate in song. -5 To sing before one (with acc.).

उद्ग्रंथ् (उत् + ग्रंथ् 1.9.U.) 1 To bind up, tie into bundles.-2 To put or sew together (as garlands &c.), to tie or fasten, intertwine. -3 To unbind, loosen (as a knot &c.).

उद्ग्रंथ: *m.* A section, chapter.

उद्ग्रंथि *a.* 1 Untied(fig.also).-2Free from worldly ties or attachments.

उद्ग्रह् (उत् + ग्रह् 9 P.) 1 To take up; lift up, elevate, erect, raise.-2 To take out, take away. -3 To deposit. -4 To cease (to rain). -5 To break off, discontinue (speaking). —*Caus.* 1 To cause to pay.-2To state, place before, adduce. -3 To extol, laud up.

उद्ग्रह: *m.*, —हणं *n.* 1 Taking up, raising. -2 An object that can be accomplished by religious or other acts. -3 Eructation.

उद्ग्राह: *m.* 1 Lifting or taking up. -2Replying in argument; rejoinder. -3 An objection.

उद्ग्राहणिका *f.* Replying in argument.

उद्ग्राहित *p. p.* (*f.* —ता) 1 Lifted or taken up. -2 Taken away. -3 Excellent; exalted. -4 Deposited, delivered. -5 Bound, tied. -6 Recalled, remembered.

उद्ग्रीव *a.* (*f.* —वा) One with the neck uplifted.

उद्घ: *m.* 1 Excellence, eminence; (at the end of comp.) गवोद्घ: *m.* An excellent bull. -2 Happiness. -3 The hollow hand. -4Fire -5 A model. -6 Organic air in the body.

उद्घट्ट् (उत् + घट्ट् 1 A.) To open. -*Caus.* (-घाटयति) 1 To open, unlock. -2 To reveal, make known. -3 To commence.

उद्घट्टनं *n.*, —ना *f.* 1 Friction, striking against. -2 Opening upwards (as a lid.)

उद्घट्टित *a.* (*f.* —ता) 1Opened, unlocked. -2 Separated.

उद्घन: *m.* A carpenter's bench or the plank on which he works.

उद्घर्षणं *n.* 1 Rubbing, rubbing up. -2 Rubbing the skin with hard substances. -3 A cudgel.

उद्घसं *n.* Flesh.

उद्घाट: *m.* A watch or guard-house.

उद्घाटक: *m.*, —कं *n.* 1 A key. -2 The rope and bucket of a well.

उद्घाटन *a.* (*f.* —नी) Opening, unlocking. —नं *n.* 1 Opening. -2 Raising, lifting up. -3 A key, any means of opening. -4 The rope and bucket of a well; a water-wheel.

उद्घाटित *p. p.* (*f.* —ता) 1 Opened, manifested. -2 Undertaken; commenced. -3 Raised, lifted up.

उद्घात: *m.* 1 Beginning, commencement. -2 Allusion, reference. -3 Striking, wounding. -4 Stroke, blow, wound. -5 Tripping, jolting, (as of a carriage). -6 Rising, elevation. -7 A club, mallet. -8 A weapon (in general). -9 A division of a book, chapter; section.

उद्घातिन् *a.* Uneven, rough.

उद्घुष् (उत् + घुष् 1 P.) To sound, cry out or shout. -10 P. 1 To proclaim. -2 To fill with cries.

उद्घोष: *m.* 1 Announcing aloud, proclaiming. -2 Popular talk.

उद्दंड *a.* (*f* —डा) 1 With the stalk

or staff raised up. -2 Formidable, terrific. -Comp. —पाल: *m.* 1 A punisher (whether king or magistrate). -2 A kind of fish. -3 A kind of serpent.

उद्दंतुर *a.* (*f.* —रा) 1 Large-toothed or having projecting teeth.-2 High, tall. -3 Terrific, formidable.

उद्दम: *m.* Subduing, overpowering.

उद्दानं *n.* 1 Binding, confinement. -2 Taming, subduing -3 The middle, the waist. -4 A fire-place. -5 The submarine fire.-6 Entrance of the sun into a zodiacal sign.

उद्दांत *a.* 1 Energetic. -2 Humble.

उद्दाम *a.* (*f.* —मा) 1 Unbound, unrestrained, free, bold. -2 Strong, powerful. -3 Violent ; intoxicated. -4 Dreadful, formidable. -5 Self-willed. -6 Large, great, excessive. -7 Proud, haughty. —म: *m.* 1 N. of Yama. -2 N. of Varuna. -मं *ind.* Violently, fiercely, strongly.

उद्दालक: *m.* -1 N. of a sage. —कं *n.* A kind of honey.

उद्दित *a.* (*f.* —ता) Tied, bound.

उद्दिनं *n.* Midday.

उद्दिश् (उत् + दिश् 6 U.) 1 To point out, mention, tell. -2 To prophesy. -3 To refer or allude to. -4 To mean, intend, aim at, assign to. -5 To teach, advise.

उद्दिश्य *ind.* 1 With reference to, in the direction of, towards. -2 For, on account of. -3 Demanding, stipulating for.

उद्दिष्ट *p. p.* (*f.* —ष्टा) 1 Mentioned, specially told. -2 Desired, wished for. -3 Taught.

उद्दीप: *m.* 1 Inflaming, lighting. -2 An inflamer. -3 That which animates or excites. —पं *n.* Bdellium (Mar. गुग्गुळ).

उद्दीपक *a.* 1 Exciting, making more intense. -2 Lighting, inflaming.

उद्दीपनं *n.* 1 Inflaming, exciting. -2 (In Rhet.) That which excites or feeds (a sentiment or *rasa*). -3 Illuminating, lighting, burning. -4 Burning of a body.

उद्दीप्त *p. p.* 1 Lighted, set on fire. -2 Shining. -3 Inflamed, excited.

उद्दीप्र *a.* (*f.* —प्रा) Shining, blazing. —प्र: *m.*, -प्रं *n.* Bdellium (Mar. गुग्गूळ).

उद्देश: *m.* 1 Pointing to, or at. -2 Mention, specification. -3 Illustration, explanation. -4 Ascertainment, inquiry, search. -5 A brief statement or account. -6 Assignment, allotment. -7 Stipulation, bargain. -8 Object, motive. -9 A spot, place. -10 (In phil.) The enunciation of a thing by its name.

उद्दंश: *m.* 1 A bug. -2 A louse. -3 A mosquito, gadfly.

उद्देशक: *m.* 1 An illustration, example. -2 An illustrator, a guide. -3 (In Math.) A question, problem.

उद्देश्य *pot. p.* (*f.* —श्या) 1 To be illustrated or explained. -2 To be intended or aimed at. -3 That to which one refers or which one has in view. -श्यं *n.* 1 The object in view, an incentive. -2 The subject of a sentence (opp. विधेय which is the predicate).

उद्देहिका *f.* The white ant (Mar. वाळवी).

उद्द्युत् (उत् + द्युत् 1 A.) To blaze up, shine.

उद्द्योत: *m.* 1 Light, lustre (lit. and fig). -2 Revelation. -3 A division of a book, chapter, section.

उद्द्राव: *m.* Flight, retreat.

उद्धत *p. p.* (*f.* —ता) 1 Raised up, elevated, lifted up. -2 Excessive, exceeding. -3 Haughty, puffed up

-4 Harsh. -5 Excited, inflamed. -6 Ill-mannered. —तः *m.* A king's wrestler. -Comp. —मनस्, -मनस्क *a.* High-minded, haughty, proud

उद्धतिः *f.* 1 Elevation. -2 Pride, haughtiness. -3 Rudeness, insolence. -4 A stroke.

उद्धमः *m.* 1 Breathing hard. -2 Blowing, sounding.

उद्धरणं *n.* 1 Taking out, taking off (clothes &c). -2 Extraction, pulling out. -3 Extricating, deliverance (from danger). -4 Destruction, extermination, dethronement. -5 Lifting, raising. -6 Taking a part or share. -7 Vomiting. -8 Anything vomited. -9 Final emancipation. -10 Acquittance of debt.

उद्धर्तृ (*nom. s.* —र्ता) 1 One who raises or lifts up. -2 A sharer, co-heir. -3 One who recovers property. -4 A destroyer, exterminator. -5 A saviour, deliverer.

उद्धर्षः *m.* 1 Great joy or delight. -2 Courage to undertake a thing. -3 A festival.

उद्धर्षणं *n.* 1 Animating. -2 Erection of the hair (on the body), thrill.

उद्धवः *m.* 1 A sacrificial fire. -2 A festival, holiday. -3 N. of a Yâdava, uncle and friend of Krishna.

उद्धस्त *a.* (*f.* —स्ता) Raising the hands.

उद्धा (उद् + हा 3 A). 1 To go or move upwards, rise (as the sun, dust &c.). -2 To depart. -3 To raise. -4 To throw up, knit (as eyebrows).

उद्धानं *n.* 1 A fireplace. -2 Ejecting, vomiting.

उद्धान्त *a.* (*f.* —न्ता) Ejected, vomited. —न्तः *m.* An elephant out of rut.

उद्धारः *m* 1 Drawing out, extraction. -2 Deliverance, saving, resting. -3 Raising, lifting up. -4 Deduction, a part to be set aside. -5 (In law) A part to be set aside from patrimony for the benefit of the eldest son. -6 The sixth part of booty taken in war which belongs to the king. -7 An obligation. -8 Debt, particularly such as bears no interest. -9 Recovering property. -10 Marching out. -11 Citing (a passage), quoting. -12 Final beatitude. -13 Prosperity, elevation. -रं *n.* A fire-place.

उद्धारकः *m.* See उद्धर्तृ.

उद्धारणं *n.* 1 Raising, elevating. -2 Rescuing from danger, delivering. -3 Sharing, dividing.

उद्धुर *a.* (*f.* —रा) 1 Unrestrained, unchecked, free. -2 Firm, bold. -3 Victorious, conquering. -4 High, loud (voice &c). -5 Heavy, full of. -6 Thick, gross. -7 Lively. -8 Able, competent.

उद्धू (उद् + धू 5. 9. U.) 1 To shake, move up, throw up, wave (as a 'chawari'); to shake or throw off. -2 To dispel, destroy. -3 To disturb, excite, rouse up.

उद्धूत *p. p.* (*f.* —ता) 1 Shaken off, raised or thrown up. -2 Exalted, high, loud.

उद्धूननं *n.* 1 Throwing upwards, raising. -2 Shaking.

उद्धूपनं *n* Fumigating.

उद्धूलनं *n.* 1 Powdering, sprinkling with dust or powder. -2 An article used to season food.

उद्धूलय् Den. P. To powder, sprinkle with powder or dust.

उद्धूषणं *n.* Erection of the hair (on the body), horripilation.

उद्धृ (उद् + धृ 1. 10. P.) 1 To draw out, raise up. -2 To save, deliver.

उद्धृ (उद् + हृ 1 P.) 1 To draw or

take out, extract, extricate. -2 To deliver from, relive of, save, rescue, protect (with abl.). -3 To uproot, extirpate, tear or pull out. -4 To pluck up (flowers &c.). -5 To raise, lift up -6 To take up, absorb. -7 To sustain, bear up -8 To separate, abstract. -9 To remove, put away. -10 To subtract. -11 To select, pick out. -12 To present, offer. -13 To prove. -14 To divide (as with partners). -15 To publish, make known.

उद्धृत *p. p.* (*f.* —ता) 1 Drawn up or out, extracted. -2 Raised, lifted up, thrown up or upwards. -3 Uprooted. -4 Separated, set apart. -5 Divided, partitioned. -6 Selected. -7 Dispersed, scattered. -8 Holding, containing. -9 Uncovered. -10 Vomited, cast up

उद्धृतिः *f.* 1 Drawing or pulling out, extracting. -2 An extract, passage selected. -3 Delivering, rescuing. -4 Delivering or purifying from sin, final liberation.

उद्ध्मानं *n.* A fire-place, stove.

उद्ध्यः *m.* N. of a river; तोयदागम इवोद्ध्यभिद्ययोः * रघुवं 11. 8.

उद्बद्ध *a.* (*f.* —द्धा) Loosened. —न्धः *m.*, —न्धनं *n.* 1 Tying up, hanging. -2 Hanging oneself.

उद्बन्धकः *m.* A man of the washerman caste.

उद्बल *a.* (*f.* —ला) Strong, powerful.

उद्बाष्प *a.* (*f.* —ष्पा) Filled or suffused with tears.

उद्बाहु *a.* 1 Having the arms raised. -2 Having the trunk upraised (as an elephant).

उद्दर्शनं *n.* Making visible.

उद्बुद्ध *p. p.* (*f.* —द्धा) 1 Awakened, aroused, excited. -2 Opened, full-blown. -3 Reminded, made to think of. -4 Recalled to memory (as an object seen before).

उद्बोधः *m.*, —धनं *n.* 1 Awakening, reminding. -2 Recalling to memory, rousing up.

उद्बोधक *a.* 1 That which reminds or calls to remembrance. -2 Exciting, rousing. -3 Discovering, exhibiting, showing. —कः *m* The sun.

उद्भट *a.* (*f.* —टा) 1 Excellent, pre-eminent. -2 Exalted, magnanimous. —टः *m.* 1 A fan for winnowing corn. -2 A tortoise.

उद्भवः *m.* 1 Creation, generation, production. -2 Source. -3 An epithet of Vishnu.

उद्भावः *m.* 1 Production, generation. -2 Magnanimity.

उद्भावनं *n.* 1 Thinking, thinking over. -2 Production, generation, creation. -3 Speaking, saying. -4 Inattention, neglect, disregard.

उद्भास् (उत् + भास् 1 A.) To shine. —*Caus.* 1 To light up, decorate, ornament. -2 (fig.) To elevate, exalt.

उद्भासः *m.* Radiance, splendour.

उद्भासिन्, उद्भासुर *a.* (*f.* —नी, —रा) Shining, radiant, splendid.

उद्भिद् (उत् + भिद् 7 U.) To break up, to send forth —*Caus.* To bring out, develop, unfold.

उद्भिद् *m.* 1 A sprout or shoot (of a plant). -2 A plant. -3 A spring, fountain. —Comp. —जः *m.* (उद्भिज्जः). 1 A plant. -2 One of the four great kingdoms of the animal creation as conceived by Hindu philosophers; see जरायुज. —उद्भिज्जविद्या *f.* The science of botany.

उद्भिद *a.* (*f.* —दा) Sprouting, germinating. —दं *n.* Culinary salt.

उद्भिन्न *p. p.* (*f.* —न्ना) 1 Produced,

generated, formed. -2 Germinated. -3 Opened, expanded, budded. -4 Breaking out, appearing.

उद्भू (उद् + भू 1. P.) 1 To arise, spring up, be produced. -2 To occur, take place. -3 To ascend, go up, mount. -4 To rise in arms, revolt, rebel. —*Caus.* 1 To cause to exist, create, produce. -2 To proclaim. -3 To use, employ, rise, elevate.

उद्भूत *p. p.* (*f.* —ता) 1 Born, produced, generated. -2 Lofty (lit. and fig.). -3 Visible, perceptible, capable of being perceived by the senses (as a गुण in वैशेषिक phil.).

उद्भूतिः *f.* 1 Generation, roduction. -2 Elevation, exaltation, prosperity.

उद्भेदः *m.*, -दनं *n.* 1 Breaking through or out. -2 Becoming visible, appearance, display, manifestation. -3 Growth, development. -4 Breaking, splitting. -5 A spring, fountain. -6 Horripilation; as in पुलकोद्भेद, रोमोद्भेद. -7 Treason, betrayal.

उद्भ्रम् (उद् + भ्रम् 1. 4. P.) To wander, roam about.

उद्भ्रमः *m.* Whirling, turning round, flourishing (as of a sword). -2 Wandering. -3 Regret.

उद्भ्रमणं *n.* 1 Moving or wandering about. -2 Rising.

उद्भ्रांत *p. p.* (*f.* —ता) 1 Agitated, bewildered. -2 Terrified, frightened. -3 Whirled, flourished, waved (as a sword). -4 Wandering upwards. —तं *n.* Flourishing a sword.

उद्यत *p. p.* (*f.* —ता) 1 Raised, lifted up. -2 Persevering, diligent, active. -3 Bent, drawn (as a bow). -4 Ready, on the point of, eager, bent on, engaged in (with dat., loc., inf., or usually in comp.) -5 Trained, disciplined.

उद्यतिः *f.* 1 Rising, elevation. -2 Effort, exertion.

उद्यम् (उद् + यम् 1 A., P. in some cases). 1 To raise, elevate, lift up. -2 To offer, give. -3 To prepare, become ready for, begin, set about (with dat., loc., or inf.). -4 To strive, be diligent. -5 To reign, manage, govern. -6 To keep back., stop, hinder. -7 To rise.

उद्यमः *m.* 1 Raising, elevation. -2 Assiduous effort, exertion, perseverance. -3 Firm resolve. -4 Preparation. -Comp. —भंगः *m.* Discouragement. —भृत *a.* Striving hard.

उद्यमनं *n.* Raising, elevation.

उद्यमिन् *a.* Diligent, active.

उद्या (उद् + या 2 P.) 1 To go up, rise, ascend. -2 To originate, arise.

उद्यानं *n.* 1 Going or walking out. -2 A garden, park, pleasure-garden. -3 Purpose, motive. -Comp. -पालः, -पालकः, -रक्षकः *m.* A gardener.

उद्यानकं *n.* A garden, park.

उद्यापनं *n.* Bringing to a conclusion, finishing (as in व्रतोद्यापन).

उद्यापित *a.* Brought to a conclusion, accomplished, finished.

उद्यामः *m.* 1 Erecting, stretching out, elevation. -2 A rope, a cord.

उद्यावः *m.* Mixing, blending.

उद्युक्त *p. p.* (*f.* —क्ता) 1 Active, perseveri g, diligent, industrious; engaged. -2 Ready.

उद्युज् (उद् + युज् 7 U.) 1 To excite, stimulate to exertion. -2 To exert, attempt, strive (with inf). -3 To prepare.

उद्योगः *m.* 1 Effort, exertion, industry. -2 Work, duty, office. -3 Perseverance. -4 Military preparations for an assault. उद्योगः प्रस्तुतः कस्मात् श्रोर्निसंतोषमिच्छति * भास. चं. रा.

उद्योगिन् *a.* (*f.* —नी) Active, diligent, industrious.

उद्रः *m.* A kind of aquatic animal.

उद्रथः *m.* 1 The pin of the axle of a carriage. (Mar. कुणी). -2 A cock.

उद्राव: *m.* A loud noise, uproar.

उद्रिक्त *p.p.* (*f.* —क्ता) 1 Excessive, abundant. -2 Distinct.

उद्रिच् (उत् + रिच् 7 U.) (Chiefly used in *pass.*) 1 To excel, surpass (with abl.). -2 To increase,exceed. -3 To abound in.

उद्रुज *a.* (*f.* —जा) 1 Destroying, breaking down. -2 Undermining (as a bank).

उद्रेकः *m.* 1 Increase, preponderance, abundance -2 Commencement, outset.

उद्वत्सरः *m.* A year.

उद्वपनं *n.* 1 A gift, donation. -2 Pouring out. -3 Up-rooting.

उद्वम् (उत् + वम् 1 P.) To throw up, vomit (fig. also).

उद्वमनं *n.* Vomiting, ejecting.

उद्वर्तः *m.* 1 A remainder, surplus. -2 Excess, preponderance. -3 Smearing the body with perfumes.

उद्वर्तक *a.* 1 Causing to rise. -2 Rubbing and cleaning the body. —कः *m.* (In Math.) The quantity assumed for the purpose of the operation.

उद्वर्तनं *n.* 1 Going up. -2 Springing up, growth (of plants, grain &c.). -3 Prosperity, elevation. -4 Turning from side to side. -5 Grinding, pounding. -6 Drawing out metal, wire-drawing. -7 Anointing, smearing. -8 Rubbing and cleaning the body with fragrant unguents, or the unguents used for this purpose or to relieve pain. -9 Bad behaviour or conduct, rudeness.

उद्वर्धनं *n.* 1 Sly or suppressed laughter. -2 Shrewdness. -3 Increase.

उद्वह् (उत् + वह् 1 P.) 1 To marry. -2 To raise up. -3 To sustain, support. -4 To experience, feel. -5 To possess, be endowed with. -6 To carry off. -7 To finish. —*Caus.* 1 To cause to marry. -2 To spread above.

उद्वहः *m.* 1 A son. -2 Who continues the lineage. -3 One (*i. e.* the 4th) of the seven courses of air. -4 The vital air which conveys nourishment upwards. -5 One of the seven tougues of fire. -6 Marriage. —हा *f.* A daughter.

उद्वहनं *n.* 1 Marrying. -2 Supporting, lifting up,carrying. -3 Possessing, having.

उद्वान *a.* (*f.* —ना) Vomited.

उद्वांत *p. p.* (*f.* —ता) 1 Vomited. -2 Out of rut (as an elephant). -3 Dropped down.

उद्वांतिः *f.* See उद्वमनं.

उद्वापः *m.* 1 Ejection, throwing out. -2 Shaving. -3 (In logic). Non-existence of a subsequent consequent on the absence of an antecedent. -4 Rooting up. -5 Raising.

उद्वासः *m.* 1 Banishment. -2 Abandonment. -3 Killing.

उद्वासनं *n.* Expelling, banishing. -2 Abandoning. -3 Taking out from the fire. -4 Killing.

उद्वाहः *m.* 1 Bearing up, supporting. -2 Marriage, wedding.

उद्वाहनं *n.* 1 Lifting up. -2 Ploughing a field twice. -3 Marriage. -4 Anxiety. —नी *f.* 1 A cord, rope. -2 A small shell, (वराटिका *mar.* कवडी).

उद्वाहिक *a.* (*f.* —की) Relating to marriage, (as a 'Mantra').

उद्वाहित *p. p.* (*f.* —ता) 1 Raised up. -2 Married. -3 Pulled up.

उद्वाहिन् *a.* 1 Raising, drawing up. -2 Marrying. —नी *f.* A rope, cord.

उद्विग्न *p. p.* (*f.* —ग्ना) 1 Sorrowful, anxious, depressed in mind, sorry. -2 Alarmed, frightened.

उद्विज् (उत् + विज् 6 A., P. epic.) 1 To be grieved. -2 To fear, shrink from, (with abl.). -3 To be disgusted with. -4 To grieve, afflict, frighten. —*Caus.* 1 To trouble, harass, afflict, terrify, frighten. -2 To produce disgust or abhorrence.

उद्वीक्ष् (उत् + वि + ईक्ष् 1 A.) 1 To look up, see, perceive, to wait for. -2 To examine, consider.

उद्वीक्षणं *n.* 1 Looking up or upwards. -2 Sight, an eye. -3 Seeing, looking.

उद्वीज् (उत् + वीज् 10. P.) 1 To fan. -2 To blow upon or towards.

उद्वीजनं *n.* Fanning.

उद्वृंहणं *n.* Increase, growth.

उद्वृत् (उत् + वृत् 1 A.) 1 To go upwards, ascend. -2 To burst out. -3 To tumble over. -4 To depart. -5 To rise, increase. -6 To be haughty. *Caus.* 1 To extirpate, destroy. -2 To throw up, elevate. -3 To roll (as eyes). -4 To anoint, smear.

उद्वृत्त *a.* (*f.* —त्ता) 1 Raised, elevated. -2 Flowing out, swollen, overflowing. -3 Grown, increased. -4 Exalted, prosperous. -5 Proud. -6 Vomited up. -7 Left as a remainder. -8 Ill-mannered, rude. -9 Agitated.

उद्वेग *a* 1 Going swiftly. -2 Steady, tranquil. -3 Ascending, mounting. —गः *m.* 1 Trembling, shaking. -2 Agitation, excitement. -3 Alarm, fear. -4 Anxiety, sorrow, distress (caused by separation from one's favourite object). -5 Admiration, astonishment. -गं *n.* A betelnut fruit. (Mar. पोफळ).

उद्वेजनं *n.* 1 Agitation, anxiety. -2 Infliction of pain, affliction. -3 Regret, sorrow for one's absence.

उद्वेदि *a* Furnished with a raised seat or altar in it.

उद्वेपः *m.* Shaking, trembling.

उद्वेल *a.* (*f.* —ला) 1 Overflowing its banks (as a river). -2 Transgressing the proper limits. -3 Excessive.

उद्वेल्लित *a.* (*f.* —ता) Shaken, tossed up. —तं *n.* Shaking.

उद्वेष्टः *m.* 1 Surrounding. -2 Besieging (as a town &c.). -3 Devastating. -4 Overcoming in battle.

उद्वेष्टन *a.* (*f.* —ना) 1 Loosened. -2 Freed from restriant, unbound. -नं *n.* 1 The act of surrounding. -2 An enclosure. -3 A pain in the buttocks or back of the body.

उद्वेष्टित *a.* (*f.* —ता) Surrounded, invested.

उधस् *n.* An udder; see ऊधस्.

उंद् 7 P. 1 To wet, moisten, bathe. -2 To flow or issue out, (as water).

उंदनं *n.* Moistening, wetting.

उंदरः, उंदुरः, उंदुरुः, उंदूरुः *m.* A mouse, rat.

उन्न *p. p.* (*f.* —न्ना) 1 Wet, wetted, moist. -2 (fig.) Kind, moved to pity.

उन्नत *a* (*f.* —ता) 1 Raised, uplifted (fig. also). -2 High (fig. also), tall, great, eminent. —तः *m.* A boa (अजगर). —तं *n.* 1 Elevation. -2 Ascension, altitude. -Comp. —आनत *a* Elevated and depressed, uneven. —शिरस् *a.* Carrying the head high, proud.

उन्नतिः *f.* 1 Elevation, height (fig also). -2 Dignity, rise, prosperity, increase. -3 Raising. -4 The wife of Garuda. -Comp. —ईशः *m.* N. of Garuda.

उन्नम् (उत् + नम् 1 P.) 1 To rise, appear. -2 To ascend. -3 To elevate, to raise (fig. also).

उन्नमनं *n.* 1 Raising up. -2 Height, elevation.

उन्नम्र *a.* (*f.* —म्रा) Erect, upright, lofty, high (fig. also).

उन्नयः *m.* 1 Raising, elevating. -2 Height, elevation. -3 Analogy, resemblance. -4 Inference.

उन्नयन *a.* With the eyes raised upwards. —नं *n.* 1 Raising, lifting up. -2 Drawing up water. -3 The vessel out of which a fluid is taken. -4 Leading away, extracting. -5 Adjusting, smoothing -6 Deliberation, discussion. -7 Inference.

उन्नस *a.* (*f.* —सा) Having a prominent nose.

उन्नादः *m.* Crying out, roaring, humming, chirping.

उन्नामः *m.* Raising, lifting up.

उन्नायः *m.* See उन्नयः.

उन्नाहः *m.* 1 Projection, rise -2 Tying up. —हं *n.* Sour gruel made from the fermentation of rice.

उन्निद्र *a.* (*f.* —द्रा) 1 Sleepless, awake. -2 Expanded, full-blown, budded (as a flower).

उन्नी (उत् + नी 1 P.) 1 To lead upwards, bring up. -2 To raise, erect, lift up (A.). -3 To free from, rescue, redeem. -4 To draw up (as water). -5 To stroke, straighten out. -6 To lead away. -7 To press out, extract. -8 To infer, ascertain, conjecture. -9 To fill completely. -10 To lead off (in singing).

उन्नेतृ *a.* 1 Raising. -2 Leading to an inference. —*m.* One of the 16 priests at a sacrifice.

उन्नेत्रं *n.* The office of the उन्नेतृ.

उन्मज्ज् (उत् + मस्ज् 6 P.) To emerge, rise up.

उन्मज्जक *a.* Emergng, rising up. —कः *m.* A kind of ascetic practising penance in water.

उन्मज्जनं *n.* Emerging, coming out of water. -नः *m.* An attendant of Siva.

उन्मत्त *a.* (*f.* —त्ता) 1 Drunk, intoxicated. -2 Insane, frantic, mad. -3 Puffed. -4 Furious, wild. -5 Possessed by an evil-spirit. -त्तः *m.* The thorn apple (धत्तूर Mar. धोतरा). N. of another tree (मुचकुंद). -Comp. —दर्शन, —रूप *a.* Maniac-like, mad in appearance. —प्रलपितं *n.* The words spoken in drunkenness or madness; words of a madman.

उन्मत्तक *a.* 1 Wild, insane, mad. -2 Drunk, intoxicated.

उन्मथ्, उन्मंथ् (उत् + मथ्, मंथ् 1, 9, P.). 1 To shake up, disturb, excite. -2 To strike, destroy. -3 Tear, peel off. -4 To mix.

उन्मथन *a.* Tearing, disturbing, paining. -नं *n.* 1 Shaking off, throwing off or down. -2 Killing, slaughter.

उन्मद् (उत् + मद् 4 P.) 1 To be, or become, mad. -2 To delight, gratify. —*Caus.* (म-मा-दयति). To madden, render drunk (lit. and fig.).

उन्मद *a* (*f.* —दा) 1 Intoxicated, drunk. -2 Mad, furious, extravagant. -3 Intoxicating. —दः *m.* 1 Insanity. -2 Intoxication, ecstacy.

उन्मदन *a.* Inflamed with love.

उन्मादिष्णु *a.* 1 Mad, insane. -2 Intoxicated, drunk. -3 In rut (as an elephant).

उन्मनस्, -नस्क *a.* (*f.* —स्का) 1 Excited or disturbed in mind, perplexed, uneasy. -2 Repining for a lost or departed friend. -3 Anxious, eager, impatient.

उन्मनाय् Den. A., To become excited or disturbed in mind, be uneasy, regret.

उन्मनीकृ 8 U To make excited, disturb.

उन्मंथः *a.* 1 Agitation, disturbance. -2 Killing, slaughter. -3 A disease of the outer ear.

उन्मंथक *a.* 1 Shaking off, agitating. -2 Throbbing, beating. —कः *m.* Inflammation of the outer ear.

उन्मंथनं *n.* 1 Shaking, agitating. -2 Killing, hurting. -3 Beating (with a stick). -4 Probing, stirring a dart, a thorn &c. lodged in the body. -5 The instrument used for this purpose

उन्मयूख *a.* (*f.* -खा)Shining, radiant.

उन्मर्दनं *n.* 1 Rubbing, kneading. -2 A fragrant essence used for rubbing. -3 Act of purifying air.

उन्माथः *m.* 1 Torment, pang. -2 Shaking, agitation. -3 Killing, slaughter -4 A snare or trap.

उन्माथिन् *a.* (*f.* —नी) 1 Shaking, agitating. -2 Tormenting.

उन्माद *a.* (*f.* —दा) 1 Mad, insane. -2 Extravagant. -दः *m.* 1 Madness, insanity. -2 Intense passion, intoxication of love. -3 Lunacy, mania (considered as a disease of the mind). -4 (In Rhet.) Madness considered as one of the 33 subordinate feelings. -2 Bloom, blossom.

उन्मादकः *m.* N. of the plant धत्तूर.

उन्मादन *a.* Maddening, exciting, intoxicating —नः *m.* One of the five arrows of Cupid.

उन्मानं *n.* 1 Weighing, measuring upwards. -2 A measure of size or quantity. -3 Price.

उन्मार्ग *a.* (*f.* —र्गा) Going to a wrong path. -र्गः *m.* 1 A wrong road, deviation from the right road (fig. also). -2 An improper conduct, evil course, —र्गे *ind.* Astray, by a wrong way. —Comp. —गत *a.* Going wrong. —गमनं *n.* Following evil courses. —गामिन्, —वर्तिन् *a.* Going wrong, erring,taking a wrong road.

उन्मार्जनं *n.* Rubbing, wiping off, removing.

उन्मित *a.* (*f.* —ता) Measured.

उन्मितिः *f.* 1 Measuring upwards.-Measure ; price.

उन्मिश्र *a* (*f.* —श्रा) Mixed with, variegated.

उन्मिष् (उत् + मिष् 6 P.) 1 To open the eyes. -2 To open (as the eyes). -3 To open, bloom, be expanded (as lotuses). -4 To begin to rise or twinkle (as stars).-5 To shine, flash (as तेजस्).-6 To arise, originate.

उन्मिष *a.* Blown, opened. —षः *m.* Opening the eyes

उन्मिषित *a.* (*f.* —ता) Opened (as eyes), blown, expanded. —तं *n.* 1 A look, glance. -2 Opening.

उन्मीनं *n.* 1 Winking. -2 Becoming visible. -3 Blowing,expanding.

उन्मील् (उत् + मील् 1 P.) 1 To open (as the eyes). -2 To be awakened or roused. -3 To expand, low (as lotus). 1 To be diffused or spread. -2 To become manifest. -3 To break forth, burst out. *-Caus.*1 To open (eyes, lotuses &c.). -2 To display, show.

उन्मीलः *m.*, -लनं *n.* 1 Opening (of the eyes), awaking. -2 Opening (in general). -3 Touching up, painting. -4 Expanding, blowing.

उन्मीलित *a.* (*f.* —ता) 1 Opened. -2 Blown, expanded, awakened. -3 Touched up, painted. -तं (In Rhet.) An open reference (to anything).

उन्मुक्त *a.* (*f.* —क्ता) Pulled off, loosened.

उन्मुख *a.* (*f.* -खी) 1 Raising the face, looking up towards.-2 Ready, on the point of, prepared for. -3 Eager, waiting for, expecting. -4 Sounding, speaking or making a sound.

उन्मुखर *a.* (*f.* —रा) Loud-sounding, noisy.

उन्मुच् (उत् + मुच् 6 U.) 1 To unfasten, pull off, take off. -2 To loosen, liberate, pay off. -3 To raise, send forth (as sound).-4 To fling, hurl (as a missile). —Caus. 1 To extricate, loosen, free. -2 To deliver.

उन्मुद्र *a.* (*f.* —द्रा) 1 Unsealed. -2 Opened, blown, expanded.

उन्मूल् (उत् + मूल् 10 P.) To pluck up by the roots, exterminate.

उन्मूलनं *n.* 1 Plucking up by the roots, destroying, uprooting.

उन्मृज् (उत् + मृज् 2 P.) 1 To rub or wipe off ; clean by washing. -2 To efface.

उन्मृष्ट *a.* (*f.* —ष्टा Rubbed off or away, cleared, removed, wiped off

उन्मेदा *f.* Corpulence, fatness.

उन्मेष: *n.*,-षणं *n.* 1 Opening the eyes, winking, twinkling (of eyes). -2 Blowing, opening, expansion. -3 Light, flash, brilliancy. -4 Awakening, becoming visible.

उन्मेय *a.* (*f.* —या) To be weighed; what is weighed. —यं *n.* Weight.

उन्मोचनं *n.* Unfastening, loosening.

उप *ind.* 1 As a prefix to verbal and nominal themes it expresses (1) nearness, contiguity *e. g* उपगच्छति goes near ; (2) power,ability *e. g.* उपकरोति ; (3) pervasion ; *e. g.* उपकीर्ण ; (4) advice, instructing as by a teacher ; *e. g.* उपदिशति, उपदेश ; (5) death, extinction ; *e. g.* उपरत; (6) defect, fault *e. g.* उपघात (7) giving *e. g.* उपनयति, उपहरति (8)beginning, commencement *e. g.* उपक्रमते, उपक्रम, (10) study *e. g.* उपाध्याय:, (11) reverence, worship *e. g.* उपस्थानं, उपचरति पितरं पुत्र:.

As unconnected with verbs and prefixed to nouns, it expresses the idea of subordination or inferiority; *e. g.* उपपुराणं A secondary Purâna. उपगुरु: *m.* An assistant master; उपाध्यक्ष: *m.*A vice-president.

It usually forms Avyayi. comp. to signify ' direction towards ' 'nearness, ' ' contiguity ' (in space, number or time) *e. g.* उपगंगं, उपकूलं, &c. Prefixed to proper nouns it means a 'younger brother'; *e. g.* उपेंद्र:.

With numerals it forms संख्याबहुव्रीहि and means ' nearly,' ' almost '; उपत्रिंशा: nearly thirty, उपविंशा: about twenty &c.

As a separable preposition with acc. it means inferiority उप हरिं सुरा: the gods are inferior to Hari. With loc. it expresses superiority, उप परार्धे हरेर्गुणा:; addition; towards, in the direction of, under, at,on, upon; upto, in, above *e. g.* उप सानुषु on or above the peaks. With the instr. it shows ' at the same time with, ' 'according to. '

उपकंठं *n.*, —ठ:, *m.* 1 Proximity, vicinity, neighb urhood. आस्तिकस्मिंश्चित्समुद्रोपकंठे महाञ्जंबूपादप: सदाफल: * पंचतं 4. -2 Space near a village or its boundary. -3 One of a horse's paces. —ठं *ind.* 1 Upon the neck, near the throat. -2 In the vicinity of, near.

उपकथा *f.* A short story or tale.

उपकनिष्ठिका *f.* The finger next to the little finger (also called अनामिका).

उपकन्या *f.* The friend of one's daughter.

उपकरणं *n.* 1 Doing service or favour, assisting. -2 Implement, instrument, means; materials. -3 A machine, apparatus. -4 Means of subsistence. -5 A means or expedient. -6 Composing, elaborating. -7 The insignia of royalty. -8 The attendants of a king.

उपकर्णनं *n.* Hearing.

उपकर्णिका *f.* Rumour, report.

उपकर्तृ *a.* (*f.* —र्त्री) One who does a service or favour.

उपकल्पनं *n.*, —ना *f.* 1 Preparation. -2 Fabricating, making.

उपकल्पित *a.* (*f.* —ता) 1 Prepared, made. -2 Secondary, substituted.

उपकार: *m.* 1 Service, help, assistance, favour, obligation. -2 Preparation. -3 Ornament, decoration. —री *f.* A royal tent, place. -2 Caravansary.

उपकारक *a.* (*f.* —रिका) Doing service or favour, helping, productive (of good results).

उपकारिका *f.* 1 Protectress, a female assistant. -2 A palace. -3 A tent, a caravansary. -4 A kind of cake.

उपकारिन् *a.* (*f.* -णी) Helping, beneficial.

उपकार्य *a.* (*f.* —र्या) 1 Deserving assistance or favour, fit to be assisted. —र्या *f.* A royal house, palace. -2 A royal tent.

उपकिरणं *n.* 1 Scattering over, covering up; burying. -2 Pervasion.

उपकुंचिः, -चिका *f.* 1 The plant Nigella Indica (कृष्णाजीरक). -2 Small cardamoms.

उपकुंभ *a.* 1 Near, proximate. -2 Solitary, retired. —भं *ind.* Near a jar.

उपकुर्वाण: *m.* A Bráhmana bachelor in a state of pupilage (ब्रह्मचारिन्) who wishes to pass on to the state of a house-holder (गृहस्थ).

उपकुल्या *f.* 1 A canal, a ditch or trench.

उपकुश: *m.* Gum-boil.

उपकूपं,-पे *ind.* Near a well.

उपकूपजलाशय: *m.* A trough near a well for watering cattle.

उपकूलं *ind.* On the shore.

उपकृ (उप + कृ 8 U.) (उपकृ) 1 To place or bring near, furnish with; do or render. -2 To assist, serve, help. -3 To take care of. -4 To wait or attend upon (with acc.). -5 To begin, (with dat.). -6 To subdue, overcome.

उपकृ (उप + कृ 8 U.) (उपस्कृ) 1 To add, supply. -2 To provide or furnish with. -3 To attend or wait on, serve. -4 To adorn, polish, perfect. -5 To care for, (with acc. of person). -6 To make efforts (with gen. of thing). -7 To furnish badly, deform. -8 To corrupt, censure. -9 To bring or call together.

उपकृत *a.* (*f.* -ता) Assisted, served. —तं *n.* Aid, favour, obligation.

उपकृतिः, उपक्रिया *f.*, Favour, obligation.

उपकॄ (उप + कॄ 6 P.) 1 To scatter or throw down; scatter or pour upon. -2 (उपस्कॄ) 1 To cut up, lop. -2 To hurt, strike.

उपक्लृप् (उप + क्लृप् 1 A.) 1 To be fit. -2 To be ready. -3 To result in, lead to (with dat.). -4 To become.

उपक्रम् (उप + क्रम् 1 A., 4 P.) 1 To go near, approach, advance towards. -2 To perform, set about. -3 To begin, commence (with inf. or dat.) (Atm.). -4 To attack, assail. -5 To make advances (of love) to. -6 To step over, traverse. -7 To treat, attend on (as a physician); cure or heal (as wounds).

उपक्रमः *m.* 1 Beginning, commencement. -2 Approach, advance. -3 An undertaking, work, enterprize. -4 A plan, means, expedient, stratagem, remedy. -5 Attendance on a patient, treatment, practice of medicine. -6 A test of honesty, trying the fidelity of a friend &c. (also called उपधा). -7 A ceremony preparatory to reading the Vedas.

उपक्रमणं *n.* 1 Approaching. -2 Undertaking. -3 Commencement. -4 (Medic.) Treatment of a patient.

उपक्रमणिका *f.* A preface, introduction.

उपक्रिया *f.* Favour, service.

उपक्रीडा *f.* A play-ground.

उपक्रुश् (उप + क्रुश् 1 P.) To blame, chide, revile.

उपक्रोश: *m.*, -शनं *n.* Censure, reproach.

उपक्रोष्टृ *m* 1 An ass. -2 One who blames or censures.

उपक्व (-क्वा-) णं *n.* The sound of a lute

उपक्षय: *m.* 1 Waste, decay, loss.-2 Expenditure.

उपाक्षिप् (उप + क्षिप् 6 P) 1 To throw, cast, hurl, to entrust, assign. -2 To insult, accuse. -3 To hint, indicate, adduce. -4 To commnce, introduce.

उपक्षीण *p. p.* 1 Decayed, consumed. -2 Powerless.

उपक्षेप: *m.* 1 Throwing. -2 Mention, allusion, suggestion. -3 A threat, accusation, charge. -4 Commencement. -5 Poetical or figurative style.

उपक्षेपणं *n.* 1 Throwing down -2 Accusing, charging.

उपग *a.* (At the end of comp. only). 1 Approaching, following, joining. -2 Receiving.

उपगण: *m.* 1 A small or subordinate class. -2 A small number less than a troop.

उपगत *p. p.* (*f.* —ता) 1 Approached, arrived, being near. -2 Occurred, happened. -3 Obtained, acquired. -4 Experienced. -5 Furnished with. -6 Promised, agreed. -7 Passed away, dead. —तं *n.* 1 Wealth acquired. -2 Receipt.

उपगति: *f.* 1 Approach. -2 Knowledge, acquaintance. -3 Acceptance, receipt. -4 Attainment, acquirement.

उपगम् (उप + गम् 1 P.) 1 To go to, approach; attain, reach (fig. also); visit. -2 To undergo, suffer. -3 To approach a woman (for sexual intercourse) -4 To attack. -5 To happen. -6 To undertake, begin. -6 To suffer, share in. -8 To agree to, allow.

उपगम: *m.*, -मनं *n.* 1 Going to, approach, advent. -2 Knowledge, acquaintance. -3 Attainment, acquiring. -4 Intercourse (as of the sexes.). -5 Society, company. -6 Undergoing, suffering, feeling. -7 Acceptance, receipt. -8 An agreement, promise.

उपगा *m.* (गा:) A priest in a sacrifice who sings the hymns.—*f.* Accompaniment of a song.

उपगातृ *m.* One who accompanies the song of the Udgatri priest; a chorister.

उपगिरि, -रं *ind* Near a mountain. —रि: *m.* N. of a country situated near a mountain in the north.

उपगु: *m.* A cow-herd.

उपगुरु: *m.* An assistant teacher. -रु *ind.* Near a teacher.

उपगुह् (उप + गुह् 1 U.) 1 To clasp, embrace. -2 To hide, conceal, encircle.

उपगूढ *p. p.* (*f.* —ढा) 1 Hidden, concealed. -2 Embraced, clasped. -3 Held, supported. -4 Suppressed. —ढं *n.* An embrace.

उपगूहनं *n.* 1 Hiding, concealing. -2 An embrace. -3 Astonishment, surprise.

उपग्रंथ: *m.* A subsidiary writing or a class of such writings.

उपग्रह् (उप + ग्रह् 9 U.) 1 To hold under, to seize, take, take possessino of. -2 To meet with, obtain.

-3 To subdue, vanquish. -4 To provide. -5 To conciliate, take as one's ally; favour, support. -6 To grasp mentally. -7 To decide, determine. -8 To accept, approve.

उपग्रहः *m.* 1 Confinement, seizure. -2 Defeat, frustration. -3 A prisoner. -4 Joining, addition. -5 Favour, encouragement, kindness, complacence. -6Use. -7 A kind of peace purchased by giving over every thing. -8 The voice or 'pada' of a verb. -9 A heap of 'kusa' grass. -10 The presiding spirit or cause which directs a planet's motion. -11 A minor planet (राहु, केतु &c.); a secondary heavenly body, such as a comet, meteor.

उपग्रहणं *n.* 1 Seizing (from below) -2 Seizure, capture. -3 Supporting, promoting. -4 Study of the Vedas.

उपग्राहः *m.* 1 Making a present. -2 A present.

उपग्राह्यः *m.*, —ह्यं *n.* 1 An offering or present. -2 Particularly, a present or offering to a great man or king.

उपघातः *m.* 1 Damage, insult, injury. -2 Destruction. -3 Touch, contact. -4 Assault.-5 Sin. -6 Disease.

उपघुष् (उप + घुष् 1. 10. P.) To fill with noise; make resonant.

उपघुष्ट *p. p.* (*f.* —ष्टा) 1 Resounding with, noisy. -2 Sounding.

उपघोषणं *n.* Proclaiming, publication, making known.

उपघ्नः *m.* 1 Contiguous support. -2 Shelter, stay, protection.

उपचक्रः *m.* A variety of the ruddy goose.

उपचक्षुस् *n.* An eye-glass, spectacles.

उपचतुर *a. pl.* Almost four, nearly four, i. e. three or five.

उपचयः *m.* 1 Accumulation, addition. -2 Increase, growth, excess.-3 Quantity, heap. -4 Prosperity, rise.

उपचर् (उप + चर् 1 P.) 1 To serve, wait or attend upon. -2 To honour, worship. -3 To deal with, act towards; entertain. -4 To treat (a patient), nurse. -5 To approach. —*pass.* To be used figuratively or metaphorically, be applied figuratively to any one (with loc.).

उपचरः *m.* 1 Cure, treatment. -2 Approach.

उपचरणं *n.* 1 Approach. -2 Cure.

उपचर्या *f.* 1 Service, attendance -2 Nursing, treating, curing.

उपचाय्यः *m.* 1 A kind of sacred fire. -2 A place for sacrificial fire; altar

उपचारः *m.* 1 Service, attendance; honouring, worshipping, entertaining. -2 Civility, politeness. -3 A merely complimentary saying, a flattering compliment. -4 Salutation, usual or customary obeisance, homage, a mode of address or salutation. -5 External show or form, ceremony. -6 A remedy, application of a cure or remedy. -7 Practice, performance, management, procedure.-8 Means of doing homage or showing respect.-9 Any necessary or requisite article(of worship, ceremony, decoration, furniture&c.). -10 Behaviour, conduct. -11 Use, employment.-12 Any religious performance, a ceremony. -13 Figurative or metaphorical use; secondary application, supposed or fancied identification founded on resemblance -14 A bribe. -15 A pretext. 16 A request, solicitation. -17 Occurrence of स् and ष् in the place of 'Visarga' (in gram.).

उपचार्य *a.* (*f.* -र्या) To be served or waited upon. —र्यः *m.* Practice of medicine. —र्यं *n.* Treatment.

उपचि (उप + चि 5 U.) 1 To gather together, collect. -2 To add, strengthen, increase. -3 To cover over with. *Pass.* 1 To be increased.-2 To be prosperous to succeed, thrive.

उपचित *p. p.* (*f.* —ता) 1 Collected, accumulated, -2 Increased, grown, full-grown. -3 Grown in power, strengthened.

उपचिति: *f.* Accumulation, collection, increase.

उपचित्रा *f.* N. of a lunar mansion. स्वाति; also हस्त.

उपचूलनं *n.* Heating, burning.

उपच्छद: *m.* A coverlet ; a cover in general.

उपच्छंद् (उप + छंद् 10 P.) 1 To flatter, entice, invite. -2 To conciliate. -3 To beseech, request. -4 To give one something.

उपच्छंदनं *n.* 1 Coaxing, persuading. -2 Inviting.

उपजन् (उप + जन् 4 A.) 1 To be born or produced, arise, grow. -2 To happen, take place, appear. -3 To be or become, be or exist. -4 To be born again. -*Caus.* (-जनयति) To produce, cause, rouse.

उपजन: *m.* 1 Addition, increase. -2 Appendage. -3 Rise,origin. -4 Addition of a letter in the formation of words. -5 Any letter, syllable or affix so added. —नं *n.* The body.

उपजप् (उप + जप् 1 P.) 1 To win over to one's party by secretly suggesting anything in the ear. -2 To instigate to rebellion or treachery. -3 To commit mischief.

उपजल्प् (उप + जल्प् 1 P.) 1 To talk to, converse with. -2 To advise.

उपजल्पनं, उपजाल्पितं *n.* A talk.

उपजात *a.* (*f.* —ता) 1 Produced, caused. -2 Happened, taken place.

उपजाति: *f.* N. of a metre.

उपजाप: *m.* 1 Secretly whispering into the ear or communicating. -2 Sowing the seeds of dissension in the party of the enemy. -3 Disunion, separation.

उपजापक *a.* 1 Instigating to rebellion. -2 Treacherous.

उपजिह्वा,-ह्विका *f.* 1 The uvula or soft palate. -2 Enlargement of the under side of the tongue. -3 A kind of ant.

उपजीव् (उप + जीव् 1 P.) 1 To live upon, subsist by, be supported by. -2 To live under, be dependent on, serve. -3 (*fig.*) To make use of, derive materials (for writing from). -4 To practise.

उपजीवक, -विन् *a.* 1 Living upon, subsisting by (instr. or in comp). -2 Depending upon, subject to. -क:, —वी *m.* A servant, a dependant. -कं *n.* Means of subsistence, profession.

उपजीवनं *n.*, -जीविका *f.* 1 Living. -2 Subsistence, livelihood. -3 A means of living.

उपजीव्य *a.* (*f.* —व्या) 1 Affording a livelihood.-2 Patronizing (as a king &c.). -3 (fig.) Supplying materials for writing ; that from which one derives his materials. —व्य: *m.* 1 A patron. -2 A source or authority (from which one derives his materials). —व्यं *n.* A means of subsistence.

उपजुष्ट *a.*(*f.* —ष्टा) 1 Approached,received with courtesy. -2 Frequented, resorted to.

उपजोष: *m.*, -षणं *n.* 1 Affection. -2 Enjoyment. -3 Frequenting, resorting to. —षं *ind.* 1 According to one's desire. -2 Silently.

उपज्ञा (उप + ज्ञा 9 A.) 1 To ascertain;to know. -2 To invent, find out,

उपज्ञा *f.* 1 Knowledge acquired by oneself and not handed down by tradition ; invention ; primitive or untaught knowledge. -2 Undertaking or commencing a thing not done before.

उपज्ञात *a.* Invented.

उपढौक् *Caus.* 1 To present (as an offering.). -2 To carry out, accomplish.

उपढौकनं *n.* A respectful offering or present.

उपतट: *m.* The skirt or border. —टं *ind.* Near the skirt.

उपतप् (उप + तप् 1 P.) 1 To heat. -2 To feel pain, become sick. -3 To cause pain.

उपताप: *m.* 1 Heat, warmth. -2 Trouble, pain, sorrow.-3 Calamity, misfortune. -4 Sickness, disease, injury. -5 Haste, hurry.

उपतापनं *n.* 1 Heating. -2 Distressing, tormenting.

उपतिष्यं *n.* 1 N. of the lunar mansion called अश्लेषा. -2 N. of another lunar mansion called पुनर्वसु.

उपत्यका *f.* A land at the foot of a mountain ; low land.

उपदंश् (उप + दंश् 1 P.) To bite or eat anything (as a relish or condiment.)

उपदंश: *m.* 1 Anything which excites thirst or appetite, a relish, condiment. -2 Biting, stinging. -3 The venereal disease, chancre.

उपदर्शक *a.* Showing. —क: *m.* 1 One who shows the way, a guide. -2 A door-keeper. -3 A witness.

उपदर्शनं *n.* A commentary.

उपदश *a.* (pl.) About or nearly ten *i. e.* nine or eleven.

उपदा (उप + दा 3 U.) 1 To give in addition. -2 To offer, grant.

उपदा *f.* 1 A present, an offering to a king or a great man. -2 A bribe.

उपदानं,-नकं *n.* 1 An oblation, a present. -2 A gift made for procuring favour or protection, such as a bribe.

उपदिश् (उप + दिश् 6 U.) 1 To instruct, explain, advise. -2 To indicate, refer to. -3 To arrange. -4 To mention, specify, tell. -5 To announce. -6 To sanction, lay down. -7 To govern, command. -8 To name, call.

उपदिश्, उपदिशा *f.* An intermediate quarter which are ऐशानी, आग्नेयी, नैर्ऋती and वायवी.

उपदिश्य *a.* Being in an intermediate quarter.

उपदिष्ट *p. p.* (*f.* —ष्टा) 1 Specified, pointed out. -2 Taught, instructed, advised. -3 Put forward as a plea or reason.-4 Initiated. -ष्टं *n.* Advice.

उपदेव: *m.*, —देवता *f.* A minor or inferior god.

उपदेश: *m.* 1 Instruction, teaching, advice, prescription. -2 Pointing out or referring to, specification, naming. -3 A plea, pretext. -4 Initiation, communication of an initiatory 'mantra' or formula.-5 (In gram.) Any word or part of a word, such as an affix, augment &c. with its *anubandhas* which show what particular grammatical rules are to be applied. -Comp. —अर्थवाक्यं, -वचनं *n.* A parable, moral fable.

उपदेशक: *m.* An instructor, a guide, preceptor.

उपदेशनं *n.* Advising, instructing. —ना *f.* Information, doctrine.

उपदेशिन् *m.* 1 A teacher, adviser. -2 A word or affix &c. in the form in which it appears in grammatical rules.

उपदेष्टृ *m.* (-ष्ट्री) A teacher, preceptor, especially a spiritual preceptor.

उपदेहः *m.* 1 An ointment. -2 A cover -3 An adventitious growth such as a boil &c. on the body.

उपदोहः *m.* 1 A nipple of the udder of a cow. -2 A milking vessel.

उपद्रवः *m.* 1 An unhappy accident, misfortune, calamity -2 Injury, trouble. -3 Outrage, violence. -4 A national distress. -5 A national disturbance, rebellion. -6 A symptom, a supervenient disease brought on whilst a person is suffering from another).

उपद्रु (उप + द्रु 1 P.) 1 To run towards. -2 To attack, assault.

उपद्रुत *p. p.* (*f.* —ता) 1 Visited by calamities ; infested. -2 (In astr.). Eclipsed. -3 Inauspicious.

उपद्वीपः *m.*, —पं *n.* An island.

उपधर्मः *m.* 1 A by-law, a secondary or minor religious precept. -2 A heretic.

उपधा (उप + धा 3 U.) 1 To place or lay upon, place under, in, or near. -2 To put to, or yoke (as a horse to a carriage &c.). -3 To cause, bring on, produce. -4 To entrust with, charge with (as a duty). -5 To lie down upon, use as a pillow. -6 To cover, conceal. -7 To communicate, impart, give, bestow. -8 (In gram.) To precede without the intervention of another syllable.

उपधा *f.* 1 Imposition, forgery, fraud; trick. -2 Trial or test of honesty. -3 A means or expedient. -4 (In gram.) A penultimate letter. -Comp. —भृतः *m.* A servant who has been guilty of dishonesty. —शुचि *a.* Tried, of approved loyalty.

उपधातुः *m.* 1 An inferior metal, semimetal. -2 A secondary secretion of the body (milk, menses, adeps, sweat, teeth, hair, and lymph).

उपधानं *n.* 1 Placing or resting upon. -2 A pillow, cushion. -3 Peculiarity, individuality. -4 Affection, kindness. -5 A religious observance. -6 Excellent quality. -7 Poison.

उपधानीयं *n.* A pillow.

उपधारणं *n*, 1 Consideration, reflection. -2 Drawing, pulling (as by a hook).

उपधाव् (उप + धाव् 1 U.) 1 To run towards -2 To resort to. -3 To run, glide (A.).

उपधावकः *m.* A follower. —नं *n.* 1 Going after, following. -2 Meditating upon.

उपधिः *m.* 1 Fraud, dishonest. -2 (In law). Suppression of the truth, a false suggestion. -3 Terror, threat, compulsion, false inducement. -4 The part of a wheel between the nave and the circumference, or the wheel itself.

उपधिकः *m.* A cheat, knave. औपधिक is the more correct form.

उपधूपित (*f.* —ता) *a.* 1 Fumigated. -2 Being at the point of death. -3 Suffering extreme pain. —तः *m.* Death.

उपधृ (उप + धृ 1, 10, P.) 1 To hold up, support, sustain. -2 To bear, carry. -3 To consider or regard as. -4 To comprehend, perceive, experience, observe. -5 To reflect or meditate upon.

उपधृतिः *f.* 1 A ray of light. -2 Holding up.

उपध्मा (उप + ध्मा 1 P.) To blow or breathe out; excite by blowing; fan.

उपध्मा *f.* 1 Blowing upon, breathing. -2 The effort of the voice which gives rise to the sound.

उपध्मानः *m.* A lip. —नं *n.* Blowing upon, breathing.

उपध्मानीयः *m.* The aspirate Visarga

before the letters प् and फ्.

उपध्वस्त *a* (*f.* —स्ता) 1 Destroyed. -2 Mixed.

उपनक्षत्रं *n.* A subordinate constellation, secondary star.

उपनगरं *n.* A suburb.

उपनत *p. p. a.* (*f.* —ता) 1 Arrived, approached. -2 Got, obtained. -3 Befallen, occurred. -4 Formed, effected. -5 Presented to, offered, given. -6 Bent down, subjected, surrendered. -7 Dependent on (for protection). -8 Approximate, near (in time or space).

उपनतिः *f.* 1 Approach. -2 Bending low, salutation.

उपनम् (उप + नम् 1 P.) 1 To arrive, approach, tend towards. -2 To occur, happen. -3 To share in. -*Caus.* 1 To lead towards, introduce. -2 To offer.

उपनयः *m.* 1 Bringing near. -2 Gaining, attaining, procuring. -3 Employing. -4 Investiture with the sacred thread. -5 The fourth member of the five-membered Indian syllogism (in logic); the application to the special case in question व्याप्तिविशिष्टस्य हेतोः पक्षधर्मता प्रतिपादकं वचनमुपनयः * तर्कको.

उपनयनं *n.* 1 Leading to or near. -2 Presenting, offering. -3 Investiture with the sacred thread.

उपनह् (उप + नह् 4 P.) 1 To tie together. -2 To bind together. -3 To inlay, set with.

उपनहनं *n.* 1 A cloth in which anything is bound up -2 Binding, tying together.

उपनागरिका *f.* A variety of वृत्यनुप्रास. It is formed by sweet-sounding letters.

उपनामन् *n.* A surname, nickname.

उपनायः *m.* Same as उपनयः q. v.

उपनायकः *m.* 1 A character in a dramatic or any other work of art next in importance to the hero *e. g.* Lakshmana in Râmâyan; Makaranda in Mâlati Mâdhava &c. -2 A paramour.

उपनायनं *n.* See उपनयनं.

उपनायिका *f.* A character in a dramatic or any other work of art next in importance to the heroine; *e. g.* Madayantikâ in Mâlati Madhav.

उपनाहः *m.* 1 A bundle. -2 An unguent applied to a wound or sore -3 The peg to which the strings of a lyre are attached and by which they are tightened. 4 Inflammation of the ciliary glands, stye.

उपनाहनं *n.* 1 Applying an unguent. -2 Anointing, plastering.

उपनिक्षेपः *m.* 1 The act of depositing or placing down -2 An open deposit, any article given in another's charge by letting him know what it is.

उपनिधा (उप + नि + धा 3 U.) 1 To put or place near ; to bring or lead near to. -2 To produce, cause. -3 To present. -4 To deposit, entrust.

उपनिधानं *n* 1 Placing near. -2 Depositing, entrusting to one's care. -3 A deposit.

उपनिधिः *m.* 1 A deposit, pledge. -2 (In law) A sealed deposit.

उपनिपातः *m.* 1 Approaching, coming near. -2 A sudden and unexpected attack or occurrence.

उपनिमंत्रणं *n.* Invitation, inauguration.

उपनिवेशित *a.* (*f.* —ता) Placed, established, colonized.

उपनिषद् *f.* 1 N. of certain mystical writings attached to the Brâhmanas, the chief aim of which is to ascertain the secret meaning of the Vedas. -2 A secret doctrine, Mystical meaning. Mystical knowledge or instruction.-3 True knowledge regarding the Supreme Spirit. -4 Sacred or religious lore. -5 Secrecy, seclusion. -6A neighbouring mansion. -7 A lonely place.

उपनिष्कर: *m.* A street, a principal road, high way.

उपनिष्क्रमणं *n.* I Coming out, issuing. -2 One of the Samskáras or religious rites *i. e.* taking out a child for the first time into the open air (which is usually performed in the fourth month of its age). -3 A main or royal road.

उपनी (उप + नी I P.) I To bring near. -2 To offer, present to. -3 To hand over, give over. -4 To expose or put to. -5 To cause, produce, accomplish. -6 To bring information, communicate. -7 To lead or reduce to -8 To take into one's possession, lead away, lead. -9 To invest with the sacred thread(Atm.). -10 To hire, employ (as hired servants.).

उपनीत *p. p.* (*f.* —ता) I Brought near. -2 Known. -3 Obtained. -4 Presented, given. -5 Adduced. —त: *m.* A youth invested with the sacred thread and led to the teacher.

उपनृत्यं *n.* A place for dancing.

उपनेतृ *a.* (*f.* —त्री) One who leads or brings near. —*m.* (ता) A preceptor who performs the उपनयन ceremony.

उपन्यस् (उप + नि + अस् 4 P.) I To place or put down; put near. -2 To commit to the care of. -3 To explain. -4 To propose, point out, state. -5 To establish argumentatively.

उपन्यस्त *p. p.* (*f.* —स्ता) I Placed near, deposited. -2 Said; proposed. -3 Pledged, entrusted. -4 Given, communicated. -5 Adduced, hinted.

उपन्यास: *m.* I Placing near, juxtaposition. -2 A deposit, pledge. -3 Statement, suggestion, proposal. -4 Preface, introduction. -5 Allusion, reference. -6 A precept, law. -7 A kind of peace. -8 Propitiating (प्रसादनं).

उपपति: *m.* A paramour.

उपपत्ति: *f.* I Happening, occurring, appearance, production, birth. -2 Cause, reason. -3 Reasoning, argument, giving a reason for the establishment of a matter. -4 Fitness, propriety. -5 Termination, end. -6 Association. -7 Acceptance. -8 Ascertainment, demonstration, demonstrated conclusion. -9 (In Arith. or Geom.) Proof, demonstration. -10 A means, an expedient. -11 Assistance. -12 Doing, effecting, accomplishment. -13 Attainment, getting. -14 Religious abstraction (समाधि).

उपपद् (उप + पद् 4 A.) I To reach, approach. -2 To be obtained. -3 To occur, happen, be produced. -4 To be possible. -5 To be suitable, fit, suit (with loc.). -6 To attack. -7 To state. —*Caus.* I To produce, to cause to arrive or be obtained. -2 To bring about. -3 To accomplish, perform. -4 To make a statement, adduce, put forward. -5 To justify. -6 To establish, prove. -7 To declare. -8 To make fit or adequate for. -9 To furnish with. -10 To find out, ascertain. -11 To examine.

उपपदं *n.* I A word prefixed or previously uttered. -2 A title, a degree; epithet of respect, such as

आर्ष, शार्ङ्ग, वर्मन् &c. -3 A secondary word of a sentence, a preposition, particle &c. prefixed to a verb or a noun derived from a verb which determines or qualifies the sense of the verb. -Comp. —तत्पुरुषः *m.* A kind of Tat. comp. in which the last member is some form of a verbal character.

उपपन्न *a.* (*f.* —न्ना) 1 Obtained, secured. -2 Accompanied by, in company with. -3 Coming presenting itself. -4 Right, proper, suitable. -5 Possible. -6 Endowed with, possessed of, furinshed with. -7 Demonstrated, proved. -8 Offered, presented. -9 Cured.

उपपरीक्षणं *n.*, उपपरीक्षा *f.*, Investigation, examination.

उपपर्शुका *f.* The false ribs.

उपपातः *m.* 1 An unexpected occurrence. -2 A calamity, accident. -3 Destruction.

उपपातकं *n.* A minor sin, a sin of the second degree.

उपपादक *a.* 1 Producing. -2 Well-reasoned.

उपपादनं *n.* 1 Effecting, accomplishing, doing. -2 Giving, delivering. -3 Proving, demonstration, establishing by arguments. -4 Examination, exposition (of a subject).

उपपादुक *a.* Self-produced, —कः *m.* A superhuman being, God.

उपपादुक *a.* Having shoes, shod (as a horse).

उपपापं *n.* See उपपातकं.

उपपार्श्वः *m.*, —र्श्वं *n.* 1 A shoulder. -2 A flank, side. -3 The opposite side. -4 One of the lesser ribs.

उपपीड् (उप + पीड् 10 P.) 1 To press down, hurt, pain. -2 To devastate, lay waste. -3 To eclipse.

उपपीडनं *n.* 1 Pressing down, devastating. -2 Inflicting pain, injuring. -3 Pain, torture.

उपपुरं *n.* A suburb.

उपपुराणं *n.* Secondary or minor Purâna.

उपपुष्पिका *f.* Yawning, gaping.

उपप्रदर्शनं *n.* Pointing out, indication.

उपप्रदानं *n.* 1 Delivering over, entrusting. -2 A bribe, present. -3 A tribute.

उपप्रलोभनं *n.* 1 Seducing, alluring. -2 A bribe, allurement.

उपप्राणः *m.* A secondary life-wind (belonging to the body).

उपप्रेक्षणं *n.* Overlooking, disregarding.

उपप्रैषः *m.* Invitation, summons.

उपप्लवः *m.* 1 Misfortune, calamity, distress. -2 An unlucky accident, trouble. -3 An obstacle, impediment. -4 Oppression, troubling. -5 Danger, fear. -6 Agitation, perturbation. -7 A portent or natural phenomenon foreboding evil. -8 An eclipse of the sun or moon. -9 N. of Râhu, the ascending node. -10 Anarchy. -11 N. of Siva.

उपप्लु (उप + प्लु 1 A.) 1 To float, swim. -2 To overwhelm, cover with. -3 To assault violently, to trouble, oppress, distress. -4 To jump or spring upon. -5 To depart from. —*Caus.* To water.

उपप्लुत *p. p.* (*f.* —ता) 1 Violently attacked, distressed, pained. -2 Harassed (by Râhu), eclipsed. -3 marked by prodigies. -4 Moistened. —ता *f.* Morbid sensibility of the uterus.

उपबंधः *m.* 1 Connection. -2 An affix.

उपबर्हः *m.*, —र्हणं *n.* 1 A pillow. -2 Pressing down, oppressing.

उपबहु *a.* A few, a tolerable number.

उपबाहुः *m.* The lower arm.

उपबृहणं *a.* Increase.

उपभंगः *m.* 1 Fleeing away, retreat. -2 A division (of a verse).

उपभाषा *f.* A secondary dialect.

उपभुक्तिः *f.* Enjoyment, use.

उपभुज् (उप + भुज् 7 U.) 1 To enjoy; taste (in all senses). -2 To eat, drink. -3 To possess. -4 To use, receive.

उपभृत् *f.* A round cup used in sacrifices.

उपभोगः *m.* 1 Enjoyment. -2 Use, application. -3 Enjoyment (of a woman), cohabitation. -4 Usufruct. -5 Pleasure, satisfaction.

उपमंत्र (उप + मंत्र 10 A.) 1 To invoke, invite. -2 To address, call to. -3 To persuade, conciliate.

उपमंत्रणं *n.* 1 The act of addressing, inviting, calling. -2 Persuading.

उपमंथनी *f.* A staff for stirring (fire.)

उपमर्दः *m.* 1 Friction, rubbing or pressing down. -2 Destruction, injury, killing -3 Reproach, abuse, insulting treatment. -4 Unhusking. -5 Refutation of a charge. -6 Stirring, shaking.

उपमर्दक *a.* Crushing, destroying. —कः *m.* Refutation of a charge.

उपमा (उप + मा 2 P., 3, 4, A.) To compare, liken.

उपमा *f.* 1 Resemblance, similarity, equality. -2 (In Rhet.). Resemblance between two things expressed in a single sentence, and unaccompanied with the statement of difference; simile, comparison. साम्यं वाच्यमवैधर्म्यं वाक्यैक उपमा द्वयोः * साहि. द. साधर्म्यमुपमा भेदे. * काव्यप्र. उपमा यत्र सादृश्य लक्ष्मीरुल्लसति द्वयोः * चंद्रालो.-3 The standard of comparison (उपमान). -4 A likeness (as a picture, portrait &c. -Comp. —द्रव्यं *n.* Any object used for a comparison. -रूपकं *n.* A figure in Rhetoric being a mixture of simile and metaphor.

उपमातृ *m.* An image-maker, a portrait-painter.

उपमातृ *f.* 1 'A second mother,' wet nurse. -2 A near female relative.

उपमानं *n.* 1 Comparison, resemblance. -2 The standard of comparison, that to which anything is compared (opp. उपमेय). -3 (In Nyáya phil.) Analogy, recognition of likeness, considered as one of the four kinds of 'Pramánas' or means of arriving at correct knowledge.

उपमितिः *f.* 1 Resemblance, comparison, similarity. 2 (In Nyâya phil.) Analogy, inference, deduction, knowledge of thing derived frOm anology, a conclusion deduced by means of an उपमान. -3 A figure of speech more commonly known as उपमा. -4 Likeness, picture

उपमेय *pot. p* (*f.* —या) Fit to be likened or compared; comparable with. —यं *n.* The subject of comparison, that which is compared (opp. उपमान). -Comp. —उपमा *f.* A figure of speech in which there are two sentences in the first of which a thing, say A, is compared to another, say B, and in the second B is compared to A. In this figure two things are alternately made Upameya and Upamâna. *e.g.* धरणिव धृतिर्धृतिरिव धरणी सततं विभाति वत यस्य * काव्यप्र.

उपयंतृ *m.* A husband, a bridegroom.

उपयंत्रं *n.* 1 A minor surgical instrument. -2 A secondary application of any kind.

उपयम् (उप + यम् 1 U) 1 To marry a wife (A. in this sense). -2 To seize, hold; take, receive, accept. -3 To show, indicate. -4 To go to (a woman). -5 To curb, restrain

उपयम: *m.* 1 Marriage.-2 Restraint.

उपयमनं *n.*1 Marrying, taking a wife. -2 Restraining curbing. -3 Placing down the fire. -4 Support.

उपयष्टृ *m.* One of the sixteen priests at a sacrifice.

उपया (उप + या 2 P.) 1 To approach, reach. -2 To attain to a particular state, meet with.

उपयाच् (उप + याच् 1 A.) To wish or ask for, solicit.

उपयाचक *a.* One who asks or solicits, suitor, beggar.

उपयाचनं *n.* Soliciting, begging, approaching with a request or prayer.

उपयाचित *p. p.* (*f.* —ता) Begged, requested. —तं *n.* 1 A request or prayer in general. -2 A present promised to a deity for the fulfilment of a desired object and generally to propitiate her. -3 A request or prayer to a deity for the accomplishment of a desired object.

उपयाचितकं *n.* See उपयाचितं.

उपयाज: *m.* Additional formulas at a sacrifice.

उपयानं *n.* Approaching, coming near.

उपयुक्त *p. p.* (*f.* —क्ता) 1 Attached &c. -2 Suited, right, proper. -3 Serviceable, useful. -4 Eaten, consumed.

उपयुज् (उप + युज् 7 A) 1 To employ, apply. -2 To enjoy, taste. -3 To devote oneself to -4 To yoke or harness (as horses to a carriage). -5 To consume, eat. —*pass.* 1 To be used or applied. -2 To be fit or proper. -3 To be taken into account.

उपयोग: *m.* 1 Employment, use, application, service. -2 Administration of medicine. -3 Fitness, suitableness, propriety. -4 Contact, proximity.

उपयोगिन् *a.* 1 Serviceable, useful. fit, proper. -2 Favourable. propitious.

उपरक्त *a.* (*f.* —क्ता) 1 Afflicted, distressed. -2 Eclipsed. -3 Tinged, coloured. —क्त: *m.* 1 The sun or moon in celipse. -2 Râhu.

उपरक्ष: *m.* A body-guard.

उपरक्षणं *n.* A guard, an out-post.

उपरंज् (उप + रंज् 4 U.) To be red; to be eclipsed. -*Caus.* 1 To colour, tint, dye. -2 To grive, distress.

उपरत *a.* (*f.* —ता) 1 Stopped, ceased. -2 Dead. -3 Abstained or retired from. -4 One who is disgusted with the world and has retired from it. -Comp. —स्पृह *a.* Void of desire, indifferent to worldly attachments or possessions.

उपरति: *f.* 1 Ceasing, stopping. -2 Death. -3 Abstaining from sexual enjoyment. -4 Indifference. -5 The conviction that ceremonial acts are futile and ceasing to rely on them.

उपरत्नं *n.* A secondary or inferior gem.

उपरम् (उप + रम् 1 P.) Sometimes A. also). 1 To cease, terminate, desist from, stop. -2 To be quiet.

उपर (-रा-) म: *m.* 1 Ceasing, stopping. -2 Abstaining from, giving up. -3 Death.

उपरमणं *n.* 1 Abstaining from pleasures of senses. -2 Refraining from ceremonial acts. -3 Ceasing, stopping.

उपरव: *m.* A sort of hole used in the extraction of Soma juice.

उपरसः *m.* 1 A secondary mineral. -2 A secondary passion or feeling. -3 A subordinate flavour.

उपरागः *m.* 1 An eclipse of the sun or moon. -2 Râhu or the ascending node. -3 Redness, red colour, colour. -4 A calamity, injury. -5 Misbehaviour. -6 Reproach, abuse.

उपराजः *m.* A viceroy.

उपरि *ind.* 1 As a separable preposition (usually with gen ; rarely with acc. or loc.) उपरि means (*a*) Above, over, upon ;(*b*) At the end of, at the head of ; (c) Beyond, in addition to ; (*d*) In connection with, with regard to, towards, upon ; (*e*) After.

उपरि joined to उपरि (with acc or gen. or by itself) means (*a*) Just above ; (*b*) higher and higher, high above.

As a separable adverb उपरि means (*a*) High, above, upon. (*b*) Besides, in addition (*c*) Afterwards, more and more, repeatedly, continuously.

Comp. —चर *a.* Moving above (as a bird). -तन, -स्थ *a.* Upper, higher. —भागः *m.* The upper portion or side. —भावः *m.* Being above or higher. —भूमिः *f.* The ground above.

उपरिष्टात् *ind.* 1 As an adverb it means (*a*) Over, above, from above; on, high (*b*) Further or later on, afterwards (*c*) Behind. -2 As a preposition it means (*a*) Over, upon (with gen., rarely acc.) (*b*) Down upon (*c*) Behind(with gen.).

उपरीतकः *m.* A particular mode or posture in sexual enjoyment.

उपरुद्ध *p. p.* (*f.* —) 1 Obstructed, stopped ; confined -2 Covered, concealed. -3 Protected, favoured. -4 Besieged, locked up

उपरुध् (उप + रुध् 7 U.) 1 To obstruct, stop, to detain. -2 To disturb, trouble, trouble with a request. -3 To overcome, subdue. -4 To besiege. -5 To lock up, confine. -6 To conceal, hide. -7 To reject.

उपरूपकं *n.* A drama of an inferior class, of which 18 kinds are enumerated.

उपरोधः *m.* 1 Obstruction, impediment, obstacle. -2 Disturbance, trouble, molestation. -3 Opposition. -4 Covering, blocking up. -5 Binding, seizing. -6 Protection, favour.

उपरोधकं *n.* An inner room, a private apartment.

उपरोधनं *n.* Obstruction, impediment.

उपलः *m.* 1 A stone, rock. -2 A precious stone, jewel. —ला *f.* 1 Refined sugar. -2 Sand.

उपलकः *m.* A stone.

उपलक्ष् (उप + लक्ष् 10 P.) 1 To look at, mark. -2 To regard or consider. -3 To put a sign upon. -4 To designate, describe. -5 To imply in addition. -6 To have in view.

उपलक्षणं *n.* 1 Looking at, beholding, marking, ascertainment. -2 A mark, distinctive feature. -3 Designation. -4 Implying something that has not been actually expressed, synecdoche of a part for the whole, of an individual for the species, or of a quality for that in which the quality exists.

उपलब्ध *a.* (*f.* —ब्धा) 1 Gained, obtained. -2 Conceived. -3 Perceived, guessed.

उपलब्धिः *f.* 1 Getting, acquisition. -2 Observation, knowledge. -3 Understanding, mind. -4 A conjecture, guess. -5 Perceptibility, appearance (recognized as a kind of proof by the Mimâmsakas).

उपलभ् (उप + लभ् 1 A.) 1 To know, understand, perceive. -2 To find out, learn. -3 To get, obtain, acquire, enjoy, experience (happiness &c.). -4 To conceive, become pregnant.

उपलंभः *m.* 1 Acquisition. -2 Direct perception or recognition, comprehension otherwise than from memory (same as अनुभव). -3 Ascertaining, knowing.

उपलंभनं *n.* 1 Apprehension. -2 Direct perception. -3 Ascertainment. -4 Knowledge.

उपला *f.* 1 Refined sugur. -2 Sand.

उपलालनं *n.* Fondling

उपलालिका *f.* Thirst.

उपलिंगं *n.* A portent, natural phenomenon, considered as boding evil.

उपलिप् (उप + लिप् 6 P.) 1 To anoint, besmear. -2 To pollute.

उपलिप्सा *f.* Desire to obtain.

उपलेपः *m.* 1 Anointing, smearing. -2 Cleaning, white-washing. -3 Becoming deadened or dull (said of senses.).

उपलेपनं *n.* 1 Smearing, anointing. -2 An ointment, unguent.

उपवनं *n.* A garden, grove, a planted forest.

उपवर्णः *m.* Minute or detailed description.

उपवर्णनं *n.* Minute description, delineation in detail.

उपवर्तनं *n.* 1 A place for exercise. -2 A district. -3 A kingdom (राज्य). -4 A bog, marshy place.

उपवस् (उप + वस् 1 P.) 1 To dwell in or at, inhabit (with acc.). -2 To abstain from food; fast. -3 To go to (a master). -4 To enter upon, learn, take to, begin. *-Caus.* To cause to fast.

उपवसथः *m.* 1 A village. -2 A fast-day.

उपवस्तं *n.* A fast.

उपवह् (उप + वह् 1 P.) 1 To lead near. -2 To bring about, commence.

उपवहनं *n.* (in music) Preliminary singing, humming a tune before beginning to sing it aloud.

उपवासः *m.* 1 A fast. -2 Kindling a sacred fire. -3 A fire-altar.

उपवाहनं *n.* Carrying to, bringing near.

उपवाह्यः *m.*, —ह्या *f.* 1 A king's riding elephant (male or female). -2 A royal vehicle (in general).

उपविद्या *f.* Profane science, inferior kind of knowledge.

उपविश् (उप + विश् 6 P.) 1 To sit down. -2 To wait upon. -3 To encamp. -4 To go down, set (as the sun). -5 To practise; as in प्रायं उपविशति. -6 To abstain from food, fast. -7 To seize.

उपविषः *m.*, -षं *n.* 1 An artificial poison. -2 A narcotic, any poisonous drug.

उपवीणय् P. To play on the Vinâ or lute (before a deity &c.).

उपवीतं *n.* 1 Investiture with the sacred thread. -2 The sacred thread worn by the first three classes of the Hindus.

उपवृंहणं *n.* Increase.

उपवृत् (उप + वृत 1 A.) 1 To go towards. -2 To return.

उपवेदः *m.* A class of writings subordinate to the Vedas.

उपवेशः *m.*, -शनं *n.* 1 Sitting down (as प्रायोपवेशन). -2 Being attached to. -3 Throwing out by stool. -4 Placing down.

उपवैणवं *n.* The three periods of the

day; *i. e.* morning, midday, and evening.

उपव्याख्यानं *n.* A supplementary explanation or interpretation.

उपव्याघ्रः *m.* A small hunting leopard.

उपशम् (उप + शम् 4 P.) 1 To become calm or quiet. -2 To cease, stop; cease to speak. —*Caus.* 1 To calm, tranquillize. -2 To appease. -3 To extinguish, to kill.

उपशमः *m.* 1 Becoming quiet, assuagement, pacification; cessation, stopping, extinction. -2 Relaxation, intermission. -3 Tranquillity, patience. -4 Control or restraint of the senses.

उपशमनं *n.* 1 Quieting, calming, appeasing. -2 Mitigation, assuagement. -3 Extinction, cessation.

उपशयः *m.* 1 Lying by the side of. -2 A lair, ambush. -3 Diagnosis by the effect of certain articles of food, or medicine (one of the five elements of निदान). -4 Allaying disease by diet, regimen &c.

उपशल्यं *n.* An open place in the vicinity of a town or village, suburb.

उपशाखा *f.* A secondary branch.

उपशांत *p. p.* (*f.* —ता) 1 Calmed, appeased, pacified. -2 Calm, tranquil. -3 Lessened, diminished.

उपशांतिः *f.* See उपशमः.

उपशांतिन् *a.* (*f.* —नी) 1 Appeased, pacified. -2 Calm, tranquil. —*m.* A tame elephant.

उपशायः *m.* Sleeping in turn, rotation for sleeping with (another who keeps watch at night).

उपशालं *n.* A place near a house, a court before a house.

उपशास्त्रं *n.* A minor science or treatise.

उपशिक्षणं *f.*, -शिक्षा *n.* Learning, training.

उपशिष्यः *m.* The pupil of a pupil.

उपशी (उप + शी 2 A.) 1 To lie near. -2 To cohabit. -3 To do good to, agree with.

उपशोभनं *n.*, -शोभा *f.* Adorning, ornamenting.

उपशोषणं *n.* Drying up, withering.

उपश्री *f.* Covering, anything thrown above or upon.

उपश्रु (उप + श्रु 5 P.) 1 To hear. -2 To promise.

उपश्रुत *a.* (*f.* —ता) 1 Heard. -2 Promised, agreed.

उपश्रुतिः *f.* 1 Hearing, listening. -2 Range of hearing. -3 A supernatural voice heard at night and personified as a nocturnal deity revealing the future. -4 Aspect of the stars, fortune-telling. -5 Promise, assent.

उपश्लिष् (उप + श्लिष् 4 P.) 1 To embrace. -2 To approach.

उपश्लिष्ट *p. p.* (*f.* —ष्टा) Placed near, contiguous, adjoining.

उपश्लेषः *m.*, -षणं *n.* 1 Juxta-position, contact. -2 An embrace.

उपसंयमः *m.* 1 Curbing, restraining, binding. -2 The end of the world, universal destruction.

उपसंयमनं *n.* See उपसंयमः.

उपसंयोगः *m.* A secondary connection, modification.

उपसंरोहः *m.* Growing together or over, cicatrizing.

उपसंवादः *m.* An agreement, a contract.

उपसंव्यानं *n.* An under-garment.

उपसंस्करणं *n.* Preparing, purifying.

उपसंस्कृ (उप + सम् + कृ 8 U.) 1 To prepare (as a meal). -2 To ornament. -3 To consecrate, purify.

उपसंहरणं *n.* 1 Withdrawing, taking back. -2 Refusing. -3 Excluding. -4 Attacking, invading.

उपसंहारः *m.* 1 Drawing in or together, contracting.-2 Drawing away, excluding, withholding. -3 A collection.-4 Summing up, winding up. -5 A preparation (of a speech &c). -6 A compendium, *résumé*. -7 Brevity, conciseness. -8 Perfection. -9 Destruction, death, end. -10 Attacking, invading -11 (In logic). Refutation.

उपसंहारिन् *a.* 1 Comprehending. -2 Exclusive. —*m.* A *hetu* (हेतु) which is not exclusive.

उपसंहित *p. p.* (*f.* —ता) 1 Connected with, endowed. -2 Accompanied by. -3 Regarding, referring to.

उपसंहृ (उप + सम् + हृ 1 P.) 1 To draw or bring together. -2 To sum or wind up. -3 To contract. -4 To withdraw, withhold. -5 To check. -6 To absorb, destroy, annihilate.

उपसंहृतिः *f.* 1 Comprehension. -2 Seizing, taking.

उपसंक्रांत *a.* (*f.* —ता) Handed down.

उपसंक्षेपः *m.* An abstract, summary, résumé.

उपसंख्यानं *n.* 1 Addition. -2 Supplementary addition, further or additional enumeration (a term applied to the *Vártikas* of Kâtyâyana which are intended to supply omissions in Pânini's Sutras, and generally to supplement them). -3 (In gram.) A substitute in form or sense.

उपसंग्रह् (उप + सम् + ग्रह् 9 P.) 1 To take upon oneself, feel, suffer. -2 To receive, accept. -3 To seize. -4 To take into custody or possession. -5 To win over, conciliate. -6 To clasp, embrace.

उपसंग्रहः *m.*, -हणं *n.* 1 Keeping pleased, supporting, maintaining. -2 Respectful salutation (as by touching the feet of the person saluted). -3 Accepting, adopting. -4 Polite address. -5 Collecting, joining. -6 Taking, accepting (as a wife); appendage, any necessary article either for use or decoration (उपकरण).

उपसत्तिः *f.* 1 Connection, union. -2 Service, worship, attendance upon. -3 Gift, donation.

उपसद् (उप + सद् 1 P., 6 P) 1 To sit near to, approach. -2 To sit at the feet of. -3 To wait upon, serve. -4 To march against. -5 To try to get or obtain. -6 To sink down. —*Caus.* 1 To place near. -2 To lead towards. -3 To get, find

उपसद् *f.* 1 Siege, assault, attack. -2 Laying up, accumulating. -3 Service, worship. -4 N. of a ceremony, forming part of the ज्योतिष्टोम ceremony. -Comp. —व्रतिन् *a.* Observing the rules of the *Upasad*; *i.e.* drinking milk in certain quantities, sleeping on the bare earth, keeping silence &c.

उपसदः *m.* 1 Approach. -2 A gift, donation. -3 The उपसद् sacrifice.

उपसदनं *n.* 1 Going near. -2 Sitting at the feet of a teacher, becoming a pupil. -3 Neighbourhood. -4 Service. -5 Partaking of.

उपसंतानः *m.* 1 Immediate connection. -2 A descendant.

उपसंधा (उप + सम् + धा 3 U.) 1 To put together, increase. -2 To join. -3 To direct towards.

उपसंधानं *n.* Adding, joining.

उपसन्न *a.* (*f.* —न्ना) 1 Approached near. -2 Worshipped, served. -3 Serving, waiting upon. -4 Easily obtainable. -5 Got, obtained.

उपसंन्यासः *m.* Laying down, giving up, resignation.

उपसमाधानं *n.* Gathering together, heaping.

उपसंपत्तिः *f.* 1 Approaching. -2 Entering into any condition.

उपसंपन्न *a.* (*f.* —न्ना) 1 Gained, obtained. -2 Arrived at. -3 Furnished with. -4 Familiar with. -5 Enough, sufficient. -6 Killed at a sacrifice (as an animal). -7 Dead, deceased. -8 Cooked, dressed (as food). —न्नं *n.* Condiment.

उपसंभाषः *m.*, —षा *f.* 1 Conversation. -2 Friendly persuasion.

उपसरः *m.* 1 Approaching (as a cow). -2 The first pregnancy of a cow.

उपसरणं *n.* 1 Going towards. -2 Rapid flowing of the blood towards the heart (as in sickness). -3 That which is approached as a refuge.

उपसर्गः *m.* 1 Sickness, disease, also a disease superinduced on another. -2 Misfortune, injury, harm. -3 Portent, a natural phenomenon foreboding evil. -4 An eclipse. -5 An indication or symptom of death. -6 Addition. -7 Possession by an evil spirit. -8 A preposition prefixed to roots. They modify or sometimes entirely alter the sense of the root.

उपसर्जनं *n* 1 Pouring on. -2 A misfortune, calamity (as an eclipse), portent. -3 Leaving. -4 Eclipsing. -5 Any person or thing subordinate to another, a substitute. -6 (In gram.) A word which either by composition or derivation loses its original independent character, while it also determines the sense of another word (opp. प्रधान)

उपसर्पः *m.* 1 Approach, access. -2 Following a person.

उपसर्पणं *n.* Going near, approaching, advancing towards.

उपसर्या *f.* A cow fit for a bull.

उपसूर्यकं *n.* The disc of the sun or its halo

उपसृ (उप + सृ 1 P.) 1 To go towards, approach. -2 To attack. -3 To have intercourse (as of a woman with a man).

उपसृज् (उप + सृज् 6 P.) 1 To pour out or on, offer (water &c.). -2 To add to, connect with, bring to. -3 To trouble oppress, infest. -4 To eclipse. -5 To come in contact with. -6 To produce, create. -7 To destroy.

उपसृप् (उप + सृप् 1 P.) 1 To approach. -2 To begin (with inf.). -3 To attack.

उपसृष्ट *p. p.* (*f.* —ष्टा) 1 Joined, accompanied by. -2 Seized or possessed by (a demon or evil spirit). -3 Troubled, injured. -4 Eclipsed. -5 Furnished with an उपसर्ग (as a root). —ष्टः *m.* The sun or moon when eclipsed. -ष्टं *n.* Sexual union.

उपसेचनं *n.*, उपसेकः *m.* 1 Pouring or sprinkling upon, watering. -2 Infusion ; juice. —नी *f.* A ladle or cup for pouring.

उपसेव् (उप + सेव् 1 A.) 1 To serve, worship, honour. -2 To practise, (as a vow). -3 To make use of. -4 To enjoy. -5 To frequent, inhabit. -6 To rub or anoint with (sandal &c.).

उपसेवक *a.* 1 Worshipping, serving. -2 Following, practising. -3 Enjoying.

उपसेवनं *n*, -सेवा *f* 1 Worshipping, honouring. -2 Service. -3 Addiction to. -4 Using, enjoying.

उपसेविन् *a.* Serving, practising.

उपस्करः *m.* 1 Any article which

serves to make anything complete, an ingredient. -2 (Hence) Condiment or seasoning for food (as mustard, peppe. &c.). -3 Furniture, apparatus, instrument. -4 Any article or implement of household use (such as a broom-stick). -5 An ornament. -6 Censure, blame.

उपस्करणं *n.* 1 Killing, injuring. -2 A collection. -3 A change. -4 An ellipsis. -5 Censure. -6 Decorating.

उपस्कार: *m.* 1 A supplement. -2 Supplying an ellipsis. -3 Beautifying, ornamenting. -4 An ornament. -5 A stroke. -6 A collection.

उपस्कृ (उप + स्कृ 8 U.) To prepare, elaborate, perfect, adorn; (see उपकृ).

उपस्कृत *p. p.* (*f.* —ता) 1 Prepared, perfected. -2 Censured. -3 Killed, injured. -4 Collected. -5 Beautified. -6 Supplied (as ellipsis). -7 Modified.

उपस्कृति: *f.* Supplement.

उपस्तंभ् (उप + स्तंभ् 5, 9, P.) To prop, support (fig. also).

उपस्तंभ: *m.*,-म्भनं *n.* 1 Stay, support. -2 Support of life (as food, sleep &c.). -3 Encouragement, incitement, aid. -4 Basis, ground, occasion.

उपस्तंभक *a.* Supporting, aiding, encouraging.

उपस्तरणं 1 Spreading out, scattering.-2 A covering.-3 A bed.-4 Anything spread out (as a covering).

उपस्तृ-स्तॄ (उप + स्तृ, स्तॄ 5, 9, U.) 1 To spread out. -2 To strew or cover with. -3 To arrange, set, in order.

उपस्त्री *f.* A concubine.

उपस्थ *a.* Near, approximate. —स्थ: *m.* 1 The lap. -2 The middle part in general. —स्थ: *m.*, -स्थं *n.* 1 The organ of generation (of men and women, particularly of the latter). -2 The anus.-3 The haunch or hip. -4 The charioteer's seat. -Comp. —दघ्न *a.* Reaching to the lap. —निग्रह: *m.* Restraint of sensual passions, continence. —पत्र:, —दल: *m.* The Indian fig-tree. —सद् *a.* Sitting in the lap.

उपस्था (उप + स्था 1 U.) 1 To stand near -2 To fall to one's share. -3 To approach. -4 To wait, serve. -5 To worship. -6 To remain near. -7 To meet, join (as a river.) -8 To form friendship with. -9 To approach with hostile intention. -10 To resort to. -11 To conciliate. -*Caus.* (—स्थापयति.) 1 To furnish with to prepare. -2 To place upon or near.-3 To produce.

उपस्थातृ *m.* 1 An attendant, a servant. -2 A sacrificial priest.

उपस्थानं *n.* 1 Presence, proximity, nearness. -2 Approaching, appearance, coming into the presence of. -3 Worshipping, waiting upon (with prayers); attendance, service. -4 Obeisance; greeting. -5 Attending to, guarding. -6 An abode. 7 Any sacred place (approached with respect). -8 An assembly. -9 Remembrance, recollection, memory. -10 Obtaining, getting.

उपस्थानीय *pot p. p.* (*f.* —या) To be kept near. -2 To be waited upon or served.

उपस्थापक *a.* 1 Placing or bringing near. -2 Explaining, teaching. -3 Causing to remember.

उपस्थापनं *n.* 1 Placing near, getting ready. -2 The awakening of memory. -3 Attendance, service.

उपस्थायक: *m.* A servant.

उपस्थित *p. p.* (*f.* -ता) 1 Approached,

arrived. -2 Close or near, at hand, drawing near. -3 Worshipped or waited upon, served.-4 Got, obtained, received without solicitation. -5 Happened, occured, fallen to the lot. -6 Caused, produced, felt. -7 Known. -8 Cleansed, clean. —तं *n* Service, worship.

उपस्थितिः *f.* 1 Approach. -2 Proximity, presence. -3 Obtaining. -4 Accomplishing. -5 Remembrance. -6 Service, attendance. [eing.

उपस्नेहः *m.* 1 Proximity. -2 Moist-

उपस्पर्शः *m.*, -र्शनं *n.* 1 Touching, contact. -2 Bathing, ablution. -3 Rinsing the mouth.

उपस्पृश् 6 P. 1 To touch (water), bathe. -2 To wash or rinse the mouth (or teeth); to sip water (and eject it.). -3 To sprinkle.

उपस्मृतिः *f.* A minor law-book.

उपस्रवणं *n.* 1 The periodical flow of a woman, menses. -2 Flow (in general).

उपस्वत्वं *n.* Revenue, profit.

उपस्वेदः *m.* Moisture, sweat.

उपहत *p. p.* (*f.* —ता) 1 Injured, struck, pained, hurt. -2 Affected by, injured, struck with, overpowered.-3 Struck by lightning &c. -4 Doomed (to destruction). -5 Censured, disregarded. -6 Vitiated, polluted. -Comp. —आत्मन् *a.* Agiated in mind, mentally affected. —दृश् *a.* Dazzled, blinded. —धी *a* Infatuated.

उपहतक *a.* Ill-fated, unfortunate.

उपहतिः *f.* 1 Stroke. -2 Killing, injuring.

उपहत्या *f.* Dazzling of the eyes.

उपहन् 2 P. 1 To strike, smite. -2 To waste, injure, destroy, kill. -3To thrust in or into. -4 To err, mistake in reciting.

उपहरणं *n.* 1 Bringing near. -2 Taking, seizing. -3 Offering gifts to superiors, deities &c. -4 Offering victims. -5 Serving out food or distributing it.

उपहवः *m.* Invitation.

उपहस् (उप + हस् 1 P.) 1 To ridicule, laugh at; (*fig.*) to excel, surpass. -2 To couple oneself with.

उपहसित *p. p.* (*f.* —ता) Ridiculed, derided. —तं *n.* Satirical laughter, ridicule.

उपहासिका *f.* A small purse (or box) containing the ingredients, necessary for betel-chewing (*e. g.* leaves, chunam, catechu, betel &c). (Mar. चंची, बटवा, झोळणा).

उपहारः *m* 1 An oblation. -2 A gift, present (in general). -3 A victim, an offering to a deity. -4 A present to a superior &c. -5 Offering of flowers &c. -6 A collection of flowers. -7 Honour. -8 Indemnity, presents given as the price of peace. -9 Food distributed to guests. -10 Exultation, merrymaking.

उपहार्य *a.* 1 Eatable. —र्यं *n.* Food to be offered to gods, manes &c.

उपहासः *m.* 1 Ridicule, derision. -2 Satirical laughter. -3 Fun, play. -Comp. —आस्पदं, -पात्रं *n.* Laughingstock, butt of ridicule.

उपहासक *a.* Ridiculing others. —कः *m.* A jester.

उपहास्य *a.* (*f.* —स्या) Ridiculous.

उपहित *p. p.* (*f.* —ता) 1 Placed, deposited. -2 Preceded by. -3 Joined, connected with. -4 Possessed of. -5 Ready; deputed to act as a spy. -6 Given.

उपहूत *a.* 1 Brought near. -2 Invited.

उपहूतिः *f.* Calling, inviting.

उपहृ (उप + हृ 1 P.) 1 To fetch,

bring near. -2 To offer, present, give (with dat. or gen.). -3 To serve out or distribute (food). -4 To offer as a victim. -5 To put down, throw. -6 To collect, gather together. -7 To take away, destroy. -8 To employ, apply, use.

उपहृत *p. p.* (*f.* —ता) 1 Offered, presented. -2 Offered as a victim. -3 Served out (as food). -4 Taken, collected.

उपह्वरं *n.* 1 A solitary or lonely place. -2 Proximity. —रः *m.* A car.

उपह्वानं *n.* 1 Calling, inviting. -2 Invoking with prayers.

उपह्वे (उप + ह्वे 1 A. P.) 1 To invoke, call.

उपांशु *ind.* 1 In a whisper. -2 Secretly, in private. —शुः *m.* 1 A prayer uttered in a low voice, muttering of prayers. -2 Silence. -3 N. of a Soma offering.

उपाकरणं *n.* 1 An invitation to begin. -2 Immolation, sacrifice of an animal. -3 Preparation, beginning, commencement. —4 Commencement of reading the Veda after the performance of the preparatory rite.

उपाकर्मन् *n.* 1 Preparation, beginning, commencement. -2 A ceremony performed before commencing to read the Veda after the monsoons.

उपाकृ (उप + आं + कृ 1 U.) 1 To bring near. -2 To invite. -3 To offer, grant, give (to another). -4 To acquire, obtain (as fame). -5 To make preparations for or to perform a rite. -6 To undertake.

उपाकृत *p. p.* (*f.* —ता) 1 Brought near. -2 Killed at a sacrifice (an animal). -3 Begun, commenced. -4 Disastrous, calamitous. —तः *m.* 1 A sacrificial animal killed during he recitation of prescribed prayers.-2 A misfortune, portent. -तं *n.* 1 Beginning, commencement. -2 The performance of the usual rites over the sacrificial animal. -3 Invitation.

उपाक्षं *ind.* Before the eyes, in the presence of.

उपाख्या (उप + आ + ख्या 2 P.) To tell, narrate, relate, with acc.).

उपाख्या *f.* 1 Observing with one's own eyes. -2 Describing

उपाख्यानं,—नकं *n.* 1 A short tale or narrative ; an episode as distinguished from the main story. -2 Repetition of a story already heard from others.

उपागत *a.* (*f.* -ता) 1 Come, approached. -2 Occurred, happened. -3 Promised. -4 Suffering, feeling, enduring.

उपागम् (उप + आ + गम् 1 P.) 1 To come, approach. -2 To go to, go to the state of. -3 To undergo, endure. -4 To obtain, get. -5 To occur, fall to the lot of.

उपागमः *m.* 1 Approach, arrival. -2 Occurrence.-3 A promise, agreement. -4 Acceptance. -5 Suffering, feeling.

उपाग्रं *n.* 1 The part next to the end or top.-2 A secondary member.

उपाग्रहणं *n.* Reading the Vedas after being initiated to them.

उपांगः *m.* A mark of sandal on the forehead. —गं *n.* 1 A subdivision, a subhead. -2 Any minor limb or member (of anything). -3 A supplement of a supplement.-4 A supplementary work. -5 A secondary portion of science; a class of writings supplementary to the Vedángas; (these are four:— पुराणन्यायमीमांसाधर्मशास्त्राणि.

उपाचर् (उप + आ + चर् 1 P.) 1 To

approach. -2 To attend upon, serve, be attached to. -3 To treat (in medicine also).

उपाचरित *p. p.* (*f.* —ता) Attached to any one's service. —तः *m.* (In gram.) That rule of Sandhi by which the sound Visarga becomes ष before क् and प्.

उपाचारः *m.* 1 Position (of a word in a sentence). -2 Procedure.

उपाजे *ind.* (Used only with the root कृ) Supporting; उपाजेकृत्य or -कृत्वा having supported.

उपाञ्जन *n.* Anointing, plastering or washing with cow-dung, chunam &c.

उपात्त *a.* (*f.* —त्ता) 1 Got, received, acquired, obtained. -2 Appropriated. -3 Taken away, seized. -4 Felt, perceived, regarded. -5 Employed, used. -6 Comprised. -7 Begun, commenced. -8 Mentioned. -9 Allowed in argument, granted, conceded. —त्तः *m.* An elephant out of rut.

उपात्ययः *m.* 1 Transgression of, deviation from established customs. -2 Disorderly conduct, rudeness.

उपादा (उप + आ + दा 3 A.) (*p. p.* उपात्त) 1 To receive, accept; take. -2 To acquire, obtain. -3 To give to, furnish with. -4 To take, assume. -5 To carry away; steal. -6 To seize, attack. -7 To take, lay hold of. -8 To assume a form. -9 To feel, perceive, experience. -10 To consider, regard. -11 To take in addition, include, comprise. -12 To employ, apply, use. -13 To begin. -14 To mention.

उपादानं *n.* 1 Taking, receiving, obtaining. -2 Taking away. -3 Employment, using. -4 Mention, enumeration. -5 Saying, speaking. -6 Including, containing. -7 Withdrawing the organs of sense and perception from the external world and its objects. -8 A cause, motive, natural or immediate cause. -9 The material out of which anything is made the material cause. -10 A mode of expression in which a word used elliptically, besides retaining its own primary sense, conveys another (in addition to that which is actually expressed). -11 Effort of body or speech. -Comp. —कारणं *n.* A material cause. -लक्षणा *f.* See अजहत्स्वार्थलक्षणा.

उपादेय *pot. p.* (*f.* -या) 1 Capable of being taken. -2 Endurable. -3 Acceptable, admissible. -4 To be selected. -5 Excellent, admirable.

उपाधा (उप + आ + धा 3 U.) 1 To place near or upon. -2 To offer, give. -3 To put on, wear. -4 To cause produce. -5 To make, effect. -6 To keep, hold.

उपाधिः *m.* 1 Fraud, deceit, trick. -2 Deception, disguise (in Vedânta). -3 Discriminative property, attribute, peculiarity. This उपाधि is of four kinds:— जाति, गुण, क्रिया, संज्ञा. -4 A title, nick-name (modern use). 5 Limitation, condition (as of time, space &c.). -6 A trace, mark. -7 A purpose, occasion, object. -8 (In logic) A special cause for a general effect. -9 A man who is careful to support his family.

उपाधिक *a.* Exceeding, supernumerary, additional.

उपाध्यायः *m.* 1 A teacher or preceptor in general. -2 Particularly a spiritual teacher, religious preceptor. -3 A sub-teacher who instructs for wages only in a part of the Veda and is inferior to an आचार्य. —या *f.* A female preceptor. —यी *f.* 1 A female preceptor. -2 The wife of a preceptor.

उपाध्यायानी f. The wife of a preceptor.

उपानह् f. (*nom. sing.* उपानत्) A sandal, shoe.

उपांत a. Near to the end, last but one. --तः m. 1 Border, edge, margin, point (of anything). -2 The corner or angle of the eye. -3 Immediate proximity, vicinity. -4 Side or slope. -5 The last letter but one.

उपांतिक a. (f. --की) Near, proximate, neighbouring. -कं n. Vicinity, proximity.

उपांत्य a. (f. --त्या) Last but one. --त्यः m. The corner of the eye. -त्यं n. Vicinity.

उपायः m. 1 Means, an expedient, remedy. -2 A plan, contrivance, stratagem. -3 A fact, circumstance. -4 Beginning, commencement. -5 Effort, exertion. -6 A means of success against an enemy; these are four:— (1) conciliation or negotiation; (2) bribery; (3) sowing dissensions and (4) punishment (open attack). -7 Joining (as in singing). -8 Approach. -Comp. --चतुष्टयं n. The four expedients against an enemy; see above. --ज्ञ a. Fertile in expedients. --तुरीयः The 4th expedient; *i. e.* दंड or punishment.

उपायनं n. 1 Going near, approach. -2 Becoming a pupil of. -3 Engaging in any religious rite. -4 Undertaking, beginning. -5 A present, gift.

उपारंभः m. Beginning, commencement.

उपारूढ a. (f. --ढा) 1 Grown, increased. -2 Attained to.

उपार्ह् (उप + अर्ह् 1 P.) To bring near to. —*Caus.* To gain, earn, acquire.

उपार्जनं, n.,-ना f. Acquiring, gaining.

उपालभ् (उप + आ + लभ् 1 A.) 1 To censure, blame, revile, scold.

उपालंभः m., --भनं n. 1 Abuse, taunt, censure. -2 Delaying, putting off.

उपावर्तनं n. 1 Coming or turning back, return. -2 Revolving, turning round. -3 Approaching. -4 Ceasing.

उपावृत् (उप + आ + वृत् 1 A.) 1 To approach. -2 To turn away from, return. -3 To give. —*Caus.* 1 To induce. -2 To cause to turn; lead or bring back. -3 To give to. -4 To produce. -5 To stretch out more and more.

उपाश्रयः m. 1 Recourse (for aid), asylum, support. -2 Receptacle, recipient. -3 Reliance, dependence upon.

उपाश्रि (उप + आ + श्रि 1 U.) To have recourse to, resort to.

उपाश्रित a. (f. --ता) 1 Relying or depending upon. -2 Supporting (fig. also), protecting.

उपास् (उप + आस् 2 A.) 1 To sit near to (with acc.), sit at the side of (as a mark of submission and respect); wait upon, serve, worship. -2 To occupy, abide in, reside. -3 To pass (as time). -4 To approach, go towards. -5 To invest or blockade (as an enemy's town). -6 To be engaged in, take part in, perform (a sacred rite). -7 To undergo, suffer. -8 To remain or continue in any state or action; oft. with a *press. p.* -9 To expect, wait for. -10 To attach oneself to, practise. -11 To resort to, apply, use. -12 To respect, recognize. -13 To practise archery.

उपासकः m. 1 A worshipper. -2 A servant, follower. -3 A Sudra.

उपासंगः *m.* 1 Proximity, vicinity. -2 A quiver.

उपासनं *n.*, -ना *f.* 1 Service, attendance upon. -2 Engaging in, performing. -3 Worship, adoration.-4 Practice of archery. -5 Religious meditation. -6 The sacred fire. -7 Harming.

उपासा *f.* 1 Service, attendance. -2 Worship, adoration. -3 Religious meditation.

उपास्तमनं *n.* Sunset.

उपास्तिः *f.* 1 Service, attendance upon (especially a deity). -2 Worship, adoration.

उपास्त्रं *n.* A minor weapon.

उपास्य *pot. p.* (*f.* —स्या) 1 To be worshipped. -2 To be performed.

उपाहारः *m.* Slight refreshment (fruits, sweetmeats &c.).

उपाहित *p. p.* (*f.* —ता) 1 Deposited, placed. -2 Put on, worn. -3 Connected, joined. -4 Ascribed or attributed to. -5 Agreed upon. —तः *m.* A fiery portent; danger or destruction from fire.

उपाइ (उप + आ + इ 1 U.) 1 To offer, give. -2 To cause, produce. -3 make, prepare. -4 To seize.

उपे (उप + इ 2 P.) 1 To approach, come near, arrive at, reach. -2 To go to (a master), become a pupil. -3 To have intercourse with (a woman), cohabit. -4 To perform, undertake, practise. -5 To go to or pass into any state, to fall into (misfortune &c.). -6 To obtain, attain to. -7 To incur, be present at. -8 To consider as, acknowledge.

उपेक्ष् (उप + ईक्ष् 1 A.) 1 To neglect, disregard. -2 To let go. -3 To abandon. -4 To despise. -5 To consider, have regard to. -6 To look at, regard, perceive.

उपेक्षणं *n.* See उपेक्षा.

उपेक्षा *f.* 1 Overlooking, disregard, neglect. -2 Indifference, contempt. -3 Leaving. -4 Endurance, patience. -5 Dissent. -6 Neglect, trick or deceit (one of the seven expedients in war).

उपेत *a.* (*f.* —ता) 1 Come near, approached, arrived. -2 Present. -3 Endowed with, having (with instr. or in comp). -4 Blockaded. -5 Fallen into.

उपेंद्रः *m.* N. of Vishnu or Krishna as the younger brother of Indra in his 5th or dwarf incarnation. -Comp. —वज्रा *f.* N. of a metre.

उपेय *a.* (*f.* —या) 1 To be gone to or approached. -2 To be effected by means -3 Assailable. -4 To be sought. -5 To be obtained.

उपोढ *a.* (*f.* —ढा) 1 Arrayed for battle (as an army). -2 Brought near. -3 Advanced, begun. -4 Married. -5 Increased, stored up, developed.

उपोत्तम *a.* (*f.* —मा) Last but one.

उपोद्ग्रहः *m.* Knowledge.

उपोद्घातः *m.* 1 A beginning. -2 An introduction, a preface. -3 An example, an apposite argument or illustration.-4 An occasion, medium, means. -5 Analysis, ascertaining the elements of anything.-6 Alluding to, mentioning.

उपोद्बलक *a.* Confirming.

उपोद्बलनं *n.* Confirmation, corroboration.

उपोषणं, उपोषितं *n.* A fast.

उपोह् (उप + उह् 1 P.) 1 To propel, push or impel towards. -2 push, insert.

उप्त *a.* (*f.* —प्ता) 1 Sown, planted (as seed). -2 Thrown cast (as dice). -3 Produced. -4 Placed. -5

Occupied. उप्तिः *f.* Sowing seed.

उब्ज् 6 P. 1 To press down, subdue. -2 To make straight.

उभ्, उंभ् 6, 9, 7 P. 1 To confine. -2 To compact together. -3 To fill with. -4 To cover or overspread with.

उभ *pron. a.* (Used only in the dual). Both.

उभय *pron. a.* (*f.* -यी) (Though dual in sense, it is used in the singular and plural only ; according to some grammarians in the dual also) Both (of persons or things). -Comp. —अर्थे *ind.* For both purposes (for earthly prosperity and heavenly happiness also). —चर *a.* Living in water and on land or in the air, amphibious. —चरः *m.* Class of birds who live both on land and in the air. —विद्या *f.* Two-fold sciences ; *i. e.* religious knowledge and knowledge about worldly affairs. -Comp-विध *a.* Of both kinds.-वेतन *a.* Treacherous, perfidious. - व्यंजन *a.* Having the marks of both sexes. —संभवः *m.* Dilemma.

उभयतस् *ind.* 1 From both sides, on both sides, to both sides (with acc). -2 In both cases. -3 In both ways. —दत्,-दंत *a.* Having a double row of teeth. —मुख *a.* 1 Looking either way. -2 Two-faced (as a house &c). —मुखी *f.* A cow.

उभयत्र *ind.* 1 In both places. -2 On both sides. -3 In both cases.

उभयथा *ind.* 1 In both ways. -2 In both cases.

उभयेद्युस् *ind.* 1 On both days.-2 On two subsequent days.

उम् *ind.* An interjection of (1) Anger.(2) Interrogation.(3)Promise or assent. (4) Cordiality or pacification.

उमः *m.* 1 A town. -2 A wharf.

उमा *f.* 1 N. of Párvati. -2 Light, splendour. -3 Fame, reputation. -4 Tranquility, calmness. -5 Night. -6 Turmeric (हरिद्रा). -7 Flax(अतसी). -Comp. —गुरुः, जनकः *m.* N. of the Himâlaya. -पतिः *m.* N. of Siva. -सुतः *m.* N. of Kârtikeya or of Ganesa.

उंब (-म्ब-) रः *m.* The upper timber of a door-frame.

उंबी *f.* The stalks of wheat or barley fried over a fire.

उरः *m.* A sheep.

उरगः (*f.*— गी) 1 A serpent, snake. -2 A Nága or semi-divine serpent usually represented in mythology with a human face. -3 Lead. —गी *f.* A female snake. -Comp. —अरिः, -अशनः,-शत्रुः *m.* 1. N. of Garuda. -2 A pea-cock. -इंद्रः, -राजः *m.* N.of Vasuki or Sesha. -भूषणः *m.* N. of Siva. -सार-चंदनः *m.*, —नं *n.* A kind of sandal-wood. —स्थानं *n.* The abode of the Nâgas; *i. e.* Pâtâla.

उरंगः,-गमः *m.* A snake.

उरच्छदं *n.* An armour.

उरणः *m.* (*f.* —णी) 1 A ram, sheep. -2 A certain demon killed by Indra. —णी *f.* A ewe.

उरणकः *m.* 1 A ram. -2 A cloud.

उरभ्रः *m.* 1 A ram. -2 The plant Cassia Alata (Mar. टाकळा).

उररी *ind.* A particle implying (1) assent, admission or acceptance (In this sense it is usually used with roots कृ, भू, or अस्, and it has the force of a गति or preposition. Hence we have उररीकृत्य not उररीकृत्वा. Other forms of the word are उरी, उररि, ऊरी and ऊररी). (2)Extension.

उररीकृ 8 U. 1 To consent, allow, accept. -2 To include.

उररीकृत *p. p.* 1 Promised, agreed, accepted. -2 Spread, extended.

उरस् *n.* (उरः) *m.* The breast, bosom.

-Comp. —कट:, —कुट: *m.* The sacrificial thread hung round the neck and upon the breast. -गामिन् *a.* Going on the breast(as a reptile),creeping, crawling. -ग्रह:, -घात: *m.* A disease of the chest, pleurisy. —छद: *m.*, —त्राणं *n.* A cuirass, breast-plate. —ज:, -भू:, —उरसिज:, —उरसिरुह: *m.* The female breast. —स्थलं *n.* The breast, bosom.

उरस्य *a.* 1 Being in the breast. -2 Pectoral. -3 Requiring an effort of the chest (as any exertion). -4 Legitimate (a son or daughter) born from a married couple of the same tribe or caste. -5 Excellent. —स्व: *m.* A son.

उरस्वत्, उरसिल *a.* Broad-chested, full-breasted.

उराह: *m* A horse of a pale colour with dark legs.

उरि *ind.* See उररी.

उरीकृ 8 U. 1 To allow, admit, accept.-2 To follow, have recourse to.

उरु *a.* (*f* —रु, -र्वी) Compar. वरीयस्, Super. वरिष्ठ). 1 Wide, spacious. -2 Great, large. -3 Excessive. -4 Excellent, precious, valuable. -Comp. —कीर्ति *a.* Renowned, well-known. —क्रम: *m.* Vishnu in the वामन incarnation. —मार्ग: *m.* A long road. —व्यचस् *m.* A malignant spirit, an imp. —सत्त्व *a.* Of mighty or great strength, powerful; magnanimous, of a noble nature. —हार: *m.* A valuable necklace.

उररी *ind.* See उररि.

उरुबु:, -बुक:,—बूक: *m.* The plant Ricinus Communis (Mar. एरंड).

उरूक: *m.* An owl.

उर्णनाभ: *m.* A spider. See ऊर्णनाभ:

उर्णा *f.* 1 Wool, felt. -2 A circle of hair between the eye brows.

उर्वट: *m.* 1 A calf. -2 A year.

उर्वरा *f.* 1 Fertile soil. -2 Land in general.

उर्वरित *a.* 1 Much, excessive. -2 Remaining after.

उर्वशी *f.* N. of an Apsaras. -Comp. —रमण:, —वल्लभ:, —सहाय: *m.* N. of Pururâvas

उर्वारु: *m.* A kind of cucumber (Mar. काकडी).

उर्वारुकं *n.* The fruit of a kind of cucumber

उर्वी *f.* 1 The earth. -2 Land, soil. -3 The open space or expanse. -Comp. —ईश:, —ईश्वर:, -पति:, -धव: *m.* A king. —धर: *m.* 1 A mountain. -2 The serpent Sesha. —भृत् *m.* 1 A king. -2 A mountain. —रुह: *m.* A tree.

उलप: *m.* 1 A creeping plant, a spreading creeper. -2 Soft grass.

उलुप: *m.* See उलप:.

उलुपिन् *m.* A guinea-pig, porpoise; so उलू (-लू-)-पिन्.

उलूक: *m.* 1 An owl. -2 N. of Indra. —कं *n.* Same as उलप.

उलूखलं *n.* A wooden mortar used for cleansing rice (from the husk &c.).

उलूखलिक *a.* (*f.* —का) Pounded in a mortar.

उलूप: *m.* A large snake, the Boa. (अजगर).

उलूप:, -पिन् *m.* A porpoise.

उलूपी *f* A Nâga princess.

उल्का *f.* 1 A fiery phenomenon in the sky, a meteor. -2 A fire-brand, torch. -3 Fire, flame. -Comp. -धारिन् *a.* A torch-bearer. —पात: *m.* The fall of a meteor. —मुख: *m.* A demon or goblin (having a mouth of fire).

उल्लुषा *f.* 1 A meteor. -2 A fire-brand.

उल्ब, -ल्वं 1 The foetus. -2 The vulva. -3 A cave.

उल्ब (-ल्व-) ण *a.* (*f.* —णा) 1 Thick

copious, abundant (blood &c.). -2 Much, excessive. -3 Strong, great. -4 Manifest, clear. -5 Gaudy, showy. —णं *ind.* Much, heavily (as sighing). -Comp. —रसः *m.* The heroic sentiment.

उल्बण्यं 1 Excess and vitiation of any one of the three humours of the body; *i. e.* phlegm, bile, or wind (त्रिदोष). -2 Any calamity.

उल्मुकः *m.* A firebrand, torch.

उल्लंघ् (उत् + लंघ् 1 A, 10 P.) 1 To leap over, pass over or beyond. -2 To transgress, disregard.

उल्लंघनं *n.* 1 Leaping or passing over. -2 Transgression, violation.

उल्लंघित *a.* (*f.* —ता) 1 Jumped over or across, passed over or beyond. -2 Transgressed, violated.

उल्लल *a.* (*f.* —ला) 1 Shaking, tremulous. -2 Covered with thick hair, shaggy. -3 Affected by many diseases.

उल्ललित *p. p.* 1 Shaken, trembling, agitated, -2 Raised up, elevated.

उल्लस् (उत् + लस् 1 P.) 1 To jump up, sport, play, flutter..-2 To glitter, sparkle; (fig.) to brighten or cheer up. -3 To rise, appear forth. -4 To be reflected. -5 To be expanded. —*Caus.* 1 To cause to jump up or play. -2 To brighten, illuminate, grace. -3 To divert, delight. -4 To shake. move.

उल्लस *a.* 1 Bright, shining. -2 Merry, happy. -3 Going out, issuing.

उल्लसनं *n.* 1 Happiness, joy. -2 Horripilation.

उल्लसित *a.* (*f.* —ता) 1 Shining, brilliant. -2 Happy, delighted. -3 Uplifted, brandishing (as sword). -4 Gleaming, fluttering.

उल्लाघ *a.* (*f.* —घा) 1 Recovered from sickness, convalescent. -2 Dexterous, clever, skilful. -3 Pure. -4 Happy, delighted. -5 Wicked. -6 Black.

उल्लापः *m.* 1 Speech, words. -2 A taunting speech, taunt. -3 Calling out in a loud voice. -4 Change of voice by emotion, sickness &c. -5 A hint, suggestion.

उल्लासः *m.* 1 Joy, delight. -2 Light, splendour. -3 (In Rhet.) A figure of speech in which a reference is made to the merits or demerits of one thing by comparing or contrasting the merits or demerits of another. -4 A division of a book, as the ten Ullâsas of the Kavyaprakâsa. -5 Beginning, commencement.

उल्लासनं *n.* Splendour.

उल्लासित *a.* (*f.* —ता) Delighted, rejoicing.

उल्लिख् (उत् + लिख् 6 P.) 1 To scratch, scrape, to furrow (as ground). -2 To rub against. -3 To grind down; polish (as a precious stone &c.). -4 To carve. -5 To paint, draw in a picture. -6 To bear, raise.

उल्लिखित *p. p.* (*f.* —ता) 1 Scratched, scraped. -2 Thrown up. -3 Written over or above. -4 Pared, made thin.

उल्लिंगित *a.* (*f.* -ता) Famous, known.

उल्लीढ *a.* (*f.* -ढा) Rubbed, polished.

उल्लुंचनं *n.* 1 Plucking out, cutting. -2 Plucking or pulling out the hair.

उल्लुंठनं *n.*, उल्लुंठा *f.* Irony.

उल्लेखः *m.* 1 Allusion, mention. -2 Description, utterance. -3 Boring or digging out. -4 (In Rhetoric). A figure of speech in which there is the description of one under different characters arising from a difference of perceivers, or from difference of the object. बहुभिर्बहुधोल्लेखादे-

कस्योल्लेख इष्यते । क्षीमिः कामोऽर्थिभिः स्वर्द्रुः कालः शत्रुभिरेषि सः * चंद्रालो. -5 Rubbing, scratching.

उल्लेखनं *n.* 1 Rubbing, scratching, digging up. -2 Vomiting. -3 Mention, allusion. -4 Raising up, elevating. -5 Writing, painting. -6 Marking out by lines (the स्थंडिल &c. in a sacrifice).

उल्लोचः *m.* A canopy, an awning.

उल्लोक *a.* (*f.* —का) Violently moving, excessively tremulous. —लः *m.* A large wave or surge

उल्वं See उल्बं. उल्वण See उल्बण.

उशनस् *m.* (Nom. sing. उशना; Voc. sing. उशनन्, उशन, उशनः) N. of Sukra, regent of the planet Venus, son of Bhrigu and preceptor of the Asuras.

उशी *f.* Wish, desire.

उशी (-षी-) रः *m.*, -रं *n.* -उशी (-षी-) रकं *n.* The fragrant root of the plant Andropogon Muricatus (वीरणमूळ, Mar. काळावाळा).

उष् 1 P. (ओषति, उवोष, ओषांचकार, ओषित-उषित-उष्ट). 1 To burn. -2 To punish, chastise. -3 To kill, injure.

उषः *m.* 1 Early morning, dawn, day-break. -2 A libidinous man. -3 Saline earth. -4 Bdellium (Mar. गुग्गूळ).

उषणं *n.* 1 Black pepper.-2 Ginger.

उषपः *m.* 1 Fire. -2 The sun.

उषरः *m.* Saline soil.

उषर्बुधः *m.* Fire.

उषस् *f.* 1 Dawn, morning. -2 Morning light; (personified as the daughter of heaven and sister of the Adityas). -3 The deity that presides over the morning and evening twilights (used in dual उषसौ or उषासौ.)

उषसी *f.* The evening, twilight.

उषा *f.* 1 Early morning, dawn. -2 Morning light. -3 Twilight. -4 Saline earth -5 A cow. -6 Night. -7 A boiler, cooking vessel (स्थाली). -8 N. of a wife of Bhava (who was a manifestation of Rudra). -9 N. of a daughter of the demon Bána and wife of Aniruddha.-*ind.* 1 Early in the morning. -2 At night. -Comp. —कलः *m.* Cock. -पतिः, -रमणः, —ईशः *m.* N. of Aniruddha, husband of Ushâ.

उषित *p.p.* (*f.* —ता) 1 Burnt, consumed. -2 Dwelt, fixed, stale. -3 Quick; expeditious. —तं *n.* Habitation.

उषितंगविन *a.* (*f.* —ना) Once occupied by cows.

उष्ट्रः *m.* 1 A camel. -2 A buffalo. -3 A bull with a hump. -4 A cart or carriage.

उष्ट्रिका *f.* 1 A she-camel. -2 An earthen wine-vessel of the shape of a camel.

उष्ट्री *f.* 1 A she-camel. -2 An earthen vessel in the shape of a camel.

उष्ण *a.* (*f.* —ष्णा) 1 Hot, warm. -2 Sharp, strict, active.-3 Pungent, acrid (as a रस). -4 Clever, sharp. -5 Choleric, warm, passionate. -ष्णः *m.*, —ष्णं *n.* 1 Heat, warmth. -2 The hot season (ग्रीष्म). -3 Sunshine. -4 A deep or feverish sigh. —ष्णः *m.* An onion. —ष्णा *f.* 1 Warmth, heat. -2 Consumption. -3 Bile. -Comp. —अंशुः, —कः, —गुः, —दीधितिः, —रश्मिः, —रुचिः *m.* The sun. —अभिगमः, —आगमः, —उपगमः *m.* Approach of heat, hot season. —कालः, —गः *m*, The hot season. —नदी *f.* The hot river, वैतरणी or the river of hell. —बाष्पः *m.* 1 Tears. -2 Hot vapour. —वारणः *m.*, —णं *n.* An umbrella, parasol.

उष्णक *a.* (*f.* —का) 1 Sharp, smart, active. -2 Sick with fever. -3 Warming, heating. -4 Bent, stooping. —कः m. 1 Fever. -2 The hot season, summer. -3 Revolving, turning round.

उष्णता f., -त्वं n. Heat, warmth.

उष्णालु a Not being able to bear heat, scorched by heat.

उष्णिका f. Rice-gruel.

उष्णीषः, -षं n. 1 Anything wound round the head. -2 Hence, a turban, diadem, crownet -3 A distinguishing mark. -4 A characteristic mark (of hair) on the head of a Buddha. [N. of Siva.

उष्णीषिन् a Wearing a diadem. m.

उष्मः, उष्मकः m. 1 Heat. -2 The hot season, summer. -3 Spring. -4 Anger, warmth of temper. -5 Ardour, eagerness, zeal. -Comp. —आगमः, —उपगमः m. The hot season. —पः m. 1 The son of Bhrigu. -2 The Manes, a deseased ancestor. —भास् m. The sun. —स्वेदः m. A vapour bath.

उष्मन् m. 1 Heat, warmth. -2 Steam, vapour. -3 The hot season. -4 Ardour, eagerness. -5 The letters श, ष, स, and ह (in gram.).

उष्मायणः m. The hot season.

उस्रः m 1 A ray (of light), beam. -2 A bull. -3 A god. -4 The two Asvini kumâras. —स्रा f. 1 Morning, dawn. -2 Light, bright sky. -3 A cow. -4 The earth. -Comp. —धन्वन् —m. N. of Indra.

उस्रिकः m. 1 A small ox. -2 An old ox. —का f. A cow.

उस्रियः m. An ox. —या f. 1 A cow. -2 Brightness, light. -3 A calf. -4 Milk.

उह् 1 P. (ओहति, उवोह, ओहित) 1 To hurt or give pain. -2 To kill, destroy. [calling.

उह, उहह ind. An interjection of

उहः m. A bull.

ऊ.

ऊ ind. 1 A particle used to introduce a sentence. -2 An interjection of calling, of compassion, of protection.

ऊढ a. (f. —ढा) 1 Carried as a load or burden. -2 Taken. -3 Married. —ढः m. A married man. -Comp. —कंकट a. Armed, mailed. —भार्य a. One who has married a wife. -वयस् m. A young man. ऊढा f. A girl who is married.

ऊतिः f. 1 Weaving, sewing. -2 Protection. -3 Enjoyment. -4 Sport, play. -5 Favour, kindness. -6 Aid, help. -7 The money given to a tailor for sewing. -8 Wish.

ऊधस् m. An udder (changed to ऊधन् in Bah. Comp.) -1 A covered secret place. -2 The bosom. -3 The breast of a mother.

ऊधन्यं, ऊधस्यं n. Milk.

ऊन a. (f. —ना) 1 Wanting, deficient, defective; incomplete. -2 Less than (in number, size or degree). -3 Fewer, smaller. -4 Weaker, inferior. -5 Minus (with *instr. e. g.* माषेणोनं.)

ऊनक a. Inferior, less.

ऊम् ind. An interjection of interrogation; anger; reproach; abuse; pride; envy.

ऊय् 1 A. To weave, sew.

ऊररी ind. See उररी.

ऊरव्यः m. A Vaisya.

ऊरी ind. See उररी.

ऊरुः m. 1 The thigh.-Comp. -उद्भव, —ज, —जन्मन्, —संभव a. Sprung from the thigh, a Vaisya. —दघ्न, -द्वयस, —मात्र a. As high as or reaching the thighs, knee-deep. —पर्वन् m., n.

The knee.—फलकं *n.* The thigh-bone, hip-bone. –स्तंभा *f.* The plantain tree.

ऊवरी *ind.* Same as ऊररी q. v.

ऊर्ज् *f.* 1 Strength, vigour. -2 Sap, juice. -3 Water. -4 Food

ऊर्जः *m.* 1 N. of the month Kártika. -2 Energy.-3 Power, strength. -4 Procreative power. -5 Life, breath. —र्जा *f.* 1 Food. -2 Strength. —र्जं *n.* 1 Water. -2 Strength.

ऊर्जस् *n.* 1 Vigour, energy.-2Food.

ऊर्जस्वत् *a.* 1 Rich in food; succulent. -2 Powerful, vigorous.

ऊर्जस्वल *a.* (*f.* —ला) Powerful, strong, mighty. -2 Excellent, preeminent.

ऊर्जस्विन् *a.* (*f.* —नी) Mighty, strong. –नी *f.*, or ऊर्जस्वि *n.* The figure of speech in which रसाभास and भावाभास become subordinate to something else.

ऊर्जित *a.* (*f.* —ता) 1 Powerful, strong, mighty. -2 Great, large, much. -3 Glorious, superior; excellent, beautiful. -4 High, noble. -5 Increased; deep, grave. —तं *n.* 1 Strength. -2 Energy.

ऊर्णं *n.* 1 Wool. -2 A woolen cloth. -Comp. —नाभः, —पटः, —वाभिः *m.* A spider.

ऊर्णा *f.* 1 Wool. -2 A circle of hair between the eyebrows. -Comp.–पिंडः *m.* A ball of wool. —मल, —वत् *a.* Woollen.

ऊर्णायु *a.* Woollen. –युः *m.* 1 A ram. -2 Spider. -3 A woollen blanket.

ऊर्णु 2 U. 1 To cover, surround, hide. -2 To cover oneself.

ऊर्दरं *n.* A vessel for measuring corn (such as a bushel). —रः *m.* 1 A hero. -2 A Ràkshasa or goblin.

ऊर्ध्व *a.* (*f.* —र्ध्वा) 1 Erect, upright, rising upwards. -2 Raised, elevated, erected. -3 High, superior. -4 Not sitting (opp. आसीन). -5 Torn (as hair) . -र्ध्वं *n.* Elevation, height. —र्ध्वं *ind.* 1 Upwards, above. -2 In the sequel. -3 In a high tone, aloud. -4 Afterwards, subsequent to (with abl.) अत ऊर्ध्वं Henceforward, hereafter. -Comp. -कचः, -केशः *m.* N. of Ketu. —कर्मन् *n.*, -क्रिया *f.* 1 Motion upwards. -2 An action for attaining a high place. —कायः *m.*, —यं *n.* The upper part of the body. —गतिः *f.*, —गमः *m.* —गमनं *n.* 1 Ascent; elevation. -2 Going to heaven. -3 Going above. (as life). —चरणः *m.* A fabulous animal called Sarabha. —जानु, —ज्ञ, —ज्ञु *a.* 1 Raising the knees, sitting on the hams. -2 Long-shanked. —दंष्ट्र (-ष्ट्रा-) केशः *m.* N. of Siva. -दृष्टि, —नेत्र *a.* 1 Looking upwards.-2. (fig.) Aspiring, ambitious. -दृष्टिः *f.* Concentrating the sight on the spot between the eyebrows (in Yoga phil). —देवः *m.* A superior deity *i. e.* Vishnu. —देहः *m.* The funeral ceremony. —पातनं *n.* Causing to ascend, sublimation (as of mercury.). —पुंड्रः, —पुंड्रकः *m.* A perpendicular sign of sandal on the forehead of a Brâhmana. —पूर्णं *ind.* Full to the brim, full to overflowing.—भागः *m.* 1 The upper part. -2 Any part of a word coming after another part. -मंथिन् *a.* Living in perpetual chastity. a Brahmachárin. —मुख *a.* Directed upwards. —मुखं *n.* The upper part of the mouth. —मौहूर्तिक *a.* Happening after a short time. —रेतस् *a.* One who lives in perpetual celibacy. —रेतस् *m.* 1. N. of Siva. -2 Bhíshma. -लिंगः *m.* N. of Siva. —लोकः *m.* Heaven. —वर्त्मन् *m.* The atmosphere. —शायिन् *a.* Sleeping with the face upwards (as a child). *m.* N. of Siva. —शोधनं *n.* Vomiting. —श्वासः

m. Expiration. —स्थिति: *f.* 1 The rearing of a horse. -2 A horse's back. -3 Elevation, superiority.

ऊर्ध्वक: *m.* A kind of drum.

ऊर्ध्वम् *ind.* 1 Upwards. -2 In the sequel. -3 Aloud. -4 Afterwards (with *abl.*).

ऊर्मि: *m. f.* 1 A wave, billow. -2 Current, flow. -3 Light. -4 Speed. -5 A fold in a garment. -6 A row, line. -7 A human infirmity. -8 Distress, uneasiness. -9 The course of a horse. -10 Missing, regretting. -11 A number, quantity. -Comp. —मालिन् *m.* The ocean.

ऊर्मिका *f.* 1 Wave. -2 A finger-ring.

ऊर्मिमत् *a.* 1 Wavy. -2 Crooked. -3 Plaited, curled (as hair).

ऊर्मिका *f.* 1 A wave. -2 A finger-ring. (shining like a wave). -3 Regret, sorrow for anything lost. -4 The humming of a bee. -5 A plait or fold in a garment.

ऊर्म्य *a.* Wavy, undulating. —र्म्या [*f.* Night.

ऊर्व: *m.* 1 Submarine fire. -2 A receptacle of water. -3 A cloud. -4 A stable for cattle. -5 An epithet of a class of the Manes or 'Pitṛs'

ऊर्वरा *f.* Fertile soil.

ऊलुपिन् *m.* A porpoise.

ऊलूक: *m.* An owl.

ऊष् 1 P. (*p. p.* ऊषित) To be diseased or disordered; be ill.

ऊष: *m.* 1 Salt ground. -2 An acid. -3 A cleft, fissure. -4 The cavity of the ear. -5 The Malaya mountain. -6 Dawn, daybreak. -7 Semen. —षा *f.* Saline earth.

ऊषकं *n.* 1 Dawn, day-break. -2 Salt. -3 Pepper.

ऊषणं *n.*, —णा *f.* 1 Black pepper. -2 [Ginger.

ऊषर *a.* (*f.* —रा) Impregnated with salt. —र: *m.*, —रं *n.* A barren spot with saline soil.

ऊषवत् *a.* See ऊषर.

ऊषा *f.* = उषा q. v.

ऊष्म *a.* Hot. —ष्म: *m.* 1 Heat. -2 [Summer.

ऊष्मन् *m.* 1 Heat, warmth. -2 The hot season, summer. -3 Steam, vapour. -4 Passion, violence. -5 (In gram.) The sounds श, ष, स, and ह. -Comp. —उपगम: *m.* The approach of summer. —प: *m.* 1 Fire. -2 A class of Manes (pl.).

ऊह् 1 U. (ऊहति-ते, ऊहांचकार-चक्रे, ऊहितुं, ऊहित) 1 To mark, observe. -2 To conjecture, infer. -3 To conceive, expect. -4 To deliberate about. -5 To reckon upon (with loc.). -6 To be regarded as.

ऊह् 1 P. 1 To change. -2 To push, remove. With अप— 1 To remove. -2 To follow immediately. अपवि— To ward off. अभि— 1 To guess. -2 To cover. उप— To bring near or down. निर्वि— To bring about, to achieve. परिसं— To sprinkle about. प्रति— 1 To deny. -2 To interrupt. प्रतिवि— To arrange an army against. वि— To arrange an army. सम्— To assemble.

ऊह: *m.* 1 A change. -2 A conjecture. -3 Examination and determination. -4 Understanding. -5 Reasoning, arguing. -6 Supplying an ellipsis. -7 Attributing, ascribing. -8 Collection. -Comp. —अपोह: *m.* Full discussion, consideration of the *pros* and *cons*.

ऊहनं *n.* Inferring, guessing.

ऊहनी *f.* A broom.

ऊहा *f.* Supplying an ellipsis.

ऊहिनी *f.* 1 An assemblage. -2 Arrangement, a multitude reduced to order.

ऊह्य *a.* (*f.* —ह्या) 1 Inferable, to be investigated. -2 To be supplied; elliptical.

ऋ.

ऋ *ind.* An interjection of (1) calling; (2) ridicule; (3) censure or abuse; (4) used at the beginning of a sentence.

ऋ 1 P. (ऋच्छति, आर, आर्षीत्, अरिष्यति, ऋत; *caus.* अर्पयति, *desid.* अरिरिषति). 1 To go, move. -2 To rise, tend towards.

ऋ 3 P. (इयर्ति, आरत्, ऋत) 1 To go. -2 To move, shake. -3 To obtain, reach, meet with. -4 To excite, rise (as voice, words &c.). -5 To display.

ऋ 5 P. (ऋणोति, ऋण) 1 To injure. -2 To attack. (—*Caus.* अर्पयति, आर्पिपत्, अर्पित). 1 To throw, fix or implant in. -2 To put on, fix upon, direct towards (as the eye &c.). -3 To insert, set or place. -4 To give in charge of, consign, deliver. -5 To give up the inherent sense. -6 To restore. -7 To penetrate.

ऋक्थं *n.* 1 Wealth. -2 Property, possessions, effects (left at death). -3 Gold. -Comp. —आदान: *m.* An inheritor, heir. —ग्रहणं *n.* Receiving or inheriting property. —ग्राह: *m.* An inheritor or receiver of property. —भाग: *m.* 1 Division of property, partition. -2 A share, inheritance. —भागिन्, —हर, -हारिन् *m.* 1 An heir. -2 A co-heir.

ऋक्ष: *m.* 1 A bear. -2 N. of a mountain. —क्ष: *m.*, —क्षं *n.* 1 A star, constellation, lunar mansion. -2 A sign of the zodiac. -3 A star under which a man happens to be born. —क्षा: (*m.* pl.) 1 The seven stars called Pleiades. -2 The seven Rishis. —ऋक्षा *f.* The north. -क्षी *f.* A female bear. -Comp. —चक्रं *n.* The circle of stars. —नाथ:, —ईश: *m.* The moon. —नेमि: *m.* N. of Vishnu. —राज्, -ज: *m.* 1 The moon. -2 Jàmbuvat, the king of bears.

ऋक्षर: *m.* 1 A priest. -2 A thorn. —रा, *f.*, —रं *n.* Shower of rain, steam.

ऋच् 6 P. (ऋचति, आनर्च, आर्चीत्, अर्चितुं). 1 To praise, celebrate. -2 To cover, screen. -3 To shine.

ऋच् *f.* 1 A hymn (in general). -2 A single verse, a verse of the Rigveda. -3 The collective body of the Rigveda (pl.). -4 Splendour. -5 Praise. -6 Worship. -Comp. -विधानं *n.* The performance of certain rites by reciting verses of the Rig-veda. -वेद: *m.* The oldest of the four Vedas, and the most ancient sacred book of the Hindus. —संहिता *f.* The arranged collection of the hymns of Rigveda.

ऋचीष: *m.* A hell. -षं *n.* A frying-pan

ऋच्छ् 6 P. (ऋच्छति, आर्च्छीत्, आनर्च्छ, अर्च्छितुं) 1 To become hard or stiff. -2 To go, move. -3 To fail in faculties.

ऋच्छका *f.* Wish, desire.

ऋज् 1 A. (अर्जते, आर्जिष्ट, अर्जितुं, आनृजे). 1 To go. -2 To obtain. -3 To be firm. -4 To be healthy or strong.

ऋञ्ज् 1 P. To acquire, earn

ऋजीषं *n.* 1 A frying-pan. -2 A hell. -3 The residue of Soma.

ऋजु *a.* (*f.* -जु or -ज्वी) (compar. ऋजीयस्, superl. ऋजिष्ठ) 1 Straight (fig. also). -2 Upright, honest. -3 Simple-minded, plain. -4 Favourable, beneficial -Comp. —ग: *m.* 1 One who is honest in his dealings. -2 An arrow. —रोहितं *n.* The straight red bow of Indra.

ऋजुक: *m.* A simpleton.

ऋजुता *f.*, —त्वं *n.* Straight direction, straightness, honesty, sincerity.

ऋज्वी *f.* 1 A straight-forward or plain woman. -2 A particular gait (of the planets).

ऋणं *n.* 1 Debt. -2 An obligation in general. -3 (In alg.) The negative sign or quantity, minus, (opp. धन). -4 A fort, strong-hold. -5 Water. -6 Land. -Comp. —अंतकः *m.* The planet Mars. —अपनयनं, -अपनोदनं, -अपाकरणं, -दानं *n.*,-मुक्तिः *f.*,-मोक्षः *m.* -शोधनं *n.* Paying off debt, discharge or liquidation of debt. —आदानं *n.* Recovery of a debt. —ग्रहः *m.* 1 Borrowing (money). -2 A borrower. —ग्राहिन् *m.* A debtor, borrower. —दातृ, -दायिन् *a.* One who pays a debt. —दासः *m* One who is bought as a slave by paying off his debts. —मत्कुणः, -मार्गणः *m.* A security, bail. —मुक्तः *m.* One released from debt. —मुक्तिः *f.* Discharge from debt. -लेख्यं *n.* 'A debt-bond,' a bond acknowledging a debt (in law; Mar. कर्जरोखा). —शोधनं *n.* Payment or discharge of a debt.

ऋणिकः *m.* A debtor.

ऋणिन् *a.* A debtor, one indebted to another (on any account).

ऋत *a.* (*f.* —ता) 1 Proper, right. -2 Honest, true. -3 Worshipped. -4 Bright. -5 Moved, affected by. —तं *ind.* Rightly, properly. —तं *n.* 1 A fixed or settled rule, law (religious). -2 Sacred custom, pious action. -3 Divine law, divine truth.-4 Absolution. -5 Water. -6 Truth (in general), right. -7 Truth.-8 Livelihood by picking or gleaning grains in a field. -Comp. —धामन् *m.* An epithet of Vishnu.

ऋतम् *ind.* Truly.

ऋतंभरः *m.* God, upholder of truth.

ऋतिः *m.* An army. —*f.* 1 Going. -2 Assault. -3 Abuse, censure. -4 Emulation, envy. -5 Prosperity. -6 Misfortune. -7 Protection.

ऋतीया *f.* 1 Censure, reproach. -2 Shame.

ऋतुः *m.* 1 A season, period of the year. commonly reckoned to be six. -2 An epoch, a period. -3 Menstruation, menstrual discharge. -4 A period favourable for conception. -5 Any fit season or right time. -6 Fixed order or rule. -7 Light, splendour. -8 A month. -9 N. of Vishnu. -10 The number 'six.' -Comp. —कालः, —समयः *m* , -वेला *f.* 1 The time of menstruation, time favourable for conception *i. e.* 16 nights from menstrual discharge. -2 The duration of a season. -गामिन् *a.* Having intercourse with a wife at the time fit for conception, *i. e.* after the period of menstruation. —धामन् *m.* N. of Vishnu. —पर्णः *m.* N. of a king of Ayodhyâ ; son of Ayutâyu, a descendant. of Ikshvâku. —पर्यायः *m.*, —वृत्तिः *f.* The revolution of the seasons. —मुखं *n.* The beginning or first day of a season. —राजः *m.* The spring. —लिंगं *n.* 1 A characteristic or sign of the season. -2 A symptom of menstruation. —स्नाता *f.* A woman who has bathed after menstruation. —स्नानं *n.* Bathing after menstruation.

ऋतुमती *f.* A woman during her courses.

ऋते *ind.* Except, without, with the exception of (usually with abl. sometimes acc. rarely instr.)

ऋतेन *ind.* Duly, rightly, truly, honestly, justly.

ऋत्विज् *m.* A priest who officiates at a sacrifice

ऋद्ध *a.* (*f.* —द्धा) 1 Prosperous, thriving, rich, splendidly furnished.

-2 Increased. -3 Stored (as grain). —द्धः *m.* N. of Vishnu. —द्धं *n.* 1 Increase, growth. -2 A demonstrated conclusion ; distinct result.

ऋद्धिः *f.* 1 Growth, increase. -2 Success, prosperity; good fortune. -3 Elevation, exaltation. -4 Extent, excellence, magnificence. -5 Supernatural power. -6 Accomplishment. -7 Prosperity personified as the wife of Kubera.

ऋध् 4, 5, P. 1 To prosper. -2 To please. With सम्— To prosper.

ऋभुः *m.* 1 A deity, divinity.

ऋभुक्षः *m.* 1 N. of Indra. -2 Heaven.

ऋभुक्षिन् *m.* (Nom.S. ऋभुक्षाः, acc. pl. ऋभुक्षः) 1 N. of Indra. -2 N. of the Maruts.

ऋल्लकः *m.* A player on a kind of musical instrument.

ऋल्लरी *f.* A kind of musical instrument.

ऋश्यः *m.* A white-footed antelope. -Comp. -केतुः, -केतनः *m.* 1 N. of Aniruddha, son of Pradyumna. -2 N. of the God of love.

ऋष् 1, 6, P. (ऋषति, आर्षीत्, आनर्ष, अर्षितुं, ऋष्ट) 1 To go, approach. -2 To injure. -3 To push.

ऋषभः *m.* 1 A bull. -2 The best or most excellent (as the last member of a comp.); पुरुषर्षभः, भरतर्षभः &c. -3 The second of the seven notes of the gamut. -4 A crocodile's tail. —भी *f.* 1 A woman with masculine features (as a beard &c) -2 A cow. -3 A widow. -Comp. —कूटः *m.* N. of a mountain. -ध्वजः *m.* N of Siva.

ऋषभतरः *m.* A small or young bull.

ऋषिः *m.* 1 An inspired poet or sage, a singer of sacred hymns. -2 A saint, an ascetic, an anchorite. -3 A ray of light. -4 An imaginary circle. -Comp. —कुल्या. *f.* A sacred river. —तर्पणं *n.* A libation offered to the Rishis. —पंचमी *f.* N. of a ceremony on the fifth day in the first half of Bhâdrapada. —लोकः *m.* The world of the Rishis. —स्तोमः *m.* 1 Praise of the Rishis. -2 A particular sacrifice completed in one day.

ऋष्टिः *m., f.* 1 A double-edged sword. -2 A sword (in general). -3 Any weapon.

ऋष्यः *m.* 1 A white-footed antelope. —ष्यं *n.* A kind of leprosy. -Comp. -अंकः, -केतनः, -केतुः *m.* N. of Aniruddha. —जिह्वं *n.* A kind of leprosy. —मूकः *m.* A mountain near the lake Pampâ which formed the temporary abode of Râma with the monkey-chief Sugrîva. —शृंगः *m.* N. of a sage.

ऋष्यकः *m.* A painted or white-footed antelope.

ॠ.

ॠ *ind.* An interjection of (1) terror ; (2) warding off ; (3) reproach or censure ; (4) compassion ; (5) remembrance.

ॠ 9 P. (*p. p.* ईर्ण) To go, to move.

ए.

ए *ind.* An interjection of (1) remembering; (2) envy; (3) compassion ; (4) calling ; (5) contempt or censure.

ए (आ + इ 2 P.). To come, approach.

एक *pron. a.* (*f.* -का) 1 One, single. -2 The same, identical. -3 Firm, unchanged -4 Single of its kind, unique, singular. -5 Chief, supreme, prominent, sole. -6 Peerless, matchless. -7 One of two or many. -8 A, an, a certain, (used like the English indefinite article) -9 True एकः -अन्यः or अपरः *m.* The one the other; it is used in the plural in the sense of some, its correlative being अन्ये or अपरे (others). -Comp. —अक्ष *a.* 1 Having one eye. -2 Having an excellent eye. —अक्षः *m.* 1 A crow. -2 N. of Siva. —अग्र *a.* 1 Closely attentive, concentrated, intent. -2 Unperplexed. -2 Single-pointed. —अंगः *m.* 1 A body-guard. -2 The planet Mercury or Mars. —अनुदिष्टं *n.* A funeral ceremony performed for only one ancestor (recently dead). —अंत *a.* 1 Solitary. -2 Exclusive. -3 Great, excessive. -4 Absolute. -5 Perpetual. -6 Worshipping only one God. —अंतः *m.* 1 A lonely or retired place, solitude. -2 Exclusiveness. -3 An invariable rule or course of conduct or action. -4 Exclusive aim or boundary. —अंतं *n.* An exclusive recourse, a settled rule or principle. —एकांतं, -तेन, —ततः, *m.* -ते *ind.* 1 Solely, invariably, always, absolutely. -2 Quite, wholly, very much. -3 Privately. —अंतर *a.* Next but one, separated by one remove. —अंतिक *a.* Final, conclusive. —अयन *a.* 1 Passable for only one (as a foot-path). -2 Closely attentive, intent. —अयनं *n.* 1 A lonely or retired place. -2 A meeting-place, rendezvous. -3 Monotheism. -4 The sole object. —अर्थ *a.* 1 Having one and the same meaning, having the same object in view. —अर्थः *m.* 1 The same thing object or intention. -2 The same meaning -अहन् (-हः) *m.* 1 The period of one day. -2 A sacrifice lasting for one day. —आतपत्र *a.* Characterized by only one umbrella (showing universal sovereignty). —आदेशः *m.* One substitute for two or more letters (got by either dropping one vowel, or by the blending of both); as in the case of the word मुरारि. —आवलिः, -ली *f.* 1 A single string of pearls, beads &c. -2 (in Rhetoric) The figure of speech in which each succeeding thing is affirmed or denied as an attribute of each preceeding thing. पूर्वं पूर्वं प्रति विशेषणत्वेन परं परं। स्थाप्यतेऽपोह्यते वा चेत्स्यात्तदेकावली द्विधा ॥ साहि. द. *e. g.* सरो विकसिताम्भोजमंभोजं भृंगसंगतं। भृंगा यत्र ससंगीताः संगीतं सस्मरोदयं ॥ —उदकः *m.* One participating by reason of blood-relationship in one and the same offering of water. A relation. —उदर्यः *m.*, -र्या *f.* Uterine, (brother or sister). —उद्दिष्टं *n.* A Srâddha or funeral rite performed for one definite individual deceased, not including other ancestors. —एक *a.* One by one, one taken singly, a single one. —एकशः *ind.* One by one, singly, severally. —ओघः *m.* A continuous current. —कार्य *a.* 1 A co-worker. -2 Answering the same end. -3 Having the same occupation. —कार्यं *n.* Sole or same business. —कालः *m.* 1 One time. -2 The same time. (-लं, -ले) *ind.* At one time, at one and the same time. —कालिक, —कालीन *a.* 1 Happening once only. -2 Contemporary, coeval. —कुंडलः *m.* N. of Kubera; of Balabhadra; and Sesha. —गम्यः *m.* The Supreme Spirit. —गुरु, —गुरुक *a.* Having the same preceptor. —चक्र *a.* 1 Having only one wheel. -2 Governed by one king only. —चक्रः *m.* The chariot of the sun. —चर *a.* 1

Wandering or living alone; alone -2 Having one attendant. -3 Living unassisted. —चरः *m.* A rhinoceros. —चारिणी *f.* A loyal wife. —चित्तं *n.* 1 Fixedness of thought upon one object. -2 Unanimity. —चेतस्, —मनस् *a.* Unanimous. —जः *m.*, —जा *f.* A brother or sister of the same parents. —जन्मन् *m.* 1 A king. -2 A Sudra. —जात *a.* Born of the same parents.-जाति *m.,f.* A Sudra. —जातीय *a.* Of the same kind or family —ज्योतिस् *m.* N. of Siva. -तान *a.* Concentrated or fixed on one object only, closely attentive. -तालः *m.* Harmony, accurate adjustment of song, dance, instrumental music. —तीर्थिन् *a.* 1 Bathing in the same holy water.-2Belonging to the same religious order. (-*m.*) A fellow-student, spiritual brother. —दंष्ट्रः, —दंतः *m.* Epithets of Ganesa. -दंडिन् *m.* N. of a class of Sannyásins or beggars (otherwise called हंस). -दृश्, दृष्टि *a.* One-eyed. (-*m.*) 1 A crow. -2 N. of Siva. -3 A philosopher. —देशः *m.* 1 One spot or place. एकदेशविभावितन्यायः *m.* An inference as to the whole when proof is given of a part. -2 A part or portion (of the whole); one side. —धर्मन्, —धर्मिन् *a.* 1 Possessing the same properties, of the same kind. -2 Professing the same religion. —धुर, —धुरावह, —धुरीण *a.* 1 Fit for but one kind of labour. -2 Fit for but one yoke (as cattle) for special burden. —नटः *m.* 1 The principal actor in a drama, the manager (सूत्रधार) who recites the prologue.—निष्ठ *a.* 1 Intently devoted or loyal (to one thing). -2 Intently fixed on one object. —पक्ष *a.* 1 Of the same side or party, an associate. -2 Partial. —पातिक *a.* Having the same husband. —पत्नी *f.* 1 A faithful wife (one perfectly chaste). -2 The wife of a man who has no other wives. -3 A co-wife. —पत्नीव्रतं *n.* The vow of perfect chastity. —पदी *f.* A foot-path. —पदे *ind.* Suddenly, all at once, abruptly. —पादः *m.* N. of Vishnu and Siva. -पादिका *f.* A kind of posture of birds. —पिंगः,-पिंगलः *m.*N of Kubera,having a yellow mark in place of one eye. —पिंड *a.* United by the offering of the funeral rice-ball. -पुत्र *a.* Having only one son. -पुरुषः *m.* 1 The Supreme Spirit (that alone truly exists). —भार्या *f.* A faithful or chaste wife. भार्यः *m.* One having one wife only. —मति *a.* 1 Fixed on one object. -2 Unanimous, thinking in the same way. -मुख *a.* Having the same aim. -3 Having one chief or head.—यष्टिः, —यष्टिका *f.* A single string of pearls. —योनि *a.* 1 Uterine. -2 Of the same family or caste. —रस *a.* 1 Finding pleasure only in one thing. -2 Of one flavour. -3 Of one feeling or sentiment only. -4 Of one tenor, stable, equable. -5 Solely or exclusively devoted (to one). —राज्, —राजः *m.* An absolute king. —रात्रं *n.* One night. —रिक्थिन् *m.* A co-heir. —रूप *a.* 1 Of one form or kind, similar. -2 Uniform, one-coloured. —लिंगः *m.* 1 A word having one gender only. -2 N. of Kubera.-वचनं *n.* The singular number. —वर्षिका *f.* A heifer one year old. —वाक्यं *n.* One or unanimous opinion. —वाक्यता *f.* Consistency in meaning, unanimity, reconciling different statements. —वारं, —वारे *ind.* 1 Only once. -2 At once, suddenly. -3 At one time. —विध *a.* Of one kind; simple. -विलोचनः *m.* 1 Kubera. -2 A crow. —विष-

पिन् *m.* A rival. —वीरः *m.* A pre-eminent warrior or hero. —वेणिः, —णी *f.* A single braid of hair (worn by a woman as a mark of her separation from her husband &c.). —शफः *m.* An animal whose hoof is not cloven (as a horse, ass &c.). —शाखः *m.* A Bráhmana of the same branch or school. —शृङ्गः *m.* 1 A unicorn; rhinoceros. -2 N. of Vishnu. —शेषः *m.* A species of Dvandva compound in which one of two or more words only is retained; *e. g.* पितरौ father and mother, parents, (=मातापितरौ); so श्वशुरौ, भ्रातरः &c. -श्रुतधरः *m.* One that keeps in mind what one has heard once. —सर्ग *a.* Closely attentive. -सर्गः *m.* Concentration. —साक्षिक *a.* Witnessed by one. -हायन *a.* One year old. —हायनी *f.* A heifer one year old.

एकक *a.* (*f.* —का) 1 Single, alone, solitary, without a co-adjutor. -2 Same, identical.

एकतमः *m.* 1 One of many. -2 One (used as an indefinete article).

एकतरः *m.* 1 One of two, either. -2 Other, different.

एकतस् *ind.* 1 From one side, on one side. -2 Singly, one by one. एकतः - अन्यतः *ind.* On one side, on the other side.

एकता *f.*, -त्वं *n.* Oneness, union, identity.

एकत्र *ind.* 1 In one place. -2 Together, all taken together. एकत्र-अपरत्र or -एकत्र *ind.* On one side, on the other, here,-there.

एकदा *ind.* 1 Once, once upon a time, at one time. -2 At the same time.

एकधा *ind.* 1 In one way. -2 Singly. -3 At once. -4 Together. -5 Once, sometimes.

एकल *a.* (*f.* —ला) Alone, solitary.

एकशस् *ind.* One by one, singly.

एकाकिन् *a.* (*f.* —नी) Alone, solitary.

एकादश *a.* (*f.* —शी) 1 Eleventh. -2 Consisting of eleven.

एकादशन् *num. a.* Eleven.

एकीकृ 8 U. 1 To collect. -2 To unite, join together, combine.

एकीभावः *m* 1 Combination. -2 Common property.

एकीभू 1 P. 1 To become one, combine.

एकीय *a.* (*f.* —या) Belonging to, or proceeding from, one —यः A partisan, an associate.

एज् 1 A. (epic, P.) 1 To tremble, shake. -2 To move stir. With अप- To drive away. उद्- To rise, go upwards.

एज् 1 P. To shine.

एजनं *n.* Trembling, shaking.

एठ् 1 A. To annoy, resist.

एड *a.* (*f.* —डा) Deaf. —डः *m.* A kind of sheep. -Comp. —मूक *a.* 1 Deaf and dumb. -2 Wicked, perverse.

एडकः *m.* 1 A ram. -2 A wild goat. —का *f.* A ewe.

एणः *m.* 1 A kind of black antelope. -2 (In astr.) Capricorn. -Comp. —आजिनं *n.* Deer-skin. -तिलकः, —भृत्, *m.* The moon. —दृश् *a.* One having eyes like those of a deer.

एणी *f.* A female black deer.

एत *a.* (*f.* एता, एनी) 1 Of a variegated colour. -2 Come, arrived. -तः *m.* 1 A deer or antelope. -2 The hide of a deer. -3 Variegated colour.

एतद् *pron. a.* (*m.* एषः, *f* एषा, *n.* एतद्) 1 This, this here, yonder (referring to what is the nearest to the speaker; the Nom. forms are used like those of इदं in the sense of 'here'; एष पृच्छामि, एष कथयामि &c. एतद् is sometimes used to give emphasis to the personal pronouns); एषोऽहं कार्यवशादायोध्यिकस्तदानींतनश्च संवृत्तः. It often refers to what precedes when it is associated with another pronoun; *e. g.* इति यदुक्तं तदेतच्चिन्त्यं. -2 It is used in connection with a relative clause. —*ind.* In this manner, thus, so, here, at this time, now.

एतदीय *a.* (*f.* —या) Belonging to this.

एतन: *m.* Breath, expiration

एतर्हि *ind.* 1 Now, at this time, now-a-days. -2 Then (correlative to यर्हि).

एतादृश्, -दृश, -दृक्ष (*f.*-शी, -क्षी) *a.* Such, such like, of this kind, similar to this.

एतावत् *a.* (*f.* —ती) So much, so great, so many, of such extent. —*ind.* So far, so much, in such a degree, thus.

एध् 1 A. 1 To grow, increase. -2 To prosper. -3 To grow strong. -4 To extend.

एधः *m.* Fuel.

एधतुः *m.* 1 Fire. -2 Man.

एधस् *n.* 1 Fuel. -2 Prosperity.

एधा *f.* Prosperity, happiness.

एनस् *n.* 1 Sin, offence, fault. -2 Mischief, crime. -3 Unhappiness. -4 Censure, blame.

एनस्वत्, एनस्विन् *a.* (*f.* —ती, —नी) Wicked, sinful.

एरंडः *m.* The castor-oil plant.

एरंडकः *m.* See एरंडः.

एलकः *m.* A ram. See एडकः.

एलवालु *n.*, एलवालुकं *n.* 1 A kind of perfume. -2 A kind of cucumber.

एलविलः *m.* N. of Kubera.

एला *f.* 1 Cardamom plant. -2 Cardamoms (the seed of the plant).

एलीका *f.* Small cardamoms.

एव 1 *ind.* Just, quite, exactly, just so. -2 Same, very, identical. -3 only, alone, merely, like. -4 Generally to emphasize a statement.

एवम् *ind.* 1 Thus, so, in this manner. एवं has sometimes an adjectival force ; एवं वचनं such words. -2 Yes, quite so (implying assent). -Comp. —अवस्थ *a.* So situated or circumstanced. —आदि, —आद्य *a.* Of such qualities or kind, such and the like. —कारं *ind.* In this manner. —गत *a.* Being in this condition or so circumstanced. एवं गते. Under these circumstances. —गुण *a.* Possessing such qualities. -प्रकार, -प्राय *a.* Of such a kind. —रूप *a.* Of such a kind or form. —विध *a.* Of this kind, such.

एष् 1 U. 1 To go or approach. -2 To attack any one. With परि — To seek.

एषणः *m.* An iron arrow. —णं *n.* 1 Seeking. -2 Wish, desire. —णा *f.* 1 Seeking ; wish, desire. -2 Begging, request. -णी *f.* 1 A goldsmith's balance. -2 A probe (of iron or steel).

एषणिका *f.* A goldsmith's balance.

एषा *f.* Wish, desire.

ऐ.

ऐ *ind.* An interjection of (1) Calling. (2) Remembrance. (3) Inviting.

ऐकध्यं *ind.* At once.

ऐकध्यं *n.* Singleness of time or occurrence. *ind.* At once.

ऐकपत्यं *n.* 1 Sole sovereignty, supreme power. -2 Absolute monarchy.

ऐकपद्यं *n.* 1 Unity of words. -2 Being formed into one word.

ऐकमत्यं *n.* Unanimity, agreement, sameness of opinion.

ऐकागारिकः *m.* 1 A thief. -2 The owner of a single house.

ऐकाग्र्यं *n.* Intentness on one object.

ऐकांगः *m.* A soldier of the body-guard.

ऐकात्म्य *n.* 1 Unity, unity of soul. -2 Identity, sameness. -3 Oneness with the Supreme Soul.

ऐकांतिक *a.* (*f.* -की) 1 Absolute, perfect. -2 Assured, certain. -3 Exclusive. -के *ind.* In private, apart from others.

ऐकान्यिकः *m.* A pupil who commits one error in reading or reciting the Vedas.

ऐकार्थ्यं *n.* 1 Sameness of aim or purpose -2 Consistency in meaning.

ऐकाहिक *a.* (*f.* -की) 1 Ephemeral. -2 Of one or the same day. -3 Lasting for one day (as a sacrifice, fever, festival &c.).

ऐक्यं *n.* 1 Oneness, harmony. -2 Unanimity. -3 Identity, sameness. -4 (Technically) The identity of the human soul or of the universe with the Deity. -5 A whole.

ऐक्षव *a.* (*f.* -वी) Made of sugar-cane, sugary. -वं *n.* 1 Sugar. -2 A kind of spirituous liquor.

ऐक्षुकः *m.* A carrier of sugar-cane.

ऐक्षुभारिकः *m.* Carrying a load of sugar-canes.

ऐक्ष्वाकः or -कुः *m.* 1 A descendant of Ikshvâku. -2 The country ruled over by the Aikshvâkus.

ऐंगुद *a.* (*f.* -दी) Produced from the इंगुदी tree. -दं *n.* The nut of the इंगुदी tree.

ऐच्छिक *a.* (*f.* -की) 1 Optional, voluntary. -2 Arbitrary.

ऐडक *a.* (*f.* -की) Belonging to a sheep. -कः *m.* A species of sheep.

ऐड (-ल-) विडः (-लः-) *m.* N. of Kub era.

ऐडु (-डू-) कं *n.* A wall &c. of bones and rubbish.

ऐण *a.* (*f.* -णी) Of an antelope or belonging to it, (as skin, wool &c.)

ऐणेयः *m.* A black antelope. -य *a.* (*f.* -यी) Belonging to an antelope.

ऐतदात्म्यं *n.* The state of having this property or peculiarity.

ऐतरेयिन् *m.* 1 A reader of the Aitareya Brâhmana. (*n.*). -2 One belonging to the ऐतरेयशाखा of the ऋग्वेद.

ऐतिहासिक *a.* (*f.* -की) 1 Traditional. -2 Historical. -कः *m.* 1 An historian. -2 One who knows or studies ancient legends.

ऐतिह्यं *n.* Traditional instruction, legendary account. (ऐतिह्य is regarded as one of the Pramânas or proofs by the Pauránikas and classed with प्रत्यक्ष, अनुमान &c.)

ऐदंपर्यं *n.* 1 The state of being इदंपर *i.e.* having this meaning, purport or scope. -2 Substance, scope, purport.

ऐनसं *n.* Sin.

ऐंदव *a.* (*f.* -वी) Lunar. -वः *m.* A lunar month, -वं *n.* 1 The asterism Mrigasiras. -2 The चांद्रायण व्रत.

ऐंद्र *a.* (*f.* -द्री) Belonging or sacred to Indra. -द्रः *m.* 1 N. of Arjuna and of Vâli. -द्रिः *m.* 1 Jayanta, son of इंद्र. -2 N. of अर्जुन. -3 N. of the monkey chief वाली. -4 A crow. -द्री *f.* 1 The east, eastern direction (presided over by Indra). -2 An epithet of शची. -3 Misfortune.

ऐंद्रजालिक (*f.* -की) 1 Deceptive, magical, illusive. -2 Familiar with magic. -कः *m.* A juggler.

ऐंद्रलुप्तिक *a.* (*f.* -की) Affected with morbid baldness of the head.

ऐंद्रशिरः *m.* A species of elephant.

ऐंद्रिय, -यक *a.* 1 Belonging to the senses, sensual. -2 Present, perceptible to the senses. -यं *n.* The world of the senses.

ऐंन्धन *a.* (*f.* —नी) Consisting of fuel. —नः *m.* N. of the sun.

ऐयत्यं *n.* Quantity, number.

ऐरावणः *m.* Indra's elephant.

ऐरावतः *m.* 1 N. of the elephant of Indra. -2 An excellent elephant. -3 The elephant presiding over the east.

ऐरावती *f.* 1 The female of Indra's elephant. -2 Lightning. -3 N. of a plant (वटपत्री). -4 N. of the river Râvi.

ऐरेयं *n.* Spirituous liquor (prepared from food).

ऐलः *m* 1 N. of Pururavas. -2 The planet Mars.

ऐलवालुकः *m.* N. of a perfume.

ऐलविलः *m.* 1 N. of Kubera. -2 The planet Mars. —कं *n.* A kind of perfume.

ऐलेयः *m.* 1 A kind of perfume. -2 Mars.

ऐश *a* (*f.*—शी) 1 Belonging to Siva. -2 Supreme, regal. -3 Divine.

ऐशान *a.* Belonging to Siva. —नी *f.* 1 The north-eastern direction. -2 N. of Durgâ.

ऐश्वर *a.* (*f.* —री) 1 Majestic. -2 Powerful, mighty. -3 Belonging to Siva. -4 Supreme, royal. -5 Divine. —री *f.* N. of Durgâ.

ऐश्वर्यं *n.* 1 Supremacy, sovereignty. -2 Might, power. -3 Dominion. -4 Affluence, greatness -5 Superhuman power. -6 The divine faculties of omnipotence,omnipresence&c.

ऐषमस् *ind.* During this year in the present year.

ऐषमस्तन,-मस्त्य *a.* Belonging to the present year.

ऐषीक *a.* Consisting of stalks; made of reeds or canes.

ऐष्टिक *a.* (*f.* —की) Sacrificial, ceremonial. -Comp. -पौर्तिक *a.* Referring to or belonging to sacrifices and charitable works.

ऐहलौकिक *a.* (*f.* —की) Happening in or belonging to this world; temporal, sublunary (opp. पारलौकिक).

ऐहिक *a.* (*f.* —की) 1 Of this world, temporal, worldly. -2 Local, of this place. —क *n.* Business (of this world).

ओ.

ओ *ind.* 1 A vocative particle(oh) -2 An interjection of (1) Calling; (2) Remembrance; (3) Compassion.

ओकः *m.* 1 A house. -2 A refuge, shelter. -3 A bird. -4 A Sudra.

ओकणः *m.* A bug. ओकणिः also.

ओकस् *n.* 1 A house, residence. -2 An asylum, refuge, a resting place.

ओकोदनी *f.* A bug.

ओख् 1 P. (ओखति, ओखांचकार, ओखितुं, ओखित). 1 To be dry. -2 To be able. -3 To adorn. -4 To refuse. -5 To ward off, prevent.

ओघः *m.* 1 A flood, stream. -2 An inundation. -3 A multitude. -4 The whole. -5 Continuity. -6 Quick time in music. -7 Tradition, traditional instruction. -8 A kind of dance.

ओंकारः *m.* The sacred syllable ओम्.

ओज् 1, 10, U. 1 To be strong or able. -2 To increase, grow.

ओज *a.* (*f.* —जा) Odd, uneven. —जं *n.* See ओजस् below.

ओजस् *n.* 1 Bodily strength, energy, ability. -2 Vitality. -3 Virility, the generative faculty. -4 Splendour, light. -5 (In Rhet.) A form of style abounding in compounds; ओजः समासभूयस्त्वमेतद्गद्यस्य जीवितम्. -6 Metallic lustre. -7 Manifestation, appearance. -8 Skill in the use of weapons.

ओजस्वत्, -ओजस्विन् *a.* 1 Strong, vigorous, powerful. -2 Splendid, bright.

ओजिष्ठ *a.* (*f.* —ष्ठा) Most strong, vehement.

ओजीयस् *a.* More vehement, stronger.

ओड्राः (*m. pl.*) N. of a people and their country (the modern Orissa). —पुष्पः *m.* The China rose. —पुष्पं *n.* The *Javâ*-flower.

ओत *a.* (*f.* —ता) Woven, sewn with threads across. -Comp. —प्रोत *a.* 1 Sewn cross-wise and lengthwise. -2 Extending in all directions. -प्रोतं *ind.* Cross-wise and lengthwise; verticallty and horizontally.

ओतुः *m.* 1 The woof or crossthreads of a web. -2 A cat (*f.* also).

ओदनः *m.*, -नं *n.* 1 Food, boiled rice. -2 Grain mashed and cooked with milk.

ओम् *ind.* 1 The sacred syllable *om*, uttered as a holy exclamation at the beginning and end of a reading of the Vedas, or previous to the commencement of a prayer or sacred work. -2 A particle implying (*a*) solemn affirmation; (b) assent or acceptance (yes, all right); (*c*) command; (*d*) auspiciousness; (*e*) removal or warding off. -3 Brahman (*n.*) -Comp. -कारः *m.* 1 The sacred syllable ओम्. -2 (fig.) Commencement.

ओंफः *m.* A hard scratch.

ओल *a.* (*f.* —ला) Wet, damp.

ओलण्ड् 1 P., 10 U. (ओलंडति, ओलंडयति, ओलंडित) To cast or throw upwards, throw up.

ओल्ल *a* (*f.* —ल्ला) Wet, damp. -ल्लः *m.* A hostage.

ओषः *m.* 1 Burning, combustion. -2 Cooking, baking.

ओषणः *m.* Pungency, sharp flavour.

ओषधिः, -धी *f.* 1 A herb, plant (in general). -2 A medicinal plant or drug. -3 An annual plant or herb which dies after becoming ripe. -Comp. —ईशः, -गर्भः, -नाथः *m.* The moon (as presiding over and feeding plants). —ज *a.* Produced from plants. -धरः, -पतिः *m.* 1 A dealer in medicinal drugs. -2 A physician. -3 The moon. —प्रस्थः *m.* The capital of Himâlaya.

ओष्ठः *m.* A lip. -Comp. —ज *a.* Labial (produced by the lips). —जाहं *n.* The root of the lip. —पल्लवः *m.*, -वं *n.* A sprout-like or tender lip. —पुटं *n.* The cavity made by opening the lips.

ओष्ठ्य *a.* 1 Being at the lips. -2 Belonging to the lips, labial (as the sounds).

ओष्ण *a.* A little warm, tepid.

औ.

औ *ind.* An interjection of (1) Calling; (2) Addressing; (3) Opposition; (4) Determination.

औक्थ्यं *n.* A peculiar mode of recitation.

औक्थिक: *m.* A Brâhmana who knows or studies or recites the *ukthas*.

औक्षं, औक्षकं *n.* A multitude of oxen.

औग्र्यं *n.* Formidableness, fierceness, dreadfulness.

औघः *m.* A flood.

औचिती *f.* 1 Aptness, fitness, propriety. -2 Fitness, as a mode of determining the exact meaning of a word in a sentence.

औचित्यं n. See औचिती.

औच्चैःश्रवसः m. N. of Indra's horse.

औजसिक a. (f. —की) Energetic, vigorous. —कः m. A hero.

औजस्यं n. Strength, vigour of life, energy.

औज्ज्वल्यं n. Brightness, brilliancy.

औड a. Wet, moist.

औडुपिकः m. A passenger in a boat or raft.

औडुंबर a. (f. —री) Made of उडुंबर tree.

औड्रः m. An inhabitant, or the king, of the Odra country.

औत्कंठ्यं n. 1 Desire, longing for. -2 Anxiety.

औत्कर्ष्यं n. Excellence, superiority.

औत्तमिः m. N. of the third of the fourteen Manus.

औत्तर a. (f.-री, -रा) Northern, living in the north. -Comp. —पथिक a. Going in the northern direction.

औत्तरेयः m. N. of Parikshit, son of Abhimanyu and Uttarā.

औत्तानपादः, —दिः m. 1 N. of Dhruva. -2 The polar star.

औत्पत्तिक a. (f. —की) 1 Inborn, natural. -2 Produced at the same time.

औत्पात a. (f. -ती) Treating of portents.

औत्पातिक a. (f. —की) Portentous, prodigious, calamitous. —कं n. A portent.

औत्संगिक a. (f. —की) Borne or placed upon the hip.

औत्सर्गिक a. (f. -की) 1 That which is liable to be abolished in exceptional cases, though generally valid (as a rule of grammar). -2 General (opp. to particular). -3 Natural, inherent. -4 Derivative.

औत्सुक्यं n. 1 Anxiety, uneasiness. -2 Ardent desine, eagerness, zeal.

औदक a. (f. —की) Referring to water.

औदंचनं a. (f. —नी) Contained in a jar.

औदनिकः m. 1 A cook. -2 One to whom rice &c. is given regularly.

औदरिक a. (f. —की) Voracious, gluttonous.

औदर्य a Being in the womb.

औदश्वितं n. Butter-milk with an equal proportion of water.

औदार्यं n. 1 Generosity, magnanimity. -2 Greatness, excellence. -3 Depth of meaning.

औदासीन्यं, औदास्यं n. 1 Indifference, apathy. -2 Solitariness, loneliness. -3 Indifference (to worldly affairs), stoicism.

औदुंबर a. (f. -री) Made of the Udumbara tree. -री f. A branch of the Udumbara. —रं n. The Udumbara tree. —रं n. 1 The Udumbara fruit. -2 A kind of leprosy. -3 Copper.

औद्गात्रं n. The office of the उद्गातृ Priest.

औद्दालकं n. A bitter and acrid substance like honey.

औद्देशिक a. (f. —की) 1 Showing, indicative of. -2 Enumerating.

औद्धत्यं n. 1 Arrogance, insolence. -2 Boldness; bold or adventurous deeds.

औद्धारिक a. (f. —की) Deducted from patrimony. -कं n. A portion or inheritance (deducted from patrimony).

औद्भिज्जं n. Fossil salt. (*Mar.* सैंधव).

औद्भिदं n. 1 Spring water. -2 Fossil salt, rock salt. (*mar.* सैंधव).

औद्वाहिक a. (f. —की) 1 Relating to marriage.-2 Obtained in marriage. —कं n. A gift made to a woman at r marriage.

औधस a. (f. —सी) Contained in the udder (as milk).

औधस्यं n. Milk (produced from the udder).

औन्नत्यं n. Height, elevation (moral also).

औपकर्णिक a. (f. —की) Being near the ears.

औपकार्यं n., —र्या f. A residence, a tent.

औपग्रस्तिकः,—ग्राहिकः m. 1 An eclipse. -2 The sun or moon in eclipse.

औपचारिक a. (f. —की) Metaphorical, figurative; secondary (opp. मुख्य).—कं n. Figurative application.

औपच्छंदसिकं n. N. of a metre.

औपजानुक a. (f. —की) Being near the knees.

औपदेशिक a. (f. —की) 1 Living by उपदेश or teaching. -2 Got by instruction (as wealth).

औपद्रष्टयं n. 1 Superintendence. -2 The state of being an eye-witness.

औपधर्म्यं n. 1 A false doctrine, heresy. -2 A degraded principle of virtue.

औपधिक a. (f. —की) Deceitful, deceptive.

औपधेयं n. The wheel of a carriage.

औपनायनिक a. (f. —की) Relating to the rite of investiture with the sacred thread.

औपनिधिकं n. A deposit or pledge, anything pledged or deposited.

औपनिषद a. (f. —दी) 1 Contained or taught in an Upanishad; scriptural, theological.-2 Based or founded on, derived from, the Upanishads; औपनिषदं दर्शनं n. means Vedânta philosphy. —दः m. 1 The Supreme Soul, Brahman (n.) -2 A follower of the doctrines of the Upanishads.

औपनीविक a. (f. -की) Being or placed near नीवि (the knot of the wearing garment of males or females).

औपपत्तिक a. (f. —की) 1 Ready at hand, within reach. -2 Fit, proper. 3 Theoretical.

औपमिक a. (f. —की) 1 Serving for a simile or comparison. -2 Shown by a simile.

औपम्यं n. Comparison, resemblance, analogy.

औपयिक a. (f. —की) 1 Proper, fit, right. -2 Obtained by efforts. —कः m., —कं n. A means, an expedient.

औपराजिक a. Belonging to a viceroy.

औपरिष्ट a. (f.—ष्टी) Produced above.

औपरो (-रौ-) धिक a.(f. -की) Proceeding from kindness. -2 Opposing, impeding.-कः m. A staff of the wood of the पीलु tree.

औपल a. (f. —ली) Stony, of stone.

औपवस्तं n. Fasting, a fast.

औपवस्त्रं n. 1 Food suitable for a fast. -2 Fasting.

औपवासिक a. (f. —की) Fit for fasting; able to fast.

औपवास्य n. Fasting.

औपवाह्य a (f. —ह्या) Serving for riding on. —ह्यः m. 1 A king's elephant. -2 Any royal vehicle.

औपवेशिक a. (f. —की) Getting livelihood by entire devotion to any employment.

औपसंख्यानिक a. (f. —की) Supplementary.

औपसर्गिक a. (f.—की) 1 Able to harm or injure. -2 Portentous. -3 Superinduced (as a disease).-4 Connected with a preposition. —कः m. Irregular action of the humours of the body, producing cold sweats &c. (वातादिसन्निपात).

औपस्थिक a. Living by fornication.

औपस्थ्यं n. Cohabitation, sexual enjoyment.

औपहारिक a. (f. —की) Serving as an oblation or offering. —कं n. An offering or oblation.

औपाधिक *a.* (*f.* —की) 1 Conditional. -2 Pertaining to attributes or properties; an effect produced.

औपाध्यायक *a.* (*f.* —की) Coming or obtained from a teacher.

औपायिक *a.* Same as औपयिक.

औपासन *a.* (*f.* —नी) Relating to गृह्याग्नि.-नः *m.* 1 A fire used for domestic worship. -2 A small rice-ball (पिंड) offered to the manes.

औम् *ind.* The sacred syllable of the Sudras (for ओम्, which is forbidden to be uttered by them).

औम, औमिक, औमक (*f.* —मी, —की) Flaxen.

औमीनं *n.* A field of flax.

औरग *a.* (*f.* —गी) Serpentine, relating to a serpent.—गं *n.* The constellation आश्लेषा.

औरभ्र *a.* (*f.* -भ्री) Belonging to or produced from a ram. —भ्रं *n.* 1 Mutton. -2 Woollen cloth, coarse woollen blanket (—भ्रः *m.* also).

औरभ्रकं *n.* A flock of sheep.

औरभ्रिक *a.* (*f.* —की) Belonging to sheep. —कः *m.* A shepherd.

औरस *a.* (*f.* —सी) Produced from breast, born of oneself, legitimate. —सः *m*, -सी *f.* A legitimate son or daughter

औरस्य *a.* (*f.* —स्यी) See औरस.

और्ण, और्णक, और्णिक *a.* (*f.* —र्णी, -की), Woollen.

और्ध्वकालिक *a.* (*f.* —की) Relating to subsequent or later time.

और्ध्वदेहं *n.* A funeral ceremony.

और्ध्वदे (-दै-) हिक *a.* (*f.* —की) Relating to a deceased person, funeral. —कं *n.* Funeral rites, obsequies.

और्व *a.* (*f.* —र्वी) 1 Relating to Aurva. -2 Produced from the thigh. -3 Relating to the earth. -र्वः *m.* 1 N. of a celebrated Rishi. -2 Submarine fire. —र्वं *n.* Fossil salt.

और्वशेयः *m.* N. of Agastya.

औलूकं *n.* A collection of owls.

औलूक्यः *m.* N. of Kanādā, the propounder of the Vaiseshika philosophy.

औशन, औशनस *a.* (*f.* —नी, -सी) Belonging or peculiar to Usanas; originating from Usanas, or taught by him. —सं *n.* The law-book on civil polity by उशनस्.

औशीनरः *m.* The son of Usínara. —री *f.* N. of the wife of king Pururavas.

औशीरं *n.* 1 The handle of a fan or 'Chowri'. -2 A bed. -3 A seat. -4 An unguent made of 'Usíra'. -5 The root of the fragrant grass उशीर (Mar. वाळा). -6 A fan.

औषणं *n.* 1 Pungency. -2 Blaek pepper. -Comp. —शौंडी *f.* Dried ginger (Mar. सुंठ).

औषधं *n.* 1 A herb; herbs taken collectively. -2 A medicament, medicinal drug, medicine in general. -3 A mineral. -4 A pot to hold a small plant (Mar. कुंडी). -5 N. of Vishnu.

औषधिः, -धी *f.* 1 A herb, plant (in general). -2 A medicinal herb. -3 An herb which emits fire. -4 An annual.

औषधीय *a.* (*f.* —या) Relating to a drug or medicine.

औषरं, -रकं *n.* 1 Rock-salt (Mar. शेंदेलोण). -2 Iron stone.

औषस *a.* (*f.* —सी) Relating to daybreak.-सी *f.* Day-break, morning.

औष्ट्र *a.* (*f.* —ष्ट्री) 1 Relating to, or produced from, a camel.-2 Abounding in camels. —ष्ट्रं *n.* The milk of a camel.

औष्ट्रक *a.* (*f.* —की) Relating to a camel.—कं *n.* A multitude of camels.

औष्ठ्य *a.* (*f.* —ष्ठ्या) Relating to

the lip, labial. -Comp. —वर्णः m. A labial letter; i. e. उ, ऊ, प्, फ्, ब्, भ्, म्, व्, and ष्. —स्थान a. Pronounced with the lips.-स्वरः m. A labial vowel.

औष्ण्यं n. Heat, warmth.

औष्ण्यं, औष्म्यं n. Heat.

क.

क The first consonant of the alphabet.

कः m. 1 Brahman (m.) -2 Vishnu. -3 Kâmadeva. -4 Fire. -5 Wind or air. -6 Yama -7 The sun. -8 The soul. -9 A king. -10 Knot or joint. -11 A peacock. -12 The king of birds. -13 A bird. -14 The mind. -15 Body. -16 Time. 17 A cloud.-18 Word, sound. -19 Hair. -20 Splendour. -21 Wealth. —कं n. 1 Happiness, joy. -2 Water. -3 The head. -Comp. —ज a. Watery, aquatic. —दः m. A cloud.

क A Taddhita affix showing diminution, deterioration, similarity, endearment; it is sometimes used to express the original meaning of the word itself. e. g. वृक्षकः, बालकः, पुत्रकः, अश्वकः &c.

कंट्य a. Happy, prosperous.

कंसः m., -सं n. 1 A drinking vessel, cup. -2 Bell-metal, white copper. -3 A measure known as आढक. —सः m. N. of a king of Mathura, son of उग्रसेन and an enemy of कृष्ण. —सा f. N. of a daughter of Ugrasena and sister of Kamsa. -Comp. -अरिः, अरातिः, जित्, कृष्, द्विष्, हन् m. Epithets of Krishna. —आस्थि n. The bell-metal. —कारः (f. -री) 1 A mixed tribe. -2 A worker in pewter or white-brass, a bell-founder.

कंसकं n. Bell-metal.

कंसीयं n. Bell-metal.

कक् 1 A. (ककते, ककित) 1 To wish. -2 To be proud. -3 To be unsteady.

ककाटिका f. A part of the back of the head.

ककुंभलः m. The Châtaka bird.

ककुद् f. 1 A summit, peak. -2 Chief, head. -3 The hump on the shoulders of the Indian bull. -4 A horn. -5 An ensign or symbol of royalty (as the छत्र, चामर &c.). -6 Any projecting corner. -7 N. of a daughter of Daksha and wife of Dharma.-Comp. —स्थः m. An epithet of Puranjaya, a king of the solar race and a descendant of Ikshvâku.

ककुदः m., -दं n. 1 The peak or summit of a monntain. -2 A hump (on the shoulders of an Indian bull). -3 Head, chief, foremost. -4 A sign or symbol of royalty. -5 A species of serpent.

ककुद्मिन् m. 1 A bull with a hump on his shoulders. -2 A mountain. -3 N. of Vishnu; and of king रैवतक. -कन्या, -सुता f. N. of Revati and wife of Balarâma.

ककुंदरं n. The cavities of the loins.

ककुभ् f. 1 A direction, quarter of the compass. -2 Splendour. -3 A wreath of Champaka flowers. -4 A sacred treatise or Sâstra -5 A summit.

ककुभः m. 1 A crooked piece of wood at the end of the lute. -2 The tree Arjuna. -3 One of the Râgas or personified musical modes. -भा f. 1 Space; quarter. -2 One of the Râginis —भं n. A flower of the Kutaja tree. -Comp. —अदनी f. A kind of fragrance or perfume.

ककेरुक: *m* A worm in the stomach.

कक्कुल: *m.* The Bakula tree.

कक्कोल:*m.*,–ली *f.*N. of a plant bearing a berry. —लं,–लकं *n.* 1 A berry of this plant. –2 A perfume prepared from its berries.

कक्खट *a.* (*f.* – टा) 1 Hard, solid. –2 Laughing.

कक्खटी *f.* Chalk.

कक्ष: *m.* 1 A hiding place.–2 The end of the lower garment. –3 A climbing plant, creeper. –4 Grass ; dry grass. –5 A forest of dead trees, dry wood. –6 The arm-pit. –7 The harem of a king. –8 The interior of a forest. –9 The side or flank (of anything). –10 A woman's girdle. –11 A surrounding wall. –12 A part of a boat. –13 The orbit of a planet. –14 A buffallo. –15 A gate. –16 The Beleric Myrobalan or Terminalia Beleria. –17 A marshy ground. – क्षा *f.* 1 Painful boil in the armpit (Mar. काखमांजरी). –2 An elephant's rope or chain. –3 A woman's girdle. –4 A surrounding wall. –5 The waist. –6 A courtyard. –7 An enclosure.–8 A private chamber. –9 A harem. –10 Similarity. –11 An upper garment –12 Objection or reply in argument, (in Logic &c.). –13 Emulation.–14 The skirt of a cloth which being carried round the waist is tucked up at the waist (Mar. कासोटा). —क्षं *n.* 1 A star. –2 Sin. –Comp. —अग्नि: *m.* Wild fire, conflagration. –अवेक्षक: *m.* 1 A superintendent of the harem. –2 A keeper of a royal garden. –3 door-keeper. –4 A debauchee. –5 A player. –6 A dyer. –7 An actor. –8 A paramour. –9 Strength of feeling or sentiment. —धरं *n.* The shoulder-joint. —प: *m.* 1 A tortoise. –2 One of the 9 treasures of Kubera.—शाय:, —शायु: *m.* A dog.

कक्ष्या *f.* 1 The girth of an elephant or horse.–2 A woman's girdle or zone. –3 The upper garment.–4 The border of a garment. –5 The inner appartment of a palace.–6 A wall, enclosure. –7 Similarity. –8 A shrub yielding the black and red berry that serves as a weight. —क्ष्यं *n.* 1 The cup or receptacle of a balance. –2 A part of a carriage. –3 The hinder part. –Comp. —अवेक्षक *m.* Same as कक्षावेक्षक.

कक्ष्या *f.* An enclosure.

कंक् 1 A. (कंकते) To go.

कंक: *m.* 1 A heron. –2 A variety of mango. –3 N. of Yama. –4 A Kshatriya.–5 A 'Vrishni'. –6 A false or pretended Brâhmana. –7 The Name assumed by Yudhishthira in the palace of Virâta. –Comp. –पंत्र: *m.* An arrow furnished with a heron's feathers. —पत्रं *n.* A heron's feather fixed on an arrow. —पत्रिन् *m.* See कंकपत्र:. —मुखं, —वदनं *n.* A pair of tongs. —शाय: *m.* A dog.

कंकट:, कंकटक: *m.* 1 Mail; defensive armour; military accoutrements. –2 An iron hook to goad an elephant (अंकुश).

कंकण: *m.*, —णं *n.* 1 A bracelet. –2 The marriage string (fastened round the wrist). –3 An ornament in general. –4 A crest. —ण: *m.* Water-spray.

कंकणी, –कंकणिका *f.* 1 A small bell or tinkling ornament. –2 An ornament furnished with bells.

कंकत:*m.*, –तं *n.*, –कंकती, –तिका *f.* A comb, hair-comb.

कंकरं *n.* Butter-milk.

कंकाल: *m.*, –लं *n.* A skeleton. –Comp

—मालिन् *m*. Siva. —शेष *a.* Reduced to a skeleton.

कंकालय: *m*. Body.

कंकेरु: *m*. 1 A kind of crow. -2 A crane.

कंकेलि: *m*. The Ashoka tree.

कंकेल्लुः *m*., –ल्लि: *f*. The Asoka tree.

कंकोली *f*. N. of a plant bearing a berry (Mar. कंकोळ).

कंखं *n*. Enjoyment, fruition.

कंगु *n*., कंगुनी *f*.A kind of Panic seed (Mar. राळा धान्य).

कंगुल: *m*. The hand.

कच् 1 P. (कचति, कचित) To sound, cry.

कच् 1 U. 1 To bind, fasten. -2 To shine.

कच: *m*. 1 Hair (especially of the head). -2 A dry or healed sore, scar. -3 A binding, band. -4 The hem of a garment. -5 A cloud. -6 N. of a son of Brihaspati. -Comp. —आचित *a*. Having dishevelled hair. —ग्रह: *m*. Seizing the hair, seizing (one) by the hair. -पक्ष:, -पाश:, -हस्त: *m*. Thick or ornamented hair. -मालः *m*. Smoke.

कचंगनं *n*. A free market (where no duty or custom is required to be paid).

कचंगल: *m*. The ocean.

कचा *f*. 1 A female elephant. -2 Beauty, lustre.

कचाकचि *ind*. ' Hair against hair ', (fighting by) pulling each other's hair.

कचाकु *a*. 1 Wicked. -2 Intolerable, unbearable. -3 Difficult to be attained. —कु: *m*. A snake.

कचाटुर: *m*. A gallinule, the दात्यूह bird.

कचु: *f*. An esculent root.

कचेलं *n*. A thread or cover containing and keeping together the leaves of a manuscript.

कच्चर *a*. 1 Bad, dirty. -2 Wicked. —रं *n*. Butter-milk diluted with water.

कच्चित् *ind*. A particle of (a) Interrogation (often translatable by ' I hope '). कच्चिन्मृगीणामनघा प्रसूति: * रघुवं. 5, 7; (*b*) Joy; (*c*) Auspiciousness.

कच्छ: *m*., —च्छं *n*. 1 Bank, margin, skirt, bordering region. -2 A marsh. -3 The hem of the lower garment tucked into the waistband. -4 A particular part of a boat. -5 The back of a tortoise. -Comp. —अंत: *m*. The border of a lake or stream; marshy place. —प: *m*. (*f*. —पी) 1 A turtle, tortoise. -2 A tumour on the palate. -3 An apparatus used in the distillation of spirituous liquor. -4 An attitude in wrestling. -5 One of the nine treasures of Kubera. —पी *f*. 1 A female tortoise. -2 A cutaneous disease, wart or blotch (Mar. खरूज, बद). -3 A kind of lute; also the lute of Sarasvati. —भू: *f*. Marshy ground morass. —रुहा *f*. A kind of grass (दूर्वा).

कच्छा *f*. 1 A cricket (Mar. रात्रकिडा). -2 The plant वाराही.

कच्छ (-च्छा-) टिका, कच्छाटी *f*. The hem of a lower garment which, after being carried round the body, is gathered up behind and tucked into the waist-band (Mar. कासोटा).

कच्छपिका *f*. 1 Pimple, blotch (Mar. खरूज). -2 A wart accompanying gonorrhœa (Mar. बद).

कच्छु:, -कच्छू: *f*. Itch, scab.

कच्छुर *a*. 1 Scabby, itchy. -2 Unchaste, libidinous. -3 Poor, wretched.

कज्जलं *n*. 1 Lamp-black or soot. -2 Collyrium applied to the eyelashes or eyelids. -2 Sulphuret of lead or antimony (used as a collyrium Mar. सुरमा). -3 Ink. -Comp. -ध्वज: *m*. A lamp. —रोचक: *m*., —कं *n*. The wooden stand on which a lamp is placed (Mar. ठाणवई).

कज्ज्वलं *n.* Lamp-black applied to the eyes).

कंचारः *m.* 1 The sun. -2 The Arka plant.

कंचुकः *m.* 1 An armour, mail. -2 The skin of a snake, slough. -3 A dress, garb, cloth (in general). -4 A robe. -5 A bodice, jacket. -6 A kind of drawers or short breeches. -7 A strap of leather. -8 Husk.

कंचुकालुः *m.* A snake.

कंचुकित *a.* (*f.* —ता) 1 Furnished with armour, mailed.

कंचुकिन् *a.* (*f.* —नी) Furnished with armour or mail. —*m.* 1 An attendant on the women's apartments, a chamberlain. -2 A libidinous man. -3 A serpent. -4 A door-keeper. -5 Barley.

कंचुलिका, कंचुली *f.* A bodice.

कंजः *m.* 1 The hair. -2 An ephithet of Brahman(*m.* . —जं *n.* 1 A lotus. -2 Ambrosia, nectar. -Comp. -जः *m.* N. of Brahman (*m.*). -नाभः *m.* N. of Vishnu.

कंजकः *m.*, —की *f.* A kind of bird Gracula Religiosa (Mar. साळुंकी).

कंजनः *m.* 1 The God of love. -2 A kind of bird (Mar. मैना).

कंजरः, कंजारः *m.* 1 The sun. -2 An elephant. -3 The belly. -4 An epithet of Brahman (*m.*) -5 A peacock. -6 A hermit.

कंजलः *m.* A kind of bird.

कटः *m.* 1 A straw mat. -2 The hip. -3 Hip and loins ; the hollow above the hips. -4 The temples of an elephant. -5 A particular throw of the dice in hazard. -6 A kind of grass. -7 Excess (as in उत्कट). -8 A corpse. -9 A hearse, bier. -10 An arrow. -11 A custom, usage. -12 A cemetery. -13 A time or season. -14 The plant Saccharum Sara (शर). -15 An annual plant. -16 Grass (in general). -17 A thin piece of wood, plank. —टी *f.* Long pepper (Mar. पिंपळी). —टं *n.* Dust of flowers. -Comp. —अक्षः *m.* A glance, a side-long look. —उदकं *n.* 1 The water for a funeral libation. -2 Rut, ichor (issuing from an elephant's temples). —कोलः *m.* A spitting-pot (Mar. पिकदाणी). —खादकः *m.* 1 A jackal. -2 A crow. -3 A glass vessel. —घोषः *m.* A hamlet inhabited by herdsmen. —पूतनः *m.*, —ना *f.* A kind of departed spirits. —प्रः *m.* 1 Siva. -2 An imp or goblin. -3 One who gambles or plays with dice. -4 A worm. -5 A kind of demi-god, (of the class of Vidyádharas). —प्रोथः *m.*, —थं *n.* The buttocks.—भंगः *m.* 1 Gleaning corn with the hands. -2 Any royal calamity or misfortune. —मालिनी *f.* Wine or any vinous liquor. —व्रणः *m.* N. of Bhîma-sena.

कटकः *m.*, —कं *n.* 1 A bracelet of gold. -2 A girdle. -3 A string. -4 The link of a chain. -5 A mat. -6 Sea-salt. -7 The side of a mountain. -8 Table-land. -9 An army, a camp. -10 A royal capital. -11 A house or dwelling. -12 A circle or wheel. -13 A ring placed as an ornament upon an elephant's tusk. -14 N. of the capital of Orissa.

कटकटः *m.* N. of Siva.

कटकिन् *m.* A mountain.

कटंकटः *m.* 1 Fire. -2 Gold. -3 N. of Ganesa. -4 N. of Siva. -5 The चित्रक tree.

कटनं *n.* The roof (or thatch) of a house.

कटंबः *m.* 1 A kind of musical instrument. -2 An arrow.

कटाहः *m.* 1 A frying-pan, a shallow boiler for oil or butter (Mar. कढई). -2 A turtle's shell. -3 A well. -4 A mound of earth. -5 A fragment of a broken jar. -6 A winnowing basket (Mar. सूप). -7 The infernal regions. -8 A heap or pile.

कटिः, -टी *f.* 1 The hip. -2 The buttocks. -3 An elephant's cheek. —टी *f.* Long pepper (Mar. पिंपळी). -Comp. —तटं *n.* The loins. —त्रं *n.* A cloth girt round the loins. —प्रोथः *m.* The buttocks. —मालिका *f.* A woman's zone or girdle. —रोहकः *m.* The rider of an elephant. —शीर्षकः *m.* The loins. —शृंखला *f.* A girdle furnished with small bells. —सूत्रं *n.* A zone or waist-band.

कटिका *f.* The hip.

कटीरः *m.*, -रं *n.* 1 A cave. -2 The cavity of the loins. —रं *n.* A hip.

कटीरकं *n.* The posteriors, hip.

कटु *a.* (*f.* -टु or -ट्वी) 1 Pungent, acrid. -2 Fragrant, exhaling strong odour. -3 Having a bad smell. -4 Bitter, caustic, disagreeable, unpleasant. -5 Envious. -6 Hot, impetuous. —टुः *m.* 1 Pungency, acerbity (one of the six flavours). —टु *n.* 1 An improper action. -2 Blaming, scandal. -Comp. —कीटः, -कीटकः *m.* A gnat, mosquito. —क्वाणः *m.* The टिट्टिभ bird. —निष्प्रावः *m.* Grain not inundated. —रवः *m.* 1 A frog. -2 A harsh word or sound.

कटुक *a.* (*f.* —का) 1 Sharp, pungent. -2 Impetuous, hot. -3 Disagreeable, unpleasant. -4 Fierce. -5 Harsh. —कः *m.* Pungency, acerbity. —कं *n.* Pungency; (at the end of comp. in a bad sense; as दधिकटुकं ' bad curds').

कटुकता *f.* Rough manners, rudness.

कटुकत्वं *n.* Pungency.

कटुकित Embittered, pained.

कट्वरं *n.* Buttermilk mixed with water.

कटोरं *n.* An earthen vessel.

कटोरा *f.* A shallow cup.

कटोल *a.* Pungent. —लः *m.* 1 A pungent flavour. -2 A man of an inferior and degraded tribe, a Chândâla.

कट्टारः *m.* A weapon, dagger.

कट्वर *a.* Despised. —रं *n.* 1 The skim or whey of curds. -2 Buttermilk with water. -3 A sauce, condiment.

कठ् 1 P., 10 U. (*pp.* कंठित, pres. कंठति, कंठयति, कंठयते) To miss, to remember with regret.

कठ् 1 A. (*pp.* कंठित, pres. कंठते) To be anxious, to long for, (with उत् and a noun in loc.).

कठः *m.* N. of a sage, pupil of Vaisampâyana, teacher of that branch of Yajurveda which is called after him. —ठाः *m.pl.* The followers of the sage कठ. -Comp. —धूर्तः *m.* Bráhmana well-versed in the कठ branch of the Yajurveda. —श्रोत्रियः *m.* A Bráhmana who has mastered the कठ branch of the Yajurveda.

कठमर्दः *m.* An epithet of Siva.

कठर *a.* Hard, stiff.

कठिका *f.* Chalk.

कठिन *a.*(*f.*-ना) 1 Hard, stiff. -2 Hard-hearted, cruel. -3 Inflexible. -4 Sharp, intense (as pain &c.). -5 Giving pain. -नः *m.* A thicket. -Comp. —पृष्ठः, -पृष्ठकः *m.* A tortoise.

कठिनिका, -कठिनी *f.* 1 Chalk. -2 The little finger.

कठेरः *m.* A needy or distressed man; a pauper.

कठोर *a.* (*f.* —रा) 1 Hard (fig. also), solid, stiff. -2 Cruel, ruthless. -3 Sharp, piercing. -4 Full-grown, of mature age; matured, refined.

कड् 1 U. 1 To be proud. -2 To unhusk. -3 To be disturbed or confused.

कड् 6 P. To eat, consume.

कड् 10 U. 1 To protect. -2 To remove the chaff or husk of grain. -3 To separate or detach, tear.

कड a. (f.—डा) 1 Dumb.-2 Hoarse. -3 Ignorant, stupid.

कडर्क n. Sea-salt.

कडंग (-क-) र: m. Straw.

कडंग (-क-) -रीय: m. An animal fed with straw, such as a cow or buffalo.

कडंग: m. A spirituous liquor.

कड (-ल-) त्रं n. A kind of vessel.

कडंदिका f. Science (also कलंडिका).

कडं (-लं-) ब: m. 1 The stem or stalk of a pot-herb). -2 The end or point.

कडार a. (f. —रा) 1 Tawny. -2 Haughty, impudent. —र: m. 1 The tawny colour. -2 A servant.

काडितुल: m. 1 A sword. -2 A sacrificial knife.

कण् 1. P. (कणति, कणित) 1 To cry (as in distress); moan. -2 To become small. -3 To go or approach.

कण् 10 P. 1 To wink, to close the eye with the lids.-2 To sigh, sound.

कण: m. 1 A grain. -2 A particle (of anything). -3 A very small quantity. -4 A grain of dust. -5 A drop (of water). -6 An ear of corn. -7 Spark (as of fire). -8 The spark or facet of a gem. —णा f. 1 A kind of fly. -2 Long pepper.-3 Cumin seed. —णी f. 1 An atom, a drop. -2 A kind of corn. -Comp. —अद:,—भक्ष:, —भुज् m. A nick-name of the philosopher who propounded the Vaiseshika system of philosophy. -भक्षक: m. A kind of bird. —लाभ: m. A whirlpool.

कणश: ind. Grain by grain, little by little, drop by drop.

कणाटीन:,—टीर:,—टारक: m. A wagtail, the खंजन Bird.

कणाद: m. 1 N. of the philosopher who founded the वैशेषिक philosophy. -2 A goldsmith.

कणिक: m. 1 A grain. -2 A small particle. -3 An ear of corn. -4 A meal of parched wheat. -5 An enemy. -6 N. of a certain ceremony. —का f. 1 An atom, a small or minute particle.-2 A drop (of water). -3 A kind of corn or rice.

कणिश: m., —शं n. An ear or spike of corn.

कणीक a. (f. —का) Small, diminutive.

कणे ind. A particle expressing the satisfaction of a desire. कणेहत्य पय: पिबति 'he drinks milk to his heart's content or till he is satisfied.'

कणेर:,—रु: m. The कर्णिकार tree.

कणेरा, रु: f. 1 A she-elephant. -2 A courtezan, harlot.

कंट a. Thorny.

कंटक: m., —कं n. 1 A thorn. -2 A prickle, a sting. -3 The point of anything. -4 (Fig.) Any troublesome fellow who is, it were, a thorn to the state and an enemy of order and good government. -5 Any source of vexation, a nuisance. -6 Horripilation. -7 A finger-nail. -8 A vexing speech. -9 A fish-bone. -10 A sharp stinging pain. -11 (In Nyaya philosophy) The detection of error. -12 Obstacle. -13 The first, fourth, seventh and tenth lunar mansions. —क: m. 1 A bamboo. -2 A work-shop, manufactory. -3 Fault. —Comp. -अशन:, भक्षक:,—भुज् m. A camel. —उद्धरणं n. 1. (lit.) Extracting thorns, weeding

-2 (Fig.) Removing annoyances. —द्रुम: *m.* 1 A tree with thorns, a thorny bush. -2 The Sâlmali tree or silk-cotton tree (Mar. सांवरी). —फल: *m.* 1 Bread-fruit tree, Panasa tree. —मर्दनं *n.* Suppressing disturbances. —विशोधनं *n.* Suppression of a source of disturbance or trouble. -श्रोणि·, -श्रेणी *f.* A porcupine.

कंटाकित *a.* (*f.* —ता) 1 Thorny. -2 Covered with erect hair, thrilled; horripilated.

कंटाकिन् *a.* (*f.* —नी) 1 Thorny, prickly.-2 Vexatious, troublesome. -Comp. —फल: *m.* The पनस tree (Mar. फणस).

कंठ् 1, 10, U. (कंठति-ते, कंटयति-ते, कंठित) 1 To grieve for. -2 To long for, remember with regret.

कंठ: *m.*, -ठं *n.* Throat. -2 The neck -3 Sound, voice. -4 The neck of a vessel &c. -5 Vicinity, (as in उपकंठ). -6 The opening of the womb. -7 Guttural sound. -Comp. —आगत *a.* Come to the throat (as the breath or soul of a dying person.) —आभरणं *n.* A neck-ornament, necklace. —कूणिका *f.* The Indian lute. —गत *a.* On the point of departing. —दघ्न *a.* Reaching to the neck. —नीडक: *m.* A kite. —नीलक: *m.* A large lamp or torch, a whisp of lighted straw &c. (Mar. मशाल). -पाश:, -पाशक: *m.* 1 A rope tied round an elephant's neck. -2 A halter in general. -मणि: *m.* 1 A jewel worn on the neck. -2 (fig.) A dear or beloved object. —वर्तिन् *a.* Being on the point of departing. —शोष: *m.* (lit.) 1 Drying up or parching of the throat. -2(fig.) Fruitless expostulation. -स्थ *a.* 1 Being in the throat. -2 Guttural (as a letter). -3 Being in the mouth, ready to be repeated by rote. -4 Learnt and ready to be repeated.

कंठाल: *m.* 1 A boat. -2 A spade, hoe. -3 War. -4 A camel. -5 An esculent root (Mar. सुरण). -6 A churning vessel.-7 A bag. —ला *f.* A churning vessel.

कंठिका *f.* A necklace of a single string or row.

कंठी *f.* 1 Neck, throat. -2 A necklace, a collar. -3 A rope round the neck of a horse. -Comp. —रव: *m.* 1 A lion. -2 An elephant in rut. -3 A pigeon. -4 Explicit declaration or mention.

कंठोल: *m.* A camel. -ल: *m.*,—ला *f.* A churning vessel.

कंटेकाल: *m.* N. of Siva.

कंठ्य *a.* (*f.* —ठ्या) 1 Relating to the throat. -2 Guttural. -Comp. —वर्ण: *m.* A guttural letter; namely अ, आ, क्, ख्, ग्, घ्, ङ् and ह्. —स्वर: *m.* A guttural vowel (अ and आ).

कंडनं *n.* 1 Threshing, separating the chaff from the grain. -2 Chaff. —नी *f.* 1 A wooden mortar in which the threshing of corn or grain is performed (Mar. उखळ). -2 A pestle. (Mar मुसळ).

कंडरा *f.* 1 A sinew. -2 A large artery, vein &c.

कंडिका *f.* 1 A short section (in Vedic works). -2 N. of a country.

कंडित *a.* Dislocated.

कंडु: *m.*, *f.*, कंडू: *f.* 1 Scratching. -2 Itching. [itch.

कंडूति: *f.* 1 Scratching. -2 Itching,

कंडूय् Den. U. (*p. p.* कंडूयित) 1 To scratch, rub gently.

कंडूयन, -नक *a.* Scratching. —नं *n.* Scratching, rubbing. -नी *f.* A brush for rubbing. —क: *m.* A tickler.

कंडूया *f.* 1 Scratching. -2 Itching.

कंडूरा *f.* N. of a plant causing itch (Mar. खाजकुयली).

कंडूल *a.* (*f.* —ला) 1 Having an itchy sensation, itchy. —ल: *m.* An esculent root (Mar. खाजरा सुरण).

कंडोल: *m.* 1 A basket for holding grain. -2 A safe, store-room. -3 A camel. —ली *f.* The lute of a Chândâla.

कंडोलक: *m.* 1 A basket. -2 A safe. store-room.

कंडोष: *m.* A caterpillar.

कण्व: *m.* 1 N. of a renowned sage, foster-father of Sakuntalâ. -Comp. —दुहितृ, -सुता *f.* Sakuntalâ, Kanva's daughter.

कत:, -कतक: *m.* The clearing-nut plant, (the nut of which clears muddy water). -तं, -तकं *n.* The nut of this tree (Mar. निवळीची बी).

कतम *pron. a.* (*f.* —मा, *n.* —मत्) Who or which of many? (sometimes it is used merely as a strengthened substitute for किम्).

कतमाल: *m.* Fire.

कतर *pron. a.* (*f.* —रा, *n.* —रत्) Who or which of two?

कतरत: *ind.* On which of the two sides?

कति *pron. a.* (always declined in the plural only; कति, कतिभि: &c.) 1 How many? -2 Some; when followed by चित, चन or अपि, कति loses its interrogative force and becomes indefinite in sense, meaning 'some', 'several', 'a few'

कतिकृत्वस् *ind.* How many times?

कतिधा *ind.* 1 How often? -2 In how many places, ways or parts?

कतिपय *a.* (*f.* —या or —यी,) 1 Some, several, a certain number.

कतिविध *a.* How many kinds?

कतिशस् *ind.* How many at a time?

कत्ता *f.* Gambling.

कत्थ् 1 A. (कत्थते, कत्थित). 1 To boast, swagger. -2 To praise, celebrate. -3 To flatter. -4 To abuse.

कत्थनं *n.*, —ना *f.* Bragging, boasting.

कत्सवरं *n.* The shoulder.

कथ् 10 U. 1 To tell, communicate. -2 To mention. -3 To converse. -4 To indicate, betray, show. -5 To describe, relate. -6 To inform, give information about, complain against. -7 To betray.

कथक *a.* (*f.* —का) A narrator, a relater. —क: *m.* 1 A chief actor, speaker of a prologue. -2 A disputant. -3 A story-teller.

कथनं *n.* Narration, description.

कथम् *ind.* 1 How? in what manner? whence?

Sometimes कथम् introduces a question when the speaker is doubtful as to the propriety of what he says.

It is often connected with the particles इव, नाम, नु, वा, or स्वित in the sense of, 'how indeed?' 'how possibly?' 'I should like to know', (where the question is generalized).

When connected with the particles चित्, चन or अपि it means 'in every way', 'on any account', 'somehow', 'with great difficulty', 'with great efforts'.

कथम् also signifies 'scarcely,' 'hardly; कथमपि भुवनेऽस्मिस्तादृशा: संभवंति * माल. मा. 2. 9.

-Comp. —कथिक: *m.* An inquisitive person—कारं *ind.* In what manner? how? —प्रमाण *a.* Of what measure? —भाव: *m.* What state? —भूत *a.* 1 How being? -2 Of what nature or kind? (oft. used by commentators). —रूप *a.* Of what shape?

कथा *f.* 1 A tale, story. -2 A fable, feigned story. -3 An account, referrence, mention. -4 Conversation, speech. -5 A variety of prose composition, often distinguished from

आख्यायिका. -6 (In phil.) Disputation. का कथा What mention? is often used in the sense of 'what need one say of', 'not to mention', 'to say nothing of', 'how much more', or 'how much less'; अभितप्तमयोपि मार्दवं भजते कैव कथा शरीरिषु * रघुवं. 8. 43.

Comp. —अनुराग: m. Taking pleasure in conversation. -अंतरं n. 1 The course of conversation. -2 Another tale. —अवशेष or कथाशेष a. One of whom only the narrative remains, i. e. deceased, dead. —आलाप: m. Speech, conversation. —उदय: m. The beginning of a tale. —उद्घात: m. The second of the five kinds of प्रस्तावना, where the first character enters the stage after over-hearing and repeating either the words of the manager (सूत्रधार) or their sense as in the case of the मुद्राराक्षस and the वेणीसंहार. -2 Commencement of a tale or narration. —उपकथनं, —उपाख्यानं n. Narration, relation, telling a story. —छलं n. 1 The device of a fable. -2 Giving a false account. —नायक:, -पुरुष: m. The hero or leading character of a story. —पीठं n. The introductory part of a tale or story. —प्रबंध: m. A tale, fiction, fable. —प्रसंग a. 1 Talkative. —प्रसंग: m. 1 Conversation, talk or course of conversation.-2 A curer of poisons (विषवैद्य). —प्राण: m. 1 An actor. -2 A professional story-teller. —मुखं n. The introductory portion of a story. —योग: m. The course of conversation or discourse. -विपर्यास: m. Changing the course of a story. —विरक्त a. Taciturn, disliking conversation. —शेष a. One of whom only an account remains; i. e. dead. —शेष: m. The remaining part of a story.

कथानकं n. A small tale; e. g. Vetâlapancha Vimsati.

कथिक: m. 1 A narrator.-2 A story-teller.

कथित pp. (f. —ता) 1 Told, narrated. -2 Expressed. —त: m. The Supreme Being. —तं n. A conversation, discourse. -Comp. —पदं n., पदता f. Tautology, repetition, considered as a fault of composition relating to a sentence, where a word is used without any purpose.

कथीकृत a. Remaining in narration (only); dead, deceased.

कद् 4 A. (कद्यते) To be confounded or confused; to suffer mentally.

कद् 1 A. (कदते) also 1 P. (कदति) 1 To cry, to weep or shed tears. -2 To grieve. -3 To call. -4 To kill or hurt.

कद् ind. This particle is often used as the first member of a comp. and expresses the senses of badness, littleness, deterioration, uselessness, defectiveness &c. of anything. -Comp. -अक्षरं n. 1 A bad letter. -2 Bad writing. —अग्नि: m. A little fire. —अध्वन् m. A bad road. —अन्नं n. Bad food. —अपत्यं n. A bad child, bad posterity. —अभ्यास: m. A bad habit or custom. —अर्थ a. Useless, unmeaning. —अर्थनं n., —ना f. Troubling, tormenting, torture. —अर्थित a. 1 Despised, disdained, ill-treated, slighted. -2 Tormented, teased. -3 Insignificant, mean, bad, vile. —अर्य a. 1 Avaricious, miserly. -2 Little, insignificant, mean. -3 Bad, disagreeable. —अर्य: m. A miser. —अश्व: m. A bad horse.—आकार a. Deformed, ugly. —आचार a. Wicked, depraved. —आचार: m. Bad conduct. -इंद्रियं n. A bad organ of sense. —उष्ट्र: m. A bad camel. —उष्ण (also

कोष्ण) *a.* Tepid, lukewarm. —उष्णं *n.* Lukewarmness. —तोयं *n.* An intoxicating drink, wine. —रथ: *m.* A bad chariot or carriage. —वद *a.* 1 Speaking ill or inaccurately or indistinctly. -2 Vile, contemptible.

कदकं *n.* A canopy, awning.

कदनं *n.* 1 Slaughter, destruction. -2 War. -3 Sin.

कदंब:,-कदंबक:*m.*1 A kind of tree(said to put forth buds at the roaring of thunder-clouds).-2 A kind of grass. -3 Turmeric. -4 The mustard-seed plant. -5 A particular mineral substance. —बं *n.* A multitude. —कं *n.* 1 A multitude, group. -2 The flower of the Kadamba tree. -3 A kind of grass (देवताड). -Comp. —अनिल: *m.* 1 A fragrant breeze (charged with the odour of Kadaba flowers). -2 Spring. —कोरकन्याय: *m.* The maxim of the कदंब buds. It is applied to denote simultaneous rise or action. —वायु: *m.* A fragrant breeze.

कदंबद: *m.* The mustard seed plant (Mar. मोहोरी).

कदर: *m.* 1 A saw. -2 An iron goad for driving an elephant. -र: *m.*,-रं *n.* A corn, a scar (Mar. घट्टा). —रं *n.* coagulated milk.

कदल:, —कदलक: *m.* The plantain tree. —ली *f.* 1 The plantain tree. -2 A kind of deer.-3 A flag carried by an elephant. -4 A flag or banner

कदलिका *f.* A banner, flag.

कदालिन् *m.* A kind of antelope.

कदलीक्षता 1 A sort of cucumber (Mar. पडवळ). -2 A beautiful woman.

कदा *ind.* When? at what time? कदा. Followed by अपि means 'now and then', 'at times', 'sometimes', 'at some time.' न कदापि Never. कदा Followed by चन means at some time', 'one day', 'at one time or another; once.' कदा Followed by चित् means 'at one time','once upon a time', 'at some time or other'. अथ कदाचित् means once upon a time. कदाचित् Followed by कदाचित् means 'now,-now'.

कद्रु *a.* (*f.* -द्रु or -द्रू) 1 Tawny. -2 Variegated, spotted. —द्रु: *m.* 1 The tawny colour. -2 The variegated colour. —द्रु:, -द्रू: *f.* Wife of Kasyapa and the mother of the Nágas. -Comp. —पुत्र:, सुत: *m.* A serpent.

कद्वरं *n.* 1 Whey.-2 Buttermilk mixed with water (Mar ताक).

कनकं *n.* Gold. -क: *m.* 1 The Palasa tree. -2 The Dhattúra tree. -3 Mountain ebony. -Comp. —अचल:, -अद्रि:, -गिरि:, शैल:. *m.* Epithets of the mountain Sumeru. —आह्व: *m.* The धत्तूर tree. —आलुका *f.* A golden jar or vase. —आह्वय: *m.* The Dhattúra tree. -क्षार: *m.* Borax(Mar. टाकणखार). —टंक: *m.* A golden hatchet. —दंड, -दंडकं *n.* The royal parasol. —निकष: *m.* A streak of gold (rubbed on a touch-stone). —पत्रं *n.* An ear-ornament made of gold. —पराग: *m.* Gold-dust. —रस: *m.* A yellow orpiment. —शक्ति: *m.* N. of Kârtikeya. —सूत्रं *n.* A gold necklace. —स्थली *f.* A gold mine.

कनकमय *a.* Made of gold, golden.

कनखलं *n.* N. of a Tírtha.

कनन *a.* One-eyed.

कनय् Den. P. To lessen, reduce in size, make small, diminish.

कनिष्ठ *a.* (*f.* —ष्ठा) (Superl. of अल्प or युवन्) 1 The smallest, least. -2 The youngest. —ष्ठ: *m.* N. of Siva. —ष्ठा *f.* 1 The little finger. -2 The wife of a younger brother.

कनिष्ठिका *f.* The little finger.

कनीनि f. 1 The little finger. -2 The pupil of the eye.

कनीयस् a. (f. —सी) (Compar. of अल्प or युवन्) 1 Smaller, less. -2 Younger.

कनीयस a. 1 Smaller, less. -2 Younger. —सं n. Copper.

कनेरा f. 1 A harlot.-2 A female elephant.

कंत a. Happy.

कंतु a. Happy. —तुः m. 1 Cupid, the God of love. -2 Heart. -3 Granary.

कंथा f. 1 A patched garment, wallet. -2 A wall. -3 A town. -Comp. —धारिन् m. A religious mendicant, Yogin.

कंदः m., -दं n. 1 A bulbous root.-2 A bulb. (fig. also as in ज्ञानकंद). -3 Garlic. -4 A knot, swelling. —दः m. 1 A cloud. -2 Camphor. -Comp. —मूलं n. A radish. —सारं n. The garden of Indra.

कंदुकः m. A palanquin.

कंदट्टं n. The white water-lily.

कंदरः m., -रं n. A cave, a valley. —रः m. A hook for driving an elephant. -रा,-री f. A cave, valley, hollow. —रं n. Dry ginger.

कंदर्पः m. 1 N. of Cupid, the God of love. 2 Love. -Comp. —कूपः m. Pudenda muliebre. —ज्वरः m. Fever of love, passion, vehement desire. —दहनः, -मथनः m. N. of Siva. —मुषलः —मुसलः m. The male organ of generation.

कंदलः m., -लं n. 1 A new shoot or sprout. -2 Reproach, censure. -3 The cheek. -4 A portent. -5 Sweet sound. -6 The plantain tree. -7 Collection. —लः m. 1 Gold. -2 War, battle. -3 Controversy. —लं n. A Kandala flower.

कंदलित a. (f. —ता) 1 Budded, blown. -2 Put forth, emitted.

कंदली f. 1 The plantain (or the Banana) tree.-2 A species of deer. -3 A flag. -4 Lotus-seed. -Comp. —कुसुमं n. 1 A mushroom. -2 The flower of the plantain tree.

कंदिरि f. N. of a plant (Mar. लाजाळू).

कंदुकः m., —कं n. A ball for playing with. —कं n. A pillow.

कंदोटः (-ट्टः) m. 1 The white lotus. -2 The blue lotus. —टं n. A blue lotus.

कंधरः m. 1 The neck. -2 A cloud. -3 A kind of grass. -4 N. of a vegetable (मारिष; Mar. तांदुळजा). —रा f. The neck.

कंधिः m. The ocean. —f. The neck.

कंबं n. 1 Sin -2 A swoon.

कन्यका f. 1 A girl. -2 A virgin, maiden -3 A technical name for a girl ten years old. -4 (In Rhet.) One of the several kinds of heroines; an unmarried girl serving as a chief character in a poetical composition. -5 The sign *Virgo*. -Comp. —छलः m. Seduction. —जनः m. A maiden. —जातः m. The son of an unmarried girl (=कानीनः).

कन्यसः m. The youngest brother. —सा f. The little finger. —सी f. The youngest sister.

कन्या f. 1 An unmarried girl or daughter. -2 A girl ten years old. -3 A virgin, maiden. -4 A woman in general. -5 The sixth sign of the zodiac, *i. e.* Virgo. -6 N. of Durgá. -7 Large cardamoms. -Comp. —अंतःपुरं n. The woman's apartments. —आट a. 1 Following after or hunting young girls. —आटः m. 1 Inner apartments of a house. -2 A man who hunts the young girls. —कुब्जः m. N. of a country.

—कुब्जं *n.* N. of an ancient city now called Kanoja. —गतं *n.* The position of a planet in the sign Virgo. —ग्रहणं *n.* Taking a girl in marriage. —दानं *n.* Giving away a girl in marriage. —दूषणं *n.* Defilement of a virgin. —दोषः *m.* A defect or blemish in a girl, bad repute (such as a disease &c.). —धनं *n.* Dowry. —पतिः *m.* A son-in-law. —पालः *m.* A dealer in slave-girls. –पुत्रः, –गर्भः *m.* The son of an unmarried daughter(called कानीन). —पुरं *n.* The women's apartments. —भर्तृ *m.* 1 A son-in-law. -2 N. of Kârtikeya. —रत्नं *n.* A very fine girl. —राशिः *m.* The sign *Virgo*. —वेदिन् *m.* A son-in-law. –शुल्कं *n.* Money given to the bride's father as her price. —स्वयंवरः *m.* The choice of a husband by a maiden. —हरणं *n.* Ravishment or seduction of a maiden.

कन्यिका *f.* 1 Young girl.-2 A virgin.

कन्युषं *n.* The hand below the wrist.

कप् 1 A. (*p. p.* कंपित, *pres.* कंपते). To move, shake, tremble. With अनु— To pity. आ–, प्र–, वि– To shake gently. समनु—To pity.

कपः *m.* 1 N. of वरुण. -2 A class of demons.

कपटः *m.*, –टं *n.* Fraud,deceit, trick. –टी *f.* A measure equal to the capacity of the hollows of the two hands joined together. -Comp. —तापसः *m.* One who pretends to be an ascetic, a pseudo-ascetic. —पटु *a.* Deceitful, crafty. —प्रबंधः *m.* A fraudulent contrivance. —लेख्यं *n.* A forged document. —वचनं *n.* A deceitful talk. —वेशः *m.* A disguise, false dress.

कपटिकः *m* A rogue, cheat.

कपर्दः, –कपर्दकः *m.* 1 A small shell or 'cowrie' (used as a coin). -2 Braided and matted hair, especially of Siva.

कपर्दिका *f.* A small shell or *cowrie* (used as a coin).

कपर्दिन् *m.* N. of Siva.

कपाटः *m.*, -टं *n.* 1 Leaf or panel of a door. -2 A door. -Comp. —उद्घाटनं *n* 1 The opening of a door. -2 A door-key. —घ्नः *m.* A house-breaker, thief. -वक्षस् *a.* Broad-chested. -संधिः *m.* The junction of the leaves of a door.

कपालः *m.*, –लं *n.* 1 The skull-bone. -2 A piece of a broken jar. -3 A multitude. -4 A beggar's bowl. -5 A cup, jar. -6 A cover or lid. -7 A treaty of peace on equal terms. –ली *f.* A beggar's bowl. -Comp. –नालिका *f.* The spindle for winding cotton &c. —पाणिः, —भृत्, —मालिन्, —शिरस् *m.* Epithets of Siva. —मालिनी *f.* N. of Durgâ. —संधिः *m.* A peace on equal terms.

कपालिका *f.* 1 A pot-sherd. -2 The tartar of the teeth.

कपालिन् *a.* 1 Furnished with or having a skull. -2 Wearing skulls. —*m.* 1 An epithet of Siva. -2 A man of low caste (offspring of a Brâhmana mother and fisherman father). —नी *f.* N. of Durgâ.

कपिः *m.* 1 An ape, a monkey. -2 An elephant. —पिः, -पी *f.* A female monkey. -Comp. —इज्यः *m* An epithet of (1) Râma; (2) of Sugriva. —इंद्रः *m.* An epithet of (1) Hanûmat (2) of Sugriva (3) of Jâmbavat. —केतनः, —ध्वजः *m.*N. of Arjuna. —जः, *m.*-तैलं, -नामन् *n.* Storax or benzoin. —प्रभुः *m.* 1 ·An epithet·of Râma; (2) Of Sugrîva. -लोहं *n.* Brass. —शीर्षकं *n.* Vermilion (Mar. हिंगुळ).

कपिंजलः *m.* 1 The Châtaka bird. -2 The Tittiri bird.

कपित्थः *m.* The wood-apple tree. —त्थं *n.* The fruit of the above tree. -Comp. —आस्यः *m.* A kind of monkey.

कपिल *a.* (*f.* —ला) 1 Tawny, reddish. -2 Having tawny hair. —लः *m.* 1 N. of a great sage. He is said to have been the founder of the Sânkhya system of philosophy. -2 A dog. -3 Benzoin. -4 Incense. -5 A form of fire. -6 The tawny colour. -7 One of the incarnations of Vishnu. —ला *f.* 1 A brown cow. -2 A kind of perfume. -3 A kind of timber. -4 The common leech. -5 N. of the female elephant of the south-east.

कपिश *a.* 1 Brown, reddish-brown. -2 Reddish. —शः *m.* 1 The brown colour. -2 Benzoin. —शा *f.* 1 The 1 The Màdhaví creeper. -2 N. of a river.

कपुच्छलं *n.*, कपुष्टिका *f.* 1 The ceremony of tonsure. -2 A patch of hair on each side of the head.

कपूय *a.* (*f.* —या) Mean, abject, low.

कपोत: *m.* 1 A dove, pigeon. -2 A bird in general. -Comp. —आंध्रिः *f.* A sort of perfume (mar. नखला). अंजनं *n.* Antimony. -अरिः *m.* A hawk, falcon. -चरणा *f.* A sort of perfume. -पालिका, -पाली *f.* An aviary, a pigeon-house, dovecot. -सारं *n.* Antimony. -हस्तः *m.* A mode of folding the hands in supplication, fear &c.

कपोतकः *m.* A small pigeon. -कं *n.* Antimony.

कपोती *f.* A female pigeon.

कपोलः *m.* A cheek. -Comp. —काषः *m.* Any object against which anything (especially the cheeks) is rubbed. —फलकः *m.* The (broad) cheeks. -भित्तिः *f.* 1 The temples and cheeks -2. Excellent (*i. e.* broad) cheeks. —रागः *m.* The colour in th cheeks.

कफः *m.* Phlegm, one of the three humours of the body (the other two being वात and पित्त) -Comp. —अरिः *m.* Dry ginger. —कूर्चिका *f.* Saliva, spittle. —क्षयः *m.* Pulmonary consumption. —घ्न,-नाशन,-हर *a.* Antiphlegmatic. —ज्वरः *m.* Fever caused by excess of phlegm.

कफल *a.* (*f.* —ला) Phlegmatic.

कफिन् *a.* (*f.* -नी) Affected with excess of phlegm, phlegmatic.

कफणिः, कफोणिः, -णी *f.* The elbow.

कबंधः, *m.*, —धं *n.* A headless trunk (especially when it retains life). —धः *m.* 1 The belly. -2 A cloud. -3 A comet. -4 N. of Ráhu. -5 Water (*n.* Also in this sense). -6 N. of a demon.

कबर,-रा,-री Usually written with व as the second letter. *a.* (*f.* -रा, —री) 1 Mixed, intermingled. -2 Inlaid, set. -3 Variegated. -रः *m*, -रं *n.* 1 Salt. -2 Sourness. -रः *m.*, -री *f.* 1 A braid or fillet of hair. -2 A lecturer (पाठक).

कबित्थः *m.* The wood-apple tree.

कबिल *a.* Tawny. -लः *m.* The tawny colour.

कम् *ind.* A particle meaning 1 Head. -2 Water. -3 Happiness.

कम् I. 10. A. (कामयते, कामित, चकमे- कामयांचक्रे, कांत) 1 To love, be in love with. -2 To wish, desire. -3 To value highly. With अभि— 1 To desire. -2 To love. नि— or प्र- To desire excessively.

कमठः *m.* 1 A tortoise. -2 A bamboo. -3 A water-jar. —ठी *f.* A female tortoise or small tortoise.

कमंडलुः *m.*,-लु *n.* A water-pot used by ascetics. -Comp. -तरुः *m.* The tree of which Kamandalus are made. —धरः *m.* An epithet Siva.

कमन a (f —ना) 1 Lustful. -2 Wishing for, desirous. -3 Lovely. —नः m. 1 Cupid. -2 The Asoka tree. -3 N. of Brahman (m.). -4 A Brâhmana. -Comp. —छद: m. A heron.

कमनीय a. (f. —या) Desirable. -2 Lovely, beautiful.

कमर a. (f. —रा) Lustful, desirous.

कमल: m. 1 The Sârasa bird. -2 A kind of deer.-3 N. of Brahman(m.). —ली f. A collection of lotuses. —लं n. 1 A lotus. -2 Water. -3 Copper. -4 A medicament, drug. -5 The Sârasa brid. -6 The bladder, the right lobe of the lungs. -Comp. —आलया f. An epithet of Lakshmí. —आसन: m. N. of Brahman (m.). —उत्तरं n. Safflower. —खंडं n. An assemblage of lotuses. —ज: m. 1 An epithet of Brahman(m.)-2The lunar asterism called Rohiṇì. —जन्मन् —भव:, -योनि:, —संभव: m. Epithets of Brahman (m.).

कमलक n. A small lotus.

कमला f. 1 An epithet of Lakshmí. -2 An excellent woman. -Comp. —पति:,-सख:m. An epithet of Vishnu.

कमलिनी f. 1 A lotus-plant. -2 An assemblage of lotuses. -3 A place abounding with lotuses.

कमा f. Beauty, loveliness.

कमितृ a. (f. —त्री) Lustful, libidinous.

कंप् 1 A. (कपते, चकंपे, कंपित) To shake, tremble, move about; (fig. also).

कंप: m. 1 Shaking, tremor. -2 A modification of the Svarita accent. —पा f. Shaking, moving. tremor. -Comp. —लक्ष्मन् m. The wind

कंपन a. (f. —ना) Trembling, shaking. -न: m. 1 'Sisira' season(November and December). -2 A kind of missile.-3 A kind of fever (सान्निपातिक). —नं m. 1 Shaking, tremor. -2 Quivering pronunciation.

कंपाक: m. Wind.

कंपिल्ल: m. N. of a tree. Also called कांपिल्ल.

कंप्र a. (f. —प्रा) 1 Shaking, moving, agitating. -2 Agile, quick.

कंब् 1 P. (कंबति, कंबित) To go, move.

कंबर a. (f. —रा) Variegated.

कंबल: m. 1 A blanket (of wool). -2 A dewlap. -3 A sort of deer. -4 An upper garment of wool. -5 A wall. -6 A small worm. -लं n. Water. -Comp. —वाह्यकं n. A kind of carriage covered with a coarse blanket.

कंबलक: m., -कं n. A blanket.

कंबलिका f. 1 A small blanket. -2 A kind of female deer.

कंबलिन् m. A bullock, ox. -Comp. —वाह्यक n. A carriage covered with blankets and drawn by oxen.

कंबि:, -बी f. A ladle or spoon.

कंबु a. (f. —बु or-बू) Spotted, variegated. —बु: m., —बु n. A conch, shell. -बु: m. 1 An elephant. -2 The neck. -3 The variegated colour. -Comp. —कंठी f. A lady having the neck like a conch-shell. —ग्रीवाf. A conch-shaped neck, (i. e. a neck marked with three lines like a shell and considered as a sign of great fortune). -2 A lady having the neck like the conch-shell.

कंबोज: m. 1 A shell. -2 A kind of elephant. -3 (pl.) N. of a country and its inhabitants.

कम्र a. (f. —म्रा) 1 Desirous. -2 Beautiful.

कर a. (-रा or -री) (Mostly at the end of comp.) Who or what does, makes or causes &c, सुख-, भयं-, दुःख- &c. —र: m. 1 A hand. -2 A ray of light, beam. -3 The trunk of an elephant. -4 A tax, toll, tribute. -5

Hail. -6 A particular measure of length equal to 24 thumbs. -7 The asterism called हस्त. -Comp. —अग्रं *n.* 1 The forepart of the hand. -2 The tip of an elephant's trunk. —आघातः *m.* A stroke or blow with the hand. —आरोहः *m.* A finger-ring. —आलंबः *m.* Supporting with the hand, giving a helping hand. —आस्फोटः *m.* 1 The chest.-2 A blow with the hand. —कंटकः *m.*, -कं *n.* A finger-nail. —कमलं, -पंकजं, -पद्मं *n.* A lotus-like hand, beautiful hand. —कलशः *m.*, -शं *n.* The hollow of the hand (to receive water). —किसलयः *m.*, -यं *n.* 1 A tender hand. -2 A finger. —कुड्मलं *n.* The finger. —कोषः *m.* The cavity of the palms; hands hollowed to receive water. —ग्रहः *m.*, -ग्रहणं *n.* 1 Levying a tax. -2 Taking the hand in marriage. -3 Marriage. —ग्राहः *m* The husband. -2 A tax-collector. —घर्षणः, —घर्षिन् *m.* The churning-stick. —जः *m.* The finger-nail. —जालं *n.* A stream of light. —तलः *m.* The palm of the hand. करतलामलकं (lit.) An *âmalaka* fruit (fruit of the Myrobalan) placed on the palm of the hand. (fig) Ease and clearness of perception, such as is natural in the case of a fruit placed on the palm of the hand. —तालः *m.*, —तालकं *n.* 1 Clapping the chands. -2 A kind of musical instrument. —तालिका, —ताला *f.* 1 Clapping the hands. -2 Beating time by clapping the hands —तोया *f.* N. of a river. —द *a.* 1 Paying taxes. -2 Tributary. -3 Giving the hand to help &c. —दक्ष *a.* Dexterous. —पत्रं *n.* 1 A saw. -2 Playing in water. —पत्रकं *n.* A saw. —पत्रिका *f.* Sporting in water. —पल्लवः *m.* 1 A ender hand. -2 A finger. —पालः *m.* —पालिका *f.* 1 A sword. -2 A cudgel. —पीडनं *n.* Marriage. —पुटः *m.* The hands joined and hollowed to receive anything. —पृष्ठं *n.* The back of the hand. -बालः, -वालः *m.* 1 Sword. -2 A finger-nail. —भारः *m.* A large amount of tribute. -भूः *m.* A finger-nail. —भूषणं *n.* An ornament worn round the wrist, such as a bracelet. —मालः *m.* Smoke. —मुक्तं *n.* A kind of weapon. -रुहः *m.* 1 A finger-nail. -2 A sword. —वीरः, -वीरकः *m.* 1 A sword or scimitar. -2 A cemetery -3 N. of a town in the S. M. country. -4 A kind of tree. —शाखा *f.* A finger. -शीकरः *m.* Water thrown out by an elephant's trunk. —शूकः *m.* A finger-nail. —सादः *m.* 1 Weakness of the hand. -2 The fading of rays. —सूत्रं *n.* A marriage-string worn rouud the wrist. —स्थालिन् *m.* An epithet of Siva.

करकः *m.*, -कं *n.* 1 The water-pot (of an ascetic). -2 The shell of the cocoa-nut (used as a pot). -कः *m.* 1 The pomegranate tree. -2 Tax. -3 A kind of bird -कः *m.*, -का *f.* -कं *n.* Hail. -Comp. —अंभस् *m.* The cocoa-nut tree. -आसारः *m.* A shower of hail. —जं *n.* Water. —पात्रिका *f.* A water-pot used by ascetics.

करंकः *m.* 1 A skeleton. -2 The skull.-3 A small pot (of cocoanut.); small box -4 Any bone of the body.

करंजः *m.* N. of a tree.

करटः *m.* An elephant's cheek. -2 Safflower. -3 A crow. -4 An atheist. -5 A degraded Bráhmana. -6 A man of a low profession. -7 The first Sràddha ceremony performed in honour of a dead man.

करटकः *m.* 1 A crow. -2 N. of कर्णीरथ the propounder of the science and art of theft.

करटिन् *m.* An elephant.

करड्डुः, -करेटुः *m.* A kind of bird (crane).

करण *a.* 1 Making, doing. —णं *n.* 1 Doing, performing, accomplishing, effecting. -2 Act. action. -3 Religious action. -4 Bus ness, trade. -5 An organ of sense. -6 The body. -7 An instrument. -8 (In Logic) The instrumental cause. -9 A cause or motive (in general). -10 The sense expressed by the instrumental case (in gram.).-11 (In law) A document, a bond. -12 The beat of the hand to keep time. -13 (In astrol.) A division of the day ; (these Karanas are eleven). -14 The Supreme Being. -Comp. —अधिपः *m.* The soul. —ग्रामः *m.* The organs of sense taken collectively. —त्राणं *n.* The head.

करंडः *m* 1 A small box or basket (of bamboo). -2 A bee-hive. -3 A sword. -4 A sort of duck (कारंडव).

करंडकः *m.*, करंडिका, करंडी *f.* A small box made of bamboo.

करभः *m.* 1 The back of the hand from the wrist to the root of the fingers. -2 The trunk of an elephant. -3 A young elephant. -4 A yong camel. -5 A camel in general. -6 A kind of perfume. —भी *f.* A she-camel. -Comp. —ऊरूः *f.* A lady whose thighs resemble the back of the fore-arm ; also a lady whose thighs resemble the trunk of an elephant.

करभकः *m.* (*f.* —भिका) A camel.

करभिन् *m* An elephant.

करंब, करंबित *a.* (*f.* —बा, —ता) 1 Mixed, intermingled, variegated. -2 Set, inlaid.

करंभः, -करंबः *m.*1 Flour or meal mixed with curds. -2 Mud.

करहाटः *m.* N. of a country. -2 The fibrous root or stem of a lotus. -3 A group of lotuses.

कराल *a.* (*f.* -ला) 1 Dreadful, frightful. -2 Gaping, opening wide. -3 Great, large.-4 Uneven, jagged; pointed. -5 Harsh. —ला *f.* A terrific form of Durgâ. -Comp. -दंष्ट्र *a.* Having terrific teeth. —वदना *f.* An epithet of Durgâ.

करालिकः *m.* 1 A tree. -2 A sword. —का *f.* N. of Durgá.

करिका *f.* Scratching.

करिणी *f.* A female elephant.

करिन् *m.* 1 An elephant. -2 The number 8 (in Math.). -Comp. —इंद्रः, —ईश्वरः, —वरः *m.* A large elephant, lordly elephant. -कुंभः *m.* The frontal globe of an elephant. -गर्जितं *n.* The roaring of an elephant. -दंतः *m.* Ivory. -दारकः *m.* A lion. -पः *m.*An elephant-driver. —पोतः, -शावः, -शावकः *m.* A young elephant. —बंधः *m.* A column to which an elephant is tied. -माचलः *m.* A lion. -मुखः *m.* An epithet of Ganesa. —वरः *m.* A big elephant. -वैजयंती *f.* A flag carried by an elephant. -स्कंधः *m.* A troop of elephants.

करीरः *m.* 1 The shoot of a bamboo. -2 A shoot in general. -3 A thorny plant without leaves.-4 A water-jar.

करीषः *m* , -करीषं *n.* Dry cow-dung. -Comp.-अग्निः*m.*Fire of dry cow-dung.

करीषंकषा *f.* A strong wind or gale.

करीषिणी *f.* The goddess of wealth.

करुण *a.* (*f.* —णा) Tender, pitiable, exciting pity. -णः *m.* 1 Pity, compassion, tenderness. -2 Pathetic sentiment, grief, sorrow (as one of the 8 or 9 sentiments in rhetoric). -Comp. —मल्ली *f.* The Mallikâ plant. —विप्रलंभः *m.* (in Rhet.) The feeling of love in separation.

करुणा *f.* Compassion, pity, tenderness. -Comp. -आत्मन् *a.* Tender-hearted. —आर्द्र *a.* Tender-hearted, moved with pity. -निधिः *m.* The store of mercy. -पर,-मय *a.* Very kind. -विमुख *a.* Merciless, cruel. -स्वनः,-ध्वनिः *m.* A cry of distress.

करेटः *m.* A finger-nail.

करेटुः *m.* See करेटः.

करेणुः *m.* An elephant in general. -2 The Karnikâra tree. —णुः, -णूः *f.* 1 A female elephant. -2 N. of the mother of Pâlakâpya. -3 N. of a medicinal plant. -Comp. —भूः, -सुतः *m.* N. of Pàlakápya the founder of the science of elephants.

करेणूः *m., f.* A male or female elephant.

करोटं *n.*, -करोटिः *f.* 1 The skull. -2 A cup.

कर्कः *m* 1 A crab. -2 Cancer, the fourth sign of the zodiac. -3 Fire. -4 A water-jar. -5 A mirror. -6 A white horse.

कर्कटः *m.* 1 A crab. -2 Cancer, the fourth sign of the zodiac. -3 The radius of a circle. -टी *f.*1 A female crab. -2 A kind of cucumber.

कर्कटकः *m.* 1 A crab. -2 Cancer, the fourth sign of the zodiac. —की *f.* A female crab.

कर्कटिः, -टी *f.* A sort of cucumber.

कर्कटिका *f.* A species of cucumber.

कर्कंधुः, -धूः *f.* 1 The jujube tree. -2 The fruit of this tree.

कर्कर *a.* (*f.* —रा) 1 Hard, solid. -2 Firm. —रः *m.* 1 A hammer. -2 A mirror. -3 A bone, broken piece (of skull); fragment. -4 A strap or rope of leather. -Comp. —अंगः *m.* The Khanjana bird. —अंधुकः *m.* A very dark well.

कर्कराटुः *m.* A side-long look.

कर्करी *f.* A water-jar with small holes at the bottom, as in a sieve.

कर्कश *a.* (*f.* —शा) 1 Hard, rough. -2 Harsh, cruel, merciless. -3 Violent, excessive. -4 Hardy, strong, robust. -5 Strict, imperative. -6 Desperate. -7 Unchaste, unfaithful (as a woman). -8 Difficult to comprehend. --शः *m.* A sword.

कर्कशिका, कर्कशी *f* Wild jujube.

कार्किः *m.* Cancer, the fourth sign of the zodiac.

कर्कोटः, -टकः *m.* One of the eight principal cobras.

कर्चूरकः *m.* A kind of fragrant tree. —रं *n.* 1 Gold. -2 Orpiment.

कर्चूरः *m.* Turmeric.

कर्ण् 10 U. (कर्णयति, कर्णित) 1 To pierce, to bore. -2 To hear. With आ- or समा- To hear, to listen to.

कर्णः *m.* 1 The ear. -2 The handle or ear of a vessel. -3 The helm or rudder of a ship. -4 The hypotenuse of a triangle. -5 (In prosody) A spondee. -6 N. of a celebrated warrior on the side of the Kauravas mentioned in the Mahábhârata. -Comp. -अंजलिः *m.* The auditory passage of the outer ear. -अनुजः *m.* Yudhishthira. —अंतिक *a.* Close to the ear. —अंदुः, -दुः *f.* An ornament for the ear, ear-ring. --अर्पण *n.* Giving ear, listening. —आस्फालः *m.* The flapping of the elephant's ears. —उपकर्णिका *f.* A rumour. —क्ष्वेडः *m.* (in medic.) A constant noise in the ear. --गोचर *a.* Audible. -ग्राहः *m.* A helmsman. —जपः *m.*(also कर्णेजपः) A tale-bearer, informer. —जाहः *m.* The root of the ear. —जित् *m.* An epithet of Arjuna, the third Pándava prince. —तालः *m.* The flapping of the elephant's ears, the noise made by it. —धारः *m.* A helmsman, a pilot. —धारिणी *f.* A female elephant. —पथः *m.* The range of hearing. —परंपरा *f.* Going from ear to ear, hearsay. —पालिः, –ली *f.* 1 The lobe of the ear. –2 The outer edge of the ear. —पाशः *m.* A beautiful ear. —पुटं *n.* The auditory passage of the ear. —पूरः *m.* 1 An ornament (of flowers &c.) worn round the ear, an ear-ring. –2 The Asoka tree. –3 The Shirisha tree. –4 The blue lotus. —पूरकः *m.* 1 An ear-ring –2 The Kadamba tree. –3 The Asoka tree. –4 The blue lotus. —प्रांतः *m.* The lobe of the ear. –भूषणं *n.*, –भूषा *f.* An ear-ornament. —मूलं *n.* The root of the ear. —मोटी *f.* A form of Durgâ. —वंशः *m.* A raised platform or *dais* of bamboo. –वर्जितः *m.* A snake. –विवरं, –छिद्रं, –पुटं, –रंध्रं *n.* The ear. —वेष्टः *m.*, —वेष्टनं *n.* An ear-ring. —शष्कुली *f.* The outer part of the ear. —शूलः *m.*, –लं *n.* Ear-ache. —श्रव *a.* Audible, loud. —स्रावः, —संस्रवः *m.* The discharge of pus or ichorous matter from the ear. —सूः *f.* Kuntí, mother of Karna. —हीनः *m.* A s ake.

कर्णाकर्णि *ind.* From ear to ear.

कर्णाटाः *m. pl.* N. of a country in the south of the Indian Peninsula. —टी *f.* 1 A woman of the above country.

कर्णिकः *m.* A steersman. —का *f.* 1 An ear-ring.–2 A round protuberance. –3 Pericarp of a lotus. –4 A small brush or pen.–5 The middle finger. –6 A fruit-stalk. –7 The tip of an elephant's trunk. –8 Chalk.

कर्णिकारः *m.* 1 N. of a tree. –2 The pericarp of a lotus. —रं *n.* A flower of the Karnikára tree.

कर्णिन् *m.* 1 An ass. –2 A kind of arrow.

कर्णी *f.* 1 An arrow of a particular shape. –2 N. of the mother of Múladeva, the father of the science and art of thieving. -Comp. —रथः *m.* A covered litter; a lady's vehicle, palanquin. —सुतः *m.* Múladeva, father of the science and art of thieving.

कर्त् 10 P. (कर्तयति, कार्तत) 1 To slacken, unloose. –2 To remove.

कर्तनं *n.* 1 Cutting, lopping off. –2 Spinning cotton or thread.

कर्तनी *f.* Scissors.

कर्तरिका, कर्तरी *f.* 1 Scissors. –2 A knife. –3 Cutlass, small sword.

कर्तव्य *a.* (*f.* —व्या) What ought to be cut or put down.

कर्तव्य *pot. p.* (*f.* —व्या) What is fit or ought to be done. —व्यं *n.* What ought to be done; a duty, obligation.

कर्तृ *m.* 1 A doer; one who does, makes; an agent. –2 (In gram). An agent. –3 The Supreme Spirit. -4 An epithet of Brahman (*m.*).-5 N. of Vishnu, and Siva also. –6 A priest. -Comp. –वाच्यः *m.* The active voice.

कर्त्री *f.* 1 A knife. –2 Scissors.

कर्दः, —कर्दटः *m.* 1 Mud. –2 Clay. –3 The fibrous root of the lotus.

कर्दमः *m.* 1 Mud, slime, mire. –2 Dirt, filth. –3 (Fig.) Sin. –4 N. of a Prajápati. —मं *n.* Flesh. -Comp. —आटकः *m.* A receptacle for filth, sewer &c.

कर्पटः *m.*, –टं *n.* 1 Old, ragged or patched garment. –2 A piece of cloth, strip. –3 A soiled garment. –4 A cloth.

कर्पटिक, –न् *a.* Wearing ragged garments.

कर्पणः *m.* A kind of weapon.

कर्परः *m.* 1 An iron sauce-pan, a

frying-pan. –2 A pot or vessel in general (as of a potter). –3 A piece of a broken jar. –4 The skull. –5 A kind of weapon. –6 A back-bone.

कर्पासः *m.*, –सं, *n.* –सी *f.* The cotton tree.

कर्पूरः *m.*, –रं *n.* Camphor. –Comp. –खंडः *m.* 1 A field of camphor. –2 A piece of camphor. –तैलं *n.* Camphor liniment.

कर्फरः *m.* A mirror.

कर्बु *a.* Variegated, spotted.

कर्बु (–र्बु–) र *a.* (*f.* –रा) 1 Variegated, or spotted. –2 Of the colour of pigeons; whitish, grey. –रः *m* 1 The variegated colour. –2 Sin. –3 An evil spirit, demon. –4 The Dhattúra plant. –5 Rice growing amidst inundation. –रा *f.* An epithet of Durgâ. –रं *n.* 1 Gold. –2 Water. –3 The Dhattúra plant.

कर्बू (–र्बू–) र *a.* Variegated.–रः *m.* 1 A demon. –2 The variegated colour. –रा *f.* A leech. –रं *n.* 1 Gold. –2 Yellow orpiment.

कर्मठ *a.* (*f.* –ठा) 1 Skilful in any work, clever. –2 Working diligently. –3 Exclusively devoted to the performance of religious rites. –ठः *m.* The director of a sacrifice.

कर्मण्य *a.* (*f.* –ण्या) Skilful, clever. –ण्या *f.* Wages. –ण्यं *n.* Activity.

कर्मन् *n.* 1 Action, work, deed. –2 Performance. –3 Business, office, duty. –4 A religious rite (it may be either नित्य, नैमित्तिक or काम्य). –5 A moral duty. –6 Performance of religious rites as opposed to speculative religion or knowledge of Brahman (opp. ज्ञान). –7 Labour. –8 Product, result. –9 A natural or active property (as maturity or heat). –10 Fate, the certain consequence of acts done in a former life. –11 (In gram.) The object of action; कर्तुरीप्सिततमं कर्म.–12 (In Vais. phil.) Motion considered as one of the seven categories of things. –13 Organ of sense. –14 (In astr.) The tenth lunar mansion. –Comp. –अक्षम *a.* Incapable of business. –अंगं *n.* Part of any act; part of a sacrificial rite (as प्रयाज of the Darsa sacrifice). –अधिकारः *m.* The right of performing religious rites. –अनुरूप *a.* 1 According to action or any particular office. –2 According to actions done in a previous existence. –अंतः *m.* 1 The end of any business or task. –2 A work, business, execution of business. –3 A barn, a store of grain &c. –4 A cultivated ground. –अंतरं *n.* 1 Difference or contrariety of action. –2 Penance, expiation. –3 Suspension of a religious action. –अंतिक *a.* Final. –अंतिकः *m.* 1 A servant, workman, one who carries a work to an end.–आजीवः *m.* One who maintains himself by some profession (as that of an artisan &c.). –आत्मन् *a.* Endowed with the principles of action;active. *m.*The soul. –इंद्रियं *n.* An organ of action, as distinguished from ज्ञानेंद्रिय (they are:– वाक्पाणिपादपायूपस्थानि). –उदारं *n.* Any valiant or noble act, magnanimity, prowess. –उद्युक्त *a.* Busy, engaged, active. –करः *m.* 1 A hired labourer (a servant who is not a slave). –2 Yama. –कर्तृ *m.* (In gram.) An agent who is at the same time the object of the action; क्रियमाणं तु यत्कर्म स्वयमेव प्रसिध्यति । सुकरैः स्वैर्गुणैः कर्तुः कर्मकर्तेति तद्विदुः ॥ –कांडः *m.*,–कांडं *n.* That department of the Veda which relates to ceremonial acts and sacrificial rites. –कारः *m.* 1 A mechanic, artisan (technically a worker not hired). -2 Any labourer in general (whether hired or not). -3 A blacksmith.-4 A bull.-कारिन् m. A labourer, artisan, workman. —कार्मुकः m., -कं, n. A strong bow.-कीलकः m. A washerman. -क्षम a. Able to perform any work or duty. —क्षेत्रं n. The land of religious acts, that is, भरतवर्ष. -गृहीत a. Caught in the very act (as a thief). —घातः m. Leaving off or suspending work. —चंडालः, -चांडालः m. I A man of very low acts or deeds; of such there are four kinds असूयकः पिशुनश्च कृतघ्नो दीर्घरोषकः । चत्वारः कर्मचांडाला जन्मतश्चापि पंचमः ॥. -2 One who commits an atrocious deed. -3 N. of Ráhu. —चोदना f. I The motive impelling one to ritual acts. -2 Any positive rule enjoining a religious act. -ज्ञः m One acquainted with religious rites. —त्यागः m. Abandonment of worldly duties or ceremonial acts. -दुष्ट a. Corrupt in action; wicked, immoral, disrespectable. -दोषः m. I Sin, vice. -2 An error (in doing an act). -3 Evil consequence of human acts. -4 Discreditable conduct. -धारयः m. N. of a compound, a subdivision of Tatpurusha, (in which the members of the compound are in apposition -ध्वंसः m. I Loss of fruit arising from religious acts. -2 Disappointment. -नामन् n. (In gram.) A participial noun: -नाशा f. N. of a river between Kásí and Vihára. -निष्ठ a. Devoted to the performance of religious acts. -न्यासः m. Renunciation of the result of religious acts. -पथः m. I The source of an action. -2 The path of religious rites (opp. ज्ञानमार्ग). -पाकः m. Ripening of actions, reward of actions done in a former life. -प्रवचनीयः m. A term for certain prepositions, particles, or adverbs when they are not connected with verbs and govern a noun in some case; e. g. आ in आ मुक्तेः संसारः is a कर्मप्रवचनीय; so अनु in जपमनु प्रावर्षत् &c. -फलं n. The fruit or reward of actions done in a former life. -बंधः m., -बंधनं n. Confinement to repeated birth, as the consequence of religious acts, good or bad (by which the soul is attached to worldly pleasures &c.) -भूः, -भूमिः f. I The land of religious rites; i. e. भरतवर्ष. -2 Ploughed ground.—मीमांसा f. The Mímámsá of ceremonial acts. -मूलं n. A kind of sacred grass called कुश. -युगं n. The fourth (the present) age of the world i. e. the Kaliyuga. —योगः m. I The performance of actions, worldly and religious rites. -2 Active exertion, industry. -वशः m. Fate considered as the inevitable result of actions done in a former life. -विपाकः m. See कर्मपाक. -शाला f. A workshop. -शील, -शूर a. Assiduous, active, laborious. -संगः m. Attachment to worldly duties and their results. -सचिवः m. A minister. —संन्यासिकः, -संन्यासिन् m. I A religious person who has withdrawn from every kind of worldly act. 2 An ascetic who performs religious deeds without looking to their reward. —साक्षिन् m. I An eye-witness. -2 One who witnesses the good or bad actions of man; (there are nine divinities which witness and watch over all human actions; सूर्यः सोमो यमः कालो महाभूतानि पंच च । एते शुभाशुभस्येह कर्मणो नव साक्षिणः ॥) —सिद्धिः f. Accomplishment of any business or desired object; success. —स्थानं n. A public office, or place of business.

कर्मंदिन् *m.* An ascetic.

कर्मार: *m.* 1 A blacksmith. -2 A bamboo.

कर्मिन् *a.* (*f.* -णी) 1 Working, active, busy -2 Engaged in any business. -3 One who performs religious deeds with the expectation of reward. -*m.* A mechanic, artisan.

कर्मिष्ठ *a.* (*f.* -ष्ठा) Skilled in business.

कर्वट: *m.* 1 The market-town (of two hundred villages). -2 Declivity of a mountain(also कर्वटक:*m.*). -टं *n.* A city.

कर्ष: *m.* 1 Drawing, dragging. -2 Attracting. -3 Ploughing. -4 A furrow, a trench. -5 A scratch. -र्ष: *m.*, -र्षं *n.* A weight of gold or silver equal to 16 Máshas. -Comp. —आपण: *m.* A coin or weight of different values.

कर्षक: *m.* A cultivator, husbandman.

कर्षणं *n.* 1 Drawing, dragging, pulling, bending (as of a bow). -2 Attracting.-3 Ploughing, tilling. -4 Injuring, -5 Emaciation. -6 Cultivated land.

कर्षिन् *m.* A ploughman. -णी *f.* The bit of a bridle.

कार्हिचित् *ind.* At any time.

कल् I. A. (कलते, कलित) 1 To count. -2 To sound.

कल् 10 U. (कलयति-ते, कलित) 1 To hold, bear, carry, wield, put on. -2 To count, reckon. -3To assume, take, possess. -4 To know, understand, take notice of, observe, think of.-5 To regard, consider. -6 To undergo, be influenced by. -7 To do, perform. -8 To go. -9 To tie on ; furnish with. -10 To impel, incite. -11 To utter a sound, murmur. With आ— 1 To take, to take hold of. -2 To bind, hold together. -3 To know, to observe, take notice of. परि— To know, to understand, to consider,to regard, to remember वि- To maim,to make defective. सम्- To sum up, to add.

कल् 10 P. (कालयति, कालित) 1 To push on,drive forward. -2 To throw,cast. -5 To proclaim the time.

कल *a.* (*f.* -ला) 1 Sweet and indistinct,soft,sweet,melodious,pleasing. -2 Making noise, jingling,tinkling &c.-3 Weak. -4 Crude; undigested. —ल: *m* 1 A low or soft tone.- 2 (In poetry) Time equal to four Mátrás.-लं*n*.Semen.-Comp.-अंकुर: *m.* Sârasa bird. -अनुवादिन् *m.* 1. The sparrow.-2. A bee. -3 The Châtaka bird. -अविकल: *m.* A sparrow. -आलाप: *m.* 1 A sweet humming sound. -2 Sweet and agreeable discourse. -3 A bee. —उत्ताल *a.* High, sharp. -कंठ *a.* Having a sweet voice. —कंठ: *m.*, -कंठी *f.* 1 The (Indian) cuckoo. -2 A goose, swan. -3 A pigeon. -कल: *m* 1 Murmuring or hum of a crowd. -2 Indistinct or confused noise. -3 N.of Shiva. -कूजिका, -कूणिका *f.* A wanton woman. —घोष: *m.* The (Indian) cuckoo. —तूलिका*f.* A wanton or lascivious woman. -धूतं *n.* Silver. -धौतं *n.* 1 Silver. -2. Gold. -3 A low or pleasing tone. कलधौतलिपि: *f.* 1 Illumination of a manuscript with gold. -2. Characters written in gold. -ध्वनि: *m.* 1 A low sweet tone. -2 A pigeon. -3 A peacock. -4 The (Indian) cuckoo. -नाद: *m.* A swan. -भाषणं *n.* The prattle of childhood. —रव: *m.* 1 A low sweet tone. -2.A dove. -3 The (Indian) cuckoo. —हंस: *m.* 1 Gander, a swan; a duck, drake. -3. The Supreme Soul. -4. An excellent king.

कलंकः *m.* 1 A spot, a mark, a dark spot (lit.). -2 (Fig.) A stain, stigma, disrepute.-3 A fault, defect. -4 Rust of iron.

कलंकषः *m.* (*f.* —षा) A lion.

कलंकुरः *m.* A whirlpool, eddy.

कलंजः *m.* 1 A bird. -2 A deer or any other animal struck with a poisoned weapon. —जं *n.* Flesh of such an animal.

कलत्रं *n.* 1 A wife. -2 The hip and loins. -3 Any royal citadel. -4 The seventh lunar mansion.

कलनं *n.* A spot, mark. -2 A defect, an offence, fault. -3 Taking, grasping. -4 Knowing, understanding, apprehension. -5 Sounding.

कलना *f.* 1 Taking, seizing, grasping. -2 Doing, effecting. -3 Understanding, comprehension. -4 Putting on, wearing.

कलंदिका *f.* Wisdom, intelligence.

कलभः *m.* (*f.* -भी) 1 A young elephant, cub. -2 An elephant 30 years old. -3 A young camel; the young of any other animal.

कलमः *m.* 1 Rice which is sown in May-June and ripens in December-January -2 A pen; a reed for writing with. -3 A thief.-4 A rogue, rascal.

कलंबः *m.* 1 An arrow. -2 The Kadamba tree.

कलंबूटं *n.* (Fresh) Butter.

कललः *m.*, -लं *n.* 1 The fœtus, uterus.

कलविंकः -गः *m.* 1 A sparrow. -2 A spot, stain.

कलशः, -सः *m* , -शं, -सं *n.* 1 A pitcher, water-pot, a jar, dish. Comp. -जन्मन् -उद्भवः *m.* N. of Agastya

कलशी, -सी *f.* A pitcher, a jar. -Comp. -सुतः *m.* N. of Agastya

कलहः *m.*, -हं *n* 1 Strife, quarrel. -2 War, battle. -3 Trick, deceit falsehood. -4 Violence, beating. -Comp. -अंतरिता *f.* A woman separated from her lover in consequence of a quarrel with him. —अपहृत *a.* Taken by main force or violence. —प्रियः *m.* An epithet of Nârada

कला *f.* A small part of anything. -2 A digit of the moon (these are sixteen). -3 Interest on capital. -4 A division of time. -5 The 60th part of one thirtieth part of a zodiacal sign; a minute of a degree. -6 Any practical art (mechanical or fine) ; there are 64 such arts, as music, dancing &c. -7 Skill, ingenuity. -8 Fraud, deceit. -9 (In Prosody) A syllabic instant. -10 A boat. -11 The menstrual discharge. -12 A term for the seven substrata of the elements of the human body. -13 An atom. -14 A term for the embryo. -Comp. -अंतरं *n.* Interest, profit. -अयनः *m.* A tumbler, a dancer.-आकुलं *n.* Deadly poison. —केलि *a.* Gay, wanton. -केलिः *m.* An epithet of Kâma. —क्षयः *m.* Waning (of the moon).-धरः, -निधिः, -पूर्णः *m.* The moon. —भृत् *m.* 1 The moon. -2 An artist &c.

कलादः,-दकः *m.* A goldsmith.

कलापः *m.* 1 A band, bundle. -2 A group or whole collection of things. -3 A peacock's tail. -4 A woman's zone or girdle ; (oft. with कांची- or रशना- &c.).-5 An ornament in general. -6 The rope round an elephant's neck. -7A quiver. -8 An arrow. -9 The moon. -10 A shrewd and intelligent man. -11 A poem written in one metre. -पी *f.* A bundle of grass

कलापकं *n.* 1 A series of four stanzas

on the same subject and forming one grammatical sentence. -2 A debt to be paid when the peacocks spread their tails. —कः *m.* 1 A band or bundle in general. -2 A string of pearls. -3 The rope round an elephant's neck. -4 A zone or girdle (= कलाप). -5 A sectarian mark on the forehead (विशेषक).

कलापिन् *m* 1 A peacock. -2 The (Indian) cuckoo. -3 The Indian fig-tree (प्लक्ष).

कलापिनी *f.* The night.

कलाय: *m.* N. of a leguminous seed (Mar. वाटाणा).

कलाविक: *m.* A cock.

कलाहक: *m.* A kind of musical instrument (काहल).

कलि: *m.* 1 Strife, quarrel, dissension, contention. -2 War, battle. -3 The fourth age of the world, the iron age. -4 Kali age personified. -5 The worst of any class. -6 The Bibhîtaka tree. -7 The side of a die which is marked with one point. -8 A hero. -9 An arrow. -*f.* A bud. -Comp. -कार:, -कारक:, -क्रिय: *m.* An epithet of Nârada. -द्रुम:, -वृक्ष: *m.* The Bibhîtaka tree. —प्रिय: *m.* 1 N. of Nârada. -2 A monkey, ape.

कलि:, कलिका *f.* 1 An unblown flower, a bud. -2 A digit, streak. -3 The bottom or peg of the Indian lute.

कलिंगा: *m.pl.* N. of a countryand its inhabitants ; (a district on the Coromandel Coast).

कलिंज: *m.* A mat, a screen.

कलित *a.* (*f.* -ता) 1 Held. -2 Full of, having. -3 Possessed. -4 Told. -5 Known. -6 Harsh. -7 Obtained.

कलिंद: *m.* 1 N. of the mountain on which the Yamunâ rises. -2 The sun. -Comp. -कन्या, -जा, -तनया, -नंदिनी -सुता *f* The river Yamuná. -गिरि: *m.* The Kalinda mountain. -गिरिजा, -गिरितनया, -गिरिनंदिनी *f.* The river Yamuná

कलिल *a.* (*f.* -ला) 1 Covered with, full of. -2 Mixed, blended with. -3 Affected by, subject to. -4 Impenetrable. —लं *n.* A large heap, confused mass.

कलुष *a.* (*f.* -षा) 1 Turbid, muddy, foul. -2 Choked, hoarse, husky. -3 Full of. -4 Angry, displeased, excited. -5 Wicked, sinful, bad. -6 Cruel, censurable. -7 Dark, opaque. -8 Idle, lazy. -ष: *m* A buffalo. —षं *n.* 1 Dirt, filth, mud. -2 Sin. -3 Wrath. -Comp. —योनिज *a.* Illegitimate, of impure origin.

कलेवर: *m.*, -रं *n* The body.

कल्क: *m.*, कल्कं *n.* 1 The viscous sediment deposited by oily substances when ground. -2 A kind of tenacious paste.-3 Dirt, filth (in general). -4 Ordure. -5 Meanness, deceit, hypocrisy. -6 Sin. -7 Levigated powder. -8 Incense. -9 The wax of the ear. -Comp. —फल: *m.* The pomegranate plant.

कल्कनं *n.* Deceiving, falsehood.

कल्कि: *m.* The tenth and last incarnation of Vishnu, the destroyer of the wicked and liberator of the world from its enemies.

कल्किन् *a.* 1 Foul, turbid, dirty. -2 Wicked. —*m.* See कल्कि: above.

कल्प *a.* (*f.* -ल्पा) 1 Practicable, possible. -2 Proper, fit, right. -3 Strong, vigorous. -4 Able, competent (with a gen., loc. ; inf. or at the end of comp.). —ल्प: *m.* 1 A sacred precept or rule, law. -2 A prescribed rule ; optional rule. प्रथम: कल्प: *m.* A very good (or best) alternative. -3 A proposal, suggestion, determination. -4 Manner of acting; procedure, way, method (in religious rites). -5 End of the world, universal destruction.-6 A day of Brahman (*m.*) covering 432 million years of mortals and measuring the duration of the world. -7 Medical treatment of the sick. -8 One of the six Vedángas, *i. e.* that which lays down the ritual and prescribes rules for ceremonial and sacrificial acts. -9 A termination added to nouns and adjectives in the sense of 'a little less than,' 'almost like,' 'nearly equal to,' (denoting similarity with a degree of inferiority). -10 The doctrine of poisons and antidotes. -11 One of the trees of paradise. —ल्पा *f.*, -ल्पं *n.* A kind of intoxicating liquor. -Comp. -अंत: *m.* End of the world, universal destruction. -अंतस्थायिन् *a.* Lasting to the end of a कल्प. -आदि: *m.* Renovation of all things in the creation.—कार: *m.* 1 The author of Kalpasútra. -2 A barber. —क्षय: *m.* The end of the world, universal destruction. —तरु:, —द्रुम:, -पादप:, -वृक्ष: *m.* 1 One of the trees of heaven or Indra's paradise. -2 A tree supposed to grant all desires. -3 (fig.) A very generous person. —पाल: *m.* 1 A protector of order. -2 A seller of spirituous liquors. —लता, -लतिका *f.* 1 A creeper of Indra's paradise. -2 A creeper supposed to grant all desires. -विद् *a.* Conversant with sacred precepts. -सूत्रं *n.* A maunal of ritual in the form of Sútras.

कल्पक: *m.* 1 A rite. -2 A barber.

कल्पनं *n.* 1 Forming, fashioning, arranging. -2 Performing, doing. -3 Clipping, cutting. -4 Fixing. -5 Anything placed upon another for decoration.

कल्पना *f.* 1 Fixing, settlement. -2 Making, performing, doing. -3 Forming, arranging.-4 Decorating, ornamenting. -5 Composition. -6 Invention.-7 Imagination, thought. -8 An idea, fancy or image. -9 Fabrication. -10 Forgery. -11 A contrivance, device. -12 (In Mím. phil.) See अर्थापत्ति. -13 Decorating an elephant.

कल्पनी *f.* Scissors.

कल्पित *a.* (*f.* -ता) Arranged, made, fashioned, formed. -त: *m* An elephant armed or caparisonedfor war.

कल्मष *a.* (*f.* -षा) 1 Sinful, wicked -2 Foul, dirty. —ष: *m.*, —षं *n.* 1 Stain, dirt, dregs. -2 The hand below the wrist. -3 Sin. -ष: *m.* Hell.

कल्माष *a.* (*f.* -षी) 1 Variegated, spotted. -2 Black and white. —ष: *m.* 1 The variegated colour. -2 A mixture of black and white. A demon, goblin. -4 The black colour. -5 A form of Agni. -6 A kind of fragrant rice. —षी *f.* N. of the river Yamuná. -2 The spotted cow of Jamadagni. -षं *n.* Stain. -Comp. —कंठ: *m.* An epithet of Siva. —पाद: *m.* N. of a king (सौदास).

कल्य *a.* (*f.* -ल्या) 1 Sound, healthy. -2 Ready, prepared. -3 Clever. -4 Agreeable, auspicious (as a discourse). -5 Deaf and dumb. -6 Instructive. —ल्यं *n.* 1 Dawn, day-break. -2 Tomorrow. -3 Spirituous liquor. -4 Congratulation, good wishes. -5 Good news. -Comp. —आश: *m.*, -जग्धि: *f.* The morning meal, breakfast. —पाल:, -पालक: *m.* A distiller. —वर्त: *m.* Morning meal, breakfast. -वर्तं *n* Anything light, trivial, or unimportant; a trifle.

कल्या *f.* 1 Spirituous liquor. -2 Congratulation. -Comp. -पालः, -पालकः *m.* A distiller.

कल्याण *a.* (*f.* -णा, or -णी) 1 Blessed, happy, fortunate. -2 Beautiful, lovely. -3 Excellent, illustrious. -4 Auspicious, salutary, good. —णं *n.* 1 Good fortune, happiness, prosperity. -2 Virtue. -3 Festival. -4 Gold. -5 Heaven. -णी *f.* 1 A cow. -2 Holy or sacred cow. -3 A young cow, heifer. -Comp. —कृत् *a.* 1 Beneficial, good. -2 Propitious, lucky. -3 Virtuous. —वचनं *n.* A friendly speech, good wishes.

कल्याणक *a.* (*f.* -णिका) Auspicious, prosperous, blessed. -णिका *f.* Red arsenic.

कल्याणिन् *a.* (*f.* -नी) 1 Happy, prosperous. -2 Lucky, fortunate, blessed. -3 Propitious, auspicious.

कल्ल *a.* (*f.* —ल्ला) Deaf.

कल्लोलः *m.* 1 A large wave, billow. -2 An enemy. -3 Joy, happiness.

कल्लोलिनी *f.* A river.

कल्हारं *n.* A white water-lily.

कव् 1 A. (कवते, कवित) 1 To praise. -2 To describe, compose (as a poem). -3 To paint, picture.

कवकः *m.* A mouthful. —कं *n.* A mushroom.

कवचः *m.*, —चं *n.* 1 An armour, coat of mail, a mail. -2 An amulet, a charm, a mystical syllable considered as a preservative like armour. -3 A kettle-drum. -Comp -पत्रः *m.* The birch tree. —हर *a.* 1 Wearing armour. -2 Old enough to wear an armour.

कवटी *f.* The leaf or panel of a door.

कव (-ब-) र *a.* (*f.* —रा, —री) 1 Mixed, intermingled. -2 Set, inlaid. -3 Variegated. —रः *m.*, —रं *n.* 1 Salt. -2 Sourness or acidity. —रः *m.* 1 A braid or fillet of hair. -2 A lecturer.

कव (-ब-) री *f.* A braid or fillet of hair. -Comp. -भरः, —भारः *m.* A fine head of hair.

कवलः *m.*, -लं *n.* 1 A mouthful. -2 A gargle.

कवलय् Den. P. To eat, devour.

कवलित *a.* (*f.* —ता) 1 Eaten. -2 Chewed. -3 Taken, seized.

कवसः *m.* 1 An armour. -2 A prickly shrub.

कवाटः *m.* The panel of a door. -Comp. —घ्नः *m.* A thief.

कवि *a.* 1 Omniscient. -2 Intelligent, clever, wise. -3 Thinking, thoughtful. -4 Praiseworthy. —विः *m.* 1 A wise man, a thinker, a sage. -2 A poet. -3 An epithet of Sukra, the preceptor of the Asuras. -4 Válmíki, the first poet. -5 Brahman (*m.*). -6 The sun. —*f.* The bit of a bridle. -Comp. —ज्येष्ठः *m.* An epithet of Válmìki, the first poet. —पुत्रः *m.* An epithet of Sukra. —राजः *m.* 1 A great poet. -2 N. of a poet, author of a poem called राघवपांडवीय. —रामायणः *m.* An epithet of Válmìki.

कविकः *m.*, —का *f.* The bit of a bridle.

कविता *f.* Poetry.

कवियं, कवीयं *n.* The bit of a bridle.

कवोष्ण *a.* (*f.* —ष्णा) Slightly warm, tepid.

कव्यं *n.* (opp. हव्य) An oblation of food to deceased ancestors. —व्यः *m.* A class of manes. -Comp. —वालः *m.* 1 Fire. -2 A class of manes. —वाह् —वाहः, —वाहनः *m.* Fire.

कशः *m.* A whip (usually in pl.). —शा *f.* 1 A whip. -2 Flogging. -3 A string, rope.

कशिपुः *m.*, —पु *n.* 1 A mat. -2 A pillow. -3 A bed. —पुः *m.* 1 Food.

-2 Clothing. -3 Food and clothing.

कशे (-से-) रु *n.*, -रुः *m.* 1 The backbone. -2 A kind of grass. —रुः *m.* One of the nine divisions of Jambudvípa.

कशेरुकः, -कसेरुकः *m.* -का *f.* A sort of grass. —का *f.* The back-bone.

कश्मल *a.* (*f.* —ला) Foul, dirty, disgraceful, ignominious. —लं *n.* 1 Dejection of mind, lowness or depression of spirits. -2 Sin. -3 A swoon. -4 Consternation, alarm.

कश्मीराः *m. pl.* N. of a country, the modern Kashmira. -Comp. -कश्मीरजः *m.*, —जं *n.*, —जन्मन् *n.* Safforn.

कश्य *a.* (*f.* -श्या) Fit to be whipped. —कश्यं *n.* Spirituous liquor.

कश्यपः *m.* 1 A tortoise. -2 N. of a Rishi, the husband of Aditi and Diti, and the father both of gods and demons. -Comp. —नंदनः *m.* An epithet of Garuda.

कष् 1 U. (कषति-ते, कषित) 1 To rub, scratch, scrape. -2 To test, try, rub on a touch-stone (as gold). -3 To injure, destroy.

कष् 10 P. (काषयति) To hurt.

कष *a.* (*f.* —षा) Rubbing, scratching. —षः *m.* 1 Rubbing. -2 A touch-stone. -Comp. —पट्टिका *f.* A touch stone.

कषणं *n.* 1 Rubbing, marking, scratching. -2 Test of gold by the touch-stone.

कषा *f.* See कशा.

कषाय *a.* (*f.* —या) 1 Astringent. -2 Fragrant. -3 Red, dark-red. -4 Sweet-sounding. -5 Brown. -6 Improper, dirty. —यः *m.*, —यं *n.* 1 Astringent flavour or taste. -2 The red colour. -3 A decoction with one part of a drug mixed with four, eight, or sixteen parts of water (the whole being boiled down until one quarter is left). -3 A fragrant unguent. -5 Perfuming the body with unguents. -6 Gum, resin, extract or exudation from a tree. -7 Uncleanness. -8 Dulness. -9 Attachment to worldly objects. -10 Decay, ruin. —यः *m.* 1 Passion, emotion. -2 The Kali Yuga.

कषायित *a.* (*f.* —ता) 1 Tinged, reddened, coloured. -2 Affected.

कषायिन् *a.* 1 Yielding a resinous exudation, astringent -2 Dyed of a red colour. -3 Worldly-minded. —*m.* N. of several plants such as खर्जूर, शाल, &c.

कषि *a.* Injurious, harmful.

कषे (-से-) रुका *f.* The backbone, the spine.

कष्ट *a.* (*f.* —ष्टा) 1 Bad, evil, ill, wrong -2 Painful, grievous.-3 Difficult. -4 Hard to subdue (as an enemy). -5 Hurtful, injurious. -6 Boding evil. -7 Sorrowful, miserable. —ष्टं *n.* 1 Difficulty, misery, hardship, pain. -2 Sin, wickedness. -3 Difficulty, effort. —कष्टेन Some how or other. —ष्टं *ind.* Alas! Ah! -Comp. —आगत *a.* Arrived or got with difficulty. —कर *a.* Troublesome. —कारः, -कारकः *m.* The world (as the scene of miseries). —तपस् *a.* One who practises hard penance. —साध्य *a.* That can be accomplished with difficulty. —स्थानं *n.* A bad station, a difficult or disagreeable place.

कष्टिः *f.* 1 Test, trail. -2 Injury, trouble, pain.

कस् 1 P. (कसति, कसित) To move, go, approach. With वि— To open, expand. निस्— To take out. -2 To drive away. प्र— or वि— To open, to cause to expand. [To destroy.

कस् 2 A (कस्ते or कंस्ते) 1 To go.-2

कसः *m.* A touchstone.

कस्तु (-स्तू-) रिका, कस्तूरी *f.* Musk. -Comp. —मृगः *m.* The musk-deer.

कह्लारं *n.* The white lotus.

कह्नः *m.* A kind of cane.

कांसीयं *n.* White copper.

कांस्य *a.* (*f.* —स्या) Made of white copper or bell-metal. —स्यं *n.* 1 Bell metal or white copper. -2 A gong of bell-metal. —स्यः *m.*, —स्यं *n.* A drinking vessel of brass; a goblet. -Comp. —कारः *m.*(*f.* —री) A brazier, a worker in bell-metal. —तालः *m.* A cymbal. —मलं *n.* Verdigris.

कांस्यकं *n.* Brass.

काकः *m.* 1 A crow. -2 (Fig.) A contemptible fellow, base or impudent person. -3 A lame man. -4 Bathing by dipping the head only into water. -5 A sectarian mark (तिलक). —की *f.* 1 A female crow. -का *f.* A multitude of crows. -Comp. —अक्षिगोलकन्यायः *m.* The maxim of the crow's eye-ball. The crow has only one eye-ball for two eye-sockets and the crow can move it from one to the other as occasion requires. The maxim is applied to a word or phrase which though used only once in a sentence, may, if occasion requires, serve two purposes. —अरिः *m.* An owl. —उदरः *m.* Snake. —उलूकिका *f.*, -उलूकीयं *n.* The natural enmity of the owl and the crow. —चिंचा *f.* The Gunjâ plant. —छदः, —छदिः *m.* 1 A wag-tail. -2 A side-lock of hair. —जातः *m.* The (Indian) cuckoo. —तालीयं *n.* Anything) taking place quite unexpectedly and accidentally; an accident. Sometimes used adverbially in the sense of 'accidentally.' -काकतालीयन्यायः *m.* The maxim of the crow and the palm-fruit. It takes its origin from the unexpected and sudden fall of a palm fruit upon the head of a crow at the very moment of its sitting on a branch of that tree. This maxim is used to denote a very unexpected and accidental occurrence whether welcome or unwelcome. —तालुकिन् *a.* Contemptible, vile. —दंतः *m.* (lit.) The tooth of a crow; (fig.) anything impossible or not existing. —दंतगवेषणं *n.* Searching after impossibilities, (said of any useless and unprofitable task). —ध्वजः *m.* The submarine fire. —निद्रा *f.* A light slumber (easily broken). —पक्षः, —पक्षकः *m.* The side-locks of hair on the temples of boys and young men especially of the Kshatriya caste. —पदं *n.* 1 The sign ^ in Mss. denoting that something has been left out. -2 An incision in the skin. —पुच्छः, -पुष्टः *m.* The (Indian) cuckoo. -पेय *a.* Shallow as in काकपेया नदी. -भीरुः *m.* An owl. —मद्गुः *m.* A gallinule. —यवः *m* Barren corn (the ear of which has no grain). —रुतं *n.* Shrill sound of a crow (considered as a sign of future good or evil under different circumstances). —वंध्या *f.* A woman that bears only one child. —स्वरः *m.* A shrill tone (as that of a crow).

काकरु (-रू-) क *a.* 1 Timid, cowardly. -2 Naked. -3 Poor, indigent. —कः *m.* 1 A hen-pecked husband. -2 (*f.* —की) An owl. -3 Fraud, deceit, trick.

काकलः, -काकालः *m.* A raven. —लं *n.* A jewel worn upon the neck.

काकलिः, -ली *f.* 1 A low and sweet tone; सवल्कीं काकलिगीतनिस्वनैः । प्रबोधयति सुप्त इवाद्य मन्मथः * ऋतुसं. १-८. अनुबद्धमुग्ध काकलीसहितं * उत्तरा. ३. -2 A musical instrument with a low tone used by thieves to ascertain whether a person is asleep or not. -3 Scissors. -4 The Gunjâ plant. -Comp. —रवः: *m.* The (Indian) cuckoo.

काकलीकः *m.* A low sweet tone.

काकालः *m.* See काकलः.

काकिणी, काकिणिका *f.* 1 A shell or *cowrie* used as a coin. -2 A sum of money equal to 20 *cowries* or to a quarter of a Pana. -3 A weight equal to a quarter of a Másha. -4 A part of a measure. -5 The beam of a balance. -6 A cubit.

काकिनी *f.* 1 A quarter of a पण. -2 A quarter of a measure. -3 'Cowrie.'

काकी *f.* A female crow.

काकुः *f.* 1 Change of the voice under different emotions, such as fear, grief, anger. -2 (Hence) A word of negation so used as to imply the contrary (affirmative), as in questions of appeal, the intended meaning being suggested by a change of the voice.

काकुत्स्थः *m.* A descendant of ककुत्स्थ, an epithet of the kings of the solar dynasty.

काकुदं *n.* The palate.

काकोलः *m.* 1 A raven. -2 A snake. -3 A boar. -4 A potter. -5 A division of the infernal regions or hell. -6 A poisonous substance.

काक्षः *m.* A side-long look, a glance. —क्षं *n.* Frown.

कागः *m.* A crow.

कांक्ष् 1 P. (Epic Atm. also) (कांक्षति, कांक्षित). 1 To wish, desire, long for. -2 To expect, wait for.

कांक्षा *f.* 1 Wish, desire. -2 Inclination, appetite as in भक्तकांक्षा.

काचः *m.* 1 Glass, crystal. -2 A loop; a swinging shelf, a string so fastened to the yoke as to support burdens. -3 An eye-disease, producing dimness of sight. -4 The string of the bálance. -Comp. —भाजनं *n.* A glass vessel. -मणिः *m.* Crystal, quartz. —मलं, —लवणं, —संभवं *n.* Black salt or soda.

काचनं, -काचनकं *n.* A string or tape which ties a parcel or bundle of papers or the leaves of a manuscript.

काचनकिन् *m.* A manuscript, writing.

काचकः *m.* 1 A cock. -2 The Chakraváka bird.

काजलं *n.* 1 A little water. -2 Bad water.

कांचन *a.* (*f.* —नी) Golden; made of gold. —नं *n.* 1 Gold. -2 Lustre, brilliancy. -3 Property, wealth. -4 The filament of a lotus. -5 Yellow orpiment. -6 A binding. —नः *m.* 1 The Dhattúra plant. -2 The Champaka tree. -Comp. —अंगी *f.* A woman with a golden (*i. e.* yellow) complexion. -कंदरः *m.* A gold mine. —गिरिः *m.* N. of the mountain Meru. —भूः *f.* 1 Golden (yellow) soil. -2 Gold-dust. —संधिः *m.* A treaty of equality.

कांचनारः (-रुः) *m.* The Kovidára tree.

कांचिः, -ची *f.* Woman's girdle furnished with small tinkling bells or other ornaments. -2 N. of a sacred ancient city in the south of India. -Comp. —पुरी, -नगरी *f.* The same as कांची. —पदं *n* The hips and loins.

काचुकायः *m.* Same as कंचुकिन्.

कांजिकं *n.* कांजिकः. कांजी *f.* कांजीकं *n.* Sour gruel.

काटुकं *n.* Acidity.

काटः *m.* A rock, stone.

काठिनं, -न्यं *n.* 1 Hardness, tightness. -2 Sternness, hard-heartedness. -3 Difficulty, obscurity (of style).

काण *a.* 1 (*f.* —णा) One-eyed. -2 Perforated, broken (as a 'cowrie'). —णः *m.* A crow.

काणेयः, -रः *m.* Son of a one-eyed woman.

काणेली *f.* 1 An unchaste or faithless woman. -2 An unmarried woman. -Comp. —मातृ *m.* The son of an unmarried woman; (a term of reproach occurring usually in the voc. case only); काणेलीमातः अपि किंचिच्चिह्नं यदुपलक्षयसि * मृच्छक. 1.

कांड: *m.*, -ड *n.* 1 A section, a part. -2 The portion of a plant from one knot to another. -3 A stem, stock, branch -4 Any division of a work such as a chapter of a book. -5 A separate department or subject, *e. g.* कर्मकांड &c. -6 A cluster, multitude. -7 An arrow. -8 A long bone, as of the arms or legs. -9 Cane, reed. -10 A stick, staff. -11 Water. -12 Opportunity, occasion. -13 Private place. -14 A kind of measure. -15 Praise, flattery. -16 A horse. -17 Vile, bad, sinful, (at the end of comp. only). -Comp —कारः *m.* A maker of arrows. -गोचरः *m.* An iron arrow. —पटः, -पटकः *m.* A screen surrounding a tent, curtain. —पातः *m.* An arrow's flight, range of an arrow. —पृष्ठः *m.* 1 One of the military profession; a soldier. -2 The husband of a Vaisya woman. -3 An adopted son, any other than one's own son. -4 (As a term of reproach) A base-born fellow, one who is faithless to his family, caste, religion, profession &c —पृष्ठं *n.* The bow of Karna & Káma -भंगः *m.* —भग्नं *n.* A fracture of the bone or limbs. —वीणा *f.* The lute of a Chándâla. -संधिः *m.* A knot or joint (as of a plant). —स्पृष्टः *m.* He who lives by arms, a warrior, soldier.

कांडालः *m.* A reed-basket.

कांडीरः *m.* An archer (sometimes used as a term of reproach).

कांडोलः *m.* A basket of reed.

काण्वः *m.* A descendant or follower of Kanva

कात् *ind* An exclamation of abuse or insult, usually in combination with कृ; कात्कृ To insult, dishonour

कातर *a.* (*f.* —रा) 1 Cowardly, timid, discouraged. -2 Distressed, afraid -3 Agitated; confused. -4 Tremulous through fear (as eyes).

कातर्यं *n.* Cowardice.

कात्यायनः *m.* 1 N. of a celebrated writer on grammar who wrote Vártikàs to supplement the Sútras of Pánini. -2 N. of a sage who wrote a work on civil and religious law.

कात्यायनी *f.* 1 An elderly or middle-aged widow. -2 N of a wife of Yájnavalkya. -3 N. of Párvati. -Comp. —पुत्रः, —सुतः *m.* Kârtikeya.

कार्थंचित्क *a.* (*f.* -त्का) Accomplished with difficulty.

काथिकः *m.* A narrator or writer of stories.

कादंबः *m.* 1 A kind of goose कलहंस). -2 An arrow. -3 A sugar-cane. -4 The Kadamba tree. —बं *n.* Flower of the Kadamba tree

कादंबरं *n.* 1 A spirituous liquor distilled from the flowers of the Kadamba tree. —री *f.* 1 A spirituous liquor distilled from the flowers of the कदंब tree. -2 Spirituous liquor or wine in general. -3 The fluid issuing from the temples of an elephant. -4 An epithet of Saraswatí, the Goddess of learning. -5 A female cuckoo. -6 The rain-water collected into clefts or hollow places. -7 A female cuckoo.

कादंबिनी *f.* A long line of clouds.

कादाचित्क *a.* (*f.* —त्की) Incidental, occasional.

काद्रवेयः *m.* A kind of snake.

काननं *n.* I A forest, a grove. -2 A house. -Comp. —अग्निः *m.* Wild fire, conflagration. —ओकस् *m.* I An inhabitant of a forest. -2 A monkey.

कानिष्ठिकं *n.* The little finger.

कानीनः *m.* The son of an unmarried woman. -2 N. of व्यास -3 N. of the warrior कर्ण.

कांत *p. p.* (*f.* —ता) I Desired, loved, dear. -2 Pleasing, agreeable. -3 Lovely, beautiful. —कांतः *m.* I A lover. -2 A husband. -3 Any beloved person. -4 The moon. -5 The spring. -6 A kind of iron. -7 A precious stone (in comp. with सूर्य -, चंद्र -, and अयस् -). -8 An epithet of Kártikeya and of Krishna. —तं *n.* I Saffron. -2 A kind of iron. -Comp. —अयसं *n.* The load-stone. —पक्षिन् *m.* A peacock. —लोहं *n.* The load-stone. —लोहं *n.* Steel.

कांता *f.* I A beloved or lovely woman. -2 A mistress; wife in general -3 The Priyangu creeper. -4 The earth. -Comp. —अंघ्रिदोहदः *m.* The Asoka tree. See अशोक.

कांतारः *m.*, —रं *n.* I A large forest. -2 A bad road. -3 A hole, cavity. —रः *m.* I A red variety of the sugarcane. -2 Mountain-ebony. -3 A bamboo.

कांतिः I *f.* Loveliness, beauty. -2 brightness, brilliance. -3 Personal embellishment. -4 Wish, desire. -5 (In Rhet.) Beauty enhanced by love. -6 A lovely or desirable woman. -7 An epithet of Durgá. -8 A digit of the moon. -Comp. कां

a. Brightening. —दं *n.* I Bile. -2 Clarified butter.

कांतिमत् *a.* Lovely, beautiful. —*m.* The moon. -2 N. of Cupid.

कांदवं *n.* Anything roasted or baked in an iron pan or oven.

कांदविकः *m.* A baker, a confectioner.

कांदिशीक *a.* I Put to fight, running away. -2 Terrified, afraid.

कान्यकुब्जः *m.* N of a country.

कापटिक *a.* (*f.* —का) I Fraudulent. -2 Wicked, perverse. —कः *m.* I A flatterer. -2 A parasite.

कापट्यं *n.* Wickedness ; deceit.

कापथः *m.* A bad road (lit. and fig.).

कापालः,-कापालिकः *m.* One of a sect who worshipped शिव and दुर्गा in their terrific forms of भैरव and चंडी. They were so called because they wore garlands of human skulls and also carried a skull in their hand to gather alms in, and drink water from. × × केचिद्रक्तपटीकृताश्च जटिलाः कापालिकाश्चापरे * पंचतं 4. 36. —लं *n.* A kind of leprosy. —ली *f.* I A wreath of skulls. -2 A clever woman.

कापालिन् *m.* N. of Siva.

कापिक *a.* (*f.* —की) Shaped or behaving like a monkey.

कापिल *a.* (*f.* —ली) I Peculiar or belonging to Kapila. -2 Taught by, or derived from, Kapila. —लः *m.* I A follower of the Sânkhya system of philosophy propounded by Kapila. -2 Tawny colour.

कापिशं *n.* A spirituous liquor.

कापिशायनं *n.* I Liquor. -2 A deity.

कापिशेयः *m.* An imp, goblin.

कापुरुषः *m.* A mean contemptible fellow.

कापेयं *n.* I The monkey species.-2

Monkey-like behaviour, monkey-tricks.

कापोत *a.* (*f.* —ती) Grey, of a dirty white colour. –तं *n.* 1 A flock of pigeons. -2 Antimony. —तः *m.* The grey colour. –Comp. –अंजनं *n.* Antimony applied to the eyes as collyrium.

काम् *ind.* An interjection used in calling out to another.

कामः *m.* 1 Wish, desire. -2 Object of desire. -3 Affection, love. -4 Love or desire of sensual enjoyments considered as one of the ends of life (पुरुषार्थ). -5 Desire of carnal gratification; lust. –6 The God of love. -7 N. of Pradyumna. -8 N. of Balaráma. -9 A kind of mango tree. -10 The Supreme Being. —मा *f.* Desire, wish. —मं *n.* 1 Object of desire. -2 Semen virile. –Comp. –अग्निः *m.* 1 The fire of love, violent or ardent love. -2 Violent desire, fire of passion. —अग्निसंदीपनं *n.* 1 Inflaming fire of love. -2 An aphrodisiac. —अंकुशः *m.* 1 A finger-nail. -2 The male organ of generation. —अंगः *m.* The mango tree. —अधिकारः *m.* The influence of love or desire. —अधिष्ठित *a.* Overcome by love. —अनलः *m.* See कामाग्निः. —अंध *a.* Blinded by love or passion. —अंधः *m.* The (Indian) cuckoo. —अंधा *f.* Musk. —अन्निन् *a.* Having food at will. —अभिकाम *a.* Libidinous, lustful. —अरण्यं *n.* A pleasant grove. –अरिः *m.* 1 An epithet of Siva. -2 A mineral substance. —अवतारः *m.* N. of Pradyumna. —अवसायः *m.* Suppression of passion or desire; stoicism. –अशनं *n.* 1 Eating at will. -2 Unrestrained enjoyment. —आतुर *a.* Love-sick, affected by love. —आत्मजः *m.* An epithet of Aniruddha, son of Pradyumna. —आत्मन् *a.* Lustful, libidinous, enamoured. —आयुधं *n.* 1 Arrow of the God of love. -2 Membrum virile. –आयुधः *m.* The mango tree. —आयुस् *m.* 1 A vulture. -2 'Garuda.' —आर्त *a.* Affected by love. —आसक्त *a.* Overcome with love or desire; impassioned, lustful. —ईप्सु *a.* Striving to obtain a desired object. —ईश्वरः *m.* 1 An epithet of Kubera. -2 The Supreme Soul. —उदकं *n.* 1 Voluntary libation of water. -2 A voluntary libation of water to deceased friends exclusive of those who are entitled to it by law. –उपहत *a.* Affected by passion. —कला *f.* N. of Rati, the wife of Káma. —काम, —कामिन् *a.* Following the dictates of passion. —कारः *m.* 1 Voluntary action, spontaneous deed. -2 Desire, influence of desire. —कूटः *m.* 1 The paramour of a harlot. -2 Harlotry. —कृत् *a.* 1 Acting as one likes. -2 Granting or fulfilling a desire. –कृत् *m.* The Supreme Soul —केलिः *m.* A paramour. -3 Copulation. —क्रीडा *f* 1 Dalliance of love, amorous sport. -2 Copulation. —ग *a.* Going of one's own accord; able to act or move as one likes. —गा *f.* An unchaste or libidinous woman. —गति *a.* Able to go to any desired place. —गुणः *m.* 1 The quality of passion, affection. -2 Satiety, perfect enjoyment. -3 An object of sense. —चर, —चार *a.* Moving freely; unrestrained. —चारः *m.* Unrestrained motion. -2 Independent or wilful action, wantonness. -3 Free-will. -4 Sensuality. -5 Selfishness. —चारिन् *a.* 1 Moving unrestrained. -2 Lustful. -3 Self-willed (*m.*). 1 'Garuda.'

-2 A sparrow. —जित् *a.* Conquering love or passion. (*m.*) An epithet of 'Skanda,' also of Siva. —तालः *m.* The (Indian) cuckoo. —द *a.* Fulfilling a desire, granting a request or desire. -दः *m.* An epithet of Skanda and of Siva.-दा *f.* =कामधेनु q. v. —दर्शन *a.* Looking lovely. -दुघ *a.* Granting every desired object. —दुघा, -दुह् *f.* A fabulous cow yielding all desires. —दूती *f.* The female cuckoo. —देवः *m.* 1 The God of love. -2 N. of Siva. -3 N. of Vishnu. —दोहिन् *a.* Granting desires. —धेनुः *f.* The cow of plenty, a heavenly cow yielding all desires —ध्वंसिन् *m.* An epithet of Siva. —पति, -पत्नी *f.* Rati, wife of Cupid. —पालः *m.* N. of Balaráma ; also of Siva. —प्रदः *m.* The Supreme Being. —प्रवेदनं *n.* Expressing one's desire, wish or hope. -प्रश्नः *m.* An unrestrained or free question. —फलः *m.* A species of the mango tree. —भोगाः *m. pl.* Sensual gratifications. —महः *m.* A festival of the God of love celebrated on the full-moon day in the month of Chaitra. —मूढ, -मोहित *a.* Influenced or infatuated by love. —रसः *m* Seminal discharge. —रसिक *a.* Lustful, libidinous. —रूप *a.* 1 Taking any form at will. -2 Beautiful, pleasing. —रूपाः *m. pl.* A district lying in the east of Bengal (the western portion of Assam). —रूपिन् *a.* 1 Taking any form at will. -2 Beautiful. —रेखा, —लेखा *f.* A harlot, courtezan. —लता *f.* Membrum virile. —लोल *a.* Overcome with passion. —वरः *m.* A gift chosen at will. -वल्लभः *m.* 1 The spring. -2 The moon. -3 The mango tree. —वल्लभा *f.* The moonlight. —वश *a.* Influenced by love. —वश्य *a.* Subject to love. —वाद *a.* Saying anything at will. —विहंतृ *a.* Disappointing desires. —वृत्त *a.* Addicted to sensual gratification. —वृत्ति *a.* Acting according to will, self-willed. —वृत्तिः *f.* Free and unrestrained action. -2 Freedom of will. —शरः *m.* 1 A love-shaft. -2 The mango tree. —शास्त्रं *n.* The science of love, erotic science. —संयोगः *m.* Attainment of desired objects. —सखः *m.* 1 The spring. -2 The month of Chaitra. -3 The mango tree. —सू *a* Fulfilling any desire. (-*m.*). N. of Vásudeva. (—*f.*) N. of Rukminí. —सूत्रं *n.* 1 N. of an erotic work by Vátsyáyana. —हैतुक *a.* Produced by mere desire without any real cause.

कामतः,-कामेन *ind.* 1 Willingly, knowingly, intentionally, wilfully, lustfully. -2 At will, freely.

कामन *a.* (*f.* —ना) Lustful, libidinous. —नं *n.* Desire, wish. —ना *f.* Wish, desire.

कामनीयं *n.* Beauty, attractiveness.

कामम् *ind.* 1 According to wish or inclination ; at will. -2 Agreeably to desire. -3 To the heart's content. -4 Willingly, joyfully. -5 Well, very well (a particle of assent), it may be that. -6 Granted or admitted (that); true that; no doubt, (generally followed by तु, तथापि, yet, still). -7 Indeed, really, (often implying unwillingness or contradiction). -8 Better, rather (usually with न).

कामयमान, कामयान, कामयितृ, *a.* Lustful, [libidinous.

कामल *a.* Lustful, libidinous. —लः *m.* 1 The spring. -2 A desert.

कामलिका *f.* Spirituous liquor.

कामावसायिता *f.* One of the supernatural faculties (सिद्धयः) supposed to be possessed by सिद्धs who are a class of semidivine beings.

कामिः *m.* A libidinous man. —*f.* N. of Rati.

कामिन् *a.* (*f.* —नी) 1 Lustful. -2 Desirous. -3 Loving, fond. —*m.* 1 A lover, a lustful person. -2 A uxorious husband. -3 A sparrow. -5 An epithet of Siva. -6 The moon. -7 A pigeon. -8 The Supreme Being. —नी *f.* 1 A loving, affectionate woman. -2 A lovely or beautiful woman. -3 A woman (in general). -4 A timid woman. -5 Spirituous liquor.

कामुक *a.* (*f.* —का or -की) 1 Wishing, desirous. -2 Lustful, libidinous. —कः *m.* 1 A lover, a libidinous man. -2 A sparrow. -3 The Asoka tree. —का *f.* A woman desirous of wealth. —की *f.* A libidinous or lustful woman.

कांपिल्लः, -कांपिलः, -कांपिल्लकः *m.* N. of a tree.

कांबलः *m.* A carriage covered with a woollen cloth or blanket.

कांबविकः *m.* 1 A vendor of shell ornaments; dealer in shells.

कांबोजः *m.* 1 A native of the Kambojas. -2 A king of the Kambojas. -3 The Punnága tree. -4 A species of horse from the Kamboja country.

काम्य *a.* (*f.* —म्या) 1 Desirable. -2 Optional, performed for some particular object. -3 Beautiful, handsome. —म्या *f.* A wish, intention, request. -Comp. —अभिप्रायः *m.* A sèlf-interested motive or purpose. —कर्मन् *n.* A rite performed for some particular object and with a view to future fruition. —गिर् *f.* An agreeable speech. —दानं *n.* 1 An acceptable gift. -2 A free-will offering, a voluntary gift. —मरणं *n.* A voluntary death, suicide. —व्रतं *n.* A voluntary vow.

काम्लक *a.* Slightly acid.

कायः *m.*, -यं *n.* 1 The body. -2 The trunk of a tree. -3 The body of a lute (the whole lute except the wires). -4 A multitude. -5 Principal, capital, -6 Residence, habitation. -7 A butt, a mark. -8 Natural temperament. —यं *n* (With or without -तीर्थ) The part of the hand just below the fingers, especially the little finger, or the last two fingers (this part being considered sacred to Prajàpati is called प्रजापतितीर्थ). —यः *m.* One of the eight forms of marriage, generally known as प्राजापत्य. -Comp. —अग्निः *m.* The digestive faculty. —क्लेशः *m.* Bodily suffering or pain. -चिकित्सा *f.* Treatment of diseases affecting the whole body. —मानं *n.* Measurement of the body. -वलनं *n.* An armour. —स्थः *m.* 1 The Supreme Being. -2 The writer-caste (proceeding from a क्षत्रिय father and a शूद्र mother). -3 A man of that caste. —स्था *f.* 1 A woman of that caste. -2 The Myrobalan tree. -स्थी *f.* The wife of a कायस्थ. —स्थित *a.* Corporeal, bodily.

कायक (*f.* -यिका), कायिक (*f.* —की) *a.* Relating to the body, bodily, corporeal. —का *f.* Interest (whatever is given for the use of money). -Comp. —वृद्धिः *f.* 1 Interest consisting in the use of any animal or capital stock pawned. -2 Interest of which the payment does not affect the principal.

कायमानं *n.* A hut made of thatch.

कार *a.* (*f.* -री) (At the end of comp.) Making, doing, working, maker, doer, author; as in ग्रंथकारः.

So कुंभकारः, सुवर्णकारः &c. -रः *m.* 1 Act, action, as in पुरुषकारः. -2 A term denoting a sound or a word which is not inflected; as अकार, ककार, फूत्कार &c. -3 Effort, exertion. -4 Religious austerity. -5 A husband, lord. -6 Determination. -7 Power, strength. -8 A tax or toll. -9 A heap of snow. -10 The Himâlaya mountain. -11 Water produced by hail. -12 Killing, slaughter. -Comp. —अवरः *m.* A man of a mixed and low caste. —कर *a.* Working, acting as agent. —भूः *f* A toll-station

कारक *a.* (*f.* —रिका) (Usually at the end of comp.) 1 Making, acting, doing. -2 An agent. -3 Intending to act or do. -कं *n.* 1 (In gram.) The relation subsisting between a noun and a verb in a sentence, (or between a noun and other words governing it); there are six such Kârakas, belonging to the first seven cases, except the genitive. (1) कर्तृ; (2) कर्मन्; (3); करण; (4) संप्रदान; (5) अपादान; (6) अधिकरण. -2 That part of grammar which treats of these relations; *i. e.* syntax. -3 Water produced from hail. -Comp. —दीपकं *n.* (in Rhet.) A figure of speech in which the same Kâraka is connected with several verbs in succession; *e. g.* निश्वसिति कूणति वेल्लति विचलति निमिषति विलोकयति तिर्यक् । अंतर्नंदति चुंबितुमिच्छति नवपरिणया वधूः शयने ॥ काव्यप्र. 10. —हेतुः *m.* The active or efficient cause (opp. ज्ञापकहेतु).

कारणं *n.* 1 A cause, reason. -2 Ground, motive, object. -3 An instrument, means. -4 (In Nyâya phil.) That which is invariably antecedent to some product and is not otherwise constituted. It is of three kinds; (1) समवायि (intimate or inherent); as threads are of cloth; (2) असमवायि (non-intimate or non-inherent), as the conjunction of the threads is of cloth; (3) निमित्त (instrumental) as the weaver's loom is of cloth. -4 The generative cause; creator; father. -6 An element, elementary matter. -6 The origin or plot of a play, poem, &c. -8 An organ of sense. -9 The body. -10 A sign, document. -11 That on which any opinion or judgment is based. -12 Action. -13 A legal instrument or document. -14 Agency, instrumentality. -15 A deity (as the proximate or remote cause of creation). -1 Killing, injuring. -णा *f.* 1 Pain, agony. -2 Urging, instigation. -Comp. —उत्तरं *n.* A special plea, denial of the cause of complaint; admission of the charge generally, but denial of the actual issue (in law). -कारणं *n.* A primary cause; an atom. —गुणः *m.* A quality of the cause. —माला *f.* (Rhet.) The figure of speech (called also हेतुमाला) in which each preceding object is spoken of as being the cause of each succeeding object परं परं प्रति यदा पूर्वपूर्वस्य हेतुता । तदा कारणमाला स्यात् ॥ साहि. द. 10. *e. g.* श्रुतं कृतधियां संगाज्जायते विनयः श्रुतात् । लोकानुरागो विनयान्न किं लोकानुरागतः ॥. —वादिन् *m.* A complainant, plaintiff. —वारि *n.* The original water produced at the beginning of the creation. -विहीन *a.* Without a cause. —शरीरं *n.* (In Vedánta phil.) The inner rudiment of the body, causal frame.

कारणिकः *m.* (*f.* —का or -की) An examiner, a judge.

कारंडवः *m.* A sort of duck

कारंधमिन् *m.* 1 Brazier. -2 A mineralogist.

कारवः *m.* A crow.

कारा *f.* 1 Imprisonment. -2 A prison-house. -3 Part of a lute below the neck. -4 Pain, affiction. -5 A female messenger. -Comp. -अगारं, -गृहं, -वेश्मन् *n.* A prison house, a jail. -गुप्तः *m.* A prisoner. -पालः *m.* A guard of a prison, jailor.

कारिः *f.* Action, act, work. -*m.* An artist, a mechanic.

कारिका *f.* 1 A female dancer. -2 A business, or trade. -3 A memorial verse. -4 Torment, torture. -5 Interest.

करीषं *n.* A heap of dried cowdung.

कारु *a.* (*f.* -रू) 1 A maker. doer, an agent, servant. -2 An artisan, mechanic, artist. -3 Terrible, horrible. -रुः *m.* 1 An epithet of विश्वकर्मन्, the architect of the gods. -2 An art, a science. -Comp. -चौरः *m.* One who commits burglary, a dacoit. -जः *m.* 1 A piece of mechanism, any product of manufacture. -2 A young elephant. -3 A hillock, an ant-hill. -4 Froth. -5 Sesamum growing spontaneously. -6 Red orpiment.

कारुकः *m.* (*f.* -का) An artisan.

कारुणिक *a.* (*f.* -की) Compassionate.

कारुण्यं *n* Compassion, kindness.

कार्कश्यं *n.* 1 Hardness.. -2 Firmness. -3 Solidity. -4 Hard-heartedness, cruelty.

कार्तवीर्यः *m.* The son of Krítavirya and king of the Haihayas, who ruled at Màhishmatí.

कार्तस्वरं *n.* Gold.

कार्तान्तिकः *m.* An astrologer, fortuneteller.

कार्तिक *a.* (*f.* -की) Belonging to the month of Kártika. -कः *m.* 1 N. of the month in which the full moon is near the कृत्तिका or Pleiades (corresponding to October-November). -2 An epithet of Skanda. -की *f.* The full moon day in the month of Kártika.

कार्तिकेयः *m.* N. of Skanda (so called because he was reared by the six Krittikás. -Comp. -प्रसूः *f.* Párvati, mother of Kârtikeya.

कार्त्स्न्यं *n.* Totality; entirety.

कार्दम, कार्दमिक *a.* (*f.* -मी, -की) Muddy, soiled or covered with mud.

कार्पटः *m.* 1 A petitioner, a suitor, a candidate. -2 A rag.

कार्पटिकः *m.* 1 A pilgrim. -2 One who maintains himself by carrying water from holy rivers. -3 A caravan of pilgrims. -4 An experienced man. -5 A parasite.

कार्पण्यं *n.* 1 Poverty, indigence. -2 Compassion; pity. -3 Niggardliness. -4 Levity

कार्पास *a.* (*f.* -सी) Made of cotton. -सः *m.*, -सं *n.* Anything made of cotton. -2 Paper. -सी *f.* The cotton plant. -Comp. -अस्थि *n.* The seed of the cotton plant. -नासिका *f.* A spindle. -सौत्रिक *a.* Made of cotton thread.

कार्पासिक *a.* (*f.* -की) Made of or from cotton.

कार्पासिका *f.* The cotton plant.

कार्मण *a.* (*f.* -णी) 1 Finishing a work well or completely. -णं *n.* Magic, witchcraft.

कार्मिक *a.* (*f.* -की) 1 Manufactured, made. -2 Embroidered, intermixed with coloured thread (as cloth). -3 Any variegated texture.

कार्मुक (*f.* -की) Fit for or able to do a work, doing it well and completely. -कं *n.* 1 A bow, -2 A bamboo. -3 The ninth sign of the zodiac. -Comp. -भृत् *m.* An archer.

कार्य *pot. p.* (*f.* -र्या) What ought

to be done, made, or performed. -र्यं *n.* 1 Work, affair, business, matter, thing. -2 Duty. -3 Occupation. -4 A religious rite or performance. -5 A motive, object, purpose. -6 Want, need, occasion, (with instr.). -7 Conduct, deportment. -8 A lawsuit, dispute. -9 An effect (opp. कारण). -10 (In gram.) Operation; विभक्तिकार्यं *n.* Declension. -11 The denouement of a drama.-12 Healthiness (in medicine). -13 Origin. -Comp. —अक्षम *a.* Incompetent. —अकार्यं *n.* Right and wrong (action). —अकार्यविचारः *m.* Discussion as to the propriety or otherwise of anything. —अधिपः *m.* 1 The superintendent of a work or affair. -2 The planet that decides any question in astrology. —अर्थः *m.* 1 The object of any undertaking, a purpose. -2 An application for employment. -3 Any object or purpose. —अर्थिन् *a.* 1 Making a request. -2 Seeking to gain one's object or purpose. -3 Seeking an employment. -4 Pleading a cause in court, going to law. -आसनं *n.* The throne sitting on which a king hears complaints and dispenses justice. This is also called धर्मासनं, व्यवहारासनं &c. तद्यावत् तत्रभवान्वयस्यः कार्यासनादुत्तिष्ठति तावदेव: * विक्रमो. 2. —ईक्षणं *n.* Superintendence of public affairs. —उद्धारः *m.* The discharge of a duty. —कर *a.* Efficacious. -कारणे *n. dual.* 1 Cause and effect; object and motive. —कारणभावः *m.* The relation of cause and effect. —कालः *m.* The time for action, season, fit time or opportunity. —गौरवं *n.* The importance of the act, or occasion. —चिंतक *a.* 1 Prudent, cautious, considerate. —चिंतकः *m.* The manager of a business, executive officer. —च्युत *a.* Out of work; out of employ, dismissed from an office. —दर्शनं *n.* 1 Inspection of work. -2 Looking into public affairs. —निर्णयः *m.* Settlement of an affair. —पुटः *m.* 1 A man who does any useless thing. -2 A mad, or crazy man. -3 An idler. —प्रद्वेषः *m.* Dislike to work, idleness, laziness. —प्रेष्यः *m.* An agent, a messenger. —वस्तु *n.* An aim or object. —विपत्तिः *f.* A reverse, misfortune.—शेषः *m.* 1 The remainder of a business. -2 Completion of an affair. -3 Part of a business. —सिद्धिः *f.* Success. —स्थानं *n.* A place of business, office. -हंतृ *a.* Obstructing or marring another's work. -2 Opposed to another's interests.

कार्यतः *ind.* 1 Through some object or motive. -2 Consequently, necessarily.

कार्श्यं *n.* 1 Thinness, emaciation, leanness. -2 Smallness, littleness, scantiness.

कार्षः, कार्षकः *m.* A husbandman, cultivator.

कार्षापणः *m.*, -णं *n.*, —पणकः -*m* A coin or weight of different values.

कार्षापणिक *a.* (*f.* —की) Worth one कार्षापण.

कार्षिकः *m.* See कार्षापण.

कार्ष्ण *a.* (*f.* —र्ष्णी) 1 Belonging to Krishna or Vishnu. -2 Belonging to Vyása. -3 Belonging to the black antelope. -4 Black.

कार्ष्णायस *a.* (*f.* —सी) Made of black iron. —सं *n.* Iron.

कार्ष्णिः *m.* An epithet of the God of love.

काल *a.* (*f.* —ली) 1 Black, of a dark or dark-blue colour. -2 Injuring.—लः *m.* 1 The black or dark-blue colour. -2 Time (in general).

-3 Proper time or occasion; (with gen., loc., dat., or inf.). -4 A period or portion of time (as the hours or watches of a day). -5 The weather. -6 Time considered as one of the nine *dravyas* by the Vaiseshikas. -7 The Supreme Spirit regarded as the destroyer of the universe, being a personification of the destructive principle. -8 Yama, the God of death. -9 Death; time of death. -10 Fate, destiny. 11 The black part of the eye. -12 The (Indian) cuckoo. -13 The planet Saturn. -14 N. of Siva. -15 A measure of time (in music or prosody).-16 A person who distils and sells spirituous liquor. -17 A red kind of plumbago. -18 Resin, pitch. -19 N. of an enemy of Siva. -ली *f.* 1 Blackness. -2 Ink, black ink. -3 An epithet of Pârvati, Siva's wife. -4 A row of black clouds. -5 A woman with a dark complexion. -6 N. of Satyavati, mother of Vyâsa. -7 Night. -8 Censure, blame. -9 One of the seven tongues of fire. -10 A form of Durgâ. कालीतनय: *m.* A buffalo. —लं *n.* 1 Iron. -2 A kind of perfume. -Comp. —अयसं *n.* Iron. —अक्षरिक: *m.* A scholar, one who can read and decipher. —अगरु *n.* A kind of sandal tree. The wood of that tree.—अग्नि:, —अनल: *m.* The destructive fire at the end of the world. —अंग *a.* Having a dark-blue body (as a sword with a dark blue edge). —अजिनं *n.* The hide of a black antelope. —अंजनं *n.* A sort of collyrium. —अंडज: *m.* The (Indian) cuckoo. —अतिक्रम: *m.*, —मणं *n.* Delay, being late. —अतिपात:, —अतिरेक: *m* Loss of time, delay. —अत्यय: *m.* 1 Delay, lapse of time. -2 Loss by lapse of time. —अध्यक्ष: *m.* 1 An epithet of the sun. -2 The Supreme Soul. —अनुनादिन् *m.* 1 A bee. -2 A sparrow. -3 The Châtaka bird. —अंतक: *m.* Time, regarded as the God of death, and the destroyer of every thing. —अंतरं *n.* 1 An interval. -2 A period of time. -3 Another time or opportunity. —अंतरावृत *a.* Hidden. —आवृत *a.* Hidden or concealed in the womb of time. —अंतरक्षम *a.* Able to bear delay. —अंतरविष: *m.* An animal venomous only when enraged, as a rat. —अभ्र: *m.* A dark watery cloud. —अवधि: *m.* Appointed time. —अशुद्धि: *f*, —अशौचं *n.* Period of mourning, ceremonial impurity caused by the birth of a child or death of a relation in the family. —आत्मन् *m.* The Supreme Spirit. —आयसं *n.* Iron. —कंजं *n.* A blue lotus. —कटंकट: *m.* An epithet of Siva. —कंठ: *m.* 1 A peacock. -2 A sparrow. -3 A wagtail. -4 A gallinule. -5 An epithet of Siva. —कंठक: —कंटक: *m.* A gallinule. —करणं *n.* Appointing or fixing time. —कर्णिका, —कर्णी *f.* A misfortune. —कर्मन् *n.* Death. —कल्प *a.* Fatal, deadly. —काल *m* The Supreme Being. —कील: *m.* Noise. —कुंट: *m.* Yama. —कूट: *m.*, —टं *n.* 1 A deadly poison. -2 The poison churned out of the ocean and drunk by Siva. —कृत् *m.* 1 The sun. -2 A peacock. -3 Supreme Spirit. —क्रम: *m.* The lapse of time, course of time; कालक्रमेण in course or process of time. —क्रिया *f.* 1 Fixing a time. -2 Death. —क्षेप: *m.* 1 Delay, loss of time. -2 Passing the time. —खंजं, —खंजनं, —खंडं *n.* The liver. —गंगा *f.* The river Yamunâ. —ग्रंथि: *m.* A year. —चक्रं *n.* 1 The wheel of time

(time being represented as a wheel always moving). -2 A cycle. -3 The wheel of fortune, the vicissitudes of life. -चिह्नं *n*. A symptom of approaching death. —चोदित *a*. Summoned by the angel of death. —ज्ञ *a*. Knowing the proper time or occasion (of any action). —ज्ञः *m*. I An astrologer.-2 A cock.-त्रयं *n*. The three times; the past, the present, and the future. —दंडः *m*. Death. —धर्मः, -धर्मन् *m*. I The line of conduct suitable to any particular time. -2 The law or rule of time. -3 Death. —धारणा *f*. Prolongation of time. —नियोगः *m*. Fate or destiny. —निरूपणं *n*. Chronology. —पक्व *a*. Ripened by time, *i.e.* spontaneously. —पाशः *m*. The noose of Yama or death. —पृष्ठं *n*. I A species of antelope. -2 A heron. —कं *n*. I N. of the bow of Karna. -2 A bow in general. —प्रभातं *n*. Autumn or 'Sarad;' (the two months following the rainy season). -भक्षः *m*. An epithet of Siva. -भृत् *m*. The sun. -भैरवः *m*. An epithet of Siva.-मानं *n* A measure of time. —मुखः *m*. A species of ape. -मेषी *f*. The Manjishtha plant. —यवनः *m*. A king of Yavanas and enemy of Krishna. —यापः *m*., -यापनं *n*. Procrastination, delay. —योगः *m*. Fate, destiny. —रात्रिः, -रात्री *f*. I A dark night. -2 A sister of Yama. -3 The Amávasyâ on which lamps are lighted (in the Divali holidays). -4 The night of destruction at the end of the world (identified with Durgâ). —लोहं, -लौहं *n* Steel. —विप्रकर्षः *m*. Prolongation of time. —वृद्धिः *f*. Periodical interest (payable monthly, quarterly, or at stated times). —वेला *f*. The time of Saturn, *i.e.* a particular time of the day (half a watch every day at which any religious act is improper. —संरोधः *m*, I Retaining for a long time. -2 Lapse of a long period of time. —सदृश *a*. Opportune, timely. —सर्पः *m*. The black and most poisonous variety of the snake. —सारः *m*. The black antelope. —रं *n*. A yellow sort of sandal wood. —सूत्रं, -सूत्रकं *n*. N. of a particular hell. —स्कंदः *m*. The Tamâla tree. —स्वरूप *a*. Terrible as death, (death-like in form). —हरः *m*. An epithet of Siva. —हरणं *n*. Loss of time, delay. —हानिः *f*. Delay.

कालकः *m*. I A mole, freckle, mark. -2 A water-snake. -3 The black part of the eye. -4 A kind of grain. —कं *n*. I The liver. -2 An unknown quantity (in alg.).

कालंजरः *m*. I N. of a mountain and adjacent country (modern Kallinjar). -2 An assembly of religious mendicants. -3 An epithet of Siva. —रा or -री *f*. An epithet of Durgâ.

कालशेयं *n*. Buttermilk (produced in a jar by churning).

काला *f*. Goddess दुर्गा.

कालापः *m*. I The hair of the head. -2 A serpent's hood. -3 A demon, an imp, a goblin. -4 A student of the Kalâpa grammar.

कालापकं *n*. I An assemblage of the pupils of Kalâpa. -2 The doctrines or teachings of Kalâpa.

कालायनी *f*. N. of Durgâ.

कालिक *a*. (*f*. —की) I Relating to time. -2 Depending on time. -3 Seasonable, timely. —कः *m*. I A crane. -2 A heron. —का *f*. I Blackness, black colour. -2 Ink, black ink. -3 Price of a commodity to be paid by instalments. -4 Periodical interest paid at stated times. -5 A multitude of clouds. -6 Flaw ('alloy &c.) in gold. -7 The liver. -8 A female crow. -9 A scorpion. -10 A spirituous liquor. -11 N. of Durgá. -12 A kind of fragrant earth. —कं n. 1 Black sandal wood. -2 Hostility.

कालिंग a. (f. —गी) Produced in, or belonging to, the Kalinga country. —गः m. 1 A king of that country. -2 A snake of that country. -3 An elephant. -4 A species of cucumber. —गाः m. pl. N. of a country. —गं n. A water-melon.

कालिंद a. (f. —दी) Connected with or coming from the mountain Kalinda or the river Yamunâ.

कालिंदी f. 1 The river Yamuná. -2 A sort of vessel. -3 N. of a wife of Krishna. —दं n. A water melon. -Comp. —कर्षणः, —भेदनः m. An epithet of Balarâma. —सूः f. Sanjnâ (संज्ञा), a wife of the sun. (—m.) The sun. —सोदरः m Yama, the God of death.

कालिमन् m. 1 Blackness. -2 Paleness.

कालियः m. N. of a large serpent inhabiting the Yamuná and killed by कृष्ण. -Comp. —दमनः, —मर्दनः m. Epithets of Krishna.

कालीकः m. A heron.

कालीन a. (f. —ना) 1 Belonging to a particular time. -2 Seasonable.

कालीयं, कालीयक n. 1 A kind of sandal-wood. -2 Saffron. -3 A kind of pigment used by women for besmearing bodies by way of enhancing beauty.

कालीयकः m., —कं n. A species of aloe wood. -2 A kind of turmeric. -3 Yellow sandal. -4 A dark kind of sandal wood. -5 Saffron.

कालुष्यं n. 1 Foulness. turbidness. (fig. also). -2 Opacity. -3 Disagreement.

कालेय a. (f. —यी) Belonging to the Kali age. —यं n. 1 The liver. -2 Black sandal-wood. -3 Saffron.

कालेयकः m. 1 A kind of aloe wood. -2 A dog. —कं n. 1 A fragrant wood. -2 The black sandal wood.

काल्पनिक a (f. —की) 1 Existing only in fancy; fictitious; fabricated.

काल्य a. (f. —ल्या) 1 Timely, seasonable. -2 Agreeable, auspicious. —ल्या f. 1 A cow fit for the bull. -2 A woman arrived at puberty or maturity. —ल्यं f. Day-break.

काल्याणकं n. Auspiciousness.

कावचिक a. (f.—की) Armorial. -कं n. A multitude of men in armour.

कावृकः m. 1 A cock. -2 The Chakraváka bird.

कावेरं n. Saffron.

कावेरी f. 1 N. of a river in the south of India. -2 A harlot. -3 Turmeric.

काव्य a. (f —व्या) 1 Possessed of the qualities of a sage or a poet. -2 Praiseworthy. -3 Prophetic, poetical. —व्यः m. N. of Sukra, preceptor of the Asuras. —व्या f. 1 Intelligence. -2 A female friend. —व्यं n. 1 A poem. -2 Poetics, poetry, poetical composition. -3 Happiness, welfare. -4 Wisdom. -5 Inspiration. -Comp. -अर्थः m. A poetical thought or idea. —चोरः m A stealer of other men's poems. —मीमांसकः m. A rhetorician, critic. —रसिकः m. One who has a taste for and can appreciate the beauties of poetry.

काव्यलिंगं n. The figure of speech in which a reason is implied in a sentence or a word. The figure in which the reason of a statement is in the form of the meaning of a word or a sentence. Poetic Cause. काव्यलिंगं हेतोर्वाक्यपदार्थता * काव्यप्र. हेतोर्वाक्यपदार्थत्वे काव्यलिंगं निगद्यते * साहि. द. त्वद्वाजिराजिनिर्धूतधूली पटलपंकिलां । न धत्ते शिरसा गंगां भूरिभारभिया हर: * साहि. द. —हास्यं *n.* A farce. —शास्त्रं *n.* The science and art of rhetoric.

काश् I A. (काशते, काशित) I To shine, look brilliant or beautiful. -2 To appear, be visible. -3 To appear, or look like. With प्र— I To be visible. -2 To shine. -3 To look like. प्रति- I To look like. -2 To shine in opposition. वि— I To expand. -2 To shine. सम्— To appear like. (*Caus.* काशयति, -ते) With निस्— I To open. -2 To take out, to present to the sight. -3 To banish. प्र— I To show, discover, disclose, reveal. -2 To illuminate. -3 To proclaim, communicate.

काश् 4 A. (*p. p.* काशित) I To shine. -2 To appear like. -3 To be visible.

काश: *m.*, -शं *n.* A kind of grass used for mats, roofs, &c. —शं *n.* A flower of that grass. —श: *m* I See कास. -2 Appearance. -3 Splendour.

काशि:, -शी *f.* N. of a celebrated city on the Ganges, the modern Benares and one of the seven sacred cities. -Comp. —यात्रा *f.* Pilgrimage to काशी. —प: *m.* An epithet of Siva. —राज: *m.* N. of a king, father of अंबा, अंबिका and अंबालिका q. v.

काशिन *a.* (*f.*—नी) (Usually at the end of comp.) Shining, appearing or looking like. जितकाशिन् *m.* One who behaves like a conqueror.

काशी *f* See काशि:. काशू: *f.* See कासू:.

काश्मरी *f.* A plant commonly called गंभारी.

काश्मीर *a.* (*f.*—री) Born in, belonging to, or coming from, Káshmíra. —रा: *m. pl.* N. of a country or its inhabitants. —रं *n.* I Saffron. -2 Root of a tree. -Comp. —जं, जन्मन् *n.* Saffron.

काश्मीर (-रि-) क *a.* Born or produced in Kásmira.

काश्मीर्यं *n.* Saffron.

काश्यं *n.* Spirituous liquor. -Comp. —पं *n.* Flesh.

काश्यप: *m.* I N. of a celebrated sage -2 N. of Kanáda. -3 An epithet of Aruna. -पी *f.* The earth. -पं *n.* Flesh. -Comp. —नंदन: *m.* I An epithet of Garuda. -2 N. of Aruna. -3 A god. -4 A demon.

काश्यपि: *m.* An epithet of Garuda and of Aruna.

काश्यपेय: *m.* I An epithet of the twelve Adityas. -2 Also of the sun. -3 Of Garuda. -4 Gods and demons.

काष: *m.* I Rubbing, scratching. -2 That against which anything is rubbed.

काषाय *a.* (*f.* —यी) Red, dyed of a reddish colour. —यं *n.* A red cloth or garment.

काष्ठं *n.* I A piece of wood, especially one used as fuel. -2 Wood or timber, in general. -3 A stick. -4 An instrument for measuring length. -Comp. —अगार: *m.*, —रं *n.* A wooden house or enclosure. —अंबुवाहिनी *f.* A wooden bucket. —कदली *f.* The wild plantain. —कीट: *m.* A small insect found in decayed wood. —कुट:, -कूट:, -कुट्ट: *m.* A wood-pecker (Mar. सुतार पक्षी). —कुद्दाल: *m.* A kind of wooden shovel used for baling water out of a boat or for scraping and cleaning its bottom. —तक्ष:, —तक्षक: *m.* A carpenter. —तंतु: *m.* A small worm found in timber. —दारु: *m.*

The Indian pine tree; also called देवदारु. -द्रु: *m.* The Palásha tree. -पुत्तलिका *f.* A wooden image. —पदानं *n.* Piling up wood, forming a funeral pile. —भारिक: *m.* A wood-carrier. —मठी *f.* A funeral pile. —मल्ल: *m.* A bier, a wooden frame on which dead bodies are carried (Mar तिरडी). —लेखक: *m.* A small worm found in wood. The same as काष्ठकूट). —लोहिन् *m.* A cudgel armed with iron. -वाट: *m* , —टं *n.* A wall made of wood.

काष्ठकं *n.* Aloe-wood.

काष्ठा *f.* 1 A quarter or region of the world, direction, region (दिश). -2 A limit, boundary. -3 The last limit, extremity, climax. -4 Race-ground, course. -5 A mark, goal. -6 The path of the wind and clouds in the atmosphere. -7 A measure of time equal to the thirtieth part of a Kalá. -8 N. of a Kasyapa and daughter of Daksha.

काष्ठिक: *m.* A bearer of wood.

काष्ठिका *f.* A small piece of wood.

काष्ठीला *f.* The plantain tree.

कास् 1 A. (कासते, कासित) 1 To shine. -2 To cough, make a sound indicating any disease.

कास: *m.*, -सा *f.* Cough, catarrh. -Comp. -कृत् *a.* Affected with cough —कुंठ: *m.* Epithet of Yama. —घ्न. -हन् *a.* Removing cough, pectoral. -मर्द: *m.* A cure of cough.

कासर: *a.* (*f.* —री) A buffalo.

कासार: *m.*, —रं *n.* A pond, pool, lake.

कासीसं *n.* Green vitriol (Mar. मोरचूद). -2 Green sulphate of iron (Mar. हिराकस).

कासू:, -काशू: *f.*1 A sort of lance. -2 Indistinct speech. -3 Light, lustre. -4 Disease. -5 Devotion. -6 Understanding

काहृति: *f.* A by-way, a secret path.

काहल *a.* (*f* —ला) 1 Dry, withered. -2 Mischievous. -3 Excessive, spacious, large. —ल: *m.* 1 A cat. -2 A cock. -3 A crow. -4 A sound in general. —लं *n.* 1 Indistinct speech. -2 A kind of musical instrument. —ल *ind.* Very much, excessively. —ला *f.* A large drum (military). —ली *f.* A young woman

काहलि: *m.* An epithet of Siva.

किंवत् *a.* Poor, insignificant.

किंशारु: *m.* 1 The beard of corn. -2 A heron. -3 An arrow.

किंशुक: *m.* A kind of tree having beautiful red blossoms but without any odour. —कं *n.* The blossom of this tree.

किंशुल (-लु-) क: *m.* The Palásha tree.

किकि: *m.* 1 The cocoa-nut tree. -2 The blue jay. -3 The Chátaka bird, (the bird is also named as किकिन, किकिदिवि, किकीदिवि.)

किखि: *m.* A monkey, an ape. —*f.* A jackal; fox.

किंकणी, किंकिणिका, किंकिणी, किंकणिका *f.* A small bell or tinkling ornament.

किंकिर: *m.* 1 A horse. -2 The (Indian) cuckoo. -3 A large black bee. -4 N. of Cupid. -5 The red colour. —रं *n.* The frontal sinus of an elephant. —रा *f.* Blood.

किंकिरात: *m.* 1 A parrot. -2 The (Indian) cuckoo. -3 Cupid. -4 The Asoka tree. -5 A species of amaranth.

किंचिलि (-लु-) क: *m.* An earth-worm (Mar. गांडूळ).

किंजं *n.*,-किंजक:,-किंजल्क: *m.* The filament or blossom of a lotus or any other plant.

किटि: *m.* A hog.

किटिभ: *m.* 1 A louse. -2 A bug.

किट्टं, -किट्टकं *n.* Secretion, excrement, sediment, dirt. -Comp. -वींजतं *n.* Semen virile.

किट्टाल: *m.* 1 A copper vessel. -2 Rust of iron.

किण: *m.* 1 A corn, callosity, a scar. -2 A wart, a mole. -3 An insect found in wood.

किण्वं *n.* Sin. —ण्व: *m.*, —ण्वं *n.* A drug or seed used to cause fermentation in the manufacture of spirits.

किण्विन् *m.* A horse.

कित् 1 P. (केतति) 1 To desire. -2 To live. -3 (चिकित्सति) To heal, cure. -4 To doubt, suspect.

कितव: *m.* (*f.* —वी) 1 A rogue, liar, cheat. -2 The Dhattùra plant. -3 A kind of perfume. -3 A gamester, gambler. -5 A mad or crazy person.

किनाटं *n.* The inner bark of a tree.

किन्नर: *m.* 1 A mythical being with a human figure and the head of a horse. -2 A bad or deformed man.

किम् *ind.* Used for कु only at the beginning of comp. to convey the senses of 'badness,' 'deterioration,' 'defect,' 'censure'. -Comp. —दास: *m.* A bad slave or servant. —नर: *m.* 1 A bad or deformed man. -2 A mythical being with a human figure and the head of a horse. —किन्नरे-श:, —श्वर: *m.* 1 An epithet of Kubera. —नरी *f.* 1 A female Kinnara. -2 A kind of lute. —पुरुष: *m.* A mythical being with a human head and the form of a horse. —पुरुषेश्वर: *m.* An epithet of Kubera. —प्रभु: *m.* A bad master or king. —राजन् *a.* Having a bad king. (—*m.*) A bad king. —सखि *m.* (nom. sing. किंसखा) A bad freind.

किम् *pron. a.* (nom. sing. क: *m.*, का *f.*, किम् *n.*) 1 Who, what, which (used interrogatively.) -2 This pronoun is often used to imply 'power or authority to do a thing' *i.e.* के आवां परित्रातुं दुष्यंतमाक्रंद् * शाकुंत 1 'who are we &c?', *i. e.* what power have we &c? Sometimes किं means 'long' as applied to time *e. g.* कोपि कालस्तस्या आगत्य गताया: What a long time has elapsed since? -2 The neuter (किं) is frequently used with instr. of nouns in the sense of 'what is the use of'? *e. g.* लोभश्चेद्गुणेन किं &c. किं तया दृष्टया what is the use of seeing her? अपि, चित्, चन, चिद्पि or स्वित् are often added to किं to give it an indefinite sense; *e. g* विवेश कश्चिज्जटिलस्तपोवनं A certain ascetic entered the penance ground. किमपि, किंचित् 'a little', 'somewhat. किमपि Also means 'indescribable.' इव is sometimes added to किम to convey the sense of 'possibly', 'I should like to know'. *e. g.* किमिव हि मधुराणां मंडनं नाकृतीनां * शाकुंत. I. 20. *-ind.* 1 A particle of interrogation; तत: किं what then? -2 A particle meaning 'why', 'wherefore.' -3 Whether(its correlatives in the sense of 'or' being किं, उत, उताहो, आहोस्वित्, वा, किंवा, अथवा). -Comp. -अपि *ind.* 1 To some extent, somewhat, to a considerable extent. -2 Inexpressibly, indescribably. -3 Very much, by far. —अर्थ *a.* Having what motive or aim? किमर्थोऽयं यत्न:. -अर्थं *ind.* Why, wherefore? -आख्य *a.* Having what name? —इति *ind.* Why indeed, why to be sure, for what purpose? —उ, -उत 1. Whether-or (showing doubt or uncertainty). -2 Why (indeed). -3 How much more, how much less. —कर: *m.* A servant, slave. —करा *f.* A female servant. -करी *f.* The wife of a servant. —कर्तव्यता, —कार्यता *f.*

Any situation in which one asks one-self what should be done; किंकर्तव्यतामूढ: 'being at a loss or perplexed whatlto do'. -कारण *a.* Having what reason or cause? -किल *ind.* What a pity (expressing displeasure or dissatisfaction). —क्षणः *m.* A lazy fellow who does not value moments. -गोत्र *a.* Belonging to what family? -च *ind.* Moreover, further. —चन *ind.* To a certain degree, a little. —चित् *ind.* To a certain degree, somewhat, a little. -चित्ज्ञ *a.* A smatterer. —चित्कर *a.* Doing something, useful. —चित्काल: *m.* Sometime, a little time. —चित्प्राण *a.* Having a little life. —चित्मात्र *a.* Only a little. -छंदस् *a.* Conversant with which Veda? -तर्हि *ind.* How then? but, however. —तु *ind.* But, yet, however, nevertheless. -दैवत *a.* Having what deity? -नामधेय, -नामन् *a.* Having what name? —निमित्त *a.* Having what cause or reason? for what purpose? -निमित्तम् *ind.* Why? wherefore? —नु *ind.* 1 Whether. -2 Much more, much less. -3 What indeed. —नु खलु *ind.* 1 How possibly? how is it that? why indeed? -2 May it be that; -पच, -पचान *a.* Miserly, niggardly. -पराक्रम *a.* Of what power or energy? —पुनर् *ind.* How much more, how much less? —प्रकारं *ind.* In what manner? —प्रभाव *a.* Possessing what power? —भूत *a.* Of what sort ot nature? —रूप *a.* Of what form or shape? -वदंति, -ती *f.* Rumour, report. -वराटक: *m.* An extravagant man. -वा *ind.* 1 An particle of interrogation. -2 Or (corr. of कि 'whether') —विद् *a* Knowing what? -व्यापार *a.* Following what occupation? —शील *a.* Of what habits? —स्वित *ind.* Whether, how?

कियत् *a.* (Nom. sing. कियान् *m.*, कियती *f.*, कियत् *n.*) 1 How great, how far? how much? how many? of what extent or qualities? -2 Of what consideration? *i.e.* of no account, worthless. -3 Some, a little; a small number, a few (having an indefinite force). -Comp, —एतिका *f.* Effort, vigorous and persevering exertion. —कालम् *ind.* 1 How long? -2 Some little time. —चिरं *ind.* How long? —दूरं *ind.* 1 How far? how distant, how long? -2 For a short time, a little way.

कियाह: *m.* A horse of a red or bay colour.

किर: *m.* A hog.

किरण: *m.* 1 A ray or beam of light, a ray. -Comp. —मय *a.* Radiant, brilliant -2 A small particle of dust. -3 The sun. -Comp. —मालिन् *m.* The sun.

किरात: *m.* 1 N. of a degraded mountain tribe who live by hunting; a mountaineer. -2 A savage, barbarian. -3 A dwarf. -4 A groom, a horseman. -5 N. of Siva in the disguise of a Kirâta. —ता: *m. pl.* N. of a country. -Comp. —आशिन् *m.* An epithet of Garuda.

किराती *f.* 1 A female Kirâta, a woman of the Kirâta tribe. -2 A woman who carries a fly-flap or 'chowri.' -3 A bawd, a procuress. -4 Párvati in the disguise of a Kiráti.

किरि: *m.* 1 A hog, boar. -2 A cloud.

किरिटि: *m* The fruit of the marshy date tree.

किरीट: *m.*, -टं *n.* A diadem, crown, crest, tiara. -Comp. —धारिन् *m.* A king. —मालिन् *m.* An epithet of Arjuna.

किरीटिन् *a.* Wearing a crown or diadem. —*m.* N. of Arjuna.

किर्मीर *a.* (*f.* —रा) Variegated, spotted. —रः *m.* 1 N. of a Rákshasa slain by Bhíma. -2 The variegated colour. -Comp. —जित्, —निषूदनः, —सूदनः *m.* Epithets of Bhíma.

किलः *m.* 1 Play, trifling. -Comp. —किंचितं *n.* Amorous agitation, weeping, laughing, being angry &c. in the society of a lover.

किल *ind.* A particle showing (1) certainty *e. g.* इदं किलाव्याजमनोहरं वपुः. (2) Report, *e. g.* बभूव योगी किल कार्तवीर्यः. (3) Dissatisfaction, dislike, *e. g.* एवं किल केचिद्वदंति. (4) Contempt *e. g.* त्वं किल योत्स्यसे. (5) Probability *e. g.* पार्थः किल विजेष्यते कुरून्. (6) Cause, reason, *e. g.* स किलेवमुक्तवान्. (7) Feigned action, *e.g.* प्रसह्य सिंहः किल तां चकर्ष.

किलकिलः *m.*, —ला *f.* A sound, or a cry expressing joy or pleasure. —लः *m.* An epithet of Siva.

किलकिलायति-ते Den. To make a chattering noise.

किलिंजं *n.* 1 A mat. -2 A thin plank of green wood, board (also किलिंचं).

किलिंजकः *m.* 1 A mat -2 A screen or twist of grass.

किल्बिषं *n.* 1 Sin. -2 A fault, injury, guilt -3 A disease, sickness.

किशलयः *m.*, —यं *n.* A sprout a young shoot.

किशोरः *m.* 1 A colt, the young of any animal. -2 A youth, lad, a boy below fifteen. -3 The sun. —री *f.* A maiden; a young woman.

किष्किंधः, —न्ध्यः *m.* 1 N. of a country. -2 N. of a mountain situated in that country. —धा, —न्ध्या *f* N. of a city, the capital of Kiskhindha.

किष्कु *a.* Vile, contemptible. —ष्कुः *m.* or *f.* 1 The fore-arm.-2 A cubit, span. -3 An instrument for measuring lengths.

किसलः *m.*, —लं *n.* —किसलयः *m.* —यं *n.* A sprout, a young and tender shoot or foliage.

कीकट *a.* (*f* —टी) 1 Poor, indigent. -2 Miserly. —टाः *m. pl.* N. of a country (Behar). —टः *m.* A horse.

कीकस *a.* (*f.* —सा) Hard, firm. —सं *n.*, —सः *m.* A bone.

कीचकः *m.* 1 A hollow bamboo. -2 A bamboo rattling or whistling in the wind. -3 N. of a people. -4 N. of the commander-in-chief of king Virâta. -Comp. —जित *m.* An epithet of Bhíma, the second Pándava prince.

कीटः *m.* 1 A worm, an insect. -2 A term expressive of contempt (generally at the end of comp.). *e g.* द्विपकीटः *m.* A wretched elephant. पक्षिकीटः *m.* A miserable bird. -Comp. —घ्नः *m.* Sulphur. —जं *n.* Silk. —जा *f.* Lac —मणिः *m.* A fire-fly.

कीटकः *m.* 1 A worm. -2 A bard of the Mâgadha tribe.

कीदृश्, कीदृश (*f.* —शी) कीदृक्ष *f* – क्षी) Of what kind or sort? of what nature? faring or doing how? (with respect to health, study. progress &c.).

कीनाश *a.* (*f.* —शा) 1 Cultivating the soil. -2 Poor, indigent. -3 Niggardly. -4 Small. little. —शः *m.* 1 An epithet of Yama. the God of death. -2 A kind of monkey.

कीरः *m.* 1 A parrot. —राः (pl.). The country and the people of Kâshmira —रं *n.* Flesh. -Comp. —इष्टः *m.* The mango tree. —वर्णकं *n.* A kind of perfume.

कीर्ण *p. p.* (*f.* —र्णा) 1 Strewn, spread, cast, scattered. -2 Covered filled. -3 Placed, put. -4 Injured, hurt.

कीर्णिः *f.* 1 Scattering. -2 Covering, concealing. -3 Injuring.

कीर्तन *n.* 1 Telling, narrating. -2 Praising, celebrating. -3 A temple; any work of art, a building. —ना *f.* 1 Narration, recital. -2 Fame, glory.

कीर्तय् *demon. verb* 1 To tell, to utter, mention. -2 To praise, to celebrate.

कीर्तिः *f.* 1 Fame, renown, glory.-2 Favour, approbation. -3 Dirt, mud. -4 Extension, expansion. -5 Light, lustre. -6 Mention, speech, report. -Comp. —भाज् *a.* Famous, celebrated. (*m.*) An epithet of Drona, the military preceptor of the Kauravas and Pándavas —शेषः *m.* Leaving nothing behind but fame; *i. e.* death; *cf.* नामशेष, आलेख्यशेष.

कील् 1 P. 1 To bind. -2 To pin. -3 To stake.

कीलः *m.* 1 A wedge, a pin. -2 A lance. -3 A post, pillar. -4 A weapon. -5 The elbow. -6 A blow with the elbow. -7 A flame. -8 A minute particle. -9 N. of Siva. -10 A gnomon,

कीलकः *m.* 1 A wedge or pin. -2 A fence. -3 A pillar, column.

कीलालः *m.* 1 A heavenly drink similar to 'Amrita'. -2 Honey. -3 A beast. —लं *n.* 1 Blood. -2 Water. -Comp. —धिः *m.* The ocean. —पः *m.* A demon, goblin.

कीलिका *f.* The pin of an axle.

कीलित *a.* (*f.*—ता) 1 Tied, bound. -2 Fixed, pinned down. -3 Staked, impaled. -4 Pierced, transfixed. -5 Set (as a stake or pole). -तं *n.* A tie.

कीशः *a.* (*f.* —शा) Naked. —शः *m.* 1 An ape, monkey. -2 The sun. -3 A bird.

कुः *f.* 1 The earth. -2 The base of a triangle or any plane figure. -Comp. —पुत्रः *m.* Mars.

कु *ind.* A prefix signifying 'badness', 'depreciation', 'sin,' 'reproach,' 'littleness,' 'deficiency' &c. Its various substitutes are कद् (कदश्व), कव (कवोष्ण), का (कोष्ण), किं (किंप्रभुः). -Comp. —कर्मन् *n.* A bad deed, a mean act. —ग्रहः *m.* An unpropitious planet. —ग्रामः *m.* A petty village or hamlet (without a king's officer, an *agnihotrin*, a physician, or a river). —चेल *a.* Wearing bad or ragged garments. —चर्या *f.* Wickedness, evil conduct, impropriety. —जन्मन् *a.* Low-born. —तनु *a.* Deformed, ugly. —तनुः *m.* An epithet of Kubera. -तंत्री *f.* A bad lute. -तर्कः *m.* A fallacious argument. -2 A heterodox doctrine. —तर्कपथः *m.* A sophistical mode of arguing. —तीर्थं *n.* A bad teacher. —दिनं *n.* An evil day. —दृष्टिः *f.* 1 Weak sight. -2 An evil eye, sinister eye (fig.). -3 An opinion or doctrine opposed to the Vedas. —देशः *m.* A country where the necessaries of life are not available or which is subject to oppression. —देह *a.* Ugly, deformed. —देहः *m.* An epithet of Kubera. —धी *a.* 1 Foolish, silly, stupid. -2 Wicked. —नटः *m.* A bad actor. —नदिका *f* A small river, rill. —नाथः *m.* A bad master. —नामन् *m.* A miser. —पथः *m.* 1 A wrong road, bad way (fig. also). -2 A heterodox doctrine. —पथ्य *a.* Unwholesome, improper. —परीक्षक *a.* Examining badly, not valuing rightly. —पुत्रः *m.* A bad or wicked son. —पुरुषः *m.* A low or wicked man. —पूय *a.* Low, vile, contemptible. —प्रिय *a.* Disagreeable, contemptible, low, mean. —प्लवः *m.*

A bad boat. —ब्रह्मः, —ब्रह्मन् *m*. A bad or degraded Brâhmana. —मंत्रः *m*. 1 A bad advice. -2 A charm used to secure success in a bad cause. -योगः *m*. An inauspicious conjunction (of planets). —योगिन् *m*. A false devotee, impostor. —रस *a*. Having bad juice or flavour. —रसः *m*. A kind of spirituous liquor. —रूप *a*. Ugly, deformed. —रूप्यं *n*. Tin. —वंगः *m*. Lead. —वचस्, —वाक्य *a*. Abusive, scurrilous; using abusive or foul language. वचस्, —वाक्यं *n*. Bad language. —वज्रक *n*. A crystal; a stone resembling a diamond. —वर्षः *m*. A sudden or violent shower. —विवाहः *m*. A degraded or improper form of marriage. —वृत्तिः *f*. Bad behaviour. -वैद्यः *m*. A bad physician, quack. —शील *a*. Rude, unmannerly; ill-tempered. —स्थलं *n*. A bad place. —सरित् *f*. A small river, rill. —सृतिः *f*. 1 Evil conduct, wickedness. -2 Conjuring, magic. -3. Roguery. —स्त्री *f*. A bad woman.

कु 1 A. (कवते) To sound.

कु 6 A. (कुवते) 1 To moan, groan. -2 To cry.

कु 2 P. (कौति) To hum, coo (as a bee).

कुकर्मं *n*. kind of spirituous liquor.

कुकीलः *m*. A mountain.

कुकु (-कू-) दः *m*. One who gives away a girl in marriage with suitable decorations and in accordance with prescribed ceremonies.

कुकुंद (-दु-) रः *m*. The cavity of the loins just above the hips (जघनकूप) See ककुंदर.

कुकुराः *m. pl*. 1 N. of a country; also called दशार्ह. -2 N. of a people, a tribe of the Yádavas.

कुकूलः *m*., -लं *n*. 1 Chaff. -2 A fire made of chaff. —लं *n*. 1 A hole, ditch (filled with stakes). -2 An armour, mail.

कुक्कुटः *m*. 1 A cock; wild cock. -2 A whisp of lighted straw, a fire-brand. -3 A spark of fire. —टी *f*. 1 A hen. -2 A small house-lizard. -3 The silk-cotton tree.

कुक्कुटिः, -टी *f*. Hypocrisy, interested observance of religious rites.

कुक्कुभः *m*. 1 A wild cock. -2 A cock in general.

कुक्कुरः *m*. (*f*. —री) A dog. -Comp. —वाच् *m*. A species of deer.

कुक्षः *m*. The belly.

कुक्षिः *m*. 1 The belly (in general). -2 The womb, the part of the belly containing the fœtus. -3 The interior of anything. -4 A cavity in general. -5 A cavern, cave. -6 The sheath of a sword. -7 N. of Bali. -8 A bay, gulf. -Comp. —शूलः *m*. Belly-ache, colic.

कुक्षिंभरि *a*. 1 'Caring to feed his own belly', selfish, gluttonous, voracious. -2 Filling or pervading the interior.

कुंकुमं *n*. 1 Saffron. -2 Saffron paint. -Comp. -अद्रिः *m*. N. of a mountain.

कुच् 6 P. (कुचति, कुचित) 1 To utter a shrill cry (as a bird). -2 To go.-3 To polish.-4 To contract, bend. -6 To stop, impede. -7 To write or delineate. -8 To mix, connect. With सम्— To be crooked or curved. -2 To be contracted. -3 To fade, to close (as a flower &c.).

कुच् 1 P. (कुंचति, कुंचित) 1 To make crooked, to bend to curve. -2 To move or go crookedly. -3 To make small, lessen. -4 To shrink, contract. With आ— To contract, to curve, to bend. वि— To contract, to curve.

कुचः *m*. The female breast, a teat,

nipple. -Comp. —अग्रं, -मुखं *n.* A nipple. —तटं *n.*, -तटी *f.* The slope of the female breast, the breast. —फलः *m.* The pomegranate tree.

कुचर *a.* (*f.* -रा, -री) 1 Going slowly, creeping. -3 Detracting, censorious. -रः *m.* A fixed star.

कुच्चं *n.* A species of lotus.

कुजः *m* 1 A tree.-2 The planet Mars. -3 N. of a demon killed by Krishna (also called नरक). —जा *f.* N. of Sitá, also of Durgá.

कुजंभलः, कुजंभिलः, -रः *m.* A thief who breaks into a house.

कुज्झटिः, कुज्झटिका, कुज्झटी *f.* A fog or mist.

कुञ्च् See कुच् 1 P. above.

कुंचनं *n.* 1 Curving, bending, contraction. -2 A certain disease of the eye.

कुंचिः *m.* A measure of capacity equal to eight handfuls.

कुंचिका *f.* 1 A key. -2 The shoot of a bamboo. -3 A sort of reed. -4 A kind of fish.

कुंचित *a.* (*f.* —ता) Contracted, curved, bent.

कुंज् 1 P. (कुंजति) To murmur

कुंजः *m.*, -जं *n.* 1 A place overgrown with plants or creepers ; a bower, an arbour. -2 The lower jaw. -3 A cave. -4 A tooth. -5 The tusk of an elephant. -Comp. —कुटीरः *m.* A bower, a place overgrown with plants and creepers.

कुंजरः *m.* 1 An elephant. -2 Any thing pre-eminent or excellent of its class (at the end of comp. only). -3 The Asvattha tree.-4 The lunar asterism called हस्त. -5 Hair. -रा, —री *f.* A female elephant. -Comp. —अनीकं *n.* The division of an army consisting of elephant-corps. -अशनः *m.* The Asvattha tree -अरातिः *m.* 1 A lion. -2 Sarabha (a fabulous animal with 8 feet). —ग्रहः *m.* An elephant-catcher.

कुट् 6 P. (कुटति, कुटित) 1 To be crooked or curved -2 To curve or bend. -3 To act dishonestly, cheat, deceive.

कुट् 4 P. (कुट्यति) To break into pieces, break asunder, split. -2 To speak indistinctly. -3 To be warm, burn.

कुटः *m.*, -टं *n.* A waterpot, a jar-pitcher. -टः *m.* 1 A fort, strong-hold. -2 A hammer. -3 A tree. -4 A house -5 A mountain. -Comp. -जः *m.* 1 N. of a tree. -2 N. of 'Agastya'. -3 N. of Drona. —हारिका *f.* A female servant.

कुटकं *n.* A plough without a pole. —कः *m.* The post round which the string of the churning stick passes.

कुटंकः *m.* A roof, thatch.

कुटंगकः *m.* 1 An arbour formed by creeping plants overrunning a tree. -2 A small house, hut or cottage.

कुटपः *m.* 1 A measure of grain (=कुडव). -2A garden near a house. -3 A sage, an ascetic.-पं *n.* A lotus.

कुटरः *m.* The post round which the rope of the churning stick passes.

कुटलं *n.* A roof, thatch.

कुटिः *m.* 1 The body. -2 A tree. -*f.* 1 A cottage, hut. -2 A curve, bend. -Comp. —चरः *m.* A porpoise.

कुटिरं *n.* A cottage, hut.

कुटिल *a.* (*f.* —ला) 1 Crooked, bent, curved, curled. -2 Tortuous, winding. -3 (fig.) Insincere, dishonest. —ला *f.* 1 N. of Sarasvati.-2 A kind of perfume. —लं *n.* 1 N. of a plant (तगर). -2 Tin. -Comp. —आशय *a.* Malevolent -पक्ष्मन् *a.* Having curved eye-lashes. —मति, -बुद्धि *a.* Evil-minded, malevolent. -स्वभाव *a.* Dishonest, malevolent.

कुटिलिका *f.* 1 *f.* Coming stealthily as a hunter on his prey, crouching. -2 A blacksmith's forge.

कुटी *f.* 1 A curve. -2 A cottage, hut. -3 A bawd, procuress. -Comp. -चक: *m.* A religious mendicant of a particular order. —चर: *m.* A kind of ascetic who entrusts the care of his family to his son and devotes himself solely to religious penance and austerities.

कुटीर: *m.*, -रं *n.*, कुटीरक: *m.* A hut, cottage.

कुटुंगक: *m.* 1 An arbour formed by creeping plants.-2 A creeper winding round a tree. -3 A thatch, roof. -4 A hut. -5 A granary.

कुटुनी *f.* A bawd, procuress.

कुटुंबं, कुटुंबकं *n.* A household; a family. -2 The duties and cares of a family. —बः *m.*, -बं *n.* 1 A kinsman, a relation by descent or marriage. -2 Offspring, progeny. -3 A name. -4 Race. -5 A group, collection. -Comp. —कलहः *m.*, -हं *n.* Internal or domestic quarrel. —भर: *m.* The burden of the family. —व्यापृत *a.* Provident and attentive to the good of the family.

कुटुंबिक:, -कुटुंबिन् *m.* 1 A house-holder, married man, a *pater familias*, one who has a family to support or take care of.

कुटुंबिनी *f.* 1 The wife of a householder, a house-wife (in charge of the house). -2 A large household or family. -3 A woman in general.

कुट्ट् 10 U. (कुट्टयति-ते, कुट्टित) 1 To cut, cut, divide. -2 To grind, pound. -3 To blame, censure.

कुट्टः *m.* (In Math.) A multiplier.

कुट्टनं *n.* 1 Cutting. -2 Pounding. -3 Abusing, censuring.

कुट्ट (-ट्टि-) नी *f.* A bawd, procuress, a go-between.

कुट्टमितं *n.* The affected repulse of a lover's endearments or caresses. (one of the 28 graces or blandishments of the heroine).

कुट्टाक *a.* (*f.* —की) Who or what divides or cuts.

कुट्टार: *m.* A mountain. —रं *n.* 1 Sexual intercourse. -2 A woollen blanket.

कुट्टिम: *m.*,-मं *n.* 1 An inlaid or paved floor ; ground paved with small stones ; pavement. -2 Ground prepared for the site of a mansion. -3 A jewel-mine. -4 The pomegranate. -5 A hut, cottage, small house.

कुट्टिमितं Same as कुट्टमितं.

कुट्टिहारिका *f.* A maid-servant, slave.

कुड्डार: *m.* A small mountain.

कुड्डीरकं *n.* A small house, hut.

कुड्मल Same as कुड्मल.

कुठ: *m.* A tree.

कुठर: *m.* The post round which the string of a churning stick winds. (Mar. घुसळ खांबा).

कुठारक: *m.*, -का *f.* An axe.

कुठार: *m.*, -री *f.* 1 An axe, or hatchet. -2 A sort of hoe or spade. -र: *m.* A tree.

कुठारक: *m.* A small axe.

कुठारिक: *m.* A wood-cutter.

कुठारिका *f.* A small axe.

कुठारु: *m.* 1 A tree. -2 An ape, a monkey. -3 An armourer.

कुठि: *m.* 1 A tree. -2 Mountain.

कुडंग: *m.* A bower, an arbour.

कुडव:, -प: *m.* A measure of grain equal to a quarter of a Prastha and containing 12 handfuls.

कुडुपः *m.* The clasp of a necklace or bracelet.

कुड्मल *a.* (*f.* —ला) Opening, full-blown, expanding, (as the blossom of a flower). —लः *m.* An opening bud. —लं *n.* A particular hell.

कुड्मलित *a.* (*f.* —ता) 1 Budded blossomed. -2 Cheerful, smiling. -3 Half-closed.

कुड्यं *n.* 1 A wall. -2 Plastering (a wall). -3 Eagerness, curiosity. -Comp. —छेदिन् *m.* A house-breaker, a thief. —छेद्यः *m.* A digger. —छेद्यं *n.* A ditch, pit, breach or opening (in a wall).

कुण् 6 P. (कुणति, कुणित) 1 To support, aid. -2 To sound.

कुणकः *m.* A young animal just born.

कुणप *a.* (*f.* —पी) Smelling like a dead body; stinking. —पः *m.*, -पं *n.* A dead body, corpse. —पः *m.* 1 A spear. -2 A foul smell, stench.

कुणिः *m.* A cripple with a withered or crooked arm. -2 A witlow (Mar. नखुर्डें).

कुंटक *a.* (*f.* —की) Fat, corpulent.

कुंठ् 1 P. (कुंठति, कुंठित) 1 To be blunted or dulled. -2 To be lame or mutilated. -3 To be dull or stupid, be idle. -4 To loosen.

कुंठ 10 P. To hide.

कुंठ *a.* (*f.* —ठा) 1 Blunt, dulled. -2 Dull, stupid. -3 Indolent, lazy. -4 Weak.

कुंठकः *m.* A fool.

कुंठित *a.* (*f.* —ता) 1 Blunted, dulled; (fig. also). -2 Stupid. -3 Mutilated.

कुंडः *m.*, -डी *f.*, -डं *n.* 1 A bow-shaped vessel, a basin. -2 A round hole in the ground for receiving water. -3 A hole in general. -4 A pool, well; especially one consecrated to some deity or holy purpose. -5 The bowl of a mendicant. —डः *m.* (*f.* —डा) A son born in adultery; the son of a woman by a man other than her husband while the husband is alive. —डा *f.* An epithet of Durgá. -Comp. —आशिन् *m.* A pander, pimp, one who depends for his livelihood on a कुंड *i. e.* a bastard, or adulterine —उधस् (कुंडोध्नी) *f.* 1 A cow with a full udder. -2 A woman with a full bosom. —कीटः *m.* 1 A keeper of concubines. -2 A follower of Chârváka; an atheist. -3 A Brâhmana born in adultery. —कीलः *m.* A low or vile man —गोलं, -गोलकं *n.* 1 Gruel. -2 A group of कुंड and गोलक (taken together).

कुंडलः *m.*, -लं *n.* 1 An ear-ring. -2 A bracelet. -3 The coil of a rope. -4 A tie, collar.

कुंडलना *f.* Encircling (as a word) to denote that it is to be left out or not considered.

कुंडलिन् *m.* (*f.* —नी) 1 Decorated with ear-rings. -2 Circular, spiral. -3 Winding, coiling (as a serpent). —*m.* 1 A snake. -2 A peacock. -3 An epithet of Varuna, also of Siva. -4 The spotted or painted deer. -नी *f.* A form of Durgâ or Sakti.

कुंडिका *f.* 1 A pitcher. -2 A student's water-pot (कमंडलु).

कुंडिन् *m.* 1 An epithet of Siva. -2 A bastard. -3 A horse.

कुंडिनं *n.* N. of a city, the capital of the Vidarbhas.

कुंडि (-डी-)र *a.* Strong. -रः *m.* A man.

कुतपः *m.* 1 A Brâhmana. -2 A twice-born man (द्विजन्मन्). -3 The sun. -4 Fire. -5 A guest. -6 An ox, a bull. -7 A daughter's son. -8 A sister's son. -9 Grain. -10 The eighth Muhúrta of the day. -11 A musical instrument. -12 A time suitable for the performance of sacrifices to the manes. —पं *n.* 1 The कुश grass.

कुतस् *ind.* 1 From where ? -2 Whence? where else? in what (other) place? -3 Why? Wherefore? From what cause or motive? -4 How? In what manner? कुतः Often makes a question of appeal. कुतः is sometimes used merely for the abl. of किम्. कुतः Becomes indefinite when connected with the particles चिद्, चन, or अपि.

कुतस्त्य *a.* 1 Whence come? -2 How happened?

कुतुकं *n.* 1 Desire, inclination. -2 Curiosity.-3 Eagerness, vehemence.

कुतुपः *m.*, कुतूः *f.* A small leathern bottle for oil. —पः *m.* 1 The eighth Muhúrta of the day.

कुतूहल *a.* (*f.* —ला) 1 Wonderful. -2 Excellent, best. -3 Praised, celebrated. —लं *n.* 1 Desire, curiosity. -2 Eagerness. -3 What excites curiosity; anything pleasing or interesting; a curiosity. -4 Delight, pleasure.

कुत्र *ind.* 1 Where? In which place? -2 In which case? कुत्र is sometimes used for the loc. sing. of किम्. When connected with the particles चित्, चन or अपि, कुत्र becomes indefinite in sense कुत्रापि, कुत्रचित् somewhere, anywhere; न कुत्रापि no where ; कुत्रचित्-कुत्राचित् in one place, in another place, here, there.

कुत्रत्य *a.* Where living or residing?

कुत्स् 10 A. (कुत्सयते, कुत्सित) To abuse, censure, condemn.

कुत्सनं *n.*, कुत्सा *f.* Abuse, reproach. —ना *f.* Expression of contempt.

कुत्सित *p. p.* (*f.* -ता) 1 Despised, contemptible. -2 Low, mean, vile. —तं *n.* Censure.

कुथः *m.* The Kusa grass.

कुथः *m.*, -थं *n.*, -था *f.* 1 A painted cloth serving as an elephant's housings. -2 A carpet (in general).

कुद्दारः, -लः, -लकः *m.* 1 A spade, hoe. -2 The Kânchana tree. -लकं *n.* A copper pitcher.

कुद्मलं *n.* See कुड्मलं *n.*

कुद्रंकः,-गः *m.* 1 A watch-house. -2 A dwelling raised on a scaffold.

कुनकः *m.* A crow.

कुंतः *m.* 1 A lance, a barbed dart, spear. -2 A small animal, an insect.

कुंतलः *m.* 1 The hair of the head, a lock of hair. -2 A drinking cup. -3 A plough. -लाः *m. pl.* N. of a country and its inhabitants.

कुंतयः (pl. of कुंति *m.*) N. of a country and its people.

कुंतिः *m.* N. of a king, son of कथ. -Comp. —भोजः *m.* N. of a Yâdava prince, king of the Kuntis, who being childless, adopted Kuntí.

कुंती *f.* N. of पृथा, daughter of a Yádava named शूर, adopted by कुंतिभोज. -2 A fragrant resin. -3 The wife of a Brâhmana.

कुंथ् I. 9. P. (कुंथति, कुथ्नाति, कुंथित) 1 To suffer pain. -2 To cling to. -3 To embrace. -4 To cling.

कुंदः *m.*, -दं *n.* A kind of jasmine (white and delicate). —दं *n.* The flower of this plant. —दः *m.* 1 An epithet of Vishnu. -2 A fragrant oleander. -3 One of the nine treasures of Kubera. -4 The number 'nine'. -5 A turner's lathe. -Comp. —करः *m.* A turner.

कुंदमः m. A cat.

कुंदिनी f. A multitude of lotuses.

कुंदुः m. A rat, mouse.

कुप् 4. P. I To be angry, (generally with the dat. of the person who is the object of anger, but sometimes with the acc. or gen. also). -2 To be excited, to gather strength, be virulent: as in दोषाः प्रकुप्यंति. With अति or परि or सम् To be angry. प्र- To be excited, to become strong or virulent.

कुपिंदः m. I A weaver. -2 A name of of the weaver caste.

कुपिनिन् m. A fisherman.

कुपिनी f. A kind of net for catching small fish.

कुप्य a. (f. -प्या) Despised, low, mean, contemptible.

कुप्यं n. I A base metal. -2 Any metal but silver and gold -Comp. —शाला f. A braziery.

कुबे (-बे-) रः m. The God of riches and regent of the northern quarter. -Comp. —अद्रिः, —अचलः m. An epithet of mountain Kailása. —दिश् f. The north.

कुब्ज a. (f. -ब्जा) Hump-backed, crooked. -ब्जः m. I A curved sword. -2 A hump on the back. —ब्जा f. A young female servant of Kamsa

कुब्जिका f. An unmarried girl eight years old.

कुभ्रं n. I A forest. -2 A hole for sacrificial fire. -3 A ring; an ear-ring. -4 A thread. -5 A cart.

कुभृत् m. I A mountain -2 A king.

कुमारः m. I A son, boy; a youth. -2 A boy below five. -3 A prince, an heir-apparent (especially in dramas). -4 N. of Kártikeya, the God of war. -5 N. of Agni. -6 A parrot. -Comp. —पालनः m. I One who takes care of children. -2 N. of king Sálivàhana. —भृत्या f. Care of young chidren. -2 Care of a woman in pregnancy or confinement; midwifery. —वाहिन्, -वाहनः m. A peacock. -व्रतं n. A vow of eternal celibacy. —सूः f. I. An epithet of Párvati. -2 An epithet of the Ganges. (-m.) An epithet of Agni.

कुमारकः m. I A child, a youth. -2 The pupil of the eye.

कुमारिक a. (f. -की), कुमारिन् (f. -णी) a. Furnished with girls, abounding in girls.

कुमारिका, कुमारी f. I A young girl, one from 10 to 12 years old. -2 A maiden, virgin. -3 A girl or daughter in general. -4 N. of Durgá. -5 The southern extremity of the Indian peninsula. -Comp. —पुत्रः m. I The son of an unmarried woman. -2 N. of Karna.

कुमुद् a. I Unkind, unfriendly. -2 Avaricious. -n. I The white water-lily. -2 The red lotus.

कुमुदः m., -दं n. I The white water-lily. -2 A red lotus. —दः m. I An epithet of Vishnu. -2 N. of the elephant supposed to guard the south. -3 Camphor. -4 A species of monkey. -5 N. of a Nâga. -Comp. —अभिख्यं n. Silver. —आकरः, —आवासः m. A pond full of lotuses. —ईशः m. The moon. -खंडं n. An assemblage of lotuses. —नाथः, —पतिः, —बंधुः, —बांधवः m. —सुहृद् m. The moon.

कुमुदिनी f. I A water-lily with white lotuse flowess. -2 A collection of lotuses. -3 A place abounding in lotuses. -Comp. —नायकः, —पतिः m. The moon.

कुमुद्वत् a. Abounding in lotuses. —ती f. I A water-lily with white flowers. -2 A collection of lotuses. -3 A place abounding in lotuses.

कुमुद्वतीशः *m.* The moon.

कुमोदकः *m.* An epithet of Vishnu.

कुंबा *f.* 1 A thick petticoat. -2 An enclosure round the sacrificial ground.

कुंभः *m.* 1 A pitcher, water-pot, jar. -2 The frontal globe on the forehead of an elephant. -3 Aquarius, the eleventh sign of the zodiac. -4 A measure of grain equal to 210 'dronas.' -5 (In Yoga phil.) Closing the nostrils and mouth so as to suspend breathing. -6 The paramour of a harlot. -7 An urn in which the bones of dead bodies are collected. -8 A kind of heart-disease. -भा *f.* A harlot, a whore. —भं *n.* A fragrant resin (गुग्गुल). -Comp —कर्णः *m.* N. of a gigantic Rákshasa, brother of Rávana and slain by Ráma. -2 An epithet of Siva. —कारः *m.* 1 A potter. -2 A mixed tribe. —जः, —जन्मन् *m.*, —योनिः, —संभवः *m.* Epithets of Agastya. -2 An epithet of Drona, the military preceptor of the Kauravas and Pándavas. -3 An epithet of Vasishtha. —दासी *f.* A bawd, procuress. —धरः *m.* The sign of the zodiac called Aquarius —राशिः *m.* The sign Aquarius. —लग्नं *n.* That time of the day in which Aquarius rises above the horizon. —मंडूकः *m.* 1 (lit.) A frog in a pitcher. -2 (fig.) An inexperienced man. —संधिः *m.* The hollow on the top of an elephant's head between the frontal globes.

कुंभकः *m.* 1 The base of a column. -2 A religious exercise (in Yoga phil.), stopping the breath by closing the mouth and both nostrils with the fingers of the right hand.

कुंभिका *f.* 1 A small pot. -2 A harlot.

कुंभिन् *m.* 1 An elephant. -2 A crocodile. -3 A fish. -4 A kind of poisonous insect. -5 A sort of fragrant resin (गुग्गुल). -Comp. —नरकः *m.* A particular hell. —मदः *m.* Rut, ichor.

कुंभिलः *m.* 1 A thief who breaks into a house. -2 A plagiarist. -3 A wife's brother. -4 A child of an imperfect impregnation or born at undue seasons.

कुंभी *f.* 1 A small water-jar. -2 An earthen cooking vessel. -3 A measure of grain. -Comp. —नसः *m.* A kind of venomous serpent. —पाकः *m.* The contents of a cooking-vessel. -2 (sing. or pl.) A particular hell in which the wicked are baked like potter's vessels.

कुंभीकः *m.* 1 The Punnâga tree. -2 A catamite. —का *f.* Swelling of the eye-lids (*mar.* रांजणवाडी).

कुंभीरः *m.* A shark.

कुंभीरकः, कुंभीलः, कुंभीलकः *m.* A thief. —लः *m.* A crocodile.

कुर् 6 P. (कुरति, कुरित) To sound.

कुरकुर् 10 A (*pr.* कुरकुरायते) To Chant, mutter. विदूषकः अद्यापि कुरकुरायत एव एषा सारिका दास्याः पुत्री * रत्नावली.

कुरंकरः, कुरंकुरः *m.* The (Indian) crane.

कुरंगः *m.* (*f.* —गी) 1 A deer in general. -2 A species of deer. -Comp. —अक्षी, —नयना, —नेत्रा *f.* A deer-eyed woman. —नाभिः *f.* Musk.

कुरंगकः, कुरंगमः *m.* See कुरंगः

कुराचिह्नः *m.* A crab.

कुरटः *m.* A shoemker.

कुरंटः, कुरंटकः, *m.* कुरंटिका *f.* The yellow amaranth (*mar.* कोन्हांटकी).

कुरंड: *m.* Enlargement of the testicles or of the scrotum, hydrocele (*mar.* अंतर्गळ).

कुरंडक: *m.* Yellow amaranth.

कुरर: (-ल:) An osprey.

कुररी *f.* 1 A female osprey (*mar.* टिटवी). चक्रंद विग्रा कुररीव भूय: * रघुवं 14. 68. -2 A ewe.

कुरल: *m.* 1 An osprey. -2 A curl, a lock of hair.

कुरव: (-ब:), कुरव (-ब-) क: *m.* A species of amaranth. —वं (-बं), —व (-ब-) कं *n.* The flower of this tree. (*mar.* तांबडी कोन्हांटी).

कुराल: (-ह:) *m.* A light bay horse with black legs.

कुरु (*m.* pl.) 1 N. of a country situated in the north of India about the site of the modern Delhi. -2 The kings of this country. —रु: *m.* 1 A priest. -2 Boiled rice. -Comp. —क्षेत्रं *n.* N. of an extensive plain near Delhi, the scene of the great war between the Kauravas and Pāndavas. -क्षेत्रयोग: *m.* A solar day in the course of which three lunar days, three asterisms and three yogas occur. -चिह्न: *m.* Crab. -जांगलं *n.* Same as कुरुक्षेत्रं. -राज् *m.*, -राज: *m.* An epithet of Duryodhana. —विस्त: *m.* A weight of gold equal to about 700 Troy grains. —वृद्ध: *m.* An epithet of Bhishma.

कुरुंट: *m.* See कुरुंटक:.

कुरुंटक: *m* Yellow or white amaranth. (*mar.* कोन्हांटी).

कुरुंटी *f.* A wooden doll or puppet.

कुरुल: *m.* A lock of hair, especially on the forehead.

कुरुवक: *m.* Same as कुरबक:.

कुरुविंद: *m.*, —दं *n.* A ruby. —दं *n.* 1 Black salt. -2 A mirror.

कुर्कुट: *m.* 1 A cock. -2 Rubbish.

कुर्कुर: *m.* A dog.

कुर्चिका *f.* See कूर्चिका.

कुर्द्, कुर्दनं See कूर्द्, कूर्दन.

कु (कू-) र्पर: *m.* 1 The knee. -2 The elbow.

कु (कू-) र्पास:, कु (कू-) र्पासक: *m.* A sort of bodice worn by women.

कुर्वत् *pres. p.* (*f.* कुर्वती) Doing &c. -*m.* 1 A servant. -2 A shoe-maker.

कुलं *n.* A race, family. -2 The residence of a family, house, an abode. -3 A high or noble family, noble descent. -4 A herd, troop, collection, -5 A gang, band (in a bad sense). -6 A country. -7 The body. -8 The front or fore part. -9 A tribe, caste, community. -10 A blue stone. —ल: *m.* The head of a guild or corporation. -Comp. —अकुल *a.* 1 Of a mixed character or origin. -2. Middling. कुलाकुलतिथि: *m f.*, The second, sixth, and the tenth lunar days of a fort-night in a month. —कुलाकुलवार: *m.* Wednesday. —अंकुर: *m.* The scion of a family. —अंगना *f.* A respectable or high-born (chaste) woman. —अंगार: *m.* A man who ruins his family. —अचल:, —अद्रि:, पर्वत:, -शैल: *m.* A principal mountain, one of a class of seven mountains which are supposed to exist in each division of the continent. They are:—महेंद्रो मलय: सह्य: शुक्तिमान् ऋक्षपर्वत: । विंध्यश्च पारियात्रश्च सप्तैते कुलपर्वता: ॥ —अन्वित *a.* Sprung from a noble family. —अभिमान: *m.* Family pride. —आचार: *m.*, -कर्मन् *n.*, -धर्म: *m.* A duty or custom peculiar to a family or caste. —आचार्य:, गुरु: *m.* 1 A family-priest or teacher. -2 A geneologist. -आलंबिन् *a.* Maintaining a family. —ईश्वर: *m.* 1 The chief of a family. -2 N. of Siva. —उत्कट *a.* High-born.

-टः *m.* A horse of a good breed. —उत्पन्न, -उद्गत, -उद्भव *a.* Sprung from a noble family, high-born. -उद्वहः *m.* The head or perpetuator of a family. -उपदेशः *m.* A family name.-कज्जलः *m.* One who is a disgrace to his family. -कंटकः *m.* One who is a thorn or trouble to his family. —कन्यका, -कन्या *f.* A girl of high birth . -करः, -कर्तृ *m.* The founder of a family. —कलंकः *m.* One who is a disgrace to his family. -क्षयः *m.* 1 Ruin of a family -2 Extinction of a family. —गिरिः, -भूभृत् *m.*, —पर्वतः,—शैलः *m.* See कुलाचल above. —ज, —जात *a.* 1 Well-born, of high birth. -2 Ancestral, hereditaty. -जनः *m.* A high-born or distinguished person. -तंतुः *m.* One who continues or perpetuates a family. -तिथिः *m.f.* An important lunar day, viz:- the 4th, 8th, 12th or 14th of a lunar fort-night. -तिलकः *m.* The glory of a family; one who does honour to his family. -दीपः —दीपकः *m.* The glory of a family. -दुहितृ *f.* See कुलकन्या. -देवता *f.* A tutelary deity; the guardian deity of a family. —धर्मः *m.* A family custom. —धारकः *m.* A son. —धुर्यः *m.* A son able to support a family; a grown-up son. —नंदन *a.* Gladdening or doing honour to a family. -नायिका *f.* A girl worshipped at the celebration of the orgies of the left-hand Sâktas. —नारी *f.* A high bred and virtuous woman. —नाशः *m.* 1 Ruin or extinction of a family. -2 A reprobate, outcast. -3 A camel. —परंपरा *f.* The series of generations comprising a race. —पतिः *m.* 1 The head or chief of a family.-2 A sage who feeds and teaches 10,000 pupils. -पांसुका *f.* An unchaste woman. —पालिः, -पालिका, -पाली *f.* A chaste, or high-born woman. —पुत्रः *m.* A nobly-born youth. —पुरुषः *m.* 1 A respectable or high-born man. -2 An ancestor. —पूर्वगः *m.* An ancestor. —भार्या *f.* A virtuous wife. —भृत्या *f.* The nursing of a pregnant woman. -मर्यादा *f.* Family honour or respectability. —मार्गः *m.* A family custom, the best way or the way of honesty. —योषित्, -वधूः *f.* A woman of good family and character. —वारः *m.* A principal day; (*i. e.* Tuesday and Friday). —विद्या *f.* 1 Knowledge handed down in a family; traditional knowledge. -2 One of the three आन्वीक्षिकी lores. —विप्रः *m.* A family-priest. —वृद्धः *m.* An old and experienced member of a family. —व्रतः *m.*, -तं *n.* A family vow. -श्रेष्ठिन् *a.* Well-born, of a good family. (—*m.*) 1 The chief of a family or a guild. -2 An artisan of noble birth. —संख्या *f.* 1 Family-respectability. -संततिः *f.* Posterity, continuation of a lineage. —संभव *a.* Of a respectable family. —सेवकः *m.* An excellent servant. -स्त्री *f.* A woman of good family; a noble woman. —स्थितिः *f.* 1 Antiquity or prosperity of a family. -2 A family custom.

कुलक *a.* (*f.* —का) Of good family. —कः *m.* 1 The chief of a guild. -2 Any artisan of eminent birth. -3 An ant-hill. —कं *n.* 1 A collection. -2 A number of verses from 5 to 15 stanzas in grammatical connection and the whole forming one sentence); *e. g.* See शिशुपा. 1 4 -10. रघुवं. 1. 5. 9; so कुमा. सं. 1. 1-16. -3 A kind of prose composition with few compounds.

कुलटा *f.* An unchaste woman. -Comp. —पतिः *m.* A cuckold.

कुलत्थः *m.* A kind of pulse.

कुलंधर *a.* One who continues or perpetuates a family.

कुलंभरः, कुलंभलः *m.* A thief.

कुलाय: *m.*, -यं *n.* The nest of a bird. -2 The body. -3 A place or spot in general. -4 A woven texture, a web. -Comp. —निलाय: *m.* The act of sitting in a nest, hatching, brooding. —स्थ: *m.* A bird.

कुलायिका *f.* A bird-cage, an aviary, dove-cot.

कुलाल: *m.* 1 A potter. -2 A wild cock. -3 An owl. -ली *f.* The wife of a potter

कुलालिका *f.* An aviary.

कुलि: *m.* A hand.

कुलिक *a.* (*f.* —का) Well-born. -क: *m.* 1 A kinsman. -2 The chief or head of a guild. -5 An artist of high birth. -Comp. -वेला *f.* Certain portions of time on each day on which it is improper to begin any good business. [sparrow.

कुलिंग: *m.* A bird in general. -2 A

कुलिन *a.* (*f.* —नी) Of good family, high-born. —*m.* A mountain.

कुलिंदा: *m. pl.* N. of a country and its rulers.

कुलिर: *m.*, -रं *n.* 1 A crab. -2 The 4th sign of the zodiac, Cancer; see कुलीरः.

कुलिश: *m.*, -शं *n.* 1 The thunder-bolt of Indra. -3 The point or end of a thing. -Comp. —धरः, -पाणि: *m* An epithet of Indra. -नायक: *m.* A particular mode of sexual enjoyment. —शासन: *m.* An epithet of Sâkyamuni.

कुली *f.* A wife's elder sister.

कुलीन *a.* (*f.*-ना) Of a high or good family; well-born. —न: *m.* A horse of a good breed.

कुलीनसं *n.* Water.

कुलीरः, -रक: *m.* 1 A crab. -2 The fourth sign of the zodiac, cancer.

कुलीनक *a.* Of a good family.

कुलीश: *m.*, -शं *n.* Indra's thunderbolt.

कुलुक्कुंजा *f.* A fire-brand.

कुलूता: *m. pl.* N. of a country and its rulers.

कुल्माषं *n.* Cruel. —ष: *m.* A kind of grain. -Comp. —अभिषुतं *n.* Gruel.

कुल्य *a.* 1 Relating to a family, race, or corporation. -2 Well-born. —ल्य: *m.* A respectable man. -ल्यं 1 *n.* Friendly inquiry after family affairs, (condolence, congratulation &c.). -2 A bone. -3 Flesh. -4 A winnowing basket. —ल्या *f.* 1 A virtuous woman. -2 A small river, canal, stream; कुल्यांभोभिः पवनचपलैः शाखिना धौतमूलाः * शाकुंत. I. 15. -3 A dike, trench.

कुल्य *a.* (*f.* —ल्या) 1 Relating to a family. -2 Well-born. —ल्य: *m.* A respectable man. —ल्य *n.* 1 A bone. -2 Flesh. -3 A winnowing basket. -4 Friendly inquiry after family affairs.

कुल्या *f.* 1 A virtuous woman. -2 A small river, canal, stream. -3 A measure of grain equal to eight 'dronas.'

कुवं *n.* 1 A flower. -2 A lotus.

कुवम: *m.* The sun

कुवर *a.* (*f.* —रा) 1 Astringent. -2 Beardless. Also see तुवर.

कुवलं *n.* 1 The water-lily. -2 A pearl. -3 Water.

कुवलयं *n.* 1 The blue water-lily. -2 A water-lily in general. -3 The earth (—*m.* also).

कुवलयिनी *f.* 1 The blue water-lily plant. -2 An assemblage of lotus es. -3 A place abounding in lotuses.

कुवाद् a. (f. —दा) 1 Detracting, undervaluing. -2 Low, vile.

कुवाहुल: m. A camel.

कुवि (-पि-) द: m. 1 A weaver. -2 N. of the weaver caste.

कुवेणी f. 1 A basket to hold fish (when caught). -2 A badly arranged tress of hair.

कुवेलं n. A lotus.

कुश: m. 1 A kind of grass considered holy and used in religious ceremonies. -2 N. of the elder son of Ráma. -3 A rope of Kusa grass for connecting the yoke of a plough with the pole. -4 One of the great 'Dvïpas.' -शा f. 1 A plank for covering anything. -2 A piece of wood. -3 A horse's bridle. —शी f. A sort of ladle.-2 Wrought iron. -3 Plough share. -4 A pod of cotton. -शं n. Water; as in कुशेशय. -Comp. -अक्ष: m. A monkey. —अग्रं n. The sharp point of a blade of the Kusa grass; hence often used in comp. in the sense of ' sharp ', ' shrewd, ' 'penetrating ' as intellect. Hence कुशाग्र बुद्धि means one having a penetrating intellect; sharp, shrewd. —अग्रीय a. Penetrating, sharp. -अंगुली -रीयं n. A ring of Kusa grass worn at religious ceremonies. -आसनं n. A mat of Kusa grass. —ध्वज: m. The younger brother of Janaka. —स्थलं n. N. of a place in the North of India. —स्थली f. N. of the town Dvârakâ.

कुशल a. (f. —ला) 1 Right, proper, good, auspicious. -2 Happy, prosperous. -3 Able, clever, proficient, with loc, or in comp. -लं n. 1 Welfare, happiness. -2 Virtue. -3 Cleverness, ability. —ल: m. An epithet of Siva. -Comp. —काम a. Desirous of happiness. —प्रश्न: m. Friendly inquiry after a person's health or welfare. —बुद्धि a. Wise, intelligent, shrewd, sharp.

कुशलिन् a. (f. —नी) Happy, prosperous.

कुशा f. 1 A rope. -2 A bridle.

कुशावती f. N. of a city, the capital of Kusa, Râma's son.

कुशिक a. (f. -का) Squint-eyed. —क: m. 1 N. of the grand father of Visvâmitra. -2 A plough-share. -3 Sediment of oil.

कुशिन् m. An epithet of Válmíkī.

कुशीदं n. Usury; also कुसीदं.

कुशीलव: m. 1 A bard, singer. -2 An actor, a dancer. -3 A newsmonger. -4 An epithet of Válmíki. m. dual. The two sons of Rama.

कुशुंभ: m. 1 The water-pot of an ascetic. -2 A jar in general.

कुशूल: m. 1 A granary, cupboard, store-room. -2 A fire made of chaff.

कुशेशयं n. A water-lily, a lotus in general. —य: m. The (Indian) crane or Sârasa bird.

कुष् 9 P. (कुष्णाति, कुषित) 1 To tear, extract, pull or draw out. -2 To test, examine. -3 To shine. With निस् To draw out.

कुषाकु: m. 1 The sun. -2 Fire. -3 An ape, monkey.

कुषीद a. Indifferent, inert. —दं n. Usury.

कुष्ठ: m., -ष्ठं n. 1 A kind of leprosy. -2 A sort of poison. -Comp. —अरि: m. Sulphur.

कुष्ठिन् a. (f. —नी) कुष्ठित (f. —ता) a. Affected with leprosy, a leper.

कुष्मांड: m. 1 A kind of pumpkin gourd. -2 A false conception. —डी f. 1 A religious ceremony. -2 An epithet of the wife of Siva

कुष्मांडकः *m.* A kind of pumpkin gourd.

कुस् 4 P. (कुस्यति, कुसित) 1 To embrace. -2 To surround.

कुसितः *m.* 1 An inhabited country. -2 One who lives on usury; see कुसीद.

कुसी (-सि-) द *a.* Lazy, slouthful. -दः *m.* (also कुशी-षी-दः) A money-lender, usurer. —दं *n.* 1 Any loan or thing lent to be repaid with interest. -2 Lending money, usury, the profession of usury. -Comp. —पथः *m.* Usury, usurious interest. —वृद्धिः *f.* Interest on money.

कुसीदा *f.* A female usurer.

कुसीदायी *f.* The wife of a usurer.

कुसीदिकः, कुसीदिन् *m.* A usurer.

कुसुमं *n.* 1 A flower. -2 Menstrual discharge. -3 A fruit. -4 A disease of the eyes. —मः *m.* A form of fire. -Comp. —अंजनं *n.* The calx of brass used as a collyrium. —अंजलिः *m.* A handful of flowers. —अधिपः, -अधिराज् *m.* The Champaka tree (bearing yellow fragrant flowers). -अवचायः *m.* Gathering flowers. -अवतंसकः *m.* A chaplet. -अस्त्रः, -आयुधः, -इषुः, -बाणः, -शरः *m.* N. of the God of love. -आकरः *m.* 1 A garden. -2 A nosegay. -3 The vernal season. —आत्मकं *n.* Saffron. -आपीडः *m.* 1 A garland or chaplet of flowers. -2 The God of love. -आसवं *n.* 1 Honey.-2 A kind of spirituous liquor (prepared from flowers). —उज्ज्वल *a.* Brilliant with blossoms. —कार्मुकः, —चापः,-धन्वन् *m.* Epithets of the God of love. —चित *a.* Heaped with flowers. —पुरं *n.* N. of the town of Pâtaliputra. —लता *f.* A creeper in blossom. -शयनं *n* A bed of flowers ; -स्तबकः *m.* A nosegay, bouquet.

कुसुमवती *f.* 1 A woman in her courses. -2 N. of the town Pátaliputra.

कुसुमालः *m.* A thief.

कुसुंभः *m.*, —भं *n.* Safflower. -2 Saffron. -3 The waterpot of an ascetic. —भं *n.* Gold. —भः *m.* Mere outward affection (compared with the colour of safflower).

कुसूलः *m.* A granary, store-house (for corn &c.).

कुस्तुभः 1 *m.* An epithet of Vishnu. -2 The ocean.

कुहः *m.* 1 Kubera, the God of riches. -2 A rogue, cheat.

कुहकः *m.* 1 A cheat,rogue, juggler. -कं *n.* —का *f.* Jugglery, deception. -Comp. -स्वनः, -स्वरः *m.* A wild cock.

कुहनः 1 A mouse. -2 A snake -ना *f.* 1 Hypocrisy. -2 Assumed and false sanctity. -3 The interested performance of religious austerities, hypocrisy. -नं *n* 1 A small earthen vessel. -2 A glass vessel.

कुहनिका *f.* Interested performance of religious austerities, hypocrisy (दंभ).

कुहरं *n.* 1 A cavity, hollow. -2 The ear. -3 The throat. -4 Proximity. 25 Copulation. -6 A hole, rent. -7 A guttural sound.

कुहरितं *n.* 1 Sound in general. -2 The cry of the (Indian) cuckoo.

कुहुः, कुहूः *f.* 1 New moon day, *i. e.* the last day of a lunar month when the moon is invisible. -2 The deity that presides over this day. -3 The cry of the (Indian) cuckoo. -4 The first day of the first quarter on which the moon rises. -Comp. —कंठः,-मुखः,-रवः,-शब्दः *m.* The(Indian) cuckoo.

कुहेडिका, कुहेडी, कुहेलिका *f.* A fog, mist.

कू 1.6 A. (कवते कुवते), also कू 9 U.

(कु-कू-नाति, कु-कू-नीते) 1 To sound, make noise, cry out in distress.

कूः *f.* A female imp.

कूचः *m.* The female breast, especially that of a young or unmarried woman. See कुच.

कूचिका, कूचा *f.* 1 A painter's brush, a small brush of hair, a pencil. -2 A key.

कूज् I. P. (कूजति, कूजित) To make any inarticulate sound, hum, coo, warble. -2 To moan, groan. -3 To fill with sounds. With नि, परि, or वि To coo, to make an indistinct noise.

कुजः *m.*, कुजनं, कुजितं *n.* 1 Cooing, warbling. -2 The rattling of wheels.

कूट *a.* (*f.* —टा) 1 False. -2 Immovable, steady. -3 Despised. -टः *m.*, —टं *n.* 1 Fraud, illusion fraudulent or roguish scheme. -2 A puzzling question, knotty or intricate point. -3 Falsehood, untruth. -4 A summit of a mountain. -5 Any projection. -6 The bone of the forehead with its projections; the crown of the head. -7 A horn. -8 End, corner. -9 Head, chief. -10 A heap, multitude. -11 A hammer, an iron mallet. -12 A plough-share, the body of a plough. -13 A trap for catching deer. -14 A concealed weapon, as a dagger in a wooden case or a sword in a stick. -15 A water-jar. -16 The door of a city. —टः *m.* 1 A house, dwelling. -2 An ox whose horns are broken. -3 An epithet of Agastya. -Comp. —अक्षः A false or loaded die. —अगारं *n.* Apartment on the top of a house. —अर्थः *m.* Ambiguity of meaning. —अर्थभाषा *f.* A tale, fiction. —उपायः *m.* A trick, stratagem. —कारः, —कारकः *m.* A rogue, a false witness. —कृत् *a.* 1 Cheating, deceiving. -2 Forging a document. -3 Bribing. (*-m.*) 1 A man of the writer caste (कायस्थ). -2 An epithet of Siva. —कार्षापणः *m.* A false कार्षापण q. v. —खड्गः *m.* A swordstick. —छद्मन् *m.* A cheat. —तुला *f.* A false pair of scales. —धर्म *a.* (A country or house) where falsehood is considered a duty. —पाकलः, —पर्वः, —पूर्वः *m.* A bilious fever to which elephants are subject, (also sometimes written as कूटपालक.) —पालकः *m.* 1 A Potter. 2 A potter's kiln. —पाशः, —बंधः *m.* A trap, snare. —मानं *n.* A false measure or weight. मोहनः *m.* An epithet of Skanda. —यंत्रं *n.* A trap, a snare for deer, birds &c. —युद्धं *n.* A treacherous or unfair warfare. —रचना *f.* A trap laid. —शाल्मलिः *f.*, *m.* 1 A species of the Sálmali tree. -2 The club of Yama. —शासनं *n.* A forged grant or decree. —साक्षिन् *m.* A false witness. —स्थ *a.* Standing at the top, occupying the highest place (said of a person who stands at the head in a geneological table). (—स्थः *m.*) The Supreme Soul (immovable, unchangeable, and perpetually the same). —स्वर्णं *n.* Counterfeit gold.

कूटक *a.* Fraudulent. —कं *n.* 1 Fraud. -2 Elevation, prominence. -3 The body of a plough, a plough-share. —कः *m.* 1 A braid or tress of hair. -2 A perfume. -Comp. —आख्यानं *n.* An invented tale.

कूटशः *ind.* In heaps or multitudes.

कूड्यं *n.* The same as कुड्यं.

कूण् 10 U. (कूणयति-ते, कूणित) 1 To speak, converse. -2 To contract, close (Atm. in this sense).

कूणिका *f.* 1 The horn of any animal. -2 The peg of a lute.

कूद्दालः *m.* Mountain ebony.

कूपः *m.* 1 A well. -2 A hole, cave

hollow, cavity. -3 A leather oil-vessel. -4 A post to which a ship is moored. -5 A tree or rock in the midst of a river. -6 A mast. -पी *f.* 1 A small well. -2 A flask, bottle -3 The navel. -Comp. —अंकः, -अंगः *m.* Horripilation. —कच्छपः, -मंडूकः, *m.* (*f.* -पी, -की) A tortoise or frog in a well; (fig.) an inexperienced person, one who has had no experience of the world at large. —यंत्रं *n.* A water-wheel, a contrivance for raising water from a well. -Comp. —यंत्रघटी(-घाटिका) *f.* A bucket or pot attached to the water-wheel to draw up water. —यंत्रघटिकान्यायः *m.* The maxim of the buckets and the water-wheel. Some of the buckets are filled with water and go up, while some buckets are being emptied and go down. The maxim is used to describe the vicissitudes of life since some men become rich and rise in society while some are becoming poor and are sinking in the social scale.

कूपकः *m.* 1 A well. -2 A hole, cavity. -3 The hollow below the loins. -4 A stake to which a boat is moored. -5 The mast of a ship. -6 A funeral pile. -7 A hole under a funeral pile. -8 A leather oil-vessel. -9 A rock or tree in the midst of a river. -10 A boat. -पिका *f.* A stone or rock in the midst of a stream.

कूपा (-वा-) रः *m.* The ocean.

कूपी *f.* 1 A small well. -2 A flask.

कूब (-व-) र *a.* (*f.* —री) 1 Beautiful, agreeable. -2 Hump-backed. -रः *m.*, —रं *n.* The pole of a carriage to which the yoke is fixed. —रः *m.* A hump-backed man. —री *f.* 1 A carriage covered with a cloth or blanket. -2 The pole of a carriage to which the yoke is fixed.

कूरः *m.*, —रं *n.* Food, boiled rice.

कूर्चः *m.*, —र्चं *n.* 1 A bunch, a bundle. -2 A handful of Kusa grass. -3 A peacock's feather. -4 The beard. -5 The tip of the thumb and the middle finger brought in contact so as to pinch &c. (Mar. चिमटी). -6 The upper part of the nose, the part (or hair) between the eyebrows. -7 A brush. -8 Deceit, fraud. -9 Boasting, bragging. —र्चः *m.* 1 The head. -2 A store-room. -Comp. —शीर्षः, -शेखरः *m.* The cocoa-nut tree.

कूर्चकः *m.* 1 A bushel. -2 A brush for cleaning the teeth. -3 A painter's brush.

कूर्चिका *f.* 1 A painting brush or pencil. -2 A key. -3 A bud, blossom. -4 Inspissated milk. -5 A needle.

कूर्द् 1 U. (कूर्दति-ते, कूर्दित) 1 To leap, jump. -2 To frolic. With उत्— To jump up.

कूर्दनं *n.* 1 Leaping. -2 Playing, sporting -नी *f.* 1 A festival in honour of Kámdeva, held on the fifteenth day of Chaitra. -2 The full moon day in Chaitra.

कूर्पः *m.* The part between the eyebrows.

कूर्परः *m.* 1 The elbow. -2 The knee.

कूर्पासः, कूर्पासकः *m.*, -सं, -कं *n.* Bodice (worn by women to cover their breasts) मनोज्ञकूर्पासकपीडितस्तनाः × × विभूषयंतीव हिमागमं स्त्रियः ॥ ऋतुसं. 5. 8.

कूर्मः 1 A tortoise. -2 Vishnu in his second or Kúrma incarnation. -3 One of the outer winds of the body. -4 A particular gesticulation with the fingers. —र्मी *f.* A female tortoise. -Comp. —अवतारः *m.* The

Kúrma incarnation of Vishnu. -पृष्ठं, —पृष्ठकं *n.* 1 The back or shell of a tortoise. -2 A lid or cover of a dish. —राज: *m* Vishnu in the shape of a tortoise in his second incarnation.

कूलं *n.* 1 A shore, bank.-2 A slope, declivity. -3 Skirt, edge, border, proximity. -4 A pond. -5 The rear of an army. -6 A heap, mound. -Comp. —चर *a.* Frequenting or grazing on the banks. —हुंडक:, -हुंडक: An eddy.

कूलवती *f.* A river.

कूलंकष *a.* Tearing away or undermining the bank. —ष: *m.* 1 The current or stream of a river. -2 The ocean, sea. —षा *f.* A river.

कूलमुद्रुज *a.* Breaking down banks, (as rivers, elephants &c.).

कूलमुद्वह *a.* Tearing up or carrying away the bank.

कूवर: *m.* See कूबर:.

कूवार: *m.* The ocean.

कूष्मांड: *m.* 1 A kind of pumpkin gourd. -2 A kind of spell or magical formula. -3 A kind of spirit or imp. —डी *f.* N. of Durgá.

कूहा A fog, mist.

कृ 5 U. (कृणोति-कृणुते) To hurt, injure, kill.

कृ 8 U. (करोति, कुरुते, चकार-चक्रे, अकार्षीत्, अकृत, कर्तुं, करिष्यति-ते, कृत) The senses of कृ are almost infinitely modified according to the noun it is joined with. 1 To do (in general). -2 To make. -3 To prepare. -4 To build, create. -5 To produce. -6 To form, arrange. -7 To write, compose. -8 To perform, be engaged in. -9 To tell, narrate. -10 To carry out, execute, obey. -11 To bring about, accomplish, effect. -12 To throw or discharge, emit. -13 To assume, put on, take, take up. -14 To send forth, utter. -15 To place or put on (with loc.). -16 To entrust (with some duty), appoint. -17 To cook (as food) as in कृतान्नं. -18 To think, regard, consider. -19 To make a sound, as in खात्कृत्य, फूत्कृत्य, भुंक्ते; so वषट्कृ, स्वाहाकृ &c. -20 To pass, spend (time). -21 To direct towards, turn the attention to, resolve on; (with loc. or dat.) as in नावमें कुरुते मन:. -22 To use, employ, make use of; as in किं तया क्रियेत धेन्वा. -23 To divide, break into parts (with adverbs ending in धा); द्विधा कृ to divide into two parts. -24 To reduce completely to (a particular condition, with adverbs ending in सात्) as in भस्मसात् कृ to reduce to ashes. -25 To secure for oneself. -26 To help, give aid. -27 To make liable. -28 To violate or outrage (as a girl). -29 To begin. -30 To order. -31 To free from. -32 To proceed with, put in practice. -33 To sacrifice. -34 To consider equal to, as in तृणीकृ.

This root is often used with nouns, adjectives, and indeclinables to form verbs from them, like the English affixes 'en' or 'fy', in the sense of 'making a person or thing to be what he or it previously is not'; *e. g.* कृष्णीकृ to make that which is not already black, black, *i e.* blacken. Sometimes such formations take place in other senses also; *e. g.* क्रोडीकृ 'to clasp to the bosom', embrace. भस्मीकृ to reduce to ashes; तृणीकृ to value as little as straw; मंदीकृ to slacken, make slow; so शूलाकृ to roast on the end of pointed lances; सुखाकृ to please; समयाकृ to spend time &c. We give below some idiomatic uses of कृ. पदं कृ To set foot (fig. also); मनसा

कृ To think of, meditate; मनसि कृ To think, to resolve or determine; सख्यं, मैत्रीं कृ To form friendship with; अस्त्राणि कृ To practise the use of weapons; दंडं कृ To inflict punishment; हृदये कृ To pay heed to; कालं कृ To die; मतिor बुद्धिं कृ To think of, intend, mean. उदकं कृ To offer libations of water to the Manes; चिरं कृ To delay; दर्दुरं कृ to play on the lute; नखानि कृ To clean the nails; कन्यां कृ To outrage or violate a maiden; विना कृ To separate from, to be abandoned by; मध्ये कृ To place in the middle, to have reference to; वशे कृ To win over, place in subjection, subdue; चमत्कृ To cause surprise; make an exhibition or a show; सत्कृ To honour, treat with respect; तिर्यक्कृ To place aside; पुरस्कृ To follow, obey. मातुराज्ञां पुरस्कृत्य वयमेतां दशां गताः * मास. म. ह्या

कृकः *m.* The throat.

कृकणः, -रः *m.* I A kind of partridge. -2 A worm. -3 An epithet of Siva.

कृकलासः, -शः *m.* A lizard, chameleon.

कृकवाकुः *m.* I A cock. -2 A peacock. -3 A lizard. -Comp. —ध्वजः *m.* An epithet of Kártikeya.

कृकाटिका *f* The raised and straight part of the neck.

कृच्छ्र *a.* (*f.* —च्छ्रा) I Causing trouble, painful. -2 Bad, miserable, wicked, sinful. -3 Being in a difficult or painful situation. —च्छ्रः *m.*, —च्छ्रं *n.* I A difficulty, trouble, hardship, calamity, danger. -2 Bodily mortification, penance, expiation. -3 Torment, torture. -4 A kind of religious penance (प्राजापत्य). —च्छ्रः *m.* Ischury- —च्छ्रं *n.* Sin. -कृच्छ्रं, कृच्छ्रेण, कृच्छ्रात् *ind.* With great difficulty, painfully, miserably. -Comp. -प्राण *a* I One whose life is in danger. -2 Breathing with difficulty. -3 Hardly supporting life. —साध्य *a.* I Curable with difficulty (as a patient or disease). -2 Accomplished with difficulty.

कृत् 6 P. (कृंतति-कृत्त) I To cut, cut off, divide, cut in pieces, destroy.

कृत् 7 P. (कृणत्ति, कृत्त) I To spin. -2 To surround. -3 To attire.

कृत् *a.* (Generallyat the end of comp.) Doer, maker, performer, manufacturer, composer. —*m.* I A class of affixes used to form derivatives (nouns, adjectives &c.) from roots. -2 A word so formed. -Comp. —अंतः *m.* A word ending with a 'krit' affix.

कृत *p. p.* (*f.*—ता) Done, performed, made, accomplished. —तं *n.* I Work, action.-2 Service, benefit.-3 Consequence, result.-4 Aim, object. -5 N. of that side of a die which is marked with four points. -6 N. of the first of the four Yugas of the world. -7 The number '4'. -8 A stake at a game. -9 Prize or booty gained in a battle. -10 An offering.-Comp. —अकृत *a.* Done and not done; *i. e.* done in part but not completed. (-तः *m.*) The Supreme Being. -अंक *a.* I Marked, branded. -2 Numbered. (-कः *m.*) That side of a die which is marked with four points. —अंजलि *a.* Folding the hands in supplication. —अनुकर *a.* Following another's example, subservient. —अनुसारः *m.* A custom, usage. -अंत *a.* Causing an end, terminating. (-तः *m.*) I Yama, the God of death. -2 Fate, destiny. -3 A demonstrated conclusion, dogma, a proved doctrine. -4 A sinful or inauspicious action. -5 An epithet of Saturn. -6 Saturday. -7 The inevitable result of former actions. -8 The second lunar mansion. -9 The number 'two.' -कृतांतजनक: *m.* The sun. -अन्न *n.* 1 Cooked food. -2 Digested food. -3 Excrement. —अपराध *a.* Guilty, criminal.. —अभय *a.* Saved from fear or danger. -अभिषेक *a.* Crowned, inaugurated. -अभ्यास *a.* Practised. —अर्थ *a.* 1 Successful. -2 Satisfied; happy, contented. -3 Clever. कृतार्थीकृ 1 To render fruitful or successful. -2 To make good. -कृतार्थयति To make fruitful. -अवधान *a.* Careful, attentive. —अवधि *a.* 1 Fixed, appointed. -2. Bounded, limited. —अवस्थ *a.* 1. Summoned, caused to be present. -2 Fixed, settled. —अस्त्र *a* 1. Armed. -2. Trained; in the science of arms or missiles; well versed in the use of missiles. वीर्योत्सिक्ता युद्धसज्जाः कृतास्त्राः राज्ञो वैरं गोषु निर्यातयन्ति * भास पंचरात्रं. -आगम *a.* Advanced, proficient, skilled. (*-m.*) The Supreme Soul. —आगस् *a* Guilty, criminal, sinful. -आत्मन् *a.* 1 Self-possessed, of a self-governed spirit. -2 Purified in mind. —आभरण *a.* Adorned. —आयास *a.* Labouring, suffering. -आह्वान *a.* Challenged. -उत्साह *a.* Diligent, energetic, spirited. —उदक *a* One who has performed his ablutions. -उद्वाह *a.* 1 Married. -2 Practising penance by standing with up-lifted hands. -उपकार *a.* 1 Favoured, befriended, assisted. -2 Friendly. -उपभोग *a.* Used, enjoyed. —कर्मन् *a.* 1. One who has done his work. -2 Skilful, clever. (*-m.*) 1 The Supreme Spirit. -2 A *Sannyasin*. -काम *a.* One whose desires are fulfilled. —कार्य *a.* 1 One who has done his work or obtained his object. -2 Not requiring another's aid. —काल *a.* 1 Fixed or settled as to time. -2 Who has waited a certain time. (-ल: *m.*) Appointed time. -कृत्य, -क्रिय *a.* 1 Who has accomplished his object. -2 Satisfied, contented. -3 Clever. -4 Having done his duty; that has done whatever is worth doing. -क्रय: *m.* A purchaser. -क्षण *a.* 1 Waiting impatiently for the exact moment. -2 One who has got an opportunity. -घ्न *a.* 1 Ungrateful. -2 Defeating all previous measures. -चूड *m.* A boy on whom the ceremony of tonsure has been performed. —ज्ञ *a.* 1 Grateful. -2 Correct in conduct. (-ज्ञ: *m.*) 1 A dog. -2 An epithet of Siva. —तीर्थ *a.* 1. One who has visited holy places. -2 One who studies with a professional teacher. -3 Fertile in means or expedients. -4 A guide. —दास: *m.* A servant hired for a stated period. -धी *a.* 1 Prudent, considerate. -2 Learned, educated, wise. -निश्चय *a.* 1 Resolute, resolved. -2 Confident, sure. —पुंख *a.* Skilled in archery. -पूर्व *a.* Done formerly. -प्रतिकृतं *n.* Assault and counter assault, attack and resistance. —प्रतिज्ञ *a.* 1 One who has made an agreement -2 One who has fulfilled his promise. -बुद्धि *a.* 1 Learned, educated, wise. -2 A man of resolute character. -3 Informed of one's duty. -मति *a.* Firm, resolute. -मुख *a.* Learned clever, wise. -युगं *n.* The first (golden) of the four ages. -लक्षण *a.* 1 Stamped, marked. -2 Branded. -3 Excellent.

amiable. -4 Defined, discriminated. -विद्य *a.* Learned, educated. -वेतन *a.* Hired, paid (as a servant). -वेदिन् *a.* Grateful. -वेश *a.* Attired, decorated. -शिल्प *a.* Skilled in art or trade. -शोभ *a.* 1. Splendid. -2 Beautiful. -3 Handy, dexterous. -शौच *a.* Purified -श्रम:, -परिश्रम: *m.* 1 One who has studied -संकल्प *a.* Resolved, determined. -संकेत *a.* Making an appointment. —संज्ञ *a.* Restored to consciousness or senses. -3 Aroused. -संनाह *a.* Clad in armour. accoutred. —सापत्निका, -सापत्नी, -सापत्नीका, सापत्नका, सपत्निका *f.* A woman whose husband has married another wife, a married woman having a co-wife or a superseded wife. -हस्त, -हस्तक *a.* 1 Dexterous, clever, skilful, handy. -2 Skilled in archery. -हस्तता *f.* Skill, dexterily. -2 Skill in archery or generally in handling arms.

कृतक *n.* (*f.* -का) 1 Done, made, prepared. -2 Artificial. -3 Feigned, false, assumed. -4 Adopted, false (as a son &c.)

कृतम् *ind.* Enough, no more of, away; (with instr.); तस्मात्कृतं चरणपातविडंबनाभि: * पंचतं 4. 9. अथवा कृतं संदेहेन *शाकुंत I; अथवा गिरा कृतं * रघुवं. II. 41.

कृति: *f.* 1 Doing, manufacturing, making, performing. -2 Action, deed. -3 Creation, work, composition. -4 Magic, enchantment. -5 Injuring, killing. -6 The number '20'. -7 An enchantress, a witch. -8 A knife. -Comp. -कर: *m.* An epithet of Râvana.

कृतिन् *a.* (*f.* -नी) 1 Satisfied, contented, happy, successful. -2 Lucky, fortunate, blessed. -3 Clever, competent, able, skilful, wise; learned. -4 Following, obeying, virtuous, doing what is enjoined.

कृते, कृतेन *ind.* (With gen. or in comp.) For, for the sake of, on account of.

कृत्त *p. p.* 1 Cut, snapped, broken, divided. -2 Desired, sought.

कृत्ति: *f.* 1 Skin, hide(in general). -2 The hide of an antelope on which a religious student sits. -3 The bark of the birch-tree used for writing. -4 One of the lunar mansions, the Pleiades. -Comp. -वास:, -वासस् *m.* An epithet of Siva.

कृत्तिका: *f. pl.* 1 The third of the 27 lunar mansions or asterisms, (consisting of 6 stars), the Pleiades. -2 Those six stars represented as nymphs nursing Kartikeya, the God of war.-Comp. -तनय:, -पुत्र:, -सुत: *m.* Epithets of Kârtikeya. -भव: *m.* The moon.

कृत्नु *a.* Working well, able to work, powerful. -2 Clever, skilful. —त्नु: *m.* A mechanic, an artist.

कृत्य (*f.* -त्या) 1 What ought to be done; right, proper, fit. -2 Feasible, practicable. - 3 Who may be seduced from allegiance, treacherous. -त्यं *n* 1. What ought to be done; duty, function. -2 Work, business. -3 Purpose, object. -4 Motive, cause. -त्य: *m.* A class of affixes forming potential (future) passive participle; these are तव्य, अनीय, य and also एलिम. —त्या *f.* 1 Action, deed. -2 Magic. -3 A female deity to whom sacrifices are offered for destructive purposes.

कृत्रिम *a.* (*f.* —मा) 1 Artificial; not spontaneous, acquired. -2 Adopted (as a child). —म: *m.* An artificial, or adopted son; a grown up son adopted without the consent of his natural parents. —मं n. I A kind of salt. -2 A kind of perfume. -Comp. —धूप:, -धूपक: m. Incense, a kind of perfume. —पुत्र: m. Same as कृत्रिम:. -पुत्रक: m. Doll, puppet. -भूमि: f. An artificial floor. —वनं n. A park, garden.

कृत्वस् ind. An affix, added to numerals to denote 'fold' or 'times'; e. g. दशकृत्व: ten times, ten fold.

कृत्सं n I Water. -2 A multitude. —त्स: m. Sin.

कृत्स्न a. (f. —त्स्ना) All, whole, entire.

कृंतत्रं n. A plough.

कृंतनं n. Cutting, cutting off, tearing asunder.

कृप: m. The maternal uncle of अश्वत्थामन्.

कृपण a. (f. —णा) I Poor, pitiable, wretched. -2 Void of judgment, unable or unwilling to discriminate or to do a thing. -3 Low, vile. -4 Miserly, stingy. -5 Avaricious. —णं n. Wretchedness. —ण: m. I A miser. -Comp. —धी, -बुद्धि a. Low-minded. —वत्सल a. Kind to the poor.

कृपा f. Pity, tenderness, compassion.

कृपाण: m. I A sword. -2 A knife.

कृपाणक: m. A sword. —णिका f. A knife. dagger.

कृपाणि f. I A pair of scissors. -2 A dagger.

कृपालु a. Merciful, compassionate, kind.

कृपी f. The sister of कृप and wife of Drona. -Comp. -पति: m. An epithet of Drona. —सुत: m. An epithet of अश्वत्थामन्.

कृपीटं n. I Underwood, forest, wood.-2 Wood, firewood.-3 Water. -4 The belly. -Comp. —पाल: m. I A rudder. -2 The ocean. -3 Air, wind. —योनि: m. Fire.

कृमि a. Full of worms, wormy. -मि: m. I A worm, an insect in general. -2 Worms (disease). -3 An ass. -4 A spider. -5 The lac (dye). -6 An ant. -Comp. —कोश:, —कोष: m. The cocoon of a silk-worm. कृमिकोशो (-षो-) त्थं n. Silken cloth. —जं, -जग्धं n. Aloe wood. -जा f. Lac, the red dye produced by insects. —जलज:, -वारिरुह: m. A shell fish, an animal (fish. &c.) living in a shell. —पर्वत:, -शैल: m. An ant-hill. —फल: m. The Udumbara tree. —शंख: m. The fish living in the conch.—शुक्ति: f. I A bivalve shell. -2 The animal living in it. -3 An oyster.

कृमिण, कृमिल a. Having worms, wormy.

कृमिका f. A fruitful woman.

कृश् 4 P. (कृश्यति, कृश) I To become lean or emaciated. -2 To wane (as the moon).

कृश a. (f. —शा Compar. क्रशीयस्; Superl. क्रशिष्ठ). I Lean, weak, feeble, emaciated. -2 Small, little, minute (in size or quantity). -3 Poor, insignificant. -Comp. —अक्ष: m. A spider. —अंग a. Lean, thin. —अंग: m. An epithet of Siva. —अंगी f. I A woman with a slender frame. -2 The Priyangu creeper. —उदर a. I Thin-waisted. -2 Having the belly reducedi n bulk.

कृशला f. Hair (of the head).

कृशानु: m. Fire. -Comp. —रेतस् m. An epithet of Siva,

कृशाश्विन् m. An actor.

कृष् 6 U. (कृषति-ते, कृष्ट) To plough, make furrows

कृष् I P. (कर्षति, कृष्ट) I To draw, drag, pull, drag away, tear. -2 To attract. -3 To lead or conduct as an army. -4 To bend (as a bow). -5 To subdue, vanquish, overpower. -6 To plough, till. -7 To obtain. -8 To deprive one of (with two acc.).

कृषकः *m.* 1 A ploughman, husbandman. -2 An ox. -3 A plough-share. —कं *n.* A plough-share.

कृषाणः *m.* A ploughman, husbandman.

कृषिः *f.* 1 Ploughing. -2 Agriculture, husbandry. -Comp. —कर्मन् *n.* Agriculture. —जीविन् *a.* Living by husbandry. —फल *n.* Agricultural produce or profit. —सेवा *f.* Agriculture, husbandry.

कृषिकः *m.* A ploughman, husbandman.

कृषीवलः *m.* One who lives by husbendry, a farmer.

कृष्करः *m.* An epithet of शिव.

कृष्ट *a.* (*f.* —ष्टा) 1 Drawn, pulled, attracted. -2 Ploughed. -Comp. —उप्त *a.* Sown on cultivated ground. —पच्य, —पाच्य *a.* 1 Ripening in cultivated ground. -2 Cultivated.

कृष्टिः *m.* A learned man. —*f.* 1 Drawing, attracting. -2 Ploughing.

कृष्ण *a.* (*f.* —ष्णा) 1 Black, dark, dark-blue. -2 Wicked, evil. —ष्णः 1 The black colour. -2 The black antelope. -3 A crow. -4 The (Indian) cuckoo. -5 The dark half of a lunar month (from full to new moon). -6 The Kâli age. -7 Vishnu in his eighth incarnation, born as the son of Vasudeva and Devakî. -8 N. of Vyása, the reputed author of the Mahâbhárata. -9 N. of Arjuna. -10 Aloe wood. -11 The Supreme Spirit. -12 Black pepper. -13 Iron. —ष्णा *f.* 1 N. of Draupadî, wife of the Pândavas. -2 N. of a river in the Deccan. -3 An epithet of Durgá. -4 One of the 7 tongues of fire. —ष्णा *f.* A dârk night. —ष्णं *n.* 1 Blackness, darkness (moral also). -2 Iron. -3 Antimony. -4 The black part of the eye. -5 Black pepper. -6 Lead. -7 An inauspicious act. -8 Money acquired by gambling. -Comp. —अगुरु *n.* A kind of sandalwood. —अचलः *m.* An epithet of the mountain Raivataka. —अजिनं *n.* The skin of the black antelope. —अध्वन्, —अर्चिस् *m.* An epithet of fire. —अयस *n.*, —अयसं, —आमिषं *n* Iron, crude or black iron —अष्टमी, जन्माष्टमी *f.* The 8th day of the dark half of Srâvana when Krishna was born; also called गोकुलाष्टमी. —आवासः *m.* The holy fig-tree. —उदरः *m.* A kind of snake.. —कंदं *n.* A red lotus. —कर्मन् *a.* Of black deeds, criminal, wicked, sinful. —काकः *m.* A raven. —कायः *m.* A buffalo. —काष्ठं *n.* A kind of sandal-wood, agallochum. —कौतूहलः *m.* A gambler. —गतिः *m.* Fire, —ग्रीवः *m.* N. of Siva. —सारः *m.* 1 A species of antelope. -2 An antelope (in general). —देहः *m.* A bee. —धनं *n.* Money got by foul means. —द्वैपायनः *m.* N. of Vyâsa. —पक्षः *m.* The dark half of a lunar mounth. —मृगः *m.* The black antelope. —मुखः, —वक्त्रः, —वदनः *m.* The black-faced monkey. —यजुर्वेदः *m.* The Taittirîya or black Yajurveda. —लोहः *m.* The loadstone. —वर्णः *m.* 1 Black colour. -2 N. of Râhu. A Sudra. —वर्त्मन् *m.* 1 Fire. -2 N. of Râhu. -3 A low man, profligate. —शकुनिः *m.* A crow. —शारः, —सारः, —सारंगः *m.* The spotted antelope. —शृंगः *m.* A buffalo. —सखः, —सारथिः *m.* An epithet of Arjuna.

कृष्णकं *n.* The hide of the black antelope.

कृष्णलः *m.* The Gunjá plant. —लं *n.* Its berry.

कृष्णश *a.* Extremely black.

कृष्णाय् Den. A. 1 To make black, blacken.-2 To behave like Krishna.

कृष्णिका *f.* Black mustard.

कृष्णिमन् *m.* Blackness.

कॄ I. 6 P. (किरति, चकार, अकारीत, अकरि-री-ष्ट, अकीर्ष्ट, करि-री-तुं,) 1 To scatter, throw about, disperse. -2 To strew, cover, fill with.

कॄ 9 U. (कृणाति, कृणीते) To injure, hurt, kill.

कॄ 10 A. (कारयते) To know, inform.

कॄत् 10 U (कीर्तयति-ते, कीर्तित) 1 To mention, utter. -2 To tell, declare, communicate. -3 To name, call. -4 To praise, commemorate.

क्लृप् 1 A. (कल्पते, चक्लृपे, अक्लृपत, अकल्पिष्ट, अकल्प्त; कल्पिष्यते, कल्प्स्यति-ते, कल्पितुं, कल्प्तुं, क्लृप्त) 1 To be fit or adequate for, bring about, accomplish, produce, tend to (with dat.); कल्पते रक्षणाय • शाकुंत. 5. 8.-2 To be well managed or regulated; to succeed. -3 To become, occur. -4 To be prepared, be ready. -5 To be favourable to. -6 To partake of. -7 To prepare, arrange. -8 To produce, cause, effect, create (with acc.). -9 To accommodate one's self to.-10 To fall to the share of. With अव— To result in, to accomplish (with a dative). उप— 1 To result in (with dat.). -2 To be prepared. प्र— 1 To happen. -2 To be successful. वि— To be doubtful. *Causal* (कल्पयति,-ते) With आ— To adorn. प्र— 1 To prepare. -2 To sketch, scheme. परि-1 To prepare. -2 To decide. वि— To doubt. सम्— 1 To intend. -2 To resolve. समुप— To prepare.

क्लृप्त *p. p.* (*f.* —प्ता) 1 Arranged, prepared, equipped. -2 Cut, pared; *e.g.* क्लृप्तकेशनखश्मश्रु With hair &c. cut. -3 Caused, produced. -4 Fixed, settled. -5 Thought of. -6 Formed. -7 Ascertained, determined. -Comp. —कीला *f.* A title-deed. —धूपः *m.* A Frankincense.

क्लृप्तिः *f.* 1 Accomplishment, success. -2 Invention, contrivance. -3 Arrangement.

क्लृप्तिक *a.* (*f.* —का) Bought, purchased.

केकयाः *m. pl.* N. of a country and its people. —यी *f.* N. of the wife of Dasaratha.

केकर *a.* (*f.* —री) Squint-eyed. —रं *n.* A squint eye. -Comp. —अक्ष *a.* Squint-eyed.

केका *f.* The cry of a peacock.

केकावलः, केकिकः, केकिन् *m.* A peacock.

केणिका *f.* A tent.

केतः *m.* 1 A house, abode. -2 Living, habitation. -3 A banner.

केतकः *m.* 1 N. of a plant. -2 A banner. —कं *n.* A flower of the Ketaka plant. —की *f.* 1 N. of a plant (केतक). -2 A flower of that plant.

केतनं *n.* 1 A house, an abode. -2 An invitation, summons. -3 Place, site. -4 A flag, banner. -5 A sign, symbol; as in मकरकेतन. -6 An indispensable act (also religious). -7 A spot, mark.

केतित *a.* (*f.* —ता) 1 Called, summoned. -2 Dwelt, inhabited.

केतुः *m.* 1 A flag, banner. -2 A chief, head, leader, foremost, any eminent person (oft. at the end of comp.). -3 A comet, meteor. -4 A sign, mark. -5 Brightness, clearness. -6 A ray of light. -7 The descending node considered as the ninth planet, and the body or trunk of the demon सैंहिकेय (the head being regarded as Ráhu); क्रूरग्रहः सकेतुश्चन्द्रमसंपूर्णमंडलमिदानीं * मुद्रा. 1.6.-Comp. —ग्रहः *m.* The descending node. —भः *m.* A cloud. —यष्टिः *f.* A flag-staff. —रत्नं *n.* Lapis lazuli, (also called वैदूर्यं). —वसनं *n.* A flag.

केदर *a* Squint-eyed.

केदारः *m.* 1 A field under water; meadow.-2 A basin for water round the root of a tree. -3 A mountain. -4 A particular mountain forming part of the Himalayas. -5 A form of Siva. -Comp. —खंडं *n.* A small dyke; earth raised to keep out water. —नाथः *m.* A particular form of Siva.

केनारः *m.* 1 The head -2 The skull. -3 A cheek. -4 A joint. -5 The temples. -6 A kind of hell.

केनिपातः *m.* A rudder, helm, a large oar used as a rudder.

केंद्रं *n.* 1 The centre of a circle. -2 The argument of a circle. -3 The argument of an equation. -4 Distance of a planet from the first point of its orbit in the 4th, 7th or 10th degree.

केयूरः *m.*, —रं *n.* A bracelet worn on the upper arm, an armlet.

केरलाः *m. pl.* N. of a country (in the south of India, the modern Malabâr) and its inhabitants. —ली *f.* A woman of the Kerala country.-2 Astronomical science. -3 A Hora or period of time equal to one hour.

केल् 1 P. (केलति, केलित) 1 To shake. -2 To sport, be frolicsome.

केलकः *m.* A dancer, tumbler.

केलाय् Den. A. To sport, play.

केलासः *m.* Crystal.

केलिः *m.*, *f.* 1 Play, sport.-2 Amorous sport, pastime. -3 Joke, jest, mirth. —लिः *f.* The earth. -Comp. —कला *f* 1 Sportive skill, wantonness, amorous address. -2 The lute of Sarasvati. —किलः *m.* The confidential companion of the hero of a drama (a kind of विदूषक or buffoon). —किलावती *f.* Rati, wife of the God of love. -कीर्णः *m.* A camel. —कुंचिका *f.* A wife's younger sister. —केषः *m.* An actor, a dancer. —गृहं, -निकेतनं, -मंदिरं, -सदनं *n.* A pleasure house, a private apartment. —नागरः *m.* A sensualist. —पर *a.* Sportive, wanton, amorous. —मुखः *m.* Joke, sport, pastime. —वृक्षः *m.* A species of Kadamba tree. —शयनं *n.* A pleasure-couch, sofa —शुषिः *f.* The earth. —सचिवः *m.* A boon companion, confidential friend.

केलिकः *m.* The Asoka tree.

केली *f* 1 Play, sport. -2 Amorous sport. -Comp. —पिकः *m.* A cuckoo kept for pleasure. —वनी *f.* A pleasure-park, pleasure-grove. —शुकः *m* A parrot kept for pleasure.

केवल *a.* (*f.* —ला) 1 Peculiar -2 Alone, mere, sole, isolated. -3 Whole, absolute, perfect. -4 Bare, uncovered (as ground). -5 Pure, unmingled. —ली *f.* Astronomical science. —लं *ind.* Only, solely, absolutely, wholly; न केवलं-अपि not only-but; वसु तस्य विभोर्न केवलं गुणवत्तापि परप्रयोजना * रघुवं. 8. 31. -Comp. —आत्मन् *a.* One whose essence is absolute unity —नैयायिकः *m.* A mere logician (not proficient in any other branch of learning)

केवलतस् *ind.* Simply, solely, wholly, merely.

केवलिन् *a.* (*f.* —नी) 1 Alone, only. -2 Devoted to the doctrine of absolute unity of the Spirit.

केशः *m.* 1 Hair in general. -2 Especially, the hair of the head. -3 The mane of a horse or lion. -4 A ray of light. -5 An epithet of Varuna. -6 A kind of perfume. -8 An epithet of Vishnu. —शी *f.* 1 A lock of hair (on the crown of the head). -2 An epithet of Durgá. -Comp. —अंतः *m.* 1 The tip of the hair. -2 Long hair hanging down, a lock or tuft of hair. -3 Cutting of the hair as a religious ceremony. —कीटः *m* A louse. —गर्भः *m.* 1 A braid of hair. -2 An epithet of Varuna. —ग्रहः *m.*, —ग्रहणं *n.* Pulling the hair, seizing (one) by the hair (both in amorous sports and in fighting). —घ्नं *n.* Morbid baldness. —छिद् *m.* A hair-dresser, barber. —जाहं *n.* The root of the hair. —पक्षः, -पाशः, -हस्तः *m.* Much (ornamented) hair. —बंधः *m.* A hair-band. —भूः, —भूमिः *f.* The head or any other part of the body on which hair grows. —प्रसाधनी *f.*, -मार्जकं, —मार्जनं *n.* A comb. —वेशः *m.* A tress or fillet of hair.

केशटः *m.* 1 A goat. -2 N. of Vishnu. -3 A bug. -4 A brother. -5 A louse. -6 An arrow of Cupid (शोषण).

केशव *a.* (*f.* —वा) Having much fine or luxuriant hair. —वः *m.* 1 An epithet of Vishnu. -2 The Supreme Being. -Comp. —आयुधः *m.* The mango tree. (-धं *n.*) A weapon of Vishnu. —आलयः, —आवसः *m.* The Asvattha tree.

केशाकेशि *ind.* ' Hair to hair': (fighting) by pulling each other's hair.

केशिक *a.* (*f.* —की) Having fine or luxuriant hair.

केशिन् *m.* 1 A lion. -2 N. of a Rákshasa slain by Krishna. -3 N. of another Rákshasa who carried Devasenâ and who was slain by Indra. -4 An epithet of Krishna. -5 One having fine hair. -Comp. -निषूदनः, —मथनः *m.* Epithets of Krishna.

केशिनी *f.* 1 A woman with a beautiful braid of hair. -2 N. of the wife of Visravas and mother of Râvana and Kumbhakarna. -3 An epithet of Durgá.

केस (-श-) रः, *m.*,-रं *n.* 1 The mane (as of a lion). -2 The filament of a flower. -3 The Bakula tree. -4 The Punnâga tree. -5 The fibre (as of a mango fruit). -6 Saffron. -7 The hair. —रं *n.* A flower of the Bakula tree. -Comp. —अचलः *m.* An epithet of the mountain Meru. —वरं *n.* Saffron.

केस (-श-) रिन् *m.* 1 A lion. -2 The best, excellent, or most prominent of a class (at the end of comp.) -3 A horse. -4 The citron plant. -5 The Punnâga tree. -6 N. of the father of Hanúmat. -Comp. —सुतः *m.* An epithet of Hanúmat.

कै 1 P. (कायति) To sound.

कैंशुकं *n. m.* A flower of the किंशुक tree.

कैकयः *m.* The king of the Kekayas; see केकयः.

कैकसः *m.* A demon, goblin.

कैकेयः *m.* A prince or ruler of the Kekayas. —यी *f.* A daughter of the prince of the Kekayas and one (the youngest) of the three wives of king Dasaratha and mother of Bharata.

कैंकिरात *a.* Made of the flowers of the yellow Ashoka tree हेमलकारभासिभिरनमितशिखैः शेखरैः कैंकिरातैः * रत्ना०. 1.

कैंकिरातः *m* An amorous person.

कैटभः *m.* N. of a demon killed by Vishnu. —भा, -भी *f.* An epithet of

Durgá. Comp. –अरिः, –जित् –रिपुः, –हन् *m.* Epithets of Vishnu.

कैतकं *n.* A flower of the Ketaka plant.

कैतवं *n.* 1 The stake in a game. -2 Gambling. -3 Falsehood, roguery, trick. -4 The *lapis lazuli.* —वः *m.* -1 A cheat, rogue. -2 A gambler. -3 The Dhattúra plant. -Comp. —प्रयोगः *m.* A trick, device. —वादः *m.* Falsehood, roguery.

कैदारः *m.* Rice, corn. —रं, कैदारकं, *n.* कैदारिका, *f.*, कैदार्यं *n.* A multitude of fields.

कैमुतिकन्यायः *m.* A maxim of 'how much more'; an argument *a fortiori* (derived from किमुत 'how much more?').

कैरवः *m.* 1 A gambler, cheat, rogue. -2 An enemy. —वं *n.* The white lotus opening at moonrise. —वी *f.* The moonlight. Comp. -बंधुः *m.* An epithet of the moon.

कैरविणी *f.* 1 A lotus plant bearing white lotuses -2 A place (pond &c.) abounding in white lotuses. -3 An assemblage of white lotuses.

कैरविन् *m.* The moon.

कैलासः *m.* N. of a mountain, a peak of the Himâlayas and residence of Siva and Kubera. Comp. -नाथः *m.* I. An epithet of Siva. -2. An epithet of Kubera.

कैवर्तः *m.* A fisherman.

कैवर्तकः *m.* A fisherman.

कैवल्यं *n.* 1 Perfect isolation, exclusiveness. -2 Individuality. -3 Detachment of the soul from matter; identification with the Supreme Spirit. -4 Final emancipation or beatitude.

कैशिक *a.* (*f.* -की) Hair-like; fine as hair. —कः *m.* The sentiment of love, lust. —कं *n.* A quantity of hair. —की *f.* A style of composition more usually and correctly written कौशिकी. -2 An epithet of Durgá.

कैशोरं *n.* Youth, childhood, tender age (below fifteen).

कैश्यं *n.* The whole mass of hair, quantity of hair.

कोकः *m.* 1 A wolf. -2 The ruddy goose (चक्रवाक). -3 A cuckoo. 4- A frog. -5 N. of Vishnu. -Comp. -देवः *m.* A pigeon.-बंधुः *m.* An epithet of the sun.

कोकनदं *n.* 1 The red lotus -2 The red water-lily.

कोकाहः *m.* A white horse.

कोकिलः *m.* (*f.* -ला) 1 The (Indian or black) cuckoo. -2 A fire-brand. -Comp. —आवासः, -उत्सवः *m.* The mango tree.

कोंकणा *f.* N. of Renukâ, wife of Jamadagni. -Comp. —सुतः *m.* An epithet of Parasurâma.

कोंकाः, कोंकणाः *m.*N. of a country, the strip of land between the Sahyâdri and the ocean.

कोजागरः *m.* N. of a festival held on the full moon night in the month of Asvina and celebrated with several games.

कोटः *m.* 1 A fort. -2 A hut, shed. -3 Crookedness (moral or physical).

कोटरः *m,* —रं *n.* The hollow space in the interior of a tree.

कोटरी, कोटवी *f.* 1 A naked woman. -2 An epithet of the Goddess Durgá.

कोटिः, -टी *f.* 1 The curved end of a bow -2 The end or extremity, edge or point in general. -3 The edge or point of a weapon. -4 The highest point, excess, climax, excellence. -5 The horns of the moon. -6 Ten millions, a crore. -7 The complement of an arc to 90° (in math.). -8 The side of a right-angled triangle (in math.). -9 A class, department, kingdom, as in मनुष्यकोटिः, प्राणिकोटिः &c. -10 One side of a question in dispute. -Comp. —ईश्वरः *m.* A millionaire. —जित *m.* An epithet of Kâlidâsa. —ज्या *f.* The co-sine of an angle in a right-angled triangle (in math.) —द्वयं *n.* Two alternatives. —पात्रं *n.* A rudder. —पालः *m.* The guard of a stronghold. —वेधिन् *a.* (lit.) Striking a point; (fig.) performing a most difficult task. —श्री *f.* An epithet of Durgá.

कोटिक *a.* (*f.* -का) Forming the highest point of anything.

कोटिरः *m.* 1 The hair collected on the forehead. -2 An ichneumon. -3 An epithet of Indra.

कोटिशः *ind.* By crores, or tens of millions; in innumerable numbers.

कोटिशस् *ind.* In hundreds of millions; in multitudes.

कोटि (-टी-) शः *m.* A harrow.

कोटीरः *m.* 1 A diadem, crown. -2 A crest. -3 The hair collected (by ascetics) on the forehead in a knot; matted hair in general.

कोट्टः *m.* A fort, castle.

कोट्टवी *f* 1 A naked woman with dishevelled hair. -2 N. of the Goddess Durgá.

कोट्टारः *m.* A fortified town, stronghold. -2 The stairs of a pond. -3 A well -4 A libertine.

कोणः *m.* 1 A corner, an angle (of anything). -2 An intermediate point of the compass. -3 The bow of a lute; a fiddle-stick. -4 The sharp edge of a sword or weapon. -5 A stick, club. -6 A drum-stick. -7 N. of the planet Mars. -8 N. of the planet Saturn. -9 A sort of musical instrument. -Comp. —आघात *m.* A mixed sound of several musical instruments —कुणः *m.* A bug.

कोणपः *m.* See कौणपः.

कोणाकोणि *ind.* From angle to angle, corner-wise, diagonally.

कोदंडः *m.*, -डं *n.* A bow. —डः *m.* An eye-brow.

कोद्रवः *m.* A species of grain eaten by the poor (Mar. हरीक).

कोपः *m.* 1 Anger, wrath, passion. -2 (In medicine) Morbid irritation or disorder of the humours of the body as in पित्तकोप, वातकोप, &c. -Comp. —आकुल, -आविष्ट *a.* Enraged, furious. —क्रमः *m.* 1 An angry or passionate man. -2 The course of anger. -पदं *n.* 1 The cause of anger. -3 Pretended anger. —वशः *m.* Subjection to anger. —वेगः *m.* Violence, fury of anger.

कोपन *a.* (*f.* —ना) 1 Passionate, irascible, angry. -2 Causing anger. -3 Irritating, causing disorder of the humours of the body. —नं *n.* Becoming angry. —ना *f.* A passionate or angry woman.

कोपिन् *a.* 1 Angry, irritated. -2 Causing anger. -3 Irritating, causing disorder of the humours of the body. —*m.* A water-pigeon.

कोमल *a.* (*f.* —ला) 1 Tender, soft, delicate (fig. also). -2 Soft, low, pleasing, sweet. -3 Handsome, beautiful

कोमलकं *n.* The fibres of the stalk of a lotus.

कोयष्टिः, कोयष्टिकः *m.* 1 The lapwing. -2 A small white crane.

कोरः *m.* 1 A movable joint (a

the fingers, the knees &c). -2 A bud.

कोरक: *m.*, —कं *n.*. 1 A bud, an unblown flower. -2 (fig.) Anything partially opened but not fully developed. -3 The fibres of the stalk of a lotus -4 A kind of perfume.

कोरदूष: *m.* See कोद्रव:.

कोरित *a* (*f* —ता) 1 Budded, sprouted. -2 Ground, pounded.

कोल: *m* 1 A hog, boar. -2 A raft, b at. -3 The breast. -4 The haunch, hip, lap. -5 An embrace. -6 The planet Saturn. -7 An out-cast, one of a degraded tribe. -8 A barbarian. -लं *n*. 1 The weight of one 'Tola.' -2 Black pepper. -3 A kind of berry. (Mar. बोर). -Comp. —अंच: *m*. N. of the country of the Kalingas. -पुच्छ: *m*. A heron.

कोलंबक: *m*. The body of a lute.

कोला, -ल:, —ली *f*. See बदरी.

कोलाहल: *m*, -लं *n*. A loud and confused noise; an uproar.

कोविद *a*. (*f*. —दा) Experienced, learned, skilled, wise, (with gen; or loc., but usually in comp.).

कोविदार: *m*., -रं *n*. N. of a tree.

कोश:, -ष: *m*, -कोशं, -षं *n*. 1 A vessel for holding liquids, a pail, bucket, cup. -2 A vessel in general. -3 A box, cupboard, drawer, trunk. -4 A sheath, scabbard. -5 A case, cover, covering. -6 A store, mass. -7 A store-room. -8 A treasury; an apartment where money is kept. -9 Treasure, money, wealth. (Fig. also as in कोशस्तपस:. -10 Gold or silver wrought or unwrought. -11 A dictionary, lexicon, vocabulary. -12 A bud. -13 The stone of a fruit. -14 A pod. -15 A nut-meg, nutshell. -16 The cocoon of a silkworm. -17 Vulva; the womb. -18 An egg. -19 A testicle or the scrotum. -20 The penis. -21 A ball, globe. -22 (In Vedânta phil.) A term for the five vestures (sheaths or cases (which successively make the body, enshrining the soul. -23 (In law) A kind of ordeal. -24 A house. -25 A kind of bandage or ligature (in surgery). -26 An oath. -Comp. —अधिपति:, -अध्यक्ष: *m*. 1. A treasurer, pay-master. -2 An epithet of Kubera. —अगार: *m*., -रं *n*. A treasury, store-room. -कार: *m*. 1 One who makes scabbards. -2 A lexicographer. -3 The silk-worm while in the coçoon. -4 A chrysalis. —कारक: *m*. A silk worm. —गृहं *n*. A treasury, store-room. —चंचु: *m*. The (Indian) crane. -नायक:, -पाल: *m*. 1 A treasurer. -2 An epithet of Kubera. —पेटक: *m*., -कं *n*. A chest in which treasure is kept, coffer. —वासिन् *m*. An animal living in a shell, a chrysalis. —वृद्धि: *f*. 1 Increase of treasure. -2 Enlargement of the scrotum. —शायिका *f*. A clasped knife; a knife lying in a sheath. —स्कृत *m*. A silk-worm. —स्थ *a*. Incased, sheathed. —स्थ: *m*. An animal living in a shell (as a snail). —हीन *a*. Deprived of riches; poor.

कोशलिकं *n*. A bribe.

कोशातकिन् *m*. 1 Trade, business. -2 A trader, merchant. -3 Submarine fire.

कोशि (-पि-) न् *m*. The mango tree.

कोष्ठ *a*. Own; one's own. -ष्ठ: *m*. 1 Any one of the vicera of the body, such as the heart, lungs &c. -2 The belly, abdomen. -3 An inner apartment. -4 A granary, store-room. —ष्ठं *n*. 1 A surrounding wall. -2 The shell of anything. -Comp. —अगारं *n*. 1 A store-house, store-room. -2 A treasury. —अग्निः *m.* The digestive faculty, gastric juice. —पालः *m.* 1 A treasurer, store-keeper. -2 A guard, watch. -3 A constable. —शुद्धिः *f.* The evacuation of the bowels.

कोष्टकः *m.* 1 A granary. -2 A surrounding wall.-कं *n.*A brick trough for watering cattle.

कोष्ण *a.* (*f* —ष्णा) Luke-warm, tepid. —ष्णं *n.* Warmth.

कोस (-श-) लाः *m. pl.* N. of a country and its people.

कोस (-श-) ला *f* The city of Ayodhyá.

कोहलः *m.* 1 A kind of musical instrument. -2 A sort of spirituous liquor.

कौक्कुटिकः *m.* 1 A poulterer. -2 A mendicant who walks always fixing his eyes on the ground for fear of treading upon worms, insects &c. -3 (Hence) A hypocrite.

कौक्ष *a.* (*f.* —क्षी) 1 Tied to or being on, the sides. -2 Abdominal.

कौक्षेय *a.*(*f.* —यी) 1 Being in the belly. -2 Being in a sheath

कौक्षेयकः *m.* A. sword, scimitar.

कौंकाः, कौंकणाः *m pl.* N. of a country and its people or rulers. Same as कोंकणाः.

कौट *a.* (*f.* —टी) 1 Living in one's own house; *i. e.* independent, free. -2 Domestic, homely, homebred.-3 Fraudulent, dishonest. —टः *m.* 1 Fraud, falsehood. -2 Giving false evidence. -Comp. —जः *m.* The Kutaja tree. —तक्षः *m.* (opp. ग्रामतक्षः) An independent carpenter, one who works at home on his own account and not for the village. —साक्षिन् *m.* A false witness. —साक्ष्यं *n.* Giving false evidence, perjury.

कौटाकिकः, कौटिकः *m.* 1 One whose business is to catch birds &c. in traps. -2 One who sells the flesh of birds, animals &c.; a butcher.

कौटिक *a.* 1 Relating to a snare or trap. -2 Dishonest, fraudulent.

कौटिलकः *m.* 1 A hunter. -2 A blacksmith.

कौटिल्यं *n.* 1 Crookedness (lit. and fig.). -2 Wickedness. -3 Dishonesty, fraud. —ल्यः *m.* 'The crooked', N. of Chánakya; a celebrated writer on civil polity and the friend and adviser of Chandragupta and a very important character in the 'Mudrârákshasa.'

कौटुंब *a* (*f.* —बी) Necessary for the family or household.-बं *n.*Family, relationship.

कौटुंबिक *a.* (*f.* —की) Constituting a family. —कः *m.* The father or master of a family; *paterfamilias.*

कौणपः *m.* A goblin, demon.-Comp. —दंतः *m.* An epithet of Bhíshma.

कौतुकं *n.*1 Desire, curiosity, wish. -2 Eagerness, vehemence, impatience. -3 Anything creating curiosity or wonder. -4 The marriage thread (worn on the wrist). -5 The ceremony with the marriage thread preceding a marriage. -6 Festivity, gaiety. -7 Particularly, auspicious festivity, solemn occasion (such as marriage). -8 Delight, joy, pleasure, happiness. -9 Sport, pastime. -10 A song, dance, show or spectacle. -11 Joke, mirth. -12 Friendly greeting, salutation. -Comp. —अगारः *m.*, —रं, —गृहं *n.* A pleasure-house. —क्रिया, —मंगलं *n.* 1 A solemn ceremony. -2 A marriage ceremony. —तोरणः *m.*, —णं *n.* A triumphal arch erected on festive occasions.

कौतूहलं (—ल्यं) *n.* 1 Desire, curio

sity, interest.-2 Eagerness.-3 Anything exciting curiosity, a wonder, curiosity. -4 A solemn ceremony.

कौंतिकः *m.* A spearman, lancer.

कौंतेयः *m.* An epithet of Yudhishthira, Bhima or Arjuna.

कौपीनं *n.* 1 The pudenda. -2 A privity, privy part. -3 A small piece of cloth (usually a small strip) worn over the privities. -4 A ragged or tattered garment. -5 Sin, an improper or wrong act.

कौमोदकी *f.* The mace of Krishna.

कौब्ज्यं *n.* 1 Crookedness. -2 Hump-backedness.

कौमार *a.* (*f.* —री) 1 Juvenile, youthful, virgin, maidenly.-2 Soft, tender. -3 Belonging to the God of war.-रं *n.* 1 Childhood (to the age of five).-रं Maidenhood (to the age of sixteen), virginity. -Comp. —बंधकी *f.* A harlot. —भृत्यं *n.* The rearing and general treatment of children.

कौमारकं *n.* Boyhood, youth, tender age.

कौमारिकः *m.* A father of girls.

कौमारिकेयः *m.* The son of an unmarried woman.

कौमुदः *m.* The month Kártika.

कौमुदी *f.* 1 Moonlight. -2 Anything causing delight and balmy coolness. -3 The full moon day in Kártika. -4 The full moon day in Asvina. -5 Festivity (in general). -6 A festive day on which temples, houses &c. are illuminated. -7 (At the end of titles of works &c.). Elucidation, throwing light on the subject as in तर्ककौमुदी, सांख्यतत्त्वकौमुदी, सिद्धांतकौमुदी &c. -Comp. —पतिः *m.* The moon. —वृक्षः *m.* The stick or stand of a lamp.

कौमोदकी, कौमोदी *f.* N. of the mace of Vishnu.

कौरव *a.* (*f.* —वी) Relating to the Kurus. —वः *m.* 1 A descendant of Kuru. -2 A ruler of the Kurus.

कौरव्यः *m.* 1 A descendent of Kuru. -2 A ruler of the Kurus.

कौर्प्यः *m.* The zodiacal sign Scorpio (a word of Greek origin).

कौल *a.* (*f.* —ली) 1 Relating to a family, ancestral, hereditary. -2 Of a noble family, well-born. —लः *m.* A worshipper of शक्ति according to the left hand ritual. -लं *n.* The doctrine and practices of the left hand Sáktas.

कौलकेयः *m.* The son of an unchaste woman; a bastard.

कौलटिनेयः *m.* 1 The son of a (chaste) female beggar. -2 A bastard.

कौलटेयः *m.* 1 The son of a female beggar (chaste or unchaste). -2 A bastard.

कौलटेरः *m.* A bastard, son or daughter of a disloyal wife. -2 The child of a beggar.

कौलिक *a.* (*f.* —की) 1 Belonging to a family. -2 Customary in a family; ancestral. —कः *m.* A weaver. -2 An imposter, a heretic. -3 A follower of the left hand Sâkta ritual.

कौलीन *a.* (*f.* —ना) Belonging to a noble family. —नः *m.* 1 The son of a female beggar. -2 A follower of the left hand Sákta ritual. —नं *n.* 1 An evil report, a scandal. मा कौलीनाद् दसितनयने मय्यविश्वासिनी भूः * मेनदू. -2 An improper act, bad or scandalous. -3 A combat of animals. -4 Cock-fighting. -5 War, battle (in general). -6 High birth. -7 A privity, the pudenda.

कौलीन्यं *n.* 1 High birth. -2 Family scandal. -3 Family honor.

कौलूतः *m.* A king of the Kulútas.

कौलेयकः *m.* A dog, hound.

कौल्य *a.* (*f.* —ल्या) 1 Noble-born, of a high birth. -2 Of the left hand Sákta secet.

कौबे (-बे-) र, (*f.* —री) Belonging to or coming from Kubera. —री *f.* The north (the direction presided over by ' Kubera ').

कौश *a.* (*f.* —शी) 1 Silken. -2 Made of Kusa grass.

कौशलं (-ल्यं) 1 Well-being, welfare, happiness, prosperity. -2 Skill, skilfulness, cleverness.

कौशलिकं *n.* A bribe.

कौशलिका, कौशली *f.* 1 A present, an offering. -2 Friendly inquiry after one's health &c.; greeting.

कौशलेय: *m.* An epithet of Ràma, son of Kausalyá.

कौशल्या *f.* The eldest wife of Dasaratha and mother of Ráma.

कौशल्यायनि: *m.* Ráma, son of Kausalyá.

कौशांबी *f.* N. of an ancient city on the Ganges in the lower part of the 'Doab'.

कौशिक *a.* (*f.* —की) 1 Incased, sheathed. -2 Coming from an owl. -3 Born of the family of Kusika. -4 Silken. —क: *m.* 1 An epithet of विश्वामित्र. -2 An owl. -3 A lexicographer. -4 Marrow. -5 Bdellium. -6 An ichneumon. -7 A snake-catcher. -8 The sentiment of love (शृंगार). -9 One who knows hidden treasures. -10 An epithet of Indra. -11 An epithet of Siva. —का *f.* A cup, drinking vessel. —की *f.* 1 N. of a river in Behár. -2 N of the Goddess Durgá. -3 N. of one of the four varieties of dramatic style. It is thus defined सुकुमारार्थसंदर्भा कौशिकी तासु बध्यते. -Comp. —अराति:, -अरि: *m.* A crow. —आत्मज: *m.* An epithet of Arjuna. —आयुध *n.* The rainbow. —फल: *m.* The cocoa-nut tree.

कौशे (-षे-) य *a.* Silk, silken. —यं *n.* 1 Silken cloth in general. -3 A woman's lower garment of silk.

कौसल्य *a.* Belonging to the people of the Kosalas. —ल्य: *m.* A prince of the Kosalas. —ल्या *f.* The wife of Dasaratha and mother of Ràma.

कौसीदं *n.* 1 The practice of usury. -2 Indolence.

कौसुम *a.* Flowery, flowering.

कौसुंभ *a.* 1 Prepared with safflower. -2 Dyed with safflower, red.

कौसृतिक: *m.* 1 A cheat, knave. -2 A juggler.

कौस्तुभ: *m.* 1 N. of gem obtained at the churning of the ocean and worn by Vishnu on his breast. -Comp. —लक्षण:, -वक्षस्, —हृदय: *m.* Epithets of Vishnu.

क्नथ् 10 P. To hurt, injure.

क्नूय् 1 A. (क्नूयते) 1 To make a creaking sound. -2 To sink.

क्रकच: *m.* A saw. —चा *f.* The Ketaka tree. -Comp. —छद: *m.* The Ketaka tree. —पत्र: *m.* The teak tree. —पाद्, —पाद:, *m.* A lizard.

क्रकर: *m.* 1 A kind of partridge. -2 A saw. -3 A poor man. -4 A disease.

क्रतु: *m.* 1 A sacrifice. -2 An epithet of Vishnu. -3 One of the ten Prajâpatis. -4 Intelligence, talent. -5 Power, ability. -6 Plan, design, purpose. -7 Resolution. -8 Desire, will. -9 Fitness. -10 Deliberation. -11 Worship. -Comp. —उत्तम: *m.* The राजसूय sacrifice. —द्रुह्, -द्विष् *m.* A demon, goblin. —ध्वंसिन् *m.* An epithet of Siva (who destroyed Daksha's sacrifice.) —पति: *m.* The performer of a sacrifice. —पशुः *m.* A sacrificial horse. —पुरुषः *m.* An epithet of Vishnu. -भुज् *m.* A god, deity. —राज्, राजः *m.* The राजसूय sacrifice.

क्रथ् I P. (क्रथति, क्राथित) To injure, hurt, kill (with gen. of person). -10 U. To delight.

क्रथकैशिकाः *m. pl.* N. of a country.

क्रथनं *n.* A slaughter. -2 Cutting.

क्रंद् I P. (क्रंदति, चक्रंद, अक्रंदीत्, क्रंदित) I To cry, weep. -2 To call out to, call out piteously to any body.

क्रंद् 10 U. (*p. p.* क्रंदित) To sound or cry continuously.

क्रंदनः *m.* A cat. —नं *n.* I A cry of distress or lamentation. -2 Mutual defiance. -3 Calling, inviting.

क्रंदितं *n.* I Cry of distress or weeping, lamentation. -2 A challange.

क्रम् I U., 4 P. (क्रामति, क्रमते, क्राम्यति, चक्राम, चक्रमे, अक्रमीत्, अक्रंस्त, क्रांत) I To walk, step, go. -2 To go to, approach (with acc). -3 To pass or go over, go across, traverse. -4 To leap, jump. -5 To ascend. -6 To cover, fill. -7 To pervade, penetrate. -8 To undertake, strive after. -9 To have full scope, be at home (with loc.) as in कृत्येषु क्रमते; क्रमतेऽस्मिञ्शास्त्राणि. -10 To succeed, have effect (Atm.). -11 To be repeated (as a letter or word. -12 To fulfil, accomplish. -13 To have sexual intercourse with.

क्रमः *m.* I A step. pace. -2 A foot. -3 Going, proceeding, course; as in कालक्रमेण, क्रमात् or क्रमेण In course of, gradually. कालक्रमेण Gradually, in course of time. -4 Performance, commencement. -5 Regular course, succession. -6 Method, manner. -7 Grasp, hold. -8 A position of attack (assumed by an animal before making a spring). -9 Preparation, readiness. -10 An enterprize. -11 The manner of proceeding. -12 Particular manner of reciting Vedic texts. -13 Power, strength. -14 N. of Vishnu. -Comp. -अनुसारः, —अन्वयः *m.* Regular order, due arrangement. -आगत,-आयात *a.* Descended or inherited lineally, hereditary. -उद्वेगः *m.* An ox. —ज्या *f.* The sine of a planet, declination.

क्रमक *a.* (*f.* —का) Orderly, methodical —कः *m.* A student who goes through a regular course of study. -2 One who knows the 'Krama' arrangement of a text.

क्रमणः *m.* I The foot. -2 A horse. —णं *n.* I A step. -2 Walking. -3 Proceeding. -4 Transgressing.

क्रमतः *ind.* Gradually, successively.

क्रमशः *ind.* I In due order, regularly, successively. -2 Gradually, by degrees.

क्रमिकः *a.* (*f.* —का) I Successive, serial. -2 Descended lineally; ancestral.

क्रमुः, क्रमुकः *m.* The betel-nut tree.

क्रमेलः, क्रमेलकः *m.* I A camel.

क्रयः *m.* Buying, purchasing. -Comp. —आरोहः *n.* A market, fair. —क्रीत *a.* Bought. —लेख्यं *n.* A deed of sale, conveyance &c. —विक्रयौ *m. dual* Trade, traffic; buying and selling. —विक्रयिकः *m.* A trader, merchant.

क्रयणं *n.* Buying, purchasing.

क्रायिकः *m.* I A trader, dealer. -2 A purchaser.

क्रय्य *a.* A thing exhibited for sale in the market; (opp. क्रेय which only means 'fit to be purchased').

क्रव्यं *n.* Raw flesh, carrion.-Comp. —अद्, -अद, -भुज् *a.* Eating raw flesh.

(-*m.*) 1 A carnivorous animal, such as a tiger &c.; -2 A demon, goblin.

क्रशिमन् *m.* Thinness, leanness.

क्राकचिक: *m.* A sawyer.

क्रांत: *m.* 1 A horse. -2 A foot, a step —दर्शिन् *a.* Omniscient.

क्रांति: *f.* 1 Going, proceeding. -2 A step, pace. -3 Surpassing. -4 Attacking, overcoming. -5 Declination of a planet. -6 The ecliptic. -Comp. —कक्ष: *m.*, —मंडलं, —वृत्तं *n.* The ecliptic. —क्षेत्रं *n.* A figure described by the ecliptic. —ज्या *f* The sine of the declination or of the ecliptic. —पात: *m.* The equinoctial points or nodes of the ecliptic. —भाग: *m.* The declination of a point of the ecliptic. —वलय: *m.* 1 The ecliptic. -2 The tropical zone.

क्राय (-यि-) क: *m.* 1 A buyer, a purchaser. -2 A trader, a dealer.

क्रिमि: *m.* 1 A worm. -2 An insect. -Comp. —जं *n.* Aloewood. —शैल: *m.* An ant-hill.

क्रिया *f.* 1 Doing, performance, accomplishment. -2 An action, act, undertaking. -3 Activity, labour. -4 Teaching, instruction. -5 Possession of some art, knowledge. -6 Practice (opp. शास्त्र theory). -7 A literary work, composition. -8 A purificatory rite. -9 An expiatory rite, expiation. -10 The ceremony of offering oblations to the deceased ancestors (श्राद्ध). Obsequies. -11 Worship. -12 Medical treatment. -13 (In gram.) Action, the general idea expressed by a verb. -14 Motion. -15 Motion as one of the seven categories of the Vaiseshikas. -16 (In law) Judicial investigation by human means (witnesses &c.) or by ordeals. -17 Burden of proof. -18 A verb. -19 A noun of action. -20 Disquistion. -21 Study. -22 Means, expedients. -23 Instrument, implement. -Comp. —अन्वित *a.* Practising ritual observances. —अपवर्ग: *m.* 1 Completion or termination of an affair; execution of a task. -2 Liberation from ceremonial acts, absolution. —अभ्युपगम: *m.* A special agreement. —अवसन्न *a.* One who loses a law-suit through the statements of the witnesses &c. —इंद्रियं *n.* Same as कर्मेंद्रिय. —कलाप: *m.* The whole body of ceremonies enjoined in the Hindu religious law. -2 All the particulars or points of any business. —कार: *m.* 1 An agent, worker. -2 A beginner, a fresh student. -3 An agreement. —द्वेषिन् *m.* A witness whose testimony is prejudicial to the cause. —निर्देश: *m.* Evidence. —पथ: *m.* A mode of medical treatment. —पदं *n.* A verb. —पर *a.* Diligent in the performance of one's duty. —पाद: *m.* The third division of a legal plaint comprising witnesses, documents and other proofs adduced by the plaintiff or complainant. —योग: *m.* 1 Connection with the verb. -2 The employment of expedients or means. —लोप: *m.* Omission or discontinuance of any of the essential ceremonies of the Hindu religion. —वश: *m.* Necessary influence of acts done. —वाचक, —वाचन् *a.* Expressing any action, as a verbal noun. —वादिन् *m.* A plaintiff, complainant. —विधि: *m.* A rule of action, manner of any rite. —विशेषणं *n.* 1 An adverb. -2 A predicative adjective. —संक्रांति: *f.* Imparting (to others) one's knowledge; teaching. —समभिहारः *m.* The repetition of any act.

क्रियावत् *a.* 1 Engaged in any work; versed in the practice of a thing.-2 Performing ceremonies in the right manner.

क्री 9. U. (क्रीणाति, क्रीणीते, क्रीत) 1 To buy, purchase. -2 To barter, exchange. With आ- To buy. निस्-To buy off, to redeem. परि— (Atmanepada) 1 To buy. -2 To hire, to purchase for a time (with *instr.* or *dat.*) *e. g.* शतेन शताय वा परिक्रीतः. -3 To return, to reply. वि— To sell (in the Atm. pada). -2 To barter, to exchange. -3 To win.

क्रीड् 1 P. (क्रीडति, क्रीडित) 1 To play, amuse oneself. -2 To gamble. -3 To jest, trifle with.-With अनु(Atm). To play, sport, amuse oneself. आ-, —परि, —सं (Atm.) To play, amuse oneself. (Parsm.) To make a noise.

क्रीडः *m.* 1 Sport, pastime, pleasure. -2 Jest, joke.

क्रीडनं *n.* 1 Playing, sporting. -2 A play-thing, toy.

क्रीडनकः *m.*, —कं, क्रीडनीयं, —यकं *n.* A play-thing, toy.

क्रीडा *f.* 1 Sport, pastime, play, pleasure. -2 Jest, joke. -Comp. —उद्देशः *m.* A play-ground. -कोपः *m.* A false or feigned anger. —गृहं, -मंदिरं *n.* A pleasure-house. -नारी *f.* A prostitute, harlot. —मयूरः *m.* A peacock kept for pleasure. -शैलः, -पर्वतः *m.* An artificial hill serving as a pleasure abode; a pleasure mountain.

क्रीत *p. p.* (*f.* —ता) Bought. —तः *m.* One of the twelve kinds of sons recognised in Hindu Law; a son purchased from his natural parents. -Comp. —अनुशयः *m.* Returning a thing purchased to the seller (admissible in some cases by law.)

क्रुंचः, —चः *m.* A curlew, heron.

क्रुध् 4 P. (क्रुध्यति, क्रुद्ध) To be angry (with the dat. of the person who is the object of anger); हरये क्रुध्यति; but sometimes with words like उपरि, प्रति &c. also; *e. g.* ममोपरि सक्रुद्धः, न मां प्रति क्रुद्धो गुरुः. With प्रति— To be angry in return. सम्— To get angry with.

क्रुध् *f.* Anger.

क्रुश् 1. P. (क्रोशति, क्रुष्ट) 1 To cry, weep, lament, mourn (for). -2 To cry out, yell, call out. With अनु— To pity. अभि— To bewail. आ— 1 To cry aloud. -2 To abuse. परि— To lament. प्रत्या— To revile in turn. वि— 1 To call aloud, to cry out. -2 To utter (with an acc.) -3 To call out to (with an *acc.*). -4 To resound. व्या— To lament.

क्रुष्ट *p. p.* (*f.* —ष्टा) 1 Cried out. -2 Called out to. -3 Abused. —ष्टं *n.* 1 Crying, a cry, yell. -2 Weeping. -3 A noise, sound.

क्रूर *a.* (*f.* —रा) 1 Cruel, wicked, hard-hearted. -2 Hard, rough. -3 Formidable, terrible. -4 Destructive, mischievous. -5 Wounded, hurt. -6 Strong. -7 Hard, solid, hardened. -8 Hot; disagreeable, sharp. —रः *m.* 1 A hawk. -2 A heron. -रं *n* 1 A wound. -2 Slaughter, cruelty. -3 Any horrible deed. -4, Any frightful appearance. -Comp. —आकृति *a.* Terrible in form. (-तिः *m.*) An epithet of Râvana. —आचार *a.* Following cruel or savage practices. —आशय *a.* 1 Containing fierce animals (as a river). -2 Of a cruel disposition. —कर्मन् *n.* 1 A bloody act. -2 Any hard labour. —कृत् *a.* Fierce, cruel, unrelenting. —कोष्ठ *a.*

Having costive bowels (unaffected by strong purgatives). --गंधः *m.* Sulphur. --दृश् *a.* 1 Evil-eyed, having a malignant look. -2 Mischievous, villainous. (*-m.*) N. of Saturn; also of Mars. --राविन् *m.* A raven. --लोचनः *m.* An epithet of the planet Saturn.

क्रेतृ *m.* A buyer, purchaser.

क्रेय *a.* Fit to be bought.

क्रौंचः *m.* N. of a mountain. The same as क्रौंच.

क्रोडः *m.* 1 A hog. -2 The hollow of a tree. -3 The chest, bosom, breast. क्रोडीकृ To clasp to the bosom. -4 The middle part of anything. -5 An epithet of the planet Saturn. --डं *n.*, -डा *f.* 1 The breast, chest, the part between the shoulders. -2 The interior of anything, a cavity. -3 The breast of a horse. -4 The lap. Comp. --अंकः, -अंघ्रिः, -पादः *m.* A tortoise. --पत्रं *n.*, A marginal writing. -2 A postscript to a letter.-3 A supplement. -4 A codicil to a will.

क्रोडीकरणं *n.* Embracing.

क्रोडीमुखः *m.* A rhinoceros.

क्रोधः *m.* 1 Anger, wrath. -2 (In Rhet.) Anger considered as the feeling which gives rise to the *raudra* sentiment. -Comp. --उज्झित *a.* Free from anger; composed, cool. --मूर्च्छित *a.* Overcome or infatuated with anger. --वश *a.* Passionate, violent.

क्रोधन *a.* (*f.* --ना) Wrathful, passionate, angry. --ना *f.* A passionate woman. -नं *n.* Being angry, anger.

क्रोधालु *a.* Wrathful, angry.

क्रोशः *m.* 1 A cry, yell, shout, scream, noise. -2 A measure of distance equal to ¼th of a Yojana, a *Koss.* Comp. --तलः, -ध्वनिः *m.* A large drum.

क्रोशन *a.* (*f.* --ना) Crying. -नं *n.* A cry.

क्रोष्टु *m.* (*f.* --ष्ट्री) A jackal (the strong cases of this word are necessarily formed from क्रोष्टृ and the weak ones optionally).

क्रौंचः *m.* 1 A curlew, heron. -2 N. of a mountain -Comp. -अदनं *n.* The fibres of the stalk of a lotus.-अरातिः, --अरिः, --रिपुः --सूदनः --दारणः, *m.* An epithet of Kártikeya; also of Parasurâma.

क्रौर्यं *n.* 1 Cruelty, hard-heartedness. -2 Terribleness.

क्लंद् 1 P. (क्लंदति, क्लंदित) 1 To call out. -2 To cry, lament, weep.

क्लंद् 1 A. (क्लंदते or क्लदते) To be confused. -2 To grieve.

क्लम् 1. 4. P. (क्लामति, क्लाम्यति, क्लांत) To be fatigued or tired ; be exhausted or depressed. -2 To feel sorry, pine for. With वि-- To be fatigued.

क्लमः, क्लमथः, क्लमथुः *m.* Fatigue, langour, exhaustion.

क्लांत *p. p.* (*f.* --ता) 1 Fatigued, tired out. -2 Withered, faded. -3 Depressed in spirits, exhausted.

क्लांतिः *f.* Fatigue. -Comp. --छिद् *a.* Refreshing, invigorating.

क्लिद् 4 P. (क्लिद्यति, क्लिन्न) To become wet.

क्लिश् 4 A. (also P.) (क्लिश्यते, क्लिष्ट or क्लिशित) 1 To be tormented, be afflicted, suffer. -2 To torment, molest.

क्लिश् 9 P. (क्लिश्नाति, क्लिष्ट, क्लिशित) 1 To torment, afflict, molest, distress.-2 To suffer, feel pain.

क्लिशित *a.* (*f.* --ता) क्लिष्ट (*f.* --ष्टा) 1 Distressed, suffering pain or misery. -2 Afflicted, tormented. -3 Faded. -4 Self-contradictory

e. g माता मे वंध्या. -5 Elaborate, artificial (as a composition.). -6 Wearied. -7 Marred, impaired. -8 Disordered. -9 Injured, hurt. —ष्टं n. A contradictory statement.

क्लिष्टि: f 1 Affliction, anguish, distress, pain. -2 Service.

क्लीब (-व) a. 1 Impotent, neuter, emasculated. -2 Unmanly, timid, weak, weak-minded. -3 Cowardly. -4 Mean, base. -5 Idle. -6 Of the neuter gender. —बः m., -बं n. (-वः,-वं) 1 An impotent man, a eunuch. -2 The neuter gender.

क्लेदः m. 1 Wetness, moisture, dampness. -2 Running or discharge from a sore. -3 Distress, suffering.

क्लेदक a Wetting, moistening —कः m. 1 Phlegm. -2 One of the fires in the body.

क्लेदन a. Wetting, making wet. —नः m. Phlegm. —नं n. 1 Wetting. -2 Trickling, oozing.

क्लेदुः m. 1 The moon. -2 Morbid combination of the three humors of the body (संनिपात).

क्लेशः m. 1 Pain, anguish, distress, worry. -2 Wrath, anger. -3 Care, trouble. -4 Worldly occupation. -Comp. —क्षम a. Capable of enduring trouble.

क्लैब्यं (-व्यं) 1 Impotence (lit.); वरं क्लैब्यं पुंसां न च परकलत्राभिगमनं * पंचतं. 1.-2 Unmanliness; timidity, cowardice. -3 Powerlessness.

क्लोमं, क्लोमन् n. The lungs. -2 The bladder.

क्व ind. 1 Whither? where? क्व-क्व when repeated in co-ordinate sentences imply 'great difference,' or 'incongruity'; क्व सूर्यप्रभवो वंशः क्व चाल्पविषया मतिः * रघुवं. 1. 2. -2 Sometimes क्व is used in the sense of the loc. of किम् ;क्व प्रदेशे i. e. कस्मिन्प्रदेशे. (a) With a following अपि it means (1) somewhere, anywhere; (2) sometimes. (b) With a following चित् it means (1) in some places; (2) in some cases; क्वचित्-क्वचित् (a) in one place-in another place, here-here; (b) now-now (referring to time).

क्वण् 1 P. (क्वणित, क्वणत) 1 To sound (indistinctly), jingle, tinkle. -2 To hum, warble (as bees &c.); sing indistinctly.

क्वणः, क्वाणः m. क्वणनं, क्वणितं n. 1 A sound in general. -2 The sound of any musical instrument.

क्वथ् 1 P. (क्वथति, क्वथित) 1 To boil, decoct. -2 To digest.

क्वथः m. A decoction, solution prepared with a continued or gentle heat.

क्वाचित्क a. (f. —त्की) Met with occasionally; rare, unusual.

क्वाथः m. A decoction, solution prepared with a continued or gentle heat. -2 Pain, sorrow, distress.

क्षः m. 1 Destruction.-2 Disappearance, loss. -3 Lightning. -4 A field. -5 A farmer. -6 Vishnu in his 4th or 'Narasimha' incarnation. -7 A demon.

क्षण् (-न्) 8 U. (क्षणोति, क्षणुते, क्षत) 1 To hurt, injure. -2 To break (to pieces); (with परा,परि,- वि- used in the same senses as क्षण्).

क्षणः, -णं n. 1 An instant, moment, measure of time equal to $\frac{4}{5}$ of a second -2 Leisure. -3 A fit moment, an opportunity. -4 An auspicious or lucky moment. -5 A festival. -6 Dependence, servitude. -7 The centre, the middle. —क्षणात्, —क्षणेन In a moment, 'at once,' 'immediately.' -Comp. —अंतरे ind. The next moment, after a little while. —क्षेप: *m.* A momentary delay. —द: *m.* An astrologer. (—दं *n*) 1 Night-blindness. -2 Water. (—दा *f.*) 1 Night. -2 Turmeric. क्षणदाकर:, -पति: =The moon. क्षणदाचर: *m.* A night-walker, a demon. क्षणदान्ध्यं *n.* The night-blindness, nyctalopsis. —द्युति: —प्रकाशा, -प्रभा *f.* Lightning. -नि:श्वास: *m.* The porpoise. —भंगुर *a.* Transient, frail, perishable. —मात्रं *ind.* For a moment. —रामिन् *m.* A pigeon. —विध्वंसिन् *m.* A class of atheistic philosophers who deny the continued identity of any part of nature, and maintain that the universe perishes and undergoes a new creation every instant.

क्षणतु: *m.* A wound, sore.

क्षणनं *n.* Injuring, killing, wounding.

क्षणिक *a.* (*f.* —का) Momentary, transient. —का *f.* Lightning.

क्षणिन् *a.* (*f.* —नी) 1 Having leisure. -2 Momentary. —नी *f.* Night.

क्षत *p. p.* (*f.* —ता) 1 Wounded, hurt, injured, bitten, torn, rent. -2 Diminished; trodden; spoiled; dirtied. -तं *n.* 1 Scratching, a scratch. -2 A wound, hurt, injury -3 Danger, destruction, peril. -Comp. —अरि *a.* Victorious. —उदरं *n.* Dysentery. —कास: *m.* A cough produced by injury. —जं *n.* 1 Blood. -2 Puss, matter. —योनि: *f.* A violated woman, a woman who is no longer a virgin. —विक्षत *a.* Mangled, covered with cuts and wounds. —वृत्ति: *f.* Destitution, being deprived of any means of support. —व्रत: *m.* A student who has violated his vow or religious engagements.

क्षति: *f.* 1 Injury, wound. -2 Destruction, cutting, tearing down. -3 (Fig.) Ruin, loss, disadvantage; decay, diminution.

क्षत्तृ *m.* 1 One who cuts or carves anything. -2 An attendant, a door-keeper. -3 A charioteer. -4 A man born of a Súdra man and Kshatriya woman. -5 The son of a female slave. -6 Brahman (*m.*). -7 A fish. -8 One who fights from a chariot. -9 The manager of a treasure.

क्षत्र: *m.*, -त्रं *n.* 1 Dominion, power, supremacy. -2 A man of the Kshatriya caste, or the Kshatriya tribe taken collectively. -2 A man of the warrior class; a soldier. —त्री *f.* 1 A woman of the military caste. -2 The rank of a member of the military caste. -Comp. —अंतक: *m.* An epithet of Parasuráma. -धर्म: *m.* 1 Bravery, military heroism. -2 The duties of a Kshatriya. —प: *m.* A governor, satrap. —बंधु: *m.* 1 A Kshatriya by caste. -2 A mere Kshatriya; vile or wretched Kshatriya (as a term of abuse).

क्षत्रिय: *m.* A member of fhe military or second cáste. —यं *n.* The rank or power of the Kshatriya class. -Comp. —हन: (ण:) *m.* An epithet of Parasurâma.

क्षत्रियका, क्षत्रिया, क्षत्रियिका *f.* A woman of the Kshatriya caste.

क्षत्रियाणी *f.* 1 A woman of the Kshatriya caste.

क्षत्रियी *f.* The wife of a Kshatriya.

क्षंतव्य *p. t. p.* 1 To be borne or endured. -2 Pardonable, fit to be forgiven.

क्षंतृ *a.* (*f.* -त्री) Patient, forbearing.

क्षप् 1 U. (क्षपति-ते, क्षपित) To fast, to be abstinent.

क्षप् 10 U. (क्षपयति-ते, क्षपित) 1 To throw, send, cast, to direct.

क्षपणः *m.* A Bauddha mendicant.

—णं *n.* 1 Defilement, impurity (अशौच). 2 Destroying, expelling.

क्षपणकः *m.* A naked Jaina mendicant.

क्षपणि *f.* 1 An oar. -2 A net.

क्षपण्युः *m.* An offence.

क्षपा *f.* 1 A night. -2 Turmeric. -Comp. -अटः *m.* 1 A night-stalker. -2 A demon, goblin. -आंध्यं *n.* Night-blindness. —करः, -नाथः *m.* 1 The moon. -2 Camphor. —घनः *m.* A dark cloud. —चरः *m.* A demon, goblin.

क्षम् 1 A., 4 P. (क्षमते, क्षाम्यति, चक्षमे, चक्षाम, क्षांत or क्षमित) 1 To permit, allow. -2 To pardon, forgive (as an offence). -3 To be patient or quiet, wait. -4 To endure, suffer. -5 To oppose, resist. -6 To be competent or able (to do anything).

क्षम *a.* 1 Patient. -2 Enduring, submissive. -3 Adequate, competent, able (with gen., loc., inf. or in comp.). -4 Appropriate, fit. -5 Bearable, endurable. -6 Favourable, friendly.

क्षमा *f.* 1 Patience, forbearance, forgiveness. -2 The earth. -3 An epithet of Durgá. -Comp. —जः *m.* The planet Mars. —भुज्, —भुजः *m.* A king.

क्षमितृ *a.* (*f.* —त्री), क्षमिन *a.* (*f.* -णी) Patient, forbearing, of a forgiving nature.

क्षयः *m.* 1 A house, residence, abode. -2 Loss, decline, waste, decay, diminuation -3 Destruction, end. -4 Pecuniary loss. 5 Fall (as of prices). -6 Removal. -7 Universal destruction (प्रलय). -8 Consumption. -9 A disease in general. -10 The negative sign or quantity, minus (in algebra). -11 Family, race. -12 The house of Yama. -Comp. —कालः *m.* 1 The time of universal destruction. -2 The period of decline. —कासः *m.* Consumptive cough. —पक्षः *m.* The dark fortnight. —युक्तिः *f.*, -योगः *m.* An opportunity of destroying. —रोगः *m.* Consumption. —वायुः *m.* The wind that is to blow at the destruction of the world. -संपद् *f.* Total loss, ruin.

क्षयथुः *m.* Consumptive cough, consumption.

क्षयिन् *a.* (*f.* —णी) 1 Diminishing, decaying, waning, wasting. -2 Consumptive. -3 Perishable, fragile. -*m.* The moon.

क्षयिष्णु *a.* 1 Wasting, decaying. -2 Perishable, fragile.

क्षर् 1 P. 1 To flow, glide. -2 To send or stream forth, pour out. -3 To drop, ooze. -4 To waste away, perish. -5 To become useless, have no effect. -6 To melt. -7 To slip from, be deprived of (with abl.) With प्र— To melt away, dissolve.

क्षर *a.* 1 Melting away. -2 Moveable. -3 Perishable. -रः *m.* A cloud. —रं *n.* 1 Water. -2 The body.

क्षरणं *n.* 1 The act of flowing, trickling, dropping, oozing. -2 The act of perspiring.

क्षरिन् *m.* The rainy season.

क्षल् 10 U. (क्षालयति-ते, क्षालित) 1 To wash, wash off, purify, cleanse. -2 To wipe away. -With वि- To wash off.

क्षवः *m.* 1 Sneezing. -2 Cough.

क्षवथुः *m.* 1 Sneezing. -2 Cough. -3 Irritation of the throat. -4 Sore throat.

क्षात्र *a.* (*f.* —त्री) Relating or peculiar to the military tribe. —त्रं *n.* 1

The Kshatriya tribe. -2 The qualifications of a Kshatriya.

क्षात्रिः *m.* The son of a Kshatriya by a woman of another caste.

क्षांत *p.p.* (*f.* —ता) 1 Patient, forbearing, enduring. -2 Forgiven. -3 Borne, endured. -4 Friendly. —तः *m.* N. of Siva. —ता *f.* The earth.

क्षांतिः *f.* 1 Patience, forbearance, forgiveness.

क्षांतु *a.* Patient, forbearing. —तुः *m.* A father.

क्षाम *a.* (*f.* —मा) 1 Scorched, singed. -2 Diminished, thin, emaciated, lean. -3 Slight, little, small. -4 Weak, infirm. —मा *f.* The earth. —मं *n.* Destruction.

क्षार *a.* (*f.* —रा) 1 Corrosive, caustic, acid, pungent, saline. -2 Flowing, oozing. —रः *m.* 1 Juice, essence. -2 Treacle, molasses. -3 Any corrosive or acid substance. (क्षारं क्षते क्षिप् 'To make bad worse', 'to add insult to injury'). -4 Glass. -5 Salt. -6 Ashes. -7 A rogue, cheat. —रं *n.* 1 Black salt. -2 Water. -Comp. —अच्छं *n.* Sea-salt. —अंजनं *n.* An alkaline unguent. —अंबु *n.* An alkaline fluid. —उदः, -उदकः, -उदधिः, -समुद्रः *m.* The salt-ocean. —त्रयं, —त्रितयं *n.* Natron, salt-petre and borax. —नदी *f.* The river of alkaline water in hell. —भूमिः *f.*, -मृत्तिका *f.* Saline soil. -मेलकः *m.* An alkaline substance. -रसः *m.* A saline flavour.

क्षारकः *m.* 1 Alkali. -2 Juice, essence. -3 A cage, basket or net for birds. -4 A washerman. -5 A blossom; fresh bud of a flower (कलिका).

क्षारणं *n.*, -णा *f.* Accusing, especially of adultery. —णं *n.* 1 Converting to alkali or ashes. -2 Distilling.

क्षारिका *f.* Hunger.

क्षारित *a.* (*f.* —ता) 1 Distilled from saline matter. -2 Falsely accused.

क्षालनं *n.* 1 Washing, cleansing (with water). -2 Sprinkling.

क्षालित *p. p.* 1 Washed, cleansed. -2 Wiped away; requited.

क्षि 1 P. (क्षयति, क्षित or क्षीण) 1 To decay or waste. -2 To rule, govern, be master of.

क्षि 5, 9. P. (क्षिणोति, क्षिणाति) 1 To destroy, ruin, corrupt. -2 To diminish, cause to waste away. -3 To kill, injure. -4 To spend, pass (as time). —*Pass.* (क्षीयते) 1 To waste, wane; decay, be diminished (fig. also) प्रतिक्षणमयं कायः क्षीयमाणो न लक्ष्यते * हितोप. 4. 66. *Caus.* (क्षययति or क्षपयति) 1 To destroy, remove, put an end to. -2 To spend or pass (as time).

क्षितिः *f.* 1 The earth. -2 A dwelling, an abode, a house. -3 Loss, destruction. -4 The end of the world. -Comp. —ईशः, —ईश्वरः *m.* A king. —कणः *m.* Dust. —कंपः *m.* An earth-quake. —क्षित् *m.* A king, prince. —जः *m.* A tree. -2 An earth-worm. -3 The planet Mars. -4 N. of the demon Naraka killed by Vishnu. (-जं *n.*) The horizon. (-जा *f.*) An epithet of Sîtâ. —तलं *n.* The surface of the earth. —देवः *m.* A Brâhmana. —धरः *m.* A mountain. —धेनुः *f.* The earth considered as a milch-cow. —नाथः, -पः, —पतिः, -पालः, -भुज्, -रक्षिन् *m.* A king, soveriegn. -पुत्रः *m.* 1 The planet Mars. -2 The demon Naraka. —प्रतिष्ठ *a.* Dwelling on the earth. —भृत् *m.* 1 A mountain. -2 A king. —मंडलं *n.* The globe. -रंध्रं *n.* A ditch, hollow. —रुह् *m.* A tree. —वर्धनः *m.* A corpse, dead body. —वृत्तिः *f.* Patient behaviour. -व्युदासः

m. A cave within the earth; an underground hole.

क्षिद्रः *m.* 1 A disease. -2 The sun. -3 A horn.

क्षिप् 6 U. (but only P. when preceded by अभि, प्रति and अपि), 4 P. (क्षिपति-ते, क्षिप्यति, क्षिप्त) 1 To throw, cast, send, let go. -2 To place, put on or upon, throw into. -3 To fix on, attach to (as a blame). -4 To cast or throw off, cast away, rid oneself of. -5 To take away, destroy; kill or slay. -6 To reject, disdain. -7 To insult, revile, abuse, scold. -8 To pour on, scatter. -9 To strike, hit.-10 To distract, afflict. —With पर्या— To bind or tie up, collect (as hair). प्र— 1 To throw at or in. -2 To interpolate. वि— 1 To throw, cast. -2 To divert. -3 To distract. सं— 1 To heap, to gather. -2 To withdraw, destroy. -3 To shorten, to abridge.

क्षिपणं *n.* 1 Sending, throwing. -2 Reviling.

क्षिपणिः, -णी *f.* 1 An oar. -2 A net. -3 A weapon.

क्षिपणुः *m.* 1 An archer. -2 A weapon. -3 Air, wind.

क्षिपण्युः *m.* 1 The body. -2 The spring season. -3 A fragrant smell.

क्षिपा *f.* 1 Sending. -2 Throwing. -3 Night.

क्षिप्त *a.* (*f.* —प्ता) 1 Thrown, scattered, cast. -2 Abandoned. -3 Disregarded, neglected, disrespected. -4 Placed. -5 Distracted, mad. -प्ता *f.* Night. —प्तं *n.* A wound caused by shooting. -Comp. —कुक्कुरः *m.* A mad dog. —चित्त *a.* Distracted in mind, absent-minded. —देह *a.* Prostrating the body, lying down.

क्षिप्तिः *f.* 1 Throwing, sending forth. -2 Explaining a hidden meaning (such as solving riddles).

क्षिप्र *a.* (*f.*-प्रा; compar. क्षेपीयस्; superl. क्षेपिष्ठ) 1 Elastic (as a bow). -2 Quick, speedy.

क्षिप्रं *n.* 1 A measure of time $=\frac{1}{15}$ of a Muhúrta. -2 The part of the hand between the thumb and the forefinger.

क्षिप्रम् *ind.* Quickly, speedily, immediately. -Comp. -कारिन् *a.* Acting quickly; prompt.

क्षिया *f.* 1 Loss, destruction, waste, decay. -2 An impropriety, offence against established customs (आचारभेद).

क्षीजनं *n.* The whistling of hollow reeds.

क्षीण *p. p.* (*f.* —णा) 1 Thin, emaciated, become lean, diminished, worn away, expended. -2 Slender, delicate. -3 Small, little. -4 Poor, miserable. -5 Powerless, weak. -6 Wasted away, lost, diminished. -7 Dead, destroyed. -8 Injured, torn. -Comp. —चंद्रः *m.* The moon on the wane. —मध्य *a.* Slender-waisted. —विक्रांत *a* Destitute of courage or prowess. —वृत्ति *a.* Deprived of the means of support; out of employ.

क्षीरः *m.*, -रं *n.* 1 Milk. -2 The milky juice or sap of plants, exudation; resin. -3 Water. -Comp. —अदः *m.* An infant, a sucking child. —अब्धिः *m.* The sea of milk. —अब्धिजः *m.* 1 The moon. -2 'Amrita' or nectar produced at the churning of the sea. -3 An epithet of Sesha. -4 A pearl. —अब्धिजं *n.* The sea-salt. —अब्धिजा, —तनया *f.* An epithet of Lakshmī. —आह्वः *m.* The pine tree. —उदः *m.* The sea of milk. —उदतनयः (-नंदनः) *m.* Moon. -उदतनया, (-सुता) *f.* An epithet of Lakshmí —ओदन: *m.* Rice boiled with milk.-कंठ:,-कंठक:*m* A young child (having milk in the throat). -जं *n.* 1 Coagulated milk. -द्रुम: *m.* The Asvattha tree. -धात्री *f.* A wet-nurse.-धि:, -निधि: *m.* The sea of milk. —धेनु: *f.* A milch cow. —नीरं *n.* 1 Water and milk. -2 Milk-like water. -3 A fast embrace. —प: *m.* A child. —वारि:, -वारिधि: *m.* The sea of milk. —विकृति: *f.* Inspissated milk. – वृक्ष: *m.* N. of the four trees न्यग्रोध, उंदुबर, अश्वत्थ and मधूक. —शूर: *m.* Cream, the skim of milk. —समुद्र: *m.* The sea of milk -सार: *m.* Butter. -हिंडीर: *m.* The foam of milk.

क्षीरिका *f.* A dish prepared with milk.

क्षीव् 1. 4. P. 1 To be drunk or intoxicated. -2 To spit, eject from the mouth.

क्षीव *a.*Excited,drunk, intoxicated.

क्षु 2 P. 1 To sneeze. -2 To cough.

क्षुण्ण *a.* (*f.* —ण्णा) 1 Pounded, crushed to pieces. -2 Powdered, pulverized, ground. -3 Beaten, trodden (as a path). -4 (Fig.) Practised, followed. -5 Violated (as vow). -6 Exercised, practised, skilful. -7 Overcome, defeated. crossed, baffled. Comp. —मनस् *a.* Penitent, repentant.

क्षुत *f.*, क्षुतं *n.*, -ता,-ति: *f.* A sneeze or sneezing.

क्षुद् 7 U. (क्षुणत्ति, क्षुंते, क्षुण्ण)To tread or trample upon, strike against, crush (under the foot), bruise, pound down. -With प्र- To crush, bruise, pound.

क्षुद्र *a* (*f.* —द्रा ; Compar. क्षोदीयस् ; superl. क्षोदिष्ठ) 1 Minute, small, little, trifling. -2 Mean, low, vile. -3 Wicked. -4 Cruel. -5 Poor, indigent. -6 Miserly, niggardly. -7 Unimportant, minor. —द्र: *m.* 1 A small particle of rice. -2 A bee or wasp. —द्रा *f.* 1 A bee. -2 A fly or gnat. -3 A woman maimed or crippled. -4 A quarrelsome woman. -5 A prostitute, whore, harlot. -6 A base or despicable woman. -7 A dancing girl. -Comp. —अंजनं *n.* A kind of unguent applied to the eyes in certain diseases. —अंत्र: *m.* The small cavity of the heart. —उलूक: *m.* A small owl. —कुष्ठं *n.* A mild form of leprosy. -घंटिका *f.* 1 A small bell. -2 A girdle of small bells. —चंदनं *n.* Red sandal-wood. —जंतु: *m.* Any small animal. —तंडुल: *m.* A grain of rice. —दंशिका *f.* A small gadfly. —बुद्धि: *a.* Low-minded, mean. —रस: *m.* Honey. -रोग: *m.* A minor disease (44 are enumerated by Susruta). —शंख: *m.* A small conch-shell. -सुवर्णं *n.* Low gold; *i. e.* brass.

क्षुद्रल *a.* (*f.*—ला) Minute, small (applied especially to disease and animals).

क्षुद्रिका *f.* 1 A small gadfly. -2 Small bells (for ornaments). [gry.

क्षुध् 4 P. (क्षुध्यति, क्षुधित) To be hun-

क्षुध्, क्षुधा *f.*, 1 Hunger. -2 Food. -Comp. —अन्वित, -आर्त, —आविष्ट *a.* Afflicted by hunger. —क्षाम *a.* Emaciated by hunger. —पिपासित *a* Hungry and thirsty. -निवृत्ति: *f.* Cessation of hunger, the appeasing of appetite (in general).

क्षुधालु *a.* Hungry.

क्षुधित *a.* Hungry.

क्षुप: *m.* A tree with small roots and branches; a shrub.

क्षुब्ध *p. p.* (*f.*—ब्धा) 1 Agitated, shaken. -2 Disturbed. -3 Afraid. —ब्ध: *m.* A churning stick.

क्षुभ् 1 [A., 4. 9. P. (क्षोभते, क्षुभ्यति, क्षुभ्नाति, क्षुभित-क्षुब्ध) 1 To shake, tremble, to be agitated or disturbed. -2 To be unsteady. -3 To stumble (fig. also). With प्र-, वि-, or सम्- To be agitated or disturbed. —*Caus.* (क्षोभयति) To agitate, stir up, excite, perturb.

क्षुभित *a.* 1 Shaken, agitated. -2 Afraid. -3 Enraged.

क्षुमा *f.* 1 Linseed; a kind of flax. -2 The Indigo plant.

क्षुर् 6 P. (क्षुरति, क्षुरित) 1 To cut, scratch. -2 To make lines or furrows.

क्षुरः *m.* 1 A razor. -2 A razor-like barb attached to an arrow. -3 The hoof of a cow or horse. -4 An arrow. -5 The foot of a bed-stead. -Comp. —कर्मन्, *n.* —क्रिया *f.* The act of shaving. -चतुष्टयं *n* The four things necessary for shaving. —धानं, —भाडं *n.* A razor-case. —धार *a.* As sharp as a razor. -प्रः *m.* 1 An arrow with a sharp horse-shoe-shaped head. -2 A sort of hoe, a weeding-spade. —मर्दिन्, मुंडिन् *m.* A barber.

क्षुरिका, क्षुरी *f.* A knife, dagger. -2 A small razor.

क्षुरिणी *f.* The wife of a barber.

क्षुरिन् *m.* A barber.

क्षुल्ल *a.* (*f.* —ल्ला) Small, little. -Comp. —तातः *m.* The younger brother of one's father; cf. क्षुल्ल.

क्षुल्लक *a.* (*f.*—का) 1 Little, minute. -2 Low, vile. -3 Wicked, malicious. -4 Poor. -5 Pained, distressed. -6 Young. —कः *m.* A small shell.

क्षेत्रं *n.* A field, ground, soil. -2 Landed property; land. -3 Place, abode, region, repository. -4 A sacred spot, a place of pilgrimage. -5 An enclosed spot of ground, circuit. -6 Fertile soil. -7 Place of origin. -8 A wife. -9 The sphere of action, the body (regarded as the field of the working of soul.) -10 The mind. -11 A house; a town. -12 A plane figure, as a triangle. -13 A diagram -14 A sign of the zodiac. -Comp. —अधिदेवता *f.* The tutelary deity of any sacred piece of ground. -आजीव -करः, —कृत् *m.* A cultivator, peasant. —गणितं *n.* Geometry. -गत *a.* Geometrical. —ज *a.* 1 Produced in a field. -2 Born from the body. (-जः *m.*) The offspring of a wife by a kinsman duly appointed to raise up issue to the husband. —जात *a.* Begotten on the wife of another. —ज्ञ *a.* 1 Knowing places. -2 Clever, dexterous. (-ज्ञः *m.*) 1 The soul. -2 The Supreme Soul. -3 A libertine. -4 A husbandman. -5 A form of Siva. -6 A witness. (-ज्ञा *f.*) A girl fifteen years old personating Durgá at a festival. —पतिः *m.* A land-owner, a landlord. —पदं *n.* A place sacred to a deity. -पालः *m.* 1 A man employed to guard a field. -2 A deity protecting fields. -3 An epithet of Siva. —फलं *n.* The area or superficial contents of a figure (in math.). —भक्तिः *f.* The division of a field. —भूमिः *f.* Cultivated land. —राशिः *m.* The quantity represented by geometrical figures. —विद् *a.* See क्षेत्रज्ञ. (—*m.*) 1 A husbandman. -2 A sage, one who has spiritual knowledge. -3 The soul. —व्यवहारः *m.* 1 Drawing a figure in geometry. -2 Geometrical demonstration. —स्थ *a.* Residing at a sacred place.

क्षेत्रिक *a.* (*f.* —की) Relating to a field. —कः *m.* 1 A farmer. -2 A husband.

क्षेत्रिन् *a.* 1 Owning a field; cultivating land. -2 Agricultural. —*m.* 1

An agriculturist, a cultivator. -2 A husband. -3 The soul. -4 The Supreme Soul.

क्षेत्रिय *a.* (*f.* —या) 1 Relating to a field. -2 Curable in a future body, or incurable in the present life ; irremediable. —यं *n.* 1 An organic disease. -2 Meadow grass, pasturage —यः *m.* 1 A medicament. -2 An incurable disease. -3 An adulterer.

क्षेपः *m*, 1 Throwing, tossing, moving about. -2 A throw, cast. -3 Sending, dispatching. -4 Depression; striking down. -5 Transgressing. -6 Passing away (time). -7 Delay, dilatoriness. -8 Insult, abuse. -9 Disrespect, contempt. -10 Pride, haughtiness. -11 A nosegay. -12 Laying on (as a paint &c.), besmearing. -13 (in arith.) Addendum.

क्षेपक *a.* (*f.* —का) A thrower, sender. -2 Interpolated, inserted (as a passage). -3 Abusive, disrespectful. —कः *m.* A spurious or interpolated passage.

क्षेपणं *n.* 1 Throwing, casting, sending.-2 Spending (as time). -3 Omitting. -4 Abusing. -5 A sling.-णिः ;-णी *f.* 1 An oar. -2 A net for fishing. -3 A sling or any instrument with which missiles are thrown.

क्षेम *a.* (*f.* —मा) 1 Conferring happiness or comfort ; beneficial. -2 Prosperous, comfortable.-3 Secure, happy. —मः *m.*, —मं *n.* 1 Peace, happiness, welfare, well-being. -2 Safety, security. -3 Preserving, protection. -4 Keeping what is acquired. -5 Final beatitude, eternal happiness. 6 Residence, resting-place. -7 A star, asterism (नक्षत्र). —मः *m.* A kind of perfume. —मा *f.* An epithet of Durgá. -Comp. —कर, —कार (also क्षेमंकर) *a.* Propitious, causing peace or security.

क्षै 1 P. To wane, waste away, decline, decay.

क्षैण्यं *n.* 1 Destruction. -2 Leanness, slenderness.

क्षैत्रं *n.* 1 A multitude of fields. -2 A field.

क्षैत्रज्ञं *n.* The knowledge of the soul.

क्षोडः *m.* The post to which an elephant is tied.

क्षोणिः, क्षोणी *f.* 1 The earth. -2 The number ' one ' (in math.).

क्षोतृ *m.* A pestle.

क्षोदः *m.* 1 Pounding, grinding. -2 The stone on which anything is powdered. -3 A mortar. -4 Any ground substance ; flour. -5 Dust, particle, any small or minute particle. -Comp. —क्षम *a.* Capable of standing a test, scrutiny or investigation.

क्षोदिमन् *m.* Minutness, smallness.

क्षोभः *m.* 1 Shaking, moving.-2 Jolting. -3 Agitation, disturbance, emotion, irritation.

क्षोभणं *n.* Agitating, disturbing. —णः *m.* One of the five arrows of Kâmadeva.

क्षोमः *m.*, —मं *n.* A room on the top of a house. —मं *n.* Woven silk.

क्षौणिः, —णी *f.* See क्षोणि. -Comp. —प्राचीरः *m.* The ocean.—भुज् *m.*,-पतिः *m.* A king -भृत, —धरः *m.* A mountain.

क्षौद्रः *m.* 1 The Champaka tree. -2 N. of a mixed caste. —द्रं *n.* 1 Smallness. -2 Meanness, lowness. -3 Honey. -4 Water. -5 A particle of dust. -Comp. —जं *n.* Wax. —धातुः *m.* A kind of mineral substance.

क्षौद्रेयं *n.* Wax.

क्षौमः *m.*, —मं *n.* 1 Silken cloth, woven silk.-2 An airy room on the top of a house. -3 The back of an edifice. -4 A fortified place before a building. —मं *n.* 1 Linen cloth. -2 Linseed. —मी *f.* Flax.

क्षौरं *n.* Shaving. —री *f.* A razor.

क्षौरिकः *m.* A barber.

क्ष्णु 2 P. (क्ष्णौति, क्ष्णुत) To whet, sharpen.-With सं-(Atm.) To sharpen (fig. also).

क्ष्मा *f.* The earth. -2 (In math.) The number 'one.' -Comp. —जः *m.* The planet Mars. -पः, -पतिः, -भुज् *m.* A king. —भृत् *m.* 1 A king. -2 A mountain.

क्ष्माय् 1 A. (क्ष्मायते, क्ष्मायित) To shake, tremble.

क्ष्विड् 1 U. (क्ष्वेडति-ते, क्ष्वेड्ढ or क्ष्वेडित) To hum, growl, murmur.

क्ष्विड् 1 A., क्ष्विद् 4 P. 1 To be wet or unctuous. -2 To emit sap, or discharge juice, ichor &c.; exude. —With प्र— To murmur, hum.

क्ष्वेडः *m.* 1 Sound, noise. -2 Venom, poison. -3 Moistening. -4 Abandonment. -5 An inarticulate sound. —डा *f.* 1 The roaring of a lion.-2 A war-cry, war-whoop. -3 A bamboo.

क्ष्वेडितः *m.*,-तं *n.* 1 Humming, murmuring. -2 A growl, roar. -3 The roaring of a lion. -4 A battle-cry.

क्ष्वेला, क्ष्वेलिका *f.* क्ष्वेलितं, क्ष्वेल्यं *n.* Play, jest, joke.

ख.

खः *m.* The sun. —खं *n.* 1 The sky. -2 Heaven. -3 Organ of sense. -4 A city. -5 A field. -6 A cipher. -7 A dot, an 'anusvára.' -8 A cavity, an aperture, hollow, hole. -9 An aperture of the human body, (of which there are 9). -10 A wound. -11 Happiness, pleasure. -12 Talc. -13 Action. -14 Knowledge. -15 Brahman (*n.*) -Comp. —अटः (खटः) *m.* 1 A planet. -2 Ráhu, the ascending node. —आपगा *f.* An epithet of the Ganges. —उल्कः *m.* 1 A meteor. -2 A planet. —उल्मुकः *m.* The planet Mars.-कामिनी *f.* N. of Durgâ.-कुंतकः *m.* The N. of Siva.-खोल्कः *m.* The 'sky meteor,' N. of the sun. —गः *m.* 1 A bird. -2 Air, wind. -3 The sun.-4 A planet. -5 A grass-hopper. -6 A deity. -7 An arrow. खगाधिपः *m.* An epithet of Garuda. खगांतकः *m.* A hawk, falcon. खगासनः *m.* 1 The eastern mountain on which the sun rises. -2 An epithet of Vishnu. खगेंद्रः,-ईश्वरः, -पतिः Epithets of Garuda. खगवती *f.* The earth खगस्थानं *n.* 1 The hollow of a tree. -2 A bird's nest -गंगा *f.* The celestial Gangá. —गतिः *f.* 1 A flight in the air. -2 The motion of a planet. -गमः *m.* A bird. (—खे) गमनः *m.* A kind of gallinule. —गोलः *m.* The celestial sphere. —विद्या *f.* Astronomy, —चमसः *m.* The moon. —चरः, -खेचरः *m.* 1 A bird. -2 A cloud. -3 The sun. -4 The wind. -5 A demon. -6 An aerial spirit. -7 A Gandharva or Vidyâdhara. -8 A planet. —जलं *n.* Dew, rain, frost &c. —ज्योतिस *m.* A fire-fly. —तमालः *m.* 1 A cloud. -2 Smoke. —तिलकः *m.* The sun. —द्योतः *m.* 1 A fire-fly. -2 The sun. —द्योतनः *m.* The sun. —धूपः *m.* A rocket. —परागः *m.* Darkness. —पुष्पं *n.* A 'sky-flower' (*lit.*); anything impossible (*fig.*). —भं *n.* A planet. —भ्रांतिः *m.* A falcon. —मणिः *m.* The 'jewel of the sky', the sun. -मूर्तिः *m.* An epithet of Siva. —वारि *n.* Rain-water, dew &c. —बाष्पः *m.* Snow, hoar-frost. —शय (also खेशय) *a.*

Resting or dwelling in . the air. —शरीरं *n.* A celestial body. —श्वास: *m.* The wind, air. —समुत्थ, -संभव *a.* Produced in the sky. —सिंधु: *m.* The moon. —स्तनी *f.* The earth. स्फटिकं *n.* The sun or moon gem. -हर *a.* Having a cipher for its denominator (in *math.*).

खक्खट *a.* Hard, solid. -टं *n.* Chalk.

खंकर: *m.* A curl, a lock of hair.

खच् I. 9. P. (खचति, खच्नाति, खाचित) 1 To come forth, appear. -2 To be born again. -3 To purify.

खच् 10 U. (खचयति, खचित) 1 To fasten, bind. -2 To set, inlay.

खचित *p. p.* (*f.* —ता) 1 Fastened, joined, intermixed with. -2 Mixed, blended. -3 Inlaid, set, studded.

खज् 1 P. (खजति, खजित) To churn, agitate.

खज: *m.* 1 A churning stick. -2 A ladle or spoon. —जा *f.* 1 A churning stick, ladle. -2 The hand with the fingers extended. -3 Churning.

खजक: *m.* A churning-stick. —जिका *f.* A ladle or spoon.

खजपं *n.* Clarified butter, ghee.

खजाक: *m.* A bird. —का *f.* A ladle.

खंज *a.* (*f.* —जा) Lame, crippled, halt. -Comp. —खेट:, —खेल: *m.* The wag-tail.

खंजन: *m.* A species of the wag-tail. —ना *f.* 1 A kind of wag-tail. -2 Mustard. —नं *n.* Going lamely. -Comp. —रतं *n.* The cohabitation of saints.

खंजनक: *m.* A wag-tail;(also खंजनिका *f.*)

खंजरीट:, -टक:, खंजलेख: *m.* The wagtail.

खट: *m.* 1 Phlegm. -2 A blind well. -3 A hatchet. -4 A plough. -5 Grass. -6 The closed fist. -Comp. —कटाहक: *m.* A spitting-box. —खादक: *m.* 1 A jackal. -2 A crow -3 An animal. -4 A glass-vessel. -5 An eater.

खटक: *m.* 1 A man whose business is to negotiate marriages. -2 The half-closed hand.

खटकामुखं *n.* A particular position of the hand in shooting. —ख: *m.* A man in the attitude of shooting.

खट (-ड-) क्किका *f.* 1 A side-door, window.

खटिक: *m.* The hand half-closed. -का *f.* Chalk. -2 The external opening of the ear.

खटिनी, खटी *f.* Chalk.

खट्टन *a.* Dwarfish. -न: *m.* A dwarf.

खट्टा *f.* 1 A bed-stead. -2 A kind of grass.

खट्टि: *m.*, *f.* A bier.

खट्टिक: *m.* 1 A butcher. -2 A hunter, fowler. —का *f.* 1 A small bedstead, a cot. -2 A bier.

खट्टेरक *a.* (*f.* —का) Dwarfish.

खट्वा *f.* 1 A bed-stead, couch, cot. -2 A swing, hammock. -3 A kind of bandage. -Comp. —अंग: *m.* 1 A club or staff with a skull at the top considered as the weapon of Siva and carried by ascetics and Yogins. -2 N. of Dilipa. -धर,-भृत् *m.* An epithet of Siva. —अंगिन् *m.* An epithet of Siva. —आप्लुत, —आरूढ *a.* 1 Low, vile. -3 Abandoned, wicked. -4 Silly, stupid.

खट्वाका, खट्विका *f.* A small bed-stead.

खड् 1 A. (खंडित, खंडते) 1 To break, tear, crush, divide. -2 To annihilate, to defeat. -3 To disappoint, to disturb, interrupt.

खड: *m.* Breaking, dividing.

खडिका, खडी *f* Chalk.

खडु:, -डू: *m.* or *f.* A bier or bed on which the corpse is carried.

खड्ग: *m.* 1 A sword. -2 The horn of a rhinoceros. -3 A rhinoceros. —ड्गं *n.* Iron. -Comp. -आधार: *n.* A sheath, scabbard. -आमिषं *m.* A buffalo's flesh. —आह्वः *m.* A rhinoceros. -कोशः *m.* A scabbard. —धरः *m.* A swordsman. -धेनुः, -धेनुका *f.* 1 A small sword. -2 A female rhinoceros. -पत्रं *n.* The blade of a sword. (-पत्रः *m.*) A tree in hell having swords for leaves. —पाणि *a.* Having a sword in hand. —पात्रं *n.* A vessel made of buffalo's horns. -पिधानं, -पिधानकं *n.* A scabbard. —पुत्रिका *f.* A knife, small sword. -प्रहारः *m.* A sword-cut. —फलं *n.* A sword-blade.

खड्गिकः *m.* 1 A swordsman. -2 A butcher. -3 The cream of buffalo's milk.

खड्गिन् *a.* (*f.* —नी) Armed with a sword. —*m.* 1 A rhinoceros. -2 An epithet of Siva.

खड्गिकं *n.* A sickle.

खंड् 10 P. (खंडयति, खंडित) 1 To break, tear, crush. -2 To defeat completely, destroy. -3 To disappoint; cross in love. -4 To disturb. -5 To cheat.

खंडः *m.*, -डं *n.* 1 A break, gap, fissure, fracture. -2 A piece, part, fragment. -3 A section of a work, chapter. -4 A multitude, an assemblage. -5 A term in an equation. —डः *m.* 1 Candied sugar. -2 A flaw in a jewel. —डं *n.* 1 A kind of salt. -2 A sort of sugar-cane. -Comp. —अभ्रं *n.* 1 Scattered clouds. -2 The impression of the teeth in amorous sports. —आलिः *f.* 1 A measure of oil. -2 A pond or lake. -3 A woman whose husband has been guilty of infidelity. —कथा *f.* A short tale. —काव्यं *n.* A small poem, such as the मेघदूत. —जः *m.* A kind of sugar. —धारा *f.* Scissors. —परशुः *m.* 1 An epithet of Siva. -2 An epithet of Parasuráma, son of Jamadagnī. -3 An epithet of Vishnu. —पर्शुः *m.* 1 N. of Siva. -2 Of Parasurma. -3 Of Rāhu. -4 An elephant with a broken tusk. —पालः *m* An confectioner. —प्रलयः *m.* A partial destruction of the universe in which all the spheres beneath Svarga are dissolved in one common ruin. —मंडलं *m.* A circle -मोदकः *m.* A kind of salt. -विकारः *m.* Sugar. —शर्करा *f.* Candied sugar. —शीला *f.* A loose woman, an unchaste wife.

खंडकः *m.*, -कं *n.* A fragment, part or piece. —कः *m.* 1 Candied sugar. -2 One who has no nails. -Comp. —आलु *n.* Sweet potato.

खंडन *a.* 1 Breaking, cutting, dividing. -2 Destroying, annihilating. -नं *n.* 1 Breaking or cutting. -2 Biting, injuring. -3 Disappointing, frustrating (as in love). -4 Interrupting. -5 Cheating, deceiving. -6 Refuting (in argument). -7 Rebellion, opposition. -8 Dismissal.

खंडलः *m.*, -लं *n.* A piece.

खंडशस् *ind.* 1 To pieces; into fragments. -2 Bit by bit, piece by piece.

खंडित *p.p.* (*f* -ता) 1 Cut, broken in pieces. -2 Destroyed, lost, decayed, rebelled, disappointed. -3 Refuted(in argument), controverted, betrayed, abandoned. -ता *f.* A woman whose husband or lover has been guilty of infidelity, and who is therefore angry with him; one of the 8 principal Nâyikâs in Sanskrit. -Comp. —विग्रह *a.* Mutilated. —वृत्त *a.* Immoral, dissolute, abandoned.

खंडिनी *f.* The earth.

खदिकाः *f. pl.* Fried or parched grain.

खदिरः *m.* 1 N. of a tree, Acacia Catechu. -2 An epithet of Indra. -3 The moon. -Comp. -सारः *m.* Catechu.

खन् 1 U. (खनति-ते, खात; *pass.* खन्यते

or खायते) To dig up, excavate. -2 To dig into the earth, bury. With. आभि- To dig. उद्— To dig out (*lit.* and *fig.*) नि— 1 To dig. -2 To bury. -3 To fix, to implant.

खनकः *m.* 1 A miner. -2 A house-breaker. -3 A rat. -4 A mine.

खननं *n.* 1 Digging, excavating. -2 Burying.

खनिः, -नी *f.* 1 A mine (of jewels). -2 A cave.

खनित्रं *n.* A spade, hoe, a pick-axe.

खनित्रकं *n*, -त्रिका *f.* A small shovel.

खपुरः *m.* The betel-nut tree. -2 Flatulence.

खर *a.* (*f.* -रा) 1 Hard, rough -2 Severe, sharp, strict. -3 Pungent, acid. -4 Dense, thick. -5 Hurtful, injurious, cutting, smart (words). -6 Sharp-edged. -7 Hot -8 Cruel. —रः *m.* 1 An ass. -2 A mule. -3 A heron. -4 A crow. -5 N. of a demon, half-brother of Ravana and slain by Râma. -Comp. -अंशुः, -करः, -रश्मिः *m.* The sun. —कुटी *f.* 1 A stable for asses. -2 A barber's shop. -कोणः, -क्वाणः *m.* The francoline partridge. -कोमलः *m.* The month Jyeshtha. -गृहं, -गेहं *n.* A stable for asses. -णस्,- णस *a.* Sharp-nosed. -दंडं *n.* A lotus. —नादः *m.* The braying of an ass. -नालं *n.* A lotus. —पात्रं *n.* An iron vessel. —पालः *m.* A wooden vessel. —प्रियः *m.* A pigeon. —यानं *n.* A donkey-cart. —शब्दः *m.* 1 The braying of an ass. -2 An osprey. -शाला *f.* A stable for asses. —स्वरा *f.* Wild jasmine.

खरिका *f.* Powdered musk.

खरिंधम, -य (*f.* -मा, -या). Drinking ass's milk.

खरी *m.* A she-ass. -Comp. -जंघः *m.* An epithet of Siva. —वृषः *m.* A jackass

खरु *a.* 1 White. -2 Foolish, stupid. -3 Cruel. -4 Desirous of prohibited things. -रुः *m.* 1 A horse. -2 A tooth. -3 Pride. -4 Cupid, the God of love. -5 Siva. -6 Likeness for prohibited things. -7 The white colour. —रुः *f.* A girl who chooses her own husband.

खर्ज् 1 P. 1 To pain, make uneasy. -2 To creak. -3 To cleanse.

खर्जिका *f.* 1 A venereal disease. -2 A relish.

खर्जुः *f.* 1 Scratching. -2 The date-tree. -3 The Dhattúra tree.

खर्जुरं *n.* Silver.

खर्जूः *f.* Itching, a scab.

खर्जूरः *m.* 1 Date-tree. -2 A scorpion. —रं *n.* 1 Silver. -2 Yellow orpiment. -3 The fruit of the date-tree. —री *f.* Date-tree.

खर्परः *m.* 1 A thief. -2 A rogue, cheat. -3 A beggar's bowl. -4 The skull. -5 A piece of a broken jar, pot-sherd. -6 An umbrella.

खर्परिका, खर्परी *f.* A kind of collyrium.

खर्ब् 1 P. (खर्बति, खर्वति) 1 To go, move, go towards. -2 To be proud.

खर्व (-र्ब) *a.* (*f.* -र्वा, -र्बा) 1 Mutilated; crippled, imperfect. -2 Dwarfish, low, short in stature. -र्वः *m.*, -र्वं *n.* A large number (10,000,000,000). -3 N. of one of the treasures of Kubera. -Comp. -शाख *a.* Dwarfish, small, short.

खर्वटः *m.*, -टं *n.* 1 A market town. -2 A village at the foot of a mountain.

खर्बु (-र्बु-) जं *n.* The water-melon.

खलः *m.*, -लं *n.* 1 A threshing floor. -2 Earth, soil. -3 Place, site. -4 A heap of dust. -5 Sediment, dregs, deposit of oil &c. -6 A mill. -7 A contest, battle. —लः *m.* 1 A wicked or mischievous person, a villain.-2 The sun. खलीकृ means (1) 'To crush';(2) 'to hurt or injure'; (3) To ill-treat,scorn'-उक्तिः f. Abuse,wicked language. —धान्यं n. A threshing floor. -पूः m. f. A sweeper, cleaner. —मूर्तिः m. Quicksilver.

खलकः m. A pitcher.

खलतिः m. Bald-headed man.

खलातिकः m. Mountain.

खलिः, -ली f. Sediment of oil or oil-cake.

खलि (-ली-) नः m., -नं n. The bit of a bridle

खलिनी f. A multitude of threshing floors.

खलीकारः m., -कृतिः f. 1 Hurting, injuring. -2 Ill-treating. -3 Evil, mischief.

खलु ind. A particle implying:— 1 Certainly, surely, verily, indeed. -2 Entreaty, conciliation ('pray'). -3 Inquiry. -4 Prohibition (with gerunds). -5 Reason (for). -6 खलु is sometimes used as an expletive. -7 Sometimes only to add grace to the sentence.

खलूर् m. Darkness.

खलूरिका f. A place for military exercise.

खलेधानी, -वाली f. The post of a threshing floor.

खल्या f. A multitude of threshing floors.

खल्लः m. 1 A stone or vessel for grinding drugs, a mill. -2 A pit. -3 Leather. -4 The Cháṭaka bird. -5 A leather-water-bag. -6 A canal, trench.

खल्लिका f. A frying-pan.

खल्लि (-ल्ली-) ट a. (f.-टा) Bald-headed.

खल्वाट a. (f. -टा) Bald, bald-headed.

खष्पः m. 1 Anger. -2 Violence, cruelty.

खसः m. 1 Itch, scab. -2 N. of a country.

खसूचिः m. f. 1 An expression of reproach (at the end of a compound); वैयाकरणखसूचिः 'A bad grammarian', 'one who has forgotten it'.

खस्खसः m. Poppy.-Comp. —रसः m. Opium.

खाजिकः m. Fried grain.

खाट् (-त्) ind. The sound made in clearing the throat; खात्कृ to clear the throat.

खाटः m., -टा, -टिका, -टी f. A bier, a bed-stead on which dead bodies are carried to the cemetery.

खाटिः f. 1 A bier. -2 A scar. -3 Caprice, whim.

खांडवः m. Sugar-candy. —वं n. N. of a forest in Kurukshetra, sacred to Indra, and burnt by Agni with the assistance of Arjuna and Krishna. -Comp. —प्रस्थः m. N. of a town.

खांडविकः, खाण्डिकः m. A confectioner.

खात a. (f. -ता) 1 Dug up, excavated, bored. -2 Torn, rent. —तं n. 1 An excavation. -2 A hole. -3 A ditch, moat. -4 An oblong pond. -5 A cavern. -6 Digging a hole. —ता f. An artificial pond. -Comp. -भूः f. A moat, ditch.

खातकः m. 1 A digger. -2 A debtor. —कं n. A moat, ditch.

खातिः f. Digging, excavating.

खात्रं n 1 A spade. -2 An oblong pond. -3 A thread. -4 A wood, forest.

खाद् 1 P. (खादति, खादित) To eat, devour feed; to prey upon, bite. -2 To hurt.

खादक a. (f. —दिका) Eating, consuming. —कः m. 1 A debtor. -2 An eater, consumer.

खादनः *m.* A tooth. -नं *n.* 1 Eating, chewing. -2 Food.

खादिर *a.* (*f.* —री) Made of, or coming from, the Khadira tree. -रः *m.* Catechu.

खादुक *a.* (*f.* —की) Mischievous, injurious.

खाद्य *a.* Eatable. —द्यं *n.* Food, victuals.

खानं *n.* 1 Digging. -2 Injury. -Comp. -उदकः *m.* The cocoa-nut tree.

खानक *a.* (*f.* —निका) One who digs; a miner.

खानिः *f.* A mine.

खानिकः *m.*, -कं *n.* A hole in a wall, breach.

खानिलः *m.* A house-breaker.

खारः *m.*, —रिः, -री *f.* A measure of grain equal to 16 *dronas.*

खारि (-री-) क *a.* Equal to or sown with a 'khâri' of grain.

खारिंपच *a.* Cooking a 'Khârî' by measure.

खार्कारः *m.* The braying of an ass.

खार्वा *f* The Tretâ age or second Yuga of the world.

खिङ्खिरः *m.* 1 A fox (*f.*—री). -2 The foot of a bed-stead.

खिद् 6 P. (खिदति, खिन्न) To strike, press down, afflict.

खिद् 4. 7. A. (खिद्यते, खिंत्ते, खिन्न) 1 To suffer pain or misery, to be afflicted or wearied, feel tired, exhausted. -2 To terrify. With परि- To suffer pain or misery.

खिद्रिरः *m.* 1 An ascetic. -2 A pauper. -3 The moon. -4 An epithet of Indra.

खिन्न *p. p.* 1 Depressed, afflicted, distressed, suffering pain. -2 Fatigued, exhausted.

खिलः *m.*, -लं *n.* 1 A piece of waste or uncultivated land, a desert, waste. -2 A gap, vacant place. -3 An additional hymn appended to the regular collection. -4 A supplement in general. -5 A compendium, compilation. -6 Vacuity. -7 Remainder. -खिलीभू 1 To become impassable, to be blocked up, be left unfrequented. -2 To be impossible, be rendered impracticable or stopped —खिलीकृ 1 To obstruct, impede, make impassable, block up. -2 To lay waste, devastate, put down or vanquish completely.

खुंगाहः *m.* A tawny (or black) horse.

खुरः *m.* 1 A hoof. -2 A kind of perfume. -3 A razor. -4 The foot of a bed-stead. -Comp. —आघातः, -क्षेपः *m.* A kick. —णस, -णस *a.* Flat-nosed. —पदवी *f.* A horse's foot-marks. —प्रः *m.* An arrow with a semi-circular head.

खुरली *f.* Military exercise or practice (as of arms, archery &c).

खुरालकः *m*- A iron arrow.

खुरालिकः *m.* 1 A razor-case. -2 An iron arrow. -3 A pillow.

खुल्ल *a.* (*f.* —ल्ला) Small, little, mean, low; see क्षुद्र. -Comp. —तातः *m.* The father's younger brother.

खेचरः *m.* See खचरः.

खेटः *m.* 1 A village, small town or hamlet. -2 Phlegm. -3 The club of Balaráma. —टः *m.*,—टं *n.* 1 Hunting, chase. -2 A shield. (*N. B.* At the end of comp. खेट expresses 'deterioration', & may be rendered by 'miserable', 'low', 'vile', 'wretched' &c.; नगरखेटं *n.* A miserable town).

खेटितालः, -लः *m.* A minstrel, whose business it is to awaken the master of the house with music and singing; (वैतालिक).

खेटिन् *m.* 1 A libertine. -2 A citizen.

खेदः *m.* 1 Depression, lassitude.-2 Fatigue, exhaustion. -3 Pain, torment. -4 Distress, sorrow.

खेय *a.* To be dug or excavated. —यं *n.* A ditch, moat.

खेल् 1 P. (खेलति, खेलित) 1 To shake. -2 To tremble. -3 To play, sport.

खेल *a.* 1 Sportive, amorous, playful. -2 Moving, shaking.-ला *f.* Sport, play, pastime.

खेलनं *n.* 1 Shaking. -2 Play, pastime. -3 A performance.

खेलि: *f.* 1 Sport, play.-2 An arrow.

खोटि: *f.* A cunning or shrewd woman.

खोड *a.* Crippled, lame, limping.

खोर (-ल) *a.* Limping, lame.

खोल: *a.* Lame. —लं *n.* Helmet.

खोलक: *m.* 1 A helmet. -2 An anthill. -3 The shell of a betel-nut. -4 Sauce-pan, pot.

खोलि: *f.* A quiver.

ख्या 2 P. (U. in non-conjugational tenses; ख्याति, ख्यात) To tell, communicate (with dat. of person). With अभि- To be known. आ - 1 To tell. -2 To call, denominate. परि- To be well-known. प्रत्या-- 1 To decline, reject. -2 To deny. -3 To interdict. -4 To surpass. वि— To be famous. व्या— 1 To explain. -2 To tell. -3 To name, call. सम्— 1 To enumerate. -2 To sum up, to calculate. *Pass*. (ख्यायते). 1 To be named or called. -2 To be known or famous. —*Caus*. (ख्यापयति-ते) 1 To make known, proclaim.-2 To tell, declare, relate. -3 To extol, make renowned, praise.

ख्यात *p. p.* (*f.* —ता) 1 Known. -2 Named, called. -3 Told. -4 Celebrated, well-known. -5 Made known, betrayed, discovered. -तं *n.* 1 Communication, mention. -2 Proclamation. -Comp. —गर्हण *a.* Notoriously vile, infamous.

ख्याति: *f.* 1 Renown, fame, celebrity. -2 A name, title. -3 Narration. -4 Praise. -5 (In phil.) Knowledge, the faculty of discriminating objects by appropriate designation.

ख्यापनं *n.* 1 Declaring, divulging. -2 Confessing, avowing publicly. -3 Making renowned, celebrating.

ग.

ग *a.* (Used only at the end of comp.) Going, moving, being, remaining, having sexual intercourse with. —ग: *m.* 1 A Gandharva. -2 An epithet of Ganesa. -3 A long syllable (used as an abbreviation of गुरु in prosody). —गं *n.* A song.

गगनं (-णं) *n.* (Some say that गगण is an incorrect form.) 1 The sky, atmosphere. -2 (In math.) A cipher. -Comp. —अग्रं *n.* The highest heavens. —अंगना *f.* An 'Apsaras'. —अध्वग: *m.* 1 The sun. -2 A planet. -3 A celestial being. —अंबु *n.* Rainwater. —उल्मुक: *m.* The planet Mars. कुसुमं,-पुष्पं *n.* A 'sky-flower'; *i. e.* an unreal thing, an impossibility. -गति *m.* 1 A deity. -2 A celestial being. -3 A planet. —चर *a.* (also गगनेचर) Moving in the air. (—र: *m.*) 1 A bird. -2 A planet. -3 A heavenly spirit. -4 A lunar mansion. -5 The zodiac (राशिचक्र). —ध्वज: *m.* 1 The sun. -2 A cloud. —सिंधु: *f.* An epithet of the Ganges. —स्पर्शन: *m.* 1 Air, wind. -2 N. of one of the eight Maruts.

गंगा *f.* I The river Ganges. -2 The Ganges personified as a goddess. -Comp.-अंबु,-अंभस् *n.* I The water of the Ganges. -2 Pure rain-water (such as falls in the month of आश्विन).-अवतार: *m.* I The descent of the Ganges on the earth. -2 N. of a sacred place.-उद्भेद: *m.* The source of the Ganges. —क्षेत्रं *n.* The river Ganges and the district two Koss on either of its banks. -चिल्ली *f.* Gangetic kite. -ज: *m.* I N. of Bhîshma.-2 Also of Kârtikeya.-दत्त: *m.* An epithet of Bhîshma. —द्वारं *n.* The place where the Ganges enters the plains (also called हरिद्वारं). —धर: *m.* I An epithet of Siva. -2 The ocean. —पुत्र: *m.* I N. of Bhîshma. -2 Of Kártikeya. -3 A man of a mixed and vile caste whose business is to remove dead bodies. -4 A Brâhmana who conducts pilgrims to the Ganges. -भृत् *m.* I N. of Siva. -2 The ocean. —यात्रा *f.* I A pilgrimage to the Ganges. -2 Carrying a sick person to the river side to die there. -सागर: *m.* The place where the Ganges enters the ocean. —सुत: *m.* I An epithet of Bhîshma. -2 Of Kártikeya.

गंगाका, गंगका, गंगिका *f.* The Ganges.

गंगोल: *m.* A precious stone also called गोमेद.

गच्छ: *m.* I A tree. -2 The period (*i. e* number of terms) of progression (in math).

गज् I P. (गजति, गजित) I To sound, roar.-2 To be drunk;to be confused or inebriated.

गज:*m.* I An elephant.-2 The number ' eight'.-3 A measure of length, a *Gaja* or yard. -4 A demon killed by Siva. -Comp. —अग्रणी *m.* I The most excellent among elephants.-2 An epithet of ऐरावत, the elephant of Indra. —अधिपति: *m.* A noble elephant. —अध्यक्ष: *m.* A superintendent of elephants. -अपसद:*m.* A common or low-born elephant. —अशन: *m.* The religious fig-tree (अश्वत्थ). (-नं *n.*) The root of a lotus. -अरि: *m.* I A lion. -2 N. or Siva who killed the demon गज. —आजीव: *m.* An elephant-driver. —आनन:, —आस्य: *m.* Names of Ganesa. —आयुर्वेद: *n.* A science of the treatment of elephants -आरोह: *m.* An elephant-driver.-आह्वं, -आह्वयं *n.* A N. of Hastinâpura -इंद्र: *m.* I An excellent elephant, a lordly elephant.-2 Airâvata, Indra's elephant.-इंद्रकर्ण: *m.* An epithet of Siva. —कूर्माशिन् *m.* N. of Garuda. -गति: *f.* I A stately and majestic gait like that of an elephant. -2 A woman with such a gait. —गामिनी *f.* A woman having a stately elephant-like gait. —दघ्न, -द्वयस *a* As high or tall as an elephant. —दंत: *m.* I An elephant's tusk. -2 An epithet of Ganesa. -3 Ivory. -4 A peg, pin, or bracket projecting from a wall. —दानं *n.* I The fluid (ichor) exuding from the temples of an elephant. -2 The gift of an elephant. —नासा *f.* The trunk of an elephant. —पुंगव: *m.* A large and excellent elephant. -पुरं *n.* N. of Hastinàpura. —बंधनी, -बंधिनी *f.* A stable for elephants. —भक्षक: *m.* The sacred fig-tree. -मंडनं *n.* The ornaments with which an elephant is decorated, particularly the coloured lines on his head. -मंडलिका, -मंडली *f.* A ring or circle of elephants. —माचल: *m.* A lion. —मुक्ता *f.*, -मौक्तिकं *n.* A pearl supposed to be found in the *kumbhas* or projections on the forehead of an elephant. -मुख:, -वक्त्र:, -वदन:, *m.* Epithets of Ganesa. -मोटन: *m.* A lion. —यूथं *n.* A herd of elephants. --योधिन् a. Fighting on an elephant. --राजः m. A lordly or noble elephant. --शिक्षा f. The science of elephants. --साह्वयं n. A N. of Hastinápura. --स्नानं n. (*Lit.*) Bathing of an elephant; (fig.) useless or unproductive efforts like the ablution of elephants which, after pouring water over their bodies, end by throwing dirt, rubbish and other foul matter.

गजता f. A multitude of elephants.

गंजः m. 1 A mine. -2 A treasury.-3 A cow-house. -4 A mart, a place where grain is stored for sale. -5 Disrespect, contempt.-जा f. 1 A hut, hovel. -2 A tavern. -3 A drinking vessel. -4 A mine, jewel-mine. -जं n. 1 A mine. -2 A treasury.

गंजन a. 1 Contemning, putting to shame, surpassing. -2 Defeating, conquering.

गंजिका f. A tavern, liquor-shop.

गड् 1 P. (गडति, गडित) 1 To distil, draw out. -2 To run (as a liquid).

गडः m. 1 A screen. -2 A fence. -3 A ditch, moat. -4 An impediment. -5 A kind of gold-fish.-Comp. -उत्थं, —देशजं, —लवणं n. Rock or fossil salt, especially that found in the district called गड.

गडयंतः, गडयित्नुः m. A cloud.

गडिः m. 1 A young steer. -2 A lazy ox.

गडु a. Crooked, hump-backed. -डुः m. 1 A hump on the back. -2 A javelin. -3 A water-pot. -4 An earth-worm. -5 Any useless object. -6 A goitre, excrescence on the neck. -7 A hump-backed person.

गडुकः m. 1 A water-pot. -5 A finger-ring.

गडुर, -लः a. Hump-backed, crooked, bent.

गडेरः m. A cloud.

गडोलः m. 1 A mouthful. -2 Raw sugar.

गडुरः, -लः m. A sheep.

गडुरिका f. 1 A line of sheep. -2 A continuous line, stream, current.

गडुकः m. A golden vase.

गण् 10 U. (गणयति-ते, गणयांचकार, अजीगणत्-त, अजगणत्-त, गणयितुं, गणित) To count, number; enumerate. -2 To calculate, compute. -3 To sum or add up, reckon. -4 To estimate, value at (with instr.); न तं तृणेनापि गणयामि. -5 To class with or among, reckon among. -6 To take into account, give consideration to. -7 To regard, consider, think or take to be. -8 To attribute to (with loc.). -9 To attend to, take notice of, mind. -10 (With a negative particle) Not to care for; not to mind. -With अभि- 1 To praise.-2 To enumerate, count. अव— To disregard. परि— 1 To count over. -2 To consider, to think. प्र- To calculate. वि- 1 To number. -2 To consider. -3 To disregard.

गणः m. 1 A multitude, group, troop, collection. -2 To A series, a class. -3 A body of followers or attendants. -4 A troop of demigods considered as Siva's attendants and under the special superintendence of Ganesa, a demigod of this troop. -5 Any assemblage or society of men formed for the attainment of the same ends. -6 A company, association. -7 A tribe, class. -8 A series of lunar mansions classed under three heads (of God, men and demons). -9 A sect (in philosophy or religion). -10 A small body of troops (a subdivision of अक्षौहिणी)

consisting of 27 chariots, as many elephants, 81 horses and 135 foot. -11 A number (in math.). -12 A foot (in prosody). -13 (In gram). A series of roots or words subject to the same rule and called after the first word of that series; *e. g.* भ्वादिगण. -14 An epithet of Ganesa. -Comp. —अग्रणी *m.* N. of Ganesa. -अधिप:, -अधिपति: *m.* 1 N. of Siva. -2 N. of Ganesa. -3 The chief of a troop of soldiers or of a class of disciples. —अभ्यंतर *a.* One of a troop or number. (-र:*m.*) The leader or member of any religious association. —ईश: *m.* N. of Ganapati, Siva's son. —ईश्वान:, —ईश्वर: *m.* 1 An epithet of Ganesa. -2 Of Siva.—उत्साह: *m.* The rhinoceros. —कार: *m.* 1 A classifier. -2 An epithet of Bhímasena. —कृत्वस् *ind.* For a whole series of times, for a number of times. -गति: *f.* A particular high number. -चक्रकं *n.* A dinner eaten in common by a party of virtuous men. —छंदस् *n.* A metre regulated and measured by feet. —दीक्षा *f.* 1 Initiation of a number or a class. -2 Performance of rites for a number of persons. -देवता: *f.pl.* Groups of deities who generally appear in classes or troops. —द्रव्यं *n.* Public property, common stock. —धर: *m.* 1 The head of a class or number. -2 The teacher of a school. —नाथ:, -नायक: *m.* 1 An epithet of Siva. -2 Of Ganesa. -नायिका *f.* An epithet of Durgá. -प:,-पति: *m.* 1 N. of Siva. -2 N. of Ganesa. -3 An epithet of Brihaspati and Indra. -4 The leader of a class or troop. —पाठ: *m.* A collection of ganas' or series of words falling under the same grammatical rule. —पीठकं *n.* The breast, bosom. —पुंगव: *m.* The head of a tribe or class. (pl.) N. of a country and its people. —भर्तृ *m.* 1 An epithet of Siva. -2 Of Ganesa. -3 The leader of a class. —यज्ञ: *m.* A rite common to all. —रात्रं *n.* A series of nights. —वृत्तं *n.* See गणच्छंदस्.

गणक *a.* (*f.* -णिका) Bought for a large sum. —क: *m.* 1 An arithmetician. -2 An astrologer. -3 An assemblage of eight stars.—की *f.* The wife of an astrologer.

गणनं *n.* 1 Counting, calculation. 2 Adding, enumerating. -3 Considering, supposing, regarding. -4 Believing, thinking. -5 Account. —ना *f.* Calculation, consideration, regard, account. -Comp. —गति: *f.* =गणगति: q. v. —पति: *m.* 1 An arithmetician. -2 An epithet of Ganesa. —महामात्र: *m.* A minister of finance.

गणशस् *ind.* In troops or flocks.

गणि: *f.* Counting.

गणिका *f.* 1 A harlot, courtezan. -2 A female elephant. -3 A kind of flower. -4 A kind of jasmine.

गणित *p. p.* (*f.* —ता) 1 Counted, numbered, calculated.-2 Regarded, cared for. —तं *n.* 1 Reckoning, calculating. -2 The science of computation, mathematics. -3 The sum of a progression. -4 A sum (In general).

गणितिन् *m.* 1 One who has made a calculation. -2 A mathematician.

गणिन् *a.* (*f.* -नी) Having a flock or troop (of anything). -*m.* A teacher (having a class of pupils).

गणेय *a.* (*f.* —या) Numerable, what may be counted.

गणेरु: *m.* The Karnikara tree. -*f.* 1 A harlot. -2 A female elephant.

गणेरुका *f.* 1 A bawd, procuress. -2 A female servant.

गंड: *m.* 1 The cheek, the whole side of the face including the temples.-2 An elephant's temple.-3 A bubble. -4 Boil, tumour, swelling, pimple. -5 Goitre and other excrescences of the neck. -6 A joint, knot. -7 A mark, spot. -8 A rhinoceros. -9 The bladder. -10 A hero, warrior. -11 Part of a horse's trappings, a stud or button fixed as an ornament upon the harness. -Comp. —अंग: *m.* A rhinoceros. —उपधानं *n.* A pillow. —कुसुमं *n.* The juice that exudes from the elephant's temples during rut, ichor. —कूप: *m.* A well on the peak or summit of a mountain. —ग्राम: *m.* Any large or considerable village. —देश:, —प्रदेश: *m.*, -स्थलं *n.*, -पाली *f.*, -पिंड: *m.* 1 The cheek, the temples of an elephant. -2 Temple-region (in general). -फलकं *n.* A broad cheek. —भित्ति: *f.* 1 The opening in the temples of an elephant from which ichor exudes during rut. -2 An excellent *i. e.* broad and expansive cheek. -माल: *m.*, -माला *f.* The inflamation of the glands of the neck. -मूर्ख *a.* Exceedingly foolish, very stupid. -शिला *f.* Any large rock. —शैल: *m.* 1 A huge rock thrown down by an earthquake or storm. -2 The forehead. —स्थलं *n.*, —स्थली *f.* The cheek. -2 The temples of an elephant.

गंडक: *m.* 1 A rhinoceros. -2 An impediment, obstacle. -3 A joint, knot. -4 A mark, spot. -5 A boil, tumour, pimple. -6 Disjunction. -7 A coin of the value of four 'cowries.' -8 A mode of reckoning by ours. -9 Astrological science. -Comp. —वती *f.* Same as गंडकी q. v.

गंडका *f.* A lump, a ball.

गंडकी *f.* 1 N. of a river flowing into the Ganges. -2 A female rhinoceros. -Comp. -पुत्र: *m.*, —शिला *f.* The Sâligrâma stone.

गंडि: *m.* 1 The trunk of a tree from the root to the beginning of the branches. -2 Goitre.

गंडिका *f.* 1 A sort of pebble. -2 A kind of beverage.

गंडीर: *m.* A hero, champion.

गंडु: (-डू:) *m.*, *f.* 1 A pillow. -2 A joint, knot.

गंडू: *f.* 1 A joint, knot. -2 A bone. -3 A pillow.-4 Oil. -Comp. —पद: *m.* A kind of worm.-पद्मवं *n.* Lead.-पदी *f.* A small गंडूपद.

गंडूष: *m.*,-षा *f.* 1 A mouthful, handful (of water). -2 The tip of an elephant's trunk. -3 A mouthful, handful in general.

गंडोल: *m.* 1 Raw sugar. -2 A mouthful.

गण्य *a.* (*f.*-ण्या) 1 Calculable, to be counted. -2 (At the end of comp.) Belonging to a multitude or class.

गत *p. p.* (*f.* —ता) 1 Gone, departed. -2 Passed away, elapsed, past. -3 Dead, deceased. -4 Gone to, arrived at, reaching to. -5 Being in, resting on, contained in ; usually in comp. *e. g.* प्रासादप्रांतगत: ; सर्वगत, existing everywhere. -6 Fallen into, reduced to, as in आपद्गत:. -7 Refrring or relating to, about, connected with (usually in comp.) *e. g.* भर्तृगतया चिंतया, पुत्रगत: स्नेह: &c. -8 Directed towards, belonging to. -9 Known, understood. —तं *n.* 1 Motion, going. -2 Gait, manner of going. -3 An event.

-4 The place where one has gone. -5 Celebration, being known, diffusion. -6 Manner. -Comp. —अक्ष a. Sightless, blind. —अध्वन् a. I One who has accomplished or finished a journey. -2 Conversant, familiar (with anything). (-f.) The time immediately preceding new moon when a small streak of the moon is still visible; (चतुर्दशीयुक्ताऽमावास्या). —अनुगतं n. Following custom or precedent. —अनुगतिक a. Doing as others do; a blind follower. —अंत a. One whose end has arrived. —अर्थ a. I Poor. -2 Meaningless (the meaning being already expressed). —असु, —जीवित, —प्राण a. Expired, dead. —आगतं n. I Going and coming, frequent visits. -2 Interchange of place. -3 The flight of a bird backward and forward. -4 Irregular course of the stars (in astronomy). —आधि a. Free from anxiety; happy. —आयुस् a. Decrepit, infirm, very old. —आर्तवा f. I A woman past her child-bearing. -2 A barren woman. —दिनं n., —दिवस: m. The past day, yesterday. —द्विनं ind. Yesterday. —प्राय a. Almost gone, nearly passed away as in गतप्राया रजनी. —भर्तृका f. A widow. —वयस्, —वयस्क a. Advanced in years, aged, old. —वर्ष: m., —र्षं n. The past year. —वैर a. At peace (with), reconciled. —शैशव a. Past child-hood. —सन्नक: m. An elephant out of rut.

गति: f. I Motion, going, moving, gait. -2 Access, entrance. -3 Scope, room. -4 Turn, course as, in दैवगतिर्हि चित्रा. -5 Going to, reaching, obtaining as in वैकुंठीया गतिः. -6 Fate, issue. -7 State, condition. -8 Position, situation, mode of existence. -9 A means, expedient, course, alternative. का गतिः What help is there? Can't help. -10 Recourse, shelter, refuge, resort. -11 Source, origin, acquisition. -12 A way, path. -13 A march, procession. -14 An event, issue, result. -15 The course of events, fortune. -16 Course of asterisms. -17 The diurnal motion of a planet in its orbit. -18 A running wound or sore. -19 Knowing; knowledge, wisdom. -20 Transmigration, metempsychosis. -21 A stage or period of life (as शैशव, यौवन, वार्धक). -22 (In gram.) A term for prepositions and some other adverbial prefixes when immediately connected with the tenses of a verb or verbal derivatives. -23 Position of a child at birth. -Comp. —अनुसर: m. Following the course of another. -हीन a. Without refuge, helpless, forlorn.

गत्वर a. (f. —री) I Going, moveable, locomotive. -2 Transient, perishable.

गद् I P. (गदति, गदित) I To speak articulately; speak, say, relate. -2 To enumerate. With नि— To declare; to say.

गद् 10 U. (गदयति-ते) To thunder.

गद: m. I Speaking, speech. -2 A -2 A sentence. -3 Disease, sickness. -4 Thunder. —दं n. A kind of poison. -Comp. —अगदौ m. dual The two Asvins, physicians of Gods. —अग्रज: m. An epithet of Krishna. —अग्रणी: m. The chief of all diseases, i.e. consumption. -अंबर: m. A cloud. —अराति: m. A drug, medicament.

गदयित्नु a. I Loquacious, garrulous, talkative. -2 Libidinous, lustful. —रथु: *m*. N. of Káma, the God of love.

गदा *f*. A mace, club. -Comp. —धर: *m*. An epithet of Vishnu. —भृत् *a*. Club-bearer, one who fights with a mace. (-*m*.) An epithet of Vishnu. —युद्धं *n*. A fight with clubs. —हस्त *a*. Armed with a club.

गदिन् *a* (*f*. —नी) 1 Armed with a club. -2 Affected with sickness; diseased. -*m*. An epithet of Vishnu.

गद्गद *a*. Stammering, stuttering, faltering. —दं *ind*. In a faltering or stammering tone. —द: *m*., —दं *n*. 1 Stammering. -2 Indistinct or convulsive speech. -Comp. —ध्वनि: *m*. A low, inarticulate sound expressive of joy or grief. —वाच् *f*. Inarticulate or convulsive speech interrupted by sobbing &c. —स्वर: *m*. A buffalo.

गद्य *pot. p*. To be spoken or uttered. —द्यं *n*. Prose, elaborate prose composition; composition not metrical yet framed with due regard to harmony.

गद्याणः (—नः, —लः.) —कः *m*. A weight equal to 48 *Gunjás*.

गंतृ *a*. (*f*. —त्री) 1 One that goes or moves. -2 Having sexual intercourse with a woman.

गंत्री *f*. A car drawn by oxen; (गंत्रीरथ in the same sense).

गंध् 10 A. (गंधयते) 1 To injure, hurt. -2 To ask, beg. -3 To move, go.

गंधः *m*. 1 Smell, odour. (गंध is changed to गंधि when as the last member of a Bah. comp. it is preceded by उद्, पूति, सु, सुरभि, or when the compound implies comparison; also when गंध is used in the sense of 'a little'). -2 Smell considered as one of the 24 properties or 'gunas' of the Vaiseshikas. -3 The mere smell of anything, a little, a very small quantity; घृतगंधि भोजनं. -4 A perfume, any fragrant substance. -5 Sulphur. -6 Pounded sandal wood. -7 Connection, relationship. -8 A neighbour. -9 Pride, arrogance. -10 An epithet of Siva. -धं *n*. 1 Smell. -2 Black aloewood. -Comp. —अधिकं *n*. A kind of perfume. —अपकर्षणं *n*. Removing smells. —अम्ला *f*. The wild lemon tree. —अश्मन् *m*. Sulphur. —अष्टकं *n*. A mixture of 8 fragrant substances offered to deities, varying in kind according to the nature of the deity to whom they are offered. —आखु: *m*. The musk-rat. —आजीव: *m*. A vendor of perfumes. —आढ्य *a*. Rich in odour, very fragrant. (—ढ्यं *n*.) The sandal-wood. —इंद्रियं *n*. The organ of smell. —इभः, —गजः, —द्विपः, —हस्तिन् *m*. 'The scent-elephant'; an elephant of the best kind. —उत्तमा *f*. Spirituous liquor. —उपजीविन् *m*. One who lives by perfumes, a perfumer. —ओतु: (forming गंधोतु: or गंधौतु:) *m*. The civet-cat. —कारिका *f*. 1 A female-servant whose business is to prepare perfumes. -2 A female artisan living in the house of another, but not altogether subject to another's control. —कालिका, —काली *f*. N. of Satyavatí, mother of Vyása. —काष्ठं *n*. Aloe-wood. —कुटी *f*. A kind of perfume. —केलिका, —चेलिका *f*. Musk. —गुण *a*. Having the property of odour. —ज्ञा *f*. The nose. —तूर्यं *n*. A musical instrument of a loud sound used in battle (as a drum or trumpet). —तैलं *n*. A kind of fragrant oil prepared with fragrant substances. —दारु *n*. Aloe-wood. —धूलि: *f*. Musk. —नकुल: *m*. The musk-rat. —नालिका,

—नाली *f.* The nose. —पः *m.* N. of a class of manes. -पलाशिका *f.* Turmeric. —पाषाणः *m.* Sulphur. —पिशाचिका *f.* The smoke of burnt fragrant resin (so called from its dark colour or cloudy nature, or perhaps from its attracting demons by fragrance). —पुष्पः *m.* 1 The 'Vetasa' plant. -2 The 'Ketaka' plant. (-पुष्पं *n.*)1 A fragrant flower. -2 Flowers and sandal offered to deities at the time of worship. —पुष्पा *f.* The indigo plant. —पूतना *f.* A kind of imp or goblin. —फली *f.* 1 The Priyangu creeper. -2 A bud of the Champaka tree. —बंधुः *m.* The mango tree. —मातृ *f.* The earth. —मादनः *m.* 1 A large black bee. -2 Sulphur. -3 An epithet of Râvana. (-नः *m.*, —नं *n.*) N of a particular mountain to the east of Meru, renownod for its fragrant forests. —मादनी *f.* Spirituous liquor. -मादिनी *f.* Lac. -मार्जारः *m.* The civet-cat. —मुखा *f.*, -मूषिकः *m.*, -मूषी *f.* The musk rat. -मृगः *m.* 1 The civet cat. -2 The musk-deer. —मैथुनः *m.* A bull. —मोदनः *m.* Sulphur. —मोहिनी *f.* A bud of the Champaka tree. -लता *f.* The 'Priyangu' creeper.-वहः *m.* The wind. —वहा *f.* The nose. -वाहः *m.* 1 The wind. -2 The musk-deer. —वाही *f.* The nose. —विह्वलः *m.* Wheat. —वृक्षकः, -वृक्षः *m.* The 'Sâla' tree. —व्याकुलं *n.* A kind of fragrant berry (कक्कोल). —शुंडिनी *f.* The musk-rat. —शेखरः *m.* Musk. —सारः *m.* 1 Sandal. - 2 A kind of jasmine. —हारिका *f.* A female servant whose business is to prepare perfumes.

गंधकः *m.* Sulphur.

गंधनं *n.* 1 Continued effort, perseverance.-2 Hurting, injury, killing. -3 Manifestation. -4 Intimation.

गंधर्वः *m.* 1 A celestial musician, a class of demi-gods regarded as the singers or musicians of gods. -2 A singer in general. -3 A horse. -4 The musk-deer. -5 The soul after death and previous to its being born again. -6 The black cuckoo. -7 The sun. -2 A sage, pious man. -Comp. -नगरं, -पुरं *n.* The city of the Gandharvas, an imaginary city in the sky. —राजः *m.* Chitraratha, the chief of the Gandharvas. —विद्या *f.* The science of music. —विवाहः *m.* One of the eight forms of marriage which proceeds entirely from love of a youth and maiden. —वेदः *m.* One of the four subordinate Vedas or *Upavedas*, which treats of music. —हस्तः, -हस्तकः *m.* The castor-oil plant.

गंधाराः *m. pl.* N. of a country and its rulers.

गंधाली *f.* 1 A wasp. -2 Continued fragrance. -Comp. —गर्भः *m.* Small cardamoms.

गंधालु *a.* Fragrant, perfumed.

गंधिक *a.* (Used only at the end of comp.) 1 Having the smell of, as in उत्पलगंधिक. -2 Having a very small quantity of, having only the smell of; भ्रातृगंधिकः *m.* A brother only in name. —कः *m.* 1 A seller of perfumes. -2 Sulphur.

गंधिन् *a.* Having a smell, smelling. —*m.* A bug.

गंधोली *f.* 1 A wasp.-2 Dried ginger.

गभस्तिः *m.*, *f.* 1 A ray of light, a sunbeam or moonbeam. —स्तिः *m.* The sun. -*f.* An epithet of 'Sváhá,' the wife of Agni. -Comp. —करः, -पाणिः, -मालिन्, -हस्तः, -मत् *m.* The sun.

गभीर *a.* (*f.* —रा) 1 Deep (in all senses). -2 Deep-sounding (as a drum). -3 Thick, dense, impervious (as a forest). -4 Profound, sagacious. -5 Grave, serious, solemn, earnest. -6 Secret, mysterious. -7 Difficult to be perceived or understood. -Comp. —आत्मन् *m.* The Supreme Soul.

गभीरिका *f.* 1 A large drum with a deep sound. -2 A gong.

गभोलिक: *m.* A small round pillow.

गम् 1 P. (गच्छति, जगाम, अगमत्, गमिष्यति, गंतुं, गत; *desid.* जिगमिषति, जिगांसते Atm.) 1 To go, move. -2 To depart, go, away, set out. -3 To go to, reach, resort to, arrive at, approach.-4 To pass, pass away, elapse (as time). -5 To go to the state or condition of, become, undergo, suffer (usually joined with nouns in the acc.). -6 To cohabit, have sexual intercourse with. With अति— To pass away. अधि— 1 To obtain. -2 To reach, to have access to. -3 To fulfil, to accomplish. -4 To know, to earn, understand. -5 To take a husband. अध्या— To find. अनु— 1 To follow, to accompany. -2 To imitate. -3 To approach, visit. अंतर्— 1 To go into. -2 To be included in. अप— To go away. अभि— 1 To approach, visit. -2 To meet by chance. -3 To have sexual intercourse with. अभ्या— 1 To approach. -2 To arrive. -3 To obtain. अभ्युत्— 1 To advance towards. -2 To rise. अभ्युप— To consent to, to accept. अव— 1 To know, to think, to understand. -2 To guess, to take for. आ— 1 To come, to approach. -2 To go to the state of. उत्— 1 To rise up. -2 To originate. -3 To be famous. उप— 1 To approach, to attain. -2 To undergo. -3 To have sexual intercourse with. -4 To go to the state of, to acquire. उपा—1 To approach. -2 To go to the state of, to attain. -3 To obtain. नि— 1 To obtain, acquire.-2 To obtain knowledge. निस्— 1 To go out, depart from. -2 To be cured of (a disease). -3 To remove. परा—1 To surround, to pervade. -2 To return. परि— 1 To walk round. -2 To surround. -3 To spread everywhere. -4 To die. -5 To obtain. -6 To know, to understand. पर्या— 1 To finish. -2 To approach. -3 To subdue. प—To advance प्रति-To advance towards.-2 To return. प्रत्या- To come back. प्रत्युत्- To advance towards as a mark of respect; to go forth to receive a visitor. वि— To disappear. -2 To pass away. विनिस्— 1 To go out. -2 To vanish. विप्र— To separate. सम्- (*Atm.*) 1 To come together, to encounter, to meet, -2 To have sexual intercourse with. समधि— 1 To approach. -2 To study. -3 To acquire. समव— To know completely. समुपा— To befall.

Caus. (गमयति, -ते) 1 To cause to go, to lead, to reduce to. -2 To explain, to expound. -3 To denote, signify. *e. g.* द्वौ नञौ प्रकृतार्थं गमयत: ' two negatives make one affirmative.' -4 To pass (as time). With अव— To convey, signify, tell. आ— 1 To bring. -2 To teach. -3 To wait वि— To pass (as time). सम्— To bring together.

गम *a.* (*f.* —मा) (At the end of comp.) Going, moving, going to reaching, getting, as in पुरोगम, हृदयंगम, &c. —म: *m.* 1 Going, moving. -2 March, -3 The march of an assailant. -4 A road. -5 Thoughtlessness. -6 Superficiality, careless perusal. -7 (Sexual) intercourse with a woman. -8 A game played with dice and men. -Comp. --आगमः *m.* Going and coming.

गमक *a.* (*f.* —मिका) 1 Indicative or suggestive; a proof or index of. -2 Convincing.

गमनं *n.* 1 Going, motion, gait. -2 Going, motion considered as one of the five *karmans* by the Vaiseshikas. -3 Approaching. -4 March of an assailant. -5 Undergoing, suffering. -6 Obtaining, attaining. -7 Cohabitation.

गमिन् *a.* (*f.* —नी) Intending to go, as in ग्रामंगमी. —*m.* A passenger.

गंभीर *a.* (*f.* —रा) See गभीर.—रः *m.* 1 A lotus.-2 A citron. -Comp. —वेदिन् *a.* Restive (as an elephant).

गम्य *a.* (*f.* —म्या) 1 Accessible, approachable. -2 Intelligible. -3 Intended, implied, meant.-4 Suitable, desirable, fit. -5 Fit for cohabitation. -6 Curable (by a drug &c.).

गयः *m.* 1 N. of the people living round Gayá and the district inhabited by them. -2 N. of an Asura. —या *f.* N. of a city in Behar which is a place of pilgrimage.

गर *a.* (*f.* —री) Swallowing. —रः *m.* 1 Any drink or fluid. -2 Sickness, disease. -3 Swallowing. —रः *m.*, —रं *n.* 1 Poison. -2 An antidote. —रं *n.* Sprinkling, wetting. -Comp. —अधिका *f.* 1 The insect called Lâkshà. -2 The red dye obtained from it. —व्रतः *m.* A peacock.

गरणं *n.* 1 The act of swallowing. -2 Sprinkling. -3 Poison.

गरभः *m.* Fœtus, embryo; see गर्भ.

गरलः *m.*, -लं *n.* 1 Poison or venom in general. -2 The venom of a snake. —लं *n.* A bundle of grass. -Comp. —अरिः *m.* An emerald.

गरिमन् *m.* 1 Weight, heaviness. -2 Importance, greatness, dignity. -3 Worth, excllence. -4 One of the eight *siddhis* or faculties of a 'Yogin' by which he can make himself heavy or great at will; see सिद्धि.

गरिष्ठ *a.* (*f* —ष्ठा) Heaviest. -2 Most important; (superl. of गुरु *a.*)

गरीयस् *a.* (*f.* —सी) Heavier, weightier, more important (compar. of गुरु *a.* q.v.).

गरुडः *m.* 1 N. of the king of birds. -2 A building shaped like Garuda. -3 N. of a particular military array. -Comp. —अग्रजः *m.* An epithet of Aruna, the charioteer of the sun. —अंकः *m.* An epithet of Vishnu. —अंकितं *n.*, —अश्मन् *m.* —उत्तीर्णं *n.* An emerald. —ध्वजः *m.* An epithet of Vishnu. —व्यूहः *m.* A particular military array.

गरुत् *m.* The wing of a bird.-2 Eating, swallowing. -Comp.-योधिन् *m.* A quail.

गरुत्मत् *a.* Winged. —*m.* 1 Gáruda. -2 A bird in general. -3 The fire.

गरुलः *m.* Garuda, the chief of birds.

गर्गः *m.* 1 N. of an old sage, one of the sons of Brahman (*m.*). -2 A bull.-3 An earth-worm. -गर्गाः *m. pl.* The descendants of Garga.

गर्गरः *m.* 1 A whirlpool, an eddy. -2 A kind of musical instrument. -3 A kind of fish. -4 A churn. -री *f.* A churn, a vessel for holding water.

गर्गाटः *m.* A kind of fish.

गर्ज् 1 P., 10 U. (गर्जति, गर्जयति-ते, गर्जित) 1 To roar, growl.-2 To thunder. With अनु- To echo, to thunder in return. प्रति- 1 To roar at or against. -2 To resist, to oppose.

गर्जः *m.* 1 The roaring of elephants.

-2 The rumbling or thundering of clouds. -3 A (roaring) elephant.

गर्जनं *n.*, -ना *f.* 1 Roaring, a roar, growl, thunder. -2 Any noise in general. -3 Passion, wrath. -4 War, battle. -5 Reproach.

गर्जा *f.*, गर्जिः *m.* The thundering of [clouds.

गर्जित *a.* Sounded, roared. -तं *n.* A thunder of clouds. -तः *m.* A roaring elephant in rut.

गर्तः *m.*, -र्ता *f.*, -र्तं *n.* 1 A hollow, hole, cave. -2 A grave. —र्तः *m.* 1 The hollow of the loins. -2 A kind of disease. -3 N. of a country, a part of the *Trigartas.*

गर्तिका *f.* Weaver's work-shop.

गर्द् 1 P., 10 U. (गर्दति, गर्दयति-ते) To sound, roar.

गर्दभः *m.*(*f.* -भी) 1 An ass. -2 Smell, odour. -भं *n.* The white water-lily. -भी *f.* 1 A she-ass. -2 An insect generated in cowdung. -Comp. -आह्वयं *n.* A white lotus. —गदः *m.* A particular disease of the skin.

गर्धः *m.* 1 Desire, eagerness. -2 Greediness.

गर्धन *a.* (*f.* —ना), -गर्धित (*f.*-ना) Covetous, greedy.

गर्धिन् *a.* (*f.* -नी) 1 Desirous, greedy, covetous. -2 Pursuing (anything) with eagerness.

गर्भः *m.* 1 The womb, the belly. -2 A foetus, embryo; act of conception, pregnancy. -3 The time of conception. -4 The child (in the womb). -5 A child, brood or offspring of birds. -6 The inside, middle or interior of anything. -7 The offspring of the sky, *i. e.* the vapours and fogs drawn upwards by the rays of the sun during 8 months and sent down again in the rainy season. -8 An inner apartment, a lying-in-chamber. -9 Any interior chamber. -10 A hole. -11 Fire. 12 Food. 13 The rough coat of the jack-fruit (पनसकंटक). -14 The bed of a river, especially of the Ganges on the fourteenth day of the dark half of Bhádrapada or in the very height of the rains when the river is fullest. 15 (In dramas) One of the *Sandhis* q. v. -Comp. —अंकः (also गर्भांकः) *m.* An interlude during an act. —अवक्रांतिः *f.* The descent of the soul into the womb. —अगारं *n.* 1 The uterus. -2 An inner and private room, the female apartments. -3 A lying-in-chamber. -4 The body or sanctuary of a temple. —आधानं *n.* 1 Impregnation. -2 One of the Samskâras or purificatory ceremonies performed after menstruation to ensure or facilitate conception. —आशयः *m.* The uterus, the womb. -आस्रावः *m.* Mis-carriage, abortion. -ईश्वरः *m.* One born rich, a sovereign or a rich man by birth. —उत्पत्तिः *f.* The formation of the embryo. -उपघातः *m.* Miscarriage of the embryo. -उपघातिनी *f.* A cow or female miscarrying from unseasonable gestation. —कालः *m.* The time of impregnation. —कोशः, -षः *m.* The uterus. —क्लेशः *m.* The pains caused by the embryo, the throes of parturition or childbirth. —क्षयः *m.* Miscarriage. —गृहं, -भवनं, -वेश्मन् *n.* 1 An inner apartment, the body of a house. -2 A lying-in-chamber. -3 The sanctuary of a temple. —च्युतिः *f.* 1 Birth, delivery. -2 Miscarriage. —दासः *m.*, —सी *f.* A slave by birth; (often used as a term of abuse or reproach.). —धरा *f.* Pregnant. -धारणं *n.*,

—धारणं f. Gestation, impregnation. —नाडी f. The umbilical cord. –पाकिन् m. Rice ripening in sixty days. —पातः m. Miscarriage after the fourth month of pregnancy. —मंडपः m. An inner apartment, a bed-chamber. —मोचनं n. Delivery, birth. —योषा f. A pregnant woman; (fig.) the Ganges overflowing its banks. —रूप a. Childish, youthful, juvenile. —रूपः,—रूपकः, m. A child, an infant, a youth. —लक्षण a. Observing the signs of the rainy season. (—णं n.) A symptom of pregnancy. —लंभनं n. A ceremony performed for the sake of facilitating and developing pregnancy. —वसतिः f., —वासः m. 1 The womb. –2 Being in the womb. —वेदना f. The throes of child-birth. —व्याकरणं n. The formation of the embryo. —शंकुः m. A kind of instrument for extracting the dead fœtus. —शय्या f. The abode of the fœtus or uterus. —स्थ a. 1 Situated in the womb. –2 Interior, internal. —स्रावः m. Abortion, miscarriage.

गर्भकः m. A chaplet of flowers worn in the hair. —कं n. A period of two nights with the intermediate day.

गर्भंडः m. Enlargement of the navel.

गर्भिणी f. A pregnant female.-Comp. —अवेक्षणं n. Mid-wifery, care and attendance of pregnant women and new-born infants. —दौहृदं n. The longings of a pregnant woman. —व्याकरणं n., –व्याकृतिः f. The 'science of the progress of pregnancy' (a particular head in medical works).

गर्भित a. Pregnant, filled with. —तं n. A defect in poetical composition.

गर्व् 1 P. (गर्वति, गर्वित) To be proud or haughty.

गर्वः m. 1 Pride, arrogance. –2 Pride considered as one of the 33 subordinate feelings in rhetoric.

गर्वाटः m. A watch-man, door-keeper.

गर्वित a. (f. —ता) 1 Proud, haughty. –2 Conceited.

गर्ह् 1. 10. A. (sometimes P.) (गर्हते, गर्हयते, गर्हित) 1 To blame, censure, reproach.–2 To accuse, charge with. –3 To be sorry for.

गर्हणं n., —णा f. Censure, blame, reproach, abuse.

गर्हा f. Abuse, censure.

गर्हित p. p. (f. —ता) Blamed. –2 Despised. –3 Contemptible.–4 Forbidden, bad, vile. —तं n. A blamable or sinful act.

गर्ह्य a. (f. —र्ह्या) Deserving censure, cencurable, blamable.

गल् 1 P. 1 To drop, drip, ooze trickle. –2 To drop or fall down. –3 To disappear, pass away, be removed. —With निस्— To ooze or flow out, trickle down. पर्या— To drop down.

गलः m. 1 The throat, neck. –2 The resin of the Sála tree. –3 A kind of musical instrument. –4 A rope. -Comp. —उद्भवः m. The tuft of hair on the neck of a horse. —कंबलः m. A bull's dewlap. —गंडः m. A goitre. —ग्रहः m., -ग्रहणं n. 1 The seizing by the throat, throttling, smothering. –2 A kind of disease. –3 N. of certain days in the dark fortnight of a month :— i. e. the 4th, 7th, 8th, 9th, 13th and the three following days. –4 A day on which a course of study is commenced but immediately preceding a day on which it is prohibited. –5 Study begun but immediately interrupted. —चर्मन् n. The gullet, throat.

—द्वारं *n.* The mouth. —वार्त *a.* Able to eat much and digest it; healthy, sound. -2 A parasite. —व्रतः *m.* A peacock. —शुंडिका *f.* The uvula.-शुंडी *f.* The swelling of the glands of the neck. —स्तनी (also गलस्तनी) *f.* A she-goat. —हस्तः *m.* 1 Seizing by the throat, throttling, collaring. -2 An arrow with a crescent-shaped head. —हस्तित *a.* Seized by the throat, throttled, strangled.

गलकः *m.* 1 The throat, the neck. -2 A kind of fish.

गलनं *n.* 1 Oozing. -2 Leaking. -3 Melting, fusing.

गलंतिका, गलंती *f.* 1 A small pitcher. -2 A small water-jar with a hole in the bottom from which the water drops upon the object of worship placed below.

गलिः *m.* A strong but lazy bull.

गलित *p. p.* (*f.* —ता) 1 Dropped or fallen down. -2 Melted. -3 Oozed, flowing. -4 Lost, vanished. -5 Untied, got loose. -6 Emptied, leaked away. -7 Filtered. -8 Decayed, impaired. -9 Decreased, exhausted. -Comp. —कुष्टं *n.* The advanced or incurable leprosy when the fingers and toes fall off. —वयस् *a.* Being in the decline of age; in declining years.

गलितकः *m.* A kind of dance.

गल्भ *a.* 1 Bold.-2 Proud, haughty.

गल्लः *m.* The cheek; especially, the part of the cheek near the corners of the mouth. -Comp. —चातुरी *f.* A small round pillow to put underneath the cheek.

गल्लकः *m.* 1 A wine-glass. -2 Sapphire.

गल्लर्कः *m.* A vessel for drinking spirituous liquor.

गल्वर्कः *m.* 1 Crystal.-2 Lapis lazuly. -3 A vessel for drinking spirituous liquor.

गल्ह् 1 A. (गल्हते, गाल्हित) To blame, censure.

गव (A substitute for गो at the beginning of certain compounds). -Comp. —अक्षः *m.* 1 An air-hole, a round window.—आक्षित *a.* Furnished with windows. —अग्रं *n.* A multitude of cows; (written as गोऽग्रं, गोअग्रं, and गवाग्रं). —अदनं *n.* A pasture or meadow grass. —अदनी *f.* 1 A pasture. -2 A manger, a trough for holding grass &c. for feeding cattle. —अधिका *f.* Lac. -अर्ह *a.* Of the value of a cow. —अविकं *n.* Cattle and sheep. —अशनः *m.* 1 A shoe-maker. -2 An out-cast. —अश्वं *n.* Bulls and horses. —आह्निकं *n.* The daily measure of food given to a cow. —इंद्रः *m.* 1 The owner of kine. -2 An excellent bull. -ईशः, -ईश्वरः *m.* An owner of cows. —उद्वः *m.* An excellent cow or bull.

गवयः *m.* A species of ox. —यी *f.* The female 'Gavaya.'

गवलः *m.* The wild buffalo. —लं *n.* Buffalo's horn.

गवांपतिः *m.* 1 The chief cattle, a bull. -2 A cowherd. -3 An epithet of the sun; also of fire.

गवाल्लूकः *m.* Same as गवयः q. v.

गाविनी *f.* A herd of cows.

गवेडुः, -धुः, -धुका *f.* A kind of grass eaten by cattle.

गवेरुकं *n.* Red chalk.

गवेष् 1 A., 10 P. (गवेषते, गवेषयति, गवेषित) 1 To seek, hunt for, inquire for. -2 To strive after, desire ardently, make efforts for.

गवेष *a.* Searching for. —षः *m.* Search, inquiry.

गवेषणं *n.*, —णा *f.* Search or inquiry

गवेषित *a.* (*f.* —ता) Searched, sought, inquired or looked for.

गव्य *a.* (*f.* —व्या) 1 Consisting of cattle or cows. -2 Coming or got from a cow (as milk, curds &c). -3 Proper or fit for cattle. -4 Sacred to the cow; worshipping the cow.—व्यं *n.* 1 Cattle, a herd of cows. -2 Pasture-land. -3 The milk of a cow. -4 A bow-string. -5 Colouring substance. —व्या *f.* 1 A herd of cows. -2 A measure of distance equal to two 'Krosas.' -3 A bow-string. -4 A colouring substance.

गव्यूतं *n.*, -ति: *f.* 1 A measure of length nearly equal to two miles or one 'Krosa.' -2 A measure of distance equal to two Krosas. -3 A pasture-ground, pasturage.

गहन *a.* (*f.* —ना) 1 Deep, dense, thick. -2 Impenetrable, impassable, inaccessible. -3 Hard to be understood, mysterious. -4 Grave, dignified. -5 Replete with love, strong. -6 Hard, difficult, causing pain or trouble. -7 Intensified. —नं *n.* 1 An abyss, depth. -2 A wood, thicket, an impenetrable forest. -3 A cave. -4 Pain, distress. -5 Water. —न: *m.* The Supreme Being.

गह्वर *a.* (-रा or -री *f.*) Deep, impervious. —रं *n.* 1 An abyss, a depth. -2 A thicket, forest. -3 A cave, cavern. -4 An inaccessible place. -5 A hiding-place. -6 A riddle. -7 Hypocrisy. -8 Weeping, crying. -9 Water. —र: *m.* An arbour, bower. —री *f.* 1 A cave, cavern.

गा *f.* A song, verse.

गांग *a.* (*f.* —गी) Being in or on the Ganges. -2 Coming from or relating to the Ganges. —ग: *m.* 1 An epithet of Bhîshma. -2 Of Kârtikeya. —गं *n.* 1 Rain-water of a peculiar kind (supposed to fall down from the heavenly Ganges). -2 Gold. —गी *f.* An epithet of Durgâ.

गांगट:, -टेय: *m.* A kind of prawn or shrimp.

गांगायनि: *m.* N. of Bhîshma or Kârtikeya.

गांगेय *a.* (*f.* —यी) Being in or on the Ganges. —य: *m.* N. of Bhîshma or Kârtikeya. —यं *n.* Gold.

गाजरं *n.* A carrot.

गांजिकाय: *m.* A quail.

गाडव: *m.* A cloud.

गाढ *p.p.* (*f.* —ढा) 1 Dived or plunged into, bathed in; deeply entered. -2 Resorted to, thickly crowded or inhabited. -3 Closely pressed together, fast, close, tight. -4 Thick, dense. -5 Deep, impervious. -6 Strong, excessive. —ढं *ind.* Closely, fast, much, heavily, vehemently, powerfully. -Comp. —आलिंगनं *n.* Close embrace. —मुष्टि *a.* Close-fisted, avaricious, miserly. —मुष्टि: *m.* A sword.

गाणपत *a.* (*f.* —ती) 1 Relating to the leader of a troop. -2 Relating to Ganesa.

गाणपत्य: *m.* A worshipper of Ganesa. —त्यं *n.* 1 Worship of Ganesa. -2 The leadership of a troop, chieftainship.

गाणिक्यं *n.* A group of harlots.

गाणेश: *m.* A worshipper of Ganesa.

गांडि (-डी-) व: *m.*, -वं *n.* 1 The bow of Arjuna. -2 A bow in general. -Comp. —धन्वन् *m.* An epithet of Arjuna.

गांडीविन् *m.* An epithet of Arjuna.

गातागतिक *a.* (*f.* — की) Caused by going or coming.

गातानुगतिक *a.* (*f.* —की) Caused by

blindly following or imitating custom or example.

गातुः *m.* 1 A song. -2 A singer. -3 A celestial chorister. -4 The male (Indian) cuckoo. -5 The large black bee. [A गंधर्व.

गातृ *m.* (*f.* —त्री) 1 A singer. -2

गात्रं *n.* 1 The body. -2 A limb or member of the body. -3 The fore-quarter of an elephant. —त्रा *f.* The earth. -Comp. —अनुलेपनी *f.* A fragrant unguent applied to the body. —आवरणं *n.* A shield. —उत्सादनं *n.* Cleaning the body with perfumes. —कर्षण *a.* Emaciating or weakening the body. —मार्जनी *f.* A towel. —यष्टिः *f* A thin or slender body. —रुहं *n.* The hair on the body. —लता *f.* A thin or tender body, slim figure. —संकोचिन् *m* The pole-cat; (so called because it contracts its body in order to spring). —संप्लवः *m.* A small bird, the diver.

गाथः *m.* A song, singing.

गाथकः, –थिकः *m.*1 A musician, singer. -2 A chanter of sacred poems or Purânas.

गाथा *f.* 1 Verse. -2 A religious verse, but not belonging to any one of the Vedas. -3 A stanza. -4 A song. -5 A Prákrita dialect. -6 N. of the Aryá metre. -Comp. —कारः *m.* A writer of Prákrita verses.

गाथिका *f.* A song, verse.

गाध् 1 A. (गाधते, गाधित) 1 To stand, stay. -2 To set out for; dive or plunge into. -3 To seek, search or inquire for. -4 Compile, string or weave together.

गाध *a.* (*f.* —धा) Fordable, not very deep; shallow. —धं *n.* 1 A shallow place, ford. -2 A place, site. -3 Desire of gain, cupidity. -4 Bottom.

गाधिः, गाधिन् *m.* N. of the father of Visvâmitra. -Comp.—जः, -नंदनः,-पुत्रः *m.* An epithet of Visvâmitra. —नगरं, -पुरं *n.* An epithet of Kányakubja, the modern Kanoja. [mitra.

गाधेयः *m.* An epithet of Vishvâ-

गानं *n.* 1 Singing. -2 A song.

गान्त्री *f.* A carriage drawn by oxen.

गांदिनी *f.* 1 An epithet of the Ganges. -2 N. of a princess, mother of Akrûra. -Comp. —सुतः *m.* An epithet (1) of Bhîshma. (2) of Kârtikeya (3) of Akrûra.

गांधर्व *a.* (-र्वी) *f.* Relating to the Gandharvas. —र्वः *m.* 1 A singer, celestial chorister. -2 One of the eight forms of marriage. In it the marital relation proceeds from the mutual inclination of the parties without ceremonies and without the sanction of seniors. -3 A subordinate Veda treating of music attached to the Sámaveda. -4 A horse. —र्वं *n.* The art of the Gandharvas; *i. e.* music, singing.-Comp. —चित्त *a.* One whose mind is possessed by a Gandharva. —शाला *f.* A music saloon, concert-hall.

गांधर्व (-र्वि-) कः *m.* A singer.

गांधारः *m.* 1 The third of the seven primary notes of the Indian Gamut (commonly denoted by ग in musical notation). -2 Red lead. -3 N. of a country between India and Persia, the modern Kandáhára. -5 A native or a ruler of that country. —रं *n.* Gum myrrh.

गांधारिः *m.* An epithet of Sakuni, Duryodhana's maternal uncle.

गांधारी *f.* N. of the daughter of Subala, king of the Gándháras and wife of Dhritaráshtra. [hana.

गांधारेयः *m.* An epithet of Duryod-

गाधिकः *m.* 1 A vendor of perfumes, a perfumer. -2 A scribe, clerk. —कं *n.* Fragrant wares, perfumes.

गामिन् *a.* (Only at the end of comp.) 1 Going, moving, walking. -2 Riding. -3 Going or reachiug to, applying to, relating to.-4 Leading or going to, accruing to. -5 United with. -6 Passing over to, devolving on.

गांभीर्यं *n.* 1 Deepness, depth (of water, sound &c.) -2 Depth, profundity (of meaning, character &c.).

गाय: *m.* Singing, a song.

गायक: *m.* A singer, musician -2 An actor.

गायत्र: *m.*, —त्रं *n.* A song or hymn.

गायत्री *f.* 1 A Vedic metre of 24 syllables. -2 N. of a very sacred verse repeated by every Brâhmana at his Sandhyá devotion. —त्रं *n.* A hymn composed and recited in the Gâyatri metre.

गायत्रिन् *a.* (*f.* —णी)One who sings hymns, especially of the Sâmaveda.

गायन: *m.* (*f.* —नी) A singer. —नं *n.* Singing, a song.-2 Practising singing as a profession.

गारुड *a.* (*f.* —डी) 1 Shaped like Garuda.-2 Coming from or relating to Garuda. —ड: *m.*, —डं *n.* 1 An emerald. -2 A charm against (snake) poison.-3 A missile presided over by Garuda.

गारुडिक: *m* A charmer, dealer in antidotes.

गारुत्मत *a.* (*f.* —ती) 1 Shaped like Garuda. -2 Sacred to, or presided over, by Garuda (as a missile). -तं *n.* An emerald.

गार्दभ *a.* (*f.* -भी) Belonging to, or coming, from an ass; asinine.

गार्ध्यं *n.* Greediness.

गार्ध *a.* (*f.* —र्धी) Derived from a vulture. —र्धः *m.* 1 Greediness. -2 An arrow. -Comp. —पक्ष:, -वासस् *m.* An arrow furnished with a vulture's feathers.

गार्भिणं, —ण्यं *n.* A number of pregnant women.

गार्हपतं *n.* The position and dignity of a householder.

गार्हपत्य: *m.* 1 One of the three sacred fires perpetually maintained by a householder. -2 The place where this sacred fire is kept. —त्यं *n.* The government of a family; position and dignity of a householder.

गार्हमेध *a.* (*f.* —धी) Fit or proper for a householder. —ध: *m.* The five Yajnas to be performed by a householder.

गार्हस्थ्यं *n.* 1 The order or stage of life of a householder (गृहस्थ). -2 Domestic affairs, the household.-3The five 'yajnas' to be daily performed by a house-holder.

गालनं *n.* 1 Straining (fluids). -2 Fusing, liquefying, melting.

गालव: *m.* 1 The Lodhra tree. -2 A kind of ebony. -3 N. of a sage, a pupil of Visvámitra.

गालि: *f.* 1 Abuse, abusive or foul language.

गालित *a.* (*f.* —ता) 1 Strained. -2 Distilled. -3 Melted, fused.

गालोड्यं *n.* The seed of a lotus.

गावल्गाणि: *m.* An epithet of Sanjaya, son of Gavalgana.

गाह् 1 A. 1 To dive or plunge into, bathe, immerse oneself into (as water). -2 To enter deeply into, penetrate ; roam or range over. -3 To stir up, agitate.-4 To be absorbed in (with lcc.). -5 To hide oneself in. -6 To destroy. With अव- (Sometimes changed to व) 1 To penetrate into, to enter. -2 To plunge into, to bathe. उप- To break in. वि- 1 To plunge into, to bathe in. -2 To agitate or stir about. -3 To enter, to pervade, to penetrate into. सं- To enter, go to or into, penetrate into.

गाहः *m.* 1 Diving into, plunging, bathing. -2 Depth, interior.

गाहनं *n.* The act of diving into, plunging, bathing.

गाहित *a.* (*f.* —ता) 1 Bathed in, plunged into. -2 Penetrated, entered into.

गिंदुकः *m.* 1 A ball for playing with. -2 N. of a tree.

गिर् *f.* (nom. sing. गीः; instr. dual गीर्भ्यां &c.) 1 Speech, words, language. -2 Invocation, praise, song. -3 N. of Sarasvati, the goddess of speech and learning. -Comp..—देवी (गीर्देवी) *f.* Sarasvati, the goddess of speech. —पतिः (written as गीःपतिः, गीष्पतिः and गीर्पतिः) *m.* 1 N. of Brihaspati, the preceptor of the gods.-2 A learned man. गीरथः *m.* N. of Brihaspati. —वा (-बा-) णः (गीर्वाणः) *m.* A god, deity. [voice.

गिरा *f.* Speech, speaking, language,

गिरि *a.* Venerable, respectable. —रिः *m.* 1 A hill, mountain, an elevation. -2 A huge rock. -3 A disease of the eyes. -4 An honorific title given to Sannyâsins; *e. g.* आनंदगिरिः. -5 (In math.) The number eight ', -6 A ball with which children play (गेंदुक). -रिः *f.* 1 Swallowing. -2 A rat ; mouse (written also गिरी in this sense). -Comp. —इंद्रः *m.* 1 A high mountain. -2 An epithet of Siva. -3. The Himâlaya mountain. -4 A term for the number ' eight '. -ईशः *m.* 1 An epithet of the Himálaya mountain. -2 An epithet of Siva. —कच्छपः *m.* A species of tortoise living in mountains. —कंटकः *m.* Indra's thunder-bolt. —कंदरः *m.* A cave, cavern. —कर्णिका *f.* The earth. —काणः *m.* A blind or one-eyed man. —काननं *n.* A mountain-grove. —कूटं *n.* The summit of a mountain. —गुडः *m.* A ball for playing with. —चर *a.* Roaming or wandering on a mountain. —चरः *m.* A thief. —ज *a.* Mountain-born. -जं *n.* 1 Talc. -2 Red chalk. -3 Benzoin. -4 Bitumen. -5 Iron. -जा *f.* 1 N. of Pârvati (the daughter of Himâlaya).-2 The hill plantain (पर्वतकदली). -3 The Mallikâ creeper. -4 An epithet of the Ganges. —जालं *n.* A range of mountains. -ज्वरः *m.* Indra's thunderbolt. -दुर्गं *n.* A hill-fort, any stronghold among mountains. -द्वारं *n.* A mountain-pass. —धातुः *m.* Red chalk. —ध्वजं *n.* Indra's thunderbolt. -णदी or -नदी *f.* A mountain-torrent, rill. —नंदिनी *f.* 1 N. of Párvati. -2 Of the Ganges. -3 A river in general (flowing from a mountain). -णितंबः (-नितंबः) *m.* The declivity of a mountain. —पुष्पकं *n.* Bitumen. —प्रपातः *m.* The declivity or slope of a mountain. —प्रस्थः *m.* The table-land of a mountain. -प्रिया *f.* A female of the Bos Grunniens. —बांधवः *m.* An epithet of Siva. —भिद् *m.* An epithet of Indra. (-*f.*) A river (breaking through a mountain). -भूः *f.* 1 An epithet of the Ganges. -2 Of Párvati. -मल्लिका *f.* The Kutaja tree. —मानः *m.* An elephant, especially a large and powerful one. —मृद् *f.*, —मृद्भवं *n.* 1 Red chalk. -2 Mountain soil. —राज् *m.* 1 A high mountain. -2 An epithet of the Himálaya. —राजः *m.* The Himalaya mountain.

—शृंगः *m.* An epithet of Ganesa (–गं *n.*) The peak of a mountain. –षद्(सद्) *m.* An epithet of Siva. —सानु *n.* Table-land. —सारः *m.* 1 Iron.–2Tin. –3 An epithet of the Malaya mountain. –सुतः *m.* The Mainâka mountain. –सुता *f.* An epithet of Pârvati. —स्रवा *f.* A mountain torrent.

गिरिकः *m.* 1 A ball for playing.

गिरि (–री–) यकः, गिरियाकः *m.* A ball for playing with.

गिरिशः *m.* An epithet of Siva. (Also गिरिशयः and गिरिशंतः).

गिल् 6 P. (गिलति, गिलित) To swallow. According to some authorities this is not a separate root.

गिल *a.* (*f.* –ला) Who or what swallows or devours.—लः *m.* 1 The citron tree. –2 A crocodile in the Ganges. –Comp. –गिलः, –ग्राहः. *m.* A crocodile, shark.

गिलनं, *n.*, गिलिः *f.* Swallowing, eating up. [throat.

गिलयुः *m.* A hard tumour in the

गिलि (–लि–) त *a.* Eaten, swallowed.

गि (गे–) ष्णुः *m.* 1 A singer. –2 Especially, a Bráhmana versed in the hymns of the Sâmaveda and who chants them.

गीत *p. p.* (*f.* —ता) 1 Sung, chanted (lit.) –2 Declared, told, said. —तं *n.* Singing, a song. –Comp. —अयनं *n.* A means or instrument of singing; *i. e.* a lute, flute &c.–ज्ञ *a.* Versed in the art of singing. –मोदिन् *m.* A Kinnara. –शास्त्रं *n.* The science of music.

गीतकं *n.* A song.

गीता *f.* A name given to certain sacred writings in verse (often in the form of a dialogue) which are devoted to the exposition of particular religious and theosophical doctrines; *e. g.* शिवगीता, रामगीता, भगवद्गीता. But the name is especially confined to the last, the Bhagavadgîtá.

गीतिः *f.* 1 A song. –2 N. of a metre.

गीतिका *f.* 1 A short song.–2 Singing.

गीतन् *a.* (*f.* —नी) One who recites in a singing manner.

गीर्ण *a.* (*f.* —र्णा) 1 Swallowed. –2 Described, praised. [Swallowing.

गीर्णिः *f.* 1 Praise. –2 Fame. –3

गु 6 P. (गुवति, गुत) To void by stool, void excrement.

गुग्गुलः, –लुः *m.* A particular fragrant gum resin.

गुच्छः *m.* 1 A bundle, bunch. –2 A bunch of flowers, a cluster of blossoms, a clump (of trees &c.). –3 The plumage of a peacock. –4 A necklace of pearls (in general). –5 A pearl necklace of 32 (or, according to some, of 70) strings. –Comp. —अर्धः *m.* A pearl necklace of 24 strings. —अर्धः *m.*, —अर्धं *n.* Half of a cluster. —पत्रः *m.* The palm tree. —फलः *m.* 1 The vine. –2 The plantain tree.

गुच्छकः *m.* The same as गुच्छः.

गुज् 1 P. (गोजति), often गुंज् 1 P. (गुंजति, गुंजित or गुञ्जित) To sound inarticulately or indistinctly, hum, buzz.

गुंजः *m.* 1 Humming. –2 A cluster of blossoms, bunch of flowers, a nosegay. –Comp. —कृत् *m.* A large black bee.

गुंजनं *n.* Sounding low, humming.

गुंजा *f.* 1 A small shrub of that name, bearing a red black berry. –2 A berry of this shrub used as a weight, measuring on an average $1\frac{5}{6}$ grains Troy, or an artificial weight called *Gunjâ* measuring about $2\frac{3}{16}$ grains. –3 Humming, a low murmuring sound.–4 A kettle-drum. -5 A tavern. -6 Reflection, meditation. [plant-

गुंजिका *f*. A berry of the Gunjá

गुंजितं *n*. Huming, murmuring.

गुटिका *f*. 1 A pill. -2 A round pebble, any small globe or ball. -3 The cocoon of the silk-worm.-4 A pearl.

गुटी *f*. The same as गुटिका q. v.

गुठ्, गुंठ् 10 U. To enclose, to surround, envelop, hide. With अव— To veil, screen.

गुडः *m*. 1 Treacle, molasses. -2 A globe, ball. -3 A ball for playing with. -4 A mouthful, bit. -5 An elephant's armour. -6 The cotton tree. -Comp. —उद्भवा *f*. Sugar. -तृणं *n*., —दारः *m*., -त्र *n*. Sugar-cane. -धेनुः *f*. A milch-cow symbolically represented by molasses and offered as a present to Bráhmanas. —फलः *m*. The Pilu tree. —शर्करा *f*. Refined sugar. —शृंगं *n*. A cupola. —हरितकी *f*. Myrobalan preserved in molasses (Mar. मुरांवळा).

गुडकः *m*. 1 A ball. -2 A mouthful. -3 A kind of drug prepared with molasses.

गुडलं *n*. Spirituous liquor distilled from molasses.

गुडा *f*. 1 The cotton plant.-2 A pill.

गुडाका *f*. 1 Sloth. -2 Sleep.

गुडाकेशः *m* 1 An epithet of Arjuna. -2 An epithet of Siva.

गुडेरः *m*. 1 A ball, globe. -2 A mouthful, bit.

गुण् 10 U. (गुणयति-ते, गुणित) 1 To multiply. -2 To advise. -3 To invite.

गुणः *m* 1 A quality (good or bad). -2 A good quality, merit, virtue, excellence, eminence. -3 Use, advantage, good. -4 Effect, result, efficacy, good result. -5 A thread or string; rope, cord. -6 The bow-string. -7 The string of a musical instrument. -8 A sinew. -9 A quality, attribute, property in general. -10 A characteristic or property of all substances, one of the seven categories or *padârthas* of the Vaiseshikas. -11 An ingredient or constituent of nature; any one of the three properties belonging to all created things; (these are सत्त्व, रजस्, and तमस्). -12 A wick cotton thread. -13 An object of sense; (these are five रूप, रस, गंध, स्पर्श, and शब्द). -14 Repetition, multiplication, denoting 'folds' or 'times', at the end of comp. after numerals, as द्विगुण. -15 A secondary element, a subordinate part(opp. मुख्य). -16 Excess, superfluity. -17 An adjective, a word subordinate to another in a sentence. -18 The substitution of ए, ओ, अर् and अल् for इ, उ, ऋ (short or long) and ऌ, or the vowels अ, ए, ओ, and अर् and अल्. -19 (In Rhet.) Quality considered as an inherent property of a *Rasa* or sentiment. -20 (In gram. and Mim.) Property considered as the meaning of a class of words. According to grammarians the meaning of words is four-fold, *viz*. जाति, गुण, क्रिया and द्रव्य, and गौः, शुक्लः, चलः, डित्थः are given as instances to illustrate these meanings. -21 (In politics) A proper course of action, an expedient. (The expedients are six:—1 संधि peace or alliance; 2 विग्रह war; 3 यान march or expedition; 4 स्थान or आसन halt; 5 संश्रय seeking shelter; 6 द्वैध or द्वैधीभाव duplicity. -22 The number 'three'. -23 The chord of an arc (in geom).

-24 An organ of sense. -25 A subordinate dish. -26 A multiplier, coefficient (iu arith.). -27 Division, subdivision, species, kind. -Comp. —अतीत *a.* Freed from all properties. (-तः *m.*) The Supreme Being. —अधिष्ठानकं *n.* The region of the breast where the girdle is fastened. —अनुरोधः *m.* Conformity or suitableness to good qualities. —आढ्य *a.* Rich in virtues. —आत्मन् *a.* Having qualities. —आचारः *m.* A virtuous or meritorious person. —आश्रय *a.* Virtuous, excellent. —ईश्वरः *m.* 1 The Supreme Being. -2 The Chitrakúta mountain. —कथनं *n.* 1 Extolling, praising. -2 A condition or state of mind of the hero of a drama to which he is reduced by Cupid. —कर्मन् *n.* 1 An unessential or secondary action. -2 (In gram.) The secondary or less immediate (*i. e.* indirect) object of an action. —कार *a.* Productive of good qualities, profitable, salutary. (-रः *m.*) 1 A cook who prepares side-dishes or any secondary articles of food. -2 An epithet of Bhîma. —गृह्य *a.* Appreciating or admiring merits (wherever they may be); appreciative. —ग्रामः *m.* A collection of virtues or merits. -घातिन् *a.* A detractor, envious, censorious. -ज्ञ *a.* Knowing how to admire or appreciate merits, apdreciative. —त्रयं, —त्रितयं *n.* The three constituent properties of nature; *i. e.* सत्त्व, रजस् and तमस्. —पदी *f.* A woman having feet as thin as cords. -लक्षणं *n.* A mark or indication of an internal property. —लयनिका, —लयनी *f.* A tent. —वचनं *n.*, —वाचकः *m.* A word which connotes an atribute or quality, an adjective, or substantive used attributively. —वृक्षः, -वृक्षकः *m.* A mast or a post to which a ship or boat is fastened. —वृत्तिः *f.* 1 A secondary or unessential condition or relation (opp. मुख्यवृत्ति). -2 The character or style of merits. —शब्दः *m.* An adjective. —संख्यानं *n.* The three essential qualities, a term applied to the Sánkhya (including the Yoga) system of philosophy. -संगः *m.* 1 Association with qualities or merits. -2 Attachment to objects of sense or worldly pleasures. —सागरः *m.* 1 A very meritorious man. -2 An epithet of Brahman (*m.*)

गुणकः *m.* 1 A calculator. -2 A multiplier (in math.)

गुणनं *n.* 1 Multiplication. -2 Enumeration. -3 Describing merits or qualities; pointing out or enumerating merits. —नी *f.* Examining books, studying; collating and correcting copies to determine the value of variants.

गुणनिका *f.* 1 Study, repeated reading; repetition. -2 Dancing, the science or profession of dancing. -3 The prologue or introduction to a drama. -4 A garland, necklace. -5 Determining the value of the various readings of a manuscript. -6 A cipher, the character in arithmetic which expresses nothing.

गुणनीय *a.* (*f.* —या) 1 To be multiplied. -2 To be enumerated. -3 To be advised. -यः *m.* Study, practice. —यं *n.* The multiplicand.

गुणिका *f.* A tumour, a swelling.

गुणित *p. p.* (*f.* -ता) 1 Multiplied. -2 Heaped together, collected. -3 Enumerated.

गुणिन् *a.* (*f.* -नी) 1 Possessed of,

or endowed with, merits ; meritorious. -2 Auspicious. -3 Familiar with the merits of anything. —नी *f.* A bow.

गुणीभूत *a.* 1 Deprived of the original meaning or importance. -2 Made secondary or subordinate. -3 Invested with attributes. -4 Having a certain force or application (as a word &c.). -Comp. —व्यंग्यं *n.* (in Rhet.) The second of the three divisions of Kávya (poetry), in which the charm of the *suggested* sense is not more striking than that of the *expressed* one.

गुंठ 10 U. (गुंठयति-ते, गुंठित) 1 To encircle, surround, envelop, enclose. -2 To hide, conceal.

गुंठनं *n.* 1 Concealing, covering, hiding. -2 Smearing.

गुंडः *m.* 1 A kind of fragrant grass. -2 Pounding, grinding.

गुंडकः *m.* 1 Dust, powder. -2 An oil-vessel. -3 A soft or low pleasing tone. -4 Dirty flour or meal.

गुंडिकः *m.* Flour, meal, powder.

गुंडित *a.* (*f.* —ता) 1 Pounded, ground. -2 Covered with dust.

गुण्य *a.* (*f.* —ण्या) Endowed with virtues. -2 To be enumerated. -3 To be described or praised. -4 To be multiplied.

गुत्सः *m.* =गुच्छः q. v.

गुत्सकः *m.* 1 A bundle, bunch. -2 A nosegay.-3 A cow-tail, 'chowrie.' -4 The section or chapter of a book.

गुदं *n.* The anus. -Comp. -अंकुरः *m.* Piles. —आवर्तः *m.* Obstruction of the bowels.-उद्भवः *m.* Piles. -ओष्ठः *m.* The opening of the anus. —कीलः, —कीलकः *m.* Piles.-ग्रहः *m.* Constipation, flatulence. -पाकः *m.* The inflammation of the anus. -भ्रंशः *m. Prolapsus ani.* -वर्त्मन् *n.* The anus. —स्तंभः *m.* Constipation.

गुंद्रलः *m.* The sound of a small oblong drum.

गुंद्रा (-द्रा-)लः *m.* The Chātaka bird.

गुप् 1 P. (गोपायति, गोपायित or गुप्त) 1 To guard, protect, defend, watch over. -2 To hide, conceal.

गुप् 1 A. (जुगुप्सते Strictly desiderative of गुप्) 1 To censure. -2 To hide, conceal (गोपते in this sense).

गुप् 4 P. (गुप्यति) To be confused or disturbed.

गुप् 10 U. (गोपयति-ते) 1 To shine. -2 To speak. -3 To conceal.

गुपिलः *m.* A king. -2 A protector.

गुप्त *p. p.* (*f.* —प्ता) 1 Protected, preserved, guarded. -2 Hidden. -3 Secret, private. -4 Invisble, withdrawn from sight. -5 Joined. —प्तः *m.* An appellation usually added to the name of a Vaisya as चंद्रगुप्तः, समुद्रगुप्तः &c. -2 An epithet of Vishnu. —प्तं *ind.* Secretly, privately, apart. —प्ता *f.* One of the principal female characters in a poetical composition, a lady married to another (परकीया) who conceals her lover's caresses and endearments. -Comp. —गतिः *m.* A spy, an emissary. —चरः *m.* 1 An epithet of Balaráma. -2 A spy, an emissary. —वेशः *m.* A disguise.

गुप्तकः *m.* A preserver.

गुप्तिः *f.* 1 Preserving, protection. -2 Concealing, hiding. -3 Covering, sheathing. -4 A hole in the ground. -5 Digging a hole in the ground. -6 A means of protection, rampart. -7 Confinement, prison. -8 The lower deck of a boat. -3 A leak in a ship. -10 Check, stoppage. -11 Secret means.

गुफ् or गुंफ 6 P. (गु-गुं-फति, गुंफित) -1

To put string or weave together, tie, wind round. -2 (fig.) To write, compose.

गुंफः *m.* I Tying, stringing together.-2 Putting together, composing; arrangement. -3 A bracelet. -4 A whisker, a mustachio.

गुंफना *f.* I Stringing together. -2 Arranging, composing. -3 Good composition.

गुं (गु-) फित *p. p.* (*f.* -ता) Strung together, tied, woven. [exertion.

गुर् 6 A. I To make an effort or

गुर् 4 A. (*p. p.* गूर्ण) I To hurt, kill, injure. -2 To go.

गुरणं *n* Effort, perseverance.

गुरु *a.* (*f.* —रु, -र्वी; compar. गरीयस्; superl. गरिष्ठ) I Heavy, weighty. (fig. also). -2 Great, large, long, extended. -3 Important, momentous, great. -4 Arduous, difficult (to bear). -5 Excessive, violent, intense. -6 Venerable, respectable.-7 Heavy, hard of digestion (as food). -8 Best, excellent. -9 Dear, beloved. -10 Haughty, proud (as a speech). -11 (In prosody) Long, as a syllables, either in itself, or being short, followed by a conjunct consonant &c. -12 Valuable, highly prized. -13 Grievous. —रुः *m.* I A father. -2 Forefather, ancestor. -3 Any venerable or respectable person; an elderly person or relative. -4 A teacher, preceptor. -5 A lord, head, superintendent, ruler. -6 N. of Brihaspati, the preceptor of the Gods. -7 The planet Jupiter. -8 The propounder of a new doctrine. -9 The lunar asterism called पुष्य. -10 N. of Drona, teacher of the Kauravas and Pándavas. -11 N. of Prabhákara, the leader of a school of the Mímámsakas (called after him Prábhâkara).-12 The Supreme Spirit. -Comp. —अर्थ *a.* Important. (-र्थः *m.*) A preceptor's fee for instructing a pupil -कारः *m.* Worship, adoration. —क्रमः *m.* Instruction handed down through a series of teachers; traditional instruction. —घ्नः *m.* White mustard. —चर्या *f.* Attendance upon a preceptor.—जनः *m.* Anyvenerable person, an elderly relative; the elders collectively. —तल्पगः, -तल्पिन् *m.* I One who violates his teacher's bed (wife). -2 One who defiles his step-mother. —दक्षिणा *f.* The fee given to a spiritual preceptor. —दैवतः *m.* The constellation पुष्य. —पूजा *f.* I The ceremonies in propitiation of Brihaspati when a work is to be preformed or undertaken. -2 The worship of one's spiritual preceptor. —भं *n.* I The constellation पुष्य. -2 A bow. -3 The sign *pisces* of the zodiac. —रत्नं *n.* I Topaz. -2 A gem brought from the Himálaya and the Indus. —लाघवं *n.* Relative importance or value. —वारः, -वासरः *m.* Thursday. —शिखरिन् *m.* An epithet of the Himálaya.

गुरुक *a.* (*f.* —की) I A little heavy. -2 Long (in prosody.)

गु (-गू-) र्जरः *m.* I The district of Gujarâth. -2 An inhabitant of Gujarâth.

गुर्विणी, गुर्वी *f.* A pregnant woman. —र्वी *f.* The wife of a preceptor.

गुलः *m* Molasses. -ली *f.* I A pill. -2 Small-pox.

गुलुच्छः, गुलुंच्छः *m.* A bunch or cluster; see गुच्छ.

गुल्फः *m.* The ankle.

गुल्मः *m.*, -ल्मं *n.* I A clump or cluster of trees, a thicket, bush. -2 A troop of soldiers, a division of an army, consisting of 45 foot, 27 horse, 9 chariots and 9 elephants. -3 A fort. -4 The spleen. -5 A chronic enlargement of the spleen. -6 A village police-station. -7 A wharf of stairs (Mar. घांट). -8 Disciplining an army; keeping it in a posture of defence. —ल्मी *f.* 1 A cluster or clump of trees. -2 A tent.

गुह् 1 U. (गूहति-ते) To cover, hide, conceal, keep secret. -2 To cover with clothes. With उप— To embrace. नि— To hide.

गुहः *m.* 1 An epithet of Kârtikeya. -2 A horse. -3 N. of a Chândâla or *Nishâda,* king of Sringavera.

गुहा *f.* 1 A cave, cavern, hiding place. -2 Hiding, concealing. -3 A pit, hole in the ground. -4 The Heart. -5 Intellect. -Comp. —आहित *a.* Placed in the heart. —चरं *n.* Brahman (*n.*). —मुख *a.* Wide-mouthed, open-mouthed. —शय: *m.* 1 A mouse.-2 A tiger or lion. -3 The Supreme Soul.

गुहिनं *n.* A wood, thickt.

गुहेर: *m.* 1 A guardian, protector. -2 A blacksmith.

गुह्य *pot. p.* (*f.* —ह्या) 1 To be concealed, covered or kept secret, private. -2 Secret, solitary, retired.-3 Mysterious. —ह्य: *m.* 1 Hypocrisy. -2 An epithet of Vishnu. -3 A tortoise. —ह्यं *n.* 1 A secret, mystery.-2 A privity, the male or female organ of generation. -3 The anus.-Comp. —गुरु: *m* An epithet of Siva. —दीपक: *m.* The fire-fly. —निष्यंद: *m.* Urine. —पुष्प: *m.* The Asvattha tree ('with concealed 'blossoms'). —मय: *m.* An epithet of Kártikeya.

गुह्यक: *m.* N. of a class of demigods.

गू: *f.* 1 Dirt. -2 Ordure.

गूढ *p. p.* (*f.* —ढा) 1 Hidden, concealed, kept secret.-2 Covered.-3 Invisible.-4 Secret, private.-5 Disguised.-ढं *n.* 1 A solitary or private place. -2 Private part.-3 A mystery.-Comp. —अंग: *m.* Tortoise. —अंघ्रि: *m.* A snake. —आत्मन् *m.* (The compound word being गूढोत्मन्). The Supreme Soul. —उत्पन्न:, —ज: *m.* One of the 12 kinds of sons in Hindu law; he is a son born secretly of a woman, when her husband is absent, the real father being unknown (गृहे प्रच्छन्न उत्पन्नो गूढजस्तु सुत: स्मृत:). —नीड: *m.* The wagtail. —पथ: *m.* 1 A hidden path. -2 A by-path. -3 The mind, intellect. —पाद्, —पाद: *m* A snake. —पुरुष: *m.* A spy, secret emissary, a disguised agent. —पुष्पक: *m.* The Bakula tree. —मैथुन: *m.* A crow. —वर्चस् *m.* A concealed witness, one placed to overhear secretly what has been said by the defendant.

गृंजन: *m.* 1 A small red variety of garlic. -2 A turnip. -3 The tops of hemp chewed to produce intoxication, the *Gânjâ.* —नं *n.* The meat of an animal destroyed by poisoned arrows.

गृध् 4 P. (गृध्यति, गृद्ध) 1 To covet, desire.-2 To long for, be desirous of.

गृधु *a.* Lustful, libidinous. —धु: *m.* The God of love.

गृधु *a.* Bad, wicked. *f.* 1 The wind escaping at the anus (अपान). -2 Reason, intellect.

गृध्नु *a.* 1 Greedy, covetous. -2 Eager, desirous.

गृध्यं *n.,*—ध्या *f.* Desire, greediness.

गृध्र *a.* (*f.* —ध्रा) Greedy, covetous. —ध्र: *m.*, —ध्रं *n.* A vulture. —ध्री *f.* The female vulture. -Comp. —कूट:

m. N. of a mountain near Râjagriha. —वाज, —वाजित *a.* Furnished with vulture's feathers (as an arrow).

गृष्टिः *f.* 1 A cow which has had only one calf, a young cow. -2 (In comp. with the names of other animals) Any young female animal; वासितागृष्टिः *f.* 'A young she-elephant.' -3 A woman who has one child only. —*m.* A boar.

गृहं *n.* 1 A house, dwelling, habitation, mansion. -2 A wife. -3 The life of a house-holder. -4 A sign of the zodiac. -5 A name or appellation. —हाः (*m. pl.*) 1 A house, dwelling. -2 A wife. -3 The inhabitants of a house, family. -Comp. —अक्षः *m.* A loop-hole, a round or oblong window. —अधिपः, -ईशः, -ईश्वरः *m.* 1 A house-holder. -2 A regent of a sign of the zodiac. —अयनिकः *m.* A house-holder. —अर्थः *m.* Domestic affairs, any household matter. -अम्लं *n.* A kind of sour gruel. —अवग्रहणी *f.* The threshold. —अश्मन् *m.* A flat oblong stone upon which condiments are ground; (Mar. पाटा). —आरामः *m.*, -वाटी, -वाटिका *f.* A garden attached to a house. —आश्रमः *m.* The second stage in the religious life of a Bráhmana. —आश्रमिन् *m.* A householder. —उत्पातः *m.* Any domestic nuisance. —उपकरणं *n.* A domestic utensil, anything required for household use. -कच्छपः *m.* See गृहाश्मन्. —करणं *n.* 1 Household affairs. -2 House-building. —कारकः *m.* A house-builder, mason. —कारिन् *m.* 1 A house-builder. -2 A kind of wasp. —गोधा, -गोधिका *f.* The small house-lizard. —चुल्ली *f.* A house with two rooms contiguous to each other, but one facing west, the other east. —छिद्रं *n.* 1 A famely-secret or scandal. -2 Family dissensions. —जः, —जातः *m.* A slave born in the house. —जालिका *f.* Deceit, disguise. —ज्ञानिन् (also गेहेज्ञानिन्) *m.* Inexperienced, stupid, foolish. —देवता *f.* The goddess of a house; (pl.) A class of house-hold deities. —नमनं *n.* Wind. —नाशनः *m.* A wild pigeon. —नीडः *m.* A sparrow. —पतिः *m.* 1 A house-holder, a man who has entered on the second stage of life; one who, after having completed his studies, is married and settled. -2 A sacrificer. —पालः *m.* 1 The guardian of a house. -2 A house-dog. —पोतकः *m.* The site of a house; the ground on which it stands and which surrounds it. —प्रवेशः *m.* A solemn entrance into a house according to prescribed rites. —बलिः *m.* A domestic oblation, offering of the remnants of a meal to all creatures, such as animals, supernatural beings, and particularly household deities. —भंगः *m.* 1 One who is driven from his house, an exile. -2 Destroying a house. -3 Breaking into a house. -4 Failure, ruin or destruction of a house, firm &c. —भेदिन् *a.* 1 Prying into domestic affairs. -2 Causing domestic quarrels. —मणिः *m.* A lamp. —मेधः *m.* 1 A householder. -2 A domestic sacrifice. —मेधिन् *m.* A house-holder, a married Brâhmana who has a household. —यंत्रं *n.* A stick or other instrument to which, on solemn occasions, flags are fastened. -वाटिका, —वाटी *f.* A garden attached to a house. —वित्तः *m.* The owner of a house. —संवेशकः *m.* A house-builder by profession. —स्थः *m.* A householder, one who has entered on the stage of a house-holder.

गृहिणी *f.* A wife, house-wife, (the lady in charge of the house).Comp. —पदं *n.* The position or dignity of the mistress of the house.

गृहिन् *m.* The master of a house, a householder.

गृहीत *p. p.* (*f.* —ता) 1 Taken, seized, caught, held. -2 Obtained, acquired, gained. -3 Received, accepted. -4 Robbed. -5 Collected. -6 Agreed, promised.-7 Perceived, understood, learnt. -8 Worn. -Comp. —गर्भा *f.* A pregnant woman. -दिश् *a.* 1 Run away, fugitive, dispersed. -2 Disappeared. —देह *a.* Incarnate.

गृहीतिन् *a.* Who has grasped or comprehended (with loc.) गृहीती षट्स्वंगेषु.

गृह्य *a.* (*f.* —ह्या) 1 To be attracted or pleased, as in गुणगृह्य. -2 Domestic. -3 Not master of oneself, dependent. -4 Tame, domesticated. -5 Situated out-side of; ग्रामगृह्यासेना *f.* 'An army out-side a village'.-6 To be takenor received.-7 To be seized. -8 To be observed, perceptible. porceivable. -9 To be acknowledged or admitted. -10 To be trusted or relied on; to be honored. -11 Dependent, subservient.—ह्यः *m.* 1 The inmate of a house. -2 A tame animal or bird. -3 The domestic fire. -ह्यं *m.* The anus.-Comp. -अग्निः *m.* A sacred fire which every Bráhmana is enjoined to maintain.

गृह्या *f.* A village adjoining to [a city.

गॄ 9 P. (गृणाति, गूर्ण) 1 To utter a sound, call out, invoke. -2 To announce, speak, utter, proclaim. -3 To relate, promulgate.-4 To praise, extol. —With अनु To encourage.

गॄ 6 P. (गिरति or गिलति) 1 To swallow, devour, eat up. -2 To send fourth, pour out, spit out or eject from the mouth. -With अव-(Atm.) To eat, devour.

गॄ 10 A. (गारयते) 1 To make known, relate. -2 To teach.

गेंडु (-दु-) कः *m.* A ball for playing with (also गेंडुकः).

गेय *a.* To be sung. -यः *m.* A singer, one who sings. —यं *n.* 1 A song, singing, also the art of singing.

गेहं *n.* A house, habitation. गेहेच्वेडिन् *a.* A coward, poltroon. गेहेदाहिन् *a.* 'Sharp at home only' *i. e.* a coward. गेहेनर्दिन् *a.* 'Shouting defiance at home only; *i. e.* a coward, dunghill-cock. गेहेमेहिन् *a.* 'Making water at home;' *i. e.* indolent. गेहेव्याडः *m.* A braggadocio, braggart; boaster. गेहेशूरः *m.* A 'house-hero', a boasting coward.

गेहिन् *a.* (*f.* —नी) Same as गृहिन्.

गेहेनी *f.* A wife, the mistress of the house.

गै 1 P. (गायति, गीत) 1 To sing, sing a song. -2 To speak or recite in a singing tone. -3 To relate, declare, tell (especialty in metrical language). -4 To describe, relate or celebrate in song. -With अनु— To follow in singing. अव— To censure. उत्— To sing aloud. उप— To sing; to sing near. परि— To sing, relate, describe. वि— To censure.

गैरेक *a.* (*f.* —की) Mountain-born. —कः *m.*, —कं *n.* Red chalk. —कं *n.* Gold.

गैरेयं *n.* Bitumen, red chalk.

गो *m., f.* (*Nom.* गौः) 1 The stars. -2 The sky. -3 The thunder-bolt of Indra. -4 A ray of light. -5 A diamond. -6 Heaven.

गो *f.* 1 A cow. -2 The earth. -3 Speech, words. -4 The goddess of speech, Sarasvatî. -5 A mother. -6

A quarter of the compass. -7 Water (pl.). -8 The eye. -9 An arrow.

गो . *m.* 1 A bull, an ox. -2 The hair of the body. -3 An organ of sense. -4 The sign Taurus of the zodiac. -5 The sun. -6 The number 'nine' (in math.). -7 An arrow.

–Comp.—कंटकः *m.*, -कं *n.* 1 A road or spot trodden down by oxen and thus made impassable.-2 The cow's hoof. -3 The print of a cow's hoof. —कर्णः *m.* 1 A cow's ear. -2 A mule. -3 A snake. -4 A span (from the tip of the thumb to that of the ring-finger). -5 N. of a place of pilgrimage in the south; sacred to Siva. —किलः, -कीलः *m.* 1 A plough. -2 A pestle. —कुलं *n.* 1 A herd of kine. -2 A cow-house. -3 N. of a village (where Krishna was brought up). —कृतं *n.* Cow-dung. -गृष्टिः *f.* A young cow which has had only one calf. —गृष्ठं,-गोष्ठं *n.* A cow-pen, cattle-shed. -ग्रंथिः *m.* 1 Dried cowdung.-2 A cow-house. —ग्रासः *m.* The ceremony of offering a morsel (of grass) to a cow when performing an expiatory rite. —घृतं *n.* 1 Rain-water. -2 Clarified butter coming from a cow. -चर *a.* 1 Grazed over by cattle. -2 Frequenting, dwelling, haunting. -3 Within the scope, power or range of. -4 Moving on earth. -5 Accessible to, attainable. -6 Circulating, having a particular meaning, prevalent. (—रः *m.*) 1 The range of cattle, pasturage. -2 A district, province, sphere, an abode, dwelling-place. -3 The range of the organs of sense, an object of sense. -4 Scope range, (in general).-5 (fig.) Grip, hold, power, influence, control. -6 Horizon. -7 The range of the planets from the Lagna or from each other. -चर्मन् *n.* 1 A cow's hide. -2 A particular measure of surface. —जरः *m.* An old ox or bull. —जलं *n.* The urine of a bull or cow. —जाम्रिकं *n.* Auspiciousness, happiness. (-कः *m*) A preparer of food, baker. —तल्लजः *m.* An exellent bull or cow. —तीर्थं *n.* A cowhouse. -त्रं *n.* 1 A cowpen. -2 A stable in general. -3 A family, race, lineage. -4 A name, appellation. -5 A multitude. -6 Increase. -7 A forest. -8 A field. -9 A road.-10 Possessions, wealth.-11 An umbrella. -12 Knowledge of futurity. -13 A genus, class. -14 A caste, tribe, caste according to families. (-त्रः *m.*) A mountain. (-त्रा *f.*) 1 A multitude of cows.-2 The earth. —दा *f.* N. of the river Godâvarî. —दंतं *n.* 1 A yellow orpiment. -2 A white fossil substance. —दानं *n.* 1 The gift of a cow.-2 The ceremony of tonsure or cutting the hair. -दारणं *n.* 1 A plough. -2 A spade, hoe. —दावरी *f.* N. of a river in the south. —दुह्, -दुहः *m.* A cowherd. —दोहः *m.* 1 The milking of cows. -2 The milk of cows. -3 The time of milking cows. —दोहनं *n.* 1 The time of milking cows. -2 The milking of cows. —दोहनी *f.* A milk-pail. —द्रवः *m.* The urine of a bull or cow. —धनं *n.* 1 A herd or multitude of cows, cattle. -2 Possession of cows. —धरः *m.* A mountain. —धुमः, -धूमः *m.* 1 Wheat. -2 The orange. —धूलिः *m.* The time of sunset or evening twilight (so called because cows, which generally return home at about sunset, raise up clouds of dust by their treading on the earth). —धेनुः *f.* A milch-cow with a calf. —ध्रः *m.* A mountain. —नर्दी *f.* The female of the Sârasa bird. —नर्दः *m.* 1 The

(Indian) crane. -2 An epithet of Siva (bellowing like a bull). -3 N. of a country. —नर्दीयः m. An epithet of Patanjali, author of the Mahâbhâshya. —नाथः m. 1 A bull. -2 An owner of land. -3 A herdsman. -4 An owner of kine. —नायः m. A cowherd.—निष्यंदः m. A cow's urine. —पः m. 1 A cowherd. -2 The chief of a cowpen. -3 The superintendent of a village. -4 A king. —पशुः m. A sacrificial cow. —पानसी f. A curved beam which supports a thatch. —पालः m. 1 A cowherd. -2 A king. -3 An epithet of Siva. -4 An epithet of Krishna. —पालकः m. 1 A cowherd. -2 A king. -3 An epithet of Siva; also of Krishna. —पालिका, -पाली f. The wife of a cowherd. —पुच्छं n. A cow's tail. (-च्छः m.) 1 A sort of monkey. -2 A sort of necklace consisting of two or four or thirty-four strings. —पुटिकं n. The head of Siva's bull. -पुरं n. 1 A city-gate. -2 A principal gate. -3 The ornamental gate-way of a temple. —प्रकांडं n. An excellent cow or bull. —प्रचारः m. Pasture-ground, pasturage for cattle. -प्रवेशः m. The time when cows return home; sunset or evening-twilight. —भृत m. A mountain. —मक्षिका f. A gadfly. -मंडलं n. 1 The globe. -2 A multitude of cows. —मतं n. Same as गव्यूति. —मतल्लिका f. A tractable cow, an excellent cow. —मथः m. A cowherd. —मायुः m. 1 A kind of frog. -2 A jackal. -3 N. of a Gandharva. —मुखः m , —मुखं n. A kind of musical instrument. (-खः m.) 1 A crocodile, shark. -2 A hole of a particular shape in a wall made by thieves. (-खं n.) 1 A house built unevenly. -2 Spreading unguents smearing. (-खं n., खी f.) A cloth-bag of the shape of a gnomon containing a rosary, the beads of which are counted by the hand thrust inside. —मूढ a. Stupid as a bull. -मूत्रं n. Cow's urine. —मृगः m. A kind of ox (गवय). —मेदः m. A kind of gem. —मेधः, -यज्ञः m. A cow-sacrifice. -रक्षः 1 Cow-herd. -2 Keeping or tending cattle. -3 The orange. -4 An epithet of Siva. —रुतं n. A measure of distance equal to two Krosas. -रोचना f. A bright yellow pigment prepared from the urine or bile of a cow, or found in the head of a cow. —लवणं a. A measure of salt given to a cow. —लांगु(-गू-) लः m. A kind of monkey with a dark body, red cheeks, and a tail like that of a cow. —लोमी f. A prostitute. —वर्धन m. A celebrated hill in वृंदावन the country about Mathurâ. —वशा f. A barren cow. —वाटं n., -वासः m. A cow-pen. —विंदः m. 1 A cow-keeper. a chief herdsman.-2 N. of Krishna. -3 Brihaspati. —विट्, -विष्ठा f. Cow-dung. —विसर्गः m. The day-break (when cows are let loose to graze in forests). —वीर्यं n. The price received for milk. —वृंदारकः m. An excellent bull or cow —वृषः, -वृषभः m. An excellent bull. —व्रजः m. 1 A cow-pen. -2 A herd of cows. -2 A place where cattle graze. —शकृत n. Cowdung. —शतं n. A present of a hundred cows to a Brâhmana. -शालं n., —ला f. A cow-stall. —षड्गवं n. Three pairs of kine. —ष्टोमः m. A kind of sacrifice lasting for one day —सर्गः m The time at which cows are usually let loose, day-break. —सूत्रिका f. A rope fastened at both ends having separate halters for each ox for cow. —स्तनः m. 1 The udder of a cow.–2 A cluster of blossoms, nosegay &c.–3 A pearl-necklace of four strings. —स्तना, –नी *f.* A bunch of grapes. —स्थानं, (–कं) *n.* A cow-pen. —स्वामिन् *m.* An owner of cows. -2 A religious mendicant.–3 An honorary title affixed to proper names. —हत्या *f.* Cow-slaughter. –हर्लं (sometimes written हर्मं) *n.* Cow-dung.

गोडुंबः *m.* The water-melon.

गोणी *f.* 1 A sack. –2 A measure of capacity equal to a Drona. –3 Ragged garment.

गोंडः *m.* 1 A fleshy navel.–2 A person with a fleshy navel. –3 A man of a low tribe, inhabiting the eastern portion of the Vindhya range.

गोतमः *m.* 1 N. of a sage belonging to the family of Angiras, father of Satânanda. –2 N. of a sage, the founder of Nyâya philosophy.

गोतमी *f.* Ahalyâ, wife of गोतम. –Comp. —पुत्रः *m.* An epithet of Satânanda.

गोधा *f.* 1 A leathern fence fastened round the left arm to prevent injury from the bow-string. –2 The alligater.

गोधिः *f.* 1 The forehead. –2 The Gangetic alligator.

गोपः *m.* (*f.* —पी) 1 One who guards or protects. –2 Hiding, concealment.–3 Abuse.–4 Flurry, agitation. –5 Light, lustre, splendour.

गोपनं *n.* 1 Guarding, protecting.–2 Hiding.–3 Abuse. –4 Flurry, hurry, alarm. –5 Light, lustre. –6 Envy. –7 Perplexity, confusion. —ना *f.* 1 Protection. –2 Light, lustre.

गोपायनं *n.* Protecting, guarding.

गोपायित *a.* (*f.* —ता) Protected.

गोप्य *a.* (*f.* —प्या) 1 To be protected. –2 To be kept secret or hidden. –3 To be taken care of. –4 To be cherished. —प्यः *m.* 1 A servant, slave. –2 A son of a female slave.

गोमय *a.* 1 Consisting of cattle. –2 Defiled with cow-dung. —यः *m.*, –यं *n.* Cow-dung. —यं *n.* Cowdung cake. (Mar. गोवरी). –Comp. —छत्रं, –प्रियं *n.* A mnshroom, a fungus.

गोमिन् *n.* Rich in herds. —*m.* 1 An owner of cattle. –2 A jackal. –3 A worshipper. –4 An attendant on a Buddha.

गोरणं *n.* Energy, perseverance.

गोर्दः *m.* Brain; (also गोद).

गोलः *m.*, –ला *f.*, –लं *n.* 1 A ball, globe. –2 The celestial or terrestrial globe. –3 A circle. –4 A sphere, anything round or globular. —लः *m.* 1 A widow's bastard.–2 The presence of seven planets in one sign.–3 Myrrh. —ला *f.* 1 A wooden ball with which children play. –2 A large globular water-jar. –3 Red arsenic. –4 Ink. –5 A woman's female friend.–6 N. of Durgá. –7 N. of the river Godâvarî.

गोलकः *m.* 1 A ball, globe. –2 A wooden ball for playing with. –3 A globular water-jar.–4 A widow's bastard. –5 A conjunction of six or more planets. -6 Molasses.

गोष्ठः *m.*, –ष्ठं *n.* (usually गोष्ठं only) 1 A cowpen, cow-station. –2 A station of cowherds. (—ष्ठः *m.*) An assembly or meeting.–3 An epithet of Siva. –गोष्ठश्वः *m.* A dog in a cowpen which barks at every one; (fig.) A slanderous person; one who stays idly at home and slanders his neighbours. गोष्ठेपंडितः *m.* 'Wise in a cow-pen,' a braggart, vain boaster. गोष्ठेक्ष्वेडिन् *m.* A boasting coward; also गोष्ठेपटु, गोष्ठेप्रगल्भः, –शूरः &c.

गोष्ठिः,-ष्ठी *f.* 1 An assembly, assemblage, meeting. -2 Society, association. -3 Conversation, discourse.-4 A multitude or collection. -5 Family connections, relatives. -6 A kind of dramatic composition in one act.

गोष्पदं *n.* 1 A cow's foot. -2 The mark or impression of a cow's foot in the soil.-3 The quantity of water sufficient to fill such an impression; *i. e.* a very small puddle. -4 As much as a cow's footstep will hold.-5 A spot frequented by cows.

गौडः *m.* 1 N. of a country. -2 A particular subdivision of Bráhmanas. —डाः *m. pl.* The inhabitants of Gauda. —डी *f.* 1 Spirit distilled from molasses. -2 One of the Râginis. -3 (In rhet.) One of the *Ritis* or *Vrittis*, or styles of poetic composition. —डं *n.* Sweetmeats.

गौडिकः *m.* Sugar-cane.

गौण *a.* (*f.* —णी) 1 Subordinate, secondary. -2 (In gram) Indirect or less immediate (opp. मुख्य or प्रधान). -3 Figurative, metaphorical, used in a secondary sense (as a word or sense). -4 Based on some similarity between the primary and secondary sense of a word; as in गौणी लक्षणा. -5 Relating to enumeration or multiplication. -6 Attributive.

गौण्यं *n.* Subordination, inferior position or rank.

गौतमः *m.* N. of (1) the sage Bhâradvâja; (2) of Satânanda, Gotama's son; (3) N. of Kripa, Drona's brother-in-law; (4) of Buddha; (5) of the propounder of the Nyâya system of philosophy. -Comp. —संभवा *f.* The river Godâvarî.

गौतमी *f.* 1 N. of Kripî, wife of Drona. -2 An epithet of the Godâvarî. -3 The teaching of Buddha. -4 The Nyâya system of philosophy propounded by Gautama. -5 Turmeric. -6 A kind of yellow pigment. -7 An epithet of Durgâ. -8 N. of the river Gomatî.

गौर *a.* (*f.* —रा or री) 1 White. -2 Yellowish, pale-red. -4 Reddish. -4 Shining, brilliant. -5 Pure, clean, beautiful. —रः *m.* 1 The white colour.-3 The reddish colour.-4 White mustard. -5 The moon. -6 A kind of buffalo. -7 A kind of deer. -8 The planet Jupiter. —रं *n.* 1 The filament of a lotus. -2 Saffron. -3 Gold. -Comp. —आस्यः *m.* A kind of black monkey, with a white face. —सर्षपः *m.* The white mustard (considered as a kind of weight).

गौरक्ष्यं *n.* The office of a herdsman.

गौरवं *n.* 1 Weight, heaviness (lit.). -2 Importance, high value or estimation. -3 Respect, regard. -4 Respectability, dignity. -5 Cumbrousness. -6 (In prosody) Length (as of a syllable). -7 Depth (as of meaning). -Comp. —आसनं *n.* A seat of honour. —ईरित *a.* Praised, famed, celebrated.

गौरवित *a.*(*f.* —ता) Highly esteemed.

गौरिका *f.* A virgin, a young girl.

गौरिलः *m.* 1 White mustard. -2 Dust of iron or steel.

गौरी *f.* 1 N. of Pârvatî. -2 A young girl eight years old. -3 A young girl prior to menstruation; virgin, maid. -4 A woman with a white or yellowish complexion.-5 The earth. -6 Turmeric. -7 A yellow pigment or dye (called गोरोचना). -8 The wife of Varuna. -9 The Mallikâ creeper. —जः *m.* N. of Kartikeya.(—जं *n.*) Talc. —पुत्रः *m.* N. of Kârtikeya. —ललितं *n.* A yellow orpiment. —सुतः *m.* N. of

कार्तिकेय. -2 The son of a girl married when 8 years old.

गौरुतल्पिकः *m.* The violator of the preceptor's bed.

गोलक्षणिकः *m.* One who knows the good or bad marks of a cow.

गौल्मिकः *m.* A single soldier of a troop.

गौशतिक *a.* (*f.* —की) Possessing a [hundred cows.

ग्मा *f.* The earth.

ग्रथ् or ग्रंथ् 1 A. (ग्रथते, ग्रंथते) 1 To be croooked. -2 To be wicked. -3 To bend.

ग्रथनं *n.* 1 Coagulation, thickening, becoming obstructed or clogged with knotty lumps. -2 Stringing together. -3 Composing.

ग्रथित *p. p.* (*f.* —ता) 1 Strung or tied together. -2 Composed. -3 Arranged, classed. -4 Thickend, coagulated. -5 Knotty. -6 Hardened. -7 Hurt, injured.

ग्रप्सः *m.* A cluster, bunch, tuft.

ग्रंथ् 1, 9. P., 10 U., 1 A. (ग्रंथति, ग्रथ्नाति ग्रंथयति-ते, also ग्रथति, ग्रथते) 1 To fasten, tie or string together. -2 To arrange, class together. -3 To wind round. -4 To write, compose. -5 To form, make. -6 To set or strew with.

ग्रंथः *m.* 1 Binding, (fig. also). -2 A work, treatise. -3 Wealth, property. -4 A verse consisting of 32 syllables, written in the Anushtubh metre. -Comp. —कर्तृ, *m.*, —कारः, —कृत् *m.* A writer, an author. —कुटी. —कूटी *f.* 1 A library. -2 A studio.

ग्रंथनं *n*-, -ना *f.* See ग्रथनं.

ग्रंथिः *m.* 1 A knot, bunch. -2 A tie or knot of a cord, garment &c. -3 The joint or knot of a reed, cane &c. -4 A joint of the body. -5 Crookedness. falsehood. -6 Swelling and hardening of the vessels of the body. -Comp. —छेदकः, -भेदः, -मोचकः *m.* A cut-purse, a pick-pocket. —बंधनं *n.* 1 The tying together the garments of the bride and the bridegroom at the marriage ceremony. —हरः *m.* A minister.

ग्रंथिकः *m.* 1 An astrologer, a fortuneteller. -2 The name assumed by Nakula when at the palace of Viráta.

ग्रंथित *a.* See ग्रथित.

ग्रंथिन् *m.* 1 One who reads books, bookish. -2 Learned, well-read. -3 Relating to books.

ग्रंथिल *a.* (*f.* —ला) Knotted, knotty.

ग्रस् 1 A. 1 To swallow, devour, eat up, consume. -2 To seize. -3 To eclipse. —With सं- To destroy.

ग्रस् 1 P. 10 U. (ग्रसति, ग्रासयति-ते) To eat, devour.

ग्रसनं *n.* 1 Swallowing, eating. -2 Seizing. -3 A partial eclipse of the sun or moon. -4 A mouthful.

ग्रस्त *a.* (*f.* —स्ता) 1 Eaten, devoured. -2 Seized, stricken, possessed. -4 Eclipsed. -5 Taken, seized. —स्तं *n.* A word or sentence half-uttered or slurred over. -Comp. —अस्तं *n.* The setting of the snn or moon while eclipsed. —उदयः *m.* The rising of the sun or moon while eclipsed.

ग्रह् 9 U. (गृह्णाति, जग्राह, अग्रहीत, ग्रहीढं, ग्रहीत; *caus.* ग्राहयति) 1 To seize, take, take hold of, catch, grasp. -2 To receive, accept; exact. -3 To apprehend, capture, take prisoner. -4 To arrest, stop, catch. -5 To attract. -6 To win over, induce to one's side. -7 To please, gratify, satisfy, propitiate. -8 To affect, seize or possess (as by a demon, spirit &c.). -9 To learn, know, recognize, understand. -10 To consider, believe, take for. -11 To catch or perceive (as by an organ of sense). -12 To master, grasp. -13 To guess, conjecture, infer.-14 To utter,mention (as a name).-15 To conceive. -16 To observe (as a fast).-17 To eclipse. -18 To include. -19 To receive hospitably (as a guest). —With अनुसं- To salute humbly. अप— To take away, tear off. अभि— To seize forcibly.

ग्रहः *m.* 1 Seizing, grasping, seizure. -2 A grasp, hold. -3 Taking, accepting. -4 Stealing, robbing. -5 Booty, spoil. -6 Eclipse. -7 A planet, (the planets are nine :—सूर्यश्चंद्रो मंगलश्च बुधश्चापि बृहस्पतिः । शुक्रः शनैश्चरो राहुः केतुश्चेति ग्रहा नव ॥). -8 Mentioning (as of a name). -9 A shark, crocodile. -10 An imp in general. -11 A particular class of evil demons supposed to seize upon children and produce convulsions. -12 Apprehension, perception. -13 An organ or instrument of apprehension. -14 Perseverance, persistence. -15 Purpose, design. -16 Favour, patronage. -17 The place of a planet in the fixed zodiac. -18 The number 'nine'. -19 The middle of a bow. -Comp. — अधीन *a.* Subject to planetary influence. —अवमर्दनः *m.* An epithet of Râhu. (-र्नं *n.*) Friction of the planets. —अधीशः *m.* The sun. -आमयः *m.* 1 Epilepsy. -2 Demoniacal possession.—आलुंचनं *n.* Pouncing on one's prey, tearing it to pieces. —ईशः *m.* The sun. —कल्लोलः *m.* An epithet of Râhu. -चिंतकः *m.* An astrologer. -दशा *f.* The aspect of a planet; the time during which it continues to exercise its influence. —नायकः *m.* 1. The sun. -2 An epithet of Saturn. —निग्रहौ *m. dual* Reward and punishment. —नेमिः *m.* The moon. —पतिः *m.* 1 The sun. -2 The moon. -पीडनं *m.*, —पीडा *f.* 1. Oppression caused by a planet. -2. An eclipse. —युतिः *f.* The conjunction of planets. -युद्धं *n.* Opposition of planets. —राजः *m.* 1 The sun. -2 The moon. -3 Jupiter. -विप्रः *m.* An astrologer. -शांतिः *f.* Propitiation of planets by sacrifices &c.

ग्रहणं *n.* 1 Seizing, catching. -2 Receiving, accepting. -3 Mentioning, uttering, as in नामग्रहणं. -4 Wearing, putting on. -5 An eclipse. -6 Understanding, comprehension, knowledge. -7 Learning, mastering. -8 An echo.-9 Taking by the hand, marrying. -10 Taking captive, imprisonment. -11 Choosing. -12 Attraction. -13 Acceptation, meaning. -14 Assent, agreement.

ग्रहणिः,-णी *f.* Diarrhœa, dysentery.

ग्रहिल *a.* (*f.* -ला) Unyielding, relentless, obstinate.

ग्रहीतृ *a.* (*f.*-त्री) 1 A taker, an accepter; as in गुणग्रहीतृ. -2 Perceiver, observant. -3 Debtor. -4 Purchaser.

ग्रामः *m.* 1 A village, hamlet. -2 A race. -3 A multitude, collection of anything. -4 A gamut, scale in music. -Comp. —अधिकृतः, —अध्यक्षः, —ईशः, —ईश्वरः *m.* The superiatendent, head, chief of a village. —अंतः *m.* The border of a village; space near a village. —आंतिकं *n.* The neighbourhood of a village. -आचारः, —आवानं *n.* Hunting. —कंटकः *m.* 1 One who is a source of trouble to the village.-2 A tale-bearer. —कूटः *m.* 1 The noblest man in a village. -2 A Súdra.-घोषिन् *m.* An epithet of Indra. —चर्या *f.* Sexual imtercourse; (स्त्रीसंभोग). -णीः *m.* 1 The leader or chief of a village or community. -2 A leader or chief in general. -3 A barber. -4 An epithet of Vishnu. -5 A libidinous man. (—*f.*) 1 A whore, harlot. -2 The indigo plant. —धर्मः *m.*

Sexual intercourse. —पाल: *m.* 1 The guardian of a village. -2 Army for the protection of a village. —मद्गुरिका *f.* A riot, fray, village tumult. —मुखं *n.* A market. —मृग: *m.* A dog. —युद्धं *n.* A riot, fray.—षंढ: *m.* An impotent man.—संघ: *m.* A village-corporation. —सिंह: *m.* A dog. —हासक: *m.* A sister's husband.

ग्रामटिका *f.* A wretched or miserable village.

ग्रामिक *a.* (*f.* —की) 1 Rural, rustic. -2 (In music) Chromatic. -3 Rude. —क: *m.* 1 The headman of a village. -2 A villager.

ग्रामिण: *m.* 1 A villager. -2 A dog. -3 A crow. -4 A hog.

ग्रामिय: *m.* A villager, boor, churl.

ग्रामेय *a.* (*f.* —यी) Village-born, rustic. —यी *f.* A harlot, prostitute.

ग्राम्य *a.* (*f.* —म्या) 1 Relating to or used in a village. -2 Living in a village, rural, rustic. -3 Domesticated, tame (as an animal). -4 Cultivated (opp. वन्य ' growing wild'). -5 Low, vulgar, used only by low people (as a word). -6 Indecent, obscene.-7 Relating to sexual pleasures. -8 Relating to a musical scale. —म्य: *m.* 1 A tame hog. -2 The first two signs of the zodiac, *Aries* and *Taurus*. —म्या *f.* The Indigo plant.-म्यं *n.* 1 A rustic speech. -2 Food prepared in a village. -3 Sexual intercourse. -4 Acceptance. -Comp. —अश्व: *m.* An ass. —कर्मन् *n.* 1 The occupation of a villager. -2 Sexual pleasure.—कुंकुमं *n.* Safflower. —धर्म: *m.* 1 The duty of a villager. -2 Sexual intercourse, copulation. -3 The right of a villager (as opp. to that of a ' recluse'), —मृग: *m.* A dog.-वल्लभा *f.* A harlot, prostitute. -सुखं *n.* Sexual intercourse, copulation.

ग्रावन् *m.* 1 A stone or rock. -2 A mountain. -3 A cloud.

ग्रास: *m.* 1 A mouthful.-2 Food, nourishment. -3 The part of the sun or moon eclipsed. -4 The morsel bitten. -5 The act of swallowing. -6 Indistinct pronunciation. -7 (In geom.) A piece cut out by the intersection of two circles. -8 An eclipse.

ग्राह *a.* (*f.*-ही) Seizing, holding, reciving —ह: *m.* 1 Seizing, grasping. -2 A crocodile, shark. -3 A prisoner. -4 Accepting. -5 Understanding, knowledge. -6 Persistence, importunity. -7 Determination, resolve. -8 A disease. -9 Any large fish or marine animal. -10 A disease. -11 Beginning, undertaking. —ही *f.* A female crocodile.

ग्राहक *a.* (*f.* —हिका) One who receives, takes &c.—क: *m.* 1 A hawk, falcon. -2 A curer of poison. -3 A purchaser. -4 A police-officer.

ग्रिवा *f.* The neck, the back part of the neck.

ग्रिवालिका *f.* See ग्रीवा.

ग्रिविन् *m.* A camel.

ग्रिष्म *a.* (*f.* —ष्मा) Hot, warm. -ष्म: *m.* 1 The summer, the hot season, corresponding to the months of Jyeshtha and Ashâdha. -2 Heat, warmth. —ष्मी *f.* The नवमल्लिका plant.

ग्रैव (*f.* -वी), ग्रैवेय (*f.* -यी) *a.* Being on or belonging to the neck. —वं *n.*, —यं *n.* 1 A collar or necklace. -2 A chain worn round the neck of an elephant.

ग्रैवेयकं *n.* 1 A neck-ornament. -2 A chain worn round the neck of an elephant.

ग्रैष्म, ग्रैष्मिक *a.* Relating to summer.

ग्रैष्मक *a*. (*f*. —ष्मिका) 1 Sown in summer. -2 To be paid in summer (as a debt). [devour.

ग्लस् 1 A. (ग्लसते, ग्लस्त) To eat,

ग्लह् 1 U., 10 U. (ग्लहति-ते, ग्लाहयति-ते) 1 To gamble, to win by gambling. -2 To take, receive.

ग्लहः *m*. 1 A dice-player. -2 A stake, wager, bet. -3 A die.-4 Gambling, playing. -5 A dice-box. -6 Cast of the dice, game at dice. -7 A chess-man.

ग्लान *p. p*. (*f*.—ना) 1 Weary, languid, tired, fatigued, exhausted. -2 Sick, ill.

ग्लानिः *f*. 1 Exhausiton, languor, fatigue. -2 Decay, decline. -3 Debility, weakness. -4 Displeasure, sickness.

ग्लास्नु *a*. Languid, wearied.

ग्लुच् 1 P. (ग्लोचति, ग्लुक्त) 1 To go, move. -2 To steal, rob. -3 To take away. [To go.

ग्लुंच् 1 P, (ग्लुंचति) 1 To rob. -2

ग्लै 1 P. (ग्लायति, ग्लान) 1 To feel aversion or dislike to do anything (with inf.). -2 To be fatigued or wearied. -3 To be dejected. -4 To wane, fade, faint away. -*Caus*. (ग्लग्लापयति, but प्रग्लापयति). 1 To cause to fade away, wither up. -5 To tire out, exhaust. -3 To injure; trouble, hurt. -4 To emaciate, waste.

ग्लौः *m*. 1 The moon. -2 Camphor. -3 The earth.

घ.

घ *a*. (Used only as the last member of comp.) Striking, killing, destroying; as in जीवघ, राजघ &c. —घः *m*. 1 A bell -2 Rattling, gurgling or tinkling noise.

घट् 1 A. 1 To be busy with; strive after, be intently occupied with anything (with inf., loc., or dat.). -2 To happen, take place, be possible. -3 To be united with. -4 To come, to reach. With प्र— 1 To be occupied in. -2 To commence. वि— 1 To be separated.-2 To be spoiled, to break down. सम्— To be united. -*Caus* (घटयति) 1 To unite, join, bring together. -2 To bring in contact with; put on.-3 To accomplish, effect. -4 To form, fashion, work out, make. -5 To prompt, impel. -6 To rub, touch.-7 Exert oneself for. -8 To move, agitate.

घट् 10 U. (घाटयति, घाटित) 1 To hurt, kill. -2 To unite, collect together. -3 To shine.

घटः *m*. A large earthen water-jar, pitcher, jar, watering pot. -2 The sign Aquarius of the zodiac. -3 An elephant's frontal sinus.-4 Suspending the breath as a religious exercise. -5 A measure equal to 20 'dronas'. -6 A part of a column.-7 A border. -8 A peculiar form of a temple. -Comp. —आटोपः *m*. The covering for a carriage or any article of furniture. —उद्भवः, —जः, —योनिः, —संभवः *m*. Epithets of the sage Agastya. —ऊधस् *f*. (forming घटोध्नी) A cow with a full udder. —कर्परः *m*. 1 N. of a poet.-2 A piece of a broken jar, potsherd. —कारः, -कृत *m*. A potter. —ग्रहः *m*. A water-bearer. -दासी *f*. A procuress. —पर्यसनं *n*. The ceremony of performing the funeral rites of an apostate during his very life-time. —भेदनकं *n*. An instrument used in making pots.-राजः *m*. A water jar of baked clay. -स्थापनं *n*. Placing a water-pot as a type of Durgâ.

घटक *a.* (*f.* —का) 1 Exerting oneself, striving for. -2 Bringing about, accomplishing. -3 Forming a constituent part; a constituent, component. —कः *m.* 1 A tree that produces fruit without apparent flowers. -2 A match-maker, an agent who ascertains genealogies and negotiates matrimonial alliances. -3 A genealogist.

घटनं *n.*, -ना *f.* 1 Effort, exertion. -2 Happening, occurring. -3 Accomplishment, bringing about, effecting. -4 Joining, union. -5 Making, forming.

घटा *f.* 1 An endeavour, effort, exertion.-2 A number, assemblage.-3 A troop of elephants assembled for martial purposes. -4 An assembly.

घटिकः *m.* A waterman. —कं *n.* The hip, the posteriors.

घटिका *f.* 1 A small water-jar, a small earthern vessel. -2 A measure of time equal to 24 minutes. -3 A water-pot used in calculating the Ghatikâs of the day. -4 The ankle.

घटिन् *m.* The sign Aquarius of the zodiac (also called कुंभ).

घटिंधम *a.* (*f.* —मा) One who blows into a water-jar or pot. —मः *m.* A potter.

घटिंधय *a.* (*f.* -या) One who drinks a pitcherful (of water &c.).

घटी *f.* 1 A small jar. -2 A measure of time equal to 24 minutes. -3 A small water-pot used in calculating the 'Ghatikâs' or time of the day. -Comp. —कारः *m.* A potter. —ग्रहः, ग्राहः *m.* A water-bearer. —यंत्रं *n.* 1 An Indian machine for raising water. -2 A contrivance (like a clepsydra) to ascertain the 'ghatikâs' or time of the day.

घट्ट् 1 A. (घट्टते), usually 10 U. (घट्टयति-ते, घट्टित) 1 To shake, stir about. -2 To touch, rub, rub the hands over. -3 To smooth, stroke. -4 To speak spitefully or malignantly. -5 To disturb. With अव— To open. परि— To strike. वि— 1 To strike. -2 To rub. -3 To open (as a door). सम्— 1 To rub, to rub against. -2. To strike. -3 To bring together ; to collect.

घट्टः *m.* 1 A landing place, steps on the side of a river leading to the waters (Mar. घाट) -2 Stirring, agitating. -3 A toll-station.-Comp. —कुटी *f.* A toll-station. घट्टकुटीप्रभातन्यायः *m.* The maxim of day-break near a toll-stoation. This maxim indicates the concurrence of what one stndiously tries to avoid.-जीविन् *m.* 1. A ferryman. -2. A man of a mixed tribe. -3. An attendant at a landing place.

घट्टनं *n.* Shaking, moving.

घट्टना *f.* 1 Shaking, moving, agitating. -2 Rubbing. -3 A means of livelihood, business, profession.

घंटः *m.* 1 N. of Siva. -2 A kind of sauce, a kind of dish.-Comp.-फलकः *m.* A shield with a ringing sound.

घंटा *f.* 1 A bell. -2 A plate of iron or mixed metal struck as a clock. -Comp. —फलकः *m.*, -कं *n.* A shield furnished with small bells. -ताडः *m.* A bellman.-पथः *m.* 1 The chief road through a village, a highway, main road. -2. N. of Mallinâtha's commentary on the 'Kirâtârjunîyam.' -शब्दः *m.* 1. Bell-metal.-2 The sound of a bell.

घंटिका *f.* A small bell.

घंटुः *m.* 1 A string of bells tied on an elephant's chest by way of ornament. -2 Heat, light.

घंड: *m.* A bee.

घन *a* (*f.*-ना) 1 Compact, firm, solid. -2 Thick, dense. -3 Thick-set, full, (as breasts). -4 Deep (as sound). -5 Uninterrupted, permanent. -6 Impenetrable.-7 Excessive, violent. -8 Complete. -9 Auspicious, fortunate. -10 Coarse, gross. -11 Engrossed by, full or replete with. कंठग्रहे प्रथमरागघने विलीय "रत्नाव. ४. —नः *m.* A cloud. -2 An iron club, a mace. -3 The body. -4 The cube of a number (in math). -5 Extension, diffusion. -6 A collection, quantity, mass, assemblage. -7 Talc. -8 Phlegm. -9 Any compact mass or substance. -10 Hardness, firmness. -11 A particular manner of reciting Vedic texts. —नं *n.* 1 A cymbal, a bell, a gong. -2 Iron. -3 Tin. -4 Skin, rind, bark. -5 A mode of dancing. -Comp. -आकरः *m.* The rainy season. —आगमः, -उदयः *m.* The rainy season. —आमयः *m.* The date-tree. —उपलः *m.* Hail. —कफः *m.* Hail. -गोलकः *m.* The alloy of gold and silver. —ज्वाला *f.* Lightning. —तोलः *m.* The Chátaka bird. —नाभिः *m.* Smoke (being supposed to be a principal ingredient in clouds). —नीहारः *m.* Thick hoar-frost or mist.—पदं *n.* The cube root. —पदवी *f.* The firmament, sky.-पाषंडः *m.* A peacock. —फलं *n.* (in geom.) The solid or cubical contents of a body or of an excavation. —मूलं *n.* The cube root (in math.). —रसः *m.* 1 A thick juice. -2 Extract, decoction. -3 Camphor. -4 Water (*m.* or *n.*). —वरं *n.* The face. —वर्गः *m.* The square of a cube, the sixth power (in math.). —वर्त्मन् *n.* The sky. —वल्लिका,-वल्ली *f.* Lightning. -वातः *m.* A thick oppressive breeze or air. —वाहनः *m.* 1 Siva. -2 Indra. —श्याम *a.* Deep-black, dark. (—मः *m.*) An epithet (1) of Râma, (2) of Krisna. —सारः *m.* 1 Camphor. -2 Mercury. -3 Water. -हस्तसंख्या *f.* The contents of an excavation or of a solid (in math).

घनाघनः *m.* 1 Indra. -2 A vicious elephant, or one in rut or intoxication.-3 A thick or raining cloud. -4 Mutual collision or contact.

घरट्टः *m.* A grinding stone.

घर्घर *a* (*f.* —रा) 1 Indistinct, purring, gurgling (as a sound). -2 Murmuring, muttering (as clouds). —रः *m.* 1 An indistinct or low murmur. -2 Noise in general. -3 A door, gate. -4 Creaking, crackling, rattling &c.-5 The pass of a mountain. -6 A sliding door, curtain. -7 Mirth, laughter. -8 An owl. -9 A fire of chaff.

घर्घरा, -री *f.* 1 A bell used as an ornament. -2 A girdle of small bells. -3 The Ganges. -4 A kind of lute. -5 A bell hanging on the neck of a horse. -6 One of the notes in music (*n.* also).

घर्घरिका *f.* 1 A bell used as an ornament. -2 A kind of musical instrument. -3 Fried grain.

घर्घरितं *n.* The grunting of a hog.

घर्मः *m.* 1 Heat, warmth. -2 The hot season, summer.-3 Sweat, perspiration. -4 A cauldron, boiler.-5 Sunshine. -6 A cavity in the earth shaped like a boiler. -7 A hot day. -Comp. —अंशुः *m.* The sun. —अंतः *m.* The rainy season. -अंबु,-अंभस्, -उदकं, -जलं *n.* Sweat, perspiration. —चर्चिका *f.* The eruptions caused by heat and suppressed perspiration.-दीधितिः *m.* The sun. —द्युतिः *m.* The sun. —पयस् *n.* Sweat, perspiration. -राशिः

m. 1 The sun. -2 Heat, radiance.

घर्षः *m.*, घर्षणं *n.* 1 Rubbing. -2 Grinding.

घस् 1. 2. P. (घसति, घास्ति, घस्त) To eat, devour (a defective root used only to form certain tenses of अद्).

घस्मर *a.* (*f.* —रा) 1 Voracious, gluttonous. -2 Devourer, destroyer.

घस्र *a.* (*f.* —स्रा) Hurtful, injurious. —स्रः *m.* 1 A day. -2 The sun. —स्रं *n.* Saffron.

घाटः *m.*, -टा *f.* The back of the neck. —टः *m.* 1 A pitcher. -2 A landing place.

घाटिकः *m.* 1 A bell-ringer. -2 A bard who sings in chorus, especially in honour of gods or kings. -3 The Dhattúra plant.

घातः *m.* 1 A blow, stroke, bruise, hit. -2 Killing, destruction, slaughter.-3 An arrow.-4 Power (in Math.) -5 The product of a sum in multiplication. -Comp. —चंद्रः *m.* The moon when in an inauspicious mansion. —तिथिः *f.* An inauspicious lunar-day. -नक्षत्रं *n.* An inauspicious constellation. —वारः *m.* An inauspicious day of the week. —स्थानं *n.* A slaughter-house, place for execution.

घातक *a.* (*f.* -तिका) Killing, destroying.

घातनः *m.* A killer, murderer. —नं *n.* 1 Striking, killing, slaughter -2 Killing (as an animal at a sacrifice), immolating.

घातिन् *a* (*f.* —नी) 1 Striking, killing. -2 Catching or killing (birds &c.) -3 Destructive. -Comp.-पक्षिन्, —विहगः *m.* A hawk, falcon.

घातुक *a.* (*f.* —की) 1 Killing, destructive, mischievous. -2 Cruel, savage. [be killed.

घात्य *a.* (*f.* —त्या) Proper or fit to

घारः *m.* Sprinkling, wetting.

घार्तिकः *m.* A kind of dish or cake prepared with clarified butter which is full of small holes.

घासः *m.* 1 Food. -2 Meadow or pasture grass. -Comp. —कुंदं, —स्थानं *n.* A pasture. [pigeon.

घुः *m.* The indistinct sound of a

घुटः *m.*,-घुटिः,-टी *f.*, घुटिकः *m.*,—का *f.* The ankle.

घुणः *m.* A particular kind of insect found in timber. -Comp. -अक्षरं *n.*, —लिपिः *f.* An incision in wood or in the leaf of a book made by an insect or worm and resembling somewhat the form of a letter.

घुणाक्षरन्यायः *m.* The maxim of letters bored by an insect in wood. It indicates any chance occurrence, taking its origin in the chance resemblance of an incision in wood or in the leaf of a book made by an insect in the form of some letters. This maxim is used to denote any fortuitous or chance occurrence.

घुंटः *m.*, -घुंटकः, घुंटिका *f.* The ankle.

घुंडः *m.* A large black bee.

घुर् 6 P. (घुराति, घुरित) 1 To sound, make a noise, grunt (as a pig, dog, &c.). -2 To be frightful or terrible, -3 To cry in distress.

घुरघुराय् Den. A. To utter gurgling sounds.

घुरी *f.* The nostrils, especially of a hog.

घुर्घुरः *m.* 1 Guinea-worm. -2 Growling, grumbling. —रा *f.* Growling &c. (as of a dog). [whisper.

घुर्घुराय् Den. A. To murmur, hum,

घुर्घुरी *f.* 1 The grunting of a hog. -2 The mole-cricket.

घुकघुलारवः *m.* A sort of pigeon.

घुष् 1 P., 10 U. (घोषति, घोषयति-ते,

घुषित, घुष्ट or घोषित) 1 To sound. -2 To proclaim aloud, announce or declare publicly; to praise. -3 To fill with cries. With आ- or उत्- To announce publicly; to proclaim loudly.

घुष् 1 A. (घुषते) To be beautiful or brilliant.

घुसृणं *n.* Saffron.

घूकः *m.* An owl. -Comp. —अरिः *m.* A crow. —नादिनी *f.* The Ganges.

घूत्कारः *m.* Hooting.

घूर्ण् 1 A., 6 P. To roll about, move to and fro, whirl, shake, reel, stagger.

घूर्ण *a.* (*f.* —र्णा) Shaking, moving to and fro.—र्णः *m.* Whirling, rolling. -Comp. —वायुः *m.* A whirlwind.

घूर्णनं *n.*, —ना *f.*, घूर्णिः *f.* Shaking, reeling, whirling or turning round.

घृ 1 P. (घरति; घृत) To sprinkle.

घृ 10 U. (घारयति-ते, घारित.). To sprinkle over, wet, moisten.

घृ 3 P. (जिघर्ति) 1 To sprinkle. -2 To shine.

घृ 5 U. (घृणोति, घृणुते) 1 To sprinkle. -2 To shine. [burn.

घृण् 8 P. (घृणोति, घृण्ण) To shine,

घृण् 1 A.(घृणते) To seize.

घृणा *f.* 1 Compassion, pity, tenderness. -2 Disgust, aversion. -3 Reproach, censure. -Comp. —अर्चिः *m.* Fire. [hearted.

घृणालु *a.* Compassionate, tender-

घृणि *a.* 1 Displeasing. -2 Shining. —णिः *m.* 1 Heat, sunshine. -2 A ray of light. -3 The sun. -4 A wave.- *n.* Water. -Comp. —निधिः *m.* The sun. (*f.*) The Ganges.

घृतं *n.* 1 Ghee, clarified butter. -2 Butter. -3 Water. -Comp. —अन्नः, —अर्चिस् *m.* Blazing fire. —आहुतिः *f.* An oblation of ghee. —आह्वः *m.* The Sarala tree. —ह्रदः *m.* The 'ocean of ghee,' one of the seven oceans.-ओदनः *m.* Boiled rice mixed whith ghee. —दीधितिः *m.* Fire. —धारा *f.* A continuous stream of ghee. —पशुः *m.* A sacrificial victim represented by ghee. —पूरः, -वरः *m.* A kind of sweet meat.-लेखनी *f.* A ladle for ghee.

घृष् 1 P. (घर्षति, घृष्ट) 1 To rub, strike against.-2 To brush, furbish, polish. -3 To crush, grind, pound. -4 To compete, rival (as in संघर्ष). With उत्- To scratch. सम्- To rival, emulate, to vie with.

घृष्टिः *m.* A hog. —*f.* 1 Grinding, pounding, rubbing. -2 Emulation, rivalry, competition.

घोटः, -घोटकः *m.* A horse. -Comp. —अरिः *m.* A buffalo.

घोटिका, घोटी *f.* A mare.

घोण (-न-) सः *m.* A sort of reptile.

घोणा *f.* 1 The nose. -2 The nose of a horse, snout (of a hog).

घोणिन् *m.* A hog.

घोंटा *f.* The jujube tree.-2 The betel-nut tree. -3 A timber tree.

घोर *a.* (*f.* —रा) 1 Terrific, frightful, horrible, awful.-2 Violent, vehement. —रः *m.* N. of Siva. —रा *f.* Night. —रं *n.* 1 Horror, awfulness. -2 Poison. -Comp. —घुष्यं *n.* Bell-metal. -घोरतरः *m.* Siva.-पुष्पं *n.* Brass. —रासनः, -रासिन्, —वाशनः, -वाशिन् *m.* A jackal. —रूपः *m.* An epithet of Siva.

घोलः *m.*, -लं *n.* Butter-milk having no water in it.

घोषः *m.* 1 Noise, tumult. -2 The thundering of clouds. -3 Proclamation. -4 Rumour, report.-5 A herdsman. -6 A hamlet, station of cowherds. -7 (In gram.) The soft sound heard in the articulation of The soft consonants.-8 A 'kâyastha.' -षं. Bell-metal -Comp.-वतीf. A lute.

घोषणं *n.*, -णा *f.* Proclamation, public announcement. -2 Speaking aloud, making a great noise.

घोषयित्नुः *m.* 1 A crier, bard, herald. -2 Bráhmana. -3 A cuckoo. -4 A captive.

घ्न *a.* (*f.* --घ्नी) (Used only at the end of comp.) Killing, destroying, curing ; *e. g.* ब्राह्मणघ्न, बालघ्न, वातघ्न, पित्तघ्न; depriving one of, taking away; *e. g.* पुण्यघ्न, धर्मघ्न &c.

घ्रा 1 P. (जिघ्रति, जघ्रौ, अघ्रात्-अघ्रासीत्, घ्रात-घ्राण; *Caus.* घ्रापयति). 1 To smell, perceive by smell. -2 To kiss.

घ्राण *p. p.* (*f.* —णा) Smelt. -णः *m.*, -णं *n.* 1 Smell. -2 Smelling. -3 The nose (also *n.*). —णं *n.* 1 The act of smelling. -2 Odour, scent. -3 The nose. -Comp. —इंद्रियं *n.* The organ or sense of smell.—चक्षुस् *a.* 'Having nose for the eyes', blind (who smells out his way).—तर्पण *a.* Grateful or pleasant to the nose, fragrant, odorous. (—णं *n.*) Fragrance, odour.

घ्रात *p. p.* (*f.* —ता) Smelled.

घ्रातिः *f.* 1 The act of smelling. -2 Smell. -3 The nose.

च.

चः *m.* 1 An epithet of Siva.-2 The moon. -3 A tortoise. -4 A thief.

च *ind.* A particle expressing 1 Copulation (and, also, as well as, moreover) used to join words or assertions together ; (in this sense it is used with each of the words or assertions which it joins together ; or it is used after the last only but it never stands first in a sentence). -2 Disjunction (but, still, yet). -3 Certainty, determination, (indeed, certainly, exactly, quite, having the force of एव). -4 Condition (if = चेत). -5 It is often used expletively (पादपूरणार्थे). When repeated in a co-ordinate sentence it expresses simultaneous action or antithesis.

चक् 1 U. (चकति-ते, चकित) 1 To be satiated, be contenled or satisfied. -2 To repel, resist: -3 To shine.

चकास् 2 P. (rarely A.) (चकास्ति-स्ते चकासांचकार, अचकासीत, चकासित) 1 To shine, be bright. -2 To be happy or prosperous. -With वि- To shine, be bright.

चकित *a.* (*f.*-ता) 1 Shaking, trembling (through fear). -2 Frightened, startled. -3 Afraid, timid; —तं *n.* 1 Trembling. -2 Alarm, fear.—तं *ind.* With fear, in a startled manner, with awe.

चकोरः *m.* A kind of bird, the Greek partridge. (चकोरकः also.).

चक्रं *n.* 1 The wheel of a carriage. -2 A potter's wheel. -3 A sharp circular missile weapon. -4 An oil-mill. -5 A circle, ring. -6 A troop, multitude, collection. -7 A realm, sovereignty. -8 A province, a group of villages. -9 A circular military array. -10 A circle or depression of the body. -11 A cycle, cycle of years. -12 The horizon. -13 An army, a host. -14 Section of a book. -15 A whirlpool.-16 An astronomical circle./-17 A particular constellation in the form of a hexagon. -18 A crooked or fraudulent contrivance. —क्रः *m.* 1 The ruddy goose (also called चक्रवाकः). -2 A multitude, troop, group. -Comp. —अंगः *m.* 1 A gander having a curved neck. -2 A carriage. -3 The ruddy goose (चक्रवाकः). (-क्री *f.*) A goose. (-क्रं *n.*) A parasol. —अटः *m.* A juggler, snake-catcher. -2 A rogue, knave, cheat. -3 A particular coin, a *dināra*. —आयुधः *m.* An epithet of Vishnu. —आवर्तः *m.* A whirling or rotatory motion. —आह्वः, -आह्वयः *m.* The ruddy goose. —ईश्वरः *m.* 1 N. of Vishnu. -2 The officer in charge of a district. —उपजीविन् *m.* An oilman. —कारकं *n.* 1 A nail. -2 A kind of perfume. —गंडुः *m.* A round pillow. —गुच्छः *m.* The Asoka tree. —ग्रहणं *n.*, -णी *f.* A rampart, an entrenchment. —चरः *m.* A juggler. —चारिन् *m.* A chariot. —चूडामणिः *m.* Round jewel in a coronet or diadem. —जीवकः, -जीविन् *m.* A potter. —तीर्थं *n.* N. of a holy place. —दंष्ट्रः *m.* A hog. —धरः *m.* 1 An epithet of Vishnu. -2 A sovereign, governor or ruler of a province. -3 A village tumbler or juggler. -4 A snake. —धारा *f.* The periphery of a wheel. —नाभिः *f.* The nave of a wheel. —नामन् *m.* 1 The ruddy goose (चक्रवाक). 2 A pyritic ore of iron. —नायकः *m.* 1 The leader of a troop. -2 A kind of perfume. —नेमिः *f.* The periphery or circumference of a wheel. —पाणिः *m.* An epithet of Vishnu. —पादः, -पादकः *m.* 1 A carriage. -2 An elephant. -पालः *m.* 1 The governor of a province. -2 An officer in charge of a division of an army. -3 The horizon. -4 A circle. -5 One who carries a discus. —बंधुः, -बांधवः *m.* The sun. —बालः, -डः, -बाटः *m.*, -लं, -डं *n.* 1 A ring, circle. -2 A collection, group, multitude, mass. -3 The horizon. (-लः *m.*) 1 A mythical range of mountains supposed to encircle the orb of the earth like a wall and to be the limit of light and darkness. -2 The ruddy goose. —बालधिः *m.* A dog. -भृत् *m.* 1 One who holds a discus. -2 N. of Vishnu. —भेदिनी *f.* Night. —भ्रमः *m.*, भ्रमिः *f.* A lathe or grindstone. —मंडलिन् *m.* A species of cobra. -मुखः *m.* A hog. -यानं *n.* A wheel-carriage. —रदः *m.* A hog. —वर्तिन् *m.* 1 An emperor, universal monarch. -2 Head, foremost. -वाकः *m.* (*f.* -की) The ruddy goose. —वाटः *m.* 1 A limit, boundary. -2 A lamp-stand. -3 Engaging in an action. —वातः *m.* A whirlwind, hurricane. —वृद्धिः *f.* 1 Interest upon interest, compound interest. -2 Wages for transporting goods in a carriage. —व्यूहः *m.* A circular array of troops. —संज्ञं *n.* Tin. (-ज्ञः *m.*) The ruddy goose. —साह्वयः *m.* The ruddy goose. -हस्तः *m.* An epithet of Vishnu.

चक्रक *a.* Wheel-shaped, circular. -कः *m* Arguing in a circle (in logic).

चक्रिकः *m.* A discus-bearer. —का *f.* 1 A heap, troop. -2 A fraudulent device.

चक्रिन् *m.* 1 An epithet of Vishnu. -2 A potter. -3 An oilman. -4 An emperor, a universal monarch. -5 The governor of a province. -6 An ass. -7 The ruddy goose. -8 An informer. -9 A snake. -10 A crow. -11 A kind of tumbler or juggler.

चक्रीवत् *m.* An ass.

चक्ष् 2 A (चष्टे) 1 To see, observe, perceive. -2 To speak, say, tell (with dat of the person). With आ- 1 To declare, teach. -2 To speak, relate. परि- 1 To declare. -2 To call. प्र- 1 To say, speak. -2 To call. प्रत्या- To repulse. व्या- To explain.

चक्षस् *m.* 1 A teacher, an instructor in sacred science. -2 An epithet of Brihaspati.

चक्षुष्य *a.* (*f.* —ष्या) 1 Good-looking, agreeable to the sight, pleasing, beautiful. -2 Good for the eyes. —ष्य: *m.*, -ष्या *f.* A collyrium or application to the eyes. —ष्या *f.* A pleasing or agreeable woman.

चक्षुस् *n.* 1 The eye. -2 Sight, look, the faculty of sight. -3 Light, clearness. -4 Lustre, splendour. -Comp. —गोचर *a.* Visible. —पथ: *m.* The range of sight, the horizon. —विषय: *m.* 1 The range of sight, presence, visibility. -2 An object of sight, any visible object. -3 The horizon.

चक्षुःश्रवस् *m.* A serpent.

चंकुण:, -र: *m.* 1 A tree. -2 A carriage. -3 A vehicle in general (*n.* also).

चंक्रमणं *n.* 1 Moving about, taking exercise. -2 Going slowly or crookedly. -3 Moving or going about, walking. -4 Going tortuously. -5 Leap, jump, spring.

चंच् 1 P. (चंचति, चंचित) 1 To move, shake. -2 To dangle about. -3 To leap, jump. -4 To go, move.

चंच: *m.* 1 A basket. -2 A measure of length equal to 5 fingers. —चा *f.* 1 Anything made of cane (as mat &c.). -2 A straw-man, doll.

चंचरिन *m.* The large black bee.

चंचरी *f.*, -चंचरीक: *m.* A large black bee.

चंचल *a.* (*f.* —ला) 1 Moving, shaking, trembling. -2 (Fig.) Inconstant, fickle, unsteady. —ल: *m.* 1 The wind. -2 A lover. -3 A libertine. —ला *f.* 1 Lightning. -2 Lakshmi, the goddess of wealth.

चंचु *a.* 1 Celebrated, renowned, known. -2 Clever (as अक्षरचंचु). —चु: *m.* A deer. —चु, -चू: *f.* A beak, bill. -Comp. —पुट: *m*, -टं *n.* The bill of a bird when shut. —भृत्, -मत्, *m.* A bird. —सूचि: *m.* The tailor-bird.

चंचुर *a.* (*f.* —रा) Clever, expert.

चटक: *m.* A sparrow.

चटका, चटिका *f.* A hen-sparrow.

चटु: *m*, -टु *n.* 1 Kind or flattering words. —टु: *m.* The belly.

चटुल *a.* (*f.* —ला) 1 Trembling, unsteady, moving about, shaking. -2 Fickle, inconstant (as a lover &c). -3 Fine, beautiful. -ला *f.* Lightning.

चण *a.* (*f.* — चणा) (At the end of comp.) Renowned, celebrated, skilled in, famous for; as अक्षरचण:. —ण: *m.* The chick-pea.

चणक: *m.* Chick-pea.

चंड *a.* (*f.* —डा) 1 Fierce, violent, impetuous, angry, wrathful. -2 Hot, warm; as in चंडांशु. -3 Active, quick. -4 Pungent, acrid. -5 Mischievous, evil. -6 Circumcised. —ड: *m.* 1 An evil being or demon. -2 Siva. -3 Skanda. -4 The tamarind tree. —डं *n.* 1 Heat, warmth. -2 Passion, wrath. -*adv.* Violently, fiercely, angrily. -Comp. —अंशु:, -दीधिति:, -भानु: *m.* The sun. -नायिका *f.* An epithet of Durgá. —मुंडा *f.* A form of Durgá. —मृग: *m.* A wild animal.

चंडा, -डी *f.* 1 An epithet of Durgá. -2 A passionate or angry woman. -Comp. —ईश्वर:, -पति: *m.* An epithet of Siva.

चंडात: *m.* The fragrant oleander.

चंडातक: *m.*, -कं *n.* A short petticoat.

चंडाल *a.* (*f.* —ला) Wicked or cruel in deeds; of black deeds. —ल: *m.* A general name for the lowest and most despised of the mixed castes originating from a Súdra father and a Bráhmana mother. -2 A man of this caste, an outcast. -Comp. —वल्लकी *f.* The lute of a Chándála; a common or vulgar lute.

चंडालिका *f.* 1 The lute of a Chándála. -2 N. of Durgá.

चंडि:, चंडिका *f.* N. of Durgâ.

चंडिमन् *m.* 1 Passion, violence, wrath. -2 Heat, warmth.

चंडिल: *m.* A barber.

चतुर् *num. a.* (always in pl.; चत्वार: *m.*, चतस्र: *f*; चत्वारि *n*) Four. -Comp. —अंग *a.* Having 4 members, quadripartite. (-गं *n.*) 1 A complete army consisting of elephants, chariots, cavalry, and infantry. -2 A sort of chess. —अंगिन् *a.* Having four parts. (-नी *f.*) A complete army. —अंत *a.* Bordered on all sides. —अंता *f.* The earth. —अशीत *a.* Eighty-fourth. —अशीति *a.* or *f.* Eighty four. —अश्र, —अस्र *a.* (for आश्रि-स्रि) 1 Four-cornered, quadrangular. -2 Symmetrical, regular or handsome in all parts. (—श्र:, -स्र: *m.*) 1 A square. -2 A quadrangular figure. -3 (In astr.) N. of the fourth and eighth lunar mansions —अहं *n.* A period of four days. —आत्मन् *m.* N. of Vishnu. —आनन:, -मुख: *m.* An epithet of Brahman (*m.*). —आश्रमं *n.* The four orders or stages of the religious life of a Brâhmana. —उत्तर *a.* Increased by four. —कर्ण (चतुष्कर्ण) *a.* Heard by two persons only. —कोण (चतुष्कोण) *a.* Square, quadrangular. (-ण: *m.*) A square, tetragon. any quadrilateral figure. —गति: *m.* 1 The Supreme Soul. -2 A tortoise. —गव: *m.* A carriage drawn by four oxen. —गुण *a.* Four times, four-fold, quadruple. -चत्वारिंशत (चतुश्चत्वारिंशत) *a.* Forty-four. —दंत: *m.* An epithet of Airávata, the elephant of Indra. —दश *a.* Fourteenth. —दशन् *a.* Fourteen. चतुर्दशविद्या: *f. pl.* The fourteen lores; (they are:- षडंगामिश्रिता वेदा धर्मशास्त्रं पुराणकं । मीमांसा तर्कमपि च एता विद्याश्चतुर्दश ॥). -दशी *f.* The fourteenth day of the lunar fortnight. -दिशं *n.* The four quarters taken collectively. —दिशं *ind.* Towards the four quarters, on all sides. —दोल: *m.*, -लं *n.* A royal litter. —नवति *a.* or *f.* Ninety-four. -पंचाशत *f.* (चतु:पंचाशत् or चतुष्पंचाशत्) Fifty-four. —पथ: (चतु:पथ: or चतुष्पथ: *m.*, -थं *n.* also) A place where four roads meet, a crossway. (-थ: *m.*) A Brâhmana.—पद: (चतुष्पद:) *m.* A quadruped. (-दी *f.*) A stanza of four lines. —पाठी (चतुष्पाठी) *f.* A school for Bráhmanas in which the four Vedas are taught and repeated. —पाणि: (चतुष्पाणि:) *m.* An epithet of Vishnu. —पाद्,-द (चतुष्पाद्, -द) *a.* 1 Quadruped. -2 Consisting of four members or parts. (-*m.*) 1 A quadruped. -2 (In law.) A judicial procedure (trial of suits) consisting of four processes; *i. e.* plea, defence, rejoinder, and judgment. -पार्श्वं *n.* The four sides of a square. —बाहु: *m.* An epithet of Vishnu. (-हु *n.*) A square. —भद्रं *n.* The aggregate of the four ends of human life (पुरुषार्थ); *i. e.* धर्म, अर्थ, काम, and मोक्ष. —भाग: *m.* The fourth part, a quarter. —भुज *a.* 1 Quadrangular. -2 Having four arms. (—ज: *m.*) 1 An epithet of Vishnu. -2 A quadrangular figure. -3 Square. (-जं *n.*) A square. -मासं *n.* A period of four months; (reckoned from the 1st day in the bright half of आषाढ to the 11th day in the bright half of कार्तिक). —मुख: *m.* An epithet of Brahman (*m.*) —युगं *n.* The aggregate of the four *Yugas* or ages of the world. —रात्रं (चतूरात्रं) *n.* An aggregate of four nights. —वक्त्र: *m.* An epithet of Brahman (*m.*). —वर्ग: *m.* The four ends of human life taken collectively (पुरुषार्थ); *i. e.* धर्म, अर्थ, काम and मोक्ष. —वर्ण: *m.* 1 The four classes or castes of the Hindus; i. e. ब्राह्मण, क्षत्रिय, वैश्य, and शूद्र. —वर्षिका f. A cow four years old. —विंश a. 1 Twenty-fourth. -2 Having twenty-four added. —विंशति a. or f. Twenty-four. —विद्य a. One who has studied the four Vedas. —विद्या f. The four Vedas. -विध a. Of four sorts or kinds, four-fold. —वेद a. Familiar with the four Vedas. (-दः m.) The Supreme Soul. —व्यूहः m. N. of Vishnu. (-हं n.) The medical science. —शालं n. (चतुःशालं, चतुश्शालं) चतुःशाली, चतुश्शाली f. A square of four buildings, a quadrangle enclosed by four buildings. -षष्टि a. or f 1Sixty-four. -2 N. for the Rigvda containing 64 Adhyâyas. चतुःषष्टि कलाः f. pl. The sixtyfour arts. —सप्तति a. or f. Seventy-four. —सीमा f. The boundaries on all four sides. -हायन,-ण a. Four years old.

चतुर a. (f. —रा) 1 Clever, skilful, ingenious. -2 Quick, swift. -3 Charming, beautiful, agreeable. -रं n. 1 Cleverness, ingenuity. -2 An elephant's stable.

चतुर्थ a. (f. -र्थी)The fourth. -र्थं n. A quarter. -Comp. —आश्रमः m. The fourth stage of a Brâhmana's religious life; *Sannyasa*. —भाज् a. Receiving a fourth part of every source of income from the subjects (as a king) on occasions of financial difficulties.

चतुर्थकः m. A fever that returns or is repeated every four days; a quartan. —चतुर्थी f. 1 The fourth day of a lunar fortnight. -2 The dative case (in gram). -Comp. —कर्मन् n. The ceremonies to be performed on the fourth night of the marriage.

चतुष्क a. (f. -ष्का) 1 Consisting of four. -2 Increased by four. —ष्कं n. 1 The number 'four.' -2 A collection of four. -3 A crossway. -4 A quadrangular courtyard. -5 A hall resting on four pillars,a hall or saloon in general. -6 A necklace of four strings. —ष्की f. 1 A large foursided pond. -2 A mosquito curtain.

चतुष्टय a. (f. —यी) Four-fold, consisting of four. —यं n. A group of four. -2 A square.

चत्वरं n. 1 A quadrangular place or courtyard. -2 A place where many roads meet. -3 A level spot of ground prepared for a sacrifice.

चत्वारिंशत f. Forty.

चत्वालः m. 1 A hole in the ground prepared for an oblation or for the sacred fire. -2 Kusa grass.

चद्रिः m.1 The moon.-2 Camphor. -3 An elephant. -4 A snake.

चन ind. Not, not also, even not (not used by itself, but found used in combination with the pronoun किम् or with कद्, कथं, क्व, कदा, कुतः to which it imparts an indefinite sense).

चंदः m. 1 The moon. -2 Camphor.

चंदनः m., -नं n. Sandal,(the tree,the wood, or any unctuous preparation of the wood). -2 Anything most excellent of its kind. -Comp. -अचलः —गिरिः, -अद्रिः m. The Malaya mountain. —पुष्पं n. Cloves. —सार m. The most excellent sandal-wood.

चंदिरः m. 1 An elephant. -2 The moon.

चंद्रः m. 1 The moon. -2 The moon as a planet. -3 Camphor. -4 The eye in a peacock's tail. -5 Water -6 Gold (n. also). -7 The numbe. 'one'. (Used at the end of comr.

चंद्र means 'excellent', 'eminent, or 'illustrious';as पुरुषचंद्रः- An excellent or illustrious man). —द्रा *f.* 1 Small cardamoms. -2 An open hall only furnished with a roof. -3 An awning, a canopy. -Comp, —अंशुः *m.* 1 Vishnu. -2 A moon-beam. —आतपः *m.* 1 Moon-light -2 Awning. -3 An open hall only furnished with a roof. —आत्मजः, —औरसः, —जः, —जातः, —तनयः —नंदनः, —पुत्रः *m.* The planet Mercury. —आनन *a.* Moon-faced. (—नः *m.*) An epithet of Kârtikeya. —आपीडः *m.* An epithet of Siva. —आह्वयः *m.*Camphor. —इष्टा *f.* A lotus plant blossoming during night. —उपलः *m* The moon-stone. -कला *f.* 1 A digit of the moon. -2 The crescent before or after the new moon. -कांतः, —मणिः *m.*The moon-stone (supposed to ooze away under the influence of the moon).(—तः *m.*, —तं *n.*) The white eatable water-lily blossoming during the night. (—तं *n.*) Sandal-wood. —कांता *f.* 1 A night. -2 The wife of the moon. -3 Moon-light. —कांतिः *f.* Moon-light. (-*n.*) Silver. —क्षयः *m.* The last day of a lunar month (अमा) when the moon is not visible. —गृहं *n.* The fourth sign of the zodiac, *Cancer.* —गोलः *m.* The lunar sphere. -गोलिका *f.* Moon-light. —ग्रहणं *n.* An eclipse of the moon.—चंचला *f.* A small fish. —चूडः, -मौलिः, -शेखरः, चूडामणिः *m.* Epithets of Siva. -दाराः(*m.pl.*)The wives of the moon, the 27 lunar mansions regarded as married to the moon. —द्युतिः *m.* Sandal-wood. (-*f.*) Moon-light. —नामन् *m.* Camphor. - पादः *m.* A moon-beam. —बाला *f.* 1 Large cardamoms -2 Moon-light —बिंदुः *m.* The sign ँ expressing nasality. —भस्मन् *n.* Camphor. —भागा *f.* N. of a river in the south. —भासः *m.* A sword. —भूति *n.* Silver. —मणिः *m.* The moon-stone. — रेखा, -लेखा *f.* The digit or streak of the moon. — रेणुः *m.* A plagiarist. —लोहकं, —लोहं, -लोहकं *n.* Silver. —वंशः *m.* The lunar race of kings, the second great line of royal dynasties in India. —व्रतं *n.* 1 A kind of vow or penance, the same as चांद्रायण. -2 A regal property or virtue. —शाला *f.* 1 A room on the top (of a house &c.). -2 Moonlight. —शालिका *f.* A room on the top of a house. —शिला *f.* The moon-stone. —संज्ञः *m.* Camphor. —संभवः *m.* N. of Budha or mercury. —हन् *m.* An epithet of Râhu. —हासः *m.* 1 A glittering sword. -2 The sword of Râvana. -3 N. of a king of Kerala, son of Sudhârmika.

चंद्रकः *m.* 1 The moon. -2 The eye in a peacock's tail. -3 A finger-nail. -4 A drop of oil thrown in water assuming the shape of the moon. --कं *n* Black pepper.

चंद्रकवत् *m.* A peacock.

चंद्रकिन् *m.* A peacock.

चंद्रमस् *m.* 1 The moon.

चंद्रिका *f.* 1 Moonlight. -2 (At the end of comp.) Elucidation, explanation of the subject treated. *e. g.* अलंकारचंद्रिका,काव्यचंद्रिका &c.-3Illumination. -4 A large cardamom. -5 The river Chandrabhágá. -6 The Malliká creeper. -Comp. —अंबुजं *n.* The white lotus opening at moonrise. —द्रावः *m.* The moon-stone. —पायिन् *m.* The Chakora bird.

चंद्रिलः *m.* 1 A barber. -2 An epithet of Siva.

चपटः *m.* Same as चपेटः.

चपल *a.* (*f.* —ला) 1 Shaking, tremulous. -2 Unsteady, fickle, inconstant. -3 Frail, transient, momentary. -4 Quick, nimble, agile. -5

Inconsiderate, rash. —लः *m.* 1 A fish. -2 Quicksilver.-3The Chátaka bird. -4 Consumption. -5 A kind of perfume. -6 Black mustard.

चपला *f.* 1 Lightning.-2 A disloyal wife. -3 Spirituous liquor. -4 Lakshmí, the goddess of wealth.-5 The tongue.-6 Long pepper.-Comp. —जन: *m.* 1 A fickle or unsteady woman. -2 The goddess of wealth.

चपेट: *m.*1 The palm of the hand with the fingers extended. -2A blow with the open hand. [open hand.

चपेटा, चपेटिका *f.* A blow with the

चम् 1 P. (चमति, चांत) 1 To drink, sip, drink off. -2 To eat. With आ- (आचामति) 1To sip,drink.-2 To dry up, remove.

चमत्करणं *n.*, चमत्कार: *m.*, चमत्कृति: *f.* 1 Admiration, surprise. -2 Show, spectacle. -3 Poetical charm, that which constitutes poetry. -4 Riot, festive or angry riot.

चमर: *m.* A kind of deer. —र: *m.*, —रं *n.* A chowric most usually made of the tail of Chamara. —री *f.* 1 A shoot, sprout (मंजरी). -2 The female Chamara. -Comp. —पुच्छं *n.* The tail of a Chamara used as a fan. (-च्छ: *m.*) A squirrel.

चमरिक: *m.* The Kovidâra tree.

चमस: *m.*, —सं *n.* 1 A vessel (can, ladle &c.) used at sacrifices for drinking the soma juice (Also चमसी). -2 A cake made of barley, rice &c.

चमाति: *f.* A kind of cake.

चमू: *f.* 1 An army (in general). -2 A division of an army consisting of 729 elephants, as many cars, 2187 horse, and 3645 foot. -Comp. —चर: *m.* A soldier, warrior. —नाथ:, -प:, -पति: *m.*The leader of an army, a commander. —हर: *m.* An epithet of Siva.

चमूरु: *m.* A kind of deer.

चंपक: *m.* 1 A tree bearing yellow, fragrant flowers. -2 A kind of perfume. —कं *n.* A flower of this tree. -Comp. —माला *f.* 1 N. of a neck-ornament worn by women. -2 A garland of Champaka flowers. -3 A kind of metre. —रंभा *f.* A species of plantain. [fruit tree.

चंपकालु: *m.* The jack or bread-

चंपकावती, चंपा, चंपावती *f.* N. of an ancient city capital of the Angas and identified with the modern Bhágalpura.

चंपालु: *m.* Same as चंपकालु:.

चंपू: *f.* A kind of elaborate and highly artificial composition in which the same subject is continued through alterations in prose and verse. *e. g.* भोजचंपू, नलचंपू, भारतचंपू &c. [wards, move.

चय् 1 A. (चयते) To go to or to-

चय: *m.* 1 An assemblage, collection, multitude, mass. -2 A mound of earth raised to form the foundation of a building. -3 A mound of earth raised from the ditch of a fort. -4 A rampart. -5 The gate of a fort. -6 A seat, stool. -7 A pile of buildings; any edifice. -8 A cover, or covering. -9 Arranging or keeping the sacred fire.

चयनं *n.* 1 The act of collecting (especially flowers &c.). -2 Piling, heaping. -3 Keeping the sacred fire. -4 Stacking wood.

चर् 1 P. (चरति, चचार, अचारीत चरितुं, चरित or sometimes चीर्ण) 1 To walk, move, go about, roam, wander. -2 To perform, do, act, practise, observe. -3 To act, behave towards, conduct oneself (oft. with loc. of the person). -4 To graze; eat, consume. -5 To live, continue to be, continue in any state. 6 To live, be, exist. With अनु— To follow. अन्वा- To imitate. अप- To disregard. अभि- 1 To deceive, betray. -2 To conjure. आ— 1 To wander over or about.-2 To act or behave towards. -3 To practise, to perform. उत्— 1 To arise, to originate. -2 To void excrement. -3 To utter, to pronounce. -4 To go up, to ascend. 5 To transgress (Atm.). -6 To treat medically. -7 To approach. दुस्— To deceive. परि— 1 To go about. -2 To serve, wait upon. -3 To nurse. प्र— 1 To walk about. -2 To be prevalent. -3 To proceed to work. वि— 1 To wander about. -2 To practise, perform. व्यभि— 1 To be faithless. -2 To act crookedly. सम्— (P. and A.) 1 To move, pass walk about. -2 To practise, perform. —*Caus.* (चारयति.) 1 To cause to move or go. -2 To send, direct. -3 To drive away. -4 To cause to perform or practise. -5 To cause to copulate. -6 To cause to graze, pasture. With उत्— To cause to utter or pronounce. प्र- To cause to wander about. वि— 1 To think, to meditate upon. -2 To form an idea of, to estimate. -3 To discuss. सम्- 1 To cause to go about, to lead. -2 To cause to spread. -3 To transmit, to communicate. -4 To turn out to graze.

चर *a.* (*f.* —री) 1 Moving, going, walking. -2 Following, practising (at the end of comp.). -3 Trembling, shaking. -4 Moveable. -5 Animate. -6 (Used as an affix) Formerly, late ; आढ्यचर ' one who was formerly rich ; so अध्यापकचर late teacher. —रः *m.* 1 A spy. -2 A wagtail. -3 A game played with dice and men.-4 A 'cowrie.' -5 The planet Mars. -6 (Hence) Tuesday. -10 The first, fourth, seventh, and tenth signs of the zodiac. -Comp. —अचर *a.* 1 Movable and immovable. (-रं *n.*) The aggregate of all created things; the world. -2 The sky, the atmosphere.-3Heaven. —द्रव्यं *n.* Movables, goods and chattels. —मूर्तिः *f.* An idol which is carried about in procession.

चरकः *m.* 1 A spy. -2 A wandering mendicant, a vagrant.

चरणः *m.*, -णं *n.* 1 A foot. -2 A support, pillar, prop. -3 The root of a tree. -4 The single line of a stanza. -5 A quarter.-6A school or branch of any of the Vedas. -7 A race. -8 (In prosody) A dactyl. —गः *m.* 1 A foot-soldier. -2 A ray of light. —णं *n.* 1 Moving, roaming, wanderring. -2 Performance, practising. -3 Conduct of life, behaviour (moral). -4 Accomplishment. -5 Eating, consuming. -Comp. -आयुधः *m.* A cock. —ग्रंथिः *m.*, —पर्वन् *n.*, The ankle. —न्यासः *m.* A footstep —पः *m.* A tree. —शुश्रूषा,-सेवा *f.* 1 Prostration. -2 Service, devotion..

चरम *a.* (*f.* —मा) 1 Last, ultimate, final ; चरमा क्रिया ' the final or funeral ceremony.' -2 Posterior, back. -3 Old (as age). -4 Outermost. -5 Western, west.-6 Lowest, least. —मं *ind.* At last, at the end. -Comp. —अचलः,-अद्रिः,-क्ष्माभृत् *m.* The western mountain behind which the sun and moon are supposed to set. —कालः *m.* The hour of death. —वयस् *a.* Old, aged.

चरिः *m.* An animal.

चरित *p. p.* (*f.* —ता) 1 Wandered, gone. -2 Performed, practised.-3 Attained.-4 Known.-5 Offered.6 Acted, behaved.-तं. *n* 1 Going, moving, course -2 Acting, doing, practice, behaviour, deeds. -3 Life, biography, history. -4 Nature. -5 Fixed law, due or proper observance. -6 The motion of a planet and the consequent position or situation of a planet. ग्रहाणांचरितं स्वप्नोऽनिमित्तान्युपयाचितं...वेणीसं२. -Comp. —अर्थ *a.* 1 That has accomplished its end or desired object; successful. -2 Satisfied, contented. -3 Accomplished. -4 Significant, true to its sense. -5 Appropriate, fit.

चरित्रं *n.* 1 Behaviour, habit, conduct, practice, acts.-2 Performance, observance. -3 History, life. -4 Nature, disposition. -5 Established or instituted observance. -त्रा *f.* The tamarind tree.

चरिष्णु *a.* Movable, active, wandering about.

चरु: *m.* 1 An oblation of rice or barley boiled for presentation to the gods and the manes. -2 A kind of vessel in which an oblation is prepared. -Comp. —स्थाली *f.* A vessel for boiling rice for presentation to the gods and the manes.

चर्च् 10. U. (चर्चयति-ते, चर्चित). To read, peruse, study.

चर्च् 6 P. (चर्चति, चर्चित) 1 To abuse, condemn. -2 To discuss. -3 To anoint, smear.

चर्च: *m.* Deliberation.

चर्चनं *n.* 1 Studying, reading repeatedly. -2 Smearing the body with unguents.

चर्चरिका, चर्चरी *f.* 1 A kind of song. -2 Striking the hands to beat time (in music). -3 The recitation of scholars. -4 Festive sport or merriment. -5 A festival. -6 Flattery. -7 Curled hair. -8 Alternate recitation of a poem by two persons.

चर्चरीक: *m.* 1 Siva. -2 Decoration or curling of the hair.

चर्चा, चर्चिका *f.* 1 Repetition, recitation, repeated reading. -2 Discussion, investigation. -3 Reflection. -4 Smearing the body with unguents. -5 An epithet of the goddess Durgá.

चर्चि: *f.* 1 Repetition. -2 Investigation.

चर्चिक्यं *n.* 1 Anointing the body.-2 An unguent.

चर्चित *p. p.* (*f.* —ता) 1 Anointed. smeared. -2 Discussed, considered. —तं *n.* Anointing, smearing.

चर्पट: *m.* The open palm of the hand with the fingers extended.

चर्पटी *f.* A thin cake of flour.

चर्भट: *m.* A kind of cucumber.

चर्भटी *f.* 1 Noise of merriment. -2 Cucumber.

चर्म *n.* A shield.

चर्मन् *n.* 1 Skin (of the body). -2 Leather, hide. -3 The sense of touch. -4 A shield. -Comp. —अंभस् *n.* Lymph. —अवकर्तनं *n.* Working in leather. —अवकार्तिन्, —अवकर्तृ *m.* A shoemaker. —कार:, —कारिन्, कृत *m.* A shoemaker, currier. —कील: *m.*, —लं *n.* A wart. —चित्रकं *n.* The white leprosy. —जं *n.* 1 Hair. -2 Blood. —तरंग: *m.* A wrinkle. —दंड: *m.*, —नालिका, —नासिका *f.* A whip. —द्रुम:, —वृक्ष: *m.* The Bhúrja tree.—पत्रा *f.* The bat, small housebat. —पादुका *f.* A leather shoe. —प्रभेदिका *f.* A shoe-maker's awl.—प्रसेवक: *m.*, —प्रसेविका *f.* A pair of bellows. —मुंडा *f.* An epithet of Durgá. —यष्टि: *f.* A whip. —वसन: *m.* N. of Siva. —संभवा *f.* Large cardamoms. —सार: *m.* Lymph, serum.

चर्मरुः, चर्मारः *m.* A shoe-maker, a worker in leather.

चार्मिक *a.* Armed with a shield.

चार्मिन् *a.* (*f.* —णी) 1 Armed with a shield. -2 Leathern. —*m.* 1 A soldier armed with a shield. -2 Plantain. -3 The Bhúrja tree.

चर्या *f.* 1 Going about, moving, walking about; driving or going in a carriage. -2 Course, motion. -3 Behaviour, conduct. -4 Practice, performance, observance. -5 Regular performance of all rites or customs. -6 Eating. -7 A custom, usage. -8 Pervading; visiting. —र्यं *n.* 1 Going about. -2 Behaviour, conduct.

चर्व् 1 P., 10 U. (चर्वति, चर्वयति-ते, चार्वित) 1 To chew, eat, browse, bite. -2 To suck up. -3 To relish, taste.

चर्वणं *n.*, -णा *f.* 1 Chewing, eating. -2 Sipping, tasting. -3 Solid food. -4 Fig.) Tasting, relishing, enjoying.

चर्वा *f.* 1 A blow with the flat of the hand. -2 Chewing.

चार्वित *p. p.* (*f.* —ता) 1 Chewed, bitten, eaten. -2 Tasted. -Comp. —चर्वणं *n.* (lit.) Chewing the chewed; (fig.) useless repetion. —पात्रं *n.* A spitting pot.

चल् 1 P. (चलति) 1 To shake; tremble, palpitate, stir. -2 To go, move (from one's place); depart, set out, start off. -3 To be disturbed, confused or disordered (as mind); be agitated. -4 To deviate or swerve (with abl.). 5 To fall off, leave.

चल् 6 P. (चलति, चलित) To sport, play, frolic about.

चल् 10 U. (चाल्यति -ते) To foster.

चल *a.* (*f.* -ला)1 Moving, trembling, shaking rolling(as eyes &c).-2 Movable(opp.स्थिर). -3 Unsteady, fickle, loose, unfixed. -4 Frail, perishable, -5 Confused. —लः *m.* 1 Trembling, agitation. -2 Wind.-3 Quicksilver. -4 The Supreme Being. —ला *f.* 1 Lakshmí, the goddess of wealth.-2 Lightning. -Comp.-अचल *a.* 1 Movable and immovable. -2 Fickle, unsteady, transitory. (-लः *m.*) A crow. —आतंकः *m.* Rheumatism. -कर्णः *m.* The true distance of a planet from the earth. —चंचुः *m.* The Chakora bird. —दलः, -पत्रः *m.* The Asvattha tree.

चलन *a.* (*f.* —ना) Moving, trembling, shaking. —नः *m* 1 A foot. -2 A deer. —नं *n* 1 Trembling, shaking or shaking motion. -2 Turning or leaving off. -3 Roaming,wandering. —नी *f.* 1 A short petticoat worn by common women. -2 The rope for tying an elephant.

चलनकं *n.* A short petticoat worn by low women. -निका *f.* Silken fringes.

चाळिः *m.* A cover, wrapper.

चलित *p. p.* (*f.* —ता) 1 Shaken, stirred, agitated. -2 Gone, departed. -3 Attained -4 Known, understood. —तं *n.* 1 Shaking, moving. -2 Going,walking.-3 A kind of dance.

चलुः *m.* A mouthful (of water).

चलुकः *m.* 1 Water taken up in the hollowed palm for rinsing the mouth. -2 A handful or mouthful (of water).

चष् 1 U. (चषति-ते) To eat.

चष् 1 P. (चषति) To kill,injure,hurt.

चषकः *m* , —कं *n.* A vessel used for drinking spirits; a goblet. -कं *n.* 1A kind of spirituous liquor.-2 Honey.

चषतिः *m.* 1 Eating -2 Killing. -3 Decay.

चषालः *m.*1 A wooden ring on the top of a sacrificial post.-2An iron-ring at the base of the post. -3 A hive.

चह् 1 P., 10 U. (चहति, चहयति-ते) 1 To be wicked. -2 To cheat. -3 To be proud. -4 To grind, pound.

चाकचक्यं *n.* Brilliancy, lustre.

चाक्र *a.* (*f* —क्री) 1 Carried on with the discus (as a fight). -2 Circular. -3 Relating to a wheel.

चाक्रिक *a.* (*f.* —की) 1 See चाक्र above. -2 Relating to a company or circle. -कः *m.* 1 A potter. -2 An oil-maker. -3 A proclaimer. -4 A bard, chorister. -5 A coachman, driver.

चाक्षुष *a.* (*f.* —षी) 1 Depending on, or produced from, sight -2 Belonging to the eye, optical. -3 Visible, to be seen. —षः *m.* N. of the sixth Manu. —षं *n.* Knowledge dependent on vision.

चांगः *m.* 1 Wood-sorrel. -2 Whiteness or beauty of the teeth.

चांचल्यं *n.* 1 Unsteadiness, rolling, tremour (as of the eyes &c.). -2 Fickleness. -3 Transitoriness.

चाटः *m.* A rogue or cheat, one who wins the confidence of the person and deceives him.

चाटुः *m.*, -टु *n.* 1 Pleasing or agreeable words; sweet speech, flattery (especially of a lover to his sweetheart). -2 Distinct or clear speech. -3 Endearing words or acts. -Comp. —उल्लोल, —कार *a.* Speaking agreeably or sweetly. —बटुः *m.* A jester, buffoon.

चाणक्यः *m.* N. of a celebrated writer on civil polity ; also known as विष्णुगुप्त, कौटिल्य.

चांडालः *m.* (*f.* —ली) An outcast.

चांडालिका *f.* 1 The lute of Chândála. 2 N. of Durgá.

चातकः (*f.* -की)N. of a bird which is supposed to live only on rain-drops. -Comp. —आनंदनः *m.* 1 The rainy season. -2 A cloud.

चातुर *a.* (*f.*-री) 1 Relating to four. -2 Clever, able, shrewd. -3 Speaking well, flattering. -4 Drawn by four (as a carriage). —रः *m.* A small round pillow. —रं *n.* A four-wheeled carriage. —री *f.* Skill, dexterity, ability.

चातुरक्षं *n.* Four casts in playing at dice. —क्षः *m.* A small round pillow.

चातुरर्थिकः *m.* (In gram.) A sufix added to words in four different senses.

चातुराश्रमिक *a.* (*f.* -की) Being in one of the four periods of the religious life of a Brâhmana.

चातुराश्रमिन *m.* (*f.*-णी) See चातुराश्रमिक.

चातुराश्रम्यं *n.* The four periods of religious life of a Bràhmana.

चातुरिकः *m.* A coachman, driver.

चातुर्थक,-चातुर्थिक *a.* (*f.* -की)1 Quartan, occurring every fourth day. —कः *m.* A quartan ague.

चातुर्थाह्निक *a.* (*f.* -की) Belonging to the fourth day.

चातुर्दश *a.* Appearing on the fourteenth day. —शं *n.* A demon.

चातुर्दशिकः *m.* One who studies on the fourteenth day of lunar fortnight (that being a day of अनध्याय).

चातुर्मास *a.* Produced in four months. -सी *f.* 1 N. of a sacrifice (इष्टि). -2 The day of full moon at this sacrifice.

चातुर्मासिक *a.*(*f.* -सिका) One who performs the Cháturmásya sacrifice.

चातुर्मास्यं *n.* N. of a sacrifice performed every four months ; *i. e.* at the beginning of कार्तिक, फाल्गुन and आषाढ.

चातुर्यं *n.* 1 Skill, cleverness, shrewdness. -2 Loveliness, beauty.

चातुर्वर्ण्यं *n.* 1 The aggregate of the four original castes of the Hindus. -2 The duties of these four castes.

चातुर्विध्यं *n.* Four kinds(collectively), a four-fold division.

चांद्र *a.* (*f.* —द्री) Relating to the moon, lunar. —द्रः *m.* 1 A lunar month. -2 The bright fortnight (शुक्लपक्ष). -3 The moon-stone. -द्रं *n.* 1 The vow called चांद्रायण. -2 Fresh ginger. -3 The lunar mansion called मृगशीर्ष. —द्री *f.* Moonlight.-Comp. —मासः *m.* A lunar month.

चांद्रकं *n.* Dried ginger.

चांद्रमस *a.* (*f.* —सी) Relating to the moon, lunar. —सी *f.* N. of the wife of Brihaspati. —सं *n.* 1 The constellation मृगशिरस्. -2 The stars in Orion.

चांद्रमसायनः, -निः *m.* The planet Mercury.

चांद्रायणं *n.* A religious observance or expiatory penance regulated by the moon's age.

चांद्रायणिक *a.* (*f.* —की) 1 One who performs the चांद्रायण vow.

चापः *m.* 1 A bow. -2 The rainbow. -3 (In geom.) An arc of a circle. -4 The sign of the zodiac called *Sagittarius.*

चापलं, —ल्यं *n.* 1 Quick motion, swiftness. -2 Fickleness, transitoriness. -3 Inconsiderate or rash conduct, rashness, rash act. -4 Boldness. -5 Agitation, tremour.

चामरः *m.*, —रं *n.* (also -रा, —री *f.* sometimes) 1 A *chowrie* or bushy tail of the Chamara (Bos Grunniens) used as a fly-flap or fan, and reckoned as one of the badges of royalty. -Comp.—पुष्पः, —पुष्पकः *m.* 1 The betelnut tree. -2 The Ketaka plant. -3 The mango tree.

चामरिन् *m.* A horse.

चामीकरं *m. n.* 1 Gold. -2 The Dhattúra plant.

चामुंडा *f.* A terrific form of Durgá.

चांपिला *f.* The river Champâ (perhaps the modern Chambal).

चांपेयः *m.* 1 The Champaka tree. -2 The Nâgakesara tree. —यं *n.* 1 Filament, especially of a lotus flower. -2 Gold. -3 The Dhattúra plant.

चाय् 1 U. (चायति-ते) 1 To observe, discern, see.-2 To worship, honour.

चारः *m.* 1 Going, walking, gait, wandering about. -2 Motion, course. -3 A spy, secret emissary. -4 Performing, practising. -5 A prison. —रं *n.* An artificial poison. -Comp. —अंतरितः *m.* A spy. —ईक्षणः, —चक्षुस् *m.* A king (or a statesman) who employs spies and sees through their medium. —चण,—चंचु *a.* Graceful in gait, of graceful carriage. —ज्या *f.* The sine of the ascensional difference. -पथः *m.* A place where two roads meet. —भटः *m.* A valorous man, warrior. —भटी *f.* Courage. —वायुः *m.* Summer-air, zephyr.

चारकः *m.* 1 A spy.-2 A herdsman. -3 A leader, driver. -4 An associate. -5 A groom, cavalier. -6 A prison. -7 A bond, fetter.-8 Going, motion. -9 A wandering Brâhmanical student.

चारणः *m.* 1 A wanderer, a pilgrim. -2 A wandering actor or singer, a dancer. -3 A celestial singer, heavenly chorister. -4 A reader of scriptures. -5 A spy.

चारितार्थ्यं *n.* Attainment of an object, successfulness.

चारित्रं (also written चारित्र्यं) *n.* 1 Conduct, behaviour, manner of acting. -2 Good name or character, reputation, uprightness, good conduct. -3 Chastity, purity of life. -4 Disposition, temperament. -5 Peculiar observance or practice.

-6 Hereditary observance —त्रा *f.* The tamarind tree.

चारु *a.* (*f.* –रु or –र्वी) 1 Agreeable, beloved, esteemed, dear (with dat. or loc.) -2 Pleasing, beautiful.-रुः *m.* An epithet of Brihaspati. —रु *n.* Saffron. -Comp. —धामा, —धारा, -रावा *f.* Sachi, Indra's wife. –नेत्रः, –नयनः *m.* A deer. —फला *f.* A vine, grape. -वर्धना *f.* A woman. -व्रता *f.* A female who fasts for a whole month. –शिला *f.* A jewel, gem.

चार्चिक्यं *n.* 1 Perfuming the person, smearing with sandal &c. -2 An unguent.

चार्म *a.* (*f.* –र्मी) 1 Leathern. -2 Covered with leather (as a car). -3 Shielded,provided with a shield.

चार्मण *a.* (*f.* –णी) Covered with skin or leather. —र्णं *n.* A multitude of hides or shields.

चार्मिक *a.* (*f.* –की)Made of leather.

चार्मिणं *n.* A number of men armed with shields.

चार्वाकः *m.* 1 N. of a philosopher who propounded the grossest form of atheism or materialism.

चार्वी *f.* 1 A beautiful woman. -2 Moonlight.-3 Intelligence.-4 Splendour, lustre,brilliancy. -5 N. of the wife of Kubera.

चाडः *m.* 1 The thatch or roof of a house. -2 The blue jay. -3 Being movable.

चालकः *m.* A restive elephant.

चालनं *n.* 1 Causing to move. -2 Loosening. -3 Muscular action. -4 Causing to pass through a sieve, sifting. -5 A sieve. -नी *f.* A sieve, strainer.

चाषः, –सः *m.* The blue jay.

चि 5 U. (चिनोति, चिनुते, चेतुं,–चित;*caus.* चाययति, चापयति also चययति, चपयति.*desid.* चिचीषति,-चिकीषति) 1 To collect,gather. -2 To search, look out for. - 3 To piie or heap up. -4 To set, inlay, cover or fill with. With अव— To gather. आ— To spread, cover. उत्— To gather. उप— To increase. नि— To spread over. निस्– To resolve; to ascertain. परि— 1 To practise. -2 To acquire. प्र— 1 To collect. -2 To increase. वि— 1 To gather. -2 To search for.विनिस्— To determine, to ascertain सम्— 1 To accumulate. -2 To arrange; to put, to place. समुत्— To collect. —*pass.* **To bear** fruit, grow, thrive, prosper.

चि 1 A. (चयते) 1 To detest, hate. -2 To revenge, take vengeance on.

चि (1 U. चायति-ते) 1 To fear,dread, be afraid of (with acc.). -2 To respect, honour. -3 To observe.

चिकित्सकः *m.* A physician, doctor.

चिकित्सनं *n.* Healing, practising medicine.

चिकित्सा *f.* 1 Administering remedies or medicine; medical treatment. -2 Therapeutics.

चिकिलः *m.* Mud, a slough, mire.

चिकीर्षा *f.* Desire of doing (anything), will, wish, desire.

चिकीर्षित *a.* (*f.* —ता) Wished, desired, purposed. —तं *n.* Design, intention, purpose.

चिकीर्षु *a.* Desirous of doing anything, desirous for.

चिकुर *a.* (*f.* —रा) 1 Moving,tremulous, fickle, unsteady -2 Inconsiderate, rash. —रः *m.* 1 The hair of the head.-2 A mountain.-3 A muskrat. -4 A reptile, snake. -Comp. —उच्चयः, —कलापः, -निकरः, -पक्षः, —पाशः, -भारः, -हस्तः *m.* A mass or tuft of hair.

चिकूरः *m.* The hair.

चिक्क *a.* Flat-nosed. —क्कः *m.* The musk-rat. —क्का *f.* 1 A mouse. -2 A betel-nut.

चिक्कण *a.* (*f.*–णा or –णी) 1 Smooth, glossy. –2 Slippery. –3 Bland. –4 Unctuous, greasy. –णः *m.* The betel-nut tree. –णा *f.* An excellent cow. –णं *n.* A betel-nut.

चिक्कणा, –णी *f.* 1 The betel-nut tree. –2 A betel-nut.

चिक्कसः *m.* Barley-meal.

चिक्किरः *m.* A mouse.

चिक्लिदं *n.* Moisture; freshness. –दः *m.* The moon.

चिंचा *f.* 1 The tamarind tree, or its fruit –2 The Gunjâ plant.

चित् 1 P., 10 A. (चेतति, चेतयते, चेतित) 1 To perceive, see, notice, observe. –2 To know, understand, be conscious of. –3 To regain consciousness.

चित् 10 U. (चिंतयति,–ते, चिंतित) 1 To think, to consider. –2 To bring before the mind. –3 To remember. –4 To discuss, to treat of. –5 To weigh, to discriminate.

चित् *f.* 1 Thought, preception. –2 Intelligence, intellect, understanding. –3 The heart, mind. –4 The soul, spirit of life. –5 Brahman (*n.*) –Comp. —आत्मन् *m.* 1 The thinking principle or faculty. –2 Pure intelligence; the Supreme Spirit. —आभासः *m.* The individual soul not freed from impurities. —घनः *m.* The Supreme Spirit or Brahman (*n.*). –प्रवृत्तिः *f.* Reflection, thinking. —रूप *a.* 1 Consisting of intelligence. –2 Wise, intelligent, of a liberal mind. –3 Amiable, good-hearted. (–पं *n.*) Pure intelligence, the Supreme Being. —शक्तिः *f.* Mental power, intellectual capacity. —स्वरूपं *n.* The Supreme Spirit.

चित् *ind.* 1 A particle added to किं and its derivatives (such as कद्, कथं, क, कदा, कुत्र, कुतः &c.) to impart to them an indefinite sense; कुत्रचित् somewhere; केचित् some &c. –2 The sound चित्.

चित *p. p.* (*f.* —ता) 1 Collected, piled up. –2 Got, acquired. –3 Covered with, full of, set or inlaid with. —तं *n.* A building.

चिता *f.* 1 A funeral pile, pyre. –2 heap, assemblage, multitude. -Comp. —अग्निः *m.* The funeral fire. —चूडकं *n.* A pyre.

चितिः *f.* 1 Collecting, gathering. –2 A heap, multitude, quantity. –3 A pile, stack. –4 A funeral pile. –5 An oblong with quadrangular sides. –6 The understanding. —*m.* The thinking mind.

चितिका *f.* 1 A pile, stack. –2 funeral pile. –3 A small chain (or girdle) worn as an ornament round the loins.

चित्त *p. p.* (*f.* —त्ता) 1 Observed. perceived, –2 Considered, reflected or meditated upon. –3 Resolved. –4 Intended, wished. –5 Visible. —त्तं *n.* 1 Observing, attending. –2 Thought, thinking, attention. –3 Intention, aim. –4 The mind. –5 The heart. –6 Reason, intellect, reasoning faculty. -Comp. —अनुवर्तिन् *a.* Acting according to one's will. —अपहारक, —आभोगः *m.* Exclusive attachment to one thing. —आसंगः *m.* Attachment, love. –उद्रेकः *m.* Pride, arrogance. –ऐक्यं *n.* Unanimity. –उन्नतिः, —समुन्नतिः *f.* 1 Noble-mindedness. –2 Pride, arrogance. —चारिन् *a.* Acting according to the will of another. —जः, —जन्मन् —भूः, –योनिः *m.*, 1 Love, passion. –2 Cupid, the god of love. —ज्ञ *a.* Knowing the mind of another. —नाशः *m.* The loss of conscience. —निर्वृतिः *f.* Contentment, happiness. —प्रशमः *m.* Tranquility of heart. –प्रसन्नता *f.* Joy, pleasure. –भेदः

m. 1 Difference of view. -2 Inconsistency, inconstancy. —मोह: m. Infatuation of the mind. —विकार: m. Change of thought or feeling.-विक्षेप: m. Distraction of the mind. —विप्लव:, -विभ्रम: m. Aberration, disturbance or derangement of mind, madness. —विश्लेष: m. Breach of friendship. —वृत्ति: f. 1 Disposition or state of the mind, inclination. -2 Thinking, imagining.-3 Inward purpose,emotion. -4 (In Yoga phil.) Inward working of the mind,mental vision. —वेदना f. Affliction, anxiety. -वैकल्यं n. Bewilderment of the mind, distraction. —संस्थ a. Pervading the heart, penetrating the soul.

चित्तवत a. 1 Reasonable, endowed with reason. -2 Kind-hearted, amiable.

चित्ति: f. 1 Thinking, reflection. -2 Understanding, wisdom. -3 Devotion. -4 Intention, purpose. -5 A wise person. -6 Fame, celebrity.

चित्यं n. 1 The place at which a corpse is burnt. -2 A monument. -त्या f. 1 A funeral pile. -2 Piling up, building (as an altar).

चित्र a. (f. —त्रा) 1 Bright, clear. -2 Variegated, spotted. -3 Amusing. -4 Various, different, manifold. -5 Surprising, wonderful, strange. —त्र: m. 1 The variegated colour. -2 A form of Yama. -3 The Asoka tree. -4 The same as चित्रगुप्त. —त्रं n. 1 A picture, painting, delineation. -2 A brilliant ornament. -3 An extraordinary appearance, wonder. -4 A sectarial mark on the forehead. -5 Heaven, sky. -6 A spot. -7 The white or spotted leprosy. -8 (In Rhet.) The last of the three divisions of *Kavya* which is of two kinds शब्दचित्र and अर्थ-वाच्य-चित्र. -9 Anything bright which strikes the eye. -10 Playing upon words, punning, using conundrums, riddles &c. —त्रं *ind.* Oh !, how strange !, what a wonder ! -Comp. —अक्षी, —नेत्रा, -लोचना f. A kind of bird commonly called Sârikâ. —अंग: m. 1 A kind of snake. -2 N. of Arjuna. (-गं n.) 1 Vermilion. -2 Yellow orpiment. —अन्नं n. Rice dressed with coloured condiments. —अर्पित a. Committed to a picture, painted resemblance, portrait. —आयसं n. Steel. —उक्ति: f. 1 Agreeable or eloquent discourse. -2 A voice from heaven. -3 A surprising tale. —कंठ: m. A pigeon. —कथालाप: m. Telling agreeable or charming stories. -कंबल: m. 1 Painted cloth used as an elephant's housing. -2 A variegated carpet. —कर: m. 1 A painter. -2 An actor. —कर्मन् n. 1 An extraordinary act.-2 Ornamenting, decorating. -3 A picture. -4 Magic. (-m.) 1 A magician,one who works wonders.-2 A painter. —काय: m. A tiger in general. -2 A leopard or panther. —कार: m. A painter. -2 N.of a mixed tribe. —कूट: m. N. of a hill and district near Prayága. —कृत a. Astonishing, surprishing. (-m.) A painter. —क्रिया f. Painting. —ग,-गत a. 1 Painted, drawn in a picture. -2 Coloured, variegated —गुप्त: m.One of the beings in Yama's world recording the vices and virtues of mankind. —जल्प: m. A random or incoherent talk, talk on various subjects. -त्वच् m. The Bhúrja tree. —तंडक: m. The cotton-plant. —न्यस्त a. Painted, drawn in a picture.-पक्ष: The francoline partridge. —पट:, -ट: m. 1 A painting, a picture. -2 A coloured or chequered cloth. -पादा *f.* The bird called Sârikâ. -पिच्छक: *m.* 1 A peacock. —पुंख: *m.* A kind of arrow. —पृष्ठ: *m.* A sparrow. -प्रतिकृति: *f.* Representation in colours, a painting, picture. —फलकं *n.* A tablet for painting, a pictureboard. —बर्ह: *m.* A peacock. —भानु *a.* Of a variegated colour, shining with light. (-नु: *m.*) 1 Fire. -2 The sun. -3 N. of Bhairava. -4 The Arka plant. -5 Siva.-6 An epithet of the Asvins. -7 The first year of the first cycle of Jupiter. —मृग: *m.* The spotted antelope. —मेखल: *m.* A peacock. —योधिन् (-*m.*) An epithet of Arjuna. —रथ: *m.* 1 The sun. -2 N. of a king of the Gandharvas, one of the sixteen sons of Kasyapa by his wife Muni. —लिखित *a.* 1 Painted. -2 Dumb, motionless (as in a picture).—लेखा *f.* 1 A portrait, picture. -2 N. of a friend and companion of Ushâ, daughter of Bâna. —लेखक: *m.* A painter. —लेखनिका *f.* A painter's brush. -वनं *n.* N. of a forest near the Gandakî. -वाज: *m.* A cock. —विचित्र *a.* 1 Variously coloured, variegated. -2 Multiform. -विद्या *f.* The art of painting. —शाला *f.* A painter's studio.-शिखंडिन् *m.* An epithet of the seven sages:— मरीचि, अंगिरस्, अत्रि, पुलस्त्य, पुलह, क्रतु and वसिष्ठ. —संस्थ *a.* Painted. —हस्त: *m.* A particular postion of the hands in fighting.

चित्रक: *m.* 1 A painter. -2 A tiger in general. -3 A small hunting leopard. -4 N. of a tree. —कं *n.* 1 A sectarial mark on the forehead. -2 A particular manner of fighting. -3 N. of a wood near the mountain Raivataka.

चित्रल *a.* (*f.* —ला) Variegated, spotted. —ल: *m.* The variegated colour.

चित्रा *f.* N. of the fourteenth lunar mansion consisting of one star. -Comp. —अटीर: *m.* The moon.—ईश: *m.* The moon. —मघा *f.* The dawn.

चित्रिक: *m.* The month Chaitra.

चित्रिणी *f.* N. for a woman, 'endowed with various talents and excellences,' one of the four divisions into which writers on erotic science class women :—पद्मिनी, चित्रिणी, शंखिनी and हस्तिनी or करिणी.

चित्रित *a.* (*f.* —ता) 1 Variegated, spotted. -2 Painted.

चित्रीय् Den. A 1 To cause wonder, to be an object of wonder. -2 To wonder.

चिंत् 10 U. (चिंतयति-ते) 1 To think, consider. -2 To think of, bring before the mind. -3 To take care of, look to. -4 To call to mind, remember. -5 To find out, discover, think out. -6 To regard as, esteem. -7 To discriminate. -8 To treat of, consider.

चिंतनं *n.*,-ना *f.* 1 Thinking, thinking of, having an idea of.-2 Thought, reflection. -3 Anxious thought.

चिंता *f.* 1 Thinking, thought. -2 Care, anxiety. -3 Reflection, consideration. -4 (In Rhet.) Anxiety, considered as one of the 33 subordinate feelings. -Comp. —आकुल *a.* Disturbed in mind, anxious. कर्मन् *n.* Anxiety. -पर *a.* Thoughtful, anxious. -मणि: *m.* 1 A fabulous gem supposed to yield to its possessor all desires ; the philosopher's stone. -2 N. of Brahman (*m.*). -वेश्मन् *n.* A council-hall.

चिंतिडी *f.* The tamarind tree.

चिंतित a. (f. —ता) 1 Thought, reflected. -2 Devised, found out.

चिंतितिः, -चिंतिया f. Consideration, reflection, thought.

चिन्मय a. Consiting of pure intelligence, spiritual (as the Supreme Spirit). —यं n. 1 Pure intelligence. -2 The Supreme Spirit.

चिन्मात्रं n. Pure intelligence.

चिंत्य pot. p. (f. -त्या) 1 To be considered or thought over. -2 To be discovered, to be devised or found out. -3 Conceivable, comprehensible. -4 Requiring consideration, doubtful, questionable.

चिपट a. (f. —टा) Flat-nosed. -टः m. Rice or grain flattened.

चिपिटः a See चिपट. -Comp. -ग्रीव a. Short-necked. —नास,-नासिक a. Flat-nosed.

चिपिटकः,-चिपटः m. Flattened rice.

चिबु (-बु-) कं n. The chin.

चिमिः m. A parrot; also चिमिकः.

चिर a. (f. —रा) Long, lasting a long time, existing from a long time, old.—रं n. A long time. *Note*.- The singular of any of the oblique cases of चिर may be used adverbially in the sense of 'long', 'for a long time,' 'after a long time,' 'long since, " at last,' 'finally,' e. g चिरं, चिरेण, चिराय, चिरात्, चिरस्य, चिरे. —Comp. —आयुस् a. Long-lived. (—m.) A god. —आरोधः m. A protracted siege, blockade. —उत्थ a. Existing for a long time. —कार, -कारिक, -कारिन्, -क्रिय a. Acting slowly, delaying, tarrying, dilatory. -कालः m. A long time. -कालिक, -कालीन a. 1 Of long standing; old, long-continued. -2 Chronic (as a disease). —जात a. Born long ago, old. -जीविन् a. Long-lived. (-m.) 1 An epithet of seven persons who are considered to be 'deathless'; अश्वत्थामा बलिर्व्यासो हनुमांश्च बिभीषणः। कृपः परशुरामश्च सप्तैते चिरजीविनः॥. -2 N. of Vishnu. -3 A crow. -पाकिन् a. Ripening late. —पुष्पः m. The Bakula tree. —मित्रं n. An old friend. —मेहिन् m. An ass. —रात्रं n. A period of many nights, a long time. —विप्रोषित a. Long banished; a long sojourner. —सूता, -सूतिका f. A cow that has borne many calves. —सेवकः m. An old servant. —स्थ, -स्थायिन्, -स्थित a. Lasting, long, enduring, continuing, durable. [epithet of Kâma.

चिरंजीव a. Long lived. —वः m. An

चिरंटी, चिरिंटी f. 1 A woman married or single who continues to reside after maturity in her father's house. -2 A young woman (in general).

चिरत्न a. (f. —त्नी) Of long standing, old, ancient.

चिरंतन (f. —नी) Of long standing, old, ancient. [tarry.

चिरय् P., चिराय् A. Den. To delay,

चिरिः m. A parrot.

चिरुः m. The shoulder-joint.

चिर्भटिः f. A sort of cucumber.

चिल् 6 P. (चिलति) To put on clothes.

चिल्मी (-मि-) लिका f. 1 A kind of necklace.-2 A fire-fly.-3 Lightning.

चिल्ल् 1 P. (चिल्लति, चिल्लित) 1 To become loose, be slack. -2 To act wantonly, sport.

चिल्लः m. 1 A bleared or sored eye. -2 The (Bengal) kite; चिल्ला f also in this sense. -Comp. —आभः m. A petty-thief, a pick-pocket.

चिल्लिका, चिल्लिका, चिल्ली f. A cricket.

चिविः f. The chin.

चिह्न् 10 U. (चिह्नयति-ते) To mark, stamp (properly a Denom. from the noun चिह्न).

चिह्नं n. 1 Mark, spot, stamp, symbol; badge, symptom. -2 A sign, indication. -3 A sign of the zodiac. -4 Stamp, print, impression. -5 Aim, direction. -Comp. —कारिन् a. 1 Marking, spotting. -2 Striking, wounding, killing. -3 Frightful, hideous.

चिह्नितं a. (f. —ता) 1 Marked, signed, stamped, bearing the badges of an office. -2 Branded. -3 Known.

चीत्कारः m. An onomatopoetic word, the cry of certain animals, particularly of the ass or elephant.

चीनः m. 1 N. of a country, the modern China. -2 A kind of deer. -3 A sort of cloth. -4 A thread. —नाः (m. pl.) The rulers or people of China. —नं n. 1 A banner. -2 A kind of bandage for the corners of the eyes. -3 Lead. -Comp. —अंशुकं, —वासस् n. China-cloth ; silk, silken cloth.

चीनाकः m. A kind of camphor.

चीरं n. 1 A rag, a tattered cloth, a long stripe. -2 A bark. -3 A cloth or garment in general. -4 A necklace of pearls consisting of four strings. -5 A stripe, stroke, line. -6 A manner of writing with strokes. -7 Lead. -8 A crest. -9 The dress of a Buddhist priest.

चीरिन् a. Clothed in bark-garments or rags.

चीरिः f. 1 A veil for covering the eyes. -2 A cricket. -3 The hem of an undergarment.

चीरि (-रु-) का f. A cricket.

चीर्ण a. (f. —र्णा) 1 Done, performed, observed. -2 Studied, repeated. -3 Split, divided. -Comp. —पर्णः m. The Kharjúra and Nimba trees.

चीलिका f. A cricket.

चीव् 1 U. (चीवति-ते) 1 To wear, cover. -2 To take or receive. -3 To seize. [-2 To speak.

चीव् 10 U. (चीवयति-ते) 1 To shine.

चीवरं n. 1 A garment (in general); a tatter, rag. -2 The dress of any mendicant, particularly of a Buddhist mendicant.

चीवरिन् m. 1 A Buddhist or Jaina mendicant. -2 A mendicant (in general).

चुक्कारः m. The roaring of a lion.

चुक्रः m. 1 A kind of cane or sorrel. -2 Sourness. —क्रं n. Sourness, acidity. -Comp. —फलं n. The tamarind fruit. —वास्तूकं n. The wood-sorrel. [sorrel.

चुक्रकं n., चुक्रिका f. A kind of wood-

चुक्रा f. The tamarind tree.

चुक्रिमन् m. Sourness.

चुचुकः m., -कं n., चुचूकं n. The nipple of the breast.

चुंचु a. (At the end of certain comp.) Celebrated, famous, renowned, skilled in. —चुः m. The muskrat or shrew. [voir.

चुंटा, -डा f. A small well or reser-

चुत् 1 P. (चोतति) To ooze, trickle.

चुतः m. The opening of the anus.

चुद् 10 U. (चोदयति-ते, चोदित) 1 To send, direct, throw forward, urge or drive on, push on. -2 To prompt, inspire, impel, animate, excite. -3 To hasten. -4 To question, ask. -5 To press with a request. -6 To put forward, adduce, (as an argument or objection.) -7 To enjoin, lay down. -8 To help on. -9 To bring or offer quickly. -10 To be quick.

चुंदी f. A procuress, bawd.

चुप् 1 P. (चोपति) To move slowly, creep or steal along.

चुबुकः m. The chin.

चुब्, चुंब् 1. 10. U. (चुंबति-ते, चुंबयति-ते, चुंबित) 1 To kiss (fig. also). -2 To touch softly, to graze. With -परि To kiss.

चुंबकः *m.* 1 A kisser. -2 A lecher, a lustful man, libertine. -3 A rogue, cheat. -4 A superficial scholar. -5 A loadstone. -6 The upper part or middle of a balance.

चुंबनं *n.* Kissing, a kiss.

चुर् 10 U. (चोरयति-ते, चोरित) 1 To rob, steal. -2 (Fig.) To bear, have, possess, take, assume.

चुरणं *n.* Robbing, theft.

चुरा *f.* Theft.

चुरिः, चुरी *f.* A small well.

चुलुकः *m.* 1 Deep mud. -2 A mouthful of water, or the hand hollowed to hold water or anything. -3 A small vessel.

चुलाकिन् *m.* A porpoise.

चुलुंप् 1 P. (चुलुंपति) 1 To swing, rock, move to and fro, agitate. —With उद्- 1 To swing. -2 To agitate.

चुलुंपः *m.* Fondling children.

चुलुंपा *f.* A she-goat.

चुल्ल् 1 P. (चुल्लति) 1 To play, sport, to make amorous gestures. -2 To conjecture.

चुल्ल *a.* Blear-eyed. -ल्लः *m.* A blear eye.

चुल्लकः *m.* The palm of the hand hollowed as in the act of holding water. -की *f.* 1 A kind of water-pot. -2 A porpoise.

चुल्लिः *f.* A fire-place.

चुल्ली *f.* 1 A fire-place. -2 A funeral pile.

चूचुकं, चूचूकं *n.* The nipple of a breast.

चूडकः *m.* A well.

चूडा *f.* 1 The hair on the top of the head, a single lock on the crown of the head (left after the ceremony of tonsure). -2 The ceremony of tonsure. -3 The crest of a cock or peacock. -4 Any crest, plume or diadem. -5 The head. -6 Top, summit. -7 A room on the top of a house. -8 A well. -9 An ornament (like a bracelet worn on the wrist). -Comp. -करणं, -कर्मन् *n.* The ceremony of tonsure. —पाशः *m.* A mass of hair. —मणिः *m.*, -रत्नं *n.* 1 A jewel worn on the top of the head, a crest jewel (fig. also). -2 Best, excellent (usually at the end of comp.). —लक्षणं *n.* Tonsure.

चूडार,-ल *a.* (*f.* —रा, -ला) 1 Having a single lock of hair on the crown of the head. -2 Crested. —लं *n.* The head.

चूतः *m.* The mango tree. —तं *n.* The anus.

चूतकः *m.* 1 The mango tree. -2 A small well.

चूतिः *f.* The anus.

चूर्ण् 10 U. (चूर्णयति-ते, चूर्णित) 1 To reduce to powder, pulverize, pound. -2 To bruise, crush. With सम्- To bruise, crush.

चूर्णः *m.*; -र्णं *n.* 1 Powder. -2 Flour. -3 Dust. -4 Aromatic powder, pounded sandal, camphor &c. —र्णः *m.* 1 Chalk. -2 Lime. -3 Pounding. -Comp. —कारः *m.* A lime-burner. —कुंतलः *m.* A curl, curly hair. —खंडः *m.*, -डं *n.* 1 Gravel, pebble. -2 Limestone nodule. —पारदः *m.* Vermilion.

चूर्णकः *m.* Grain fried and pounded. —कं *n.* 1 A fragrant powder. -2 A style of prose-composition which is easy, does not contain hard letters, and has very few compounds. -3 Explaining in prose the purport of a foregoing verse.

चूर्णनं *n.* Crushing, pounding.

चूर्णिः, -र्णी *f.* 1 Pounding, powder. -2 A sum of hundered 'cowries.' -3 N. of Patanjali's Mahâbháshya on the Sútras of Pánini. -4 A selection of an unanswerable argument. -Comp. —कृत m. 1 An epithet of Patanjali. -2 An annotator, commentator.

चूर्णिका f. 1 Grain fried and powdered. -2 A style of prose composition.

चूर्णित a. (f. —ता) 1 Pounded, pulverized. -2 Crushed, bruised, shattered to pieces.

चूल: m. Hair. —ला f. 1 An upper room. -2 A crest. -3 The crest of a comet.

चूलिका f. 1 The crest or comb of a cock. -2 The root of an elephant's ear. -3 (In dramas) The hinting or indication of the occurrence of any event by characters behind the stage. [suck up or out.

चूष् 1 P. (चूषति, चूषित) To drink,

चूषा f. 1 A leathern girth (for an elephant). -2 Sucking. -3 A girdle.

चूष्यं n. Any article of food to be sucked.

चृत 6 P. (चृतति) 1 To hurt, kill. -2 To tie, bind or connect together.

चृत 1 P., 10 U. (चर्तति, चर्तयति-ते) To light, kindle.

चेकितान: m. 1 An epithet of Siva. -2 N. of a Yádava prince.

चेट: (-ड:) m. A servant.

चेटक: m. 1 A servant, any one who does a set task -2 A paramour.

चेटि (-डि-) का, चेटि: (-टी), (-डी) f. A female slave or servant.

चेत् ind. If, provided that, although, (never used at the beginning of a sentence), इति चेत् न 'If it be urged that... (we reply) not so' (frequently used in controversial works). अथ चेद् But if.

चेतन a. (f. —नी) Animate, alive, living, sentient, feeling. —न: m. 1 A sentient being, a man. -2 Soul, mind. -3 The Supreme Soul. -4 An animal in general. —ना f. 1 Sense, consciousness. -2 Understanding, intelligence. -3 Life, vitality, animation. -4 Wisdom, reflection. —नं n. 1 Appearance. -2 The mind.

चेतस् n 1 Consciousness, sense. -2 Thinking soul, reasoning faculty. -3 The mind, heart, soul. -4 Will. -Comp. —जन्मन्, -भव:, -भू: m. 1 Love, passion. -2 The god of love. -विकार: m. The disturbance of the mind, emotion, agitation.

चेदि: m. (m, pl. चेदय:) N. of a country. -Comp. -पति:, -भूभृत m., -राज् m., -राज: m. N. of Sisupála, son of Damaghosha and king of the Chedis.

चेल् 1 P. (चेलति) 1 To go, move. -2 To shake, tremble

चेलं n. 1 A garment. -2 (At the end of comp.) Bad, wicked, vile; भार्याचेलं 'A bad wife.' -Comp. —प्रक्षालक: m A washerman.

चेलिका f. A bodice.

चेष्ट् 1 A (चेष्टते, चेष्टित) 1 To move about, stir, be active. -2 To strive, endeavour, exert oneself. -3 To perform, do (anything). -4 To behave, act. -With वि— 1 To stir, move, move about. -2 To act, behave.

चेष्टनं n. 1 Motion. -2 Effort, exertion. -3 Performing, doing.

चेष्टा f. 1 Motion, movement. -2 Gesture, action. -3 Effort, exertion. -4 Behaviour. -5 Action, deed. —नाश: m. The destruction of the world. —निरूपणं n. Observing a person's movements.

चेष्टित p. p. (f. —ता) Moved, stirred &c. —तं n. 1 Motion, gesture, act. -2 Doing, action, behaviour.

चैतन्यं n. 1 Spirit, life, intelligence,

vitality, sensation. -2 Soul, spirit, mind. -3 Consciousness, sensation, sense. -4 (In Vedânta phil.) The Supreme Spirit considered as the essence of all being and source of all sensation. —न्यः *m.* N. of a modern reformer of the Vaishnava faith.

चैत्यः *m.* 1 The individual soul. -2 A pile of stones forming a landmark. -3 A monument, tomb-stone. -4 A sacrificial shed. -5 A place of religious worship, temple. -6 A reflection. -7 A religious fig-tree or any tree growing by the side of streets. -Comp. —तरुः, -द्रुमः, -वृक्षः *m.* A fig-tree standing on a sacred spot. —पालः *m.* The guardian of a sanctuary. —मुखः *m.* A hermit's waterpot. —अग्निः *m.* The sacred and sacrificial fire kept burning in चैत्य which is a sacred place. This चैत्याग्नि is generally known as गार्हपत्य, आहवनीय and दाक्षिण. Any fire other than चैत्याग्नि is लौकिकः अग्निः ordinary fire.

चैत्रः *m.* 1 N. of a lunar month in which the full moon stands in the constellation Chitrâ (corresponding to March-April). -2 A Buddhist mendicant. -3 One of the seven ranges of mountains dividing the continent into 'Varshas.' —त्रं *n.* A temple, monument for the dead. -Comp. —आवलिः *f.* The full-moon-day of Chaitra. —सखः *m.* An epithet of the god of love.

चैत्रिः, चैत्रिकः, चैत्रिन् *m.* The month called Chaitra.

चैत्री *f.* The day of full-moon in the month of Chaitra.

चैत्ररथं (-थ्यं) *n.* N. of the garden of Kubera.

चैद्यः *m.* N. of Sisupâla.

चैलं *n.* A piece of cloth, garment. -Comp. —धावः *m.* A washerman.

चोक्ष *a.* (*f.* —क्षा) 1 Pure, clean. -2 Honest. 3 Clever, skilful. -4 Pleasing; delightful. -5 Sharp, pungent, keen.

चोचं *n.* 1 A bark, rind. -2 Skin, hide. -3 The cocoa-nut.

चोटी *f.* A petticoat.

चोडः *m.* A bodice; चोडी *f.* also.

चोदनं *n.* 1 The act of driving. -2 Invitation. -3 Order, rule, precept.

चोदना *f.* 1 Sending, directing, throwing. -2 Urging onward. -3 Promoting, encouraging, inspiration. -4 A precept, sacred commandment. Comp. —गुडः *m.* A ball for playing with.

चोदित *a.* (*f.* —ता) 1 Sent, directed. -2 Urged on, driven. -3 Incited, prompted, inspired. -4 Put forward as an argument. -5 Thrown, cast. -6 Appointed -7 Ordered, directed.

चोद्यं *n.* 1 Objecting, asking a question. -2 An objection. -3 Wonder, surprise.

चो (चौ-) रः *m.* 1 A thief, robber. -2 Any dishonest dealer. -3 One that steals or captivates the heart. -Comp. —कर्मन् *n.* Theft. —गत *a.* Robbed. —रूपः *m.* A clever thief.

चो (चौ-) रिका *f.* Theft, robbery.

चोरित *a.* Stolen, robbed. —तं *n.* Theft.

चोरितकं *n.* 1 Petty theft, larceny. -2 Anything stolen.

चोलः *m* (*m.pl.* चोलाः) N. of a country in southern India, the modern Tanjore. —लः *m.*, —ली *f.* 1 A short jacket, a bodice. -2 A garment reaching to the feet. —लं *n.* A garment.

चोलकः *m.* 1 A breast-plate. -2 A bark-dress. -3 A bodice. —कं *n.* Bark, rind.

चोलकिन् *m.* 1 A soldier armed with a breast-plate. -2 The orange tree.

चोलं (-लों-) डुकः *m.* A fillet for the head, a turban, tiara or diadem.

चोषः *m.* 1 Sucking. -2 Inflammation (in medicine). -3 Drying up.

चोष्यं *n.* The same as चूष्य q. v.

चौड (*f.* —डी), चौल (*f.* —ली) *a.* 1 Crested. -2 Relating to tonsure. -डं, -लं *n.* The ceremony of tonsure.

चौर्यं *n.* 1 Theft, robbery. -2 Trickery. -3 Secrecy, concealment. -Comp. —रतं *n.* A secret sexual enjoyment. —वृत्तिः *f.* The habit of robbery.

च्यवनं *n.* 1 Moving, motion. -2 Loss, deprivation. -3 Dying, perishing. -4 Sinking, falling. -5 Departure, deviation. -6 Flowing, trickling.

च्यु 1 A. (च्यवते, च्युत) 1 To fall or drop down, slip, sink (fig. also). -2 To flow or issue from, drop, trickle or stream forth from. -3 To swerve from, fall off or away from (duty &c., with abl.). -4 To lose, be deprived of. -5 To disappear, perish. -6 To decrease. -*Caus.* (च्यावयति-ते).

च्यु 10 P. (च्यावयति) 1 To suffer, bear. -2 To laugh.

च्युत् 1 P. (च्योतति) 1 To drop, flow, trickle, stream forth. -2 To drop or fall down. -3 To cause to drop or stream forth. -4 To moisten.

च्युत *p. p.* (*f.* —ता) 1 Fallen down. -2 Removed, expelled. -3 Deviated from. -4 Deprived. -5 Broken, disordered. -6 Dropped, oozed out. -7 Lost, gone, perished. -8 Moved, shaken. -Comp. —आत्मन् *a.* Of a depraved soul, evil-minded.

च्युतिः *f.* 1 Falling down, a fall. -2 Deviation from. -3 Dropping, oozing. -4 Losing, deprivation. -5 Vanishing, perishing. -6 The vulva. -7 The anus. -8 Quick motion.

च्यूतः *m.* The mango tree.

छ.

छगः *m.* (*f.* —गी) A goat.

छगलः *m.* 1 A goat. -2 N. of the sage Atri. -3 N. of a country. —ला, —ली *f.* A she-goat. -लं *n.* A blue cloth.

छगलकः *m.* A goat.

छटा *f.* 1 Mass, number, assemblage. -2 A collection of rays of light, lustre, splendour, light. -3 A continuous line, streak. -Comp. —आभा *f.* Lightning. —फलः *m.* The betel-nut tree.

छत्रः *m.* A mushroom. —त्रं *n.* 1 A parasol, an umbrella. -Comp. —धारणं *n.* 1 Carrying or bearing an umbrella. -2 Carrying an umbrella as a type of royal authority. —पतिः *m.* 1 A king over whom an umbrella is carried as a mark of dignity, a sovereign, emperor. -2 N. of an ancient king in जंबुद्वीप. —भंगः *m.* 1 'Destruction of the royal parasol', loss of dominion, deposition. -2 Dependence. -3 A forlorn condition, widowhood.

छत्रकः *m.* 1 A temple in honour of Siva. -2 A bee-hive of a conical form. -3 A king-fisher. —त्रिका *f.* Mushroom. —कं *n.* A mushroom.

छत्रा *f.* छत्राकः *m.* A mushroom; also छत्राकी-कं.

छत्रिकः *m.* The bearer of an umbrella.

छत्रिन् *a.* (*f.* —णी) Having or bearing an umbrella. —*m.* A barber.

छत्वरः *m.* 1 A house. -2 A bower.

छद् 1, 10 U. (छदति-ते, छादयति-ते, छन्न, छादित) 1 To cover, cover over, veil.

-2 To hide, conceal. (fig.); To keep secret.

छद: *m.*, -छदनं *n.* 1 A covering, cover. -2 A wing. -3 A leaf. -4 A sheath, case. -Comp. —पत्र: *m.* The Bhúrja tree.

छदि: *f.*, —छदिस् *n.* 1 The roof of a carriage. -2 The roof or thatch of a house.

छद्म *n.* 1 A deceptive dress, a disguise. -2 A plea, pretext, guise. -3 Fraud, dishonesty, trick. -4 The thatch or roof of a house. -Comp. —तापस: *m.* A religious hypocrite. —रूपेण *ind.* In disguise. —वेशिन् *m.* A player, a cheat, one dressed in disguise.

छद्मिन *a.* (*f.* —नी) 1 Fraudulent, deceitful. -2 Disguised (at the end of comp.) *e. g.* ब्राह्मणछद्मिन् Disguised as a Brâhmana.

छनच्छन *ind.* An imitative sound, expressive of the noise of falling drops &c.

छंद् 10 U. (छंदयति-ते, छंदित) 1 To please, gratify. -2 To persuade, coax. -3 To cover. -4 To be delighted in.

छंद: *m.* 1 Wish, desire; fancy, liking, will. -2 Free will, whim, free or wilful conduct. स्वच्छंदं *ind.* According to one's free will, independently. -3 Subjection, control. -4 Meaning, intention. -5 Poison. -6 Appearance, look, shape. -7 Pleasure, delight. -Comp.—अनुवृत्तं *n.*, -त्ति: *f.* Indulgence of whims, humouring, compliance.

छंदस् *n.* 1 Wish, desire, will, pleasure. -2 Free will, free or wilful conduct. -3 Meaning, intention. -4 Fraud, deceit. -5 The Vedas, the sacred text of the Vedic hymns. -6 A metre. -7 Metrical science, prosody (regarded as one of the six Vedângas or auxiliaries to the Vedas, the other five being शिक्षा, व्याकरण, कल्प, निरुक्त and ज्योतिष), -Comp. —कृतं *n.* Any metrical part of the Vedas or other sacred compositions. —ग: (छंदोग:) *m.* 1 A reciter in metre. -2 A student or chanter of the Sâmaveda. -भंग: *m.* A violation of the laws of metre. —वृत्तं *n.* A metre in general.

छन्न *a.* (*f.* -न्ना) 1 Covered. -2 Secret, concealed.

छमंड: *m.* 1 An orphan. -2 A single man ; one who has no relative.

छर्द् 10 U. (छर्दित) To vomit.

छर्द: *m.*, छर्दनं *n.*, छर्दि:, छर्दिका *f.* Vomiting.

छर्दिस् *f.* Vomiting.

छल: *m.*, —लं *n.* 1 Fraud, trick, deceit, deception. -2 Roguery, knavery. -3 A plea, pretext, guise, semblance (often used in this sense to denote an उत्प्रेक्षा). -4 Intention. -5 Wickedness. [cheat.

छलय् Den. P. To outwit, deceive,

छलनं *n.*, -ना *f.* 1 Deceiving, cheating, outwitting. -2 Fraud, trick.

छालिक्यं *n.* A kind of drama or dancing.

छलिन् *m.* A cheat, rogue.

छल्लि:, -ल्ली *f.* 1 Bark, rind. -2 A spreading creeper. -3 Offspring, progeny, posterity.

छवि: *f.* 1 Hue, colour of the skin, complexion. -2 Colour in general. -3 Beauty, splendour, brilliance. -4 Light, lustre. -5 Skin, hide.

छाग *a.* (*f.* —गी) Retating to a goat or she-goat. —ग: *m.* (*f.* -गी) 1 A goat. -2 The sign Aries of the zodiac. —गं *n.* 1 The milk of a she-goat. -2 An oblation. -Comp. —भोजिन् m. A wolf. —मुखः m. An epithet of Kârtikeya. -रथः, -वाहनः m. An epithet of Agni, the god of fire.

छागणः m. A fire of dried cowdung.

छागल a. (f. -ली) Coming from or relating to a goat. —लः m. A goat.

छागिका f. A she-goat.

छात a. (f. -ता) 1 Cut, divided. -2 Feeble, thin, emaciated (p. p. of छो q. v.).

छात्रः m. A pupil, disciple. —त्रं n. A kind of honey. -Comp. —गंडः m. An indifferent student of poetry knowing only the beginnings of stanzas. —दर्शनं n. Fresh butter prepared from millk one day old. —व्यंसकः m. A roguish or dull-witted pupil.

छादं n. A thatch, roof.

छादनं n. 1 A cover, screen (fig. also). -2 Concealing. -3 A leaf. -4 Clothing. -5 Darkening. —नी f. Hide, skin.

छादित a. (f. —ता) See छन्न.

छाद्मिकः m. A rogue.

छांदस a. (f. -सी)1 Vedic, peculiar to the Vedas. -2 Studying or familiar with the Vedas. -3 Metrical. —सः m. A Brâhmana versed in the Vedas.

छाया f. Shade, shadow (changed at the end of Tat. comp. into छायं when बाहुल्य or thickness of shade is meant. -2 A reflected image, a reflection. -3 Resemblance, likeness. -4 A hallucination. -5 Blending of colours. -6 Lustre, light -7 Colour. -8 Colour of the face, complexion. -9 Beauty. 10 Protection. -11 A row, line. -12 Darkness. -13 A bribe. -14 N. of Durgâ. -15 N. of a wife of the sun, mother of Saturn. -Comp. —अंकः m. The moon. -आत्मन् m. A reflected image or form. -करः m. The bearer of an umbrella. -ग्रहः m. A mirror. —तनयः, —सुतः आत्मजः m. Saturn, son of छाया. -तरुः, -द्रुमः m. A large umbrageous tree. -द्वितीय a. 'Accompanied only by one's shadow', alone. -पथः m. The galaxy, the atmosphere. -भृत् m. The moon. —मानः m. The moon. (-नं n.) A measure of shadow. —मित्रं n. A parasol. —मृगधरः m. The moon. -यंत्रं n. Sun-dial.

छिः f. Abuse, reproach.

छिक्का f. Sneezing.

छित a. (f. —ता) See छात.

छितिः f. Cutting, dividing.

छित्वर a. (f. —री) 1 Fit for cutting.-2 Hostile, fraudulent, roguish.

छिद् 7 U. (छिनत्ति, छिंत्ते, छेत्तुं, छिन्न) 1 To cut, cut or lop off, hew, mow, tear, pierce, break, asunder, split, divide. -2 To disturb, interrupt (as sleep). -3 To drive off, destroy, annihilate. -4 To take away, remove, deprive one of.

छिद् a. (At the end of comp.) Cutting, dividing, destroying, removing. -m. The divisor, denominator.

छिद्कं n. 1 Indra's thunderbolt.-2 A diamond.

छिदा f. Cutting, dividing.

छिदिः f. 1 An axe. -2 Indra's thunderbolt. -3 Cutting off.

छिदिरः m. 1 An axe. -2 A sword. -3 Fire. -4 A rope, cord.

छिदुर (f. -रा) 1 Cutting. -2 Easily breaking. -3 Broken, disordered. -4 Hostile. -5 Roguish, knavish.

छिद्र a. (f. —द्रा) Pierced, containing holes. —द्रं n. 1 A hole, crack, cleft, fissure, rent, pit, opening.-2 A defect, blemish. -3 A vulnerable or weak point, weak side, imperfection, foible -4 (Astr.) N. of the eighth house. -Comp. —अनुजीविन्, –अनुसंधानिन्, –अनुसारिन्, –अन्वेषिन् *a.* 1 Looking out for faults or flaws. -2 Seeking the weak points of another. —अंतर् *m.* A cane, reed. —आत्मन् *a.* One who exposes his weak points to the attack of others. -कर्ण *a.* Having the ear pierced. —दर्शन *a* 1 Exhibiting faults. -2 Seeking the weak points. —दर्शिन् *a.* Observing faults.

छिद्रित *a.* (*f.* —ता) 1 Having holes. -2 Bored, perforated.

छिन्न *p. p.* (*f.*—न्ना) 1 Cut, divided, torn, broken. -2 Destroyed, removed. -3 Decaying, declining. -4 Exhausted, fatigued. —न्ना *f.* A whore, harlot. -Comp. —केश *a.* Shorn, shaven. —द्वैध *a.* Whose doubt is dispelled. —भिन्न *a.* Cut up through and through, mutilated, cut up. -मस्त: -मस्तक *a.* Decapitated. (*f.* -स्ता, -का) A headless form of Durgâ.-श्वास: *m.* A kind of asthma. —संशय *a.* 'One whose doubt is dispelled' free from doubt, confirmed.

छुछुंदर: *m.* (*f* -री)The musk-rat.

छुप: *m.* 1 Touch.-2 A shrub, bush. -3 Combat, war. -4 Air, wind.

छुर् 1 P. (छोरति, छुरित) 1 To cut, divide. -2 To engrave.

छुर् 6 P. (छुरति, छुरित) 1 To cover, smear, inlay. -2 To intermix. —*Caus.* (छोरयति, छुरयति) 1 To inlay, set with mosaic ornaments. -2 To overspread. -3 To besmear.

छुरणं *n.* 1 Smearing, anointing. -2 Overspreading.

छुरा *f.* Lime.

छुरिका *f.* A knife.

छुरित *p. p.* (*f.* -ता) 1 Set inlaid, strewed, interset with. -2 Overspread, coated, covered over with. -3 Blended, intermixed.-4 Besmeared, anointed. -5 Cut.

छुरी, छुरिका, छूरी *f.* A knife.

छृद् 1 P., 10 U. (छर्दति, छर्दयति-ते)To kindle.

छृद् 7 P. (छृणत्ति, छृण्ण) 1 To play. -2 To shine. -3 To vomit. —*Caus.* (छर्दयति-ते) 1 To pour out. -2 To spit out, eject, vomit. -3 To kindle, light.

छेक *a.* (*f.* —का) 1 Tame, domesticated (as a beast). -2 Town-bred, trained in the acuteness and vice of towns. —क: *m.* 1 A bee. -Comp. —अनुप्रास: *m.* One of the several kinds of अनुप्रास. This kind of अनुप्रास consists in a single repetition of two or more consonants. —अपह्नुति: *f.* A figure of speech ; one of the varieties of अपह्नुति. The Chandrâloka thus defines and illustrates it :- छेकापह्नुतिरन्यस्य शंकातस्तस्य निह्नवे । प्रजल्पन्मत्पदे लग्नः कांतः किं न हिं नूपुरः. -उक्ति: *f.* Insinuation, *double entendre.*

छेद: *m.* 1 Cutting, breaking, dividing. -2 Solving, removing, clearing; as in संशयछेद. -3 Destruction, interruption. -4 Cessation, end, disappearance, as in धर्मच्छेद. -5 A distinguishing mark. -6 A cut, an incision. -7 Deprivation, want, deficiency. -8 Failure as in संततिच्छेद. -9 A piece, bit, fragment, section. -10 (In math.) A divisor, the denominator of a fraction. -Comp. —कर: *m.* A wood-cutter.

छेदक *a.* Cutting off, dividing. —क *m.* The denominator of a fraction.

छेदनं *n.* 1 Cutting asunder, dividing, splitting.-2Cutting, tearing, cutting off, dividing. -3 A section, portion, bit, part. -4 Destruction, removal. -5 Division.

छेदि: *m.*1 A carpenter. -2 Indra's [thunderbolt.

छेद्य *p. p.* (*f.* —द्या To be cut or divided, divisible.-द्यं *n.* Amputation.

छेमंड: *m.* An orphan.

छेलक: *m.* A goat.

छेदिक: *m.* A cane.

छो 4 P. (छ्यति, अच्छात्-अच्छासीत्, छात, or छित, *caus.* छाययति) To cut, mow, reap.

छोटिका *f* Snapping the thumb and fore-finger together (Mar. चुटकी or चिटकी).

छोरणं *n.* Abandoning, leaving.

ज.

ज *a.* 1 (At the end of comp.) Born from or in, produced or caused by, living or being at or in. -ज: *m.* 1 A father. -2 Production, birth. -3 Poison. -4 An imp or goblin. -5 A conqueror.

ज: *m.* (In prosody) One of the eight syllabic feet (गण).

जकुट: *m.* 1 The Malaya mountain. -2 A dog.

जक्ष् 2 P. (जक्षिति, जक्षित or जग्ध) To eat, eat up, destroy, consume.

जक्षणं *n.*, जक्षि: *f.* Eating, consuming.

जगत् *a.* (*f.* -ती) Moving, movable. -*n.* The world, the universe. —ती *n. dual* Heaven and the lower world. -Comp. —अंबा,-अंबिका *f.* N. of Durgâ. —आत्मन् *m.* The Supreme Spirit. —आदि:, -आदिज: *m.* The Supreme Deity.-आदिज: *m.* An epithet of Siva. —आधार: *m.* 1 Time. -2 Air, wind. —आयु:, -आयुस् *m.* Wind. —ईश:, -पति: *m.* The lord of ' the universe, ' the Supreme Deity; an epithet of Vishnu and Shiva. —उद्धार: *m.* Salvation of the world. -कर्तृ, -धातृ *m.* 1 The creator of the world. -2. Brahman (*m.*) -3 Vishnu. —चक्षुस् *m.* The sun. —दीप: *m.* The sun. -धात्री *f.* 1 Durgâ. -2 Sarasvatî. —नाथ: *m.* 1 The lord of the universe. -2 Vishnu.-3 Dattâtreya. -4 N. of a country. -5 N. of an idol at Jagannâtha. -6 N. of a poet. -निवास: *m.* 1 The Supreme Being. -2 An epithet of Vishnu. -प्राण:,-बल: *m.* The wind. -मातृ *f.* 1 Durgâ. -2 Lakshmî. —योनि: *f.* 1 The Supreme Being. -2 An epithet of Vishnu.-3 of Siva.-4 of Brahman (*m.*)(-नि: *f.*) The earth.—वहा *f.* The earth. —साक्षिन् *m.* 1 The Supreme Spirit. -2 The sun. —सेतु: *m.* The Supreme Being.

जगती *f.* The earth. -2 People, mankind. -3 A cow. -4 A kind of metre. -Comp. —अधीश्वर:, -ईश्वर: *m.* A king. —धर: *m.* A mountain. -रुह् *m.* A tree.

जगनु: (-नू:) *m.* 1 Fire. -2 An insect. -3 An animal.

जगर: *m.* An armour.

जगल *a.* (*f.* —ला) Roguish, tricky, knavish. -लं *n.* 1 Cowdung. -2 An armour. -3 A kind of liquor (*m.* also in the last two senses.).

जग्ध *a.* (*f.* —ग्धा) Eaten.

जग्धि: *f.* 1 Eating.-2Food, victuals.

जग्मि: *m.* Wind, air.

जघनं *n.* 1 The hip and the loins, the buttocks. -2 The pudenda. -3 Rear-guard, the reserve of an army. -Comp. —अर्ध: *m.* 1 The hinder part. -2 Rear-guard. —कूपकौ *m. dual* The hollows of the loins of a handsome woman. —चपला *f.* 1 An unchaste or libidinous woman. -2 A woman active in dancing.

जघन्य *a.* (*f.* —न्या) 1 Hindmost, last. -2 Worst, vilest, base, lowest, -3 Of low origin or rank. —न्य: *m.*

A Sudra. —Comp. —जः *m.* 1 A younger brother. -2 A Sudra.

जाघ्निः *m.*1 A weapon (offensive).

जघ्नु *a.* Striking, killing.

जंगम *a.* (*f.* —मा) Moving, living, movable (opp. immovable स्थावर). —मं *n.* A movable thing.—Comp- —इतर *a.* Immovable. —कुटी *f.* An umbrella.

जंगलं *n.* 1 A desert, dreary ground, waste land. -2 A thicket, forest.-3 A secluded or unfrequented place.

जंगालः *m.* A ridge of earth running along the edge of a field to collect water and form a passage over it; land-mark.

जंगुलं *n.* Poison, venom.

जंघा *f.* 1 Leg from the ankle to the knee, the shank. -2 The upper part of the leg, the part about the loins. -3 A part of a bed-stead. -Comp. —करः,-करिकः,-कारः, -कारिकः *m.* A runner, courier, an express.-त्राणं *n.* An armour for the legs.

जंघाल *a.* (*f.* —ला) Running swiftly, rapid. —लः *m.* 1 A courier. -2 A deer, an antelope.

जंघिल *a.* (*f.* —ला) Running swiftly, rapid, quick.

जज्, जंज् 1 P. (जजति or जंजति) To fight.

जट् 1 P. (जटति) To clot, become twisted or matted together(as hair).

जटा *f.* 1 The hair matted and twisted together, matted or clotted hair. -2 A fibrous root. -3 A particular manner of reciting Vedic texts. -4 A root in general. -5 A branch. -6 The शतावरी plant. -Comp. —चीरः,-टंकः, -टीरः,-धरः *m.* Epithets of Siva. —जूटः *m.* 1 A mass of twisted hair (in general). -2 The twisted hair of Siva. -ज्वालः *m.* A lamp. —धर *a.* Wearing matted hair. (-रः *m.*) A mendicant or ascetic.

जटायुः,जटायुस् *m.* A son of Syeni and Aruna, a semi-divine bird.

जटाल *a.* (*f.* -ला) 1 Wearing a coil of twisted hair. -2 Collected together (like matted hair). —लः *m.* The (Indian) fig-tree. -2 Bdellium.

जटिः (-टी) *f.* 1 The (Indian) fig-tree. -2 Clotted hair. -3 An assemblage, multitude.

जटिन् (*f.* -नी) *a.* Having twisted hair. —*m.* 1 An epithet of Siva. -2 The waved-leaf fig-tree (प्लक्ष). -3 An elephant sixty years old.

जटिल *a.* (*f.* —ला) 1 Wearing matted or twisted hair (as an ascetic). -2 Complicated, confused, intermixed, intermingled, irregularly mixed. -3 Dense, impervious. —लः *m.* 1 A lion. -2 A goat. -3 An ascetic. -4 A Brâhmana in the first period of his life.

जठर *a.* (*f.* —रा) 1 Hard, stiff, firm. -2 Old. -3 Bound, tied. —रः *m* , -रं *n.* 1 The stomach, belly, abdomen. -2 The womb. -3 A hole, cavity. -4 The interior of anything. -5 The bosom. -6 Morbid affection of the bowels. -Comp. —अग्निः *m.* The digestive fire of the stomach, the gastric fluid. -आमयः *m.* Dropsy. -ज्वाला, -व्यथा *f.* Belly-ache, colic. —यंत्रणा, -यातना *f.* The pain endured by the child in the womb.

जड *a.* (*f.* -डा) 1 Cold, frigid, chilly. -2 Dull,motionless, benumbed. -3 Dull, senseless, stupid, irrational, dull-witted. -4 Dulled,made senseless; devoid of appreciation or taste. -5 Stunning, benumbing, stupefying. -6 Dumb. -7 Unable to learn the Vedas. —डः *m.* 1 Cold, frost, winter. -2 Idiocy, stupidity.

-3 Dulness, apathy, sluggishness. —डं n. 1 Water. -2 Lead.

जडता f.,-त्वं n. 1 Dulness, slothfulness. -2 Ignorance, stupidity. -3 (In Rhet.) Dulness, regarded as one of the 33 subordinate feelings. -4 Stupefaction, numbness, stupor. -5 Dulness, timidity.

जाडिमन् m. 1 Frigidity. -2 Stupidity. -3 Dulness, apathy. -4 Stupor, stupefaction.

जतु n. The red resin of certain trees. -Comp. -अश्मन् n. Red arsenic. —पुत्रकः m. A man at chess &c. —रसः m. Lac.

जतुकं n. Lac.

जतुका f 1 Lac. -2 A bat.

जतुनी, जतुका f. A bat.

जत्रु n. The collar-bone, The clavicle (जत्रुकं also).

जन् 4 A. (जायते, जात. *Caus.* जनयति ; *Pass.* जन्यते, जायते). 1 To be born or produced. -2 To grow, to be, to become. With अनु— 1 To be born afterwards. -2 To be born similar to. अभि— 1 To be born or produced. -2 To be or become. -3 To be turned into. -4 To be born of a high family. उप— 1 To grow, to arise. -2 To be born. -3 To be or become. प्र—, वि—, सम्—1 To grow, arise. -2 To be born or produced.

जनः m. 1 A person (male of female). In this sense जन may stand for the 1 st *pers. pron.* -2 The people, the populace. -3 The world beyond the महर्लोक ; The heaven of deified mortals. -Comp. -अतिग a. Extraordinary, uncommon, superhuman. —अधिपः, -अधिनाथः m. A king. -अंतः m. 1 A place removed from men ; an uninhabited place. -2 A region. -3 An epithet of Yama. -अंतिकं n. Secret communication, whispering —अंतिकं ind. Aside (in theatrical language). —अर्दनः m. An epithet of Vishnu or Krishna -अशनः m. A wolf. —आकीर्ण a. Crowded, full of people. —आश्रयः m. A pavilion. -इंद्रः, -ईशः, ईश्वरः m. A king. —इष्ट a. Liked by people. (-ष्टः m.) A kind of jasmine. —उदाहरणं n. Glory, fame. —ओघः m. A crowd, a mob. —कारिन् m. Lac. —चक्षुस् n. The sun. —ता f. 1 A number of men; a community, mankind. -2 The subjects of a king collectively. -3 Birth. -त्रा f. An umbrella. —देवः m. A king. -पदः m. A nation, a community, (*sing or pl.*) -2 An empire, an inhabited country. -3 The subject (*opp.* to king). -4 Country (*opp.* to the town or city). —पदिन् m. The ruler of a country. -प्रवादः m. 1 Rumour, report. -2 A scandal —रवः m. 1 Rumour. -2 Calumny, scandal. -लोकः m. One of the seven divisions of the universe situated above महर्लोक. जनवादः, जनेवादः m 1 News, rumour. -2 Scandal. -व्यवहारः m. Popular usage. -श्रुत a. Famous -श्रुति f. Rumour, report. —संबाध a. Densely crowded by people. -स्थानं n. N. of a part of the Dandakâ forest.

जनक a. (f. —निका) Producing, causing, generating. (-कः m) 1 A father -2 N of a famous king of Videha. —आत्मजा, -तनया, -सुता, -नंदिनी, -कन्या f. An epithet of Sita, daughter of king Janak.

जननं n. 1 Birth. -2 Life, duration of life. -3 Race, family. -4 Rise, production, origin, creation. -5 Appearance, manifestation.

जनानिः f. 1 A mother. -2 Birth.

जननी f. 1 A mother. -2 Mercy,

tenderness, compassion. -3 A bat. -4 Lac.

जनायितृ a. (f. —त्री) Producing, begetting, creator. -m. A father.

जनायित्री f. A mother.

जनर्, जनस् n. The world beyond महर्लोक; The heaven of deified mortals.

जनि:, जनिका, जनी f. 1 Birth, creation, production. -2 A woman. -3 A mother. -4 A wife. -5 A daughter-in-law.

जनित a. (f. -ता) 1 Given birth to. -2 Produced, created. -3 Occasioned, caused.

जनितृ m. A father.

जनित्री f. A mother.

जनु: (-नू:) f. Birth, production.

जनुस् n. 1 Birth. -2 Creation, production. -3 Life, existence. -4 Nativity. -5 Birth-place. -6 A creature, being. -7 Genus, kind. -Comp. जनुरंध a. Blind from birth, born blind.

जंतु: m. 1 A creature, a living being, man. -2 The (individual) soul. -3 An animal of the lowest organization. -Comp. —कंबु: m. 1 A snail's shell. -2 A snail. —फल: m. The Udumbara tree.

जंतुका f. Lac.

जन्मं n. Birth.

जन्मन् n. 1 Birth. -2 Origin, rise, production, creation. -3 Life, existence. -4 Birth place. -5 Nativity. -6 A father, progenitor. —Comp. —आधिप: m. 1 An epithet of Siva. -2 The regent of a constellation under which a person is born (in astrology). —अंतरं n. 1 Another life. -2 The preceding life, former birth. -3 Regeneration. -4 The other world. —अंतरिय a. Belonging to or done in another life. —अंध: a. Born blind. —अष्टमी f. The eighth day of the dark fortnight of Srâvana, the birth-day of Krishna. —कील: m. An epithet of Vishnu. —कुंडली f. A diagram in a horoscope in which the positions of different planets at the time of one's birth are marked. —कृत m. A father. —क्षेत्रं n. Birth-place. —तिथि: m., f., —दिनं n. —दिवस: m. Birth-day. —द: m. A father. —नक्षत्रं, -भं n. The natal star. That lunar mansion through which the moon passes on the day on which a person is born. जन्मनक्षत्रक्रिया f. The ceremony of performing religious rites befitting such a day. -नामन् n. The name received on the 12th day after birth. —प: m. The regent of a planet under which a person is born. —पत्रं n.; -पत्रिका f. A horoscope. -पादप: m. A family-tree. -प्रतिष्ठा f. 1 A birth-place. -2 A mother. —भाज्, -भृत m. A creature, living being. —भाषा f. A mother-tongue. -भूमि: f. Birth-place, native country. —योग: m. A horoscope. —रोगिन् a. Sickly from birth. —लग्नं n., -राशि: m. Sign of the zodiac under which a person is born. -वर्त्मन् n. The vulva. —शोधनं n. Discharging the obligations derived from birth. —साफल्यं n. Attainment of the ends of existence. —स्थानं n. Birth-place, native country, home. -2 The womb. —हेतु: m. The cause of birth, author of one's being.

जन्मिन् m. A creature, a living being.

जन्य a. (f. -न्या) 1 To be born or produced. -2 Born, produced. -3 (At the end of comp.) Born from, occasioned by. -4 Belonging to a race or family. -5 Vulgar, common. -6 National. —न्य: m. 1 A father.

-2 A friend, attendant or relative of a bridegroom. -3 A common man. -4 A report, rumour. —न्यं *n.* 1 Birth, production, creation. -2 A created thing, an effect(opp. जनक). -3 The body. -4 A portent occurring at birth. -5 A market, a fair. -6 War, battle. -7 Censure, abuse. -8 A community, nation. -9 People. -10 Report, rumour. -न्या *f.* 1 The friend of a mother. -2 The relation of a bride; a bride, a bride's maid. -3 Pleasure, happiness. -4 Affection.

जन्युः *m.* 1 Birth. -2 A creature, living being. -3 Fire. -4 The creator or Brahman.(*m.*).

जप् 1 P. 1 To utter in a low voice, repeat internally, mutter. -2 To mutter prayers or spells. -3 To pray to one or invoke in a low voice. With उप— To whisper into the ears ; to bring over to one's party by secretly suggesting anything in the ear, to rouse to rebellion.

जपः *m.* 1 Muttering prayers, repeating prayers &c. in an undertone. -2 Repeating passages of the Veda or names of deites &c. -3 A muttered prayer. -4 Counting silently the beads of a rosary &c. -Comp. -परायण *a.* Engaged in muttering prayers. -माला *f.* A rosary of beads. —यज्ञः, -होमः *m. m.* Muttering prayers as a sacrifice.

जपनं *n.* The muttering of prayers.

जपा *f.* The China rose (the plant or its flower.).

जप्य *a.* (*f.* —प्या) To be repeated in a low voice, to be muttered, or whispered. —प्यः *m.*, -प्यं *n.* A muttered prayer.

जभ्, जंभ् 1 P. (जभति; जंभति) To copulate.

जभ् 1 A. (जभते, जंभते) 1 To yawn, gape. -2 To snap at ; seize with the mouth. -*Caus.* (जंभयति) To crush, destroy, dispel.

जम् 1 P. (जमति) To eat.

जमदग्निः *m.* A Bráhmana and descendant of Bhrigu and father of Parasurâma.

जमनं *n.* Same as जेमनं.

जंपती *m. dual.* Husband and wife.

जंबालः *m.* 1 Mud. -2 Moss. -3 The Ketaka plant.

जंबालिनी *f.* A river.

जंबीरः *m.* The citron tree. —रं *n.* A citron.

जंबुः, -बूः *f.* 1 The rose apple tree and its fruit. -Comp. —खंडः,-द्वीपः, -पर्वतः *m.* N. of one of the seven continents surrounding the mountain Meru. —नदी *f.* One of the seven heavenly rivers.

जंबु (-बू-) कः (*f.* -की) 1 A jackal. -2 A low man. -3 The rose apple tree. -4 An epithet of Varuna.

जंबुमत् *m.* 1 A mountain. -2 A monkey. —ती *f.* A heavenly nymph.

जंबुलः, जंबूलः *m.* 1 kind of tree. -2 The Ketaka plant. —लं *n.* Jests addressed to the bride and the bridegroom by their friends and female relatives. -Comp. —मालिका *f.* The same as above.

जंभः *m.* 1 The jaws (usually in pl.). -2 A tooth. -3 Eating. -4 Biting asunder. -5 A part, portion. -6 A quiver. -7 The chin. -8 Yawning, gaping. -9 N. of a demon killed by Indra. -10 The citron tree. -Comp. -अरातिः, -द्विष्, -भेदिन्, -रिपुः *m.* Epithets of Indra. -अरिः *m.* 1 Fire. -2 Indra's thunderbolt. -3 Indra. [or citron.

जंभकः *m.* 1 Yawning. -2 A lime

जंभका, जंभा, जंभिका *f.* A yawn, gaping. [tree.

जंभ (-भी-) रः *m.* The lime or citron.

जयः *m.* Conquest, triumph, victory, success, winning (in battle, game or a law-suit). -2 Restraint, curbing, conquest as in इंद्रियजय. -3 N. of the sun. -4 N. of Jayanta, son of Indra. -5 N. of Yudhishthira the first Pândava prince. -6 N. of an attendant of Vishnu. -7 An epithet of Arjuna.-Comp. आवह *a.* Conferring victory. —आशिस् *f.* 1 A prayer for victory. -2 Congratulations after victory; a cheer of victory. —उद्धुर *a.* Exulting in victory. —कोलाहल: *m.* 1 A shout of victory. -2 A kind of game with dice. —घोषः *m*, -घोषणं *n.* —णा *f.* A proclamation of victory. —ढक्का *f.* A kind of drum beaten as a sign of victory. -दत्तः *m.* N. of Jayanta, Indra's son. -पत्रं *n.* Record of victory. —पालः *m.* 1 A king. -2 An epithet of Brahman (*m.*) -3 An epithet of Vishnu. —पुत्रकः *m.* A kind of dice. —मंगलः *m.* 1 A royal elephant. -2 A remedy for fever. (-लं *n.*) A cheer of victory. —यज्ञः *m.* The अश्वमेध sacrifice. -लक्ष्मीः,-श्रीः *f.* The goddess of victory. —वाहिनी *f.* An epithet of Sachi. —शब्दः *m.* 1 A shout of victory. -2 The exclamation '*jaya*' (hail! glory!) uttered by bards &c. -शृंगं *n.* A horn blown to announce a victory. -स्तंभः *m.* A trophy, a column erected to commemorate a victory, a triumphal column. -स्वामिन् *m.* An epithet of Siva.

जयत्सेनः *m.* A name assumed by Nakula while living at Viráta's house.

जयद्रथः *m.* A king of the Sindhu district and brother-in-law of Duryodhan.

जयद्बलः *m.* A name assumed by Sahadeva.

जयनं *n.* 1 Conquering, subduing. -2 Armour for cavalry, elephants. &c. -Comp. -युज् *a.* 1 Caparisoned. -2 Victorious.

जयंतः *m.* 1 N. of the son of Indra. -2 N. of Siva. -3 The moon. -4 N. of Vishnu. -5 A name assumed by Bhima at the court of Viráta. -Comp. —पत्रं *n.* (in law) 1 The written award of the judge in favour of either party.-2 The label on the fore-head of a horse turned loose for the Asvamedha sacrifice.

जयंती *f.* 1 A flag or banner. -2 N. of the daughter of Indra. -3 N. of Durgá.

जया *f.* 1 N. of Durgâ. -2 N. of an attendant of the goddess Durgâ. -3 A kind of banner. -4 The third, eighth or thirteenth lunar days of any of the two lunar fortnights.

जयिन् *a.* (*f.* —नी) 1 Conquering, vanquishing. -2 Successful, winning a law-suit. -3 Fascinating, captivating. -*m.* A victor, a conqueror.

जय्य *a.* (*f.* -य्या) Conquerable, vulnerable, that can be conquered.

जरठ *a.* (*f.* —ठा) 1 Hard, solid. -2 Old, aged. -3 Decayed, decrepit, infirm. -4 Bent, bowed down, drooping. -5 Pale, yellowish-white. -6 Full-grown, ripe, matured. -7 Hard-hearted, cruel. —ठः *m.* 1 N. of Pandu, father of the five Pándavas. -2 Old age.

जरण *a.* (*f.* —णा) 1 Old, decayed, infirm. -2 Promoting digestion.-णः *m.*, —णं *n.* Cummin seed. -णा *f.* 1 Old age. -2 Praise. -णं *n.* 1 Old age. -2 One of the ten ways in which an eclipse is supposed to end.

जरंड *a.* Decayed, old.

जरत् *a.* (*f.* —ती) Old, aged, decayed.-2Infirm, decrepit. -*m*. An old man. -Comp. -कारुः *m*. N. of a great sage who married a sister of the serpent Vâsuki.—गवः *m*. An old ox.

जरतः *m*. 1 An old man. -2 A buffalo.

जरतिका, जरती *f*. An old woman.

जरा *f*. (The word जरस् is optionally substituted for जरा before vowel terminations after acc. dual). 1 Old age. -2 Decrepitude, infirmity consequent on old age. -3 Digestion. -4 N. of a female demon. -Comp. -अवस्था *f*. Decrepitude.-जीर्ण *a*. Old through age, debilitated, infirm. -भीरुः *m*. The God of love, Cupid.-संधः *m*. N. of a celebrated king and warrior, son of Brihadratha.

जरायणिः *m*. N. of Jarâsandha.

जरायु *n*. 1 The slough or cast-off skin of a serpent. -2 The outer skin of the embryo. -3 The uterus, womb. -Comp. —ज *a*. Born from the womb, viviparous.

जरित *a*. (*f*. —ता) 1 Old, aged. -2 Decayed, infirm.

जरिन् *a*. (*f*. -णी) Old, aged. -*m*. An old man.

जरूथं *n*. Flesh.

जर्जर *a*. (*f*. -रा) 1 Old, infirm, decayed. -2 Worn out, torn, shattered, broken to pieces, split up into thin particles. -3 Wounded, hurt. -4 Pained, tormented. -5 Dull, hollow (as the sound of a broken vessel). -रं *n*. 1 The banner of Indra. -2 Moss.

जर्जरित *a*. (*f*. —ता) 1 Old, decayed, infirm. -2 Worn out, torn to pieces, shattered. -3 Completely disabled.

जर्जरीक *a*. (*f*. -का) 1 Old, decayed. -2 Ragged, full of holes, perforated.

जर्तुः *m*. 1 The vulva.-2 An elephant.

जल *a* (*f*. -ला) 1 Dull, cold, frigid. -2 Stupid, idiotic. -लं *n*. 1 Water. -2 A kind of fragrant medicinal plant or perfume (ह्रीवेर). -3 The embryo or uterus of a cow. -5 The constellation called पूर्वाषाढा. -Comp. —अंचलं *n*. 1 A spring. -2. A natural water-course. -3. Moss. —अंजलिः *m*. 1 A handful of water. -2 A libation of water presented to the manes of a deceased person. —अटनः *m*. A heron. —अटनी *f*. A leech. —अणुकं, -अंडकं *n*. The fry of fish. —अंतकः *m*. A shark. —अत्ययः *m*. Autumn (शरद्). —आधिदैवतः *m*., -तं *n*. An epithet of Varuna. (—तं *n*.) The constellation called पूर्वाषाढा. —अधिपः *m*. An epithet of Varuna. —अंबिका *f*. A well. —अर्कः *m*. The image of the sun reflected in water. —अर्णवः *m*. 1 The rainy season. -2 The ocean of sweet water. —अर्थिन् *a*. Thirsty. —अवतारः *m*. A landing-place at a river-side. —अष्ठीला *f*. A large square pond. —असुका *f*. A leech.—आकरः *m*. A spring, fountain, well. —आकांक्षः, -कांक्षः, -कांक्षिन् *m*. An elephant. —आखुः *m*. An otter. —आत्मिका *f*. A leech. —आधारः *m*. A pond, lake, reservoir of water. —आयुका *f*. A leech. —आर्द्र *a*. Wet. (-र्द्रं *n*.) Wet garment or clothes. (-द्रा *f*.) A fan wetted with water. —आलोका *f*. A leech. —आवर्तः *m*. An eddy, whirl-pool. —आशयः *m*. 1 A pond, lake, reservoir. -2. A fish.-3 The ocean. -4. The fragrant root of a plant (उशीर). —आश्रयः *m*. 1 A pond. -2 A water-house. -आह्वयं *n*. A lotus. —इंद्रः *m*. 1 An epithet of Varuna. -2 The ocean. —इंधनः *m*. The submarine fire. —इभः *m*. A water elephant. -इभः,-ईश्वरः *m.* 1 An epithet of Varuna. -2 The ocean. —उच्छ्वासः *m.* 1 A channel made for carrying off excess of water, a drain. -2 Overflow of a river. —उदरं *n.* Dropsy. —उद्भव *a.* Aquatic. (-वा *f.*) Benzoin.—उरगा, *f.*, -ओकस् *m.*, -ओकसः *m.* A leech. —कंटकः *m.* A crocodile. —कपिः *m.* The Gangetic porpoise. —कपोतः *m.* A water-pigeon. —करंकः *m.* 1 A shell. -2. Cocoa-nut. -3. A cloud. -4 A wave. -5 A lotus.-कल्कः *m.* Mud. —काकः *m.* The diver-bird. —कांतः *m.* The wind. —कांतारः *m.* An epithet of Varuna.-किराटः *m.* A shark. —कुक्कुटः *m.* A water-fowl. (—टी *f.*) The black-headed gull. -कुंतलः,-कोशः *m.* Moss. —कूपी *f.* 1 A spring, well. -2 A pond. -3 A whirlpool. -कूर्मः *m.* The porpoise. -केलिः *m.* or *f.*, —क्रीडा *f.* Playing in water. -केशः *m.* Moss. -क्रिया *f.* Presenting libations of water to the manes of the deceased. -गुल्मः *m.* 1 A turtle. -2 A quadrangular tank.-3 A whirlpool. —चरः *m.* 1 An aquatic animal. -2 A fish. -3 Any kind of water-fowl. -चारिन् *m.* 1 An aquatic animal. -2 A fish. -ज *a.* Born or produced in water. (-जः *m.*) 1 An aquatic animal. -2 A fish. -3 Sea-salt. -4 A collective name for several signs of the zodiac. -5 Moss. -6 The moon. -जः *m.*, -जं *n.* 1 A shell. -2 The conch-shell. (-जं *n.*) A lotus. -जंतुः *m.* 1 A fish. -2 Any aquatic animal. -जंतुका *f.* A leech. -जन्मन् *n.* A lotus. -जिह्वः *m.* A crocodile. —जीविन् *m.* A fisherman. -तरंगः *m.* 1 A wave. -2 A metal cup filled with water producing harmonic notes like a musical glass. —ताडनं *n.* (lit.) ' Beating water', (fig.) any useless occupation. —त्रा *f.* An umbrella. —त्रासः *m.* Hydrophobia. —दः *m.* 1 A cloud. -2 Camphor. —दागमः *m.* The rainy season.-दर्दुरः *m.* A kind of musical instrument. -देवः *m.* The constellation पूर्वाषाढा. -देवता *f.* A naiad, water-nymph. —द्रोणी *f.* A bucket. —धरः *m.* 1 A cloud. -2 The ocean. -धिः *m.* 1 The ocean. -2 A hundred billions -3 The number ' four '. -नकुलः *m.* An otter. —नरः *m.* A merman. -नाडी,-ली *f.* A water-course. —निधिः *m.* 1 The ocean. -2 The number 'four.'-निर्गमः *m.* 1 A drain, water-course. -2 A water-fall, descent of a spring &c. into a river below. —नीलिः *f.* Moss. -पक्षिन् *m.* A water-fowl.-पटलं *n.* A cloud. -पारावतः *m.* A water-pigeon. —पित्तं *n.* Fire. —पुष्पं *n.* An aquatic flower. —पूरः *m.* 1 A flood of water. -2 A full stream of water. —पृष्ठजा *f.* Moss. —प्रदानं *n.* Presenting libations of water to the manes of the deceased. —प्रलयः *m.* Destruction by water. —प्रांतः *m.* The bank of a river. -प्रायं *n.* A country abounding with water. -प्रियः *m.* 1 The Châtaka bird. -2 A fish. (-या *f.*) An epithet of Dákshâyani. —प्लवः *m.* An otter. —प्लावनं *n.* A deluge, an inundation. —बंधः, -बंधकः *m.* A dam, dike; rocks or stones impeding a current. —बंधुः *m.* A fish. —बालकः, -वालकः *m.* The Vindhya mountain. —बालिका *f.* Lightning. —बिडालः *m.* An otter. —बिंबः *m.*, -बं *n.* A bubble. —बिल्वः *m.* 1 A (quadrangular) pond; lake. -2 A tortoise. -3 A crab. -भीतिः *f.* Hydrophobia. —भू *a.* Produced in water. —भूः *n.* 1 A cloud. -2 A place for holding water. -3 A kind of camphor. -भृत् *m.* 1 A cloud. -2 A jar. -3 Camphor. —मक्षिका *f.* A water-insect.

—मंडूकं *n*. A kind of musical instrument (=जलदर्दुर). —मद्गुः *m*. A kingfisher. —मार्जारः *m*. An otter. —मुच् *m*. 1 A cloud. -2 A kind of camphor. —मूर्तिः *m*. An epithet of Siva. —मूर्तिका *f*. Hail. —यंत्रं *n*. 1 A machine for raising water. -2 A water-clock, clepsydra. -3 A fountain. —यात्रा *f*. A voyage —यानं *n*. A ship. —रंकुः *m*. A kind of gallinule. —रंकः, -रंडः *m*. 1 A whirlpool. -2 A drop of water, drizzle, thin sprinkling. -3 A snake. —रसः *m*. The sea-salt. —राशिः *m*. The ocean. —रुह्, -हं *f*. A lotus. -रूपः *m*. A crocodile. —लता *f*. A wave, billow. —वाद्यं *n*. A kind of musical instrument. -वायसः *m*. The diver-bird. —वाहः *m* 1 A cloud. -2 A water-bearer. -3 A kind of camphor. —वाहकः, -नः *m*. A water-carrier. —वाहनी *f*. An aqueduct. —विषुवं *n*. The autumnal equinox. —वृश्चिकः *m*. A prawn. —व्यालः *m*. 1 A water-snake. -2 A marine monster. —शयः, -शयनः, -शायिन् *m* An epithet of Vishnu. —शुक्तिः *f*. A bivalve shell. -शूकं *n*. Moss. -शूकरः *m*. A crocodile. -शोषः *m*. A drought. -सर्पिणी *f*. A leech. -सूचिः *f*. 1 The Gangetic porpoise. -2 A kind of fish. -3 A crow. -4 A water-nut. -5 A leech. —स्थानं *n*., -स्थाश्रयः *m*. A pond, lake, reservoir. —हं *n*. A small water-house (a kind of summer-house) furnished with artificial fountains. —हस्तिन् *m*. A water-elephant. -हारिणी *f*. A drain. —हासः *m*. 1 Foam. -2 Cuttle-fish-bone considered as the foam of the sea.

जलमसिः *m*. 1 A cloud. -2 Camphor

जलाका, जलालुका, जलिका, जलुका, जलूका, जलोका, जलौकिका *f*. A leech.

जलेजं, जलेजातं *n*. A lotus.

जलेवाहः *m*. A diver. [Vishnu.

जलेशयः *m*. 1 A fish. -2 N. of

जल्प् 1 P. (जल्पति, जल्पित) 1 To speak or converse (with another.) -2 To murmur, speak inarticulately -3 To chatter, prattle. -4 To praise.

जल्पः *m*. 1 Talk, speech. -2 Discourse, conversation. -3 Prattling, gossip. -4 Debate, discussion.

जल्पक *a*. (*f*. -ल्पिका), जल्पाक *a*. (*f*. -का) Talkative, garrulous.

जव *a*. (*f*. —वा) Swift, expeditious. —वः *m*. 1 Speed, swiftness, quickness, rapidity. -2 Haste, hurry. -Comp. —अधिकः *m*. A fleet horse, a courser. —अनिलः *m*. A strong wind, hurricane.

जवन *a*. (*f*. —नी) Quick, swift, fleet. —नः *m*. A courser, a swift horse. —नं *n*. Speed, quickness, velocity.

जवनिका, जवनी *f*. 1 A screen of cloth surrounding a tent. -2 A curtain in general. -3 The sail of a boat.

जवसः *m*. Pasture-grass.

जवा *f*. The China rose, see जपा.

जष् 1 U. (जषति,-ते) To injure, hurt, kill.

जसु 4 P. (जस्यति) 1 To set free, release. -2 To be exhausted or tired. -3 To go.

जस् 1, 10. P. (जसति, जासयति) 1 To hurt, injure, strike. -2 To disregard, slight.

जहकः *m*. 1 Time. -2 A child. -3 The slough of a snake. —का *f*. A kind of pole-cat.

जहत् *a*. (*f*. -ती) Leaving, abandoning. -Comp. —लक्षणा, —स्वार्था *f*. That kind of लक्षणा in which the primary sense of a word is wholly abandoned and a new one is substituted. When it is said मंचाः क्रोशन्ति the word मंचाः signifies, not a cot, but a child sleeping or lying on it. [world.

जहानकः *m*. Total destruction of the

जहुः *m*. A young animal.

जह्नुः *m*. N. of an ancient king, son of Suhotra, who adopted the river Gangâ as his daughter.-Comp. —कन्या, —जा, —तनया *f*. The Ganges.

जागर *a* Awake, watchful. —रः *m*. 1 Wakefulness, waking, keeping awake. -2 A vision in a waking state. -3 An armour, mail.

जागरणं *n*. 1 Waking, wakefulness. -2 Watchfulness, vigilance. -3 Sitting up at night as a part of a religious ceremony.

जागरा *f*. See जागरणं.

जागरित *a*.(*f*.-ता) One who has been long awake. —तं *n*. Waking.

जागरितृ *a*. (*f*. -त्री), जागरूक *a*. (*f*. -का) 1 Wakeful, waking, sleepless. -2 Watchful, vigilant.

जागर्तिः, जागर्या, जागिर्या *f*. Wakefulness, keeping awake.

जागुडं *n*. Saffron.

जागृ 2 P. (जागर्ति, जागरित) 1 To be awake, be watchful or attentive(fig. also).-2 To sit up during the night. -3 To be roused from sleep, awake. -4 To foresee, be provident.

जाघनी *f*. 1 A tail. -2 The thigh.

जांगल *a*. (*f*. -ली) 1 Rural, picturesque.-2 Wild.-3 Savage, barbarous. -4 Arid, desert. —लः *m*. The francoline partridge. —लं *n*. Flesh, flesh of deer &c. [charmer.

जांगलिः, जांगलिकः *m*. A snake-

जांगुलं *n*. Poison, venom. —ली *f*. 1 Knowledge of poisons, possession of charms or drugs as antidotes.-2 An epithet of Durgâ.

जांगुलिः, जांगुलिकः *m*. A snake-doctor, a dealer in antidotes (विषवैद्य).

जांघिकः *m*. 1 A courier, an express. -2 A camel.

जाजिन् *m*. A warrior, combatant.

जाठर *a*. (*f*. -री) Belonging to or being in the stomach; stomachic, abdominal. —रः *m*. 1 The digestive faculty, gastric fluid. -2 'Offspring of the womb', a child.

जाड्यं *n*. 1 Coldness, frigidity. -2 Apathy, sluggishness, inactivity. -3 Dulness of intellect; folly, stupidity.-4 Tastelessness of the tongue. -Comp. —अरिः *m*. The citron tree.

जात *p. p.* (*f*. -ता) 1 Brought into existence, engendered, produced. -2 Grown, arisen. -3 Caused, occasioned. -4 Felt, affected by. -5 Happened. —तः *m*. 1 A son, male offspring (in dramas often used as a term of endearment). -2 A living being. —ता *f*. A daughter, mostly used in addressing. —तं *n*. 1 A creature, living being. -2 Production, origin. -3 Kind, sort, class, species. -4 A collection of things forming a class. -5 A child, a young one. -6 Individuality, specific condition. -Comp. —अपत्या *f*. A mother. —इष्टिः *f*. A sacrifice performed at the birth of a child. —उक्षः *m*. A young bullock. —कर्मन् *n*. A ceremony performed at the birth of a child. —कलाप *a*. Having a tail (as a peacock). —पुत्रा *f*. A woman who has borne a son or sons. -प्रत्यय *a*. Inspired with confidence. —मात्र *a*. Just born. —रूप *a*. Beautiful, brilliant. (—पं *n*.) 1 Gold. -2 The form in which a person is born, *i. e.* nakedness.-3 The thorn apple. —वेदस् *m*. An epithet of fire (or of the sun). —वेदसी *f*. An epithet of Durgâ. —वासगृहं, -वेश्मन् *n*. The lying-in-chamber.

जातक *a*. (*f*. -का) Born, produced. —कः *m*. 1 A new-born infant. -2 A mendicant. —कं *n.* 1 A ceremony performed after the birth of a child (जातकर्मन्). -2 Astrological calculation of a nativity. -3 An aggregate of similar things. -Comp. —छ्यानि: *m.* A leech.

जाति: *f.* 1 Birth, production. -2 Race, lineage, rank. -3 A caste, tribe or class (of men). -4 A class, genus, kind, species. -5 The properties which are peculiar to a class and distinguish it from all others; the essential characteristics of a species. -6 A fire-place. -7 Nutmeg. -8 The Jasmine plant or its flower (written also as जाती in the last two senses). -9 (In Nyâya) Futile answer. -10 (In music) The seven primary notes of the Indian gamut. -11 Reduction of fractions to a common denominator. -12 False generalization. -13 A class of metres.-Comp. -अंध *a.* Born blind.-कोश:,-ष:*m.*, -शं,-षं *n.* The nutmeg. —कोशी, -षी *f.* The outer skin of the nutmeg. —धर्म: *m.* 1. The duties of a caste. -2 A generic property. —ध्वंस: *m.* The loss of caste or its privileges. -पत्री *f.* The outer skin of the nutmeg. —फलं *n.* A nutmeg. —ब्राह्मण: *m.* A Brâhmana only by birth, but not by knowledge or religious austerities; an ignorant Brâhmana. —भ्रंश: *m.* Loss of caste. —भ्रष्ट *a.* Outcast. —मात्रं *n.* 1 'Mere birth,' position in life obtained by mere birth. -2 Caste only (but not the performance of duties pertaining to it). -3. A species, genus. —लक्षणं *n.* Generic distinction, a characteristic of a class. —वाचक *a.* Expressing a genus, generic (as a word). —वैरं *n.* Instinctive or natural hostility. —वैरिन् *m.* A born enemy. —शब्द: *m.* A name conveying the idea of a genus, a generic word, common noun. —संकर: *m.* Admixture of caste; mixed blood. -संपन्न *a.* Belonging to a noble family. —सारं *n.* Nutmeg. —स्मर *a.* Remembering one's condition in a former life. —स्वभाव: *m.* Generic character or nature. —हीन *a.* Of low birth, outcast.

जाती *f.* The jasmine plant (मालती).

जातु *ind.* A particle meaning :—1, At all, ever, at any time, possibly. -2 Perhaps, sometimes. -3 Once, once upon a time, sometime, at some day. -4 Used with the potential mood जातु has the sense of 'not allowing or not putting up with'. -5 Used with a present indicative it denotes 'censure.'

जातुधान: *m.* A demon, imp.

जातुष *a.* (*f.* -षी) 1 Made of, or covered with, lac. -2 Sticky, adhesive.

जातूः *m.* A thunderbolt.

जात्य *a.* (*f.* —त्या) 1 Of the same family, related.-2 Noble, well-born. sprung from a noble family. -3 Lovely, beautiful, pleasing.-4 Best, excellent. -5 (Math.) Rectangular.

जानकी *f.* N. of Sitâ, wife of Râma.

जानपद: *m.* 1 An inhabitant of the country; a rustic, boor, peasant (opp. पौर). -2 A country.

जानि A substitute for जाया at the end of Bah. comp.

जानु *n.* The knee. -Comp. —दघ्न *a.* Reaching to, or as high as, the knees; knee-deep. -फलकं,-मंडलं *n.* The knee-pan.—संधि: *m.* The knee-joint.

जाप: *m.* 1 Muttering prayers, murmuring. -2 A muttered prayer.

जाबाल: *m.* A goat-herd.

जामदग्न्यः *m.* N. of Parasurâma.

जामा *f.* 1 A daughter. -2 A daughter-in-law.

जामातृ *m.* 1 A son-in-law. -2 A lord, master. -3 The sun-flower.

जामिः *f.* 1 A sister. -2 A daughter. -3 A daughter-in-law. -4 A near female relative. -5 A virtuous and respectable woman. -*n.* 1 Blood-relationship, relation of sister and brother. -2 Relation (in general), descent.

जामित्रं *n.* The seventh zodiacal sign from the natal sign (लग्न).

जामेयः *m.* A sister's son.

जांबवं *n.* 1 Gold. -2 The fruit of the Jambu tree.

जांबवत् *m.* N. of a king of bears who was of signal service to Ráma at the siege of Lankâ. He was also noted for his medical skill.

जांबीरं (-लं) *n.* A citron.

जांबूनदं *n.* 1 Gold. -2 A golden ornament. -3 The Dhattùra plant.

जाया *f.* A wife. As last member of Bah.comp. जाया is changed to जानि *e.g.* सीताजानिः 'One who has Sîtâ for his wife'; so युवजानिः, वामार्धजानिः. -Comp. -अनुजीविन् *m.*, -आजीवः *m.* 1 An actor, a dancer. -2 The husband of a harlot. -3 A needy man, pauper. -4 A kind of crane (बक). —पती *m. dual* The husband and wife. (The other forms of the comp. are दंपती and जंपती).

जायिन् *a.* (*f.* -नी) Conquering, subduing. -*m.* The burden of a song (in music).

जायुः *m.* 1 Medicine. -2 A [physician.

जारः *m.* 1 A paramour, gallant, lover. -2 A confidential friend.

जारिणी *f.* An adulteress.

जालं *n.* 1 A net, snare. -2 A web, cob-web. -3 A coat of mail, a helmet made of wire. -4 An eye-hole, lattice, window. -5 A collection, an assemblage, mass. -6 Magic. -7 Illusion, deception. -8 An unblown flower. -9 The membrane which unites the toes of many water-birds. -10 A disease of the eyes. -11 Pride, arrogance. —लः *m.* The Kadamba tree. -Comp. —अक्षः *m.* A loop-hole, window. —कर्मन् *n.* The occupation of catching fish, fishing. —कारकः *m.* 1 A net-maker. -2 A spider. -गोणिका *f.* A kind of churning vessel. -पाद्, -पादः *m.* A goose. —प्राया *f.* Mail, armour.

जालकं *n.* 1 A net. -2 A multitude, collection. -3 A lattice, window. -4 A bud, an uublown flower. -5 A kind of ornament (worn in the hair). -6 A nest. -7 Illusion, deception. -8 A plantain or the fruit. —कः *m.* A window, lattice. -Comp. —मालिन् *a.* Veiled.

जालकिन् *m.* A cloud.

जालकिनी *f.* A ewe.

जालिक *m.* 1 A fisherman. -2 A fowler, bird-catcher. -3 A spider. -4 The governor or chief ruler of a province. -5 A rogue, cheat. -6 A conjurer, juggler. —का *f.* 1 A net. -2 A chain armour. -3 A spider. -4 A leech. -5 A widow. -6 Iron. -7 Plantain. -8 A veil, woollen cloth.

जालिनी *f.* A room ornamented with pictures.

जाल्म *a.* (*f.* -ल्मी) 1 Cruel, severe, harsh. -2 Rash, inconsiderate. -ल्मः *m.* (*f.* -ल्मी) 1 A rogue, rascal, villain, wretch, miscreant. -2 A poor man, a low or degraded man. -3 One who reads or recites badly.

जाल्मक *a.* (*f.* -ल्मिका) Despised, low, contemptible.

जावन्यं *n.* 1 Speed, swiftness. [Haste, hurry

जाहं *n.* A termination added to nouns expressive of the parts of the body in the sense of the root of ; कर्णजाहं *n.* The root of the ear.

जाह्नवी *f.* An epithet of the river Ganges.

जि I P. (Atm. when preceded by परा and वि) (जयति, जिगाय, जिग्ये,अजैषीत्-अजेष्ट, जेतुं, जित) 1 To conquer, defeat, vanquish, subjugate. -2 To surpass, excel -3 To win (by conquest, in gambling or in a law-suit), acquire by conquest.-4 To curb, restrain, (as passions) -5 To be victorious, be supreme or pre-eminent (generally used in benedictory stanzas or salutations). -6 To convict. -7 To overcome or get the better of (as a disease &c.) -8 To expect from (with abl.). -*Caus.* (जापयति) To cause to win or conquer. -*Desid.* (जिगीषति) -With अधि- To conquer, defeat, vanquish. With निस्- 1 To conquer, defeat. -2 To win, acquire by conquest. परा- 1 To defeat, subjugate. -2 To lose, to be deprived of. -3 To be overcome by (with an *abl.*) *e. g.* अध्ययनात् पराजयते. वि- To conquer. -3 To be victorious, to be pre-eminent.

जि: *m.* A demon (पिशाच).

जिगत्नु: *m.* Breath, life.

जिगीषा *f.* 1 Desire of conquering, subduing or overcoming.-2 Emulation, rivalry. -3 Eminence. -4 Exertion, profession. -5 Eminence. -6 Military ardour, warlike spirit.

जिगीषु *a.* 1 Desirous of conquering. -2 Vying or contending with.

जिघत्सा *f.* 1 Desire of eating, hunger. -2 Striving for.

जिघत्सु *a.* Hungry.

जिघांसा *f.* Desire of killing. -2 Malice, revenge.

जिघांसु *a.* Desirous of killing, murderous. —सु: *m.* An enemy, king.

जिघृक्षा *f.* Desire of taking or seiz-

जिघ्र *a.* (*f.* —घ्रा) 1 Suspecting. -2 Conjecturing, guessing; observing.

जिज्ञासा *f.* 1 Desire of knowing; curiosity, inquisitiveness.-2 Search, investigation, test, examination.

जिज्ञासित *a.* (*f.* —ता) Investigated, asked, inquired into.

जिज्ञासु *a.* 1 Desirous of knowing, inquisitive, curious. 2 Desirous of getting absolution (मुमुक्षु).

जित् *a.* (At the end of comp.) Conquering, defeating, winning &c., *e. g.* शत्रुजित्, कंसजित्.

जित *p. p.* (*f.* —ता) 1 Conquered, subdued. -2 Won, got, obtained (by conquest). -3 Surpassed, excelled. -4 Enslaved or influenced by, *e. g.* कामजित ; स्त्रीजित &c. —तं *n.* Victory. -Comp. —अक्षर *a.* Reading well or readily. —आत्मन् *a.* One who has conquered his foes, triumphant. -2 He who has subdued his passions. (-त्म: *m.*) N. of Vishnu. —अरि *a.* He who has conquered his enemies or passions. (-रि: *m.*) An epithet of Buddha. —आत्मन् *a.* Self-subdued, void of passion. —आहव *a.* Victorious. —इन्द्रिय *a.* He who has conquered his passions or subdued the senses. —काशिन् *a.* Appearing victorious, proud of victory, assuming the airs of a victor —क्रोध, —मन्यु *a.* Imperturbable, not excitable. —क्रोध: *m.* An epithet of Vishnu. —नेमि: *m.* A staff made of the Asvattha tree. —लोक *a.* One who has won heaven (epithet of a class of manes). —शत्रु *a.* Victorious. —स्वर्ग *a.* One who has won heaven.

जिति: *f.* 1 Victory. -2 Obtaining.

जितुमः, मिथुनः m. The sign Gemini of the zodiac.

जित्वर a. (f. -री) Victorious, conquering. —री f. N. of the city Benares.

जिन a. (f. —ना) Victorious, triumphant. -2 Very old. —नः m. 1 A generic term applied to a chief Bauddha or Jaina saint. -2 N. applied to the Arhats of the Jainas. -3 A very old man. -4 An epithet of Vishnu. -Comp. —इंद्रः,-ईश्वरः m. 1 A chief Bauddha saint. -2 An Arhat of the Jainas. —सद्मन् n. A Jaina temple or monastery.

जिवाजिवः m. The châtaka bird.

जिष्णु a. 1 Victorious, triumphant. -2 Winning, gaining. -3 (At the end of comp.) Canquering, excelling. —ष्णुः m. The sun. -2 N. of Indra. -3 N. of Vishnu. -4 N. of Arjuna.

जिह्म a. (f. —ह्मा) 1 Sloping, athwart, oblique. -2 Crooked, awry. -3 Going irregularly. -4 Curved, bent. -5 Morally crooked, deceitful, wicked. -5 Dim, dark, pale-coloured. -6 Slow, lazy. —ह्मं n. Dishonesty, falsehood. -Comp. —अक्ष a. Crooked-eyed, squinting.-ग a. Moving slowly. (-गः m.) A snake.-गति a. Going tortuously. -मेहनः m. A frog. —योधिन् a. Fighting unfairly. (-m.) An epithet of Bhima. —शल्यः m. The Khadira tree.

जिह्वः m. The tongue.

जिह्वल a. (f.-ला) Voracious, greedy.

जिह्वा f. 1 The tongue. -2 The tongue of fire i. e. a flame. -Comp. —पः m. 1 A dog. -2 A cat. -3 A tiger. -4 A leopard. -5 A bear. —मूलीय a. A term particularly aplied to the Visarga before क् and ख् and also to क्, ख् and the guttural class of consonants (in gram.). -रदः m. A bird. -लिह् m. A dog. —लौल्यं n. Greediness. —शल्यः m. The Khadira tree.

जीन a. (f. -ना) Old, aged, decayed. (-नः m.) A leather bag.

जीमूतः m. 1 A cloud. -2 A mountain. -3 A nourisher, sustainer. -4 An epithet of Indra. -Comp. -कूटः m. A mountain. -केतुः m. An epithet of Siva. —वाहनः m. 1. N. of Indra. -2 N. of a king of the Vidyádharas, hero of the play called Nâgánanda. —वाहिन् m. A smoke.

जीर m. 1 A sword. -2 Cumin-seed. -3 An atom.

जीरकः, जीरणः m. Cumin-seed.

जीर्ण p. p. (f. —र्णा) 1 Old, ancient. -2 Worn out, ruined, wasted, decayed, tattered (as clothes.) -3 Digested. —र्णः m. 1 An old man. -2 A tree. -3 Cumin-seed. —र्णा f. Large cumin-seed. -र्णं n. 1 Benzoin. -2 Old age, decrepitude. -Comp. —उद्धारः m. Repairs, especially of a temple or any chartable or religious institution. —ज्वरः m. A lingering fever. —पर्णः m. The Kadamba tree —वज्रं n. A particular gem.

जीर्णक a. (f. -का) Almost dried up or withered.

जीर्णिः f. 1 Old age, decrepitude, decay, infirmity. -2 Digestion.

जीव् 1 P. (जीवति, जीवित) 1 To live, be alive. -2 To revive, come to life. -3 To live by, subsist on, make a livelihood by (with instr). -4 (Fig.) To live or prey upon, depend upon as one's source of existence (with loc.). With अति- To surpass in living; to live more happily or pompously. अनु—1 To imitate the life of. -2 To live for, to serve, to live by or by means of (with an an *acc.*). -3 To survive, to out-live. आ- To get a living from (with *acc*). अनु- To return to life, to revive. उप- To maintain oneself by (with *acc.* of the person or profession). -*Caus.* 1 To restore to life. -2 To nourish, nurture, bring up.

जीव *a.* (*f.* -वा) Living, existing. —वः *m.* 1 The principle of life, the vital breath, life, soul.-2 The individual or personal soul (called जीवात्मन् as opposed to परमात्मन् the Supreme Soul). -3 Life, existence. -4 A creature, living being. -5 Livelihood, profession. -6 N. of Karna. -7 N. of one of the Maruts. -8 The constellation पुष्य. -9 N. of Brihaspati. -10 The third lustrum in the cycle of Jupiter.-11 Association of cause and effect. -12 N. of Vishnu. -Comp. —अंतकः *m.* 1 A bird-catcher, fowler.-2A murderer, slayer. —आत्मन् *m.* The individual soul '(as opposed to परमात्मन् the Supreme Soul ').-आदानं *n.* Abstracting healthy blood, bleeding; (in medic.).-आधानं *n.* Preservation of life. -आधारः *m.*The heart.-उत्सर्गः*m.* Voluntary death, suicide. —उपाधिः *m.* The three states *i. e.* waking, dreaming and sleeping. —ऊर्णा *f.* The wool of a living animal. —गृहं, -मंदिरं *n*. The body. —ग्राहः *m.* A prisoner taken alive. —घनः *m.* Brahman (*m.*). —जीवः (also जीवंजीवः) *m.* The Chakora bird.-तोका *f.*A woman whose children are living. -दः *m.* 1 A physician.-2An enemy. -दशा *f.* Mortal existence. —धनं *n.* Property in the shape of living creatures, live-stock.—धनी *f.* The earth. —पतिः, -पत्नी *f.* A woman whose husband is alive. —पितृ, -पितृक *a.* (A son or daughter) whose father is still alive. —पुत्रा, -वत्सा *f.* A woman whose son is living. —मातृका *f.* The seven mothers or female divinities; (कुमारी धनदा नंदा विमला मंगला बला । पद्मा चेति च विख्याताः सप्तैता जीवमातृकाः). —लोकः *m.* 1 The world of mortals, the world or worldly existence. -2 Living beings, mankind. —वृत्तिः *f.* Breeding or keeping cattle. —शेष*a.* One to whom only life is left,escaping only with life and nothing more. —संक्रमणं *n.* The transmigration of the soul. —साधनं *n.* Grain, corn. —साफल्यं *n.* The relization or attainment of the chief end of human existence. —सूः *f.* A woman whose children are living.-स्थानं*n.*1 A joint, articulation. -2 The vital parts. -3 The heart.

जीवकः *m.* 1 A living being. -2 A servant.-3 A Buddhist mendicant, any mendicant who lives by begging. -4 A usurer. -5 A snake-catcher.

जीवत् *a.* (*f.* -ती) Living, alive. -Comp. —तोका *f.* A woman whose children are living.—पतिः *f.*, -पत्नी *f.* A woman whose husband is living. —मुक्त *a.* One who, being purified by a true knowledge of the Supreme Spirit, is freed from the future birth and all ceremonial rites while yet living. —मुक्तिः *f.* Final liberation in the present state of life.-मृत *a.* He who, though alive, is as good as dead and useless to the world (said of a mad man or one whose character is lost).

जीवथः *m.* 1 Life, existence. -2 A tortoise. -3 A peacock.-4 A cloud.

जीवन *a* (*f.* -नी) Enlivening, giv

ing life. -नः m. 1 A living being. -2 Wind. -3 A son. -4 The Supreme Being. —नं n. 1 Life, existence (fig. also). -2 The principle of life, vital energy. -3 Water. -4 Livelihood, profession, means of existence (fig. also). -5 Butter made from milk one day old. -6 Marrow. -7 Enlivening, making alive. -Comp. —अंत: m. Death. —आघातं n. Poison. —आवास: m. 1 An epithet of Varuna, the regent of water. -2 The body. —उपाय: m. Livelihood. —औषधं n. 1 The elixir of life. -2 A life-giving medicine.

जीवनकं n. Food.

जीवनीयं n. 1 Water. -2 Fresh milk.

जीवंत: m. 1 Life, existence. -2 A drug, medicament.

जीवंतिक: m. A fowler.

जीवा f. 1 Water. -2 The earth. -3 A bow-string. -4 The chord of an arc. -5 Means of living. -6 The tinkling of metallic ornaments. -7 N. of a plant (वचा). -8 Life, existence.

जीवातु: m., -तु n. 1 Food. -2 Life, existence (fig. also). -3 Restoration to life, revival. -4 A medicine for restoring life.

जीविका f. 1 Means of living, livelihood. -2 The life-giving element, *i. e.* water.

जीवित p. p. (f. -ता) 1 Living, existent, alive. -2 Returned to life, revived. -3 Animated, enlivened. -4 Lived through (as a period). -तं n. 1 Life, existence. -2 Duration of life. -3 Livelihood. -4 A living being. -Comp. -अंतक: m. An epithet of Siva. —आशा f. The hope of life, love of life. —ईश: m. 1 A lover, husband. -2 An epithet of Yama. -3 The sun. -4 The moon. —काल: m. The duration of life. —ज्ञा f. An artery. —नाथ: m. A husband. —व्यय: m. Sacrifice of life. —संशय: m. Risk of life, jeopardy, danger to life.

जीविन् a. (f. -नी) (Generally at the end of comp.) 1 Living, alive, existing. -2 Living upon or by. -m. A living being.

जीव्यं n. Life. —व्या f. A means of livelihood.

जुगुप्सनं n., जुगुप्सा f. 1 Censure, reproach. -2 Dislike, aversion, disgust, abhorrence. -3 (In Rhet.) Disgust considered as the feeling which gives rise to the 'Bibhatsa' sentiment.

जुटकं n. A braid of hair.

जुटिका f. A tuft of hair on the top of the head.

जुष् 6 A. (जुषते, -जुष्ट) 1 To be pleased or satisfied. -2 To be favourable or propitious. -3 To like, take pleasure or delight in, enjoy. -4 To devote or attach oneself to, practise, undergo, suffer. -5 To frequent, visit, inhabit. -6 To enter, seat oneself on, resort to. -7 To choose. -8 To enjoy, possess, have. -9 To happen to.

जुष् 1 P., 10 U. (जोषति, जोषयति-ते) 1 To reason, think. -2 To investigate, examine. -3 To hurt. -4 To be satisfied.

जुष् a. (At the end of comp.) 1 Liking, enjoying, taking delight in. -2 Visiting, approaching, going to, resorting to.

जुष्ट p. p. (f. —ष्टा) 1 Pleased, gratified. -2 Practised, resorted to, visited, suffered. -3 Furnished or endowed with. -4 Liked, loved. -5 Served, worshipped. -6 Shared, partaken in. —ष्टं n. The remants of meal (उच्छिष्ट).

जुहुराण *a.* Making crooked or acting crookedly. –णः *m* 1 The fire. –2 The moon.

जुहूः *f.* 1 A crescent-shaped wooden ladle used for pouring the sacrificial ghee into the fire. –2 A tongue (especially of Agni) *i. e.* a flame.

जुहोतिः *m.* A technical name for those sacrificial ceremonies to which the verb जुहोति is applied as distinguished from those to which यजति is applied. (सर्वज्ञनारायण shortly renders जुहोति by उपविष्टहोम and यजति by तिष्ठद्धोम).

जूः *f.* 1 Speed. –2 Atmosphere. –3 A female demon. –4 An epithet of Sarasvatī.

जूकः *m.* The sign Libra of the [zodiac.

जूटः *m.* The mass of twisted or matted hair.

जूटकं *n.* Matted hair.

जूतिः *f.* 1 Going on, moving. –2 Quickness, speed. –3 Uninterrupted motion.

जूर् 4 A. (जूर्यते, जूर्ण) 1 To hurt, injure, kill. –2 To be angry with (with dat.). –3 To grow old.

जूर्तिः *f.* 1 Fever. –2 Feverish heat.

जृ 1 P. (जरति) 1 To make low or humiliate. –2 To excel.

जृभ्, जृंभ् 1 A. (जृम्भते, जृंभते, जृंभित, जृब्ध) 1 To gape, yawn. –2 To open, expand (as a flower &c.). –3 To increase, extend every where. –4 To appear, rise, become visible or manifest. –5 To recoil or fly back (as a bow). With वि- 1 To open the mouth, gape, yawn. –2 To open or expand (as a flower). –3 To spread. –4 To pervade, to appear. समुत्- To endeavour, to attempt.

जृंभः *m.*, –भा *f.*, –भं *n.* 1 Yawning, gaping. –2 Opening, blossoming, expanding. –3 Expansion. –4 Bursting open.

जृंभणं *n.* 1 Gaping, yawning. –2 Stretching (the limbs). –3 Blossoming, blooming.

जृंभिका *f.* Gaping, yawning.

जृंभित *p. p.* (*f.* —ता) 1 Yawned, gaped. –2 Opened, expanded. –3 Opened, blown (as a flower). –4 Done, exerted. –5 Enlarged, increased. —तं *n.* 1 Gaping. –2 Expansion blooming. –3 Appearing, becoming manifest.

जॄ 1. 4. 9. P., 10 U. (जरति, जीर्यति, जृणाति, जारयति-ते, जरि-री-तुं, जीर्ण or जारित) 1 To grow old, wear out, wither away, decay. –2 To perish, be consumed (fig. also). –3 To be digested. –4 To break up or fall to pieces. –*Caus.* (ज-जा-रयति).

जेतृ *m.* 1 A conqueror, victor. –2 An epithet of Vishnu.

जेताकः *m.* A heated chamber for inducing perspiration ; a dry hot bath.

जेमनं *n.* 1 Eating. –2 Food.

जैत्र *a.* (*f.* –त्री) 1 Victorious, successful, leading to victory. –2 Superior. –त्रः *m.* 1 A victor, conqueror. –2 Quick-silver. –त्रं *n.* A victory, triumph. –3 Superiority. –*Comp.* –रथः *m.* A victor.

जैनः *m.* 1 A Jaina, a follower of Jaina doctrines. –2 A Buddha.

जैमिनिः *m.* N. of a celebrated sage and philosopher, founder of the Mimámsá school of philosophy.

जैवातृक *a.* (*f.* –की) 1 Long-lived, one for whom long life is desired. –2 Thin, lean. –कः *m.* 1 The moon.

-2 Camphor. -3 A son. -4 A drug, medicament. -5 A peasant.

जैवेय: *m.* An epithet of Kacha, son of Brihaspati. [falsehood.

जैह्म्यं *n.* Crookedness, deceit,

जोंगट: *m.* The longings of a pregnant woman (दोहद).

जोटिंग: *m.* 1 An epithet of Siva.-2 A devotee who practises the most rigid austerities.

जोष; *m.* 1 Satisfaction, enjoyment, happiness, pleasure. -2 Silence. --ष: *m.* Happiness. -षं *ind.* 1 According to one's wish, with ease. -2 Silently.

जोषणं *n.*,-ष्णा *f.* 1 Liking.-2Satisfaction, approval. -3 Choosing.

जोषा, जोषित *f.* A woman.

जोषिका *f.* 1 A cluster of young buds. -2 A woman.

ज्ञ *a.* (*f.* —ज्ञा) (At the end of comp.) 1 Knowing, familiar with, as in कार्यज्ञ, निमित्तज्ञ, शास्त्रज्ञ, सर्वज्ञ &c. -2 Wise: as in ज्ञम्मन्य *a.* Thinking oneself to be wise. —ज्ञ: *m.* 1 A wise and learned man. -2 The sentient soul. -3 The planet Mercury. -4 The planet Mars. -5 An epithet of Branman (*m.*).

ज्ञपित (*f.* —ता), ज्ञप्त (*f.* —प्ता) *a.* Made known, informed, expounded, taught.

ज्ञप्ति: *f.* 1 Understanding. -2 Intellect. -3 Promulgating. -4 Praise.

ज्ञा 9 U. (जानाति, जानीते, ज्ञातुं, ज्ञात), 1 To konw (in all senses), to learn, become acquainted with. -2 To know, be aware of, be familiar or conversant with. 3 To find out, ascertain, investigate. -4 To apprehend, understand, feel, experience; as in दु:खज्ञ, सुखज्ञ &c.-5 To test, try. -6 To recognise. -7 To regard, consider, know to be. -8 To act, engage in (with gen. of the instrument) ; सर्पिषो जानीते ' He engages in sacrifice with clarified butter (सर्पिष: =सर्पिषा). With अनु- 1 To permit, to allow, to assent to. -2 To promise. -3 To acknowledge. अप— (In the *Atm.*) To conceal. अभि— 1 To know, to understand, to be acquainted with. -2 To regard, to consider, to know as. -3 To recognize. अव— To disregard, neglect. आ— To know, understand, to ascertain. परि— 1 To know, to be acquainted with, to be aware of. -2 To learn, ascertain. प्रति— (*Atm.*) 1 To promise. -2 To confirm. वि— 1 To know, to be aware of. -2 To understand, to learn, ascertain. -3 To consider, regard, know as. सम्— (*Atm.*) 1 To recognize.-2 To agree together, to live in harmony (used with the *acc.* or *instr.*) *e.g.* पित्रा पितरं वा संजानीते. -3 To know, to understand -4 To watch for. -5 (*Parasm.*) To think of, remember; *e. g.* मातरं मातुर्वा संजानाति.

-Caus. (ज्ञापयति, ज्ञपयति). 1 To announce, inform, make acquainted with, make known, notify. -2 To request, ask (Atm.). *—Desid.* (जिज्ञासते) 1 To desire to know, investigate, ascertain. -2 To conjecture, suppose, guess.

ज्ञात *a.* (*f.* —ता) Known, ascertained, understood, learnt. —तं *n.* Knowledge. —Comp. -सिद्धांत: *m.* A man completely versed in any Sástra.

ज्ञातव्य *pot. p.* (*f.* —व्या) 1 To be known or understood. -2 Conceivable, comprehensible.

ज्ञाति: *m.* A paternal relation, a

father, brother &c. ; agnate relatives collectively. -Comp. —कर्मन् *n.*, —कार्यं *n.* The duty of a kinsman. —भावः *m.* Relationship.-भेदः *m.* Dissension among relatives.

ज्ञातृ *m.* 1 A wise man. -2 An acquaintance. -3 A bail, surety.

ज्ञातेयं *n.* Relationship.

ज्ञानं *n.* 1 Knowing, understanding, becoming acquainted with, proficiency. -2 Knowledge, learning. -3 Consciousness, cognizance, knowledge. -4 Sacred knowledge; especially, knowledge derived from meditation on the higher truths of religion and philosophy which teaches man how to understand his own nature and how he may be reunited to the Supreme Spirit (opp. कर्मन्). -5 The organ of intelligence, sense, intellect. -6 Conscience. -7 The Supreme Spirit. -8 An epithet of Vishnu.-9 The Vedas taken collectively. -Comp. —अनुत्पादः *m.* Ignorance, folly. —आत्मन् *a.* All-wise. —इंद्रियं *n.* An organ of perception ; (these are five त्वच्, रसना, चक्षुस्, कर्ण and घ्राण; the skin, tongue, eye, ear and nose. -कांडं *n.*, -डः *m.* The esoteric portion of Veda which treats of the knowledge of the Supreme Spirit, as distinguished from the knowledge of ceremonial rites (opp. कर्मकांड). —कृत *a.* Done knowingly or intentionally. —गम्य *a.* Attainable by the understanding. —चक्षुस् *n.* The eye of intelligence, the mind's eye, intellectual vision (opp. चर्मचक्षुस्). (-*m.*) A wise and learned man. —तत्त्वं *n.* True knowledge, knowledge of God.—तस् *ind.* Knowingly, intentionally. -तपस् *n.* Penance consisting in the cultivation of true knowledge. -दः *m.* A preceptor. —दा *f.* An epithet of Sarasvatî. —दुर्बल *a.* Wanting in knowledge. —निष्ठ *a.* Intent on acquiring true (spiritual) knowledge. —यज्ञः *m.* A man possessed of true or spiritual knowledge, philosopher. —योगः *m.* Contemplation as the principal means of attaining the Supreme Spirit or acquiring true or spiritual knowledge. —लक्षणं *n.*, -णा *f.* 1 Indication, sign, a means of knowing or inferring. -2 (In logic) Sign or proof of knowledge. —शास्त्रं *n.* The science of fortune-telling. —साधनं *n.* 1 A means of acquiring true or spiritual knowledge. -2 An organ of perception.

ज्ञानमय *a.* 1 Consisting of knowledge; spiritual. -2 Containing knowledge. -यः *m.* 1 The Supreme Spirit. -2 An epithet of Siva.

ज्ञानिन् *a.* (*f.* -नी) Intelligent, wise. —*m.* 1 An astrologer, a fortuneteller. -2 A sage, one possessed of true or spiritual knowledge.

ज्ञापक *a.* (*f.* -का) Making known, informing, indicating. —कः *m.* 1 A teacher.-2 A commander, a master. —कं *n.* (In phil.) A significant expression, a suggestive rule or precept, said of such rules as imply something more than what is actually expressed by the words of those rules themselves.

ज्ञापनं *n.* Making known, informing, announcing, indicating.

ज्ञापित *a.* (*f.* —ता) Made known, informed, announced, declared.

ज्ञीप्सा *f.* The desire of knowing.

ज्ञेय *pot. p.* (*f.* —या) 1 To be investigated, or learnt or understood. -2 To be regarded as.-3 Perceptible, cognizable.

ज्या 9. P. (जिनाति) 1 To overpower, oppress. -2 To grow old.

ज्या *f.* 1 A bow-string. -2 The chord of an arc. -3 The earth. -4 A mother.

ज्यानि: *f.* 1 Old age, decay. -2 Quitting, abandoning. -3 A river, stream.

ज्यायस् *a.* (*f.*—सी); (compar. of प्रशस्य, and वृद्ध) 1 Elder, senior. -2 Superior, more excellent or worthy. -3 Larger, greater. -4 (In law) One come of age and responsible for his own action.

ज्यायिष्ठ *a.* (irreg.) 1 The most excellent. -2 Noblest, first, best.

ज्येष्ठ *a.* (*f.* -ष्ठा) (Superl. of प्रशस्य and वृद्ध). 1 Eldest, most senior. -2 Most excellent, best. -3 Pre-eminent, first, chief, highest. —ष्ठ: *m.* 1 An elder brother. -2 An epithet of the Supreme Being. -3 N. of a lunar month (ज्यैष्ठ q. v.). —ष्ठा *f.* 1 An eldest sister. -2 N. of the eighteenth lunar mansion (consisting of three stars.) - 3 The middle finger. -4 A small house-lizard. -5 An epithet of the Ganges. -6 The goddes of misfortune, elder sister of Lakshmi. -श्री *f.* A small house-lizard. —ष्ठं *n.* 1 The most excellent, the first or head. -2 Tin. -Comp. —अंश: *m.* 1 The eldest brother's share. -2 The right of the eldest brother to a larger share of the patrimonial property. -3 The best share. —अंबु *n.* 1 Water in which grain has been washed. -2 The scum of boiled rice. —आश्रम: *m.* 1 The highest or most excellent order in the religious life of a Brâhmana ; *i. e.* that of a householder.-2 A house-holder. —तात: *m.* The father's eldest brother. -वर्ण: *m.* 1 The highest caste (that of Brâhmanas). -2 A Bráhmana. —वृत्ति: *f.* The duties of seniority. —श्वश्रू: *f.* 1 A wife's eldest sister.-2 The eldest mother-in-law.

ज्यैष्ठ: *m.* N. of a lunar month in which the full moon stands in the constellation ज्येष्ठा (corresponding to May-June). —ष्ठी *f.* 1 The full-moon day in the month of ज्यैष्ठ. -2 A small house-lizard.

ज्यैष्ठ्यं *n.* 1 Precedence, priority of birth, primogeniture, seniority. -2 Pre-eminence, sovereignty.

ज्यो 1 A. (ज्यवते) 1 To advise, instruct. -2 To observe any religious obligation (such as a vow).

ज्योतिर्मय *a.* Consisting of stars, starry.

ज्योतिष *a.* (*f.* -षी) 1 Astronomical or astrological. —ष: *m.* An astronomer or astrologer. -षं *n.* 1 Astronomy, astrology. -2 One of the six Vedângas (being a short tract on Astronomy).-Comp. -विद्या *f.* Astronomical or astrological science.

ज्योतिषी *f.*, ज्योतिष्क: *m.* A planet, star, luminary. —ष्कं *n.* N. of the shining peak of Meru.

ज्योतिष्मत् *a.* (*f.* —ती) 1 Luminous, bright, shining. -2 Celestial. -*m.* 1 The sun. -2 N. of the third foot of Brahman (*m.*). -ती*f.* 1 The night (as illuminated by the stars). -2 (In phil.) A state of mind pervaded by सत्त्वगुण *i. e.* a tranquil state of mind.

ज्योतिस् *n.* 1 Light, lustre, brightness, flash. -2 Light of Brahman(*n.*); light regarded as the Supreme Spirit. -3 Lightning. -4 A heavenly body. -5 A luminary (planet, star &c.) -6 Bright.

ness of the sky, day-light (opp. तमस्.) -7 The sun and moon(dual). -8 Light as the divine principle of life, intelligence. -9 The science of the course of heavenly bodies; astronomy. -10 The faculty of seeing. -11 The celestial world. —*m.* 1 The sun. -2 Fire. -3 An epithet of Vishnu. -Comp. —इंगः, —इंगणः *m.* The fire-fly. -गणः *m.* 1 The heavenly bodies collectively. —चक्रं *n.* 1 The zodiac. —ज्ञः *m.* An astronomer or astrologer. —मंडलं *n.* The stellar sphere. —रथः (ज्योतीरथः) *m.* The polar star.-लोकः *m.* The Supreme Spirit.-विद् *m.* An astronomer or astrologer. —विद्या *f.*,—शास्त्रं (ज्योतिश्शास्त्रं) *n.* Astronomy or astrology. —स्तोमः (ज्योतिष्टोमः)*m.* 1 A Soma sacrifice considered as the type of a whole class of sacrificial ceremonies. -हस्ता *f.* N. of Durgâ.

ज्योत्स्ना *f.* 1 Moonlight. -2 Light (in general). -Comp. —ईशः *m.* The moon. -प्रियः *m.* The Chakora bird. —वृक्षः *m.* A lamp-stand, a candlestick.

ज्योत्स्नी *f.* A moonlight-night.

ज्योः *m.* The planet Jupiter, (a word connected with Greek Zeus).

ज्यौतिषकः *m.* An astronomer or astrologer.

ज्वर् 1 P. (ज्वरति, जूर्ण) 1 To be hot with fever or passion, be feverish. -2 To be diseased.

ज्वरः *m.* 1 Fever, feverish heat (in medicine used fig. *e. g.* दर्पज्वरः, मदनज्वरः, मदज्वरः &c. -2 Fever of the soul, mental pain, affliction, distress. -Comp. —अग्निः *m.* The paroxysm of fever. — अंकुशः *m.* A febrifuge. —प्रतीकार *m.* A cure of fever, febrifuge.

ज्वरित (*f.* —ता), ज्वरिन् *a.* (*f.* -णी) Attacked with fever.

ज्वल् 1 P. (ज्वलति, ज्वलित) 1 To burn brightly, blaze, glow, shine. -2 To be burnt up, be consumed or afflicted (as by fire). -3 To be ardent. -4 To burn (as a wound). -*Caus.* ज्वलयति-ते, ज्वालयति-ते but प्रज्वलयति) 1 To set on fire, light, kindle. -2 To irradiate, illuminate, brighten.

ज्वलका *f.* A large flame of fire.

ज्वलन *a.* (*f.* -ना) 1 Flaming, shining. -2 Combustible. —नः *m.* 1 Fire. -2 Corrosive alkali. -3 The number 'three'—नं *n.* Burning, blazing, shining. -Comp. -अश्मन् *m.* The sun-stone.

ज्वलित (*f.* -ता) 1 Burnt, kindled, illuminated. -2 Flaming, blazing.

ज्वालः *m.* 1 A flame, light. -2 A torch.

ज्वाला *f.* 1 A blaze, flame, illumination. -2 Burnt rice.-Comp.-जिह्वः, -ध्वजः *m.* Fire. -मुखी *f.* A volcano. -वक्त्रः *m.* An epithet of Siva

ज्वालिन् -*m.* An epithet of Siva.

झ.

झः *m.* 1 Beating time. -2 Jingling, clanking sound. -3 Wind accompanied by rain. -4 N. of Brihaspati. —झा *f.* The descent of a cascade, waterfall.

झगझगायते Den. A. To flash, sparkle.

झग (-गि-) ति *ind.* Quickly, at once.

झंकारिणी *f.* The river Ganges.

झंकृतिः *f.* A clanking or jingling sound as of metal ornaments.

झंगारः *m.*, झंकृतं *n.* A low murmuring sound, as the buzzing of bees.

झंजनं *n.* 1 Jingling and clanking of metal ornaments. 2 A rattling sound.

झंझा *f.* 1 The noise of the wind or of falling rain. -2 Hurricane. -3 A clanking sound, jingling. -4 Raining in large drops. -Comp. —अनिलः, -मरुत्,-वातः *m.* Wind with rain, a storm.

झटिति *ind.* Quickly, at once.

झणझणं *n.*, —णा *f.* Jingling sound.

झणझणायित *a.* (*f.* —ता) Tinkling.

झण(-न-)त्कारः *m.* Jingling, tinkling or clinking, as of metallic ornaments.

झंपः *m.*, —झंपा *f.* A spring, jump.

झंपाकः, झंपारुः, झंपिन् *m.* A monkey.

झरः *m.*, झरा, झरी *f.* A cascade.

झर्झरः *m.* 1 A sort of drum. -2 The Kali age. -3 A cane-staff. -4 An iron instrument used in cooking. -5 A cymbal. —रा *f.* A whore, harlot. —री *f.* A sort of drum. -रं *n.* A sound as of splashing or dropping.

झर्झरावती *f.* The Ganges.

झर्झरिन् *m* An epithet of Siva.

झलज्झला *f.* The noise of falling drops or of the flapping of an elephant's ears. [shine, splendour.

झला *f.* 1 A girl, daughter. -2 Sun-

झलिः *f.* The areca-nut.

झल्लः *m.* 1 A prize-fighter. -2 N. of one of the degraded classes.—ल्ली *f.* A kind of drum.

झल्लकं *n.*, -की *f.* Cymbal.

झल्लकंठः *m.* A pigeon.

झल्लिका *f.* 1 Dirt rubbed off the body by the application of perfumes. -2 Light, lustre.

झषः *m.* 1 A fish in general. -2 A large fish. -3 The sign pisces of the zodiac. -4 Heat, warmth. -5 The sign Capricornus of the zodiac. —षं *n* 1 A forest, wood. -2 A desert, dreary forest. -Comp. -अंकः, -केतनः, -केतुः, -ध्वजः *m.* N. of the God of love. -अशनः *m.* A porpoise. -उदरी *f.* An epithet of Satyavatí, mother of Vyása.

झांकृतं *n.* 1 A tinkling ornament worn round the feet. -2 A splashing sound (as of falling cascades).

झाटः *m.* 1 An arbour, bower. -2 A wood, thicket. -3 Cleaning sores. —टा, —टी *f.* The Jasmine plant.

झिरिका, झिरी, or झीरिका *f.* A cricket.

झिल्लिः *f.* 1 A cricket. -2 A kind of musical instrument.

झिल्लिका *f.* 1 A cricket. -2 The sound or cry of a cricket. -3 The light of sunshine.

झिल्ली *f.* 1 A cricket. -2 A kind of musical instrument, cymbal. -3 The wick of a lamp. -4 Sunshine. -5 Light, lustre.

झीरुका *f.* A cricket.

झुंटः *m.* 1 A tree. -2 A shrub, bush.

झोंडः *m.* The betel-nut tree.

ट.

टंक् 10 U. (टंकयति-ते, टंकित) 1 To bind, tie. -2 To cover. -With उद्- 1 To scrape, scratch. 2 To pierce through.

टंकः *m.*, —कं *n.* 1 A hatchet, an axe, a stone-cutter's chisel. -2 A sword. -3 The sheath a sword. -4 A peak shaped like the edge of a hatchet ; the slope or declivity of a hill. -5 Anger. -6 Pride. -7 The leg. -8 A chasm, cleft. 9 A spade, -का *f.* The leg.

टंककः *m.* A stamped coin, especially of silver. -Comp. —पतिः *m.* A mint-master. —शाला *f.* A mint.

टंकणं (-नं) *n.* 1 Borax. -2 Binding, tying. —णः (-नः) *m.* A species of horse. -Comp. —क्षारः *m.* Borax.

टंकारः *m.* 1 The twang of a bow-string. -2 A howl, cry, shout.

टंकारिन् *a.* (*f.* —णी) Twanging, making a hissing or twanging sound.

टंगः *m.*,—गं *m.* 1 A spade, hoe. —णः *m.* 1 Borax. -2 A weight of four Mashas,

टंगणः *m.*, —णं *n.* Borax.

टंगा *f.* The leg.

टट्टरी *f.* 1 A kind of musical instrument. -2 A joke, jest.

टिक् 1 A. (टेकते) To go, move.

टिटि (-ट्टि-) भः *m.* (*f.* -भी) A kind of bird. also टिट्टिभक.

टिप्पणी (-नी) *f.* A gloss, a comment.

टांकारः *m.* A clang, twang.

टीक् 1 A. (टीकते) To move, go, -With आ- To go, move, go about.

टीका *f.* A commentary, gloss.

टुंटुक *a.* 1 Small,. -2 Vile, cruel. -3 Harsh.

ठ.

ठक्करः *m.* 1 An idol, a deity. -2 An honorific title added to the name of a distinguished person.

ठालिनी *f.* A girdle.

ड.

डमः *m.* A low and mixed caste.

डमरः *m.* 1 Riot, tumult, affray. -2 Petty warfare between villages. -3 Terrifying an enemy by shouts and gestures. —रं *n.* Runing away through fear.

डमरुः *m.* A sort of small drum.

डंबर *a.* (*f.* —रा) Famous. —रः *m.* 1 An assemblage, mass. -2 Show, pomp. -3 Resemblance, appearance. -4 Pride, arrogance.

डाकिनी *f.* A kind of female imp.

डामर *a.* (*f.*-रा) 1 Terrific. -2 Riotous -3 Lovely, beautiful. —रः *m.* 1 An uproar, rout, affray, riot. -2 The bustle and confusion of festivity or strife. -3 Any surprising sight.

डाडिमः *m.* Same as दाडिमः.

डिंडिमः *m.* A kind of small drum.

डिंडी (-डि-) रः *m.* 1 Cuttle-fish-bone considered as the foam of the sea. -2 Foam (in general).

डित्थः *m.* 1 A wooden elephant. 2 A good-looking, dark-colored young man proficient in every science.

डिमः *m.* A kind of drama.

डिंबः *m.* 1 Affray, riot. -2 Sound occasioned by terror. -3 A young child or animal. -4 An egg. -5 A globe or ball. -6 Globular blossom. -7 A chrysalis. -8 Embryo. -9 The spleen. 10 The uterus. [-2 A bubble.

डिंबिका *f.* 1 A libidinous woman.

डिंभः *m.* 1 A young child. -2 A young animal such as a cub. -3 A fool, a block-head. -भा *f.* An infant.

डिंभकः *m.* (*f.* —भिका) 1 A young child. -2 Any young animal.

डी 1. 4. A. (डयते, डीयते, डयितुं, डीन) 1 To fly, pass through the air. -2 To go. -With प्र- To fly up.

डयनं *n.* 1 Fight. -2 A litter carried upon men's shoulders, palanquin.

डीन *p. p.* (*f.* —ना) Flown up. -नं *n.* The flight of a bird.

डुंडुभ,—भः *m.* A kind of snake.

डोमः, डोंब *m.* A man of a low caste

डोरः *m.* A fillet of thread (tied round the arm). -2 The string with which a packet or parcel is tied.

ढ.

ढक्का *f.* A large or double drum.

ढामरा *f.* A goose.

ढालं *n.* A shield.

ढालिन् *m.* A warrior with a shield.

ढुंढिः *m.* An epithet of Ganesa.

ढोलः *m.* A large drum or tabor.

ढौक् 1 A (ढौकते, ढौकित) To go, approach. -*Caus.* (ढौकयति-ते) 1 To bring near, cause to approach. -2 To present, offer. -With उप- To present.

ढौकनं *n.* 1 Offering. -2 A present.

त.

तक् 1 P. To live in distress.-2 To laugh at, deride.-3 To bear, endure.

ताकिल a. (f. —ला) Fraudulent, crafty. —ला f. A medicament, drug.

तक्रं n. Butter-milk. -Comp. —अट: m. A churning-stick. —सारं n. Fresh butter.

तक्ष् 1. 5 P. (तक्षति, तक्ष्णोति, तष्ट) 1 To chop, cut off, pare, chisel, slice, split. -2 To fashion, shape, form (out of wood &c.). -3 To make, create in general. -4 To invent, form in the mind. 5 To peel. -6 To make thin. -With निस्-1 To slice off.-2 To form

तक्षक: m. 1 A carpenter, wood-cutter (whether by caste or profession). -2 The chief actor in the prelude of a drama (i.e. the सूत्रधार). -3 N. of the architect of the gods. -4 N. of one of the principal Nâgas, son of Kasyapa and Kadru.

तक्षणं n. Paring, cutting. —णी f. A carpenter's adze.

तक्षन् m. 1 A carpenter, wood-cutter (whether by caste or profession). -2 N. of the architect of the gods.

तगर: m. A kind of plant.

तंक् 1 P. (तंकति, तंकित) To endure, bear. -2 To laugh. -3 To live in distress.

तंक: m. 1 Living in distress, a miserable life. -2 Grief produced by separation from a beloved object. -3 Fear. -4 A stone-cutter's chisel.

तंकनं n. Living in distress, miserable living.

तंच् 7 P. (तनक्ति, तंचित) To contract, shrink.

तंच् 1 P. (तंचति) To go.

तंज् 7 P. See तंच्.

तट: m. 1 A slope, declivity, precipice. -2 The sky or horizon. -3 An epithet of Siva. —ट: m., टा f., —टी, f., टं n. 1 The shore or bank, declivity, slope. -2 A term applied to certain parts of the body which have, as it were, sloping sides. e. g. जघनतट, कटितट, श्रोणितट, कुचतट, कंठतट, ललाटतट &c. —टं n. A field. -Comp. —स्थ a. 1 (lit.) Situated on a bank or or declivity. -2 (fig.) Standing aloof, neutral, indifferent. (—स्थ: m.) An indifferent person, one neither a friend nor a foe. (—स्थं n) That property or लक्षण of a thing which is distinct from its nature, and yet is the property by which it is known; e. g. गंधवत्त्व in the case of पृथ्वी.

तटग: m. See तडाग:.

तटाक: m., —कं n. A pond (deep enough for the lotus and other aquatic plants).

तटिनी f. A river.

तड् 10 U. (ताडयति,-ते; ताडित) 1 To beat, strike (in general), dash against. -2 To beat, strike, punish by beating. -3 To strike, beat (as a drum). -4 To play on, strike the wires of (a musical instrument). -5 (In astr.) To strike against, touch, obscure or eclipse partially. -8 (In Math.) To multiply.

तडग: m. Same as तडाग:.

तडाक: m. A pond, pool. —का f. 1 A blow. -2 A bank, shore.

तडाग: m., —गं n. 1 A pond, tank

तडाघात: m. See तटाघात:.

तडित् f. Lightning. -Comp. —गर्भ: m. A cloud. —लता f. Forked lightning. —लेखा f. A streak of lightning.

तडित्वत् m. A cloud.

तंड् 1 A. (तंडते, तंडित) To strike.

तंडक: m. 1 A juggler, a cheat. -2 Froth, foam. -3 A wagtail.

तंडुलः *m.* Grain after threshing, unhusking and winnowing ; (especially rice.). -Comp. —अंबु *n.* Gruel. —उत्थं (—कं) *n.* Rice-gruel.

तत *a.* 1 Spread. -2 Commenced.-तं *n.* Any stringed musical instrument.

ततस् (ततः) *ind.* 1 From that (person or place &c.), thence. -2 There, thither. -3 Then, thereupon, afterwards.-4 Therefore, for that reason. -5 Then, in that case (as a corr. of यदि) -6 Beyond that (in place), further more, more over.-7 Than that, other than that. -8 Sometimes used for the ablative forms of तत. यतः-ततः Means where-there, since-therefore. यतो यतः—ततस्ततः Wherever-there. ततः किं 'what then'?, 'of what use is it?' 'what avails it?' ततस्ततः 'here and there', 'to and fro' (2) 'what next? 'what further? well proceed (occurring in dramas). ततः प्रभृति Thence forward (corr. of यतः प्रभृति).

ततस्त्य *a.* (*f.* —स्त्या) Coming or proceeding from thence.

ततिः *f.* 1 A series, row, line. -2 A troop.-3 A sacrifical act, a ceremony.

तति *pron. a.* (Declined only in plural; nom. and acc. तति) So many.

तत्त्वं (Sometimes written as तत्वं) *n.* 1 True state or condition, fact. -2 Truth, reality. -3 True or essential nature. -4 The real nature of the human soul or the material world as being identical with the Supreme Spirit pervading the universe. -5 A true or first principle. -6 An element, a primary substance.-7 The mind.-8 Sum and substance. -9 Slow time in music. -10 An element or elementary property. -11 The Supreme Being. - 12 A kind of dance. -13 The three qualities or constituents of every thing in nature (सत्त्व, रजस् and तमस्).-Comp. —अभियोगः *m.* A positive charge or declaration. -अर्थः *m.* Truth, reality. -ज्ञ, -विद् *a.* 1 A philosopher.-2 Knowing the true nature of Brahman (*n.*). -3 Knowing the true nature of anything. -4 Acquainted with the true principles of science. —ज्ञः *m.* A Bráhmana. —ज्ञानं *n.* 1 Knowledge of the truth. -2 A thorough knowledge of the principles of a science. -3 Philosophy. -न्यासः *m.* N. of a ceremony performed in honour of Vishnu.

तत्त्वतः, तत्त्वेन *ind.* Truly, really.

तत्र *ind.* 1 In that place. -2 On that occasion, under those circumstances, then, in that case. -3 For that, in that. -4 Often used for the loc. case of तत. तत्रापि 'Even then', 'nevertheless' (corr. of यद्यपि). तत्र तत्र 'In various places or cases, 'here and there,' 'to every place'. -Comp. —भवत *a.* (*f.* -ती) His honour, his reverence. A title given in dramas to persons not near the speaker. —स्थ *a.* Standing or being there, belonging to that place.

तत्रत्य *a.* (*f.* —त्या) Belonging to that place.

तथा *ind.* 1 So, thus, in that manner. -2 And also, so also, as well as. -3 True, just so, exactly so. -4 As surely as (preceded by यथा). तथापि (oft. corr. of यद्यपि) 'Even then,' 'still', 'yet', 'never-the-less'. तथेति shows 'assent' or 'promise'. तथैव 'Even so', 'just so'; 'exactly so'. तथैव च 'In like manner'. तथा च 'And also', 'and likewise', 'in like manner', 'so it has been said.' तथाहि 'For so', 'as for instance', 'for this (it has been said).-Comp. —गत *a.* 1 Being in such a state or condition. -2 Of such a quality. (—तः *m.*) 1 Buddha. -2 A Jina. —गुण *a.* Endowed with such qualities. —भावः *m.* 1 That state or condition. -2 Reality. —भूत *a.* 1 Of such qualities or nature. -2 So circumtanced, in that conditon. —राजः *m.* An epithet of Buddha. —रूप, -रूपिन *a.* Thus shaped, looking thus. -विध *a.* Of such a sort. -विधं *ind.* 1 Thus, in this manner.-2 Likewise,equally. —विधेय *a.* Of such a sort.

तथात्वं *n.*, तथाता *f.* 1 Such a state, being so. -2 True state or nature.

तथ्य *a.* (*f.* —थ्या) True, real, genuine. —थ्यं *n.* Truth, reality.

तद् *pron. a.* (Nom. sing. *m.* सः , *f.* सा, *n.* तत्) 1 That,referring to something not present. -2 He, she, it ; (oft. as corr. of यद्). -3 That, *i.e.* well-known.-4 The same, identical, that very ; usually with एव. When repeated तद् has the sense of 'several, ' various '. तेन Instr. of तद् is often used with adverbial force in the sense of 'therefore', 'on that account' 'in that case', 'for that reason'. तेन हि If so, well then. -*ind.* 1 There, thither. -2 Then, in that case, at that time. -3 For that reason. -4 Then (corr. of यदि). -*n.* 1 The Supreme Spirit or Brahman (*n.*).-2 This world. -Comp. —अनंतर *a.* Next to that. (-*ind.*) Immediately after that, thereupon. —अनु *ind.* After that, afterwards. —अंत *a.* Perishing in that, ending thus. —अर्थ, -अर्थीय *a.* 1 Intended for that. -2 Having that meaning. —अवधि *ind.* 1 So far, upto that period, till then. -2 From that time, since then. -एकचित्त *a.* Having the mind solely fixed on that. -कालः *m.* 1 The current moment, present time. -2 That time. —कालं *ind.* 1 Instantly, immediately. -2 At that time, at a certain time. —क्षणः *m.* 1 Present time, time being, present or current moment. -2 The same moment.-3 A measure of time.-क्षणं, -क्षणात् *ind.* Immediately, directly, instantly. -क्रिय *a.* Working without wages. —गत *a.* Gone or directed to that,intent on that, devoted to that, belonging to that. (—तः *m.*) The continued multiplication of four or more like quantities. —गुण *a.* Possessing those qualities.(-णः *m.*) 1 The quality or virtue of anything. -2(In *Rhet.*) The figure of speech in which an object is represented as giving up its own quality and assuming the quality of another excellent thing that is near. तद्गुणः स्वगुणत्यागादत्युत्कृष्टगुणग्रहः । *साहि० द० *e.g.* नीतोनासान्तिकं तन्व्या मालत्याः कुसुमोत्करः । बंधूकभावमानिन्ये रागेणाधरवर्तिना ॥ —ज *a.* Immediate, instantaneous.-ज्ञः *m.* A knowing or intelligent man, wise man,philosopher. —तृतीय *a.* Doing that for the third time. —धन *a.* Niggardly. —पदार्थः *m.* The Supreme Being. —पर *a.* 1 Following that, coming after that, inferior. -2 Having that as the highest object, closely intent on, exclusively devoted to, eagerly engaged in. -3 Diligent. —परायण *a.* Solely devoted or attached to anything. —पुरुषः *m.* 1 The original or Supreme Spirit. -2 N. of a class of compounds in which the last member is defined or qualified by the first, without losing its original independence. —पूर्व *a.* 1 Happening or occurring for the first time. -2 Former. -प्रथम *a.* Doing that for the first time.

–चक्रः *m.* A kind of arrow. —मात्रं *n.* 1 Merely that, only a trifle, a very small quantity. –2 (In phil.) A subtle and primary element (such as शब्द, रस, स्पर्श, रूप and गंध). —वाचक *a.* Denoting or signifying that. –विद् *a.* 1 Knowing that.–2 Knowing the truth.–विध *a.* Of that kind or sort.

तदा *ind.* 1 Then, at that time. –2 Then, in that case. यदा यदा–तदा तदा 'Whenever.' तदाप्रभृति 'Since then,' 'thenceforward,' –Comp. —मुख *a.* Begun. (—खं *n.*) Beginning.

तदानीं *ind.* Then, at that time.

तदानींतन *a.* Belonging to that time, contemporary of that time.

तदीय *a.* (*f.* —या) Belonging to that, his, hers, its, theirs.

तद्वत *a.* Containing or possessed of that. *ind.* 1 Like that, in that manner. –2 Equally, in like manner.

तन् 8 U. (तनोति, तनुते, तनिष्ठुं,तत; *pass.* तन्यते or तायते ; *desid.* तितंसति, तितांसति, तितनिषति) 1 To stretch, extend, lengthen. –2 To spread, diffuse. –3 To cover, fill. –4 To cause, produce. –5 To perform, do, accomplish (as a sacrifice). –6 To compose, write (as a work &c.) –7 To stretch or bend (as a bow). –8 To spin out, weave. –9 To propagate, or be propagated. –10 To protract, prolong, augment. With अव— 1 To cover. –2 To descend. आ– 1 To stretch. –2 To cause, make, create. –3 To spread, diffuse. —प्र 1 To spread. –2 To cause, to create. –3 To perform (as a sacrifice). –4 To cover. –5 To show, to exhibit. वि— 1 To cover. To spread. –3 To form. –4 To stretch (as a bow). –5 To cause, give. –6 To perform (as a sacrifice). –7 To compose (as a work). सम्– To continue.

तन् 1 P., 10 U. (तनति, तानयति,–ते) 1 To confide, trust, place confidence in. –2 To help, assist. –3 To pain or afflict with disease. With वि— To spread, extend.

तनयः *m.* 1 A son. –2 A male descendant. –3 (In astrol.) N. of the fifth lunar mansion. —या *f.* A daughter. —यं *n.* Posterity, offspring.

तनिमन् *m.* Thinness, slenderness, minuteness. —*n.* The liver.

तनु *a.* (*f.* —नु,–न्वी) 1 Thin, lean, emaciated. –2 Delicate, slender (as limbs). –3 Fine, delicate(as cloth). –4 Small, little, scanty, few. –5 Trifling, unimportant, little. –6 Shallow (as a river).–नुः *f.* 1 The body, the person. –2 Outward form, manifestation. –3 Nature, the form or character of anything. –4 Skin –Comp. —अंग *a.* Having slender limbs, delicate. (–गी *f.*) A delicate woman. —अनः *m.* The wind. –कूपः *m.* A pore of the skin. —छदः *m.* An armour. (–जः) *m.* A son. —जा *f.* A daughter. —त्यज् *a.* 1 Risking one's life. –2 Giving up one's person, dying. —त्याग *a.* Spending little, sparing, niggardly. —त्रं, –त्राणं *n.* An armour. —भवः *m.* A son. —भवा *f.* A daughter. —भस्त्रा *f.* The nose. —भृत *m.* Any being furnished with a body, a living being ; particularly a human being. —मध्य *a* Having a slender waist. –रसः *m.* Perspiration. —रुह्, –रुहं *n.* The hair of the body. —वारं *n.* An armour. —व्रणः *m.* A pimple.–संचारिणी *f.* A young woman, a girl ten years old. —सरः *m.* Perspiration. —ह्रदः *m.* The anus.

तनुल *a.* (*f.* –ला) Spread, expanded.

तनुस् *n.* The body.

तनू *f.* The body.–Comp.–उद्भवः, –नः *m.* A son. –उद्भवा,–जा *f.* A daughter.

—जनिः, —आत्मज *m.* A son. —नपं *n.* Clarified buttter, ghee.—नपात *m.*Fire. —रुहं *n.* 1 The hair of the body (*-m.* also). -2 The wing of a bird, a feather. —रुहः *m.* A son. —ह्रदः *m.* The anus, the rectum.

तंतिः *f.* 1 A cord, line, string. -2 A row, series. -3 Extension, expansion. -4 A cow. 5 A weaver. -Comp. —पालः *m.* 1 A guardian of (the rows of) cows. -2 N. assumed by Sahadeva when living at the house of Viráta.

तंतुः *m.* 1 A thread, cord, wire, string, line.-2 A cob-web. -3 A filament. -4 An offspring, issue, race. -Comp. —काष्ठं *n.* A piece of wood or brush used by weavers for cleaning threads. -कीटः *m.* A silk-worm. —नागः *m.* A (large) shark. —निर्यासः *m.* The palmyra tree. —नाभः. *m.* A spider.-भः *m.* 1 The mustard seed. -2 A calf. —वाद्यं *n.* Any stringed musical instrument. -वानं *n.* Weaving. —वापः *m.* 1 A weaver. -2 A loom. -3 Weaving. —वायः *m.* 1 A spider. -2 A weaver. -3 Weaving. —विग्रहा *f.* A plantain. —शाला *f.* A weaver's workshop.-संतत *a.* Woven, sewn. (-तं *n.*) Woven cloth. -संततिः, -संतानः *m.* Weaving. —सारः *m.* The betel-nut tree.

तंतुकः *m.* The mustard seed. —की *f.* A vein or any tubular vessel of the body.

तंतुनः,-णः *m.* A shark.

तंतुरं,-लं *n.* The fibrous root of a [lotus.

तंत्र् 10 U. (तंत्रयति,-ते, तंत्रित) 1 To rule, control, govern. -2 To perform or go through in order. -3 To maintain by discipline, keep in order. -4 (A.) To support, maintain (as a family).

तंत्रं *n.* 1 A loom. -2 A thread. -3 The warp or threads extended lengthwise in a loom. -4 Posterity. -5 An uninterrupted series. -6 The regular order of ceremonies and rites, system, framework, ritual. -7 Main point. -8 Principal doctrine, rule,theory,science.-9Subservience, dependence, as in स्वतंत्र, परतंत्र. -10 A scientific work. -11 A chapter, section, as of a work. -12 A religious treatise teaching magical and mystical formularies.-13The cause of more than one effect. -14A spell. -15 A chief remedy or charm. -16 A drug, medicament. -17 An oath, ordeal. -18 Raiment. -19 The right way of doing anything. -20 Royal retinue. -21 A realm, country, authority. -22 Government, ruling, adminstration,machinery of government. -23 An army. -24 A heap, multitude. -25 A house. -26 Decoration. -27 Wealth. -28 Happiness.-29 Providing for the security and prosperity of a kingdom. -Comp —काष्ठं *n.* The same as तंतुकाष्ठ. —वापः *m.*, —पं *n.* 1 Weaving. -2 loom. —वायः *m.*, —यं *n.* 1 Weaving. -2 A loom. —वायः *m.* 1 A spider.-2 A weaver (तंत्रवापः also).

तंत्रकः *m.* A new garment (unbleached cloth).

तंत्रणं *n.* Maintenance of order,discipline, government.

तंत्रिः, -त्री *f.* 1 A string, cord. -2 A bow-string. -3 The wire of a lute. -4 A sinew. -5 A tail. -6 A lute.

तंद्रा *f.* 1 Lassitude, weariness-fatigue. -2 Sleepiness,sluggishness.

तंद्रालु *a* 1 Tired, exhausted. -2 Sleepy, slothful.

तंद्रिः,-द्री *f.* 1Sleepiness,drowsiness. -2 Exhaustion, fainting.

तंद्रिका *f.* Sloth, sleepiness.

तन्मय *a.* (*f.* —यी) 1 Made up of that. -2 Wholly absorbed in that. -3 Identical with that.

तन्वी *f.* A thin and delicate woman.

तप् 1 P. rarely A, 4. P. (तपति, तप्यति ; तप्त). (Intransitively used). 1 To shine, blaze (as fire or sun). -2 To be hot or warm, give out heat. -3 To suffer pain. -4 To undergo penance (with तपस्).-5(Transitively used). To make hot, heat, warm. -6 To burn. -7 To hurt, injure, damage, pain, distress. -8 To undergo penance (with तपस्). With अनु- 1 To repent. -2 To grieve. उत्- (Atm. when used intransitively or has a limb of the body for its object). 1 To scorch, burn, heat. -2 To cousume, torture by heat. -3 To melt. निस्- To purify. पश्चात्- To repent. वि- (Atm.) 1 To shine. -2 To warm. सम्- 1 To heat. -2 To be sorry. -3 To repent.

तप् 10 U. (तापयति-ते, तापित) 1 To heat, make warm. -2 To pain, distress. With निस् 1 To heat. -2 To purify. -3 To burnish. वि— 1 To shine (Atm.). -2 To warm, heat.

तप *a.* (*f.* —पा) 1 Burning, consuming by heat. -2 Causing pain or trouble, distressing. —पः *m.* 1 Heat, fire, warmth. -2 The sun. -3 The hot season.-4 Penance.-Comp. -अत्ययः,-अंतः*m.*The end of hot season.

तपती *f.* The river Tâptî.

तपनः *m.* 1 The sun. -2 The hot season. -3 The sun-stone. -4 N. of a hell. -5 An epithet of Siva. -6 The Arka plant. 7 N. of Agastya. —नं *n.* 1 Heat, burning. -2 Paining, grieving. -3 Mental agony.-Comp. —अंशुः, -करः,-दीधितिः *m.* 1 The sun. -2 A sun-beam. —आत्मजः, -तनयः *m.* An epithet (1) of Yama. (2) of Karna. (3) of Sugrîva. —आत्मजा, -तनया*f.* An epithet of the Yamunâ and of the Godâvarî. —इष्टं *n.* Copper. —उपलः, -मणिः *m* The sun-stone. —छदः *m.* The sun-flower.

तपनी *f.* 1 The river Godâvarî or the river Tâptî. -2 Heat.

तपनीयं *n.* Gold ; especially gold purified with fire. (Also तपनीयकं.).

तपस् *n.* 1 Warmth, heat, fire. -2 Pain, suffering.-3 Penance, religious austerity. -4 Meditation connected with the practice of personal self-denial or bodily mortification. -5 Moral virtue, merit. -6 Special observance of any particular caste. -7 One of the seven worlds ; *i. e* the region above the world called जनस्. -8 The month of religious austerities.-9A long period of time Kalpa. -10 (In astr.) The ninth lunar mansion. -*m.* 1 The month of Mâgha. -2 An epithet of Agni. —*m.*, -*n.* 1 The cold season (शिशिर). -2 The winter (हेमंत). -3 The hot season (ग्रीष्म).-Comp.-अनुभावः *m.* Influence of religious penance.—अवटः *m.* The Brahmâvarta country. —चरणं *n*, -चर्या *f.* The practice of penance. —तक्षः *m.* An epithet of Indra. —धनः *m.* An ascetic, devotee. —निधिः *m.* An eminently pious man, an ascetic. —निष्ठ *a.* Performing penance. —प्रभावः *m.*, -बलं *n.* The power acquired by religious austerities ; efficacy or potency of devotion. —राशिः *m.* An ascetic. -लोकः *m.* The region above the world called जनस्. —वनं *n.* A penance-grove, a sacred grove in which ascetics practise penance. —विशेषः *m.* Excellence of devotion; pre-eminent religious austerities. —वृद्ध *a.* Very ascetic or devout. —समाधि: *m.* The practice of penance or religious austerities. —स्थली *f.* 1 A seat of religious austerity.-2N. ofBenares.

तपस: *m.* 1 The sun. -2 The moon. -3 A bird.

तपस्य् Den. P. To practise penance.

तपस्य: *m.* 1 The month of Phâlguna. -2 An epithet of Arjuna. —स्या *f.* Religious austerity, penance.

तपस्विन् *a.* (*f.* —नी) 1 Practising penance,devout. -2 Poor,miserable, helpless, pitiable.-*m.* 1 An ascetic. -2 A mendicant, pauper. -3 An epithet of Nârada. -4 A sparrow. —नी *f.* 1 A female ascetic. -2 A poor or wretched woman. -Comp. —पत्र: *m.* The sun-flower.

तप्त *p. p.* (*f.* -प्ता) 1 Heated,burnt. -2 Red-hot, hot. -3 Melted, fused. -4 Distressed, afflicted. -5 Practised (as penance).-Comp.—कांचनं *n.* Gold purified with fire. —कृच्छ्रं *n.* A kind of penance. —रूपं, -रूपकं *n.* Purified silver.

तम् 4 P. (ताम्यति, तांत) 1 To choke, be suffocated. -2 To be exhausted or fatigued. -3 To be distressed (in body or mind),be uneasy or pained, waste away. With उत्- To be impatient.

तमं *n.* 1 Darkness. -2 The tip of the foot. —म: *m.* 1 A N. of Râhu. -2 The Tamâla tree.-3Darkness.

तमस् *n.* 1 Darkness. -2 The gloom or darkness of hell.-3 Mental darkness, illusion, error. -4 (In Sân. phil.). Darkness or ignorance, as one of the three qualities or constituents of nature (the other two being सत्त्व and रजस्). -5 Grief, sorrow. -6 Sin. —*m.*, -*n.* An epithet of Râhu. -Comp.-अपह *a* Removing darkness or ignorance, illumining, enlightening. (-ह: *m.*) 1 The sun. -2 The moon.-3 Fire.-4A Buddha. -अरि: *m.* 1 The sun.-2 The moon.-3 Fire. -कांड:*m.*, -डं *n.*Great or spreading darkness. —घ्न: *m.* 1 The sun. -2 The moon. -3 Fire. -4 Vishnu. -5 Siva. -6 Knowledge. -7 A Buddha. —ज्योतिस् *m.* A fire-fly. —ततिः *f.* Spreading darkness. —नुद् *m.* 1 The sun. -3 The moon. -4 Fire. -5 A lamp, light. —नुद: *m.* 1 The sun. -2 The moon. -3 The Supreme Being. —भिद्, -मणि: *m.* A fire-fly.—विकार: *m.* Sickness, disease. —हन्, -हर: -*m.* 1 The sun. -2 The moon.

तमस: *m.* 1 Darkness, -2 A well. —सा *f.* N. of a river. -सं *n.* 1 Darknees. -2 A city.

तमस्वती *f.* 1 Night. -2 Turmeric.

तमस्विनी, तमा *f.* A night.

तमाल: *m.* 1 N. of a tree with a very dark bark. -2 A sectarial mark of sandal upon the forehead. -3 A sword, scimitar. -4 The bark of the bamboo. -Comp. -पत्रं *n.* 1 A sectarial mark upon the forehead. -2 Tamâla leaf.

तमि:, -मी *f.* 1 Night, especially a dark night.-2A swoon,-3Turmeric.

तमिस्र *a.* (*f.* -स्रा) Dark. --स्रं *n.* 1 Darknnss. -2 Mental darkness, illusion. -3 Anger, wrath.-स्र: *m.* The dark half of the month.-Comp.-पक्ष: *m.* The dark fortnight (of a lunar month).

तमिस्रा *f.* 1 A dark night. -2 Extensive darkness.

तंबा, तंबिका *f.* A cow.

तय् 1 A. (तयते) 1 To go, move.-2 To guard, protect.

तर *a.* 1 Crossing. -2 Surpassing. -3 Conquering. —र: *m.* 1 Passing over, crossing, passage.-2 Freight.

-3 A road. -4 A ferry-boat.-5 Fire. -Comp. -पण्यं *n*. The freight. -पण्यिकः *m*. One who receives the freight. —स्थानं *n*. A landing-place, wharf.

तरक्षः, -क्षुः *m*. A hyena.

तरंगः *m*. 1 A wave. -2 A section or part of a work (as of the कथासरित्सागर). -3 A leap, jump, gallop, jumping motion (as of a horse).-4 Cloth or clothes. -5 Waving, moving to and fro.

तरंगित *a*. (*f*. -ता) 1 Wavy. -2 Overflowing. -3 Tremulous. —तं *n*. Waving.

तरंगिन् *a*. (*f*. -णी) Wavy, undulating, unsteady. —णी *f*. A river.

तरणः *m*. 1 A boat, raft. -2 *Svarga* or heaven. —णं *n*. 1 Crossing over. -2 Conquering, -3 An oar.

तरणिः *m*. 1 The sun. -2 A ray of light.-3 The *Arka* plant.-4 Copper. —णिः, -तरणी *f*. A raft, boat. -Comp. —पेटकः *m*. An oval bowl of wood for baling a boat. —रत्नं *n*. A ruby.

तरंडः *m*., -डा, -डी *f*., -डं *n*. A boat. -डः *m*., -डं *n*. 1 A raft or float made of bamboos tied together and floated on jars or inverted hollow gourds. -2 The float of a fishing-line. -3 An oar -Comp. —पादा *f*. A kind of boat.

तरंतः *m*. 1 The ocean. -2 A hard shower.-3 A frog. -4 A Rákshasa. -5 A devotee. —ती *f*. A boat.

तरल *a*. (*f*. —ला) 1 Trembling, waving, shaking, tremulous. -2 Fickle, unsteady. -3 Sparkling, glittering.-4 Liquid.-5 Libidinous, wanton. -6 Hollow. -7 Extensive, wide. —लः *m*. 1 The central gem of a necklace. -2 A necklace. -3 A level surface. -4 Bottom, depth. -5 A diamond. -6 Iron. -7 Thorn-apple. —ला *f*. 1 Rice-gruel. -2 Spirituous liquor. -3 A bee.

तरलय् Den. P. To cause to shake, to wave, move to and fro.

तरलाय् Den A. To tremble, shake, move to and fro.

तरलायितः *m*. A large wave, surf. —तः *m*., —तं *n*. Fickleness.

तरलित *a*. (*f*. —ता) Shaking, tremulous, undulating.

तरवारिः *m*. A sword.

तरस् *n*. 1 Speed, velocity. -2 Vigour, strength, energy.-3 A bank, a place of crossing. -4 A float, raft. -5 A monkey. -6 A disease.

तरसं *n*. Meat, flesh.

तरसानः *m*. A boat.

तरस्वत् *a*. 1 Quick, swift. -2 Sick. -3 Energetic, strong, powerful.

तरस्विन् *a*. (*f*.—नी) 1 Swift, quick.-2 Strong, powerful, courageous, mighty.-*m*. 1 A courier, an express.-2 A hero. -3 Air, wind.-4 N. of Garuda.

तरांधुः, तरालुः *m*. A large flat-bottomed boat.

तरिः, -तरी *f*. 1 A boat. -2 A box for clothes. -3 The hem of a garment. -Comp. —रथः *m* An oar.

तरिकः *m*. 1 A ferry-man.2 A float, raft. —का *f*. 1 A boat. -2 Cream.

तरिकिन् *m*. A ferry-man.

तरित्रं *n*., तरित्री, तरिणी *f*. A boat, ship.

तरिषः *m*. 1 A boat, raft. -2 The ocean. -3 A fit or competent person. -4 Heaven. -5 Work, business, profession. -6 A fine shape or form. -7 Decorating. -8 Dry cow-dung. —षी *f*. N. of a daughter of Indra.

तरुः *m*. 1 A tree. -Comp. -खंडः *m*., —डं *n*., -षंडः *m*., —डं *n*. Assemblage or clump of trees. —जीवनं *n*. The root of a tree. —तलं *n* The ground about the foot of a tree, foot of a tree. —नख: *m.* A thorn. —मृग: *m.* A monkey. —राग: *m.* 1 A bud or blossom. -2 A young shoot, sprout. -राज:*m.* The Tâla tree.-रुहा *f.* A parasitical plant. -विलासिनी *f.* The Navamallikâ creeper. —शायिन् *m.* A bird.

तरुण *a.* (*f.* —णी) 1 Young, youthful, juvenile (as a man). -2 Young, newly-born or produced, tender, soft. -3 Newly risen, not high in the sky (as the sun).-4 New, fresh. —ण: *m.* A young man, youth. -2 The castor-oil plant. -3 Large cumin-seed. —णी *f.* A young or youthful woman. णं *n.* 1 Cartilage. -2 A sprout. -Comp. —अस्थि *n.* Cartilage. —ज्वर: *m.* Fever lasting for a week. —दधि *n.* Coagulated millk five days old. —पीतिका*f.* Red arsenic.

तरुणकं *n.* A sprout.

तरुणिमन् *m.* Youth, juvenility. [tory.

तरुष: *m.* A conqueror. —षा *f.* Vic-

तर्क् 10 U. (तर्कयति-ते, तर्कित) 1 To suppose, guess, suspect, believe. conjecture. -2 To reason, speculate about, reflect. -3 To consider or regard as (with two acc.). -4 To intend, mean, have in view. -5 To ascertain. -6 To shine. -7 To speak. With. प्र— 1 To reason, to reflect. -2 To think, believe, suppose. वि— 1 To guess. -2 To think, belive.-3To reflect.

तर्क: *m.* 1 Supposition, conjecture, guess. -2 Reasoning, speculation, discussion. -3 Doubt. -4 Logic, the science of logic. -5 (In logic) Reduction to absurdity, a conclusion opposed to the premises, a ***reductio ad absurdum.*** -6 A system of doctrine founded on pure reasoning or free thinking, a philosophical system (particularly one of the six principal ' darsanas '). -7 A name for the number ' six '. -8 Supplying an ellipsis. -9 Cause, motive. -10 Wish, desire. —र्का *f.* Speculation, reasoning. -Comp. —आभास: *m.* Fallacious reasoning, fallacy in drawing conclusions. —विद्या *f.* Logic. —शास्त्रं *n.* 1 Logic. -2 A philosophical work.

तर्कक: *m.* 1 A suitor, an inquirer, a petitioner. -2 A logician.

तर्कु: *m.*, *f.* A spindle, an iron pin upon which cotton is first drawn out. -Comp.—पिंड: *m.*,—पीठी *f.*, -पीठ:, *m.*, —पाठी *f.* A ball at the lower end of a spindle.

तर्क्षु: *m.* A hyena.

तर्क्ष्य: *m.* Nitre, salt-petre.

तर्ज् 1 P., 10 A. (often P. also) (तर्जति, तर्जयति-ते, तर्जित) 1 To threaten, menace, terrify. -2 To scold, censure, blame. -3 To mock, deride.

तर्जनं *n.*, —ना *f.* 1 Threatening, frightening. -2 Censuring.-3 Pointing at (in ridicule or contempt). -4 Putting to shame, excelling, surpassing. -5 Anger. —नी *f.* The fore-finger.

तर्ण:, तर्णक: *m.* A calf.

तर्णि: *m.* 1 A raft. -2 The sun.

तर्द् 1 P. (तर्दति) 1 To injure, hurt, -2 To kill, cut through.

तर्पणं *n.* 1 Pleasing, satisfying. -2 Satisfaction, pleasure. -3 Satiety, fulness. -4 One of the five daily Yajnas; presenting libations of water to the Manes of the deceased ancestors (पितृयज्ञ). -5 Fuel for the sacred fire. -Comp. —इच्छु: *m.* An epithet of Bhishma. [post.

तर्मन् *n.* The top of the sacrificial

तर्ष: *m.* 1 Thirst, wish, desire. -2 The ocean. -3 A boat.

तर्षण *a.* (*f.* —णा), तर्षुल *a.* (*f.* —ला) 1 Thirsty. -2 Wishing.

तर्षितं *n.* Thirst.

तर्हि *ind.* 1 At that time, then. -2 In that case. यदा-तर्हि 'When-then'. यदि-तर्हि 'If-then'; कथं तर्हि 'How then'.?

तल: *m.*, —लं *n.* 1 A surface; sometimes used at the end of comp. without much alteration of meaning. *e.g.* महीतलं 'surface of the earth' *i. e.* (earth itself). -2 The palm of the hand. -3 The sole of the foot. -4 The fore-arm. -5 A slap with the hand. -6 Lowness, inferiority of position. -7 A lower part, base, foot, bottom. -8 The ground under tree or any other object, shelter, shadow &c. afforded by anything. -9 A hole, pit. -10 A span. —क: *m.* 1 The hilt of a sword. -2 The palmyra tree. —लं *n.* 1 A pond. -2 A forest, wood. -3 Cause, origin, motive. -4 A leathern fence worn round the left arm (तला also in this sense). -Comp. —अंगुलि: *f.* A toe. —अतलं *n.* Fourth of the seven divisions of hell. —ईक्षण: *m.* The hog. —उदा *f.* A river. —घात: *m.* A slap with the palm of the hand. —ताल: *m.* 1 A kind of musical instrument. -2 The clapping of the hands. —त्रं, -त्राणं, —वारणं *n.* A leathern glove of an archer. —लोक: *m.* The nether world (पाताल). —सारकं *n.* A martingale.

तलकं *n.* A large pond.

तलत: *ind.* From the bottom.

तलवारणं *n.* A sword.

तलाचा *f.* A mat.

तलिका *f.* A martingale.

तलितं *n.* Fried meat.

तलिन *a.* (*f.* —ना) 1 Thin, meagre, spare. -2 Small, little. -3 Clear, clean. -4 Situated under or beneath. —नं *n.* A bed, couch.

तलिमं *n.* 1 Paved ground, a pavement. -2 A bed, cot, couch. -3 An awning. -4 A large sword or knife.

तलुन: *m.* 1 A youth. -2 Wind, air. —नी *f.* A girl, young woman.

तल्कं *n.* A forest.

तल्प: *m.*, —ल्पं *n.* 1 A couch, bed, sofa. -2 (Fig.) A wife (as in गुरुतल्पग). -3 The seat of a carriage. -4 An upper story, a turret, tower.

तल्पक: *m.* One whose business it is to make or prepare beds.

तल्लज: *m.* 1 Excellence, superiority, happiness. -2 (At the end of comp.) Excellent; in this sense the word is always masculine, whatever be the gender of the first member of the compound). गोतल्लज: *m.* 'An excellent cow'; so कुमारितल्लज: *m.* 'An excellent maiden'.

तल्लिका *f.* A key.

तल्ली *f* A youthful woman.

तष्ट *a.* (*f.* -ष्टा) 1 Hewn, cut, chiselled, split. -2 Fashioned.

तष्टृ *m.* 1 A carpenter in general. -2 The architect of gods (विश्वकर्मन्).

तस्कर: *m.* 1 A thief, robber. -2 (At the end of comp.) Anything bad or contemptible.

तस्थु *a.* Stationary, immoveable.

ताक्ष्णय:, ताक्ष्ण: *m.* The son of a carpenter.

ताच्छीलिक: *m.* N. of an affix used to denote a particular inclination, tendency or habit.

ताच्छील्यं *n.* The act of being accustomed to that. [a large ear-ring.

ताटंक: *m.* An ornament for the ear,

ताटस्थ्यं *n.* 1 Proximity. -2 Indifference, disregard, neutrality.

ताड: *m.* 1 A blow, knock, chastisement. -2 Noise, sound. -3 A sheaf. -4 A mountain. -Comp. —घ:, —घात: *m.* An artificer who beats or hammers; a smith.

ता(-ट-)डका *f.* 1 N. of a female fiend,

daughter of Suketu, wife of Sunda and mother of Mârîcha. -2 The large dark-green pumpkin.

ताडकेयः *m.* An epithet of the demon Márîcha, son of Tàdaká.

ताडङ्कः *m.*, ताडपत्रं *n.* An ornament for the ear; a large ear-ring.

ताडनं *n.* 1 Beating, flogging. -2 (In astr.) Touching, partial eclipse. —ना *f.* Striking. —नी *f.* A whip.

ताडिः, -डी *f.* 1 A kind of palm. -2 A kind of ornament.

ताड्यमान *a.* (*f.* —ना) Being beaten or struck. —नः *m.* A musical instrument struck with a stick &c. (as a drum).

ताण्डवः *m.*, -वं *n.* 1 Dancing in general. -2 Frantic or violent dance of Siva. -3 The art of dancing. -4 A sort of grass. -5 (In prosody) A foot of three short syllables. -Comp. —तालिकः *m.* An epithet of Nandin, the door-keeper of Siva. —प्रियः *m.* N. of Siva.

तातः *m.* 1 A father. -2 A term of affection, endearment or pity, applied to any person, usually to inferiors or juniors, pupils, children &c -3 A term of respect applied to elders or other venerable personages. -Comp. —जु *a.* 1 Agreeable to a father. -2 Paternal. (-जुः *m.*) A paternal uncle.

तातनः *m.* The Khanjana or wagtail.

तातलः *m.* 1 A disease. -2 An iron club or spike. -3 Cooking, maturing. -4 Heat. -5 A relative who may be regarded as a father.

तातिः *m.* Offspring. —तिः *f.* Continuity, succession, as in अरिष्टतातिः or शिवतातिः.

तात्कालिक *a.* (*f.* —की) 1 Simultaneous. -2 Immediate. -3 Relating to any particular time.

तात्काल्यं *n.* Simultaneity.

तात्पर्यं *n.* 1 Purport, meaning, scope. -2 Aim, object, intended reference to any object, purpose, intention (with loc.). -4 The object or intention of the speaker (in using particular words in a sentence) as in वक्तुरिच्छा तु तात्पर्यं परिकीर्तितं -5 Explanation. -6 Entire devotion to or absorption in any object.

तात्त्विक *a* (*f.* —की) True, real, essential.

तादर्थ्यं *n.* 1 Identity of aim, object. -2 Relation to. -3 Sameness of meaning. -4 Purpose, aim.

तादात्म्यं *n.* Sameness of nature, identity, unity.

तादृक्ष *a.* (*f.* -क्षी) तादृश् *a.*, तादृश *a.* (*f.* —शी) Such-like, like him, her or it, like that. तादृश coupled with यादृश means 'common', 'ordinary,' 'low.' यादृशस्तादृशः *m.* Any body whoever, common or ordinary man, *e. g.* उपदेशो न दातव्यो यादृशे तादृशे जने.

तानः *m.* 1 A thread, fibre. -2 (In music) A protracted tone, a key-note. -3 A monotonous tone. —नं *n.* 1 Expanse, extension. -2 An object of sense.

तानवं *n.* Thinness, smallness.

तानूरः *m.* A whirlpool.

तान्त *a.* (*f.* -न्ता) 1 Wearied, fatigued. -2 Troubled. -3 Faded, withered.

तान्तव *a.* (*f.* —वी) Made of threads. —वं *n.* 1 Spinning, weaving. -2 A web. -3 A woven cloth.

तान्त्रिक *a.* (*f.* —की) 1 Well-versed in any science or doctrine. -2 Relating to the Tantras. -3 Taught or contained in them. —कः *m.* A follower of Tantra doctrines.

तापः *m.* 1 Heat, glow. -2 Torment, pain, affliction, misery. -3 Sorrow, distress. -Comp. —त्रयं *n.* The three kinds of miseries which human beings have to suffer in this world. *i. e.* आध्यात्मिक, आधिदैविक and आधिभौतिक.

तापनः *m.* 1 The sun. -2 The hot season. -3 The sun-stone. -4 N. of one of the arrows of Cupid. —नं *n.* 1 Burning. -2 Distressing. -3 Chastising. -4 A division of hell. -5 Gold.

तापस *a.* (*f.* —सी) 1 Relating to religious penance or to an ascetic. -2 Devout. -सः *m.* (*f.* -सी) A hermit, devotee, an ascetic. -Comp. —इष्टा, —प्रिया *f.* A grape. —तरुः, —द्रुमः *m.* The tree of ascetics; also called इंगुदी.

तापस्यं *n.* Asceticism.

तापिच्छः *m.* The Tamâla tree or its flower (*n.*) (तापिंज used in the same sense).

तापी *f.* 1 N. of the river Táptî, which joins the sea near Surat. -2 The river Yamunâ.

तापिजं *n.* Sulphuret of iron

तामः *m.* 1 An object of terror. -2 A fault, defect. -3 Anxiety, distress. -4 Desire. -5 Exhaustion, fatigue.

तामरं *n.* 1 Water. -2 Clarified butter.

तामरसं *n.* 1 The red lotus. -2 Gold. -3 Copper. —सी *f.* A lotus-pond.

तामस *a.* (*f* —सी) 1 Dark, consisting of darkness. -2 Affected by or relating to तमस् or the quality of darkness (the third of the three qualities of nature. -3 Ignorant. -4 Vicious. —सः *m.* 1 A malignant person, an incendiary, a villain. -2 A snake. -3 An owl. -4 N. of a son of Ráhu. —सं *n.* Darkness. -सी *f.* 1 Night, a dark night. -2 Sleep. -3 An epithet of Durgâ.

तामसिक *a.* (*f.* —की) 1 Dark. -2 Belonging to, derived from, or connected with तमस्.

तामिस्रः *m.* 1 A division of hell. -2 The dark fortnight of a month. -3 Hatred. -4 Anger. -5 A demon, Rákshasa (going about in the dark).

तांबूलं *n.* 1 The areca-nut. -2 The leaf of piper-betel. -Comp. —करंकः *m.*, —पेटिका *f.* A betel box. —वल्ली *f.* The betel-plant.

तांबूलिकः *f.* A seller of betel.

तांबूली *f.* The betel-plant.

ताम्र *a.* (*f.* —म्रा) 1 Made of copper. -2 Of a coppery red colour, red. —म्रः *m.* A kind of leprosy with red spots. —म्रं *n.* 1 Copper. -2 A dark or coppery red. —म्री *f.* A copper pot having a small hole at the bottom used in measuring time by placing it in a water-vessel. -Comp. —अक्षः *m.* 1 A crow. -2 The (Indian) cuckoo. —अर्धः *m.* Bell-metal. -अश्मन् *m.* kind of jewel (पद्मराग). —आभं *n.* Red sandal (रक्तचंदन). —उपजीविन् *m.* A coppersmith. -ओष्ठः *m.* (forming ताम्रोष्ठ or ताम्रौष्ठ) A red or cherry lip. —कारः, -कुट्टः *m.* A brazier, coppersmith. -कृमिः *m.* A kind of red insect (इंद्रगोपः). —गर्भं *n.* Sulphate of copper. —चूडः *m.* A cock. —त्रपुजं *n.* Brass. -द्रुः *m.* The red sandalwood. —पट्टः *m.*, -पत्रं *n.* A copper-plate on which grants of land were frequently inscribed. —पर्णी *f.* N. of a river rising in Malaya, celebrated for its pearls. -पल्लवः *m.* The Asoka tree. -मुखः *m.* A Frank or European. —लिप्तः *m.* N of a country. (-ताः *m. pl*) Its people or rulers. -वृक्षः *m.* A species of sandal. —शिखिन् *m.* A cock.

ताम्रिक *a.* (*f.* -की) Made of copper, coppery. —कः *m.* A brazier, coppersmith.

ताम्रिमन् *m.* Redness, the colour of [copper.

ताय् 1 A (तायते, तायित) 1 To spread, extend. -2 To protect, preserve.

-With वि- To spread, create.

तार a. (f. -रा) 1 High (as a note). -2 Loud, shrill (as a sound). -3 Shining, radiant, clear. -4 Good, excellent, well-flavoured. -5 Clear, clean. —रः m. 1 The bank of a river. -2 The clearness of a pearl. -3 A beautiful or big pearl.-4 An epithet of (1) Vishnu, (2) Siva. 5 The mystical syllable ओम् (प्रणव). -6 Protection. -7 A high tone or note. -8 Crossing, passing over. —रः m., -रं n. 1 A star or planet. -2 The pupil of the eye; (said to be m. also). -3 A pearl (said to be f. also). -Comp. —अभ्रः m. Camphor. —अरिः m. A pyritic ore of iron. —पतनं n. The falling of a star or meteor. -पुष्पः m. The Kunda or jasmine creeper.-वायुः m. A lound-sounding wind, a whistling breeze. -शुद्धिकरं n. Lead.

तारकः m. N. of a demon killed by Kârtikeya. -Comp. —अरिः, -जित् m. An epithet of Kârtikeya.

तारक a. (f. -रिका) 1 Carrying over. -2 Protecting, preserving, rescuing. -3 Helping another through a difficulty. -कः m. 1 A pilot, helmsman. -2 A deliverer, saviour. -3 N. of Siva. —कः m., -कं n. A boat, raft. —कं n. 1 The pupil of the eye. -2 The eye (also f.).

तारका f 1 A star. -2 A meteor, falling star. -3 The pupil of the eye. -4 N. of the wife of Brihaspati.

तारकिणी f. A starry night, night during which stars are visible.

तारकित a. (f. —ता) Starry, star-spangled.

तारणः m. 1 N. of Siva; also of Vishnu. -2 A boat, raft. —णं n. 1 Crossing. -2 Conquering. -3 Carrying or conveying across. -4 Rescuing, delivering, liberating.

तारणिः, -णी f. A float, raft.

तारतम्यं n. 1 Gradation, proportion, relative importance, comparative value. -2 Difference, distinction.

तारलः m. 1 A libidinous man, lecher, libertine.-2 The companion of a dissolute man (विट).

तारल्यं n. 1 Tremulousness. -2 Libidinousness, dissoluteness.

तारा f. 1 A star or planet in general. -2 A fixed star. -3 The pupil of the eye, the eye-ball. -4 A pearl. -5 N. of the wife of Váli, king of the monkeys, and mother of Angada.-5 N. of the wife of Brihaspati, the preceptor of the gods. -Comp. —अधिपः m. The moon. -2 Siva. -3 Brihaspati. -4 Váli. -5 Sugriva. —आपीडः m. The moon. —आभः m. Quicksilver. —पतिः m. 1 The moon. -2 Váli.-3 Brihaspati. -4 Siva. —पथः m. The atmosphere, firmament. —प्रमाणं n. The sidereal measure, sidereal time. —भूषा f. The night. —मंडलं n. 1 The starry region, the zodiac. -2 The pupil of the eye. —मृगः m. The constellation मृगशिरस्.

तारिकं n. Fare, freight.

तारुण्यं n. 1 Youth, youthfulness. -2 Freshness (fig.)

तारेयः m. 1 The planet Mercury.-2 An epithet of Angada, son of Vâli.

तार्किकः m. 1 A dialectician, logician. -2 A philospher.

तार्क्षः m. N. of the sage कश्यप.

तार्क्ष्यः m. 1 An epithet of Garuda. -2 N. of Garuda's elder brother Aruna. -3 A car. -4 A horse. -5 A snake.-6 A bird in general.-Comp. —ध्वजः m. An epithet of Vishnu. —नायकः m. An epithet of Garuda.

तार्तीय a. (f. —या) 1 The third. -2

Belonging to the third. —यं *n.* A third part.

तार्तीयिक *a.* (*f.* —का) The third.

तालः *m.* The palmyra tree. -2 A banner formed of the palm. -2 A Slapping or clapping the hands together; the noise made by it. -4 Flapping in general. -5 Flapping of the ears of an elephant.-6 Beating time (in music). -7 A musical instrument made of bell-metal. -8 The palm of the hand. -9 A lock, bolt. -10 The hilt of a sword. -11 An epithet of Siva. -12 (In prosody) A trochee. -13 A particular measure of height. -14 A short span. -लं *n.* 1 The nut of the palmyra tree. -2 Yellow orpiment. -Comp. -अंकः *m.* 1 N. of Balaráma. -2 The palm-leaf used for writing. -3 A book. -4 A saw. -अवचरः *m.* A dancer, an actor. -केतुः *m.* An epithet of Bhīshma. -क्षीरकं *n.*, -गर्भः *m.* The exudation of the palm. -ध्वजः, —भृत *m.* An epithet of Balaráma. पत्रं *n.* 1 The palm-leaf used for writing.-2A kind of ear-ornament. -बद्ध, -शुद्ध *a.* Measured, rhythmical, regulated by musical time. —मर्दलः *m.* A kind of musical instrument, a cymbal. —यंत्रं *n.* 1 A kind of surgical instrument. -2 A lock, a lock and key. —रेचनकः *m.*A dancer, an actor. -लक्षणः *m.* An epithet of Balaráma. -वृंतं*n.*A fan (alsoतालवृंतकः.

तालकं *n.* 1 Yellow orpiment. -2 A fragrant earth. -3 A belt, latch. -Comp. —आभ *a.* Green. (—भः *m.*) The green colour.

तालंकः *m* A kind of ear-ornament (The same as ताडंकः q. v.).

तालव्य *a.* (*f.* -व्या) Relating to the palate,palatal.-Comp.वर्णः*m.*A palatal letter ; *i. e.* इ, ई, च्, छ्, ज्, झ्, ञ्, and य्. —स्वरः *m.* A palatal vowel ; *i. e.* इ and ई.

तालिकः *m.* 1 The open palm of the hand. -2 Clapping the hands(तालिका *f.* also). -3 A tie, seal.

तालितं *n.* Coloured cloth. -2 Any musical instrument.-3A string,tie.

तालिन् *m.* N. of Siva.

ताली *f.* 1 A species of the mountain-palm, palm-tree. -2 The common toddy (*tadi.*). -3 Fragrant earth. -4 A sort of key.

तालु *n.*The palate -Comp.—जिह्वः*m.* A crocodile. —स्थान *a.* Palatal. (—नं *n.*) The palate.

तालूरः *m.* A whirlpool, an eddy.

तालूषकं *n.* The palate.

तावक *a.* (*f.* -की), तावकीन *a.*(*f.* -ना) Thy, thine.

तावत् *a.* (Correlative of यावत्) 1 So much, that much, so many. -2 So great, so large. -3 All (expressing totality) *e. g.* यावद्दत्तं तावद्भुक्तं. -*ind.*1 First(before doing anything else) ; आर्ये इतस्तावदागम्यतां *शाकुंत. 1 -2On one's part, in the meanwhile. -3 Just, now as in गच्छ तावत्. -4 Indeed,(to emphasize an expression). -5 Truly (to express assent). -6 As for, with respect to ; विग्रहस्तावदुपस्थितः. -7 Completely. -8 Surprise (oh ! what a wonder!). -Comp. -कृत्वस् *ind.* So many times. -मात्रंJust so much.-वर्ष*a.*So many years old.

तावतिक, तावत्क *a* (*f.* —का, -त्का) Bought for so much, worth so much.

तावुरिः *m* The sign Taurus of the Zodiac, (a word borrowed from the Greek *Tauros.*)

तिक्त *a.* (*f.* —क्ता) 1 Bitter, pungent. -2 Fragrant. —क्तः *m.* 1 Bitter taste. -2 The Kutaja tree. -3 Pungency. -4 Fragrance. -Comp. -धातुः *m.* Bile. —फलः, -मरिचः *m.* The clearing-nut plant.

तिग्म *a.* (*f.* —ग्मा) 1 Sharp, pointed (as a weapon). -2 Violent.-3Hot, scorching. -4 Pungent, a d. -5 Fiery, passionate. —ग्मं *n.* 1 Heat. -2 Pungency. -Comp. —अंशुः *m.* 1 The sun. -2 Fire. -करः,-दीधितिः,-रश्मिः, -रुच् *m.* The sun. —यातना *f.* Acute or violent pain.

तिज् 1 A. (तितिक्षते, तितिक्षित) 1 To endure, bear. -2 To put up with, suffer patiently or with courage.

तिज् 10 U. (तेजयति-ते, तेजित) 1 To sharpen, whet. -2 To stir up, excite, instigate.

तितउः *m.*1 A sieve.-उ *n.*A parasol.

तितिक्षा *f.* Endurance, patience, resignation, forbearance.

तितिक्षु *a.* Patient, forbearing.

तितिभः *m.* 1 A fire-fly -2 kind of insect (इंद्रगोप).

तित्तिरः, तित्तिरिः *m.* The francoline partridge.

तित्तिरिः *m.* 1 The francoline partridge. -2 N. of a sage said to be the first teacher of the *black* Yajurveda. [dge.

तित्तिरिकः*m.* The francoline partri-

तिथः *m.* 1 Fire. -2 Love. -3 Time. -4 The rainy season or autumn.

तिथिः *m.* or *f.* 1 A lunar day. -2 The number '15'. -Comp. —ईशः *m.* The regent of a lunar day. -क्षयः *m.* 1 The day of new moon. -2 The day on which a *tithi* begins and ends without one sunrise or between two sunrises. —पत्री *f.* An almanac. —प्रणीः *m.* The moon. —वृद्धिः *f.* The day in which a *tithi* is completed under two suns (one which comprises two sunrises). [तिथ्स.

तिनिशः *m.* A particular tree. *Mar.*

तिंतिडः *m.*, -डी, तिंतिडिका *f.*, तिंतिडिकः *m.* The tamarind tree. —कं *n.* 1The fruit of the tamarind. -2 A sour sauce. [arind tree.

तिंतिली, तिंतिलि (-ली-) का*f.* The tam-

तिंदुः, तिंदुकः, तिंदुलः *m.* N. of a tree.

तिम् 1 P. (तेमति, तिमित) To make wet or damp, moisten.

तिम् 4 P. (तिम्यति) 1 To become wet. -2 To become quiet or tranquil, be calm.

तिमिः *m.* The ocean. -2 A kind of whale or fish of an enormous size. -3 A fish in general. -Comp. -कोषः *m.* The ocean. —जं *n.* A kind of pearl.

तिमिंगिलः *m.* 1 A kind of fish which swallows a *timi.* [-2 Wet, moist.

तिमित *a.* (*f.* —ता) 1 Motionless.

तिमिर *a.* (*f.* —रा) Dark. —रः *m.*,- रं *n.* 1 Darkness. -2 Blindness. -3 Iron-rust. -Comp. —अरिः,-नुद् -रिपुः *m.* Sun.

तिरय् Den. P. 1 To conceal. -2 To stop, obscure. -3 To conquer.

तिरश्री *f.* See तिर्यंची.

तिरश्रीन *a.* (*f.* —ना) 1 Oblique, sideways, awry. -2 Irregular.

तिरस् *ind.* 1 Crookedly, obliquely, awry.-2 Secretly, covertly, invisibly. -4 Indireetly, badly. (In classical literature तिरस् is rarely used by itself, but chiefly occurs in composition with कृ, धा, and भू). -Comp. —गत *a.* Vanished, disappeared.

तिरस्कर *a.* Surpassing, excelling.

तिरस्क (-स्का-) रिणी *f.* 1 A curtain, veil. -2 A screen of cloth. -3 A kind of magical veil (or spell) rendering the wearer invisible.

तिरस्कारः *m.*, तिरस्कृतिः, तिरस्क्रिया *f.* 1

Contempt, disrespect. -2 Censure. reproach. -3 Concealment.

तिरस्कृ (तिरः + कृ)8 U.1 To despise, contemn.-2 To blame, scold, abuse. -3 To surpass, excel. -4 To cover, conceal.-5 To set aside, remove.

तिरस्कृत *p. p.* (*f.* —ता) 1 Disregarded despised. -2 Abused, condemned. -3 Concealed, covered. -4 Disappeared, vanished. -5 Surpassed.

तिरोधा (तिरस् + धा 3 U.) 1 To disappear, vanish.-2 To conceal, hide. -3 excel. -4 To overpower, defeat. -5 To set aside, remove. -6 To hide one's self from (with abl.).

तिरोधानं *n.* 1 Disappearance, removal. -2 A covering, veil.

तिरोभावः *m.* Disappearance.

तिरोभू (तिरस् + भू 1 P.) To disappear, vanish.

तिरोहित *p. p.* (*f.* —ता) 1 Concealed, removed form sight. -2 Vanished, disappeared.

तिर्यक् *ind.* Obliquely, crookedly, in a slanting or oblique direction.

तिर्यच् *a.* (तिरश्ची *f.*, rarely तिर्यची) 1 Oblique, horizontal. -2 Crooked, curved. -3 Crossing over, traversing. -4 Winding. -5 Lying in the middle or between. *-m.*, *-n.* 1 An animal (going horizontally, as distinguished from man who walks erect); a lower or irrational animal. -2 A bird. -Comp. —अंतरं (तिर्यगंतरं) The intermediate space measured across, breadth. —अयनं *n.* The annual revolution of the sun. —ईक्ष *a.* Looking obliquely. —जातिः *f.* The brute kind (opp. man).-प्रमाणं *n.* The breadth. —यानः *m.* A crab. —योनिः *f.* The animal creation or race. —स्रोतस् *m.* 1 The animal world. -2 An animal, a beast or bird.

तिर्यची *f.* The female of an animal.

तिलः *m.* 1 The sesamum plant. -2 The seed of this plant. -3 A mole, spot. -4 A small particle, as much as a sesamum-seed. -Comp. -अंबु, -उदकं *n.* Water with sesamum seed offered to the dead as a libation. —उत्तमा *f.* N. of an Apsaras. —कल्कः *m.* Dough made of ground sesamum. -कल्कजः *m.* The oil-cake made of the sediment of ground sesamum. —कालकः *m.* A mole, a dark spot under the skin.—किट्टं *n*, -खलिः, -खली *f*, -चूर्णं *n.* The caky sediment of sesamum after the oil is extracted. —तंडुलकं *n.* An embrace (so called because in it the two bodies are united together like rice mixed up with sesamum-seed). —पर्णः *m.* Turpentine. (-र्णं *n.*) Sandal-wood. —पर्णी *f.* 1 The sandal tree.-2 Frankincense. -3 Turpentine. —पर्णिका *f.*, -पर्णि (-र्ण-) कं *n.* Sandal-wood. -पिंडः *m.* An oilman. -रसः, —स्नेहः *m.* Sesamum oil. —होमः *m.* A burut offering of sesamum.

तिलकः *m.* 1 A species of tree with beautiful flowers. -2 A freckle or natural mark under the skin. -3 The sesamum tree. —कः *m.*, —कं *n.* 1 A mark made with sandalwood or unguents &c. -2 The ornament of anything (used at the end of comp. in the sense of 'best', 'chief' or 'distinguished').-3 The burden of a song (ध्रुवक). —का *f.* A kind of necklace. —कं *n.* 1 The bladder. -2 The lungs.-3 A kind of salt.-4 Alliteration -Comp. -आश्रयः *m.* The forehead.

तिलंतुदः *m.* An oilman.

तिलशः *ind.* In pieces as small as sesamum-seed; in very small quantities.

तिलित्सः *m.* A large snake.

तिल्वः *m.* The *lodhra* tree.

तिष्ठद्गु *ind.* At the time when cows stand up to be milked (*i.e.* an hour or an hour and a half after evening).

तिष्यः *m.* 1 The eighth of the 27 constellations, (also called पुष्यः). -2 The lunar month Pausha. —ष्यं *n.* The Kali Yuga.

तीक् 1 A (तीकते) To go, move.

तीक्ष्ण (*f.* —क्ष्णा) 1 Sharp (in all senses); pungent. -2 Hot, warm (as rays). -3 Fiery, passionate.-4 Hard, forcible, strong (as उपाय).-5 Rude, cross. -6 Severe, harsh. -7 Injurious, inauspicious. -8 Keen. -9 Intelligent, clever. -10 Zealous, energetic. -11 Devoted, self-abandoning.-12 Unfriendly.-13 Devout, ascetic, pious. —क्ष्णः *m.* 1 Nitre. -2 Long pepper. -3 Black pepper. -4 Black mustard. —क्ष्णं *n.* 1 Iron. -2 Steel. -3 Heat, pungency. -4 War, battle. -5 Poison. -6 Death. -7 A weapon. -8 Sea-salt.-9 Haste. -10 Plague, pestilence. -Comp. —अंशुः *m.* 1 The sun. -2 Fire. —अग्निः *m.* Dyspepsia, heart-burn.-आयसं *n.* Steel. —उपायः *m.* A forcible means, strong measure. -कंदः *m.* The onion. —कर्मन् *a.* Active, zealous, energetic. (*n.*) A clever work. —कल्कः *m.* Coriander. —तंडुला *f.* Long pepper. -दंष्ट्रः *m.* A tiger. -दंष्ट्रकः *m.* A leopard. -धारः *m.* A sword. —पुष्पं *n* Cloves. -पुष्पा *f.* 1 The clove tree -2 The Ketaka plant. —फलं *n.* 1 Coriander. -2 Black mustard. -बुद्धि *a.* Sharp-witted, acute, clever. —मंजरी *f.* The betel-plant. —रश्मिः *m.* The sun. -रसः *m.* 1 Saltpetre. -2 Any poisonous liquid, a poison. —लौहं *n.* Steel. —शूकः *m.* Barley. —सारः *m.* Iron. [moist.

तीम् 4 P. (तीम्यति) To be wet or

तीरं *n.* 1 A shore, bank.-2 Margin, brim, edge. -रः *m.* 1 A sort of an arrow. -2 Lead. -3 Tin.

तीरित *a.* (*f.* —ता) Settled, adjusted, decided according to evidence. —तं *n.* 1 Completion of any affair. -2 Non-infliction of a sentence owing to bribery or other unfair means.

तीर्ण (*f.*-र्णा) Crossed, passed over. -2 Spread. -3 Surpassed, excelled.

तीर्थं *n.* 1 A passage, road, ford. -2 A descent into a river, the stairs a landing-place (Mar. घाट). -3 A place of water. -4 A holy place of pilgrimage; especially on or near the bank of a sacred river &c. -5 A channel, medium, means. -6 A remedy, expedient. -7 A sacred or holy personage, an object of veneration; a fit or proper recipient. -8 A sacred preceptor, a teacher. -9 Source, origin. -10 A sacrifice. -11 A minister. -12 Advice, instruction. -13 Right place or moment. -14 The right or usual manner. -15 Certain parts of the hand sacred to deities, manes &c. 16 A school of philosophy. -17 Pudendum muliebre. -18 Menstrual courses of a woman. 19 A Bráhmana.-20 Fire. -21 Ascertainment of a disease.-22 A science (शास्त्र).-र्थः *m.* An honorary affix added to the names of ascetics, saints &c. Comp.-करः *m.* 1 A Jaina Arhat, sanctified teacher or saint of the Jainas; (also तीर्थंकर). -2 An ascetic. -3 The founder of a new religious or philosophical school. -4 N. of Vishnu. -काकः,-ध्वांक्षः, -वायसः *m.* A very greedy person. —यात्रा *f.* A visit to a holy place, a pilgrimage. —राजः *m.* N. of Prayága. -राजिः, -राजी *f.* An epithet of Benares. -वाकः *m.* The hair of the head.-सेविन् *m.* 1 A pilgrim. -2 A crane.

तीर्थिकः *m.* A pilgrim, an ascetic Bráhmana (visiting holy places). -तीर्थ्य *a.* Relating to a sacred place. —र्थ्यः *m.* An ascetic.

तीवरः *m.* 1 The ocean. -2 A hunter. -3 The adulterine offspring of a Rájaputri by a Kshatriya.

तीव्र *a.* (*f.* -व्रा) 1 Severe, intense, sharp, acute, violent, impetuous. -2 Hot, warm. -3 Endless, unlimited. -4 Horrible, dreadful. —व्रः *m.* 1 Sharpness. -2 Siva. -व्रं *n.* 1 Heat, pungency. -2 A shore.-3Iron,steel. -4 Tin. -व्रं *ind.* Violently, sharply. -Comp. -आनंदः *m.* An epithet of Siva. -संवेग *a.* 1 Of strong impulse, resolute. -2 Very poignant or sharp.

तु *ind.* (Never used at the beginning of a sentence.) 1 An adversative particle meaning 'but', 'on the contrary', 'on the other hand', 'nevertheless' (in this sense तु is often added to किं and परं, but किंतु and परंतु are, unlike तु, always used at the beginning of a sentence).-2 And now, on one's part, and. -3As to, as regards, as for. -4 It sometimes marks a difference (भेद) or superior quality. -5 Sometimes it is used as an emphatic particle.-6 Sometimes it is used as a mere expletive.

तुक्खारः, तुखारः, तुषारः *m.* N. of a people inhabiting the Vindhya mountain.

तुंग *a.* (*f.* -गा) 1 High, elevated, tall, lofty, prominent. -2 Long. -3 Vaulted. -4 Chief, principal. -5 Strong, passionate. —गः *m.* 1 A height, elevation. -2 A mountain. 3 Top, summit. -4 The planet Mercury. -5 A rhinoceros. -6 The cocoa-nut tree. -7 The aphelion of a planet. -8 (Fig.) A throne. -9A wise man. -गं *n.* The stamina of the lotus blossoms. -Comp. -बीजः *m.* Quicksilver. -भं *n.* The apsis of a planet. -भद्रः *m.* A restive elephant, an elephant in rut. —भद्रा *f.* N. of a river flowing into the Krishná.-मुखः *m.* A rhinoceros. —वेणा *f.* N. of a river. —शेखरः *m.* A mountain.

तुंगी *f.* 1 Night. -2 Turmeric. -Comp. —ईशः *m.* 1 The moon. -2 The sun.-3 An epithet of Krishna. —ईश्वरः *m.* 1 An epithet of Siva. -2 A temple of Siva. —पतिः *m.*The moon.

तुच्छ *a.* (*f.* —च्छा) 1 Empty,void, vain, light. -2 Small, trifling. -3 Abandoned. -4 Low, mean, contemptible,worthless.-5Poor,wretched. -च्छं *n.* Chaff. -Comp. -द्रुः *m.*The castor-oil tree. —धान्यः, -धान्यकः *m.* Straw, chaff.

तुज् 1 P. (तोजति) To hurt, injure.

तुडुमः *m.* A mouse, rat.

तुण् 6. P (तुणति) 1To curve,bend. -2 To act fraudulently. -3 To be crooked.

तुंडं *n.* 1 Mouth, face, beak, snout (of a hog). -2 The trunk of an elephant.-3The point of an instrument.

तुंडकेरिका *f.* The cotton plant.

तुंडिः *m.* 1 Face, mouth. -2 A beak. —डिः *f.* The navel.

तुंडिन *m.* N. of the bull of Siva.

तुंडिभ *a.* See तुदिंभ.

तुंडिल *a.* (*f.* —ला) 1 Talkative, loquacious. -2 Having a prominent navel. 3 Talking severely.

तुत्थः *m.* 1 Fire. -2 A stone. —त्थं *n.* Sulphate of copper. —त्था *f.* 1 Small cardamoms. -2 The indigo plant.

तुद् 6 U. (तुदति-ते, तुन्न) 1 To strike, wound, hit. -2 To prick, goad. -3

To bruise, hurt. -4 To pain, afflict. With प्र— To strike, wound. -*Caus.* (तोदयति,-ते) -With प्र— To press, to request repeatedly.

तुंदं *n.* The belly, a corpulent or protuberant belly. —दः *m.*,दी *f.* The navel. -Comp. —कूपिका, -कूपी *f.* The cavity of the navel. -परिमार्ज, -परिमृज्, —मृज *a.* Lazy, sluggish.

तुंदवत *a.* Corpulent, fat.

तुंदि :*f.*,-दि*n.* The belly.*f.* The navel.

तुंदिक, तुंदित, तुंदिप, तुंदिभ, तुंदिल *a.* (*f.* -का,-ता,-भी,-भा,-ला) 1 Having a protuberant belly. -2 Corpulent. -3 (Fig.) Filled or laden with.-4 Great.

तुंदिकरः *m.*, तुंदिका *f* The navel.

तुन्न *p.p.*(*f.*-न्ना) 1 Struck, hurt, wounded. -2 Tormented. -3 Cut, broken. -4 Pricked. -Comp.-वायः:*m.* A tailor.

तुभ् 4. 9 P. (तुभ्यति, तुभ्नाति) To hurt, injure, strike.

तुमुल *a.* (*f.* —ला) Tumultuous, noisy. -2 Fierce, raging. -3 Excited. -4 Perplexed, confused. —लः*m.* —लं *n.* 1 An uproar, a tumult -2 A confused combat, melee.

तुंबः *m.* A kind of gourd. —बा *f.* 1 A kind of long gourd. -2 A milch cow. -3 A milk-vessel.

तुंबरः *m.* N.of a Gandharva.-रं *n.* A kind of musical instrument.

तुंबिः,-बी *f.* A sort of gourd.

तुंब (-बु-) रुः*m.*N. of a 'gandharva.'

तुरगः *m.* 1 A horse. -2 The mind, thought. —गी *f.* A mare. -Comp. —आरोहः *m.* A horseman. —उपचारकः *m.* A groom. —प्रियः *m.*, —यं *n.* Barley. —ब्रह्मचर्यं *n.* Forced or compulsory celibacy.

तुरंगः *m.* 1 A horse.-2 The number ' seven '. -3 The heart, mind. —गी *f.* A mare. -Comp. —अरिः *m* A buffalo. —आरूढः *m.* A horseman. —द्विषणी *f.* A she-buffalo. —प्रियः*m.*,—यं *n.* Barley.—मेधः*m.* A horse-sacrifice. —यायिन्, —सादिन् *m.* A horseman. -वक्त्रः, -वदनः *m.* 1 A Kinnara. -शाला*f.*, -स्थानं *n.* A horse-stable. -स्कंधः *m.* A troop of horses.

तुरंगकः *m.* A horse.

तुरंगमः *m.* A horse.

तुरायणं *n.* 1 Non-attachment to any object or pursuit. -2 A kind of sacrifice.

तुरासाह् *m.* (Nom. sing. तुराषाद्,-ड्) N. of Indra, also of Vishnu.

तुरी *f.* 1 The fibrous stick used by weavers to clear and separate the threads of the woof. -2 A shuttle. -3 A painter's brush.

तुरीय *a.* (*f.* —या) The fourth. -यं *n.* 1 A quarter, a fourth part, fourth. -2 (In Vedánta phil.) The fourth state of the soul in which it becomes one with Brahman (*n.*) or the Supreme Spirit. -Comp.-वर्णः*m.* A Súdra.

तुरुष्काः (*m. pl.*) N. of a people, the Turks.

तुर्य *a.* Fourth. —र्यं *n.* 1 A quarter, a fourth part. -2 (In Vedánta phil.) The fourth state of the soul in which it becomes one with Brahman (*n.*).

तुल् 1 P., 10 U. (तोलति-तोलयति-ते; also तुलयति-ते which some suppose to be a denominative from तुला *f*). 1 To weigh, measure. -2 To weigh in the mind, ponder, consider. -3 To raise, lift up. -4 To bear up, support. -5 To compare, equal, liken (with instr.). -6 To be equal to (with acc.). -7 To make light of, contemn, despise. -8 To suspect. -9 To try, reduce to a wretched state. -10 To outweigh. -11 To attain or reach to.

तुलनं *n.* 1 Weight. -2 Lifting. -3 Comparing, likening. —ना *f.* 1

Comparison. -2 Weighing. -3 Lifting, raising. -4 Assessing, estimating. -5 Examining.

तुलसी *f.* The holy basil held in veneration by the Hindus, especially by the worshippers of Vishnu. -Comp —पत्रं *n* (lit. A Tulasi leaf). (fig.) A very small gift.—विवाहः *m.* The marriage of an image of Bálakrishna with the holy basil, performsd on the 12th day of the bright half of Kârtika.

तुला *f.* 1 A balance or the beam of a balance. -2 A measure, weight. -3 Weighing. -4 Resemblance, equality, (with gen., instr. or in comp.). -5 Libra, the seventh sign of the zodiac. 6 A sloping beam or timber in the roof of a house. -7 A measure of gold or silver equal to 100 *palas*. -Comp. —कूटः *m.* A false weight. —कोटिः,—टी *f.* 1 An ornament (an anklet or नूपुर) worn on the feet by women. -2 A hundred millions (अर्बुद). —कोशः,-कोषः *m.* 1 Ordeal by weighing. -2 A place where a balance is kept.-दानं *n.* The gift to a Bráhmana of as much gold or silver as equals the weight of one's body. -धटः *m.* 1 The scale of a balance. -2 An oar. —धरः *m.* 1 A trader, merchant. -2 The sign *Libra* of the zodiac. -धारः *m.* 1 A dealer, trader, or merchant. -2 The string of a balance. -3 The beam. -4 The sign *Libra* of the zodiac. -परीक्षा *f.* 1 The ordeal by the balance. —पुरुषः *m.* Gold, jewels or other valuable things equal to a man's weight (given to a Brâhmana as a gift). -प्रग्रहः,-प्रग्राहः *m.* The string or beam of a balance. -मानं *n.*, —यष्टिः *f.* The beam of a balance. -बीजं *n.* The berry of the Gunjá plant.-सूत्रं *n.* The string of a balance

तुलित *p. p.* (*f.* -ता) 1 Weighed, counterpoised.-2 Compared, likened, equalled.

तुल्य *a.* (*f.* —ल्या) 1 Of the same kind or class, well-matched, similar, equal (with gen., instr., or in comp.) -2 Fit for. -3 Identical, same. -4 Indifferent. -Comp. -दर्शन *a.* Regarding with the same or indifferent eyes. —पानं *n.* Drinking together, compotation. -भावना *f.* (In arith.) Combination of like sets of magnitude. —योगिता *f.* (In Rhet.) The figure of speech in which objects in hand (i. e. प्रस्तुतs) or others (i. e. अप्रस्तुतs) are associated with one and the same attribute. The figure in which relevant things or irrelevant things have but one attribrute. पदार्थानां प्रस्तुतानामन्येषां वा यदा भवेत् । एकधर्माभिसंबंधः स्यात्तदा तुल्ययोगिता ॥ साहि· द.10 *e.g.* त्वदंगमार्दवं द्रष्टुः कस्य चित्ते न भासते । मालतीशशभृल्लेखाकदलीनां कठोरता॥ -रूप *a.* Like, similar, analogous.

तुवर *a.* (*f.* -रा) 1 Astringent. -2 Beardless; also तूवर.

तुष् 4P. (तुष्यति,तुष्ट) 1 To be pleased, or satisfied, be contented (usually with instr.) -2 To become calm or quiet. With परि- To be contented, satisfied or delighted. सम्- To be contented or satisfied.

तुषः *m.* The husk or chaff of grain. Comp. —अग्निः,-अनलः *m.* Fire of the chaff or husk of corn. —अंबु, -उदकं,-उत्थं *n.* Sour rice-gruel or barley gruel. —ग्रहः,—सारः *m.* Fire.

तुषार *a.* Cold, frigid, dewy. —रः *m.* 1 Frost, cold. -2 Ice, snow. -3 Dew. -4 Mist, thin rain, spray of cold water. -5 A kind of camphor. -Comp. —अद्रिः, —गिरिः, -पर्वतः *m.* The Himâlaya mountain. —करः *m.* 1

The moon.-2Camphor.-कालः m Winter. -किरणः, -रश्मिः m. The moon.

तुषिताः (m. pl.) A class of subordinate deities, 12 (or36) in number.

तुष्ट p. p. (f. —ष्टा)1 Pleased, satisfied, delighted, contented. -2 Contented with what one possesses and indifferent to everything else.

तुष्टिः f. 1 Satisfaction, gratification, pleasure, contentment. -2 (In Sân. phil.) Acquiescence, indifference to everything except what is possessed.

तुष्ठुः m. A jewel worn in the ears.

तुसः m. The same as तुषः.

तुहिन a. (f. —ना) Cold, frigid. -नं n. 1 Snow, ice. -2 Dew or frost. -3 Moonlight. -4 Camphor. -Comp. —अंशुः, — करः, -किरणः, -गुः, -द्युतिः,-रश्मिः m. 1 The moon. -2Camphor.-अचलः, —आद्रिः, —शैलः m. The Himâlaya mountain. —शर्करा f. Ice.

तूण् 10 U. (तूणयति-ते) To contract.

तूण् 10 A. (तूणयते) To fill, fill up.

तूणः m. A quiver.

तूणी f. A quiver. -Comp. -धरः,-धारः m. An archer.

तूणीरः m., —रं n. A quiver.

तूबरः m. 1 A beardless man. -2A bull without horns. -3 Astringent flavour. -4 A eunuch. -री f. A fragrant earth.

तूर् 4 A.(तूर्यते, तूर्ण) 1To go quickly, make haste. -2 To hurt, kill.

तूरं n. A kind of musical instrument. —री f. A thorn-apple.

तूर्ण a. (f. -र्णा) Quick, rapid, fleet. —र्णं n. Rapidity, quickness. -र्णं ind. Rapidly.

तूर्णिः f. Speed.

तूर्यः m.,-र्यं n. A kind of musical instrument. -Comp.-ओघः m. A band of instruments.-खंडः m. A sort of tabor.

तूलः m.,-लं n. Cotton.-लं n. 1 The sky, air. -2 A tuft of grass. -3 The mulberry. —ला f. 1 The cotton tree. -2 The wick of a lamp. -ली f. 1 Cotton. -2 The wick of a lamp. -3 A weaver's fibrous stick or brush. -4 A painter's brush. -5 The Indigo plant. -Comp. —कार्मुकं, —धनुस् n. A cotton-bow i. e. a bow used for cleaning cotton. —नाली (-लिः),-नालिका f. A thick roll of cotton drawn out in spinning. —शर्करा f. A seed of the cotton plant. —सेचनं n. The act of spinning.

तूलकं n. Cotton.

तूलिः f. A painter's brush.-Comp. —फला f. The silk-cotton tree.

तूलिका f. 1 A painter's brush; a pencil. -2 A wick of cotton either for a lamp or for applying unguents. -3 A mattress filled with cotton, a down or cotton-bed. -4 A boaring instrument, a probing rod. -5 An ingot mould.

तूलिनी f. See तूलिफला.

तूवर a. Same as तुवर q. v.

तूष्णीक a. (f. —का)Silent, taciturn.

तूष्णीम् ind. In silence, silently, quickly, without speaking or noise. -Comp. —भावः m. Silence, taciturnity. —शील a. Silent, taciturn.

तूस्तं n. 1 Matted hair. -2 Dust. -3 Sin. -4 An atom.

तृह् 6 P. (तृंहति) To kill, hurt.

तृंहणं n. Hurting, killing.

तृणं n. 1 Grass in general. -2 A blade of grass, reed, straw. -3Anything made of straw (as a mat for sitting); often used as a symbol of worthlessness. -Comp. —अंजनः m. A chameleon. —आवर्तः m. A whirlwind. —इंद्रः m. The palmyra tree. hay, a fire-brand made of straw.

—ओकस् *n.* A hut of straw. —काण्ड: *m.*, -कं *n.* A heap of grass. -कुटी *f.*, -कुटीरकं *n.* A hut of straw. —केतु: *m.* 1 The palmyra tree. -2 A bamboo. —गोधा *f.* A kind of chameleon. —ग्राहिन् *m.* A sapphire. —चर: *m.* A kind of gem (गोमेद). —जलायुका, —जलूका *f.* A caterpillar. —द्रुम: *m.* 1 The palm tree. -2 The cocoa-nut tree. -3 The betel-nut tree. -4 The Ketaka tree. -5 The date-tree. —धान्यं *n.* Grain growing wild or without cultivation. -ध्वज: *m.* 1 The palmyra tree. -2 A bamboo. -पीडं *n.* A hand-to-hand fighting. -पूली *f.* A mat, seat made of reeds. —प्राय *a.* Worth a straw, worthless, insignificant. —बिंदु: *m.* N. of a sage. —मणि: *m.* A sort of gem (amber). —मत्कुण: *m.* A bail or surety (perhaps a wrong reading for ऋणमत्कुण). —राज: *m.* 1 The cocoa-nut tree.-2The bamboo -3 The sugar-cane. -4 The palmyra tree. —वृक्ष: *m.* 1 The fan-palm-tree. -2 The date-tree. -3 The cocoa-nut tree. -4 The areca-nut tree. —शीतं *n.* A kind of fragrant grass. -सारा *f.* The plantain tree. —सिंह: *m.* An axe.

तृंढ *a.* (*f.* —ढा) Hurt, injured, killed (*p. p.* of तृह्).

तृण्या *f.* A heap of grass or straw.

तृतीय *a.* (*f.* -या) The third.-यं *n.* A third part. -Comp. -प्रकृति: *m.* or *f.* 1 A eunuch. -2 The neuter gender.

तृतीयक: *m.* A fever returning every third day.

तृतीया *f.* 1 The third day of a lunar fortnight. -2 (In gram.) The instrumental case or its terminations. -Comp. —कृत *a.* (*f.* —ता) Thrice ploughed (as a field). -प्रकृति: *m.*, *f.* 1 A eunuch.-2A hermaphrodite. -3 The neuter gender.

तृतीयिन् *a.* (*f.* -नी) 1 Entitled to a third portion (of inheritance &c). -2 Occupying the third rank.

तृद् 1 P., 7 U. (तर्दति, तृणत्ति, तृंते, तृण्ण) 1 To split, pierce.-2 To kill, destroy. -3 To set free. -4 To disregard.

तृप् 4. 5. 6. P. (तृप्यति, तृप्नोति, तृपति, तृप्त) 1 To become satisfied, to be contented (usually with instr ; but sometimes with gen. or loc. also). -2 To please, gratify. -*Caus.* To gratify, please. -*Desid.* तितृप्सति, तितर्पिषति.

तृप् 1 P , 10 U. (तर्पति, तर्पयति-ते) 1 To light up, kindle. -2 (Atm.) To be satisfied. -3 To please, satisfy. -4 To gladden, refresh.

तृप्त *a.* (*f.* —प्ता) Satiated, satisfied, contented. —प्तं *n.* Satisfaction.

तृप्ति: *f.* 1 Satisfaction, contentment. -2 Satiety, disgust. -3 Pleasure, gratification.

तृष् 4 P. (तृष्यति, तृषित) 1 To be thirsty. -2 To wish, be eager or greedy.

तृष् *f.* (nom. sing. तृट्-ड्) 1 Thirst. -2 Strong desire, eagerness.

तृषा *f.* See तृष्. -Comp. —आर्त *a.* Suffering from thirst, thirsty. —भू: *f.* The bladder. —हं *n.* Water.

तृषित *p. p.* (*f.* —ता) 1 Thirsty. -2 Greedy, desirous of gain. —तं *n.* Thirst, desire.

तृष्णज् *a.* Covetous, greedy, thirsting.

तृष्णा *f.* 1 Thirst (lit. and fig.) -2 Desire, strong desire, greed, desire of gain

तृष्णालु *a.* Very thirsty.

तृह् 7 P., 10 U., 6 P. (तृणेढि, तर्हयति-ते, तृहति, तृढ ; *desid.* तितृक्षति, तितर्हिषति, तितृंहिषति) To injure, hurt, kill, strike.

तॄ 1 P. (तरति, ततार,अतारीत, तरि-री-ष्यति, तीर्ण) 1 To cross over, cross. -2 To cross over, traverse (as a way). -3 To sail across : navigate (as a river). -4 To float, swim. -5 To surmount: overcome, overpower, subdue, destroy, become master of. -6 To go to the end of, master completely. -7 To fulfil, accomplish, perform (as a promise). -8 To be saved or rescued, escape from. -9 To acquire, gain. -10 To live through (a definite period). With अति- 1 To cross over. -2 To overcome. अव- 1 To descend. -2 To enter, enter into, to come to. -3 To overcome. -4 To descend into the world of mortals in the shape of a mortal. उद्- 1 To get out of, to rise from. -2 To overcome, -3 To cross over. निस्- 1 To cross over. -2 To accomplish, to attain.-3 To get over, to go to the end of. प्र- To cross over. वि- 1 To cross over. -2 To give, grant, to favour with. -3 To cause. व्यति- To overcome. सम्- 1 To cross over. -2 To float. -3 To go to the end of. —*Pass*. तीर्यते. -*Caus* तारयति-ते. -*Desid*. तितीर्षति तितरिषति, तितरीषति.

तेजनं *n*. 1 A bamboo.-2 Sharpening. whetting.-3 Kindling.-4 Rendering bright, polishing. -5 A reed. -6 The point of an arrow, the edge of a weapon. -नी *f*. 1 A mat. -2 A tuft. -3 A tuft of hair on the head of a horse.

तेजलः *m* The francoline partridge.

तेजस् *n*. 1 Sharpness. -2 The sharp edge (of a knife &c.).-3 The point or top of a flame. -4 Heat, glow, glare, light, brilliance, splendour. -5 Heat or light considered as the third of the five elements of creation (the other four being पृथिवी अप्, वायु, and आकाश). -6 The bright appearance of the human body, beauty. -7 Fire of energy. -8 Might, strength, courage, heroic lustre. -9 One possessed of heroic lustre. 10 Spirit, energy. -11 Strength of character, not bearing insult or ill-treatment with impunity. 12 Majesty, dignity, authority. 13 Semen virile. -14 The essential nature of any thing. -15 Spiritual, moral, or magical power. -16 Fire. -17 Marrow. -18 Bile. -19 Fresh butter.-20 Gold. -Comp. —भंगः *m*. 1 Disgrace. -2 Depression, discouragement. —मंडलं *n*. A halo of light. —मूर्तिः *m*. The sun. —रूपं *n*, 1 The Supreme Spirit, Brahman (*n*.).

तेजस्वत्, तेजोवत् *a*. 1 Bright.-2 Sharp, pungent. -3 Brave. -4 Energetic.

तेजस्विन् *a*. (*f*. -नी) 1 Brilliant, bright. -2 Powerful, strong. -3 Dignified, noble. -4 Famous, illustrious. -5 Violent. -6 Haughty.

तेजित *a*. (*f*. -ता) 1 Sharpened, whetted. -2 Excited, stimulated.

तेमः *m*. Becoming wet or moist, moisture.

तेमनं *n*. 1 Wetting, moistening. -2 Moisture. -3 A sauce, condiment. —नी *f*. A fire-place.

तेवनं *n* 1 Play, pastime.-2 A playground.

तैजस *a*. (*f*. —सी) 1 Bright, splendid, luminous. -2 Consisting of light. -3 Metallic. -4 Passionate. -5 Vigorous, energetic. -6 Powerful, intense. —सः *m* The highly refined or subtle essence (Vedânta phil.). -सं *n*. 1 Any metal.-2 Ghee. -3 Intensity, severity. -4 Vigour. -Comp —आवर्तनी *f*. A crucible.

तैतिक्ष *a*. (*f*. -क्षी) Patient.

तैतिरः *m*. A partridge.

तैतिलः *m* 1 A rhinoceros.-2 A god.

तैत्तिरः *m.* 1 A partridge. -2 A rhinoceros. -रं *n* A flock of partidges.

तैत्तिरीयाः *m. pl.* The followers of the Taittirîya school of the Yajurveda. -यः *m* The Taittirîya branch of the Yajurveda (कृष्णयजुर्वेद).

तैमिरः *m.* A disease of the eyes (dimness).

तैर्थिकः *m.* 1 An ascetic. -2 One who propounds a new religious or philosophical doctrine. -कं *n.* Holy water brought from a sacred bathing-place.

तैलं *n.* 1 Oil. -2 Benzoin. -Comp. —अटी *f.* A wasp. —अभ्यंगः *m* Anointing the body with oil. —कल्कजः *m.* Oil-cake. —पर्णिका, -पर्णी *f.* 1 Sandal. -2 Incense. -3 Turpentine.-पिपीलिका *f.* The small red ant. -फलः *m.* 1 The Ingudî tree. -2 The sesamum plant. —भाविनी *f.* Jasmine. —माली *f.* The wick of a lamp. -स्फटिकः *m.* A kind of gem.

तैलंगः *m.* N. of a. country, the modern Telangana or Carnatic. —गाः *m. pl.* The people of this country.

तैलिकः, **तैलिन्** *m.*An oilman.

तैलिनी *f.* The wick of a lamp.

तैलीनं *n.* A field of sesamum.

तैषः *m.* N. of the month Pausha.

तोकं *n.* An offspring, a child.

तोककः *m.* The 'Châtaka' bird.

तोडनं *n.* 1 Splitting, dividing. -2 Tearing. -3 Hurting, injuring.

तोत्रं *n.* A goad for driving cattle or elephants.

तोदः *m.* Pain, anguish, torture.

तोदनं *n.* 1 Pain, anguish. -2 A goad. -3 Face, mouth.

तोमरः *m* , -रं *n.* 1 An iron club. -2 A javelin. -Comp.-धरः *m.* 1 Fire (considered as a deity). -2 A warrior armed with a club.

तोयं *n.* 1 Water. -2 The constellation पूर्वाषाढा or its regent. -Comp. —अधिवासिनी *f.* The trumpet-flower. —आधारः,—आशयः *m.* A lake, well,any reservoir of water. -ईशः *m.* An epithet of Varuna. (—शं *n.*) The constellation called पूर्वाषाढा. —कर्मन् *n.* 1 The ablutions of various parts of the body performed with water. -2 The libations of water to the deceased. —कृच्छ्रः *m.*,—चक्रं *n.* A kind of penance, drinking nothing but water for a fixed period. —गर्भः *m.* The cocoanut. —चरः *m.* An aquatic animal.—डिंबः,-डिंभः *m.* Hail. —दः *m.* A cloud.-धरः *m.* A cloud.-धिः,-निधिः *m.* 1 The ocean. 2 The number 'four.'-नीवी *f.* The earth.-प्रसादनं *n.*The clearing-nut tree or its nut. —मलं *n.* Sea-foam. —मुच् *m.* A cloud. —यंत्रं *n.* 1 A water-clock. -2 An artificial jet or fountain of water.—राज् *m.* 1 The ocean. -2 Varuna, the regent of waters. -राशिः *m.* The ocean. -वेला *f.* The edge of water, shore. —व्यतिकरः *m.* The confluence (as of rivers). -शुक्तिका *f.* An oyster. -सर्पिका *f.*,-सूचकः *m.* A frog.

तोरणः *m.*, -णं *n.* 1 An arched doorway, a portal. -2 An outer door or gatway. -3 Any temporary and ornamental arch. -4 An elevated place near a bathing-place. —णं *n.* The neck, throat.

तोलः *m.*,-लं *n.* 1 Weight or quantity measured by the balance. -2 A weight of gold or silver equal to 12 mâshas or a tolâ.

तोलनं *n.*Raising, lifting, weighing.

तोषः *m.* Satisfaction,contentment, pleasure.

तोषणं *n.* 1 Satisfaction, gratification, contentment.-2Anything that gives satisfaction.

तोषलं *n.* A club (मुसल). [the zodiac.

तौक्षिकः *m.* The sign Sagittarius of

तौतिकः *m.* The pearl-oyster. —कं *n.* A pearl.

तौर्यं *n.* The sound of musical instruments. -Comp. —त्रिकं *n.* The union of song, dance, and instrumental music; triple symphony.

तौलं *n.* A balance.

तौलिकः, तौलिकिकः *m.* A painter.

तौलिन् *m.* 1 A weigher. -2 The sign *Libra* of the zodiac.

त्यक्त *p. p.* (*f.* —क्ता) 1 Abandoned, left.-2 Resigned, surrendered, avoided. -Comp. —अग्निः *m.* A Bráhmana who has given up household fire. —जीवित, —प्राण *a.* Ready to abandon life, willing to run any risk.

त्यज् 1 P. (त्यजति, तत्याज, अत्याक्षीत्, त्यक्ष्यति, त्यक्त) 1 To leave (in all senses), abandon, quit. -2 To dismiss, discharge. -3 To shun, avoid. -4 To get rid of, free oneself from. -5 To set aside, disregard. -6 To except. -7 To distribute, give away. -8 To shoot off. With परि- 1 To abandon. -2 To resign, renounce. -3 To except. सम्- 1 To abandon. -2 To avoid. -3 To give up, renounce. -4 To except.-*Desid.* (तित्यक्षति) To wish to leave.

त्यागः *m.* 1 Leaving, abandoning, deserting, separation. -2 Giving up, resigning, renouncing. -3 Gift, donation. -4 Liberality, generosity. -5 Secretion, excretion. -Comp. —पत्रं *n.* A bill of divorcement.—युत, —शील *a.* Liberal, generous.

त्यागिन् *a.* (*f.*-नी) 1 Leaving, abandoning.-2 A donor.-3 Heroic, brave. -4 Liberal. -5 One who does not look to any reward or result from the performance of ceremonial rites.

त्याज्य *a.* (*f.* —ज्या) 1 To be left, shunned or expelled. -2 To be given up or relinquished. -3 To be excluded.

त्रप् 1 A. (त्रपते, त्रपित) To be ashamed or abashed, be embarrassed. With अप- To turn away or retire through shame.

त्रपा *f.* 1 Bashfulness, modesty. -2 Shame (in a good or bad sense). -3 A libidinous or unchaste woman. -4 Fame, celebrity. -Comp.-रण्डा *f.* A harlot.

त्रपिष्ठ *a.* (*f.*-ष्ठा; superl. of तृप्र) Highly satisfied.

त्रपीयस् *a.* (*f.* -सी compar. of तृप्र) More satisfied.

त्रपु *n.* 1 Tin. -2 Lead.

त्रपुलं, -षं, त्रपुस्, त्रपुसं *n.* Tin.

त्रप्स्यं *n.* Diluted curds.

त्रय *a.* (*f.* -यी) Triple, three-fold, treble, divided into three parts, of three kinds. -यं *n.* A triad, a group or collection of three.

त्रयस् (*Nom. pl. m.* of त्रि) Three. -Comp. —चत्वारिंश *a.* Forty third. चत्वारिंशत् *a.* or *f.* Forty-three. —त्रिंश *a.* Thirty third.-त्रिंशत् *a.* or *f.* Thirty-three. —दश *a.* 1 Thirteenth. -2 Having thirteen added. —दशन् *a. pl.* Thirteen. —दशक *a.* Consisting of thirteen. (-कं *n.*) The number thirteen. —दशम *a.* Thirteenth. —दशी *f.* The thirteenth day of a lunar fortnight. —नवतिः *f.* Ninety-three. —पंचाशत् *f.* Fifty-three.—विंश *a.* 1 Twenty-third. -2 Consisting of twenty-three. —विंशतिः *f.* Twenty-three.—षष्टिः *f.* Sixty-three. —सप्ततिः *f.* Seventy-three.

त्रयी *f.* 1 The three Vedas taken collectively (ऋग्यजुःसामानि). -2 A triad, triplet. -3 A matron or married woman whose husband and children are living. 4 Intellect, understanding. -Comp. —तनुः *m.* 1 An epithet of the sun. -2 An epithet of Siva. —धर्मः *m.* The duty enjoined by the three Vedas. —मुखः *m.* A Brâhmana.

त्रस् I. 4. P. (त्रसति, त्रस्यति; त्रस्त) 1 To tremble, shake, start with fear. -2 To fear, dread, be afraid of (with abl., gen or instr.). -3 To run away, run from.

त्रस् 10 U. (त्रासयति,-ते) To go, move. -2 To hold. -3 To take, seize. -4 To oppose.

त्रस *a* (*f.* —सा) Movable, locomotive. —सः *m.* The heart. —सं *n.* 1 A wood, forest. -Comp. —रेणुः *m.* 1 An atom, the mote or atom of dust which is seen moving in a sunbeam.-2 N. of a wife of the sun.

त्रसरः *m.* A shuttle.

त्रसुर, त्रस्नु *a.* (*f.* —रा) Fearful, timid.

त्रस्त *p. p.* (*f.* —स्ता) 1 Frightened, terrified, alarmed. -2 Timid, fearful. -3 Quick.

त्राण *a.* (*f.* —णा) Protected, preserved, saved. —णं *n.* 1 Protection. defence.-2 Shelter, help. -3 Protecting, preserving.-4 An armour.

त्रात *p. p.* (*f.* —ता) Preserved, saved, protected.

त्रातृ *m.* A guardiau. defeneer, protector.

त्रास *a* (*f.* —सा) 1 Movable, moving. -2 Frightening. —सः *m.* 1 Fear. alarm. -2 Alarming. -3 A flaw or defect in a jewel.

त्रासन *a.* (*f.*—ना)Terrifying, frightening. -नं *n.* The act or means of frightening, any cause of alarm.

त्रासित *a.* (*f.* —ता) Frightened, alarmed.

त्रि *num.* (declined in pl. only, nom. *m.* त्रयः, *f.* तिस्रः, *n.* त्रीणि) Three. -Comp. —अंशः *m.* 1 A three-fold share. -2 A third part. -3 Three-fourths. —अक्षः, -अक्षकः *m.* An epithet of Siva. -अक्षरः *m.* 1 The mystic syllable ओम् consisting of three letters; see under अ. -2 A match-maker or घटक (that word consisting of three syllables.). -3 A genealogist.-अंकटं, —अंगटं *n.* A pole with three strings suspended to either end for carrying burdens (*mar.* कावड). -2 A sort of collyrium.—अंजलं, -लि *n.* Three handfuls taken collectively. —अधिष्ठानः *m.* The soul. (-नं *n.*) Spirit, life (चैतन्य). -अध्वगा,-मार्गगा,-वर्त्मगा *f.* Epithets of the river Ganges (flowing through the three worlds). —अंबकः (also त्रियंबकः) *m.* N. of Siva. त्र्यंबकसखः *m.* An epithet of Kubera. -अंबका *f.* An epithet of Párvati. —अब्द *a.* Three years old. (-ब्दं *n.*) Three years taken collectively.—अशीत *a.* Eighty-third.-अशीतिः *f.* Eighty-three. —अष्टन *a.* Twenty-four. —अश्र,—अस्र *a.* Triangular.(-स्रं *n.*) A triangle.-अहः *m.* 1 A period of three days. -2 A festival lasting three days. —आह्निक *a.* 1 Performed or produced in three days. -2 Recurring after the third day, tertian, (as fever.) -3 Having provision for three days. —ऋचं (तृचं also) *n.* Three *Riks* taken collectively. —ककुद् *m.* 1 N. of the mountain Trikuta.-2N. of Vishnu or Krishna. -3 The highest chief. -4A sacrifice lasting for ten nights. -कर्मन् *n.* The three chief duties of a Brâhmana *i. e.* sacrifice, study of the Vedas, and making gifts or charity. (-*m.*) One who engages in these three duties (as a Brâhmana). -कायः *m.* N. of Buddha. —काण्डं *n.* 1 The three-times; the past, the present, and the future, or morning, noon and evening. -2 The three tenses (the past, present, and future) of a verb. (-लं) *ind.* Three times, thrice. त्रिकालज्ञ, -दर्शिन *a.* Omniscient. (*m.*) 1 A divine sage, seer. -2 A deity. -3 N. of Buddha. —कूट: *m.* N. of a mountain in Ceylon on the top of which was situated Lanká, the capital of Rávana. -कूर्चकं *n.* A knife with three edges. —कोण *a.* Triangular, forming a triangle. (-ण: *m.*) 1 A triangle. -2 The vulva. —खट्वं *n.*, —खट्वी *f.* Three bedsteads taken collectively. —गण: *m* An aggregate of the three objects of worldly existence *i. e.* धर्म, अर्थ and काम. —गत *a.* 1 Tripled. -2 Done in three days. —गर्ता: *m. pl.* 1 N. of a country, also called जलंधर, in the north-west of India. -2 The people or rulers of that country. -गर्ता *f.* 1 A lascivious woman, wanton. -2 A woman in general. —गुण *a.* 1 Consisting of three threads. -2 Thrice, treble, threefold, triple. -3 Containing the three 'Gunas' सत्त्व, रजस् and तमस्. (-णं *n.*) The Pradhâna (in Sân. phil.). (-*ind.*) Three times; in three ways. (-णा: *m. pl.*) The three qualities or constituents of nature (-णा *f.*) 1 Mâyâ or illusion (in Vedânta phil.). -2 An epithet of Durgá. —चक्षुस् *m* An epithet of Siva. -चतुर *a.* (pl.) Three or four. —चत्वारिंश *a.* Forty-third.-चत्वारिंशत *f.* Forty-three. —जगत् *n.*,-जगती *f.* The three worlds. —जट: *m.* An epithet of Siva. —जटा *f.* N. of a female demon. —जीवा,-ज्या *f.* The sine of three signs or 90°; a radius. —णता *f.* A bow. —णव, -णवम *a.* pl. Three times nine *i. e.* 27 —तक्षं *n.*, तक्षी *f.* Three carpenters taken collectively. —दंडं *n.* 1 The three staves of a *Sannyasin* (who has resigned the world) tied together so as to form one. -2 The triple subjection of thought, word, and deed. (-ड: *m.*) The state of a religious ascetic. —दंडिन *m.* 1 A religious mendicant or *Sannyásin*. -2 One who has obtained command over his mind, speech, and body (or thought, word, and deed). -दशा: *m. pl.* 1 Thirty. -2 Thirty-three gods. (-श: *m.*) A god; an immortal. त्रिदशांकुश: *m.*, त्रिदशायुधं *n.* Indra's thunderbolt. —दिनं *n.* Three days collectively. —दिवं *n.* 1 The heaven. -2 Sky, atmosphere. -3 Paradise. -4 Happiness. (—वा *f.*) Cardamoms. —दृश् *m.* An epithet of Siva. —दोषं *n.* Vitiation or derangement of the three humours of the body, *i. e.* वात, पित्त and कफ. —धारा *f.* The Ganges. —णयन: (= नयन:), —नेत्र: -लोचन: *m.* Epithets of Siva. —नवत *a.* Ninety-third. -नवति: *f.* Ninety-three. —नयना *f.* Pârvatî. -नाभ: *m.* Vishnu. —पंच *a.* Three-fold five, *i. e.* fifteen. —पंचाश *a.* Fifty-third. —पंचाशत *f.* Fifty-three. —पटु: *m* Glass (काच). —पताक: *m.* 1 The hand with three fingers stretched out or erect. -2 The forehead marked naturally with three horizontal lines. —पत्रक: *m.* The Palása tree. —पथं *n.* 1 The three paths taken collectively, *i. e.* the sky, atmosphere and the earth, or the sky, earth and the lower world. -2 A place where three roads meet. (-था *f.*) An epithet of Mathurá. त्रिपथगा *f.* An epithet of the Ganges. —पद *a.* Three-footed. (-दं *n.*) A tripod. —पदिका *f.* 1 A tripod. -2 A stand with three feet. -पदी *f.* 1 The girth of an elephant. -2 The Gáyatrî metre. -3 A tripod. —पर्णः *m.* The Kimsuka tree. -पाद्ः *m.* 1 Vishnu in his dwarf incarnation. -2 Fever. -पुट *a* Triangular. (-टः *m.*) 1 An arrow -2 The palm of the hand. 3 A cubit. -4 A bank or shore. -पुटकः *m.* A triangle. —पुटा *f.* An epithet of Durgá —पुंड्ं, -पुंड्रकं *n.* A mark on the forehead consisting of three lines of ashes. —पुरं *n.* 1 A collection of three cities. -2 The three cities of gold, silver, and iron in the sky, air and earth built for demons by Maya. (—रः *m.*) N. of a demon or demons presiding over these cities. त्रिपुरांतकः *m.* Epithet of Siva. -प्रस्नुतः *m.* An elephant in rut. -फला *f.* The three myrobalans tak'n collectively (Mar. हिरडा, बेहडा and आंवळकाठी). —बंधनः *m.* The individual soul. -बलिः, -बली, -वालिः, -वली *f.* 1 The three folds or wrinkles of skin above the navel of a woman (regarded as a mark of beauty). —भद्रं *n.* Sexual union, cohabitation. —भुजं *n.* A triangle. —भुवनं *n.* The three worlds. —भूमः *m.* A palace with three floors. -मार्गा *f.* The Ganges. -मुकुटः *m.* The Trikúta mountain. -मुखः *m.* An epithet of Buddha. —मूर्तिः *m.* 1 The united form of Brahman (*m.*), Vishnu, and Mahesa, the Hindu triad. -2 Buddha, or Jina. -यष्टिः *m.* A necklace of three strings. -यामा *f.* Night. योनिः *f.* A law-suit (in which a person engages from anger, covetousness, or infatuation). —रात्रं *n.* A period of three nights. -लिंग *a.* An adjective. -2 Possessing the three Gunas. (—गी *f.*) The three genders taken collectively. -लोकं *n.* The three worlds.

—लोकी *f.* The three worlds taken collectively, the universe. —लोचनः *m.* Siva. —वर्गः *m.* 1 The three objects of worldly existence, *i. e.* धर्म अर्थ, and काम. -2 The three qualities of nature, *i. e.* सत्व, रजस् and तमस्. -3 The three higher castes. —वर्णकं *n.* The first three of the four castes of Hindus taken collectively. —वारं *ind.* Three times, thrice. —विक्रमः *m.* Vishnu in his fifth or dwarf incarnation. —विद्यः *m.* A Bráhmana versed in the three Vedas. -विध *a.* Of three kinds, three-fold. —विष्टपं, -पिष्टपं *n.* 1 The world of Indra, heaven. -2 The three worlds. -वेणिः, -णी *f.* The place near Prayága where the Ganges joins the Yamuná and receives under ground the Sarasvatî. —वेदः *m* A Bráhmana versed in the three Vedas. —शंकुः *m.* 1 N. of a celebrated king of the Solar race. -2 The Châtaka bird. -3 A cat. -4 A grass-hopper. -5 A fire-fly. -शत *a.* Three hundred. (-तं *n.*) 1 One hundred and three. -2 Three hundred. -शालं *n.* A house with three halls or chambers —शिखं *n.* 1 A trident. -2 A crown or crest (with three points). -शिरस् *m.* 1 N. of a demon killed by Râma. -2 An epithet of Kubera. -3 Fever. —शूलिन् *m.* An epithet of Siva. -शृंगः *m.* 1 The Trikuta mountain. -2 A triangle -षष्टिः *f.* Sixty-three. -संध्यं *n.*, -संध्यी *f.* The three periods of the day, *i. e.* dawn, noon, and sunset. —संध्यं *ind.* At the time of the three Sandhyás. —सप्तत *a.* Seventy third. -सप्ततिः *f.* Seventy-three. -सप्त, -सप्त *a. pl.* Three times 7, *i. e.* 21. -सम *a.* (in geom.) Equilateral. -साम्यं *n.* Equilibrium of the three (qualities).

-स्थली *f*. The three sacred places काशी, प्रयाग and गया. —स्रोतस् *f*. The Ganges. —सीत्य, -हल्य *a*. Ploughed thrice (as a field). —हायण *a*. Three years old.

त्रिंश *a*.(-शी *f*.) 1 Thirtieth. -2 Joined with thirty; *e. g*. त्रिंशं शतं one hundred and thirty. -3 Consisting of thirty.

त्रिंशक *a*. 1 Consisting of thirty. -2 Bought for thirty.

त्रिंशत *f*. Thirty. -Comp. —पत्रं *n*. A lotus opening at moonrise.

त्रिंशतिः *f*. Thrity.

त्रिंशत्कं *n*. An aggregate of thirty.

त्रिक *a*. (*f*. —का) 1 Triple, three-fold. -2 Forming a triad. -3 Three per cent. -4 Happening the third time. —कं *n*. 1 A triad. -2 A place where three roads meet. -3 The lower part of the spine, the part about the hips. -4 The part between the shoulder-blades. -5 The three spices. —का *f*. 1 A contrivance for raising water (like a wheel) over which passes the rope of the bucket. -2 The cover of a well.

त्रितय *a*. (*f*. -यी) Consisting of three parts, three-fold. —यं *n*. A triad, a group of three. [parts.

त्रिधा *ind*. In three ways, or in three

त्रिस् *ind*. Thrice, three times.

त्रुट् 4. 6. P. (त्रुट्यति, त्रुटति, त्रुटित) To tear, break, be split (fig. also).

त्रुटिः, —टी *f*. 1 Cutting, breaking. -2 A small part, an atom. -3 A very minute space of time equal to 1/4 of a *Kshana* or 1/2 of a *Lava*. -4 Doubt, uncertainty. -5 Loss, destruction. -6 Small cardamoms (the plant).

त्रेता *f*. 1 A triad, triplet. -2 The three sacred fires taken collectively. -3 A particular throw at dice, a cast of three or trey -4 The second of the four Yugas of the Hindus. [parts.

त्रेधा *ind*. Trebly, in three ways or

त्रै 1 A. (त्रायते, त्रात or त्राण) To protect, rescue or save from. (usually with abl.).

त्रैकालिक *a*. (*f*. की) Relating to the three times, *i. e*. past, present, and future.

त्रैकाल्यं *n*. The three times, past, present, and future, or sunrise, noon and sunset.

त्रैगुण्यं *n*. 1 The state of consisting of three threads, qualities &c. -2 Triplicity. -3 The three Gunas or properties (सत्त्व, रजस् and तमस्) taken collectively.

त्रैपुरः *m* 1 The Tripura country. -2 A ruler or inhabitant of that country. [mana.

त्रैमातुरः *m*. An epithet of Laksh-

त्रैमासिक *a*. (*f*. -की) 1 Three months old. -2 Lasting for or occurring every three months. -3 Quarterly.

त्रैमास्यं *n*. A period of three months.

त्रैराशिकं *n*. The rule of three (in math.).

त्रैलोक्यं *n*. The three worlds taken collectively.

त्रैवर्णिक *a*. (*f*. —की) Relating to the first three castes. —कः *m*. A member of the first three castes.

त्रैविक्रम *a*. (*f*. —मी) Belonging to Trivikrama or Vishnu. —मं *n*. The three steps of Vishnu.

त्रैविद्यं *n*. 1 The three Vedas. -2 The study of the three Vedas. -3 An assembly of Bráhmanas familiar with the three Vedas. —द्यः *m*. A Bráhmana versed in the three Vedas.

त्रैविष्टपः, त्रैविष्टपेयः *m*. A god.

त्रैशंकवः *m*. An epithet of Harischandra, son of Trisanku.

त्रोटकं *n.* 1 A species of drama thus defined:—समाप्तसप्तपंचांकं दिव्यमानुषसंश्रयं। त्रोटकं नाम तत्प्राहुः प्रत्यंकं सविदूषकं ॥ साहि. द.

त्रोटि:, —टी *f.* A bill, beak. -Comp. —हस्त: *m* A bird.

त्रोत्रं *n.* A goad.

त्वक्ष् 1 P. (त्वक्षति, त्वष्ट) 1 To pare, hew. -2 To make thin.

त्वंकार: *m.* Addressing disrespectfully with a 'thou'; theeing and thouing.

त्वंग् 1 P. (त्वंगति) 1 To go, move. -2 To jump; gallop.-3 To tremble.

त्वच् *f.* 1 Skin, hide. -2 Bark; rind. -3 Any cover or coating. -4 The sense of touch.-Comp.-अंकुर: *m.* Horripilation. —इंद्रियं *n.* The organ of touch. —कंडुर: *m.* A sore. —गंध: *m.* The orange. —छेद: *m.* 1 A skin-wound, scratch, bruise. -2 Circumcision.-जं *n.* 1 Blood.-2 Hair (on the body).-तरंगक: *m.* A wrinkle. —त्रं *n.* An armour. —दोष: *m* A disease of the skin, leprosy. —पुष्प: *m.* Horripilation. -सार: (or त्वचिसार:) *m.* A bamboo. —सुगंध: *m.* An orange.

त्वचं *n.* 1 Skin. -2 Bark.

त्वचस् *n.* Skin.

त्वचा *f.* The same as त्वच्.

त्वदीय *a.* (*f.* -या) Thy, thine, your, yours.

त्वाद्विध *a.* (*f.* -धा) Like thee or you.

त्वर् 1 A. (त्वरते, त्वरित-तूर्ण) To hurry, make haste.

त्वरा, त्वरि: *f.* 1 Haste, hurry, speed. -comp. —आरोह: *m.* A pigeon.

त्वरित *p. p.* (*f.* —ता) Quick, swift, speedy. —तं *n.* Despatch; haste. -*ind.* Quickly.

त्वष्टृ *m.* 1 A carpenter. -2 Visvakarman, the architect of the gods.

त्वादृश्, त्वादृश (*f.* शी) *a.* Similar to thee or you; of thy or your kind.

त्विष् 1 U. (त्वेषति-ते) To shine.

त्विष् *f.* 1 Light, splendour. -2 Beauty. -3 Authority, weight. -4 Wish, desire. -5 Custom, practice. -6 Violence. -7 Speech. -Comp. —ईश:, त्विषांपति: त्विषामीश: *m.* The sun.

त्विषा *f.* Splendour; lustre, light.

त्विषि: *m.* 1 A ray of light. -2 Beauty.

त्सरु: *m.* 1 Any creeping animal. -2 The hilt or handle of a sword or any other weapon.

थ.

थ: *m.* 1 A mountain. —थं *n.* 1 Protection.

थुत्कार: *m.* The sound थुत made in spitting.

थुर्व् 1 P. (थु-थुर्वति) To hurt.

थूत्कार: *m.*, थूत्कृतं *n* The sound थूत made in spitting.

थैथै *ind.* The imitative sound of a musical instrument.

द.

द *a.* (*f.*-दा) (At the end of comp.) Giving, causing; destroying. *e g.* धनद, अन्नद, गरद, तोयद, अनलद &c. -द: *m* 1 A gift. -2 A mountain. -दं *n.* A wife.

दंश् 1 P. (दशति, दष्ट; *desid.* दिदंक्षति) To bite, sting.

दंश् 1 P, 10 U. (दंशति, दंशयति,-ते) 1 To speak. -2 To shine.

दंश: *m.* 1 Biting, stinging. -2 The sting of a snake.-3 A bite, the spot bitten. -4 Cutting, tearing. -5 A gad-fly. -6 A flaw, fault, defect (in a jewel). -7 A tooth.-8 Pungency. -9 An armour. 10 A joint, limb. -Comp. —भीरुः, —भीरुकः *m.* A buffalo. —वदनः *m.* A heron.

दंशकः *m.* 1 A dog.-2 A gad-fly. -3 A fly.

दंशनं *n.* 1 The act of biting or stinging. -2 An armour, mail.

दंशित *a.* (*f.* —ता) 1 Bitten. -2 Mailed, furnished with an armour. —तं *n.* A bite.

दंशिन् *m.* See दंशक.

दंशी *f.* A small gad-fly.

दंष्ट्रा *f.* A large tooth, tusk, fang. -Comp. —अस्त्रः, —आयुधः *m.* A wild boar. —विषः *m* A kind of snake.

दंष्ट्राल *a.* (*f.* —ला) Having large tusks.

दंष्ट्रिका *f.* Same as दंष्ट्रा.

दंष्ट्रिन् *m.* 1 A wild boar. 2 A snake. -3 A hyena. -4 Any animal with tusks.

दक्ष *a.* (*f.* —क्षा) 1 Able, competent, clever, skilful.-2 Fit, suitable. -3 Ready, careful, prompt. -4 Honest, upright. —क्षः *m.* 1 N. of a celebrated Prajápati.-2 A cock. -3 Fire. -4 The bull of Siva. -5 A lover attached to many mistresses. -6 An epithet of Siva ; also of Vishnu. -7 Mental power, ability, capacity. -8 The right side or part. —क्षा *f.* 1 The earth. -2 The Ganges. —क्षं *n.* Strength, vigour. -Comp. —कन्या, —जा, —तनया *f.* 1 An epithet of Durgâ. -2 A lunar mansion.-सुतः *m.* A god. (-ता *f.*) A lunar mansion.

दक्षाय्यः *m.* 1 A vulture. -2 An epithet of Garuda.

दक्षिण *a.* (*f.* —णा) 1 Able, skilful, clever. -2 Right (opp. वाम). -3 Situated on the right side. -4 South, southern. -5 Situated to the south. -6 Sincere, honest. -7 Pleasing, amiable. -8 Courteous. -9 Submissive. -10 Dependent. —णः *m.* 1 The right hand or arm. -2 A civil or courteous person. (In dram.) A lover who professes attachment to one mistress, while his heart has been entirely taken up by another. -3 An epithet of Siva or Vishnu. -4 The southern sacred fire. —णः *m.*, —णं *n.* 1 The right side. -2 The Deccan. -Comp. —अग्निः *m.* The southern fire, the sacred fire placed southwards. —अचलः *m.* The southern mountain, Malaya. —अभिमुख *a.* Facing the south. —अयनं *n.* The sun's progress south of the equator, the half year in which the sun moves from the north to the south, the winter solstice. —अर्धः *m.* 1 The right hand. -2 The right or southern side. -आचार *a* 1 Honest, well-behaved. -2 A worshipper of Sakti according to the right hand ritual. —आशा *f.* The south. —इतर *a.* 1 Left (as hand or foot). -2 Northern. (—रा *f.*) The north. —उत्तर *a.* Turned or lying to the south and the north. —स्थः *m.* A charioteer.

दक्षिणतः *ind.* 1 From the right or south.-2 To the right hand.-3 To the south or southward (with gen.).

दक्षिणा *ind.* 1 On the right or south of. -2 In the southern direction (with abl.).—णा *f.* 1 A present or gift to Brâhmanas. -2 Dakshinâ regarded as a dughter of Prajápati and as the wife of Sacrifice personified. -3 A gift or donation in general. -4 A good milch-cow, prolific cow. -5 The south.-6 The southern country, the Deccan. -7 Fame.-8 A kind of heroine. -Comp.-आवर्त: *m.* The Deccan. —पथ: *m.* The southern part of India, the south or Deccan.

दक्षिणाहि *ind.* 1 Far on the right. -2 Far in the south, to the south of (with abl.)

दाक्षिणीय:, दक्षिण्य: *m.* A Bráhman worthy of or desrving a sacrificial gift.

दाक्षिणेन *ind.* On the right side of (with acc. or gen.).

दग्ध *p p.* (*f.*—ग्धा) 1 Burnt. consumed by fire. -2 (Fig.) Consumed by grief; distressed. -3 Famished. -4 Inauspicious, as in दग्धयोग. -5 Dry. tasteless. -6 Wretched, accursed, vile (used as a term of abuse before a word); e. *g.* दग्धदेह:, दग्धोदरं, दग्धजठरं.-7 Cunning (विदग्ध).-Comp. —काक: *m.* A raven.

दग्धिका *f.* Scorched rice.

दघ्न *a.* (*f.*-घ्नी) A termination added to nouns in the sense of ' reaching to ', ' as high or deep as ', ऊरुदघ्न. गुल्फदघ्न.

दंड् 10 U. (दंडयति-ते, दंडित) To punish. chastise; (this is one of the roots that govern two accusatives) *e. g.* तान् सहस्रं च दंडयेत.

दंड: *m*, डं *n.* 1 A stick. club, cudgel. -2 The sceptre of a king. -3 The staff given to a twice-born man at the time of investiture with the sacred thread. -4 The staff of a संन्यासिन or ascetic. -5 The trunk of an elephant. -6 The stem or stalk (as of a lotus,tree &c.),the handle (as of an umbrella). -7 The oar of a boat. -8 The staff or pole of a banner, a tent &c. -9 The stick with which an instrument is played. -10 A churning-stick.-11 Fine. -12 Chastisement. -13 Imprisonment.-14 Attack,assault,the last of the four expedients of a king. -15 An army. -16 A form of military array. -17 Subjection, control, restraint. -18 A measure of length equal to4'Hastas.'19 The penis.-20 Pride. -21 The body. -22 An epithet of Yama.-23N.of Vishnu;of Siva. -24 An attendant on the sun. -25 A row or series,a line. 26 Standing upright or erect. —Comp. -आजिनं *n. sing.* 1 The staff and hide (as outer badges of devotion). -2. (fig.) Hypocrisy, deceit. -अधिप: *m.* The chief mágistrate. -अनीकं *n.* A detachment or division of an army.-अपूपन्याय: *m.* The maxim of the stick and cakes. It is used to show that what happens to one thing happens to anotheer connected to it in a particular way. -अलसिका *f.* Cholera. -आज्ञा *f.* A judicial sentence. -आहतं *n.* Buttermilk. -कर्मन् *n.* Infliction of punishment, chastisement. -काक: *m.* A raven. -काष्ठं *n.* A wooden club or staff.-ग्रहणं*n.*Becoming a mendicant. -चक्र: *m.* A division of an army. -छदनं *n.* A room in which utensils of various kinds are kept. -ढक्का *f.* A kind of drum. -दास: *m.* He who has become a slave from non-payment of a debt. -देवकुलं *n.* A court of justice. -धर,-धार *a.* 1 Carrying a staff, staff-bearer.,-2 Punishing, chastising. -3 Exercising judicial authority. (-र: *m.*) 1 A king. -2 N. of Yama.-3 A judge, supreme magistrate. -4 A mendicant carrying a staff. -5 A potter. -नायक:*m.*1 A judge,a head police-officer, a magistrate.-2 The leader of an army, a general. -3 A king. —नीतिः f. 1 The administration of justice, judicature. -2 The system of civil and military administration, the science of politics, polity. -नेतृ m. 1 A king.-2Yama. -3 Judge. -पः m. A king. -पाशुलः m. A porter; door-keeper. -पाणिः m. An epithet of Yama.-पातः m. The infliction of punishment. -पारुष्यं n. 1 Assault, violence. -2 Hard or cruel infliction of punishment. -पालः, -पालकः m. 1 A head magistrate. -2 A door-keeper, porter. -पोणं n. A strainer furnished with a handle. —प्रणामः m. 1 Bowing without bending the body, (keeping it erect like a stick). -2 Falling flat or prostrate on the ground. —बालधिः m. An elephant. —भंगः m. The non-execution of a sentence.-भृत m. 1A potter.-2 An epithet of Yama. -माथः m.A principal road,high way.-यात्राf. 1 A solemn procession,(particularly bridal). -2 Warlike expedition, conquest (of a region). —यामः m. 1 An epithet of Yama;also of Agastya. -3 A day. —वधः m. The capital punishment. —वासिकः m. A door-keeper, warder. —वासिन m. 1 A door-keeper. -3 A magistrate, —वाहिन m. A police officer. -विधिः,-उद्यमः m. I The rule of punishment -2Criminal law. —विष्कंभः m. The post to which the string of a churning-stick is fastened. —व्यूहः m. A particular arrangement troops. —शास्त्रं n. The criminal law. —हस्तः m. 1 A door-keeper,warder, porter. -2 An epithet of Yama.

दंडकः m. 1 A stick, staff. -2 A line, row. -3 N. of a metre. -कः m., -का f., -कं n. N. of an ancient celebrated district in the Deccan situated between the rivers Narmadá and Godâvari.

दंडनं n. Punishing, chastising, fining

दंडादंडि ind ' Stick against stick, ' fighting with sticks and staves.

दंडारः m.1 A carriage.-2 A potter's wheel. -3 A raft, boat. -4 An elephant in rut. -5 A bow or any other instrument.

दंडिकः m. A staff-bearer, a mace-bearer

दाडिका f. 1 A stick -2 A row,line, series. -3 A string of pearls, a necklace. -4 A rope.

दंडिन m. 1 A Bráhmana of the fourth order, a Sannyasin. -2 A door-keeper,porter.-3 An oarsman. -4 A Jaina ascetic -5 An epithet of Yama. -6 A king.-7 A religious mendicant (Bhikshu). -8 An epithet of Siva. -9 N. of a poet, author of the Kavyâdarsa and Dasakumára-charita.

दत m. A tooth; (a word obtionally substituted for दंत in all the case-forms after the acc. dual. It has no forms for the first five inflections.-Comp-च्छदः (दच्छदः)m. The lip.

दत्त p. p. (f. —त्ता) 1 Given, presented. -2 Made over. delivered,assigned. -3 Placed, stretched forth. -4 Preserved,guarded p.p. of दाq.v. -त्तः m. 1 One of the twelve kinds of sons in Hindu-law ;-(also called दत्त्रिम). -2 A title added to the names of Vaisyas ; e. g. वसुदत्त. -3 N. of a son of Atri and Anasuyá दत्तात्रेय also. —त्तं n. Gift, donation. -Comp. —अनप (-पा-) कर्मन्,-अप्रदानिकं n Non delivery or resumption of gifts, one of the 18 titles of Hindu law. —अवधान a. Attentive —आत्रेयः m. N. of a sage, son of Atri and Anasúyá considered as an incarnation of Brahman (*m*.), Vishnu and Mahesa. —आदर *a.* 1 Showing respect, respectful. -2 Treated with respect. —शुल्का *f.* A bride for whom a dowry has been paid. —हस्त *a.* 1 Supported by the hand (of); शंभुना दत्तहस्ता *मेघदू. 'leaning on Sambhu's arm. 2 (fig.) Being given a helping hand, supported, aided, assisted.

दत्तकः *m.* An adopted son.

दत्तिः *f.* 1 A gift, donation. -2 An offering, an oblation.

दत्तेयः *m.* N. of Indra.

दत्रिमः *m.* One of the twelve kinds [of sons.

दद् 1 A. (ददते) To give.

दद *a.* (*f.* —दा) Giving, offering.

ददनं *n.* A gift, donation.

दध् 1 A. (दधते) 1 To hold. -2 To have, possess. -3 To give, present.

दधि *n.* 1 Coagulated milk, thick sour milk. -2 Turpentine. -3 A garment. -Comp. -उत्तरं, —उत्तरकं (-गं) *n.* The skim of curdled milk, whey. —उदः, -उदकः *m.* The ocean of coagulated milk. —कूर्चिका *f.* A mixture of boiled and coagulated milk.-चारः *m.* A churning-stick. —जं *n.* Fresh butter. —फलः *m.* The wood-apple (कपित्थ). —मंडः *m.*, —वारि *n.* Whey. -मंथनं *n.* Churning coagulated milk. —शोणः *m.* A monkey. —सक्तु *m. pl.* Barley-meal mixed with coagulated milk. —सारः, —स्नेहः *m.* Fresh butter. —स्वेदः *m.* Buttermilk

दधित्थः *m.* The wood-apple (कपित्थ).

दधिषाय्यः *m.* Clarified butter.

दधीचः, —चिः *m.* N. of a celebrated sage.-Comp. -अस्थि *n.* 1 The thunderbolt of Indra. -2 A diamond.

दनुः *f.* N of a daughter of Daksha given in marriage to Kasyapa and mother of the *Dánavas.* -*m.* N. of a monster, Killed by Ráma and Lakshmana. -Comp. —जः, -पुत्रः, -संभवः, -सूनुः *m.* Demon.

दंतः *m.* 1 A tooth, tusk, fang (as of serpents, beasts &c.). -2 An elephant's tusk, ivory. -3 The point of an arrow.-4 The peak of a mountain.-5 The side or ridge of a mountain.-6 The number thirty-two.-7 A bower, an arbour (कुंज). -Comp. —अग्रं *n.* The point of a tooth. -अर्बुदः *m.*, -दं *n.* Gum-boil. —आघातः *m.* A bite. —आयुधः *m.* A hog. —आलयः *m.* The mouth. —आलिका, —आली *f.* A horse's bridle. —उलूखलिकः, —उलूखलिन् *m.* An anchorite of a particular order, who uses his teeth for a mortar, (grinding grain between his teeth). —कर्षणः *m.* The lime or citron tree. —कारः *m.* An artist who works in ivory. —काष्ठं *n.* A piece of stick or twig used as a tooth-brush. —क्रूरः *m.* A fight. —ग्राहिन् *a.* Injuring the teeth, causing them to decay. -घर्षः *m.* Chattering or grinding the teeth. —चालः *m.* Looseness of the teeth. —छदः *m.* The lip. —जात *a.* (A child) that is teething. —जाहं *n.* The root of a tooth. —धावनं *n.* 1 Cleaning or washing the teeth.-2 A tooth-brush. (-नः *m.*) 1 The Bakula tree. -2 The Khadira tree. —पत्रं *n.* A sort of ear-ornament. —पत्रकं *n.* 1 An ear ornament. -2 A Kunda flower. —पत्रिका *f.* 1 An ear-ornament. -2 Kunda. —पवनं *n.* 1 A tooth brush. -2 Cleaning or washing the teeth. -पांचालिका *f.* An ivory doll.—पातः *m.* The falling out of the teeth. —पाली *f.* 1 The point of a tooth -2 Gum. -पुप्पुटः, (-टकः) *m.* A gum-boil.-पुष्पं *n.* 1 The Kunda flower. -2 The fruit of the clearing-nut plant. (कतकफल). —फलः *m.* The wood-apple tree. (—ला *f.*) The long pepper. —भागः *m.* The fore-part of an elephant's head (where the tusks appear). —मलं, —रजस् n. The tartar of the teeth. —मांसं, -मूलं, —वल्कं n. Gums. -मूलीयाः m. pl. The dental letters, viz. -लृ, त्, थ्, द्, ध्, न्, ल्, and स्. —वल्कं n. The enamel of the teeth. —वस्त्रं, —वासस् n. The lip. -बीजः, -वीजः,-बीजकः,-वीजकः m. The pomegranate tree. —वीणा f. 1 A kind of musical instrument or harp. -2 Chattering of the teeth. —वेष्टः m. 1 The gums. -2 A ring round the tusk of an elephant. -3 A tumor of the gums. —वैदर्भः m. The loosening of the teeth through external injury. -व्यसनं n. The fracture of the teeth. —शंकुः m. A pair of pincers for drawing out teeth. —शठ a. Sour, acid. (—ठः m.) 1 Sourness, acidity. -2 The citron tree. —शर्करा f. The tartar of the teeth. —शाणः m. A kind of tooth-powder, dentifrice. —शोधनिः f. A tooth-pick. -शोफः m. A swelling of the gums.-संघर्षः m. The gnashing or rubbing together the teeth. —हर्षः m. The morbid sensitiveness of the teeth.-हर्षकः m. The citron tree.

दंतकः m. 1 A tooth (at the end of comp.). -2 A peak, summit. -3 Pin or shelf projecting from a wall, bracket.

दंतादंति ind. ' Tooth against tooth,' biting one another.

दंतावलः, दंतिन् m. An elephant.

दंतुर (f.-रा) 1 Having long or projecting teeth. -2 Dentated, notched, serrated, uneven (fig. also) -3 Undulatory. -4 Rising, bristling (as hair). -5 Overspread, covered with. -Comp.-छदः m. The lime tree.

दंतुरित a. (f. —ता) 1 Having long or projecting teeth. -2 Notched, serrated, bristling. -3 Besmeared, covered with.

दंत्य a. (f. -त्या) 1 Dental.-2 Suitable to the teeth. —त्यः (i. e. वर्णः) m. A letter of the dental class.

दंदशः m. A tooth.

दंदशूक a. (f. —का) 1 Biting, venomous. -2 Mischievous. —कः m. 1 A serpent, snake.-2 A reptile in general. -3 A demon, a Râkshasa.

दभ्, 1, 5 P. (दभति or दभ्नोति, दब्धः desid. धिप्सति, दिदंभिषति) 1 To injure, hurt.-2 To deceive, cheat.-3 To go.

दभ्र a. (f. —भ्रा) Little, small. -भ्रः m. The ocean. —भ्रं ind. A little, to some extent.

दम् 4 P. (दाम्यति: दमित, दांत) 1 To be tamed. -2 To be calm or tranquil. -3 To tame, subdue, restrain. -4 To pacify. -Caus. (दमयति,-ते).

दमः m. 1 Taming, subduing -2 Self-command, self-restraint,-3 Curbing the evil propensities of the mind.-4 Firmness of mind. -5 Punishment, fine. -6 Mire, mud.

दमथः, -थुः m. 1 Subduing the passions, self-restraint. -2 Punishment.

दमन a. (f.-नी) 1 Taming, subduing. -2 Tranquil, passionless.-नः m. 1 A charioteer. -2 A warrior. -3 The Kunda plant. -नं n. 1 Taming, subjugation, restraint. -2 Punishing, chastising.-3 Self-restraint.-4 Slaying, killing.

दमयंती f. N. of the daughter of Bhîma, king of the Vidarbhas.

दमयितृ m. 1 A chastiser.-2 An epithet of Vishnu, also of Siva.

दमित a. (f. —ता) 1 Tamed, calmed, tranquillized. -2 Conquered, curbed, subdued.

दमु (-मू-) नस् m. Fire.

दंपती m. du. Husband and wife.

दंभ् 10 U. (दंभयति,-ते) To impel, propel, drive onward.

दंभः *m.* 1 Deceit, fraud, trickery. -2 Religious hypocrisy. -3 Arrogance, pride. -4 Sin, wickedness. -5 The thunderbolt of Indra. -6 An epithet of Siva.

दंभनं *n.* Cheating, deceiving, deceit.

दंभिन् *m.* A hypocrite, an impostor.

दंभोलिः *m.* 1 Indra's thunderbolt. -2 A diamond.

दम्य *a.* (*f.*-म्या) 1 To be trained or tamed. -2 To be punished, punishable. --म्यः *m.* 1 A young bullock (requiring training and experience). -2A steer that has to be tamed.

दय् 1 A. (दयते, दयित) 1 To feel pity for, pity, sympathise (with gen.). -2 To love, like, be fond of. -3 To protect. -4 To go, move. -5 To grant, give. -6 To hurt.

दया *f.* Pity, tenderness, sympathy, compassionate. Comp. —कूटः, —कूर्चः *m.* Epithets of Buddha. —वीरः *m.* (in Rhet.) The sentiment of heroic compassion; the sentiment of heroism arising out of compassion.

दयालु *a.* Kind, tender, merciful, compassionate.

दयित *p. p.* (*f.*—ता) Beloved, desired, liked. —तः *m.* A husband, lover, a beloved person. —ता *f.* A wife, one's beloved woman. दयिताजितः *m.* A hen-pecked husband.

दरः *m.*, —दरं *n.* 1 A cave, cavity, hole. -2 A conch-shell. -रः *m.* 1 Fear, terror, dread. -2 A stream. —रं *ind.* A little, slightly (in comp.). Comp. —तिमिरं *n.* The darkness of fear. —दः *m.*, —दं *n.* Vermilion.

दरणं *n* Breaking, splitting.

दरणिः *m.*, *f.*, दरणी *f.* 1 An eddy. -2 A current. -3 Surf. -4 Breaking.

दरथः *m.* 1 A cavity. -2 Fleeing away. -3 Over-running the country for forage.

दरद् *f.* 1 The heart. -2 Terror, fear. -3 A mountain. -4 A precipice. -5 A bank or mound.

दरदाः *m. pl.* A country bordering on Kashmîra. —दः *m.* Fear, terror. —दं *n.* Red lead.

दरिः,-री *f.* A cave, cavern, valley.

दरिद्र *a.* (*f.*—द्रा) Poor, needy.

दरिद्रा 2 P. (दरिद्राति, दरिद्रित; *caus.* दरिद्रयति; *desid.* दिदरिद्रासति, दिदरिद्रषति) 1 To be poor or needy. -2 To be in distress. -3 To become thin.

दरोदरः *m.* 1 A gamester. -2 A stake at play. -रं *n.* 1 Gambling. -2 A die, dice.

दर्दरः *m.* 1 A mountain. -2 A jar slightly broken.

दर्दरीकः *m.* 1 A frog. -2 A cloud. 3 A kind of musical instrument. —कं *n.* A musical instrument in general.

दर्दुरः *m.* 1 A frog. -2 A cloud. -3 A kind of musical instrument such as a flute. -4 A mountain. -5 N. of a mountain in the south. -6 The sound of a drum. -7 A sort of rice.

दद्रूः (-द्रूः) *f.* A kind of leprosy.

दद्रु (-द्रू-) ण *a.* Herpetic.

दर्पः *m.* 1 Pride, arrogance, haughtiness. -2 Rashness. -3 Vanity, conceit -4 Sullenness, sulkiness. -5 Heat. -6 Musk.

दर्पक *a.* Making proud, inflaming. —कः *m.* N. of Kâmadeva, the god of love.

दर्पणः *m* 1 A looking-glass, mirror. -2 N. of a mountain inhabited by Kubera. —णं *n.* 1 The eye. -2 Kindling. inflaming, making proud.

दर्पित, दर्पिन् *a.* (*f.*-ता, -णी.) Proud, arrogant, haughty.

दर्भः *m.* A kind of sacred grass (Kusa grass) used at sacrificial ceremonies &c. -Comp. —अंकुरः *m.* Pointed blade of *darbha* grass. —अनूपः *m.* A watery plâce full of *darbha*.

grass. —आह्वय: *m.* The Munja grass.

दर्मटं *n* A private apartment, a retired room.

दर्वः *m.* 1 A mischievous or harmful person. -2 A demon, goblin.

दर्वटः *m.* 1 A village constable, a police-officer. -2 A door-keeper.

दर्वरीकः *m.* 1 An epithet of Indra. -2 A kind of musical instrument. -3 Air, wind.

दार्विकः *m.*, -का *f.* A ladle, spoon.

दर्वी (-र्विः) *f.* 1 A ladle, spoon. -2 The expanded hood of a snake. -Comp. —करः *m.* A snake, serpent.

दर्शः *m.* 1 Sight, view, appearance. -2 Ocular evidence or proof. -3 The day of the new moon (अमावास्या). -4 The new moon. -5 The half-monthly sacrifice, a sacrificial rite performed on the day of the new moon. -Comp. -पः *m.* A god. —यामिनी *f.* The night of the new moon.—विपद् *m.* The moon.

दर्शक *a.* (-का or -र्शिका *f.*) 1 Seeing, observing. -2 Showing, pointing out. -3 Examining, looking out for. 4 Explaining, making clear, elucidating. —कः *m.* 1 One who shows or exhibits. -2 A door-keeper, warder. -3 A skilful man, one proficient in any art or science.

दर्शनं *n.* 1 Looking at, seeing, observing. -2 Knowing, understanding, foreseeing. -3 Sight, vision. -4 The eye. -5 Inspection, examination. -6 Showing, displaying. -7 Becoming visible. -8 Visit, paying a visit. -9 Colour, aspect, appearance. -10 Appearance, (in court.) -11 A vision, dream. -12 Discernment, intellect. -13 Judgment, apprehension. -14 Religious knowledge. -15 A doctrine or theory prescribed in a system. -16 A system of philosophy. -17 A mirror. 18 Virtue, moral merit. -19 Opinion. -20 Intention. -21 Demonstration. -22 A sacrifice. -Comp. —उज्ज्वला *f.* The great white jasmine. —पथः *m.* The range of sight or vision ; horizon. —प्रतिभूः *m.* A bail or surety for appearance.

दर्शनीय *pot. p.* (*f.* —या) 1 To be seen, visible, perceptible. -2 Fit to be seen, good-looking, handsome. -3 To be produced in a court of justice.

दर्शयितृ *m.* 1 A warder, door-keeper. -2 A guide (in general).

दर्शित *p. p.* (*f.* -ता) 1 Shown, exhibited. -2 Explained, demonstrated, proved. -3 Apparent, visible.

दर्शिन् *a.* (*f.* —नी) (At the end of comp.) Seeing, observing, knowing, showing, exhibiting.

दल् 1 P (दलति, दलित) 1 To burst open, split, crack. -2 To expand, bloom, open (as a flower). —*Caus.* (द-दा- लयति) 1 To tear asunder. -2 To cut, divide, split. -3 To dispel, drive or chase away. -4 To wither.

दलः *m.*, -लं *n.* 1 A piece, portion, part, fragment. -2 Tearing, cutting. -3 A degree. -4 A half, the half. -5 A sheath, scabbard. -6 A small shoot or blade, a petal, leaf. -7 The blade of any weapon -8 A heap, quantity. -9 A detachment, a body of troops. -10 Alloy or adulteration. Comp. —आढकः *m.* 1 Foam. -2 A cuttle-fish-bone. -3 A ditch, moat. -4 A hurricane, high wind. -5 Red chalk. -6 Wild sesamum. -7 Kunda creeper. -8 A Sudra. -9 The headman of a village. -10 An elephant's ear. —कोषः *m.* The Kunda creeper. —निर्मोकः *m.* The Bhúrja tree. -पुष्पा *f.* The Ketaka plant. —सूचिः, -ची *f.* A thorn. -स्नसा *f.* The fibre or vein of a leaf.

दलनं *n.* Bursting, breaking, dividing, crushing, splitting.

दलपः *m.* 1 A weapon. -2 Gold. -3 Sástra.

दलशः *ind.* By pieces.

दालिकं *n.* Timber, a piece of wood.

दलित *p. p.* (*f.* -ता) 1 Broken, torn, burst, split. -2 Opened, expanded. -3 Bisected. -4 Driven asunder, scattered. -5 Trodden down, destroyed. -6 Manifested, displayed.

दल्भः *m.* 1 A wheel. -2 Fraud, dishonesty. -3 Sin.

दवः *m.* 1 A wood, forest. -2 A forest-conflagration. -3 Fire, heat. -4 Fever, pain. -Comp. —आग्निः, -दहनः *m.* A forest-conflagration.

दवथुः *m.* 1 Fire, heat. -2 Pain, anxiety. -3 Inflammation of the eye.

दविष्ठ *a.* (*f.* —ष्ठा, Superl. of दूर) Most distant.

दवीयस् *a.* (*f.* -सी, Compar. of दूर) More distant or remote.

दशक *a.* (*f.* -का) Consisting of ten, ten-fold. -कं *n.* A group of ten; decade.

दशत *f.*, दशतिः *f.* A group of ten, a decade.

दशधा *ind.* 1 In ten ways. -2 In ten parts.

दशन् *num. a.* (pl.) Ten. -Comp. —अंगुल *a.* Ten fingers long. (-लं *n.*) A water-melon. —अर्ध *a.* Five. -अर्धं *n.* Five. —अर्धः *m.* An epithet of Buddha. —अर्हः *m.* 1 An epithet of Krishna or Vishnu. -2 Buddha. —अवताराः *m. pl.* The ten incarnations of Vishnu. —अवर *a.* Consisting of at least ten. —अश्वः *m.* The moon. -आननः,-आस्यः *m.* Epithets of Rávana. —आमयः *m.* An epithet of Rudra. -ईशः *m.* A superintendent of 10 villages. -एकादशिक *a.* Who lends 10 and receives 11 in return *i. e.* who lends money at ten per cent. —कंठः, -कंधरः, *m.* Epithets of Rávana. -गुण *a.* Ten-fold, ten times larger. —ग्रामपतिः, -ग्रामिकः, -ग्रामिन्, -पः *m.* A superintendent of ten villages. -ग्रीवः *m.* See दशकंठ. -पारमिताध्वरः *m.* An epithet of Buddha. —पुरं *n.* N. of an ancient city, capital of king Rantideva. -बलः, -भूमिगः *m.* Epithets of Buddha. —मालिकाः *m. pl.* 1 N. of a country. -2 The people or rulers of this country. —मास्य *a.* 1 (A child) ten months in the womb (as a child before birth). —मुखः *m.* An epithet of Râvana. —रथः *m.* N. of a celebrated king of Ayodhyâ, and father of Ráma, and his three brothers. —रात्रं *n* A period of ten nights. (-त्रः *m.*) A particular sacrifice lasting for ten days. —रूपभृत *m.* An epithet of Vishnu. —लक्षणकः *m.* Religion. -वक्त्रः, -वदनः *m.* The same as दशमुखः. —वाजिन् *m.* The moon. —वार्षिक *a.* Happening after, or lasting for, ten years. —विध *a.* Of ten kinds. —शतं *n* 1 A thousand. -2 One hundred and ten. —शती *f.* A thousand. -स (-सा-)हस्रं *n.* Ten thousand. —हरा *f.* 1 An epithete of the Ganges. -2 A festival in honour of the Ganges held on the 10th day of Jyeshtha. -3 A festival in honour of Durgá held on the tenth of Asvina.

दशनः *m.*, -नं *n.* 1 A tooth. -2 Biting. —नः *m.* The peak of a mountain. —नं *n.* An armour (also *m.*). Comp. —अंकः *m.* A tooth-mark, bite. -उच्छिष्टः *m.* 1 A lip. -2 A kiss. -3 A sigh. —छदः,-वासस् *a.* 1 A lip. -2 A kiss. —पदं *n.* A bite, tooth-mark. -बीजः *m.* The pomegranate tree.

दशम *a.* (*f.* —मी) Tenth. —मं *n.* A tenth part.

दशमिन् *a.* (*f.* —नी) Very old.

दशमी *f.* 1 The tenth day of a lunar fortnight. -2 The tenth decade of the human life. -3 The last ten years of a century. -Comp. —स्थ,—दशमीगत *a.* Above ninety years old.

दशा *f.* 1 The threads at the end of a piece of woven cloth, the fringe of a garment, the skirt, edge or hem of a garment. -2 The wick of a lamp. -3 Age or time of life. -4 A period or stage of life; asबाल्य, यौवन &c. -5 A period in general. -6 State, condition, circumstances. -7 State or condition of the mind. -8The result of actions,fate.-9 The aspect or position of planets (at birth). -10 The mind, understanding. -Comp. —आधिपतिः,—ईशः *m.* The sun. —अंतः *m.* 1 The end of a wick. -2 The end of life. —अंतरं *n.* The different states, vicissitudes of life. —अंतरः *m.* A lamp. -कर्षः, -कर्षिन् *m.* 1 The end of a garment. -2 A lamp. —पाकः, —विपाकः *m.* 1 The fulfilment of fate. -2 A changed condition of life. —विपर्यासः *m.* Ill luck.

दशार्णाः *m.pl.* 1 N. of a country. -2 The people of this country.

दशिन् *a.* (*f.* -नी) 1 Divided into ten parts. -2 Having ten. —*m.* A superintendent of ten villages.

दशेर *a.*(*f.* -रा) 1 Biting.-2 Noxious, hurtful. —रः *m.* A mischievous or venomous animal.

दशे (-से-) रकः *m.* A young camel

दष्ट *p. p.* (*f.*—ष्टा) Bitten, stung.

दस्युः *m.* 1 N. of a class of evil beings or demons, enemies of gods and men, and slain by Indra,(mostly Vedic in this sense). -2 An outcast, a Hindu who has become an outcast by neglect of the essential rites. -3 A thief, robber, bandit. -4 A villain, miscreant -5 A desperado, oppressor.

दस्र*a.*(*f.*-स्रा)Savage,fierce, destructive.-स्रौ (*m.dual*) 1 The two Asvins, the physicians of the gods. -2 The number 'two.' —स्रः *m.* 1 An ass. -2 A robber. —स्रं *n.* 1 The cold season.-2 The lunar mansion Asvinî. -Comp. —देवता *f.* The constellation Asvinî. —सूः *f.* संज्ञा Wife of the sun and mother of the Asvins,

दह् 1 P.(दहति, ददाह, अधाक्षीत, धक्ष्यति, दग्धुं, दग्ध; *desid.* दिधक्षति.) 1 To burn, scorch (fig. also). -2 To pain, torment, distress. -3 To cauterize (in medicine). With निस्— 1 To burn, consume. -2 To torment, pain. परि— To burn, scorch. प्र— 1 To burn. -2 To burn completly. -3 To pain, torment,trouble, tease. सं- To burn.

दहः *m.* 1 Cavity of the heart, or the heart itself.-2 Fire.-3 A forest-conflagration.

दहन *a* (*f.*-नी) 1 Burning,consuming by fire. -2 Destructive, injurious. —नः *m.* 1 Fire. -2 A pigeon. -3 The number three. -4 A bad man. -5 The *Bhallātaka* plant. -6 The constellation कृत्तिका. —नं *n.* 1 Burning, consuming by fire (fig. also). -2 Cauterizing. -Comp. —अरातिः *m.* 1 Water. —उपलः *m.* The sun-stone. —उल्का *f.* A fire-brand. —केतनः *m.* Smoke. -प्रिया *f.* Svâhâ, wife of Agni. —सारथिः *m.* Wind.

दहर *a.* (*f.* -रा) Small,subtile, fine, thin.-2Young in age. -3 Unintelligible.-रः *m.* 1 A child or any young animal. -3 A younger brother. -4 The cavity of the heart, or the heart itself. -5 A mouse or rat.

दा 1 P. (यच्छति, दत्त)To give,grant, —With प्रति —To exchange.

दा 2. P. (दाति,) To cut.

दा 3 U. (ददाति, दत्ते,ददौ-ददे,अदात्-आदित, दास्यति,-ते,दातुं, दत्त; but with आ the *p.p.* is आत ; with उप, उपात्त ; with नि, निदत्त. or नीत्त, and with प्र, प्रदत्त or प्रत्त) 1 To give, bestow, offer, impart, present (usually with acc. of the thing and dat., sometimes gen. or loc. also of the person). सेचनघटैः बालपादपेभ्यः पयो दातुमित एवाभिवर्तते * शकुंत. 1 To pay (as debt, fine &c.). -2 To hand or deliver over. -3 To restore, return. -4 To give up, surrender. -5 To put, place, apply, plant; *e.g.* कर्णे करं ददाति. -7 To give in marriage.-8To allow, permit (usually with inf.); बाष्पस्तु न ददात्येनां द्रष्टुं चित्रगतामपि *शाकुंत6. 21. The meanings of this root may be variously modified or extended according to the noun with which it is connected. We give below some instances. मनोदा To direct the mind to anything. अवकाशं दा To make room. कर्णं दाTo give ear to or listen. दर्शनं दा To show oneself to, grant audience to. आत्मानं खेदाय दा To expose oneself to trouble. आतपे दा To expose to the sun's heat. आज्ञांor -निदेशं दा To issue orders, command. आशिषं दा To pronounce a blessing. चक्षुः or दृष्टिं दा To cast a glance, see. वाचं दा To address a speech to.प्रतिवचः, प्रतिवचनंor प्रत्युत्तरं दाTo give reply. श्राद्धं दा To perform a Sraddha. मार्गं दा To make way for. संग्राम दाTo fight. अर्गलं दा To bolt, fasten or secure with a latch निगडं दा To put in chains,fetter संकेतं दा To make an appointment शापं दा To curse. अग्निंor पावकं दा To set on fire. --*Caus.* दापयति,-ते. —*Desid.* दित्सति-ते.

दाक्षायणी *f.* 1 Any one of the 27 lunar mansions. -2 N. of Diti, wife of Kasyapa and mother of the demons. -3 N. of Pârvatî. -4 The lunar constellation called Revatî. -5 N. of Kadru or Vinatá. -6 N. of Aditi, mother of the gods. -Comp. —पतिः *m.* An epithet of Siva. -2 The moon.—पुत्रः *m.* A god.

दाक्षाय्यः *m.* A vulture.

दाक्षिण *a.* (*f.* -णी) 1 Relating to a sacrificial gift or to a gift in general. -2 Relating to the south. —णं *n.* A collection of sacrificial gifts.

दाक्षिणात्य *a.* (*f.* —त्या) Belonging to or living in the south; southern. —त्यः *m.* A southerner, a native of the Deccan. -2 The cocoa-nut.

दाक्षिणिक *a.* (*f.* —की) Connected with a sacrificial gift.

दाक्षिण्यं *n.* 1 Politeness, courtesy, kindness.-2The state of relating to or coming from the south. -3 Honesty, candour.-4Talent, cleverness.

दाक्षेयः *m* A metronymic of Pànini.

दाक्ष्यं *n.* 1 Cleverness, skill,fitness, dexterity,ability.-2Probity,honesty.

दाघः *m.* Burning.

दाडकः *m.* A tooth, tusk.

दाडि (-लि-)मः*m.*,-मा *f.* 1 The pomegranate tree. -2 Small cardamoms. —मं *n.* The fruit of the pomegranate tree.-Comp.-प्रियः,-भक्षणः*m.* A parrot.

दाडिंबः *m.* The pomegranate tree.

दाढा *f.* 1 A large tooth or tusk.-2 A multitude. -3 Wish, desire.

दाढिका *f.* The beard.

दाण्डाजिनिक *a.* (*f* —की) Carrying a staff and hide (as mere outward signs of religious devotion). -कः *m.* A hypocrite, impostor.

दाण्डिकः *m*. A chastiser, punisher.

दात *a.* (*f.* —ता) 1 Divided. -2 Cleaned, washed, purified.

दातिः *f.*1 Giving.-2Cuting,destroying. -3 Distribution.

दातृ *a.* (*f.* —त्री) 1 Giving granting. presenting, bestowing. -2 Liberal. —*m.* 1 A giver (in general). -2 A donor. -3 A lender, creditor. -4 A teacher. -5 A cutter.

दात्यूहः *m.* 1 The gallinule. -2 The Chátaka bird. -3 A cloud. -4 A water-crow. (also दात्यौहः).

दात्रं *n.* 1 An instrument of cutting, a sort of sickle or knife.

दादः *m.* A gift, donation. -Comp. —दः *m.* A donor.

दान् 1 U. (दानति,-ते) To cut, divide. —*Desid.* (दीदांसति,-ते) To make straight; (*desid.* in form, but not in sense).

दानं *n.* 1 Giving, granting. -2 Delivering, handing over. -3 A gift, present. -4 Liberality, munificence. -5 Ichor or the juice that exudes from the temples of an elephant in rut. -6 Bribery, as one of the four Upáyas or expedients of overcoming one's enemy.-7 Cutting, dividing.-8 Purification, cleaning.-9 Protection.-10 Pasture.-11 Adding. Comp.-धर्मः *m.* Alms-giving, charity. —पतिः *m.* 1 An exceedingly liberal man. -2 Akrúra, a friend of Krishna. —पत्रं *n.* A deed of gifts. —पात्रं *n.* A Bráhmana fit to receive gifts. —प्रातिभाव्यं *n.* Security for payment of a debt. —भिन्न *a.* Made hostile by bribes. —वीरः *m.* 1 A very liberal man. -2 (In Rhet.) The sentiment of heroism arising out of liberality, the sentiment of chivalrous liberality. -शील, -शूर, -शौंड, *a.* Exceedingly liberal or munificent.

दानकं *n.* A mean or unworthy gift.

दानवः *m.* A demon, a Rákshasa. -Comp. —अरिः *m.* 1 A god. -2 An epithet of Vishnu. —गुरुः *m.* An epithet of Sukra.

दानवेयः *m.* See दानवः.

दांत *p. p* (*f.* —ता) 1 Tamed, subdued, restrained, bridled. -2 Docile, tame, mild. -3 Self-possessed, self-controlled. -4 Subdued, vanquished. -5 Resigned. -6 Liberal. -7 Patient of bodily mortifications or austerities &c.-तः *m.* 1 A tamed ox. -2 A donor.-3 N. of a tree (दमनक).

दांतिः *f.* 1 Self-restraint, subjection. -2 The patient endurance of bodily mortifications, religious austerities &c. -3 Humiliation.

दांतिक *a.* (*f.* -की) Made of ivory.

दापनं *n.* Causing or obliging (one) to pay or give.

दापित *p. p.* (*f.* —ता) 1 Caused to be given. -2 Condemned to pay a fine, fined. -3 Adjudged. -4 Assigned, awarded.

दामन् *n.* 1 A string, thread, fillet, rope. -2 A chaplet, a garland in general. -3 A line, streak (as of lightning). -4 A large bandage.-5 A girdle. -Comp. —अंचलं,-अंजनं *n.* A foot-rope for horses &c. -उदरः *m.* An epithet of Krishna.

दामनी *f.* A foot-rope.

दामिनी *f.* Lightning.

दांपत्यं *n.* Matrimony, the matrimonial relation.

दांभिक *a.* (*f.* —की) 1 Deceitful, hypocritical. -2 Proud, imperious. -3 Ostentatious, sanctimonious.-कः *m.* 1 A cheat. -2 A hypocrite.

दायः *m.* 1 A gift, present, donation. -2 A nuptial present (given to the bride or the bridegroom). -3 Share, inheritance, patrimony. -4 A part or share in general. -5 Delivering, handing over.-6 Dividing, distributing. -7 Loss, destuction. -8 Irony. -9 Site, place.

-10 Alms given to a student at his initiation, &c. -Comp. —अपवर्तनं *n.* Forfeiture of inheritance. —अर्ह *a.* Claiming inheritance. -आद: *m.* 1 One entitled to a share of patrimony, an heir.-2 A son. -3 A relative, kinsman near or remote.-4 A claimant or pretender in general. —आदा,—दी *f.* 1 An heiress. -2 A daughter. —आद्यं *n.* 1 Inheritance. -2 The state of being an inheritor. -कालः *m.* The time of the partition of an inheritance. -बंधुः *m.* 1 A partner in the inheritance. -2 A brother. —भागः *m.* Division of property among heirs, partition (of inheritance).

दायक *a.* (*f.* -यिका) Giving, granting, bestowing &c. (at the end of comp.). —कः *m.* 1 An heir, inheritor. -2 A donor.

दारः *m.* 1 A rent, gap, cleft, hole. -2 A ploughed field.-राः *m. pl.* A wife. -Comp. —अधीन *a.* Dependent on a wife. -उपसंग्रहः, -ग्रहः,-परिग्रहः *m.*, -ग्रहणं *n.* Marriage. —कर्मन् *n.*, —क्रिया *f.* Marriage. [splitting.

दारक *a.*(*f.*-रिका) Breaking, tearing, -कः *m.* 1 A boy, a son. -2 A child, infant. -3 Any young animal. -4 Village hog. -Comp. —आचार्यः *m.* A school-master.

दारणं *n.* 1 Splitting, tearing, rending, opening. -2 The fruit of the clearing-nut plant.

दारदः *m.* 1 Quicksilver. -2 The ocean. -दः *m.*, -दं *n.* Vermilion.

दारिका *f.* 1 A daughter. -2 A harlot. -3 A rent, cleft.

दारित *p. p.* (*f.* -ता) Torn, rent.

दारिद्यं, दारिद्रं *n.* Poverty, indigence.

दारी *f.* 1 A cleft. -2 A kind of disease.

दारुः *m.* 1 A liberal or munificent man. -2 A donor. -3 An artist. -रु *n.* 1 Wood, a piece of wood, timber. -2 A block. -3 A lever. -4 A bolt. -5 The pine or Devadâru tree. -6 Ore. -7 Brass. -Comp. —अंडः *m.* The peacok. —आघाटः *m.* The woodpecker. —गर्भा *f.* A wooden puppet. —जः *m.* A kind of drum. —पात्रं *n.* A wooden vessel, such as a trough. —पुत्रिका, —पुत्री *f.* A wooden doll. -मुस्याह्वया, -मुस्याह्वा *f.* A lizard. —यंत्रं *n.* 1 A wooden puppet moved by strings.-2 Any machinery of wood. —वधूः *f.* A wooden doll. —सारः *m.* Sandal. -हस्तकः *m.* A wooden spoon.

दारुकः *m.* 1 The Devadâru tree. -2 N. of Krishna's charioteer. —का *f.* 1 A puppet. -2 A wooden figure.

दारुण *a.* (*f.*-णा) 1 Hard, rough. -2 Harsh, pitiless. -3 Fierce, terrible, frightful. -4 Heavy, intense, agonizing. -5 Sharp, severe (as words). -6 Atrocious, shocking. —णः *m.* The sentiment of horror (भयानक). —णं *n.* Severity, cruelty, horror.

दार्ढ्यं *n.* 1 Hardness, firmness, tightness. -2 Confirmation, corroboration. -3 Strength, energy.

दार्दुरः *m.*, -रं *n.* A conch-shell the valve of which opens to the right.

दार्भ *a.* (*f.* -र्भी) Made of *darbha* grass.

दार्व *a.* (*f.* -र्वी) Wooden.

दार्वटं *n.* A council-house, court.

दार्शनिकः *m.* One familiar with the Darsanas or systems of philosophy.

दार्षद *a.* (*f.* -दी) 1 Stony, mineral. -2 Ground on a flat stone.

दार्ष्टांत *a.* (*f.* -ती), दार्ष्टांतिक *a.* (*f.* -की) Explained or illustrated by a दृष्टांत (*i. e.* a similar case).

दालिमः *m.* Same as दाडिमः.

दाल्मिः *m*. N. of Indra.

दावः *m*. Same as दव *q. v.* -Comp. -आग्निः,-अनलः,-दहनः *m*. A forest-conflagration.

दाशः *m*. 1 A fisherman. -2 A servant (same as दास). -Comp. -ग्रामः *m*. A village mostly inhabited by fishermen. —नंदिनी *f*. An epithet of Satyavatî, mother of Vyâsa.

दाशरथः, दाशरथिः 1 A son of Dasaratha in general. -2 N. of Râma and his three brothers, but especially of Râma.

दाशेरः *m*. 1 The son of a fisherman. -2 A fisherman. -3 A camel.

दाशेरकः *m*. The Mâlava country. —काः (*m. pl.*) The rulers or inhabitants of that country.

दाश्व *a*. Liberal, giving.

दासः *m*. 1 A slave, servant in general. -2 A fisherman. -3 A Súdra, a man of the fourth caste. -4 A savage, barbarian (opp. आर्य). -5 A word added to the name of a Súdra. -Comp.—अनुदासः *m*. A slave of a slave, the humblest of the servants; (sometimes used by the speaker as a mark of humility). —जनः *m*. A servant or slave. दासस्य कुलं *n*. The mob or the common people. [slave.

दासिका *f*. A female servant or

दासी *f*. 1 A female servant or slave. -2 The wife of a fisherman. -3 The wife of a Súdra. -4 An altar. -5 A harlot. -Comp. —पुत्रः, -सुतः *m*. The son of a female slave. —सभं *n*. A collection of female slaves. (The gen. sing. दास्याः enters into some compounds, but loses its literal sense; *e. g.* दास्याः पुत्रः, -सुतः *m*. A whore-son, used as a term of abuse, but दास्याः सदृशी *f*. means behaving like a female slave.

दासेयः *m*. The son of a female slave.

दासेरः,-रकः *m*. 1 The son of a female slave. -2 A Súdra. -3 A fisherman. -4 A camel.

दास्यं *n*. Servitude, slavery, service.

दास्रं *n*. The first of the 27 lunar mansions.

दाहः *m* 1 Burning, conflagration. -2 Glowing redness(as of the sky). -3 The sensation of burning. -4 Feverish or morbid heat. -Comp. —अगुरु *n*., —काष्ठं *n*. A kind of agallochum. —आत्मक *a*. Destructive, having power to burn, combustible. —ज्वरः *m*. Inflammatory fever. —सरः *m*., -सरस् *n*., —स्थलं *n*. A place where dead bodies are burnt, cemetery.

दाहक *a*. (*f*. -हिका)1 Burning, kindling. -2 Incendiary, inflammatory. -3 Cauterizing. —कः *m*. 1 Fire. -2 The Chitraka plant.

दाहनं *n*. 1 Burning, reducing to ashes. -2 Cauterizing.

दाह्य *a*. (*f*. -ह्या) 1 To be burnt. -2 Combustible. [twenty years old.

दिक्कः *m*. A young elephant (करभ)

दिग्ध*a*.(*f*.-ग्धा) 1 Smeared, anointed. -2 Soiled, polluted.-3 Poisoned (as an arrow). -ग्धः *m*. 1 Oil, ointment. -2 Any oily substance or unguent. -3 Fire. -4 A poisoned arrow. -5 A story (true or fictitious.)

डिंडिः, डिंडिरः *m*. A kind of musical instrument. [divided.

दित *a*. (*f*. -ता) Cut, torn, rent,

दितिः *f*. 1 Cutting, dividing. -2 Liberality. -3 N. of a daughter of Daksha, wife of Kasyapa and mother of the demons or *daityas*. -Comp. —जः, —तनयः *m*. A demon, a Ràkshasa.

दित्यः *m*. A demon.

दित्सा *f*. Desire of giving.

दिदृक्षा *f*. Desire of seeing.

दिदृक्षु *a.* Desirous of seeing.

दिधिषु: *m.* The second husband of a woman married again or twice. —*f.* A virgin widow remarried.

दिधि (—धी—) षू: *f.* 1 A woman twice married. -2 An unmarried elder sister whose younger sister is married. -Comp. —पति: *m.* A man who has a sexual intercourse with the widow of his brother.

दिन: *m.*, -नं *n.* 1 Day (opp.रात्रि). -2 A day (including the night), a period of 24 hours. -Comp. —अंहं *n.* Darkness. —अत्यय:, —अंत: *m.*, —अवसानं *n.* Evening, sunset. —अधीश: *m.* The sun. —अर्ध: *m.* Midday, noon. —आगम: —आदि:, —आरंभ: *m.* Daybreak, morning. -ईश:, -ईश्वर: *m.* The sun. -कर:, -कर्तृ, —कृत *m.* The sun. —केशर: (—व:) *m.* Darkness. —क्षय:, —पात: *m.* Evening. —चर्या *f.* Daily occupation, daily routine of business —ज्योतिस् *n.* Sunshine. —दु:खित: *m.* The Chakravâka bird. —प:,—पाते:, —बंधु:. -प्रणी:, -मणि:, -मयूख:, -रत्नं *n.* The sun. —मुखं *n.* Morning. —मूर्द्धन् *m.* The eastern mountain behind which the sun is supposed to rise. —यौवनं *n.* Noon.

दिनिका *f.* A day's wages.

दिरिपक: *m.* A ball for playing with.

दिलीप: *m.* A king of the Solar race.

दिलीरं *n.* A mushroom.

दिव् 4 P. (दीव्यति, द्यूत or द्यून) 1 To shine, be bright. -2 To throw, cast (as a missile). -3 To gamble, play with dice (with acc. or instr. of the dice'); अक्षैरक्षान्वा दीव्यति -4 To play, sport. -5 To joke, trifle with, make sport of (with acc.). -6 To stake, make a bet. -7 To sell, deal in(with gen.); अदेवीद्बंधुमोगानां (but with acc. or gen. when the root is preceded by a preposition; शतं शतस्य वा परिदीव्यति). -8 To squander, make light of. -9 To praise. -10 To be glad, rejoice. -11 To be mad or drunk. -12 To be sleepy. -13 To wish for.

दिव् 1 P., 10 U. (देवति; to देवयति,-ते) 1 To cause to lament, to pain, vex, torment. -2 To ask, beg.

दिव् 10 A. (देवयते) To suffer pain, lament, moan. -With परि— To lament, moan, suffer pain.

दिव् *f.* (Nom. sing. द्यौ:) 1 The heaven. -2 The sky. -3 A day. -4 Light, brilliance. -5 Fire, glow of fire. दिवस्पति: *m.* An epithet of Indra. दिवस्पृथिव्यौ *f. dual.* The heaven and earth. दिविज:, दिविष्ठ:, दिविस्थ:, दिविस(-ष-)द् *m.* दिवोकस् दिवोकस,-स: *m.*, A god. दिवस्पृश् *m.* The Supreme Being. दिविस्पृश् *a.* Reaching or pervading the sky दिवोल्का *f.* A meteor. दिवौकस् *m.* 1 A god. -2 The Châtaka bird. -3 A deer. -4 A bee. -5 An elephant.

दिवं *n.* 1 Heaven. -2 The sky. -3 A day. -4 A forest, wood, thicket.

दिवस: *m.*,-सं *n.* A day. -Comp -ईश्वर:, -कर:,-नाथ: *m.* The sun.-मुखं *n.* Morning, daybreak. —मुद्रा *f.* A day's wages. —विगम: *m.* Evening, sunset.

दिवा *ind.* By day, in the day time. दिवा भू To become day. *e. g.* दिवाभूता रात्रि:-Comp.-अटन: *m.* A crow. -अंध: *m.* An owl.-अंधकी, —आंधिका *f.* The musk-rat. —कर: *m.* 1 The sun. -2 A crow.-3The sun-flower. —कीर्ति: *m.* 1 Chándála, man of low caste. -2 A barber. -3 An owl. —निशं *ind.* By day and night. —पुष्ट:, -मणि: *m.* The sun. —प्रदीप: *m.* A lamp by day *i. e.* obscure man. —भीत:, भीति: *m.* 1 An owl. -2 A white lotus (opening at night). -3 A thief, house-breaker. —मध्यं *n.* Midday. —रात्रं *ind.* Day and night· —वसु: *m*· The sun· —शय *a*. Sleeping by day. —स्वप्न:,-स्वाप: *m*. Sleep during day-time. (-स्वाप: *m*·) An owl·

दिवातन *a*· (*f*.-नी) Of or belonging to the day. [दिव:)

दिविः *m*. he Chásha bird; (also

दिव्य *a*· (*f*.-व्या) I Divine, celestial· -2 Supernatural, wonderful· -3 Brilliant· -4 Charming, beautiful. -व्य:*m*. I A superhuman or celestial being· -2 Barley. -3 An epithet of Yama. -4 A philosopher. —व्यं *n*. I Celestial nature, divinity. -2 The sky. -3 An ordeal (of which there are 10 kinds). -4 An oath,a solemn declaration. -5 Cloves. -6 A kind of sandal.-7A kind of water.-Comp. —अंशु: *m*. The sun. —अंगना, -नारी, -स्त्री *f*· A heavenly nymph, celestial damsel, an *apsaras*. -आदिव्य*a*. Partly human and partly divine (as a hero, such as Arjuna). -उदकं*n*·Rain water· —कारिन् *a*. Taking an oath. -2 Undergoing an ordeal. —गायन: *m*. A Gandharva. —चक्षुस् *a*. I Having divine vision, heavenly-eyed. -2 Blind. (-*m*·) A monkey. (-*n*·) A divine or prophetic eye, supernatural vision, the power of seeing what is invisble by the human eye· -ज्ञानं *n*. Supernatural knowledge. -दृश् *m*. An astrologer. -प्रश्न: *m*. Inquiry into celestal phenomena or future course of events, augury. -मानुष: *m*. A demi-god. -रत्नं *n*. A fabulous gem said to grant all desires of its possessor, the philosopher's stone. -रथ: *m*. A celestial car moving through the air. —रस: *m*. Quicksilver. -वस्त्र: *m*. I Sunshine. -2 A kind of sun-flower. —सरित् *f*· The celestial Ganges. —सार:*m*.The Sâla tree.

दिश्6 U. (दिशति,-ते, दिष्ट ; *desid*. दिदिक्षति-ते) I To produce (as a witness). -2 To assign, allot. -3 To give, grant. -4 To pay (as tribute). -5 To consent to. -6 To direct, command. -7 To allow, permit. With अति— To extend by anlogy, to extend the application of. अप- I To tell, say, announce. -2 To pretend. -3 To refer to. आ— I To order, command. -2 To point out,to single out.-3 To instruct,advise.-4 To lay down, rescribe. उत—I To refer to. -2To direct towrads· -3 To denote, to mean. -4 To teach· उप— I To advise, instruct. -2 To prescribe, sanction. -3 To announce. -4 To refer to. निस्-- I To point out· -2 To predict. -3 To assign to,to give. -4 To allude to. प्र— I To point out, assign. -2 To grant, give· प्रत्या— I To repulse, reject. -2 To defeat, to put into the back ground. व्यप– I To name, to call -2 To call or name falsely.-3 To pretend. सम्— I To give, to make over. -2 To order, direct, instruct. -3 To send (as a messenger). -*Caus*. (देशयति,-ते) I To show, allot,assign. -2 To teach, tell. inform. -3 To direct, order. -4 To confer,bestow.

दिश् *f*. (Nom. sing. दिक्,-ग्) I A direction, cardinal point, point of the compass, quarter of the sky. -2 Indication (of the general lines), manner, method. -3 Region, space, place in general· -4 A foreign or distant region.-5 A point of view, manner of considering a subject· -6 A precept, order· -7 The number ' ten. ' -8 A side or party. -9 The mark of a bite. -Comp. —अंत: *m*· The end of the direction or horizon, remote distance,remote place.-अंतरं*n*·

1 Another direction. -2 The intermediate space, atmosphere, space. -3 A distant or foreign country. -अंबर *a.* Naked, unclothed (-रः *m.*) 1 A naked mendicant (of the Jaina or Buddha sect). -2 A mendicant, an ascetic. -3 An epithet of (1) Siva; (2) Of Skanda. -4 Darkness. (-री *f.*) An epithet of Durgâ. —ईशः, -ईश्वरः *m.* The regent of a quarer. —करः *m.* 1 A youth. -2 An epithet of Siva. —करिका, -करी *f.* A young girl or woman. -करिन्, -गजः, -दंतिन्, वारणः *m.* One of the eight elephants said to guard and preside over the eight cardinal points. -ग्रहणं *n.* The observation of the quarters of the compass. —चक्रं *n.* 1 The horizon. -2 The whole world. -जयः,-विजयः *m.* The conquest of various countries in all directions, conquest of the world. —तटं *n.* The horizon. —दर्शनं *n.* 1 Showing merely the direction, pointing out only the general mode or manner. -2 A general outline or survey. -3 A compass. —नागः *m.* 1 An elephant of the quarter of the compass. -2 N. of a poet said to be a contemporary of Kâlidâsa. —पतिः, —पालः *m.* The regent or guardian of a quarter. —पथः *m.* The surrounding region. —मंडलं *n.* 1 Horizon. 2- The whole world. -मात्रं *n.* The mere direction or indication. -मुखं *n.* Any quarter or part of the sky. -वस्त्रः *m.* Stark naked, unclothed. (-स्त्रः *m.*) 1 A jain or Buddhist mendicant of the दिगंबर class. -2 An epithet of Siva. —विभाव्रित *a.* Renowned or celebrated in all quarters.

दिशा *f.* Direction, quarter of the compass. -Comp. -गजः, -पालः *m.* See दिग्गजः, दिक्पालः.

दिश्य *a.* (*f.* —श्या) Belonging to or situated towards any quarter of the compass.

दिष्ट *p. p.* (*f.* —ष्टा) 1 Shown, indicated. -2 Described, referred to. -3 Fixed, settled. -4 Directed, ordered. -ष्टः *m.* Time. -ष्टं *n.* 1 Assignment, allotment. -2 Fate, destiny. -3 Order, direction, command. -4 Aim, object. -Comp. -अंतः *m.* Death.

दिष्टिः *f.* 1 Assignment, allotment. -2 Direction, command, instruction, precept. -3 Fate, destiny. -4 Good fortune, any auspicious event. -5 A sort of measure of length.

दिष्ट्या *ind.* (Instr. sing. of दिष्टि) Fortunately, luckily; how fortunate! (an exclamation of joy or gratulation). (दिष्ट्या वृध् To be congratulated upon ; *e. g.* दिष्ट्या धर्मपत्नीसमागमेन पुत्रमुखदर्शनेन चायुष्मान्वर्धते *शाकुंत. 7).

दिह् 2 U. (देग्धि, दिग्धे, दिग्ध; *desid.* दिधिक्षति) 1 To anoint, smear. -2 To defile, pollute. -3 To increase, augment. With सम्- 1 To doubt, to be uncertain about. -2 To raise an objection. -3 To mistake for.

दिह् *f.* 1 Anointing, smearing. -2 Pollution, soiling.

दी 4 A. (दीयते, दीन) 1 To perish, waste, decay.

दीक्ष् 1 A. (दीक्षते, दीक्षित) 1. To consecrate or prepare oneself for the performance of a sacred rite. -2 To dedicate oneself to. -3 To initiate a pupil. -4 To invest with the sacred thread.

दीक्षकः *m.* A spiritual guide.

दीक्षणं *n.* Initiation, consecration.

दीक्षा *f.* 1 Consecration for a religious ceremony; initiation in general. -2 Receiving the initiatory *mantra.* 3 A ceremony preliminary to a sacrifice.

-4 A ceremony or religious rite in general.-5 Investiture with the sacred thread.-6 Dedicating oneself to a particular object. -Comp. —अंत: m. A supplementary sacrifice made to atone for the defects in a preceding one.

दीक्षित p. p. (f.-ता) 1 Consecrated, initiated. -2 Prepared for a sacrifice. -3 Prepared for, having taken a vow of. -4 Crowned. -5 Performed (as the दीक्षा ceremony). —त: m. 1 A priest engaged in a Dîkshâ. -2 A pupil. -3 An appellation affixed to the name of a person who or whose ancestors may have performed a grand sacrificial ceremony, such as ज्योतिष्टोम.

दीदिवि: m. Boiled rice.

दीधिति: f. 1 A ray of light. -2 Splendour, brightness. -3 Bodily lustre, energy.

दीधितिमत् m. The sun.

दीधी 2 A. (दीधीते) 1 To shine, to seem, to appear.

दीन a. (f -ना) Poor, indigent. -2 Distressed, ruined, wretched. -3 dejected melancholy, sad.-4 Timid, frightened. -5 Mean, piteous. —न: m. A poor person, one in distress or misery.-Comp. -बंधु m. A friend of the poor.

दीनार: m. 1 A particular gold coin. -2 A coin in general.

दीप् 4 A. (दीप्यते, दीप्त) 1 To shine, blaze, (fig. also). -2 To burn. be lighted. -3 To glow, be inflamed or excited, increase (fig. also). -Caus. (दीपयति,-ते) 1 To kindle, inflame. -2 To illuminate.

दीप: m. 1 A lamp, light. -Comp. -अन्विता f. The day of new moon (अमा) -आराधनं n. Worshipping an idol by waving a light before it. -आलि., -ली, —आवली f., —उत्सव: m. 1 A row of lights, nocturnal illumination. -2 The festival called *Diwali* held on the night of new moon in आश्विन. —कलिका f. The flame of a lamp. -किट्टं n. Lamp-black, soot. -कूपी, —खोरि f. The wick of a lamp. -ध्वज: m. 1 Lamp-black. -2 Lamp-stand. -पुष्प: m. The Champaka tree. —भाजनं n. A lamp. —माला f. An illumination. —शत्रु: m. A moth. —शिखा f. 1 The flame of a lamp. -2 Lamp-black. —शृंखला f. A row of lights, illumination.

दीपक a (f. -पिका) 1 Kindling, inflaming. -2 Illuminating, making bright. -3 Beautifying, making illustrious. -4 Exciting. -5 Simulating digestion; digestive. —क: m. 1 A light, lamp. -2 A falcon. -3 An epithet of Kámadeva, (also. दीप्यक:). -कं n. 1 Saffron.-2(In Rhet.) The figure of speech in which a thing which is the subject in hand (प्रकृत) and another which is not the subject in hand are connected with same attribute. दीपक also means the figure of speech when the same case(कारक) is connected with more than one verb. अप्रस्तुतप्रस्तुतयोर्दीपकं तु निगद्यते। अथ कारकमेकं स्यादनेकासु क्रियासु चेत् *साहि. द. e.g. मदेन भाति कलभ: प्रतापेन महीपति:

दीपनं n. 1 Kindling, inflaming. -2 A tonic stimulating digestion. -3 Exciting, stimulating. -4 Lighting, illuminating. -5 Promoting digestion. -6 Saffron. [Moonlight.

दीपिका f. 1 A light, torch. -2

दीपित p. p. (f. —ता) 1 Set on fire. -2 Inflamed. -3 Illuminated. -4 Manifested. -5 Excited, stimulated.

दीप्त *p. p.* (*f.* —प्ता) 1 Lighted, kindled. -2 Glowing, radiant. -3 Illuminated. -4 Excited. -5 Luminous, bright.-6 Heated by the sun, exposed to sunshine. —प्तः *m.* 1 A lion. -2 The citron tree. —प्तं *n.* Gold. -Comp. -अंशुः *m.* The sun. —अक्षः *m.* A cat. —अग्निः *m.* N. of अगस्त्य. —अंगः *m.* A peacock. -आत्मन् *a.* Having a fiery nature. —उपलः *m.* 1 The sun-stone. —किरणः *m.* The sun. -कीर्तिः,-वर्णः,-शक्तिः *m.* Epithets of Kârtikeya. —जिह्वा *f.* A vixen. —तपस् *a.* Fervent in devotion. —लोचनः *m.* A cat. —लोहं *n.* Brass, bell-metal.

दीप्तिः *f.* 1 Brightness, brilliance, lustre. -2 Brilliancy of beauty, extreme loveliness. -3 Lac. -4 Brass.

दीप्र *a.* (*f.* —प्रा) Shining,brilliant, radiant. —प्रः *m.* Fire.

दीर्घ *a.* (*f.* —र्घा Compar. द्राघीयस्, Superl. द्राघिष्ठ) 1 Long reaching, far. -2 Of long duration, lasting long. -3 Deep (as a sigh). -4 Long (as a vowel). -5 Lofty, high, tall. —र्घः *m.* 1 A camel. -2 A long vowel. -3 The fifth, sixth, seventh, and eighth signs of the zodiac. —र्घा *f.* A long lake or oblong tank. —र्घं *ind.* 1 Long, for a long time. -2 Deeply. -3 Far. -Comp. -अध्वगः *m.* 1 A messenger. -2 A camel. -अहन् *m.* Summer (ग्रीष्म). —आयुधः *m.* 1 A spear. -2 A hog. —आस्यः *m.* An elephant. -कंठः, -कंठकः, -कंधरः *m.* The (Indian) crane. —काय *a.* Tall (in stature). —काष्ठं *n.* A beam. —केशः *m.* A bear. -गतिः, -ग्रीवः,-घाटिकः *m.* A camel. -जंघः *m.* 1 A camel. -2 A crane. -जिह्वः *m.* A snake, serpent. —तपस् *m.* An epithet of Gautama, husband of Ahalyá. -तरुः, -द्रुः. The palm tree. —दुंदी *f.* The musk-rat. -दंडः *m.* The palm tree. -2 The castor-oil tree. —दर्शिन् *a.* 1 Provident, far-seeing, long-sighted. -2 Sagacious, wise. (-*m.*) 1 A vulture. -2 A bear. -3 An owl -दृष्टि *a* Far-sighted,shrewd, prudent.-नादः *m.* 1 dog. -2 A cock. -3 A conch-shell. —निद्रा *f.* 1 Long sleep. -2 The sleep of death. —पत्रः *m.* The palm tree. -पादः, -प (-पा-) द् *m.* A heron. —पादपः *m.* 1 The cocoa-nut tree. -2 The areca-nut tree.- 3The plam tree. -पृष्ठः *m.* A snake. —वाला *f.* A kind of deer (चमरी) of whose tails chowries are made. —मारुतः *m.*An elephant. -रदः *m.* A hog. -रसनः *m.* A snake. -रोमन् *m.* A bear. —वक्त्रः *m.* An elephant. —सक्थ *a.* Having long thighs. —सत्रं *n.* A long-continued Soma sacrifice. (—त्रः *m.*) One who performs such a sacrifice. —सुरतः *m.* A dog. —सूत्र, -सूत्रिन् *a.* Working slowly, slow, dilatory

दीर्घिका *f.* 1 A long or oblong lake. -2 A well or lake in general.

दीर्ण *a* (*f.*—र्णा) 1 Torn, rent. -2 Frightened.

दु 5. P. (दुनोति, दुत or दून) 1 To burn, consume with fire. -2 To torment, distress. -3 To pain, excite sorrow.-4 To be afflicted or pained.

दुःख *a.* 1 Painful, unpleasant. -2 Dfficult, uneasy. —खं *n.* 1 Sorrow, grief, distress, pain. -2 Trouble, difficulty. (दुःखं and दुःखेन are used as adverbs in the sense of 'hardly', 'with great difficulty or trouble.' -Comp. —अतीत *a.* Freed from pain. —अंतः *m.* Final emancipation. -ग्रामः *m.* Worldly existence. —क्लिष्ट *a.* 1

Tough, hard. -2 Pained, distressed. —प्राय, बहुल a Full of trouble or grief. -भाज् a. Unhappy. -लोकः m. Worldly life, the world as a scene of constant suffering. —शील a. 1 Hard to please or manage, bad-tempered. -2 Accustomed to the misery of.

दुःखित a. (f. —ता) 1 Distressed, afflicted, pained. -2 Poor, unhappy, miserable.

दुःखिन a. (f. —नी) 1 Distressed, afflicted, pained. -2 Difficult, painful. -3 Poor, miserable.

दुकूलं n. Woven silk, a silk-garment, a very fine garment.

दुग्ध p. p. (f. —ग्धा) 1 Milked, milked out. -2 Extracted, drawn out. -ग्धं n. 1 Milk. -2 The milky juice of plants. -Comp. —अग्रं, -अग्रं, —तालीयं n. The skim of milk, cream. -दा f. A milch cow. —पाचनं n. A vessel for boiling milk. —पोष्य a. Living on the mother's milk (as a child); a suckling. —समुद्रः, -अब्धिः m. The ocean of milk, one of the seven oceans.

दुघ a (f. -घा. At the end of comp.) Milking, yielding, granting, as in कामदुघ -घा f. A milch-cow.

दुडिः f. A small tortoise.

दुंडुक a. (f. -का) Dishonest, bad-hearted, fraudulent.

दुंडुभः m. See डुंडुभः.

दुड्रुमः m. A green onion.

दुंदमः m. A kind of drum.

दुंदुभः m. 1 A kind of large kettle-drum. -2 A kind of water-snake.

दुंदुभिः m., f. 1 A sort of large kettle-drum. -m. 1 An epithet of Vishnu. -2 Of Krishna. -3 N. of Varuna.

दुंदुमा f. A sound (as of a drum).

दुर् ind. (A prefix substituted for दुस् before words beginning with vowels or soft consonants in the sense of 'bad', 'hard or difficult'. -Comp. —अक्षः m. 1 A loaded or false die. -2 Dishonest gambling. -अतिक्रम a. 1 Difficult to be overcome or conquered. -2 Insurmountable. -3 Inevitable. -अत्यय a. 1 Difficult to be overcome. -2 Hard to be attained or fathomed. —अदृष्ट n. Ill-luck, misfortune. —आधिग, —आधिगम a. 1 Hard to reach or attain, unattainable. -2 Insurmountable. -3 Hard to be studied or understood. —आविष्ठित a. Badly performed, managed or executed. —अध्यय a. 1 Dfficult of attainment. -2 Hard to be studied. -अध्यवसायः m. A foolish undertaking. —अध्वः m. A bad road. —अंत a. 1 Endless, infinite. -2 Ending ill or in misery; unhappy. -3 Hard to be understood or known. -4 Insurmountable. —अन्वय a. 1 Difficult to be passed along. -2 Hard to be carried out or followed. 3 Difficult to be attained or understood. (-यः m.) 1 A wrong conclusion, one wrongly inferred from given premisses. -2(In gram.) A false agreement. —आभिमानिन् a. Vain-glorious. -अवगम a. Incomprehensible. -अवग्रह a. 1 Difficult to be restrained or subjugated. -2 Disagreeable. -अवबोध a. Unintelligible. -अवस्थ a. Badly or poorly circumstanced. -अवस्था f. A wretched or miserable state. —आक्रम a. 1 Invincible, unconquerable. -2 Difficult to be passed. -आक्रमणं n. 1 An unfair attack. -2 Difficult approach. -आगमः m. An improper or illegal acquisition. —आग्रहः m. Foolish obstinacy. -आचर a. 1 Hard to be performed. -2 Incurable (as a disease). —आचार a. 1 Ill-conducted, badly behaved (—रः m.) Bad practice, wickedness

—आत्मन् a. Evil-natured,low,wicked, mean. (-m.) A rascal, scoundrel. —आधर्ष a. 1 Hard to be approached or assailed. -2 Not to be attacked with impunity. -3 Haughty. —आनम Difficult to bend or draw. —आप a. 1 Difficult to be obtained. -2 Difficult to be approached. -3 Hard to be overocome. —आराध्य a. Difficult to be propitiated. -आरोह a. Difficult of ascent. (-हः m.) 1 The cocoanut tree. -2 The palm tree. -3The date tree. —आलापः m. 1 A curse, imprecation. -2 Abusive language. —आलोक a. Difficult to be seen or perceived; dazzling. —आशय a. 1 Evil-minded. —आशा f. 1 A bad or wicked desire. -2 Hoping against hope. —आसद् a. 1 Unassailable,unconquerable; unapproachable. -2 Difficult to be found or met with. -3 Unequalled, unparalleled.-4 Insupportable. —इत a. 1 Difficult. -2 Sinful. (-तं n.) 1 A bad course, evil, sin. -2 A difficulty, danger. -3 A calamity, evil. —इष्टं n. 1 A curse, imprecation. -2 A spell or sacrificial rite performed to injure another person. —ईशः m. A bad lord or master. —ईषणा,—एषणा f. 1 A curse, an imprecation. -2 An evil eye. —उक्तं n., —उक्तिः f. Offensive speech, abuse, censure. -उत्तर a. Unanswerable. —उदाहर a. Difficult to be pronounced or composed. —उद्वह a. Burdensome, unbearable —ऊह a. Abstruse. —ग a. 1 Difficult of access, impassable. -2 Unattainable. -3 Incomprehensible. (-गः m., -गं n.) 1 A difficult or narrow passage through a wood or over a stream, mountain &c; a defile. -2 A citadel, fortress. -3 Rough ground. -4 Difficulty, adversity, calamity. (-गः m.) 1 Bdellium. -2 The Supreme Being. (-र्गा f.) An epithet of Párvati,wife of Siva. —गत a. 1 Unfortunate, in bad circumstances. -2 Indigent, poor. -3 Distressed. —गतिः f. 1 Misfotune, poverty, indigence. -2 A difficult situation or path. -3 Hell. —गंध a. Ill-smelling. (-धः m.) 1 Bad odour, stink. -2 Any ill-smelling substance. -3 An onion. -4 The mango tree. —गंधि, —गंधिन् a. Ill-smelling. —गम n. 1 Impassable, inaccessible. -2 Unattainable, difficult of attainment. -3 Hard to be understood. —ग्रह a. 1 Difficult to be gained or accomplished. -2 Difficult to be conquered or subjugated. -3 Hard to be understood. -घट a. 1 Difficult. -2 Impossible. —घोषः m. 1 A harsh cry. -2 A bear. —जन a. 1 Wicked, bad, vile. -2 Slanderous,malicious. (-नः m.) A bad or wicked person. —जय a. Invincible. —जात a. 1 Unhappy, wretched.-2 Bad-tempered. -3 Not genuine. (-तं n.) 1 A misfortune, calamity, difficulty. -2Impropriety. —जाति a. 1 Bad-natured, vile, wicked. -2 Out-cast. (-तिः f.) Misfortune, ill-condition. —ज्ञान,-ज्ञेय a. Difficult to be known, incomprehensible. —णयः,-नयः m., —नीतिः f. 1 Bad conduct. -2 Impropriety. -3 Injustice. —णामन्, -नामन् a.Having a bad name. -नीर्त n Misconduct. -दम, -दमन, -दम्य a. Difficult to be subdued, untamable. —दर्श a. 1 Difficult to be seen. -2 Dazzling. —दर्शन a. Ugly, ill-looking. —दशा f. A misfortune, calamity. —दांत a. 1 Hard to be tamed. -2 Intractable, proud, insolent. (—तः m.) 1 A calf. -2 A strife, quarrel. -दिन a. Cloudy, rainy. (-नं n.) 1 A bad day in general. -2 A rainy or cloudy day, stormy or rainy weather. -4 Thick darkness. —दिवसः m. A dark or rainy day.—दृष्ट a. Ill judged or seen, wrongly decided. -दैवं n. Ill-luck, misfortune. -द्यूतं n. An unfair game. —द्रुमः m. Onion. -धर a. 1 Irresistible. -2 Difficult to be borne or suffered. (-रः m.) Quicksilver. —धर्ष a. 1 Inviolable, unassailable. -2 Inaccessible. -3 Fearful, dreadful. -4 Naughty. -धी a. Stupid, silly. -नामकः m. Piles. —निहित a. Carelessly put or placed on the ground. -निमित्तं n. A bad omen. -2 A bad pretext. -निवार, -निवार्य a. Difficult to be checked or warded off, irresistible. -नीतं n. Misconduct, bad policy. -नीतिः f. Mal-administration. —बल a. 1 Weak, feeble. -2 Enfeebled, spiritless. -3 Thin, lean. -4 Small, scanty. -बाल a. Bald-headed. -बुद्धि a. 1 Silly, foolish, stupid. -2 Perverse, evil-minded, wicked. -बोध a. Unintelligible, inscrutable. -भग a. 1 Unfortunate, unlucky. -2 Ill-looking. —भगा f. 1 A wife disliked by her husband. 2 An ill-tempered woman. —भर a. Insupportable, burdensome. —भाग्य a. Unfortunate, unlucky. (-ग्यं n.) Ill-luck.-भिक्षं n. 1 Scarcity of provisions, dearth, famine. -2 Want in general. —भृत्यः m. A bad servant. —मति a. 1 Silly, stupid, foolish, ignorant.-2 Wicked, evil-minded. —मनस् a. Troubled in mind, discouraged.—मनुष्यः m. A bad or wicked man. —मंत्रः m., -मंत्रितं n., -मंत्रणा f. An evil advice, bad counsel. —मरणं n. A violent or unnatural death. मल्लिका,-मल्ली f. A minor drama, comedy, farce. —यशस् n. Ill-repute, dishonour. —योध, योधन a. Invincible, unconquerable. (-नः m.) The eldest of the 100 sons of Dhritarâshtra and Gândhâri. —योनि a. Of a low birth. —लक्ष्य a. Difficult to be seen or perceived, hardly visible. -लभ a. 1 Difficult to be attained, or accomplished.-2 Difficult to be found or met with, scarce, rare. -3 Excellent, eminent. -4 Dear, beloved. -5 Costly. -ललित a. 1 Spoilt by fondling, fondled too much, hard to please. -2 Way-ward, ill-bred.—लेख्यं n. A forged document. -वच a. 1 Difficult to be described. -2 Not to be talked about. -3 Speaking improperly, abusing. (-चं n.) Abuse, censure, foul language. —वचस् n. Abuse, censure. —वर्ण a. Bad coloured. (-र्णं n.) 1 Silver. -2 A kind of leprosy. —वह a. Heavy, difficult to be borne. -वाच्य a. 1 Difficult to be spoken or uttered. -2 Abusive. -3 Harsh, cruel (as words).(-च्यं n.) 1 Censure, abuse. -2 Slandar, ill-repute. -वादः m. Slander, defamation, calumny. -वार,-वारण a. Irresistible, unbearable. -वासना f. 1 Evil propensity. -2 A chimera. -वासस् m. N. of a very irascible saint or Rishi, son of Atri and Anasûyâ. —विदग्ध a. 1 Unskilled, raw, foolish, stupid, silly. -2 Wholly ignorant. -3 Vainly proud. -विध a. 1 Base, low. -2 Wicked, vile. -3 Poor, indigent. -4 Stupid, foolish, silly. —विनयः m. Imprudence. —विनीत a. 1 Badly educated, ill-behaved, wicked, rude. -2 Stubborn, obstinate. (-तः m.) 1 A restive or untrained horse. -2 A wayward person, reprobate. -विपाक a. Producing bad fruit. (-कः m.) 1 Bad result or consequence. -विलसितं n. A wayward act, rudeness, naughtiness. -विलासः m. A bad or evil turn of fate. -विध a. Ill-natured, malignant. -वृत्त *a.* 1 Vile, wicked, ill-behaved. -2 Roguish. -व्यवहारः *m.* A wrong judgment in law. -व्रत *a.* Not conforming to rules, disobedient. -हुतं *n.* A badly offered sacrifice. -हृद् *a.* Ill-disposed, inimical. -हृदय *a.* Evil-minded, evil-intentioned.

दुरोदरः *m.* 1 A gamester.-2 A dice-box. -3 A stake.—रं *n.* 1 Gambling. -2 A die.

दुल् 10 U. (दोलयति,-ते, दोलित) 1 To swing, shake to and fro. -2 To move or shake upwards, throw up.

दुलिः *f.* A small or female tortoise.

दुष् 4 P. (दुष्यति, दुष्ट) 1 To be bad or corrupted, be spoiled or suffer damage. -2 To be defiled or violated. -3 To sin, be wrong. -4 To be unchaste or faithless. *Caus.* (दूषयति,-ते; but दूषयति,-ते or दोषयति,-ते in the sense of ' making depraved ' or ' corrupting ') 1 To corrupt, spoil, cause to perish, taint, contaminate, vitiate, pollute (lit. and fig.). -2 To demoralize. -3 To violate or dishonour (as a girl or another's wife). -4 To abrogate, annul. -5 To blame, speak ill of, accuse. -6 To adulterate. -7 To falsify. -8 To refute, disprove.

दुष्ट *p. p.* (*f.* -ष्टा) 1 Spoiled, damaged, ruined. -2 Tainted, violated. -3 Depraved, corrupted. -4 Vicious, wicked. -5 Guilty, culpable. -6 Low, vile. -7 Faulty or defective, as a हेतु in logic. -8 Painful. -9 Worthless. —ष्टा *f.* 1 A bad or unchaste woman. -2 A harlot. -ष्टं *n.* 1 Sin, crime, guilt. -2 A kind of leprosy. -Comp. -वृषः *m.* A strong but stubborn ox which refuses to draw; a vicious ox. -व्रणः *m.* 1 A dull boil or sore. -2 A sinus.

दुष्टिः *f.* Corruption, depravity.

दुष्ठु *ind.* 1 Ill, bad. -2 Improperly, incorrectly, wrongly.

दुष्यन्तः *m* N. of a king of the lunar race husband of शकुंतला and father of भरत.

दुस् *ind.* A prefix to nouns and sometimes to verbs meaning 'bad, evil, wicked, inferior, hard or difficult, &c. ' (N. B. The स् of दुस् is changed to र् before vowels and soft consonants; to a Visarga before sibilants; to श् before च् and छ्, and to ष् before क् and प्). -Comp. -कर *a.* Hard to be done or accomplished, arduous, difficult. (-रं *n.*) 1 A difficult or painful task or act. -2 Atmosphere, ether. -कर्मन् *n.* 1 Any bad act, sin, crime.-2 Any difficult or painful act. —कालः *m.* 1 Bad times.-2 The time of universal destruction. -कुलं *n.* A bad or low family. —कृत् *m.* A wicked person.-कृतं *n.*, -कृतिः *f.* A sin, misdeed.-क्रिया *f.* A misdemeanour, bad act. —चर *a.* 1 Hard to be performed, difficult. -2 Unapproachable. -3 Behaving wickedly. (-रः *m.*) 1 A bear. -2 A bi-valve shell.-च्यवनः *m.* An epithet of Indra.-परिग्रहः *m.* A bad wife. -पार *a.* 1 Difficult to be crossed.-2 Difficult to be accomplished. -प्रकाश *a.* Obscure, dark, dim. -प्रजस् *a.* Having bad progeny. -प्रज्ञ *a.* (दुष्प्रज्ञ) Weak-minded, stupid. -प्रधर्ष,-प्रधृष्य *a.* 1 Unassailable. —प्रमेय *a.* Immeasurable. —प्रवादः *m.* Slander, calumnious report, scandal. —प्रसह (दुष्प्रसह) *a.* 1 Irresistible, terrible. -2 Hard to bear or endure. -प्राप,-प्रापण *a.* Unattainable, hard to get. —शक, -शक्त *a.* Powerless, weak. —शला *f.* N. of the only daughter of धृतराष्ट्र given in marriage to Jayadratha. —शासन *a.* Difficult to be managed or governed, intractable. (-नः *m.*) N. of one of the100 sons of धृतराष्ट्र.-शील(दुश्शील) *a.* Ill-mannered or ill behaved, reprobate. —शृंगी *f.* A disloyal wife. —षम (दुःषम or दुष्षम), -सम (दुःसम or दुस्सम) *a.* 1Uneven,unlike, unequal. -2 Adverse, unfortunate. -3 Evil, improper, bad. —संधान, -संधेय*a.*Difficult to be united or reconciled.-सह (दुस्सह) *a.* Unbearable, irresistible, insupportable. —साक्षिन् *m.* A false witness. —साध, -साध्य *a.* 1 Difficult to be accomplished or managed.-2 Difficult to be cured. -3 Difficult to be conquered. —स्थ,-स्थित *a.*(written also दुस्थ and दुस्थित) 1 Ill-conditioned, miserable. -2 Unhappy, distressed. -3 Unwell, ill -4 Unsteady, disquieted. -5 Foolish, unwise, ignorant. -स्थितिः *f.* 1 Bad condition or situation. -2 Instability. —स्पृष्टं *n.* 1 Slight touch or contact. -2 Slight touch or action of the tongue which produces the sounds य, र, ल् and व. -स्मर *a.* Hard or painful to remember.

दुह् 2 U. (दोग्धि, दुग्धे, दोग्धुं, दुग्ध) 1 To milk or squeeze out, extract (with two acc.); भास्वंति रत्नानि महौषधीश्च पृथूपदिष्टां दुदुहुर्धरित्रीं * कुमा. सं. 1, 2. -2 To draw anything out of another (with two acc.). -3 To drain a thing of its contents, to make profit out of ; दुदोह गां स यज्ञाय शस्याय मघवा दिवं * रघुवं. 1, 26. -4 To yield or grant (any desired object). कामान्दुग्धे विप्रकर्षत्यलक्ष्मीं *उत्तर. रा. 5. 31. -5 To enjoy. *-Caus.* दोहयति,-ते. *Desid.* दुधुक्षति,-ते.

दुहितृ *f.* A daughter. -Comp. -पतिः *m.* A son-in-law (also दुहितुःपतिः).

दू 4 P. (दूयते,-दून 1 To be afflicted, suffer pain, be sorry. -2 To give or cause pain.

दूतः, दूतकः*m.* A messenger, an envoy, an ambassador. -Comp. -मुख *a.* Speaking by an ambassador.

दूतिका, दूती *f.* 1 A female messenger, a confidante. -2A go-between, procuress. -3 A gossiping or mischief-making woman. (N.B. The ती of दूती is sometimes shortened.).

दूत्यं *n.*1 Employment of a messenger. -2 An embassy. -3A message.

दून *a.* (*f.* -ना)Pained, distressed.

दूर *a.* (*Compar.* दवीयस् , *superl.*दविष्ठ) Distant, remote, a long way off, long. -रं *n.* Distance, remoteness. [N. B. Some of the oblique cases of दूर are used adverbially as follows:— दूरं 1 Far away, far or distant from (with abl or gen.); ग्रामात् or ग्रामस्य दूरं. -2 High above. -3 Far below. -4 Highly, very much; नेत्रे दूरमनंजने. -5 Entirely, completely. दूरेण 1 Far,from afar. -2 In a high degree. दूरात् 1 From afar. -2 In a remote degree. -3 From a remote period. दूरे Far, far away, in a distant place]. दूरीकृ means 1 To remove to a distance, remove, take away. -2 To deprive (one) of. -3 To prevent, ward off.-4To surpass, excel, distance. दूरीभू To be away or removed, be separated from, be at a distance ; दूरीभूते मयि सहचरे चक्रवाकीमिवैकां * मेघदू.-Comp.-अंतरित*a.*Separated by a long distance. —ईरितेक्षण *a.* Squint-eyed. —ग्रहणं *n.* The supernatural faculty of seeing objects though situated at a distance.-दर्शन, —दृश् *a.* Far-seeing. (-नः *m.*) 1 A vulture. -2 A learned man. (-नं*n.*) Prudence, foresight. —दर्शिन् *a.* Far seeing, prudent. (*-m.*) 1 A vulture. -2 A learned man. -3 A seer, prophet, sage. —दृष्टि: *f.* 1 Longsightedness.-2 Prudence, foresight. —पात्र *a.* Having a wide channel or bed (as a river). —पार *a.* 1 Very broad (as a river.) -2 Difficult to be crossed. —भाज् *a.* Distant, remote -वस्त्रक *a.* Naked. -वेधिन *a.* Piercing from afar. —संस्थ *a.* Being at a distance, remote, far away.

दूरत: *ind.* 1 From afar, from a distance. -2 Far away, to a distance.

दूर्यं *n.* Feces, ordure.

दूर्वा *f.* Bent grass, panic grass (considered as a sacred article of worship and offered to deities &c.). -Comp. -अंकुर: *m.* Tender Durvâ grass.

दूलिका, दूली *f.* The Indigo plant.

दूषक (*f.* —षिका) 1 Corrupting, spoiling. -2 Violating, seducing.-3 Offending, trespassing.-4 Disfiguring. -5 Sinful, wicked(as an action).

दूषणं *n.* 1 Spoiling, corrupting, vitiating, polluting. -2 Violating, breaking (as an agreement). -3 Seducing, dishonouring (as a woman). -4 Abuse, censure. -5 Detraction, disparagement. -6 Adverse argument or criticism, objection. -7 Refutation. -8 A fault, defect, sin, crime. —ण: *m.* N of a demon, one of the generals of Râvana slain by Râma. -Comp. —अरि: *m.* An epithet of Râma.

दूषः *m.*,-षी *f.* The rheum of the eyes.

दूषिका *f* 1 A pencil,paint-brush.-2 A kind of rice.-3Rheum of the eyes.

दूषित *a.*(*f.*-ता)1 Corrupted spoiled. -2Hurt, injured,spoiled,frustrated. -3Damaged, demoralized. -4 Blamed, censured. -5 Falsely accused, traduced.

दूष्य *a.* (*f.* -ष्या) 1 Corruptible. -2 Condemnable, culpable, blamable. -ष्यं *n.* 1 Matter, pus. -2 Poison. -3 Cotton. -4 A garment, clothes. -5 A tent. —ष्या *f.* Leathern girth of an elephant.

दृ 6. A.(द्रियते, दृत, *desid.* दिदृरिषते) (Rarely used by itself,usually found in combination with आ-) 1 To respect, honor, reverence. -2 To care for, mind, usually with न. -3 To have regard for. -4 To desire.

दृंहित *p. p.* (*f.* —ता) 1 Made firm, strengthened. -2 Grown,increased.

दृकं *n.* A hole, an opening.

दृढ *a.*(*f.* -ढा)1 Fixed,firm,strong, untiring. -2 Solid, massive. -3 Confirmed, established. -4 Steady, persevering. -5 Firmly fastened. -6 Compact. -7 Close,dense.-8Strong, great, excessive, mighty, severe, powerful. -9 Tough. -10 Difficult to be drawn or bent (as a bow). -11 Reliable. -12 Certain, sure.-13 Hard-hearted, cruel. -14 Secure. -15 (In Math.) Reduced to the smallest number by a common divisor.—ढं *n.* 1 Iron. -2 A fortress. -3 Excess, abundance. -4 Anything fixed firm or solid. -ढं *ind.* 1 Firmly, fast. -2 Very much, excessively, vehemently. -3 Thoroughly. -Comp. —अंग *a.* Strong-limbed, stout. (-गं *n.*) A diamond. -काण्ड:, -ग्रंथि:,-पत्र: *m.* A bamboo. -ग्राहिन् *a.* Seizing firmly,pursuing an object with untiring energy, resolute. —दंशक: *m.* A shark.-क्षण: *m.* An epithet of Buddha. -धन्वन्,-धन्विन् *m.* A good archer. -निश्चय *a.* 1 Of firm resolve; resolute, firm. -2 Confirmed. -नीर:, -फल: *m.* The cocoanut tree. -प्रतिज्ञ *a.* Firm to a promise, true to one's word, faithful to an agreement. -प्रत्यय:m. Firm confidence, settled conviction -प्ररोह: m. The holy fig tree.-प्रहारिन् a. 1 Striking hard. 2 Hitting firmly, shooting surely.-भक्ति a. Faithful, devoted. -मति a. Resolute, strong-willed, firm. -मुष्टि a. Close-fisted, miserly, niggardly. (-ष्टिः m.) A sword. —मूल:, —वृक्ष: m. The cocoa-nut tree. —लोमन् m. A wild hog.—वैरिन् m. A relentless foe, an inveterate enemy. -व्रत a. 1 Firm in religious austerity. -2 Firm, faithful. -3 Persevering, persistent. -संधि a. 1 Firmly united, closely joined. -2 Close, compact.

दृतिः m., f. 1 A leathern bag for holding water &c. -2 A fish. -3 A skin, hide. -4 A pair of bellows. Comp. -हरि: m. A dog. [bolt.

दृन्फू: f. 1 A snake -2 Thunder-

दृन्भू: m. 1 The thunderbolt (of Indra). -2 The sun. -3 A king. -4 Yama, god of death (अंतक).

दृप् 1 P., 10 U. (दर्पति, दर्पयति,-ते) To light, inflame, kindle.

दृप् 4 P. (दृप्यति, दृप्त) 1 To be proud, be arrogant or insolent. -2 To be greatly delighted. -3 To be wild or extravagant. -4 To be mad or foolish.

दृप्त a. (f. -प्ता) 1 Proud, arrogant. -2 Mad, wild.

दृप्र a. (f. —प्रा) 1 Proud, arrogant. -2 Strong, powerful.

दृश् 1 P. (पश्यति, द्रष्टुं, दृष्ट) 1 To see, look at, observe, behold, perceive. -2 To regard, consider. -3 To visit, wait or call upon. -4 To learn, know, understand. -5 To inspect, discover. -6 To search, examine, decide. -7 To see by divine intuition. -8 To look helplessly on (without power to prevent what is taking place). With उत्— To expect, to foresee. सम्— To see, behold, see well.

Pass. (दृश्यते) 1 To be seen or perceived, become visible or manifested. -2 To appear like; seem, look. -3 To be found or seen, occur (as in a book &c). -4 To be considered or regarded. सामान्यप्रातिपदिपूर्वकमिर्य दारेषु दृश्या त्वया * शाकुंत. 4.16.

-Caus. (दर्शयति,-ते) 1 To cause any one (acc., dat. or gen.) to see anything (acc.), to show, point out; *e. g.* दर्शयति भक्तान् हरिं; प्रत्यभिज्ञानरत्नं च रामायादर्शयत्कृती * रघुवं. -2 To prove, demonstrate. -3 To display, make visible. -4 To produce (as in a court of justice). -5 To adduce (as evidence). -6 (Atm.) To show oneself, appear, show anything belonging to oneself. [to see.

--Desid. (दिदृक्षते) To wish or desire

दृश् a. (At the end of comp.) 1 Seeing, surveying. -2 Discerning, knowing. -3 Looking like, appearing. -*f.* 1 Seeing, perceiving. -2 The eye, sight. -3 Knowledge. -4 The number 'two'. -5 The aspect of a planet. -Comp. -अध्यक्ष: m. The sun. —कर्ण: m. A snake. —गोचर a. Visible. (-र: m.) The range of sight. —क्षेप: m., —ज्या f. The sine of the zenith-distance. —तुल्य a. Coincident with observation, or an observed place (in astr.). -पथ: m. The range of sight. —पात: m. A look, glance.—प्रिया f. Beauty, splendour. -भक्ति:f. A look of love, an amorous glance. —लंबनं n. Vertical parallax. —विष: m. A snake. -वृत्तं n. A vertical circle. —श्रुति: m. A snake, serpent.

दृषद् f. A stone. -Comp. -वती f. N. of a river in the north of India.

दृशा f. The eye. -Comp. -आकांक्ष्यं n. A lotus. —उपमं n. A white lotus.

दृशानः *m.* 1 A spiritual teacher. -2 A Brâhmana. -3 A guardian of the world (लोकपाल). —नं *n.* Light, brightness.

दृशिः,-शी *f.* 1 The eye.-2 A Sástra. -3 Light. —शिः *f.* Seeing, viewing.

दृश्य *pot. p.* (*f.* —श्या) 1 To be seen, visible. -2 To be looked at. -3 Beautiful, lovely. —श्यं *n.* A visible object.

दृश्वन् *a.* (*f.* -री) (At the end of comp.) 1 Seeing, perceiving. -2 (Fig.) Familiar or conversant with. *e. g.* श्रुतपारदृश्वा * रघुवं. 5 24. विद्यानां पारदृश्वनः * रघुवं 1. 23.

दृषद् *f.* 1 A rock, large stone. -2 A mill stone, a flat stone for grinding condiments upon.-Comp.-उपलः *m.* A grind-stone for grinding condiments upon. दृषदिमाषकः *m.* A tax raised from mill-stones.

दृष्ट *p p.* (*f.*—ष्टा) 1 Seen, perceived, observed.-2 Visible, observable. -3 Regarded, considered.-4 Occurring, found. -5 Appearing, manifested. -6 Known, understood. -7 Determined, decided. -8 Valid. -9 Experienced, suffered, endured, felt. -ष्टं *n.* 1 Perception, observation. -2 Danger from dacoits. -Comp. -अंतः *m.*, -तं *n.* 1 An example, illustration, parable. -2 (In Rhet.) The figure of speech in which the assertion in one sentence is illustrated by an assertion in the second sentence, the two assertions stating facts related as a thing and its reflexion. दृष्टान्तस्तु सधर्मस्य वस्तुनः प्रतिबिंबनं * साहि. द. -3 A Sâstra or science. -4 Death. —अर्थ *a.* 1 Having the object or meaning obvious or quite apparent. -2 Practical. -3 Having a clear idea about anything. -कूटं *n.* A riddle, an enigma. —दोष *a.* Considered to be faulty. -2 Vicious. -3 Exposed, detected. —प्रत्यय *a.* 1 Of proved confidence, manifested. -2 Convinced.-रजस् *f.* A girl arrived at puberty. —व्यतिकर *a.* 1 One who has experienced a misfortune. -2 One who foresees evil.

दृष्टिः *f.* 1 Seeing, viewing. -2 Seeing with the mental eye. -3 Knowing, knowledge. -4 The eye, the faculty of seeing; sight. -5 A look, glance.6 View, notion.7 Consideration, regard. -8 Intellect, wisdom, knowledge.-9 (In astr.) Aspect of the stars. -10 Light (प्रकाश). -Comp. -कृत, -कृतं *n.* A kind of lily (स्थलपद्म). -क्षेपः *m.* A glance, look. —गुणः *m.* A mark for archers, butt, target. —गोचर *a.* Within the range of sight, in sight, visible. (-रः *m.*) The range of sight. —पातः *m.* 1 A look, glance. -2 Act of seeing, function of the eye. —पथः *m.* The range of sight. -पूत *a.* Kept pure by the sight, watched that no impurity is contracted; *e. g.* दृष्टिपूतं न्यसेत्पादं. -बंधुः *m.* A fire-fly. -विक्षेपः *m.* A side-glance, leer, oblique look. —विभ्रमः *m.* An amorous glance, a coquettish look. —विषः *m.* A serpent.

दृह्, दृंह् 1 P. (दर्हति, दृंहति) 1 To be fixed or firm. -2 To grow, increase, prosper.

दॄ 4. 9. P. (दीर्यति, दृणाति, दीर्ण) 1 To burst or break asunder, split open. -2 To cause to burst, tear, divide, pull to pieces. —*Pass.* (दीर्यते) 1 To burst, break open. -2 To separate. -3 To be afraid, to fear. -*Caus.* (द-दा-रयति,-ते) 1 To split, tear asunder; divide by digging. -2 To disperse, scatte-.

दॄ 1 P. (दरति) To fear, be afraid of.

दे 1 A. (दयते, दात. *Desid.* दित्सते) To

protect, cherish. [resplendent.

देदीप्यमान *a.*(*f.* -ना) Bright, blazing,

देय *a.* (*f.* —या) 1 To be given or presented.-2 Fit to be given, proper for a gift. -3 To be returned or restored.

देव् 1 A. (देवते) 1 To sport, play, gamble. -2 To lament. -3 To shine. -4 To throw, cast. -With परि— To lament, mourn.

देव *a.* (*f.* —वी) 1 Divine, celestial. -2 Shining. -3 Fit to be worshipped. —वः *m.* 1 A god, deity. -2 The god of rain, an epithet of Indra.-3 A cloud.-4 A divine man, a Bráhmana. -5 A king, ruler, as in मनुष्यदेव. -6 A title affixed to the names of Bráhmanas; as in गोविंददेव, पुरुषोत्तमदेव &c. -7 (In dramas) A title of honour used in addressing a king. -8 The Supreme Spirit. -Comp-अंशः *m.* A partial incarnation of god. —अगारः *m.*, -रं *n.* A temple. -अंगना *f.* A celestial damsel, an *apsaras*. —आतिदेवः, अधिदेवः *m.* 1 A The highest god. -2 An epithet of (1) Siva. (2) Buddha. (3) Vishnu. —अधिपः *m.* 1 An epithet of Indra. -2 The supreme god.—अंधस्, -अन्नं *n.* The food of gods, divine food, ambrosia. -2 Food that has been first offered to an idol. -अभीष्ट *a.* 1 Liked by or dear to gods. -2 Sacred or dedicated to a deity. (—ष्टा *f.*) Piper betel. —अरण्यं *n.* The garden of gods, the Nandana garden -अरिः *m.* A demon. —अश्वः *m.* An epithet of उच्चैःश्रवस्, the horse of Indra. -आक्रीडः *m.* Nandana garden. —आजीवः, —आजीविन् *m.* 1 An attendant upon an idol. -2 A low Bráhmana subsisting by attendance upon an idol and upon the offerings made to it. —आत्मन् *m.* The holy fig-tree. —आयतनं *n.* A temple. —आयुधं *n.* 1 A divine weapon. -2 Rainbow. —आलयः *m.* 1 Heaven. -2 A temple. —आवासः *m.* 1 Heaven. -2 The holy fig-tree (अश्वत्थ). -3 A temple. -4 The Sumeru mountain. —आहारः *m.* Nectar, ambrosia. -इज्यः *m.* An epithet of Brihaspati, preceptor of the gods. -इंद्रः *m.* An epithet of Indra. -2 Of Siva. —इष्ट *a.* Dear to gods. (—ष्टः *m.*) Bdellium. (—ष्टा *f.*) The wild lime tree. —ईशः *m.* An epithet of (1) Indra. (2) Siva. (3) Vishnu. (4) Brahman (*m.*). (—शी *f.*) N. of Durgá; also of Devakí, mother of Krishna. —ऋषिः (देवर्षिः) *m.* 1 A deified saint, divine sage, such as अत्रि, भृगु, पुलस्त्य &c.-2 An epithet of Nárada. —ओकस् *n.* The mountain Sumeru. —कन्या *f.* A nymph. —कर्मन्, —कार्यं *n.* 1 A religious act or rite. -2 The worship of gods. —काष्ठं *n.* The Devadâru tree. -कुटं *n.* A temple. —कुंडं *n.* A natural spring. —कुलं *n.* 1 A temple. -2 A race of gods. -3 A group of gods. —कुल्या *f.* The celestial Ganges. —कुसुमं *n.* Cloves. -खातं, -खातकं *n.* 1 A natural hollow among mountains. -2 A natural pond or reservoir. -3 A pond near a temple. —गणिका *f.* An *apsaras*. —गंधर्वः *m.* An epithet of Nárada. —गर्जनं *n.* Thunder. -गायनः *m.* A celestial chorister, a Gandharva. -गिरिः *m.* N. of a mountain. —गुरुः *m.* 1 An epithet of Kasyapa (the father of gods). -2 Of Brihaspati (the preceptor of gods). —गुही *f.* An epithet of Sarasvatí.-गृहं *n.* 1 A temple. -2 The palace of a king. -3 A planetary sphere. —चर्या *f.* The worship or service of gods. -चिकित्सकौ *m. dual* Asvins, the twin physicians of gods. —छंदः *m.* A pearl necklace having a hundred strings. -तरुः m. 1 The holy fig-tree. -2 One of the trees of paradise,(*i.e.* मंदार, पारिजात, संतान, कल्प, and हरिचंदन). —ताडः *m.* 1 Fire. -2 An epithet of Râhu. —दत्तः *m.* N. of the conch-shell of Arjuna. —दारुः *m.*, -रु *n.* A species of pine. -दासी *f.* 1 A female in the service of gods or a temple. -2 A courtezan (employed as a dancer in a temple). -3 The wild citron tree. -दीपः *m.* The eye.-दुंदुभिः *m.* 1 A divine drum. -2 The holy basil with red flowers. -3 An epithet of Indra. —दूतः *m.* A divine envoy or messenger, an angel.-देवः *m.* 1 An epithet of Brahman (*m.*). -2 Of Siva. -3 Of Vishnu. —द्रोणी *f.* A procession with idols. —नदी *f.* 1 The Ganges. -नंदिन् *m.* N. of the door-keeper of Indra. -नागरी *f.* N. of the character in which Sanskrit is usually written. -निकायः *m.* Paradise,heaven. -निंदकः *m.*A blasphemer, unbeliever, heretic, atheist. —पथः *m.* Heaven, firmament. -2 The milky way. —पशुः *m.* Any animal consecrated to a deity. —पूज्यः *m.* An epithet of Brihaspati. —प्रतिकृतिः, —प्रतिमा *f.* An idol —प्रश्नः *m.* Astrology, fortune-telling. —प्रियः *m.* An epithet of Siva. (देवानांप्रियः *m.* Is an irreg. comp. meaning. 1 A goat. -2 A fool, one like a brute beast. -3An ascetic or one who renounces the world). —बलिः *m.* An oblation to the gods. —ब्रह्मन् *m.* An epithet of Nárada. —ब्राह्मणः -*m.* 1 A Bráhmana who lives on the proceeds of a temple.-2A venerable Bráhmana. —भवनं *n.* 1 The heaven. -2 A temple. -3 The holy fig-tree. —भूमिः *f.* Heaven. —भूतिः *f.* An epithet of the Ganges. -भूयं *n.* Divinity, godhead. —भृत्*m.* 1 An epithet of Vishuu. -2 Of Indra. —मणिः *m.* 1 The jewel of Vishnu called कौस्तुभ. -2 The sun. -3 A curl of hair on a horse's neck. —मातृक *a.* Having the clouds as foster-mother *i. e.* watered only by the clouds,depending on rain-water and not on irrigation (as a country). —मानकः *m.* The jewel of Vishnu called कौस्तुभः. —मासः *m.*The eighth month of pregnancy. —मुनिः *m.* A divine sage. —यजनं *n.* A sacrificial place, a place where a sacrifice is performed.-यजि *a.* Making oblations to gods. —यज्ञः *m.* A sacrifice to the superior gods made by oblations to fire, or through fire to the gods ; (one of the five daily sacrifices of a Bráhmana) —यात्रा *f.* 'An idol-procession ', any sacred festival when the idols are carried in procession. —यानं *n.*, —रथः *m.* A celestial car. —युगं *n.* 1 The first of the four ages of the world ; also called कृतयुग. -2 An age of the gods comprising four ages of men.-योनिः *m.* 1 A superhuman being,a demigod. -2 A being of divine origin. —योषा *f.* An *apsaras*. —राज्,-राजः *m.* 1 An epithet of Indra. -2 A king. -3 N. of Buddha. —लता *f.* The Navamallikâ or double jasmine plant. -लिंगं *n.* The image or statue of a deity. —लोकः *m.* Heaven, paradise. -वक्त्रं *n.* An epithet of fire. —वर्त्मन् *n.* The sky. —वर्धकिः, —शिल्पिन् *m.* Visvakarman, the architect of gods. -वाणी *f.* 'A divine voice',a voice from heaven. —वाहनः *m.* An epithet of Agni. -विमानः*m.* The nothern hemisphere. -वृक्षः *m.* The Mandàra tree. —व्रतं *n.* A religious observance, any religious vow. (—तः *m.*) An epithet of 1 Bhîshma. -2 Kârtikeya. —शत्रुः *m.* A demon.

—शुनी *f.* An epithet of Saramá, the bitch of the gods. -शेषं *n.* The remnants of a sacrifice offered to gods. —श्रुतः *m.* An epithet of 1 Vishnu. -2 Nârada. -3 A sacred treatise. -4 A god in general. —सभा *f.* 1 An assembly of the gods (सुधर्मन्). -2 A council of a king, council-chamber. -3 A gambling-house. —सायुज्यं *n.* Identification or unification with a deity, conjunction with the gods, deification. —सेना *f.* 1 The army of gods. -2 N. of the wife of Skanda. —स्वं *n.* Property applicable to religious purposes or endowments. -हविस् *n.* An animal offered to gods at a sacrifice. —हूतिः *f.* 1 Invocation of the gods. -2 N. of a daughter of Manu Svâyambhuva and wife of Kardama.

देवकी *f.* N. of a daughter of Devaka and wife of Vasudeva and mother of Krishna. -Comp. -नंदनः, -पुत्रः,-मातृ *m.*, -सूनुः *m.* Epithets of Krishna.

देवटः *m.* An artizan.

देवता *f.* 1 Divine dignity or power of divinity. -2 A deity, god. -3 The image of a deity. -4 An idol. -5 An organ of sense.-Comp.-अगारः *m.*, -रं *n.*, -आगारः *m.*, -रं *n.* -गृहं, -स्थानं *n.* A temple. —अधिपः *m.* An epithet of Indra. -आयतनं *n.*, -आलयः *m.*, -वेश्मन् *n.* A temple or chapel.-प्रतिमा *f.* The image of a god, an idol. -स्नानं *f.* The ablution of an idol.

देवन् *m.* The younger brother of the husband.

देवनः *m.* A die. —नं *n.* 1 Beauty, splendour,lustre.-2 Gaming,gambling, a game at dice. -3 Play,sport, pastime. -4 A pleasure-ground, a garden. -5 A lotus. -6 Emulation. -7 Affair, business. -8 Praise. -9 Grief, lamentation, sorrow. —ना *f.* 1 Gambling, a game at dice. -2 Sport, pastime. -3 Lamentation.

देवयानी *f.* N. of the daughter of Sukra, preceptor of the *Asuras.*

देवरः *m.* The husband's brother (elder or younger).

देवलः *m.* 1 An attendent upon an idol, a low Bráhmana who subsists upon the offerings made to an idol. -2 A virtuous man.-3N.of Nárada. -4 The husband's brother.

देवसात् *ind.* To or into the nature of a god or gods.

दैविक *a.* (*f.* -की), दैविल *a.* (*f.* -ला) 1 Divine, godly. -2 Derived from a god. -3 Virtuous, pious.

देवी *f.* 1 A female deity, a goddess. -2 N. of Durgâ. -3 N. of Sarasvatî. -4 N. of Sâvitrî. -5 A queen, especially a crowned queen. -6 A respectful title applied to a lady of the first rank.

देवृ *m.* A husband's brother (especially younger).

देशः *m.* 1 A place or spot in general. -2 A country, province, territory. -3 A department, portion (as of a whole) as in एकदेश, एकदेशिय. -4 An institute, an crdinance. -5 Range,compass as in दृष्टिदेशः.-Comp. —अतिथिः *m.* A foreigner. —अंतरं *n.* Another country. —अंतरिन् *m.* A foreigner. —आचारः, —धर्मः *m.* A local law or custom,the usage or custom of any country. —कालौ (*m. dual*) Time and place. (-लं) *ind.* According to time and place. —कालज्ञ *a.* Knowing the proper place and time. —ज, —जात *a.* 1 Native, indigenous.-2 Produced in the right country. -3 Of genuine descent.

—भाषा *f.* The dialect of a country. —कर्म *n.* Propriety, fitness. —व्यवहारः *m.* A local usage, custom of the country.

देशकः *m.* 1 A ruler, governor. -2 An instructor, a preceptor.

देशना *f.* Direction, instruction.

देशिक *a.* (*f.* -का) Local, native. —कः *m.* 1 A spiritual teacher (गुरु). -2 A traveller. -3 A guide. -4 One familiar with places.

देशिनी *f.* The fore-finger.

देशी *f.* The dialect of a country.

देशिय *a.* (*f.* —या) 1 Belonging to a province, provincial. -2 Native, local. -3 Inhabiting any country (at the end of comp.) ; as in मगधदेशिय, तद्देशिय, बंगदेशीय &c. -4 Not far or distant from, almost, bordering on (used as an affix at the end of words); अष्टादशवर्षदेशीया कन्या 'a girl about 18 years old (whose age borders on 18).

देश्य *a.* (*f.* -श्या) 1 To be pointed out or proved.-2 Local, provincial -3 Born in a country, native. -4 Genuine, of genuine descent. -5 Being on the spot or place (where anything is due). -6 Not far from, almost. —श्यः *m.* 1 An eye-witness of anything. -2 The inhabitant of a country. —श्यं *n.* The statement of a question or argument, the thing to be proved or substantiated (पूर्वपक्ष).

देहः *m.*, —हं *n.* The body. -Comp. —अंतरं *n.* Another body. -आत्मवादः *m.* Materialism, the doctrines of Chârvâka. -आत्मवादिन् *m.* A materialist, a Chârvâka. —आवरणं *n.* An armour, dress. -ईश्वरः *m.* The soul. —उद्भव, -उद्भूत *a.* Born in the body, inborn, innate. —कर्तृ *m.* The sun. -2 The Supreme Soul. -3 Father. -कोषः *m.* 1 The covering of the body. -2 A feather, wing &c. -3 Skin. —गत *a.* Incarnate, embodied.-जः *m.* A son. —जा *f.* A daughter. —त्यागः *m.* 1 Death (in general).-2 Voluntary death ; resigning the body. —दः *m.* Quicksilver. -दीपः *m.* The eye. -धर्मः *m.* The function of the body. -धारकं *n.* A bone. —धारणं *n.* Living, life. —धिः *m.* A wing. —धृष् *m.* Air, wind.-बद्ध *a.* Embodied, incarnate. —भाज् *m.* Any being possessed of a body or life, especially a man. —भुज् *m.* 1 The soul. -2 The sun. —भृत् *m.* 1 A living being, especially a man.-2 An epithet of Siva. -3 Life, vitality. —यात्रा *f.* 1 Dying, death. -2 Nourishment, food. —लक्षणं *n.* A mole, a black or dark spot upon the skin. —वायुः *m.* One of the five vital airs or life-winds. -सारः *m.* Marrow.

देहंभर *a.* Gluttonous.

देहला *f.* Spirituous liquor.

देहलिः,—ली *f.* The threshold of a door, the sill or lower part of the wooden frame of a door. -Comp. -दीपः *m.* A lamp suspended over the threshold. देहलीदीपन्यायः *m.* The maxim of the lamp over the threshold. Such a lamp illumines the rooms on either side of the threshold. Hence this maxim is applied to indicate something serviceable in a double capacity.

देहवत् *a.* Embodied. -*m.* 1 A man. -2 The soul.

देहिन् *a.* (*f.* —नी) Incarnate, embodied. -*m.* 1 A living being, especially a man. -2 The soul, spirit. -नी *f.* The earth.

दै 1 P. (दायति, दात) 1 To purify, cleanse. -2 To be purified. -3 To protect -With अव— 1 To whiten, brighten. -2 To purify.

दैतेयः m. 'A son of Diti,' a Rákshasa, demon. -Comp. -इज्यः, -गुरुः, -पुरोधस्, पूज्यः m. Epithets of Sukra, the preceptor of the Asuras. —मेदजा f. The earth.

दैत्यः m. Same as दैतेयः. -Comp. —अरिः m. 1 A god. -2 An epithet of Vishnu. —देवः m. 1 An epithet of Varuna. -2 Wind. -पतिः m. An epithet of Hiranyakasipu.

दैत्या f. 1 A drug. -2 Spirituous liquor.

दैन (f. -नी), दैनंदिन (f. -नी), दैनिक (f. -की) a. Diurnal, daily.

दैनिकी f. Daily wages, day's hire.

दैन्, -न्यं n. 1 Poverity, poor and pitiable condition. -2 Affliction, grief. -3 Feebleness. -4 Meanness.

दैव a. (f. —वी) Relating to gods, divine, celestial. -वः (i. e. विवाहः) m. One of the eight forms of marriage; that in which the daughter is given away at a sacrifice to the officiating priest. —वं n. 1 Fate, destiny, luck, fortune, (e. g. दैवात् By chance, luckily, accidentally). -2 A god, deity. -3 A religious rite or offering, an oblation to gods. -4 A kind of Sráddha ceremony. -5 Parts of the hands sacred to the gods, i. e. The tips of the fingers. -वी f. A woman married according to the form of marriage called *daiva*. -Comp. —अत्ययः m. An evil resulting from unusual natural phenomena. -अधीन, -आयत्त a. Dependent on fate. —अहोरात्रः m. A day of the gods i. e. the human year. —उपहत a. Ill-fated, unfortunate. -कर्मन् n. Offering oblations to gods. -कोविदः, —चिंतकः, -ज्ञः m. An astrologer, a fortune-teller. —गतिः f. Turn or course of fate. -दीपः m. The eye. —दुर्विपाकः m. Hardness of fortune, adverseness or unpropitiousness of fate, an evil turn of fate. -पर a 1 Fatalistic. -2 Predestined. -प्रश्नः m. 1 Fortune-telling, astrology. -2 A voice from heaven. -युगं n. 'A Yuga of the gods', said to consist of 12000 divine years. -योगः m. A lucky coincidence, chance; (दैवयोगेन, दैवयोगात् Fortunately, accidentally). —लेखकः m. A Fortune-teller, an astrologer. —वशः m., -शं n. The power of destiny, subjection to fate. —वाणी f. 1 A voice from heaven. -2 The Sanskrit language.

दैवकः m. A god, deity.

दैवत a. (f. -ती) 1 Divine. -2 (At the end of an adj. comp.) Honouring or worshipping as one's deity, as in सूर्यदैवता जनाः.-तं n. A god, deity, divinity. -2 A number of gods, the whole class of gods. -3 An idol. (The word is said to be m. also but is rarely used in that gender.) -4 N. of the third Kânda of Yâska's Nirukta.

दैवतस् ind. By chance, fortunately.

दैवत्य a. (f. —त्या) Addressed or sacred to a deity. —त्यं n. A deity.

दैवलः, —लकः m. The servant of an evil spirit.

दैवारिपः m. A conch-shell (शंख).

दैवासुरं n. The natural enmity subsisting between the gods and the demons.

दैविक a. (f. —की) Relating to the gods, divine. -कं n. An invitable accident.

दैविन् m. An astrologer.

दैव्य a. (f.-व्या or -व्यी) Divine. -व्यं n. 1 Fortune, fate. -2 Divine power.

दैशिक a (f. —की) 1 Local, provin

cial. -2 National, belonging to the whole country. -3 Belonging or having reference to space.-4 Acquainted with any place. -5 Teaching, directing, showing. —कः *m*. 1 A teacher, preceptor. -2 A guide

दैष्टिक *a* (*f*. -की) Fated, predestined. —कः *m*. A fatalist.

दैहिक *a*. (*f*. -की) Bodily, corporeal.

दैह्य *a*. (*f*. -ह्या) Bodily. —ह्यः *m*. The soul.

दो 4 P. (द्यति, दित; *caus*. दापयति. *desid*. दित्सति) 1 To cut, divide. -2 To mow, reap. -With अव- To cut or lop off.

दोग्धृ *m*. 1 A cow-herd, a milkman. -2 A calf. -3 A panegyrist who writes verses for reward. -4 One who performs any thing from interested motives.

दोग्ध्री *f*. 1 A cow which yields milk. -2 A wet nurse.

दोधः *m*. A calf.

दोरः *m*. A rope.

दोरकं *n*. A string for fastening the wires of a lute.

दोलः *m*. 1 Swinging, rocking, oscillating. -2 A swing, litter. -3 A festival held on the fourteenth or full-moon day of the month of Phálguna when figures of 'young Krishna' (बालकृष्ण) are swung in a swing.

दोला, दोलिका *f*. A litter, palanquin. -2 A swing, hammock (fig. also). -3 Swinging, fluctuation.-4 Doubt, uncertainty. -Comp. —अधिरूढ, -आरूढ *a*. (Lit.) Mounted on a swing. (fig.) Uncertain, irresolute, disquieted. —युद्धं *n*. Uncertainty of success, a fight with varying success

दोलाय Den. A. 1 To swing, oscillate, vacillate (fig. also). -2 To be restless or uneasy.

दोलायमान *a* (*f*. -ना) 1 Swinging, oscillating. -2 Wavering, vacillating. -3 Perplexed, doubtful.

दोलायित, दोलित *a*. (*f*. -ता) Swung, shaken, oscillating. [swing.

दोलिका, दोली *f*. 1 A cradle. -2 A

दोषः *m*. 1 A fault, blame, censure, defect, blemish. -2 An error, a mistake. -3 A crime, sin, guilt, offence. -4 Noxious quality, injurious nature or quality; as in आहारदोष. -5 Harm, evil, danger, injury. -6 Bad or injurious consequence. -7 Morbid affection, disease. -8 Disorder of the three humours of the body, or the three humors when in a disordered state. -9 (In Nyâya &c.) A fault of a definition; (*i e* अव्याप्ति, अतिव्याप्ति and असंभव). -10 (In Rhet.) A fault or defect of composition (such as पददोष, पदांशदोष, वाक्यदोष, रसदोष and अर्थदोष). -11 A calf. -12 Refutation -13 Evening, dusk. -Comp. —आरोपः *m*. A charge, accusation. -एकदृश् *a*. Fault-finding, censorious. —कर,-कारिन,-कृत *a*. Causing evil, hurtful.—ग्रस्त *a*. 1 Convicted, guilty. -2 Full of faults or defects. -ग्राहिन् *a*. 1 Malicious, malignant.-2 Censorious.-ज्ञ *a*. Knowing faults. (—ज्ञः *m*.) 1 A wise or learned man. -2 A physician. —त्रयं *n*. Vitiation of the three humours of the body ; (*i*. *e*. वात, पित्त and कफ). -दृष्टि *a*. Censorious. -प्रसंगः *m*. Attaching blame, condemnation, censure. —भाज् *a*. Guilty, wrong.

दोषकः *m*. A calf.

दोषणं *n*. A charge, an accusation.

दोषन् *m*., *n*. (This word has no forms for the first five inflections, *i*. *e*. before. acc. pl.) An arm.

दोषल *a*. (*f*. -ला) Faulty, defective, corrupt, sinful.

दोषस् *f.* Night. -*n.* Darkness.

दोषा *ind.* At night.—*f.*1 The arm. -2 The darkness of night, night. -Comp. —आस्य:, —तिलक: *m.*A lamp. -कर: *m.* The moon. [turnal.

दोषातन *a.* (*f.* —नी) Nightly, noc-

दोषिक *a.* (*f.* -की) Faulty, defective, bad. -क: *m.* Sickness, disease.

दोषित *a.* (*f.* -णी) 1 Impure, contaminated. -2 Faulty, defective. -3 Criminal, sinful, guilty.

दोस् *m.*, *n.* (दोषन् is optionally substituted for this word after acc. dual) 1 The fore-arm, the arm. -2 The part of an arc defining its sine. -3 The side of a triangle or square. -Comp. —मडु (दोर्मडु) *a.* Crooked-armed. —ग्रह (दोर्ग्रह) *a.* Strong, powerful. (-ह: *m.*) Pain in the arm. —ज्या (दोर्ज्या) *f.*The sine of the base. -दंड: (दोर्दंड:) *m.* A stick-like arm, strong arm. —मूलं (दोर्मूलं) *n.* The arm-pit. —युद्धं (दोर्युद्धं) *n.* A duel. —शालिन् (दो:शालिन्) *a.* Possessed of strong arms, warlike, brave. -शिखरं (दो:शिखरं) *n.* The shoulder. -सहस्रभृत(दो:सहस्रभृत)*m.* 1 An epithet of the demon Bâna.-2An epithet ofSahasrárjuna. —स्थ:(दोस्थ:)*m.* 1A servant. 2 Service.-3A player.-4Play, sport.

दोह: *m.* 1 Milking. -2 Milk. -3 A milk-pail. -4 Making profit out of anything, satisfaction, success. -Comp. -अपनय: *m.*, -जं *n.* Milk.

दोहद: *m.*, -दं *n.* The longing of a pregnant woman, the object desired by a pregnant woman. -3 Pregnancy. -4 The desire of plants at budding time (as for instance, of the Asoka to be kicked by young ladies, of the Bakula to be sprinkled by mouthfuls of liquor &c.). -5 Vehement desire.-6 Wish or desire in general. -Comp. —लक्षणं *n.* 1 The foetus, the embryo. -2 The period of passing from one stage of life to another.

दोहन *a.* (*f.* —ना) 1 Milking. -2 Yielding or granting (desired objects). —नं *n.* 1 Milking. -2 A milk-pail. —नी *f.* A milk-pail.

दोहल: *m.* See दोहद:.

दोहली *f.* The Asoka tree.

दोह्य *a.* (*f.* —ह्या) To be milked, milkable. -ह्यं *n.* Milk. -ह्या *f.*A cow.

दौ:शील्यं *n.* Bad temper, wickedness, wicked disposition.

दौ:साधिक: *m.* 1 A door-keeper, porter. -2 The superintendent of a village. [women.

दौ:स्त्रं *n.* Wrangling between

दौकू (-कू-) ल: *m.* A car covered with silk cloth.-लं *n.* Fine silk cloth.

दौत्यं *n.* Message, mission, duty or work of a messenger.

दौरात्म्यं *n.* 1 Wickedness, evil or wicked temper.-2 Mischievousness.

दौर्गत्यं *n.* 1 Poverty, want.-2 Wretchedness, distress.

दौर्गन्ध्यं*n.*Bad or disagreeable smell.

दौर्जन्यं *n.* Wickedness, depravity.

दौर्जीवित्यं *n.* A wretched or miserable life. [weakness.

दौर्बल्यं, -लं *n.* Impotency, debility,

दौर्भागिनेय: *m.* The son of a woman disliked by her husband.

दौर्भाग्यं *n.* Ill-luck, misfortune.

दौर्भ्रात्रं *n.* A quarrel or disagreement between brothers.

दौर्मनस्यं *n.*1 Evil disposition.-2 Affliction, dejection. -3 Despair.

दौर्मन्त्र्यं *n* Evil advice, bad counsel.

दौर्वचस्यं *n.* Evil speech, bad language.

दौर्हृदं, दौहृदं *n.* 1 Evil disposition of the mind, enmity; (also दौर्हार्दं in-this sense). -2 Pregnancy. -3 The longing of a pregnant woman. -4 Desire in general. [enmity.

दौर्हृदयं n. Evil disposition of mind,

दौलेयः m. A tortoise.

दौल्मिः m. An epithet of Indra.

दौवारिकः (f. -की) A door-keeper, warder.

दौष्कुल a. (f. -ली), दौष्कुलेय a. (f. -यी) Sprung from a low family, born in a contemptible family.

दौश्चर्यं n. 1 Evil conduct, wickedness. -2 A bad deed.

दौष्ट्यं, दौष्ठवं n. Badness, wickedness. [shyanta.

दौष्यं (-ष्मं-) -न्तिः m. A son of Du-

दौहित्रः m. A daughter's son. -त्रं n. Sesamum seed. [er's son.

दौहित्रायणः m. The son of a daught-

दौहित्री f. A daughter's daughter.

दौहृदिनी f. A pregnant woman.

द्यविद्यवी f. A day.

द्यु 2 P. (द्यौति) To advance towards, attack, assail.

द्यु n. 1 A day. -2 The sky. -3 Brightness. -4 Heaven. -5 Sharpness. -m. Fire. (द्यु is a substitute for दिव् f. before terminations beginning with consonants and in compounds). -Comp. -गः m. A bird. -चरः m. 1 A planet. -2 A bird. —जयः m. Attainment of heaven. —निवासः m. A deity, god. —पतिः m. 1 The sun. -2 An epithet of Indra. —मणिः m. The sun. —सरित् f. The Ganges. [A crow.

द्युकः m. An owl. -Comp. —अरिः m.

द्युत् 1 A. (द्योतते, द्युतित or द्योतित; desid. दिद्युतिषते, दिद्योतिषते) To shine, be bright or brilliant. With वि- To shine. -Caus. (द्योतयति,-ते) 1 To illuminate, irradiate. -2 To make clear, explain, elucidate. -3 To express, mean.

द्युतिः f. 1 Splendour, lustre, beauty. -2 Light, a ray of light. -3 Majesty, dignity. -Comp. -करः m. The polar star or the sage Dhruva.

द्युमत् a. 1 Bright. -2 Clear, loud -3 Strong, vigorous. -4 Calm, serene. -Comp. -गानं n. A mode of chanting the Sâmaveda. -सेनः m. N of a king of Sálva, and father of Satyavat, husband of Sâvitrí.

द्युम्नं n. 1 Splendour, lustre. -2 Energy, power. -3 Wealth, property

द्युवन् m. The sun.

द्यूतः m., -तं n. 1 Play, gambling playing with dice. -2 (fig.) A battle, fight. -3 The prize won. -Comp —अधिकारिन् m. The keeper of a gambling-house. -करः, -कृत् m. A gamester, a gambler. -कारः, -कारक m. 1 The keeper of a gambling house. -2 A gambler. -पूर्णिमा, -पौर्णिमा f. The day of full moon in the month of Asvina (also called कोजागर) when games of chance are played in honour of Lakshmí the goddess of wealth. -प्रतिपद् f The first day of the bright half of Kártika (usually spent in gambling.) —बीजं n. A *cowrie*, a shell used in playing. —वृत्तिः m. 1 A professional gambler. -2 The keeper of a gambling-house.

द्यै 1 P. (द्यायति) To despise, treat with contempt.

द्यो f. (Nom. sing. द्यौः) Heaven paradise, the sky. द्यावापृथिव्यौ, द्यावाभूमी, द्यावाक्षमे f. dual. ' Heaven and earth '. -Comp. -भूमिः m. A bird -सद् (द्योसद्) m. A god.

द्योतः m. 1 Light, lustre, brilliance as in खद्योत. -2 Sunshine. -3 Heat

द्योतक a. (f. -का) 1 Shining. -

Illuminating. -3 Explaining, making manifest.

द्योतनः *m.* A lamp. —नं *n.* 1 Shining. -2 Illuminating -3 Explaining.

द्योतनिका *f.* Explanation, elucidation.

द्योतित *p. p.* (*f.* —ता) 1 Illuminated. -2 Illustrated.

द्योतिस् *n.* 1 Light, lustre. -2 A star. -Comp. —इंगणः *m.* (द्योतिरिंगणः) A fire-fly.

द्रंक्षणं *n.* A measure of weight.

द्रढय् Den. P. 1 To make firm, fasten, tighten. -2 To strengthen, confirm, corroborate.

द्रढिमन् *m.* 1 Tightness, firmness. -2 Confirmation, corroboration. -3 Assertion, affirmation. -4 Heaviness.

द्रप्सः *m.* 1 A drop. -2 A spark (of fire). -प्सं *n.* Diluted sour milk, diluted curds; (also द्रप्स्यं).

द्रम् 1 P. (द्रमति) To go about, run.

द्रम्मं *n.* A drachma; (a word of Greek origin).

द्रव *a.* (*f.* -वा) 1 Running (as a horse). -2 Dropping, oozing, wet, dripping. -3 Flowing, fluid. -4 Liquid (opp. कठिन). -5 Melted; liquefied. -वः *m.* 1 Going, walking about, motion. -2 Dropping, trickling. -3 Flight, retreat. -4 Play, amusement, sport. -5 Fluidity, liquefaction. -6 A fluid. -7 Juice; essence. -8 Decoction. -9 Speed, velocity. -Comp —आधारः *m.* 1 A small vessel or receiver. -2 The hands joined together and hollowed (चुलुक). —जः *m.* Treacle. —रसा *f.* 1 Lac. -2 Gum. -3 Extract.

द्रवंती *f.* A river.

द्रविडाः *m. pl.* N. of a country on the east coast of the Deccan(-डः *m. sing.*) An inhabitant or native of that country. -3 N. of a degraded tribe.

द्रविणं *n.* 1 Wealth, property, substance. -2 Gold. -3 Strength, power. -4 Valour. -5 A thing, matter, material. -6 That of which anything is made. -Comp. -आधिपतिः, -ईश्वरः *m.* An epithet of Kubera.

द्रव्यं *n.* 1 A thing, object, matter. -2 The ingredient or material of anything. -3 A material to work upon. -4 A fit or suitable object (to receive instruction &c.) -5 An elementary substance, one of the seven categories of the Vaiseshikas; (the *dravyas* are nine viz. पृथिव्यप्तेजोवाय्वाकाशकालदिगात्ममनांसि). -6 Any possession, wealth, property, money. -7 A medicinal substance or drug. -8 Modesty. -9 Bell-metal. -10 Spirituous liquor. -11 A wager, stake. -12 An ointment. -13 Extract, gum. -Comp. —परिग्रहः *m* The possession of property or wealth. —वाचकं *n.* A substantive.

द्रष्टव्य *pot. p.* (*f.* —व्या) 1 To be seen, visible. -2 Perceptible. -3 Fit to be seen or examined. -4 Pleasing to the sight, beautiful. -5 Deserving to be regarded or considered as.

द्रष्टृ *m.* 1 A seer, one who sees mentally; *e.g.* ऋषयो मंत्रद्रष्टारः. -2 A judge.

द्रहः *m.* A deep lake.

द्रा 2 P. (द्राति द्राण) 1 To sleep. -2 To run, make haste, fly away. -With नि- To sleep. वि- To run away.

द्राक् *ind.* Quickly, forthwith, immediately. -Comp. -भृतकं *n.* Water just drawn from a well.

द्राक्षा *f.* Vine, grape, (the creeper or the fruit). -Comp. -रसः *m.* Grape-juice, wine.

द्राघय् Den. P. 1 To lengthen, stretch, extend. -2 To increase, intensify -3 To tarry, delay.

द्राघिमन् *m*. 1 Length. -2 A degree of longitude.

द्राघिष्ठ *a*. (*f*. —ष्ठा) Longest, very long (superl. of दीर्घ).

द्राघीयस् *a*. (*f*. -सी) Longer, very long (compar. of दीर्घ).

द्राण *a*. (*f*. -णा) 1 Flown, run away. -2 Sleeping, sleepy. —णं *n*. 1 Retreat, running away. -2 Sleep.

द्राप: *m*. 1 Mud, mire. -2 Heaven, sky. -3 A fool, an idiot. -4 An epithet of Siva. -5 A small shell.

द्रामिल: *m* N. of Chânakya.

द्राव: *m*. 1 Flight, retreat.-2 Speed. -3 Running, flowing. -4 Heat. -5 Liquefaction, melting.

द्रावक: *m*. 1 A flux used to assist the fusion of metals. -2 The load-stone. -3 Moon-stone. -4 A thief. -5 A sharp or clever man, wit.-6 A libertine, lecher. —कं *n*. Wax.

द्रावणं *n*. 1 Putting to flight. -2 Melting, fusing. -3 Distilling. -4 The clearing-nut.

द्राविड:*m* 1 A Dravidian,a Dravida. -2 A general name for a Brâhmana of any of the five southern tribes (the पंचद्राविड) द्राविड, कर्णाट गुर्जर, महाराष्ट्र and तैलंग. —डा: *m. pl*. The Dravid country and its people.-डी *f* Cardamoms

द्राविडक: *m*. Zedoary. —कं *n*. Black [salt.

द्रु 1 P. (द्रवति, द्रुत) 1 To run, run away, retreat, fly (often with acc.). -2 To attack, assault quickly. -3 To become fluid, dissolve, melt, (fig. also). With अनु- To follow, to run after. अभि- To attack. 2 To befall. उप- 1 To attack. -2 To hurt. प्र- To run away. प्रति— To run to. वि— 1 To run away.-2 To go, move.

द्रु 5 P. (द्रुणोति) 1 To hurt, injure. -2 To go. -3 To repent.

द्रु: *m*., द्रु *n*. 1 Wood. -2 Any instrument made of wood. -द्रू:*m*. 1 A tree. -2 A branch. —*f*. Motion. -Comp. -किलिमं *n*. The Devadâru tree.—घण: *m*. 1 A mallet, wooden mace. -2 An iron weapon made like a carpenter's hammer.-3 An axe,a hatchet. -4 An epithet of Brahman (*m*.). —घ्नी *f*. A hatchet.—नख: *m*. A thorn.

द्रुण: *m*. 1 A scorpion. -2 A bee. -3 A rogue. —णं *n*. 1 A bow. -2 A sword. -Comp. -ह: *m*. A sheath, scabbard.

द्रुणा *f*. A bow-string.

द्रुणि:, -णी *f*. 1 A small or female tortoise.-2 A bucket.-3A centipede.

द्रुत *p. p*. (*f*. -ता) 1 Quick, speedy. -2 Flown, run away, escaped. -3 Melted, dissolved. -4 Scattered, diffused. -5 Indistinct. -6 Moved, softened. —त: *m*. A scorpion. -2 A tree. -3 A cat. -तं *ind*. Quickly, swiftly,immediately.-Comp. -विलंबितं *n*. N. of a metre.

द्रुति: *f*. 1 Melting, dissolving. -2 Going, running away.

द्रुपद: *m*. N. of a king of the Pânchâlas. Comp. —आत्मज: *m*. An epithet of शिखंडिन, and of धृष्टद्युम्न. -आत्मजा *f*. An epithet of द्रौपदी.

द्रुम: *m*. 1 A tree. -2 A tree of Paradise. -Comp. —अरि: *m*. An elephant.-आमय: *m*. Lac, gum. -आश्रय: *m*. A lizard. —ईश्वर: *m*. 1 The palm tree. -2 The moon. -3 The पारिजात tree.—उत्पल: *m*. The Karnikâra tree. —नख:, —नर: *m*. A thorn. — व्याधि: *m*. Lac. gum. —श्रेष्ठ: *m*. The palm tree- —षंड *n*. A grove of trees.

द्रुमिणी *f*. An assemblage of trees.

द्रुवय: *m*. A measure (मानं).

द्रुह् 4 P. (द्रुह्यति, द्रुग्ध) 1 To bear malice or hatred.-2 To seek to injure, meditate mischief; (generally with the dat. of the object of hatred).

द्रुह् *a.* (At the end of comp).(Nom. sing. ध्रुक्, -ग, ध्रुट्, -ड्) Injuring, hurting, acting as an enemy against —*f.* Injury, damage.

द्रुहः *m.* 1 A son. -2 A lake. —ही *f.* A daughter.

द्रुहणः, द्रुहिणः *m* N. of Brahman (*m.*).

द्रूः *m* Gold

द्रूघणः *m.* A hammer, iron club.

द्रूणः *m.* A scorpion.—णं *n.* A bow.

द्रोणः *m.* A lake 400 poles long. -2 A cloud abounding in water. -3 A raven or a carrion crow. -4 A scorpion. -5 A tree (in general). -6 A tree bearing (white) flowers. -7 N. of the preceptor of the Kauravas and Pāṇḍavas. —णः *m.*, —णं *n.* A measure of capacity, either the same as an Adhaka or equal to 4 'Adhakas' or $\frac{1}{16}$ of a 'khāri,' or 32 or 64 *shers.* —णं *n.* 1 A wooden vessel or cup; bucket. -2 A tub. -Comp. —आचार्यः *m.* See द्रोणः above. — काकः, —काकलः *m.* A raven.-क्षीरा, -घा, —दुग्धा, -दुघा *f.* A cow yielding a *drona* of milk. — मुखं *n.* The capital of 400 villages.

द्रोणिः, —णी *f.* 1 An oval vessel of wood used for holding or pouring out water; a bucket. basin; baling-vessel. -2 A water-reservoir (जलाधार). -3 A trough for feeding cattle. -4 A measure of capacity equal to 128 *shers.* -5 The valley or chasm between two mountains. -6 N. of the wife of Drona.

द्रोहः *m.* 1 Plotting against, seeking to hurt or assail; mischief, malice. -2 Treachery, perfidy. -3 Wrong, offence. -4 Rebellion. -Comp. -अटः *m* 1 A religious impostor, hypocrite, impostor. -2 A hunter.

द्रौणायनः,-निः, द्रौणिः *m.* An epithet of Asvatthâman.

द्रौणी *f.* A tub, trough.

द्रौपदी *f.* N. of the daughter of Drupada.

द्रौपदेयः *m.* A son of Draupadi.

द्वंद्वः *m.* A plate on which hours are struck. —द्वं *n.* A pair, couple.

द्वंद्वं *n.* 1 A pair, a couple. -2 A couple of animals (including even men) of different sexes *i. e.* male and female. -3 A couple of opposite conditions or qualities, (such as सुख and दुःख, शीत and उष्ण). -4 A strife, dispute, fight. -5 A duel. -6 Doubt, uncertainty. -7 A fortress. -8 A secret. —द्वः *m.* 1 (In gram.) One of the four principal kinds of compounds, in which two or more words are joined together which, if not compounded, would stand in the same case and be connected by the copulative conjunction 'and'. -2 The sign Gemini of the zodiac. -Comp. —चर, —चारिन् *a.* Living in couples. (-रः, -री *m.*) The ruddy goose. -मोहः *m.* The trouble caused by doubt. —युद्धं *n.* A duel, a single combat.

द्वय *a.* (*f.* -यी) Two-fold, double, of two kinds or sorts.—यं *n.* 1 Pair, couple(usually at the end of comp.). -2 Two-fold nature, duplicity. -3 Untruthfulness. -4 (In gram.) The masculine and feminine gender. —यी *f.* A pair, couple. -Comp. -अतिग *a.* One whose mind is freed from the influence of the two bad qualities रजस् and तमस्; a saint or a virtuous man.-वादिन् *a.* Double-tongued, insincere. —हीन *a.* Of the neuter gender.

द्वयस *a.* (*f.* —सी) A termination

added to nouns to signify 'reaching to', 'as high or deep as', ' as far as'.

द्वापरः *m.*, -रं *n.* 1 N. of the third Yuga of the world. -2 The side of a die marked with two points. -3 Doubt, suspense, uncertainty.

द्वार् *f.* 1 A door, gate. -2 Access, way. -3 A means, an expedient. (द्वारा ' By means of, ' ' through'). -Comp. --स्थः, --स्थितः (द्वाःस्थः; द्वास्थः द्वाःस्थितः, द्वास्थितः) *m.* A door-keeper.

द्वारं *n.* 1 A door, gateway. -2 A passage,entrance, -3 An aperture of the human body. (The mouth, the two ears, the two nostrils, and the organs of excreetion and generation.) -4 Way, medium means. --री *f.* A door. -Comp. -अधिपः *m.* A porter, door-keeper. --कंटकः *m.* The bolt of a door. --कपाटः *m.*, --टं *n.* The leaf or panel of a door. -गोपः, -नायकः --पः, -पालः, -पालकः *m.* A door-keeper, porter, warder. --दारुः *m.* Teak-wood. -पट्टः *m.* 1 The panel of a door.-2 The curtain of a door. --पिंडी *f.* The threshold of a door. --पिधानः *m.* The bolt of a door. -बलिभुज् *m.* 1 A crow -2 A sparrow. -बाहुः *m.* A door-post,jamb. -यंत्रं *n.* A lock, bolt. --शाखा *f.* The leaf of a door. --स्थः *m.* A door-keeper.

द्वार (-रि-) का *f.* N. of the capital of Krishna on the western point of Gujarath. -Comp. --ईशः,--नाथः,-पतिः *m.* Epithets of Krishna.

द्वारवती, द्वारावती *f.* See द्वारका.

द्वारिकः,द्वारिन्*m.* A porter,door-keeper.

द्वि *num. a.* (Nom. du. द्वौ *m.*, द्वे *f.*, द्वे *n.*) ' Two , both. (N. B. In comp. द्वा is substituted for द्वि necessarily before दशन्, विंशति and त्रिंशत्, and optionally before चत्वारिंशत, पंचाशत षष्टि, सप्तति and नवति, द्वि remaining unchanged before अशीति). Comp. -अंगुल *a.* Two fingers long. --अणुकं *n.* An aggregate or molecule of two atoms; a diad.--अर्थ *a.* 1 Having two senses. -2 Ambiguous, equivocal. -3 Having two objects in view. --अशीत *a.* Eighty-second. --अशीतिः *f.* Eighty-two. --अष्टं *n.* Copper. --अहः *m* A period of two days. --आत्मक *a* 1 Having a double nature. -2 Being two. --आमुष्यायणः *m.* A son of two persons or fathers; an adopted son who remains heir to his natural father though adopted by another. --ऋचं (द्वृचं or द्व्यर्चं) *n.* A collection of two 'riks' or verses. --कः, -ककारः *m.* 1 A crow (there being two कs in the word काक). -2 The ruddy goose (there being two कs in the word कोक). --ककुद् *m.* A camel. -गु *a.* Exchanged for two cows. (-गुः *m.*) A sub-division of the Tatpurusha compound in which the first member is a numeral. --गुण *a.* Double, twofold.(द्विगुणाकृ To plough twice. द्विगुणीकृ To double, increase; द्विगुणीभूत *a.* Doubled, augmented). -गुणित *a.* 1 Doubled, multiplied by two. -2 Folded double. -3 Enveloped. --चत्वारिंश *a.* (द्वि-द्वा-चत्वारिंश) Forty-second. --चत्वारिंशत *f.* (द्वि-द्वा-चत्वारिंशत) Forty-two.--जः *m.* ' Twice-born ,' 1 A man of any of the first three castes of the Hindus (a Bráhmana, Kshatriya or Vaishya). -2 Brâhmana (over whom the Samskâras or purificatory rites are performed) -3 Any oviparous animal, such as a bird, snake, fish &c. -4 A tooth.--जन्मन्, -जातिः*m.* 1 A man of any of the first three castes of the Hindus.-2A Brâhmana.-3A bird.-4 A tooth. --जातीय*a.* 1 Belonging to the first three castes of the Hindus. -2 Of a twofold nature.-3 Of mixed origin, mongrel. (-यः *m*) A mule. -जिह्व *a.* 1 Double-tongued -2 (fig. also). Insincere. (-ह्वः *m.*) 1 A snake. -2 An informer. -3 An insincere person. -4 A thief. —ठः *m.* The sign *visarga* consisting of two dots. —त्राः *a. pl.* Two or three. —त्रिंश (द्वात्रिंश) *a.* 1 Thirty-second. -2 Consisting of thirty-two. —त्रिंशत् (द्वात्रिंशत्) *f.* Thirty-two. —दंडि *ind* Stick against stick. —दल *a.* Having two parts, two-leafed. —दश *a. pl.* Twenty. —दश *a.* (द्वादश) 1 Twelfth. -2 Consisting of twelve. -दशन् (द्वादशन्) *a. pl.* Twelve. —दशी (द्वादशी) *f.* The twelfth day of a lunar fortnight. —दशं (द्वादशं) *n.* A collection of twelve. —देवतं *n.* The constellation विशाखा. —देहः, -मातुः *m.* An epithet of Ganesa. —नवत (द्वि-द्वा नवत) *a* Ninety-second. —नवतिः (द्वि-द्वा-नवतिः) *f.* Ninety-two. —पः *m.* An elephant. —पक्षः *m.* 1 A bird. -2 A month. —पंचाश (द्वि-द्वा पंचाश) *a.* fifty-second. —पंचाशत् *f.* (द्वि-द्वा-पंचाशत्) Fifty-two. —पथं *n.* Two ways. -2 A cross-way. —पद् *m.* See द्विपाद् below. —पद् *a* Having two feet (as a verse). —पदः *m.* A biped; a man. -पाद्, -पादः *m.* 1 A biped, man. -2 A bird. -3 A god. —पायिन् *m.* An elephant. —बिंदुः *m.* A Visarga (:). —भुजः *m.* An angle. —भूम *a.* Having two floors (as a house). —मातृ, -मातृजः *m.* An epithet of 1 Ganesa. -2 Of King Jarâsandha. —मात्रः *m.* A long vowel (having two syllabic instants.) —मार्गी *f.* A cross-way. —मुखा *f.* A leech. —रः *m.* 1 A bee. —रदः *m.* An elephant. —रसनः *m.* A snake. —रात्रं *n.* Two nights. —रेतस् *m.* A mule. —रेफः *m.* A large black bee (there being two *ra's* in the word भ्रमर) —वचनं *n.* The dual number (in Gram.). —वाहिका *f.* A swing. —विंश (द्वाविंश) *a.* Twenty-second. —विंशतिः *f.* (द्वाविंशतिः) Twenty-two. —विध *a.* Of two kinds or sorts. —शतं *n.* 1 Two hundred. -2 One hundred and two. —शफ *a.* Cloven-footed. (—फः *m.*) Any cloven-footed animal. —शीर्षः *m.* An epithet of Agni. —षष्ट (द्विषष्ट, द्वाषष्ट) *a.* Sixty-second. —षष्टिः *f.* (द्विषष्टिः, द्वाषष्टिः) Sixty-two. —सप्तत (द्वि-द्वा-सप्तत) *a.* Seventy-second. —सप्ततिः *f.* (द्वि-द्वा-सप्ततिः) Seventy-two. —सप्ताहः *m.* A fortnight. —सहस्र, -साहस्र *a.* Consisting of 2000 —सीत्य, —हल्य *a.* Ploughed in two ways, *i. e.* first length-wise and then breadth-wise. —हप *m.* An elephant. —हायन, —वर्ष *a.* Two years old. —हीन *a.* Of the neuter gender. —हृदया *f.* A pregnant woman. —होतृ *m.* An epithet of Agni.

द्विक *a.* (*f.* -का) 1 Two-fold, forming a pair, consisting of two. -2 Second. -3 Happening the second time. -4 Increased by two, two per cent.

द्वितय *a.* (*f.* -यी) Consisting of, or divided into, two; double, two-fold. —यं *n.* A pair, couple.

द्वितीय *a.* (*f.* -या) Second. —यः *m.* 1 The second in a family, a son. -2 A companion, partner. —या *f.* 1 The second day of a lunar fortnight. -2 A wife, companion, partner. -3 (In gram.) The accusative case. —यं *n.* The half. —यं *ind.* A second time, again. -Comp. —आश्रमः *m.* The second stage or period of the religious life of a Brâhmana *i e.* गार्हस्थ्य.

द्वितीयक *a.* 1 Second; (also द्वितीयिक). -2 Happening the second time. -3 Returning every second day (as a fever).

द्वितीयाकृ 8 U. To plough twice

द्वितीयाकृत *a.* Ploughed twice (as a field).

द्वितीयिन् *a.* (*f.* -नी) Occupying the second place. [two ways.

द्विधा *ind.* 1 In two parts. -2 In

द्विष् 2 U (द्वेष्टि, द्विष्टे, द्विष्ट) To hate, dislike, be hostile towards.

द्विष् *a.* Hostile, hating, inimical. —*m.* An enemy.

द्विषः *m.* An enemy. (द्विषंतप *a.* Harassing an enemy, retaliating).

द्विषत् *m.* An enemy.

द्विष्ट *p. p.* (*f.* -ष्टा) 1 Hostile. -2 Hated, disliked. —ष्टं *n.* Copper.

द्विस् *ind.* Twice. -Comp. —आगमनं (द्विरागमनं) *n.* The ceremony of the second entrance of the bride into her husband's house. —आपः (द्विरापः) *m.* An elephant. —उक्त *a.* (द्विरुक्त) 1 Spoken twice; repeated. -2 Said in two ways.-3 Tautologous, superfluous. (—क्तं *n.*) Repetition. —उक्तिः *f.* (द्विरुक्तिः) 1 Repetition.-2 Superfluity, uselessness. -3 Twofold way of narration. —ऊढा (द्विरूढा) *f.* A woman married twice. —भावः*m.*,—वचनं *n.* Reduplication.

द्वीपः *m.*, —पं *n.* 1 An island. -2 A place of refuge or protection. -3 A division of the terrestrial world. —पं *n.* The skin of a tiger. -Comp. —कर्पूरः *m.* Camphor from China.

द्वीपवत् *a* Full of islands. —*m.* 1 A river. -2 The ocean. —ती *f.* 1 The earth. -2 A river.

द्वीपिन् *m.* 1 A tiger in general. -2 A leopard, panther. [twice.

द्वेधा *ind.* In two parts, in two ways,

द्वेषः *m.* 1 Hate, dislike, repugnance, distaste. -2 Enmity, hostility.

द्वेषणः *m.* An enemy. —णं *n.* Hate, hatred, enmity, dislike.

द्वेष्य *pot. p.* (*f.* -ष्या) 1 To be hated. -2 Odious, disagreeble.—ष्यः *m.* An enemy.

द्वैगुणिकः *m.* A usurer who charges cent. per cent. interest.

द्वैगुण्यं *n.* 1 Double amount or value.-2 Duality.-3 The possession of two out of the three qualities सत्त्व, रजस् and तमस्.

द्वैतं *n.* 1 Duality. -2 Dualism in philosophy; the assertion of two distinct principles. The doctrine that spirit and matter, Brahman(*n.*) and the universe, or the Individual and the Supreme Soul, are different from each other -3 N. of a forest. -Comp. —वनं *n.* N. of a forest. —वादः *m.* The doctrine of dualism. —वादिन् *m.* A philosopher who maintains the *dvaita* doctrine.

द्वैतिन् *m.* A philosopher who maintains the *dvaita* doctrine.

द्वैतीयीक *a.* (*f.* -की) Second.

द्वैध *a.* (*f* -धी) Two-fold, double. —धं *n.* 1 Duality, two-fold nature or state. -2 Separation into two parts. -3 Double resource. -4 Diversity, conflict, variance. -5 Doubt, uncertainty. -6 Double-dealing, one of the six modes of foreign policy. -7 Contradiction. —धं *ind.* 1 In two parts. -2 In two ways, doubly.

द्वैधीभावः *m.* 1 Duality, double state or nature.-2Separation into two, difference, diversity. -3 Doubt, uncertainty, suspense. -4 A dilemma. -5 One of the six modes of foreign policy. -6 A contest, dispute. -7 Falsehood, duplicity.

द्वैप *a.* (*f.* -पी) 1 Relating to or living on an island. -2 Belonging to a tiger; made of or covered with a tiger's skin. —पः *m.* A car covered with a tiger's skin —र्पं n. The skin of a tiger.

द्वैपक्षं n. Two parties. [Vyâsa.

द्वैपायन: m. 'The island-born,' N. of

द्वैप्य a. (f. -प्या, -प्यी). Living on or relating to an island

द्वैमातुरः m. 1 N. of Ganesa. -2 N. of Jarâsandha.

द्वैमातृक a. (f. —की) Nourished by rain and rivers (as a country).

द्वैरथं n. 1 A single combat in chariots. -2 A single combat in general. —थः m. An adversary.

द्वैराज्यं n. A dominion divided between two kings

द्वैविध्यं n. 1 Duality, two-fold nature. 2 Variance, difference.

ध.

धः m. 1 An epithet of Brahman (m.). -2 N. of Kubera. -3 Virtue, moral merit. —धं n. Wealth, property.

धक्क् 10 U. (धक्कयति,-ते) To destroy or annihilate.

धटः m. 1 A balance, a pair of scales. -2 The sign Libra of the zodiac.

धटकः m. A kind of weight equal to 42 Gunjâs.

धटिका, धटी f. 1 Old cloth or raiment. -2 A strip of cloth fastened round the loins or over the privities.

धटिन् m. 1 An epithet of Siva. -2 The sign Libra of the zodiac. -3 A dealer, trader.

धण् 1 P. (धणति) To sound.

धत्तूरः m., धत्तूरकः m., —का f. The white thorn-apple, (Mar. धोतरा).

धन् 1 P. (धनति) To sound.

धनं n. 1 Property, wealth, riches, money (gold, chattels &c.). Fig. also, as in तपोधन, विद्याधन &c. -2 Any valued possession, an object of affection or endearment. -3 A valuable article. -4 Capital (opp वृद्धि or interest). -5 A booty, spoil. -6 The reward given to a victor in a combat; the prize won in a game. -7 A contest for prizes, a match. -8 The lunar mansion called धनिष्ठा. -9 Surplus, residue. -10 (In math) The affirmative quantity or plus (opp. ऋण). -Comp. —अधिकारः m. The right to property; right of inheriting property. -अधिकारिन् m.,-अधिकृतः m. 1 A treasurer. 2 An heir. —अधिगोप्तृ, —अधिपः, —अधिपतिः,-अध्यक्षः m. 1 An epithet of Kubera. -2 A treasurer. —अपहारः m. 1 Fine. -2 Plunder. -अर्चित a. 1 Kept contented by valuable presents. -2 Wealthy, opulent. —अर्थिन् a Desiring or seeking for wealth; covetous, miserly. -आढ्य a. Rich.-आधारः m A treasury. —ईशः, -ईश्वरः m. 1 A treasurer. -2 An epithet of Kubera. —उष्मन् m. The warmth of wealth i. e. The power acquired by the possession of wealth. —एधिन् m. A creditor who claims his money. —केलिः m. An epithet of Kubera. —दः m. 1 A liberal or munificent man. -2 An epithet of Kubera. -3 N. of fire. —दंडः m. A punishment in the shape of a fine. —दायिन् m. Fire. —पतिः m. 1 An epithet of Kubera. -2 A treasurer. —पालः m. 1 A treasurer. -2 An epithet of Kubera. —पिशाचिका, —पिशाची f. The demon of wealth, an avaricious desire of wealth; greed, avarice. —प्रयोगः m. Usury. —मूलं n. Principal, capital —हरः m. 1 An heir. -2 A thief. -3 A kind of perfume.

धनकः m., - धनाया f. Avarice, greed, covetousness.

धनंजयः *m.* 1 N of Arjuna. -2 An epithet of fire. -3 N. of Vishnu. -4 A k nd of vital air nourishing the body.

धनवत् *a.* (*f.* —ती) Rich, wealthy. —ती *f.* N. of the constellation धनिष्ठा.

धनिकः *m.* 1 A rich or wealthy man. -2 A money-lender, creditor. -3 A husband. -4 An honest trader. -का *f.* 1 A virtuous woman. -2 A wife, young woman.

धनिन् *a.* (*f.* -नी) Rich, wealthy. —*m.* 1 A wealthy man. -2 A creditor. -3 The possessor of anything.

धनिष्ठ *a.* Very rich (Superl. of धनिन् or धनवत्). —ष्ठा *f.* N. of the twenty-third lunar mansion (consisting of four stars).

धनी, धनीका *f.* A young girl.

धनुः *m.* A bow (perhaps for धनुस्).

धनुस् *a.* Armed with a bow. —*n.* 1 A bow. -2 A measure of length equal to four *hastas*. -3 An arc of a circle. -4 The sign Sagittarius of the zodiac. -5 A desert. -Comp. —कर (धनुष्कर) *a.* Having, or armed with, a bow. (रः *m.*) A bow-maker. -कांडं (धनुःकांडं) *n.* A bow and arrow. —खंडं (धनुःखंडं) *n.* Part of a bow. —गुणः (धनुर्गुणः) *m.* A bow-string. —ग्रहः (धनुर्ग्रहः),— ग्राहः *m.* An archer. —ज्या (धनुर्ज्या) *f.* A bow-string. —द्रुमः (धनुर्द्रुमः) *m.* A bamboo. -धरः, -भृत् *m* An archer.-धारिन् *m.* An archer. -पाणि *a.* (धनुष्पाणि) Armed with a bow, having a bow in hand. —मत् (धनुष्मत्) *m.* An archer. —मार्गः (धनुर्मार्गः) *m.* A line curved like a bow, a curve. —विद्या (धनुर्विद्या) *f.* The science of archery. - वृक्षः (धनुर्वृक्षः) *m.* 1 A bamboo. -2 The अश्वत्थ tree. —वेदः (धनुर्वेदः) *m.* The science of archery, one of the four *Upavedas*.

धनू *f.* A bow. —*m.* A store of grain.

धन्य *a.* (*f.* —न्या) 1 Bestowing wealth. -2 Wealthy.-3 Blessed, fortunate, lucky, happy. -4 Excellent, virtuous. —न्यः *m.* 1 A lucky or blessed man, a fortunate being. -2 An infidel, an atheist. —न्या *f.* 1 A nurse. -2 Coriander.-न्यं *n.* 1 Wealth, treasure. -2 Coriander. -Comp. -वादः *m.* 1 An expression of thanks, thanks-giving. 2 Praise, applause.

धन्यंमन्य *a.* Considering oneself to be blessed or fortunate.

धन्याकं *n.* 1 A plant bearing a small pungent seed used as a condiment. -2 The seed of this plant (coriander).

धन्वं *n.* A bow (rarely used in classical literature). -Comp. —धिः *m.* A bow-case.

धन्वन् *m.*, *n.* 1 A dry soil, desert, waste. -2 Shore, firm land. -3 The sky -Comp. —दुर्गं *n.* A fort inaccessible on account of a surrounding desert.

धन्वंतरं *n.* A measure of distance or length equal to four *hastas*.

धन्वंतरिः *m.* N. of the physician of the gods. (He was produced at the churning of the ocean with a cup of nectar in his hand).

धन्विन् *a.* (*f.* -नी) 1 Armed with a bow. -2 Cunning, shrewd. —*m.* 1 An archer.-2 An epithet of Arjuna. -3 Of Siva. -4 Of Vishnu. -5 The sign Sagittarius of the zodiac.

धान्विनः *m.* A hog (शूकर).

धम *a.* (*f.* -मा or -मी) At the end of a comp.) 1 Blowing, *e. g.* अग्निधम, नाडिंधम. -2 Melting, fusing. —मः *m.* 1 The moon. -2 An epithet of Krishna. -3 Of Yama, the god of death. -4 Of Brahman(*m.*).

धमकः *m.* A blacksmith.

धमधमा *ind.* An onomatopoetic word expressive of the sound made by blowing with a bellows or a trumpet.

धमन *a.* (*f.* –ना) 1 Blowing. –2 Cruel. —नः *m.* A kind of reed.

धमनिः, —नी *f.* 1 A reed, blow-pipe. –2 A tube or canal of the human body (*i. e.* a vein, a nerve, &c) –3 Throat, neck.

धमिः *f.* The act of blowing.

धम्मलः, धम्मिलः, धाम्मिल्लः *m.* The braided and ornamented hair of a woman intermixed with flowers, pearls, &c.

धय *a.* (*f.* –या. At the end of comp.) Drinking, sucking, as in स्तनंधय.

धर *a.*(*f.* –रा or –री) (Usually at the end of comp.) Holding, carrying, wearing, containing, possessing. preserving, observing &c. as in अंशुधर, गदाधर, गंगाधर, महीधर, दिव्यांबरधर, &c. –रः *m.* 1 A mountain.–2 A flock of cotton. –3 A frivolous or dissolute man (विट). –4 The king of the tortoises *i. e.* Vishnu in his Kúrma incarnation.

धरण *a.* (*f.* –णी) Bearing, holding. —णः *m.* 1 A ridge of land serving the purpose of a bridge; the side of a mountain. –2 The world. –3 The sun. –4 The female breast. –5 Rice, corn. –6 The Himálaya. (as king of mountains). —णं *n.* 1 Supporting, sustaining.–2Possessing, bringing.–3 Prop, stay, support. –4 Security. –5 A measure of weight equal to ten *palas*.

धरणिः, –णी *f.* 1 The earth. –2 Ground, soil.–3 A beam for a roof.–4 A vein. -Comp. -कीलकः *m.* A mountain -जः,-पुत्रः, -सुतः *m.* 1 An epithet of Mars. –2 Of the demon Naraka. —जा, —पुत्री, —सुता *f.* An epithet of Sitâ, daughter of Janaka (as born from the earth). —धरः *m.* 1 An epithet of Sesha.–2 Of Vishnu. –3 A mountain. –4 A tortoise. –5 A king. –6 An elephant fabled to support the earth. —धृत *m.* 1 A mountain. –2 An epithet of Vishnu. –3 Of Sesha. –पतिः *m.* A king. -पूरः, —प्लवः *m.* The ocean. —भृद्‌ः *m.* 1 A king. –2 A mountain. –3 Vishnu. –4 Sesha. —मंडलं *n.* The globe. —रुहः *m.* A tree.

धरा *f.* 1 The earth. –2 A vein. –3 Marrow.–4 The womb or uterus.–5 A mass of gold or other valuables given as a present to Bráhmanas. -Comp. —अमरः, –देवः, —सुरः *m.* A Bráhmana. —आत्मजः, —पुत्रः, सूनुः *m.* 1 Epithet of the planet Mars. –2 Epithets of the demon Naraka. —आत्मजा *f.* An epithet of Sítá. —धरः *m.* 1 A mountain. -2 An epithet of Vishnu or Krishna. –3 Of Sesha. —भुज् *m.* A king. —भृत *m.* A mountain.

धरित्री *f.* 1 The earth. –2 Ground, soil.

धरिमन् *m.* A balance, pair of scales.

धत्तूरः *m.* The Dhattúra plant.

धर्त्रं *n.* 1 A house. –2 A prop, stay. –3 A sacrifice. –4 Virtue, moral merit.

धर्मः *m.* 1 Religion; the customary observances of a caste, sect &c. –2 Law, practice, custom. –3 Religious or moral merit, virtue, good works. –4 Duty, prescribed course of conduct. –5 Right, justice. –6 Piety, propriety, decorum. –7 Morality. –8 Nature, disposition, character. –9 An essential quality, peculiarity, characteristic property, (peculiar) attribute. –10 Manner, likeness. -11 A sacrifice. -12 Good company, associating with the virtuous. -13 Devotion. -14 Manner, mode. -15 An *Upanishad*. -6 N. of Yudhishthira, the eldest Pándava. -17 N. of Yama, the god of death. -18 (In astrol.) N. of the ninth lunar mansion. -19 The soul. -Comp. —अंगः *m.* (-गा *f.*) The Indian crane. —अधिकरणं *n.* 1 Administration of the laws.-2 A court of justice. (—णः *m.*) A judge, —अधिकरणिकः, अधिकारिन् *m* A judge, magistrate. —अधिकरणिन् *m.* A judge magistrate. —अधिकारः *m.* 1 Superintendence of religious affairs. -2 Administration of justice. -3 The office of a judge. —अधिष्ठानं *n.* A court of justice. —अध्यक्षः *m.* 1 A judge. -2 An epithet of Vishnu.—अनुष्ठानं *n.* Acting according to religion ; virtuous or moral conduct. —अनुसारः *m.* Conformity to virtue or justice. —अपेत *a.* Deviating from virtue; wicked, immoral. (-तं *n.*)Immorality, injustice. —अरण्यं *n.* A sacred or penance grove. —अर्थं *ind.* 1 For religious purposes. -2 Justly, according to justice or right. —अलीक *a.* Having a false character. —आगमः *m.* A religious statute, law-book. —आचार्यः *m.* 1 A religious teacher. -2 A teacher of law or customs. —आत्मजः *m.* A epithet of Yudhishthira. —आत्मन् *a.* Just, righteous, virtuous. (—*m.*) A saint, a pious man. —आसनं *n.* The throne of justice, court of justice, tribunal. —इंद्रः *m.* An epithet of Yudhishthira. —ईशः *m.* An epithet of Yama. —उत्तर *a.* Very just and impartial.—उपदेशः *m.* 1 Instruction in law or duty. -2 The collective body of law. —कर्मन्, —कार्य *n.*, —क्रिया *f.* 1 Any act of duty or religion; a religious act or rite. -2 Virtuous conduct. —कथादरिद्रः *m.* The *Kali* age. —कायः *m.* An epithet of Buddha. —कीलः *m.* A grant, royal edict or decree. —केतुः *m.* An epithet of Buddha. —कोशः, —षः *m.* The collective body of laws or duties. —क्षेत्रं *n.* 1 Bharatavaraha (the land of religion). -2 N. of a plain near Delhi, the scene of the great battle between the Kauravas and Pándavas. (-त्रः *m.*) A virtuous or pious man. —घटः *m.* A jar of fragrant water offered daily (to a Brahmana) in the month of Vaisákha.—चर्या *f.* Observance of the law, performance of religious duties. —चारिणी *f.* 1 A wife. -2 A chaste or virtuous wife. —चिंतनं *n.*, —चिंता *f.* The study of virtue; consideration of moral duties; moral reflection. —जः *m.* 1 A legitimate son.-2 N. of युधिष्ठिर. —जन्मन् *m.* N. of युधिष्ठिर. —जिज्ञासा *f.* An inquiry into religion or the proper course of conduct. —जीवन *a.* One who acts according to the rules of his caste and fulfils prescribed duties. (-नः *m.*) A Bráhmana who maintains himself by assisting other men in the performance of their religious rites. —ज्ञ *a.* 1 Knowing what is right; conversant with civil or religious law. -2 Righteous, pious. —त्यागः *m.* Apostacy. —दाराः (*m. pl.*) A lawful wife. —द्रोहिन् *m.* A demon. —धातुः *m.* An epithet of Buddha. —ध्वजः, —ध्वजिन् *m.* A religious hypocrite, an impostor. —नंदनः *m.* An epithet of युधिष्ठिर —नाथः *m.* A legal protector; rightful master. —नाभः *m.* An epithet of Vishnu. —निवेशः *m.* Religious devotion. —निष्पत्तिः *f.* 1

Discharge or fulfilment of duty. -2 Moral or religious observance. -पत्नी *f.* A lawful wife. -पथः *m.* The way of virtue, a virtuous course of conduct. -पर *a* Religiously-minded, righteous. --पाठकः *m.* A teacher of civil or religious law.--पालः *m.* Punishment or chastisement. --पीडा *f.* An offence against law. --पुत्रः *m.* A lawful son, a son begotten from a sense of duty and not from mere sensual pleasure. -2 An epithet of युधिष्ठिर. 3 Any one regarded as a son for religious purposes, a spiritual son. --प्रवक्तृ *m.* I An expounder of the law; a legal adviser. -2 A religious teacher, preacher. --प्रवचनं *n.* I The science of duty. -2 Expounding the law. (-नः *m.*) An epithet of Buddha.. -बाणिजिकः, -वाणिजिकः *m.* I One who tries to make profit out of his virtue like a merchant. --भगिनी *f.* I A lawful sister. -2 A daughter of the spiritual preceptor. -3 A spiritual sister, any one regarded as a sister from discharging the same religious duties. -भागिनी *f.* A virtuous wife. --भाणकः *m.* A public reader of sacred books like the Bhârata, Bhágavata &c. --भ्रातृ *m.* I A fellow religious student;a spiritual brother.-2 Any one regarded as a brother from discharging the same religious duties. -महामात्रः *m.* A minister of religion. -मूलं *n.* The foundation of civil or religious law: the Vedas. --युगं *n* The Krita age. --यूपः *m.* An epithet of Vishnu. -रति *a.* 'Delighting in virtue or justice,' righteous, just.--राजः *m.* An epithet of I Yama. -2 Jina. -3 युधिष्ठिर. -4 A king. --राजन् *m.* N. of युधिष्ठिर. --लक्षणं *n.* The essential mark of law. -2 The Vedas. (-णा *f.*) The Mîmâmsá philosophy. --वासरः *m.* The day of full moon. --वाहनः *m.* I An epithet of Siva. -2 A buffalo (being the vehicle of Yama).-विद्या *f.* Knowledge of the law.-विधिः *m.* A legal precept or injunction. -विप्लवः *m.* Violation of duty, immorality. --वीरः *m.* (in Rhet.) The sentiment of heroism arising out of virtue or piety; the sentiment of chivalrous piety. --वृद्ध *a.* Advanced in virtue or piety. --वैतंसिकः *m.* One who gives away money unlawfully acquired in the hope of appearing generous. --शाला *f.* I A court of justice, tribunal. -2 Any charitable institution. -शासनं, -शास्त्रं *n.* A code of laws;jurisprudence. --शील *a.* Pious, virtuous. -संहिता *f.* A code of laws (especially compiled by sages like Manu, Yájnavalkya &c.). --संगः *m.* I An attachment to justice or virtue. -2 Hypocrisy. -सभा *f.* A court of justice. --स्थः *m.* A judge.

धर्मयु *a.* Virtuous, pious.

धर्मिन् *a.* (*f.* -णी) I Virtuous, pious. -2 Knowing one's duties. -3 Obeying the law. -4Having the peculiar properties or characteristics of any thing (at the end of comp.).-5 Following the habits of any person. --*m.* An epithet of Vishnu.

धर्मीपुत्रः *m.* An actor, player.

धर्म्य *a.* (*f.* --र्म्या). I Righteous, lawful, legal. -2 Religious (as an act). -3 Just, fair. -4 Legitimate. -5 Usual.

धर्षः *m.* I Boldness, haughtiness, impudence. -2 Pride, arrogance.-3 Impatience. -4 Restraint. -5 Violation, seduction (of a woman). -6 Wrong,insult.-7 A eunuch.-Comp. --कारिणी *f.* A violated woman.

धर्षक *a.* (*f.* —का) 1 Assailing, assaulting. -2 Violating, seducing. -3 Impatient. —कः *m.* 1 A seducer, an adulterer. -2 An actor, dancer.

धर्षणं *n.*,-णा *f.* 1 Boldness; insolence. -2 Insult. -3 An assault, seduction. -4 Copulation. 5 Contempt, disrespect.-6 Abuse.-7 Arrogance.

धर्षणिः,-णी *f.* A disloyal or wanton woman, a harlot.

धर्षित *a.* (*f.*-ता) 1 Seduced; outraged. -2 Overpowered, defeated. -3 Ill-treated, insulted. —तं *n.* 1 Pride. -2 Cohabitation. -3 Impatience. —ता *f.* A harlot, unchaste woman.

धवः *m.* 1 Shaking, trembling.-2 A man. -3 A husband, as in विधवा. -4 A master, lord. -5 A cheat. -6 A kind of tree.

धवल *a.* (*f.* -ला) 1 White. -2 Handsome. -3 Clear, pure.—लः *m.* 1 The white colour.-2 An excellent bull. 3 China camphor.-4 N. of a tree (धव). —लं *n.* White pepper. —ला *f.* A woman with a white complexion.—ली *f.* A white cow (धवला also) -Comp. —गिरिः *m.* N. of the highest peak of the Himâlaya mountain. —गृहं *n.* A house whitened with chunam; a palace. —पक्षः *m.* 1 A goose. -2 The bright half of a lunar month. —मृत्तिका *f.* Chalk.

धवलित *a* (*f.* —ता) Whitened.

धवलिमन् *m.* 1 Whiteness, white colour. -2 Paleness.

धवित्रं *n.* A fan made of the deer's skin (Also धुवित्रं.).

धा 3 U (दधाति, धत्ते,धातुं, हित; *pass* धीयते; *Caus.* धापयति,-ते *desid.* धित्सति,-ते 1 To put, place, lay on or upon. -2 To direct (the mind or thoughts &c.) towards (with dat. or loc.). -3 To grant, confer, present (with dat., gen. or loc.) -4 To hold, contain. -5 To wear, put on, bear. --To assume, exhibit, possess; *e. g.* काचः कांचनसंसर्गाद्धत्ते मारकतीं द्युतिं. -7 To sustain, bear up. -8 To support, maintain. -9 To cause, produce, make. -10 To suffer, incur. -11 To perform, do. -12 To appoint, fix. [The meanings of this root, are variously modified according to the word with which it is connected; *e. g.* मनः, मतिं, धियं &c. धा To fix the mind or thoughts upon, resolve upon. पदं धा To set foot on, to enter]. With अतिसम्— To deceive. अंतर्— 1 To cover, conceal. -2 To obscure, to put into the background अनुसम्- 1 To search, investigate. -2 To collect. अपि— (Sometimes अ is dropped). 1 To cover, conceal, shut. -2 To hinder, obstruct, bar. अभि— 1 To speak, declare, communicate. -2 To signify directly or primarily. *e.g.* हरि शब्दो विष्णुमेवाभिधत्ते. अभ्या- To throw under. अभिसम्- 1 To aim at, to have in view. 1 To deceive. -2 To win over; to make friendship with. -4 To fix (as an arrow). अव— To give attention to, to be attentive. आ— (Usually Atm.) 1 To put, place. -2 To fix upon, to direct towards. -3 To bear, support, uphold. -4 To create, produce. -5 To take, to assume. -6 To employ, to appoint. -7 To perform (as a व्रत). आविस्— To manifest. उप-1 To place under, in, or on. -2 To employ, to apply; *e. g.* क्रिया हि वस्तूपहिता प्रसीदति * रघुवं.3.29, 3 To make over to. -4 To use as a pillow. -5 To cover. उपा— 1 To put on. -2 To create. तिरस्— 1 To hide. -2 (Atm.) To disappear. नि— 1 To place, put down. -2 To bury, to conceal. -3 To deposit. -4 To entrust. -5 To restrain, to allay. परि— 1 To put on (as a garment) -2 To surround. -3 To direct towards. पुरस्— 1 To put at the head of. -2 To take as a family-priest. प्रणि— 1 To lay down, to put down, to prostrate. -2 To set, put in, to fix. -3To stretch out, to extend. -4 To direct towards. -5 To send out spies. प्रवि— 1 To do, make. -2 To divide. प्रतिवि— 1 To despatch, to dispose of. -2 To undo, repair, retaliate. वि— 1 To do, cause, effect, accomplish.-2 To command, to lay down (as a rule). -3 To form, to manufacture, shape. -4 To perform. -5 To appoint. व्यव— 1 To intervene, to screen. सम्— 1 To combine, to join, unite. -2 To make an alliance, to enter into a treaty. -3 To direct towards, to fix upon. -4 To put on the bow (as an arrow). -5 To produce, cause. -6 To be a match for. समा— 1 To put, place, apply. -2 To place on the throne. -3 To fix or concentrate upon. -4 To tranquilize. -5 To redress. -6 To satisfy, to remove a doubt or objection. -7 To think, ponder over. संनि— 1 To place,put, keep. -2 To draw near, approach.

धाकः *m.* 1 An ox. -2 A receptacle, reservoir. -3 Food.-4 A post,pillar, column. -5 A supporter.

धाटी *f.* Assault, attacking.

धाणकः *m.* A gold coin (part of a Dînâra).

धातुः *m.* 1 A constituent or essential part, an ingredient. -2 An element *i. e.* पृथिवी, अप्, तेजस्, वायु and आकाश. -3 A secretion, primary fluid or juice of the body (which are considered to be 7:—रसासृङ्मांसमेदोऽस्थिमज्जाशुक्राणि धातवः).-4 A humour or affection of the body (*i. e.* वात, पित्त and कफ). -5 A mineral, metal. -6 A verbal root. -7 The soul. -8 The Supreme Spirit. -9 An organ of sense. -10 Any one of the properties of the five elements. *i. e.* रूप, रस, गंध, स्पर्श and शब्द.-11 A bone. -12 A part, portion. -13 A fluid mineral of a red colour. -Comp. —उपलः *m.* Chalk. —काशीसं, —कासीसं *n.* Red sulphate of iron. —क्रिया *f.* Metallurgy, mineralogy. —क्षयः *m.* Waste of the bodily humours, a kind of consumption. —जं *n.* Bitumen. —द्रावकः *m.* Borax.—पः *m* The alimentary juice, the chief of the seven essential ingredients of the body. -पाठः*m.*A list of roots arranged according to Pânini's grammatical system. —भृत *m.* A mountain. —मलं *n.* 1 Impure excretion of the essential fluids of the body. -2 Lead. —माक्षिकं *n.* Sulphuret of iron. —मारिन *m.* Sulphur. —राजकः*m.*, -कं *n.* Semen. —वल्लभं *n.* Borax. —वादः *m.* Mineralogy, metallurgy. —वादिन *m.* A mineralogist. —वैरिन *m* Sulphur. —शेखरं *n.* Green sulphate of iron, green vitriol. —शोधनं ,-संभवं *n.* Lead.—साम्यं *n* Good health.—हन् *m.* Sulphur.

धातृ *m.* 1 A maker.creator,author -2 A bearer, supporter. -3 An epithet of Brahman (*m.*), the creator of the world. -4 An epithet of Vishnu. -5 The soul. -6 N. for the seven sages (सप्तर्षि) being the first creation of Brahman(*m.*). -7 A married woman's paramour.-8

An arranger.-9One who nourishes.

धात्रं *n.* A vessel for holding anything, a receptacle.

धात्री *f.* 1A nurse, wet-nurse, foster-mother.-2 A mother.-3 The earth.-4 The tree called आमलक.-Comp.-पुत्रः *m.* 1. A foster brother. -2 An actor. -फलं *n.* An Amalaka fruit.

धात्रेयिका, धात्रेयी *f* 1 A foster-sister. -2A nurse. wet-nurse.

धानं *n.*,-नी*f.*1 A receptacle, seat. *e.g.* मसिधानी, राजधानी, यमधानी.-2Nourishing, nourishment. —नी *f.* 1 The site of a habitation. -2 Coriander.

धानाः *f. pl.* 1 Fried barley or rice. -2 Grain fried or powdered.-3 Corn, grain. -4A bud, shoot.-5Coriander.

धानुर्दंडिक, धानुष्कः *m.* An archer (living by the bow); a bowman.

धानुष्यः *m.* Bamboo.

धान्धा *f.* Cardamoms.

धान्यं *n.* 1 Grain, corn. Corn before thrashing, winnowing and unhusking. -2 Coriander.-3 A measure equal to four sesamum seeds. -Comp. -अस्थि *n.* Husk, chaff.—उत्तमः *m.* The best of grain *i. e.* rice. —कल्कं *n.*1 Bran. -2 Chaff, straw. -कोशः, -कोष्ठकं *n.*, -कः *m.* A granary. —चमसः *m.* Rice flattened by thrashing after it has been steeped and fried in the husk. -त्वच् *f.* The husk of corn.—मायः *m.* A corn-dealer. —राजः *m.* Barley. —वर्धनं *n.* Lending grain at interest, usury with grain. —वीरः *m.*A sort of pulse (माष). —शीर्षकं *n.*An ear of corn. -शूकं *n.* The beard or awn of corn. —सारः *m.* Thrashed corn.

धान्या *f*, धान्याकं *n.* Coriander.

धान्वन *a.* (*f.* -नी) Situated in a desert.

धामकः *m.* A sort of weight (the same as माष).

धामन् *n.* 1 A dwelling-place, residence, house. -2 A place, site. -3 The inmates of a house. members of a family. -4 A ray of light. -5 Light, luster. -6 Majestic glory, dignity.-7 Power, strength, energy. -8 Birth. -9 The body.-10 A troop, host. -11 A class. -Comp.—कोशेर, —निधिः *m.* The sun.

धामनिका, धामनी *f.* Same as धमनी.

धार *a.* (*f.* -रा) 1 Holding supporting. -2 Streaming, flowing. -रः *m.* 1 An epithet of Vishnu. -2 A sudden and violent shower of rain. -3 Snow, hail. -4 A deep place. -5 Debt. -6 A boundary, limit. -7 A sort of stone.

धारकः *m.* 1 A vesssel of any kind (box, trunk &c.); a water-pot. -2 A debtor.

धारण *a.*(*f.*-णी)Holding, carrying, preserving, protecting, having, assuming. —णं *n.* 1 The act of holding, supporting, preserving, or keeping back. -2 Possessing, possession.-3Observing or holding a fast. -4 Retaining in the memory. -5 Being indebted (to any one). -6 Steady abstraction of the mind. -7 Restraining. -8 (In gram.) Pronouncing imperfectly. —णी *f.* 1 A row or line. -2 A vein or tubular vessel. -3 Steadiness.

धारणकः *m.* A debtor.

धारणा *f.* 1 The act of holding, supporting or preserving.-2 The faculty of retaining in the mind, retentive memory. -3 Memory in general. -4 Holding the breath suspended; steady abstraction of mind; परिचेतुमुपांशु धारणां *रघुवं.8,18. -5 Fortitude, firmness, steadiness. -6 A fixed precept or injunction, a settled rule, conclusion; इतिधर्मस्य धारणा * मनुस्मृ. 8

184. -7 Understanding, intellect.-8 Propriety, decorum.-9 Abstraction. -Comp. —शक्तिः f. A retentive memory.

धारयित्री f. The earth.

धारा f. 1 A stream or current of water, a line of descending fluid.-2 A shower, a hard or sharp-driving shower. -3 A continuous line or series. -4 A leak or hole in a pitcher. -5 The pace of a horse. -6 The margin or border of anything. -7 The sharp edge of a sword, axe or of any cutting instrument. -8 The edge of a mountiain or precipice. -9 A wheel or the periphery of a wheel -10 A garden-wall, fence, hedge. -11 The front line of an army. -12 The highest point, excellence. -13 A multitude. -14 Fame. -15 Night. -16 The tip of the ear. -17 Speech.-18 Rumour, report.-Comp. —अग्रं n. The broad-edged head of an arrow. —अंकुरः m. 1 A drop of rain. -2 Hail. -3 Advancing before the line of an army. —अंगः m. A sword. —अटः m. 1 The Chátaka bird. -2 A horse. -3 A cloud. -4 A furious elephant, one in rut. —ऊधिरूढ a. Raised to the highest pitch. —अवनिः f. Wind. —अश्रु n. A flood of tears. —आसारः m. A heavy down-fall of rain. —उष्ण a. Warm from a cow (as milk). —गृहं n. A bath room with water-jets.—धरः m. 1 A cloud.-2 A sword. —निपातः, -पातः m. 1 A fall of rain, a hard or pelting shower.-2 A stream of water. —यंत्रं n. A fountain, jet (of water). -वर्षः m.,-र्षं n.,-संपातः m. A hard incessant shower. —वाहिन् a. incessant, continuous. —विषः m. A crooked sword.

धारिणी f. The earth.

धारित्र a. (f. -णी) 1 Carrying, bearing; sustainiug, holding, supporting. -2 Keeping in one's memory, possessed of retentive memory. -3 Edged.

धार्तराष्ट्रः m. 1 A son of Dhritarâshtra. -2 A sort of goose with black legs and bill.

धार्मिक a. (f. -की) 1 Righteous, just, virtuous. -2 Resting on right, equitable. -3 Religious.

धार्मिणं n. An assemblage of virtuous men.

धार्ष्ट्यं n. Arrogance, insolence, impudence, rudeness.

धाव् 1 P. (धावति, धावित) 1 To run, advance, move, glide. -2 To advance against, assault, encounter. -3 To flow, stream or flow forth. -4 To run or flee away. -5 To give milk (as a cow).

धाव् 1 U. (धावति,-ते, धौत or धावित) 1 To wash, cleanse, purify, rub off. -2 To brighten. With निस्- To wash off. polish. -3 To rub into one's person (Atm.).

धावकः m. 1 A washerman. -2 N. of a poet.

धावनं n. 1 Running, galloping. -2 Flowing. -3 Attacking. -4 Cleansing, rubbing, washing off. -5 Rubbing with anything.

धावल्यं n. 1 Whiteness. -2 Paleness.

धि 6 P. (धियति) To hold, have, possess.-With सं- To make peace, treat with.

धिः (At the end of comp. only) A receptacle, reservoir, as in उदधि, इषुधि, जलधि &c.

धिक् ind. An interjection of censure, menace or displeasure; ('fie' 'shame,' 'out upon,' 'what a pity' &c. usually with acc. and sometimes with nom., voc. and gen. also.

–Comp. -कारः *m*, –कृतिः *f*. Reproach, contempt, disregard. –दंडः *m*. A reprimand, censure. –पारुष्यं *n*. Abuse, reproach, reviling.

धिक्ष 8 U. To despise, disregard, reproach.

धिन्व् 5 P. (धिनोति) To delight, to please.

धिप्सु *a*. Wishing to deceive.

धिषण: *m*. N. of Brihaspati, preceptor of the gods. –णं *n*. A dwelling-place, a residence. –णा *f* 1 Speech. –2 Praise, hymn. –3 Intellect, understanding. –4 Earth. –5 A cup, bowl. –Comp. –अधिप: *m*. N. of Brihaspati.

धिष्ण्य: *m*. 1 A place for the sacrificial fire –2 N. of Sukra, preceptor of the demons. –3 The planet Venus. –4 Power, strength. –ष्ण्यं *n*. 1 A seat, site, place, house. –2 A meteor. –3 Fire (*m*. also). –4 A star, an asterism.

धी: *f*. 1 Intellect, understanding. –2 Mind. –3 Idea, fancy, conception. –4 A thought, purpose, propensity. –5 Devotion, prayer. –6 Knowledge, science. –Comp. –इंद्रियं *n*. An organ of perception (ज्ञानेंद्रिय). –पति: (धियांपति:) *m*. Brihaspati, the preceptor of the gods. –मत (धीमत) *a*. Wise, intelligent, learned —*m*. An epithet of Brishaspati. –मंत्रिन *m*.. –सचिव: *m*. 1 A minister for counsel (opp. कर्मसचिव a minister for action or execution). –2 A wise or prudent adviser. –शक्ति: *f*. Intellectual quality or faculty. –सख: *m*. An adviser, minister.

धीत *a*. (*f*. –ता) 1 Sucked, drunk. –2 Thought about. –3 Propitiated.

धीति: *f*. 1 Drinking, sucking. –2 Thirst.

धीर *a*. (*f*. –रा) 1 Brave, bold, courageous. –2 Steady, firm, lasting constant. –3 Persevering, resolute of firm purpose. –4 Composed calm. –5 Sober, solemn. –6 Strong energetic. –7 Prudent, intelligent sensible, learned, clever. –8 Deep grave, loud, hollow (as sound). –9 Well-behaved. –10 Gentle, agreeable, pleasing (as a breeze). –11 Lazy, dull. –12 Daring. –13 Headstrong. –र: *m*. 1 The ocean. –2 An epithet of Buddha. –3 The soul (चिदात्मन्). –4 An epithet of king Bali. –रं *n*. Saffron. –रं *ind*. Boldly, firmly, steadfastly, steadily –Comp. –उदात्त: *m*. The hero of a poetic composition (*i. e*. a play or poem) who is brave and noble minded. –उद्धत: *m* The hero of a poetic composition who is brave but haughty. –प्रशांत: *m*. The hero of a poetic composition who is brave and calm. –ललित: *m*. The hero of a poetic compostion who is firm and brave, but sportive and reckless –स्कंध: *m*. A buffalo.

धीरता *f*. 1 Fortitude, courage strength of mind. –2 Gravity, solemnity (as shown by silence &c.) –4 Steadiness, firmness. –5 Wisdom cleverness. –6 Refusal. (For other meanings see धैर्य).

धीरा *f* The heroine of a poetic composition who though jealous of her husband or lover, suppresses all outward manifestation or expression of her resentment in his presence. –Comp. –अधीरा *f*. The heroine of a poetic composition who, being jealous of her husband or lover alternately expresses and conceals her jealousy.

धीलटिः,-टी *f.* A daughter.

धीवरः *m.* A fisherman. -रं *n.* Iron. —री *f.* 1 A fisherman's wife. -2 A fish-basket.

धु 5 U. (धुनोति, धुनुते, धुत) See धू.

धुक्ष् 1 A. (धुक्षते, धुक्षित) 1 To be kindled. -2 To be weary. —With सं- To be kindled or excited (fig. also). (*Caus.* धुक्षयति,-ते) To kindle, inflame, excite.

धुत *a.* (*f.* —ता) 1 Shaken.-2 Abandoned.

धुनय् Den. P. 1 To sound, roar. -2 To flow.

धुनिः,-नी *f.* A river. -Comp. -नाथः *m.* The ocean.

धुर् *f.* (Nom. sing. धूः) 1 A yoke. (lit.) -2 That part of a yoke which rests on the shoulder. -3 The foremost part of the pole where the yoke is fixed. -4 The pin at both ends of an axle for fastening the nave of the wheel. -5 The shaft or pole of a carriage. -6 A load, burden (fig. also); responsibility, duty, task. -7 The front, top, head. -Comp.-गत (धुर्गत) *a.* 1 Standing on the pole of a chariot.-2 Standing at the head, chief, head, foremost. —जटिः (धूर्जटिः) *m.* An epithet of Siva. —धर (धूर्धर, also धुरंधर) *a.* 1 Bearing the yoke. -2 Fit to be harnessed. -3 Laden with good qualities or important duties. -4 Foremost, pre-eminent. (—रः *m.*) 1 A beast of burden. -2 A man of business. -3 A chief, leader. —वह (धूर्वह) *a.* 1 Carrying or bearing a burden. -2 Managing affairs. (-हः *m.*) A beast of burden.

धुरंधर See धूर्धर above.

धुरा *f* A burden, load.

धुरीण, धुरीय *a.*(*f* —णा,—या) 1 Able to bear or carry a burden. -2 Fit to be harnessed. -3 Charged with important duties. —णः, —यः *m.* 1 A beast of burden. -2 A man of business. -4 Chief, leader.

धुर्य *a.* (*f.* —र्या) 1 Fit for, or able to bear, a burden. -2 Fit to be entrusted with important duties. -3 Chief, foremost. —र्यः *m.* 1 A beast of burden. -2 A horse or bullock yoked to the pole of a carriage. -3 One who bears a responsibility. -4 A leader, head. -5 One who is charged with important duties. -र्यं *n.* The forepart of a pole.

धुवित्रं *n.* A sort of fan (made of deer-skin) used in kindling the sacred fire.

धुस्तु (-स्तू-) रः *m.* N. of a plant (=धत्तूर q. v.)

धू 6. P., 1. 5. 9. 10. U. (धुवति, धवति-ते, धूनोति, धूनुते, धूनाति, धूनीते, धूनयति-ते, धूत-धून) 1 To shake, cause to move or tremble. -2 To shake off, throw off; destroy. -3 To kindle, excite, (as fire). -4 To treat roughly, hurt, injure. -5 To oppose.

धूः *f.* Shaking, trembling, agitating.

धूत *p. p.* (*f.* —ता) 1 Shaken. -2 Shaken off, removed. -3 Fanned. -4 Abandoned.-5 Disregarded, treated with contempt. -6 Guessed.

धूतिः *f.* 1 Shaking -2 Fanning.

धून *p. p.* (*f.* —ना) Shaken.

धूननः *m.* Wind. —नं *n.* Shaking.

धूनिः *f.* Shaking, agitating.

धूप् 1 P. (धूपायति, धूपायित) 1 To heat. -2 To be heated.

धूप् 10 U (धूपयति,-ते, धूपित) 1 To fumigate, perfume, to make fragrant. -2 To shine. -3 (In astr.) To obscure with mist; to eclipse.

धूपः *m.* 1 Incense, frank-incense, perfume, any fragrant substance.

-2 The vapour proceeding from any fragrant substance. -3 A fragrant powder -Comp. —अगुरु n. A kind of agallochum used for incense. —अंग: m. 1 Turpentine. -2 The Sarala tree. —अर्हं n. A black kind of agallochum. —वास: m. Fumigating, perfuming.

धूप (-पि-) कः m. A perfumer.

धूपनं m. 1 Fumigation, perfuming. -2 Incense.

धूम: n. 1 Smoke, vapour. -2 Mist, haze. -3 A meteor or the fall of a meteor. -4 A cloud. -5 Smoke inhaled (as a sternutatory). -6 Belch, eructation. -Comp. —उत्थं n. Ammoniac. —उद्गार: m. 1 Issuing of smoke or vapour. -2 Eructation, belch. —ऊर्णा f. N. of the wife of Yama. —केतन:, -केतु: m. 1 Fire. -2 A meteor, comet, falling star. -3 Ketu. -ग्रह: m. Rāhu. —ज: m. A cloud. —ध्वज: m. Fire. -पथ: m. 1 A sacrifice. -2 Seeking salvation by religious works. -3 An air-hole, a window. —पानं n. Inhaling smoke or vapour. —महिषी f Fog, mist. —योनि: m. A cloud.

धूमल a (f. —ला) Smoke-coloured, brownish-red, purple.

धूमिका f. Vapour, fog, mist.[of fire.

धूमिनी f N. of one of the tongues

धूम्या f. A volume or cloud of smoke, thick smoke.

धूम्र a. (f. —म्रा) 1 smoke-coloured, smoky. -2 Dark red. -3 Dark, obscured. —म्र: m. 1 A mixture of red and black. -2 Incense. -3 Purple (the colour). —म्रं n. Sin, vice, wickedness. -Comp. —लोचन: m. A pigeon. —लोहित a. Dark-red, deep-purple. (—त: m.) An epithet of Siva. —शूक: m. A camel.

धूम्रक: m. A camel

धूर्त a. (f. —र्ता) 1 Cunning, roguish, crafty. -2 Mischievous, injurious. -4 Gay, licentious. —र्त: m. 1 A cheat, swindler. -2 A gamester. -3 A lover, gallant, gay deceiver. -4 The thorn-apple (धतूर). -5 Hurting, injuring. -Comp. —कृत a. Crafty, dishonest. (-m.) The Dhattura plant. —जंतु: m. A man.

धूर्तक: m. 1 A jackal. -2 A rogue.

धूर्वी f. The fore-part or pole of a carriage.

धूलकं n. Poison.

धूलि: m. f, धूली f. 1 Dust. -2 Powder. -Comp. —कुट्टिमं n., —केदार: m. 1 A mound, rampart of earth. -2 A ploughed field. —ध्वज: m. Wind. —पटल: m., —अं n. A cloud of dust. —पुष्पिका, —पुष्पी f. The Ketaka plant.

धूलिका f. Fog, mist.

धूसर a. (f. —रा) Of a greyish colour, grey —र: m. 1 The grey colour. -2 A donkey. -3 A camel. -4 pigeon. -5 An oilman.

धृ 6 A. (ध्रियते, धृत) 1 To be or exist, live. -2 To remain, continue. -3 To resolve upon.

धृ 10 U. (धारयति, -ते, धृत, धारित) 1 To hold, bear, carry. -2 To maintain, support, sustain. -3 To possess, have, keep. -4 To assume, take (as a form, disguise &c.) to wear, put on, use (clothes, ornaments &c.). -5 To curb, restrain, detain. -6 To fix upon, direct towards (with dat. or loc.) e. g. मनोदधे राजसूयाय. -7 To suffer, undergo. -8 To allot, assign. -9 To owe anything to a person (with dat. ; rarely gen. of person, 10 only in this sense) e. g वृक्षसेचने द्वे धारयासि मे * शाकुंत. 1; तस्मै-तस्य वा धनं धारयाते. -10 To hold, contain. -11 To observe, practise. (The senses of this root may be variously modified according to the noun with which it is connected ; *e. g.* मनसा धृ To bear in mind, remember. शिरसा or मूर्ध्नि धृ To bear on the head, respect highly. अंतरे धृ To pledge, deposit anything as surety. दंडं धृ To punish, chastise, use force. जीवितं, प्राणान्, शरीरं, गात्रं, देहं &c. धृ To continue to live. व्रतं धृ To observe a vow. मनः, मतिं, चित्तं, बुद्धिं धृ To fix the mind upon, think of, resolve upon.) With अव- 1 To fix, determine. -2 To know, understand. उत्— 1 To save, lift up. -2 To draw out. निस्- To verify, determine accurately. वि— 1 To seize. -2 To wear, bear. -3 To maintain, support. सम्— 1 To hold, bear. -2 To restrain, curb. -3 To retain in the mind. समुद् – 1 To pull out by roots, to take out. -2 To deliver. संप्र— To consider, think of. -2 To ascertain, determine.

धृत *p. p.* (*f.* —ता) 1 Held, carried, supported. -2 Possessed. -3 Kept, retained. -4 Seized, grasped. -5 Worn, used, put on. -6 Placed, deposited. -7 Practised, observed. -8 Weighed. -Comp. —आत्मन् *a.* Firm-minded, steady. —दीधितिः *m.* Fire. —राजन् *m.* A country governed by a good king. -राष्ट्रः *m.* 1 A good king -2 A country ruled by a good king. -3 N. of the eldest son of Vyása by a widow of विचित्रवीर्य. —वर्मन् *a.* Clad in armour, mailed. —व्रत *a.* 1 Observing vows, performing religious rites. -2 Devoted, attached. -3 Of a fixed law or order. (-तः) *m.* An epithet of (1) Indra, (2) Varuna. (3) Agni.

धृतिः *f.* Taking, seizing. -2 Firmness, steadiness, constancy.-3 Fortitude, courage, self-command. -4 Satisfaction, contentment, pleasure, happiness, joy.-5 Satisfaction considered as one of the 33 subordinate feelings (In rhetoric).

धृतिमत् *a.* 1 Firm, steady, resolute. -2 Satisfied, happy, glad

धृत्वन् *m.* 1 An epithet of Vishnu. -2 Of Brahman (*m.*). -3 Virtue, morality. -4 The sky. -5 The sea. -6 A clever man.

धृष् 1 P. (धर्षति, धर्षित) 1 To come together, be compact. -2 To hurt, to injure.

धृष् 1 P., 10 U. (धर्षति, धर्षयति,-ते) 1 To offend, injure. -2 To insult, treat with indignity. -3 To assail, overcome, over-power, destroy. -4 To dare to attack, challenge, defy. -5 To violate or outrage (as a woman).

धृष् 5 P. (धृष्णोति, धृष्ट) 1 To be bold or courageous. -2 To be confident. -3 To be proud or overbearing. -4 To be impudent.-5 To dare, venture (with inf). -6 To brave, challenge. -7 To treat with contumely.

धृष् 10 A. (धर्षयते) To assail, attack, outrage.

धृष्ट *p. p.* (*f.* —ष्टा) 1 Bold, courageous, confident.-2 Impudent, shameless, insolent. -3 Forward, presumptuous. -4 Profligate, abandoned. —ष्टः *m.* A faithless husband or lover. —ष्टा *f* A disloyal woman. -Comp. —द्युम्नः *m.* N. of a son of Drupada and brother of Draupadî. —मानिन् *a.* Having too high an opinion of oneself, presumptuous [Shameless.

धृष्णज् *a.* 1 Bold, confident. -2

धृष्णिः *m.* A ray of light.

धृष्णु *a.* 1 Bold, courageous, powerful. -2 Shameless, impudent.

धे I P. (धयति, धीत; *Caus.* धापयति; *desid.* धित्सति) 1 To suck, drink, absorb (fig. also). -2 To suck out, draw or take away. -3 To approprite. -*Caus.* To suckle, nourish.

धेनः *m.* 1 The ocean. -2 A male river (नद).

धेनुः *f.* 1 A cow, milch-cow. -2 The female of a species (affixed to the names of other animals in this sense); as खड्गधेनुः, वडवधेनुः &c. (Sometimes at the end of comp. धेनु forms a diminutive; as असिधेनुः, खड्गधेनुः).

धेनुकः *m.* N. of a demon killed by Balarâma.

धेनुका *f.* 1 A female elephant. -2 A milch-cow. -3 A female animal in general.

धेनुष्या *f.* A cow who or whose milk has been pledged.

धैनुकं *n.* 1 A herd of cows. -2 A particular mode of sexual enjoyment.

धैर्यं *n.* 1 Firmness, strength, constancy, stability, fortitude.-2 Calmness, composure. 3 Gravity, patience. -4 Inflexibility. -5 Forwaredness.

धैवतः *m.* The sixth of the seven primary notes of the Indian gamut.

धैवत्यं *n.* Cleverness. [poisonous.

धोडः *m.* A species of snakes not

धोर् I P (धोरति) To go quickly, run, trot. -2 To be skilful (in general).

धोरणं *n.* 1 A vehicle in general (as a horse, elephant &c.) -2 Going well or quickly. -3 A horse's trot.

धोरणिः, -णी *f.* 1 An uninterrupted series or continuity. -2 Tradition.

धोरितं *n.* 1 Injuring, hurting, striking. -2 Going, motion. 3 A horse's trot

धौत *p. p.* (*f.* —ता) 1 Washed, cleaned, purified. -2 Polished, brightened. -3 Bright, white, glistening. —तं *n.* Silver. -2 Cleaning, washing. -Comp. —कटः *m.* A bag of coarse cloth. —कौशं.-कौषेयं *n.* Bleached or purified silk. —खंडी Sugar candy. —शिलं *n.* Rock-crystal.

धौम्रः *m.* 1 Greyness. -2 A place for building (prepared in a particular way.)

धौरितकं *n.* A horse's trot.

धौरेय *a.* (*f.* —यी) Fit for a burden. —यः *m.* 1 A beast of burden, a horse. -2 A chief, leader.

धौर्तकं, धौर्तिकं, धौर्त्यं *n.* Fraud, dishonesty, roguery.

ध्मा I P. (धमति, ध्मात ; *Caus.* ध्मापयति) 1 To blow, breathe out -2 To blow (as a wind-instrument). -3 To excite fire by blowing. -4 To manufacture by blowing. -5 To cast or throw away.

ध्माकारः *m.* A blacksmith, smith.

ध्मां (ध्वां-) क्ष् I P. (ध्मांक्षति) 1 To crow or caw. -2 To desire.

ध्मात *p. p.* (*f.* —ता) 1 Blown (as a wind-instrument). -2 Inflamed, blown, fanned, excited. -3 Inflated, puffed up.

ध्मानं *n.* Blowing.

ध्मापनं *n.* Inflating, swelling by blowing into. [to cinder.

ध्मापित *a.* Reduced to ashes, burnt

ध्यात *p. p.* (*f.* —ता) Thought of, reflected upon.

ध्यानं *n.* 1 Meditation, reflection, contemplation. -2 Religious meditation. -3 Divine intuition or discernment. -4 Mental representation of the personal attributes of a deity. -Comp. —योगः *m.* Profound meditation. -स्थ *a.* Absorbed in meditation, lost in thought.

ध्यानिक *a.* (*f.* —का) Sought or obtained by pious contemplation or abstract meditatio

ध्याम *a.* (*f.* —मा) Unclean, dirty. —मं *n.* A kind of grass.

ध्यामन् *m.* 1 Measure. -2 Light.-*n.* Meditation.

ध्यै 1 P. (ध्यायति, ध्यातः *desid.* दिध्यासति; *pass.* ध्यायते) To think of, meditate upon, contemplate, imagine, call to mind. With अनु— To think of, remember, wish well to' अप— or अव — To disregard. अभि- To desire. नि- To think of, remember. to meditate deeply upon. निस्-To think, of meditate upon.

ध्राडिः *m.* Gathering flowers(पुष्पचय).

ध्रुव *a.* (*f.* -वा) 1 Fixed, firm, immovable, stable, constant, unchangeable, everlasting, eternal. -2 Certain, sure, inevitable. -3 Retentive, tenacious; *e. g.* ध्रुवा स्मृतिः. —वः *m.* 1 The polar star. -2 The pole of any great circle. -3 The distance of a planet from the beginning of the sidereal Zodiac, polar longitude. -4 The Indian fig tree.-5 A post, stake. -6The stem or trunk(of a tree lopped off).-7 The introductory stanza of a song (repeated as a chorus; see any अष्टपदी of Jayadeva).-8 Time, epoch, era.-9 An epithet of Brahman (*m.*). -10 Of Vishnu. -11 Of Siva. -12 A constant arc. -13 The tip of the nose. -14 A sacrificial vessel. -15 N. of the son of Uttánapáda and grandson of Manu. —वं *n.* 1 The sky, atmosphere. -2 Heaven. —वा *f.* A sacrificial ladle (of wood). -2 A virtuous woman. -3 A cow who stands still when being milked. —वं *ind.* Certainly, surely. -Comp. —आवर्तः *m.* The point on the crown of the head from which the hair radiates. -तारा *f.*, —तारकं *n.* The polar star.

ध्रुवकः *m.* 1 The introductory stanza of a song (repeated as a sort of chorus). -2 A trunk, stem. -3 A post. -4 Polar longitude.

ध्रौव्यं *n.* 1 Fixedness, firmness, stability. -2 Duration. -3 Certainty.

ध्वंस् 1 A.(ध्वंसते, ध्वस्त) 1 To fall to pieces, be reduced to dust or powder. -2 To sink, despond. -3 To perish, be decayed.-4 To be eclipsed. -5 To be covered with dust. -6 To sprinkle over. *-Caus.* (ध्वंसयति) To destroy, ruin, remove. With प्र- To perish; to be destroyed. वि-1 To fall to pieces. -2 To be dispersed. -3 To perish; to be destroyed.

ध्वंसः *m.* 1 Falling down, falling to pieces. -2 Disappearance. -3 Loss, ruin. -सी *f.* A mote in the sun-beam.

ध्वंसनं *n.* 1 Perishing, dying. -2 Loss, destruction. -3 Falling

ध्वांक्षि: *f.* The hundredth part of a Muhúrta.

ध्वजः *m.* 1 A flag, banner, ensign. -2 A distinguished or eminent person, the flag or ornament (at the end of comp.)as in कुलध्वजः 'the head' ornament or distinguished person of a family. -3 A flag-staff. -4 A mark, sign, as in वृषभध्वज. -5 The attribute of a deity. -6 The sign of a tavern; any trade-mark. -7 The organ of generation, (of any animal, male or female). -8 A keeper of a liquor-shop. -9 A house situated to the east of any object. -10 Pride. -11(In prosody). An iambic foot. (ध्वजीकृ to hoist a flag. (Fig.) To use as a plea or pretext . -Comp. —आहृत *a.* Taken possession of on the battle-field. -उत्थानं *n.* A festival in honour of Indra. —द्रुमः *m.* The palm tree. —प्रहरणः *m.*

Air, wind. -यंत्रं *n.* Any contrivance to which a flag-staff is fastened.

ध्वजवत् *a.* 1 Adorned with flags. -2 Having a mask. -3 Having the mark of a criminal, branded. —*m.* 1 A standard-bearer. -2 A vendor of spirituous liquors, distiller.

ध्वजिन् *a.* (*f.* -नी) 1 Bearing or carrying a flag. -2 Having as a mark. -3 Having the mark of a liquor-vessel. —*m.* 1 A standard-bearer. -2 A distiller or vendor of spirituous liquors. -3 A car, carriage, chariot. -4 A mountain. -5 A snake. -6 A peacock. -7 A horse. -8 A Brâhmana. —नी *f.* An army.

ध्वजीकरणं *n.* 1 Hoisting a flag. -2 Setting up as a pretext or claim, making anything a plea.

ध्वन् 1 P. (ध्वनति, ध्वनित) To sound, buzz, hum, echo, thunder, roar. -*Caus.* (ध्वनयति) To cause to sound, ring (as a bell); but ध्वानयति 'to cause to articulate indistinctly.'

ध्वनः *m.* 1 Sound, tune. -2 Hum, buzz. -Comp. -मोदिन् *m.* A bee.

ध्वननं *n.* 1 Sounding. -2 Hinting at, suggesting or implying (as a meaning). -3 (In Rhet.) The same as व्यंजना q. v., or that power of a word or sentence by virtue of which it conveys a sense different from its primary or secondary meaning; suggestive power. -4 Humming, indistinct utterance.

ध्वनिः *m.* 1 Sound, echo, noise. -2 Tune, note, tone. -3 The sound of a musical instrument. -4 The thunder of a cloud. -5 Word. -6 Hint, implied meaning. -7 (In Rhet) The suggested or implied sense of a काव्य, as distinguished from the expressed sense. By some rhetoricians ध्वनि is divided into three kinds वस्तुध्वनि, अलंकारध्वनि, and रसध्वनि. A ध्वनिकाव्य is that काव्य in which the implied or *suggested* sense is more striking than the *expressed* sense; or where the *expressed* sense is subordinate to the *suggested* sense. -Comp. —ग्रहः *m.* 1 The ear. -2 Hearing. —विकारः *m* A change of voice caused by fear, grief &c.

ध्वनित *p. p.* (*f.* —ता) 1 Sounded. -2 Implied, suggested. —तं *n.* 1 A sound. -2 The roar or thunder of a cloud.

ध्वस्त *pp.* (*f.* —स्ता) 1 Fallen. -2 Destroyed. -3 Lost. -4 Covered. -5 Eclipsed.

ध्वस्तिः *f.* Ruin, loss, destruction.

ध्वाङ्क्षः *m.* 1 A crow. (Sometimes used at the end of comp. to show contempt; *e. g.* तीर्थध्वाङ्क्षः). -2 A beggar -3 An impudent fellow. -4 A gull, crane. -5 A carpenter. -Comp. —अरातिः *m.* An owl. —पुष्टः *m* The (Indian) cuckoo.

ध्वानः *m.* 1 Sound (in general). -2 Buzzing, humming.

ध्वान्तं *n.* Darkness. -Comp. -उन्मेषः, -चित्तः *m.* A fire-fly. -शात्रवः, -अरातिः *m.* 1 The sun. -2 The moon. -3 Fire. -4 The white colour.

न.

न *ind.* A particle of negation equivalent to 'not' 'no' 'nor,' 'neither.' -2 Used with the potential mood न may sometimes have the force of 'lest' 'for fear lest 'that not' *e.g.* क्षिप-

यैर्धार्यते शस्त्रं नार्तशब्दो भवेदिति. -3 In argumentative writings न often comes after इति चेत and means 'not so.' -4 When a negative has to be repeated in successive clauses of the same sentence or in different sentences, न may be simply repeated or may be used with particles. -5 Sometimes न may not be expressed in the second and the following clauses, but represented only by च. -6 न is frequently joined with a second न or any other negative particle to intensify or emphasize an assertion; *e. g.* न पुनरलंकारश्रियं न पुष्यति शाकुंत.; नांदज्यो नाम राज्ञोऽस्ति. -7 In a few cases न is retained at the beginning of a negative Tatpurusha compound; *e. g.* नाक, नासत्य, नकुल.-8 न is often joined with other particles; नच, नवा, नैव, नतु, नचेत, नखलु &c. &c.

a. (*f.* —ना) 1 Thin, spare. -2 Vacant, empty. -3 Identical, the same. —नः *m.* 1 A name of Ganesh. -2 A pearl. -3 Wealth; prosperity. -Comp —असत्यौ (*m. du.*) Asvins, the twin physicians of the gods. —एक *a.* More than one, several, various. (-कः *m.*) 1 An epithet of Vishnu. -2 N. of the Supreme Being.

नकुटं *n.* The nose.

नकुलः *m.* 1 The mungoose, an ichneumon.-2 N.of the fourth Pândava prince. -3 A son. -4 An epithet of Siva. —ली *f.* 1 A female mungoose. -2 Saffron.

नक्तं *n.* 1 Night. -2 Eating only at night, as a sort of religious vow or penance. -Comp. —अंध *a.* Blind at night. —चारिन् *m.* 1 An owl. -2 A cat. -3 A thief.-4 A demon,goblin, evil spirit. —भोजनं *n.* Supper. —मालः *m.* N. of a tree. —मुखा *f.* Evening. —व्रतं *n.* 1 Fasting by day and eating at night. -2 Any penance or religious rite observed at night.

नक्तं *ind.* At night, by night; -Comp. —चरः *m.* 1 Any animal that goes about at night. -2 A fiend, demon, goblin. -3 A thief. —चर्या *f.* Wandering by night. —चारिन् *m.*See —नक्तचारिन्. —दिनं *n.* Night and day. —दिनं,—दिवं *ind.* Night and day.

नक्तकः *m.* Dirty or ragged cloth.

नक्रः *m.* 1 A crocodile, an alligator. -2 The sign Scorpio of the zodiac. —क्रं *n.* 1 The upper timber of a door. -2 The nose. —क्रा *f.* 1 The nose. -2 A swarm of bees or wasps.

नक्षत्रं *n.* 1 A star in general. -2 An asterism in the moon's path, lunar mansion, (they are twenty-seven). -3 A pearl. -4 A necklace of 27 pearls -Comp. —ईशः, -ईश्वरः, —नाथः, —पः, —पतिः, —राजः *m.* The moon. —चक्रं *n.* 1 The sphere of the fixed stars. -2 The lunar asterisms taken collectively. —दर्शः *m.* An astronomer or astrologer. —नेमिः *m.* 1 The moon. -2 The pole-star. -3 An epithet of Vishnu. (-मिः *f.*) Revati, the last asterism. —पथः *m.* The starry sky. —पाठकः *m.* An astrologer. —माला *f.* 1 A group of stars. -2A necklace of twentyseven pearls. -3 The table of the asterisms in the moon's path.-4 A neck ornament of elephants. —योगः *m.* The conjunction of the moon with the lunar mansions.—लोकः *m.* The starry region, the firmament. —वर्त्मन् *n.* The sky. —विद्या *f.* Astronomy or astrology. —वृष्टिः *f.* Falling stars. —सूचकः *m.* A bad astrologer.

नक्षत्रिन् *m.* The moon. -2 An epithet of Vishnu.

नखः *m.*, —खं *n.* 1 A nail of a finger or of a toe, claw, talon. -2 The number 'twenty'. —खः *m.* A part, portion. -Comp. -अंकः *m* A scratch, nail-mark. —आघातः *m.* A scratch, nail-wound. -आयुधः *m* 1 A tiger -2 A lion. -3 A cock. —आशिनः *m.* An owl. —कुट्टः *m.* A barber. —जाहं *n.* The root of a nail. —दारणः *m.* A falcon, hawk. (—णं *n.*) A pair of nail-scissors. —निकृंतनं *n.*, — रंजनी *f.* A pair of nail-scissors, nail-parer —मुचः *m.* A bow. —लेखकः *m.* A nail-painter. —लेखा *f* 1 A nail-mark. -2 Nail-painting. —विषः *m.* A man. —विष्किरः *m.* A bird of prey (tearing with claws). -शंखः *m.* A small shell.

नखंपच *a.* Nail-scorching.

नखरः *m.*, -रं *m.* A finger-nail, claw, talon. -Comp. —आयुधः *m.* 1 A tiger. 2 A lion. -3 A cock. —आह्वः *m.* Fragrant oleander.

नखानखि *ind.* Nail against nail.

नखिन् *a.* (*f.* —नी) 1 Having or armed with nails or claws. -2 Thorny. —*m.* 1 A tiger. -2 A lion.

नगः *m.* 1 A mountain. -2 A tree. -3 The sun. -4 A serpent. -5 The number 'seven.' -Comp —अटनः *m.* A monkey. —अधिपः, —अधिराजः, -इंद्रः *m.* 1 Himálaya (the lord of mountains). -2 The Sumeru mountain. —अरिः *m.* An epithet of Indra. —ओकस् *m* 1 A bird (in general). -2 A crow. -3 A lion. -4 The fabulous animal called शरभः. —जः *m.* An elephant. -जा, -नंदिनी *f.* Epithets of Parvati. -पतिः *m.* 1 The Himálaya mountain. -2 The moon. —भिद् *m.* 1 An axe. -2 An epithet of Indra. -3 A crow. —मूर्धन् *m.* The crest or brow of a mountain. —रंध्रकरः *m.* An epithet of Kártikeya. -वाहनः *m.* An epithet of Siva.

नगरं *n* A town, city (opp. ग्राम). -Comp. —अधिकृतः, —अधिपः, —अध्यक्ष *m.* 1 The chief magistrate of a town. -2 The governor or superintendent of a town. —उपांतः *m.* A suburb, the skirt of a town. —काकः *m.* A vile fellow, (an expression of contempt). —घातः *m.* An elephant. -प्रदक्षिणा *f.* Carrying an idol round a city in procession. -प्रांतः *m.* A suburb. —मार्दिन् *m.* An intoxicated elephant. —मार्गः *m.* A principal road, highway. -रक्षिन् *m.* 1 The superintendent of a town. -2 A town-watchman.

नगरी *f.* Same as नगरं. -Comp. —काकः *m.* The (Indian) crane. —बकः *m.* A crow.

नग्न *a.* (*f.* —ग्ना) 1 Naked, nude, bare. -2 Uncultivated, uninhabited, desolate. —ग्नः *m.* A naked mendicant. -2 A Buddhist mendicant (क्षपणक). -3 A bard accompanying an army; or a wandering bard. —ग्ना *f.* 1 A naked, shameless or wanton woman. -2 A girl before menstruation, or less than 12 or 10. -Comp. -अटः, -अटकः *m.* 1 One who goes about naked. -2 A Jaina or Buddhist mendicant (of the दिगंबर class.)

नग्नक *a.* (-ग्निका *f.*) Naked, nude. -कः *m.* 1 A naked mendicant. -2 A Jania or Buddihist mendicant (of the दिगंबर class). -3 A bard.

नग्नका, नग्निका *f.* 1 A naked, shameless or wanton woman -2 A girl before menstruation.

नंगः *m.* A lover, paramour (जार).

नचिकेतस् *m.* An epithet of Agni.

नचिर *a.* See अचिर.

नञ् *ind.* The technical term for the negative particle न.

नट् 1 P. (नटति, the न is not changed to ण after प्र in the sense of 'hurting') 1 To dance. -2 To act -3 To injure (by a deceptive trick). —*Caus.* (नाटयति,-ते) 1 To, act, represent dramatically (in dramas). -2 To imitate, copy. (N. B. नट् forms नटयति in the sense of 'causing to dance').

नट् 10 U. (नाटयति,-ते) 1 To drop or fall. -2 To shine.-3 To injure.

नटः *m.* 1 A dancer. -2 An actor. -3 The son of a degraded Kshatriya. -4 The Asoka tree. -Comp. -अंतिका *f.* Shame, modesty. —ईश्वरः *m.* An epithet of Siva. —चर्या *f.* The performance of an actor. —भूषणः, —मंडनः *m.* (Yellow) orpiment -रंगः *m.* A theatrical stage. —वरः *m.* The Sútradhára of a drama. —संज्ञकं *n.* Yellow orpiment (—कः *m.*) An actor, dancer.

नटनं *n.* 1 Dancing, dance. -2 Acting, dramatic representation.

नटी *f.* 1 An actress. -2 The chief actress (regarded as the wife of the Sútradhára). -3 A courtezan, harlot. -4 Red arsenic.

नट्या *f.* A company of actors.

नडः *m.*, नडं *n.* A species of reed. -Comp. —प्राय *a.* Abounding in reeds. —भक्तं *n.* A place abounding in reeds. —संहतिः *f.* A collection or quantity of reeds.

नडश *a.* (*f.* -शी) Covered with [reeds.

नडिनी *f.* 1 A quantity of reeds. -2 A reed-bed, a river abounding in reeds.

नाडिल *a.* (*f.* —ला),नड्वत *a.* (*f.* -ती) Abounding in or covered with reeds; reedy.

नड्या *f.* A quantity of reeds.

नड्वल *a.* (*f.* —ला) Abounding in reeds. —लं *n.*, -ला *f.* A quantity or a bed of reeds. A place full of reeds उत्कंपितकादंबककदंबकाश्रीयमणोपकूलनड्वलं ×× तदेवाच्छोदमाससाद * कादंब. उ० भा०.

नत *p. p.* (*f.* -ता) 1 Bent, bowed, inclined. -2 Sunk, depressed. -3 Crooked, curved. —तं *n.* The distance of any planet from the meridian. -2 The zenith distance at a meridian transit. -Comp. —अंशः *m.* The zenith distance. —अंगी *f.* 1 A woman with stooping limbs. -2 A woman in general.-भ्रूः *f.* A woman with curved eye-brows.

नतिः *f.* 1 Bending, stooping, bowing. -2 Curvature, crookedness. -3 Bending the body in salutation; a bow. -4 Parallax in latitude (in astronomy). -5 The change of a dental to a lingual letter.

नद् 1 P. (नदति, नदित) 1 To sound, thunder (as a cloud &c.). -2 To speak, shout, roar, (with शब्द, स्वन, नाद &c as a cognate object).-3 To vibrate. With उत्—To roar, to cry. नि— To sound. प्र— To sound, resound. —*Caus.* (नादयति,-ते) 1 To fill with noise, make resonant. -2 To cause to make a sound.

नद् 1 P. (नंदति) To be glad, to be satisfied with, to be glad of any thing. With अभि—1 To be glad, or satisfied. -2 To desire, to wish for, to like. -3 To greet, to congratulate. -4 To praise, approve of. आ— To be glad. प्रति— 1 To bless. -2 To congratulate.-*Caus.*(नंदयति,-ते) To gladden, to please, make happy. With आ— To please, gladden.

नदः *m.* 1 A river, great river. -2 A stream, rivulet. -3 The ocean.

-Comp. —पतिः, -राजः *m.* The ocean.

नदथुः *m.* 1 Noise, roaring. -2 The roaring of a bull. -3 Crying.

नदी *f.* A river, any flowing stream. -Comp. —इनः, -ईशः, -कांतः *m.* The ocean. —जः *m.* 1 An epithet of Bhishma. -2 Antimony. —तरस्थानं *n.* A landing-place, ferry. —दोहः *m.* Freight, river-toll, fare. -धरः *m.* An epithet of Siva. —पतिः, -ईनः *m.* 1 The ocean. -2 An epithet of Varuna. -पूरः *m.* A river which has overflown its banks. -भवं *n.* River-salt. —मातृक *a.* Watered by rivers, irrigated, supplied with the water of rivers, canals &c. (as a country &c.). —रयः *m.* The current of a river. —वंकः *m.* The bend or arm of a river. —स्नाः (स्नः) *m.* 1 Bathing in rivers. -2 Knowing the dangerous spots in rivers, their depth, course &c. -3(Hence) Experienced, clever. —सर्जः *m.* The Arjuna tree.

नद्ध *p. p.* (*f.* —द्धा) 1 Tied, bound; put on. -2 Covered, inlaid, interwoven. -3 Joined, connected. —द्धं *n.* A tie, bond, knot.

नद्धी *f.* A leather-strap.

ननंद, ननांद *f.* A husband's sister. -Comp. ननांदपतिः (also ननांदुःपतिः)The husband of a husband's sister.

ननु *ind.* A particle implying :—1 Inquiry or interrogation. -2 Surely certainly, indeed (with an interrogative force). -3 Of course, indeed, certainly. -4 It is used as a vocative particle meaning 'O', 'Oh.' -5 It has the sense of ' pray ', ' be pleased. ' -6 It is sometimes used as a corrective word like the English ' why?' or ' ' I say ' । ननु पदे परिवृत्य भण *मृच्छक. -7 In argumentative discussions ननु is frequently used to advance a contrary proposition.

नंद् 1 P. (नंदति, नंदित) To be glad, be pleased, delighted or satisfied, to rejoice at (anything). -*Caus.* (नंदयति,-ते) To please, gladden, make happy. See नद्.

नंदः *m* 1 Happiness, pleasure, joy. -2 A kind of lute. -3 A frog. -4 N. of Vishnu. -5N. of a cowherd who was the foster-father of Krishna -6 N. of the founder of the Nanda dynasty; or of nine brother-kings of Pátaliputra killed by the machinations of Chánakya, the minister of Chandragupta. -7 One of the nine treasures of Kubera. -दी *f.* An epithet of Durgá. -Comp. —आत्मजः, -नंदनः *m.* An epithet of Krishna. —पालः *m.* An epithet of Varuna.

नंदक *a.* (*f.* —का) 1 Rejoicing, gladdening. -2 Delighting or rejoicing in. -3 Gladdening a family. -कः *m.* 1 A frog. -2 N. of the sword of Krishna. -3 A sword in general. -4 Happiness. -5 Nanda, the foster-father of Krishna.

नंदकिन *m.* An epithet of Vishnu.

नंदथुः *m.* Happiness, pleasure.

नंदन *a.* (*f.* —ना) Delighting, pleasing, gladdening. —नः *m.* 1 A son. -2 A frog. -3 An epithet of Vishnu. -4 N. of Siva. —ना *f.* A daughter. —नं *n.* 1 N. of the garden of Indra. -2 Rejoicing, being glad. -3 Joy. -Comp. —जं *n.* Yellow sandal-wood (हरिचंदन).

नंदंतः *m.* A son. -ती *f.* A daughter.

नंदा *f.* 1 Delight, happiness. -2 Wealth, prosperity. -3 A small earthen water-jar. -4 A husband's sister. -5 The first, sixth and eleventh days of a lunar fortnight (considered as auspicious). -6 An epithet of Gaurí.

नांदि: *m. f.* Joy, pleasure, delight. —दि: *m.* 1 An epithet of Vishnu. -2 Of Siva. -3 N. of an attendant of Siva. -4 The speaker of a prelude or benediction(in a drama.) -Comp. —आवर्त: *m.* A building in the form of a quadrangle without a western gate (*n.* also).—ईश:, -ईश्वर: *m.* 1 An epithet of Siva. —ग्राम: *m.* N. of a Village where Bharata lived during Râma's banishment —घोष: *m.* N. of the chariot of Arjuna. —वर्धन: *m.* 1 An epithet of Siva. -2 A friend. -3 The end of a lunar fortnight *i. e.* the day of new or full moon. -4 A son.

नांदिक: *m* 1 Joy, pleasure. -2 A small water-jar. -3 An attendant of Siva. -Comp. —ईश:, -ईश्वर: *m.* 1 N. of one of Siva's chief attendants. -2 N. of Siva.

नांदिन् *a.* (*f.* —नी) 1 Happy, delighted. -2 Gladdening, giving delight. -3 Taking delight in, liking. *-m* 1 A son. -2 The speaker of a prelude or benediction in a drama. -3 N. of the door-keeper of Siva. —नी *f.* 1 A daughter. -2 A husband's sister. -3 A fabulous cow, daughter of *Surabhi,* yielding all desires (कामधेनु) and in the possession of the sage Vasishtha. -4 An epithet of the Ganges. -5 The holy basil.

नपुंस्, नपुंस: *m.* Not a man, a eunuch.

नपुंसक: *m.*, -कं *n.* 1 A hermaphrodite. -2 An impotent man, a eunuch. -3 A coward. —कं *n.* 1 A word in the neuter gender. -2 The neuter gender.

नप्तृ *m.* A grandson (a son's or daughter's son).

नप्त्री *f.* A grand daughter (a son's daughter or a daughter's daughter).

नभ: *m.* The month Srávana. —भं *n.* The sky, atmospher. —भा *f.* A spitting-pot.

नभस् *n.* 1 The sky, atmosphere. -2 A cloud. -3 Fog, vapour. -4 Water. -5 Period of life, age. —*m.* 1 The rainy season. -2 The nose, smell. -3 N. of the month of Srâvana. -4 The fibres in the root of the lotus. -5 A spitting-pot. *-Dual* Both the worlds, heaven and earth. -Comp. —अंबुप: *m.* The Châtaka bird. —कांतिन् A lion. —गज: *m.* A cloud. —चक्षुस् *m.* The sun. —चमस: *m.* 1 The moon. -2 Magic. —चर: *m.* 1 A god or demi-god. -2 A bird. —दुह: *m.* A cloud. —दृष्टि *a.* 1 Blind. -2 Looking towards the sky. —दीप:, -धूम: *m.* A cloud. —नदी *f.* The celestial Ganges. —प्राण: *m.* Wind —मणि: *m.* The sun. —मंडलं *n.* The firmament, the atmosphere. रजस् *n.* Darkness. -रेणु: *f.* Fog, mist. —लय: *m.* Smoke. —लिह् *a.* Licking the sky, lofty, very high. —श्वास: *m.* Wind. —सद् *m.* 1 A bird. -2 A star. -3 A god. —सरित *f.* 1 The milky way. -2 The celestial Ganges. —स्थली *f.* The sky. —स्पृश् *a.* Reaching the sky, lofty.

नभस: *m.* 1 The sky. -2 The rainy season. -3 The ocean.

नभसंगम: *m.* A bird.

नभस्य: *m.* N. of the month Bhádrapada.

नभस्वत् *a.* 1 Vaporous, misty, cloudy.-2 Young.*-m* The wind, air.

नभाक: *m.* 1 Darkness. -2 An epithet of Râhu.-3 A cloud.-4 The sky.

नभ्राज् *m.* A dark cloud.

नम् 1 P. Sometimes A. (नमति,-ते, ननाम, अनंसीत, नंस्यति, नत; *caus.* नमयति,-ते or नामयति,-ते, but with a preposition नमयति only; *desid.* निनंसति) 1 To bow to, to salute (as a mark of respect) (with acc. or dat.). -2 To submit or subject oneself.-3 To bend, sink; go down. -4 To stoop, be inclined. -5 To be bent or curved. With अभ्युद्- To rise; to elevate. अव -1 To bend.-2 To bend one-self, to go down. उद्— 1 To rise, spring up, arise. -2 To ascend, go up (*lit.* and *fig.*).-3 To raise. उप— 1 To fall to one's share, to occur, happen. -2 To present one with, to present, to offer. -3 To approach. परि— 1 To stoop (said of an elephant about to strike with his tusks). -2 To bend down. -3 To be changed into, to appear in a different form.-4 To be developed, to be aged, to grow old, decay. -5 To be digested (as food). प्र— To bow to, to salute (with *acc.* or *dat.*). साष्टांगं प्रणम् To make obeisance by throwing oneself on the ground so that eight parts of the body touch the ground (See अष्टांग). दंडवत् प्रणम्— To make obeisance by throwing oneself on the ground flat (prostrate like a stick). वि— 1 To bend oneself. -2 To be bent विपरि— To change for worse. सम्— 1 To subject oneself to. -2 To bend.

नमत *a.* (*f* —ता) Bent, bowed, crooked, curved. -तः *m.* 1 An actor. -2 Smoke. -3 A master, lord. -4 A cloud.

नमनं *n.* 1 Bowing down, bending, stooping. -2 Sinking. -3 A bow, salutation.

नमस् *ind.* 1 A bow, salutation, adoration ; (this word is, by itself, invariably used with dat.; but with कृ, generally with acc., but sometimes with dat. also. The word has the sense of a noun, but is treated as an indeclinable) -Comp. —कार *m*, —कृतिः *f.*, —करणं *n.* Bowing, respectful salutation. —कृत *a.* 1 Saluted. -2 Revered, worshipped. —गुरुः *m.* 1 A spiritual teacher.-2 A Bráhmana. —वाकं *ind.* Uttering the word नमस् *i. e.* making a low obeisance; इदं कविभ्यः पूर्वेभ्यो नमोवाकं प्रशास्महे *उत्तर रा. 1. 1. —वृध *m.* A sacrifice.

नमस *a.* (*f.* -सा) Favourable, kindly disposed.

नमसित, नमस्यित *a.* (*f.* -ता, -ता) Revered, respected, saluted.

नमस्य Den. P. To bow down to, pay homage to, worship.

नमस्य *a.* (*f.* —स्या) 1 Entitled to obeisance, respectable, adorable.-2 Respectful, humble. —स्या *f.* Worship, reverence, obeisance.

नमित *a.* (*f.* —ता) Bowed, bent down.

नमुचिः *m.* 1 N. of a demon slain by Indra. -2 N. of the god of love. —Comp. —सूदनः, -द्विष्, -हन् *m.* Epithets of Indra.

नमेरुः *m.* N. of a tree (रुद्राक्ष or सुरपुंनाग).

नम्र *a.* (*f.* —म्रा) 1 Bowing, bowing down, bent, hanging down. 2 Making a low obeisance. -3 Humble, reverential ; as in भक्तिनम्रः * मेघदू. -4 Crooked, curved -5 Worshipping. -6 Devoted or attached to.

नम्रित *a.* Bent or bowed down.

नय् I A. (नयते) 1 To go. -2 To protect.

नयः *m.* 1 Guiding, leading, managing. -2 Behaviour, conduct, way of life, as in दुर्नय. -3 Prudent conduct, virtue. -4 Foresight, circumspection.-5 Policy, statesmanship, state-policy. -6 Morality, justice, equity. -7 A design, scheme. -8 A maxim, principle. -9 Method, manner.

-10 A philosophical system. -11 A doctrine, opinion. Comp कोविद्,-ज्ञ a. Skilled in policy, prudent. -चक्षुस् a. Wise prudent. —नेतृ m. A master in politics. —वादिन् m. A politician. —विद्, -विशारदः m. A politician, statesman —शास्त्रं n. 1 The science of polities. -2 Any work on politics or political economy, or on morality.

नयनं n. 1 Leading, guiding, managing. -2 Taking, carrying, bringing to or near. -3 Ruling, governing -4 The eye. -5 Passing, spending (as time). -Comp. —उत्सवः m 1 A lamp. -2 Delight of the eyes. -3 Any lovely object. —उपांतः m. The corner of the eye. -गोचर a. Visible, within the range of sight. —छदः m. eyelid. —जलं, -वारि n. Tears. —पथः m. The range of sight. —पुटं n. The Cavity of the eye. -विषयः m. 1 Any visible object. -2 The horizon. -3 The range of sight.

नरः m. 1 A man, person. -2 A male. -3 A man or piece at chess. -4 The pin of a sun dial. -5 The Supreme Spirit. -6 Man's length (=पुरुष).-7 N. of a primitive sage. -8 N. of Arjuna. -9 A horse. -Comp —अंगः m. 1 The penis. -2 Eruption on the face. —अधमः m. A wretch, miscreant. —अधिपः, —अधिपतिः, -इन्द्रः, -ईश्वरः, -देवः, पतिः, -पालः m. A king. —अंतकः m. Death. —अयनः m. An epithet of Vishnu. —अशः m A demon, goblin. —इंद्रः m. 1 A king. -2 A physician, curer of poisons. —उत्तमः m. 1 An epithet of Vishnu -2 Of Buddha. —ऋषभः m. 'The chief of men', a prince, king. —कीलकः m. The murderer of a spiritual preceptor. —केसरिन् m. 1 Vishnu in his fourth incarnation (नरसिंह). -2 The chief of men. -क्षितिः m. The world. —द्विष् m. A demon, goblin. —नारायणः m. N. of Krishna. (-णौ m. dual.) नर and नारायण are two sages mentioned in the vedas. In later writings they are always mentioned together being called देवौ, पूर्वदेवौ, तापसौ, ऋषिसत्तमौ &c. They are also spoken of as incarnations of विष्णु. Afterwards they came to be identified with Arjuna and Krishna. —पशुः m. 'A beast-like man', a beast in human form -पुंगवः m 'Best of men', an excellent man. —मानिका, -मानिनी, -मालिनी f. A woman with a beard, masculine woman or an amazon. —मेधः m. A human sacrifice. —यंत्रं n Sun-dial. —यानं n., —रथः m., —वाहनं n. A vehicle drawn by men. —लोकः m. 1 'The world of men,' the earth, terrestrial world. -2 Mankind. —वाहनः m. An epithet of Kubera. —व्याघ्रः, -शार्दूलः m. An eminent man. —शृंगं n. An impossibility, a chimera, non-entity. —सखः m. An epithet of Nárâyana. —सिंहः, -हरिः m. Vishnu in his fourth incarnation. —स्कंधः m. A multitude or body of men.

नरकः m., —कं n. Hell (including several places of torture which are said to be 21). -कः m. N. of a demon killed by Krishna. -Comp. -अंतकः, —अरि, -जित् m. Epithets of Krishna. —आमयः m. 1 The soul after death. -2 A ghost, spirit. —कुंडं n. A pit in hell where the wicked are tormented. —स्था f. The Vaitarini river.

नरंगं n. 1 The penis. -2 Eruption on the face. See नरांग.

नरंधिः m. Worldly life or existence.

नरी f. A woman.

मर्कुटकं n. Nose.

नर्तः *m*. Dancing. a dance.

नर्तकः *m*. 1 A dancer; a dancing master.-2 An actor, an actor in a farce in which scenes from actual life are represented by gestures; a masker; a buffoon. -3 A bard, herald. -4 An elephant.-5 A peacock. -6 An epithet Siva. —की *f*. 1 A female dancer, a singing girl, an actress. -2 A female elephant. -3 A pea-hen.

नर्तनः *m* A dancer.-नं *n*. Gesticulation, dancing, dance -Comp. -प्रियः *m*. 1 An epithet of Siva. -2 A peacock.

नर्तयितृ *m*. A dancing-master.

नर्तित *a*. (*f* —ता) 1 Danced, made to dance. -2 Dancing, moving to and fro.

नर्द् 1 P. (नर्दति, नर्दित) 1 To bellow, roar. -2 To go, move.

नर्द *a*. (*f*. —र्दा) 1 Bellowing, roaring. -2 Celebrating, praising aloud.

नर्दनं *n*. 1 Bellowing, roaring.

नर्दितः *m*. A kind of die or a throw at dice. —तं *n*. A roar, bellowing.

नर्मटः *m*. 1 A pot-sherd.-2 The sun.

नर्मठः *m*. 1 A jester. -2 A rake, libertine. -3 Sport, amusement. -4 Copulation, coition. -5 The chin. -6 The nipple.

नर्मन् *n*. 1 Sport, amusement, pleasure, amorous pastime or sport. -2 Jest, joke, wit. -Comp. —कीलः *m*. A husband. —गर्भ *a*. Humorous, full of humour, witty. (—गर्भः *m*.) A secret lover. -द *a*. Delighting making happy. (-दः *m*.) A jester. -दा *f*. N of a river which rises in the Vindhya mountain, and falls into the gulf of Cambay. —द्युति *a*. Bright with joy, cheerful, merry. (-द्युतिः *f*.) Enjoyment of a joke. — सचिवः, -सुहृद् *m*. An associate of the amusements of a prince or a man of rank.

नर्मरा *f*. 1 A valley, cavity. -2 A bellows -3 An old woman past menstruation.

नलः *m*. 1 A kind of reed. -2 N. of a celebrated king of the Nishadhas. -3 N. of a monkey-chief. son of Visvakarman, who built the bridge of stones(now called 'Adam's bridge') over which Ráma passed to Lankâ with his army. —लं *n* 1 A lotus. -2 Smell, odour. -Comp. —कीलः *m* The knee. —कूबर (-व-) रः *m* N. of a son of Kubera. —दं *n*. 1 A fragrant root (उशीर). -2 The honey of a flower. -पट्टिका *f*. A sort of mat of reeds. -मीनः *m*. A shrimp or prawn.

नलकं *n*. 1 Any long bone of the body. -2 The radius of the arm.

नलकिनी *f*. 1 The knee-pan.-2 The leg.

नलिनः *m*. The (Indian) crane. -नं *n*. 1 A lotus-flower, water-lily. -2 Water.-3 The Indigo plant. Comp.

नलिनेशयः *m*. An epithet of Vishnu.

नलिनी *f*. 1 A lotus-plant. -2 An assemblage of lotuses. -3 A pond or place abounding in lotuses. -Comp. —खंडं, —षंडं *n*. A group or assemblage of lotuses. —रुहः *m*. An epithet of Brahman(*m*.). (-रुहं *n*.) A lotus-stalk, the fibres of a lotus.

नल्वः *m*. A measure of distance equal to 400 *hastas* or cubits.

नव *a*. (*f*. —वा) 1 New, fresh, young. -2 Modern. —वः *m*. A crow. —वं *ind*. Recently, newly, lately, not long ago. -Comp. —अन्नं *n*. 1 New rice or grain -2 A ceremony performed on first eating the new rice. —अंबु *n*. Fresh water. —अहः *m*.

The first day of a fortnight. —इतर *a.* Old. -उद्धृतं *n.* Fresh butter. -ऊढा, -पाणिग्रहणा *f.* 1 A newly married woman, a bride. -2 A kind of heroine (In dramas) -कारिका, -कालिका, -फलिका *f.* 1 A woman newly married. -2 A woman in whom menstruation has recently commenced. —छात्रः *m.* A fresh student, novice, tyro. -नी *f.*, -नीतं *n.* Fresh butter. —नीतकं *n.* 1 Clarified butter. -2 Fresh butter. —पाठकः *m.* A new teacher. -मल्लिका, —मालिका *f.* A kind of jasmine. —यौवनं *n.* Fresh youth, bloom or prime of youth. (-ना *f.*) A young woman. —वधूः, -वरिका *f.* 1 A newly married girl. -2 A daughter-in-law. —वल्लभं *n.* A kind of sandal. —शस्यं *n.* The first fruits of the year's harvest —शशिभृत *m.* An epithet of Siva. -सूतिः -सूतिका *f.* 1 A milch-cow. -2 A woman recently delivere

नवकं *n.* The aggregate of nine.

नवत *a.* (*f.* -ती) Ninetieth. -तः *m.* 1 An elephant's painted housings. -2 A woollen cloth, blanket.

नवतिः *f.* Ninety.

नवतिका *f.* 1 Ninety. -2 A paint-brush (said to contain 90 hairs).

नवधा *ind.* In nine ways, ninefold.

नवन् *num. a.* (always *pl.*). Nine (At the beginning of comp. नवन् drops its final न). -Comp. -अशीतिः *f.* Eighty-nine. —अर्चिस्, —दीधितिः *m.* The planet Mars. -कृत्वस् *ind.* Nine times. -ग्रहाः (*m. pl.*) The nine planets; see under ग्रह. —चत्वारिंशत *a.* Forty-nine. —छिद्रं, -द्वारं *n.* The body (having nine apertures). -त्रिंश *a.* Thirty ninth. —त्रिंशत *f.* Thirty-nine —दश *a.* Nineteenth. —दशन् *pl.* Nineteen. —नवतिः *f.* Ninety-nine. -निधयः *m.pl.* The nine treasures of Kubera *i. e.* महापद्मश्च पद्मश्च शंखो मकरकच्छपौ । मुकुंदकुंदनीलाश्च खर्वश्च निधयो नव ॥ —पंचाश *a.* Fifty-ninth. -पंचाशत *f.* Fifty nine. —रत्नं *n.* The nine precious jewels *i. e.* मुक्तामाणिक्यवैडूर्यगोमेदा वज्रविद्रुमौ । पद्मरागो मरकतं नीलश्चेति यथाक्रमं ॥ -2 The nine gem's or poets at the court of king Vikramaditya. —रसाः (*m. pl.*) The nine sentiments in poetry. They are शृंगार, वीर, करुण, अद्भुत, हास्य, भयानक, बीभत्स, रौद्र and शांत. —रात्रं *n.* 1 A period of nine days. -2 The first nine days of the month of Asvina held sacred to Durgá. —विंश *a.* Twenty-ninth. -विंशतिः *f.* Twenty-nine. —विध *a.* Nine-fold, of nine kinds or sorts. —शतं *n.* 1 One hundred and nine. -2 Nine hundred. —षष्टिः *f.* Sixty-nine. —सप्ततिः *f.* Seventy-nine.

नवम *a.* (*f.* -मी) Ninth. -मी *f.* The ninth day of a lunar fortnight.

नवशः *ind.* By nines.

नवीन *a.* (*f.* -ना), नव्य *a.* (*f.* -व्या) 1 New, fresh, recent. -2 Modern.

नश् 4 P. (नश्यति, ननाश, अनशत, नंक्ष्यति नशिष्यति, नष्ट; *caus.* नाशयति; *desid.* निनंक्षति, निनाशिषति) 1 To be lost, to vanish, become invisible. -2 To perish, die, be ruined. -3 To run away, fly away, escape. -4 To become unsucessful.

नश् *f.*, नशः *m*, नशनं *n.* Destruction, perishing, loss, disappearing.

नश्यत्प्रसूतिका *f.* A woman who brings forth a dead child.

नश्वर *a.* (*f.* -री) 1 Perishable, transitory, frail. -2 Destructive, mischievous.

नष्ट *p. p.* (*f.* -ष्टा) 1 Lost, vanished, invisible. -2 Dead, destroyed. -3 Spoiled, wasted. -4 Fled or run away. -5 Deprived of, free from (in comp.). -6 Corrupted, debauched. -ष्टं *n.* 1 Destruction, loss. -2 Disappearance. -Comp. -अग्निः *m.* A house-holder who has lost his consecrat ed fire (it being extinguished). —अर्थ *a*. Reduced to poverty. -आतंकं *ind*. Without anxiety or fear. -आत्मन् *a*. Deprived of sense. -आमिषं *n*. Booty, plunder. -आशंक *a*. Fearless, secure, free from fear. -इंदुकला *f*. The day of new moon. -इंद्रिय *a*. Deprived of senses. —चेतन, -चेष्ट, -संज्ञ *a*. One who has lost his senses, fainted. -चेष्टता *f* Universal destruction.

नस् *f*. The nose (optionally substituted for नासिका after acc. dual). -Comp. -क्षुद्र *a*. Small-nosed

नसा *f*. The nose.

नस्तः *m*. The nose. -स्तं *n*. A sternutatory, snuff. -स्ता *f*. A hole bored in the septum of th nose.-Comp —उतः *m*. An ox led by a string through the nose.

नस्तकं *n*. A hole bored in the septum of the nose (of cattle).

नस्तस् *ind*. From the nose.

नस्तित *a*, (*f*. -ता) Nozzled (with a string through the nose).

नस्य *a*. (*f*. -स्या) Nasal. —स्यं *n*. 1 The hairs in the nose. -2 A sternutatory -स्या *f*. 1 The nose -2 The string through the nose of an animal.

नह् 4 U. (नह्यति,-ते, नद्ध; *desid*. निनत्सति,-ते) 1 To tie, bind, gird round. -2 To put on (oneself), to dress, arm oneself (Atm). -With अप- To untie. —अपि (अपि being sometimes changed to पि) 1 To fasten, gird round, bind. -2 To put on, wear. -3 To cover, envelop. उद्— To tie up, to bind up. परि— To entwine, surround सम्- 1 To tie, bind, fasten. -2 To put on, to dress. -3 o put on an armour; to arm oneself. -4 (Atm.) To prepare oneself, to be ready.

नहि *ind*. Surely or certainly not, by no means, not at all.

नहुष: *m*. N. of a king of the lunar race, son of Ayus and grandson of Purúravas and father of Yayáti.

ना *ind*. (Another form of न *q v*.).

नाक: *m*. 1 Heaven. -2 The upper sky, firmament. -Comp. -ईशः, -ईश्वरः *m* N. of Indra. —चरः *m*. 1 A god. -2 A demi-god. —नाथ:, —नायक: *m*. An epithet of Indra. —वनिता *f*. An *Apsaras*. —सद् *m*. A god.

नाकिन् *m*. A god.

नाकु: *m*. 1 An ant-hill.-2 A mountain.

नाक्षत्रं *n*. A month computed by the moon's passage through the 27 lunar mansions, a month of 30 days of sixty Ghatis each.

नाक्षत्रिक: *m*. A month of 27 days (each day being the period of the moon's passage through a lunar asterism).

नाग: *m*. 1 A snake in general, particularly the cobra. -2 A semi-divine being having the face of a man and the tail of a serpent and said to inhabit the Pâtála. -3 An elephant. -4 A shark. -5 A cruel or tyrannical person. -6 (At the end of comp.) Any pre-eminent or distinguished person *e. g*. पुरुषनाग:. -7 A cloud. -8 A peg projecting from a wall to hang anything upon. -9 Piper betel.-10 One of the five vital airs of the body; that which is expelled by eructation. -11 The number 'seven.' —गं *n*. 1 Tin. -2 Lead. -3 The asterism called आश्लेषा. —गी *f*. 1 A female Nâga.-2 A female elephant.-Comp. —अंगं *n*. Hastinápura. —अंगना *f*. 1 A female elephant. -2 The proboscis of an elephant. —अंजना *f*. A female elephant. —अधिपः *m*. An epithet of

Sesha. -अंतकः, -अरातिः, -अरिः *m.* 1 An epithet of Garuda. -2 A peacock. -3 A lion. —अशनः *m.* 1 A peacock. -2An epithet of Garuda. -3 A lion. —आननः *m.* An epithet of Ganesa. —आह्वः *m.* Hastinâpura. —इंद्रः *m.* 1 A lordly or superior elephant. -2 Airávata, Indra's elephant. -3 An epithet of Sesha. —ईशः *m.*1 An epithet of Sesha. -2 N. of the author of Paribhâshendusekhara and several other works. -3 N. of Patanjali. —उदरं *n.* 1 A breast-plate. -2 A peculiar disease of pregnancy. —कर्णः *m.* The castor-oil plant. -किंजल्कः, —केसरः *m.* N. of a tree with fragrant flowers. —गर्भं *n.* Red lead. —चूडः *m.* An epithet of Siva. —जं *n.* 1 Red lead. -2 Tin. —जिह्विका *f.* Red arsenic. -जीवनं *n.* Tin. -दंतः,-दंतकः *m.* Ivory. -2 A peg or bracket projecting from a wall and used to hang things upon. —दंती *f.* 1 A species of sunflower. -2 A harlot. —नक्षत्रं, —नायकं *n.* The constellation called Asleshâ. —नामकं *n.* Tin. —नामन् *m.* The holy basil. —नासा *f.* The proboscis of an elephant. —नियूहः *m.* A large pin or bracket projecting from a wall. —पंचमी *f.* 1 N. of a festival on the fifth day in the bright half of Srâvana. -2 The fifth day in the dark half of Ashádha. —पदः *m.* A mode of sexual enjoyment (रतिबंध). -पाशः *m.* 1 A sort of magical noose used in battle to entangle an enemy. -2 N. of the noose or weapon of Varuna. —पुरं *n.* 1 Hastinápura. -2 N. of a city in Pátála. —पुष्पः *m.* 1 The Champaka tree. -2 The Punnâga tree. —बंधकः *m.*An elephant-catcher. -बंधुः *m.* The holy fig-tree. -बलः *m.* An epithet of Bhîma. -भूषणः *m.* An epithet of Siva. -मंडलिकः *m.* 1 A snake-keeper. -2 A snake-catcher. -मल्लः *m.* An epithet of Airâvata. नागमुद्राविधानं *n.* The ceremony of placing something bearing the diagram of a snake on a water jar, and reciting some mystic words, in order to make the water an antidote against snake-poison. —यष्टिः *f.*, —यष्टिका *f.* 1 A graduated pole or post for showing the depth of water in a newly-dug pond. -2 A boring-rod driven into the earth. —रक्तं *n.*, —रेणुः *m.* Red lead. —रंगः *m.* The orange. —राजः *m.* 1 An epithet of Sesha. -2 A large elephant. —रुकः *m.* The orange tree. —लता, —वल्लरी, -वल्ली *f.* The piper betel. —लोकः *m.* The world of serpents, one of the regions below the earth ealled Pátâla. —वारिकः *m.* 1 A royal elephant. -2 An elephant-driver. -3 A peacock -4 An epithet of Garuda. -5 The chief of a herd of elephants. -6The chief person in an assembly. -वीथिः *f.* The part of the moon's path which contains the asterisms अश्विनी, भरणी and कृत्तिका. -संभवं, -संभूतं *n.* Red lead. —साह्वयं *n.* Hastinâpura.

नागर *a.* (*f.* -री) 1 Town-born, town-bred. -2 Relating to a town. -3 Spoken in a town. -4 Polite, civil. -5 Clever, sharp. -6 Spoiled by the vices of a town.—रः *m.* 1 A citizen. -2 A husband's brother. -3 A lecturer. -4 An orange. -5 Fatigue; hardship. -6 Desire of final beatitude. -7 Denial of knowledge. -रं *n.* Dry ginger. —री *f.* 1 The character in which Sanskrit is generally written. -2 A clever, intriguing or shrewd woman.

नागरक, नागरिक *a.* (*f.*—की) 1 Town-bred, town-born. -2 Polite, courteous. -3 Clever, shrewd, cunning. —कः *m.* 1 A citizen. -2 A polite or courteous man. -3 He who has been spoiled by the vices of a town. -4 A thief. -5 An artist. -6 The chief of the police. —कं *n.* I Dry ginger.

नागरिट:, नागर्वट: *m.* 1 A libertine, rake. -2 A paramour. -3 A match-maker.

नागरङ्क: *m.* Orange.

नागर्यं *n.* Shrewdness, cleverness.

नाचिकेत: *m.* Fire.

नाट: *m.* 1 Dancing, acting. -2 N. of the Karnátaka country.

नाटकं *n.* 1 A play, drama (in general). -2 One of the 10 principal kinds of dramatic composition. -क: *m.* An actor, a dancer. [dramatic.

नाटकीय *a.* Pertaining to a drama,

नाटार: *m.* The son of an actress or a dancing girl.

नाटिका *f.* A short or light comedy, one of the Uparúpakas, *e. g.* the Ratnâvalí, Priyadarsikâ or Viddhasálabhanjiká.

नाटितकं *n.* A mimic representation, a gesture, gesticulation.

नाटेय:,-र: *m.* The son of an actress or dancing girl.

नाट्यं *n.* 1 Dancing. -2 Dramatic representation, gesticulation, acting. -3 The science or art of dancing or acting. -4 The costume of an actor. -ज्ञ: *m.* An actor. -Comp. —आचार्य: *m.* A dancing preceptor. —उक्ति: *f.* Dramatic phraseology. -धर्मिका,-धर्मी *f.* The rules of dramatic representation. —प्रिय:*m.* An epithet of Siva. —शाला *f.* 1 A dancing-hall. -2 A theatre. -शास्त्रं *n.* 1 The dramatic science, dramaturgy. -2 A work on dramatic representation

नाडि:, —डी *f.* 1 The tubular stalk of any plant. -2 The hollow stalk of a lotus &c. -3 Any tubular organ of the body (such as an artery, vein). -4 A pipe, flute. -5 A sinus. -6 The pulse at the hand or foot.-7 A measure of time equal to twenty-four minutes or equal to half a Muhurta. -9 A sort of bent grass. -10 A juggling trick.-Comp. —चरण: *m.* A bird. —चीरं *n.* A small reed. —नाडिंधम: *m.* A gold-smith. —मंडलं *n.* The celestial equator. —यंत्रं *n.* Any tubular instrument. —व्रण: *m.* An ulcer, a fistula.

नाडिका *f.* Same as नाडि:.

नाडीका *f.* The wind-pipe or throat.

नाणकं *f.* A coin, any thing stamped with an impression.

नातिचिर *a.* Of no long duration.

नातिदूर *a.* Not very far or distant.

नातिवाद: *m.* Avoiding abusive language.

नाथ् 1 P. (नाथति, sometimes A. also) 1 To ask, beg, solicit for anything (with dat. or two acc.) -2 To have power, be master, prevail. -3 To harass, trouble. -4 To bless, give blessings to (said to be Atm. only in this sense).

नाथ: *m.* 1 A lord, master, protector, leader.-2A husband. -3 A rope passed through the nose of a draft-ox. -Comp. —हरि: *m.* A beast. सनाथ-Having a master; hence full of.

नाथवत् *a.* 1 Possessed of a lord or protector. -2 Dependent, subject.

नाद: *m.* 1 A loud roar, cry, shout. -2 A sound in general. -3 (In Yoga phil.) The nasal sound represented by a semi-circle. -4 One who praises.

नादिन् a. (f. —नी) 1 Sounding, resonant. -2 Bellowing, roaring.

नादेय (f. -यी) River-born, aquatic, marine. —यं n. Rock-salt.

नाना ind. 1 In different places, in different ways, variously. -2 Distinctly, separately. -3 Without(=विना). (with acc., instr. or abl.). -4(Used as an adjective at the beginning of comp.) Manifold, various, different, diverse. -Comp. —अत्यय a. Of different kinds. —अर्थ a. 1 Having different aims or obiects.-2Having different meanings, homonymous (as a word). —आत्मवादिन् a. Maintaining the Sánkhya doctrine that each individual has a soul distinct from the universal spirit. —कारं ind. Having done variously. —रूप a. Of different forms, multiform, various. —वर्ण a. Of different colours. —विध a Of various sorts, manifold.-विधं ind. In various ways.

नानान्द्रः m. A husband's sister's son.

नान्त a. Endless, infinite.

नान्तरीयक a. (f. —का) Inseparable, invariably connected.

नान्द्रं n. Praise, eulogy.

नान्दिकरः, नान्दिन् m. The speaker of the नान्दी or benediction.

नान्दी f. 1 Joy, delight. -2 Prosperity. -3 Praise of a deity at the commencement of a religious observance. -4 The benedictory verse or verses recited at the beginning of a drama; benediction.-Comp. -करः, m. Same as नान्दिन्. —निनादः, —नादः, —रवः m. A shout of joy or rejoicing. —पटः m. The lid or cover of a well. —मुख a. (The class of manes or deceased ancestors)to whom the नान्दीमुखश्राद्ध is offered. This is a Sráddha ceremony performed in memory of the manes, preliminary to any festive occasion such as marriage &c. —मुखः m. The cover or lid of a well. —मुखी f. A female ancestor entitled to a share in the above Sráddha. —वादिन् m. 1 The speaker of a prologue to a drama.-2 A drummer.

नापितः m. A barber, shaver.-Comp. —शाला f. A barber's shop, a hair-cutting saloon.

नापित्यं n. The trade of a barber. —त्यः m The son of a barber.

नाभिः m., f., नाभी f. 1 The navel. -2 Any navel-like cavity. —नाभिः m. 1 The nave of a wheel. -2 The centre, focus, chief point. -3 A leader, head. -4 Near relationship. -5 A paramount sovereign or lord. -6 A near relation.-7 A Kshatriya. —नाभिः f. Musk (मृगनाभि). (N. B. नाभि at the end of Bah. comp. becomes नाभ when the comp. is used as an epithet, as पद्मनाभः.). -Comp. —आवर्तः m. The cavity of the navel. -अः,-जन्मन्,-भूः m. Epithets of Brahman (m.). -नाडी f., -नालं n. The umbilical cord. —वर्धनं n. 1Cutting or division of the umbilical cord. -2 Rupture of the navel. -3 Corpulency.

नाभिक a. (f. —का) Relating to or coming from a navel. [-2 Pain.

नाभीलं n. 1The cavity of the navel.

नाभ्य a. (f. —भ्या) Relating to, proceding from, being in, the navel, umbilical. —भ्यः m. An epithet of Siva.

नाम ind. A particle used in the following senses:—1 Named, called, by name. -2Indeed, certainly, truly, to be sure, as is well-known. -3 Probably, perhaps. -4 Possibility, frequently used with अपि in the sense of ' I wish ', ' would that ', is it likely that &c? ' -5 A feigned or pretended action, pretence *e. g.* परिश्रमं नाम विनीय च क्षणं * कुमा. सं.5. 32-6 (With imperatives) Granted, though, well, it may be ; *e. g.* एवं नामास्तु ' be it so,if you like.' -7 Anger or censure. 8 Wonder. -9 Recollection. नाम is often used with the interrogative pronoun and its derivatives कथं, कदा &c. in the sense of ' possibly ',' indeed,"I should like to know '; *e.g.* को नाम राज्ञां प्रियः; को नाम पाकाभिमुखस्य जंतुर्द्वाराणि दैवस्य पिधातुमीष्टे * उत्त. रा 7. 4.

नामत: *ind.* By name, namely.

नामन् *n.* 1 A name, appellation, personal name (opp. गोत्र). -2 The mere name; तस्य पयसो नामापि न ज्ञायते * भर्तृहरि: ' Not even the name, *i. e.* no trace or mark is seen. ' -3 (In gram.) A noun, substantive (opp. आख्यात). -4 A word, name, synonymous word as in इति वृक्षनामानि -5 Substance (opp. गुण). -Comp. —अनुशासनं, -अभिधानं *n.* 1 Declaring one's name. -2 A dictionary, lexicon. —अपराध: *m.* Abusing (a respectable man) by name, calling names. —आवली *f.* A list of names (of a god). —करणं, -कर्मन् *n.* 1 The ceremony of naming a child after birth. -2 A nominal affix. —ग्रह: *m.*, -ग्रहणं *n.* Addressing or mentioning by name; utterance of the name,calling to mind the name.

ग्राहं *ind.* By naming, by mentioning the name.—धातु:*m.*A verbal base derived from a noun(*e.g.* तपस्य् from तपस्).-धारक, -धारिन्*a.* Bearing only the name, in name only, nominal. —धेयं *n* 1 A name, appellation. -2 The ceremony of naming a child. —निर्देश: *m.* Pointing out by name. -मात्र *a.* Having only the name, nominal, in name. (-त्रं *n.*) The mere name or mention (of a thing). -माला *f.*, —संग्रह: *m.* A vocabulary or glossary (of nouns). —मुद्रा *f.* A seal-ring, signet-ring. —वर्जित *a.* 1 Nameless. -2 Stupid, foolish. —वाचक *a.* Expressing a name. (—कं *n.*) A proper name. —शेष *a.* Having only the name left, remaining in name only, dead, deceased.

नामि: *m.* An epithet of Vishnu.

नामित *a.* (*f.*-ता)Bent,bowed down.

नाय: *m.* 1 A leader,guide.-2 Guiding, directing. -3 Policy.-4 Means, expedient.

नायक: *m.* 1 A leader, conductor.-2 A chief, master, lord. -3 A preeminent or distinguished personage. -4 A general, commander. -5 (In Rhet.) The hero of a poetic composition.According to साहित्यदर्पण there are four main kinds of नायक:- धीरोदात्त, धीरोद्धत, धीरललित and धीरप्रशांत) The Rasamanjarí mentions 3 classes पति, उपपति and वैशिक). -6 The central gem of a necklace.-7 A paradigm or leading example *e. g.* दृशेते क्षिपु नायका:. -8 An epithet of Sâkyamuni. -Comp. —अधिप: *m.* A king, sovereign.

नायिका *f.* A mistress. -2 A wife. -3 The heroine of a poetic composition. (According to साहित्यदर्पण she is of three kinds स्वा or स्वीया, अन्या or परकीया and साधारणस्त्री).

नार: *m.* 1 A calf. -2 Water. —रं *n.* 1 A multitude or assemblage of men. -2 Dry ginger.

नारक *a.* (*f.* -की)Hellish, infernal. —क: *m.* 1 The infernal regions, hell. -2 An inhabitant of hell.

नारकिक:, नारकिन् (*nom. sing.* —की

नारकीय: *m.* An inhabitant of hell.

नारंग: *m.* 1 The orange tree. -2 A libertine. -3 A twin. —गं, -गकं *n.* The fruit of the orange tree. -2 A carrot. -3 The juice of the pepper plant. [*varshi·*

नारद: *m.* N. of a celebrated *De-*

नारसिंह: *m.* An epithet of Vishnu.

नाराच: *m.* An iron arrow. -2 An arrow in general. -3 Water-elephant.

नाराचिका, नाराची *f.* A goldsmith's scales.

नारायण: *m.* An epithet of Vishhu. -2 N. of an ancient sage said to be a companion of Nara and to have produced Urvasi from his thigh. —णी *f.* 1 An epithet of Lakshmi, the goddess of wealth.-2 An epithet of Durgâ. -Comp. —प्रिय: *m.* 1 N. of Siva. -2 Yellow sandal-wood.

नारिकेर:, -ल: *m.* The cocoa-uut. (The word is also written नारिकेलि,-ली, नारी-केलि,-ली, नाडि (-डी-) केर, नालिकेलि, -ली). -ली *f.* Fermented liquor made from the water of the cocoa-nut.

नारी *f.* 1 A woman. -Comp. -तरंगक: *m.* 1 A paramour. -2 A libertine. —दूषणं *n.* woman's vice (they are:- पानं दुर्जनसंसर्ग: पत्या च विरहोऽटनम् । स्वप्नोन्यगृहवासश्च नारीणां दूषणानि षट्.—प्रसंग: *m.* Lechery, libertinism. -रत्नं *n.* A jewel of a woman, an excellent woman.

नार्यंग: *m.* The orange tree.

नाल *a.* (*f.* —ला) Consisting or made of reeds. —लं *n.* 1 A hollow stalk, especially the stalk of the lotus. (-*m.* also in this sense). -2 Any tubular vessel of the body.-3 Yellow orpiment. -4 A handle. -ल: *m.* A canal, drain.

नालंबी *f.* The lute of Siva.

नाला *f.* A hollow stalk, especially that of the lotus.

नालि:, -ली *f.* 1 Any tubular vessel of the body. -2 A hollow stalk, especially that of the lotus. -3 A period of 24 minutes (घटिका). -4 An instrument for boring an elephant's ear. -5 A canal, drain. -6 A lotus flower.-7 A piece of metal on which the hours are struck (घटी).

नालिक: *m.* A buffalo. —का *f.* 1 The stalk of lotus. -2 A tube. -3 An instrument for boring an elephant's ear. -4 A period of 24 minutes. —कं *n.* A lotus-flower. -2 A flute. -3 Myrrh.

नालिकेर: *m.* नालिकेलि,-ली *f.* See नारिकेर.

नालीक: *m.* 1 An arrow. -2 A javelin. -3 A lotus. -4 The fibrous stalk of a lotus. -5 A water-pot made of the cocoa-nut. —कं *n.* An assemblage of lotus-flowers.

नालीकिनी *f.* 1 A multitude or assemblage of lotus flowers. -2 A lotus-pond.

नाविक: *m.* 1 The helmsman of a vessel, a pilot.-2 A navigator, sailor. -3 A passenger on board a ship.

नाविन् *m.* A boatman.

नाव्य *a.* (*f.* —व्या) 1 Accessible by a boat or ship, navigable (as a river &c.). -2 Praiseworthy. —व्यं *n.* Newness.

नाश: *m.* 1 Disappearance. 2 Frustration, destruction, ruin, loss. -3 Death. -4 Misfortune, calamity. -5 Abandonment, desertion. -6 Flight, retreat.

नाशनं *n.* 1 Destruction, ruin. -2 Removing, removal, expulsion. -4 Perishing, death. -5 Forgetting.

नाशिन् *a.* (*f.* —नी) 1 Destructive, destroying, removing.-2 Perishing, perishable. [lost.

नाष्टिक: *m.* The owner of anything

नासत्यौ *m. dual* The two Asnvini Kumâras.

नासा *f.* 1 The nose. -2 The trunk of an elephant.-3 The upper timber of a door.-Comp.-छिद्रं,-रंध्रं,-विवरं *n.* A nostril. -दारु *n.* The upper timber of a door-frame. —परिस्राव: *m.* The running at the nose; a running cold. —पुट:*m.*, पुटं*n.* Nostril.—मर्यादा *f.* The septum of the nose. -वंश: *m.* The bridge of the nose.-स्राव: *m.* A running cold.

नासिकंधम *a.* Blowing or breathing through the nose.

नासिकंधय *a.* Drinking through the nose.

नासिका *f.* 1 The nose.-2 Any nose-shaped object. -3 The trunk of an elephant. -4 The upper timber of a door. -5 A projection. -6 An epithet of the nymph Asvini. -Comp. —मल: *m.* The mucus of the nose.

नासिक्य *a.* (*f.* —क्या) Nasal. -क्य: *m.* A nasal sound. -क्यौ *m. dual* An epithet of the Asvins. —क्यं *n.* The nose.

नासीरं *n.* Advancing in front of an army. —र: *m.* 1 The van or front (of an army &c.). -2 A champion who advances before the line.

नास्ति *ind.* Non-existence, as in नास्तिक्षीरा. -Comp. -वाद: *m.* Assertion of the non-existence of God, atheism, infidelity.

नास्तिक: *m.* An atheist, unbeliever, one who denies the authority of the Vedas and a future life or the existence of a supreme ruler or creator of the universe.

नास्तिक्यं *n.* Atheism, infidelity.

नास्तिद: *m.* The mango tree.

नास्यं *n*. A nose-cord.

नाह: *m.* 1 Binding, confinement. -2 A trap or snare.

नाहुष:,-षि:*m.* An epithet of Yayâti.

नि *ind.* It is used in the following senses. 1 Lowness, as in निषद्. -2 A group or collection as in निकर.-3 Intensity as in निकाम.-4 Command, order, as in निदेश. -5 Continuance, permanence, as in निविशते.-6 Skill, as in निपुण. -7 Restraint, confinement, as in निबंध.-8 Inclusion, as in निपीतमुदकं.-9 Proximity, as in निकट. -10 Insult, wrong, as in निकृति.-11 Showing, as in निदर्शन.-12 Cessation as in निवृत्त.-13 Resort, refuge as in निलय.-14 Doubt. -15 Certainty. -16 Affirmation &c.

नि:शेष *a.* Whole, complete, entire. —षं:,-षेण *ind.* Wholly, entirely.

नि:श्रय (-यि-) णी, नि:श्रेणी *f.* A ladder, staircase.

नि:श्रेयसं *n.* Final beatitude, absolution.

नि:श्वसनं *n.* Breathing out, sighing.

नि:श्वास:, निश्वास: *m.* Breathing out, expiration.-2 Sighing, a sigh, breath.

नि:सह *a.* (*f.* —हा) 1 Unable to bear, impatient. -2 Powerless, spiritless, fatigued. 3 Unbearable, irresistible.

नि:सरणं *n.* 1 Going out, exit. -2 An outlet from a house. -3 Final departure, death. -4 A remedy.-5 Final beatitude.

नि:सार: *m* Going forth or out, exit.

नि:सारणं *n.* 1 Expelling, turning out. -2 The outlet from a house.

नि:स्व: *m.* Remainder, surplus.

नि:स्राव: *m.* 1 Expense, expending, expenditure. -2 The water of boiled rice.

निकट *a.* (*f.* —टा) Near, close, proximate. —ट: *m.*, -टं *n.* Proximity. (निकटे means near, at hand, hard by or close).

निकर: *m.* 1 A heap, pile. -2 A multitude, collection. -3 A bundle. -4 Sap, pith, essence. -5 A suitable gift. -6 A treasure.

निकर्तनं *n.* Cutting down or off.

निकर्षणं *n.* 1 An open space for recreation or a play-ground in or near a town. -2 A court at the entrance of a house.-3An unploughed plot of ground.

निकषः (--सः) 1 *m.* A touch-stone, whet-stone. -2 (Fig.) Anything serving as a test. -3 A line of gold made on a touch-stone. -Comp. —उपलः, —ग्रावन्, -पाषाणः *m.* A touchstone, whetstone.

निकषा *f.* N. of the mother of Râvana or of imps in general. —*ind.* 1 Near, close by (with acc.) *e. g.* निकषा सौधभित्तिं, विलंघ्य लंकां निकषा हनिष्यति. शिशुपा. I. 68. -Comp. -आत्मजः *m.* A demon. [ant.

निकाम *a.* (*f.* -मा) Copious, abund-

निकामम् *ind.* 1 According to wish or desire. -2 To one's satisfaction, to one's heart's content.-3 Exceedingly. (This word is also treated as a noun (*n.*). As the first member of a compound it loses its final म्.

निकायः *m.* 1 A heap, an assemblage, a multitude, group in general. -2 A congregation, an association of persons who perform like duties. -3 A house, habitation, abode. -4 The body. -5 Aim, mark. -6 The Supreme Being.

निकाय्यः *m* A dwelling, a house.

निकारः *m.* 1 Winnowing corn. -2 Killing, slaughter.-3 Humiliation, subjugation. -4 Insult, wrong, offence. -5 Abuse, disrespect. -6 Wickedness, malice.-7 Opposition, contradiction.

निकारणं *n.* Killing, slaughter.

निकाशः, -सः*m*.1 Appearance, sight. -2 Proximity, vicinity. -3Likeness, resemblance (at the end of comp.).

निकाषः *m.* Scratching, rubbing.

निकुंचकः *m.* A measure of capacity equal to ¼ of a *Kudava* (also निकुंचक).

निकुंजः *m.*, -जं *n.* 1 A bower, an arbour, a place over-grown with shrubs and creepers. -2 A vault.-3 A cavern.

निकुंभः *m.* 1 N. of an attendant of Siva. -2 N. of the father of Sunda and Upasunda.

निकुंभिला *f.* 1 A cave or grove at the western gate of Lankâ. -2 An image of Bhadrakâlî on the west side of Lanká. -3 A place where oblations are offered.

निकुरं (-रं-) बं *n.* A flock, collection, multitude.

निकुलीनिका*f.* Family art, one inherited by birth, any skill or art peculiar to a race.

निकृत *p. p.* (*f.* -ता) 1 Humbled, humiliated. -2 Insulted, offended. -3 Deceived, cheated. -4 Afflicted, injured. -5 Wicked, dishonest. -6 Base, vile. —तं *n.* Humiliation. -Comp. —प्रज्ञः *a.* Evil-minded. —मति *a.* Depraved in mind, base.

निकृतिः*f.*1 Baseness, wickedness. -2 Dishonesty, fraud, deception, deceit. -3 Insult, offence, humiliation. -4 Abuse, reproach. -5 Rejection, removal. -6 Poverty, indigence. -7 The earth. -8 N. of one of the eight Vasus. -Comp. —प्रज्ञ, नैकृतिक*a.* Evil-minded, deceitful.

निकृतिन् *a.* Base, dishonest, wicked.

निकृंतन *a.* (*f.* नी) Cutting down, destroying. —नं *n.* Cutting, cutting off, destruction. -2 An instrument of cutting.

निकृष्ट *p. p.* (*f.* -ष्टा) 1 Low, base, vile. -2 Outcast. -3 Vulgar. -4 Near. -ष्टं *n.* Proximity.

निकेतः, —तनः *m.* 1 A house, mansion, abode. -2 A mark, countersign.

निकेतनः *m.* An onion. **—नं** *n.* A mansion, house, abode.

निकोचनं *n.* Contraction, compres- [sion.

निक्वणः, निक्वाणः *m.* 1 A musical tone or sound. -2 A sound in general.

निक्षा *f.* A nit (perhaps a wrong form for लिक्षा).

निक्षिप्त *p. p.* (*f.*-प्ता) 1 Thrown or put down, thrown into. -2 Deposited, pledged, pawned. -3 Rejected, abandoned.

निक्षेपः *m.* 1 Throwing or casting on (with acc.); अलं मान्यानां व्याख्यानेषु कटाक्षनिक्षेपेण * साहित्य द. -2 A deposit, pledge. 3 Anything deposited without a seal in trust or as a compensation ; an open deposit. -4 Sending away. -5 Abandoning. -6 Wiping, drying.

निक्षेपणं *n.* 1 Putting down, placing down (the feet). -2 A means by which anything is kept.

निखननं *n.* Digging in, burying as in स्थूणानिखननन्याय.

निखर्व *a.* (*f.* —र्वा) Dwarfish. **—र्वं** *n.* A billion.

निखात *p. p.* (*f.* —ता) 1 Dug up, excavated. -2 Fixed, infixed. -3 Dug in, buried.

निखिल *a.* (*f.* —ला) Complete, entire, all.

निगड *a.* (*f* —डा) Fettered, chained. **—डः** *m.*, **—डं** *n.* An iron chain for the feet of an elephant. -2 A fetter, chain or shackle.

निगडित *a.* (*f.* —ता) Fettered.

निगणः *m.* The smoke of a sacrificial fire or burnt offering.

निगदः, निगादः *m.* 1 Recitation, audible recitation of prayers. -2 A prayer repeated aloud. 3 Discourse. -4 Learning anything without knowing the meaning. -5 Mention.

निगदितं *n.* A discourse, speech.

निगमः *m.* The Veda. -2 Any word or words quoted from the Vedas, a Vedic sentence. -3 A work explanatory of the Vedas. A sacred precept, the words of a god or holy man. -5 A root (as the source of a word). -6 Certainty, assurance. -7 Logic. -8 Trade, traffic. -9 A market, fair. -10 A caravan of wandering merchants. -11 A road, market-road. -12 A city.

निगमनं *n.* 1 Quotation of a word or words from the Veda. -2 (In logic) The conclusion in a syllogism, a deduction (the fifth member of the five-membered Indian syllogism).

निगरः, निगारः, *m.* Swallowing.

निगरणं *n.* 1 Swallowing, devouring. -2 (Fig.) Completely absorbing. **—णः** *m.* 1 The throat. -2 The smoke of a sacrificial fire.

निग (-गा-) लः *m.* 1 Swallowing; devouring. -2 The throat or neck of a horse. **निगालवत्** *m.* A horse.

निगीर्ण *p. p.* (*f.* —र्णा) 1 Swallowed, devoured. -2 (Fig.) Completely swallowed up or absorbed.

निगु *a.* Pleasing. **-गुः** *m.* 1 The mind. -2 Dirt, excrement. -3 A root. -4 Painting.

निगूढ *a.* (*f.* —ढा) 1 Hidden, concealed, private, obscure. **—ढं** *ind.* Secretly, privately.

निगूहनं *n.* Concealing, hiding.

निगृहीत *p. p.* 1 Seized, arrested. -2 Restrained, curbed, checked, subdued. -3 Attacked. -4 Defeated in argument, caught.

निगृहीतिः *f.* 1 Restraint, check. -2 Overpowering, subjection.

निग्रंथनं *n.* Killing, slaughter.

निग्रहः *m.* 1 Keeping in check, curbing, subjection. -2 Suppression, obstruction, putting down. -3 Overtaking, capturing. -4 Imprisonment. -5 Defeat, overthrow. -6 Destruction, removing. -7 Punishment (opp. अनुग्रह). -8 Rebuke, blame. -9 Aversion, dislike, disgust. -10 (In Nyâya phil.) A flaw in an argument, a fault in a syllogism. 11 A handle. -12 A limit, boundary.

निग्रहण *a.* (*f.* —णा) Holding back or down, suppressing. -णं *n.* 1 Subduing. -2 Capture, confinement. -3 Punishment in general. -4 Defeat.

निग्राहः *m.* 1 Punishment. -2 An imprecation; as in निग्राहस्ते भूयात 'Confusion seize thee!'

निघ *a.* (*f.* —घा) As high as broad. —घः *m.* 1 A ball. -2 Sin.

निघंटुः *m.* 1 A vocabulary or glossary of words. -2 Particularly the glossary of Vedic words explained by Yâska in his Nirukta. [tion.

निघर्षः *m.*, निघर्षणं *n.* Rubbing, friction.

निघसः *m.* 1 Eating. -2 Food.

निघातः *m.* 1 A blow, stroke. -2 Suppression or absence of accent. -3 A vowel having a grave accent.

निघातिः *f.* An iron club.

निघुष्टं *n.* Sound, noise.

निघर्षः *m.*, निघर्षणं *n.* 1 Rubbing; friction. -2 Grinding.

निघ्न *a.* (*f.* —घ्ना) 1 Dependent, subservient, obedient. -2 Docile, tractable. -3 Dependent on, *i. e.* following the gender &c. of, a substantive. -4 (After a numeral) Multiplied by.

निचयः *m.* 1 A collection, heap, multitude. -2 Store, stock. -3 An assemblage of parts constituting a whole. -4 Certainty.

निचायः *m.* A heap.

निचिकी, नैचिकी *f.* An excellent cow.

निचित *p. p.* (*f.* —ता) 1 Covered, overcast, overspread. -2 Full of, filled. -3 Raised up, heaped up.

निचुलः *m.* 1 A kind of reed. -2 N. of a poet and friend of Kâlidâsa. -3 An upper garment, cover.

निचुलकं *n.* 1 A breast-plate, cuirass. -2 An outer garment.

निचोलः *m.* 1 A cover, wrapper. -2 A bed-cover. -3 The cover of a litter.

निचोलकः *m.* 1 A jacket, bodice. -2 A soldier's jacket serving as a cuirass.

निच्छविः *m.* N. of a district, the modern Tirhut.

निच्छिविः *m.* N. of one of the degraded castes (sprung from outcast Kshatriyas)

निज् 3. U. (नेनेक्ति, नेनिक्ते, प्रणेनेक्ति, निक्त) 1 To wash, cleanse, purify. -2 To wash or clean oneself, to be purified (A.). -3 To nourish. -With अव— To wash, sprinkle water. -निस् -To wash, clean, purify.

निज *a.* (*f.* —जा) 1 Innate, native, inborn, congenial. -2 Own, one's own party or country. -3 Peculiar. -4 Continual, perpetual.

निंज् 2 A. (निंक्ते) To wash. -With प्र- To wash (प्रणिंक्ते).

निटलं *n.* (Sometimes written निटिलं) The forehead. Comp. —अक्षः *m.* N. of Siva.

निडीनं *n.* The downward flight or swoop of birds. See डीन.

नितंबः *m.* 1 The buttocks, posteriors (of a woman), the circumference of the hip and loins. -2 The ridge, side or flank of a mountain. -3 A precipice -4 The sloping bank of a river. -5 The shoulder. -Comp. -बिंबं *n.* Round or circular hips.

नितंबिन a. (*f.* —नी) 1 Having beautiful buttocks. -2 Having beautiful sides (as a mountain). -नी *f.* 1 A woman with large and handsome hips. -2 A woman in general.

नितरां *ind.* 1 Wholly, completely. -2 Exceedingly, very much.-3 Continually, always, eternally. -4 At all events. -5 Certainly.

नितलं *n.* One of the seven divisions of the lower regions.

नितांत *a.* (*f.* —ता) Extraordinary, excessive, very much. —तं *ind.* Excessively, very much, in a high degree.

नित्य *a.* (*f.* —त्या) 1 Continual, perpetual, constant. -2 Imperishable, indestructible. -3 Invarible, regular, not optional, regularly prescribed (opp. काम्य). -4 Necessary, obligatory, 5 Ordinary; usual (opp. नैमित्तिक). -6 (At the end of comp.) Constantly dwelling in, perpetually engaged in or busy with; *e. g.* अरण्यनित्य, तपोनित्य. —त्यः *m.* The ocean. —त्या *m.* An epithet of the goddess Durgâ —त्यं *n.* An indispensable or inevitable act. —त्यं *ind.* Daily, always, perpetually, eternally. -Comp. —अनध्यायः *m.* Invariable suspension of Vedic studies. —आनित्य *a.* Eternal and perishable. —ऋतु *a.* Regularly recurring at the seasons. —कर्मन्, -कृत्यं *n.*, —क्रिया *f.* Any daily and necessary rite, a constant act or duty. —गतिः *m.* Air, wind. —दानं *n.* Daily alms-giving. —नियमः *m.* An invariable rule. -नैमित्तिकं *n.* Any ceremony constantly performed to accomplish a particular object (*e.g.* a पर्वश्राद्ध) —प्रलयः *m.* Sleep. —मुक्तः *m.* The Supreme Spirit. —यौवना *f.* An epithet of Draupadi. —शंकित *a.* Perpetually alarmed, ever suspicious. —समासः *m.* A compound the meaning of which cannot be expressed by its constituent members used separately (the separate ideas having merged into one); *e. g.* जमदग्नि, जयद्रथ &c.

नित्यदा *ind.* Perpetually, constantly, eternally.

नित्यशस् *ind.* Constantly, always.

निदुः *m.* A man.

निदर्शक *a.* (*f.* —का) 1 Seeing, perceiving. -2 Pointing out, proclaiming, indicating.

निदर्शनं *n.* 1 View, insight, looking into, sight, vision. -2 Pointing to, showing. -3 Proof; evidence. -4 An instance; illustration. -5 A scheme, system. -6 A precept, scriptural authority. -7 The third member of an Indian syllogism (usually called उदाहरण). —ना *f.* The figure in which is stated a possible, or as is sometimes the case, even an impossible connection of things, implying a relation of type and prototype. संभववस्तुसंबंधोऽसंभवन्वापि कुत्रचित । यत्र बिंबानुबिंबत्वं बोधयेत्सा निदर्शना. * साहि. द.

निदाघः *m.* 1 Heat, warmth. -2 The hot season, (the months of ज्येष्ठ and आषाढ). -3 Sweat, perspiration. -Comp. —करः *m.* The sun. —सिंधुः *m.* A river in hot season (nearly dry).

निदानं *n.* 1 A rope; halter. -2 A primary cause, the first or essential cause. -3 A cause in general. -4 (In medicine) Inquiry into the causes of a disease, pathology. -5 Diagnosis of a disease. -6 End, termination.-7 Purity, purification.

निदिग्ध *p. p.* (*f.* -ग्धा). 1 Smeared, anointed. -2 Increased; accumulated. —ला *f.* Small cardamoms.

निदिध्यासः *m.*, निदिध्यासनं *n.* Profound and repeated meditation.

निदेशः *m.* 1 Order, command, instruction. -2 Speech, narration, conversation. -3 Vicinity; neighbourhood. -4 A vessel.

निदेशिन् *f.* 1 A quarter, point of the compass. -2 A region.

निद्रा *f.* 1 Sleep, sleepiness. -2 Shutting, budding state. -Comp. -वृक्षः *m.* Darkness.-संजननं *n.* Phlegm, phlegmatic humour.

निद्राण *a.* (*f.* —णा) 1 Sleeping; asleep. -2 Shut, closed (as a bud).

निद्रालु *a.* Sleeping, asleep. —लुः *m.* An epithet of Vishnu.

निद्रित (*f.* —ता) Asleep, slept.

निधन *a.* (*f.* -ना) Poor, indigent. -नः *m.*, -नं *n.*1 Destruction, annihilation, death, loss. -2 The *finale* (in music). -3 Conclusion, end, termination. —नं *n.* Family, race.

निधनता *f.* Indigence, poverty.

निधानं*n.*1Putting down, depositing. -2 Keeping, preserving. -3 A place where anything is placed, a receptacle, reservoir. -4 Treasure. -5 Store, property, wealth.

निधिः *m.* 1 Abode, receptacle, reservoir. -2 A store-house, treasury. -3 A treasure, store, hoard. -4 The ocean.-5 An epithet of Vishnu. -Comp -ईशः,-नाथः *m.* An epithet of Kubera.

निधुवनं *n.* 1 Agitation, trembling. -2 Coition. -3 Pleasure, enjoyment, sport.

निध्यानं *n.* Seeing, beholding, sight.

निध्वानः *m.* Sound.

मिनक्षु *a.* 1 Wishing to die. -2 Wishing to escape or fly away.

निन (-ना-) दः *m.* 1 Sound, noise. -2 Buzzing, humming (of bees &c.). -3 A sound like that of a chariot.

निनयनं *n.* 1 Performance.-2 Pointing out.

निंद् 1 P. (निंदति, निंदित, प्रणिंदति) To blame, censure, reproach, condemn.

निंदक *a.* (*f.* —का) Blaming, censuring, abusing.

निंदनं *n.*, निंदा *f.* 1 Blame, censure, reproach, abuse, defamation.-2 Injury, wickedness. निंदास्तुतिः *f.* 1 Ironical praise, irony. -2 Covert praise.

निंदित *p. p.* (*f.* -ता) 1 Blamed, censured, abused. -2 Low, despicable.-3 Prohibited, forbidden.

निंदुः *f.* A woman bearing a dead [child.

निंद्य *a.* (*f.* —द्या) 1 Blamable, censurable, reprehensible, vile.-2 Forbidden, prohibited.

निपः *m.*,-पं *n.* A water-jar. —पः *m.* The Kadamba tree.

निप (-पा-) ठः *m.*, निपठनं *n.* निपठितिः *f.* Reading, reciting, studing.

निपतनं *n.* 1 Falling down, descendine, alighting. -2 Flying down.

निपत्या *f.* 1 Slippery ground. -2 A battle-field.

निपातः *m.*1 Falling or coming down, descending, alighting.-2 Attacking, falling upon, a spring, leap.-3 Casting, discharging, -4 Descent, fall. -5 Death. -6 Accidental occurrence or mention. -7 An irregular form, putting down as irregular or exceptional.-8 A particle, an indeclinable. -9 The opposite extremity, the lower end.

निपातनं *n.* 1 Throwing down, beating or knocking down. -2 Overthrowing, destroying, killing. -3 An irregular form of a word, irregularity, exception.-4 Falling down.

निपानं *n.* 1 Drinking. -2 Any reservoir of water, pool. -3 A place or trough near a well for watering cattle. -4 A well.-5 A milk-pail.

निपीडनं *n.* 1 Squeezing, pressing. -2 Hurting, injuring. -ना *f.* Oppression, hurt, injury.

निपुण *a.* (*f.* —णा) 1 Clever, shrewd, skilful. -2 Proficient or skilled in, conversant or familiar with (with loc. or instr.) वाचि निपुण: वाचा निपुण:.-3 Experienced.-4 Kindly or friendly towards. -5 Acute, delicate, minute, sharp. -6 Complete, perfect, accurate. —णं or निपुणेन *ind.* 1 Skilfully, cleverly. -2 Perfectly, completely, totally. -3 Exactly, carefully, accurately, minutely. -4 In a delicate manner.

निबंध: *m.* 1 Binding, fastening. -2 Attachment.-3 Composing, recording, writing down. -4 A literary composition or treatise, work. -5 A compendium. -6 Restraint, confinement. -7 Suppression of urine. -8 A bond, fetter. -9 A grant of property, an assignment of cattle, money &c. for support. -10 Fixed property. -11 Foundation, origin. -12 Cause, reason,

निबंधनं *n.* 1 The act of fastening. -2 Constructing, building. -3 Restraining, checking. -4 A bond, fetter. -5 A support, stay. -6 Dependence, connection. -7 Cause, motive, basis, foundation.-8 Abode, receptacle.-9 Composing, arrangement. -10 A literary composition. -11 A grant (of land), an assignment. -12 The peg of a lute. -13. (In gram.) Syntax. -14 A commentary.

निबंधनी *f.* A bond, fetter, tie.

निब (-ब-) र्हणं *n.* Killing: destruction, slaughter.

निबिड *a.* (*f.* -डा) Dense, thick.-2 Hard, difficult.

निभ *a.* (*f.* —भा) (At the end of comp. only) Like, similar, resembling. —भ: *m.*,-भं *n.* 1 Appearance, light, manifestation. -2 Pretence, disguise. -3 Trick, fraud.

निभालनं *n.* Seeing, sight, perception.

निभृत *a.* (*f.* -ता) 1 Very much frightened. -2 Gone, past.

निभृत *a.* (*f.* -ता) 1 Placed down, deposited, lowered. -2 Filled with, full of. -3 Concealed, out of sight, unobserved. -4 Secret, covert. -5 Still, silent, fixed, immovable, motionless. -6 Mild, gentle. -7 Modest, humble. -8 Firm, resolute. -9 Lonely, solitary. -10 Shut, closed (as a door). -11 True, faithful, firmly attached. -तं *n.* Modesty, humility.—तं *ind.* 1 Secretly, unperceived, quietly.-2 Out of sight, in a corner. -Comp. —आत्मन्*a.* Firm, resolute.

निमग्न *p. p.* (*f.* —ग्ना) 1 Plunged, immersed, submerged, sunk (fig. also). -2 Gone down, set (as the sun). -3 Overwhelmed, covered. -4 Depressed, not prominent.

निमज्जथु: *m.* 1 The act of diving or entering into, plunging. -2 Plunging into the bed, sleeping, going to bed.

निमज्जनं *n.* Bathing, diving, plunging (lit. and fig.)

निमंत्रणं *n.* 1 Invitation. -2 Summoning, calling. -3 A summons.

निमंत्राणिक: *m.* A Brâhmana invited to dinner.

निमय: *m.* Barter, exchange.

निमानं *n.* 1 Measure. -2 Price.

निमिः *m.* 1 Winking, twinkling (of the eyes). -2 N. of one of the descendants of Ikshváku, and ancestor of the line of kings who ruled in Mithilá.

निमित्तं *n.* 1 A motive, ground, reason. -2 The instrumental or efficient cause (opp. उपादान). -3 Any apparent cause, pretext. -4 A sign, token. -5 A mark, target. -6 An omen, prognostic (good or bad). -Comp. —अर्थः *m.* The infinitive mood (in gram.). —आवृत्तिः *f.* Dependence on a special cause. —कारणं *n.*, —हेतुः *m.* An instrumental or efficient cause. —कालः *m.* A specific time. —कृत *m.* A crow. —धर्मः *m.* 1 Expiation. -2 An occasional rite. —विद् *m.* An astrologer.

निमिषः *m.* 1 Winking, shutting the eye, twinkling. -2 Twinkling of the eye, as a measure of time, a moment. -3 The shutting (of flowers). -4 Morbid twinkling of the eye. -Comp. —अंतरं *n.* The interval of a moment.

निमीलनं *n.* 1 Shutting the eyelids, winking. -2 Death. -3 (In astr.) Total eclipse.

निमीला, निमीलिका *f.* 1 Shutting the eyes. -2 Winking, conniving at anything. -3 Fraud, pretence.

निमीलित *p. p.* (*f.* —ता) 1 Shut, closed. -2 Obscured, darkened. -3 Benumbed, stupefied. -4 Disappeared.

निमूलं *ind.* Down to the root *e. g.* निमूलकाषं कषति.

निमेयः *m.* Barter, exchange.

निमेषः *m.* Twinkling of the eye, a moment. -Comp. —कृत *f.* Lightning. —रुच् *m.* A fire-fly.

निम्न *a.* (*f.* —म्ना) 1 Deep (lit. and fig.) -2 Low, depressed. —म्नं *n.* 1 Depth, low ground, low land. -2 A slope, declivity. -3 A gap, chasm in the ground. -4 A depression, low part. -Comp. —उन्नत *a.* Low and high, depressed and elevated, uneven —वर्तं *n.* A low place. —गा *f.* A river, a mountain-stream.

निंबः *m.* A tree with bitter fruits. -Comp. —तरुः *m.* 1 The Mandára tree. -2 The Nimba tree.

निंबू *f.* A kind of जंबीर (lime).

निंबूकः *m.* The common lime..

निम्लुक्तिः *f.*, **निम्लोचः** *m.* Sunset.

नियत *p. p.* (*f.* —ता) 1 Curbed, restrained. -2 Subdued, controlled, self-governed. -3 Abstemious, temperate. -4 Attentive, intent. -5 Fixed, constant, steady. -6 Certain, settled. -7 Inevitable. -8 Positive, definite. -9 Forming the subject of consideration, relevant or irrelevant. -10 Maintained, observed (as a vow &c.). —तं *ind.* 1 Always, constantly. -2 Positively, certainly, surely. -3 Forcibly.

नियतिः *f.* 1 Restraint, restriction. -2 Destiny, fate, fortune (good or bad). -3 A religious duty or obligation. -4 Self-command, self-restraint.

नियंतृ *m.* 1 A charioteer, driver. -2 A governor, ruler, master. -3 A punisher. -4 The Supreme Being.

नियंत्रणं,—णा *f.* 1 Checking, reserve, restraint ; अनियंत्रणानुयोगो नाम तपस्विजनः श. 1. -2 Restricting, confining (to a particular sense; (अनेकार्थस्य शब्दस्यैकार्थनियंत्रणं *साहि. द. -3 Guiding, governing. -4 Defining.

नियंत्रित *p. p.* 1 Curbed, restrained, checked -2 Guided, governed. -3 Restricted, confined to (a particular sense, as a word).

नियमः *m.* 1 Restraining, checking. -2 Taming, subduing. -3 Confining, preventing. -4 A restraint, check. -5 Restriction, limitation. -6 A rule or precept, law (in general) usage. -7 Regularity. 8 Certainty. -9 An agreement, vow, engagement. -10 Necessity, obligation. -11 Any voluntary or self-imposed religious observance. -12 Penance, religious austerities. -13 (In Mim. phil.) A rule or precept which lays down something which, in the absence of that rule, would be *optional*. -14 (In Yoga phil.) Restraint of the mind, the second of the 8 principal steps of meditation in *yoga*. -15 (In Rhet.) A poetical convention, as the peacock's cry in the rains &c. (नियमेन As a rule, invariably). -Comp. —निष्ठा *f.* Rigid observance of prescribed rites. -पत्रं *n.* A written agreement. —स्थितिः *f.* Steady observance of religious obligations.

नियमनं *n.* 1 Checking, punishing, subduing. -2 Restriction, limitation. -3 Humiliation. -4 A precept. -5 Binding, tying down.

नियमवती *f.* A woman having the monthly courses.

नियमित *p. p.* (*f.* —ता) 1 Checked, restrained. -2 Moderated, tempered. -3 Removed, lessened. -4 Governed, guided. -5 Regulated, prescribed. -6 Fixed, stipulated. -7 Bound, confined. -8 Observed (as a vow or penance).

नियातनं *n.* Throwing down, knocking down.

नियामः *m.* 1 Restraint. -2 A religious vow. -3 A boatman.

नियामक *a.* (*f.* -मिका) 1 Restraining, checking. -2 Subduing, overpowering. -3 Limiting, defining more closely. -4 Guiding, governing. —कः *m.* 1 A master, ruler. -2 A charioteer. -3 A boatman, sailor. -4 A pilot.

नियुक्त *p. p.* (*f.* —क्ता) 1 Directed, instructed, commanded. -2 Authorised, appointed. -3 Permitted to raise issue; see नियोग (7) below. -4 Attached to. -5 Ascertained. —क्तः *m.* A officer; any one charged with some business.

नियुक्तिः *f.* 1 Injunction, command. -2 Appointment, commission, charge.

नियुतं *n.* 1 A million. -2 A hundred thousand. -3 Ten thousand crores.

नियुद्धं *n.* Close fight, personal struggle, wrestling.

नियोक्तृ *m.* An employer, a master.

नियोगः *m.* 1 Employment, use, application. -2 A command, direction, commission, charge, any business committed to one's care. -3 Fastening or attaching to. -4 Necessity, obligation. -5 Effort, exertion. -6 Certainty, ascertainment. -7 A practice in ancient times by which a childless widow was permitted to have intercourse with the brother or any near kinsman of her deceased husband to raise up issue to him, the son so born being called क्षेत्रज. (Vyása begot पांडु and धृतराष्ट्र on the widows of विचित्रवीर्य in this way).

नियोगिन् *m.* An officer, dependant, minister, functionary.

नियोज्यः *m.* A lord, master.

नियोजनं *n.* 1 Fastening, attaching. -2 Ordering, prescribing. -2 Urging, impelling. -4 Appointing. -नी *f.* A halter.

नियोजित *a.* (*f.* —ता) 1 Directed, ordered. -2 Appointed. -3 Joined to. -4 Instigated, incited. -5 Used, employed.

नियोज्यः *m.* One charged with any duty, an officer, a servant.

नियोद्धृ *m.* 1 A combatant, wrestler. -2 A cock.

निर् *ind.* A substitute for निस् before vowels and soft consonants and used to convey the senses of 'out of', 'away from', 'without', 'free from', &c. -Comp. —अंश *a.* 1 Whole, entire. -2 Not entitled to any share of the ancestral property. —अक्षः *m.* The place of no latitude (in astronomy). -अंकुश *a.* Uncontrolled, unruly, independent, completely free. -अजिन *a.* Skinless. —अंजन *a.* 1 Without collyrium. -2 Unstained, untinged. -3 Free from falsehood. -4 Simple, artless. (—नः *m.*) 1 An epithet of Siva. -2 N. of the Supreme Being. —अतिशय *a.* Unsurpassed, matchless, unrivalled. (—यः *m.*) The Supreme Being. —अत्यय *a.* 1 Free from danger, secure, safe. -2 Free from fault, unblamable, faultless. -3 Completely successful. —अध्व *a.* One who has lost one's way. —अनुक्रोश *a.* Pitiless, merciless, hard-hearted. (—शः *m.*) Mercilessness, hard-heartedness. —अनुग *a.* Having no followers. —अनुनासिक *a.* Not nasal. —अनुरोध *a.* 1 Unfavourable, unfriendly. -2 Unkind, unamiable. —अंतर *a.* 1 Constant, perpetual, uninterrupted, incessant. -2 Having no intermediate space, having no interval, close, closely contiguous. -3 Compact, dense. -4 Faithful, true (as a friend). -5 Not hidden from view. -6 Not different, similar, identical. -7 Sincere, sympathetic. (-रं *ind.*) 1 Without interruption, continually, incessantly. -2 Without interval. -3 Closely, firmly. -4 Immediately. —अंतराल *a.* 1 Without an intervening space, close. -2 Narrow. —अन्वय *a.* Having no progeny, childless. -2 Unconnected, unrelated. -3 Not agreeing with the context (as a word in a sentence). -4 Having no logical connection or regular sequence, unmethodical. -5 Without being seen, out of sight. -6 Unaccompanied. -7 Sudden, unexpected. —अपत्रप *a.* 1 Shameless, impudent. -2 Bold. —अपाय *a.* 1 Free from harm or evil. -2 Free from decay, imperishable. -3 Infallible. —अपेक्ष *a.* 1 Not depending on, independent of, having no need of (with loc.). -2 Taking no notice of. -3 Free from desire. -4 Indifferent to worldly attachments or pursuits. -5 Disinterested, not expecting any reward from another. (-क्षा *f.*) Indifference, disregard. —अभिभव *a.* 1 Not subject to humiliation or disgrace. -2 Not to be surpassed, unrivalled. —अभिमान *a.* 1 Free from self-conceit. -2 Void of self-respect. -3 Unconscious. —अभिलाष *a.* Indifferent to. -अभ्र *a.* Cloudless. —अंबु *a.* 1 Abstaining from water. -2 Waterless, destitute of water. —अर्गल *a.* Without a bolt, unbarred, unobstructed, completely free. (-लं *ind.*) Freely. —अर्थ *a.* 1 Void of wealth, poor, indigent. -2 Meaningless, unmeaning (as a word or sentence). -3 Nonsensical. 4 Purposeless. (-र्थः *m.*) 1 Loss, detriment. -2 Nonsense. —अर्थक *a.* 1 Unmeaning, nonsensical. -3 (A consonant) not followed by a vowel. (—कं *n.*) An expletive.

—अवकाश *a.* 1 Without free space. -2 Without leisure. -अवग्रह *a.* 1 Unrestrained, unchecked, irresistible. -2 Free, independent. -3 Self-willed, headstrong. (-हं *ind.*) 1 Uninterruptedly. -2 Intensely, strongly. -अवद्य *a.* 1 Blameless, unblamable, unobjectionable. -2 The Supreme Being. —अवधि *a.* Having no end, unlimited.-2 Continuous. -अवयव *a.* 1 Without parts.-2 Indivisible.-3 Without limbs —अवलंब *a.* 1 Unsupported. -2 Not affording support. -3 Not depending or relying on. —अवशेष *a.* Complete, entire. (निरवशेषेण *ind.* Completely, fully.) —अव्यय *a.* Eternal, immutable. —अशन *a.* Abstaining from food. (—नं *n.*) Fasting. —अहंकार, अहंकृति *a.* Free from egotism or pride, humble, lowly. —अहम् *a.* Free from egotism or self-conceit. —आकांक्ष *a.* 1 Wishing nothing, free from desire. -2 Wanting nothing to fill up or complete (as the sense of a word or sentence). -आकार *a.* 1 Formless, without form. -2 Ugly, deformed. -3 Disguised. -4 Modest. (-रः *m.*) 1 The universal spirit, Almighty. -2 An epithet of Siva. -3 Of Vishnu. —आकृतिः *m.* A religious student who has not duly gone through a course of study, or who has not properly read the Vedas. -2 A Bráhmana who has neglected the duties of his caste by not going through a regular course of study. —आकाश *a.* Leaving no free space, completely filled or occupied. —आक्रोश *a.* Unaccused, unreviled. —आगम *a.* Not derived from the Vedas. —आगस् *a.* Faultless, innocent, sinless. —आचार *a.* Without approved customs or usages, lawless, barbarian. —आडंबर *a.* 1 Without drums. -2 Without show, unostentatious. -आतंक *a.* 1 Free from fear. -2 Comfortable, healthy. -3 Not causing pain. -4 Unchecked, unhampered. (—कः *m.*) An epithet of Siva. —आतप *a.* Sheltered from heat, shady. (—पा *f.*) The night. -आदानः *m.* An epithet of Buddha. —आधार *a.* 1 Without a receptacle. -2 Without support, supportless (fig. also). —आधि *a.* Secure, free from anxiety. —आपद् *a.* Free from misfortune or calamity. (-*f.*) Prosperity. -आबाध *a.* 1 Unvexed, unmolested. -2 Unobstructed. -3 (In law) Frivolously vexatious (as a suit or cause of complaint). —आमय *a.* 1 Free from disease or illness, healthy. -2 Untainted, pure. -3 Free from defects or blemishes. -4 Full, complete. -5 Infallible. -6 Not liable to failure or miscarriage. (-यः *m.*, -यं *n.*) Freedom from disease or illness, health, welfare, happiness. (-यः *m.*) 1 A wild goat. -2 A hog or boar. —आमिष *a.* 1 Fleshless. -2 Having no sensual desires or covetousness. -3 Receiving no wages or remuneration. —आय *a.* Profitless. —आयत *a.* Full-stretched or extended. -आलंब *a.* 1 Having no prop or support (fig. also). -2 Not depending on another, independent. -3 Self-supported, friendless, alone. —आलोक *a.* 1 Not looking about or seeing. -2 Deprived of sight. 3 Depived of light, dark. 5 Invisible. (-कः *m.*) An epithet of Siva. -आश *a.* 1 Devoid of hope, despairing or despondent of. -आशंक *a.* Fearless. —आशिस् *a.* 1 Without a boon or blessing. -2 Without any desire, wish or hope, indifferent. —आश्रय *a.* 1 Without a support. -2 Friendless, destitute. —आहार *a.* Abstaining from food. (-रः *m.*) Fasting. —इच्छ *a.* Without wish or desire ; indifferent. —इंद्रिय *a.* Mutilated, maimed. —ईति *a.*Free from the calamities of the season. —ईश्वर *a.* Godless, atheistic. —ईषं *n.* The body of a plough. —ईह *a.* 1 Desireless, indifferent. -2 Inactive. (—हा *f.*) 1 Inactivity. -2 Indifference. —उच्छ्वास *a.* 1 Breathless,without breathing. -2 Narrow,contracted. (—सः *m.*) Absence of breath. —उत्तर *a.* 1 Answerless, without a reply.-2 Unable to answer,silenced. -3 Having no superior. —उत्सव *a.* Without festivites. —उत्साह *a.* 1 Inactive, indolent. -2 Devoid of energy. (—हः *m.*) 1 Absence of energy. -2 Indolence. —उत्सुक *a.* 1 Indifferent. -2 Calm, tranquil.-उदक *a.* Waterless. -उद्यम, -उद्योग *a.* Effortless,inactive. -उद्वेग *a.* Free from excitement or perturbation ; sedate, calm. —उपक्रम *a.* Without a commencement. —उपद्रव *a.* 1 Free from calamity or affliction ; happy, unmolested. -उपाधि*a.* Guileless, honest. —उपपत्ति *a.* Unsuitable. —उपपद *a.* 1Without any title or designation. -2 Unconnected with a subordinate word. —उपप्लव *a.* 1 Free from disturbance or calamity; unharmed. -2 Not causing any affliction. —उपम *a.* Peerless, incomparable. —उपसर्ग *a.* Free from portents. —उपस्कृत *a.* Not corrupted ; pure. —उपाख्य *a.* 1 Unreal, false (as वंध्यापुत्र). -2 Immaterial. -3 Invisible. (-ख्यं *n.*) Brahman (*n.*) —उपाय *a.* 1 Helpless. -2 Unsuccessful. —उपेक्ष *a.* 1 Free from trick or fraud. -2 Not neglectful. —गंध *a.* Scentless, unfragrant. —गुण *a.* 1 Stringless (as a bow). -2 Devoid of all properties. -3 Devoid of good qualities; bad, worthless. -4 Without attributes.(-णः *m.*) The Supreme Spirit. —ग्रंथ *a.* 1 Freed from all ties or hindrances. -2 Poor, beggarly. -3 Alone, unassisted. (—थः *m.*) 1 An idiot, a fool. -2 A gambler. -3 A saint or devotee who wanders about naked and lives as a hermit. —ग्रंथिक *a.* Clever. (—कः *m.*) A naked mendicant, a Jaina mendicant of the Digambara class. —घट्टं *n.* 1 A free market. -2 A crowded market. —घृण *a.* 1 Cruel,pitiless. -2 Shameless, immodest. —घृणा *f.* Cruelty. —जन *a.* Lonely, desolate. (—नं *n.*) A solitude, lonely place. -जर *a.* 1 Young, fresh. -2 Imperishable, immortal. (-रः *m.*) A deity, god; (nom. pl. निर्जराः,-निर्जरसः).(-रं *n.*)Ambrosia, nectar. —जल *a.* 1 Waterless,desert, destitute of water. -2 Not mixed with water. (-लः *m.*) A waste, desert. —जिह्वः *m.* A frog. —दंडः *m.* A Súdra. —दय *a.* 1 Merciless,unkind. -2 Passionate.-3 Excessive,violent. —दयं *ind.* 1 Unmercifully, cruelly. -2Violently, excessively. —दश *a.* More than ten days old. —द्रव्य *a.* 1 Immaterial. -2 Without property; poor. —द्वंद्व *a.* 1 Indifferent in regard to opposite pairs of feelings (pleasure or pain), neither glad nor sorry. -2 Independent. -3 Free from jealousy or envy. -4 Not contested; undisputed. —धनः *m.* An old ox. —नमस्कार *a.* 1 Not courteous or civil, not respecting any one. -2 Disrespected, despised. -नर *a.* Abandoned by men,deserted. -नाभि

a. Going or reaching beyond the navel. —बंधु *a.* Without kindred or relation; friendless. —बलं *n.* Powerless, feeble. —बाध *a.* 1 Unobstructed. -2 Lonely, solitary. -3 Unmolested. —बुद्धि *a.* Stupid, ignorant, foolish. —बुष, —बुस *a.* Unhusked, freed from chaff. —भर *a.* 1 Excessive, violent, much, strong. -2 Ardent. -3 Fast, close (as embrace). -4 Sound, deep (as sleep). -5 Filled with (at the end of comp.). (-रं *ind.*) 1 Excessively, exceedingly, intensely. -2 Soundly. —भृति *a.* Without wages. —मक्षिक *a.* Undisturbed, private, lonely. (—कं) *ind.* Lonely, privately. —मद *a.* 1 Not intoxicated; sober, quiet. -2 Not proud; humble. -3 Sad, sorry. -4 Not in rut (as an elephant.) —मम *a.* 1 Free from all connection with the outer world; who has renounced all worldly ties. -2 Unselfish, disinterested. -3 Indifferent to (with loc.). -4 An epithet of Siva. —मर्याद *a.* 1 Boundless, immeasurable. -2 Unrestrained, unruly, sinful, criminal. -3 Confused. -4 Insolent, immodest. —मल *a.* 1 Free from dirt or impurities; stainless, unsullied (fig. also). -2 Resplendent, bright. -3 Sinless, virtuous. (-लं *n.*) 1 Talc. -2 The remainings of an offering made to a deity. —मुट: *m.* 1 A tree bearing large blossoms. -2 The sun. -3 A rogue. (-टं *n.*) A large free market or fair. —मूल *a.* 1 Rootless (as a tree). -2 Baseless, unfounded (as a statement, charge &c.). -3 Eradicated. —मेध *a.* Without understanding; foolish, dull. —मोह *a.* Free from illusion. (-ह: *m.*) An epithet of Siva. —यंत्रण *a.* 1 Unrestrained, uncontrolled, unrestricted. -2 Unruly. (-णं *n.*) 1 Squeezing out. -2 Independence. —यूथ *a.* Separated from the herd; strayed from the flock (as an elephant). —रजस् (नीरजस्) *a.* Unsullied. (-*f.*) A woman not menstruating. —रव *a.* (नीरव) Not making any noise. —रस *a.* (नीरस) 1 Tastless, flavourless. -2 (Fig.) Insipid, without any poetic charm. -3 Sapless, without juice; withered or dried up. -4 Disagreeable. 5 Cruel, merciless. (-स: *m.*) The pomegranate. —रुज्, —रुज *a.* (नीरुज्, नीरुज) Free from sickness; healthy. *e. g.* नीरुजस्य किमौषधैः. —रूप *a.* (नीरूप) Formless, shapeless. (-प: *m.*) 1 Air, wind. -2 A god. (-पं *n.*) Ether. —रोग *a.* (नीरोग) Free from sickness or disease; healthy. —लक्षण *a.* 1 Ill-featured. -2 Undistinguished. -3 Unimportant, insignificant. -4 Unspotted. -5 Having a white back. —लेप *a.* 1 Unsmeared, unanointed. -2 Stainless, sinless. (-प: *m.*) A sage. —वंश *a.* Without posterity; childless. —वचन *a.* 1 Not speaking; silent. -2 Unobjectionable, blameless. —वाच्य *a.* 1 Not fit to be said. -2 Blameless, unobjectionable. —वात *a.* Free or sheltered from wind; calm, still. (-त: *m.*) A place sheltered from wind. —वार्य *a.* 1 Irresistible. -2 Acting fearlessly or boldly. —विकल्प, —विकल्पक *a.* 1 Not admitting an alternative. -2 Being without determination or resolution. -3 Not capable of mutual relation. -4 Conditioned. -5 Undeliberative. -6 Recognizing no such distinction as that of subject and object, or of the knower and the known; as applied to समाधि or contemplation, it is an exclusive concentration upon the one entity without distinct and separate consciousness of the knower, the known, and the knowing, and without even self-consciousness. -7 (In phil.) Not arising from the relation of the qualifier and the qualified. said of knowledge not derived from the senses, as घटत्व. (—ल्पं) *ind.* Without hesitation of wavering. —विकार *a.* 1 Unchanged, immutable. -2 Not disposed. -3 Disinterested. (—रः *m.*) The Supreme Deity. —विघ्न *a.* Uninterrupted, free from impediments. (-घ्नं *n.*) Absence of impediment. -विचिकित्स *a.* Free from doubt or reflection. —विचेष्ट *a.* Motionless, insensible. —वितर्क *a.* Unreflecting. —विंध्या *f.* N. of a river in the Vindhya hills. —विमर्श *a.* Void of reflection; thoughtless. -विवाद *a.* 1 Not contending or disagreeing. -2 Undisputed, not contradicted or disputed, universally acknowledged. —विवेक *a.* Indiscreet, void of judgment, wanting in discrimination ; foolish. —विशंक *a.* Fearless, undaunted, confident. —विशेष *a.* 1 Showing or making no difference; without distinction. -2 Having no difference ; same, like, not differing from. -3 Indiscriminate, promiscuous. (—षः *m.*) Absence of difference. (निर्विशेषं and निर्विशेषेण are used adverbially in the sense of 'without difference', 'equally', 'indiscriminately'). -विषय *a.* 1 Expelled or driven away from one's home, residence or proper place. -2 Having no scope or sphere of action. -3 Not attached to sensual objects (as mind). —वीर *a.* 1 Deprived of heroes, *e.* g. निर्वीरमुर्वीतलं. -2 Cowardly. —वीरा *f.* A woman whose husband and children are dead. -वीर्य *a.* Powerless, feeble, impotent. -वेतन *a.* Honorary, unsalaried. —वेद *a.* Not acknowleding the Vedas, an atheist, infidel. —वेष्टं *n.* A weaver's shuttle. —वैर *a.* Free from enmity; amicable, peaceable. (-रं *n.*) Absence of enmity. -व्यंजन *a.* 1 Straight-forward. -2 Without condiment. (—नं *ind.*) Plainly, in a straight-forward or honest manner. -व्यपेक्ष *a.* Indifferent to, regardless of. —व्यलीक *a.* 1 Not hurting or offending. -2 Without pain. -3 Pleased, doing anything willingly. -4 Sincere, genuine, undissembling. —व्याज *a.* 1 Candid, upright, honest, plain. -2 Without fraud ; genuine. -3 Got by heroism or daring deeds (not by fraud or cowardly conduct). -4 Not hypocritical. (—जं *ind.*) Plainly, honestly, candidly. -व्यापार *a.* 1 Without employment or business, free from occupation. -2 Motionless. -व्रत *a.* Not observing vows. —हिमं *n.* Cessation of winter. —हेतु *a.* Causeless, having no cause or reason. —ह्रीक *a.* 1 Shameless, impudent. -2 Bold, daring.

निरत *a.* (*f.* —ता) 1 Engaged or interested in. -2 Attached to. -3 Pleased. -4 Rested, ceased.

निरतिः *f.* Strong attachment, fondness, devotion.

निरयः *m.* Hell.

निरवहानि (-लि-) का *f.* A fence, an outer wall.

निरस *a.* (*f.* —सा) Tasteless, insipid, dry. —सः *m.* 1 Insipidity, tastelessness. -2 Want of juice, dryness. -3 Want of passion or feeling.

निरसन *a.* (*f.* —नी) Expelling,

driving away. -2 Vomiting. —र्सं n. 1 Expelling, ejecting, removal. -2 Denial, contradiction, refusal. -3 Refutation.-4 Vomiting forth, spitting out. -5 Checking, suppressing. -6 Destruction, extirpation.

निरस्त p. p. (f. —स्ता) 1 Cast away, thrown away, repudiated, driven, banished. -2 Dispelled, destroyed. -3 Abandoned. -4 Deprived or void of. -5 Discharged (as an arrow). -6 Refuted. -7 Vomited, spit out. -8 Uttered rapidly. -9 Torn out, destroyed.-10 Suppressed, checked. -11 Broken (as an agreement &c.). 12 Offered, given. —स्त: m. An arrow discharged. —स्तं n. 1 Rejecting, refusal. -2 Dropping or leaving out; rapid pronunciation. -Comp. —भेद a. Having all differences removed; same, identical. —राग a. One that has renounced all worldly attachments.

निराक: m. 1 Cooking. -2 Sweat. -3 The recompense of a bad action.

निराकरणं n. 1 Repudiating, expelling. -2 Banishing. -3 Obstruction, contradiction, opposition, rejection. -4 Refutation, reply. -5 Contempt. -6 Neglecting the chief sacrificial duties.

निराकरिष्णु a. 1 Repudiating, turning out, expelling. -2 Obstructive. -3 Spurning, disdaining. -4 Seeking to deprive one of a thing. -5 Forgetful.

निराकार: m. Reproach, censure.

निराकुल a. (f. —ला) 1 Full of, filled or covered with. -2 Distressed.

निराकृत p. p. (f. —ता) 1 Expelled. -2 Refuted. -3 Despised.

निराकृति:, निराक्रिया f. 1 Repudiation. -2 Refusal, rejection. -3 Obstruction, interruption.

निराग a. (f. —गा) Passionless dispassionate.

निरादिष्ट a. (f. —ष्टा) Paid off (as a debt).

निरादेश: m. Complete payment (of a debt).

निरामालु: m. The wood-apple (कपित्थ).

निरास: m. 1 Ejection, expulsion, removal. -2 Vomiting. -3 Refutation, contradiction. -4 Opposition. -5 Dropping (a sound or letter &c).

निरिंगिणी,—णी f. A veil.

निरीक्षणं n., निरीक्षा f. 1 A look. -2 Looking at, regarding, beholding. -3 Looking out for, searching. -4 Consideration, regard. -5 Hope, expectation.

निरीशं (—षं) n. A plough-share.

निरुक्त a. (f. —क्ता) 1 Expressed explained, defined. -2 Loud, distinct. —क्तं n. 1 Explanation, derivation, etymological interpretation. -2 N. of that Vedánga which contains glossarial explanation of obscure words, especially those occuring in the Vedas. -3 N. of the commentary on the Nighantus by Yâska. -Comp. —ज: m. One of the twelve kinds of sons allowed by the old Hindu law (= क्षेत्रज q. v.).

निरुक्ति: f. 1 Derivation, etymological interpretation of words. -2 (In Rhet.) An artificial explanation of the derivation of a word. -3 N. of Yâska's commentary on the Nighantus.

निरुत्सुक a. (f. —का) 1 Exceedingly anxious. -2 Unconcerned, indifferent.

निरुद्ध p. p. (f. —द्धा) 1 Obstructed, checked, curbed. -2 Confined, imprisoned.-Comp.-कंठ a. Having one's breath obstructed; choked, suffocated. —गुदः *m.* Obstruction of the rectum.

निरूढ *a.* (*f.* —ढा) 1 Conventional, accepted (as the meaning of a word, as opposed to its यौगिक or etymological sense). -2 Unmarried. -3 Drawn out, purged. -4 (In Rhet.) The accepted and popular meaning of a word. -Comp. —लक्षणा *f.* A *lakshaná* or secondary use of a word which is based not on the *vivakshá* or particular intention of the speaker, but on its accepted and popular sense.

निरूढिः *f.* 1 Fame, celebrity. -2 Familiarity, proficiency. -3 Confirmation. -4 Same as निरूढलक्षणा.

निरूपणं *n.*, -णा *f.* 1 Form, shape. -2 Sight, seeing. -3 Looking for, searching. -4 Ascertaining, investigation. -5 Definition.

निरूपित *p. p.* (*f.* -ता) 1 Seen, beheld. -2 Appointed, selected. -3 Weighed, considered. -4 Ascertained, determined.

निरूहः *m.* 1 An enema not of an oily kind. -2 Logic, disputation. -3 Certainty, ascrtainment. -4 A purging clyster. -5 A sentence having no ellipsis; a complete sentence.

निर्ऋतिः *f.* 1 Decay, destruction, dissolution. -2 A calamity, evil, adversity. -3 An imprecation, a curse. -4 The goddess of death or destruction, the regent of the south-western quarter. -5 The bottom of the earth.

निरोधः *m.*, **निरोधनं** *n.* 1 Confinement, imprisonment. -2 Restraint, check, suppression, control. -3 Obstruction, oppostion. -4 Hurting, punishing, injuring. -5 Annihilation, complete destruction. -7 Aversion, dislike. -8 Disappointment, frustration of hopes (in dramatic language). -9 (With the Buddhists) Suppression of pain.

निर्गः *m.* Country, region, place.

निर्गत *p. p.* (*f.* —ता) 1 Come forth or out, appeared. -2 Gone away, departed. -3 Disappeared. -4 Freed from. -5 Removed.

निर्गंधनं *n.* Killing, slaughter.

निर्गमः *m.* 1 Going forth or out, going away. -2 Departure, passing away. -3 A door, an outlet. -4 Exit, issue.

निर्गमनं *n.* 1 Going out or forth. -2 A door.

निर्गुंडः *m.* The hollow of a tree.

निर्ग्रंथनं *n.* Killing, slaughter.

निर्घंटः *m.*, -टं *n.* 1 A vocabulary. -2 A table of contents (सूचिपत्र).

निर्घर्षणं *n.* Rubbing, friction.

निर्घर्षणकं *n.* A dentifrice.

निर्घातः *m.* 1 Destruction. -2 A violent gust of wind; hurricane. -3 The noise of contending winds in the sky. -4 An earth-quake. -5 A thunder-stroke. -6 A stroke in general.

निर्घातनं *n.* Forcing out, bringing out.

निर्घोषः *m* 1 A sound in general. -2 A loud noise.

निर्जयः *m.*, **निर्जितिः** *f.* Complete victory; subjugation, vanquishing.

निर्झरः *m.*, -रं *n.* A spring, waterfall, cataract, mountain-torrent. -रः *m.* 1 Burning chaff. -2 An elephant. -3 A horse of the sun.

निर्झरिणी, **निर्झरी** *f.* A river, mountain-torrent.

निर्झरिन् *m.* A mountain.

निर्णयः *m.* 1 Removing, removal. -2 Complete ascertainment, decision, affirmation, determination, settlement. -3 Deduction, inference, demonstration (in logic). -4 Discussion, investigation.-5 Sentence, verdict, judgment. -6 (In Rhet.) Narration of events.-Comp.-पादः *m.* Sentence, decree, verdict (in law).

निर्णयनं *n.* 1 Ascertainment, determination. -2 Positive conclusion, settlement.

निर्णायक *a.* 1 Settling, conclusive. -2 Determining.

निर्णायनं *n.* 1 Making certain. -2 The outer angle of the elephant's ear.

निर्णिक्त *p. p.* (*f.* —क्ता) 1 Washed, purified, cleansed. -2 Expiated, atoned.

निर्णिक्तिः *f.* 1 Washing. -2 Expiation, atonement.

निर्णीत *p p.* (*f.* —ता) Settled, decided; resolved.

निर्णेकः *m.* 1 Washing, cleaning. -2 Ablution. -3 Atonement, expiation.

निर्णेजकः *m.* A washerman.

निर्णेजनं *n.* 1 Ablution. -2 Expiation, atonement (for an offence).

निर्णेतृ *m.* 1 A judge. -2 A voucher. -3 A guide.

निर्णोदः *m.* Removal, banishment.

निर्दंट,-ड *a.* (*f.* -टा, —डा) 1 Unkind, unmerciful. -2 Rejoicing over the faults of others. -3 Envious. -4 Slanderous.-5 Useless, unnecessary. -6 Violent. -7 Mad, intoxicated.

निर्दरः, —निर्दरिः *m.* 1 A cave, cavern. -2 A waterfall, spring. -र *n.* Essence (सार).

निर्दलनं *n.* Splitting, breaking, destroying.

निर्दहनं *n.* Burning, consuming.

निर्दातृ *m.* 1 A digger up of weeds, weeder. -2 A donor.-3 A husbandman, reaper.

निर्दारित *a.* (*f.* —ता) 1 Torn, rent. -2 Opened.

निर्दिग्ध *p. p.* (*f.* —ग्धा) 1 Anointed, smeared. -2 Well-fed, corpulent.

निर्दिष्ट *p. p.* (*f.* —ष्टा) 1 Pointed out, shown, indicated, particularized. -2 Described. -3 Assigned allotted.-4 Asserted, declared.-5 Ascertained, determined. -6 Ordered.

निर्देशः *m.* 1 Pointing out, showing, indicating. -2 Order, direction. -3 Advice, instruction. -4 Telling, declaring. -5 Particularization, specification, specific mention. -6 Ascertainment. -7 Vicinity, proximity.-8 Description, designation.

निर्देष्टृ *m.* An authority, a guide.

निर्धारः *m.*, निर्धारणं *n.* 1 Specifying or separating one out of many.-2 Determining, deciding. -3 Certainty, ascertainment.

निर्धारित *p. p.* (*f.* —ता) Determined, ascertained, fixed, settled.

निर्धूत *p. p.* (*f.* —ता) 1 Shaken off, removed, dispelled. -2 Deserted, rejected. -3 Deprived of, bereft. -4 Refuted. -5 Destroyed, divided.-तः *m.* A man deserted by his relations and friends.

निर्धौत *p. p.* (*f.* —ता 1 Washed off, cleansed. -2 Polished, bright.

निर्बंधः *m.* 1 Insisting upon, persistence, intentness, pertinacity; निर्बंधसंजातरुषा (गुरुणा) * रघुवं 5. 21. -2 Importunity, a pressing demand or request; urgency. -3 Obstinacy. -4 Accusation. -5 A contest, dispute.

निर्बर्हणं *n.* Same as निबर्हण.

निर्भट *a.* (*f.* —टा)Hard, firm.

निर्भर्त्सनं *n.*,-ना *f.* 1 Threat, menace. -2 Abuse, reproach, reviling, blame. -3 Malignity. -4 Red paint, lac.

निर्भेदः *m.* 1 Bursting, splitting asunder. -2 A split, rent. -3 Disclosure, betrayal. -4 Explicit mention or declaration. -5 The bed of a river.-6 Determination of an affair, event.

निर्भेद्य *a.* (*f.* —द्या) 1 Having no rent. -2 Not to be pierced through. -3 Disappointed.

निर्मथः *m.*, निर्मथनं *n.*, निर्मन्थः *m.*, निर्मन्थनं *n.* 1 Rubbing, churning, stirring. -2 The wood used for producing fire by friction. -3 Rubbing two pieces of wood together to produce fire. -4 Destruction, havoc.

निर्मन्थ्यं *n.* The wood used for producing fire by friction.

निर्माणं *n.* 1 Measuring, meting out. -2 Full measure, reach or extent. -3 Making, creation, formation, manufacture. -4 A created thing or object. -5 A form, shape, figure. -6 Composition, work. -7 (With Buddhists) Transformation. —णा *f.* Fitness, propriety, decorum.

निर्माल्यं *n.* 1 Purity, stainlessness. -2 The remains of an offering to a deity, such as flowers. -3 Flowers used and cast off; faded or withered flowers. -4 Remains in general.

निर्मित *p. p.* (*f.* —ता) 1 Constructed, built, formed. -2 Artificial.

निर्मितिः *f.* Production, creation, any artistic production.

निर्मुक्त *p. p.* (*f.* —क्ता) 1 Set free, freed, liberated. -2 Freed from worldly attachments.-3 Separated, disjoined. —क्तः *m.* A snake which has lately cast off its skin.

निर्मुक्तिः *f.* Freedom, liberation.

निर्मूलनं *n.* Eradication, uprooting, extirpation (fig. also).

निर्मृष्ट *p. p.* (*f.* —ष्टा) Wiped off, washed out.

निर्मोकः *m.* 1 Setting free, liberating. -2 A hide, skin, especially, the slough of a serpent.-3 Armour, mail. -4 The sky, heaven. -5 Atmosphere.

निर्मोक्षः *m.* Liberation, deliverance.

निर्मोचनं *n.* Liberation, deliverance.

निर्याणं *n.* 1 Exit, issue, departure. -2 Vanishing, disappearing. -3 Death. -4 Eternal emancipation, final beatitude.-5 The outer corner of the eye of an elephant. -6 A rope for tying cattle or the feet of a calf; a foot-rope in general.

निर्यातनं *n.* 1 Returning, restoring, restitution (as of a deposit). Payment of a debt.-3 Gift, donation Retaliation, requital, revenge (as in वैरनिर्यातन). -5 Killing, slaughter.

निर्यातिः *f.* 1 Exit, departure. -2 Dying, death.

निर्यामः *m.* A salior, pilot, boatman.

निर्यासः *m.*, —सं *n.* 1 Exudation of trees or plants; gum, juice, resin. -2 Extract, infusion, decoction. -3 Any thick fluid substance.

निर्यूहः *m.* 1 A pinnacle, turret, projection (on columns or gates). -2 A chaplet, crest. -3 A peg projecting from a wall.-4 A piece of wood placed in a wall for pigeons to build their nests or to perch upon. -5 A door, gate. -6 Extract, decoction.

निर्लुञ्चनं *n.* Pulling out or off, tearing off, peeling.

निर्लुण्ठनं *n.* 1 Robbing, plundering. -2 Tearing off.

निर्लेखनं *n.* 1 Scraping, scratching, -2 An instrument for scraping, a scraper.

निर्ल्वयनी *f.* The slough of a snake.

निर्वचनं *n.* 1 A proverbial expression; proverb. -2 Etymological interpretation, etymology.-3 A vocabulary, an index.

निर्वपण *a*. (*f*. —णी) 1 Relating to oblations. -2 Pouring out, scattering. -3 Giving, bestowing. —णं *n*. 1 Pouring out, offering. -2The presention of funeral offerings to the Manes ; a libation. -3 Bestowing presents. -4 Gift, donation. -5 A vessel (ladle &c.) for pouring.

निर्वयनी *f*. The slough of a snake.

निर्वर्णनं *n*. Looking at, seeing, sight, observing carefully.

निर्वर्तक *a*. (*f*. -र्तिका) 1 Completing, accomplishing, performing. -2 Desisting.

निर्वर्तनं *n*. Accomplishment, completion. -2 Desisting.

निर्वर्तिन् *a*. (*f*. —नी) 1 Completing, accomplishing. -2 Acting rudely.

निर्वहणं *n*. 1 End, completion. -2 Maintaining, carrying to the end, sustaining. -3 Destruction, annihilation. -4 (In dramas) The catastrophe, the denouement.

निर्वाण *p*. *p*. (*f*. —णा) 1 Blown or put out, extinguished (as a lamp or fire). -2 Lost, disappeared. -3 Dead; deceased. -4 Liberated from existence. -5 Set (as the sun). -6 Calmed, quieted. -7 Plunged. -णं *n*. 1 Extinction. -2 Vanishing from sight, disappearance. -3 Dissolution, death. -4 Final emancipation from matter and reunion with the Supreme Spirit ; eternal bliss. -5 (With Buddhists) Absolute extinction or annihilation. -6 Perfect and perpetual calm, repose. -7 Complete satisfaction or pleasure. -8 Cessation, desisting.-9 Vacuity. -10 Union, association, confluence. -11 The bathing of an elephant; as in अनिर्वाणस्य दंतिनः * रघुवं.1, 71. -12 Instruction in sciences. -Comp. -भूयिष्ठ *a*. Almost vanished or departed. -मस्तकः *m*. Final emancipation final beatitude.

निर्वादः *m*. 1 Blame, reproach. -2 Scandal, obloquy. -3 Decision of a controversy. -4Absence of dispute. -5 Rumour, report.

निर्वापणं *n*. 1 An offering, oblation. a funeral oblation. -2 A gift, donation. -3 Putting out, extinguishing. -4 Pouring out, scattering, sowing (as seed). -6 Offering, giving. -6 Allaying , pacification. -7 Annihilation. -8 Killing, slaughter. -9 Cooling refreshing. -10 A cooling applcation.

निर्वासः *m*., निर्वासनं *n*. 1 Expulsion, banishment. -2 Killing, slaughter. -3 Leaving one's home, living abroad (निर्वासः only in this sense).

निर्वाहः *m*. 1 Accomplishng, performing. -2 Completion, end. -3 Carrying to the end, steadfast adherence, perseverance ; निर्वाहः प्रतिपन्नवस्तुषु सतामेतद्धि गोत्रव्रतं * मुद्रारा.2. 18.-4 Subsisting on. -5 Competent provision, competency. -6 Describing, narrating.

निर्वाहणं *n*. See निर्वहणं.

निर्विण्ण *p*. *p*. (*f*. —ण्णा) 1 Despondent, depressed. -2 Overcome with fear or sorrow. -3 Emaciated with grief. -4 Abused, degraded. -5 Disgusted with anything. -6 Impaired, decayed.

निर्विष्ट *p*. *p*. (*f*. -ष्टा 1 Enjoyed, attained, experienced.-2 Fully enjoyed or used. -3 Obtained as wages. -4 Married.

निर्वृत *p*. *p*. (*f*. —ता) 1 Satisfied, contented, happy. -2 Free from care or anxiety; at ease. -3 Ceased, ended.

निर्वृतिः *f.* 1 Satisfaction, happiness, bliss. -2 Rest, repose. -3 Final emancipation or liberation from worldly existence. -4 Completion, accomplishment.

निवृत्त *p. p.* (*f.* —त्ता) Accomplished, attained.

निवृत्तिः *f.* 1 Accomplishment, fulfilment. -2 Completion, end.

निर्वेदः *m.* 1 Disgust, loathing. -2 Satiety. -3 Depression of spirits, despondency. -4 Humiliation. -5 Grief. -6 Complete indifference to worldly objects considered as the feeling which gives rise to the sentiment called शांत (quietude).-7 Self-disparagement or humiliation (regarded as one of the 33 subordinate feelings). -8 Shame.

निर्वेशः *m.* 1 Gaining, obtaining. -2 Wages, hire. -3 Eating, enjoyment. -4 Return of payment. -5 Expiation, atonement. -6 Marriage. -7 Fainting, swooning.

निर्वेष्टनं *n.* A weaver's shuttle.

निर्व्यथनं *n.* 1 Extreme pain, afflicting. -2 A hole, chasm.

निर्व्यूढ *p. p.* (*f.* —ढा) 1 Completed, finished. -2 Grown, developed. -3 Vindicated; fully shown; carried out faithfully or to the end. -4 Deserted, abandoned.

निर्व्यूढिः *f.* 1 End, completion. -2 A helmet, crest. -3 A door, gate. -4 A peg or bracket projecting from a wall. -5 Decoction.

निर्व्यूहः *m.* 1 A turret. -2 A crest. -3 A door. -4 A peg projecting from a wall. -5 Decoction.

निर्हरणं *n.* 1 Carrying out dead bodies to be burnt. -2 Taking forth, carrying or drawing out, extracting. -3 Rooting up.

निर्हादः *m.* Evacuation, voiding excrement.

निर्हारः *m.* 1 Taking away, removal. -2 Drawing out, rooting up, destruction. -3 Carrying out a dead body to be burnt. -4 Accumulation of a private store of wealth; private hoard. -5 Evacuation of the natural excrements of the body (opp. आहार). -6 Setting aside, excluding, leaving.

निर्हारिन् *a.* (*f.* —णी) 1 Crrying out. -2 Spreading wide (as fragrance). -3 Fragrant.

निर्हृतिः *f.* Taking out of one's way, removal.

निर्ह्रादः *m.* A sound in general.

निलयः *m.* 1 A hiding place, the lair or den of animals; a nest (of birds). -2 An abode, residence, house. -3 Total destruction. -4 Setting, disappearance; दिनांते निलयाय गंतुं *रघुवं. 2 15 (where the word is used in sense 2 also).

निलीयनं *n.* 1 Settling in a place, alighting. -2 A place of refuge, house, habitation.

निलिंपः *m.* 1 A god. -2 A troop of Maruts.-Comp. -निर्झरी *f.* The celestial Ganges.

निलिंपा, निलिंपिका *f.* A cow.

निलीन *p. p.* (*f.* —ना) 1 Melted or fused into. -2 Hidden into. -3 Involved, surrounded. -4 Destroyed, perished. -5 Changed, transformed. -6 Full.

निवचने *ind.* Not speaking; ceasing to speak, holding the tongue (regarded as a गति or preposition, or a separate word, when used with कृ; *e. g.* निवचनेकृत्य, निवचने कृत्वा).

निवपनं *n.* 1 Scattering or pouring

down. -2 Sowing. -3 An offering to deceased ancestors.

निवरा f. A virgin, an unmarried girl.

निवर्तक a. (f. —का) 1 Returning, turning back. -2 Stopping, ceasing. -3 Abolishing, removing. -4 Bringing back.

निवर्तनं n. 1 Returning, turning or coming back. -2 Not happening, ceasing. -3 Desisting or abstaining from (with abl.) -4 Desisting from work, inactivity (opp. प्रवर्तनं). -5 Bringing back. -6 A desire to improve. -7 A measure of land (equal to 20 rods), -8 Keeping back from (with abl.).

निवर्तिन् a. 1 Turning back, returning. -2 Abstaining from. -3 Allowing to return or turn back.

निवसतिः f. A habitation, abode, residence.

निवसथः m. A village.

निवसनं n. 1 A house, habitation. -2 A garment.

निवहः m. 1 A multitude, quantity, group, heap. -2 N. of one of the seven winds. -3 N. of one of the seven tongues of fire.

निवात a. (f. —ता) 1 Protected from the wind; not windy; calm. -2 Unhurt, uninjured. -3 Safe, secure. -4 Accoutred in strong mail. —तः m. 1 A refuge, an asylum. -2 An impenetrable coat of mail. —तं n. 1 A place sheltered from the wind. -2 Calm, stillness. -3 A secure spot. -4 A strong armour.

निवान्या f. A cow whose calf is dead and who is milked by means of another calf.

निवापः m. 1 Seed, grain. -2 An offering to the Manes of deceased parents or other relatives; a libation of water &c. at the Srâddha ceremony. -3 A gift or offering in general.

निवापकः m. A sower, scatterer.

निवारः m., निवारणं n. 1 Keeping off, preventing, warding off. -2 Prohibition, impediment.

निवासः m. 1 Living, residing. -2 A house; habitation, resting place. -3 Passing the night. -4 A dress, garment. -5 Night-quarters. -6 Refuge, asylum.

निवासनं n. 1 Residence. -2 Sojourn. -3 Spending time.

निवासिन् a. 1 Dwelling, residing. -2 Wearing, clothed in. -m. A resident, an inhabitant.

निवि (-वि-) ड a. (f. —डा) 1 Without space or interstices; close, compact. -2 Firm, fast. -3 Thick, impervious, dense, impenetrable. -4 Gross, coarse. -5 Crooked-nosed.

निविरी (-डी-) श,—स a. (f. -शा,-सा) 1 Compact, close. -2 Coarse, gross. —शा, —सा f. A crooked nose.

निविशेष a. (f. —षा) Not different; alike. —षः m. Want of difference, sameness.

निविष्ट p. p. (f. —ष्टा) 1 Seated, sitting upon. -2 Encamped. -3 Fixed or intent upon. -4 Concentrated, subdued, controlled. -5 Initiated. -6 Arranged. -7 Entered.

निवीतं n. 1 Wearing the sacred thread round the neck like a garland. -2 The thread so worn. —तः m., —तं n. A veil, mantle.

निवृत p. p. (f. —ता) Surrounded, enclosed. —तः m., —तं n. A veil, mantle, wrapper.

निवृतिः f. Covering, enclosing.

निवृत्त p. p. (f. —त्ता) 1 Returned, turned back. -2 Gone, departed.

vanished, disappeared. -3 Ceased, abstained from, stopped, desisted. -4 Abstracted from this world; quiet. -5 Repenting of improper conduct. -6 Finished, completed, whole. —त्तं *n.* 1 Return. -2 A mind free from the influence of passions. -Comp. —आत्मन् *m.* 1 A sage. -2 An epithet of Vishnu. —कारण *a.* Having no further cause or motive. (—णः *m.*) A virtuous man, a man uninfluenced by worldly desires. —मांस *a.* One who abstains from eating meat. —राग *a.* Of subdued passions. —वृत्ति *a.* Quitting any practice or occupation. —हृदय *a.* With relenting heart.

निवृत्तिः *f.* 1 Returning or coming back, return. -2 Disappearance, termination, suspension. -3 Abstaining from work; inactivity (opp. प्रवृत्ति). -4 Abstaining from. -5 Leaving off. -6 Resignation, discontinuance of worldly acts or emotions; separation from the world. -7 Repose, rest. -8 Felicity, beatitude. -9 Denial, refusal. -10 Abolition, prevention. -11 Ceasing to be binding (as a rule). -12 Completion.

निवेदनं *n.* 1 Making known, proclaiming; a communication, announcement. -2 Delivering, entrusting. -3 Dedication. -4 Representation. -5 An offering or oblation.

निवेदित *p. p.* (*f.* —ता) 1 Made known, announced, communicated. -2 Delivered, entrusted.

निवेद्यं *n.* Offering of food to an idol; cf. नैवेद्यं.

निवेशः *m.* 1 Entering, entrance. -2 Encamping, halting. -3 A halting place, encampment. -4 A house, dwelling. -5 Expanse, contour (of the breast). -6 Depositing, delivering. -7 Marrying, settling in life. -8 Impression, copy. -9 Military array. -10 Ornament, decoration. -11 Founding (a town).

निवेशनं *n.* 1 Entering, entrance. -2 Halting, encamping. -3 Marrying. -4 Entering in writing, inscribing. -5 An abode, house. -6 A camp. -7 A town or city. -8 A nest. —नी *f.* The earth.

निवेष्टः *m.* A cover, an envelope.

निवेष्टनं *n.* Covering, enveloping.

निश् *f.* (This word is optionally substituted for निशा in all cases after acc. dual; it has no forms for the first five inflections). 1 Night. -2 Turmeric.

निशमनं *n.* 1 Looking at, beholding. -2 Seeing, sight. -3 Hearing. -4 Becoming aware of.

निश (-शा-) रणं *n.* Killing, slaughter.

निशा *f.* 1 Night. -2 Turmeric. -3 A dream. -4 A collective name for the zodiacal signs Aries, Taurus, Gemini, Cancer, Sagittarius, and Capricorn. -Comp. —अटः, —अटनः *m.* 1 An owl. -2 A demon, ghost, goblin. —अदः *m.* A Nisháda. —अंध *a.* Blind at night. (—धा *f.*) The creeper called जतुका. — अधीशः, —ईशः, —नाथः, —पतिः, —मणिः *m.*, रत्नं *n.* 1 The moon. -2 Camphor. —अर्धकालः *m.* The first part of the night. —आख्या, —आह्वा *f.* Turmeric. —आदिः *m.* The evening twilight. —उत्सर्गः *m.* End of night, daybreak. —करः *m.* 1 The moon. -2 A cock. -3 Camphor. —केतुः *m.* The moon. —गृहं *n.* A bed-chamber. —चर *a.* (-रा, -री *f.*) Moving about by night, night-stalker. (-रः *m.*) 1 A fiend, goblin, an evil spirit. -2 An epithet of Siva. -3 A jackal. -4 An owl. -5 A snake. -6 The ruddy goose. -7 A thief. (-री *f.*) 1 A female fiend. -2 A woman going to meet her lover at night by appointment. -3 A harlot. -चर्म्म *m.* Darkness. —जर्क *n.* Dew, frost. —दर्शिन *m.* An owl. -निशं *ind.* Every night, always. —पुष्पं *n.* The white water-lily (opening at night). -2 Hoar-frost, dew. —मुखं *n.* The beginning of night. —मृगः *m.* A jackal. —वनः *m.* Hemp (शन). —विहारः *m.* A demon, goblin, a Rákshasa. -वेदिन *m.* A cock. —हसः *m.* The white water-lily (opening at night).

निशात *p. p.* (*f.* —ता) 1 Sharpened, whetted. -2 Polished, burnished.

निशादः *m.* A man of low caste.

निशानं *n.* Sharpening, whetting.

निशांत *p. p.* (*f.* —ता) Tranquil, quiet. —तं *n.* A house, dwelling. -Comp.—नारी *f.* A housewife.

निशामः *m.* Observing, perceiving.

निशामनं *n.* 1 Seeing, beholding. -2 Sight. -3 Hearing -4 Repeated observation. -5 A shadow, reflection.

निशारुक: *m.* One of the seven Rúpakas in music. —कं *n.* An air, a sort of musical composition played as an accompaniment to dancing.

निशित *a.* (*f.* —ता) 1 Sharpened, whetted, sharp. -2 Stimulated. -तं *n.* Iron. —ता *f.* Night.

निशीथः *m.* 1 Midnight. -2 Night in general.

निशीथिनी, निशीथ्या *f.* Night.

निशुंभः *m.* 1 Killing, slaughter. -2 Breaking, bending (as of a bow). -3 N. of a demon killed by Durgâ.

निशुंभनं *n.* Killing, slaying.

निश्चयः *m.* 1 Ascertainment, inquiry. -2 A fixed opinion ; settled or firm conviction; firm belief. -3 A determination, resolution. -4 Certainty, positive conclusion. -5 Fixed intention; design, purpose, aim. -6 A figure of speech in which there is the denial of the fancied character of a thing and the emphatic establishing of its real character. अन्यन्निषिध्य प्रकृतस्थापनं निश्चयः पुनः *साहि. द. *e. g.* वदनमिदं न सरोजं नयने नेन्दीवरे एते । इह सविधे मुग्धदृशो भ्रमर मुधा किं परिभ्रमसि ॥

निश्चल *a.* (*f.* —ला) 1 Immovable, steady, still. -2 Invariable, unchangeable. —ला *f.* The earth. -Comp. —अंग *a.* Firm. (-गः *m.*) 1 A species of crane. -2 A rock or mountain.

निश्चायक *a.* (*f* —का) Who or what ascertains or determines; decisive.

निश्चारकं *n.* 1 Evacuation by stools. -2 Air, wind. -3 Obstinacy, wilful nature.

निश्चित *p. p.* (*f.* —ता) 1 Ascertained, determined, decided, (used actively also). -2 Pronounced (as a sentence). -तं *n.* Certainty, decision. —तं *ind.* Decidedly, certainly.

निश्चितिः *f.* 1 Ascertainment, settling. -2 A determination, resolution.

निश्रमः *m.* Labour bestowed upon anything ; continued practice or labour.

निश्रयणी, निश्रोणि, निश्रेणी *f.* A ladder, a staircase. [sighing.

निश्वासः *m.* Inspiration, inhaling,

निषंगः *m.* 1 Attachment, clinging to. -2 Union, association. -3 A quiver. -4 A sword.

निषंगथिः *m.* 1 An embrace. -2 A bowman. -3 A charioteer.

निषंगिन —*m.* 1 An archer, a bowman. -2 A quiver. -3 A swordbearer.

निषण्ण *p. p.* (*f.* —ण्णा) 1 Seated.

reclined. -2 Supported. -3 Dejected, afflicted, down-cast.

निषण्णकं *n.* A seat.

निषद्या *f.* 1 A small bed or couch. -2 The hall of a merchant, a trader's shop. -3 A market-place, market.

निषद्वरः *m.* 1 Mud, mire. -2 The god of love. —री *f.* Night.

निषध *a.* Hard, solid. —धाः (*m. pl.*) N. of a people and their country governed by Nala. —धः *m.* 1 A ruler of the Nishadhas. -2 N. of a mountain. -3 A musical note. -धा *f.* N. of Nala's capital.

निषादः *m.* 1 N. of one of the wild aboriginal tribes in India; a mountaineer. -2 A man of a degraded tribe in general; an outcast, a Chândâla. -3 Especially, the son of a Brâhmana by a Sudra woman. -4 (In music) The last or seventh note of the Hindu gamut.

निषादित *p.p.* (*f.* —ता) 1 Made to sit down. -2 Afflicted, distressed.

निषादिन् *a.* (*f.* —नी) Sitting or lying down, resting. —*m.* An elephant-driver.

निषिक्त *p.p.* (*f.* —क्ता) 1 Sprinkled upon. -2 Infused, instilled, impregnated.

निषिद्ध *p. p.* (*f.* —द्धा) Forbidden, prohibited, prevented.

निषिद्धिः *f.* 1 Prohibition, warding or keeping off. -2 Defence.

निषूदनं *n.* Killing, slaughter. —नः *m.* A killer; as in बलवृत्रनिषूदनः &c.

निषेकः *m.* 1 Sprinkling, infusion. -2 Dripping, trickling, distilling. -3 Effusion, discharge. -4 Infusion of semen; impregnation; seed. -5 The ceremony performed upon impregnation. -6 Irrigation. -7 Water for washing. -8 Seminal impurity. -9 Dirty water.

निषेधः *m.* 1 Prohibition, keeping off, stopping, prevention. -2 Negation, denial. -3 The particle of negation; *e. g.* द्वौ निषेधौ प्रकृतार्थं गमयतः. -4 A prohibitive rule (opp. विधि). -5 Exception.

निषेवक *a.* (*f.* —का) 1 Practising, following, devoted to, fond of. -2 Frequenting, resorting to. -3 Enjoying.

निषेवणं *n.*, निषेवा *f.* 1 Serving, service, waiting upon. -2 Worship, adoration. -3 Practice, performance. -4 Attachment to. -5 Living in, enjoying, using. -6 Familiarity with, use.

निषेवित *p. p.* (*f.* —ता) 1 Served, waited upon, honoured. -2 Visited, frequented. -3 Practised, observed (as a vow &c.)

निष्क् 10 A. (निष्कयते) To weigh, measure.

निष्कः *m.*, —कं *n.* 1 A golden coin generally taken to be equal to one *Karsha* or Suvarna of 16 Mâshas. -2 A weight of gold equal to 108 or 150 Suvarnas. -3 A golden ornament for the neck or the breast. -4 Gold in general. -5 A golden vessel. —ष्कः *m.* A Chândâla.

निष्कर्षः *m.* 1 Drawing out, extraction. -2 The essence, the chief or main point; pith. -3 Measuring. -4 Certainty, ascertainment.

निष्कर्षणं *n.* 1 Drawing out, extracting, pulling off. -2 Deducting.

निष्कालनं *n.* 1 Driving away (cattle &c.). -2 Killing, slaughter.

निष्कासः (—शः) *m.* 1 Exit, egress, issue. -2 A portico. -3 Day-break. -4 Disappearance.

निष्कासित *p. p.* (*f.* —ता) 1 Expelled, driven out. -2 Gone forth or out. -3 Placed, deposited. -4 Stationed, appointed. -5 Opened, expanded. -6 Reviled, reproached.

निष्कासिनी *f.* A female slave not restrained by her master.

निष्कुटः *m.* 1 A pleasure-grove near a house. -2 A field. -3 The harem of a king. -4 A door, gate. -5 The hollow of a tree. [(एका.)

निष्कुटिः,—टी *f.* Large cardamoms

निष्कुषित *p. p.* (*f.* —ता) 1 Torn off, forced or drawn out. -2 Expelled.

निष्कुहः *m.* The hollow of a tree.

निष्कृत *p.p.* (*f.* —ता) 1 Taken away, removed. -2 Expiated, absolved, pardoned. -3 Disregarded, overlooked. -तं *m.* 1 Expiation or atonement. -2 A place of rendezvous.

निष्कृतिः *f.* 1 Expiation, atonement; ब्रह्मघ्ने च सुरापे च चौरे भग्नव्रते तथा। निष्कृतिर्विहिता सद्भिः कृतघ्ने नास्ति निष्कृतिः * पंचतं. -2 Acquittance, requital, discharge of a debt or obligation; *e.g.* न तस्य निष्कृतिः शक्या कर्तुं वर्षशतैरपि. Removal. -4 Restoration, cure. -5 Avoiding, escaping from. -6 Neglecting. -7 Bad conduct, roguery.

निष्कृष्ट *p. p.* (*f.* —ष्टा) 1 Pulled or drawn out, extracted. -2 Summed up.

निष्कोषः *m.*, निष्कोषणं *n.* 1 Tearing, drawing off or out, extracting, extirpating. -2 Husking, shelling.

निष्क्रमः *m.* 1 Going out, coming forth. -2 Departure, exit. -3 The ceremony of taking out a child for the first time into the open air (performed in the fourth month of its age). -4 Degradation, loss of caste, inferiority of tribe. -5 Intellectual faculty.

निष्क्रमणं *n.* 1 Going forth or out. -2 The ceremony of taking an infant out for the first time in the fourth month after delivery.

निष्क्रमणिका *f.* The ceremony explained in निष्क्रमणं (2.).

निष्क्रयः *m.* Redemption, ransom. -2 Reward. -3 Hire, wages. -4 Return, aquittance. -5 Fxchange, barter. -6 Sale. -7 Purchase.

निष्क्रयणं *n.* Redemption, ransom.

निष्क्राथः *m.* 1 Decoction. -2 Broth.

निष्टपनं *n.* Burning, scorching.

निष्टानकः *m.* 1 Roar, murmur. -2 Sound of lamentation.

निष्टापः *m.* Burning, slight heating.

निष्ट्यः *m.* An outcast, a Chândâla or Mlechchha.

निष्ठ *a.* (Usually at the end of comp.). 1 Being in or on, situated on. -2 Depending or resting on, referring or relating to. -3 Devoted or attached to, intent on; as in सत्यनिष्ठ. -4 Skilled in. -5 Believing in, as in धर्मनिष्ठ. —ष्ठा *f.* 1 Position, condition, state. -2 Basis, foundation. -3 Fixity, steadiness. -4 Devotion, close attachment. -5 Belief, faith, as in शास्त्रेषु निष्ठा. -6 Excellence, skill, perfection. -7 Conclusion, end, termination. -8 The catastrophe of a drama. -9 Accomplishment, completion (समाप्ति). -10 The culminating point. -11 Death, destruction. -12 Fixed knowledge, certainty. -13 Suffering, distress, anxiety. -4 (In gram.) A technical term for the past participial termination.

निष्ठानं *n.* Sauce, condiment.

निष्ठित *p. p.* (*f.* —ता) 1 Being in or on. -2 Devoted to. -3 Versed or skilled in. -4 Firm, fixed. -5 Certain, ascertained.

निष्ठी (-ष्ठे-) वः *m.*, -वंन., निष्ठी (-ष्ठे-) वनं; निष्ठीवितं *n.* Spitting out, spitting.

निष्ठुर *a.* (*f.* -रा) 1 Hard, coarse,

rough. -2 Severe, sharp. -3 Cruel, harsh. -4 Motionless, stiff. -5 Contumelious. —रं n. A harsh speech.

निष्ठ्यूत p. p. (f. —ता) 1 Spit out, cast or thrown out. -2 Uttered. -तं n. Spitting out.

निष्ठ्यूति: f. Spitting out.

निष्ण a. (f. —ष्णा), निष्णात a. (f. -ता). 1 Clever, skilful, versed, skilled, expert. -2 Fully accomplished. -3 Superior, perfect.

निष्पक्व a. (f. —क्वा) 1 Decocted, infused. -2 Well-cooked.

निष्पतनं n. Rushing out, issuing quickly.

निष्पत्ति: f. 1 Birth, production. -2 Ripeness, maturity. -3 Perfection. -4 Completion, termination.

निष्पंद a. (f. —दा) Motionless, immovable, fixed.

निष्पन्न p. p. (f.-न्ना) 1 Born, arisen, produced. -2 Effected, accomplished. -3 Ready.

निष्पवनं n. Winnowing.

निष्पादनं n. 1 Effecting, accomplishing. -2 Concluding.-3 Producing, causing.

निष्पाव: m. 1 Winnowing, cleaning corn &c. -2 The wind caused by the winnowing sieve or basket. -3 Wind.

निष्पिष्ट p. p. (f. —ष्टा) 1 Pounded. -2 Harassed, oppressed.

निष्पीडित p. p. (f. —ता) Squeezed, pressed together or out.

निष्पेष: m., निष्पेषणं n. 1 Rubbing together, grinding, bruising. -2 Striking, hitting against, friction. -3 The sound produced by striking or clashing.

निष्प्रवाणि, -णि n. New unbleached [cloth.

निस् ind. 1 As a prefix to verbal themes it implies separation (away from, outside of) (e. g. निर्गम्); certainty, (e.g. निश्चि); completeness or fulness (e. g. निर्जित); enjoyment, (e. g. निर्विश्); crossing over, transgressing (e. g. निष्क्रम् &c.).

As a prefix to nouns, not directly derived from verbs, it forms nouns or adjectives, and has the sense of out of, away from, as in निष्कौशाम्बि ; or not, without , नि:शेष:, निर्जन &c.N.B. In a compound the स् of निस् is changed to र् before vowels and soft consonants ;to a visarga before sibilants ; to श् before च् and छ्; and to ष् before क् and प्.

-Comp. —कंटक (निष्कंटक) a. 1 Thornless. -2 Free from enemies, danger or nuisance). —कपट (निष्कपट) a. Guileless, sincere. —करुण (निष्करुण) a. Merciless, cruel. —कल (निष्कल) a. 1 Without parts, undivided, whole. -2 Decayed, diminished. -3 Impotent, barren. -4 Maimed. (—ल:m.)- 1 A receptacle. -2 The pudendum muliebre. -3 N. of Brahman (m.). (-ला, -ली) f. An elderly woman, one who is past child-bearing, or one in whom menstruation has ceased. —कलंक, —कल्मष (निष्कलंक, निष्कल्मषं) a. Stainless, spotless. -कषाय(निष्कषाय) a. Free from dirt or impure passions. -काम (निष्काम) a. 1 Free from wish or desire; disinterested, unselfish. -2 Free from all worldly desires. (-मं ind.) 1 Without wish or desire. -2 Unwillingly. —कारण (निष्कारण) a. 1 Causeless, unnecessary. -2 Disinterested, free from any motive. -3 Groundless, not proceeding from any cause. (—णं ind.) Without any cause or reason, needlessly. —कालक: (निष्कालक:) m.A penitent shaven and smeared with clarified but ter. -कालिक (निष्कालिक) *a.* 1 One whose term of life is over or elapsed. -2 One who has no conqueror ; invincible (अजय्य). —किंचन (निष्किंचन) Poor, indigent. -किल्बिष (निष्किल्बिष) *a.* Sinless, faultless —कुल (निष्कुल) *a.* Having no kindred. -निष्कुल,—कुलीन (निष्कुलीन) *a.* Of low family. -कूट (निष्कूट) *a.* Free from deceit, honest. -कृप (निष्कृप) *a.* Pitiless, merciless, cruel. —कैवल्य (निष्कैवल्य) *a.* 1 Pure, absolute. -2 Deprived of final beatitude. (मोक्षहीन). —कौशाबि (निष्कौशाबि) *a.* Who has gone out of Kausâmbi. —क्रिय (निष्क्रिय) *a.* 1 Inactive. -2 Not performing ceremonial rites. —क्षत्र (निःक्षत्र), -क्षात्रिय (निःक्षात्रिय) *a.* Destitute of the military tribe. —क्षेप: (निक्षेप:) *m.* 1 Throwing upon. -2 Abandoning, sending away. -3 Wiping, drying. -4 A deposit. —चक्रं (निश्चक्रं) *ind.* Completely. —चक्षुस् (निश्चक्षुस्) *a.* Blind, eyeless.—चत्वारिंश (निश्चत्वारिंश) *a.* Past forty. —चिंत (निश्चिंत) *a.* 1 Free from anxiety, unconcerned, secure. -2 Thoughtless, unthinking. —चेतन (निश्चेतन) *a.* Unconscious. —चेतस् (निश्चेतस्) *a.* Not in one's right senses; mad. —चेष्ट (निश्चेष्ट) *a.* Motionless, powerless. —चेष्टाकरण (निश्चेष्टाकरण) *a.* Causing motionlessness (said of one of the arrows of Cupid. —छंदस् (निश्छंदस्) *a.* Not studying Scriptures. —छिद्र (निश्छिद्र) *a.* 1 Without holes. -2 Without defects or weak points. -3 Uninterrupted, unhurt. —तंतु *a.* Having no offspring, childless. -तंद्र, -तंद्रि *a.* Not lazy; fresh, healthy. —तमस्क, -तिमिर *a.* 1 Free from darkness, bright. -2 Freed from sin or moral impurities. -तर्क्य *a.* Unimaginable, inconceivable. -तल *a.* 1 Round, globular. -2 Moving, trembling, shaking. -3 Bottomless. -4 Down, below. (—ला *f.*) A pill, round ball. —तुष *a.* 1 Freed from chaff. -2 Purified, cleansed. -3 Simplified. —तुषित *a.* Husked. -2 Made thin. -3 Abandoned. —तेजस् *a.* Destitute of fire, heat or energy; impotent. -2 Spiritless, dull. -3 Obscure. —त्रप *a.* Impudent, shameless. —त्रिंश *a.* 1 More than thirty. -2 Pitiless, cruel (-श: *m.*) A sword. -त्रैगुण्य *a.* Destitute of the three qualities (सत्त्व, रजस्, and तमस्). —पंक (निष्पंक) *a.* Free from mud, pure. —पताक (निष्पताक) *a.* Having no flag or banner. —पतिसुता (निष्पतिसुता) *f.* A woman having no husband and no sons. —पत्र (निष्पत्र) *a.* 1 Leafless. -2 Unfeathered, featherless. [निष्पत्राकृ To pierce with an arrow so that the feathers come through on the other side; to cause excessive bodily pain (fig.) *e. g.* निष्पत्राकरोति मृगं व्याधः]. —पद (निष्पद) *a.* Having no foot. (-दं *n.*) A vehicle moving without feet. —पराक्रम (निष्पराक्रम) *a.* Powerless. —परिकर (निष्परिकर) *a.* Without preparations. —परिग्रह (निष्परिग्रह) *a.* Having no property or possessions. (-ह: *m.*) An ascetic without family, dependents or other belongings. —परिच्छद (निष्परिच्छद) *a.* Having no retinue or train. —परीक्ष (निष्परीक्ष) *a.* Not examining or testing accurately. —परिहार (निष्परिहार) *a.* Not observing caution. —पर्यंत (निष्पर्यंत), —पार (निष्पार) *a.* Boundless, unbounded. —पाप (निष्पाप) *a.* Sinless, guiltless, pure.—पुत्र (निष्पुत्र) *a.* Sonless, childless. —पुरुष (निष्पुरुष) *a.* 1 Unpeopled, desolate. -2 Without male issue. -3 Not male; feminine, neuter. (-षः *m.*) 1 A eunuch. -2 A coward. --पुलाक (निष्पुलाक) *a.* Freed from chaff. —पौरुष (निष्पौरुष) *a.* Unmanly. —प्रकंप (निष्प्रकंप) *a.* Steady, motionless. —प्रकारक (निष्प्रकारक) *a.* 1 Without distinction of species; absolute (as knowledge). —प्रकाश (निष्प्रकाश) *a.* Not transparent; dark. —प्रचार (निष्प्रचार) *a.* 1 Not moving away; remaining in one place. -2 Concentrated, intently fixed. -प्रति-(-ती-) कार (निष्प्रति-ती-कार), -प्रतिक्रिय (निष्प्रतिक्रिय) *a.* 1 Incurable, irremediable. -2 Unobstructed, uninterrupted. (-रं) *ind.* Uninterruptedly. -प्रतिघ(निष्प्रतिघ) *a.* Unobstructed, unimpeded. —प्रतिद्वंद्व (निष्प्रतिद्वंद्व) *a.* 1 Without enemies; unopposed. -2 Matchless, unrivalled, unequalled. -प्रतिभ (निष्प्रतिभ) *a.* 1 Devoid of splendour. -2 Having no intelligence; dull, stupid. -3 Apathetic. —प्रतिभान (निष्प्रतिभान) *a.* Cowardly, timid. -प्रतीप(निष्प्रतीप) *a.* 1 Looking straight forward; not turned backwards. -2 Unconcerned (as a look.)—प्रत्यूह (निष्प्रत्यूह) *a.* Unobstructed. —प्रपंच (निष्प्रपंच) *a.* 1 Without extension. -2 Without deceit; honest. —प्रभ (निःप्रभ or निष्प्रभ) *a.* 1 Pale-looking. -2 Powerless. -3 Obscure, dim, dark. —प्रमाणक (निष्प्रमाणक) *a.* Without authority. —प्रयत्न (निष्प्रयत्न) *a.* Inactive, dull. -प्रयोजन (निष्प्रयोजन) *a.* 1 Not influenced by any motive. -2 Causeless, groundless. -3 Useless. -4 Needless, unnecessary. (-नं) *ind.* Causelessly, without reason, without any object. —प्राण (निष्प्राण) *a.* Lifeless, dead. —फल (निष्फल) *a.* 1 Fruitless; (fig. also) unsuccessful; futile. -2 Useless, profitless, vain. -3 Barren (as a tree). -4 Meaningless (as a word). -5 Seedless, impotent. (—ला,-ली *f.*) A woman past child-bearing. —शंक *a.* Free from fear or risk; secure, fearless. -शब्द (निःशब्द) *a.* Inaudible. (-ब्दः *m.*, -ब्दं *n.*) Silence, a calm. —शरण *a.* (निःशरण) Helpless, forlorn. —शलाक (निःशलाक) *a.* Lonely, solitary, retired. (-कं *n.*) A retired place, solitude. —शल्य *a.* 1 Free from arrows.-2 Free from thorns or darts. —शोध्य (निःशोध्य) *a* Washed, pure, clean. —श्रीक *a.* 1 Deprived of lustre, or beauty.-2 Unhappy. -श्रेयस *a.* The best, most excellent. (-सः *m.*) An epithet of Siva. (—सं *n.*) 1 Final beatitude, eternal bliss. -2 Devotion, faith, belief. -3 Apprehension, conception. -4 Happiness (in general); welfare. —संशय (निःसंशय) *a.* 1 Certain. -2 Not doubtful, not suspecting or doubting. (—यं) *ind.* Doubtlessly, undoubtedly, certainly. —संग (निःसंग) *a* 1 Not attached or devoted to; regardless of, indifferent to. -2 One who has renounced all worldly attachments. -3 Separated, detached. -4 Unobstructed. (-गं) *ind.* Unselfishly. -संज्ञ (निःसंज्ञ) *a.* Unconscious. —सत्त्व (निःसत्त्व) *a.* 1 Unenergetic, impotent. -2 Insignificant, low. -3 Non-existent, unsubstantial. -4 Deprived of living beings. (-त्त्वं *n.*) 1 Absence of power or energy. -2 Non existence. -3 Insignificance. —संतति (निःसंतति), -संतान (निःसंतान) *a.* Childless. —संदिग्ध (निःसंदिग्ध), —संधि (निस्संधि, निःसंधि) Having no joints perceptible; compact, firm, close. —सपत्न (निःसपत्न) *a.* 1 Having no rival or enemy. -2 Belonging exclusively to one possessor. -3 Having no foes. —सर्गं (निःसर्गं) *ind.* 1 Unseasonably, at a wrong time -2 Wickedly. —संपात (निःसंपात) *a.* Affording no passage; blocked up. (-तः *m.*)The darkness of midnight; thick darkness. —संबाध (निःसबाध) *a.* Not contracted; spacious. -निःसह *a.* Unable to bear, sustain, or support; nerveless.- सार *a.* 1 Sapless, pithless. -2 Vain, unsubstantial. -सीम (निःसीम), —सीमन् (निःसीमन्) *a.* Immeasurable, boundless. —स्नेह (निःस्नेह) *a.* 1 Not unctuous or greasy; dry. -2 Not showing affection; unkind, indifferent. -3 Not loved, not cared for. -4 Not longing for; indifferent to. —स्पंद (निःस्पंद, or निस्स्पंद)*a* Motionless, steady. —स्पृह (निःस्पृह) *a.* 1 Free from desire -2 Regardless of, indifferent to. -3 Content, unenvious. -4 Free from any worldly ties. —स्व (निःस्व) *a* Poor, indigent. -स्वादु (निःस्वादु) *a.* Tasteless, insipid.

निसंपात *a.* Blocked up. (-तः *m.*) Thick darkness.

निसर्गः *m.* 1 Bestowing, granting. -2 A grant. -3 Evacuation, voiding excrement. -4 Abandoning, relinquishing. -5 Creation. -6 Nature, natural state or condition. (निसर्गतः, निसर्गेण *ind.* 'By nature', or 'naturally'.) -7 Exchange, barter. -Comp. —ज, —सिद्ध *a.* Innate, inborn, natural. —भिन्न *a.* Different by nature. —विनीत *a.* 1 Naturally discreet. -2 Naturally well-behaved.

निसारः *m.* A multitude (समूह).

निसूदन *a* (*f.* -ना) Killing, destroying. —नं *n.* Killing, slaughter.

निसृष्ट *p. p.* (*f.* —ष्टा) 1 Delivered, given, bestowed. -2 Abandoned, left. -3 Dismissed. -4 Permitted, allowed. -5 Central, middle. -Comp. —अर्थ *a.* To whom the management of an affair is entrusted. (—र्थः *m.*) 1 An envoy, ambassador. -2 A messenger, an agent. निसृष्टार्थदूती *f.* A female who brings about the union of two lovers of her own accord.

निस्तनी *f.* A pill, bolus,

निस्तब्ध *a.* (*f.* -ब्धा) 1 Paralysed. -2 Stopped, fixed.

निस्तरणं *n.* Going out or forth. -2 Crossing over. -3 Rescue, deliverance, getting rid of. -4 A means, plan. -5 Accomplishing, mastering.

निस्तर्हणं *n.* Killing, slaughter.

निस्तारः *m.* 1 Crossing or passing over. -2 Release, escape, rescue. -3 Final emancipation. -4 Discharge or payment of a debt; acquittance, requital. -5 A means, expedient.

निस्तारणं *n.* 1 Passing or conveying across. -2 Conquering, overcoming. -3 Delivering liberating.

निस्तीर्ण *p. p.* (*f.* —र्णा) 1 Rescued, delivered saved. -2 Crossed (fig). also

निस्तोदः *m.* Pricking; stinging.

निस्त्रुटी *f.* Card moms.

निस्नावः *m.* Residue of articles after [a sale.

निस्पंद *a* (*f* —दा) Immovable, steady. —दः *m.* Trembling, throbbing, motion.

निस्यं (-ष्यं-) दः *m.* 1 Flowing forth or down, dripping, streaming, oozing. -2 A discharge, sap, juice. -3 A flow, stream. -4 Necessary consequence or result. -5 Uttering, declaring.

निस्यंदिन *a.* (*f.* -नी) 1 Trickling or flowing down, oozing. -2 Dropping or pouring down.

निस्रवः, निस्रावः *m.* 1 A stream, torrent. -2 The scum of boiled rice. -3 Flowing forth.

निस्वनः, निस्वानः *m.*, निस्वनितं *n.* I Noise, voice. -2 The whistling sound of an arrow (only निस्वान in this sense).

निहत *p. p.* (*f.* -ता) I Struck down, killed, slain. -2 Struck into, infixed. -3 Attached or devoted.

निहननं *n.* Killing, slaughter.

निहंतृ *a.* I Killing. -2 Destructive, murderous.

निहवः *m.* Invocation, summoning, calling.

निहाका *f.* I The Gangetic alligator. -2 A storm.

निहारः *m* I Fog, mist. -2 Hoar-frost, heavy dew. -3 Evacution.

निहिंसनं *n.* Killing, slaughter.

निहित *p. p.* (*f.* -ता) I Laid, lodged, situated, deposited. -2 Delivered, entrusted. -3 Bestowed upon ; applied to. -4 Inserted, infixed. -5 Treasured up. -6 Held. -7 Laid down (as dust). -8 Uttered in a deep tone.

निहीन *a.* (*f.* -ना) Low, vile. —नः *m.* A low man ; one of vile origin.

निह्नवः *m.* I Denial, concealment of knowledge. -2 Secrecy, concealment. -3 A secret. -4 Mistrust ; doubt, suspicion. -5 Wickedness. -6 Atonement, expiation -7 Excuse, exculpation. -Comp. —उत्तरं *n.* An evasive reply. —वादिन् *m.* A defendant or witness who prevaricates or gives evasive replies.

निह्नुत *p. p.* (*f.* -ता) I Denied, disowned. -2 Concealed, dissembled.

निह्नुतिः *f.* I Denial, concealment of knowledge. -2 Dissimulation, reserve. -3 Secrecy, concealment in general.

निह्रादः *m.* A sound.

नी I U. (नयति,-ते, निनाय, निन्ये, अनैषीत्, अनेष्ट, नेष्यति,-ते, नेतुं, नीत) (One of the roots that govern two accusatives, *e. g.* अजां ग्रामं नयति) I To carry, bring, convey, take, conduct. -2 To guide, direct, govern. -3 To lead away to, carry or bring away. -4 To carry off. -5 To carry off for oneself (Atm). -6 To spend or pass (as time) नीत्वा मासान्कतिचित् ; *मेघ. 2 संविष्टः कुशशयने निशां निनाय * रघुवं. I 25. -7 To reduce any person to any state or condition ; *e. g.* दुःखं नी To reduce to misery ; वशं नी To reduce to subjection, win over ; अस्तं नी To cause to set ; विनाशं नी To destroy ; परितोषं नी To gratify, please ; साक्ष्यं नी To admit as a witness ; दंडं नी To inflict punishment upon, to punish ; पुनरुक्ततां नी To render superfluous ; विक्रयं नी To sell ; भस्मतां-भस्मसात्-नी To reduce to ashes &c. -8 To ascertain, inquire into, settle, decide. -9 To trace, track, find out. -10 To marry. -11 To exclude from. -12(Atm). To instruct, give instruction in ; *e. g.* शास्त्रे नयते. With अनु— I To conciliate, to please. -2 To beg, supplicate. -3 To cherish, love. अप— I To lead away, to cause to retire. 2 To rob, plunder. -3 To remove. -4 To extract. अभि— I To bring on, to conduct to. -2 To adduce, to quote. -3 To represent by gesticulation ; to exhibit dramatically. अभिवि— To instruct well. आ— I To bring. -2 To bring on, produce. -3 To reduce to any state or condition. उद्— (Atm.) To raise, lift up. -2 To lead out or aside. -3 To conjecture, ascertain. उप— I To raise. -2 To bring near. -3 To bring about, to cause. -4 (Atm.) To invest with the sacred thread.

-5 To bring into any state.-6 (Atm. To hire, to employ for wages. उपा— To lead, to reduce oneself to. नि— 1 To take near or towards. -2 To incline, bend. निस्– To investigate, settle, decide. परि- 1To lead round. -2 To marry. -3 To investigate, प्र— 1 To offer, to present. -2 To consecrate by reciting *mantras*. -3 To inflict.-4To perform,to effect.-5 To promulgate, to instiute,to teach. -6 To compose, write.प्रति -To carry back, take back.वि— 1 To remove, to take away. -2 To train, to educate. -3 To tame, govern, subjugate. -4 (Atm.) To appease (anger &c.). -5 To present, offer. -6 To spend, pass. -7 (Atm.)To spend (as money). -8 (Atm.) To pay, pay off. सम्— 1 To bring together. -2 To guide, govern. -3 To bring back, restore, to give back. समा— To join.

—*Caus.* (नाययति,-ते) (with instr. of agent) ; तेन मां सरस्वतीमनाययत्.*Desid.* (निनीषति,-ते).

नीः *m.* (At the end of comp.) A leader, guide, as in सेनानी,ग्रामणी,अग्रणी.

नीका *f.* A channel for irrigation.

नीकारः *m.* 1 Winnowing corn. -2 Killing, slaughter. -3 Injury, insult, offence. -4 Abuse, wickedness, malice. -5 Opposition, contradiction.

नीकाश *a.* (*f.* —शा) Like, similar. —शः *m.* 1 Appearance, sight. -2 Proximity.

नीच *a.* (*f.* -चा) 1 Low, short, little, dwarfish. -2 Situated below, being in a low position. -3 Lowered, deep (as a voice). -4 Mean, base, vile, worst. -5 Worthless, insignificant. —चा *f.* An excellent cow. -चं *n.* The lowest point of a planet. -Comp. —उक्तिः *f.* A low or vulgar expression. —उच्चवृत्तं *n.* An epicycle. —उपगत *a.* Situated low in the sky. -ग *a.* 1 Going down-wards,descending (as a river). -2 Low, base, vile. (—गा) *f.* A river. (-गं).*n.* Water. —गृहं *n.* (In astr.) The part of the heavens in which a planet stands at its lowest point. —भोज्यः *m.* An onion. —योनि *a.* Of low origin, low-born ; so नीचजाति. —वज्रः *m.*,-ज्रं *n.* A kind of gem (वैक्रान्त).

नीचक *a.* (*f.* —का) 1 Low, short, dwarfish. -2 Low, soft (as the voice). -3 Base, mean, vile.

नीच (-चि-) का *f.* An excellent cow ; (also नैचिकी).

नीचकिन् *m.* 1 The top of anything. -2 The head of an ox. -3 The owner of a good cow.

नीचकैस् *ind.* See नीचैस् below.

नीचैस् *ind.* (Often used with the force of an adjective) 1 Low,below, underneath, down, downwards (opp.उपरि).-2 Bowing down humbly or modestly.-3 Gently, softly.-4In a low tone. -5 Short,dwarfish.-*m.*N.of a mountain. -Comp. -गतिः *f.* Slow pace. -मुख *a.* With downcast countenance.

नीडः *m.*, -डं *n.* 1 A bird's nest. -2 A bed, couch. -3 A lair, den. -4 The interior of a carriage. -5 A place in general ; a resting place. -Comp. -उद्भवः,—जः *m.* A bird.

नीडकः *m.* 1 A bird. -2 A nest.

नीत *p. p.* (*f.* -ता) 1 Carried, conducted, led.-2 Gained, obtained.-3 Brought. -4 Spent, passed away. -5 Well-behaved, correct. —तं *n.* 1 Wealth. -2 Corn, grain.

नीतिः *f.* 1 Guidance, direction,

management. -2 Conduct, behaviour, course of action.-3 Propriety, decorum. -4 Policy, wisdom, right course. -5 A plan, scheme. -6 Politics, political science. -7 Righteousness, moral conduct, morality. -8 The science of morality, ethics, moral philosophy. -9 Acquirement, acquisition -10 Giving, presenting. -11 Relation, support. -Comp. —कुशल,-ज्ञ, -निपुण, विद् *a.* 1 One versed in politics; a politician. -2 Prudent, wise. —घोषः *m.* N. of the car of Brihaspati. —दोषः *m.* An error of conduct, mistake in policy. —बीजं *n.* A germ or source of intrigue. —विद्या *f.* 1 Political science, political economy.-2 Moral science, ethics. —विषयः *m.* The sphere of morality or prudent conduct. —व्यतिक्रमः *m.* A transgression of the rules of moral or political science. -2 An error of conduct, mistake in policy. —शास्त्रं *n.* The science of ethics or of politics; morality.-संधिः *m.* A method of policy.

नीध्रं (-ध्रं) *n.* 1 The edge of the thatch or roof. -2 A wood. -3 The circumference of a wheel. -4 The moon. -5 The asterism रेवति.

नीपः *m.* 1 The foot of a mountain. -2 The Kadamba tree (said to blossom in the rainy season). -3 A species of Asoka. -4 N. of a family of kings. -पं *n.* The flower of the Kadamba tree.

नीरं *n.* 1 Water. -2 Juice, liquor. -Comp. —ज *a.* Aquatic. (—जः *m.*) 1 An otter. -2 A kind of grass (उशीर.) (-जं *n.*) 1 A lotus. -2 A pearl. —दः *m.* A cloud. —धरः *m.* A cloud. —धिः,—निधिः *m.* The ocean. —प्रियः *m.* A kind of reed. —रुहं *n.* A lotus.

नीराजनं *n.*, —ना *f.* 1 Lustration of arms; a kind of military and religious ceremony performed by kings or generals of armies in the month of Asvina before they took the field. -2 Waving lights before an idol as an act of adoration.

नील *a.* (—ला,-ली *f.* The former in relation to clothes &c., the latter in relation to animals, plants &c.) 1 Blue, dark-blue. -2 Dyed with indigo. —लः *m.* 1 The dark-blue or black colour. -2 Sapphire. -3 The Indian fig-tree. -4 N. of a monkey-chief in the army of Râma. -5 N. of one of the principal ranges of mountains.-6 One of the nine treasures of Kubera. -7 —ला *f.* 1 The indigo plant. -2 A Raginî. —ले *f. dual* 1 The two arteries in front of the neck. (for other senses see नीली). —लं *n.* 1 Black-salt. -2 Blue vitriol. -3 Antimony. -4 Poison. -5 Indigo, indigo dye.-6 Darkness. -Comp. —अक्षः *m.* A goose. —अंगः *m.* The Sârasa bird.—अंजनं *n.* 1 Antimony. -2 Blue vitriol. -अंजना,-अंजसा *f.* Lightning. —अब्जं,-अंबुजं,-अंबुजन्मन्, उत्पलं *n.* The blue lotus. —अभ्रः *m.* A dark cloud. —अंबर *a.* Dressed in dark-blue clothes. (-रः *m.*) 1 A demon, goblin.-2 The planet Saturn. -3 An epithet of Balaráma. -अरुणः *m.* Early dawn; the first dawn of day. —अश्मन् *m.* A sapphire. —उपलः *m.* The blue stone; *lapis lazuli*.-कंठः *m.* 1 A peacock. -2 An epithet of Siva. -3 A kind of gallinule. -4 A blue-necked jay. -5 A wag-tail. -6 A sparrow. -7 A bee. (-ठं *n.*) A radish. —केशी *f.* The indigo plant. —ग्रीवः *m.* An epithet of Siva. —छदः *m.* 1 The date-tree. -2 An epithet of Garuḍa. —तरुः m. The cocoanut tree. -तालः,-ध्वजः m. The Tamâla tree. —पंकः m., —पंकं n. Darkness. —पटलं n. A dark mass; a black coating or covering. -पद्मं n. The blue water-lily. —पिच्छः m. A falcon. —पुष्पिका f. The indigo plant. —भः m. 1 The moon. -2 A cloud. -3 A bee. —मणिः m., —रत्नं n. 1 The sapphire. -2 An epithet of Krishna. —मीलिकः m. A fire-fly. —मृत्तिका f. 1 Iron pyrites. -2 Black earth. —राजिः f. A line of darkness; thick darkness. -लोहित a. Dark-blue, purple. (—तः m.) 1 A purple colour. -2 An epithet of Siva. —वर्णं n. A radish. —वृंतकं n. Cotton.

नीलकं n. 1 Black salt. -2 Blue steel. -3 Blue vitriol. —कः m. 1 A dark-coloured horse. -2 (In alg.) The third unknown quantity (corresponding to z of European Algebra).

नीलं (-लं-) गुः m. 1 A kind of insect. -2 An insect in general.

नीलिका f. The indigo plant; (also नीलिनी). [blueness.

नीलिमन् m. Blue colour, darkness,

नीली f. 1 The indigo plant. -2 A species of blue fly. -3 A kind of disease. -Comp. —रागः m. 1 An affection as unchangeable as the colour of indigo; unalterable or unswerving love. -2 A firm and constant friend. —संधानं n. Fermentation of indigo.

नीवरः m. 1 Trade, traffic. -2 A trader. -3 A religious mendicant. -4 A place fit for the site of a house. -5 A dwelling, residence. -6 Mud. —रं n. Water.

नीवाकः m. 1 Increased demand for grain in times of dearth. -2 Famine; scarcity.

नीवारः m. Rice growing wild or without cultivation (also नीवारक).

नीविः, -वी f. 1 A cloth worn round a woman's waist; the ends of the cloth tied into a knot in front; the knot of the wearing garment. -2 The outer tie of a packet in which the offerings of a Súdra at funeral obsequies are presented. -3 Capital, principal, stock. -4 A stake, wager.

नीवृत् m. Any inhabited country, realm, kingdom.

नीशारः m. 1 A warm cloth, a blanket. -2 A mosquito-curtain. -3 An outer tent or screen.

नीहारः m. 1 Fog, mist. -2 Hoar-frost, heavy dew. -3 Evacuation.

नु ind. 1 A particle having an interrogative force and implying 'doubt', or 'uncertainty'. -2 It is very often compounded with the interrogative pronoun and its derivatives in the sense of 'possibly,' indeed.

नु 2 P. (नौति, प्रणौति; नुत; -Caus. नावयति; desid. नुनूषति) 1 To praise, commend. [extolled.

नु (-नू-) त p.p (f. —ता) Praised,

नुतिः f. 1 Praise, eulogium, panegyric. -2 Worship, reverence.

नुत्त (-न्न) p.p. (f. -त्ता,-न्ना) 1 Pushed, driven onward, propelled. -2 Driven away, dispelled.

नुद् 6 U (नुदति,-ते, नुत्त or नुन्न, प्रणुदते) 1 To push, push or drive on, propel. -2 To prompt, urge on. -3 To remove, drive away, dispel. -4 To throw, cast, send. With अप- To drive away. वप- To drive away, remove. निस्- 1 To reject. -2 To remove. प्र- To dispel, drive off, remove. वि- 1 To strike. -2 To play (on a musical instrument) सम्— 1 To collect. -2 To find.

—Causal नोदयति,-ते To push on, drive, incite. With वि- 1 To drive away. -2 To spend (time). -3 To divert, amuse, entertain.

नुद a. (f —दा) (At the end of comp.)Pushing, impelling, driving away.

नू 6 P. (नुवति) See नु.

नूतन, नूत्न a. (f. —ना, -त्ना) 1 New. -2 Fresh, young. -3 Present. -4 Instantaneous. -5 Recent, modern. -6 Curious, strange.

नूनं *ind.* Certainly, surely, indeed. -2 Most probably, in all probability.

नूपुरः m.,-रं n. An anklet, an ornament for the feet.

नृ (Nom. sing. ना; gen. pl. नृणां or नॄणां) 1 A person whether male or female. -2 Mankind. -3 A piece at chess. -4 The pin of a sun-dial. -5 A masculine word; *i. e. g.* संधिर्ना विग्रहो यानं* अमरको.-6 A leader.-Comp. —केसरिन् m. 'Man-lion', Vishnu in his Narasimha incarnation. —मलं n. Human urine. —देवः m. A king. —धर्मन् m. An epithet of Kubera. —पः m. A ruler of men; king, sovereign. नृपाध्वरः m. N. of a sacrifice (Rájasúya) performed by an emperor or lord paramount, in which all the offices are performed by tributary princes. नृपाभीरं, नृपमानं n. Music played at the royal meals. नृपामयः m. Consumption. नृपनीतिः f. Politics, royal policy, state-craft. नृपप्रियः m. The mango tree.-पतिः, -पालः m. 1 A king. -2 N. of Kubera. -3 A Kshatriya. —पशुः m. A beast in the form of a man; a brute of a man. -मिथुनं n. The sign Gemini (twins) of the zodiac. -मेधः m. A human sacrifice. -यज्ञः m. Hospitality; reception of guests (one of the five daily Yajnas.) —लोकः m. The world of mortals, the earth. -वराहः m. Vishnu in the boar-incarnation. —वाहनः m. An epithet of Kubera. —शृङ्गं n. 'man's horn', *i. e.* an impossibility. —सदनं (नृषदनं) n. The hall of sacrifice. -सद् (-षद्) m. The Supreme Being. -सिंहः, -हरिः m. 1 'A lion-like man', a chief among men. -2 Vishnu in his fourth incarnation. -3 A particular mode of coition. -सेनं, -सेना f. An army of men. —सोमः m. An illustrious man, great man

नृगः m. A son of Manu Vaivasvata who was cursed by a Bráhmana to be a lizard.

नृत 4. P. (नृत्यति, प्रणृत्यति, नृत्त) 1 To dance, move about. -2 To act on the stage. -3 To gesticulate, play. With उप- or प्र- To dance. 2 To dance before somebody. प्रति— To mock by dancing in return. -*Caus.* (नर्तयति,-ते).

नृतिः f. Dancing; dance.

नृत्तं, नृत्यं f. Dancing, acting, a dance, gesticulation. -Comp. —प्रियः m. 1 An epithet of Siva. -2 A peacock. —शाला f. A dancing hall. —स्थानं n. A stage, dancing room.

नृशंस a. (f. —सा) 1 Wicked, malicious, cruel, mischievous.

नृशंस्य a. (f. -स्या) Wicked, malicious. -स्यं n. Maliciousness, wickedness.

नेजकः m. A washerman.

नेजनं n. Washing, cleansing.

नेतृ m. (*nom. sing.* नेता) 1 A leader, conductor, manager, guide. -2 A director, preceptor. -3 A chief, master, head. -4 An owner.-5 The hero of a drama -6 The numeral 'two'.

नेत्रं n. 1 Leading, conducting. -2 The eye. -3 The string of a churning-stick. -4 Woven silk, a fine silken garment. -5 The root of a tree.-6 An enema-pipe. -7 A carriage in general. -8 The number 'two'. -9 A leader. -Comp. -अंजनं n. A collyrium for the eyes. -अंतः m. The outer corner of the eye. -अंबु, -अंभस् n. Tears. -आभिष्यंदः m. The running of the eyes; a kind of eye-disease. -आमयः m. Ophthalmia. -उत्सवः m. Any pleasing or beautiful object.-उपमं n. The almond fruit. -कनीनिका f. The pupil of the eye. -कोषः m. 1 The eye-ball. -2 The bud of a flower. -गोचर a. Perceptible, visible. -छदः m. The eyelid. -जं,-जलं,-वारि n. Tears. -पर्यंतः m. The outer corner of the eye.-पिंडः m. 1 The eye-ball. -2 A cat. -मलं n. The mucus of the eyes. -योनिः m. 1 An epithet of Indra. -2 The moon. -रंजनं n. A collyrium. -रोमन् n. The eyelash. -वस्तिः m., f. A clyster-pipe with a bag. -वस्त्रं n. A veil over the eye, the eyelid. -विष् f. Excretion of the eyes. -स्तंभः m. Rigidity of the eyes.

नेत्रिकं n. 1 A pipe. -2 A ladle.

नेत्री f. 1 A river. -2 A vein. -3 An epithet of Lakshmi.-4 A female leader.

नेदिष्ठ a. (f. -ष्ठा) Nearest, next, very near (Superl. of अंतिक).

नेदीयस् a. (f. -सी) Nearer, very near (compar. of अंतिक q. v.).

नेपः m. A family-priest. -पं n. Water.

नेपथ्यं n. 1 Decoration, an ornament. -2 Dress, costume. -3 The costume of an actor. -4 The tiring-room, where the actors attire themselves and which is always behind the curtain). -Comp. -विधानं n. The arrangements of the tiring-room.

नेपालः m. N. of a country in the north of India. -लाः m. pl. The people of this country.-लं n. Copper. -ली f. 1 The wild date tree or its fruit. -2 Red arsenic. -Comp. -जा, -जाता f. Red arsenic. -मूलकं n. A radish.

नेपालकं n. Copper.

नेपालिका f Red arsenic.

नेम a. (Nom. pl. नेमे,-नेमाः)1 Half. -मः m. 1 A part. -2 A period, time, season. -3 A boundary, limit. -4 An enclosure. -5 The foundation of a wall. -6 Fraud, deceit.-7 Evening. -8 A hole, ditch.

नेमिः, -मी f. 1 The circumference, ring or felly of a wheel. -2 Edge, rim. -3 A windlass. -4 A circumference (in general).-5 A thunderbolt. -6 The earth. -Comp. -वृत्ति a. Following the course of, or acting like, the outer rims of the wheel.

नेष्टृ m. One of the sixteen officiating priests at a Soma sacrifice.

नैःश्रेयस a. (f. -सी), नैःश्रेयसिक a. (f. -की) Leading to happiness or final beatitude. [indigence.

नैःस्वं, नैःस्व्यं n. Destitution, poverty,

नैक a. (न-एक) Not one or alone; (mostly in comp.).-Comp, -चर a. Living n society,gregarious. -भावाश्रय a. Fickle, changeable. -भेद a. Various.

नैकटिक a. (f. -की) Adjacent, contiguous. -कः m. An ascetic or Bhikshu.

नैकधा ind. In various ways

नैकशस् ind. 1 In great numbers.-2 Repeatedly, often, frequently.

नैकट्यंn. Proximity,neighbourhood.

नैकषेयः m. A demon, a Rákshasa.

नैकृतिक a. (f. —की) 1 Dishonest, false.-2 Low,vile,wicked.-3Morose.

नैगम a. (f. —मी) Relating to or occurring in the Veda or holy writings. —मः m. 1 An interpreter of the Vedas or sacred writings. -2 An Upanishad q. v. -3 A means. an expedient· -4 Prudent conduct· -5 A citizen, towns-man. -6 A trader, merchant.

नैगमिक a. (f. -की) Connected with or peculiar to the Vedas derived from the Vedas.

नैघंटुकं n· N. of the glossary of Vedic words commented upon and explained by Yáska in his Nirukta.

नैच (-चि-) की f. An excellent cow.

नैचिकं n. The head of an ox.

नैज a. (f. —जी) Own, one's own.

नैतलं n. The lower or infernal regions.

नैत्यं n. Eternity, perpetuity.

नैत्यक a. (f. —की), नैत्यिक a. (f· -की) 1 Regularly recurring, constantly repeated. -2 Indispensable, constant, obligatory·

नैदाघः m· Summer. [philologist.

नैदानः m. 1 An etymologist. -2 A

नैदानिकः m. A pathologist.

नैदेशिकः m. One who executes orders; a servant.

नैपातिक a. (f. —की) Mentioned incidentally or by the way.

नैपुण्यं n.(-ण्यं) 1 Dexterity, skill, cleverness, proficieney. -2 Strictness, exactness· -3 Anything that requires skill;a delicate matter. -4 Totality, completeness. [Secrecy.

नैभृत्यं n. 1 Modesty, humility. -2

नैमंत्रणकं n. A banquet, feast.

नैमयः m. A trader, merchant.

नैमित्त a. (f. —त्ती) Relating to signs, marks &c.

नैमित्तिक a. (f.- की) 1 Produced by, connected with, or dependent on, any particular canse· -2 Occasional, accidental, produced by some cause (opp. नित्य). —कः m. An astrologer, prophet. —कं n. 1 An effect (opp. निमित्त 'cause'). -2 An occasional rite, a periodical ceremony.

नैमिष a· (f. -षी) Momentay, transient. -षं n. N. of a sacred forest celebrated as the residence of certain sages to whom Sauti related the Mahabhârata.

नैमेयः m· Barter, exchange.

नैयग्रोधं n. The fruit of न्यग्रोध, the Indian fig-tree.

नैयत्यं n. Restraint, self-command.

नैयमिक a. (f. —की) Conformable to rule or precept; regular. —कं n. Regularity.

नैयायिकः m. A logician, a follower of the Nyâya system of philosophy·

नैरंतर्यं n. ·1 Uninterruptedness, close succession, continuity. -2 Closeness, contiguity (in space).

नैरपेक्ष्यं n. Disregard, indifference.

नैरयिकः m. An inhabitant of hell.

नैरर्थ्यं n. Senselessness, nonsense.

नैराश्यं n· 1 Hopelessness, despair, despondency. -2 Absence of wish or expectation·

नैरुक्तः, नैरुक्तिकः m. One who knows the etymology of words; an etymologist.

नैरुज्यं n. Health.

नैर्ऋतः m. 1 A demon· -2 The regent of the south-western direction· —तं n. The lunar mansion called Mula.

नैर्ऋती f. 1 An epithet of Dúrgá.

-2 The south-western direction.

नैर्गुण्यं *n.* 1 Absence of qualities or properties. -2 Absence of good qualities.

नैर्घृण्यं *n.* Pitilessness, cruelty.

नैर्देशिकः *m.* A servant.

नैर्मल्यं *n.* Cleanness, purity, spotlessness, (physical as well as moral).

नैर्लज्जयं *n.* Shamelessness, impudence.

नैल्यं *n.* Blueness, dark-blue colour.

नैवि (-बि-) डयं *n.* Compactness, thickness, denseness.

नैवेद्यं *n.* An offering of eatables presented to a deity or idol.

नैवेशिकं *n.* 1 Any vessel or implement forming part of domestic furniture. -2A present to a Brâhmana householder, *e. g.* a girl or ornaments given with her.

नैश *a.* (*f.* —शी), नैशिक *a.* (*f.* —की) 1 Nocturnal, nightly. -2 To be observed at night.

नैश्चल्यं *n.* Fixedness, fixity.

नैश्चित्यं *n.* 1 Determination, certainty. -2 A fixed ceremony.

नैषधः *m.* 1 A king of the Nishadhas. -2 An epithet of king Nala -3 A native or inhabitant of Nîshadha. -4 N. of a Mahâkâvaya by Srîharsha, treating of the adventures of Nala, king of the Nishadhas.

नैष्कर्म्यं *n.* 1 Idleness, inactivity.-2 Exemption from acts or their consequences. -3 The salvation obtained by abstraction.

नैष्कशातिक *a.* (*f.* —की) Worth a hundred *Nishkas.*

नैष्किक *a.* (*f.* —की) Bought with or made of a Nishka q. v. —कः *m.* A mint-master.

नैष्ठिक *a.* (*f.* —की) 1 Final, last, concluding. -2 Decided, conclusive (as a reply.) -3 Fixed, constant. -4Highest, perfect.-5 Completely versed in. -6 Vowing perpetual abstinence and chastity. -कः *m.* A perpetual religious student who continues with his spiritual preceptor even after the prescribed period and vows life-long abstinence and chastity.

नैष्ठुर्यं *n.* Cruelty, harshness, severity.

नैष्ठ्यं *n.* Constancy, firm belief, steadfastness.

नैसर्गिक *a.* (*f.* —की) Natural, inherent.

नैस्त्रिंशिकः *m.* A swordsman.

नो *ind.* No, not ; often used like न.

नो चेत् *ind.* If not, otherwise.

नोदनं *n.* 1 Impelling, urging onward. -2 Driving away, dispelling. -3 Cutting, splitting.

नोधा *ind.* Ninefold, in nine parts.

नौः *f.* 1 A ship, boat. -2 N. of a constellation. -Comp. —आरोहः (नावारोहः) *m.* 1 A passenger on board a ship. -2 A sailor. —कर्णधारः *m.* A helmsman, pilot. —कर्मन् *n.* The occupation of a sailor. —चरः, -उपजीवनः, —जीविकः *m.* A sailor, boatman. —तार्य *a.* Navigable, to be traversed in a ship. —दंडः *m.* An oar. —यानं *n.* Navigation. —यायिन् *a.* Going in a boat, a passenger. -वाहः *m.* A steersman, pilot, captain. —व्यसनं *n.* Shipwreck, naufrage. —साधनं *n.* Fleet, navy.

नौका *f.* A small boat ; a boat in general. -Comp. —दंडः *m.* An oar.

न्यक् *ind.* An adverb, prefixed to कृ or भू, to imply 'contempt', 'degradation' or 'humiliation'.

न्यक्करणं *n.*, न्यक्कारः *m.* Humiliation, degradation, contempt, insult.

न्यक्ष *a.* (*f.* —क्षा) 1 Low, inferier.

-2 Whole, entire. -क्षः *m.* 1 A buffalo. -2 An epithet of Paraśurâma. —क्षं *n.* 1 The whole. -2 A kind of grass.

न्यग्भावः *m.* 1 Humiliation, degradation. -2 Making inferior, subordination.

न्यग्भावित *a* 1 Humiliated, slighted. -2 Surpassed, excelled.

न्यग्रोधः *m.* 1 The (Indian) fig-tree. -2 A fathom (measured by the arms extended). -Comp. —परिमंडलः *m.* A man being a fathom in circumference. —परिमंडला *f.* An excellent woman.

न्यंकुः *m.* A kind of antelope.

न्यंगः *m.* 1 A mark, sign. -2 A kind, sort.

न्यच्छं *n.* A mole upon the body.

न्यंच् *a.* (*f.* नीची) 1 Going or turned downwards, turned down. -2 Lying on the face. -3 Low, contemptible, vile. -4 Slow, lazy. -5 Whole, entire.

न्यंचनं *n.* 1 A curve. -2 A hiding place. -3 A hollow. —नी *f.* The lap.

न्ययः *m.* Loss, destruction; decay.

न्यसनं *n.* (*f.* —स्ता) Depositing, lying down. -2 Delivering, giving up.

न्यस्त *p. p.* (*f.*—स्ता) 1 Cast down, thrown or laid down, deposited. -2 Put in, inserted, applied. -3 Depicted, drawn, as in चित्रन्यस्त. -4 Consigned, transferred to. -5 Leaning, resting on. -6 Given up, resigned. -7 Mystically touched.

न्याक्यं *n.* Fried rice.

न्यादः *m.* Eating, feeding.

न्याय. *m.* 1 Method, manner, way, rule, system, plan. -2 Fitness, decorum. -3 Law, justice, virtue, righteousness, honesty. -4 A lawsuit, legal proceeding. -5 Judicial sentence, judgment. -6 Policy, good government. -7 Likeness, analogy. -8 A popular maxim, an illustration, as काकतालीयन्याय, घुणाक्षरन्याय, देहलीदीपन्याय &c. -9 A Vedic accent. -10 (In gram.) A universal rule. -11 A system of Hindu philosophy founded by the sage Gautama. -12 The science of logic, logical philosophy. -13 A complete argument or syllogism (consisting of five members; *i. e.* प्रतिज्ञा, हेतु, उदाहरण, उपनय and निगमन). 14 An epithet of Vishnu. -Comp. —पथः *m.* The Mîmâmsá philosophy. —वादिन *a.* One who speaks what is right or just. —शास्त्रं *n.* 1 The philosophical system of the Nyáya school. -2 The science of logic. —सारिणी *f.* Proper or suitable behaviour. —सूत्रं *n.* The aphorisms of Nyáya philosophy by Gautama.

न्यायतः *ind.* 1 In a fitting manner, suitably, fitly. -2 Justly, rightly.

न्याय्य *a.* (*f.* —य्या) 1 Just, right, proper, fit, suitable. -2 Customary, usual.

न्यासः *m.* 1 Placing, putting down or upon, planting. -2 An impression, mark, print. -3 Depositing. -4 A pledge, deposit; प्रत्यर्पितन्यास इवांतरात्मा * शाकुंत. 4 21. 5 Entrusting, committing, delivering, consigning. -8 Painting, writing down. -7 Giving up, abandoning, relinquishing. -9 Bringing forward, adducing. -9 Digging in, seizing (as with claws). -10 Assignment of the various parts of the body to different deities, accompanied with prayers and corresponding gesticulations. -11 Lowering the tone or voice. -Comp. —अपह्नवः *m.* Repudiation of a deposit. —धारिन् *m.* The holder of a deposit, a mortgagee.

न्यासिन् *m.* One who has renounced all worldly ties ; a Sannyásin.

न्युं (-न्यूं-) ख *a.* (*f.* -खा) 1 Charming, beautiful, lovely. -2 Proper.

न्युब्ज *a.* (*f.* —ब्जा) 1 Turned or bent down-wards, lying on the face. -2 Bent, crooked. -3 Hump-backed.—ब्ज: *m.* 1 The Nyagrodha tree. -2 A kind of ladle made of Kusa grass. —ब्जं *n.* A vessel used in Srâddhas. -Comp. -खड्ग: *m.* A crooked sword, sabre.

न्यून *a.* (*f.* —ना) 1 Lessened, shortened. -2 Defective, inferior, wanting, destitute of ; as in अर्थन्यून. -3 Less (opp. अधिक). -4 Defective (in some organ) as in पादन्यून. -5 Low, wicked, despicable. -नं *ind.* Less, in a less degree. -Comp. -अंग *a.* Maimed, mutilated. —अधिक *a.* More or less, unequal. —धी *a.* Deficient in intellect, foolish.

न्योजस् *a.* Crooked (fig. also), wicked, vile.

प.

प *a.* (*f.* —पा) (At the end of comp.) 1 Drinking ; as in द्विप, अनेकप. -2 Guarding, protecing, as in गोप, नृप, क्षितिप. -प: *m.* 1 Air, wind. -2 A leaf. -3 An egg.

पक्कण: *m.* The hut of a savage or a barbarian.

पक्ति: *f.* 1 Cooking. -2 Digesting, digestion. -3 Ripening, maturity. -4 Fame, dignity. -5 The place of digestion. -Comp. —शूलं *n.* Violent pain of the bowels arising from indigestion.

पक्तृ *m.* 1 Fire (especially in the stomach). -2 A cook.

पक्त्रं *n.* 1 The state of house-holder who keeps the sacred fire. -2 The sacred fire so maintained.

पक्त्रिम *a.* (*f.* —मा) 1 Ripe, ripened. -2 Matured. -3 Cooked.

पक्व *a.* (*f.* —क्वा) 1 Cooked, roasted, boiled ; as in पक्वान्न. -2 Digested. -3 Baked, burned. -4 Mature, ripe. -5 Fully developed, perfect, matured ; as in पक्वधी. -6 Experienced, shrewd. -7 Perished, decaying, ripe to meet one's doom. —क्वं *n.* Cooked food. -Comp. —अतिसार: *m.* Chronic dysentery. —अन्नं *n.* Cooked or dressed food. —आधानं *n.*, -आशय: *m.* The stomach, abdomen. —इष्टका *f.* A baked brick. —रस: *m.* Wine or any spirituous liquor. —वारि *n.* The water of bolied rice (कांजिक); sour rice-gruel.

पक्कश: *m.* N. of a barbarous tribe, a Chándála.

पक्ष् 1 P., 10 U. (पक्षति, पक्षयति,-ते) 1 To take, seize. -2 To accept. -3 To side with.

पक्ष: *m.* 1 A wing, pinion. -2 The feather or feathers on each side of an arrow. -3 The flank or side of a man or animal ; the shoulder. -4 The side of anything, a flank. -5 The wing or flank of an army. -6 The half of anything. -7 A fortnight (comprising 15 days);(there are two such *pakshas*, शुक्लपक्ष: the bright or light half, and कृष्ण-तामिस्र-पक्ष: the dark half). -8 A party in general, faction, side. 9 A family, race. -10 A follwer, partisan. -11 A class, host, any number of adherents.-12 One side of an argument, an alternative, one of two cases; [पक्षे 'in the other case, on the other hand'.] -13 A case or supposition in general; as in पक्षांतरे.-14 A point under discussion, a thesis; an argument to be maintained -15 The subject of a syllogism or conclusion (the minor term); संदिग्धसाध्यवान् पक्षः -16 A symbolical expression for the number 'two.' -17 A bird. -18 A state, condition. -19 The body. -20 A limb of the body. -21 A royal elephant.-22 An army. -23 A wall. -24 Opposition. -25 Rejoinder, reply. -26 A mass, quantity (in composition with words meaning 'hair' *e.g.* केशपक्षः)-27 Place, position. -28 A view, notion, idea. -29 The side of an equation in a primary division. -Comp.-अंतः *m.* 1 The 15 th day of either half month, *i. e.* the day of new or full moon. -2 The end of the wings of an army. —अंतरं *n.* 1 Another side. -2 A different side or view of an argument. -3 Another supposition. —आघातः *m.* 1 Palsy or paralysis of one side; hemiplegia.-2 Refutation of an argument. —आभासः *m.* 1 A fallacious argument. -2 A false plaint. —आहारः *m.* Eating food only once in a fortnight. -ग्रहणं *n.* Choosing a party. —घातः *m.* See पक्षाघातः above.-चरः *m.* 1 An elephant strayed from the herd. -2 The moon. -3 An attendant. —छिद् *m.* An epithet of Indra. —जः *m.* The moon. -द्वयं *n* 1 Both sides of an argument. -2 A couple of fortnights, *i. e.* a month. -द्वारं *n.* A side door, private entrance. —धर *a.* 1 Winged. -2 Siding with any one. (-रः *m*) 1 A bird. -2 The moon. -3 A partisan. -4 An elephant strayed from the herd. —नाडी *f.* A quill. —पातः *m.* 1 Siding with any one.-2 Liking, desire, affection (for a thing). -3 Partisanship, partiality. -4 The moulting of birds. -5 A partisan. —पातिन् *a.* 1 Siding with, adhering to a party, attached to a particular cause. -2 Sympathizing. —पालिः *m.* A private door.—पुटः *m.* A wing. —बिंदुः *m.* A heron —भागः *m.* 1 The side or flank. -2 Especially, the flank of an elephant. -भुक्तिः *f.* The course traversed by the sun in a fortnight. —मूलं *n.* The root of wing. —वादः *m.* 1 An exparte statement. -2 Stating a case, expression of opinion. -वाहनः *m.* A bird. —व्यापिन् *a.* 1 Embracing the whole of an argument. -2 Pervading the minor term. -हत *a.* Paralysed on one side. —हरः *m.* A bird. —होमः *m.* 1 A sacrificial rite lasting for a fortnight. -2 A rite to be performed every fortnight.

पक्षकः *m.* 1 A side-door. -2 A side. -3 An associate, a partisan (at the end of comp.).

पक्षतिः *f.* 1 The root of a wing. -2 The first day of a lunar fortnight.

पक्षस् *n.* 1 A wing. -2 The side-part of a carriage. -3 The leaf of a door. -4 The wing of an army -5 A half or division.-6 A half month. -7 The shore of a river. -8 A side in general.

पक्षालुः *m.* A bird.

पक्षिणी *f.* A female bird. -2 A night with the two days enclosing it, (द्वावह्नावेकरात्रिश्च पक्षिणीत्यभिधीयते) (in religious law.).-3 The day of full moon.

पक्षिन् *a.* (*f.* -णी) 1 Winged. -2

Furnished with wings. -3 Adhering to the party of. -*m.* 1 A bird. -2 An arrow. -3 An epithet of Siva. -Comp. —इंद्रः, -प्रवरः, -राज्, -राजः, -सिंहः, स्वामिन् *m.* Epithets of Garuda. -कीटः *m.* An insignificant bird. -पतिः *m.* An epithet of Sampâti. -पानीयशालिका *f.* A trough or reservoir for watering birds. -पुंगवः *m.* An epithet of Jatâyu. —शाला *f.* 1 A nest. -2 An aviary.

पक्षिलः *m.* N. of the saint Vâtsyâyana.

पक्षीय *a.* (At the end of comp.). Belonging to a side or party as in कुरुपक्षीयाः &c.

पक्ष्मन् *n.* 1 An eye-lash. -2 The filament of a flower. -3 The point of a thread ; a thin thread. -4 A wing. -5 The leaf of a flower.

पक्ष्मल *a.* (*f.* —ला) 1 Having strong, long or beautiful eye-lashes. -2 Hairy, shaggy.

पक्ष्यः *m.* A partisan, follower, friend, ally.

पंकः *m.*, —कं *n.* 1 Mud, clay, mire. -2 A thick mass, large quantity. -3 A slough, quagmire. -4 Sin. -5 Ointment, unguent. -Comp. —कीरः *m.* Lapwing. —क्रीडः, -क्रीडनकः *m.* A hog. —ग्राहः *m.* A Makara or crocodile. —छिद् *m.* The clearing-nut tree (कतक). —जं *n.* A lotus. (-जः) *m.* The Sárasa bird. -जजः, -जजन्मन् *m.* An epithet of Brahman (*m.*). -जनाभः *m.* An epithet of Vishnu. -जन्मन् *n.* A lotus. (-*m.*) The Sárasa bird. -मंडुकः *m.* A bivalve conch. —रुह्, —रुहं *n.* A lotus. —वासः *m.* A crab. —शू (-सू-) रणः *m.* The fibrous edible root of a lotus.

पंकजिनी *f.* 1 A lotus-plant. -2 A group of lotus plants or lotuses. -3 A place abounding with lotuses. -4 The flexible stalk of a waterlily.

पंकणः *m.* The hut of a Chândala ; see पक्कण.

पंकारः *m.* Moss. -2 A dam, dike. -3 Stairs, flight of steps.

पंकिल *a.* (*f.* —ला) Muddy, foul, turbid, dirty. —लः *m.* A boat.

पंकेजं *n.* A lotus.

पंकेरुह्, -हं *n.* A lotus. —हः *m.* The crane or Sârasa bird.

पंकेशय *a.* Dwelling in mud.

पंक्तिः *f.* 1 A line, row, series. -2 A group, flock, troop. -3 A row of people (of the same caste) sitting down to a meal; a company or party at dinner of the same caste. -4 The living generation. -5 The earth. -6 Fame, celebrity. -7 A collection of five. -8 The number 'ten' as in पंक्तिरथ, पंक्तिग्रीव. -Comp. —ग्रीवः *m.* An epithet of Râvana. -चरः *m.* An osprey. -दूषः, -दूषकः *m.* A person with whom it is improper to associate at dinner-time. —पावनः *m.* A respectable Brâhmana who, being very learned, always gets the seat of honour at dinner parties, or who purifies by his presence the पंक्ति or persons who sit in the same row to dine with him. —रथः *m.* N. of Dasaratha.

पंगु *a.* (*f* गु or —ग्वी) Lame, halt, crippled. —गुः *m.* 1 A lame man. -2 An epithet of Saturn. -Comp. —ग्राहः *m.* 1 A crocodile (मकर) -2 The tenth sign of the zodiac ; Capricornus (मकर).

पंगुक *a.* (*f.* —का) Lame, crippled.

पंगुल *a.* (*f.* —ला) Lame, crippled. —लः *m.* A horse of silvery-white colour.

पच् I U. (पचति,-ते, पपाच,-पेचे, अपाक्षीत्-अपक्त, पक्ष्यति, ते, पक्तुं, पक्वः; *Passive* पच्यते

Caus. पाचयति,-ते; *desid.* पिपक्षति). 1 To cook, roast, dress (as food &c.). -2 To bake, burn (as bricks). -3 To digest (as food) -4 To ripen, mature. -5 To bring to perfection, develop (as understanding). -6 To melt (as metals). -7 To cook (for oneself) (Atm.). —With परि- To ripen, mature, develop. वि— 1 To mature, develop, ripen, bear fruit. -2 To digest. -3 To cook thoroughly [or evident.

पच् 1. A. (पचते) To make clear

पच *a.* (*f.* —चा) 1 Cooking, roasting. -2 Digesting. —चः *m.*, —चा *f.* 1 Cooking. -2 Maturing.

पचकः *m.* A cook.

पचतः *m.* 1 Fire. -2 The sun. -3 N. of Indra. —तं *n.* Cooked food.

पचन *a.* (*f.* —ना) Cooking, dressing, maturing. —नः *m.* Fire. —ना *f.* Becoming ripe, ripening. —नी *f.* The wild citron tree.-नं *n.* 1 Cooking, dressing, maturing. -2 A means or instrument for cooking as a vessel, fuel &c. -3 Ripening, maturing. -4 Becoming cooked or ripe.

पचपचः *m.* An epithet of Siva.

पचा *f.* The act of cooking.

पचिः *m.* 1 Fire. -2 Cooking.

पचेलिम *a.* (*f.* —मा) 1 Cooking or ripening quickly. -2 Fit to be matured. -3 Ripening spontaneously or naturally.-मः *m.* 1 Fire.-2 The sun.

पचेलुकः *m.* A cook.

पञ्झाटिका *f.* A small bell.

पंचक *a.* (*f.* —का) 1 Consisting of five, relating to five. -3 Made of five. -4 Bought with five. -5 Taking five per-cent. —कः *m.*, —कं *n.* A collection or aggregate of five as in यतिपंचक. [five.

पंचत *f.* A pentad, an aggregate of

पंचतयः *a.* Fivefold.

पंचता *f.*, —त्वं *n.* 1 Five-fold state. -2 A collection of five. -3 The five elements taken collectively. -4 Death, dissolution ; पंचतां, -त्वं गम्, -या &c. 'To be resolved into the five elements of which the body consists', 'to die or perish'; पंचतां, —त्वं नी 'To kill or destroy'.

पंचथुः *m.* 1 Time. -2 The (Indian) cuckoo.

पंचधा *ind.* 1 In five parts, -2 In five ways.

पंचन् *num a.* (Always pl. ; nom. and acc. पंच) Five. (As the first member of comp. पंचन् drops its final न्.) -Comp. -अंशः *m.* The fifth part, a fifth. -अग्निः *m.* 1 An aggregate of five sacred fires ; *i. e.* (अन्वाहार्यपचन or दाक्षिण, गार्हपत्य, आहवनीय, सभ्य; and आवसथ्य) - 2 A house-holder who maintains the five sacred fires. -3 The five mystic fires supposed to exist in the body.-अंग *a.* Five-membered ; having five parts or divisions ; consisting of five branches; manifested by five parts of the body. पंचांगः अभिनयः *m.* Gesticulation with five limbs of the body (hands, feet, and the head. पंचांगः प्रमाणः *m.* A salutation with the arms, the knees, the breast and the head. शिरसा वक्षसा दृशा). (—गः *m.*) 1 A tortoise or turtle. -2 A kind of horse with five spots in different parts of his body. (-गी *f.*) A bit for horses. (-गं *n.*) 1 A collection or aggregate of five parts. -2 Five modes of devotion.-3 The five parts of a tree, the bark, leaves, flowers, the fruit and the root.-4 A calender or almanac, so called because it treats of five things:-(तिथिर्वारश्च नक्षत्रं योगः करणमेव च). पंचांगगुप्तः *m.* A turtle.-अंगुलः *m.* The castor-oil plant. -अ(-आ-)जं *n*. The five products of the goat. —अप्सरस् *n*. N. of a lake, said to have been created by the sage Mandakarni. —अमृतं *n*. An aggregate of any five drugs. -2 The collection of five sweet things used in worshipping deities (दुग्धं च शर्करा चैव घृतं दधि तथा मधु). —आर्चिस् *m*. The planet Mercury. —अवयव *a*. Five-membered (as a syllogism, the five members being प्रतिज्ञा, हेतु, उदाहरण:, उपनय and निगमन). —अवस्थ: *m*. A corpse; (so called because it is resolved into the five elements). —आविकं *n*. The five products of the sheep. -अशीति: *f*. Eighty-five.—अह: *m*. A period of five days. —आतप *a*. Doing penance with five fires (*i. e*, with four fires and the sun). —आत्मक *a*. Consisting of five elements (as body). —आनन:, —आस्य:, —मुख:, —वक्त्र: *m*.1 Epithets of Siva. -2 A lion (so called because its mouth is generally wide open). (often used at the end of names of learned men to express great learning or respect; *e*. g.—न्यायपंचानन, —तर्कपंचानन&c.,*e.g*. जगन्नाथतर्कपंचानन). -3 The sign Leo of the zodiac.—आम्नाया: (*m. pl.*) Five Sâstras supposed to have proceeded from the five mouths of Siva. -इंद्रियं *n*. An aggregate of the five organs (of sense or actions; see इंद्रियं). —इषु:, —बाण:, —शर: *m*. Epithets of the god of love; (so called because he has five arrows which are:— अरविंदमशोकं च चूतं च नवमल्लिका। नीलोत्पलं च पंचैते पंचबाणस्य सायका:; the five arrows are also thus named :—संमोहनोन्मादनौ च शोषणस्तापनस्तथा। स्तंभनश्चेति कामस्य पंचबाणा: प्रकीर्तिता:॥). —उष्मन् *m. pl*. The five digestive fires supposed to be in the body. —कर्मन् *n*. (In medicine) The five kinds of treatment; *i. e*. 1 वमन 'Giving emetics'; -2 रेचन 'Purging'; -3 नस्य 'Giving strenutatories'; -4 अनुवासन 'Administering an enema which is oily', and -5 निरूह 'Administering an enema which is not oily'. —कृत्वस् *ind*. Five times. -कोण: *m*. A pentagon. -कोलं *n*. The five spices taken collectively.-कोशा: (*m. pl.*) The five vestures or wrappers supposed to invest the soul; they are:-अन्नमयकोष or स्थूलशरीर, प्राणमयकोष, मनोमयकोष, विज्ञानमयकोष and आनंदमयकोष. -क्रोशी*f*.1A distance of five Krosas.-2 N. of the city Benâres. -खट्वं, -खट्वी *f*. A collection of five beds. -गत *a*. (In alg.) Raised to the fifth power. —गवं *n*. A collection of five cows. —गव्यं *n*. The five products of the cow taken collectively; *i. e*. milk, curds, clarified butter or ghee, urine, and cowdung (क्षीरं दधि तथा चाज्यं मूत्रं गोमयमेव च).-गु *a*. Bought with Five cows.-गुण *a*. Five-fold (-णा: *m. pl.*) The five objects of sense (रूप, रस, गंध, स्पर्श and शब्द) (—णी *f*.) The earth. —गुप्त: *m*. 1 A tortoise.-2 The materialistic system of philosophy, the doctrines of the Chárvâkas. —चत्वारिंश *a*. Forty fifth. —चत्वारिंशत् *f*. Forty-five. -जन: *m*. 1 A man, mankind. -2 N. of a demon who had assumed the form of a conch-shell, and was slain by Krishna. -3 The soul. -4 The five classes of beings; *i. e*. gods, men, Gandharvas, serpents and pitris. -5 The four primary castes of the Hindus (ब्राह्मण, क्षत्रिय, वैश्य and शूद्र) with the Nishâdas or barbarians as the fifth; *pl*.

in these two senses). (-नी *f.*) An assemblage of five persons. -जनीन *a.* Devoted to the five races.(-नः *m.*) An actor, a mimic, buffoon. —ज्ञानः *m.* 1 An epithet of Buddha. -2 A man familiar with the doctrines of the Pásupatas. —तक्षं *n.*, —क्षी *f.* A collection of five carpenters.-तत्त्वं *n.* 1 The five elements taken collectively *i. e.* पृथ्वी, अप्, तेजस्, वायु and आकाश. -2 (In the Tantras) The five essentials of the Tántrikas, also called पंचमकार because they all begin with म ; *i. e.* मद्य, मांस, मत्स्य, मुद्रा and मैथुन. —तंत्रं *n.* N. of a well-known collection in five books containing moral stories and fables. —तन्मात्रं *n.* 1 The five subtle and primary elements (such as शब्द, रस, स्पर्श, रूप and गंध).—तपस् *m.* An ascetic who in summer practises penance sitting in the middle of four fires with the sun burning right over his head. —तय *a.* Five-fold. (-यः *m.*) A pentad. —त्रिंश *a.* Thirty-fifth. -त्रिंशत्, -त्रिंशतिः *f.* Thirty-five. —दश *a.* 1 Fifteenth. -2 Increased by fifteen as in पंचदशं शतं ' one hundred and fifteen '. —दशन् *a. pl.* Fifteen. —दशिन् *a.* Consisting of fifteen. -दशी *f.* The fifteenth day of a lunar fortnight. -दीर्घं *n.*The five long parts of the body. —नखः *m.* 1 Any animal with five claws. -2 An elephant. -3 A turtle. -4 A lion or tiger. —नदः *m.* The modern Punjab (the five rivers being शतद्रु, विपाशा, इरावती, चंद्रभागा and वितस्ता). (-दाः *m. pl.*) The people of this country. —नवतिः *f.* Ninety-five. -नीराजनं *n.* Waving five things before an idol and then falling prostrate before it ; (the five things are a lamp, lotus, cloth, mango and betel-leaf)- —पंचाश *a.* Fifty-fifth.-पंचाशत् *f.* Fifty-five. —पदी *f.* Five steps. -2 The five strong cases, *i. e.* the first five inflections. —पात्रं *n.* 1 Five vessels taken collectively. -2 A Sráddha in which offerings are made in five vessels. -पितरः (*m. pl.*) The five fathers:—जनकश्चोपनेता च यश्च कन्यां प्रयच्छति । अन्नदाता भयत्राता पंचैते पितरः स्मृताः ॥.-प्राणाः (*m. pl.*)The five life-winds or vital airs ; प्राण, अपान, व्यान, उदान and समान. —प्रसादः *m.* A temple of a particular size with four pinnacles and a steeple). -बाणः,-वाणः, -शरः *m.* Epithets of the god of love.-भुजः *m.* A pentagon. —भूतं *n.* The five elements ; पृथ्वी, अप्, तेजस्, वायु and आकाश. —मकारं *n.* The five essentials of the left hand Tantra ritual of which the first letter is म; see पंचतत्त्व (2). -महापातकं *n.* The five great sins. They are ब्रह्महत्या सुरापानं,स्तेयं, गुर्वंगनागमः, एतेषां संसर्गश्च. -महायज्ञाः *m. pl.* The five daily sacrifices enjoined to be performed by a Brâhmana ; see महायज्ञ. —रत्नं *n.* A collection of five gems ; (they are variously enumerated ; one enumeration is कनकं हीरकं नीलं पद्मरागश्च मौक्तिकम्। पंचरत्नमिदं प्रोक्तमृषिभिः पूर्वदर्शिभिः ॥-रात्रं *n.* A period of five nights ; a period of five days and five nights. -2 A particular school of philosophy commonly known as नारदनीति. —राशिकं *n.* The rule of five (in math.). -लक्षणं *n.* Purána ; so called because it deals with five important topics:-सर्गश्च प्रतिसर्गश्च वंशो मन्वंतराणि च। वंशानुचरितं चैव पुराणं पंचलक्षणं॥-लवणं *n.* Five kinds of salt *i. e.* काचक, सैंधव, सामुद्र, बिड and सौवर्चल.-वटः *m.* The sacred or sacrificial thread worn across the breast (यज्ञोपवीत).-वटी *f.*

1 The five fig-trees *i. e.* अश्वत्थ, बिल्व, वट, धात्री and अशोक-2 N. of a part of the Dandakâ forest where the Godavarî rises and where Râma dwelt for a considerable time with his wife and brother. -वर्षदेशीय *a.* About five years old.-वर्षीय *a.* Five years old.-वल्कलं *n.* A collection of the barks of five kinds of trees : namely न्यग्रोध, उदुंबर, अश्वत्थ, प्लक्ष and वेतस). —विंश *a.* Twenty-fifth. -विंशतिः *f.* Twenty-five. —विंशतिका *f.* A collection of twenty five; as in वेतालपंचविंशतिका.-विध *a.* Five-fold, of five kinds. -शत *a.* Amounting to five hundred.(-तं *n.*) 1 One hundred and five. -2 Five hundred.-शाखः *m.* 1 The hand. -2 An elephant. -शिखः *m.* A lion.-ष *a.* (pl.) Five or six. —षष्ट *a* Sixty-fifth. -षष्टिः *f.* Sixty five. -सप्तत *a.* Seventy-fifth. —सप्ततिः *f.* Seventy-five. —सूनाः *f.* The five things in a house by which animal life may be accidentally destroyed ; they are:-पंचसूना गृहस्थस्य चुल्लीपेषण्युपस्करः कंडनी चोदकुंभश्च. -हायन *a.* Five years old.

पंचनी *f.* A chequered cloth for playing at draughts.

पंचम *a.* (*f.* —मी) 1 The fifth. -2 Forming a fifth part.-3 Dexterous, clever. -4 Beautiful, brilliant. —मः *m.* 1 The fifth (or in later times the seventh) note of the Indian gamut. -2 N. of a Râga or musical mode. -3 The fifth consonant of a class *i. e.* a nasal. —मं *n.* 1 A fifth. -2 Sexual intercourse. —मी *f.* 1 The fifth day of a lunar fortnight. -2 The ablative case (in gram.). -3 An epithet of Draupadî. -4 A chequered board for playing at draughts. -Comp. -आस्यः *m.* The cuckoo.

पंचशः *ind.* Five by five, by fives.

पंचालाः *m.pl.* 1 N. of a country and its people. —लः *m.* A king of the Panchâlas.

पंचालिका *f.* A doll, puppet.

पंचाली *f.* 1 A doll, puppet. -2 A kind of song. -3 Chequered board for playing at draughts, chess-board &c.

पंचवटः *m.* The sacrificial cord worn across the shoulder.

पंचाश *a.* (*f.* —शी) Fiftieth.

पंचाशत्, पंचाशतिः *f.* Fifty.

पंचाशिका *f.* 1 A collection of fifty. -2 A collection of fifty verses.

पंजरं *n.* A cage ; an aviary. -रः *m.*, -रं *n.* 1 Ribs. -2 A skeleton. -रः *m.* 1 The body. -2 The Kali-yuga. -3 A purificatory ceremony performed on cows.-Comp.-आखेटः *m.* A sort of basket or trap for catching fish.

पंजरकः *m.*, —कं *n.* A cage.

पंजिः, -जी *f.* 1 The ball of cotton from which thread is spun. -2 A record, journal, register. -3 A calender, an almanac. -Comp. —कारः, —कारकः *m.* 1 A writer, scribe.-2 An almanac-maker.

पंजिका *f.* 1 A running commentary which explains and analyses every word. -2 A journal, a book in which accounts of receipts and expenditure are entered. -3 The record or register of human actions kept by Yama. -Comp. -कारकः *m.* A scribe ; a man of the Kâyastha tribe.

पट् 1 P. (पटति) To go or move. —*Caus.* or 10 U. (पाटयति,-ते) 1 To split, tear up, tear open. -2 To break, break open. -3 To pierce, prick, penetrate. -4 To eradicate. -5 To pluck out. With उद्— 1 To pull out, to extract. -2 To tear out. -3 To eradicate. वि— 1 To tear. -2 -2 To pull out.

पट् 10 U. (पटयति,-ते) 1 To string or weave. -2 To clothe, envelop. -3 To surround, encircle.

पटः *m.*, -टं *n.* 1 A garment, cloth, a piece of cloth. -2 Fine cloth. -3 A veil, screen. -4 A tablet, plate or piece of cloth for writing or painting upon.-टः *m.* Any thing well made or polished. -टं *n.* A thatch, roof.-Comp. -कटजं *n.* A tent.-कर्मन् *n.* Weaving ; business of the loom. —कारः *m.* 1 A weaver. -2 A painter. -कुटी *f.*, —मंडपः, -वापः *m.*, -वेश्मन् *n.* A tent. —वासः *m.* 1 A tent.-2 A petticoat. -3 A kind of perfumed powder. -वासकः *m.* Perfumed powder.

पटकः *m.* 1 A camp, an encampment. -2 Cotton-cloth.

पटच्चरः *m.* A thief. -रं *m* Old or ragged clothes.

पटत्कः *m.* A thief.

पटपटा *ind.* An imitative sound.

पटलं *n.* 1 A roof, thatch.-2 A cover, covering. -3 A film or coating over the eyes. -4 A heap, mass, quantity. -5 A basket. -6. Retinue, train. -7 A mark on the forehead or any other part of the body. -लः *m.*, —ली *f.* 1 A tree.-2 A stalk. —लः *m.*, —लं *n.* A section or chapter of a book. -Comp. -प्रांतः *m.* The edge of a roof.

पटहः *m.* 1 A kettle-drum, a war-drum, drum, tabor. -2 Beginning, undertaking. -3 Injuring, killing. -Comp.-घोषकः *m.* A crier (who beats a drum and then makes the proclamation). —भ्रमणं *n.* Going about with a drum to call people together.

पटालुका *f.* A leech.

पटिः,-टी *f.* 1 The curtain of a stage. -2 A cloth. -3 Coarse cloth, canvas. -4 A screen of cloth surrounding a tent. -Comp. —क्षेपः *m.* Tossing aside the curtain (of the stage); (a stage-direction to denote the hurried entrance of a character on the stage).

पटिमन् *m.* 1 Dexterity, cleverness. -2 Sharpness.-3 Acidity. -4 Harshness, roughness. -5 Violence.

पटीरः *m.* 1 A ball for playing with. -2 Sandal-wood. -3 Cupid, the god of love. -रं *n.* 1 Catechu. -2 A sieve. -3 The belly. -4 A field. -Comp. —जन्मन् *m.* Sandal-tree.

पटु *a.* (*f.* -टु or-ट्वी ; compar. पटीयस् superl. पटिष्ठ) 1 Clever, skilful, proficient (usually with a loc). *e. g.* वाचि पटुः &c.-2 Sharp, pungent. -3 Sharp, smart (as intellect) ; intelligent. -4 Violent, strong. -5 Shrill, sharp-sounding. -6 Apt, disposed to. -7 Harsh, hard-hearted. -8 Crafty, roguish. -9 Healthy, sound. -10 Active, busy. -11 Eloquent. -12 Blown, expanded.-13 Rough, fierce. -14 Contumelious (as a speech). —टुः *m.*, —टु *n.* A mushroom. —टु *n.* Salt.

पटोलः *m.* A species of cucumber (Mar. पडवळ). —लं *n.* A kind of cloth.

पटोलकः *m.* An oyster.

पट्टः *m.*, -ट्टं *n.* 1 A slab, tablet (for writing upon), plate in general. -2 A royal grant or edict. -3 A tiara, diadem. -4 A strip. -5 Silk. -6 Fine cloth, cloth in general. -7 An upper garment. -8 A turban. -9 A throne. -10 A chair or stool. -11 A shield. -12 A grinding stone. -13 A place where four roads meet.

-14 A city, town. -15 A bandage, ligature. -Comp. —अभिषेकः *m.* The consecration of the tiara. —अर्हा *f.* The principal queen. —उपाध्यायः *m.* A writer of royal grants and other documents. —जं *n.* A sort of cloth. —देवी,-महिषी,-राज्ञि *f.* The principal queen. —वस्त्र, —वासस् *a.* Attired in woven silk or coloured cloth.—सूत्रकारः *m.* A silk-weaver.

पट्टकः *m.* 1 A plate of metal used for inscriptions or royal edicts. -2 A bandage.-3 A document(also *n.*).

पट्टनं *n.*, -नी *f.* A city.

पट्टिका *f.* 1 A tablet, plate. -2 A document.-3 A piece or fragment of cloth. -4 A piece of silken cloth. -5 A ligature, bandage. -Comp. —वायकः *m.* A silkweaver.

पट्टि (-ट्टी-) शः, (-सः) *m.* A kind of spear with a sharp edge (Mar.पट्टा).

पट्टोलिका *f.* 1 A kind of bond or lease. -2 A written legal opinion.

पठ् 1 P.(पठति, पठित) 1 To read aloud, recite, rehearse. -2 To read or recite to oneself ; study, peruse.-3 To invoke (as a deity). -4 To cite, quote(as in a book).-5 To declare, describe, express. -6 To learn from (with abl.). -With परि- To mention, declare. सं— To read, learn. -*Caus* (पाठयति,-ते) —*Desid.* (पिपठिषति).

पठनं *n.* 1 Reading, reciting. -2 Mentioning. -3 Studying,perusing.

पठिः *f.* Reading, perusal.

पठित *p. p.* 1 Recited, repeated.-2 Studied, perused.

पण् 1 A. (पणते,-पणित) To deal in, barter, purchase. -2 To bargain. -3 To bet or stake at play (usually with gen. of the thing staked, but sometimes with acc.). -4 To risk or hazard (a battle). -5 To win anything at play.

पण् 1 A., 10 U. (पणते, पणायति,-ते) 1 To praise. -2 To honour.

पणः *m.* 1 Playing with dice or for a stake. -2 A game played for a stake ; bet, wager. -3 The thing staked. -4 A condition, compact, agreement. -5 Wages, hire. -6 Reward. -7 A sum in coins or shells. -8 A particular coin equal in value to 80 *cowries*. -9 Price. -10 Wealth. -11 A commodity for sale. -12 Business, transaction. -13 A shop. -14 A seller. -15 A distiller. -16 A house.-17 Expense of an expedition. -18 A handful of anything. -Comp. —अंगना,-स्त्री *f.* A prostitute, harlot. —ग्रंथिः *m.* A market, fair. —बंधः *m.* 1 Making a treaty or peace.-2 An agreement,stipulation.

पणनं *n.* 1 Bartering, purchasing. -2 Betting. -3 Sale. -4 Traffic.

पणवः *m.* A kind of musical instrument ; a small drum or tabor.

पणसः *m.* An article of a sale, a commodity.

पणाया *f.* 1 Transaction, business, dealing. -2 A market-place. -3 Profits of a trade. -4 Gambling. -5 Praise.

पणिः *f.* A market. -*m.* 1 A miser, niggard. -2 An impious man.

पणित *p. p.* 1 Transacted (as business). -2 Betted. —तं *n.* A bet, wager.

पणिज् *m.* A trader, dealer.

पंड् 1 A. (पंडते, पंडित) To go or move.

पंड् 10 U. (पंडयति,-ते) To collect, heap together.

पंडः *m.* A eunuch.

पंडा *f.* 1 Wisdom, understanding. -2 Learning, science.

पंडावत् *a.* Wise.-*m* A learned man.

पंडित *a.* (*f.* —ता) 1 Learned, wise. -2 Shrewd, clever. -3 Skilled in, proficient, skilful (generally with loc. or in comp.).-तः *m.* 1 A scholar, learned man. -2 Incense. -3 An adept, expert. -Comp. —मानिक, -मानिन्, also पंडितंमन्य *a.* Fancying oneself to be learned, a conceited person. —वादिन् *a.* Pretending to be wise.

पंडितिमन् *m.* Learning, scholarship, wisdom.

पण्य *a.* (*f.* —ण्या) 1 Saleable. -2 To be transacted. —ण्यः *m.* 1 A ware, an article, a commodity. -2 Trade, business. -3 Price. -Comp. —अंगना, —योषित, —विलासिनी, —स्त्री *f.* A harlot, a courtezan. —आजिरं *n.* A market. —आजिवः *m.* A trader. -आजीवकं *n.* A market, fair. —पतिः *m.* A great merchant. —भूमिः *f.* A warehouse. —वीथिका, -वीथी, -शाला *f.* 1 A market. -2 A stall, shop.

पत् 1 P. (पतति, पतित) 1 To fall, fall down, descend, drop down. -2 To fly. -3 To set, sink below the horizon . -4 To cast oneself at, throw oneself down. -5 To fall (in a moral sense), lose one's caste, forfeit one's rank or position. -6 To be reduced to wretchedness-7 To go down into hell; go to perdition. -8 To occur, come to pass, take place. -9 To be directed to, light or fall upon (with loc.). -10 To fall to one's lot or share. With अनु— 1 To fly to. -2 To run, run on. अभि- 1 To fly or hasten near. -2 To assail. -3 To overtake in flying. अभ्युत्— To fall upon, to attack. आ— 1 To fly towards, to rush upon. -2 To happen, to befall. -3 To assail. -4 To approach. उत्— 1 To fly up, jump up. -2 To rise, originate. नि— To fall upon, to alight, descend. -2 To throw oneself down.-3 To assault, assail. -4 To fall into, to become fixed in -5 To be directed to or towards. -6 To happen. निस्— To issue from, to come out of. परा— To return, arrive. परि— 1 To fly round or about, to hover about. -To run in all directions. -3 To attack, to fall upon. प्र— 1 To fly, fly about. -2 To come down, to fall away from. प्रणि— To salute (with *dat.* or *acc.*). प्रोत्— To fly into. सम्— 1 To fly together, to meet together. -2 To assail, to attack. -3 To go or roam about. -3 To happen.

Caus. पातयति,-ते, rarely पतयते. *Desid.* पिपतिषति or पित्सति.

पतः *m.* 1 Flying, flight. -2 Going, falling, alighting. -Comp. —गः *m.* A bird.

पतंगः *m.* 1 A bird. -2 The sun. -3 A moth, locust or grass-hopper. -4 A bee.-5 A ball for playing with. —गं *n.* 1 Quicksilver. -2 A kind of sandal wood.

पतंगमः *m.* 1 A bird. -2 A moth.

पतंगिका *f.* 1 A small bird. -2 A kind of small bee.

पतंगिन् *m.* A bird.

पतंचिका *f.* The string of a bow.

पतंजलिः *m.* 1 N. of the celebrated author of the Mahâbháshya, the great commentary on Panini's Sútras. N. of a philosopher, the propounder of the Yoga philosophy.

पतत् (*f.* —न्ती) Flying, descend

ing, alighting, coming down. *-m.* A bird. -Comp. —ग्रहः *m.* 1 The reserve of an army. -2 A spitting pot, spittoon. —भीरुः *m.* A hawk, falcon.

पतत्रं *n.* 1 A wing, pinion. -2 A feather. -3 A vehicle.

पतत्रिः *m.* A bird.

पतत्रिन् *m.* 1 A bird. -2 An arrow -3 A horse. -Comp. —केतनः *m.* An epithet of Vishnu. —राजः *m.* N. of Garuda.

पतनं *n.* The act of flying or coming down, alighting, throwing oneself down at. -2 Setting (as of the sun). -3 Going down to hell. -4 Apostacy. -5 Falling from dignity, virtue &c. -6 Fall, decline, adversity (opp. उदय or उच्छ्राय). -7 Miscarriage. -8 (In arith.) Subtraction. -9 The latitude of a planet.

पतनीयं *n.* A degrading crime or sin.

पतयः, पतसः *m.* 1 The moon. -2 A bird. -3 A grass-hopper.

पतयालु *a.* Prone to fall, liable to fall.

पताका *f.* 1 A flag, banner (fig. also) -2 A flag-staff. -3 A sign, emblem, mark, symbol. -4 An episode or episodical incident in a drama. -5 Auspiciousness, good fortune or luck. -Comp. —अंशुकं *n.* A flag. —स्थानकं. *n.* (In dramaturgy) Intimation of a subordinate incident. (यत्रार्थे चिंतितेऽन्यस्मिंस्तल्लिंगोऽन्यः प्रयुज्यते । आगंतुकेन भावेन पताकास्थानकं तु तत्* साहि. द.

पताकिक *a.* (*f.* —का) Having or carrying a banner.

पताकिन् *m.* 1 An ensign, standard-bearer. -2 A flag. -3 A scheme or figure for casting a nativity. —नी *f.* An army.

पतिः *m.* 1 A master, lord. -2 An owner, possessor, proprietor. -3 Governor, ruler. -4 A husband. -Comp. —घातिनी, —घ्नी *f.* 1 A woman who murders her husband. -2 A line on the hand showing that a woman will be faithless to her husband. —देवता, -देवा *f.* One who is loyally devoted to her husband ; a chaste woman. —धर्मः *m.* The duty (of a wife) towards a husband. —प्राणा *f.* A chaste wife. —लोकः *m.* The world of husbands in a future life. —व्रता *f.* A devoted, faithful and loyal wife ; a chaste and virtuous wife. —सेवा *f.* Devotion to a husband.

पतिंवरा *f.* A woman who is about to choose a husband.

पतित *p. p.* (*f.* —ता) 1 Fallen, descended. -2 Dropped. -3 Fallen (in a moral sense) ; wicked. -4 Apostate. -5 Degraded. -6 Defeated or overthrown. —तं *n.* Flying.

पतिवत्नी *f.* A wife whose husband is living.

पतीयंती *f.* A woman wishing or fit for a husband.

पतेरः *m.* 1 A bird. -2 A hole or pit. -3 A kind of measure(आढक q.v.)

पत्तनं *n.* 1 A town, city (opp. ग्राम). -2 A musical instrument, मृदंग.

पत्तिः *m.* 1 A footman, a foot-soldier. -2 A pedestrian. -3 A hero. *-f.* 1 The smallest division of an army, consisting of one chariot, one elephant, three horsemen and five foot-soldiers. -2 Going, walking. -Comp. —कायः *m.* Infantry. —गणकः *m.* An officer whose business it is to muster the infantry. —संहतिः *f.* A body of infantry, infantry.

पत्तिक *a.* Going on foot, pedestrian.

पत्तिन् m. A foot-soldier, foot-man.

पत्नी f. 1 A wife. -Comp.—आटः m. Women's apartments. —संनहनं n. 1 Girdling a wife. -2 The girdle of a wife.

पत्रं n. 1 A leaf (of a tree). -2 The leaf of a flower, lotus &c. -3 A leaf for writing upon, a paper. -4 A letter, document. -5 Any thin leaf or plate of metal, a gold-leaf. -6 The wing of a bird, a pinion. -7 A feather of an arrow. -8 A vehicle in general (car, horse, camel &c.). -9 Painting the person (particularly the face) with musk, sandal-juice or other fragrant substances. -10 The blade of a sword, knife &c. -11 A knife, dagger. -Comp. —अङ्गं n. The Bhúrja tree. —अङ्गुलिः f. Drawing lines of painting with the finger on the person with coloured sandal, saffron or any other fragrant substance. —अञ्जनं n. Ink. —आवलिः f. 1 A row of leaves. -2 The lines of painting drawn on the body with coloured substances as a decoration. —ऊर्णं n. A silk-garment. —काहला f. The noise or sound made by the flapping of wings or rustling of leaves. —कृच्छ्रं n. A sort of penance, drinking the infusion of leaves of various plants. -दारकः m. A saw. -नाडिका f. The fibre of a leaf. -परशुः m. A file. -पालः m. A dagger, large knife. -पाली f. 1 The feathered part of an arrow. 2 A pair of scissors. —पाश्या f. An ornament (a gold-leaf) on the forehead. -पुटं n. A vessel of leaves. —पुष्पा f. The holy basil. —बा (-वा-) लः m. An oar. -भङ्गः m., —भङ्गिः, -भङ्गी, —लेखा f. The lines or figures of various forms painted on the cheeks, breasts, arms &c. of women with fragrant and coloured substances, such as musk, saffron, sandal juice, yellow pigment &c. as a mark of decoration. -यौवनं n. A young leaf or sprout. —रञ्जनं n. Embellishing a page. —रथः m. A bird. —लता f. A long knife or poniard. -रे(-ले-)खा, -वल्लरी, —वल्लिः, —वल्ली f. See पत्रभङ्ग above. -वाज a. Furnished with feathers (as an arrow). —वाहः m. 1 A bird. -2 An arrow. -3 A letter-carrier. -विशेषकः m. See पत्रभङ्ग. -वेष्टः m. A kind of ear-ring. —शाकः m. A vegetable consisting chiefly of leaves. —श्रेष्ठः m. The Bilva tree. —सूचिः f. Thorn. —हिमं n. Wintry or snowy weather.

पत्रकं n. 1 A leaf. -2 Drawing lines or figures on the body as a decoration.

पत्रणा f. 1 Drawing lines or figures of painting on the body as a decoration. -2 Feathering an arrow.

पत्रिका f. 1 A leaf for writing upon. -2 A letter, document.

पत्री f. Writing.

पत्रिणी f. A sprout, shoot.

पत्रिन् a. (f. —णी) 1 Winged, feathered. -2 Having leaves or pages. —m. 1 An arrow. -2 A bird. -3 A falcon. -4 A mountain. -5 A chariot. -6 A tree. -Comp. —वाहः m. A bird.

पत्सलः m. A way, road.

पथः m. A way, road; reach, course (at the end of comp.). -Comp. —अतिथिः m. A traveller. —कल्पना f. Juggling tricks. —दर्शकः m. A guide.

पथकः m. A guide, one knowing the way.

पथिकः m. 1 A traveller, way-farer. -2 A guide. -Comp. —आश्रयः m. An asylum for travellers, inn. —संततिः,

—संहतिः *f.*, —सार्थः *m.* A company of travellers, a caravan.

पथिन् *m.* (Nom. पंथाः, पंथानौ, पंथानः, acc. pl. पथः, instr. pl. पथिभिः &c. ; the word is changed to पथ at the end of comp.) 1 A road, way, path. -2 Journey. -3 Range, reach as in कर्णपथ.-4 Manner of action, line of conduct. -5 A sect, doctrine. -6 A division of hell. -Comp. —देयं *n.* A toll levied on public roads. —द्रुमः *m.* The Khadira tree. -प्रज्ञ *a.* Acquainted with roads. —वाहक *a.* Cruel. (-कः *m.*) 1 A hunter, fowler. -2 A burden-bearer, porter.

पथिकः *m.* A traveller, way-farer.

पथ्य *a.* (*f.*—थ्या,) 1 Salutary, wholesome, beneficial (said of a medicine, diet, advice &c.) -2 Fit, proper ; suitable (in general) -थ्या*f.* A road, way.-थ्यं *n.*1 A wholesome diet. 4. -2 Welfare, well-being. -Comp.-अपथ्यं*n.* The class of things that are considered wholesome or hurtful in a disease.

पद् 10 A. (पदयते) To go or move.

पद् 4 A. (पद्यते, पन्न ; *caus.* पादयति,-ते; *desid.* पित्सते) 1 To go, move. -2 To go to, approach (with acc.).-3 To attain, obtain. -4 To observe, practise. With अनु— 1 To follow. -2 To be fond of. -3 To notice, to understand. -4 To have recourse to. अभि— 1 To go to, to approach, to draw near.-2To take to be, to know as, to consider. -3 To assist, to come to the assistance of. -4 To attack, to catch, to over-power. -5 To take possession of. -6 To accept, to assume. अभ्युप— 1 To protect. -2 To assent to. आ— 1 To walk towards, to go near to, to approach. -2 To enter into. -3 To fall into misfortune. -4 To happen. उत— 1 To arise, to originate, to be produced, to be born. उप— 1 To arrive at, to approach.-2 To occur, to happen, to be produced, to be present. -3 To be possible or probable. -4 To be fit or adequate for. -5 To be obtained or gained. निस्- To spring from, to be brought about or effected. प्र- 1 To go to or towards, to reach, to attain to, resort to. -2 To take refuge with, to fly to for safety. -3 To come to a particular state, to arrive at a condition. -4 To obtain, to attain, to gain. -5 To deal with, to act or behave towards.-6To allow, to admit, to agree to. प्रति— 1 To set on foot, to step upon, to go towards. -2 To get, obtain, share. -3 To take refuge with, to resort to. -4 To recover, to re-obtain. -5 To become aware of, to perceive. -6 To know, understand, to be acquainted with. -7 To affirm, to admit, to acknowledge. -8 To consider, to regard, to deem. -9 To perform, practise, to observe. -10 To undertake. -11 To do any thing to any one (with a *loc.* or *gen.*). वि— 1 To fall into a bad state, to fall into misfortune. -2 To be disabled. -3 To perish, to die. सम्— 1 To be accomplished, to succeed, to be prosperous.-2 To amount to, to be completed (as a number). -3 To become. -4 To come together, to meet with, to unite, to be possessed of (with *instr.*). -5 To attain to, to obtain acquire. -6 To bring about, to tend to (with *dat.*). समा— 1 To take place. -2 To attain to.

Causal पादयति,-ते. With आ— 1 To bring to the state of, to lead to, to reduce to. -2 To bring into subjection. -3 To bring on, to produce, to cause. उत्— 1 To produce, to create. -2 To beget. उप— 1 To lead to. -2 To offer, to present. -3 To accomplish, to achieve. -4 To justify, to make conformable to, to give reasons for. निस्— 1 To produce, to manufacture, to prepare. प्रति— 1 To give, to present, to bestow upon. -2 To substantiate by proof, to establish, to prove. -3 To consider, to regard as, to declare to be. व्या— 1 To kill. सम्— 1 To accomplish, to bring about, to effect. -2 To make ready, to prepare, to manufacture.-3 To obtain, to attain, to acquire. 4 To strike a bargain

पद् *m.* (This word has no forms for the first five inflections; it is optionally substituted for पद after acc. dual) 1 A foot. -2 A quarter, a fourth part. -Comp. -काषिन् *a.* 1 Rubbing or scratching the feet. -2 Going on foot, pedestrian. (-*m.*)A footman. -ग:(पद्गः) *m.*A foot-soldier. —ज: (पज्ज:) *m.* 1 A footman. -2 A Sûdra. —भद्रा,-भद्री *f.* A shoe, boot. —रथ: (पद्रथ:) *m.* A foot-soldier, footman. -हतिः,-ती (पद्धतिः,-ती)*f.*1 A way, path, road, course (fig. also). -2 A line, row, range. -3 A surname, title or epithet; a word denoting caste or profession in compounds which are used as proper names ; *e. g.* गुप्त, दास,दत्त &c. - हिमं (पद्धिमं) *n.* Coldness of the feet.

पदं *n.*,-द: *m.* 1 A foot. [—पदेन *ind.* On foot.-पदं कृ 1 To set foot in, on or over (lit.).2 To enter upon or into, take possession of, occupy (fig.) मूर्ध्नि पदं कृ 'To mount on the head of', 'to humble'. पदं धा,-आधा, or -निधा To set foot on, to step into, to gain a footing. गले पदं कृ To plant foot on the neck of ; to defy.] -2 A step. pace, stride. पदे पदे *ind.*At every step. -3 A foot-step, foot-print, foot-mark. -4 A trace, mark, impression, vestige. -5 A place, position, station, -6 Dignity, rank, office, station or position. -7 Cause, subject, occasion, thing, matter, business, affair. -8 Abode, object, receptacle. -9 A quarter or line of a stanza, verse. -10 A complete or inflected word. -11 A name for the base of nouns before all consonantal case-terminations except nom. singular. -12 Detachment of the Vedic words from one another ; separation of a Vedic text into its several constituent words. -13 A pretext. -14 A square root. -15 A part, portion or division (as of a sentence). 16 A measure of length. -17 Protection, preservation.-18 A square or house of a chess-board. -19 (In Arith.) Any one in a set of numbers the sum of which is required. -द: *m.* A ray of light. -Comp. —अंगुष्ठ: *m.* The great toe; thumb (of the foot).-अध्ययनं *n.* Study of the Vedas according to the पदपाठ. -अनुग *a.* 1 Following closely, being at the heels of (gen.). -2 Suitable, agreeable to. (-ग: *m.*) A follower, companion. —अनुराग: *m.* 1 A servant. -2 An army. —अनुशासनं *n.* The science of words; grammar. —अंत: *m.* 1 The end of a line of a stanza. -2 The end of a word. -अंतरं *n.* Another step, the interval of one step. —अब्जं, —अंभोजं, —अरविंदं, -कमलं, —पंकजं, -पद्मं, *n.* A lotus-like foot. —अर्थ: *m.* 1 The meaning of a word. -2 A thing or object. -3 A head or topic (of which the Naiyâyikas enumerate 16 sub-heads). -4 Anything which can be named (अभिधेय), a category or predicament; these categories, according to the Vaiseshikas, are seven; according to the Sânkhyas, twenty-five (or twenty seven according to the followers of Patanjali), and two according to the Vedântins.-आजि: *m.* A foot-soldier. —आसनं *n.* A foot-stool. -ग: *m.* A foot-soldier. -गति: *f.* The gait, manner of going. —छेद:, —विच्छेद:, —विग्रह: *m.* Separation of words, resolution of a sentence into its constituent parts. —च्युत *a.* Dismissed from office, deposed.-न्यास: *m.* 1 Stepping, tread, step. -2 A foot-mark.-3 Position of the feet in a particular attitude. —पंक्ति: *f.* 1 A line of footsteps. -2 A line or arrangement of words; a series of words. -3 A sacred brick.—पाठ: *m.* An arrangement of the Vedic text in which each word is written and pronounced in its original form and independently of phonetic changes (opp. संहितापाठ). —भंजनं *n.* Analysis of words, etymology. —भंजिका *f.* 1 A commentary which separates the words and analyses the compounds of a passage. -2 A register, journal. -3 A calendar. -वृत्ति: *f.* The hiatus between two words. —संघात:(-ट:) *m.* 1 Connecting the words which are separated in the संहिता. 2 A writer, an annotator. -स्थ *a.* 1 Going on foot. -2 Being in a position of authority or high rank.

पदकं *n.* A step, position, office. —क: *m.* 1. An ornament of the neck. -2 One conversant with the पदपाठ. -3 A निष्क or weight of gold.

पदवि:,-वी *f.* A way, road, course (fig. also). -2 Position, station, rank, dignity, office, post. -3 A place, site. -4 Good conduct or behaviour.

पदात:, पदाति: *m.* 1 A foot-soldier. -2 A pedestrian.

पदातिक:, पदातीय: *m.* A foot-man.

पदातिन् *a.* 1 Having foot-soldiers (as an army). -2 Being or going on foot. —*m.* A foot-soldier.

पदिक *a.* (*f.* —का) 1 Going on foot, pedestrain. -2 One *pada* long. -3 Containing only one division. —क: *m.* A footman. —कं *n.* The point of the foot.

पद्मं *n.* 1 A lotus (*m.* also in this sense). -2 A lotus-like ornament. -3 The form or figure of a lotus.-4 The root of a lotus. -5 The coloured marks on the trunk and face of an elephant. -6 An army arrayed in the form of a lotus.-7 The number one thousand billions.-8 Lead. -9 A mark or mole on the human body. -10 A spot. -11 N. of a particular part of a column. —द्म: *m.* 1 An elephant. -2 A species of serpent.-3 An epithet of Râma.-4 One of the nine treasures of Kubera. -5 A mode of sexual enjoyment. —द्मा *f.* N. of Lakshmi, the goddess of fortune and wife of Vishnu.-Comp. —अक्ष *a.* Lotus-eyed. (-क्ष: *m.*) An epithet of Vishnu or the sun. (-क्षं *n.*) The seed of a lotus. —आकर: *m.* 1 A large tank or pond abounding in lotuses. -2 A pond or pool of water in general. -3 A lotus-pool. -4 An assemblage of lotuses. —आलय: *m.* An epithet of Brahman (*m.*) the creator. (-या *f.*) 1 An epithet of Lakshmi. -2 Cloves. —आसनं *n.* 1 A lotus-seat. -2 A particular posture in religious meditation. (-भः *m.*) 1 An epithet of Brahman (*m.*). -2 Of Siva. -3 Of the sun. —आह्वं *n.* Cloves. -उद्भवः *m.* An epithet of Brahman (*m.*) -करः,-हस्तः *m.* An epithet of Vishnu. -3 N. of the sun. (-रा,-स्ता *f.*) N. of Lakshmî. —कर्णिका *f.* 1 The pericarp of a lotus. -2 The central part of an army arrayed in the form of a lotus. -कलिका *f.* A lotus-bud, an unblown lotus. -केसरः *m.*,-रं *n.* The filament of a lotus. -कोशः,-कोषः *m.* The calyx of a lotus. —खंडं,-षंडं *n.* A multitude of lotuses. -गंध, -गंधि *a.* Lotus-scented, or as fragrant as or smelling like a lotus. —गर्भः *m.* 1 An epithet of Brahman (*m.*) -2 Of Vishnu. -3 Of Siva. -4 The sun. -5 The inside or middle of a lotus. —गुणा, —गृहा *f.* An epithet of Lakshmî, the goddess of wealth. -जः, -जातः —भवः, —भूः, —योनिः, संभवः *m.* Epithets of Brahman (*m.*). —तंतुः *m.* The fibrous stalk of a lotus. —नाभः, -नाभिः *m.* An epithet of Vishnu.-नालं *n.* A lotus-stalk. —पाणिः *m.* 1 An epithet of Brahman. (*m.*). 2N. of Buddha. -3 N. of the sun.-4 Of Vishnu. —पुष्पः *m.* The Karnikára plant. —बंधः *m.* That kind of artificial composition in which the words are arranged in the form of a lotus-flower. —बंधुः *m.* 1 The sun. -2 A bee.-मालिनी *f.* The goddess of wealth. —रागः *m.*, -गं *n.* A ruby. —रूपा *f.* An epithet of the goddess of wealth. —रेखा *f.* A form of a lotus on the palm of the hand which indicates the acquisition of great wealth. -लांछनः *m.* 1 An epithet of Brahman (*m.*). -2 Kubera. -3 The sun. -4 A king. (—ना *f.*) 1 An epithet of Lakshmí, the goddess of wealth.-2 Of Sarasvatî, the goddess of learning. -वासा *f.* An epithet of Lakshmî.

पद्मकं *n.* 1 An army arrayed in the form of a lotus-flower.-2 The coloured spots on the trunk and face of an elephant.-3 A particular posture in sitting.

पद्माकिन् *m.* 1 An elephant. -2 The *Bhûrja* or birch tree.

पद्मावती *f.* 1 An epithet of Lakshmì. -2 N. of a river.

पद्मिन् *m.* 1 An elephant. -2 An epithet of Vishnu.

पद्मिनी *f.* 1 The lotus plant. -2 An assemblage of lotus flowers. -3 A pond or lake abounding in lotuses. -4 The fibrous stalk of a lotus. -5 A female elephant. -6 A woman of the first of the four classes into which writers on erotical science divide women. -Comp. -ईशः, -कांतः, -वल्लभः *m.* The sun. -खंडं, -षंडं *n.* A multitude of lotuses; a place abounding in lotuses.

पद्मेशयः *m.* An epithet of Vishnu.

पद्यः *m.* 1 A Súdra. -2 A part of a word. —द्या *f.* 1 A footpath, path, way. -2 Sugar. —द्यं *n.* 1 A stanza or verse (consisting of four lines). -2 Praise, panegyric.

पद्रः *m.* A village.

पद्वः *m.* 1 The world of human beings (भूलोक). -2 A car. -3 A road.

पन् 1 U. (पनायति,-ते, पनायित or पनित) 1 To praise, extol. -2 (Atm.) To rejoice at, be glad of.

पनसः *m.* 1 The bread-fruit tree.-2 A thorn. —सं *n.* The fruit of the bread-fruit tree.

पंथक *a.* (*f.* —का) Produced in or on the way.

पन्न *p. p.* (*f.* -न्ना) 1 Fallen, gone down, descended. -2 Gone.-Comp. -गः *m.* A snake, serpent. (-गं *n.*) Lead. पन्नगारिः, पन्नगाशनः, पन्नगनाशनः *m.* Epithets of Garuda.

पपिः *m.* The moon.

पपी *m.* 1 The sun. -2 The moon.

पपु *a.* Fostering, protecting. -पुः *f.* A foster-mother.

पंपा *f.* 1 N. of a lake in the Dandaká forest. -2 N. of a river in the south of India.

पयस् *n.* 1 Water. -2 Milk. -3 Semen virile. (पयस् is changed to पयो before soft consonants). -Comp. —कः, -गडः *m.* 1 Hail.-2 An island. —घनं *n.* Hail. -चयः (पयश्चयः) *m.* A reservoir or lake. —जन्मन् *m.* A cloud. —दः *m.* A cloud. —सुहृद् *m.* A peacock. —धरः *m.* 1 A cloud. -2 A woman's breast. -3 An udder. -4 The cocoa-nut tree. -5 The backbone or spine (कशेरुक).-धस् *m.* 1 The ocean. -2 A pond, lake, a piece of water.-3 A rain-cloud. -धारागृहं *n.* A bath-room with flowing water. -धिः, -निधिः *m.* The ocean.-मुच् *m.* A cloud. -राशिः *m.* The ocean. —वाहः *m.* A cloud. -व्रतं *n.* Subsisting on mere milk (as a vow).

पयस्य *a.* (*f.* —स्या) 1 Milky ; made of milk. -2 Watery. -स्यः *m.* A cat. —स्या *f.* Curds.

पयस्वल *a.* (*f.* —ला) Rich in milk, yielding copious milk. —लः *m.* A goat.

पयस्विन् *a.* (*f.* —नी) Milky, juicy. —नी *f.* 1 A milch-cow. -2 A river. -3 A she-goat. -4 Night.

पयोष्णी *f.* N. of a river rising in the Vindhya mountain (identified by some with the modern Tâpti river, but more correctly with Purna, a feeder or that river).

पर *a.*(*f.* —रा)(Declined optionally like a pronoun in nom. and voc. pl., and abl. and loc. sing. when it denotes relative position) 1 Other, different, another. -2 Distant, remote. -3 Beyond, further, on the other side of ; म्लेच्छदेशस्ततःपरः.-4 Subsequent, following, next to, future, after, (usually with abl.) ; बालात्परामिव दशां मदनोऽध्युवास * रघुवं. 5. 63.-5 Higher, superior ; *e. g.* इंद्रियाणि पराण्याहुरिंद्रियेभ्यः परं मनः । मनसस्तु परा बुद्धिः * भगवद्गीता 3. 42. -6 Highest, greatest, pre-eminent, best, principal, *e. g.* न त्वया द्रष्टव्यानां परं दृष्टं*शाकुंतल.-7 Having as a following letter or sound, followed by (in comp.). -8 Alien, stranger. -9 Hostile, adverse.-10 Having a surplus or remainder, left over ; as in परं शतं ' exceeding a hundred.' -11 Final, last. -12 (At the end of comp.) Absorbed or engrossed in, intent on, solely devoted to, wholly engaged or occupied in , as in ध्यानपर, शोकपर, दैवपर, चिंतापर &c. —रः *m.* 1 A stranger, foreigner ; oft. in pl. in this sense. -2 An enemy, adversary ; उत्तिष्ठमानस्तु परो नोपेक्ष्यः पथ्यमिच्छता *शिशुपा. 2.10. -रं *n.*1 The highest point or pitch. -2 The Supreme Spirit. -3 Final beatitude. -4 The secondary meaning of a word.-4(In logic) One of the two kinds of सामान्य or generality of notion ; more extensive kind (comprehending more objects) ; *e g.* पृथ्वी is पर with respect to a घट).

The acc, instr. and loc. singulars of पर are used adverbially ; acc. परं 1 Beyond, over, out of (with abl) ; वर्त्मनः परं.-2 After (with abl.) as in अस्मात्परं, ततः परं &c. -3 Thereupon, thereafter.-4 But, however. -5 Otherwise. -6 Very much, completely, quite ; परं दुःखितोऽस्मि &c. -7 Most willingly. -8 Only. -9 At the utmost. Instr. परेण 1 Farther, beyond, more than ; किं वा भृत्यो: परेण विधास्यति. -2 Afterwards. -3 After (with abl.) as in स्तन्यत्यागात्परेण.Loc. परे 1. Afterwards, thereupon as in अथ तेन दशाहतः परे * रघुर्व. -2 In future.

-Comp. —अंगं n. The hinder part of the body. —अंगदः m. An epithet of Siva. —अदनः m. A horse found in the country of Persia or Arabia. —अधीन a. Dependent on another, subject, subservient. —अंताः m. pl. N. of a people.-अंतकः m. An epithet of Siva. -अन्न a. Living or subsisting on another's food. (-न्नं n.) The food of another. -अपर a. 1 Far and near; remote and proximate. -2 Prior and posterior.-3Before and beyond;earlier and later.-4 Higher and lower; best and worst.(-रः m.) A *Guru* of an intermediate class. (-रं n.) (In logic) A property intermediate between the greatest and smallest numbers,a species (as existing between the genus and individual); e. g. पृथ्वी which is पर with respect to a घट is अपर with respect to द्रव्य. —अमृतं n. Rain. — अयण (अयन) a. 1 Attached or devoted to -2 Depending on, subject to. -3 Intent on, solely devoted to or absorbed in (at the end of comp.) e. g. प्रभुर्धनपरायणः.-4 Connected with. -5 Leading or conducive to. (-णं n.) 1 The chief aim, best or last resort. -2 Essence, sum. —अर्थ a. 1 Having another aim or meaning.-2 Intended or designed for another, done for another. (-र्थः m.) 1 The highest interest or advantage. -2 The interest of another (opp. स्वार्थ). -3 The chief or highest meaning. -4 The highest object (-र्थं,-र्थे) *ind.*For the sake of another. —अर्धं n. 1 The other part (opp. पूर्वार्ध); the latter half. -2 A particular high number; i. e. 100, 000, 000, 000, 000, 000. —अर्ध्य a. 1 Being on the farther side or half. -2 Most distant in number. -3 Most excellent, best, highly esteemed, highest supreme. -4 Most costly. -5 Most beautiful or lovely, finest. (-र्ध्यं n.) 1 A maximum. -2 An infinite number. —अवर a. 1 Far and near. -2 Earlier and later. -3 Prior and posterior or subsequent. -4 Higher and lower. -5 Traditional. -6 All-including. (-रं n.) 1 Cause and effect. -2 The whole extent of an idea. -3 The universe. -4 Totality. —अहः m. The next day. —अह्णः m. The afternoon. —आचित a. Fostered or brought up by another. (-तः m.) A slave.—आत्मन् m. The Supreme Spirit. —आयत्त a. Dependent on another. —आयुस् m. An epithet of Brahman (m.). —आविद्धः m. 1 An epithet of Kubera. -2 Of Vishnu. —आश्रयः m. Dependence upon another. —आसंगः m. Dependence upon another.-आस्कंदिन् m. A thief,robber. -इतर a. 1 Other than inimical i. e. friendly, kind. -2 One's own. -ईशः m. 1 An epithet of Brahman (m.).-2 Of Vishnu. -इष्टिः m. N. of Brahman(m.).-उपकारः m. Benevolence, beneficence, charity. -उपजापः m. Causing dissension among enemies. —उपरुद्ध a. Besieged by an enemy. —ऊढा f. Another's wife. —एधित a. Fostered or brought up by another. (-तः m.) 1 A servant. -2 The (Indian) cuckoo. —क्रांतिः f. Inclination of the ecliptic. -क्षेत्रं n. 1 Another's body. -2 Another's field. -3 Another's wife. —गामिन् a. 1 Being with another. -2 Relating to another.-3 Beneficial to another. —ग्रंथिः m. A joint (as of a finger). —चक्रं n. 1 The army of an enemy. -2 Invasion by an enemy, one of the six ītis.-3 A hostile prince.-छंदः m. 1 The will of another. -2 Dependence.-छिद्रं n. A weak or vulnerable point of another a defect in another. —जनः m. A stranger (opp. स्वजन).-जात a. 1 Born of another. -2 Dependent on another for livelihood. (-तः m.) A servant.-जित a. 1 Conquered by another.-2 Maintained by another. (-तः m.) The (Indian) cuckoo. —तंत्र a. Dependent on another, dependent, subservient. —दाराः (m. pl.) Another's wife. —दारिन् m. An adulterer. —देवता f. The Supreme Being.-देशः m. A foreign country. —देशिन् m. A foreigner. —द्रोहिन्, —द्वेषिन् a. Hating others, hostile, inimical. —ध्यानं n. Absolute meditation or contemplation. -निपातः m. The irregular posteriority of a word in a compound; e. g. राजदंतः m. Which signifies दंतानां राजा &c.-पक्षः m. The side or party of an enemy. -पदं n. 1 The highest position, eminence.-2 Final beatititude.-पुरुषः m. 1 Another man, a stranger. -2 The Supreme Spirit.-3 Vishnu.-4 The husband of another woman. -पुष्ट a. Fed or nourished by another. (-ष्टः m.) The (Indian) cuckoo. -पुष्टा f. 1 The (Indian) cuckoo.-2 A parasitical plant. -3 A harlot, prostitute. -पूर्वा f. A woman who has had a former husband.-प्रेष्यः m. A slave, menial servant -ब्रह्मन् n. The Supreme Spirit. —भागः m. 1 Another's share. -2 Superior merit. -3 Good fortune, prosperity. -4 Excellence, superiority. -5 Excess, abundance, height.-6 The last part, remainder. —भाषा f. A foreign tongue. -भृत् m. A crow (said to nourish the cuckoo). -भृत a. Nourished by another.—भृतः m., -ता f. The (Indian) cuckoo; (so called because it is nourished by a crow). —मर्मज्ञ a. Knowing the secrets of another.—मृत्युः m. A crow. —लोकः m. The next (or future) world. —वश, —वश्य a. Subject to another, dependent. — वाच्यं n. A fault or a defect. —वाणिः m. 1 A judge. -2 A year. -3 N. of the peacock of Kârtikeya. —वादः m. 1 Rumour, report. -2 Objection, controversy. —वादिन् m. A disputant, controversialist. —वेश्मन् n. The abode of the Supreme Being. —व्रतः m. An epithet of Dhritarâshtra. —श्वस् ind. The day after tomorrow. —संज्ञकः m. The soul. —सवर्ण a. Homogeneous with a following letter (in gram.). —सात् ind. Into the hands of another. —सूता f. A woman given in marriage. —सेवा f. Service of another. —स्त्री f. Another's wife. —स्वं n. Another's property. -हन् a. Killing enemies. —हित a. 1 Benevolent. -2 Profitable to another. (-तं n.) The welfare of another.

परकीय a. (f. —या) 1 Belonging to another. -2 Stranger, hostile. —या f. Another's wife, a woman not one's own, one of the three main kinds of heroines.

परंजः m. 1 An oil-mill. -2 The blade of a sword. -3 Foam. [runa.

परंजनः, परंजयः m. An epithet of Va-

परतस् *ind.* 1 From another.-2 From an enemy. -3 Further, more(than), over (often with abl.). -4 Otherwise. -5 Differently. -6 Further, afterwards.

परत्र *ind.* 1 In another world, in a future birth-2 Further or later on. -3 Hereafter, in future.-त्रं *n.* Future world. -Comp. -भीरु: *m.* One who stands in awe of the future world and lives a pious and religious life.

परत्वं *n.* The following of another letter, posteriority. -2 Distinction, difference. -3 Remoteness. -4 Consequence, result. -5 Enmity. -6 Priority of place or time, proximity, one of the 24 'gunas' of the Vaisehikas.

परंतप *a* Annoying or vexing others ; subduing one's enemy.—प: *m* A hero, conqueror.

परम *a* (*f*— मा) 1 Most distant, last.-2 Highest, best, most excellent.-3 Chief, principal, supreme. -4 Exceeding, extreme. -5 Sufficient. —मं*n.* The utmost or highest ; the chief or prominent part. —मं *ind.* 1 A particle expressing assent, acceptance or agreement, (well, very well, yes, be it so). —2 Exceedingly, very much; परमक्रुद्ध: &c. -Comp. -अंगना *f.* An excellent woman.-अणु: *m.* An infinitesimal particle, an atom.-अद्वैतं *n.*1 The Supreme Spirit. -2 Pure unitarianism. —अन्नं *n.* Delicious, rich food ; rice boiled in milk. -अपम: *m.* The inclination of a planet's orbit to the ecliptic. —अर्थ: *m.* 1. The highest or most sublime truth, true spiritual knowledge, knowledge about Brahman or the Supreme Spirit.-2 Truth, reality, earnestness.-3 Any excellent or important object. -4 The best sense. -5 The best kind of wealth. -विद् *m.* A philosopher. -अर्थत: *ind.* Truly, really, exactly, accurately. -अह: *m* An excellent day.-आत्मन् *m.* The Supreme Spirit or Brahman(*m.*).-आनंद: *m.* Supreme felicity ; Supreme Spirit. —ईश: *m* 1 An epithet of Vishnu. -ईश्वर: *m* An epithet of Vishnu.-2 Of Indra.-3 Of Siva.-4 The Almighty god, the Supreme Being. —गति: *f.* 1 Any chief object or refuge (as a god) .-2 Final beatitude, emancipation. —गव: *m.* An excellent bull or cow. -पदं *n.* 1 The best position, highest rank. 2 Final beatitude. —पुरुष:,-पूरुष: *m.* The Supreme Spirit. —प्रख्य *a.* Celebrated, renowned. —ब्रह्मन् *n.* The Supreme Spirit. —रस: *m.* Butter-milk mixed with water. —हंस: *m.* An ascetice of the highest order; one who has controlled and subdued all his senses by abstract meditation.

परमत: *ind.* In the highest degree, exceedingly, very much.

परंपदं *n.* 1 The abode of Vishnu. -2 Eternal felicity. -3 A high position.

परमेष्ठ *a.* Superior, supreme. -ष्ठ: *m.*1 An epithet of Brahman (*m.*). --2 A deity.

परमेष्ठिन् *m.* 1 An epithet of Brahman. (*m.*). -2 Of Siva. -3 Of Vishnu. -4 Of Garuda. -5 Of Agni. -6 Any spiritual teacher. -7 (with Jainas) An Arhat.

परंपर *a.*1 One following the other. -2 Successive, repeated.-र: *m.* 1 A great-grandson. -2 A kind of deer. -रा *f.* 1 An uninterrupted series, regular series, succession. -कर्णपरंपरया

From ear to ear, by hear-say. परंपरया आगम् 'To be handed down in regular succession'. -2 A row, line, collection, assemblage (of regular things). -3 Method, order, due arrangement. -4 Race, family, lineage. -5 Injury, killing. -र ind. Successively, one after another.

परंपराकं n. Immolating an animal at a sacrifice.

परंपरीण a. 1 Obtained by succession or descent, hereditary. -2 Traditional.

परवत a. (f. —वती) 1 Dependent upon another, ready to obey; (oft. with instr. or loc. of person). -2 Deprived of strength, rendered powerless. -3 Overpowered or overcome. -4 Devoted to.

परवत्ता f. Subjection to another, dependence.

परशः m. A kind of stone or gem the touch of which is said to turn other metals, such as iron, into gold.

परशुः m. 1 An axe, a hatchet, a battle-axe. -2 A weapon in general. -3 A thunderbolt. -Comp. —धरः m. 1 An epithet of Parasuráma. -2 Of Ganesa. -3 A soldier armed with an axe. —रामः m. 'Ráma with the axe', N. of a celebrated Bráhmana warrior, son of Jamadagni and the sixth incarnation of Vishnu.

परश्व (-स्व-) धः m. A hatchet, a battle-axe.

परस् ind. (Rarely used by itself in classical Sanskrit). 1 Beyond, further, more than. -2 On the other side of. -3 Far away, at a distance. -4 With the exception of. -Comp. —कृष्ण a. Extremely black. —पुरुष a. Higher than a man. —शत a. More than a hundred. —श्वस ind. The day after tomorrow. —सहस्र a. More than a thousand.

परस्तात् ind. 1 Beyond, on the other side of, further than (with gen.). -2 Hereafter, afterwards. -3 Higher than. -4 Aside, apart.

परस्पर a. Mutual. —pron. a. Each other, one another (used in the sing. only; often in comp.) परस्परस्योपरि पर्यचीयत * रघुवं 3. 24. *Note.* The acc. and abl. singulars are often used adverbially in the sense of 'mutually', 'reciprocally', 'by, from, or to one another' &c. -Comp. —ज्ञः m. A friend.

परस्मैपदं n., परस्मैभाषा f. 'A voice for another', one of the two voices in which verbs in Sanskrit are conjugated.

परा ind. A prefix to verbs and nouns in the sense of 'away, back, in an inverted order, aside, towards'. These are the senses of परा. 1 Killing, injuring &c. (as in पराहत). -2 Going (as in परागत). -3 Seeing, encountering (as in परादृष्ट). -4 Prowess (as in पराक्रांत). -5 Direction towards (as in परावृत्त). -6 Excess (as in पराजित). -7 Dependence (as in पराधीन). -8 Liberation (as in पराकृत). -9 Inverted order, backwards (as in पराङ्मुख). -10 Setting aside, disregarding.

पराकः m. 1 A sacrificial sword. -2 A kind of penance. -3 A kind of disease.

पराकरणं n. The act of setting aside; disregading, disdaining.

पराक्रमः m. 1 Heroism, prowess, valour. -2 Marching against, attack. -3 Attempt, enterprise. -4 N. of Vishnu.

पराक्रांत *p. p.* (*f.* —ता) 1 Strong, valiant, energetic. -2 Attacked. -3 Turned back.

परागः *m.* 1 The pollen of a flower. -2 Dust in general. -3 Fragrant powder used after bathing.-4 Sandal.-5 An eclipse of the sun or moon. -6 Fame. -7 Independence.

परांगवः *m.* The ocean.

परा (-रां-) च् *a.* (*f.* -ची) 1 Situated beyond or on the other side. -2 Having the face turned away (पराङ्मुख). -3 Unfavourable, adverse. -4 Distant. -5 Directed outwards. -6 Turned away, averted. -7 Departing or returning from. -8 Inverted, reversed. -Comp. —मुख *a.* (पराङ्मुख) 1 Having the face turned away or averted.-2 Averse from. -3 Shunning, avoiding.-4 Unfavourable. -5 Regardless of. (-खः *m.*) A magical formula pronounced over weapons.

पराचीन *a.* (*f.* -ना) 1 Turned in an opposite direction; averted. -2 Disinclined to. -3 Not caring about. -4 Happening subsequently or afterwards. -5 Situated on the other side. —नं *ind.* 1 Away from, beyond. -2 More than.

पराजयः *m.* 1 Overpowering, conquering, subjugating; defeat. -2 Being overcome by, not being able to suffer (with abl.) as in अध्ययनात्पराजयः. -3 Losing, loss, failure (as in a law-suit).-4 Deprivation. -5 Desertion.

पराजित *p. p.* (*f.* —ता) 1 Conquered, defeated. -2 Condemned by law; defeated (as in a law-suit).

पराजिष्णु *a.* 1 Victorious. -2 Conquered, defeated.

परांजः *m.* 1 An oil-mill. -2 Foam. -3 The blade of a sword or knife.

परात्परः *m.* The Supreme Being.

पराण (-न-) सा *f.* Medical treatment; practice of medicine.

पराभवः *m.* 1 Defeat, discomfiture, overthrow.-2 Mortification, humiliation.-3 Disregard, disrespect.-4 Destruction.-5 Disappearance, separation(sometimes written पराभाव).

पराभूत *p. p.* (*f*—ता) 1 Defeated, overcome. -2 Treated with contempt; dishonoured.

पराभूतिः *f.* See पराभवः.

परामर्शः *m.* 1 Seizing, pulling. -2 Bending or drawing (as a bow). -3 Violence, attack, assault. -4 Disturbance. -5 Calling to mind, recollection. -6 Consideration, reflection, thought. -7 Judgment. -8 (In logic) Deduction, ascertaining that the पक्ष or subject possesses the हेतु; व्याप्तिविशिष्टपक्षधर्मताज्ञानं परामर्शः *तर्कसं. -9 Touching, striking gently. -10 Affection (by disease).

परामृष्ट *p. p.* (*f.*—ष्टा) 1 Touched, seized, grasped. -2 Roughly treated, violated. -3 Weighed, considered. -4 Endured. 5 Connected with. -6 Afflicted by (a disease).

परायण See under पर (पर + अयन).

परारि *ind.* The year before the last.

परारुकः *m.* A stone or rock.

परावर्तः *m.* 1 Turning back, retreat. -2 Exchange, barter.-3 Restoration. -4 Reversal of a sentence (in law).

परावृत्तिः *f.* 1 See परावर्तः above. -2 Recoiling. -3 Not taking effect.

परावृत्त *p. p.* (*f.*—त्ता) 1 Returned, turned back. -2 Revolved. -3 Exchanged. -4 Reversed (as a judgment).-5 Restored, given back.

पराशरः *m.* N. of a celebrated sage.

पराशरिन् *m.* A beggar, mendicant.

परासः m. The range of anything thrown.—सं n. Tin.

परासनं n. Killing, slaughter.

परासु a. Lifeless, dead.

परास्कंदिन् m. A thief.

परास्त p. p. (f. -स्ता) 1 Thrown away. -2 Expelled. -3 Repudiated. -4 Refuted, rejected. -5 Defeated, overcome.

पराहत p. p. (f. —ता) 1 Struck down or back. -2 Driven back, repulsed. -3 Assailed, attacked. —तं n. A stroke.

परि ind. (Sometimes changed to परी, as परिवाह or परीवाह, परिहास or परीहास).

परि as a prefix to verbs and nouns derived from them, means 1 Round, round about.-2 In addition to, further. -3 Opposite to, against. -4 Much, excessively.

परि as a separable preposition means 1 Towards, in the direction of, to, opposite to; (with an acc.) as in वृक्षं परि विद्योतते विद्युत्. -2 Successessively, severally (with an acc.) as in वृक्षं वृक्षं परि सिंचति ' he waters tree after tree. ' -3 To the share or lot of (Showing भाग or participation); with acc. यदत्र मां परि स्यात् what may fall to my lot'.-4 From, out of. -5 Except, outside of, with the exception of (with abl.).-6 After the lapse of. -7 In consequence of. -8 Beyond, more than. -9 According to. -10 Above, over.

परि as an adverbial prefix to nouns not directly connected with verbs means 'very, ' very much,' 'excessively ' as in पर्यश्रु ' bursting into tears.'

परि at the beginning of adverbial compounds means (1) without, except, outside, with the exception of.

परि may be used at the end of adverbial comp. after अक्ष, शलाका and numeral to denote ' loss or defeat in a game by an unlucky or adverse cast of dice' e. g. अक्षपरि, शलाकापरि, एकपरि. (2) Round about, as in पर्यग्नि.

परिकथा f. A work giving the history and adventures of a fabulous person.

परिकंपः m. 1 A great terror.-2 Violent tremour or trembling.

परिकरः m. 1 Retinue, attendants, followers. -2 A multitude, crowd. -3 A beginning, commencement. -4 A girth, waist-band, cloth worn round the loins. परिकरं बंध् or कृ To gird up one's loins, to make oneself ready, prepare oneself for any action'. कृतपरिकर a. That has become ready for fight &c. कृतपरिकरस्य भवादृशस्य त्रैलोक्यमपि न क्षमं परिपंथीभवितुं *वेणिसं. 3. -5 A sofa. -6 (In Rhet.) The figure of speech in which there is a number of significant epithets; उक्तिर्विशेषणैः साभिप्रायैः परिकरोमतः *साहि. द.10 e. g. सुधांशुकलितोत्तंसस्तापं हरतु वः शिवः *चंद्रालोकः -7 (In dramaturgy) Covert or indirect intimation of coming events in the plot of a drama. -8 Judgment. -9 A helper, colleague, co-worker.

परिकर्तनं n.1 Cutting off.-2 A shooting pain.

परिकर्तिका f. A sharp shooting pain, especially in the rectum.

परिकर्तृ m. A priest who performs the marriage ceremony of a younger brother whose elder brother is not yet married.

परिकर्मन् m. A servant. —n.1 Painting or perfuming the body; personal decoration; toilet. -3 Worship adoration. -4 (In Yoga phil.) A means of purifying the mind.-5 Ar arithmetical operation (of which there are 8 divisions).

परिकर्मिन् *m.* An assistant, a servant.

परिकर्षः *m.*, —कर्षणं *n.* Dragging out, extraction.

परिकल्कनं *n.* Deceit, cheating.

परिकल्पनं *n.*, -ना *f.* 1 Settling, fixing, determining. -2 Inventing, forming, arranging. -3 Providing, furnishing.

परिकल्पित *p. p.* (*f.* —ता) 1 Settled, decided. -2 Invented. -3 Prepared. 4 Distributed. -5 Provided, furnished (with).

परिकांक्षितः *m.* A religious mendicant or ascetic; a devotee.

परिकीर्ण *p. p.* (*f.*—र्णा) 1 Spread, scattered about. -2 Surrounded. -3 Crowded with.

परिकीर्तनं *n.* 1 Proclaiming. -2 Boasting. -3 Naming.

परिकीर्तित *p. p.* (*f.* -ता) 1 Proclaimed, announced. -2 Boasted of. -3 Declared to be.

परिकूटं *n.* A barrier; a trench before the gate of a town.

परिकोपः *m.* Great anger, fury.

परिक्रमः *m.* 1 Roaming about. -2 Passing over. -3 Circumambulating. -4 Walking for pleasure. -5 Series, order. -Comp. —सहः *m.* A goat.

परिक्रयः *m.*, —क्रयणं *n.* 1 Wages, hire. -2 Employing on hire. -3 Purchasing. -4 Barter, exchange. -5 Anything purchased.

परिक्रांत *p. p.* (*f.*—ता) Walked round. —तं *n.* 1 The place on which any one has walked about. -2 A footstep, foot-print.

परिक्रांतिः *f.* Revolution, perambulation.

परिक्रिया *f.* 1 Enclosing with a fence or ditch. -2 Encircling or surrounding in general. -3 (In dramaturgy) A covert intimation of coming events in the plot of a drama. -4 Attention.

परिक्लांत *a.* (*f.* —ता) Fatigued.

परिक्लिष्ट *p. p.* (*f.* -ष्टा) 1 Vexed, troubled. -2 Fatigued. -ष्टं *n.* Pain, vexation.

परिक्लेदः *m.* Wetness, dampness.

परिक्लेशः *m.* Fatigue, trouble, pain.

परिक्षतिः *f.* Injury, harm.

परिक्षयः *m.* 1 Decay, destruction. -2 Disappearing, ceasing. -3 Ruin, failure.

परिक्षाम *a.* (*f.* —मा) Emaciated, lean.

परिक्षालनं *n.* 1 Washing, cleansing. -2 Water for washing.

परिक्षित् *m.* 1 N. of a king, son of Abhimanyu and father of Janamejaya. -2 An epithet of Agni.

परिक्षिप्त *p. p.* (*f.* —प्ता) 1 Scattered, diffused. -2 Encircled, surrounded. -3 Intrenched. -4 Overspread. -5 Left, abandoned.

परिक्षीण *p. p.* (*f.* —णा) 1 Vanished. -2 Decayed. -3 Emaciated, exhausted. -4 Quite ruined. -5 Diminished. -6 (In law) Insolvent.

परिक्षीव *a.* (*f.*-वा) Quite intoxicated.

परिक्षेपः *m.* 1 Moving about. -2 Scattering, spreading. -3 Surrounding, encircling circumfluence. -4 That by which anything is surrounded. -5 Abandoning. -6 An organ of sense.

परिखा *f.* A moat, trench round a fort or town.

परिखातं *n.* 1 A moat, ditch. -2 A furrow. -3 Digging round.

परिखिन्न *p. p.* (*f.* —न्ना) Afflicted, troubled.

परिखेदः *m.* Fatigue, exhaustion, lassitude.

परिख्यातिः *f.* Fame, reputation.

परिगणनं *n.*, -ना *f.* Complete enume

ration; accurate statement or calculation.

परिगत *p. p.* (*f.* —ता) 1 Surrounded, enclosed, encircled.-2 Diffused, spread. -3 Known, understood. -4 -4 Filled or covered with. -5 Got, obtained.-6 Remembered. -7 Overcome, overwhelmed. -8 Afflicted (with).

परिगमः *m.*, परिगमनं *n.* 1 Going round, surrounding. -2 Spreading, diffusing. -3 Obtaining. -4 Knowing, ascertaining.

परिगर्हणं *n.* Excessive blame.

परिगलित *p. p.* (*f.* —ता) 1 Sunk. -2 Dropped down. -3 Vanished. -4 Melted. -5 Flowing.

परिगीति *f.* A kind of metre.

परिगूढ *p. p.* (*f.* -ढा) 1 Quite secret. -2 Incomprehensible.

परिगृहीत *p. p.* (*f.* —ता) 1 Grasped, seized. -2 Embraced, surrounded. -3 Accepted, received. -4 Assented or consented to. -5 Patronized, favoured. -6 Followed, obeyed, observed. -7 Married.

परिगृहीता *f.* A married woman.

परिग्रहः *m.* 1 Seizing, holding, grasping. -2 Surrounding, encircling, fencing round.-3 Putting on, wrapping round (as a dress). -4 Assuming, taking. -5 Receiving, acceptance. -6 Possessions, property. -7 Taking in marriage, marriage. -8 A wife, queen. -9 Taking under one's protection. 10 Followers, train, retinue, suite. -11 A household, family. -12 The seraglio or household of a king. -13 A present. -14 Assent, consent. -15 A claim. -16 Entertaining (a guest &c.). -17 Assistance. -18 A husband. -19 Grace, favour. -20 Comprehension, understanding. -21 Undertaking, performing. -22 Dominion. -23 Punishment. -24 Summing up; totality.-25 A house, residence.-26 A curse. -27 Root, origin. -28 The eclipse of the sun or moon. -29 An oath. -30 The rear of an army. -31 N. of Vishnu.

परिग्रहणं *n.* Wrapping round, putting on.

परिग्रहीतृ *m.* 1 A husband. -2 An assistant. -3 An adoptive father.

परिग्राहः *m.* The fencing round of the sacrificial altar.

परिग्लान *p. p.* (*f.*-ना) 1 Languid, exhausted. -2 Disinclined to.

परिघः *m.* 1 An iron or wooden beam or bar used for locking or shutting a gate (अर्गल). -2 (Hence) A barrier, hindrance, obstacle. -3 A stick or club studded or tipped with iron. -4 An iron club in general. -5 A water-jar, pitcher. -6 A glass-pitcher. -7 A house, dwelling. -8 Killing, destroying. -9 A stroke or blow. -10 A child which assumes a peculiar cross position in birth. -11 The gate of a palace, town or house.

परिघट्टनं *n.* Stirring up, stirring round.

परिघर्मः *m.* A vessel for preparing the hot sacrificial beverage.

परिघातः *m.*, परिघातनं *n.* 1 Killing, striking, getting rid of. -2 An iron bludgeon or club.

परिघोषः *m.* 1 Noise. -2 Improper speech. -3 Thunder.

परिचतुर्दशन् *a.* Fully fourteen.

परिचयः *m.* 1 Accumulation. -2 Acquaintance, familiarity, intimacy. -3 A study, practice, frequent repetition. -4 Recognition.

परिचरः *m.* 1 A servant, follower, an attendant. -2 A body-guard. -3

A guard or patrol in general. -4 Homage, service.

परिचरणः *m.* A servant, an attendant. —णं *n.* 1 Serving, attending or waiting upon. -2 Going about.

परिचर्या *f.* 1 Service, attendance. -2 Adoration, worship.

परिचाय्यः *m.* Sacrificial fire (arranged in a circle).

परिचारः *m.* 1 Service, attendance. -2 A Servant. -3 A place for walking.

परिचारकः, परिचारिकः, परिचारिन् *m.* A servant, an attendant.

परिचारिका *f.* 1 A female servant. -2 (plu.) Fried grain.

परिचित *p. p.* (*f.*—ता) 1 Heaped up, accumulated. -2 Familiar with. -3 Learnt, practised.

परिचितिः *f.* Acquaintance, familiarity, intimacy.

परिचिंतनं *n.* Thinking (of), remembering.

परिचुंबनं *n.* Kissing passionately.

परिच्छद् *f.* 1 Retinue, train. -2 Paraphernalia.

परिच्छदः *m.* 1 A covering, cover. -2 A garment, dress. -3 Train, retinue, attendants. -4 Paraphernalia, exteranl appendage (as छत्र, चामर). -5 Goods and chattles, personal property, all one's possessions or belongings (utensils, implements &c.). -6 Necessaries for travelling.

परिच्छंदः *m.* Train, retinue.

परिच्छन्न *p. p.* (*f.*—न्ना) 1 Enveloped, covered, clad. -2 Overspread or overlaid. -3 Surrounded. -4 Concealed.

परिच्छित्तिः *f.* 1 Accurate definition. -2 Partition; division.

परिच्छिन्न *p. p.* (*f.*—न्ना) 1 Cut off, divided. -2 Accurately defined, ascertained. -3 Limited, circumscribed, confined.

परिच्छेदः *m.* 1 Cutting, separating, dividing. -2 Accurate definition or distinction, accurate determination. -3 Discrimination, judgment, discernment. -4 A limit, boundary, circumscribing. -5 A section, chapter or division of a work. -6 A segment. -7 Remedying. -8 A measure.

परिच्छेदकं *n.* Limitation.

परिच्छेदनं *n.* 1 Discriminating. -2 Dividing.

परिच्छेद्य *a.* (*f.*—द्या) 1 To be accurately defined; definable. -2 To be weighed or estimated.

परिच्युतिः *f.* 1 Falling down. -2 Swerving, deviating.

परिजनः *m.* Attendants or servants taken collectively. -2 The retinue, or train of females; the maids of a lady. -3 A single servant.

परिजाल्पितं *n.* A covert indication (as by a servant) of one's own skill, superiority &c, by pointing out the cruelty, deceitfulness and such other faults of his master; Ujjvalamani thus defines it:—
प्रभोर्निर्दयताशाठ्यचापलाद्युपपादनात्। स्वविचक्षणताभिव्यक्तिर्भंग्या स्यात्परिजाल्पितम्॥

परिज्ञप्तिः *f.* 1 Conversation, discourse. -2 Recognition.

परिज्ञा *f.*, परिज्ञानं *n.* 1 Thorough knowledge; complete acquaintance. -2 Recognition.

परिज्ञेय *a.* (*f.*—या) 1 To be recognised or ascertained. -2 Comprehensible, conceivable.

परिडीनं *n.* The fight of a bird in circles.

परिणत *p. p.* (*f.*-ता) 1 Bent or bowed down; stooping. -2 Declining, old (as age). -3 Ripe, matured, ripened, fully developed. -4 Full-grown, advanced, perfected. -5 Digested (as food). -6 Transformed or changed into (with instr) -7 Ended, come to a close, terminated -8 Set (as the sun) —त m An elephant stooping to strike with his tusks, or giving a side blow with his tusks (तिर्यग्दन्तप्रहारस्तु गजः परिणतो मतः *हलायुध)

परिणति f 1 Bending or stooping down -2 Ripeness maturity development -3 Change, transformation -4 Fulfilment -5 Result, consequence -6 End, close, termination -7 Close of life, old age -8 Digestion (of food)

परिणद्ध p p (f —द्धा) 1 Bound or wrapped round -2 Broad, large

परिणमनं n Change, transformation

परिणय m, णयनं n Marriage

परिणहनं n Girding on, wrapping round

परि (-री-) णाम m 1 Change transformation -2 Digestion -3 Result, issue, effect 4 Ripening, maturity, full development -5 End close, decline -6 Old age e g परिणामे तहि दिलीपवंशजाः *रघुवंश 8 11 -7 Lapse (of time) 8 (In Rhet) The figure in which what is superimposed serves the purpose in hand as being identified with the subject of superimposition (viz the उपमेय) In this figure the object superimposed is commuted into the nature of the subject of superimposition, विषयात्मतयारोप्ये प्रकृतार्थोपयोगिनी । परिणामो भवेत्तुल्यातुल्याधिकरणो द्विधा। *साहि०द० परिणाम क्रियार्थश्चेद्विषयी विषयात्मना।प्रसन्नेन दृगब्जेन वीक्षते मदिरेक्षणा॥ *चन्द्रालोक -Comp -दर्शिन् a Prudent fore sighted —दृष्टि a Prudent (-ष्टिः f) Prudence providence —पथ्य a Salutary in the end —शूल n Violent or painful indigestion, colic flatulence with pain

परिणामक a Causing a change

परि (-री-) णाय m 1 Moving a piece at chess, draughts &c -2 A move (at chess)

परिणायक m 1 A leader -2 A husband

परि (-री) णाह m 1 Circumference, expanse extent, breadth, width -2 Periphery or circumference of a circle

परिणाहवत् a (f—ती) Large big, expansive

परिणाहिन् a Large, big

परिणिंसक a (f —का) 1 Tasting, eating -2 Kissing

परिणिष्ठा f Perfect skill

परिणीत p p (f —ता) Married —ता f A married woman

परिणेतृ m A husband

परितप्त p p (f —प्ता) 1 Heated burnt -2 Tormented, pained

परितप्ति f Excessive pain anguish

परितर्पण n Gratifying

परितस् ind (Usually with a noun in the acc, sometimes by itself) 1 All around, on all sides in all directions every where on every side -2 Towards, in the direction of

परि(री)ताप m 1 Extreme or scorching heat -2 Pain, agony, anguish -3 Lamentation wailing -4 Trembling, fear -5 Hell

परितुष्ट p p (f —ष्टा) 1 Completely satisfied -2 Pleased, delighted

परितुष्टि f 1 Contentment complete satisfaction -2 Delight, joy

परितोष m 1 Contentment -2 Complete satisfaction, gratification आपरितोषाद्विदुषां न साधु मन्ये प्रयोगविज्ञानं *शाकुंतल 1 2 -3 Pleasure, delight liking (for) (with loc)

परितोषणं n Satisfaction

परित्यक्त *p. p.* (*f.* -क्ता) 1 Left, abandoned. -2 Deprived or bereft (of) (with instr.). -3 Discharged (as an arrow). -4 Wanting.

परित्यजनं *n.* Abandoning, giving up, leaving.

परित्यागः *m.* 1 Abandonment, desertion, repudiation (as of a wife &c.). -2 Neglect, omission. -3 Giving away, liberality. -4 Loss, privation. -5 A sacrifice.

परित्रस्त *a.* (*f.* —स्ता) Frightened, [afraid.

परित्राणं *n.* Protection, rescue, defence, deliverance. परित्राणाय साधूनां विनाशाय च दुष्कृतां * भगवद्गीता 4. 8. -2 Self-defence.

परित्रासः *m.* Fear, terror, fright.

परिदंशित *a.* (*f.* —ता) Covered with mail.

परिदरः *m.* A disease of the gums in which the skin peels off and bleeds.

परिदानं *n.* 1 Barter, exchange. -2 Devotion. -3 Restitution or restoration of a deposit.

परिदायिन् *m.* A father who gives his daughter in marriage to a man whose elder brother is not yet married.

परि (-री-) दाहः *m.* 1 Burning. -2 Anguish, pain, sorrow.

परिदेवः *m* Wailing, lamentation.

परिदेवनं *n.*, -ना *f.*, परिदेवितं *n.* 1 Lamentation, complaint, bewailing. -2 Repentance, regret.

परिद्यून *a.* (*f.* -ना) Sorrowful, miserable.

परिधर्षणं *n.* 1 An assault, attack. -2 Insult, affront, abuse. -3 Ill-treatment, rough usage.

परि (-री-) धानं *n.* 1 Putting on a garment, dressing. -2 A garment; especially an under-garment; clothes in general.

परिधानीयं *n.* An under-garment. -या *f.* A concluding hymn.

परिधायः *m.* 1 Train, retinue. -2 A receptacle, a reservoir. -3 The posteriors.

परिधायकः *m.* A hedge, fence.

परिधारणं *n.* Suffering, enduring.

परिधिः *m.* 1 A wall, fence, an enclosure. -2 A misty halo round the sun or moon ; परिधेर्मुक्त इवोष्णदीधितिः * रघुवं 8. 30. -3 A circle of light. -4 The horizon. -5 The circumference. -6 The periphery of a wheel. -7 A stick (of a sacred tree like पलाश) laid round the sacrificial fire. -8 A covering. -9 A branch of a sacred tree to which the sacrificial victim tied. -Comp. —पतिखेचरः *m.* An epithet of Siva. —स्थः *m.* 1 A guard. -2 An officer attendant on a king or a general.

परिधूपित *a.* (*f.* —ता) Richly perfumed or scented.

परिधूसर *a.* (*f.* -रा) Quite grey.

परिधेयं *n.* An under garment.

परिध्वंसः *m.* 1 Distress, disaster. -2 Failure. -3 Destruction. -4 Loss of caste.

परिनिर्वपणं *n.* Distributing, giving.

परिनिर्वाण *a.* (*f.* —णा) Completely extinguished. —णं *n.* Final extinction (of the individual).

परिनिर्वृतिः *f.* Final liberation or complete emancipation of the soul from the body and exemption from future transmigration.

परिनिष्ठा *f.* 1 Complete knowledge (of anything). -2 Complete accomplishment. -3 Extreme limit.

परिनिष्ठित *p. p.* (*f.*—ता) Completely skilled in.

परिन्यासः *m.* 1 Completing the sense

of a passage. -2 Alluding to the development of the origin of the dramatic plot.

परिपक्व *p. p.* (*f.*—क्वा) 1 Completely cooked. -2 Completely baked or burnt. -3 Quite ripe; perfected (fig. also). -4 Highly cultivated ; very sharp or shrewd. -5 Fully digested. -6 Being on the point of decay or death.

परिपणं,-नं *n.* Capital, principal, stock.

परिपणनं *n.* Plighting, promising.

परिपणित *p. p.* (*f.*—ता) Plighted, pledged, promised.

परिपतनं *n.* Flying round or about.

परिपंथः *m.* An antagonist, enemy.

परिपंथकः *m.* An antagonist, adversary.

परिपंथिन् *a.* (*f.*—नी) Standing in the way, obstructing, hindering. -*m.* 1 An antagonist ; one who spreads evil reports about another; an enemy, an opponent. -2 A robber. thief, highwayman. [about way.

परिपरः *m.* A tortuous or round-

परिपवनः *m.* 1 Winnowing corn. -2 A winnowing basket.

परि (-री-) पाकः *m.* 1 Being completely cooked or dressed.-2 Digestion. -4 Ripening, development, perfection. -4 Fruit, consequence. -5 Cleverness, skilfulness.

परिपाटल *a.* (*f.*—ला) Pale red.

परिपाटिः,—टी *f.* 1 Method, course. -2 Arrangement, order, succession. -3 Arithmetic.

परिपाठः *m.* Complete enumeration.

परिपार्श्व *a.* (*f.*—र्श्वा) Near, at the side, hard by.

परिपालनं *n.* 1 Protecting, maintaining, keeping, sustaining.-2 Nourishment, nurture.

परिपिष्टकं *n.* Lead.

परिपीडनं *n.*, परिपीडा *f.* 1 Squeezing, pressing out. -2 Injuring, hurting; harm.

परिपुटनं *n.* 1 Removing the bark. -2 Losing the bark.

परिपूजनं *n.*, परिपूजा *f.* Honouring, worshipping, adoring.

परिपूत *p. p.* (*f.*—ता) 1 Purified, quite pure. -2 Completely winnowed or threshed ; freed from chaff.

परिपूरणं *n.* 1 Filling. -2 Perfecting, making complete.

परिपूर्ण *p. p.* (*f.* —र्णा) 1 Quite full. -2 Self-satisfied, content.

परिपूर्तिः *f.* Completion, fulness.

परिपेलव *a.* (*f.*—वा) Very delicate, excessively tender. —वं *n.* A kind of fragrant grass.

परिपोटः, —पोटकः *m.* A particular disease of the ear (in medicine) (by which the ear loses its skin).

परिपोषणं *n.* 1 Feeding, nourishing. -2 Furthering, promoting.

परिप्रश्नः *m.* Inquiry, interrogation, question.

परिप्राप्तिः *f.* Acquisition, obtaining.

परिप्रेषणं *n.* 1 Sending away. -2 Banishing, abandoning.

परिप्रेष्यः *m.* A servant.

परिप्लुत *p. p.* (*f.*—ता) 1 Flooded, inundated. -2 Overwhelmed. -3 Wetted, bathed. —तं *n.* A spring, jump. —ता *f.* Spirituous liquor.

परिप्लुष्ट *p. p.* (*f.*—ष्टा) Burnt, scorched.

परिब्र (-व-) र्हः *m.* 1 Retinue, train, attendants. -2 Furniture. -3 Royal insignia. -4 The necessaries of life. -5 Property, wealth.

परिब (-व-) र्हणं *n.* 1 Retinue, train. -2 Attire, trim. -3 Growth. -4 Worship.

परिबाधा *f.* 1. Trouble, annoyance.

-2 Fatigue, hardship.

परिबृं (-बृं-) हणं *n.* 1 Prosperity, welfare. -2 Appendix, supplement.

परिबृं (-बृं-) हित *p.p.* (*f.* -ता) 1 Increased, augmented. -2 Grown prosperous. -3 Accompanied by, furnished with. -तं *n.* The roar of an elephant.

परिभंगः *m.* Shattering, breaking to pieces. [ing.

परिभर्त्सनं *n.* Threatening, menac-

परि (-री-) भवः *m.* 1 Insult, injury, disrespect, degradation, disgrace. -2 Defeat, discomfiture. -comp. —आस्पदं, -पदं *n.* 1 An object of contempt. -2 A disgrace or disgraceful situation. -विधिः *m.* Humiliation.

परिभविन् *a.* (*f.* —नी) 1 Humiliating, treating with contempt.-2 Suffering disrespect.

परिभावः *m.* See परिभव.

परिभावनं *n.* Union, cohesion. -नं *n.*, -ना *f.* Contemplation, meditation.

परिभावित *p. p.* (*f.* -ता) 1 Contained, included.-2 Pervaded.-3 Penetrated. -4 Conceived.

परिभाविन् *a.* (*f.* -नी) 1 Treating with contempt.-2 Putting to shame, excelling. -3 Setting at naught, defying.

परिभाषणं *n.* 1 Speaking, discourse, talking, chatting, gossiping. -2 Expression of censure ; admonition, reproof, abuse. -3 Rule, precept.

परिभाषा *f.* 1 Speech, discourse. -2 Censure, blame, abuse. -3 An explanation. -4 Terminology, technical phraseology ; technical terms (used in a work). -5 Any general rule, precept or definition which is applicable throughout. -6 A list of abbreviations or signs used in any work.-7 (In gram.) An explanatory Sátra mixed up with the other Sútras of Pânini, which teaches the method of applying them. -8 (In medicine) Prognosis.

परिभुक्त *p. p.* (*f.* -क्ता) 1 Eaten. -2 Used, enjoyed. -3 Possessed.

परिभुग्न *a.* (*f.*—ग्ना) Bowed, curved.

परिभूतिः *f.* Contempt, insult, disrespect, humiliation.

परिभूषणः *m.* (*scil.* संधि) Peace obtained by the cession of the whole revenue of a land.

परिभोगः *m.* 1 Enjoyment. -2 Especially, sexual enjoyment. -3 Illegal use of another's goods.

परिभ्रंशः *m.* 1 Escape. -2 Falling (from).

परिभ्रंशनं *n.* Falling (from).-Loss.

परिभ्रमः *m.* 1 Wandering, going about.-2 Rambling discourse, periphrasis. -4 Error, delusion.

परिभ्रमणं *n.* 1 Going about, roaming, wandering. -2 Revolving, turning round. -3 Circumference.

परिभ्रष्ट *p. p.* (*f.* -ष्टा) 1 Fallen or dropped off.-2Escaped. -3 Degraded. -4 Deprived of, devoid of with abl. or instr.) -5 Vanished. -6 Lost.

परिभ्रांत *a.* (*f.*—ता) That has rambled about somewhere.

परिमंडल *a.* (*f.* —ला) 1 Globular, round, circular. -2 Of the measure of an atom. -लं *n.* 1 A globe, sphere. -2 A ball. -3 A circle.

परिमंथर *a.* (*f.* -रा) Extremely slow.

परिमंद *a.* (*f.* -दा) 1 Very dull or dim ; quite faint. -2 Very slow. -3 Very weak. -4 Very little.

परिमरः *m.* 1 Destruction. -2 The wind.-3 A magical rite for the destruction of enemies.

परिमर्दः *m.*, परिमर्दनं *n.* 1 Rubbing, grinding. -2 Crushing, trampling. -3 Destruction. -4 Hurting. -5 Embracing, pressing.-6 Using up, consuming.

परिमर्शः *m.* 1 Friction. -2 Contact. -3 Consideration, reflection.

परिमर्षः *m.* 1 Envy, dislike. -2 Anger.

परिमलः *m.* 1 Fragrance, perfume. -2 Pounding of fragrant substances.-3 A fragrant substance.-4 Copulation. -5 A meeting of learned men. -6 A stain, spot.

परिमलित *a.* (*f.* -ता) 1 Perfumed.-2 Soiled, despoiled of beauty.

परि (-री-) माणं *n.* 1 Measuring, measure. -2 Weight, number, value.-3 Size, dimension.

परिमाथिन् *a.* (*f.* -नी) Torturing.

परिमार्गः *m.*, परिमार्गणं *n.* 1 Searching for. -2 Touch, contact. -3 Cleaning, wiping.

परिमार्जः *m.*1 Cleaning.-2 Rubbing.

परिमार्जनं *n.* 1 Cleaning, wiping off. -2 A dish of honey and oil.

परिमित *p. p.* (*f.* —ता) 1 Moderate, sparing. -2 Limited. -3 Measured, meted out. -4 Regulated, adjusted. -Comp. —आभरण *a.* Moderately adorned.-आयुस् *a.*Short-lived. -आहार, -भोजन *a.* Eating little food. -कथ *a.* Speaking little; using measured words.

परिमितिः *f.* 1 Measure, quantity. -2 Limitation.

परिमिलनं *n.* 1 Touch, contact. -2 Combination.

परिमुखं *ind.* About the face, round.

परिमुग्ध*a.*(*f.*-ग्धा)1 Artlessly lovely. -2 Fascinating but foolish.

परिमृदित *p. p.* (*f.* -ता) 1 Trodden or trampled down, squeezed, crushed, roughly handled, squeezed. -2 Embraced, clasped. -3 Rubbed, ground.

परिमृष्ट *p. p.* (*f.* —ष्टा) 1 Washed, cleaned,purified.-2 Rubbed, touched. -3 Embraced. -4 Spread, filled with. -5 Invested.

परिमेय *a.* (*f.* —या) 1 Few, limited. -2 Measurable. -3 Finite.

परिमोक्षः *m.* 1 Removing, relieving. -2 Liberation, deliverance. -3 Emptying evacuation. -4 Escape. -5 Final beatitude (निर्वाण).

परिमोक्षणं *n.* 1 Liberation, deliverance. -2 Untying.

परिमोषः *m.* Stealing, theft.

परिमोषिन् *m.* A thief, robber.

परिमोहनं *n.* 1 Beguiling, alluring, fascinating. -2 Bewildering.

परिम्लान *p. p.* (*f.* —ना) 1 Faded, withered. -2 Languid, dull. -3 Impaired, diminished. -4 Soiled, stained.

परिरक्षकः *m.* A protector, guardian.

परिरक्षणं *n.*, परिरक्षा *f.* 1 Protection, preservation, guarding. -2 Keeping, maintaining, adhering to. -3 Deliverance,rescuing.

परिरथ्या *f.* A street, road.

परि (-री-) रंभः *m.*, —भणं *n.* Embracing ; an embrace.

परिराटिन् *a.* (*f.*—नी) Crying aloud, screaming.

परिलघु *a.* 1 Very light (lit.). -2 Very light or easy to digest. -3 Very small.

परिलुप्त *p. p.* (*f.*—प्ता) 1 Interrupted, disturbed diminished. -2 Lost, disappeared.

परिलेखः *m.* 1 An outline, a delineation, sketch. -2 A picture.

परिलेखनं *n.* Drawing lines on the altar.

परिलोपः *m.* 1 Injury. -2 Neglect, omission.

परिवत्सरः *m.* A year, a full year.

परिवदनं *n.* 1 Reviling. -2 Clamouring.

परिवर्जनं *n.* 1 Leaving, abandoning. -2 Giving up, resigning. -3 Killing, slaughter.

परि (-री-) वर्तः *m.* 1 Revolving, revolution (as of a planet).-2 A period, lapse or expiration of time. -3 The expiration of a Yuga. -4 Repetition. -5 Change. -6 Retreat, flight.-7 A year.-8 Repeated birth, transmigration. -9 Barter, exchange. -10 Requital, return. -11 An abode. -12 A chapter or section of a work.-13 N. of the Kúrma or second incarnation of Vishnu.

परिवर्तनं *n.* 1 Moving to and fro, rolling about. -2 Turning round, whirling round. -3 Revolution, end of a period of time. -4 Change. -5 Exchange, barter. -6 Inverting. -7 Requital, return.

परिवर्तिका *f.* Phimosis or contraction of the prepuce (in medicine).

परिवर्तित *a.* (*f.*—ता) 1 Revolved. -2 Exchanged. -3 Inverted. -4 Returned, retreated.

परिवर्तिन् *a.* (*f.*—नी) 1 Moving or turning round, revolving. -2 Coming round again and again.3Changing. -4 Being or remaining near; moving round about. -5 Retreating, flying. -6 Exchanging. -7 Recompensing, requiting.

परिवर्धनं *n.* 1 Increasing, enlarging. -2 Rearing, breeding. -3 Growing; growth.

परिवर्धित *a.* (*f.*—ता) 1 Increased. -2 Cut, excavated.

परिवर्मन् *a.* Clad in mail; armed.

परिवसथः *m.* A village.

परिवहः *m.* 1 N. of one of the seven courses of wind. -2 One of the seven tongues of fire.

परि (-री-) वादः *m.* 1Blame, censure, abuse.-2 Scandal,stigma,ill-repute. -3 Charge, accusation. -4 An instrument with which the lute is played.

परिवादकः *m.* 1 A plaintiff,complainant, accuser. -2 One who plays on the lute.

परिवादिन् *a.* (*f.*—नी) 1 Reviling, censuring, slandering. -2 Accusing. -3 Screaming, crying aloud. -4 Censured, slandered. —*m.* An accuser, a plaintiff, complainant. —नी *f.* A lute(वीणा)of seven strings.

परि (-री-) वापः *m.* 1 Shaving, shearing. -2 Sowing.-3 A reservoir,pool, pond. -4 Furniture. -5 Train, retinue.-6 Fried grains of rice. -7 Coagulated milk.

परिवापणं *n.* Shaving.

परिवापित *a.* (*f.*—ता) Shaven, shorn.

परि (-री-) वारः *m.* 1 Train, retinue, attendants or followers.-2 A cover, covering. -3 A sheath, scabbard.

परिवारणं *n.* 1 An envelope, a cover. -2 Train, retinue. -3 Warding off, keeping off.

परिवारित *p. p.* (*f.*—ता) Surrounded, encircled.

परिवासः *m.* 1 Residence, stay. -2 Fragrant odour.

परि (-री-) वाहः *m.* 1 Overflowing (of a tank &c.); inundation; overflow,(natural or artificial).2A watercourse, a channel to carry off excess of water.

परिविण्णः (-न्नः), परिवित्तः, परिवित्तिः *m.* An unmarried elder brother whose younger brother is married.

परिविद्धः *m.* An epithet of Kubera.

परिविंदकः, परिविंदत् *m.* A younger

brother married before the elder.

परिविहारः *m.* Walking about; walking for pleasure.

परिविह्वल *a.* (*f.*—ला) Extremely confused, agitated or bewildered.

परिवीत *p. p.* (*f.*—ता) 1 Surrounded. -2 Pervaded, overspread. —तं *n.* The bow of Brahman (*m.*)

परिवृढः *m.* A master, owner, head, chief.

परिवृत *p. p.* (*f.*—ता) 1 Surrounded, encircled, attended. -2 Concealed.-3 Pervaded, overspread.-4 Known. -5 Completely gained.

परिवृतिः *f.* Surrounding.

परिवृत्त *p. p.* (*f.*—त्ता) Revolved, turned round. -2 Retreated, turned back. -3 Exchanged, bartered -4 Finished,ended.-त्तं *n* An embrace.

परिवृत्तिः *f.* 1 Revolution. -2 Return; turning back. -3 Barter, exchange. -4 End, termination. -5 Surrounding. -6 Staying in a place. -7 Contraction of the prepuce.-8(In Rhet.) The figure in which is described the exchange of a thing for another which is equal, or less, or greater in value. परिवृत्तिर्विनिमयः समन्यूनाधिकैर्भवेत् *साहि॰द॰. दत्त्वा कटाक्षमेणाक्षी जग्राह हृदयं मम। मया तु हृदयं दत्त्वा गृहीतो मदनज्वरः ॥ -9 Substitution of one word for another without affecting the sense.

परिवृद्धिः *f.* Growth, increase.

परिवेत्तृ, परिविंदकः *m.* A younger brother married before the elder.

परिवेदः *m.* Accurate knowledge.

परिवेदनं *n.* 1 The marriage of a younger brother before the elder.-2 Marriage in general. -3 Complete or accurate knowledge. -4 Gain, acquisition. -5 Keeping the household fire (अग्न्याधान). -6 Pervasion on all sides, universal pervasion or existence. -7 Misery, pain. —ना *f.* 1 Shrewdness, wit. -2 Prudence, foresight.

परिवेदनीया, परिवेदिनी *f.* The wife of a younger brother who is married before the elder.

परि (-री-) वेशः,(-षः) *m.* 1 Waiting at meals, distributing food. -2 A circle, circlet, halo (of lustre &c.). -3 The halo round the sun or moon. -4 The circumference of a circle. -5 The disc of the sun or moon. -6 Anything which surrounds or protects.

परिवेषकः *m.* A waiter at meals.

परिवेषणं *n.* 1 Serving up meals; distributing food. -2 Enclosing, surrounding. -3 A halo round the sun or moon. -4 Circumference.

परिवेष्टृ *m.* One who serves up meals.

परिवेष्टनं *n.* 1 Surrounding, enclosing. -2 Circumference. -3 A cover, covering. -4 A bandage.

परिव्ययः *m.* 1 Cost. -2 Condiment, spices.

परिव्याधः m. A species of reed.

परिव्रज्या *f.* 1 Strolling, wandering from place to place. -2 Turning a recluse. -3 Renunciation of the world; religious austerity.

परिव्राज्, परिव्राजः, -जकः *m.* A wandering mendicant; an ascetic.

परिशाश्वत *a.* (*f.*—ती) Perpetually the same.

परिशिष्ट *a.* (*f.*—ष्टा) 1 Left, remaining. -2 Finished. —ष्टं *n.* A supplement, an appendix.

परिशीलनं *n.* 1 Touch, contact (lit.). -2 Constant contact, intercourse, or correspondence. -3 Study, application to a thing; steady or fixed pursuit.

परिशुद्धिः *f.* I Complete purification. -2 Justification; acquittal.

परिशुष्क *p. p.* (*f.*—ष्का) I Thoroughly dried; completely dried or parched up. -2 Withered, shrivelled, —ष्कं *n.* A kind of fried meat.

परिशून्य *a.* (*f.*—न्या) I Quite empty. -2 Quite free from, completely devoid of.

परिशृतः *m.* Ardent spirits.

परि (-री-) शेषः*m.* I Remainder, remnant. -2Supplement. -3 Termination, completion. (परिशेषेण *ind.* I With the residue.-2 Completely;in full.).

परिशेषणं *n.* Remainder, residue.

परिशोधः *m.*, परिशोधनं *n.* I Purifying, cleansing. -2 Rectifying, correcting. -3 Discharging or paying off (a debt or obligation).

परिशोषः *m.* Act of being completely dried or parched up.

परिश्रमः *m.* I Fatigue, trouble, pain. -2 Exertion, labour. -3 Close application to or study of; being constantly occupied with.

परिश्रयः *m.* I A meeting, an assembly. -2 Refuge, asylum.

परिश्रांतिः *f.* I Fatigue, weariness, exhaustion. -2 Labour, exertion.

परिश्लेषः *m.* An embrace.

परिषद् *f.* I An assembly, an audience. -2 A religious assembly. -3 A group, collection, circle.

परिषदः, परिषद्यः, परिषद्वलः *m.* A member of an assembly (councillor, assessor &c.)

परिषेकः *m.*, परिषेचनं *n.* I Sprinkling or pouring over; moistening. -2 Water for watering trees (परिषेचनं).

परिष्कण्ण (-न्न) *n.* (*f.*—ण्णा) Fostered by another.—ण्णः *m.* A foster-child,

परिष्कं (-स्कं-) द *a.* (*f.* —दा,) Fostered by another. -दः *m.* I A foster-child. -2 A servant.

परिष्करः *m.* Decoration, ornamentation.

परिष्कारः *m.* I Decoration, embellishment. -2 Dressing, cooking. -3 Initiation, purification by initiatory rites. -4 Furniture; (also परिस्कार in this sense).

परिष्कृत *p. p.* (*f.* —ता) I Adorned, decorated. -2 Cooked, dressed. -3 Purified by intiatory ceremonies; also परिस्कृत -4 Prepared, equipped. -5 Highly polished.

परिष्कृतिः *f.* I Polishing. -2 Cleansing.

परिष्क्रिया *f.* Adoring, decorating; embellishment.

परिष्पं (-स्पं-) -दः *m.* I A train, retinue. -2 Decorating the hair (with flowers &c.). -3 Ornament or decoration in general. -4 Throbbing, vibration. -5 Provision.

परिष्यंदः *m.* I A stream, river. -2 Moisture.

परिष्वक्त *p. p.* (*f.* —क्ता) Clasped, embraced.

परिष्वंगः*m.*, परिष्वं (-स्वं-) जनं or परिष्वजनं*n.* I An embrace. -2 Touch, union.

परिसंवत्सर *a.* A whole year old.-रः*m.* A whole year. परिसंवत्सरात् 'After the expiration of one whole year'.

परिसंख्या *f.* I Enumeration, computation. -2 Sum, total, number. -3 Recapitulation. -4 (In Mim. phil.) Exclusion, specification, limitation to that which is enumerated or expressly mentioned, so that everything else is excluded; (परिसंख्या is opposed to विधि which lays down a rule for the first time, and to नियम which restricts 'the choice to an alternative which is expressly stated when several such alternatives are possible). -5 (In Rhet)

The figure of speech in which, with or without a query, there is, owing to the very mention of a thing, the exclusion of some thing else similar to it, whether that exclusion be expressed or implied. प्रश्नादप्रश्नतोवापि कथिताद्वस्तुनो भवेत । ताद्दगन्यव्यपोहश्चेच्छाब्द आर्थोऽथवा तदा ॥परिसंख्या *e g*. किमाराध्यं सदा पुण्यं कश्च सेव्यः सदागमः। को ध्येयो भगवान्विष्णुः। किं कांम्यं परमं पदं ॥

परिसंख्यात *p. p.* (*f.* -ता) 1 Enumerated, reckoned up. -2 Specified exclusively.

परिसंख्यानं *n.* 1 Enumeration, total, number.-2 Exclusive specification. -3 Correct judgment.

परिसंचारः*m.* Time of universal destruction.

परिसभ्यः *m.* A member of an assembly.

परिसमाप्त *p. p.* (*f.* प्ता) 1 Finished, completed. -2 Comprehended.

परिसमापनं *n.*, परिसमाप्तिः *f.* Finishing, completing.

परिसमूहनं*n.*1 Heaping up.-2Sprinkling water (in a particular way) round the sacrificial fire.

परिसरः *m.* 1 Verge, border, neighbourhood, environs (of a river, mountain, town &c.) -2 Position, site. -3 Width, breadth. -4 Death. -5 A rule, precept.

परिसरणं *n.* Running about.

परिसर्पः *m.* 1 Going or moving about.-2 Going in search of, pursuing. -3 Surrounding.

परिसर्पणं *n.* 1 Walking or creeping about.-2 Running to and fro, flying about, constantly moving.

परि (-री-) सर्या *f.*, परि (-री-) सारः *m*, Wandering or moving about; perambulation.

परिस्तरः*m.* Strewing round or heaping together.

परिस्तरणं *n.* 1 Strewing or spreading round, scattering about. -2 A covering, cover.

परिस्थानं *n.* 1 Abode. -3 Fixedness, solidity. -3 Firmness.

परिस्फुट *a.* (*f.* —टा) 1 Quite plain, distinctly visible.-2 Fully developed, blown or grown.

परिस्फुरणं *n.* 1 Quivering, shooting. -2 Budding.

परिस्पंदः *m.* 1 Oozing, trickling. -2 A flow, stream. -3 A train, retinue. -4 Decoration.

परिस्रवः *m.* 1 Flowing, streaming. -2 Gliding down. -3 A river, torrent. -4 Birth of a coild.

परिस्रावः *m.* 1 Effluxion, efflux.

परिस्रावणं *n.* A filtering vessel.

परिस्रुत् *f.* 1 A kind of intoxicainig liquor. -2 Trickling, flowing.

परिहृत *a.* (*f.*—ता)Loosened.

परि (-री-) हासः *m.* 1 Joking, jesting, jest, mirth, merriment. [परिहासपूर्वं *ind* ' Jokingly or in jest'] -2 Ridiculing, deriding. -Comp. -वेदिन् *m.* A buffoon, jester, a witty person.

परिहस्तः *m.* A ring for the hand.

परिहाणिः (-निः) *f.* 1 Decrease, deficiency, loss. -2 Decay. -3 Neglect.

परिहीण *p. p.* (*f.*—णा) Waned, wasted -2 Deprived of. -3 Wanting or deficient in.

परिहरणं *n.* 1 Leaving, abandoning. -2 Avoiding, shunning. -3 Refuting. -4 Seizing, taking away.

परि (-री-) हारः *m.* 1 Leaving, abandoning. -2 Removing, taking, away ; as in शिरोषपरिहार. -3 Shunning, avoiding. -4 Refutiug. -5 Omission to mention. leaving out. -6 Reserve, concealment. -7 A tract of common land round a village or town. -8 A special grant or immunity, privilege ; exemption from taxes. -9 Contempt, disrespect. -10 An objection. -11 Seizing, keeping back. -12 Bounty. -13 (In gram.) The repetition of a word before and after इति. -14 Atoning for any improper action.

परिहार्य a. (f.—र्या) To be shunned or avoided, to be escaped from; to be taken off or away. —र्यः m. A bracelet.

परिहृत p. p. (f.—ता) 1 Shunned, avoided. -2 Left, abandoned. -3 Refuted (as a charge, objection &c.). -4 Taken, seized.

परीत p. p. (f.—ता) 1 Surrounded. -2 Elapsed. -3 Departed. -4 Seized, filled with.

परीक्षकः m. An examiner, investigator, a judge.

परीक्षणं n. Putting to test, testing, examining.

परीक्षा f. 1 Examination, test, trial. -2 Trial by various kinds of ordeals (in law).

परीक्षित p. p. (f.—ता) Examined, tried, tested.

परीक्षित m. N. of a king, son of Abhimanyu and grandson of Arjuna.

परीणाहः m. 1 circumference, extent, bre?dth. -2 A piece of common land encircling a village.

परीताप, परीपाक, परीवार-ह, परीहास &c. See परिताप &c.

परीप्सा f. 1 Desire of obtaining. -2 Haste, hurry.

परीरं n. A fruit.

परीरणं n. 1 A tortoise. -2 Stick. -3 A garment.

परीष्टिः f. 1 Research, investigation. -2 Service, attendance. -3 Respect, homage. -4 Willingness, readiness.

परुः m. 1 A joint, knot. -2 A limb, member.-3 The ocean.-4 Heaven. -5 A mountain.

परुत् ind. Last year.

परुद्वारः m. A horse.

परुष a. (f.—षा) 1 Hard, rough, rugged, (opp. मृदु or श्लक्ष्ण). -2 Harsh, abusive, unkind, cruel, (as words). -3 Harsh or disagreeable to the ear (as a sound &c.). -4 Coarse, rough to the touch, shaggy (as hair). -5 Violent, strong, keen, piercing (wind &c.). —षं n. A harsh or abusive speech. -Comp. —उक्तिः f., वचनं n. Abusive or harsh language.

परुस् n. 1 A joint, knot. -2 A limb or member of the body.

परेत p. p. (f.—ता) Deceased, dead. —तः m. A spirit, a ghost. -Comp. —भर्तृ, -राज् m. The god of death, Yama.-भूमिः f.,-वासः m. A cemetery.

परेद्यवि, परेद्युस् ind. The other day.

परेष्टुः, परेष्टुका f. A cow that has often calved.

परोक्ष a. (f.—क्षा) 1 Out of sight, invisible. -2 Absent. -3 Secret, unknown. —क्षः m. An ascetic. —क्षं n. 1 Absence, invisibility. -2 (In gram.) Past time or tense (not witnessed by the speaker) as in परोक्षे लिट्. *Note*. The acc. and loc. singulars *i. e* परोक्षं, परोक्षे are used adverbially in the sense of 'in one's, absence', 'out of sight' 'behind one's back', with or without a *gen*. -Comp.

—अर्थ *a.* Having a secret meaning —कृता *f.* A hymn in which a deity is spoken of in the third person. —भोगः *m.* Enjoyment of anything in the absence of the owner. —वृत्ति *a.* Living out of sight. —वृत्तिः *f.* An unseen or obscure life.

परोष्टिः, परोष्णी *f.* A cock-roach.

पर्जन्यः *m.* 1 A rain-cloud; a cloud in general. -2 Rain. -3 The god of rain *i. e.* Indra.

पर्ण् 10 U. (पर्णयति,-ते) To make green or verdant.

पर्ण *n.* 1 A pinion, wing. -2 The feather of an arrow. -3 A leaf. -4 The betel leaf. —र्णः *m.* The Palâsa tree. -Comp. —अशनं *n.* Feeding on leaves. (-नः) A cloud. —आसिः *m.* A kind of basil. —आहार *a.* Feeding upon leaves. —उटजं *n.* A hut of leaves, a hermitage. —कारः *m.* A vendor of betel-leaves. —कुटिका, -कुटी *f.* A hut made of leaves. —कृच्छ्रः *m* A kind of penance which consists in living upon an infusion of leaves and Kusa grass only for five days. —खंडः *m.* A tree without apparent blossoms. (-डं) *n.* A collection of leaves. -चीरपटः *m.* An epithet of Siva. —चोरकः *m.* A kind of perfume. —नरः *m.* The figure of a man made of leaves and burnt in place of a lost corpse. —मेदिनी *f.* The Priyangu creeper. —भोजनः *m.* A goat. —मुच् *m.* The winter season (शिशिर). —मृगः *m.* A wild animal living in the boughs of trees &c. —रुह् *m.* The spring season (वसंत). —लता *f.* The betel-plant. —वीटिका *f.* Pieces of areca-nut mixed with other spices and rolled up in betel leaves. —शय्या *f.* A couch of leaves. —शाला *f.* A hut made of leaves; a hermitage.

पर्णक *a.* (*f.*—का) Full of leaves, leafy.

पर्णसिः *m.* 1 A house standing in the midst of water, a summer-house. -2 A lotus. -3 A vegetable. -4 Decoration, toilet, adorning.

पर्णिन् *m.* A tree.

पर्णिक *a.* (*f.* —का) Leafy; full of leaves.

पर्द् 1 A. (पर्दते) To break wind.

पर्दः *m.* A quantity of hair, thick hair. -2 A fart, breaking wind (पर्दनं also in this sense).

पर्पः *m.* 1 Young grass. -2 A seat for cripples (पंगुपीठं), wheel-carriage in which cripples are moved about. -3 A house.

पर्परीकः *m.* 1 The sun. -2 Fire. -3 A reservoir, tank.

पर्पिकः *m.* (*f.* की) A cripple who moves about in a chair.

पर्यक् *ind.* Round about, in every direction.

पर्यंकः, पल्यंकः *m.* 1 A bed, sofa. -2 A palanquin, -3 A cloth girt round the back, loins, and knees (by a person) when sitting on his hams; cf अवसक्थिका. -4 A particular kind of posture in meditation; it is the same as वीरासन which is thus defined by Vasistha:—एकं पादमथैकस्मिन् विन्यस्योरौ तु संस्थितं। इतरस्मिंस्तथैवोरुं वीरासनमुदाहृतं॥ -Comp. —बंधः *m.* Sitting on the hams, the posture called पर्यंक. —भोगिन् *m.* A kind of serpent.

पर्यटनं, पर्यटितं *n.* Wandering or roaming about.

पर्यनुयोगः *m.* 1 An inquiry with the object of contradicting or refuting a statement. -2 Asking, inquiring. -3 Censure, reproach.

पर्यंत *a.* (*f.* -ता) Bounded by, or extending as far as. —तः *m.* 1 Circuit circumference. -2 Skirt, border, boundary.-3 Side, flank.-4 End, termination.-Comp.-देशः m., -भूः, -भूमिः f. An adjoining district or region. —पर्वतः m. An adjoining hill.

पर्यंतिका f. Loss of good qualities; depravity, moral turpitude.

पर्यन्यः m. Same as पर्जन्यः

पर्ययः m. 1 Revolution, lapse, expiration. -2 Change, alteration. -3 Inversion, irregularity. -5 Deviation from customary observances; neglect of duty. -6 Opposition.

पर्ययणं n. 1 Walking round, circumambulation.-2A horse's saddle.

पर्यवदात a. (f. —ता) Perfectly pure or clean.

पर्यवरोधः m. Obstruction.

पर्यवशेषः m. End, termination.

पर्यवष्टंभनं n. Surrounding, investing.

पर्यवसानं n. 1 End, conclusion. -2 Determination, ascertainment.

पर्यवसित p. p. (f.—ता) 1 Finished, completed. -2 Perished, lost. -3 Determined.

पर्यवस्था f., पर्यवस्थानं n. 1 Opposition, obstruction. -2 Contradiction.

पर्यवस्थातृ m. An adversary, antagonist.

पर्यश्रु a. Bathed in tears; shedding tears; tearful.

पर्यसनं n. 1 Casting, throwing about.-2 Sending or throwing away.

पर्यस्त p. p. (f. स्ता) 1 Thrown round, scattered about.-2 Surrounded, encompassed. -3 Upset, overturned. -4 Dismissed, laid aside.

पर्यस्तिः, पर्यस्तिका f. Sitting upon the hams. See पर्यंक (3).

पर्याकुल a. (f. —ला) 1 Turbid (as water). -2 Confused, frightened. -3 Disordered, dishevelled. -4 Excited, bewildered. -5 Filled (with).

पर्याणं n. A saddle.

पर्याप्त p. p. (f. —प्ता) 1 Obtained, gained. -2 Finished, completed. -3 Full, whole, entire, all. -4 Able, competent, adequate, sufficient. -5 Large, spacious. -6 Abundant. copious, many. —प्तं ind. 1 Willingly, readily. -2 To one's satisfaction, sufficiently. -3 Fully, ably, competently.

पर्याप्तिः f. 1 Obtaining, acquisiton. -2 End, close. -3 Fulness, sufficiency. -4 Satisfaction. -5 Preserving; warding off a blow. -6 Fitness, competency. -7 Willingness, readiness.

पर्यायः m. 1 Going round, revolution. -2 Lapse, course, expiration (of time). -3 Regular recurrence or repetition. -4 Turn, due or regular order. -5 Method, arrangement. -6 Manner of proceeding. -7 A synonym, a convertible term. -8 An opportunity, occasion. -9 Creation, preparation, manufacture. -10 Comprehensiveness. -11 A strophe of a hymn. -12 Property, quality. -13 (In Rhet.) A figure of speech in which it is said that one thing is found, or is made to be found, in other things successively. The second variety of this figure is when many things are successively found, or made to be found, in one thing. (Note:-पर्यायेण is often used adverbially in the sense of:—1 In turn or succession, by regular gradation. -2 Occasionally, now and then.-Comp. —उक्तं n. (In Rhetoric) The figure of speech in which the thing desired to be made known to others is conveyed by words which do not express it but only suggest it. A round-about way of expressing a thing. Circumlocution. Periphrasis. पर्यायोक्तं विना वाच्यवाचकत्वेन यद्वचः *काव्यप्र. पर्यायोक्तं यदा भंग्या गम्यमेवाभिधीयते *साहि. द. —च्युत *a.* Supplanted, superseded. —वचनं *n.*, —शब्दः *m.* A synonym. —शयनं *n.* Alternate sleeping and watching. —सेवा *f.* Service by rotation.

पर्यारिणी *f.* A cow afflicted with diseases.

पर्याली *ind.* A particle expressing 'harm or injury', (हिंसन) and used with कृ, भू or अस्. पर्यालीकृत्य =हिंसित्वा.

पर्यालोचनं *n.*, —ना *f.* 1 Circumspection, attentive observation, mature reflection. -2 Knowing, recognition.

पर्यावर्तः *m.*, पर्यावर्तनं *n.* Coming back, return.

पर्याविल *a.* (*f.* ला) Very muddy or turbid; much soiled.

पर्यासः *m.* 1 End, conclusion, termination. -2 Rotation, revolution. -3 Inverted position.

पर्यासनं *n.* Revolution.

पर्याहारः *m.* 1 A yoke worn across the shoulders in carrying a load. -2 Conveying. -3 A load or burden. -4 A pitcher. -5 Storing grain.

पर्युक्षणं *n.* Sprinkling round water silently and without uttering any ritual fromulæ or Mantras.

पर्युत्थानं *n.* Standing up.

पर्युत्सुक *a.* (*f.* —का) Sorrowful, sorry, regretting, sad. -2 Anxious, anxiously longing for. -3 Agitated, excited.

पर्युदंचनं *n.* 1 Debt. -2 Raising up, drawing out.

पर्युदस्त *p. p.* (*f.* —स्ता) 1 Excluded, excepted. -2 Prohibited (as a ceremony).

पर्युदासः *m.* An exception, a prohibitive rule or precept.

पर्युपस्थानं *n.* Serving, waiting upon, attendance.

पर्युपासक, -सिन्, -सितृ *m.* A worshipper.

पर्युपासनं *n.* 1 Worship, service. -2 Friendliness, courtesy. -3 Sitting round.

पर्युप्तिः *f.* Sowing.

पर्युषणं *n.* Worship, adoration, service.

पर्युषित *a.* (*f.*—ता) Stale, not fresh. -2 Insipid. -3 Stupid. -4 Vain.

पर्येषणं, —णा *f.* 1 Investigation by reasoning. -2 Search. -3 Homage, worship.

पर्येष्टिः *f.* Search, inquiry.

पर्वकं *n.* The knee-joint.

पर्वणी *f.* 1 The full-moon day or the day of new moon. -2 A festival. -3 A particular disease of the juncture or संधि of the eye.

पर्वतः *m.* 1 A mountain, hill, a rock. -2 The number 'seven'. -3 A tree. -4 A kind of vegetable. -Comp. —अरिः *m.* An epithet of Indra. —आत्मजः *m.* An epithet of the mountain Mainâka. —आत्मजा *f.* An epithet of Pârvati. —आधारा *f.* The earth. —आशयः *m.* A cloud. —आश्रयः *m.* A fabulous animal called Sarabha. —आश्रयिन्, —आश्रयः *m.* A mountaineer. —काकः *m.* A raven. —जा *f.* A river. —पतिः *m.* An epithet of the Himâlaya mountain. —मोचा *f.* A kind of plantain. —राज्, —राजः *m.* 1 A large mountain. -2 The Himâlaya mountain. -वासिनी *f.* 1 N. of Durgâ. -2 Of Gàyatri.

पर्वन् *n.* 1 A knot, joint (sometimes changed to पर्व at the end of Bah. comp; as in कर्कशांगुलिपर्वणा *रघुवं. 12. 41). -2 A limb, member, a knuckle. -3 A portion, part, division. -4 A book, section (as of the

Mahábhárata). -5 The step of a staircase. -6 A period, fixed time. -7 Particularly, the days of the four changes of the moon, i. e. the eighth and the fourteenth days of each half month, and the days of the full and the new moon. -8 A sacrifice performed on the occasion of a change of the moon. -9 The day of new or full moon. -10 An eclipse of the sun or moon. -11 A festival, holiday, an occasion of joy. -12 An opportunity or occasion. -13 A particular period of the year (as the equinox, solstice). -14 The moment of the sun's entering a new sign. -Comp. —काल: *m.* 1 A periodic change of the moon. -2 The time at which the moon at its conjunction or opposition passes through the node. —कारिन् *m.* A Bráhmana who from motives of gain performs on common days ceremonies which ought to be performed on periodical occasions, such as अमावास्या &c. —गामिन् *m.* One who has sexual intercourse with his wife at particular times or occasions when such intercourse is prohibited by the Sâstras. —धि: *m.* The moon. —योनि: *m.* A cane or reed. —रुह् *m.* A pomegranate tree. -संधि:*m.* The junction of the fifteenth and first days of a lunar fortnight.

पर्शु: *m.* 1 An axe, a hatchet. -2 A weapon in general. -3 A rib. -Comp.—पाणि: *m.* An epithet of Ganesa. -2 Of Parasurâma.

पर्शुका *f.* A rib.

पर्श्वध: *m.* See परश्वध:.

पर्षद् *f.* 1 An assembly, a meeting. -2 A religious synod or assembly.

पल: *m.* Straw, husk. —लं *n.* 1 Flesh, meat. -2 A particular weight equal to four *karshas.* -3 A particular measure of fluids. -4 A particular measure of time. —Comp. —अग्नि: *m.* Bile.—अंग: *m.* A tortoise. —अद:, —अशन: *m.* A demon, Râkshasa. —क्षार: *m.* Blood. -गड: *m.* A plasterer, mason. -प्रिय: *m.* A demon. -2 A raven. —भा *f.* The equinoctial shadow at midday.

पलंकट *a.* Timid, bashful.

पलंकर: *m.* Bile, gall.

पलंकष: *m.* 1 A demon, goblin. -2 Bdellium. -3 The किंशुक tree. —षा *f.* A fly.

पलल: *m.* A demon, goblin, an evil spirit. —लं *n* 1 Flesh. -2 Mire, mud. -3 A sweetmeat made of ground sesamum and sugar. —Comp. —ज्वर: *m.* Gall, bile. —प्रिय: *m.* A reven. -2 A demon.

पलव: *m.* A kind of net or basket for catching fish.

पलस: *m.* See पनस:.

पलांडु: *m.*, —डु *n.* An onion.

पलाप: *m.* 1 The temples of an elephat. -2 A halter, rope.

पलायनं *n.* Running away, retreat, flight, escape. -2 A saddle.

पलायित *p. p.* (*f.* —ता) Fled, retreated, run away, escaped.

पलाल:*m.*, -लं*n.* Straw, husk.-Comp. —दोहद: *m.* The mango tree.

पलाश *a.* (*f.* —शा) 1 Green.-2 Unkind.—शव: *m.* A demon.-2 N. of the Magadha country. -3 N. of a tree. Butea Frondosa (also called किंशुक). —शं *n.* 1 The flower or blossom of this tree. -2 A leaf or petal in general. -3 The green colour. —शी *f.* Lac.

पलाशिन् *a*. Leafy. —*m*. A tree.

पलिक्नी *f*. 1 An old grey-haired woman. -2 A cow which has calved for the first time.

पलिघः *m*. 1 A glass-vessel, pitcher. -2 A wall or rampart. -3 An iron club. -4 A cow-pen (गोगृह). -5 The gateway of a building.

पलित *a*. (*f*. —ता) Grey, hoary, old. —तं *n*. 1 Grey hair or the greyness of hair caused by old age. -2 Much or ornamented hair. -3 A tuft of hair (केशपाश). -4 Mud, mire. -5 Heat. -6 Benzoin.

पलितंकरण *a*. Rendering grey.

पलितंभविष्णु *a*. Becoming grey.

पल्यंकः *m*. A bed.

पल्ययनं *n*. 1 A saddle. -2 A rein, [bridle.

पल्लः *m*. A large granary.

पल्लवः *m*., —वं *n*. 1 A sprout, sprig, twig. -2 A bud, blossom. -3 Expansion, dilating. -4 The red dye called Alakta. -5 Strength, power. -6 A blade of grass. -7 A bracelet, an armlet. -8 Love, amorous sport. -9 The end of a robe or garment. -10 Unsteadiness. -वः *m*. A libertine. -Comp. —अदः *m*. A deer. —अस्त्रः *m*. A epithet of the god of love. -आहित *a*. 1 Putting forth sprouts. -2 Dealing with trifles. -3 Diffusive or superficial. -द्रुः *m*. The Asoka tree.

पल्लवकः *m*. 1 A libertine. -2 A catamite. -3 The parmour of a harlot. -4 The Asoka tree. -5 A kind of fish. -6 A sprout (*n*. also).

पल्लविकः *m*. 1 A libertine, a gallant. -2 A catamite.

पल्लवित *a*. (*f*. -ता) 1 Sprouting, having young shoots or sprouts. -2 Spread, extended. -3 Dyed red with lac. -तः *m*. Lac-dye.

पल्लविन् *a*. (*f*. -नी) Having young shoots or leaves. —*m*. A tree.

—पल्लिः, -पल्ली *f*. 1 A small village. -2 A hut. -3 A house, station. -4 A city or town (at the end of names of towns). -5 A house-lizard. -6 A creeping plant.

पल्लिका *f*. 1 A small village or station. -2 A house-lizard.

पल्वलं *n*. A small pond, a puddle, tank. -Comp. —आवासः *m*. A tortoise.

पवः *m*. 1 Wind. -2 Purification. -3 A marsh. -4 Winnowing corn. -वा *f*. Purification. -वं *n*. Cow-dung.

पवन *a*. (*f*. —ना) Clean, pure. -नः *m*. 1 Air, wind. -2 N. of Vishnu. -3 A householder's sacred fire. -नं *n*. 1 Purification. -2 Winnowing. -3 A sieve, strainer. -4 Water. -5 A potter's kiln (*m*. also). -नी *f*. A broom. -Comp. —अशनः, —भुज् *m*. A serpent. —आत्मजः *m*. 1 An epithet of Hanumat. -2 Of Bhîma. -3 Fire. —आशः *m*. A serpent, snake. —तनयः, —सुतः *m*. 1 Epithets of Hanumat. -2 Of Bhîma. —वाहनः *m*. Fire. -व्याधिः *m*. 1 An epithet of Uddhava, a friend and counsellor of Krishna. -2 Rheumatism.

पवमानः *m*. 1 Air, wind. -2 The sacred fire called गार्हपत्य.

पवाका *f*. A whirl-wind, a hurricane.

पविः *m*. The thunderbolt of Indra.

पवित्र *a*. (*f*. —त्रा) 1 Sacred, holy, sinless, sanctified (persons or things). -2 Purified by the performance of religious rites. -4 Purifying, removing sin. —त्रं *n*. 1 An instrument for cleansing or purifying. -2 Two blades of Kusa grass used at sacrifices in purifying and sprinkling ghee. -3 A ring of Kusa grass worn on the fourth finger on certain religious occasions. -4 The sacred thread worn by members of the first three castes of the Hindus. -5 Copper -6 Rain. -7 Water. -8 Rubbing, cleansing. -9 A vessel in which the *arghya* is presented. -10 Clarified butter. -11 Honey. —त्रा *f.* 1 The holy basil. -2 Turmeric. -Comp. —आरोपणं, आरोहणं *n.* Investiture with the sacred thread. —धान्यं *n.* Barley. —पाणि *a.* Holding *darbha* grass in the hand.

पवित्रकं *n.* A net or rope made of hemp or pack-thread.

पशव्य *a.* 1 Fit or suitable for cattle -2 Relating to cattle, or to a herd or drove. -3 Possessed of cattle. -4 Brutish.—व्यं *n.* 1 A herd of cattle. -2 A stall for cattle.

पशुः *m.* 1 Cattle (both singly and collectively). -2 An animal in general. -3 A sacrificial animal, such as a goat; an oblation, a victim. -4 A brute, beast; as added to words meaning 'man' it shows contempt ; पुरुषपशोश्च पशोश्च को विशेषः -5 N. of a subordinate deity and one of Siva's followers.-6 An uninitiated person. -7 The Supreme Spirit. -8 A sacrifice in which an animal is killed. -9 Fire. -Comp. —अवदानं *n.* A sacrifice of an animal.-क्रिया *f.* 1 The act of animal-sacrifice. -2 Copulation. —गायत्री *f.* A Mantra whispered into the ear cf an animl which is about to be sacrificed; (It is this:— पशुपाशाय विद्महे शिरश्छेदाय धीमहि । तन्नो जीवः प्रचोदयात्.). —धर्मः *m.* 1 The nature or characteristics of cattle. -2. Treatment of cattle. -3. Promiscuous cohabitation. -4. The marrying of widows. —नाथः *m.* An epithet of Siva. —पः *m.* A herdsman. —पतिः *m.* 1 An epithet of Siva. -2 A herdsman, owner of cattle. -3. N. of a philosopher who taught the philosophical doctrine called पाशुपत. —पालः, —पालकः *m.* A herds-man. —पाशः *m.* 1 The cord with which the sacrificial animal is bound. -2 An animal-sacrifice. -3. The bonds which enchain the individual soul. —मारं *ind.* According to the manner of slaughtering animals. —यज्ञः, —यागः, *m.* An animal-sacrifice. —राजः *m.* A lion.

पशुका *f.* Any small animal.

पशुता *f.* 1 Brutality.-2 The sacrifice of an animal.

पश्च *a.* 1 Being behind.-2 Posterior, later. -3 Western.

पश्चात् *ind.* (Used by itself or with gen. or abl.) 1 From behind, from the back. -2 Backwards, towards the back (opp. पुरः) -3 Afterwards, subsequenly. -4 Lastly, finally. -5 From the west. -6 Towards the west. -Comp. -कृत *a.* Surpassed, thrown into the back-ground, defeated. —तापः *m.* Repentance, contrition. —वातः *m.* A west wind.

पश्चार्धः *m.* 1 The hinder part or side (of the body). -2 The latter half. -3 The western side.

पश्चिम *a.* 1 Being behind, hindmost. -2 Last (in time or space). Western, westerly. (पश्चिमेन Is used adverbially in the sense of 'in the west ;' or 'after, behind'; with acc. or gen ; so पश्चिमे 'In the west'). -Comp. —अर्धः *m.* 1 The latter half. -2. The hinder part. —उत्तर *a.* North-western. —रात्रः *m.* The latter part of the night.

पश्चिमा *f.* The west· -Comp· —उत्तरा *f.* The north-west.

पश्यत् *a.* (*f.*—न्ती) Seing, beholding, observing·

पश्यतोहर: *m.* A robber, highwayman (one who steals before a person's eyes, or in the very sight of the possessor).

पश्यंती *f.* 1 A harlot, courtezan. -2 A particular sound·

पस्त्यं *n.* 1 A house, habitation. -2 Household, family. —स्त्या *f.* The goddess presiding over domestic affairs·

पस्पश: *m.* 1 N. of the first Ahnika of the first chapter of Patanjali's Mahábhàshya. -2 (Fig.) An introductory chapter in general(उपोद्घात)·

पह्लवा:, पह्लिका: (*m. pl.*) N. of a people; (Perhaps the Persians).

पा 1 P. (पिबति, पीत; pass. पीयते). I To drink, quaff· -2 To kiss. -3 To inhale. -4 To drink in (with the eyes or ears); feast on, look at or listen to intently. -5 To drink or swallow up. With अनु— To drink after. आ— 1 To drink· -2 To drink up, to soak. -3 To feast on (with the eyes or ears). नि— 1 To drink. -2 To feast on (with the eyes or ears). -*Caus*· पाययति,-ते -*Desid.* पिपासति.

पा 2 P. (पाति, पात) 1 To protect, guard, defend, preserve.-2 To rule, govern. —*Caus.* (पालयति,-ते) 1 To protect, guard, keep, preserve. -2 To rule, govern· -3 To observe, keep, fulfil (as a vow or promise). -4 To nourish, maintain· -5 To wait for. -With परि- 1 To preserve, to protect, to defend against· -2To bring up, nourish. -3 To rule, govern. -4 To keep to, to persevere in, to continue -5 To wait for. प्रति- 1 To protect, preserve. -2To obey, to execute. -3 To wait for, await.

पा *a.* (At the end of comp.) 1 Drinking, quaffing; as in सोमपा:; अग्रेपा: &c. -2 Protecting, guarding, keeping as in गोपा.

पांस (-श-) न *a.* (*f.*-ना or —नी) (Usually at the end of comp.) 1 Disgracing, dishonouring, defiling. -2 Vitiating, spoiling. -3 Wicked, contemptible. -4 Infamous. —नं *n.* Contempt.

पांस (-श-) व *a.* (*f.* —वा) Consisting of dust.

पांसु:, -शु: *m.* 1 Dust, crumbling soil. -2 A particle of dust·-3Dung, manure. -4 A kind of camphor. -Comp. —कासीसं *n.* Sulphate of iron· —कुली *f.* A high-road, highway. —कूलं *n.* 1 A dust-heap. -2 A legal document not made out in any particular person's name. —कृत *a.* Covered with dust.—क्षारं,-र्जं *n.* A kind of salt· -चत्वरं *n.* Hail· -चंदन:, *m.* An epithet of Siva. —चामर: *m.* 1 A heap of dust. -2 A tent. -3 A bank covered with Durvá grass. -4 Praise. —जालिक: *m.* An epithet of Vishnu· -पटलं *n.* A mass or coating of dust. —मर्दन: *m.* As excavation for water round the root of a tree; a basin.

पांसुका *f.* A menstruous woman.

पांसु (-शु-) र: *m* 1 A· gad-fly. -2 A cripple moved about in a wheelchair.

पांसु (-शु-) ल *a.* (*f.* —ला) 1 Dusty, covered with dust. -2 Sullied, stained· -3 Disgracing, dishonouring, as in कुलपांसुल —ल: *m.* 1 A profligate or licentious person, libertine. -2 One of the weapons of Siva. -3 An epithet of Siva. -ला f. 1 A menstruous woman. -2 An unchaste woman. -3 The earth.

पाकः m. 1 Cooking, baking, dressing, boiling. -2 Burning (as bricks), baking. -3 Digestion (as of food). -4 Ripeness. -5 Perfect development. -6 Completion, fulfilment. -7 Consequence, fruit, fruition (fig. also). -8 Development of the consequences of acts done. -9 Grain, corn. -10 A domestic fire. -11 An owl. -12 A child, young one. 13 N. of a demon killed by Indra. -14 An abscess, ulcer. -15 A cooking-utensil. -16 General fear and panic such as causes a revolution or some national calamity. -Comp. -अगारः m., -रं n.-आगारः m., -रं n. -शाला f.,-स्थानंn. A kitchen. —अतीसारः -m. Chronic dysentery. —अभिमुख a. 1 Ready for ripeness or development. -2 Inclined to favour. —ज a. Produced by heat. (-जं n.) 1 Black salt. -2 Flatulence. —पात्रं, —भांडं n. A cooking utensil. —पुटी f. A potter's kiln. —यज्ञ m. A simple or domestic sacrifice (of which there are several varieties). —शुक्ला f. Chalk. —शासनः, -द्विष्, -हंतृ m. Epithets of Indra. —शासनिः m. 1 An epithet of Jayanta, son of Indra. -2 Of Váli. -3 Of Arjuna. —स्थानं n. 1 A kitchen. -2 A potter's kiln.

पाकलः m. 1 Fire. -2 Wind. -3 A fever to which elephants are subject.

पाकिम a. (f. -मा) 1 Cooked; dressed. -2 Ripened (naturally or artificially). -3 Got by boiling (as salt).

पाकुः, पाकुकः m. A cook.

पाक्य a. (f. —क्या) To be cooked, dressed, matured &c. -क्यः m. Saltpetre.

पाक्ष a. (f. -क्षी) 1 Belonging to a lunar fortnight; fortnightly. -2 Relating to a party.

पाक्षपातिक a.(f.-की)Partial, factious.

पाक्षिक a. (f. की) 1 Belonging to a fortnight, fortnightly. -2 Belonging to a bird. -3 Favouring a party or faction. -4 Belonging to an argument. -5 Optional, allowed but not specifically laid down; नियमः पाक्षिके सति. —कः m. 1 A fowler. -2 An alternative.

पाखंडः m. A heretic.

पागल a (f. -ला) Mad, demented.

पांक्तेय, पांक्त्य a. (f.-या, -क्त्या) 1 Fit to sit in the same row at a dinner-party. -2 Fit to be associated with.

पाचक a. 1 Cooking, baking. -2 Maturing, bringing to maturity. -3 Digestive, tonic. —कः m. 1 A cook. -2 Fire. —कं n. Gall, bile. -Comp. —स्त्री f. A female cook.

पाचन a. (f. -नी) 1 Cooking. -2 Ripening. -3 Digestive. -4 Softening, relaxing. -5 Suppurative. -नः m. 1 Fire. -2 Acidity. -नं n. 1 The act of cooking. -2 The act of ripening. -3 A digestive medicine. -4 Causing a wound to close. -5 Penance, expiation (प्रायश्चित्त).

पाचनकः m. Borax.-कं n. 1 A sort of diet drink. -2 Causing a wound to close.

पाचनिका f. Cooking, maturing.

पाचलः m. 1 A cook. -2 Fire. -3 Wind. -4 A thing dressed without the aid of fire.

पाचा, पाचिः f. Cooking.

पांचकपाल a. (f, -ली) Relating to an oblation offered in five cups (कपाल).

पांचजन्यः *m.* N. of the conch of Krishna. -Comp. -धरः *m.* An epithet of Krishna.

पांचदश *a.* (*f.* -शी), पांचदश्य (*f.* -श्यी) Relating to the fifteenth day of a month.

पांचदश्यं *n.* A collection of fifteen.

पांचनद *a.* (*f.* -दी) Prevalent in the पंचनद or Punjâb.

पांचभौतिक *a.* (*f.* की) Composed of the five elements or containing them.

पांचयज्ञिक *a.* (*f.* की) 1 Belonging to the five great sacrifices. -कं *n.* Any one of the five great sacrifices.

पांचवर्षिक *a.* (*f.* -की) Five years old.

पांचशब्दिकं *n.* 1 Music of five kinds. -2 Musical instruments in general.

पांचार्थिकः *m.* A follower or votary of Siva.

पांचाल *a* (*f.* -ली) Belonging to or ruling over the Panchálas. —लः *m.* 1 The country of the Panchálas. -2 A prince of the Panchâlas.—लाः (*m. pl.*) 1 The people of the Panchâlas. -2 An association of five guilds (*i. e.* of a carpenter, weaver, barber, washerman, and shoe-maker).

पांचालिका *f.* A doll, puppet.

पांचाली *f.* 1 A woman or princess of the Panchâlas. -2 N of Draupadi, the wife of the Pândavas. -3 A doll, puppet. -4 (In Rhet.) One of the four styles of composition.

पाट् *ind.* An interjection used in calling.

पाटः *m.* 1 Extension, breadth. -2 (In geometry) The intersection of a prolonged side and perpendicular, or the figure formed by such intersection. —टा *f.* A series, order.

पाटकः *m.* 1 A splitter, divider. -2 Part of a village. -3 A kind of musical instrument. -4 A shore. -5 A flight of steps leading to the water. -6 Loss of capital or stock. -7 A long span. -8 Throwing dice.

पाटच्चरः *m.* A thief, robber.

पाटनं *n.* Splitting, breaking, cleaving, destroying.

पाटल *a.* (*f.* —ला) Pale-red, of a pink or pale-red colour. —लः *m.* The pale-red or pink colour. -2 The trumpet-flower, Bignonia Suaveolens. -लं *n.* 1 The flower of this tree. -2 A kind of rice ripening in the rains. -3 Saffron. -Comp. -उपलः *m.* A ruby. —द्रुमः *m.* The trumpet-flower.

पाटला *f.* 1 The red *lodhra.* -2 The trumpet flower (the tree or its blossom). -3 An epithet of Durgá.

पाटलिः *f.* The trumpet-flower. -Comp. -पुत्रं *n.* N. of an ancient city, the capital of Magadha, situated near the confluence of the Sona and the Ganges, and identified by some with the modern Pátnâ. It is also known by the names of पुष्पपुर, कुसुमपुर.

पाटलिक *a.* (*f.* —की) 1 Knowing the secrets of others. -2 Knowing time and place. —कः *m.* A pupil.

पाटलिमन् *m.* Pale-red colour.

पाटल्या *f.* A multitude of Pátala flowers.

पाटवं *n.* 1 Sharpness, acuteness. -2 Cleverness, skill, proficiency. -3 Energy. -4 Quickness, rashness. -5 Health.

पाटविक *a.* (*f.* —की) 1 Clever, skilful. -2 Cunning, crafty.

पाटी *f.* Arithmetic. -Comp. -गणितं *n.* Arithmetic.

पाटीरः *m.* A 1 Sandal. -2 A field. -3 Tin. -4 A cloud. -5 A sieve. -6 The manna of the bamboo. -7 Catarrh.

पाठः *m.* 1 Reciting, repeating. -2 Study; what is to be recited by actor; the part assigned to each actor in the representation of a drama. -3 Studying or reciting the Vedas (ब्रह्मयज्ञ), one of the five daily Yajnas or sacrifices to be performed by Bráhmanas. -4 The text of a book, a reading, variant. -Comp. --अंतरं *n.* Another reading, a variant. —छेदः *m.* A pause, caesura. —दोषः *m.* False reading. —निश्चयः *m.* Determining the text of a passage. —भूः *f.* A place where the Vedas are learnt.-मंजरी, -शालिनी *f.* The Sárikâ bird.—शाला *f.* A school, collage, seminary. —शालिन् *m.* A pupil.

पाठकः *m.* 1 A teacher, lecturer, preceptor. -2 A public reader of the Puránas or other sacred books. -3 A spiritual teacher. -4 A pupil, student. -5 The text of a book.

पाठनं *n.* Teaching, lecturing.

पाठित *p. p.* (*f.*—ता) Taught, instructed.

पाठिन् *m.* 1 One who has read or studied any subject. -2 A Brâhmana who has finished hia studies.

पाठीनः *m.* 1 A public reader of the Puránas or other mythological books. -2 A kind of fish.

पाणः *m.* 1 Trade, traffic. -2 A trader. -3 A game. -4 A stake at play. -5 An agreement. -6 Praise. -7 The hand.

पाणिः *m.* 1 The hând. पाणिं ग्रह् or पीड् 'To take the hand of, lead to the altar, marry.' पाणौ कृ To hold by the hand, marry; पाणीकरणं *n.* Marriage. —णिः *f.* A market. Comp. —कर्मन् *m.* 1. N. of Siva. -2. One playing on a drum. —गृहीती *f.* A wife. -ग्रहः *m.*, -ग्रहणं *n.* -ग्राहः *m.* Marrying, marriage, nuptial.-ग्रहणिक,-ग्रहणीय *a.* Matrimonial. (-यं *n.*) A nuptial gift. —ग्रहीतृ,—ग्राहः *m.* A bridegroom, husband. —घः *m.* drummer. -2 A workman, handicraftsman. —घातः *m.* 1 A blow with the hand. -2 Boxing. -3 A boxer. —जः *m.* A finger-nail. -तलं *n.* The palm of the hand. —धर्मः *m.* Due form of marriage. —पल्लवः *m.* 1 A sprout-like hand. -2 The fingers. —पीडनं *n.* Marriage. —प्रणयिनी *f.* A wife.-बंधः *m.* Marriage —भुज् *m.* The sacred fig-tree. —मुक्त *n.* A missile thrown with the hand. —मुखाः *m. pl.* The manes. —रुह्,-रुहः *m.* A finger-nail. —वादः *m.* 1 Clapping the hands together. 2 Playing on a drum.-सर्ग्या,-सर्या *f.* A rope, —स्वनिक *a.* Playing musical instruments with the hands.

पाणिक *a.* (*f.*—की) Got by playing at stake. —कः *m.* A merchant.

पाणिनिः *m.* N. of a celebrated grammarian.

पाणिनीय *a*, (*f*—या) Relating to or composed by Pánini. —यः *m.* A follower of Pánini. —यं *n.* The grammar of Pánini.

पाणिंधम,-य *a.* 1 Blowing through the hands. -2 Chilly, as a road or journey. -3 Obscure, dark.

पांडर *a.* (*f.*—रा) Whitish, pale-white. —रं *n.* 1 Red-chalk. -2 The blossom of the Jasmine.

पांडवः *m.* 1 A son or descendant of Pandu. -2 N. of any one of the five sons of Pándu *i. e.* युधिष्ठिर, भीम, अर्जुन, नकुल and सहदेव. -Comp.—आभीलः

m. N. of Krishna. —श्रेष्ठः *m*. N. of Yudhishthira.

पांडवायनः *m*. An epithet of Krishna.

पांडवीय *n*. (*f*.—या) Belonging to the Pándavas.

पांडवेयः *m*. Same as पांडवः.

पांडित्यं *n*. 1 Scholarship, learning, erudition.-2 Skill, dexterity, sharpness.

पांडु *a*. Pale-white, pale, yellowish. —डुः *m*. 1 The pale white or yellowish-white colour. -2 Jaundice. -3 A white elephant. -4 N. of the father of the Pándavas. -Comp. —आमयः *m*. Jaundice.—कंबलः *m*. 1 A white blanket. -2 A warm upper garment. -3 The housing of a royal elephant. —कंबलिन् *m*. 1 A carriage covered with a woollen blanket.-2 The housings of a royal elephant. —पुत्रः *m*. A son of Pándu; any one of the five Pândavas. -मृत्तिका *f*. 1 White or pale soil. -2 The opal. -मृद् *f*. Chalk. -रागः *m*. Whiteness, pallor. —रोग *m*. Jaundice. —लेखः *m*. A sketch made with chalk; a rough draft or sketch made on the ground, board &c.-शर्करा *f*. Light coloured gravel (प्रमेहभेद). —शर्मिला *f*. An epithet of Draupadí. —सोपाकः *m*. N. of a mixed tribe.

पांडुकः *m*. 1 The yellowish-white colour.-2 Jaundice. -3 N. of Pându.

पांडुर *a*. (*f*. —रा) Whitish, pale, white, yellowish-white, pale. —रं *n*. The white leprosy. -Comp. -इक्षुः *m*. A species of sugar-cane.

पांडुरिमन् *m*. Paleness, white or pale colour.

पांड्याः (*m.pl.*) N. of a country and its inhabitants. -ड्यः *m*. A king of that contry.

पातः *p. p.* (*f*.-ता) Protected.

पातः *m*. 1 Flying, flight.-2 Alighting, descending. -3 Falling down. downfall (fig. also). -4 Destruction, dissolution, ruin. -5 A blow, stroke, as in खड्गपातः. -6 Shedding, discharging. -7 A cast, throw, shot, as in दृष्टिपात. -8 An attack, inroad. -9 Happening, occurrence. -10 A failing, defect. -11 An epithet of Râhu. -12 (In astr.) An inauspicious or malignant position or aspect. -13 The node in a planet's orbit.

पातकः *m*., —कं *n*. Sin, crime (According to Hindu law-givers the five great sins are:—ब्रह्महत्या सुरापानं स्तेयं गुर्वंगनागमः । महांति पातकान्याहुः संसर्गश्चापि तैस्सह)

पातंगिः *m*. 1 An epithet of Saturn. -2 Of Yama. -3 Of Karna. -4 Of Sugrîva.

पातंजल *a*. (*f*. -ली) Composed by Patanjali. —लं *n*. The Yoga system of philosophy tought by Patanjali.

पातनं *n*. 1 Causing to fall down, throwing down. -2 Humbling, lowering. -3 Removing.

पातालं *n*. 1 The last of the seven regions or worlds under the earth, said to be peopled by Nágas; the seven regions are:—अतल, वितल, सुतल, रसातल, तलातल, महातल and पाताल. -2 The lower world in general. -3 An excavation, a hole.-4 Submarine fire. -5 (In astr.) The fourth house or sign from that in which the sun is present. -लः *m*. 1 A kind of instrument for distillation or the calcination and sublimation of metals. -2 N. of Jupiter's year (of 361 days). -Comp. —ओकस्, —निलयः, —निवासः, —वासिन् *m*. 1 A demon. -2 A Nâga or a serpent-demon.

पातिकः *m.* The Gangetic porpoise.

पातित *p. p.* (*f.* -ता) 1 Cast down, struck down. -2 Overthrown, humbled. -3 Lowered.

पातित्यं *n.* Loss of caste or position.

पातिन् *a.* (*f.*-नी) 1 Going to, descending. -2 Falling, sinking. -3 Being contained in. -4 Throwing down. -5 Pouring forth, discharging.

पातिली *f.* 1 A snare, trap. -2 An earthen vessel. -3 A woman of a particular class.

पातिव्रत्यं *n.* Fidelity to a husband; [chastity.

पातुक *a.* (*f.* —की) 1 Falling frequently. -2 Apt or disposed to fall. -3 Losing one's caste. -4 Going to hell. —कः *m.* 1 The declivity of a mountain; a precipice. -2 The water-elephant.

पात्रं *n.* 1 A drinking-vessel, jar. -2 A vessel or pot in general; any sacrificial vessel or utensil. -3 A receptacle of any kind. -4 A fit or worthy person, a person fit or worthy to receive instruction of any kind or any gift. -5 An actor, a *dramatis perosona.*-6 A king's minister.-7 The channel or bed of a river. -8 Fitness, propriety. -9 An order, command. -9 A leaf. —त्रः *m.* A kind of measure (आढक). -त्री *f.* 1 A vessel, plate, dish.-2A small furnace. -3 N. of Durgâ. Comp. —पालः *m.* 1 A large paddle used as a rudder. -2 The rod of a balance —भृत् *m.* A servant. -संस्कारः *m.* 1 The cleaning or purification of a vessel. -2 The current of a river.

पात्रकं *n.* A vessel, pot.

पात्रटीरः *m.* 1 A competent minister. -2 A vessel of iron, brass or silver. -3 Mucus running from the nose.

पात्रसात् *ind.* In the possession of worthy persons.

पात्रिक *a.* (*f.* —की) 1 Measured out with any vessel or a measure called आढक. -2 Fit, adequate, appropriate. —कं *n.*, -की *f.* A vessel, cup, dish.

पात्रीण *a.* (*f.* —णा) Measured, sown or cooked with a Pátra.

पात्रीय, पात्र्य *a.* (*f.*—या,-त्र्या) Worthy to partake of a meal.

पात्रीयं *n.* A sacrificial vessel or utensil.

पात्रीरः *m.*, —रं *n.* An oblation.

पात्रेबहुलः, पात्रेसमितः *m.* 1 'Constant at meals or dinner-time', a parasite. -2 A treacherous or hypocritical fellow.

पाथः *m.* 1 Fire. -2 The sun. -थं *n.* Water.

पाथस् *n.* 1 Water. -2 Air, wind.-3 Food. -4 The sky. -Comp. -जं *n.* 1 a lotus. -2 A conch. —दः, -धरः *m.* A cloud. —धिः,-निधिः,-पतिः *m.* The ocean.

पाथेयं *n.* 1 Provisions for a journey. -2 The sign *virgo* of the zodiac.

पादः *m.* 1 The foot whether of men or animals). (The word पाद at the end of comp. is changed to पाद् after सु and numerals; *i. e.* सुपाद्, द्विपाद्, त्रिपाद् &c.; and also when the first member is used as a standard of comparison, but is a word other than हस्ति &c. *e. g.* व्याघ्रपाद्. The nom. pl. of पाद is often added to names of persons or titles of address to show veneration). 2A ray of light. -3 The foot or leg of an inanimate object, as of a bed-stead. -4 The foot or root of a tree; as in पादप. -5 The foot of a mountain. -6 Quarter, fourth part. -7 The fourth part of a stanza, a line. -8 The fourth part of a chapter or book. -9 A part in general. -10 A column, pillar. -11 A foot as a measure equal to twelve Angulis. -12 The quadrant of a circle. -Comp. -अंगदं *n.*,-दी *f.* An ornament for the foot, an anklet. —अंगुष्ठः *m.* The great toe. —अंतः *m.* The extremity of the feet. —अंतरं *n.* The interval of a step, the distance of a foot. (-रे) *ind.* 1 After the interval of a step. -2 Close or near to. —अंबु *n.* Butter-millk containing a fourth part of water. -अंभस् *n.* Water in which the feet (of revered persons) have been washed. —अरविंदं,-कमलं, -पंकजं, -पद्मं *n.* A lotus-like foot. -अर्घ्यं *n.* A gift to a Brâhmana or a venerable person. —आकिंदी *f.* A boat. —अङ्गदः The anklet. —आघातः *m.* A kick. -अवनत *a.* Prostrate, fallen at the feet of. —आवर्तः *m.* 1 A wheel worked by the feet for raising up wat r from a well. -2 A square foot -आसनं *n.* A foot-stool. -आस्फालनं *n.* Flound ring. —आहत *a.* Kicked. —आहतिः *f.* 1 Treading or trampling. -2 A kick. —उदकं, —जलं *n.* 1 Water for washing the feet. -2 Water in which the feet of sacred and revered persons are washed and which is thus considered holy. —उदरः *m.* A serpent. —कटकः *m.*, —कं *n.*, -कीलिका *f.* An anklet. —क्षेपः *m.* A foot-step.—गंडीरः *m.* A morbid swelling of the legs and feet. —ग्रंथिः *m.* The ankle. -ग्रहणं *n.* Seizing or clasping the feet (as a mark of respectful salutation). -चतुरः, -चत्वरः *m.* 1 A slanderer. -2 A goat. -3 The fig-tree. -4 A sand-bank. -5 Hail. —चारः *m.* Going on foot, walking. -चारिन् *m.* 1 A pedestrian. -2 A foot-soldier. -जः *m.* A Súdra. —जलं *n.* Butter-milk mixed with one-fourth of water. —जाहं *n.* The tarsus. —तलं *n.* The sole of the foot. -त्रः *m.*, -त्रा *f.*, -त्राणं *n.* A boot or shoe. —पः *m.* 1 A tree. -2 A foot-stool. —पद्धतिः *f.* A track. —पालिका *f.* An anklet. —पाशः *m.* 1 A foot-rope for cattle. -2 An anklet of small bells &c. -पाशी *f.* 1 A fetter. -2 A mat. -3 A creeper. —पीठः *m.*, -ठं *n.* A foot-stool. —पूरणं *n.* 1 Filling out a line. -2 An expletive. —प्रतिष्ठानं *n.* A foot-stool. -प्रधारणं *n.* A shoe. -प्रहारः *m.* A kick.-बंधनं *n.* 1 A chain, fetter. -2 A stock of cattle. —भागः *m.* A quarter. —मुद्रा *f.* A foot-print. -मूलं *n.* The tarsus. -2 The sole of the foot. -3 The heel. -4 The foot of a mountain. -5 A polite way of speaking of a person; *e. g.* देवपादमूलमागताः. -रजस् *n.* The dust of the feet. —रज्जुः *f.* A tether for the feet of an elephant. —रथी *f.* A shoe, boot. —रोहः *m.*, रोहणः *m.* The (Indian) fig-tree. —वल्मीकः *m.* Elephantiasis. —विरजस् *f.* A shoe, boot. (*-m.*) A god. —शाखा *f.* A toe. -शौचं *n.* Washing the feet. -सेवनं *n.*, -सेवा *f.* 1 Showing respect by touching the feet. -2 Service. —स्फोटः *m.* Chilblain.

पादविकः *m.* A traveller.

पादात् *m.* A foot-soldier.

पादातः *m* A foot-soldier. -तं *n.* Infantry.

पादातिः, पादातिकः, पादाविकः *m.* A foot-soldier.

पादिक *a.* (*f.* —की) Amounting to a quarter or fourth.

पादुक *a.* (*f.*-का,-की) Going on foot. —का *f.* A wooden-shoe, sandal. -Comp. —कारः *m.* A shoe-maker.

पादू *f.* A shoe. -Comp. —कृत *m.* A shoe-maker.

पाद्य *a.* (*f.* -द्या) Belonging to the foot. —द्यं *n.* Water for washing the feet.

पानं *n.* 1 Drinking,kissing (a lip). -2 Drinking spirituous liquors. -3 A drink in general. -4 A drinking vessel. -5 Sharpening, whetting. -6 Protection, defence. -7 A canal. —नः *m.* 1 A distiller. -2 Breath. -Comp. —अगारः,—आगारः *m.*, -रं *n.* A tavern. -अत्ययः *m.* Hard drinking. —गोष्ठिका, —गोष्ठी *f.* 1 A drinking party. -2 A tavern. —प *a.* Drinking spirituous liquors. —पात्रं, -भाजनं, —भांडं *n.* A drinking vessel, a goblet. —भूः,—भूमिः, —भूमी *f.* A drinking room. —मंडलं *n.* A drinking party.-वणिज् *m.* A vender of spirits. —विभ्रमः *m.* Intoxication. —शौंडः *m.* A hard drinker.

पानकं *n.* A drink, beverage.

पानिकः *m.* 1 A vender of spiritual liquors.

पानिलं *n.*A drinking vessel;goblet.

पानीयं *n.* 1 Water. -2 A drink, beverage.-Comp. —नकुलः *m.* An otter. —वर्णिका *f.* Sand. —शाला, —शालिका *f.* A place where water is distributed to travellers.

पान्थः *m.* 1 A traveller,a way-farer. -2 The sun.

पाप *a.* (*f.* —पा) Sinful, wicked, vicious.-2 Mischievous,destructive. 3 Low,vile.-4 Inauspicious, foreboding evil (as in पापग्रह).—पं *n.* 1 Evil, bad fortune or state. (The phrase शांतं पापं means 'may the evil be averted', 'god forbid'; often used in dramas). -2 Sin, crime, guilt. —पं *ind.* Badly, sinfully, wrongly. —पः *m.* A wretch, a wicked or profligate person. -Comp. —अधम *a.* Exceedingly wicked. —अपनुत्तिः *f.* Expiation —अहः *m.* An unlucky day. —आचार *a.* Living a sinful life; vicious, wicked. —आत्मन् *a.* Evil-minded, sinful, wicked. (-*m.*) A sinner. —आरंभ *a.* Villainous, committing murderous deeds —आशय, -चेतस् *a.* Evil-intentioned, wicked-minded. —क्षयः *m.* Removal or destruction of sin. —ग्रहः *m.* A planet of evil or malignant aspect, such as Mars, Saturn, Râhu or Ketu. -घ्नः *m.* The sesamum plant. -चर्यः *m.* A sinner. -2 A demon. —दृष्टि *a.* Evil-eyed. —धी *a.* Evil-minded, wicked. —नापितः *m.* A cunning or vile barber. —नाशनः *m.* 1 N. of Siva. -2 Of Vishnu. (—नं *n.*) Expiation, atonement. —पतिः *m.* A paramour. — पुरुषः *m.* A villainous person. —भक्षणः *m.* N. of Kâlabhairava. —भाज् *a.* Sinful, sinning. —योनि *a.* Low-born. (—निः *f.*)Birth in an inferior condition.-शील *a.* Wicked by nature,evil-minded. -संकल्प *a.* Evil-minded, wicked. (-ल्प *m.*) A wicked thought.

पापर्द्धिः *f.* Hunting, chase.

पापिन् *a.* (*f.* —नी) Sinful, wicked bad. —*m.* A sinner.

पापिष्ठ *a.* (*f.* —ष्ठा) Most sinful, worst,very wicked (superl. पापq.v.).

पापीयस् *a.* (*f.* —सी) Worse, more vile or wicked (compar. पाप q. v.).

पाप्मन् *m.* 1 Sin, crime,wickedness, guilt. -2 Evil, bad fortune or state.

पामन् *m.* A kind of skin-disease, scab. -Comp. —घ्नः *m.* Sulphur.

पामन *a.* (*f.* —ना) Diseased with scab.

पामर *a.* (*f.* -रा) 1 Vile, wicked.-2 Low,vulgar,base.-3 Foolish,stupid. -4 Poor, helpless. -रः *m.* 1 A fool, an idiot. -2 A wicked man. -3 One engaged in the most degrading occupation.

पामा *f.* See पामन् above. -Comp. -अरिः *m.* Sulphur.

पाय्यं *n.* Water.

पायनं *n.* Giving or causing to drink. —ना *f.* 1 Causing to drink. -2 Watering, moistening. -3 Sharpening, whetting.

पायस *a.* (*f.*—सी) Made of water or milk. —सः *m.*, -सं *n.* 1 Rice boiled in milk. -2 Turpentine. -3 An oblation of milk, rice and sugar. —सं *n.* Milk. -2 Nectar.

पायिकः *m.* A foot-soldier.

पायुः *m.* The anus.

पाय्यं *n.* 1 Water. -2 Drinking. -3 Protection. -4 A measure (परिमाण). -5 Practice, profession.

पारः *m.*; —रं *n.* 1 The opposite bank of a river or ocean. -2 The further or opposite side anything. -3 The furthermost or concluding limit. -4 The fullest extent, the totality of anything. (पारं गम्, -इ, -या 1 To cross over, surmount, get over. -2 To accomplish, fulfil; as in प्रतिज्ञायाः पारं गतः. -3 To master fully, become proficient in, as in सकलशास्त्रपारं गतः. पारं नी Means 'to bring to a close.'). -रः *m.* Quick-silver. (पारे meaning 'on the other side of', 'beyond' sometimes stands as the first member of a comp.; *e. g.* पारेगंगं, पारेसमुद्रं beyond the Ganges or the ocean). -Comp. -अपारं, -अवारं *n.* Both banks, the nearer and the further bank. (-रः *m.*) The sea, ocean. -अयणं *n.* 1 Going across. -2 Reading through, perusal, thorough study. -3 The whole; completeness, or totality of anything; as in मंत्रपारायणं &c. —अयणी *f.* 1 N. of the goddess Sarasvatī. -2 Meditation. -3 An act, action. -4 Light. —ग *a.* 1 Crossing over, ferrying across. -2 One who has gone to the end (of); one who has completely mastered anything (with gen. or in comp.). -3 Profoundly learned. (—गं *n.*) Keeping, fulfilling. —गत, -गामिन् *a.* One who has gone to the other side or shore. (—तः *m.*) A Jaina. —दर्शक *a.* 1 Showing the opposite bank. -2 Transparent. —दृश्वन् *a.* 1. Far-seeing, prudent. -2 One who has seen the other side of anything; one who has completely mastered or has become familiar with anything.

पारक *a.* (*f.* -की) 1 Enabling to cross. -2 Saving, delivering. -3 Pleasing, satisfying.

पारक्य *a.* (*f.*—क्या) 1 Alien, belonging to another. -2 Hostile, inimical. —क्यः *m.* An enemy, adversary. —क्यं *n.* Doing anything for future happiness (परलोकसाधन); pious conduct.

पारग्रामिक *a.* (*f.* -की) Alien, hostile, inimical.

पारज् *m.* Gold.

पारजायिकः *m.* An adulterer.

पारटीटः, -नः *m.* A stone or rock.

पारण *a.* (*f.*—णा) 1 Carrying across. -2 Saving, delivering. -णः *m.* 1 A cloud. -2 Satisfaction. —णं *n.* 1 Accomplishing, fulfilling. -2 Reading through, perusal. -3 Eating after a fast; concluding a fast. -4 The complete text of a book. —णा *f.* 1 Eating after a fast concluding a fast. -2 Eating (in general).

पारणीय *a.* (*f.*—या) Capable of being completed or finished.

पारतः *m.* Quick-silver.

पारतंत्र्यं *n.* Dependence, subjection.

पारत्रिक *a.* (*f.* -की) 1 Belonging to the next world. -2 Useful in the future life.

पारत्र्यं *n.* Reward in a future life.

पारदः *m.* Quick-silver. —दाः *m. pl.* N. of a barbarous tribe.

पारदारिकः *m.* An adulterer (intriguing with the wife of another).

पारदार्यं *n.* Adultery, intriguing with another's wife.

पारदेशिक *a.* (*f.* —की) Foreign, outlandish. —कः *m.* 1 A foreigner.-2 A traveller.

पारदेश्य *a.* (*f.* —श्यी) Belonging to a foreign country; foreign. —श्यः *m.* 1 A foreigner. -2 A traveller.

पारभृतं *n.* A present (perhaps a misreading for प्राभृत).

पारमहंस्यं *n.* Most sublime asceticism or meditation.

पारमार्थिक *a.* (*f.* —की) 1 Relating to परमार्थ or the highest truth or spiritual knowledge. -2 Real, truly or really existent. -3 Loving truth or right. -4 Excellent, best.

पारमिक *a.* (*f.*—की) Supreme, best chief, principal.

पारमेष्ठ्यं *n.* 1 Supremacy, highest position. -2 Royal insignia.

पारंपरीण *a.* (*f.*—णी) Handed down from father to son; hereditary, ancestral.

पारंपरीय *a.* (*f.* —या) Handed down, traditional.

पारंपर्यं *n.* 1 Hereditary succession, continuous order. -2 Traditional instruction. -3 Intermediation. -Comp. —उपदेशः *m.* Tradtional instruction, tradition, (regarded by the Pauránikas as a प्रमाण or proof).

पारयिष्णु *a.* 1 Pleasing, gratifying. -2 Able to accomplish anything.

पारलोक्य *a.* (*f.* —क्या) Relating to the next world.

पारलौकिक *a.* (*f.* —की) Relating to or useful in the next world. —कं *n.* Obsequies, funeral rites.

पारवतः *m.* A pigeon.

पारवश्यं *n.* Dependence, subjection, subservience.

पारशव *a.* (*f.* —वी)1 Made of iron. -2 Relating to or derived from an axe. —वः *m.* 1 Iron. -2 The son of a Bráhmana by a Súdra woman.-3 An adulterine, a bastard.

पारश्वधः, पारश्वधिकः *m.* A man armed with an axe.

पारस *a.* (*f.* —सी) Persian.

पारसिकः *m.* 1 Persia. -2 A horse of Persian breed.

पारसी *f.* The Persian language.

पारसीकः *m.* 1 Persia. -2 A Persian horse. —काः (*m. pl.*) The Persians.

पारस्करः *m.* 1 N. of a certain district. -2 N. of a sage, the author of the Grihya Sútras.

पारस्त्रैणेयः *m.* An adulterine, a bastard.

पारहंस्य *a.* (*f.* -स्या) Relating to an ascetic who has subdued all his senses.

पारा *f.* N. of a river.

पारापतः *m.* 1 A pigeon.

पारापारीणः *m.* 1 One who goes to both sides. -2 Perfectly familiar (with).

पारायणिकः *m.* 1 A lecturer, reader of the Puránas or mythological works. -2 A pupil, scholar.

पारावतः *m.* 1 A pigeon, turtle-dove, dove.-2 A monkey.-3 A mountain.

पारावारीणः *m.* 1 One who goes to both sides.-2 One who is completely conversant with.

पाराशरः, पाराशर्यः *m.* An epithet of Vyása, son of Parásara.

पाराशरिः *m.* 1 An epithet of Suka. -2 N. of Vyása.

पाराशरिन् *m.* 1 A religious mendicant. -2 Particularly, such religious mendicants or ascetics as study the Sârîra Sutras of Vyàsa (pl.).

पारिकांक्षिन् *m.* An ascetic who devotes himself to abstract meditation.

पारिक्षितः *m.* A patronymic of Janamejaya, great-grandson of Arjuna, and son of Parîkshit.

पारिखेय *a.* (*f.* -यी) Surrounded by a ditch.

पारिग्रामिक *a.* (*f.* -की) Situated round a village.

पारिजातः, पारिजातकः *m.* 1 N. of one of the five trees of Paradise (said to have been produced at the churning of the ocean). -2 The coral tree. -3 Fragrance.

पारिणाय्य *a.* (*f.* -य्यी) 1 Relating to marriage. -2 Obtained on the occsion of marriage. —य्यं *n.* 1 Property received by a woman at the time of marriage. -2 Marriage settlement.

पारिणाह्यं *n.* Household furniture and utensils.

पारितथ्या *f.* A string of pearls for binding the hair.

पारितोषिक *a.* (*f.*-की) Pleasing, gratifying, consolatory. —कं *n.* A present, reward.

पारिध्वजिकः *m.* A standard-bearer.

पारींद्रः *m.* A lion. [man.

पारिपंथिकः *m.* A robber, highway-

पारिपाट्यं *n.* 1 Mode, method, manner. -2 Regularity.

पारिपार्श्वं *n.* Retinue, attendants, followers.

पारिपार्श्वकः, पारिपार्श्विकः *m.* 1 A servant or an attendant. -2 An assistant of the manager of a play who is one of the interlocutors in the prologue.

पारिपार्श्विका *f.* A female attendant, a chamber-maid.

पारिप्लव *a. f.* (*f.*—वा) Moving, rolling, shaking, unsteady, tremulous. -2 Swimming, floating. -3 Bewildered, disturbed or perplexed. —वः *m.* A boat. —वं *n.* Restlessness, uneasiness.

पारिप्लाव्यः *m.* A goose. —व्यं *n.* 1 Perplexity, agitation. -2 Tremour, tremulousness.

पारिबर्हः *m.* A wedding present.

पारिभद्रः *m.* 1 The coral tree. -2 The *Devadáru* tree. -3 The *Sarala* tree. -4 The *Nimba* tree.

पारिभाव्यं *n.* 1 Bail, security, surety. -2 A kind of drug.

पारिभाषिक *a.* (*f.* —की) 1 Current, common, universally received. -2 Technical (as a word &c.).

पारिमांडल्य *n.* An atom, a mote in a sun-beam; the measure of an atom. [pass.

पारिमाण्य *n.* Circumference, com-

पारिमित्यं *n.* Limit, limited extent or number.

पारिमुखिक *n.* (*f.* -की) Being before the face, being near or present.

पारिमुख्यं *n.* Presence.

पारिया (-पा-) त्रः *m.* N. of one of the seven principal mountain ranges.

पारिया (-पा-) त्रिकः *m.* 1 An inhabitant of the Páriyâtra mountain. -2 The Páriyâtra mountain.

पारियानिकः *m.* A travelling carriage.

पारिरकः *m.* A religious mendicant, an ascetic.

पारिवित्त्यं, पारिवेत्र्यं *n.* Being unmarried while a younger brother is married.

पारिव्राजकं, पारिव्राज्यं *n.* The wandering life of a religious mendicant; asceticism.

पारिशेष्यं *n.* That which is left over; the remainder.

पारिषद *a.* (*f.* -दी) Belonging to an assembly or council. -दः *m.* 1 A person present at an assembly, a member of an assembly. -2 A king's companion. —दाः (*m. pl.*) The retinue of a god. —दं *n.* Taking part in an assembly.

पारिषद्यः *m.* One present at an assembly ; a spectator.

पारिहारिकी *f.* A kind of enigma or riddle.

पारिहार्यः *m.* A bracelet.

पारिहास्यं *n.* Jest, joke, fun.

पारी *f.* 1 A rope for tying an elephant's feet. -2 A quantity of water. -3 A drinking vessel, water-jar, cup. -4 Milk-pail. -5 Pollen (of flowers).

पारीक्षितः *m.* A N. of Janamejaya great grandson of Arjuna.

पारीण *a* (*f.*—णा) 1 Being on or going over to the opposite side. -2 (At the end of comp.) Thoroughly versed in ; well acquainted with. -3 Fulfilling, completing, accomplishing.

पारीणह्यं *n.* Household furniture or utensils.

पारींद्रः *m.* 1 A lion. -2 A large serpent.

पारीय *a.* (At the end of comp.) Completely versed in or conversant with.

पारीरणः *m.* 1 A tortoise. -2 A stick, staff. -3 A garment.

पारुः *m.* 1 The sun. -A fire.

पारुष्यं *n.* 1 Roughness, hardness. -2 Harshness, cruelty. -3 Abusive language, reproach, insult. -4 Violence (in word or deed). -5 The garden of Indra. -6 Aloe wood. —ष्यः *m.* An epithet of Brihaspati.

पारोक्ष *a.* (*f.* -क्षी) Unintelligible, mysterious, obscure.

पारोक्ष्यं *n.* Mystery, secrecy.

पारोवर्यं *n.* Tradition.

पार्घटं *n.* Dust or ashes.

पार्जन्य *a.* (*f.*—न्या) Belonging to rain.

पार्ण *a.* (*f.* र्णी) 1 Relating to or made of leaves ; leafy. -2 Raised from leaves (as a tax).

पार्थः *m.* 1 A metronymic of Yudhishthira, Bhima and Arjuna, but especially of Arjuna. -2 A king. -Comp. —सारथिः *m.* An epithet of Krishna.

पार्थक्यं *n.* Severalty, separateness, separation.

पार्थवं *n.* Greatness, immensity, [width.

पार्थिव *a.* (*f.*—वी) 1 Earthen, terrestrial, relating to the earth. -2 Ruling the earth. -3 Princely, royal. —वः *m.* 1 An inhabitant of the earth. -2 A king, sovereign. -3 An earthen vessel. -4 The body. —वं *n.* An earthly substance.

पार्थिवी *f.* 1 An epithet of Sitâ, daughter of the earth. -2 An epithet of Lakshmî.

पार्परः *m.* 1 A handful of rice. -2 Consumption (क्षयरोग). -3 Ashes. -4 A filament of Kadamba. -5 N. of Yama.

पार्यंतिक *a.* (*f.* -की) Final, last, conclusive.

पार्वण *a.* (*f.*—णी). 1 Belonging

or relating to a *Parvan.* -2 Increasing (as the moon.) -र्वं *n.* The ceremony of offering oblations to all the Manes at a *Parvan.*

पार्वत *a.* (*f.* —ती) 1 Living on a mountain.-2 Growing on or coming from a mountain. -3 Mountainous.

पार्वतिकं *n.* A mountain-range.

पार्वती *f.* 1 N. of Durgá, born as the daughter of the Himâlaya mountain. -2 A female cow-herd. -3 An epithet of Draupadî.-4 A mountain-stream.-5 A kind of fragrant earth. -Comp. —नंदन: *m.* 1 An epithet of Kârtikeya. -2 Of Ganesa.

पार्वतीय *a.* (*f.* -यी) Dwelling in a mountain. —यः *m.* A mountaineer. -2 N. of a particular mountain tribe (pl.).

पार्वतेय *a.* (*f.* -यी) Mountain-born. —यं *n.* Antimony.

पार्श्वधः *m.* A warrior armed with an axe.

पार्शुका *f.* A rib.

पार्श्व *a.* (*f.*— र्श्वा) Near, proximate. -र्श्वः *m.*, —र्श्वं *n.* 1 The part of the body below the arm-pit; the region of the ribs. -2 The side, flank (in general) (of an animate or inanimate object).-3 Vicinity.-र्श्वः *m.* An epithet of Jina. —र्श्वं *n.* 1 A multitude of ribs. -2 A fraudulent or dishonourable means.-3 The extremity of the fore-axle of a wheel.

पार्श्वं is used adverbially in the sense of'near to','by the side of,'towards '. So पार्श्वात् ' from the side of, away from'. पार्श्वे 'Near, 'at hand, 'at the side'.

-Comp. -अनुचरः *m.* An attendant, a servant. —अस्थि *n.* A rib. —आयात *a.* One who has come very near.-आसन्न *a.* Standing by the side. —उदरप्रियः *m.* A crab. —ग, -गम, —चर, —स्थित *a.* Being close to, standing by the side of. —गः *m.* An attendant, a servant. —गत *a.* 1 Being at the side. —चरः *m.* A servant, an attendant. —दः *m.* An attendant, a servant. —देशः *m.* The side (of the human body). —नाथः*m.* The Jaina pontiff. —परिवर्तनं *n.* 1 Turning round from one side to the other in a bed.-2 N. of a festival on the eleventh day of the first half of Bhâdrapada (when Vishnu is supposed to turn upon the other side in his sleep). — भागः *m.* The side or flank. —वक्त्रः *m.* An epithet of Mahâdeva. —वर्तिन् *a.* 1 Being by the side, waiting upon.-2 Adjacent. -शय *a.* 1 Sleeping on the side. -2 Sleeping by the side. —शूलः *m.*, —लं *n.* 1 A shooting pain in the side. -2 Pleurisy. —सूत्रकः *m.* A kind of ornament. —स्थः *m.* 1 A Companion. -2 An assistant of a stage-manager.

पार्श्वकः *m.* (*f.*-की) A swindler, thief.

पार्श्वतस् *ind.* Near, at hand, by the side, close to.

पार्श्विक *a.* (*f.* —की) Belonging to the side. —कः *m.* 1 A partisan. -2 A companion, an associate. -3 A juggler. -4 A thief.

पार्षत *a.* (*f.* -ती) Belonging to the spotted antelope.-तः *m.* A patronymic of king Drupada, and also of his son Dhrishtadyumna.

पार्षती *f.* 1 An epithet of Draupadî. -2 Of Durgâ.

पार्षद् *f.* An assembly.

पार्षदः *m.* 1 A companion, an attendant. -2 A train, retinue. -3 One present at an assembly; a spectator.

पार्षद्यः *m.* A member of an assembly ; an assessor.

पार्ष्णिः *m., f.* 1 The heel. -2 The rear of an army. -3 The back or rear in general. -4 A kick. -5 Inquiry. —*f.* 1 A licentious woman. -2 An epithet of Kuntí. -Comp.-ग्रहः *m.* A follower. —ग्रहणं *n.* Attacking an enemy in the rear. -ग्राहः *m.* An enemy in the rear. -2 A general commanding the rear of an army. -3 An ally who supports a prince. —घातः *m.* A kick. —त्रं *n.* A rear guard; a body of forces in the rear.

पालः *m.* 1 A protector, guardian, as in गोपालः,वृष्णिपालः &c. -2 A herdsman. -3 A king. -4 A spitting-pot. -Comp. —घ्नः *m.* A mushroom.

पालकः *m.* 1 A guardian, protector. -2 A prince, ruler. -3 A groom, horse-keeper. -4 A horse. -5 The Chitraka tree. -6 A foster-father.

पालकाप्यः *m.* N. of a sage, son of Karenu; he taught the science of elephants. -प्यं *n.* The science of elephants.

पालक्यः *m.*, —क्या *f.* Incense.

पालंकः *m.* 1 The olibanum tree. -2 A hawk.

पालनं *n.* 1 Protecting, guarding, nourishing. -2 Maintaining, observing, keeping (as a promise, vow &c.). -3 The milk of a cow that has recently calved.

पालयितृ *m.* A protector, guardian.

पालाश *a.* (*f.* —शी) 1 Belonging to or coming from the Palásha tree.-2 Made of the wood of the Palásha tree. -3 Green. —शः *m.* The green colour. -Comp. —खंडः, -षंडः *m.* An epithet of the Magadha country.

पालिः, -ली *f.* 1 The tip of the ear. -2 The edge, margin. -3 The edge, or point of anything. -4 Boundary, limit. -5 A line, row. -6 A spot, mark. -7 A causeway, bridge. -8 The lap or bosom. -9 An oblong pond. -10 Maintenance of a pupil by his teacher during the period of his studies. -11 A louse. -12 Praise. -13 A woman with a beard. -14 The hip. -15 A measure of capacity (प्रस्थ).-16 The circumference. —ली *f.* A pot, boiler.

पालिका *f.* The tip of the ear. -2 The sharp edge of any cutting instrument.-3 A butter-knife.

पालित *p. p.* (*f.* —ता) 1 Protected, guarded, preserved. -2 Observed, fulfilled.

पालित्यं *n.* Greyness of hair on account of old age.

पाल्लवा *f.* A game with twigs.

पाल्वल *a.* (*f.* —ली) Coming from or belonging to a pool.

पावक *a.* Purifying. —कः *m.* 1 Fire. -2 Agni or the God of fire. -3 A flash of lightning. -4 The Chitraka tree. -5 The number 'three'. -6 A person purified by religious abstraction; a saint, sage. -Comp. —आत्मजः *m.* 1 An epithet of Kârtikeya.

पावकिः *m.* An epithet of Kârtikeya.

पावन *a.* (*f.* -नी) 1 Purifying; freeing from sin; sanctifying. -2 Sacred, holy, pure. —नः *m.* 1 Fire. -2 Incense. -3 A kind of demi-god or Siddha. -4 N. of the poet Vyâsa. -5 N. of Vishnu. —नं *n.* 1 Purifying, purification. -2 Penance. -3 Water. -4 Cow-dung. -5 A sectarial mark. -6 Any means of purification. -7 Atonement. -8 Incense. -Comp. —ध्वनिः *m.* A conch-shell.

पावनी *f.* 1 The holy basil. -2 A cow. -3 The river Ganges.

पावमानी *f.* An epithet of particular Vedic hymns.

पावरः *m.* 1 The side of a die which is marked with two points. -2 A particular throw of the die.

पाशः *m.* 1 A cord, chain, fetter, noose. -2 A snare or net for catching birds and beasts. -3 A noose used as a weapon. -4 A die. -5 At the end of comp. पाश expresses (*a*) contempt or depreciation as in छात्रपाशः *m.* A bad pupil. (*b*) Beauty or admiration as in कर्णपाशः. (*c*) Abundance, mass, or quantity (after a word signifying 'hair') as in केशपाशः. -Comp. —अंतः *m.* The back of a garment. —क्रीडा *f.* Gambling, playing with dice. —धरः, -पाणिः *m.* An epithet of Varuna. —बद्ध *a.* Caught in a snare or net; noosed. —बंधः *m.* A noose, halter. —बंधकः *m.* A bird-catcher. -बंधनं *n.* A snare. -भृत *m.* An epithet of Varuna. -रज्जुः *f.* A fetter, rope. -हस्तः *m.* An epithet of Varuna.

पाशकः *m.* 1 A die, dice. -2 (At the end of comp.) A snare, trap as in कंठपाशक &c. -Comp. -पीठं *n.* A gambling house or table.

पाशनं *n.* 1 A noose, net. -2 A cord, lash. -3 Ensnaring, entrapping.

पाशिकः *m.* A bird-catcher.

पाशित *a.* (*f.* —ता) Bound, fettered.

पाशिन् *m.* 1 An epithet of Varuna. -2 Of Yama. -3 A deer-catcher; a fowler.

पाशव *a.* (*f.* -वी) Relating to animals. -वं *n.* A flock, herd. -Comp. —पालनं *n.* Pasturage or meadow-grass.

पाशुपत *a.* (*f.* -ती) Relating or sacred to Pashupati.—तः *m.* 1 A follower and worshipper of Siva. -2 A follower of the doctrines of Pashupati. —तं *n.* The Pâsupata-doctrines. -Comp. -अस्त्रं *n.* N. of a missile presided over by पशुपति or Siva.

पाशुपाल्यं *n.* The breeding or rearing of cattle.

पाश्चात्य *a.* (*f.* —त्या) 1 Hinder. -2 Western. -3 Posterior, later. -4 Subsequent. —त्यं *n.* The hinder part.

पाश्या *f.* 1 A net. -2 A collection of ropes.

पाषंडः *m.* A heretic, an unbeliever, a hypocrite. -डः *m.*, -डं *n.* Heresy.

पाषंडकः, पाषंडिन्, पाषांडिकः *m.* A heretic, a religious hypocrite.

पाषाणः *m.* A stone. —णी *f.* 1 A small stone used as a weight. -2 A spear. -Comp. —चतुर्दशी *f.* N. of a festival on the 14th day of the month of Mârgasîrsha, in honour of Gaurí. —दारकः, —दारणः *m.* A stone-cutter's chisel. -संधिः *m.* A cave or chasm in a rock. —हृदय *a.* Cruel, relentless.

पि 6 P. (पियति) To go, move.

पिकः *m.* The (Indian) cuckoo. -Comp. —आनंदः, —बांधवः *m.* The spring. —बंधुः, -रागः, -वल्लभः *m.* The mango tree.

पिक्कः *m.* 1 An elephant twenty years old. -2 A young elephant in general.

पिंग *a.* (*f.* —गा) Reddish-brown, yellow-red. -गः *m.* 1 The tawny colour. -2 A buffalo. -3 A rat. -गा *f.* 1 Turmeric. -2 Saffron. -3 A kind of yellow pigment. -4 An epithet of Durgá. -5 A bow-string. —गं *n.* A young animal. -Comp.—अक्षः *m.* 1 An ape. -2 An epithet of Siva. —ईक्षणः *m.* An epithet of Siva.—ईशः *m.* An epithet of fire. —कपिशा *f.* A species of cock-roach. —चक्षुस् *m.* A crab. —जटः *m.* An epithet of Siva.

—सारः *m.* A yellow orpiment.-स्फटिकः *m.* A kind of gem (गोमेद).

पिंगल *a.* (*f.* —ला) Reddish-brown, tawny.—लः *m.* 1 The tawny colour. -2 Fire. -3 A monkey. -4 An ichneumon. -5 A small owl. -6 A kind of snake. -7 N. of an attendant on the sun. -8 N. of one of Kubera's treasures. -9 N. of a reputed sage, the father of Sanskirt prosody. -लं *n.* 1 Brass. -2 Yellow orpiment. —ला *f.* 1 A kind of owl.-2 The Sisu tree. (शिंशपा).-3 A kind of metal. -4 A particular vessel of the body. -5The female elephant of the south. -6 N. of a courtezan remarkable for her piety and virtuous life. -Comp. -अक्षः *m.* An epithet of Siva. —लोहं *n.* Brass.

पिंगलिका *f.* 1 A kind of crane.-2 A kind of owl.

पिंगाशः *m.* 1 The headman of a village.-2 A kind of fish. -शं *n.* Virgin gold. —शी *f.* The Indigo plant.

पिचंडः *m.*, -डं *n.*, पिचिंडः *m.*, -डं *n.* 1 The belly. -2 A limb of an animal.

पिचंडकः *m.* A glutton.

पिचं (-चिं-) डिन्, पिचं (-चिं-)डि(-क, -ल) *a.* Big-bellied, corpulent.

पिचव्यः *m.* The cotton plant.

पिचिंडिका *f.* 1 The calf of the leg. -2 The instep (also पिचंडिका in these senses.).

पिचुः *m.* 1 Cotton. -2 kind of weight.-3 A kind of leprosy. -4 A kind of grain. -Comp. —तूलं *n.* Cotton. —मंदः,-मर्दः *m.* The *Nimba* tree.

पिचुलः *m.* 1 Cotton. -2 A kind of cormorant or sea-crow.

पिचुटः *m.* Inflamation of the eyes, ophthalmia.-टं *n.* 1 Tin.-2 Lead.

पिच्चा *f.* A string of 16 pearls weighing a *dharana* (a particular measure of pearls).

पिच्छं *n.* 1 A feather of a tail (as of a peacock). -2 The tail of a peacock. -3 The feathers of an arrow. -4 A wing. -5 A crest. —च्छः *m.* A tail in general.—च्छा *f.* 1 A sheath, covering. -2 The scum of boiled rice. -3 A row, line. -4 A heap, multitude. -5 The gum or exudation of the silk-cotton tree. -6 A plantain. -7 An armour. -8 The calf of the leg. -9 The venomous saliva of a snake. -10 A betel-nut. -11 A diseased affection of a horse's feet.-Comp. —बाणः *m.* A hawk.

पिच्छिका *f.* The feathers of a peacock's tail tied in a bunch.

पिच्छल *a.* (*f.*-ला) Slimy, slippery.

पिच्छिल *a.* (*f.*—ला) 1 Slimy, slippery. -2 Having a tail. —लः *m.*, -ला *f.*, -लं *n.* 1 The scum of boiled rice. -2 Sauce mixed with rice-gruel. -3 Broth, soup. -Comp. —त्वच् *m.* The orange tree or its peel.

पिंज् 2 A. (पिंक्ते) 1 To tinge, dye. -2 To touch. -3 To adore. -4 To sound. -5 To join.

पिंज् 10 U. (पिंजयति,-ते) 1 To give. -2 To take. -3 To shine. -4 To be strong or powerful. -5 To live, dwell. -6 To hurt, kill. -7 To speak.

पिंजः *m.* 1 The moon -2 A species of camphor. -3 Killing, slaughter. -4 A heap, collection. —जं *n.* Strength, power. —जा *f.* 1 Injury, hurting. -2 Turmeric. -3 Cotton. -4 A switch.

पिंजटः *m.* The mucus of the eyes.

पिंजनं *n.* A bow-shaped instrument used for cleaning cotton.

पिंजर *a.* (*f.*—रा) Reddish yellow, gold-coloured.-रः *m.* 1 The reddish-yellow colour. -2 The yellow colour. —रं *n.* Gold. -2 Yellow orpiment.-3 A skeleton. -4 A cage (for पंजर). -5 The ribs or the cavity formed by them ; the thorax.

पिंजरकं *n.* Orpiment.

पिंजरित *a.* (*f.*—ता) Coloured yellow; tinged brown.

पिंजल *a.* (*f.*—ला) 1 Over-come with terror; extremely confounded or perplexed. -2 Panic-struck (as an army). —लं *n.* 1 Yellow orpiment. -2 The leaf of the Kusa-grass. -ली *f.* Two blades of Kusa grass used in holding certain articles at a sacrifice.

पिंजालं *n.* Gold.

पिंजिका *f.* A roll of cotton from which threads are spun.

पिंजूष: *m.* The wax of the ear.

पिंजेट: *m.* The excretion or mucus of the eyes.

पिंजोला *f.* The rustling of leaves.

पिट: *m.* A box, basket. —टं *n.* 1 A house, hovel. -2 A roof.

पिटक: *m.*, -कं *n.* 1 A box, basket.-2 A granary.-3 A small boil or ulcer; (also पिटका or पिटिका in this sense). -4 An ornament on the banner of Indra. -5 A collection of writings. —का *f.* A small boil or pimple.

पिटक्या *f.* A multitude of boxes.

पिटाक: *m.* A basket, box.

पिट्टकं *n.* The tartar of the teeth (दंतकिट्ट).

पिठ: *m.* Affliction, distress.

पिठर: *m.*, —रं *n.* A pot, pan, boiler (also पिठरी in this sense). —रं *n.* A churning-stick. —र: *m.* An addition to a building shaped like a hollow vessel.

पिठरक: *m.*, -कं *n.*A pot,pan.-Comp. —कपाल: *m.*,-लं *n.* A pot-sherd.

पिडक: *m.*,-का *f.* A small boil, pimple, pustule.

पिंड् 1 A,10 U.(पिंडते,पिंडयति,-ते;पिंडित). 1 To roll into a lump or ball, put together. -2 To join, unite. -3 To heap or accumulate.

पिंड *a.* (*f.* -डी) 1 Solid (घन.) -2 Compact, dense, close. —ड: *m.*, -डं *n.* 1A round mass,ball, globe. -2 A lump, clod (of earth &c). -3 A morsel, mouthful. -4 A ball or lump of rice offered to the Manes at obsequial ceremonies or Sráddhas. 5 Food in general.-6 Livelihood, subsistence. -7 Alms. -8 Flesh, meat. -9 The fœtus or embryo in an early stage of gestation. -10 The body, corporeal frame.-11 A heap, multilude. -12 The calf of the leg. -13 Anything round, thick or solid. -14 An object in general. -15 A particular part of a house. -16 (In astr.) A sine expressed in numbers. -17 The twenty-fourth part of the quadrant of a circle. -18 The frontal sinus of an elephant. -19 A portico or shed in front of the door.-20 Incense,frank-incense. -21 (In arith.) Sum, amount. -22 (In geom.) Thickness. —डं *n.* 1 Power, strength. -2 Iron. -3 Fresh butter. -4 An army. -Comp. —अन्वाहार्य *a.* To be eaten after the funeral rice-ball has been offered to the Manes. —अन्वाहार्यकं *n.* A meal in honour of the Manes. —अभ्रं *n.* Hail. -अयसं *n.*Steel. -अलक्तक: *m.* A red dye. —अशन:, -आश:, -आशक:, -आशिन् *m.* A beggar. —उदकक्रिया *f.* An oblation of obsequial rice-balls and water to the deceased. —उद्धरणं *n.* Participating in funeral-offerings. —गोस: *m.* Gum-myrrh. —तैल

n., —तैलकः *m.* Incense. —द *a.* 1 One who gives food; one who supplies with bread or with any other means of subsistence. -2 One who is qualified to give the funeral rice-balls to deceased ancestors. (-दः *m.*) 1 The nearest male relation who offers the funeral rice-ball. -2 A master, patron. —दानं *n.* 1 Presentation of the obsequial rice-balls. -2 The funeral oblation made to deceased ancestors on the day of new-moon. —निर्वपणं *n.* Presenting obsequial rice-balls to the Manes. —पातः *m.* Giving alms. —पातिकः *m.* One who lives on alms.—पादः,—पाद्यः *m.* An elephant. —पुष्पः *m.* 1 The Asoka tree. -2 The China rose. -3 The pomegranate.(-ष्पं *n.*) 1 The blossom of the Asoka tree. -2 The flower of the China-rose.-3 A lotus. —भाज् (-जः *m. pl.*) The deceased ancestors or Manes. —भृतिः *f.* Livelihood, means of subsistence. —मूलं, —मूलकं *n.* A carrot. —यज्ञः *m.* The presentation of the obsequial rice-balls to the deceased ancestors. —लेपः *m.* The fragments of the obsequial rice-balls which cling to the hand; (these are offered to the three ancestors immediately preceding the great grandfather).-लोपः *m.* 1 Interruption in offering the funeral rice-balls(as through failure of issue). -2 Neglect in offering the funeral rice-balls (to the deceased ancestors). —संबंधः*m.* Relationship between a living person and one deceased sufficiently near to qualify the former to offer the obsequial rice-ball to the latter.

पिंडकः *m.*, -कं *n.* 1 A lump, globe. -2 A round swelling. -3 A lump of food. -4 The calf of the leg. -5 Incense. -6 Carrot. -7 (In astr.) A sine expressed in numbers. —कः *m.* A goblin, demon.

पिंडनं *n.* Forming globes. -नः *m.* A mound or bank.

पिंडलः *m.* 1 A bridge, cause-way. -2 A mound, ridge.

पिंडसः *m.* A beggar; a mendicant living on alms.

पिंडातः *m.* Incense.

पिंडारः *m.* 1 A religious mendicant. -2 A cow-herd.-3 A buffalo-herdsman. -4 The *Vikankata* tree.-5 An expression of censure.

पिंडिः, -डी *f.* 1 A round mass. -2 The nave of a wheel. -3 The calf of the leg. -4 The Asoka tree. -5 The long gourd. -6 A house. -7 A species of palm. -8 A stool or seat. -9 A pedestal for the image of a deity. -Comp. —पुष्पः *m.* The Asoka tree. —लेपः *m.* A kind of unguent. —शूरः *m.* A braggart, cowardly boaster, poltroon.

पिंडिका *f.* 1 A round or fleshy swelling. -2 The calf of the leg.

पिंडित *a.* (*f.* —ता) 1 Pressed or rolled into a ball or lump.-2 Thick, lumpish. -3 Heaped together.(पिंडितार्थः*m.* Compressed sense, sum and substance).-4 Mixed with.-5 Added, multiplied. -6 Counted, numbered. -तः *m.* Incense.

पिंडिन् *m.* 1 A beggar. -2 One who offers funeral rice-balls to the Manes.

पिंडिलः *m.* 1 A bridge, cause-way. -2 An astronomer or astrologer.

पिंडीर *a.* (*f.* —रा) Sapless, insipid, dry.-रः *m.* 1 The pomegranate tree.-2 Cuttle-fish-bone. -3 Foam of the sea.

पिंडोलि: *f.* 1 Fragments dropped from the mouth. -2 The leavings of a meal.

पिण्याकः *m.*, --कं *n.* 1 Oil-cake. -2 Incense. -3 Saffron. -4 Residue of seeds ground for oil.

पितामहः *m.* (*f.* -ही) 1 A paternal grandfather.-2 An epithet of Brahman (*m.*). -हाः *m. pl.* The Manes.

पितृ *m.* A father. -रौ *dual* Parents; father and mother.-रः *m. pl.* 1 Forefathers, ancestors, fathers. -2 Paternal ancestors taken collectively. -3 The Manes. -Comp. —अर्जित *a.* (Property) acquired by a father paternal (as property). —कर्मन्, —कार्यं,—कृत्यं *n.*,—क्रिया *f.* Oblations or sacrifice offered to deceased ancestors ; obsequial rites. -कल्पः *m.* The performance of the Srâddha ceremony in honor of the Manes.-काननं *n.* A cemetery.-कुल्या *f.* N. of a river rising in the Malaya mountain. —गणः *m.* 1 The whole body of ancestors taken collectively. -2 A class of Manes or deceased progenitors who were sons of the Prajâpatis. —गृहं *n.* 1 A paternal mansion.-2 A cemetery, burial-ground. —घातकः,-घातिन् *m.* A parricide. -तर्पणं *n.* 1 An oblation to the Manes. -2 The act of throwing water out of the right hand (as at the time of ablutions) as an offering to the Manes or deceased ancestors. -3 Sesamum. -4 Gifts given at Sráddhas or funeral rites. -5 The part of the hand between the thumb and the fore-finger (sacred to the Manes). —तिथिः *f.* The day of new-moon (अमावास्या).—तीर्थं *n.* 1 N. of Gayá where the performance of funeral rites is considered to be particularly meritorious. -2 The part of the hand between the fore-finger and the thumb (considered to be sacred to the Manes). —दानं *n.* An offering to the Manes. —दायः *m.* Patrimony. —दिनं *n.* The day of new-moon (अमावास्या). —देव *a.* 1 Worshipping a father. -2 Relating to the worship of the Manes. (-वाः *m. pl.*) The divine Manes. —देवत *a.* 1 Presided over by the Manes.-2 Relating to the worship of the Manes. (-तं *n.*) N. of the tenth lunar mansion (मघा).—दैवत्य *a.* Belonging to the worship of the Manes. (-त्यं *n.*) A sacrifice offered to the Manes on the day called अष्टका. —द्रव्यं *n.* Patrimony. —पक्षः *m.* 1 The paternal side, paternal relationship.-2 A relative by the father's side. -3 N. of the dark half of Bhâdrapada which is particularly appointed for the celebration of obsequial rites to the Manes. —पतिः *m.* An epithet of Yama. —पदं *n.* The world of the Manes. —पितृ *m.* A paternal grandfather. —पुत्रौ (पितापुत्रौ *m. dual.*) Father and son. (पितुः पुत्रः *m.* means 'the son of a renowned father'). —पूजनं *n.* Worship of the Manes. —पैतामह *a.* (*f.* -ही) Inherited from ancestors, hereditary. (-हाः *m. pl.*) Ancestors. —प्रसूः *f.* 1 A paternal grandmother. -2 Evening twilight. —प्राप्त *a.* 1 Inherited from a father. -2 Inherited patrimonially. —बंधुः *m.* A kinsman by the father's side. (-धु *n.*) Relationship by the father's side. —भक्त *a.* Dutifully attached to a father. —भक्तिः *f.* Filial duty.-भोजनं *n.* Food offered to the Manes. -भ्रातृ *m.* Paternal uncle. —मंदिरं *n.* 1 A paternal mansion. -2 A cemetery.

—मेध: *f.* Obsequial offerings.-यज्ञ: *m.* 1 Obsequial offerings. -2 Offering libations of water every day to the deceased ancestors; it is one of the five daily Yajnas. --राज् , --राज:, —राजन् *m.* An epithet of Yama.-रूप: *m.* An epithet of Siva. —लोक: *m.* The world of the Manes. —वंश: *m.* The paternal family. —वनं *n.* A cemetery. (°पितृवनेचर: *m.* 1 A demon, goblin. -2 An epithet of Siva). —वसति *f.*,—सद्मन् *n.* A cemetery. -व्रत: *m.* A worshipper of the Manes. (-तं *n.*) Obsequial rites. —श्राद्धं *n.* Obsequial rites in honour of a father or deceased ancestor.—स्वसृ, पितृष्वसृ, पितुःस्वसृ, पितुःष्वसृ *f.* A father's sister. —ष्वस्रीय *m.* A paternal aunt's son. —संनिभ: *a.* Fatherly, paternal. —सू: *f.* 1 A paternal grandmother. -2 Evening twilight.—स्थान:, —स्थानीय: *m.* A guardian (who is in the place of a father).—हत्या *f.* Parricide. -हन् *m.* A parricide.-हू: *m.* The right ear.

पितृक *a.* (*f.* -का) 1 Paternal, ancestral. -2 Obsequial.

पितृव्य: *m.* 1 A father's brother, paternal uncle.-2 Any elderly male relation.

पित्तं *n.* Bile, one of the three humours of the body (the other two being वात and कफ).-Comp.—अतीसार: *m.* A bilious form of diarrhœa. —अभिष्यंद: *m.* A bilious form of ophthalmia. —उपहत *a.* Affected by bile. —क्षोभ: *m.* A derangement of the bilious humour. -ज्वर: *m.* A bilious fever. -प्रकृति *a.* Of a bilious temperament. —प्रकोप: *m.* A vitiation of the bilious humour. —रक्तं *n.* Plethora. —वायु: *m.* The flatulence caused by the vitiation of the bilious humour. —शमन, -हर *a.* Antibilious.

पित्तल *a.* (*f.* -ला) Bilious. -लं *n.* 1 Brass. -2 A species of birch tree.

पित्र्य *a.* (*f.* -त्र्या) 1 Paternal, patrimonial, ancestral. -2 Relating or sacred to the deceased ancestors. -3 Obsequial. -त्र्य: *m.* 1 The eldest brother. -2 The month of Maghâ. --त्र्या *f.* 1 The constellation called Maghá. -2 The day of full as well as new moon. -त्र्यं *n.* 1 The lunar mansion called Maghá. -2 The part of the hand between the fore-finger and the thumb (sacred to the Manes).

पित्सत *m.* A bird.

पित्सल: *m.* A road, path.

पिधानं *n.* 1 Covering, concealing. -2 A sheath.-3 A wrapper, cloak. -4 A lid or top. [-2 A lid.

पिधानकं *n.* 1 A sheath, scabbard.

पिधायक *a.* (*f.* -का) Covering, hiding, concealing.

पिनद्ध *p. p.* (*f* —द्धा) 1 Fastened, tied on. -2 Dressed. -3 Hid, concealed. -4 Pierced, penetrated. -5 Wrapped, enveloped.

पिनाक: *m.*, -कं *n.* 1 The bow of Siva. -2 A trident. -3 A bow in general. -4 A staff or stick. -5 A shower of dust. -Comp. —गोप्तृ,-धृक् -धृत,-पाणि: *m.* Epithets of Siva.

पिनाकिन् *m.* An epithet of Siva.

पिपतिषत *m.* A bird.

पिपतिषु *a.* Being about to fall. -षु: *m.* A bird.

पिपासा *f.* Thirst.

पिपासित (*f.* -ता), पिपासिन् (*f.* -नी), पिपासु *a.* Thirsty.

पिपीतकी *f.* The twelfth day of the light half of Vaisâkha.

पिपील: *m.*, पिपीली *f.* An ant.

पिपीलक: *m.* A large black ant.

पिपीलिक: *m.* An ant.

पिपीलिका *f.* A female ant.

पिप्पलः *m.* 1 The holy fig-tree. -2 A nipple. -3 The sleeve of a jacket or coat. -4 A bird kept free (not confined in a cage). —लं *n.* 1 A berry in general. -2 A berry of the holy fig-tree. -3 Sensual enjoyment.

पिप्पलिः,-ली *f.* Long pepper.

पिप्पिका *f.* The tartar of the teeth.

पिप्लुः *m.* A mark, mole, freckle.

पियालः *m.* N. of a tree. —लं *n.* The fruit of this tree.

पिल् 10 U. (पिलयति,-ते) 1 To throw, cast. -2 To send, direct. -3 To incite, prompt.

पिलुः *m.* See पीलु.

पिल्ल *a.* (*f.* —ल्ला) Blear-eyed. —ल्लं *n.* A bleared eye.

पिल्लका *f.* A female elephant.

पिशंग *a.* (*f.* -गी) Reddish-brown; of a tawny colour. —गः *m.* The tawny colour.

पिशंगकः *m.* An epithet of Vishnu or his attendant.

पिशंगिल *a.* (*f.* -गी) Brown, tawny.

पिशाचः *m.* A fiend, goblin, malevolent being. -Comp. -आलयः *m.* Phosphorescence. -द्रुः *m.* A kind of tree. -बाधा *f.*,-संचारः *m.* Demoniacal possession.-भाषा *f.* One of the lowest Prákrita dialects used in plays. -सभं *n.* 1 An assemblage of fiends. -2 Pandemonium.

पिशाचकिन् *m.* An epithet of Kubera, the god of wealth.

पिशाचिका *f.* 1 A she-demon, a female imp. -2 (At the end of comp.) Devilish or diabolical fondness for a thing; किमनया आयुधपिशाचिकया devilish fondness for fighting; (पिशाची is used in the same sense).

पिशितं *n.* 1 Flesh.-2 A small piece or part. -Comp. —अशनः, -आशः, -आशिन्, —भुज् *m.* 1 A flesh-eater, a demon, goblin. -2 A cannibal. -3 A wolf.

पिशुन *a.* (*f.*-ना) 1 Indicating, manifesting, displaying, indicative of.-2 Memorable for, commemorating ; क्षेत्रं क्षत्रप्रधनपिशुनं कौरवं तद्भजेथाः * मेघदूत 48. -2 Slanderous, back-biting. -3 Betraying, treacherous. -4 Harsh, unkind. -5 Wicked, malignant. -6 Low, vile. -7 Foolish, stupid. —नः *m.* 1 A back-biter, base informer, traitor. -2 Cotton. -3 An epithet of Nârada. -4 A crow. -5 N. of a goblin (said to be dangerous to pregnant women). -नं *n.* 1 Betraying. -2 Saffron. -Comp. —वचनं, —वाक्यं *n.* Detraction, calumny.

पिष् 7. P. (पिनष्टि, पिष्ट) 1 To pound, grind, crush. -2 To injure, destroy, kill. With निस्— 1 To pound, to powder. -2 To injure, to bruise.

पिष्ट *p.p.* (*f.* -ष्टा) 1 Ground, powdered, crushed. -2 Rubbed together, clasped (as the hands). -3 Kneaded. -ष्टं *n.* 1 A ground substance. -2 Flour, meal. -3 Lead. -Comp. -उदकं *n.* Water mixed with flour. —पचनं *n.* A pan for parching flour. —पशुः *m.* An effigy of a beast made with flour. —पाकभृत *m.* A boiler. -पाचकं *n.* A boiler. -पिंडः *m.* A cake or ball of flour. —पूरः *m.* See घृतपूर. —पेषः *m.*,—पेषणं *n.* 'Grinding flour' *i. e.* doing any useless work, a vain or profitless repetition. (पिष्टपेषणन्यायः *m.* The maxim of grinding flour *i. e.* doing any useless work). -मेहः *m.* A variety of diabetes. —वर्तिः *m.* A kind of small ball made of the flour of barley, pulse or rice. —सौरभः *m.* (Pounded) sandal-wood.

पिष्टकः *m.*, -कं *n.* 1 A cake made of the flour of any grain. -2 A baked cake, bread. -3 A disease of the eye, opacity of the cornea. -कं *n.* Pounded sesamum-seeds.

पिष्टपः *m.*, -पं *n.* A division of the universe.

पिष्टातः *m.* Scented or perfumed powder (*mar.* बुक्का).

पिष्टिकं *n.* A cake made of rice-flour.

पिस् 1 P. (पेसति) To go, move.

पिस् 10 U. (पेसयति,-ते) 1 To go. -2 To be strong. -3 To dwell. -4 To hurt, injure. -5 To give or take.

पिहित *p. p.* (*f.* -ता) 1 Shut, barred. -2 Covered, hidden. -3 Filled or covered with. —तं *n.* (Rhet.) A figure of speech which consists in insinuating to a person that one knows his secrets पिहितं परवृत्तान्ताज्ञातुः साकूतचेष्टितं । प्रिये गृहागते प्रातः कान्ता तल्पमकल्पयत् ॥ * चंद्रालोक.

पी 4 A (पीयते) To drink.

पीचं *n.* The chin.

पीठं *n.* 1 A seat, a stool, chair, bench, sofa &c. -2 The seat of a religious student made of Kusa grass. -3 The seat of a deity. -4 A pedestal, basis. -5 A particular posture in sitting. -6 (In geometry.) The complement of a segment. -Comp. —केलिः *m.* A male confidant, a parasite. —ग *a.* Lame, crippled. —गर्भः *m.* The cavity in the pedestal of an idol. —चक्रं *n.* A carriage. -नायिका *f.* A girl of fourteen who represents Durgá at the festival of that goddess. —भूः *f.* Basement. -मर्दः *m.* 1 A companion, one who assists the hero of a drama in great undertakings, *e. g.* in securing his mistress. (So पीठमर्दिका *f.* A lady who assists the heroine in securing her lover). -2 A dancing master who instructs courtezans in the art of dancing. —सर्प *a.* Lame, crippled.

पीठकः *m.*,-कं *n.* A seat.

पीठिका *f.* 1 A seat (bench, stool). -2 A pedestal. -3 A section or division of a book.

पीड् 10 U. (पीडयति,-ते, पीडित) 1 To torment, harm, injure, annoy, molest. -2 To oppose resist. -3 To besiege (as a city). -4 To press or squeeze, compress, pinch. -5 To suppress, destroy. -6 To neglect. -7 To cover with anything inauspicious. -8 To overpower. With उद्- To press out of ; to press upwards. उप- To harass, to molest. नि— 1 To squeeze, to hold fast, to press together. -2 To harass, molest, punish. निस्— To press out. परि- 1 To press, to squeeze. -2 To annoy, molest. प्र- 1 To press. -2 To harass. सम्— To press.

पीडकः *m.* An oppressor.

पीडनं *n.* 1 Paining, distressing, inflicting pain. -2 Squeezing, pressing. -3 Pressure. -4 An instrument for pressing. -5 Taking, seizing as in करपीडन or पाणिपीडन q. v. -6 Laying waste, devastation. -7 Threshing corn. -8 An eclipse as in ग्रहपीडनं. -9 Suppressing sounds, a fault in the prounciation of vowels.

पीडा *f.* 1 Pain, trouble, suffering, annoyance. -2 Injury, damage, harm. -3 Devastation, laying waste. -4 Violation, transgression, -5 Restriction. -6 Pity, compassion. -7 Eclipse. -8 A chaplet, garland for the head. -9 The *Sa-*

rala tree. -10 A kind of box or basket.

पीडित *p. p.* (*f.* -ता) 1 Harassed, tormented, oppressed, pained. -2 Squeezed, pressed. -3 Espoused, seized. -4 Violated, broken. -5 Devastated. -6 Eclipsed. -7 Bound, tied. -तं *n.* 1 Paining, harassing. -2 A particular mode of sexual enjoyment. -तं *ind.* Fast, closely, firmly.

पीत *a.* 1 Drunk, quaffed.-2 Steeped, filled or saturated with. -3 Absorbed, drunk up, evaporated. -4 Sprinkled with water. -5 Yellow. —तः *m.* 1 Yellow colour. -2 Topaz. -3 Safflower. -4 A yellow pigment.-तं *n.* 1 Gold.-2 Yellow orpiment. -Comp. —अब्धिः *m.* An epithet of Agastya. —अंबरः *m.* 1 An epithet of Vishnu. -2 An actor. -3 A religious mendicant wearing yellow garments. —अरुण *a.* Yellowish red. -अश्मन् *m.* Topaz.-कदली *f.* A species of banana.-कंदं *n.*The carrot. —कावेरं *n.* 1 Saffron. -2 Brass. -गंधं *n.* Yellow sandal. —चंदनं *n.* 1 A species of sandal-wood. -2 Saffron. -3 Turmeric. —चंपकः *m.* A lamp. —तुंडः *m.* The Kârandava bird. -दारु *n.* A kind of pine or *Sarala* tree. -दुग्धा *f.* A milch cow. -द्रुः *m.* The *Sarala* tree. -पादा *f.* A kind of bird (Mar. मैना). -मणिः *m.* A topaz.-माक्षिकं *n.* A kind of mineral substance. -मूलकं *n.* The carrot. -रक्तं *n.* A kind of yellow gem, the topaz. -रागं *n.* 1 The yellow colour. -2 Wax. -3 The fibres of a lotus. --लोहं *n.* Brass. -वालुका *f.* Turmeric. -वासस् *m.* An epithet of Krishna.-सारः *m.* 1 The topaz. -2 The sandal tree. (-रं *n.*) Yellow sandal wood. —सारि *n.* Antimony. -स्कंधः *m.* A hog.-स्फटिकः *m.* The topaz.-हरित *a.* Yellowish green.

पीतकः *m.* The Asoka tree. -कं *n.* 1 Yellow orpiment. -2 Brass. -3 Saffron. -4 Honey. -5 Aloe-wood. -6 Sandal-wood. -7 Yellow sandal.

पीतनः *m.* 1 A species of fig-tree. -2 The hog-plum tree. -नं *n.* 1 Yellow orpiment. -2 Saffron. -3 The *Sarala* tree.

पीतल *a.* (*f.* -ला) Yellow. -लः*m.*The yellow colour. —लं *n.* Brass.

पीतलकं *n.* Brass.

पीतिः *m.* A horse. -*f.* 1 Draught, drinking. -2 A tavern. -3 The proboscis of an elephant.

पीतिका *f.* 1 Saffron. -2 Turmeric. -3 Yellow jasmine.

पीतुः *m.* 1 The sun.-2 Fire. -3The chief elephant of a herd.

पीथः *m.* 1 The sun. -2 Time. -3 Fire. -थं *n.* 1 Water. -2 Ghee.

पीथिः *m.* A horse.

पीन *a.* (*f.* -ना) 1 Fat, corpulent. -2 Plump, thick. -3 Full, round. -4 Swollen, big. -5 Brawny. -6 Profuse, excessive. -Comp. —ऊधस् *f.* (पीनोध्नी) A cow with full udders. -वक्षस् *a.* Full-chested, having a full bosom.

पीनसः *m.* 1 Cold affecting the nose. -2 Cough, catarrh.

पीयुः *m.* 1 crow. -2 The sun. -3 Fire. -4 An owl. -5 Time. -6 Gold.

पीयूषः*m.*, -षं*n.*1 Nectar,ambrosia.-2 Milk in general. -3 The milk of a cow during the first seven days after calving.-4 The first milk given by a cow after calving. -Comp. —महस्, -रुचिः *m.* 1 The moon. -2 Camphor. -वर्षः *m.* 1 A shower of nectar. -2 The moon. -3 Camphor.

पीलकः *m.* The large black ant.

पीलुः *m.* 1 An arrow. -2 An atom

-3 An insect. -4 An elephant. -5 The stem of the palm. -6 A flower. -7 A group of palm trees. -8 A kind of tree. -9 The central part of the hand. -लु *n.* The fruit of the Pilu tree.-Comp. —पर्णी *f.* A kind of drug. —पाकवादिन् *m.* A Vaiseshika ;(one who maintains the doctrine that heat acts only on the atoms of matter, as of a jar, and not on the whole body).

पीलुकः *m.* An ant.

पीव् I P. (पीवति) To be fat or corpulent.

पीवन् *a.* (*f.* पीवरी) 1 Full,fat,large. -2 Stout, strong. -*m.* Wind.

पीवर *a.* (-रा or -री *f.*) 1 Fat,large, fleshy, corpulent. -2 Plump, thick. -रः *m.* A tortoise.-री *f.* 1 A young woman. -2 A cow.

पीवा *f.* Water.

पुंस् 10 U. (पुंसयति,-ते) 1 To crush, grind. -2 To pain, trouble, punish.

पुंस् *m.* (Nom. पुमान्, पुमांसौ,पुमांसः; Instr. du. पुंभ्यां; Voc. sing.पुमन्) 1 A male,male being.-2 A man, human being. -3 Man, mankind. -4 A servant, an attendant. -5 A word in the masculine gender. -6 The masculine gender.-7 The soul.-Comp.-अनुज(पुंसानुज)*a* Having an elder brother. —अनुजा (पुमनुजा) *f.* A girl born after a male child *i. e.* a girl having an elder brother. —अपत्यं (पुमपत्यं) *n.* A male child. —अर्थः (पुमर्थः) *m.* 1 The aim of man. -2 Any one of the four ends of human existence *i. e.* धर्म, अर्थ, काम and मोक्ष. —आख्या (पुमाख्या) *f.* A designation of a male being. —आचारः (पुमाचारः) *m.* A usage of men. -कटिः *f.* A man's hip. -कामा *f.*A woman wishing for a huaband. —कोकिलः *m.* A male cuckoo. —खेटः (पुंखेटः) *m.* A male plant.—गवः(पुंगवः) *m.* 1 A bull, an ox. -2 (At the end of comp.) Chief, most excellent, distinguished or pre-eminent of any class as in वाल्मीकिर्मुनिपुंगवः, गजपुंगवः, नरपुंगवः &c. (पुंगवकेतुः *m.* An epithet of Siva).—चलः (पुंश्चलः) *m.* An adulterer. —चली (पुंश्चली) *f.* A harlot, an unchaste woman. -चलीयः (पुंश्चलीयः) *m.* The son of a harlot.-चिह्नं (पुंश्चिह्नं) *n.*The characteristic of a male, the membrum virile. -जन्मन् (पुंजन्मन्) *n.* The birth of a male child. -दासः (पुंदासः) *m.* A male slave. —ध्वजः (पुंध्वजः) *m.* 1 The male of any species of animal. -2 A mouse. —नक्षत्रं (पुंनक्षत्रं)*n.* A male asterism.-2 An asterism under which male children are born. —नागः (पुंनागः) *m.* A distinguished man. -2 A white elephant.-3 A white lotus.-4 Nutmeg. -5 N. of a tree called नागकेसरः. -नाटः, -डः (पुंनाटः,-डः) *m.* N. of a tree.—नामधेयः (पुंनामधेयः) *m.* A male. —नामन् पुंनामन् *a.* Having a masculine name. (—*m.*) 1 The tree called पुंनाग. -2 N. of a hell. —पुत्रः *m.* A male child. —प्रजननं *n.* The male organ of generation. -भूमन् (पुंभूमन्) *m.* A word of the masculine gender used only in the plural number ; *e. g.* दाराः पुंभूम्नि चाप्सुतः"अमरकोषः.-योगः (पुंयोगः)*m.* 1 Cohabitation with men. -2 Reference to a male or husband *e. g.* पुंयोगे क्षत्रियी. -रत्नं (पुंरत्नं) *n.* An excellent man.—राशिः (पुंराशिः) *m.* A male sign of the zodiac. —रूपं (पुंरूपं) *n.* The form of a man. —लिंग (पुंलिंग) *a.* Of the masculine gender.-2 Virility, manhood. -3 The male organ. —वत्सः (पुंवत्सः) *m.* A bull-calf. —वृषः (पुंवृषः) *m.* The musk-rat. —वेषः *a.* (पुंवेषः) Clad in male attire. -सवनं (पुंसवनं) *n.* The ceremony performed on a woman's perceiving the first signs of a living conception with a view to the birth of a son. -2 Fœtus. -3 Milk.

पुंस्त्वं *n.* 1 The characteristic of a male; virility, masculineness. -2 Semen virile. -3 The masculine gender.

पुंवत् *ind.* 1 Like a man. -2 In the masculine gender.

पुक्कश *a.* (*f.* -शी), पुक्कस *a.* (*f.* -सी) Low, vile. —शः, -सः *m.* N. of a degraded mixed caste, the offspring of a Nishâda by a Súdra woman. -शी, -सी *f.* 1 A bud. -2 The indigo plant. -3 A woman of the Pukkasa caste.

पुंखः *m.*, -खं *n.* 1 The feathered part of an arrow. -2 A falcon, heron.

पुंखित *a.* (*f.* -ता) Furnished with feathers (as an arrow).

पुंगः *m.*, -गं *n.* A heap, collection.

पुंगलः *m.* The soul.

पुच्छः *m.*, -च्छं *n.* 1 A tail.-2 A hairy tail. -3 A peacock's tail. -4 The hinder part. -5 The end of anything. -Comp. -अग्रं,—मूलं *n.* The tip of the tail. -कंटकः *m.* The scorpion. —आद्यं *n.* The root of the tail.

पुच्छटिः, -टी *f.* Cracking the fingers.

पुच्छिन् *a.* Having a tail. —*m.* 1 A Cock. -2 The *Arka* plant.

पुंजः *m.* A heap, mass, collection.

पुंजिः *f.* A heap, quantity, mass. -Comp. -ष्ठ *a.* (*f.* -ष्ठा) Heaped.

पुंजिकः *m.* Hail.

पुंजित *a.* (*f.* -ता) 1 Heaped, collected, heaped together.-2 Pressed together.

पुट् 6 P. (पुटति) 1 To embrace, clasp. -2 To intertwine.

पुट् 10 U. (पुटयति,-ते) 1 To be in contact with. -2 To bind together; fasten. -3 (पोटयति,-ते) 1 To grind, reduce to powder. -2 To speak. -3 To shine.

पुट् 1 P. (पोटति) 1 To grind. -2 To rub.

पुटः *m.*, -टं *n.* 1 A fold. -2 A cavity, concavity. -3 A cup made of a leaf folded or doubled; a vessel of leaves. -4 Any shallow receptacle.-5 The pod or capsule which envelops young shoots.-6A sheath, covering.-7 An eyelid. (पुटी also in all these senses).-8 A horse's hoof. -टः *m.* 1 A casket. -2 Contraction. -3 Anything folded so as to form a cup —टं *n.* 1 A nutmeg. -2 Two vessels joined together used in medical preparations.-Comp. -उटजं *n.* A white umbrella.-उदकः *m.* A cocoa-nut. -ग्रंथिः *m.* A pot, pitcher. -2 A copper-vessel. -पाकः *m.* That method of preparing drugs, in which the various ingredients are wrapped up in leaves and are covered with clay and then roasted in the fire. -भेदः *m.* 1 A town, city. -2 A kind of musical instrument (आतोद्य.).-3 A whirl-pool or eddy. —भेदनं *n.* A town, city.

पुटकं *n.* 1 A fold. -2 Any shallow cup or cavity. -3 A vessel made of a leaf. -4 A lotus. -5 Nutmeg.

पुटकिनी *f.* 1 A lotus. -2 A group of lotuses.

पुटिका *f.* Cardamoms.

पुटित *a.* (*f.* -ता) 1 Rubbed, ground. -2 Contracted. -3 Stitched, sewn.-4 Split.-तं *n.* The hollow of the hands.

पुटी *f.* A small piece of cloth worn over the privities; (for other senses see पुट).

पुंड् 1 P. (पुंडति) To grind, to pound

पुंडः *m.* A sign, mark.

पुंडरीकं *n.* 1 A lotus-flower, especially a white lotus. -2 A white umbrella.-कः *m.* 1 The white colour. -2 N. of the elephant presiding over the south-east direction. -3 A tiger. -4 A kind of serpent. -5 A species of rice.-6 A kind of leprosy. -7 A fever in an elephant. -8 A kind of mango tree. -9 A pitcher, water-pot. -10 Fire. -11 A sectarial mark on the fore-head. -Comp. —अक्षः *m.* An epithet of Vishnu. —प्लवः *m.* A kind of bird. —मुखी *f.* A kind of leech.

पुंडर्यं *n.* 1 A plant, creeper. -2 A kind of medicinal plant.

पुंड्रः *m.* 1 A kind of sugar-cane. -2 A lotus in general. -3 A white lotus. -4 A sectarial mark on the fore-head. -5 A worm. -6 The *Atimukta* creeper. -ड्राः *m. pl.* N. of a country and its inhabitants. -Comp. -केलिः *m.* An elephant.

पुंड्रकः *m.* 1 A variety of sugar-cane. -2 A sectarial mark. -3 One who lives by breeding silk-worms.

पुण्य *a.* (*f.* —ण्या) 1 Holy, sacred. -2 Meritorious, virtuous, just. -3 Auspicious, lucky, favourable (as a day).-4 Pleasing, lovely, beautiful. -5 Sweet, fragrant (as odour). -6 Solemn, festive.—ण्यं *n.* 1 Virtue, religious or moral merit. -2 A virtuous or meritorious act.-3 Purity, purification. -4 A trough for watering cattle. -5 A particular religious ceremony.-ण्या *f.* The holy basil. -Comp. -अहं (for अहन्) *n.* A happy or auspicious day as in पुण्याहं भवंतो ब्रुवंतु। अस्तु पुण्याहं. (पुण्याहवाचनं *n.* Repeating 'this is an auspicious day' three times at the commencement of religious ceremonies).-उद्यान *a.* Having beautiful gardens. -कालः *m.* An auspicious time. —कीर्ति *a.* Of auspicious fame, celebrated.-कृत *a.* Virtuous, meritorious. —क्षेत्रं *n.* 1 A holy place, place of pilgrimage. -2 N. of Aryávarta. —गंध *a.* Sweet-scented. (-धः *m.*) The Champaka tree. —गंधि *a.* Sweet-scented. —गृहं *n.* 1 An alms-house. -2 A temple. —जनः *m.* 1 A virtuous man. -2 A demon, goblin. -3 A Yaksha. -जित *a.* Attained by merit or good works. -तीर्थं *n.* A holy place of pilgrimage. —दर्शन *a.* 1 Beautiful. -2 Of sacred appearance. (-नः *m.*) The blue jay. (-नं *n.*) Visiting holy shrines. —पुरुषः *m.* A pious man. —प्रतापः *m.* The efficacy of virtue or moral merit. -फलं *n.* The reward of good works. (-लः *m.*) A grove. —भाज् *a.* Virtuous, meritorious.—भूः, -भूमिः *f.* Aryâvarta. —रात्रः *m.* 1 An auspicious night. -2 A night on which any religious ceremony is held. -लोकः *m.* Paradise. -शकुनं *n.* An auspicious omen. (-नः *m.*) A bird of good omen. -शील *a.* Of a virtuous disposition; virtuous, pious. —श्लोक *a.* Of good fame. (-कः *m.*) An epithet of Nala (of Nishadha), Yudhishthira, and Janárdana ; पुण्यश्लोको नलो राजा पुण्यश्लोको युधिष्ठिरः। पुण्यश्लोका च वैदेही पुण्यश्लोको जनार्दनः॥ (—का *f.*) An epithet of Sítá and Draupadî. -स्थानं *n.* A sacred or holy place ; a place of pilgrimage.

पुण्यकं *n.* 1 A religious or viritu-ous act (such as fasting &c.). -2 A religious rite or ceremony.

पुण्यवत् *a.* 1 Meritorious, virtuous.

-2 Lucky, fortunate. -3 Blessed. -4 Pleasing, beautiful.

पुत् *n.* A particular division of Hell to which childless persons are said to be condemned; see पुत्र below.-Comp. —नामन् *a.* Called पुत्; the same as पुत्.

पुत्तलः *m.*, —ली *f.* 1 An image, a statue, effigy. -2 A doll, puppet. -Comp. —दहनं *n.*, —विधिः *m.* Burning an effigy in place of the body of one whose corpse is lost. —पूजा *f.* Idolatry.

पुत्तलकः *m.*, पुत्तलिका *f.* The same as पुत्तल *q. v.*

पुत्तिका *f.* 1 A small kind of bee. -2 The white ant.

पुत्रः *m.* 1 A son; (the word is thus derived by Manu:—पुन्नाम्नो नरकाद्यस्मात्त्रायते पितरं सुतः। तस्मात्पुत्र इति प्रोक्तः स्वयमेव स्वयंभुवा॥ The word should hence be correctly written पुत्त्रः -2 A child; the young one of an animal. -3 A dear child (a term of endearment in addressing young persons). -4 (At the end of comp.) Anything little or small of its kind; as in असिपुत्रः, शिलापुत्रः &c.). —त्रौ (*m. dual*) A son and daughter.-Comp. —अन्नादः *m.* 1 One who is maintained by his son. -2 A mendicant of a particular order. —अर्थिन् *a.* Wishing for a son. —आदिनी *f.* 1 An unnatural mother.-2 A tigress. —इष्टिः, —इष्टिका *f.* 1 A sacrifice performed to obtain male issue. —काम *a.* Desirous of sons. -कार्यं *n.* A ceremony relating to a son.-कृतकः *m.* An adopted son. —गंधी *f.* An unnatural mother(who eats her own children). —जात *a.* One to whom a son is born. —दारं *n.* Son and wife. —धर्मः *m.* Filial duty. -पौत्रं *n. sing.* or -पौत्राः *m. pl.* Sons and grand-sons. —पौत्रिण *a.* Transmitted from son to son, hereditary. -प्रतिनिधिः *m.* A substitute for a son (*e. g.* an adopted son). —वधूः *f.* A daughter-in-law. —सखः *m.* One who is fond of children.

पुत्रकः *m.* 1 A little son or boy, (often used as a term of endearment). -2 A doll, puppet. -3 A rogue, cheat. -4 A locust, grasshopper. -5 A fabulous animal with eight feet (शरभ).

पुत्रका, —पुत्रिका *f.* 1 A daughter. -2 A doll, puppet. -3 A daughter appointed to raise male issue for a father who has no sons. -4 (At the end of comp.) Anything little or small of its kind; as in असिपुत्रिका, खड्गपुत्रिका &c. -Comp. -पुत्रः, —सुतः *m.* 1 A daughter's son who by agreement becomes the son of her father. -2 A daughter who, being regarded as a son, returns to her father's house. -3 A grandson. —प्रसूः *f.* A mother of daughters. —भर्तृ *m.* A son-in-law.

पुत्रिन् *a.* (*f.* —णी) Having a son or sons. —*m.* The father of a son. —णी *f.* 1 The mother of a son. -2 A parasitical plant.

पुत्रिय, पुत्रीय, पुत्र्य *a.* (*f.* -या, -या, -त्र्या) Relating to a son; filial.

पुत्री *f.* 1 A daughter. -2 N. of Durgâ.

पुत्रीया *f.* The desire of a son.

पुद्गल *a.* (*f.* —ला) Lovely, handsome. —लः *m.* 1 An atom. -2 The body, matter. -3 The soul. -4 An epithet of Siva.

पुनर् *ind.* 1 Again, once more. -2 Back, in an opposite direction (mostly with verbs). -3 On the other hand, on the contrary, but howerer, nevertheless, still (with an adversative force) -4 Further, besides. पुनः पुनः 'Again and again' 'repeatedly', 'frequently'. किंपुनः 'How much more', or 'how much less ?' पुनरपि Again, once more, and also; on the other hand. -Comp. —अर्थिता f. A repeated request.-आगत a. Come back, returned. —आगमः m., —मनं n. Coming back, return. -आदानं, —आधेयं n. Renewing the consecrated fire. —आवर्तः m. I Return. -2 Repeated birth. —आवृत, —आवृत्तिः f. I Repetition. -2 Return to worldly existence; repetition of birth. -3 Revision, another edition (of a book &c).—उक्त a. I Said again, repeated. -2 Superfluous, unnecessary. (—क्तं n.) I Repetition. -2 Superfluity, redundancy, uselessness. पुनरुक्तजन्मन् m. A Brâhmana (द्विजन्मन्). पुनरुक्तवदाभासः m. (Rhet.) A figure of speech consisting in the appearance of repetition. —उक्तिः f. I Repetition. -2 Superfluity, uselessness. —उत्थानं n. Rising again, resurrection.—उत्पत्ति f. I Reproduction. -2 Return of birth, metempsychosis. —उपगमः m. Return.-उपोढा, —ऊढा f. A woman married again. —गमनं n. Return, going again. —जन्मन् n. Repeated birth, metempsychosis. -जात a. Born again.—णवः, -नवः m. A finger-nail. —दारक्रिया f. Marrying again, taking a second wife. —प्रत्युपकारः m. Returning one's obligations; requital. —भवः m. Transmigration, repeated or recurring birth; metempsychosis. -2 A finger-nail. —भाविन् m. The sentient soul.-भावः m. New birth, repeated birth. -भूः f. I A widow remarried. -2 Re-existence. —वसुः m. (Usually dual). I The seventh lunar mansion (consisting of two or four stars). -2 An epithet of Vishnu. -3 Of Siva. —विवाहः m. Remarriage. -संस्कारः (पुनःसंस्कारः) m. Repetition of any Samskára or purificatory ceremony. —संगमः m., -संधानं (पुनःसंधानं) n. I Reunion.-2 Rekindling the sacred fire when it has been extinguished. —संभवः (पुनःसंभवः) m. Being born again (into the world); metempsychosis.

पुप्फुटः m. N. of disease of the palate and gums.

पुप्फुलः m. Flatulency or wind (in the stomach).

पुप्फुसः m. The lungs. -2 The pericarp of a lotus.

पुर् f. (Nom. sing. पूः; instr. du. पूर्भ्यां) I A town, fortified town. -2 A fortress. -3 A wall, rampart. -4 The body. -5 Intellect. -Comp. —द्वार् f.,-द्वारं n. (पुर्द्वारं) The gate of a city.

पुरं n. I A town, city (surrounded by a ditch, and not less than one Krosa in extent). -2 A castle, fortress. -3 A house, residence. -4 The body. -5 The female apartment.-6 N. of पाटलिपुत्र. -7 The calyx of a flower or any cup formed of leaves. -8 The skin. -9 Bdellium. -10 An upper story. -11 A storehouse. -12 A fragrant grass (नागरमुस्ता). -Comp. —अट्टः m. A turret on a city-wall. —अधिपः, —अध्यक्षः m. The governor of a town. —अरातिः, -अरिः, —असुहृद्, -रिपुः m. Epithets of Siva. —अर्धविस्तारः m. A small village. —उत्सवः m. A festival held in a city. -उद्यानं n. A city-garden, park. —ओकस् m. An inhabitant of a town. —कोट्टं n. A citadel. —जित्,-द्विष्, -भिद्, m. Epithets of Siva. —ज्योतिस् m. I

An epithet of fire. -2 The world of Agni. -नटी f. A small market-town ; small village. -तोरणं n. The outer gate of a city.—द्वारं n. A city-gate. —निवेशः m. The founding of a city. -पाल: m. 1 The commandant of a fortress. -2 The soul.—मथन: m. An epithet of Siva. -रक्षः, -रक्षकः, —रक्षिन् m. A constable, police-officer. —रोधः m. The siege of a fortress. —वासिन् m. A citizen, a townsman. —वास्तु n. Ground fit for the foundation of a town —शासनः m. 1 An epithet of Vishnu. -2 Of Siva. —हन् m. 1 An epithet of Vishnu. -2 Of Siva.

पुरग a. (f -गा) Favourably inclined.

पुरंजनः m. The soul.-नी f. Intellect, understanding.

पुरंजरः m. The arm-pit.

पुरटं n. Gold.

पुरणः m. The sea, ocean.

पुरतस् ind. 1 Before, in front, in the presence of. -2 Afterwards.

पुरंदरः m. 1 N. of Indra.-2 An epithet of Siva. -3 Of Agni. -4 N. of Vishnu. -5 N. of the eighteenth lunar mansion (ज्येष्ठा). -6 A thief, house-breaker. -रा f. An epithet of the Ganges.

पुरंध्रिः, —ध्री f. An elderly married woman; a respectable matron. -2 A woman whose husband and children are living.

पुरला f An epithet of Durgā.

पुरस् ind. 1 Before (in time or space); in front, in the presence of, before the eyes. (In this sense it is often prefixed to कृ, भू and गम्; hence such forms as पुरस्कृत्य &c. often used). -2 In the east, from the east -3 Eastward. -Comp. -अनुवाक्या (पुरोऽनुवाक्या) f. An introductory verse or hymn. -करणं n., -कारः m. 1 Placing before or in front. -2 Preference. -3 Treating with honour, showing respect. -4 Worshipping. -5 Accompanying, attending. -6 Preparing, arranging. -7 Making complete or perfect. -8 Attacking. -9 Accusation. -10 Consecrating. -11 Expecting. -12 Acceptance. —कृत a. 1 Placed in front. -2 Honoured. -3 Chosen, followed -4 Adored. -5 Provided with, having. -6 Got ready. -7 Consecrated. -8 Accused. -9 Made complete. -10 Expected. -11 Appointed. -12 Attacked. -13 Sprinkled with holy water. -14 Initiated. —क्रिया f. 1 Showing respect. -2 A preparatory or initiatory rite. —ग, —गम (पुरोग, -गम) a. 1 Leading, foremost. -2 Led or presided over by (at the end of comp.); e.g. इंद्रपुरोगमाः देवाः the Gods with Indra at the head. -गत a. 1 Standing in front of. -2 Preceded. —गतिः f Precedenece. (-तिः f.) A dog.-गंतृ, -गामिन् a. 1 Going before or in front. -2 Chief, leading. (-m.) 1 A leader. -2 A dog. -चरणं (पुरश्चरणं) n. 1 A preparatory or initiatory rite. -2 Initiation. -3 Repetition of the name of a deity accompanied with burnt offerings. —छदः (पुरश्छदः) m. A nipple. —जन्मन् (पुरोजन्मन्) a. Born before. —डाश् m., —डाशः (पुरोडाश्, -शः) m. 1 A sacrificial oblation made of ground rice and offered in *kapālas* or vessels. -2 An oblation in general. -3 An oblation of ghee with cakes of ground meal. -4 A kind of sacrificial ladle. -5 The leavings of an oblation. -6 The Soma juice. -7 A prayer (मंत्र) recited in offering oblations.—पाक a. Near fulfilment; about to be fulfilled. —प्रहर्तृ m One who fights in the front line.—फल a. Promising fruit in the near future. —भाग (पुरोभाग) a. 1 Obtrusive, officious. -2 Fault-finding. -3 Jealous of. (-गः m.) 1 The front part, forepart, van. -2 Officiousness. -3 Jealousy. —भागिन् a. 1 Self-willed, naughty. -2 Obtrusive, officious.-3 Fault-finding. -4 Envious, jealous. —मारुतः, -वातः(पुरोमारुतः,-वातः) m. Forewind, wind blowing in front.-वर्तिन् a. Being in front or in the presence of. —सर a. Going or moving in front. (-रः m.) 1 A fore-runner, harbinger. -2 A follower, attendant, servant.-3 A leader; one who is foremost or pre-eminent. -4 (At the end of comp.) Attended or precded by or with; as मानपुरःसरं, प्रणामपुरःसरं, &c. -स्थायिन् a. Standing in front.

पुरस्तात् ind. 1 Before, in front of. (oft. with gen., abl. or used by itself. -2 At the head of, foremost. -3 In the first place. -4 Formerly, previously. -5 Eastward -6 Later or further on, in the sequel.

पुरा ind. 1 In former times, formerly, in the olden time. -2 Upto the present time. -3 At first, in the first place. -4 In a short time, soon, shortly (in this sense usually with a present tense to which it gives a future sense) as in पुरा दूषयति स्थलीं ' Will pollute the place. -Comp. —उपनीतa. Formerly possessed. -कथा f. An old legend. -कल्पः m. 1 A former creation. -2 A story of the past. -3 A former age. -कृत a. Done formerly. (-तं n.) Actions done in a former life. —योनि a. Of ancient origin. (-निः m.) An epithet of Siva. —वसुः m. An epithet of Bhishma. —विद् a. Knowing the events of former times. —वृत्त a. 1 Relating to ancient times. -2 Old, ancient. (-त्तं n.) 1 History.-2 An old or legendary event.

पुरा f. 1 An epithet of the Ganges. -2A kind of perfume. -3 The east. -4 A castle.

पुराण a. (f. -णा or -णी) 1 Old, ancient. -2 Aged, primeval. -3 Decayed, worn out. —णं n. 1 A past event or occurrence. -2 A legend. -3 N. of certain well-known sacred works; these are 19; they are ascribed to Vyása; they contain the whole body of Hindu mythology. (पुराण is thus defined: —सर्गश्च प्रतिसर्गश्च वंशो मन्वंतराणि च। वंशानुचरितं चैव पुराणं पंचलक्षणं॥). -णः m. A coin equal to 80 cowries. -Comp. —अंतः m. An epithet of Yama. —उक्त a. Enjoined by or laid down in the Puránas.—कल्पः m. See पुराकल्पः under पुरा.-गः m. 1 An epithet of Brahman (m.).-2 A reciter or reader of the Puránas. —पुरुषः m. 1 An epithet of Vishnu. -2 An old man.

पुरातन a. (f. -नी) 1 Old, ancient. -2 Aged, primeval. -3 Worn out, decayed. —नः m. An epithet of Vishnu. -2 (—नाः m. pl.) The ancients. (-नं n.) An ancient story.

पुरिः f. 1 A city. -2 A river. -3 A king.

पुरिशय a. Reposing in the body.

पुरी f. 1 A city, town.-2 A stronghold. -3 The body. -Comp. —मोहः m. The Dhattúra plant.

पुरीतत् m., n. 1 A particular intestine near the heart. -2 The entrails in general; (also पुरितत् but it appears to be a wrong form).

पुरीषं n. 1 Feces, excrement, ordure. -2 Rubbish, dirt. -Comp. —आधानं n. The rectum. —उत्सर्गः m. Voiding excrement. —निग्रहणं *n.* Obstruction of the bowels.

पुरीषणः *m.* Feces, ordure. —णं *n.* Evacuation by stool.

पुरीषमः *m.* The black kidney-bean.

पुरु *a.* (*f.* -रु, -र्वी) Much, abundant, many. -रुः *m.* 1 The pollen of flowers. -2 Heaven. -3 N. of a demon killed by Indra. -4 N. of a prince, the sixth monarch of the lunar race. —*ind.* 1 Much, exceedingly. -2 Repeatedly, often. -Comp —जित् *m.* 1 An epithet of Vishnu. -2 N. of king Kuntibhoja or his brother. -दं *n.* Gold. —दंशकः *m.* A goose. —लंपट *a.* Very lustful or lascivinus. -हः,-हु *a.* Much, many. —हूत *a.* Invoked by many. (-तः *m.*) An epithet of Indra.

पुरुषः *m.* 1 A male being, man. -2 Men, mankind. -3 A representative of a generation. -4 An officer, agent, servant. -5 The height or measure of a man (considered as a measure of length). -6 The soul. -7 The Supreme Being, God (Soul of the universe). -8 A person (in grammar); प्रथमपुरुषः the third person मध्यमपुरुषः the second person, and उत्तमपुरुषः the first person. -9 The pupil of the eye. -10 (In Sán. phil.) The soul (opp प्रकृति). -11 The seven divine or active principles of which the universe was formed. —षी *f.* A woman. -षं *n.* An epithet of the mountain Meru. -Comp. -अंगं *n.* The male organ of generation. —अदः, —अद् *m.* A cannibal, goblin. —आधिकारः *m.* 1 A manly office or duty. -2 A calculation or estimation of men. —अयणः, -अर्थः *m.* 1 Any one of the four principal objects of human life; *i. e.* धर्म, अर्थ, काम and मोक्ष. -2 Human effort or exertion (पुरुषकार). —अस्थिमालिन् *m.* An epithet of Siva. —आद्यः *m.* 1 An epithet of Vishnu. -2 A demon. -आशिन् *m.* A demon, goblin. —इंद्रः *m.* A king. —उत्तमः *m.* 1 An excellent man. -2 The highest or Supreme Being, an epithet of Vishnu or Krishna. -कारः *m.* Manliness, prowess (opp. दैव). -2 Manhood, virility. -केसरिन् *m.* An epithet of Vishnu in his fourth incarnation. -दघ्न, -द्वयस *a.* Of the height of a man. -द्विष् *m.* An enemy of Vishnu. —नाथः *m.* 1 A general, commander. -2 A king. -नियमः *m.* (In gram.) A restriction to a person. -पुंगवः, -पुंडरीकः *m.* A superior or eminent man. —पुरं *n.* N. of the capital of Candahára. -वरः *m.* An epithet of Vishnu. -वाहः *m.* 1 An epithet of Garuda. -2 An epithet of Kubera. —व्याघ्रः, -शार्दूलः, -सिंहः *m.* A distinguished or eminent man. -2 A hero, brave man. —सूक्तं *n.* N. of the 90th hymn of the 10th Mandala of the Rigveda (regarded as a very sacred hymn).

पुरुषकः *m.*, —कं *n.* Standing on two feet like a man; the rearing of a horse.

पुरुषायितं *n.* 1 Playing the man, acting a manly part, a manly conduct. -2 A kind of coitus in which the woman plays the man.

पुरूरवस् *m.* The son of Budha and Ilâ and founder of the lunar race of kings.

पुरोटिः *m.* 1 The current of a river. -2 The rustling noise of leaves.

पुरोडाशः *m.* 1 An oblation. -2 A sacrificial cake of ground rice.

पुरोधस् *m.* A family priest (esp. of a king).

पुरोधानं *n.* 1 Placing in front. -2 Ministration by a priest.

पुरोधिका *f.* A favourite wife (preferred to all others).

पुरोहित *p. p.* (*f.* —ता) 1 Placed in front.-3 Appointed, entrusted. —तः *m.* 1 One charged with a business, an agent. -2 A family-priest.

पुल *a.* (*f.* —ला) Great, large, wide, extensive. —कः *m.* Horripilation.

पुलकः *m.* 1 Erection or bristling of the hairs of the body, through joy or fear), horripilation. -2 A kind of gem. -3 A flaw or defect in a gem. -4 A kind of mineral. -5 A ball of food with which elephants are fed. -6 Yellow orpiment. -7 A wine-glass. -8 A species of mustard. -Comp. —अंगः *m.* The noose of Varuna. —आलयः *m.* An epithet of Kubera.

पुलकित *a.* (*f.* —ता) Having the hairs of the body erect, thrilled with joy; rejoiced, enraptured.

पुलकिन् *a.* (*f.* -नी) Having the hairs of the body erect. -*m.* A species of Kadamba tree.

पुलस्तिः,-स्त्यः *m.* N. of a sage, one of the mind-born sons of Brahman (*m.*).

पुलहः *m.* N. of a sage, one of the mind-born sons of Brahman (*m.*).

पुला *f.* The soft palate, uvula.

पुलाकः *m.*, -कं *n.* 1 Empty, bad or shrivelled grain. -2 A lump of boiled rice. -3 A compendium. -4 Brevity.-5 Rice-water.-6 Despatch, celerity. -7 Smallness.

पुलाकिन् *m.* A tree.

पुलायितं *n.* A horse's gallop.

पुलिनः *m.*, -नं *n.* 1 A sand-bank, sandy beach (sometimes used in pl.) -2 A small island left in the bank of a river by the passing off of the water; an islet. -3 The bank of a river.

पुलिनवती *f.* A river.

पुलिंदः, पुलिंदकः *m.* 1 N. of a barbarous tribe (usually in pl.). -2 A man of this tribe, a barbarian.

पुलिरिकः *m.* A snake.

पुलोमन् *m.* N. of a demon, the father-in law of Indra. -Comp. -अरिः, -जित, -भिद्, -द्विष् *m.* Epithets of Indra. —जा, -पुत्री *f.* Sachi, daughter of Puloman and wife of Indra.

पुलोमा *f.* N. of the wife of Bhrigu and mother of Chyavana.

पुष् 1, 4, 9. P. (पोषति, पुष्यति, पुष्णाति, पुष्ट or पुषित) 1 To nourish, rear, bring up. -2 To support, maintain, bear. -3 To cause to thrive or grow, to develop, bring into relief. -4 To increase, further, promote, enhance. -5 To possess, have, enjoy. -6 To show, display. -7 To be increased or nourished, to thrive, prosper.-8 To magnify, extol.-9 To bloom, to blossom. -*Caus.* or 10 U. पोषयति,-ते)1 To nourish, bring up. -2 To increase. -3 To provide for. -4 To put on, wear.

पुष्करं *n.* 1 A blue lotus. -2 The tip of an elephant's tongue. -3 The skin of a drum *i. e.* the place where it is struck. -4 The blade of a sword; the sleath of a sword. -6 An arrow. -7 Sky, atmosphere. -8 A cage. -9 Water.-10 Intoxication. -11 The art of dancing. -12 War, battle. -13 N. of a elebrated place of pilgrimage in the district of Ajmere.-14 The bowl of a spoon. —रः *m.* 1 A lake, pond. -2 A kind of serpent. -3 A kind of drum. -4 The sun. -5 A kind

clouds said to cause dearth or famine. -6 An epithet of Krishna. -7 The Sárasa bird. -8 An inauspicious conjunction of planets. —रः *m*., -रं *n*. N. of one of the seven great divisions of the universe. -Comp. -अक्षः *m*. An epithet of Vishnu. -आख्यः, -आह्वः *m*. The (Indian) Crane. -तीर्थः *m*. N. of a sacred bathing place.-प्रियः*m*.Wax.-बीजंn. Lotus-seed. -व्याघ्रः *m*. An alligator. --शिखा *f*. The root of a lotus. --स्थपतिः *m*. An epithet of Siva. (-रौ *m. dual*) N. of the two Asvinî Kumâras.

पुष्करिणी *f*. 1 A female elephant.-2 A lotus-pool. -3 A piece of water, a lake or pool in general. -4 The lotus-plant.

पुष्करिन् *a*. (*f*. -णी) Abounding in lotuses. —*m*. An elephant.

पुष्कल *a*. (*f*. -ला) 1 Much, abundant. -2 Full, complete. -3 Magnificent, splendid. -4 Excellent, eminent. -5 Loud, resonant. -लः *m*. 1 A kind of drum.-2 N. of mount Meru. -लं *n*. 1 A particular measure of capacity= 64 handfuls. -2 Alms to the extent of four morsels of food.

पुष्कलकः *m*. 1 The musk-deer. -2 A bolt, pin. -3 A Buddhist mendicant.

पुष्ट *p. p.* (*f*. —ष्टा) 1 Nourished, reared. -2 Thriving, strong, fat. -3 Cared for. -4 Rich, magnificently provided. -5 Complete, perfect. -6 Full-sounding, loud. -7 Eminent. -ष्टः *m*. N. of Vishnu. -ष्टं*n*. Nourishment.

पुष्टिः *f*. 1 Nourishing, breeding, rearing.-2 Nourishment, growth, increase. -3 Strength, plumpness. -4 Prosperity, thriving. -5 Maintenance, support. -6 Wealth, property. -7 Richness, magnificence. -8 Development, perfection. -Comp. —कर्मन् *n*.A religious ceremony performed for the attainment of worldly prosperity. —कांतः *m*. An epithet of Ganesa. -वर्धन *a*. Promoting welfare, causing prosperity. (-नः *m*.) A cock.

पुष्टिका *f*. An oyster.

पुष्प् 4. P. (पुष्प्यति) To open, blow, expand, bloom.

पुष्पं *n*.1 A flower, blossom.-2 The menstrual discharge.-3 A topaz.-4 A disease of the eyes (albugo). -5 The vehicle of Kubera. -6 Gallantry, politeness (in erotic poetry). -7 Expanding, blossoming (said to be *m*. in this sense). -Comp. -अंजनं *n*. Calx of brass used as a collyrium. —अभिषेकः *m*. Bathing with flowers. —अंबुजं *n*. The sap of flowers. —अवचायिन् *m*. A garland-maker.-अस्त्रः *m*. An epithet of the God of love. —आकर *a*. Abounding in flowers. —आगमः *m*. The spring. —आजीवः *m*. A florist, garland-maker. —आपीडः *m*. A chaplet of flowers. —आयुधः, -इषुः *m*. The God of love. -आसवं *n*. Honey. —आसारः *m*. A shower of flowers. —उद्गमः *m*. The appearance of flowers. —उपजीविन् *m*. A florist, gardener, garland-maker. —कालः *m*. 1 The spring. -2 The time of the menses.—कासीसं *n*. Green (or black) sulphate of iron. —कीटः *m*. A large black bee. —केतनः *m*. The God of love. —केतुः *m*. The God of love. (-*n*.) 1 The calx of brass. -2 Vitriol (used as a collyrium). —घातकः *m*. The bamboo. —चापः *m*.The God of love —चामरः *m*. A kind of cane. —जं *n*. The juice of flowers. -द्रुः *m*. A tree. —दंतः *m*. 1 N. of an attendant of Siva. -2 N. of the author of the

'Mahimna stotra'.-3 N. of the elephant presiding over the north-west. —दंतौ *m. dual* The sun and moon. —द्रव: *m.* The sap or exudation of flowers. -2 An infusion of flowers. -द्रुम: *m.* A flowering tree. -ध: *m.* The offspring of an outcast Bráhmana. — धनुस्,-धन्वन् *m.* The God of love —धारण: *m.* An epithet of Vishnu. —ध्वज: *m.* The God of love. —लिट्: *m.* A bee. —निर्यास:, -निर्यासक: *m.* The sap, nectar or juice of flowers. -नेत्रं *n.* The tube of a flower.-पत्रिन्*m.* The God of love. -पथ: *m.* The vulva. —पुट: *m.* The calyx of a flower. —पुरं *n.* N. of Pátaliputra. -प्रचायिका *f.* Gathering of flowers. —प्रस्तार: *m.* A bed or couch of flowers. —बाण:, -बाण: *m.* An epithet of the God of love. —भव: *m.* The nectar or juice of flowers. —मंजरिका *f.* A blue lotus. —मास: *m.* 1 The month of Chaitra. -2 The spring. —रजस् *n.* The pollen. —रथ: *m.* A carriage for travelling or for pleasure (but not for war). —रस: *m.* The nectar or juice of flowers. —राग:, —राज:*m.* A topaz. —रेणु: *m.* Pollen. —लोचन: *m.* The Nâgakesara tree. -लाव: *m.* A flower-gatherer. (—वी *f.*) A female flower-gatherer. —लिक्ष:, -लिह् *m.* A bee. -वटुक: *m.* A gallant. —वर्ष: *m.*, -वर्षणं *n.* A shower of flowers. -वाटिका, —वाटी *f.* A flower-garden. —वृक्ष: *m.* A tree bearing flowers. -वृष्टि: *f.* A shower of flowers. -वेणी *f.* A garland of flowers.-शकटी*f.*A heavenly voice,voice from heaven. -शय्या*f.* A flowery bed, a couch of flowers. -शर:, -शरासन:, -सायक: *m.* The God of love. —समय: *m.* The spring. -सार:, -स्वेद: *m.* The nectar or honey of flowers.-सारा *f.* The holy basil.-स्नानं *n.* A kind of inauguration. -हास: *m.* 1 An epithet of Vishnu. -2 The blooming of flowers. -हासा *f.* A woman in her courses. -हीना *f.* A woman past child-bearing.

पुष्पकं *n.* 1 flower.-2 Calx of brass. -3 A cup of iron. -4 The car of Kubera. -5 A bracelet. -6 A kind of collyrium. -7 A particular disease of the eyes. -8 A bracelet of jewels. -9 A small earthen fireplace.

पुष्पंधय: *m.* A bee.

पुष्पलक: *m.* A post,wedge, pin.

पुष्पवत् *n.* (*f.* -ती) 1 Blooming, flowery. -2 Set off with flowers. —वंतौ *m. dual* The sun and moon. -ती *f.* A woman in her courses.

पुष्पा *f.* N. of the town Champâ, the modern Bhâgalpur.

पुष्पिका *f.* 1 The tartar of the teeth. -2 The last words of a chapter which state the subject treated therein.

पुष्पिणी *f.*A woman in her courses.

पुष्पित *a.* (*f.* -ता) 1 Flowered,full of flowers, blooming. -2 Florid, flowery (as speech). -3 Abounding or rich in; as in सुवर्णपुष्पिता पृथ्वी. -4 Fully developed, completely manifested. -5 Spotted, variegated. -ता *f.* A woman in her courses.-Comp. -अग्रा *f.* N. of a metre.

पुष्पिन् *a.* (*f.* -णी) 1 Bearing flowers,blooming,blossoming.-2 Rich or abounding in flowers.

पुष्य: *m.* 1 The Kali age. -2 The month called पौष. -3 The eighth lunar mansion (consisting of three stars),written also तिष्य. -ष्या *f.* The asterism called पुष्य. -Comp. -अभिषेक:*m.*, स्नानं *n.* A ceremony of coronating a king &c. when the moon stands in the asterism Pushya. -योगः m. The moon when in conjunction with Pushya. -रथः m. A carriage for travelling or for pleasure.

पुष्यलकः m. 1 The musk-deer. -2 A bolt, a pin.

पुस्तं n. 1 Plastering, painting, anointing. -2 Clay work, clay model. -3 Anything made of clay, wood or metal. -4 A book, manuscript. -Comp.-कर्मन् n. Plastering, painting, clay-modelling. पुस्तमय a. Anything made of clay. स्तंभित इव लिखित इवोत्कीर्ण इव पुस्तमय इव×× तूष्णीमभवो मुक्तसतस्थौ *कादंब.

पुस्तकः m.,-कं n., पुस्ती f. A book, manuscript. -2 A military register in which in ancient times were noted down the names of those soldiers that had distinguished themselves by deeds of heroism &c.

पू 1,4 A., 9 U. (पवते पूयते, पुनाति, पुनीते; पूतः caus. पावयति; desid. पुपूषति, पिपविषते) 1 To make pure, cleanse, purify (lit. and fig.). -2 To refine. -3 To winnow. -4 To expiate, atone for. -5 To discern, discriminate. -6 To devise, invent. -7 To become clear or pure (Atm.).

पूगः m. 1 A heap, collection, quantity. -2 An association, corporation. -3 The areca or betelnut-tree. (पूगी f. also). -4 Nature, property. -गं n. Areca-nut, betelnut. -Comp. —कृत a. Heaped up, collected. -पात्रं n. 1 A spitting-pot, spittoon. -2 A betel-box. -पीठः m.,-ठं n. A spitting-pot. -पुष्पिका f. Betel-nut and flowers given to guests at a marriage ceremony. -फलं n. The areca nut. -वैरं n. Enmity against many men.

पूज् 10 U (पूजयति,-ते; पूजयांचकार,-चक्रे, अपूपुजत,-त, अपपूजत,-त, पूजयितुं, पूजित) 1 To adore, worship, receive with respect. -2 To honour with.

पूजक a. (f.-जिका) Honouring, worshipping, respecting.

पूजनं n. 1 Worshipping, adoring. -2 Treating with respect, hospitality. -3 An object of reverence. -नी f. A hen-sparrow.

पूजा f. Worship, honour, respect, homage. -Comp. -अर्ह a. Venerable, respectable, worthy of reverence.

पूजित a. (f. -ता) 1 Honoured, respected, revered. -2 Acknowledged. -3 Endowed. -4 Recommended. -5 Frequented.

पूजिल a. (f. -ला) Venerable, respectable. -लः m. A god.

पूज्य a. (f. -ज्या) Deserving respect, worthy of honour, venerable. -ज्यः m. A father-in-law.

पूण् 10 U. (पूणयति,-ते) To heap together, accumulate, amass.

पूत् ind. An imitative word expressive of hard breathing or blowing.

पूत a. (f. -ता) 1 Cleaned, washed, purified. -2 Threshed, winnowed. -3 Contrived, composed. -4 Foul-smelling, putrid.

पूत p. p. (f. —ता) 1 Purified, cleansed, washed (fig. also). -2 Threshed, winnowed. -3 Expiated. -4 Invented. -5 Fetid, foul-smelling. -तः m. 1 A conch-shell. -2 White Kusa grass. —तं n. Truth. —ता f. An epithet of Durgâ. -Comp. -आत्मन् m. 1 An epithet of Vishnu. -2 A purified man, saint, sage. -क्रतायी f. Sachi, the wife of Indra. —तृणं n. White Kusa grass. -द्रुः m. The bread-fruit tree. -पलाशं, -धान्यं n. Sesamum. -पाप, -पाप्मन् a. Freed from sin. -फलः m. The bread-fruit tree (पनस).

पूतनः m. A dead body in a cemetery. -ना f. 1 N. of a female demon killed by Krishna. -2 A demoness, or Rakshasi in general. -Comp. -अरिः, -सूदनः,-हन् m. Epithets of Krishna.

पूति a. Putrid, stinking, foul-smelling. —तिः f. 1 Purification. -2 Stink, stench. -3 Putrefaction. -n. 1 Filthy water. -2 Pus, matter. -3 The substance called civet.-Comp. —अंडः m. A musk deer.—काष्ठं n. The Devâdaru tree. -काष्ठकः m. The *Sarala* tree. —गंध a. Foul-smelling, stinking. (-धः m.) 1 Stench, fetid odour. -2 The Ingudi plant. -3 Sulphur. -गंधि a. Stinking, foul-smelling. -गंधिक a. Stinking, fetid. —नस्यं n. A kind of disease of the nose in which it emits offensive breath. —नासिक a. Having a fetid nose. -वक्त्र a. Having offensive breath. —वातः m. A fart. -व्रणं n. A foul ulcer (discharging pus).

पूतिक a. (f. -का) Stinking, fetid, foul. -कं n. Ordure, excrement.

पूतिका f. 1 A kind of herb. -2 A civet-cat. -Comp. —मुखः m. A bivalve shell.

पून a. (f. —ना) Destroyed.

पूपः m. A sort of bread.

पूपला (-ली), पूपालिका, पूपाली, पूलिका, पूपिका f. A sort of sweet cake.

पूयः m.,-यं n. Pus, discharge from an ulcer or wound. -Comp. —अरिः m. The Nimba tree. -रक्तः m. A kind of disease of the nose.(-रक्तं n.) 1 Ichor, sanies. -2 Discharge of sanies from the nostrils.

पूयनं n. The same as पूय.

पूर् 4 A. (पूर्यते, पूर्ण) 1 To fill, fill out. -2 To please, satisfy.

पूर् 10 U. (पूरयति,-ते, पूरित) 1 To fill. -2 To blow into or fill with wind, blow (as a conch-shell). -3 To cover, surround.-4 To fulfil, satisfy. -5 To intensify, strengthen (as sound). -6 To make resonant. With आ— 1 To fill, to fill up, to make full. -2 To blow, to fill with wind. -3 To cover, envelop, intertwine. परि— To fill completely. प्र— 1 To fill. -2 To enrich, to load with riches. सम्— To fill.

पूरः m. 1 Filling, making full. -2 Satisfying, making content. -3 Pouring in, supplying. -4 The swelling of a river or of the sea. -5 A stream, flood. -6 The healing or cleansing of wounds -7 A kind of cake. -8 Drawing in breath slowly through the nose. —रं n. A kind of incense. -Comp. —उत्पीडः m. A flood or excess of water.

पूरक a. (f. —का) 1 Filling up.-2 Satisfying, making content. —कः m. 1 The citron tree. -2 A cake of meal offered at the conclusion of the oblantions to the Manes.-3 (In arith.) The multiplier. -4 Closing the right nostril and inhaling air through the left, (a religious ceremony).

पूरण a. (f. -णी) 1 Filling up, completing. -2 Ordinal as applied to numbers (द्वितीय, तृतीय &c.). -3 Satisfying. -4 Drawing (as a bow). -णः m. 1 A bridge, dam, causeway. -2 The ocean. -3 The *Salmali* tree. —णी f. 1 The silk-cotton tree. -णं n. 1 Filling.-2 Filling up, completing. -3 Puffing or swelling. -4 Accomplishing. -5 A sort of cake. -6 A funeral cake. -7 Rain, raining. -8 Warp (in a loom).-9 Multiplication (in math.). -10 Injection of fluids (in Medic.). -11 Drawing, bending (as a bow). -12 Decorating, adorning. -Comp.—प्रत्ययः *m.* An affix forming an ordinal number.

पूरिकः *m.*, -का *f.* A kind of cake.

पूरित *p. p.* (*f.* —ता) 1 Filled, complete. -2 Overspread. -3 Mnultiplied.

पूरुषः *m.* The same as पुरुषः.

पूर्ण *p. p.* (*f.* —र्णा) Filled, full of. -2. Whole, full, complete. -3 Fulfilled, accomplished.- 4 Completed. -5 Past, elapsed. -6 Satisfied, contented. -7 Full-sounding, sonorous. -8 Strong, powerful. -9 Selfish. -10 Drawn, bent (as a bow). —र्णा *f.* 1 An epithet of the fifteenth digit of the moon. -2 N. of the fifth, tenth, and fifteenth lunar days or 'tithis'. -Comp. —अंकः *m.* An integer. -अमृता *f.* An epithet of the sixteenth digit of the moon. -अवतारः *m* N. of the fourth, seventh and eighth incarnations of Vishnu. —आनकं *n.* A drum. -2 The sound of a drum. -3 A vessel. -4 A moon-beam. -5 A present to a person who brings a good news (पूर्णालक also in this sense).—आनंदः *m.* The Supreme Being. —उपमा (In Rhet.) A full or complete simile *i.e.* one in which the four requisites उपमान, उपमेय, साधारणधर्म and उपमाप्रतिपादक are all expressed; (opp. लुप्तोपमा). —ककुद् *a* Full-humped. —काम *a.* Satisfied, contented. (-मः *m.*) The Supreme Being. -कुंभः *m.* 1 A full jar. -2 A vessel full of water. -3 A particular mode of fighting. -4 A hole (in a wall) of the shape of a water-jar. —पात्रं *n.* 1 A full cup or jar. -2 A cupful. -3 A measure of capacity (equal to 256 handfuls). -4 A vessel filled with valuable things (such as clothes, ornaments &c.) and scrambled for by servants or relatives on festive occasions or distributed as presents. -5 A present made to one who brings a happy news. -6 A vessel full of rice presented to the priests at the end of the sacrifice. —बी (-वी-) जः *m.* The citron. -मासः *m.* The moon. -2 A monthly sacrifice performed on the day of full moon.-मासी *f.* The day of full moon.

पूर्णकः *m.* 1 A kind of tree. -2 A cock. -3 The blue jay.

पूर्णिमा, पूर्णिमासी, पूर्णमा *f.* The day of full moon.

पूर्त *a.* (*f.* —र्ता) 1 Full, complete. -2 Concealed, covered. -3 Nourished, protected. —र्तं *n.* 1 Fulfilment. -2 Nourishing. -3 Granting. -4 A reward, merit. -5 A class of acts of pious liberality. पूर्त is thus defined:——वापीकूपतडागादि देवतायतनानि च। अन्नप्रदानमारामः पूर्तमित्यभिधीयते. पूर्त is opposed to इष्ट which is thus defined अग्निहोत्रं तपः सत्यं वेदानां चैव पालनम्। आतिथ्यं वैश्वदेवश्च इष्टमित्यभिधीयते).

पूर्तिः *f.* 1 Filling. -2 Completion, accomplishment. -3 Satiety. -4 A reward. -5 Multiplying.

पूर्व *a.* (*f.* -र्वा) (Declined like a pronoun when it implies relative position in time or space, but optionally so in nom. pl., and abl. and loc. sing.) 1 Being in front of, first, foremost. -2 Eastern, easterly. -3 Previous to, earlier than. -4 Old, ancient. -5 Former, previous, (opp. उत्तर). -6 Aforesaid, beforementioned. -7 Established of long standing. -8 Early, prime, as in पूर्वे वयसि 'in early age or prime of life.' -9 (At the end of comp.) Preceded by, accompanied by, attended with; पुण्यःशब्दो मुनिरिति मुहुः केवलं राजपूर्वः

*शाकुंत. 2, 14. तान् स्मितपूर्वमाह * कुमा. सं. 7. 47.दशपूर्वरथं यमाख्यया दशकंठारिगुरुं विदुर्बुधाः *रघुवं. 8. 29 मतिपूर्वं = 'intentionally', 'knowingly'. अबोधपूर्वं ='unconsciously'. —जः m An ancestor, a forefather. —र्वं n. The forepart. -र्वा f. 1 The east.-2 N. of a country to the east of Madhydesa. —र्वं ind. 1 Before (with abl.)as in मासात्पूर्वं. -2 Formerly, previously, at first, beforehand. -3 Immemorially. (पूर्वेण 'in front, ' before', ' to the east of', with gen. or acc;.अद्य पूर्वं 'till now', hitherto'. पूर्वः... ततः, पूर्वं...पश्चात्, पूर्वं... उपरि 'first ..then,''first... afterwards' 'previously... subsequently', पूर्वं... अधुना or अद्य'formerly...now.'-Comp. —अग्निः m. The sacred fire kept in the house (आवसथ्य). -अचलः, —अद्रिः m. The eastern mountain behind which the sun and moon are supposed to rise. —अंतः m. The end of a preceding word.-अपर a. 1 Eastern and western. -2 First and last. -3 Prior and subsequent, preceding and following. -4 Connected with another. (-रं n.) 1 What is before and behind. -2 Connection. -3 The proof and the thing to be proved. —अभिमुख a. Turned towards or facing the east. -अंबुधिः m. The eastern ocean. -आर्जित a. Attained by former works. (-तं n.) Ancestral property. —अर्धः m.,-र्धं n. 1 The first half. -2 The upper part (of the body).-3 The first half of a hemistich. -अह्नः m. The earlier part of the day, forenoon, (पूर्वाह्णतन, पूर्वाह्णिक: पूर्वाह्णेतन a. Relating to the forenoon). —आवेदकः m. A plaintiff. —आषाढा f. N. of the 20th lunar mansion consisting of two stars. —इतर a. Western. —उत्तर a. North-eastern. (-रा f.) The north-east. (-रे dual) The preceding and following; antecedent and subsequent. -कर्मन् n. 1 A former act or work.-2 The first thing to be done. -3 Actions done in a former life. -4 Preparations. -कल्पः m. Former times. -कायः m. 1 The fore-part of the body of animals. -2 The upper part of the body of men. —कालिक, —कालीन a. Ancient. -काष्ठा f. The east, eastern quarter. —कृतं n. An act done in a former life. -कोटिः f. The starting point of a debate, or the पूर्वपक्ष. -गंगा f. N. of the river Narmadâ. -चोदित a. 1 Aforesaid, above-mentioned. -2 Previously stated or advanced (as an objection). -ज a. 1 Born or produced before or formerly, first-born. -2 Ancient, old. -3 Eastern. (—जः m.) 1 An elder brother. -2 The son of the elder wife. -3 An ancestor, a forefather. (—जा f.) An elder sister. —जन्मन् n. A former birth. (-m.) An elder brother. —जातिः f. A former birth. -ज्ञानं n. Knowledge of a former life.-दक्षिण a. South-eastern. (-णा f.) The south-east. -दिक्पतिः m. Indra.-दिनं n. The forenoon. -दिश् f. The east. -दिश्य a. Situated towards the east, eastern. -दिष्टं n. The award of destiny. -देवः m. 1 An ancient deity. -2 A demon or Asura. -3 A progenitor (पितृ). -4 -देवौ m. dual) An epithet of Nara-Nârâyana. -देशः m. The eastern country, or the eastern part of India. -निपातः m. The irregular priority of a word in a compound. —पक्षः m. 1 The fore-part or side. -2 The first half of a lunar month. -3 The *prima facie* argument or view of a question. -4 The first objection to an argument. -5 The statement of the plaintiff. -6 A suit at law. -7 An assertion, a proposition. -पदं *n.* The first member of a compound or sentence. -पर्वतः *m.* The eastern mountain behind which the sun is supposed to rise. -पांचालक *a.* Belonging to the eastern Pânchálas. -पाणिनीयाः (*m. pl.*)The disciples of Pânini living in the east. --पितामहः *m.* A forefather, an ancestor. —पुरुषः *m.* An epithet of Brahman (*m.*). -2 Any one of the first three ancestors, beginning with the father (पितृ, पितामह, and प्रपितामह). -3 An ancestor in general. —पूर्व *a.* Each preceding one. (-र्वाः *m. pl.*) Forefathers. —फल्गुनी *f.* The eleventh lunar mansion containing two stars. —भागः *m.* 1 The forepart -2 The upper part. —भाद्रपदा *f.* The twenty-fifth lunar mansion containing two stars. —भावः *m.* 1 Priority. -2 Prior or antecedent existence. -3 (Rhet.) Disclosing an intention. —भुक्तिः *f.* Prior occupation or possession. —भूत *a.* Preceding, previous. -मीमांसा*f.* 'The prior or first Mîmâmsá', an inquiry into the first or ritual portion of the Veda, as opposed to the उत्तरमीमांसा or वेदांत. —रंगः *m.* The commencement or prelude of a drama, the prologue. —रागः *m.* The dawning or incipient love. —रात्रः *m.* The first part of the night. —रूपं *n.* Indication of an approaching change. -2 A symptom of occurring disease. -3 The first of two concurrent vowels or consonants that is retained. -4 (in Rhet.) A figure of speech which consists in describing anything as suddenly resuming its former state —वयस् *n.* Youth. -वर्तिन् *a.* Existing before, previous.—वादः *m.* The first plea or commencement of an action at law. —वादिन् *m.* The complainant or plaintiff. —वैरिन् *m.* One who first commences hostilities; an aggressor.-शारद *a.*Relating to the first half of autumn.-शैलः *m.* The same as पूर्वपर्वत.-सक्थं *n.*The upper part of the thigh. -संध्या *f.* Daybreak,dawn.-सर *a.* Going in front. —सागरः *m.* The eastern ocean.-साहसः *m.* The first or heaviest of the three fines (in law).

पूर्वक *a.* (*f.* -र्विका) (At the end of comp.) 1 Preceded by, attended with. -2 Preceding,antecedent. -3 Previous, former, prior. -4 First. —कः *m.* An ancestor, a forefather.

पूर्वंगम *a.* Going before, preceding.

पूर्वतन *a.* Former, old, ancient.

पूर्वतस् *ind.* 1 In the east, to the east. -2 Before,in front of.-3 First, in the first place. [previously.

पूर्वत्र *ind.* In the preceding part,

पूर्ववत् *a.* 1 Having an antecedent or a cause. -2 Relating to something preceding. -*n.* One of the three kinds of अनुमान, inference of the effect from the cause. —*ind.* As before.

पूर्विन *a.* (*f.* -णी), पूर्वीण *a.* (*f.* —णा 1 Ancient. -2 Ancestral.

पूर्वेद्युस् *ind.* 1 On the former day. -2 On the day before; yesterday. -3 During the first part of the day. -4 Early, betimes.

पूल् 1 P, 10 U. (पूलति, पूलयति,-ते) To heap up, collect, gather.

पूलः, पूलकः *m.* A bundle, pack.

पूलाकः *m.* The same as पुलाक.

पूलिका *f.* A kind of cake.

पूषः, पूषकः m. The mulberry tree.

पूषन् m. (nom पूषा,-षणौ,-षणः) The sun. -Comp. —असुहृद् m. An epithet of Siva. —आत्मजः m. 1 A cloud. -2 An epithet of Indra. —भासा f. The city of Indra.

पृ 6 A. (प्रियते, पृत) To be busy or active (mostly with व्या-) *Caus.* (पारयति,-ते) 1 To cause to work, engage upon, appoint to (usually with loc.). -2 To place, fix, direct, cast.

पृ 3 U. (पिपर्ति, पूर्ण) 1 To bring or carry over. -2 To deliver from, bring out of.-3 To fill. -4 To protect, sustain.-5 To promote, advance.

पृ 5 P. (पृणोति) 1 To please, gratify. -2 To be pleased or delighted.

पृ 9 P. (पृणाति) To protect.

पृ 10 U. (पारयति,-ते) 1 To carry over or across, ferry over. -2 To reach the other side of anything; accomplish, achieve, bring to a conclusion (a vow &c.).-3 To be able or capable.-4 To deliver, save. -5 To oppose. -6 To live.

पृक्त p. p. (f. —क्ता) Mixed, mingled. -2 Touched, touching, united. -3 Filled, full. —क्तं n. Property, wealth.

पृक्तिः f. Touch, contact, union.

पृक्थं n. Property, wealth, possessions.

पृच् 2 A. (पृक्ते, पृक्ण) To come in contact with.

पृच् 7 P. (पृणक्ति, पृक्त) 1 To bring in contact with, unite. -2 To mix, mingle. -3 To touch.-4 To satisfy, fill, satiate.-5 To augment, increase.

पृच् 1 P. 10 U. (पर्चति, पर्चयति,-ते) 1 To touch -2 To hinder, oppose.

पृच्छकः m. An inquirer, an investigator.

पृच्छनं n. Asking, inquiring.

पृच्छा f. 1 Questioning, asking, inquiring.-2 An inquiry into the future.

पृंज् 2 A. (पृंक्ते) To come in contact with, touch.

पृत् f. An army. (This word has no forms for the first five inflections and is optionally substituted for पृतना after acc. dual).

पृतना f. 1 An army (in general). -2 A division of an army consisting of 243 elephants, as many chariots, 729 horses and 1215 foot. -3 Battle, encounter. -4 A hostile army. -Comp. —साहः m. An epithet of Indra.

पृथ् 10 U. (पर्थयति,-ते).1 To extend. -2 To throw, cast. -3 To send, direct.

पृथक् ind. 1 Separately, singly. -2 Different, separate, distinct. -3 Apart, aside, alone. -4 Apart from, except, without; (with acc., instr., or abl.) as in पृथग्रामेण or रामात् or -रामं.-Comp. —आत्मता f. 1 Severalty, separateness).-2 Distinction, difference. -3 Discrimination, judgment. -आत्मन् a. Distinct, separate. —आत्मिका f. Individual existence, individuality.—करणं n., —क्रिया f. 1 Separating, distinguishing. -2 Analysing. —कुल a. Belonging to a different family.-क्षेत्राः (m. pl.) Children of one father by different wives, or by wives of different classes. -चर a. Going alone or separately. —जनः m. 1 A low man, a vulgar man, the mob, low people; न पृथग्जनवच्छुचो वशं वशिनामुत्तम गंतुमर्हसि * रघुवं 8. 90. -2 A fool, a blockhead, an ignorant man. -3 A wicked man, sinner. —भावः m. Separateness, individuality, (so पृथक्त्वं). —रूप a. Of different shapes or kinds. -विध *a.* Of different kinds, diverse, various. -शय्या *f.* Sleeping apart. -स्थितिः *f.* Separate existence.

पृथक्त्वं *n.* 1 Separateness, severalty.-2 Individuality.

पृथवी *f.* The same as पृथिवी.

पृथा *f.* N. of Kuntî, one of the two wives of Pându. -Comp. -जः, -तनयः, -सुतः, -सूनुः *m.* An epithet of the first three Pândava princes, but generally applied only to Arjuna. -पतिः *m.* An epithet of Pându.

पृथिका *f.* A centipede.

पृथिवी *f.* 1 The earth : (sometimes written पृथिवि also).-2 Ground, soil. -3 The earth considered as one of the nine substances or five primary elements. -Comp. -इंद्रः, -ईशः, -क्षित्, -पालः, -पालकः, -भुज्, -शक्रः *m.* A king. -पतिः *m* 1 A king. -2 Yama, the God of death. -मंडलः *m.*, -लं *n.* The circuit of the earth.-रुहः *m.* A tree. -लोकः *m.* The terrestrial world.

पृथु *a.* (*f.* -थु or -थ्वी, compar. प्रथीयस्, superl. प्रथिष्ठ *a.* 1 Broad, wide, spacious. -2 Copious, abundant. -3 Large, great. -4 Detailed. -5 Numerous. -6 Smart, clever. -7 Important. -8 Various. -थुः *m* 1 N. of fire or Agni. -2 N. of Vishnu. -3 Of Mahâdeva. -4 N. of a king. -थुः *f.* Opium. -Comp. -उदर *a.* Big-bellied, corpulent. (-रः *m.*) A ram. -पत्रः *m.*, -त्रं *n.* Red garlic. -प्रथ, -यशस् *a.* Far-famed, widely renowned. -रोमन् *m.* A fish. -स्कंधः *m.* A hog.

पृथुकः *m.*, -कं *n.* Rice parched and flattened (Mar. पोहे).-कः *m.* A child. -का *f.* A girl. [wide.

पृथुल *a.* (*f.* -ला) Broad, large,

पृथ्वी *f.* 1 The earth. -2 The earth as one of the five elements. 3 Large cardamoms. -4 N. of a metre. -Comp. -ईशः, -पतिः, -पालः, -भुज् *m.* A king, sovereign. -खातं *n.* A cavern. -गर्भः *m.* An epithet of Ganesa. -गृहं *m.* A cave, grotto.-जः *m.* 1 A tree.-2 The planet Mars. -धरः *m.* A mountain. [Small cardamoms.

पृथ्वीका *f.* 1 Large cardamoms. -2

पृदाकुः *m.* 1 A scorpion.-2 A tiger. -3 A serpent. -4 A tree. -5 An elephant. -6 A panther.

पृश्नि (-श्णि) *a.* 1 Short, dwarfish.-2 Delicate, feeble. -3 Spotted. -श्निः *f.* 1 A ray of light. -2 The earth. -3 N. of Devaki, mother of Krishna. -Comp. -गर्भः, -धरः, -भद्रः *m.* Epithets of Krishna. -शृंगः *m.* 1 An epithet of Krishna. -2 Of Ganesa.

पृश्नि (-श्णि-) का, पृश्नी (-श्णी) *f.* N. of an aquatic plant.

पृषत् *m.* The spotted antelope.-*n.* 1 A drop of water or of any other liquid ; (said to be used only in pl.). -Comp. -अंशः, -अश्वः *m.* 1 Wind, air. -2 An epithet of Siva. -आज्यं *n.* Ghee mixed with coagulated milk. -पतिः (पृषतांपतिः) *m.* Wind. -बलः *m.* N. of the horse of wind.

पृषतः *m.* 1 The spotted antelope. -2 A drop of water. -3 A spot, mark. -Comp. -अश्वः *m.* Air, wind.

पृषत्कः *m.* An arrow.

पृषंतिः *m.* A drop of water.

पृषभाषा *f.* The same as पृषभासा.

पृषाकरा *f.* A small stone.

पृषातकं *n.* Mixture of ghee and coagulated milk.

पृषोदरः *m.* Wind, air. (The word is supposed to be compounded of पृषत् and उदर, the त of पृषत being dropped as an irregular case. The word is thus taken as the type of a whole class of such irregular compounds).

पृष्ट *p. p.* (*f.* -ष्टा) 1 Asked, inquired, questioned. -2 Sprinkled.

पृष्टहायन: *m.* 1 A species of grain.-2 An elephant.

पृष्टि: *f.* 1 Inquiry, interrogation.

पृष्ठं *n.* 1 The back, hinder part, rear. -2 The back of an animal. -3 The surface or upper side. -4 The back side (of a letter, document &c.). -5 The flat roof of a house. -6 The page of a book. (पृष्ठेन, पृष्ठे 'Behind, from behind'). -Comp. —अस्थि *n.* The back-bone. —गोप:, -रक्ष: *m.* A soldier who protects the rear of a warrior while he is fighting.-ग्रंथि *a.* Hump-backed. -चक्षुस् *m.* A crab. -दृष्टि *m.* 1 A crab.-2 A bear. —फलं *n.* The superficial contents of a figure. —मांसाद:, —मांसादन: *m.* A back-biter. —यानं *n.* Riding. —वंश: *m.* The back-bone. -वास्तु *n.* The upper story of a house.-वाह्,-वाह्य: *m.* A draught-ox. -शृंग: *m.* A wild goat. -शृंगिन् *m* A ram. -2 A buffalo. -3 A eunuch. -3 An epithet of Bhīma.

पृष्ठकं *n.* The back.(पृष्ठके कृ 1 To put off, postpone.-2 To resign, give up, discard).

पृष्ठतस् *ind.* 1 Behind, behind the back, from behind. -2 Towards the back, back-wards. -3 On the back. -4 Behind the back, secretly, covertly. (पृष्ठत: कृ 1 To place on the back, leave behind. -2 To neglect, forsake. -3 To renounce, desist from, resign. पृष्ठतो गम् To follow. पृष्ठतोऽस्तु 1 To stand at the back. -2 To be disregarded).

पृष्ठ्य *a.* (*f.* -ष्ठ्या) Relating to the back. —ष्ठ्य: *m.* A pack-horse. —ष्ठ्या *f.* A mare for draught.

पृष्णि: *f.* 1 The hell. -2 A ray of light.

पृ 3, 9. P. (पिपर्ति, पृणाति, पति-री-तुं, पूर्ण) 1 To fill, fill up, complete. -2 To fulfil, gratify (as hopes &c.) -3 To fill with wind, blow (as a conch, flute &c.). -4 To satisfy, refresh, please.-5 To rear, bring up.

पेचक: *m.* 1 An owl. -2 The root of an elephant's tail.-3 A couch, bed. -4 A cloud. -5 A louse.

पेचकिन्, पेचिल: *m.* An elephant.

पेंजूष: *m.* The wax of the ear.

पेट: *m.* (-टा, -टी *f.*,-टं *n.* also) 1 A bag, basket. -2 A chest. -3 A mulititude. -4 A retinue, train. -ट: *m.* The open hand with the fingers extended.

पेटक: *m.*, -कं *n.* 1 A basket, box, bag. -2 A multitude, quantity.

पेटक: *m.*,-टं *n.* A bag, basket, box.

पेटिका, पेटी *f.* A small bag, a basket.

पेडा *f.* A large bag.

पेय *a.* (*f.* -या) Drinkable, fit to be drunk.-यं *n.* A drink, beverage. -या *f.* Rice-gruel.

पेरु: *m.* 1 The sea. -2 Fire. -3 The sun.

पेयूष: *m.*, -षं *n.* 1 Nectar. -2 The milk of a cow that has calved within seven days.-3 Fresh ghee.

पेरा *f.* A kind of musical intrument.

पेल् 1 P, 10 U. (पेलति, पेलयति,-ते) 1 To go or move. -2 To shake or tremble.

पेल: *m.* 1 Going. -2 A small part. -लं *n.*,-पेलक: *m.* A testicle.

पेलव *a.* (*f.* -वा) 1 Delicate, soft, tender. -2 Lean, thin, slender.

पेलि:, पेलिन् *m.* A horse.

पेश (-ष,-स-) ल *a.* (*f.* -ला) 1 Soft, tender, delicate. -2 Thin, slender, (as waist). -3 Lovely, charming. -4 Clever, skilful. -5 Crafty, frau_ dulent. -6 Decorated, adorned. -लं *n.* Beauty.

पेशिः,-शी *f.* 1 A piece of flesh. -2 A ball or mass of flesh. -3 An egg. -4 A muscle. -5 The fœtus shortly after conception. -6 A bud on the point of blowing. -7 The thunderbolt of Indra. -8 A kind of musical instrument. -9 The shell or rind (of fruits). -10 A sheath. -11 A shoe. -Comp. —कोशः, -षः *m.* A bird's egg.

पेषः *m.* Grinding, pounding, crushing.

पेषणं *n.* 1 Pounding, pulverizing. -2 A threshing-floor. -3 A stone and muller.

पेषाणिः, पेषणी *f.*, पेषाकः *m.* A mill-stone, gind-stone, muller.

पेस्वर *a.* (*f.* -रा) 1 Gòing, moving. -2 Destructive.

पै 1 P. (पायति) To dry, wither.

पैंगिः *m.* A patronymic of Yâska.

पैंजूषः *m.* The ear.

पैठर *a.* (*f.* -री) Boiled in a पिठर (a kind of vessel.).

पैठीनसिः *m.* N. of an ancient sage, author of a system of laws.

पैंडिक्यं, पैंडिन्यं *n.* Living on alms, mendicity.

पैतामह *a.* (*f.* -ही) Relating to a paternal grandfather. -2 Inherited or derived from a paternal grandfather. -3 Relating to Brahman (*m.*). -हाः (*m. pl.*) Ancestors, forefathers.

पैतामहिक *a.* (*f.* -की). Relating to a paternal grandfather.

पैतृक *a.* (*f.* -की) 1 Relating to a father. -2 Coming from a father, ancestral, paternal. -3 Sacred to the Manes. —कं *n.* A Sráddha performed in honour of the deceased ancestors.

पैतृमत्यः *m.* The son of an unmarried woman.

पैतृष्वसेयः, पैतृष्वस्रीयः *m.* The son of a paternal aunt.

पैत्त (*f.*-त्ती), पैत्तिक *a.* (*f.* -की) Bilious.

पैत्र *a.* (*f.* -त्री) 1 Relating to a father or ancestors; paternal, ancestral. -2 Sacred to the Manes. —त्रं *n.* 1 The part of the hand between the forefinger and the thumb. -2 A year, month, or day sacred to the 'Pitris'.

पैलव *a.* (*f.* -वी) Made of the wood of the Pilu tree.

पैशल्यं *n.* Mildness, affability.

पैशाच *a.* (*f.* -ची) Demoniacal, infernal. -चः *m.* 1 The eighth of the eight forms of marriage in Hindu law; in it a lover ravishes a maiden without her consent when she is sleeping, or intoxicated or deranged in intellect. -2 A kind of demon or पिशाच.-ची *f.* 1 A present made at a religious ceremony. -2 Night. -3 The lowest Prâkrit dialect spoken on the stage by demons.

पैशाचिक *a.* (*f.* -की) Infernal, demoniacal.

पैशुनं, -न्यं *n.* 1 Back-biting, slandering. -2 Roguery. -3 Wickedness, malignity.

पैष्ट *a.* (*f.*-ष्टी) Made of flour or meal.

पैष्टिक *a.* (*f.* -की) Made of flour or meal. —कं *n.* 1 A number of cakes. -2 A spirituous liquor distilled from meal.

पैष्टी *f.* A spirituous liquor distilled from meal.

पोगंड *a.* (*f.* —डा) 1 Young; not adult or full-grown. -2 Having a deficient or redundant member. -3 Deformed. -डः *m.* A boy, one from his 5th to his 16th year.

पोटः *m.* 1 The foundation of a house. -2 Putting together.-Comp. —गलः *m.* 1 A kind of reed (नल). -2 A kind of grass (काश). -3 A kind of fish.

पोटकः *m.* A servant.

पोटा *f.* 1 masculine woman;a woman with a beard.-2 A hermaphrodite.

पोटिकः *m.* A boil.

पोटी *f.* 1 A large alligator.-2 The rectum.

पोट्टलिका, पोट्टली *f.* A bundle, packet.

पोतः *m.* 1 The young of any animal. (वीरपोतः *m.* A young warrior). -2 An elephant ten years old. -3 A ship, raft, boat. -4 A garment, cloth. -5 The young shoot of a plant. -6 The site or foundation of a house. Comp.—आच्छादनं *n.* A tent. -आधानं *n.* A shoal of small fish. —धारिन् *m.* The master of a vessel. -प्लवः *m.* A mariner,seaman.-भंगः *m.* A ship-wreck.-रक्षः *m.* The rudder of a boat or ship. -वणिज् *m.* A sea-faring merchant.-वाहः *m.* Rower,steersman.

पोतकः *m.* 1 The young of an animal. -2 A young plant. -3 The site of a house.

पोतासः *m.* A kind of camphor.

पोतृ *m.* One of the sixteen officiating priests at a sacrifice.

पोत्या *f.* A multitude of boats.

पोत्रं *n.* 1 The snout of a hog. -2 A boat, ship. -3 A plough-share. -4 The thunder-bolt.-5 A garment. -6 The office of the 'Potri'. -Comp. —आयुधः *m.* A hog, boar.

पोत्रिन् *m.* A hog, boar.

पोथः *m.* 1 A heap. -2 Bulk,magnitude.

पोलिका, पोली *f.* A kind of cake (of wheat).

पोलिंदः *m.* The mast of a ship.

पोषः *m.* 1 Nourishing, maintaining. -2 Growth, increase, advance. -3 Prosperity, abundance.

पोषकः *m.* One who maintains or nourishes.

पोषणं *n.* Nourishing, fostering, supporting, maintaining.

पोषयित्नुः *m.* The cuckoo.

पोष्यः *a.* (*f.* —ष्या) To be fed, nourished or supported. -Comp. —पुत्रः, —सुतः *m.* An adopted son. —वर्गः *m.* A class of relatives, who must be nourished and protected.

पौंश्चलीय *a.* (*f.* —यी) Relating to harlots.

पौंश्चलेयः *m.* The son of a harlot.

पौंश्चल्यं *n.* Harlotry, female incontinence.

पौंसवनं *n.* See पुंसवन.

पौंस्न *a.* (*f.*—स्नी) 1 Fit for a man. -2 Manly, virile. -3 Human. —स्नं *n.* Manhood, virility.

पौगंड *a.* (*f.* -डी) Boyish. -डं, पौगंडकं *n.* Boyhood (from the 5th to the 16th year).

पौंड्रः *m.* 1 N. of a country. -2 A king or inhabitant of that country. -3 A kind of sugarcane. -4 A sectarial mark. -5 N. of the conch-shell of Bhîma.

पौंड्रकः *m.* 1 A kind of sugarcane. -2 A mixed caste.

पौंड्रिकः *m.* A kind of sugarcane.

पौतवं *n.* A measure.

पौतिकं *n.* A kind of honey.

पौत्र *a.* (*f.* -त्री) Relating to a son. —त्रः *m.* A grandson, son's son. -त्री *f.* A grand-daughter. —त्रं *n.* The office of a 'Potri'.

पौत्रिक *a.* (*f.* —की) Belonging to a son or grandson.

पौत्रिकेयः *m.* The son of a daughter appointed to raise issue for her father.

पौनःपुनिक *a.* (*f.* -की) Frequently repeated.

पौनःपुन्यं *n.* Frequent or constant repetition.

पौनरुक्तं, पौनरुक्त्यं *n.* 1 Repetition. -2 Superfluity, redundancy.

पौनर्भव *a.* (*f.* -वा) 1 Relating to a

widow who has married a second husband. -2 Repeated, superfluous. -वः *m.* The son of a widow remarried, one of the twelve sons recognised by the old Hindu law. -2 The second husband of a woman.

पौर *a.* (*f.*-री) 1 Relating to a town, civic. -रः *m.* A townsman, citizen (opp. जानपदः). -री *f.* The language of the servants in a palace.-Comp. —अंगना, —योषित्,-स्त्री *f.* A woman living in a town. —कार्यं *n.* Public business. —जनः,-लोकः *m.* 1 A citizen.-2 Citizens. —जानपद *a.* Belonging to town and country. (-दाः *m. pl.*) Citizens and rustics; townsmen and country people. —वृद्धः *m.* An eminent citizen, an elderly man.

पौरकं *n.* 1 A garden near a house. -2 A garden near a town.

पौरंदर *a.* (*f.* -री) Derived from, or sacred to, Indra. -रं *n.* The lunar mansion called ज्येष्ठा.

पौरव *a.* (*f.* -वी) Descended from Puru. -वः *m.* 1 A descendant of Puru. -2 N. of a country or people in the north of India.-3 An inhabitant or ruler of that country.

पौरवीय *a.* (*f.* -यी) Devoted to Paurava'.

पौरस्त्य *a.* (*f.* —स्त्या) 1 Eastern. -2 Fore-most. -3 Prior, first, preceding.

पौराण *a.* (*f.* -णी) 1 Belonging to the past, ancient. -2 Relating to the Purânas or derived from them. -3 Former, previous.

पौराणिक *a.* (*f.* -की) 1 Belonging to the past; ancient. -2 Belonging to the Purânas or derived from them. -3 Versed in the legends of the past. —कः *m.* 1 A Bráhmana well versed in the Purânas. -2 A public reader of the Purânas. -3 A mythologist.

पौरुष *a.* (*f.* —षी) 1 Relating to man, human. -2 Manly, virile. -3 Sacred to *Purusha*. -षः *m.* A weight which can be carried by one man. -षी *f.* A woman. -षं *n.* 1 Human action, exertion, effort. -2 Heroism, valour, manliness, courage. -3 Strength, vigour. -4 Virility. -5 Semen virile. -6 Penis. -7 The full height of a man with both arms raised up and the fingers extended. -8 Sun-dial.

पौरुषेय *a.* (*f.* -यी) 1 Derived from or made, established or propounded by man. -2 Manly, virile. -3 Spiritual. -यः *m.* 1 Man-slaughter (पुरुष वध). -2 A crowd of men. -3 A day-labourer. -4 Human action, man's work. -5 Law as affecting persons. —यं *n.* Human work, action of man.

पौरुष्यं *n.* Manliness, courage.

पौरेय *a.* (*f.* -यी) Civic, town-bred.

पौरोगवः *m.* A superintendent of the royal kitchen.

पौरोडाशः *m.* A 'Mantra' recited upon making an oblation of ghee.

पौरोभाग्यं *n.* 1 Fault-finding. -2 Envy; jealousy -3 A mishievous deed. -4 Obtrusiveness.

पौरोहित्यं *n.* The office of a family-priest.

पौर्णमास *a.* (*f.* -सी) Relating to the full moon. —सः *m.* A ceremony performed on the full moon day by one who maintains the sacred fire (अग्निहोत्रिन्). —सं *n.* A day of full moon.

पौर्णमासी, पौर्णमी *f.* A day of full moon.

पौर्णमास्यं *n.* A sacrifice performed on the full-moon day.

पौर्णिमा *f.* A day of full moon.

पौर्तिक *a.* (*f.* —की) Relating to acts of pious charity.

पौर्व *a.* (*f.* -र्वी) 1 Relating to the

past. -2 Relating to the east ; eastern.

पौर्वदे (-दै-) हिक *a.* (*f.* —की) Relating to a former existence.

पौर्वपदिक *a.* (*f.* -की) Relating to the fiıst member of a compound.

पौर्वापर्य *n.* 1 The relation of prior and posterior. -2 Due order.

पौर्वाह्णिक *a.* (*f.* —की) Relating to the forenoon.

पौर्विक *a.* (*f.* -की) 1 Previous, former, prior. -2 Ancestral. -3 Old, ancient.

पौलस्त्य:*m.* 1 An epithet of Ràvana. -2 Of Kubera. -3 Of Bibhishana. -4 The moon.

पौलि: *m.*, *f.*, पौली *f.* A kind of cake.

पौलोमी *f.* 1 Relating to or descended from Puloman or Pulomá. -2 Sachî, daughter of Puloman and wife of Indra. -Comp. —संभव: *m.* An epithet of Jayanta.

पौष: *m.* N. of a lunar month in which the moon is in the Pushya asterism (corresponding to December-January). —षी *f.* The day of full moon in the month of Pausha.

पौष्करिणी *f.* A lotus pool or pond.

पौष्कल: *m.* A species of grain.

पौष्कल्यं *n.* 1 Maturity, full growth. -2 Abundance.

पौष्टिक *a.* (*f.* -की) 1 Promoting growth or welfare. -2 Nourishing, nutritive, invigorating.

पौष्णं *n.* The lunar mansion called Revatî.

पौष्प *a.* (*f.* -ष्पी) Floral, flowery. -ष्पी *f.* 1 N. of the town पाटलिपुत्र. -2 A kind of spirituous liquor (made from flowers).

प्याट् *ind.* A particle of calling (ho! holla !).

प्यान *a.* (*f.* —ना) Fat, grown fat.

प्याय् 1 A (प्यायते, प्यान or पीन) To swell, grow. See प्यै below.

प्यायन *a.* 1 Invigorating. -2 Promoting strength or growth. —नं *n.* Increase, growth.

प्यायित *a.* (*f.* —ता) 1 Grown, increased. -2 Grown fat. -3 Refreshed, strengthened.

प्यै 1 A (प्यायते, पीन) 1 To grow, increase, swell. -*Caus.* (प्याययति,-ते) 1 To increase, make fat or comfortable. -2 To gratify.

प्र *ind.* 1 As a prefix to verbs it means ' forward', 'forth', 'in front', ' onward', ' before ', ' away '. -2 With adjectives it means ' very ', ' excessively ', ' very much' &c. -3 With nouns whether derived from verbs or not, it is used to signify (1) Beginning, commencemet, as in प्रयाणं, प्रस्थानं, प्रह्व (2) Length. (3) Power, as in प्रभु (4) Intensity, excess as, in प्रवाद, प्रकर्ष, प्रच्छाय, प्रगुण. (5) Source or orgin, as in प्रभव, प्रपौत्र.(6) Completion, perfectness, satisfaction, as in प्रभुक्तमन्नं (7) Destitution, separation, being without, as in प्रोषिता, प्रपर्णोवृक्ष: (8) Apart,as in प्रज्ञु. (9) Excellence,as in प्राचार्य (10) Purity,as in प्रसन्नं जलं (11) Wish, as in प्रार्थना (12) Cessation, as in प्रशम (13)Adoration,respect,as in प्रांजलि: (14) Prominence,as in प्रणस, प्रवाल.

प्रकट *a.* (*f.* -टा) 1 Evident plain, clear, apparent, manifest. -2 Undisguised, public. -3 Visible. —टं *ind.* Clearly, manifestly. -2 Publicly, openly. -Comp —प्रतिवर्धन: *m.* An epithet of Siva. [disclosing.

प्रकटनं *n.* The act of manifesting,

प्रकटित *p. p.* (*f.* —ता), 1 Manifested, unfolded. -2 Publicly exhibited

प्रकंपः *m.* Trembling, shaking, violent motion.

प्रकंपनः *m.* 1 Wind, violent wind or gust. -2 N. of a hell. —नं *n.* Excessive trembling, violent motion.

प्रकरः *m.* 1 A multitude, quantity, collection. -2 A nosegay, bunch of flowers. -3 Assistance, friendship. -4 Usage, practice. -5 Respect. -6 Seduction, abduction. -रं *n.* Aloe-wood.

प्रकरणं *n.* 1 Explaining, discussing. -2 A subject, topic, a subject (of representation). -3 A subject of treatment. -4 A section, chapter or any smaller division of a work. -5 An opportunity, occasion. -6 An introduction, prologue. -7 A species of drama with invented or fictitious plot.

प्रकराणिका, प्रकरणी *f.* A drama of the same character as the प्रकरण.

प्रकरिका *f.* An interlude or episode inserted in a drama to explain what is to follow.

प्रकरी *f.* 1 An interlude or episode inserted in a drama to explain what is to follow. -2 Theatrical dress. -3 An open piece of ground. -4 A place where four roads meet. -5 A kind of song.

प्रकर्षः *m.* 1 Excellence, superiority. -2 Intensity, high degree, excess. -3 Strength power. -4 Absoluteness. -5 Length, protraction. -6 Speciality. -7 Universality. (प्रकर्षेण and प्रकर्षात are used adverbially in the sense of 'exceedingly', 'pre-eminently', 'in a high degree').

प्रकर्षकः *m.* An epithet of the God of love.

प्रकर्षणं *n.* 1 The act of drawing away. -2 Ploughing. -3 Duration, extension. -4 Excellence, superiority. -5 Distraction.

प्रकला *f.* A minute portion.

प्रकल्पना *f.* Settlement, fixing, allotment.

प्रकल्पित *p. p.* (*f.* -ता) 1 Made, formed. -2 Settled, allotted. -3 Intended or wished to be obtained. -4 Formed or shed (as a tear). --ता *f.* A kind of riddle.

प्रकांडः *m.*, -डं *n.* 1 The trunk of a tree from the root to the branches. -2 A branch, shoot. -3 (At the end of comp.) Anything excellent or pre-eminent of its kind *e. g.* दंतप्रकांड, ऊरुप्रकांड &c. —डः *m.* The upper part of the arm.

प्रकांडकः *m.* See प्रकांड.

प्रकांडरः *m.* A tree.

प्रकाम *a.* (*f* —मा) 1 Amorous. -2 Excessive, much, to the heart's content. —मः *m.* Desire, pleasure. satisfaction. —मं *ind.* 1 Very much, exceedingly. -2 Sufficiently, to the heart's content. -3 Voluntarily, willingly.

प्रकारः *m.* 1 Manner, way, fashion. -2 Sort, variety, species. -3 Similitude. 4 Special property or quality.

प्रकाश *a.* (*f.* —शा) 1 Bright, brilliant. -2 Visible, manifest. -3 Distinct, perspicuous. -4 Renowned, celebrated. -5 Open, public. -6 Cleared of trees. -7 Blown, expanded. -8 (At the end of comp.) Looking like, resembling. —शः *m.* 1 Splendour, brightness. -2 (Fig.) Explanation (mostly at the end of titles of works) as in काव्यप्रकाश, भावप्रकाश, तर्कप्रकाश &c. -3 Sunshine. -4 Display, manifestation. -5 Renown, glory. -6 Expansion, diffusion. -7 Open spot or air. -8 A golden mirror. -9 A chapter or section (of a book). —शं n. Bell-metal, brass. -शं *ind.* 1 Openly, publicly. -2 Aloud, audibly (used as a stage direction in dramas ; opp. आत्मगतं). —शे *ind.* 1 Openly, publicly. -2 Visibly. -3 In the presence of. -Comp. -आत्मक *a.* Shining, brilliant. —आत्मन् *a.* Bright, shining, (*-m.*) An epithet of (1) Vishnu. (2) Of Siva. (3) The sun. —इतर *a.* Invisible. —क्रयः *m.* An open purchase. —नारी *f.* A public woman, harlot.

प्रकाशक *a.* (*f.* —शिका) Illuminating, giving light. -2 Making apparent, displaying. -3 Expressing, indicating. -4 Explaining, expounding. -5 Bright, brilliant. -6 Noted, renowned. —कः *m.* 1 The sun. -2 A discoverer. -3 An expounder. -4 A publisher. -Comp. —ज्ञातृ *m.* A cock.

प्रकाशनं *n.* 1 Making known or manifest; disclosing. -2 Displaying, manifesting. -3 Illuminating, making bright. -4 Announcement, declaration. —नः *m.* N. of Vishnu. —ना *f.* Fxplaining, teaching.

प्रकाशित *p. p.* (*f.* —ता) 1 Made clear or manifest; displayed, manifested. -2 Published. -3 Illuminated, enlightened. -4 Visible, apparent. —तं *n.* Light, clearness.

प्रकिरणं *n.* Scattering about, strewing.

प्रकीर्ण *p.p.*(*f.*-र्णा) 1 Scattered about, thrown about, dispersed. -2 Published, promulgated. -3 Waved, waving. -4 Disordered, dishevelled. -5 Incoherent. -6 Agitated, excited. -7 Miscellaneous, mixed : as the प्रकीर्णकांड of Bhattikávya. -8 Expanded, opened. -9 Standing alone. —र्णं *n.* 1 A miscellany, any miscellaneous colleection. -2 A chapter containing miscellaneous rules. -3 A chapter or section of a book.

प्रकीर्णक *a.* (*f.* —का) Scattered about. —कः *m.*, -कं *n.* 1 A chowrie, fly-flap (चामर). -2 A tuft of hair used as an ornament for horses. —कः *m.* A horse. —कं *n.* 1 A miscellany, any collection of miscellaneous things. -2 A miscellaneous chapter. -3 A case not provided by the Sâstras and to be decided by the judge or king.

प्रकीर्तनं *n.* 1 Proclaiming, announcing. -2 Praising, extolling. —ना *f.* Mentioning, naming.

प्रकीर्तिः *f.* 1 Celebration, praise. -2 Fame, celebrity. -3 Declaration.

प्रकुंचः *m.* A particular measure of capacity.

प्रकुपित *p. p.* (*f.* -ता) 1 Very angry, incensed. -2 Excited. -3 Disordered, deranged.

प्रकुलं *n.* A handsome body.

प्रकुष्मांडी *f.* An epithet of Durgâ.

प्रकृत *p. p.* (*f.* —ता) 1 Accomplished, completed. -2 Commenced. -3 Appointed. -4 Genuine, real. -5 Forming the subject of discussion; that which is under consideration ; the subject in hand (often used in works on Alankára for उपमेय). -6 Important, interesting. —तं *n.* The original subject, the matter or subject in hand. -Comp. —अर्थः *m.* The original sense.

प्रकृतिः *f.* 1 The natural condition or state of anything; nature, natural form (opp. विकृति which is a change or effect). -2 Natural disposition ; nature, constitution. -3 Form, figure. -4 Extraction, descent. -5 Origin, original or material cause, the material of which anything made.-6(In Sân. phil.)Nature (as distinguished from पुरुष), the original source of the material world, consisting of the three essential qualities सत्व, रजस्, and तमस्. -7 (In gram.) The radical or crude form of a word to which caseterminations and other affixes are applied. -8 A model, standard, (especially in ritualistic works). -9 A woman. -10 The personified will of the Supreme Spirit in the creation (identified with माया or illusion). -11 The male or female organ of generation.-12 A mother. -13 (In arith.) A co-efficient, or multiplier. -14 (In anatomy)Temperament of the humours. -15 An animal. -16 The Supreme Being.-*f. pl.* 1 A king's ministers; the ministry. -2 The subjects (of a king). -3 The constituent elements of the state (सप्तांगानि), which are स्वाम्यमात्यसुहृत्कोशराष्ट्रदुर्गबलानि च. -4 The various sovereigns to be considered in case of war. -5 The eight elements out of which everything else is evolved according to the Sákhyas. -6 The five primary elements of the creation. called पंचमहाभूतानि which are पृथ्वी,अप्, तेजस्, वायु and आकाश. -Comp. -कृपण *a.* Naturally slow or unable to discern. —पुरुष: *m.* A minister, a functionary (of the state). —मंडलं *n.* The entire kingdom, the whole empire. —सिद्ध *a.* Inborn, innate, natural. —स्थ *a.*1 Being in the natural state or condition; natural, genuine. -2 Innate, incidental to nature. -3 Healthy, in good health. -4 Recoverd. -5 Come to oneself. -6 Stripped of everything; bare.

प्रकृष्ट *p. p.* (*f.*—ष्टा) 1 Drawn forth or out. -2 Protracted, lengthy. -3 Superior, excellent, exalted. -4 Chief, principal. -5 Distracted,disquieted. -6 Strong, excessive.

प्रक्लृप्त *p. p.* (*f.* -प्ता) Prepared, arranged.

प्रक्लेद: *m.* Putrefaction, putridity.

प्रकोप: *m.* 1 Wrath, rage. -2 Great excitement ; irritation. -3 Rebellion, mutiny. -4 An attack. -5 (Medic.) Excess, superabundance.

प्रकोष्ठ: *m.* 1 The fore-arm, the part above the wrist. -2 A room near the gate of a palace. -3 A court in a house, a quadrangle or square (surrounded by buildings).

प्रकोष्ठक: *m.* A room near the gate of a palace (= प्रकोष्ठ).

प्रक्खर:, प्रखर: *m.* 1 An armour for the defence of a horse or elephant. -2 A dog. -3 A mule.

प्रक्रम: *m.* 1 A step, stride. -2 A pace considered as a measure of distance. -3 Commencement. -4 Stepping forward. -5 Procedure, course. -6 Leisure, opportunity. -7 Regularity, order, uniformity ; continuity. -8 Degree, proportion, measure. -9 The reading of the Kramapátha.-Comp.-भंग: or भग्नप्रक्रम: *m.* A fault in composition occuring when there is a breach of the uniformity or regularity of expression; this breach may either be in regard to expression or construction. e. g. नाथे निशाया नियतेर्नियोगादस्तं गते हंत निशापि याता. Here गते requires the sequence of गता instead of याता.

प्रक्रांत *p. p.* (*f.* —ता) 1 Commenced, begun. -2 Gone, proceeded. -3

In hand, under discussion. -4 Surpassed. -5 Brave.

प्रक्रिया *f.* 1 Way, manner, conduct. -2 A ceremony. -3 The bearing of royal insignia. -4 High position, elevation. -5 A chapter or section (of a book) as in उणादिप्रक्रिया. -6 (In gram.) Etymological formation. -7 An introductory chapter of a work. -8 Rules for the formation of words.

प्रक्रीडः *m.* Play, pastime, sport.

प्रक्लिन्न *p. p.* (*f.* -न्ना) 1 Moist, humid, wet -2 Satisfied. -3 Moved with pity.

प्रक्लेदः *m.* Moistness, wetness.

प्रक्वणः, प्रक्वाणः *m.* The sound of a lute.

प्रक्षयः *m.* Ruin, destruction.

प्रक्षरः *m.* See प्रक्खर.

प्रक्षरणं *n.* Trickling out, oozing.

प्रक्षालनं *n.* 1 Washing, washing off. -2 Cleansing, cleaning, purifying. -3 Bathing. -4 Anything used for purifying. -5 Water for washing.

प्रक्षालित *p. p.* (*f.* —ता) 1 Washed, cleansed. -2 Purified. -3 Expiated.

प्रक्षिप्त *p. p.* (*f.* —प्ता) 1 Thrown at, hurled. -2 Projected. -3 Interpolated, spurious.

प्रक्षीण *p. p.* (*f.* —णा) 1 Decayed, declining. -2 Destroyed. -3 Expiated. -4 Vanished, disappeared.

प्रक्षीबित *a.* (*f.* —ता) 1 Drunken, intoxicated.

प्रक्षुण्ण *p. p.* (*f.* -ण्णा) 1 Crushed. -2 Pierced through. -3 Incited.

प्रक्षेपः *m.* 1 Throwing forward, projecting. -2 A throw, cast. -3 Spurious insertion, interpolation. -4 The sum deposited by each member of a commercial company.

प्रक्षेपणं *n.* 1 Throwing, hurling. -2 Pouring upon, throwing into.

प्रक्षोभणं *n.* Exciting, agitating.

प्रक्ष्वेडनः *m.* (*f.* —ना) 1 An iron arrow. -2 Clamour, hubbub.

प्रक्ष्वेडित *a.* (*f.* —ता) Clamorous, shouting, noisy.

प्रखर *a.* (*f.* —रा) 1 Very hot. -2 Very acrid or pungent, sharp. -3 Very hard or rough. -रः *m.* See प्रक्खर.

प्रख्य *a.* (*f.* —ख्या) 1 Clear, visible, distinct. -2 Looking like, resembling (at the end of comp.).

प्रख्या *f.* 1 Perceptibility, visibility. -2 Renown, celebrity. -3 Disclosure. -4 Resemblance, similitude (in comp.). -5 Look, appearance.

प्रख्यात *p. p.* (*f.* —ता) 1 Famous, celebrated, renowned. -2 Claimed by right of pre-emption -3 Happy, pleased. -4 Acknowledged. -Comp. -वप्तृ *a.* Having a celebrated father.

प्रख्यातिः *f.* 1 Fame, celebrity. -2 Praise. -3 Perceptibility.

प्रख्यानं *n.* 1 Reporting. -2 A report, information.

प्रख्यापनं *n.* 1 Publishing, making public. -2 Communicating.

प्रगंडः *m.* The upper part of the arm from the elbow to the shoulder.

प्रगंडी *f.* The outer wall (of a city).

प्रगत *p. p.* (*f.* —ता) 1 Gone forth or forward. -2 Separate, apart. -Comp. —जानु, -जानुक *a.* Bandy-legged, bow-legged.

प्रगमः *m.* The first manifestation [of love.

प्रगमनं *n.* 1 Advance, progress. -2 The first advance in courtship.

प्रगर्जनं *n.* Roaring.

प्रगल्भ *a.* (*f.* —ल्भा) 1 Bold, confident. -2 Spirited, courageous. -3 Bold in speech; eloquent. -4 Ready-witted, prompt. -5 Resolute, energetic. -6 Mature (as age). -7 Full-grown, strong. -8 Skilful. -9

Arrogant, officious, proud. -10 Shameless. -11 Illustrious, eminent. —ल्भा *f.* 1 A bold woman. -2 A shrew, scolding woman. -3 A bold woman experienced in love-matters, considered as a character in poetic composition. -4 An epithet of Durgâ.

प्रगाढ *a.* (*f.* —ढा) 1 Much, excessive. -2 Hard, difficult. -3 Firm. —ढं *n.* Privation. —ढं *ind* Exceedingly. -2 Firmly. -3 A strophe, a combination of two verses (ऋच्).

प्रगातृ *m.* An excellent singer.

प्रगुण *a.* (*f.*-णा) 1 Straight, honest, upright (lit. and fig.). -2 Being in the right state or condition, having excellent qualities. -3 Worthy, meritorious. -4 Efficient. -5 Skilful, clever. प्रगुणीकृ 1 To make straight, put in order, arrange. -2 To make smooth. -3 To nourish, bring up.

प्रगुणित *a.* (*f.* —ता) 1 Made even or straight. -2 Made smooth.

प्रगृहीत *p. p.* (*f.* —ता) 1 Held forth or out. -2 Received, accepted. -3 Pronounced separately without observing the rules of euphony (संधि).

प्रगृह्यं *n.* A word which is allowed to be written and pronounced separately without observing the usual rules of *Sandhi*.

प्रगे *ind.* Early in the morning, at day-break. -Comp. —तन *a.* To be performed in the morning. —निश, -शय *a.* Who is asleep at day-break.

प्रगोपनं *n.* Protection, preservation.

प्रग्रथनं *n.* Stringing together, weaving.

प्रग्रहः *m.* 1 Stretching forth, holding out. -2 Grasping, seizing. -3 The commencement of an eclipse. 4 A rein, bridle. 5 A whip, scourge. -6 A check, restraint. -7 Binding, confinement. -8 A prisoner. -9 Taming, breaking (as an animal). -10 A ray of light. -11 The string of a balance. -12 A vowel not subject to the rules of *Sandhi* or euphony. -13 The arm.

प्रग्रहणं *n.* Seizing, grasping. -2 The commencement of an eclipse. -3 A rein, bridle. -4 A check, restraint. -5 Binding, confining.

प्रग्राहः *m.* 1 Seizing, taking. -2 Bearing, carrying. -3 The string of a balance. -4 A rein, bridle.

प्रग्रीवः *m.*, -वं *n.* 1 A wooden fence round a building. -2 A window. -3 A stable. -4 The top of a tree. -5 A pleasure-house.

प्रघटकः, प्रघट्टकः *m.* A rule, doctrine, [precept.

प्रघटा *f.* The first elements or rudiments of a science. -Comp. —विद् *m.* A superficial reader, smatterer.

प्रघणः (-नः), प्रघाणः (-नः) *m.* 1 A porch before the door of a house, portico. -2 A copper-pot. -3 An iron mace, crow-bar.

प्रघस *a.* (*f.* -सा) Voracious. —सः *m.* 1 A demon. -2 Gluttony.

प्रघातः *m.* 1 Killing. -2 A combat.

प्रघुणः *m.* A guest.

प्रघूर्णः *m.* A guest.

प्रघोषः *m.* 1 Sound, noise. -2 Up- [roar.

प्रचक्रं *n.* 1 An army in motion. -2 A foraging army.

प्रचक्षस् *m.* 1 The planet Jupiter. -2 An epithet ot Brihaspati.

प्रचंड *a.* (*f.* -डा) 1 Excessively violent, impetuous. -2 Strong, powerful. -3 Very hot, stifling (as heat). -4 Furious. -5 Bold, confident. -6 Terrible, terrific. -7 Intolerable, unbearable. -Comp. -घोण *a.* Large-nosed.

प्रच (-चा-) यः *m.* 1 Collecting, gathering (as flowers). -2 A multitude, quantity, number. -3 Growth, increase. -4 Slight union. -5 The neutral accentless tone.

प्रचयनं *n.* Collecting, gathering.

प्रचरः *m.* 1 A road, path, way. -2 A custom, usage.

प्रचल *a.* (*f.*-ला) 1 Trembling, shaking. -2 Prevailing, customary. -3 Going well or widely.

प्रचलाकः *m.* 1 Archery. -2 A peacock's tail. -3 A snake.

प्रचलाकिन् *m.* A peacock.

प्रचलायित *a.* (*f.* —ता) Rolling about, tossing. —तं *n.* Nodding the head (while asleep in a sitting posture).

प्रचायिका *f.* 1 Gathering (flowers &c.) in turn. -2 A female who gathers.

प्रचारः *m.* 1 Going forth, walking about, wandering. 2 Appearance, manifestation. -3 Prevalence, use, being used or applied. -4 Conduct, behaviour. -5 Custom, usage. -6 A play-ground. -7 A parturage. -8 A passage, path.

प्रचालः *m.* The neck of the Indian lute.

प्रचालनं *n.* Stirring, shaking, a stir.

प्रचित *p. p.* (*f.* —ता) 1 Gathered, plucked. -2 Accumulated. -3 Covered, filled.

प्रचुर *a.* (*f.* -रा) 1 Much, ample, abundant, plentiful. -2 Great, extensive. -3 (At the end of comp.) Abounding in, filled with. —रः *m.* A thief. -Comp. -पुरुष *a.* Populous. (-षः *m.*) A thief.

प्रचेतस् *m.* 1 An epithet of Varuna. -2 N. of an ancient sage and lawgiver.

प्रचेतृ *m.* A charioteer.

प्रचेलं *n.* Yellow sandal wood.

प्रचेलकः *m.* A horse.

प्रचोदः *m.* 1 Driving onward, urging, inciting. -2 Instigating.

प्रचोदनं *n.* 1 Driving onward, urging. -2 Instigating. -3 Enjoining, prescribing. -4 A rule, precept, commandment.

प्रचोदित *p. p.* (*f.* -ता) 1 Urged, incited. -2 Instigated. -3 Ordered, prescribed. -4 Sent, despatched. -5 Decreed, determined.

प्रच्छ् 6 P. (पृच्छति, पप्रच्छ अप्राक्षीत्, प्रक्ष्यति, प्रष्टुं, पृष्ट ; *caus.* प्रच्छयति ; *pass.* पृच्छ्यते) 1 To ask, question, inquire of (with two acc.). -2 To ascertain, learn by inquiry. -3 To seek, seek for. With अनु—To question about. आ- 1 To ask, question. -2 (Atm.) To take leave of, bid adieu to. परि- To ask, inquire.

प्रच्छदः *m.* A cover, wrapper, coverlet, bed-cover. -Comp. —पटः *m.* Bed-clothes, coverlet.

प्रच्छनं *n.*,-ना *f.* A question, inquiry.

प्रच्छन्न *p. p.* (*f.* —ना) 1 Covered, wrapped. -2 Private, secret. -3 Concealed, hidden. -4 Clothed, clad. -न्नं *n.* 1 A private door. -2 A loop-hole, window. —न्नं *ind.* Secretly. -Comp. —तस्करः *m.* An unseen thief.

प्रच्छर्दनं *n.* 1 Vomiting. -2 An emetic.

प्रच्छर्दिका *f.* Vomiting.

प्रच्छादनं *n.* 1 Covering, concealing. -2 An upper garment. -Comp. -पटः *m.* A wrapper, cover, coverlet.

प्रच्छादित *p. p.* (*f.* —ता) 1 Covered, enveloped, clothed. -2 Hidden, concealed.

प्रच्छायं *n.* Thick or dense shade, a shadowy place.

प्राच्छिल *a.* (*f.* —ला) Dry, waterless.

प्रच्यवः *m.* 1 Fall, ruin. -2 Improvement, advancement, growth. -3 Withdrawal.

प्रच्यवनं *n.* 1 Departing, withdrawal. -2 Loss, deprivation. -3 Oozing, dropping.

प्रच्युत *p. p.* (*f.* —ता) 1 Fallen off or from. -2 Strayed, deviated. -3 Displaced, degraded. -4 Banished, expelled. -5 Routed, put to flight.

प्रच्युतिः *f.* 1 Withdrawal. -2 Loss, deprivation, falling down from. -3 Fall, ruin.

प्रजः *m.* A husband.

प्रजनः *m.* 1 Impregnating, begetting, production -2 The impregnation of cattle -3 Bringing forth, bearing. -4 A generator, progenitor.

प्रजननं *n.* 1 Procreation, generation, conception in the womb. -2 Birth, delivery. -3 Semen. -4 The male or female organ of generation. -5 Offspring. -6 Pregnancy of cattle.

प्रजनिका *f.* A mother.

प्रजनुकः *m.* The body.

प्रजल्पः *m.* Prattle, gossip, heedless or frivolous words (used in greeting a lover). [Prattle, gossip.

प्रजल्पनं *n.* 1 Talking, speaking. -2

प्रजविन् *a.* Rapid, swift speedly. -*m.* An express, a courier.

प्रजा *f.* (Changed to प्रजस् at the end of a Bah. compound, when the first member is अ, सु or दुस्) 1 Procreation, generation, birth, production. -2 Offspring, progeny, children, brood (of animals). -3 Posterity, descendants. -4 A creature. -5 Subjects, people, mankind. -6 Semen. -Comp. —अंतकः *m.* Yama, the God of death. —ईशः, -ईश्वरः *m.* The lord of men, a king, sovereign. —काम *a.* Desirous of progeny. -कारः *m.* The author of the creation. —तंतुः *m.* A line of descendants; lineage, race. -दानं *n.* Silver. -नाथः *m.* 1 An epithet of Brahman (*m.*). -2 A king, sovereign, prince. -निषेकः *m.* 1 Impregnation, seed (implanted in the womb). -2 Offspring. —पतिः *m.* 1 The God presiding over creation. -2 An epithet of Brahman (*m.*). -3 An epithet of the ten lords of created beings first created by Brahman(*m.*). -4 An epithet of Visvakarman, the architect of Gods. -5 The sun. -6 A king. -7 A son-in-law. -8 An epithet of Vishnu. -9 A father, progenitor. -10 The penis. -11 A sacrifice. —पालः, -पालकः *m.* A king, sovereign. —पालिः *m.* An epithet of Siva. —सृज् *m.* An epithet of Brahman (*m.*). —हित *a.* Beneficial to children or pepople. (-तं *n.*) Water.

प्रजागरः *m.* 1 Lying awake at night, sleeplessness. -2 Vigilance, carefulness. -3 A guardian. -4 An epithet of Krishna.

प्रजात *p. p.* (*f* —ता) Born, produced. -ता *f.* A woman who has borne a child.

प्रजातिः *f.* 1 Procreation, production. -2 Delivery. -3 Procreative power. -4 Travail, labour.

प्रजावत् *a.* 1 Having subjects or children. -2 Pregnant. -3 Abounding in progeny, prolific -ती *f.* 1 A brother's wife. -2 A matron, mother. -3 An elder brother's wife.

प्रजिनः *m.* Wind, air.

प्रजीवनं *n.* Livelihood, subsistence.

प्रजुष्ट *a.* (*f.* —ष्टा) Attached or devoted to; intent on.

प्रज्ञ *a.* (*f.* —ज्ञा) 1 Wise, intelligent, learned. -2 (At the end of comp.) Conversant with. —ज्ञः *m.* A wise or learned man.

प्रज्ञप्तिः *f.* 1 Agreement, engagement. -2 Teaching, communicating. -3 A doctrine. -4 Intellect.

प्रज्ञा *f.* 1 Intelligence, understanding, intellect, wisdom. -2 Discernment, judgment. -3 Device, design. -4 A wise or learned woman. -5 N. of the Goddess Sarasvatī. -Comp. —चक्षुस् *a.* Blind. (-*m.*) An epithet of Dhritarâshtra. (-*n.*) The mind's eye, mental eye; the mind. —वादः *m.* A wise saying. —वृद्ध *a.* Old in wisdom. —सहाय *a.* Intelligent, wise.

प्रज्ञात *p. p.* (*f.* —ता) 1 Known, understood. -2 Distinguished, discerned. -3 Distinct, clear. -4 Famous, well-known.

प्रज्ञानं *n.* 1 Intelligence, knowledge, wisdom. -2 A mark, token. -3 Discernment, judgment.

प्रज्ञाल (*f.* —ला), प्राज्ञिन् (*f.* -नी), प्रज्ञिल (*f.* —ला) *a.* Wise, intelligent, prudent.

प्रज्ञु *a.* Bow-legged, bandy-legged.

प्रज्वलनं *n.* 1 Blazing up, burning. -2 Kindling.

प्रज्वलित *p. p.* (*f.* —ता) 1 Being in flames, flaming, blazing. -2 Bright, shining. -3 Burnt.

प्रडीनं *n.* 1 Flying in every direction. -2 Flying forward. -3 Taking flight.

प्रण *a.* (*f.* —णा) Old, ancient.

प्रणखः *m.* The point of a nail.

प्रणत *p. p.* (*f.* —ता) 1 Bending, stooping. -2 Saluting. -3 Humble. -4 Skilful, clever. -5 Crooked.

प्रणतिः *f.* 1 A salutation, obeisance. -2 Submissiveness, humility. -3 Bending, stooping.

प्रणदनं *n.* Sounding, a sound.

प्रणयः *m.* 1 Espousing, seizing (as in marriage.) -2 Love, affection, attachment. -3 A wish, desire. -4 Friendship, intimacy. -5 Familiarity, confidence. -6 Favour, kindness. -7 An entreaty, request. -8 Reverence, obeisance. -9 Final beatitude. -10 Conduct, guidance. (प्रणयेन Confidentially, candidly; without reserve or ceremony. प्रणयात् Openly, frankly). -Comp. -अपराधः *m.* An offence against friendship or love. —उन्मुख *a.* Impatient through love. —कलहः *m.* A lover's quarrel, a mock or feigned quarrel. —कुपित *a.* Feigning anger. —कोपः *m.* Feigned anger of a mistress towards her lover. —प्रकर्षः *m.* Excessive love, intense attachment. —भंगः *m.* 1 Breach of friendship. -2 Faithlessnes . -वचनं *n.* A declaration of love. —विमुख *a.* 1 Averse from love. -2 Disinclined to friendship. —विहतिः *f.*, -विघातः *m.* Non-compliance, refusal (of a request &c.).

प्रणयनं *n.* 1 Bringing, fetching. -2 Conducting, conveying. -3 Carrying out, performing. -4 Writing, composing. -5 Sentencing, awarding ; as in दंडस्य प्रणयनं. -6 Adducing. -7 Distributing.

प्रणयिन् *a.* (*f.* —नी) 1 Loving, kind, attached. -2 Beloved. -3 Desirous of. -4 Familiar, intimate. -*m.* 1 A friend, companion, favourite. -2 A husband, lover. -3 A supplicant, suitor. -4 A worshipper ; devotee. —नी *f.* A mistress, beloved wife. -2 A female friend.

प्रणवः *m.* 1 The sacred syllable *om.* -2 A kind of musical instrument (drum or tabor). -3 An epithet

executed or accomplished. -3 To be setted or fixed.

प्रणोदः *m.* 1 Driving. -2 Directing.

प्रतत *p. p.* (*f.* —ता) 1 Spread over, covered. -2 Stretched out, diffused. —तं *ind.* Continuously.

प्रततिः *f.* 1 Extension, expansion, diffusion. -2 A creeper.

प्रतन *a* (*f.* —नी) Old, ancient.

प्रतनु *a.*(*f.*-नू or-न्वी) 1 Very thin or minute, delicate. -2 Very small, limited, narrow. -3 Slender, emaciated. -4 Insigmificant, trifling.

प्रतपनं *n.* Warming, making warm.

प्रतप्त *p. p.* (*f.* —प्ता) 1 Heated. -2 Hot. -3 Tortured.

प्रतमकः *m.* A kind of asthma.

प्रतरः *m.* Crossing, going over.

प्रतर्कः *m.* Conjecture, supposition.

प्रतर्कणं *n.* 1 Reasoning, discussion. -2 Doubt. -3 Logic.

प्रतलं *n.* One of the seven divisions of the lower world. -लः *m.* The open hand with the fingers extended.

प्रतानः *m.* 1 A shoot, tendril. -2 A low spreading plant. -3 Branching out, ramification. -4 Epilepsy. -5 Extension.

प्रतानिनी *f.* A spreading creeper.

प्रतापः *m.* 1 Heat, warmth. -2 Glowing heat. -3 Splendour, brilliancy. -4 Dignity, glory. -5 Courage, heroism. -6 Vigour, energy. -7 Ardour, zeal.

प्रतापनं *n.* 1 Burning, heating. -2 Paining; inflicting punishment. -नः *m.* N. of a hell.

प्रतापवत *a.* 1 Glorious, dignified. -2 Valorous, powerful, mighty. —*m.* 1 An epithet of Siva. -2 Of Vishnu.

प्रतारः *m.* 1 Carrying or bearing over. -2 Deceit, fraud. [postor.

प्रतारकः, प्रतारित *m.* A cheat, an impostor.

प्रतारणं *n.* 1 Carrying over. -2 Deceiving, cheating. —णा *f.* Deceit, knavery, roguery, hypocrisy.

प्रतारित *a.* (*f.* —ता) Cheated, deceived.

प्रति *ind.* 1 As a prefix to verbal themes it means (*a*) In the direction of. (*b*) In return, back again. (*c*) In opposition to, against. (*d*) Upon, down upon.

As a prefix to nouns not immediately derived from verbs it means (*a*) Likeness, resemblance. (*b*) Opposite, of the opposite side, as in प्रतिबल which means ' the opposing force'. (*c*) Rivalry ; as in प्रतिचंद्रः *m.* ' A rival moon.'

As a separable preposition (with acc.) it means(*a*) Towards, to. (*b*) Against, in opposition to, opposite. (*c*) In comparison with, on a par with, in proportion to. (*d*) In the vicinity of, at, by, in, on. (*e*) At the time, about, during. (*f.*) In favour of, to the lot of. (*g*) In each, in or at every, severally (used in a distributive sense) as in वृक्षं वृक्षं प्रति सिंचति. (*h*) With reference to, in relation to, regarding, about, as to. (*i*) According to, in conformity with. (*j*) Before, in the presence of. (*k*) For, on account of.

As a separable preposition (with abl.) it means either (*a*) A representative of, in place of, instead of. (*b*) In exchange or return for, as in तिलेभ्यः प्रति यच्छति माषान.

As the first member of Avyayibhâva compounds it means (*a*) In or at every ; as in प्रतिसंवत्सरं 'every year', प्रतिक्षणं every moment ; प्रत्यहं every day. (*b*) Towards, in the direction of, as in प्रत्यग्नि शलभा डयंते. Some times used as the last member of Avyayí. comp. to signify ' a little'; as in सूपप्रति, शाकप्रति.

-Comp. —अक्षरं *ind.* At every syllable or letter. —अग्नि *ind.* Towards the fire. -अंगं *n.* A secondary or minor limb (of the body), as the nose. -2 A division, chapter.-3 Every limb. -4 A weapon. (—गं *ind.*) 1 On or at every limb of the body. -2 For every subdivision. -3 In each case (in grammar). -अनंतर *a.* 1 Being in immediate neighbourhood. -2 Standing nearest (as an heir). -3Immediately following, closely connected with. (-रं *ind.*) 1 Immediately after. -2 Next in succession. —अनिलं *ind.* Towards or against the wind. —अनीक *a.* 1 Hostile, opposed, inimical. -2 Opposing. (-कः *m.*) An enemy. (-कं *n.*) 1 Hostility, hostile attitude or position,-2 A hostile army.-3 (In Rhet.) The figure of sheech in which somebody unable to avenge himself on his enemy is represented as doing harm to somebody else connected with the enemy, and by doing such a harm proving his enemy's superiority. प्रत्यनीकमशक्तेन प्रतीकारे रिपोर्यदि । तदीयस्य तिरस्कारस्तस्यैवोत्कर्षसाधकः * साहित्यदर्पण. *e. g.* मध्येन तनुमध्या मे मध्यं जितवतीत्ययं । इभकुंभौ भिनत्त्यस्याः कुंचकुंभनिभौ हरिः . —अनुमानं *n.* A contrary deduction. -अंत *a.* Contiguous, adjacent. (-तः *m.*) 1 A border, frontier. -2 A bordering country ; especially, a country occupied by barbarians or Mlechchhas. —अपकारः *m.* Retaliation, injury in return. -अब्दं *ind.* Every year. —आमित्र *a.* Hostile. (-त्रः *m.*) An enemy. (-त्रं *ind.*) Towards an enemy. —अर्कः *m.* A mock sun. —अवयवं *ind.* 1 In every limb. -2 In every particular, in detail. —अवर *a.* 1 Lower, less honoured. -2 Very low or degrading, very insignificant. —अश्मन् *m.* Red chalk. —अहं *ind.* Every day, daily ; day by day. —आकारः *m.* A scabbard, sheath. —आघातः *m.* 1 A counter-stroke. -2 Reaction. —आचारः *m.* Suitable conduct or behaviour. —आत्मम् *ind.* Singly, severally. —आत्मक *a.* Belonging to oneself. -आदित्यः *m.* A mock-sun. -आरंभः *m.* 1 A recommenncement, second beginning. -2 Prohibition. —आशा *f.* 1 Hope, expectation. -2 Trust, confidence. —उत्तरं *n.* A reply. -उलूकः *m.* 1 A crow. -2 A bird resembling an owl. —ऋचं *ind.* In each *Rik.* —एक *a.* Each, each one, every single one. (—कं *ind.*) 1 One by one, one at a time, singly, in every one, to every one. —कंचुकः *m.* An adversary. —कंठं *ind.* 1 Severally, one by one.-2Near the throat. —कश, —कष *a.* Not obeying the whip. —कायः *m.* 1 An effigy, image. -2 An adversary. -3 A target, butt, mark. —कितवः *m.* An opponent in a game. —कूपः *m.* A moat, ditch. —कूल *a.* 1 Unfavourable, contrary, hostile, opposite. -2 Harsh, unpleasant, disagreeable. -3 Inauspicious. -4 Contradictory. -5 Reverse, inverted. -6 Cross, peevish, stubborn. —कूलं *ind.* 1 Adversely, contrarily.-2 In inverted order. -क्षणं *ind.* At every moment or instant ; constantly. —गजः *m.* A hostile elephant.-गात्रं *ind.* In every limb. -गिरिः *m.* 1 An opposite mountian. -2 An inferior mountain. -गृहं,—गेहं *ind.* In every house. —ग्रामं *ind.* In every village. -चंद्रः *m.* A mock-moon.-चरणं

ind. 1 In every (Vedic) school or branch. -2 At every foot-step. -छाया *f.* 1 A reflected image, reflection, shadow.-2 An image, picture.-जंघा *f.* The forepart of the leg. -जिह्वा,-जिह्विका *f.* The soft palate. —तंत्रं *ind.* According to each Tantra or opinion. —तंत्रसिद्धांतः *m.* A conclusion adopted by one of the disputants only. —त्र्यहं *ind.* For three days at a time. —दिनं *ind.* Every day. —दिशं *ind.* In every direction, all round, everywhere. —देशं *ind.* In every country. -देहं *ind.* In every body. —दैवतं *ind.* For every deity. -द्वंद्वः *m.* 1 An antagonist, opponent, rival. -2 An enemy. (-द्वं *n.*)Opposition, hostility. —द्वंद्विन् *a.* 1 Hostile, inimical. -2 Adverse -3 Rivalling, vying with. (-*m.*)An opponent, adversary, rival. -द्वारं *ind.* At every gate. —धुरः *m.* A horse harnessed by the side of another. -नप्तृ *m.* A great-grandson. -नव *a.* 1 New, young, fresh. -2 Newly blown or budded. —नाडी *f.* A branch-vein. —नायकः *m.* The adversary of the hero of any poetie composition; as रावण in the Râmáyana, शिशुपाल in Mágha Kávya &c. —पक्ष *a.* Like, similar. (-क्षः *m.*) 1 The opposite side, party or faction; hostility. -2 An enemy, rival, often used in comp. in the sense of 'equal' or 'similar'. -3 A defendant or respondent (in law). -पाक्षित *a.* 1 Containing a contradiction. -2 Nullified by a contradictory premiss;(as a *hetu* in न्याय). -पाक्षिन् *m.* An opponent, adversary. —पथं *ind.* Along the road, towards the way. -पदं *ind.* 1 At every step. -2 At every place, everywhere. -3 Expressly. -4 In every word. —पादं *ind.* In each quarter. —पात्रं *ind.* As regards each part or character; प्रतिपात्रमाधीयतां यत्नः * शाकुंत. 1 'Let care be taken of each character'. —पाप *a.* Requiting evil for evil. -पु (-पू-) रुषः *m.* 1 A like or similar man. -2 A substitute, deputy. -3 A companion. -4 The effigy of a man pushed by thieves into the interior of a house before entering it themselves (to ascertain if any body is awake). -5 An effigy in general. (-षं *ind.*) Man by man, for each man. -पूर्वाह्णं *ind.* Every forenoon. —प्रभातं *ind.* Every morning. —प्राकारः *m.* An outer wall or rampart. —प्रियं *n.* A kindness or service in return —बंधुः *m.* An equal in rank or station. —बल *a.* 1 Able, powerful.-2 Equal in strength. (-लं *n.*) 1 A hostile army. -2 Strength. —बाहुः *m.* The forepart of the arm. -बिं (-विं-) बः *m.*, -बं *n.* 1 A reflection, reflected image. -2 An image, a picture. —भट *a.* Vying with, rivalling. (-टः *m*) 1 A rival, an opponent. -2 A warrior on the opposite side. —भय *a* 1 Fearful, terrible, frightful. -2 Dangerous. (-यं *n.*) A danger. -मंडलं *n.* 1 A secondary disc (of the sun &c.). -2 An eccentric orbit. —मल्लः *m.* An antagonist, a rival.-माया *f.* A counter-spell or charm. -मासं *ind.* Every month, monthly. —मित्रं *n.* An enemy, adversary. —मुख *a.* 1 Standing before the face, facing. -2 Near, present. (—खं *n.*) A secondary plot or incident in a drama which tends either to hasten or retard the catastrophe. (—खं *ind.*)1 Towards. -2 In front, before. —मुद्रा *f.* A counter-seal. —मुहूर्तं *ind.* Every moment. —मूर्तिः *f.* An image, a likeness. —रथः *m.* An adversary in war (lit. in fighting in a war-chariot). —राजः *m.* A hostile king. —रात्रं*ind.* Every night. —रूप *a.* 1 Corresponding, similar. -2 Beautiful. -3 Suitable, proper. (-पं *n.*) A piecture, a likeness. —रूपकं *n.* 1 A picture, an image. -2 A forged edict. -3 A reflection. —लक्षणं *n.* A mark, sign, token. —लिपिः *f.* A transcript, written copy. —लोम *a.* 1 Contrary to the natural order, inverted, reverse (opp. अनुलोम). -2 Contrary to caste (said of the children of a woman who is of a higher caste than her husband). -3 Hostile. -4 Low, base. -5 Left (वाम). -6 Obstinate, perverse. 7 Unpleasant. (-मं *n.*) Any injurious or unpleasant act. (-मं*ind.*) Inversely, invertedly. —लोमकं *n.* Inverted order. -वत्सरं *ind.* Every year. -वर्षं*ind.* Every year. —वस्तु *n.* An equivalent, a counter-part. -2 Anything given in retnrn. -3 A parallel. -वस्तूपमा*f.* The figure of spaech in which, in two sentences, the resemblance of which is implied, the same common attribute is differently expressed. प्रतिवस्तूपमा सास्या-द्वाक्ययोर्गम्यसाम्ययोः । एकोऽपिधर्मः सामान्यो यत्र निर्दिश्यते पृथक्*साहित्यदर्पण. 10. —वातः *m.* A contrary wind. (-तं *ind.*) Against the wind. -वासरं *ind.* Every day. —वेदं *ind.* In or for every Veda. —विषं *n.* An antidote. —विष्णुकः *m.* The 'Muchakunda' tree. -वीरः *m.* An antagonist. -वेलं *ind.* On every occasion. -वेशः *m.* 1 A neighbouring house, neighbourhood. -2 A neighbour -वेशिन् A neighbour. -वेश्मन् *n.* A neighbour's house. -वेश्यः *m.* A neighbour. -वैरं *n.* Revenge. -शब्दः *m.* 1 Echo, reverberation. -2 A roar. -शशिन् *m.* A mock-moon. -शाखं *ind.* For every branch or school (of the Veda). -संवत्सरं *ind.* Every year. -सव्य *a.* In an inverted order. —सायं *ind.* Every evening. —सूर्यः, -सूर्यकः *m.* 1 A mock-sun. -2 A lizard, chameleon. -सेना *f.* A hostile army. —स्थानं *ind.* In every place, every-where. -स्रोतस् *ind.* Against the stream. -हस्तः, —हस्तकः *m.* A deputy, an agent.

प्रतिक *a.* (*f.*-का) Worth or bought for a 'Kárshâpana'.

प्रतिकरः *m.* Requital, compensation.

प्रतिकर्तव्य, -कार्य *a.* (*f.* —व्या, —र्या) 1 To be retaliated, returned or paid (as a debt &c.). -2 To be counteracted. -3 To be cured or treated (by a physician). -र्यं *n.* Retribution, retaliation.

प्रतिकर्तृ *a.* (*f.* -र्त्री) Requiting, recompensing. -*m.* An opponent, adversary.

प्रतिकर्मन् *n.* 1 Retaliation. -2 Remedy, counter-action. -3 Personal decoration, dress, toilet. -4 Opposition, hostility.

प्रतिकर्षः *m.* 1 Aggregation. -2 Anticipation (of a word) occurring later on.

प्रतिकषः *m* 1 A leader. -2 An assistant. -3 A messenger (वार्ताहर).

प्रति (-ती-) कारः *m.* 1 Requital, reward, return. -2 Revenge, retaliation. -3 Counter-action, prevention, remedy. -4 Opposition, obstruction. -5 Help. -6 A kind of treaty where one party requites the services of the other.

प्रति (-ती-) काशः *m.* 1 A reflection. -2 Appearance, resemblance.

प्रतिकुंचित *a.* (*f.* —ता) Bent, curved.

प्रतिकृत *p. p.* (*f.* —ता) 1 Returned, repaid, retaliated.–2 Counter-acted, remedied –तं *n.* 1 Recompense. -2 Opposition.

प्रतिकृतिः *f.* 1 Revenge, retaliation. –2 Return, requital. –3 A reflected image. -4 A likeness, statue, picture, an image. -5 A substitute. -6 Resistance.

प्रतिकृष्ट *p. p.* (*f.* —ष्टा) 1 Twice ploughed. -2 Repulsed, rejected. -3 Hidden.-4 Low, abject. [any one.

प्रतिकोपः, प्रतिक्रोधः *m.* Anger against

प्रतिक्रमः *m.* Inverted order.

प्रतिक्रिया *f.* 1 Recompense, requital. -2 Retaliation, revenge. -3 Remedying, removal. -4 Opposition. -5 Personal decoration; dress. -6 Protection. -7 Help. -8 A fence.

प्रतिक्रुष्ट *a.* (*f.*—ष्टा) Miserable, poor.

प्रतिक्षयः *m.* A guard, an attendant.

प्रतिक्षिप्त *p. p.* (*f.* —प्ता) 1 Turned away, dismissed. -2 Repelled, repulsed, opposed. -3 Abused, reviled.–4 Sent, despatched.–5 Hurt, injured. -6 Despised. -7 Falsely accused. —प्तं *n.* Medicine.

प्रतिक्षुतं *n.* Sneezing.

प्रतिक्षेपः *m.*, प्रतिक्षेपणं *n.* 1 Not acknowledging, rejection. -2 Opposing, contradiction. -3 Contest.

प्रतिख्यातिः *f.* Renown, fame.

प्रतिगत *p. p.* (*f.* —ता) Flying backward and forward, wheeling about. [return.

प्रतिगमनं *n.* Returning, going back,

प्रतिगर्जना *f.* Roaring against, answering roar..

प्रतिगर्हित *p. p.* (*f.* —ता) Blamed, reviled.

प्रतिगृहीत *p. p.* (*f.* —ता) 1 Taken, received, accepted. -2 Admitted, assented to. -3 Married.

प्रतिग्रहः *m.* 1 Receiving, accepting. -2 Receiving or accepting a donation. -3 The right of accepting a donation.-4 The right of receiving gifts (which is a peculiar prerogative of Brâhmaṇas). -5 A present, donation. -6 A receiver (of a gift). -7 Kind or friendly reception. -8 Favour, grace. -9 Marrying. -10 Listening to. -11 The rear of an army. -12 A spittoon. -13 The sun near the moon's node.

प्रतिग्रहणं *n.* 1 Receiving presents. -2 Reception. -3 Marrying. 4 -A vessel.

प्रतिग्रहीतृ *m.* 1 A receiver.-2 A husband ; one who marries.

प्रतिग्राहः *m.* 1 Accepting gifts. -2 A spitting-pot, spittoon.

प्रतिग्राह्य *a.* (*f.* —ह्या) Acceptable, admissible.

प्रतिघः *m.* 1 Opposition. -2 Combat, mutual beating. -3 Anger. -4 Fainting. -5 An enemy.

प्रति (-ती-) घातः *m.* 1 Warding off, repulse. -2 Resistance. -3 A counter-blow. -4 Rebound, reaction. -5 Prohibiting.

प्रतिघातनं *n.* 1 Repulsing, warding off. -2 Killing, slaughter.

प्रतिघ्नं *n.* The body. [or revenge.

प्रतिचिकीर्षा *f.* Desire of retaliation

प्रतिचिंतनं *n.* Meditating upon.

प्रतिच्छदनं *n.* A cover, a piece of cloth for covering.

प्रतिच्छंदः, प्रतिच्छंदकः *m* 1 A likeness, picture, statue. -2 A substitute.

प्रतिच्छन्न *p. p.* (*f.* -न्ना) 1 Covered, enveloped. -2 Hidden. -3 Furnished with. -4 Hemmed in. -5 Clothed or dressed. [tion.

प्रतिच्छेदः *m.* Resistance, opposi-

प्रतिजागरः *m.* Watchfulness, vigilance.

प्रतिजीवनं *n.* Resuscitation.

प्रतिज्ञा *f.* 1 Admission, acknowldgment. -2 A vow, promise, solemn declaration. -3 A statement, affirmation. -4 (In Nyâya phil.)A proposition, statement of the proposition to be proved, the first member of the five-membered Indian syllogism. -5 A plaint, an indictment. -Comp. —अंतरं *n.* (In logic.) A subsequent proposition on failure of the first. -पत्रं,-पत्रकं *n.* A bond, written contract or document. —विराधः *m.* 1 Breaking an agreement, acting contrary to promise. -2 denial of a logical proposition. —संन्यासः *m.* 1 Breaking a promise. -2 (In logic) Abandonment of the original proposition.

प्रतिज्ञात *p. p.* (*f.* —ता) 1 Declared, asserted. -2 Promised, agreed. -3 Acknowledged. -4 Agreeable, desirable. -तं *n.* A promise.

प्रतिज्ञानं *n.* 1 Asserting, affirmation. -2 A promise. -3 Admission. -4 Bringing forward or adducing.

प्रतितरः *m.* An oarsman, a sailor.

प्रतिताली *f.* The key of a door.

प्रतिदर्शनं *n.* Seeing, perceiving.

प्रतिदानं *n.* 1 Restoration, giving back, restitution (as of a deposit). -2 An exchange. [Splitting.

प्रतिदारणं *n.* 1 Fighting, battle. -2

प्रतिदिवन *m.* 1 A day. -2 The sun.

प्रतिदृष्ट *p. p.* (*f.* —ष्टा) 1 Beheld. -2 Come in sight, become visible.

प्रतिधानं *a.* 1 Putting on. -2 Taking measures.

प्रतिधावनं *n.* 1 Assailing, attacking.

प्रतिध्वनिः, प्रतिध्वानः *m.* An echo, reverberation. [cast.

प्रतिध्वस्त *p. p.* (*f.* —स्ता) Down-

प्रतिनंदनं *n.* 1 Congratulating, welcoming. -2 Thanks-giving. [tion.

प्रतिनादः *m.* An echo, a reverbera-

प्रति (-नी-) नाहः *m.* A flag, banner.

प्रतिनिधि *m.* 1 A representative, substitute. -2 A deputy, vicegerent. -3 Substiution. -4 A surety. -5 An image, picture. [destined.

प्रतिनियत *a.* (*f.* -ता) Settled, pre-

प्रतिनियमः *m.* A general rule.

प्रतिनिर्जित *p. p.* (*f.*-ता) 1 Vanquished. -2 Rescinded.

प्रतिनिर्दिष्ट्य *a.* (*f.*—ष्टया) That which, though before expressed, is repeated in order to state something more about it.

प्रतिनिर्यातनं *a.* 1 Retribution, retaliation. -2 Returing, giving back.

प्रतिनिवर्तनं *n.* Returning. -2 Turning away from.

प्रतिनिविष्ट *a.* (*f.* —ष्टा) Perverse, obstinate, hardened. -Comp. -मूर्खः *m.* A perverse fool, a confirmed blockhead.

प्रतिनोदः *m.* Repelling, repulse.

प्रतिपत्तिः *f.* 1 Getting, gain. -2 Perception, consciousness, (right) knowledge. -3 Assent, compliance, acceptance. -4 Admission, acknowledgment. -5 A statement. -6 Undertaking, beginning, commencing. -7 A proceeding, knowledge of what to do : procedure. -8 Performance, doing, proceeding with. -9 Resolution, determination. -10 News, intelligence. -11 Honour, mark of distinction, respectful behaviour. -12 A method, means, remedy. -13 Intellect, intelligence. -14 Use, application. -15 Promotion, exaltation. -16 Fame. -17 Boldness, confidence. -18 Conviction, proof. -19 A rite from which no advantage accrues. -Comp. —पटहः *m.* A kind of kettle-drum. —विशारद *a.* Knowing how to act; skilful, clever.

प्रतिपद् *f.* 1 Access, way. -2 Beginning, commencement. -3 Intelligence, intellect. -4 The first day of a lunar fortnight. -5 A kettle-drum. -6 An introductory stanza. -7 Rank. -Comp. —चंद्रः *m.* The new moon particularly revered and saluted by people. —तूर्यं *n.* A kind of kettle-drum.

प्रतिपदा,-दी *f.* The first day of a lunar fortnight.

प्रतिपन्न *p. p.* (*f.* —न्ना) 1 Gained. -2 Done, accomplished. -3 Undertaken, commenced. -4 Promised, engaged. -5 Assented to; admitted, to be accepted as acknowledged. -6 Known, understood. -7 Answered. -8 Proved. -9 Approached. -10 Conquered. -11 Proficient in.

प्रतिपादक *a.* (*f.* —दिका) 1 Granting, bestowing. -2 Demonstrating, proving, establishing. -3 Explaining, illustrating. -4 Promoting, advancing. -5 Effective, accomplishing.

प्रतिपादनं *n.* 1 Giving, bestowing. -2 Demonstrating, establishing. -3 Explaining, expounding, illustrating. -4 Effecting, accomplishing, fulfilment. -5 Causing, producing. -6 Repeated action -7 Commencement. -8 Giving back. -9 Entrusting, appointing.

प्रतिपादयितृ *m.* 1 A teacher, instructor. -2 A bestower. -3 A demonstrator.

प्रतिपादित *p. p.* (*f.* —ता) 1 Given, bestowed, presented. -2 Proved, demonstrated. -3 Explained, expounded. -4 Declared, asserted. -5 Caused, produced.

प्रतिपालकः *m.* A protector, guardian.

प्रतिपालनं *n.* 1 Guarding, defending. -2 Observance, following, practising.

प्रतिपीडनं *n.* Oppressing, molesting.

प्रतिपूजनं *n.*, प्रतिपूजा *f.* 1 Doing homage, showing respect. -2 Mutual salutation.

प्रतिपूरणं *n.* 1 Filling, filling up. -2 Injecting (a fluid &c.).

प्रतिप्रणामः *m.* An obeisance in return.

प्रतिप्रदानं *n.* 1 Returning, restoring. -2 Giving in marriage.

प्रतिप्रयाणं *n.* Return, retreat.

प्रतिप्रसवः *m.* 1 A counter-exception, an exception to an exception. -2 A contrary effect.

प्रतिप्रस्थानं *n.* Joining the opposite party; going over to the enemy.

प्रतिप्लवनं *n.* Leaping back.

प्रतिफलः *m.*, प्रतिफलनं *n.* 1 A reflection, an image or shadow. -2 Remuneration, requital. -3 Retaliation.

प्रतिफुल्लक *a.* (*f.* —का) Blossoming, full blown.

प्रतिबद्ध *p. p.* (*f.* —द्धा) 1 Bound, tied. -2 Connected with. -3 Hindered. -4 Set, inlaid. -5 Furnished with, possessing. -6 Entangled. -7 Kept at a distance. -8 Excluded, cut off. -9 (In phil.) Invariably and inseparably connected and implied (as fire in smoke).

प्रतिबंधः *m.* 1 Binding or tying to. -2 Obstruction, obstacle. -3 Resistance. -4 Blockade, siege. -5 Connection. -6 Cessation. -7 (In phil.) Invariable and inseparable connection.

प्रतिबंधक *a.* (*f.* —धिका) 1 Binding, fastening. -2 Obstructing, hindering. -3 Resisting, opposing. —कः *m.* A branch, shoot.

प्रतिबंधनं *n.* 1 Binding, tying. -2 Confinement. -3 Obstructing, impeding.

प्रतिबंधिः, —धी *f.* 1 An objection. -2 An argument which equally affects the other side; (प्रतिबंधिः *m.* also in this sense).

प्रतिबाधनं *n.* Repelling, keeping off, rejecting.

प्रतिबिंबनं *n.* 1 Reflection. -2 Comparison as in दृष्टांतः पुनरेतेषां सर्वेषां प्रतिबिंबनं.

प्रतिबिंबित *a.* (*f.* -ता) Reflected, mirrored.

प्रतिबुद्ध *p. p.* (*f.* —द्धा) 1 Awakened, roused. -2 Restored to consciousness. -3 Opened, blown. -4 Illuminated, enlightened. -5 Recognized, observed. -6 Celebrated, known.

प्रतिबुद्धिः *f.* 1 Awakening. -2 Hostile purpose or intention.

प्रतिबोधः *m.* 1 Waking, being awakened. -2 Perception, knowledge. -3 Instruction. -4 Reason, reasoning faculty. -5 Recollection.

प्रतिबोधनं *n.* 1 Awakening. -2 Instructing, informing. -3 Knowledge, enlightenment.

प्रतिबोधित *p. p.* (*f.* -ता) 1 Awakened. -2 Instructed, taught.

प्रतिभा *f.* 1 An appearance, a look. -2 Light, splendour. -3 Intellect, understanding. -4 Genius. -5 That power whereby the poet sees the subjects of his poem as steeped in beauty and gives his readers in apt language a vivid picture of the beauty he has seen, vivid imagination. -6 An image, reflection.

प्रतिभागः *m.* 1 Division. -2 A share, portion (given to a king as a tax).

प्रतिभात *p p.* (*f.* —ता) 1 Bright, luminous. -2 Known, understood.

प्रतिभानं *n.* 1 Light, splendour. -2 Intellect or understanding, brightness of conception. -3 Readiness of wit, presence of mind. -4 Confidence, boldness.

प्रतिभावः *m.* Corresponding disposition.

प्रतिभाषा *f.* An answer, a reply.

प्रतिभासः *m.* 1 Occuring to, or flashing across, the mind at once; (sudden) perception. -2 A look, appearance. -3 Illusion.

प्रतिभासनं *n.* Look, appearance.

प्रतिभिन्न *p. p.* (*f.* —न्ना) 1 Pierced through. -2 Closely connected with. -3 Divided.

प्रतिभूः *m.* A bail, surety, guarantee.

प्रतिभेदः *m.* 1 Splitting, dividing, [-2 Discovery.

प्रतिभेदनं *n.* 1 Piercing, penetrating. -2 Cutting, splitting. -3 Putting out (as the eyes). -4 Dividing.

प्रतिभोगः *m.* Enjoyment

प्रतिमा *f.* 1 An image, a likeness, statue, figure, an idol. -2 Resemblance, similitude. -3 A reflected image. -4 A measure, extent. -5 The part of an elephant's head between the tusks. -6 A symbol. -Comp. —गत *a.* Present in an idol. —परिचारकः *m.* An attendant upon an idol.

प्रतिमानं *n.* 1 A model, pattern. -2 An image, idol. -3 Likeness, similarity. -4 A weight -5 The part of an elephant's head between the tusks. -6 A reflection. -7 A picture.

प्रतिमुक्त *p. p.* (*f.* —क्ता) 1 Put on, worn. -2 Tied, fastened. -3 Armed. accoutred. -4 Liberated, released. -5 Restored, returned. -6 Flung, hurled, thrown, cast.

प्रतिमोक्षः *m.*, प्रतिमोक्षणं *n.* Liberation, deliverance.

प्रतिमोचनं *n.* 1 Loosening. -2 Requital, retaliation, retribution. -3 Liberation, release.

प्रतियत्नः *m.* 1 An effort, endeavour. -2 Preparation, elaboration. -3 Making complete or perfect. -4 Imparting a new quality or virtue. -5 Wish, desire. -6 Opposition, resistance. -7 Retaliation, revenge. -8 Making prisoner. -9 Favour. -10 Acting well or properly. -11 Comprehension.

प्रतियातनं *n.* Requital, retaliation; as in वैरप्रतियातनं. [statue.

प्रतियातना *f.* A picture, an image,

प्रतियानं *n.* Return, retreat.

प्रतियोगः *m.* 1 Being or forming a counter-part of anything. -2 Opposition, resistance. -3 Contradiction. -4 Co-operation. -5 An antidote, a remedy.

प्रतियोगिक *a.* Antithetical, correlative, relative.

प्रतियोगिन् *a.* (*f.* —नी) 1 Opposing, impeding. -2 Being or forming a counter-part (of anything); as a घट is the प्रतियोगी of घटाभाव. -3 Co-operating with. -4 Equally matched. —*m.* 1 An adversary, opponent. -2 A counterpart, match. -3 A partner. -4 An object dependent upon another. -5 A counter-part.

प्रतियोधः, प्रतियोधिन्, प्रतियोद्धृ *m.* An adversary, opponent.

प्रतिरक्षणं *n.*, प्रतिरक्षा *f.* Safety, preservation, protection.

प्रतिरंभः *m.* Passion, rage. [Echo.

प्रतिरवः *m.* 1 Quarrel, contest. -2

प्रतिरुद्ध *p. p.* (*f.* —द्धा) 1 Impeded, obstructed. -2 Interrupted. -3 Impaired. -4 Disabled. -5 Blockaded.

प्रतिरोधः *m.* 1 Impediment, hindrance. -2 Siege, blockade. -3 An opponent. -4 Concealing. -5 Theft, robbery. -6 Censure.

प्रतिरोधक, प्रतिरोधिन्, -द्धृ *a.* 1 An opponent. -2 A robber, thief. -3 An obstacle.

प्रतिरोधनं *n.* Opposing, obstructing.

प्रतिलंभः *m.* 1 Getting, obtaining, receiving. -2 Censure, abuse.

प्रतिलाभः *m.* Taking back, taking, getting.

प्रतिवचनं *n.* 1 An answer, reply. -2 An echo. -3 A dependent or final clause in a sentence. [echo.

प्रतिवचस् *n.* 1 An answer. -2 An

प्रतिवर्तनं *n.* Returning.

प्रतिवसथः *m.* A village.

प्रतिवहनं *n.* Leading back.

प्रतिवाक्यं *n.* A reply.

प्रतिवाच् *f.* 1 An answer, reply. -2 Calling out to.

प्रतिवादः *m.* 1 A rejoinder, reply. -2 Refusal, rejection.

प्रतिवादिन् *m.* 1 A defendant, respondent (in law). -2 An opponent in general.

प्रतिवापः *m.* Addition of substances to medicines either during or after decoction.

प्रतिवारः *m.*, प्रतिवारणं *n.* Warding or keeping off. [news, tidings.

प्रतिवार्ता *f.* Account, information,

प्रतिवासिन् *a.* (*f.* —नी) Dwelling near, neighbouring. —*m.* A neighbour. [fending.

प्रतिविघातः *m.* Striking back, de-

प्रतिविधानं *n.* 1 Counteracting, taking steps against.-2 Arrangement, array. -3 Prevention. -4 Substituted ceremony. [remedy.

प्रतिविधिः *m.* 1 Retaliation. -2 A

प्रतिविशिष्ट *a.* (*f.* —ष्टा) Most excellent.

प्रतिवेशः *m.* 1 A neighbour. 2 The house of a neighbour.-3 Neighbourhood

प्रतिवेशिन *a.* (*f.* —नी) A neighbour.

प्रतिवेश्यः *m.* A neighbour.

प्रतिवेष्टित *p. p.* (*f.* -ता) Rolled back, reverted.

प्रतिव्यूढ *p. p.* (*f.* -ढा) Drawn out in battle-array.

प्रतिव्यूहः *m.* 1 Arraying an army against an enemy.-2 A multitude, collection.

प्रतिशमः *m.* Cessation.

प्रतिशयनं *n.* The act of lying down without food before a deity to secure some desired object.

प्रतिशापः *m.* A curse for a curse ; a curse in return.

प्रतिशासनं *n.* 1 Giving orders ; sending on an errand. -2 Despatching an inferior after calling him to attend. -3 Counter-manding. -4 A rival command or authority.

प्रतिशिष्ट *p. p.* (*f.* —ष्टा) 1 Ordered, sent. -2 Dismissed, rejected. -3 Famous, celebrated.

प्रतिश्या *f.*,प्रतिश्यानं *n.*, प्रतिश्यायः *m.* A catarrh or cold.

प्रतिश्रयः *m.* 1 A shelter, asylum -2 A house, residence. -3 An asembly. -4 A sacrificial hall. -5 Help, assistance. -6 A promise. -7 A receptacle.

प्रतिश्रवः *m.* 1 Assent, agreement, promise. -2 An echo.

प्रतिश्रवणं *n.* 1 Listening to.-2 Promising, agreeing. -3 A promise.

प्रतिश्रुत्, प्रतिश्रुतिः *f.* 1 A promise. -2 An echo, reverberation.

प्रतिश्रुत *p. p.* (*f.* —ता) Promised, agreed.assented to.-तं *n.* A promise.

प्रतिषिद्ध *p. p.* (*f.* —द्धा) 1 Forbidden, prohibited, disallowed. -2 Contradicted.

प्रतिषेधः *m.* 1 Keeping or warding off. -2 Prohibition. -3 Denial, refusal. -4 Contradiction. -5 A negative particle. -6 An exception. -Comp -उपमा *f.* One of the several kinds of Upamá mentioned by Dandin.

प्रतिषेधनं *n.* 1 Keeping or warding off. -2 Prohibition. -3 Denial, refusal.

प्रतिष्कः, प्रतिष्कसः *m.* A spy, messenger. [A whip.

प्रतिष्कशः *m.* 1 A spy, emissary. -2

प्रतिष्कषः *m.* A whip, leather thong.

प्रतिष्टंभः *m.* Obstruction,resistance, obstacle.

प्रतिष्ठा *f.* 1 Situation, position. -2 A house, residence. -3 Fixity, strength,firm foundation.-4 Basis, foundation, site ; as in गृहप्रतिष्ठा.-5 A support. -6 High position, preeminence,high authority. -7 Fame, celebrity.-8 Installation, inauguration. -9 Attainment of a desired object. -10 Tranquillity, rest. -11 A receptacle. -12 The earth. -13 The consecration of an idol or image. -14 A boundary.

प्रतिष्ठानं *n.* 1 Basis, foundation. -2 Site, situation. -3 A resting-place. -4 The foundation of a city. -5 N. of a town at the confluence of the Ganges and Yamuná. -6 N. of a town on the Godâvari and capital of Sáliváhana.

प्रतिष्ठित *p. p.* (*f.* —ता) 1 Erected. -2 Fixed, established. -3 Placed, situated. -4 Inaugurated, consecrated. -5 Completed. -6 Prized, valued. -7 Famous. -8 Settled, determined. -9 Included. -10 Established in life, married. -11 Conversant with.

प्रतिसंविद् *f* An accurate knowledge of anything.

प्रतिसंहार: *m.* 1 With-drawing. -2 Diminution, compression. -3 Inclusion. -4 Yielding, giving up.

प्रतिसंहृत *p. p.* (*f.* —ता) 1 Taken back, withdrawn. -2 Comprehended, included. -3 Compressed.

प्रतिसंक्रम: *m.* 1 Re-absorption. -2 Reflection

प्रतिसंख्या *f.* Consciousness.

प्रतिसंचर: *m.* 1 Moving back-wards. -2 Re-absorption. -3 The re-absorption (of the world) back into 'Prakriti' *i.e.* universal destruction.

प्रतिसंधानं *n.* 1 Joining together, uniting. -2 The period of transition between two ages. -3 A means, remedy. -4 Restraint of feelings or passions. -5 Praise.

प्रतिसंधि: *m.* 1 Reunion. -2 Entering into the womb. -3 The period of transition between two ages. -4 Cessation.

प्रतिसमाधानं *n.* Cure, remedy.

प्रतिसमासनं *n.* 1 Being a match for. -2 Resisting, withstanding.

प्रतिसर: *m.*, -रं *n.* 1 A cord worn round the wrist or neck as an amulet. -2 An ornament. -3 A watch-guard. —र: *m.* 1 A servant, follower. -2 A bracelet, marriage-string. -3 A garland, wreath. -4 Day-break. -5 The rear of an army. -6 A form of incantation. -7 Heaiing or dressing a wound. —रा *f.* 1 A female servant. -2 A thread, fillet.

प्रतिसर्ग: *m.* 1 Secondary creation (as by the agents of one Supreme Being). -2 Dissolution. -3 Continued creation out of primitive matter.

प्रतिसांधानिक: *m.* A bard, panegyrist.

प्रतिसारणं *n.* 1 Dressing the edges of a wound. -2 An instrument used for anointing a wound.

प्रतिसीरा *f* A screen, curtain, a wall of cloth.

प्रतिसृष्ट *p. p.* (*f.* —ष्टा) 1 Sent, despatched. -2 Celebrated. -3 Repulsed. -4 Intoxicated.

प्रतिस्नात *p. p.* (*f.* —ता) Bathed.

प्रतिस्नेह: *m.* Love in return.

प्रतिस्पंदनं *n.* Throbbing.

प्रतिस्पर्धा *f.* Rivalry, emulation.

प्रतिस्पर्धिन् *m.* A rival, competitor.

प्रतिहत *p. p.* (*f.* —ता) 1 Struck or beaten back. -2 Driven away. -3 Opposed, obstructed. -4 Sent, despatched. -5 Hated, disliked. -6 Disappointed, frustrated. -7 Fallen, overthrown. -Comp. —मति *a* Hating, disliking.

प्रतिहति: *f.* 1 Striking or knocking back. -2 Rebound, recoil. -3 Disappointment, frustration. -4 Anger.

प्रतिहननं *n.* Striking or knocking back, returning a blow.

प्रतिहरणं 1 Avoiding, shunning. -2 Striking back, repelling.

प्रतिहस्तिन् *m.* The keeper of a brothel.

प्रति (-ती-) हार: *m.* 1 Striking back. -2 A door, gate. -3 A porter, door-keeper. -4 A juggler. -5 A juggling trick. -6 (In gram.) The hard contact of the tongue with the edge of the teeth in pronouncing dental letters. —री *f.* A female door-keeper. -Comp. —भूमि: *f.* The threshold

(of a house &c.). -रक्षी *f.* A female door-keeper.

प्रतिहारकः *m.* A juggler.

प्रतिहिंसा *f.* Retaliation, revenge.

प्रतिहार्यं *n.* Juggling, jugglery.

प्रतिहित *p. p.* (*f.* —ता) 1 Fitted to, put close to.

प्रतीक *a.* (*f.* —का) 1 Directed towards.-2 Inverted, reverse.-3 Unfavourable, adverse. -कः *m.* 1 A limb, member. -2 A part, portion.-कं *n.* 1 An image. -2 Mouth, face. -3 The front (of anything) -4 The first word (of a verse, sentence &c.).

प्रतीकारः *m.* See प्रतिकारः.

प्रतीकाशः *m.* See प्रतिकाशः.

प्रतीक्षणं *n.*, प्रतीक्षा *f.* 1 Waiting for. -2 Expectation, hope. -3 Regard, attention. -4 Looking at, considering. -5 Fulfilment, observance (of a vow, promise &c).

प्रतीक्ष्य *pot. p.* (*f.* —क्ष्या) 1 To be waited for. -2 Worthy of regard. -3 Respectable. -4 To be maintained or to be fulfilled.

प्रतीघातः *m.* See प्रतिघातः.

प्रतीची *f.* The west. -Comp. —ईशः *m.* N. of Varuna.

प्रतीचीन *a.* (*f.* —ना) 1 Western, westerly. -2 Future, subsequent.

प्रतीच्छकः *m.* A receiver.

प्रतीच्य *a.* (*f.* —च्या) Living in the west; western, westerly.

प्रतीत *p. p.* (*f.* —ता) 1 Set forth, started. -2 Gone by. -3 Believed, trusted. -4 Proved, established. -5 Acknowledged, recognised. -6 Called, named. -7 Renowned, famous. -8 Firmly resolved. -9 Convinced. -10 Believing, trusting -11 Pleased, delighted. -12 Respectful. -13 Clever, wise.

प्रतीति *f.* 1 A settled belief. -2 Knowledge, clear or distinct perception. -3 Fame, renown. -4 Respect. -5 Delight.

प्रतीत्त *a.* (*f.* —त्ता) Given back, restored.

प्रतीनाहः *m.* A flag, banner.

प्रतीन्धकः *m.* N. of a country called विदेह.

प्रतीप *a.* (*f.* -पा) 1 Contrary, unfavourable, adverse. -2 Reverse, out of order. -3 Against the current, retrograde. -4 Disagreeable. -5 Disobedient, obstinate, perverse. -6 Averted. -7 Hindering.—पः *m.* N. of a king, father of Santanu and grand-father of Bhishma. —पं *n.* The figure of speech (I) in which things usually taken as standards of comparison (*i. e.* are उपमानs) are themselves turned into objects of comparison (*i. e.* into उपमेयs); or (II) in which things which are standards of comparison (*i. e.* which are usually उपमानs) are declared to be useless, because the purpose that they (*i. e.* उपमानs) serve can very well be served by other things (*i. e.* by the उपमेयs). *ind.* 1 On the contrary. -2 In an inverted order. -3 Against, in opposition to. -Comp. -ग *a.* 1 Going against. -2 Adverse, unfavourable. —गमनं *n.*, —गतिः *f.* Retrograde motion. —तरणं *n.* Going or sailing against the stream. —दर्शिनी *f.* A woman. —वचनं *n.* 1 Contradiction. -2 A perverse or evasive manner of speaking.

प्रतीरं *n.* A shore, bank.

प्रतीवापः *m.* 1 Adding to, inserting (as an ingredient). -2 Fluxing metals. -3 An epidemic disease, a plague.

प्रतीवेश See प्रतिवेश. प्रतीहार See प्रतिहार. प्रतीहास See प्रतिहास.

प्रतीवेशिन् *a.* See प्रतिवेशिन्.

प्रतीहारी *f.* 1 A female door-keeper. -2 A door-keeper in general.

प्रतीहास: *m.* A fragrant oleander.

प्रतुद: *m.* 1 An epithet of a class of birds (such as hawks, parrots, crows &c.). -2 An instrument for pricking.

प्रतुष्टि: *f.*, प्रतोष: *m.* Gratification, satisfaction.

प्रतूर्ण *a.* (*f.* -र्णा) Speedy, quick, fleet.

प्रतोद: *m.* 1 A goad.-2 A long whip. -3 A pricking instrument.

प्रतोली *f.* A principal street through a town.

प्रत्त *p. p.* (*f.* -त्ता) 1 Given, given away, presented, offered. -2 Given in marriage, married.

प्रत्न *a.* (*f.* —त्ना) 1 Old, ancient. -2 Former. -3 Traditional, customary.

प्रत्यक् *ind.* 1 In an opposite direction. -2 Against. -3 Westward, to the west of (with abl.). -4 In the interior. -5 Formerly, in old times.

प्रत्यक्ष *a.* (*f.* —क्षा) 1 Perceptible (to the eye); visible, in sight, before the eye.-2 Cognizable by any organ of sense.-3 Distinct, evident, clear. -4 Direct, immediate.-5 Explicit, express. -6 Corporeal. —क्षं *n.* 1 Perception, apprehension by the senses considered as a प्रमाण or mode of proof. -2 Explicitness, distinctness. (The forms प्रत्यक्षं, प्रत्यक्षेण, प्रत्यक्षत:, प्रत्यक्षात् are used adverbially to signify (1) In the presence of. -2 Openly, publicly. -3 Directly.-4 Personally.-5 Explicitly, clearly.-6 Literally. प्रत्यक्षे In the sight of. -Comp. —ज्ञानं *n.* The knowledge obtianed by direct perception. —दर्शन:, —दर्शिन् *m.* An eye-witness. —दृष्ट *a.* Personally seen. -प्रमा *f.* Correct knowledge obtained by direct perception through the senses.—प्रमाणं *n.* 1 An ocular proof, evidence of the senses.-2 An organ of perception.-फल *a.* Having evident or visible consequences. -वादिन् *m.* A Buddhist who admits no other evidence than ocular proof or perception. —विहित *a.* Explicitly enjoined. —सिद्ध *a.* Determined by ocular proof.

प्रत्यक्षता *f.*,-त्वं *n.* 1 Perceptibility, ocular proof. -2 Standing face to face. -3 Explicitness.

प्रत्यक्षिन् *m.* An eye-witness.

प्रत्यग्र *a.* (*f.* -ग्रा) 1 Fresh, young new. -2 Repeated.-3 Pure. -Comp. —वयस् *a.* Young in age, youthful.

प्रत्यंच्, प्रत्यच् *a.* (*f.* —प्रतीची or according to some प्रत्यंची also).1 Turned or directed towards. -2 Being behind. -3 Following, subsequent. -4 Turned away, turning back. -5 Western. -6 Interior. -7 Equal to, a match for. —*m.* 1 The individual soul. -2 Future time. -Comp. प्रत्यगक्षं *n.* An inner organ. प्रत्यगात्मन् *m.* The individual soul. प्रत्यगानंद *a.* Inwardly joyful. प्रत्यगाशापति: *m.* The regent of the western direction, an epithet of Varuna. प्रत्यगुदच् *f.* The north-west. प्रत्यग्दक्षिणत: *ind.* Towards the south-west. प्रत्यग्दृश् *f.* An inward glance, a glance directed inwards. प्रत्यङ्मुख *a.* 1 Facing the west. -2 Having the face averted. प्रत्यक्स्रोतस् *a.* Flowing towards the west. (-*f.*) An epithet of the river Narmadâ.

प्रत्यंचित *a.* (*f.* —ता) Honoured, worshipped.

प्रत्यभिज्ञा *f.* Knowing, recognition.

प्रत्यभिज्ञात *p. p.* (*f.* —ता) Recognised.

प्रत्यभिज्ञानं *n.* 1 Recognition. -2 A token of recognition (in return).

प्रत्यभिभूत *p. p.* (*f.*—ता) Overcome, conquered.

प्रत्यभियुक्त *p. p.* (*f.* -क्ता) Accused [in return.

प्रत्यभियोगः *m.* A counter-charge; an accusation in return.

प्रत्यभिवादः *m.*, प्रत्यभिवादनं *n* Returning a salutation.

प्रत्यभिस्कंदनं *n.* A counter-plaint or [charge.

प्रत्ययः *m.* 1 Conviction, settled belief. -2 Faith, confidence. -3 Conception, notion, opinion.-4 Surety, certainty. -5 Knowledge, experience. -6 A means of action. -7 Fame, renown.-8 An affix or suffix. -9 An oath. -10 A dependant, assistant; associate. -11 A usage, practice. -12 A hole. -13 Intellect. -14 (With Buddhists) A co-operating cause. -15 Religious contemplation. -16 A house-holder who keeps a sacred fire. -Comp. -कारक, —कारिन् *a.* Convincing. (-णी *f.*) A seal, signet-ring.

प्रत्ययित *a.* (*f.* -ता) 1 Relied upon, confided in.-2 Trusty; confidential.

प्रत्ययिन् *a.* 1 Trusting, believing. -2 Trustworthy, confidential.

प्रत्यर्थ *a.* (*f.* -र्था) Useful, expedient. -र्थं *n.* 1 A reply, an answer.-2 Hostility, opposition.

प्रत्यर्थकः *m.* An opponent.

प्रत्यर्थिन् *a.* (*f.* -नी) 1 Hostile, inimical to. -2 Emulating. —*m.* 1 An opponent; enemy. -2 An equal, match. -3 (In law) A defendant. -4 An obstacle or impediment.

प्रत्यर्पणं *n.* Giving back, restoring.

प्रत्यर्पित *p. p.* (*f.* —ता) Restored, given back.

प्रत्यवमर्शः,-र्षः *m.* 1 Profound meditation or contemplation. -2 Counsel, advice. -3 A counter-conclusion.-4 Patience, forbearance.

प्रत्यवरोधनं *n.* Obstruction, hindrance.

प्रत्यवसानं *n.* Eating or drinking.

प्रत्यवसित *a.* (*f.* -ता) Eaten, drunk, consumed.

प्रत्यवस्कंदः *m.*, -दनं *n.* (In law) Admitting a fact but qualifying it in such a manner that it may not appear as a count of accusation.

प्रत्यवस्थातृ *m.* An opponent, adversary.

प्रत्यवस्थानं *n.* 1 Removal. -2 Hostility, opposition. -3 *Status quo.*

प्रत्यवहारः *m.* 1 Withdrawal. -2 Universal destruction; dissolution (of the world).

प्रत्यवायः *m.* 1 Decrease; diminution. -2 An obstacle. -3 A contrary course, contrariety. -4 A sin, sinfulness. -5 Disappointment. -6 Disappearance of an existing thing. -7 Non-production of what does not exist.

प्रत्यवेक्षणं *n.*, प्रत्यवेक्षा *f.* Taking care of, regard for, looking after.

प्रत्यस्तमयः *m.* 1 Setting (of the sun). -2 End, cessation.

प्रत्याक्षेपक *a.* (*f.* -पिका) Deriding, treating scornfully.

प्रत्याख्यात *p. p.* (*f.* —ता) 1 Refused, denied. -2 Prohibited. -3 Set aside, rejected. -4 Repulsed. -5 Surpassed.

प्रत्याख्यानं *n.* 1 Repulse, rejection. -2 Denial, disavowal.-3 Disregard. -4 Reproach. -5 Refutation.

प्रत्यागतिः *f.* Coming back, return.

प्रत्यागमः *m.*, प्रत्यागमनं *n.* 1 Return, coming back. -2 Arrival.

प्रत्यादानं *n.* Receiving back, resumption.

प्रत्यादिष्ट *p. p.* (*f.* —ष्टा) 1 Rejected, repulsed. -2 Removed, set aside. -3 Thrown into the shade. -4 Warned, cautioned. -5 Declared.

प्रत्यादेशः *m.* 1 A command. -2 Refusal, denial, rejection, repulse. -3 Obscuring, putting to shame or throwing into shade. -4 Caution, warning. -5 Divine caution, supernatural warning. -6 Reproach.

प्रत्यानयनं *n.* Bringing back, recovery.

प्रत्यापत्तिः *f.* 1 Return. -2 Indifference to worldly objects.

प्रत्याम्नायः *m.* 1 The fifth member of a complete syllogism (the repetition of the first proposition निगमन). -2 Contrary determination.

प्रत्यायः *m.* 1 A toll, tax. -2 Revenue, income.

प्रत्यायनं *n.* 1 Leading home (a bride); marrying. -2 Setting (of the sun). —नं *n.*, —ना *f.* 1 Producing confidence. -2 Explaining. -3 Proving, demonstrating.

प्रत्यायितः *m.* A confidential agent.

प्रत्यालीढं *n.* A particular attitude in shooting.

प्रत्यावर्तनं *n.* Returning, coming back.

प्रत्याश्वस्त *p. p.* (*f.* —स्ता) Consoled, revived, refreshed.

प्रत्याश्वासः *m.* 1 Respiration, recovery (of breath). -2 Consolation.

प्रत्याश्वासनं *n.* Consolation.

प्रत्यासत्तिः *f.* 1 Close proximity or contiguity (in time or space). -2 Close contact. -3 An analogy.

प्रत्यासन्न *p. p.* (*f.* —न्ना) 1 Proximate, contiguous. -2 Imminent.

प्रत्यास (-सा-) रः *m.* 1 The rear of an army. -2 A form of array, one array being behind another.

प्रत्याहत *a.* (*f.* —ता) Distracted, repelled.

प्रत्याहरणं *n.* 1 Bringing or taking back. -2 Withholding. -3 Restraining the organs of sense.

प्रत्याहारः *m.* 1 Marching back, retreat. -2 Withholding. -3 Restraining the organs of sense. -4 Dissolution of the world. -5 (In gram.) The inclusion of several letters or affixes into one syllable, effected by combining the first letter of a 'Sutra' with its final letter, or in the case of several 'Sutras', with the final letter of the last member : *e. g.* अण्, अच्, हल्, अल् &c. -6 Abridgment.

प्रत्युक्त *p. p.* (*f.* —क्ता) Answered, replied.

प्रत्युक्तिः *f.* A reply, an answer.

प्रत्युच्चारः *m.*, प्रत्युच्चारणं *n.* Repetition.

प्रत्युज्जीवनं *n.* 1 Reviving, restoring to life, resuscitation (fig. also). -2 Coming to life.

प्रत्युत *ind.* 1 On the contrary. -2 Rather, even. -3 On the other hand.

प्रत्युत्क्रमः *m.*, —क्रमणं *n.*, —क्रान्तिः *f.* 1 An undertaking. -2 Preparations for war. -3 Marching out to attack an enemy. -4 A secondary act or effort tending to a main object. -5 The first step in any business.

प्रत्युत्थानं *n.* 1 Rising against. -2 Preparing for war. -3 Rising from one's seat to welcome a visitor. -4 Preparing for any undertaking.

प्रत्युत्थित *p. p.* (*f.* —ता) Risen to meet or encounter (a friend, foe, &c.).

प्रत्युत्पन्न *p. p.* (*f.*-न्ना) 1 Reproduced, regenerated. -2 Prompt, quick. -3 (In math.) Multiplied. -4 Present, existing at present. -न्नं *n.* Multiplication. -Comp. -मति *a.* 1 Possessed of presence of mind; ready-witted. -2 Bold, confident. -3 Subtle, sharp.

प्रत्युदाहरणं *n.* A counter-illustration, an example to the contrary.

प्रत्युद्गत *p. p.* (*f.* -ता) 1 Risen from one's seat to greet or welcome a guest. -2 Gone forth against.

प्रत्युद्गतिः *f.*, प्रत्युद्गमः *m.*, प्रत्युद्गमनं *n.* Going out or rising from one's seat to meet or greet a guest.

प्रत्युद्गमनीयं *n.* A clean pair of garments.

प्रत्युद्धरणं *n.* 1 Recovering, re-obtaining. -2 Raising up again.

प्रत्युद्यमः *m.* 1 Counterbalance, counterpoise. -2 A counteraction.

प्रत्युद्यात *a.* (*f.* —ता) 1 Risen from one's seat to greet a visitor.-2 Gone forth against.

प्रत्युपपन्न *a.* (*f.* —न्ना) See प्रत्युत्पन्न

प्रत्युपमानं *n.* 1 A counterpart of a resemblance. -2 A pattern, model. -3 A counter-comparison ; a counter standard of comparison ; उपमानस्यापि सखे प्रत्युपमानं वपुस्तस्याः *विक्रमो*2.3.

प्रत्युपलब्ध *p. p.* (*f.* -ब्धा) Got back, recovered.

प्रत्युपवेशः, -षः *m.*, -वेशनं *n.* Besetting any one in order to bring him to compliance.

प्रत्युपस्थानं *n.* Vicinity, neighbourhood.

प्रत्युपहारः *m.* 1 A respectful offering. -2 Giving back, restoring.

प्रत्युप्त *p. p.* (*f.* —प्ता) 1 Inlaid, set with, studded. -2 Sown. -3 Fixed, firmly fixed or lodged.

प्रत्युषः *m.*, प्रत्युषस् *n.* Morning, day-break, dawn.

प्रत्यूषः *m.*, -षं *n.* Day-break, morning, dawn. —षः *m.* 1 The sun. -2 N. of one of the eight Vasus.

प्रत्यूषस् *n.* Day-break, morning, dawn.

प्रत्यूहः *m.* Impediment, obstacle.

प्रथ् 1 A. (प्रथते, प्रथित) 1 To increase (as wealth &c.). -2 To spread abroad (as fame, rumour &c.) -3 To become celebrated. -4 To appear, arise, come to light. -5 To occur (to mind),

प्रथ् 10 U. (प्रथयति,-ते, प्रथित) 1 To spread abroad, proclaim.-2 To display, indicate. -3 To enlarge, augment. -4 To disclose.-5 To spread, extend. -6 To throw, cast.

प्रथनं *n.* 1 Spreading.-2 Scattering. -3 Throwing, projecting.-4 Evincing, displaying. -5 A place where anything is spread.-6 Celebrating, proclaiming.

प्रथम *a.* (*f.* —मा) (Nom. *pl. m.* प्रथमे or प्रथमाः)1 First, foremost.-2 Chief, most excellent or eminent. -3 Earliest, most ancient. -4 Previous, former. -5 (In gram.) The first person (= third person according to European phraseology). —मः *m.* 1 The first (third) person. -2 The first consonant of a class. —मा *f.* The nominative case. —मं *ind.* 1 First, firstly, at first.-2 Previously, formerly. -3 At once,immediately. -4 Before.-5 Newly,recently. प्रथमं... अनंतरं or ततः or पश्चात First, afterwards. प्रथमात् Firstly, for the first time. प्रथमतः 1 At first,firstly.-2 Previously. -3 Immediately. -4 Before, in preference to (*gen.*).-Comp.-आश्रमः *m.* The first of the four stages in the religious life of a Bráhmana; *i. e.* Brahmacharya. —इतर *a.* The second.—कल्पः *m.* 1 The best course to adopt. -2 An excellent suggestion or idea.-कल्पित *a.* 1 First thought out. -2 First in rank or importance. —ज *a.* 1 First-born. -2 Original, primary.-दर्शनं *n.* 1 First sight. -पुरुषः *m.* The first person (= the third person according to the English system of treating Sanskrit grammar). —यौवनं *a.* Early youth or age; youthful state. —वयस् *n.* Early age, youth. —वृत्तांतः *m.* The antecedents, former circumstances. —वैयाकरणः *m.* 1 The most distinguished grammarian. -2 A beginner in grammar. —साहसः *m* The first of the three degrees of punishment or fine. —सुकृतं *n.* Former kindness or service.

प्रथा *f.* 1 Fame, celebrity.

प्रथित *p. p.* (*f.* -ता) 1 Increased, extended. -2 Published, proclaimed. -3 Shown, manifested, evinced. -4 Renowned, well-known.-5 Devoted to. -6 Spread, stretched.

प्रथितिः *f.* Celebrity, fame.

प्रथिमन् *m.* Breadth, greatness, magnitude.

प्राथिविः *f.* The earth.

प्रथिष्ठ *a.* (*f.* -ष्ठा) Largest, widest, broadest ; (superl. of पृथु).

प्रथीयस् *a.* (*f.* —सी) Larger, wider, broader ; (compar. of पृथु),

प्रथु *a.* Wide, wide-spread.

प्रथुकः *m.* Rice parched and flattened.

प्रद *a.* (At the end of comp.) 1 Giving, bestowing, yielding. -2 Liberal, bountiful. —दा *f.* A gift.

प्रदक्षिण *a.* (*f.* —णा) 1 Being placed on the right; moving to the right. -2 Respectful, reverential. -3 Auspicious, favourable. —णः *m.*, —णा *f.*, —णं *n.* A reverential salutation made by walking round a person or an idol so that the right hand is towards the object of salutation. —णं *ind.* 1 From left to right. -2 Towards the right side, so that the right side is always turned towards the person or object circumambulated. -3 Towards the south.-Comp. —अर्चिस् *a.* Having the flames turned towards the right. (-*f.*) Flames turned towards the right. —क्रिया *f.* Going round from left to right, keeping the right side towards one as a mark of respect. —पट्टिका *f.* A court-yard.

प्रदग्ध *a.* (*f.* -ग्धा) Burnt, consumed.

प्रदत्त *a.* (*f.* —त्ता) The same as प्रत्त.

प्रदरः *m.* 1 Rending, tearing. -2 A fracture, crack, crevice. -3 Breach, hole. -3 The dispersion of an army. -4 An arrow. -5 A particular disease of women.

प्रदर्पः *m.*, प्रहासिः *f.* Pride, arrogance.

प्रदर्शः *m.* 1 Look, appearance. -2 Direction, order.

प्रदर्शक *a.* 1 Showing, exhibiting. -2 Foretelling. -3 Presenting. -4 Proclaiming. -5 Teaching, instructing. —कः *m.* 1 A prophet. -2 A teacher. -3 A doctrine, precept.

प्रदर्शनं *n.* 1 Look, appearance. -2 Manifesting, show, exhibition. -3 Teaching, explaing. -4 An example. -5 Prophesying.

प्रदर्शित *p. p.* (*f.* —ता) 1 Exhibited, manifested. -2 Made known. -3 Taught. -4 Explained, declared.-5 Foretold.

प्रदलः *m.* An arrow.

प्रदवः *m.* Burning, inflaming.

प्रदव्यः *m.* A forest conflagration.

प्रदातृ *m.* 1 A giver, donor. -2 A

liberal man. -3 One who gives a daughter in marriage. -4 An epithet of Indra.

प्रदानं *n.* 1 Giving, bestowing, offering. -2 Giving away in marriage. -3 Instructing. -4 A donation, present.-5 A goad. -6 An oblation. -Comp. —शूरः *m.* A very munificent man, donor. [present.

प्रदानकं *n.* An offering, a donation,

प्रदायं *n.* A present, gift.

प्रदिः, प्रदेयः *m.* A present, gift.

प्रदिश् *f.* 1 Pointing out. -2 An order, command. -3 A direction, quarter. -4 An intermediate point of the compass such as नैर्ऋती, आग्नेयी, ऐशानी and वायवी.

प्रदिष्ट *p. p.* (*f.* —ष्टा) 1 Shown, pointed out. -2 Directed, ordered. -3 Ordained, appointed.

प्रदीपः *m.* 1 A lamp, light (fig. also) -2 Elucidation; especially at the end of titles of works; as in महाभाष्यप्रदीपः, काव्यप्रदीपः &c.

प्रदीपकः *m.*, प्रदीपिका *f.* A small lamp.

प्रदीपन *a.* (*f.* —नी) 1 Kindling. -2 Illuminating. -3 Stimulating, exciting. —नं *n.* The act of kindling or lighting. —नः *m.* A kind of mineral poison.

प्रदीप्त *p. p.* (*f.* —प्ता) 1 Kindled, lighted, illuminated. -2 Blazing, shining. -3 Raised, expanded. -4 Stimulated, excited (as hunger &c.). -Comp. —प्रज्ञ *a.* Of a bright or sharp intellect.

प्रदीप्तिः *f.* Lustre, brilliancy.

प्रदुष्ट *p. p.* (*f.* —ष्टा) 1 Spoiled, corrupted. -2 Wicked, sinful.-3Licentious, wanton.

प्रदूषणं *n.* 1 Corrupting, spoiling. -2 Polluting, defiling.

प्रदूषित *p. p.* (*f.* —ता) 1 Corrupted, spoiled, depraved. -2 Polluted

प्रदेय *a.* 1 To be given, imparted, or communicated. -2 To be given in marriage. —यः *m.* gift.

प्रदेशः *m.* 1 Pointing out, indicating. -2 A place, region, territory, district. -3 A span measured from the tip of the thumb to that of the fore-finger. -4Decision, determination. -5 A wall. -6 An example (in grammar).

प्रदेशनं *n.*1 Pointing out -2 Advice, instruction. -3 A gift. an offering (to Gods, superiors &c.)

प्रदेश (-शि-)नी *f.* The fore-finger, the index finger.

प्रदेहः *m.* 1 Anointing, plastering, unction. -2 A plaster, thick ointment.

प्रदोषः *m.* 1 A fault, sin, offence. -2 Transgression, violation. -3 Disordered condition. -4 Evening; the first part of the night. -Comp. —आगमः *m.* Nightfall. —कालः, —समयः *m.*, -वेला *f.* Evening-time, nightfall. —तिमिरं *n.* The dusk of early night

प्रदोहः *m.* Milking. [God of love

प्रद्युम्नः *m.* An epithet of Cupid, the

प्रद्योतः *m.*1 Lighting, illuminating. -2 Light, lustre. -3 A ray of light. -4 N. of a king of Ujjayini, whose daughter Vatsa married.

प्रद्योतनं *n.* 1 Blazing, shining. -2 Light. —नः *m.* The sun.

प्रद्रवः *m.* Running.

प्रद्रावः *m.* 1 Running away, flight, retreat, escape. -2 Going quickly or fast.

प्रद्वार् *f.*, प्रद्वारं *n.* A place near a door or gate. [aversion.

प्रद्वेषः *m.*, प्रद्वेषणं *n.* Dislike, hatred,

प्रधनं *n.* 1 A fight, war, contest. -2

Spoil taken in battle. -3 Destruction. [A sternutatory.

प्रधमनं n. 1 Blowing in or into. -2

प्रधर्षः m. 1 Assaulting, attacking. -2 Outrage.

प्रधर्षणं n., —णा f. 1 An assault. -2 An outrage, insult.

प्रधर्षित p. p. (f. —ता) 1 Assaulted. -2 Injured. -3 Haughty.

प्रधान a. (f. —ना) 1 Chief, principal, pre-eminent; most excellent. -2 Prevalent, predominant. —नं n. 1 The most important thing; head, chief. -2 The source of the material world; the primary germ out of which all material appearances are evolved according to the Sánkhya philosophy. -3 The Supreme Spirit. -4 Intellect. -5 The principal member of a compound. —नः m., —नं n. 1 The principal attendant or companion of a king (his minister or confidant). -2 A noble, courtier -3 An elephant-driver. -4 The commander-in-chief.-Comp. —अंगं n. 1 The principal part of anything. -2 The chief member of the body. -3 The principal person in a state. —अमात्यः m. The prime-minister, premier. —आत्मन् m. An epithet of Vishnu. —धातुः m. The chief element of the body i. e. semen virile. —पुरुषः m. 1 The principal or most eminent person (in a state &c.). -2 An epithet of Siva. —मंत्रिन् m. The prime-minister. —वासस् n. A principal garment —वाससी n. dual The two chief garments. —वृष्टिः f. A heavy shower of rain.

प्रधावनः m. Air, wind. -नं n. Rubbing; rubbing or washing off.

प्रधिः m. 1 The periphery of a wheel. -2 A well.

प्रधी a. Pre-eminently intelligent. -f. Great intelligence.

प्रधूपित p. p. (f. -ता) 1 Fumigated, perfumed. -2 Heated, burned. -3 Inflamed. -4 Afflicted, distressed.-ता f. 1 A woman in trouble. -2 The quarter to which the sun proceeds.

प्रधृष्ट p. p. (f. —ष्टा) 1 Treated with contumely. -2 Proud, arrogant, haughty.

प्रध्यानं n. Deep thought, reflection.

प्रध्वंसः m. Utter destruction, total annihilation. -Comp. —अभावः m. Non-existence caused by destruction.

प्रध्वस्त p. p. (f- —स्ता) Annihilated, destroyed.

प्रनप्तृ m. The son of a grandson a great-grand-son.

प्रनष्ट a. (f. —ष्टा) 1 Lost. -2 Disappeared. -3 Perished, ruined, annihilated.

प्रनायकः m. (f. -का) Destitute of a leader or guide. [प्रणाली.

प्रनालः m., -ली f. See प्रणाल and

प्रनिघातनं n. Killing, slaughter.

प्रनृत्त a. (f. —त्ता) Dancing. —त्तं n. A dance.

प्रपक्षः m. The extremity of a wing (as of an army).

प्रपंचः m. 1 Display, manifestation. -2 Expansion, extension. -3 Amplification, explanation.-4 Diffuseness, copiousness -5 Manifoldness, diversity. -6 Heap, quantity. -7 A phenomenon. -8 Illusion, fraud. -9 The world considered as the expansion of the primary germ and as the scene of manifold action. -10 Analysis. -Comp. -बुद्धि a. Cunning, deceitful. —वचनं n. A prolix discourse, diffuse talk.

of Vishnu or the Supreme Being.

प्रणस *a.* (*f.*—सा) Having a prominent nose, large-nosed.

प्रणाडी *f.* Intervention, interposition, medium.

प्रणाद: *m.* 1 A loud noise, shout. -2 Roaring, a roar. -3 Neighing, braying. -4 A burst of applause; huzza. -5 A cry for help. -6 A particular disease of the ear (a buzzing sound in the ear).

प्रणाम: *m.* 1 Bending, stooping. -2 A reverential salutation, prostration, bow (used with dat.). -Comp. —अंजलि: *m.* A respectful salutation with the hands folded together.

प्रणायक: *m.* 1 A leader or commander (of an army). -2 A guide, head, chief.

प्रणाय्य *a.* (*f.* —य्या) 1 Dear, beloved. -2 Upright, straight-forward. -3 Disliked, disapproved. -4 Indifferent to worldly attachments.

प्रणाल: *m.*,—ली, प्रणालिका *f.* 1 A channel, water-course, drain. -2 Succession, uninterrupted series.

प्रणाश: *m.* 1 Cessation, loss, disappearance. -2 Death, destruction.

प्रणाशनं *n.* Destruction, annihilation.

प्रणिंसित *a.* (*f.* —ता) Kissed.

प्रणिधानं *n.* Employing, application, use. -2 Great effort, energy. -3 Profound religious meditation. -4 Respectful behaviour towards (with loc.). -5 Renunciation of the fruit of actions. -6 (With Buddhists) A prayer, an entreaty

प्रणिधि: *m.* 1 Observing, spying out. -2 Sending out spies. -3 A spy, an emissary. -4 An attendant, a follower. -5 Care, attention. -6 Entreaty, request.

प्रणिनाद: *m.* A deep sound.

प्रणिपतनं *n.*, प्रणिपात: *m.* 1 Falling at one's feet, prostration. -2 Salutation, reverential bow. -Comp. -पुर:-सरं, —पूर्वकं *ind.* With an obeisance. —रस: *m.* A magical formula pronounced over weapons.

प्रणिहित *p. p.*(*f.*-ता) 1 Laid on, applied. -2 Deposited. -3 Stretched forth. -4 Consigned, entrusted. -5 Having the attention fixed upon one object. -6 Determined, decided. -7 Cautious, wary. -8 Obtained, attained. -9 Spied out. -10 Applied, directed.

प्रणीत *p. p.* (*f.* —ता) 1 Advanced, presented. -2 Delivered, given, presented. -3 Brought into, reduced to. -4 Executed, performed. -5 Taught, prescribed. -6 Sent, discharged. -7 Brought to, set. -8 Written, composed. -9 Removed. -10 Agreeable or pleasing. -11 Inflicted (as punishment). —त: *m.* Fire consecrated by prayers. -ता *f.* A sacrificed vessel. —तं *n.* Anything cooked or dressed, such as a condiment.

प्रणुत *p. p.* (*f.* —ता) Praised, [lauded.

प्रणुत्त *p. p.* (*f.* —ता) 1 Driven away, repelled. -2 Scared away.

प्रणुन्न *p. p.* (*f.*-न्ना) 1 Driven or sent away. -2 Set in motion. -3 Scared away. -4 Shaking, trembling. -5 Sent, despatched.

प्रणेजनं *n.* 1 Washing or wiping away. -2 Bathing. -3 Water for washing.

प्रणेतृ *m.* 1 A leader. -2 A maker, creator. -3 The promulgator of a doctrine. -4 An author.

प्रणेय *a.* (*f.* —या) 1 Tractable, submissive, obedient. -2 To be

प्रपंचनं *n.* 1 Display, development. -2 A detailed explantion or amplification.

प्रपंचित *p. p.* (*f.* —ता) 1 Displayed. -2 Expanded, amplified. -3 Fully explained. -4 Erring, mistaken. -5 Deceived, tricked.

प्रपतनं *n.* 1 Flying forth or away. -2 Falling down, alighting. -3 Death, destruction. -4 A precipice.

प्रपदं *n.* 1 The forepart of the foot. -2 Tip of the toe.

प्रपदीन *a.* (*f.* —ना) Relating to the forepart of the foot.

प्रपन्न *p. p.* (*f.* -न्ना) 1 Reaching or going to. -2 Resorting to. -3 Seeking protection with, submissive to. -4 Adhering to. -5 Furnished with, possessed of. -6 Got, obtained. -7 Poor, distressed. -Comp. —पाल: *m.* An epithet of Krishna.

प्रपन्नाड: *m.* See प्रपुनाट.

प्रपर्णं *n.* A fallen leaf.

प्रपलायनं *n.* Flight, retreat.

प्रपा *f.* 1 A place where water is distributed to travellers or to cattle. -2 A well or cistern. -3 A supply of water. -4 A draught. -Comp. -पालिका *f.* A woman who distributes water to travellers. —वनं *n.* A cool grove.

प्रपाक: *m.* 1 Ripening (of a boil &c.). -2 Inflamation.

प्रपाठक: *m.* A lesson, lecture. -2 A chapter or subdivision of a work.

प्रपाणि: *m* 1 The forepart of the hand. -2 The palm of the extended hand.

प्रपात: *m.* 1 Going away, departure. -2 Falling down, a fall. -3 A sudden attack. -4 A cascade, waterfall. -5 A bank, shore. -6 A precipice. -7 Emission, discharge, as in वीर्यप्रपात. -8 Throwing oneself down from a rock. -9 A particular mode of flight.

प्रपातनं *n.* Throwing down (on the ground).

प्रपाथ: *m.* A road, way.

प्रपादिक: *m.* A peacock.

प्रपानं *n.* 1 Drinking. -2 The under part of a horse's upper lip.

प्रपानकं *n.* A kind of drink.

प्रपितामह: *m.* 1 A paternal great-grand-father. -2 An epithet of Krishna. -3 Of Brahman (*m.*). -4 Of the Supreme Spirit. -ही *f.* A paternal great-grand-mother.

प्रपितृव्य: *m.* A paternal grand-uncle.

प्रपीडनं *n.* 1 Pressing, squeezing. -2 An astringent.

प्रपीन (—न) *a.* (*f.* -ना, -ना) Swollen up, distended.

प्रपुत्र: *m.* A grandson.

प्रपुना (-न्ना-) ट:,-ड: *m.* N. of a tree. (चक्रमर्द).

प्रपूरणं *n.* 1 Filling, filling up, completing. -2 Inserting, injecting. -3 Satisfying, satiating.

प्रपूरित *p. p.* (*f.* —ता) Filled up.

प्रपौत्र: *m.* A great-grand-son. -त्री *f.* A great-grand-daughter.

प्रप्यायनं *n.* Swelling.

प्रफुल्त *p. p.* (*f.* —ल्ता) Blooming, blossomed, full-blown.

प्रफुल्ति: *f.* Blooming, blossoming.

प्रफुल्ल *p. p.* (*f.* —ल्ला) 1 Full-blown, blossoming, blooming. -2 Smiling. -3 Shining. -4 Gay, cheerful. -Comp. -नयन, -नेत्र, -लोचन *a.* Having eyes expanded with joy. —वदन *a.* Having a beaming or cheerful look.

प्रबद्ध *p. p.* (*f.* —द्धा) 1 Bound, fastened. -2 Stopped, suppressed, checked.

प्रबंद्धृ *m.* An author.

प्रबंधः *m* 1 A bond, tie. -2 Continuity, uninterrupted series or succession. -3 A continued or connected narrative or discourse. -4 Any literary work or composition. -5 Arrangement, plan, scheme, as in कपटप्रबंधः -Comp. —कल्पना *f*. A feigned story ; a work of imagination founded on fact.

प्रबंधनं *n*. Bond, tie.

प्रबभ्रः *m*. An epithet of Indra.

प्रब (-व-) र्ह *a*. (*f*. —र्ही) Most excellent, best.

प्रबल *a*. (*f*. -ला) 1 Very strong or mighty, valorous (as a man). -2 Violent, strong, excessive. -3 Important. -4 Abounding with. -5 Dangerous, destructive. —लः *m*. 1 N. of a Daitya. -2 A sprout. -लं *ind*. Exceedingly, much.

प्रब (-व-) ह्लिका *f* See प्रहेलिका.

प्रबाधक *a*. 1 Repelling, repulsive. -2 Harassing, oppressive. -3 Keeping off or back. -4 Refusing, rejecting.

प्रबाधनं 1 Oppressing, tormenting. -2 Refusing, denying. -3 Keeping off.

प्रबा (-वा-) लः *m*., —लं 1 A sprout, shoot, new leaf -2 Coral. -3 The neck of the Indian lute. —लः *m*. 1 A pupil. -2 An animal. -Comp. —अश्मंतकः *m*. 1 The red Asmantaka tree. -2 The coral tree. —पद्मं *n*. A red lotus. —फलं *n*. Red sandalwood. —भस्मन् *n*. Calx of coral.

प्रबाहुः *m*. The fore-arm.

प्रबाहुकं *ind* 1 On high. -2 At the same time.

प्रबुद्ध *p p*. (*f*. —द्धा) 1 Awakened, roused. -2 Wise, learned, clever. -3 Knowing, conversant with. -4 Full-blown, expanded. -5 Beginning to work or take effect (as a charm). -6 Enlivened, lively.

प्रबुधः *m*. A great sage.

प्रबोधः *m*. 1 Awaking (fig. also), awakening ; regaining one's consciousness. -2 Blowing, expanding (of flowers). -3 Wakefulness, sleeplessness. -4 Watchfulness. -5 Knowledge, wisdom, removal of delusion, real knowledge. -6 Consolation. -7 Reviving the fragrance of a perfume. -8 Explaining. -Comp. —उत्सवः *m*. N. of a festival observed from the tenth to the day of full-moon in the month of Kártika.

प्रबोधन *a*. (*f* -नी) Awakening, rousing. —नं *n*. 1 Waking. -2 Awakening, rousing. -3 Regaining one's consciousness. -4 Knowledge, wisdom. -5 Instructing. -6 Reviving the scent of a perfume.

प्रबोध (-धि-) —नी *f*. The eleventh day of the bright half of Kârtika on which Vishnu awakes from his four months' sleep.

प्रबोधित *p. p*. (*f*. —ता) 1 Awakened, roused. -2 Instructed, taught. -3 Persuaded.

प्रभंगः *m*. 1 Breaking, crushing. -2 Destruction ; complete defeat.

प्रभंजनं *n*. Breaking to pieces. —नः *m*. Wind, hurricane.

प्रभद्रः *m*. The Nimba tree.

प्रभव *a*. (*f*. —वा) 1 Excellent, distinguished. -2 Powerful. —वः *m*. 1 Source, origin. -2 Birth, production. -3 The source of a river. -4 The origin of being (as father, mother &c.). -5 The author, creator. -6 Birth-place. -7 Power, valour, majestic dignity. -8 An epithet of Vishnu. -9 (At the end of comp.) Arising or originating from, derived from.

प्रभवितृ *m.* A ruler, great lord.

प्रभविष्णु *a.* 1 Strong, mighty, powerful, able to achieve any object. -2 Pre-eminent, distinguished. —ष्णुः *m.* 1 A lord, master. -2 An epithet of Vishnu.

प्रभविष्णुता *f.* Might; all-reaching authority or power to control.

प्रभा *f.* 1 Light, lustre, splendour. -2 A ray of light. -3 The shadow of the sun on a sun-dial. -4 An epithet of Durgá. -5 N. of the city of Kubera. -6 N. of an Apsaras. -Comp. —करः *m.* 1 The sun. -2 The moon. -3 Fire. -4 The ocean. -5 An epithet of Siva. -6 N. of a learned writer, the founder of that school of Mimâmsá philosophy which is called after him. —कीटः *m.* A fire-fly. —तरल *a.* Tremulously radiant. —प्ररोहः *m.* A ray or flash of light. —मंडलं *n.* A circle or halo of light. —लेपिन् *a.* Covered with lustre.

प्रभागः *m.* 1 Division. -2 The fraction of a fraction (in math.).

प्रभात *p. p.* (*f.* —ता) Begun to become clear or light. —तं *n.* Day-break, dawn.

प्रभानं *n.* Light, lustre, splendour.

प्रभावः *m.* 1 Lustre, brilliance. -2 Dignity, majesty, grandeur. -3 Valour, power. -4 Regal power(one of the three 'Saktis' q. v.) -5 A superhuman or divine power or faculty with which all the inhabitants of heaven are endowed, and which enables them to know things outside the reach of the senses, to create any thing at pleasure &c. -6 Magnanimity. -7 Extension, circumference. -Comp. —ज *a.* Proceeding from regal power.

प्रभावना *f.* Disclosing, revealing.

प्रभाषणं *n.* Explantion, interpretation.

प्रभासः *m.* Splendour, beauty, lustre. -सः *m.*, —सं N. of a well-known place of pilgrimage near Dvárakâ.

प्रभासनं *n.* Illumining, brightening.

प्रभास्वर *n.* (*f.* रा) Brilliant, bright, shining.

प्रभिन्न *p. p.* (*f.* —न्ना) 1 Severed, cleft, divided. -2 Broken to pieces. -3 Detached. -4 Budding, opened. -5 Changed, altered. -6 Deformed, disfigured. -7 Loosened. -8 Intoxicated; in rut. -9 Pierced, bored. -10 Different, distinct. —न्नः *m.* An elephant in rut. -Comp. —अंजनं *n.* A kind of collyrium mixed with oil. —करट *a.* Intoxicated (as an elephant).

प्रभु *a.* (—भु, —भ्वी *f.*) 1 Mighty, strong, powerful. -2 Able, competent, having power to (with inf. or in comp.) -3 A match for *e. g.* प्रभुर्मल्लो मल्लाय. -भुः *m.* 1 A lord, master. -2 A governor, ruler. -3 An owner, proprietor. -4 Quick-silver. -5 N. of Vishnu. -6 Of Siva. -7 Of Brahman (*m.*). -8 Of Indra. -Comp. —भक्तः *m.* A good horse. —भक्तिः *f.* Devotion to one's lord; loyalty, faithfulness.

प्रभुता *f.*, -त्वं *n.* 1 Lordship, ascendancy, authority. -2 Ownership.

प्रभूत *p. p.* (*f.* -ता) 1 Sprung from, produced. -2 Much, abundant, numerous, many. -3 Mature, perfect. -4 High, lofty. -Comp. —वयस् *a.* Advanced in age, old, aged.

प्रभूतिः *f.* 1 Source, origin. -2 Power, strength. -3 Sufficiency.

प्रभूष्णु *a.* Able, powerful, strong.

प्रभृतिः *f.* Beginning, commen

cement; generally as the last member of Bah. compound as in इन्द्रप्रभृतयो देवाः &c. —*ind.* From, ever since, beginning with (with abl.) अद्य प्रभृति henceforward; ततः प्रभृति,अतः प्रभृति &c.

प्रभेदः *m.* 1 Splitting, opening. -2 Division,separation. -3 The flowing of rut or ichor from the temples of an elephant. -4 Difference, distinction. -5 A kind, a sort.

प्रभेदक *a.* 1 Tearing asunder,piercing. -2 Distinguishing.

प्रभ्रंशः *m.* Fall, falling off.

प्रभ्रंशथुः *m.* A disease of the nose.

प्रभ्रष्ट *p. p.* (*f.* —ष्टा) 1 Fallen off, fallen or dropped down.-2 Broken -ष्टं *n.* A garland of flowers suspended from the lock of the head.

प्रभ्रष्टकं *n.* See प्रभ्रष्टं above.

प्रमग्न *p. p.* (*f.* -ग्ना) Drowned, immersed.

प्रमण (-न-) स् *a.* 1 Happy, cheerful, delighted. -2 Good-natured. -3 Attentive.

प्रमत *p.p.* (*f.* —ता) 1 Thought out. -2 Wise, prudent.

प्रमत्त *p. p.* (*f.* —त्ता) 1 Intoxicated, drunk. -2 Mad, insane.-3 Inattentive, regardless (generally with loc.). -4 Swerving from,failing to do (with abl.). -5 Blundering. -6 Wanton, lascivious. -Comp. —गीत *a.* Sung carelessly.-चित्त*a.* Careless.

प्रमत्तता *f.* Inattention, carelessness.

प्रमत्तवत् *a* Inattentive, careless.

प्रमथः *m.* 1 A horse. -2 N. of a class of Beings attending on Siva. -Comp. —अधिपः,—नाथः,-पतिः *m.* An epithet of Siva. —आलयः *m.* Hell.

प्रमथनं *n.* 1 Hurting, tormenting. -2 Killing, slaughter.-3 Churning, stirring about.

प्रमथित *p. p.* (*f.* —ता) 1 Tormented, distressed. -2 Trampled down. -3 Slain,killed. -4 Well churned. -तं *n.* Butter-milk without water.

प्रमद *a.* (*f.* -दा) 1 Drunk, intoxicated (fig also). -2 Impassioned. -3 Careless. -4 Violent, strong. -दः *m.* 1 Joy, pleasure, delight. -2 The Dhattúra plant. -Comp. -काननं, -वनं *n.* A pleasure-garden attached to the royal harem.

प्रमदनं *n.* Amorous desire.

प्रमदा *f.* 1 A young handsome woman. -2 A wife or woman in general.-3 The sign *virgo* of the zodiac -Comp.-काननं,-वनं *n.* A pleasure garden attached to the royal harem -जनः *m.* 1 A young woman. -2 Woman-kind.

प्रमद्वर *a.* (*f.* -रा) Careless, inattentive.

प्रमनस् *a.* Delighted, cheerful, in good spirits.

प्रमन्यु *a.* 1 Enraged, incensed against (with loc.). -2 Distressed, sorrowful.

प्रमयः *m.* 1 Death. -2 Ruin. -3 Killing, slaughter.

प्रमर्दनं *n.* Crushing, destroying. —नः *m.* An epithet of Vishnu.

प्रमा *f.* 1 Consciousness, perception. -2 (In logic) Correct apprehension,true and certain knowledge, accurate conception.

प्रमाणं *n.* 1 A measure (of length, breadth &c.). -2 Extent, magnitude. -3 Scale, standard. -4 Limit, quantity. -5 Evidence, proof. -6 Authority ; one who judges or decides; one whose word is an authority, as in आर्यमिश्राः प्रमाणं, व्याकरणे पाणिनिः प्रमाणं ; sometimes *pl.* as in वेदाः प्रमाणाः. -7 A true or acccurate conception or notion. -8 A mode of proof, a means of arriving at correct knowledge ; they are six according to the Mimánsakas:- प्रत्यक्ष, अनुमान, उपमान, शब्द, अनुपलब्धि and अर्थापत्ति The Naiyâyikas recognize only the first four ; the Sankhyas recognize प्रत्यक्ष, अनुमान and शब्द only. -9 Principal, capital. -10 Unity. -11 Sacred authorily. -12 Cause, reason. -13 Sanction, precept. -14 The first term in a rule of three. -15 The prosodial length of a vowel. —णः *m.*, —णी *f.* A rule, standard, authority. -Comp. -ज्ञ *a.* Knowing the modes of proof, (as a logician). (—ज्ञः *m.*) An epithet of Siva. —दृष्ट *a.* Sanctioned by authority. —पत्रं *n.* A written warrant. —पुरुषः *m.* An arbitrator, an umpire. -भूत (-णीभूत) *a.* Authoritative. —वचनं, —वाक्यं *n.* An authoritative statement. —शास्त्रं *n.* 1 Scripture. -2 The science of logic. —सूत्रं *n.* A measuring cord.

प्रमाणक *a.* (At the end of comp.) Measuring, extending to, as far as.

प्रमाणय् Den. P. 1 To regard as an authority. -2 To hold up as a model. -3 To prove, show.

प्रमाणिक *a.* (*f.* —का) 1 Forming a measure. -2 Forming an authority.

प्रमाणीकृ 8 U. 1 To confide, believe. -2 To regard as an authority. -3 To dispense, deal or meet out. -4 To obey. -5 To prove, to establish. -6 To take the consent of. -7 To take into account.

प्रमातामहः *m.* A maternal great-grand-father. —ही *f.* A maternal great grand-mother.

प्रमातृ *m.* An authority, proof.

प्रमाथः *m.* 1 Tormenting, torturing. -2 Agitating, churning. -3 Killing, destruction. -4 Rape, outrage, forcible abduction. -थाः *m. pl.* Epithet of the fiends attendant upon Siva.

प्रमाथिन् *a.* (*f.* —नी) 1 Torturing, afflicting. -2 Killing, destroying. -3 Agitating, setting in motion. -4 Striking down, cutting down. —*m.* N. of a year.

प्रमादः *m.* 1 Negligence, inattention, oversight. -2 Intoxication. -3 Swoon. -4 Insanity, madness. -5 A mistake, mistaken judgment. -6 A mishap, calamity, danger.

प्रमादिका *f.* 1 A careless woman. -2 A deflowered girl.

प्रमादिन् *a.* (*f.* —नी) 1 Inattentive, negligent. -2 Insane, mad. -3 Intoxicated, drunk.

प्रमापकः *m.* An authority.

प्रमापणं *n.* Killing, slaughter.

प्रमापयितृ *m.* A murderer, killer.

प्रमार्जनं *n.* Wiping off, rubbing or washing off.

प्रमित *p. p.* (*f.* —ता) 1 Measured. -2 Measured off, limited, few, little. -3 Known, understood. -4 Proved, demonstrated. -5 (At the end of comp.) Of such and such extent or measure.

प्रमितिः *f.* 1 Measurement. -2 True knowledge, accurate notion or conception. -3 Knowledge acquired by any one of the Pramânas or means of knowledge. -4 True inference or analogy.

प्रमीढ *a.* (*f.* —ढा) 1 Thick, dense, compact. -2 Passed as urine.

प्रमीला *f.* Sleepiness, lassitude.

प्रमीलित *p. p.* (*f.* -ता) With closed eyes.

प्रमुक्त *p. p.* (*f.* —क्ता) 1 Loosened. -2 Set free. -3 Renounced. -4 Cast, hurled. -Comp. —कंठं *ind.* Bitterly.

प्रमुख *a.* (*f.* —खा) 1 Facing. -2 Chief, principal, formost, first. -3 Respectable, honourable. -4 (At the end of comp.) 1 Headed by, having as chief or at the head. -2 Accompanied by. —खः *m.* 1 A respectable man. -2 A heap, multitude. -3 The tree called Punnâga. —खं *n.* 1 The mouth. -2 The beginning of a chapter or section. -3 The time being, the present time. (प्रमुखतस् and प्रमुखे are used adverbially to signify 'in front of, ' before', 'opposite.').

प्रमुग्ध *a.* (*f.* —ग्धा) 1 Fainting, unconscious. -2 Extremely charming.

प्रमुद् *f.* Extreme joy.

प्रमुदित *p. p.* (*f.* —ता) Delighted, pleased, happy.

प्रमुषित *p. p.* (*f.* —ता) 1 Stolen, taken away. -2 Distracted, unconscious. -ता *f.* A kind of riddle.

प्रमूढ *p. p.* (*f.* —ढा) 1 Bewildered, infatuated. -2 Stupid, foolish.

प्रमेय *a.* (*f.* —या) 1 Measurable, finite. -2 To be proved or demonstrated. —यं *n.* 1 An object of certain knowledge, a demonstrated conclusion. -2 The topic to be proved or discussed.

प्रमेहः *m.* A urinary disease in general.

प्रमोक्षः *m.* 1 Letting fall. -2 Discharging, liberating.

प्रमोचनं *n.* 1 Liberating. -2 Emitting, shedding.

प्रमोदः *m.* 1 Joy, delight, pleasure. -2 A strong perfume.

प्रमोदनं *n* 1 Gladdening, making glad. -2 Gladness. —नः *m.* An epithet of Vishnu.

प्रमोदित *p. p.* (*f.* —ता) Pleased, delighted, joyful, happy. -तः *m.* An epithet of Kubera.

प्रमोहः *m.* 1 Stupefaction, insensibility. -2 Infatuation, bewilderment.

प्रमोहित *p. p.* (*f.* —ता) Infatuated, bewildered.

प्रम्लान *a.* (*f.* —ना) 1 Faded, withered away. -2 Soiled, dirty.

प्रयत *p. p.* (*f.* —ता) 1 Restrained, self-subdued, devout. -2 Purified by austerities or religious observances; keeping the organs of sense under restraint. -3 Zealous. -4 Submissive. -5 Careful, prudent. -तः *m.* A holy or pious person.

प्रयत्नः *m.* 1 Effort, endeavour. -2 A continued effort; perseverance. -3 Labour, difficulty. -4 (In gram.) Effort of the mouth in the production of articulate sounds. (प्रयत्नतः, प्रयत्नेन, प्रयत्नात् &c. *ind.* 1 With great effort, diligently. -2 Assiduously. -3 Hardly, scarcely. -4 Particularly, specially).

प्रयस्त *p. p.* (*f.* —स्ता) Seasoned, dressed with condiments.

प्रयागः *m.* 1 A sacrifice. -2 An epithet of Indra. -3 A horse. -4 N. of a celebrated place of pilgrimage. (*n.* also in this sense). -Comp. —भवः *m.* An epithet of Indra.

प्रयाचनं *n.* Begging, requesting, imploring.

प्रयाजः *m.* A principal sacrificial ceremony.

प्रयाणं *n.* 1 Setting out, departure. -2 A march, journey. -3 Progress, advance. -4 An attack, invasion, expedition. -5 Commencement. -6 Death. -7 The back of a horse. -8 The hinder part of any animal.

प्रयाणकं *n.* 1 A journey, march. -2 Going, motion.

प्रयात *p. p.* (*f.* —ता) 1 Advanced, departed. -2 Deceased, dead. -तः

m. 1 An invasion. -2 A precipice, steep rock.

प्रयापनं (-णं) *n.* 1 Sending.-2 Expelling,driving away.

प्रयापित *p. p.* (*f.* —ता) 1 Made to advance or go forward. -2 Made to go away.

प्रयामः *m.* 1 Restraining,checking. -2 Dearth, scarcity, (of water,corn &c.) -3 Length. -4 Competition of buyers on account of dearth.

प्रयासः *m.* 1 Effort, endeavour. -2 Labour, difficulty.

प्रयुक्त *p. p.* (*f.*-क्ता) 1 Yoked, harnessed.-2 Used,employed(as a word &c.) -3 Applied. -4 Appointed, nominated.-5 Acted, represented. -6 Arising or resulting from, produced by,consequent on.-7 Endowed with. -8 Lost in meditation, abstracted. -9 Lent or put to interest (as money).-10 Prompted, instigated,urged. -11 Directed,hurled at. -12 Shaken, set in motion. -13 Inflicted upon.-14 Connected with. -15 Thick, compact,closely united. —क्तं *n.* A cause. -Comp. —संस्कार *a.* Polished (as a gem).

प्रयुक्तिः *f.* 1 Use, employment, application.-2 Instigation.-3 Motive, main object or end, occasion. -4 Activity, effort, exertion.

प्रयुत *a.* (*f.* —ता) 1 Joined, united. -2 Separated. —तं *n.*A million.

प्रयुत्सुः *m.* 1 A warrior.-2 A ram. -3 Wind, air. -4 An ascetic. -5 N. of Indra.

प्रयुद्धं *n.* A battle, fight.

प्रयोक्तृ *m.* 1 One who uses or employs (as a means, word &c.).-2 One who directs ; an executor. -3 One who instigates. -4 An author, an agent. -5 One who acts or represents (a drama). -6 A money-lender. -7 One who shoots (an arrow).-8 The agent of an action. -9 A reciter.

प्रयोगः *m.* 1 Use, application, employment ; as in शब्दप्रयोगः-2 A general usage. -3 Hurling, throwing, dicharging (opp. संहारः), प्रयोगसंहारविभक्तमंत्रं *रघुवं. 5. 57. -4 Exhibition, performance, representation of a dance, a drama &c. -5 Practice, experimental portion(of a subject); (opp. शास्त्र 'theory'). -6 Course of procedure. -7 An act, action. -8 Recitation, delivery. -9 Commencement. -10 A contrivance, scheme. -11 A means, instrument. -12 Consequence, result. -13 Combination, connection. -14 Addition. -15 (In gram.) A usual form. -16 Offering, presenting.-17 Principal, loan bearing interest. -18 A sacred text or authority. -19 A cause, motive. -20 An example. -21 Application of magic, magical rites. -22 A horse. -Comp. -अतिशयः *m.* Bringing a character on the stage unexpectedly at the moment when his name is incidentally pronounced. -Comp. —बंधः *m.* A dramatic composition.

प्रयोगतः *ind.* 1 By the use of, through the employment of. -2 In action, actually.

प्रयोजकः *m.* 1 An employer, one who uses or employs. -2 An author. -3 An institutor or founder. -4 A money-lender. -5 A law-giver. -6 An instigator.

प्रयोजनं *n.* 1 Use, employment, application. -2 Use, need, necessity (with instr. of that which is needed and gen. of the user). -3

End, object, purpose. -4 A means of attaining. -5 A cause, motive, occasion. -6 Profit, interest.

प्रयोज्य *pot. p.* (*f.* -ज्या) 1 To be employed. -2 To be practised. -3 To be produced or caused. -4 To be appointed. -5 To be thrown or discharged (as a missile). -6 To be set to work. —ज्य: *m.* A servant, an employe'. —ज्यं *n.* Capital, principal.

प्ररुदित *p. p.* (*f.*-ता) Crying bitterly, weeping.

प्ररूढ *p. p.* (*f.*—ढा) 1 Full-grown. -2 Born, produced. -3 Increased. -4 Germinated, rooted ; as is प्ररूढमूल. -5 Grown long ; as in प्ररूढकेश, प्ररूढश्मश्रु.

प्ररूढि: *f.* Growth, increase.

प्ररोचनं *n.* 1 Exciting, or stimulating. -2 Illustration, explanation. -3 Seduction. -4 Exhibition (of a person) for approval. -5 Favourable description of that which is to follow (in dramaturgy). -6 Representation of the end as all but accomplished (प्ररोचना also in the last two senses).

प्ररोह: *m.* 1 Sprouting, germination. -2 A sprout, shoot (fig. also). -3 A shoot of light. -4 A new leaf or branch, twig, spray.

प्ररोहणं *n.* 1 Growing, germination. -2 Budding, sprouting. -3 A twig, sprout, shoot, spray.

प्रलपनं *n.* 1 Talking, speaking, talk, words, conversation. -2 Prating, incoherent or nonsensical talk *e.g.* इदं कस्यापि प्रलपितं. -3 Lamentation, wailing.

प्रलपितं *n.* 1 Talk. -2 A nonsensical talk.

प्रलब्ध *p. p.* (*f.* -ब्धा) Deceived, cheated.

प्रलंब *a.* (*f.* -बा) 1 Pendulous, hanging down. -2 Prominent as in प्रलंबनासिक:. -3 Slow, dilatory. —ब: *m.* 1 Anything hanging down. -2 A branch. -3 A garland worn round the neck. -4 A kind of necklace. -5 The female breast. -6 N. of a demon killed by Balaráma. -7 A verse (गाथा). -Comp. —अंड: *m.* A man with hanging testicles. —घ्न:, —मथन:, —हन् *m.* Epithets of Balarâma.

प्रलंबक: *m.* A kind of fragrant grass.

प्रलंबनं *n.* Hanging down, depending.

प्रलंबित *a.* (*f.* —ता) Pendulous, hanging down, suspended.

प्रलंभ: *m.* 1 Obtaining, gaining, attaining. -2 Deceiving, cheating, over-reaching.

प्रलंभनं *n.* Deceiving, cheating.

प्रलय: *m.* 1 Destruction, annihilation, dissolution. -2 The destruction of the whole universe (at the end of a *kalpa*). -3 Any extensive destruction or devastation. -4 Death. -5 Swoon, fainting. -6 (In Rhet.) Loss of consciousness considered as one of the 33 subordinate feelings. -7 The mystic syllable *om*.

प्रललाट *a.* (*f.* —टा) Having a prominent fore-head.

प्रलव: *m.* 1 A fragment, chip. -2 The sheath of a leaf.

प्रलवित्रं *n.* An instrument for cutting off.

प्रलाप: *m.* 1 Talk, conversation. -2 Prating, prattling, nonsensical talk. -3 Lamentation, wailing. -Comp. -हन् *m.* A sort of collyrium.

प्रलापिन् *a.* 1 Talking, speaking. -2 Prating, prattling.

प्रलीन *p. p.* (*f.* -ना) 1 Melted, dissolved. -2 Annihilated. -3 Insensible; unconscious.

प्रलून *p. p.* (*f.* -ना) Cut off. [ment.

प्रलेपः *m.* An unguent, an ointment.

प्रलेपक *a.* (*f.* —का) Anointing, smearing. -कः *m.* 1 An anointer, a plasterer. -2 A kind of slow fever.

प्रलेहः *m.* A kind of broth.

प्रलोठनं *n.* 1 Rolling(on the ground). -2 Heaving, tossing.

प्रलोभः *m.* 1 Cupidity, covetousness. -2 Allurement, seduction.

प्रलोभनं *n.* 1 Attracting. -2 An allurement, temptation. -3 A lure, bait.

प्रलोभिन् *a.*(*f.*-नी) 1 Greedy of.-2 Alluring, enticing.

प्रलोभिनी *f.* Sand.

प्रलोभ्य *a.* (*f.* —भ्या) To be desired or coveted, attractive, alluring.

प्रलोलः *a.* (*f.* -ला) Greatly agitated.

प्रवक्तृ *m.* 1 A speaker, declarer. -2 A teacher, expounder. -3 An orator, eloquent man.

प्रवगः, प्रवंगः, प्रवंगमः *m.* A monkey. See प्लवग, प्लवंग, प्लवंगम.

प्रवचनं *n.* 1 Declaration, announcement. -2 Teaching, expounding.-3 Exposition, explanation, interpretation. -4 Eloquence. -5 A sacred treatise or writing. -6 An expression, a term. -7 The fundamental doctrine of the Buddhists. -Comp. —पटु *a.* Skilled in talking, eloquent.

प्रवटः *m.* Wheat.

प्रवण *a.* (*f.* —णा) 1 Sloping down, inclined, flowing downwards. -2 Steep, precipito[illegible] Crooked, bent. -4 Incli[illegible]sed to. -5 Devoted or a[illegible]o, intent on; full of. -6 Favou[illegible]y inclined towards.-7 Eager, ready.-8 Endowed with, possessed of. -9 Humbled, humble, submissive. -10 Decaying, wasting, waning. -11 Generous. -णः *m.* A place where four roads meet. —णं *n.* 1 A steep descent, precipice. -2 The side of a hill, declivity. -3 The belly.

प्रवत्स्यत् *a.*(-ती or-न्ती *f.*) About to go on a journey. -Comp.-पतिका *f* The wife of one who intends to go on a journey (one of the 8 Nâyikás in erotic poetry).

प्रवप *a.* Very fat.

प्रवयणं *n.* 1 The upper part of a piece of woven cloth. -2 A goad.

प्रवयस् *a.* 1 Advanced in age, aged, old. -2 Ancient; old.

प्रवर *a.* (*f.* —रा) 1 Chief, most excellent, best; exalted. -2 Eldest. -रः *m.* 1 A call, summons. -2 A particular invocation addressed to Agni by a Brâhmana at the consecration of his fire. -3 A line of ancestors. -4 A race, family, lineage. -5 An ancestor. -6 A noble ancestor who contributes to the credit of a particular *gotra* or family. -7 Offspring, descendants.-8 A cover, covering. -9 An upper garment.-10 One of the 42 Gotras. -रा *f.* N. of a river falling into the Godâvarî.-रं *n.* Aloe-wood. -Comp. —वाहनौ *m. dual.* An epithet of the two Asvins.

प्रवर्गः *m.* 1 The sacrificial fire. -2 An epithet of Vishnu.

प्रवर्ग्यः *m.* A ceremony introductory to the *Soma* sacrifice.

प्रवर्जनं *n.* The perforr[illegible] प्रवर्ग्य ceremony.

प्रवर्तः *m.* 1 Undertaking, engaging in. -2 Excitement, stimulus.

प्रवर्तक *a.* (*f.* -र्तिका) 1 Setting on foot, founding. -2 Promoting, furthering. -3 Producing, causing. -4 Inducing, instigating (in a bad sense). —कः *m.* 1 An originator, founder, author. -2 A prompter, instigator. -3 An arbiter, umpire. —कं *n.* The entrance of a character on the stage.

प्रवर्तनं *n.* 1 Going on, moving forward. -2 Commencement. -3 Establishing, founding. -4 Urging, inciting. -5 Applying oneself to. -6 Happening. -7 Activity, action. -8 Behaviour; procedure. -9 Directing, superintending. -10 Exhortation. —ना *f.* Inciting or prompting to action.

प्रवर्तित *p. p.* (*f.* —ता) 1 Caused to turn, made to go or roll onwards. -2 Founded, established. -3 Prompted, instigated. -4 Kindled. -5 Caused, made. -6 Purified. -7 Informed.

प्रवर्धनं *n.* Increasing, augmenting.

प्रवर्षः *m.* Heavy rain. [rain.

प्रवर्षणं *n.* 1 Raining. -2 The first

प्रवलाकिन् *m.* 1 A peacock. -2 A snake.

प्रवसनं *n.* Going or journeying abroad; going on a journey.

प्रवहः *m.* 1 Flowing forth. -2 Wind (in general). -3 N. of one of the seven courses of wind (said to cause the motion of the planets). -4 A reservoir into which water is carried off.

प्रवहणं *n.* 1 A covered carriage or litter (for women). -2 A carriage or a vehicle in general. -3 A ship.

प्रवह्लि: —ह्ली *f.* See प्रहेलिका.

प्रवाकः *m.* A proclaimer.

प्रवाच् *a.* Eloquent, oratorical. -2 Garrulous. [quent

प्रवाचक *a.* 1 Explanatory. -2 Elo-

प्रवाचनं *n.* 1 Proclamation, declaration. -2 A designation.

प्रवाच्यं *n.* A literary composition.

प्रवाणं *n.* The trimming or edging of a piece of woven cloth.

प्रवाणि:,—णी *f.* A weaver's shuttle.

प्रवात *p. p.* (*f.* —ता) Exposed to stormy wind. —तं *n.* 1 A fresh or free breeze of air. -2 A stormy wind. -3 An airy place.

प्रवादः *m.* 1 Mentioning, declaring. -2 Discourse, conversation. -3 Report, rumour, popular belief. -4 A fable or myth. -5 Litigious language. -6 Mutual defiance. [ing.

प्रवारः, प्रवारकः *m.* A cover, cover-

प्रवारणं *n.* 1 Satisfying (a desire). -2 Priority of choice. -3 Prohibition, opposition. -4 A voluntary gift (काम्यदा).

प्रवाल See प्रबाल.

प्रवासः *m.* Going or journeying abroad; foreign residence. -2 A temporary sojourn. -Comp -गत, —स्थ, —स्थित *a.* Journeying abroad; being absent from home.

प्रवासनं *n.* 1 Living abroad; temporary sojourn. -2 Exile, banishment. -3 Killing, slaughter. [ed.

प्रवासित *a.* (*f.* —ता) Banished, exil-

प्रवासिन् *m.* A traveller, wayfarer.

प्रवाहः *m.* 1 Flowing or streaming forth. -2 A stream, a current. -3 Running water. -4 Unbroken succession, continuity. -5 Course of events (rolling onward like a stream). -6 A pond, lake. -7 An excellent horse. प्रवाहे मूत्रितं *n.* Means (lit.) making water in a stream; (fig.) doing a useless action.

प्रवाहकः *m.* A goblin, an imp.

प्रवाहनं *n.* 1 Driving forth. -2 Evacuation by stool.

प्रवाहिका *f.* Diarrhœa.

प्रवाही *f.* Sand.

प्रविकीर्ण *p. p.* (*f.* —र्णा) 1 Scattered or strewed about. -2 Dispersed, diffused.

प्रविख्यात *p. p.* (*f.* —ता) 1 Named, called. -2 Famous, celebrated.

प्रविख्यातिः *f.* Fame, reputation, renown, celebrity.

प्रविचयः *m.* Examination, investigation.

प्रविचरः *m.* Discernment, discrimination.

प्रवितत *p. p.* (*f.* -ता) 1 Spread out, expanded. -2 Dishevelled (as hair).

प्रविदारः *m.* Bursting asunder, opening.

प्रविदारणं *n.* 1 Tearing, breaking, bursting asunder. -2 Budding. -3 War, battle. -4 Crowd. -5 Confusion, tumult.

प्रविद्ध *p. p.* (*f.* —द्धा) Cast away, thrown off.

प्रविद्रुत *p. p.* (*f.* —ता) Dispersed, scattered.

प्रविधानं *n.* 1 Thinking upon. -2 Doing.

प्रविध्वस्त *a.* (*f.* —स्ता) 1 Thrown away. -2 Agitated, disturbed.

प्रविभक्त *p. p.* (*f.* —क्ता) 1 Severed, separated. -2 Apportioned, partitioned, divided, distributed.

प्रविभागः *m.* 1 Division, distribution.

प्रविरः *m.* Yellow sandal.

प्रविरल *a.* (*f.* —ला) 1 Separated by an interval; isolated. -2 Very few or rare, very scanty.

प्रविलयः *m.* 1 Melting away. -2 Complete dissolution or absorption.

प्रविलुप्त *p. p.* (*f.* —प्ता) Cut off, fallen off, rubbed off; removed.

प्रविवादः *m.* Dispute, quarrel, wrangling.

प्रविविक्त *a.* (*f.* —क्ता) 1 Very solitary. -2 Separated, detached.

प्रविश्लेषः *m.* Separation.

प्रविषण्ण *a.* (*f.* —ण्णा) Dejected, spiritless.

प्रविष्ट *p. p.* (*f.* —ष्टा) 1 Gone or entered into. -2 Engaged in, occupied with. -3 Begun.

प्रविष्टकं *n.* 1 Entrance on the stage. -2 Entering a room.

प्रविस्तरः (-स्तारः) *m.* Extent, circumference, compass.

प्रवीण *a.* (*f.* —णा) Clever, skilled or versed in, conversant with.

प्रवीर *a.* (*f.* —रा) 1 Most excellent or distinguished. -2 Strong, heroic. -रः *m.* 1 A hero, warrior. -2 A chief, a distinguished personage.

प्रवृत्त *p. p.* (*f.* —त्ता) 1 Begun, commenced. -2 Engaged in, occupied with. -3 Fixed, settled, determined. -4 Unimpeded, undisputed. -6 Round. —त्तः *m.* A round ornament. —त्तं *n.* An action, undertaking.

प्रवृत्तकं *n.* Entrance on the stage.

प्रवृत्तिः *f.* 1 Continued advance. -2 Rise, origin, flow (of words &c.). -3 Appearance, manifestation. -4 Advent, commencement. -5 Application or addiction to; inclination towards. -6 Conduct; behaviour. -7 Occupation, activity. -8 Use, employment, currency (as of a word). -9 Continued effort. -10 Signification or acceptation (of a word). -11 Continuance, prevalence. -12 Active life, taking an active part in worldly affairs (opp. निवृत्ति.) -13 Tidings, intelligence. -14 Applicability or validity of a rule. -15 Fate, luck. -16 Direct perception or apprehension. -17 Ichor exuding from the temples of an elephant in rut. -18 N. of the city of उज्जयिनी. -Comp. —ज्ञः *m.* A spy. —निमित्तं *n.* A reason for the use of any term in a particular significa-tion. —मार्गः *m.* Worldly life ; attachment to the business and pleasures of the world.

प्रवृद्ध *p. p.* (*f.* —द्धा) 1 Full-grown. -2 Increased, augmented, expanded. -3 Full, deep. -4 Haughty. -5 Violent. -6 Large.

प्रवृद्धिः *f.* 1 Increase, growth. -2 Rise, prosperity, elevation.

प्रवेक *a.* (*f.* —का) Best, chief, most excellent.

प्रवेगः *m.* Great speed, velocity.

प्रवेटः *m.* Barley.

प्रवेणिः,-णी *f.* 1 A braid of hair (in general). -2 The hair twisted and unadorned (worn by wives in the absence of their husbands).-3 The housings of an elephant. -4 A piece of coloured woollen cloth.-5 The current or stream (of a river).

प्रवेतृ *m.* A charioteer. [ing.

प्रवेदनं *n.* Making known, proclaim-

प्रवेपः, प्रवेपकः, प्रवेपथुः *m.*, प्रवेपनं *n.* Trembling, shaking, tremour.

प्रवेरित *a.* (*f.* —ता) Cast hither and thither.

प्रवेलः *m.* A kind of kidney-bean.

प्रवेशः *m.* 1 Entrance, penetration. -2 Access, approach. -3 Entrance on the stage. -4 The door (of a house &c.). -5 Income, revenue.-6 Close application (to a pursuit). -7 The entrance of the sun into a sign of the zodiac. -8 Coming on, setting in (of night).-9 The syringe of a clyster-pipe.

प्रवेशकः *m.* An interlude acted by inferior characters for the purpose of acquainting the audience with events not represented on the stage, but a knowledge of which is necessary for the proper understanding of what follows ; it never occurs at the beginning of the first act or at the end of the last.

प्रवेशनं *n.* 1 Entrance, penetration. 2 Introducing, conducting. -3 An entrance to the main door of a house, the gate. -4 Sexual intercourse.

प्रवेशित *p. p.* (*f.* —ता) Introduced, brought in.

प्रवेष्टः *m.* 1 An arm. -2 The wrist or fore-arm. -3 The fleshy part of an elephant's back (where the rider sits). -4 An elephant's gums. -5 An elephant's housings.

प्रव्यक्त *p. p.* (*f.* —क्ता) Apparent, manifest, evident. [ance.

प्रव्यक्तिः *f.* Manifestation, appear-

प्रव्याहारः *m.* Prolongation of discourse.

प्रव्रजनं *n.* 1 Going abroad, sojourning. -2 Going into exile. -3 Turning a recluse.

प्रव्रजित *p. p.* (*f.* —ता) 1 Gone abroad or into exile. -2 Turned a recluse. —तः *m.* 1 A religious mendicant or ascetic in general. -2 A Bráhmana who has entered on the fourth (भिक्षु) order. -3 The pupil of a Jaina or Buddhist mendicant. -ता *f.* 1 A female ascetic.-2 A spikenard(*mar.* जटामांसी).-तं *n.* Turning a recluse; the life a of religious mendicant.

प्रव्रज्या *f.* 1 Going abroad, migration. 2 Wandering about as a religious mendicant -3 The order of a religious mendicant; a mendicant's life; the fourth (or भिक्षु) order in the religious life of a Bráhmana. -Comp. -अवसितः *m.* A religious mendicant who has renounced his order.

प्रव्रश्चः *m.* A knife for cutting wood.

प्रव्राज्, प्रव्राजकः *m.* A religious mendicant, recluse. —जिका f. A female ascetic.

प्रव्राजनं n. Banishing, exile, sending into exile.

प्रशंसनं n. Praising, extolling.

प्रशंसा f. 1 Praise, applause. -2 Description, reference to; as in अप्रस्तुतप्रशंसा. -3 Glory, fame. -Comp. -उपमा f. One of the several kinds of उपमा mentioned by Dandin.

प्रशंसित p. p. (f. -ता) Praised, applauded.

प्रशत्वन् m. The ocean.

प्रशत्वरी f. A river.

प्रशमः m. 1 Calmness, tranquillity, composure. -2 Peace, rest. -3 Extinction, abatement. -4 End, destruction. -5 Appeasement.

प्रशमन a. (f. -नी) 1 Tranquillizing, pacifying. -2 Curing, healing. -नं n. 1 Calming, pacifying. -2 Allaying, soothing. -3 Extinguishing, suppressing. -4 Cessation, abatement. -5 Bestowing on fit objects. -6 Securing, keeping safe, guarding, -7 Killing, slaughter.

प्रशमित p. p. (f. —ता) 1 Pacified, appeased, allayed. -2 Extingushed, quenched. -3 Atoned for, expiated.

प्रशस्त p. p. (f. -स्ता) 1 Praised, eulogised. -2 Praiseworthy, commendable. -3 Best, excellent. -4 Blessed, auspicious. -Comp. —अद्रिः m. N. of a mountain.

प्रशस्तिः f. 1 Praise, laudation. -2 Description. -3 A small poem written in praise of any one (e. g a patron). -4 Excellence, eminence. -5 Benediction. -6 Guidance, rule for guidance.

प्रशस्य a. (f.—स्या. Compar. श्रेयस् or ज्यायस्; superl. श्रेष्ठ or ज्येष्ठ) Praiseworthy, commendable.

प्रशाख a. (f. —खा) 1 Having many or spreading branches. -2 Being in the 5th stage of formation (as an embryo). —खा f. A small branch or twig.

प्रशाखिका f. A small branch.

प्रशांत p. p. (f. —ता) 1 Calmed, tranquillized. -2 Calm, quiet, sedate, still. -3 Tamed, subdued. -4 Ended, ceased. -5 Dead, deceased.

प्रशांतिः f. 1 Calmness, tranquillity, quiet, repose. -2 Cessation, abatement. -3 Allaying, quenching, extinction.

प्रशामः m. 1 Tranquillity, composure. -2 Quenching, extinction. -3 Cessation.

प्रशासनं n. 1 Governing, ruling. -2 Enjoining, exacting. -3 Government.

प्रशास्तृ m. 1 A king, governor. -2 A director, adviser.

प्रशिथिल a. (f. —ला) Very loose.

प्रशिष्यः m. The disciple of a disciple.

प्रशुद्धिः f. Clearness, purity.

प्रशोषः m. Becoming dry, drying up, aridity.

प्रश्चोतनं n. Sprinkling, oozing.

प्रश्नः m. 1 A question, an inquiry. -2 A judicial inquiry or investigation. -3 A subject of controversy, controverted or disputed point. -4 A problem for solution or calculation. -5 Inquiry into the future. -6 A section of a work. -Comp. —उपनिषद् f. N. of an Upanishad consisting of six questions and six answers. —दूतिः,-ती f. A riddle, an enigma. —विवाकः m. An arbitrator, umpire.

प्रश्रथः m. Laxity, relaxation.

प्रश्रब्धिः f. Trust, confidence.

प्रश्रयः *m.*, प्रश्रयणं *n.* 1 Respect, courtesy, politeness, humility. -2 Love, affection, regard.

प्रश्लथ *a.* (*f.* —था) 1 Very loose or flaccid. -2 Spiritless, unnerved.

प्रश्लिष्ट *p. p.* (*f.* —ष्टा) 1 Twisted, entwined. -2 Reasonable, well argued or reasoned (युक्तियुक्त).

प्रश्लेषः *m.* 1 Close contact, pressing hard against -2 Euphonic coalition of vowels.

प्रश्वासः *m.* Breath, respiration.

प्रष्ठ *a.* (*f.* —ष्ठा) 1 Standing or being in front. -2 Chief, principal, foremost, best. -Comp. —वाह् *m.* A young bull being trained for the plough.

प्रसू 1.4 A. (प्रस-स्य-ते) 1 To bring forth young. -2 To spread, diffuse, expand, extend.

प्रसक्त *p. p.* (*f.* —क्ता) 1 Attached to, connected with. -2 Excessively fond. -3 Adhering or sticking to.-4 Devoted or addicted to, engaged in. -5 Contiguous, near. -6 Constant, uninterrupted.-7 Got, obtained, gained. -8 Expanded, opened. —क्तं *ind.* Incessantly, continuously.

प्रसक्तिः *f.* 1 Attachment, devotion, devotedness.-2 Connection, association. -3 Applicability, bearing, application.-4 Energy, perseverance. -5 Conclusion, deduction. -6 A topic or subject of discourse.-7 Occurrence of a possibility.-8 Acquisition, gain.

प्रसंख्या *f.* 1 Total number, sum. -2 Reflection, contemplation.

प्रसंख्यानः *m.* Payment, liquidation. —नं *n.* 1 Enumeration. -2 Deep meditation, abstract contemplation. -3 Fame, reputation.

प्रसंगः *m.* 1 Addiction, devotedness. -2 Union, association, connection. -3 Illicit intercourse. -4 Occupation, being engaged or occupied with. -5 A subject or topic (of discourse or controversy). -6 An occasion, incident.-7 Conjuncture, opportunity. -8 A contingency, occurrence of a possibillity. -9 Connected reasoning. -10 A conclusion, an inferrence. -11 Inseparable application or connection (= व्याप्ति q. v.) -12 Mention of parents. (प्रसंगेन, प्रसंगतः, प्रसंगात् are used adverbially in the sense of 1 In relation to. -2 In consequence of, on account of, by way of. -3 Occasionally. -4 In course of). -Comp. —निवारणं *n.* Prevention or obviation of similar contingencies in future. —वशात् *ind.* By the force of circumstances.

प्रसंगिन् *a.* (*f.* —नी) 1 Attached or devoted to. -2 Dependent on, contingent on. -3 Incidental.-4 Subordinate.

प्रसज्य *a.* (*f.* —ज्या) 1 To be attached to. -2 Applicable, holding good. -3 Contingent, possible.

प्रसंजनं *n.* 1 Act of connecting, uniting. -2 Bringing into use.

प्रसत्तिः *f.* 1 Favour, complacency. -2 Clearness, transparency.

प्रसंधानं *n.* Combination, union.

प्रसन्न *p. p.* (*f.* —न्ना) 1 Pure, clear, pellucid, limpid, transparent. -2 Pleased, delighted, soothed. -3 Kindly disposed, gracious, propitious. -4 Plain, easily intelligible (as meaning). -5 True, correct *e. g.* प्रसन्नस्ते तर्कः. -6 Tranquil. —न्ना *f.* 1 Propitiation, pleasing. -2 Spirituous liquor. -Comp. —ईरा *f.* Spirituous liquor.

प्रसभः *m* Force, violence, impetuosity. —भं *ind.* 1 Violently, forcibly. -2 Very much, exceedingly. -3 Importunately. -Comp. —हरणं *n.* Forcible abduction.

प्रसमीक्षणं *n.*, प्रसमीक्षा *f.* Deliberation, judgment

प्रसयनं *n.* 1 Binding, fastening. -2 A net.

प्रसरः *m.* 1 Advancing. -2 Free motion, free scope, access or course. -3 Spreading, extension, expansion. -4 Extent, great quantity. -5 Prevalence, influence. -6 A stream, flood. -7 A group, multitude. -8 War, battle. -9 An iron arrow. -10 Speed. -11 Affectionate solicitation.

प्रसरणं *n.* 1 Going forth, streaming forth. -2 Escaping, running away. -3 Spreading forth or abroad -4 Surrounding an enemy. -5 Amiability.

प्रसरणिः, —णी *f.* Surrounding an enemy.

प्रसर्पः *m.* Going to the part of the sacrificial enclosure called सदस्.

प्रसर्पणं *n.* 1 Going forward, advancing. -2 Pervading. -3 Entering the सदस्.

प्रस (-श-) लः *m.* The cold season (हेमंत).

प्रसवः *m.* 1 Procreation, birth, production. -2 Child-birth, delivery. -3 Offspring, young ones, children. -4 Source, birth-place (*fig.* also). -5 Flower, blossom. -6 A fruit, product. -7 A current, stream. -Comp. —गृहं *n.* A lying-in-chamber. —बंधनं *n.* The foot-stalk of a leaf or flower; peduncle. —वेदना, -व्यथा *f.* The pangs of child-birth. —स्थली *f.* A mother. —स्थानं *n.* 1 A place for delivery. -2 A nest.

प्रसवकः *m.* The 'Piyâla' tree.

प्रसवनं *n.* 1 Bringing forth. -2 Bearing children; fecundity.

प्रसवंतिः, -ती *f.* A woman in labour.

प्रसवितृ *m.* A father, procreator.

प्रसवित्री *f.* A mother.

प्रसव्य *a.* (*f.* —व्या) 1 Contrary, reverse. -2 Unfavourable.

प्रसह *a.* (*f.* —हा) Withstanding, bearing up. —हः *m.* 1 A beast or bird of prey. -2 Resistance, opposition.

प्रसहनः *m.* A beast or bird of prey. —नं *n.* 1 Withstanding, resisting, bearing up. -2 Defeating, overcoming. -3 Embracing, an embrace.

प्रसह्य *ind.* 1 Forcibly, violently. -2 Exceedingly, much. -Comp. -चौरः *m.* A plunderer, highwayman. —हरणं *n.* Violent or forcible seizure, plundering.

प्रसातिका *f.* A kind of rice.

प्रसादः *m.* 1 Favour, kindness, propitiousness. -2 Graciousness of disposition. -3 Tranquillity, composure, absence of excitement. -4 Clearness, brightness, transparency, purity (as of water, mind &c.). -5 Perspicuity, clearness of style. -6 The remnants of food offered to idols. -7 A free gift. -8 Any propitiatory offering. -9 Well-being, welfare. -Comp. —पराङ्मुख *a.* 1 Withdrawing favour from any one. -2 Not caring for any body's favour. —पात्रं *n.* An object of favour. —स्थ *a.* 1 Kind, propitious. -2 Serene, happy.

प्रसादक *a.* (*f.* —दिका) 1 Purifying, clearing. -2 Soothing, calming. -3 Gladdening. -4 Courting favour, propitiating.

प्रसादन *a.* (*f.* —नी) 1 Purifying, rendering pure or clear. -2 Soothing, calming. -3 Cheering, gladdening. —नः *m.* A royal tent. -नं *n*

1 Clearing from impurities; purifying. -2 Soothing, tranquillizing. -3 Pleasing, gratifying. -4 Propitiating, courting favour. —ना *f.* 1 Service, worship.-2 Purifying.

प्रसादित *p.p.*(*f.*-ता) 1 Purified, cleared.-2 Appeased, propitiated.-3 Worshipped. -4 Calmed, soothed.

प्रसाधक *a.* (*f.* —धिका) 1 Accomplishing or perfecting. -2 Purifying, cleansing. -3 Decorating. —कः *m.* An attendant who dresses his master.

प्रसाधनं *n.* 1 Accomplishing, bringing about. -2 Arranging. -3 Ornamenting, embellishing; toilet, dress. -4 A decoration, ornament. -नः *m.*, —नं *n.*,—नी *f.* A comb. -Comp.-विधिः *m.* Act of decoration or embellishment.-विशेषः *m.* The highest decoration.

प्रसाधिका *f.* 1 A lady's maid; a female attendant who dresses her mistress. -2 Wild rice.

प्रसाधित *p. p.* (*f.* —ता) 1 Accomplished, perfected. -2 Decorated. -3 Proved.

प्रसारः *m.* 1 Spreading, extending. -2 Diffusion, extension, expansion. -3 Spreading over the country to forage.

प्रसारणं *n.* 1 Spreading abroad, extending, expanding. -2 Stretching out. -3 Surrounding an enemy. -4 Spreading over the country for fuel and grass. -5 The change of a semivowel (य,र and व) into a vowel.

प्रसारिणी *f.* Surrounding an enemy.

प्रसारित *p. p.* (*f.* -ता) 1 Expanded, spread, extended. -2 Stretched out (as hands.). -3 Exhibited, exposed (for sale).

प्रसाहः *m.* Overpowering, defeating.

प्रसित *p. p.* (*f.* —ता) 1 Bound, fastened. -2 Devoted to, occupied with. -3 Intent on, craving after (with instr. or loc.).-4 Very clear. —तं *n.* Pus, matter.

प्रसितिः *f.* 1 A net. -2 A tie, fetter. -3 An attack, assault. -4 A throw, shot. -5 Reach, extent.-6 A series, succession.

प्रसिद्ध *p. p.* (*f.* —द्धा) 1 Renowned, celebrated. -2 Decorated, adorned.

प्रसिद्धिः *f.* 1 Fame, celebrity, renown. -2 Success, accomplishment.-3 Ornament, decoration.

प्रसीदिका *f.* A small garden.

प्रसुप्त *p. p.* (*f.* —प्ता) 1 Asleep, sleepy. -2 Fast asleep.

प्रसुप्तिः *f.* 1 Sleepiness. -2 Paralysis.

प्रसू *a.* 1 Bringing forth, bearing, giving birth to. —*f.* 1 A mother. -2 A mare.-3 A spreading creeper -5 A young shoot.

प्रसूका *f.* A mare.

प्रसूत *p. p.* (*f.* —ता) 1 Begotten, engendered. -2 Brought forth, born, produced. —तं *n.* 1 A flower. -2 Any productive source. —ता *f.* A woman recently delivered.

प्रसूतिः *f.* 1 Procreation, generation. -2 Bringing forth, giving birth to. -3 Calving. -4 Laying eggs. -5 Birth, production. -6 Appearance, coming forth, growth (of flowers &c.). -7 A product, production. -8 Offspring, progeny, issue. -9 A producer, generator. -10 A mother. -Comp. —जं *n.* Pain resulting as a necessary consequence of birth. —वायुः *m.* Wind produced in the womb during the pangs of travail.

प्रसूतिका *f.* A woman recently delivered.

प्रसून *p.p.* (*f.* —ना) Produced, born. —नं *n.* 1 A flower. -2 A bud, blossom. -3 A fruit. -Comp. —इषुः, -बाणः, -वाणः *m.* Epithets of the God of love. -वर्षः *m.* A shower of flowers.

प्रसूनकं *n.* 1 A flower. -2 A bud, blossom.

प्रसृत *p.p.* (*f.* —ता) 1 Gone forward. -2 Stretched out, extended. -3 Spread, diffused. -4 Long, lengthened -5 Engaged in, attached to. -6 Swift or quick. -7 Manifested, displayed. -8 Modest. —तः *m.* The palm of the hand stretched out and hollowed. —तः *m.*, -तं *n.* A measure equal to two *palas.* -ता *f.* The leg. -Comp. —जः *m.* An adulterine (कुंडगोलककप).

प्रसृतिः *f.* 1 Advance, progress. -2 Flowing. -3 The palm of the hand stretched out and hollowed. -4 A handful (considered as a measure equal to two *palas.*).

प्रसृमर *a.* (*f.* —रा) Flowing forth, dropping, distilling.

प्रसृष्ट *p.p.* (*f.* —ष्टा) 1 Dismissed. -2 Hurt, injured. —ष्टा *f.* A finger stretched forth or extended.

प्रसेकः *m.* 1 Flowing forth, oozing -2 Sprinkling, wetting. -3 Emission, discharge. -4 Vomiting. -5 Watering of the mouth or nose. -6 The bowl of a spoon or ladle.

प्रसेदिका *f.* A small garden.

प्रसेवः, प्रसेवकः *m.* 1 A sack for grain. -2 A leathern bottle. -3 A small instrument of wood placed under the neck of the lute to make the sound deeper.

प्रस्कंदनं *n.* 1 Springing across or over. -2 Evacuation by stool; diarrhœa. —नः *m.* An epithet of Siva.

प्रस्कंदिका *f.* Dysentery.

प्रस्कन्न *p.p.* (*f.* —न्ना) 1 Sprung forth. -2 Fallen, dropped. -3 Defeated. —न्नः *m.* 1 An outcast. -2 A sinner, transgressor.

प्रस्कुंदः *m.* An altar of a circular shape.

प्रस्खलनं *n.* 1 Staggering. -2 Stumbling, falling.

प्रस्तरः *m.* 1 A couch of leaves and flowers. -2 A couch or bed in general -3 A flat surface; level plain. -4 A stone. -5 A precious stone, a gem. -6 A section of a work. -7 A handful of *darbha* grass.

प्रस्तरणं *n.*, —णा *f.* 1 A bed, couch. -2 A seat.

प्रस्तारः *m.* 1 Spreading out, covering. -2A bed of leaves and floweres. -3 A bed or couch in general. -4 Flat surface. -5 A thicket, wood. -6 (In prosody) A tabular representi n of the long and short vowels of a metre with all possible varieties. -7 A process in preparing minerals.

प्रस्तावः *m.* 1 Beginning, commencement, anything that has been commenced; the situation. -2 An introduction. -3 Mention, refererence. -4 An occasion, season; fit or proper time. -5 The occasion of a discourse, subject, topic -6 The prologue of a drama. (प्रस्तावे *ind.* On a suitable occasion, seasonably. प्रस्तावेन 1 Incidentally, occasionally. -2 Suitably). -Comp. —यज्ञः *m.* A conversation in which each interlocutor takes a part.

प्रस्तावना *f.* 1 Beginning, commencement. -2 An introduction, preface, exordium (in general). -3 An introductory dialogue at the beginning of a drama between the manager and one of the actors.

प्रस्तावित *a.* (*f.*-ता) 1 Begun, continued. 2 Mentioned.

प्रस्तिरः *m.* A bed of leaves and flowers.

प्रस्तीत,-म *a.* 1 Sounded. -2 Crowded together.

प्रस्तुत *p. p.* (*f.* —ता) 1 Praised, panegyrised. -2 Begun, commenced. -3 Done, effected. -4 Happened. -5 Approached. -6 Under discussion, taken in hand. —तं *n.* 1 The matter in hand, the subject under discussion or consideration. -2 (In Rhet.) Forming the subject of discussion ; the उपमेय. -Comp. —अंकुरः *m.* The figure of speech in which a reference is made to a passing circumstance to bring out something latent in the hearer's mind.

प्रस्थ *a.* (*f.* —स्था) 1 Going to, visiting, abiding in. -2 Going on a journey. -3 Spreading, expanding. -4 Firm, stable. —स्थः *m.*, -स्थं *n.* 1 A level expanse, level plain. -2 Table-land or the peak of a mountain. -3 A particular measure of capacity equal to thirty-two *palas*. -4 Anything measuring a *Prastha*. -Comp. —पुष्पः *m.* A variety of holy basil.

प्रस्थंपच *a.* Cooking a *Prastha*.

प्रस्थानं *n.* 1 Going forth, departure, moving, walking. -2 Procession, march; the march of an army or assailant. -3 A method, system. -4 Death, dying. -5 An inferior kind of drama.

प्रस्थापनं *n.* 1 Sending away, despatching. -2 Appointment to an embassy. -3 Proving, demonstrating. -4 Using, employing. -5 Carrying off cattle. —ना *f.* Sending away, despatching.

प्रस्थापित *p. p.* (*f.* -ता) 1 Sent away, despatched. -2 Established, proved. -3 Urged, pushed on.

प्रस्थित *p. p.* (*f.* —ता) Set out, gone forth, gone on a journey.

प्रस्थितिः *f.* 1 Going forth, departure. -2 A march, journey.

प्रस्नः *m.* A vessel for bathing.

प्रस्नवः *m.* 1 Flowing, pouring forth. -2 A stream or flow.

प्रस्निग्ध *a.* (*f.* —ग्धा) Very oily or greasy.

प्रस्नुत *p. p.* (*f.* —ता) Dropping, pouring forth. -Comp. -स्तनी *f.* One whose breasts distil milk (through excess of maternal love).

प्रस्नुषा *f.* The wife of a grandson.

प्रस्पंदनं *n.* Palpitating, vibrating, trembling.

प्रस्फुट *a.* (*f.* —टा) 1 Blown, expanded (as a flower). -2 Published, spread abroad (as a report). -3 Plain, manifest, evident.

प्रस्फुरित *p. p.* (*f.* —ता) Quivering, trembling, tremulous.

प्रस्फोटनं *n.* 1 Expanding, blooming. -2 Making clear or manifest, revealing. -3 Splitting. -4 Causing to bloom or blow. -5 Threshing corn. -6 A winnowing basket. -7 Striking, beating. -8 Wiping away, rubbing out.

प्रस्यंदः *m*, -दनं *n.* Flowing forth, trickling out, oozing.

प्रस्रंसिन् *a.* (*f.* —नी) Miscarrying.

प्रस्रवः *m.* 1 Trickling forth, flowing or oozing out. -2 A flow, stream. -3 Milk flowing from the breast or udder. -4 Urine -5 The overflowing scum of boiling rice. —वाः *m. pl.* Falling or gushing tears.

प्रस्रवणं *n.* 1 Flowing or gushing forth, trickling, oozing, dripping. -2 Flow or discharge of milk from the breast or udder.-3 A cascade, cataract. -4 A spring, fountain. -5 Sweat, perspiration. -6 Voiding urine. —णः *m.* N. of a mountain.

प्रस्रावः *m.* 1 Flowing, oozing. -2 Urine. -3 A spout. [issued.

प्रस्रुत *p. p.* (*f.* —ता) Oozed, trickled,

प्रस्व (–स्वा–) नः *m.* A loud noise.

प्रस्वापः *m.* 1 Sleep. -2 A dream. -3 A missile which brings on sleep.

प्रस्वापनं *n.* 1 Causing or inducing sleep. -2 A missile which induces sleep in the person attacked.

प्रस्विन्न *p. p.* (*f.* —न्ना) Sweated, perspired.

प्रस्वेदः *m.* Excessive perspiration.

प्रस्वेदित *p. p.* (*f.* —ता) 1 Covered with sweat. -2 Causing perspiration, hot.

प्रहणनं *n.* Killing, slaughter.

प्रहत *p. p.* (*f.* —ता) 1 Wounded, killed, slain. -2 Beaten, struck (as a drum). -3 Repulsed, defeated. -4 Spread, expanded. -5 Contiguous. -6 Beaten, frequented (as a track). -7 Accomplished ; learned.

प्रहरः *m.* The eighth part of a whole day ; a watch (a period of roughly. -3 hours). [the hours.

प्रहरकः *m.* 1 A watch. -2 Striking

प्रहरणं *n* 1 Striking, beating. -2 Casting, throwing. -3 Assailing, attacking. -4 Hurting. -5 Removing ; expelling. -6 A weapon, missile. -7 War, fight. -8 A covered litter or car. -9 The box of a carriage.

प्रहरणीयं *n.* A missile, weapon.

प्रहरिन् *m.* 1 A watchman. -2 A bell-man.

प्रहर्तृ *m.* (*f* -र्त्री) 1 One who strikes or beats ; an assailant. -2 Fighting, a fighter. -3 A shooter, an archer.

प्रहर्षः *m.* 1 Extreme joy, exultation. -2 Erection of the male organ.

प्रहर्षणं *n.* Enrapturing, making extremely glad. —णः *m.* The planet Mercury. [of a metre.

प्रहर्ष (-र्षि-) णी *f.* 1 Turmeric. -2 N.

प्रहर्षुलः *m.* The planet Mercury.

प्रहसनं *n.* 1 Loud or violent laughter, laughing, mirth. -2 Ridicule, mockery, irony, joke. -3 Satire, satirical writing. -4 A farce, a kind of low comedy.

प्रहसन्ती *f.* 1 A kind of jasmine. -2 A large fire-pan.

प्रहसितं *n.* Laughter, mirth.

प्रहस्तः *m.* 1 The open hand with the fingers extended. -2 N. of a general of Râvana. [quitting.

प्रहाणं *n.* Abandoning, omiting.

प्रहाणिः *f.* 1 Abandoning. -2 Deficiency, want.

प्रहारः *m.* 1 Striking, beating. -2 Wounding, killing. -3 A stroke, blow, knock. -4 A cut or thrust, as in खड्गप्रहारः. -5 A kick, as in पादप्रहारः. -6 Shooting. –Comp. –आर्त *n.* Acute pain caused by a wound.

प्रहारणं *n.* A desirable gift.

प्रहासः *m.* 1 Violent laughter. -2 Ridicule, derision -3 Irony, satire. -4 A dancer, an actor. -5 N. of Siva. -6 N. of a place of pilgrimage.

प्रहासकः *m.* A jester, buffoon.

प्रहासिन् *m.* A jester, buffoon.

प्रहिः *m.* A well.

प्रहित *p. p.* (*f.* –ता) 1 Placed or put forth -2 Extended, stretched out. -3 Sent, despatched. -4 Discharged, shot (as an arrow). -5 Appointed. -6 Appropriate, suitable. —तं *n.* A sauce, condiment.

प्रहीण *p. p* (*f.* —णा) Left, quitted,

abandoned. —णं Destruction, removal, loss.

प्रहुतः *m.*, —तं *n.* An offering of food to all created beings (भूतयज्ञ). One of the five daily Yajnas consisting in the offerings of food to all created beings (भूतयज्ञ).

प्रहूतिः *f.* An excellent oblation.

प्रहृत *p. p.* (*f.*—ता) Beaten, struck, hit, wounded. -तं *n.* A blow, stroke.

प्रहृष्ट *p. p.* (*f.* —ष्टा) 1 Delighted, pleased, overjoyed. -2 Thrilling, bristling (as hair). -Comp. —आत्मन्, —चित्त, —मनस् *a.* Rejoiced at heart.

प्रहृष्टकः *m.* A crow.

प्रहेणकं *n.* 1 A kind of cake.-2 Sweetmeats distributed at festivals

प्रहेलकः *m.* 1 A kind of cake or sweetmeat. -2 A riddle.

प्रहेला *f.* Loose conduct, playful dalliance.

प्रहेलिः, प्रहेलिका *f.* A riddle, an enigma, a conundrum. There are several kinds of these.

प्रह्ला (-ह्ला-) दः *m.* 1 Great joy, delight, happiness. -2 Sound. -3 N. of a son of the demon Hiranya-Kasipu.

प्रह्ला (-ह्ला-) दन *a.* (*f.* -ना) Gladdening, delighting. —नं *n.* Causing joy or delight, gladdening, delighting.

प्रह्रासः *m.* 1 Diminution, decrease. -2 Languishing, fading away.

प्रह्लन्न *p. p.* (*f.* —न्ना) Delighted, joyful, pleased.

प्रह्लत्तिः *f.* Pleasure, delight.

प्रह्व *a.* (*f.* —ह्वा) 1 Sloping, slanting, inclined. -2 Stooping, bent down ; bowing humbly down. -3 Submissive, humble. -4 Devoted to, engaged in, engrossed by. Comp. —अंजलि *a.* Bowing with the palms of the hand joined and put to the forehead as a mark of respect.

प्रह्वलिका *f.* See प्रहेलिका.

प्रह्वायः *m.* A call, summons, invitation.

प्रांशु *a.* 1 High, tall, lofty, of tall stature. -2 Long, extended. —शुः *m.* A tall man.

प्राक् *ind.* 1 Before (usually with abl.). -2 At first, already. -3 Before, previously, in a previous portion (as of a book). -4 In the east, to the east of. -5 In front. -6 As far as, up to. -7 At dawn or daybreak.

प्राकट्यं *n.* Manifestation, publicity, notoriety.

प्राकरणिक *a.* (*f.* —की) Pertaining to the subject of discussion, relevant to the matter in hand (often used in the sense of उपमेय in works on Rhetoric).

प्राकर्षिक *a.* (*f.* —की) Entitled to preference.

प्राकर्षिकः *m.* 1 A catamite. -2 A man supported by another's wife.

प्राकाम्यं *n.* 1 Freedom of will. -2 Wilfulness -3 Irresistible will, considered as one of the eight attributes or *siddhis* of Siva or the Supreme Being.

प्राकारः *m.* 1 A fence, an enclosure. -2 A rampart.

प्राकारीय *a.* (*f.* -या) 1 Fit for a wall. -2 Enclosed by a wall, walled.

प्राकाश्यं *n.* 1 Being known, publicity. -2 Fame, renown.

प्राकृत *a.* (*f.* -ता, -ती) 1 Original, natural, unmodified. -2 Usual, common, ordinary. -3 Uncultivated, vulgar, illiterate. -4 Insignificant, trifling. -5 Derived from 'Prakriti'. -6 Provincial, vernacular (as a dialect). —तः *m.* A low, ordinary or vulgar man. —तं *n.* A vernacular or provincial dialect derived from Sanskrit. (Many of these dialects are spoken by the female characters and inferior personages of Sanskrit plays). -Comp. —अरिः *m.* A natural enemy *i. e.* the ruler of an adjacent country. —उदासीनः *m.* A natural neutral *i. e.* a ruler whose dominions lie beyond those of the natural ally. —ज्वरः *m.* A common or ordinary fever. —प्रलयः *m.* Total dissolution of the universe. —मित्रं *n.* A natural ally *i. e.* a ruler whose dominions lie immediately beyond those of the natural enemy.

प्राकृतिक *a.* (*f.* —की) 1 Natural, derived from nature. -2 Illusory.

प्राक्तन *a.* (*f.* —नी) 1 Former, previous. -2 Old, ancient, early. -3 Relating to a former life. —नं *n.* Fate, destiny.

प्राखर्यं *n.* 1 Sharpness.-2 Pungency. -3 Wickedness. -4 Ardour, zeal.

प्रागल्भ्यं *n.* 1 Boldness, confidence. -2 Pride, arrogance.-3 Proficiency, skill. -4 Development, maturity. -5 Manifestation, appearance. -6 Eloquence. -7 Pomp, rank. -8 Resoluteness, determination. -9 Impudence.

प्रागारः *m.* A house, building.

प्राग्रं *n.* The highest point.-Comp. —सर *a.* First, foremost. —हर *a.* Chief, principal.

प्राग्राटः *m.* Thin coagulated milk.

प्राग्र्य *a.* (*f.* —ग्र्या) Chief, foremost, most excellent.

प्राघातः *m.* War, battle, [oozing.

प्राघारः *m.* Trickling out, dropping,

प्राघुणः प्राघूणकः, प्राघुणिकः, प्राघूर्णकः, प्राघूर्णिकः *m.* A guest, visitor.

प्राङ्गं *n.* A small kind of drum (पणव).

प्राङ्गणं (—नं) *n.* 1 A court, courtyard. -2 A floor (as of the house). -3 A kind of drum.

प्राच् *a.* (*f.*—ची) 1 Turned towards the front, in front, foremost. -2 Eastern, easterly. -3 Prior, previous, former. —*m. pl.* 1 The people of the east. -2 Eastern grammarians. -Comp. —अग्र *a.* (प्रागग्र) Having the point turned towards the east. —अभावः (प्रागभावः) *m.* Antecedent non-existence, non-existence of a thing previous to its production. —अभिहित (प्रागभिहित) *a.* Mentioned before. —अवस्था(प्रागवस्था) *f.* The former state. —आयत (प्रागायत) *a.* Extending towards the east. -उक्तिः *f.* (प्रागुक्तिः) Previous utterance.-उत्तर(प्रागुत्तर) *a.*,—उदंच् *a.* (प्रागुदंच्) North-eastern.-उदीची (प्रागुदीची) *f.* The north-east.-कर्मन्(प्राक्कर्मन्) *n.* An action done in a former life. —कालः (प्राक्कालः) *m.* A former age. —कालीन (प्राक्कालीन) *a.* Belonging to the former times, old, ancient. —कूल (प्राक्कूल) *a.* Having the points turned towards the east (said of Kusa grass). -कृतं (प्राक्कृतं) *n.* An act done in a former life. —चरणा (प्राक्चरणा) *f.* The female organ of generation. —चिरं (प्राक्चिरं) *ind.* Before too late. -जन्मन् (प्राग्जन्मन्) *n.* —जातिः (प्राग्जातिः) *f.* A former birth. —ज्योतिषः (प्राग्ज्योतिषः) *m.* 1 N. of country, also called Kâmarupa. -2 The people of this country (*m. pl.*). (-षं *n.*) N. of a city. -दक्षिण *a.* (प्राग्दक्षिण) South-eastern. —देशः (प्राग्देशः). *m.* The eastern country. —द्वार, -द्वारिक *a.* (प्राग्द्वार, प्राग्द्वारिक) *a.* Having doors facing the east. —न्यायः (प्राङ्न्यायः) *m.* The plea of a former trial, *res judicata.* —पदं (प्राक्पदं) *n.* The first member of a compound. —फलः (प्राक्फलः) *m.* The bread-fruit tree. -फ (-फा-)

ल्गुनी (प्राक्फ-फा-ल्गुनी) *f.* The eleventh lunar mansion. -फ (-फा-) ल्गुनी-भवः *m.* 1 The planet Jupiter. -2 N. of Brihaspati. —फाल्गुनः, —फाल्गुनेयः (प्राक्फाल्गुनः, प्राक्फाल्गुनेयः) *m.* Planet Jupiter. —भक्तं (प्राग्भक्तं) *n.* Taking medicine before meals. —भागः (प्राग्भागः) *m.* 1 The front. -2 The fore-part. —भारः (प्राग्भारः) *m.* 1 The top or summit of a mountain.-2The front part, fore-part or end (of anything). -3 A large quantity, heap, multitude, flood.-भावः (प्राग्भावः)*m.* 1 Previous existence. -2 Excellence, superiority. —मुख (प्राङ्मुख) *a.* 1 Turned towards or facing the east. -2 Inclined towards, wishing,desirous of. —वंशः (प्राग्वंशः) *m.* 1 A kind of sacrificial room having its columns turned towards the east; aparticular apartment in the sacrificial pavilion. -2 A former dynasty or generation.—वृत्तांतः (प्राग्वृत्तांतः) *m.* A former event. -शिरस्,-स, -शिरस्क (प्राक्शिरस् &c.) *a.* Having the head turned towards the east. -संध्या (प्राक्संध्या) *f.* The morning twilight. —सवनं (प्राक्सवनं) *n* A morning libation or sacrifice. —स्रोतस् (प्राक्स्रोतस्) *a.* Flowing eastward. (-*f.*) A river.

प्राचंड्यं *n.* 1 Vehemence, passion. -2 Fierceness.

प्राचिका *f.* 1 A mosquito. -2 A female falcon.

प्राची *f.* The east. -Comp. —पतिः *m.* An epithet of Indra. -मूलं *n.* The eastern horizon.

प्राचीन *a.* (*f.* —ना) 1 Turned towards the front or east; eastern, easterly. -2 Previous, previously mentioned. -3 Old, ancient. -नः*m*, —नं. *n.* A fence, wall. —नं *ind.* 1 In front. -2 Eastward (abl.).-3 Before. -Comp. —अग्र *a.* Having the point turned towards the east. —आवीतं *n.* The sacred thread (यज्ञोपवीत) worn over the right shoulder and passed under the left arm, as at a Srâddha. —आवीतिन्, —उपवीत *a.* Wearing the sacred thread over the right shoulder and under the left arm. -कल्पः *m.* A former कल्प. -गाथा *f.* Ancient story. —तिलकः *m.* The moon. —पनसः *m.* The An Bilva tree —बर्हिस् *m.* An epithet of Indra. -मतं.*n.* An ancient opinion.

प्राचीरं *n.*An enclosure,fence, wall.

प्राचुर्यं *n.* 1 Abundance, copiousness, plenty. -2 Multitude.

प्राचेतसः*m.*1A patronymic of Manu. -2 Of Daksha. -3 Of Válmiki.

प्राच्य *a.* (*f.* —च्या) 1 Situated in front. -2 Being or living in the east, eastern, easterly. -3Prior, previous. -4 Ancient, old. —च्याः *m. pl.* 1 The country south or east of the river Sarasvatî. -2 The people of this country. -Comp. —भाषा *f.* The eastern dialect; language spoken in the east of India.

प्राच्यक *a.* (*f.*-का) Eastern,easterly.

प्राछ् *a* (Nom. sing. प्राट्-ड्)Asking, questioning; as in शब्दप्राट्. -Comp. —विवाकः (प्राड्विवाकः) *m.* A judge, the presiding officer in a court of law.

प्राजकः *m.* A charioteer, coachman.

प्राजनः *m.*, —नं *n.* A whip, goad.

प्राजापत्य *a.* (*f.* —त्या) 1 Sacred to Prajápati. -2 Born of Prajápati (Brahman), (*m.*). -3 Belonging to Prajâpati.-त्यः *m.* 1 One of the eight forms of marriage in Hindu law, in which the father gives his daughter to the bridegroom with out taking any present from him in order that the two may live happily and faithfully together. -2 N. of the confluence of the Ganges and Yamunâ (प्रयाग), (also *n.*) -3 A kind of fast or penance. —त्या *f.* Giving away the whole of one's property before entering upon the life of an ascetic.

प्राजिकः, प्राजिन् *m.* A hawk.

प्राजितृ *m.* A charioteer, driver, coachman.

प्राजेशं, -षं *n.* The constellation [Rohini.

प्राज्ञ *a.* (*f.*-ज्ञा or -ज्ञी) 1 Intellectual. -2 Wise, learned, clever. -ज्ञः *m.* 1 A wise or learned man. -2 A kind of parrot. —ज्ञा *f.* 1 Intelligence, understanding. -2 A clever or intelligent woman. —ज्ञी *f.* 1 A clever or learned woman. -2 The wife of a learned man. -3 N. of a wife of the sun (सूर्यपत्नी).

प्राज्य *a.* (*f.* —ज्या) 1 Abundant, plentiful, much, many. -2 Great, large. -3 Lofty. [-2 Straight, erect.

प्रांजल *a.* (*f.* -ला) 1 Honest, sincere.

प्रांजलि *a.* Folding the hands in supplication, as a mark of respect or humility.

प्रांजलिक, प्रांजलिन् (*f.* —का, -नी) Same as प्रांजलि.

प्राणः *m.* 1 Breath, respiration. -2 The breath of life; vitality, principle of life (usually pl. in this sense, the Pránas being five viz. प्राण, अपान, समान, व्यान and उदान). -3 The first of the five life-winds or vital airs (which has its seat in the lungs). -4 Wind, air inhaled. -5 Energy, strength, power. -6 The spirit or soul (opp. शरीर). -7 The Supreme Spirit. -8 An organ of sense. -9 The life or essence of poetry; poetical talent or genius inspiration. -10 Aspiration as in महाप्राण or अल्पप्राण. -11 Digestion. -12 A breath as a measure of time. -13 Gum-myrrh. -Comp. —अतिपातः *m.* Killing a living being. —अधिनाथः *m.* A husband. —अधिपः *m.* The soul. —अंतः *m* Death. -अंतिक *a.* 1 Fatal, mortal. -2 Lasting to the end of life; ending with life. -3 Dangerous. -4 Capital (as a sentence). (-कं *n.*) Murder. —अयनं *n.* An organ of sense. —आघातः *m.* Destruction of life; killing a living being. —आचार्यः *m.* A physician to a king. —आत्मन् *m.* The vital or animal soul. —आद *a.* Fatal, mortal, causing death. -आबाधः *m.* Injury to life. —आयामः *m.* Restraining the breath during the mental recitation of the names or attributes of a deity. —आहुतिः *f.* An oblation to the five 'Pránas'. —ईशः, —ईश्वरः *m.* 1 A lover, husband. -2 Wind. -ईशा, -ईश्वरी *f.* A wife, a beloved mistress. —उत्क्रमणं *n.*, —उत्सर्गः *m.* Departure of the soul; death. —उपहारः *m.* Food, life. —ग्रहः *m.* The nose. —छेदः *m.* Murder. —त्यागः *m.* 1 Suicide. -2 Death. —दं *n.* 1 Water. -2 Blood. —दक्षिणा *f.* Gift of life. प्राणदक्षिणां दा To grant one his life. —दंडः *m.* Capital punishment. —दयितः *m.* A husband. —दानं *n.* 1 Resigning life. -2 The gift of life, saving one's life. —दुरोदरं, —द्यूतं *n.* Fighting for life. —द्रोहः *m.* An attempt upon any body's life. —धारणं *n.* 1 Maintenance or support of life. -2 Vitality. -3 A means of supporting life. -नाथः *m.* 1 A lover, husband. -2 An epithet of Yama. —पतिः *m.* 1 A lover, husband. -2 The soul. -प्रियः *m.* A lover, husband. —भक्ष a. Feeding on air only. —भास्वत् m. The ocean. —भृत् m. A living being. —मोक्षणं n. 1 Departure of life; death. -2 Suicide.—यात्रा f. 1 Support of life; maintenance, livelihood. — रंध्रं n. 1 The mouth. -2 A nostril.—सद्मन् n. The body.

प्राणकः m. 1 A living being. -2 Myrrh.

प्राणथः m. 1 Breathing. -2 Air, wind. -3 A sacred bathing place. -4 The lord of created beings.

प्राणनः m. 1 The throat. -2 Water. —नं n. 1 Respiration, breathing. -2 Life, living.

प्राणंतः m. Air, wind.

प्राणंती f. 1 Hunger. -2 Sobbing. -3 Sneezing.

प्राणमय a. Living, breathing. -Comp. —कोशः m. The vesture of the vital airs.

प्राणित a. Kept alive, being animated.

प्राणिन् m. 1 A living being. -2 A man. -Comp.-जातं n. A whole class of animals.—द्यूतं n. Gambling with fighting animals (cock-fighting, ram-fighting &c.) -पीडा f. Cruelty to animals. —हिंसा f. Injury to life, doing harm to living creatures.

—हिता f. A shoe, boot.

प्राणीत्यं n. Debt.

प्रातर् ind. 1 At day-break, at dawn. -2 The next or tomorrow morning. Comp. —अह्नः m. The early part of the day; forenoon.—आशः m. Breakfast. —आशिन् m. One who has breakfasted. —कालः (प्रातःकालः) m. Morning time. —गेयः m. A minstrel whose duty it is to wake up his lord in the morning with appropriate songs. —त्रिवर्गा (प्रातस्त्रिवर्गा) f. The river Ganges. —दिनं n. Forenoon. —प्रहरः (प्रातःप्रहरः) m. The first watch of the day. —भोक्तृ m. A crow.-संध्या (प्रातःसंध्या) f. 1 The morning twilight.-2 The morning devotions or Sandhyâ adoration of a Brâhmana.

प्रातस्तन a. (f. —नी) Relating to the morning.

प्रातस्तरां ind. Very early in the morning.

प्रातस्त्य a. (f.—स्त्या) Matutinal.

प्रातिः f. 1 The span of the thumb and the forefinger. -2 Filling.

प्रातिका f. The China rose (जवा).

प्रातिकूलिक a. (f. —की) Opposed, contrary.

प्रातिकूल्यं n. Adverseness, opposition, unfavourableness, unfriendliness.

प्रातिजनीन (f. —नी) Suitable against an adversary.

प्रातिज्ञं n. The topic under discussion.

प्रातिदैवसिक a. (f. —की) Occurring daily.

प्रातिपक्ष a. (f. —क्षी) Contrary, adverse, inimical.

प्रातिपक्ष्यं n. Enmity, hostility.

प्रातिपद a. (f. —दी) 1 Forming the commencement.-2 Produced in, or belonging to, the day called प्रतिपद्.

प्रातिपदिकः m. Fire.—कं n. The crude form of a substantive; a noun in its uninflected state (before receiving the case-terminations); अर्थवद्धातुरप्रत्ययः प्रातिपदिकं.

प्रातिपौरुषिक a. (f. —की) Relating to manliness or valour.

प्रातिभ a. (f. —भी) 1 Relating to divination or genius. -2 Intellectual, mental. —भं n. Genius or vivid imagination.

प्रातिभाव्यं n. Becoming answerable for the appearane of a debtor and for paying his debt.

प्रातिभासिक *a.* (*f.* —की) 1 Existing only in appearance : not real. -2 Looking like.

प्रातिलोमिक *a.* (*f.* —की) Adverse, hostile, disagreeable.

प्रातिलोम्यं *n.* 1 Inversion, inverted or reverse order.-2Hoslility,hostile feeling.

प्रातिवेशिकः, प्रातिवेश्मकः, प्रातिवेश्यकः *m.* A neighbour.

प्रातिवेश्यः *m.* 1 A neighbour (in general). -2 A next door neighbour.

प्रातिशाख्यं *n.* A grammatical treatise teaching the phonetic changes which words in any Sákhá of the Vedas undergo and teaching the mode of pronouncing the accents &c.

प्रातिस्विक *a.* (*f.* —की) 1 Peculiar; not common to others : one's own. -2 Granting to every one what is his due.

प्रातिहंत्रं *n.* Vengeance, revenge.

प्रातिहारः, प्रातिहारकः, प्रातिहारिकः *m.* A juggler, conjurer.

प्रातिहार्यं *n.* 1 Juggling, conjuring. -2Working miracles.-3 A miracle.

प्रातीतिक *a.* (*f.* —की) Mental, existing in the mind or imagination.

प्रातीपः *m.* A patronymic of Santanu.

प्रातीपिक *a.* (*f.*—की) Reverse,retrograde.

प्रात्यंतिकः *m.* A prince of the Pratyantas.

प्रात्ययिक *a.* (*f.* —की) 1 Confidential, trusty. -2 Standing bail for the trustworthiness of a debtor.

प्रात्यहिक *a.* (*f.* —की) Occurring every day : daily.

प्राथमकल्पिकः *m.* 1 A student who has just entered on the study of the Vedas. -2 A Yogin just commencing his course.

प्राथमिक *a.* (*f.* —की) 1 Primary, initial. -2 Former, previous. -3 Happening for the first time.

प्राथम्यं *n.* Being first, precedence, priority.

प्रादक्षिण्यं *n.* Going round a person or object from left to right keeping the right side towards the object circumambulated.

प्रादुर्भावः *m.* 1 Coming into existence, arising. -2 Becoming visible. -3 Becoming audible. -4 The appearance of a deity on earth.

प्रादुर्भूत *a.* (*f.* —ता) Appeared, manifested, displayed.

प्रादुस् *ind.* Visibly, evidently manifestly, in sight (used chiefly with भू, कृ and अस्).

प्रादुष्करणं *n.* Manifestation, making visble.

प्रादुष्यं *n.* Manifestation.

प्रादेशः *m.*1 The span of the thumb and forefinger.-2 A spot, region.

प्रादेशनं *n.* A gift, donation.

प्रादेशिक *a.* (*f.* —की) 1 Having precedents, precedented. -2 Limited, local. -3 Significant. -कः *m.* The owner of a district.

प्रादेशिन *a.* (*f.* —नी) A span long.

प्रादेशिनी *f.* The forefinger.

प्रादोष *a.* (*f.* -षी), प्रादोषिक *a.* (*f.*-की) Relating to the evening.

प्राधनिकं *n.* A destructive weapon. any war-implement.

प्राधानिक *a.* (*f.* —की) 1 Most eminent or excellent, pre-eminent. -2 Relating to or derived from Pradhâna.

प्राधान्यं *n.* 1 Pre-eminence, prominence. -2 Ascendancy, supremacy. -3 A chief or principal cause. (प्राधान्येन, प्राधान्यात्, प्राधान्यतः 'Chiefly',

' especially ', ' principally').

प्राधीत *a.* (*f.* —ता) Well-read, highly educated.

प्राध्ययनं *n.* Reading, studying.

प्राध्व *a.* (*f.* —ध्वा) 1 Distant, remote, long. -2 Bent, inclined. -3 Fastened, bound. -4. Favourable. —ध्वः *m.* A carriage. —ध्वं *ind.* 1 Favourably, suitably. -2 Crookedly.

प्रांतः *m.* 1 Edge, border, skirt. -2 Corner (as of the lips, eyes &c.) -3 Boundary, extremity. -4 Extreme verge, end. -5 A point, tip. -6 The back part. -Comp. —दुर्गं *n.* A suburb outside the walls of a town; a town near a fort. —शून्य *a.* A long road without shade.

प्रांतरं *n.* 1 A long, lonesome or solitary path. -2 A road without shade. -3 A forest, wilderness. -4 The hollow of a tree. -Comp. -शून्यः *m.* A long dreary road without trees.

प्राप *a.* (*f.* —पा) Arriving at, reaching, obtaining, as in दुष्प्राप.

प्रापक (*f.* —पिका) 1 Leading to, conveying. -2 Providing with. -3 Establishing, making valid. -4 Obtaining.

प्रापणं *n.* 1 Reaching, extending to. -2 Obtaining, attainment. -3 Coveying, leading to. -4 Procuring.

प्रापणिकः *m.* A trader, a merchant.

प्राप्त *p. p.* (*f.* —प्ता) 1 Obtained, won, acquired. -2 Attained to. -3 Met with, found. -4 Incurred, suffered. -5 Arrived, present. -6 Completed. -7 Proper, right. -8 Following from a rule. -Comp. —अनुज्ञ *a.* Allowed to depart. —अर्थ *a.* Successful. —कारिन् *a.* Doing what is right. —काल *a.* Opportune, seasonable ; suitable. —जीवन *a.* Revived, restored to life. —पंचत्व *a.* Dead. —प्रसवा *a.* 1 Delivered of a child. -2 Near her confinement. —भारः *m.* A beast of burden. —मनोरथ *a.* One who has obtained his desired object. —यौवन *a.* Arrived at the age of puberty; youthful. —रूप *a.* 1 Handsome, beautiful. -2 Wise, learned. -3 Fit, proper, worthy. —व्यवहार *a.* Able and legally authorised to manage his own affairs (opp. ' minor').

प्राप्तिः *f.* 1 Acquisition, gain, profit. -2 Arrival, coming to. -3 A guess, conjecture. -4 Lot, share, portion. -5 Fortune, luck. -6 Rise, production. -7 The power of obtaining anything (one of the eight Siddhis). -8 Union, collection (संहति). -9 The result of actions done in a former life. -10 Fate, destiny. -11 Application (as of a rule). -12 The successful termination of a plot (सुखागम). -Comp. —आशा *f.* The hope of obtaining anything (regarded as part of the development of the plot of a play).

प्राबल्यं *n.* 1 Ascendancy, superiority. -2 Power, force, might.

प्राबा (-वा-) लिकः *m.* A dealer in [coral.

प्राबोध (-बि-) कः *m.* 1 Dawn, daybreak. -2 A minstrel whose duty it is to wake his lord in the morning by singing appropriate songs.

प्राभंजनं *n.* The lunar mansion Svâti.

प्राभंजनिः *m.* 1 An epithet of Hanumat. -2 Of Bhîma.

प्राभवं *n.* Superiority, supremacy, predominance.

प्राभवत्यं *n.* Supremacy, authority, [power.

प्राभाकरः *m.* A follower of the Prabhâkara school of Mîmâmsâ philosophy.

प्राभातिक *a.* (*f.* —की) Relating to the morning; matutinal.

प्राभृतं, प्राभृतकं *n.* 1 A present, gift. -2 An offering to a deity or to a king. -3 A bribe.

प्रामाणिक *a.* (*f.* —की) 1 Established by proof; founded on authority. -2 Founded on the authority of scriptures. -4 Authentic, credible. -4 Relating to a प्रमाण. —कः *m.* 1 One who accepts proof. -2 One who is versed in logic; a logician. -3 The head of a trade.

प्रामाण्यं *n.* 1 Credibility, authenticity. -2 Proof, evidence, authority.

प्रामादिक *a.* (*f.* —की) Faulty, incorrect.

प्रामाद्यं *n.* 1 Error, fault, mistake. -2 Madness, frenzy. -3 Intoxication.

प्रामित्यं *n.* 1 Debt. -2 Death.

प्रायः *m.* 1 Departure; departure from life. -2 Seeking death by fasting; sitting down and abstaining from food with some object in view (generally in constructions with words like आस्, उपविश् &c.). -3 The largest portion; majority; majority of cases. -4 Excess, abundance, plenty. -5 A condition of life. (At the end of comp. प्राय may be translated by 'for the most part,' 'generally', 'mostly,' 'almost,' 'nearly,' *e. g.* मृतप्रायः 'almost dead', or by 'abounding or rich in,' 'full of', 'abundant', कमलामोदप्राया वनानिलाः 'full of the fragrance' &c.; or by 'like', 'resembling'; वर्षशतप्रायं दिनं, अमृतप्रायं वचनं &c.).-Comp. —उपगमनं, —उपवेशनं *n.*, उपवेशः *m.*, —उपवेशनिका *f.* Sitting down and abstaining from food with a view to die; fasting oneself to death. —उपेत *a.* Prepared to die by abstaining from food. —उपविष्ट, —उपवेशिन *a.* Fasting oneself to death; who sits without food at the door of another to exact compliance with his demands. —दर्शनं *n.* An ordinary phenomenon.

प्रायणं *n.* 1 Entrance, beginning, commencment. -2 The path of life. -3 Voluntary death. -4 Taking refuge.

प्रायणीय *a.* (*f.* —या) Introductory, initiatory. —यं *n.* The first. —यः *m.* 1 An introductory libation at a Soma sacrifice. -2 The first day of a Soma sacrifice.

प्रायशस् *ind.* Generally, for the most part, in all probability.

प्रायश्चित्तं *n.*, प्रायश्चित्तिः *f.* 1 Atonement, expiation, a religious act to atone for sin. -2 Satisfaction, amends (in general).

प्रायश्चित्तिन् *m.* One who makes an atonement.

प्रायस् *ind.* 1 Mostly, generally, as a general rule. -2 Most likely, probably, perhaps. -3 Abundantly, largely.

प्रायाणिक, प्रायात्रिक *a.* (*f.* -की) Necessary or suitable for a journey.

प्रायिक *a.* (*f.*—की) Usual, common.

प्रायुद्धेषिन् *m.* A horse.

प्रायेण *ind.* 1 Mostly, as a general rule. -2 Probably.

प्रायोगिक *a.* (*f.* —की) 1 Applied. -2 Applicable.

प्रारब्ध *p. p.* (*f.*—ब्धा) Begun, commenced. —ब्धं *n.* 1 What is begun, an under-taking. -2 Fate, destiny.

प्रारब्धिः *f.* 1 Beginning, commencement. -2 A rope for fastening an elephant.

प्रारंभः *m.* 1 Beginning, commencement. -2 An undertaking, enterprize

प्रारंभणं *n.* Commencing, beginning.

प्रारोहः *m.* A shoot, a new leaf.

प्रार्णं *n.* A chief debt.

प्रार्थक *a.* (*f.* —र्थिका) Asking, begging, soliciting, entreating, wishing. —कः *m.* A suitor, petitioner.

प्रार्थनं *n.*, -ना *f.* 1 A request, prayer, solicitation, a suit. -2 A wish.

प्रार्थनीय *pot. p.* (*f.* —या) 1 To be prayed for or solicited. -2 To be desired. —यं *n.* The third or Dvápara age.

प्रार्थित *p. p.* (*f.* —ता) 1 Begged, requested, sought for, solicited. -2 Wished, desired. -3 Attacked. -4 Killed, hurt.

प्रालंबः *m.* 1 A kind of pearl-ornament. -2 A female breast. —बं *n.* A garland worn round the neck and reaching to the breast.

प्रालंबकं *n.* See प्रालंबं.

प्रालंबिका *f.* A kind of gold neck- [lace.

प्रालेयं *n.* Snow, frost, hoar frost, dew. -Comp. —अद्रिः, —शैलः *m.* The Himálaya. —अंशुः, —करः, —रश्मिः *m.* 1 The moon. -2 Camphor. —लेशः *m.* A hail-stone.

प्रावटः *m.* Barley.

प्रावर्णं *n.* A spade, hoe, shovel.

प्रावरः *m.* 1 A fence, an enclosure. -2 An upper garment. -3 N. of a country.

प्रावरणं *n.* A garment, covering, upper garment, mantle.

प्रावरणीयं *n.* An upper garment.

प्रावारः *m.* 1 An upper garmant, a mantle. -2 N. of a district. -Comp. —कीटः *m.* A kind of white ant.

प्रावारकः *m.* An upper garment, mantle.

प्रावारिकः *m.* A maker of upper gar- [ments.

प्रावास *a.* (*f.* -सी) Relating to a journey.

प्रावासिक *a.* (*f.* —की) Suitable or fit for a journey.

प्रावीण्यं *n.* Cleverness, skilfulness, [dexterity.

प्रावृत *p. p.* (*f.* —ता) Enclosed, surrounded, covered, screened. —तः *m.*, -तं *n.* A veil, mantle.

प्रावृतिः *f.* 1 An enclosure, a hedge. -2 Spiritual darkness.

प्रावृत्तिक *a.* (*f.* —की) 1 Secondary. -2 Well-informed. —कः *m.* A messenger.

प्रावृष् *f.* The rainy season, monsoon (the months आषाढ and श्रावण).

प्रावृषः *m.*, -षा *f.* The rainy season, monsoons.

प्रावृषिक, प्रावृषीण *a.* (*f.* —की, —णा) Produced in the rainy season. —कः *m.* A peacock.

प्रावृषेण्य *a.* (*f.* —ण्या) 1 Produced in or relating to the rainy season. -2 Abundant, copious. -3 To be paid in the rainy season (as a debt &c.). —ण्यः *m.* 1 The Kadamba tree. -2 The Kutaja tree. —ण्यं *n.* Abundance, plenty.

प्रावृष्यः *m.* 1 A kind of Kadamba tree. -2 The Kutaja tree. —ष्यं *n.* Lapis lazuli.

प्रावेण्यं *n.* A fine woollen covering.

प्रावेशन *a.* (*f.* —नी) To be given or done on entering. -नं *n.* A workshop, manufactory.

प्रावेशिक *a.* (*f.* —की) Relating to or connected with entrance (into a house or upon the stage).

प्राव्रज्यं *n.*, प्राव्राज्यं *n.* 1 The life of a religious mendicant or recluse. -2 Vagrancy; wandering habit.

प्राशः *m.* 1 Eating, feeding on. -2 Food.

प्राशनं *n.* 1 Eating, feeding upon. -2 Causing to eat or taste. -3 Food.

प्राशनीय *a.* (*f.* —या) Eatable, serving as food. -यं *n.* Food. [nence.

प्राशस्त्यं *n.* Excellence, pre-emi-

प्राशित *p. p.* (*f.* —ता) Eaten, tasted, consumed. -तं *n.* 1 A daily offering of rice and water to the Manes. -2 Eating.

प्राशित्रं *n.* 1 The portion of oblation partaken by Brahman (*m.*) at a sacrifice. -2 The vessel in which this oblation is placed. -3 Anything eatable,

प्राश्निकः *m.* 1 An examiner. -2 An umpire, a judge.

प्रासः *m.* 1 Throwing, discharging. -2 A barbed missile. -3 Insertion.

प्रासकः *m.* 1 A barbed missile. -2 A die.

प्रासंगः *m.* A yoke for cattle.

प्रासंगिक *a.* (*f.* —की) 1 Proceeding from close connection. -2 Connected with; innate. -3 Incidental, occasional. -4 Relevant. -5 Seasonable, opportune. -6 Episodical.

प्रासंग्यः *m.* A draught-ox.

प्रासादः *m.* 1 A palace, mansion. -2 A royal mansion. -3 A temple, shrine. -4 A raised platform for spectators. -Comp. —अंगनं *n.* The court-yard of a palace or temple. —कुक्कुटः *m.* A tame pigeon. —तलं *n.* The surface or flat roof of a palace. —पृष्ठः *m.* A balcony on the top of a palace. -प्रतिष्ठा *f.* The consecration of a temple. —प्रस्तरः *m.* The flat roof of a house. -मंडना *f.* The kind of orpiment. -शृंगं *n.* The spire or pinnacle of a palace or temple; a turret.

प्रासादिक *a.* (*f.* —की) 1 Given as a favour. -2 Kind, friendly. -3 Beautiful, lovely.

प्रासूतिक *a.* (*f.* -की) Relating to delivery or child-birth.

प्रास्त *p. p.* (*f.*-स्ता) 1 Thrown, cast, discharged. -2 Expelled, turned out.

प्रास्ताविक *a.* (*f.* —की) 1 Introductory, prefatory. -2 Seasonable, opportune, timely. -3 Relevant (to the matter in hand).

प्रास्तुत्यं *n.* Being under discussion.

प्रास्थानिक *a.* (*f.* —की) 1 Relating to or proper at the time of departure. -2 Favourable to a departure.

प्रास्थिक *a.* (*f.* —की) 1 Weighing a *Prastha.* -2 Bought for a *Prastha.* -3 Containing a *Prastha.* -4 Sown with a ***Prastha.*** [dancing.

प्राह्नः *m.* Instruction in the art of

प्राह्णः *m.* The forenoon.

प्राह्णेतन *a.* (*f.* -नी) Relating to or happening in the forenoon.

प्राह्णेतरां, -मां *ind.* Very early in the morning.

प्रिय *a.* (*f.*-या; compar. प्रेयस्; superl. प्रेष्ठ) 1 Dear, beloved, favourite. -2 Pleasing, agreeable. -3 Dear, expensive. -यः *m.* 1 A lover, husband. -2 A kind of deer. -या *f.* 1 A beloved (wife), wife, mistress. -2 A woman in general. -3 Small cardamoms. -4 News, information. -5 Spirituous liquor. -6 A kind of jasmine. -यं *n.* 1 Love. -2 Kindness, favour. -3 Pleasing or gladsome news. -4 Pleasure -यं *ind.* In a pleasing or agreeable manner. -Comp. —अंबुः *m.* The mango tree. —आख्य *a.* Announcing good news. —आत्मन् *a.* Amiable, pleasant, agreeable. —उपपत्तिः *f.* A happy or pleasant occurrence. —एषिन् *a.* 1 Desirous of pleasing or doing service. -2 Friendly, affectionate. —कर *a.* Giving or causing pleasure. -कामः *a.* Desirous of rendering service. —कृत् *m.* 1 A friend, benefactor. -2 N. of

Vishnu. -जनः m. A beloved or dear person.-जानिः m. A husband who dearly loves his wife. -दर्श a. Agreeable to look at. —दर्शन a. Good-looking, lovely, handsome. (-नः m.) 1 A parrot. -2 A kind of date tree. -3 N. of a prince of the Gandharvas. —देवन a. Fond of gambling. —धन्वः m. An epithet of Siva. —पुत्रः m. A kind of bird. —प्रसादनं n. The conciliation of a husband. -प्राय a. Exceedingly kind or courteous. (-यं n.) Eloquence in language. -प्रायस n. A lover's speech.-भाषिन् a. Speaking sweet words. —रण a. Warlike, heroic. —वक्तृ a. Flattering, a flatterer. —वर्णी f. The plant called प्रियंगु. —वाच् a. Speaking kindly, affable in address. —वादिका f. A kind of musical instrument. -वादिन a. Speaking kind or pleasing words. (-नी f.) A kind of bird. -संदेशः m. 1 A friendly message, the message of a lover. -2 The tree called चंपक.

प्रियंवद a. Sweet-speaking, affable in address; agreeable. —दः m. 1 A kind of bird.-2 N. of a Gandharva.

प्रियकः m. 1 A kind of deer. -2 The tree called नीप.-3 The creeper प्रियंगु. -4 A bee. -5 A kind of bird. -6 Saffron. —कं n. A flower of the *asana* tree.

प्रियंकर, प्रियंकरण, प्रियंकार a 1 Acting kindly or affectionately. -2 Agreeable. -3 Amiable.

प्रियंगुः m., f. 1 N. of a creeper (said to put forth blossoms when touched by women).-2 Long pepper. -गु n. Saffron.

प्रियतमः m. A lover, husband. —मा f. A wife, mistress, beloved.

प्रियंभविष्णु, प्रियंभावुक a. Amiable, dearly loved. [—का f. A vine.

प्रियालः m. The tree called Piyâl.

प्री 9 U. (प्रीणाति, प्रीणीते, प्रीत) 1 To please, satisfy, gladden. -2 To be pleased, take delight in. -3 To act kindly towards. -4 To be cheerful or gay.

प्री 4 A (प्रीयते) 1 To be satisfied or pleased, be gratified. -2 To feel affection for love.-3 To be satisfied.

प्री 1 P. To please, gratify.

प्रीण a. (f. —णा) 1 Pleased, satisfied, gratified. -2 Old, ancient. -3 Previous.

प्रीणनं n. 1 Pleasing, satisfying. -2 That which pleases or satisfies.

प्रीत p. p. (f. —ता) 1 Pleased, delighted, gladdened. -2 Glad, joyful. -3 Content. -4 Dear, beloved. -5 Kind, affectionate.

प्रीतिः f. Pleasure, happiness, satisfaction, delight, gratification. -2 Favour, kindness. -3 Love, affection. -4 Liking or fondness for. -5 Friendliness, amity.-6 Conciliation. -7 N. of a wife of Cupid and rival of Rati. -Comp. —कर्मन् n. A kind action. —जुषा f. N. of the wife of अनिरुद्ध. —दृश् m. N. of Cupid. -दः m. A jester or buffoon in a play. —दत्तं n. The property given to a female by her relatives, particularly by her father-in-law or mother-in-law at the time of marriage. -पात्रं n. An object of love, any beloved person or object.-पूर्व,-पूर्वकं ind. Kindly, affectionately. —युज् a. Dear, affectionate, beloved. —विवाहः m. A love-marriage. —श्राद्धं n. A sort of Sráddha or obsequial ceremony performed in honour of the Manes of both parents.

प्रुष् 1 P. (प्रोषति, प्रुष्ट) 1 To burn, consume. -2 To reduce to ashes.

प्रुष् 9. P. (प्रुष्णाति) 1 To become wet or moist.-2 To pour out, sprinkle. -3 To fill.

प्रुष्ट *p. p.* (*f.* —ष्टा) Burnt, consumed, reduced to ashes.

प्रुष्वः *m.* 1 The rainy season. -2 The sun. -3 A drop of water.

प्रेक्षकः *m.* A spectator, looker on.

प्रेक्षणं *n.* 1 Viewing, seeing. -2 A view, appearance. -3 The eye. -4 Any show or spectacle, a show. -5 A dramatic representation. -6 A place where public exhibitions are held. -Comp. -कूटं *n.* The eyeball.

प्रेक्षणकं *n.* A show, spectacle.

प्रेक्षणिका *f.* A woman fond of seeing shows.

प्रेक्षणीय *pot. p.* (*f*, —या) 1 To be seen or gazed at, visible, apparent. -2 Fit to be seen, beautiful to look at.-3 To be considered or regarded.

प्रेक्षणीयकं *n.* A show, sight, spectacle.

प्रेक्षा *f.* 1 Viewing, beholding. -2 A look, sight, appearance. -3 Any public spectacle or show; a sight. 4 A theatrical show; dramatic performance, play. -5 Intellect, understanding. -6 Reflection, deliberation. -7 The branch of a tree.-Comp. —अ (-आ-) गारः *m.*, -रं, -गृहं, -स्थानं *n.* 1 A theatre or playhouse. -2 A council-chamber. -कारिन् *a.* Wise, prudent, circumspect. —समाजः *m.* An audience, a crowd of spectators, assembly.

प्रेक्षित *p. p.* (*f.* -ता) Seen, viewed, beheld; gazed or looked at. -तं *n.* A look, glance.

प्रेंख् 1 P. To vibrate, shake, tremble. swing to and fro; oscillate.

प्रेंखः *m.*, -खं *n.* A swing.

प्रेंखण *a.* (*f.* -णा) Wandering, moving, going towards, entering. -णं *n.* 1 Swinging. -2 A swing. -3 A minor drama in one act having no Sutradhâra, hero &c.

प्रेंखा *f.* 1 A swing. -2 Dancing. -3 Wandering, travelling. -4 A kind of building or house. -5 A particular pace of a horse.

प्रेंखित *p. p.* (*f.* -ता) Swung, shaken, oscillated.

प्रेंखोल् 10 U. (प्रेंखोलयति,-ते) To swing, shake, oscillate.

प्रेंखोलः *m.*, प्रेंखोलनं *n.* 1 Swinging, shaking, oscillating. -2 A swing.

प्रेत *p. p.* (*f.* —ता) Departed from this world, dead. —तः *m.* 1 The departed spirit, the spirit before obsequial rites are performed. -2 A ghost, evil spirit. -Comp. —अधिप *m.* An epithet of Yama.-अन्नं *n.* Food offered to the Manes. —आवासः *m.* A burial-ground, cemetery. -ईशः, -ईश्वरः *m.* An epithet of Yama. -उद्देशः *m.* An offering to the Manes. —कर्मन्, —कृत्यं *n.*, -कृत्या *f.* Obsequial or funeral rites. —गत *a.* Dead. -गृहं *n.* A cemetery.-गोपः *m.* The keeper of the dead. —चारिन् *m.* An epithet of Siva. -नदी *f.* The river वैतरणी. -नरः *m.* A goblin, ghost. —निर्यातकः, —निर्हारकः A man employed or carry out dead bodies. -पक्षः *m.* N. of the dark half of Bhâdrapada when offerings in honour of the Manes are usually performed. —पतिः *m.* Yama. —पुरं *n.* The city of Yama.—भावः *m.* Death. —भूमिः *f.* A cemetery. —मेधः *m.* A funeral sacrifice. —राक्षसी *f.* The holy basil (तुलसी).-राजः *m.* An epithet of Yama. -लोकः *m.* The world of the dead. -वनं *n.* An cemetery.

-शुद्धि *f.*,-शौचं *n.* A purification after the death of a relative. —श्राद्धं *n.* An obsequial offering made to a departed relative during the year of his death. -हारः *m.* 1 One who carries out a dead body. -2 A near relative.

प्रेतिकः *m.* A ghost, spirit.

प्रेत्य *ind.* Having departed (from this world); after death, in the next world. -Comp.—जातिः *f.* Position in the next world. —भावः *m.* The condition of soul after death.

प्रेत्वन् *m.* 1 Wind. -2 An epithet of Indra.

प्रेप्सा *f.* 1 Desire of obtaining. -2 Desire (in general). -3 Supposition, assumption.

प्रेप्सु *a.* 1 Desirous of obtaining, longing for. -2 Aiming at.

प्रेमन् *m., n.* 1 Love, affection. -2 Favour, kindness, tender regard. -3 Sport, pastime. -4 Joy, delight, gladness. -*m.* 1 A jest, joke. -2 Wind, air. -3 An epithet of Indra. -Comp. -पर *a.* Affectionate, loving. —पातनं *n.* 1 Tears (of joy). -2 The eye (that sheds them). —पात्रं *n.* Any beloved person or thing. -बंधः *m.*, -बंधनं *n.* A bond or tie of affection.

प्रेमिन् *a.* (*f.* -णी) Loving, affectionate.

प्रेयस् *a.* (*f.* -सी) Dearer, more agreeable (comper. of प्रिय). —*m.* 1 A lover, husband. -2 A dear friend. —*m.*, —*n.* Flattery.—सी *f.* A wife, mistress. -Comp. —अपत्यः *m.* (प्रेयोपत्यः) A heron (fond of offspring.

प्रेरक *a.* (*f.* —रिका) 1 Impelling, urging. -2 Sending, directing.

प्रेरणं *n* , -णा *f.* 1 Driving or urging on, inciting, instigation. -2 Impulse, passion. -3 Throwing, casting. -4 Sending, despatching. -5 Order, direction. -6 (In gram.). The sense of the causal form. -7 Activity, exertion.

प्रेरित *p. p.* (*f.*-ता) 1 Impelled, urged, instigated. -2 Excited, prompted. -3 Sent, despatched. -4 Ordered. -5 Directed, cast. -6 Touched. -तः *m.* An envoy, a messenger.

प्रेषः *m.* 1 Urging on. -2 Affliction, pain, sorrow.

प्रेषणं *n.*,-णा *f.* 1 Sending, despatching. -2 Sending on a mission, directing, commissioning. -3 Executing a commission.

प्रेषित *p. p.* (*f.* -ता) Despatched (on an errand).-2 Ordered, directed. -3 Turned, fixed upon, directed towards, cast (as eyes). -4 Banished. -5 Sent away.

प्रेष्य *a.* (*f.* -ष्या) To be ordered or despatched.-ष्यः *m.* 1 A servant, slave. -2 A messenger. —ष्या *f.* A female servant, hand-maid. -ष्यं *n.* 1 Sending on a mission.-2 Servitude. -Comp. —भावः *m.* Servitude, bondage. -वर्गः *m.* The body of servants, suite, train.

प्रेष्ठ *p. p.* (*f.* -ष्ठा) Dearest, most beloved. (superl. of प्रिय q. v.). -ष्ठः *m.* A lover, husband. -ष्ठा *f.* 1 A wife, mistress. -2 A leg.

प्रेहि (Second person sing. of the imperative of इ with प्र)-Comp. -कटा *f.* A rite in which no mats are allowed.-कर्दमा *f.* A rite in which no impurity is allowed. -द्वितीया *f.* A rite at which no second person is allowed to be present. —वाणिजा *f.* A rite at which no merchants are allowed to be present.

प्रैयं *n.* Being kind, kindness, love.

प्रैषः *m.* 1 Sending, directing. -2 An order, invitation. -3 Affliction. -4 Madness, frenzy. -5 Crushing, squeezing.

प्रैष्यः *m.* A servant, menial, slave. —ष्या *f.* A female servant. -ष्यं *n.* Servitude, slavery.

प्रोक्षणं *n.* 1 Sprinkling. -2 Consecration by sprinkling. -3 Killing of animals at a sacrifice. -4 A text to be repeated at an animal-sacrifice. —णी, -प्रोक्षणिः *f.* Water for consecrating. -2 The vessel containing holy water.

प्रोक्षणीयं *n.* Water for consecrating.

प्रोक्षित *p. p.* (*f.* -ता) 1 Purified or consecrated by sprinkling. -2 Immolated at a sacrifice. -3 Offered in sacrifice.

प्रोग्रंड *a.* (*f.* —डा) Exceedingly frightful or terrible.

प्रोच्चारित *a.* Sounding loudly.

प्रोच्चैस् *ind.* 1 Very loudly, aloud. -2 In a very high degree.

प्रोच्छून *a.* (*f.* —ना) 1 Dilated. -2 Swollen. [elevated.

प्रोच्छ्रित *p. p.* (*f.* —ता) High, lofty,

प्रोज्जासनं *n.* Killing, slaughter.

प्रोज्झनं *n.* Abandoning, quitting, leaving.

प्रोज्झित *p. p.* (*f.*—ता) Abandoned, quitted, forsaken, avoided.

प्रोञ्छनं *n.* 1 Wiping away, wiping out, effacing. -2 Picking up remnants. [away.

प्रोड्डीन *a.* (*f.* -ना) Flown up or

प्रोंठः *m.* A spitting-pot, spittoon.

प्रोत *p. p.* (*f.* -ता) 1 Sewn, stitched. -2 Extended lengthwise or perpendicularly (opp. ओत). -3 Tied, bound, fastened. -4 Pierced, transfixed. -तं *n.* A garment, woven cloth. -Comp. -उत्सादनं *n.* 1 An umbrella. -2 A cloth-house, a tent.

प्रोत्कंठ *a.* (*f.* -ठा) Lifting up or stretching out the neck.

प्रोत्कुष्टं *n.* A loud noise or uproar.

प्रोत्तुंग *a.* (*f.* -गा) Very high or lofty.

प्रोत्फुल्ल *a.* (*f.* -ल्ला) 1 Full-blown, expanded. -2 Fully dilated, wide open.

प्रोत्सारणं *n.* Getting rid of, clearing away, expelling.

प्रोत्सारित *p. p.* (*f.* —ता) Removed, expelled. -2 Urged forward. -3 Relinquished.

प्रोत्साहः *m.* 1 Zeal, ardour. -2 An incentive, a stimulus.

प्रोत्साहकः *m.* 1 An inciter, instigator. -2 (In law) An instigator of a crime.

प्रोत्साहनं *n.* Inciting, stimulating.

प्रोथ् 1 U. (प्रोथति,-ते) To be equal to, be a match for, withstand (with dat. or gen) *e. g.* पुप्रोथास्मै न कश्चन.

प्रोथ *a.* (*f.* —था) 1 Famous, well-known. -2 Placed, fixed -3 Setting out on a journey. -थः *m.*, -थं *n.* 1 The nose or nostrils of a horse. -2 The snout of a hog. -थः *m.* 1 The hip, buttocks. -2 An excavation. -3 A garment. -4 Embryo. -5 Terror, fright.

प्रोथिन् *m.* A horse.

प्रोद्घुष्ट *p. p.* (*f.*-ष्टा) 1 Resounding, resonant. -2 Making a loud noise.

प्रोद्घोषणं *n.*, -णा *f.* 1 Proclaiming, proclamation. -2 Sounding aloud.

प्रोद्दीप्त *p. p.* (*f.* —प्ता) Set on fire, burning, blazing.

प्रोद्भिन्न *p. p.* (*f.* -न्ना) 1 Germinated, shot up. -2 Burst forth.

प्रोद्भूत *p. p.* (*f.* —ता) Sprung up, arisen.

प्रोद्यत *p. p.* (*f.* -ता) 1 Lifted up. -2 Active, industrious.

प्रोद्वाहः *m.* Marriage.

प्रोन्नत *p. p.* (*f.* -ता) 1 Very high or lofty. -2 Projecting. -3 Superior to. -4 Powerful, strong.

प्रोन्मीलनं *n.* Disclosing ; opening.

प्रोल्लाघित *a.* (*f.* -ता) 1 Recovered from sickness. -2 Robust.

प्रोल्लेखनं *n.* Scratching ; marking.

प्रोष: *m.* Burning, combustion.

प्रोषित *p. p.* (*f.* -ता) Gone abroad, living abroad, away from home, living in a foreign country.-Comp. -भर्तृका *f.* A woman whose husband is gone abroad ; one of the eight Nâyikás in erotic poetry.

प्रो (प्रौ-) ष्ठ: *m.* 1 A bull, an ox. -2 A bench, stool. -3 A kind of fish (-ष्ठी *f.* also). -Comp. —पद: *m.* The month भाद्रपद. (-दा *f.*) The 25th and 26th lunar mansions ; पूर्वाभाद्रपदा and उत्तराभाद्रपदा. —पाद् *a.* Born under the above Nakshatra.

प्रो (प्रौ-) ह: *m.* 1 Reasoning, logic. -2 An elephant's foot or ankle. -3 A knot, joint.

प्रौ (-प्रो-) ढ *a.* (*f.* -ढा) 1 Full-grown, developed, matured, ripened, full (as moon &c.). -2 Adult, old, grown up ; veteran. -3 Thick, dense. -4 Mighty, strong. -5 Violent, impetuous. -6 Proud. -ढा *f.* A bold and grown-up woman, one of the four principal female characters in poetic compositions. -Comp. -अंगना *f* A bold woman. -उक्ति: *f.* A pompous sheech.-प्रताप *a.* Of great or mighty valour.-यौवन *a.* Advanced in youth. -वाद: *m.* An arrogant or bold assertion.

प्रौ (प्रो-) ढि: *f.* 1 Full development, maturity, perfection. -2 Growth, increase. -3 Greatness, elevation, dignity. -4 Boldness, audacity. -5 Pride, arrogance.-6 Zeal, exertion, enterprize.-Comp.-वाद: *m.* 1 A pompous speech. -2 A bold assertion.

प्रौण *a* (*f.* -णा) Clever, learned, skilful.

प्रौष्ठपद: *m.* N. of the month Bhâdrapada. -दी *f.* The full moon in the month of Bhâdrapada.

प्लक्ष: *m.* 1 The Indian fig-tree. -2 One of the seven Dvîpas or continents of the world. -3 A private entrance. -4 The space at the side of a door. -Comp. -जाता, -समुद्रवाचका *f.* An epithet of the river Sarasvatî. -तीर्थ, -प्रस्रवणं *n.*, -राज् *m.* The place where the Sarasvatî rises.

प्लव *a.* (*f.* —वा) 1 Swimming, floating. -2 Jumping, leaping. -व: *m.* 1 Swimming, floating -2 Flood, swelling of a river. -3 A jump. -4 A float, small boat. -5 A frog. -6 A monkey. -7 A declivity, slope. -8 An enemy. -9 A sheep -10 A Chândála. -11 A snare for catching fish. -12 The fig-tree. -13 The Kârandava bird, a kind of duck. -14 Five or more stanzas syntactically connected (=कुलक). -15 The prolated utterance of a vowel.-Comp.-ग: *m.* A monkey.-2. A frog. -3 The diver. -4 The tree शिरीष. -5 N. of the sun's charioteer. (-गा *f.*) The sign of the zodiac called *Virgo*.-गति: *m.* A frog.

प्लवक: *m.* 1 A frog. -2 A jumper, rope-dancer. -3 The holy fig-tree. -4 A Chándála, an outcast. -5 A monkey.

प्लवंग: *m.* 1 An ape, a monkey. -2 A deer. -3 The fig-tree.

प्लवंगम: *m.* 1 A monkey.-2 A frog. -Comp.-इंदु: *m.* An epithet of Hanumat.

प्लवनं *n.* 1 Swimming. -2 Bathing,

plunging into. -3 Flying. -4 Jumping. -5 A deluge. -6 A declivity. -7 One of a horse's paces (capering).

प्लवाका *f.* A float, raft.

प्लविक *a.* (*f.* -का) Taking over in a boat, a ferry-man.

प्लाक्षं *n.* The fruit of प्लक्ष.

प्लाव: *m.* 1 Flowing over. -2 Jumping. -3 Straining a liquid (to remove impurities &c.). -4 Submersion.

प्लावनं *n.* 1 Bathing. -2 Overflowing, inundating. -3 A flood, deluge.

प्लावित *p. p.* (*f.* —ता) 1 Made to swim, float or overflow. -2 Deluged. -3 Moistened, sprinkled. -4 Covered with, smeared.

प्लिह् 1 A. (प्लेहते) To go, move.

प्ली 9. P. (प्लिनाति) To go, move.

प्लीहन्, प्लिहन् *m.* The spleen or its enlargement. -Comp. -उदरं *n.* An enlargement of the spleen. -उदरिन् *a.* Affected with enlargement of the spleen.

प्लीहा *f.* The spleen.

प्लु 1 A (प्लवते, प्लुत) 1 To float, swim. -2 To cross in a boat. -3 To swing to and fro, vibrate. -4 To leap, jump. -5 To plunge into. -6 To fly or haste away. -7 To blow (as the wind). -8 To fade away. -9 To hover about. -10 To be lengthened (as a vowel). With अभि- 1 To overflow. -2 To overwhelm, overcome. अव- To jump up. आ- 1 To bathe. -2 To jump up. उत् -1 To float. -2 To swim. -3 To spring, to leap. उप -1 To float. -2 To attack. -3 To harass. परि -1 To swim, float. -2 To bathe. -3 To overwhelm. -4 To jump. -5 To flood, inundate. -6 To cover with. वि- 1 To float about, to fluctuate. -2 To be scattered about. -3 To be confused. -4 To be ruined. सम्- 1 To float about, fluctuate. -2 To meet *e. g.* आप: संप्लवते. -*Caus.* प्लावयति,-ते.

प्लुत *p. p.* (*f.* -ता) 1 Swimming, floating. -2 Inundated, overflowed. -3 Leaped, jumped. -4 Lengthened, protracted (as a vowel). -5 Covered with, filled with. -6 Bathed in. —तं *n.* 1 A jump. -2 Capering, one of the paces of a horse. -3 Bounding, vaulting. -Comp. —गति: *m.* A hare. (-*f.*) 1 Going by leaps. -2 A gallop, bounding motion.

प्लुति: *f.* 1 A flood, inundation. -2 A leap, jump. -3 Capering, one of the paces of a horse. -4 Prolation or protraction of a vowel.

प्लुष् 1. 4. 9. P. (प्लोषति, प्लुष्यति, प्लुष्णाति, प्लुष्ट) To burn, scorch.

प्लुष् 9 P. (प्लुष्णाति) 1 To sprinkle, wet. -2 To anoint. -3 To fill.

प्लुष्ट *p. p.* (*f.* —ष्टा) Scorched, burnt.

प्लेव् 1 A (प्लेवते) To serve, attend or wait upon.

प्लोष:, प्रोष: *m.* Burning, combustion.

प्लोषण, प्रोषण *a.* (*f.* —णी) Burning, scorching. —णं *n.* Burning, scorching.

प्सा 2 P. (प्साति, प्सात) To eat, devour.

प्सानं *n.* 1 Eating. -2 Food.

फ.

फक्क् 1 P. (फक्कति, फक्कित) 1 To move slowly, go softly. -2 To behave ill.

फक्किका *f.* 1 An argument to be proved ; a thesis or assertion to be maintained. -2 A preconceived opinion. -3 A sophistical argument. -4 A trick, fraud. -5 Logical exposition.

फट् *ind.* An onomatopoetic word used mystically in incantations; *e. g.* अस्त्राय फट्.

फटः *m*, फटा *f.* 1 The expanded hood of a snake.

फड़िंगा *f.* A cricket, locust or grasshopper.

फण् 1 P. (फणति, फणित) 1 To move, move about. -2 To produce easily or without exertion.

फणः *m.*, -णा *f.* The expanded hood of a cobra or any serpent. -Comp. —करः *m.* A serpent. —धरः *m.* 1 A serpent. -2 N. of Siva. —भृत् *m.* A serpent. —मणिः *m.* A jewel said to be found in the hood of a serpent. —मंडलं *n.* The rounded body of a serpent.

फणिन् *m.* 1 A hooded serpent; a serpent in general. -2 An epithet of Râhu. -3 An epithet of Patanjali, the author of the Mahâbhâshya. -Comp. —इंद्रः, —ईश्वरः *m.* 1 An epithet of the serpent-demon Sesha. -2 Of Ananta, the lord of serpents. -3 Of Patanjali. —खेलः *m.* A quail. —तल्पगः *m.* An epithet of Vishnu. (who uses Sesha as his couch). —पतिः *m.* 1 An epithet of Sesha or of Vâsuki. -2 Of Patanjali. —प्रियः *m.* Wind. —फेनः *m.* Opium. —भाष्यं *n.* Mahâbhâshya (the commentary of Patanjali on Pánini's Sútras). —भुज् *m.* 1 A peacock. -2 An epithet of Garuda.

फत्कारिन् *m.* A bird.

फरं *n.* A shield.

फरुवकं *n.* A betel-box.

फर्फरीकः *m.* The palm of the hand with the fingers extended. —कं *n.* 1 A young shoot or branch. -2 Softness. —का *f.* A shoe.

फल् 1 P. (फलति, फलित) 1 To bear fruit; yield or produce fruit. -2 To be fruitful, to be successful, to succeed. -3 To result, produce results or consequences. -4 To ripen. -5 To fall to the lot of; befall. -6 To be useful.

फल् 1 P. (फलति, फुल्ल or फुल्त in the first sense, and फलित in other senses). 1 To burst open, burst, cleave. -2 To be reflected. -3 To go.

फलं *n.* 1 Fruit (fig. also). -2 Crop, produce. -3 A result, consequence, effect. -4 Reward, recompense, retribution (good or bad). -5 An act actually done (opp. words). -6 Aim, object, purpose. -7 Use, profit, advantage; the enjoyable part. -8 Profit or interest on capital. -9 Progeny, offspring. -10 A kernel (of a fruit). -11 A tablet or board (as in शारिफलं). -12 A blade (of a sword). -13 The point or head of an arrow, a barb. -14 A shield. -15 A testicle. -16 A gift. -17 The result of a calculation (in Math.). -18 Menstrual discharge. -19 Nutmeg. -20 A ploughshare. -21 The second term in a rule-of-three sum. -22 Correlative equation. -23 The area of a figure. -Comp. —अनुबंधः *m.* The succession or sequence of fruits or results. —अनुमेय *a.* Inferable from the results or consequences. —अंतः *m.* A bamboo. —अशनः *m.* A parrot. —अस्थि *n.* A cocoa-nut. —आगमः *m.* The fruit season; autumn. —आढ्या *f.* A kind of plantain. —आरामः *m.* A fruit garden, orchard. —आसक्त *a.* Acting for the sake of reward. —उत्तमा *f.* A kind of grapes (having no stones). —केसर: *m.* The cocoanut tree. -कोश:, -ष:, -कोशक: *m.* The scrotum (covering of the testicles). -ग्रहि, —ग्राहिन् *a.* (also फलेग्रहि and फलेग्राहिन्) Fruitful, yielding or bearing fruit in season. (-*m.*) A fruit-tree. —त्रयं, —त्रिकं *n.* The three myrobalans (त्रिफला). —निवृत्ति: *f.* Cessation of consequences. —पाकांता, —पाकावसाना *f.* An annual plant. —पूर:, —पूरक: *m.* The common citron tree.—प्रदानं *n.* 1 The giving of fruits. -2 A ceremony at weddings. -प्रिया *f.* The Priyangu plant.-बंधिन् *a.* Forming or developing fruit. —भूमि: *f.* A place where one receives the reward or recompense of his deeds (*i. e.* heaven or hell).—मत्स्या *f.* The aloe plant.-योग: *m.* 1 The attainment of fruit or the desired object. -2 Wages, remuneration. —राजन् *m.* A water-melon. —वर्तुलं *n.* A water-melon. —वृक्षक: *m.* The bread-fruit tree. -शाडव: *m.* The pomegranate tree. —शैशिर: *m.* The Badara tree. —श्रेष्ठ: *m.* The mango tree. —स्नेह: *m.* A walnut tree. —हारी *f.* An epithet of Kâlî or Durgá.

फलकं *n.* 1 A board, plank, tablet.-2 Any flat surface. -3 A shield. -4 A tablet, leaf or page for writing upon. -5 The buttocks, hips. -6 Fruit, result, consequence. -7 Profit, gain. -8 Menstruation. -9 The head of an arrow. -10 A broad and flat bone (of the forehead).-Comp. —पाणि *a.* Armed with a shield (as a warrior). —यंत्रं *n.* An astronomical instrument invented by Bháskarácharya.

फलनं *n.* 1 Bearing fruit, fructifying. -2 Producing results or consequences.

फलवत् *a.* (*f.* -ती) 1 Fruitful, fruitbearing.-2 Successful, profitable.-3 Containisg the result or end of a plot. —*m.* A fruit tree. —ती *f.* The plant called प्रियंगु. [tree.

फलस: (-श:) *m.* The bread-fruit

फलित *p. p.* (*f.* —ता) 1 Fruitful. -3 Accomplished, realized (as a desire). —त: *m.* A fruit-tree. —ता *f.* A menstruous woman. —तं *n.* A sort of perfume (शैलेय).

फलिन् *a.* (*f.* —नी) 1 Fruit-bearing or yielding fruit (fig also). -2 Profitable. —*m.* A tree.

फलिन *a.* (*f.* —ना) Fruitful, bearing fruit. -न: *m.* The bread-fruit tree. [per.

फलिनी, फली *f.* The Priyangu cree-

फल्गु *a.* 1 Pithless, unsubstantial. -2 Worthless, unimportant. -3 Small, minute. -4 Vain, unmeaning. -5 Weak, feeble. -6 Untrue.-7 Beautiful, lovely. —ल्गु: *f.* 1 The spring season. -2 The opposite-leaved fig-tree. -3 N. of a river at Gayá. -4 A red powder of wild ginger (Mar. गुलाल). -Comp.-उत्सव: *m* The vernal festival commonly called *Holi*. —वाटिका *f.* The opposite-leaved fig-tree.

फल्गुन: *m.* 1 The month of Phâlguna. -2 N. of Indra. -3 Of Arjuna.

फल्गुनी *f.* N. of a constellation. -Comp. —भव: *m.* The planet Jupiter.

फल्यं *n.* A flower.

फाटकी *f.* Alum.

फाणि: *f.* 1 Molasses.-2 Flour mixed with curds (करंभ).

फाणितं *n.* Raw sugar.

फांट *a.* (*f.* -टा) Made by an easy process, readily or easily prepared

(as a decoction). —टः m., —टं n. An infusion, decoction. -टं n. The first particles of butter produced by chruning.

फांटक: m. A decoction, infusion.

फाँडं n. The belly.

फाल: m., -लं n. 1 A plough-share. -2 Separation of the hair on each side of the head (सीमंतभाग). -3 A sort of spade. -4 A bundle. -5 The forehead (for भाल). -लः m. 1 An epithet of Balaráma. -2 Of Siva. -3 The citron tree. -लं n. 1 A garment of cotton. -2 A ploughed field. -Comp. —कृष्ट: m. N. of Balaráma.

फाल्गुन: m. 1 N. of a Hindu month (corresponding to February-March) -2 An epithet of Arjuna. -3 N. of a tree, also called अर्जुन. -Comp.-अनुज: m. 1 The month Chaitra. -2 The vernal season (वसंतकाल).-3 An epithet of नकुल and सहदेव.

फाल्गुनी f. The full-moon day of the month फाल्गुन. -Comp. -भव: m. An epithet of the planet Jupiter.

फिरंग: m. 1 The country of the Franks (i.e. of Europeans). -2 A disease of the Franks; syphilis.

फिरंगिन् m. A Frank (i. e. a European).

फुक: m. A bird.

फुट: m. The expanded hood of a snake.

फु (फू-) त ind. An onomatopoetic word used in composition with कृ, and imitative of the sound made by blowing into liquids &c.; sometimes it expresses disregard or contempt. -Comp. —कार: m., —कृतं n., —कृति: f. 1 Blowing into.-2 Hissing, whizzing.-3 The hiss of a serpent. -4 Sobbing. -5 Screaming, a yell.

फुप्फुस: m., —सं n. The lungs.

फुल्ल् 1 P. (फुल्लति, फुल्लित) 1 To bloom, expand, blow (as a flower). -2 To swell, expand.

फुल्ल p. p. (f. —ल्ला) 1 Expanded, opened, blown. -2 Blossomed. -3 Expanded, wide opened (as eyes). -4 Smiling, gay. -Comp. —तुवरी f. Alum. —लोचन: m. A kind of deer. —फाल: m. The wind raised in winnowing corn.

फेत्कार: m. A shriek, howl.

फेण:, -न: m. Foam, froth.-2 Foam of the mouth. -3 Saliva. -4 White cuttle-fish bone. -Comp. —अशनि: m. N. of Indra. —वाहिन् m. A filtering cloth.

फेण (-न-) क: m. See फेन.

फेनि (-न-) ल a. (f. -ला) Foamy, frothy.

फेरः, फेरंड: m. A jackal.

फेरव: m. 1 A jackal. -2 A rogue, cheat. -3 A demon, goblin.

फेरु: m. A jackal.

फेलं n., फेला, फेलिका, फेली f. Remnants of food, leavings of a meal.

ब.

बंह् 1 A (बंहते, बंहित) To increase, grow.

बंहिमन् m. Abundance, multitude.

बंहिष्ठ a. (f.-ष्ठा) Most abundant, very great, excessive (superl. of बहुल).

बंहीयस् a. (f. —सी) More numerous or abundant, much more (compar. of बहुल).

बक: m. 1 The Indian crane. -2 A cheat, rogue, hypocrite (the crane being a very cunning bird). -3 N. of a demon killd by Bhíma. -4 N. of another demon killed by Krishna. -5 N. of Kubera. —की *f.* The demoness called also पूतना. -Comp. —चरः,—वृत्तिः,—व्रतचरः,—व्रातिकः, —व्रतिन् *m.* A false devotee, religious hypocrite. —जित्,—निषूदनः *m.* 1 Epithets of Bhíma. -2 Of Krishna. —यंत्रं *n.* A kind of retort. —व्रतं *n.* Hypocrisy.

वकुलः *m.* 1 A kind of tree (said to put forth blossoms when sprinkled by young women with mouth-fuls of wine). -2 A kind of drug.—लं *n.* The fragrant flower of this tree.

बकेरुका *f.* A small crane.

बकोटः *m.* A crane.

बटुः *m.* 1 A boy, lad; sometimes used to show contempt as in चाणक्यबटुः &c. -2 A young Brahmachârin.

बडि (-लि-) शं *n.* A fish-hook.

बत *ind.* A particle expressing 1 Sorrow, regret (alas !). -2 Pity or compassion.-3 Addressing,calling. -4 Joy or satisfaction -5 Wonder or surprise. -6 Censure. With a preceding अहो, बत shows joy, surprise, regret or address.

बदरः *m.* 1 The jujube tree.-2 The kernel of the fruit of the cotton-plant. -रं *n.* 1 The fruit of jujube. -2 The pod of the cotton-shrub. -3 The berry used as a weight. -Comp. —कुणः *m.* The time when the fruit of the jujube becomes ripe. —पाचनं *n.* N. of a sacred bathing-place.

बदरिः *f.* The jujube tree.

बदरिका *f.* 1 The jujube tree or its fruit.-2 N. of one of the many sources of the Ganges and of the neighbouring hermitage of the sages Nara and Nárâyana.

बदरी *f.* The jujube tree. -2 The cotton-shrub.-Comp. -तपोवनं *n.* The penance-grove at Badarî. —नाथः *m.* N. of a temple at Badarî. -नारायणः *m.* N. of a place. -पत्रं *n.* A kind of perfume (नखी). -फलं *n.* A fruit of the jujube tree. -वासा *f.* An epithet of Durgá. —शैलः *m.* A rocky eminence at Badarî.

बद्ध *p. p.* (*f.* —द्धा) 1 Bound,tied, fastened. -2 Chained, fettered. -3 Captured, caught. -4 Confined,imprisoned. -5 Put or girt on. -6 Restrained, withheld. -7 Formed, built. -8 Cherished,entertained. -9 Combined, united.-10 Firmly rooted,firm. -11 Composed (as verses). -12 Formed, contracted. -13 Congealed, clotted (as blood).-14 Formed, produced. -Comp. -अंजलि *a.* Folding the hands together in supplication. —अनुराग *a.* Feeling or manifesting love for. —आयुध *a.* Accoutred with arms. —उत्सव *a.* Enjoying or observing a festival or holiday. —उद्यम *a.* Making united efforts. —कक्ष,-कक्ष्य *a.* Having the girdle girt up *i.e.* prepared,ready. —चित्त,—मनस् *a.* Having the mind intently fixed on. —दृष्टि, —नेत्र, -लोचन *a.* Looking with a steadfast gaze at.-परिकर *a.* Having the girdle girded on *i. e.* ready, prepared. -प्रतिज्ञ *a.* 1 One who has made a vow or promise. -2 Firmly resolved. -भाव *a.* Enamoured of (with loc.). -मुष्टि *a.* 1 Having a closed fist.-2 Close-fisted, covetous. —मूल *a.* Deep-rooted, striking root firmly. —मौन *a.* Keeping silence, silent. —राग *a.* Enamoured, impassioned. -वाच् *a.* Maintaining silence.-वैर *a.* One who has contracted confirmed hostility. -शिख *a.* 1 One whose hair is tied up. -2 One who is still in childhood;

young. -स्नेह *a* conceiving affection for.

बभ्र् 1 A. (बीभत्सते) To abhor, detest, be disgusted with (with abl.).

बधिर *a.* (*f.* -रा) Deaf.

बधिरित *a.* (*f.*-ता) Made deaf, deafened.

बाधिरिमन् *m.* Deafness.

बंदिन *m.* See बांदिन्.

बंदिः, -दी *f.* 1 Confinement. -2 A prisoner, captive.

बंध् 9 P. (बध्नाति, बद्धुं, बद्ध ; *pass.* बद्ध्यते) 1 To bind, tie; fasten.-2 To capture, imprison, ensnare. -3 To check, suppress ; as in बद्धकोप,बद्धकोष &c. -4 To put on, wear. -5 To attract, arrest (as eyes &c.). -6 To direct towards (as the eyes or mind); cast upon (with loc.). -7 To construct,form, arrange. -8 To compose, contruct (a poem, verse &c.). -9 To produce,bear(as fruit &c.).-10 To entertain,cherish, feel. -11 To strike (as root). Some idiomatic uses of बंध् are given below ; भ्रुकुटिं बंध् To frown. अंजलिं बंध् To fold the hands together in supplication. चित्तं, चित्तं, मनः, हृदयं बंध् To set the heart on. प्रीतिं, भावं, रागं बंध् To be enamoured of. वैरं बंध् To conceive hatred, contract enmity. सख्यं, सौहृदं बंध् To form friendship. मंडलं बंध् To form a circle, sit or stand in a circle. मौनं बंध् To maintain silence. परिकरं, कक्षां बंध् To gird up one's loins, prepare one-self for anything.

With अनु- 1 To be attached to. -2 To follow. -3 To press, to importune. आ-1 To form,to compose. -2 To fix on or upon. -3 To bind, to tie उद्- To tie to raise up and tie. नि- 1 To bind, to fasten, to chain, -2 To fix, to rivet. -3 To build, form, construct, compose. -4 To compose verses. निस्- To press, to insist upon, to urge परि- 1 To bind.-2 To put on, to encircle. -3 To stop, to interrupt. प्रति- 1 To bind, to tie. -2 To set, to incase. -3 To fix, to direct. -4 To obstruct, to keep off, to shut out, exclude, cut off. सम्- 1 To bind together, to unite. -2 To attach, to connect. -3 To form, construct.

बंधः *m* 1 A tie, bond. -2 A hair-band, fillet. -3 A chain, fetter. -4 Confinement, imprisonment. -5 Capturing,catching hold of.-6 Constructing, arranging as in सर्गबंधो महाकाव्यं. -7 Building, erecting. -8 Conceiving, cherishing. -9 Union, intercourse. -10 Joining or folding together, combining. -11 A bandage, ligature. -12 Agreement, harmony. -13 Manifestation, exhibition. -14 Confinement to this world (opp. मुक्ति).-15 A position,posture. -16 A particular mode of sexual intercourse -17 A border, frame-work.-18 Arrangement of a stanza in a particular shape *e. g.*-खड्गबंध, पद्मबंध, मुरजबंध.-19 A sinew,tendon.-20 The body. -21 A deposit, pledge. -22 An embankment or bridge across (a river). -23 A disease of the eyes.-Comp.-तंत्रं *n.* A complete army containing the four necessary elements *i.e.* elephants,horses, chariots and footmen. -पारुष्यं *n.* A forced construction of words. -स्तंभः *m.* A post to which an animal (*e.g.* an elephant) is tied.

बंधकः *m.* 1 A binder.-2 A catcher. -3 A band, tie, rope, tether. -4 A dike, bank, dam. -5 A pledge, deposit. -6 A posture of the body. -7 Barter, exchange. -8 A violator, ravisher. -9 A promise. -10 A city. -11 A part or portion. —कं *n.* Binding, confinement. —की *f.* 1 An unchaste woman, a harlot -2 A female elephant. -3 A barren woman.

बंधनं *n.* 1 The act of binding, fastening, tying. -2 Binding on or round, clasping. -3 A bond, tie (fig. also). -4 Chaining, confining. -5 A chain, fetter, halter. -6 A place of confinement, prison. -7 Building, construction. -8 Connecting, uniting. -9 A stalk, stem, peduncle. (of a flower). -10 A sinew, muscle. -11 A bandage. -12 A barrier. -13 An embankment, a bridge.—नं *n.*, -नी *f.* 1 A bond, tie. -2 A rope, cord. -3 A string, thread. -4 A chain, fetter. -5 A bondage. -Comp.-अ (-आ-) गार: *m.*,-रं *n.*,-आलय: *m.* A prison, jail. —पालक:, —रक्षिन् *m.* A jailor. —वेश्मन *n.* A prison. —स्थ: *m.* A captive, prisoner.—स्तंभ: *m.* A tying-post. —स्थानं *n.* A stable, stall (for horses &c.).

बंधित *a.* (*f.* —ता) 1 Bound, fastened. -2 Confined, imprisoned.

बंधित्र: *m.* 1 The God of love. -2 A leathern fan. -3 A spot, mole.

बंधु: *m.* 1 A relation, kinsman; a relative in general. -2 Any one associated with another, a brother *e.g.* प्रवासबंधु: *m.* A brother-traveller. धर्मबंधु: *m.* A spiritual brother. -3 (In law) A cognate kinsman, one's own kindred or kinsmen generally. -4 A friend (in general). -5 A husband. -6 A father. -7 A mother. -8 A brother. -9 The tree called बंधुजीव. -10 One who belongs to a tribe, caste or class but does not do the duties pertaining thereto (often used by way of contempt) as in ब्रह्मबंधु:, क्षत्रबंधु:. -Comp. -कृत्यं *n.* 1 The duty of a kinsman. -2 A friendly or kind act or service.-जन: *m.* 1 A relative: kinsmen taken collectivly. —जीव:, —जीवक: *m.* N. of a tree. -दग्ध: *m.* An abandoned wretch (हतक). -दत्तं *n.* A property given to a girl by her relatives at the time of marriage.

बंधुक: *m.* 1 The tree called बंधुजीव. -2 A bastard. —का, -की *f.* An unchaste woman.

बंधुता *f.* 1 Relatives, kindred (taken collectively). -2 Relationship, affinity.

बंधुत्वं *n.* Relationship, brotherhood, affinity.

बंधुदा *f.* An unchaste woman.

बंधुर *a.* (*f.* —रा) 1 Undulating, wavy, uneven. -2 Bent, inclined. -3 Crooked, curved. -4 Pleasing, beautiful, lovely. -5 Deaf. -6 Injurious, mischievous.—र: *m.* 1 A goose. -2 A crane. -3 A drug. -4 An oil-cake. -5 The vulva. -6 The बंधुजीव tree. —रा: *m. pl.* Parched corn or meal there-of. —रा *f.* An unchaste woman. —रं *n.* A diadem.

बंधुल *a.* (*f.* —ला) 1 Bent, curved, inclined. -2 Pleasing, attractive, beautiful. -ल: *m.* 1 A bastard. -2 An attendant in a harlot's chamber. -3 The tree called बंधूक.

बंधूक: *m.* N. of a tree. -कं *n.* A flower of this tree.

बंधूर *a.* (*f.* —रा) 1 Undulating, uneven. -2 Bent, inclined, bowed. -3 Pleasing, delightful, lovely. -रं *n.* A hole.

बंधूलि: *m.* The बंधुजीव tree.

बंध्य (*f.* —ध्या) 1 To be bound

fettered, confined or imprisoned. -2 To be joined or bound together. -3 To be formed, built or constructed. -4 Detained. -5 Barren, unproductive, fruitless, useless. -6 Not having the menstrual discharge.

बंध्या *f.* 1 A barren woman. -2 A barren cow. -3 A kind of perfume (बाल). -Comp. —तनयः, —पुत्रः, —सुतः *m.*, or दुहितृ, —सुता *f.* The son or daughter of a barren woman *i. e.* an impossibility ; anything that does not and cannot exist.

बंध्रं *n.* A bond, tie.

बभ्रवी *f.* An epithet of Durgâ.

बभ्रु *a.* (*f.* -भ्रु or —भ्रू) Tawny, reddish-brown. -2 Bald-headed through disease. —भ्रुः *m.* 1 Fire. -2 An ichneumon. -3 The tawny colour. -4 A man with tawny hair. -*n.* 1 A tawny or brown colour. -2 Any object of a brown colour. -Comp. —धातुः *m.* 1 Gold. -2 Red chalk (गैरिक), a kind of ochre. -वाहनः *m.* N. of a son of Arjuna by Chitrángadà.

बंर् 1 P. (बंरति) To go, move.

बंभरः *m.* A bee.

बंभराली *f.* A fly.

बरटः *m.* A kind of grain.

बर्ब् 1 P. (बर्बति) To go, move.

बर्बटः *m.* A kind of grain (राजमाष).

बर्बटी *f.* 1 A kind of grain (राजमाष). -2 A harlot, prostitute.

बर्बणा *f.* A blue fly.

बर्बरः *m.* 1 A barbarian, low fellow. -2 A fool, block-head.

बर्बुरः *m.* N. of a tree (Mar. बाभुळ).

बर्ह् 1 A. (बर्हते) 1 To speak. -2 To give. -3 To cover. -4 To destroy. -5 To spread. -6 To be preeminent or excellent.

बर्ह् 10 U. (बर्हयति,-ते To hurt, injure. —With नि— To kill, destroy.

बर्हः *m.*, -र्हं *n.* 1 A peacock's tail. -2 The tail of a bird. -3 A tail-feather (especially of a peacock). -4 A leaf. -5 A train, retinue. -Comp. —भारः *m.* 1 A peacock's tail. -2 A tuft of peacock's feathers.

बर्हणं *n.* A leaf.

बर्हिः *m.* Fire. —र्हि *n.* The Kusa grass.

बर्हिणः *m.* A peacock.-Comp.-बाणः *m.* An arrow feathered with a peacock's plumes. -वाहनः *m.* An epithet of Kártikeya.

बर्हिन *m.* A peacock. -Comp. —कुसुमं, —पुष्पं *n.* A kind of perfume. —ध्वजा *f.* An epithet of Durgâ.-यानः, -वाहनः *m.* An epithet of Kàrtikeya.

बर्हिस् *m.*, *n.* Kusa grass. -*m.* 1 Fire. -2 Light, splendour. -*n.* 1 Water.-2 Sacrifice. -Comp. —केशः, —ज्योतिस् *m.* An epithet of fire.-मुखः (बर्हिर्मुखः) *m.* 1 An epithet of fire. -2 A God.-शुष्मन् *m.* An epithet of fire. —सद् (बर्हिःषद्) *a.* Seated on Kusa grass. (-*m. pl.*) The Manes.

बल् 1 P. (बलति) 1 To breathe or live. -2 To hoard grain.

बल् 1 U. (बलति,-ते) 1 To give. -2 To hurt, kill. -3 To speak. -4 To see, mark.

बलं *n.* 1 Strength, power, might, vigour. -2 Force, violence. -3 An army, troops. -4 Bulkiness (of the body). -5 Body, figure, shape. -6 Semen virile. -7 Blood. -8 Gum myrrh. -9 A shoot, sprout. (बलेन 'On the strength of'. 'by means or virtue of'. बलात् Forcibly', ' violently', ' against one's will'.)—लः *m.* 1 A crow. -2 N. of the elder brother of Krishna. -3 N. of a demon killed by Indra. -Comp. —अर्थ

न. Excessive strength or force.(-अ: m. The head of an army. -अंभक: m. The spring. —अंचिता f. The lute of Balarâma.-अट: m. A kind of bean. -अध्यक्ष: m. 1 A general or commander of an army. -2 A war-minister. -अनुज: m. An epithet of Krishna. -अबलं n. 1 Comparative strength and want of strength; relative strength and weakness.-2 Relative significance and insignificance;comparative importance and unimportance.-3 Pros and cons, arguments for and against; the importance of both sides of a question. -अभ्र: m. An army in the form of a cloud. —अराति: m. An epithet of Indra. —अश:, -अस: m. 1 Consumption. -2 The phlegmatic humour (कफ).-3 A swelling in the throat. —अश्मिका f. A kind of sun-flower (हस्तिशुंडी).-आहं n. Water. -ओघ: m. A multitude of troops, numerous army. —क्षोभ: m. A disturbance in the army; mutiny, revolt. -चक्रं n. 1 Dominion,sovereignty.-2An army. -ज a. Produced by power. (-जं n.) 1 A city-gate, gate. -2 A field. -3 Grain, a heap of grain. -4 War, battle. -5 Marrow, pith. -6 A pretty figure. (-जा f.) 1 The earth. -2 A handsome woman. -3 A kind of jasmine (Arabian). —द: m. An ox, a bullock. —देव: m. 1 Air, wind. -2 N. of the elder brother of Krishna. --द्विष्, --निषूदन: m. Epithets of Indra. -पति: m. 1 A general, commander.-2 An epithet of Indra. —प्रसू: f. N. of Rohini,mother of Balarâma. —भद्र: m. 1 A strong or powerful man -2 A kind of ox.-3 N. of Balarâma. -4 The tree called लोध्र. -5 N. of Ananta. (-द्रा f.) A maiden. —भिद् m. An epithet of Indra. —मुद् a. Strong, powerful —राम: m. N. of the elder brother of Krishna. —विन्यास: m. Array or arrangement of troops. —सूदन: m. An epithet of Indra.-स्थ: m. A warrior, soldier. —स्थिति: f. 1 A camp; an encampment. -2 A royal camp.-हन् m. 1 An epithet of Indra.-2 Of Balaráma. -3 Phlegm.

बलक्ष a. (f. -क्षा) White.

बलल: m. An epithet of Indra.

बलवत् ind. 1 Foribly, powerfully,strongly. -2 Well, in a high degree. a. 1 Powerful,strong, mighty. -2 Dense,thick (as darkness &c.). -3 Predominant, prevailing. -4 More important. -5 Accompained by an army.

बला f. N. of a particular incantation (taught by Visvámitra to Ráma and Lakshmana).

बलाक: m., -का f. A crane. -का f. A mistress, beloved woman.

बलाकिका f. A small kind of crane.

बलाकिन् a. (f. -नी) Abounding in cranes.

बलात्कार: m. 1 Employing force -2 Outrage, force, oppression. -3 Injustice. -4 (In law.) Detention of the person of a debter by the creditor. [come.

बलात्कृत a. (f. -ता) Forced, over-

बलाहं n. Water.

बलाहक: m. 1 A cloud. -2 A kind of crane. -3 A mountain. -4 N. of one of the seven clouds appearing at the destruction of the world. -5 One of the four horses of Vishnu.

बलि:m. 1 An oblation;a gift or offering. -2 The offering of a portion of the daily meal to all creatures,one of the five daily Yajnas to be performed by a householder. -3 Worship adoration. -4 Fragments of food left at a meal. -5 A victim offered to a deity.-6 A tax, impost. -7 The handle of a chowrie. -8 N. of a celebrated demon. —लि: *f.* 1 A fold, wrinkle. -2 The fold of skin in stout persons or females. -3 The ridge of a thatched roof.-Comp. —कर्मन् *n.* 1 Offering oblations to all creatures. -2 The act of worshipping. -3 Payment of tribute. —दानं *n.* 1 Presentation of an offering to a deity. -2 Offering oblations to creatures. —ध्वंसिन् *m.* An epithet of Vishnu. —नंदन:,-पुत्र:,-सुत: *m.* Epithets of Bâna, the son of Bali.-पुष्ट:, -भोजन:*m.*A cr_w.-प्रिय:*m.*The Lodhra tree.-बंधन: *m.* An epithet of Vishnu. --भुज् *m.* 1 A crow. -2 A sparrow. -3 A crane. --मंदिरं, -वेश्मन,-सद्मन् *n.* The lower regions, the abode of Bali. —मुख: *m.* A monkey. —हन् *m.* An epithet of Vishnu.-हरणं *n.*An offering of oblations to all creatures.

बलिन् *a.*(*f.*—नी) 1 Strong, powerful, mighty.-2 Stout, robust.—न: *m.* 1 A buffalo. -2 A hog. -3 A camel. -4 A bull. -5 A soldier. -6 A kind of jasmine. -7 The phlegmatic humour. -8 An epithet of Balaráma.

बलिन, बलिभ *a*. (*f.* -ना,-भा) Wrinkled, shrivelled.

बलिंदम: *m.* An epithet of Vishnu.

बलिमन् *m.* Strength, might, power.

बलिवर्द: *m.* An ox, a bull.

बलिष्ठ *a*. (*f.* —ष्ठा) Most powerful, very powerful (superl. of बलवत् or बलिन्). —ष्ठ: *m.* A camel.

बलिष्णु *a.* Dishonoured, degraded, despised.

बलीक: *m.* The edge of a thatched roof.

बलीन: *m.* A scorpion.

बलीयस् *a.* (*f.* —सी) 1 Stronger, more powerful. -2 More effective. -3 More important (compar. of बलवत्, or बलिन् —*adv.* Powerfully, very much.

बली (-री) बर्द: *m* A bull, an ox.

बल्य *a.* (*f.* —ल्या) 1 Strong, powerful. -2 Giving strength. —ल्य: *m.* A Buddhist mendicant. —ल्यं *n.* Semen virile.

बल्लव: *m.* 1 A cowherd. -2 A cook. -3 The name assumed by Bhima when serving as a cook at the court of Viráta. —वी *f.* A cowherdess.

बल्वज: *m.*,—जा *f.* A kind of coarse grass.

बल्हिका:,बल्हीका: *m.pl.* N. of a country and its inhabitants.

बष्कय: *m.* Full-grown (as a calf).

बष्कय (-यि-) णी, (-णी) *f.* 1 A cow whose calf is full-grown. -2 A prolific cow(one bearing many calves).

बस्त: *m.* A goat. -Comp. —कर्ण: *m.* The Sâla tree. —गंधा *f.* A shrubby basil.

बहल *a* (*f.* -ला) 1 Very much, abundant, plentiful, great, strong. -2 Thick, dense. -3 Shaggy (as a tail). -4 Hard, compact. -5 Harsh (as a sound). —ल: *m.* A kind of sugar-cane. —ला *f.* Large cardamoms. -Comp. —गंध: *m.* A kind of sandal.

बहिष्कार: *m.*1 Expulsion, exclusion. -2 Excommunication.

बाहिष्टात् *ind.*On the outside, abroad.

बहिस् *ind.* 1 Out of, outside (with abl.). -2 On the outside, out of doors (opp. अंत:). -3 Outwardly. -4 Separately. -5 Beside, except. -Comp. —उपाधि: *m.* An external condition or circumstance. —द्वारं *n.* An outer door.—लापिका *f.* A kind of enigma. —विकारः *m.* Syphilis. —व्यसनं *n.* Licentiousness, immorality, evil or lewd practices. -व्यसनिन् *a.* Dissolute, lewd.

बहु *a.*(-हु,-ह्वी *f.* compar. भूयस् ; superl. भूयिष्ठ) 1 Much, plentiful, abundant. -2 Many, numerous. -3 Frequented, repeated. -4 Large, great. -5 Abounding or rich in (as first member of comp.). —*ind.* 1 Much, very much, exceedingly, in a high degree. (किं बहुना ' Why say much?' ' in short'.)-Comp. —उदकः *m.* A kind of mendicant. —ऋच् *a.* Having many verses. (-*f.*) A term applied to the Rigveda. -करः *m.* 1 A sweeper, cleaner. -2 A camel. (-री *f.*) A broom. —कालं *ind.* For a long time.—कालीन *a.* Of long standing; old, ancient. —कूर्चः *m.* A kind of cocoa-nut tree. —गंध *a.* Strong-scented. (-धं *n.*) Cinnamon. —गंधदा *f.* Musk.—जल्प *a.* Talkative, loquacious. —तृणं *n.* 1 Anything much like grass. -2 What is unimportant or contemptible.-त्वक्कः, -त्वच् *m.* A kind of birch tree.—दर्शक, -दर्शिन *a.* Prudent, circumspect, provident -दुग्धः *m.* Wheat.-दृश्वन् *a.* Greatly experienced, a great observer. —दृष्ट *a.* Very experienced. —धारं *n.* The thunderbolt of Indra.-पादः *m.* A conch-shell.-पत्रः *m.* An onion.-पत्री *f.* The holy basil.-पद्,-पाद्,-पादः *m.* The fig-tree. —पुष्पः *m.* 1 The coral tree. -2 The Nimba tree. —प्रजः *m.* 1 A hog. -2 The *munja* grass. -प्रतिज्ञ *a.* 1 Comprising many statements or assertions; complicated. -2 (In law) Involving many counts, as a plaint.—फल *a.* Rich in fruits (-ल. *m.*) The Kadamba tree. -बलः *m.* A lion. —भुजा *f.* An epithet of Durgá. —मंजरी *f.* The holy basil. -मत *a.* 1 Highly esteemed or prized; valued, respected.-2 Having different opinions. —मलं *n.* Lead. -माय *a.* Artful, deceitful, treacherous.-मार्गगा *f.* 1 N. of the river Ganges. -2 A wanton or unchaste woman. —मुख *a.* Much, excessive. —मूर्धन् *m.* An epithet of Vishnu. —राशि *a.* (In arith.) Consisting of many terms. —रूपः *m.* 1 A lizard, chameleon. -2 Hair. -3 The sun. -4 N. of Siva. -5 of Vishnu.-6 Of Brahman(*m.*).-7 Of the God of love. -रेतस् *m.* An epithet of Brahman(*m.*)-रोमन् *m.* A sheep. —वचनं *n.* The plural number (in gram.). -वारं *ind.* Many times, often. -विध *a.* Of many kinds, manifold, diverse. -वी (-बी-) जं *n.* The custard apple. —व्रीहि *a.* Possessing much rice. (-हिः *m.*) One of the four principal kinds of compounds in Sanskrit. -शत्रुः *m.* A sparrow. —शल्यः *m.* Species of Khadira. —शृंगः *m.* An epithet of Vishnu. -श्रुत *a.* 1 Well-informed, very learned. -2 Well-versed in the Vedas. —संततिः *m.* A kind of bamboo. -सार *a.* Possessed of great pith or essence; substantial. (-रः *m.*) The Khadira tree. —सूः *f* 1 A mother of many children. -2 A sow. -सूतिः *f.* 1 A mother of many children. -2 A cow that often calves.-स्वन *a.* Vociferous (-नः *m.*) An owl.

बहुकः *m.* 1 The sun. -2 The sun-plant (अर्क). -3 A crab. -4 A kind of gallinule. -5 The digger of a tank.

बहुतिथ *a.* Much, long, many. -थं *ind.* Greatly, in a high degree.

बहुश *ind.* In many ways or places.

बहुथा *ind.* In several ways.

बहुधा *ind.* 1 In many ways, diversely, multifariously. -2 In different forms or ways. -3 Frequently, repeatedly. -4 In various places or directions.

बहुल *a.* (*f.* -ला; *compar.* बंहीयस् ; *superl.* बंहिष्ठ) 1 Thick, dense, compact. -2 Wide, capacious, ample, large. -3 Abundant, plentiful. -4 Numerous, many. -5 Full of, abounding in. -6 Accompanied by. -7 Born under the Pleiades. -8 Black. -लः *m.* 1 The dark half of a month (कृष्णपक्ष). -2 An epithet of fire. -ला *f.* 1 A cow. -2 Cardamoms. -3 The indigo plant. -4 (-लाः *f. pl.*) The Pleiades. -लं *n.* 1 The sky. -2 White pepper. -लं *ind.* Often, frequently. -Comp. -गंधा *f.* Cardamoms.

बहुलिका: *f. pl.* The Pleiades.

बहुलीकृ 8 U. 1 To make public, disclose, divulge. -2 To make dense or compact. -3 To increase, extend. -4 To thresh.

बहुलीभू 1 P. 1 To increase, multiply. -2 To become public or generally known.

बहुशस् *ind.* 1 Much, abundantly, plentifully. -2 Frequently, oftentimes. -3 Generally, commonly.

बाकुलं *n.* The fruit of the Bakula tree.

बाड् 1 A (बाडते) 1 To bathe. -2 To emerge.

बाडव: *m.* See वाडव.

बाडवेय: *m.* See वाडवेय.

बाडव्यं *n.* See वाडव्य.

बाढ *a.* (*f.*—ढा; compar. साधीयस्; superl. साधिष्ठ) 1 Firm, strong. -2 Much. -3 Loud. —ढं *ind.* 1 Certainly, surely, really. -2 Very well, be it so, good. -3 Very much.

बाण: *m.* 1 An arrow, shaft. -2 A mark for arrows -3 The feathered end of an arrow. -4 The udder of a cow. -5 A kind of plant. -6 N. of a demon, son of Bali. -7 N. of a celebrated poet who is the author of कादंबरी, हर्षचरित and of some other works. -8 A symbolical expression for the number 'five'.-Comp. -असनं *n.* A bow —आवलि:,—ली *f.* 1 A series of arrows.-2 A series of five verses forming one sentence. —आश्रय: *m.* A quiver. —गोचर: *m.* The range of an arrow. —जालं *n.* A number of arrows. —जित *m.* An epithet of Vishnu. —तूण:, -धि: *m.* A quiver. -पथ: *m.* The range of an arrow. —पात: *m* 1 An arrow-shot (as a measure of distance). -2 The range of an arrow. —योजनं *n.* A quiver. —वार: *m.* A breast-plate, an armour. -सुता *f.* An epithet of Ushá, daughter of Bána.-हन् *m.* An epithet of Vishnu.

बाणिनी *f.* 1 An excellent woman. -2 A shrewd woman.-3 A dancing girl. -4 A drunken woman.

बादर *a.* (*f.* —री) 1 Belonging to the jujube tree. -2 Made of cotton. -र: *m.* The cotton shrub. -रं *n.* 1 The jujube. -2 Silk. -3 Water. -4 A garment of cotton. -5 A conch-shell winding from left to right.-रा *f.* The cotton shrub.

बादरायण: *m.* N. of a sage the author of the Sârîraka Sútras of the Vedânta philosophy. -Comp. —सूत्रं *n.* The Vedânta aphorisms. -संबंध: *m.* (A modern formation) An imaginary or far-fetched relation.

बादरायणि: *m.* N. of Suka, son of Vyása.

बादरिक *a.* (*f.*-की) One who gathers jujube fruits.

बाध् 1 A (बाधते, बाधित) 1 To torment, annoy, trouble, disturb, vex, pain (persons or things).-2 To resist, thwart, check, obstruct, interfere with. -3 To assault, assail. -4 To wrong, violate. -5 To hurt, injure. -6 To repel, remove. -7 To suspend, annul, annihilate, conquer. -With अभि- 1 To injure. -2 To vex, harass, torment. आ— To vex, injure. परि— To trouble, afflict. सं- To trouble, torment.

बाधः *m.*, -धा *f.* 1 Pain, suffering, affliction. -2 Disturbance, annoyance. -3 Harm, damage, hurt. -4 Danger, peril. -5 Resistance, opposition.-6 An objection.-7 Contradiction, refutation. -8 Suspension, annulment. -9 A flaw in a syllogism, one of the five forms of हेत्वाभास or fallacious middle term. —धा *f.* Refutation.-Comp. —अपवादः *m.* A denial of an exception.

बाधक *a.* (*f.* —धिका) 1 Tormenting, oppressing. -2 Vexing, annoying. -3 Annulling. -4 Suspending, contradicting (as a rule &c.). —कः *m.* A particular disease of women.

बाधनं *n.* 1 Oppression, annoyance, disturbance, pain. -2 Annulment. -3 Removal, suspension. -4 Refutation, contradiction. -5 Opposing, hindering. —ना *f.* Pain, trouble, anxiety, disturbance.

बाधित *p. p.* (*f.* -ता) 1 Harassed, annoyed. -2 Pained, afflicted. -3 Opposed, obstructed. -4 Checked, arrested. -5 Set aside, suspended. -6 Refuted. -7 (In logic) Contradicted, inconsistent (and hence futile).

बाधिर्यं *n.* Deafness.

बांधकिनेयः *m.* A bastard.

बांधवः *m.* 1 A relation, kinsman. -2 A maternal relation.-3 A friend. -4 A brother. -Comp. —जनः *m.* Kinsmen (taken collectively).

बांधव्यं *n.* Consanguinity, relationship.

बाभ्रवी *f.* An epithet of Durgâ.[ish.

बाभ्रुक *a.* (*f.* —की) Brown, brown-

बार्हीरः *m.* 1 The kernel of the mango-fruit. -2 Tin. -3 A young shoot. -4 The son of a harlot.

बार्ह *a.* (*f.* -र्ही) Made of the feathers of a peacock's tail.

बार्हद्रथः, बार्हद्रथिः *m.* A patronymic of king Jarâsandha.

बार्हस्पत *a.* (*f.* -ती) Related to, descended from or sacred to, Brihaspati.

बार्हस्पत्य *a.* (*f.* -त्या) Relating to Brihaspati. -त्यः *m.* 1 A pupil of Brihaspti. -2 A follower of Brihaspati who taught a form of materialism; a materialist. -3 An epithet of Agni —त्यं *n.* 1 The constellation Pushya. -2 Morality.

बार्हिण *a.* (*f.* —णी) Derived from or relating to a peacock.

बाल *a.* (*f.* -ला) 1 Young, infantine, not full-grown (said of persons or things). -2 Newly risen, young (as the sun or its rays). -3 New, waxing (as the moon). -4 Ignorant, unwise. -5 Pure (as an animal fit for sacrifice). —लः *m.* 1 A child, an infant.-2 A boy, a young person. -3 A minor (under 16 years of age). -4 A colt, foal. -5 A fool, simpleton. -6 A tail. -7 Hair. -8 An elephant five years old. -9 A kind of perfume. -Comp. —अभ्यासः *m.* A study during childhood; early application (to study). —अरुण *a.* Red like early dawn. (-णः *m.*) Early dawn, morning sun. -इष्:

m. The jujube tree. —उपवीतं *n*. 1 A piece of cloth used to cover the privities. -2 The sacrificial cord. —कांडं *n*. The first book of the Râmâyana. —कृमिः *m*. A louse. —कृष्णः *m*. Krishna as a boy. —क्रीडनकं *n*. A child's toy. (-कः *m*.) 1 A ball. -2 An epithet of Siva.-क्रीडा *f*. A child's play; childish or juvenile sport. —खिल्यः *m*. A class of divine personages of the size of a thumb. —गर्भिणी *f*. A cow with calf for the first time. —गोपालः *m*. An epithet of Krishna,as the boy-cowherd. —ग्रहः *m*. A demon teasing or injuring children. —चर्यः *m*. N. of Kârtikeya. (—र्या *f*.) The behaviour of a child. —तनयः *m*. The Khadira tree. -तंत्रं *n*. Midwifery. -दलकः *m*. The Khadira. —धिः *m*. A hairy tail. —पत्रः, —पत्रकः *m*. The Khadira tree —पाश्या *f*. 1 An ornament worn in the hair when parted. -2 A string of pearls binding the braid of hair. —पुष्टिका, -पुष्टी, -पुष्पी *f*. A kind of jasmine.—भावः *m*. Childhood, infancy. —भैषज्यं *n*. A kind of collyrium.—भोज्यः *m*. Pease. -यज्ञोपवीतकं *n*. The sacred thread worn across the breast.-राजं *n*. Lapis lazuli. —वत्सः *m*. 1 A young calf. -2 A pigeon.—वायजं *n*. Lapis lazuli. -वाह्यः *m*. A wild goat. -व्यजनं *n*. A *chowrie* made of the tail of the *Bos Grunniens* (an item in royal insignia). —संध्या *f*. Early twilight.-सूर्यः, -सूर्यकः *m*. The Lapis lazuli. —हस्तः *m*. A hairy tail.

बालक *a*. (*f*. —लिका) 1 Childlike, young. -2 Ignorant. —कः *m*. 1 A child, boy. -2 A minor (in law). -3 A finger-ring. -4 A fool. -5 A bracelet. -6 The tail of a horse or elephant. -7 Hair.—कं *n*. 1 A finger-ring. -2 A bracelet.

बाला *f*. 1 A girl, a female child. -2 A young woman under sixteen years of age. -3 A young woman (in general).-4 A variety of jasmine.-5 The cocoa-nut. -6 The plant घृतकुमारी. -7 Small cardamoms.-8 Turmeric.

बालिः *m*. N. of a celebrated monkey-king.-Comp. —हन्, —हंतृ *m*. An epithet of Râma.

बालिका *f*. 1 A girl. -2 A kind of ear-ring. -3 Small cardamoms. -4 Sand. -5 The rustling of leaves.

बालिन् *m*. N. of a monkey.

बालिनी *f*. The constellation Asvini.

बालिमन् *m*. Childhood, boyhood.

बालिश *a*. (*f*. —शा) 1 Childish, silly. -2 Young. -3 Foolish, ignorant -4 Careless. -शः *m*. 1 A fool, blockhead. -2 A child, boy. -शं *n*. A pillow.

बालिश्यं *n*. 1 Youth, boyhood. -2 Ignorance, silliness, folly.

बाली *f*. A kind of ear-ring.

बालीशः *m*. Retention of urine.

बालुः *m*., बालुकं *n*. A kind of perfume.

बालुका *f*. 1 Sand. -2 Camphor. -3 A sand-cloth.-4 A kind of cucumber.

बालुकी, बालुंकी, बालुंगी *f*. A kind of cucumber.

बालूकः *m*. A kind of poison.

बालेय *a*. (*f*. —यी) 1 Fit for an offering.-2 Tender, soft. -3 Descended from Bali. -यः *m*. An ass.

बाल्यं *n*. 1 Boyhood, childhood. -2 A state of waxing(as of the moon). -3 Immaturity of understanding, folly.

बाल्हकाः, बाल्हिकाः, बाल्हीकाः *m. pl*. N. of a people. —कः *m*. 1 A king of the

Bâlhikas. -2 A horse of the Balkh breed. —कं *n.* 1 Saffron. -2 Asa Fœtida.

बाल्हिः *m.*N. of a country (Balkh).

बाष्पः *m.*, —ष्पं *n.* 1 A tear. -2 Vapour, steam, mist. -3 Iron.-Comp. —कंठ *a.* Choked with tears. —दुर्दिनं *n.* A flood of tears.

बास्तः *n.* (*f.* -स्ती) Coming or derived from a goat.

बाहः *m.* 1 The arm. -2 A horse

बाहा *f.* The arm. -Comp. —बाहवि *ind.* Hand to hand, arm against arm.

बाहीक *a.* (*f.* -की) External, outer. —काः *m. pl.* The people of the Punjab. —कः *m.* 1 An inhabitant of the Punjab. -2 An ox.

बाहुः *m.* 1 The arm. -2 The fore-arm.-3 The fore-foot of an animal. -4 A door-post. -5 The base of a right-angled triangle (in geom). —हू *m. dual* The lunar mansion Ardrâ. -Comp. —उत्क्षेपं *ind.* Having raised or tossed up the arms. —कुंथः *m.* A wing (of a bird) —चापः *m.* The distance measured by the extended arms. —जः *m.* 1 A man of the Kshatriya caste. -2 A parrot.—ज्या *f.* A sine (in math.). —त्रः *m.*,—त्रं *n.*, —त्राणं *n.* Vant-brass (armour for the arms).—पाशः *m.* 1 A particular attitude in fighting.-2 An embrace. —प्रहरणः *m.* A boxer.—बलं *n.* Strength of arm, muscular strength.—भेदिन् *m.* An epithet of Vishnu. —मूलं *n.* 1 The armpit. -2 The shoulder-blade.—योधः,—योधिन *m.* A pugilist, boxer. —लता *f.* An arm-like creeper. —शालिन *m.* 1 An epithet of Siva -2 Of Bhima. —शिखरं *n.* The upper part of the arm, the shoulder. —संभवः *m.* A man of the Kshatriya caste.—सहस्रभृत *m.* An epithet of king Kârtavîrya (also called सहस्रार्जुन).

बाहुक *a.*1 Swimming with the arms. -2 Servile, dependent.-3 Dwarfish. —कः 1 A monkey. -2 A name assumed by Nala after his transformation into a dwarf by Karkotaka.

बाहुदंतिन्, बाहुदंतेयः *m.* An epithet of Indra.

बाहुदा *f.* N. of river.

बाहुभाष्यं *n.* Garrulity, loquaciousness, talkativeness.

बाहुरूप्यं *n.* Manifoldness, variety.

बाहुलः *m* 1 Fire. -2 The month Kârtika. —लं *n.* 1 Manifoldness. -2 An armour forthe arms,vant-brass. —ली *f.* The day of full moon in the month of Kârtika. Comp. -ग्रीवः *m.* A peacock.

बाहुलकं*n.*A Manifoldness.-2 The indeterminate applicability of a rule.

बाहुलेयः *m.* An epithet Kârtikeya.

बाहुल्यं *n.* 1 Abundance, plenty. -2 Manifoldness, multiplicity. -3 The common order of things.

बाहुबाहवि *ind.* Arm to arm, hand to hand, in close encounter.

बाह्य *a.* (*f.*-ह्या) 1 Outer .exteral,exterior.-2 Foreign,strange.-3 Excluded from;out of the pale of.-4 An outcast. —ह्यः *m.* 1 A stranger,foreigner. -2 One who is excommunicated;an outcast. —ह्यं, —बाह्येन, बाह्ये *ind.* Outside. on the outside,externally.

बाह्वृच्यं *n.* Traditional teaching of the Rigveda

बिट् 1 P. (बेटति) 1 To swear, To curse. -2 To shout, exclaim.

बिटकः *m.*, —कं *n.*, बिटका *f.* A boil.

बिडं *n.* A kind of salt, salt-petre.

बिडालः*m.*A The eyeball.—ली *f.*A female cat. -Comp. -पद *m.*, —पदकं *n*

A measure of weight equal to sixteen Máshas.

बिडालकः *m.* 1 A cat. -2 Application of ointment to the eye. —कं *n.* Yellow orpiment.

बिडौजस् *m.* An epithet of Indra.

बिद्, बिंद् 1 P. (बिंदति) 1 To split -2 To divide.

बिदलं *n.* 1 A slip, a chip. -2 A twig. -3 A split bamboo.-4 A basket of bamboos.

बिंदुः *m.* 1 A drop, a particle -2 A dot, point. -3 A zero or cypher. -4 The dot over a letter representing the अनुस्वार.-5 (In dramas)The sudden development of a secondary incident. -Comp. —चित्रकः *m.* The spotted antelope. —जालं, -जालकं *n.* 1 A number of drops. -2 Marks of coloured paint on the trunk and face of an elephant.-तंत्रः *m.*1 A die. -2 A chess-board. —देवः *m.* An epithet of Siva.-पत्रः*m.* A kind of birch tree. -फलं *n.* A pearl.-रेखकः *m.* 1 An 'anusvara'.-2 A kind of bird. -रेखा *f.*A line of dots.-वासरः *m.*The day of conception.

बिब्बोकः *m.* 1 Affectation of indifference towards a beloved object through pride. -2 Haughty indifference in general. -3 Playful or amorous gestures.

बिभित्सा *f.* A wish to break, a desire to pierce or penetrate.

बिभित्सु *a.* Desirous of penetrating.

बिभीषण *a.* 1 Frightening. -2 Terrible. -3 Blustering (as language). —णं *n.*, -णा *f.* 1 Terrifying. -2 An object of terror. -णः *m.* N. of a *Rakshasa* and brother of Rávana.

बिभ्रुः *m.* Fire.

बिभजिषुः *m.* Fire.

बिंबः *m.*,-बं *n.* 1 The disc of the sun or moon. -2 Any disc-like surface, as in नितंबबिंब &c. -3 An image, shadow.-4 A mirror.-5 A jar. -6 An object to which another is compared (opp. प्रतिबिंब). -बः *m.* A lizard. -बं *n.* The fruit of a tree (which, when ripe, is red and the lips of young women are often compared to it). -Comp. —ओष्ठ *a.* (बिंबो-बौ-ष्ठ) Having lips as red and plump as the Bimba fruit.

बिंबकं *n.* 1 The disc of the sun or moon. -2 The fruit of the Bimba.

बिंबिका *f.* 1 The disc of the sun or moon. -2 The Bimba plant.

बिंबित *a.* (*f.* -ता) 1 Reflected, shadowed. -2 Pictured.

बिल् 6 P., 10 U. (बिलति, बेलयति,-ते) To split, break, divide.

बिलं *n.* 1 A hole, cavity. -2 A pit, chasm. -3 An opening, outlet. -4 A cave, hollow. -5 The vagina. -लः *m.* N. of उच्चैःश्रवस् the horse of Indra. -Comp.—ओकस् *m.* Any animal that lives in holes. —कारिन् *m.* A mouse. -वासः *m.* A pole-cat. —वासिन् (also बिलेवासिन्) *m.* A snake. —शायिन् *m.* Any animal living in burrows.

बिलंगमः *m.* A serpent, snake.

बिलेशयः *m.* 1 A snake.-2 A mouse, rat. -3 Any animal that lives in burrows. -4 A hare.

बिल्लं *n.* 1 A pit. -2 A basin for water round the foot of a tree. -3 The plant Asa Fœtida. -Comp.-सूः *f.* A mother of ten children.

बिल्वः *m.* A species of tree. -ल्वं *n.* 1 The fruit of this tree. -2 A particular weight (equal to one pala). -Comp. -दंडः *m.* An epithet of Siva. —पेशिका, —पेशी *f.* The shell of the Bilva fruit.

बिल्वकीया *f.* A place planted with Bilva trees.

बिस् 4 P. (बिस्यति) 1 To go, move. -2 To urge on; instigate. -3 To throw, cast. -4 To split. -5 To grow.

बिसं n. 1 The fibre of a lotus. -2 The fibrous stalk of a lotus.-Comp. —कंठिका f.,—कंठिन् m. A small crane. —कुसुमं,-पुष्पं, -प्रसूनं n. A lotus.-खादिका f. Eating the fibres of a lotus. —जं n. A lotus-flower, lotus. -नाभिः f. The lotus-plant (पद्मिनी).—नासिका f. A sort of crane. [bud.

बिसलं n. A young shoot, sprout,

बिसिनी f. 1 The lotus-plant. -2 Lotus-fibres. -3 An assemblage of lotuses.

बिसिल a. (f. —ला) Coming from or relating to the fibres of a lotus.

बिस्तः m. A weight of 80 *gunjás* of gold.

बिह्लणः m. N. of a poet, the author of the Vikramánkadevacharita.

बीजं n. 1 Seed (fig. also); corn, grain. -2 A germ, element. -3 Origin, cause.-4 Semen virile.-5 The germ of the plot of a play, story &c. -6 Marrow. -7 Algebra.-8 The mystical letter forming the essential part of the *mantra* of a deity. -जः m. The citron tree. -Comp. -अक्षरं n. The first syllable of a *mantra*. —अंकुरः m. A seed-shoot, first shoot. —अंकुरन्यायः m. The maxim of seed and shoot; the maxim takes its origin from the mutual relation of causation that exists between seed and shoot and is applied to cases in which two objects stand to each other in the relation of both cause and effect. —अध्यक्षः m. An epithet of Siva.—अश्वः m. A stallion.—आढ्यः, —पूरः, —पूरकः m. The citron tree. —आकृत a. First sown and the ploughed.-उत्कृष्टं n. A good seed.-उदकं n. Hail.—कर्तृ m. An epithet of Siva. —कोशः, -कोषः m. 1 The seed-vessel. -2 The seed-vessel of the lotus. -गणितंn. The science of Algebra.-गुप्तिः f. A pod, legume.-दर्शकः m. A stage-manager. —न्यासः m. Making known the germ of the plot of a play. —पुरुषः m. The progenitor of a family. —पुष्पः,—पूरणः m. The citron tree. —फलकः m. The citron tree. -मंत्रः m. The mystical syllable with which a Mantra begins. —मातृका f. The pericarp of a lotus. —रुहः m. Grain, corn. —वापः m. 1 A sower of seed. -2 Sowing seed. —वाहनः m. An epithet of Siva.-सूः f. The earth. —सेक्तृ m. A procreator, progenitor. —हरा, -हारिणी f. A witch.

बीजकः m. 1 The citron tree. -2 A lemon or citron. -3 The position of the arms of a child at birth. -कं n. Seed. [seed.

बीजल a. (f. -ला) Furnished with

बीजिक a. (f. —का) Abounding in seeds.

बीजिन् a. (f. -नी) Possessed of seed; seedy. —m. 1 The real father (opp. क्षेत्रिन् the owner or husband of the क्षेत्र or woman). -2 A father in general. -3 The sun.

बीज्य a. (f. —ज्या) Of a good or respectable family; nobly-born.

बीभत्स a. (f. —त्सा) 1 Loathsome, nauseous, hideous, revolting. -2 Envious, mischievous. -3 Cruel, ferocious. -4 Estranged in mind. -5 Loathing, detesting.-6 Wicked. —त्सः m. 1 Abhorrence, detestation. -2 The sentiment of disgust, one of the 8 or 9 *rasas* in poetry. -3 N. of Arjuna.

बीभत्सुः m. An epithet of Arjuna.

बुक् *ind* An imitative word.-Comp. -कार: *m.* 1 The roaring of a lion. -2 The cry of an animal.

बुक्क् 1 P., 10 U. (बुक्कति,-बुक्कयति,-ते) 1 To bark. -2 To speak, talk. -3 To sound in general.

बुक्कः *m.*, -क्कं *n.* 1 The heart.-2 The bosom, chest. -3 Blood. -क्कः *m.* 1 A goat. -2 Time (समय).-क्का *f.* Blood.

बुक्कन् *m.* The heart.

बुक्कनं *n.* 1 Barking. -2 The noise made by animals in general.

बुक्कसः *m.* A Chândâla.

बुक्का, -क्की *f.* The heart.

बुद्ध *p. p.* (*f.*-द्धा) 1 Known, understood. -2 Awakened. -3 Observed. -4 Enlightened, wise. —द्धः *m.* 1 A wise man, a sage. -2 (With Buddhists) A saint who, by perfect knowledge of the truth, has attained liberation from all existence and who reveals to the world the method of obtaining the final emancipation before obtaining it himself. -3 N. of Sákyasimha, the celebrated founder of the Bauddha religion. -Comp. -आगमः *m.* The doctrines and tenets of the Bauddha religion. —गया *f.* N. of a sacred place of pilgrimage. -मार्गः *m.* The doctrines and tenets of Buddha; Buddhism.

बुद्धिः *f.* 1 Perception. -2 Intellect, intelligence, talent. -3 Information, knowledge. -4 Discrimination, discernment. -5 Mind. -6 Presence of mind. -7 A belief, idea, feeling.-8 Purpose, design. (बुद्ध्या 'Intentionally', 'purposely', 'deliberately'). -9 Return to consciousness', recovery from a swoon. -10 (In Sân. phil.) Intellect, the second of the 25 elements of the Sânkhyas. -Comp.—अतीत *a.* Beyond the reach of the intellect. —इन्द्रियं *n.* An organ of perception (opp. कर्मेन्द्रिय); (these are five:— the ear, skin, eye, tongue, and nose; to these sometimes मनस् is added). —योगिन् *a.* Rational. —तत्त्वं *n.* The second element of the Sânkhya philosophy. —पूर्व *a.* Intentional. -पूर्वं, —पूर्वकं, -पुरःसरं *ind.* Intentionally, purposely.—योगः *m.* Intellectual communion with the Supreme Spirit. —सखः, -सहायः *m.* A counsellor.

बुद्धिमत *a.* (*f.* —ती) 1 Intelligent, rational.-2 Wise, learned.-3 Sharp, clever. -4 Humble, docile.

बुद्बुदः *m.* 1 A bubble. -2 Anything very transitory. -3 Embryo five days old.

बुध् 1 U., 4 A. (बोधति,-ते बुध्यते, बुद्ध) 1 To know, understand.-2 To perceive, recognise, mark. -3 To regard, consider. -4 To attend to. -5 To think, reflect. -6 To awake. -7 To regain consciousness, to come to one's senses. -8 To advise, admonish. With अनु— 1 To know, learn; understand. -2 To be aware of. अव— To know, learn. उद्— 1 To awake. -2 To expand. नि— 1 To know, learn, understand. -2 To regard as, to consider as. प्र— 1 To wake up. -2 To blow, to expand. प्रति- 1 To wake. सम्- To know, to understand, to learn. -*Caus.* बोधयति, -ते.-*Desid.* बुबु-बो-धिषति,-ते, बुभुत्सते.

बुध *a.* (*f.* —धा) 1 Wise, clever, learned. -2 Intelligent. —धः *m.* A wise or learned man. -2 A God.-3 The planet Mercury. -Comp. -तातः *m.* The moon. —दिनं *n.*,—वारः, -वासरः *m.* Wednesday.-रत्नं*n.* The emerald. —सुतः *m.* An epithet of Purúravas.

बुधानः *m.* 1 A wise man, sage. -2 A holy teacher, spiritual guide.

बुधित *a.* (*f.* —ता) Known, understood.

बुधिल *a.* (*f.* —ला) Learned, wise.

बुध्नः *m.* 1 The bottom of a vessel. -2 The foot of a tree. -3 The lowest part. -4 An epithet of Siva (Also बुध्न्य in the last sense).

बुभुक्षा *f.* Desire of eating, hunger. -2 The desire of enjoyment.

बुभुक्षित *a.* (*f.* —ता) 1 Hungry, starving.

बुभुक्षु *a.* 1 Hungry.-2 Desirous of worldly enjoyments(opp. मुमुक्षु).

बुभूषा *f.* Wish to be or become.

बुभूषु *a.* Wishing to be or become.

बुलिः *f.* Fear.

बुस् 4 P. (बुस्यति) 1 To discharge, pour forth.-2 To divide, distribute.

बुसं (-षं) *n.* 1 Chaff. -2 Rubbish, refuse.-3 Dry cow-dung.-4 Wealth. -5 The thick part of sour curds.

बुस्त 10 U. (बुस्तयति,-ते) 1 To honour, respect. -2 To disrespect.

बुस्तं *n.* 1 Baked flesh. -2 The shell of fruit.

बूकं *n.* See बुक.

बृशी, बृषी (-सी) *f.* The seat of an ascetic or holy sage.

बृंह् 6. P. (बृंहति, बृंहित) 1 To grow, increase. -2 To roar.

बृंह् 1 P., 10 U. (बृंहति, बृंहयति,-ते) 1 To speak. -2 To shine.

बृंहणं *n.* 1 Nourishing.-2 The roaring noise (of an elephant).

बृंहितं *n.* The roaring of an elephant.

बृह् 1. 6. P. (बर्हति, बृहति) 1 To grow, increase. -2 To roar. -With उद्— 1 To lift, raise. नि— To destroy, remove.

बृहत् *a.* (*f.* —ती) 1 Large, great, bulky. -2 Wide, extensive. -3 Ample, abundant.-4 Strong, powerful. -5 Long, tall. -6 Full-grown. -7 Compact, dense. -8 Eldest or oldest. —ती *f.* 1 A large lute. -2 The lute of Nârada. -3 A mantle, wrapper. -4 A reservoir. -5 N. of a metre. -*n.* 1 The Veda. -2 N. of a Sâman.-3 Brahman (*n.*). Comp.—अंगः *m.* A large elephant. —आरण्यं,—आरण्यकं *n.* N. of a celebrated Upanishad, forming the last six chapters of the Satapatha Brâhmana. —केतुः *m.* An epithet of Agni. —गोलं *n.* A water-melon. —चित्तः *m.* The citron tree. —नटः,-नलः *m.*, ला *f.* The name assumed by Arjuna when residing as dancing and music master at the court of Virâta. -पादः *m.* The fig-tree. —पालः *m.* The Indian fig-tree. —भट्टारिका *f.* An epithet of Durgá. —भानुः *m.* Fire. —रथः *m.* 1 An epithet of Indra. -2 N. of a king, father of Jarâsandha. -रात्रिचरः *m.* A kind of small owl.

बृहतिका *f.* An upper garment, a mantle, wrapper.

बृहस्पतिः *m.* 1 N. of the preceptor of the gods. -2 The planet Jupiter. -3 N. of the author of a Smriti. -Comp.—पुरोहितः *m.* An epithet of Indra. —वारः,-वासरः *m.* Thursday.

बेडा *f.* A boat.

बेह् 1 A. (बेहते) To endeavour, attempt.

बैजिक *a.* (*f.* —की) 1 Seminal. -2 Original. -3 Relating to conception. -4 Relating to sexual union. —कः *m.* A sprout, young shoot. -कं *n.* 1 Cause, origin. -2 The soul.

बैडाल *a.* (*f.* —ली) 1 Relating to a cat. -2 Peculiar to cats. -Comp. —व्रतं *n.* Concealing evil designs under the garb of piety or virtue. —व्रतिः *m.* One who leads a chaste life simply from want of female company. —व्रतिकः,—व्रतिन् *m.* A religious hypocrite.

बैदल *a.* Made of bamboos. —लं *n.* A basket made of bamboos.

बैंबिकः *m.* A gallant, lover.

बैल्व *a.* (*f.* -ल्वी) *m.* 1 Relating to or made of the Bilva tree or its wood. -2 Covered with Bilva trees. —ल्वं *n.* The fruit of the Bilva tree.

बोधः *m.* 1 Perception, knowledge, apprehension,conception.-2 Understanding, intelligence, wisdom. -3 Waking up, conscioueness. -4 Blooming, expanding. -5 Advice, admonition. -6 An epithet, designation. -Comp. -अतीत *a.* Incomprehensible. —करः *m.* 1 A bard or minstrel who wakes up his master by singing appropriate songs in the morning. -2 An instructor, a teacher. -पूर्व *a.* Intentional, concious. -वासरः *m.* The eleventh day in the bright half of Kârtika when Vishnu is supposed to rise from his four months' sleep.

बोधक *a.* (*f.* -धिका) 1 Informing, apprising. -2 Instructing, teaching. -3 Indicative of. -4 Awakening,rousing. —कः *m.* 1 A spy. -2A teacher, instructor. -3 A minstrel, bard.

बोधनः *m.*The planet Mercury(बुध). —नं *n.* 1 Informing, teaching, instruction. -2 Denoting, signifying. Observing, perceiving. -4 Waking, being awake. -5 Making attentive. -6 Burning incense.—नी *f.* 1 The eleventh day in the bright half of Kártika when Vishnu rises from his four months' sleep. -2 Long pepper.

बोधानः *m.* 1 A wise man. -2 An epithet of Brishapati.

बोधिः *m.* 1 Perfect wisdom or enlightenment. -2 The enlightened intellect of a Buddha. -3 The sacred fig tree. -4 A cock. -5 An epithet of Buddha. -Comp. —तरुः, —द्रुमः, —वृक्षः *m.* The sacred fig-tree. —दः *m.* An *arhat* (of the Jainas). —सत्वः *m.* A Buddhist saint, who has only a certain number of births to undergo before attaining to the state of a Supreme Buddha and complete annihilation.

बोधित *p. p.* (*f.*-ता) 1 Made known, informed. -2 Reminded. -3 Advised, instructed.

बौद्ध *a.* (*f.* —द्धी) 1 Relating to *Buddhi* or understanding. -2 Relating to Buddha.-द्धः *m.* A follower of the religion taught by Buddha.

बौधः *m.* An epithet of Purúravas.

बौधायनः *m.* N. of an ancient author of a सूत्र.

ब्रध्नः *m.* 1 The sun. -2 The root of a tree. -3 A day. -4 The *arka* plant. -5 An epithet of Siva or Brahman (*m.*). -6 The point of an arrow.

ब्रह्मं *n.* The Supreme Spirit.

ब्रह्मण्य *a.* (*f.* —ण्या) 1 Relating to Brahman (*m.*). -2 Relating to Brahman (*m.*) -3 Relating to the acquisition of sacred knowledge,holy, pious. -4 Fit for a Brâhmana. -5 Friendly, favourable or hospitable to a Bráhmana. -ण्यः *m.* 1 One well versed in the Veda.-2 The mulberry tree.-4The palm tree. -4 Munja grass. -5 The planet Saturn. -6 An epithet of Vishnu -7 Of Kârtikeya.—ण्या *f.* An epithet of Durgá. -Comp. —देवः *m.* An epithet of Vishnu.

ब्रह्मण्वत् *m.* An epithet of Agni.

ब्रह्मन् *n.* 1 The Supreme Being, regarded as impersonal; the all-pervading soul and spirit of the universe;the essence from which all created things emanate and to which they return.. -2 A hymn of praise. -3 A sacred text. -4 The Vedas. -5 The mystic syllable *om*.-6 The priestly or Bráhmanical class (collectively). -7 The power or energy of a Bráhmana. -8 Religious penance or austerities. -9 Celibacy, chastity. -10 Final beatitude. -11 Sacred learning, religious knowledge. -12 The Brâhmana portion of the Veda. -13 Wealth.-14 Food. -15 A Brâhmana. -16 Truth. —*m.* 1 The Supreme Being; the Creator; the first deity of the sacred Hindu Trinity, on whom falls the duty of creating the world.-2 A Brâhmana. -3 A devout man. -4 One of the four priests employed at a Soma sacrifice. -5 One conversant with sacred knowledge. -6 The sun. -7 Intellect. -8 An epithet of the seven Prajápatis:—मरीचि, अत्रि, अंगिरस्, पुलस्त्य, पुलह, क्रतु and वसिष्ठ. -9 An epithet of Brihaspati. -10 Of Siva. —Comp. —अक्षरं *n.* The sacred syllable *om*.-अंजलिः *m.* 1 Salutation with folded hands while repeating the Veda. -2 Obeisance to a preceptor (at the beginning and conclusion of the repetition of the Veda).-अंडं *n.* The primordial egg from which the universe sprang ; the world, universe. —अधिगमः *m.*, —अधिगमनं *n.* A study of the Vedas.-अंभस् *n.* The urine of a cow. —अभ्यासः *m.* The study of the Vedas. —अयणः, —नः *m.* An epithet of Nárâyana. —अर्पणं *n.* 1 The offering of sacred knowledge, -2 Devoting oneself to the Supreme Spirit. -3 N. of a spell. -4 A mode of performing the Sráddha in which no 'Pindas' or rice-balls are offered. —आत्मभूः *m.* A horse. -आनंदः*m.* The rapture of absorption into Brahman (*n.*).-आरंभः *m.* Beginning to repeat the Vedas.-आवर्तः *m.* N. of the tract between the rivers Sarasvati and Drishadvatî (north-west of Hastinápura).-आसनं *n.* Sitting down for profound meditation. —आहुतिः *f.* 1 The offering of prayers. -2 The study of the Vedas.-उज्झता *f.* Forgetting or neglecting the Vedas. -उद्यं *n.* A discussion of theological problems. —उपदेशः *m.* Instruction in the Vedas or sacred knowledge. —ऋषिः (ब्रह्मर्षिः or ब्रह्मऋषिः) *m.* A Brâhmanical sage.-कन्यका *f.* An epithet of Sarasvatî.-करः *m.* A tax paid to the Bráhmanas.-कर्मन् *n.* 1 The religious duties of a Brâhmana.-2 The office of Brahman,one of the four principal priests at a sacrifice.—कल्पः *m.* An age of Brahman(*m.*).-काष्ठः*m.*The mulberry tree. —कूर्चं *n.* A kind of penance.—कृत *m.* An epithet of Vishnu.—गुप्तः *m.* N. of an astronomer born in 598 A.D.—गोलः *m.* The universe. —ग्रंथिः *m.* A particular joint of the body. —ग्रहः, —पिशाचः, —पुरुषः, —राक्षसः *m.*, —रक्षस् *n.* The ghost of a Bráhmana,who while living indulges in a haughty spirit and carries away the wives of others and the property of Bràhmanas. -घातकः, —घातिन् *m.* The murderer of a Bràhmana. -घातिनी *f.* A woman on the second day of her courses. —घोषः *m.*1 The recital of the Veda.-2 The Vedas collectively. —घ्नः *m.* The murderer of a Bràhmana. —चर्यं *n*

1 Religious studentship, the life of celibacy passed by a Bràhmana boy while studying the Vedas ; the first stage or order of his life. -2 Chastity, abstinence, continence.(-र्यः *m.*) A religious student.(-र्या *f.*) Chastity, celibacy. —चारिकं *n.* The life of a religious student.-चारिन् *m.* A Bràhmana in the first order of his life, who lives with his spiritual guide from the investiture with sacred thread and does the duties belonging to his order till he settles in life. -2 One who vows to lead the life of a celibate.-3 An epithet of Siva. -4 Of Skanda. -चारिणी *f.* 1 An epithet of Durgâ. -2 A woman who observes the vow of chastity. —जः *m.* An epithet of Kârtikeya. —जारः *m.* The paramour of a Brâhmana's wife. -जीविन् *m.* A Brâhmana who lives by sacred knowledge. —ज्ञ, -ज्ञानिन् *a.* One who knows Brahman (*n.*). (-ज्ञः *m.*) 1 An epithet of Kârtikeya. -2 Of Vishnu. —ज्ञानं *n.* Divine knowledge, knowledge of the identity of the universe with Brahman (*n.*) -ज्येष्ठः *m.* The elder brother of Brahman (*m.*). —ज्योतिस् *n.* 1 The light of the Supreme Being. -2 An epithet of Siva. -तत्त्वं *n.* The true knowledge of the Supreme Spirit. -तेजस् *n.* 1 The glory which surrounds a Brâhmana. -दः *m.* A spiritual teacher. -दंडः *m.* 1 The curse of a Bráhmana. -2 A tribute paid to a Bráhmana. -3 An epithet of Siva. —दानं *n.* The gift of sacred knowledge. -दायः *m.* Instruction in the Vedas.-2 The sacred knowledge received as an inheritance. -3 The earthly possesion of a Bráhmana. —दायादः *m.* 1 A Bràhmana who receives the Vedas as his hereditary gift); a Bráhmana.-2 The son of a Bràhmana. —दारुः *m.* The mulberry tree. —दिनं *n.* A day of Brahman (*m.*). —देय *a.* Married according to the Bráhma form of marriage. —दैत्यः *m.* A Bráhmana changed into a demon. —द्विष्, -द्वेषिन् *a.* 1 Hating Bràhmanas.-2 Hostile to religion and piety. —द्वेषः *m.* Hatred of Brâhmanas. —नदी *f.* An epithet of the river Sarasvati. -नाभः *m.* An epithet of Vishnu. —निर्वाणं *n.* Absorption into the Supreme Spirit. -निष्ठ *a.* Intent on the contemplation of the Supreme Spirit.(-ष्ठः *m.*) The mulberry tree. —पदं *n.* 1 The rank or position of a Bráhmana. -2 The place of the Supreme Spirit. —पवित्रः *m.* The Kusa grass. —परिषद् *f.* An assembly of Bráhmanas. —पादपः, —पत्रः *m.* The Palása tree. —पारायणं *n.* A complete study of the Vedas. —पाशः *m.* N. of a missile presided over by Brahman(*m.*). —पितृ *m.* An epithet of Vishnu. -पुत्रः *m.* 1 A son of Brahman (*m.*). -2 N. of a (male) river which rises in the Himálaya and falls with the Ganges into the Bay of Bengal. (-त्री *f.*) An epithet of the river Sarasvati. -पुरं *n.*, -पुरी *f.* The city of Bráhman (*m.*) in heaven. -2 N. of Benares. —पुराणं *n.* N. of one of the eighteen Puránas. —प्रलयः *m.* The universal destruction in which even the Supreme Being is supposed to be swallowed up. —प्राप्तिः *f.* Absorption into the Supreme Spirit. -बंधुः *m.* 1 A contemptuous term for a Bráhmana; an unworthy Brâhmana; a wretched or stupid Bráhmana ; one who is a Bráhmana

only by caste but not by qualifications. -बीजं *n.* 1 The mystic syllable *om*. -2 The mulberry tree. —ब्रुवः, -ब्रवाणः *m.* One who pretends to be a Brâhmana. —भागः *m.* The mulberry tree. -भावः *m.* Absorption into the Supreme Spirit. -भूत *a.* Become one with the Supreme Spirit. —भूतिः *f.* Twilight. -भूयं *n.* 1 Absorption into Brahman (*m.*). -2 Bráhmanahood, the state or rank of a Bráhmana. -भूयस् *n.* Absorption into Brahman(*n.*). —मंगलदेवता *f.* An epithet of Lakshmí. -मीमांसा *f.* The Vedanta philosophy which inquires into the nature of the Supreme Spirit. -मूर्ति *a.* Having the form of Brahman (*m.*). -मूर्धभृत *m.* An epithet of Siva. —मेखलः *m.* The 'Munja' plant.—यज्ञः *m* One of the five daily Yajnas or sacrifices. -योगः *m.* The cultivation of spiritual knowledge. —रत्नं *n.* A valuable present made to a Bráhmana. -रंध्रं *n.* An aperture in the crown of the head through which the soul is said to escape on its leaving the body. —राक्षसः *m.* Same as ब्रह्मग्रहः.—रातः *m.* An epithet of Suka. -राशिः *m.* 1 The whole mass or circle of sacred knowledge. -2 An epithet of Parasurâma. -रीतिः *f.* A kind of brass. -रे(-ले-) खा *f.* —लिखितं *n.*, -लेखः *m.* The predestined lot of any man. —लोकः *m.* The world of Brahman (*m.*). -वक्तृ *m.* An expounder of the Vedas. -वद्यं *n.* A knowledge of Brahman (*n.*). -वर्चस्, -वर्चसं *n.* 1 Spiritual pre-eminence or holiness resulting from sacred knowledge. -2 The natural sanctity a Brâhmana. -वर्चसिन्, -वर्चस्विन् *a.* Holy on account of the study of the Vedas. (-*m.*) An eminent or holy Brâhmana.—वर्तः *m.* See ब्रह्मावर्त. —वर्धनं *n.* Copper. —वादिन् *m.* 1 One who teaches or expounds the Vedas. -2 A follower of the Vedânta philosophy. (-नी *f.*) An epithet of Gáyatrî. -वासः *m.* The abode of Bráhmanas. -विद्, -विद *a.* 1 Knowing the Supreme Spirit. (-*m.*) A sage, philosopher. -विं (-बिं-) -दुः *m.* The drop of saliva sputtered while reciting the Vedas. —विवर्धनः *m.* An epithet of Indra. -वृक्षः *m.* 1 The Palâsa tree. -2 The Udumbara tree. -वेदः *m.* 1 Knowledge of the Vedas. -2 Knowledge of Brahman (*n.*). -3 The Veda of the Brâhmanas (opp. क्षत्रवेद). -4 N. of the Atharvaveda. —वेदिन् *a.* Knowing the Vedas. —वैवर्तं *n.* N. of one of the eighteen Purânas.-व्रतं *n.* A vow of chastity. —शिरस्, -शीर्षन् *n.* N. of a particular missile. -संसद् *f.* An assembly of Bráhmanas. —सती *f.* An epithet of the river Sarasvatì. —सत्रं *n.* 1 Repeating and teaching the Vedas. -2 Absorption into the Supreme Spirit. -सदस् *n.* The residence of Brahman (*m.*). -सभा *f.* The hall or court of Brahman(*m.*). - संभवः *m.* N. of Nárada. -सर्पः *m.* A kind of snake. -सायुज्यं *n.* Complete identification with the Supreme Spirit.-सार्ष्टिका *f.* Identification with Brahman (*n.*). -सावर्णिः *m.* N. of the tenth Manu.-सुतः *m.* 1 N.of Nárada, Marîchi &c. -2 A kind of *Ketu*. -सूः *m.* 1 N. of Aniruddha. -2 N of the God of love. -सूत्रं *n.* 1 The sacred thread worn by the Bráhmanas or the twice-born over the shoulder. -2 The aphorisms of the Vedanta philosophy by Bâdarâyana. -सूत्रिन *a.* Invested with the sacred thread. -सूत्र *m.* An epithet of Siva. -स्तंव: *m.* The world, universe. -स्तेयं *n.* Acquiring holy knowledge by unlawful means.-स्वं *n.* The property or possessions of a Brâhmana. -स्वरूप *a.* Of the nature of the Supreme Spirit. -हुतं *n.* One of the five daily Yajanas or sacrifices, which consists in offering the rites of hospitality to guests.-हृदय: *m.*,-यं *n.* N. of the star Capella.

ब्रह्मवत *a.* Possessing spiritual knowledge.

ब्रह्मसात *ind.* 1 To the state of Brahman (*n.*) or the Supreme Spirit. -2 To the care of Brâhmanas.

ब्रह्माणी *f.* 1 The wife of Brahman (*m.*). -2 An epithet of Durgâ. -3 A kind of perfume. -4 A kind of brass.

ब्राह्मिष *a.* Relating to Brahman(*n.*). -*m.* An epithet of Vishnu.

ब्राह्मिष्ठ *a.* (*f.* -ष्ठा) Thoroughly proficient in the Vedas. -ष्ठा *f.* An epithet of Durgâ.

ब्रह्मी *f.* N. of a medicinal plant.

ब्रह्मेशय: *m.* 1 An epithet of Kartikeya. -2 Of Vishnu.

ब्राह्म *a.* (*f.* -ह्मी) 1 Relating to Brahman (*m.*) or the creator, or to the Supreme Spirit. -2 Belonging to Brâhmanas. -3 Relating to sacred knowledge or study.-4 Vedic. -5 Holy, divine. -6 Presided over by Brahman (*m.*).-7 Fit for a divine state or godhead. -ह्म: *m.* 1 One of the eight forms of marriage in Hindu law. -2 N. of Nârada. -3 Quicksilver. -4 The duty or prescribed course of conduct of a king. —ह्मं *n.* 1 The part of the hand under the root of the thumb. -2 Holy or sacred study. -3 N. of a Purâna. -4 N. of the constellation Rohini. -Comp.—अहोरात्र: *m.* A day and night of Brahman (*m.*). —देया *f.* A girl to be married according to the Brâhma form. -मुहूर्त: *m.* The early part of the day.

ब्राह्मण *a.* (*f.* —णी) 1 Belonging to or befitting a Brâhmana. -2 Given by a Brâhmana.-3 Relating to religious worship.-ण: *m.* 1 A man of the first of the four original castes of the Hindus; a Bráhmana. -2 An epithet of Agni. -3 N. of the twenty-eighth Nakshatra. —णं *n.* 1 A society of Brâhmanas. -2 That portion of the Veda which states rules for the employment of the 'mantras' at the various sacrifices, their origin and detailed explanation, with illustrations in the shape of legends or stories. -3 N. of that class of the Vedic works which contain the Bráhmana portion.-Comp.—अभ्युपपत्ति: *f.* Preservation of,or kindness shown to,a Bráhmana. —चाण्डाल: *m.* 1 A degraded or outcast Bráhmana. -2 The son of a Sudra father by a Bráhmani woman. —जातं *n.*,-जाति: *f.* The Bráhmana caste. -जीविका *f.* The means of livelihood prescribed for a Bráhmana. —त्रा *ind.* To or to the disposition of a Bráhmana. —द्रव्यं; -स्वं *n.* A Bráhmana's property. -ब्रुव: *m.* One who pretends to be a Bráhmana; one who is a Brâhmana only in name and neglects the duties of his caste.

ब्राह्मणक: *m.* 1 A bad or unworthy Bráhmana. -2 A family of such a Bráhmana. -3 N. of a country inhabited by warlike Bráhmanas.

ब्राह्मणत्रा *ind.* Among or to Bráhmanas. [Bráhmanas.

ब्राह्मणसात *ind.* In the possession of

ब्राह्मणाच्छंसिन् *m*. A particular priest at a *soma* sacrifice.

ब्राह्मणायनः *m*. A Bráhmana descended from learned and hcly progenitors.

ब्राह्मणी *f*. 1 A woman of the Bráhmana caste. -2 The wife of a Bráhman. -3 Intellect. -4 A kind of lizard.-5 A kind of wasp.-6 A kind of grass.

ब्राह्मण्य *a*. (*f*. —ण्या) Befitting a Bráhmana. —ण्यः *m*. An epithet of the planet Saturn. —ण्यं *n*. 1 The station or rank of a Bráhmana. The nature or temperment of a Bráhmaan. -2 A collection of Brâhmanas

ब्राह्मी *f*. 1 The personified female energy of Brahman(*m*.).-2Sarasvatî, the goddess of speech. -3 Speech. -4 A tale or narrative. -5 A pious custom. -6 N. of the constellation Rohiní. -7 N. of Durgá. -8 A woman married according to the *Bráhma* form of marriage. -9 The wife of a Brâhmana. -10 A certain medicinal plant. -11 A kind of brass. -12 N. of a river.

ब्राह्म *a*. (*f*. —ह्मी) 1 Relating to Brahman (*m*.). -2 Relating to the Supreme Spirit. -3 Relating the Brâhmanas. -ह्मं *n*. 1 Wonder, astonishment.-2 Worship of the Brâhamanas. -Comp. -मुहूर्तः *m*., -र्तं *n*. A particular period of the early part of the day. -हुतं *n*. Hospitality to guests.

ब्रुव, ब्रुवाण *a*. Professing or pretending to be (at the end of comp.)as in ब्राह्मणब्रुवः, क्षत्रियब्रुवः &c.

ब्रू 2 U. (ब्रवीति, ब्रूते or आह ; this root is defective in the non-conjugational tenses, its forms being made up from वच्). 1 To say, tell, speak (with two acc). -2 To say or speak about, refer to (a person or thing). -3 To proclaim, publish, prove. -4 To name, designate. With अनु— To say, speak, declare. निस्— To explain, derive. प्र— To say, speak, tell. प्रति— To answer or reply. वि— 1 To say, speak. -2 To speak falsely or wrongly.

ब्लेष्कं *n*. A snare, net, noose.

भ.

भः *m*. 1 The planet Venus. -2 Error, delusion. -भं *n*. 1 A star. -2 A lunar mansion. -3 A planet. -4 A sign of the zodiac. -5 The number twenty-seven. -6 A bee. -Comp. -गणः, -वर्गः *m*. 1 The group of stars or asterisms.-2 The zodiac. -3 Revolution of the planets in the zodiac. —गोलः *m*.The starry sphere. —चक्रं *n*., -पंजरः *m*., -मंडलं *n*. The zodiac -पतिः *m*. The moon. -सूचकः *m*. An astrologer.

भांकिका *f*. A cricket.

भक्त *p*. *p*. (*f*. —क्ता)1 Distributed, allotted. -2 Divided. -3 Served, worshipped. -4 Engaged in, attentive to.-5 Devoted to, loyal,faithful. -6 Dressed, cooked (as food). —क्तः *m*. A worshipper, adorer, devotee, a faithful attendant. -क्तं *n*. 1 A share, portion. -2 Food. -3 Boiled rice. -4 Any eatable grain, boiled with water. -5 Adoration, worship. -Comp. —अभिलाषः *m*. The desire of food, appetite. —उपसाधक *m*. A cook. -कंसः *m*. A dish of food.

—कर: *m.* Incense prepared from various fragrant resins and perfumes.-कारः *m.* A cook.-छंदं *n.* Appetite.-जा *f.* Nectar.-दासः *m.* A slave who receives his meals as a return for his services. -द्वेषः *m.* Loss of appetite. —मंडः *m.* The scum of boiled rice. -रोचन *a.* Exciting appetite. —वत्सल *a.* Kind to worshippers or devotees. —शाला *f.* 1 An audience chamber. -2 A dining-hall.

भक्तिः *f.* 1 Separation, division. -2 Devotion, attachment, loyalty, faithfulness. -3 Faith, belief, pious faith. -4 Worship, homage. -5 Texture, arrangement. -6 Embellishment. -7 An attribute. -Comp. -पूर्वं, —पूर्वकं *ind.* Devoutly, reverentially. —भाज् *a.* 1 Devout, fervid. -2 Devoted, faithful, loyal.-मार्गः *m.* The devotion to god as the way to the attainment of final emancipation and eternal bliss. -योगः *m.* Loving faith, loyal devotion.

भाक्तिलः *m.* A faithful horse.

भक्ष् 10 U. (भक्षयति,-ते, भक्षित) 1 To eat, devour.-2 To use up, consume. -3 To waste, destroy. -4 To bite.

भक्षः *m.* 1 Eating. -2 Food.

भक्षक *a.* (*f.* —क्षिका) 1 One who eats or lives (upon.). -2 Gluttonous, voracious —कः *m.* Food.

भक्षण *a.* (*f.* —णी) One who eats or devours. —णं *n.* Eating, feeding or living upon.

भक्षिका *f.* A meal.

भक्ष्यं *n.* 1 Anything eatable, an article of food, food (fig. also). -2 Water. -Comp. —कारः (also भक्ष्यंकारः) *m.* A baker, cook.

भगः *m.* 1 One of the twelve forms of the sun; the sun. -2 The moon. -3 A form of Siva. -4 Good fortune, happiness. -5 Prosperity.-6 Fame, glory. -7 Loveliness, beauty. -8 Excellence, distinction. -9 Love. -10 Amorous dalliance or sport. -11 The pudendum muliebre. -12 Virtue, morality. -13 Effort, exertion. -14 Indifference to worldly objects. -15 Final beatitude. -16 Strength. -17 Omnipotence. (*n.* also in the last 14 senses).-18 The power of becoming as small as an atom, one of the eight *Siddhis* or powers of Siva. —गं *n.* 1 The asterism called उत्तरा फल्गुनी.-2 The perinæum of males. -Comp. —अंकुरः *m.* (In medicine) Clitoris. —आधानं *n.* Granting matrimonial happiness. —घ्नः *m.* An epithet of Siva. —देवः *m.* A thorough libertine.-देवता *f.* The deity presiding over marriage. —दैवतं *n.* The constellation उत्तरा फल्गुनी. —नंदनः *m.* An epithet of Vishuu. —भक्षकः *m.* A pander, procurer. [pudendum.

भगंदरः *m.* A fistula in the anus or

भगवत *a.* (*f.* —ती) 1 Glorious, illustrious. -2 Revered, venerable, holy. —*m.* 1 A deity.-2 An epithet of Vishnu. -3 Of Siva. -4 Of Jina. -5 Of Buddha. -Comp -गीता *f.* N. of a celebrated sacred work consisting of a dialogue between Krishna and Arjuna.

भगवती *f.* 1 N. of Durgá. -2 Of Lakshmî.-3 Any venerable woman.

भगवदीयः *m.* A worshipper of Vishnu.

भगालं *n.* A skull.

भगालिन् *m.* An epithet of Siva.

भगिन् *a.* (*f.* -नी) 1 Prosperous, fortunate. -2 Grand, splendid.

भागिनिका *f.* A sister.

भगिनी *f.* 1 A sister.-2 A fortunate

woman. -3 A woman in general. -Comp. —पतिः, —भर्तृ *m.* A sister's husband.

भगिनीयः *m.* A sister's son.

भगीरथः *m.* N. of an ancient king of the solar dynasty, who brought down, by the most austere penance, the celestial river Ganges from heaven to the earth and from the earth to the lower regions to purify the ashes of his 60,000 ancestors the sons of Sagara. -Comp. -पथः, —प्रयत्नः *m.* The path or effort of Bhagîratha (used to denote any great or Herculean effort). —सुता *f.* An epithet of the Ganges.

भग्न *p. p.* (*f.* -ग्ना) 1 Broken, shattered, torn. -2 Frustrated, disappointed.-3 Arrested, suspended. -4 Marred, impaired.-5 Routed, completely vanqished. -घ्नं *n.* Fracture of the leg.-Comp.-आपद् *a.* One who has surmounted difficulties or misfortunes.-आश *a.* Disappointed, frustrated. -उत्साह *a.* Discouraged damped. -उद्यम *a.* Disappointed, baffled.-क्रमः *m.* A violation of symmetry in construction or expression (a fault in composition. See प्रक्रमभंगः). -चेष्ट *a.* Disappointed, frustrated. -दर्प *a.* Crest-fallen. -पार्श्व *a.* Suffering from a pain in the sides. —पृष्ठ *a.* 1 Having a broken back. -2 Coming in front. -प्रक्रमः *m.* 1 Disorder, confusion. -2 Absence of regularity or symmetry. -मनस् *a.* Discouraged, disappointed. -मनोरथ *a.* Disappointed in expectations. -संकल्प *a.* One whose designs are frustrated.

भग्नी *f.* A sister.

भंका (-या-) री *f.* A gad-fly.

भंक्तिः *f.* Breaking, fracture.

भंगः *m.* 1 Breaking, shattering, splitting, dividing. -2 A fracture, breach. -3 Lopping off. -4 Separation, analysis. -5 A portion, fragment. -6 Downfall, destruction, ruin. -7 Breaking up, dispersion.-8 Discomfiture, rout. -9 Disappointment, frustration. -10 Rejection, refusal. -11 A chasm.-12 Obstacle, disturbance. -13 Suspension, stoppage. -14 Taking to flight, flight. -15 A bend, fold. -16 A wave. -17 Contraction, knitting as in ग्रीवाभंगः, भ्रूभंगः. -18 Going, motion. -19 Paralysis. -20 Fraud, deceit. -21 A canal, water-course. -22 A roundabout way of speaking or acting. -23 Hemp. -Comp. —नयः *m.* A removal of obstacles. —वासा *f.* Turmeric. —सार्थ *a.* Dishonest, fraudulent.

भंगा *f.* 1 Hemp. -2 An intoxicating drink prepared from hemp. -Comp. —कटं *n.* The pollen of hemp.

भंगिः, -गी *f.* 1 Breaking, breach, division. -2 Undulation. -3 Bending, contracting. -4 A wave, a current. -5 A crooked path, tortuous course. -6 A round-about way of speaking or acting, periphrasis. -7 A trick, pretext, disguise. -8 Irony, a repartee, wit. -9 A step. -10 An interval. -11 Modesty. -Comp. —भक्तिः *f.* Division into a series of waves or wave-like steps; a wavy staircase. [transient.

भंगिन् *a.* (*f.* —नी) Frail, fragile,

भंगिमन् *m.* 1 Fracture, breach. -2 Bending, undulation. -3 Curliness. -4 Disguise, deceit. -5 Wit, irony.

भंगिलं *n.* A defect in the organs of sense.

भंगुर *a.* (*f.* —रा) 1 Fragile,brittle. -2 Frail, transitory, perishable. -3 Crooked, bent. -4 Curved, curled. -5 Dishonest, crafty. —रः *m.* The bend of a river.

भज् 1 U. (भजति,-ते) 1 To share, distribute, assign, allot, apportion. -2 (Atm.) To obtain for oneself, share in, partake of. -3 To accept, receive. -4 To resort to, betake oneself to, have recourse to, follow, observe. -5 To enjoy, possess, have, experience, entertain. -6 To wait or attend upon, serve. -7 To adore, honour, worship (as a God). -8 To select, perfer, accept. -9 To take possession of. -10 To fall to the lot of any one.-11 To decide in favour of, declare for. -12 To love, court (affection). -13 To be engaged in. -14 To cook, dress (food). (The meanings of this root are variously modified according to the noun with which it is connected:—*e. g.* निद्रां भज् To go to sleep &c.). With वि- 1 To divide, to distribute. -2 To effect a partition. -3 To distinguish. संवि— To admit to a share.

भज् 10 U. (भाजयति,-ते) 1 To cook. -2 To give.

भजकः *m.* A divider, distributer. -2 A worshipper, devotee.

भजनं *n.*1 Sharing,dividing.-2 Possession. -3 Service, worship, attending upon.

भजमान *a.*(*f.* —ना) Fit, right, proper.

भंज् 7 P. (भनक्ति, भंक्तुं, भग्न ; *desid.* बिभंक्षति) 1 To break, shatter, break to pieces,split.-2 To make a breach (in a fortress). -3 To foil, disappoint, baffle.-4 To arrest, interrupt, suspend, as in भग्ननिद्रः— -5 To defeat, vanquish. —With अव— To break down, shatter. प्र- 1 To break down, splinter. -2 To stop, arrest, suspend. -3 To disappoint.

भंज् 10 U. (भंजयति,-ते) 1 To brighten, illuminate. -2 To speak. -3 To shine.

भंजक *a.* (*f.* —जिका) Breaking, dividing.

भंजन *a.* (*f.*—नी) 1 Breaking.splitting. -2 Arresting, checking. -3 Frustrating -4 Causing violent pain.-नं *n.* 1Breaking down,destroying. -2 Removing, driving away. -3 Routing, vanquishing.-4 Checking, interrupting, disturbing. -5 Afflicting. paining. -नः *m.* Decay of the teeth.

भंजनकः *m.* A particular disease of the mouth.

भंजरः *m.* A tree growing near a temple.

भट् 1 P. (भटति, भटित) 1 To nourish, maintain. -2 To hire. -3 To receive wages.

भट् 10 U. (भटयति,-ते) To speak, converse.

भटः *m.* 1 A warrior, soldier, combatant. -2 A mercenary, a hireling. -3 An outcast, a barbarian. -4 A demon.

भटित्र *a.* (*f.* —त्रा) Roasted on a spit.

भट्टः *m.* 1 A lord, master (used in addressing princes.). -2 A title used with the names of learned Bràhmanas. as in भट्टगोपालः, कुमारिलभट्टः &c. -3 Any learned man or philosopher. -4 A kind of mixed caste.-5 A bard,panegyrist. -Comp. -प्रयागः *m.* The same as प्रयागः.

भट्टार *a.* (*f.* —रा) 1 Revered,worshipful. -2 A title of respect used with proper names -रः *m.* A noble lord.

भट्टारक *a.* (*f.* —रिका) Venerable, worshipful.—कः *m.* 1 A sage, saint. -2 The sun. -3 A God, deity. -4 (In dramas) A king.-5 An epithet applied to great and learned men. -Comp. —वारः, -वासरः *m.* Sunday.

भट्टारिका *f.* A noble lady.-2 A goddess, tutelary deity.

भट्टिनी *f.* 1 A queen not crowned, a princess ; (often used in dramas by maid-servants in addressing a queen). -2 A lady of high rank.-3 The wife of a Brâhmana.

भडः *m.* N. of a mixed caste.

भडिलः *m.* 1 A hero, warrior. 2 An attendant, servant.

भण् 1 P. (भणति, भणित) 1 To say, speak, describe. -2 To name, call.

भणनं, भणितं *n.*, भणितिः *f.* Speaking, talk, discourse, conversation.

भंड् 1 A. (भंडते) 1 To chide, upbraid. -2 To mock, deride. -3 To speak. -4 To joke.

भंड् 10 U. (भंडयति,-ते) 1 To make fortunate. -2 To cheat. -3 To be fortunate.

भंडः *m.* 1 A buffoon, jester, an actor. -2 N. of a mixed caste. -Comp. -तपस्विन् *m.* A pseudo ascetic. -हासिनी *f.* A harlot, courtezan.

भंडकः *m.* A wag-tail.,

भंडनं 1 *n.* Mail, armour. -2 War, battle. -3 Mischief, wickedness.

भंडिः,—डी *f.* A wave.

भंडिल *a.* (*f.* —ला) Happy, auspicious, fortunate. —लः *m.* 1 Good fortune, happiness. -2 A messenger -3 A workman, artisan.

भदंतः *m.* 1 A term of respect applied to a Buddhist. -2 A Buddhist mendicant.

भदाकः *m.* Prosperity, good fortune.

भद्र *a.* (*f.* —द्रा) 1 Happy, prosperous, auspicious, blessed. -2 Foremost, best, chief. -3 Favourable, propitious. -4 Gracious, friendly, good; often used in voc. sing. in the sense of 'my good sir', or 'my good friend',' my good lady.'-5 Lovely, beautiful.-6 Laudable, praisewothy. -7 Beloved, dear.-8 Plausible, hypocritical. -द्रं *n.* 1 Happiness, welfare, blessing, prosperity ; often used in pl. in this sense, as in सर्वो भद्राणि पश्यतु. -2 Gold. -3 A fragrant grass. -4 Iron, steel. -द्रः *m.* 1 A bullock. -2 A wag-tail. -3 A term applied to a particular kind of elephants.-4 An impostor, a hypocrite. -5 N. of Siva. -6 An epithet of mount Meru. -7 A kind of tree. (भद्राकृ Means ' to shave', भद्राकरणं shaving). -Comp. -अंगः *m.* An epithet of Balarâma. —आत्मजः *m.* A sword. —आश्रयः *m.* The sandal tree. —आसनं *n.* 1 A chair of state, a throne. -2 A particular posture in meditation. —ईशः *m.* An epithet of Siva. —एला *f.* Large cardamoms. -कपिलः *m.* An epithet of Siva. -काली *f.* N. of Durgâ —कुंभः *m.* A golden jar filled with water from a holy place, particularly from the Ganges.-गणितं *n.* The construction of magical diagrams.—घटः,-घटकः *m.* A vessel from which a lottery is drawn. —दारुः *m.*, -दारु *n.* A sort of pine. -नामन् *m.* 1 A wag-tail. -2 The wood-pecker. -पीठं *n.* 1 A splendid seat, chair of state, throne. -2 A kind of winged insect. -बलनः *m.* An epithet of Balarâma. —मृगः *m.* An epithet of a particular kind of elephant. —रेणुः *m.* N. of Indra's elephant. —वर्मन् *m.* A kind of jasmine. —शाखः *m.* An epithet of Kârtikeya -श्रयं.-श्रियं *n.*

Sandal-wood.-श्रीः *f.* The sandal tree. -सोमा *f.* An epithet of the Ganges.

भद्रक *a.* (*f.* —द्रिका) 1 Good, auspicious. -2 Handsome, beautiful. -कः *m.* The Devadáru tree. -2 A kind of bean.

भद्रंकर *a.* Causing prosperity.

भद्रवत् *a.* Auspicious. *-n.* The Devadáru tree.

भद्रा *f.* 1 A cow. -2 N. of the second, seventh and twelfth days of a lunar fortnight. -3 The celestial Ganges. -Comp. —श्रयं *n.* Sandal-wood.

भाद्रिका *f.* 1 An amulet. -2 N. of the second, seventh and twelfth days of a lunar fortnight.

भंद्रिकं *n.* 1 Prosperity, good fortune.-2 Tremulous motion.

भंभः *m.* 1 A fly. -2 Smoke.

भंभरालिका, भंभराली *f.* 1 A gadfly. -2 A gnat.

भंभारवः *m.* The lowing of a cow.

भयं *n.* 1 Fear, alarm, dread, terror. (oft. with abl.). -2 A danger, hazard. —यः *m.* Sickness, disease -Comp. -आवह *a* 1 Causing fear, formidable. -2 Risky. —उत्तर *a.* Attended with or succeeded by fear —कर (also भयंकर) *a.* 1 Frightening, terrible, fearful. -2 Dangerous, perilous. -डिंडिमः *m.* A drum used in battle. —प्रद *a.* Inspiring fear, fearful, terrible.-प्रस्तावः *m.* An occasion of fear. -ब्राह्मणः *m.* A timid Brâhmana, a Brâhmana who declares his caste to save himself.-व्यूहः *m.* A particular array of troops when they are threatened with danger.

भयानक *a.* (*f.* —का) Horrible, terrible, frightful. —कः *m.* 1 A tiger. -2 N. of Râhu. -3 The sentiment of terror, one of the eight or nine sentiments in poetry. -कं *n.* Terror, fear.

भरः *m.* 1 A burden, load, weight. -2 A great number, large quantity. -3 Bulk, mass. -4 Excess. -5 A particular measure of weight.

भरटः *m.* 1 A potter. -2 A servant.

भरण *a.* (*f.*-णी) Maintaining, supporting, nourishing. —णं *n.* 1 The act of nourishing, maintaining or supporting. -2 The act of bearing or carrying. -3 Wearing, putting on. -4 Bringing or procuring. -5 Nutriment. -6 Hire, wages. —णः *m.* The constellation Bharanî.

भरणी *f.* N. of the second constellation containing three stars. -Comp.-भूः *m.* An epithet of Râhu. —भंडः *m.* 1 A master, lord. -2 A prince, king. -3 An ox, a bull.

भरण्यं *n.* 1 Supporting, maintaining. -2 Wages, hire. -3 The lunar mansion Bharanî. -ण्या *f.* Wages, hire. -Comp. —भुज् *m.* A hired servant, hireling.

भरण्युः *m.* 1 A master.-2 A protector. -3 A friend. -4 Fire. -5 The moon. -6 The sun.

भरतः *m.* 1 N. of the son of Dushyanta and Sakuntalâ. -2 N. of a brother of Râma, son of Kaikeyî, the youngest wife of Dasaratha. -3 N. of an ancient sage, the founder of the science of music and dramaturgy. -4 An actor, a stage-player. -5 A hired soldier, mercenary. -6 A barbarian, mountaineer. -7 An epithet of Agni.-8 A weaver. -9 N. of the sage Jadabharata. -Comp. -अग्रजः *m.* An epithet of Râma. -खंडं *n.* N. of a part of India. —ज्ञ *a.* Knowing the science of

Bharata or the dramatic science. —पुत्रकः *m.* An actor. —वर्षः *m.* India. —वाक्यं *n.* The last verse or verses in a drama, a sort of benediction.

भरथः *m.* 1 A sovereign, king. -2 Fire. -3 A deity presiding over one of the regions of the world.

भरद्वाजः *m.* 1 N. of one of the seven sages. -2 A sky-lark.

भरित *a.* (*f.* -ता) 1 Nourished, maintained. -2 Filled with, full of.

भरुः *m.* 1 A husband. -2 A lord. -3 N. of Siva. -4 Of Vishnu. -5 Gold. -6 The sea.

भरुजः (*f.* —जा or —जी) A jackal.

भरुटकं *n.* Fried meat.

भर्गः *m.* 1 N. of Siva. -2 Of Brahman (*m.*). -3 Radiance, lustre.

भर्ग्यः *m.* An epithet of Siva.

भर्जन *a.* (*f.* -ना) Roasting, frying, baking. -2 Annihilating. —नं *n.* 1 The act of roasting or frying. -2 A frying-pan.

भर्तृ *m.* 1 A husband. -2 A lord, master. -3 A leader, commander. -4 A supporter, protector. -5 The creator. -6 N. of Vishnu. -Comp —घ्नी *f.* A woman who murders her husband.—दारकः *m.* A crown-prince, prince royal, young prince, an heir-apparent (a term of address chiefly used in dramas).—दारिका *f.* A young princess (a term of address in dramas). —व्रतं *n.* Fidelity or devotion to a husband. (—ता *f.*) A virtuous and devoted wife. -हरिः *m.* N. of the celebrated author of the three Satakas (शृंगार, नीति, and वैराग्य) and also वाक्यपदीय and भट्टिकाव्य.

भर्तृमती *f.* A married woman whose husband is living.

भर्तृसात् *ind.* In the possession of a husband.

भर्त्री *f.* 1 A mother. -2 A female supporter.

भर्त्स् 10 A (भर्त्सयते. Sometimes P. भर्त्सयति) 1 To menace, threaten. -2 To revile, abuse. -3 To deride.

भर्त्सकः *m.* A threatener, reviler.

भर्त्सनं *n.*, भर्त्सना *f.* 1 Threatening, reviling. -2 A threat, menace. -3 Reproach, abuse. -4 A curse.

भर्त्सितं *n.* 1 Reviling, threatening. -2 A threat, reproach, abuse. -3 A curse.

भर्म *n.* 1 Wages, hire. -2 Gold. -3 The navel.

भर्मण्या *f.* Wages, hire.

भर्मन् *n* 1 Support, maintenance, nourishment. -2 Wages, hire. -3 Gold. -4 Gold coin. -5 The navel. -6 A burden, load. -7 A house.

भल् 10 A. (भालयते, भालित) To see, behold.

भल्ल् 1 A. (भल्लते, भल्लित) 1 To describe, narrate, tell. -2 To wound, kill. -3 To give.

भल्लः *m.*, -ल्ली *f.*, -ल्लं *n.* A kind of missile or arrow. —ल्लः *m.* 1 A bear. -2 An epithet of Siva. -3 The marking-nutplant; भल्ली also).

भल्लकः *m.* A bear.

भल्लातः, भल्लातकः *m.* The marking-nut plant (also *n.*)

भल्लुकः *m* A bear.

भल्लूकः *m* 1 A bear. -2 A dog.

भव *a.* (At the end of comp.) Arising or produced from, originating in.—वः *m.* 1 Being, state of being, existence. -2 Birth, production. -3 Source, origin. -4 Woldly existence, worldly life, life. -5 The world. -6 Well being, health, prosperity. -7 Excellence, superiority. -8 N. of Siva.—वौ *Dual* Siva and Bhavâni. Comp. -अंतकृत् *m.* 1 N. of Buddha. -2 An epithet of Brahman (*m.*). -अंतरं *n.* Another existence (previous or future). —आब्धिः, -अर्णवः, -समुद्रः, -सागरः-:

सिंधुः *m.* The ocean of worldly life.—अभीष्टं *n.* Bdellium. —अयना, —नी *f.* The Ganges. —अरण्यं *n.* The forest in the form of worldly existence. —आत्मजः *m.* An epithet of Ganesa or Kartikeya. —क्षितिः *f.* The place of birth. —चस्मरः *m.* A forest conflagration —च्छिद् *a.* Preventing recurrence of birth. —च्छेदः *m.* Prevention of recurring birth. —दारु *n.* The *devadâru* tree. —नाशिनी *f.* N. of the river Sarayu.—भूतिः *m.* N. of a celebrated poet. —मोचनः *m.* N. of Krishna. —रुद् *m.* A drum beaten at funeral ceremonies. —वीतिः *f.* 1 Liberation from worldly existence. -2 End of the world.

भवत् *a.* (*f.*—न्ती) 1 Being, becoming, happening. -2 Present.—*pron. a.* (*f.* ·ती) A respectful or honorific pronoun, translated by ' your honour', ' your lordship,' ' your worship or highness ' ; (oft. used in the sense of the second personal pronoun, but with the third person of the verb). It is often joined to अत्र or तत्र (See the words) and sometimes to स also.

भवती *f.* 1 Your ladyship, lady. -2 A poisoned arrow.

भवदीय *a.* (*f.* —या) Your honour's, your, thine.

भवनं *n.* Being, existence. -2 Production, birth. -3 An abode, mansion. -4 A site, receptacle. -5 A house, building. -6 A field. -7 Nature. -Comp.-उदरं *n.* The interior of a house. —पतिः, —स्वामिन् *m.* The lord of the house, a *pater familias.*

भवंतः, -तिः *m.* The time being, present time.

भवंती *f.* 1 A virtuous wife. -2 Time being, present time. -3 (In gram.) A technical term for the present tense.

भवादृक्ष *a.* (*f.* —क्षी), भवादृश् *a.* भवादृश *a.* (*f.* —शी) Like your honour, like you.

भवानी *f.* N. of Pârvati, wife of Siva. —गुरुः *m.* An epithet of the mountain Himâlaya. —पतिः *m.* An epithet of Siva.

भविक *a.* (*f.* —की) 1 Beneficial, suitable, useful. -2 Happy, prosperous. —कं *n.* Prosperity, welfare.

भवितव्य *pot. p.* (*f.* —व्या) About to take place, likely to be. —व्यं *n.* What is destined to happen.

भवितव्यता *f.* Necessary consequence. fate, destiny.

भवितृ *a.* (*f.*-त्री) 1 About to become, future. -2 Imminent, impending. -3 Being or faring well.

भविनः *m.* A poet.

भविलः *m.* 1 A paramour. -2 A sensualist, voluptuary.

भविष्णु *a.* 1 To be about to become or take place. -2 Future.

भविष्य *a.* (*f.* -ष्या) 1 Future. -2 Imminent, impending. —ष्यं *n.* The future, futurity. -Comp. —कालः *m.* The future tense. —पुराणं *n.* N. of one of the 18 Purânas.

भविष्यत् *a.* (*f.* —ती or न्ती) About to be, become or come to pass ; future. -*n* The future time. -Comp. -आक्षेपः *m.* 1 Denying the occurrence of a possible future event. -2 A kind of Alankâra or figure of speech. —कालः *m.* Futurity. —वक्तृ, -वादिन् *a.* Prophesying.

भव्य *a.* (*f.* —व्या) 1 Existing, being, being present. -2 Future. -3 Likely to become. -4 Suitable, worthy. -5 Good, excellent. -6 Auspicious, fortunate, happy. -7

Lovely, beautiful. -8 Calm, tranquil. -9 True. -व्या *f.* N. of Párvatî. —व्यं *n.* 1 Existence. -2 Future time. -3 Result, fruit. -4 Good result, prosperity. -5 A bone.

भष् 1 P. (भषति) 1 To bark, growl. -2 To abuse,) revile, to rail at.

भषः, भषकः *m.* A dog.

भषणः *m.* A dog. —णं *n.* The barking of a dog, a growl.

भसद् *m.* 1 The sun. -2 Flesh. -3 A kind of duck. -4 Time. -5 A float (प्लव). -6 The hinder parts. -7 Pudendum muliebre.

भसनः *m.* A bee.

भसंतः *m.* Time.

भसित *a.* (*f.* -ता) Reduced to ashes. —तं *n.* Ashes.

भस्त्रका, भस्त्रा, भस्त्रिः *f* 1 A bellows. -2 A leathern vessel for holding water. -3 A pouch, leathern bag.

भस्त्रिका *f.* A little bag.

भस्मकं *n.* 1 Gold or silver. -2 Morbid appetite from over-digestion of food. -3 A kind of disease of the eyes.

भस्मन् *n.* 1 Ashes. -2 Sacred ashes (smeared on the body). (भस्मनि हु 'To sacrifice in ashes' *i.* e. to do a useless work). -Comp. —आह्वयः *m.* Camphor. —कारः *m.* A washerman. —गंधा, —गंधिका, —गंधिनी *f.* A kind of perfume. —तूलं *n.* 1 Frost, snow. -2 A shower of dust. -3 A number of villages. —प्रियः *m.* An epithet of Siva. -भूत *a.* Dead. —मेहः *m.* A sort of gravel. —रोगः *m.* A kind of disease. -वेधकः *m.* Camphor. -शायिन् *m.* N. of Siva. -स्नानं *n.* Purification by ashes.

भस्मसात् *ind.* 1 To the state of [ashes.

भस्मीकरणं *n.* 1 Reducing to ashes. -2 Completely consuming or burning. -3 Calcining.

भा 2 P. (भाति, भात) 1 To shine; be bright or splendid. -2 To seem, appear. -3 To be. exist. -4 To show oneself. With अभि- To shine on every side. आ- To shine, to appear bright. निस्- 1 To shine forth. -2 To proceed. प्र- To shine, to be bright. प्रति- 1 To shine, to be bright. -2 To appear, to seem. -3 To be present to the memory. वि-1 To shine, to be bright. -2 To seem, to appear. व्याति- (Atm.) To shine forth brightly.

भा *f.* 1 Light, splendour, lustre, beauty. -2 A shadow, reflection. -3 Likeness, resemblance. -Comp —कोशः, -षः *m.* The sun. —गणः *m.* The whole group of constellations. -नेमिः *m.* The sun. -मंडलं *n.* A halo of light. -रूपः *m.* The soul.

भाःकरः *m.* See भास्करः.

भाक्त *a.* (*f.* —क्ती) 1 Regularly fed by another, a dependant, retainer. -2 Fit for food. -3 Secondary, indirect. भाक्त = लाक्षणिक or गौण as opp. to मुख्य. -4 Used in a secondary sense.

भाक्तिकः *m.* A retainer, dependant.

भाक्ष *a* (*f.* —क्षी) Voracious, gluttonous.

भागः *m* 1 A part, share, division. -2 Allotment, partition. -3 Lot, fate. -4 A part of any whole, a fraction. -5 The numerator of a fraction. -6 A quarter, one-fourth part. -7 A degree or the 360th part of the cicrumference of a circle. -8 The 30th part of a zodiacal sign. -9 The quotient. -10 Room, spot, region, place. -Comp. —अर्ह *a.* Entitled to a share or inheritance. -कल्पना *f.* Allotment of shares. -जातिः *f.* Reduction of fractions to a common denominator (in math.). -धेयं *n.* 1 A share, part, portion. -2 Fortune, destiny, luck. -3 Good fortune or luck. -4 Property. -5 Happiness. —धेय: *m* 1 A tax. -2 An heir. —भाज् *a.* Interested, a sharer or partner.—भुज् *m.* A king, sovereign. —लक्षणा *f.* A kind of लक्षणा or secondary use of a word by which it partly loses and partly retains its primary meaning ; also called जहदजहल्लक्षणा. -हर: *m.* 1 A co-heir. -2 Division (in math.). —हार: *m.* Division (in math).-हारिन् *a.* Entitled to a share, inheriting. (*m.*) 1 An heir. -2 Division.

भागवत *a.* (*f.* -ती) 1 Relating to or worshipping Vishnu. -2 Pertaining to a god. -3 Holy, divine, sacred. —त: *m.* A follower or devotee of Vishnu or Krishna. —तं *n.* N. of one of the 18 Purânas.

भागशस् *ind.* 1 In parts or portions, part by part. -2 According to the share.

भागिक *a.* (*f.* -का) 1 Relating to a part. -2 Forming a part. -3 Fractional. -4 Bearing interest. (भागिकं शतं ' one part in a hundred' *i. e.* one per cent.).

भागिन् *a. f.* —नी) 1 Consisting of shares or parts.-2 Having a share. -3 Sharing in, partaking of. -4 Concerned in, affected by. -5 A possessor, owner. -6 Entitled to a share. -7 Lucky, fortunate. -8 Inferior, secondary. —*m.* A co-heir. —नी *f.* A co-heiress.

भागिनेय: *m.* A sister's son. —यी *f.* A sister's daughter.

भागीरथी *f.* 1 N. of the river Ganges. -2 N. of one of the three main branches of the Ganges.

भाग्यं *n* 1 Fate, destiny, luck, fortune. -2 Good fortune or luck. -3 Prosperity. -4 Happiness, welfare. -Comp. —क्रम: *m.* Course or turn of fortune. —योग: *m.* A lucky or fortunate juncture. —विप्लव: *m.* Ill-luck, adverseness of fate. -वशात *ind.* Through the will of fate, luckily, fortunately.

भाग्यवत *a.* 1 Fortunate, blessed, happy. -2 Prosperous. [hempen.

भांग *a.* (*f.* -गी) Made of hemp,

भांगक: *m.* A tattered cloth, shred, rag.

भांगिनं *n.* A field of hemp.

भाज् 10 U. (भाजयति,-ते) To divide, distribute.

भाज् *a.* (At the end of comp.) 1 Sharing or participating in. -2 Having, enjoying, possessing, obtaining. -3 Entitled to. -4 Feeling, experiencing. -5 Devoting oneself to.-6 Living in, inhabiting. -7 Resorting to, seeking. -8 Worshipping. -9 Falling to the lot of. -10 What must be done.

भाजक: *m.* 1 Dividing. -2 (In arith.) A divider.

भाजनं *n.* 1 Sharing, dividing. -2 Division (in arith). -3 A vessel, cup. -4 (Fig.) A receptacle, recipient. -5 A fit or deserving person. -6 Representation. -7 A Measure equal to 64 *palas*.

भाजितं *n.* A share, portion.

भाजिन् *m.* A servant.

भाजी *f.* Rice, gruel.

भाज्यं *n.* 1 A portion, share. -2 An inheritance. -3 (In arith.) The dividend.

भाटं, भाटकं *n.* Wages, hire, rent.

भाटिः *f.* 1 Wages, hire. -2 The earnings of harlots.

भाट्टः *m.* A follower of the Bhatta school of the Mimâmsâ philosophy.

भाणः *m.* A species of dramatic composition in which only one character is introduced on the stage.

भाणकः *m.* A declarer, proclaimer.

भांडं *n.* 1 A vessel, pot, utensil.-2 A box, trunk, case.-3 Any tool or instrument.-4 A musical instrument. -5 Goods, merchandise. -6 A bale of goods. -7 (Fig.) Any valued possession, treasure. -8 The bed of a river. -9 Trappings of a horse. -10 Buffoonery (from भंड). -11 An ornament in general. —डाः *m. pl.* Wares, merchandise. -Comp. —अ (-आ-) गारः *m.*, -रं *n.* 1 A store-house, store-room. -2 Treasury. -3 A collection, store, magazine. —आगारिकः *m.* 1 A store-keeper.-2 A treasurer. —पतिः *m.* A merchant. —पुटः *m.* A barber. -प्रतिभांडकं *n.* Barter, computation of the exchange of goods. —मूल्यं *n.* Capital in the form of wares. -शाला *f.* A store-house, store-

भांडकः *m.*, -कं *n.* A small vessel, cup. —कं *n.* Goods, merchandise, wares.

भांडारं *n.* A store-house, store.

भांडारिकः *m.* See भांडागारिकः.

भांडारिन् *m.* The keeper of a store-house.

भांडिः *f.* A razor-case. -Comp. -वाहः *m.* A barber. —शाला *f.* A barber's shop.

भांडिकः, -लः *m.* A barber. [utensil.

भांडिका *f.* An implement, a tool,

भांडिनी *f.* A chest, basket.

भांडीरः *f.* The Indian fig-tree.

भात *p. p.* (*f.* —ता) Shining, brilliant, bright. -तः *m.* Dawn, morning.

भातिः *f.* 1 Light, lustre, splendour. -2 Perception, knowledge.

भातुः *m.* The sun.

भाद्रः, भाद्रपदः *m.* N. of a lunar month (August, September). -दा (*f. pl.*) N. of the 25th and 26th lunar mansions (पूर्वा भाद्रपदा and उत्तरा भाद्रपदा).

भाद्रपदी, भाद्री *f.* The day of full moon in the month of Bhâdrapada.

भाद्रमातुरः *m.* The son of a virtuous or good mother.

भानं *n.* 1 Appearing, being visible -2 Light, lustre.-3 Perception, knowledge.

भानुः *m.* 1 Light, lustre, brightness. -2 A ray of light. -3 The sun. -4 Beauty. -5 A day. -6 A king, sovereign. -7 An epithet of Siva. -*f.* A handsome woman. -Comp. —केश (-स-) रः *m.* The sun. -जः *m.* The planet Saturn. -दिनं *n.*, -वारः *m.* Sunday.

भानुमत् *a.* (*f.* —ती) 1 Bright, splendid. -2 Beautiful, handsome. -*m.* 1 The sun. —ती *f.* N. of the wife of Duryodhana.

भामः *m.* 1 Brightness, lustre, splendour. -2 The sun. -3 Passion, anger. -4 A sistsr's husband. —मा *f.* 1 A passionate woman. -2 N. of one of the wives of Krishna, usually called सत्यभामा.

भामिनी *f.* 1 A beautiful young woman. -2 A passionate woman. -Comp. -विलासः *m.* N. of a poem by Jagannátha Pandit.

भारः *m.* 1 A load, burden, weight (fig. also). -2 The thickest part (as of a battle). -3 Excess, pitch. -4 Labour, toil; trouble.-5 A large quantity.-6 A weight equal to 2000 *palas* of gold. -7 A yoke for carrying burdens.-8 An epithet of Vishnu. -Comp. —उद्वहः *m.* A porter, burden-carrier. —उपजीवनं *n.* Living by carrying burdens. —भृत् m. An epithet of Vishnu. -यष्टिः f. A pole for carrying burdens. -वाह् a. (f. भारौही) Bearer of burdens.—वाहः m. A burden-carrier, porter. -वाहनः m. A beast of burden. (-नं n.) A cart, waggon. —वाहिकः m. A porter. —सह a. Very strong or powerful. —हरः,-हारः m. A burden-bearer, porter. —हारिन् m. An epithet of Krishna.

भारकं n. A load, burden, weight.

भारंगी f. A female supporter.

भारंडः m. A kind of fabulous bird. (Also भारुंड).

भारत a. (f. -ती) Belonging to or descended from Bharata. -तः m. 1 A descendant of Bharata. -2 An inhabitant of *Bharatavarsha* or India. -3 An actor. -4 An epithet of the sun shining on the south of Meru. —तं n. 1 India, the country of Bharata. -2 N of the most celebrated epic poem in Sanskrit giving the history of the descendants of Bharata. It is attributed to Vyása or कृष्णद्वैपायन. -3 The science of music and dramaturgy founded by Bharata. —ती f. Speech, voice, eloquence. -2 The goddess of speech, Sarasvatí. -3 N. of a particular kind of style. -4 A quail. -5 The dramatic art in general.

भारद्वाजः m. 1 N. of Drona, the military preceptor of the Kauravas and Pándavas. -2 Of Agastya. -3 The planet Mars. -4 One of the seven Rishis. -5 A sky-lark. —जं n. A bone. [sacred basil.

भारवं n. A bow-string. -वी f. The

भारविः m. N. of the author of the Kirâtârjunîya.

भारिः m. A lion.

भारिक, भारिन् a. 1 Bearing or carrying a load. -2 Heavy. —m. A burden-carrier, porter.

भार्गः m. A king of the Bhargas.

भार्गवः m. 1 N. of Sukra, regent of the plant Venus and preceptor of the Asuras. -2 N. of Parasuráma. -3 An epithet of Siva. -4 An archer. -5 An elephant. -6 A epithet of Jamadagni. -7 Of Márkandeya. -8 N. of an eastern country. -Comp. —प्रियः m. A diamond.

भार्गवी f. 1 The Dúrvá grass. -2 An epithet of Lakshmî. -3 Of Párvatî. -4 Of Devayáni.

भार्यः m. A servant, a dependant (to be supported).

भार्या f. 1 A lawful wife. -2 The female of an animal. -Comp. —आट a. Living by the prostitution of his wife.—ऊढ a. Married (as a man). —जितः, —आटिकः m. A hen-pecked husband. [adulterer.

भार्यारुः m. 1 A kind of deer. -2 An

भालं n. 1 The forehead, brow. -2 Light. -3 Darkness. -Comp. —अंकः m. 1 A man born with lucky lines on his forehead. -2 An epithet of Siva. -3 A saw. -4 A tortoise. -चंद्रः m. 1 An epithet of Siva. -2 Of Ganesa. —दर्शनः m. N. of Siva.—दर्शनं n. Red lead. —दर्शिन् m. A servant who is attentive to his master's wishes. —दृश् m., -लोचनः m. An epithet of Siva. -पट्टः m.,-ट्टं n. The forehead

भालुः m. The sun. [bear.

भालु (-लू-) कः, भल्लु (-ल्लू-) कः m. A

भावः m. 1 Being, existing, existence. -2 Occurring, taking place. -3 Condition, state of being. -4 Manner, mode. -5 Rank, position. -6 True condition, truth, reality. -7 Sincerity, devotion. -8 Nature, temperament. -9 Idea, thought, opi nion, supposition.-10 Feeling, emotion, sentiment. (In poetic compositions generally *Bhāvas* are either स्थायिन् primary or व्यभिचारिन् subordinate). -11 Love, affection, attachment. -12 Purport, gist, substance. -13 Resolution, determination. -14 The heart, soul, mind.-15 An object, a thing, substance. -16 A living creature. -17 Abstract meditation.contemplation.-18 Conduct, movement. -19 Gesture, behaviour ; gesture of love. -20 Birth. -21 The world, universe. -22 The womb. -23 Will. -24 Superhuman power. -25 Advice, instruction. -26 (In dramas) A learned or venerable man (a term of address). -27 (In gram.) The abstract idea conveyed by a word. -28 A term for an impersonal, passive or neuter verb. -29 (In astr.) An astronomical house. -30 A lunar mansion. -31 An organ of sense.-Comp. -अनुग *a.* Natural : not forced. (-गा *f.*) A shadow. —अर्थः *m.* 1 The obvious meaning or import (of a word or phrase). -2 The subject-matter. —आकूतं *n.* The thoughts of the mind.-आत्मक *a.* Real, actual. —आभासः *m.* Simulation of a feeling, a feigned or false emotion. —आलीना *f.* A shadow. -उदयः *m.* The figure of speech in which an emotion (भाव) is described as occurring or as being in process of evolution. —ग्राहिन् *a.* 1 Understanding the sense.-2 Appreciating the sentiment. -जः *m.* 1 Love. -2 The God of love. —दर्शिन *m.* A servant attentitive to the wishes of his master. —बंधन *a.* Fettering the heart ; linking together the hearts. —बोधक *a.* Indicating or revealing any feeling. —मिश्रः *m.* A worthy person (used in dramas). -रूप *a.* Real, actual. -वचनं *n.* Denoting an abstract idea —वाचकं *n.* An abstract noun. —शबलत्वं *n.* A mixture of various emotions. —भावशबलः *m.* 1 The figure of speech in which many emotions (भावs) are represented as successively taking the place of each preceeding one. -संधिः *m.* The union or co-existence of two emotions. -2 The figure of speech in which two emotions (भावs) opposed to each are described as competing with each other. —समाहित *a.* Abstracted in mind, devout. —सर्गः *m.* The creation of the faculties of the human mind and their affections (opp. भौतिकसर्ग or material creation).-स्निग्ध *a.* Affectionately disposed.sincerely attached.

भावक *a.* (*f.* -का) 1 Effecting, bringing about. -2 Promoting any one's welfare. -3 Fancying, imagining.-4 Having a poetic taste.-कः *m.* 1 A feeling, sentiment. -2 The external manifestation of one's sentiments (especially of love).

भावन *a.* (*f.* -नी) See भावक above. -नः *m.* 1 An efficient cause. -2 A creator. -3 An epithet of Siva. -4 Of Vishnu. -नं *n.*, -ना *f.* 1 Creating, manifesting.-2Promoting any one's interests. -3 Imagination, fancy, thought, idea. -4 Feeling of devotion, faith.-5 Abstract meditation. -6 A supposition, hypothesis. -7 Observing, investigating. -8 Settling, determining. -9 Remembering. -10 Direct knowledge, perception or cognition. -11 Proof, argument. -12 Saturating a dry powder with fluid. -13 Decorating with flowers and perfumes. -नं *n.* Apprehension, perception.

भावाटः *m.* 1 Emotion, sentiment. -2 A manifestation of the feeling of love. -3 A pious or holy man. -4 An amorous man. -5 An actor. -6 Decoration, dress.

भाविक *a.* (*f.* -की) 1 Natural, real, innate. -2 Sentimental, full of feeling or sentiment. -3 Future -कः *m.* (*Math.*) An equation involving the products of unknown quantities. -कं *n.* 1 Language full of love or passion. -2 (In Rhet.) The figure of speech in which a wonderful object whether past or future is so represented as to strike the mind as if it were present. अद्भुतस्य पदार्थस्य भूतस्याथ भाविष्यतः । यत्प्रत्यक्षायमाणत्वं तद्भाविकमुदाहृतं ॥ *साहित्य द. E. g. मुनिर्जयति योगींद्रो महात्मा कुंभसंभवः । येनैकचुलुके दृष्टौ दिव्यौ तौ मत्स्यकच्छपौ ॥ Another instance, आसीदंजनमत्रेति पश्यामि तव लोचने। भाविभूषणसंभारां साक्षात्कुर्वे तवाकृतिं ॥.

भावित *p. p.* (*f.* —ता) 1 Produced, obtained, got. -2 Displayed, exhibited. -3 Cherished, fostered. -4 Imagined, supposed, presented to the imagination. -5 Recognized, acknowledged. -6 Thought of, meditated upon. -7 Transformed into. -8 Sanctified by meditation as in भावितात्मन्. -9 Proved, established. -10 Saturated with, inspired by. -11 Perfumed, scented. -12 Mixed with. -13 (In math.) Involving the porducts of unknown quantities -तं *n.* Product obtained by multiplication, a factum. -Comp. —आत्मन्, —बुद्धि *a.* 1 One whose soul is purified by meditating on the Supreme Spirit. -2 Pure, devout. -3 Thoughtful, meditative. -4 Occupied with. (*-m.*) A sage, saint.

भावितकं *n.* The product of a multiplication, a factum.

भावित्रं *n.* The three worlds (heaven, earth and lower regions).

भाविन् *a.* (*f.* -नी) 1 Being, becoming. -2 To be or to happen in future. -3 Future. -4 Capable of taking place. -5 What is destined to happen, predestined. -6 Beautiful, illustrious. -7 Devoted to -8 Possessed of. —नी *f.* 1 A handsome woman. -2 A noble or virtuous lady. -3 A wanton woman.

भावुक (*f.* —का) 1 About to be or happen. -2 Becoming. -3 Prosperous, happy. -4 Auspicious. -5 Having a poetic taste. —कः *m.* A sister's husband (In theatrical language). -कं *n.* Welfare, prosperity. -2 Language full of passion.

भाव्य *a.* (*f.* —व्या) 1 About to be or happen (often used impersonally like भवितव्यं). -2 Future. -3 To be accomplished. -4 To be conceived or imagined. -5 To be demonstrated. -6 To be investigated. -भाव्यं *n.* 1 What is destined to happen. -2 Futurity.

भाष् I A. (भाषते, भाषित) 1 To say, speak. (oft. with two acc.) -2 To speak to, address. -3 To tell. -4 To name, call. -5 To describe. -With अनु— 1 To speak, say. -2 To communicate, announce. अप-To abuse; to censure. अभि— 1 To address; to speak to. -2 To tell. -3 To use or employ (as a word). आ— To speak to, to address. परि— To make a convention; to speak conventionally. प्र- To speak, to speak to. प्रति— 1 To reply. -2 To speak what one has heard. -3 To name, to call. वि— To lay down as optional. सं— To converse, to speak together.

भाषणं *n.* 1 Speaking, talking, saying. -2 Speech, talk. -3 Kind words.

भाषा *f.* 1 Speech, talk. -2 Language, tongue. -3 A vernacular dialect (opp. to Sanskrit language). -4 Definition, description. -5 An epithet of Sarasvatí, the goddess of speech. -6 (In law) The first of the four stages of a law-suit; the plaint, charge or accusation. -Comp. —अंतरं *n.* 1 Another dialect or language. -2 Translation (modern use). —पादः *m.* A charge, plaint. —समः *m* A sentence that can be read either as Sanskrit or Prákrita *e.g.* किं त्वां भणामि विच्छेददारुणायासकारिणि। कामं कुरु वरारोहे देहि मे परिरंभणं (which is in Sanskrit or Sauraseni).

भाषिका *f.* Speech, language.

भाषित *p. p.* (*f.* —ता) Spoken, said. —तं *n.* Speech, language. -Comp. -पुंस्कः *m.*, -पुंस्कं *n.* A *fem.* or *neuter* word, of which a masculine also exists and the meaning of which differs only by the notion of gender (in *gram.*).

भाष्यं *n.* 1 Speaking, talking. -2 Any work in the vernacular language. -3 Exposition, commentary. -4 A commentary which explains *Sutras* or aphorisms word by word with comments of its own. -5 N. of the great commentary of Patanjali on Pánini's Sútras. -Comp. -कारः, -कारः, -कृत *m.* 1 A commentator, scholiast. -2 N. of Patanjali.

भास् 1 A.(भासते, भासित) 1 To shine. -2 To become clear or evident, come into the mind. -3 To appear. With अव-1 To shine. -2 To appear, to appear like. आ— To appear like. उद्- 1 To shine. -2 To appear like. प्रति- 1 To appear like. -2 To shine. वि- To shine. Causal. भासयति,-ते 1 To brighten, to illuminate. -2 To make clear or evident.

भास् *f.* 1 Light, lustre, brightness. -2 A ray of light. -3 A reflection, an image. -4 Majesty, glory, splendour. -5 Wish, desire. -Comp. —करः *m.* 1 The sun. -2 A hero. -3 fire. -4 An epithet of Siva. -5 N. of a celebrated Hindu astronomer. (-रं *n.*) Gold. भास्करप्रियः *m.* A ruby. भास्करसप्तमी *f.* The seventh day in the bright half of Màgha. —करिः *m.* The planet Saturn.

भासः *m.* 1 Brightness, lustre. -2 Fancy. -3 A cock. -4 A vulture. -5 A cow-shed(गोष्ठ). -6 N. of a poet.

भासक *a.* (*f.* —सिका) 1 Brightening, illuminating. -2 Showing, making evident. -3 Making intelligible. —कः *m.* N. of a poet.

भासनं *n.* 1 Shining, glittering. -2 Illuminating.

भासंत *a.* (*f.* —ती) 1 Shining. -2 Beautiful, handsome. —तः *m.* 1 The sun. -2 The moon. -3 An asterism, a star. -4 The bird भास. —ती *f.* An asterism (नक्षत्र).

भासुः *m.* The sun.

भासुर *a.* (*f.* —रा) 1 Shining, bright, splendid. -2 Terrible. —रः *m.* 1 A hero. -2 A crystal.

भास्वत् *a.* Bright, shining, luminous. -*m.* 1 The sun. -2 Light, splendour. -3 A hero. —ती *f.* The city of the sun.

भास्वर *a.* (*f.* —रा) Shining, bright, brilliant. —रः *m.* 1 The sun. -2 A day. -3 Fire.

भास्मन a. (f. -नी) Consisting or made of ashes, ashy.

भिक्ष् 1 A. (भिक्षते, भिक्षित) 1 To ask, beg or ask for (with two acc.). -2 To beg (as alms). -3 To ask without obtaining. -4 To be weary or distressed

भिक्षणं n. Begging, mendicancy.

भिक्षा f. 1 Asking, begging. -2 Any thing given as alms; alms. -3 Wages, hire. -4 Service. -Comp. —अटनं n. Going about for alms. (—नः m.) A beggar, mendicant. -अयनं (-णं) n. Going about for alms. -अर्थिन् a. Begging for alms or charity. (-m.) A beggar. -अर्ह a. A fit object of charity. -आशिन् a. 1 Subsisting on alms. -2 Dishonest. -आहारः m. Begged food. —उपजीविन् a. Living on alms, a beggar. —करणं. n. Asking alms, begging. -चरः, -चारः m. A beggar or mendicant. -चरणं. -चर्यं n. -चर्या f. Wandering about begging for alms. -पात्रं n. A begging-bowl, an alms-dish; so भिक्षाभांडं, भिक्षाभाजनं. -माणवः m. A young beggar (used as a term of contempt). -वृत्तिः f. Living by begging; a mendicant's life.

भिक्षाकः a. (f. की) A beggar, mendicant.

भिक्षित p. p. (f. —ता) Solicited.

भिक्षुः m. 1 A beggar, mendicant in general. -2 A religious mendicant, a Bràhmana in the fourth order of his religious life; a *sannyásin*. -3 The fourth order or stage in the religious life of a Bràhmana (संन्यास). -4 A Buddhist mendicant. -Comp. -चर्या f. A mendicant's life. -संघः m. A society of Buddhist mendicants. —संघाती f. Old or tattered clothes.

भिक्षुकः m. A beggar, mendicant. —की f. A female mendicant.

भित्तं n. 1 A part, portion. -2 A fragment, bit. -3 A wall, partition.

भित्तिः f. 1 Breaking, dividing. -2 A wall, partition. -3 A fragment, bit, portion. -4 Anything broken. -5 A rent, fissure. -6 A mat. -7 A flaw, defect. -8 An opportunity. -Comp. —खातनः m. A rat. -चौरः m. A house-breaker. —पातनः m. 1 A kind of rat. -2 A rat.

भित्तिका f. 1 A wall, partition. -2 A small house-lizard.

भिद् a. (At the end of comp.) Breaking, splitting; destroying.

भिद् 1 P. (भिंदति) To divide, to cut into parts.

भिद् 7 U. (भिनत्ति, भिंत्ते, भेत्तुं, भिन्न) 1 To break, cut asunder, rend, pierce. -2 To dig or tear up, excavate. -3 To pass through. -4 To divide, separate. -5 To displace. -6 To violate, transgress, break. -7 To remove, take away, interrupt. -8 To expand, cause to open or blossom, open (as a flower). -9 To disperse, scatter away. -10 To set at variance. -11 To loosen, relax, dissolve. -12 To disclose, divulge. -13 To perplex, distract. -14 To distinguish, discriminate. With अनु— To break down. उद्— To grow, to germinate. निस्— 1 To tear up. प्र— To break, to tear. -2 To flow from the temples of an elephant. प्रति— 1 To pierce through. -2 To disclose. -3 To censure. -4 To reject; to disown. वि— 1 To break. -2 To pierce. 3 To interrupt. -4 To disperse. सम्— 1 To break to pieces. -2 To bring together, to join, combine, to mix.

Passive-भिद्यते. *Causal*- -भेदयति,-ते.

भिदकः m. A sword. -कं n. 1 A diamond. -2 Indra's thunderbolt.

भिदा *f.* 1 Breaking, rending, tearing. -2 Separation.-3 Difference.-4 Kind, sort. -5 Coriander.

भिदिः *m.*, भिदिरं *n.*, भिदुः *m.* Indra's thunderbolt.

भिदुर *a.* (*f.* -रा) 1 Breaking, bursting. -2 Fragile, brittle. -3 Variegated, mixed, mingled. -रः *m.* The *Plaksha* tree. -रं *n.* A thunderbolt.

भिद्यः *m.* 1 A rushing river. -2 N. of a particular river.

भिद्रं *n.* A thunderbolt.

भिंद् (-दि-) पालः *m.*1 A small javelin thrown from the hand. -2 A sling, an instrument like a sling for throwing stones (*mar.* गोफण).

भिन्न *p. p.* (*f.*—न्ना) 1 Broken, torn, rent. -2 Divided, separated.-3 Disjoined. -4 Expanded, blown, opened.5 Different from, other than(with abl.) as in तस्मादयं भिन्नः. -6Different, varied.-7Loosened, scattered about. -8Mingled, blended. -9 Deviating from. -10 Changed. -11 Furious, in rut (as an elephant). -12 Deprived of. -न्नः *m.* A flaw in a gem. —न्नं *n.* 1 A bit, fragment, part. -2 A blossom. -3 A wound.-4 A fraction. -Comp. —अंजनं *n.* A kind of collyrium made of many pounded ingredients. --अर्थ *a.* Perspicuous, intelligible.-उदरः*m.* A half brother, a brother by a different mother. -कटः, —करटः *m.* An elephant in rut. —कूट *a.* Deprived of a leader (as an army). —गुणनं *n.* Multiplication of fractions. —घनः *m.* The cube of a fraction. —मर्मन् *a.* Wounded in vital parts ; mortally wounded. -मर्याद *a.* 1 Disrespectful. -2 Unrestrained, uncontrolled. —लिंगं, -वचनं *n.* Incongruity of gender or number in a composition. —वर्गः *m.* The square of a fraction. —वर्चस्, वर्चस्क *a.* Voiding excrement. —वर्ण *a.* 1 Discoloured, pale. -2Of a different caste or tribe. —वृत्त *a.* Leading a bad life, following evil courses. -2 Having different feelings or tastes or emotions. -3 Having different occupations. -व्यवकलितं *n.* Subtraction of fractions. -संकलनं, —संकलितं *n.* Addition of fractions. —स्वर *a.* 1 Having a changed voice, faltering. -2 Discordant.

भिल्लः *m.* N. of a wild tribe. —ल्ली *f.* The *lodhra* tree. Comp. —गवी *f.* The female of the *Bos gavoeus* -तरुः *m.* The *lodhra* tree. —भूषणं *n.* The *gunjá* plant.

भिल्लोटः,-टकः *m.* The *lodhra* tree.

भिषज् *m.* 1 A physician, doctor. -2 N. of Vishnu. -3 Medicine, a remedy. -*m. dual.* The two Asvins(physicians of gods). -Comp. -जितं *n.* A drug or medicine. -पाशः*m.* A quack doctor. -वरः *m.* An excellent physician. (-रौ *m. dual.*) The two Asvins.

भिषज्यं *n.* 1 Healing, curing. -2 A remedy, cure.

भिष्मा, भिष्मिका -टा, भिस्सटा, भिस्सिटा *f.* Parched or fried grain.

भिस्सा *f.* Boiled rice.

भी 3 P. (बिभेति, भीत) 1 To fear, dread, be afraid of. -2 To be anxious about.

भी *f.* Fear, dread, fright, terror.

भीत *p. p.* (*f.* -ता) 1 Frightened, terrified, alarmed, afraid of (with abl.) as in न भीतो मरणादस्मि.-2 Fearful, timid. -3 Placed in danger, imperiled. -तं *n.* Fear, dread. -Comp. —भीत *a.* Exceedingly afraid.

भीतंकार *a.* Making (one) afra.

भीतंकारं *ind.* Calling(one) a coward.

भीतिः *f.* 1 Fear, dread, terror. -2 Shaking tremour. -3 Danger, risk. -Comp. —नाटितकं *n.* A gesticulation or representation of fear.

भीम *a.* (*f.* -मा) Fearful, terrible, dreadful. -मः *m.* 1 An epithet of Siva. -2 The Supreme Being.-3 The sentiment of terror (= भयानक q. v.) -4 N. of the second Pândava prince. —मं *n.* Horror, terror. -Comp. —उदरी *f.* An epithet of Umá. -एकादशी *f.* The eleventh day in the light half of Màgha. -तिथिः *f.* = भीमैकादशी. -नादः *m.* 1 A loud or dreadful sound. -2 A lion. -3 N. of one of the seven clouds that will appear at the destruction of the world. -पुरं *n.* N. of Kundinapura. —रथी *f.* N. of the 7th night in the 7th month of the 77th year of a man's life (said to be a very dangerous period).-विक्रांतः *m.* A lion -विग्रह *a.* Gigantic, of terrific form. —शासनः *m.* An epithet of Yama. -सेनः *m.* 1 N. of the second Pândava prince.-2 A kind of camphor.

भीमरं *n.* War, battle.

भीमा *f.* 1 An epithet of Durgá. -2 A kind of perfume (रोचना). -3 A whip. -4 N. of a river.

भीरु *a.* (*f.* -रु or -रू) 1 Timid, fearful. -2 Afraid of, as in -पापभीरु &c. —रुः *m* 1 A jackal. -2 A tiger. -रु *n.* Silver. —*f.* 1 A timid woman. -2 A goat. -3 A shadow. -4 A centipede. -Comp. —चेतस् *m.* A deer. -रंध्रः *m.* An oven, a furnace. -हृदयः *m.* A deer.

भीरु (-लु-) क *a.* (*f.* -का) 1 Timid, timorous. -2 Shy. -3 Afraid. -4 Formidable. —कः *m.* 1 A tiger.-2 A jackal. -3 A bear. -4 An owl. -5 A kind of sugar-cane. —कं *n.* A forest.

भीरू (-लू) *f.* A timid woman.

भीलु (-लु-)कः *m.* A bear.

भीषण *a.* (*f* -णा) Terrific, dreadful, horrible. —णः *m.* 1 The sentiment of terror (in rhetoric). -2 N. of Siva. -3 A pigeon, dove. -4 The olibanum tree. —ण *n.* 1 Anything exciting terror.-2 Terrifying, causing terror.

भीषा *f.* 1 The act of frightening or intimidating. -2 Fright, terror.

भीषित *a.* Frightened, terrified.

भीष्म *a.* (*f.* -ष्मा) Terrible, frightful, fearful.-ष्मः *m.* 1 The sentiment of terror (in rhetoric).-2 A demon, a fiend, goblin. -3 An epithet of Siva. -4 N. of the son of Santanu by Gangâ —ष्मं *n.* Horror, horribleness. -Comp. —अष्टमी *f.* The eighth day in the light half of Màgha (when Bhishma died). —जननी *f.* An epithet of the Ganges. -पंचकं *n.* N. of the five days from the eleventh to the fifteenth of the bright half of Kàrtika (sacred to Bhîshma). -सूः *f.* An epithet of the river Gànges.

भीष्मकः *m.* 1 N. of a son of Santanu by Gangà. -2 N. of a king of the Vidarbhas.

भुक्त *p. p.* (*f.* —क्ता) 1 Eaten. -2 Enjoyed, used. -3 Suffered, experienced. -4 Possessed, occupied (in law). -5 Passed (as time). -क्तं *n.* 1 The act of eating or enjoying. -2 Anything eaten, food. -3 The place where any one has eaten. -Comp. —भोग *a.* 1 One who has enjoyed or suffered (anything).-2 That which has been used, enjoyed or employed. —सुप्त *a.* Sleeping after a meal.

भुक्ति *f.* 1 Eating, enioyment. -2 In law) Possession, usufruct.

-3 Food. -4 The diurnal motion of a planet. -5 A limit.

भुग्न *p p.* (*f.* -ग्ना) 1 Bent, bowed. -2 Crooked, curved. -3 Broken.

भुज *a.* 1 (At the end of comp.) Eating, enjoying, suffering. -2 Ruling, governing. -3 Useful, serviceable. -*f.* 1 Enjoyment. -2 Profit, advantage.

भुज् 6 P. (भुजति, भुग्न) 1 To bend.-2 To curve; make crooked.

भुज् 7 U. (भुनक्ति, भुंक्ते, भुक्त) 1 To eat, devour (Atm). -2 To enjoy, use, possess (land &c). -3 To enjoy carnally (Atm). -4 To rule, govern, protect (Paras.). -5 To suffer, endure. -6 To pass (as time). —*Caus.* भोजयाति,-ते; *Desid.* बुभुक्षति,-ते.

भुजः *m.* 1 The arm. -2 The hand. -3 The trunk of an elephant. -4 A bend, curve.-5 The side of a mathematical figure. -6 The base of a triangle.-7 A branch (of a tree). -8 (In Astr.) The base of a shadow. -Comp. -अग्रं *n.* 1 The hand.-2 The shoulder. —अंतरं,—अंतरालं *n.* The bosom, breast. —आपीडः *m.* Embracing in the arms. —कोटरः *m.* The arm-pit. —गः *m.* A snake. —ज्या *f.* The base sine. —दंडः *m.*, -दंडं *n.* The hand. -प्रतिभुजं *n.* The opposite sides in a plane figure. —मध्यं *n.* The breast. -मूलं *n.* The shoulder. —शालिन् *a.* Possessing strong arms. -शिखरं, -शिरस् *n.* The shoulder. -सूत्रं *n.* The base-sine (in Astr.).

भुजगः *m.* A snake, serpent. -गी *f.* The Asleshâ Nakshatra. -Comp. —अंतकः, —अशनः, -आभोजिन्, -दारणः, -भोजिन् *m.* Epithets of 1. Garuda.-2 A peacock. -3 An ichneumon. -ईश्वरः, -राजः *m.* Epithets of Sesha.

भुजंगः *m.* 1 A serpent, snake. -2 A paramour, gallant. -3 A husband or lord in general. -4 A catamite. -5 The dissolute friend of a king.-6 The constellation आश्लेषा.-7 The number 'eight'. -Comp. —इंद्रः *m.* An epithet of Sesha, the lord of snakes. —ईशः 1 *m.* An epithet of Vásuki.-2 Of Sesha. -3 Patanjali. -4 Of the sage Pingala. —भं *n.* The asterism आश्लेषा. -भुज् *m.* 1 An epithet of 1 Garuda. -2 A peacock. —लता *f.* Betel-pepper (तांबूली). -हन् *m.* An epithet of Garuda.

भुजंगमः *m.* 1 A snake. -2 An epithet of Râhu.-3 The number 'eight'. -4 The constellation आश्लेषा. —मी *f.* A female snake. —मं *n.* Lead.

भुजा *f.* 1 The arm. -2 The hand. -3 The coil of a snake (भोग). -4 Winding. -Comp. -कंटः *m.* A finger-nail. —दलः *m.* The hand. —मध्यः *m* 1 The elbow. -2 The breast. —मूलं *n.* The shoulder.

भुजिष्यः *m.* 1 A slave, servant. -2 A companion. -3 The string worn round the wrist.-4 A disease (रोग). —ष्या *f.* 1 A maid-servant, female slave. -2 A harlot, prostitute.

भुर्भुरिका, भुर्भुरी *f.* A kind of sweat-meat or eatable.

भुवनं *n.* 1 A world : (they are three, or on other authorities, fourteen). -2 The earth. -3 Heaven. -4 Water. -5 The number 'fourteen'. -Comp. -ओकस् *m.* A god. —त्रयं *n.* The three worlds (the earth, atmosphere and heaven). —पावनी *f.* An epithet of the Ganges.—शासिन् *m.* A king, ruler.

भुवन्युः *m*, 1 A master, lord. -2 The sun. -3 Fire. -4 The moon.

भुवर्, भुवस् *ind.* 1 The atmosphere, (the second of the three worlds, the one immediately above the earth). -2 A mystical word.

भुविस् *m.* The ocean.

भुशुंडिः, -डी *f.* A sort of weapon or missile.

भू 1 P. (Rarely A.) (भवति, भविष्टं. भूत) 1 To be, become. -2 To be born or produced. -3 To proceed from, arise. -4 To happen, occur. -5 To live, exist. -6 To be living, breathe. -7 To be in any state or condition. fare. -8 To abide ; remain. -9 To be possible (usually with a future tense in this sense) *e. g.* भवति भवान याजयिष्यति.-10 To lead to, conduce to, (with dat.) as in वाताय कपिला विद्युत. or न तस्या रुचये बभूव. -11 To be on the side of, assist.-12 To belong to (in English translated by 'have') तस्य ह शतं जाया बभूवुः He had a hundred wives. -13 To be occupied (with loc.) as in दाने तपसि सत्ये च भव. In combination with a preceeding noun or adjective भू is used to form verbs in the sense of 'becoming what it previously is not' or 'becoming in general' as in कृष्णीभू To become black. पयोधरीभू To become or serve the purpose of teats'. क्षपणीभू To be or become a mendicant. आर्द्रीभू To melt. भस्मीभू To be reduced to ashes. विषयीभू To form the subject of.

In combination with certain adverbs भू shows various idiomatic senses: *e. g.* पुनर्भू To marry again. आविर्भू To appear, arise, to be evident or clear. तिरोभू To disappear. प्रादुर्भू To arise, be visible. अग्रेभू To be in front, to take the lead, अंतर्भू To be included (in). दोषाभू To grow evening. अन्यथा भू To be otherwise, be changed. पुरो भू To come forward, stand forth. मिथ्या भू To turn out false. वृथा भू To become useless &c.

With अति— To excell, surpass. अनु— 1 To experience, enjoy, suffer. -2 To notice, perceive, understand. अभि— 1 To attack, overcome, defeat; to humiliate. -2 To rise. -3 To spread. उद्— To spring up, arise. परा— 1 To defeat; overcome, to overpower. -2 To hurt, injure. परि— 1 To overcome, conquer, subdue. -2 To treat with disrespect; to despise, insult. -3 To injure. -4 To grieve. -5 To disgrace. प्र— 1 To originate, to arise, spring up. (with abl.). -2 To appear, be visible. -3 To increase, multiply. -4 To be powerful, prevail. -5 To have power over(with *gen.loc, dat*). -6 To prevail, to be a match for (with *dat.*) as in प्रभवति मल्लो मल्लाय. -7 To be able, to have power for (generally with an *ind.*). -8 To be useful. -9 To beseech, implore. -10 To be contained in. सम्— 1 To arise, spring up, ensue, to be born or engendered. -2 To take place, occur. -3 To be united or joined with. -4 To be, become or exist. -5 To be adequate for, to be competent to. -6 To be consistent. -7 To be possible. -8 To be capable of holding.

Caus. (भावयति,-ते) 1 To cause to be or become, call into existence. -2 To cause, produce. -3 To manifest, exhibit. -4 To cherish, support, preserve. -5 To think, consider, imagine. -6 To consider or regard as. -7 To prove, establish. -8 To purify. -9 To get, obtain. -10 To mingle or mix. -11 To

lying on the earth. —शुद्धिः *f.* Purification of the ground by sweeping &c. -श्रवस् *m.* An ant-hill.—सुरः *m.* A Bràhmana. -स्पृश् *m.* 1 A man. -2 Mankind.-3A Vaisya. -स्वर्गः *m.* An epithet of the mountain Meru. —स्वामिन् *m.* A landlord.

भूकः *m.*, —कं *n.* 1 A cavity, chasm. -2 The spring. -3 Time —कः *m.* Darkness.

भूकलः *m.* A restive horse.

भूत *pp* (*f.*—ता). 1 Become, produced,formed. -2 Really happened, true.-3Right,fit.-4 Past,gone.-5Obtained. -6 Mixed or joined with. -7 Being like, similar. (See भू). —तः *m.* 1 A son, child. -2 An epithet of Siva -3 The fourteenth day of the dark half of a lunar month. -4 A great devotee. -5 N. of a priest of the gods. -6 The dark fortnight of a month (कृष्णपक्ष). -तं *n.* 1 Any being or creature. -2 A spirit, ghost, a devil(*m.* also in these senses.) -3 An element (they are five, *i.e.* पृथ्वी, अप्, तेजस्, वायु and आकाश).-4 An actual occurrence,a fact.5 The past time, past.-6 The world. -7 Well-being, welfare. -8 A symbolical expression for the number 'five.' -Comp. -अंतकः *m.* The God of death, Yama. -अर्थः *m.* The fact, the truth, reality —आत्मक *a.* Cousisting or composed of the elements.-आत्मन *a.* One whose soul is purified. (—*m.*) 1 The individual (as opposed to the Supreme) soul. -2 An epithet of Brahman (*m.*).-3 Of Siva.-4 Of Vishnu. -5 An elementary substance. -6 The body. -7 War, conflict. -आदिः *m.* 1 The Supreme Spirit. -2 An epithet of *Ahankára* (in Sánkhya phil.).—आर्त *a.*. Possessed by a devil. —आवासः *m.* 1 The body. -2 An epithet of Siva. -3 Of Vishnu. -आविष्ट *a.* Possessed by a devil or evil spirit. —आवेशः *m.* Demoniac possession. —इज्यं *n.*, —इज्या *f.* Making oblations to the Bhútas. —इष्टा *f.* The fourteenth day of a lunar fortnight. —ईशः *m.* 1 An epithet of Brahman (*m.*). -2 Of Vishnu. -3 Of Siva.-ईश्वरः *m.* An epithet of Siva. —उन्मादः *m.* Demoniac poesession. —उपसृष्ट, -उपहत *a.* Possessed by a devil. —ओदनः *m.* A dish of rice. —कर्तृ, —कृत *m.* An epithet of Bráhman (*m.*). —कालः *m.* 1 Past time. -2 (In gram.) The past or preterite time. —केशी *f.* The white basil.-क्रांतिः *f.* Possession by a devil. —गणः *m.* 1 The aggregate of created beings -2 The whole class of spirits or devils. —ग्रस्त *a.* 1 Possessed by a devil. -ग्रामः *m.* 1 The whole multitude of living beings. -3 A multitude of spirits. -3 The body. —घ्नः *m.* 1 A camel. -2 Garlic. —घ्नी *f.* The holy basil. —चतुर्दशी *f.* The fourteenth day of the second half of Kàrtika. —चारिन् *m.* An epithet of Siva. —दया *f.* Universal benveolence. —धरा, —धात्री, —धारिणी *f.* The earth. —नाथः *m.* An epithet of Siva.-नायिका *f.* An epithet of Durgâ. —नाशनः *m.* 1 The marking-nut plant. -2 Mustard.-3 Pepper. (—नं *n.*) 1 Asa Fœtida. -3 A bead used for rosaries (रुद्राक्ष). —निचयः *m.* The body. —पक्षः *m.* The dark fortnight. —पतिः *m.* 1 An epithet of Siva. -2 Of Agni. -3 The sacred basil. -पत्री *f.* The holy basil. —पूर्णिमा *f.* The full-moon day in the month of Asvina. —पूर्व *a.* Existed before, former. —पूर्वं *ind.*

Formerly. —प्रकृतिः *f.* The origin of all beings. —बलिः *m.* An offering to all beings. —ब्रह्मन *m.* A low Bráhmana who subsists upon the offerings made to an idol. —भर्तृ *m.* An epithet of Siva. —भावनः *m.* An epithet of Brahman (*m.*) -2 Of Vishnu. —भाषा *f.*, —भाषितं *n.* The language of demons. -महेश्वरः *m.* An epithet of Siva. —यज्ञः *m.* An oblation to all created beings, one of the five daily Yajnas to be performed by a house holder. —योनिः *m.* The origin of all created beings. —राज् *m.* An epithet of Siva. -वर्गः *m.* The whole class of spirits. -वासः *m.* The Bibhîtaka tree. —वाहनः *m.* An epithet of Siva. —विक्रिया *f.* 1 Epilepsy. -2 Possession by evil spirits. -विज्ञानं *n.*, —विद्या *f* Demonology. —वृक्षः *m.* The Bibhîtaka tree. —संसारः *m.* The world of mortals. —संचारः *m.* Demoniac possession. —संप्लवः *m.* Universal deluge or destruction. —सर्गः *m.* 1 The creation of the world. -2 The creation of the elements, —साधनी *f.* The earth. —सूक्ष्मं *n.* A subtle element. —स्थानं *n.* The abode of living beings.-2The abode of demons. —हरः *m.* Bdellium.

भूतकं *n.* 1 Camphor. -2 Sandalwood. -3 N. of a medicinal plant (Mar. कायफळ.).

भूतमय *a.* 1 Including all beings. -2 Formed out of the elements or created beings.

भूतिः *f.* 1 Being, existence.-2 Birth, production. -3 Welfare, happiness, prosperity. -4 Success, good fortune. -5 Wealth, fortune. -6 Dignity, majesty. -7 Ashes. -8 Decoration of elephants with coloured stripes. -9 The superhuman power attainable by the practice of austerity or magical rites. -10 Fried meat. -11 The rutting of elephants. —तिः *m.* 1 An epithet of Siva. -2 Of Vishnu.-3 Of a class of Manes. -Comp. —कर्मन् *n.* A festive rite. -कामः *m.* 1 A minister of state. -2 An epithet of Brihaspati. —कीलः *m.* 1 A hole, pit. -2 A moat. -3 A cellar. —कृत् *m* An epithet of Siva. -गर्भः *m.* A epithet of Bhavabhúti. -दः *m.* An epithet of Siva. —निधानं *n.* The lunar mansion धनिष्ठा, —भूषणः *m.* An epithet of Siva. —वाहनः *m.* An epithet of Siva.

भूमन् *m.* 1 A great quantity, abundance, large number. -2 Wealth. —*n* 1 The earth. -2 A piece of ground. -3 A being, creature. -4 Plurality (of number) as in आपः स्त्री भूम्नि * अमरकोशः.

भूमय *a.* (*f* -यी) Earthen, earthly.

भूमिः *f.* 1 The earth. -2 Soil, ground. -3 A district, country, land. -4 A spot, ground, plot of ground. -5 A site, situation. -6 Land, landed property. -7 A story or the floor of a house ; as in सप्तभूमिकाः प्रासादाः. -8 Attitude, posture. -9 A character or part (in a play). -10 Subject, object, receptacle as in विश्वासभूमि, स्नेहभूमि &c.-12 The tongue. -13 The number ' one '. -Comp. —अंतः *m.* A king of an adjacent district. —कदंबः *m.* A kind of Kadamba. —कंपः *m.* An earthquake. —गृहं *n.* A cellar. —चलः *m.*, —चलनं *n.* An earth-quake. —जः *m.* 1 The planet Mars. -2 An epithet of the demon Naraka.-3 A man. (—जा *f.*) An epithet of Sîtà. —जीविन *a.* An agriculturist (-*m.*) A Vaisya.-देवः*m.* Bràhhmana. -धरः *m.* 1 A mountain.-2 A king. -3 The number ' seven '. —पक्षः *m.* A swift or fleet horse. —पिशाचं *n* The wine palm. —पुत्रः *m.* The planet Mars. -भृत् *m* 1 A mountain. -2 A king. —मंडा *f.* A kind of jasmine.-रक्षः *m.* A swift or fleet horse. —रुहः *m.* A tree. —लाभः *m.* Death (figuratively). -लेपनं *n.* Cow-dung. —वर्धनः *m.*,-नं *n.* A dead body, corpse. —शयः *m.* A wild pigeon. -2 A child, boy.—संभवः,—सुतः *m.* 1 The planet Mars. -2 An epithet of the demon Naraka. (-वा, -ता *f.*) An epithet of Sítâ. -संनिवेशः *m.* The configuration of a country. —स्पृश् *m.* 1 A man. -2 Mankind. -3 A Vaisya. -4 A thief.

भूमिका *f.* 1 Earth, ground, soil. -2 A place, spot (of ground). -3 A story, floor (of a house). -4 Step, degree. -5 A board for writing. -6 A part or character in a play. -7 Theatrical dress ; an actor's costume. -8 Decoration (as of an image).-9A preface or introduction to a book.

भूमी *f.* The earth. -Comp. --पतिः, -भुज् *m.* A king. -रुह्, -रुहः *m.* A tree.

भूयं *n.* The state of being or becoming ; as in ब्रह्मभूयं, दाशरथिभूयं &c.

भूयशस् *ind.* 1 Mostly, generally. -2 Exceedingly. -3 Again ; further.

भूयस् *a.* (*f.* -सी)1 More numerous or abundant. -2 Greater, larger. -3 Very great or large, much, many, numerous.-4Rich or abounding in. —*ind.* 1 Much, exceedingly, largely, greatly. -2 More-over.-3 Repeatedly. (The form भूयसा is used adverbially in the sense of 1 Very much, in a high degree, exceedingly. -2 As a general rule). -Comp. —भूयस् *ind.* Again and again, repeatedly. —विद्य *a.* 1 More learned. -2 Very learned.

भूयिष्ठ *a.* (*f.* —ष्ठा) 1 Most, most numerous or abundant. -2 Most important. -3 Very great or large, many, numerous. -4 Mostly composed or consisting of, chiefly filled with (at the end of comp.) अभिरूपभूयिष्ठा परिषद् *शाकुंत. -5 Almost, nearly (usually after a past passive participle) as in अये उदितभूयिष्ठ एष तपनः. -ष्ठं *ind.* 1 For the most part, mostly.-2 Exceedingly, very much.

भूर् *ind.* 1 One of the three Vyàhritis. -2 The lowest of the seven lower worlds.

भूरि *a.* 1 Much, abundant, numerous. -2 Great, large. -रिः *m.* 1 An epithet of Vishnu. -2 Of Brahman (*m.*).-3 Of Siva. -4 Of Indra. -रि *n.* Gold. -*ind.* 1 Very much, exceedingly. -2 Often, repeatedly. -Comp. -गमः *m.* An ass.-तेजस् *m.* Fire. -दक्षिण *a.* 1 Attended with rich presents or rewards. -2 Munificent. —प्रयोग *a.* In common use (as a word). —प्रेमन् *m.* The ruddy goose. —भाग *a.* Prosperous. —मायः *m.* A jackal or fox. —रसः *m.* The sugar-cane. —श्रवस् *m.* N. of a warrior on the Kaurava side slain by Sâtyaki.

भूरिज् *f.* The earth.

भूर्जः *m.* The birch-tree. -Comp. —कंटकः *m.* The offspring of an outcast Bráhmana by a woman of the same class. -पत्रः *m.* The birch tree.

भूर्णि: *f.*1 The earth.-2 A desert.

भूष् 1 P., 10 U.(भूषति,भूषयति,-ते,भूषित) 1 To adorn, decorate. -2 To decorate oneself (Atm.). -3 To strew with, overspread. -With अभि— or वि— To adorn, grace, decorate.

भूषणं *n.* 1 Ornamenting, decoration. -2 An ornament, an article of decoration. —णः *m.* N. of Visnnu.

भूषा *f.* 1 Decorating, adorning. -2 An ornament. -3 A jewel.

भूषित *p. p.* (*f.* -ता) Adorned, ornamented.

भूष्णु *a.* 1 Being, becoming. -2 Wishing for wealth or prosperity.

भृ 1, 3 U. (भरति,-ते: बिभर्ति, बिभृते,भर्तुं, भृतः *pass.* भ्रियते. *desid.* बिभरिषति,-ते or बुभूर्षति,-ते) 1 To fill.-2 To fill up, fill with. -3 To bear, support, bear up. -4 To cherish, protect, nourish. -5 To bear, possess, have. -6 To wear, to have on. -7 To experience, suffer, endure, feel. -8 To confer, bestow, give. -9 To retain (as in memory). -10 To hire. With उद्- To support, bear. सम्— 1 To collect, to hoard, to place together. -2 To make ready, prepare. -3 To present, offer. -4 To maintain, nourish. -5 To effect, accomplish, produce, bring on. [female attire.

भृकुंशः (-सः) *m.* A male actor in

भृकुटिः,—टी *f.* Knitting of the eye brows.

भृश *ind.* An imitative word expressive of the crackling sound of fire.

भृगुः *m.* 1 N. of a sage, regarded as the ancestor of the family of the Bhrigus, and also regarded as one of the ten patriarchs created by the first Manu. -2 N. of the sage Jamadagni. -3 An epithet of Sukra. -4 The planet Venus. -5 A cliff, precipice. -6 The level summit of a mountain. -7 N. of Krishna. -8 An epithet of Siva. -9 Friday. -Comp. -उद्वहः *m.* An epithet of Parasurâma. -जः, —तनयः *m.* 1 An epithet of Sukra. -2 The planet Venus. —नंदनः *m.* 1 An epithet of Parasurâma. -2 Of Sukra. —पतिः *m.* An epithet of Parasuráma. —वंशः *m.* N. of a family descended from Parasurâma. -वारः, —वासरः *m.* Friday. —शार्दूलः, —श्रेष्ठः, —सत्तमः *m.* Epithets of Parasuráma. —सुतः, —सूनुः *m.* 1 An epithet of Parasuráma. -2 Of Venus or Sukra.

भृंगः *m.* 1 A large black bee.-2 A kind of wasp. -3 A kind of bird. -4 A lecher, a libertine. -5 A vase or jar. —गं *n.* Talc. —गी *f.* The female of the large black bee.-Comp. —अभीष्टः *m.* The mango tree. -आनंदा *f.* The Yúthikâ creeper. —जं *n.* 1 Aloe-wood. -2 Talc. —पर्णिका *f.* Small cardamoms. —प्रिया *f.* The Mádhavî creeper. -राज् *m.* 1 A kind of large bee. -2 N. of a shrub.-रिटिः, —रीटिः *m.* N. of one of the attendants of Siva. —रोलः *m.* A kind of wasp. -वल्लभः *m.* A species of Kadamba.

भृंगारः *m.*,-रं *n.* 1 A golden pitcher. -2 A pitcher of a particular shape (Mar. झारी). -3 A vase used at the coronation of a king. -गं *n.* 1 Gold. -2 Cloves.

भृंगालिका, भृंगारी *f.* A cricket.

भृंगिन् *m.* 1 The fig-tree.-2 N. of an attendant of Siva.

भृंगिरि (-री-) टिः *m.* N. of one of the attendants of Siva.

भृंगेरिटिः *m.* N. of an attendant of Siva.

भृज् 1 A. (भर्जते) To roast, fry.

भृंटिका *f.* A species of plant.

भृत *p. p.* (*f.* -ता) 1 Borne. -2 Supported, maintained. -3 Endowed or furnished with. -4 Full of, filled with. -5 Hired. —तः *m.* A hired servant.

भृतक *a.* (*f.* -का) Hired, paid.—कः *m.* A hired servant. -Comp.—अध्यापकः *m.* A hired teacher. -अध्यापितः *m.* A student who pays his teacher for his labour (a paying student).

भृतिः *f.* 1 Bearing, supporting. -2 Cherishing, maintaining. -3 Bringing, leading to. -4 Support, maintenance. -5 Food. -6 Wages, hire. -7 Service for hire.-8 Capital, principal. -Comp.—अध्यापनं *n.* Teaching (especially the Vedas) for hire. —भुज् *m.* A hired servant. —रूपं *n.* A reward in lieu of the wages due.

भृत्यः *m.* 1 Any one requiring to be supported. -2 A servant ; a slave. -3 A minister of state. -4 A subject. —त्या *f.* 1 Maintenance, support. -2 A means of substenance, food. -3 Wages. -4 Service. -जनः *m.* 1 A servant, dependant. -2 Servants taken collectively. —वर्गः *m.* The body of servants. —वात्सल्यं *n.* Kindness to servants.-वृत्तिः *f.* Maintenance of servants or dependants.

भृत्रिम *a.* (*f.* -मा) Supported, nourished. [-2 Whirlwind.

भृमिः *m.* 1 An eddy, a whirlpool.

भृश् 4 P. (भृश्यति) To fall down.

भृश *a.* (*f.* —शा ; compar. भ्रशीयस्, superl. भ्रशिष्ठ) 1 Strong, powerful, intense, excessive, very much. -2 Frequent. —शं *ind.* 1 Much, excessively, intensely, violently, in a high degree, greatly. -2 Repeatedly. -3 In a better or superior manner. -Comp. —कोपन *a.* Highly choleric or irascible.

भृष्ट *p. p.* (*f.*—ष्टा) Fried, roasted, parched. -Comp.—अन्नं *n.* Rice boiled and fried. —यवाः *m. pl.* Parched rice.

भृष्टिः *f.* 1 Frying, parching, roasting. -2 A deserted garden.

भॄ 9 P. (भृणाति, भूर्ण) To bear, support, maintain. -2 To fry. -3 To blame, censure.

भेकः *m.* 1 A frog.-2 A timid man. -3 A cloud. -की *f.* 1 A small frog. -2 A female frog. -Comp. —भुज् *m.* A serpent. -रवः,-शब्दः *m.* The croaking of frogs.

भेडः *m* 1 A ram, sheep. -2 A raft, float. -डी *f.* A ewe.

भेड्रः *m.* A ram.

भेदः *m.* 1 Breaking, splitting, cleaving. -2 Hitting (as a mark). -3 Piercing through, perforation. -4 Difference, dissension, quarrel, dispute. -5 Breach, rupture. -6 Disturbance, interruption. -7 A chasm, gap. -8 A hurt, injury, wound. -9 Difference, distinction. -10 A change, modification, as in बुद्धिभेदः. -11 Disclosure, betrayal, as in रहस्यभेदः. -12 Treachery, treason. -13 A kind, variety. -14 Dualism. -15 (In polities) Sowing dissensions in an enemy's party, one of the four Upàyas or means of success against an enemy. -16 Defeat. -17 (In medicine) Evacuation of the bowels. -Comp. —कर, -कृत *a.* Sowing dissensions. -दर्शिन्, -दृष्टि, -बुद्धि *a.* Considering the universe as distinct from the Supreme Spirit. -प्रत्ययः *m.* Belief in dualism. —वादिन् *m.* One who maintains the doctrine of dualism. —सह *a.* 1 Capable of being divided or separated -2 Seducible.

भेदक *a.* (*f.* -दिका) Splitting, dividing, separating. -2 Piercing. -3 Destroying. -4 Distinguishing, discriminating.-5 Defining.-6 Evacuating the bowels, purgative. -कः *m.* An adjective or differentiating attribute.

भेदनं *n.* 1 Splitting, breaking. -2 Dividing, separating. -3 Distinguishing. -4 Creating discord. -5 Dissolving, loosening. -6 Disclosing. -7 Disunion. -8 Asa Foetida. -9 (In astr.) Passing through a constellation.-नः *m.* A hog.

भेदिरं, भेदुरं *n.* A thunderbolt.

भेद्यं *n.* A substantive. -Comp. —रोगः *m.* A disease treated by incision. —लिंग *a.* Distinguished by the gender.

भेरः *m.* A kettle-drum.

भेरिः,—री *f.* A kettle-drum.

भेरुंड *a.* (*f.* —डा) Terrible, fearful. —डः *m.* A species of bird. —डं *n.* Conception, pregnancy.

भेरुंडकः *m.* A jackal.

भेल *a.* (*f.* —ला) 1 Timid. -2 Foolish, ignorant. -3 Unsteady, inconstant. -4 Tall. —लः *m.* A boat, raft, float.

भेलकः *m.*,—कं *n.* A boat, raft.

भेष् 1 U. (भेषति,-ते) To fear, be afraid.

भेषजं *n.* 1 A medicine, medicament. -2 A remedy or cure in general. -3 A kind of fennel. -Comp. —अ (-आ-) गारः *m.*,-रं *n.* An apothecary's shop. —अंगं *n.* Anything taken after medicine.

भेषज्य *a.* (*f.* -ज्या) Curative, having healing properties.

भैक्ष *a.* (*f.* —क्षी) Living on alms. —क्षं *n.* 1 Begging, mendicancy. -2 Anything got by begging. -Comp. —आशिन् *m.* A beggar, mendicant. —आहारः *m.* A beggar. -चरणं, -चर्यं *n.*, —चर्या *f.* Going about begging; begging; collecting alms. -जीविका, -वृत्तिः *f.* Mendicancy. —भुज् *m.* A beggar, mendicant.

भैक्षवं *n.*, भैक्षुका *f.* 1 A number of beggars.

भैक्ष्यं *n.* Food got by begging; alms, charity.

भैमी *f.* 1 'The daughter of Bhíma,' a patronymic of Damayantî, wife of Nala. -2 The eleventh day of the bright half of Màgha or the festival performed on that day.

भैमसेनिः,-न्यः *m.* Son of Bhîmasena.

भैरव *a.* (*f.* -वी) 1 Terrible, frightful. -2 Miserable. -2 Relating to Bhairava. -वः *m.* 1 A form of Siva. -2 The sentiment of terror (भयानक). -3 Fear, terror. -4 N. of a musical mode (राग). —वी *f.* 1 A form of Durgâ. -2 N. of a Ráginí. -3 A young girl representing Durgà at the Durgá festival. —वं *n.* Terror, horror. -Comp. —ईशः *m.* An epithet of Vishnu. —यातना *f.* A purificatory torment inflicted by Bhairava of Benares on those who die there,to make their spirits fit for absorption into the Supreme Spirit.

भैषजं *n.* A medicine, drug. —जः *m.* A kind of quail.

भैषज्यं *n.* 1 Administering medicines, medical treatment. -2 A medicine, drug. -3 Healing power, curativeness.

भैष्मकी *f.* A patronymic of Rukmini, wife of Krishna.

भोक्तृ *a.* (*f.*—क्त्री) 1 Possessing. -2 Enjoying or making use of. -3 Feeling, enduring, experiencing. -4 Protecting, ruling. -*m.* 1 A possessor, enjoyer. -2 A husband. -3 A king, ruler. -4 A lover.

भोगः *m.* 1 Eating, consuming. -2 Enjoyment, fruition.-3 Possession. -4 Utility, advantage. -5 Ruling, governing. -6 Use as of a deposit. -7 Suffering, experiencing. -8 Feeling, perception. -9 Sexual enjoyment. -10 An object of enjoyment or pleasure. -11 A repast, feast, banquet. -12 Food. -13 Food offered to an idol. -14 Profit, gain. -15 Income, revenue. -16 Wealth. -17 The wages of prostitution. -18 A coil, winding. -19 The (expanded) hood of a snake. -20 A snake. -21 The body. -22 The passing (of an asterism). -23 The part of the ecliptic occupied by each of the 27 Nakshatras. -Comp. —अर्हं *n.* Property, wealth. —अर्ह्यं *n.* Corn, grain. —आधिः *m.* A pledge that may be used until redeemed. —आवली *f.* The panegyric of a bard. —आवासः *m.* The apartments of women, harem. —गुच्छं *n.* Wages paid to prostitutes. —गृहं *n.* The women's apartments, harem. -तृष्णा *f.* 1 Thirst for worldly enjoyments. —देहः *m.* The subtle body which a dead person carries with him. —धरः *m.* A serpent. —पतिः *m.* The ruler of a district or province. -पाकः *m.* A groom. —पिशाचिका *f.* Hunger. -भृतकः *m.* A servant who works for mere maintenance. -स्थानं *n.* 1 The body, as the seat of enjoyment. -2 Women's apartments.

भोगवत् *a.* (*f.* -ती) 1 Delightful. -2 Happy, prosperous. -3 Having curves; coiled. -*m.* 1 A snake. -2 A mountain. -3 Dancing, acting, and singing together. (—ती *f.*) 1 An epithet of the Ganges of Pàtála or the lower world. -2 A female snake-demon. -3 N. of the city of the snakes in the lower regions. -4 The night of the second day of a lunar month

भोगिकः *m.* A groom.

भोगिन् *a.* (*f.* —नी) 1 Eating. -2 Enjoying. -3 Suffering, experiencing. -4 Using, possessing. -5 Having curves. -6 Devoted to sensual pleasures. -7 Rich, opulent. -*m.* 1 A snake. -2 A king. -3 A voluptuary. -4 A barber. -5 The headman of a village. -6 The lunar mansion आश्लेषा. —नी *f.* The concubine of a king. -Comp. —इंद्रः, —ईशः *m.* Sesha or Vâsuki. —कांतः *m.* Wind, air. -भुज् *m.* 1 An ichneumon. -2 A peacock. -वल्लभं *n.* Sandal.

भोग्य *a.* (*f.* —ग्या) 1 To be enjoyed. -2 To be suffered or endured. -3 Profitable. —ग्यं *n.* 1 Any object of enjoyment. -2 Wealth, property, possessions. -3 Corn, grain. —ग्या *f.* A harlot, courtezan.

भोजः *m.* 1 N. of a king of Mâlvà. -2 N. of a country. -3 N. of a king of the Vidarbhas. —जाः *m. pl.* N. of a people. -Comp. —अधिप· *m.* An epithet of 1 Kamsa. -2 Karna. -पतिः *m.* 1 King Bhoja. -2 An epithet of Kamsa.

भोजनं *n.* 1 Eating. -2 Food. -3 Giving (food) to eat, feeding. -4 Using, enjoying. -5 Any object of enjoyment. -6 That which is enjoyed. -7 Property, wealth, possessions. -Comp. —अधिकारः *m.* Superintendence over food or provisions, stewardship. —विशेषः *m.* A dainty, delicacy. —वृत्तिः *f.* A meal, food.

भोजनीयं *n.* Food.

भोज्य *pot. p.* (*f.* —ज्या) 1 To be eaten. -2 To be enjoyed or possessed. -3 To be suffered or experienced. -4 To be enjoyed carnally. —ज्यं *n.* 1 Food, meal. -2 A store of provisions. -3 A dainty. -4 Enjoyment. -5 Advantage, profit. -6 Food given to the Manes. -Comp. —कालः *m.* Meal-time. —संभवः *m.* The primary juice of the body.

भोज्या *f.* A princess of the Bhojas.

भोटः *m.* N. of a country(probably the same as Tibet). -Comp. -अंगः *m*. The country called Bhootâna.

भोटीय *a.* (*f.* —या) Tibetan.

भोमीरा *f.* Coral.

भोलिः *m.* A camel.

भोस् *ind.* 1 A particle used in addressing translated by ' oh,' ' sir,' ' oh ,' ' ah ;' (it drops its final *visarga* before vowels and soft consonants). -2 भोस् is also used to express the senses of ' sorrow ' and ' interrogation'

भौजंगं *n.* The lunar mansion called आश्लेषा.

भौट्टः *m.* A Tibetan.

भौत *a.* (*f.* —ती)1 Relating to living beings. -2 Elemental, material. -3 Demoniacal. —तः *m.* 1 A worshipper of demons and spirits. -2 An attendant upon an idol. —तं *n.* A collection of evil spirits. —ती *f.* Night.

भौतिक *a.* (*f.* -की) 1 Belonging to created or living beings. -2 Elemental, material. -3 Relating to evil spirits. -4Possessed by evil spirits. —कः *m.* N. of Siva. -कं *n.* 1 A pearl. -2 Anything elemental. -Comp. —मठः *m.* A monastery. —विद्या *f.* Sorcery, witchcraft.

भौम *a.* (*f.* —मी) 1 Belonging to the earth. -2 Earthly, terrestrial. -3 Earthy. -4 Relating to Mars. -मः *m.* 1 The planet Mars. -2 An epithet of the demon Naraka. -3 Water. -4 Light. -5 The atmosphere. -6 N. of Atri. -Comp. —दिनं *n.*, —वारः, -वासरः *m.* Tuesday. -रत्नं *n.* Coral.

भौमनः *m.* N. of Visvakarman, architect of the gods.

भौमिक *a.* (*f.* —की), भौम्य *a.* (*f.*-म्या) Earthly ; earthy.

भौरिकः *m.* The superintendent of gold in a royal treasury. -2 A treasury-officer, a treasurer.

भौवनः *m.* An epithet of Vishwakarman, architect of Gods.

भौवादिक *a.* (*f.* —की) Belonging to that class of roots which begin with भू in Pânini's grammar.

भ्रंश् 1 A., 4 P. (भ्रंशते, भ्रश्यति, भ्रष्ट ; with abl. in most cases) 1 To fall or drop down. -2 To deviate or swerve from. -3 To be deprived of, lose. -4 To flee from. -5 To decay, decrease. 6 To vanish, depart. With परि— 1 To drop down, to tumble. -2 To go astray. -3 To fall away from. -4 To be deprived of. वि- 1 To drop down. -2 To be free from. -3 To go astray. -*Caus.* भ्रंशयति,-ते.

भ्रंशः,-सः *m.* 1 Falling off, dropping down. -2 Decline, decay. -3 Fall, ruin, overthrow. -4 Running away. -5 Disappearance. -6 Losing, loss.-7 Swerving or deviating from. -8 Abandoning, deserting.

भ्रंशथुः *m.* A disease of the nose.

भ्रंश (-स-) नं *n.* 1The act of dropping down. -2 Falling from, being deprived of, losing.

भ्रंशिन् *a.* (*f.* —नी) 1 Falling off or down, falling from. -2 Decaying. -3 Straying away from. -4 Ruining, destroying.

भ्रंस् See भ्रंश्.

भ्रकुंशः *m.* An actor in female dress.

भ्रक्ष् 1 U. (भ्रक्षति,-ते) To eat, devour.

भ्रज्जनं n. The act of frying, roasting or parching.

भ्रभंग: m. See भ्रूभंग:.

भ्रम् 1, 4 P. (भ्रमति, भ्रम्यति, भ्राम्यति, भ्रमितुं,भ्रांत) 1 To roam or wander about,rove,ramble (fig also). (भिक्षां भ्रम् To go about begging). -2 To whirl round,move in a circle.-3 To go astray,swerve,deviate. -4 To prevail, be current. -5 To reel, stagger ; be in doubt or suspense; waver. -6 To err, be mistaken. -7 To flutter, move unsteadily. -8 To surround. With उद्— 1 To be confused, to be mad. -2 To err, to fall into error. -3 To wander about. परि-1 To wander about, rove, to ramble. -2 To hover. -3 To whirl round, revolve. -4 To describe a circle round. वि— 1 To wander about. -2 To hover. -3 To scatter, to frighten away. -4 To be disarranged, to be confused, to be bewildered. सम्— 1 To wander about. -2 To err, be confused, to be perplexed. —*Caus*. (भ्रमयति,-ते or भ्रामयति,-ते) 1 To cause to wander, cause to revolve or turn round, whirl round. -2 To cause to err ; to mislead, confuse, embarrass ; cause to stagger. -3 To wave,brandish.

भ्रम: m. 1 Moving about, roving.-2 Whirling, revolving. -3 Circular motion, rotation. -4 Straying, deviating. -5 A mistake, delusion. -6 Perplexity, embarrassment. -7 A whirlpool.-8 A potter's wheel.-9 A grind-stone. -10 A lathe. -11 Giddiness. -12 A fountain, water-course. -Comp. -आसक्त: m.A sword-cleaner, an armourer.

भ्रमणं n. 1 Moving about, roaming about. -2 Revolution.-3 Deviation, swerving. -4 Tottering ; unsteadiness. -5 Erring. -6 Giddiness. -7 A tour, excursion. -8 The orbit of a planet. -णी f. 1 A kind of game. -2 A leech.

भ्रमत्कुटी f. A kind of umbrella.

भ्रमर: m. 1 A bee,large black bee. -2 A gallant, libertine. -3 A potter's wheel. -4 A young man. -री f. 1 A bee. -2 Lac. —रं n. Giddiness, vertigo. -Comp. —अतिथि: m. The Champaka tree.-अलक:m. A curl on the forehead. -इष्ट: m. The श्योनाक tree. -उत्सवा f.The Mádhavî creeper. —करंड: m. A small box containing bees (used by thieves to extinguish light in a house by letting the bees escape). -कीट: m. A species of wasp. —प्रिय: m. A kind of Kadamba tree. —विलसितं n. 1 The sporting of bees. -2 N. of a metre.

भ्रमरक: m. 1 A bee. -2 A whirlpool, an eddy. —क: m.,—कं n. 1 A lock of hair hanging down on the forehead. -2 A ball for playing with. -3 A humming top.

भ्रमरिका f. Wandering in all directions.

भ्रमि: f. 1 Whirling,circular movement ; revolution. -2 A potter's wheel. -3 A turner's lathe. -4 A whirlpool. -5 A whirlwind. -6 A circular arrangement of troops. -7 An error, a mistake.

भ्रशू See भ्रंशू.

भ्रशिमन् m. Violence, vehemence.

भ्रष्ट a. (f. -ष्टा) 1 Dropped down, fallen off. -2 Ruined, decayed. -3 Lost. -4 Deprived of. -5 Strayed from (with an abl.). -6 Vicious, depraved. -Comp. —गुद a. Suffering from *prolapsus ani*.

भ्रस्ज् 6. U. (भृज्जति, भृष्ट) To fry, roast,parch. (fig. also).

भ्राज् I A (भ्राजते) To shine, glitter. -With वि— To shine brilliantly or intensely.

भ्राजः *m*. N. of one of the seven suns. -जं *n*. N. of a Sâman.

भ्राजक *a*. (*f*. —जिका) Illuminating, irradiating. -कं *n*. Bile, gall.

भ्राजथुः *m*. Lustre, brilliance.

भ्राजिष्णु *a*. Shining, bright, radiant. —ष्णुः *m*. I An epithet of Siva. -2 Of Vishnu.

भ्रातृ *m*. I A brother. -2 An intimate friend. -3 A near relative in general. -4 A term of friendly address. (-*Dual*.) A brother and sister. -Comp. —गंधि, —गंधिक *a*. Having only the name of a brother, a brother in mere name. -जः *m*. A brother's son. -जा I *f*. A brother's daughter. —जाया (also भ्रातुर्जाया) *f*. A brother's wife, a sister-in-law. -दत्तं *n*. Property given by a brother to a sister at the time of her marriage. -द्वितीया *f*. The second day of the bright half of Kàrtika (when sisters entertain their brothers who in their turn give them presents). —पुत्रः (also भ्रातुष्पुत्रः) *m*. A brother's son. (-त्री *f*.) A niece. —वधूः *f*. A brother's wife. —श्वशुरः *m*. An elder brother of the husband.

भ्रातृक *a*. (*f*. —का) Relating to a brother.

भ्रातृव्यः *m*. I A nephew. -2 An enemy, adversary.

भ्रात्रीयः, भ्रात्रेयः *m*. A brother's son, a nephew.

भ्रात्र्यं *n*. Fraternity, brotherhood.

भ्रांत *p. p*. (*f* —ता) I Wandered or roamed about. -2 Whirled, revolved. -3 Mistaken, gone astray. -4 Confused. -5 Moving about, wheeling. -6 Whirling round, roaming about. —तः *m*. I An elephant in rut. -2 A kind of thorn-apple. -तं *n*. I Roaming, moving about. -2 A mistake, an error.

भ्रांतिः *f*. I Moving or wandering about. 2 Turning round. -3 A circular or rotatory movement. -4 An error, a mistake ; false idea or impression. -5 Confusion, perplexity. -6 Doubt, uncertainty. -7 Unsteadiness. -Comp. —नाशनः *m*. An epithet of Siva. -हरः *m*. A counsellor, minister.

भ्रांतिमत् *a*. I Revoling, turning round. -2 Mistaking, being under a delusion. -*m*. A figure of speech in which, on account of resemblance, an object is wrongly apprehended to be what it is really not साम्यादतस्मिंस्तद्बुद्धिर्भ्रांतिमान् प्रतिभोत्थितः*साहित्य द. *e. g*. कपाले मार्जारः पय इति करान् लेढि शशिनः.

भ्रामः *m*. I Roaming about. -2 Delusion, error, mistake.

भ्रामकः *m*. I A sun-flower. -2 A kind of loadstone. -3 A deceiver, cheat. -4 A jackal.

भ्रामर *a*. (*f*. -री) Relating to a bee. -रः *m*., -रं *n*. A kind of loadstone. -रं *n*. I Whirling round. -2 Giddiness. -3 Epilepsy. -4 Honey. -5 A kind of coitus. -6 A village. -री *f*. I An epithet of Durgá. -2 Walking round from left to right (=प्रदक्षिणा).

भ्रा (भ्ला-) श् I. 4. A. (भ्राशते, भ्राश्यते, भ्लाशते, भ्लाश्यते) To shine, glitter.

भ्राष्ट्रः *m*., -ष्ट्रं *n*. A frying-pan. -ष्ट्रः *m*. I Light. -2 Ether.

भ्राष्ट्रकं *n*., -कः *m*. A frying-pan.

भ्राष्ट्रमिंध *a*. One who fries or roasts.

भ्रा (भ्ला-) स् I, 4 A. (भ्रासते, भ्रास्यते, भ्लासते, भ्लास्यते) To shine, to glitter.

भ्रुकंसः, भ्रूकंसः, भ्रुकुंसः, भ्रूकुंसः *m.* A male actor in female attire.

भ्रुकुटिः, -टी *f.* The knitting of eye-brows ; a frown.

भ्रूः *f.* Brow,eyebrow.-Comp. -कुटिः, -टी *f.* Contraction or knitting of the eyebrows, a frown. भ्रुकुटिं बंध् or रच् To knit the eyebrows, to frown. —क्षेपः Contraction of the eyebrows. —जाहं *n.* The root of the eyebrow. —भंगः,—भेदः *m.* Contraction or knit-ting of the eyebrows, a frown. -मंडलं *n.* The arch of the eyebrow. —मध्यं *n.* The space between the eye-brows. —लता *f.* An arched or curv-ing eyebrow. —विचेष्टितं *n*-, -विभ्रमः,-वि-लासः *m.* A graceful or playful move-ment of the eyebrows.

भ्रूणः *m.* I An embryo, fœtus. -2 A child, boy. -Comp. —घ्न, —हन् *a.* One who causes abortion. —हतिः, —हत्या *f.* Killing an embryo, caus-ing abortion.

भ्रेज् I A (भ्रेजते) To glitter, shine.

भ्रे (भ्ले-) ष् I U. (भ्रेषति,-ते, भ्लेषति, -ते) I To go, move. -2 To fall, tot-ter. -3 To fear. -4 To be angry.

भ्रेषः, भ्रेशः *m.* I Moving. -2 Waver-ing, slipping. -3 Swerving, aberra-tion. -4 Trespass, sin. -5 Loss, deprivation.

भ्रौणहत्यं *n.* The killing of an em-bryo.

म्लक्ष् I U. (म्लक्षति,-ते) To eat, to devour.

म्लाश् I, 4 A To shine, glitter.

म.

मः *m.* I A magical formula. -2 N. of Brahman (*m.*) -3 (In pro-sody) A syllabic foot (गण) con-sisting of three long syllables. -4 N. of the fifth (मध्यम) note in music.

मकरः *m.* I A kind of sea-animal resembling a crocodile. (Makara is regarded as an emblem of the God of love). -2 The sign *capricor-nus* of the zodiac. -3 An array of troops in the form of a Makara. -4 An ear-ring in the shape of a Ma-kara. -5 The hands folded in the form of a Makara. -6 One of the nine treasures of Kubera. -Comp. —अंकः *m.* An epithet of (I) the God of love and of (2) the ocean. —अश्वः *m.* An epithet of Varuna. —आकरः —आलयः, —आवासः *m.* The ocean.-कुंडलं *n.* An ear-ring in the shape of a Makarā. -केतनः, -केतुः, -केतुमत् *m.* Epi-thets of the God of love. —ध्वजः *m.* I An epithet of the God of love. -2 A particular array of troops. —राशिः *m.* The sign *capricornus* of the zodiac.—संक्रमणं *n.* The passsage of the sun into the sign *capricornus*. —सप्तमी *f.* The seventh day in the bright half of Mágha.

मकरंदः *m.*I The honey of flowers.-2 A kind of jasmine. -3 The Indian cuckoo. -4 A bee. -5 A kind of mango tree. —ई *n.* A filament.

मकरंदवत् *a.*(*f.*-ती) Filled with honey, -ती *f.* The *Pátalá* creeper or its flo-wer.

मकरिन् *m.* The ocean.

मकरी *f.*The female of a crocodile. -Comp. -पत्रं *n.*, —लेखा *f.* A figure of a Makarî on the face of Lakshmî. —प्रस्थः *m.* N. of a town.

मकुटं *n.* A crown, a tiara.

मकुतिः *f.* I A government order addressed to the Súdras.

मकुरः *m.*I A mirror -2 The *Bakula* tree. -3 A bud. -4 The Arabian jasmine.-5 The handle of a potter's wheel. [bud.

मकुलः *m.* 1 The *Bakula* tree. -2 A

मकूलकः *m.* A bud.

मक्क् 1 A. (मक्कते) To go, move.

मक्कलः *m.* A kind of abscess in the abdomen (of lying-in women).

मक्कुलः *m.* Benzoin, red chalk.

मक्कोलः *m.* Chalk.

मक्ष् 1 P. (मक्षति) 1 To heap, collect. -2 To be angry.

मक्षः *m.* 1 Wrath. -2 Hypocrisy. -3 A multitude, collection. -Comp. —वीर्यः *m.* The पियाल tree.

मक्षिकः *m.*, माक्षि (-क्षी-) का *f.* A fly, bee. -Comp. —मलं *n.* Wax.

मखः *m.* A sacrificial rite. -Comp. —अंशभाज् *m.* A God. —असुहृद् *m.* An epithet of Siva. —त्रातृ *m.* An epithet of Râma. —द्विष् *m.* A demon, a Râkshasa. —द्वेषिन् *m.* An epithet of Siva. -हन् *n.* An epithet of Indra. -2 Of Siva.

मगधः *m.* 1 N. of a country, the southern part of modern Behar. -2 A bard, minstrel. —धाः *m. pl.* The people of Magadha. —धा *f.* 1 The town of the Magadhas. -2 Long pepper.-Comp.-उद्भवा *f.* Long pepper. —पुरी *f.* The city of Magadha. —लिपिः *f.* Writing or character of the Magadhas.

मग्न *a* (*f.* -ग्ना) 1 Plunged. -2 Immersed.-3 Absorbed. (*pp.* of मस्ज्).

मघः *m.* 1 N. of one of the divisions of the universe. -2 N. of a country. -3 A kind of medicine. -4 Pleasure. -5 N. of the tenth lunar mansion. —घं *n.* A kind of flower.

मघवः, मघवत् *m.* N. of Indra.

मघवन् *m.* (Nom. sing. मघवा; acc.pl. मघोनः) 1 N. of Indra. -2 An owl.-3 N. of Vyâsa.

मघा *f.* N. of the tenth lunar mansion containing five stars. -Comp. —त्रयोदशी *f.* The thirteenth day of the dark half of Bhâdrapada. -भवः, -भूः *m.* The planet Venus.

मंक् 1 A. (मंकते) 1 To go, move. -2 To decorate, adorn.

मंकिलः *m.* A forest-conflagration.

मंकुरः *m.* A mirror. [greaves.

मंक्षणं *n.* An armour for the legs,

मंक्षु *ind.* 1 Immediately, quickly, soon. -2 Exceedingly, very much. -3 Truly, really.

मंगल *a.* (*f.* —ला) 1 Auspicious, lucky, fortunate. -2 Prosperous. -3 Brave. —लं *n.* 1 Auspiciousness, propitiousness ; good luck or fortune, welfare, good (also *m.* in these senses). -2 A good omen. -3 A blessing, benediction.-4 An auspicious object. -5 An auspicious occasion, event, ceremony, or rite. -6 Any ancient custom. -7 Turmeric. -लः*m.* The planet Mars.-Comp. —अक्षताः (*m. pl.*) Rice thrown over persons by Brâhmanas when pronouncing blessings.-अष्टकं *n.* A benedictory verse or verses repeated by priests over the bride and bridegroom to promote their good luck. —आह्निकं *n.* A daily rite performed for good luck. —आचरणं *n.* 1 An auspicious introduction in the form of a prayer at the beginning of any undertaking or of any work of composition. -2 Pronouncing a blessing. —आचारः *m.* 1 An auspicious ceremony. -2 A benediction. —आरंभः *m.* An epithet of Ganesa. —आलंभनं *n.* Touching anything auspicious. —आलयः, —आवासः *m.* A temple. —करणं *n.* Reciting a prayer for the success of any undertaking.

—घट: *m.*, —पात्रं *n.* A pot filled with water offered to the Gods on festive occasions —छाय: *m.* The *plaksha* tree. —देवता *f.* A tutelary deity. -प्रतिसर: *m.*, -सूत्रं *n.* The auspicious thread worn by a married woman round her neck as long as her husband lives.-2The cord of an amulet. —प्रस्थ: *m.* N. of a mountain. —वार:, —वासर: *m.* Tuesday. —सूत्रं *n.* The marriage string worn by married women.—स्नानं *n.* Solemn or auspicious ablution.

मंगलीय *a.* (*f.* -या) Auspicious; fortunate.

मंगल्य *a.* (*f.* —ल्या) 1 Auspicious, lucky, prosperous. -2 Pleasing, beautiful. -3 Holy; pure. —ल्य: *m.* 1 The sacred fig tree. -2 The cocoanut tree. -3 A sort of pulse.-4 The Bilva tree. —ल्या *f.* 1 A species of fragrant sandal.-2 N. of Durgá.-3 A kind of aloe-wood. -4 A particular perfume. -5 A particular yellow pigment. -ल्यं *n.* 1 Auspicious water for the coronation of a king (brought from various holy places). -2 Sandal-wood.-3 Red lead. -4 Sour curds.

मंगल्यक: *m.* A kind of pulse (मसूर).

मचर्चिका *f.* A word used at the end of a noun to denote ' excellence ' or ' the best of its kind ' ; as गोमचर्चिका *f.* 'An excellent cow or bull'.

मच्छ: *m.* A fish.

मज्जन *m.*1 The marrow of the bones and flesh. -2 The pith of plants. -Comp. —कृत *n.* A bone. —समुद्भव: *m.* Semen virile.

मज्जनं *n.*1 Sinking,plunging,immersion. -2 Deluging. -3 Bathing, ablution. -4 Drowning. -5 The marrow of the bones and flesh.

मज्जा *f.*1 The marrow of the bones and flesh. -2 The pith of plants. -Comp. —जं *n.* Semen virile. —रजस् *n.* A particular hell. -रस: *m.* Semen virile. —सार: *m.* A nutmeg.

मञ्जूषा *f.* See मंजूषा.

मंच: *m.* 1 A bed-stead.-2 A raised seat, a *dais*.-3 An elevated shed in a field (for a watch-man).-4 A pulpit. -5 A stage, platform.

मंचकं *n.*, —क: *m.* 1 A sofa. -2 A raised seat or platform.-3 A stand for holding fire. -Comp. —आश्रय: *m.* A bug.

मंचिका *f.* 1 A chair.-2 A trough, tray.

मंजरं *n.* 1 A cluster of blossoms. -2 A pearl. -3 The plant Tilaka.

मंजरि:, -री *f.* 1 A shoot, sprout. -2 A cluster of blossoms.-3 A flower-stalk. -4 A line or row.-5 A pearl. -6 A creeper. -7 The holy basil. -8 The plant *Tilaka*. -Comp. —चामरं *n.* A fan-like sprout. —नम्र: *m.* The plant called वेतस.

मंजा *f.* 1 A she-goat. -2 A cluster of blossoms. -3 A creeper.

मंजि:,-जी *f.*1 A cluster of blossoms. -2 A creeper. -Comp. —फला *f.* The plantain tree.

मंजिका *f.* A prostitute, courtezan.

मंजिमन् *m* Beauty, loveliness.

मंजिष्ठा *f.* Bengal or Indian madder. -Comp. —राग: *m.* 1 The colour of the Indian madder. -2 (Fig.) Attachment as durable as the colour of the madder *i. e.* durable or permanent attachment.

मंजीर: *m.*,-रं *n.* An anklet or ornament for the foot. -रं *n.* A post round which the string of the churning-stick passes.

मंजील: *m.* 1 A village mostly inhabited by washermen.-2 An anklet.

मंजु *a.* 1 Lovely, beautiful, pleasing. -Comp. —कोशिन् *m.* An epithet of Krishna. —ममता *f.* 1 A goose. -2 A flamingo. —मर्तः *m.* N. of Nepâl. —माशी *f.* 1 An epithet of Durgá. -2 Of Sachi, wife of Indra. —पाठकः *m.* A parrot. —प्राणः *m.* An epithet of Brahman (*m.*).

मंजुल *a.* (*f.* -ला) Agreeable, charming, sweet. -लः *m.* 1 A kind of gallinule. -लं *n.* 1 An arbour, a bower. -2 A spring, well.

मंजूषा *f.* 1 A box, casket, chest. -2 A large basket. -3 Madder. -4 A stone.

मटची, मटती *f.* Hail.

मटस्फटिः *m.* Incipient pride.

मट्टकं *n.* The ridge of a roof.

मठः *m.*, -ठं *n.* 1 The hut of an ascetic. -2 A monastry. -3 A seminary, place of learning. -4 A temple. -5 A carriage drawn by oxen. -ठी *f.* 1 A cell. -2 A cloister. -Comp. —आयतनं *n.* A monastery, college.

मठर *a.* (*f.* -रा) Intoxicated, drunk.

मठिका *f.* 1 A small cell. -2 A college.

मडुः, मड्डुकः *m.* A kind of drum. [mur-

मण् 1 P. (मणति) To sound, mur-

मणिः *m.* (*f.* rarely) 1 A jewel, gem. -2 An oranment in general. -3 Anything best of its kind. -4 A magent, loadstone. -5 The wrist. -6 A water-pot. -7 Clitoris. -8 Glans penis. -9 A crystal. -10 The fleshy excrescence on the neck of a goat (The word is also written मणी in the feminine). -Comp. —इंद्रः, —राजः *m.* A diamond. —कंठः *m.* The blue jay. —कंठकः *m.* A cock. —कर्णिका, —कर्णी *f.* N. of a sacred pool in Benares. —काचः *m.* The feathered part of an arrow. —काननं *n.* The neck. —कारः *m.* A jeweller. —तारकः *m.* The crane or Sárasa bird. —दर्पणः *m.* A jewelled mirror. —द्वीपः *m.* 1 The hood of the serpent Ananta. -2 N. of an island in the ocean of nectar. —धनुः *r* , —धनुस् *n.* A rainbow. —पाली *f.* A female keeper of jewels. —पुष्पकः *m.* N. of the conch-shell of Sahadeva. -पूरः *m.* 1 The navel. -2 A kind of bodice richly adorned with jewels. (-रं *n.*) N. of a town in Kalinga. —बंधः *m.* The wrist. —बंधनं *n.* 1 String or ornament of pearls. -2 That part of a ring or bracelet where the jewels are set; a collet. -3 The wrist. —बीजः, —वीजः *m.* The pomegranate tree. —भित्तिः *f.* N. of the palace of Sesha. —मंडपः *m.* N. of the residence of Sesha. —मंथं *n.* Rock-salt. —माला *f.* 1 A string or necklace of jewels. -2 Splendour, beauty. -3 A circular impression left by a bite (in amorous sports). -4 N. of Lakshmî. -5 N. of a metre —यष्टिः *m.*, *f.* A jewelled stick. —रत्नं *n.* A jewel, gem. -रागः *m.* The colour of jewels. (-गं *n.*) Vermilion. —सरः *m.* A necklace.

माणिकः *m.*, -कं *n.* 1 A water-jar. -कः *m.* 1 A crystal palace. -2 A jewel.

माणितं *n.* An inarticulate murmuring sound uttered at cohabitation.

माणिमत् *m.* 1 The sun. -2 N. of a mountain. -3 N. of a place of pilgrimage. [moon-stone.

मणिचकः *m.* A king fisher. -कं *n.* The

मणिवकं *n.* A flower.

मंठः *m.* A kind of sweet-meat.

मंडः *m.*, -डं *n.* 1 The scum forming on the surface of any liquid. -2 The scum of boiled rice. -3 Cream (of milk). -4 Foam, scum in general. -5 Ferment. -6 Gruel. -7 Pith, essence. -8 The head. -9 The spirituous part of wine. —डः *m.* 1 An ornament. -2 A frog. -3 The castor-oil tree. —डा *f.* 1 Spirituous liquor. -2 The emblic myrobalan tree. -Comp. —डदर्कं *n.* 1 Decorating walls, floors &c. on festive occasions. -2 Mental excitement. -हारकः *m.* A distiller of spirits.

मंडकः *m.* A kind of baked flour.

मंडनं *n.* 1 Act of ornamenting. -2 An ornament. —नः (or मंडनमिश्रः) *m.* N. of a philosopher who was defeated in controversy by Sankarâchârya.

मंडपः *m.* 1 A temporary hall erected on ceremonial occasions. -2 A tent, pavilion. 3 An arbour, a bower. -4 A building consecrated to a deity.

मंडयंतः *m* 1 An ornament, a decoration. -2 An actor. -3 Food. -4 An assembly of women. —ती *f.* A woman.

मंडलः *m.* 1 A circular array of troops -2 A dog. -3 A kind of snake. -लं *n.* 1 A globe, wheel, ring, circumference. -2 The disc of the sun or moon. -3 The halo round the sun or moon. -4 The orbit of a heavenly body. -5 A multitude, assemblage, company. -6 An association. -7 The visible horizon. -8 A district or province. -9 (In politics) The circle of a kings's near and distant neighbours. -10 A particular position of the feet in shooting. -11 A kind of mystical diagram used in invoking a divinity. -12 A division of the Rigveda (the whole collection being divided into ten Mandalas or eight Ashtakas). -13 A kind of leprosy with round spots. -14 A kind of perfume. —ली *f.* 1 A circle, orb. -2 A group, assemblage. -3 Circular motion. -Comp. —अग्रः *m.* A bent sword, scimitar. —आधिपः, —अधीशः, —ईशः, -ईश्वरः *m.* 1 The ruler or governor of a district or province. -2 A king, sovereign. —कार्मुक *a.* Having a circular bow. —न्यासः *m.* The drawing of circle. —पुच्छकः *m.* A kind of insect. —वटः *m.* A fig-tree forming a circle. —वर्तिन *m.* The ruler of a small province. -वर्षः *m.* The rain over the whole of a territory; general rain-fall.

मंडलकं *n.* 1 A circle. -2 A disc. -3 A district, province. -4 A collection. -5 A circular array of troops. -6 White leprosy with round spots. -7 A mirror. —कः *m.* A dog.

मंडलायित *a.* (*f.* -ता) Round, circular. —तं *n.* A ball, globe.

मंडलित *a.* (*f.* -ता) Rounded, made round.

मंडलिन *a.* (*f.* —नी) 1 Forming a circle, made up into a coil. -2 Ruling a country. —*m.* 1 A particular kind of snake. -2 A snake in general. -3 A cat. -4 The pole-cat. -5 A dog. -6 The sun. -7 The fig-tree. -8 The ruler of a province.

मंडलीकः *m.* A tributary king.

मंडित *p. p.* (*f.* —ता) Adorned.

मंडूकः *m.* A frog. -कं *n.* A kind of coitus. —की *f.* 1 A female frog. -2 A wanton woman. -Comp. —अनुवृत्तिः, -प्लुतिः *f.* Skipping over any portion or omitting it. —योगः *m.* A kind of abstract meditation in which the person who meditates sits motionless like a frog.

मंडूरं *n.* Rust of iron used as a medicine.

मत *p. p.* (*f.* -ता) 1 Thought, supposed. -2 Considered, regarded, deemed. -3 Honoured, respected

-4 Commended, valued. -5 Conjectured.-6 Meditated upon, perceived, recognised. -7 Thought out. -8 Intended, aimed at. -9 Approved. -10 Hoped for. -11 Known, understood. -तं *n.* 1 A thought, opinion, idea, belief, view. -2 Doctrine, creed, religious belief. -3 Counsel, advice. -4 Intention, purpose. -5 Approbation, commendation. -Comp. —अक्ष *a.* Skilled in dice. —अंतरं *n.* 1 A different view -2 A different creed. —अवलंबनं *n.* The holding of a particular opinion.

मतंगः *m.* 1 An elephant.-2 A cloud. -3 N. of a sage.

मतंगजः *m.* An elephant.

मताल्लिका *f.* A word used at the end of a compound to denote anything best of its kind'; *e.g.* गोमताल्लिका *f.* 'An excellent cow.'

मतल्ली *f.* See मताल्लिका.

मतिः *f.* 1 Intellect, understanding, knowledge, judgment. -2 Mind, heart. -3 Belief, opinion, notion, impression, view.-4 Intention, purpose. -5 Resolution, determination. -6 Esteem, respect. -7 Wish, desire. -8 Counsel, advice. -9 Remembrance, recollection. (मतिं कृ, -धा, -आधा 'To set the heart on', 'resolve upon', 'think of'. मत्या Is used adverbially in the sense of 1 Knowingly; intentionally, wilfully. -2 Under the impression that; व्याघ्रमत्या पलायंते).-Comp.-ईश्वरः *m.* An epithet of Visvakarman.—गर्भ *a.* Intelligent, clever.-द्वैधं *n.* Difference of opinion. —निश्चयः *m.* A firm conviction. —पूर्व, —पूर्वकं *ind.* Purposely, intentionally. —प्रकर्षः *m.* Superiority of intellect; cleverness. -भेदः *m.* A change of opinion. —भ्रमः,—विपर्यासः *m.* 1 Delusion, confusion of mind. -2 An error, a mistake, misapprehension. —विभ्रमः,—विभ्रंशः *m.* Madness, frenzy.

मतिमत् *a.* (*f.* -ती) Clever, intelligent.

मत्क *a.* (*f.* -त्का) My, mine. —त्कः *m.* A bug.

मत्कुणः *m.* 1 A bug. -2 An elephant without tusks.-3 A small elephant. -4 A beardless man. -5 A buffalo. -6 The cocoa-nut tree. —णं *n.* An armour for the legs or the thighs. -Comp. —अरिः *m.* Hemp.

मत्त *p. p.* (*f.* -त्ता) 1 Intoxicated, drunk, inebriated (fig. also). -2 Mad, insane. -3 In rut, furious (as an elephant). -4 Proud, arrogant. -5 Delighted, over-joyed. -6 Amorous, wanton.-त्तः *m.* 1 A drunkard. -2 A mad man. -3 An elephant in rut.-4 A cuckoo.-5 A buffalo. -6 The thorn-apple or Dhattūra plant.-त्ता *f.* Spirituous or vinous liquor. -Comp. —आलंबः *m.* A fence round a mansion. —काशि (-सि-) नी *f.* A handsome and very fascinating woman. —कीशः *m.* An elephant. -वारणः *m.*, -वारणं *n.* 1 A fence round a large building or mansion. -2 A small room on the top of a large building. -3 A veranda. -4 A pavilion. —वारणं *n.* Pounded betel-nuts.

मत्यं *n.* 1 A harrow.-2 The means of acquiring knowledge. -3 The exercise of knowledge.

मत्सः *m.* 1 A fish. -2 A king of the Matsyas.

मत्सर *a.* (*f.* —रा) 1 Jealous, envious. -2 Greedy, covetous. -3 Niggardly. -4 Wicked. -5 Selfish. -रः *m.* 1 Envy, jealousy. -2 Hostility, enmity. -3 Pride. -4 Greediness.-5

Anger, passion. -6 The Soma. -रः *m.*, -रा *f.* A gnat.

मत्सरिन् *a.* (*f.* -णी) 1 Envious, jealous. -2 Hostile, inimical.-3 Selfishly addicted to (with loc.). -4 Wicked.

मत्स्यः *m.* 1 A fish. -2 A particular variety of fish. -3 A king of the Matsyas. —त्स्यौ *m dual* The sign *Pisces* of the zodiac. —त्स्याः *m. pl.* N. of a country and its inhabitants; the country of Viráta. -Comp. -अवतारः *m.* The first of the ten incarnations of Vishnu. -असुरः *m.* N. of a demon. —आधानी, —धानी *f.* A fish-basket (used by fishermen). —उदरिन् *m.* An epithet of Viráta. -उदरी *f.* An epithet of Satyavatî. उदरीयः *m.* An epithet of Vyása. —उपजीविन्, —आजीवः *m.* A fisherman. —गंधा *f.* N. of Satyavatî. —घंटः *m.* A kind of fish-sauce. —घातिन्, -जीवत्, --जीविन् *m.* A fisherman. —द्वादशी *f.* N. of the twelfth day in the month of मार्गशीर्ष. -नारी *f.* An epithet of Satyavatî. -नाशकः, -नाशनः *m.* An osprey. -पुराणं *n.* N. of one of the eighteen Purâ-nas. —बंधः, -बंधिन् *m.* A fisherman. —बंधनं *n.* A fish-hook, an angle. -बंधा(-धि.)नी *f.* A fish-basket. -रंकः,-रंगः -रंगकः *m.* A halcyon, king-fisher.-राजः *m.* 1 The Rohita fish. -2 N. of Viràta. -वेधनं *n.*, -वेधनी *f.* The angle. —वेधनी *f.* A cormorant. —संघातः *m.* A shoal of fish.

मत्स्यंडिका, मत्स्यंडी *f.* Coarse or unrefined sugar.

मथ् See मंथ्.

मथः = माथः q. v.

मथन *a.* (*f.* -नी) 1 Churning, stirring up. -2 Hurting, injuring. -3 Killing, destroying, a destroyer.-4 Rubbing. -नः *m.* N. of a tree used in producing fire by attrition. —नं *n.* 1 Churning, agitating. -2 Rubbing, friction. -3 Injury, hurting, destruction. -Comp. —अचलः, —पर्वतः *m.* A N. of the mountain Mandara.

माथिः *m.* A churning-stick.

मथित *p. p.* (*f.* -ता) 1 Churned, stirred round, shaken about. -2 Ground, pinched. -3 Distressed, oppressed. -4 Killed, destroyed. -5 Dislocated. —तं *n.* Pure butter-milk (without water).

मथिन् *m.* (Nom. sing. मंथाः, acc.pl. मथः) 1 A churning-stick. -2 Wind. -3 A thunderbolt. -4 The penis.

मथु (-थू-) रा *f.* N. of an ancient city on the right bank of the Yamuná. -Comp. -ईशः, —नाथः *m.* Epithets of Krishna.

मद् A form of the first personal pronoun in the singular number used at the beginning of comps.; as मदर्थे 'for me,' 'for my sake'; मत्सादृश्यं 'my likeness'.

मद् 4 P. (माद्यति, मत्त) 1 To be drunk or intoxicated. -2 To be mad. -3 To delight in. -4 To be glad or rejoiced. With उद्— 1 To be intoxicated (used figuratively also).-2 To be mad. प्र- 1 To be intoxicated.-2 To be careless about, to be negligent (generally with a loc.).-3 To swerve from (with abl.). -4 To err, to go wrong. सम्— 1 To be glad. -2 To be intoxicated.

मद् 10 A. (मादयते) To please, gratify.

मद् 1 P. (मदति) 1 To be proud.-2 To be poor.

मदः *m.* 1 Intoxication, drunkenness. -2 Madness, insanity.-3 Lustful passion, lasciviousness.-4 Rut, ichor, (which exudes from the temples of an elephant in rut). -5 Love, desire, ardour. -6 Pride, arrogance. -7 Excessive delight. -8 Spirituous liquor. -9 Honey. -10 Musk. -11 Semen virile. -12 Soma. -13 Any beautiful object. -14 A river (नद). —दी *f.* 1 A drinking-cup. -2 Any agricultural implement (such as a plough &c.). -Comp. —अत्ययः, —आतंकः *m.* A disorder resulting from drunkenness. —अंध *a.* 1 Blind through intoxication or passion. -अंबरः *m.* 1 An elephant in rut. -2 N. of Airâvata, the elephant of Indra. —आढ्यः *m.* The palm tree. —आम्नातः *m.* A kettle-drum carried on the back of an elephant. —आलापिन् *m.* A cuckoo.—आह्वः *m.* Musk. —उत्कटः *m.* 1 An elephant in rut. -2 A dove. —उत्कटा *f.* Spirituous liquor. —उल्लापिन् *m.* The cuckoo. —कटः *m.* A eunuch. -कल *a.* Speaking softly or inarticulately, speaking indistinctly. -2 Uttering low sounds of love. -3 Drunk with passion. -4 Indistinct yet sweet.-5 Ruttish, furious. -6 Furious, mad. (-लः *m.*) An elephant in rut.-कोहलः *m.* A bull set at liberty (to roam at will). —गंधा *f.* 1 An intoxicating drink. -2 Hemp. —गमनः *m.* A buffalo. —च्युत् *a.* 1 Distilling rut (as an elephant). -2 Lustful, wanton, drunk. -3 Exhilarating. (-*m.*) An epithet of Indra.—च्युतौ *m. dual* An epithet of the Asvins. —द्विपः *m.* A furious elephant, an elephant in rut.—रक्त *a.* Affected with passion. —रागः *m.* 1 Cupid. -2 A cock. -3 A drunkard. —विक्षिप्त *a.* 1 In rut, furious. -2 Agitated by lust or passion. -वृंदः *m.* An elephant.—शौंडकं *n.* Nutmeg. —सारः *m.* The cotton shrub. —स्थलं, —स्थानं *n.* An ale-house, a tavern.

मदन *a.* (*f.* —नी) 1 Intoxicating, maddening. -2 Delighting, exhilarating. -नः *m.* 1 The God of love, Cupid. -2 Love, sexual love, lust. -3 The spring season. -4 A bee. -5 Bees'-wax. -6 A kind of embrace. -7 The Dhattúra plant.-8 The Khadira tree. -9 The Bakula tree. —ना, -नी *f.* 1 Spirituous liquor. -2 Musk, -3 The *atimukta* creeper.(-नी only in these two senses).-नं *n.* 1 Intoxicating. -2 Delighting. -Comp. -अग्रकः *m.* A species of grain (कोद्रव).-अंकुशः *m.* 1 The penis. -2 A wound made by a nail in cohabitation. -अंतकः, —अरिः, —दमनः, —दहनः, —नाशनः, —रिपुः *m.* Epithets of Siva. —आयुधं *n.* 1 Pudendum muliebre. -2 A very lovely woman.—आलयः *m.*,-यं *n.* 1 Pudendum muliebre. -2 A lotus. -3 A king.-इच्छाफलं *n.* A kind of mango. —उत्सवः *m.* The vernal festival held in honour of Cupid. —उत्सवा *f.* An *apsaras.* —कंटकः *m.* Horripilation caused by the feeling of love. -काकुरवः *m.* A dove or pigeon. —गृहं *n.* Pudendum muliebre. —गोपालः *m.* An epithet of Krishna. —चतुर्दशी *f.* The fourteenth day in the bright half of Chaitra, or the festival celebrated on that day in honour of Cupid. —त्रयोदशी *f.* The thirteenth day in the bright half of Chaitra, or the festival celebrated on that day in honour of Cupid. -नालिका *f.* A faithless wife.-पक्षिन् *m.* The Khanjana brid. —पाठकः *m.* The Indian cuckoo.—पीडा,-बाधा *f.* Pangs or torments of love. —महोत्सवः *m.* A festival in honour of Cupid.-मोहनः *m.* An epithet of Krishna. -ललितं *n.* Amorous sport or dalliance. —लेखः *m.* A love-letter. —शलाका *f.* 1 The female of the Indian cuckoo. -2 An aphrodisiac.

मदनकः *m.* N. of a plant (दमनक).

मदयंतिका, मदयंती *f.* A kind of jasmine (Arabian).

मदयित्नु *a.* Intoxicating, maddening. -2 Gladdening. —त्नुः *m.* 1 The God of love. -2 A cloud. -3 A distiller of spirituous liquors. -4 A drunken man. -5 Spirituous liquor (*n.* also in this sense).

मदारः *m.* 1 An elephant in rut. -2 A hog. -3 A thorn-apple or Dhattúra. -4 A lover, libertine. -5 A kind of perfume -6 A cheat.

मदिः *f.* A kind of harrow.

मदिर *a.* (*f.* -रा) 1 Intoxicating, maddening.-2 Delighting,gladdening. —रः *m.* A kind of Khadira tree. -Comp. —अक्षी, —ईक्षणा, —नयना, —लोचना *f.* A woman with fascinating or bewitching eyes.

मदिरा *f.* 1 Spirituous liquor. -2 A kind of wag-tail. -3 N. of Durgâ. -Comp —सखः *m.* The mango tree.

मदिष्ठा *f.* Spirituous liquor.

मदीय *a.* (*f.* -या) My,mine, belonging to me.

मद्गुः *m.* 1 A kind of aquatic bird,a cormorant or diver. -2 A kind of snake.-3 A kind of wild animal.-4 A kind of war-vessel.-5 N. of a degraded mixed tribe ; the offspring of a Brâhmana by a woman of the bard class. -6 An outcast.

मद्गुरः *m* 1 A diver, pearl-fisher. -2 A kind of sheat-fish. -3 N. of a degraded mixed tribe.

मद्य *a.* (*f.* -द्या) 1 Intoxicating. -2 Gladdening. —द्यं *n.* Any intoxicating drink. -Comp. —आमोदः *m.* The *Bakula* tree. —कीटः *m.* A kind of insect. —द्रुमः *m.* A kind of tree (माडवृक्ष). —पः *m.* A drunkard. —पुष्पा *f.* The plant called Dhâtakî. -बी(-बी-)जं *n.* Drug used to cause fermentation, leaven. —मंडः *m.* Yeast. -संधानं *n.* Distillation of spirit.

मद्रः *m.* 1 N. of a country. -2 A ruler of that country.-द्राः*m. pl.* The inhabitants of Madra. —द्रं *n.* Joy, happiness (मद्राकृ To shave or shear). -Comp. —कार *a.* (Also मद्रंकार) Producing delight.

मद्रकः *n* . A ruler or inhabitant of Madra. —काः *m. pl.* N. of a degraded tribe in the south.

मधव्यः *m.* The month Vaisákha.

मधु *a.* (-धु or -ध्वी *f*) Sweet,agreeable, delightful. —धु *n.* 1 Honey. -2 The juice or nectar of flowers. -3 Spirituous liquor. -4 Water. -5 Sugar. -6 Sweetness. -7 Anything sweet. —धुः *m.* 1 The spring or vernal season. -2 The month of Chaitra. -3 N. of a demon killed by Vishnu. -4 N. of another demon, father of Râvana and killed by Satrughna. -5 The Asoka tree. -6 N. of king Kártavîrya. -Comp. —अष्ठीला *f.* A lump of honey. -आधारः *m.* Wax. —आपात *a* Having honey at the first taste. —आम्रः *m.* A kind of mango tree. —आलु, —अलुकं *n.* Sweet potato. —आवासः *m.* The mango tree. -आसवः *m.* Sweet spirituous liquor (made from honey). —आहुतिः *f.* A sacrificial offering of sweet things. —उच्छिष्टं, —उत्थं, —उत्थितं *n.* Bees'-wax. —उत्सवः *m.* The spring or vernal festival. —उदकं *n.* Water mixed with honey,hydromel. —उद्यानं *n.* A spring-garden. —उपघ्नं *n.* An epithet of Mathurâ. —कंठः *m.* The Indian cuckoo. -करः *m.* 1 A large black bee. -2 A lover, liber-

change or transform into. -12 To devote oneself to. With उद्— To produce. वि— 1 To contemplate, to think of. -2 To see, perceive. -3 To decide. सम्— 1 To consider. -2 To establish. -3 To conjecture. -4 To honour. -5 To ascribe to.

भू 1 U. (भवति,-ते To get, obtain.

भू 10 A. (भावयते) To obtain, gain.

भू 1 U. (भावयति,-ते) 1 To think, reflect. -2 To mix, mingle. -3 To be purified.

भू a. (At the end of comp.) Being, existing, springing from, arising from, as in चित्तभू, आत्मभू, कमलभू, मनोभू &c.-*m.* 1An epithet of Vishnu. -2The sacrificial fire.

भूः *f.*1 The earth. -2 The universe, globe. -3 Ground, floor as in मणिभयभुवः (प्रासादाः).-4 Land, landed property. -5 A place, plot of ground. -6 Matter, subject-matter. -7A symbolical expression for the number ' one '. -8 The base of a geometrical figure. -9 A sacrificial fire. -10 The first of the three Vyâhritis or mystic syllables (representing the earth) repeated by every Bráhmana at the commencement of his daily Sandhyâ.-Comp. —उत्तमं *n.* Gold. —कदंबः *m.* A species of Kadamba tree.-कंपः *m.* An earthquake. —कर्णः *m.* The diameter of the earth. —कश्यपः *m.* An epithet of Vasudeva, Krishna's father. —काकः *m.* 1 A kind of heron. -2 The curlew. -3 A kind of pigeon. —केशः *m.* The Indian fig-tree. -केशा *f.* A female demon. —क्षित *m.* A hog. —गं *n.* A particular poison. —गर्भः *m.* 1 N. of Vishnu. -2 An epithet of Bhavabhúti. -गृहं, —गेहं *n.* A cellar, a room under-ground. —गोलः *m.* The terrestrial globe. -गोलविद्या *f.* Geography. -घनः *m.* The body. —चक्रं *n.* The equator. —चरः *m.* The land-animal (opp जलचर). -2 An epithet of Siva. —चर्या, -छाया, *f.*, -छायं *n.* 1 Earth's shadow (vulgarly called Ràhu). -2 Darkness. -जंतुः *m.* An elephant. -जंबुः,—बूः *f.* Wheat. —तृणः, -भूस्तृणः *m.* A kind of fragrant grass. —दारः *m.* A hog. —देवः, —सुरः *m.* A Bráhmana. -धनः *m.* A king. —धरः *m.* 1 A mountain. -2 An epithet of Siva. -3 Of Krishna. -4 The number 'seven'. —ध्रः *m.* A mountain. —नागः *m.* A kind of earth-worm. -नेतृ *m.*A sovereign, ruler, king. -पः *m.* A sovereign, king. —पतिः *m.* 1 A king. -2 An epithet of Siva. -3 Of Indra. —पदः*m.* A tree. -पदी *f.* A kind of jasmine. —परिधिः *m.* The circumference of the earth.-पवित्रं*n.*Cow-dung. —पालः *m.* 1 A king, sovereign. -2 An epithet of king Bhoja. -पुत्रः,-सुतः *m.* 1 The planet Mars. -2 N. of the demon Naraka. —पुत्री, -सुता *f.* An epithet of Siva. -प्रकंपः *m.* An earth-quake. —प्रदानं *n.* A gift of land. —बिंबः *m.*, —बिं *n.* The terrestrial globe. —भर्तृ *m.* A king. —भागः *m.* A region, place, spot. —भुज् *m.* 1 A mountain. -2 A king, sovereign. -3 An epithet of Vishnu. —मंडलं*n.* 1 The earth, the terrestrial globe. -2 The circumference of the earth. —रुह्, -रुहः *m.* A tree. —लोकः (भूर्लोकः) *m.* 1 The terrestrial globe.-2 The country on the southern part of the equator. —वल्लभः *m.* A king, sovereign. —वृत्तं *n.* The equator. —शक्रः *m.* A king, sovereign. —शयः *m.* 1 An epithet of Vishnu. -2 Any animal

tine. (-री *f.*) A female bee. -कर्कटी *f.* 1 Sweet lime, a kind of citron. -2 A kind of date. —कारः, -कारिन् *m.* A bee. —कुक्कुटिका, -कुक्कुटी *f.* A sort of citron tree. —कुल्या *f.* A stream of honey. —कृत् *m.* A bee. —केशटः *m.* A bee. —कोशः, -षः *m.* 1 A bee-hive. -2 A honey-comb. —क्रमः *m.* 1 A bee-hive. -2 A honey-comb. —क्रमाः *m. pl.* Carousals. —क्षीरः, -क्षीरकः *m.* The Kharjûra tree. —गायनः *m.* The cuckoo. —ग्रहः *m.* A libation of honey. —घोषः *m.* The Indian cuckoo. -जं *n.* Bees'-wax. -जा *f.* 1 Sugar-candy. -2 The earth. -जंबीरः *m.* A kind of citron. -जित्, -द्विष्, -निषूदनः,-निहंतृ, -मथः, -मथनः, -रिपुः, -शत्रुः, —सूदनः *m.* Epithets of Vishnu. —तृणः *m.*, -णं *n.* Sugar-cane. -त्रयं *n.* The three sweet things *i. e.* sugar, honey and clarified butter. —दीपः *m.* The God of love. —दूतः *m.* The mango tree. -दोहः *m.* The extracting of honey. -द्रः *m.* 1 A bee. -2 A libertine. -द्रुमः *m.* The mango tree. -धातुः*m.* A kind of yellow pyrites. —धूलिः *f.* Molasses. —नालिकेरकः *m.* A kind of cocoa-nut. —नेतृ *m.* A bee. —पः *m.* 1 A bee. -2 A drunkard. —पटलं *n.* A bee-hive. —पतिः *m.* An epithet of Krishna. -पर्कः *m.* 1 A respectful offering made to a guest or to the bridegroom on his arrival at the door of the father of the bride.-2 The ceremony of receiving a guest. -पर्क्य *a.* Worthy of *madhuparka*. -पर्णिका, —पर्णी *f.* The Indigo plant. -पायिन् *m.* A bee. -पुरं *n.*, -री *f.* An epithet of Mathurâ -पुष्पः *m.* 1 The Asoka tree. -2 The Bakula tree. -3 The Dantî tree.-4The Sirîsha tree.-प्रमेहः *m.* Diabetes, saccharine urine. —प्राशनं *n.* One of the sixteen purificatory Samskâras (which consists in putting a little honey into the mouth of a new-born male child). —प्रियः *m.* An epithet of Balaráma. -फलः *m.*A kind of cocoa-nut. -फलिका *f.* A kind of date —बहुला *f.* The Mâdhavî creeper. -बी (-वी-) जः *m.* A pomegranate tree. -बी(-वी-) जपूरः *m.* A kind of citron. —मक्षः *m.*, -क्षा, —मक्षिका *f.* A bee. -मज्जनः *m.* The tree called आखोट. -मल्लिः, -ल्ली *f.* The Málatî creeper. -माधवी *f.* 1 A kind of intoxicating drink. -2 Any spring-flower. -माध्वीकं *n.* A kind of intoxicating liquor. -मारकः *m.* A bee. -मेहः *m.* See मधुप्रमेह. -यष्टिः, -ष्टी *f.* Sugar-cane. -रसः *m.* 1 The wine palm. -2 Sugar-cane.-3 Sweetness. (-सा *f.*) 1 A bunch of grapes. -2 Vine. -लग्नः *m.* N. of a tree. -लिह्, -लेह्, लेहिन्, -लोलुपः *m.* A bee.—वनं *n.* 1 N. of the forest inhabited by the demon Madhu. -2 N. of the forest of Sugrîva. (-नः *m.*) The cuckoo. -वाराः *m. pl.* Drinking often and often;carousing. -व्रतः *m.* A bee. -शर्करा *f.* Honey-sugar. -शाखः *m.* A kind of tree.-शिष्टं, -शेषं *n.*Wax.-सखः, -सहायः,-सारथिः,-सुहृद् *m.* The God of love. -सिक्थकः *m.* A kind of poison. -सूदनः *m.* 1 A bee. -2 An epithet of Vishnu. —स्थानं *n.* A bee-hive. -स्रवा *f.* 1 Liquorice. -2 N. of the third day in the bright half of Srâvana. —स्वरः *m.* The cuckoo. —हन् *m.* 1 A destroyer or collector of honey. -2 A kind of bird of prey. -3 A sooth-sayer. -4 An epithet of Vishnu.

मधुकः *m.* 1 N. of a tree (= मधूक). -2 The Asoka tree. -3 A kind of bird. -4 The liquorice-root. —कं *n.* 1 Tin. -2 Liquorice.

मधुमत *a.* (*f.* —ती) 1 Sweet. -2 Pleasant, agreeable. -3 Mixed with honey ; honied. -4 Rich in honey (as a flower).

मधुर *a.* (*f.* —रा) 1 Sweet. -2 Honied, mellifluous. -3 Pleasant, agreeable. -4 Melodious (as a sound). —रः *m.* 1 The red sugar-cane. -2 Rice. -3 A kind of sugar, molasses (गुड).-4 A kind of mango. -5 Cumin-seed. —रा *f.* 1 Liquorice. -2 Sour rice-water.-3 N. of the city Mathurà. —री *f.* A kind of musical instrument. —रं *n.* 1 Sweetness. -2 A sweet drink, syrup. -3 Poison. -4 Tin. -रं *ind.* Sweetly, agreeably. -Comp. —अम्लकः *m.* The hog-plum. —त्रयं *n.* See मधुत्रयं. —फलः *m.* A sort of jujube tree (राजबदर). —स्रवा *f.* A kind of date tree.

मधुरिमन् *m.* Sweetness, agreeableness.

मधूलं *n.* An intoxicating drink, spirituous liquor.

मधुलिका *f.* Black mustard.

मधूकः *m.* 1 A bee. -2 N. of a tree. —कं *n.* 1 A flower of the Madhúka tree. -3 Liquorice.

मधूलिका *f.* A kind of tree.

मध्य *a.* (*f.* —ध्या) 1 Middle, central. -2 Intervening, intermediate. -3 Moderate, modiocre. -4 Neutral, impartial. -5 Just, right. -6 Mean (in astr.). —ध्यः *m.*, —ध्यं *n.* 1 The middle, centre, middle or central part. -2 The middle of the body, the waist. -3 The belly, abdomen. -4 The interior of anything. -5 A middle state or condition. -6 The flank of a horse. -7 Mean time in music. -8 The middle term of a progression. -9 Cessation, pause, interval. —ध्या *f.* 1 The middle finger. -2 A young woman, one arrived at puberty. —ध्यं *n.* Ten thousand billions. (The *acc.sing.* मध्यं is used as an *adv.* to signify 'into the midst of,"into.'The *instr.sing.* मध्येन signifies 'through'or 'between.' The *abl. sing.* मध्यात्signifies'out of,'from among, 'from the midst' (with gen.) as in तेषां मध्यात् काकः प्रोवाच. The *loc.sing.* मध्ये signifies 'in the middle,' 'between','among,'in the midst','in,"into', 'within,' 'inside.' मध्ये*loc. sing.* stands as the first member of adverbial compounds ; *e.g.*मध्येगंगं Into the Ganges. मध्येनगरं Inside the city).

-Comp. -अंगुलिः, -ली *f.* The middle finger.—अह्नः (for अहन्) *m.* Mid-day, noon. —कर्णः *m.* A radius. —गत *a.* Middle, being in the middle. —गंधः *m.* The mango tree. —दिनं (also मध्यंदिनं) *n* 1 Midday,noon. -2A midday offering. —दीपकं *n.* A variety of the figure called Dípaka, in which the common attribute that throws light on the whole description is placed in the middle. -देशः *m.* 1 The middle part of anything. -2 The waist. -3 The belly. -4The meridian -5 The country lying between theHimâlaya and Vindhya mountains. -देहः *m.* The trunk of the body ; the belly. —पद्लोपिन् *m.* See मध्यमपदलोपिन्. —पातः *m.* 1 Comunion, intercourse. -2 (in astr.) The mean occurrence of the aspect. —भागः *m.* 1 The middle part. -2 The waist. —भावः *m.* Mediocrity. —यवः *m.* A weight of six white mustard-seeds. -रात्रः *m.*, -रात्रिः *f.* Midnight.-रेखा *f.* The first meridian. -लोकः *m.* The earth or world of mortals. —वर्तिन् *m.* An arbitrator, a mediator. -वृत्तं *n.* The navel. -सूत्रं *n.* The central meridian. —स्थः *m.* 1 An umpire, arbitrator, a mediator. -2 An epithet of Siva. —स्थलं *n.* 1 The middle or centre. -2 The middle space or region. -3 The waist. -4 The hip. —स्थानं n. A neutral region.

मध्यतस् *ind.* 1 From the middle or midst, out of. -2 Among, between.

मध्यंदिन *a.* 1 Middle, central. -2 Meridional, belonging to noon.

मध्यम *a.* (*f.* -मा) 1 Being or standing in the middle; middle, central. -2 Intermediate, intervening. -3 Middling, mediocre, moderate. -4 Middle-sized. -5 Impartial, neutral. -6 Mean (in astr.). -7 Belonging to the meridian. —मः *m.* 1 The fifth note in music. -2 A particular musical mode. -3 The mid-land country. -4 The second person (in grammar). -5 A neutral sovereign. -6 The governor of a province. —मा *f.* 1 The middle finger. -2 A girl arrived at the age of puberty. -3 The pericarp of a lotus. -4 One of the classes of heroines (Nâyikás) in poetic compositions. -5 A central blossom. -मं *n.* 1 The middle. -2 The waist. -Comp. -आहरणं *n.* (In alg.) The elimination of the middle term in an equation. -कक्षा *f.* The middle court-yard. -खंडं *n.* The middle term of an equation. —पदलोपिन् *m.* A subdivision of the Tatpurusha compound in which the middle word is omitted in composition *e.g.* शाकपार्थिवः which means शाकप्रियः पार्थिवः where the middle word प्रिय is omitted. -पांडवः *m.* An epithet of Arjuna. -पुरुषः *m.* The second person (in grammar). -भृतकः *m.* A cultivator (who works both for himself and for his landlord). -रात्रः *m.* Mid-night. -रेखा *f.* 1 The central meridian of the earth. -लोकः *m.* The middle world, the earth. —वयस् *n.* The middle age. —वयस्क *a.* Middle-aged. —संग्रहः *m.* Intrigue of a middling character, such as sending presents of flowers &c. to another's wife. —साहसः *m.* The second of the three penalties or modes of punishment. (-सः *m.*, -सं *n.*) An outrage or offence of the middle class.

मध्यमक *a.* (*f.* —मिका) 1 Middle, middle-most. -2 Common (property &c.).

मध्यमिका *f.* A girl arrived at puberty.

मध्ये *ind.* 1 In the middle, in the midst. -2 Within, in. Comp. —गंगं *ind.* In the Ganges. —नगरं *ind.* Inside the city. -नदि *ind.* In the middle of the river. —पृष्ठं *ind.* On the back. —भक्तं *n.* A medicine to be taken whilst eating. —सभं *ind.* In or before an assembly.

मध्वः *m.* N. of the founder of the sect of Vaishnavas and author of a Bhâshya on the Vedânta Sutras.

मध्वकः *m.* A bee.

मध्विजा *f.* Any intoxicating drink, spirituous liquor.

मन् 1 P. (मनति) 1 To be proud or arrogant. -2 To worship.

मन् 10 A. (मानयते) To be proud.

मन् 4. 8. A. (मन्यते, मनुते, मंतुं, मत) 1 To think, believe, fancy, conceive. -2 To regard, look upon, take (one) for, take to be. -3 To honour, respect, esteem, prize. -4 To know, understand, observe, have regard to. -5 To agree or consent to, act up to. -6 To think upon. -7 To wish or hope for. -8 To set the heart on. -9 To mention, declare. -10 To devise, invent. -11 To be regarded as, seem, appear like. With अनु- To permit, allow, approve of, assent to.

आभि— 1 To approve of, to like. -2 To think, to regard, to esteem. अव– To disregard, to contemn, to think lightly of. सम्– 1 To think, to regard. -2 To approve of, to like. -3 To esteem, to think highly of. -4 To allow, permit.

We give here some phrases containing मन्. बहु मन् To think highly or much of, value greatly, esteem. लघु मन् To think lightly of, despise. अन्यथा मन् To think otherwise; doubt. साधु मन् To think well of, approve, consider satisfactory. तृणाय मन् or तृणवत् मन् To value lightly, make light of. नमन् To disregard, not to mind).

-Caus. (मानयति,-ते) To honour, esteem, respect, value. With अनु– To take the permission of. प्रति— 1 To get the approval of.-2 To allow, permit, grant. वि– To disregard, to disesteem. सम्— To honour, value, to respect.

Desid. (मीमांसते) 1 To reflect upon, examine, investigate, inquire into. -2 To doubt, call in question (with loc.).

मननं *n.* 1 Thinking, reflection, meditation. -2 Intelligence, understanding. -3 Determination by reasoning. -4 A guess, conjecture.

मनस् *n.* 1 The mind, understanding, perception, intelligence.-2 (In phil.) The internal organ of perception and cognition, the instrument by which objects of sense affect the soul. -3 The faculty of discrimination or judgment.-4 Thought, idea, imagination, conception.-5 Purpose intention. -6 Desire, inclination, wish. (The words मनस् and काम are used with the infinitive form with the final म् dropped, and form adjectives meaning wishing or having a mind to do what is indicated by the root; *e. g.* प्रष्टुमनाः, प्रष्टुकामः 'Having a mind to ask'). -7 Reflection. -8 Disposition, temper. -9 Energy, mettle. -10 An epithet of the lake Mànasa. -11 Breath or living soul.

We give some idiomatic uses of मनस्. मनसा गम् or व्रज् To think of, contemplate, remember. मनः कृ To fix the mind upon (with dat. or loc.). मनो बंध् To fix the heart or affection upon. मनः समाधा To collect oneself. मनसि कृ To think, to bear in mind; to resolve, determine, think of.

-Comp.-अधिनाथः *m.* A lover, husband.-अनुग *a.* Suiting the mind, agreeable. -अभिनिवेशः *m.* Tenacity of purpose.-अभिराम *a.* Delighting the heart. —आप *a* Attractive, pleasing. -कांत *a.* (मनस्कांत or मनःकांत) Dear to the mind, agreeable. -कारः *m.* Perfect perception, full consciousness (of pleasure or pain). —क्षेपः (मनःक्षेपः) *m.* Distraction of the mind. —गत *a.* 1 Concealed in the breast, internal, inward, secret. -2 Affecting the mind, desired. (-तं *n.*) 1 A wish, desire. -2 A thought, notion, opinion. —गतिः *f.* Desire of the heart. —गवी *f.* Wish, desire.—गुप्ता *f.* Red arsenic. -ग्रहणं *n.* Captivating the mind. —ग्राहिन् *a.* Captivating or fascinating the mind.-जः,-जन्मन् *m.* The God of love.-जव *a.* 1 Quick or swift as thought. -2 Quick in thought or conception. -3 Fatherly, pateral.-जवस *a.* Resembling a father, fatherly. -जात *a.* Arisen or produced in the mind. —जिघ्र *a.* Guessing the thoughts. -ज्ञ *a.* Lovely, agreeable, charming. (-ज्ञः *m.*) N. of a Gandharva. (-ज्ञा *f.*) 1 Red arsenic. -2 An intoxicating drink.-3 A princess.—तोका *f.* An epithet of Durgâ. —दंडः *m.* Complete control over the mind or thoughts. —दत्त *a.* Mentally dedicated. —नाशः *m.* Loss of the mind or understanding; dementedness. -नीत *a.* Approved, chosen. -पतिः (मनःपति) An epithet of Vishnu.-पूत *a.* (मनःपूत) 1 Approved by one's conscience. -2 Of a pure mind, conscientious.-प्रणीत *a.* (मनःप्रणीत) Agreeable or pleasing to the mind.-प्रीतिः *f.* (मनःप्रीति) Joy, delight. -भवः,—भूः *m.* 1 The God of love, Cupid. -2 Love, passion, lust. —मथनः *m.* The God of love. —मय *a.* Mental, spiritual. —यायिन् *a.* Swift, quick as thought. -योगः *m.* Close application of the mind, close attention. —योनिः *m.* The God of love —रथः *m.* 1 A wish, desire. -2 A desired object. -3 (In dramas) A hint, a wish expressed indirectly or covertly. -रथदायकः *m.* N. of a Kalpataru. —रम *a.* Attractive, agreeable, lovely, beautiful. (-मा *f.*) 1 A lovely woman. -2 A kind of pigment. -राज्यं *n.* A castle in the air. —लयः *m.* Loss of consciousness. —विकारः *m.*, विकृतिः *f.* Emotion of the mind. —वृत्तिः *f.* 1 Volition. -2 Disposition, temper. -शिलः *m.*, -ला *f.* Red arsenic. —संगः *m.* Attachment of the mind (to any thing). —सुख *a.* Agreeable to the mind. -हत *a.* Disappointed. —हर *a.* Pleasing, attractive, lovely. (-रः *m.*) A kind of jasmine. (-रं *n.*) Gold. —हारी *f.* A unchaste or unfaithful woman.-ह्वा *f.* A red arsenic.

मनसा *f.* N. of a daughter of Kasyapa, sister of the serpent king, Ananta and wife of the sage जरत्कारु. Comp. -देवी *f.* The same as मनसा.

मनसिजः *m.* 1 The God of love. -2 Love, passion. -3 The moon.

मनसिशयः *m.* 1 The God of love. -2 The moon.

मनस्तः *ind.* From the mind or [heart.

मनस्विन् *a.* 1 Wise, intelligent, high-souled, high-minded. -2 Attentive. -3 Resolute, determined. -*m.* The fabulous animal called Sarabha. —नी *f.* 1 A high-minded or proud woman. -2 A wise or virtuous woman. -3 N. of Durgà. -4 N. of the mother of the moon.

मनाक् *ind* 1 A little, slightly, in a small degree. -2 Slowly, tardily. -3 Only, merely. -Comp. -कर *a.* Doing little. (-रं *n.*) A kind of fragant aloe-wood.

मनाका *f.* A female elephant.

मनायी (-वी) *f.* The wife of Manu.

मनोकं *n.* Collyrium, eye-salve.

मनीषा *f.* 1 Desire, wish. -2 Intelligence, understanding.-3 A thought, idea.

मनीषिका *f.* Understanding, intelli- [gence.

मनीषित *a.* (*f.* —ता) 1 Desired, liked, loved, dear. -2 Agreeable. -तं *n.* A wish, desire, desired object.

मनीषिन् *a.* (*f.* —णी) 1 Wise, learned, intelligent, prudent. -*m.* 1 A wise or learned person ; a sage.

मनुः *m.* 1 N. of a divine sage regarded as the father of the human race. -2 A term applied to the fourteen successive progenitors or sovereigns of the earth. They are:— 1 स्वायंभुव, 2 स्वारोचिष, 3 औत्तमि 4 तामस, 5 रैवत, 6 चाक्षुष, 7 वैवस्वत, 8 सावर्णि, 9 दक्षसावर्णि, 10 ब्रह्मसावर्णि, 11 धर्मसावर्णि, 12 रुद्रसावर्णि, 13 देवसावर्णि and 14 इंद्रसावर्णि. -3 The number 'fourteen'

-4 A man, mankind(opp. evil spirits). -5 A prayer, sacred text or spell (मंत्र). -नुः *f.* The wife of Manu. -Comp. —अंतरं *n.* The period or age of a *manu* (this period comprises 4,320,000 human years). —जः *m.* A man, mankind. —जा *f.* A woman. —जातः *m.* A man. -ज्येष्ठः *m.* A sword. —भूः *m.* A man, mankind. —राज् *m.* An epithet of Kubera. -श्रेष्ठः *m.* An epithet of Vishnu. —संहिता *f.* The code of laws ascribed to the first Manu, the institutes of Manu.

मनुष्यः *m.* 1 A man, human being, mortal. -2 A male. -Comp. —देवः *m.* 1 Brâhmana. -2 A king. -धर्मन् *m.* An epithet of Kubera. -यज्ञः *m.* Hospitable reception of guests, one of the five daily acts of a house-holder. -लोकः *m.* The world of mortals, the earth. —विश्, —विशा, *f.*, —विशं *n.* Human race, mankind.

मंतुः *m.* 1 A fault, an offence. -2 Mankind. -3 Lord of men (प्रजापति). —तुः *f.* Understanding, intellect.

मंतृ *m.* A wise man, an adviser or counsellor.

मनोमय *a.* Mental, spiritual.-Comp. -कोशः, -षः *m.* The second of the five vestures or sheaths which are supposed to enshrine the soul.

मंत्र् 10 A. (मंत्रयते, but sometimes मंत्रयति also ; मंत्रित) 1 To consult, deliberate, ponder over. -2 To advise, counsel. -3 To enchant with spells or charms. -4 To say, speak, talk, mutter. With अनु— 1 To win over.-2 To consecrate by *mantras.* -3 To take leave of. अभि— To consecrate by *mantras.* आ- 1(Atm.) 1 To say, speak, tell. -2 To invite. -3 To consecrate by '*mantras.* ' -4 (Atm.) To take leave of. उप— T persuade. नि— To invite. परि— To consecrate by *mantras.* सम्— To consult, deliberate.

मंत्रः *m.* 1 A Vedic hymn or sacred prayer (addressed to any deity), a sacred text ; (it is called ऋच् if metrical and intended to be loudly recited । यजुस् if in prose and muttered in a low tone ; and सामन् if, being metrical, it is intended for chanting). -2 The संहिता portion of the Veda as distinguished from the *Bráhmana* (*n.*).-3 A charm, spell, an incantation. -4 A formula (of prayer) sacred to any deity. -5 Consultation, counsel, advice. resolution, plan.-6A secret.-7Policy, statesmanship. -Comp. —आराधनं *n.* Striving to obtain by spells or incantations. —उदकं, -जलं, —तोयं, -वारि *n.* Water consecrated by means of spells; charmed water. —उपष्टंभः *m.* Encouragement by advice. —करणं *n.* 1 Vedic texts. -2 Composing or reciting sacred texts. -कारः *m.* The author of Vedic hymns.-कालः *m.* The time of consultation or deliberation.-कुशल *a.* Skilled in giving advice. —कृत *m.* 1 A composer of Vedic hymns.-2 One who recites a sacred text. -3 A counsellor, an adviser. -4 An ambassador. —गंडकः *m.* Knowledge, science. -गुप्तिः *f.* Secret counsel. —गूढः *m.* A spy, a secret emissary or agent. —जिह्वः *m.* An epithet of fire. —ज्ञः *m.* 1 A counsellor, adviser. -2 A learned Bráhmana. -3 A spy. —दः, दातृ *m.* A spiritual preceptor or teacher. -दर्शिन् *m.* 1 A seer of Vedic hymns. -2 A Brâhmana versed in the Vedas. —दीधितिः *m.* Fire. —दृश् *m.* 1 A see of Vedic hymns. -2 An adviser, a counsellor. -देवता *f.* The deity invoked in a sacred text or *mantra.* —धरः, -धारिन् *m.* A counsellor. -निर्णयः *m.* Final decision after deliberation. —पदं *n.* The words of a sacred text. —पूत *a.* Purified by *mantras.* -प्रयोगः *m.*, -युक्तिः *f.* Application of spells. -बीं (-बी-) जः *m.* The first syllable of a spell. -भेदः *m.* Breach or betrayal of counsel. —मूर्तिः *m.* An epithet of Siva. —मूलं *n.* Magic. —यंत्रं *n.* A mystical diagram with a magical formula. -योगः *m* 1 Employment or application of spells. -2 Magic. —वर्जं *ind.* Without the use of spells. -वादिन् *m.* 1 A reciter of sacred texts. -2 An enchanter, a conjurer. -विद् *m.* A Brâhmana learned in the Vedas. —विद्या *f.* The science of spells, magic. -संस्कारः *m.* Any Samskára or rite performed with sacred texts. -संहिता *f.* The whole body of Vedic hymns.-साधकः *m.* A magician, conjurer. —साधनं *n.* 1 Subduing by magic.-2 A spell, an incantation -3 Attainment of supernatural or magical powers (by muttering spells). —साध्य *a.* 1 To be effected or subdued by magic or spells. -2 Attainable by consultation -सिद्धिः *f.* 1 The accomplishment of a spell. -2 The power which the possession or knowledge of a spell gives to a person. -हीन *a.* Destitute of or contrary to sacred hymns.

मंत्रणं *n.*, -णा *f.* 1 Deliberation, consultation. -2 Advising, counselling.

मंत्रवत *a.* 1 Attended with spells or incantations.-2 Initiated.-*ind.* 1 According to sacred texts. -2 According to the rules of consultation.

मंत्रिः *m.* A minister of state.

मंत्रित *p. p* (*f.* -ता) 1 Consulted. -2 Counselled. -3 Said, spoken. -4 Charmed, consecrated by *mantras.* -5 Settled, determined. -तं *n.* Advice, counsel.

मंत्रिन् *m.* 1 A minister, counsellor, a king's minister. -2 A conjurer, an enchanter. -Comp. -धुर *a.* Able to bear the burden of a minister's office. -पतिः, -प्रधानः, -प्रमुखः, -मुख्यः, -वरः, -श्रेष्ठः *m* The prime minister, premier. —प्रकांडः *m.* An excellent or eminent minister. —श्रोत्रियः *m.* A minister conversant with the Vedas.

मंथ्, मथ् 1, 9. P. (मंथति, मथति, मथ्नाति, मथित; *pass.* मथ्यते) 1 To churn, to produce by churning (oft. with two acc.) -2 To agitate, stir up, turn up and down ; (fig also). -3 To crush, grind. -4 To oppress, afflict, trouble, destroy, kill, to tear off, to dislocate.

मंथः *m.* 1 Churning, stirring, agitating. -2 Killing, destroying. -3 A mixed beverage. -4 A churning-stick. -5 The sun. -6 A ray of the sun -7 Excretion from the eyes. -8 An instrument for kindling fire by attrition. 9 A kind of antelope. -Comp -अचलः,-अद्रिः,-गिरिः, -पर्वतः,-शैलः *m.* The Mandara mountain. -उदकः, -उदधिः *m.* The sea of milk.-गुणः *m.* A churning-cord. -जं *n.* Butter. —दंडः, -दंडकः *m.* A churning-stick.

मंथनः *m.* A churning-stick. -नं *n.* 1 Churning, agitating, stirring about. -2 Kindling fire by attrition. -नी *f.* A churning vessel -Comp. -घटी *f.* A churning vessel.

मंथर *a.* (*f.* -रा) 1 Slow, dull, lazy, inactive. -2 Foolish, silly. -3 Having a low tone. -4 Large, bulky wide, big.-5 Bent, crooked,curved. -रः *m*. 1 A store, treasure. -2 The hair of the head.-3 Anger.-4 Fresh butter. -5 A churning-stick. -6 Hinderance. -7 A stronghold. -8 Fruit. -9 A spy. -10 The month Vaisâkha. -11 The mountain Mandara. -12 An antelope. -रा *f*. N. of a hump-backed nurse of Kaikeyí. -रं *n*. Safflower. -Comp. —विवेक *a*. Slow to discriminate. [a *chowrie*.

मंथरुः *m*. The wind produced from

मंथानः *m*. 1 A churning stick. -2 An epithet of Siva.

मंथानकः *m*. A kind of grass.

मंथिन् *m*. Semen virile. -नी *f*. A churning-vessel.

मंद *a*. (*f*.-दा)1 Slow,inactive, lazy, dull. -2 Indifferent, apathetic. -3 Stupid, foolish,ignorant.-4 Hollow (as sound). -5 Faint, gentle; as in मंदस्मित. -6 Small, little, slight,as in मंदोदरी. -7 Weak, feeble, as in मंदाग्नि. -8 Unlucky, unhappy. -9 Faded. -10 Wicked, vile. -11 Addicted to drinking. -दः *m*. 1 The planet Saturn. -2 An epithet of Yama. -3 The dissolution of the world. -4 A kind of elephant.-5 The apsis of a planet's course. -दं *ind*. 1 Slowly, gradually, by degrees. -2 Gently, softly. -3 Weakly, lightly. -4 In a low tone. -Comp.-अक्षं *n*. Shame,modesty,bashfulness. -आक्रांता *f*. N. of a metre. -आत्मन् *a*. Dull-witted, silly, ignorant.-उच्चः*m*. The upper apsis of the course of a planet. -उदरी *f*.N. of the wife of Râvana. -उष्ण *a*. Tepid, lukewarm.(-ष्णं*n*.)Gentle heat.-कांतिः *m*. The moon. -कारिन् *a*. Acting slowly or foolishly. —गः *m*. Saturn. —छाय *a*. Lustreless. —जननी *f*. The mother of Saturn. —फलं *n*. Equation of the apsis.

मंदटः *m*. The coral tree.

मंदनं *n*. Praise, eulogium.

मंदयंती *f*. An epithet of Durgá.

मंदर *a*. (*f*. -रा) 1 Slow, tardy, dull. -2 Thick, dense. -3 Large, bulky. -रः *m*. 1 N. of a mountain (used by the gods and demons as a churning-stick when they churned the ocean for nectar). -2 A necklace of pearls (of 8 or 16 strings). -3 Heaven. -4 A mirror. -5 One of the five trees in Indra's paradise. -Comp. -आवासा, -वासिनी *f*. N. of Durgà. —सानुः *m*. 1 Sleep. -2 Life. [Praise.

मंदाकः *m*. A current, stream. -2

मंदाकिनी *f*. 1 The river Ganges. -2 The celestial Ganges.

मंदारः *m*. 1 The coral tree, one of the five trees in Indra's paradise. -2 The plant Arka. -3 The Dhatúra plant. -4 Heaven. -5 An elephant. -रं *n*. A flower of the coral tree.Comp.—षष्ठी *f*. The sixth day in the bright half of Mágha. [tree.

मंदारकः, मंदारवः, मंदारुः *m*. The coral

मंदिमन् *m*. 1 Slowness, tardiness.-2 Dulness, stupidity, folly.

मंदिरं *n*. A dwelling house, a mansion. -2 A town. -3 A camp. -4 A temple. —रः *m*. 1 The sea. -2 The hollow of the knee, ham. Comp. —पशुः *m*. A cat. —मणिः *m*. An epithet of Siva.

मंदिरा *f*. 1 A stable.

मंदुरा *f*.1 A stable for horses.-2 A stable in general. -3 A bed, mattress.

मंद्र *a*. (*f*. —द्रा) Deep, hollow, rumbling (as sound). —द्रः *m*. 1 A deep sound. -2 A kind of drum. -3 A kind of elephant.

मन्मथः *m*.1 Cupid,the God of love.

-2 Love, amorous passion. -3 The wood apple.—था *f.* N. of Dâkshàyanî. -Comp. —आनंदः *m.* A kind of mango tree.—आलयः *m.*1 The mango tree. -2 Pudendum muliebre. —कर *a.* Exciting love. —युद्धं *n.* Copulation. —लेखः *m.* A love letter.

मन्मनः *m.* 1 Confidential whispering. -2 The God of love.

मन्य *a.* (At the end of Comp.) 1 Thinking oneself to be, as in पंडितंमन्य. -2 Appearing as.

मन्या *f.* 1 The nape or back of the neck. -2 Knowledge.

मन्युः *m.* 1 Anger, resentment, indignation. -2 Grief, affliction. -3 Wretched or miserable state; meanness. -4 A sacrifice. -5 An epithet of Siva. -6 Of Agni.

मम (Gen. sing. of अस्मद् the first personal pronoun) My, mine. -Comp.- कारः *m.*,—कृत्यं *n.* Interesting oneself about anything; self interest.

ममता *f.* 1 Self-interest, selfishness. -2 Pride, arrogance. -3 Individuality.

ममत्वं *n.* 1 Sense of ownership. -2 Affectionate regard.-3 Arrogance.

ममापतालः *m.* An object of sense.

मम्मटः *m.* N. of the author of the Kâvyaprakâsa.

मय् 1 A. (मयते) To go, move.

मय *a.* (*f.* —यी) An affix indicating 'made of,' consisting or composed of,' 'full of,' as in सुवर्णमय, काष्ठमय, तेजोमय, जलमय &c. —यः *m.* 1 N. of a demon, the architect of the demons. -2 A horse. -3 A camel. -4 A mule. —यी *f.* A mare.

मयटः *m.* A hut of grass or leaves.

मय (-यु-) ष्टकः *m.* A kind of bean.

मयुः *m.* 1 A *Kinnara*, a celestial musician. -2 A deer, an antelope. -Comp. —राजः *m.* An epithet of Kubera.

मयूखः *m.* 1 A ray of light; brightness. -2 Beauty. -3 A flame. -4 The pin of a sun-dial.

मयूरः *m.* 1 A peacock. -2 A kind of flower. -3 N. of a poet (author of the सूर्यशतक).-4 A kind of instrument for measuring time. -री *f.* A pea-hen. -Comp. —अरिः *m.* An lizard —केतुः *m.* An epithet of Kârtikeya. —ग्रीवकं *n.* Blue vitriol. —चटकः *m.* The domestic cock. —तुत्थं *n.* Blue vitriol. —पत्रिन् *m.* An arrow feathered with peacock's feathers. -रथः *m.* An epithet of Kàrtikeya. -व्यंसकः *m.* A cunning peacock.-शिखा *f.* A peacock's crest. -2 A cock's comb.

मयूरकः *m.*1 A peacock.-2 A cock's comb. -कः *m.*, -कं *n.* Blue vitriol.

मरकः *m.* A plague, an epidemic.

मरकतं *n.* An emerald. (Sometimes written मरक्त).-Comp.-मणिः *m.*,*f.* An emerald. -शिला *f.* An emerald slab.

मरणं *n.* 1 Dying, death. -2 A kind of deadly poison. -Comp. —अंत, —अंतक *a.* Ending in death. -अभिमुख, -उन्मुख *a.*On the point of death, moribund. -आत्मक *a.* Fatal.-धर्मन् *a.* Mortal. -शील *a.* Mortal.

मरतः *m.* Death.

मरंदः,-दकः *m.* The juice of flowers. -Comp. -ओकस् *n.* A flower.

मरारः *m.* A granary.

मराल *a.* (*f.* -ला) 1 Soft, greasy -2 Bland, tender. -लः *m.*(*f.* -ली) 1 A swan, flamingo, goose. -2 A kind of duck (कारंडव). -3 A horse. -4 A cloud. -5 Collyrium. -6 A grove of pomegranate trees. -7 A rogue, cheat.

मरि (-री-) चः *m.* The pepper-shrub· —चं *n.* Black pepper.

मरीचिः *m.*, *f.* 1 A ray of light. -2 A particle of light. -3 Light· -4 Mirage. -चिः *m.* 1 N. of a Prajàpati. -2 N. of a law-giver. -Comp. ·तोयं *n.* A mirage. —मालिन् *m.* The sun·

मरीचिका *f.* Mirage·

मरीचिन्, मरीचिमत् *m.* The sun.

मरीमृज *a.* (*f.* -जा) Repeatedly rubbing.

मरुः *m.* 1 A desert, sandy desert, a wilderness, a region destitute of water. -2 A mountain or rock. -*m. pl.* N. of a country or its inhabitants.-Comp.-उद्भवा *f.* 1 The cotton shrub. -2 A cucumber· —कच्छः *m.* N. of a district· -जः *m.* A kind of perfume.-देशः *m.* 1 N. of a district. -2 Any region destitute of water. -द्विपः, -प्रियः *m.* A camel. -धन्वः, -धन्वन् *m.* A wilderness, desert. —पथः *m.*, —पृष्ठं *n.* A sandy desert, wilderness. -भू (*pl.*) The country called Màrwâr. -भूमिः *f.* A desert, sandy desert. -संभवः *m.* A kind of horse-radish.

मरुकः *m.* A peacock.

मरुत् *m* 1 Wind, air, breeze. -2 The God of wind.-3 A God, deity. -4 A kind of plant (मरुवक). -Comp. —आंदोलः *m.* A kind of fan (of a deer's or buffalo's skin). —करः *m.* A kind of bean. —कर्मन् *n.*, -क्रिया *f.* Flatulency. —कोणः *m.* The north-west quarter. —तनयः, —पुत्रः, —सुतः, —सूनुः *m.* 1 Epithets of Hanumat. -2 Of Bhima. —ध्वजं *n.* The down of cotton floating in the air. —पटः *m.* A sail. —पतिः,—पालः *m.* An epithet of Indra. —पथः *m.* Sky, atmosphere. —प्लवः *m.* A lion. —फलं *n.* Hail. —बद्धः *m.* 1 An epithet of Vishnu. -2 A kind of sacrificial vessel. —रथः *m.* 1 A car in which idols of Gods are moved about. 2 A horse· —लोकः *m.* The world of the Maruts. —वर्त्मन् *n.* Sky, atmosphere· -वाहः *m.* 1 An epithet of fire. -2 Of Indra.-सखः *m.* 1 Indra. -2 Fire·

मरुतः *m.* 1 Wind.-2 A God. [race.

मरुत्तः *m.* N. of a king of the solar

मरुत्तकः *m.* The Marubaka plant.

मरुत्वत् *m.* 1 A cloud. -2 N. of Indra. -3 N. of Hanumat.

मरुलः *m.* A kind of duck.

मरूकः *m.* 1 A peacock. -2 A kind of stag.

मरूयः *m.* 1 N. of a plant. -2 An epithet of Ráhu.

मरुव (-ब-) कः *m.* 1 A kind of plant (Marjoram). -2 A variety of lime. -3 A tiger. -4 Ràhu. -5 A crane.

मरोलिः, -लिकः *m.* The sea-monster Makara.

मर्कटः *m.* 1 An ape, a monkey. -2 A spider· -3 A kind of crane. -4 A kind of coitus. -5 A kind of poison. -Comp.-आस्य *a.* Monkey-faced.(-स्यं *n.*) Copper.-इंदुः *m.* Ebony. —तिंदुकः *m.* A kind of ebony. —वासः *m.* A cobweb. —शीर्षं *n.* Vermilion.

मर्कटकः *m.* 1 An ape. -2 A spider. -3 A kind of fish.-4 A kind of grain.

मर्करा *f.* 1 A pot, vessel. -2 A subterranean hole, cavity, cavern, hollow· -3 A barren woman.

मर्च् 10 U. (मर्चयति,-ते) 1 To take. -2 To cleanse. -3 To sound. -4 To go, move.

मर्जुः *m.* 1 A washerman.-2 A catamite. —*f.* Cleansing, washing, purification·

मर्तः *m* A man, human being, mortal. -2 The earth, the world of mortals·

मर्त्य *a.* (*f.* -र्त्या) Mortal. —र्त्यः *m.* 1 A mortal, a man. -2 The world of mortals, the earth. -र्त्यं *n.* The body. -Comp. —धर्मन् *a.* Mortal. —भुवनं *n.* The earth. —महितः *m.* A God. — मुखः *m.* A *kinnara.* -लोकः *m.* The world of mortals, the earth.

मर्दः *m.* 1 Grinding, pounding. -2 A violent stroke.

मर्दनं *n.* 1 Crushing, grinding. -2 Rubbing, shampooing. -3 Anointing (with unguents &c.).-4 Pressing,kneading.-5 Tormenting,afflicting. -6 Destroying. -7 Opposition of planets.

मर्दलः *m.* A kind of drum.

मर्मन् *n.* 1 A vital part of the body, weak or tender point (of the body). -2 Any weak or vulnerable point. -3 The core, quick. -4 Any joint (of a limb). -5 The secret or hidden meaning, the pith or essence (of anything). -Comp. —अतिग *a.* Piercing deeply into the vital parts. —आवरणं *n.* An armour, a coat of mail. -कीलः *m.* A husband -घ्न *a.* Excessively painful. -चरं *n.* The heart. —ज्ञ, -विद् *a.* 1 Knowing the weak or vulnerable points of another. -2 Knowing the most secret portions of a subject.-3 Having a deep insight into anythig ; exceedingly acute or clever. (-ज्ञः *m.*) A clever or learned man. -त्रं *n.* A coat of mail. —भेदनः, —भेदिन् *m.* An arrow.

मर्मर *a.* (*f.* —रा) 1 Rustling (leaves,garments &c.).-2 Murmuring. -रः *m.* 1 A rustling sound. -2 A murmur. [-2 Turmeric.

मर्मरी *f.* 1 A species of pine tree.

मर्मरीकः *m.* 1 A poor man, pauper. -2 A wicked man.

मर्या *f.* 1 A limit, boundary.

मर्यादा *f.* 1 A limit, boundary, border, frontier. -2 End, termination. -3 A shore, bank.-4 A mark, landmark. -5 Any fixed usage or established rule; moral law. -6 A contract, an agreement.

मर्यादिन् *m.* A neighbour, border.

मर्व् 1 P. (मर्वति) 1 To go, move. -2 To fill.

मर्शः *m.* 1 Deliberation.-2 Advice, counsel. -3 A sternutatory.

मर्शनं *n.* 1 Rubbing. -2 Examination, inquiry. -3 Deliberation. -4 Advising, counselling. -5 Removing, rubbing off. -6 Explaining.

मर्षः *m.*,मर्षणं *n.* Endurance, forbearance, patience.

मर्षित *p. p.* (*f.* -ता) 1 Endured, patiently borne. -2 Excused, forgiven. -तं *n.* Endurance,patience.

मल् 1 A., 10 U. (मलते, मलयति,-ते) To hold, possess.

मलः *m.*, -लं *n.* 1 Dirt,impurity,any impure matter. -2 Refuse, sediment, excrement, dung. -3 Dross (of metals), rust, alloy. -4 Moral impurity, sin.-5 Any impure secretion of the body. -6 Camphor. -7 Cuttle-fish bone.-8 Tanned leather; a leather garment. -9 The three humours of the body (वात, पित्त and कफ). -लं *n.* A kind of base metal. -Comp. -अरिः *m.* A kind of natron. —आकर्षिन् *m.* A sweeper, a scavenger. —आशयः *m.* The stomach. -कर्षण *a.* Cleansing. —घ्नः *m.* The bulbous root of शाल्मली. (-घ्नी *f.*) N. of a plant (नागदमनी.)—जं *n.* Pus, matter. —द्रवः *m.* Purging, diarrhœa. -द्राविन् *m.* The Jayapála tree. —धात्री *f.* A nurse who attends to a child's necessities. —धारिन् *m.* A religious mendicant of the Jaina sect. —पृष्ठं

n. The first (or outer) page of a book. —भुज *m*. A crow. —मल्लकः *m*. A strip of cloth covering the privities (कौपीन). —मास: *m*. An intercalary month. —वासस् *f*. A woman in her courses. [*m*. A tent.

मलनं *n*. Crushing, grinding. —नः

मलयः *m*. 1 N. of a mountain-range in the south of India, abounding in sandal trees. -2 N. of the country lying to the east of the Malaya range; Malabar. -3 A garden. -4 The garden of Indra. -5 The side of a mountain. -Comp. —उद्भवं *n*. Sandal-wood.—जः *m*. A sandal tree. (-जः *m*., —रुहं *n*) Sandal-wood. (-जं *n*.) An epithet of Râhu. —द्रुमः *m*. A sandal tree. -वासिनी *f*. An epithet of Durga.

मलाका *f*. An amorous or lustful woman. -2 A female messenger, confidante. -3 A female elephant.

मलिन *a*. (*f*. —ना) 1 Dirty, filthy, impure, unclean, stained, sullied (fig. also). -2 Black, dark (fig. also). -3 Sinful, wicked, depraved. -4 Clouded, obscured. -नं *n*. 1 Sin, fault, guilt. -2 Butter-milk. -3 Borax. -ना,-नी *f*. A woman during menstruation. -Comp. -अंबु *n*. Ink. -मुखः *m*. 1 Fire. -2 A ghost, an evil spirit. -3 A kind of monkey (गोलांगूल).

मलिनय् Den. P. 1 To make dirty, soil, stain, sully, spoil (fig. also). -2 To corrupt, deprave.

मलिनिमन् *m*. 1 Dirtiness, impurity. -2 Blackness, darkness. -3 Moral impurity, sin.

मलिम्लुचः *m*. 1 A robber, thief. -2 A demon. -3 A gnat, mosquito. -4 An intercalary month. -5 Air, wind. -6 Fire. -7 A Bráhmana who neglects the five daily Yajnas or sacrifices. -8 The Chitraka tree.-9 Frost, snow.

मलिष्ठा *f*. A woman in her courses.

मलीमस *a*. (*f*. -सा) 1 Dirty, impure, unclean, soiled. -2 Dark, of a black colour. -3 Wicked, sinful, unrighteous. —सः *m*. 1 Iron. -2 Green vitriol.

मल्ल् 1 A. (मल्लते) To hold, possess.

मल्ल *a*. (*f*. -ल्ला) 1 Strong, robust. -2 Good; excellent. —ल्लः *m*. 1 A strong man.-2 An athlete, a boxer, wrestler.-3 A drinking-vessel, cup. -4 The remnants of an oblation. -5 The cheek and temple. -6 N. of a mixed tribe. -7 N. of a country. -Comp. —अरिः *m*. 1 An epithet of Krishna. -2 Of Siva. -क्रीडा *f*. 1 Boxing or wrestling match. -2 Athletic or gymnastic exercise. -घटी *f*. A kind of dance. -जं *n*. Black pepper. —तूर्यं *n*. A kind of drum. —नागः *m*. 1 Indra's elephant. -2 A letter-carrier. —युद्धं *n*. A wrestling or boxing match. -विद्या *f*. The art of wrestling.-शाला *f*. A gymnasium.

मल्लकः *m*. 1 A lamp-stand. -2 An oil-vessel, a lamp-vessel. -3 A lamp. -4 A cup made out of a cocoa-nut shell. -5 A tooth. -6 A kind of jasmine.

मल्लारः *m*. N. of one of the six Rágas.

मल्लिः,-ल्ली *f*. A kind of jasmine. -Comp. —गंधि *n*. A kind of agallochum. -नाथः *m*. N. of a celebrated commentator. —पत्रं *n*. A mushroom.

मल्लिकः *m*. 1 A kind of goose with brown legs and bill. -2 The month Mâgha. -3 A shuttle. -Comp.-अक्षः, -आख्यः *m*. 1 A kind of goose with brown legs and bill. -2 A particular breed of horses (with white spots on the eyes). (-क्षी *f.*) A female dog (with white spots on the eyes). —अर्जुनः *m.* N. of a *Linga* of Siva on the mountain Srîsaila. —आख्या *f.* A kind of jasmine.

मल्लिका *f.* 1 A kind of jasmine. -2 A flower of this jasmine. -3 A lamp-stand. -4 An earthen vessel of a particular form. -Comp. -गंधं *n.* A kind of agallochum. —छदू, -छदनं *n.* A shade for a lamp.

मल्लीकरः *m.* A thief.

मल्लः *m.* A bear.

मल्लूरः *m.* Rust of iron.

मश् 1 P. (मशति) 1 To buzz, hum. -2 To be angry.

मशः *m.* 1 A mosquito. -2 Hum, humming. -3 Anger. -Comp. -हरी *f.* A mosquito-curtain.

मशकः *m.* 1 A mosquito, gnat. -2 A particular disease of the skin. -3 A leather water-bag. -Comp. -कुटिः, -टी *f.*, —वरणं *n.* A whisk for scaring away mosquitos. -हरी *f.* A mosquito-curtain.

मशकिन् *m.* The *Udumbara* tree.

मशी *f.* See मसी.

मशुनः *m.* A dog.

मष् 1 P. (मषति) To injure, kill.

मषिः,-षी *f.* See मसी.

मस् 4 P. (मस्यति) 1 To weigh, measure. -2 To change form.

मसः *m.* A measure, weight.

मसनं *n.* 1 Measuring, weighing. -2 A species of medicinal plant. -3 Hurting.

मसरा *f.* A kind of pulse.

मसारः, मसारकः *m.* An emerald.

मसिः *m.*, *f.* 1 Ink.-2 Lamp-black, soot. -3 A black powder used to paint the eyes. -Comp. -पण्यः *m.* A writer, scribe. -पथः *m.* A pen. -प्रसूः *f.* 1 A pen. -2 An ink-bottle. -वर्धनं *n.* Myrrh.

मसिकः *m.* A serpent's hole.

मसी *f.* See मसिः above.

मसु (-सू-) रः *m.* 1 A kind of pulse. -2 A pillow. —रा *f.* 1 A lentil. -2 A harlot.

मसूरकः *m.* A pillow. -कं *n.* A kind of ornament on Indra's banner.

मसूरिका *f.* 1 A kind of small-pox. -2 A mosquito-curtain. -3 A procuress, bawd.

मसूरी *f.* A kind of small-pox.

मसृण *a.* (*f.*-णा) 1 Unctuous, oily. -2 Soft, smooth. -3 Mild, sweet. -4 Lovely, charming. —णा *f.* Linseed.

मस्क् 1 P. (मस्कति) To go, move.

मस्करः *m.* 1 A bamboo. -2 A hollow bamboo. -3 Going, motion. -4 Knowledge (ज्ञान).

मस्करिन् *m.* 1 An ascetic or religious mendicant; a Bráhmana in the fourth order.

मस्ज् 6 P. (मज्जति, मग्न; caus. मज्जयति; *desid.* मिमंक्षति) 1 To bathe, plunge, throw oneself into water. -2 To sink, sink into or down, plunge.-3 To be drowned, perish (in water). -4 To sink into misfortune. -5 To be discouraged.

मस्तं *n.* The head. -Comp. -दारु *n.* The *devadâru* tree. —मूलकं *n.* The neck.

मस्तकः *m.*, -कं *n.* 1 The head, skull. -2 The head or top of anything, peak, summit. -3 The tuft of leaves growing at the top of palm trees. -Comp. —आख्यः *m.* The top of a tree. -पिंडकः *m.*, -कं *n.* A round protuberance on the temples of an elephant in rut. —मूलकं *n.* The neck. -लुंगः *m.* The membrane surrounding the brain. -स्नेहः *m.* The brain.

मस्तिकं *n.* The head.

मस्तिष्कं *n.* The brain. -Comp.-त्वच्

f. The membrane surrounding the brain.

मस्तु *n*. 1 Sour cream. -2 Whey. -Comp. -लुंगः *m*., -र्ष *n*.,-लुंगकः *m*., -ष्कं *n*. The brain.

मह् 1 P., 10 U. (महति, महयति,-ते, महित) 1 To honour, respect, revere, worship, value greatly. -2 To gladden. -3 To increase, to grow.

मह् 1 A. (महते) To grow, increase.

महः *m*. 1 A festival, festive occasion. -2 A sacrifice.-3 A buffalo. -4 Light, lustre.

महकः *m*. 1 An eminent man. -2 A tortoise. -3 N. of Vishnu.

महत् *a*. (*f*. —ती ; Compar. महीयस् ; superl. महिष्ठ ; nom. महान्, महान्तौ, महान्तः, acc. pl. महतः) 1 Great, large, big, vast, copious, abundant, numerous, extended, extensive. -2 Strong, powerful, mighty. -3 Intense, excessive. -4 Gross, thick, dense, as in महान्धकारः. -5 Important, weighty. -6 Eminent, noble ; distinguished. -7 Loud. -8 Early or late ; as in महति प्रत्यूषे 'early in the morning'; महत्यपराह्णे 'late in the afternoon.' -*m*. 1 A camel. -2 An epithet of Siva. -3 (In Sán. phil.) The second of the twenty-five elements or *tattvas* recognized by the Sânkhyas. -4 The superior of a monastery.-*n*. 1 Greatness, infiniteness, numerousness. -2 Kingdom, dominion.-3 Sacred knowledge. *Ind*. Greatly, excessively, exceedingly. -Comp. —कथ *a*. Talked of or mentioned by the great, in great men's mouths. -तत्त्वं *n*. The second of the 25 principles of the Sánkhyas.-बिलं *n*. The atmosphere.

महती *f*. 1 A kind of lute. -2 N. of the lute of Nârada. -3 A kind of plant. -4 Greatness, importance.

महत्तरः *m*. 1 The most respectable person.-2 A chamberlain.-3 A courtier. -4 The head-man of a village.

महत्तरकः *m*. A courtier, chamberlain.

महत्त्वं *n*. 1 Greatness, largeness. -2 Mightiness, majesty. -3 Importance. -4 Exalted position. -5 Intensity, high degree.

महनीय *a*. (*f*. —या) Worthy of honour, illustrious, glorious, noble.

महंतः *m*. The superior of a monastery.

महर् *ind*. The fourth of the seven worlds rising one above the other from the earth (महर्लोक also in this sense).

महल्लः, महल्लिकः *m*. A eunuch in a king's harem (a word from Arabic).

महल्लक *a*. (*f*. -ल्लिका) Weak, feeble, old. -कः *m*. 1 A eunuch in a king's harem. -2 A large house.

महस् *n*. 1 A festival, a festive occasion. -2 A sacrifice. -3 Light, lustre. -4 The fourth of the seven worlds ; see महर्.

महस्वत्, महस्विन् *a*. 1 Splendid, brilliant, lustrous. -2 Great, mighty.

महा *f*. A cow.

महा *a*. The substitute of महत् at the beginning of Karmadháraya and Bahuvríhi compounds, and also at the beginning of some other irregular words. -Comp. —अक्षः *m*. An epithet of Siva. —अंगः *m*. 1 A camel. -2 A kind of rat. -3 N. of Siva. —अंजनः *m*. N. of a mountain. —अध्वनिक *a*. Dead. —अनसं *n*. 1 A heavy carriage. -2 Cooking utensils. (—सी *f*.) A kitchen-maid. (—सः *m*., -सं *n*.) A kitchen. —अनुभाव *a*. 1 Of great prowess glorious, magnanimous, illustrious. -2 Virtuous, righteous, just. (-वः *m.*) A worthy or respectable person. —अंतकः *m.* 1 Death. -2 An epithet of Siva. —अंध्राः *m. pl.* N. of a people and their country.-अन्वय, —अभिजन *a.* Nobly-born, of noble birth. (—यः, -नः *m.*) Noble birth, high descent. -अभिषवः *m.* The great extraction of Soma. -अमात्यः *m.* The chief or prime minister (of a king). --अंबुकः *m.* An epithet of Siva. -अंबुजं *n.* A billion. —अम्लं *n.* The fruit of the tamarind tree.-अर्घ *a.* Very costly. (-र्घः *m.*) A kind of quail. -अर्घ्य *a.* Valuable, precious. —अर्णवः *m.* 1 The great ocean. -2 N. of Siva. —अर्बुदं *n.* One thousand millions. —अर्ह *a.* 1 Very valuable, very costly. -2 Invaluable, inestimable. (-र्हं *n.*) White sandal-wood.—अवरोहः *m.* The fig tree. —अशनिध्वजः *m.* A great banner in the form of the thunder-bolt.—अश्मन् *m.* A precious stone, ruby. —अष्टमी *f.* The eighth day in the bright half of Asvina sacred to Durgâ. —असुरी *f.* N. of Durgá. —अह्नः *m.* The afternoon. —आचार्यः *m.* 1 A great teacher. -2 An epithet of Siva.—आढ्य *a.* Wealthy, very rich. (-ढ्यः *m.*) The Kadamba tree.—आत्मन् *a.* 1 High-souled, magnanimous, noble. -2 Exalted, eminent. (—*m.*) 1 The Supreme Spirit. -2 The great principle *i. e.* intellect of the Sánkhyas. —आनंदः, —नंदः *m.* The great bliss of final beatitude. (-दा *f.*) 1 Spirituous liquor. -2 A festival on the ninth day in the bright half of Màgha.—आयुधः *m.* An epithet of Siva. -आरंभ *a.* Enterpizing. (-भः *m* .) Any great enterprize. —आलयः *m.* 1 A temple, a sanctuary, an asylum. -2 A great dwelling. -3 A place of pilgrimage.-4 The world of Brahman (*m.*).-5 The Supreme Spirit. —आशय *a.* High-souled, magnanimous. —आस्पद *a.* Mighty, powerful. —इच्छ *a.* 1 Noble-minded. -2 Ambitious. —इंद्रः *m* 1 N. of Indra. -2 A chief or leader in general. -3 N. of a mountain range. -इषुः *m.* A great archer. —इष्वासः *m.* A great archer, a great warrior. -ईशः, —ईशानः *m.* N. of Siva. —ईश्वरः *m.* 1 A great lord, sovereign. -2 N. of Siva. -3 Of Vishnu. (-री *f.*) 1 N. of Durgá. -2 A kind of bell-metal. —उत्पलः *m.* The Sàrasa bird. —उत्सवः *m.* 1 A great festival. -2 The God of love. -उत्साह *a.* Energetic, persevering. —उदधिः *m.* 1 The great ocean.-2 An epithet of Indra —उदय *a.* Very glorious or splendid; of great prosperity. (-यः *m.*) 1 Greatness, prosperity, good luck. -2 Final beatitude. -3 A lord, master. -4 N. of the district called Kânyakubja or Kanouja. -5 N. of the capital of Kanouja. -6 Sour milk mixed with honey. —उदरं *n.* Dropsy. —उद्यम *a.* See महोत्साह. -उन्नतः *m.* The palmyra tree. —उरस्कः *m.* An epithet of Siva. —ऋषिः *m.* 1 A great sage or saint. -2 One of the ten *Prajápatis* or patriarchs of mankind.-3 N. of Siva. -4 Of Buddha. —ओष्ठ (महोष्ठ) *a.* Having large lips. (-ष्ठः *m.*) An epithet of Siva. —ओजसं *n.* The discus of Vishnu. —औषधिः *f.* 1 A sovereign drug. -2 The Dúrvá grass. —औषधं *n.* 1 A panacea. -2 Ginger. -3 Garlic. -4 A kind of poison (वत्सनाभ). -कच्छः *m.* 1 The sea. -2 N. of Varuna. -3

A mountain. —कंदः *m*. Garlic. -कला *f*. The night of the new moon.-कांता *f*. The earth. —कार्तिकी *f*. The night of full-moon in the month of Kàrtika. -कालः *m*. 1 Siva in his charater as the destroyer of the world. -2 N. of a celebrated shrine. -3 An epithet of Vishnu. -4 N. of a kind of gourd. -5 N. of Siva's servant (नंदि). -काली *f*. An epithet of Durgá in her terrific form. —काव्यं *n*. A great or classical poem. —कुमारः *m*. The eldest son of a reigning prince ; heir-apparent. —क्रतुः *m*. A great sacrifice *e. g.* a horse-sacrifice.—क्षीरः *m*. Sugar-cane. —खर्वः *m*., —खर्वं *n*. A particular high number. -गर्तः, —गर्भः,-गीतः *m*. N. of Siva. -गल *a*. Long-necked.-गवः *m*. *Bos gavæus*. -गृष्टिः *f*. A cow with a large hump. -ग्रहः *m*. An epithet of Ráhu. —ग्रीवः *m*. 1 A camel. -2 An epithet of Siva. -ग्रीविन *m*. A camel.-चक्रवर्तिन *m*. A universal monarch. -छायः *m*. The fig-tree. -जनः *m*. 1 A multitude of men; a great many beings; the general populace or public.-2 A great man, a distinguished or eminent man. -3 The chief of a caste or trade. -4 A merchant, tradesman. -ज्यैष्ठी *f*. The day of full-moon in the month of Jyeshtha. -तलं *n*. N. of one of the seven lower regions.-देवः *m*. N. of Siva. (-वी *f*.) 1 N. of Pàrvatì. -2 The chief queen. -नटः *m*. An epithet of Siva. -नंदा *f*. 1 Spirituous liquor. -2 N. of a river.-नरकः *m*. N. of one of the 21 hells. -नवमी *f*. The ninth day in the bright half of Asvina. -निद्रा *f*. The great sleep, death. -निर्वाणं *n*. Total extinction of individuality (according to the Buddhists). -निशा *f*. 1 The dead of night, the second and third watches of the night. -2 An epithet of Durgâ. -नीचः *m*. A washerman.-नेमिः *m*. A crow.-न्यायः *m*. The chief rule. -पद्मः *m*. 1 A particular high number. -2 N. of Nârada. -3 N. of one of the nine treasures of Kubera. -4 N. of the southernmost elephant supporting the world.(—द्मं *n*.) 1 A white lotus. -2 N. of a city. —पराह्नः *m*. A late hour in the afternoon. -पातकं *n*. A great sin, a heinous crime. —पात्रः *m*. A prime minister. -पृष्ठः *m*. A camel. -प्रलयः *m*. The total annihilation of the universe at the end of the life of Brahman (*m*.).-प्रस्थानं *n*. Departing this life, death. -प्राणः *m*. 1 The hard breathing or aspirate sound made in the pronunciation of the aspirates. -2 The aspirated letters themselves (pl.) ; they are:—ख्, घ्, छ्, झ्, ठ्, ढ्, थ्, ध्, फ्, भ्, श्, ष्, स्, ह्. -3 A raven. —बलं *n*. Lead. —बिलं (-विलं) *n*. 1 The atmosphere. -2 The heart. -3 A water-jar, pitcher. -4 A hole, cave. —बी (-वी -) जः *m*. Epithet of Siva. —बोधिः *m*. 1 The great intelligence of a Buddha. -2 A Buddha. —ब्रह्मं, -ब्रह्मन् *n*. The Supreme Spirit. —भाग *a*. 1 Very fortunate or blessed. -2 Distinguished, glorious. -3 Very pure or holy, highly virtuous. -भारतं *n*. N. of the celebrated epic which describes the rivalries and contests of the sons of Dhritaráshtra and Pándu. —भाष्यं *n*. 1 A great commentary. -2 The great commentary of Patanjali on the Sutras of Pánini.-भूतं *n*. A great or primary element. (—तः *m*.) 1 The Supreme Being. -2 A great creature. -मनस्, -मनस्क *a*. Noble-minded, magnanimous. -2 Liberal. -3. Proud, haughty. (-m.) A fabulous animal called शरभ. —मंत्रः m. 1 Any sacred text of the Vedas. -2 A powerful spell. —मंत्रिन् m. The prime-minister, premier. -महोपाध्यायः m. 1 A very great preceptor. -2 A title given to learned men and reputed scholars. —मात्रः m. 1 A great officer of state, a high state-official, a chief minister. -2 An elephant-driver or keeper. -3 A superintendent of elephants. —माया f. Worldly illusion which makes the material world appear really existent. —मारी f. 1 Cholera, an epidemic. -2 An epithet of Durgâ. -मुखः m. A crocodile. —मूलं n. A large radish. (-लः m.) A kind of onion. —मूल्यः m. A ruby. —मेदः m. The coral tree. —यज्ञः m. 1 One of the five daily sacrifices or acts of piety to be performed by a house-holder. -2 N. of Vishnu. —यात्रा f. The pilgrimage to Benares. —युगं n. A great युग consisting of the four *Yugas* of mortals, or comprising 4,320,000 years of men. -योगिन् m. A cock. -रथः m. 1 A great chariot. -2 A great warrior or hero. -3 A desire, longing. —राजः m. 1 A great king, sovereign or supreme ruler. -2 A respectful mode of addressing kings or other great personages. -3 A deified Jaina teacher. -4 A finger-nail. —राजिकः m. N. of Vishnu. —राजिकाः m. pl. An epithet of a class of Gods (said to be 220 or 236 in number). -2 N. of Durgá. —रात्रं n. Midnight, dead of night. -रात्रिः f. 1 Midnight. -2 The eighth night in the bright half of Asvina. -राष्ट्रः m. N. of a country in the west of India, the country of the Marâthás. (-ष्ट्री f.) N. of the principal Prákrita dialect. —रौरवः m. N. of one of the 21 hells. —लक्ष्मी f. 1 The great Lakshmî or Sakti of Nârâyana. -2 A young girl who represents the goddess Durgâ at the Durgá festival. —कोलः m. A crow. —कोहं n. A mag…et. —वराहः m. An epithet of Vishnu in his third or boar incarnation. —वाक्यं n. A long sentence. -2 Any literary work. -3 A great proposition, principal sentence; such as तत्वमसि, ब्रह्मैवेदं सर्वं &c. —विभाषा f. A rule giving a general option or alternative. —विषः m. A serpent having two mouths. —विषुवं n. The vernal equinox. —व्याधिः f. 1 A great disease. -2 A very bad kind of leprosy (black leprosy). -व्याहृतिः f. A great mystical word, *i. e.* भुर्, भुवस् and स्वर्. —शंखः m. 1 A great conch-shell. -2 The temporal bone, forehead. -3 A particular high number. -5 One of Kubera's treasures. —शालः m. A great householder. -शिरस् m. A kind of serpent. —शुक्तिः f. A pearl-shell. —श्मशानं n. An epithet of Benares. —श्रमणः m. An epithet of Buddha. -श्वासः m. A kind of asthma. —श्वेताः f. 1 An epithet of Sarasvatî. -2 Of Durgá. -3 White sugar. —संक्रांतिः f. The winter solstice. —सत्यः m. An epithet of Yama. —सत्त्व a. 1 Noble. -2 Very strong or powerful. -? Just, righteous. (-त्त्वः m.) 1 A large animal. -2 N. of Sákya muni. -3 An epithet of Kubera. -संधिविग्रहः m. The office of the minister of peace and war. -सर्जः m. The bread-fruit or jack-tree. —साधनभागः m. A great executive officer. —सांतपनः m.

A kind of very rigid penance. -सांधि-विग्रहिकः *m.* A minister of peace and war. -सारः *m.* A kind of Khadira tree. -सारथिः *m.* An epithet of Aruna. —साहसिकः *m.* A dacoit, highwayman. -सिंहः *m.* The fabulous animal called Sarabha. -सिद्धिः *f.* A kind of magical power. -स्कंधः *m.* A camel. -स्थली *f.* The earth. -हविस् *n.* Clarified butter.

महिका *f.* Frost, mist.

महित *p. p.* (*f.* -ता) Honoured, worshipped. -तं *n.* The trident of Siva.

महिमन् *m.* 1 Greatness (fig. also). -2 Glory, majesty. -3 Exalted rank or position, dignity. -4 One of the 8 *Siddhis*, the power of increasing size at will. [plant.

महिरः *m.* 1 The sun. -2 The Arka

महिला *f.* 1 A woman. -2 An amorous woman. -3 The creeper called Priyangu. -4 A kind of perfume or fragrant plant (रेणुका). -Comp. —आह्वया *f.* The Priyangu creeper.

महिलारोप्यं *n.* N. of a city in the south.

महिषः *m.* 1 A buffalo; (considered as the vehicle of Yama). -2 N. of a demon killed by Durgá. -Comp. अर्दनः *m.* An epithet of Kàrtikeya.

महिषी *f.* 1 A she-buffalo, buffalo-cow. -2 The principal queen, queen consort. -3 A queen in general.

महिष्मत् *a.* (*f.* -ती) Possessing, rich or abounding in, buffaloes.

महिष्ठ *a.* (*f.* -ती) Greatest, largest (superl of महत्.)

मही *f.* 1 Earth. -2 Ground, soil. -3 Landed property or estate, land. -4 A country, kingdom. -5 N. of a river falling into the gulf of Cambay. -6 (In geom.) The base of any plane figure. -Comp. —धरः *m.* 1 A mountain. -2 An epithet of Vishnu. —ध्रः *m.* 1 A mountain. -2 A symbolical expression for the number, ' seven '. -3 An epithet of Vishnu. -पतनं *n.* Humble obeisance (as by falling on the ground). —पुत्रः, —सुतः, —सूनुः, *m.* 1 The planet Mars. -2 Epithets of the demon Naraka. —प्ररोहः, -रुह्, -रुहः *m.* A tree. -प्राचीरं *n.*, -प्राचारः *m.* The sea. -भर्तृ *m.* A king. -भृत *m.* 1 A mountain. -2 A king, sovereign. —सुरः *m.* A Bráhmana.

महीयस् *a.* (*f.* -सी) Greater, more powerful or weighty, mightier, stronger (compar of महत q. v.). -*m.* A great or noble-minded man.

महीला, महेला, महेलिका *f.* A woman, a female.

मा *ind.* 1 A particle of prohibition or negation usually joined with the Imperative or with the Aorist, when the augment अ is dropped; Imperfect (the augment being dropped here also); the Future, or Potential mood, in the sense of ' lest', ' that not'; or the Present Participle when a curse is implied or with potential passive participles. मा is sometimes used without any verb; मा तावत 'oh ! do not (say or do) so'; मैवं. Sometimes मा is followed by स्म and is used with the Aorist or Imperfect with the augment dropped, and rarely with the potential mood as in क्लैब्यं मा स्म गमः पार्थ, मा स्म प्रतीपं गमः &c. -Comp. -चिरं —विलंबं, -विलंबितं *ind.* Without delay, shortly, quickly.

मा *f.* 1 The goddess of wealth, Lakshmî. -2 A mother. -3 A measure. -Comp. -पः, —पतिः *m.* Epithets of Vishnu.

मा 2 P.; 3. 4 A. (माति, मिमिते or मीयते,मित) 1 To measure.-2 To measure or mark off, limit. -3 To compare with (in size). -4 To be contained or comprised in. With उप— To compare with.

मांस् n. 1 Flesh. (This word has no forms for the first five inflections, and is optionally substituted for मांस after *acc. dual*).

मांसं n. Flesh, meat. -2 The fleshy part of a fruit. —सः m. 1 A worm. -2 N. of a mixed tribe selling meat. -Comp. —अर्गलः m., -लं n. A piece of flesh hanging down from the mouth. -अष्टका f.N. of the eighth day in the dark half of Mágha. -उपजीविन् m. A dealer in flesh.-कच्छपः m. A fleshy abscess on the palate. -कारिन् n. Blood. —ग्रंथिः m. A gland. —जं, —तेजस् n. Fat.—द्राविन् m. A kind of sorrel. —पित्तं n. A bone. --पेशी f. 1 A muscle. -2 A piece of flesh. -3 The fœtus form the 8th to the 14th day.-योनिः m. A creature of flesh and blood.-सारः, —स्नेहः m. Fat. —हासा f. Skin.

मांसल a. (f. —ला) 1 Fleshy. -2 Muscular, brawny. -3 Fat, strong, powerful. -4 Deep (as sound). -5 Pulpy (as fruit). -6 Dense, thick.

मांसिकः m. A butcher.

माकंदः m. The mango tree. -दी f. 1 The myrobalan tree. -2 Yellow sandal.-3N. of a city on the Ganges.

माकर a. (f. -री) Belonging to the sea-monster Makara. —री f. N. of the seventh day in the bright half of Mâgha.

माकरंद a. (f. —दी) Derived from, relating to, or full of, the juice of flowers.

माकलिः m. 1 N. of Màtali, the charioteer of Indra. -2 The moon.

माक्षि (-क्षि-) क a. (f. -की) Coming from a bee. —कं n. 1 Honey. -2 A kind of mineral substance. -Comp. —आश्रयं n. 1 Bees'-wax. -2 Honeycomb. -जं n. Bees'-wax. —फलः m. A kind of cocoa-nut.—शर्करा f. A candied sugar.

मागध a. (f.—धी) Relating to or living in the country of Magadha. —धः m, 1 A king of the Magadhas. -2 N.of a mixed tribe (who are professionally bards).-3 A bard or panegyrist in general. —धाः m. pl. N. of a people, the Magadhas. -धा f. 1 A princess of the Magadhas. -2 Long pepper. —धी f. 1 A princess of the Magadhas. -2 A kind of Prákrita. -3 Long pepper. -4 White cumin. -5 Refined sugar.-6 A kind of jasmine. -7 A kind of cardamoms.

मागधा, मागधिका f. Long pepper.

माघः m. 1 N. of a lunar month (corresponding to January-February). -2 N. of the author of the Sisupâlavadha. —घी f. The day of full moon in the month of Mágha.

माघमा f. A female crab.

माघवत a. (f. -ती) Belonging to Indra. -ती f. The east. -Comp.-चापं n. The rain-bow.

माघवन a. (f -नी) Belonging to or ruled by Indra.

माघ्यं n. The flower of the *kunda* creeper.

मांक्ष् 1 P. (मांक्षति) To wish.

मांगलिक a. (f. —की) 1 Auspicious. -2 Fortunate.

मांगल्यं n. 1 Auspiciousness, welfare, good fortune.-2 A blessing or benediction.-3 A festivity,festival. -4 Any auspicious rite.-5 An amulet

माच॰ *m.* A way, road. [crocodile.

माचकः *m.* 1 A thief, robber. -2 A

माचिका *f.* A fly.

मांजिष्ठ *a.* (*f.* —ष्ठी) 1 Red as madder. -2 Dyed with madder. —ष्ठं *n.* Red colour.

मांजिष्ठिक *a.* (*f.* -की) Dyed or tinged with madder.

माठः *m.* A road.

माठरः *m.* 1 N. of Vyâsa. -2 A Brâhmana. -3 A distiller. -4 One of the attendants on the sun.

माठी *f.* An armour, mail.

माडः *m.* 1 A species of tree. -2 Weight, measure.

माढिः *f.* 1 The young leaf before it opens. -2 Poverty.-3 Anger, passion. -4 The hem of a garment. -5 A double tooth.

माणवः *m.* 1 A lad, boy, youngster. (used contemptuously or in endearment).-3 A pearl-necklace of sixteen (or twenty) strings. -4 A young Brâhmana.

माणवकः *m.* 1 A youth, boy, youngster (oft. used contemptuously).-2 A little man, dwarf.-3A silly fellow. -4 A religious student. -5 A pearl-necklace of sixteen (or twenty) strings.

माणवीन *a.* (*f.* -ना) Boyish, childish.

माणव्यं *n.* 1 A company of lads or boys.

माणिका *f.* A particular weight (equal to eight *palas.*)

माणिक्यं *n.* A ruby.

माणिक्या *f.* A house-lizard.

माणिबंधं, माणिमंथं *n.* Rock-salt.

मांडलिक *a.* (*f.* —की) Relating to, or ruling, a province.

मातंगः *m.* An elephant. -2 A man of the lowest caste, a Chándala. -3 A mountaineer or barbarian. -4 (At the end of comp.) Any thing the best of its kind; *e. g.* बलाहकमातंगः -Comp. -दिवाकरः *m.* N. of a poet. —नक्रः *m.* A crocodile as large as an elephant [boaster.

मातरिपुरुषः *m.* A poltroon, cowardly

मातरिश्वन् *m.* Wind.

मातलिः *m.* N. of the charioteer of Indra. -Comp.-सारथिः *m.* An epithet of Indra.

माता *f.* A mother.

मातामहः *m.* A maternal grandfather. -हौ *m.* *dual* The maternal grand-father and grand-mother. -ही The maternal grand-mother.

मातिः *f.* 1 Measure. -2 An idea, conception.

मातुलः *m.* 1 A maternal uncle. -2 The Dhattúra plant. -3 A kind of snake. -Comp. -पुत्रकः *m.* 1 The son of a maternal uncle. -2 The fruit of the Dhattúra plant.

मातुलकः *m.* 1 A maternal uncle. -2 The thorn-apple.

मातुला, मातुलानी, मातुली *f.* 1 The wife of a maternal uncle. -2 Hemp.

मातुलिंगः, मातुलुंगः *m.* A kind of citron tree. —गं *n.* The fruit of this tree, a citron.

मातुलेयः (*f.* -यी) The son of a maternal uncle.

मातृ *f.* 1 A mother. -2 Mother as a term of respect or endearment. -3 A cow. -4 An epithet of Lakshmí. -5 An epithet of Durgá. -6 Ether, sky. -7 The earth. -8 A divine mother. -9 An epithet of Revatí. —मातरः *f. pl.* 1 An epithet of the divine-mothers, said to attend on Siva (They are eight according to some).

Comp. -केशटः *m.* A maternal uncle. -गंधिनी *f.* An unnatural mother. -गामिन् *m.* One who has committed incest with his mother. -गोत्रं *n.* A mother's family. -घात:, -घातक:, -घातिन्, -घ्न: *m.* 1 A matricide. —घातुक: *m.* 1 A matricide. -2 An epithet of Indra. -देव *a* Revering a mother like a God. —नंदन: *m.* An epithet of Kârtikeya.-पक्ष *a.* Belonging to the mother's side or line. (-क्ष: *m.*) Maternal kinsmen. मातापितरौ or मातरपितरौ *m. dual* Parents. —पुत्रौ (मातापुत्रौ) *m. dual* Mother and son. -पूजनं *n.* Worship of the divine mothers. —बंधु:, -बान्धव: *m.* Maternal kinsmen.(-धव,-वा:*pl.*)Relative on the mother's side. —मातृ *f.* An epithet of Pàrvatí. —मुख:, —शासित: *m.* A foolish fellow, a simpleton. -यज्ञ:*m.*A sacrifice, offered to the divine mothers. -वत्सल: *m.* An epithet of Kârtikeya. —स्वसृ *f.* (मातृष्वसृ or मातु: स्वसृ) A mother's sister, a maternal aunt. -स्वसेय: *m.* (मातृष्वसेय:) A mother's sister's son. (-यी *f.*) The daughter of a maternal aunt ; so मातृष्वस्रीय,-या.

मातृक *a.* (*f.* -का) 1 Coming or inherited from a mother. -2 Maternal. -क: *m.* A maternal uncle. -का *f.* 1 A mother. -2 A grand-mother. -3 A nurse. -4 A source, origin. -5 A divine mother. -6 N. of certain diagrams written in characters supposed to have a magical power. -8 The alphabet (*pl.*).

मात्र *a.* (*f.*-त्रा,-त्री) An affix added to nouns in the sense of 'measuring,' 'as much as,' 'as high or long, or broad as,' reaching as far as,' as in ऊरुमात्र So high as the thigh. —त्रं *n.* 1 A measure, of any kind. अंगुलिमात्रं The 'finger's breadth'. क्रोशमात्रे 'At the distance of a Krosa.' So क्षणमात्रं, निमिषमात्रं 'The space of an instant.' So गजमात्रं 'As high or big as an elephant'. -2 The full measure of anything, the whole ; as in जीवमात्रं or प्राणिमात्रं 'The entire class of living beings'. -3 The one thing and no more, often translateable by 'mere,' 'only', 'even'; as in वर्णमात्रेण कृष्ण: Black only in colour.

मात्रा *f.* 1 A measure ; the word is used in all the senses of मात्र *q. v.*). -2 A standard of measure. -3 The correct measure. -4 A unit of measure. -5 A moment. -6 A particle, an atom. -7 A part, portion. -8 A small portion, a little. -9 Account, consideration ; राजेति कियती मात्रा 'Of what account or consideration is a king, ?' *i. e.* I hold him of no account. -10 Money, property. -11 (In prosody).A syllabic instant.-12 An element. -13 The material world, matter. -14 The upper part of the Nâgarí characters. -15 An ear-ring. -16 An ornament ; a jewel. -17 A measure of time (in music). -18 Function of the organs (इंद्रियवृत्ति). -Comp. —अर्धं *n.* The half of a prosodial instant. —छंदस्, वृत्तं *n.* A metre regulated by the number of prosodial instants it contains, *e. g.* the Aryà. —भस्त्रा *f.* A money-bag.-बस्ति:*m.* An oily clyster. —संग: *m.* Attachment to household possessions. —स्पर्श: *m* Contact of the organs of sense with material elements.

मात्रिका *f.* A syllable or prosodial [instant.

मात्सर *a.* (*f.*-री), मात्सरिक *a.* (*f.*-की) Jealous, envious.

मात्सर्य *n.* 1 Envy, jealousy, spite, malice. -2 Displeasure.

मात्स्यकः *m.* A fisherman.

माथः *m.* 1 Stirring, churning. -2 Killing, destruction. -3 A road.

माथुर *a.* (*f.* —री) 1 Coming from Mathurá. -2 Produced in Mathurá. -3 Dwelling in Mathurâ.

मादः *m.* Intoxication. -2 Joy, delight. -3 Pride, arrogance.

मादक *a.* (*f.* —दिका) 1 Intoxicating, stupefying. -2 Gladdening. —कः *m.* A gallinule.

मादन *a.* (*f.* -नी) See मादक. -नः *m.* 1 The God of love. -2 The thorn-apple. —नं *n.* 1 Intoxication.-2 Delighting. -3 Cloves.

मादनीयं *n.* An intoxicating drink.

मादृक्ष *a.* (*f.* —क्षी) मादृश् *a.*, मादृश *a.* (*f.* —शी) Like me, resembling me.

माद्रकः *m.* A prince of the Madras.

माद्रवती *f.* N. of the second wife of Pándu.

माद्री *f.* N. of the second wife of Pándu. -Comp. -नंदनः*m.* An epithet of Nakula and Sahadeva. —पतिः *m.* An epithet of Pándu.

माद्रेयः *m.* An epithet of Nakula and Sahadeva.

माधव *a.* (*f.* -वी) 1 Honey-like, sweet. -2 Made of honey.-3 Vernal, relating to the spring. -4 Relating to the descendants of Madhu. -वः *m.* 1 N. of Krishna. -2 The spring season. -3 The month called Vaisákha. -4 N. of Indra. -5 N. of Parasuráma. -6 N. of the Yâdavas (pl.). -7 N. of a celebrated author. He was a very reputed scholar. -Comp.—श्रीः *f.* Vernal beauty.

माधवकः *m.* A kind of spirituous liquor.

माधविका *f.* N. of a creeper.

माधवी *f.* 1 Candied sugar. -2 A kind of drink made from honey. -3 A spring creeper (with white fragrant flowers. -4 The sacred basil. -5 A procuress, bawd.

माधवीय *a.* (*f.* —या) Relating to Mâdhava.

माधुकरी *f.* 1 Collecting alms by begging from door to door, as a bee collects honey from flower to flower. -2 Alms obtained from five different places. [creeper.

माधुरं *n.* The flower of the Mallikà

माधुरी *f.* 1 Sweetness, sweet taste. -2 Spirituous liquor.

माधुर्यं *n.* 1 Sweetness, gracefulness. -2 Exquisite beauty. -3 (In Rhet.) Sweetness, one of the three chief 'Gunas' in poetic compositions. -4 Kindness, amiability.

माध्यंदिन *a.* (*f.* -नी) 1 Midday, meridional. -2 Middle, central. —नः *m.* N. of a branch of Vâjasaneyins. —नं *n.* A branch of the शुक्ल or white Yajurveda (followed by the Màdhyandinas).

माध्यम *a.* (*f.* —मी), Belonging to the middle; central, middle, middlemost.

माध्यमक *a.* (*f.* —मिका), माध्यमिक *a.* (*f.* —की) Middle, central.

माध्यस्थं, माध्यस्थ्यं *n.* 1 Impartiality. -2 Indifference, unconcern. -3 Intercession, mediation. [to noon.

माध्याह्निक *a.* (*f.* —की) Belonging

माध्व *a.* (*f.* —ध्वी) Sweet. -ध्वः *m.* A follower of Madhva. —ध्वी *f.* 1 A beverage made from honey. -2 The creeper called Mádhaví.

माध्वकं *n.* An intoxicating drink made from honey.

माध्वीकं *n.* 1 A kind of liquor from the flowers of the tree Madhúka. -2 Wine from grapes. -3 A grape.

-Comp. —फलं *n*. A kind of cocoa-nut. q. v.).

मान् I A. (मीमांसते =desid. of मन्

मान् I P., 10 U. =Cuas of मन् q. v.

मानः *m*. I Respect,honour, respectful consideration. -2 Pride self-reliance, self-respect. -3 Haughtiness, conceit. -4 A wounded sense of honour. -5 Anger excited by jealousy (especially in women). -नं *n*. I Measuring.-2 A measure,standard. -3 Dimension. -4 Proof, means of proof or demonstration. -5 Likeness, resemblance. -Comp. —उन्नतिः *f*. Great respect or honour. —क्षितिः *f*., —भंगः *m*.,—हानिः *f*. Humiliation, mortification, insult, indignity. —ग्रंथिः *m*. Injury to honour or pride. —धन *a*. Rich in honour. —धानिका *f*. A cucumber. —महत *a*. Geatly proud. -योगः *m*. The correct mode of measuring or weighing. —रंध्रा *f*. A perforated water-vessel, which, placed in water and gradually filling, serves to measure time. —सूत्रं *n*. I A measuring-cord. -2 A chain (of gold &c.) worn round the body. [red arsenic.

मानःशिल *a*. (*f*. -ली) Consisting of

माननं *n*., -ना *f*. I Honouring, respecting. -2 Killing.

माननीय *a*.(*f*. -या) Fit to be honoured, worthy of honour (with gen.).

मानव *a*. (*f*. -वी) I Relating to, or descended from, Manu. -2Human. —वः *m*. I A man, human being.-वी *f*. A woman. -वं *n*. A particular fine. -Comp. —धर्मशास्त्रं *n*. The institutes of Manu.

मानवत *a*. (*f*. -ती) Proud, arrogant, haughty or high-spirited. —ती *f*. A haugty woman angry through jealous pride.

मानवीयं *n*. A particular fine.

मानव्यं *n*. A number of boys or youths.

मानस *a*. (*f*. —सी) Pertaining to the mind, mental, spiritual (opp. शारीर).-2 Produced from the mind. -3 Only to be conceived in the mind ; conceivable. -4 Tacit, implied. -5 Dwelling on the lake Mánasa. —सः *m*. A form of Vishnu. —सं *n*. I The mind, heart, soul. -2 N. of a sacred lake on the mountain Kailâsa. -3 (In law) Tacit or implied consent. -4 A kind of salt. -Comp. —आलयः *m*. A swan, goose. -ओकस्, -चारिन् *m*. A swan. -जन्मन् *m*. I The God of love. -2 A swan.

मानसिक *a*. (*f*. की) Mental, spiritual. —कः *m*. An epithet of Vishnu.

मानिका *f* I A kind of spirituous liquor. -2 A kind of weight.

मानित *p*. *p*. (*f*. —ता) Honoured, esteemed.

मानिन् *a*.(*f*.-नी) IFancying,considering,regarding (at the end of comp.); as in पंडितमानिन्. -2 Honouring, respecting (at the end of comp.).-3 Haughty, proud. -4 Entitled to respect. -5 Disdainful, angry. -6 Being regarded or considered as. -*m*. A lion. -नी *f*. I A woman possessed of self-respect;a strong-minded, resolute woman (in a good sense). -2 An angry woman or one offended with her husband (through jealous pride) -3 A kind of odoriferous plant.

मानुष *a*. (*f*. —षी) Human. -2 Humane, kind. -षः*m*. I A man, human being. -3 An epithet of the three signs of the zodiac, Gemini, Virgo, and Libra. -षी *f*. I A woman. -2 Administering drugs and herbs.

-षं *n.* 1 Humanity, -2 Human effort or action. [tal.

मानुषक *a.* (*f.* —की) Human, mortal.

मानुष्यं, मानुष्यकं *n* 1 Human nature, humanity. -2 A mortal frame, human body. -3 Mankind.-4 A collection of men.

मानोज्ञकं *n.* Beauty, loveliness.

मांत्रिकः *m.* A conjurer, sorcerer.

मांदारः, मांदारवः *m.* A kind of tree.

मांद्यं *n.* 1 Dulness, laziness.-2 Stupidity. -3 Weakness, feeble state, as in अग्निमांद्यं. -4 Apathy. -5 Sickness, illness.

मांधातृ *m.* N. of a king of the solar race, son of Yuvanâsva.

मान्य *pot. p.* (*f.* -न्या) 1 To be revered or respected. -2 Respectable, honourable.

मापत्यः *m.* The God of love.

माम *a.* (*f.* —मी) 1 My, mine. -2 Uncle (used in voc.).

मामक *a.* (*f.* —मिका) 1 My, mine, belonging to my side. -3 Selfish, covetous, greedy. -कः *m.* 1 A misėr. -2 A maternal uncle.

मामकीन *a.* (*f.* —ना) My, mine.

मायः *m.* 1 A conjurer, juggler. -2 A demon, an evil spirit.

माया *f.* 1 Deceit, fraud, trick, a device, an artifice. -2 Jugglery, witchcraft, enchantment.-3 A phantom, illusion, unreal apparition.-4 A diplomatic feat. -5 (In Vedânta phil.) Unreality, the illusion by virtue of which one considers the unreal universe as really existent and as distinct from the Supreme Spirit. -6 (In Sán. phil.) The Pradhâna or Prakriti. -7 Wickedness. -8 Pity, compassion. -9 N. of the mother of Buddha.-10 N. of the city Gayâ. -11 N. of Lakshmi. -Comp. -कारः, -कृत्,-जीविन् *m.* A conjurer, juggler. -चण *a.* 1 Noted for juggling. -2 Deceptive. -दः *m.* A crocodile. -देवि *f.* N. of the mother of Buddha. -धर *a.* Deceitful, illusive. -फलं *n.* A gall-nut. -वादः *m.* The doctrine of illusion (a term applied to Buddhism). -सुतः *m.* An epithet of Buddha.

मायामय *a.* (*f.* -यी) 1 Illusive, deceitful. -2 False, unreal. -3 Magical.

मायावत् *a.* (*f.* -ती) 1 Deceitful, fraudulent. -2 Illusory, deceptive. -3 Skilled in magical arts. -*m.* An epithet of Kamsa. -ती *f.* N. of the wife of Pradyumna.

मायाविन *a.* (*f.* -नी) 1 Deceitful, fraudulent. -2 Skilled in magic. -3 Unreal, illusory.-*m.* 1 A magician. conjurer. -2 A cat. -*n.* A gall-nut.

मायिक *a.* (*f.* -का) 1 Deceitful, fraudulent. -2 Illusory, unreal. -कः *m.* A juggler. -कं *n.* A gall-nut.

मायिन् See मायाविन्.

मायुः *m.* 1 The sun.-2 Bile, bilious humour (*n.* also in this sense).

मायूर *a.* (*f.* -री) 1 Belonging to or arising from a peacock. -2 Made of the feathers of a peacock. -3 Drawn by a peacock (as a car). -4 Dear to a peacock. -रं *n.* A flock of peacocks. [catcher.

मायूरकः, मायूरिकः *m.* A peacock-

मारः *m.* 1 Killing, slaughter, slaying. -2 A hindrance, opposition. -3 The God of love. -4 Love, passion. -5 The thorn-apple (धत्तूर). -6 The devil, the evil one (according to Buddhists).-7 Death.-Comp. -अंक *a.* Displaying signs of love. -अभिभूः *f.* An epithet of a Buddha. -अरिः, —रिपुः *m.* Siva. —आत्मक *a*

Murderous. -जित् *m.* A epithet of Siva. -2 Of a Buddha.

मारकः *m.* 1 A pestilential disease, plague, epidemic. -2 The God of love. -3 A murderer; a destroyer in general. -4 A hawk.

मारकत *a* (*f.* -ती) Belonging to an emerald.

मारणं *n.* 1 Killing, slaying, slaughter, destruction. -2 A magical ceremony performed for destroying an enemy -3 Calcination. -4 A kind of poison. [Killing, ruin.

मारिः *f.* 1 A pestilence, plague. -2

मारिका *f.* A plague, pestilence.

मारिच *a.* (*f.* ची) Made of pepper.

मारिषः *m.* A respectable, worthy or venerable man (in dramas a respectful mode of address by the Sútradhâra to his assistant.

मारी *f.* 1 Plague, pestilence. -2 The goddess presiding over plagues.

मारीचः *m.* 1 N. of a demon. -2 A large elephant. -3 A kind of plant. -चं *n.* A collection of pepper shrubs.

मारुंडः *m.* 1 A serpent's egg. -2 Cow-dung. -3 A way, road. -4 A place covered with cow-dung.

मारुत *a.* (*f.* ती) 1 Relating to the Maruts. -2 Relating to wind; windy. —तः *m.* 1 Wind. -2 The God of wind. -3 Breathing. -4 Vital air, one of the three essential humours of the body. -5 The trunk of an elephant. -ती *f.* The north-west quarter. -तं *n.* The lunar mansion Sváti. -Comp. -अशनः *m.* A snake. -आत्मजः, -सुतः, -सूनुः *m.* 1 Epithets of Hanumat. -2 Of Bhíma.

मारुतिः *m.* 1 An epithet of Hanumat. -2 Of Bhíma.

मार्कंडः, मार्कंडेयः *m.* N. of an ancient sage. -Comp. —पुराणं *n.* N. of one of the eighteen Puránas (composed by this sage).

मार्ग् 1 P., 10 U. (मार्गति, मार्गयति,-ते) 1 To seek, seek for. -2 To hunt after, chase. -3 To strive after. -4 To ask for. -5 To ask in marriage. -6 To seek through, trace out.

मार्ग् 10 U. (मार्गयति,-ते) 1 To go, move. -2 To decorate, adorn. -With परि- To seek, look out for.

मार्गः *m.* 1 A way, path (fig. also). -2 A passage; the tract passed over. -3 Reach, range. -4 A scar, mark (as of a wound &c.). -5 The path of a planet. -6 Search, inquiry. -7 A canal, channel. -8 A means, way. -9 The right way or course, proper course. -10 Mode, method, course. -11 Style, direction. -12 Custom, practice. -13 Tracing out game. -14 A ground for litigation. -15 A high style of acting, dancing and singing. -16 (In dramaturgy) Indicating how anything is to happen. -17 (In geom.) A section. -18 The anus. 19 Musk. -20 The constellation called मृगशिरस्. -21 The month called मार्गशीर्ष. -Comp. -तोरणं *n.* A triumphal arch erected on a road. -धेनुः *m.*, -धेनुकं *n.* A measure of distance equal to 4 'krosas.' —रक्षकः *m.* A road-keeper, guard. —हर्म्यं *n.* A palace on a high road.

मार्गकः *m.* The month called मार्गशीर्ष.

मार्गणं *n.*, —णा *f.* 1 Begging, soliciting. -2 Searching -3 Investigating, inquiry. —णः *m.* 1 A beggar, supplicant, mendicant. -2 An arrow. -3 The number 'five'.

मार्गणकः *m.* A beggar, supplicant.

मार्गशिरः, मार्गशिरस्, मार्गशीर्षः *m.* N. of the ninth month of the Hindu year (corresponding to November,

December, in which the full moon is in the constellation मृगशिरस्.

मार्गशिरी, मार्गशीर्षी *f.* The full-moon day in the month of मार्गशीर्ष.

मार्गिकः *m.* 1 A traveller. -2 A hunter.

मार्गित *p. p.* (*f.* -ता) 1 Sought, inquired after. -2 Hunted after, desired, solicited.

मार्ज् 10 U. (मार्जयति.-ते) 1To purify, cleanse, wipe. -2 To sound.

मार्जः *m.* 1 Cleaning, purifying. -2 A washerman. -3 An epithet of Vishnu.

मार्जक *a.* (*f.* —र्जिका) Cleansing, purifying, scouring.

मार्जनं *n.* 1 Cleansing, cleaning, purifying. -2 Wiping off. -3 Effacing. -4 Cleansing the person by rubbing it with unguents. -5 Sprinkling the body with consecrated water. —नः *m.* The Lodhra tree. —ना *f.* 1 Cleansing, purifying, cleaning. -2 The sound of a drum. —नी *f.* A broom, brush.

मार्जारः (—लः) *m.* 1 A cat. -2 A pole-cat. -Comp. —कंठः *m.* A peacock. —करणं *n.* A particular mode of sexual enjoyment. —कर्णिका, -कर्णी *f.* N. of Châmundâ.

मार्जारकः *m.*1 A cat. -2 A peacock.

मार्जारी *f.* 1 A female cat. -2 A civet-cat.-3 Musk.

मार्जारीयः *m.* 1 A cat. -2 A Sudra.

मार्जित *p. p.* (*f.* -ता) 1 Cleansed, purified. -2 Swept, brushed. -3 Clean, bright. -4 Washed away, removed. [spices.

मार्जिता *f.* Curds with sugar and

मार्तंडः *m.* 1 The sun.-2 The Arka tree. -3 A hog. -4 The number twelve (Also मार्तांड).

मार्तिक *a.* (*f.* —की) Made of clay, earthen. —कः *m.* 1 A kind of pitcher. -2 The lid of pitcher. -कं *n.* A clod or lump of earth.

मार्त्य *n.* Mortality. [city, town.

मार्दंगः *m.* A drummer. —गं *n.* A

मार्दंगिकः *m.* A drummer.

मार्दवं *n.* 1 Softness (lit. and fig.), weakness.-2 Mildness, indulgence, leniency.

मार्द्वीक *a.* (*f.* -की) Made of grapes. —कं *n.* Wine. [into-

मार्मिक *a.* Having a deep insight

मार्षः *m.* The same as मारिषः.

मार्ष्टिः *f.* Cleansing, purifying.

मालः *m.* 1 N. of a country in the west or south-west of Bengal. -2 N. of a tribe of barbarians. -3 N. of Vishnu. —लं *n.* 1 A field. -2 A rising or elevated ground. -3 A wood near a village. -4 Fraud, deceit. -Comp. —चक्रकं *n.* The hip-joint.

मालकः *m.* 1 The *Nimba* tree. -2 A wood near a village.-3 A pot made of a cocoa-nut shell. —का *f.*, -कं *n.* A garland. [cal mode.

मालकोशः *m.* N. of a Râga or musi-

मालतिः, -ती *f.* 1 A kind of jasmine. -2 A flower of this jasmine. -3 A bud, blossom (in general.) -4 A young woman. -5 Night. -6 Moonlight. -Comp. —क्षारकः *m.*, —तीरजं *n.* Borax. —पत्रिका *f.* The shell of a nutmeg. —फलं *n.* A nutmeg. -माधवं *n.* N. of a celebrated drama by Bhavabhûti.

मालय *a.* (*f.* —यी) Coming from the Malaya mountain.-यः *m.* Sandal wood.

मालवः *m.* 1 N. of a country, the modern Mâlvâ in central India. -2 N. of a Râga or musical mode -वाः *m. pl.* The people of Mâlvâ.

मालवकः *m.* 1 The country of the Mâlavas. -2 An inhabitant of Mâlvâ.

मालसी *f.* N. of a plant.

माला *f.* 1 A garland, chaplet. -2 A row, line, series. -3 A cluster, collection. -4 A string, necklace. -5 A rosary, chain, as in अक्षमाला. -6 A streak, as in ताडिन्माला, विद्युन्माला. -7 (In dramas) The offering of several things to obtain a wish. -Comp. —उपमा *f.* An Upamá or simile, in which the same *Upameya* is compared to several *Upamânas*; *e. g.* अनयेनेव राज्यश्रीर्दैन्येनेव मनस्विता। मम्लौ साथविषादेन पद्मिनीव हिमाम्भसा. —करः, -कारः *m.* 1 A garland-maker, gardener. -2 The caste of gardeners. -गुणः *m.* A necklace. -तृणं *n.* A kind of fragrant grass. -दीपकं *n.* A figure of speech in which several objects are in succession connected with the same attribute. तन्मालादीपकं पुनः। धर्मिणामेकधर्मेण संबंधोयद्यथोत्तरं ॥ * साहि. द. *e. g.* त्वयि संगरसंप्राप्ते धनुषासादिताः शराः। शरैरिशिरस्तेनभूस्तया त्वं त्वया यशः ॥

मालिकः *m.* 1 A florist, gardener. -2 A painter. -3 A garland-maker.

मालिका *f.* 1 A garland. -2 A row, series. -3 A necklace. -4 A variety of jasmine. -5 Linseed. -6 A daughter. -7 A palace. -8 A kind of bird. -9 An intoxicating drink.

मालिन् *a.* (*f.* —नी) 1 Wearing a garland. -2 Crowned or wreathed with, encircled by, as in अंशुमालिन् मरीचिमालिन्, ऊर्मिमालिन् &c. —*m.* 1 A gardener. -2 A garland-maker, florist. —नी *f.* 1 A female florist, the wife of a garland-maker. -2 N. of the city of Champâ. -3 A girl seven years old representing Durgá at the Durgá festival. -4 N. of Durgá. -5 The celestial Ganges -6 N. of a metre. -7 N. of the mother of Bibhîshana. -8 N. asumed by Draupadî while residing at the Court of Viráta. -9 N. of a river.

मालिन्यं *n.* 1 Dirtiness, impurity. -2 Pollution, defilement. -3 Sinfulness. -4 Blackness. -5 Trouble, affliction.

मालुः *f.* 1 A kind of creeper. -2 A woman. -Comp. —धानः *m.* A kind of snake. [*Kapittha* tree.

मालूरः *m.* 1 The *Bilva* tree. -2 The

मालेया *f.* Large cardamoms.

माल्यं *n.* 1 A garland, wreath. -2 A flower. -3 A chaplet or garland worn on the head. -Comp. —जीविकः *m.* A florist, garland-maker. —पुष्पः *m.* A kind of hemp. —वृत्तिः *m.* A florist.

माल्यवत् *a.* (*f.* -ती) Wreathed. —*m.* 1 N. of a mountain or mountain range. -2 N. of a demon, son of Suketu.

माल्लः *m.* N. of a particular mixed tribe.

माल्लवी *f.* A wrestling match.

माषः *m.* 1 A bean; (the sing. being used for the plant and the pl. for the fruit or seed). -2 A particular weight of gold. -3 A fool, blockhead. -4 A kind of pulse. -5 A cutaneous eruption resembling beans. -Comp. —अदः, -आदः *m.* A tortoise. —आज्यं *n.* Beans cooked with ghee. —आशः *m.* A horse. —ऊन *a.* Less by a Mâsha. -वर्धकः *m.* A goldsmith.

माषिक *a.* (*f.* -की) Worth a Mâsha.

माषीणं *n.* A field of beans.

माष्यं *n.* A field of beans.

मास् *m.* The same as मास (This word has no forms for the first five inflections and is optionally substituted for मास after acc. dual.) -2 The moon.

मासः *m.*, -सं *n.* 1 A month (either चांद्र, सौर, सावन, नाक्षत्र or बार्हस्पत्य).-2 The number 'twelve'.-Comp. -अनुमासिक *a.* Monthly.-अंतः *m.* The day of new moon.-उपवासिनी *f.* 1 A woman who fasts for a whole month. -2 A procuress; a lascivious or lewd woman (*fig*). —जात *a.* A month old. —ह्वः *m.* A. kind of gallinule. —देय *a.* To be paid in a month. —प्रमितः *m.* The new-moon.—प्रवेशः *m.* The beginning of a month. —मानः *m.* A year.

मासकः *m.* A month.

मासरः*m.*1 The scum of boiled rice, rice-gruel. -2 The meal of parched barley mixed with sour milk.

मासलः *m.* A year.

मासिक *a.* (*f.* -की) 1 Relating to a month. -2 Monthly. -3 Lasting for a month. -4 Payable in a month. -5 Engaged for a month. —कं *n.* A funeral rite or Srâddha performed every new-moon day (during the first year of a man's death).

मासीन *a.* (*f.* -ना) 1 One month old. -2 Monthly.

मासुरी *f.* A beard.

माह् 1 U. (माहति, —ते) To measure.

माहाकुल *a.* (*f.* -ली), महाकुलीन *a.* (*f.*-नी) 1 Nobly born, of illustrious descent.

माहाजनिक *a.* (*f.* -की), माहाजनीन *a.* (*f.* -नी) 1 Fit for merchants. -2 Fit for great persons.

माहात्मिक *a.* (*f.*-की) High-minded, magnanimous, dignified, glorious.

माहात्म्यं *n.* 1 Magnanimity, noble-mindedness. -2 Majesty, exalted position. -3 The peculiar virtue of any divinity. -4A work giving an account of the merits of divinities or shrines; as देवीमाहात्म्य, शनिमाहात्म्य &c.

माहानस *a.* (*f.* -सी) 1 Belonging to a large carriage. -2 Relating to a kitchen.

माहाराजिक *a.* (*f.* -की) Fit for a great king; imperial, royal.

माहाराज्यं *n.* Sovereignty.

माहाराष्ट्री *f.* The same as महाराष्ट्री.

माहिरः *m.* An epithet of Indra.

माहिष *a.*(*f.* -षी) Coming or derived from a buffalo or a buffalo-cow.

माहिषकः *m.* A buffalo-keeper.

माहिषिकः *m.* 1 A buffalo-keeper. -2 The paramour of an unchaste woman. -3 One who lives by the prostitution of his wife.

माहिष्मती *f.* N. of a city.

माहिष्यः *m* A mixed caste sprung from a Kshatriya father and Vaisya mother.

माहेंद्र *a.* (*f.* -द्री) 1 Relating to or fit for Indra. -2 Eastern. —द्री *f.* 1 The east.-2A cow.-3 N. of Indrânî.

माहेय *a.* (*f.* -यी) 1 Terrestrial. -2 Made of earth, earthen. —यः *m.* 1 The planet Mars. -2 The demon Naraka. -3 Coral.

माहेयी *f.* A cow.

माहेश्वर *a.* (*f.* -री) 1 Belonging to a great lord or to Siva. -2 Worshipping Siva. —रः *m.* A worshipper of Siva. —री *f.* N. of Párvatî or Durgá.

मि 5 U. (मिनोति, मिनुते; rarely used in classical literature) 1 To cast, scatter. -2 To build, erect. -3 To measure. -4 To observe, perceive.

मिच्छ् 6 P. (मिच्छति) 1 To hinder, obstruct. -2 To annoy.

मित *p. p.* (*f.* —ता) 1 Measured, measured out. -2 Measured off, limited. -3 Moderate, little, scanty, sparing, brief (words &c.).-4 Investigated, examined.-Comp. -अक्षर a. 1 Brief, short, concise. -2 Metrical. (-रा f.) N. of a commentary by Vijnânesvara on Yâjnavalkya's Smriti. -अर्थक: m. A cautious envoy.

मितंगम: m. An elephant.

मितंपच a. 1 Cooking little.-2 Sparing, niggardly, stingy.

मिति: f. 1 Measuring, a measure, weight. -2 Accurate knowledge. -3 Proof, evidence. -4 Determination.

मित्र: m. 1 The sun. -2 N. of a Vedic deity. -त्रं n. 1 A friend. -2 An ally, the next neighbour of a king. -Comp. -आचार: m. Conduct towards a friend. -कर्मन्,-कार्यः,-कृत्यं n. A friendly act or service. -घ्न a. Treacherous. -द्रोहिन् a. Treacherous to a friend. -सप्तमी f. N. of the seventh day in the bright half of मार्गशीर्ष. -सह a. Kind or indulgent to friends. [A friend.

मित्रयु a. Friendly-minded -युः m.

मिथ् 1 U. (मेथति,-ते) 1 To associate with. -2 To unite, copulate. -3 To hurt, kill.-4 To understand. -5 To wrangle.

मिथस् ind. 1 Mutually, reciprocally. -2 Secretly, privately.

मिथिल: m. N. of a king. -ला: m.pl. N. of a people. -ला f. N. of a city, capital of the country called Videha

मिथुनं n. 1 A pair, couple.-2 Union, junction. -3 Sexual union, copulation. -4 The sign *Gemini* of the zodiac. -5 (In gram.) A root compounded with a preposition.

मिथुनीभाव: m. Cohabitation, sexual union. [वाक).

मिथुनेचर: m. The ruddy goose (चक्र-

मिथ्या ind. 1 Falsely, wrongly, incorrectly.-2 Invertedly, contrarily. -3 In vain, fruitlessly. (मिथ्या कृ 1 To falsify. -2 To contradict. मिथ्या भू To turn out false, be false ; मिथ्या ग्रह् To misunderstand, mistake). At the beginning of comp. मिथ्या may be translated by 'false,' 'untrue.' 'unreal.' 'sham,' 'pretended.' -Comp.-अध्यवसिति: f. A paricular figure of speech. -अपवाद: m. A false charge.-अभिधानं n. A false assertion. -अभियोग: m. A false or groundless charge. -अभिशंसनं n. Calumny, false accusation. -अभिशाप: m. 1 A false diction.-2 A false or unjust claim. -उत्तरं n. A false or prevaricating reply. -कर्मन् n. A false act. -ग्रह: m., -ग्रहणं n. Misconception, mis-understanding. -चर्या f. Hypocrisy. -ज्ञानं n. A mistake, error, misapprehension. -दर्शनं n. Heresy. -दृष्टि: f. Heresy, holding atheistic doctrines. -पुरुष: m. A man only in appearance. -वार्ता f. A false report. -साक्षिन् m. A false witness.

मिद् 1 A., 4. 10 U. (मेदते, मेद्यति,-ते, मेदयति,-ते) 1 To be unctuous or greasy. -2 To melt. -3 To be fat. -4 To love, feel affection.

मिद् 1 U. (मेदति,-ते) See मिथ्.

मिद्धं n. 1 Sloth, indolence. -2 Sleepiness, dulness.

मिन्व् 1 P. (मिन्वति) 1 To moisten. -2 To honour, worship.

मिल् 6 U. (मिलति,-ते, मिलित) 1 To join, be united with, accompany. -2 To come together, gather, assemble. -3 To encounter (as in fighting). -4 To happen.-5 To embrace, clasp.

मिलनं n. 1 Joining, meeting, assembling together. -2 Encountering. -3 Contact, coming in contact with.

मिलित p. p. (f. -ता) 1 Assembled,

encountered, combined. -2 Met, encountered. -3 Mixed -4 Put together, taken in all.

मिलिन्द: *m.* A bee.

मिलिन्दक: *m.* A kind of snake.

मिशृ 1 P. (मेशति) 1 To make a sound or noise. -2 To provoke.

मिश्र 10 U. (मिश्रयति,-ते) 1 To mix, mingle, unite, combine.-2To add to.

मिश्र *a.* (*f.* —श्रा) 1 Mixed, mingled, combined. -2 Associated, connected. -3 Manifold, diverse. -4 Intertwined. —श्र: *m.* 1 A title of respect affixed to the names of scholars and great men, as in कृष्णमिश्र, मित्रमिश्र &c. -2 A kind of elephant -3 The group of the constellations कृत्तिका and विशाखा. —श्रं *n.* 1 A mixture. -2 A kind of radish. -Comp. —ज: *m.* A mule. —शब्द: *m.* A mule.

मिश्रक: *m.* 1 A compounder.-2 An adulterator of mercantile goods.-कं *n.* Salt produced from salt soil.

मिश्रणं *n.* 1 Mixing, combining. -2 (In arith.) Addition.

मिश्रित *p. p.* (*f.*-ता) 1 Mixing, combined. -2 Added. -3 Respectable.

मिष् 6 P. (मिषति) 1 To open the eyes, wink.-2 To look at, look helplessly. -3 To rival, emulate

मिष् 1 P. (मेषति) To wet, moisten, sprinkle.

मिष: *m.* Emulation, rivalry. —षं *n.* Pretext, deceit, false or outward appearance (aften used like छल to indicate an उत्प्रेक्षा).

मिष्ट *a.* (*f.* —ष्टा) 1 Sweet. -2 Dainty, savoury. -3 Moistened, wetted. -ष्टं *n.*1 A sweet-meat.-2A dainty or savoury dish.-ष्ट:*m.*Sweetness.

मिह् 1 P.(मेहति,मीढ)1To make water. -2 To wet, moisten, sprinkle. -3 To emit semen.

मिहिका *f.* Mist, snow.

मिहिर: *m.* 1 The sun.-2 A cloud.-3 The moon. -4 Wind, air. -5 An old man. -6 The *Arka* plant.

मिहिराण: *m.* An epithet of Siva.

मी 9 U.(मीनाति,मीनीते) 1 To kill, hurt, injure.-2To diminish.-3To change, alter. -4 To violate. -5 To disappear, be lost. -6 To stray, go astray.

मी P., 10 U. (मयति, माययति,-ते) 1To go, move. -2 To know, understand.

मी 4 A. (मीयते) To die, perish.

मीढ *p.p.* (*f.* —ढा) 1 Urined, watered. -2 Passed (as urine).

मीढुष्टम: *m.* 1 An epithet of Siva.-2 The sun. -3 A thief.

मीढ्वस् *a.* 1 Bountiful, liberal. -2 Discharging semen.

मीन: *m.* 1 A fish. -2 The twelfth sign of the zodiac (*Pisces*). -3 The first incarnation of Vishnu.-Comp. —अंडं *n.* A fish-spawn. —आघातिन्, —घातिन् *m.* 1 A fisherman. -2 A crane. —केतन: *m.* The God of love. —गंध: *f.* An epithet of Satyavatî. —गंधिका *f.* A pond, pool of water. —रंक:, —रंग: *m.* A king-fisher.

मीनर: *m.* The sea-monster *Makara.*

मीम् 1 P. (मीमति) 1 To go, move. -2 To sound.

मीमांसक: *m.* 1 One who investigates or inquires into; an investigator, examiner. -2 A follower of the system of philosophy called मीमांसा.

मीमांसा *f.* 1 Inquiry, examination, investigation. -2 N. of one of the six chief *darsanas* or systems of Indian philosophy. -Comp. —कार:, —कृत *m.* N. of Jaimini.

मीर: *m.* 1 The ocean. -2 A limit, boundary.

मील् 1 P. (मीलति, मीलित) 1 To close (as the eyes), wink, twinkle. -2

ing. -6 Unloosing, opening.-7 Discharge, paying off (as a debt). -Comp. —क्षेत्रं n. An epithet of Benaras. —मार्गः m. The way to final beatitude.—मुक्तः m. Frank-incense.

मुखं n. 1 The mouth (fig. also). -2 The face, countenance. -3 The snout or muzzle (of any animal). -4 The front, van, forepart ; head, top.-5 The tip, point (of an arrow), head. -6 The edge or sharp point (of any instrument). -7 A teat, nipple. -8 The beak or bill of a bird. -9 A direction, quarter. -10 Opening, entrance, mouth. -11 An entrance to a house, a door.-12 Beginning, commencement. -13 Introduction. -14 The chief, the principal or prominent ; as in इंद्रमुखा देवाः &c. -15 The upper side. -16 A means.-17 A source, cause.-18 The Vedas, scripture.-19 (In Rhet.) The original source of the action in a drama. -20 The first term in a progression (in arith.). -21 The side opposite to the base of a figure. -Comp. —अग्निः m. 1 A forest conflagration. -2 A sort of goblin. -3 The consecrated or sacrificial fire. -4 Fire put into the mouth of a corpse at the time of lighting the funeral pile. -5 A Brâhmana. —अनिलः, —उच्छ्वासः m. Breath. —अस्त्रः m. A crab. —आकारः m. Look, mien, appearance. —आस्रवः, —स्रावः m. Spittle, saliva. —उल्का f. A forest-conflagration.—खुरः m. A tooth. —गंधकः m. An onion. —चीरिः f. The tongue. —जः m. Brâhmana. —जाहं n. The root of the mouth. —दूषणः m. An onion. —निरीक्षकः m. A lazy fellow, an idler. —निवासिनी f. An epithet of Sarasvatî. —पाकः m. Inflammation of the mouth. —पूरणं n. 1 A mouthful of water, a mouthful in general. —प्रसादः m. A pleased countenance, graciousness of aspect. —प्रियः m. An orange.—बंधः m. A preface, an introduction. —बंधनं n. 1 A preface. -2 A lid, cover. —यंत्रणं n. The bit of a bridle. —रागः m. The colour or complexion of the face. —लांगलः m. A dog. —वल्लभः m. The pomegranate tree. -वासः, —वासनः m. A perfume used to scent the breath. —विलुंठिका f. A she-goat. —शफ a. Foul-mouthed, scurrilous. —शुद्धिः f. Washing or purifying the mouth. —शेषः m. An epithet of Ráhu. -शोधन a. 1 Ceansing the mouth. -2 Pungent, sharp. (—नः m.) The sharp flavour, pungency. (-नं n.) 1 Cleansing the mouth -2 Cinnamon. —शोधिन् m. The citron tree. —श्रीः f. A lovely face. —संभवः m. A Brâhmana. —स्रावः m. Saliva.

मुखंपचः m. A beggar, mendicant.

मुखर a. (f. -रा) 1 Talkative, garrulous. -2 Noisy, tinkling, jingling (as an anklet &c.).-3 Sounding, resonant or resounding with (usually at the end of comp.). -4 Expressive or indicative of.-5 Foul-mouthed, abusive, scurrilous. —रः m. 1 A crow. -2 A leader, the chief or principal person. -3 A conch-shell. —री f. The bit of a bridle.

मुखरय् Den. P. 1 To make noisy, cause to sound or echo. -2 To make (one) talk or speak. -3 To notify, declare, announce.

मुखरिका f. 1 The bit of a bridle. -2 Conversation.

मुखरित a. (f. -ता) Made noisy, [ringing with.

मुख्य a. (f. -ख्या) 1 Relating to the mouth or the face. -2 Chief, foremost, pre-eminent, prominent. —स्थ: *m.* A leader, guide. —स्थं *n.* 1 A principal rite or ordinance. -2 Reading or teaching the Vedas. —Comp. —अर्थ: *m.* The primary or original (as opp. गौण) meaning of a word. -चांद्र: *m.* The chief lunar month. —नृप:, -नृपति: *m.* A paramount sovereign. —मंत्रिन् *m.* The prime minister.

मुग्रहः *m.* A kind of gallinule.

मुग्ध *a.* (*f.* -ग्धा) 1 Stupefied, fainted. -2 Perplexed. -3 Foolish, silly, stupid. -4 Simple, artless. -5 Erring, mistaken. -6 Attractive by youthful simplicity. -7 Beautiful, lovely, pretty.-ग्धा *f.* A pretty young maiden ; (regarded as a variety of Nâyikà in poetic compositions). -Comp. -अक्षी *f.* A lovely-eyed woman. —आनना *a.* Lovely-faced woman.-आलोक *a.* Lovely to look at. —बुद्धि, —मति *a.* Silly, foolish, stupid, simple. —भाव: *m.* Simplicity, silliness. [cheat.

मुच् 1 A. (मोचते) To deceive,

मुच् 6 U. (मुंचति,-ते, मोक्तुं, मुक्त) 1 To loose, set free, liberate. -2 To set free, loosen (as the voice). -3 To abandon, quit. -4 To set apart, take away, except. -5 To dismiss, send away. -6 To cast, throw, discharge. -7 To emit, drop, let fall (tears &c.). -8 To utter. -9 To grant, bestow. -10 To . . d (as excrement).

मुचक: *m.* Lac.

मुच (-चु-) कुंद: *m.* 1 N. of a tree. -2 N. of an ancient king, son of Mândhâtri. -Comp. -प्रसादक: *m.* An epithet of Krishna. [Wind, air.

मुचिर: *m.* 1 A deity. -2 Virtue. -3

मुचिलिंद: *m.* A kind of flower.

मुचुटी *f.* 1 Snapping the fingers. -2 A fist. -3 A pair of forceps.

मुज्, मुंज् 1 P., 10 U. (मोजति, मुजंति, मोजयति,-ते, मुंजयति,-ते) 1 To cleanse, purify. -2 To sound.

मुंज: *m.* 1 A sort of rush or grass (of which the girdle of a Brâhmana is made). -2 The sacred cord or girdle itself. -3 N. of a king of Dhârà the uncle of the celebrated Bhoja. -Comp. —केश: *m.* 1 An epithet of Siva. -2 Of Vishnu. —कोशिन् *m.* An epithet of Vishnu. —बंधनं *n.* Investiture with the sacred thread (or gridle). —मेखलिन् *m.* 1 N. of Siva. -2 Of Vishnu. -वासस् *m.* An epithet of Siva. [lotus.

मुंजरं *n.* The fibrous root of the

मुंट् 1 P. (मुंटति) To crush, grind.

मुंड् 1 P. (मुंडति) To shave, shear.

मुंड् 1 P. (मुंडते) To sink.

मुंड *a.* (*f.* -डा) 1 Shaved, bald. -2 Stripped of top-leaves. -3 Blunt, pointless. -4 Low, mean. —ड: *m.* 1 A man with a shaved or bald head. -2 A bald or shaven head. -3 The forehead. -4 A barber. -5 The trunk of a tree stripped of its leaves and branches. -6 An epithet of Rahu. —डं *n.* 1 The head. -2 Myrrh. -3 Iron. -Comp. —अयसं *n.* Iron. —फल: *m.* A cocoa-nut tree. —लोहं *n.* Iron. —शालि: *m.* A kind of rice.

मुंडक: *m.* 1 A barber. -2 The trunk of a tree stripped of its branches. —कं *n.* The head. -Comp. -उपनिषद् *f.* N. of an Upanishad of the Atharvaveda.

मुंडनं *n.* Shaving the head, tonsure.

मुंडित *p. p.* (*f.* -ता) 1 Shaved. -2 Lopped. —तं *n.* Iron.

मुंडिन् *m.* 1 A barber. -2 An epithet of Siva.

मुत्यं *n.* A pearl.

मुद् 10 U. (मोदयति,-ते) 1 To mix. -2 To cleanse, purify.

मुद् 1 A. (मोदते, मुदित) To rejoice, be glad or happy, be delighted.

मुद्, मुदा *f.* Joy, pleasure,gladness, satisfaction.

मुदित *p. p.* (*f.* -ता) Pleased,rejoiced ; delighted, joyous.—तं*n.* 1 Pleasure, delight, happiness. -2 A kind of sexual embrace.—ता *f.* Joy, delight.

मुदिरः *m.* 1 A cloud. -2 A lover, libertine. -3 A frog.

मुदी *f.* Moon-light.

मुद्गः *m.* 1 A kind of kidney-bean. -2 A lid, cover. -3 A kind of sea-bird. -Comp. —भुज्, —भोजिन *m.* A horse.

मुद्गरः *m.* 1 A hammer, mallet. -2 A club, mace.-3 A staff for breaking clods of earth. -4 A kind of dumb-bell. -5 A bud. -6 A kind of jasmine (*n.* also in this sense).

मुद्गलः *m.* N. of a sage. —लं *n.* A kind of grass.

मुद्गष्टः *m.* A kind of bean.

मुद्रणं *n.* 1 Sealing, printing, marking -2 Closing, shutting.

मुद्रा *f.* 1 A seal, a seal ring,signet ring, (fig. also). -2 A mark, impression. -3 A pass, pass-port.-4 A stamped coin, coin,piece of money. -5 A medal.-6 An image, a badge, token. -7 Shutting, closing. sealing. 8 A mystery. -9 N. of certain positions of the fingers practised in devotion or religious worship. -Comp. —अक्षरं *n.* A letter of the seal. —मार्गः *m.* An opening in the crown of the head through which the soul is said to escape at death. —राक्षसं *n.* N. of a drama by Visâkha-datta.

मुद्रिका *f.* 1 A little seal.-2 A seal-ring. -3 A stamp or impression.-4 A stamped coin, coin. -5 A signed or sealed paper.-6 A particular surgical instrument.

मुद्रित *a.* (*f.* —ता) 1 Sealed, marked, stamped. -2 Closed, sealed up. -3 Unblown. -4 Printed.

मुधा *ind.* 1 In vain, uselessly, unprofitably. -2 Wrongly, falsely.

मुनिः *m.* 1 A sage, devotee, an ascetic. -2 N. of the sage Agastya. -3 Of Vyása. -4 Of Buddha. -5 Of Pánini. -6 N. of several plants. -7 The mango-tree. -8 The number ' seven '. -Comp.-इन्द्रः *m.* 1 An epithet of Sâkyamuni. -2 Of Bharata. -3 Of Siva. -ईशः, —ईश्वरः. *m.* 1 A great sage. -2 An epithet of Vishnu. -3 Of Buddha. —त्रयं *n.* The triad of sages *i. e.* Pânini, Kátyäyana, and Patanjali (who are considered to be inspired saints). —पित्तलं *n.* Copper.-पुत्रकः *m.* 1 A wagtail. -2 The *damanaka* tree. —भेषजं *n.* 1 The fruit of the yellow myrobalan. -2 Fasting.

मुंथ् 1 P. (मुंथति) To go, move.

मुमुक्षा *f.* Desire of liberation or final emancipation.

मुमुक्षु *a.* Desirous of releasing or liberating.2 Wishing to discharge. -3 About to shoot (arrows &c.). -4 Wishing to be free from worldly existence. —क्षुः *m.* A sage striving after final emancipation or beatitude.

मुमुचानः *m.* A cloud.

मुमूर्षा *f.* Desire of death.

मुमूर्षु *a.* Being on the point of death, about to die.

मुर् 6 P. (मुरति) To encircle, surround, entwine.

मुरः *m.* N. of a demon slain by Krishna. -रं *n.* Encompassing, surrounding. -Comp. —अरिः *m.* 1 An epithet of Krishna. -2 N. of the author of Anargharághava. —जित्, -द्विष्, -भिद्, —मर्दनः,-रिपुः,-वैरिन्, -हन् *m.* Epithets of Krishna or Vishnu.-द्ः *m.* The discus of Vishnu.

मुरजः *m.* 1 A kind of drum or tabor. -2 A stanza in the form of a drum ; also called मुरजबंध. -Comp. —फलः *m.* The jack-fruit tree.

मुरजा *f.* 1 A large drum. -2 N. of Kubera's wife.

मुरंदला *f.* N. of a river identified with Narmadâ.

मुरला *f.* N. of a river in the Keralas.

मुरली *f* A flute, pipe. -Comp. -धरः *m.* The epithet of Krishna.

मुर्छ् 1 P. (मूर्छति, मूर्छित or मूर्त) 1 To settle into a sound form, to congeal. -2 To swoon, become senseless. -3 To grow, increase, become powerful.-4 To take effect on. -5 To prevail against.-6 To pervade, penetrate. -7 To be a match for. -8 To be frequent. -9 To cause to sound loudly.

मुर्मुरः *m.* 1 A fire made of chaff. -2 The God of love. -3 N. of one of the horses of the sun.

मुश (-स-) ली *f.* A small house-lizard.

मुष् 9 P. (मुष्णाति; मुषित) To steal, plunder, carry off (governs two acc) *e. g.* देवदत्तं शतं मुष्णाति. -2 To remove, drive off. -3 To ruin, undo. -4 To eclipse, envelop, conceal.-4 To surpass, excel.

मुष् 1 P. (मोषति) 1 To hurt, kill.

मुष् 4 P (मुष्यति) 1 To steal. -2 To break, destroy.

मुषकः *m.* A mouse.

मूषा, मूषी *f.* A crucible.

मुषिः *f.* Stealing, theft.

मुषित *p. p.* (*f.* —ता) 1 Robbed, stolen, plundered. -2 Carried off, ravished. -3 Cheated, deceived.

मुषितकं *n.* Stolen property.

मुष्कः *m.* 1 A testicle.-2 The scrotum. -3 A robust man. -4 A mass, multitude. -5 A thief. -Comp. —शून्यः *m.* A eunuch, a castrated person.

मुष्टिः *m., f.* 1 The clenched hand, fist. -2 A handful. -3 A hilt. -4 A particular measure (*pala*). -5 A measure of capacity equal to one handful. -6 The penis. -Comp. —देशः *m.* The middle of a bow.

मुष्टिकः *m.* 1 A goldsmith. -2 A particular position of the hands. -3 N. of a demon.—कं *n.* A pugilistic encounter, fisticuffs. -Comp. —अंतकः *m.* An epithet of Balaráma.

मुष्टिका *f.* The fist.

मुष्टिंधयः *m.* A child, baby, infant.

मुष्टीमुष्टि *ind.* Fist-to-fist, hand-to-hand fighting.

मुसकः *m.* Black mustard.

मुसलः *m.*, -लं *n.* 1 A mace, club. -2 A pestle (used for cleaning rice). -Comp. —आयुधः *m.* An epithet of Balarâma.

मुसलामुसलि *ind.* Club against club.

मुसलिन् *m.* 1 An epithet of Balaráma. -2 Of Siva.

मुसल्य *a.* (*f.* —ल्या) To be pounded or put death with a club.

मुस्त् 10 U. (मुस्तयति,-ते) To heap up, accumulate.

मुस्तः *m.*, —स्ता *f.*, —स्तं *n.* A kind of grass. -Comp. -अदः,-आदः *m.* A hog.

मुर्श *n.* 1 A pestle. -2 A tear.

मुह् 4 P. (मुह्यति, मुग्ध or मूढ) 1 To faint, swoon. -2 To be perplexed or bewildered. -3 To be foolish. -4 To fail. -5 To err, mistake.

मुहिर a. (f. —रा) Silly, foolish, stupid. —रः m. 1 The God of love. -2 A fool, block-head.

मुहूर्क n. Ved. A moment.

मुहुस् ind. 1 Constantly, repeatedly, frequently. -2 For a time or moment, awhile. मुहुर्मुहुः ind. Again and again, repeatedly. -Comp. -भाषा f., —वचस् n. Repetition, tautology. —भुज् m. A horse.

मुहूर्तः m., -र्तं n. 1 A moment, an instant. -2 A period, time (auspicious or otherwise). -3 A period of 48 minutes. —र्तः m. An astrologer.

मुहूर्तकः m. 1 An instant, a moment. -2 A period of 48 minutes.

मूक a. (f. —का) 1 Dumb; silent, mute, speechless. -2 Poor, wretched. —कः m. 1 A mute. -2 A poor man. -3 A fish.

मूकिमन् m. Dumbness, silence.

मूढ p. p. (f. -ढा) 1 Stupefied, infatuated. -2 Bewildered. -3 Foolish, stupid, ignorant. -4 Mistaken, deceived. -5 Abortive. -6 Confounding. -ढः m. A fool, blockhead. -Comp. —गर्भः m. 1 A dead fœtus. -2 Difficult delivery. —ग्राहः m. 1 A misconception. -2 Infatuation.

मूत a. (f. —ता) 1 Bound, tied. -2 Confined.

मूत्रं n. Urine. -Comp. —कोशः m. The scrotum.—पतनः m. A civet-cat. —पुटं n. The lower belly.

मूत्रल a. Promoting the secretion of urine, diuretic.

मूर्ख a. (f.—र्खा) Stupid, foolish, silly. -र्खः m. 1 A fool. -2 A kind of bean. -Comp. —भूयं n. Stupidity, ignorance.

मूर्च्छन a. (f. -नी) 1 Stupefying, producing insensibility or stupor (an epithet applied to one of the five arrows of Cupid). -2 Increasing, augmenting, strengthening. -नं n., -ना f. 1 Fainting, swooning. -2 Prevalence, increase (usually n. only in this sense). -3 Calcining quicksilver with sulphur. -4 (In music) Rise and fall of sounds.

मूर्च्छा f. 1 Fainting, swooning. -2 Spiritaul ignorance. -3 A process in calcining metals.

मूर्च्छाल a. (f. -ला) Fainted.

मूर्च्छित p. p. (f. -ता) 1 Fainted. -2 Foolish.-3 Increased.-4 Intensified. -5 Perplexed, bewildered.-6 Filled. -7 Calcined. -8 Rising upwards, lofty. -तं n. A kind of song or air.

मूर्त a. (f. -र्ता) 1 Fainted, insensible. -2 Stupid, foolish. -3 Embodied, incarnate. -4 Material, corporeal. -5 Solid, hard. -6 Real.

मूर्तिः f 1 Anything which has a definite shape. -2 A form, body, figure. -4 An incarnation, personification, manifestation. -4 An image, idol. -5 Beauty. -6 Solidity, hardness.-Comp.-पः m. A worshipper of an image; one who is in charge of an idol.

मूर्तिमत् a. (f. —ती) 1 Material, corporeal. -2 Embodied, incarnate. -3 Hard, solid. -m. The body.

मूर्धन् m. 1 The forehead, brow. -2 The head in general. -3 The most prominent part, top, summit. -4 (Hence) A leader, head, chief, foremost; prominent. -5 Front, van, forepart; the thick of the fight. -6 (In geom.) The base. -Comp. —अभिषिक्त a. (f. —क्ता)Consecrated, crowned, inaugurated. (-क्तः m.) 1 A consecrated king. -2 A man of the Kshatriya caste. -3 A minister. —अभिषेकः m. Censecration, inauguration. -अवसिक्तः m. 1 N. of a particular mixed tribe sprung from a Bráhmana father and Kshatriya mother. -2 A consecrated king. -कर्णी, -कर्परी f. An umbrella. -जः m. 1 The hair (of the head). -2 The mane. -ज्योतिस् n. A hole in the crown of the head from which the soul is supposed to escape. -पुष्पः m. The Sirîsha tree. -रसः m. The scum of boiled rice. -वेष्टनं n. A turban, diadem.

मूर्धन्य a. (f. -न्या) 1 Being in or on the head. -2 Cerebral, a term applied to the letters ऋ, ॠ, ट, ठ, ड, ढ, ण, र and ष. -3 Chief, pre-eminent.

मूर्र्धिन m. See मूर्धन्.

मूर्वा, -र्वी, मूर्विका f. A kind of creeper (from which bow-strings and the girdle of Kshatriyas are made).

मूल् 1 U. (मूलति,-ते) To take or strike root, be firm, stand fast.

मूल् 10 U. (मूलयति,-ते मूलित) 1 To plant, rear. -2 Grow, germinate.

मूलं n. 1 A root (fig. also). -2 To lowest edge or extremity of anything. -3 The end of anything by which it is joined to something else e. g. पादमूलं, कर्णमूलं, ऊरुमूलं &c. -4 Beginning, commencement. 5 Basis, foundation, origin. -6 The bottom of anything. -7 The text or original passage (as distinguished from the commentary or gloss). -8 Vicinity, neighbourhood. -9 Capital, principal, stock. -10 A hereditary servant. -11 A square root. -12 A king's own territory. -13 A vendor who is not the true owner. -14 The nineteenth lunar mansion containing eleven stars. -15 A thicket. -16 The root of long pepper. -17 A particular position of the fingers. -18 A capital city. -19 An aboriginal inhabitant. -20 A bower, an arbour. (In a comp. मूल may be translated by ' first, original, chief, principal). -Comp. -आधारं n. The navel. -आभं n. A radish. -आशिन a. Living upon roots. -आह्वं n. A radish. -कर्मन् n. Magic. -कारिका f. A furnace, an oven. -कृच्छ्रः m., -च्छ्रं n. A kind of penance, living only upon roots. -केशरः m. A citron. -गुणः m. The co-efficient of a root. -जः m. A plant growing from a root. (-जं n.) A green ginger. -देवः m. An epithet of Kamsa. -द्रव्यं, -धनं n. Stock, capital. -धातुः m. Lymph. -पुरुषः m. The male representative of a family. -प्रकृतिः f. The Prakriti or Pradhâna of the Sànkhyas. -फलदः m. The bread-fruit tree. -भृत्यः m. An old or hereditary servant. -विभुजः m. A chariot. -शाकटः m., -शाकिनं n. A field planted with edible roots. -स्थानं n. 1 Foundation. -2 The Supreme Spirít. -3 Wind, air.

मूलकः m., -कं n. 1 A radish. -2 An esculent root. -कः n. A kind of poison. -Comp. -पोतिका f. A radish.

मूला f. 1 N. of a plant. -2 The asterism *mûla*.

मूलिकः n. A devotee, an ascetic.

मूलिन् m. A tree.

मूलिन a. (f. -ना) Growing from a root. -नः m. A plant, tree.

मूली f. A small house-lizard.

मूलेरः m. 1 A king. -2 The Indian spikenard.

मूल्यं n. 1 Price, worth, cost. -2 Wages, hire, salary. -3 Gain. -4 Capital, principal.

मूष् I A. (मूषति, मूषित) To steal.

मूषः *m.* I A rat, mouse. -2 A window, an air-hole. -3 A crucible.

मूषकः *m.* I A rat, mouse. -2 A thief. -Comp. —अरातिः *m.* A cat. —वाहनः *m.* An epithet of Ganesa.

मूषणं *n.* Stealing, pilfering.

मूषा, मूषिका *f.* I A female rat. -2 A crucible. -3 An air-hole.

मूषिकः *m.* I A rat. -2 A thief. -3 The Sirisha tree. -4 N. of a country. -Comp. —अंकः, —अंचनः, —रथः *m.* Epithets of Ganesa. —अदः *m.* A cat. —अरातिः *m.* A cat. —उत्करः *m.*, —स्थलं *n.* A mole-hill.—विषाणं *n.* An impossibility.

मूषिकारः *m.* A male rat. [mouse.

मूषी *f.*, मूषिकः *m.*, मूषीका *f.* A rat,

मूषिकरणं *n.* Melting in a crucible.

मृ 6. A. (but P. in the Perfect, the two Futures and the Conditional) (म्रियते, ममार, अमृत, मरिष्यति, मर्तुं, मृत) To die, perish. With अनु— To die after. -*Caus.* (मारयति,-ते) To kill, slay. —*Desid.* (मुमूर्षति) I To wish to die. -2 To be about to die, be on the point of death.

मृक्ष् I P. (मृक्षति) To be heaped up.

मृग् 4 P., 10 A. (मृग्यति, मृगयते, मृगित) I To seek, search for, seek after. -2 To hunt, pursue. -3 To strive after. -4 To examine, investigate. -5 To ask for.

मृगः *m.* I A quadruped, an animal in general. -2 A deer, an antelope. -3 Game in general. -4 Musk. -5 Seeking, search. -6 Pursuit, chase. -7 Inquiry, investigation. -8 Asking, soliciting. -9 A kind of elephant. -10 N. of a particular class of men. -11 The lunar mansion called मृगशिरस्. -12 The lunar month called मार्गशीर्ष. -13 The sign *Capricornus* of the zodiac. -14 N. of a district in Sàkadvîpa. -Comp. —अंकः *m.* I The moon. -2 Camphor. -3 The wind. —अंगना *f.* A doe. —अजिनं *n.* A deer's skin. —अंडजा *f.* Musk. —अद्, —अदनः, —अंतकः *m.* A small tiger or hunting leopard, hyena. —आधिपः, —अधिराजः *m.* A lion. —अरातिः *m.* I A lion. -2 A dog.—अरिः *m.* I A lion. -2 A dog. -3 A tiger. —अशनः *m.* A lion. —आजीवः *m.* I A hunter. -2 A hyena. —आविधः *m.* A hunter.—आस्यः *m.* The sign *Capricornus* of the zodiac.—इंद्रः *m.* I A lion. -2 A tiger. -3 The sign *Leo* of the zodiac. —ईश्वरः *m.* I A lion. -2 The sign *Leo* of the zodiac. -उत्तमं, -उत्तमांगं *n.* The constellation मृगशिरस्. —जलं *n.* Mirage. —जीवनः *m.* A hunter, fowler. -तृष्, -तृषा, -तृष्णा, -तृष्णिः, -तृष्णिका *f.* Mirage. —दंशः, —दंशकः *m.* A dog. -द्युः *m.* A hunter. —द्विष् *m.* A lion. —धरः *m.* The moon. —धूर्तः, -धूर्तकः *m.* A jackal. -नाभिः *m.* I Musk. -2 The musk-deer. —पतिः *m.* I A lion. -2 A roe-buck. -3 A tiger. —पालिका *f.* The musk-deer. —पिप्लुः *m.* The moon. -पोतः, —पोतकः *m.* The fawn. —प्रभुः *m.* A lion. -ब (-व-) धाजीवः *m.* A hunter. —बंधिनी *f.* A net for catching deer. —मदः *m.* Musk. —मंद्रः *m.* N. of a class of elephants. —मातृका *f.* A doe. —मासः *m.* The month of Márgasírsha. —मुखः *m.* The sign *Capricornus* of the zodiac. —राज् *m.* I A lion. -2 A tiger. -3 The sign *Leo* of the zodiac. —राजः *m.* I A lion. -2 The sign *Leo* of the zodiac. -3 A tiger. -4 The moon. —रिपुः *m.* A lion. -लांछनः, -लक्ष्मन् *m.* The moon. —वाहनः *m.* Wind. -व्याधः *m.* I A hunter. -2 Sirius or the dog-star. -3 An epithet of Siva. —शिरः, -शिरस् *n.*, -शिरा *f.* N. of the fifth lunar mansion consisting of three stars. —शीर्षं *n.* The constellation मृगशिरस्. (-र्षः *m.*) The lunar month Màrgasîrsha. —शीर्षन् *m.* The constellation मृगशिरस्. -श्रेष्ठः *m.* 1 A tiger. —हन् *m.* A hunter.

मृगणा *f.* 1 Searching, looking out for. -2 Investigation, inquiry.

मृगया *f.* Hunting, chase.

मृगयुः *m.* 1 A hunter, fowler. -2 A jackal. -3 An epithet of Brahman (*m.*) [A target.

मृगव्यं *n.* 1 The chase, hunting. -2

मृगी *f.* 1 A female deer, doe. -2 Epilepsy. -3 N. of a particular class of women. -Comp. -पतिः *m.* An epithet of Krishna.

मृग्य *a.* (*f.* —ग्या) To be sought or inquired after; to be hunted.

मृज् 2 P., 10 U. (मार्ष्टि, मार्जयति,-ते मार्जितुं, मार्ष्टुं, मार्जयितुं, मृष्ट, मार्जित) 1 To wipe or wash off, cleanse, clean (fig also).-2 To rub, stroke. -3 To make smooth, curry (as a horse). -4 To deck, adorn. -5 To purify, wash. -6 To sharpen.

मृजः *m.* A kind of drum.

मृजा *f.* 1 Cleansing, purifying. washing, ablution. -2 Cleanliness, purity. -3 Complexion.

मृजित *a.* (*f.* —ता) Wipped off or away, cleansed.

मृडः *m.* An epithet of Siva.

मृडा, मृडानी, मृडी *f.* An epithet of Párvatí.

मृण् 6 P. (मृणाति) To kill, slay.

मृणालः *m.*, —लं *n.* The fibrous root of a lotus, a lotus-fibre. —लं *n.* The root of a fragrant grass (वीरणमूल).

मृणालिका, मृणाली *f.* A lotus stalk or fibre.

मृणालिन् *m.* A lotus.

मृणालिनी *f.* 1 A lotus-plant. -2 An assemblage of lotuses. -3 A place abounding with lotuses.

मृत *p. p.* (*f.* —ता) 1 Dead, deceased. -2 Useless, inefficacious.-2 Calcined, reduced. —तं *n.* 1 Death. Food obtained by begging, alms. -Comp.-अंगं *n.* Corpse.—अंडः *m.* The sun. —अशौचं *n.* Impurity contracted through the death of a relative. —उद्भवः *m.* The sea, ocean. —गृहं *n.* A grave. —जीवनं *n.* Reviving the dead. —मत्तः, —मत्तकः *m.* A jackal. —संस्कारः *m.* Funeral or obsequial rites.—संजीवनं *n.*, —नी *f.* The revival of a dead person. (-नी *f.*) A charm for reviving the dead.-सूतकं *n.* Bringing forth a still-born child. -स्नानं *n.* Ablution after a death or funeral.

मृतकः *m.*, -कं *n.* A dead person, a corpse. —कं *n.* 1 Impurity contracted through the death of a relation. -2 Death. -Comp. —अंतकः *m.* A jackal.

मृतंडः *m.* The sun.

मृतिः *f.* Death, dying.

मृत्तिका *f.* 1 Clay, earth. -2 A kind of fragrant earth.

मृत्युः *m.* 1 Death, decease. -2 Yama, the God of death. -3 An epithet of Brahman (*m.*). -4 Of Vishnu. -5 Of Mâyà. -6 Of Kali. -7 The God of love. -Comp.—नाशकः *m.* Quicksilver. -पः *m.* An epithet of Siva. —पुष्पः *m.* The sugar-cane. -बीजः,-वीजः *m.* A bamboo-cane. -राज् *m.* Yama, the God of death. -लोकः *m.* 1 The world of the dead, the world of Yama. -2 The world of mortals. —सूतिः *f.* A female crab.

मृत्युंजयः *m.* An epithet of Siva.

मृत्सा, मृत्स्ना *f.* 1 Earth, clay -2

Good earth or clay. -3 A kind of fragraut earth

मृद् 9 P. (मृद्गाति,मृदित) 1 To squeeze, press, rub. -2 To tread upon; crush, destroy, pound, bruise. -3 To rub, stroke. -4 To overcome, surpass. -5 To wipe away. -6 (In astr.) To pass through (as a constellation).

मृद् f. 1 Clay, earth, loam. -2 A lump of clay.-3 A mound of earth. -4A kind of fragrant earth.-Comp. -करः m. A potter. —कांस्यं n. An earthen vessel. —गः m. A kind of fish. —पचः m. A potter. —शकटिका (मृच्छकटिका) f. A small car of earth, a toy-cart; (it is the name of a celebrated play by Súdraka).

मृदंगः m. 1 A kind of drum. -2 A bamboo-cane. -Comp. —फलः m. The bread-fruit tree.

मृदर a. (f.-री) 1 Sporting, sportive. -2 Transient, evanescent.

मृदा f. See मृद् -Comp. -करः m. A thunder-bolt.

मार्दिनी f. Good or soft earth.

मृदु a. (-दु or -द्वी f. compar. म्रदीयस् superl. म्रदिष्ठ) 1 Soft, tender, delicate. -2 Mild, gentle. -3 Weak, feeble. -4 Moderate. -5 Blunt. -6 Slow. —दुः m. The planet Saturn. -दु n. Softness, gentleness. -दु ind. Softly, gently, in a sweet manner. -Comp. -चर्मिन्, -छदः,-त्वच्, -त्वचः m. A kind of birch tree.-पत्रः m. A rush or reed. —पर्वकः, -पर्वन् m. A reed, cane. —पुष्पः m. The *Sirīsha* tree. -रोमन्, -रोमकः m. A hare. -वर्गः,-गणः m. The group of the Nakshatras अनुराधा, मृगशिरस्, चित्रा and रेवती.

मृदुत्नकं n. Gold.

मृदुल a. (f. -ला) 1 Soft, tender, delicate. -2 Mild, gentle. -लं n. 1 Water. -2 A variety of aloe-wood.

मृद्वी, मृद्वीका f. A vine or bunch of grapes.

मृध् 1 U. (मर्धति, -ते) To moisten.

मृधं n. War, battle, fight.

मृन्मय (-एम-) य a. Earthen.

मृश् 6 P. (मृशति,मृष्ट) 1 To touch. -2 To rub, stroke. -3 To consider, deliberate.

मृष् 1 P. (मर्षति) To sprinkle.

मृष् 1 U. (मर्षति,-ते) 1 To bear, endure (Atm.) -2 (Par.) To sprinkle

मृष् 4. 10. U. (मृष्यति,-ते, मर्षयति,-ते, मर्षित) 1 To suffer, bear, endure. -2 To allow,permit. -3 To pardon, forbear. -4 To forget, neglect.

मृषा ind. 1 Falsely, wrongly, untruly.-2 In vain, uselessly.-Comp. —अध्यायिन् m. A kind of crane. -अर्थकं n. An absurdity, an impossibility. -उद्यं n. A false statement. -वाच् f. An untrue or satirical speech, satire, irony. -वादः m. 1 An untrue speech,a lie,falsehood.-2Insincere speech,flattery. -3 Irony, satire.

मृषालकः m. The mango tree.

मृष्ट p. p. (f. -ष्टा) 1 Cleansed, purified. -2 Besmeared. -3 Dressed, cooked. -4 Touched.-5 Considered, deliberated. -6 Savoury, agreeable. -7 Sprinkled. —ष्टं n. Pepper. -Comp. —गंधः m. A savoury or agreeable smell.

-ष्टिः f. 1 Cleansing, purifying. -2 Cooking, dressing. -3 Touch. -4 Sprinkling.

मे 1 A (मयते, मित, *desid.* मित्सते) To exchange or barter. -With नि- or विनि-To exchange or barter.

मेकः m. A goat.

मेकलः m.1 N. of a mountain (also मेखल). -2 To goat. -Comp. —अद्रिजा, -कन्यका,-कन्या f. The river Narmadá.

मेखला *f.* 1 A belt, girdle, waist-band, zone in general (fig. also).-2 The triple girdle worn by the first three castes. -3 The slope of a mountion.-4 The hips.-5 A sword-belt. -6 The girth of a horse. -7 N. of the river Narmadá. -Comp. -पदं *n.* The hips.

मेखलिन् *m.* 1 An epithet of Siva. -2 A Brahmachárin.

मेघ: *m.* 1 A cloud. -2 A mass, multitude. -3 N. of one of the six Rágas (in music). -4 A fragrant grass. -घं *n.* Talc. —Comp. -अध्वन्, -पथ:, -मार्ग: *m.* The atmosphere. —अंत: *m.* The autumn. —अग्नि: *m.* The wind. —आस्थि *n.* Hail. -आख्यं *n.* Talc. —आगम: *m.* The rainy season.-आटोप: *m.* A dense or thick cloud. -आडंबर: *m.* Thunder. -आनंदा *f.* A kind of crane. -आनंदिन् *m.* A peacock. —आस्पदं *n.* The atmosphere. -कफ: *m.* Hail.-चिंतक: *m.* The Châtaka bird.-ज: *m.* A large pearl. -जालं *n.* 1 A dense mass of clouds. -2 Talc. -जीवक:, —जीवन: *m.* The Châtaka bird. -ज्योतिस् *m., n.* Lightning. -डंबर: *m.* Thunder. —दीप: *m.* Lightning. —दूतं *n.* N. of a celebrated poem by Kâlidâsa.-द्वारं *n.* The sky, atmosphere.-नाद: *m.* Thunder. -2 An epithet of Varuna. -3 N. of Indrajit, son of Râvana. -4 The Palâsa tree. —पुष्पं *n.* 1 Water. -2 Hail. -3 River-water. -प्रसव: *m.* Water. —भूति: *m.* A thunder-bolt. —मंडलं *n.* The firmament, sky. -योनि: *m.* Fog, smoke. -वर्णा *f.* The Indigo plant. —वर्त्मन् *n.* The atmosphere. —वह्नि: *m.* Lightning.-वाहन: *m.* 1 An epithet of Indra. -2 An epithet of Siva. —विस्फूर्जितं *n.* 1 Thunder. -2 N. of a metre.—वेश्मन् *n.* The atmosphere. -सार: *m.* A kind of camphor. -सुहृद् *m.* A peacock.-स्तनितं Thunder.

मेचक *a.* (*f.* -का) Black, dark-blue, dark-coloured. -क: *m.* 1 Blackness. -2 An eye of a peacock's tail. -3 A cloud. -4 Smoke. -5 A nipple. -6 A kind of gem. —कं *n.* 1 Darkness. -2 Sulphuret of antimony. -Comp. -आपगा *f.* An epithet of the Yamuná.

मेठ: *m.* 1 A ram. -2 An elephant-driver or keeper.

मेठि:, मेथि: *m.* 1 A pillar. -2 A pillar in the midst of a threshing-floor to which oxen are bound. -3 A post to which cattle are bound. -4 A prop for supporting the shafts of a carriage.

मेढ्र: *m.* A ram. —ढ्रं *n.* The male organ of generation.

मेढ्रक: *m.* 1 A ram.-2 The penis.

मेंठ:, मेंड: *m.* An elephant-keeper.

मेंढ:, मेंढक: *m.* A ram.

मेंढ्र: *m.* See मेढ्र.

मेथ् 1 U. (मेथति,-ते) 1 To meet.-2 To meet one another (Atm.). -3 To revile.-4 To know, understand. -5 To hurt, injure, kill.

मेथिका, मेथिनी *f.* A kind of grass.

मेद: *m.* 1 Fat.-2 A particular mixed trible.

मेदस् *n.* 1 Fat, marrow. -2 Corpulence. -Comp. —कृत् *m., n.* Flesh.-जं, —तेजस् *n.* A bone.

मेदस्विन् *a.* (*f.* -नी) 1 Fat, corpulent. -2 Strong, robust.

मेदिनी *f.* 1 The earth. -2 Ground, soil. -3 N. of a lexicon (मदिनीकोश). -Comp. —ईश:, —पति: *m.* A king. -द्रव: *m.* Dust.

मेदुर: *a.* (*f.* -रा) 1 Fat.-2 Smooth, unctuous, soft. -3 Thick, dense, full of, covered with. [thick.

मेद्य *a.* (*f.* -द्या) 1 Fat. -2 Dense,

मेद् I U. See मेथ्.

मेधः m. I A sacrifice. -2 A sacrificial animal.-Comp. —जः m. An epithet of Vishnu.

मेधा f. (This word is changed to मेधस् in Bah. comp. after सु, दुस् and the negative particle अ) I Retentive faculty, retentiveness (of memory). -2 Intellect ; intelligence. -3 A sacrifice. -Comp. -रुद्रः m. An epithet of Kâlidása. [gent.

मेधावत a. (f. -ती) Wise, intelli-

मेधाविन् a. (f. -नी) Very intelligent ; having a good memory. -m. I A learned man. -2 A parrot. -3 An intoxicating drink. -नी f. The wife of Brahman (m.).

मेधिः f. A pillar to which beasts are tethered.

मेध्य a. (f. —ध्या) I Fit for a sacrifice. -2 Relating to a sacrifice, sacrificial. -3 Sacred, holy. —ध्यः m. I A goat.-2 The Khadira tree.-3 Barley.

मेनका f. I N. of an *Apsaras* (mother of Sakuntalá.) -2 N. of the wife of Himàlaya. -Comp. —आत्मजा f. N. of Párvatî.

मेना f. N. of the wife of Himâlaya. -2 N. of a river.

मेनाद: m. I A peacock. -2 A cat. -3 A goat.

मेंधिका, मेंधी f. N. of a plant (Mar. मेंदी) (from the leaves of which a reddish dye is extracted).

मेय a. (f. -या) I Measured. -2 Capable of being estimated.-3Capble of being known.

मेरु: m. I N. of a fabulous mountain (round which all the planets are said to revolve).-2 The central bead in a rosary. -3 The central gem of a necklace. -Comp. -धामन् m. An epithet of Siva. -पृष्ठं n. The sky.

मेरुकः m. Incense.

मेलः m. I Meeting,union.-2 A fair.-3 An assembly.

मेलनं n. I Union, junction. -2 Association. -3 Mixture. -4 A fight.

मेला f. I Union, intercourse. -2 A company, society. -3 Antimony.-4 The indigo plant. -5 Ink. -6 A musical scale. -Comp. -अंधुकः,-अंबुः,-नंदः, m., —नंदा, —मंदा f. An ink-stand, ink-bottle.

मेषः m. I A ram, sheep. -2 The sign *Aries* of the zodiac. -Comp. —अंडः m. An epithet of Indra. -कंबलः m. A woollen blanket or rug. -वालः, -पालकः m. A shepherd. -यूथं n. A flock of sheep.

मेषा f. Small cardamoms.

मेषिका, मेषी f. A ewe.

मेहः m. I Making water, passing urine. -2 Urine. -3 A urinary disease. -4 A ram.-5 A goat. -Comp. -घ्नी f. Turmeric.

मेहनं n. I Passing urine. -2 Urine. -3 The penis.

मैत्र a. (f. —त्री) I Belonging to a friend. -2 Given by a friend. -3 Amicable, kind. -4 Relating to the God Mitra.—त्रः m. I A high or perfect Bràhmaṇa. -2 N. of a particular mixed tribe. -3 The anus. -4 A friend. -त्री f. I Friendship.-2 Intimate association, union, contact. -3 The lunar mansion called अनुराधा. -त्रं n. I Friendship. -2 Voiding or evacuation of excrement. -3 A prayer addressed to Mitra. -4 The lunar mansion अनुराधा.

मैत्रकं n. Friendship.

मैत्रावरुणः m. An epithet of Vàlmíki. -2 Of Agastya. -3 N. of one of the officiating priests at a sacrifice. -4 N. of Vasishtha.

मैत्रावरुणिः *m.* 1 An epithet of Agastya. -2 Of Vasishtha. -3 Of Válmîki.

मैत्रेय *a.* (*f.* —यी) Relating to a friend, friendly. -यः *m.* N. of a mixed tribe.

मैत्रेयकः *m.* N. of a mixed tribe.

मैत्रेयिका *f.* A contest between friends or allies.

मैत्र्यं *n.* Friendship, alliance.

मैथिलः *m.* A king of Mithilá. -लाः *m. pl.* The people of Mithilâ. -ली *f.* N. of Sità.

मैथुन *a.* (*f.* -नी) 1 Paired, coupled. -2 United by marriage. -3 Relating to copulation. —नं *n.* 1 Copulation, sexual union. -2 Marriage. -3 Union, connection. -4 Consecrating the fire (अग्न्याधान).

मैथुनिका *f.* Union by marriage, matrimonial alliance.

मैधावकं *n.* Wisdom, intelligence.

मैनाकः *n.* N. of a mountain, son of Himâlaya. -Comp. —स्वसृ *f.* An epithet of Párvatî.

मैनालः *m.* A fisherman.

मैंदः *m.* N. of a demon killed by Krishna.

मैरेयः *m.*, -यं *n.*, मैरेयकः *m.*, -कं *n.* A kind of intoxicating drink.

मैलिंदः *m.* A bee.

मोकं *n.* The cast-off skin of an animal.

मोक्ष् 1 P., 10 U. (मोक्षति, मोक्षयति,-ते) 1 To release, liberate. -2 To untie, undo. -3 To wrest away. -4 To hurl, fling. -5 To detach, extract.

मोक्षः *m.* 1 Liberation, escape, freedom. -2 Deliverance. -3 Final emancipation. -4 Death. -5 Dropping down, falling off. -6 Loosening, unbinding. -7 Shedding. -8 Shooting, discharging. -9 Scattering, strewing. -10 Acquittance of an obligation (debt &c.). -11 (In astr.) The end of an eclipse -12 N. of a tree (पाटलि). -Comp. —देवः *m.* An epithet applied to Hiouen Thsang, the celebrated Chinese traveller. —द्वारं *n.* The sun. —पुरी *f.* An epithet of the town called कांची.

मोक्षणं *n.* 1 Releasing, liberating, deliverance. -2 Loosening. -3 Abandoning, resigning. -4 Shedding. -5 Discharging, casting.

मोघ *a.* (*f.* —घा) 1 Fruitless, unprofitable. -2 Left, abandoned. -3 Idle. —घः *m.* A fence, an enclosure. —घा *f.* The trumpet flower. -घं *ind.* In vain, uselessly. -Comp. —पुष्पा *f.* A barren woman.

मोघोलिः *m.* A hedge, fence.

मोचः *m.* The plantain tree. -चा *f.* 1 The plantain tree. -2 The cotton shrub. -3 The indigo plant. —चं *n.* A plantain fruit.

मोचकः *m.* 1 A devotee, an ascetic. -2 Emancipation, deliverance. -3 A plantain tree.

मोचन *a.* (*f.* —नी) Releasing, freeing from. —नं *n.* 1 Releasing, liberating, emancipating. -2 Discharging, emitting. -3 Acquittance of a debt or obligation. -Comp. —पट्टकः *m.* A filter.

मोचाटः *m.* 1 The pith or fruit of the banana. -2 Sandal-wood.

मोटकः *m.*,-कं *n.* A pill. -कं *n.* A couple of broken blades of Kusa grass given at a Sráddha.

मोटनं, मोटनकं *n.* Crushing, pressing, grinding, breaking. —नः *m.* Wind, air.

मोट्टायितं *n.* Manifestation of love on the part of a woman in the absence of her lover.

मोदः *m.* 1 Delight, joy.-2 Perfume, fragrance. -Comp. —आढ्यः *m.* The mango tree.

मोदकः *m.*, —कं *n.* A sweetmeat in general.-कः *m.* N. of a mixed tribe

मोदनं *n.* 1 Joy, pleasure. -2 The act of pleasing.

मोदयंतिका, मोदयंती *f.* A kind of jasmine (Arabian).

मोदिनी *f.* 1 A kind of jasmine. -2 Musk. -3 A spirituous liquor.

मोरटः *m.* 1 A kind of plant. -2 The milk of a cow recently calved. —टं *n.* The root of the sugar-cane. —टा *f.* Hemp used for bow-strings.

मोषः *m.* 1 A thief, robber. -2 Theft, robbery. -3 Plundering, stealing. -4 Stolen property.

मोषकः *m.* A robber, thief.

मोषणं *n.* 1 Robbing, plundering, stealing.-2 Cutting. -3 Destroying.

मोषा *f.* Theft, robbery.

मोहः *m.* 1 A swoon, insensibility. -2 Perplexity, embarrassment, confusion. -3 Folly, infatuation. -4 Error, mistake. -5 Wonder, astonishment. -6 Affliction, pain. -7 A magical art employed to confound an enemy. -8 (In phil.) Delusion of mind which prevents the discernment of truth. -Comp. —कलिलं *n.* The thick net or snare of delusion. -निद्रा *f.* Over-weening confidence. -मंत्रः *m.* A deluding spell. -रात्रिः *f.* The night when the whole universe will be destroyed

मोहन *a.* (*f.* – नी) 1 Stupefying.-2 Bewildering, puzzling.-3 Deluding. -4 Enrapturing. —नः *m.* 1 An epithet of Siva. -2 N. of one of the five arrows of Cupid.-3 The thorn-apple (धत्तूर). -नं *n.* 1 Stupefying. -2 Bewildering.-3 Stupor ; loss of sensation. -4 Infatuation. -5 A seduction, temptation. -6 Sexual intercourse. -7 A means employed in perplexing others. -8 A magical charm employed to bewilder an enemy. -Comp. —अस्त्रं *n.* A missile which fascinates or bewitches the person against whom it is used.

मोहनकः *m.* The month of Chaitra.

मोहित *p. p.* (*f.* —ता) 1 Stupefied. -2 Perplexed, bewildered. -3 Fascinated, infatuated, beguiled.

मोहिनी *f.* 1 N. of an *Apsaras.* -2 Vishnu in the form of a fascinating woman.-3 The flower of a kind of jasmine.

मौक (-कु-) लिः *m.* A crow.

मौक्तिकं *n.* A pearl. -Comp. -शुक्तिः *f.* A pearl-oyster.

मौचं *n.* The fruit of the plantain [tree.

मौंज *a.* (*f.* -जी) Made of Munja grass.

मौंजी *f.* The gridle of a Brâhmana made of a triple string of Munja grass. -Comp. -निबंधनं, -बंधनं *n.* Binding on the Munja grass girdle; investiture with the sacred thread.

मौत्रं *n.* A quantity of urine.

मौदकिकः *m.* A confectioner.

मौद्गलिः *m.* A crow.

मौनं *n.* Silence, taciturnity.-Comp. -मुद्रा *f.* The attitude of silence. -व्रतं *n.* A vow of silence.

मौनिन *a.* (*f.* -नी) Observing a vow of silence ; silent, taciturn. -*m.* A holy sage, an ascetic, a hermit.

मौरजिकः *m.* A drummer.

मौर्ख्यं *n.* Folly, stupidity.

मौर्यः *m.* N. of a dynasty of kings beginning with Chandragupta.

मौर्वी *f.* 1 A bow-string. -2 A girdle made of Múrvâ grass (to be worn by a Kshatriya).-3 (In geom.) The chord of an arc.

मौल *a.* (*f.* —ला, -ली) 1 Radical, original. -2 Ancient, old. -4 Nobly born. -4 Brought up in the service of a king for generations. —लः *m.* An old or hereditary minister.

मौलिः *m.* 1 The head. -2 The top of anything. -3 The Asoka tree. -लिः ., *f.* 1 A crown, diadem, tiara. -2 Hair on the crown of the head. -3 Braided hair. -लिः, -ली *f.* The earth.

मौल्यं *n.* Price.

मौष्टा *f.* A boxing or pugilistic en- [counter.

मौष्टिकः *m.* A rogue, cheat, sharper.

मौसल *a* (*f.* -ली) 1 Formed like a club. -2 Fought with clubs (as a battle). —लः *m.* A kind of *madhuparka.*

मौहूर्तः *m.* An astrologer.

मौहूर्तिकः *m.* An astrologer.

म्ना 1 P. (मनति, म्नात) 1 To repeat (in the mind). -2 To learn diligently. -3 To remember. With आ— 1 To proclaim, to speak of. -2 To study. समा— 1 To prescribe. -2 To repeat

म्नात *p. p.* (*f.*—ता) 1 Repeated. -2 Learnt, studied.

म्रक्षः *m.* Hypocrisy, dissimulation.

म्रक्षणं *n.* 1 Smearing the body with unguents. -2 Smearing in general. -3 Heaping up. -4 Oil, ointment.

म्रद् 1 A. (म्रदते; *caus.* म्रदयति,-ते) To pound, grind, crush, trample upon.

म्रदिमन् *m.* 1 Tenderness, softness. -2 Mildness, weakness.

म्लान *p. p.* (*f.*-ना) 1 Faded, withered. -2 Made white by tanning.

म्लान *p. p.* (*f.* -ना) 1 Faded, withered. -2 Wearied, weary. -3 Weak, feeble, faint. -4 Dejected, melancholy. -5 Black. -6 Foul, dirty. -Comp. —अंगी *f.* A woman during her menses.

म्लानिः *f.* 1 Withering, decay. -2 Langour, weariness. -3 Sadness, dejection. -4 Foulness.

म्लास्नु *a.* 1 Becoming faded. -2 Growing thin or emaciated. -3 Growing languid or weary.

म्लिष्ट *a.* (*f.* —ष्टा) 1 Spoken indistinctly ; indistinct. -2 Withered, faded. -ष्टं *n.* An indistinct speech.

म्लेच्छ् or म्लेछ् 1 P. 10 U. (म्लेच्छति, म्लेच्छयति,-ते, म्लिष्ट, म्लेच्छित) To speak indistinctly.

म्लेच्छः *m.* 1 A barbarian, (applied to a person outside the pale of Hinduism); a foreigner in general. -2 An outcast. -3 A sinner. -च्छं *n.* Copper. -Comp. —आस्यं *n.* Copper.—आशः *m.* Wheat. -आस्यं, -मुखं *n.* Copper. —कंदः *m.* Garlic. —जातिः *f.* A savage or barbarian race ; a mountaineer. —भोजनः *m.* Wheat. (—नं *n.*)Barley.

म्लेच्छित *p. p.* (*f.* —ता) Spoken indistinctly or barbarously. —तं *n.* 1 A foreign tongue. -2 An ungrammatical word or speech.

म्लै 1 P. (म्लायति, म्लान) 1 To fade, wither. -2 To grow weary or languid; to be exhaustad. -3 To be dejected, be dispirited. -4 To become emaciated. -5 To disappear, vanish. -6 To decline, become less.

य.

यः *m.* 1 A goer, mover. -2 One of the eight syllabic feet (गण) consisting of one short syllable followed by two long ones.

यकन् *n* The liver. (This word has no forms for the first five inflections, and is optionally substituted for यकृत after acc. dual).

यकृत *n*. The liver or any affection of it. -Comp. —आत्मिका *f.* A kind of cock-roach. -उदरं *n*. An enlargement of the liver.

यक्षः *m*. 1 N. of a class of demigods, attendants of Kubera and employed in guarding his treasures. -2 A ghost or spirit. -3 The palace of Indra. -Comp. —अधिपः,-अधिपतिः, —इंद्रः *m*. Kubera, the lord of Yakshas. —आवासः *m*. The fig-tree. —कर्दमः *m*. A kind of ointment -ग्रहः *m*. The being possessed by Yakshas or evil spirits. -तरुः *m*. The fig-tree. —धूपः *m*. Resin, incense. —रसः *m*. A kind of intoxicating drink. -राज् *m*. 1 N. of Kubera.-2 A place prepared for wrestling and boxing. —राजः *m*. N. of Kubera. —रात्रिः *f*. The festival called Dipâli. -वित्तः *m*. One who stores up wealth but never uses it.

यक्षिणी *f*. 1 A female Yaksha. -2 N. of the wife of Kubera. -3 A certain female fiend attendant on Durgâ. -4 A fairy.

यक्षी *f*. A female Yaksha.

यक्ष्मः, यक्ष्मन् *m*. Pulmonary disease in general. -Comp. —घ्नी *f*. A grape.

यज् 1 U. (यजति,-ते, यष्टुं, इष्ट) 1 To sacrifice,(often with instr.of words meaning ' a sacrifice') *e. g.* यजेत राजा क्रतुभिः. -2 To make an oblation to (with acc. of the deity and instr. of the oblation; *e. g.* पशुना रुद्रं यजते). -3 To worship, honour, revere. -4 To consecrate, dedicate. -5 To give, bestow.

यजातिः *m*. A name for those sacrifices to which the verb यजाति is applied as distinguished from those rites to which the verb जुहोति is applied.

यजत्रः *m*. A Brâhmana who maintains the sacred fire. -त्रं *n*. Maintenance of the sacred fire.

यजनं *n*. 1 The act of sacrificing. -2 A sacrifice. -3 A place of sacrifice.

यजमानः *m*. 1 A person who performs a regular sacrifice and pays its expenses. -2 A person who employs a priest or priests to sacrifice for him. -3 A host, patron, rich man. -4 The head of a tribe. -Comp.-शिष्यः *m* The pupil of a Bràhmana who performs a sacrifice.

यजिः *m*. 1 A sacrificer.-2 A sacrifice.

यजुस् *n*. 1 A sacrificial prayer. -2 A text of the Yajurveda. -3 N. of the Yajurveda. -Comp.-वेदः *m*. The second of the three principal Vedas, which is a collection of sacred texts in prose :elating to sacrifices. It is two-fold:-the तैत्तिरीय or कृष्णयजुर्वेद and वाजसनेयि or शुक्लयजुर्वेद.

यज्ञः *m*. 1 A sacrifice. -2 A pious or devotional act. -3 N. of Agni. -4 Of Vishnu. -Comp. -अंगं *n*. 1 A part of a sacrifice.-2 Any means of a sacrifice.(-गः *m*.) 1 The उदुंबर tree. -2 The Khadira tree. -3 N. of Vishnu. —अशनः *m*. A God. —आत्मन्, —ईश्वरः *m*. N. of Vishnu. -उपवीतं *n*. The sacred thread worn by members of the first three classes over the left shoulder and under the right arm. —कल्प *a*. Of the nature of a sacrifice or sacrificial offering. -कीलकः *m*. The post to which the sacrificial victim is fastened. —कुंडं *n.* A hole in the ground made for receiving the sacrificial fire. —क्रतुः *m.* 1 A sacrificial rite. -2 A complete rite or chief ceremony. -3 An epithet of Vishnu. —दीक्षा *f.* 1 Admission or initiation to a sacrificial rite.-2 The performance of a sacrifice. —द्रव्यं *n.* Anything used for a sacrifice. —पतिः *m.* 1 One who institutes a sacrifice.-2 N. of Vishnu. -पुंस्, -पुमान्,-पुरुषः, —फलदः *m.* Epithets of Vishnu. —भुज् *m.* A God.—योगः *m.* The Udumbara tree. —वराहः *m.* Vishnu in his boar incarnation. —वल्लिः, —ल्ली *f.* The Soma plant. —वाहनः *m.* 1 An epithet of Vishnu. -2 A Brâhmana. -3 N. of Siva. —वृक्षः *m.* The fig-tree. —वेदिः, -दी *f.* The sacrificial altar. —शरणं *n.* A sacrificial shed or hall. —शाला *f.* A sacrificial hall. —श्रेष्ठा *f.* The Soma plant. —सदस् *n.* A number of people at a sacrifice. —सूत्रं *n.* See यज्ञोपवीत. —सेनः *m.* An epithet of king Drupada.

याज्ञिकः *m.* The Palása tree.

यज्ञिय *a.* (*f.* -या) 1 Belonging to or fit for a sacrifice.-2 Holy,sacred. -3 Adorable. -4 Devout, pious.-यः *m.* 1 A God, deity. -2 The third or Dvápara age.

यज्ञीय *a.* (*f.* —या) Sacrificial. -यः *m.* The Udumbara tree. -Comp. —ब्रह्मपादपः *m.* The विकंकत tree.

यज्वन् *a.* (*f.* —यज्वरी) Sacrificing, worshipping. —*m.* 1 One who performs sacrifices in accordance with Vedic precepts.

यत् 1 A .(यतते, यतित) 1 To attempt (usually with inf. or dat.). -2 To strive after. -3 To exert oneself, labour. -4 To be watchful. —With निस्- or प्रति- To requite. वि— To punish. —*Caus.* (यातयति,-ते) To requite, recompense, restore. -2 To despise, censure. -3 To encourage, animate. -4 To torture. -5 To prepare, elaborate. -6 To cause to be returned or restored.

यत *p. p.* (*f.* —ता) 1 Restrained, subdued. -2 Limited, moderate. -तं *n.* The spurring of an elephant by means of the rider's feet. -Comp. -व्रत *a.* 1 Observing vows. -2 Keeping to one's engagements.

यतनं *n.* Exertion, effort.

यतम *a.* (*f.* -मा, *n.* -मत्) Who or which of many.

यतर *a.* (*f.* -रा, *n.* -रत) Who or which of two.

यतस् *ind.* 1 From whence, from which place or quarter. -2 Wherefore, in consequence of which. -2 As, since, because. -4 From which time forward, ever since. -5 That, so that. यतस्ततः *ind.* 1 From any quarter whatever. -2 From any person whatever.-3 Anywhere soever,on all sides,in any direction. यतो यतः *ind.* 1 From whatever place.-2From whom soever, from any person whatever. -3 Wherever, in whatever direction. यतः प्रभृति *ind.* From which time forward.-Comp. -भव *a.* Arising from which. —मूल *a.* Sprung from which.

यति *pron a.* (declined only in pl.; nom. acc. यति) As many, as often, how many.

यतिः *f.*1 Restraint,control.-2 Stopping, ceasing. -3 Guidance. -4 A pause in music.-5 (In prosody) A caesura.-6 A widow. -तिः *m.* 1 An ascetic.-2 N. of Vishnu.

यतित *p. p.* (*f.*—ता) Tried,attempted, striven after.

यतिन् *m.* An ascetic

यतिनी *f.* A widow.

यत्न: *m.* 1 An effort, exertion. -2 Diligence, perseverance. -3 Care, vigilance. -4 Trouble, difficulty.

यत्र *ind.* 1 Where, in which place. -2 When, as in यत्र काले.-3 Whereas, because. (यत्र यत्र 'Wherever'. यत्र तत्र In whatever place, everywhere. यत्र-कुत्र or यत्रक्वचन or यत्रक्वापि 1 Where-so-ever.-2 When-so-ever, at whatever time. -3 Whenever, as often as.-4 Hither and thither.

यत्रत्य *a.* (*f.*—त्या) Of which place, dwelling in which place.

यथा *ind.* I (Used by itself) 1 As, in the manner mentioned.-2Namely: as follows. -3 As, like (showing comparison). -4 As for example, for instance. -5 That (used to introduce direct assertions with or without इति at the end). -6 So that, in order that. (Used correlatively with तथा). 1 As, so (in which case एवं and तद्वत् often take the place of तथा). -2 So that. -3 Since-therefore, as (because) so. -4 If-then, as surely as-so surely. यथा यथा-तथा तथा The more the more, the less the less. यथातथा In any manner, in whatever way. यथा कथंचित् Any how, some how or other.

As the first member of Avyayibhava Comp. यथा is usually translated by ' according to,"according as,'in accordance with,"in conformity to,' 'in proportion to,' 'not exceeding '.

-Comp.-अंशं,-अंशतस् *ind.* In due proportion, proportionately. -अनुपूर्वं,-अनुपूर्व्यं,-अनुपूर्व्या *ind.* In regular order or succession, successively. -अनुभूतं *ind.* 1 According to experience. -2 By previous experience. -अनुरूपं *ind.* In exact conformity, properly. -अभिप्रेत, -अभिमत, -अभिलषित, —अभीष्ट *a.* As wished, intended or desired. —अभिरुचित *a.* Pleasant, agreeable. —अर्थ *a.* 1 True, real, correct. -2 True to the sense, right, appropriate, significant. -2 Fit, suitable. —अर्ह *a.* 1 According to merit, as deserved. -2 Appropriate, suitable, just. -अवकाशं *ind.* 1 According to room or space. -2 As occasion may occur, according to occasion. -3 In the proper place. -आगत *a.* Foolish, stupid. -आगमं *ind.* According to tradition, as handed down from generation to generation. —आम्नातं, -आम्नायं *ind.* As laid down in the Vedas. -इच्छ, -इष्ट, -ईप्सित *a.* According to wish or desire, as much as desired, as desired or wished for.-उक्त, -उदित *a.* As said or told above, afore-said, above-mentioned. -उचित *a.* Suitable, proper, due, fit. -उत्तरं *ind.* In regular order or succession, one after another. -उद्दिष्ट *a.* As indicated or described. -काम *a.* Conformable to desire. —मं *ind.* Agreeably to desire, at will or pleasure, to the heart's content. —कामिन् *a.* Free, unrestrained. —कालं *ind.* At the right time, opportunely, seasonably. —क्रमं, -क्रमेण *ind.* In due order or succession, regularly.-जात *a.* 1 Foolish, senseless, stupid. -2 Barbarous, outcast. —ज्ञानं *ind.* To the best of one's knowledge or judgment. -ज्येष्ठं *ind.* According to rank, by seniority. -तत्त्वं *ind.* 1 According to actual facts, actually. -तथ *a.* 1 True, right. -2 Accurate, exact. (-थं *n.*) A detailed or minute account. (-थं *ind.*) 1 Exactly, precisely. -2 Properly, as the case really may be.–दिक्,–दिशं *ind.* In all directions. –न्यायं *ind.* Justly, rightly, properly. –पुरं *ind.* As before, as on previous occasions. –पूर्व *a.* –पूर्वक *a.* Being as before, former. (–र्वं,–पूर्वकं *ind*) 1 As before. –2 In due order or succession, one after another. –3 According to direction or precept. –प्राप्त *a.* Suitable to circumstances. –बलं *ind.* To the best of one's power, with all one's might. –बुद्धि, –मति *ind.* To the best of one's knowledge. –भागं, –भागशः *ind.* 1 According to the share of each, proportionately. –2 Each in his respective place. –3 In the proper place. –भावः *m.* Destiny. –भूतं *ind.* According to what has taken place, according to truth, truly, exactly. –यथं *ind.* 1 As is fit, fitly, properly. –2 In regular order, each in its proper place. –3 By degrees, gradually. –युक्तं, –योगं *ind.* According to circumstances, suitably. –योग्य *a.* Suitable, fit, proper, right. –वस्तु *ind.* As the fact stands, accurately. –विधि *ind.* According to rule or precept; properly. –शक्ति, –शक्त्या *ind.* To the best of one's power, as far as possible. –शास्त्रं *ind.* According to the scriptures, as the law ordains. –शीघ्रं *ind.* As quickly as possible. –श्रुत *a.* According to the report. –श्रुतं, –श्रुति *ind.* 1 As heard or reported. –2 (यथाश्रुति *ind*) According to Vedic precepts. –श्रेष्ठं *ind.* In the order of precedence or merit. –संख्यं *n.* The figure of speech in which several things are mentioned in a certain order and then other things are shown to be related to them in the same order. यथासंख्यमनुद्देशउद्दिष्टानां क्रमेण यत् *सा.द्. द. *e. g.* मृगमीनसज्जनानां तृणजलसंतोषविहितवृत्तीनां। लुब्धकधीवरपिशुना निष्कारणवैरिणो जगति ॥ –संभावित *a.* Suitable, appropriate. –सुखं *ind.* 1 At will or pleasure –2 At ease, comfortably. –स्थानं *ind.* 1 In the proper place; duly, properly. –2 Instantly. –3 According to rank. –स्थित *a.* According to circumstances or actual facts, as it stands. –2 Right, proper, fit. –स्वं *ind.* 1 Each his own, respectively. –2 Individually. –3 Properly, rightly.

यथावत् *ind.* 1 Duly, fitly, properly, rightly (oft. with the force of an adjective). –2 According to rule or precept 3 Exactly, truly.

यद् *pron.* (*nom. sing.* यः *m.*, या *f.*, यत् *n.*) A *relative pron.* correspounding to the English 'who', 'which' or 'what' The correlative of यद् is तद्, एतद्, इदं or अदस्. Sometimes this correlative is omitted. When यद् is repeated, it means 'whoever' or 'whatever'. यद् is often joined with the interrogative pronoun or its derivatives to signify 'any', 'whatever'. यत्किंचन or यत्किंचित means 'a trifle', 'a worthless thing.' As an *ind.* यद् is use (with or without इति) at the beginning of a subordinate sentence in the sense of the Eng. conjunction 'that'. –2 As an *ind.* यद् means 'because', 'since'. In this use यद् is often followed by तद् or ततः; when यद् is followed by अपि it means 'although' 'not-with-standing.' यदर्थं, यदर्थे *ind.* 1 On which account, wherefore, why. –2 Since, because. यत्कारणं *ind.* 1 On which account, for which reason. –2 Because. यत्कृते *ind.* Wherefore, why, for whom. यद्वा *ind.* Or, or else, whether. यत्सत्यं *ind.* To speak the truth, to be sure, verily.

Comp. —भाविष्य: *m.* A fatalist.

यदा *ind.* 1 When. यदा यदा *ind.* Whenever. यदैव तदैव *ind.* At the very time, as soon as. यदाप्रभृति – तदाप्रभृति *ind.* From what time-from that time forward. -2 If (= यदि). -3 Whereas, since, as.

यदि *ind.* 1 If, in case.-2 Whether, if. -3 Povided that, when. -4 Perhaps. यद्यपि Means 'though', 'although.' यदिवा Means'or','or rather'.

यदीय *a.* (*f.* —या) Whose,of whom or what.

यदुः *m.* 1 N. of an ancient king. -2 N. of a country near Mathurá. Comp. —कुलोद्भवः, -नंदनः, —श्रेष्ठः *m.* Epithets of Krishna.

यदृच्छा *f.* 1 Self-will, independence (of action). -2 Chance, accident (usually used in the instrumental singular in this sense). -Comp. —अभिज्ञः *m.* A self-offered witness. —संवादः *m.* 1 Accidental conversation. -2 Spontaneous or accidental meeting.

यदृच्छातस् *ind.* Accidentally, by chance.

यंतृ *m.* 1 A governor, ruler. -2 A driver (as of an elephant,carriage, &c.); a coachman,charioteer.-3 An elephant-driver or rider.

यंत्र् I 10 U. (यंत्राति,-ते, यंत्रयाति,-ते) 1 To restrain,check. -2 To bind, fasten. -3 To force, oblige, compel.

यंत्रं *n.* 1 A prop or support,a stay. -2 A fetter, tie. -3 A surgical instrument,especially a blunt instrument (opp. शस्त्र). -4 Any instrument or contrivance ; implement in general. -5 A bolt, lock.. -6 Restraint,force.-7 An amulet.-Comp. —उपलः *m.* A mill, mill-stone. —करंडिका *f.* A kind of magical basket. —कर्मकृत *m* An artist, artisan. -गृहं *n.*1 An oil-mill.-2 A manufactory. -चेष्टितं *n.* Any magical work. -नालं *n.* A mechanical pipe or tube. -पुत्रकः *m.*, —पुत्रिका *f.* A mechanical doll, a puppet fitted with contrivances for moving the limbs. —मार्गः *m.* A canal or an aqueduct —शरः *m.* A missile shot off by means of machinery.

यंत्रकः *m.* One well acquainted with machinery. -कं *n.* 1 A bandage (in medic).-2 A turner's lathe.

यंत्रणं *n.*, -णा *f.* 1 Restraining. -2 A restraint, restriction ; check. -3 Fastening, binding. -4 Constraint, trouble. -5 Guarding, protecting. -6 A bandage.

यंत्रणी, यंत्रिणी *f.* A wife's younger sister.

यंत्रिन् *m.* 1 A horse furnished with harness or trappings -2 A tormentor. -3 One having an amulet.

यम् I P. (यच्छति,यंतुं, यत) 1 To check, restrain, subdue, suppress. -2 To offer,give, bestow. -3 To raise, lift up. -4 To extend, stretch. -5 To go.-6 To exhibit, show.

यमः *m.* 1 Restraining, curbing.-2 Control, restraint. -3 Self-control. -4 Any great moral or religious duty or observance (opp. नियम).-5 The first of the eight *angas* or means of attaining 'Yoga.' -6 The God of death, death personified.-7 A twin.-8 One of a pair or couple a fellow. -9 N. of Saturn. -10 A crow. -11 A symbolical expression for the number 'two'. —मं *n.* A pair or couple. —मी *f.* N. of the river Yamunâ. -Comp. —अनुगः,-अनुचरः *m.* A servant or attendant of Yama. —अंतकः *m.* An epithet of Siva. —ज *a.* Twin-born, twin.

-दूतः, -दूतकः *m.* 1 A messenger of Death. -2 A crow. —देवता *f.* The asterism Bharaṇī. —द्वितीया *f.* The second day in the bright half of Kârtika when sisters entertain their brothers.-धानी *f.* The abode of Yama. —भगिनी *f* N. of the river Yamunâ. —राज् *m.* Yama, the God of death. —वाहनः, -रथः *m.* A buffalo. —सूर्यं *m.* A building with two halls, one facing the west and the other facing the north.

यमकः *m.* 1 A restraint. -2 A twin; one of a pair, a fellow.-कं *n.*1 A double bandage.-2 (In Rhet.) Repetition in the same stanza (in any part of it) of words or syllables similar in sound, but different in meaning; a kind of rhyme.

यमन *a.* (*f.* -नी) Restraining, governing. -नं *n.* 1 The act of curbing or binding. -2 Stopping, ceasing. -3 Cessation, rest. -4 Governing, managing. -नः *m.* The God of death, Yama.

यमानिका *f.* A curtain, screen.

यमल *a.* (*f.* -ला) Twin, one of a couple. -लः *m.* The number ' two '. -लौ *m. dual* A pair. -लं *n.*, -ली *f.* A pair, couple. -ली*f.* A dress consisting of two pieces.

यमवत् *a.* (*f.* -ती) 1 Self-controlled. -2 Temperate, moderate.

यमसात् *ind.* In the hands of Yama, to the power of Yama.

यमुना *f.* N. of a celebrated river (regarded as a sister of Yama). -2 N. of Durgâ.

ययातिः *m.* N. of a celebrated king of the lunar race, son of Nahusha.

ययावरः *m.* See यायावरः

ययिः, ययी *m.* 1 A horse. -2 A road.

ययुः *m.* A horse fit for a sacrifice.

यर्हि *ind.* 1 When, while, whenever. -2 Because, as, since ; (its proper correlative is तर्हि or एतर्हि, but it is rarely used in classical literature.)

यवः *m.* 1 Barley. -2 A barley-corn or the weight of a barley-corn. -3 A measure of length equal to 1/6 or 1/8 of an *angula.* -4 (In palmistry) A mark on the fingers of the hand resembling a barley-corn. -Comp. -आग्रयणं *n.* The first fruits of barley. —क्षारः, —आह्वः, -नालजः, -जः *m.* Saltpetre, nitre, nitrate of potash. -फलः *m.* A bamboo. -क्षासः *m.* Saltpetre, nitre.

यवनः *m.* 1 A Greek, an Ionian. -2 Any foreigner. -3 A carrot.

यवनानी *f.* The writing of the Yavannas.

यवनिका, यवनी *f.* 1 A Yavana female. -2 A curtain.

यवसं *n.* Grass, fodder, meadow-grass.

यवागू *f.* Rice-gruel, sour gruel made from rice &c.

यवानिका, यवानी *f.* A kind of bad barley.

यविष्ठ *a.* (*f.* -ष्ठा) Youngest, very young (superl. of युवन q. v.). -ष्ठः *m.* 1 The youngest brother. -2 N. of Agni.

यवीयस् *a.*(*f.* -सी) Younger, very young (compar. of युवन q. v.). -*m.* 1 A younger brother. -2 A Súdra.

यशस् *n.* Fame, reputation, glory, renown. -Comp. -काम *a.* Eager for fame.-दः *m.* Quicksilver.(-दा *f.*) N. of the wife of Nanda and foster-mother of Krishna. -पटहः (यशःपटहः) *m.* A double drum. -शेषः *a.* Remaining only in fame *i. e.* dead.

यशस्य *a.* (*f.* —स्या) 1 Leading to glory or distinction. -2 Renowned famous, glorious.

To close, be closed or shut (as eyes or flowers). -3 To fade, disappear, vanish.-4 To be collected. With उद्— 1 To open the eyes. -2 To spring up. नि— 1 To shut the eyes. -3 To die. -3 To be closed. -4 To disappear. सम्— To be shut.

मीलनं n. 1 Winking, twinkling. -2 Closing the eyes. -3 The closing of a flower.

मीलित p. p. (f. -ता) 1 Shut, closed. -2 Twinkled. -3 Half-opened, unblown. -4 Disppeared. 5 Assembled, gathered. -तं n. (In Rhet) The figure of speech in which something is concealed or covered up by another possessing a similar characteristic.

मीवरः m. The leader of an army, a general. [Wind.

मीवा f. 1 The tapeworm. -2

मुः m. 1 An epithet of Siva. -2 Bondage, confinement. -3 Final emancipation.

मुकंदकः m. An onion.

मुकुः m. 1 Liberation, deliverance, -2 Final emancipation.

मुकुटं n. 1 A crown, tiara, diadem. -2 A crest. -3 A peak, point.

मुकुटी f. Cracking or snapping the fingers.

मुकुंदः m. 1 N. of Vishnu or Krishna. -2 Quicksilver. -3 A kind of precious stone. -4 N. of one of the nine treasures of Kubera.-5 A kind of drum.

मुकुरः m. 1 A mirror, looking-glass. -2 A bud. -3 The handle of a potter's wheel. -4 The Bakula tree.

मुकुलः m.,—लं n. 1 A bud. -2 Anything like a bud. -3 The body. -4 The soul or spirit.

मुकुलित a. (f. -ता)1 Having buds, budded,blossoming.-2 Half-closed, half-shut. -3 Closed, shut.

मुकुष्ठः, मुकुष्ठकः m. A kind of bean.

मुक्त p. p. (f. —क्ता) 1 Loosened, relaxed. 2 Set free, liberated. -3 Abandoned, given up, set aside.-4 Discharged, hurled.-5 Fallen down. -6 Drooping, unnerved. -7 Given, bestowed. -8 Sent forth, emitted.-9 Finally emancipated. -10 Ejected, spit out. -11 Deprived. -12 Absolved or emancipated. —क्तः m. One who is finally emancipated from the bonds of worldly existence ; one who has renounced all worldly attachments and secured final beatitude ; an absolved saint. —क्तं n. The spirit released from worldly existence -Comp. —अंबरः m. A Jaina ascetic of the *digambara* class. —कच्छः m. A Buddhist. —कंचुकः m. A snake that has cast off its slough. —कर,—हस्त a. Open-handed, liberal. —चक्षस् m. A lion.

मुक्तकं n. 1 A missile. -2 Simple prose. -3 A detached stanza the meaning of which is complete in itself.

मुक्ता f. 1 A pearl. -2 A harlot, courtezan. -Comp. —अगारः, —आगारः m. The pearl-oyster. —पुष्पः m. A kind of jasmine.—प्रसूः f. The pearl-oyster. —फलं n. 1 A pearl. -2 A kind of flower. -3 The custard-apple. -4 Camphor. -मणिः m., -रत्नं n. A pearl. —मातृ f. The pearl-oyster. -शुक्तिः f.,-स्फोटः m. The pearl oyster.

मुक्तिः f. 1 Release, liberation, deliverance. -2 Freedom, emancipation. -3 Final beatitunde ; absolution of the soul from metempsychosis. -4 Leaving, abandoning, avoiding. -5 Letting off, discharg-

यशस्विन् *a.* (*f.* -नी) 1 Famous, glorious, renowned. -2 Excellent, best.

यष्टिः, यष्टी *f.* 1 A stick, staff. -2 A cudgel, mace, club. A column, pillar. -4 A perch, as in वासयष्टिः. -5 A stem, support. -6 A stalk, stem. -7 A branch, twig. -8 A string, thread (as of pearls), a necklace. -9 Any creeping plant. -10 Anything thin or slender (at the end of comp. after words meaning 'the body' as in अंगयष्टिः slender or delicate frame. Comp. -निवासः *m.* 1 A stick or rod serving as a perch for peacocks &c.-2 A pigeon-house resting on upright poles. -प्राण *a.* 1 Feeble or powerless. -2 Out of breath.

यष्टिकः *m.* 1 A lap-wing.-2 A kind of water-fowl.

यष्टिका *f.* 1 A staff, stick, pole, club. -2 A pearl necklace (of one string) -3 An oblong pond or tank.

यष्टी *f.* See यष्टि.

यष्टृ *m.* A worshipper, sacrificer.

यस् I. 4. P. (यसति, यस्यति, यस्त) To strive, endeavour, labour. With आ— 1 To endeavour. -2 To be afflicted. प्र- To strive, to endeavour.

या 2 P. (याति, यातुं, यात) 1 To go, move, walk, proceed. -2 To invade. -3 To set out for (with acc., dat. or with प्रति). -4 To withdraw, depart -5 To pass away or by, elapse (as time). -6 To last. -7 To happen, come to pass. 8 To be reduced to any state, be or become (usually with the acc. of abstract noun). -9 To have carnal intercourse with. -10 To request, implore. -11 To find out, discover. -12 To behave, act. With अति- 1 To transgress. -2 To surpass. अपि- To escape. अभि-1 To approach. -2 To invade. परि-To surround. प्रत्युद्- To go out to meet, to welcome.

Caus. (यापयति,-ते) 1 To cause to go or proceed. -2 To remove, drive away. -3 To spend, pass (time). -4 To live or spend time with. -5 To support, nourish.

यागः *m.* 1 An offering, a sacrifice, an oblation. -2 Any ceremony in which oblations are presented.

याच् 1 A. (याचते; rarely याचति याचित) 1 To beg, ask, request, implore (with two acc.) as in बलिं याचते वसुधां. -2 To demand in marriage.

याचकः *m.* (*f.* -की) 1 A mendicant; beggar. -2 A petitioner, suppliant.

याचनं *n.*,-ना *f.* 1 Asking, begging, entreating. -2 A request, an entreaty, a petition.

याचनकः *m.* A beggar, suitor, petitioner. [soliciting.

याचिष्णु *a.* Habitually begging or

याचित *p. p.* (*f.* -ता) 1 Asked, begged, entreated.-2 Requisite, necessary. -तं *n.* 1 The profession of a beggar.

याचितकं *n.* A thing go by begging.

याच्ञा *f.* 1 Begging, asking. -2 Mendicancy. -3 Request, solicitation, entreaty. -4 Making an offer of marriage.

याजः *m.* 1 A sacrificer. -2 Boiled rice. -3 Food in general.

याजकः *m.* 1 A sacrificer, a sacrificing priest. -2 A royal elephant. -3 An elephant in rut.

याजिः *m.* The institutor of a sacrifice -*f.* A sacrifice.

याज्ञवल्क्यः *m.* N. of a celebrated sage, author of a code of laws.

याज्ञसेनी *f.* A patronymic of Draupadi.

याज्ञिक *a*. (*f*. -की) Belonging to a sacrifice. -कः *m*. 1 A sacrificer or a sacrificing priest. -2 A ritualist.

याज्ञिय: *m*. One skilled in sacrificial rites.

याज्य *a*. (*f*. ज्या) 1 To be sacrificed. -2 Sacrificial. -3 One for whom a sacrifice is performed -4 One who is allowed by Sàstras to sacrifice. —ज्यः *m*. 1 A sacrificer. -2 The performer of a sacrifice for another. -ज्यं *n*. The presents or fee received for officiating at a sacrifice.

यात *p.p*. (*f*. —ता) 1 Gone, marched, walked. -2 Passed, gone away. -3 Passed by, elapsed. -4 Reduced or gone to(a state &c.).-तं*n*.1 Going, motion -2 A march. -3 The past time. -Comp. -याम,-यामन् *a*. 1 Stale, spoiled, become useless. -2 Raw, half cooked (as food). -3 Aged, exhausted, worn out.

यातनं *n*. 1 Requital,recompense,retaliation, as in वैरयातनं-2 Vengeance, revenge.-ना *f*. 1 Requital, recompense, return. -2 Torment, acute pain,anguish.-3 The torments inflicted by Yama upon sinners ; the tortures of hell (pl.).

यातु: *m*. 1 A traveller. -2 Wind. -3 Time. -4 An evil spirit, a demon. -*n*. 1 An evil spirit, a demon. -2 A weapon. -Comp.-धान: *m*. An evil spirit, a demon.

यातृ *f*. A husband's brother's wife -*m*. 1 A goer, a traveller. -2 A driver.

यात्रा *f*. 1 Going, motion, journey. -2 The march of an army, expedition. -3 Going on a pilgrimage, as in तीर्थयात्रा. -4 A company of pilgrims. -5 A festival, fair. -6 A procession, festive train.-7 A road. -8 Livelihood, maintenance -9 Passing away (time). -10 Intercourse. -11 A means, expedient. -12 A custom, usage, practice, way. -13 A vehicle in general. -14 A kind of dramatic entertainment.

यात्रिक *a*. (*f*. -की) 1 Marching. -2 Relating to a journey or campaign. -3Requisite for the support of life. -4 Usual, customary.-कः *m*.1 A traveller. -2 A pilgrim. —कं *n*. 1 A march, an expedition -2 Provisions, supplies (for a march).

याथातथ्यं *n*. 1 Reality,truth.-2 Rectitude, propriety.

याथार्थ्यं *n*.1 Real or correct nature, truth, true character. -2 Suitableness.-3 Accomplishment or attainment of an object.

यादव: *m*. 1 A descendant of Yadu. -2 N. of Krishna.

यादस् *n*. Any large aquatic animal, sea-monster -2 Water. -Comp. —पति:, -नाथ: (also यादसांपतिः and यादसांनाथः *m*.) The ocean. -2 N. of Varuna.

यादृक्ष *a*. (*f*. —क्षी) यादृश्, यादृश *a*. (*f*. -शी) What like, of which sort or nature

यादृच्छिक *a*. (*f* —की) 1 Voluntary, independent. -2 Accidental, unexpected.

यानं *n*. 1 Going, moving, walking, riding. -2 A voyage, journey. -3 Attacking. -4 A procession, train. -5 A conveyance,vehicle, carriage, a litter, palanquin. -Comp. -पात्रं *n*. A ship, boat. —मुखं *n*. The yoke of a carriage.

यापनं *n* , —ना *f*. 1 Driving out, expulsion, removal. -2 Cure or alleviation (of a disease). -3 Passing time. -4 Support, maintenance. -5 Practice, exercise. -6 Loitering.

याप्य *a.* (*f.* —प्या) Low, contemptible, unimportant. -Comp. -यानं *n.* A palanquin.

यामः *m.* 1 Restraint, forbearance. -2 A watch, a period of three hours. -Comp.-घोषः *m.* 1 A cock.-2 A gong on which night-watches are struck. —यमः *m.* A stated occupation for every hour. —वृत्तिः *f.* The being on watch or guard.

यामवती *f.* Night.

यामलं *n.* A pair, couple.

यामिः, यामी *f.* 1 A sister. -2 Night. -3 A daughter-in-law.

यामिकः *m.* A watchman, one on guard at night.

यामिका, यामिनी *f.* Night. -Comp. —पतिः *m.* 1 The moon.-2 Camphor.

यामुन *a.* (*f.* —नी) Belonging to, or coming from, the Yamunâ.-नं *n.* A kind of collyrium.

यामुनेष्टकं *n.* Lead.

यामेयः *m.* A sister's son.

याम्य *a.* (*f.* —म्या) 1 Southern. -2 Belonging to or resembling Yama. —म्यं *n.* The Bharanî Nakshatra. -Comp. —अयनं *n.* The winter solstice. —उत्तर *a.* Going from south to north,

याम्या *f.* 1 The south. -2 Night.

याययूकः *m.* A performer of frequent sacrifices.

यायावरः *m.* A vagrant mendicant, saint. —रं *n.* The life of a vagrant mendicant.

यावः *m.* 1 Food prepared from barley. -2 Lac, red dye.

यावकः *m.*, -कं. *n.* 1 Food prepared from barley. -2 Lac, red lac.

यावत् *a.* (*f.* —ती) (As a correlative of तावत्) 1 As much as, as many as. -2 As great, as large, how great or large. -3 All, whole, as in यावद् दत्तं तावद्भुक्तं.

As an independent adv. यावत् means, 'just now,' or 'in the meantime'. -2 'Till', 'during', 'as far as' (with an acc.).

As a relative of तावत् it means 1 So long as, as long as.-2 As soon as, no sooner than. -3 While, during. -Comp. —अंतं, —अंताय *ind.* To the last. —अर्थ *a.* As much or as many as necessary for the meaning. (—र्थं) *ind.* 1 As much as useful. -2 In all senses. -इष्टं,-ईप्सितं *ind.* As much as is desired. —इत्थं *ind.* As much as is necessary. —जन्म, -जीवं, -जीवेन *ind.* For life, throughout life. -बलं *ind.* To the best of one's power. -मात्र *a.* Insignificant, trifling, little. -शक्यं, —शक्ति *ind.* As far as possible, to the best of one's power.

यावनः *m.* Incense.

यावसः *m.* 1 A heap of grass. -2 Fodder, provisions.

याष्टीकः *m.* A warrior armed with a club.

यास्कः *m.* N. of the author of the [Nirukta.

यु (2 P. यौति; युत) 1 To join, unite. -2 To mix, combine.

यु 3 P. (युयोति) To detach, separ[ate.

यु 9 U. (युनाति, युनीते) 1 To bind, fasten. -2 To join, unite. -3 To mix, combine.

युक्त *p. p.* (*f.* —क्ता) 1 Joined, united. -2 Yoked, harnessed. -3 Fitted out, arranged. -4 Accompanied. -5 Absorbed or engaged in, devoted to (with loc.). -6 Adapted, fitted. -7 Appointed -8 Active, diligent. -9 Fit, proper, right, suitable (with gen. or loc.). -10 Primitive, not derived (from another word). —क्तः m. 1 A saint who has become one with the Supreme Spirit.–क्तं n. 1 A team, yoke.–2 Money lawfully obtained. —क्तं ind. Fitly, properly, justly. –Comp. —अर्थ a. Sensible, significant. —मनस् a. Attentive. —रूप a. Fit, proper, suitable (with gen. or loc.).–3 Fit for, corresponding to.

युक्तिः f. 1 Union, combination. –2 Use, employment. –3 Yoking, harnessing. –4 A practice, usage. –5 A means, a plan. –6 Propriety, fitness, suitableness. –7 Skill, art. –8 Reasoning, an argument. –9 Inference, deduction. –10 Reason, ground. –11 Arrangement. –12 (In law.) Probability. –13 (In dramas) The regular chain or connection of events.–14 Sum, total.–15 Alloying of metals. –Comp.–कर a. 1 Suitable, fit. –2 Proved.

युगं n. 1 A yoke (m. also in this sense).–2 A pair, couple.–3 A couple of stanzas forming one sentence.–4 An age of the world (the Yugas are four:—कृत or सत्य, त्रेता, द्वापर and कलि). –5 (Hence) A long period of years. –6 A generation, life. –7 An expression for the number 'four'. –8 A period of five years. –9 A measure of length equal to four *Hastas*. –10 A part of a chariot or plough. –Comp. —अंतः m. 1 The end of the yoke. –2 The end of an age, end or destruction of the world. –3 Meridian, midday. —कीलकः m. The pin of a yoke. —धरः m. The pole of a carriage.–पार्श्वग a. Going to the side of the yoke (said of an ox while being broken in to the yoke). –बाहु a. Long-armed.

युगंधरः m ,—रं n. The pole of a carriage to which the yoke is fixed.

युगपद् ind. Simultaneously, all at once, at the same time.

युगलं n. A pair, couple.

युगलकं n. 1 A pair. –2 A couple of verses forming one sentence.

युग्म a. (f. —ग्मा) Even. —ग्मं n. 1 A pair, couple. –2 Junction, union. –3 Confluence (of rivers). –4 Twins.–5 A couple of stanzas forming one grammatical sentence. –6 The sign *Gemini* of the zodiac. –7 Mixing, uniting. –Comp. —ज a. Twin, twin-born. —पत्रः m. Mountain ebony.

युग्य a. (f. –ग्या) 1 Fit to be yoked. –2 Belonging to a yoke. –3 Yoked, harnessed. –4 Drawn by, as in अश्वयुग्यो रथः.–ग्यः m. Any yoked or draught animal. —ग्यं n. A vehicle, carriage.

युज् 7 U (युनक्ति, युंक्ते, योक्तुं, युक्त) 1 To join, unite, add.–2 To yoke, harness. –3 To use, employ, apply. –4 To appoint, set (with loc.). –5 To fix upon (as the mind &c.).–6 To prepare, make ready or fit. –7 To give, bestow, confer (a blessing). –8 To think or meditate upon.

युज् 1 P., 10 U. (योजति, योजयति,–ते) To unite, join, yoke.

युज् m. 1 A joiner, one who unites or joins. –2 A sage, one who devotes himself to abstract meditation –3 A pair, couple (n. also in this sense). –m. dual. 1 The sign *Gemini* of the zodiac. –2 The two Asvins.

युंजानः m 1 A driver, charioteer. –2 A Brâhmana who is engaged in the practice of Yoga. –3 A Brâhmana.

युत p. p. (f. —ता) 1 United, joined or united with. –2 Provided or endowed with.-3 Accompanied by.

युतकं *n.* 1 A pair. -2 Union, friendship. -3 A nuptial gift. -4 A sort of dress worn by women.

युतिः *f.* 1 Union, junction. -2 Being endowed with.-3 Gaining possession of. -4 Sum, addition. -5 (In astr.) Conjunction.

युद्धं *n.* 1 War, battle, fight, struggle, combat.-2 (In astr.) The opposition or conflict of planets. —द्यूतं *n.* The chance of war. —भूः, —भूमिः *f.* A battle-field. —रंगः *m.* 1 A battle-field, battle-arena. -2 N. of Kártikeya. —वीरः *m.* 1 A warrior, hero, champion.-2 (In Rhet). The sentiment of heroism arising out of military prowess. —सारः *m.* A horse.

युध् 4 A (युध्यते, युद्ध) 1 To fight, contend with, wage war. -2 To conquer or overcome in fight.- With नि- To restle, box. प्रति- To encounter in fight, oppose.

युध् *f.* War, battle, fight, contest. —*m.* A hero, soldier.

युधाजित् *m.* N. of a king of the Kekayas and maternal uncle of Bharata.

युधानः *m.* 1 A warrior, a man of the warrior caste. -2 An enemy.

युधिष्ठिरः *m.* N. of the eldest Pândava prince, also called 'Dharma', ' Dharmarâja '.

युयुः *m.* A horse. [intention.

युयुत्सा *f.* Desire of fighting, hostile

युयुत्सु *a.* 1 Wishing to fight, hostile. —त्सुः *m* A combatant.

युयुधानः *m.* 1 N. of Indra. -2 A Kshatriya, a warrior. -3 N. of Sátyaki.

युवति,-ती *f.* 1 A young woman. (whether of men or animals). -ती *f.* The sign *virgo* of the zodiac.

युवन् *a.* (*f.* युवतिः,-ती or यूनी compar. यवीयस् or कनीयस्; superl. यविष्ठ or कनिष्ठ) 1 Young, youthful, arrived at puberty. -2 Strong, healthy. -3 Excellent, good.—*m.* (nom. युवा, युवानौ, युवानः, acc. pl. यूनः) 1 A young man, a youth. -2 A younger descendant (the elder being still alive). -Comp. —खलति *a.* (*f.*-तिः,-ती) Bald in youth —गंडः *m.* An eruption on the cheeks or face of young men. —जरत *a.* (*f.* -ती) Prematurely old, —राज्, -राजः *m.* An heir-apparent, a prince-royal, crown-prince.

युष्मद् *pron.* The second personal pronoun; (*nom.* त्वं, युवां ,यूयं) Thou, you.

युष्मदीय *a.* (*f.* -या) Your, yours.

युष्मादृश्,-श *a.* (*f.* —शी) Like you.

यूकः *m.*, यूका *f.* A louse.

यूतिः *f.* Mixing, union, connection.

यूथं *n.* 1 A herd, multitude, a number of beasts. —नाथः, -पः, -पतिः *m.* 1 The leader of a troop or band. -2 The head of a flock or herd (usually of elephants).

यूथिका, यूथी *f.* A kind of jasmine or its flower.

यूपः *m.* 1 A sacrificial post to which the victim is fastened. -2 A trophy.

यूषः *m.*, यूषं *n.*, यूषन् *m.*, *n.* Soup, broth, pease soup. (यूषन् has no forms for the first five inflections, and is optionally substituted for यूष after acc. dual).

येन *ind.* (Instr. sing. of यद् used adverbially) 1 Whereby, by which, wherefore, on which account, by means of which. -2 So that. -3 Since, because.

योक्तृ *m.* 1 One who yokes, joins, or unites. -2 A coachman. -3 An exciter, instigator.

योक्त्रं *n.* A cord, rope, thong, halter.

योगः *m.* 1 Joining, uniting. -2 Union, combination. -3 Contact, touch. -4 Application, use. -5 Manner, course, means. -6 Consequence, result. -7 A yoke. -8 A vehicle, carriage. -9 An armour. -10 Putting on armour. -11 Propriety, suitableness. -12 An occupation, a business. -13 A trick, device. 14 Diligence, assiduity. -15 Remedy, cure. -16 A charm, spell. -17 Acquisition. -18 The equipment of an army. -19 Fixing, putting on -20 A side; an argument. -21 An opportunity. -22 Possibility, occurrence. -23 Wealth, substance. -24 A precept. -25 Regular order or connection, dependence of one word upon another. -26 Etymology of a word. -27 The etymological meaning of a word (opp. रूढि). -28 Deep and abstract meditation, contemplation of the Supreme Spirit. -29 The system of philosphy established by Patanjali. -30 (In arith.) Addition. -31 (In astr.) Conjunction, lucky conjunction. -32 A combination of stars. -33 N. of a particular astronomical division of time. -34 The principal star in a lunar mansion. -35 Devotion, pious seeking after God. -36 A spy. -37 A traitor. -Comp. —अंगं *n.* A means of attaining *Yoga*. —अंजनं *n.* A healing ointment. —अनुशासनं *n.* The doctrine of the *Yoga*. -आचारः *m.* 1 The practice or observance of *Yoga*. -2 A follower of that Buddhist sect which maintains the eternal existence of intelligence alone. -आचार्यः *m.* 1 A teacher of magic. -2 A teacher of the *Yoga* philosophy. —आधमनं *n.* A fraudulent pledge. —आसनं *n.* A posture suited to profound and abstract meditation. -इंद्रः —ईशः, -ईश्वरः *m.* 1 A master of *Yoga*. -2 One who has obtained superhuman faculties. -3 A magician. -4 An epithet of Siva. -5 A Vetàla. -6 An epithet of Yájnavalkya. —क्षेमः *m.* 1 Keeping safe of property. -2 The charge for securing property from accidents, insurance. -3 Welfare, well-being, prosperity. -4 Property, profit, gain. (-मौ *m. dual.* —मे *n. dual*, -मं *n. sing.*) Acquisition and preservation (of property), gain and security, preserving the old and acquiring the new. —चक्षुस् *m.* A Bráhmana. —चूर्णं *n.* A magical powder. —तारका, -तारा *f.* The chief star in a *Nakshatra* or constellation. —दानं *n.* 1 Communicating the Yoga doctrine. -2 A fraudulent gift. —धारणा *f.* Perseverance in devotion. —नाथः *m.* 1 An epithet of Siva. -2 Of Datta. -निद्रा *f.* 1 A state between sleep and wakefulness *i. e.* light sleep. -2 The sleep of Vishnu at the end of a Yuga. -3 N. of Durgá. —पट्टं *n.* A cloth thrown over the back and knees of an ascetic during abstract meditation. —बलं *n.* 1 The power of abstract meditation. -2 Power of magic. —माया *f.* 1 The magical power of the *Yoga*. -2 The power of God in the creation of the world personified as a deity. -3 N. of Durgá. —रंगः *m.* The orange. —रूढ *a.* Having an etymological as well as a special or conventional meaning (said of a word). —रोचना *f.* A kind of magical ointment. —वर्तिका *f.* A magical lamp or wick. —वासिष्ठं *n.* N. of a work treating of the means of obtaining final beatitude by means of *Yoga.* —वाहिन् *m., n.* A medium for mixing medicines *e. g.* honey. —वाही *f.* 1 An alkali. -2 Honey. -3 Quicksilver. —विक्रयः *m.* A fraudulent sale.—विद् *a.* 1 Knowing the proper method ; skilful, clever. -2 Conversant with *Yoga.* (*-m.*) 1 An epithet of Siva. -2 A practiser of *Yoga.* -3 A follower of the *Yoga* doctrines.-4 A magician. -5 A compounder of medicines. —शास्त्रं *n.* The *Yoga* philosophy. —समाधिः *m.* The absorption of the soul in profound and abstract contemplation. —सारः *m.* A universal remedy ; a panacea. —सूत्रं *n* Aphorisms of the *Yoga* system of philosophy. —सेवा *f.* The practice of abstract meditation.

योगिन् *m.* 1 A saint, a devotee, an ascetic. -2 A magician, sorcerer. -3 A follower of the *Yoga* system of philosophy. -4 N. of Yàjnavalkya. —नी *f.* 1 A female magician. -2 A female devotee. -3 N. of a class of female attendants on Siva or Durgá. -4 N. of Durgá. -Comp. —इन्द्र, -ईशः *m.* 1 N. of Yâjnavalkya.

योग्य *a.* (*f.* —ग्या) 1 Fit, suitable, appropriate. -2 Fit or suitable for, capable of, able to (with loc., dat. or gen. or in comp.). -3 Useful, serviceable.-4 Fit for *Yoga* or abstract meditation. -5 (In Nyáya phil.) Capable of being directly cognized. —ग्यः *m* 1 A calculator of expedients. -2 The asterism Pushya. —ग्या *f.* 1 Exercise or practice in general. -2 Martial exercise; drill. —ग्यं *n.* 1 A carriage, vehicle. -2 Sandal-wood. -3 A cake. -4 Milk.

योग्यता *f.* 1 Ability, capability. -2 Fitness, propriety.-3 Appropriateness. -4 Fitness or compatibility of sense, the absence of absurdity in the mutual connection of the things signified by the words.

योजनं *n.* 1 Joining, uniting yoking. -2 Applying, fixing. -3 Preparation, arrangement.-4 Construing the sense of a passage. -5 A measure of distance equal to four *Krosas.* -6 Exciting, instigation.-7 Concentration of the mind. —ना *f.* 1 Junction, union, connection. -2 Grammatical construction -Comp. —गंधा *f.* 1 Musk.-2 N. of Satyavatí.

योत्रं *n.* See योक्त्रं.

योद्धृ *m.* A warrior, combatant.

योधः *m.* 1 A warrior, soldier combatant. -2 War, battle. -Comp. —धर्मः *m.* The law of soldiers, a military law. —संरावः *m.* Mutual defiance of combatants, a challenge,

योधनं *n.* 1 War, battle contest.-2 A weapon. —नः *m.* A warrior, combatant.

योधिन् *m.* A warrior, soldier, combatant.

योनिः *m., f.* 1 Womb, uterus, the female organ of generation. -2 Any place of birth or origin ; generating cause, spring, fountain. -3 A mine. -4 An abode, a repository, seat, receptacle. -5 A family, stock, race, birth, form of existence ; as in मनुष्ययोनिः.-6 The asterism पूर्वफल्गुनी. -7 Water. -Comp. —गुणः *m.* The quality of the womb or place of origin. —ज *a.* Born of the womb, viviparous. -रंजनं *n*. The menstrual discharge. —लिंगं *n*. The clitoris. —संकरः *m*. A mixture of caste by unlawful intermarriage.

योनी *f*. See योनि.

योपनं *n*. Effacing, blotting out. -2 Anything used for effacing.-3 Molesting, oppressing, destroying.

योषणा *f*. A young, girl, maiden.

योषा, योषित्, योषिता *f* A woman, a girl, a young woman.

यौक्तिक *a*. (*f*. —की) 1 Suitable, fit, proper. -2 Based on argument or reasoning. -3 Usual, customary. —कः *m*. A king's boon companion.

यौगः *m*. A follower of the *Yoga* philosophy.

यौगपद्यं *n*. Simultaneity.

यौगिक *a*. (*f*. —की) 1 Useful, serviceable, proper. -2 Usual. -3 Derivative, etymological, (opp. रूढ or 'conventional'). -4 Remedial. -5 Relating to or derived from *Yoga*. -Comp. —रूढ *a*. Etymological and conventional, as उद्भिद्.

यौतक *a*. (*f*. -की) *n*. Rightfully belonging to any one. -कं *n*. A woman's dowry or private property.

यौतवं *n*. A measure.

यौनं *n*. Marriage.

यौवतं *n*. 1 An assemblage of young women. -2 The state of being a young woman.

यौवनं *n*. 1 Youth (fig. also), youthfulness. -2 A number of young persons, especially women.

यौवनकं *n*. Youth.

यौवनाश्वः *m*. N. of Mândhâtri, son of Yuvanâsva. [an heir-apparent.

यौवराज्यं *n*. The rank or rights of

यौष्माक *a*. (*f*. —की), यौष्माकीण *a*. (*f*. -णा) Your, yours.

र.

रंह् 1 P. (रंहति) 1 To move or go with speed, hasten.-2 Flow.

रंह् 10 U. (रंहयति,-ते) 1 To cause to move or flow rapidly, urge on. -2 To go. -3 To speak.

रंहतिः *f*. Speed, velocity.

रंहस् *n*. 1 Speed, velocity. -2 Violence, vehemence.

रक्त *p. p*. (*f*. —क्ता) 1 Coloured, dyed, tinged. -2 Red, crimson. -3 Impassioned, affected with love. -4 Lovely, charming, pleasant. -5 Fond of play, playful. —क्तः *m*. 1 Red colour. -2 Safflower. —क्ता *f*. 1 Lac. -2 The plant गुंजा. —क्तं *n*. 1 Blood. -2 Copper. -3 Saffron. -4 Vermilion. -Comp. —अक्ष *a*. 1 Red-eyed. -2 Fearful. (-क्षः *m*.) 1 A buffalo.-2 A pigeon.-3 A crane (सारस). -4 The Chakora bird. —अंकः *m*. A coral. —अंगः *m* 1 A bug. -2 The planet Mars. —अंबरः *m*. A vagrant devotee wearing red garments. —अर्बुदः *m*. A bloody tumour. -आधारः *m*. The skin. —आशयः *m*. Any viscus containing or secreting blood (as the heart, spleen, or liver). —उपलं *n*. Red chalk, red earth. -कंठः,-कंठिन् *m*. The cuckoo. —कंदः, —कंदलः *m*. A coral.—चंदनं *n*. 1 Red sandal. -2 Saffron. —चूर्णं *n*. Vermilion. —जिह्वः *m*. A lion. —तुंडः *m*. A parrot. —धातुः *m*. 1 Red chalk, orpiment. -2 Copper. —पल्लवः *m*. The Asoka tree. -पायिन् *m*. A bug. —पायिनी *f*. A leech. -प्रमेहः *m*. The passing of blood in the urine. —फलः *m*. The fig tree. -लोचनः *m*. A pigeon. -वटी, —वरटी *f*. Small-pox. —बी (-बी-) जः *m*. The pomegranate tree. -संध्यकं *n.* The red lotus. —सारं *n.* Red sandal.

रक्तक *a.* (*f.* -क्ता) 1 Red. -2 Impassioned, enamoured. -3 Pleasing, amusing. -4 Bloody. -कः *m.* 1 A red garment -2 An amorous person.-3 A sporter. -कं *n.* 1 Blood. -2 A red garment.

रक्तिः *f.* 1 Pleasingness, loveliness. -2 Attachment, loyalty, devotion.

रक्तिका *f.* The *gunjá* plant or its seed used as a weight.

रक्तिमन् *m.* Redness.

रक्ष् 1 P. (रक्षति, रक्षित)1 To protect, guard, watch, tend (as cattle); rule, govern (as earth). -2 To keep secret, not to divulge. -3 To preserve, save, spare(often with abl.). -4 To avoid.

रक्षः *m.* A guard, protector.

रक्षक *a.* (*f.* —क्षिका) Guarding, protecting. -कः *m.* A protector, guard, watchman.

रक्षणं *n.* Protecting, protection, watching, guarding. -णी *f.* A rein, bridle. —णः *f.* 1 A protector. -2 N. of Vishnu. -णा *f.* Protecting.

रक्षस् *n.* 1 An evil spirit, a demon, a goblin.

रक्षा *f.* 1 Protection, preservation; guarding. -2 Care, security. -3 A guard, watch. -4 An amulet. -5 A tutelary deity. -6 Ashes. -7 A piece of silk or thread fastened round the wrist on particular occasions, especially on the full-moon-day of Srávana, as an amulet or preservative ; (रक्षी also in this sense). -7 Lac. -Comp. -अपेक्षकः *m.* 1 A porter; door-keeper.-2 A guard of the women's apartments. -3 A catamite. -4 An actor. -करंडः *m.*, -करंडकं *n.* A preservative casket, an amulet.-गृहं *n.* A lying-in-chamber. -पालः,-पुरुषः *m.* A watchman, guard. -प्रदीपः *m.* A lamp kept burning as a sort of protection against evil spirits.-भूषणं *n.*, -मणिः *m.*, —रत्नं *n.* An ornament or jewel worn as an amulet against evil spirits.

रक्षिका *f.* 1 A female guardian. -2 An amulet, charm.

रक्ष्णः *m.* Protection.

रघुः *m.* 1 N. of a celebrated king of the solar race, son of Dilîpa and father of Aja. -2 रघवः *m. pl.* The Raghus or descendants of Raghu. -Comp. —नंदनः,—नाथः, -पतिः, —श्रेष्ठः, -सिंहः *m.* Epithets of Ráma. -वंशं *n.* N. of a celebrated classical poem by Kálidâsa.

रंक *a.* (*f.* -का) 1 Mean, poor, wretched, miserable. -2 Slow. -कः *m.* A beggar, wretch.

रंकुः *m.* A deer, an antelope.

रंगः *m.* 1 Colour, dye, paint. -2 A stage, theatre, an arena, any place of public amusement. -3 A place of assembly. -4 The audience. -5 A field of battle. -6 Dancing, singing, acting. -7 Mirth, diversion. -गः *m.*,-गं *n.* Tin.-Comp. -अंगनं(-णं)*n.* Arena, an amphitheatre. —अवतरणं *n.* 1 Entrance on the stage. -2 An actor's profession. -अवतारकः, -अवतारिन् *m.* An actor. -आजीवः *m.* 1 An actor. -2 A painter ; (so -उपजीविन् *m.*).-चरः *m.* 1 An actor, a player. -2 A gladiator. -जं *n.* Red lead. —जीवकः *m.* 1 An actor. -2 A dyer, colourist. -दः *m.* 1 Borax. -2 An extract of Khadira. -देवता *f.* The goddess supposed to preside over sports and public diversions generally. -द्वारं *n.* 1 A stage-door. -2 The prologue of a play. -भूतिः *f.* 1

The night of full moon in the month of Asvina. -भूमिः *f.* 1 A stage, theatre. -2 An arena, battle-field. -मंडपः *m.* A theatre. -मल्ली *f.* A lute. -मातृ *f.* 1 Lac, red-dye; or the insect which produces it. -2 Bawd, procuress.—शाला *f.* A dancing-hall, theatre, play-house

रच् 10 U. (रचयति,-ते, रचित) 1 To arrange, make ready, contrive, plan. -2 To effect, create, produce. -3 To write, compose, put together (as a work).-4 To place in or upon. fix on. -5 To adorn, decorate. -6 To direct (the mind &c.) towards.

रचनं *n.*, -ना *f.* 1 Arrangement, preparation. -2 Formation, creation, production. -3 Completion accomplishment.-4 A literary work, a composition. -5 Dressing the hair. -6 An arrangement of troops.-7 A creation of the mind, an artificial image. -8 Stringing together(flowers &c.).

रजः *m.* See रजस्.

रजकः *m.* 1 A washer-man. -2 A parrot. -की *f.* 1 A washer-woman. -2 An epithet of a woman on the third day of her courses.

रजका *f.* A washer-woman.

रजत *a.* (*f.* -ता) 1 Silvery, made of silver. -2 Whitish. -तं *n.* 1 Silver. -2 Gold. -3 A pearl-ornament or necklace. -4 Blood. -5 Ivory. -6 An asterism, a constellation. -7 A mountain. -Comp. —अद्रिः *n.* N. of Kailâsa. —प्रस्थः *m.* N. of Kailâsa.

रजनिः,—नी *f.* 1 Night.-2 Turmeric. -3 Red lac. -4N. of Durgá.-Comp. —करः *m.* 1 The moon. -2 Camphor. —चरः *m.* 1 A night-stalker, demon, goblin. -2 A thief. -3 A night-watcher. -4 N. of the moon. -जलं *n.* Night-dew, hoar-frost. -पतिः, -रमणः *m.* The moon. -मुखं *n.* Night-fall, evening.

रजनिमन्य *a.* Passing for or looking like night (as a day).

रजस् *n.* 1 Dust, powder, dirt. -2 The dust or pollen of flowers. -3 A small particle (of matter). -4 A Ploughed or cultivated land, arable field. -5 Gloom, darkness. -6 Moral or mental darkness. -7 The second of the three Gunas or constituent qualities of all material substances (the other two being सत्व and तमस्). -8 Menstrrual discharge, menses.-9 Safflower.-10 Tin. -Comp.-गुणः *m.* See 7 above.—तमस्क *a.* Being under the influence of both *rajas* and *tamas.*—तोकः *m.*, -कं *n.* -पुत्रः *m.* 1 Greediness, avarice. -2 'The child of Passion', a term applied to a person to show that he is quite insignificant.-दर्शनं *n.* The first appearance of the menstrual excretion.

रजसानुः *m.* A cloud. -2 Soul, heart.

रजस्वल *a.* (*f.*-ला) 1 Dusty, covered with dust. -2 Full of passion (रजस्) or emotion. -लः *m.* A buffalo. -ला *f.* 1 A woman during the menses. -2 A marriageable girl; one above ten years of age.

रज्जुः *f.* A rope, cord, string. -2 N. of a sinew proceeding from the vertebral column. -3 A lock of braided hair. -Comp. -दालकः *m.* A kind of wild fowl —पेडा *f.* A rope-basket.

रंज् 1, 4. U. (रजति,-ते, रज्यति,-ते, रक्त.) 1 To be dyed or coloured, to become red, glow. -2 To dye, tinge. -3 To be attached or devoted to (with loc). -4 To fall in love with, feel passion or affection for. -5 To be pleased, satisfied or delighted.

Caus. (रंजयति,-ते) I To dye, tinge, redden, paint. -2 To gratify, propitiate (रजयति also in this sense). -3 To conciliate, win over. -4 To hunt deer (रजयति only in this sense).

रंजकः *m.* I A painter, dyer. -2 An exciter, a stimulus. —कं *n.* I Red sandal.-2 Vermilion.-नं *n.* I Colouring, dyeing, painting. -2 Colour, dye. -3 Pleasing, delighting, gratifying. -4 Red sandal-wood. -5 The Munja grass. -6 (In gram.) nasalizing (a sound.). [meric.

रंजनी *f.* I The Indigo plant.-2 Tur-

रट् I P. (रटति, रटित) I To shout, scream, yell, cry, howl. -2 To call out, proclaim loudly. -3 To shout with joy.

रटनं *n.* I The act of crying, screaming or shouting. -2 A shout of applause.

रटंती *f.* N. of the fourteenth day in the dark half of Mâgha.

रण् I P. (रणति, रणित) I To sound, ring, tinkle. -2 To go.

रणः *m.*, —णं *n.* I War, combat, fight. -2 A battle-field. —णः *m.* I Sound, noise. -2 The bow of a lute. -3 Motion, going. -Comp. —अंगं *n.* A weapon. —अभियोगः *m.* Engaging in battle. —धुरा *f.* The front or van of battle. —पंडितः *m.* A warrior. -प्रियः *m.* A falcon.-मत्तः *m.* An elephant.-रंकः *m.* The space between the tusks of an elephant. —रणः *m.* A gnat, mosquito. (-णं *n.*) I. Longing, anxious desire. -2 Regret for a lost object.-रणकः *m.*, -कं *n.* Anxiety, uneasiness, regret. -2. Love, desire. (—कः *m.*) The God of love.—संकुलं *n.* The confusion of battle -सज्जा *f.* Military accoutrement. —सहायः *m.* An ally. —स्तंभः *m.* A monument of war, trophy.

रणत्कारः *m* I A rattling, clanking, or jingling sound. -2 A sound in general.-3 Humming (as of bees).

रणितं *n.* Rattling, ringing, a rattling or jingling sound.

रंडः *m.* I A man who dies without male issue. -2 A barren tree. —डा *f.* I A slut, whore..

रत *p. p.* (*f.*-ता) I Pleased, delighted, gratified. -2 Pleased, fondly attached. -3 Inclined to, disposed. -4 Loved, beloved. -5 Intent on, engaged in, devoted to. -तं *n.* I Pleasure. -2 Sexual union. -3 The private parts. -Comp. —अयनी *f.* A prostitute, harlot. —उद्वहः *m.* The (Indian) cuckoo. —ऋद्धिकं *n.* I A day. -2 The eight auspicious objects. -3 Bathing for pleasure. —कीलः *m.* A dog. —ज्वरः *m* A crow. —ताली *m.* A libertine, sensualist. —ताली *f.* A procuress, bawd. -नारीचः *m.* I A voluptuary. -2 The God of love, Cupid. -3 A dog. -4 Lascivious murmur. -वर्णः *m.* A dog.-शायिन् *m.* A dog. —हिंडकः *m.* I A ravisher or seducer of women. -2 A voluptuary.

रतिः *f.* I Pleasure, delight, satisfaction. -2 Fondness for, devotion or attachment to, (with loc.). -3 Love, affection. -4 Sexual pleasure. -5 Sexual union. -6 The goddess of love, the wife of Kâma or Cupid. -7 The pudenda.-8 N. of the sixth digit (कला) of the moon. -Comp. —अंगं,—कुहरं *n.* Pudendum muliebre. —कर्मन् *n.* Sexual union. —गृहं, -भवनं, —मंदिरं *n.* I A pleasure-house. -2 A brothel. -3 Pudendum muliebre.

—तस्करः *m.* A seducer, ravisher. -पतिः, —प्रियः, -रमणः *m.* The God of love.

रत्नं *n.* 1 A gem, jewel. -2 Anything valuable or precious, any dear treasure. -3 Anything best or excellent of its kind ; (mostly at the end of comp.). -4 A magnet. -Comp. —अनुविद्ध *a.* Set or studded with jewels. —आकरः *m.* 1 A mine of jewels. -2 The ocean. —कंदलः *m.* A coral —करः *m.* N. of Kubera. -गर्भः *m.* 1 Kubera. -2 The sea. (—र्भा *f.*) The earth. —निधिः *m.* 1 The ocean. -2 N. of Vishnu. -3 Of Meru. -4 A wag-tail. —प्रभा *f.* The earth. —मुख्यं *n.* A diamond. —राज् *m.* A ruby. —राशिः *m.* 1 A heap of gems. -2 The ocean. —सानुः *m.* N. of the mountain Meru. —सूः,—सूतिः *f.* The earth.

रत्निः *m., f.* 1 The elbow. -2 The distance from the elbow to the end of the closed fist; a cubit. -*m.* The closed fist.

रथः *m.* 1 A carriage, chariot, car, a war-chariot.-2 A hero (for रथिन्). -3 A foot. -4 A limb, part, member. -5 The body. -6 A reed. -7 Pleasure, delight. -Comp. —अक्षः *m.* 1 A carriage-axle. -2 A measure of length. —अंगं *n.* 1 Any part of a carriage. -2 The wheels of a carriage. -3 A discus, especially of Vishnu. -4 A potter's wheel. (-गः *m.*) The ruddy goose. —ईशः *m.* A warrior fighting from a chariot. —ईशः, —षा *f.* The pole of a carriage. —उद्वहः, -उपस्थः *m.* The seat of a chariot, the driving-box. —कट्या, —कड्या *f.* An assemblage of chariots. —कल्पकः *m.* An officer who is in charge of a king's chariots. —कुटुंबिकः, —कुटुंबिन् *m.* A charioteer, coachman. —कूबरः *m.*, -रं *n.* The pole or shaft of a carriage. -गर्भकः *m.* A litter, palanquin —गुप्तिः *f.* A fence of wood or iron with which a chariot is provided as a protection from collision. —चरणः, -पादः *m.* 1 A chariot-wheel. -2 The ruddy goose. —चर्या *f.* Chariot exercise, travelling by carriage. —नाभिः *f.* The nave of the wheel of a chariot. —महोत्सवः *m.*, —यात्रा *f.* The solemn procession of an idol placed in a car (usually drawn by men). —योजकः *m.* A charioteer, harnesser of a chariot. —वर्त्मन् *n.*, —वीथिः *f.* A highway, main-road. —वाहः *m.* 1 A carriage-horse. -2 A charioteer. —शक्तिः *f.* The staff which supports the banner of a war-chariot. -सप्तमी *f.* The seventh day in the bright half of Mágha.

रथारथि *ind.* 'Chariot against chariot', in close fight.

रथिक *a.* (*f.*-की) 1 Riding in a carriage.-2 The owner of a carriage.

रथिन् *a.* (*f.*—नी) 1 Riding or driving in a carriage.-2 Possessing or owning a carriage-*m.* 1 An owner of a carriage.-2 A warrior who fights from a chariot. -नी *f.* A number of carriages or chariots.

रथिन *a.* See रथिन् above.

रथिर *a.* 1 Possessing a carriage. -2 Riding in a carriage. -3 Quick, speedy. -रः *m.* = रथिन् *m.*

रथ्यः *m.* 1 A chariot-horse. -2 A part of a chariot.

रथ्या *f.* 1 A road for carriages (hence) a high-way, main road. -2 A place where many roads meet. -3 A number of carriages or chariots.

रदः *m*. 1 Splitting, scratching. -2 A tooth ; tusk (of an elephant). -Comp. —च्छदः *m*. A lip.

रदानिन् रादिन् *m*. An elephant.

रध्, रंध् 4 P. (रध्यति, रद्ध) 1 To hurt, torment, kill, destroy. -2 To subdue. -3 To become subject to (any one).

रन्तिदेवः *m*. N. of a king of the lunar race. -2 N. of Vishnu. -3 A dog.

रन्तुः *f*. 1 A way, road. -2 A river.

रन्धनं *n*., रन्धिः *f*. 1 Injuring, destroying. -2 Cooking.

रन्ध्रं *n*. 1 A hole, an aperture, a chasm, fissure.-2A weak or vulnerable point, fault, an imperfection. -3 A symbolical expression for the number ' nine '. -Comp. —बभ्रुः *m*. A cat.—वंशः *m*. A hollow bamboo.

रभ् 1 A. (रभते, रब्ध) 1 To begin. -2 To clasp, embrace. -3 To long for, be eager. -4 To act rashly.

रभस् *n*. 1 Violence, vehemence. -2 Rashness. -3 Force, strength.

रभस *a*. (*f*. —सा) 1 Violent, fierce, wild. -2 Strong, vehement, ardent, eager (as desire &c.). -3 Joyful, glad. —सः *m*. 1 Violence, force, haste, speed, vehemence. -2 Rashness, headlong haste. -3 Passion, rage. -4 Regret, sorrow. -5 Joy, pleasure, delight. -6 Ardent desire, eagerness.

रम् 1 A. (रमते, but Paras. when preceded by वि, आ, परि, and उप ; रेमे, रंतुं, रत) 1 To be pleased, to rejoice, be gratified. -2 To rejoice at, take delight in. -3 To play, sport, amuse oneself with. -4 To have sexual intercourse with. -5 To remain, stay, pause. -6 To remain quiet. -7 To gladden, delight.

रमः *m*. 1 Joy, delight. -2 A lover, husband. -3 The God of love.

रमठं *n*. Asa Fœtida. -Comp.-ध्वनिः *m*. Asa Fœtida.

रमण *a*. (*f*. —णी) Pleasing, delightful, charming. —णः *m*. 1 A lover, husband -2 The God of love. - 3 An ass. -4 A testicle. —णं *n*. 1 Sporting. -2 Dalliance, amorous sport. -3 Love, sexual union. -4 Joy or pleasure in general. -5 The hip and the loins.

रमणा *f*. 1 A wife, mistress. -2 A lovely woman.

रमणी *f*. 1 A lovely young woman. -2 A wife, mistress. -3 A woman in general.

रमणीय *a*. (*f*. -या) 1 Pleasant, delightful. -2 Lovely, charming.

रमा *f*. 1 A wife, mistress. -2 N. of Lakshmî, the wife of Vishnu, and Goddess of wealth. -3 Riches. -4 N. of the eleventh day in the dark half of Kártika. Comp. -कांतः, -नाथः, -प्रियः, -पतिः *m*. Epithets of Vishnu. —वेष्टः *m*. Turpentine.

रंभा *f*. 1 A plantain tree. -2 N. of Gaurî.-3 N. of an *apsaras*. -Comp. —ऊरु *a*. (*f*. -रु, or -रू). Having thighs like the interior of a plantain tree *i. e.* full, round, and hence lovely.

रम्य *a*. (*f*. —म्या) 1 Pleasing, agreeable. -2 Beautiful, lovely.-म्यः *m*. The tree called चंपक. —म्यं *n*. Semen virile.

रय् 1 A. (रयते, रयित) To go, move.

रयः *m*. 1 The stream of a river, current. -2 Speed, velocity. -3 Zeal ; ardour, vehemence.

रल्लकः *m*. 1 A woollen cloth, blanket. -2 An eye-lash. -3 A kind of deer.

रवः *m*. 1 A cry, shriek, scream, yell, roar (of animals &c). -2 Singing, humming. -3 Clamour. -4 Noise or sound in general.

रवण *a.* (*f.* -णा) 1 Crying, roaring. -2 Sonorous, sounding. -3 Sharp, hot. -4 Fickle, unsteady. -5 Jesting. —णः *m.* 1 A camel. -2 The cuckoo. —णं *n.* Bell-metal.

रविः *m.* 1 The sun. -2 The number 'twelve'. Comp. —कांतः *m.* The sun-stone (सूर्यकांत).—जः, -तनयः,-पुत्रः,-सूनुः *m.* I. The planet Saturn. -2. Epithets of Karna. -3 An epithet of Váli.-4 Of Manu Vaivasvata.-5 Of Yama. -6Of Sugrîva. -दिनं *n.*, -वारः, -वासरः*m.*, -वारं *n.* Sun-dây. -संक्रांतिः *f.* The sun's entrance into any zodiacal sign.

रशना, रसना *f.* I A rope, cord. -2 A rein, bridle. -3 A zone, girdle, woman's girdle. -4 The tongue. Comp. —उपमा *f.* A variety of the figure उपमा; it is 'a string or series' of comparisons, which consists in making the *Upameya* in the first comparison the *Upamána* in the second, and so forth.

रश्मिः *m.* 1 A string, cord, rope. -2 A bridle, rein.-3 A goad, whip. -4 A beam, ray of light. -Comp. —कलापः *m.* A pearl-necklace of 54 threads. —मुचः *m.* The sun.

रश्मिम (-व-) त *m.* The sun.

रस् 1 P. (रसति, रसित) 1 To roar, yell, scream. -2 To tinkle, jingle. -3 To resound, reverberate.

रस् 10 U. (रसयति,-ते,रासित) To taste, relish.

रसः *m.* 1 Sap, juice (of trees). -2 A liquid, fluid. -3 Water. -4 Liquor, drink. -5 A draught, potion. -6 Flavour, relish (fig. also) (considered in Vais. Phil. as one of the 24 *gunas*; the *rasas* are six कटु, अम्ल, मधुर, लवण, तिक्त, and कषाय) -7 A condiment. -8 An object of taste. -9 Taste or inclination for a thing, liking, desire. -10 Love, affection. -11 Pleasure, delight. -12 Charm, beauty. -13 Pathos, emotion, feeling. -14 (In poetic compositions) A sentiment. (The *rasas* are usually eight:— शृंगार, हास्य, करुण, रौद्र, वीर, भयानक, बीभत्स, अद्भुत; and शांत, वात्सल्य, and भक्ति according to some). The Rasas constitute the very essence of poetry, in the opinion of most writers on rhetoric. -15 Essence, pith. -16 A constituent fluid of the body. -17 Semen virile. -18 Mercury.-19A poison,poisonous drink. -20 Any mineral substance. -21 A symbolical expression for the number ' six '. -Comp. —अम्लः *m.* 1 A kind of sorrel. -2 Sour sauce. -अयनं *n.* 1 An elixir of life (elixir vitae), any medicine supposed to prolong life and prevent old age. -2 Alchemy or chemistry. -3 Any medicinal compound. (-नः *m.*) 1 An alchemist. -2N. of Garuda. -आभासः *m.* 1 The semblance or mere appearance of a sentiment. -2 An improper manifestation of a sentiment. -इंद्रः *m.* 1 Mercury. -2 The philosopher's stone (the touch of which is said to turn iron into gold). —उद्भवं *n.* 1 A pearl. -2 Vermilion. —उपलं *n.* A pearl. —ऊनं *n.* Garlic. —कर्पूरं*n.* Sublimate of mercury. -कर्मन् *n.* Preparation of quicksilver. —केसरं *n.* Camphor. —गंधः *m.*, —धं *n.* Gum myrrh. —ग्रह *a.* 1 Perceiving flavours. -2 Appreciating or enjoying pleasures. (-हः *m.*) The organ of taste. —जं *n.* Blood. —ज्ञ *a.* 1 One who appreciates the flavour or excellence of ; one who knows the taste of. -2 Capable of discerning the beauty of things. (—ज्ञा *f.*) The tongue. —धातु *n.* Quick-silver. —पाचकः *m.* 1 A cook.—प्रबंधः *m.* Any poetical composition, particularly a drama. —फलः *m.* The cocoa-nut tree.—भंगः *m.* An interruption or cessation of a sentiment. —राजः *m.* Quick-siver.—सिद्धिः *f.* Skill in alchemy.

रसनं *n.* 1 Crying, roaring ; tinkling noise or sound in general. -2 Thunder, rumbling or muttering of clouds. -3 Taste, flavour. -4 The organ of taste, the tongue. -5 Perception, appreciation, sense. —नः *m.* Phlegm.

रसना *f.* 1 The tongue. -2 A zone, a woman's girdle. -Comp. —रदः *m.* A bird. —लिह् *m.* A dog.

रसवत् *a.* (*f.* -ती) 1 Juicy, succulent. -2 Tasteful, savoury, well-flavoured. -3 Moist, well-watered. -4 Charming, elegant. -5 Full of feeling or sentiment. -6 Full of affection, possessed of love. -7 Spirited, witty. —ती *f.* A kitchen. *m.* The figure of speech in which there is a principal रस (sentiment), and its development is furthered by another रस which is subordinate to it.

रसा *f.* 1 The lower or infernal regions, hell. -2 The earth, ground, soil. -3 The tongue. -Comp. —तलं *n.* 1 N. of one of the seven regions below the earth.-2 The lower world or hell in general. —पायिन् *m.* A dog.

रसालः *m.* 1 The mango tree. -2 The olibanum tree. -3 The bread-fruit-tree. -4 The sugar-cane. —ला *f.* 1 The tongue. -2 Curds mixed with sugar and spices. -3 A vine or grape. —लं *n.* 1 Gum-myrrh. -2 Frankincense.

रसिक *a.* (*f.*—का) 1 Savoury, tasteful. -2 Graceful, elegent. -3 Impassioned. -4 Apprehending flavour or excellence,possessed of taste, appreciative.-5 Finding pleasure or taking delight in,delighting in, devoted to. -6 Humourous, witty. —कः *m.* 1 A man of taste or feeling,an appreciator of excellence or beauty. -2A libertine.-3 An elephant.-4 A horse. -5 The Sârasa bird. —का *f.* 1 The juice of sugar-cane,molasses. -2The tongue.-3A woman's girdle.

रसित *p. p.* (*f.* -ता). 1 Tasted. -2 Having flavour or sentiment. -3 Gilded. -4 Sounded, making indistinct sound. —तं *n.* 1 Wine or liquor. -2 A cry, roar, roaring noise, sound or noise in general.

रसोनः *m.* A kind of garlic.

रस्य *a.* (*f.* —स्या) Juicy, savoury, sapid. palatable.—स्यं *n.* Blood.

रह् 1 P., 10 U. (रहति, रहयति,-ते, रहित) To leave, abandon, desert.

रहणं *n.* Desertion, quitting, separation.

रहस् *n.* 1 Solitude, privacy, retirement, secrecy. -2 A lonely place, hiding-place.-3 A secret, mystery. -4 Copulation. -5 A privity. —*ind.* Secretly, privately.

रहस्य *a.* (*f.*-स्या) 1 Secret, private. -2 Mysterious. —स्यं *n.* 1 A secret (fig. also). -2 A mystic spell or incantation,the mystery (of a missile). -3 The secret of conduct, mystery.-4 An esoteric teaching, a mystic doctrine.. -5 An Upanishad. —स्यं *ind.* Secretly, privately. Comp. —व्रतं *n.* 1 A secret vow or penance

-2 The mystic science of obtaining command over magical weapons.

रहित *p. p.* (*f.*-ता) 1 Abandoned, deserted. -2 Separated from, deprived of, without (with instr. or at the end of comp.). -3 Lonely, solitary. —तं *n.* Secrecy, privacy.

रा 2 P. (राति, रात) To give, grant, bestow.

राका *f.* 1 The full moon day, particularly the night. -2 A girl in whom menstruation has just commenced. -3 Itch, scab.

राक्षस *a.* (*f.* —सी) Belonging to or like an evil spirit ; demoniacal. —सः *m.* 1 A demon, an evil spirit, a fiend. -2 One of the eight forms of marriage in Hindu Law, in which a girl is forcibly seized and carried away after the defeat or destruction of her relatives in battle. -3 One of the astronomical *Yogas.* -4 N. of a minister of Nanda, an important character in the Mudràrákshasa. —सी *f.* A female demon.

राक्षा *f.* An incorrect form of लाक्षा.

रागः *m.* 1 Colouring, dyeing, tinging. -2 Colour, dye. -3 Red colour, redness. -4 Love, affection, amorous or sexual feeling. -5 Joy, pleasure. -6 Anger, wrath. -7 Loveliness, beauty -8 A musical mode or order of sound ; (there are six primary *Râgas.* Each *râga* has six *ráginís* and their union gives rise to several musical modes).-9 Musical harmony, melody. -10 Regret, sorrow. -11 Greediness, envy. -Comp.—चूर्णः *m.* 1 Acasia Catechu or Khadira tree. -2 Red lead. -3 Lac. -4 Red powder thrown by people over one another at the festival called *holi.* -5 The God of love. —पुष्पः *m.* A ruby. —सूत्रं *n.* 1 A coloured thread. -2 A silk-thread. -3 The string of a balance.

रागिन् *a.* (*f.* -णी)1 Coloured, dyed. -2 Red. -3 Full of passion or feeling, impassioned. -4 Full of love. -5 Devotedly attached to, desirous of. -*m.* 1 A painter. -2 A lover. -3 A libertine, sensualist. —णी *f.* 1 A modification of a musical mode (राग), of which 30 or 36 kinds are enumerated. -2 A wanton and intriguing woman.

राघवः *m.*1 A descendant of Raghu, especially Râma.

रांकव *a.* (*f.* -वी) Belonging to the species of deer called *ranku* or made from its hair ; woollen. —वं *n.* 1 A woollen cloth made of deer's hair; a woollen garment.-2 A blanket.

राज् 1 U. (राजति,-ते, राजित) 1 To shine, glitter, be eminent. -2 To appear or look (like), shine (like).

राज्,राजः *m.* 1 A king, chief, prince. -2 Anything best of its kind.

राजकः *m.* A little king, a petty prince. —कं *n.* A number of kings or princes.

राजत *a.* (*f.* —ती) Silvery, made of silver. —तं *n.* Silver.

राजन् *m.* 1 A king, prince, chief. -2 A man of the military caste, a Kshatriya. -3 N. of Yudhishthira. -4 N. of Indra. -5 The moon. -6 A Yaksha. -Comp. —अधिराजः, -इंद्रः *m.* A king of kings, a supreme king, paramount sovereign, an emperor. —अधिष्ठानं *n.* The capital of a king, metropolis. —अध्वन् *m.* A principal or royal road, main street. —अनकः *m.* 1 An inferior king, petty prince. -2 A title of respect formerly given to distinguished scholars and poets. —अपसदः *m.* An unworthy or degraded king. —अभिषेकः *m.* The coronation of a king. —अर्हं *n.* A species or sandal. —अर्हणं *n.* A royal gift of honour. —आवलिः, —ली *f.* A royal dynasty or genealogy. —आसनं *n.* A throne. —उपकरणं *n.* The paraphernalia of a king, the insignia of royalty (used in the *pl.*). -ऋषिः (राजऋषिः or राजर्षिः) *m.* A royal sage, a saint-like prince; a Kshatriya who, by his pious life and austere devotion, has become a sage or *rishi.* —करः *m.* A tax or tribute paid to the king. —कुलं *n.* 1 A royal family, a king's family. -2 The court of a king. -3 A court of Justice -4 A royal palace. —गृहं *n.* 1 A royal dwelling, royal place. -2 N. of a chief city in Magadha. —चिह्नं *n.* The insignia of royalty, regalia. —तरंगिणी *f.* N. of a celebrated historical poem treating of the kings of Kâshmîra by Kalhana. -तालः,-ताली *f.* The betel-nut tree. -दंडः *m.* 1 A king's sceptre. -2 Royal authority. -3 Punishment inflicted by a king. -4 Fine payable to a king. —दंतः *m.* The front tooth. -धर्मः *m.* 1 A king's duty. -2 A law or rule relating to kings (oft. in pl.). —धानं, —धानकं *n.*,—धानिका,-धानी *f.* The king's residence, the capital, metropolis, the seat of goverment. —धुर्, -धुरा *f.* The burden or responsibility of government. -नयः *m.*,—नीतिः *f.* Administration of a state, administration of government, politics, statesmanship. —नीलं *n.* An emerald. —पट्टः *m.* 1 A diamond of inferior quality. -2 A royal fillet.-पथः *m.*, —पद्धतिः *f.* A main road, a public street. —पुत्रः *m.* 1 A prince. -2 A Kshatriya, a man of the military tribe. -3 The planet Mercury. -4 N. of a mixed caste. —पुरुषः *m.* 1 A king's servant.-2 A minister.-बीजिन्, —वंश्य *a.* A scion of royalty; of royal descent. —भृतः *m.* A king's soldier. —भृत्यः *m.* 1 A royal servant or minister. -2 Any public or government officer. —भोगः *m.* A king's meal, royal repast. —भौतः *m.* A king's fool or jester.—मंत्रधरः, —मंत्रिन् *m.* A king's counsellor. -मार्गः *m.* A highway, high road, a royal or main road, principal street. -2 The way, method or procedure of kings.-मुद्रा *f.* The royal seal. -यक्ष्मः, -यक्ष्मन् *m.* Pulmonary consumption; consumption in general. —योगः *m.* 1 The configuration of planets at the birth of a man which indicates that he is destined to be a king. -2 An easy mode of religious meditation as distinguished from the more rigorous one called हठयोगः. -रंगं *n.* Silver. —राजः *m.* 1 A supreme king, an emperor. -2 N. of Kubera. -3 The moon. —रीतिः *f.* Bell-metal. —लक्षणं *n.* 1 Any mark on a man's body indicating future kingship. -2 Royal insignia.-लक्ष्मीः, -श्रीः *f.* The fortune or prosperity of a king. —लेखः *m.* A royal edict. —लोकः *m.* A collection of princes or kings.-वंशावली *f.* Royal pedigree. -विद्या *f.* State-policy, statesmanship. —विहारः *m.* A royal convent. -शासनं *n.* A royal edict. —शृंगं *n.* A royal umbrella with a golden handle. —संसद्, -सभा *f.* A court of justice. —सायुज्यं *n.* Sovereignty. —सारसः *m.* A peacock. —सूयः *m.*,-यं *n.* A great sacrifice performed by a universal monarch at the time of his coronation as a mark of his undisputed sovereignty. -स्कंधः m. A horse. -स्वं n. 1 Royal property. -2 Tribute, revenue. -हंसः m. A flamingo (a sort of white goose with red legs and bill). -हस्तिन् m. A royal elephant ; a lordly and handsome elephant.

राजन्यः m. 1 A man of the Kshatriya caste; royal personage. -2 A noble or distinguished personage. -न्या f. A lady of royal rank.

राजन्यकं n. A collection of warriors or Kshatriyas.

राजन्वत् a. (f. -ती) Governed by a just or good king (as distinguished from राजवत which simply means 'having a ruler').

राजस a. (f. -सी) Relating to or influenced by the quality 'rajas'; endowed with the quality *rajas* or passion.

राजिः, राजी f. 1 A streak, line, row, range. -2 Black mustard.

राजिका f. 1 A line, row, range. -2 A field. -3 Black mustard. -4 Mustard (used as a weight).

राजिलः m. A species of innocent and poisonless snakes.

राजीवः m. 1 A kind of deer. -2 A crane. -3 An elephant. -वं n. A blue lotus. -Comp. -अक्ष a. Lotus-eyed.

राज्ञी f. A queen, the wife of a king.

राज्यं n. 1 Royalty, sovereignty, royal authority. -2 A kingdom, an empire. -3 Rule, reign, administration of a kingdom. -Comp. -अंगं n. A constituent member of the state; (these are usually said to be seven:-स्वाम्यमात्यसुहृत्कोषराष्ट्रदुर्गबलानि च). -अधिकारः m. 1 Authority over a kingdom. -2 A right to sovereignty. -अभिषेकः m Inauguration or coronation of a king. -करः m. The tribute paid by a tributary prince. -तंत्रं n. The science of government, system of administration. -धुरा f., -भारः m. The yoke or burden of government ; the responsibility or administration of government. -व्यवहारः m. Government business. -सुखं n. The sweets of royalty.

राढा f. N. of a district in Bengal, as also of its capital.

रात्रिः, रात्री f. Night. -Comp. -अटः m. 1 A goblin, demon, ghost. -2 A thief. -करः m. The moon. -चरः m. (also रात्रिंचर) (f. -री) 1 A robber, a thief. 1 A watchman, patrol, guard. -2 A demon, ghost, evil spirit. -चर्या f. 1 Night-roving. -2 A nightly act or ceremony. -जं n. A star, constellation. -जलं n. Dew. -जागरः m. 1 Night-watching, wakefulness or sitting up at night. -2 A dog. -तरा f. The dead of night. -रक्षः, -रक्षकः m. A watchman, guard. -रागः m. Darkness, obscurity. -वासस n. 1 Night-dress. -2 Darkness. -विरामः m. Break of day, dawn, day-light. -वेदः, -वेदिन् m. A cock.

रात्रिंदिवं, रात्रिंदिवा ind. By night and day.

रात्रिंमन्य a. Looking like night (as a cloudly or dark day).

राद्ध p. p. (f. -द्धा) 1 Propitiated, pleased, conciliated. -2 Effected, accomplished, achieved, performed. -3 Dressed, cooked (as food). -4 Prepared. -5 Obtained, got. -6 Successful, fortunate, happy. -7 Perfect in magical power. -8 Fallen to the lot of. -Comp. -अंतः m. A proved or established fact ; a demonstrated conclusion or truth; an ultimate conclusion, doctrine; dogma. —अंतिम *a.* Demonstrated, established by proof, logically proved.

राद्धिः *f.* Perfection, accomplishment. -2 Prosperity, success.

राध् 5 P. (राध्नोति, राद्ध) 1 To propitiate, conciliate, please -2 To accomplish, complete, achieve. -3 To prepare, make ready. -4 To fall to the lot of any one (also 4 P.). -5 To injure, destroy.

राध् 4 P. (राध्यति, राद्ध) 1 To be favourable or merciful. -2 To be accomplished or finished. -3 To propitiate, look to the welfare of (any one, with dat.).-4 To succeed, prosper. -5 To be ready.-6 To kill, destroy.

राधः *m.* The month called Vaisákha. —धी *f.* The day of full moon in the month of Vaisâkha.

राधा *f.* 1 Prosperity, success. -2 N. of a celebrated Gopî or cowherdess loved by Krishna. -3 N. of the foster-mother of Karna. -4 The lunar mansion called विशाखा. -5 Lightning. -6 The full-moon-day in the month of Vaisàkha.

राधिका *f.* See राधा.

राधेयः *f.* An epithet of Karna.

राम *a.* (*f.* -मा) 1 Pleasing, delighting, rejoicing. -2 Beautiful, charming. -3 Obscure. -4 White. -मः *m.* 1 N. of three celebrated personages; (*a*) Parasurâma, son of Jamadagni; (*b*) Balarâma, son of Vasudeva and brother of Krishna (*c*) Râmachandra or Sîtâram, a son of Dasaratha and Kausalyá and the hero of the Râmâyana. -2 A kind of deer. Comp. —अनुजः *m.* N. of a celebrated founder of a Vedántic sect and author of several works. —अयनं (-णं *n.*) 1 The adventures of Ràma. -2. N. of a celebrated epic by Válmíkí. —ईश्वरः *m.* N. of a sacred place of pilgrimage. —गिरिः *m.* N. of a mountain. —चंद्रः, —भद्रः *m.* N. of Râma, son of Dasaratha. —नवमी *f.* The ninth day in the bright half of Chaitra, the anniversary of the birth of Râma. —सेतुः *m.* The bridge of sand between the Indian peninsula and Ceylon now called Adam's bridge.

रामठः *m.*, -ठं *n.* Asa Foetida (हिंगु).

रामणीयक *a.* (*f.*-की) Lovely, beautiful, pleasing. —कं *n.* Loveliness, beauty.

रामा *f.* 1 A beautiful woman. -2 A woman in general. -3 A woman of low origin. -5 Vermilion. -6 Asa Foetida.

राम्भः *m.* A bamboo-staff carried by a religious student or ascetic.

रालः *m.* The resin of the Sála tree.

रावः *m.* 1 A cry, scream, shriek, the cry of any animal. -2 Sound in general.

रावण *a.* (*f.*-णी) Crying, screaming, bewailing. —णः *m.* N. of a celebrated demon, king of Lankâ and the chief of the Rákshasas.

रावणिः *m.* N. of Indrajit.

राशिः *m.* 1 A heap, mass, collection, quantity, multitude. -2 The numbers or figures put down for any artihmetical operation. -3 A sign of the zodiac. -Comp. —अधिपः *m.* The regent of an astrological house. —चक्रं *n.* The zodiac. -त्रयं *n.* The rule of three. —भागः *m.* A fraction. —भोगः *m.* 1 The passage of the sun, moon, or any planet through a sign of the zodiac

राष्ट्रं *n.* 1 A kingdom, realm, empire. -2 A district, territory, country. -3 The people, nation, subjects. -इः *m.*, इं *n.* Any national or public calamity.

राष्ट्रिकः *m.* 1 An inhabitant of a kingdom or country; a subject. -2 The ruler of a kingdom.

राष्ट्रियः *m.* 1 The ruler of a kingdom, king. -2 The brother-in-law of a king (queen's brother).

रास् 1 A. (रासते) To cry, scream.

रासः *m.* 1 An uproar, a din, confused noise. -2 A sound in general. -3 A kind of dance practised by Krishna and the cowherds but particularly the *gopis* or cowherdesses of Vrindâvana. -Comp. —क्रीडा *f.*, —मंडलं *n.* A sportive dance, the circular dance of Krishna and the cowherdesses of Vrindàvana.

रासकं *n.* A kind of minor drama in one act.

रासभः *m.* An ass, a donkey.

राहित्यं *n.* Being without anything; destitution ; destituteness.

राहुः *m.* 1 N. of a demon, son of Viprachitti and Simhikâ. -2 An eclipse, or the moment of occultation. -Comp. -ग्रसनं *n.*, -ग्रासः *m.*, -दर्शनं *n.*,-पीडा *f.*,-संस्पर्शः *m.* An eclipse (of the sun or moon). —सूतकं *n.* The birth of Ráhu *i. e.* an eclipse (of the sun or moon).

रि 6 P. (रियति, रीण) To go, move.

रिक्त *p. p.* (*f.* —क्ता) 1 Emptied, evacuated. -2 Empty, deprived of, without. -3 Indigent. —क्तं *n.* 1 An empty space, vacuum. -2 A forest, wilderness.

रिक्तक *a.* See रिक्त.

रिक्ता *f.* N. of the fourth, ninth, and fourteenth days of a lunar fortnight.

रिक्थं *n.* 1 Inheritance, bequest, property left at death. -2 Property in general, wealth, possessions. -3 Gold. -Comp. -आदः, -ग्राहः, -भागिन्, -हरः *m.* An heir. -हारिन् *m.* 1 An heir. -2 A maternal uncle.

रिंख्, रिंग् 1 P. (रिंखति, रिंगति) 1 To crawl, creep. -2 To go slowly.

रिंखणं, रिंगणं *n.* 1 Crawling, creeping. -2 Deviating (from rectitude).

रिच् 7 U. (रिणक्ति, रिंक्ते, रिक्त) 1 To empty, evacuate, purge. -2 To make destitute of. -3 To separate, divide. -4 To give up, part with.

रिच् 1. 10. P. (रेचति, रेचयति, रेचित) 1 To divide, separate, disjoin. To -2 abandon, leave. -3 To join, mix.

रिटिः *m.* N. of an attendant of Siva.

रिपुः *m.* 1 An enemy, a foe, an opponent. -2 A hostile planet. -3 N. of the sixth astrological house. Comp. —भवनं, -स्थानं *n.* N. of the 6th astrological house.

रिरंसा *f.* 1 Desire to sport. -2 Desire of pleasure, lustfuleness, libidinousness.

रिष् 1, 4. P. (रेषति, रिष्यति, रिष्ट) 1 To injure, hurt, harm. -2 To kill or destroy.

रिष्ट *p. p.* (*f.* —ष्टा) 1 Injured, hurt. -2 Unlucky. -ष्टं *n.* 1 Mischief, injury. -2 Misfortune. -3 Destruction, loss. -4 Sin -5 Good luck, prosperity.

रिष्टिः *f.* See रिष्टं *n.* above. —*m.* A sword.

री 4 A. (रीयते) To trickle, drip, ooze, flow.

री 9 U. (रिणाति, रिणीते, रीण) 1 To go, move. -2 To hurt, injure, kill. -3 To howl.

रीज्या *f.* 1 Censure, reproach, blame. -2 Shame, modesty.

रीढकः *m.* The back-bone.

रीढा *f.* Disrespect, contempt, irreverence.

रीण *p. p.* (*f.* -णा) Oozed, flowed.

रीतिः *f.* 1 Moving, flowing.-2 Motion, course. -3 A stream, river.-4 A line, boundary. -5 A mode, manner, way, fashion, general way. -6 Usage, custom, practice. -7 Style, diction (They are वैदर्भी, गौडी, पाञ्चाली, and लाटिका or मागधी). -8 Brass, bell-metal, (रीती also in this sense). Rust of iron. -10 The oxide formed on the surface of metals. -11 Calx of brass. -Comp.—पुष्पं *n.* The calx of brass.

रु 2 P. (रौति, रवीति, रुत) To cry, scream, shout, roar; to hum (as bees); to sound in general.

रुक्म *a.* (*f.* —क्मा) Bright, radiant. —क्मः *m.* 1 A golden ornament.-क्मं *n.* 1 Gold. -2 Iron. -Comp. -कारकः *m.* A goldsmith. —रथः, —वाहनः *m.* N. of Drona.

रुक्मिणी *f.* The daughter of Bhishmaka of Vidarbha.

रुग्ण *p. p.* (*f.* -ग्णा) 1 Broken, shattered. -2 Bent, curved. -3 Injured, hurt. -4 Diseased, sick. -Comp. —रय *a.* Checked in an onset, foiled in an attack.

रुच् 1 A. (रोचते, रुचित) 1 To shine look splendid, be resplendent. -2To be agreeable to, please (used with *dat.* of the person and sometimes with *gen.* of the person.). With अभि- To please. वि- To shine.

रुच्, रुचा *f.* 1 Light, lustre, brightness. -2 Splendour, loveliness, beauty.-3 Colour, appearance. -4 Liking, desire.

रुचक *a.* (*f.* —का) 1 Agreeable, pleasing. -2 Sharp, acrid. —कः *m.* 1 The citron. -2 A pigeon. —कं *n.* 1 A tooth. -2 A golden ornament especially for the neck. -3 A tonic. -4 A wreath, garland. -5 A curl on a horse's neck.

रुचा *f.* See रुच्.

रुचिः (*f.* —ची) 1 Light, splendour, brightness. -2 A ray of light. -3 Appearance, colour, beauty. -4 Taste, relish. -5 Hunger, appetite. -6 Wish, desire. -7 Liking, taste. -8 Close application to any object. -9 A kind of yellow pigment. -Comp. —कर *a.* 1 Tasteful, savoury, palatable. -2 Exciting desire. -3 Stomachic, tonic. —धामन् *m.* The sun. —भर्तृ *m.* 1 The sun. -2 A husband.

रुचिर *a.* (*f.* -रा) 1 Bright, shining. -2 Tasteful, palatable. -3 Sweet, dainty. -4 Stomachic, exciting appetite. -5 Cordial, restorative. -रा *f.* 1 A kind of yellow pigment. -2 N. of a metre. —रं *n.* 1 Saffron. -2 Cloves.

रुच्य *a.* (*f.* —च्या) Bright, lovely. See रुचिर. —च्यः *m.* 1 A lover, husband. -2 Rice. —च्यं *n.* A tonic.

रुज् 1,6 P. (रुजति, रुग्ण) 1 To break to pieces, destroy. -2 To pain, injure, afflict with disease.-3To bend.

रुज् 10 U. (रोजयति,-ते) To hurt, kill.

रुज्, रुजा *f.* 1 Breaking, fracture.-2 Pain, torment.-3 Sickness, disease. -4 Fatigue, toil, effort, trouble. -Comp. —प्रतिक्रिया *f.* Treatment of disease, curing, practice of medicine. —सद्मन् *n.* Feces, excrement.

रुंडः *m.*, रुंडं *n.* A headless body, trunk.

रुतं *n.* A cry, yell, roar, sound or noise in general; humming (of bees). -Comp. —ज्ञः *m.* An augur.

रुद् 2 P. (रोदिति, रुदित) 1 To cry, weep, lament, mourn. -2 To howl, roar, scream.

रुदनं, रुदितं *n.* Weeping, crying. lamentation.

रुद्ध *p. p.* (*f.* —द्धा) 1 Obstructed, impeded, opposed. -2 Besieged, enclosed. -3 Kept, detained, withheld. -4 Covered, occupied, inhabited.

रुद्र *a.* (*f.* -द्रा) Dreadful, terrific, formidable.—द्रः *m.* 1 N. of a group of Gods, (eleven in number), supposed to be inferior manifestations of Siva.-2 N. of Siva. -3 The number 'eleven'. -Comp. —अक्षः *m.* A kind of tree. (-क्षं *n.*) 1 A rosary. -2 The berry of this tree, used for rosaries. -आक्रीडः *m.* A cemetery. -आवासः *m.* The mountain Kailás. -2 N. of Benares. -3 A cemetery.

रुद्राणी *f.* N. of Pârvati, wife of Rudra.

रुध् 7 U. (रुणद्धि, रुंद्धे, रोद्धुं, रुद्धः; *desid.* रुरुत्सति,-ते) 1 To obstruct, stop, arrest, oppose, prevent. -2 To hold up, keep, sustain (from falling). -3 To shut up, lock or block up, shut, close. -4 To surround, fence or hem in, confine. -5 To besiege, blockade. -6 To obscure, conceal. -7 To torment. With अनु— (also A.) 1 To comply with, approve. -2 To obey.-3 To love. अव— To infix. उप— 1 To Confine, restrain. -2 To obstruct, block up. -3 To molest. नि—1 To obstruct, stop. -2 To confine. वि— 1 To oppose, quarrel with. —सं To obstruct, check. -2 To fetter.

रुधिर *a.* (*f.*-रा) Red, red-coloured. —रं *n.* 1 Blood. -2 Saffron. —रः *m.* 1 The red colour. -2 The planet Mars. -Comp.—अशनः *m.* A demon, an evil spirit. —आमयः *m.* Hemorrhage, piles. —पायिन् *m.* A demon.

रुमा *f.* N. of the wife of Sugríva.

रुरुः *m.* 1 A kind of deer.

रुश् 6 P. (रुशति) To hurt, kill, tease, vex.

रुष् 4 P. (रुष्यति; रुषित, रुष्ट) To be angry, to be vexed or annoyed.

रुष् 1 P. (रोषति) 1 To hurt, kill. -2 To vex, annoy.

रुष्, रुषा *f.* Anger, wrath.

रुह् 1 P. (रोहति, रोढुं, रूढ) 1 To grow, germinate. -2 To be developed, increase. -3 To rise, mount upwards, ascend.-4 To grow over, heal up (as a wound). -5 To reach to, attain.

रुहा *f.* The Dúrvà grass.

रूक्ष *a.* (*f.* -क्षा) 1 Rough, harsh. -2 Astringent (taste). -3 Rough, austere. -4 Sullied, dirtied. -5 Cruel, harsh. -6 Parched up, dry, dreary.

रूक्षणं *n.* 1 Making dry or thin. -2 A treatment for reducing fat (of the body).

रूढ *p. p.* (*f.* —ढा) 1 Grown, germinated. -2 Born, produced. -3 Grown up, increased, developed. -4 Risen, ascended. -5 Large, great, strong. -6 Diffused, spread about. -7 Become current or widely known. -8 Traditional, conventional, popular (as the meaning of a word or the word itself). -9 Certain, ascertained.-10 Obscure.

रूढिः *f.* 1 Growth, germination.-2 Birth, production. -3 Increase, growth, spread. -4 Rise, ascent. -5 Fame, notoriety.-6 A tradition, traditional usage. -7 General prevalence,common currency.-8 Conventional acceptation of a word.

रूप् 10 U. (रूपयति,-ते, रूपित) 1 To form, fashion. -2 To represent on the stage, gesticulate. -3 To observe carefully,behold. With नि— 1 To represent, to gesticulate. -2 To look out, to see.-3 To consider, to ponder. -4 To investigate. -5 To appoint. वि— To disfigure.

रूपं *n.*1 Form,figure,appearance.-2 Form or the quality of colour(one of the 24 gunas of the Vaiseshikas). -3 Any visible object or thing. -4 A beautiful form, beauty,elegance. -5 Natural state, property, characteristic, essence.-6 Mode, manner. -7 A sign, feature. -8 Kind, sort, species. -9 An image, a reflected image. -10 Similitude, resemblance. -11 Type, pattern. -12 The form of a noun or a verb derived from inflection. -13 The number one, an arithmetical unit. -14 An integer. -15 A drama, play, see रूपक. -16 Acquiring familiarity with any book by learning it by frequent recitation. -17 Cattle. -18 A sound, a word. -19 An affix to nouns and adjeictives meaning 'formed or composed of,' 'consisting of,' 'in the form of,' 'namely', 'having the appearance or colour of:' as in धर्मरूपः सखा &c.) -Comp. —अभिबोधः *m.* The perception of form or colour of any object by the senses. —आजीवा *f.* A prostitute, courtezan. -इंद्रियं *n.* The organ which perceives form and colour; the eye. —कारः, -कृत *m.* A sculptor. -तत्त्वं *n.* Inherent property, essence.

रूपकः *m.* A particular coin, a *ruppee.* —कं *n.* 1 Form, shape. -2 Any manifestation or representation. -3 A sign, feature. -4 A kind, species. -5 A dramatic composition. -6 (In Rhet.) A figure of speech in which the उपमेय is represented as being identical with the उपमान. -6 A kind of weight (three *gunjás*). Comp.-तालः *m.* A particular time in music.

रूपणं *n.* 1 Metaphorical or figurative description. -2 Investigation, examination.

रूप्य *a.*(*f.*-प्या)1 Beautiful,lovely.-2 Stamped; impressed.-प्यं *n.* 1 Silver. -2 A stamped coin, a rupee. -3 Wrought gold.

रूष् 1 P. (रूषति, रूषित) 1 To adorn, decorate. -3 To anoint, cover (as with dust).

रूष् 10 U. (रूषयति,-ते) 1 To tremble. -2 To burst.

रे *ind.* A vocative particle.

रेखा *f.* 1 A line, streak. -2 A small portion, as much as a line. -3 A row, line, series. -4 Delineation, drawing. -5 The first or prime meridian of the Indian astronomers drawn from Lanká to Meru through Ujjayinî. -6 Fulness, satisfaction. -7 Deceit,fraud.-Comp. —अंशः *m.* A degree of longitude.-अंतरं *n.* Distance east or west from the first meridian, longitude of a place.-आकार *a.* Formed in lines, striped. —गणितं *n.* Geometry.

रेचक (*f.* -चिका) 1 Emptying, purging.-2 Purgative,aperient.-3Emptying the lungs, emitting the breath. -कः *m.* 1 Emission of breath,especially through one of the nostrils(opp.

पूरक which means 'inhaling breath'). -2 A syringe. -3 Nitre, salt-petre. -कं n. A Purgative, cathartic.

रेचनं n., —ना f. 1 Emptying or diminishing. -2 Emitting the breath. -3 Purging. -4 Evacuation.

रेचित a. (f. ता) Emptied, cleared, —तं n. horse's gallop.

रेणुः m. f. 1 Dust; an atom of dust, sand &c. -2 The pollen of flowers.

रेणुका f. The wife of Jamadagni and mother of Parasuráma.

रेतस् n. 1 Semen virile, seed.-2 Progeny, offspring.

रेप a. (f.-पा) 1 Contemptible, low, vile. -2 Cruel.

रेफ a. (f.-फा) Low, contemptible. —फः m. 1 A burr, grating sound. -2 The letter र्. -3 Passion.

रेवती f 1 N. of the 27 th constellation which contains thirty-two stars. -2 N. of the wife of Balaràma.

रेवा f. N. of the river Narmadá.

रेष् 1 A. (रेषते, रेषित,) To roar, howl, neigh. [riches.

रै m. (Nom. राः, रायौ, रायः) Wealth,

रैवतकः m. N. of a mountair near Dvàrakâ.

रोकं n. 1 A hole. -2 A boat, ship. -3 Moving shakihg.

रोगः m. A disease, sickness.-Comp. —आयतनं n. Body. —भूः f. The body.

रोचकं n. 1 Hunger. -2 Any medicine restoring appetite, a stimulant, tonic. -3 A worker in glass or artificial ornaments.

रोचन a. (f. -ना or -नी) I Enlightening, illuminating. -2 Bright, beautiful, pleasing. -3 Stomachic.-नः m. 1 A stomachic. -2 N. of one of the five arrows of Cupid. —नं n. 1 Raising a desire for.-2 The bright sky, firmament.

रोचना f. 1 The bright sky, firmament. -2 A handsome woman. -3 A kind of yellow pigment. -4 A red lotus-flower.

रोचिष्णु a. 1 Bright, brilliant. -2 Gay, blooming. -3 Exciting appetite.

रोचिस् n. Light, flame.

रोदनं n. 1 Weeping. -2 A tear or tears.

रोदस् n., रोदसी f. Always used in the dual. रोदसी n. dual, रोदस्यौ f. dual). Heaven and earth.

रोधः m. 1 Stopping, arresting. -2 Obstruction, hindrance, prohibition. -3 Closing, shutting up, blockade, siege.-4 A dam, bank.

रोधनः m. The planet Mercury.—नं n. Stopping, checking.

रोधस् n. A bank, an embankment. a dam. -Comp. -वक्रा, -वती f. 1 A river. -2 A rapid river. -वप्रः m., A rapid river.

रोध्रः m. A kind of tree.-ध्रः m. ध्रं n. Sin. -ध्रं n. Offence, injury.

रोपः m. 1 The act of raising. -2 Planting. -3 An arrow.

रोपणं n. 1 The act of setting up or raising.-2 Planting.-3 Healing. -4 A healing application.

रोमकः m 1 The city of Rome.-2 A Roman, an inhabitant of Rome (usually in pl.) -Comp.-पत्तनं n. The city of Rome. -सिद्धांत m. One of the five chief Siddhântas or systems of astronomy.

रोमन् n. The hair on the body of men and animals. -Comp. —अंचः m. Horripilation. -अंतः m. The hair on the back or upper side of the hand -उद्गम, -उद्भेदः m. Thrill.-कूपः m.,-पं n.-गर्तः m. A pore of the skin. -केशरं, —केसरं

–गुच्छं *n*. A whisk, *chowrie*. –भूमिः *f*. The skin. –रंध्रं *n*. A pore of the skin.–हर्षण *a*. Causing thrill or horripilation, thrilling. (–णः *m*) N. of Súta, a pupil of Vyása. (–णं *n*.) Erection of hair on the body, thrill.

रोमंथः *m*. 1 Ruminating, chewing the cud. –2 Frequent repetition.

रोमश *a*. (*f*. –शा) Hairy, shaggy, woolly. –शः *m*. 1 A sheep, ram. –2 A hog, boar.

रोरुदा *f*. Violent weeping, excessive lamentation.

रोलंबः *m*. A bee.

रोषः *m*. Anger, wrath.

रोषण *a*. (*f*. –णी) Angry, wrathful, passionate. –णः *m*. 1 A touchstone. –2 Quicksilver. –3 A desert soil containing salt.

रोहः *m*. 1 Rising, height, altitude. –2 The raising of anything (as of a number from a smaller to a higher denomination). –3 Growth. –4 Bud, blossom.

रोहणः *m*. N. of a mountain in Ceylon. –णं *n*. 1 The act of mounting, ascending. –2 Growing over, healing. –Comp. –द्रुमः *m*. The sandal tree.

रोहिः *m*. 1 A kind of deer. –2 A religious man. –3 A tree.

रोहिणी *f*. 1 A red cow. –2 A cow in general. –3 N. of the fourth lunar mansion (containing five stars). –4 N. of a wife of Vasudeva and mother of Balarâma. –5 A young girl in whom menstruation has just commenced. –6 Lightning. –7 Inflammation of the throat. –Comp. –अष्टमी *f*. The eighth day in the month of Bhâdrapada. –पतिः, –प्रियः, –वल्लभः *m*. The moon. –शकटः *m*. The constellation Rohiní figured by a cart. –सुतः, –भवः *m*. Mercury.

रोहित *a*. (*f*. रोहिता or रोहिणी) Red, red-coloured. –तः *m*. 1 Red colour. –2 A kind of deer. –3 N. of Harischandra's son. –4 A kind of fish. –तं *n*. 1 Blood. –2 Saffron. –3 A straight rain-bow. –Comp. –अश्वः *m*. Fire.

रोहिषः *m*. 1 A kind of fish. –2 A kind of deer.

रौद्र *a*. (*f*. –द्रा,–द्री) 1 Violent, wrathful. –2 Fierce, terrible, wild. –द्रः *m*. 1 A worshipper of Rudra. –2 Heat, warmth, passion. –3 The sentiment of wrath or furiousness. –4 N. of Yama. –5 Winter. –द्रं *n*. 1 Wrath, rage. –2 Fierceness, savageness. –3 Heat, warmth.

रौप्य *a*. (*f*. –प्या) Made of silver, like silver. –प्यं *n*. Silver.

रौरव *a*. (*f*. –वी) 1 Made of the hide of 'Ruru'. –2 Dreadful, terrible. –3 Fraudulent, dishonest. –वः *m*. 1 A savage. –2 N. of one of the hells.

रौहिणेयः *m*. 1 A calf. –2 N. of Balarâma. –3 The planet Mercury. –4 The planet Saturn. –यं *n*. An emerald.

रौहिष *m*. A kind of deer.

रौहिषः *m*. A kind of deer. –षं *n*. A kind of grass.

ल.

लः *m*. 1 An epithet of Indra. –2 A short syllable (in prosody). –3 A technial term used by Pânini for the ten tenses and moods.

लकः *m*. 1 The forehead. –2 An ear of wild rice.

लकचः, लकुचः m. A kind of bread-fruit tree. -चं n. The fruit of this tree.

लकुटः m. A club, cudgel; cf. लगुडः.

लक्तकः m. 1 Lac. -2 A tattered cloth, a rag.

लक्तिका f. A lizard.

लक्ष् 1 A. (लक्षते, लक्षित) To perceive, observe, see.

लक्ष् 10 U. (लक्षयति,-ते, लक्षित) 1 To observe, see, perceive. -2 To mark, indicate. -3 To define. -4 To signify in a secondary sense. -5 To aim at. -6 To consider, think.

लक्षं n. 1 One hundred thousand (m. also in this sense). -2 A mark, butt, target. -3 A sign, mark. -4 Show, pretence.

लक्षक a. (f. -का) Indicating indirectly, expressing secondarily. -कं n. One hundred thousand.

लक्षणं n. 1 A mark, sign, indication, characteristic. -2 A symptom (of a disease). -3 An attribute, a quality. -4 A definition. -5 A lucky or auspicious mark on the body. -6 Any mark or features of the body (indicative of good or bad luck). -7 A name, designation. -8 Excellence, merit. -9 An aim, an object. -10 A fixed rate(as of duties). -11 Form, kind, nature. -12 Effect operation. -13 Cause, occasion. -14 Head, topic, subject. -15 Observation, seeing. -णः m. The crane. -णा f. 1 An aim, object. -2 (In Rhet.) The power that a word has of signifying a meaning that is not the same as the expressed meaning. -3 A goose. -Comp. -लक्षणा f. See जहल्लक्षणा. -संनिपातः m. Branding, stigmatizing.

लक्षण्य a. (f. -ण्या) 1 Serving as a mark. -2 Having good marks.

लक्ष्मण a. (f. -णा) 1 Having marks. -2 Fortunate, lucky. -3 Prosperous, thriving. -णः m. 1 The crane. -2 N. of a son of Dasaratha by his wife Sumitrà. -णा f. A goose. -णं n. 1 A name, an appellation. -2 A mark, sign, token.

लक्ष्मन् n. 1 A mark, sign. -2 A speck, spot. -3 Definition. -4 The chief, principal. -m. 1 The crane or Sârasa bird. -2 N. of Lakshmana.

लक्ष्मीः f. 1 Fortune, prosperity, wealth. -2 Good fortune, good luck. -3 Success, accomplishment. -4 Beauty, grace, charm, lustre. -5 The goddess of fortune, prosperity and beauty, regarded as the wife of Vishnu. -6 Sovereign power, dominion. -7 The wife of a hero. -8 A pearl. -9 N. of the eleventh digit of the moon. -Comp. -ईशः m. 1 An epithet of Vishnu. -2 The mango tree. -3 A prosperous or fortunate man. -गृहं n. The red lotus flower. -तालः m. A kind of palm. -पुत्रः m. 1 A horse. -2 N. of Kusa and Lava. -3 N. of Cupid or Káma. -पुष्पः A ruby. -पूजनं n. The ceremony of worshipping Lakshmi (performed by the bridegroom in company with his bride after she has been brought home). -पूजा f. The worship of Lakshmi performed on the day of new moon in the month of Asvina. -फलः m. The Bilva tree. -वसतिः f. The red lotus flower. -वारः m. Thursday. -सहजः, -सहोदरः m. 1 The moon. -2 Camphor. -3 N. of the horse of Indra.

लक्ष्मीवत् a. (f -ती) 1 Fortunate, lucky. -2 Wealthy, rich. -3 Handsome, lovely, beautiful. -m. The bread fruit tree.

लक्ष्य *pot. p.* (*f.* -क्ष्या) 1 To be looked at or observed, perceptible. -2 Indicated or recognizable. -3 To be known or found out, traceable. -4 To be marked. -5 To be defined. -6 To be aimed at. -7 To be expressed or denoted indirectly. -8 To be regarded or considered as. —क्ष्यं *n.* 1 An aim, a butt, mark, target, mark aimed at (fig also). -2 A sign, token. -3 The thing defined (opp. लक्षण). -4 An indirect or secondary meaning. -5 A pretence, disguise. -6 A 'lac', one hundred thousand. -Comp. -क्रम *a.* The method or order of which is (indirectly) preceptible, as a 'dhavni'. —भेदः, -वेधः *m.* Hitting the mark. -सुप्त *a.* Feigning sleep.

लग् 1 P. (लगति, लग्न) 1 To adhere or stick to. -2 To come in contact with. -3 To affect, have an effect on. -4 To become united. -5 To follow closely, happen immediately. -6 To detain, occupy (one).

लग् 10 U. (लागयति,-ते) 1 To taste. -2 To obtain.

लगड *a.* (*f.* —डा) Lovely, beautiful.

लगित *a.* (*f.* -ता) 1 Adhered or clung to. -2 Attached to. -3 Got, obtained.

लगुडः, लगुरः, लगुलः *m.* A club, cudgel.

लग्न *p. p.* (*f.* -ग्ना) 1 Adhered to, held fast. -2 Coming in contact with. -3 Connected with. -4 Sticking to, remaining on. -5 Cutting, meeting (as lines). -6 Following closely. -7 Occupied about. -8 Fastened on, directed towards. -9 Auspicious. -ग्नः *m.* 1 A bard, minstrel. -2 An elephant in rut. -ग्नं *n.* 1 The point where the horizon and the ecliptic or the path of planets meet. -2 The point of the ecliptic which at any given time is at the horizon or on the meridian. -3 The rising of the sun or the planets. -4 The moment of the sun's entrance into a zodiacal sign. -5 A figure of the twelve zodiacal signs. -6 An auspicicous moment. -7 A decisive moment, time for action. -Comp. —अहः *m.*, -दिनं *n.*, —दिवसः, —वासरः *m.* An auspicious day chosen for the performance of any work. —कालः, —मुहूर्तः *m.*, -वेला *f.* —समयः*m.* The time fixed upon (by astrologers &c.) as auspicious for the performance of any thing. -नक्षत्रं *n.* An auspicious asterism. —मंडलं *n.* The zodiac. —मासः *m.* An auspicious month. —शुद्धिः *f.* Auspiciousness of the zodiacal signs &c. for the performance of any work.

लग्नकः *m.* A surety, bail, bondsman.

लग्निका *f.* See नग्निका.

लघिमन् *m.* 1 Lightness, absence of weight. -2 Littleness, smallness. -3 Lowness or meanness of spirit. -4 Thoghtlessness, frivolity. -5 The supernatural power of assuming excessive lightness at will, one of the eight *Siddihis*.

लघिष्ठ *a.* (*f.* —ष्ठा) Lightest, lowest, very light.

लघीयस् *a.* (*f.* -सी) Lighter, lower, very light.

लघय् (*Den. present* लघयति) 1 To make light. -2 To diminish. -3 To make inferior or low.

लघु *a.* (*f.* -घु or -घ्वी) 1 Light, not heavy. -2 Little, small. -3 Short, brief. -4 Trifling, insignificant. -5

Low, mean, debased or degraded. -6 Weak, feeble. -7 Wretched, frivolous. -8 Active, nimble. -9 Swift, rapid. -10 Easy. -11 Light (as food). -12 Short (as a vowel in prosody). -13 Soft, low, gentle. -14 Agreeable, desirable. -15 Handsome, beautiful. -16 Young, younger. *-m.* N. of the Nakshatras Hasta, Pushya, and Asvini. *-ind.* 1 Lightly, contemptuously. -2 Quickly, swiftly. -Comp. —आशिन्, -आहार *a.* Moderate in diet, abstemious. —कायः *m.* A goat. —चित्त, -चेतस्, —मनस्, -हृदय *a.* 1 Low-hearted, little-minded, mean-hearted. -2 Frivolous. -3 Fickle, unsteady. —पाक, —पाकिन् *a.* Easily digested.—बदरः *m.*, —बदरी *f.* A kind of jujube. -मांसः *m.* A kind of partridge. -मूलकं *n.* A radish. —विक्रम *a.* Having a quick step, quick-footed. —वेधिन् *a.* Making a clever hit. -हस्त *a.* 1 Light-handed, clever, dexterous.-2 Active, agile. (—स्तः *m.*) An expert or skilful archer.

लघ्वी *f.* 1 A delicate woman. -2 A light carriage.

लंका *f.* 1 N. of the capital and residence of Râvana and identified with the island of Ceylon or the chief town in it. -2 An unchaste woman, a prostitute. -3 A branch. -4 A kind of grain.

लंखनी *f.* The bit of a bridle.

लंगः *m.* 1 Lameness.-2 Union, association. -3 A lover, paramour.

लंगकः *m.* A lover, paramour.

लंगलं *n.* A plough.

लंगूलं *n.* The tail of an animal.

लंघ् 1 U. (लंघति,-ते, लंघित) 1 To go by leaps.-2 To ascend.-3 To transgress. -4 To fast, abstain from food. -5 To dry, dry up (Paras.). -6 To diminish, lessen. -7 To attack, injure.

Caus. (लंघयति,-ते) 1 To leap over, go beyond. -2 To traverse (as distance).-3 To ascend.-4 To violate, transgress, disobey. -5 To disrespect, disregard.-6 To stop, avoid, avert. -7 To seize upon, injure. -8 To eat, browse. -9 To surpass, outshine, eclipse.-10 To cause to fast.

लंघनं *n.* 1 Leaping, jumping, traversing, going, ascending. -2 Assaulting, capturing. -3 Exceeding, overstepping, transgression. -4 Disregarding, slighting. -5 An offence, affront, insult. -6 A harm, an injury. -7 Fasting, abstinence. -8 One of the paces of a horse.

लज् 6 A. (लजते) To be ashamed.

लज् 1 P.(लजति) To blame.

लज् 10 P. (लजयति) 1 To seem, appear, shine. -2 To cover, conceal.

लज्ज् 6 A. (लज्जते, लज्जित) To be ashamed, to blush.

लज्जका *f.* The wild cotton-tree.

लज्जा *f.* 1 Shame. -2 Bashfulness, modesty. -3 The sensitive plant.

लज्जालु *a.* Modest, bashful.-लुः *m., f.* The sensitive plant.

लज्या *f.* See लज्जा.

लंजः *m.* 1 A foot.-2 The end of the lower garment tucked up into the waist-band. -3 A tail.

लट् 1 P. (लटति) To be a child. -2 To act like a child. -3 To talk like a child, prattle. -4 To cry.

लटः *m.* 1 A fool, blockhead. -2 A fault, defect. -3 A robber. [villain.

लटकः *m.* A cheat, rogue, rascal,

लटभः *a.* (*f.*—भा) Charming, beautiful, lovely.

लट्टः *m.* A rogue, rascal.

लट्वः *m.* 1 A horse. -2 A dancing boy. -3 N. of a Râga in music. -ट्वा *f.* 1A kind of bird.-2 A curl on the forehead. -3 A s arrow. -4 A kind of musical instrument. -5 A game. -6 Safflower. -7 An unchaste woman. [dally.

लड् 1 P. (लडति) To play, sport,

लड् 1 P., 10 P. (लडति, लडयति) 1 To throw, toss. -2 To blame. -3 To loll the tongue.-4 To harass, annoy.

लड् 10 P. (लाडयति,-ते) 1 To fondle. caress. -2 To annoy. [some.

लडह *a.* (*f.* -हा) Beautiful, hand-

लड्डूः *m.* See लटकः.

लड्डुः, लड्डुकः *m.* A kind of sweetmeat.

लंडं *n.* Excrement, ordure.

लता *f.* 1 A creeper, creeping plant (often used as the last member of compounds, to denote beauty, tenderness, thinness &c. as in भुजलता, बाहुलता, भ्रूलता, विद्युल्लता).-2 A branch.-3 The creeper called *Priyangu.* -4 The Mâdhavì creeper. -5 Musk-creeper. -6 A whip. -7 A string of pearls.-8 A slender woman.-Comp. —अंतं *n.* A flower. —अंबुजं *n.* A kind of cucumber. —अर्कः *m.* A green onion.—अलकः *m.* An elephant.-आननः *m.* A particular position of the hands in dancing. -करः *m.* A particular position of the hands in dancing. —कस्तूरिका, -कस्तूरी *f.* The musk-creeper. —जिह्वः, —रसनः *m.* A snake. —पनसः *m.* The water-melon. —मणिः *m.* Coral. —मृगः *m.* A monkey. —यावकं *n.* A shoot, sport. —वृक्षः *m.* The cocoa-nut tree. —वेष्टनं, —वेष्टितकं *n.* A kind of embrace.

लतिका *f.* 1 A small creeper. -2 A string of pearls.

लत्तिका *f.* A kind of lizard.

लप् 1 P. (लपति) 1 To speak, talk (in general). -2 To chatter. -3 To wail, lament. -With अनु- To speak again and again. अप— 1 To conceal. -2 To deny. आ— 1 To talk, speak. -2 To converse. उद्— To call out loudly to. प्र— 1 To speak, say. -2 To speak wildly or at random. वि— 1 To lament. -2 To say, speak. विप्र— To dispute, contradict. सम्— To converse.

लपनं *n.* 1 Talking, speaking. -2 The mouth.

लपित *p. p.* (*f.* -ता) Spoken, said, chattered. —तं *n.* Speech, voice.

लब्ध *p.p.* (*f.*-ब्धा) Obtained, acquired, received, perceived, apprehended. -ब्धा*f.* A woman whose husband or lover is faithless. —ब्धं *n.* That which is secured or got. -Comp. —अंतरं *a.* 1 One who has found an opportunity. -2 One who has got access or admission. —अवकाश, -अवसर *a.* 1 One who has found an opportunity. -2 (Anything) that has gained a scope (for work). -3 One who has obtained leisure. -क्षण *a.* One who has found leisure time; one whose time is disengaged. —नामन्, -शब्द *a.* Renowed, celebrated. —प्रशमनं *n.* 1 Securing safe what has been acquired.-2 Bestowing on a worthy recipient. -लक्ष, -लक्ष्य *a.* 1 One who has hit the mark. -2 Skilled in the se of missiles. —वर्ण *a.* 1 Learned, wise. -2 Famous, renowned, celebrated.

लब्धिः *f.* 1 Acquisition, acquirement. -2 Profit, gain. -3 (In arith.) The quotient.

लब्धिम *a.* Obtained, acquired.

लभ् 1 A. (लभते, लब्धुं, लब्ध) 1 To get, obtain, acquire. -2 To possess, be in possession of. -3 To take, receive. -4 To take hold of. -5 To meet with. -6 To recover, regain. -7 To perceive, understand. -8 To be able or be permitted (to do a thing) (with inf.). With. आ— I To touch.-2To offer as a sacrifice. -3 To obtain. उप— I To obtain. -2 To perceive. उपा— I To chide, blame. -2 To know, learn. प्रति— I To obtain.-2 To recover,to regain. विप्र— I To cheat. -2 To insult, disregard. -3 To recover, regain. सम्- To obtain.

लभनं *n.* I The act of getting, obtaining. -2 Act of conceiving.

लभसः *m.* I Wealth, riches. -2 One who solicits ; a solicitor. —सं *n.* A rope for tying a horse. (-*m.* also).

लभ्य *a.* (*f.* —भ्या) I Capable of being acquired or obtained. -2 Fit, suitable, proper. -3 Intelligible.

लमकः *m.* A lover, parmour.

लंपट *a.* (*f.* —टा) I Greedy, covetous. -2 Lustful, addicted to licentious pleasures. -टः *m.* A libertine, profligate.(लंपाकः in the same sense).

लंफः *m.* A leap, jump, spring.

लंफनं *n.* Leaping, jumping.

लंब् I A. (लंबते, लंबित) I To hang down, hang from. -2 To be attached to, stick to, rest on. -3 To go down, sink (as the sun). -4 To lag behind. -5 To delay. -6 To sound. With अव- I To hang from, descend. -2 To cling to, to support oneself by. -3To depend upon. -4 To hold. -5 To bear up aganist sorrow or calamity. -6 To assume, to take. आ— I To rest upon, to hang from, to depend from. -2 To support. -3 To take refuge with. -4 To take hold of. -5 To assume, take. वि- I To hang from. -2 To stay, remain. -4 To delay.

लंब *a.* (*f.* —बा) I Hanging down or from, attached to. -2 Great, large, spacious, long, tall. —बः *m.* I A perpendicular. -2 Co-latitude, the arc between the pole of any place and the zenith, complement of latitude. -3 A bribe. -Comp. (-उदरः *m.*) I N. of Ganesa. -2 A glutton. —ओष्ठः *m.* (-कंबो -बौ- ष्ठः) A camol. —कर्णः *m.* I An ass. -2 A goat. -3 An elephant. -4 A falcon. -5 A demon or Râkshasa. —स्फिच् *a.* Having fat or protuberant buttocks.

लंबकः *m.* I A perpendicular (in geom.). -2 The complement of latitude,co-latitude (in astr.).

लंबनः *m.* I An epithet of Siva. -2 The phlegmatic humour. —नं *n.* I Hanging down. -2 Fringe. -3 The parallax in longitude(of the moon). -4 A sort of long necklace. -5 A mode of fighting.

लंबा *f.* I An epithet of Durgâ. -2 Of Lakshmí.

लंबिका *f.* The soft palate.

लंबुषा *f.* A necklace of seven strings.

लंभः *f.* I Attainment, acquirement. -2 Meeting with. -3 Recovery. -4 Gain. [-2 Recovery.

लंभनं *n.*I Attainment, acquirement.

लंभित *p. p.* (*f.* -ता) I Procured, obtained. -2 Given. -3 Improved. -4 Employed, applied. -5 Cherished. -6 Addressed.

लय् I A. (लयते) To go, move.

लयः *m.* I Sticking, adherence. -2 Hiding. -3 Fusion,melting. -4 Disappearance, extinction, universal destruction. -5Deep concentration, exclusive devotion (to any one object). -6 Time in music. -7 A pause in music. -8 Rest, repose. -9 A place of rest, habitation. -10 Mental inactivity -11 An embrace. -12 The supreme being. -13 The union of song, dance, and instrumental music.-Comp.-आरंभः,-आरंभः m. An actor, a dancer. -कालः m. The time of destruction (of the world). -पुत्री f. An actress, a female dancer.

लयनं n. 1 Adhering, clinging, sticking. -2 Rest, repose. -3 A place of rest, house. [frolic.

लल् 1 U. (ललति,-ते) To play, sport,

लल् 10 U. (लालयति,-ते, लालित) 1 To cause to sport or play; caress, fondle. -2 To desire.

लल् 10 U. (ललयति,-ते) 1 To fondle. -2 To loll the tongue. -3 To desire.

लल a. (f. -ला) 1 Playful, sportive. -2 Lolling. -3 Wishing, desirous. -Comp. —जिह्वः m 1 A dog. -2 A camel.

ललनं n. 1 Sport, dalliance. -2 Lolling the tongue. —नः m. 1 A child. -2 The Sàla and Piyála trees.

ललना f. 1 A woman (in general). -2 A wanton woman. -3 The tongue. -Comp. —प्रियः m. The *Kadamba* tree. [woman.

ललनिका f. A little or miserable

ललन्तिका f. 1 A long necklace. -2 A lizard or chameleon.

ललाकः m. The penis.

ललाटं n. The forehead.-Comp. -अक्षः m. An epithet of Siva. —तटं n. The slope of the forehead, the forehead itself. -पट्टः m., —पट्टिका f. 1 The flat surface of the forehead ; the forehead. -2 A tiara, fillet. —रेखा f. 1 A line on the forehead.-2 A wrinkled brow. -3 A coloured sectarial mark on the forehead.

ललाटकं n. 1 The forehead. -2 A beautiful forehead.

ललाटंतप a. 1 Burning or scorching the forehead. -2 (Hence) Very painful. -पः m. The sun.

ललाटिका f. 1 An ornament worn on the forehead. -2 A mark made with sandal or any other fragrant powder on the forehead.

ललाटूल a. (f. -ला) Having a high or handsome forehead.

ललाम a. (f. -मी) Beautiful, charming. -मं n. 1 An ornament for the forehead; an ornament or decoration in general (-मः m. also in this sense). -2 Anything the best of its kind. -3 A mark on the forehead. -4 A sign, a mark in general. -5 A banner, flag. -6 A row, series, line. -7 A tail.-8 A mane. -9 Eminence, dignity, beauty. -10 A horn. -मः m. A horse.

ललामकं n. A chaplet of flowers worn on the forehead.

ललामन् n. 1 An ornament. -2 Anything the best of its kind. -3 A banner, flag. -4 A sectarial mark, sign, symbol. -5 A tail.

ललित a. (f. -ता) 1 Playing, sporting. -2 Amorous, voluptuous. -3 Lovely, elegant, graceful. -4 Pleasing, charming, agreeable. -5 Desired. -6 Soft, gentle. -7 Tremulous, trembling. —तः m. N. of a musical scale. —तं n. 1 Sport, play. -2 Amorous pastime; gracefulness of gait ; any languid or amorous gesture in a woman. -3 Beauty, charm. -4 Any natural or artless act. -5 Simplicity, innocence. -Comp. —अर्थ a. Having a pretty or amorous meaning. —पद a. 1 Elegantly composed. -2 Consisting of amorous words —प्रहार *m* A soft or gentle blow

ललिता *f* 1 A woman (in general) -2 A wanton woman -3 Musk 4 A form of Durgâ 5 N of various metres Comp —पंचमी *f* The fifth day in the bright half of Asvina —सप्तमी *f* The seventh day in the bright half of Bhâdrapada

लव *m* 1 Plucking mowing reaping gathering (of corn) 2 A piece fragment bit particle drop small quantity 3 Wool hair 4 Sport 5 A minute division of time(-the sixth part of a twinkling) -6 The numerator of a fraction 7 A degree (in astr) 8 Loss destruction -9 N of a son of Râma one of the twins the other being Kusa 10 A kind of quail -ङ *n* 1 Cloves -2 Nutmeg -लं *ind* A little

लवङ्ग *m* The clove plant —ङ *n* Cloves -Comp —कलिका *f* Cloves

लवंगक *n* Cloves

लवण *a* (*f* -णा) 1 Saline saltish 2 Lovely handsome -णः *m* 1 Saline taste 2 The sea of salt water 3 N of a demon 4 N of a hell —णं *n* 1 Salt sea salt -2 A factitious salt -Comp —अंबुराशि *m* The ocean —आलय *m* The ocean —आकर *m* 1 A salt mine 2 The sea -3 (fig) A mine of beauty —अर्णव *m* The ocean —उत्तम *n* 1 Rock-salt 2 Nitre —जल —जलधि —जलः *m* The ocean —मेह *m* A kind of urinary disease

लवणिमन् *f* Lustre beauty

लावण्य *m* 1 Saltness 2 Beauty loveliness grace

लवनं *n* 1 Mowing reaping (of corn &c) 2 An instrument for mowing a sickle, scythe

लवली *f* A kind of creeper

लवित्र *n* An instrument for mowing a sickle

लशुन (-न) *m* -नं *n* Garlic

लष् I 4 U (लषति ते लष्यति ते लषित) To wish desire long for (usually with the preposition अभि)

लषित *p p* (*f* —ता) Wished desired

लसक *m* An actor a dancer

लस् I P (लसति लसित) 1 To shine glitter 2 To appear arise 3 To embrace 4 To frolic about skip about dance 5 To sound resound With उद्— 1 To shine 2 To arise appear 3 To blow expand open वि 1 To shine glitter -2 To appear arise 3 To play sport 4 To sound echo

लसा *f* 1 Saffron 2 Turmeric

लसिका *f* Spittle saliva

लसित *p p* (*f* -ता) Played sported manifested

लसीका *f* 1 Saliva 2 Pus matter 3 The juice of the sugar-cane 4 Lymph

लस्ज् I A (लज्जते लज्जित) 1 To be ashamed feel shame 2 To blush

लग्न *a* (*f* —ग्ना) 1 Embraced clasped -2 Skilful skilled

लस्तक *m* The middle of a bow

लस्तकिन् *m* A bow

लहरि लहरी *f* A wave a large wave or billow [ob a a

ला 2 P (लाति) To take receive

लागुडिक *a* (*f* —की) Armed with a club or cudgel -क *m* A sentinel watchman

लाङ्गली *f* N of Sitâ

लाक्षणिक *a* (*f* —की) 1 Acquainted with marks or signs 2 Characteristic indicatory 3 Used in a secondary sense (as a word as distinguished from वाच्य and व्यंजक).-4 Indirect or figurative. -5 Secondary, inferior. -6 Technical. —कः *m.* A technical term.

लाक्षण्य *a.* (*f.* —ण्या) One who is able to explain or interpret signs.

लाक्षा *f.* A kind of red dye obtained from the cochineal insect and from the resin of a particular tree. -2 The insect which produces red dye. -Comp. —तरुः, -वृक्षः *m.* N. of the tree *Butea Frondosa*. —प्रसादः, —प्रसाधनः *m.* The red *Lodhra* tree.

लाक्षिक *a.* (*f.* —की) 1 Relating to, made of, or dyed with, lac. -2 Relating to a lac (लक्ष).

लागुडिक *a.* (*f.* —की) Armed with a club. —कः *m.* A sentinel.

लाघ् 1 A. (लाघते) To be equal to; to suffice; to be competent.

लाघवं *n.* 1 Smallness, littleness. -2 Levity, lightness. -3 Thoughtlessness, frivolity. -4 Disrespect, dishonour. -5 Quickness, rapidity. -6 Ease, facility. -7 Good health or constitution. -8 Activity, dexterity, readiness. -9 Brevity, conciseness (of expression). -10 Shortness of a syllable (in prosody).

लांगलं *n.* 1 A plough. -2 A plough-shaped beam or timber. -3 The palm tree. -4 The membrum virile. -5 A kind of flower. -6 A particular appearance of the moon. -7 A kind of timber (used in building houses). -Comp. —ग्रहः *m.* A ploughman, peasant. —दंडः *m.* The pole of a plough. —ध्वजः *m.* N. of Balaráma. —पद्धतिः *f.* A furrow. —फालः *m.* A plough-share.

लांगलिन् *m.* 1 N. of Balarâma. -2 The cocoa-nut tree. -3 A snake.

लांगली *f.* The cocoa-nut tree.

लांगलीषा *f.* The pole of a plough.

लांगुलं *n.* 1 A tail. -2 Membrum virile.

लांगूलं *n.* 1 A tail. -2 The membrum virile. -3 A granary.

लांगूलिन् *m.* A monkey, an ape.

लाज्, लांज् 1 P. (लाजति; लांजति) 1 To blame, censure. -2 To roast, fry.

लाजः *m.* Wetted grain. —जाः *m. pl.* Parched or fried grain (*f.* also).

लांछ् 1 P. (लांछति) 1 To distinguish, mark, characterize. -2 To deck, decorate.

लांछनं *n.* 1 A sign, a characteristic mark. -2 A name, an appellation. -3 A stain, a mark of ignominy. -4 The spot on the moon. -5 A land-mark.

लांछित *p. p.* (*f.* —ता) 1 Marked, distinguished, characterised. -2 Named, called. -3 Decorated. -4 Furnished with.

लाटाः *m. pl.* N. of a country and its inhabitants. —टः *m.* 1 A king of the Látas. -2 Old, worn out clothes. -3 Clothes in general. -4 Childish language. -Comp. —अनुप्रासः *m.* One kind of alliteration; the repetition of a word or words in the same sense but in a different application.

लाटक *a.* (*f.* -टिका) Relating to the Látas.

लाटिका, लाटी *f.* 1 A particular style of composition. -2 N. of a Prákrita dialect.

लाड् 10 U. (लाडयति,-ते) 1 To fondle, caress. -2 To blame, censure. -3 To throw, toss.

लांठनी *f.* An unchaste woman (कुलटा).

लापः *m.* 1 Speaking, talking. -2 Chattering, prating.

लापिका *f.* A sort of enigma or riddle.

लावः, लावकः *m.* A sort of quail.

लाबुः (-बूः) *m.* A kind of gourd.

लाबुकी *f.* A kind of lute.

लाभः *m.* 1 Gaining, obtaining, acquistion. -2 Gain, profit. -3 Enjoyment. -4 Perception, knowledge, apprehension.

लाभकः *m.* Gain, profit.

लामज्जकं *n.* The root of a particular fragrant grass (वीरणमूल).

लाम्पट्यं *n.* Lasciviousness, lustfulness, lewdness.

लालन *a.* (*f.* —नी) Fondling, coaxing, caressing. —नः *m.* A sort of poisonous mouse. -नं *n.* Caressing, fondling, coaxing.

लालस *a.* (*f.* -सा) 1 Ardently longing for, eagerly desirous of. -2 Devoted to, fond of, absorbed in.

लालसा *f.* 1 Longing or ardent desire, eagerness. -2 Solicitation, entreaty. -3 Regret, sorrow. -4 The longing of a pregnant woman.

लालसीकं *n.* Sauce.

लाला *f.* Saliva, spittle. -Comp. —भक्षः *m.* A spider. —स्रावः *m.* 1 A flow of saliva. -2 A spider.

लालाटिक *a.* (*f.* —की) 1 Being on or relating to the forehead. -2 Arising from or dependent on fate. -3 Useless; low, vile. -4 Attentive, vigilant. —कः *m.* 1 An attentive servant (who watches his master's countenance and learns by it what is necessary to be done). -2 An idler, a useless person. -3 A kind of embrace.

लालाटी *f* The forehead.

लालिकः *m.* A buffalo. —का *f.* A jesting reply.

लालित *p. p.* (*f.* —ता) 1 Caressed, fondled, indulged. -2 Seduced. -3 Loved, desired. —तं *n.* Pleasure, love, joy.

लालितकः *m.* A fondling or darling, a pet, a little favourite.

लालित्यं *n.* 1 Loveliness, charm, grace, sweetness. -2 Amorous gestures.

लालिन् *m.* A seducer.

लालिनी *f.* A wanton woman.

लालुका *f.* A kind of necklace.

लाव *a.* (*f.* —वी) 1 Cutting, lopping off. -2 Plucking, gathering. -3 Cutting down, destroying. —वः *m.* 1 Cutting. -2 A quail.

लावकः *m.* 1 A cutter, divider. -2 A reaper. -3 A quail.

लावण *a* (*f.* —णी) 1 Salt. -2 Salted; dressed with salt.

लावणिक *a.* (*f.* —की) 1 Salted, dressed with salt. -2 Dealing in salt. -3 Lovely, beautiful, charming. —कः *m.* A salt-merchant. —कं *n.* A salt-vessel, salt-cellar.

लावण्यं *n.* 1 Saltness. -2 Beauty, charm. -Comp. —अर्जितं *n.* The private property of a married woman given to her at her marriage by her father or mother-in-law.

लावाणकः *m.* N. of a district near Magadha.

लाविकः *m.* A buffalo.

लाबुक *a.* (*f.* -का or —की) Covetous, avaricious.

लासः *m.* 1 Jumping, sporting, dancing. -2 Dalliance, wanton sport. -3 Dancing as practised by women. -4 Soup, broth.

लासक *a.* (*f.* —सिका) 1 Playing, sporting. -2 Moving hither and thither. —कः *m.* 1 A dancer. -2 A peacock. -3 Embracing. -4 N. of Siva. —कं *n.* A room on the top of a building; a turret.

लासकी *f.* A female dancer.

लासिका *f.* 1 A female dancer. -2 A

wanton or unchaste woman. -3 A kind of dramatic performance.

लास्यं *n.* 1 Dancing ; a dance. -2 A dance accompanied with singing and instrumental music.-3A dance in which the emotions of love are represented mimically. —स्यः *m.* A dancer, an actor. —स्या *f.* A dancing girl.

लिकुचः *m.* See लकुच.

लिक्षा, लिक्ष्या *f.* 1 A nit, the egg of a louse. -2 A very minute measure of weight.

लिक्षिका *f.* A nit.

लिख् 6 P. (लिखति, लिखित) 1 To write, write down, inscribe, draw a line, engrave. -2 To draw, portray, delineate, paint. -3 To scratch, rub, tear up. -4 To make smooth. -5 To unite sexually with a female.

लिखनं *n.* 1 Writing, inscribing. -2 Drawing, painting. -3 Scratching. -4 A written document or manuscript.

लिखित *p. p.* (*f.* -ता) Written, painted, scratched. —तः *m.* N. of a writer on law. —तं *n.* 1 A writing, document. -2 Any book or composition.

लिख्यः *m.* A nit, the egg of a louse.

लिगुः *m.* 1 A deer. -2A fool, blockhead. -*n.* The heart. [move.

लिङ्ग् 1 P. (लिंगति, लिंगित) 1 To go,

लिंग् 10 U. (लिंगयति,-ते) 1 To paint, variegate. -2 To inflect (a noun) according to its gender.

लिंगं *n.* 1 A mark, sign, token; an emblem, a symbol, characteristc. -2 A guise,disguise.-3 A symptom, mark of disease. -4 A means of proof, a proof, evidence. -5 (In logic) The *hetu* or middle term in a syllogism. -6 The sign of gender or sex. -7 Sex. -8 The male organ of generation. -9 Gender (in gram.). -10 The genital organ of Siva worshipped as a representative of him.-11The image of a God, an idol. -12 One of the relations or indications (such as संयोग, वियोग, साहचर्य) which serve to fix the meaning of a word in any particular passage. -13 (In Vedánta phil.) The subtle frame or body ; the indestructible original of the gross or visible body. -14 A spot, stain. -15 The nominal base, the crude form of a noun (प्रातिपदिक). -16 (In Sán. phil.) Pradhána or Prakriti. -Comp. —देहः *m.*, —शरीरं *n.* The subtle frame or body. —परामर्शः *m.* The finding out or consideration of a sign or characteristic (in logic), *e. g.* that smoke is a sign of fire. —पुराणं *n.* N. of one of the 18 Purânas. —वृत्ति *a.* Hypocritical. —वृत्तिः *m.* A religious hypocrite.

लिंगकः *m.* The *Kapittha* tree.

लिंगनं *n.* Embracing.

लिंगिन् *a.* (*f.* -नी) 1 Having a mark or sign. -2 Characterized by. -3 Wearing the marks or badges of, disguised as, hypocritical, wearing false badges (at the end of comp.). -4 Furnished with a *linga*. -*m.* 1 A religious student, Bráhmana ascetic. -2 A worshipper of Siva's *linga*. -3 A hypocrite or pseudo-ascetic. -4 An elephant. -5 (In logic) That which possesses the *linga* or middle term ; *i. e.* वह्नि is the लिंगिन् in the instance पर्वतो वह्निमान् धूमात्. -6 The subject of a proposition.

लिप् 6 U. (लिंपति,-ते, लिप्त) 1 To anoint, smear, besmear. -2 To cover, overspread. -3 To pollute, defile. -4 To inflame, kindle.

लिपिः,लिपी *f.* 1 Anointing, smearing. -2 Writing, hand-writing. -3 The written characters, letters, alphabet. -4 The art of writing. -5 A writing (as a letter, document, &c.). -6 Painting, drawing.-Comp. -करः *m.* 1 A plasterer, white-washer, mason. -2 A writer, scribe. -3 An engraver (also लिपिंकर). —कारः *m.* A writer, scribe. —ज्ञ *a.* One who can write. -फलकं *n.* A writing tablet or board. -शाला *f.* A writing school. —सज्जा *f.* Writing materials or apparatus.

लिपिका *f.* See लिपी.

लिप्त *p. p.* (*f.* —ता) 1 Anointed, besmeared. -2 Polluted, defiled. -3 Poisoned, envenomed (as an arrow). -4 Eaten. -5 United, joined.

लिप्तकः *m.* A poisoned arrow.

लिप्सा *f.* 1 Desire of getting. -2 Desire in general.

लिप्सु *a.* Desirous of getting.

लिबिः, लिबी *f.* See लिपिः, लिपी.

लिबिंकरः *m.* A scribe, writer, copyist.

लिंपः *m.* Smearing, anointing.

लिंपट *a.* Libidinous, lustful. -टः *m.* A libertine, lecher.

लिंपाकः *m.* 1 The citron or lime tree. -2 An ass. —कं *n.* A citron or lime.

लिंपिः, लिंबिः *f.* See लिपि.

लिश् I 6 P. (लिशति) 1 To go, move. -2 To hurt.

लिश् 4 U. (लिश्यति,-ते) To become small, be decreased.

लिष्ट *p. p.* (*f.* —ष्टा) Become small, lessened, decreased.

लिष्वः *m.* An actor, a dancer.

लिह् 2 U. (लेढि, लीढे, लेढुं, लीढ, *desid.* लिलिक्षति,-ते) 1 To lick. -2 To lick up, sip.

ली 1 P. (लयति) To melt, dissolve.

ली 9 P. (लिनाति) 1 To adhere. -2 To melt, (usually with वि).

ली 4 A (लीयते, लीन) 1 To stick or adhere firmly to. -2 To clasp, embrace. -3 To lie or rest on, stay or dwell in, lurk, cower. -4 To be dissolved, melt away. -5 To be viscous. -6 To be absorbed in, be attached to. -7 To vanish, disappear.

लीः *f.* 1 Adhering, clinging to. -2 Embracing. -3 Melting, dissolving.

लीक्षा *f.* A nit.

लीढ *p. p.* (*f.* -ढा) Licked, sapped, tasted, eaten.

लीन *p. p.* (*f.* —ना) 1 Clung or adhered to. -2 Hid, concealed. -3 Resting or reclining on. -4 Melted, dissolved. -5 Completely swallowed up in, intimately united with. -6 Devoted or given up to.

लीला *f.* 1 Play, sport, diversion, pleasure, amusement. -2 Amorous or playful sport. -3 Ease, facility. -4 Appearance, semblance. -5 Beauty, charm, grace. -6 Pretence, disguise. -Comp. —अ (-आ-) गारः *m.*, रं, —गृहं, -वेश्मन् *n.* A pleasure-house. —अवतारः *m.* The descent (of Vishnu) on the earth for amusement. —उद्यानं *n.* 1 A pleasure-garden. -2 Indra's paradise. —नटनं *n.* A sportive dance. —मनुष्यः *m.* A sham man, a man in disguise. —मात्रं *n.* Child's play, absence of the least effort. —वापी *f.* A pleasure-tank. —शुकः *m.* A parrot kept for pleasure. -साध्य *a.* To be effected with ease, easy of accomplishment.

लीलायितं *n.* Play, sport, amusement, pleasure.

लीलावती *f.* 1 A charming or handsome woman. -2 An amorous or wanton woman. -3 N. of Durgá. -4 N. of a well-known mathematical work by Bháskaráchârya. -5 N. of the wife of the demon Maya.

लुङ् A technical term used by Pânini to denote the Aorist or its terminations.

लुंच् 1 P. (लुंचति, लुंचित) 1 To pluck, peel, pare. -2 To tear off, pluck out.

लुंचः m., लुंचनं n. Peeling, plucking out.

लुंचित p.p. (f.-ता) 1 Peeled, plucked, plucked out, torn off.

लुट् I. 1 A (लोटते) 1 To resist, repel, oppose. -2 To shine. -3 To suffer pain. [-2 To shine.

लुट् 10 U. (लोटयति,-ते) 1 To speak.

लुट् 1, 4 P. (लोटति, लुट्यति) 1 To roll, wallow on the ground. -2 To take away, rob, plunder.

लुट् A technical term used by Pánini to denote the First or Periphrastic Future or its terminations.

लुठ् 1 P. (लोठति) To strike, knock down.

लुठ् 1 A (लोठते) To roll on the ground. -2 To go, move. -3 To resist, oppose. [der.

लुठ् 10 U. (लोठयति,-ते) To rob, plun-

लुठ् 6 P. (लुठति) 1 To roll about, roll on the ground, wallow, move to and fro. -2 To agitate, move, stir.

लुठनं n. Rolling, wallowing.

लुठित p. p. (f. -ता) Rolled down, rolling or wallowing on the ground.

लुड् 1 P. (लोडति) To stir, agitate, churn, disturb. *-Caus.* (लोडयति,-ते) To stir, churn, agitate (used with वि in the same sense).

लुड् 6. P. (लुडति) 1 To adhere. -2 To cover.

लुंट् 1 P. (लुंटति) 1 To go. -2 To steal, plunder. -3 To be lame or crippled. -4 To be idle or lazy.

लुंट् 1 P., 10 U. 1 To rob, plunder, steal. -2 To disregard, despise.

लुंटाक a. (f. -की) Stealing (fig. also), robbing, plundering. —कः m. 1 A thief. -2 A crow.

लुंठ् 1 P. (लुंठति) 1 To go. -2 To stir up. -3 To be idle. -4 To be lame. -5 To rob, plunder. -6 To resist.

लुंठकः m. A robber, thief. [ing.

लुंठनं n. Plundering, robbing, steal-

लुंठा f. 1 Robbing, plundering, -2 Rolling.

लुंठाकः m. 1 A robber. -2 A crow.

लुंठिः, लुंठी f. Plundering, robbing.

लुंड् 10 U. (लुंडयति,-ते) To plunder, rob, pillage.

लुंडिका f. 1 A round mass or ball. -2 Proper conduct. [duct.

लुंडी f. Proper or becoming con-

लुंथ् 1 P. (लुंथति) 1 To strike, hurt. -2 To be afflicted.

लुप् 4 P. (लुप्यति) 1 To confound, perplex. -2 To be perplexed or confounded. -3 To be suppressed or destroyed.

लुप् 6 U. (लुंपति,-ते, लुप्त) 1 To break, violate, destroy, injure. -2 To take away, rob, plunder. -3 To seize. -4 To cause to disappear.

लुप्त p. p. (f. —ता) 1 Broken, injured, destroyed. -2 Lost, deprived of. -3 Robbed, plundered. -4 Dropped, disappeared (in gram.). -5 Omitted, neglected. -6 Obsolete, disused, out of use. —प्तं n. Stolen property, booty. -Comp. —उपमा f. An *upamá* in which one, two, or even three of the four requisites of a simile are omitted.

लुब्ध p. p. (f. —ब्धा) 1 Greedy, covetous, avaricious. -2 Desirous of, greedy of. —ब्धः m. 1 A hunter. -2 A libertine, lecher.

लुब्धकः *m.* 1 A hunter, fowler. -2 A covetous or greedy man. -3 A libertine. -4 The star Sirius. -5 The hinder part.

लुभ् 4 P. (लुभ्यति, लुब्ध) 1 To covet, long for, desire eagerly (with dat. or loc.). -2 To allure, entice. -3 To be bewildered or perplexed, go astray. —*Caus.* (लोभयति,-ते) 1 To make greedy; to produce or excite desire for. -2 To excite lust. -3 To seduce, allure, attract. -4 To derange, disorder, disturb.

लुंब् 1 P., 10 U. (लुंबति, लुंबयति,-ते) To torment, harass.

लुंबिका *f.* A kind of musical instrument.

लुल् 1 P. (लोलति, लुलित) 1 To roll about, move to and fro. -2 To agitate, make tremulous, disturb. -3 To press down, crush.

लुलापः, लुलायः *m.* A buffalo.

लुलित *p. p.* (*f.* -ता) 1 Shaken, moved to and fro, waving. -2 Disturbed, touched. -3 Disarranged, dishevelled (as hair). -4 Pressed down, crushed. -5 Pressing on, touching. -6 Fatigued, unnerved. -7 Elegant, beautiful.

लुष् 1 P. (लोषति) 1 To steal, plunder. -2 To injure, kill.

लुषभः *m.* An elephant in rut.

लुह् 1 P. (लोहति) To covet, desire or long for.

लू 9 U. (लुनाति, लुनीते, लून ; *caus.* लावयति,-ते) 1 To cut, lop, divide, pluck, gather (flowers &c). -2 To cut off, annihilate. —With आ— To pluck (gently). विप्र— To cut, lop or pluck off.

लूता *f.* 1 A spider. -2 An ant. -Comp. -तंतुः *m.* A cobweb. -मर्कटकः *m.* 1 An ape. -2 A kind of jasmine.

लूतिका *f.* A spider.

लून *p. p.* (*f.* —ना) 1 Cut, lopped, severed, cut off. -2 Plucked, gathered (flowers &c.). -3 Destroyed. -4 Bitten, nibbled at. -5 Wounded. —नं *n.* A tail.

लूमं *n.* A tail. -Comp. —विषः *m.* An animal that stings with its tail.

लूष् 1 P. (लूषति) To adorn, decorate.

लूष् 10 U. (लूषयति,-ते) 1 To hurt, injure. -2 To rob, steal.

लेखः *m.* A writing, document, a letter. -2 A God, deity. -Comp. —अधिकारिन् *m.* The secretary (of a king &c.). —अर्हः *m.* A kind of palm tree. —ऋषभः *m.* N. of Indra. —हारः, —हारिन् *m.* A letter carrier.

लेखकः *m.* 1 A writer, copyist. -2 A painter. —कं *n.* Writing down, transcribing. -Comp.-दोषः -प्रमादः *m.* A slip of the scribe ; a copyist's mistake.

लेखनः *m.* A kind of reed of which pens are made. —नं *n.* 1 Writing, transcribing. -2 Scratching, scraping. -3 Grazing, touching. -4 Making thin or emaciated. -5 An instrument for scraping. -6 A palm-leaf (for writing upon). —नी *f.* 1 A pen, writing-reed, reed-pen. -2 A spoon.

लेखनिकः *m.* 1 A letter-carrier. -2 One who signs by a proxy (being unable to write). -3 A writer, scribe.

लेखा *f.* 1 A line, streak. -2 A stroke, furrow, stripe. -3 Writing, drawing lines, painting. -4 A streak of the moon. -5 A figure, an impression, a mark. -6 Hem, border, skirt. -7 The crest.

लेखिनी *f.* 1 A pen. -2 A spoon.

लेख्यं *n.* 1 The art of writing. -2 Writing, transcribing. -3 A letter, document. -4 An inscription. -5 Painting, drawing. -6 A painted figure. -Comp. —आरूढ, -कृत *a.* Committed to writing, done in writing. —गत *a.* Painted, drawn in picture. —चूर्णिका *f.* A paint-brush, writing-pencil. —पत्रं, -पत्रकं *n.* 1 A writing, letter, document. -2 A palm-leaf —प्रसंग: *m.* A document.

लेंडं *n.* Excrement, feces.

लेत: *m.*, लेतं *n.* Tears.

लेप् 1 P. (लेपते) 1 To go, move.-2 To worship.

लेप: *m.* 1 Smearing, plastering, anointing. -2 An ointment, salve. -3 A plaster of any kind (such as white-wash, mortar &c.) -4 The wipings of the hand (or the remnants of the food sticking to the hand), after offering funeral oblations to the first three ancestors (पितृ, पितामह and प्रपितामह) (these wipings being offered to the three ancestors after the great-grand-father *i. e.* to paternal ancestors in the 4th, 5th and 6th degrees). -5 A stain, defilement, pollution. -6 Sin. -7 Food. -Comp. —भागिन्, —भुज् *m.* A paternal ancestor in the 4th, 5th and 6th degree.

लेपक: *m.* 1 A plasterer, mason, white-washer. -2 One who moulds or models.

लेपन: *m.* Incense. -नं *n.* Anointing, smearing, plastering.-2 A plaster, an ointment. -3 Mortar, white-wash. -4 Flesh.

लेप्यं *n.* 1 Plastering, smearing. -2 Moulding, modeling, making models -Comp. —कृत *m.* 1 A model-maker. brick-layer.—स्त्री *f.* A woman covered with unguents or perfumed ointments.

लेप्यमयी *f.* A doll, puppet.

लेलायमाना *f.* One of the seven tongues of fire.

लेलिह: *m.* A snake or serpent.

लेलिहान: *m.* 1 A snake or serpent. -2 An epithet of Siva.

लेश: *m.* 1 A particle, an atom, a very small quantity.-2 A measure of time (equal to two *kalâs*). -3 (In Rhet.) A figure of speech in which what is usually considered as an advantage is represented to be a disadvantage and *vice versa.* -Comp. —उक्त *a.* Suggested or hinted at, insinuated.

लेश्या *f.* Light.

लेष्टु: *m.* A clod, a lump of earth. -Comp. —भेदन: *m.* An instrument for breaking clods.

लेसिक: *m.* A rider of an elephant.

लेह: *m.* 1 Licking; a sipper, as in मधुनो लेह: -2 Tasting. -3 Food. -4 One of the ways in which an eclipse occurs. -ही *f.* A disease of the tips of the ears.

लेहनं *n.* Licking, sipping with the [tongue.

लेहिन: *m.* Borax.

लेह्य *a.* (*f.* —ह्या) To be licked, or lapped up. —ह्यं *n.* 1 Anything to be eaten by licking (as an article of food). -2Nectar.-3Food in general.

लैंगं *n.* N. of one of the eighteen Purâṇas.

लैंगिक *a.* (*f.* —की) 1 Depending on or relating to a sign or mark. -2 Inferred (अनुमित). —क: *m.* A statuary.

लोक् 1 A. (लोकते, लोकित)To view, perceive. With अव- To see, perceive. आ— To see, look at, view.

लोक् 10 U. (लोकयति;-ते, लोकित) 1 To

look, behold, perceive. -2 To be aware of. -3 To shine. -4 To seek.

लोकः *m.* 1 The world, a divison of the universe; there are three *lokas* स्वर्ग, पृथ्वी and पाताल. But according to fuller classification the *lokas* are fourteen, seven higher regions above the earth, and seven below the earth. -2 The earth. -3 The human race, mankind, men. -4 The people or subjects (opp. the king). -5 A collection, group, company. -6 A district, province. -7 Common life, ordinary practice (of the world). -8 Common or worldly usage (opp. Vedic usage or idiom). -9 Sight, looking. -10 The number 'seven', or 'fourteen'. -Comp. —आतिग *a.* Extraordinary, supernatural. —आतिशय *a.* Extraordinary. —अधिपः *m.* 1 A king. -2 A God or deity. —अनुरागः *m.* Universal love, general benevolence, philanthropy. —अंतरं *n*, The next world, future life. —अपवादः *m.* Public scandal, popular censure. —अभिभाविन् *a.* 1 Overcoming the world. -2 Pervading the whole world (as light). -अभ्युदयः *m.* 1 Public weal or welfare. -अयनः *m.* N. of Náráyana. -अलोकः *m.* N. of a mythical mountain which divides the visible world from the regions of darkness. (-कौ *m. dual*) The visible and the invisible world. -आचारः *m.* Common practice; ways of the world. -आत्मन् *m.* The soul of the universe. —आदिः *m.* The beginning of the world. -2 The creator of the world. —आयत *a.* Atheistical, materialistic. (-तः *m.*) A materialist, an atheist. (-तं *n.*) Materialism, atheism. -आयतिकः *m.* An atheist, a materialist. —ईशः *m.* A king. -2 Brahman (*m.*). -3 Quick-silver. -उक्तिः *f.* 1 A proverb, popular saying. -2 Public opinion. —उत्तर *a.* Extraordinary, uncommon, unusual. (-रः *m.*) A king. -एकबंधुः *m.* An epithet of Sâkyamuni. —एषणा *f.* Desire for heaven. —कंटकः *m.* 1 A troublesome or wicked man. -2. An epithet of Râvana. —कथा *f.* A popular legend. —गाथा *f.* A song handed down among people. -चक्षुस् *n.* The sun. —चारित्रं *n.* The ways of the world. —जननी *f.* An epithet of Lakshmi —जित *m.* An epithet of Buddha. -ज्येष्ठः *m.* An epithet of Buddha. —तत्त्वं *n.* Knowledge of mankind. —तुषारः *m.* Campher. —द्वारं *n.* The gate of heaven. -धातुः *m.* A particular division of the world. —धातृ *m.* An epithet of Siva. —नाथः *m.* 1 Brahman (*m.*). -2 Vishnu. -3 Siva. -4 A king, sovereign. -5 A Buddha. -नेतृ *m.* An epithet of Siva. -पः, -पालः *m.* 1 A regent or guardian of a quarter of the world. -2 A king, sovereign. —पक्तिः *f.* Esteem of mankind, general respectability. -पतिः *m.* 1 An epithet of Brahman (*m.*) -2 Of Vishnu. -3 A king, sovereign. -पथः, -पद्धतिः *f.* The general or usual way; the universally accepted way. -पितामहः *m.* An epithet of Brahman (*m.*). -प्रकाशनः *m.* The sun. —प्रवादः *m.* Popular talk. -बंधुः, -बांधवः *m.* 1 The sun. -2 Siva. -बाह्य *a.* 1 Excommunicated. -2 Eccentric, singular. (-ह्यः *m.*) An outcast. -मातृ *f.* An epithet of Lakshmí. -यात्रा *f.* 1 The course of worldly life, business of the world. -2 A popular usage or custom. -3 Worldly existenc. -4 Support of life, maintenance. —वार्ता *f.* Public rumour. -श्रुतिः *f.* 1 A popular report.-2 World-wide fame. —संसृतिः *f.* Fate, destiny. —संग्रहः *m.* 1 The whole universe. -2 The welfare of the world. -3 Worldly experience. -4 Propitiation of mankind. —साक्षिक *a.* Attested by witnesses. —साक्षिन् *m.* 1 An epithet of Brahman (*m.*). -2 Fire. —सिद्ध *a.* 1 Usual, customary. -2 Generally received or accepted. —हास्य *a.* The butt of general ridicule.

लोकनं *n.* Seeing, beholding.

लोकंपृण *a.* Filling or pervading the world.

लोक् 1 A. (लोकते) To see, view, [perceive.

लोक् 10 U. or *Caus.* (लोकयति, -ते) To cause to see.

लोर्च *n.* Tears.

लोचकः *m.* 1 A stupid person. -2 The pupil of the eye. -3 Lampblack, collyrium.-4 A kind of earring. -5 A dark or blue garment. -6 A bow-string. -7 A particular ornament worn on the forehead. -8 A lump of flesh. -9 The slough of a snake. -10 A wrinkled skin. -11 The wrinkled brow. -12 A plantain tree.

लोचनं *n.* 1 Seeing, sight, viewing. -2 The eye. -Comp. —गोचरः, —पथः, —मार्गः *m.* The range of sight, sphere of vision. —हिता *f.* Blue vitriol.

लोट् 1 P. (लोटति) To be mad or foolish.

लोठः *m.* Rolling on the ground, wallowing. [shaking about.

लोडनं *n.* Disturbing, agitating,

लोणारः *m.* A kind of salt.

लोत्रं *n.* Stolen property, booty.

लोधः, लोध्रः *m.* N. of a tree with red or white flowers.

लोपः *m.* 1 Deprivation, robbing, plundering. -2 Loss, destruction. -3 Abolition, disappearance, disuse. -4 Violation, transgression. -5 Want, absence. -6 Omission, dropping. -7 Elision, dropping (in gram.).

लोपनं *n.* 1 Violation, transgression. -2 Omission, dropping.

लोपा, लोपामुद्रा *f.* N. of a daughter of the king of Vidarbha and wife of the sage Agastya.

लोपाकः, लोपापकः *m.* A kind of jackal.

लोपाशः, लोपाशकः *m.* A jackal, fox.

लोप्त्रं *n.* Booty, stolen property.

लोभः *m.* 1 Avarice, greed, cupidity. -2 Desire for, longing after.

लोभनं *n.* 1 Allurement, temptation, enticement. -2 Gold. [the body.

लोमः *m.* 1 A tail. -2 The hair on

लोमकिन् *m.* A bird.

लोमन् *n.* The hair on the body of men or animals. -Comp. —अंचः *m.* See रोमांचः. -2 Wool, down. -3 A tail. —आलिः, -आली, —आवलिः, -ली, —राजिः *f.* The line of hair from the breast to the navel. —कर्णः *m.* A hare. -कीटः *m.* A louse. —कूपः, -गर्तः *m.*, —रंध्रं, —विवरं *n.* A pore of the skin. —घ्नं *n.* Morbid baldness. -पादः *m.* N. of a king of the Angas.—मणिः *m.* An amulet made of hair. -संहर्षण *a.* Thrilling, causing horripilation. —सारः *m.* An emerald.-हर्षः *m.*, -हर्षणं *n.* Horripilation. —हृत् *m.* Yellow orpiment.

लोमश *a.* (*f.* -शा)1 Hairy, woolly. -2 Woollen. —शः *m.* A sheep, ram. -शा *f.* 1 A fox. -2 A female jackal. -3 An ape.-4 Green vitriol.-Comp. -पुष्पकः *m.* The Sirisha tree. —मार्जारः *m.* The civet-cat.

लोमाशः *m.* A jackal.

लोमाशिका *f.* The female of the jackal or fox.

लोल a. (f. —ला) 1 Shaking, rolling, tremulous, dangling, trembling; flowing, waving, disturbed, restless, uneasy. -2 Fickle, inconstant, changing, unsteady, transient. -3 Longing or anxious for, eager for. -4 Greedy, lustful. —ला f. 1 N. of Lakshmî. -2 Lightning. -3 The tongue. -Comp. —आक्षिका f. A woman with rolling eyes. —जिह्व a. Greedy.

लोलुप a. (f. —पा) 1 Very eager or desirous, greedy of. —पा f. Ardent longing, eagerness.

लोलुभ a. (f. —भा) Ardently desirous, covetous.

लोष्ट् 1 A. (लोष्टते) To heap up, accumulate.

लोष्ट m., लोष्टं n. A clod, a lump of earth —ष्टं n Rust of iron. -Comp. —घ्नः, —भेदनः m. —घ्नं n. An instrument for breaking clods, a harrow.

लोष्टुः m. A clod, lump of earth.

लोह a. (f. —हा) 1 Red, reddish. -2 Made of copper. -3 Made of iron. —हः m, —हं n. 1 Copper. -2 Iron. -3 Steel. -4 Any metal. -5 Gold. -6 Blood. -7 A weapon. —हः m. The red goat. —हं n. Aloe-wood. -Comp. —अजः m. The red goat. —अभिसारः, —अभिहारः m. N. of a military ceremony resembling नीराजन. —उत्तमं n. Gold. —कान्तः m. A loadstone, magnet. —कारः m. A blacksmith. —किट्टं n. Rust of iron. —घातकः m. A blacksmith. —चूर्णं n. Iron-filings, rust of iron. —जं n. 1 Bell-metal. -2 Iron-filings. —जालं n. A coat of mail. —जित् m. A diamond. —द्राविन् m. Borax. —नालः m. An iron arrow. —पृष्ठः m. A heron. —प्रतिमा f. 1 An anvil. -2 An iron image. —मुक्तिका f. Red pearl. —रजस् n. Rust of iron. —राजकं n. Silver. —वरं n. Gold. —वर्मन् n. Iron-armour, mail. —शंकुः m. An iron spike. —श्लेषणः m. Borax.

लोहल a. (f. —ला) 1 Made of iron. -2 Speaking indistinctly.

लोहिका f. An iron vessel.

लोहित a. (f. लोहिता or लोहिनी) 1 Red, red-coloured. -2 Copper, made of copper. —तः m. 1 The red colour. -2 The planet Mars. -3 A serpent. -4 A kind of deer. —ता f. N. of one of the seven tongues of fire. —तं n. 1 Copper. -2 Blood. -3 Saffron. -4 Battle. 5 A kind of sandal. -6 An imperfect form of a rainbow. -Comp. —अक्षः m. 1 A kind of snake. -2 The (Indian) cuckoo. -3 An eipthet of Vishnu. —अंगः m. The planet Mars. —अयस् n. Copper. —अशोकः m. A variety of *Asoka* (having red flowers). —अश्वः m. Fire. —आननः m. An ichneumon. —आर्द्र a. Dripping with blood. —ग्रीवः m. An epithet of Agni. —चंदनं n. Saffron. —पुष्पकः m. The granate tree. —मृत्तिका f. Red chalk. —शतपत्रं n. A red lotus-flower.

लोहितकः m. 1 A ruby. -2 The planet Mars. -3 A kind of rice. —कं n. 1 Bell-metal. -2 Calx of brass.

लोहितिमन् m. Redness.

लोहिनी f. A woman with a red complexion.

लौकायतिकः m. A follower of Chárvàka; an atheist, a materialist.

लौकिक a. (f. —की) 1 Worldly, terrestrial, earthly. -2 General, common, ordinary, popular, customary. -3 Temporal, secular (opp. आर्ष or शास्त्रीय). -4 Not sacred, profane (as a word or its sense). —कं n. Any general or worldly custom.

लौक्य a. (f. —क्या) 1 Worldly, terrestrial, human. -2 Common, ordinary, usual. [or mad.

लौड् 1 P. (लौडति) To be foolish

लौल्यं *n.* 1 Fickleness, unsteadiness. -2 Eagerness, greediness; excessive passion or desire.

लौह *a.* (*f.* -ही) 1 Made of iron, iron. -2 Coppery. -3 Metallic. -4 -4 Copper-coloured. -हं *n.* Iron. -हा *f.* A kettle. -Comp. —आत्मन *m.*, -भूः *f.* A boiler, kettle, caldron. -कारः *m.* A blacksmith. -जं *n.* Rust of iron. —मलं *n.* Rust of iron. -शंकुः *m.* An iron spike.

लौहित: *m.* The trident of Siva.

लौहित्य: *m.* N. of a river, the Brahmaputrâ. -त्यं *n.* Redness.

ल्पी, ल्यी 9 P. (ल्पिनाति, ल्यिनाति) To join, unite.

ल्वी 9 P. (ल्विनाति) To go, move, approach.

व.

वंशः *m.* 1 A bamboo. -2 A race, dynasty, lineage. -3 A shaft. -4 A flute, pipe. -5 A collection, multitude. -6 A cross-beam. -7 A joint (in a bamboo). -8 A sort of sugar-cane. -9 The back-bone. -10 The Sâla tree.-11 A particular measure of length (ten *hastas*). -12 The central projecting part of a sabre. -13 Bamboo-manna. —Comp. -अनुकीर्तनं *n.*,-अनुक्रमः *m.* Genealogy.-अनुचरितं *n.* The history of a dynasty or family.-आवली *f.* A pedigree, genealogy. —आह्वः *m.* Bamboo. -कठिनः *m.* A thicket of bamboos. — कर *a.* 1 Founding a family. -2 Perpetuating a race. (-रः *m.*) 1 A son. -2 An ancestor. —कर्पूररोचना,-रोचना,-लोचना *f.* Bamboo-manna. -कृत *m.* The founder or perpetuator of a family. —क्षीरी *f.* Bamboo-manua. चिंतकः *m.* A genelogist. -जः *m.* 1 Progeny, lineal descendant.-2 The seed of the bamboo. (-जं *n.*) Bomboo-manna. (-जा *f.*) Bamboo-manna.-नर्तिन् *m.* A buffoon. -नेत्रं *n.* The root of sugar-cane. -पूरकं *n.* The root of sugar-cane. -विततिः *f.* 1 A family, descent. -2 A thicket of bamboos. -शर्करा *f.* Bamboo-manna. -शलाका *f.* A small bamboo peg at the lower end of a Vînâ.

वंशकः *m.* 1 A kind of sugar-cane. -2 The joint in a bamboo. -3 A kind of fish. -कं *n.* Aloe-wood.

वांशिकं *n.* Aloe-wood. [wood.

वंशिका *f.* 1 A kind of flute.-2 Aloe-

वंशी *f* 1 A flute, pipe. -2 A vein or artery. -3 Bomboo-manna. -4 A Particular weight.

वंश्य *a.* (*f.* -श्या) 1 Relating to the main beam. -2 Connected with the spine. -3 Belonging to a family. -4 Born in a good family. -5 Lineal, genealogical. -श्यः *m.* 1 A descendant, posterity. -2 A forefather, an ancestor.-3 Any member of a family.-4 A cross-beam. -5 A bone in the arm or leg. -6 A pupil. -7 A kinsman from seven generations above and seven below.

वंह् See बंह्.

वकः *m.* See बकः.

वकरः *m.* The bend of a river.

वकुलः *m.* See बकुलः.

वक्तव्य *pot. p.* (*f.* -व्या) 1 Fit to be said, told or declared. -2 To be spoken about. -3 Blameable, censurable. -4 Low, vile. -5 Responsible.-6 Dependent. -व्यं *n.* 1 Speaking, speech. -2 A precept, rule. -3 Reproach.

वक्तृ m. 1 A speaker.-2 An orator. -3 A teacher.-4 A learned or wise man in general.

वक्त्रं n. 1 The mouth. -2 The face. -3 Snout, muzzle, beak. -4 The point (of an arrow); the spout of a vessel. -5 N. of a metre similar to *anushtubh*. -Comp. --आसवः m. Saliva. --खुरः m. A tooth. --जः m. A Brâhmana. --तालं n. A musical instrument played with the mouth. --दलं n. The palate. -पटः m. A veil. --पट्टः m. A bag of corn tied round a horse's neck. --वासः m. An orange. --शोधनं n. 1 Cleansing the mouth. -2 A lime, citron. --शोधिन् n. A citron. (-m.) A citron tree

वक्र a. (f --क्रा) 1 Crooked (fig. also); curved, tortuous. -2 Indirect, evasive, equivocal, ambiguous (as a speech). -3 Curled, curling (as hair). -4 Retrograde (as motion). -5 Dishonest, fraudulent. -6 Malignant (as a planet). -7 Prosodially long. --क्रः m. 1 The planet Mars.-2 The planet Saturn. -3 N. of Siva. -4 N of the demon Tripura. --क्रं n. 1 The bend or arm of a river. -2 Retrograde motion (of a planet). -Comp. --अंगः m. 1 A goose. -2 The ruddy goose. -3 A snake. --उक्तिः f. A figure of speech consisting in the use of evasive speech either by means of a pun or by an affected change of tone. -2 Equivocation, insinuation, inuendo. -3 Sarcasm. -कंटः m. The jujube tree. --कंटकः m. The Khadira tree. --ग्रीवः m. A camel. --चंचुः m. A parrot. --तुंडः m. 1 An epithet of Ganesa. -2 A parrot. -दंष्ट्रः m. A boar. --नक्रः m. 1 A parrot. -2 A low man. --नासिकः m. An owl.-पुच्छः, -पुच्छिकः m. A dog.-पुष्पः m. The palâsa tree. -वालधिः, -लांगूलः m. A dog. -भणितं n. Prevarication, evasion. --वक्त्रः m. A hog.

वक्रिन् m. A Jaina or Buddha.

वक्रिमन् m. 1 Crookedness, curvature. -2 Equivocation, ambiguity ; tortuous, round about or indirect nature (as of a speech). -3 Duplicity, craftiness.

वक्रोष्ठिः, वक्रोष्ठिका f. A gentle smile.

वक्ष् 1 P. (वक्षति) 1 To grow. -2 To be powerful. -3 To be angry. -4 To accumulate.

वक्षस् n. 1 The bosom, chest. -Comp. --जः, -रुह्, -रुहः (वक्षोजः, वक्षोरुह्, वक्षोरुहः) m. The female breast. --स्थलं (वक्षस्थलं or वक्षःस्थलं) n. The breast or bosom.

वगाहः m. See अवगाहः.

वंकः m. 1 The bend of a river. -2 Crookedness, a bend, a curve.

वंका f. The pummel of a saddle.

वंकिलः m. A thorn.

वंक्रिः f. 1 A rib.-2 The timber of a roof. -m., -n. A kind of musical instrument.

वंक्षुः f. A small arm or branch of the Ganges.

वंगाः m. N. of Bengal proper and its inhabitants. -गः m. 1 Cotton. -2 The egg-plant.-गं n. 1 Lead.-2 Tin. -Comp. --अरिः m. A yellow orpiment. --जं n. 1 Brass. -2 Red lead. --जीवनं n. Silver. --शुल्वजं n. Bell-metal (कांस्य).

वच् 2 P. (A. also in non-conjugational tenses ; in conjugational tenses it is said to be defective in the third person plural by some authorities, or in the whole plural by others ; वक्ति, उवाच, अवोचत्, वक्ष्यति, वक्तुं, उक्त) 1 To say, speak. -2 To relate, describe.-3 To tell, declare. -4 To name, call. -5 To signify, (as sense). -6 To recite, repeat. -7 To censure. With अनु-To recite. निस्— 1 To explain etymologically. -2 To explain (in general). प— 1 To say, speak. -2 To call, name. -3 To announce. प्रति— To answer. -*Caus* (वाचयति,-ते) 1 To cause to speak. -2 To read. -3 To tell, declare.-4 To promise.—*Desid.* (विवक्षति) To wish to speak, intend to say (something).

वचः *m.* 1 A parrot. -2 The sun. —चा *f.* 1 A kind of talking bird. -2 A kind of aromatic root. —चं *n.* Speaking, talk.

वचनं *n.* 1 The act of speaking, saying. -2 Speech, sentence -3 Repeating, recitation. -4 A rule, precept, a passage of a sacred book, as in शास्त्रवचनं, श्रुतिवचनं, स्मृतिवचनं &c. -5 An order, a direction.-6 Advice, instruction. -7 Declaration, affirmation. -8 Pronunciation (of a letter) (in gram.). -9 The signification of a word. -10 Number (in gram.) (there are three numbers, singular, dual and plural). -11 Dry ginger. -Comp. —मात्रं *n.* An unsupported assertion. —स्थित *a.* (वचनेस्थित also) Obedient, compliant.

वचनीय *a.* (*f.* —या) 1 To be said or related. -2 Censurable, blameable. —यं *n.* Blame, reproach.

वचरः *m.* 1 A cock. -2 A rogue, a cheat.

वचस् *n.* 1 A speech, word, sentence. -2 A command, a precept, an injunction. -3 Advice, counsel. -4 A hymn. -5 Singing, a song of birds. -6 (In gram.) Number. -Comp. —कर *a.* 1 Obedient, compliant. -2 Executing the orders of another. —क्रमः *m.* Discourse. -ग्रहः *m.* The ear.

वचसांपतिः *m.* An epithet of Brihaspati, or the planet Jupiter.

वज् 1 P. (वजति) To go, move.

वज् 10 U. (वाजयति,-ते) 1 To trim, prepare. -2 To feather an arrow. -3 To go, move.

वज्रः *m* ,वज्रं *n.* 1 A thunderbolt, the weapon of Indra.-2 Any weapon like the thunderbolt. -3 An instrument for perforating jewels. -4 A diamond in general.-5 Sour gruel.-ज्रः *m.* 1 A form of military array. -2 A kind of Kusa grass. —ज्रं *n.* 1 Steel.-2 A kind of talc.-3 Thunder-like or severe language. -4 A child. -Comp. —अंगः *m.* A snake. —अशनिः *m., f.* The thunderbolt of Indra. —आख्यः *m.* A kind of mineral spar. —आघातः *m.* 1 A stroke of thunder or lightning.-2 (Fig.) Any sudden shock or calamity. —आयुधः *m.* An epithet of Indra. —कंकटः *m.* An epithet of Hanumat. —कीलः *m.* A thunderbolt. —कूटः *m.* A mountain consisting of diamonds. -क्षारं *n.* An alkaline earth. —गोपः *m.* See इंद्रगोपः. —चंचुः *m.* A vulture. —चर्मन् *m.* A rhinoceros. —जित *m.* N. of Garuda. —ज्वलनं *n.*, —ज्वाला *f.* Lightning. —तुंडः *m.* 1 A vulture. -2 A mosquito, gnat. -3 N. of Garuda. -4 Of Ganesa. -तुल्यः *m.* *Lapis Lazuli* or azure stone.-दंतः *m.* 1 A hog. -2 A car. —दशनः *m.* A rat. —धरः *m.* 1 An epithet of Indra. —नाभः *m.* The discus of Krishna. -निर्घोषः,-निष्पेषः *m.* A peal of thunder. —पाणिः *m* 1 An epithet of Indra. -2 An owl.-पातः *m.*,-पतनं *n.* A stroke of lightning, a fall of thunderbolt. —पुष्पं *n*. The blossom of sesamum. -सुत *m*. An epithet of Indra. -मणिः *m*. A diamond, an adamant. -मुष्टिः *m*. An epithet of Indra. -रद: *m*. A hog. -लेपः *m*. A kind of very hard cement. -लोहकः *m*. A magnet. -व्यूहः *m*. A kind of military array. -शल्यः *m*. A porcupine. —सार *a*. Having the strength of the thunderbolt. -सूचिः, —सूची *f* A diamond-needle.

वज्रिन् *m*. 1 N. of Indra. -2An owl.

वंच् 1 P. (वंचति) 1 To go. -2 To wander over. -3 To go secretly. -4 To go crookedly. -*Caus*. (वंचयति,-ते) 1 To avoid, evade. -2 To deceive, defraud. -3To deprive one of.

वंचक *a*. (*f*. -चिका) 1 Fraudulent, crafty. -2 Cheating, deceiving. -कः *m*. 1 A rogue, cheat, swindler. -2 A jackal. -3 Musk-rat. -4 A tame ichneumon.

वंचतिः *m*. Fire.

वंचथः *m*. 1 Cheating, trickery. -2 A cheat, a rogue. -3 The cuckoo.

वंचनं *n*., —ना *f*. 1 Cheating -2 A trick, deception, trickery.-3 An illusion, delusion. -4 Loss. -5 A hindrance.

वंचित *p*. *p* (*f*. —ता) 1 Deceived, cheated. -2 Deprived (of). -ता *f*. A sort of riddle or enigma.

वंचुक *a*. (*f*. —की) Deceitful, dishonest. —कः *m*. A jackal.

वंजुलः *m* 1 The cane or reed. -2 kind of flower -3 The Asoka tree. -4 A kind of bird. —ला *f*. A cow that yields much milk.-Comp. —द्रुमः *m*. The Asoka tree. —प्रियः *m*. The ratan.

वट् 1 P. (वटति) To surround.

वट् 10 U. (वटयति,-ते) 1 To tell. -2 To divide, partition. -3 To surround. -4 To tie, connect. -*Caus*. (वटयति) To speak.

वटः *m*. The fig-tree. -2 A small ball, pill. -3 A round figure, a cipher. -4 A kind of cake. -5 A string, rope (*n*. also in this sense). -7 Equality in shape. -Comp. —पत्रं *n*. A variety of the white basil. (-त्रा *f*.) A jasmine. —वासिन् *m*. A Yaksha.

वटकः *m*. 1 A kind of cake. -2 A small lump, ball, pill.

वटरः *m*. 1 A cock.-2 A mat. -3 A turban. -4 A thief. -5 A churning-stick. -6 Fragrant grass.

वटाकरः, वटारकः *m*. A cord, string.

वटिकः *m*. A pawn at chess.

वटिका *f*. 1 A pill. -2 A chessman. -3 A kind of cake.

वटिन् *a*. Circular. -*m*. A pawn at chess. [pill, bolus.

वटी *f*. 1 A rope or string. -2 A

वटुः *m*. 1 A boy, lad. -2 A religious student or Brahmachárin.

वटुकः *m*. 1 A boy, lad. -2 A Brahmachárin. -3 A fool or blockhead.

वठ् 1 P. (वठति) 1 To be strong or powerful. -2 To be fat.

वठरः *m*. A fool or blockhead. -2 A rogue, a vile fellow. -3 A physician. -4 A water-pot.

वडभिः, —भी *f*. 1 A turret, a balcony, a top-room. -2 The wooden frame of a roof.

वडवा *f*. 1 A mare. -2 The nymph Asviní who assumed the form of a mare and bore to the sun two sons, the Asvins. -3 A female slave. -4 A harlot, prostitute. -5 A woman of the Bráhmana caste. -Comp.-अग्निः, -अनलः *m*. The submarine fire. -2 N. of Siva.

वडा *f*. A kind of cake.

वडिलं *n*. See वडिशं.

वड् *a.* (*f*. —ड्डा) Large ; big, great.

वण् 1 P. (वणति) To sound.

वणिज् *m*. 1 A merchant, trader. -2 The sign *Libra* of the zodiac. -*f*. Merchandise, trade. -Comp. —पथः *m*. 1 Trade, traffic. -2 A merchant. -3 A merchant's shop. -4 The sign *Libra* of the zodiac. —वृत्तिः *f*. Trade, traffic. —सार्थः *m*. A caravan.

वणिजः *m*. 1 A merchant, trader. -2 The sign *Libra* of the zodiac.

वणिजकः *m*. A merchant.

वणिज्यं *n*., वणिज्या *f*. Trade, traffic.

वंट् 1 P., 10 U. (वंटति, वंटयति,-ते) To divide, to partition.

वंटः *m*. 1 A part, portion, share. -2 The handle of a sickle. -3 An unmarried man, a bachelor.

वंटकः *m*. 1 Dividing, distributing. -2 A distributer. -3 A part, share.

वंटनं *n*. Partitioning, dividing.

वंटालः, वंडालः *m*. 1 A contest of heroes. -2 A shovel, hoe. -3 A boat.

वंठ *a*. (*f*. —ठा) 1 Unmarried. -2 Dwarfish. -3 Crippled. —ठः *m*. 1 An unmarried man, a bachelor. -2 Javelin, dart. -3 A dwarf.

वंठरः *m*. 1 The sheath that envelops the young bamboo. -2 The shoot of the palm. -3 A rope for tying. -4 The tail of a dog. -5 A cloud. -6 The female breast.

वंड् I. 1 A. (वंडते) 1 To divide, share, apportion. -2 To surround, encompass.

वंड् 10 U. (वंडयति,-ते) To share, divide, apportion.

वंड *a*. (*f*. -डा) 1 Crippled, maimed. -2 Unmarried. -3 Emasculated. -डः *m*. A man who has no prepuce. -डा *f*. An unchaste woman. [eunuch.

वंडरः *m*. 1 A stingy person. -2 A

वत *a*. 1 An affix added to nouns to show 'possession'; *e. g.* धनवत् possessed of wealth ; रूपवत beautiful. -2 Added to the base of the past passive participle वत turns it into a past active participle. —*ind*. An affix added to nouns or adjectives to denote ' likeness ' or ' resemblance ' and may be translated by ' like ', ' as '.

वत *ind*. See बत.

वतंसः *m*. See अवतंसः.

वतोका *f*. A barren or childless woman ; a woman or cow miscarrying from accident.

वत्सः *m*. 1 A calf, the young of an animal. -2 A boy, son (in this sense often used in the voc. as a term of endearment and translatable by 'my dear ', 'my darling', ' my dear child'). -3 Offspring or children in general. -4 A year. -5 N. of a country. -त्सा *f*. 1 A female calf. -2 A little girl. —त्सं *n*. The breast. -Comp. —अक्षी *f*. A kind of cucumber. —अदनः *m*. A wolf. —ईशः, -राजः *m*. A king of the *Vatsas*. —तंत्री *f*. A rope for tying calves. -दंतः *m*. A kind of arrow. —नाभः *m*. 1 N. of a tree. -2 A kind of very strong poison. - पालः *m*. N. of Krishna or Balaràma.

वत्सकः *m*. 1 A little calf, calf in general. -2 A child. -कं *n*. Green or black sulphate of iron.

वत्सतरः *m*. A weaned calf, a steer, a young ox. —री *f*. A heifer.

वत्सरः *m*. 1 A year. -2 N. of Vishnu. -Comp. —अंतकः *m*. The month *Phâlguna*. —ऋणं *n*. A debt to be paid by the end of a year.

वत्सल *a*. (*f*. -ला) 1 Child-loving, affectionate towards children or offspring. -2 Affectionate towards, devoted to, fond of. -लः m. 1 A fire fed with grass. -2 N. of Vishnu.-3 The sentiment of affection. -लं n. Affection, fondness.

वात्सिमन् m. Youth, childhood.

वत्सीपः m. A cowherd.

वद् 1 P. (वदति, but Atm. in certain senses and with certain prepositions ; वदति, -ते, उद्यते, उदित) 1 To say, speak, utter, speak to.-2 To tell, communicate, inform. 3 To describe. -4 To state.-5 To name, call. -6 To indicate, bespeak.-7 To utter a cry, sing. -8 To be an authority on (Atm.) -9 To shine, look splendid or bright (Atm.). -10 To maintain, affirm. -11 To toil, exert, labour (Atm.). With अनु— 1 To repeat after, to say again what has been said. -2 To resound. -3 To ratify, confirm. -3 (Atm) To imitate. अप— (Atm.) 1 To hate (with a *dat.*) -2 To revile, reproach. अभि- 1 To speak, express.-2 (*Atm*). To salute (with reverence). उप— (*Atm.*) 1 To flatter. -2 To conciliate, persuade. परि— To speak ill of. प्र- To call, consider. प्रति— 1 To speak in reply. -2 To speak in general. वि— (*Atm.*) 1 To dispute. -2 To litigate. विप्र— (U.) To dispute. विसम्— 1 To fail. -2 To be inconsistent with. सम्— 1 To converse. -2 To speak to. -3 To call, to name. -4 To coincide, resemble (with *instr.*). संप्र— (*Atm.*) To speak loudly together.—*Caus.* (वादयति,-ते) 1 To cause to speak or say. -2 To play on a musical instrument. -3 To speak, recite.

वदनं n. 1 The face. 2 The mouth. -3 Look, appearance. -4 The front point -5 First term (in a series). -6 The summit or apex of a triangle. -Comp. —आसवः m. Saliva.

वदंती f. Speech, discourse.

वदन्य a. (f.-न्या)See वदान्य.

वदरः m. See बदरः.

वदान्य a. (f. --न्या) 1 Speaking fluently, eloquent -2 Speaking kindly. -3 Liberal, generous. —न्यः m. A liberal or generous person.

वदामः m. An almond.

वदालः m. 1 A whirlpool.-2 A kind of sheat-fish.

वदावद a. (f. -दा) Eloquent, talkative, garrulous.

वदि *in l.* In the dark half (of a lunar month) ; as in ज्येष्ठवदि (opp. शुदि.)

वद्य a. (f. -द्या) 1 Fit to be spoken; not blamable. -2 Dark or second fortnight of a lunar month. —द्यं n. Speech, speaking about.

वध् 1 P. (वधति) To slay, kill (not used in classical Sanskrit except as a substitute for हन् in the Aorist and Benedictive).

वधः m. 1 Killing, murder, slaughter. -2 A blow, stroke.-3 Paralysis. -4 Multiplication (in math.). -Comp. —अंगकं n. A poison. —जीविन् m. 1 A hunter. -2 A butcher. -दंडः m. 1 Corporeal punishment (as whipping &c.) -2 Capital punishment. —स्तंभः m. The gallows.

वधकः m. (f. -धका,-धिका) 1 An executioner, a hangman. -2 A murderer.

वधत्रं n. A deadly weapon.

वधित्रं n 1 The God of love.-2 Sexual passion, lust.

वधुः, वधुका f. 1 A daughter-in-law. -2 A young woman in general.

वधूः *f.* 1 A bride.-2A wife, spouse. -3 A daughter-in-law. -4 A woman in general -5 The wife of a younger relation, a younger female relation. -6 The female of any animal. -Comp. —गृहप्रवेशः, -प्रवेशः *m.* The ceremony of a bride's entrance into her husband's house. —जनः *m.* A wife, a woman. —पक्षः *m.* The party of the bride (at a wedding).—वस्त्रं *n.* The bridal apparel.

वधू (- धु-) टी *f.* 1 A young woman or female. -2 A daughter-in-law.

वध्य *a.* (*f.* —ध्या) 1 To be killed or slain. -2 Sentenced to be killed. -3 To be subjected to corporeal punishment. —ध्यः *m.* 1 A victim. -2 An enemy. -Comp. —पटहः *m.* A drum beaten at the time of execution. —भूः. -भूमिः *f.*, -स्थलं, -स्थानं *n.* A place of execution. -माला *f.* A garland of flowers placed on a person who is about to be executed.

वध्या *f.* Slaughter, murder.

वध्रं *n.* 1 A leathern strap.-2 Lead. —ध्री *f.* A leathern thong.

वध्रि *a.* Castrated, emasculated.

वध्रयः *m.* A shoe.

वन् 1 P. (वनति) 1 To honour, worship. -2 To aid. -3 To sound. -4 To be engaged.

वन् 8 U. (वनोति, वनुते, usually वनुते only) 1 To beg, request. -2 To seek, to obtain.-3 To conquer, possess.

वन् 1 P., 10 U. (वनति, वानयति,-ते) 1 To favour, aid. -2 To hurt, injure. -3 To sound. -4 To confide in.

वनं *n.* 1 A forest, wood, thicket of trees. -2 A group, a quantity of plants growing in a thick bed. -3 A place of residence, house. -4 A fountain, spring (of water.). -5 Water in general. -6 A wooden vessel. -7 Wood, timber. -8 Dwelling in a forest, living abroad -Comp. —अंतः *m.* 1 The skirts or borders of a forest. -2 A forest, wood. -अंतरं *n.* 1 Another wood. -2 The interior of a forest. -अरिष्टा *f.* Wild turmeric. —अलक्तं *n.* Red earth. —अलिका *f.* A sun flower. —आखुः *m.* A hare. -आखुकः *m.* A kind of bean. —आपगा *f.* A forest-stream. —आर्द्रका *f.* Wild ginger. —आश्रमः *m.* The third stage in the religious life of a Brâhmana. -आश्रमिन् *m.* An anchorite, a hermit. -आश्रयः *m.* 1 An inhabitant of the wood. -2 A sort of crow or raven. -उत्साहः *m.* A rhinoceros. -उद्भवा *f.* The wild cotton plant. -उपप्लवः *m.* A forest-conflagration. ओकस् *m.* 1 An inhabitant of a wood, forester. -2 An anchorite, a hermit. -8 A wild animal such as a monkey, boar &c.. —कणा *f.* Wild pepper. —कदली *f* A wild plantain. —खंडं *n.* A forest. —गवः *m.* The wild ox. -गहनं *n.* The thick part of a forest. -गुप्तः *m.* A spy. —गुल्मः *m.* A forest shrub. —गोचरः *m.* 1 A hunter. -2 A forester. (-रं *n.*) A forest. —चंदनं *n.* 1 The Devadâru tree. -2 Aloe-wood. —चंद्रिका, —ज्योत्स्ना *f.* A kind of jasmine. -चंपकः *m.* The wild Champaka tree. —चर *a.* Living in a forest. (—रः *m.*) 1 A forester, forest-dweller. -2 A wild animal. -3 The fabulous eight-legged animal called Sarabha. -चर्या *f.* Roaming about or residence in a forest. —छागः *m.* 1 A wild goat. -2 A boar. —जः *m.* 1 An elephant. -2 A kind of fragrant grass. -3 The wild citron tree. (-जं *n.*) A blue lotus-flower. —जा *f.* 1 Wild ginger. -2 The wild cotton tree. -जीविन् *m.*

A forester. —दः *m.* A cloud. —देवता *f.* A sylvan deity. —द्रुमः *m.* A tree growing wild in a forest. -धारा *m.* An avenue of trees. —धेनुः *f.* The female of the wild ox or *Bos gavœus.* —पः *m.* A woodman. —पांसुलः *m.* A hunter. —पूरकः *m.* The wild citron tree. -प्रस्थः *m.* A wood situated on a table-land. -प्रियः *m.* The cuckoo. (-यं *n.*)The cinnamon tree. —मक्षिका *f.*A gad-fly. —मल्ली *f.* Wild jasmine.-माला *f.*A garland of flowers reaching to the knees such as that worn by Krishna -मालिन् *m.*An epithet of Krishna.-मालिनी *f.* N. of the town Dvârakâ —मुच्, -मूतः *m.* A cloud. —मुद्गः *m.* A kind of kidney-bean. —मोचा *f.* Wild plantain. —राजः *m.* The lion. —रुहं *n.* A lotus-flower. —लक्ष्मी *f.*1 An ornament or beauty of the wood. -2 The plantain.-वासः *m.* 1 Living in a wood.-2 A wild or nomadic life.-3 A forest-dweller.-वासनः *m.* A civet-cat.-वासिन् *m.* 1 A forest-dweller.-2 A hermit.-वीजः,-वीजकः *m.* The wild citron tree. —शोभनं *n.* A lotus.-श्वन् *m.* 1 A jackal.-2 A tiger. -3 A civet-cat. -संकटः *m.* A kind of pulse. —सद्, —संवासिन् *m.* A forester. —सरोजिनी *f.* The wild cotton plant. -स्थः *m.* 1 A deer. -2 A hermit. -स्था *f.* The holy fig-tree.

वनस्पतिः *m.* 1 A large forest tree, especially one that bears fruit apparently without any blossoms. -2 A tree in general.

वनायुः*m.*N. of a district.-Comp.-जः *m.* A horse produced in Vanàyu.

वनिः *f.* Desire, wish.

वनिका *f.* A little wood, as in अशोकवनिका.

वनिता *f.* 1 A woman in general. -2 A wife, mistress. -3 Any beloved woman.-4The female of an animal.

वनिष्णु *a.* Begging, requesting.

वनी *f.* A forest, wood, grove.

वनीपकः, वनीयकः *m.* A beggar, mendicant.

वनेकिंशुका: *m. pl.* Anything found unexpectedly; (also वनेबिल्वका: *m. pl.* In the same sense.).

वनेचरः *m.* 1 A forester, woodman. -2 An ascetic, a hermit. -3 A wild beast. -4 A sylvan, satyr. -5 A demon.

वंद् 1 A. (वंदते, वंदित) 1 To salute, pay homage to. -2 To adore, worship. -3 To praise, extol. -With अभि— To salute, greet respectfully.

वंदथः *m.* A bard, panegyrist.

वंदनं *n.* 1 Saluation. -2 Adoration. -3 Obeisance paid to a Bràhmana &c. -4 Praising, extolling. -ना *f.* 1 Worship, adoration. -2 Praise -नी *f.* 1 Worship, adoration. -2 Praise. -3 Solicitation.-4 A drug for reviving the dead. -Comp. -माला, -मालिका *f.*A garland suspended across gateways.

वंदनीया *f.* Yellow pigment.

वंदा *f.* A female beggar.

वंदारु *a.* 1 Praising.-2 Reverential, polite, civil. -*n.* Praise.—*m.* A panegyrist, bard.

वंदिन् *m.* 1 A bard, an encomiast, a herald. -2 A captive, prisoner.

वंदी *f.* See बंदी. -Comp. -पालः *m.* A keeper of prisoners, jailer.

वंद्य *a.* (*f.* -द्या) 1 Adorable, venerable.-2 To be respectfully saluted. -3 Laudable, praiseworthy. -द्या *f.* 1 A parasitical plant. -2 Yellow pigment.

वंद्रः *m.* A worshipper, votary. —द्रं *n.* Prosperity.

वंधुर *a.* See बंधुर.

वंध्य, वंध्या *a.* See वंध्य,वंध्या.

वन्य *a.* (*f.*-न्या) 1 Belonging to or growing in a forest. -2 Not tamed or domesticated.-3 Wooden. -न्यः *m.* 1 A wild animal. -2 A wild plant.-न्यं *n.* Forest-produce. -Comp. —इतर *a.* Tame, domesticated.

वन्या *f* 1 A large forest, a number of thickets. -2 A flood, deluge.

वप् 1 U. (वपति,वपते, उप्त, *pass.* उप्यते) 1 To sow, scatter (as seed), plant. -2 To beget, produce.-3 To weave. -4 To shear, shave. With नि- 1 To make offerings to the manes.-2 To scatter seed. -3 To kill. निस्— 1 To scatter. -2 To perform. -3 To offer libations to the dead. प्रति— 1 To sow. -2 To pierce.

वपः *m.* 1 Sowing seed.-2 A sower. -3 Shaving. -4 Weaving.

वपनं *n.* 1 Sowing seed. -2 Shaving, shearing. -3 Semen virile, seed.-नी *f.* 1 A barber's shop. -2 A weaving instrument.-3 A weaver's shop.

वपा *f.* 1 Fat, marrow. -2 A hole. -Comp. -कृत *m.* Marrow.

वपिलः *m.* A procreator, father.

वपुनः *m.* A God, deity.

वपुष्मत् *a.* (*f.* -ती) 1 Embodied, incarnate. -2 Beautiful,handsome.

वपुस् *n.* 1 Body, person. -2 Form, figure, appearance. -3 Beauty, a beautiful form.-Comp. —गुणः, -प्रकर्षः *m.* Excellence of form. —धर *a.* 1 Embodied. -2 Beautiful. —स्रवः *m.* A humour of the body.

वप्तृ *m.* 1 A sower (of seed). -2 A father, procreator. -3 A poet.

वप्रः *m.*, वप्रं *n.* 1 A rampart, mud-wall. -2 A bank or mound of any kind (against which bulls and elephants butt).-3 The slope, summit, peak, table-land on a mountain.-4 The bank of a river.-5 The foundation of a building. -6 The gate of a fortified town. -7 A ditch. -8 A field -9 The butting of an elephant or bull.-प्रः *m* A father.—प्रं *n.* Lead. -Comp.-क्रिया,-क्रीडा *f.* The playful butting of an elephant (or bull) against a bank or mound.

वप्रिः *m.* 1 A field. -2 The ocean.

वर्मी *f.* A hillock.

वभ्र् 1 P. (वभ्रति) To go.move.

वम् 1 P. (वमति,वांत; *caus.*वामयति, वमयति) 1 To vomit, eject from the mouth. -2 To pour out, give out, (fig. also). -3 To reject.

वमः *m.* 1 Ejecting, vomiting.

वमथुः *m.* 1 Ejecting, vomiting. -2 Water ejected by an elephant from his trunk.

वमनं *n.* 1 Ejecting, vomiting. -2 Taking or geting out. -3 An emetic. -4 Offering oblations. —नः *m.* Hemp. -नी *f.* A leech.

वमनीया *f.* A fly.

वमिः *m.* 1 Fire.-2 A rogue.—मिः *f.* 1 Sickness, nausea. -2 An emetic.

वमी *f.* Vomiting.

वंभः *m.* A bamboo (वंश).

वंभारवः *m.* The lowing of cattle.

वम्रः *m.*, वम्री *f.* An ant. -Comp. —कूटं *n.* An ant-hill.

वय् 1 P. (वयते) To go, move.

वयः *m.* A weaver.

वयनं *n.* Weaving.

वयस् *n.* 1 Age, any time or period of life. -2 Youth, the prime of life. -3 A bird. -4 A crow. -Comp. -परिणतिः *f.*, —परिणामः *m.* Advanced or old age. -वृद्ध (वयोवृद्ध) Advanced in years.-स्थ *a.*(वयस्थः or वयस्थ) 1 Youthful. -2 Grown up,mature.-3 Strong, powerful.—हानिः *f.* (वयोहानिः) 1 Loss or decline of youth.-2 Loss of youthful vigour.

वयस्य *a.* 1 Being of the same age. -2 Contemporary.-स्यः *m.* A friend, companion, an associate. -स्या *f.* A female companion or friend.

वयुनं *n.* 1 Knowledge, wisdom.-2 A temple (*m.* also in this sense).

वयोवस् *m.* A young or middle-aged man.

वयोरंगं *n.* Lead. [choose.

वर् 10 U. (वरयति,-ते) 1 To ask for,

वर *a.* (*f.* -रा) 1 Best, excellent, finest. -2 Better than,preferable to. -रः *m.* 1 The act of choosing, selecting. -2 Choice,selection.-3 A boon, favour. -4 A gift, reward. -5 A wish. -6 Solicitation. -7 Charity. alms. -8 Surrounding, enclosing, checking. -9 A bride-groom, husband. -10 A suitor, wooer. -11 A dowry.-12 A son-in-law.-13A libertine. -14 A sparrow. -रं *n.* Saffron. -Comp. -अंगः *m.* 1 An elephant. (-गं *n.*) 1 The head. -2 The best part. -3 An elegant form. -4 The female pudendum. -5 Green cinnamon. —आगमिवित् *m* An astrologer. —आरोह *a.* Having fine hips. (-हः *m.*) 1 An excellent rider. -2 A rider on an elephant or horse. -3 Riding. (-हा *f.*) An elegant or a beautiful woman. -आलिः *m.* The moon.-ऊरुः, —रूः *f.* A beautiful woman (lit. having beautiful thighs).-ऋतुः*m.* An epithet of Indra.-तनुः*f.* A beautiful woman. —तंतुः *m.*N. of an ancient sage.-त्वचः *m.* The *Nimba* tree. -द *a.* 1 Granting or fulfilling a boon. -2 Propitious. (-दः *m.*) A benefactor. (-दा *f.*) 1 N of a river. -2 A maiden, girl. —दक्षिणा *f.* 1 A present to the bridegroom by the father of the birde. —द्रुमः *m.* Agallochum.—निश्चयः *m.* The choice of a bridegroom —पक्षः *m.* The party of the bridegroom (at a wedding). —प्रस्थानं *n.*, -यात्रा*f.* The setting out of the bridegroom in procession towards the the house of the bride for the celebration of marriage. —फलः *m.* The cocoa-nut tree. —बाह्लिकं *n.* Saffron. —रुचिः *m.* N. of a poet and grammarian. —लब्धः *m.* The *Champaka* tree. —वत्सला *f.* A mother-in-law. —वर्णं *n.* Gold. —वर्णिनी *f.* 1 An excellent woman. -2 A woman in general. -3 Turmeric. -4 Lac. -5 N. of Lakshmí. -6 Of Durgá. -7 Of Sarasvatí. -8 The creeper called *Priyangu.* -9 A yellow pigment. —स्रज् *f.* The garland put by the bride round the neck of the bridegroom.

वरकः *m.* 1 A wish, request. -2 A cloak. -3 A kind of wild bean. -4 One who asks a female in marriage. —कं *n.* The cover of a boat.

वरटः *m.* 1 Gander. -2 A kind of grain.-3 A kind of wasp.—टा,-टी *f.* 1 A goose. -2 A kind of wasp. —टं *n.* The *kunda* flower.

वरणं *n.* 1 Choosing. -2 Soliciting, requesting.-3 Encircling.-4Screening, protecting. -5 The choice of a bride. —णः *m.* 1 A rampart. -2 A bridge. -3 The tree Varuna. -4 A camel. -Comp. -माला, —स्रज् *f.* Same as वरस्रज्.

वरणसी *f.* See वाराणसी.

वरंडः *m.* 1 A multitude. -2 A pimple on the face. -3 A veranda. -4 A heap of grass. -5 The string of a fish-hook.-6 Packet.-7 A long rod (according to some); a projecting wall (according to others.).

वरंडकः *m.* 1 A mound of earth. -2 The seat on an elephant. -3 A wall. -4 An eruption on the face.

वरंडा *f.* 1 A dagger, knife. -2 A kind of bird (सारिका). -3 The wick of a lamp.

वरत्रा *f.* 1 A strap, a leather thong. -2 The girth of an elephant or horse.

वरम् *ind* Rather, better than, preferably to, it is better that. (Used either absolutety or with an *abl.* In the former case it is generally followed by न, नच, नतु or न पुनः in the second clause).

वरलः *m.* A kind of wasp. —ला *f.* 1 A goose. -2 A kind of wasp.

वरा *f.* 1 A kind of perfume. -2 Turmeric. -3 N. of Pârvatî.

वराक *a.* (*f.* —की) 1 Poor, pitiable, unhappy, unfortunate. -कः *m.* War, battle. [cord.

वराटः *m.* 1 A *cowrie*. -2 A rope,

वराटकः *m.* 1 A *cowrie*. -2 The seed-vessel of the lotus-flower. -3 A string, rope (*n.* also in this sense). -Comp. —रजस् *m.* The tree नागकेशर.

वराटिका *f.* 1 A *cowrie*.

वराणः *m.* An epithet of Indra.

वराणसी *f.* See वाराणसी.

वरारकं *n.* A diamond.

वरालः, वरालकः *m.* Cloves.

वराशिः, (—सिः) *m.* A coarse cloth.

वराहः *m.* 1 A boar, hog. -2 A ram. -3 A bull. -4 A cloud. -5 A crocodile. -6 An array of troops in the form of a boar. -7 N. of Vishnu in the third or boar-incarnation. -8 N. one of the 18 Purànas. -Comp. —अवतारः *m.* The boar or third incarnation of Vishnu. —कर्णः *m.* A kind of arrow. -कर्णिका *f.* A kind of missile. —कल्पः *m.* The period during which Vishnu assumed the form of a boar. —मिहिरः *m.* N. of a celebrated astronomer. —शृंगः *m.* N. of Siva. [ence.

वरिमन् *m.* 1 Excellence, pre-emin-

वरिवसि (-स्यि-) त *a.* (*f.* —ता) Worshipped, revered.

वरिवस्या *f.* Worship, honour, devotion, attendance.

वरिष्ठ *a.* (*f.* —ष्ठा) 1 Best, pre-eminent. -2 Largest, greatest. -3 Widest. -4 Heaviest. —ष्ठः *m.* 1 The francoline partridge. -2 The orange tree. -ष्ठं *n.* 1 Copper. -2 Pepper. [sun.

वरी *f.* N. of Chhàyá, wife of the

वरिमन् *m.* Excellence, pre-eminence.

वरीयस् *a.* (*f.* -सी) 1 Better, more excellent, preferable. -2 Most excellent. -3 Larger, more extensive.

वरी (-ली-) वर्दः *m.* An ox, a bull.

वरीषुः *m.* N. of Cupid, the God of love.

वरुणः *m.* 1 N. of an *Aditya* (usually associated with Mitra). -2 The regent of the ocean and of the western quarter. -3 The ocean. -4 Firmament. -5 The Sun. -6 The Varuna tree. -Comp —अंगरुहः *m.* An epithet of Agastya. —आत्मजा *f.* Spirituous liquor. —आलयः, -आवासः *m.* The ocean. -पाशः *m.* 1 A shark. -2 The noose of Varuna. —लोकः *m.* 1 The world of Varuna. -2 Water.

वरुणानी *f.* Varuna's wife.

वरुत्रं *n.* A cloak, an outer garment.

वरूथं *n.* 1 A sort of wooden fence with which a chariot is provided as a defence against collision (*m.* also in this sense). -2 An armour, a coat of mail. -3 A shield. -4 A group, multitude. -थः *m.* 1 The cuckoo. -2 Time.

वरूथिन् *a.* (*f.* —नी) 1 Wearing an

armour; mailed. -2 Furnished with a protecting plank. -3 Protecting, sheltering. -*m*. 1 A chariot. -2 A guard, defender. —नी *f*. An army.

वरेण्य *a*. (*f*.—ण्या) 1 To be wished for, most excellent, pre-eminent, chief. —ण्यं *n*. Saffron.

वरोटः *m*. The Marubaka plant. -टं *n*. Its flower.

वरोलः *m*. A kind of wasp.

वर्करः *m*. 1 A lamb. -2 A goat. -3 Any young beast. -4 Mirth, sport, pastime. -5 Jest, joke. -Comp. -कर्करः *m*. A strap or rope of leather to bind a lamb or goat with.

वर्कराटः *m*. 1 A side-glance. -2 The marks of a lover's finger.

वर्कुटः *m*. A pin, a bolt.

वर्गः *m*. 1 A class, division, company, society, a collection (of similar things). -2 A class of words grouped together; as मनुष्यवर्गः, वनस्पतिवर्गः &c. -3 A class of consonants in the alphabet. -4 A section, chapter, division of a book. -5 The square power. -6 Strength. -Comp. —अंत्यं, -उत्तमं *n*. The last letter of each of the first five classes of consonats *i. e*. a nasal. —पदं, -मूलं *n*. The square root.

वर्गणा *f*. Multiplication.

वर्गशस् *ind*. In groups, according to classes.

वर्ग्यः *m*. One belonging to the same class or company; a colleague, class-fellow, fellow-student.

वर्च् 1 A. (वर्चते) To shine.

वर्चस् *n*. 1 Vigour, energy, power. -2 Light, splendour. -3 Form, shape. -4 Ordure, feces. -5 Semen virile. -Comp. —ग्रहः *m*. Constipation.

वर्चस्कः *m*. 1 Brightness, lustre. -2 Vigour. -3 Feces.

वर्चस्विन् *a*. (*f*. —नी) 1 Vigorous, active. -2 Bright, brilliant.

वर्जः *m*. Leaving, abandoning.

वर्जनं *n*. 1 Leaving, abandoning. -2 Exception, exclusion. -4 Hurt, injury, killing.

वर्जं *ind*. To the exclusion of, excluding, except (at the end of comp.).

वर्जित *a*. (*f*. —ता) 1 Left out, excepted. -2 Abandoned, relinquished. -3 Excluded. -4 Destitute of, without.

वर्ज्य *a*. (*f*. —वर्ज्या) 1 To be avoided, excluded or left out. -2 With the exception of.

वर्ण् 10 U. (वर्णयति,-ते, वर्णित) 1 To paint, dye. -2 To describe, explain, delineate, illustrate. -3 To praise; extol. -4 To spread, extend. -5 To illuminate.

वर्णः *m*. 1 A colour, hue, complexion, beauty. -2 A class of men, tribe, caste (especially applied to the four principal castes, ब्राह्मण, क्षत्रिय, वैश्य and शूद्र). -3 A letter, character, sound. -4 A word, syllable. -5 Fame, glory, renown. -6 Praise. -7 Decoration. -8 Outward appearance, form, figure. -9 A cloak, mantle. -10 The order or arrangement of a subject in a song (गीतक्रम). -11 The housings of an elephant. -12 A quality, property. -13 A religious observance. -र्णं *n*. 1 Saffron. -2 A coloured unguent or perfume. -Comp. —अंका *f*. A pen. —अपसदः *m*. An outcast. —अपेत *a*. Devoid of any caste, outcast, degraded. -अर्हः *m*. A kind of bean. -आगमः *m*. Addition of a letter. —आत्मन् *m*. A word. —आश्रमाः *m. pl*. The (four) castes and stages of life. —उदकं *n*. Coloured water. —कूपिका *f*. An ink-stand.

—क्रमः 1 The order of castes or colours. -2 Alphabetical order or arrangement. —चारकः m. A painter. —ज्येष्ठः m. A Brâhmana.-तूलिः, -तूलिका, —तूली f. A pencil, paint-brush. —दं n. A kind of fragrant yellow wood —दात्री f. Turmeric. —दूतः m. A letter. —धर्मः m. The peculiar duties of a caste. —पातः m. The omission of a letter. —पुष्पं n. The flower of the globe-amaranth. —पुष्पकः m. The globe-amaranth. —प्रसादनं n. Aloe-wood. —मातृ f. A pen, pencil. -मातृका f. N. of Sarsvati. —माला, —राशिः The alphabet. —विपर्ययः m. The substitution or change of letters. —विलासिनी f. Turmeric. -विलोडकः m. 1 A house-breaker. -2 A p agiarist. —वृत्तं n. A metre regulated by the number of syllables it contains (opp. मात्रावृत्त). —व्यवस्थितिः f. The intitution of caste. —श्रेष्ठः m. A Bráhmana. —संयोगः m. Marriage between persons of the same caste. —संकरः m. 1 Confusion of castes through intermarriage. -2 Mixture or blending of colours. —संघातः, -समाम्नायः m. The alphabet.

वर्णकः m. 1 A dress of an actor. -2 A paint, a colour for painting. -3 Anything used as an unguent or pigment. -4 A bard, panegyrist.-5 Vermilion. -6 Sandal (the tree). -7 A letter, syllable. —का f. 1 A mask.-2 A paint, a colour for painting -3 Fine gold. -4 Vermilion. -5 A cloak, mantle —कं n. 1 A paint, pigment. -2 Sandal. -3 A chapter, division. -4 A circle, orb.

वर्णनं n., —ना f. 1 Painting. -2 Description, representation. -3 Writing. -4 A statement, an assertion. -5 Praise, commendation. (—ना only in this sense).

वर्णवती f. Turmeric.

वर्णसिः m. Water.

वर्णाटः m. 1 A painter.-2A singer. -3 One who maintains himself by his wife. -4 A lover.

वर्णिका f. 1 The mask or dress of an actor. -2 A colour, paint. -3 Ink. -4 A pen, pencil. -5 Chalk. -Comp. —परिग्रहः m. The assumption of a character or mask.

वर्णित p. p. (f. -ता) 1 Painted. -2 Described, represented. -3Praised.

वर्णिन् a. (f. —नी) (At the end of comp.) 1 Having the colour or appearance of. -2 Belonging to the caste of. -m. 1 A painter. -2 A scribe, writer.-3 A Brahmachárin. -4 A person of any one of the four principal castes. -Comp. —लिंगिन् a. Wearing the marks of a religious student.

वर्णिनी f. 1 A woman (in general). -2 A woman belonging to any one of the four principal castes. -3 Turmeric.

वर्णुः m. The sun.

वर्ण्य n. Saffron.

वर्त: (Usually at the end of comp.) Living, livelihood. -Comp. -जन्मन् m. A cloud. -लोहं n. Bell-metal.

वर्तकः m. 1 A quail. -2 A horse's hoof. कं n. Bell-metal.

वर्तका, वर्तकी f. A kind of quail.

वर्तन a. (f. —ना) 1 Living, staying, being. -2 Stationary. -नः m. A dwarf. -नी f. 1 A road, way -2 Living, life. -3 Pounding, grinding. -4 A spindle. —नं n. 1 Living, being. -2 Staying, residing. -3 Mode or manner of living. -4 Subsisting(at the end of comp.). -5 Livelihood. -6 Turning round, revolving.-7 A profession, occupation.

-8 Conduct, behaviour, proceeding. -9 Wages, salary, hire. -10 Commerce, traffic. -11 A spindle. -12 A globe, ball.

वर्तनिः *m* 1 The eastern part of India; the eastern country. -2 A hymn. —**नि:** *f.* 1 A way, road. -2 The eye-lashes.

वर्तमान *a.* (*f.* —**ना**) 1 Being, existing, being alive, contemporary. -2 Turning or moving round. -3 Dwelling in. —**नः** *m.* The present tense (in gram.). —**नं** *n.* Presence.

वर्तरूकः *m.* 1 A pool, puddle. -2 An eddy, a whirlpool. -3 A door-keeper. -4 N. of a river.

वर्तिः, वर्ती *f.* 1 A pad, a roll. -2 An unguent, eye-salve, collyrium or any cosmetic. -3 The wick of a lamp. -4 The projecting threads (of a cloth); the fringe. -5 The protuberance round a vessel. -6 A surgical instrument. -7 A streak, a line.

वर्तिकः *m.* A kind of quail.

वर्तिका *f.* 1 A paint-brush. -2 The wick of a lamp. -3 Colour, paint. -4 A quail.

वर्तिन् *a.* (*f.* —**नी**) (Usually at the end of comp.) 1 Resting, staying, situated. -2 Going, turning. -3 Acting, behaving. -4 Performing, practising.

वर्तिष्णु *a.* 1 Revolving. -2 Being. -3 Circular. -4 Stationary, fixed.

वर्ती (-र्ति-) रः *m.* A kind of quail.

वर्तुल *a.* (*f.*—**ला**) 1 Round, circular, globular. -**लः** *m* 1 A kind of pulse, a pea. -2 A ball. —**लं** *n.* A circle.

वर्त्मन् *n.* 1 A way, road, passage. -2 (Fig.) A course, an established usage, the manner or course of conduct. -4 Scope for action. -5 An eye-lid. -6 An edge, a border. -Comp. —**बंधः**, —**बंधकः** *m.* An affection of the eye-lids.

वर्त्मनिः, -नी *f.* A road, way, path.

वर्ध् 10 U. (**वर्धयति,-ते**; also **वर्धापयति**) 1 To cut, divide. -2 To fill.

वर्धः *m.* 1 Cutting, dividing. -2 Increase, augmentation. —**र्धं** *n.* 1 Lead. -2 Red lead.

वर्धकः *m.* 1 A carpenter.

वर्धकिः, वर्धकिन् *m.* A carpenter.

वर्धन *a.* (*f.* **ना**) 1 Increasing, enlarging, magnifying. -**नः** *m.* 1 A bestower of prosperity. -2 A tooth growing over another tooth. N. of Siva. —**नी** *f.* 1 A broom. A water-jar of a particular shape. —**नं** *n.* 1 Growing, thriving. Growth, increase, prosperity. -3 Elevation. -4 Exhilaration (of spirits). -5 Educating, rearing. -6 Cutting, dividing. -7 A restorative.

वर्धमान *a.* (*f.* —**ना**) Growing, increasing. —**नः** *m.* 1 The castor-oil plant. -2 A kind of riddle. -3 N. of Vishnu. -4 N. of a district (perhaps the modern Bardvâna). -5 Sweet citron. —**नः** *m.*, —**नं** *n.* 1 A pot or dish of a particular shape &c. -2 A kind of mystical diagram. -3 A house having no door on the south side. -**ना** *f.* N. of a district (the modern Bardvâna).

वर्धापनं *n.* 1 Cutting, dividing. -2 The ceremony of cutting the umbilical cord. -3 A festival on which wishes for prosperity and other congratulatory expressions are offered.

वर्धित *p. p.* (*f.* —**ता**) 1 Grown, increased. -2 Cut.

वर्धिष्णु *a.* Growing, increasing.

वर्ध्रं *n.* 1 A leather strap or thong. -2 Leather. -3 Lead.

वार्ध्रिका, ध्री f. A leather strap or thong.

वर्मणः m. The orange tree.

वर्मन् n. 1 An armour, a coat of mail. -2 Shelter, protection -3 Bark, rind. -m. An affix added to the names of Kshatriyas; as चंद्रवर्मन्. -Comp. -हर a. 1 Wearing armour. -2 Old enough to wear armour.

वर्मिः m. A kind of fish.

वर्य a. (f. -र्या) 1 To be chosen or selected. -2 Excellent, chief (mostly at the end of comp.). -र्यः m. The God of love. —र्या f. 1 A girl choosing her own husband. -2 A girl in general.

वर्वटः m. See बर्बटः.

वर्वणा f. See बर्बणा.

वर्वरः m. 1 A barbarian. -2 A blockhead. -3 An outcast. -4 Curly hair. -5 The clash of weapons. -6 A mode of dancing. -रं n. 1 Yellow sandal-wood. -2 Vermilion. -3 Gum-myrrh.

वर्वरकं n. A kind of sandal-wood.

वर्वरीकः m. 1 Curly hair. -2 A kind of basil.

वर्वू (-र्बु-) रः m. A kind of tree.

वर्षः m., वर्षं n. 1 Raining, rain, a shower of rain -2 Sprinkling, a shower of anything. -3 Seminal effusion. -4 A year (usually only n.). -5 A division of the world, a continent. -6 India (भारतवर्ष). -7 A cloud (only m.). -Comp. —अंशः, —अंशकः, -अंगः m. A month. -आर्चिस् m. The planet Mars. —आघोषः m. A frog. -आमदः m. A pea-cock. -उपलः m. Hail. -करः m. A cloud. -करी f. A cricket. —कोशः, -कोषः m. 1 A month. -2 An astrologer. -गिरिः, -पर्वतः m. A mountain-range supposed to separate the different divisions of the world from one another (they are seven). -धरः m. 1 A cloud. -2 A eunuch, an attendant on the women's apartments. -पूगः m. A series or collection of years. -प्रतिबंधः m. A drought. —प्रियः m. The Châtaka bird. -वरः m. A eunuch, an attendant on the women's apartments. -वृद्धिः f A birth-day. -वर्द्धनं n. A religious ceremony, performed every year on the birth-day, which is supposd bring on an increase of the duration of life.

वर्षणं n. 1 Raining, rain. -2 Sprinkling, showering down (fig. also).

वर्षणिः f. 1 Raining. -2 A sacrifice. -3 An act, action. -4 Living, abiding.

वर्षा f. (sing. or pl.) 1 The rainy season, the monsoon. -2 Rain (sing. in this sense). -Comp. -भूः m. 1 A frog. -2 A kind of insect (इंद्रगोप). —भूः, -भ्वी f. A female frog or a little frog. -रात्रः m. 1 A night in the rainy season. -2 The rainy season.

वार्षिकं n. Aloe-wood.

वर्षिष्ठ a. (f. -ष्ठा) 1 Oldest, very old. -2 Strongest. -3 Largest.

वर्षीयस् a. (f. सी) 1 Older, very old, -2 Stronger.

वर्षुक a. (f. -की) Raining, pouring down water. -Comp. -अब्दः, -अंबुदः m. A rain-cloud.

वर्ष्म n. The body.

वर्ष्मन् n. 1 Body, form. -2 A measure, height. -3 A handsome or lovely form.

वर्ह वर्ह वर्हण वर्हिण वार्हिन् वार्हिस्	See बर्ह्, बर्ह, बर्हण, बर्हिण, बर्हिन्, बर्हिस्.

वल् 1 A. (वलते, rarely वलति, वालित) 1 To go, hasten. -2 Turn, move round

–3 To be drawn or attracted towards. –4 To increase.–5 To cover, enclose. –6 To be enclosed or surrounded. –With वि– To move to and fro, roll about. सं– To mix, blend, connect, unite with.

वलं *n*. See बलं.

वलक्ष *a*. See बलक्ष.

वलग्नः *m*., –ग्नं *n*. The waist.

वलनं *n*.1 Moving, turning towards, moving round in a circle. –2 (In astr) Deflection. –3 Agitation, excitement.

वलभिः, –भी *f*. (Also frequently writen बडभिः, -भी) 1 The sloping roof, the wooden frame of a thatch. –2 The topmost part (of a house). –3 N. of a town in Saurâshtra.

वलंबः *m*. See अवलंबः.

वलयः *m*., यं *n*.1 A bracelet, armlet. –2 A ring, coil. –3 The zone or girdle of a married woman.–4 A circle, circumference. –5 An enclosure, a bower. —यः *m*. 1 A fence, hedge. –2 A branch. –3 A sore throat.

वलयित *a*. (*f*.—ता) 1 Surrounded, enclosed. 2 Whirling round.-3 Curled.

वलाक See बलाक.

वलाकिन् See बलाकिन्. [frog.

वलासकः *m*. 1 The cuckoo. –2 A

वलाहकः See बलाहक.

वलिः, –ली *f*. (Also written बलिः, बली) 1 A fold or wrinkle. -2 The ridge of a thatched roof. -3 A line made on the body with fragrant unguents. -Comp —मुद् *a*. Having curls (as hair). -मुखः, -वदनः *m*. A monkey.

वलिकः *m*., –कं *n*. The edge of a thatched roof.

वलित *p. p*. (*f*. -ता) 1 Moving. –2 Moved, turned round. –3 Surrounded. –4 Wrinkled. –5 Cast, darted.

वलिन, वलिभ *a*. (*f*.–ना,–भा) Wrinkled, shriveled.

वलिमत *a*. (*f*. -ती) Wrinkled.

वलिर *a*. (*f*. रा) Squint-eyed.

वलिशं *n*., –शी *f*. A fish-hook. [roof.

वलीकं *n*. The edge of a thatched

वलुकः *m*. A kind of bird. –कं *n*. 1 The root of lotus.

वलुल *a*. (*f*. –ला) Strong, powerful.

वल्कः *m*., वल्कं *n*. 1 The bark of a tree. –2 The scales of a fish. –3 A part, fragment (खंड). –Comp. –तरुः *m*. A kind of tree. –द्रुमः *m*. The birch tree.

वल्कलः *m*., -लं *n*. 1 The bark of a tree -2 A bark-garment. –Comp. —संवीत *a*. Clad in bark.

वल्किलः *m*. A thorn.

वल्कुटं *n*. Bark, rind.

वल्ग् 1 U. (वल्गति, -ते, वल्गित) 1 To go, move –2 To leap, bound, gallop (fig. also). –3 To be pleased. –4 To eat. –5 To swagger, vaunt.

वल्गनं *n*. Leaping, galloping.

वल्गा *f*. 1 A bridle, rein.

वल्गु *a*. 1 Lovely, beautiful, attractive. -2 Sweet. -ल्गुः *m*. A goat. -Comp —पत्रः *m*. A kind of wild pulse. [chest.

वल्गुलिका *f*. 1 A cock roach. –2 A

वल्मिक, वल्मिकि *m*., *n*. See वल्मीक.

वल्मी *f*. An ant. -Comp. —कूटं *n*. An ant-hill.

वल्मीकः *m*.,-कं *n*. An ant-hill, a hillock thrown up by white ants, moles &c. -कः *m*. Elephantiasis. -2 The poet Válmiki.

वल्ल् 1 A. (वल्लते)1 To cover. –2 To go, move.

वल्लः *m*.1 Covering.-2 A weight of three *Gunjâs*. –3 Another weight of one *Gunjâ* and a half ; or of two *Gunjâs* (in medicine).-4 Prohibiting. –5 Winnowing corn. –6 A Mâsha of silver.

वल्लकी *f.* The (Indian) lute.

वल्लभ *a.* (*f.* -भा) 1 Beloved, dear. -2 Supreme. -भः *m.* 1 A lover, husband. -2 A favourite. -3 An overseer. -4 A chief herdsman. -5 A good horse (one with auspicious marks). —भा *f* A beloved female, mistress, wife. -Comp. —आचार्यः *m.* N. of the celebrated founder of a Vaishnava sect. -पालः *m.* A groom.

वल्लभायितं *n.* A mode of sexual enjoyment.

वल्लं *n.* 1 Aloe-wood. -2 A bower. -3 A thicket. -4 A branching foot-stalk.

वल्लरिः, —री *f.* 1 A creeping plant. -2A branching foot-stalk.

वल्लवः *m.* (*f.* -वी) See बल्लव.

वल्लिः *f.* 1 A creeper, a creeping or winding plant.-2The earth.-Comp. —दूर्वा *f.* A kind of grass.

वल्ली *f.* A creeping plant, creeper. -Comp. —जं *n.* Pepper. -वृक्षः *m.* The *Sála* tree.

वल्लूरं *n.* 1 A bower, an arbour. -2 A wood, thicket. -3 A branching foot-stalk.-4 An uncultivated field. -5 A desert, wild, wilderness. -6 Dried flesh.

वल्लूरः *m.* 1 Dried flesh. -2 The flesh of a hog. -रं *n.* 1 A thicket. -2 An uncultivated field. -3 Salt soil. -4 A desert.

वल्ह् 1 A (वल्हते) 1 To be pre-eminent. -2 To kill, hurt.-3To speak. -4 To give. [-2 To shine.

वल्ह् 10 U. (वल्हयति) 1 To speak.

वल्हिक, वल्हीक See बाल्हिक, बल्हीक.

वश् 2 P. (वष्टि, उशित) 1 To wish, desire. -2 To favour. -3 To shine.

वश *a.* (*f.* —शा) 1 Influenced by, under the influence or control of, as शोकवशः मृत्युवशः &c. -2 Submiss ve, compliant. -3 Humbled, tamed. -4 Fascinated.5Subdued by charms.-शः *m.*,-शं *n.* 1 Wish.-2Influence,control, authority, submission. वशात् (abl.) 'Through the force, power or influence of','on account of',for the purpose of'.-3Being tamed.-4 Birth. -शः *m.* The residence of harlots.-Comp.- —अनुग, -ग, -वर्तिन् (also वशंवत) *a.* Obedient to the will of another, submissive, subject. (*m.*) A servant. —आल्यकः *m.* 1 A porpoise. -ग *a* Subject, obedient. (—गा *f.*) An obedient wife.

वशंवद *a.* (*f.* -दा) Submissive, subject,under the influence of (lit. and fig.).

वशका *f.* An obedient wife.

वशा *f.* 1 A woman. -2 A wife. -3 A daughter. -4 A husband's sister. -5 A cow. -6 A barren woman. -7 A barren cow. -8 A female elephant.

वशिः *m.* Subjugation.

वशिक *a.* (*f.* -का) Void, empty. —का *f.* Aloe-wood.

वशिन् *a.* (*f.* -नी) 1 Powerful. -2 Being under control, subdued, submissive. -*m.* A sage.

वशिनी *f.* The Samī tree.

वशिरः *m.* A sort of pepper. —रं *n.* Sea-salt.

वशिष्ठः *m* See वसिष्ठः.

वशीकरणं *n.* 1 Fascinating, attracting. -2 A cause of attraction or allurement. -3 Subduing, subjugation.

वश्य *a.* (*f.* —श्या) 1 Capable of being subdued, controllable, governable. -2 Subdued, conquered. -3 Tamed,humbled.-4 Subject,dependent. —श्यः *m.* A servant, dependant. —श्या *f.* An humble or obedient wife. —श्यं *n*. Cloves.

वश्यका *f*. See वश्या.

वष् 1 P. (वषति) To hurt, kill.

वषट् *ind*. An exclamation used on offering an oblation to a deity, (with dat. of the deity) ; इंद्राय वषट्, पूष्णे वषट् &c. -Comp. —कर्तृ *m*. The priest who makes the oblation with the exclamation वषट्. —कार *m*. The formula or exclamation वषट्.

वष्क् 1 A. (वष्कते) To go, move.

वष्कयः *m*. A calf one year old.

वष्कयणी, वष्कायिणी *f*. A cow that has full-grown calves.

वस् 1 P. (वसति ; sometimes वसते, वस्तुं, उषित) 1 To dwell, live, reside (usually with loc ; but sometimes acc.) -2 To be, exist. -3 To spend, pass (as time) (with acc.).

वस् 2 A. (वस्ते) To wear, put on.

वस् 4 P. (वस्यति) 1 To be straight. -2 To be firm, -3 To fix.

वस् 10 U. (वासयति,-ते) 1 To cut, divide -2 To love. -3 To accept. -4 To hurt, kill. -5 To offer.

वस् 10 U. (वासयति,-ते) To scent, perfume.

वसतिः,—ती *f*. 1 Dwelling, residing. -2 A house, habitation. -3 A receptacle, reservoir (fig.). -4 A camp, halting place (शिबिर). -5 A Jai a monastery.

वसथं *n*. An abode, dwelling, a nest of birds).

वसनं *n*. 1 Dwelling, residing. -2 A house, residence. -3 Dressing, clothing. -4 A garment, clothes. -5 An ornament worn round the loins.

वसंतः *m*. 1 The spring, vernal season. -2 Spring personified and regarded as a companion of Kámadeva. -3 Dysentery. -5 Small-pox. -5 In dramas) A nick-name for the Vidúshaka or buffoon. -Comp. —उत्सवः *m*. The vernal festival. —घोषिन् *m*. A cuckoo. —जा *f*. 1 The Vâsanti or Màdhavi creeper. -2 The spring festival. —तिलकः *m*, -का *f*., —कं *n*. N. of a metre. —दूतः *m*. 1 The cuckoo. -2 The month called Chaitra. -3 The musical mode हिंदोल. -4 The mango tree —दूती *f*. The trumpet-flower. —द्रुः, -द्रुमः *m*. The mango tree. —पंचमी *f*. The fifth day in the bright half of Mágha. —बंधुः, —योधः, —सखः *m* Epithets of the God of love.

वसा *f*. 1 The marrow of the flesh, fat. -2 Brain. -Comp. —आढ्यः, -आढ्यकः *m*. The Gangetic porpoise. —छटा *f*. The mass of the brain. -पायिन् *m*. A God.

वसिः *m*. 1 Clothes. -2 A dwelling.

वसित *p. p*. (*f*. —ता) 1 Worn, put on. -2 Stored (as grain). —तं *n*. Abode, residence.

वसिरं *n*. Sea-salt.

वसिष्ठः (also वशिष्ठः) *m*. N. of a sage, the family priest of the solar roce of kings and author of several Vedic hymns. -2 N. of the author of a Smriti.

वसु *n*. 1 Wealth, riches. -2 A jewel, gem. -3 Gold. -4 Water. -5 A thing, substance. -6 A kind of salt. -7 A medicinal root (वृद्धि). -8 A yellow kind of kidney-bean. —वसुः *m*. 1 N. of a class of deities (usually pl. in this sense); the *Vasus* are eight in number. -2 The number 'eight'. -3 N. of Kubera. -4 Of Siva. -5 Of Agni. -6 A tree. -7 A lake. -8 A rein. -9 The tie of a yoke. -10 A ray of light. -11 The sun. —*f*. 1 A ray of light. -2 Radiance. -3 A medicinal root (वृद्धि).

-Comp. —ओकसारा *f.* I N. of Amarávatí, the city of Indra. -2 Of Alakâ the city of Kubera. -3 Of a river attached to Amarâvtí and Alakâ. —कीटः, —कृमिः *m.* A beggar. —दा *f.* The earth. -देवः *m.* N. of the father of Krishna. -देवता, —देव्या *f.* The asterism called Dhanishthá. -देव्या *f.* The ninth day of a lunar fortnight. —धर्मिका *f.* A crystal. —धा *f.* The earth. —धारा, -भारा *f.* The capital of Kubera. -प्राणः *m.* An epithet of Agni. — रेतस् *m.* Fire. -रोचिस् *m.* A sacrifice. -श्रेष्ठं *n.* 1 Wrought gold. -2 Silver. -षेणः *m.*N. of Karna. -स्थली *f.* N. of the city of Kubera.

वसु (-स्-) कः *m.* The plant called Arka.-कं *n.* I Sea-salt.-2 Fossil-salt.

वसुंधरा *f.* The earth.

वसुमती *f.* The earth.

वसुलः *m.* A God, deity.

वस्रा *f.* A harlot, prostitute.

वस्क् I A. (वस्कते) To go, move.

वस्कयः *m.* See वष्कयः.

वस्कयणी *f.* See वष्कयणी.

वस्कराटिका *f.* A scorpion.

वस्त 10 U. (वस्तयति,-ते) I To hurt, kill.-2To beg,solicit.-3To go,move.

वस्तं *n.* An abode. -स्तः *m.* A goat.

वस्तकं *n.* An artificial salt.

वस्तिः *m.*, *f.* 1 Dwelling, staying. -2 The abdomen. -3 The pelvis -4 The bladder. -5 A syringe, clyster. -Comp. -मलं *n.* Urine. -शिरस् *n.* The pipe of a clyster.-शोधनं *n.* Aiduretic.

वस्तु *n.* I A really existing thing, a reality. -2 A thing in general, article, matter. -3 Wealth, possessions.-4 Essence, natural or essential property. -5 Stuff (of which a thing is made),ingredients(fig.also). -6 The plot of a drama or of any poetic composition. -उत्थापनं *n.* The production of any incident in a drama by means of magic. -उपमा *f.* A variety of Upamâ according to Dandin where the साधारणधर्म or common quality is omitted.

वस्तुतस् *ind.* I In fact; really, actually. -2 Essentially, substantially. -3 As a matter of course, indeed.

वस्त्यं *n.* A house, an abode.

वस्त्रं*n.*A garment, clothes, raiment, apparel. -Comp. -अगारः *m.*,-अगारं *n.*, -गृहं*n.* A tent.-कुट्टिमं *n.*I A tent.-2 An umbrella. —निर्णेजकः *m.* A washerman. —पुत्रिका *f.* A doll, puppet. —भेदकः, —भेदिन *m* A tailor.

वस्नं *n.*I Hire, wages (in this sense *m.* also). -2 Dwelling, abiding. -3 Wealth, substance. -4 A cloth, clothes. -5 A skin. -6 Price.

वस्ननं *n.* A girdle, zone.

वस्नसा *f.* A tendon, nerve.

वंह् 10 U. (वंहयति,-ते) To cause to shine.

वह् 10 U. (वहति, ते, वोढुं, ऊढ ; *pass.* उह्यते) I To carry, bear, convey, (oft with two acc.)-2 To cause to move onward. -3 To bear, support, sustain.-4 To carry off, take away. -5 To marry. -6 To have, possess. -7 To assume, exhibit. -8 To look to, attend to.-9 To feel, experience. -10 (Intransitive in this and the following senses) To be borne or carried on. -11 To flow (as rivers). -12 To blow (as wind). -13 To breathe.

With अति— To pass (as time). अप— I To remove, carry off. -2 To deduct. आ— I To cause, to bring about. -2 To flow. -3 To have, to possess. उद्— I To raise, to bear up, to elevate. -2 To marry. -3 To bear, to bear the burden of. -4 To wear. -5 To possess, to have. उप—

To bring about, to commence. नि— To bear up, to support. निस्— To be finished. परि— To overflow. प्र— 1 To draw, carry. -2 To blow. -3 To flow. -4 To carry, waft (as scent). -5 To bear the burden of. वि— To marry. सम्— 1 To bear along.-2 To marry, to take a wife. -3 To press together. -4 To display, to manifest.

Causal (वाहयति,-ते) 1 To cause to draw or carry. -2 To go over, to traverse. With. अति—To lead (life). आ— To invoke. निस्— To perform, manage, complete. सम्— To press together, to rub.

वहः *m.* 1 Bearing, supporting. -2 The shoulder of an ox.-3 A vehicle or conveyance in general. -4 A horse. -5 Air, wind. -6 A way, road. -7 A male river (नद). -8 A measure of four *Dronas*.-9A current.

वहतः *m.* 1 A traveller. -2 An ox.

वहतिः *m.* 1 An ox. -2 Air, wind. -3 A friend, adviser.

वहती, वहा *f.* A river, stream in general.

वहतुः *m.* An ox.

वहनं *n.* 1 Carrying, conveying. -2 Supporting. -3 Flowing. -4 A vehicle. -5 A boat.

वहंतः *m.* 1 Wind. -2 An infant.

वहल *a.* (*f.* —ला) See बहल. —लः *m.* A boat.

वहित्रं, वहित्रकं *n.*, वहित्री *f.* A raft, boat, vessel.

वाहिष्क *a.* (*f.* -ष्का)Outer, external.

वहिस् *ind.* See बहिस्.

वहेडकः *m.* The Bibhítaka tree.

वह्निः *m.* 1 The digestive faculty. -2 Digestion, appetite. -Comp. —काष्ठं *n.* A kind of agallochum.-गंधः *m.* 1 Incense. -2 Resin. —गर्भः *m.* 1 A bamboo. -2 The Samî tree. —दीपकः *m.* Safflower.—भोग्यं *n.* Clarified butter. —मित्रः *m.* 1 Air, wind. —रेतस् *m.* 1 An epithet of Siva. -2 Gold. —लोहं, -लोहकं *n.* Copper. -वर्णं *n.* The red water-lily. -वल्लभः *m.* Resin. —वीजं *n.* 1 Gold. -2 The common lime. -शिखं *n.* 1 Saffron. -2 Safflower. —सखः *m.* The wind.

वह्यं *n.* 1 A carriage. -2 A vehicle in general.

वाल्हिकाः, वल्हीकाः *m. pl.* N. of a country and its people.

वा *ind.* (This word cannot stand at the beginning of a sentence , or, either...or ; (in this sense वा is) like च, repeated after each word or clause, or is placed after the last). -2 And, as well, also. -3 Like, as. -4 Optionally (in this sense वा occurs in Grammatical sútras of Pánini). -5 Sometimes वा is merely an expletive.

Sometimes वा is added to interrogative pronoun and its derivatives like इव or नाम, and may be translated by ' possibly', 'I should like to know'.

When repeated वा has the sense of ' either-or, ' ' whether-or '. अथवा or, or rather, or else. न वा not,neither, nor; यदि वा or if; यद्वा or,or else; किंवा whether.

वा 2 P. (वाति, वात or वान) 1 To blow. -2 To go, move. -3 To strike, injure. —*Caus* (वापयति,-ते) 1 To cause to blow. -2 (वाजयति,-ते) To shake. With. निस्— 1 To put out,to extinguish. -2 To alleviate, to cool. आ— To blow. निस्— 1 To blow. -2 Cool,to be cool.-3 To be extinguished, to be extinct. प्र—, वि– To blow.

वांशी *f.* Bamboo manna.

वांश *a.* (*f.* -शी) Made of bamboo.

वाकं *n.* A flight of cranes. —कः *m.* Speech,uttering; as in नमोवाकं प्रशास्महे.

वाकुलं *n.* See बाकुल.

वाक्यं *n.* 1 Speech, a saying. -2 A sentence, period (complete utterance of a thought).-3 An argument or syllogism (in logic). -4 A precept, rule, an aphorism. -Comp. —अर्थोपमा *f.* A variety of Upamá according to Dandin. —आलापः *m.* A discourse. —खंडनं *n.* Refutation of an assertion or argument.—पद्धतिः *f.* Diction, style. —प्रबंधः *m.* A treatise, connected composition. —प्रयोगः *m.* Employment of speech, use of language.

वागरः *m.* 1 A sage. -2 A learned Brâhmana. -3 A hero. -4 A touch-stone, whet-stone. -5 An impediment. -6 Submarine fire.-7 A wolf.

वागा *f.* A bridle.

वागुरा *f.* A trap, snare. -Comp. —वृत्तिः *f.* Livelihood obtained by catching wild animals. [catcher.

वागुरिकः *m.* A fowler, hunter, deer-

वाग्मिन् *a.* (*f.* —नी) 1 Eloquent, oratorical. -2 Talkative. -3 Verbose, wordy. —*m* 1 An orator, an eloquent man. -2 N. of Brihspati. -3 N. of Vishnu.

वाग्य *a.* (*f* —ग्या) 1 Speaking little, speaking cautiously. -2 Speaking truly. —ग्यः *m.* Modesty, humility.

वांकः *m.* The ocean

वांछ् 1 P. (वांछति) To wish, desire.

वाङ्मय *a.* (*f.* —यी) Consisting of words. 2 Relating to speech or words. -3 Endowed with speech. -4 Eloquent, oratorical. —यं *n.* 1 Speech, language. -2 Eloquence. -3 Rhetoric. -यी *f.* The Goddess Sarasvatî.

वाच् *f.* 1 A word, an expression (opp. अर्थ). -2 Language, speech. -3 A voice, sound.-4 An assertion, a statement.-5 An assurance, a promise.-6 A phrase, proverb, saying. -7 N. of Sarasvatî, the Goddess of speech.-Comp.-अर्थः(वागर्थ) *m.* A word and its meaning. —आडंबरः (वागाडंबरः) *m.* Verbosity, bombast. -ईशः (वागीशः) *m.* 1 An orator, an eloquent man. -2 An epithet of Brihaspati. -3 An epithet of Brahman (*m.*). -4 The lunar mansion called Pushya) (-शा *f.*) N. of Sarasvatî. -ईश्वरः (वागीश्वरः) *m.* 1 An orator, eloquent man. -2 An epithet of Brahman (*m.*). (री *f.*) Sarasvati, the Goddess of speech. -ऋषभः (वागृषभः) *m.* An eloquent or learned man.-कीरः (वाक्कीरः) *m.* A wife's brother. —गुलिः, —गुलिकः *m.* The betel-bearer of a king &c. —चपल *a.* Frivolous or inconsiderate in talk. —चापल्यं *n.* Idle or frivolous talk. —छलं (वाक्छलं) *n.* An evasive reply. —जालं (वाग्जालं) *n.* Empty talk. -डंबरः *m.* 1 Bombast. -2 Eloquent language. —दंडः *m.* 1 A reprimand, reproof. -2 Control over words. -दत्त (वाग्दत्त) *a.* Promised, affianced, betrothed. —दलं (वाग्दलं) *n.* A lip. —दानं *n* Betrothal. —देवता, —देवी *f.* Sarasvatî, the Goddess of speech. —निश्चयः (वाङ्निश्चयः) *m.* A marriage contract. —पटु *a.* Skilful in speech, eloquent. —पतिः *m.* 1 N of Brihspati (in this sense वाचस्पतिः is also used) -2 The constellation Pushya. -प्रलापः *m.* Eloquence.-मुखं *n.* The introduction of a speech, an exordium, a preface.—यमः *m.* One who has controlled his speech, a sage. —यामः *m.* A dumb man. —युद्धं *n.* A war of words, (hot) debate or discussion, controversy. —विदग्धः *a.* Skilled in speech. —संयमः *m.* Restraint or control of speech.

वाचः *m.* 1 A kind of fish. -2 The plant मदन.

वाचंयम *a.* Silent, taciturn. -मः *m.* A sage who maintains rigid silence.

वाचक *a.* (*f.* —का) 1 Speaking, declaring, explanatory. -2 Expressing, signifying, denoting. -3 Verbal. -कः *m.* 1 A speaker.-2 A reader. 3 A significan word. -4 A messenger. -Comp. —पदं *n.* A significant word.

वाचनं *n.* 1 Reading, reciting. -2 Declaration, proclamation.

वाचनकं *n.* A riddle.

वाचनिक *a.* (*f.*—की) Verbal, expressed by words.

वाचस्पतिः *m.*1 An epithet of Brihaspati, preceptor of the Gods. -2The constellation Pushya. [oration.

वाचस्पत्यं *n.* An eloquent speech,

वाचा *f.* 1 Speech. -2 A text, an aphorism. -3 An oath. [rulous.

वाचाट *a.* (*f.* —टा) Talkative, gar-

वाचाल *a.*(*f.* -ला) 1 Noisy. -2 Talkative, garrulous. -3 Boasting.

वाचिक *a.* (*f.* का, -की) 1 Expressed by words. -2 Oral, verbal. —कं *n.* 1 A message, an oral communication. -2 News, tidings.

वाचोयुक्ति *a.* Skilled in speech, eloquent. —क्तिः *f.* 1 A declaration, announcement, speech. -2 Good or clever speech.

वाच्य *a.* (*f.* -च्या) 1 To be spoken, told or said. -2 To be spoken to or addressed. -3 To be predicated, attributive. -4 Expressed (as the meaning of a word). -4 Blamable. -च्यं *n.* 1 Blame, censure. -2 The expressed meaning of a word. -3 A predicate. -4 The voice of a verb. -Comp. -अर्थः *m.* The expressed meaning. -चित्रं *n.* One of the two kinds of the third or lowest (अधम) kind of *Kávya* or poetry in which the charm lies in the expression of a striking or fanciful idea (opp. शब्दचित्र).-वर्जं*n.* Harsh language.

वाजः *m.* 1 A wing. -2 A feather. -3 The feather of an arrow. -4 Battle. -5 Sound. —जं *n.* 1 Clarified butter.-2 An oblation of rice offered at an obsequial ceremony. -3 Water. -4 A prayer or *mantra* with which a sacrifice is concluded. -5 Speed. -Comp.-पेयः *m.*, -यं *n.* N. of a particular sacrifice. -सनः *m.* 1 N. of Vishnu. -2 Of Siva. —सानिः *m.* The sun.

वाजसनेयः*m.* N. of Yàjnavalkya, the author of the Sukla Yajurveda.

वाजसनेयिन् *m.* 1 N. of Yájnavalkya, the author and founder of the white or Sukla Yajurveda. -2 One belonging to the sect of the Vâjasaneyins.

वाजिन् *m.* 1 A horse. -2 An arrow. -3 A bird. -4 A follower of the Vâjasaneyin branch of the Yajurveda —नी *f.* 1 A mare. -2 N. of Ushas (dawn). -Comp. —पृष्ठः *m.* The globe-amaranth. —भक्षः *m.* A chickpea -भोजनः *m.* A kind of kidney-bean. -मेधः *m.* A horse-sacrifice. -शाला *f.* A stable.

वाजीकरणं *n.* Stimulating or exciting desire by aphrodisiacs.

वांछ् 1 P. (वांछति, वांछित) 1 To wish, desire. -2 To seek for, pursue.

वांछनं *n.* Wishing, desiring.

वांछा *f.* A wish, desire.

वांछित *p. p.* (*f.* —ता) Wished, desired. -तं *n.* A wish, desire.

वाटः *m.*, वाटं *n.* 1 An enclosure. -2 A garden, park. -3 A road. -4 The groin. -5 A sort of grain. -Comp. —धानः *m.* The descendant of an outcast Bráhmana by a Bràhmana female.

वाटिका *f.* 1 The site of a house. -2 An orchard, a garden.

वाटी *f.* 1 The site of a house. -2 A house. -3 A court, an enclosure. -4 A garden, park. -5 A road. -6 The groin. -7 A kind of grain.

वाट्या *f.*, वाट्यालः *m.*, वाट्याली *f.* N. of the plant अतिबला.

वाड्ड 1 A. (वाडते) To bathe, dive,

वाडव: *m.* 1 Submarine fire. -2 A Brâhmana. —वं *n.* A stud or collection of mares. [two Asvins.

वाडवेय: *m.* A bull. -यौ *m. dual*, The

वाडव्यं*n.* A collection of Bráhmanas.

वाढ *a.* (*f.*-ढा) See बाढ.

वाण: *m.* See बाण:.

वाणि:*f.* 1 Weaving.-2 A weaver's loom.-3Speech. -4 N. of Sarasvatí.

वाणिज: *m.* A merchant.

वाणिजिक: *m.* 1 A merchant.-2 A cheat, rogue.-3The submarine fire.

वाणिज्यं *n.* Trade, traffic.

वाणिनी *f.* 1 A clever or intriguing woman. -2 A dancing girl, an actress. -3 A wanton woman.

वाणी *f.* 1 Speech, language. -2 Power of speech. -3 Sound, voice. -4 A literary production, a work or composition. -5 Praise. -6 Sarasvatí, the Goddess of learning.

वात *p. p.* (*f.* —ता) 1 Blown. -2 Desired or wished for. —त: *m.* 1 Air, wind. -2 The God of wind. -3 Wind, as one of the three humours of the body. -4 Gout, rheumatism. -5 A faithless lover. -Comp. -अट: *m.* 1 An antelope. -2 A horse of the sun. -अंड: *m.* A disease of the testicles. -अतिसार: *m.* Dysentery caused by some derangement or vitiation of the bodily wind. —अर्थ *n.* A leaf. —अयन: *m.* A horse. (-नं *n.*) 1 A window, an air-hole. -2 A porch, portico. -3 A pavilion. -अयु: *m.* An antelope. —अरि: *m.* The castor-oil tree. -2 N. of several plants. -अश्व: *m.* A very fleet or swift horse. -आमोदा *f.* Musk. -आलि:, —ली *f.* A whirl-wind. —आहत *a.* 1 Shaken by the wind. -2 Affected by gout. -आहति: *f.* A violent gust of wind. -ऋद्धि: *f.* 1 Excess of wind. -2 A mace, stick tipped with iron. -कर्मन् *n.* Breaking wind. —कुंडलिका *f.* A painful flow of urine. -कुंभ: *m.* The part of an elephant's forehead below the frontal sinuses. —केतु: *m.* Dust. -केलि: *m.* 1 Amorous discourse. -2 The marks of finger-nails on the person of a lover. —गामिन् *m.* A bird. —गुल्म: *m.* 1 A high wind. -2 Rheumatism. -ज्वर: *m.* Fever arising from vitiated wind. -ध्वज: *m.* 1 A cloud. -2 Dust. -प्रमी *m. f.* A swift antelope. -मंडली *f.* A whirl-wind.-मृग: *m.* A swift antelope. —रक्तं,—शोणितं *n.* Acute gout. —रंग: *m.* The fig-tree. —रूप: *m.* 1 A storm.-2 The rainbow. -3 A bribe. —वस्ति: *f.* Suppression of urine.-वृद्धि: *f.* Swelled testicle. —वैरिन् *m.* The castor-oil tree. —शीर्षं *n.* The lower belly. -शूलं *n.* Colic with flatulence. —सारथि:*m.* Fire. [a plant.

वातक: *m.* 1 A paramour. -2 N. of

वातकिन् *a.* (*f.* —नी) Gouty.

वातर *a.* (*f.* —रा) 1 Stormy,windy. -2 Swift.

वातरायण: *m.* 1 An arrow.-2 An arrow's flight. -3 A peak, summit. -4 A saw. -5 A mad or intoxicated man.-6 An idler. -7 The Sarala or pine tree.

वातल *a.* (*f.* —ली) 1 Stormy,windy. -2 Flatulent. —ल: *m.* 1 Wind. -2 The chickpea (चणक).

वातापि: *m.* N. of a demon said to have been eaten up and digested by Agastya. -Comp. -द्विष्,-सूदन:,-हन् *m.* Epithets of Agastya.

वाति: *m.* 1 The sun. -2 Wind, air. -3 The moon. -Comp. —ग:,-गम: *m.* 1 A mineralogist -2 The egg-plant (वातिगण: in the same sense).

वातिक *a.* (*f.* -की) 1 Stormy,windy. -2 Gouty, rheumatic. -2 Mad. -क:

m. Fever caused by a vitiated state of the wind.

वातीयं *n.* Rice-gruel.

वातुल *a.* (*f.*-ला) 1 Affected by wind-disease.-2 Mad.-लः *m.* A whirl-wind.

वातुलिः *m.*, *f* A large bat.

वातूल *a.* See वातुल.

वातृ *m.* Air, wind.

वात्या *f.* A hurricane.-Comp -चक्रं *n.* A whirl-wind.

वात्सकं *n.* A herd of calves.

वात्सल्यं *n.* 1 Affection (towards one's offspring.affection in general. -2 Fondness,affection or partiality.

वात्सिः, वात्सी *f.* The daughter of a Sudra woman by a Brâhmana.

वात्स्यायनः *m.* 1 N. of the author of the Kâmasútras. -2 N. of the author of a commentary on the Nyâya Sútras.

वादः *m.* 1 Talking, speaking. -2 Speech, talk. -3 A statement, an assertion. -4 An account. -5 Discussion, controversy. -6 A replay. -7 An exposition, explanation.-8A theory, doctrine (as in परिणामवादः *m.* The theory of evolution. नास्तिकवादः *m.* The doctrine of atheism). -9 Sounding, sound. -10 Report, rumour.-11 A plaint (in law). -Comp. —अनुवादौ *m. dual* Plaint and reply, accusation and defence. -2 Dispute,controversy. -ग्रस्त *a.* Disputed, in dispute. —चंचु *a.* Clever in repartees. —प्रतिवादः *m.* Controversy. —युद्धं *n.* A dispute, controversy. —वादिन् *m.* A Jaina. —विवादः *m.* Disputation, discussion. [speaker.

वादकः *m.* 1 A musician. -2 A

वादनं *n.* 1 Sounding. -2 Instrumental music.

वादर *a.* (*f.* —री) Made or consisting of cotton. —रा *f.* The cotton shrub. -रं *n.* Cotton cloth.

वादरंगः *m.* The sacred fig-tree.

वादरायणः *m* See बादरायण.

वादि *a.* Wise, learned.

वादित *p.p.*(*f.* -ता) 1 Made to speak. -2 Played, sounded.

वादित्रं *n.* 1 A musical instrument. -2 Instrumental music.

वादिन् *a.* (*f.* -नी) 1 Speaking, discoursing -2 Disputing. -*m.* 1 A speaker. -2 A disputant. -3 An accuser, a plaintiff.

वादिशः *m.* A learned man, scholar.

वाद्यं *n.* 1 A musical instrument. -2 The sound of a musical instrument. -Comp. -करः *m.* A musician. —भांडं *n.* 1 A number of musical instruments. -2 A musical instrument.

वाध्, वाध, वाधक,वाधनः,-ना, वाधा See बाध् बाध, बाधक, बाधन, बाधना, बाधा.

वाधू (-धू-) क्यं *n.* Marriage.

वाध्रीणसः *m.* The rhinoceros.

वान *a.* (*f.* —ना) 1 Blown. -2 Dried by wind —नं *n.* 1 Dry or dried fruit (*m.* also). -2 Blowing. -3 Living. -4 A perfume, fragrance. -5 A number of groves or thickets. -6 Weaving. -7 A mat of straw. -8 A hole in the wall of a house.

वानप्रस्थः *m.* 1 A Bráhmana in the third stage of his religious life. -2 An anchorite. -3 The Madhúka tree. -4 The Palâsa tree.

वानरः *m.* A monkey, an ape. -री *f.* A female monkey. -Comp. —अक्षः *m.* A wild goat. —आघातः *m.* The Lodhra tree.—इंद्रः *m.* N. of Sugrîva or of Hanumat.

वानलः *m.*A kind of holy basil.

वानस्पत्यः *m.* A tree the fruit of which is produced from flower.

वाना *f.* A quail.

वानायुः *m.* N. of a country. -Comp. —जः *m.* Vanáyu horse.

वानारिः *m.* A sort of cane or ratan.

वानीरकः *m.* The *Munja* grass, a kind of rush.

वानेयं *n.* N. of a fragrant grass.

वांत *p. p.* (*f.* -ता) I Vomited. -2 Emitted, ejected. -Comp. —अदः *m.* A dog.

वांतिः *f.* I Vomiting. -2 Ejecting.

वान्या *f.* A multitude of groves or woods.

वापः *m.* I Sowing seed.-2Weaving. -3 Shaving, shearing. -Comp. -दंडः *m.* A weaver's loom.

वापिः, वापी *f.* A well. -Comp. —हः *m.* The *Châtaka* bird.

वापित *p. p.* (*f.* -ता) I Sown. -2 Shaven.

वाम *a.* (*f.* —मा or —मी) I Left(opp. दक्षिण). -2 Being on the left side. -3 Reverse, adverse, unfavourable. -4 Vile, wicked, low.-5 Lovely, charming. -6 Short. -मः *m.* I A sentient being, an animal. -2 N. of Siva. -3 Of Cupid. -4 A snake. -5 An udder, a breast. -मं *n.* Wealth, possessions. -Comp. —आचारः, -मार्गः *m.* The left-hand ritual or doctrine of the *Tantras*. -आवर्तः *m.* I A conch-shell, the spiral of which runs from right to left. -ऊरु, -ऊरू *f.* A woman with handsome thighs. —दृश् *f.* A woman (with lovely eyes). —देवः *m.* I N. of a sage. -2 N. of Siva. -लोचना *f.* A woman with lovely eyes. —शील *a.* Of a perverse nature, cross-tempered. (-लः *m.*) An epithet of the God of love.

वामक *a.* (*f.* -का) I Left. -2 Adverse, contrary.

वामन *a.* (*f.* —ना) I Short in stature. -2 Small, short, little. -3 Bent down, bent low. -4 Vile, low, base. —नः *m.* I A dwarf.-3 N. of Vishnu in his fifth incarnation. -3 N. of the elephant that presides over the south. -4 N. of the author of the Kásikávritti. -5 The tree अंकोट. -Comp. -पुराणं *n.* N. of one of the 18 Purânas.

वामनिका *f.* A female dwarf.

वामनी *f.* I A female dwarf. -2 A mare

वामलूरः *m.* An ant-hill, a mole-hill.

वामा *f.* I A woman. -2 A lovely woman. -2 N. of Gaurì.-4 Of Lakshmî. -5 Of Sarasvatî.

वामिल *a* (*f.* —ला) I Beautiful. -2 Haughty. -3 Cunning.

वामी *f.* I A mare. -2 A she-ass. -3 female elephant. -4 The female of the jackal.

वायः *m.* Weaving. -Comp. -दंडः *m.* A weaver's loom.

वायकः *m.* I A weaver. -2 A heap, multitude, collection.

वायनं, वायनकं *n.* A present of sweetmeats made to a Bràhmana on festive occasions

वायव *a.* (*f.* -वी) I Relating to or given by Vâyu. -2 Aerial. —वी *f.* The north-west quarter (presided over by Vàyu).

वायवीय, वायव्य *a.* (*f.* —या, —व्या) Relating to the wind. -Comp. -पुराणं *n.* N. of a Purâna.

वायसः *m.* I A crow. -3 Fragrant aloe-wood, agallochum.-3 Turpentine. -Comp. —अरातिः, —अरिः *m.* An owl. —आह्वा *f.* A kind of esculent vegetable.

वायुः *m.* I Air, wind. -2 The God of wind. -3 A life-wind or vital air of which five kinds are enumerated viz.-प्राण, अपान, समान, व्यान, and उदान. -4 Vitiation of the windy humour.

-Comp. -आस्पदं *n.* The sky, atmosphere. —केतुः *m.* Dust. —कोणः *m.* The north-west. —गंडः *m.* Flatulence. —गुल्मः *m.* 1 A hurricane, storm. -2 A whirlpool. —गोचरः *m.* The range of the wind. -जातः,-तनयः,-नंदनः, -पुत्रः, -सुतः, -सूनुः *m.* Epithets of Hanumat or Bhima. —दारुः *m.* A cloud. -निघ्न *a.* Mad,frantic.-पुराणं *n.* N. of a Purâna. —फलं *n.* 1 Hail. -2 The rainbow. —भक्षः, भक्षणः, -भुज् *m.* 1 An ascetic. -2 A snake. -रोषा *f.* Night. —वर्त्मन *m.*, *n.* The sky, atmosphere. -वाहः *m.* Smoke. -वाहिनी *f.* A vein,an artery. -सखः, सखिः *m.* Fire.

वार् *n.* Water. -Comp. -आसनं *n.* A reservoir of water. -किटिः (वाःकिटि) *m.* A porpoise. -चः *m.* 1 A goose, gander. -दः *m.* A cloud. -दं *n.* 1 Water. -2 Silk. -3 Speech. -4 The seed of the mango. -5 A curl on a horse's neck. -6 A conch shell. -धिः *m.* The ocean. -पुष्पं (वाःपुष्पं) *n.* Cloves. —भटः *m.* An alligator. -मुच् *m.* A cloud. —राशिः *m.* The ocean. -वटः *m.* A ship, boat. -सदनं (वाःसदनं *n.* A reservoir of water, a cistern.

वारः *m.* A cover. -2 A multitude, large number. -3 A heap, quantity. -4 A herd, flock. -5 A day of the week. -6 Time, turn. -7 An occasion, opportunity. -8 A door, gate. -9 The opposite bank of a river. -10 N. of Siva. —रं *n.* 1 A vessel for holding spirituous liquor. -2 A mass of water (जलसंच).-Comp. —अंगना, —नारी, —युवतिः, योषित, —वनिता, विलासिनी, —सुंदरी, -स्त्री *f.* A harlot, prostitute. -कीरः *m.* 1 A wife's brother. -2 The submarine fire. -3 A hairdresser or comb. -4 A louse.-5 A courser. -6 A porter. -बु (-बू) षा *f.* The plantain tree. -मुख्या *f.* The chief of a number of harlots. -वा (-बा-) णः *m.*, -णं *n.* Armour,a coat of mail. -वाणिः *m.* 1 A piper, player on a flute. -2 A musician. -3 A year. -4 A judge. (-णिः *f.*) A harlot. -वाणी *f.* A harlot. —सेवा *f.* 1 Harlotry, prostitution. -2 A number of harlots.

वारकः *m.* 1 A kind of horse. -2 A horse in general. -3 One of the paces of a horse. -कं *n.* 1 The seat of pain. -2 A kind of perfume.

वारकिन् *m.* An enemy -2 The ocean. -3 A kind of horse, one with good marks. -4 An ascetic living on leaves.

वारंकः *m.* A bird.

वारंगः *m.* The handle of a sword, knife &c.

वारटं *n.* 1 A field. -2 A number of fields. -टा *f.* A goose.

वारणं*n.*1 Warding off,obstructing. -2An obstacle.-3Defending,guarding, protecting. —णः *m.* 1 An elephant. -2 An armour, mail-coat. -Comp. —बुषा, —सा, -वल्लभा *f.* The plantain tree. —साह्वयं *n.* N. of Hastinápura.

वारणसी *f.* See वाराणसी.

वारणावतः *m.*, -तं *n.* N. of a town.

वारत्रं *n.* A leather thong.

वारंवारं *ind.* Often times, again and again.

वारला *f.* 1 A wasp. -2 A goose.

वाराणसी *f.* The holy city of Benares.

वारांनिधिः *m.* The ocean.

वाराह *a.* (*f.* -ही) Relating to a boar. —हः *m.* 1 A boar. -2 A kind of tree. -Comp. —कल्पः *m.* N. of the present *Kalpa* (that in which we are at present living). —पुराणं *n.* N. of one of the 18 Puránas.

वाराही *f.* 1 A sow. -2 The earth. -3 The Sakti of Vishnu in the form of a boar. -4 A measure.

वारि *n.* 1 Water. -2 A fluid. -3 A kind of perfume. —रिः, -री *f.* 1 A place for fastening an elephant. -2 A rope for fastening an elephant. -3 A hole or trap for catching elephants. -4 A captive, prisoner. -5 A water-pot. -6 N. of Sarasvatí. -7 Speech -Comp. —ईशः *m.* 1 The ocean. -2 N. of Vishnu. -उद्भवं *n.* A lotus. -ओकः *m.* A leech. —कर्पूरः *m.* The इलीश fish. —क्रिमिः *m.* A leech. -चरः *m.* 1 A fish. -2 Any aquatic animal. -जः *m.* 1 A conch-shell. -2 Any bivalve shell. (-जं *n.*) 1 A lotus. -2 A kind of salt. -3 A kind of plant (गौरसुवर्ण). -4 Cloves. -तस्करः *m.* 1 A cloud. -2 The sun. -त्रा *f.* An umbrella. -दः *m.* A cloud. —द्रः *m.* The *Chátaka* bird. —धरः *m.* A cloud. -धारा *f.* A shower of rain. -धिः *m.* 1 The ocean. -2 A jar or pot. -नाथः *m.* 1 The ocean. -2 An epithet of Vishnu. -3 A cloud. —निधिः *m.* The ocean. —मसिः, -मुच्, -रः *m.* A cloud. -राशिः *m.* 1 The ocean. -2 A lake. —रुहं *n.* A lotus. -लोमन् *m.* N. of Varuna. -वासः *m.* A dealer in spirituous liquors. -वाहः, —वाहनः *m.* A cloud. —शः *m.* N. of Vishnu. —संभवः *m.* 1 Cloves. -2 A kind of antimony.

वारी *f.* See वारि (*f.*).

वारीटः *m.* An elephant.

वारुः *m.* A war-elephant.

वारुठः *m.* A bier.

वारुण *a.* (*f.* —णी) 1 Belonging to Varuna. -2 Sacred to Varuna. -3 Given to Varuna. —णः *m.* N. of one of the nine divisions of Bharatavarsha. -णं *n.* Water.

वारुणिः *m.* 1 N. of Agastya. -2 Of Bhrigu.

वारुणी *f.* 1 The west. -2 Any spirituous liquor. -3 The asterism शतभिषज्. -4 Dúrvâ grass. -5 N. of the wife of Varuna. -6 A kind of Dúrvâ. -Comp. -वल्लभः *m.* An epithet of Varuna.

वारेंड्रः *m.* The chief of the serpent-race. -डः *m*, -डं *n.* The rheum or excretion of the eyes. -2 The ear-wax. -3 A vessel for baling water out of a boat. —डी *f.* A door-step.

वारेंद्री *f.* N. of part of Bengal now called राजशाही.

वार्क्ष *n.* A forest.

वार्णिकः *m.* A scribe, writer.

वार्त्त *a.* (*f.* -र्त्ता) 1 Healthy. -2 Light, weak, unsubstantial. -3 Following a profession. -र्त्तं *n.* 1 Welfare, good health. -2 Skill, dexterity. -3 Chaff.

वार्त्ता *f.* 1 Staying. -2 Tidings, news. -3 Livelihood, profession. -4 Agriculture. -5 The egg-plant. -Comp. —आरंभः *m.* A commercial undertaking. -वहः, -हरः *m.* 1 A messenger. -2 A chandler. -वृत्तिः *m.* One who lives on agriculture.

वार्ताकः *m.*, वार्ताकिः *f.*, वार्ताकिन *m*, वार्ताकी *f.*, वार्ताकुः *m.*, *f.* The egg-plant.

वार्त्तायनः *m.* A news-bearer, spy, an emissory.

वार्त्तिक *a.* (*f.*-की) 1 Relating to news. -2 Bringing news. -3 Explanatory. -कः *m.* 1 A spy. -2 A husbandman (a man of the third tribe). —कं *n.* An explanatory or supplementary rule or सूत्र intended to correct, modify, or supplement an original सूत्र.

वार्त्तिका *f.* A kind of quail.

वार्त्रघ्नः *m.* N. of Arjuna.

वार्धकं *n.* 1 Old age. -2 The infirmity of old age. -3 A number of old men.

वार्द्धक्यं *n.* 1 Old age. -2 The infirmity of old age.

वार्द्धुषि:, वार्द्धुषिक:, वार्द्धुषिन् *m.* A usurer.

वार्द्धुष्यं *n.* Usury, high or exorbitant interest.

वार्ध्र *n.*, वार्ध्री *f.* A leather thong.

वार्ध्रीणस: *m.* A rhinoceros.

वार्यं *n.* A blessing, boon.

वार्वणा *f.* A kind of blue fly.

वार्षिक *a.* (*f.* -की) 1 Belonging to the rains or rainy season. -2 Annual, yearly. -3 Lasting for one year. -कं *n.* N. of a medicinal plant.

वार्षिला *f.* Hail.

वार्षुक *a.* (*f.* -की) Raining, pouring down.

वार्ष्णेय: *m.* 1 A descendant of Vrishni. -2 An epithet of Krishna. -3 N. of the charioteer of Nala.

वार्ह, वार्हद्रथ, वार्हद्राथि, वार्हस्पत, वार्हस्पत्य, वार्हिण, वाल, वालक } See बार्ह, बार्हद्रथ, बार्हद्राथि, बार्हस्पत, बार्हस्पत्य, बार्हिण, बाल, बालक.

वालखिल्य: *m.* See बालखिल्य:.

वालि: *m.* N. of a celebrated monkey chief, who was slain by Râma at the desire of Sugrîva, his younger brother.

वालुका *f.* 1 Sand, gravel. -2 Powder. -3 Camphor in general. —का, -की *f.* A kind of cucumber.

वालेय See बालेय.

वाल्क *a.* (*f.* —ल्की) Made of the bark of trees.

वाल्कल *a.* (*f.* —ली) Made of the bark of trees. —लं *n.* A bark-garment. —ली *f.* Spirituous liquor.

वाल्मीक:, वाल्मीकि: *m.* N. of a celebrated sage, and author of the Râmâyanâ.

वावदूक *a.* (*f.* -का) 1 Talkative. -2 Eloquent.

वावय: *m.* A kind of basil.

वावुट: *m.* A boat, raft.

वावृत् 4 A. (वावृत्यते) 1 To choose, select, love. -2 To serve.

वावृत्त *a.* (*f.* -त्ता) Chosen, selected.

वाश् 4 A. (वाश्यते, वाशित) 1 To roar, scream, howl, hum (as birds), sound in general. -2 To call.

वाशनं *n.* 1 Roaring, howling. -2 The humming (of bees &c.).

वाशि: *m.* 1 Fire. -2 The God of fire.

वाशितं *n.* 1 The cry of birds. -2 Calling out, calling.

वाशिता *f.* 1 A female elephant. -2 A woman.

वाष्प: *m.*, वाष्पं *n.* See बाष्प.

वास् 10 U. (वासयति, -ते) 1 To perfume, fumigate, make fragrant. -2 To steep, infuse. -3 To spice, season.

वास् 4 A. See वाश्.

वास: *m.* 1 Perfume. -2 Living, dwelling. -3 A habitation, house. -4 Site, situation. -5 Clothes, dress. -Comp. —अ (-आ-) —गार: *m.*, (-रं), -गृहं, —वेश्मन् *n.* The inner apartments of a house; bed-chamber. -कर्णी *f.* 1 A hall for public exhibitions. -2 A sacrificial hall. —तांबूलं *n.* Betel mixed with other fragrant spices. -यष्टि: *f.* A roosting perch. -योग: *m.* A kind of fragrant powder. —सज्जा *f.* See वासकसज्जा.

वासक *a.* (*f.* -सका or -सिका) 1 Scenting, perfuming, fumigating. -2 Causing to dwell. -कं *n.* Clothes. -Comp. —सज्जा, -सज्जिका *f.* A woman who dresses herself in all her ornaments in expection of her lover,

(one of the several classes of a Nàyikà).

वासनं *n.* 1 Perfuming, scenting. -2 Infusing. -3 Dwelling, abiding.-4 An abode, a dwelling. -5 Any receptacle such as a basket, box, &c. -6 Knowledge. -7 Clothes. -8 An envelope. -9 A kind of posture practised by ascetics in abstract meditation.

वासना *f.*1 Knowledge derived from memory. -2 The impression on the mind by past good or bad actions, which produces pleasure or pain. -3 Fancy, imagination. -4 False idea -5 A wish. desire.-6 Respectful regard. -7 Perfuming,scenting.

वासंत *a.* (*f,* -ती) 1 Vernal. -2 In the spring or prime of life, youthful. -3 Attentive (in the performance of duties).—तः *m.*1 A camel. -2 A young elephant. -3 A cuckoo. -4 The south wind. -5 A kind of bean. -6 A dissolute man. —ती *f.* 1 A kind of jasmine. -2 Long pepper. -3 The trumpet-flower. -4 N. of a festival held in honour of Cupid. -5 The spring creeper.

वासंतिक *n.* (*f.* —की) Vernal. -कः *m.* 1 The Vidúshaka or buffoon in a drama. -2 An actor.

वासरः *m.*, -रं *n.* A day (of the week).-Comp.—संगः *m.* The morning.

वासव *a.* (*f.* -वी) Belonging to Indra. -वः *m.* N. of Indra. —वं *n.* The constellation Dhanishthà.

वासवी *f.* N. of the mother of Vâysa.

वासस् *n.* A garment, clothes. -Comp. —कुटी (वासःकुटी) *f.* A tent.

वासिः *m.*, *f.* An adze, a hatchet, chisel. —सिः *m.* Dwelling, abiding.

वासित *p. p.* (*f.* -ता) 1 Perfumed, scented. -2 Seasoned, spiced. -3 Dressed, clothed. -4 Peopled, populous. -5 Famous, celebrated. -तं *n.* 1 The cry or hum of birds. -2 Knowledge.

वासिता *f.* See वाशिता.

वासि (-शि-) ष्ठ *a.* (*f.* -ष्ठी) Belonging to or composed by Vasishtha. -ष्ठः *m.* A descendant of Vasishtha.

वासुः *m.* 1 The soul. -2 The Supreme Being. -3 N. of Vishnu. -4 The constellation पुनर्वसु.

वासुकिः, वासुकेयः *m.* N. of a celebrated serpent, king of snakes.

वासुदेवः *m.*1 Any descendant of Vasudeva. -2 An epithet of Krishna.

वासुरा *f.* The earth. -2 Night. -3 A woman.-4 A female elephant.

वासूः *f.* A young girl, maiden(used chiefly in dramas).

वास्त See वास्त.

वास्तव *a.* (*f.* —वी) 1 Real, true, substantial. -2 Determined, fixed. -वं *n.* Anything fixed or determined.

वास्तवा *f.* Dawn.

वास्ताविक *a.* (*f.* —की) 1 True, real, substantial. -2 Demonstrated, established.

वास्तव्य*a.*(*f* -व्या)1 Dwelling, inhabiting.-2 Fit to be dwelt in. -व्यः *m.*1 A resident, an inhabitant. —व्यं *n.* 1 A habitable place, house. -2 A residence (वसाति).

वास्तिकं *n.* A collection of goats.

वास्तुः*m.*,वास्तु *n.*1 The site of a house. -2 A house. -Comp. -यागः *m.* A sacrifice performed on the occasion of laying the foundation of a house. —संशमनं *n.*, —शांतिः *f.* A religious rite performed on the occasion of laying the foundation of a new house or on the occasion of entering it.

वास्तेय *a.* (*f.* -यी) 1 Habitable, fit to be inhabited. -2 Abdominal.

वास्तोष्पतिः *m.* 1 N. of a Vedic deity. -2 N. of Indra.

वास्त्रः *m.* A carriage covered with cloth.

वाह् 1 A (वाहते) To exert oneself, [endeavour.

वाहः *m.* 1 Carrying, bearing. -2 A porter. -3 A beast of burden. -4 A house. -5 A bull. -6 A buffalo. -7 A carriage, conveyance. -8 The arm. -9 Air, wind. -10 A measure equal to four Bhāras. -Comp. —द्विषत *m.* A buffalo. —श्रेष्ठः *m.* A horse.

वाहकः *m.* 1 A porter. -2 A horseman.

वाहनं *n.* 1 Bearing, conveying. -2 A vehicle, conveyance of any kind. -3 An animal used in riding or draught, as a horse. -4 An elephant.

वाहसः *m.* 1 A water-course. -2 A large serpent; the boa.

वाहिकः *m.* 1 A large drum. -2 A car drawn by oxen. -3 A carrier of loads.

वाहितं *n.* A heavy burden.

वाहित्थं *n.* The part of an elephant's forehead below the frontal globes.

वाहिन् *m.* A chariot.

वाहिनी *f.* 1 An army. -2 A detachment of an army consisting of 81 elephants, as many chariots, 243 horse, and 405 foot. -3 A river.

वाहीक See वाहिक.

वाहुक See वाहूक.

वाह्यः *m.* A beast of burden, an ox &c. —ह्यं *n.* A carriage.

वाह्लिः *f.* N. of a country (the modern Balkh). -Comp. —जः *m.* A Balkh-bred horse.

वाह्लि (-ह्ली-) कः *m.* 1 N. of a country (the modern Balkh). -2 A horse from this country; a Balkh-bred horse. —कं *n.* 1 Saffron. -2 Asa Fœtida.

वि *ind.* As a prefix to verbs and nouns it expresses-Separation. -2 The reverse of an action. -3 Division.-4 Distinction.-5 Discrimination. -6 Order, arrangement. -7 Opposition. -8 deliberation. -9 Intensity.

As a prefix to nouns or adjectives not immediately connected with roots वि expresses (1) Negation or privation. (2) Intensity, greatness. (3) Variety. (4) Difference. (5) Manifoldness. (6) Contrariety, opposition. (7) Change. (8) Impropriety.

विः *m.*, *f.* 1 A bird. -2 A horse.

विंश *a.* (*f.*—शी) Twentieth.-शः *m.* A twentieth part.

विंशक *a.* (*f.* -की) Twenty.

विंशतिः *f.* Twenty, a score.

विंशतितम *a.* (*f.* —मी) Twentieth.

विंशिन् *m.* 1 Twenty. -2 A lord or ruler of twenty villages.

विकं *n.* The milk of a cow that has recently calved.

विकंकटः, -तः *m.* A kind of tree.

विकच *a* (*f.* -चा) 1 Blown, expanded (as a lotus-flower &c.). -2 Spread about, scattered over. -3 Destitute of hair. -4 Manifested. -चः *m.* A Buddhist mendicant.

विकट *a.* (*f.* -टा) 1 Hideous, ugly. -2 Frightful, horrible. -3 Great, large, broad, wide. -4 Beautiful. -5 Frowning. -6 Obscure. -7 Changed in appearance. —टं *n.* A boil, tumour.

विकत्थन *a.* (*f.* —ना) 1 Boasting, vaunting. -2 Praising ironically.

-नं *n.* 1 Vaunting, boasting. -2 Irony, false praise.

विकत्था *f.* 1 Boasting, vaunt, brag. boast. -2 Praise. -3 False praise, irony.

विकर: *m.* Sickness, disease.

विकरण: *m.* The conjugational sign placed between the root and the termination.

विकराल *a.* (*f.* —ला) Very dreadful or formidable.

विकर्ण: *m.* N. of a Kuru prince.

विकर्तन: *m.* 1 The sun. -2 The *Arka* plant. -3 A son who has usurped his father's kingdom.

विकर्मन् *n.* 1 An unlawful or prohibited act. -2 Retiring from business.

विकर्ष: *m.* 1 Pulling apart. -2 An arrow.

विकर्षण: *m.* N. of one of the five arrows of Cupid. —णं *n.* 1 Drawing, pulling asunder. -2 A cross throw.

विकल *a.* (*f.* -ला) 1 Defective, imperfect, maimed. -2 Frightened, alarmed. -3 Devoid or destitute of (in comp.). -4 Agitated, dispirited. -5 Ineffective, useless. -6 Withered; decayed. —ला, -ली *f.* A woman during her courses. -Comp. —करुण *a.* Helpless, piteous. -पाणिक: *m.* A cripple.

विकला *f.* The sixtieth part of a *Kalá*.

विकल्प: *m.* 1 Doubt, uncertainty, hesitation. -2 Suspicion. -3 Contrivance, art. -4 Option, alternative (in gram.)! -5 Sort, variety. -6 An error, a mistake. (*Rhet.*) The figure of speech in which there is an ingenious or striking oppostion of two things of equal force. -Comp. -उपहार: *m.* An optional offering. —जालं *n.* *n.* An dilemma.

विकल्पनं *n.* 1 Admitting of a doubt -2 Allowing an option. -3 Indecision.

विकस: *m.* The moon.

विकसित *p. p.* (*f.* -ता) Blown, fully opened or expanded.

विकस्व (-स्व-) र *a.* (*f.* -रा) 1 Opening, expanding. -2 Loud, distinctly audible.

विकार: *m.* 1 Change of form or nature. -2 Sickness, disease. -3 Change of mind or purpose. -4 A feeling, an emotion. -5 Agitation, excitement. -6 Contortion, contraction (as of the features of the face). -7 (In Sân phil.) That which is evolved from a previous source or Prakriti. -8 A wound. -Comp. -हेतु: *m.* A temptation, cause of perturbation.

विकारिन् *a.* (*f.* —णी) 1 Liable to change, susceptible of emotion. -2 Changing, modifying.

विकाल:, विकालक: *m.* Evening, evening twilight, the close of day.

विकालिका *f.* A perforated copper-vessel which, placed in water, marks the time by gradually filling.

विकाश: *m.* 1 Manifestation, display, exhibition. -2 Blowing, expanding. -3 An open or direct course. -4 An oblique course. -5 Joy, pleasure. -6 Sky, heaven. -7 Eagerness. -8 Retreat, privacy.

विकाशनं *n.* 1 Manifestation, display, exhibition. -2 Blowing, expanding (of flowers &c.).

विकाशि (-सि-) न् *a.* (*f.* —नी) 1 Becoming visible. -2 Expanding, opening. -3 Shining.

विकास: *m.* 1 Blowing, expanding, blooming. -2 Increase, growth.

—विकिरः *m.* 1 A scattered portion -2 A bird. -3 A well. -4 A tree.

विकिरणं *n.* 1 Scattering. -2 Spreading abroad.-3 Tearing up. -4 Killing (हिंसन). -5 Knowledge. -णः *m.* The *Arka* tree.

विकीर्णः *p. p.* (*f.* —र्णा) 1 Scattered, dispersed. -2 Diffused. -3 Celebraed. -Comp. —र्णं *n.* A kind of perfume.

विकुंठः *m.* N. of Vishnu's heaven.

विकुंठित *a.* (*f.* —ता) 1 Obtuse, blunt. -2 Weak.

विकुर्वाण *a.* (*f.* —णी) 1 Undergoing or causing a change. -2 Delighted, rejoiced.

विकुस्रः *m.* The moon.

विकूजनं *n.* Cooing, humming.

विकूणनं *n.* A side-glance, leer.

विकूणिका *f.* The nose.

विकृत *p. p.* (*f.* —ता) 1 Changed, altered. -2 Sick, diseased. -3 Mutilated. disfigured. -4 Incomplete, imperfect. -5 Affected by passion or emotion. -6 Loathsome. -7 Strange, extraordinary. -8 Unnatural. तं *n.* 1 Change, modification. -2 Sickness. -3 Aversion, disgust.

विकृतिः *f.* See विकारः.

विकृष्ट *p. p.* (*f.* —ष्टा) 1 Dragged asunder. -2 Drawn, pulled. -3 Extended, protracted. -4 Making a noise.

विकशी *f.* 1 A woman with loose hair. -2 A small tress of hair tied up separately and then collected into the larger braid of *Veni.*

विकोश,-ष *a.* (*f.* -शा,-षा) 1 Without husk. -2 Unsheathed, uncovered.

विक्कः *m.* A young elephant.

विक्रमः *m.* 1 A step, stride, pace.-2 Stepping over, walking. -3 Overcoming. -4 Heroism, prowess. -5 N.of a celebrated king ef Ujjaynii. -6 N. of Vishnu.-7 Strength,power. -Comp.—कर्मन् *n.* A heroic deed,feat of valour.

विक्रमणं *n.* A stride (of Vishnu).

विक्रमिन् *m.* 1 A lion. -2 A hero. -3 An epithet of Vishnu.

विक्रांत *p. p.* (*f.* —ता) 1 Stepped or passed beyond. -2 Heroic, valiant. -3 Victorious, overpowering (one's enemies). —तः *m.* 1 A hero, warrior. -2 A lion.—तं *n.* 1 A pace, stride. -2 Heroism.

विक्रांतिः *f.* 1 Stepping, striding. -2 A horse's gallop. -3 Heroism.

विक्रांतृ *m.* 1 A lion. -2 A hero, victor.

विक्लवः *m.* The moon.

विक्रयः *m.* Sale, selling. -Comp. —अनुशयः *m.* A rescission of a sale. —पत्रं *n.* A bill of sale, sale-deed.

विक्रायिकः,विक्रयिन् *m.* A dealer,seller.

विक्रिया *f.* 1 Change, modification, alteration. -2 Agitation, excitement. -3 Anger. -4 Reverse, evil. -5 Any sudden movement, as in रोमाविक्रिया.-6 A disease.-7 Violation, vitiation (of the proper duties).-8 A preparation or dish of rice &c.

विक्रुष्ट *n.*1 A cry for help.-2Abuse.

विक्रेय *a.* (*f.* —या) Saleable, vendible (as an article.)

विक्रोशनं *n.* 1 Calling out. -2 Abusing.

विक्लव *a.* (*f.* —वा) 1 Overcome with fear. -2 Timid. -3 Affected by, overcome with. -4 Agitated, excited, bewildered. -5 Distressed. -6 Averse from. -7 Faltering.

विक्लिन्न *p. p.* (*f.* —न्ना) 1 Thoroughly wetted. -2 Decayed, withered up. -3 Old.

विक्लिष्ट *p. p.* (*f.* —ष्टा) 1 Afflicted, distressed. -2 Injured, destroyed. —ष्टं *n.* A fault in pronunciation.

विक्षत *p. p.* (*f.*—ता) Wounded, hurt. —तं *n.* Wounding, a wound.

विक्षाव: *m.* 1 Cough, sneezing. -2 A sound.

विक्षिप्त *p. p.* (*f.* —प्ता) 1 Scattered, thrown about. -2 Discarded. -3 Sent, despatched. -4 Bewildered, agitated. -5 Refuted.

विक्षिणकः *m.* 1 N. of an attendant of Siva. -2 An assembly of the Gods.

विक्षिरः *m.* The *Arka* tree.

विक्षेपः *m.* 1 Scattering about. -2 Discharging (opp. संहारः). -3 Moving to and fro. -4 Sending, despatching. -5 Confusion, perplexity. -6 Alarm, fear. -7 Refutation of an argument. -8 Polar latitude.

विक्षोभः *m.* 1 Shaking, agitation, movement. -2 Agitation of mind, alarm. -3 Conflict, struggle.

विख्र
विखु
विख्य
विख्न
विख्नु
विग्र } *a.* Noseless.-Comp. -नस् *m.* An epithet of Bráhman (*m.*)

विखानसः *m.* A kind of hermit

विखासा *f.* The tongue.

विखुरः *m.* 1 A demon. -2 A thief.

विख्यात *p. p.* (*f.* — ता) 1 Renowned, famous. -2 Called, named. -3 Avowed, confessed.

विख्यातिः *f.* Celebrity, fame.

विगणनं *n.* 1 Reckoning. -2 Deliberating. -3 Paying off a debt.

विगंधकः *m.* The tree called इंगुदी.

विगत *p. p.* (*f.* —ता) 1 Departed, disappeared. -2 Separated. -3 Dead. -4 Destitute or devoid of. -5 Lost. -6 Dark, obscured. -Comp. —आर्तवा *f.* A woman past child-bearing.

विगमः *m.* 1 Departure, disappearance, end. -2 Loss, destruction. -3 Death. -4 Separation.

विगरः *m.* 1 A nakcd ascetic. -2 A mountain.

विगर्हणं *n.*, -णा *f.* Censure, blame, abuse.

विगर्हित *p. p.* (*f.*-ता) 1 Censured, abused. -2 Disdained. -3 Condemned, prohibited. -4 Low, vile. -5 Wicked -तं *n.* Censure.

विगलित *p. p.* (*f.* -ता) 1 Trickled, oozed. -2 Disappeared. -3 Dropped down. -4 Melted away, dissolved. -5 Dispersed. -6 Slackened, untied. -4 Loose, dishevelled.

विगाढ *p. p.* (*f.* —ढा) 1 Plunged into, immersed. -2 Deep, excessive.

विगाहः *m.* Plunging into, bathing.

विगुण *a.* (*f.* —णा) 1 Destitute of merits, worthless. -2 Having no string.

विगूढ *p. p.* (*f.* -ढा) 1 Secret, hidden. -2 Reproached.

विगानं *n.* 1 Censure, reproach. -2 contradiction, inconsistency.

विगीत *p. p.* (*f.* —ता) 1 Censured, abused. -2 Contradictory, inconsistent.

विगीतिः *f.* 1 Censure, abuse. -2 A [contradiction.

विगृहीत *p. p.* (*f.* —ता) 1 Divided, analysed. -2 Seized. -3 Encountered, opposed.

विग्रहः *m.* 1 Extension, expansion. -2 Form, figure, shape, -3 The body. -4 Resolution, dissolution, analysis. -5 Quarrel, strife. -6 War, battle. -7 Disfavour. -8 A part, divsion.

विघट्टनं *n.* Ruin, destruction.

विघटित *p. p.* (*f.* —ता) 1 Separated. -2 Divided. -3 Broken.

विघटिका *f.* A measure of time equal to one-sixtieth part of a Ghatiká.

विघट्टनं *n.*,–ना *f.* 1 Striking asunder –2 Striking against, friction. –3 Separating, untying. –4 Offending, hurting.

विघट्टित *p. p.* (*f.* –ता) 1 Severed, separated, dispersed. –2 Loosened, opened. –3 Rubbed, touched. –4 Shaken about. –5 Hurt, offended

विघन: *m.* A mallet, hammer.

विघस: *m.* 1 The residue or leavings of food eaten. –2 Food in general. –सं *n.* Bees'-wax.–Comp.–आश:, –आशिन् *m.* One who eats the remains of an offering or of food eaten.

विघात: *m.* 1 Destruction, warding off. –2 Killing, slaying. –3 An obstacle. –4 A blow, stroke. –5 Abandoning.–Comp. –सिद्धि: *f* The removal of obstacles.

विघूर्णित *p. p.* (*f.* –ता) Shaken about, rolling (as eyes).

विघृष्ट *p. p.* (*f.* –ष्टा) 1 Rubbed excessively. –2 Sore.

विघ्न: *m.* (rarely *n.*) 1 An obstacle, interruption. –2 Difficulty, trouble. –Comp. –ईश:, –ईशान:,–ईश्वर: *m.* Epithets of Ganesa. –नायक:, –नाशक: –नाशन: *m.* Epithets of Ganesa. –राज: –विनायक:, –हारिन *m.* Epithets of Ganesa. –सिद्धि: *f.* Removal of obstacles.

विघ्नित *a.* (*f.* –ता) 1 Impeded, hindered, opposed. –2 Obscured, blinded.

विङ्ख: *m.* A horse's hoof.

विच् 3 7. U. (वेवेक्ति, वेविक्ते, विनक्ति, विंक्ते, विक्त) 1 To separate. –2 To distinguish, discern. –3 To remove from (with instr.). With वि– 1 To separate, to divide. –2 To discriminate. –3 To describe, 4 To tear up, remove.

विचकिल *m.* 1 A kind of jasmine. –2 N. of the tree called *Madana.*

विचक्षण *a.* (*f.* –णा) 1 Farseeing, circumspect. –2 Wise, clever. –3 Skilful able.–ण: *m.* A learned man.

विचक्षस् *m* A spiritual teacher, preceptor.

विचक्षुस् *a.* 1 Blind. –2 Perplexed, sad.

विचार: *m.* 1 Thought, consideration. –2 Examination, investigation. –3 Trial, (of a case).–4 Judgment, discernment, exercise of reason. –5 Decision, determination. –6 Selection. –7 Doubt, hesitation. –8 Prudence. –Comp. –भू *f.* 1 A tribunal, seat of justice, –2 The judgment-seat of Yama. –स्थलं *n.* 1 A tribunal. –2 A logical discussion.

विचारक: *m.* A judge, an examiner

विचारणं *n.* 1 Discussion, considera tion, investigation. –2 Doubt, hesitation

विचारणा *f.* 1 Examination, investigation. –2 Consideration, thought. –3 Hesitation, doubt. –4 The Mîmâmsa system of philosophy.

विचारित *p. p.* (*f.* –ता) 1 Considered, examined, discussed. –2 Decided, determined. –तं *n.* Deliberation, thought.

विचर्चिका *f.* Itch, scab.

विचर्चित *a.* (*f.* –ता) Anointed, smeared.

विचल *a.* (*f.* –ला) 1 Shaking, tottering, unsteady (fig. also). –2 Conceited, proud

विचलनं *n.* 1 Moving. –2 Deviation. –3 Unsteadiness. –4 Conceit, pride.

विचयः *m.* 1 Search, seeking, looking out for. -2 Investigation.

विचयनं *n.* Searching, seeking, investigating.

विचिः *m.*, *f.*, विची *f.* A wave.

विचिकित्सा *f.* 1 Doubt, hesitation, uncertainty. -2 Mistake, error.

विचित *p. p.* (*f.* —ता) Searched.

विचितिः *f.* 1 Searching, search, seeking for. -2 Inquiry.

विचित्र *a.* (*f.* -त्रा) 1 Spotted, speckled. -2 Various, varied. -3 Painted. -4 Beautiful. -5 Wonderful, strange. —त्रा *f.* A white deer. -त्रं *n.* 1 Variegated colour. -2 Surprise. -Comp. —अंगः *m.* 1 A peacock. -2 A tiger. —देहः *m.* A cloud. —रूप *a.* Diverse. —वीर्यः *m.* N. of a king of the lunar race.

विचित्रकः *m.* The birch tree. —कं *n.* Wonder, surprise.

विचिन्वकः *m.* 1 Search. -2 Investigation. -3 A hero.

विचीर्ण *a.* (*f.* —र्णा) 1 Wandered through. -2 Entered.

विचेतन *a.* (*f.* —ना) 1 Senseless, unconscious, dead. -2 Inanimate.

विचेतस् *a.* 1 Stupid, ignorant. -2 Perplexed, sorry. -3 Wicked.

विचेष्टित *p. p.* (*f.* —ता) 1 Striven, struggled. -2 Investigated. -3 Done foolishly. —तं *n.* 1 An act, a deed. -2 Undertaking, enterprise. -3 Gesture. -4 Machination.

विच्छ् 6 P. (विच्छति. also विच्छायति,-ते) 1 To go, move.

विच्छ् 10 U. (विच्छयति,-ते) 1 To shine. -2 To speak.

विच्छंदः, विच्छंदकः *m.* A large building having several stories.

विच्छर्दकः *m.* A large building.

विच्छर्दनं *n.* Vomiting, ejecting.

विच्छर्दित *p. p.* (*f.* —ता) 1 Vomited, ejected. -2 Neglected, disregarded. -3 Abandoned, left. -4 Impaired, lessened.

विच्छाय *a.* (*f.* —या) Pale, dim. —यः *m.* A gem, jewel. —यं *n.* The shadow of a flock of birds.

विच्छित्तिः *f.* 1 Cutting off, tearing off. -2 Dividing, separating. -3 Disappearance, absence. -4 Cessation. -5 Colouring the body with paints and unguents. -6 Limit, boundary (of a house &c.). -7 A pause in a verse. -8 A kind of amorous gesture.

विच्छिन्न *p. p.* (*f.* —न्ना) 1 Cut off. -2 Broken, separated. -3 Interrupted. -4 Ended, terminated. -5 Variegated. -6 Hidden. -7 Smeared with unguents. -8 Crooked, curved.

विच्छुरित *p. p.* (*f.* —ता) 1 Covered, coated. -2 Inlaid. -3 Besmeared, anointed.

विच्छेदः *m.* 1 Cutting, dividing. -2 Breaking. -3 Break, interruption, discontinuance. -4 Removal, prohibition. -5 Dissension. -6 A section of a book. -7 Interval, space.

विच्छेदनं *n.* See विच्छेदः.

विच्युत *p. p.* (*f.* -ता) 1 Fallen down. -2 Displaced. -3 Swerving from.

विच्युतिः *f.* 1 Falling down from, separation. -2 Decline, downfall. -3 Deviation. -4 Miscarriage, failure.

विज् 1, 3 U. (वेवेक्ति, वेविक्ते, विक्त) 1 To separate, divide. -2 To distinguish, discriminate. With उद्- 1 To be afraid of. -2 To be disgusted. -3 To be sorry. -4 To afflict; to frighten.

विज् 6 A., 7 P. (विजते, विनक्ति, विग्न) 1 To shake, tremble. -2 To be agitated. -3 To be afraid. -4 To be afflicted.

विजन *a.* (*f.* —ना) Lonely, solitary. —नं *n.* A solitary place, retreat.

विजननं *n.* Birth, procreation, delivery.

विजन्मन् *m.* A bastard. —*n.* Birth.

विजपिलं *n.* Mud.

विजय: *m.* 1 Conquest, victory, triumph. -2 A celestial chariot. -3 N. of Arjuna. -4 An epithet of Yama. -5 N. of the first year of Jupiter's cycle. -6 N. of an attendant of Vishnu. -Comp. —कुंजर: *m.* A war-elephant. —छंद: *m.* A necklace of 500 strings. —नगरं *n.* N. of a town. —मर्दल: *m.* A large military drum. —सिद्धि: *f.* Success, victory.

विजयंत: *m.* N. of Indra.

विजया *f.* 1 N. of Durgâ. -2 N. of a lore taught by Visvámitra to Râma. -3 Hemp. -4 N. of a festival; see विजयोत्सव below. -Comp. —उत्सव: *m.* A festival in honour of Durgá held on the 10th day of the bright half of Asvina. -दशमी *f.* The tenth day of the bright half of Asvina.

विजयिन् *m.* A conqueror, victor.

विजरं *n.* A stalk.

विजल्प: *m.* 1 Prattle, idle or foolish talk, speech in general. -2 A malignant speech.

विजल्पित *p.p.* (*f.* —ता) 1 Spoken, talked. -2 Prated, babbled.

विजात *p. p.* (*f.* —ता) 1 Base-born. -2 Born, produced. -3 Transformed. -ता *f.* A mother, a woman who has borne children.

विजाति: *f.* 1 Different origin. -2 Different kind, species or tribe.

विजातीय *a.* (*f.* —या) 1 Dissimilar, unlike. -2 Of a different caste or tribe. -3 Of mixed origin.

विजिगीषा *f.* 1 Desire to conquer. -2 Emulation, competition, ambition.

विजिगीषु *a.* 1 Wishing to conquer. -2 Emulous, ambitious. —षु: *m.* 1 A warrior, a hero. -2 An opponent.

विजित *p.p.* (*f.* —ता) Subdued, conquered, defeated. -Comp. -आत्मन् *a.* Self-subdued, self-controlled. -इंद्रिय *a.* Having the organs of sense subdued.

विजिति: *f.* Conquest, victory.

विजिन: *m.*, -नं *n.*, **विजिल:** *m.*, -लं *n.* A sauce (mixed with gruel).

विजिह्म *a.* (*f.* -ह्मा) 1 Crooked, bent. -2 Dishonest.

विजुल: *m.* The silk-cotton tree.

विजृंभणं *n.* 1 Gaping, yawning. -2 Blossoming, opening. -3 Exhibiting, displaying. -4 Amorous sport.

विजृंभित *p. p.* (*f.* —ता) 1 Gaped, yawned. -2 Opened, blown, expanded. -3 Displayed. -4 Sported. —तं *n.* 1 Sport, pastime. -2 Wish, desire. -3 Display. -4 An action, conduct. -5 Fruit, result.

विज्जलं, -लं *n.* 1 A kind of sauce. -2 An arrow.

विज्जिल: *m.* See विजिन:.

विज्जुलं *n.* Cinnamon.

विज्ञ *a.* (*f.* —ज्ञा) 1 Knowing, wise, learned. -2 Clever, skilful. —ज्ञ: *m.* A wise or learned man.

विज्ञप्त *p. p.* (*f.* —प्ता) 1 Respectfully told, requested. -2 Informed.

विज्ञप्ति: *f.* 1 A respectful communication, an entreaty. -2 An announcement.

विज्ञात *p.p.* (*f.*-ता) 1 Known, perceived. -2 Famous.

विज्ञानं *n.* 1 Knowledge, intelligence, understanding, -2 Discrimination, discernment. -3 Skill, proficiency. -4 Knowledge derived from worldly experience (opp. ज्ञान which is 'knowledge of Brahman (*n.*) or Supreme Spirit'). -5 Business, employment. -6 Music. -7 Knowledge of the fourteen lores. -Comp. —ईश्वरः *m.* N. of the author of the Mitâksharâ. —पादः *m.* N. of Vyâsa. —मातृकः *m.* An epithet of Buddha. —वादः *m.* The doctrine taught by Buddha.

विज्ञानिक *a.* (*f.* -का) Wise, learned.

विज्ञापकः *m.* 1 An informant. -2 An instructor.

विज्ञापनं *n.*,-ना *f.* 1 Respectful statement or communication, an entreaty. -2 Information. -3 Instruction.

विज्ञापित *p. p.* (*f.* —ता) 1 Respectfully told or communicated. -2 Requested. -3 Informed. -4 Instructed.

विज्ञाप्तिः *f.* See विज्ञप्तिः.

विज्ञाप्यं *n.* A request.

विंजामरं *n.* The white of the eye.

विंजोलिः,-ली *f.* A line, row.

विट् 1 P. (वेटति) 1 To sound. -2 To curse.

विटः *m.* 1 A paramour.-2 A voluptuary, sensualist. -3 (In dramas) The companion of a prince or a dissolute young man or of a courtezan.-4 A rogue, cheat.-5 A catamite. -6 A rat. -7 The Khadira tree. -8 The orange tree. -9 A branch together with its shoot. -10 A mineral salt. -Comp. —माक्षिकं *n.* A kind of mineral. —लवणं *n.* A medicinal salt.

विटंकः *m.* 1 An aviary, dove-cot. -2 The loftiest point.

विटंककः *m.* See विटंकः.

विटंकित *a.* (*f.* —ता) Marked, stamped.

विटपः *m.* 1 A branch, (of a creeper or tree). -2 A bush. -3 A new shoot or sprout.-4 A clump, thicket. -5 The septum of the scrotum.

विटपिन् *m.* 1 A tree. -2 The fig-tree. -Comp. —मृगः *m.* A monkey, an ape.

विट्ठ (-ट्ठ-) लः *m.* N. of a form of Vishnu or Krishna (worshipped at Pandharpur).

विठंक *a.* (*f.* —का) Bad, vile, low.

विठरः *m.* N. of Brihaspati.

विड् 1 P. (वेडति) 1 To curse, revile. -2 To cry out against.

विडं *n.* A kind of artificial salt.

विडंगः *m* , —गं *n.* N. of a vegetable and medicinal substance.

विडंबः *m.* 1 Imitation. -2 Distressing, molesting.

विडंबनं *n.*, -ना *f.* 1 Imitation. -2 An imposture. -3 Deception, fraud. -4 Vexation, mortification. -5 Paining, distressing. -6 Disappointing. -7 Ridiculousness.

विडंबित *p. p.* (*f.* —ता) 1 Imitated. -2 Mocked. -3 Deceived. -4 Vexed, mortified. -5 Frustrated. -6 Low, abject. -तं *n.* An object of ridicule.

विडारकः *m.* A cat.

विडालः,विडालकः *m.* See बिडालः, बिडालकः.

विडीनं *n.* One of the several modes of flight of birds.

विडुलः *m.* A sort of cane.

विडूरजं *n.* *Lapis lazuli.*

विडौ (-डौ-) जस् *m.* N. of Indra.

वितंसः *m.* 1 A bird-cage. -2 A fetter to catch or confine beasts or birds.

वितंडः *m.* 1 An elephant. -2 A sort of bolt.

वितंडा *f.* 1 A frivolous or fallacious argument.-2 Wrangling, captious criticism in general. -3 A spoon, ladle. -4 Benzoin.

वितत *p. p.* (*f.*-ता) 1 Spread out, extended. -2 Large, broad. -3 Performed, accomplished, effected. -4 Covered. -5 Diffused. —तं *n.* Any stringed instrument.-Comp.-धन्वन् *a.* One who has fully drawn his bow.

विततिः *f.* 1 Extension, expansion.

-2 Quantity, cluster.-3 A line,row.

वितथ *a.* (*f.* —था) Untrue, false. -2 Vain, futile.

वितथ्य *a.* (*f.* —थ्या) False.

वितद्रुः *f.* N. of a river in the Panjab.

वितनु *a.* 1 Delicate. -2 Beautiful.

वितंडः *f.* A good horse. -*f.* A widow.

वितरणं *n.* 1 Crossing over. -2 A gift, a donation. -3 Leaving, abandoning.

वितर्कः *m.* 1 Argument, reasoning. -2 A conjecture.-3 Fancy,thought. -4 Doubt. -5 Deliberation, discussion.

वितर्कणं *n.* 1 Reasoning.-2 Conjecturing. -3 Doubt. -4 Discussion.

वितर्दिः, —र्दी, वितर्दिका *f.* 1 A raised seat of a rectangular form in a court-yard.-2 A balcony,verandah.

वितर्द्धिः —र्द्धी, वितर्धिका *f.* See वितर्दिः.

वितलं *n.* The second of the seven lower regions under the earth.

वितस्ता *f.* N. of a river in the Punjab called Hydaspes by the Greeks and now called Jhelum or Betustâ.

वितस्तिः *m.*, *f.* A measure of length equal to twelve *angulas.*

वितान *a.* (*f.* —ना) 1 Vacant, empty. -2 Dull, stupid. -3 Wicked. —नः *m.*, —नं *n.* 1 Spreading out, expansion. -2 An awning, a canopy. -3 A cushion. -4 A quantity, an assemblage. -5 A sacrifice ; an oblation.-6 The sacrifical altar. -7 An opportunity. —नं *n.* Leisure, rest.

वितानकः *m.*, —कं *n.* 1 An expanse. -2 A collection, mass. -3 An awning, a canopy. -4 The tree called Máda.

वितीर्ण *p. p.* (*f.* —र्णा) 1 Crossed over. -2 Given, bestowed. -3 Gone down, descended. -4 Conveyed. -5 Subdued, overcome.

वितुन्नं *n.* 1 A pot-herb. -2 The plant called शवाल.

वितुन्नकं *n.* 1 Coriander-seed. -2 Blue vitriol. —कः *m.* The plant called तामलकी.

वितुष्ट *p. p.* (*f.* —ष्टा) Dissatisfied, discontented.

वितृष्ण *a.* (*f.* —ष्णा) Free from desire, contented.

वित्त् 10 U. (वित्तयति,-ते; वित्तापयति,-ते also according to some) To give away, give as alms.

वित्त *p. p.* (*f.* —त्ता) 1 Found, discovered. -2 Gained, acquired. -3 Investigated. -4 Famous. —त्तं *n.* 1 Wealth, property, substance. 2 Power. -Comp.—ईशः *m.* An epithet of Kubera.

वित्तवत् *a.* (*f.* —ती) Rich, wealthy.

वित्तिः *f.* 1 Knowledge -2 Judgment. -3 Gain, acquisition.

वित्रासः *m.* Fear, alarm.

वित्सनः *m.* An ox, a bull.

विथुरः *m.* 1 A demon. -2 A thief. —रा *f.* A widow.

विद् 2 P. (वेत्ति or वेद, वेत्तुं, विदित) 1 To know, understand, learn, find out, discover. -2 To experience. -3 To regard, to know or take to be. With सम्— 1 To recognise. -2 To know, to be aware of.

विद् 4 A (विद्यते, वित्त) 1 To be, to exist. -2 To happen.

विद् 6 U. (विंदति,-ते,वित्त) 1 To obtain, gain. -2 To find, discover, recognise. -3 To feel, experience. -4 To marry.

विद् 7. A (विंते, वित्त or विन्न) 1 To know, understand. -2 To consider, regard, take for. -3 To find, meet with. -4 To reason, reflect. -5 To inquire into.

विद् 10 A (वेदयते) 1 To tell, communicate. -2 To feel, experience. -3 To dwell.

विद् *Caus.* (वेदयति,-ते) To make known, to inform. With आ— 1 To tell, to communicate. -2 To show, to exhibit. नि— 1 To communicate, tell, narrate. -2 To announce. -3 To present, to make an offering. -4 To commit to the care of. प्रति— To inform.

विद् *a.* (At the end of comp.) Conversant with as in वेदविद् &c. —*m.* 1 The planet Mercury. -2 A learned man, wise man. —*f.* 1 Knowledge. -2 Understanding, intellect.

विदः *m.* 1 A learned man, a wise man. -2 The planet Mercury. —दा *f.* 1 Knowledge, learning. -2 Understanding.

विदंशः *m.* Pungent food that excites thirst.

विदग्ध *p. p.* (*f.* —ग्धा) 1 Burnt up. -2 Cooked.-3 Digested. -4 Destroyed, decomposed. -5 Clever, shrewd. -6 Crafty. -7 Lovely, charming. —ग्धः *m.* 1 A scholar. -2 A libertine. —ग्धा *f.* A shrewd and artful woman.

विदथः *m.* 1 A learned man, scholar. -2 An ascetic.

विदरः *m.* Breaking, bursting. —रं *n.* The prickly pear.

विदर्भाः (*m. pl.*) 1 N. of a district, the modern Berar. -2 The natives of Vidarbha. -र्भः *m. sing.* 1 A king of the Vidarbhas. -2 A desert soil. -Comp. —जा,-तनया, -राजतनया,-सुभ्रूः *f.* Epithets of Damayantī, daughter of the king of the Vidarbhas.

विदल *a.* (*f.* —ला) 1 Split. -2 Opened, blown. —लः *m.* 1 Dividing, splitting. -2 A cake. -3 Mountain ebony. —लं *n.* 1 A basket of bamboos. -2 The bark of pomegranate.

विदलनं *n.* Splitting, cutting.

विदारः *m.* 1 Cutting asunder, splitting. -2 War, battle. -3 An inundation. —री *f.* A swelling in the groin.

विदारकः *m.* 1 A divider. -2 A tree or rock in the middle of a stream (which divides its course). -3 A hole sunk in the bed of a dry river for water. —कं *n.* Alkaline earth.

विदारणः *m.* 1 A tree or rock in the middle of a stream (to which a boat is fastened). -2 War, battle. -3 The Karnikára tree. —णा *f.* War, battle. -णं *n.* 1 Splitting, tearing. -2 Afflicting, tormenting. -3 Killing, slaughter.

विदारुः *m.* A lizard.

विदित *p. p.* (*f.* —ता) 1 Known, understood. -2 Informed. -3 Renowned, well-known. -4 Promised, agreed to. —तः *m.* A learned man. —तं *n.* 1 Knowledge, information. -2 Fame.

विदिश् *f.* An intermediate point of the compass.

विदिशा *f.* 1 N. of the capital of the district called दशार्ण. -2 N. of a river in Málvá. -3 An intermediate point of the compass.

विदीर्ण *p. p.* (*f.* —र्णा) 1 Torn, split open. -2 Opened, expanded.

विदुः *m.* 1 The middle of the frontal globes on an elephant's forehead. -2 A hippopotamus.

विदुर *a.* (*f.* —रा) Wise, intelligent. —रः *m.* 1 A wise or learned man. -2 A crafty man. -3 N. of the young brother of Pându.

विदुलः *m.* 1 A kind of reed or ratan. -2 Gum-myrrh.

विदून *p. p.* (*f.* —ना) Afflicted, tormented, distressed.

विदूर *a.* (*f.* —रा) Remote, distant. —रः *m.* N. of a mountain or city from which the Vaidurya jewel or *lapis lazuli* is brought. (The forms विदूरं विदूरेण, विदूरतस् or विदूरात् are used adverbially in the sense of ' from a distance, ' ' from afar '; ' at a distance'). -Comp.-जं *n*. The *lapis lazuli*.

विदूषक *a*. (*f*. —का) 1 Contaminating, corrupting. -2 Detracting, abusing. -3 Humorous, jocular. —कः *m*. 1 A jester, buffoon. -2 The humorous companion and confidential friend of the hero in a play. -3 A libertine, lecher.

विदूषणं *n*. 1 Pollution, corruption. -2 Abuse detraction

विदृतिः *f*. A seam.

विदेशः *m*. A foreign land or country.

विदेशिक, विदेशीय *a*. (*f*. —नी, —या) Foreign, exotic. —*m*. A foreigner.

विदेह *a*. 1 Bodiless, incorporeal. -2 Trunkless. -हाः (*m. pl*.) 1 N. of a country, the ancient Mithilâ. -2 The natives of this country. —हः *m*. 1 The district Videha. -2 N. of Janaka. —हा *f*. N. of a district, the ancient Mithilâ.

विद्ध *p. p*. (*f*. —द्धा) 1 Pierced, wounded. -2 Beaten, lashed. -3 Thrown, directed, sent. -4 Opposed. -5 Resembling. -द्धं *n*. A wound.

विद्या *f*. 1 Knowledge, learning, science. -2 Spiritual knowledge. -3 A spell, an incantation. -4 The Goddess Durgâ. -5 Magical skill. -Comp. —अर्थः *m*. Seeking for knowledge. —आर्थिन् *m*. A student, scholar, pupil. —आलयः *m*. A school, college, any place of learning. —करः *m*. A learned man. —चण, -चंचु *a*. Famous for one's learning. -दलः *m*. The Bhúrja tree. —देवी *f*. The Goddess of learning. -धनं *n*. Wealth in the form of learning. —धरः *m*. (—री *f*.) A class of demigods or semi-divine beings. —वृद्ध *a*. Old in knowledge, advanced in learning. —व्यसनं *n*., —व्यवसायः *m*. Pursuit of knowledge. —व्रतस्नातकः, —स्नातकः *m*. A Brâhmana who has finished his course of religious studentship.

विद्युत् *f*. 1 Lightning. -2 A thunderbolt. -Comp. —उन्मेषः *m*. A flash of lightning. -जिह्वः *m*. A kind of demon or Râkshasa. —प्रियं *n*. Bell-metal. —लता, -लेखा (विद्युल्लता, विद्युल्लेखा) *f*. A streak of lightning.

विद्युत्वत् *m*. A cloud.

विद्योतन *a*. (*f*. —नी) 1 Illuminating. -2 Illustrating, elucidating.

विद्रः *m*. 1 Tearing, piercing. -2 A hole, a cavity.

विद्रधिः *m*. An abscess.

विद्राण *a*. (*f* —णा) Roused from sleep, awakened.

विद्रवः *m*. 1 Running away, retreat. -2 Flowing out. -3 Melting, liquefaction.

विद्रावः *m*. See विद्रवः.

विद्रावणं *n*. 1 Driving away, putting to flight, defeating. -2 Liquefying.

विद्रुत *p. p*. (*f*. —ता) 1 Fled away, (in panic). -2 Agitated, frightened. -3 Liquid, fluid, liquefied.

विद्रुमः *m*. 1 The coral tree (bearing reddish precious gems called corals). -2 A coral. -3 A young shoot or sprout. -Comp. —लता *f*. 1 A branch of coral. -2 A kind of perfume. —लतिका *f*. A kind of perfume (नालिका).

विद्वस् *a*. (Nom. sing. *m*. विद्वान्, *f*. विदुषी, *n*. विद्वत्) 1 Knowing. -2 Wise, learned. —*m*. A learned or wise man, scholar. -Comp. —कल्प, -देशीय, —देश्य *a*. (विद्वत्कल्प, विद्वद्देशीय, विद्वद्देश्य) Slightly learned, a little learned.

विद्विष् *m.*, विद्विष: *m.* An enemy, a foe.

विद्विष्ट *p.p.* (*f.* —ष्टा) Hated, disliked. [tempt.

विद्वेष: *m.* 1 Enmity, hatred.-2 Con-

विद्वेषण: *m.* A hater, an enemy. -णी *f.* A woman of a resentful temper. —णं *n.* 1 Causing hatred or enmity. -2 Enmity, hatred.

विद्वेषिन्, विद्वेष्टृ *m.* A hater, an enemy.

विध् 6 P. (विधति) 1 To pierce, cut. -2 To honour, worship. -3 To rule, govern.

विध् 1 A. (वेधते) To ask, beg.

विध: *m.* 1 Kind, sort. -2 Mode, manner. -3 Fold (at the end of comp., especially after numerals *e.g.* त्रिविध, अष्टविध &c.). -4 The food of elephants. -5 Prosperity. -6 Penetration. [trembling.

विधवनं *n.* 1 Agitating. -2 Tremor,

विधव्यं *n.* Tremor, agitation.

विधवा *f.* A widow. -Comp. —आवेदनं *n.* Marrying a widow. —गामिन् *m.* One who has sexual intercourse with a widow. [creator.

विधस् *m.* N. of Brahman (*m.*) the

विधा *f.* 1 Mode, manner. -2 Kind, sort. -3 Prosperity. -4 The food of elephants. -5 Penetration. -6 Hire, wages.

विधातृ *m.* 1 A maker, creator. -2 N. of Brahman (*m.*).-3 A giver, bestower. -4 Fate, destiny. -5 N. of Visvakarman. -6 N. of the God of love. -7 Spirituous liquor. -Comp. —आयुस् *m.* 1 Sunshine. -2 The sunflower. -भू:*m.* An epithet of Nárada.

विधात्री *f.* Long pepper.

विधानं *n.* 1 Arranging. -2 Making, doing. -3 Creation, creating.-4 Use, application. -5 Enjoining, ordering. -6 A precept, a sacred injunction. -7 Mode, manner. -8 A means or expedient. -9 A rite, ceremony. -10 Affixing, prefixing (as terminations, suffixes &c.).-11 The food given to elephants (to make them intoxicated).-12 Wealth.-13 Pain, agony, torment, distress. -Comp. —ग:, -ज्ञ: *m.* A wise or learned man.

विधानकं *n.* Distress, affliction.

विधायक *a.* (*f.* —यिका), विधायिन् *a.* (*f.* —नी) 1 Arranging, disposing. -2 Doing, making. -3 Creating. -4 Prescribing, laying down. -5 Consigning (to the care of).

विधि: *m.* 1 Doing, performance, an act. -2 A manner, way, mode. -3 A rule, any precept which enjoins something for the first time (as distinguished from नियम and परिसंख्या). -4 A sacred precept or rule, a sacred command, religious commandment (opp. अर्थवाद which means ' an explanatory statement and illustrations').-5 Any religious rite or ceremony. 6 Behaviour, conduct. -7 Condition. -8 Creation, formation. -9 The creator. -10 Fate, luck. -11 The food of elephants. -12Time.-13A physician. -14 N. of Vishnu. -Comp. —ज्ञ: *m.* A Bráhmana versed in the ritual ; a ritualist. —दृष्ट,-विहित *a.* Enjoined by law. -द्वैधं*n.* A variance of precept or commandment.-पूर्वकं*ind.* According to rule, -प्रयोग: *m.* Application of a rule.-वधू:*f.* An epithet of Sarasvatí.

विधित्सा *f.* 1 Desire to do or perform. -2 Design, purpose, desire in general.

विधित्सितं *n.* Intention, design.

विधु: *m.* 1 The moon. -2 Camphor. -3 A demon, fiend. -4 An expiatory oblation. -5 N of Vishnu. -6 N. of Brahman(*m.*).-7N. of Siva.-Comp.

—क्षय: *m.* The period of the dark fortnight of a month. —पंजर: (also पिंजर:) *m.* A scimitar, sabre. —प्रिया *f.* A *Nakshatra* or lunar mansion.

विधुत *a.* (*f.* -ता) See विधूत.

विधुति: *f.* Shaking, tremor.

विधुननं *n.* 1 Shaking, agitating. -2 -2 Trembling.

विधुंतुद: *m.* N. of Ráhu.

विधुर *a.* (*f.* —रा) 1 Afflicted, miserable. -2 Love-lorn, suffering separation from a wife or husband. -3 Deprived or destitute of, free from. -4 Adverse, unfriendly. —र: *m.* A widower. —रं *n.* 1 Alarm, anxiety. -2 Separation from a wife or husband. [and spices.

विधुरा *f.* Curds mixed with sugar

विधुवनं *n.* Shaking, trembling.

विधूत *p. p.* (*f* —ता) 1 Shaken about. -2 Tremulous. -3 Shaken off, removed. -4 Unsteady. -5 Abandoned. —तं *n.* Repugnance.

विधूति: *f.*, विधूननं *n.* Shaking, tremor, agitation.

विधृत *p. p.* (*f.*—ता) 1 Held, grasped. -2 Kept asunder or separate. -3 Assumed, possessed. -4 Restrained. -5 Supported, borne up. —तं *n.* 1 Disregard of a command. -2 Dissatisfaction. [tion.

विधृति: *f.* Arrangement, regula-

विधेय *pot. p.* (*f.* -या) 1 To be done or performed. -2 To be enjoined or prescribed. -3 Dependent on, influenced or controlled by. -4 Obedient, compliant, submissive. -5 To be predicated (in gram. &c). —यं *n.* 1 What ought to be done, a duty.-2The predicate of a sentence, the subject being called the अनुवाद्य. -य: *m.*A servant, dependant.-Comp. -अविमर्श: *m.*A fault(दोष) consisting in giving a subordinate place to the predicate in a sentence. Called also अविमृष्टविधेयांशदोष. -ज्ञ *a.* One who knows one's duty. -पदं *n.* 1 The object to be accomplished. -2 he predicate.

विध्वंस: *m.* 1 Ruin, destruction. -2 Enmity, dislike. -3 An insult, offence.

विध्वस्त *p. p.* (*f.* —स्ता) 1 Ruined, destroyed. -2 Scattered about. -3 Obscured, darkened.

विनत *p. p.* (*f.* -ता) 1 Bent down, bowed. -2 Sunk down, depressed. -3 Crooked, curved. -4 Humble, modest.

विनता *f.* 1 N. of the mother of Aruna and Garuda. -2 A kind of basket

विनति: *f* 1 Bowing down, stooping. -2 Modesty, humility. -3 A request. [a tree.

विनद: *m.* 1 Sound, noise. -3 N. of

विनमनं *n.* Bending, bowing.

विनम्र *a.* (*f.* —म्रा) 1 Bent down, stooping. -2 Depressed, sunk down. -3 Modest, humble. [tree.

विनम्रकं *n.* The flower of the *Tagara*

विनय *a.* (*f.* —या) 1 Cast, thrown. -2 Secret. -3 Ill-behaved. —य: *m.* 1 Moral training. -2 Decorum, decency, good breeding or manners. -3 Modesty, humility. -4 Courtesy, obeisance. -5 Conduct in general. -6A man who has subdued his senses. -7 A trader, merchant.

विनयनं *n.* 1 Removing, taking away. -2 Education, instruction, discipline.

विनशनं *n.* Perishing, loss, disappearance. —न: *m.* N. of the place where the river Sarasvati is lost in the sand.

विनष्ट *p. p.* (*f.* -ष्टा) 1 Perished. -2 Disappeared, lost. -3 Spoiled, corrupted.

विनस *a.* (*f.* -सा or -सी) Noseless.

विना *ind.* Without, except (with acc; instr. or abl.) (विनाकृ 'to leave, abandon, bereave, deprive of). -Comp.-उक्तिः *f.* The figure of speech in which a thing in the absence of another is represented as not disagreeable or as disagreeable.

विनाडिः, विनाडिका *f.* The sixtieth part of a Ghatikâ or a period of time equal to 24 seconds.

विनायकः *m.* 1 A N. of Ganesa. -2 A Buddhist deified teacher. -3 N. of Garuda. -4 An obstacle, impediment. [Removal.

विनाशः *m.* 1 Destruction, ruin. -2

विनाशनं *n.* Destruction, ruin. -नः *m.* A destroyer.

विनास (-सि-) क *a.* Noseless.

विनाहः *m.* A cover for the mouth of a well. [ing forth.

विनिक्षेपः *m.* Throwing down, send-

विनिग्रहः *m.* 1 Restraining, subduing. -2 Mutual opposition or antithesis.

विनिद्र *a.* (*f.*-द्रा) 1 Sleepless, awake (fig. also). -2 Full-blown, expanded.

विनिपातः *m.* 1 Falling down, a fall. -2 A calamity, loss, destruction. -3 Decay, death. -4 Hell, perdition. -5 Occurrence, happening. -6 Disrespect.

विनिमयः *m* 1 Exchange, barter. -2 A pledge, deposit.

विनिमेषः *m.* Twinkling (of the eyes).

विनियत *p. p.* (*f.* -ता) Controlled, restrained.

विनियमः *m.* Control, restraint.

विनियुक्त *p. p.* (*f.* -क्ता) 1 Separated, detached. -2 Attached to, appointed. -3 Commanded, enjoined.

विनियोगः *m.* 1 Separation, parting. -2 Abandoning. -3 Employment, use, application. -4 Appointment to a duty, commission, charge. -5 An impediment. [Departure.

विनिर्गमः *m.* 1 Disappearance. -2

विनिर्णयः *m.* 1 Complete settlement, full decision. -2 Certainty. -3 A settled rule.

विनिर्बंधः *m.* Persistence.

विनिर्मित *p. p.* (*f.* -ता) 1 Formed, made, created. -2 Celebrated, observed (as a feast).

विनिवृत्त *p. p.* (*f.* —त्ता) 1 Returned, turned away. -2 Stopped. -3 Retired.

विनिवृत्तिः *f.* 1 Cessation, stopping, removing. -2 End, stop, termination.

विनिवेशः *m.* 1 Entrance, settling down in a place. -2 An impression.

विनिश्चयः *m.* 1 Ascertainment. -2 A decision, resolution.

विनिश्वासः *m.* Sighing, a sigh.

विनिष्पेषः *m.* Bruising, grinding.

विनिहत *p. p.* (*f.* —ता) 1 Struck down, wounded. -2 Killed. -3 Completely overcome. —तः *m.* 1 Any great or unavoidable calamity. -2 A portent, comet.

विनीत *p. p.* (*f.*-ता) 1 Taken away, removed. -2 Educated, disciplined. -3 Well-behaved. -4 Modest, meek. -5 Decorous. -6 Sent away, dismissed. -7 Tamed. -8 Self-subdued. -9 Chastised, punished. -10 Tractable, governable. -11 Lovely. —तः *m.* 1 A trained horse. -2 A trader.

विनीतकं *n.* 1 A vehicle as a litter &c. -2 A carrier, bearer. [Sin, crime.

विनीयः *m.* 1 Sediment, dregs. -2

विनेतृ *m.* 1 A leader, guide. -2 A teacher. -3 A king, ruler. -4 A chastiser, punisher.

विनोदः *m.* 1 Removing, driving away. -2 A diversion, an amusement. -3 Play, pastime. -4 Eagerness. -5 Pleasure, gratification.

विनोदनं *n.* See विनोदः.

विंदु *a.* 1 Intelligent, wise. -2 Liberal. —दुः *m.* See विंदुः.

विंध्यः *m.* 1 N. of a range of mountains which separates Hindustán proper from the Deccan or south. -2 A hunter. -Comp. —अटवी *f.* The great Vindhya forest. —कूटः, —कूटनः *m.* Epithets of the sage Agastya. —वासिनी *f.* An epithet of Durgà.

विन्न *p. p.* (*f.* —न्ना) 1 Known. -2 Got, obtained. -3 Discussed, investigated. -4 Placed, fixed. -5 Married.

विन्नकः *m.* N. of Agastya.

विन्यस्त *p. p.* (*f.* —स्ता) 1 Placed or put down. -2 Inlaid, paved -3 Arranged. -4 Delivered. -5 Presented, offered. -6 Deposited.

विन्यासः *m.* 1 Entrusting, depositing. -2 A deposit. -3 Arrangement, composition. -4 A collection. -5 A site or receptacle.

विपक्त्रिम *a.* (*f.* —मा) 1 Fully ripened or matured. -2 Developed, fulfilled.

विपक्वः *a.* (*f.* —क्वा) 1 Fully ripened or matured. -2 Developed, fulfilled. -3 Cooked.

विपक्ष *a.* (*f.* -क्षा) Hostile, adverse, contrary. —क्षः *m.* 1 An enemy, a rival, an adversary. -2 A disputant. -3 (In logic) A negative instance (*i. e.* that in which the साध्य or major term is not found.). -4 (In gram.) An exception.

विपंचिका, विपंची *f.* 1 A lute. -2 Play, sport, pastime.

विपणः *m.*, विपणनं *n.* 1 Sale. -2 Petty trade.

विपणिः *m.*, *f.*, —णी *f.* 1 A market, market-place. -2 Trade, traffic.

विपणिन् *m.* A merchant, shop-keeper.

विपत्तिः *f.* 1 A calamity, misfortune. -2 Death, destruction. -3 Agony, torment. —त्तिः (*m.*) An excellent or distinguished foot-soldier.

विपथः *m.* A wrong road, bad way (lit. and fig.).

विपद् *f.* 1 A calamity, misfortune.

विपदा *f.* See विपद्.

विपन्न *p. p.* (*f.* —न्ना) 1 Dead. -2 Lost, destroyed. -3 Unfortunate, distressed. -4 Declined. -5 Disabled. —न्नः *m.* A snake.

विपरिणमनं *n.*, विपरिणामः *m.* 1 A change or an alteration. -2 Change of form, transformation.

विपरिवर्तनं *n.* 1 Turning about, rolling.

विपरीत *a.* (*f.* —ता) 1 Reversed, inverted. -2 Contrary, reverse, inverse. -3 Wrong, contrary to rule, untrue. -4 Unfavourable. -5 Disagreeable, inauspicious. —तः *m.* A particular mode of coitus. —ता *f.* 1 An unchaste wife. -2 A perverse woman.

विपर्णकः *m.* The 'palâsha tree.

विपर्ययः *m.* 1 Contrariety, inversion. -2 Change. -3 Absence or non-existence. -4 Loss, annihilation. -5 Exchange, barter. -6 Error, mistake. -7 A calamity. -8 Hostility, enmity. -9 Perverseness, opposition.

विपर्यस्त *p. p.* (*f.* —स्ता) 1 Changed, reversed. -2 Opposite, contrary. -3 Erroneously considered to be real.

विपर्यायः *m.* See विपर्ययः above.

विपर्यासः *m.* 1 Change, reverse. -2 Being unfavourable. -3 Interchange, exchange. -4 A mistake.

विपलं *n.* An extremely small division of time equal to one-sixtieth part of a *pala*. [ing.

विपलायनं *n*. Running away, retreat-

विपश्चित *a*. Learned, wise. —*m*. A learned or wise man,a sage.

विपाक: *m*. 1 Cooking, boiling. -2 Digestion. -3 Ripening, maturiy, (fig. also). 4 The result of actions either in this or in a former birth. -5 Distress, calamity. -6 Difficulty, embarrassment. -7 Flavour, taste.

विपाटनं *n*. 1 Splitting, tearing up. -2 Spoliation. -2 Eradication.

विपाठ: *m* A kind of large arrow.

विपांडु *a* Pale, pallid.

विपादिका *f*. 1 A sore or tumour on the foot. -2 An enigma, a riddle.

विपाशु, विपाशा *f*. N. of one of the five rivers in the Panjab (now called the Beas).

विपिन *n*. A wood, grove thicket.

विपुल *a*. (*f*. —ला) 1 Large, extensive. -2 Much, abundant. -3 Deep, profound. -ल: *m*. 1 N. of the mountain Meru. -2 Of Himálaya. -3 A respectable man. -Comp. —रस: *m*. The sugar-cane.

विपुला *f*. The earth.

विपुय: *m*. The *Munja* grass.

विप्र: *m*. 1 A Brâhmana. -2 The Asvattha tree. -Comp. —प्रिय: *m*. The 'Palása' tree. -स्वं *n*. The property of a Bràhmana.

विप्रकर्ष: *m*. Distance, remoteness.

विप्रकार: *m*. 1 Insult, abuse. -2 Injury, offence. -3 Wickedness. -4 Opposition, counteraction. -5 Retaliation.

विप्रकीर्ण *a* (*f*. —र्णा) 1 Scattered. -2 Loose, dishevelled. -3 Broad, expanded.

विप्रकृत *p*. *p*. (*f*. -ता) Hurt, offended. -2 Insulted, abused. -3 Opposed. -4 Retaliated.

विप्रकृति: *f*. 1 Injury, offence. -2 An insult, abuse. -3 Retaliation.

विप्रकृष्ट *p*. *p*. (*f* -ष्टा) 1 Drawn away, removed. -2 Distant remote. -3 Lengthened, extened.

विप्रतिकार: *m*. 1 Counteraction, opposition, contradiction.-2 Retaliation.

विप्रतिपत्ति: *f*. 1 Contest,conflict,dispute, opposition. -2 Dissent, objection. -3 Perplexity, confusion. -4 Mutual relation.

विप्रतिपन्न *p*. *p*. (*f*. -न्ना) 1 Mutually opposed, dissentient. -2 Confused, perplexed. -3 Contested, disputed. -4 Mutually connected.

विप्रतिषेध: *m*. 1 Keeping under control. -2 The opposition of two courses of action which are equally important. -3 (In gram.) The conflict of two equally important rules. -4 Prohibition.

विप्रति (-ती-) सार: *m*. 1 Repentance. -2 Anger. -3 Wickedness, evil.

विप्रदुष्ट *p*. *p*. (*f*. -ष्टा) 1 Vitiated, dissolute. 2 Corrupt.

विप्रमुक्त *p*. *p*. (*f*. —क्ता) 1 Set free. -2 Shot, discharged.

विप्रयुक्त *p*. *p*. (*f*. —क्ता) 1 Separated. -2 Freed or released from. -3 Deprived or destitute of.

विप्रयोग: *m*. 1 Separation, dissociation. -2 Quarrel, disagreement.

विप्रलब्ध *p*. *p*. (*f*. -ब्धा) 1 Deceived cheated. -2 Disapointed. -3 Hurt, injured. —ब्धा *f*. A woman disappointed by her lover's breaking his appointment (In poetic composition).

विप्रलंभः *m.* 1 Deceiving, deceit, or deceiving by false statement or by not keeping promises. -2 Quarrel, disagreement. -3 Disunion, separation. -4 The separation of lovers. -5 (In Rhet.) The feeling or sentiment of love in separation.

विप्रलयः *m.* Annihilation.

विप्रलापः *m.* 1 Idle or unmeaning talk, nonsense. -2 Contradictory statement. -3 A dispute. -4 Breaking one's word.

विप्रलुप्तः *p. p.* (*f.* —प्ता) 1 Snatched away. -2 Disturbed, interrupted.

विप्रलोभक्ष *m.* The Ashoka tree.

विप्रवासः *m.* Dwelling in a foreign country.

विप्राश्निका *f.* A female fortune-teller.

विप्रहीण *a.* (*f.* —णा) Deprived or destitute of.

विप्रिय *a.* (*f.* —या) Disagreeable, unpleasant. -यं *n.* Offence, a disagreeable act.

विप्रुष् *f* 1 A drop (of water or any other liquid). -2 A mark,dot,spot.

विप्रोषित *p. p.* (*f.* -ता) 1 Staying abroad, away from, absent. -2 Banished. -Comp. —भर्तृका *f* A woman whose husband is absent from home.

विप्लवः *m.* 1 Floating or drifting about. -2 Opposition, contrariety. -3 Confusion,perplexity.-4 Tumult, affray.-5 Predatory warfare; danger from an enemy. -6 Extortion. -7 Loss, destruction. -8 An evil turn. -9 The rust on a mirror or dust on its surface. -10 An evil, a calamity. -11 Sin, wickedness.

विप्लावः *m.* Deluging, inundating. -2 A horse's gallop.

विप्लुत *p. p.* (*f.* —ता) 1 Drifted about. -2 Drowned, deluged. -3 Confounded, disturbed. -4 Devastated. -5 Lost, disappeared. -6 Disgraced. -7 Depraved,dissolute. -8 Contrary, reverse. -9 Turning out false.

विप्लुष् *f.* See विप्रुष्.

विफल *a.* (*f.* —ला) 1 Fruitless,vain. -2 Idle, unmeaning.

विबंधः *m.* 1 Constipation. -2 Obstruction.

विबाधा *f.* Pain, torment, agony.

विबुद्ध *p. p.* (*f.* —द्धा) 1 Aroused, awakened. -2 Expanded, blossomed. -3 Clever, skilful. -4 Unconscious.

विबुधः *m.* 1 A wise or learned man. -2 A God, deity. -3 The moon.

विबुधानः *m.* 1 A learned man. -2 A teacher.

विबोधः *m.* 1 Awakening. -2 Perceiving, discovering. -3 Intelligence. -4 Becoming conscious(one of the 33 subordinate feelings in Rhetoric). -5 Inattention, absence of mind.

विब्बोकः *m.* See बिब्बोकः.

विभक्त *p. p.* (*f.* —क्ता) 1 Divided, partitioned (as property &c.) -2 Divided, separated in interest (in law). -3 Separated,made distinct. -4 Different, multifarious. -5 Secluded. -6 Regular, symmetrical. -7 Ornamented. -8 Measured. —क्तः *m.* N.of Kârtikeya. -क्तं *n.* 1 Solitude, retirement. -2 Separation.

विभक्तिः *f.* 1 Separation, division, partition. -2 Separation in interest. -3 A share of inheritance. -4 (In gram.) Inflection of nouns ; a case or case-termintion.

विभंगः *m.* 1 Breaking, fracture. -2 Obstruction, stoppage. -3 Contraction (as of the eye-brows). -4 A fold, wrinkle. -5 A step, stair. -6 Division.

विभवः *m.* 1 Wealth, property. -2 Might, prowess, greatness. -3 High rank, dignity. -4 Magnanimity. -5 Final beatitude.

विभा *f.* 1 Light, lustre. -2 A ray of light. -3 Beauty; splendour. -Comp. —करः *m.* 1 The sun. -2 The *arka* plant. -3 The moon. -4 Fire. -वसुः *m.* 1 The sun. -2 Fire. -3 The moon. -4 A kind of necklace.

विभागः *m.* 1 Division, partition. -2 The share of an inheritance. -3 A part or share in general. -4 Division, separation (regarded in Nyâya phil. as a Guna). -5 The numerator of a fraction. -Comp. -धर्मः *m.* The law of inheritance. -पत्रिका *f.* A deed of partition. —भाज् *m.* One who shares in a property already distributed.

विभाजनं *n.* Dividing, distributing.

विभाज्य *a.* (*f.* -ज्या) 1 Portionable, to be divided. -2 Divisible.

विभातं *n.*, —ती *f.* Day-break, dawn.

विभावः *m.* 1 (In Rhet.) Any condition which produces or develops a particular state of body or mind (one of the three main divisions of Bhâvas, the other two being अनुभाव and व्यभिचारिभाव). -2 A friend, an acquaintance.

विभावनं *n.*, -ना *f.* 1 Clear perception, discrimination, judgment. -2 Investigation. -3 Conception, imagination. -ना *f.* (In Rhet.)A figure of speech in which an effect is represented as taking place though the usual cause is absent.

विभावरी *f.* 1 Night. -2 Turmeric. -3 A bawd. -4 A harlot. -5 A perverse woman. -6 A talkative woman. -7 N. of a metre.

विभावित *p. p.* (*f.* -ता) 1 Manifested, made visible. -2 Understood, ascertained. -3 Seen, conceived. -4 Judged, discriminated. -5 Inferred, indicated. -6 Proved, established.

विभाषा *f.* 1 An option, alternative. -2 Optionality of a rule.

विभासा *f.* Light, lustre.

विभिन्न *p.p.* (*f.*—न्ना) 1 Broken, split. -2 Pierced, wounded. -3 Driven away, dispersed. -4 Perplexed. -5 Moved to and fro. -6 Disappointed. -7 Different, various. -8 Variegated. -9 Manifested, displayed. -न्नः *m.* N. of Siva.

विभीतः (-तकः) *m.*, विभीतं (-तकं) *n.*, विभीतकी, विभीता *f.* N. of a tree, Terminalia Belerica.

विभीषिका *f.* 1 Terror. -2 A means of terrifying.

विभु *a.* (*f.* -भु,-भ्वी) 1 Mighty, powerful. -2 Eminent, supreme. -3 Able to, capable of (with inf.). -4 Self-controlled. -5 (In Nyâya phil.) Eternal, all-pervading. -6 Firm, hard. -भुः *m.* 1 Ether. -2 Space. -3 Time. -4 The soul. -5 A master, sovereign. -6 The supreme ruler. -7 A servant. -8 N. of Brahman (*m.*). -9 Of Siva. -10 Of Vishnu.

विभुग्न *a.* (*f.* —ग्ना) Bent.

विभूतिः *f.* 1 Might, power. -2 Prosperity, welfare. -3 Exalted rank. -4 Plenty, magnificence, splendour. -6 Superhuman power consisting of eight faculties, अणिमन्, लघिमन्, प्राप्ति, प्राकाम्य, महिमन्, ईशिता, वशिता and कामावसायिता. -7 Ashes of cow-dung.

विभूषणं *n.* Ornament, decoration.

विभूषा *f.* 1 Ornament, decoration. -2 Light, lustre. -3 Beauty.

विभूषित *p. p.* (*f.*—ता) Adorned, ornamented.

विभृत *p. p.* (*f.* -ता) Upheld, supported, maintained.

विभ्रंश: *m.* 1 Falling away or off. -2 Decay, ruin -3 A precipice.

विभ्रम: *m.* 1 Roaming about. -2 Whirling round, rolling about. -3 Error. -4 Hurry, confusion, perturbation. -5 Any amorous or sportive movement. -6 Beauty, charm. -7 Doubt, apprehension. -8 Caprice, whim.

विभ्रमा *f.* Old age.

विभ्रष्ट *p. p.* (*f.* -ष्टा) 1 Fallen off, separated. -2 Decayed, ruined. -3 Disappeared. -4 Deprived of.

विभ्राज् *a.* Shining, bright.

विभ्रांत *p. p.* (*f.* -ता) 1 Whirled about. -2 Agitated, confused. -3 Mistaken, erring. -Comp, —शील: *m.* 1 A monkey. 2 The disc of the sun or moon.

विभ्रांति: *f.* 1 Whirling round. -2 Hurry. -3 Error. -4 Coufusion.

विमत *p. p.* (*f.* -ता) 1 Disagreeing. -2 Inconsistent. -3 Slighted, neglected. —त: *m.* An enemy.

विमति *a.* Stupid, foolish. —ति: *f.* 1 Dissent, difference of opinion. -2 Dislike. -3 Stupidity.

विमत्सर *a.* (*f.* —री) Free from jealousy.

विमद *a.* (*f.* -दा) 1 Free from intoxication. -2 Sad, cheerless.

विमनस्, विमनस्क *a.* (*f.* —स्का) 1 Sad, sorry, discomposed. -2 Absent-minded. -3 Perplexed. -4 Displeased. [Free from grief.

विमन्यु *a.* 1 Free from anger. -2

विमय: *m.* Exchange, barter.

विमर्द: *m.* 1 Crushing, bruising. -2 Rubbing together, friction. -4 Touch contact. -5 Rubbing the person with saffron or other unguents. -6 War, battle. -7 Destruction, devastation. -8 Conjunction of the sun and moon.

विमर्दक: *m.* 1 Grinding, pounding, bruising. -2 The trituration of perfumes. -3 An eclipse. -4 The conjunction of the sun and moon. -5 Destroying.

विमर्दनं *n.*, -ना *f.* 1 Pounding, crushing -2 Rubbing together, friction. -3 Destuction. -4 An eclipse.

विमर्श: *m.*, विमर्शनं *n.* 1 Deliberation, discussion, thoughtfulness, reflection. -2 Reasoning. -3 A conflicting judgment. -4 Hesitation, doubt. -5 The impression left on the mind by past good or bad actions.

विमर्ष: *m.* 1 Thought, deliberation. 2 Non-forbearance. -3 Dissatisfaction. -4 (In dramas) A change in the prosperous course of a love-story caused by some unforeseen reverse (one of the five *Sandhis* in a drama) (often writtien विमर्श: in all these senses).

विमल *a.* (*f.* —ला) 1 Pure, stainless (fig. also). -2 Clear, transparent (as water). -3 White, bright. -लं *n.* 1 Silver-gilt. -2 Talc. -Comp. —मणि: *m.* A crystal.

विमांस: *m.*, -सं *n.* Unclean meat.

विमातृ *f.* A step-mother. Comp. —ज: *m.* A step-mother's son.

विमान: *m.*, -नं *n.* 1 Disrespect, dishonour. -2 A measure. -3 A heavenly car (moving through the skies). -4 A vehicle in general. -5 A seven-storied palace. -6 A horse.

विमानना *f.* Disrespet, humiliation.

विमार्ग: *m.* 1 A bad road. -2 Evil conduct or course, immorality. -3

A broom, a brush. [for.

विमार्गणं *n.* Searching, looking out

विमिश्र, विमिश्रित *a.* (*f.* —श्रा, —ता) Mixed, mingled.

विमुक्त *p. p* (*f.* —क्ता) 1 Released, liberated. -2 Given up, left. -3 Freed from. -4 Hurled, discharged. -5 Given vent to.

विमुक्तिः *f.* 1 Release, liberation. -2 Separation. -3 Final liberation.

विमुख *a.* (*f.* —खी) 1 With the face averted or turned away from. -2 Averse, disinclined. -3 Adverse. -4 Devoid of. [wildered.

विमुग्ध *a.* (*f.* —ग्धा) Confused, bewildered.

विमुद्र *a.* (*f.* —द्रा) 1 Unsealed. -2 Opened, blown (as a flower).

विमूढ *p. p.* (*f.* —ढा) 1 Confounded, bewildered. -2 Tempted, beguiled. -3 Stupid.

विमृष्ट *p. p.* (*f.* —ष्टा) Considered, pondered over.

विमोक्षः *m.* 1 Release, liberation. -2 Discharging. -3 Final emancipation.

विमोक्षणं *n.*, —णा *f.* 1 Liberating, setting free. -2 Discharging. -3 Leaving, abandoning.

विमोचनं *n.* 1 Unloosing. -2 Release, freedom. -3 Liberation, emancipation.

विमोहनं *n.*, —नः *m.* N. of a division of Hell. —नं *n.* 1 Seducing, tempting. 2 Infatuation.

विंबः *m.*, विंबं *n.* See बिंब.

विंबकं *n.* See बिंबकं.

विंबटः *m.* The mustard plant.

विंबा, विंबी *f.* N. of a creeper.

विंबिका *f.* See बिंबिका.

विंबुः *m.* The betel-nut tree.

वियत् *n.* The sky, atmosphere. -Comp. —गंगा *f.* 1 The heavenly Ganges. -2 The galaxy. —चारिन् (वियच्चारिन्) *m.* A kite. —भूतिः *f.* Darkness. —मणिः (वियन्मणिः) *m.* The sun.

वियातिः *m.* The bird.

वियमः *m.* 1 Restraint, control. -2 Distress, affliction. -3 Cessation.

वियात *a.* 1 Bold. -2 Shameless, impudent.

वियामः *m.* See वियमः.

वियुक्त *p. p.* (*f.* —क्ता) 1 Detached, separated. -2 Deserted by. 3 Free from, deprived of.

वियुत *p. p.* (*f.* —ता) 1 Separated from. -2 Devoid of.

वियोगः *m.* 1 Separation, disunion. -2 Absence, loss. -3 Subtraction.

वियोगिन *m.* The ruddy goose.

वियोगिनी *f.* 1 A woman separated from her lover or husband. -2 N of a metre.

वियोजित *p. p.* (*f.* —ता) 1 Separated. -2 Deprived of.

वियोनि., वियोनी *f.* 1 Manifold birth. -2A debased or ignominious birth

विरक्त *p. p.* (*f.* —क्ता) 1 Very red, ruddy. -2 Discoloured. -3 Changed in mind, displeased. 4 Free from passion or worldly attachment. -5 Impassioned.

विरक्तिः *f.* 1 Change of disposition, dissatisfaction, disaffection -2 Estrangement. 3 Freedom from passion or worldly attachment.

विरचनं *n.*, —ना *f.* 1 Arrangement. 2 Contriving, constructing. -3 Formation, creation. -4 Composition, compilation.

विरचित *p. p.* (*f.* —ता) 1 Arranged, formed, prepared. -2 Constructed -3 Written, composed. 4 Trimmed, embellished, ornamented. -5 Put on, worn. -6 Set, inlaid.

विरज *a.* (*f.* —जा) Free from dust or passion. —जः *m.* An epithet of Vishnu.

विरजस्, विरजस्क *a.* (*f.* -स्का) 1 Free from dust. -2 Free from passion. -3 Free from menstrual excretion.

विरजस्का *f.* A woman who has ceased to menstruate.

विरंचः, -चिः *m.* N. of Brahman (*m.*).

विरटः *m.* A kind of black agallochum.

विरणं *n.* A kind of fragrant grass.

विरत *p. p* (*f.* -ता) 1 Ceased or desisting from (with abl.).-2 Stopped, ceased. -3 Ended, concluded.

विरतिः *f.* 1 Cessation. -2 Rest, end, pause. -3 Indifference to worldly attachment.

विरमः *m.* 1 Cessation, stop. -2 Sunset.

विरल *a.* (*f.* -ला) 1 Having interstices, separated by intervals, thin. -2 Rare, scarcely found, unfrequent. -3 Few, litlle (referring to number or quantity). -4 Remote, distant, long (as time, distance etc.) -लं *n.* Curds, coagulated milk. -लं *ind.* Scarcely, rarely. -Comp. —जानुक *a.* Bandy-legged, bow-kneed. -द्रवा *f.* A kind of gruel.

विरस *a.* (*f.* -सा) 1 Tasteless, flavourless. -2 Disagreeable, painful. —सः *m.* Pain.

विरहः *m.* 1 Separation. -2 The separation of lovers.-3 Absence, want. -4 Abandonment, relinquishment. -5 Loneliness.

विरहिणी *f.* 1 A woman separated from her lover or husband. -2 Wages, hire.

विरहित *p. p.* (*f.* -ता) 1 Abandoned, forsaken. -2 Separated from. -3 Lonely, solitary. -4 Destitute of, free from.

विरहिन् *a.* (*f.* —णी) Absent from, being separated from a mistress or lover.

विरागः *m.* 1 Change of colour. -2 Change of disposition, discontent, dissstisfaction. -3 Disinclination. -4 Indifference to worldly pursuits.

विराज् *m.* 1 Beauty, splendour. -2 A man of the Kshatriya tribe. -3. The first progeny of Brahman (*m.*). -4 The body.-*f.* N. of a Vedic metre.

विराजः *m.* See विराज्.

विराजित *p. p.* (*f.* —ता) Illuminated -2 Manifested.

विराटः *m.* 1 N. of a district in India. -2 N. of a king of the Matsyas. -Comp. —जः *m.* A sort of inferior diamond. -पर्वन् *n.* The fourth book of the Mahábhârata.

विराटकः *m.* A sort of inferior diamond.

विराणिन् *m.* An elephant.

विरुद्ध *p. p.* (*f.* —द्धा) 1 Opposed, counteracted. -2 Offended, injured.

विराधः *m.* 1 Opposition. -2 Vexation, molestation.-3 N. of a Rákshasa slain by Ráma.

विराधनं *n.* 1 Opposing. -2 Injuring, offending. -3 Pain.

विरामः *m.* 1 Cessation, discontinuance. -2 End, conclusion.-3 Pause, stop. -4 The stop of the voice. -5 A small oblique stroke marking the end of sentence.

विरालः *m.* See बिडालः.

विरावः *m.* Noise, sound.

विराविणी *f.* 1 Weeping. -2 A broom.

विरिंचः, विरिंचनः, *m.* 1 N. of Brahman (*m.*).

विरिंचिः *m.* 1 N. of Brahman (*m.*). -2 Of Vishnu. -3 Of Siva.

विरुग्ण *p. p.* (*f.* —ग्णा) 1 Broken to pieces, destroyed.-2 Bent. -3 Blunted, dulled.

विरुत *p. p.* (*f.* -ता) 1 Screamed. -2 Filled with cries. -तं *n.* 1 Crying, shrieking. -2 Cry, noise. -3 Singing, humming.

विरुदः *m.*, -दं *n.* 1 Proclaiming. 2 Crying aloud. -3 A panegyric.

विरुदितं *n.* Loud lamentation.

विरुद्ध *p.p.* (*f.* —द्धा) 1 Hindered, obstructed. -2 Confined or shut up, blockaded. -3 Inconsistent with, incongruous. -4 Contrary, opposite, opposed in quality. -5 Contradictory. -6 Adverse, inimical. -7 Unfavourable, unpropitious. -8 Prohibited. -9 Unlawful, improper. -द्धं *n.* 1 Opposition, hostility. -2 Disagreement. -Comp.—अन्नं *n.* Forbidden food.

विरूक्षणं *n.* 1 Roughening. 2 Blame, censure. -3 A curse, an imprecation.

विरूढ *p.p.* (*f.* -ढा) 1 Grown, germinated. -2 Produced. -3 Grown, increased. -4 Budded, blossomed. -5 Ascended, mounted.

विरूप *a.* (*f* -पा or -पी) 1 Deformed, ugly, misshapen, unnatural, monstrous. -2 Multiform, diverse. —पं *n.* 1 Deformity, ugliness. -2 Variety of form, nature or character.-Comp. -अक्ष *a.* Having deformed eyes -अक्षः *m.* N. of Siva. —चक्षुस् *m.* An epithet of Siva.

विरूपिन् *a.* (*f.* —णी) Deformed; disfigured. -*m.* A pole-cat.

विरेकः *m.* 1 Evacuation of the bowels, purging. -2 A purgative.

विरेचनं *n.* See विरेकः.

विरेचित *a.* (*f.* -ता) Purged, evacuated.

विरेफः *m.* 1 A river, stream. -2 Absence of the letter र.

विरोकः *m.*,-कं *n.* A hole, chasm. कः *m.* A ray of light.

विरोचनः *m* 1 The sun. -2 The moon. -3 Fire. -4 N. of the son of Prarháda. -Comp -सुतः *m.* An epithet of Bali.

विरोधः *m.* 1 Opposition, impediment. -2 Siege, investment. -3 Restraint, check. -4 Contradiction.-5 Antithesis, contrast.-6 Enmity, hostility.- 7 A quarrel. -8 A misfortune. (In Rhet.) The figure of speech in which there is a mention of an incongruity (which is only apparent) between things. This figure is also called विरोधाभासः. -Comp. -उक्तिः *f.*, -वचनं *n.* Contradiction, opposition. —आभासः *m.* See above.

विरोधनं *n.* 1 Opposing, obstructing. -2 Besieging, blockading. -3 Resistance. -4 Contradiction.

विरोधिन् *a.* (*f.* -नी) Resisting. -2 Besieging. -3 Contradictory. -4 Hostile. -5 Quarrelsome. -*m.* An enemy.

विरोप (-इ-) णं *n.* 1 Healing (as a sore). 2 Planting.

विरोहः *m* Growing, shooting forth.

विल् 6 P. (विलति) 1 To cover, conceal. -2 To break, divide.

विलं *n.* See बिलं.

विलक्ष *a.* (*f.* —क्षा) 1 Having no distinguishing marks.-2 Bewildered. -3 Astonished. -4 Ashamed, abashed.

विलक्षण *a.* (*f.* —णा) 1 Having no distinguishing marks. -2 Different, other. -3 Strange, unusual. -4 Possessed of inauspicious marks.

विलक्षित *p.p.* (*f.* —ता) 1 Distinguished, seen, discovered. -2 Discernible (by). -3 Dismayed, embarrassed.

विलग्न *a.* (*f.* —ग्ना) 1 Sticking to, fastened on. -2 Thin, slender, delicate. —ग्नं *n.* 1 The waist. -2 The hips.-3 The rising of a constellation.

विलंघनं *n.* 1 Transgressing, overstepping. -2 Transgression, injury

विलंघित *p. p.* (*f.* -ता) 1 Gone over. -2 Transgressed. -3 Surpassed, excelled. -4 Overcome, defeated.

विलज्ज *a.* (*f.* -ज्जा) Shameless, unabashed.

विलपनं *n.* 1 Talking.-2 Chattering, prattle. -3 Lamenting.-4 The sediment of any oily substance. [wail.

विलपितं *n.* 1 Lamentation. -2 A

विलंबः *m.* 1 Hanging over, pendulousness. -2 Delay.

विलंबनं *n.* 1 Hanging down, depending. -2 Delay.

विलंबिका *f.* Constipation.

विलंबित *p. p.* (*f.* —ता) 1 Hanging depending. -2 Pendulous. -3 Depending on, closely connected with. -4 Delayed, retarded. -5 Slow (as time in music). —तं *n.* Delay. -तं *ind.* Slowly, tardily.

विलंबिन् *a.* (*f.* —नी) 1 Hanging down, pendent. -2 Delaying, dilatory. [donation.

विलंभः *m.* 1 Liberality. -2 A gift,

विलयः *m.* 1 Dissolution, liquefaction. -2 Destruction, death. -3 Dissolution of the world.

विलयनं *n.* 1 Dissolving, liquefying, dissolution. -2 Corroding. -3 Removing, taking away. -4 Attenuating [ing, dallying.

विलसनं *n.* 1 Glittering. -2 Sport-

विलसित *p. p.* (*f.* —ता) 1 Glittering, shining.-2 Manifested.-3 Sportive, wanton. —तं *n.* 1 Glittering, gleaming. -2 A gleam, flash. -3 Appearance, manifestation. -4 Sport, amorous or wanton gesture (fig. also). [moan.

विलापः *m.* Lmentation, a wail,

विलालः *m.* 1 A cat. -2 An instrument, a machine.

विलासः *m.* 1 Sport, play. -2 Amorous pastime. -3 Coquetry, affectation. -4 Grace, charm. 5 Flash, gleam.

विलासनं *n.* 1 Sport, pastime -2 Wantonness, dalliance. [woman.

विलासवती *f.* A wanton or amorous

विलासिका *f.* A drama in one act full of love-incidents.

विलासिन् *a.* (*f.* -नी) Sportive, playful, wanton, coquettish. —*m.* 1 A sensualist -2 Fire. -3 The moon. -4 A snake. -5 An epithet of Krishna or Vishnu. -6 Of Siva. -7 Of the God of love.

विलासिनी *f.* 1 A woman (in general). -2 A coquettish or wanton woman. -3 A harlot. [writing.

विलिखनं *n.* Scratching, scraping.

विलिप्त *p. p.* (*f.* -प्ता) 1 Besmeared, smeared over. -2 Stained, defiled.

विलीन *p. p.* (*f.* -ना)1 Sticking to, attached to.-2Contiguous to, in contact with. -3 Melted, dissolved, liquefied. -4 Disappeared, vanished withered up.

विलुंचनं *n.* Tearing off, peeling

विलुंठनं *n* Robbing, plundering.

विलुप्त *p. p.* (*f.* —प्ता) 1 Broken or torn off -2 Snatched away, carried off. -3 Robbed, plundered. 4 Destroyed, ruined. -5 Impaired, mutilated.

विलुंपकः *m.* A thief, robber, ravisher.

विलुलित *p. p.* (*f.* —ता) 1 Moving to and fro, tossed about. -2 Disordered, disarranged -3 Fickle, unsteady [asunder.

विलून *p. p.* (*f.* —ना) Cut off, cut

विलेखनं *n.* 1 Scaratching, making a mark or furrow. -2 Digging. -3 Uprooting -4 Dividing, splitting.

विलेपः *m.* 1 An unguent, an ointment. -2 Mortar. -4 Plaster (in general). -4 Anointing, plastering.

विलेपनं n. 1 Smearing, anointing. -2 An ointment, unguent.

विलेपनी f. 1 A woman scented with perfumes. -2 A woman beautifully dressed. -3 Rice gruel.

विलेपिका, विलेपी f., विलेप्यः m. Rice-gruel.

विलोकनं n. 1 Seeing, looking at, observing. -2 Sight, observation.

विलोकित p. p. (f. -ता) 1 Seen, observed, viewed, beheld. -2 Examined, thought about. -तं n. A look, glance. [n. Tears.

विलोचनं n. The eye. -Comp. —अंबु

विलोडनं n. Agitating, stirring up.

विलोडित p. p. (f. -ता) Shaken, stirred. —तं n. Butter-milk.

विलोपः m. 1 Taking away, carrying off, plunder. -2 Loss, destruction, disapperance.

विलोपनं n. 1 Cutting off. -2 Carrying away. -3 Destroying, destruction.

विलोभः m. Attraction, allurement.

विलोभनं n. 1 Enticing, alluring. -2 A temptation, seduction. -3 Praise, flattery.

विलोम a. (f. —मी) 1 Inverted, reverse, inverse. -2 Produced in the reverse order. -3 Backward. -मः m. 1 Reverse order, inversion. -2 A dog. -3 A snake. -4 N. of Varuna. —मं n. A machine for raising water from a well. -Comp. -उत्पन्न, —ज, —जात, —वर्ण a. Born of a mother whose caste is superior to the father's. -क्रिया f., —विधिः m. A rule of inversion (in math.). -जिह्वः m. An elephant.

विलोमी f. The emblic myrobalan.

विलोल a. (f. —ला) 1 Shaking about, tremulous, unsteady, rolling, waving. -2 Loose, disordered, dishevelled (as hair).

विलोहितः m. N. of Rudra. —ता f. One of the tongues of fire.

विल्लं n. See बिल्लं.

विल्वः m. See बिल्वः.

विवक्षा f. 1 A desire to speak. -2 Wish, desire. -3 Meaning, sense. -4 Intention, purpose.

विवक्षित a. (f. —ता) 1 Intended to be said or spoken. -2 Meant, intended, purposed. -3 Wished, desired. -4 Favourite. —तं n. 1 Purpose, intention. -2 Sense, meaning

विवक्षु a. Wishing or about to speak.

विवत्सा a. A calf-less cow.

विवधः m. 1 A yoke for carrying burdens. -2 A road, high-way. -3 A load, burden. -4 A pitcher.

विवधिकः m. 1 A carrier of loads, porter. -2 A pedlar, a hawker.

विवरं n. 1 A fissure, hole, cavity, vacuity. -2 An interval, intervening space. -3 A solitary place. -4 A fault, defect, a weak point. -5 A breach, wound. -6 The number 'nine.' -Comp. —नालिका f. A flute, a pipe.

विवरणं n. 1 Displaying, unfolding, opening. -2 Laying bare or open. -3 Explanation, comment, interpretation. -4 Describing, description. -5 A sentence.

विवर्जनं n. Leaving, excluding, abandoning.

विवर्जित p. p. (f. -ता) 1 Left, abandoned. -2 Deprived of, destitute of. -3 Given, distributed.

विवर्ण a. (f. —र्णा) 1 Pale, pallid. 2 Low, vile. -3 Ignorant, stupid. —र्णः m. A man of a low caste.

विवर्तः m 1 Turning round, revolving, moving round. -2 Rolling back, returning. -3 Dancing. -4 Alteration, change of form, altered state. -6 (In Vedânta phil.) An unreal appearance caused by अविद्या or human error. -7 A heap, collection, an assemblage.-Comp. —वादः *m.* The doctrine of the Vedántins that the visible world is illusory and Brahman (*n.*) alone is the real entity.

विवर्तनं *n.* 1 Revolving, revolution, whirling round, turning round. -2 Rolling back, returning. -3 Existing, abiding. -4 Reverential salutation. -5 Passing through various states or existences. -6 An altered condition.

विवर्धनं *n.* 1 Increasing, augmentation, growth. -2 Enlargement, aggrandisement.

विवर्धित *p, p.* (*f.* —ता) 1 Increased, augmented. -2 Promoted, furthered. -3 Gratified, satisfied.

विवश *a.* (*f.* -शा) 1 Uncontrolled, unsubdued. -2 Subject; under control (of another), helpless. -3 Insensible, not master of oneself. -4 Dead, perished. 5 Desirous of death.

विवसन *a.* (*f.* —ना) Naked, unclothed.

विवस्वत *m.* The sun. -2 N. of Aruna. -3 N. of the present Manu. -4 A God. -5 The *Arka* plant.

विवहः *m.* N. of one of the seven tongues of fire.

विवाकः *m.* A judge.

विवादः *m.* 1 A dispute, controversy, discussion, quarrel, strife, argumentation. -2 Contradiction. -3 A law-suit, contest at law. -4 Crying aloud. -Comp. —अर्थिन् *m.* 1 A litigant. -2 A plaintiff, complainant, prosecutor. — पदं *n.* A title of dispute. —वस्तु *n.* The subject of dispute, the matter at issue.

विवादिन् *a.* (*f.* —नी) 1 Disputing, quarrelling. -2 Litigating. -*m.* A litigant, a party in a law-suit.

विवारः *m.* 1 Opening, expansion. -2 Expansion of the throat in articulation.

विवासः *m.*, विवासनं *n.* Banishment, expulsion.

विवासित *p. p.* (*f.* —ता) Banished. exiled.

विवाहः *m.* Marriage. -Comp. —दीक्षा *f.* The marriage ceremony or rite.

विवाहित *p. p.* (*f.* —ता) Married.

विवाह्यः *m.* 1 A son-in-law. -2 A bridegroom.

विविक्त *p. p.* (*f.* —क्ता) 1 Separated. detached. -2 Lonely, solitary. -3 Single, alone. -4 Distinguished. discriminated. -5 Judicious. -6 Pure, faultless. —क्तं *n.* 1 A lonely or solitary place. -2 Loneliness, privacy. —क्ता *f.* A woman disliked by her husband.

विविग्न *a.* (*f.* —ग्ना) 1 Very much agitated or terrified.-2 Very angry.

विविध *a.* (*f.* —धा) Various, manifold, multiform, sundry.

विवीतः *m.* An enclosed pasture-land

विवृक्त *p. p.* (*f.* —क्ता) Left, abandoned. —क्ता *f.* A woman disliked by her husband.

विवृत *p. p.* (*f.* —ता) 1 Displayed, manifested, expressed. -2 Evident. -3 Uncovered, laid bare. -4 Proclaimed. -5 Expounded, commented upon. -6 Large, spacious. —तं *n.* Open articulation. —तं *ind.* Openly. -Comp. —अक्षः *m.* A cock.

विवृतिः *f.* 1 Display, manifestation. -2 Expansion. -3 Exposure, discovery. -4 Comment, interpretation.

विवृत्त *p. p.* (*f.* —त्ता) 1 Turned round. -2 Revolving, rolling.

विवृत्तिः *f.* 1 Turning round, whirling -2 (In gram.) A hiatus.

विवृद्ध *p. p.* (*f.* —द्धा) 1 Grown up. -2 Increased. -3 Copious, plentiful.

विवृद्धिः *f.* 1 Growth, increase, development. -2 Prosperity.

विवेकः *m.* 1 Discrimination, judgment, discretion. -2 Consideration, investigation. -3 Distinction, difference. -4 (In Vedánta phil.) The power of separating reality from mere semblance or illusion. -5 True knowledge. -6 A basin, reservoir. -Comp. —पदवी *f.* Reflection, consideration.

विवेकिन् *a.* (*f.* —नी) Discriminating, judicious. *m.* 1 A judge. -2 A philosopher.

विवक्तृ *m.* 1 A judge. -2 A sage, philosopher.

विवेचनं *n.*, —ना *f.* 1 Discrimination. -2 Discussion, decision.

विवोढृ *m.* 1 A bridegroom, husband. -2 A son-in-law.

विव्वोकः *m.* See बिब्बोक.

विश् 6 P. (विशति, वेष्टुं, विष्ट) 1 To enter. -2 To come into the possession of, fall to the share of. -3 To settle down upon. -4 To penetrate, pervade. -5 To undertake. With अनु— 1 To enter after some one. -2 To enter. अनुप्र— 1 To enter into; to adapt or accommodate oneself to. अभिनि— (*Atm.*) To resort to, to take possession of, to go to. आ— 1 To enter. -2 To approach. -3 To occupy. उप— 1 To sit down. -2 To encamp. -3 To enter. नि— (*Atm.*) To sit down. -2 To enter. -3 To be intent on. -4 To marry. निस्— 1 To enjoy. -2 To embellish. प्र— 1 To enter. -2 To begin. सम्— 1 To enter. -2 To have sexual intercourse with. -3 To sleep, lie down. समा— 1 To enter. -2 To approach.

Causal. (वेशयति,-ते) To cause to enter. With नि-1 To apply the mind. -2 To draw, portray. -3 To put, place. -4 To enter on, to commit. प्र— 1 To usher. विनि- To put, to fix.

विश् *m.* 1 A Vaisya. -2 A man in general. -3 People. -*f.* 1 People, subjects. -2 A daughter. -Comp. -पण्यं *n.* Goods, merchandise. —पतिः (also विशांपतिः) *m.* 1 A king. -2 A son-in-law. -3 A head-merchant.

बिसं *n.* The fibres of the stalk of a lotus. -Comp. -कंठा *f.*, -कंठिका *m.* A crane.

विशंकट *a.*(*f.* -टा, -टी) 1 Great, large. -2 Strong, powerful.

विशद *a.* (*f.* -दा) 1 Clear, pure, spotless. -2 White. -3 Bright, beautiful. -4 Evident, manifest. -5 Free from anxiety, at ease. —दः *m.* The white colour.

विशयः *m.* 1 Doubt, uncertainty. -2 Refuge, asylum.

विशरः *m.* 1 Splitting, bursting. -2 Slaughter, killing.

विशल्य *a.* (*f.* —ल्या) 1 Free from trouble or anxiety. -2 Free from thorns or darts.

विशसनं *n.* 1 Killing, slaughter. -2 Ruin. —नः *m.* A sword.

विशस्त *p. p.* (*f.* —स्ता) 1 Cut up. -2 Ill-mannered. -3 Praised, celebrated.

विशस्तृ *m.* 1 An immolator. -2 A Chándâla.

विशस्त्र *a.* (*f.* —स्त्रा) Weaponless, unarmed, defenceless.

विशाखः *m.* 1 N. of Kártikeya. -2 A particular attitude in shooting (in which the archer stands with the feet a span apart). -3 A beggar, a petitioner.-4 A spindle.-5 N of Siva. -Comp. —ग: *m.* The orange tree. [in shooting.

विशाखलं *n.* A particular attitude

विशाखा *f.* (-खे usually in the dual) N. of the 16 th lunar mansion consisting of two stars).

विशाय:*m.* The rest enjoyed in rotation by the sentinels on watch.

विशारण *n.* 1 Splitting, cutting. -2 Killing, slaughter.

विशारद *a.* (*f.* —दा) 1 Clever, proficient in. -2 Learned, wise. -3 Famous, celebrated. -4 Bold, confident. —द: *m.* The Bakula tree.

विशाल *a.* (*f.* -ला) 1 Large, extensive, broad, wide. -2 Rich or abounding in. -3 Illustrious, celebrated. —ल: *m.* 1 A kind of deer. -2 A kind of bird. —ला *f.* N. of the town Ujjayinî. -2 N. of a river. -Comp. —अक्ष: *m.* 1 N. of Vishnu. -2 Of Garuda. -3 Of Siva. (-क्षी *f.*) An epithet of Pàrvatî.

विशिख: *m.* 1 An arrow. -2 A kind of reed. -3 An iron crow.

विशिखा *f.* 1 A spade. -2 A spindle. -3 A needle or pin. -4 A minute arrow.-5 A highway.-6 A barber's wife.

विशित *a.* (*f.* —ता) Sharp, acute.

विशिप *n.* 1 A temple. -2 A house.

विशिष्ट *p. p.* (*f.* —ष्टा) 1 Distinguished, distinct. -2 Special, peculiar, distinctive. -3 Endowed with, possessed of, having. -4 Eminent, excellent. -Comp. -अद्वैतवाद: *m.* The doctrine of Râmânuja which regards Brahman (*n.*) and Prakriti as identical and real entities. -बुद्धि: *f.* A distinguishing knowledge.

विशीर्ण *p. p.* (*f.* —र्णा) 1 Shattered, broken to pieces. -2 Decayed, withered. -3 Fallen down. -4 Shrunk, shrivelled. -Comp. -पर्ण: *m.* The Nimba tree. —मूर्ति: *m.* An epithet of the God of love.

विशुद्ध *a.* (*f.* द्धा) 1 Purified, cleansed. -2 Free from vice or sin. -3 Stainless. -4 Correct, accurate. -5 Virtuous, honest. -6 Humble.

विशुद्धि: *f.* 1 Purification. 2 Complete purity. -3 Correctness, accuracy. -4 Removal of error. -5 Similarity, equality. [spear.

विशूल *a.* (*f.* —ला) Without a

विशृंखल *a.* (*f.* —ला) 1 Without fetters (lit.). -2 Unchecked, unrestrained (fig.). -3 Dissolute.

विशेष *a.* (*f.* —षा) 1 Peculiar. -2 Copious, abundant. —ष: *m.* Discrimination, distinguishing between.-2 Distinction, difference.-3 Characteristic difference, special property, speciality, differentia. -4 A change for the better, a favourable turn (as in sickness). -5 A limb, member. -6 A special sort. -7 A different or various object. various particulars (pl.). -8 Excellence, superiority, as in आकृतिविशेषा: ' excellent forms ', अतिथिविशेष: ' a distinguished guest ' &c. -9 A peculiar attribute. -10 Individuality, particularity, a particular instance. -11 A category, predicament. -12 A mark on the forehead with sandal, saffron &c. -13 A word which limits the sense of another. -14 N. of the mundane egg. -15 (In Rhet.) A figure of speech (I) in which something which is dependent on another as its support is represented as existing without it; (II) in which an object is spoken of as being present in many places simultaneously or (III) in which somebody in bringing about one result unexpectedly accomplishes something else also, which is impossible. Comp. —अतिदेशः *m*. A special supplementary rule. —उक्तिः *f*. The figure of speech in which the effect is said to be absent although the cause is present. —लक्षणं, -लिंगं *n* A characteristic mark. —वचनं *n*. A special text or precept. —विधिः *m*., —शास्त्रं *n*. A special rule.

विशेषकः *m*., —कं *n*. 1 A distinguishing feature or characteristic -2 A distinguishing quality. -3 A mark on the forehead with sandal, saffron &c. -4 Painting on the face and person with coloured unguents, and cosmetics. -कं *n*. A group of three stanzas forming one grammatical sentence.

विशेषणं *n*. 1 Distinguishing, discrimination. -2 Distinction, difference. -3 A word which qualifies or defines another, an adjective. -4 A distinguishing feature or mark. -5 Species, kind.

विशेषतस्, विशेषेण, विशेषात् *ind*. Especially, particularly.

विशेषित *p. p.* (*f.* —ता) 1 Distinguished. -2 Defined, particularized. -3 Distinguished by an attribute. -4 Superior, excellent.

विशेष्यं *n*. The word qualified or limited by an adjective; a noun.

विशोक *a*. (*f*. -का) Free from grief. —कः *m*. The Asoka tree. —का *f*. Exemption from grief.

विशोधनं *n*. 1 Cleaning, clearing(fig. also). -2 Purifying, freeing from sin, defect &c. -3 Expiation.

वैशोध्यं *n*. A debt.

विशोषणं *n*. Drying up, dessication

विश्रः *m*. Lustre, splendour.

विश्रणनं, विश्राणनं *n*. Giving away bestowing: a grant, gift, donation

विश्रब्ध *p. p.* (*f.*—ब्धा) (also written विस्रब्ध) 1 Confided in, entrusted. -2 Fearless, confiding. -3 Trusty, confidential. -4 Tranquil, free from anxiety. -5 Firm, steady. -6 Meek, lowly. -7 Excessive. —ब्धं *ind*. Confidently, fearlessly, without fear or hesitation.

विश्रमः 1 Rest, repose. -2 Relaxation, cessation.

विश्रंभः *m*. 1 Trust, confidence. -2 A confidential matter, secret. -3 Rest: relaxation. -4 An affectionate inquiry. -5 A love-quarrel. -6 Killing. -Comp. —पात्रं *n*., —भूमिः *f*., -स्थानं *n*. An object of confidence a confidant, trusty person.

विश्रवस् *m*. N. of The father of Kubera.

विश्राणित *a*. (*f*. —ता) Given away, bestowed.

विश्रांत *p. p.* (*f*. — ता) 1 Ceased, stopped. -2 Rested, reposed. -3 Calm, composed.

विश्रांतिः *f*. 1 Rest: repose -2 Cessation: stop.

विश्रामः *m*. 1 Cessation, stop. -2 Rest, repose. -3 Tranquillity; composure.

विश्रावः *m*. 1 Dropping: flowing forth. -2 Celebrity, renown.

विश्रुत *p. p.* (*f*. —ता) 1 Renowned, celebrated -2 Pleased, delighted. -3 Flowing forth.

विश्रुतिः *f*. 1 Fame, celebrity. -2 Flowing, oozing.

विश्लथ *a*. (*f*. —था) 1 Loose, untied. -2 Languid, drooping

विश्लिष्ट *p. p.* (*f* —ष्टा) Disjoined, separated, disunited, dishevelled.

विश्लेषः *m*. 1 Disunion, disjunction.

-2 Separation.-3 Absence,bereavement. -4 A chasm.

विश्लेषित *p. p.* (*f.* —ता) Severed, separated, disunited.

विश्व *pron. a.* (*f.* —श्वा ; *Nom. pl. m.* विश्वे) 1 All, whole, entire, universal. -2 N. of a particular group of deities, ten in number. —श्वं *n.* 1 The universe, the (whole) world. -2 Dry ginger. -Comp. —आत्मन् *m.* 1 The Supreme Being (soul of the universe). -2 An epithet of Brahman (*m.*). -3 Of Siva. -4 Of Vishnu. —ईशः, -ईश्वरः *m.* 1 The Supreme Being. -2 An epithet of Siva. —कद्रुः *m.* 1 A hound trained for the chase. -2 Sound. -3 A wicked man. —कर्मन् *m.* 1 N. of the architect of gods. -2 An epithet of the sun. —कृत *m.* An epithet of Visvakarman. —केतुः *m.* An epithet of Aniruddha. —गंधः *m.* An onion. (-धं *n.*) Myrrh. —गंधा *f.* The earth. -जनं *n.* Mankind. —जनीन, -जन्य, -जनीय *a.* Good for all men, beneficial to all men. -जित *m.* 1 N. of a particular sacrifice. -2 The noose of Varuna. -3 N. of Vishnu. -धारिणी *f* The earth. -धारिन् *m.* A deity. —पः *m.* 1 The protector of all. -2 The sun. -3 The moon. -4 Fire. -पावनी, —पूजिता *f.* The holy basil. -रसः *m.* 1 A god.-2 The sun. -3 The moon. -4 An epithet of Agni. -5 N. of Visvakarman. -भेषजं *n.* Dry ginger. (-जः *m.*) A universal remedy. —मूर्ति *a.* Existing in all forms, all-pervading, omnipresent. —योनिः *m.* 1 An epithet of Brahman (*m.*). -2 Of Vishnu. -राज्,-राजः *m.* A universal sovereign. —रूप *a.* Omnipresent. (-पः *m.*) An epithet of Vishnu. (-पं *n.*) Agallochum.—रेतस् *m.* An epithet of Brhman (*m.*). -वाह् *a.* (विश्वौही *f.*) All-sustaining. -सहा *f.* The earth. —सृज् *m.* An epithet of Brahman (*m.*).

विश्वतस् *ind.* On all sides, everywhere. -Comp. -मुख *a.* Having a face on every side.

विश्वथा *ind.* Everywhere.

विश्वंभरः *m.* 1 The all-pervading being, the Supreme Spirit. -2 An epithet of Vishnu. 3 Of Indra. -रा *f.* The earth.

विश्वसनीय *pot. p.* (*f.* -या) 1 To be relied upon. -2 Capable of inspiring confidence.

विश्वस्त *p. p.* (*f.* —स्ता) 1 Believed in, trusted. -2 Confiding, relying on.-3 Fearless, confident. -4 Trustworthy, reliable. —स्ता *f.* A widow.

विश्वावसु *m.* A God, deity.

विश्वामित्रः *m.* N. of a celebrated sage.

विश्वासः *m.* 1 Trust, confidence, reliance.-2 A confidential communication.-Comp.-घातः,-भंगः *m.* Treachery, perfidy. -घातकः,-घातिन् *m.* A treacherous fellow, traitor.—पात्रं *n.*, -भूमिः *f.* -स्थानं *n.* A reliable or trusty person, a confidant.

विश्वासनं *n.* Producing confidence.

विश्वावसुः *m.* N. of a Gandharva.

विष् *f.* Feces, excrement, ordure. -Comp. —कारिका (विट्कारिका) *f.* A kind of bird. -ग्रहः *m.* (विड्ग्रहः) Constipation. —चरः, —वराहः (विट्चरः, विड्वराहः) *m.* A tame or village hog. -पतिः *m.* A son-in-law.-लवणं (विड्लवणं) *n.* A kind of medicinal salt. —संगः (विट्संगः) *m.* Constipation. —सारिका (विट्सारिका) *f.* A kind of bird.

विषं *n.* 1 Poison, venom (*m.* also in this sense). -2 Water. -3 The fibres of a lotus-stalk.-4 Gum myrrh. -Comp. —अंकुरः *m.* 1 A spear. -2 A poisoned arrow. -अंतकः m. An epithet of Siva. —आननः, —आयुधः, —आस्यः m. A snake. —कंठः m N. of Siva. -कृमिः m. A worm generated in poison. -कृमिन्यायः m. The maxim of a worm in poison. It is used to dencte a state of things which, though fatal to others, is not so to those who are born therein or are naturalized to it. —ज्वरः m. A buffalo. -दः m. A cloud. (-दं n.) Green vitriol. -दंतकः m. A snake. —दर्शनमृत्युकः, -मृत्युः m. A kind of bird (said to be Chakora). —धरः m. A snake. —पुष्पं n. The blue lotus. -मंत्रः m. 1 A spell for curing snake-bites. -2 A snake-charmer, conjurer. -वेगः m. The circulation or effect of poison. —शालूकः m. The root of the lotus. —शूकः, —शृंगिन्, —सूचक m. A wasp.

विषक्त p. p. (f. -क्ता) 1 Fixed firmly or closely. -2 Clinging closely to.

[stalk.

विषंडं n. The fibres of the lotus-

विषण्ण p. p. (f. —ण्णा) Dejected, sad, spiritless, despondent.-Comp. —मुख, —वदन a. Looking sad.

विषम a. (f. —मा) 1 Uneven, rough, rugged.-2 Irregular, unequal.-3 Odd as a number). -4 Hard to understand, mysterious. -5 Impassable, inaccessible. -6 Coarse, rough. -7 Oblique. -8 Painful, troublesome. -9 Very powerful, vehement. -10 Dangerous, fearful. -11 Adverse, unfavourable. -12 Unusual, unparalleled. -13 Dishonest, crafty. -14 Intermittent (as fever). -15 Wicked. -16 Different. —मं n. 1 Unevenness. -2 Oddness. -3 A precipice. -4 A Dfficulty, misfortune -5 Rough or uneven ground. -6 (In Rhet.) The figure of speech in which the qualities or actions of a cause and its effect are said to be opposed to each other; or in which the effort fails and some evil result follows or in which there is an association between two things that are incongruous.-Comp. -अक्षः, -ईक्षणः, —नयनः, —नेत्रः, —लोचनः m. Epithets of Siva —अन्नं n. Irregular food. -आयुधः, —इषुः, —शरः m. Epithets of the God of love. -कालः m. An unfavourable season. —चतुरस्रः, —चतुर्भुजः m. An unequal quadrilateral figure. —छदः m. The tree सप्तपर्ण. —ज्वरः m. Remittent fever. —स्थ a. 1 Being in an inaccessible position. -2 Being in difficulty or misfortune.

विषमित a. (f. -ता) 1 Made rough, uneven or crooked. -2 Made difficult or inaccessible.

विषयः m. 1 An object of sense (these are five, corresponding to the five organs of sense, रूप, रस, गंध, स्पर्श and शब्द, corresponding to the eye, tongue, nose, skin and ear). -2 A worldly concern, an affair, a transaction. -3 The pleasures of sensual objects (usually in pl.). -4 An object, a thing, matter. -5 An object or thing aimed at, a mark. -6 Range, reach, compass. -7 Department, province, element. -8 A subject, matter, topic. -9 The topic or subject to be explained, the first of the five members of an Adhikarana. -10 A place, spot. -11 A realm, domain, kingdom. -12 A refuge. -13 A collection of villages. -14 A lover, husband. -15 Semen virile. -16 A religious observance. (विषये means 'with regard or reference to', 'in respect of.', 'in the case of', 'regarding'). -Comp.

—आसक्त, -निरत *a.* Addicted to sensual objects. —प्रसंगः *m.* Addiction to pleasures of sense. -पाविन् *a.* Addicted to worldly objects. -ग्रामः *m.* The collection of the objects of sense.

विषयायिन् *m.* 1 A sensualist. -2 A man of the world. -3 The God of love. -4 A king. -5 An organ of sense. -6 A materialist.

विषयिन् *m.* 1 A man of the world. worldling. -2 A king. -3 The God of love. -4 A sensualist. -*n.* 1 An organ of sense. -2 Knowledge.

विषलः *m.* Poison, venom.

विषह्य *a.* (*f.* -ह्या) 1 Endurable, bearable. -2 Possible to be settled or determined.

विषा *f.* 1 Ordure. feces. -2 Intellect, understanding.

विषाण *m.*,-णं *n.*, -णी *f.* 1 A horn.-2 The tusk of an elephant or boar.

विषाणिन् *a.* (*f.* -नी) Having horns or tusks. -*m.* 1 Any animal having horns or tusk. -2 An elephant. -3 A bull.

विषादः *m.* 1 Dejection, depression of spirits, sorrow, -2 Disappointment. -3 Drooping state. -4 Dullness, stupidity, insensibility.

विषादिन् *a.* (*f.* -नी) Dejected, sad, disconsolate.

विषारः *m.* A snake.

विषालु *a.* Poisonous, venomous.

विषु *ind.* 1 In two equal parts, equally. -2 Differently, variously. -3 Same, like.

विषुपं *n.* The equinox.

विषुवं *n.* The first point of *Aries* or *Libra* into which the sun enters at the vernal or autumnal equinox, the equinoctial point. -Comp. -छाया *f.* The shadow of the gnomon at noon. —दिनं *n.* The day of the equinox. -रेखा *f.* The equinoctial line. —संक्रांतिः *f.* The sun's equinoctial passage

विषुवत् *n.* The equinox. -2 The central day in a sacrificial session. -Comp. विषुवन्मंडलं, विषुवद्वृत्तं *n.* The equinoctial line. विषुवत्संक्रांतिः *f.* The sun's equinoctial passage.

विषूचिका *f.* Cholera.

विष्क् 10 U. (विष्कयति,-ते) 1 To kill, hurt, injure (Atm. only in this sense). -2 To see, perceive.

विष्कंदः *m.* 1 Dispersing. -2 Going away.

विष्कंभः *m.* 1 Obstacle, impediment -2 The bolt or bar of a door. -3 The supporting beam of a house. -4 A post, pillar. -5 A tree. -6 (In dramas) An interlude between the acts of a drama performed by one or more inferior characters, who briefly explain to the audience what has occurred in the intervals of the acts or what is likely to happen later on. -7 The diameter of a circle. -8 A particular posture practised by Yogins.-9 Extension, length. -10 The first of the twenty-seven astronomical periods (योग

विष्कंभकः *m.* The same as विष्कंभः.

विष्कंभित *a.* (*f.* —ता) Hindered, obstructed.

विष्कंभिन् *m.* The bolt of a door.

विष्किरः *m.* 1 Scattering about tearing up. -2 A cock. -3 A bird

विष्टपः *m.*, -पं *n.* A world. -Comp. —हारिन् *a.* One who pleases all.

विष्टब्ध *p.p.* (*f.* -ब्धा) 1 Fixed firmly; well supported. -2 Obstructed, hindered. -3 Made motionless.

विष्टंभः *m.* 1 Fixing firmly. -2 Obstruction, impediment. -3 Obstruction of the urine or ordure. -4 Paralysis. -5 Stopping, staying.

विष्टरः *m.* 1 A seat, a stool, a chair. -2 A layer, bed (as of Kusa grass). -3 A handful of Kusa grass. -4 The seat of the presiding priest at a sacrifice. -5 A tree. -Comp —श्रवस् *m.* An epithet of Vishnu or Krishna.

विष्टा *f.* Excrement, feces, ordure.

विष्टिः *f.* 1 Pervading. -2 An act, occupation. -3 Hire, wages. -4 Unpaid labour. -5 Sending. -6 Residence in hell to which one is condemned.

विष्ठलं *n.* A place situated at a distance. [-2 The belly

विष्ठा *f.* 1 Feces, ordure, excrement.

विष्णुः 1 The second deity of the sacred Triad, regarded as the preserver of the world. -2 N. of Agni. -3 A pious man. -4 N. of the author of the Smriti called विष्णुस्मृति. -5 N. of one of the 'Vasus.' -6 The lunar mansion called Sravana. -Comp. —कांची *f.* N. of a town. -क्रमः *m.* The step or stride of Vishnu. —गुप्तः *m.* N. of Chânakya. —तैलं *n.* A kind of medicinal oil. —दैवत्या *f.* N. of the eleventh and twelfth days of each fortnight (of a lunar month). —पदं *n.* 1 The sky, atmosphere. -2 The sea of milk. -3 The foot of Vishnu (worshipped at Gayâ). -4 A lotus. —पदी *f.* An epithet of the Ganges. -पुराणं *f n.* N. of one of the eighteen Purânas. -प्रीतिः *f.* Land granted rent-free to Brâhmanas to maintain Vishnu's worship. -माया *f.* N. of Durgâ. रथः *m.* An epithet of Garuda. —लोकः *m.* Vishnu's world. -वल्लभा *f.* 1 An epithet of Lakshmî. -2 The holy basil.

-वाहनः, -वाह्यः *m.* Epithets of Garuda

विष्पंदः *m.* Throbbing, palpitation

विष्फारः *m.* 1 The twang of a bow -2 Vibration [by poison.

विष्य *a.* (*f.* -ष्या) Deserving death

विष्यंदः *m.* Flowing, tricking. [ous

विष्व (*f.* -ष्वा) Hurtful, mischiev-

विष्वच्, विष्वंच् *a.* (Nom. sing. *m* विष्वङ् *f.*, विषूची, *n.* विष्वक्) 1 Going or being everywhere, all pervading -2 Separating into parts. -3 Different. -4 Alternately. (विष्वक् is used adverbially in the sense of everywhere, on all sides. -Comp. -सेनः (विष्वक्सेनः or विष्वक्षेणः) *m* An epithet of Vishnu.

विष्वणनं *n.*, विष्वाणः *m.* Eating.

विष्वद्र्य (-द्र्यं) -च् *a* (*f.* विष्वद्रीची Going everywhere, all-pervading.

विस् 4 P. (विस्यति) To cast, throw, send.

विसं *n.* See बिसं. [separated

विसंयुक्त *p. p.* (*f.* -क्ता) Disjoined.

विसंयोगः *m.* Disjunction, separation.

विसंवादः *m.* 1 Deception, breaking one's promise, disappointment. -2 Inconsistency, disagreement. -3 Contradiction.

विसंवादिन् *a.* (*f.* -नी) 1 Disappointing, deceiving. -2 Contradictory. -3 Differing, disagreeing. -4 Disputing, contesting. -5 Fraudulent, crafty.

विसंस्थुल *a.* (*f.* -ला) 1 Unsteady, agitated. -2 Uneven.

विसंकट *a.* (*f.* -टा) Frightful, dreadful. -टः *m.* 1 A lion. -2 The Ingudi tree. [unharmonious.

विसंगत *a.* (*f.* -ता) Incongruous,

विसंज्ञ (*f.*-ज्ञा) Insensible, unconscious.

विसंधिः *m.* Bad or disagreeable *sandhi* (euphony) or absence of Sandhi, regarded as a fault in composition.

विसरः *m.* 1 Going forth. -2 Spreading, extending. -3 Crowd, multitude, herd, flock.-4 A large quantity, heap.

विसर्गः *m.* 1 Sending forth, emission -2 Pouring down, dropping. 3 Casting, discharge -4 Giving away, a gift, donation. -5 Sending away. -6 Abandonment. -7 Voiding; evacuation. -8 Departure, separation -9 Final beatitude. -10 Light, splendour. -11 A symbol in writing, representing a distinct hard aspiration and marked by two perpendicular dots. -12 The sun's course to the south.

विसर्जनं *n.* 1 Sending forth or away, pouring down. -2 Giving away, a gift, donation.-3 Voiding. -4 Quitting, abandoning. -5 Allowing (the deity invoked) to go (opp. आवाहन). -6 Setting a bull at liberty on certain occasions.

विसर्जनीयः *m.* See विसर्गः.

विसर्जित *p. p.* (*f.* —ता) 1 Emitted, sent forth. -2 Given away. -3 Left, abandoned. -4 Sent, despatched. -5 Dismissed.

विसर्पः *m.* 1 Creeping about, moving to and fro, circulation. -2 An unexpected or unwished for consequence of an act. -3 A dry spreading itch. -Comp. —घ्नं *n.* Wax.

विसर्पणं *n.* Creeping along, gliding, spreading, extending.

विसर्पिः *m.*, **विसर्पिका** *f.* A kind of spreading itch.

विसलं *n.* See बिसलं.

विसारः *m.* 1 Expansion, diffusion. -2 Creeping, gliding. -3 A fish. -रं *n.* 1 Wood. -2 Timber. —री *f.* The region of the winds.

विसारिन् *a.* (*f.* —णी) 1 Spreading, diffusing. -2 Creeping, gliding.-*m* A fish.

विसिनी *f.* See बिसिनी.

विसिल *a.* (*f.* —ला) See बिसिल.

विसूचिका *f.* Cholera.

विसूरणं *n.*, —णा *f.* Distress, sorrow

विसूरितं *n.* Repentance, distress —ता *f.* Fever.

विसृत *p. p.* (*f.* —ता) 1 Spread out, extended, stretched. -2 Uttered, spoken.

विसृत्वर *a.* (*f.* —री) 1 Spreading about, being diffused. -2 Creeping, gliding.

विसृमर *a.* (*f.* —रा) Creeping along, gliding, moving gently.

विसृष्ट *p. p.* (*f.* —ष्टा) 1 Emitted, sent forth, despatched. -2 Created, emanated. -3 Shed, cast. -4 Dismissed, let go, discharged, abandoned, removed, hurled.-5 Given, bestowed, granted.

विसृष्टिः *f.* 1 Emitting, sending forth. -2 Abandoning. -3 Giving

विस्तः *m.* See बिस्तः.

विस्तरः *m.* 1 Extension, expansion. -2 Detailed description, minute particulars. -3 Prolixity, diffuseness. -4 Abundance, quantity, multitude, number. -5 A bed, layer. -6 A seat, stool. विस्तरेण In detail, fully.

विस्तारः *m.* 1 Extension, expansion. -2 Amplitude, breadth. -3 Expanse, vastness, magnitude. -4 Full particulars. -5 The diameter of a circle. -6 A shrub. -7 The branch of a tree with new shoots.

विस्तीर्ण *p. p.* (*f.* -र्णा) 1 Spread out, expanded, extended. -2 Wide broad. -3 Large, extensive.-Comp. —पर्णं n. A kind of root.

विस्तृत p. p. (f. —ता) 1 Diffused, spread, extended.-2 Broad, expanded. -3 Ample. -4 Diffuse, prolix.

विस्तृतिः f. 1 Extension, expansion. -2 Breadth, width, magnitude. -3 The diameter of a circle.

विस्पष्ट a. (f. —ष्टा) 1 Plain, clear, intelligible. -2 Manifest, obvious, open, apparent.

विस्फारः m. 1 Vibration, trembling. -2 The twang of a bow.

विस्फारित p. p. (f. —ता) 1 Made to vibrate. -2 Trembling, tremulous. -3 Twanged. -4 Dilated, expanded. -5 Manifested, -6 Apparent, manifest.

विस्फुरित p. p. (f. -ता) 1 Tremulous. -2 Swollen.

विस्फुलिंगः m. 1 A spark of fire. -2 A kind of poison.

विस्फूर्जथुः m. 1 Roaring, thundering. -2 A clap of thunder. -3 A thunderlike sudden appearance or stroke. -4 Rolling (as of waves).

विस्फूर्जितं n. 1 Roar, shout. -2 Rolling. -3 Fruit, result.

विस्फोटः m., -टा f. 1 A boil, tumour. -2 Small-pox.

विस्मयः m. 1 Wonder, astonishment. -2 (In Rhet.) Astonishment or wonder, being the feeling which produces the *adbhuta* sentiment. -3 Pride, arrogance. -4 Uncertainty, doubt. -Comp. —आकुल, —आविष्ट a. Astonished, struck with wonder.

विस्मयंगम a. (f. —मा) Astonishing, causing wonder.

विस्मरणं n. Forgetting, forgetfulness.

विस्मापन a. (f. —नी) Astonishing. —नः m. 1 The God of love. -2 A deceit, Illusion. -नं n. 1 Causing wonder. -3 Anything causing wonder. -4 A city of the Gandharvas (—नः m. also.).

विस्मित p. p. (f -ता) 1 Astonished, wonder-struck. -2 Proud.

विस्मितिः f. Astonishment, wonder surprise.

विस्मृत p. p. (f. —ता) Forgotten.

विस्मृतिः f. Forgetfulness, oblivion

विस्मेर a. (f. -रा) Surprised, astonished.

विस्रं n. A smell like that of raw meat. -Comp. —गंधिः m. A yellow orpiment.

विस्रंसः m., —सा f. 1 Falling down. -2 Decay, weakness, debility.

विस्रंसन a. (f. -ना) 1 Causing to drop down. -2 Untying, loosening. -नं n Falling down. -2 Untying, loosening. -3 A laxative, purgative.

विस्रब्ध, विस्रंभः See a. विश्रब्ध, विश्रंभः

विस्रसा f. Decay, weakness.

विस्रस्त p. p. (f. —स्ता) 1 Loosened. -2 Weak, infirm.

विस्रवः, विस्रावः m Flowing, dropping, trickling.

विस्रावणं n. 1 Bleeding. -2 Distilling. -3 A kind of spirit distilled from molasses.

विस्रुतिः f. Flowing forth, oozing.

विस्वर a. (f. —रा) Discordant.

विहगः m. 1 A bird. -2 A cloud. -3 An arrow. -4 The sun. -5 The moon. -6 A planet in general.

विहंगः m. 1 A bird. -2 A cloud. -3 An arrow. -4 The sun. -5 The moon -Comp. —इंद्रः, —ईश्वरः, —राजः m. Epithets of Garuda.

विहंगमः m. 1 A bird. -2 The sun.

विहंगमा, विहंगिका f A pole for carrying burdens.

विहत p. p. (f. —ता) 1 Struck, killed -2 Hurt -3 Opposed —त *m* A Jaina temple

विहति *m* 1 A friend companion *f* 1 Killing striking 2 Failure 3 Defeat

विहनन *n* 1 Killing striking 2 Hurt 3 Obstruction 4 A bow for cleaning cotton

विहर *m* 1 Taking away remov ing 2 Separation -3 Changing

विहरण *n* 1 Removing taking away 2 Taking a walk 3 Pleasure pastime

विहरु *m* 1 A roamer 2 A robber

विहर्ष *m* Great joy rapture

विहसन विहसित *n* विहास *m* A gentle laugh smile

विहस्त *a* (*f* —स्ता) 1 Handless 2 Bewildered overpowered 3 Dis abled -4 Learned wise

विहा *ind* Heaven paradise

विहापित *p p* (*f* —ता) Caused to abandon or to be given up —त *n* A gift donation [*m* A bird

विहायस् *m* *n* Sky atmosphere

विहायस *m* See विहायस्

विहार *m* 1 Removing taking away 2 Roaming for pleasure -3 Sport recreation pleasure 4 Movement (of hands feet &c) 5 A park garden -6 The shoulder 7 A Jaina or Buddhist convent 8 A temple

विहारिका *f* A convent

विहित *p p* (*f* ता) 1 Done made acted -2 Arranged settled -3 Ordered, decreed -4 Constructed 5 Placed, deposited 6 Fit to be done 7 Distributed —तं *n* An order a decree

विहिति *f* 1 Performance action 2 Arrangement

विहीन *p p* (*f* —ना) 1 Left for saken 2 Destitute or deprived of -3 Low inferior

विहृत *p p* (*f* —ता) 1 Sported played 2 Expanded —त *n* 1 One of the ten modes of indicating love used by women 2 Sport play

विहृति *f* 1 Taking away 2Sport pleasure 3 Expansion

विहेठ *m* 1 Hurt injury 2 Afflicting [calumniator

विहेठक *n* 1 An injurer -2 A

विहेठन *n* 1 Injuring hurting 2 Rubbing grinding 3 Afflicting 4 Pain torment

विह्वल *a* (*f* —ला) 1 Agitated confused -2 Alarmed -3 Delirious -4 Afflicted distressed 5 Desponding 6 Fused liquid

वी 2 P (वेति rarely used in classical literature) 1 To go 2 To pervade -3 To throw 4 To eat -5 To be born 6 To shine be beautiful 7To desire

वीक *m* 1 Wind 2 A bird 3 The mind

वीकाश *m* See विकाश

वीक्ष *n* 1 A visible object -2 Surprise astonishment —क्ष *m* —क्षा *f* Seeing gazing at

वीक्षणं *n* —णा *f* Seeing looking at sight —ण *n* An eye

वीक्षित *n* A look, glance

वीक्ष्य *a* (*f* —क्ष्या) 1 To be looked at 2 Visible —क्ष्य *m* 1 A dancer an actor -2 A horse —क्ष्यं *n* 1 Anything to be looked at a visible object -2 Wonder surprise

वीङ्खा *f* 1 Going moving 2 One of the paces of a horse -3 Dancing

वीचि *m* *f* वीची *f* 1 A wave -2 Pleasure delight 3 Rest leisure -4 A ray of light -5 Little -Comp —माकर् *m* The ocean

वीज् 1 A (वीजते) To go.

वीज् 10 U. (वीजयति,-ते) To fan, cool by fanning -With अभि-, उप-, परि- To fan.

वीजनः *m.* 1 The ruddy goose. -2 A sort of pheasant. -नं *n.* 1 Fanning. -2 A fan.

वीज, वीजक, वीजल, वीजिक, वीजिन, वीज्य } See बीज, बीजक, बीजल, बीजिक, बीजिन्, and बीज्य.

वीटा *f.* A small piece of wood struck with a stick or bat in a game played by boys (Marathi विटीदांडूचा खेळ).

वीटिः, वीटिका, वीटी *f.* 1 The betel plant. -2 A preparation of betel (Mar. विडा). -3 A tie, knot (of a wearing garment).

वीणा *f.* 1 The (Indian) lute. -2 Lightning. -Comp. —आस्यः *m.* An epithet of Nârada. —दंडः *m.* The neck of a lute. —वादः, -वादकः *m.* A lutanist.

वीत *p. p.* (*f.* ता) 1 Gone, departed. -2 Let go, set free. -3 Excepted, exempt. -4 Approved, liked. -5 Unfit for war. -6 Tame, quiet. -7 Freed from, devoid of. -8 Desired, wished for. -तः *m.* An elephant or horse unfit for war. —तं *n.* Pricking (an elephant) with the goad. -Comp. —भयः *m.* An epithet of Vishnu. —शोकः *m.* The Asoka tree. —सूत्रं *n.* The sacred thread.

वीतंसः *m.* 1 A cage for confining beasts or birds. -2 An aviary. -3 A place for preserving game.

वीतनौ (*m. dual*) The sides of the larynx or throat.

वीतिः *m.* A horse. -तिः *f.* 1 Going, motion. -2 Enjoyment. -3 Eating. -4 Light, lustre. Comp. —होत्रः *m.* 1 Fire. -2 The sun.

वीथिः, वीथी *f.* 1 A road, way. -2 A row, line. -3 A market, a shop in a market. -4 A terrace in front of a house. -5 A variety of drama.

वीथिका *f.* 1 See वीथि: -2 A picture-gallery. -3 A large scroll of paper or a wall (on which pictures are drawn).

वीध्र *a.* (*f.* —ध्रा) Pure, clean. —ध्रं *n.* 1 The sky. -2 Wind, air. -3 Fire.

वीनाहः *m* The cover of a well.

वीपा *f.* Lightning.

वीप्सा *f.* 1 Pervasion. -2 Repitition of words to imply continuous or successive action : e. g. वृक्षं वृक्षं सिंचति He sprinkles every tree. -3 Repetition.

वीभ् 1 A. (वीभते) To boast, brag.

वीर *a.* (*f.* -रा) Heroic, brave, powerful. -3 Excellent, eminent. —रः *m.* 1 A hero, warrior. -2 The sentiment of heroism (in rhetoric). -3 An actor. -4 Fire. -5 The sacrificial fire. -6 A son. -7 A husband. -8 N. of Vishnu. —रं *n.* 1 A reed. -2 Pepper. -3 Rice-gruel. -Comp. —आशंसनं *n.* 1 Keeping watch. -2 The post of danger in battle. -3 A forlorn hope. —आसनं *n.* A kind of posture practised in meditation. -2 A field of battle. -3 The station of a sentinel. —ईशः, -ईश्वरः *m.* 1 Epithets of Siva. -2 A great hero. —उज्झः *m.* A Bráhmana who omits to offer oblations to the sacrificial fire. —कीटः *m.* A contemptible warrior. —जयंतिका *f.* A war-dance. -2 War, battle. —तरः *m.* 1 The Bilva tree. 2 The Arjuna tree.

—धन्वन् *m.* An epithet of the god of love. —पानं (or -पाणं) *n.* An exciting or refreshing drink taken by soldiers either before or after a battle. —बाहुः *m.* N. of Vishnu. —भद्रः *m.* 1 N. of a hero created by Siva from his matted hair. -2 A distinguished hero. -3 A horse fit for the Asvamedha sacrifice. -4 A kind of fragrant grass. —मुद्रिका *f.* A ring worn on the middle toe. —रजस् *n*, Red lead. —रसः *m.* 1 The sentiment of heroism. -2 A war-like feeling. —रेणुः *m.* N. of Bhìmasena. —सूः *f.* The mother of a hero. —सेनः *m.* N. of the father of Nala. -सैन्यं *n.* Garlic. -स्कंधः *m.* A buffalo. —हन् *m.* A Bráhmana who has neglected his domestic fire. -2 N of Vishnu.

वीरणं *n.* N. of a fragrant grass.

वीरणी *f.* 1 A side look. -2 A deep place.

वीरतरः *m.* 1 A great hero. -2 An arrow. —रं *n.* A kind of fragrant grass.

वीरंधरः *m.* 1 A peacock. -2 Fighting with beasts. -3 A leather-jacket.

वीरा *f.* 1 The wife of a hero. -2 A wife. -3 A mother. -4 A kind of perfume (called Murâ). -5 Spirituous liquor. -6 The plantain tree.

वीरिणं *n.* See ईरिणं.

वीरुध्,-धा *f.* 1 A spreading creeper. -2 A creeper (in general). -3 A branch, shoot. -4 A plant which grows after being cut.

वीर्यं *n.* 1 Heroism, valour. -2 Vigour, energy, courage, strength.-3 Virility, semen virile. -4 Potency, efficacy (of medicines). -5 Splendour, lustre.

वीवधः *m.* 1 A yoke for carrying burdens. -2 A burden. -3 Storing corn. -4 A way, road.

वीवधिकः *m.* 1 A man who carries loads by means of a yoke. -2 A general dealer.

वीहारः *m.* 1 A Buddhist or Jaina convent. -2 A sanctuary.

वूर्ण *a.* (*f.* —र्णा) Chosen, selected.

वृ 1 5 9 U. (वरति,-ते, वृणोति, वृणुते, वृणाति वृणीते, वृत, *pass.* व्रियते) 1 To choose, select as a boon. -2 To choose in marriage, woo, court. -3 To solicit, ask for. -4 To cover, conceal, envelop. -5 To surround. -6 To keep away, restrain, check.-7 To hinder, obstruct. With अप— To show. अपा- To open. आ— 1 To conceal. -2 To fill. -3 To choose. -4 To beg, solicit. -5 To restrain. नि— To be satisfied, to be happy. परि- To surround. प्र- 1 To cover. -2 To wear, to put on. -3 To choose. प्रा- To put on, wear. वि- 1 To open. -2 To reveal. -3 To explain, expound. -4 To choose. सम्- 1 To hide, cover. -2 To shut. -3 To restrain.

Causal (वारयति,-ते) 1 To cover, conceal. -2 To prevent, to keep off, to avert from (with an *abl.*) -3 To suppress, restrain. With नि-To keep away from, to avert from (with an *abl.*). विनि— To oppose, ward off.

वृ 10 U. (वरयति,-ते) 1 To choose, select. -2 To choose in marriage. -3 To beg, solicit (with two acc.).

वृंहितं *n.* See बृंहितं.

वृकः *m.* 1 A wolf. -2 A hyena. -3 A jackal. -4 A crow. -5 An owl.-6 A robber. -7 A Kshatriya. -8 Turpentine. -9 A mixture of various fragrant articles. -10 N. of a demon.-11 N. of a fire in the stomach.

-Comp· —अरातिः, —अरिः *m.* A dog. —उदरः *m.* 1 An epithet of Brahman (*m.*). -2 Of Bhíma the second Pàndava prince. —दंशः *m.* A dog. —धूपः *m.* 1 Turpentine. -2 A compound perfume. —धूर्तः *m.* A jackal.

वृक्कः *m.*, वृक्का *f* 1 The heart. -2 A kidney (in dual in this sense).

वृक्ण *p. p.* (*f.* -क्णा) Cut, divided, torn, broken.

वृक्त *p. p.* (*f.* —क्ता) 1 Cleaned, cleared, purified. -2 Spread, strewn.

वृक्ष् 1 A (वृक्षते) 1 To select. -2 To cover.

वृक्षः *m.* 1 A tree. -Comp· —अदनः *m.* 1 A carpenter's chisel. -2 A hatchet. -3 The fig-tree. -4 The *Piyála* tree. —आलयः *m.* A bird. —आवासः *m.* 1 A bird. -2 An ascetic. —आश्रयिन् *m.* 1 A kind of small owl. -2 A bird. —कुक्कुटः *m.* A wild cock. —खंडं *n.* A grove or clump of trees. —चरः *m.* A monkey. -छाया *f.* The shade of trees. (-यं *n.*) Thick shade, the shade of many trees. -धूपः *m.* Turpentine. —नाथः *m.* The Indian fig-tree. -निर्यासः *m.* Gum, resin. -पाकः *m.* The fig-tree. -भिद् *f.* An axe. —भेदिन् *m.* 1 A hatchet. -2 A carpenter's chisel. -मर्कटिका *f.* A squirrel. -वाटिका, -वाटी *f.* A garden, grove of trees. -शः *m.* A lizard. —शायिका *f.* A squirrel.

वृक्षकः *m.* 1 A small tree. -2 A tree (in general). -3 The Kutaja tree.

वृच् 7 P. (वृणक्ति) To choose.

वृज् 2 A (वृक्ते) To avoid, shun, abandon.

वृज् 7 P. (वृणक्ति) 1 To avoid, abandon. -2 To choose. -3 To atone for, efface, purify. -4 To avert.

वृज् 1 P. 10 U (वर्जति, वर्जयति,-ते, वर्जित) 1 To shun, avoid. -2 To abandon. -3 To exclude. With आ— To bend, to incline. -2 To offer. परि— To avoid. वि- 1 To avoid. -2 To be destitute of.

वृजनः *m.* Hair. -नं *n.* 1 Sin. -2 A calamity. -3 Sky. -4 An enclosure, a field cleard for pasture or agriculture.

वृजिन *a.* (*f.* -ना) 1 Crooked, curved. -2 Wicked, sinful. -नः *m.* 1 Hair, curled hair. -2 A wicked man. -नं *n.* Sin.

वृण् 8 U. (वृणोति, वृणुते) To eat, consume.

वृत् 4 A. (वृत्यते) To choose. -2 To divide.

वृत् 10 U. (वर्तयति,-ते) To shine.

वृत् 1 A. (वर्तते but Paras. also in the Aorist, second Future and Conditional; also in the Desiderative) 1 To be, exist, remain, subsist, stay. -2 To happen, come to pass. -3 To proceed in regular course. -4 To live on, subsist by (fig. also). -5 To roll on, revolve. -6 To be occupied or engaged in (with loc.). -7 To act, conduct or demean oneself towards, do, perform, practise (usually with loc. or by itself). -8 To enter upon a particular course of conduct. -9 To abide by, follow. -10 To be used in the sense of. -11 To tend or conduce to (with dat.). -12 To rest or depend upon. With अति— 1 To overcome. -2 To surpass. -3 To neglect, to violate. -4 To pass away (as time). -5 To injure, to slight. -6 To be delayed अनु— 1 To follow. -2 To wait upon, to follow the inclination. -3 To seek. -4 To obey. अप— 1 To turn away from. -2 To be overturned. अभि— 1 To go to, to turn towards. -3 To be eminent. -2 To be, to exist.

आ— 1 To come. -2 To return. उद्— To overflow. उप— 1 To go near. -2 To return. नि- 1 To return. -2 To refuse. -3 To absta[n] from. -4 To escape (with abl.). -5 To be withheld. निस्— 1 To be accomplished. -6 Not to take place. परा— To turn back. परि— 1 To be, to become. -2 To turn round. -3 To change. -4 To interchange. -5 To wande[r] about. प्र— 1 To begin. -2 To happen. -3 To prosper. -4 To hold good. -5 To act towards (with *loc*.). -6 To subsist. -7 To arise. -8 To prevail. -9 To set about, to undertake. -10 To turn. प्रतिनि- 1 To return. -2 To turn round. वि- 1 To roll, to revolve. -2 To be, to become. विनि— 1 To return. -2 To abstain from. -3 To cease. विपरि— To revolve. व्यप— To return. व्या— To turn back. सम्- 1 To be, to become. -2 To be produced. -3 To be accomplished.

Caus. (वर्तयति,-ते) 1 To cause to be or exist. -2 To cause to turn round. -3 To brandish. -4 To practice, exhibit. -5 To attend to. -6 To spend (as time). -7 To subsist. -8 To relate. -With नि— 1 To cause. -2 To send back. निस्— To finish. प्र— 1 To proceed with. -2 To introduce. व्या— To exclude.

वृत् 4 A. (वृत्यते) 1 To choose. -2 To divide.

वृत 10 U. (वर्तयति,-ते) To shine.

वृत *p. p*, (*f*. —ता) 1 Chosen. -2 Covered. -3 Hidden. -4 Surrounded. -5 Assented to. -6 Hired. -7 Spoiled.

वृतिः *f*. 1 Choosing. -2 Concealing. -3 Asking, soliciting. -4 A request. -5 Surrounding. -6 A fence.

वृतिंकर *a*. Surrounding, passing. —रः *m*. The tree विकंकत.

वृत्त *p. p*. (*f*. —त्ता) 1 Existed. -2 Happened. -3 Completed. -4 Done, acted. -5 Past. -. Circular. -7 Dead. -8 Firm, fixed. -9 Read through, studied. -10 Derived from. -11 Famous. -12 Covered. -13 Turned. —त्तः *m*. A tortoise. —त्तं *n*. 1 An event, occurrence. -2 History. -3 News. -4 Practice, profession, occupation. -5 Conduct, action. -6 Good or virtuous conduct. -7 A us[a]ge, law, custom. -8 A circle, circumference of a circle. -9 A metre, especially a metre regulated by the number of syllables it contains (opp. जाति). -Comp. —अनुवर्तिन् *a*. Obedient. —अनुसारः *m*. 1 Conformity to prescribed rules. -2 Conformity to metre. —अंतः *m*. 1 An incident, event. 2 News. -3 Account, tale. -4 A subject, topic. -5 A kind, sort. -6 Mode, manner. -7 State, condition. -8 Totality. -9 Leisure. -10 Solitude. —इर्वारुः *m*., —कर्कटी *f*. The water-melon. —गंधि *n*. N. of a kind of prose (having only the name of metre). —पुष्पः *m*. 1 A cane (वानीर). -2 The *Sirisha* tree. -3 The *kadamba* tree. —फलः *m*. 1 The jujube tree. -2 The pomegranate tree. (—लं *n*.) Black pepper. —शस्त्र *a*. One who has mastered the science of arms.

वृत्तिः *f*. 1 Being, existence. -2 Attitude, being in a particular state -3 State, condition. -4 Action, movement. -5 A method. -6 Behaviour. -7 Profession, mode of leading life. -8 Maintenance. -9 Wages, hire. -10 Cause of activity. -11 Respectful treatment. -12 Commentary, exposition.-13 Revolving, turning round. -14 The circumference of a wheel or circle. -15 (In gram.) A complex formation. -16 The power of a word by which it expresses, indicates or suggests a meaning: (these are three, अभिधा, लक्षणा and व्यंजना) -17 A style in composition (these are four; कैशिकी, भारती, सात्वती and आरभटी) -18 Manner of thinking. -Comp. —अनुप्रासः m. A kind of alliteration. —उपायः m. A means of subsistence. —कर्षित a. Distressed for want of livelihood. —स्थ a. 1 Being in employment. -2 Of good behaviour. (—स्थः m.) A lizard, chameleon.

वृत्रः m. 1 N. of a demon killed by Indra. -2 A cloud. -3 Darkness. -4 An enemy. -5 Sound. -6 A wheel. -7 N. of Indra. -8 A mountain. -Comp. —अरिः, -द्विष्, —शत्रुः, -हन् m. Epithets of Indra.

वृथा ind. 1 Uselessly, unprofitably. -2 Unnecessaily. -3 Foolishly, idly. -4 Wrongly; improperly. -Comp. दानं n. A gift that may be revoked. मांसं n. Flesh not intended for the Gods or Manes.

वृद्ध a. (f. —द्धा) (Compar. ज्यायस् or वर्षीयस्, superl. ज्येष्ठ or वर्षिष्ठ) 1 Increased. -2 Full grown. -3 Old, advanced in years; advanced in any respect. -5 Great, large. -6 Accumulated. -7 Wise, learned.-द्धः m. 1 An old man. -2 A worthy or venerable man.-3 A sage, saint. -4 A male descendant. -द्धं n. Benzoin. -Comp. —अंगुलिः f. 1 The thumb. -2 The great toe. —आचारः m. An ancient or long-standing custom. —काकः m. A raven. -नाभि a. Corpulent. —वाहनः m. The mango tree. —श्रवस् m. An epithet of Indra. —सूत्रकं n. A flock of cotton.

वृद्धा f. An old woman. -2 A female descendant.

वृद्धिः f. 1 Growth, increase. -2 Increase of the digits of the moon. -3 Prosperity, affluence.-4 Success, rise. -5 Wealth, property. -6 A heap, quantity. -7 Interest; as in सरलवृद्धि, चक्रवृद्धि &c. -8 Usury. -9 Profit.-10 Enlargement of the scrotum. -11 (In politics) Extension of power or revenue.-12 (In gram.) The lengthening of vowels, the change of अ, इ, उ, ऋ, short or long, and लृ to आ, ऐ, औ, आर्, and आल् respectively. -13 The impurity caused by childbirth in a family. -14 (In law) Forfeiture (as of property). -Comp. —आजीवः, —आजीविन् m. A usurer, money-lender. -जीवनं, -जीविका f. The profession of usury. —पत्रं n. A kind of razor. —श्राद्धं n. An offering made to the Manes on prosperous occasions.

वृध् 1 A. (but Paras. also in the Second Future, Aorist and Conditional, also in the Desiderative) (वर्धते, वृद्ध; desid. विवृत्सति, or विवर्धिषते) 1 To grow, increase, thrive, prosper. -2 To continue, last.-3 To ascend.-4 To be joyfulor, have cause for congratulation, usually with दिष्ट्या. With अभि- To increase. परि— To grow up, increase. प्र— To grow, increase. वि— To grow, prosper increase.

Caus. (वर्धयति,-ते, also वर्धापयति,-ते) 1 To cause to grow; amplify, enhance. -2 To cause to prosper; glorify, exalt. -3 To congratulate, felicitate (वर्धापयति in this sense).

वृध् 10 U. (वर्धयति,-ते) 1 To speak. -2 To shine.

वृधसान *m* A man

वृधसानु *m* 1 A man 2 A leaf -3 An act or action

वृन्त *n* 1 The foot stalk of a leaf or fruit a stalk -2 The stand of a water-jar -3 A teat, nipple

वृन्ताक *m*, -की *f* The egg-plant

वृन्तिका *f* A small stalk

वृन्दं *n* 1 A large number group heap, quantity -2 Ten hundred millions

वृन्दा *f* 1 The holy basil -2 N of Rådhika -3 N of a forest near *Gokula* Comp —अरण्य वन *n* 1 N of a forest near Gokula -2 A raised mound of earth to plant and pre serve the holy basil —वनी *f* The holy basil

वृन्दार *a* (*f* —रा) 1 Much great large 2 Best excellent 3 At tractive beautiful

वृन्दारक *a* (*f* —रका or —रिका) 1 Much great many -2 Best, excell lent 3 Pleasing 4 Respectable —क *m* A god deity

वृंदिष्ठ *a* (*f* —ष्ठा) 1 Very great or large -2 Very handsome (superl of वृन्दारक)

वृन्दीयस् *a* (*f* —सी) 1 Greater larger 2 More handsome or beautiful (compar of वृंदारक)

वृश् 4 P (वृश्यति) To choose, select [illegible] *n* Ginger

वृश *m* A rat —शी *f* A drug -श

वृश्चिक *m* 1 A scorpion -2 The sign *scorpio* of the zodiac -3 A crab -4 A centipede 5 A kind of beetle -6 The month when the sun is in *Scorpio*

वृष् 1 P (वर्षति वृष्ट) 1 To rain 2 To rain or pour down shower down -3 To give bestow 4 To produce engender 5 To have supreme power With अभि- 1 To shower, rain

वृष् 10 A (वर्षयते) 1 To be power ful or eminent -2 To have the power of production

वृष *m* 1 A bull 2 The sign *Taurus* of the zodiac -3 The chief or best of a class as in मुनिवृष, कपिवृष &c -4 The God of love -5 A strong or athletic man -6 A lustful man -7 An enemy 8 A rat -9 The bull of Siva -10 Mor ality justice -11 Virtue a pious or meritorious act 12 N of Karna -13 N of Vishnu -14 The prin cipal die —षं *n* A peacock s plu mage -Comp -अङ्क *m* 1 An epithet of Siva -2 A pious or virtuous man -3 The marking-nut plant -4 A eunuch —अञ्चन *m* An epithet of Siva —अन्तक *m* An epithet of Vishnu —आहार *m* A cat —उत्सर्ग *m* Setting free a bull on the occa sion of a funeral rite or as a re- ligious act generally —दंश, —दंशक *m* A cat —ध्वज *m* 1 An epithet of Siva 2 An epithet of Ganesa -3 A pious man —पति *m* 1 An epi thet of Siva 2 A bull set at liber ty —पर्वन् *m* 1 An epithet of Siva. -2 N of a demon —भाषा *f* The residence of Indra and the gods *i e* Amaravati —राजकेतन *m* N of Siva —वाहन *m* A cat —वृषभ *m* An epithet of Siva —स्कंध *a* Hav ing shoulders as lusty as those of a bull

वृषण *m* The scrotum, the bag containing the testicles

वृषणश्व *m* A horse of Indra.

वृषभ *m* 1 A bull 2 The sign *Taurus* of the zodiac -3 The chief of a class 4 Pain sorrow 5 Insensibility to pain. -6 N. of Indra. 7 N. of Karna.

वृषभ: *m.* 1 A bull. -2 Any male animal. -3 Any thing best of its class. -4 The sign *Taurus* of the zodiac. -5 An elephants' ear. -6 The orifice or hollow of the ear. -Comp. —गति:, —ध्वज: *m.* Epithets of Siva.

वृषभी *f.* A widow.

वृषय: *m.* Refuge, shelter.

वृषल: *m.* 1 A Súdra. -2 A horse. -3 Garlic. -4 A sinner. -5 An outcast. -6 N. of Chandragupta.

वृषलक: *m.* A contemptible Súdra.

वृषली *f.* 1 An unmarried girl remaining unmarried at her father's house in whom menstruation has commenced. -2 A woman during menstruation.-3 A barren woman. -4 The mother of a still-born child. -5 A Súdra female or the wife of a Súdra. -Comp.—पति: *m.* The husband of a Súdra woman.

वृषसृक्की *f.* A wasp.

वृषस्यंती *f.* 1 A woman longing for sexual intercourse. -2 A libidinous or lascivious woman. -3 A cow in heat.

वृषाकपायी *f.* 1 An epithet of Lakshmí. -2 Of Gaurî. -3 Of Sachí. -4 Of Svâhà, wife of Agni. -5 Of the wife of the sun. -6 Of the mother of Indra.

वृषाकपि: *m.* 1 An epithet of the sun. -2 Of Vishnu. -3 Of Siva. 4 Of Indra. -5 Of Agni. [A sparrow.

वृषायण: *m.* 1 An epithet of Siva. -2

वृषिन् *m.* A peacock.

वृषी *f.* The seat of an ascetic or religious student (made of Kusa grass.).

वृष्ट *p. p.* (*f.* -ष्टा) 1 Rained.-2 Raining. -3 Showering, pouring down.

वृष्टि: *f.* 1 Rain, a shower of rain. -2 A shower (of anything).-Comp. —काल: *m.* The rainy season. —जीवन *a.* Watered by rain (as a country). (-न: *m.*) The Châtaka bird. —भू: *m.* A frog. —संपात: *m.* A shower of rain.

वृष्णि *a.* 1 Heretical. -2 Angry. —ष्णि: *m.* 1 A cloud. -2 A ram. -3 A ray of light. -4 N. of an ancestor of Krishna. -5 N. of Krishna. -6 Of Indra. -7 Of Agni. -8 Air, wind. -9 A heretic. -Comp. —गर्भ: *m.* N. of Krishna.

वृष्य *a.* (*f.* —ष्या) 1 To be showered down. -2 Stimulating amorous desire. —ष्य: *m.* A kind of kidney-bean. -ष्यं *n.* Stimulating amorous desires.

वृह, वृहत, वृहतिका } See बृह, बृहत, and बृहतिका.

वृहती *f.* 1 The lute of Nârada. -2 The number 'thirty six'. -3 A wrapper. -4 Speech. -5 A reservoir (as of water). -Comp. -पति: *m.* An epithet of Brihaspati.

वृहस्पति: *m.* See बृहस्पति.

वॄ 9 U. (वृणाति, वृणीते, वूर्ण; *pass;* वूर्यते, *desid.* वुवूर्षति,-ते or विवरिषति,-ते or विवरीषति,-ते). The same as वृ.

वे 1 U. (वयति,-ते, उत; *caus.*वाययति,-ते) 1 To weave. -2 To braid, plait. -3 To sew. -4 To cover. -5 To string together. With प्र— 1 To set, to fix. -2 To tie, fasten.

वेकट: *m.* 1 A buffoon. -2 A jeweller. -3 A youth.

वेग: *m.* 1 Impulse, impetus. -2 Speed, rapidity. -3 Agitation. -4 Violence, force. -5 A current. -6 Energy. -7 Power, strength. -8 Circulation, working, effect (as of poison). -9 Haste. -10 The flight of an arrow. -11 Passion. -12 Delight, pleasure. -13 Evacuation of the feces. -14 Semen virile. -Comp. —अनिलः *m.* 1 A blast caused by speed. -2 A violent wind. —आघातः *m.* 1 A check of speed. -2 Constipation. —नाशनः *m.* The phlegmatic humour. —सरः *m.* A mule.

वेगिन् *a.* (*f* —नी) Swift, violent, rapid. *m.* 1 A courier. -2 A hawk. —नी *f.* A river.

वेंकटः *m.* N. of a mountain.

वेचा *f.* Hire, wages.

वेडं *n.* A kind of sandal.

वेडा *f.* A boat.

वेण्, वेन् 1 U. (वेणति,-ते, वेनति,-ते) 1 To go, move. -2 To know, perceive. -3 To consider. -4 To take. -5 To play on an instrument. -6 To praise, worship.

वेणः *m.* 1 A musician by caste. -2 N. of a king. [Krishna).

वेणा *f.* N. of a river (joining the

वेणिः, वेणी *f.* 1 Braided hair, a braid of hair. -2 Hair twisted into a single unornamented braid and allowed to fall on the back, worn by women whose husbands are away). -3 A current, stream. -4 The confluence of two or more rivers. -5 The confluence of the Ganges, Yamunâ and Sarasvatí. -6 N. of a river. -Comp. —बंधः *m.* Hair twisted into a braid. —वेधनी *f.* A leech. —वेधिनी *f.* A comb. —संहारः *m.* 1 Tying the hair into a braid. -2 N. of a drama by Bhatta Nárá yana.

वेणुः *m.* 1 A bamboo. -2 A reed. -3 A flute-pipe. -Comp. —जः *m.* The bamboo-seed. —ध्मः *m.* A flute-player, piper. —निष्कृतिः *m.* The sugar cane. —यवः *m.* The bamboo-seed. —वाद्ः, —वादकः *m.* A piper, fltue-player. —बीजं *n.* The bamboo-seed.

वणुकं *n.* A goad with a bamboo-handle.

वेणुनं *n.* Black pepper.

वेतः *m.* A cane, reed.

वेतं (-दं-) डः *m.* An elephant.

वेतनं *n.* 1 Hire, wages, salary. 2 Livelihood, subsistence. -Comp. —अदानं, —अनपाकर्मन् *n.* —अनपक्रिया *f.* 1 Non-payment of wages. -2 An action for non-payment of wages. —जीविन् *m.* A stipendiary.

वेतसः *m.* The ratan, reed, cane.

वेतसी *f.* The ratan. [reeds.

वेतस्वत् *a.* (*f.* -ती) Abounding in

वेतालः *m.* 1 A kind of ghost occupying a dead body. -2 A door keeper. [an espouser.

वेत्तृ *m.* 1 A sage. -2 A husband

वेत्रः *m.* 1 The cane, ratan. -2 A staff, particularly that of a door-keeper. -Comp. —आसनं *n.* A cane-seat. —धरः, —धारकः *m.* 1 A door-keeper. -2 A mace-bearer. —यष्टिः *f.* A staff of reed. [reeds

वेत्रकीय *a.* (*f.* —या) Abounding in

वेत्रवती *f.* 1 A female door-keeper. -2 N. of a river. [-2 Staff-bearer.

वेत्रिन् *m.* 1 A door-keeper, warder.

वेदः *m.* 1 Knowledge. -2 Sacred knowledge, the scriptures of the Hindus. (Originally there were only three *Vedas.* ऋग्वेद, यजुर्वेद and सामवेद, to which a fourth, the अथर्ववेद. was subsequently added). -3 A bundle of Kusa grass. -4 N. of Vishnu. -Comp. —अंगं *n.* N. of certain classes of works auxiliary to the Vedas. The *Vedângas* are six in number 1 शिक्षा 'The science of proper articulation and pronunciation'. 2

छंदस ' The science of prosody. ' 3 व्याकरण ' Grammar.' 4 निरुक्त ' Etymological explanation of difficult Vedic words'.5 ज्योतिष 'Astronomy and 6 कल्प ' Ritual or ceremonial '. —अधिगमः *m.*, -अध्ययनं *n.* The study of the Vedas. -अंतः *m.* 1 An *Upanishad*. -2 The last of the six principal *Darsanas* or systems of Hindu philosophy. —अंतिन् *m.* A follower of the Vedânta philosophy. —अवतारः *m.* The revelation of the Vedas. आदि *n.* -आदिवर्णः, —आदिबीजः *m. n.* The sacred syllable *om.* —उक्त *a.* Scriptural, taught in the Vedas. -कौलेयकः *m.* An epithet of Siva. -गर्भः *m.* 1 An epithet of Brahman (*m.*). -2 A Bráhmana versed in the Vedas. -3 N. of Vishnu. -त्रयं *n.*, -त्रयी *f.* The three Vedas collectively. —पारगः *m.* A Brâhmana skilled in the Vedas. मातृ *f.* N. of a very sacred Vedic verse called *Gâyatri*. -वचनं, -वाक्यं *n.* A Vedic text. -वदनं *n.* Grammar. —वासः *m.* A Bràhmana. —बाह्य *a.* Contrary to, or not founded on the Veda. -विद् *m.* 1 A Brahmana versed in the Vedas.-2N.of Vishnu. —विहित *a.* Enjoined by the Vedas. —व्यासः *m.* An epithet of Vyâsa. -संन्यासः *m.* Discontinuance of the ritual of the Vedas. —संमत, —संमित *a.* Sanctioned by the Vedas.

वेदनं *n.*, वेदना *f.* 1 Knowledge. -2 Feeling, sensation. -3 Pain. -4 Acquisition, wealth, property. -5 Marriage. 6 Presenting, giving. -7 The marriage of a Súdra woman with a man of a higher caste.

वेदारः *m.* A chameleon.

वेदिः *m.* A learned man, sage. -दिः, -दी *f.* 1 An altar especially one prepared for a sacrifice. -2 A quadrangular spot in the court-yard of a temple or palace. -3 A seal-ring. -4 N. of Sarasvatí. -Comp. —जा *f* An epithet of Draupadí who was born from the midst of an altar.

वेदिका *f.* 1 A sacrificial altar. -2 An elevated spot of ground. 3 A seat in general. -4 A heap, mound. -5 An open shed in the middle of a court-yard. -6 An arbour, a bower.

वेदिन् *m.* 1 A knower.-2 A teacher. -3 A learned Brâhmana. -4 An epithet of Brahman (*m.*)

वेद्य *a.* (*f.* -द्या) 1 To be known. 2 To be taught or explained. -3 To be married.

वेधः *m.* 1 Penetrating, piercing.-2 A wound. -3 An excavation. -4 The depth (of an excavation). -5 A particular division of time.

वेधकः *m.* 1 N. of one of the divisions of hell. -2 Camphor —कं *n.* Rice in the ear.

वेधनं *n.* Piercing. -2 Penetration -3 Evacuation. -4 Wounding. -5 Depth (of an evacuation).

वेधनिका *f.* A pointed instrument for perforating shells and jewels.

वेधनी *f.* 1 An instrument for piercing an elephant's ear. -2 A sharp instrument for perforating shells and jewels. -3 Depth (in measurement).

वेधस् *m.* 1 A creator. -2 N. of Brahman (*m.*). -4 N. of Siva. -5 Of Vishnu. -6 The sun. -7 The *Arka* plant.

वेधसं *n.* The part of the hand under the root of the thumb.

वेन 1 U. (वेनति,-ते) See वेण्.

वेनः *m.* See वेणः.

वेना *f.* See वेणा.

वेप् 1 A (वेपते, वेपित) To tremble.

वेपथुः *m.* Tremor, trembling.

वेपनं *n.* Trembling.

वेमः *m.*, वेमन् *m.n.* A loom.

वेरः *m.*, वेरं *n.* 1 The body. -2 Saffron. -3 The egg-plant.

वेरटः *m.* A man belonging to an inferior caste. —टं *n.* The fruit of the jujube.

वेल् 1 P. (वेलति) 1 To go, move. -2 To shake, tremble.

वेल् 10 U. (वेलयति,-ते) To count the time.

वेलं *n.* A garden, grove.

वेला *f.* 1 Time. -2 Season, opportunity. -3 Leisure. -4 Tide, current. -5 The sea-coast, sea-shore. -6 Boundary. -7 Speech. -8 Easy death. -9 The gums. -Comp. —कूलं *n.* N. of a district called Tâmralipta. —मूलं *n.* The sea-shore.

वेल्ल् 1 P. (वेल्लति) 1 To move -2 -2 To tremble, move about.

वेल्लः *m.* 1 Going, moving. -2 Trembling.

वेल्लनं *n.* Shaking, moving. -2 Rolling (on the ground).

वेल्लहलः *m.* A libertine.

वेल्लिः *f.* A creeper.

वेल्लित *p. p.* (*f.* —ता) 1 Trembling, tremulous, shaken. -2 Crooked. —तं *n.* Going, moving. -2 Shaking.

वेशः *m.* 1 Entrance. -2 Ingress, access. -3 A house. -4 A residence of prostitutes. -5 Dress, apparel (also वेष). -Comp. —दानः *m.* The sunflower. —धारिन् *a.* Disguised. (*-m.*) 1 A hypocrite, false ascetic. -2 An actor. —नारी, —वनिता *f.* A harlot.

वेशकः *m.* A house.

वेशनं *n.* 1 Entering. -2 A house.

वेशिका *f.* Entrance, ingress. [Fire.

वेशंतः *m.* 1 A small pond, pool. -2

वेशरः *m.* A mule.

वेश्मन् *n.* A house, a mansion. -Comp. —कर्मन् *n.* House-building. —कलिंगः *m.* A kind of sparrow. —नकुलः *m.* The musk-rat. —भूः *f.* The site of a habitation.

वेश्या *f.* The habition of harlots.

वेश्मन *n.* A prostitute, concubine. -Comp. —आचार्यः *m.* 1 The keeper of prostitutes. -2 A pimp. -3 A catamite.

वेश्वरः *m.* A mule.

वेषः *m.* See वेशः.

वेषणं *n.* Occupation, possession.

वेष्ट् 1 A. (वेष्टते) 1 To surround, envelop. -2 To twist round. -3 To dress. -With आ- To fold. परि-, सं- To clasp or wind round.

वेष्टः *m.* 1 Surrounding. -2 An enclosure. -3 A turban. -4 Gum, resin. -5 Turpentine. -Comp. —वंशः *m.* A kind of bamboo. —सारः *m.* Turpentine.

वेष्टकः *m.* 1 An enclosure. -2 A pumpkin-gourd. —कं *n.* 1 A turban. -2 A wrapper. -3 Gum, exudation. -4 Turpentine.

वेष्टनं *n.* 1 Surrounding. -2 An envelope, a cover, case. -3 A turban. -5 An enclosure. -5 A girdle, zone. -6 A bandage. -7 The outer ear. -8 Bdellium.

वेष्टनकः *m.* A particular position in copulation.

वेष्टित *p. p.* (*f.* —ता) 1 Surrounded, enveloped. -2 Wrapped up. -3 Stopped. -4 Blockaded. —तं *n.* 1 Surrounding. -2 One of the attitudes of dancing.

वेष्पः, वेष्यः *m.* Water.

वेष्या *f.* See वेश्या.

वेसरः *m.* A mule.

वेस (-श-) वारः *m* A particular condiment (consisting of ground coriander, mustard, pepper, ginger &c.).

वेह्ल् I A (वेह्लते) See बेह्.

वेहत् *f.* A barren cow.

वेहारः *m.* N. of a country (Behár).

वेह्ल I P.(वेह्लते) To go, move.

वै I P. (वायति)I To dry, be dried. -2 To be weary, be exhausted.

वै *ind.* A particle of affirmation or certainty (indeed, truly, forsooth), but it is generally used as an expletive. It is also said to be a vocative particle, and sometimes shows entreaty or persuasion (अनुनय).

वैंशतिक *a.* (*f* —की) Bought for [twenty.

वैकक्षं *n.* I A garland worn over one shoulder and under the other. -2 An upper garment, a mantle.

वैकक्षकं, वैकक्षिकं *n.* A garland worn over the left shoulder and under the right arm.

वैकटिकः *m.* A jeweller.

वैकर्तनः *m.* N. of Karna.

वैकल्पं *n.* I Optionality. -2 Ambiguity, uncertainty, indecision.

वैकल्पिक *a.* (*f.* —की) I Optional. -2 Doubtful, uncertain.

वैकल्यं *n.* I Defect, imperfection. -2 Mutilation. -3 Incompetency. -4 Agitation, excitement. -5 Non-existence.-6 Weakness, imbecility.

वैकारिक *a.* (*f.* —की) I Relating to modification. -2 Modifying. -3 Modified.

वैकालः *m.* Afternoon, evening,

वैकालिक *a.* (*f.*-की), वैकालीन *a.* (*f.*-नी) Relating to or occurring in the evening.

वैकुंठः *m.* I An epithet of Vishnu. -2 Of Indra. -3 Holy basil. —ठं *n.* I The heaven of Vishnu. -2 Talc. -Comp. —चतुर्दशी *f.* The fourteenth day of the bright half of Kârtika. —लोकः *m.* The world of Vishnu.

वैकृत *a.* (*f.* —ती) I Changed. -2 Modified. —तं *n.* I Change, modification. -2 Aversion. -3 Disfigurement. -4 An event foreboding evil. -Comp. —विवर्तः *m* A miserable condition.

वैकृतिक *a.* (*f.* —की) I Changed, modified. -2 Belonging to a Vikriti (in Sânkhya phil.).

वैकृत्यं *n.* I Change, alteration. -2 miserable plight. -3 Disgust.

वैक्रांतं *n.* A kind of gem.

वैक्लवं, वैक्लव्यं *n.* I Confusion, bewilderment. -2 Commotion, tumult. -3 Affliction.

वैखरी *f.* I Articulate utterance. -2 The faculty of speech. -3 Speech in general.

वैखानस *a.* (*f.* —सी) Relating to a hermit. —सः *m.* Bràhmana in the third order of his religious life.

वैगुण्यं *n.* I Absence of qualities or attributes. -2 A fault, an imperfection. -3 Diversity, contrariety. -4 Inferiority, lowness. -5 Unskilfulneass. [ciency.

वैचक्षण्यं *n.* Skill, cleverness, profi-

वैचित्यं *n.* Grief, sorrow.

वैचित्र्यं *n.* I Variety, diversity. -2 Manifoldness. -3 Strangeness, strikingness. [nancy.

वैजननं *n.* The last month of preg-

वैजयंतः *m.* I The palace of Indra. -2 The banner of Indra. -3 A banner in general. -4 N. of Indra.

वैजयंतिकः *m.* A standard-bearer.

वैजयंतिका *f.* I A banner, flag (fig. also). -2 A kind of necklace of pearls.

वैजयंती *f.* I A banner, flag. -2 A garland, necklace. -3 The necklace of Vishnu.

वैजात्यं *n.* I Difference of kind or

species. -2 Difference of caste. -3 Exclusion from caste. -4 Wantonness.

वैजिक *a.* See बैजिक.

वैज्ञानिक *a.* (*f.* — की) Clever, skilful, proficient.

वैडाल *a.* See बैडाल.

वैणः *m.* A maker of bamboo-work.

वैणव *a.* (*f.* —वी) 1 Made of or produced from a bamboo. —वः *m.* 1 A bamboo-staff. -2 A worker in bamboo or wicker-work. —वी *f.* Bamboo-manna. —वं *n.* The seed or fruit of the bamboo.

वैणविकः *m.* A piper, flute-player.

वैणविन् *m.* An epithet of Siva.

वैणिकः *m.* A lutanist.

वैणुकः *m.* A flute-player. —कं *n.* A goad.

वैतंसिकः *m.* A vendor of flesh.

वैतंडिकः *m.* A disputatious man.

वैतथ्यं *n.* Falseness.

वैतनिक *a.* (*f.* —की) Living on wages. —कः *m.* 1 A hired labourer 2 A stipendiary.

वैतरणिः,-णी *f.* 1 N. of the river of hell.-2 N. of a river in the country of the Kalingas.

वैतस *a.* (*f.* —सी) 1 Pertaining to a cane. -2 Humble, yielding. —सः *m.* A kind of cane.

वैतान *a.* (*f.* —नी) Sacrificial, sacred. —नं *n.* 1 A sacrificial rite. -2 A sacrificial oblation.

वैतानिक *a.* (*f.* -की)See वैतान. कं *n.* A burnt offering.

वैतालिकः *m.* 1 A bard, minstrel. -2 A conjurer. -3 The servant of a Vetála.

वैत्रक *a.* (*f.* —की) *a.* Cany, reedy.

वैदः *m.* A learned man.

वैदग्धं *n.*, वैदग्धी *f.*, वैदग्ध्यं *n.* 1 Skill, proficiency. -2 Skill in arrangement. -2 Shrewdness.

वैदर्भः *m.* 1 A king of Vidarbha. -2 A gum-boil. —र्भं *n.* Crafty speech. —र्भी *f.* 1 N. of Damayantī. -2 Of Rukminí. -3 A particular style of composition.

वैदल (*f.* —ली) Made of wicker or cane. —लः *m.* 1 A kind of cake. -2 Any leguminous vegetable or grain. —लं *n.* 1 A shallow cup of a religious mendicant. -2 Any seat or vessel of wicker-work.

वैदिक *a.* (*f.* —की) 1 Derived from or conformable to the Vedas. -2 Sacred, scriptural. —कः *m.* A Bráhmana well-versed in the Vedas. -Comp. —पाशः *m.* One possessing an imperfect knowledge of the Vedas.

वैदुषी *f.*, वैदुष्यं *n.* Learning, wisdom.

वैदूर्य *a.* (*f.* —री or —र्यी) Brought from, or produced in, Vidúra. —र्यं *n.* *Lapis lazuli.*

वैदेशिक *a.* (*f.* —की) Foreign, exotic. —कः *m.* A foreigner.

वैदेश्यं *n.* Foreignness.

वैदेहः *m.* 1 A king of Videha. -2 An inhabitant of Videha. -3 A trader by caste. -4 The son of a Vaisya by a Brâhmana woman. —हाः (*m. pl.*) The people of Videha. —ही *f.* N. of Sitâ.

वैदेहकः *m.* A trader.

वैदेहिकः *m.* A merchant.

वैद्य *a.* (*f.* —द्यी) 1 Relating to the Vedas, spiritual. -2 Relating to medicine, medical. —द्यः *m.* 1 A learned man. -2 A physician. -3 A man of the medical caste, (the offspring of a Bráhmana by a *Vaisya* woman). -4 A man of a lower mixed tribe (the offspring of a Sudra father by a Vaisya mother).

वैद्यकः *m.* A doctor, physicion. —कं *n.* The science of medicine.

वैद्युत *a.* (*f.* —ती) Belonging to or proceeding from lightning, electric. -Comp. —अग्निः, —अनलः, —वह्निः *m.* The fire of lightning.

वैध *a.* (*f.* —धी), वैधिक *a.* (*f.* —की) 1 Conformable to rule, ritual. -2 Legal, lawful.

वैधर्म्यं *n.* 1 Dissimilarity. -2 Difference of duty or obligation. -3 Unlawfulness, injustice.

वैधवेयः *m.* The son of a widow.

वैधव्यं *n.* Widowhood.

वैधुर्यं *n.* 1 Bereavement. -2 Agitation, tremor.

वैधेय *a.* (*f.* यी) 1 According to rule, prescribed. -2 Foolish —यः *m.* A fool.

वैनतेयः *m.* 1 N. of Garuda. -2 N. of Aruna.

वैनयिक *a.* (*f.* —की) 1 Pertaining to modesty, decorum, moral conduct or discipline. -2 Enforcing proper conduct. —कः *m.* A war-carriage.

वैनायक *a.* (*f.* —की) Belonging to Ganesa.

वैनायिकः *m.* 1 The doctrines of a Buddhist school of philosophy. -2 A follower of that school.

वैनाशिकः *m.* 1 A slave.-2 A spider. 3 An astrologer.-4 The doctrines of the Buddhists. -5 A follower of those doctrines.

वैनीतकं *n.* See विनीतकं.

वैपरीत्यं *n.* Opposition. -2 Inconsistency.

वैपुल्यं *n.* 1 Spaciousness, largeness. -2 Plenty, abundance.

वैफल्यं *n.* Uselessness, fruitlessness.

वैबोधिकः *m.* A watchman.

वैभवं *n.* 1 Greatness, magnificence, wealth. -2 Power, might.

वैभाषिक *a.* (*f.* —की) Optional.

वैभं *n.* The heaven of Vishnu.

वैभ्राजं *n.* N. of a celesstial grove or garden.

वैमत्यं *n.* 1 Dissension, dissent. -2 Dislike.

वैमनस्यं *n.* 1 Distraction of mind, sorrow, sadness. -2 Sickness.

वैमात्रः, वैमात्रेयः *m.* A step-mother's son.

वैमात्रा, वैमात्री, वैमात्रेयी *f.* A step-mother's daughter.

वैमानिक *a.* (*f.* -की) Borne in divine cars. —कः *m.* An aeronaut.

वैमुख्यं *n.* 1 Flight, retreat. -2 Aversion, disgust.

वैमेयः *m.* Exchange, barter.

वैयग्र्यं, वैयग्र्यं *n.* 1 Distraction, bewilderment. -2 Complete absorption in any object.

वैयर्थ्यं *n.* Uselessness.

वैयधिकरण्यं *n.* The state of being in different case-relations or positions.

वैयाकरण *a.* (*f.* —णी) Grammatical.—णः *m.* A grammarian.-Comp. —पाशः *m.* A bad grammarian.—भार्यः *m.* One whose wife is a grammarian.

वैयाघ्र *a.* (*f.* —घ्री) 1 Tiger-like or covered with a tiger's skin. —घ्रः *m.* A cart covered with a tiger's skin.

वैयात्यं *n.* Immodesty, absence of shame.

वैयासिकः *m.* A son of Vyâsa.

वैरं *n.* Hostility, enmity, opposition, quarrel.-2 Heroism, prowess. -Comp. —अनुबंधः *m.* Commencement of hostilities. —आतंकः *m.* The Arjuna tree. —आनृण्यं, —निर्यातनं, —साधनं *n.*, —उद्धारः, —प्रतीकारः *m.*, —प्रतिक्रिया, —यातना, —शुद्धिः *f.* Requital of enmity, taking ravenge, retaliation —कारः, —कारः, —कृत् *m.* An enemy.

वैरक्तं, वैरक्त्यं *n.* 1 Indifference to worldly attachments. 2 Dislike, aversion.

वैरंगिकः *m.* An ascetic.

वैरल्यं *n.* 1 Scarceness, rareness. -2 Looseness. -3 Fineness.

वैरागं *n.* See वैराग्यं.

वैरागिकः, वैरागिन् *m* An ascetie

who has subdued his passions and desires.

वैराग्यं *n*. 1 Asceticism.-2 Dissatisfaction, discontent. -3 Dislike.

वैराट *a*. (*f*. —टी) Belonging to Viráta. -टः *m*. A kind of earth worm (इंद्रगोप).

वैरिन् *a*. (*f*. —णी) Hostile. -*m*. 1 An enemy. -2 A brave person.

वैरूप्यं *n*. 1 Deformity. -2 Diversity of form.

वैरोचनः, वैरोचनिः,वैरोचिः *m*. A patronymic of the demon Bali.

वैलक्षण्यं *n*. 1 Strangeness- -2 Contrariety. -3 Divergence.

वैलक्ष्यं *n*. 1 Embarassment. -2 Affectation.-3 Shame.-4 Contrariety, inversion.

वैलोम्यं *n*. Opposition, contrariety.

वैल्व *a*. See बैल्व.

वैवधिकः *m*. 1 A pedlar, hawker.-2 A load carrier.

वैवर्ण्यं *n*. 1 Change of colour, paleness. -2 Diversity. -3 Deviation from caste.

वैवस्वतः *m*. 1 N. of the seventh Manu who is now reigning. -2 N. of Yama. -3 N. of Agni. -4 One of the eleven Rudras. -5 The planet Saturn. —तं *n*. The present age or Manvantara. [N. of Yamunâ.

वैवस्वती *f*. The southern quarter.-2

वैवाहिक *a*. (*f*. —की) Relating to marriage.—कः *m*., —कं *n*. A marriage. —कः The father of a son's wife or daughter's husband.

वैशद्यं *n*. 1 Clearness. purity (fig. also). -2 Perspicuity. -3 Whiteness. -4 Calmness, cemposure (of mind). [of Vyâsa.

वैशंपायनः *m*.N.of a celebrated pupil

वैशसं *n*. 1 Destruction, slaughter. -2 Distress, suffering.

वैशस्त्रं *n*. 1 Defencelessness. -2 Government, rule.

वैशाखः *m*. 1 N. of the second lunar month (corresponding to April-May). -2 A churning-stick. —खं *n*. A particular attitude in shooting —खी *f*. The full-moon day in the month of Vaisákha.

वैशिकः *m*.A person who associates with harlots. —कं *n*. Harlotry. arts of harlots.

वैशिष्टं *n*. See वैशिष्ट्यं.

वैशिष्ट्यं *n*. 1 Distinction; difference. -2 Peculiarity. -3 Excellence.

वैशेषिक *a*. (*f*. —की). 1 Characteristic. -2 Belonging to the Vaiseshika doctrine. —कः *m*. A follower of the Vaiseshika doctrine. —कं *n*. One of the six principal Darsanas or systems of Hindu philosophy.

वैश्यः *m*. 1 A man of the third tribe whose business is trade and agriculture. -Comp. —कर्मन् *n*., —वृत्तिः *f*. The business or occupation of a Vaisya.

वैश्रवणः *m*. 1 N. of Kubera the god of wealth. -2 N. of Râvana.-Comp. —आलयः, —आवासः *m*. The abode of Kubera. -2 The fig-tree. —उदयः *m*. The fig-tree.

वैश्वदेवं *n*. 1 An offering made to the Visvedevas. -2 An offering to all deities. —वी *f*. The eighth day of the second half of Mágha.

वैश्वानरः *m*. 1 An epithet of fire. -2 The fire of digestion. -3 The Supreme Being. 5 The Chitraka tree.

वैश्वासिक *a*. (*f*. —की) Trusty, confidential.

वैषम्यं *n*. 1 Unevenness. -2 Roughness. -3 Inequality. -4 Injustice.-5 Difficulity,misery, calamity.-6Solitariness.

वैषयिक *a.* (*f.* —की) 1 Relating to an object. -2 Pertaining to objects of sense, sensual. —कः *m.* A sensualist.

वैहुतं *n.* The ashes of a burnt offering.

वैहुः *m.* 1 Heaven,sky.-2Air,wind. -3 A division of the universe.

वैष्णव *a.* (*f.* -वी) 1 Relating to Vishnu. -2 Worshipping Vishnu. -वः *m.* 1 One of the three important modern Hindu sects, the other two being Saiva and Sákta sects.-2 N. of the asterism Sravana. -वी *f.* 1 The personified Sakti or energy of Vishnu. -2 N. of Durgâ. —वं *n.* 1 The residence of Vishnu. -2 The ashes of a burnt offering.

वैसारिणः *m.* A fish.

वैसूचनं *n.* Assuming the part of a female by a man (in dramas).

वैहायस *a.* (*f.* -सी) Being in the air.

वैहार्य *a.* (*f.* —र्या) To be sported with,to be made the suject of jokes (said of the brother of one's wife or of the wife's relatives).

वैहासिकः *m.* A jester, buffoon.

वोड: *m.* 1 A kind of snake. -2 A kind of fish.

वोड्री *f.* The fourth part of a 'Pana'.

वोढ़ः *m.* 1 A bearer, porter. -2 A leader.-3 A husbaud. -4 A bull. -5 A charioteer. -6 A draught-horse.

वोन्टः *m.* A stalk, stem.

वोद *a.* (*f.* —दा) Moist,wet,damp.

वोदालः *m.* The sheat-fish.

वोर (-ल-) कः *m.* A scribe, writer.

वोरन्टः *m.* A kind of jasmine(कुंद).

वोलः *m.* Gum-myrrh.

वोल्लाहः *m.* A kind of horse.

वौद्र *a.* See वौद्र.

वौषट् *ind.* An exclamation used in offering an oblation to the gods or Manes.

व्यंशकः *m.* A mountain.

व्यंसकः *m.* A cheat.

व्यंसनं *n.* Cheating.

व्यक्त *p.p.* (*f.* —क्ता) 1 Manifested. -2 Developed. -3 Plain, distinct. -4 Distinguished. -5 Individual.-6 Wise, learned. —क्तं *n.* That which is developed as the product of अव्यक्त. —क्तं *ind.* Clearly, certainly.-Comp. -गणितं *n,* Arithmetic. -दृष्टार्थः *m* An eye-witness.

व्यक्तिः *f.* 1 Manifestation, clear perception. -2 Clearness, distinctness. -3 Distinction, discrimination. -4 True character. -5 An individual (opp. जाति) -6 Gender (in gram.). -7 Inflection

व्यग्र *a.* (*f.* -ग्रा) 1 Bewildered,perplexed. -2 Frightened. -3 Eagerly or intently occupied in (with loc., instr. or in comp.).

व्यंग *a.* (*f.* -गा) 1 Bodiless.-2 Deformed, maimed, crippled. -3 Ill-arranged. -4 Lame. —गः *m.* 1 A cripple. -2 A frog. -3 Dark spots on the cheek. -Comp.—अर्थः *m.* Suggested or implied sense.

व्यंगुलं *n.* A measure of length equal to one-sixtieth part of an *angula.*

व्यंग्यं *n.* Suggested sense, insinuation (opp. वाच्य the expressed meaning ' and लक्ष्य ' the secondary meaning '). -Comp.-उक्तिः *f.* Covert expression, insinuation.

व्यच् 6 P. (विचति, *pass.* विच्यते) 1 To cheat. -2 To surround, pervade.

व्यजः *m.* A fan.

व्यजनं *n.* A fan.

व्यंजक *a.* (*f.* —जिका) 1 Making clear, manifesting, showing, indicating. -2 Suggesting a meaning (applied to a word or sense and opp. वाचक and लाक्षणिक). —कः *m.* Gesticulation indicating internal feeling ; dramatic gesture.

व्यंजनं *n.* 1 Making clear, manifesting, indicating. -2 A mark, a sign, token.-3 A mark of the sex *i.e.* the male or the female organ of generation. 4 A consonant.-5 A mark of the sex *i. e.* the male or female organ. -6 Insignia. -7 A mark or sign of puberty 9 The beard. -10 A limb, member. 10 A condiment, sauce, spices; a seasoned article.-11 The last of the three powers of a word by which it suggests or insinuates a sense. (व्यंजना *f.* also in this sense). -Comp.-संधिः *m.* The junction or coalition of consonants.

व्यंजना *f.* 1 See व्यंजनं (I) above.

व्यंजित *p. p.* (*f.* -ता) 1 Made clear, manifested, indicated. -2 Marked, characterized.-3 Suggested.

व्यड्वकः, व्यडंबनः *m.* The castor-oil plant.

व्यतिकरः *m.* 1 Mixture, blending together. -2 Contact, combination. 3 Striking against. -4 Obstruction. -5 An occurrence, affair, a matter. -6 An opportunity. -7 Misfortune, calamity. -8 Mutual relation, reciprocity. -9 Alternation.

व्यतिकीर्ण *p. p.* (*f*, -र्णा) Mixed or blended together.

व्यतिक्रमः *m.* 1 Transgressing, deviating. -2 Violation, breach, non-performance. -3 Disregard, omission. -4 Inversion, reverse. -5 Sin, vice, crime. -6 Adversity.

व्यतिक्रांत *p. p.* (*f.* —ता) 1 Passed over, transgressed, violated.-2 Inverted, reversed. -3 Elapsed, passed away (as time).

व्यतिरिक्त *p. p.* (*f.* —क्ता) 1 Separated from. -2 Surpassing, excelling. -3 Withheld. -4 Excepted. —क्तं *ind.* With the exception of. except, without.

व्यतिरेकः *m.* 1 Distinction, difference. -2 Separation from. -3 Exclusion, exception. -4 Surpassing, excelling. -5 Contrast. -6 (In logic) Logical discontinuance (opp. अन्वय). -7 (In Rhet.) The figure of speech in which the उपमेय is represented as excelling or falling short of the उपमान (व्यतिरेकेण means 'except, without' ; व्यतिरेके ' on the contrary supposition').

व्यतिरेकिन् *a.* (*f.* —णी) 1 Different. -2 Surpassing, excellng. - 3 Excluding. excepting. -4 Showing negation or non-existence.

व्यतिषक्त *p. p.* (*f.* -क्ता) 1 Linked or joined together. -2 Intermixed.

व्यतिषंगः *m.* 1 Reciprocal connection. -2 Intermixture. -3 Union. -4 Tying together.

व्यति (-ती-) हारः *m.* 1 Exchange, barter. -2 Reciprocity, interchange.

व्यतीत *p. p.* (*f.* —ता) 1 Passed, gone, elapsed. -2 Dead. -3 Abandoned. -4 Departed from. -5 Disregarded, omitted.

व्यतीपातः *m.* 1 A portent foreboding a great calamity. -2 Disrespect, contempt.-3 The seventeenth of the astronomical Yogas. -4 The day of full-moon (when it falls on a Monday). -5 A malignant or evil aspect of the sun and moon.

व्यत्ययः *m.* 1 Passing over. -2 Inverted order, inversion -3 Interchange, transmutation.-4 Obstruction.

व्यत्यस्त *p. p.* (*f.* —स्ता) 1 Reversed, inverted. -2 Contrary, opposite -3 Incoherent.

व्यत्यासः *m.* 1 Inverted order. 2 Opposition, contrariety.

व्यथ् 1 A (व्यथते, व्याथित) 1 To be sorry, to be vexed or afflicted, to be agitated or disquieted ; be disturbed or agitated -3 To be afraid. -4 To dry, become dry.

Caus. (व्यथयति,-ते) 1 To distress vex, annoy. -2 To frighten, terrify.

व्यथक *a.*(*f.*थिका) Painful, distressing.

व्यथनं *n.* Giving pain, tormenting.

व्यथा *f.* 1 Pain, agony, anguish. 2 Fear, alarm. -3 Agitation, disquietude. -4 Disease.

व्यथित *p. p.* (*f.* -ता) 1 Afflicted, distressed, pained. -2 Alarmed -3 Agitated, disquieted, troubled.

व्यधं 4 P. (विध्यति,विद्ध) 1 To pierce hurt, stab, kill. -2 To bore, perforate. -3 To pick. -4 To wave or brandish in triumph (as the tail &c.). With अनु— 1 To pierce. to wound. 2 To intertwine. अप— 1 To throw away. -2 To pierce. आ— 1 To throw. -2 To pierce. परि— 1 To pierce. -2 To wound.

व्यधः *m.* 1 Piercing. -2 Wounding. 3 Perforating.-4 A stroke,wound.

व्यधिकरणं *n.* Subsisting in different receptacles or substrata. व्यधिकरणबहुव्रीहिः *m.*A Bahuvrihi compound, the first member of which is not in apposition,but stands in a different case relation to the second.

व्यध्वः *m.* A butt,a mark to aim at.

व्यध्वः *m.* A bad or wrong road.

व्यनुनादः *m.* Reverberation, loud echo. [-2 To diminish.

व्यप् 10 U. (व्यापयति,-ते) 1 To throw.

व्यपकृष्ट *p. p.* (*f.* —ष्टा) Drawn aside, taken away, removed.

व्यपगत *p. p.* (*f.*-ता) 1 Gone away. -2 Removed. -3 Deprived of, free from.

व्यपगमः *m.* Departure. [pudent.

व्यपत्रपः *a.* (*f.* —पा) Shameless,im-

व्यपदिष्ट *p. p.* (*f.* —ष्टा) 1 Named. -2 Shown, signified. -3 Pleaded as a pretext.

व्यपदेशः *m.* 1 Representation,notice. -2 Designation by name. 3 A name, a title. -4 A family, race.-5 Fame, renown. -6 A pretext, device. -7 Fraud, craft. -8 Concealment, dissimulation.

व्यपरोपणं *n.*1 Uprooting. -2 Expelling, driving away. -3 Tearing out, plucking.

व्यपवर्तनं *n.* Return.

व्यपाकृतिः *f.* 1 Expelling, driving away -2 Denial.

व्यपायः *m.* End, disappearaece.

व्यपाश्रयः *m.* 1 Succession, -2 Taking refuge with. -2 Depending on.

व्यपेक्ष *a.* (*f.* -क्षा) 1 Expecting. -2 Eager. -3 Regarding, minding.

व्यपेक्षणं *n.* Expecting. expectation.

व्यपेक्षा *f.* 1 Expectation, hope. -2 Regard, consideration. -3 Interdependence. -4 Mutual regard. -5 Application. -6 (In gram.) The mutual application of two rules.

व्यपेक्षित *p. p.* (*f.* -ता) 1 Hoped, expected. -2 Regarded, minded. -3 Mutally connected. 4 Applied, used.

व्यपेत *p. p.* (*f.* -ता) 1 Separated, severed. -1 Gone away. -3 Contraary, opposed to.

व्यपोढ *p. p.* (*f.* -ढा) Expelled, removed. -2 Contrary, opposite. -3 Displayed, shown.

व्यपोहः *m*. Expelling, keeping off.

व्यभि (-भी-) चारः *m*. 1 Going away from, deviation, following improper courses. -2 Transgression. -3 Error, crime, sin. -4 Separableness. -5 Faithlessness (of a wife or husband), unchastity. -6 An irregularity, exception (to a rule.) -7 (In logic) A fallacious *hetu*, one without the *sádhya*.

व्यभिचारिणी *f*. An unchaste wife, adulteress.

व्यभिचारिन् *a*. (*f*. -णी) 1 Deviating from, going astray. -2 Irregular, anomalous. -3 Untrue. -4 Unchaste, adulterous. -5 Wanton. -6 Having several secondary meanings (as a word). -भावः *m*. A transitory feeling, an accessory (opp. स्थायिन् or स्थायिभाव).

व्यय् 10 U. (व्यययति,-ते) 1 To go, move. -2 To expend, give away, bestow.

व्यय् 1 U. (व्ययति,-ते) To go, move.

व्यय् 10U.(व्ययति,-ते, also व्याययति,-ते) 1 To throw. cast. -2 To drive.

व्यय *a*. (*f*. —या) Liable to change, perishable. —यः *m*. 1 Loss. -2 Hindrance, obstacle. -3 Decay, downfall. -4 Expenditure. -5 Prodigality. -Comp. —शुद्धिः *f*. Defraying of expenses.

व्ययित *p. p*. (*f*, —ता) 1 Expended, spent. -2 Fallen into decay.

व्यर्थ *a*. (*f*. —र्था) 1 Useless, vain, unprofitable. -2 Meaningless, idle.

व्यलीक *a*. (*f*. -का) 1 False, untrue. -2 Disagreeable, displeasing. —कः *m*. 1 A libertine. -2 A catamite. —कं *n*. 1 Anything disagreeable or displeasing. -2 Pain, sorrow, grief. -3 A fault, any improper act. -4 Fraud. -5 Falsehood, -9 Inversion, contrariety.

व्यवकलनं *n*. 1 Separation. -2 (In math.) Subtraction.

व्यवक्रोशनं *n*. 1 Mutual abuse. -2 Abuse in general.

व्यवच्छिन्न *p. p*. (*f*. —न्ना) 1 Cut off, torn off. -2 Separated, divided. -3 Specified. -4 Marked, distinguished. -5 Interrupted.

व्यवच्छेदः *m*. 1 Cutting off. -2 Dividing, separating. -3 Particularizing. -4 Distinguishing. -5 Contrast. -6 Determination. -7 Letting fly (as an arrow). -8 A chapter or section of a work.

व्यवधा *f*. 1 That which intervenes. -2 A screen, partition. -2 Concealment.

व्यवधानं *n*. 1 Interposition, separation. -2 Hiding from view. -3 Concealment. -4 A screen, partition. -5 A cover, covering. -6 Interval, space. -7 (In gram.) The intervention of a syllable or letter.

व्यवधिः *m*. See व्यवधानं.

व्यवसायः *m*. 1 Effort, exertion, perseverance. -2 Resolution, determination. -3 An action, performance. -4 Business, a particular profession or trade. -5 Conduct, behaviour. -6 A stratagem. -7 Boasting. -8 N. of Vishnu. 9 Of Siva.

व्यवसित *p. p*. (*f*. -ता) 1 Attempted. -2 Undertaken. -3 Determined, settled. -4 Devised, planned. -5 Endeavouring, resolving. -6 Persevering, energetic. -7 Cheated. —तं *n*. Ascertainment, determination.

व्यवस्था *f*. 1 Arrangement, settlement, definiteness. -2 Firm basis.

-3 Relative position. -4 A settled rule or law; written declaration of the law (where contradictory texts have to be properly adjusted). -5 An agreement. -6 State, condition. -7 State or order of things.

व्यवस्थानं *n.*, व्यवस्थितिः *f.* 1 Arrangement, settlement, decision. -2 A rule, a decision. -3 Steadiness. -4 Firmness, perseverance. —नः *m. N.* of Vishnu.

व्यवस्थापक *a.* (*f.* —पिका) 1 Arranging, adjusting, establishing, deciding. -2 One who gives a legal opinion.

व्यवस्थापनं *n.* 1 Arranging properly. -2 Settling, deciding.

व्यवास्थित *p. p.* (*f.* —ता) Adjusted. arranged. -2 Settled, fixed. -3 decided. -4 Extracted.

व्यवास्थितिः *f.* See व्यवस्थानं.

व्यवहर्तृ *m.* 1 The manager of a business. -2 A litigant, plaintiff. -3 A judge.

व्यवहारः *m.* 1 Conduct, action. -2 A business, work. -3 Profession, occupation. -4 A transaction. -5 Commerce. -6 Dealing in money, usury. -7 An established rule or practice. -8 Connection. -9 Administration of justice. -10 A legal dispute. -11 An occasion of litigation. -Comp. —अंगं *n.* The body of civil and criminal law. —आसनं *n.* The tribunal of justice; judgment-seat. -ज्ञः *m.* 1 One who understands business. -2 A youth come of age. -3 One who is acquainted with judicial pocedure. —दर्शनं *n.* Trial, judicial investigation. —पदं *n.* An occasion of litigation ; a head of legal procedure. —पादः *m.* The fourth stage in the conduct of a law-suit ; that which concerns the decision. —मातृका *f.* 1 A legal process in general. -2 Any act or subject relating to the administration of justice. —विधिः *m.* A rule of law; any code or law. —विषयः *m.* (so —पदं *n.*, —मार्गः *m.*, —स्थानं *n.*) A subject or head of legal procedure. —स्थितिः *f.* Judicial procedure.

व्यवहारकः *m.* A dealer, trader.

व्यवहारिक *a.* (*f.* -का or -की) 1 Relating to business. -2 Engaged in business. -3 Judicial. -4 Usual, customary.

व्यवहारिका *f.* 1 Usage, custom. -2 A broom. -3 The *Ingudi* plant.

व्यवहारिन् *a.* (*f.* -णी) 1 Transacting business. -2 Engaged in a law-suit. -3 Usual, customary.

व्यवाहित *p. p.* (*f.* —ता) 1 Placed apart. -2 Separated. -3 Interrupted, obstructed. -4 Screened, hidden. -5 Not immediately connected. -6 Done, performed. -7 Omitted. -8 Surpassed, excelled.

व्यवहृतिः *f.* 1 Practice. -2 Performance.

व्यवायः *m.* 1 Separation, decomposition. -2 Covering, concealment. -3 Intervention, interval. -4 An impediment, obstacle. -5 Copulation. -7 Purity. -यं *n.* Light, lustre.

व्यवायिन् *m.* 1 A sensualist. -2 An aphrodisiac.

व्यवेत *p, p.* (*f.* —ता) 1 Separated, decomposed. -2 Different.

व्यष्टिः *f.* 1 Individuality, singleness. -2 Distributive pervasion. -3 (In Vedànta phil.) A whole viewed as made up of many separate bodies (opp. समष्टि).

व्यसनं *n.* 1 Separating, dividing. -2 Violation, infraction. -3 Loss, defeat. -4 A calamity, misfortune.

-5 Setting (as of the sun &c.). -6 Vice, an evil habit. -7 Close or intent application. -8 Crime, sin. -9 Punishment. -10 Inability, incompetency. -11 Fruitless effort. -12 Air, wind.

व्यसनिन् *a.* (*f.* —नी) 1 Addicted to any vice. -2 Unlucky. -3 Intently attached to anything.

व्यसु *a.* Dead, lifeless.

व्यस्त *p. p.* (*f.* —स्ता) 1 Tossed about. -2 Dispersed, scattered. -3 Separated, divided. -4 Taken or considered separately, taken singly (opp. समस्त). -5 Simple, uncompounded (as a word). -6 Manifold, different. -7 Expelled. -8 Agitated. -9 Disarranged. -10 Upset. -11 Inverse (as ratio). -12 Pervading, inherent in.

व्यस्तारः *m.* The issue of rut from the temples of an elephant.

व्याकरणं *n.* 1 Analysis, decomposition. -2 The science of grammar. -3 Explaining, expounding.

व्याकारः *m.* 1 Change of form. -2 Deformity.

व्याकीर्ण *p. p.* (*f.* —र्णा) 1 Scattered about. -2 Disordered.

व्याकुल *a.* (*f.* —ला) 1 Agitated, bewildered. -2 Frightened. -3 Intently engaged in.

व्याकुलित (*f.* —ता) *a.* Agitated, perplexed.

व्याकूतिः *f.* Fraud, deception.

व्याकृत *p. p.* (*f.* —ता) 1 Analysed, separated. -2 Explained, expounded. -3 Disfigured, deformed.

व्याकृतिः *f.* 1 Analysis. -2 Exposition, explanation. -3 Change of form. -4 Grammar.

व्याकोश (-ष) *a.* (*f.* -शा, -षा) 1 Expanded, blown, blossomed. -2 Developed.

व्याक्षिप्त *p. p.* (*f.* -प्ता) 1 Tossed about. -2 Torn asunder, distracted. -3 Upset, uneasy.

व्याक्षेपः *m.* 1 Tossing about. -2 Obstruction. -3 Delay. -4 Distraction.

व्याख्या *f.* 1 Relation, narration. -2 Explanation, comment.

व्याख्यात *p. p.* (*f.* —ता) 1 Related, narrated. -2 Explained.

व्याख्यानं *n.* 1 Communication, narration. -2 Speech, lecture. -3 Explanation.

व्याघट्टनं *n.* 1 Churning. -2 Friction.

व्याघातः *m.* 1 A blow, stroke. -2 An obstacle. -3 Contradiction. -4 The figure of speech in which a certain thing which is done by one man by a certain means is described as being undone by another by the same means.

व्याघ्रः *m.* (*f.* व्याघ्री) 1 A tiger. -2 (At the end of comp.). Best, pre-eminent, chief ; as in नरव्याघ्रः, पुरुषव्याघ्रः. -3 The red variety of the castor-oil plant. —घ्री *f.* A tigress. -Comp. -अटः *m.* A sky-lark. -आस्यः *m.* A cat. —दलः, -पुच्छः *m.* The castor-oil plant. —नखः *m.*, -नखं *n.* 1 A tiger's claw. -2 A kind of perfume. -3 The impression of a finger-nail. —नायकः *m.* A jackal.

व्याजः *m.* 1 Deceit, deception, fraud. -2 Art, cunning. -3 A pretext, semblance. -4 A device, contrivance. -Comp. —उक्तिः *f.* 1 The figure of speech in which there is described the artful concealment of a thing though discovered. -2 Covert allusion, insinuation. —सुप्त *a.* Feigning to be asleep. -स्तुतिः *f.* The figure of speech in which from blame expressed praise is understood or from praise expressed blame is understood. The figure in which from apparent blame is understood praise and from apparent praise is understood blame. -2 Irony.

व्याडः *m.* 1 A carnivorous animal. -2 A rogue. -3 A snake. -4 N. of Indra.

व्याडिः *f.* N. of a celebrated grammarian.

व्यात्त *p. p.* (*f.* —त्ता) Opened, expanded. —त्तं *n.* The open mouth.

व्यात्युक्षी *f.* Mutual splashing and sporting in water.

व्यादानं *n.* Opening.

व्यादिशः *m.* An epithet of Vishnu.

व्याधः *m.* 1 A hunter, fowler. -2 A wicked man. -Comp. —भीतः *m.* A deer.

व्याधामः, व्याधावः *m.* Indra's thunderbolt.

व्याधिः *m.* 1 Sickness, ailment, disease (usually physical, and opp. to आधि which means 'mental distress or anxiety'). -2 Leprosy.

व्याधित *a.* (*f.* —ता) Diseased, sick.

व्याधूत *p. p.* (*f.* —ता) Shaken about, tremulous.

व्यानः *m.* One of the five life-winds in the body (which is diffused through the whole body).

व्यापक *a.* (*f.* -पिका) Pervading, extending over the whole of anything. —कः *m.* An attribute which is invariably concomitant or inherent. -कं *n.* An invariably concomitant or inherent property.

व्यापत्तिः *f.* 1 Ruin, misfortune. -2 Substitution of one thing for another. -3 Death.

व्यापद् *f.* 1 Calamity, misfortune. -2 Disease. -3 Derangement. -4 Death.

व्यापनं *n.* 1 Pervading, penetrating. -2 Covering.

व्यापन्न *p. p.* (*f.* —न्ना) 1 Fallen into misfortune, ruined. -2 Failed. -3 Hurt. -4 Dead, deceased. -5 Deranged. -6 Substituted, changed.

व्यापिन् *a.* (*f.* —नी) Pervading, filling. -2 All-pervading, co-extensive. -3 Covering. -*m.* 1 An epithet of Vishnu. -2 A pervading property.

व्यापादः *m.*, व्यापादनं *n.* 1 Killing. -2 Ruin. -3 Evil design, malice.

व्यापादित *p. p.* (*f.* —ता) 1 Killed, destroyed. -2 Ruined, hurt.

व्यापारः *m.* 1 Employment, engagement. -2 Application. -3 Profession, trade. -4 An act, performance. -5 Operation, action. -6 Exertion, effort. -7 Meddling.

व्यापारित *p. p.* (*f.* —ता) Employed, appointed.

व्यापारिन् *m.* A dealer, trader.

व्यापृत *p. p.* (*f.* —ता) Engaged, occupied or busy with, (with loc). —*m.* An employe', a minister.

व्यापृतिः *f.* 1 Employment, engagement, business. -2 Operation, action. -3 Exertion. -4 Profession, practice.

व्याप्त *p. p.* (*f.* —प्ता) 1 Spread through, pervaded, extended over, covered. -2 Pervading, extending over all. -3 Filled with, full of. -4 Surrounded. -5 Obtained, possessed. -6 Included. -7 Invariably accompanied (in logic). -8 Famous, celebrated.

व्याप्तिः *f.* 1 Pervasion, permeation. -2 (In logic) Universal pervasion, universal accompaniment of the middle term by the major. -3 A universal rule. -4 Fulness. -5 Omnipresence, (as a divine attrbute). -Comp. —ग्रहः *m.* Apprehension of universal concomitance. —ज्ञानं *n.* Knowledge of invariable concomitance.

व्याप्यं *n.* The sign or middle term of a syllogism (in logic).

व्याप्यत्वं *n.* Invariableness.–Comp. —असिद्धिः *f.* Imperfect inference, where the हेतु itself is false or non-existent.

व्याभ्युक्षी *f.* See व्यात्युक्षी.

व्यामः *m.*, व्यामनं *n.* A measure of length equal to the space between the tips of the fingers of either hand when the arms are extended.

व्यामर्षः *m.* 1 Impatience. –2 Erasure, wiping out. [termixed.

व्यामिश्र *a.* (*f.* —श्रा) Mingled, in-

व्यामोहः *m.* 1 Infatuation. –2 Bewilderment, embarrassment.

व्यायत *p p.* (*f.* —ता) 1 Long, extended. –2 Expanded, wide open. –3 Exercised, disciplined. –4 Engaged, occupied. –5 Hard, firm. –6 Strong, excessive.–7Mighty,powerful.

व्यायामः *m.* 1 Stretching out. –2 Gymnastic or athletic exercise. –3 Fatigue, labour. –4 Effort, exertion. –5 Contention, struggle. –6 Business, occupation. –7 A measure of distance (= व्याम).

व्यायामिक *a.* (*f.* —की), व्यायामिन् *a.* (*f.* —नी) Athletic, gymnastic.

व्यायोगः *m.* A kind of dramatic composition in one act, having a famous and well-known person for its hero, having a very small number of female characters, having a large number of male characters, describing fighting and wrestling (not orginating in the love of any woman), and having the action extending over the period of only one day.

व्याल *a.* (*f.* —ला) 1 Wicked, vicious. –2 Villainous. –3 Cruel, fierce, savage. —कः *m.* 1 A vicious elephant.–2 A beast of prey.–3A snake. –4 A tiger. –5 A leopard. –6 A king. –7 A cheat, rogue. –8 N. of Vishnu.

व्यालकः *m.* A vicious elephant.

व्यालंबः *m.* A kind of castor-oil plant.

व्यालोल *a.* (*f.* –ला) 1 Shaking about, tremulous. –2 Disordered,dishevelled.

व्यावकलनं *n.*Subtraction (in math.).

व्यावक्रोशी, व्यावभाषी *f.* Mutual abuse.

व्यावर्तः *m.* 1 Surrounding. –2 Going round. –3Ruptured navel.

व्यावर्तक *a.* (*f.* –र्तिका) 1 Surrounding. –2 Excluding, restricting. –3 Turning away from. –4 Turning round.

व्यावर्तनं *n.* 1 Surrounding, encompassing. –2 Revolving, turning round. –6 A fold, band.

व्यावहारिक *a.* (*f.* –की) 1 Relating to business. –2 Legal, judicial. –3 Custumary, usual. –4 Relating to the world of illusion. —कः *m.* A counsellor, minister. —कं *n.* Use.

व्यावहारी *f.* Mutual seizing.

व्यावहासी *f.* Mutual derision or laughter.

व्यावृत *p. p.* (*f.* —ता) 1 Covered, hid. –2 Obstructed. –3 Opened. –4 Excluded. [sion.

व्यावृतिः *f.* 1 Covering. –2 Exclu-

व्यावृत्त *p. p.* (*f.* ता) 1 Turned away from. –2 Singled out. –3 Excluded, different from, not existing in, absent from. –4 Revolved. –5 Surrounded. –6 Ceased from.

व्यावृत्तिः *f.* 1 Screening. –2 Exclusion, separation. –3 Absence from. –4 Surrounding –5 Rolling backwards. –6 Praise.

व्यासः *m.* 1 Separation into parts. -2 Analysis of a compound.-3 Distinction. -4 Extension. -5 Width, breadth. -6 The diameter of a circle. -7 A fault in pronunciation. -8 Arrangement, compilation. -9 An arranger, a compiler. -10 N. of a celebrated sage. -11 A Brâhmana who recites or expounds the Purânas in public.

व्यासक्त *p. p.* (*f.*-क्ता) 1 Closely adhering to. -2 Attached or devoted to, occupied or busy with (with loc.). -3 Detached, disjoined. -4 Confused, bewildered.

व्यासंगः *m.* 1 Intent attachment or application. -2 Devotion. -3 Diligent study. -4 Attention. -5 Separation.

व्यासिद्ध *p. p.* (*f.*-द्धा) 1 Prohibited, forbidden. -2 Contraband.

व्याहत *p. p.* (*f.*—ता) 1 Obstructed. -2 Repulsed. -3 Disappointed. -4 Bewildered, alarmed. -Comp.-अर्थता *f.* One of the faults of composition.

व्याहरणं *n.* 1 Utterance, pronunciation.-2 Speech, narration.

व्याहारः *m.* 1 Speech, utterance. -2 Voice, sound. -3 Jest, joke.

व्याहृत *p. p.* (*f.* —ता) Said, uttered.

व्याहृतिः *f.* 1 Utterance, speech. -2 Statement. -3 A mystic word uttered by every Brâhmana in performing his daily Sandhyà adoration ; (these Vyâhritis are three भूर्, भुवस् and स्वस् or स्वर्; according to some they are seven in number).

व्युच्छित्तिः *f.*, व्युच्छेदः *m.* Cutting off, destruction.

व्युत्क्रमः *m.* 1 Transgression. -2 Inverted order. -3 Disorder.

व्युत्क्रांत *p. p.* (*f.* -ता) 1 Transgressed, overstepped. -2 Departed. -3 Neglected. —ता *f.* A kind of riddle.

व्युत्थानं *n.*, व्युत्थितिः *f.* 1 Great activity. -2 Rising up against. -3 Following one's own bent of mind. -4 The completion of religious abstraction (in Yoga phil.).-5 A kind of dance. -6 Contradicting.

व्युत्पत्तिः *f.* 1 Origin, production.-2 Derivation, etymology. -3 Scholarship, learning.

व्युत्पन्न *p. p.* (*f.* —न्ना) 1 Produced. -2Formed by derivation. -3 Traced to its etymology, as a word. -4 Completed. -5 Learned, erudite.

व्युदस्त *p. p.* (*f.* -स्ता) Thrown aside, rejected.

व्युदासः *m.* 1 Rejection. -2 Exclusion (in gram.). -3 Prohibition. -4 Disregard, indifference. -5 Killing, destruction.

व्युपदेशः *m.* Pretext, pretence.

व्युपरमः *m.* Cessation, stop, close.

व्युपशमः *m.* 1 Non-cessation. -2 Inquietude. -3 Complete cessation.

व्युष्ट *p. p.* (*f.* —ष्टा) 1 Burnt. -2 Dawned, become day-light. -3 Become bright or clear. -4 Dwelt. -5 Passed. -ष्टं *n.* 1 Day break. -2 Day. -3 Fruit, result.

व्युष्टिः *f.* 1 Dawn. -2 Prosperity. -3 Praise. -4 Fruit, consequence.

व्यूढ *p. p.* 1 Expanded, broad, wide. -2 Firm, compact. -3 Placed in order, marshalled (as an army); forcibly borne up or scattered. -4 Disarranged. -5 Married.-6 Large, great. -Comp. -कंकट *a.* Mailed, clad in armour.

व्यूढिः *f.* Orderly arrangement.

व्यूत *a.* (*f.* —ता) Interwoven, sewn.

व्यूतिः *f.* 1 Weaving, sewing. -2 The wages of weaving.

व्यूहः *m.* 1 A military array. -2

An army. -3 A large quantity, a multitude. -4 A subhead. -5 The body. -6 Structure, formation. -7 Reasoning, logic. -8 Separation, distribution. -9 (In phil.) A peculiar arrangement of the senses. -Comp. —पार्ष्णिः *f*. The rear of an army. —भंगः, —भेदः *m*. Breaking an array.

व्यूहनं *n*. 1 Arraying of troops. 2 Structure of the members of the body.

व्यृद्ध *p. p.* (*f*. —द्धा) 1 Unlucky, unfortunate. -2 Exclued from. -2 Imperfect, deficient.

व्यृद्धिः *f*. 1 Ill-luck, misfortune.

व्ये 1 U. (व्ययति,-ते, उत) 1 To cover. -2 To sew.

व्योकारः *m*. A blacksmith.

व्योमन् *n*. 1 The sky, atmosphere. -2 Water. -3 A temple sacred to the sun. -4 Talc. -Comp. —उदकं *n*. Rain-water, dew. —केशः, —केशिन् *m*. An epithet of Siva. —गंगा *f*. The heavenly Ganges. -चारिन् *m*. 1 A God. -2 A bird. -3 A saint. -4 A Bráhmana. -5 A heavenly body. —धूमः *m*. A cloud. -देवः *m*. N. of Siva. —नाशिका *f*. A kind of quail. —मंजरं, —मंडलं *n*. A flag, banner. —मुद्गरः *m*. A gust of wind. —यानं *n*. A celestial car. —सद् *m*. 1 A deity, God. -2 A *Gandharva*. -3 A spirit. —स्थली *f*. The earth. —स्पृश् *a*. Very lofty.

व्रज् 1 P. (व्रजति) 1 To go, proceed. -2 To approach, visit. -3 To depart. -4 To pass away (as time). -5 To go to the state of. -6 To obtain, gain. With अनु- 1 To follow. -2 To perform. परि— To wander about as a mendicant. प्र- 1 To go into exile. -2 To renounce the world, to enter on the fourth stage of life, to become a संन्यासिन्. प्रति— To go to or towards. प्रत्युद्— To go out to meet.

व्रजः *m*. 1 A multitude, flock, group. -2 A station of cowherds. -3 A cow-pen, cow-shed. -4 A resting-place. -5 A road. -6 A cloud. -7 N. of a district near Mathurá. -जं *n*. Wandering, going. -Comp. -अंगना, —युवतिः *f*. A woman of Vraja, a cowherdess. —अजिरं *n*. A cow-pen. —किशोरः, —नाथः, —मोहनः, —वरः, -वल्लभः *m*. Epithets of Krishna.

व्रजकः *m*. A religious mendicant wandering about for alms.

व्रजनं *n*. 1 Roaming. -2 Exile.

व्रज्या *f*. 1 Wandering about as a religious mendicant. -2 An attack, a march. -3 A flock, tribe, class. -4 A theatre.

व्रण् 1 P. (व्रणति) To sound.

व्रण् 10 U. (व्रणयति,-ते) To hurt, wound.

व्रणः *m*., व्रणं *n*. 1 A wound, hurt. -2 A boil, an ulcer. -3 A fracture, scar. Comp.—अरिः *m*. Gum myrrh. —कृत् *m*. The marking-nut tree. —विरोपण *a*. Sore-healing. —शोधनं *n*. The cleansing or dressing of a wound. -हः *m*. The castor-oil plant.

व्रणित *a*. (*f*. -ता) Wounded, bruised.

व्रतः *m*., व्रतं *n*. 1 A religious act of devotion or austerity, a vow in general. -2 A vow, resolve. -3 Object of devotion or faith, devotion. -4 A rite, an observance. -5 Mode of life, course of conduct. -6 A law, rule. -7 Sacrifice. -8 An act, a work. -9 A design, plan.-Comp. —आचरणं *n*. The observance of a vow.-आदेशः *m*. Investiture of a youth with the sacred thread. —चर्यः *m*. A religious student. -चर्या *f*. An observance or practice of a religious vow.-पारणं *n*., -पारणा *f*. The conclusion of a vow or fast; eating after a fast. --भंगः m. 1 Breach of a vow. -2 Breach of a promise.-भिक्षा f. Begging alms as part of the ceremony of investiture with the sacred thread. -वैकल्यं n. The incompletion of a religious vow. --स्थ a. Practising any vow. --स्नातकः m. A Bràhmana who has completed the first stage of his religious life i. e. that of a religious student.

व्रततिः, व्रतती f. 1 A creeper. -2 Expansion, extension.

व्रतिन् a. Observing a vow, practising penance, devout, pious. -m. 1 A religious student. -2 An ascetic, a devotee. -3 One who institutes a sacrifice.

व्रश्चः m. See व्रश्चः.

व्रश्च् 6. P. (वृश्चति, वृक्ण) 1 To cut, tear. -2 To wound.

व्रश्चनः m. 1A small saw. -2 A fine file used by goldsmiths. -3 The juice trickling from an incision in a tree. --नं n. 1 Cutting, wounding. -2 A cut, an incision.

व्रांजिः f. A gust of wind.

व्रातः m. A group, flock, an assemblage. -तं n. 1 Bodily labour. -2 Day-labour. -3 Casual employment. -4 The company at a marriage feast.

व्रातीन a. (f. -ना) 1 Living by day-labour. -2 Hired for labour. -नः m. A hired labourer, coolie. -2 One living by violence.

व्रात्यः m. 1 A man of the first three classes on whom the purificatory rites have not been performed ; an outcast. -2 A low or vile person in general. -त्या f. The daughter of an outcast. Comp. -ब्रुवः m. One who calls himself a Vràtya. -स्तोमः m. N. of a sacrifice.

व्री 4 A. (व्रीयते, व्रीण) 1 To go, move. -2 To be chosen. -3 To cover, screen.

व्रीड् 4 P. (व्रीड्यति) 1 To be ashamed, feel shame. -2 To throw, send forth.

व्रीडः m., व्रीडा f. 1 Shame. -2 Modesty, bashfulness.

व्रीडित p. p. (f. -ता) Put to shame, ashamed.

व्रीस् 1 P., 10 U. (व्रीसति, व्रीसयति, -ते) To injure, kill.

व्रीहिः m. 1 Rice. -2 A grain of rice.

व्रुड् 6 P. (व्रुडति) 1 To cover. -2 To be heaped up. -3 To heap. -4 To sink, go down.

व्रूस् 1 P., 10 U. See व्रीस्.

व्रैहेय a. (f. —यी) 1 Fit for rice. -2 Sown with rice. -यं n. A field of rice; a field fit for growing rice.

ब्ली 9 P. (ब्लिनाति rarely ब्लीनाति) 1 To go, move. -2 To support, hold. -3 To choose, select.

श.

शः m. 1 A cutter, destroyer. -2 A weapon. -3 N. of Siva. शं n. Happiness.

शंयु a. Happy, prosperous.

शंवः m. 1 Ploughing in the regular direction. -2 The thunder-bolt of Indra. -3 The iron head of a pestle.

शंस् 1 P. (शंसति, शस्त ; pass. शस्यते) 1 To praise, approve of. -2 To tell, announce, (with dat. or sometimes gen. of person or by itself). -3 To indicate, bespeak, show. -4 To repeat, recite. -5 To hurt, injure. -6 To revile, traduce. With अभि— To curse. आ- (Atm.) 1 To hope, expect. -2 To desire (Parsm.). -3 To tell. प्र— To praise.

शंसनं *n.* 1 Praising. -2 Telling, relating. -3 Reciting.

शंसा *f.* 1 Praise. -2 Wish, desire, hope. -3 Narrating. -4 Reciting.

शंसित *p. p.* (*f.*—ता) 1 Praised, extolled. -2 Told, declared. -3 Wished, desired. -4 Ascertained, determined. -5 Falsely accused.

शंसिन् *a.* (*f.* —नी) (Usually at the end of comp.) 1 Praising. -2 Telling, communicating. -3 Indicating, bespeaking. -4 Presaging, foretelling.

शक् 5 P.(शक्नोति,शक्त) 1 To be able, to have power to effect (usually with an inf. and translateable by 'can').-2 To bear, endure.-3To be powerful.

शक् 4 U. (शक्यति,-ते, शक्त) 1 To be able, have power to effect. -2 To endure.

शक: *m.* 1 N. of a king usually understood to be Sáliváhana). -2 An epoch, era (especially that of Sáliváhana). —का: (*m. pl.*) 1 N. of a country. -2 N. of a particular tribe or race of people. -Comp. —अंतक:, —अरि: *m.* Epithets of king Vikramáditya who is said to have exterminated the Sakas. —अब्द: *m.* A year of the Saka era. —कर्तृ, —कृत् *m.* The founder of an era.

शकट: *m.*, शकटं *n.* A cart, carriage. -ट: *m.* 1 A form of military array resembling a wedge. -2 A measure of capacity, equal to 2000 *palas.* -3 N. of a demon slain by Krishna when quite a boy. -4 N. of a tree (तिनिश). -5 An implement for preparing grain. -Comp. —अरि:, —हन् *m.* Epithets of Krishna. —आह्वा *f.* The lunar asterism Rohinì. -विल: *m.* A gallinule.

शकटिका *f.* A small cart, a toy-cart.

शकटी *f.* A small cart. -2 A cart employed to carry sacrificial implements from one place to another, or to bring the सोमराजा into the sacrificial pandal.

शकन् *n.* Ordure, feces, especially of animals; (this word has no forms for the first five inflections, and is optionally substituted for शकृत after acc. dual).

शकल: *m.*, शकलं *n.* 1 A part, fragment, bit. -लं *n.* 1 Bark. -2 The scales (of a fish).

शकलित *a.* (*f.* —ता) Reduced to fragments.

शकलिन् *m.* A fish.

शकलीकृ 8 U. To reduce to fragments or pieces, cut to pieces, divide.

शकार: *m.* The brother of a king's concubine, the brother-in-law of a king by a wife not regularly married.

शकुन: *m.* 1 A bird (in general). -2 A vulture or kite.-3 A kind of song (sung at festivals). —नं *n.* 1 A prognostic, any omen presaging good or evil. -2 An auspicious omen. -Comp. -ज्ञ *a.* Knowing omens. (—ज्ञा *f.*) A small house-lizard.

शकुनि: *m.* 1 A bird. -2 A vulture, kite or eagle. -3 A cock. -4 N. of the maternal uncle of Duryodhana. -5N. of a demon killed by Krishna. -Comp. —ईश्वर: *m.* N. of Garuda. —प्रपा *f.* A trough for watering birds. —वाद: *m.* 1 The cry or sound of a bird.-2 The crowing of a cock.

शकुनी *f.* 1 A hen-sparrow. -2 A kind of bird.

शकुंत: *f.* 1 A bird in general. -2 The blue jay. -3 A kind of bird.-4 A sort of insect.

शकुंतक: *m* A bird.

शकुंतला *f.* N. of the daughter of Visvámitra by the nymph Menaká.

शकुंतिः *m.* A bird.

शकुंतिका *f.* 1 A bird. -2 A kind of bird. -3 A locust, cricket.

शकुलः *m.*, शकुली *f.* A kind of fish. -Comp. —अर्भकः *m.* A kind of fish.

शकृत *n.* Ordure, excrement, especially of animals. -Comp. —करिः *m.*, *f.*, —करी *f.* A calf. —द्वारं *n.* The anus.

शक्करः, शक्करिः *m.* A bull.

शक्करी *f.* 1 A river. -2 A girdle, zone. -3 A woman of impure caste. -4 A finger.

शक्त *p. p.* (*f.* —क्ता) 1 Able, capable, competent (with gen. or loc. or inf.). -2 Strong, powerful. -3 Rich, opulent. -4 Significant, expressive. -5 Clever, intelligent. -6 Speaking kindly or agreeably.

शक्तिः *f.* 1 Power, ability, strength, energy, capacity. -2 Regal power which consits of three parts or elements viz. प्रभुशक्ति or प्रभावशक्ति the 'majesty or pre-eminent position of the king himself'; 2 मंत्रशक्ति 'the power of good counsel', and 3 उत्साहशक्ति 'the power of energy'. -3 The power of composition, poetic power or genius. -4 The active power of a deity. -5 A kind of missile. -6 A spear, dart, lance. -7 (In phil.) The relation of a term to the thing designated. -8 The power inherent in cause to produce its necessary effect. -9 (In Rhet.) The power or signification of a word; (these are three अभिधा, लक्षणा and व्यंजना). -10 The expressive power or denotation of a word (opp. लक्षणा and व्यंजना). -11 The female organ, worshipped by the Sâktas. -12 A sword. -13 An implement in gambling. -Comp. —अर्धः *m.* Perspiring and panting through fatigue or exertion. —ग्रह *a.* 1 Apprehending the force or meaning. -2 Armed with a spear. (—हः *m.*) 1 Apprehension of the force, meaning or acceptation of a word. -2 A spear-man, lancer. -3 An epithet of Siva. -4 Of Kártikeya. —ग्राहकः *m.* An epithet of Kârtikeya. -त्रयं *n.* The three constituent elements of regal power. —धर *a.* Strong, powerful. (-रः *m.*) 1 A spear-man.-2 An epithet of Kàrtikeya. -पाणिः, —भृत *m.* 1 A spear-man.-2 An epithet of Kârtikeya. -पातः *m.* Prostration of strength. -पूजकः *m.* A Sâkta.-पूजा *f.* The worship of Sakti. -हेतिकः *m.* A lancer, spearman.

शक्तुः *m.*, *n.* The flour or meal of barley or barley-meal.

शक्र (*f.* —क्रा), शक्रु *a.* Speaking kindly or agreeably.

शक्य *pot. p.* (*f.* -क्या) 1 Possible, practicable, capable of being done or effected (generally with an inf.). -2 Fit, easy to be effected. -3 Directly conveyed or expressed (as the meaning of a word). (The form शक्यं is sometimes used adverbially with a *noun* in any gender, and an *inf.* -Comp. —अर्थः *m.* The meaning directly expressed.

शक्रः *m.* 1 N. of Indra. -2 The Arjuna tree. -3 The Kutaja tree. -4 An owl. -5 The asterism ज्येष्ठा. -6 The number 'fourteen'. -7 N. of Siva. -Comp. —अशनः *m.* The Kutaja tree. -आह्वयः *m.* An owl. -आत्मजः *m.* 1 Jayanta, son of Indra.-2 Arjuna. —उत्थानं *n.*, —उत्सवः *m.* A festival in honour of Indra on the 12th day of the bright half of Bhâdrapada. —गोपः *m.* A kind of red insect. -जः, —जातः *m.* A crow. —जित, —भिद् *m.* Epithets of Meghanâda, son of Râvana. —द्रुमः *m.* The Devadàru tree. —धनुस,-शरासनं *n.* The rain-bow. —ध्वजः *m.* A post with a flag erected in honour of Indra. —पर्यायः *m.* The Kutaja tree. —पादपः *m.* 1 The Kutaja tree. -2 The Devadâru tree. —भवनं, —भुवनं *n.*, -वासः *m.* Heaven, paradise. —मातृका *f.* A wooden post for supporting Indra's banner. —मूर्धन् *m.*, —शिरस् *n.* An ant-hill, a hillock. —लोकः *m.* The world of Indra. —वाहनं *n.* A cloud. —शाखिन *m.* The Kutaja tree. —शाला *f.* A sacrificial ground. —सारथिः *m.* An epithet of Mâtali, Indra's charioteer. —सुतः *m.* 1 An epithet of Jayanta. -2 Of Arjuna.-3 Of Vàli.

शक्राणि *f.* N. of Sachî, wife of Indra.

शक्रिः *m.* 1 A cloud.-2 The thunder-bolt of Indra. -3 A mountain. -4 An elephant.

शक्वरः *m.* A bull, an ox.

शंक् 1 A (शंकते, शंकित) 1 To doubt, be uncertain, be doubtful. -2 To dread, be afraid (with abl.).-3 To mistrust, distrust. -4 To believe, fancy, think probable, suspect, fear. -5 To raise a doubt or objection (about). With अभि— To doubt, to be doubtful. आ— 1 To fear, suspect, to think, to believe. -2 To expect. -3 To entertain doubts about. परि— 1 To doubt. -2 To suspect, believe. वि— To fear, suspect.

शंकः *m.* A draught-ox.

शंकर *a.* (*f.* -रा, -री) Conferring happiness or prosperity; propitious. —रः *m.* N. of Siva. —री *f.* 1 N. of Pàrvatî, wife of Siva. -2 Bengal madder. -3 The Samí tree. -Comp. —आवासः *m.* 1 The Kailàsa.-2 A kind of camphor.

शंका *f.* 1 Doubt, uncertainty. -2 Hesitation. -3 Suspicion, misgiving. -4 Fear, dread, alarm. -5 Hope, expectation. -6 (Mistaken) belief, (wrong) impression. -7 An objection started in disputation.

शंकित *p. p.* (*f.* -ता) 1 Doubted, feared. -2 Suspicious, suspecting, distrustful. -3 Uncertain. -4 Fearful, alarmed. -5 Weak, unsteady. -Comp. —वर्णः *m.* A thief.

शंकिन् *a.* (*f.* —नी) 1 Doubting, suspecting, fearing, believing (at the end of comp). -2 Full of danger.

शंकुः *m.* 1 A dart, spear, dagger.-2 A stake, pillar.-3 A nail, pin, peg.-4 The pointed head of an arrow, barb. -5 The trunk (of a lopped tree), stump. -6 The pin of dial. -7 A measure of twelve fingers. -8 A measuring-rod. -9 The sine of altitude (in astr.). -10 Ten billions. -11 The fibres of a leaf. -12 An ant-hill. -13 The penis. -14 The skate-fish. -15 A demon. -16 Poison. -17 Sin, crime. -18 An aquatic animal, particularly, a goose. -19 A kind of perfume (नखी). -20 N. of Kâma, the God of love. -Comp. —कर्णः *m.* An ass.—जीवा *f.* (In astr.) The gnomon sine. —तरुः, —वृक्षः *m.* The Sála tree.

शंकुला *f.* 1 A kind of knife. -2 A pair of scissors. -Comp. —खंडः *m.* A piece cut off with scissors.

शंखः *m.*, शंखं *n.* 1 The conch-shell, a shell. -2 The bone on the fore-head. -3 The part between the tusks of an elephant.-4 A hundred billions. -5 A military drum. -6

A kind of perfume (नखी). -7 One of the nine treasures of Kubera. -8 N. of a demon slain by Vishnu. -Comp. —उदकं *n.* The water poured into a conch-shell. —कारः, -कारकः *m.* A shell-cutter. —क्षीरं *n.* An impossibility. —चरी, —चर्चा *f.* A mark made with sandal (on the forehead). —चूर्ण *n* Power produced from shells. —ध्मः, -ध्मा *m.* A shell-blower; conch-blower. —ध्वनिः *m.* I The sound of a conch. -2 A cry of alarm or despair. —भृत् *m.* An epithet of Vishnu.-मुखः *m.* An alligator.

शंखकः *m.*, शंखकं *n.* A conch-shell. —कः *m.* I A disease of the head. -2 The temporal bone. —कं *n.* A bracelet (made of conch-shell).

शंखनकः (—खः) *m.* A small conch or shell.

शंखिन् *m.* I The ocean. -2 An epithet of Vishnu. -3 A conch-blower. -4 A worker in shells.

शंखिनी *f.* I A woman of one of the four classes into which writers on erotic science divide women. -2 A female spirit, or a kind of fairy.

शच् I A. (शचते) To speak, say.

शचिः, शची *f.* N. of the wife of Indra. -Comp. —पतिः, -भर्तृ *m.* Epithets of Indra.

शंच् I A. (शंचते) To go, move.

शट *a.* (*f.* -टा) Sour, acid, astringent. [ascetic.

शटा *f.* The matted hair of an

शठ् I P. (शठति) I To deceive, defraud. -2 To hurt. kill. -3 To suffer pain.

शठ *a.* (*f.* -ठा) I Crafty, deceitful, dishonest. -2 Wicked depraved. —ठः *m.* I A rogue, cheat. -2 A false or deceitful lover. -3 A fool, blockhead. -4 A mediater, arbitrator. -5 The Dhattùra plant. -6 An idler, a lazy fellow. —ठं *n.* I Iron. -2 Safforn.

शणं *n.* Hemp. -Comp. —सूत्रं *n.* I A hempen cord or string. -2 A net made of hemp. -3 Cordage.

शंडः *m.* I An impotent man. -2 A bull. -3 A bull at liberty to move. —डं *n.* A multitude.

शढः *m.* I An impotent man. -2 A male attendant in the harem emasculated for the purpose. -3A bull. -4 A bull at liberty to move. -5 A mad-man.

शतं *n.* I A hundred. -2 Any large number; as in शतपत्रं. -Comp. —अक्षी *f.* I Night. -2 The Goddess Durgâ. —अंगः *m.* I A car, carriage. -2 A war-chariot. —अनीकः *m.* An old man. —अरं, —आरं *n.* The thunderbolt of Indra. —आनंदः *m.* I N. of Brahman(*m.*). -2 Of Vishnu or Krishna. -3 Of the car of Vishnu. -4 Of a son of Gautama and Ahalyâ. —आयुस् *a.* Lasting or living for a hundred years. —आवर्तः, -आवर्तिन *m.* N. of Vishnu. —ईशः *m.* I The ruler of a hundred -2 The ruler of a hundred villages. —कुंभः *m.* N. of a mountain. (—भं) *n.* Gold. —कृत्वस् *ind.* A hundred times. —कोटिः *m.* Indra's thunderbolt. (*f.*) A hundred crores. —क्रतुः *m.* An epithet of Indra. —खंडं *n.* Gold. —गु *a.* Possessed of a hundred cows. —गुण, —गुणित *a.* A hundred-fold. —ग्रंथिः *f.* The Dúrvá grass. —घ्नी *f.* I A kind of weapon used as a missile. -2 A female scorpion. -3 A disease of the throat. —जिह्वः *m.* An epithet of Siva. —तारका, —भिषज्, —भिषा *f.* N. of the 24th lunar mansion containing one hundred stars. —द्रुः *f.* I N. of a river in the Panjáb now called Sutlej. -2 N. of the Ganges. —धारं *n.* The thunderbolt of Indra.— धृतिः *m.* 1 An epithet of Indra. -2 Of Brahman (*m.*). -3 Heaven or *Svarga.* —पत्रः *m.* 1 A peacock. -2 The (Indian) crane.-3 A wood-pecker. -4 A parrot or a species of it. (-त्रा) *f.* A woman. (-त्रं *n.*) A lotus. -पत्रकः *m.* The wood-pecker. --पथब्राह्मणं *n.* N. of a well-known Bráhmana of the Sukla Yajurveda. —पत्रं *n.* 1 A lotus with a hundred petals. -2 The white lotus. --पर्वन् *m.* A bamboo. (-*f.*) 1 The full-moon day in the month of Asvina. -2 Dúrvâ grass. —भीरुः *f.* The Arabian jasmine. -मखः, -मन्युः *m.* 1 Epithets of Indra. -2 An owl. —मुख *a.* 1 Having a hundred ways.-2 Having a hundred outlets, mouths or openings. (-खी *f.*) A brush, broom. --यष्टिकः *m.* A necklace of one hundred strings. —रूपा *f.* N. of a daughter of Brahman (*m.*). —वेधिन् *m.* A kind of sorrel. --ह्रदा *f.* 1 Lightning.-2 The thunderbolt of Indra.--ह्रादा *f.* The thunderbolt.

शतक *a.* (*f.* -का) 1 A hundred. -2 Containing a hundred. --कं *n.* 1 A century. -2 A collection of one hundred stanzas.

शततम *a.* (*f.* -मी) One-hundredth.

शतधा *ind.* 1 In a hundred ways. -2 Into a hundred parts or pieces. -3 A hundred-fold. -*f.* The Dúrvà grass.

शंतनुः *m.* N. of a king of the lunar race.

शतशस् *ind.* 1 By hundreds. -2 A hundred times. -3 A hundred-fold, variously.

शतिक *a.* (*f.* -की), शत्य *a.* (*f.* -त्या) 1 Containing a hundred. -2 Relating to a hundred. -3 Effected with a hundred. -4 Bought with a hundred. -5 Changed with or for a hundred. -6 Bearing tax or interest per hundred. -7 Indicative of (the acquisition of) a hundred.

शतिन् *m.* The owner of a hundred.

शत्रिः *m.* An elephant.

शत्रुः *m.* 1 A destroyer, conqueror. -2 An enemy, an adversary. -3 A rival neighbouring king. -Comp. —उपजापः *m.* The treacherous overtures of an enemy. —घ्नः *m.* An epithet of a brother of Ráma and twin brother of Lakshmana being a son of Sumitrâ. —पक्षः *m.* 1 The side of an enemy. -2 An opponent, antagonist.

शत्रुंजयः *m.* 1 An elephant. -2 N. of a mountain.

शत्रुंतप *a.* (*f.* —पा) Overcoming or destroying one's foes.

शत्वरी *f.* Night.

शद् I. 1 P. (but A. in conjugational tenses. शीयते, शन्न) 1 To fall, perish, decay. -2 To go.

शाद्रिः *m.* 1 An elephant. -2 Cloud. -3 N. of Arjuna.

शद्रु *a.* 1 Going, moving. -2 Falling, perishing.

शनकैस् *ind.* Slowly.

शनिः *m.* 1 The planet Saturn (the son of sun and represented as of a black colour or dressed in dark-coloured clothes). -2 Saturday. -Comp. --जं *n.* Black pepper. -प्रदोषः *m.* The (evening) worship of Siva performed on the thirteenth day of a lunar fortnight when it falls on a Saturday. --प्रसूः *f.* An epithet of Chháyá, wife of the sun. --प्रियं *n.* A sapphire. -वारः, -वासरः *m.* Saturday.

शनैस् *ind.* 1 Slowly, gently. -2 Gradually, little by little. -3 Mildly, softly. -4 Tardily, sluggishly. -Comp. —चर *a.* Going or moving slowly. (-रः *m.*) The planet Saturn.

शप् I. 4. U. (शपति,-ते, शप्यति,-ते,शप्त) 1 To curse, execrate.-2 To swear, say on oath. -3 To blame, revile, abuse. —*Caus.* (शापयति,-ते) To bind by an oath, conjure. [oath.

शपः *m.* शपत्रं *n.* 1 A curse. -2 An

शपथः *m.* 1 Cursing. -2 A curse, anathema. -3 An oath, asseveration by oath or ordeal. -4 Conjuration, binding by oaths. -Comp. —पत्रं *n.* An affidavit, statement on oath.

शपनं *n.* See शपथः.-2Reviling;abuse.

शप्त *p. p.* (*f.* —प्ता) 1 Cursed. -2 Sworn. -3 Reviled, abused.

शफः*m.*,शफं *n.* 1 A hoof.-2 The root of a tree.

शफरः *m.* (*f.* -री) A kind of small glittering fish. -Comp. —अधिपः *m.* The fish called Ilîsha.

शब (-व-) रः *m.* 1 A mountaineer, barbarian. -2 N. of Siva. -3 The hand. -4 Water. -5 N. of a commentator and writer on Mîmâmsâ. —री *f.* 1 A Sabara female. -2 A female Kirâta who was an ardent devotee of Râma.

शब (-व-) ल *a.* (*f.* —ला) 1 Spotted, variegated. -2 Varied, divided into various parts. -3 Articulate; imitative. —लः *m.* A variegated colour. —ला, —ली *f.* 1 A spotted cow. -2 The cow of plenty or Kâmadhenu. —लं *n.* Water.

शब्द् 10 U. (शब्दयति,-ते, शब्दित) 1 To sound, make a noise. -2 To speak, call out to.-3 To name,call. With अभि— To name. प्र— To explain. —सं To call out to.

शब्दः *m.* 1 Sound, note, noise. -2 The sound of a musical instrument. -3 A word, significant word. -4 A declinable word, a noun, substantive. -5 A title, an epithet. -6 The name, mere name. -7 Verbal authority (regarded by the Naiyâyikas as a Pramàna). -8 Grammar. -Comp. —अतीत *a.* Indescribable.—अधिष्ठानं *n.* The ear.—अध्याहारः *m.* Supplying an ellipsis. —अनुशासनं *n.* The science of words; *i.e.*grammar. -अर्थः *m.* The meaning of a word. -अलंकारः *m.*A figure of speech which depends on sound or words and vanishes if the words which constitute the figure are replaced by others of the same meaning (opp.अर्थालंकार). —आख्येय *a.* Fit to be communicated in words. (-यं *n.*) An oral communication. —आडंबरः *m.* Bombast, verbosity, grandiloquent words. —कोशः *m.* A lexicon, dictionary. -गत *a.* Inherent or residing in a word. -ग्रहः *m.*1 Catching the sound.-2 The ear. -चातुर्यं *n.* Cleverness of style, eloquence.-चित्रं *n.* One of the two subdivisions of the lowest class of poetry (wherein the charm lies in the use of words which please the ear simply by their sound. —चोरः *m.* A plagiarist. —तन्मात्रं *n.* The subtle element of sound. —पतिः *m.* A lord in name only, nominal lord. —बोधः *m.* Knowledge derived from verbal testimony. —ब्रह्मन् *n.* 1 The Vedas. -2 The property of words called स्फोट. —भेदिन् *a.* 1 An epithet of Arjuna. -2 The anus. -3 A kind of arrow. —विद्या *f.* —शास्त्रं *n.* The science of words; *i. e.*grammar.-विरोधः *m.* Opposition of words (in a sentence). —वृत्तिः *f.* The function of a word (in Rhet.).—वेधिन् *a.* Hitting an invisible mark the sound of which is only heard. (—*m.*) 1 A kind of arrow. -2 An archer. -3 An epithet of Arjuna. —शक्तिः *f.* The force or expressive power of a word; signification of a word. -श्लेषः *m.* A play or pun upon words.-संग्रहः *m.* A vocabulary, lexicon.— सौष्ठवं *n.* Elegance of words, a graceful or elegant style. -सौकर्यं *n.* Ease of expression.

शब्दन *a.* (*f.* —ना) Sounding, making a sound. -नं *n.* 1 Sounding, making a noise, uttering a sound. -2 A sound, noise. -3 Calling out, calling. -4 Naming.

शब्दाय् Den. A. 1 To make a noise, sound. -2 To cry, yell. -3 To call, call out to.

शब्दित *p. p.* (*f.* -ता) 1 Sounded, made to give out a sound, played upon (as a musical instrument). -2 Uttered, articulated. -3 Called, called out to. -4 Designated. —तं *n.* Noise, cry.

शम् *ind.* A particle meaning welfare, happiness, prosperity, health, and used to express a blessing or pious wish, (with dat. or gen.). शं देवदत्ताय or देवदत्तस्य. -Comp. —कर *a.* Causing happiness. —ताति *a.* Conferring happiness, propitious, auspicious. —पाकः *m.* 1 Lac, red dye. -2 Cooking, maturing. —भुः *m.* 1 A name of Brahman (*m.*). -2 Of Siva. -3 A sage, a venerable man.

शम् 4 P. (शाम्यति, शांत) 1 To be calm, be appeased (as a person). -3 To cease, come to an end. -3 To be extinguished or quenched. -4 To desist, leave off (speaking &c.). -5 To put an end to, destroy, kill (also 9 P. in this sense). With उप— 1 To become quiet or calm. -2 To cease, to be extinguished. नि— To hear, know. प्र— 1 To be calm or tranquil. -2 To be shoothed. -2 To cease, to be extinguished. सं— To be allayed, to be extinguished.

Caus. (शमयति,-ते but शामयति,-ते in the sense of ' seeing ') 1 To appease, tranquillize, pacify, sooth. -2 To put an end to, stop. -3 To subdue, tame, defeat. -4 To desist, cease.

शम् 10 U. (शामयति,-ते) 1 To see, look at, inspect. -2 To show, display.

शमः *m.* 1 Tranquillity, calmness. -2 Rest, repose, cessation. -3 Absence or restraint of passions, mental quietness. -4 Allayment, mitigation, satisfaction, pacification (of grief, thirst, hunger &c.). -5 Peace. -6 Final emancipation from all wordly illusions and attachments). -7 The hand. -Comp. —अंतकः *m.* The God of love.

शमथः *m.* 1 Tranquillity, calmness, absence of passion. -2 A counsellor, minister.

शमनं *n.* 1 Appeasing, soothing, conquering, alleviation. -2 Calmness, tranquillity. -3 End, stop, destruction. -4 Hurting, injuring. -5 Killing animals for sacarifice. -6 Swallowing, chewing. -नः *m.* 1 A kind of deer, an antelope. -2 N. of Yama, the God of death. -Comp. —स्वसृ *f.* An epithet of the river Yamuná.

शमनी *f.* Night. -Comp. -सदः (-षदः) *m.* A demon, goblin.

शमलं *n.* 1 Feces, excrement. -2 Impurity, sediment. -3 Sin. -4 A calamity, misfortune.

शमित *p. p.* (*f.* —ता) 1 Appeased,

soothed, calmed. -2 Cured, relieved. -3 Relaxed, -4 Calm, sedate. -5 Moderated, tempered.

शमिन् *a.* (*f.* —नी) 1 Calm, tranquil, pacific.-2 One who has subdued his passions.

शमिः, शमी *f.* 1 N. of a tree.-2 A pod, legume. -Comp.—गर्भः *m.* 1 An epithet of fire. -2 A Bráhmana, one belonging to the sacerdotal or priestly class. —धान्यं *n.* Any pulse or grain growing in pods; leguminous grain.

शमि (-मी-) रः *m.* A small variety of the Samí tree.

शंपा *f.* Lightning.

शंब् I. 1 P. (शंबति) To go, move.

शंब् 10 P. (शंबयति) To collect, heap together.

शंब *a.* (*f.* -बा) 1 Happy, fortunate.-2 Poor, indigent. -बः *m.* 1 The thunderbolt of Indra. -2 The iron head of a pestle. -3 An iron chain worn round the loins. -4 Ploughing in the ordinary or the regular direction. (शंबाकृ means to plough twice').

शंबरः *m.* 1 N. of a demon killed by Pradyumna. -2 A mountain. -3 A kind of deer. -4 War. —रं *n.* 1 Water. -2 A cloud. -3 Wealth. -4 A religious observance. -Comp. —अरिः, -सूदनः *m.* Epithets of Pradyumna or the God of love.

शंबरी *f.* Illusion, jugglery.

शंबलः *m*, शंबलं *n.* 1 A bank, shore. -2 Provisions for a journey; viaticum. -3 Envy, jealousy.

शंबली *f.* A procuress.

शंबुः, शंबुकः, शंबुक्कः *m.* A bivalve [shell.

शंबूकः *m.* 1 A bivalve shell. -2 A small conch-shell. -3 A snail. -4 The frontal protuberance of an elephant. -5 N. of a Súdra (who practised penance contrary to the duties of his caste and was in consequence slain by Ráma).

शंभः *m.* 1 A happy man. -2 The thunder-bolt of Indra. -3 The iron head of a pestle.

शंभली *f.* A bawd, procuress.

शंभु *a.* Causing happiness, granting prosperity. —भुः *m.* 1 N. of Siva. -2 Brahman (*m.*). -3 A sage, venerable man. -4 A kind of Siddha. -Comp. —तनयः, -नंदनः, -सुतः *m.* Epithets of Kârtikeya or Ganesa. —प्रिया *f.* N. of Durgá. -2 Emblic myrobalan (आमलकी). —वल्लभं *n.* The white lotus.

शम्या *f.* 1 A wooden stick or post. -2 A staff. -3 The pin of a yoke. -4 A kind of cymbal. -5 A sacrificial vessel.

शय *a.* (*f.* -या,-यी) Lying down, sleeping (usually at the end of comp.). —यः *m.* 1 Sleep. -2 A bed, couch. -3 A hand. -4 A sort of snake. -5 Abuse, curse.-6 A stake.

शयथः *m.* 1 Death. -2 A kind of snake. -3 A boar. -4 A fish.

शयनं *n.* 1 Sleeping, lying down. -2 A bed, couch. -3 Copulation. -Comp. -अ (-आ-) -गारः *m.*, -रं. *n.*, -गृहं *n.* A bed-chamber. —एकादशि *f.* The eleventh day of the bright half of Ashâdha when Vishnu lies down to enjoy his four months' repose.

शयनीयं *n.* A bed, couch.

शयानकः *m.* 1 A chameleon. -2 A kind of snake.

शयालु *a.* Sleepy, slothful. —लुः *m.* 1 A kind of snake. -2 A dog. -3 A jackal.

शयित *p. p.* (*f.* —ता) 1 Sleeping, asleep. -2 Lying down. -तं *n.* Sleep, sleeping.

शयुः, शयुनः *m.* A large snake.

शय्या *f.* 1 A bed, couch. -2 Sleeping. -3 Tying, stringing together. -Comp. —अध्यक्षः, -पालः *m.* The superintendent of a king's bed-chamber. —उत्संगः *m.* The side of a bed.

शरः *m.* 1 An arrow, a shaft. -2 A kind of white reed or grass. -3 The cream of slightly curdled milk. -4 Hurt, injury, wound. -5 The number 'five'. -रं *n.* Water. -Comp. —अग्र्यः *m.* An excellent arrow. —अभ्यासः, -आघातः *m.* Archery. -असनं, -आस्यं *n.* A bow. —आक्षेपः *m.* A flight of arrows. —आरोपः, -आवापः *m.* A bow. -आश्रयः *m.* A quiver. -इषीका *f.* An arrow. —इष्टः *m.* The mango-tree. —कांडः *m.* 1 A reed-stalk. -2 A shaft of an arrow. —जं *n.* Fresh butter. —जः *m.* N. of Kârtikeya. —जन्मन् *m.* An epithet of Kârtikeya. —धिः *m.* A quiver. —पातः *m.* An arrow's flight. —पुंखः *m.*, -पुंखा *f.* The feathered end of an arrow. —प्रवेगः *m.* A swift arrow. —फलं *n.* The blade of an arrow. —भंगः *m.* N. of a sage whom Râma visited in the Dandaka forest. —भूः *m.* N. of Kârtikeya. —भृष्टिः *f.* The point of an arrow. —मल्लः *m.* An archer. —वनं (-वणं) *n.* An thicket of reeds. -वाणिः *m.* 1 The head of an arrow. -2 An archer. -3 A maker of arrows. -4 A foot-soldier. —संधानं *n.* Taking aim with an arrow. —संबाध *a.* Covered with arrows. —स्तंबः *m.* A clump of reeds.

शरटः *m.* 1 A chameleon. -2 A safflower.

शरणं *n.* 1 Protection, help, defence. -2 Refuge, shelter. -3 A place of refuge, an asylum (applied to persons also). शरणं इ, गम् or या To take shelter with, to submit to. -4 A sanctuary, an apartment. -5 A house, habitation. -6 Lair, resting-place. -7 Injuring, killing. -Comp. —अर्थिन्, -एषिन् *a.* Seeking refuge or protection. —आगत, -आपन्न *a.* Gone to for refuge or protection.

शरंडः *m.* 1 A bird. -2 A chameleon. -3 A cheat, rogue. -4 A libertine. -5 A kind of ornament.

शरण्य *a.* (*f.* -ण्या) Yielding protection, helping. -2 Needing protection, miserable. —ण्यः *m.* An epithet of Siva. -ण्यं *n.* 1 A place of refuge, shelter. -2 A protector. -3 Protection, defence. -4 Injury, hurt.

शरण्युः *m.* 1 A protector. -2 A cloud. -2 Wind.

शरद् *f.* 1 The autumn, (comprising the two months आश्विन and कार्तिक). -2 A year. -Comp. —अंतः *m.* The end of autumn, winter. —अंबुधरः *m.* An autumnal cloud. —उदाशयः *m.* An autumnal lake. —कामिन् *m.* A dog. —घनः, मेघः *m.* An autumnal cloud. —पद्मः *m.*, पद्मं *n.* The white lotus. —पर्वन् *n.* The festival called *Kojagara*. -मुखं *n.* The commencement of autumn.

शरदा *f.* 1 Autumn. -2 A year.

शरदिज *a.* (*f.* —जा) Autumnal.

शरभः *m.* 1 A young elephant. -2 A fabulous animal said to have 8 legs and to be stronger than a lion. -3 A camel. -4 A grass-hopper. -5 A locust.

शरयुः (-यूः) *f.* N. of a river flowing by अयोध्या. See सरयुः (-यूः).

शरल *a.* (*f.* —ला) 1 See सरल.

शरलकं *n.* Water.

शरव्यं *n.* A butt or mark (for arrows), target (fig. also.)

शरारु *a.* Hurtful, injurious. -रुः *m.* A mischievous animal.

शरावः *m.*, शरावं *n.* 1 A shallow dish, an earthen-ware vessel. -2 A cover, lid. -3 A measure equal to two Kudavas.

शरावती *f.* N. of a town of which Lava was made ruler by Râma.

शरिमन् *m.* Bearing, bringing forth.

शरीरं *n.* 1 The body (of animate or inanimate objects). -2 The constitutent element. -3 A dead body. -Comp. —अंतरं *n.* Another body. —आवरणं *n.* The skin. —कर्तृ *m.* A father. —जः *m.* 1 Sickness. -2 Lust, passion. -3 The God of love. -4 A son, offspring. —दंडः *m.* 1 Corporal punishment. -2 Mortification of the body (as in penance). -पतनं *n.*, -पातः *m.* Death. -बद्ध *a.* Embodied, incarnate. -बंधकः *m.* A hostage. —भाज् *-m.* A creature, an embodied being. -यष्टिः *f.* A slender body, delicate figure. -यात्रा *f.* Means of bodily sustenance. —विमोक्षणं *n.* The emancipation of the soul from the body. —वृत्तिः *f.* Maintenance or support of the body. —वैकल्यं *n.* Sickness, disease. —संस्कारः *m.* 1 Decoration of the person. -2 Purification of the body by purificatory *Samskáras*. —संपत्तिः *f.* The prosperity of body, good health. -संबंधः *m.* Relation by marriage. -सादः *m.* Leanness of body.

शरीरकं *n.* 1 The body. -2 A small body. —कः *m.* The soul.

शरीरिन् *a.* (*f.* -णी). 1 Embodied, incarnate. -2 Living. -*m.* 1 Anything endowed with a body (whether animate or inanimate). -2 A sentient being. -3 A man. -4 The soul.

शरुः *m.* 1 An arrow. -2 A weapon. -3 The thunderbolt of Indra. -4 Anger, passion. -5 Practice of archery.

शर्करजा *f.* Candied sugar.

शर्करा *f.* 1 Candied sugar. -2 A pebble, small stone. -3 Gravelly mould. -4 Soil abounding in stony fragments, sand. -5 A piece, fragment. -6 A potsherd. -7 Any hard particle, as in जलशर्करा 'a ball of water' *i. e.* hail. -8 The disease called gravel. -Comp. —सप्तमी *f.* N. of an observance on the 7th day in the bright half of Vaisâkha.

शर्करिक *a.* (*f* —की), शर्करिल *a.* (*f.* -ला) शर्करावत *a.* (*f.* -ती) Stony, gravelly, gritty

शर्करी *f.* 1 A river. -2 A girdle.

शर्धः *m.* 1 Breaking wind, flatulence (*n.* also in this sense). -2 A multitude. -3 Strength, power.

शर्धजहः *m.* A kind of pulse or bean.

शर्धनं *n.* The act of breaking wind.

शर्मन् *m.* 1 An affix added to the name of a Bráhmana, as in विष्णुशर्मन्. -*n.* 1 Pleasure, delight. -2 A blessing. -3 Protection. -4 A house, receptacle (mostly Vedic in this sense).

शर्मरः *m.* A sort of garment.

शर्मिष्ठा *f.* N. of one of the wives of Yayáti and daughter of Vrishaparvan. the king of the Daityas.

शर्या *f.* 1 Night. -2 A finger.

शर्व् 1 P. (शर्वति) 1 To go. -2 To hurt, kill.

शर्वः *m.* 1 N. of Siva. -2 N. of [Vishnu.

शर्वरः *m.* N. of the God of love. —रं *n.* Darkness.

शर्वरी *f.* 1 A night. -2 Turmeric. -3 A woman. -Comp.—ईशः *m.* The moon.

शर्वाणि *f.* N. of Párvatî or Durgâ, wife of Siva.

शर्शरीकः *m.* A rogue, mischievous [man.

शल् 1 A. (शलते) 1 To shake, agitate. -2 To tremble. -3 To cover.

शल् 1 P. (शलति) 1 To go. -2 To run fast.

शल् 10 A. (शालयते) To praise.

शलः *m.* 1 A dart, spear. -2 A stake. -3 N. of Brahman (*m.*) -4 A camel. —लं *n.* The quill of a porcupine.

शलकः *m.* A spider.

शलंगः *m.* A king, sovereign.

शलभः *m.* 1 A grass-hopper, locust. -2 A moth.-3 N. of an Asura.

शललं *n.* The quill of a porcupine. —ली *f.* 1 The quill of a porcupine. -2 A small porcupine.

शलाका *f.* 1 A small stick,rod, pin, thin bar (of anything). -2 A small stick (used in painting the eyes with collyrium). -3 An arrow. -4 A javelin. -5 A kind of pointed surgical instrument. -6 A rib (as of an umbrella). -7 A bone (forming the root of the fingers and toes). -8 A sprig, shoot. -9 A paint-brush. -10 A tooth-brush.-11 A porcupine. -12 An oblong piece of ivory used in gambling. -13 A ruler. -14 The Sáriká bird.-Comp. शलाकधूर्तः *m.* A swindler, sharper. —परि *ind.* An unlucky throw or movement of one of the pieces at a game played with Salákas.

शलाटः *m.* A cart-load. [of root.

शलाटु *a.* Unripe. —टुः *m.* A kind

शलाभोलिः *m.*A camel.

शल्कं, शल्कलं *n.* 1 The scale of a fish. -2 Bark, rind (of trees). -3 A portion, fragment.

शल्कलिन्, शल्किन् *m.* A fish.

शल्भ् 1 A (शल्भते) To praise.

शल्मलिः, -ली *f.* The silk-cotton tree.

शल्यं *n.* 1 A spear, javelin, dart. -2 An arrow, a shaft. -3 A thorn, splinter. -4 A pin, stake (said to be *m.* also in these four senses). -5 Any extraneous substance lodged in the body and giving it very great pain. -6 (Fig.) Any cause of poignant grief. -7 A bone. -8 Difficulty.-9 Sin, crime.-10 Poison. -11 Abuse. —ल्यः *m.* 1 A porcupine, hedge-hog. -2 Extraction of splinters. -3 A fence, boundary. -4 N. of a king of Madra and brother of Mâdrî, the second wife of Pàndu. -Comp. —अरिः *m.* An epithet of Yudhishthira. —कंठः *m.* A porcupine. —लोमन् *n.* The quill of a porcupine. —हर्तृ *m.* A weeder.

शल्यकः *m.* 1 A dart, javelin. -2 A splinter, thorn. -3 A porcupine.

शल्ल् 1 P. (शल्लति) To go, move.

शल्लः *m.* A frog. —ल्लं *n.* Bark, rind.

शल्लकः *m.* N. of a tree.—कं *n.* Bark, rind.

शल्लकी *f.* 1 A porcupine.-2 A kind of tree (of which elephants are very fond). -Comp. —द्रवः *m.* Incense.

शल्वः *m.* N. of a country.

शव् 1 P. (शवति) 1 To go,approach. -2 To alter, change.

शवः *m.*, शवं *n.*A corpse,dead body. —वं *n.* Water.-Comp.—आश *a.* Feeding on corpses. —काम्यः *m.* A dog.

शवर } See शबर, शबल.
शवल }

शवसानः *m.*1 A traveller.-2 A way, road. —नं *n.* A cemetery.

शशः*m.*1 A hare,rabbit.-2The spots on the moon (which are suppsosed to resemble the form of a hare). -3 One of the four classes into which men are divided by erotic writers. -4 The Lodhra tree.-5 Gum-myrrh. -Comp. —अंकः *m.* 1 The moon.

-2 Camphor. —अदः m. 1 A hawk, falcon.-2 N. of a son of Ikshváku, father of पुरंजय. -अदनः m. A hawk, falcon. —धरः m. 1 The moon. -2 Camphor. —प्लुतकं n. A scratch with a finger-nail. —भृत् m. The moon. —लक्ष्मणः m. An epithet of the moon. —लांछनः m. 1 The moon. -2 Camphor. —विं (-विं-) दुः m. 1 The moon. -2 An epithet of Vishnu. —विषाणं, -शृंगं n. A hare's horn (used to denote an utter impossibility). -स्थली f. The country between the Ganges and the Yamuná.

शशाकः m. A hare, rabbit.

शशिन् m. 1 The moon.-2 Camphor. -Comp. —ईशः m. An epithet of Siva. —कला f. A digit of the moon. —कांतः m. The moon-gem. (—तं n.) A lotus. —कोटिः f. A horn of the moon. —ग्रहः m. An eclipse of the moon. -जः m. An epithet of Budha or Mercury. —प्रभं n. 1 A water-lily. -2 A pearl. —भूषणः,-भृत्,-मौलिः, -शेखरः m. Epithets of Siva. -लेखा f. A digit of the moon.

शशिनी f. N. of one of the sixteen digits of the moon.

शश्वत् ind. 1 Perpetually, for ever. -2 Constantly. शश्वच्छांतिः f. Eternal tranquillity.

शष्कु (-स्कु-) ली f. 1 The orifice of the ear. -2 A kind of baked cake. -3 Rice-gruel.-4 A disease of the ear.

शष्पः, शस्पः m. Loss of intellect —ष्पं n. Young grass.

शस् 1 P. (शसति) To cut up, kill, destroy.

शस् 2 P. (शस्ति) To sleep.

शसनं n. 1 Wounding, killing. -2 Immolation (of an animal at a sacrifice).

शस्त p. p. (f. —स्ता) 1 Praised. -2 Auspicious. -3 Right, best. -4 Repeated, recited. -5 Best, excellent. -6 Wounded, injured. -7 Killed. —स्तं n. 1 Happiness, welfare. -2 Auspiciousness. -3 The body. -4 A finger-guard.

शस्तिः f. 1 Praise, eulogy. -2 A hymn of praise.

शस्त्रं n. 1 A weapon. -2 An instrument, a tool in general. -3 Iron. -4 Steel. -5 A hymn of praise (स्तोत्र). -6 Repetition, recitation. -Comp. —अयसं n. 1 Steel. -2 Iron. —अस्त्रं n. 1 Weapons for striking and throwing, arms and missiles. -2 Arms or weapons generally.-आजीवः, -उपजीविन् m. A professional soldier. —उपकरणं n. Arms or instruments of war, military apparatus. —कारः m. An armourer. —कोषः m. The sheath or scabbard of any weapon. —ग्राहिन् a. Taking up or wearing arms (for battle). —जीविन्, —वृत्तिः m. One living by the use of arms, a professional soldier. —पूत a. Rendered pure or absolved from guilt by being killed with a weapon on the battle-field.—भृत् m. 1 A soldier, warrior.-2 An armed man. —विद्या f., —शास्त्रं n. The science of arms. —संहतिः f. 1 A collection of arms.-2 An arsenal.-संपातःm. A sudden fall of a number of weapons. —हस्त a. Armed (—स्तः m.) An armed man.

शस्त्रकं n. 1 Steel. -2 Iron. -3 An instrument, a tool, weapon.

शस्त्रिका f. A knife.

शस्त्रिन् a. (f. —णी) Bearing arms or weapons; armed.

शस्त्री f. A knife.

शस्य a. (f. —स्या) 1 Best, excellent. -2 Praiseworthy, laudable.

शस्यं *n.* 1 Corn or grain in general. -2 The produce or fruit of a plant or tree. -3 A merit. -Comp. —भक्षक *a.* Granivorous. —मंजरी *f.* 1 An ear of corn. -2 A fruit-stalk. —शालिन्, —संपन्न *a.* Abounding in corn. —शूकं *n.* A beard of corn. —संब (-व-) रः *m.* The Sâla tree.

शाकः *m.*, शाकं *n.* A vegetable, a herb, any edible leaf, fruit or root used as a vegetable. —कः *m.* 1 Power, energy. -2 The teak tree. -3 The Sirisha tree. -4 N. of a people. -5 An era ; especially the era of Sâlivâhana. -6 N. of the sixth Dvìpa.-Comp.-अंगं *n.* Pepper. —आख्यः *m.* The teak tree. (-ख्यं *n.*) A vegetable. —चुक्रिका *f.* The tamarind. —तरुः *m.* The teak tree. —पणः *m.* 1 A measure equal to a handful. -2 A handful of vegetables. —पत्रः *m.* The *Sigru* tree. —पार्थिवः *m.* A king fond of an era. —प्रति *ind.* A little of herbs. —योग्यः *m.* Coriander. —वृक्षः *m.* The teak tree. —शाकटं, -शाकिनं *n.* A field of vegetables, a kitchen-garden.

शाकट *a.* (*f.* —टी) 1 Relating to a cart. -2 Going in a cart. —टः *m.* 1 A draught-ox. -2 The tree called श्लेष्मातक. —टं *n.* A field.

शाकटायनः *m.* N. of a philologist and grammarian mentioned by Pânini and Yáska.

शाकटिक *a.* (*f.* —की) 1 Belonging to a car. -2 Going in a car.

शाकटीनः *m.* A cart-load, a measure of load equal to 20 *tulâs*.

शाकंभरी *f.* 1 An epithet of Durgá. -2 N. of a city.

शाकलः *m.* A school of the Rigveda or the followers of this school. -Comp. —प्रातिशाख्यं *n.* N. of the Rigveda Prátisákhya. —शाखा *f.* The recension or traditional text of the Rigveda as represented by the Sákalas.

शाकल्यः *m.* N. of an ancient grammarian.

शाकारी *f.* One of the lowest forms of Prâkrita.

शाकिनी *f.* 1 A field of vegetables. -2 A kind of female demon attendant on Durgâ.

शाकुन *a.* (*f.*-नी) 1 Relating to birds. -2 Relating to omens. -3 Ominous.

शाकुनिकः *m.* A fowler, bird-catcher. —कं *n.* The interpretation of omens.

शाकुनेयः *m.* A small owl.

शाकुंतलः, शाकुंतलेयः *m.* A metronymic of Bharata (son of Sakuntalâ). -लं *n.* The drama called अभिज्ञानशकुंतला of Kâlidâsa.

शाकुलिकः *f.* A fisherman.

शाक्करः *m.* An ox.

शाक्त *a* (*f.*-क्ती) 1 Relating to power. -2 Relating to *Sakti* or the female personification of divine energy.-क्तः *m.* A worshipper of *Sakti*.

शाक्तिकः *m.* 1 A worshipper of *Sakti*. -2 A spearman, lancer.

शाक्तीकः *m.* A spearman, lancer.

शाक्तेयः, शाक्त्यः *m.* 1 A worshipper of *Sakti*. -2 N. of Parásara.

शाक्यः *m.* 1 N. of the family of Buddha.-2 N. of Buddha.-Comp. -भिक्षुकः *m.* A Buddhist religious mendicant. —मुनिः, -सिंहः *m.* Epithets of Buddha.

शाक्री *f.* 1 N. of Sachî, wife of Indra. -2 Of Durgá.

शाक्करः *m* An ox.

शाखा *f.* 1 A branch (as of a tree). -2 An arm. -3 A party, faction. -4 A part or subdivision of a work. -5 A school, branch, sect. -Comp. -चक्रमणं *n.* Irregular study. -चंद्रन्यायः

m. The maxim of the moon and a bough. It is adduced in illustration when an object has its position assigned to it from the appearance of contiguity. —नगरं, —पुरं *n.* A suburb. —पित्तः *m.* Inflammation of the extremities of the body *e.g.* hands, shoulders &c. —भृत *m.* A tree. -भेदः *m.* Difference of (Vedic) school. —मृगः *m.* 1 A monkey; an ape. -2 A squirrel. —रंडः *m.* A Bráhmana who has changed his own school of the Vedas. —रथ्या *f.* A branch-road. —शिफा *f.* A root growing from a branch (as of the fig-tree).

शाखालः *m.* A sort of cane (वानीर).

शाखिन् *a.* (*f.* —नी) 1 Having branches (fig. also). -2 Branching. -3 Belonging to any branch or school (as of the Veda). —*m.* 1 A tree.-2 A Veda.-3 A follower of any Vedic school or recension.

शाखोटः, शाखोटकः *m.* N. of a tree.

शांकरः *m.* A bull.

शांकरिः *m.* 1 N. of Kártikeya. -2 Of Ganesa. -3 Fire.

शांखिकः *m.* 1 A shell-cutter. -2 N. of mixed tribe.-3 A shell-blower.

शाटः *m.*, शाटी *f.* 1 A garment,cloth. -2 A petticoat.

शाटकः *m.*, शाटकं *n.* Cloth, garment, petticoat.

शाठ्यं *n.* 1 Dishonesty, trickery, villainy. -2 Art, skill, cunning.

शाणः *m.* 1 A touchstone. -2 A whetstone. -3 A saw. -4 A weight of four Màshas. —णं *n.* 1 Sack-cloth, coarse cloth.-2 A hempen garment. -Comp.—आजीवः *m.* An armourer.

शाणिः *m.* A plant from the fibres of which a coarse cloth is prepared.

शाणित *p. p.* (*f.* —ता) Whetted, ground, sharpened (on a whetstone).

शाणी *f.* 1 A touchstone.-2 A whetstone. -3 A saw.-4 A hempen garment. -5 A ragged garment. -6 A small screen or tent. -7 A sign made with the hands or eyes. -8 A weight of four Mâshas.

शाणीरं *n.* A bank or spot of ground in the Sona river.

शांडिल्यः *m.* 1 N. of a sage the author of a law-book. -2 The *Bilva* tree.

शात *p. p.* (*f.* —ता) 1 Sharpened, whetted.-2 Thin,slender.-3 Weak, feeble. -4 Beautiful. -5 Cut down. -6 Happy, thriving. —तः *m.* The Dhattúra plant. —तं *n.* Pleasure, delight. -Comp. —उदरी *f.* A woman with a slender waist. —शिख *a.* Sharp-pointed.

शातकुंभं *n.* 1 Gold. -2 The thorn-apple (धत्तूर).

शातनं *n.* 1 Whetting, sharpening. -2 Destroyer. -3 Becoming thin or small, thinness. -4 Withering, decaying.

शातपत्रकः *m.*, -की *f.* Moonlight.

शातभीरुः *f.* A kind of Mallikà.

शातमान *a.* (*f.* —नी) Bought for one hundred.

शात्रव *a.* (*f.* —वी) 1 Relating to an enemy. -2 Hostile, inimical. —वः *m.* An enemy. —वं *n.* 1 A collection of enemies. -2 Hostility.

शात्रवीय *a.* (*f.* -या) 1 Relating to an enemy. -2 Hostile, inimical.

शादः *m.* 1 Young grass. -2 Mud. -Comp. —हरितः *m.*, —तं *n.* A place green with young grass; a place clad in verdure.

शाद्वल *a.* (*f.* —ला) 1 Grassy. -2 Abounding in young green grass.

-3 Green, verdant. —लः *m* A grass-plot, meadow.

शान् I U, (शिशांसति,-ते) To sharpen, whet.

शानः *m*. 1 A touch-stone. -2 A whet-stone. -Comp. —पादः *m*. 1 A stone for grinding sandal. -2 The Páriyátra mountain.

शांत *p. p.* (*f.* —ता) 1 Appeased, calmed,satisfied, pacified.-2 Cured, alleviated. -3 Abated, put an end to, extinguished. -4 Ceased, stopped. -5 Dead, deceased. -6 Stilled, hushed. -7 Undisturbed, tranquil, still. -8 Tamed. -9 Free from passions. -10 Shaded. -11 Gentle. -12 Purified. -13 Meek, humble. -14 Auspicious, (in augury).(The phrase शांतं पापं is a phrase or interjection showing fear of some calamity, disapproval of some event or remark &c. It means ' oh no !' ' how can it be ? ', ' God forbid such an untoward or unlucky event !').-तः *m*. 1 A man who has subdued his passions; an ascetic. -2 Tranquillitity, the sentiment of quietism, the predominant feeling of which is indifference to worldly objects and pleasures. —तं *n*. Appeasing, pacifying. —तं *ind*. Enough, no more, not so, God forbid! -Comp. —रसः *m*. The sentiment of quietism. See शांत above.

शांतनवः *m*. ' The son of Santanu', N. of Bhîshma.

शांता *f*. N. of the daughter of Dasaratha, adopted by the sage Lomapáda and subsequently married by Rishyasringa.

शांतिः *f*. 1 Pacification, alleviation, removal. -2 Tranquillity, quiet, repose. -3 Cessation of hostility. -4 Cessation, stop. -5 Indifference to all worldly enjoyments. -6 Consolation, solace. -7 Reconciliation. -8 Satisfaction of hunger. -9 A propitiatory rite for averting evil.-10 Good fortune,auspiciousness. -11 Exculpation from blame. -12 Preservation. -13 N. of Durgà. -Comp. -उदं, -उदकं, -जलं *n*. Soothing or propitiatory water. —गृहं *n*. A room for rest or retirement.—होम. *m*. A sacrifice to avert or remove an evil.

शांतिक *a*. (*f*.—की) Expiatory, propitiatory. —कं *n*. Observances or ceremonies to remove clamities.

शापः *m*. 1 A curse, an anathema. -2 An oath. -3 Abuse, calumny. -4 A ban. -Comp. —अस्त्रः *m*. A sage, saint. —उत्सर्गः *m*. An utterance of a curse. —उद्धारः *m*., —मुक्तिः *f*., —मोक्षः *m*. A release or deliverance from a curse. —मुक्त *a*. Released from a curse. —यंत्रित *a*. Restrained by a curse.

शाफरिकः *m*. A fisherman.

शाबर (-व-) *a*. (*f*.—री) 1 Savage, barbarous. -2 Low, base. —रः *m*. 1 An offence, a fault. -2 Sin, wickedness. -3 The tree called Lodhra. —री *f*. A low form of the Prâkrita dialect. -Comp. —भेद्याख्यं (also भेद्राक्षं *n*.) Copper.

शाब्द *a*. (*f*.—ब्दी) 1 Relating to or derived from a word. -2 Relating to or depending on sound (opp. आर्थ). -3 Verbal, oral.-4 Sounding, sonorous. -5 Nominal (as inflection). —ब्दः *m*. A grammarian. —ब्दी *f*. N. of Sarasvatî.-Comp. —बोधः *m*. Perception or apprehension of the sense of words. —व्यंजना *f*. Insinuation founded on words.

शाब्दिक *a.* (*f.* —की) 1 Verbal, oral. -2 Relating to sounds or words. -3 Sounding. —कः *m.* A grammarian.

शामनः *m.* N. of Yama. -नं *n.* 1 Killing, slaughter. -2 Tranquillity. peace. -3 End. -नी *f.* The southern direction.

शामित्रं *n.* 1 Sacrificing -2 Killing animals at a sacrifice. -3 Tying up cattle for sacrifice -4 A sacrificial vessel.

शामिली *f.* A sacrificial ladle.

शामीनं *n.* 1 Ashes.-2 A sacrificial ladle.

शामीलं *n.* Ashes.

शामीली *f.* A chaplet, garland.

शांबरी *f.* 1 Jugglery, sorcery. -2 A sorceress.

शांबविकः *m.* A dealer in shells.

शांबु (-बू-) कः *m.* A bivalve-shell.

शाम्भव *a.* (*f.* —वी) Belonging to Siva. —वः *m.* A worshipper of Siva. -2 A son of Siva. -3 Camphor. -4 Bdellium. -5 A kind of poison. —वं *n.* The *Devadáru* tree.

शाम्भवी *f.* 1 N. of Párvatî. -2 The opening in the crown of the head through which the soul is said to escape.

शायकः *m.* 1 An arrow.-2 A sword.

शार् 10 U. (शारयति,-ते) 1 To weaken. -2 To be weak.

शार *a.* (*f.* —रा) 1 Variegated, spotted.-2 Yellow.-रः *m.* 1 A variegated colour. -2 Air, wind. -3 A chessman. -4 Injuring, hurting.

शारंगः *m.* 1 The *Ghâtaka* bird. -2 A peacock. -3 A bee. -4 A dear.-5 An elephant.

शारंगी *f.* A particular musical instrument.

शारद *a.* (*f.* —दी in the first sense and —दा in the other senses). 1 Belonging to autumn, autumnal. Annual. -3 New, recent.-4 Young, fresh. -5 Modest, bashful. -6 Not bold. —दः *m.* 1 A year. -2 An autumnal sickness. -3 Autumnal sunshine.-4 A kind of kidney-bean. -5 The Bakula tree. —दी *f.* The full-moon day in the month of Kártika. —दं *n.* 1 Corn, grain.-2 The white lotus. —दा *f.* 1 A kind of Vîná or lute. -2 N. of Durgá.-3 Of Sarasvati.

शारदिकः *m.* 1 Autumnal sickness. -2 Autumnal sunshine or heat. -कं *n.* An autumnal Srâddha.

शारदीय *a.* (*f.* —या) Autumnal.

शारिः *m.* 1 A chessman. -2 A small round ball. -3 A kind of die. —रिः *f.* 1 The bird called Sârikà. -2 Fraud, trick. -3 An elephant's housings. -Comp.—पट्टः *m.*, —फलं *n.*, —फलकः *m.*, -कं *n.* A chequered cloth for playing at chess, draughts &c.

शारिका *f.* 1 A kind of bird. -2 A bow or stick for playing any stringed instrument. -3 Playing at chess &c. -4 A piece at chess.

शारी *f.* A kind of bird.

शारीर *a.* (*f.* —री) Relating to the body, corporeal. —रः *m.* 1 The incorporate or embodied spirit (जीवात्मन्); human or individual soul. -2 A bull.

शारीरक *a.* (*f.* —की) Relating to the body, corporeal. —कं *n.* 1 The embodied spirit. -2 The inquiry into the nature of the spirit (a term applied to the Bháshya of Sankará-chàrya on the Brahmasútras). -Comp. —सूत्रं *n.* The aphorisms of the Vedanta philosophy.

शारीरिक *a.* (*f.* -की) Bodily, corporeal, material.

शारुक *a.* (*f.*-की) Noxious, hurtful.

शार्कर *a.* (*f.*—री) 1 Made of sugar, sugary. -2 Stony, gravelly. —रः *m.* 1 A gravelly place. -2 The froth of milk. -3 Cream. -4 Molasses.

शार्ङ्ग *a.* (*f.* —ङ्गी) 1 Made of horn, horny. -2 Having a bow, armed with a bow. -ङ्गः *m.*, -शार्ङ्गं *n.* 1 A bow (in general). -2 The bow of Vishnu.—ङ्गं *n.* Wet ginger. -Comp. —धन्वन्, -धरः, -पाणिः, -भृत् *m.* Epithets of Vishnu.

शार्ङ्गिन् *m.* 1 An archer, a bowman. -2 An epithet of Vishnu.-3 Of Siva.

शार्दूलः *m.* 1 A tiger. -2 A leopard or panther.-3 A demon, *Râkshasa.* -4 (At the end of comp.) An eminent or distinguished person, foremost, as in नरशार्दूल. -Comp.-विक्रीडितं *m.* 1 A tiger's play.-2 N. of a metre.

शार्वर *a.* (*f.* —री) 1 Nocturnal. -2 Mischievous, pernicious.-रं *n.* Darkness, thick gloom. —री *f.* Night.

शाल् 1 A. (शालते) 1 To praise, flatter. -2 To shine. -3 To be endowed with. -4 To tell.-5 To boast, vaunt.

शालः *m.* 1 N. of a tree (very tall and stately). -2 A tree in general -3 An enclosure.-4 A kind of fish. -5 N. of king Sâlivâhana. -Comp. —ग्रामः *m.* A kind of sacred stone typical of Vishnu. -जः, — निर्यासः *m.* Exudation of the Sâla tree, resin. —भंजिका *f.* 1 A doll, puppet, statue. -2 A courtezan, harlot. —भंजी *f.* A doll, puppet. —वेष्टः *m.* The resin of the Sála tree.

शालक्षः *m.* The *Lodhra* tree.

शाला *f.* 1 A room, saloon, hall. -2 A house. -Comp. —आजिरः *m.*, -रं *n.* A hollow earthen cup. —मृगः *m.* A jackal. —वृकः *m.* 1 A dog. -2 A wolf. -3 A deer. -4 A cat. -5 A jackal.-6 A monkey. —चतुःशालं *n.* A quadrangular house.

शालाकः *m* N. of Pânini.

शालाकिन् *m.* 1 A lancer, spearman. -2 A surgeon. -3 A barber.

शालातुरीयः *m.* An epithet of Pánini. (written also शालोत्तरीय).

शालारं *n.* 1 A ladder. -2 A bird-cage. -3 The claw of an elephant.

शालिः *m.* 1 Rice. -2 The civet-cat. -Comp. —ओदनः *m.*, —नं *n.* A boiled rice (of a superior kind). —गोपी *f.* A female appointed to watch a rice-field.-चूर्णः *m.*,-चूर्णं *n.*Rice-flour. —पिष्टं *n.* crystal. -भवनं *n.* A rice-field. —वाहनः *m.* N. of a celebrated sovereign of India whose era commences with 78 A. D. —होत्रः *m.* 1 writer on veterinary subjects. -2 A horse. —होत्रिन् *m.* A horse.

शालिकः *m.* 1 A weaver. -2 A toll, tax. -3 A village of artisans.

शालिन *a.* (*f.* -नी) (Usually at the end of comp.) 1 Endowed with, possessing, shining with.-2 Domestic.

शालिनी *f.* 1 A mistress of the house, housewife. -2 N. of a metre.

शालीन *a.* (*f.* -ना) 1 Modest, shy. -2 Like, resembling. —नः *m.* A house-holder. (शालीनी कृ To make humble, humiliate).

शालुः *m.* 1 A frog. -2 A kind of perfume. -3 A kind of astringent substance. -लुः *n.* The water-lily.

शालु (-लू-) कं *n.* 1 The root of the water-lily. -2 Nutmeg. —कः *m.* 1 A frog. -2 The root of the water-lily. (शालूक only in this sense).

शालुं (-लू-) रः *m.* A frog.

शालेयं *n.* A field of rice.

शालोत्तरीयः *m.* An epithet of Pánini.

शाल्मलः *m.* 1 The silk-cotten tree. -2 One of the seven great divisions of the earth. -3 The gum of the cotton-tree.

शाल्मलिः *m.*, *f.* 1 The silk-cotton tree.-2 One of the seven great divisions of the earth.-3N. of a kind of hell. -Comp. —स्थः *m.* An epithet of Garuda.

शाल्मलिन् *m.* N. of Garuda.

शाल्मलिनी *f.* The silk cotton tree.

शाल्मली *f.* 1 The silk-cotton tree. -2 N. of a river in Pátâla. -3 A kind of hell. -Comp. —वेष्टः, -वेष्टकः *m.* The gum of the silk-cotton tree.

शाल्वः *m.* 1 N. of a country. -2 A king of Sâlva.

शाव *a.* (*f.* —वी) 1 Relating to a dead body; caused by the death (of a relative). -2 Tawny, dark-yellowish. —वः *m.* 1 The young of any animal; a fawn, cub.-2 A dark-yellowish colour. [mal.

शावकः *m.* The young of any ani-

शावर, शाबर *a.* (*f.* —री) 1 Barbarous. -2 Low, vile. —रः *m.* 1 Sin, wickedness. -2 A fault, offence, -3 The *lodhra* tree. -Comp. —भेदाख्यं *n.* Copper.

शाश्वत *a.* (*f.* —ती) 1 Eternal, perpetual. -तः *m.* 1 N. of Siva. -2 Of Vyâsa. -3 The sun. —तं *n.* Heaven. —तं *ind.* Eternally, perpetually.

शाश्वतिक *a.* (*f.* —की) Eternal, perpetual, constant.

शाश्वती *f.* The earth.

शाष्कुल *a.* (*f.* —ली) Eating flesh (or fish). [cakes.

शाष्कुलिकं *n.* A quantity of baked

शास् 2 P. (शास्ति, शासितुं, शिष्ट) 1 To teach, instruct, train (governing two accusatives) -2 To rule, govern. -3 To command, enjoin.-4 To tell, communicate (with dat.). -5 To advise. -6 To enact. -7 To punish, correct. -8 To tame, subdue. -9 To wish, desire.

शासनं *n.* 1 Instruction, teaching, discipline. -2 Rule, government. -3 An order, a command, direction. -4 An edict, enactment. -5 A precept, rule.-6 A royal grant (of land &c.). -7 A written agreement. -8 Control of passions. -Comp. —पत्रं *n.* 1 A plate (usually of copper) on which a grant of land &c. is inscribed.-2 A sheet of paper on which an order is written. —हरः *m.* A royal messenger. —हारिन् *m.* An envoy, a messenger.

शासित *p. p.* (*f.* —ता) 1 Ruled, governed.-2 Punished. [A chastiser.

शासितृ *m.* 1 A ruler, governor. -2

शास्तिः *f.* 1 Governing, ruling. -2 A command. -3 Chastisement, punishment.

शास्तृ *m.* 1 An instructor. -2 A ruler, king. -3 A father. -4 A Buddha or Jina or a deified teacher of the Bauddhas or Jainas.

शास्त्रं *n* 1 A command, a precept. -2 A scriptural injunction. -3 A religious or sacred treatise. -4 Any department of knowledge, science. -5 What is learnt, knowledge. -6 A scientific work or treatise. -7 Theory (opp. प्रयोग or parctice). -Comp. —अनुष्ठानं *n.*, -अनुसारः *m.* Conformity to or observance of sacred precepts. —अर्थः *m.* 1 The meaning of a sacred precept. -2 A scriptural precept or statement. —आचरणं *n.* 1 Observance of sacred precepts. -2 The study of Sâstras. (-णः *m.*) 1 One versed in scriptures. -2 A student of the Vedas. -उक्त *a.* Prescribed by sacred laws. -कोविद *a.* Versed in the Sâstras. —गंडः *m.* A superficial reader of books, a superficial scholar. —चक्षुस् *n.* Grammar. —तत्त्वं *n.* Truth as taught in the Sástras; scriptural truth —दृष्टि: *f.* Scriptural point of view. —योनि: *m.* The source of the Sâstras. —विधानं *n.*, —विधि: *m.* A sacred precept, scriptural injunction. —विरुद्ध *a.* Contrary to the Sàstras; illegal, unlawful. —व्युत्पत्ति: *f.* Intimate knowledge of the sacred writings; proficiency in the Sàstras. —शिल्पिन् *m.* The country of Kásmira. -सिद्ध *a.* Established by sacred authority.

शास्त्रिन् *a.* (*f.*—णी) Versed or skilled in the Sâstras. —*m.* 1 One who has mastered the Sâstras; a learned man. -2 A teacher of sacred science. [Scientific.

शास्त्रीय *a.* (*f.* —या) 1 Scriptural.-2

शास्य *a.* (*f.* —स्या) 1 To be taught or advised. -2 To be regulated or governed. -3 Deserving punishment.

शि 5 U. (शिनोति, शिनुते) 1 To whet, sharpen. -2 To make thin. -3 To excite. -4 To be attentive. -5 To be sharp.

शि: *m.* 1 Auspiciousness, good fortune.-2 Composure, tranquillity. -3 An epithet of Siva.

शिंशपा *f.* 1 N. of a tree (शिशु). -2 The Asoka tree.

शिक्कु *n* Idle, lazy.

शिक्थं *n.* Bee's wax.

शिक्यं *n.*, शिक्या *f.* 1 A loop or swing (made of rope). -2 A burden or load carried in a sling. -3 The strings of a balance. [study.

शिक्ष् 1 A. (शिक्षते, शिक्षित) To learn,

शिक्षक: *m.* (*f.* शिक्षका or शिक्षिका) 1 A learner. -2 A teacher, instructor.

शिक्षणं *n.* 1 Learning, acquiring knowledge. -2 Teaching.

शिक्षा *f.* 1 Learning, study. -2 Desire of being able to do anything; wish to prevail.-3 Teaching, training. -4 One of the six Vedángas, the science which teaches the proper pronunciation of words and laws of euphony. -5 Modesty, humility. -6 Science. -Comp. —कर: *m.* 1 A teacher, an instructor. -2 N. of Vyása. —गुरु: *m.* A religious preceptor. —नर: *m* An epithet of Indra. —शक्ति: *f.* Skill.

शिक्षित *p. p.* (*f.* —ता) 1 Learnt, studied. -2 Taught, instructed. -3 Trained, disciplined. -4 Tame, docile.-5 Skilful, clever.-6 Modest. -Comp. —अक्षर: *m.* 1 A teacher. -2 A pupil. —आयुध *a.* Skilled in the use of weapons. [scholar.

शिक्षमाण:, शिक्ष्यमाण: *m.* A pupil,

शिखंड: *m.* 1 A lock of hair left on the crown or sides of the head at tonsure. -2 A peacock's tail. -3 A crest.

शिखंडक: *m.* 1 A lock of hair left on the crown of the head at tonsure. -2 Locks of hair left on the sides of the head.-3 A crest, tuft, plume. -4 A peacock's tail.

शिखंडिक: *m.* A cock.

शिखंडिका *f.* A lock of hair on the crown of the head.

शिखंडिन् *m.* 1 A peacock.-2 A cock. -3 An arrow. -4 A peacock's tail. -5 A kind of jasmine. -6 N. of Vishnu.-7 N. of a son of Drupada.

शिखंडिनी *f.* 1 A pea-hen.-2 A kind of jasmine. -3 N. of the daughter of Drupada.

शिखर: *m*, शिखरं *n.* 1 The top, summit of a mountain. -2 The top of a tree -3 Crest, tuft. -4 The edge of a sword. -5 Top, peak, point in general. -6 The arm-pit. -7 Bristling of the hair. -8 The bud of the Arabian jasmine.-9 A kind of gem. -Comp. —वासिनी *f.* An epithet of Durgâ.

शिखरिणी *f.* 1 An excellent woman. -2 A dish of curds and sugar with spices. -3 A line of hair extending across the navel. -4 N. of a plant. -5 N. of a metre.

शिखरिन् *a.* (*f.* —णी) 1 Crested, tufted. -2 Pointed, peaked.-*m.* 1 A mountain.-2 A hill-fort. -3 A tree. -4 The lapwing.

शिखा *f.* 1 A lock of hair left on the crown of the head. -2 A crest, top-knot. -3 Tuft, plume. -4 Top, peak. -5 Sharp end or edge in general. -6 The end of a garment. -7 A flame. -8 A ray of light. -9 A peacock's crest or comb. -10 A branch in general, especially one taking root. -11 The head or chief of anything. -12 The excitement of love. -13 The point of the foot. -Comp. -तरुः *m.* A lamp-stand. -धरः *m.* 1 A peacock. -2 A Jaina deified saint. —धारः *m.* A peacock. —मूलं *n.* 1 A carrot. -2. A turnip. —वरः *m.* The jack-fruit tree. —वलः *m.* A peacock. —वृक्षः *m.* A lamp-stand. -वृद्धिः *f.* A kind of usurious interest daily increasing.

शिखालुः *m.* The crest of a peacock.

शिखिन् *a.* (*f.* —नी) 1 Pointed. -2 Crested, tufted. -3 Proud. -*m.* 1 A peacock. -2 Fire. -3 A cock. -4 An arrow. -5 A tree. -6 A lamp. -7 A bull. -8 A horse. -9 A mountain. -10 A Brâhmana. -11 A religious mendicant. -12 N. of Ketu. -13 The number 'three'. -Comp. —कंठं, -ग्रीवं *n.* Blue vitriol. —ध्वजः *m.* 1 An epithet of Kârtikeya.-2 Smoke. —पिच्छं, -पुच्छं *n.* A peacock's tail. —यूपः *m.* An antelope. —वाहनः *m.* An epithet of Kártikeya. —शिखा *f.* 1 A flame. -2 A peacock's crest.

शिग्रुः *m.* 1 A pot-herb. -2 A kind of tree.

शिंघ् 1 P. (शिंघति) To smell.

शिंघाणः *m.* 1 Froth, foam.-2 Phlegm. —णं *n.* 1 The mucus of the nose.-2 Rust of iron. -3 A glass-vessel.

शिंघाणकः *m.*, -कं *n.* The mucus of the nose. —कः *m.* Phlegm.

शिंज् 1. 2. A., 10 U. (शिंजते, शिंक्ते, शिंजयति,-ते, शिंजित) 1 To tinkle, jingle, rattle. -2 To roar, bellow.

शिंजः *m.* Tinkle, jingle of ornaments such as anklets.

शिंजंजिका *f.* A chain worn round the loins.

शिंजा *f.* 1 Tinkle, jingle. -2 A bow-string.

शिंजित *p. p.* (*f.* -ता) Tinkling, jingling. —तं *n.* Tinkling, jingling. (of ornaments &c.). -2 Clanking (of chains).

शिंजिनी *f.* 1 A bow-string. -2 An anklet (worn round the feet).

शिट् 1 P.(शटति) To despise, disregard.

शित *p. p.* (*f.* -ता) 1 Sharpened, whetted. -2 Thin, emaciated. -3 Wasted, declined.-4 Weak, feeble. -Comp. —अग्रः *m.* A thorn. —धार *a.* Sharp-edged. —शूकः *m.* 1 Barley. -2 Wheat.

शितद्रुः *f.* The river Sutlej.

शिति *a.* 1 White. -2 Black. —तिः *m.* The birch tree. -Comp. —कंठः *m.* 1 An epithet of Siva. -2 A peacock. -3 A gallinule. —छदः, —पक्षः *m.* A goose. —रत्नं *n.* Sapphire. —वासस् *m.* An epithet of Balarâma.

शिथिल *a* (*f.* -ला) 1 Loose, loosen.

ed, slackened, unfastened. -2 Severed, fallen from the stalk. -3 Languid, unnerved. -4 Flaccid, flabby. -5 Dissolved. -6 Decayed. -7 Ineffective, futile. -8 Inattentive, careless. -9 Loosely done, not rigidly performed. —लं *n.* 1 Laxity, looseness. (शिथिली कृ To loose, unfasten, untie, slacken. -2 To weaken. -3 To abandon. शिथिली भू 1 To be slackened or relaxed. -2 To fall off from.

शिथिलय् Den. P. 1 To relax, slacken, loosen. -2 To give up, abandon. -3 To allow to cool down.

शिथिलाय् Den. A. To become loose or flaccid.

शिथिलित *a.* (*f.* —ता) 1 Loosed. -2 Relaxed, loosened. -3 Dissolved.

शिनिः *m.* N. of a warrior of the Yádava family.

शिपिः *m.* A ray of light. -*f.* Skin, leather. शिपि *n.* Water. -Comp. -विष्ट *a.* (written शिपाविष्ट or शिविपिष्ट also). 1 Pervaded by rays. -2 Bald.-3 Leprous. (-ष्टः *m.*) 1 An epithet of Vishnu. -2 A man without prepuce. -3 A leper. [laya.

शिप्रः *m.* N. of a lake on the Himá-

शिप्रा *f.* 1 N. of a river flowing by Ujjayiní. -2 A visor or helmet.

शिफः *f.* See शिफा.

शिफा *f.* 1 A fibrous root. -2 The root of water-lily. -3 A root in general. -4 A stroke with a whip. -5 A mother. -6 A river. -7 Turmeric. -8 Spikenard. -Comp. -कंदः *m.*,—कंदं *n.* The root of a water-lily. —धरः *m.* A branch. -रुहः *m.* The (Indian) fig-tree.

शिफाकः *m.* The root of a water-lily.

शिबिः, शिविः *m.* 1 A beast of prey. -2 The birch tree. -3 N. of a king.

शिबि (-वि-) का *f.* 1 A palanquin, litter. -2 A bier. -3 A raised platform.

शिबि (-वि-) रं *n.* 1 A camp. -2 A royal camp or residence. -3 An intrenchment for the protection of an army. -4 A kind of grain.

शिबि (-वि-) रथः *m.* A palanquin, litter.

शिंबा *f.* A pod, legume; (also शिंबिः *f.* in this sense).

शिंबिका *f.* 1 A pod, legume. -2 A kind of kidney-bean.

शिंबी *f.* 1 A pod, legume. -2 A kind of plant.

शिरं *n.* 1 The head. -2 The root of the pepper plant. —रः *m.* 1 A bed. -2 A large serpent. -Comp. —जं *n.* The hair.

शिरस् *n.* 1 The head. -2 Skull. -3 A peak, top (as of a mountain). -4 The top of a tree. -5 The top of anything. -6 The highest point. -7 The forepart, van (as of an army). -8 Chief, principal. -Comp. —अस्थि *n.* (शिरोस्थि) The skull. —कपालिन् *m.* An ascetic who carries about a human skull. —गृहं (शिरोगृहं) *n.* A room on the top of a house, turret, garret. -ग्रहः(शिरोग्रहः) *m.* An affection of the head, head-ache.-छेदः *m.*, —छेदनं *n.* Beheading, decapitation.-तापिन् *m.* An elephant.-त्रं, -त्राणं *n.* 1 A helmet. -2 A head-dress. —धरा *f.*, -धिः *m.* The neck. —प्रावरणं *n.* A turban. -फलः *m.* The cocoa-nut tree.—भूषणं *n.* An ornament for the head. —मणिः *m.* 1 A jewel worn on the head. -2 A crest-jewel. -3 A title of respect conferred on learned men. -मर्मन् *m.* A hog. —मालिन् *m.* An epithet of Siva. —रुह्, -रुहः *m.* (also शिरसिरुह्,-हः) The hair of the head. —वर्तिन् *a.*

(शिरोवर्तिन्) Being at the head. (*-m.*) A chief, any one at the head of affairs. —वल्ली (शिरोवल्ली) *f.* The crest of a peacock. —वृत्तं *n.* Pepper. -वेष्टः *m.*, —वेष्टनं *n.* A head-dress, turban. —शूलं *n.* Head-ache. —हारिन् *m.* An epithet of Siva.

शिरसिजः *m.* The hair of the head.

शिरस्कं *n.* 1 A helmet. -2 A turban, head-dress.

शिरस्का *f.* A palanquin.

शिरस्तस् *ind.* From the head.

शिरस्य *a.* (*f.* —स्या) Belonging to, or being on, the head. —स्यः *m.* Clean hair.

शिरा *f.* Any tubular vessel of the body (as a nerve, vein, or artery). -Comp. —पत्रः *m.* The wood-apple. —वृत्तं *n.* Lead.

शिराल *a.* (*f.* —ला) Sinewy, veiny.

शिरिः *m.* 1 A sword. -2 A killer, murderer. -3 An arrow. -4 A locust.

शिरीषः *m.* N. of a tree. —षं *n.* A flower of this tree.

शिल् 6 P. (शिलति) To glean.

शिलः *m.*, शिलं *n.* Gleaning ears of corn. -Comp. —उंछः *m.* Gleaning ears of corn.

शिला *f.* 1 A stone, rock. -2 A grind-stone. -3 The lower timber of a door. -4 A tendon, vein (for शिरा). -5 Red arsenic. -6 Camphor. -Comp. —अटकः *m.* 1 A hole. -2 A fence. -3 A room on the top of a house. —आत्मजं *n.* Iron. —आत्मिका *f.* A crucible. —आरंभा *f.* The wild plantain. —आसनं *n.* 1 A slab of stone used as a seat. -2 Benzoin. —आह्वं *n.* Bitumen. —उच्चयः *m.* A mountain, a huge rock. —उत्थं *n.* Benzoin. —उद्भवं *n.* 1 Benzoin. -2 A kind of sandal wood. —ओकस् *m.* An epithet of Garuda. —कुट्टकः *m.* A stone-cutter's hatchet. —कुसुमं, -पुष्पं *n.* Benzoin. —जं *n.* 1 Bitumen. -2 Benzoin. -3 Petroleum. -4 Iron. -5 Any fossil production. —जतु *n.* 1 Bitumen. -2 Red chalk. —जित् *f.*, —दद्रुः *m.* Bitumen. -धातुः *m.* 1 Chalk. -2 Red chalk. —पट्टः *m.*, -पट्टकः *m.* 1 A flat stone for grinding &c. -2 A slab (of stone) used as a seat. —पुत्रः, -पुत्रकः *m.* A small flat stone for grinding condiments upon. -प्रतिकृतिः *f.* An image of stone. -फलकं *n.* A stone-slab. —भवं *n.* Benzoin. —भेदः *m.* A stone-cutter's chisel. —रसः *m.* 1 Benzoin. -2 Incense. —वृष्टिः *f.* 1 A shower of stones. -2 Hail. —वेश्मन् *n.* A rocky recess. —व्याधिः *m.* Bitumen. —सारं *n.* Iron.

शिलिः *m.* The birch tree. —लिः *f.* 1 The lower timber of a door. -2 A female frog.

शिलिंदः *m.* A kind of fish.

शिली *f.* 1 The lower timber of a door. -2 A kind of earth-worm. -3 An arrow. -4 A female frog. -Comp. —मुखः *m.* 1 A bee. -2 An arrow.

शिलींध्रः *m.* 1 A kind of fish. -2 A kind of tree. —ध्रं *n.* A mushroom, fungus. -2 The flower of the plantain tree. -3 Hail.

शिलींध्रकं *n.* A mushroom, fungus.

शिलींध्री *f.* 1 Earth, clay. -2 A small earthworm.

शिल्पं *n.* 1 A fine or mechanical art. -2 Skill (in any art); craft. -3 A kind of ladle or spoon used at sacrifices. -4 A ceremonial act. -Comp. —कर्मन् *n.*, -क्रिया *f.* Handicraft. —कारः, -कारकः, -कारिन् *m.* An artisan. -शाकं *n.*, -शाला *f.* A work-shop, manufactory. —शास्त्रं *n.* 1 A book on any art, fine or mechanical -2 mechanics.

शिल्पकं *n.* A kind of drama.

शिल्पिन् *a.* (*f.* —नी) 1 Relating to a fine or mechanical art. -2 Mechanical. -*m.* 1 An artisan, a mechanic. -2 One who is skilled in any art.

शिव *a.* (*f.* —वा) 1 Auspicious, propitious, lucky. -2 Happy, prosperous, fortunate. —वः *m.* 1 N. of the third God of the Hindu Trinity. -2 The penis. -3 An auspicious planetary conjunction.-4 The Veda. -5 Final beatitude. -6 A post to which cattle are tied. -7 A God, deity. -8 Quick-silver.-9 Bdellium. -10 The black variety of thorn-apple.-वौ (*m. dual*) Siva and Pârvatî. —वं *n.* 1 Prosperity, welfare, happiness. -2 Bliss, auspiciousness. -3 Final beatitude. -4 Water. -5 Sea-salt.-6 Rock-salt.-7 Refined borax. -Comp. —अक्षं *n.* See रुद्राक्षं. —आत्मकं *n.* Rock-salt. —आदेशकः *m.* 1 The bearer of auspicious news. -2 A fortune-teller. —आलयः *m.* 1 Siva's abode. -2 The red basil. (-यं *n.*) 1 A temple of Siva.-2 A cemetery. —इष्टा *f.* Dúrvá grass. —कर (शिवंकर also) *a.* Auspicious.—चतुर्दशी *f* The fourteenth day of the dark half of Mágha. —ताति *a.* 1 Having an auspicious end; propitious. -2 Tender, merciful, not demoniacal. (-तिः *f.*) Auspiciousness, happiness. —दत्तं *n.* The discus of Vishnu. —दारु *n.* The Devadâru tree. —द्रुमः *m.* The Bilva tree. —द्विष्टा *f.* The Ketaka tree.-धातुः *m.* Quick-silver. -पुरं *n.*, -पुरी *f.* N. of Benares. —पुराणं *n.* N. of one of the eighteen Puránas.—प्रियः *m.* 1 A crystal.-2 The thorn-apple. (-यं *n.*) See रुद्राक्ष. -मल्लकः *m.* The Arjuna tree. —रसः *m.* The water of boiled rice —राजधानी *f.* N. of Benares. —रात्रिः *f.* The fourteenth day of the dark half of Mâgha sacred to Siva. —लिंगं *n.* 1 Siva, worshipped in the form of a Phallus. -2 A temple dedicated to the worship of the *Linga.* —लोकः *m.* The world of Siva. —वल्लभः *m.* The mango tree. —वाहनः *m.* A bull. —वीजं *n.* Quick-silver. —शेखरः *m.* 1 The moon. -2 The thorn-apple. -सायुज्यं *n.* Final emancipation.-सुंदरी *f.* An epithet of Durgâ.

शिवकः *m.* 1 A post to which cattle in general are tied. -2 A post for cattle to rub against.

शिवा *f.* 1 N. of Párvatî. -2 A jackal. -3 A fortunate woman. -4 Final beatitude. -5 The Samî tree. -6 The yellow myrobalan.-7 Dúrvá grass.-8 A kind of yellow pigment. -9 Turmeric. -Comp. —अरातिः *f.* A dog. —प्रियः *m.* A goat. —फला *f.* The Samî tree. —रुतं *n.* The howling of a jackal.

शिवानी *f.* Pârvatî, wife of Siva.

शिवालुः *m.* A jackal.

शिविका, शिविर See शिबिका, शिबिर.

शिशिर *a.* (*f.*-रा) Cool, cold. -रः *m.*, -रं *n.* 1 Dew, hoar-frost.-2 The cold season (comprising the two months Mágha and Phâlguna). -Comp. —अंशुः, -करः, -किरणः, -दीधितिः, -रश्मिः *m.* The moon. —अत्ययः, -अपगमः *m.* The spring season.—कालः, -समयः *m.* The cold season. —घ्नः *m.* An epithet of Agni.

शिशुः *m.* 1 A child, an infant. -2 The young of any animal. -3 A boy under eight or sixteen years of age. -4 A pupil, scholar. -Comp. —गंधा *f.* A kind of jasmine (double jasmine). —चांद्रायणं *n.* A lunar penance of children. —पालः *m.* N. of a king of the Chedis and son of Damaghosha. —मारः *m.* The Gangetic porpoise.-वाहकः,वाह्यकः *m.* A wild goat.

शिशुकः *m.* 1 A child, an infant. -2 The young of any animal. -3 A tree. -4 A porpoise. -5 A fish resembling a porpoise.

शिश्नं, शिस्नं *n.* The male organ of generation.

शिश्विदान *a.* (*f.* -ना) 1 Virtuous, holy. -2 Wicked, sinful.

शिष् 1 P. (शेषति) To hurt, kill.

शिष् 1 P. 10 U. (शेषति, शेषयति,-ते) To leave as a remainder, spare.

शिष् 7 P. (शिनष्टि, शिष्ट) 1 To leave as a remainder; to leave.-2 To distinguish or discriminate from others. -*Caus.* (शेषयति,-ते).

शिष्ट *p. p.* (*f.*—ष्टा) 1 Left, remaining, rest. -2 Ordered, commanded. -3 Trained, disciplined. -4 Tamed, docile.-5 Wise,learned.-6 Respectable. -7 Civil, polite. -8 Chief, excellent, eminent. -ष्टः *m.* 1 An eminent or distinguished person.-2 A wise man. -3 A counsellor.-Comp. —आचारः *m.* 1 The practice of wise men. -2 Good breeding. —सभा *f.* 1 A council of state. -2 An assembly of learned men.

शिष्टिः *f.* 1 Rule, government. -2 Order, command.-3 Chastisement.

शिष्यः *m.* 1 A pupil, scholar. -2 Anger, passion. -3 Violence, force. -Comp. —परंपरा *f.* A succession of pupils.

शिह्लः, शिह्लकः *m.* Benzoin.

शी 2 A. (शेते, शयित) 1 To lie, lie down, rest. -2 To sleep (fig. also). -3 To rest, repose.

शी *f.* Sleep, repose. -2 Tranquillity.

शीक् 1 A (शीकते) 1 To wet, sprinkle. -2 To go or move gently.

शीक् 1 P. 10 U. (शीकति, शीकयति,-ते) 1 To be angry. -2 To moisten.

शीकरः *m.* 1 Spray, drizzle, mist. -2 A drop of water or rain. —रं *n.* 1 The *Sarala* tree. -2 The resin of this tree.

शीघ्र *a.* (*f.* —घ्रा) Quick, rapid. -घ्रः *m.* Conjunction (in astr.). —घ्रं *ind.* Quickly, rapidly. -Comp. —उच्चः *m.* A conjunction (in astr.). —चेतनः *m.* A dog.—वेधिन् *m.* A good archer.

शीघ्रिय *a.* Quibk. —यः *m.* 1 N. of Vishnu. -2 Of Siva. -3 The fiting of cats.

शीत् *ind.* A sound made to express a sudden thrill of pleasure or pain.

शीत *a.* (*f.* —ता) 1 Cool, cold. -2 Dull, sluggish, sleepy. -तः *m.* 1 A kind of reed. -2 The Nimba tree. -3 The cold season (*n.* also). -4 Camphor. —तं *n.* 1 Cold, coldness, chillness. -2 Water. -3 Cinnamon. -Comp. —अंशुः *m.* 1 The moon. -2 Camphor. —अदः *m.* A diseased state of the gums. —अद्रिः *m.* The Himàlaya mountain. —अश्मन् *m.* The moon-stone. — उत्तमं *n.* Water. —करः *m.* 1 The moon. -2 Camphor. —कालः *m.* The cold season, winter. —कालीन *a.* Wintry. -कुंभः *m.* The fragrant oleander.—कृच्छ्रः *m.*,-कृच्छ्रं *n.* A kind of religious penance. —क्षारः *m.* Refined borax. —गंधः *m.* White sandal.-गुः *m.* 1 The moon. -2 Camphor. —चंपकः *m.* 1 A lamp. -2 A mirror. —दीधितिः *m.* The moon.-पुष्पः *m.* The Sirisha tree. —पुष्पकं *n.* Benzoin. —प्रभः *m.* Camphor. —भानुः *m.* The moon. —भीरुः *m.* A kind of jasmine (Arabian). —मयूखः,-मरीचिः -रश्मिः *m.* 1 The moon. -2 Camphor. —रम्यः *m.* A lamp. —रुच् *m.* The moon.-वल्कः *m*. The *Udumbara* tree. -वीथकः *m*. The fig-tree.-शिवः *m*. The *Sami* tree. (-वं *n*.)1 Rocksalt. -2 Borax. —शूकः *m*. Barley.

शीतक *a*. (*f*. -का) Cold. -कः *m*. 1 A cold thing. -2 The cold season. -3 A dilatory person. -4 A man free from cares or anxieties. -5 A scorpion.

शीतल *a*. (*f*. -ला) Cool, cold, chill. -लः *m*. 1 The moon. -2 A kind of camphor. -3 Turpentine. -4 The Champaka tree.-5 A kind of religious observance.—लं *n*. 1 Cold, coolness. -2 The cold season. -3 Benzoin. -4 White sandal. -5 A pearl. -6 Green sulphate of iron. -7 A lotus. -Comp. -छदः *m*. The Champaka tree. -जलं *n*. A lotus. -प्रदः *m*., -प्रदं *n*. Sandal. -षष्ठी *f*. The sixth day of the bright half of Mâgha.

शीतलकं *n*. A white lotus.

शीतला *f*. 1 Small-pox.-2 The Goddess presiding over small-pox.

शीतली *f*. Small-pox.

शीता *f*. See सीता.

शीतालु *a*. Suffering from cold, [chilled.

शीत्य *a*. (*f*. -त्या) See सीत्य.

शीधुः *m*., शीधु *n*. 1 Any spirituous liquor,rum.-2 Wine.-Comp.-गंधः *m*. The *Bakula* tree. -पः *m*. A drinker of spirits.

शीन *a*. (*f*. -ना) Thick, congealed. -नः *m*. 1 A blockhead. -2 A large snake (अजगर).

शीभ्यः *m*. 1 A bull. -2 N. of Siva.

शीरः *m*. A large snake.

शीर्ण *p*. *p*. (*f*. -र्णा) 1 Withered, decayed. -2 Shattered, shivered. -3 Thin, emaciated. -4 Slender. —र्णं *n*. A kind of perfume. -Comp. —अंघ्रिः, -पादः *m*. 1 Epithets of Yama. -2 Of the planet Saturn. -पर्णः *m*. The *Nimba* tree. -वृंतं *n*. A water-melon.

शीर्वि *a*. 1 Destructive, hurtful, injurious. -2 Savage.

शीर्ष *n*. 1 The head. -2 The black aloe-wood.-Comp. -रक्षं *n*. A helmet.

शीर्षकः *m*. An epithet of Râhu. -कं *n*. 1 The head. -2 Skull. -3 A helmet. -4 A head-dress. -5 A judicial sentence.

शीर्षण्यः *m*. Clean or unentangled hair. -ण्यं *n*. 1 A helmet. -2 A head-dress.

शीर्षन् *n*. The head. (This word has no forms for the first five inflections, and is optionally substituted for शिरस् or शीर्ष after acc.dual.)

शील् 1 P. (शीलति) 1 To meditate, contemplate. -2 To serve, honour. -3 To do, practise.

शील् 10 U. (शीलयति,-ते) 1 To honour, worship. -2 To practise repeatedly, exercise, study, ponder over. -3 To put on, wear. -4 To go to, visit. -With अनु-,परि- The same as शील्.

शीलः *m*. 1 A large serpent -लं *n*. 1 Disposition, character, tendency, habit, custom. (In compounds शील means 'habituated to' 'prone to' 'apt' as in दयाशील,कलहशील.-2Conduct, behaviour. -3 Good disposition. -4 Virtue ; good conduct, virtuous life, chastity, uprightness.-5 Beauty, good form.-Comp. -धारिन् *m*. An epithet of Siva.-वृत्तिः *f*. Virtue.

शीलनं *n*. 1 Repeated practice, exercise, study -2 Constant application. -3 Honouring, serving. -4 Wearing.

शीलित *p*. *p*. (*f*. —ता) 1 Practised, exercised.-2 Worn on.-3 Frequented, visited.-4 Skilled in.-5 Endowed with, possessed of. —त्वं *n*. Practice, conduct.

शीवन् *m*. A large snake.

शुंशुमारः *m*. A porpoise.

शुक् 1 P. (शोकति) To go, move.

शुकः *m*. 1 A parrot. -2 The Sirîsha tree. -3 N. of a son of Vyása. —कं *n*. 1 Cloth, clothes. -2 A helmet. -3 A turban. -4 The hem of a garment. -Comp. —अदनः *m*. The pomegranate tree. —तरुः, -द्रुमः *m*. The Sirîsha tree. —नास *a*. Having an aquiline nose. -नासिका *f*. An aquiline nose. —पुच्छः *m* Sulphur. -पुष्पः,-प्रियः *m*. The Sirîsha tree. —प्रिया *f*. The rose-apple. -वल्लभः The pomegranate. —वाहः *m*. An epithet of Cupid.

शुक्त *p. p.* (*f.* -क्ता) 1 Bright, pure, clean. -2 Acid, sour. -3 Harsh, hard, severe. -4 United. -5 Deserted, lonely. —क्तं *n*. 1 Flesh. -2 Sour gruel. -3 A kind of acid liquid.

शुक्तिः *f*. 1 An oyster-shell, pearl-oyster. -2 A conch-shell. -3 A small shell, muscle. -4 A portion of the skull. -5 A curl of hair on a horse's breast (or neck). -6 A kind of perfume. -7 A weight equal to two *Karshas*. -Comp. —उद्भवं, -जं *n*. A pearl. -पुटं *n*., -पेशी *f*. A pearl-oyster-shell. —वधूः *f*. The pearl-oyster. —बीजं *n*. A pearl.

शुक्तिका *f*. A pearl-oyster.

शुक्रः *m*. 1 The planet Venus. -2 N. of the preceptor of the Asuras. -3 The month of Jyeshtha. -4 N. of Agni or fire. -5 N. of the plant Chitraka. —क्रं *n*. 1 Semen virile. -2 The essence of anything. -3 Male and female energy. -Comp. —अंगः *m*. A peacock. —करः *m*. The marrow of the bones. —भुज् *f*. A peahen. —भूः *m*. The marrow of the bones. —वारः, -वासरः *m*. Friday. -शिष्यः *m*. A demon.

शुक्रल, शुक्रिय *a*. (*f*. -ला, -या) 1 Seminal. -2 Increasing the seminal flow.

शुक्ल *a*. (*f*. —क्ला) White, pure, bright. -क्लः *m*. 1 The white colour. -2 The bright half of a lunar month. -3 N of Siva. —क्लं *n*. 1 Silver. -2 A disease of the white part of the eye. -3 Fresh butter. -4 Sour gruel. -Comp. —अंगः,-अपांगः *m*. A peacock. —अम्लं *n*. A kind of sorrel. —उपला *f*. Candied sugar. —कंठकः *m*. A kind of gallinule. —कुष्ठं *n* White leprosy. —धातुः *m*. Chalk. —पक्षः *m*. The bright half of a month. —वायसः *m*. A crane.

शुक्लक *a*. (*f*. -का) White. —कः *m*. 1 White colour. -2 The bright half of a lunar month.

शुक्लल *a*. (*f*. -ला) White.

शुक्ला *f*. 1 N. of Sarasvati. -2 Candied sugar. -3 A woman having a white complexion.

शुक्लिमन् *m*. Whiteness.

शुक्षिः *m*. 1 Air, wind. -2 Light, lustre. -3 Fire.

शुंगः *m*. 1 The (Indian) fig-tree. -2 The hog-plum. -3 The awn of corn.

शुंगा *f*. 1 The sheath of a young bud. -2 The awn of barley or corn. -3 The waved-leaf-fig.

शुंगिन् *m*. 1 The (Indian) fig-tree. -2 The *Plaksha* tree.

शुच् 1 P. (शोचति) 1 To be sorry, bewail, mourn. -2 To regret, repent. With अनु— To bewail. परि— To bewail.

शुच् 4 U. (शुच्यति,-ते) 1 To be afflicted. -2 To be wet. -3 To shine. -4 To be pure or clean.

शुच्, शुचा *f*. Grief, affliction, distress.

शुचि *a.* 1 Clean, pure, clear. -2 White. -3 Bright. -4 Pious, unsullied. -5 Purified, hallowed. -6 Honest, faithful, true. -7 Correct, accurate. —चिः *m.* 1 The white colour. -2 Purification. -3 Innocence, goodness, uprightness. -4 Correctness, accuracy. -5 The condition of a religious student. -6 A pure man. -7 A Brâhmana. -8 The hot season. -9 The months of Jyeshtha and Ashâdha. -10 A faithful or true friend. -11 The sun. -12 The moon. -13 Fire. -14 The sentiment of love. -15 The planet Venus. -16 The Chitraka tree. -17 N. of Siva. -Comp. —द्रुमः *m.* The sacred fig tree. —मणिः *m.* 1 A crystal. -2 A jewel worn on the head. —मल्लिका *f.* A kind of jasmine (Arabian). —रोचिस् *m.* The moon. —व्रत *a.* Holy, virtuous.

शुचिष्मत् *a.* (*f.* —ती) Bright. —*m.* An epithet of Agni.

शुचिस् *n.* Light, lustre.

शुच्य् 1 P. (शुच्यति) 1 To bathe. -2 To squeeze out (as juice). -3 To distill. -4 To churn.

शुटीरः *m.* A hero.

शुठ् I. 1 P. (शोठति) 1 To be impeded or hindered. -2 To be lame. -3 To resist.

शुठ् 10 U. (शोठयति,-ते) To be idle or dull.

शुंठिः, शुंठी *f.*, शुंठ्यं *n.* Dry ginger.

शुंडः *m.* 1 The juice issuing from the temples of an elephant in rut. -2 An elephant's trunk.

शुंडकः *m.* 1 Distiller. -2 A kind of military musical instrument.

शुंडा *f.* 1 An elephant's trunk. -2 Spirituous liquor. -3 A tavern. -4 The stalk of the lotus. -5 A courtezan, harlot. -6 A bawd, procuress. -Comp.—पानं *n.* A tavern, dram-shop.

शुंडारः *m.* 1 A distiller. -2 An elephant's trunk or proboscis.

शुंडालः *m.* An elephant.

शुंडिका *f.* See शुंडा.

शुंडिन् *m.* 1 A distiller. -2 An elephant.-Comp.-मूषिका *f.* The musk-rat.

शुतुद्रिः, शुतुद्रूः *f.* The river Sutlaj.

शुद्ध *p. p.* (*f.* —द्धा) 1 Pure, clean, purified. 2 Holy, chaste, innocent. -3 Bright -4 Stainless.-5 Innocent, guileless.-6 Genuine, true, upright. -7 Faultless. -8 Cleared, acquitted. -9 Mere, only. -10 Simple, pure, unmixed (opp. मिश्र). -11 Unequalled. -12 Authorized. -13 Whetted, sharpened. -14 Not nasal. —द्धः *m.* An epithet of Siva. —द्धं *n* 1 Anything pure. -2 The pure spirit. -3 Rock-salt.-4 Black pepper.-Comp. —अंतः *m.* A king's female apartments.—अंता *f.* A king's wife, queen. -अपह्नुतिः *f.* A figure of speech.-ओदनः *m.* (शुद्धोदनः) N. of the father of the celebrated Buddha. -कोटिः *f.* One of the sides of a right-angled triangle. —जंघः *m.* An ass.

शुद्धिः *f.* 1 Purity, cleanness. -2 Brightness, lustre. -3 Sanctity, holiness.-4 Purification, atonement. -5 A purificatory or expiatory rite. -6 Paying off (of expenses). -7 Retaliation. -8 Innocence (established by trial). -9 Truth, correctness. -10 Rectification. -11 Subtraction.-12 N. of Durgá.-Comp. —पत्रं *n.* 1 A list of errata or corrigenda. -2 A certificate of purification by penance or atonement.

शुध् 4 P. (शुध्यति, शुद्ध) 1 To become pure or purified (fig. also). -2 To be auspicious or favourable. -3 To be made clear, have the doubts removed.-4 To be defrayed or cleared. With परि-, वि-, or सम्- To be purified.

—*Caus.* (शोधयति,-ते) I To purify, wash off. -2 To clear, pay off (as a debt). -3 To filter.-4 To correct. -5 To acquit.

शुन 6 P. (शुनति) To go, move.

शुनःशेप: (-फः) *m.* N. of a Vedic sage, son of Ajīgarta.

शुनकः *m.* I N. of a sage.-2 A dog. -3 A young dog.

शुनाशी (-सी-)रः *m.* I An epithet of Indra. -2 An owl.

शुनिः *m.* A dog.

शुनी *f.* A female dog, a bitch.

शुनीरः *m.* A number of female dogs.

शुंध् I. 10. U. (शुंधति,-ते, शुंधयति,-ते) I To be purified.-2 To purify.

शुंध्युः *m.* I Air, wind.

शुन्य *a.* See शून्य. शुन्यं *n.* I A number of bitches. -2 A cypher.

शुभ् I A. (शोभते) I To look beautiful or handsome. -2 To appear to advantage. -3 To become or befit (with gen.). -4 To be gay or happy. -5 To be victorious. With वि- To shine.

—*Caus.* (शोभयति,-ते) To decorate, adorn, grace.

शुभ *a.* (*f.* —भा) I Shining, bright. -2 Beautiful, handsome. -3 Auspicious, fortunate.-4 Good, virtuous. -5 Learned, versed in the Vedas. —भं *n.* I Auspiciousness, good fortune, happiness, prosperity. -2 An ornament. -3 A kind of fragrant wood. -Comp. —अक्षः *m.* An epithet of Siva. -अपांगा *f.* A beautiful woman. —आनना *f.* A handsome woman. —आवह *a.* Tending to welfare, conducive to good. -इतर *a.* I Evil, bad.-2 Inauspicious. —उदर्क *a.* Having a happy end. —कर *a.* Auspicious, propitious. —कर्मन् *n.* I A virtuous act.-2 An honourable occupation. -ग *a.* I Elegant, graceful. -2 Propitious, fortunate. —गंधकं *n.* Gum-myrrh. —ग्रहः *m.* An auspicious planet. —द: *m.* The sacred fig-tree. —क्षणः *m.*, -क्षणं *n.* A lucky or auspicious moment. —वासनः *m.* A perfume for the mouth. —स्थली *f.* I A hall in which sacrifices are performed.-2 An auspicious place.

शुभंयु *a.* Auspicious, fortunate, blessed.

शुभंकर *a.* I Auspicious. -2 Promoting happiness.—री *f.* N. of Durgá.

शुभंभावुक *a.* Decorated, ornamented, bright.

शुभा *f.* I Lustre, light. -2 Beauty. -3 Desire. -4 Yellow pigment. -5 The Samí tree. -6 An assembly of Gods. -7 Durvâ grass. -8 Bamboo-manna. -9 The Priyangu creeper.

शुभ्र *a.* (*f.* —भ्रा) I Shining, bright. -2 White. —भ्रः *m.* I The white colour. -2 Sandal. —भ्रं *n.* I Silver. -2 Talc. -3 Rock-salt. -4 Green vitriol. -Comp. —अंशुः, -करः *m.* I The moon. -2 Camphor. -रश्मिः *m.* The moon.

शुभ्रा *f.* I The Ganges. -2 A crystal. -3 Bamboo-manna.

शुभ्रिः *m.* An epithet of Brahman (*m.*).

शुंभः *m.* N. of a demon killed by [Durgà.

शुल्क् 10 U. (शुल्कयति,-ते) I To gain. -2 To pay, give. -3 To create. -4 To tell, narrate. -5 To leave, abandon.

शुल्कः *m.*, शुल्कं *n.* I A toll, tax, duty. -2 Gain, profit. -3 Money advanced to ratify a bargain. -4

Purchase-price (of a girl), money given to the parents of a bride. -5 A nuptial present. -6 Marriage dowry. -7 Present given by the bride-groom to his bride. -Comp. —वंचनं *n*. Defrauding government of its due revenue. [Copper.

शुल्लं *n*. 1 A cord, rope, string. -2

शुल्व्, शुल्ब् 10 U. (शुल्ब-ल्व यति,-ते) 1 To give, bestow. -2 To send away. -3 To measure. -4 To create, produce.

शुल्वं, शुल्बं *n*. 1 A rope, string. -2 Copper. -3 A sacrificial rite or act. -4 A place near water. -5 A rule, law, an institute. —ल्वा, -ल्वी *f*. A rope, string. -Comp. —अरिः *m*. Sulphur. —जं *n*. Brass.

[illegible] *f*. A mother.

शुश्रूषकः *m*. A servant, an attendant.

शुश्रूषणं *n*., शुश्रूषणा *f*. 1 Desire to hear. -2 Service, attendance. -3 Obedience, dutifulness.

शुश्रूषा *f*. 1 Desire to hear. -2 Service, attendance. -3 Dutifulness, obedience. -4 Reverence. -5 Telling, saying.

शुश्रूषु *a*. 1 Desirous to hear. -2 Desirous of serving or attending. -3 Obedient, attentive.

शुष् 4 P. (शुष्यति, शुष्क) 1 To be dried, become dry. -2 To be withered. -3 To languish, be emaciated. -4 To be afflicted or distressed. -With परि— To dry up, to wither. सम् -To be dried up.

Caus. (शोषयति,-ते) 1 To dry up, wither, parch. -2 To emaciate. -3 To destroy. -4 To exhaust, empty.

शुषः *m*., शुषी *f*. 1 Drying, drying up. -2 A hole in the ground.

शुषिः *f*. 1 Drying up. -2 A hole. -3 The hollow in the fang of a snake.

शुषिर *a*. (*f*. -रा) Full of holes, perforated. —रः *m*. 1 Fire. -2 A rat or mouse. —रं *n*. 1 A hole. -2 The atmosphere. -3 A wind-instrument.

शुषिरा *f*. 1 A river. -2 A sort of perfume.

शुषिलः *m*. Air, wind.

शुष्क *p. p*. (*f*. —ष्का) 1 Dry, dried up. -2 Shrivelled, emaciated. -3 Feigned, pretended. -4 Useless, unproductive. -5 Groundless, causeless. -6 Offensive, harsh. -Comp. —अंगी *f*. A lizard. —अन्नं *n*. Rice in the husk. —आर्द्रं *n*. Dry ginger. -व्रणं *n*. A healed wound ; a scar.

शुष्कलः *m*., शुष्कलं *n*. 1 Dried flesh. -2 Flesh in general.

शुष्णः *m*. 1 The sun. -2 Fire.

शुष्मः *m*. 1 The sun. 2 Fire -3 Air, wind. -4 A bird. —ष्मं *n*. 1 Prowess, strength. -2 Light, lustre.

शुष्मन् *m*. 1 Fire. -2 The Chitraka tree. —*n*. 1 Strength, prowess. -2 Light, lustre.

शूकः *m*., शूकं 1 *n*. The awn of barely &c., beard. -2 A bristle. -3 Point, tip, sharp end. -4 Tenderness, compassion. -5 A kind of poisonous insect. -Comp. —धान्यं *n*. Any awned grain, (as barely). —पिंडिः, -पिंडी, -शिंबा, -शिंबिका, -शिंबी *f*. Cowach (कपिकच्छु).

शूककः *m*. 1 A kind of grain. -2 Tenderness, compassion.

शूकरः *m*. A hog. Comp. —इष्टः *m*. A kind of grass (मुस्ता).

शूकलः *m*. A restive horse.

शूद्रः *m*. A man of the fourth or the last of the four principal tribes of Hindus. -Comp. —आर्ता *f*. The Priyangu plant. -आह्निकं *n*. The daily ceremonics of a Súdra. —प्रियः *m*. An onion. —प्रेष्यः *m*. A man of any of the three higher castes who has become a servant to a Súdra. -सेवनं *n.* Being the servant of a Súdra.

शूद्रकः *m.* N. of a king, the reputed author of the Mrichchhakatika.

शूद्रा *f.* A woman of the Súdra tribe. -Comp. —वेदनं *n.* Marrying a Súdra woman.

शूद्राणी, शूद्री *f.* The wife of a Súdra.

शून *p. p.* (*f.* —ना) 1 Swollen. -2 Increased, prospered. -3 Morbidly swollen.

शूना *f.* 1 The soft palate, uvula. -2 A slaughter house.-3 Any piece of household furniture which is likely to destroy life (these are five ; a fire place,a grind-stone,a broom, a mortar, and a water-pot).

शून्य *a.* (*f.* —न्या) 1 Empty, void. -2 Vacant-minded, listless. -3 Non-existent. -4 Lonely, desolate. -5 Dejected, dispirited. -6 Utterly devoid of, without, wanting in (with instr. or in comp.). -7 Indifferent. -8 Guileless. -9 Nonsensical, unmeaning -10 Bare, naked. —न्यं *n.* 1 A vacuum, void. -2 The sky, atmosphere. -3 A cipher, dot. -4 Non-entity, nonexistence. -Comp. —मनस्, -मनस्क *a.* Absent-minded, listless. -मुख, -वदन *a.* Having a downcast countenance. -वादः *m.* The doctrine of a Buddhist sect. —वादिन् *m.* 1 An atheist. -2 A Buddhist. —हृदय *a.* 1 Absent-minded. -2 Open-hearted,unsuspecting.

शून्या *f.* 1 A hollow reed. -2 A barren woman.-3 The prickly pear.

शूर् 10 U. (शूरयति,-ते) 1 To act the hero, to be powerful. -2 To make vigorous exertions.

शूर *a.* (*f.* —रा) Brave, valiant, mighty. —रः *m.* 1 A hero, a valiant man. -2 A lion. -3 A boar. -4 The sun. -5 The Sàla tree. -6 N. of a Yádava.-Comp. -कीटः *m.* A contemptible warrior. —मानं *n.* Arrogance, vaunting. —मानिन् *m.* A boaster. —सेनाः *m. pl.* N. of the country about Mathurá or the inhabitants of that country.

शूरणः *m.* A kind of esculent root.

शूरंमन्य *a.* (*f.* —न्या) One who fancies himself to be a hero.

शूर्पः *m.*,शूर्पं *n.* A winnowing-basket. —र्पः *m.* A measure of two Dronas. -Comp. —कर्णः *m.* An elephant. —णखा (for नखा) *f.* N. of a sister of Ràvana.—वातः *m.* A wind produced by shaking a winnowing-basket. —श्रुतिः *m.* An elephant.

शूर्पी *f.* 1 A small winnowing-basket or fan. -2 N. of Súrpanakhá.

शूर्मः *m.*, शूर्मिः *m.*, *f.*, शूर्मिका, शूर्मी *f.* 1 An iron-image. -2 An anvil.

शूल् 1 P. (शूलति) 1 To be ill. -2 To make a noise.

शूलः *m.*, शूलं *n.* 1 A pike, spear. lance.-2 The trident of Siva.-3 An iron-spit (for roasting meat upon). -4 A stake for impaling criminals. -5 Any acute pain. -6 Colic. -7 Gout, rheumatism. -8 Death. -9 A banner.(शूला कृ 'To roast on an iron-spit '). -Comp. -ग्रंथिः *f.* A kind of Dúrvá grass. —घातनं *n.* Iron-filings. —द्विष् *m.* Asa fœtida. —धन्वन्, —धरः, -धारिन्, -धृक्, -पाणिः,-भृत् *m.* Epithets of Siva. -शत्रुः *m.* The castor-oil plant. —हंत्री *f.* A kind of barley. -हस्तः *m.* A lancer. -हृत् *m.* Asa fœtida.

शूलकः *m.* A restive horse.

शूला *f.* 1 A stake for impaling criminals. -2 A harlot.

शूलाकृतं *n.* Roasted meat.

शूलिक *a.* (*f.*—का) 1 Having a pike. -2 Roasted on a spit. -कः *m.* A hare. -कं *n*. Roasted meat.

शूलिन् *a*. (*f*. -नी) 1 Armed with a spear. -2 Suffering from colic. -*m*. 1 A spearman. -2 A hare. -3 N. of Siva.

शूलिकः *m*. The (Indian) fig tree.

शूल्य *a*. (*f*. -ल्या) 1 Roasted on a spit. -2 Deserving impalement. -ल्यं *n*. Roasted meat.

शूष् 1 P. (शूषति) 1 To beget. -2 To bring forth.

शृकालः *m*. A jackal. See शृगाल below.

शृगालः *m*. 1 A jackal. -2 A cheat, swindler. -3 A coward. -4 An ill-natured man. -5 N. of Krishna. -Comp. -जंबुः, -जंबूः *f*. A kind of cucumber. -रूपः *m*. An epithet of Śiva.

शृगालिका, शृगाली *f*. 1 A female jackal. -2 A fox. -3 Flight, retreat.

शृंखलः *m*., -ला *f*., -लं *n*. 1 An iron-chain, fetter. -2 A fetter in general (fig. also). -3 A chain for tying the feet of an elephant. -4 A chain worn round the waist. -5 A measuring chain. -6 A chain, series, succession.

शृंखलकः *m*. A chain. -2 A camel.

शृंखलित *a*. (*f*. —ता) Chained, fettered.

शृंगं *n*. 1 A horn. -2 The summit of a mountain. -3 The top of a building, turret. -4 Elevation, height. -5 Lordship, supremacy. -6 A horn of the moon. -7 A point or projection in general. -8 A horn used for blowing. -9 A syringe. -10 Rising of desire. -11 A mark, sign. -12 A lotus. -13 A fountain of water. -Comp. -उच्चयः *m*. A lofty summit. -जः *m*. An arrow. (-जं *n*.) Aloe-wood. —प्रियः *m*. An epithet of Siva. —मोहिन् *m*. The Champaka tree. —वेरं *n*. 1 N. of a town. -2 Ginger. —वेरकं *n*. Ginger.

शृंगकः *m*., शृंगकं *n*. 1 A horn. -2 A horn of the moon. -3 Any pointed thing. -4 A syringe.

शृंगवत् *m*. A mountain.

शृंगाटः *m*. 1 N. of a mountain. -2 N. of a plant. —टं *n*. A place where four roads meet.

शृंगाटकः *m*. A mountain with three peaks. —कं *n*. 1 A place where four roads meet. -2 A door.

शृंगारः *m*. 1 The sentiment of love, the erotic sentiment. -2 Love, sexual love. -3 A dress suited to amorous interviews. -4 Sexual union. -5 Marks made with red-lead on the body of an elephant. -6 A mark in general. —रं *n* 1 Clove, -2 Red-lead. -3 Undried ginger. -4 A fragrant powder for the dress or body. -5 Agallochum. -Comp. —भूषणं *n*. Red-lead. —योनिः *m*. An epithet of the God of love. —रसः *m*. The sentiment of love. —विधिः, —वेशः *m*. A dress suited for amorous purposes. —सहायः *m*. An assistant in love-affairs.

शृंगारकः *m*. Love. —कं *n*. Red-lead.

शृंगारित *a*. (*f*. —ता) 1 Affected by love. -2 Adorned.

शृंगारिन् *m*. 1 An impassioned lover. -2 A ruby. -3 An elephant. -4 Dress, decoration. -5 A preparation of betel-leaves and pieces of areca-nut.

शृंगिः *m*. Gold for ornaments. —*f*. The sheat-fish.

शृंगिकं *n*. A kind of poison.

शृंगिणः *m*. A ram.

शृंगिणी *f*. 1 A cow. -2 The Arabian jasmine.

शृंगिन् *a*. (*f*. —णी) 1 Horned. -2 Crested, peaked. —*m*. 1 A mountain. -2 An elephant. -3 A ram. -4 A tree. -5 N. of Siva. -6 N. of one of Siva's attendants.

शृंगि *f.* 1 Gold used for ornaments. -2 A kind of poison. -3 The sheat-fish. -Comp. —कनकं *n.* Gold used for ornaments.

शृणिः *f.* A hook for goading an elephant, a goad. [Boiled.

शृत *p. p.* (*f.* —ता) 1 Cooked. -2

शृध् 1 A. (But Paras. also in the Second Future, Aorist, and Conditional) (शर्धते) To break wind downwards.

शृध् 1 U. (शर्धति,-ते) 1 To moisten, wet. -2 To cut off.

शृध् 10 U. (शर्धयति,-ते) 1 To strive. -2 To take, grasp. -3 To mock, ridicule.

शृधुः *m.*, *f.* 1 Intellect. -2 The anus.

शॄ 9 P. (शृणाति, शीर्ण) 1 To tear to pieces. -2 To hurt, injure. -3 To kill, destroy. —*Pass.* (शीर्यते) 1 To be shattered. -2 To wither, waste away. -With अव- or वि- To seize away.

शेखरः *m.* 1 A crest, chaplet, a garland of flowers worn on the head. -2 A diadem, crown. -3 A summit. -4 The best or most distinguished of a class (at the end of comp.). -5 A kind of *Dhruva* or burden of a song. —रं *n.* Cloves.

शेपः *m.*, शेपस् *n.*, शेफः *m.*, शेफं *n.*, शेफस् *n.* 1 The penis. -2 A testicle. -3 A tail. [plant.

शेफालिः, -ली, शेफालिका *f.* A kind of

शेमुषी *f.* Intellect, understanding.

शेवः *m.* 1 The penis. -2 A snake. -3 Height, elevation. -4 Happiness. -5 Wealth, treasure. —वं *n.* 1 The penis. -2 Happiness.-Comp. —निधिः *m.* A valuable treasure.

शेवलं *n.* 1 The green moss-like substance growing on the surface of water. -2 A kind of plant.

शेवलिनी *f.* A river.

शेवालं *n.* See शेवलं.

शेष *a.* (*f.*-षा) Remaining, rest, all the other. —षः *m.*, -षं *n.* 1 Remainder, residue. -2 Anything left out or omitted to be said. —षः *m.* 1 Result, effect. -2 End, conclusion. -3 Death, destruction. -4 N. of a celebrated serpent, having one thousand heads. -5 N. of Balaráma. -6 An elephant. -षा *f.* The remains of offerings made to an idol. —षं *n.* The remnants of food, remains of an offering. (शेषे is used adverbially in the sense of 1 'At last', 'finally'. -2 In other cases. —Comp. —अवस्था *f.* Old age. —रात्रिः *f.* The last watch of the night. —शयनः, —शायिन् *m.* Epithets of Vishnu.

शैक्षः *m.* 1 A student who studies Sikshâ or the science of prouncia-tion. -2 (Hence) A novice, tyro.

शैक्षिकः *m.* One skilled in Sikshá.

शैक्ष्यं *n.* Learning, proficiency.

शैघ्र्यं *n.* Quickness, rapidity.

शैत्यं *n.* Cold, frigidity.

शैथिल्यं *n.* 1 Looseness, laxity.. -2 Slackness.-3 Dilatoriness, inattention.

शैनेयः *m.* N. of Sátyaki. [Sini.

शैन्याः *m. pl.* The descendants of

शैब्यः *m.* See शैव्यः.

शैलः *m.* 1 A mountain, hill. -2 A dike, dam. -3 A rock, big stone. -जं *n.* 1 Borax, benzoin. -2 Bitumen. -3 A kind of collyrium. -Comp. -अग्रः *m.* N. of a country. —अटः *m.* 1 A mountaineer, a barbarian. -2 An attendant on an idol. -3 A lion. -4 A crystal. —आधिपः, -अधिराजः, -इन्द्रः,

—पतिः, –राजः *m*. Epithets of the Himâlaya. —आख्यं *n*. 1 Benzoin. -2 A fragrant resinous substance. —गंधं *n*. A kind of sandal. —जं *n*. 1 Benzoin. -2 Bitumen. —जा, –तनया, –पुत्री, –सुता *f*. Epithets of Pârvatî. —धन्वन् *m*. An epithet of Siva. —धरः *m*. An epithet of Krishna.—निर्यासः *m*. Benzoin. —पत्रः *m*. The Bilva tree.–भित्तिः *f*. An instrument for cutting stones. —रंध्रं *n*. A cave, cavern.–बीजं *n*. The marking-nut plant. —शिबिरं *n*. The ocean. —सार *a*. As strong as a mountain.

शैलर्कं *n*. 1 Benzoin. -2 Bitumen.

शैलादिः *m*. N. of Nandin, Siva's attendant.

शैलाकिन् *m*. An actor, a dancer.

शैलिक्यः *m*. A hypocrite, an impostor, a cheat.

शैली *f*. 1 A short explanation of a grammatical aphorism. -2 A mode of interpretation. -3 Behaviour, conduct, course.

शैलूषः *m*. 1 An actor, a dancer. -2 A musician.-3 One who beats time at a concert. -4 A rogue. -5 The *Bilva* tree.

शैलूषिकः *m*. One who follows the profession of an actor. —की *f*. An actress.

शैलेय *a*. (*f*. –यी) 1 Mountainous.-2 Produced from rocks.-3 Mountain-like, hard. –यः *m*. 1 A lion. -2 A bee. –यं *n*. 1 Benzoin. -2 Fragrant resin. -3 Rock-salt. —यी *f*. N. of Pârvatì.

शैल्यं *n*. Rockiness, hardness.

शैव *a*. (*f*. –वी) Relating to the God Siva. —वः *m*. 1 N. of one of the three principal Hindu sects. -2 A member of the Saiva sect. —वं *n*. N. of one of the eighteen Purânas.

शैवलः *m*. A kind of aquatic plant, moss. —लं *n*. A kind of fragrant wood.

शैवलिनी *f*. A river.

शैवालं *n*. See शैवलः.

शैव्यः *m*. 1 N. of one of the four horses of Krishna. -2 N. of a warrior in the Pándava army. -3 A horse (in general).

शैशवं *n*. Childhood, infancy.

शैशिर *a*. (*f*. –री) Belonging to the cold or dewy season. –रः *m*. A kind of Châtaka bird.

शैष्योपाध्यायिका *f*. Instruction or tuition of young pupils.

शो 4 P. (श्यति, शात or शित, *pass*. शायते; *caus*. शाययति) 1 To sharpen, whet. -2 To make thin, attenuate.

शोकः *m*. Sorrow, distress, affliction, lamentation, deep anguish. -Comp. –अपनोदः *m*. Removal of grief.–आरः *m*. The Kadamba tree. —चर्या *f*. Indulgence in grief. —नाशः *m*. The Asoka tree. —परायण, –लासक *a*. Engrossed in grief; wholly given up to grief.

शोचनं *n*. Grief, sorrow, mourning.

शोचनीय *a*. (*f*. —या) Lamentable, mournful.

शोच्य *a*. (*f*. —च्या) 1 To be lamented or mourned; pitiable. -2 Vile, wicked.

शोचिस् *n*. 1 Light, lustre. -2 A flame. -Comp. —केशः (शोचिष्केशः) *m*. An epithet of fire.

शोटीर्यं *n*. Valour, heroism.

शोठ *a*. (*f*. –ठा) 1 Foolish. -2 Low, wicked. -3 Idle, lazy. —ठः *m*. 1 A fool. -2 An idler.-3 A low or wicked man. -4 A rogue, cheat.

शोण् 1 P. (शोणति) 1 To go, move. -2 To become red.

शोण *a*. (*f*.–णा or –णी) Red, crimson. —णः *m*. 1 The red colour. -2 Fire.

-3 A kind of red sugar-cane. -4 A bay horse. -5 N. of a male river, falling into the Ganges near Pâtaliputra. -6 The planet Mars. —णं n. 1 Blood. -2 Red lead. -Comp. —अंबुः m. N. of a cloud which would rise at the destruction of the world. -अश्मन्, -उपलः m. 1 A red stone. -2 A ruby. —पद्मं n. A red lotus. -रत्नं n. A ruby.

शोणित a. (f. —ता) 1 Red, purple crimson.—णं n. 1 Blood.-2 Saffron. -Comp. —आह्वयं n. Saffron. —उपलः m. A ruby. -चंदनं n. Red sandal. -पुरं n. N. of the city of the demon Bâna.

शोणिमन् m. Redness.

शोथः m. Swelling, intumescence. -Comp. - रोगः m. Dropsy. —हृत् m. The marking-nut plant.

शोधः m. 1 Purification. -2 Correction, rectification. -3 Acquittance, (as of debts). -4 Retaliation, requital.

शोधक a. (f.-का or -धिका) 1 Purificatory. -2 Purgative. -3 Corrective. —कः m. 1 A purifier. -2 (In arith. and alg.) The subtrahend. —कं n. A kind of earth.

शोधन a. (f. —नी) Purifying.-नं n. 1 Purifying, cleansing, washing (as of a wound). -2 Correction. -3 Exact determination. -4 Payment, acquittance. -5 Atonement. -6 Refining of metals. -7 Retaliation, requital, punishment. -8 Subtraction (in math.) -9 Green vitriol. -10 Feces, ordure. -नः m. The lime.

शोधनकः m. An officer in a criminal court.

शोधनी f. A broom.

शोधित p. p. (f. —ता) 1 Purified, cleansed. -2 Refined. -3 Filtered. -4 Corrected. -5 Paid off. -6 Requited, retaliated. -7 Acqitted, absolved.

शोध्यः m. An accused person; one who has to answer a charge brought against him.

शोफः m. Swelling, tumour, intumescence. -Comp. —जित्, -हृत् m. The marking-nut plant.

शोभन a. (f. -नी) 1 Shining, beautiful, auspicious, fortunate. -2 Richly decorated. -3 Moral, virtuous. —नः m. 1 N. of Siva. -2 A planet. -3 A burnt offering for the production of happy results. —ना f. 1 Turmeric. -2 A beautiful or virtuous woman. -3 A sort of yellow pigment (गोरोचना). —नं n. 1 Beauty, lustre, brilliance. -2 A lotus.

शोभा f. 1 Light, brilliance, radiance. -2 Splendour, beauty. -3 Natural beauty, grandeur (as of a mountain). -4 Turmeric. -5 A kind of pigment. -Comp. -अंजनः m. N. of a tree. [-2 Beautiful.

शोभित p. p. (f. -ता) 1 Adorned.

शोषः m. Drying up, dryness. -2 Emaciation, withering up. -3 Pulmonary consumption or consumption in general -Comp. —संभवं n. The root of long pepper.

शोषण a. (f. -णी) 1 Drying up. -2 Causing to wither up. —णः m. N. of one of the arrows of Cupid. —णं n. 1 Drying up. -2 Sucking up, absorption.-3 Exhaustion. -4 Emaciation, withering up.-5 Dry ginger.

शोषित p. p. (f. —ता) 1 Dried up. -2 Emaciated, withered up. -3 Exhausted.

शौकं n. A flock of parrots.

शौक्त a. (f. —क्ती) Acid, acetic.

शौक्तिक a. (f. —की) 1 Relating to a pearl. -3 Acid, acetic.

शौक्तिकेयं, शौक्तियं n. A pearl.

शौक्र a. (f. —क्री) Seminal.

शौक्लिकेयः m. A sort of poison.

शौक्ल्यं n. Whiteness, clearness.

शौचं n. 1 Purity, clearness.-2 Purification from defilement caused by voiding excrement, but particularly by the death of a relative. -3 Cleansing, purifying. -4 Evacuation of excrement. -5 Uprightness, honesty. -Comp. —आचारः m., —कर्मन् n.—कल्पः m. A purificatory rite.-कूपः m. A privy.

शौचेयः m. A washer-man.

शौटीर a (f.— रा) Proud, haughty. -रः m. 1 A hero, a champion. -2 A proud man. -3 An ascetic. -4 An upstart.

शौटीर्यं n. 1 Arrogance, haughtiness. -2 Prowess, heroism.

शौंड a. (f. —डी) 1 Addicted to drinking. -2 Excited, intoxicated. (fig.).-2 Skilled in (with loc. or in comp., as in अक्षशौंड, दानशौंड. &c.).

शौंडर्यं n. Pride, arrogance.

शौंडिकः, शौंडिन् m. A distiller and seller of spirituous liquors. —की, -नी f. A female vintner.

शौंडिकेयः m. A demon.

शौंडी f. Long pepper.

शौंडीर a. (f. -रा) 1 Proud, haughty. -2 Elevated.

शौद्धोदनिः m. An epithet of Buddha, son of शुद्धोदन.

शौद्र a. (f. -द्री) 1 Relating to a Súdra or his tribe. —द्रः m. The son of a man of any of the first three castes by a Sudra woman.

शौनं n. Meat kept at a slaughter-house.

शौनकः m. N. of a great sage, the reputed author of the Rigveda Prátisákhya.

शौनिकः m. 1 A butcher. -2 A bird catcher, hunter. -3 Hunting, chase.

शौभः m. 1 God, divinity. -2 The betel-nut tree.

शौभांजनः m. N. of the शोभांजन tree.

शौभिकः m. 1 A juggler, conjurer. -2 A hunter, fowler.

शौरसेनी f. N. of a Prákrita dialect.

शौरिः m. 1 N. of Vishnu or Krishna.-2 Of Balarâma.-3 The planet Saturn.

शौर्यं n. 1 Heroism, valour. -2 Strength, might. -3 Representation of supernatural events on the stage.

शौल्कः, शौल्किकः m. A superintendent of tolls; a custom-officer.

शौल्विकः (-ल्बि-)कः m. A copper-smith.

शौवन a. (f. -नी) Canine. -नं n. 1 The nature of a dog. -2 The progeny of a dog.

शौवस्तिक a. (f. —की) Belonging to or lasting till to-morrow.

शौष्कलः m. A vendor of flesh —लं n. The price of dried meat.

श्चुत् 1 P. (श्चोतति) To ooze, trickle, exude.

श्च्युत् 1 P. (श्च्योतति) 1 To trickle, ooze, flow. -2 To shed, scatter. -With नि— To flow, ooze, trickle.

श्चो (-श्चो-) तः m., श्चो (-श्च्यो-) तनं n. Oozing, flowing, exuding.

श्मशानं n. A cemetery. -Comp. —निवासिन्, —वर्तिन्, -वासिन् m. A ghost. —भाज्, —वासिन् m. Epithets of Siva. —वेश्मन् m. 1 An epithet of Siva. -2 A spirit, ghost.-वैराग्यं n. Temporary despondency.

श्मश्रु n. The beard. -Comp. -मुखी f. A woman with a beard. —वर्धकः m. A barber.

श्मश्रुक a. (f. -का) Having a beard, bearded.

श्मील् 1 P. (श्मीलति) To wink, contract the eyelids.

श्यान *p. p.* (*f.* —ना) 1 Gone, -2 Congealed. -3 Thick, viscous. -4 Shrunk, dry. —नं *n.* Smoke.

श्याम *a.* (*f.* —मा) 1 Black, dark-coloured.-2 Shady,dusky. -3 Dark-green. —मः *m.* 1 The black colour. -2 The green colour. -3 A cloud.-4 The cuckoo. -5 N. of a sacred fig-tree at Allahabad. —मं *n.* 1 Sea-salt. -2 Black pepper. -Comp. —अंगः *m.* The planet Mercury. -कंठः *m.* 1 An epithet of Siva. -2 A peacock. -कर्णः *m.* A horse suitable for a horse-sacrifice.—पत्रः *m.* The *tamâla* tree. —सुंदरः *m.* An epithet of Krishna.

श्यामल *a.* (*f.* -ला) Black, blackish. -लः *m.* 1 Black colour.-2 Black pepper. -3 A large bee. -4 The sacred fig-tree. -ला *f.* N. of Durgâ.

श्यामालिका *f.* The indigo plant.

श्यामालिमन् *m.* Blackness.

श्यामा *f.* 1 Night, particularly a dark night. -2 Shade, shadow. -3 A dark woman. -4 A kind of woman. -5 A woman who has borne no children.-6 A cow.-7 Turmeric. -8 The female cuckoo. -9 The Priyangu creeper. -10 The indigo plant. -11 The holy basil. -12 The seed of the lotus. -13 N. of the Yamunâ.

श्यामाकः *m.* A kind of grain or [corn.

श्यामाय् Den. A. To become black.

श्यामिका *f.* 1 Blackness, darkness. -2 Impurity, alloy (of metals &c.).

श्यालः *m.* A wife's brother.

श्यालकः *m.* A wife's brother. -2 A wretched brother-in-law.

श्यालकी, श्यालिका, श्याली *f.* A wife's sister.

श्याव *a.* (*f.* —वा or —वी) 1 Dark-brown, dusky.-2 Bay, brown.—वः *m.* The brown colour. -Comp. -तैलः *m.* The mango tree.

श्येत *a.* (*f.*-ता or -नी) White -तः *m.* The white colour.

श्येनः *m.* The white colour. -2 Whiteness. -3 A hawk, falcon. -4 Violence. -Comp. —करणं *n.*,-करणिका *f.* 1 Burning on a separate funeral pile. -2 A rash and desperate act.

श्यै 1 A. (श्यायते, श्यान, शित or शीन) 1 To go, move. -2 To be congealed or coagulated. -3 To dry up, wither.

श्येनंपाता *f.* Hawking, hunting, [chase.

श्योणाकः, श्योनाकः *m.* N of a tree.

श्रण् 1 P., 10 U. (श्रणति, श्राणयति,-ते) To give, bestow, usually with वि.

श्रत् *ind.* A prefix used with the root धा. To believe, have faith in.

श्रथ् 1. 9. P. (श्रथति, श्रथ्नाति) To hurt, injure, kill.

श्रथ् 1 P., 10 U. (श्रथति, श्राथयति,-ते) 1 To hurt, kill.-2 To untie, loosen. liberate, release.

श्रथ् 10 U. (श्रथयति,-ते) 1 To make efforts. -2 To be infirm. -3 To be glad.

श्रद्धा *f.*1 Trust, belief, confidence. -2 Belief in divine revelation. -3 Respect, reverence. -4 Strong or vehement desire. -5 Respect, reverence.

श्रद्धालु *a.* 1 Believing, full of faith. -2 Desirous, longing or wishing for (anything). —लुः *f.* A pregnant woman longing for anything.

श्रंथ् 1 A. (श्रंथते) 1 To be weak. -2 To be loose or relaxed.-3 To be loosened.

श्रंथ् 9 P. (श्रथ्नाति) 1 To be loosen. release. -2 To delight repeatedly.

श्रंथः *m.* 1 Loosening.-2 Looseness. -3 Tying together.-4 N. of Vishnu.

श्रपणं *n.*, श्रपणा *f.* Causing to boil.

boiling, seething.

श्रपित *p. p.* (*f.* —ता) Boiled or caused to be boiled. -2 Seethed.

श्रम् 4 P. (श्राम्यति, श्रांत) 1 To exert oneself, toil, labour.-2 To perform austerities. -3 To be wearied. -4 To be afflicted or distressed.

श्रमः *m.* 1 Toil, labour, effort. -2 Weariness, exhaustion. -3 Affliction. -4 Penance. -5 Exercise. -6 Military exercise, drill. -7 Hard study. -Comp. —स्थानं *n.* A drill-ground, gymnasium &c.

श्रमण *a.* (*f.*-णा, -णी) 1 Labouring. toiling. -2 Low, base, vile. —णः *m.* 1 An ascetic, a devotee. -2 A Buddhist ascetic. -3 A beggar. —णा, -णी *f.* 1 A female devotee or mendicant.-2 A handsome woman. -3 A woman of low caste. -4 Bengal madder.

श्रंभ् 1 A. (श्रंभते, श्रब्ध) 1 To be careless or inattentive. -2 To err. With वि— To confide in. [asylum.

श्रयः *m.*, श्रयणं *n.* Refuge, shelter,

श्रवः *m.* 1 Hearing. -2 The ear.-3 The hypothenuse of a triangle.

श्रवणः *m.*, -णं *n.* 1 The ear. -2 The hypothenuse of a triangle. —णः *m.*, -णा *f.* 1 N. of a lunar mansion containing three stars. —णं *n.* 1 The act of hearing. -3 Fame, glory. -4 That which is heard or revealed, the Veda. -Comp. —इंद्रियं *n.* The organ of hearing; the ear. —उदरं *n.* The hollow of the outer ear. —गोचर *a.* Within the range of hearing. (—रः *m.*) Ear-shot, as in श्रवणगोचरे तिष्ठ. —पथः, -विषयः *m.* The reach or range of the ear.—पालिः, -पाली *f.* The tip of the ear. —पाशः *m.* A beautiful ear. [Wealth.

श्रवस् *n.* 1 The ear. -2 Fame. -3

श्रवस्यं *n.* Fame, glory, renown.

श्रवाय्यः, —य्यः *m.* An animal fit for sacrifice.

श्रविष्ठा *f.* N. of a lunar asterism, also called *Dhanishthâ.* -2 The asterism called श्रवणा. -Comp. —जः *m.* The planet Mercury.

श्रा 2 P. (श्राति, श्राण or श्रात) 1 To cook, boil, ripen. -2 To sweat or cause to sweat, heat.

श्राण *a.* (*f.*-णा) 1 Cooked, dressed, boiled. -2 Wet, moist.

श्राणा *f.* Rice gruel.

श्राद्ध *a.* (*f.* —द्धा) Faithful, believing.—द्धं *n.* 1 A funeral rite or ceremony performed in honour of dead relatives.-2 An obsequial oblation. -Comp. —कृत *m.* The performer of a funeral rite. —दः *m.* The offerer of a Sráddha or funeral oblation —दिनः *m.*, -दिनं *n.* The anniversary of the death of a relative in whose honour a Srâddha is performed. —देवः *m.*, -देवता *f.* A deity presiding over funeral rites. -2 An epithet of Yama.-3 A Visvadeva, a deceased ancestor. —भुज्, -भोक्तृ *m.* A deceased ancestor.

श्राद्धिक *a.* (*f.* -की) Relating to a Sráddha. —कः *m.* The recipient of an obsequial offering. —कं *n.* A present given at a Sráddha.

श्राद्धीय *a.* (*f.* —या) Relating to a Srâddha.

श्रांत *p. p.* (*f.* —ता) 1 Wearied, fatigued. -2 Calmed, tranquil —तः *m.* An ascetic.

श्रांतिः *f.* Fatigue, weariness.

श्रामः *m.* 1 A month. -2 Time. -3 A temporary shed.

श्रायः *m.* Shelter, asylum.

श्रावः *m.* Hearing, listening.

श्रावकः *m.* 1 A hearer. -2 A pupil

disciple. -3 A class of Buddhist saints or votaries. -4 A Buddhist votary in general. -5 A crow.

श्रावण *a.* (*f.* -णी) 1 Relating to the ear.-2 Born under the asterism Srâvana. —णः *m.* 1 N. of a lunar month (July-August). -2 A heretic. -3 An impostor. -4 N. of a Vaisya ascetic.

श्रावणिक *a.* (*f.* —का) Relating to the month Srâvana. -कः *m.* The month Srávana.

श्रावणी *f.* 1 The day of full moon in Srávana. -2 N. of a certain annual ceremony performed on this day.

श्रावस्तिः, -स्ती *f.* N. of a city founded by king Srâvasta.

श्रि 1 U. (श्रियति,-ते ; श्रयितुं, श्रितं, *caus.* श्राययति,-ते) 1 To go to, approach. -2 To reach, undergo, assume (as a state). -3 To cling to, depend on. -4 To dwell in, inhabit. -5 To worship. With अधि— To ascend. आ— 1 To take refuge with. -2 To enter. -3 To undergo, assume, to take. -4 To follow. -5 To choose. -6 To inhabit. -7 To depend upon.-8 To use. उद्-To raise. सम्— 1 To have recourse to. -2 To depend on. -3 To obtain. -4 To see. उप— To request.

श्रित *p. p.* (*f.* -ता) 1 Gone to, approached for refuge or protection. -2 Resting or sitting on. -3 United with. -4 Protected. -5 Honoured.served.-6 Subservient,auxiliary. -7 Covered with, overspread. -8 Contained. -9 Assembled.-10 Having, possessing.

श्रितिः *f.* Resort, recourse,approch.

श्रियंमन्य *a.* 1 Thinking oneself worthy. 2 Proud. [also श्रियावासिन्.

श्रियांपतिः *m.* An epithet of Siva.

श्रिष् 1 P. (श्रेषति) To burn.

श्री 9 U. (श्रीणाति, श्रीणीते) To cook, dress, boil.

श्रीः *f.* 1 Wealth, riches, prosperity, plenty. -2 Royalty, majesty. -3 Dignity. -4 Beauty, splendour. -5 Colour, aspect. -6 The goddess of wealth, Lakshmí. -7 Any virtue or excellence. -8 Decoration. -9 Intellect, understanding. -10 Superhuman power. -11 The three objects of human existence taken collectively (धर्म, अर्थ and काम). -12 The Sarala tree.-13 The Bilva tree. -14 Cloves. -15 A lotus. -16 Fame, glory. —*m.* N. of one of the six *Rágas* or musical modes. (The word श्री is often used as an honorific prefix to the names of deities and eminent persons *e. g.* श्रीकृष्णः, श्रीरामः, श्रीवाल्मीकिः, श्रीजयदेवः. Also to the names of celebrated works, generally of a sacred character *e. g.* श्रीभागवत, श्रीरामायण &c. It is also used as an auspicious sign at the commencement of letters, manuscripts &c.-Comp.-आह्वं *n.* A lotus. —ईशः *m.* An epithet of Vishnu.-कंठः *m.* An epithet of Siva. -2 Of the poet Bhavabhúti. —करं *n.* Red lotus. —करणं *n.* A pen. —कांतः *m.* An epithet of Vishnu. —कारः *m.* The word 'श्री' written at the top of a letter. —कारिन् *m.* A kind of antelope. —खंडः *m.*, —खंडं *n.* Sandalwood. —गदितं *n.* A kind of minor drama.—गर्भः 1 *m.* An epithet of Vishnu. -2 A sword.-ग्रहः *m.* A trough or place for watering birds. —घनं *n.* Sour curds. (—नः *m.*) Buddhist saint. —चक्रं *n.* 1 The circle of the earth; the globe. -2 A wheel of Indra's car. —जः *m.* An epithet of Kâma. —दः *m.* An epithet of Kubera. —द्रविनः, -धरः *m.* Epithets of Vishnu. —नगरं *n.* N. of a city. -नंदनः *m.* An epithet of Káma. —निकेतनः, —निवासः *m.* Epithets of Vishnu. —पतिः *m.* 1 An epithet of Vishnu. -2. A king, sovereign. —पथः *m.* A main road. —पर्णं *n.* A lotus. —पर्वतः *m.* N. of a mountain. —पिष्टः *m.* Turpentine. —पुष्पं *n.* Cloves. —फलः *m.* The *Bilva* tree. (—लं *n.*) The *Bilva* fruit. —फला, -फली *f.* 1 The indigo plant. -2 Emblic myrobalan. —भ्रातृ *m.* 1 The moon. -2 A horse. -मस्तकः *m.* Garlic. —मुद्रा *f.* A particular mark on the forehead by the Vaishnavas. —मूर्तिः *f.* 1 An idol. —युक्त, -युत *a.* 1 Fortunate, happy.-2 Wealthy, prosperous. -3 Famous, illustrious. —रंगः *m* An epithet of Vishnu. —रसः *m.* 1 Turpentine. -2 Resin. —वत्सः *m.* 1 An epithet of Vishnu. -2 A mark or curl of hair on the breast of Vishnu. —वत्सांकिन् *m.* A horse having a curl of hair on his breast. —वल्लभः *m.* A favourite of fortune, a happy or fortunate person —वासः *m.* 1 An epithet of Vishnu. -2 Of Siva. -3 A lotus. -4 Turpentine. —वासस् *m.* Turpentine. —वृक्षः *m.* 1 The *Bilva* tree. -2 The Asvattha or sacred fig-tree. -3 A curl of hair on the breast and forehead of a horse. —वेष्टः *m.* 1 Turpentine.-2 Resin.-संज्ञं *n.* Cloves. —सहोदरः *m.* The moon. —सूक्तं *n.* N. of a Vedic hymn. —हरिः *m.* An epithet of Vishnu. —हस्तिनी *f.* The sun-flower.

श्रीमत् *a.* (*f.* —ती) Wealthy, rich. -2 Fortunate,prosperous.-3 Beautiful. -4 Famous, dignified. -5 A title applied to any venerable person. -*m.* 1 An epithet of Vishnu. -2 Of Kubera. -3 Of Siva. -4 The *Tilaka* tree. -5 The Asvattha tree.

श्रील *a.* (*f.* -ला) 1 Rich, wealthy. -2 Fortunate,prosperous.-3 Beautiful. -4 Famous.

श्रु 1 P. (श्रवति) To go, move.

श्रु 5 P. (शृणोति, श्रोतुं, श्रुत) 1 To hear, listen to. -2 To learn, study. -3 To obey. (इति श्रूयते 'It is so heard', *i. e.* is enjoined in the scriptures). With अनु- 1 To hear. अभि— To listen to, hear. आ— To promise. उप— 1 To hear. -2 To learn from. प्रति— To promise. सम्— To hear.

Caus. (श्रावयति,-ते) To cause to hear, tell, relate, inform.

Desid. (शुश्रूषते) 1 To wish to hear. -2 To be attentive to, to obey. -3 To serve; wait or attend upon.

श्रुत *p. p.* (*f.* -ता) 1 Heard, listened to. -2 Heard of. -3 Learnt, ascertained, understood. -4 Famous, renowned. -5 Named, called. —तं *n.* 1 That which was heard by revelation *i. e.* the Veda. -2 Learning in general. -Comp. —अन्वित *a.* Conversant with the Vedas. —अर्थः *m.* A fact verbally or orally communicated. —कीर्ति *a.* Famous, renowned.(-र्तिः *m.*) 1 A generous man.-2 A divine sage.(-*f.*) N. of the wife of Satrughna. —देवी *f.* N. of Sarasvatî. —श्रवस् *m.* N. of the father of Sisupâla.

श्रुतवत् *a.* (*f.* —ती) Knowing the Veda; learned in the Vedic lore.

श्रुतिः *f.* 1 Hearing. -2 The ear. -3 Rumour, news. -4 A sound in general. -5 The Veda. -6 A Vedic or sacred text. -7 (In music) A quarter tone or interval. -8 The constellation Sravana. -9 The diagonal of a tetragon; the hypothenuse of a triangle. -Comp. —अनुप्रासः *m.* A kind of alliteration. —कटः *m.* 1 A snake. -2 A penance, expiation. —चोदनं *n.*, -ना *f.* A scriptural injunction. —जीविका *f.* A law-book or code of laws. -निदर्शनं *n.* Evidence of the Vedas. —पथः *m.* The range of the ear. —प्रामाण्यं *n.* Authority or sanction of the Vedas.—मंडलं *n.* The outer ear.-मूलं *n.* 1 The root of the ear. -2 A Vedic text. —वर्जित *a.* 1 Deaf. -2 Not knowing the Vedas. —विषयः *m.* 1 The object of the organ of hearing. *i. e.* sound. -2 The reach or range of the ear. -3 The subject-matter of the Veda. -4 Any sacred ordinance. —स्मृती *f. dual* Revelation and legal institutes, Veda and law.

श्रुवः *m.* A sacrifice.

श्रुवा *f.* A sacrificial ladle.-Comp. —वृक्षः *m.* The *Vikankata* tree.

श्रेढी *f.* A progression (in math). -Comp. —फलं *n.* The sum of a progression.

श्रेणिः *m.*, *f.*, श्रेणी *f.* 1 A line, row. -2 A multitude, group. -3 A company of traders, artisans &c., a corporate body. -4 A bucket. -Comp. —धर्माः *m. pl.* The customs of trades or guilds.

श्रेणिका *f.* A tent.

श्रेधी *f.* 1 A succession of distinct things. -2 (In math.) Progression. -3 Sequence.

श्रेयस् *a.* 1 Better, preferable, superior. -2 Most excellent. -3 More happy or fortunate.-4 More blessed, dearer (compar. of प्रशस्य). *-n.* 1 Virtue, righteous deeds. -2 Bliss, good fortune, welfare. -3 Any good or auspicious occasion. -4 Final beatitude. -Comp.—अर्थिन *a.* 1 Seeking happiness. -2 Wishing well. —कर *a.* 1 Promoting happiness. -2 Propitious, auspicious.

श्रेष्ठ *a.* (*f.*—ष्ठा) 1 Best, pre-eminent. -2 Most happy or prosperous. -3 Most beloved. -4 Oldest, senior -ष्ठः *m.* 1 A Brâhmana. -2 A king. -3 N. of Kubera. -4 N. of Vishnu. -ष्ठं *n.* Cow's milk. -Comp.-अम्लं *n.* The fruit of the tamarind. —आश्रमः *m.* 1 The order of a house-holder. -2 A house-holder. —वाच् *a.* Eloquent.

श्रेष्ठिन् *m.* The head or president of a mercantile or other guild.

श्रै 1 P. (श्रायति) 1 To sweat, perspire. -2 To cook, boil.

श्रोण *a.* (*f.* —णा) Crippled, lame. —णः *m.* A kind of disease.

श्रोणा *f.* 1 Rice-gruel. -2 The constellation Sravana.

श्रोणिः, श्रोणी *f.* 1 The hip or loins; the buttocks. -2 A road, way. -Comp. —तटः *m.* The slope of the hips. —फलकं *n.* 1 The broad hips. -2 The buttocks.-नितंबः *m.* The hinder part of the waist; the buttocks. —बिंबं *n.* 1 The round hips. -2 A waist-band.-सूत्रं *n.* 1 A string worn round the loins. -2 A sword-belt.

श्रोतस् *n.* 1 The ear. -2 The trunk of an elephant. -3 An organ of sense. -4 The stream or current. -Comp. —रंध्रं *n.* An aperture of the trunk, a nostril.

श्रोतृ *m.* 1 A hearer.-2 A pupil.

श्रोत्रं *n.* 1 The ear. -2 Proficiency in the Vedas.-3 The Veda.-Comp. —पेय *a.* To be attentively heard. —मूलं *n.* The root of the ear.

श्रोत्रिय *a.* (*f.* -या) Proficient or versed in the Veda. —यः *m.* A Brâhmana well versed in the *Vedas*. -Comp. —स्वं *n.* The property of a learned Brâhmana.

श्रौत *a*. (*f* —ती) 1 Relating to the ear. -2 Relating to, or prescribed by, the Veda. -3 Sacrificial. —तं *n*. 1 Any observance prescribed by the Vedas. -2 Ritual enjoined by the Vedas. -3 Preservation of the sacred fire. -4 The three sacred fires collectively *i. e.* गार्हपत्य, आहवनीय and दक्षिण . -Comp. —कर्मन् *n*. A Vedic rite. —सूत्रं *n*. N. of a class of Sútra writings based on the Veda.

श्रौत्रं *n* 1 The ear. -2 Proficiency in the Vedas.

श्रौषट् *ind*. An exclamation used in making an offering to the Gods or departed spirits.

श्लक्ष्ण *a*. (*f*.-क्ष्णा) 1 Soft, gentle.-2 Smooth, polished.-3 Fine, delicate. -4 Beautiful. -5 Candid, frank.

श्लक्ष्णकं *n*. The Areca nut.

श्लथ् 10 U. (श्लथयति,-ते) 1 To be loosed.-2 To be weak.-3 To slacken (fig. also). -4 To hurt, kill.

श्लथ *a*. (*f*. -था) 1 Untied.-2 Loose, loosened.-3 Dishevelled (as hair).

श्लाघ् 1 A (श्लाघते) 1 To praise, applaud. -2 To be proud of. -3 To flatter, coax (with dat).

श्लाघनं *n*. 1 Praising. -2 Flattering.

श्लाघा *f*. 1 Praise. -2 Self-praise.-3 Flattery.-4 Service.-5 Wish, desire.

श्लाघ्य *a*. (*f*.-घ्या) 1 Praised, praiseworthy. -2 Respectable, venerable. -3 Laudable.

श्लिकुः *m*. 1 A debauchee, libertine. -2 A slave, dependent. —*n*. Astronomy, astrology.

श्लिक्युः *m*. 1 A libertine. -2 A servant.

श्लिष् 1 P. (श्लेषति) To burn.

श्लिष् 4 P. (श्लिष्यति, श्लिष्ट) 1 To embrace.-2 To cling to.-3 To unite, join.

श्लिष् 10 U. (श्लेषयति,-ते) To join, connect.

श्लिषा *f*. 1 An embrace. -2 Clinging, adherence.

श्लिष्ट *p. p*. (*f*. -ष्टा) 1 Embraced. -2 Adhered to. -3 Resting on. -4 Involving a pun; susceptible of a double interpretation.

श्लिष्टिः *f*. 1 Embrace. -2 Adherence.

श्लीपदं *n*. Swelled leg, elephantiasis. -Comp. -प्रभवः *m*. The mango tree.

श्लीक *a*. (*f*. —का) See श्रीक.

श्लेषः *m*. 1 An embrace. -2 Clinging to. -3 Union. -4 Pun, paronomasia. (*Reht*.) The figure of speech which occurs when in one sentence words bear more meanings than one. Paronomasia. -5 A society, an association.-Comp.-भित्तिक *a*. Depending on a Slesha.

श्लेष्मकः *m*. Phlegm.

श्लेष्मण *a*. (*f*. —णा) Phlegmatic.

श्लेष्मन् *m*. Phlegmatic humour.

श्लेष्मल *a*. (*f*. —ला) Phlegmatic.

श्लेष्मातः, श्लेष्मातकः *m*. A kind of tree.

श्लोक् 1 A. (श्लोकते) 1 To praise in verse. -2 To acquire. -3 To abandon.

श्लोकः *m*. 1 Praising in verse. -2 A verse of praise. -3 Celebrity. -4 An object of praise. -5 A proverb or saying. -6 A stanza or verse in general. -7 A stanza or verse in the Anushtubh metre.

श्लोकय् Den. P. To praise in song.

श्लोणः *m*. A lame man.

श्वन् *m*. 1 (Nom. श्वा, श्वानौ, श्वानः ; acc. pl. शुनः; *f*. शुनी) A dog.-Comp. —अश्वः *m*. An epithet of Bhairava. —क्रीडिन् *m*. A keeper of sporting dogs. —गणिकः *m*. 1 A hunter. -2 A dog-feeder. —धूर्तः *m*. A jackal. -पच्, —पचः *m*. 1 A man of a low and degraded caste. —पदं *n.* A mark like a dog's foot (to be branded on the forehead of a thief). —पाकः *m.* A Chândála. —फलं *n.* Lime or citron. —भीरुः *m.* A jackal.—यूथ्यं *n.* A pack of dogs. -वृत्तिः *f.* 1 The life of a dog. -2 Servitude. -व्याघ्रः *m.* 1 A beast of prey. -2 A tiger. -3 A leopard.-हन् *m.* A hunter.

श्वभ्र् 10 U. (श्वभ्रयति,-ते) 1 To go, move. -2 To make a hole. -3 To live in misery.

श्वभ्रं *n.* 1 A hole, chasm. -2 A den.

श्वयः *m.*, श्वयनं *n.* Swelling, increase.

श्वयथुः *m.* Swelling, intumescence.

श्वयीची *f.* Sickness, disease.

श्वशुरः *m.* A father-in-law, wife's or husband's father.-रौ *m. dual* The father-in-law and mother-in-law.

श्वशुरकः *m.* A father-in-law.

श्वशुर्यः *m.* A brother-in-law,a wife's or husband's brother.

श्वश्रूः *f.* A mother-in-law, a wifs's or husband's mother.-Comp. -श्वशुरौ *m. dual* Mother-in-law and father-in-law.

श्वस् *ind.* 1 Tomorrow. -2 Future (at the beginning of comp.). -3 A particle implying auspiciousness. -Comp. —भूत *a.* (श्वोभूत) Being tomorrow. -वसीय,-वसीयस् (श्वोवसीय, श्वोवसीयस्) *a.* Happy, auspicious, fortunate. (-*n.*) Happiness, good fortune. —श्रेयस (श्वश्रेयस) *a.* Happy, prosperous. (-सं *n.*) 1 Happiness, prosperity. -2 An epithet of Brahman (*n.*).

श्वस् 2 P. (श्वसिति, श्वस्त or श्वसित) 1 To breathe,draw breath.-2 To sigh, pant. -3 To hiss. With आ— 1 To recover. -2 To take courage. -3 To sigh. उद्— 1 To breathe. -2 To sigh. -3 To open, expand. -4 To upheave. नि— To sigh. निस्— To sigh. वि— 1 To confide in. -2 To be fearless. समा— To take heart, to calm oneself.

Caus. (श्वासयति,-ते) With आ- To console, to comfort. With वि -To inspire confidence. समा- To cheer up, encourage.

श्वसनः *m.* 1 Air,wind.-2 N. of a demon killed by Indra. —नं *n.* 1 Breathing, respiration. -2 Sighing. -Comp. —अशनः *m.* A serpent. -ईश्वरः *m.* The Arjuna tree. —उत्सुकः *m.* A serpent. —ऊर्मिः *f.* A gust of wind.

श्वसितं *n.* 1 Breathing, respiration. -2 Sighing.

श्वस्तन *a.* (*f.* -नी), श्वस्त्य *a.* (स्त्या) Relating to the morrow; future. -नं *n.* The future.

श्वाकर्णः *m.* The ear of a dog.

श्वागणिकः *m.* A dog-keeper.

श्वाग्निकः *m.* 1 A hunter. -2 A dog-keeper.

श्वादंतः *m.* A dog's tooth.

श्वानः *m.* A dog. -Comp. —निद्रा *f.* A very light sleep. -वैखरी *f.* Angry or currish snarling.

श्वापद *a.* (*f.* —दी) Savage, ferocious. —दः *m.* 1 A beast of prey, wild beast. -2 A tiger.

श्वापुच्छः *m.*,श्वापुच्छं *n.* A dog's tail.

श्वाविध् *m.* A porcupine.

श्वासः *m.* 1 Breathing, breath. -2 A sigh, panting. -3 Air, wind. -4 Asthma. -Comp. —उच्छ्वासः *m.* Exhalation and inhalation; respiration. —कासः *m.* Asthma. —कुठारः *m.* A drug used to cure asthma. -रोधः *m.* Suspension or obstruction of breath.-हिक्का *f.* A kind of hiccough. —हेतिः *f.* Sleep.

श्वासिन् *m.* 1 Air, wind. -2 A breathing animal.

श्वि I P. (श्वयति, श्वयितुं, शून) I To grow, increase (fig. also), to swell (as the eye). -2 To thrive, prosper. -3 To go, approach, move towards. With उद्— I To swell, increase, grow.-2 To be puffed up with pride.

श्वित I A. (श्वेतते) To become [white.

श्वित a. (f. -ता) White. —तं n. Whiteness.

श्विति: f. Whiteness.

श्वित्य, श्वित्न्य a. (f. -त्या,-त्न्या) White.

श्वित्रं n. I White leprosy. -2 A leprous spot. [A leper.

श्वित्रिन् a. (f. —णी) Leprous. -m.

श्वेत a. (f. श्वेता or श्वेनी) White. —तः m. I The white colour. -2 A conch-shell. -3 A cowrie. -4 The planet Venus. -5 Sukra, the regent of the planet. -6 A white cloud. -7 Cumin seed. -8 N. of a range of mountains. -9 N. of a division of the world. —तं n. Silver. -Comp. —अंबरः, -वासस् m. A class of Jaina ascetics. —इक्षुः m. A kind of sugar-cane. —उदरः m. An epithet of Kubera. —कुंजरः m. An epithet of Airàvata, the elephant of Indra. —कुष्ठं n. White leprosy. —कोलः m. A kind of fish (शफर). —गजः, -द्विपः m. The elephant of Indra. —गरुत्, -गरुतः m. A goose.-छदः m. I A goose. -2 A kind of basil. --द्वीपः m. N. of one of the eighteen minor divisions of the known continent. —धातुः m. I A white mineral. -2 Chalk. -3 The milk-stone. -धामन् m. I The moon. -2 Camphor. -3 The foam of the sea. -4 Cuttle-fish-bone. —नीलः m. A cloud. —पत्रः m. A goose. -पाटला f. The white trumpet-flower. —पिंगः m. A lion. -पिंगलः m. I A lion. -2 An epithet of Siva. —मरिचं n. White pepper. —मालः m. I A cloud. -2 Smoke. —रंजनं n. Lead. —रथः m. The planet Venus. -रोचिस् m. The moon. -रोहितः m. An epithet of Garuda. —वल्कलः m. The glomerous fig-tree. —वाजिन् m. I The moon. -2 An epithet of Arjuna. —वाह् m. An epithet of Indra. —वाहः m. I An epithet of Arjuna. -2 Of Indra. —वाहनः m. I An epithet of Arjuna. -2 The moon.-3 A marine monster (मकर). —वाहिन् m. An epithet of Arjuna. —शुंगः, -शृंगः m. Barley.-हयः m. I The horse of Indra. -2 An epithet of Arjuna. -3 N. of Indra. —हस्तिन् m. Indra's elephant.

श्वेतकः m. A cowrie. -कं n. Silver.

श्वेता f. I A cowrie. -2 White Dúrvâ grass. -3 A crystal. -4 Candied sugar. -5 Bamboo-manna. -6 N. of one of the tongues of fire.

श्वेतौही f. N. Sachî, wife of Indra.

श्वेत्रं n. White leprosy.

श्वैत्यं n. I Whiteness. -2 White leprosy.

श्वैत्रं, श्वैत्र्यं n. White leprosy.

ष.

षः m. I Loss, destruction. -2 Rest, remainder. -3 Final emancipation.

षट्क a. (f. -का) Six-fold. षट्कं n. An aggregate of six.

षड्धा ind. See षोढा.

षंडः m. I A bull. -2 A eunuch. -3 A group, miltitude. (n. also in this sense). -डः m., -डं n. A flock (of goats &c.).

षंडकः m. A eunuch.

षंडाली *f.* 1 A pond, pool -2 A wanton or unchaste woman.

षंढः *m.* A eunuch. -Comp. --तिलः *m.* Barren sesamum.

षष् *num. a.* (Used in pl., nom. षट्; gen. षण्णां) Six. -Comp. षडंगं *n.* 1 Six parts of the body taken collectively. -2 The six works auxiliarly to the Veda. -3 Six auspicious things obtained from a cow. -4 Any set of six articles. षडंघ्रिः *m.* A bee. षडभिज्ञः *m.* A Buddhist deified saint. षडशीत *a.* Eighty-sixth. षडशीतिः *f.* Eighty-six. षडहः *m.* A period of six days. षडाननः, षड्वक्त्रः, षड्वदनः *m.* Epithets of Kártikeya. षडाम्नायः *m.* The six-fold Tantra. -ऊषणं *n.* Six spices taken collectively. षट्कर्ण *a.* Heard by six ears; *i. e.* by a third person. (-र्णः *m.*) A kind of lute. षट्कर्मन् *n.* 1 The six acts or duties enjoined on a Brâhmana. -2 The six acts allowable to a Brâhmana for his subsistence. -3 The six acts that may be performed by means of magic. -4 The six acts belonging to the practice of Yoga. (*-m.*) 1 A Brâhmana skilled in the above six acts. -2 One well-versed in the Tantra magical rights. षट्कोण *a.* Hexangular. (--णं *n.*) 1 A hexagon. -2 The thunderbolt of Indra. षड्गवं *n.* 1 A team or yoke of six oxen. -2 A yoke of six. (Sometimes after the names of other animals; *e. g.* हस्तिषड्गवं, अश्वषड्गवं). षड्गुण *a.* 1 Sixfold. -2 Having six attributes. (-णं *n.*) 1 An assemblage of six qualities. -2 The six expedients to be used by a king in foreign politics. षंड्ग्रंथिका *f.* Zedoary (शठी). षट्चक्रं *n.* The six mystical circles of the body. षट्चत्वारिंशत् *a.* Forty-six. षट्चरणः *m.* 1 A bee. -2 A locust. -3 A louse. षड्जः *m.* The fourth (or first according to some), of the seven primary notes of the Indian gamut. षड्विंशत् *f.* Thirty-six. षट्त्रिंश *a.* Thirty-sixth. षड्दर्शनं *n.* The six principal systems of Hindu philosophy. षड्दुर्गं *n.* The six kinds of forts taken collectively. षण्णवतिः *f.* Ninety-six. षट्पंचाशत् *f.* Fifty-six. षट्पदः *m.* 1 A bee. -2 A louse. -3 A verse consisting of six *padas.* षट्पदी *f.* 1 A stanza consisting of six lines. -2 A female bee. -3 A louse. षट्प्रज्ञः *m.* 1 One who is well acquainted with six subjects; *i. e.* the four *Purushárthas* or objects of human existence, the nature of the world, and the nature of the Supreme Spirit. -2 A lustful or licentious man. षड्बिंदुः *m.* An epithet of Vishnu. षड्भागः *m.* A sixth part, one-sixth. षड्भुज *a.* 1 Six-armed. -2 Six-sided, hexagonal. (—जः *m.*) A hexagon. (—जा *f.*) 1 An epithet of Durgâ. -2 The water-melon. षण्मासः *m.* A period of six months षण्मासिक *a.* Half-yearly, occurring every six months. षण्मुखः *m.* An epithet of Kàrtikeya. (—खा *f.*). A water-melon. षड्रसं *n.* The six flavours taken collectively. षड्रात्रं *n.* A period of six nights. षड्रेखा *f.* A water-melon. षड्वर्गः *m.* 1 An aggregate of six things. -2 The six enemies of mankind (also called षड्रिपु; they are काम, क्रोध, लोभ, मोह, मद, and मत्सर). षड्विंशतिः *f.* Twenty-six. षड्विंश *a.* Twenty-sixth. षड्विध *a.* Of six kinds, sixfold. -षट्शास्त्रिन् *m.* One conversant with the six Sástras or 'darsanas'.

षट्षष्टिः *f.* Sixty-six. षट्सप्ततिः *f.* Seventy-six.

षष्टिः *f.* Sixty. षाष्टितम *a.* Sixtieth. -Comp.-भाषः *m.* An epithet of Siva. -मत्तः *m.* An elephant who has reached the age of sixty and is in rut at that time.-योजनी *f.* A journey or extent of sixty *Yojanas*. -संवत्सरः *m.* A period of sixty years. —हायनः *m.* 1 An elephant (sixty years old).-2 A kind of rice.

षष्टिक *a.* (*f.* —का) Bought with sixty. —कः *m.*,-का *f.* A kind of rice of quick growth.

षष्ठ *a.* (*f.* —ष्ठी) Sixth, the sixth. -Comp. —अंशः *m.* 1 A sixth part in general. -2 The sixth part of the produce of fields &c. which the king takes from his subjects as land-tax. षष्ठांशवृत्तिः *m.* A king. -अन्नं *n.* The sixth meal.

षष्ठी *f.* 1 The sixth day of a lunar fortnight. -2 The sixth or genitive case (in gram.). -3 An epithet of Durgá. -Comp. —तत्पुरुषः *m.* The genitive Tatpuresha compound; one in which, when dissolved, the first member usually stands in the genitive case.—पूजनं *n.*,-पूजा *f.* Worship of the goddess षष्ठी performed on the sixth day after a woman's delivery.

षहसानुः *m.* 1 A peacock. -2 A sa[crifice.

षाट् *ind.* A vocative particle.

षाट्कौशिक *a.* (*f.* —की) Enveloped in six sheaths.

षाट्पौरुषिक *a.* (*f.* —की) Belonging to six generations.

षाडवः *m.* 1 Passion, sentiment. -2 Singing, music. -3 (In music) A *Rága* in which six of the seven primary notes are used.

षाड्गुण्यं *n.* 1 The collection of six qualities. -2 Six measures of royal policy. -3 Multiplication of anything by six.

षाण्मातुरः *m.* An epithet of Kârtikeya.

षाण्मासिक *a.* (*f.* -की) 1 Six monthly. -2 Six months' old.

षाष्ठ *a.* (*f.* -ष्ठी) Sixth.

षिड्गः *m.* 1 A libidinous man. -2 An inconsistent lover.

षुः *m.* Delivery, child-bearing.

षोडश *a.* (*f.* —शी) The sixteenth.

षोडशन् *num. a. pl.* Sixteen. -Comp. —अंग *a.* Having 16 parts or ingredients. (-गः *m.*) A kind of perfume. —अंघ्रिः *m.* A crab. —आर्चिस् *m.* The planet Venus. —आवर्तः *m.* A conch-shell. —उपचाराः *m. pl.* The sixteen ways of doing homage to a deity &c.—भुजा *f.* A form of Durgâ.

षोडशधा *ind.* In sixteen ways.-मातृकाः *f. pl.* The sixteen divine mothers.

षोडशिक *a.* (*f.* -की) Consisting of sixteen parts; sixteen-fold.

षोडशिन् *m.* A kind of sacrifice.

षोढा *ind.* In six ways. -Comp. —न्यासः *m.* The six ways of touching the body with mystical texts. —मुखः *m.* N. of Kártikeya.

ष्ठिव् 1. 4. P. (ष्ठीवति, ष्ठीव्यति, ष्ठ्यूत) 1 To spit. -2 sputter.

ष्ठीवनं, ष्ठेवनं *n.* 1 Spitting out. -2 Saliva, spittle.

ष्ठ्यूत *p. p.* (*f.* -ता) Spit, ejected.

स.

स *ind.* A prefix substituted for सह or सम्, सम, तुल्य or सदृश and एक or समान, and compounded with nouns to form adjectives and adverbs; *e. g.* सपुत्र With son; सधन- Wealthy, -सरोषं Angrily. -सजाति Of the same class or kind. सः -*m.* 1 A snake. -2 Air, wind. -3 A bird. -4 A short name for the musical note षड्ज. -5 N. of Siva. -6 Of Vishnu. -7 (In prosody) A foot consisting of two short syllables followed by a long one. सा *f.* 1 An epithet of Gaurí. -2 The goddess Lakshmí.

संयः *m.* A skeleton.

संयत् *f.* A battle, fight. -Comp. —वरः *m.* A king, prince.

संयत *p. p.* (*f.* —ता) 1 Restrained, subdued. -2 Tied up. -3 Fettered. -4 Captive. -5 Ready. -6 Arranged. —तः *m.* 1 One who has restrained his passions; an ascetic. -2 N. of Siva. -Comp. —अंजलि *a.* One who has folded his hands in supplication. —उपस्कर *a.* One who has a well-regulated house.

संयत्त *a.* (*f.* —त्ता) Prepared, ready, being on guard.

संयमः *m.* Restraint, control. -2 Concentration of mind. -3 Humanity, feeling of compassion.

संयमनं *n.* 1 Restraining. -2 Drawing in. -3 Tying up. -4 Confinement. -5 Self-denial. -6 A religious vow or obligation. -7 A square house with a central quadrangle. —नः *m.* One who restrains or regulates; a ruler. —नी *f.* N. of the city of Yama.

संयमिन् *a.* (*f.* —नी) One who curbs or restrains. -*m.* One who controls his passions; a sage, an ascetic.

संयानः *m.* A mould. —नं *n.* 1 Going along with, accompanying. -2 Travelling. -3 Carrying out a dead body.

संयामः *m.* See संयमः.

संयावः *m.* A kind of cake of wheaten flour.

संयुक्त *p. p.* (*f.* —क्ता) 1 Joined, united. -2 Blended, mingled. -3 Accompanied by. -4 Possessed of. -5 Consisting of.

संयुगः *m.* 1 Conjunction, union, mixture. -2 Fight, battle. -Comp. —गोष्पदं *n.* 'A contest in a cow's footstep' *i. e.* an insignificant or trifling quarrel.

संयुत *a.* (*f.*-ता) 1 Joined together. -2 Furnished with.

संयोगः *m.* 1 Conjunction, union. -2 Possession. -3 Alliance between two kings for a common object. -4 (In gram.) A conjunct consonant. -5 (In astr.) The conjunction of two heavenly bodies. -6 An epithet of Siva. -Comp. —विरुद्धं *n.* Any eatables causing disease by being mixed.

संयोजनं *n.* 1 Union, conjunction. -2 Sexual union.

संरक्षः *m.* Protection, care.

संरक्षणं *n.* 1 Protection. -2 Charge, custody.

संरक्त *p. p.* (*f.* —क्ता) 1 Coloured, red. -2 Fired with passion. -3 Angry. -4 Enamoured. -5 Charming.

संरब्ध *p. p.* (*f.* —ब्धा) 1 Excited. -2 Exasperated, enraged. -3 Augmented. -4 Swelled. -5 Overwhelmed. -6 Closely joined.

संरंभः *m.* 1 Beginning. -2 Turbulence, impetuosity, violence. -3 Agitation. -4 Ardent desire. -5 Anger. -6 Arrogance. -7 Swelling with heat and inflammation. -Comp. —वेगः *m.* The impetuosity of anger.

संरंभिन् *a.* (*f.* —णी) 1 Excited, agitated. -2 Angry, enraged. -3 Arrogant.

संरागः *m.* 1 Colouring. -2 Passion, affection. -3 Anger.

संराधनं *n.* 1 Propitiation, conciliation. -2 Accomplishing. -3 Profound meditation.

संरावः *m.* Tumult, uproar.

संरुग्ण *p. p.* (*f.* -ग्णा) Shattered, broken to pieces.

संरुद्ध *p. p.* (*f.* —द्धा) 1 Checked, opposed.-2 Blocked up.-3 Blockaded. -4 Covered over, concealed. -5 Refused.

संरूढ *p. p.* (*f.* —ढा) 1 Grown together. -2 Healed (as in संरूढव्रण). -3 Sprouted, germinated. -4 Firmly grown. -5 Bold, confident.

संरोधः *m.* 1 Complete obstruction or impediment, check.-2 Blockade, siege. -3 Bond, fetter. -4 Sending forth.

संरोधनं *n.* Obstructing, stopping.

संलक्षणं *n.* Marking, characterizing.

संलग्न *p. p.* (*f.* -ग्ना) 1 Closely attached, adhering to. -2 Come to blows.

संलयः *m.* 1 Lying down, sleep. -2 Dissolution. -3 Universal destruction.

संललित *p. p.* (*f.* —ता) Fondled, caressed.

संलापः *m.* 1 Conversation. -2 Confidential talk. -3 (In dramas) A kind of dialogue.

संलापकः *m.* A kind of minor drama, said to be of a controversial kind.

संलीढ *p. p.* (*f.* —ढा) Licked up. -2 Enjoyed.

संलीन *p. p.* (*f.* —ना) 1 Adhered.-2 Hidden. -3 Contracted, shrunk. -Comp. —मानस *a.* Depressed in mind.

संवत् *ind.* 1 A year. -2 A year of the Vikramáditya era.

संवत्सरः *m.* 1 A year. -2 A year of Vikramádity's era. -3 N. of Siva. -Comp. —भ्रामि *a.* Completing one revolution in a year (said of the sun).

संवदनं *n.* 1 Conversing. -2 Communication of tidings.-3 Examination. -4 Subduing by magic. -5 A charm, an amulet.

संवरः *m.* 1 Covering. -2 Comprehension. -3 Compression, contraction. -4 A causeway, dam, bridge. -5 A kind of deer. — रं *n.* 1 Concealment.-2 Self-control. -3 Water. -4 A particular religious observance of Buddhists.

संवरणं *n.* 1 Covering. -2 Concealment. -3 A pretext. -4 A secret.

संवर्जनं *n.* 1 Appropriating to oneself. -2 Consuming, devouring.

संवर्तः *m.* 1 Turning towards.-2 Dissolution.-3 The periodical destruction or dissolution of the world. -4 A cloud. -5 A cloud of a particular class. -6 A year. -7 A collection, multitude.

संवर्तकः *m.* 1 A kind of cloud.-2 The fire that is to destroy the world at the time of universal destruction. -3 Sub-marine fire. -4 N. of Balarâma.

संवर्तकिन् *m.* N. of Balaráma.

संवर्तिका *f.* 1 The new leaf of a water-lily. -2 The petal near the filament. -3 The flame of a lamp.

संवर्धक *a.* (*f.* —र्धिका) 1 Causing growth or prosperity; augmenting. -2 Welcoming, hospitable.

संवलनं *n.* 1 Combination, union.-2 Being mixed or charged with.

संवलित *p. p.* (*f.* —ता) 1 Met together, mixed.-2 Sprinkled with. -3 Associated. -4 Broken. -5 Surrounded.

संवाल्गित *a.* (*f.* —ता) Overrun.

संवसथः *m.* A place where people live together; a village; an inhabited place.

संवहः *m*.N. of the third of the seven courses or Márgas of the wind.

संवादः *m*. 1 Speaking together, conversation. -2 Discussion. -3 Communication of tidings. -4 Assent.-5 Agreement, correspondence. -6 Encounter.

संवादिन् *a*. (*f*. —नी) 1 Speaking, conversing. -2 Resembling, corresponding.

संवारः *m*. 1 Covering, closing up. -2 Contraction of the throat in the pronunciation of letters; obtuse articulation. -3 Diminution. -4 Protecting.

संवासः *m*. 1 Domestic intercourse. -2 A house. -3 An open space for meeting or recreation. -4 Association, company.

संवाहः *m*. 1 Bearing or carrying along. -2 Pressing together. -3 Shampooing.-4 A servant employed to rub and shampoo the body.

संवाहकः *m*. A shampooer.

संवाहनं *n*.,-ना *f*. 1 Carrying or bearing a burden. -2 Shampooing; gentle rubbing. -3 Bearing along.

संविक्त *a*. (*f*. —क्ता) That which is separated or individualised.

संविग्न *p. p*. (*f*. —ग्ना) 1 Agitated, excited, disturbed, distracted. -2 Terrified, frightened.

संविज्ञात *p. p*. (*f*.-ता) 1 Universally known. -2 Generally recognised or allowed.

संवित्तिः *f*. 1 Perception, consciousness, feeling. -2 Understanding, intellect. -3 Recognition, recollection. -4 Harmony, mutual reconciliation.

संविद् *f*. 1 Understanding, intellect. -2 Consciousness, perception. -3 An agreement, contract, promise. -4 Assent, consent. -5 A prescribed custom. -6 War, battle. -7 A war-cry, watch-word. -8 A name, an appellation. -9 A sign, signal. -10 Pleasing, delighting. -11 Sympathy, participation. -12 Meditation. -13 Conversation. -14 Hemp. —Comp. —व्यतिक्रमः *m*. A breach of promise; violation of a contract.

संविदा *f*. An agreement or promise, covenant.

संविदित *p. p*. (*f*. —ता) 1 Known, understood.-2 Rocognised.-3 Well-known. -4 Explored. -5 Agreed upon. -6 Advised, admonished.

संविधा *f*. 1 Arrangement, preparation, plan. -3 Means of leading life.

संविधानं *n*. 1 Arrangement. -2 Performance. -3 Plan, mode. -4 Arrangement of incidents (in a plot).

संविधानकं *n*. 1 The plot of a drama &c. -2 A strange act, an unusual occurrence.

संविभागः *m*. 1 Partition, dividing. -2 A part, portion, share.

संविभागिन् *m*. (*f*. —नी) A partner, sharer, participator.

संविष्ट *p p*. (*f*. —ष्टा) 1 Sleeping, lying down. -2 Seated together. -3 Dressed, clothed.

संवीक्षणं *n*. 1 Looking about in all directions; looking for anything lost. -2 Looking attentively.

संवीत *p. p*. (*f*. —ता) 1 Clothed. -2 Covered over, overlaid.-3 Adorned. -4 Surrounded, shut in. -5 Overwhelmed.

संवृक्त *p. p*. (*f*. —क्ता) 1 Devoured, consumed. -2 Destroyed.

संवृत *p. p*. (*f*. —ता) 1 Covered, covered up. -2 Hidden, concealed. -3 Retired, secluded. -4 Contracted, compressed. -5 Confiscated, sequestered.-6 Surrounded. -7 Filled with, full of. -8 Accompanied by. -तं *n* 1 A secret or retired place. -2 A particular mode of pronunciation. -Comp. —आकार *a.* One who conceals all outward manifestation of feeling.

संवृतिः *f.* 1 Covering, covering up. -2 Concealment.-3 Secret purpose.

संवृत्त *p. p.* (*f.* —त्ता) 1 Become, happened. -2 Accomplished. -3 Heaped together. -4 Past, gone. -5 Covered. -6 Furnished with.—त्तः *m.* N. of Varuna.

संवृत्तिः *f.* 1 Happening, occurrence. -2 Accomplishment.

संवृद्ध *p. p.* (*f.* -द्धा) 1 Full-grown, augmented.-2 Big,large. -3 Blooming, flourishing.

संवेगः *m.* 1 Agitation, excitement. -2 Impetuosity, vehemence. -3 Haste, speed. -4 Agonising pain.

संवेदः *m.* 1 Perception, knowledge, consciousness, understanding.

संवेदनं *n.*, -ना *f.* 1 Perception, knowledge. -2 Sensation,feeling, experiencing.-3 Passing on, transferring.

संवेशः *m.* 1 Sleep. -2 A dream. -3 A seat, a chair, stool. -4 A particular mode of coition.

संवेशनं *n.* Coition, sexual union.

संव्यवहारः *m.* 1 Business. -2 Mercantile transaction.

संव्यानं *n.* 1 Covering, wrapping.-2 Cloth, garment. -3 An upper garment.

संशप्तकः *m.* 1 A warrior sworn never to recede from a contest and kept to prevent the flight of others. -2 A picked warrior. -3 A conspirator bound by oath to kill another.

संशयः *m.* 1 Doubt, uncertainty, hesitation. -2 Doubt or indecision (in Nyàya).-3 Danger, peril, risk. -4 Possibility. -Comp. —आत्मन् *m.* A sceptic.

संशयान, संशयालु, संशयित् *a.* Doubtful, irresolute, uncertain.

संशरणं *n.* Commencement of a combat; attack, charge.

संशित *p. p.* (*f.* -ता) 1 Sharpened, aroused. -2 Sharp, acute. -3 Thoroughly accomplished. -4 Decided, determined.

संशुद्धिः *f.* 1 Complete purification. -2 Correction, rectification. -3 Acquittance (of debt). -4 Purity, cleanness.

संशोधनं *n.* See संशुद्धिः.

संश्वत *n.* Trick, jugglery, illusion. —*m.* A juggler.

संश्यान *p. p.* (*f.* -ना) 1 Contracted, shrunk up. -2 Frozen, congealed. -3 Rolled up. -4 Collapsed.

संश्रयः *m.* 1 A dwelling place, residence. -2 Seeking protection with, fleeing for refuge, leaguing together for mutual protection, one of the six gunas or expedients in politics. -3 Refuge, asylum,shelter.

संश्रवः *m.* 1 Hearing attentively.-2 A promise.

संश्रवणं *n.* 1 Hearing. -2 The ear.

संश्रुत *p. p.* (*f.* -ता) 1 Promised, agreed to. -2 Well-heard.

संश्लिष्ट *p. p.* (*f.* -ष्टा) 1 Clasped together, joined, united. -2 Embraced. -4 Adjoining. -5 Furnished or endowed with. -6 Connected together. [-2 Union.

संश्लेषः *m.* 1 Embracing, an embrace.

संश्लेषणं *n.*, -णा *f.* 1 Pressing together. -2 Means of binding together. -3 A tie, bond.

संसक्त *p. p.* (*f.* -क्ता) 1 Adhered or stuck together. -2 Joined or linked together. -3 Contiguous, adjoining. -4 Confused, mixed, mingled. -5 Intent on. -6 Endowed with.-7 Restrained.

संसक्तिः *f.* 1 Close adherence. -2 Proximity. -3 Intimate acquaintance. -4 Tying together. -5 Devotion, addiction (to anything)

संसद् *f.* 1 An assembly, meeting. -2 A court of justice.

संसरणं *n.* 1 Going, proceeding, revolution. -2 Wordly life. -3 Birth and re-birth.-4 The unresisted march of troops. -5 The commencement of battle. -6 A highway. -7 A resting-place for passengers near the gates of a city.

संसर्गः *m.* 1 Commixture, union. -2 Contact, association. -3 Proximity. -4 Intercourse, familiarity. -5 Copulation. -6 Co-existence, intimate relation. -7 Equal extent, co-existence (*log.*). -Comp. -अभावः *m.* Relative non-existence, which is of three kinds. viz. prior, incidental and final (In Nyáya phil.).

संसर्जनं *n.* 1 Commingling. -2 Abandoning. -3 Voiding.

संसर्पः *m.* 1 Creeping along, gentle motion. -2 The intercalary month occurring in a year in which there occurs a *Kshaya-mása.*

संसर्पणं *n.* 1 Creeping along. -2 An unexpected attack, a sally.

संसर्पिन् *a.* (*f.* -णी)Creeping along, moving near.

संसादः *m.* An assembly.

संसारः *m.* 1 Course, passage. -2 The course of worldly life, mundance existence;the world.-3 Transmigration, metempsychosis, succession of births. -4 Worldly illusion. -Comp. —गुरुः *m.* An epithet of the God of love. —मार्गः *m.* 1 The course of worldly affairs; worldly life. -2 The vulva. -मोक्षः *m.*, -मोक्षणं *n.* Final liberation or emancipation from worldly life.

संसारिन् *m.* 1 A sentient being, creature. -2 The embodied spirit, the individual soul(जीवात्मन्).

संसिद्ध *p. p.* (*f.* —द्धा) 1 Fully accomplished. -2 One who has obtained final emancipation.

संसिद्धिः *f.* 1 Complete accomplishment or attainment. -2 Final beatitude. -3 A natural disposition, state or quality. -4 A passionate or intoxicated woman.

संसूचनं *n.* 1 Showing plainly, proving. -2 Informing, telling. -3 Hinting. -4 Reproaching.

संसृतिः *f.* 1 Course, current, flow. -2 The worldly life. -3 Metempsychosis, transmigration.

संसृष्ट *p. p.* (*f.* —ष्टा) 1 Commingled, mixed together, conjoined. -2 Associated as partners.-3 Composed. -4 Reunited. -5 Involved in. -6 Created. -7 Cleanly dressed.

संसृष्टता *f.*, —त्वं *n.* 1 Association, union. -2 (In law) Voluntary reunion in pecuniary interest of kinsmen.

संसृष्टिः *f.* 1 Combination, union. -2 Association, co-partnership. -3 Living in one family. -4 A collection. -5 (In Rhet.) The figure of speech in which two or more figures of speech whether of words or of sense exist independently of each other in one sentence. The figures thus coming together may all be those of words or all of sense, or some of words and some of sense.

संसृष्टिन *m.* 1 A reunited kinsman. -2 A copartner.

संस्कर्तृ *m.* 1 One who cooks or prepares (food &c.). -2 One who consecrates or initiates.

संस्कार: *m.* 1 Making perfect, refining, polishing. -2 Refinement, grammatical purity (as of words). -3 Education, training (as of the mind). -4 Making ready; preparation. -5 Cooking, dressing (as of food &c.). -6 Embellishment, ornament. -7 Sanctification. -8 Impression, form, operation, influence. -9 Idea, conception. -10 Any faculty or capacity. -11 Merit of action. -12 The self-reproductive quality, one of the 24 qualities or 'gunas' recognised by the Vaiseshikas; it is of three kinds :-भावना, वेग, and स्थितिस्थापकता. -13 The faculty of recollection. -14 A purificatory sacred rite or ceremony. -15 Purification, purity. -16 A rite or ceremony in general. -17 Investiture with the sacred thread. -18 Obsequial ceremonies. -19 A polishing stone.

संस्कृत *p. p.* (*f.* —ता) 1 Made perfect, refined, polished. -2 Artificially made; carefully or accurately formed. -3 Dressed, cooked. -4 Consecrated, hallowed. -5 Initiated into worldly life, married. -6 Cleansed, purified. -7 Adorned. -8 Excellent, best. —त: *m.* 1 A word formed according to the rules of grammar; a regular derivative. -2 A man of any one of the first three castes who has received all the purificatory rites. -3 A learned man. —तं *n.* 1 Refined or highly polished speech, the Sanskrit language. -2 A sacred usage. -3 An offering, oblation, sacrifice.

संस्क्रिया *f.* 1 A purificatory rite. · Consecration. -3 A funeral ceremony.

संस्तंभ: *m.* 1 Support, prop. -2 Confirming, fixing. -3 Stop, stay. -4 Paralysis. [sacrifice.

संस्तर: *m.* 1 A couch, a bed. -2 A

संस्तव: *m* 1 Praise. -2 Acquaintance, familiarity. -3 Agreement, harmony.

संस्ताव: *m.* 1 Praise, celebration. -2 Hymning in chorus. -3 The place for repeating hymns and prayers at a sacrifice.

संस्तुत *p. p* (*f.* —ता) 1 Praised -2 Agreeing together, harmonious. -3 Intimate, familiar.

संस्तुति: *f.* Praise.

संस्त्याय: *m.* 1 A collection, heap. -2 Vicinity. -3 Diffusion, expansion. -4 A residence, habitation.

संस्थ *a.* (*f.*—स्था) 1 Staying, abiding, lasting. -2 Dwelling, being, situated (at the end of comp.). -3 Tame, domesticated. -4 Stationary. -5 Perished, dead. -6 Completed. —स्थ: *m.* 1 An inhabitant. -2 A neighbour, countryman. -3 A spy.

संस्था *f.* 1 An assemblage, assembly. -2 Situation, state or condition of being. -3 Form, nature. -4 Occupation, business. -5 Proper conduct. -6 End. -7 Stop, stay. -8 Destruction. -9 Destruction of the world. -10 Resemblance. -11 A royal decree or ordinance. -12 A form of Soma sacrifice.

संस्थानं *n.* 1 A collection, quantity. -2 The aggregation of primary atoms. -3 Configuration, position. -4 Form, appearance, disguise. -5 Construction, formation -6 Vicini ty. -7 Common place of abode. -8 Situation. -9 Any place or station. -10 A place where four roads meet. -11 A characteristic sign. -12 Death.

संस्थापनं *n.* 1 Placing together, collection. -2 Fixing, regulating. -3 Establishment. -4 Confirmation. -5 Restraining. -6 A statute, regulation. —ना *f.* 1 Restraining, curbing. -2 A means of calming.

संस्थित *p. p.* (*f.* —ता) 1 Being together. -2 Being, staying. -3 Adjacent. -4 Resembling, like. -5 Collected. -6 Settled, established. -7 Placed in or on, being in. -8 Stationary. -9 Stopped, ended. -10 Dead.

संस्थितिः *f.* 1 Being together, staying with. -2 Contiguity. -3 Residence, resting-place. -4 Accumulation, heap. -5 Duration, continuance. -6 Condition of life. -7 Restraint. -8 Death. -9 Destruction of the world.

संस्पर्शः *m.* 1 Contact, mixture. -2 Being touched or affected. -3 Perception, sense.

संस्पर्शा *f.* A kind of fragrant plant.

संस्फालः *m.* 1 A ram. -2 A cloud.

संस्फेटः, संस्फोटः, संस्फोटिः *m.* War, battle.

संस्मरणं *n.* Remembering, calling to mind.

संस्मृतिः *f* Remembranece, recollection.

संस्रवः, संस्रावः *m* 1 Flowing, oozing. -2 A stream. -3 The remains of a libation. -4 A kind of offering or libation.

संहत *p. p.* (*f.* —ता) 1 Wounded. -2 Closed, shut. -3 Firmly united. -4 Closely allied. -5 Compact, firm, solid. -6 Combinned, joined, being very close. -7 Of one accord. -8 Assembled. -Comp. -जानु *a.* Knock-kneed. -भ्रू *a.* Knitting the eyebrows.

संहतता *f.*, -त्वं *n.* 1 Close contact. -2 Compactness. -3 Agreement. -4 Harmony.

संहतिः *f.* 1 Firm or close union. -2 Combination. -3 Compactness, firmness. -4 Bulk, mass. -5 Agreement, harmony. -6 A collection. -7 Strength. -8 The body.

संहननं *n.* 1 Compactness, firmness. -2 The body, person. -3 Strength. -4 Rubbing the limbs. -5 Killing.

संहरणं *n.* 1 Gathering. -2 Seizing. -3 Contracting. -4 Restraining. -5 Destroying. -6 Withdrawing.

संहर्षः *m.* 1 Horripilation, a thrill of joy or fear. -2 Pleasure, delight. -3 Rivalry. -4 Wind. -5 Rubbing together.

संहातः *m.* One of the 21 hells.

संहारः 1 Drawing or bringing together. -2 Compression, abridgment. -3 Withholding, withdrawal (opp. प्रयोग or विक्षेप). -4 Restraining. -5 Destruction, especially universal destruction. -6 End, conclusion. -7 A group. -8 A fault in pronunciation. -9 A spell for withdrawing magical weapons. -10 Practice, skill. -11 A division of hell. -Comp. —मुद्रा *f.* N. of a particuler posture in the *Tantra* worship.

संहित *p. p.* (*f.* —ता) 1 Placed together, united. -2 Conformable to, in accordance with. -3 Relating to. -4 Collected. -5 Furnished, endowed, accompanied. -6 Caused by. -7 Placed, fixed. -8 Compiled.

संहिता *f.* 1 Combination, conjunction. -2 A compilation, compendium. -3 Any systematically arranged collection of texts or verses

-4 A compilation of laws; a code, digest, as in मनुसंहिता. -5 The continuous hymnical text of the Veda as formed out of the Padas or individual words by proper phonetic changes according to different Sákhás or schools. -6 (In gram.) The junction of letters according to the rules of Sandhi or euphony. -7 The Supreme Being. -Comp. —पाठः *m.* The continuous text of the Veda (opp. पदपाठ).

संहूतिः *f.* Clamour; tumultuous exultation.

संहृत *p. p.* (*f.* —ता) 1 Drawn together. -2 Contracted, abridged.-3 Withdrawn.-4 Collected.-5 Seized. -6 Restrained. -7 Destroyed.

संहृतिः *f.* 1 Contraction, compression. -2 Destruction. -3 Seizure.-4 Restraint. -5 Collection.

संहृष्ट *p. p.* (*f.* —ष्टा) 1 Thrilled or horripilated with joy. -2 Bristling, shuddering.-3 Fired with emulation.

संह्रादः *m.* 1 A loud noise. -2 Noise in general.

संह्रीण *a.* Modest, bashful.

सकट *a.* (*f.* —टी) Bad, vile.

सकंटकः *m.* The aquatic plant शैवल.

सकर्ण *a.* (*f.* -र्णा or -र्णी) 1 Having ears. -2 Hearing, listening. [agent.

सकर्तृक *a.* (*f.* —का) Having an

सकर्मक *a.* (*f.* —का) 1 Having or performing any act. -2 (In gram.) Having an object, transitive (as a verb).

सकल *a.* (*f.* —ला) 1 Together with the parts. -2 All, whole, entire. -3 Having all the digits, full (as the moon). -4 Having a soft or low sound. -Comp. —वर्ण *a.* Having the letters क & ल *i. e.* quarrelling.

सकल्प *a.* (*f.* —ल्पा) Attended with the ritual or ceremonial part of the Veda. —ल्पः *m.* N. of Siva. [hells.

सकाकोलः *m.* N. of one of the 21

सकाम *a.* (*f.* —मा) 1 Full of love, impassioned. -2 Amorous. -3 One who has got his desired object; contented. —मं *ind.* 1 With pleasure. -2 Contentedly. -3 Surely, indeed.

सकाल *a* (*f.* —ला) Seasonable, opportune. —लं *ind.* Seasonably, betimes, early in the morning.

सकाश *a.* (*f.* —शा) Having appearance; visible, present, near. —शः *m.* Presence, vicinity. (सकाशम् and सकाशात् are used adverbially in the sense of 1 near. -2 from near, from, from the presence of).

सकुक्षि *a.* Having the same womb, born of the same mother, uterine (as a brother &c.).

सकुल *a.* (*f.* —ला) 1 Belonging to a noble family. -2 Belonging to the same family. —लः *m.* 1 A kinsman. -2 A kind of fish (सकुली also).

सकुल्यः *m.* 1 One of the same family. -2 An ancestor in the 4th, 5th or 6th or even in the 7th, 8th, or 9th degree (in law). -3 A remote relation in general.

सकृत् *ind.* 1 Once -2 Formerly. -3 At once. -4 Always. -*f.* Feces, excrement. -Comp. —गर्भा *f.* 1 A mule.-2 A woman who is pregnant only once. —प्रजः *m.* A crow. -प्रसूता, -प्रसूतिका *f.* 1 A woman who has borne only one child. -2 A cow that has calved once. —फला *f.* The plantain tree.

सक्त *p. p.* (*f* —क्ता) 1 Attached to, in contact with. -2 Devoted or attached to. -3 Relating to.

सक्तिः *f.* 1 Contact, touch. -2 Union, junction. -3 Attachment, devotion (to anything).

सक्तुः *m.* (Always सक्तवः *m. pl.*) The flour of barley first fried and then ground; barley-meal.

सक्थि *n.* 1 The thigh ; (changed in comp. to सक्थ after उत्तर, पूर्व and मृग or when the compound implies comparison. -2 A bone. -3 The pole or shafts of a carriage.

सक्षण *a.* (*f.* -णा) Being at leisure.

सखि *m.* (nom. सखा, सखायौ, सखायः) A friend, an associate. (At the end of comp. सखि is changed to सख).

सखी *f.* 1 A female friend or companion. -2 A lady's maid.

सख्यं *n.* 1 Friendship, alliance. -2 Equality. —ख्यः *m.* A friend.

सगंध *a.* (*f.* —धा) Fragrant. —धः *m.* A kinsman, relation.

सगर *a.* (*f.* -रा) Poisonous, having poison. —रः *m.* N. of a king of the Solar race whose great-grandson brought the Ganges from heaven to the earth. [blood.

सगर्भः, सगर्भ्यः *m.* A brother of whole

सगुण *a.* (*f.* —णा) 1 Possessed of qualities or attributes. -2 Possessed of good qualities, virtuous. -3 Worldly. -4 Furnished with a string (as a bow).

सगोत्र *a.* (*f.* -त्रा) Being of the same family or kin, related. —त्रः *m.* 1 A kinsman sprung from a common ancestor. -2 A kinsman of the same family, connected by funeral oblations of food and water. -3 A distant kinsman.—त्रं *n.* Family, race, lineage.

सग्धिः *f.* Eating together.

संकट *a.* (*f.* —टा) 1 Contracted, narrow, strait. -2 Impervious, impassable. -3 Full off, crowded with, beset with. —टं *n.* 1 A narrow passage. -2 A difficulty, danger.

संकथनं *n.* Narration.

संकथा *f.* Conversation, talk.

संकरः *m.* 1 Commingling, intermixture. -2 Confusion or mixture (of castes), unlawful intermarriage resulting in mixed castes. -3 (*Rhet.*) That figure of speech in which in one sentence two or more figures of speech or figures of words are subservient to each other *i. e.* stand in the relation of principal and subordinate ; or when they reside in one and the same phrase ; or when there is a doubt as to which figure the poet means.

संकरी *f.* A girl recently deflowered; a new bride.

संकर्षणं *n.* 1 The act of drawing together, contracting. -2 Attracting. -3 Ploughing. —णः *m.* N. of Balarâma. [ition.

संकलः *m.* 1 Accumulation. -2 Add-

संकलनं *n.*, —ना *f.* 1 The act of heaping together. -2 Contact, junction. -3 Collision. -4 Blending. -5 Addition (in math.).

संकलित *p. p.* (*f.* —ता) 1 Heaped up, piled up. -2 Intermixed. -3 Seized, laid hold of. -4 Added. -तं *n.* Addition.

संकल्पः *m.* 1 Will, volition, mental resolve. -2 Purpose, intention, determination. -3 Wish, desire. -4 Thought, idea, reflection. -5 A fixed thought ; final opinion ; an idea. -6 Imagination, fancy. -7 The mind, heart. -8 A solemn vow to perform an observance. -9 Expectation of advantage from a holy act. -Comp. —जः, -जन्मन्, -योनिः *m.* Epithets of the God of love.

संकसुक *a.* (*f.* —का) 1 Unsteady,

changeable, inconstant. -2 Uncertain, doubtful. -3 Bad, wicked. -4 Weak, feeble.

संकारः *m.* 1 Dust, sweepings. -2 The crackling of flames.

संकारी *f.* A girl recently deflowered.

संकाश *a.* (*f.*—शा) 1 Like, similar, resembling (at the end of comp.). -2 Near, close, at hand. —शः *m.* 1 Appearance, presence. -2 Vicinity.

सांकिलः *m.* A. fire-brand, burning torch.

संकीर्ण *p. p.* (*f* —र्णा) 1 Mixed together, intermingled; miscellaneous -2 Shattered, spread, crowded. -3 Indistinct. -4 In rut, intoxicated. -5 Of mixed caste, of impure origin. -6 Impure, adulterated. -7 Narrow, contracted.—र्णः *m.* 1 A man of a mixed caste. -2 A mixed note or mode. -3 An elephant in rut. —र्णं *n.* A difficulty. —र्णा *f.* A kind of riddle. -Comp. —जाति, -योनि *a.* Of a mongrel breed (as a mule).

संकीर्तनं *n.*, -ना *f.* 1 Praising, applauding, extolling. -2 Glorification (of a deity). -3 Repeating the name of a deity as a devotional act.

संकुचित *p. p.* (*f.* -ता) 1 Contracted abridged. -2 Shrunk, wrinkled. -3 Closed, shut.

संकुल *a.* (*f.* -ला) 1 Confused. -2 Crowded or filled with, full of. -3 Disordered, perplexed. -4 Inconsistent.—लं *n.* 1 A crowd, throng. -2 A confused fight, melee. -3 An inconsistent or contradictory speech.

संकेतः *m.* 1 An intimation, allusion, sign, gesture, hint; an indicatory sign. -2 Agreement, convention. -3 Engagement, appointment, assignation (made by a mistress or lover). -4 A place of meeting (for lovers), rendezvous. -5 Condition, provision. -6 A short explanatory rule (in gram.).

संकेतकः *m.* 1 Agreement, convention. -2 Appointment, assignation. -3 Rendezvous. -4 A lover or mistress who makes an appointment.

संकेतित *a.* (*f.*-ता) 1 Agreed upon, fixed by convention. -2 Invited, called.

संकोचः *m.* 1 Contraction, shrinking up. -2 Abridgment, compression. -3 Terror, fear. -4 Shutting up, closing. -5 Binding. -6 A kind of skate-fish. —चं *n.* Saffron.

संक्रंदनः *m.* N. of Krishna

संक्रमः *m.* 1 Concurrence, going together. -2 Transition, traversing, transfer, progress. -3 Offshoot (as of lustre of some jewel). -4 The passage of a planetary body through the zodiacal signs. -5 Moving, travelling. —मः *m.*, -मं *n.* 1 A difficult or narrow passage. -2 A causeway, bridge. -3 A medium or means of attaining any object.

संक्रमणं *n.* 1 Concurrence. -2 Transition, passing from one point to another. -3 Passage. -4 The sun's passage from one zodiacal sign to another. -5 The day on which the summer solstice begins.

संक्रांत *p. p.* (*f.* —ता) 1 Passed through or into, entered into. -2 Transferred, entrusted. -3 Seized, affected. -4 Depicted.

संक्रांतिः *f.* 1 Going together, union. -2 Passage from one point to another, transition. -3 The passage of the sun or any planetary body from one zodiacal sign into another

-4 Transference, giving over. -5 The power of imparting (instruction to another). -6 Image, reflection. -7 Depicting.

संक्रामः *m.* See संक्रमः.

संक्लेदः *m.* 1 Dampness, moisture. -2 The rudiment of the fœtus, its form in the first month after conception.

संक्षयः *m.* 1 Destruction. -2 Complete destruction or consumption. -3 Loss, ruin. -4 Destruction of the world.

संक्षिप्त *p. p.* (*f.* —प्ता) 1 Heaped together. -2 Compressed, contracted. -3 Abridged. -4 Diminished. -5 Concise, short. -6 Thrown, despatched. -7 Seized, grasped.

संक्षिप्तिः *f.* 1 Throwing together. -2 Compressing, abridging. -3 Throwing, sending. -4 Ambuscade.

संक्षेपः *m.* 1 Throwing together. -2 Abridgment. -3 Conciseness. -4 A brief exposition. -5 Throwing, sending. -6 Taking away. -7 Assisting in another's duty. (संक्षेपेण, संक्षेपतस् 'Briefly', 'concisely', 'shortly').

संक्षेपणं *n.* 1 Heaping together. -2 Abridgment, abbreviation. -3 Sending.

संक्षोभः *m.* 1 Agitation, trembling. -2 Disturbance, commotion. -3 Upsetting, overturning. -4 Pride, arrogance.

संख्यं *n.* War, battle, fight.

संख्या *f.* 1 Enumeration, calculation. -2 A number. -3 A numeral. -4 Sum. -5 Reason, understanding. -6 Deliberation. -7 Manner. -Comp. —अतिग, अतीत *a.* Innumerable, countless. —वाचकः *m.* A numeral.

संख्यात *p. p.* (*f.*—ता) 1 Enumerated. -2 Calculated, reckoned up. -तं *n.* A number. — ता *f.* A kind of riddle.

संख्यानं *n.* Numbering, calculation.

संख्यावत् *a.* (*f.* —ती) 1 Numbered. -2 Possessed of reason. *-m.* A learned man.

संगः *m.* 1 Coming together, joining. -2 Meeting, union, confluence (as of rivers). -3 Touch, contact. -4 Association, friendly intercourse. -5 Attachment, fondness. -6 Attachment to worldly ties. -7 Encounter, fight. -8 Hindrance.

संगणिका *f.* An excellent or incomparable discourse.

संगत *p. p.* (*f.* —ता) 1 Joined or united with, associated with. -2 Assembled, met together. -3 Joined in wedlock, married. -4 Sexually united. -5 Fitted together, appropriate. -6 In conjunction with (as planets). -7 Shrunk up, contracted. —तं *n.* 1 Union, meeting, alliance. -2 Association, company. -3 Friendship, intimacy. -4 A harmonious or consistent speech.

संगतिः *f.* 1 Union, conjunction. -2 Company, association, intercourse. -3 Sexual union. -4 Visiting, frequenting. -5 Appropriateness, applicability. -6 Accident, accidental occurrence. -7 Knowledge. -8 Questioning for further knowledge.

संगमः *m.* 1 Meeting, union. -2 Association, society, intercourse. -3 Contact, touch. -4 Sexual union. -5 Confluence (of rivers). -6 Fitness, adaptation. -7 Encounter, fight. -8 Conjunction (of planets).

संगरः *m.* 1 A promise, an agreement. -2 Accepting, undertaking -3 A bargain. -4 War, battle, fight -5 Misfortune. -6 Poison.

संगवः *m*. N. of a particular Muhúrta after early dawn and forming the second of the five divisions of the day.

संगित *p. p.* (*f.*—ता) Sung together, sung in chorus. —तं *n*. 1 Chorus, a song sung by many voices. -2 Singing accompanied by instrumental music and dancing; triple symphony. -3 A concert. -4 The art of singing with music and dancing. -Comp. —अर्थः *m*. 1 The subject of a musical performance. -2 The materials or necessary apparatus for a musical concert.-शाला *f*. A concert-hall.

संगीतकं *n*. 1 Concert, symphony. -2 A public entertainment consisting of songs attended with music and dancing. [Conversation.

संगीतिः *f*. 1 Concert, harmony. -2

संगीर्ण *p. p.* (*f.* —र्णा) 1 Agreed or assented to. -2 Promised, vowed.

संग्रहः *m*. 1 Seizing, grasping. -2 Reception, admission.-3 Guarding, protection. -4 Propitiating supporting -5 Accumulation.-6 Governing, controlling. -7 Conglomeration. -8 Agglomeration (a kind of संयोग).-9 Inclusion, comprehension. -10 Compilation. -11 Summary, abridgment. -12 Sum, amount, totality. -13 A catalogue, list. -14 A store-room. -15 An effort. -16 Mention, reference. -17 Greatness, elevation.

संग्रहणं *n*. 1 Seizing, grasping. -2 Supporting, encouraging. -3 Compiling, collecting. -4 Blending. -5 Incasing, setting. -6 Sexual union. -7 Adultery. -8 Hoping. -9 Accepting, receiving.-णी *f*. Dysentery.

संग्रहीतृ *m*. A charioteer.

संग्रामः *m*. War, battle, fight.

संग्राहः *m*. 1 Laying hold of, grasping. -2 Forcible seizure. -3 Clenching the fist. -4 The fist. -5 The handle of a shield.

संग्राहकः *m*. A collector, compiler.

संघः *m*. 1 A collection, multitude, flock. -2 A number of people living together. -3 Close combination. —चारिन् *m*. A fish. —जीविन् *m*. A hired labourer.

संघटना *f*. Joining together, union.

संघट्टः *m*. 1 Friction, rubbing together. -2 Collision.-3 Conflict. -4 Meeting, collision or rivalry (as of wives). -5 Embracing.

संघट्टनं *n*., -ना *f*.1 Rubbing together, friction. -2 Collision. -3 Adherence to. -4 Contact. cohesion. -5 The intertwining of wrestlers. -6 Encounter in general. -7 The embrace of lovers.

संघर्षः *m*. 1 Rubbing together, friction. -2 Grinding. -3 Collision. -4 Contest for superiority. -5 Envy, jealousy. -6 Flowing gently.

संघाटिका *f*. 1 A pair, couple. -2 A bawd, procuress. -3 Smell.

संघातः *m*. 1 Union, an association. -2 A multitude. -3 Killing, slaughter. -4 Phlegm. -5 N. of a division of hell.

सचकित *a*. (*f*. -ता) Startled, timid. —तं *ind*. Tremblingly, in an alarmed or startled manner.

सचिः *m*. 1 A friend. -2 Friendship, intimacy. —*f*. The wife of Indra ; see शची.

साचिल्लक *a*. (*f*. —का) Blear-eyed.

सचिवः *m*. 1 A friend, companion. -2 A minister, counsellor.

सची *f*. See शची.

सचेतन *a*. (*f*. —ना) 1 Sentient, animate, rational. -2 Conscious, sensible. [sed of feeling.

सचेतस् *a.* 1 Intelligent. -2 Posses-

सचेष्टः *m.* The mango tree

सजन *a.* (*f.* -ना) Having men or living beings. —नः *m.* A man of the same family; a kinsman.

सजंबाल *a.* (*f.* -ला) Muddy.

सजाति, सजातीय *a.* (*f.* -या) 1 Of the same kind, class or species. -2 Like, similar. —*m.* A son of a man and woman of the same caste.

सजुष् (स्) *a.* Loving, attached to. -2 Associated together. -*m.* (Nom. सजूः, सजुषौ, सजुषः; *instr. Dual* सजूर्भ्याम्). A friend, companion. —*ind.* With, together with.

सज्ज *a.* (*f.* -ज्जा) 1 Ready, got ready. -2 Dressed, clothed. -2 Accoutred, equipped, armed. -4 Fortified.

सज्जनं *n.* 1 Fastening, tying on. -2 Dressing. -3 Preparing, arming, equipping. -4 A guard, sentry. -5 A ferry. —नः *m.* A good man. —ना *f.* Decoration, accoutrement, equipment.

सज्जा *f.* 1 Dress. -2 Equipment. -3 Military accoutrement, armour, mail.

सज्जित *a.* (*f.* -ता) 1 Dressed. -2 Decorated. -3 Made ready, equipped. -4 Accoutred, armed.

सज्य *a.* (*f.* -ज्या) 1 Furnished with a bow-string. -2 Strung (as a bow).

संचः *m.* A collection of leaves for writing upon. [Cheating, deceit.

संचत *m.* 1 A cheat, juggler. -2

संचयः *m.* 1 Heaping up, gathering. -2 A heap, stock, store. -3 A large quantity, collection.

संचयनं *n.* 1 Gathering, collecting. -2 Collecting the ashes and bones of a body after it has been burnt.

संचरः *m.* 1 Passage, transit from one zodiacal sign to another. -2 A way, path. -3 A narrow road, a difficult passage. -4 Entrance, gate. -5 The body. -6 Killing. [ling.

संचरणं *n.* Going, motion, travel-

संचलनं *n.* Agitation, shaking.

संचाय्यः *m.* N. of a particular sacrifice.

संचारः *m.* 1 Going, movement, roaming through. -2 Passing through, passage, transit. -3 A way, road, pass. -4 A difficult journey. -5 Difficulty, distress. -6 Transmission of contagion. -7 A gem said to be found in the hoods of serpents. -8 The entrance of the sun into a new sign. [An instigator.

संचारकः *m.* 1 A leader, guide. -2

संचारिका *f.* 1 A female messenger. -2 A procuress. -3 A pair, couple. -4 Smell, odour.

संचारिन् *a.* (*f.* —णी) 1 Moving, movable. -2 Roaming, wandering. -3 Unsteady, fickle. -4 Inaccessible. -5 Evanescent, as a ' Bhâva '. -6 Influencing. -7 Hereditary (as a disease). -8 Contagious. -9 Impelling. -*m.* 1 Wind, air. -2 Incence. -3 A transient or evanescent feeling which serves to strengthen the prevailing sentiment.

संचाली *f.* The Gunjâ shrub.

संचित *p. p.* (*f.* —ता) 1 Heaped up, accumulated. -2 Laid by, stored. -3 Enumerated, reckoned. -4 Full of, furnished with. -5 Impeded, obstructed. -6 Dense, thick (as a wood).

संचितिः *f.* A collection.

संज् 1 P. (सजति, सक्त; the स of the root is changed to ष after a preposition ending in इ or उ) 1 To adhere to, cling to -2 To go, move. -3 To fasten. With अनु— To associate, accompany. अव— 1 To adhere to. -2 To assign to. आ — 1 To fasten. -2 To take up, bear. -3 To assign to, delegate. -4 To be attached to. वि – 1 To adhere to. -2 To be attached to. प्र — 1 To cling to. -2 To be relevant, to be applicable. व्यति— To link together.

Pass. (सज्यते) To be attached to, cling or adhere to. With अव— To prepare, to be ready. प्र— To apply to, to be applicable, to follow.

संजः *m*. 1 N. of Brahman (*m*.). -2 N. of Siva.

संजयः *m* N. of the charioteer of king Dhritarâshtra. It was he who narrated the events of the great Bhâratî war to the blind king Dhritarâshtra.

संजल्पः *m*. 1 Conversation. -2 Confused talk. -3 An uproar.

संजवनं *n*. A quadrangle; a group of four houses forming a court.

संजा *f*. A she-goat.

संजीवनं *n*. 1 Living together. -2 Bringing to life, resuscitation. -3 N. of one of the 21 hells. -4 A group of four houses; a quadrangle. -नी *f*. 1 A kind of elixir. -2 Restoring life. -3 Food.

संज्ञ *a*. (*f*.-ज्ञा) 1 Knock-kneed. -2 Being conscious. -3 Named, called. —ज्ञं *n*. A yellow fragrant wood.

संज्ञा *f*. 1 Consciousness. (संज्ञा लभ्, To recover consciousness, come to one's senses). -2 Knowledge, understanding. -3 Intellect, mind. -4 A hint, token, gesture. -5 A name, designation. -6 (In gram.) Any name or noun having a meaning peculiar to itself; a proper name. -7 The technical name for an affix. -8 The Gâyatrî verse. -9 N. of the daughter of Visvakarman and wife of the sun. -Comp. —अधिकारः *m*. A leading rule which gives a peculiar name to the rules falling under it and which influences them. —विषयः *m*. An epithet, an attribute. —सुतः *m*. An epithet of Saturn.

संज्ञापनं *n*. 1 Informing. -2 Teaching. -3 Killing, slaughter.

संज्ञित *a*. (*f*. —ता) Named; called, denominated.

संज्ञु *a*. Knock-kneed.

संज्वरः *m*. 1 Great heat, fever. -2 Heat. -3 Indignation.

सटं *n*., सटा *f*. 1 An ascetic's matted hair. -2 The mane (of a lion). -3 Bristles of a boar. -4 A braid of hair. -5 A crest. -Comp. —अंकः *m*. A lion.

सटीक *a*. (*f*. —का) Accompanied or explained by a commentary.

सट्टकं *n*. A kind of minor drama in Prâkrita.

सट्वा *f*. 1 A kind of bird. -2 A musical instrument.

सठ् 10 U. (साठयति,-ते) 1 To finish. -2 To leave unfinished. -3 To go, move. -4 To adorn.

सणसूत्रं *n*. A hempen cord or thread.

संडः *m*. A eunuch. [pers.

संडिशः *m*. A pair of tongs or nip-

संडीनं *n*. One of the several modes of flight of birds.

सत *a*. (*f*.—ती) 1 Being, existing. -2 Real, essential, true. -3 Good, virtuous. -4 Noble, worthy. -5 Right, proper. -6 Best, excellent. -7 Respectable. -8 Learned. -9 Beautiful. -10 Firm, steady. —*m*.

A good or virtuous man, a sage. —*n.* I That which really exists; entity, existence, essence. -2 The reality. -3 Good. -4 Brahman (*n*). (सत्कृ I To respect, receive hospitably. -2 To honour, worship. -3 To adorn). -Comp. —असत् (सदसत्) *a.* I Existent and non-existent.-2 Real and unreal. -3 True and false. -4 Good and bad, right and wrong. -5 Virtuous and wicked. (-*n. du.*) I Entity and non-entity.-2 Good and evil; right and wrong. —आचारः *m* I Good manners, moral conduct.-2 Approved usage ; traditionary observances. -उत्तरं *n.* A proper or good reply.-कांडः *m.* A hawk, kite.-कारः *m.* I A kind or hospitable treatment.-2 Reverence, respect. -3 Care, attention. -4 A meal. -5 A festival, religious observance. —कुलीन *a.* Nobly born, of noble descent. -कृत *a.* I Done well or properly. -2 Hospitably received. -3 Respected, honoured. -4 Worshipped. -5 Entertained, welcomed. (-तः *m.*) An epithet of Siva.(-तं *n.*) I Hospitality. -2 Respect. -3 Virtue, piety. —कृतिः *f.* I Treating with respect, hospitality.-2 Virtue, morality. —क्रिया *f.* I Virtue, goodness. -2 A good or virtuous action. -3 Hospitality. -4 Salutation. -5 Any purificatory ceremony. -6 Obsequies. —गतिः *f.* A good or happy state, beatitude. —गुण *a.* Possessed of good qualities, virtuous.(-णः *m.*) Virtue, excellence, goodness, good quality. —चरित, -चारित्र *a.* Well-conducted, virtuous, righteous. (-*n.*) I Virtuous conduct. -2 History or account of the good. —चारा *f.* Turmeric. -चित् *n.* The Supreme Spirit. —चिदानंदः *m.* I Entity, knowledge and joy. -2 An epithet of the Supreme Spirit. —जनः *m.* A good or virtuous man. —पत्रं *n.* The new leaf of a water-lily. —पथः *m.* A good road. -2 The right path of duty. -3 An orthodox doctrine. —पशुः *m.* A victim fit for a sacrifice, a good sacrificial victim. -पात्रं *n.* A worthy or virtuous person. —प्रतिपक्षः *m.* (In logic) One of the five kinds of *hetvábhâsas* or fallacious *hetus*; a *hetu* along which there exists another equal *hetu* on the opposite side. —फलः *m.* The pomegranate tree. —भावः *m.* I Existence, being, entity. -2 Actual existence, reality. -3 Amiability. -4 The quality of goodness. —मातुरः *m.* The son of a virtuous mother. —मात्रः *m.* 'Consisting of mere entity', the soul. —मानः *m.* Esteem of the good. —वचस् *n.* An agreeable or pleasing speech. —वस्तु *n* I A good thing.-2 A good plot or story.—विद्य *a.* Well-educated, having good learning. —वृत्त *a.* I Well-behaved, virtuous, upright. -2 Perfectly circular, well-rounded. (-त्तं *n.*) I Virtuous conduct. -2 An agreeable disposition. —शील *a.* I Good-tempered. -2 Benevolent, kindly disposed (towards others). —संसर्गः, -संनिधानं, -संगः, -संगतिः, -समागमः *m.* Association with the good. —संप्रयोगः *m.* Right application. —सहाय *a.* Having virtuous friends. (-यः *m.*) A good companion. —सार *a.* Having good sap or essence. (-रः *m.*) I A kind of tree. -2 A poet. -3 A painter. —हेतुः *m.* A faultless or valid *hetu* or middle term.

सतत *a.* (*f.* -ता) Eternal, everlasting, perpetual. —तं *ind.* Constantly, eternally, always. -Comp. —गः, -गतिः *m.* Wind.

सातिः *f.* 1 A gift, donation.-2 End, destruction.

सती *f.* 1 A virtuous or good woman (or wife). -2 A female ascetic. -3 N. of the goddess Durgâ. -4 A kind of fragrant earth.

सतीत्वं *n.* Chastity.

सतीनः *m.* 1 A kind of pulse. -2 A bamboo.

सतीर्थः, सतीर्थ्यः *m.* A fellow student.

सतीलः *m.* 1 A bamboo. -2 Air, wind. -2 Pease, pulse (-ला *f.* also).

सतेरः *m.* Husk, chaff.

सत्ता *f.* 1 Existence, being.-2 Reality.-3 The highest 'Játi' or generality. -4 Goodness, excellence.

सत्त्रं, सत्रं *n.* 1 A sacrificial session, especially one lasting from 13 to 100 days.-2 A sacrifice in general. -3 An oblation, offering or gift.-4 Liberality, munificence. -5 Virtue. -6 A house, residence. -7 Covering. -8 Wealth. -9 A forest.-10 A tank, pond. -11 Fraud, cheating. -12 A place of refuge, asylum. -13 A place where houseless people are housed and fed. -Comp. —अयनं (-णं *n.*) A long sacrificial session. —शाला *f.* An alms-house.

सत्रा *ind.* With, together with. -Comp. —हन् *m.* An epithet of Indra.

सत्रिन् *m.* A liberal house-holder. -2 A priest superintending or performing a sacrifice.

सत्त्रिः *m.* 1 A cloud. -2 An elephant.

सत्त्वं *n.* (-त्त्वः *m.* Also in the first ten senses) 1 Being, entity.- 2 Nature, essence. -3 Inborn disposition. -4 Life, vitality. -5 Consciousness, mind, sense. -6 An embryo. -7 Substance, thing, wealth. -8 An elementary substance, such as earth, air, fire &c. -9 A living or sentient being, an animal. -10 Demon, ghost.-11 Goodness, virtue, excellence. -12 Truth, reality. -13 Strength, energy, courage, the stuff of which a person is made. -14 Wisdom, good sense. -15 The quality of goodness or purity (the highest of the three Gunas). -16 A characteristic. -17 A noun, substantive. -Comp. -अनुरूप *a.* 1 According to inborn disposition or inherent character. -2 According to one's means or wealth. —उद्रेकः *m.* 1 Excess of the quality of goodness. -2 Pre-eminence in strength or courage.—लक्षणं *n.* Signs of pregnancy. —विप्लवः *m.* Loss of consciousness. —विहित *a.* 1 Caused by nature. -2 Caused by goodness. -3 Virtuous, upright.—संशुद्धिः *f.* Purity of nature. —संपन्न *a* 1 Endowed with goodness. -2 Even-minded. —संप्लवः *m.* 1 Loss of vigour. -2 Universal destruction.-सारः *m.* 1 Essence of strength. -2 A very powerful person.-स्थ *a.* 1 Being in the nature of things. -2 Inherent in animals. -3 Animate. -4 Good, excellent.

सत्त्वमेजय *a.* Terrifying animals or living beings.

सत्त्ववत् *a.* (*f.*-ती) 1 Living, existing. -2 Possessed of true essence. -3 Good, virtuous. -4 Endowed with energy or courage.

सत्य *a.* (*f.* —त्या) 1 True, real. -2 Honest, truthful, faithful. -3 Fulfilled, realized.-4 Virtuous, upright. —त्यः *m.* 1 The uppermost of the seven worlds or *lokas* above the earth. -2 The Asvattha tree. -3 N.

of Râma. -4 Of Vishnu. -5 The deity presiding over the rite नांदीमुखश्राद्ध. —त्यं n. 1 Truth. -2 Sincerity. -3 Goodness, virtue, purity. -4 An oath, a promise, solemn asseveration.-5 A demonstrated truth or dogma. -6 The first of the four Yugas or ages of the world; the golden age or the age of truth and purity. -7 The Suprme Spirit. —त्यं ind. Truly, really, indeed. -Comp. -अग्निः m. N. of the sage Agastya.-अनृत a. 1 True and false. -2 Apparently true, but really false. (-तं n. sing., -ते n. dual) 1 Truth and falsehood. -2 Practice of truth and falsehood; i. e. trade, commerce. —अभिसंध a. True to one's promise, sincere. -आत्मन् a. True. -उत्कर्षः m. 1 Pre-eminence in truth.-2 True excellence. —उद्य a. Speaking the truth. —कामः m. A lover of truth.-दर्शिन् a. Truth-seeing, fore-seeing truth. —वृत्ति a. Strictly truthful. —पुरं n. The world of Vishnu. —पूत a. Purified by truth (as words). —भामा f. N. of the daughter of Satrájit and the favourite wife of Krishna. —भारतः m. N. of Vyàsa.—युगं n. The golden age. —वचस् a. Truthful, veracious. (-m) 1 A saint, a 'rishi'.-2 A seer. (-n.) Truth, veracity. —वद्य a. Veracious. (—द्यं n.) Truth, veracity. —वाच् a. Truthful. (-m.) 1 A saint, seer. -2 A crew. —व्रत, -संगर, -संध a. 1 True or faithful to an agreement, promise or word.- संगरः m. N. of Kubera. —संधः m. 1 An epithet of Râma. -2 Of Bharata -3 Of king Janamejaya. (—धा f.) An epithet of Draupadî.

सत्यंकारः m. 1 Making true or good, ratification of a contract or bargain. -2 Earnest money.

सत्यवत् m. N. of a king, husband of Sàvitrî. —ती f. 1 N. of the daughter of a fisherman, who became mother of Vàysa by the sage Parâsara. -2 N. of the wife of Nàrada.-3 Of the wife of Richìka.

सत्या f. 1 Truthfulness. -2 N. of Sítâ. -3 Of Draupadî. -4 Of Satyavatí, mother of Vyása.-5 Of Durgâ. -6 Of Satyabhâmâ, wife of Krishna. -7 Of the mother of Vishnu.

सत्याकृतिः f. Earnest money.

सत्रं n. See सत्त्रं. —त्रं ind. With, together.

सत्राजित् m. N. of a son of Nighna and father of Satyabhâmâ.

सत्वर a. (f.-रा) Quick, speedy, expeditious.-रं ind. Quickly, speedily.

सथूत्कारः m. Speech accompanied with sputtering.

सद् 1 P. (6 P. also according to some) (सीदति, सन्न ; the स of सद् is changed to ष after any preposition ending in इ or उ except प्रति) 1 To sit, sit down, lie down, settle. -2 To sink down, plunge into. -3 To live, reside.-4 To be low-spirited, to despair.-5 To decay, waste away.-6 To be in distress, be helpless. -7 To be impeded. -8 To be fatigued, to droop. With अव-1 To sink down, to be exhausted, to faint. -2 To be disheartened.-3 To perish, to come to an end. आ— 1 To sit down, to sit or be near. -2 To place. -3 To approach, to meet with, to find. -4 To attack, encounter. उद्- 1 To sink down, to fall into ruin or decay. -2 To leave off. -3 To rise up. उप— 1 To approach. -2 To worship. वि— 1 To sit down. -2 To be afflicted. प्र— 1 To be pro pitious, to favour, to be gracious. -2 To be soothed, to be appeased. -3 To be clear (*lit.* and *fig.*). -4 To take effect, to succeed. वि— 1 To be exhausted. -2 To be afflicted, to be sorrowful, to despair.

Caus. (सादयति,-ते) 1 To cause to sit down, rest. -2 To throw or cast down, place, put. -3 To weary, exhaust. -4 To cause to perish. With आ— 1 To find out, obtain, get, be in possession of. उद्— To destroy, annihilate. प्र— To propitiate, to get the favour of. वि— To cause to despair.

Desid. (सिषत्सति) To wish to sit down.

सदः *m.* The fruit of trees.

सदंशकः *m.* A crab.

सदंशवदनः *m.* A heron.

सदनं *n* 1 A house, mansion. -2 Sinking down, decaying. -3 Exhaustion, fatigue. -4 Water. -5 A sacrificial hall. -6 The abode of Yama. -7 Sitting, a seat.

सदस् *n.* 1 Seat, residence, dwelling. -2 An assembly. -Comp. -गृहं *n.* An assembly-hall, council-room.

सदस्यः *m.* 1 Any person present at an assembly, a member of an assembly. -2 An assistant at a sacrifice.

सदा *ind.* Always, perpetually. -Comp. —आनंदः *m.* An epithet of Siva. —गतिः *m.* 1 Wind. -2 The universal spirit. -3 The sun. -4 Final beatitude. —तोया, -नीरा *f.* 1 N. of the *Karatoyá* river. -2 A river always bearing water. —दानः *m.* 1 A ruttish elephant. -2 A scent-elephant. -3 N. of the elephant of Indra. -4 N. of Ganesa. —नर्तः *m.* The wagtail. —फलः *m.* 1 The cocoa-nut tree. -2 The 'Bilva' tree. -3 The jack tree. -4 The glomerous fig-tree. —शिवः *m.* N. of Siva.

सदातन *a.* Perpetual, eternal. —नः *m.* An epithet of Vishnu.

सदृक्ष (*f.* -क्षी), सदृश्, सदृश *a.* (-शी *f*) 1 Like, similar, of the same rank, (with gen. or loc., but usually in comp.). -2 Fit, right, suitable. -3 Worthy, becoming.

सदेश *a.* (*f.* —शा) 1 Possessing a country. -2 Belonging to the same country. -3 Neighbouring.

सद्मन् *n.* 1 A house, a dwelling. -2 A place, station. -3 A temple. -4 An altar. -5 A seat.

सद्यस् *ind.* 1 To-day. -2 Instantly, immediately. -3 Quickly, promptly. -4 A short time back. -Comp. —कालः *m.* The present time. -कालीन *a.* Recent. —सद्योजात Newly born. (—तः *m.*) 1 A calf. -2 An epithet of Siva. -भाविन् -*m.* A calf. -शुद्धिः, *f.* -शौचं *n.* Immediate purification.

सद्यस्क *a.* (*f.*—स्का) 1 New, recent. -2 Instantaneous.

सद्रु *a.* 1 Resting, staying. -2 Going.

सद्वंद्व *a.* (*f.* —द्वा) Quarrelsome, contentious.

सद्वसथः *m.* A village.

सधर्मन् *a.* 1 Having similar properties. -2 Having similar duties. -3 Of the same sect or caste. -4 Like, resembling. -Comp. —चारिणी *f.* A legally married wife.

सधर्मिणी *f.* A wife married according to proper rites.

सधर्मिन *a.* (*f.* —णी) See सधर्मन्.

सध्र्यंच् *a.* (*f.* सध्रीची) Going along with, accompanying. -*m.* A companion, a confidant.

सध्रीची *f.* A female companion, or confidant.

सन् 1 To love, like. -2 To worship, honour. -3 To obtain. -4 To receive graciously. -5 To honour with gifts, give, bestow.

सनः *m.* The flapping of an elephant's ears.

सनकः *m.* N. of one of the four sons of Brahman (*m.*).

सनत् *m.* An epithet of Brahman (*m.*). -*ind.* Always, perpetually. -Comp. —कुमारः *m.* N. of one the four sons of Brahman (*m.*).

सनसूत्रं *n.* 1 A net made of hemp. -2 A hempen cord.

सना *ind.* Always, perpetually.

सनात् *ind.* Always.

सनातन *a.* (*f.* —नी) 1 Perpetual, permanent. -2 Firm, fixed. -3 Primeval, ancient. —नः *m.* 1 The primeval being, Vishnu. -2 N. of Siva. -3 Of Brahman (*m.*). —नी *f.* 1 N. of Lakshmî. -2 Of Durgá or Párvatî. -3 Of Sarasvatí.

सनाथ *a.* (*f.* —था) 1 Having a lord or husband. -2 Possessed of a guardian. -3 Occupied by, possessed by. -4 Possessing, endowed with, full of. —था *f.* A woman whose husband is living.

सनाभि *a.* 1 Connected by the same navel or womb; uterine. -2 Kindred, related. -3 Like, resembling. -4 Affectionate. —भिः *m.* 1 A uterine brother; a near kinsman. -2 A relation, kinsman. -3 A relation as far as the seventh degree.

सनाभ्यः *m.* A relation as far as the 7th degree.

सनिः *m.* 1 Worship, service. -2 A donation. -3 An entreaty, a respectful solicitation (*f.* also in this sense).

सनिष्ठीवं, सनिष्ठेवं *n.* Speech accompanied with emission of saliva.

सनी *f.* 1 A respectful entreaty. -2 A quarter or point of the compass.

संतः *m.* The two hands opened and the palms joined.

संतक्षणं *n.* Sarcastic language, sarcasm.

संतत *p. p.* (*f.* —ता) 1 Stretched, extended. -2 Uninterrupted, regular. -3 Lasting, eternal. -4 Much, many. —तं *ind.* Always, constantly, perpetually.

संततिः *f.* 1 Stretching across. -2 Extent, expanse, extension. -3 A series, succession, continuity. -4 Uninterrupted continuance. -5 A lineage, family. -6 Offspring, progeny. -7 A heap, mass.

संतपनं *n.* 1 Heating; inflaming. -2 Torturing.

संतप्त *p. p.* (*f.* —प्ता) 1 Heated, glowing. -2 Afflicted, tormented.

संतर्पणं *n.* 1 Satisfying, satiating. -2 Gratifying, delighting. -3 That which gives delight.

संततमस्, संततमसं *n.* 1 Universal darkness, great darkness. -2 Great darkness or delusion of the mind (महामोह).

संतानः *m.*, -नं *n.* 1 Stretching, extension, expanse, spread. -2 Continuity, succession, continuance. -3 Family, race. -4 Progeny, issue. -5 One of the five trees of Indra's paradise.

संतानकः *m.* One of the five trees of Indra's paradise or its flower.

संतानिका *f.* 1 Froth, foam. -2 Cream. -3 A cob-web. -4 The blade of a knife or sword.

संतापः *m.* 1 Heat, inflammation. -2 Distress, suffering, agony, anguish. -3 Passion, rage. -4 Remorse. -5 Penance.

संतापनः *m*, N. of one of the 5 arrows of Cupid. —नं *n.* 1 Burning, scorching. -2 Paining, afflicting. -3 Exciting passion. [gift.

संतिः *f.* 1 End, destruction. -2 A

संतुष्ट *p. p.* (*f.* —ष्टा) Satisfied, contented.

संतुष्टिः *f.* Complete satisfaction.

संतोषः *m.* 1 Satisfaction, contentment. -2 Pleasure, joy. -3 The thumb and forefinger.

संतोषणं *n.* Pleasing, comforting.

संत्रासः *m*, Fear, terror, alarm.

संदंशः *m.* 1 A pair of tongs.-2 Too great compression of the teeth in the pronunciation of vowels (or letters). -3 N. of a hell.

संदंशकः *m.* A pair of tongs.

संदंशिका *f.* A pair of pincers.

संदर्भः *m.* 1 Stringing together, weaving. -2 Uniting, mixture. -3 Consistency, regular connection.-4 Construction. -5 A literary work.

संदर्शनं *n.* 1 Beholding, viewing, looking steadfastly. -2 Seeing one another. -3 Sight, appearance. -4 Regard, consideration. -5 Showing, display.

संदानं *n.* 1 A rope, cord, chain, fetter. -2 Cutting, dividing. —नः *m.* That part of an elephant's temples whence ichor exudes.

संदानित *a.* (*f.* -ता) Bound, tied, chained.

संदानिनी *f.* A cow-pen (गोष्ठ).

संदावः *m.* Flight, retreat.

संदाहः *m.* Burning up, consuming.

संदिग्ध *p. p.* (*f* —ग्धा) 1 Besmeared, covered. -2 Dubious, uncertain. -3 Mistaken for. -4 Doubted, questioned. -5 Unintelligible. -6 Dangerous, unsafe. -7 Envenomed. —ग्धं *n.* 1 A doubt, uncertainty. -2 Besmearing.

संदिष्ट *p. p.* (*f.* —ष्टा) 1 Pointed out, indicated. -2 Assigned. -3 Narrated, communicated.-4 Agreed to, promised. —ष्टः *m.* One entrusted with, a message; a messenger, herald. -ष्टं *n.* Information, news, tidings.

संदित *a.* (*f.*—ता) Bound, fettered.

संदी *f* A small bed-stead, couch.

संदीपनः *m.* One of the five arrows of Cupid. — नं *n.* 1 Kindling, inflaming. -2 Exciting, stimulating.

संदीप्त *p. p.* (*f.* — प्ता) 1 Kindled, inflamed. -2 Excited, stimulated. -3 Instigated, prompted.

संदूषणं *n.* Corrupting, vitiating.

संदेशः *m.* 1 Information, news, tidings. -2 A message, an errand. -3 Commission, command.-Comp. —अर्थः *m.* The subject of a message. —हरः, -हारकः *m.* A news-bearer, messenger, an envoy, ambassador.

संदेहः *m.* 1 Doubt, uncertainty, suspense. -2 Risk, peril. -3 (In Rhet.) The figure of speech in which the object under discussion is poetically suspected to be something else. (this figure is also called ससंदेह). -Comp. —दोला *f.* The swing of uncertainty *i.e.* a state of suspense, a dilemma.

संदोहः *m.* 1 Milking. -2 A multitude, heap, mass.

संद्रावः *m.* Flight, retreat.

संधा *f.* 1 Union, intimate union, close connection. -2 State, condition. -3 An agreement, a promise, compact. -4 Limit, boundary. -5 Steadiness. -6 Twilight. -7 Distillation. -8 Steady continuance in any state.

संधानं *n.* 1 Joining, uniting, junction, combination. -2 Compounding (of medicines &c.). -3 Restoration, repairing. -4 Fitting, fixing

(as an arrow to the bow-string). -5 Alliance, league, friendship, peace. -6 A joint. -7 Attention. -8 Direction. -9 Supporting. -10 Distillation (of liquors). -11 Spirituous liquor or a kind of it.-12 Some thing eaten to excite thirst. -13 Preparation of pickles. -14 Contraction of the skin by means of astringents. -15 Sour rice-gruel.

संधानित *a.* (*f.* —ता) 1 United, strung together. -2 Bound, tied.

संधानिनी *f.* A cow-house, cow pen.

संधिः *m.* 1 Union, connection. -2 A compact, an agreement.-3 Alliance, league, (one of the six expedients to be used in foreign politics.). -4 A joint, articulation (of the body).-5 A fold (of a garment). -6 A breach, hole. -7 A chasm or opening made by thieves in a wall or underneath a building. -8 Separation, division. -9 Euphonic junction or coalition(in gram.). -10 An interval. -11 A critical juncture. -12 An opportune moment. -13 A period at the expiration of each *Yuga* or age. -14 A division or joint (in a drama).-15 The vulva.-16 Distillation. -Comp. —अक्षर *n.* A diphthong. —चोरः *m.* A house-breaker. —जीवकः *m.* One who lives by dishonest means (particularly as a go-between). —दूषणं *n.* The violation of a treaty.-बंधनं *n.* A ligament, tendon, nerve. —विचक्षणः *m.* One skilled in negotiating treaties.—वेला *f.* 1 The time of twilight. -2 Any connecting period. —हारकः *m.* A house-breaker.

संधिकः *m.* A kind of fever.

संधिका *f.* Distillation (of liquors).

संधित *a.* (*f.* -ता) 1 United, joined, tied. -2 Reconciled, allied. -3 Fixed, fitted.-4 Pickled, preserved. -तं *n.* 1 Pickles.-2 Spirituous liquor.

संधिनी *f.* 1 A cow (united with the bull or impregnated by him.-2 A cow milked unseasonably.

संधिला *f.* 1 A breach made in a wall, a pit, chasm. -2 A river. -3 Spirituous liquor.

संधुक्षणं *n.* 1 Kindling, inflaming. -2 Exciting, stimulating.

संधुक्षित *p. p.* (*f.* —ता) 1 Kindled, inflamed. -2 Excited.

संधेय *a.* 1 To be united or joined. -2 Capable of being reconciled. -3 To be made peace with. -4 To be aimed at.

संध्या *f.* 1 Union.-2 Joint,division. -3 Morning or evening twilight. -4 The time intervening between the expiration of one *Yuga* and the commencement of another. -5 The morning, noon and evening prayers of a Bráhmana. -6 A promise. -7 A boundary, limit, -8 Meditation. -9 A kind of flower. -10 N. of a river. -11 N. of the wife of Brahman (*m.*) -Comp. —उपासना *f.* Sandhyâ adoration. —नाटिन् *m.* An epithet of Siva. -पुष्पी *f.* 1 A kind of jasmine. -2 A nutmeg. —बलः *m.* A demon.—रागः *m.* Red lead. —रामः *m.* An epithet of Brahman (*m.*).

सन्न *p. p.* (*f.*—न्ना) 1 Sitting down, lying. -2 Dejected, downcast. -3 Drooping. -4 Weak, low, feeble. -5 Decayed. -6 Perished. -7 Still, motionless. -8 Adjacent, near. —न्नः *m.* The tree called पियाल. —न्नं *n.* A little, a small quantity.

संनत *p. p.* (*f.* —ता) 1 Bent down. -2 Downcast. -3 Contracted.

संनतिः *f.* 1 Respectful salutation,

reverence. -2 Crouching.-3 Humility. -4 A kind of sacrifice. -5 A sound.

संनद्ध *p. p.* (*f.* —द्धा) 1 Bound together, girded on. -2 Dressed in armour, mailed. -3 Prepared for battle, fully equipped.-4 Arranged in general. -5 Pervading. -6 Closely attached ; bordering, near. -7 Ready to burst or blossom.

संनय: ***m.*** 1 A multitude, quantity, number. -2 Rear, rear-guard (of an army).

संनहनं *n.* 1 Equipping, arming oneself. -2 Preparation. -2 Binding tightly -4 Industry, exertion.

संनाह: *m.* 1 Putting on armour. -2 Warlike preparation. -3 Armour, mail.

संनाह्य: ***m.*** A war-elephant.

संनिकर्ष: *m.* 1 Bringing near. -2 Vicinity, presence. -3 Connection, relation. -4 (In Nyáya phil.) Connection of an organ of sense (इंद्रिय) with its object (विषय).

संनिकर्षणं *n.* 1 Bringing near. -2 Approaching, approximating. -3 Proximity.-4 Relation,connection. -5 Connection of an organ of sense with its object.

संनिकृष्ट *p. p.* (*f.* —ष्टा) 1 Approximate. -2 Adjacent, near. —ष्टं *n.* Proximity, vicinity.

संनिधातृ *m.* 1 One who brings near. -2 One who deposits. -3 A receiver of stolen goods. -4 An officer who introduces people at court.

संनिधानं *n.*, संनिधि: ***m.*** 1 Putting down together, juxta-position. -2 Proximity, vicinity, presence.-3 Perceptibility, appearance. -4 A receptacle. -5 Taking charge of. -6 Combination. -7 Depositing. -8 The object of an organ of sense (इंद्रियविषय).

संनिपात: *m.* 1 Alighting, descent. -2 Meeting: confluence. -3 Collision, contact. -4 Union, mixture. -5 An assemblage, a multitude, number. -6 Arrival. -7 A morbid state of the three humours of the body causing fever which is of a dangerous kind. -Comp. —ज्वर: *m.* Fever arising from a vitiated state of the three humours of the body.

संनिबंध: *m.* 1 Binding firmly. -2 Connection, attachment. -3 Effectiveness.

संनिभ *a.* (*f.* —भा) Like, similar (at the end of comp.).

संनिवृत्त *p. p.* (*f.*—त्ता) 1 Returned. -2 Stopped. -3 Withdrawing.

संनिवृत्ति: *f.* 1 Return. -2 Desisting from. -3 Check, forbearance.

संनिविष्ट *p. p.* (*f.* —ष्टा) 1 Entered into. -2 Assembled. -3 Absorbed in. -4 Resting in. -5 Contiguous. -6 Encamped.

संनिवेश: *m.* 1 Ardent devotion,close application. -2 A multitude. -3 Arrangement. -4 Site, place. -5 Vicinity, proximity. -6 Form, figure. -7 A dwelling-place. -8 Giving seats to; an encampment. -9 Insertion. -10 An open space near a town where people assemble for amusement or exercise. -11 The collective position of an asterism.

संनिहित *p. p.* (*f.* —ता) 1 Placed near, neighbouring. -2 Proximate, at hand. -3 Present. -4 Placed, deposited. -5 Prepared, ready. —तं *n.* Proximity, vicinity. -Comp. —अपाय *a.* Frail, transitory.

संन्यसनं *n.* 1 Resignation. -2 Complete renunciation of the world. -3

Entrusting to the care of. -4 Depositing.

संन्यस्त *p. p.* (*f.* —स्ता) 1 Laid down. -2 Deposited. -3 Entrusted, consigned, -4 Relinquished. -5 Encamped.

संन्यास: *m.* 1 Abandonment. -2 Complete renunciation of the world. -3 A deposit, rust. -4 A wager in a game. -5 Giving up the body, death. -6 Indian spikenard.

संन्यासिन् *m.* 1 One who lays down or deposits.- 2 One who completely renounces the world; an ascetic.

सपक्ष *a.* (*f.* —क्षा) 1 Winged, having wings. -2 Having a side or party. -3 Belonging to the same side or party. -4 Like, similar (fig.). -5 Containing the पक्ष or subject of an inference. —क्ष: *m.* 1 An adherent, a partisan. -2 A kinsman.-3 (In logic) An instance on the same side; a similar instance.

सपत्न: *m.* An enemy, adversary, a rival.

सपत्नी *f.* A rival or fellow wife, rival mistress.

सपत्नीक *a.* (*f.* —का) Attended by [a wife.

सपत्राकरणं *n.* 1 Wounding in such a manner that the feathered part of the arrow enters the body. -2 Causing excessive pain.

सपत्राकृति: *f.* Great agony or pain; excessive affliction or torment.

सपदि *ind.* 1 Instantly, immediately. -2 Quickly, swiftly.

सपर्या *f.* 1 Worship, honouring. -2 Service, attendance.

सपाद *a.* (*f.* —दा) 1 Having feet. -2 Increased by a fourth part.

सपिंड: *m.* ' Having the same पिंड or funeral rice-ball offering ', a kinsman connected by the offering of the funeral rice-ball to the Manes of certain relations.

सपिंडी *f.* The *shráddha* in honour of the deceased relatives called Sapinda. (See सपिंड and सपिंडीकरणं).

सपिंडीकरणं *n.* 1 The performance of a particular Sráddha in honour of deceased relatives called सपिंड, to be performed at the end of one full year after the death of a relative, but now usually performed on the 12th day after death as part of the funeral obsequies.-2 Giving a person the rights of a 'Sapinda' or kinsman.

सपीति: *f.* Drinking together or in company.

सप्तक *a.* (*f.* -का or -की) 1 Containing seven. -2 Seven. -3 Seventh. —कं *n.* A collection of seven things.

सप्तकी *f.* A woman's girdle or zone.

सप्तन् *num a.* (Always *pl.* सप्त nom. and acc.) Seven. -Comp. —अंशु. *m.* N. of Agni. —अर्चिस् *a.* 1 Having seven tongues or flames. -2 Evil-eyed; of inauspicious look. (-*m.*). 1 N. of fire. -2 Of Saturn. —अशीति: *f.* Eighty-seven. —अश्रं *n.* A heptagon. —अश्व: *m.* The sun. —अह: *m.* Seven days *i. e.* a weak. —आत्मन् *m.* An epithet of Brahman (*m.*). —ऋषि: (सप्तर्षय: *m. pl.*). 1 The seven sages *i. e.* मरीचि, अत्रि, अंगिरस्, पुलस्त्य, पुलह, क्रतु, and वसिष्ठ. -2 The constellation called Ursa Major (the seven stars of which are said to be the seven sages mentioned above) —कोण *a.* Septangular. -चत्वारिंशत् *f.* Forty-seven. —जिह्व:, -ज्वाल: *m.* Fire —तंतु: *m.* A sacrifice. -त्रिंशत् *f.* Thirty-seven.—दशन् *a.* Seventeen.-दीधिति *m.* N. of fire. —द्वीपा *f.* The earth —धातु *m.* सप्तधातव: (*m.pl.*) The seven constituent elements of the body ; *i. e*, chyle, blood, flesh, fat, bone, marrow and semen. —नवतिः *f.* Ninety-seven. —नाडीचक्रं *n.* An astrological diagram used as a means of foretelling rain. —पदी *f* The ceremony of walking together round the nuptial fire after which the marriage becomes irrevocable. –पर्णः *m.* (so सप्तच्छदः, सप्तपत्रः) N. of a tree. —प्रकृतिः *f.* (प्रकृतयः *f. pl.*) The seven constituent parts of a kingdom, viz. king, ministers, ally, territory, fortress, army and treasury). —भूमिक, —भौम *a.* Seven stories high (as a palace). —रात्रं *n.* A period of seven nights. —विंशतिः *f.* Twenty-seven. —विध *a.* Seven-fold, of seven sorts. –शतं *n.* 1 Seven hundred. –2 One hundred and seven. (—ती *f.*) An aggregate or colleciion of 700 verses or stanzas. —शलाकः *m.* An astronomical diagram used for indicating auspicious days for marriages. –सप्तिः *m.* An epithet of the sun.

सप्ततिः *f.* Seventy.

सप्तधा *ind.* 1 Seven-fold, –2 In seven parts.

सप्तम *a.* (*f.* –मी) The seventh. –मी . The seventh or locative case (in gram.). –2 The seventh day of a lunar fortnight.

सप्तला *f.* A kind of jasmine.

सप्तिः *m.* 1 A yoke. –2 A horse. –3 A yoke-fellow.

सफरः *m.*, –री *f.* A small glittering fish.

सफल *a.* (*f.* –ला) 1 Fruitful, productive (fig. also). –2 Fulfilled, successful.

सबंधु *a.* 1 Closely connected. –2 Having a friend. –3 Of the same family. –धुः *m.* A relation, kinsman.

सबलिः *m.* Evening twilight.

सब्रह्मचर्यं *n.* Fellow-studentship.

सब्रह्मचारिन् *m.* 1 A fellow-student. –2 A fellow-sufferer. –3 One of the same kind.

सभर्तृका *f.* A woman, whose husband is living.

सभा *f.* 1 An assembly, a couucil. –2 Council chamber or hall. –3 A court of justice. –4 A public audience. –5 A gambling-house. –7 A much frequented place. –Comp. —आस्तारः *m.* 1 An assistant at an assembly. –2 A member of a society. —सद् *m.* 1 An assistant at an assembly or meeting. –2 A member of an assembly or meeting –3 An assessor, a juror.

सभाज् 10 U. (सभाजयति,–ते) 1 To salute, greet, render homage to; congratulate. –2 To worship, respect. –3 To please, gratify. –4 To adorn, grace. –5 To show.

सभाजनं *n.* 1 Salutation, honouring. –2 Congratulation. –3 Courtesy, politeness. –4 Service.

सभावनः *m.* N. of Siva.

सभि (–भी–) कः *m.* The keeper of a gaming-house.

सभ्य *a.* (*f.* –भ्या) 1 Belonging to an assembly. –2 Fit for society. –3 Refined. –4 Polite, courteous. –5 Trusty, faithful. –भ्यः *m.* 1 An assessor. –2 An assistant at an assembly. –3 A person of honourable parentage. –4 The keeper of a gaming-house. –5 The servant of the keeper of a gaming-house. –6 N. of one of the five sacred fires.

सम् *ind.* 1 (As a prefix to verbs and verbal derivatives) With, together with, together. Sometimes it intensifies the meaning of the simple root, and may be translated by 'very', 'quite', 'greatly', thoroughly', 'very much'. It also expresses completeness, perfection, or beauty. -2 As prefixed to nouns to form compounds, it means 'like', 'same', 'similar', as in समर्थ. -3 Sometimes it means 'near' 'before', as in समक्ष.

सम a. (f. -मा). 1 Same, identical. -2 Equal, as in समलोष्टकाञ्चनः -3 Like, similar, resembling. -4 Even, level, plain. -5 Even (as number) -6 Impartial, fair. -7 Honest, upright, virtuous. -8 Ordinary, common. -9 Mean, middling. -10 Straight. -11 Suitable, convenient. -12 Unaffected by passion. -13 All, whole, complete. —मः m. 1 N. of certain zodiacal signs (वृषभ, कर्क, कन्या, वृश्चिक, मकर and मीन). -2 A mode of measuring time in music. -मं n. 1 A flat country. -2 (In rhet.). The figure of speech in which the thing in hand is described as being fitly associated with another. -3 (In geometry) A mean proportional segment. -मं ind. 1 With, together with, in company with, accompanied by (with instr.). -2 Equally. -3 In the same manner. -4 Entirely. -5 At the same time, together. -Comp. —अंतर a. Parallel. —आचारः m. 1 Equal or similar conduct. -2 Proper practice. —उदकं n. A mixture of half butter-milk and half water. —कन्या f. A fit or suitable girl (fit to be married). —कर्णः m. An equi-diagonal tetragon. —कालः m. The same time or moment. (-लं ind.) At the same time. —कालीन a. Contemporary, coevel. —कोलः m. A serpent, snake. —क्षेत्रं n. (In astr.) An epithet of a particular arrangement of the Nakshatras. —खातः m. An equal excavation, a parallelopipedon. —चतुरस्र a. Square. (-स्रं n.) An equilateral tetragon. —चतुर्भुजः m., -जं n. A rhombus. —चित्त a. 1 Equanimous. -2 Indifferent. —छेद, छेदन a. Having the same denominator. -ज्ञा f. Fame. —त्रिभुजः m., -जं n. An equilateral triangle. -दर्शन, -दर्शिन् a. Impartial. -दुःख a. Sympathising. a fellow-sufferer. —दृश्, -दृष्टि a. Impartial. —द्विभुजः m. A rhomboid. —बुद्धि a. 1 Impartial. -2 Indifferent, stoical. —भाव a. Having the same nature or property. (-वः m.) Equability. —मंडलं n. (In astr.) The prime vertical line. -मय a. Of like origin. -रेख a. Straight. —लंबः m., -बं n. A trapezoid. —वर्तिन् a. Impartial. (-m.) Yama, the God of death —वृत्तं n. A stanza the lines of which have all the same number of feet. —वृत्ति a. Equable, fair. —वेधः m. Mean depth. —शोधनं n. Subtraction of the same quantity on both sides of an equation. —संधिः m. Peace on equal terms. —सुप्तिः f. Universal sleep. -सूत्र, —सूत्रस्थ a. Situated on the same diameter. -स्थ a. 1 Equal, uniform. -2 Level. -3 Like. -स्थली f. The Doab or country between the Ganges and Yamunā

समक्ष a. (f. -क्षा) Being before the eyes, visible, present. -क्षं ind. In the presence of, before the very eyes.

समग्र a. (f. -ग्रा) All, entire, complete.

समंगा f. Bengal madder (मंजिष्ठा).

समजः m. 1 A herd, flock. -2 A number of fools. -जं n. A wood, forest.

समज्या f. 1 A meeting, an assembly. -2 Renown, celebrity.

समंजस a. (f. -सा) 1 Proper, right, fit. -2 Correct, accurate. -3 Clear, intelligible. -4 Virtuous, just. -5

Experienced. -6 Healthy. -सं *n.* 1 Propriety, fitness. -2 Accuracy. -3 Correct evidence.

समतीत *p. p.* (*f.* -ता) Gone, past (as time).

समाधिक *a.* (*f.* -का) 1 Exceeding.-2 Abundant, plentiful. —कं *ind.* Very much exceedingly.

समनुज्ञानं *n.* Assent, consent, full concurrence.

समंत *a.* (*f* -ता) 1 Being on every side. -2 Complete, entire. -तः *m.* Limit, boundary. (समंतं, समंततः, समंतात are used adverbially in the sense of ' from every side ', ' all around ', ' on all sides ', ' wholly ', ' completely') -Comp. -पंचकं *n.* N. of the district called Kurukshetra or of a place near it. —भद्रः *m.* A Buddha or the Buddha. -भुज् *m.* Fire.

समन्वयः *m.* 1 Regular succession or order. -2 Connected sequence, mutual connection,oneness of purport. -3 Conjunction.

समन्वित *p.p.* (*f.* —ता) 1 Connected with. -2 Followed. -3 Endowed with, full of. -4 Affected by.

समभिव्याहारः *m.* 1 Mentioning together. -2 Association, company. -3 Proximity to a word the meaning of which is clearly ascertained or understood.

समभिहारः *m.* 1 Repetition. -2 Surplus, excess.

समभ्यर्चनं *n.* Worshipping, reverencing.

समभ्याहारः *m.* Accompaniment, association.

समयः *m.* 1 Time in general. -2 Opportunity. -3 Proper time or season -4 An agreement. -5 A conventional usage. -6 A customary duty; a ceremonial custom. -7 A convention of poets; (*e. g.* The dance of peacocks on the appearance of clouds &c.). -8 An assignation. -9 A stipulation.-10 Instruction, precept. -11 Emergency. -12 An oath. -13 A hint, indication. -14 Limit, boundary. -15 A demonstrated conclusion, tenet.-16 End, termination.-17 Success,prosperity. (समयेन ' on condition, conditionally '). -Comp. -अध्युषितं *n.* A time at which neither the stars nor the sun is visible. —अनुसारेण, —उचितं *ind.* Suitably to the occasion. -आचारः *m.* Conventional practice, usage. —परिरक्षणं *n.* The observance of a compact, treaty or agreement.—भेदः,-व्यभिचारः *m.* Violation or breach of contract.

समया *ind.* 1 At a fixed or appointed time. -2 In the midst, within, between. -3 Near (with acc.) *e.g.* समया सौधभित्तिं.

समरः *m.*, समरं *n.* War, battle,fight. -Comp. —उद्देशः *m.*, -भूमिः *f.* Battlefield. —मूर्धन् *m.*, —शिरस् *n.* The front or van of battle.

समर्चनं *n.* Worshipping, adoration.

समर्ण *a.* (*f.* —र्णा) 1 Afflicted, wounded. -2 Asked, solicited.

समर्थ *a* (*f.*—र्था) 1 Strong, powerful. -2 Competent, qualified. -3 Fit, suitable.-4 Made fit, prepared. -5 Having the same meaning. -6 Significant. -7 Being in apposition. —र्थः *m.* 1 A significant word (in gram.). -2 The coherence of words together in a significant sentence.

समर्थकं *n.* Aloe-wood.

समर्थनं *n.*, समर्थना *f.* 1 Establishing, corroborating. -2 Justifying. -3 Pleading, advocating.-4 Considering, imagining. -5 Deliberation. -6 Adequacy, capability.-7 Energy, perseverance.-8 Allaying disputes. -9 Objection.

समर्धक *a.* (*f.* —का) 1 Granting a boon. -2 Causing to prosper.

समर्पणं *n.* Giving over to, consigning.

समर्याद *a.* (*f.* —दा) 1 Limited, bounded. -2 Proximate. -3 Keeping within bounds of propriety. -4 Respectful, courteous.

समल *a.* (*f.*—ला) 1 Dirty, impure. -2 Sinful. —लं *n.* Excrement, feces.

समवकारः *m.* A kind of drama.

समवतारः *m.* 1 A descent. -2 A descent into a river or sacred bathing place.

समवस्था *f.* 1 Fixed condition. -2 Similar condition or state.-3 State or condition in general.

समवाप्तिः *f.* Obtaining, acquisition.

समवायः *m.* 1 Combination, collection. -2 A multitude, heap. -3 Close connection, cohesion. -4 (In Vais. phil.) Intimate union, constant and inseparable connection, (one of the seven categories of the Vaiseshikas). -Comp.-संबंधः *m.* Intimate and inseparable relation.

समवायिन् *a.* (*f.* —नी) 1 Intimately connected.-2Multitudinous.-Comp. —कारणं *n.* An inseparable cause, the material cause (one of the three kinds of कारण mentioned in Vaiseshika phil.).

समवेत *p. p.* (*f.* —ता) 1 Come together, united, joined.-2 Intimately united or inherent. -3 Comprised or contained in a larger number.

समष्टिः *f.* 1 An aggregate which is considered as made up of parts each of which is consubstantially the same with the whole (opp. व्यष्टि). -2Totality.

समसनं *n.* 1 Joining together. -2 Formation of compound words. -3 Contraction.

समस्त *p. p.* (*f.* -स्ता) 1 Combined. -2 Compounded. -3 Pervading the whole of anything. -4 Abridged, condensed. -5 All, whole, entire.

समस्या *f.* 1 Proposing part of a stanza to another to be completed, -2 The part of a stanza so given to be completed. -3 (Hence) Completing or filling up what is incomplete.

समा *f.* (Generally in pl,but used by Pánini in sing. also, *e. g.* समां समां). A year. -*ind.* With; together with.

समांसमीना *f.* A cow bearing a calf every year.

समाकर्षिन् *a.* (*f.* —णी) 1 Attracting. -2 Diffusing fragrance. -*m.* A scent spreading afar.

समाकुल *a.* (*f.* —ला) 1 Full of, crowded. -2 Greatly agitated.

समाक्रमणं *n.* 1 Treading. -2 Assailing.

समाख्या *f.* 1 Fame, reputation, celebrity.-2 An appellation.

समाख्यात *p. p.* (*f.*—ता) 1 Counted, summed up.-2 Declared, proclaimed. -3 Celebrated, famous.

समागतिः *f.* 1 Union, meeting. -2 Arrival. -3 Similar condition or progress.

समागमः *m.* 1 Union, meeting. -2 Intercourse, association, society. -3 Approach, arrival. -4 Conjunction (in astr.).

समाघातः *m.* 1 Killing, slaughter. -2 War, battle.

समाचारः *m.* 1 Proceeding, going.

-2 Practice, behaviour. -3 Proper conduct. -4 Report, tidings.

समाजः *m.* 1 An assembly, a meeting. -2 A society, an association. -3 A multitude, collection. -4 A convivial meeting.-5 An elephant.

समाजिकः *m.* 1 A member of an assembly. -2 A spectator in general.

समाज्ञा *f.* Fame, reputation.

समादानं *n.* 1 Receiving fully. -2 Receiving suitable gifts. -3 The daily observances of the Jaina sect.

समादेशः *m.* Command, order, instruction.

समाधा *f.*, समाधानं *n.* 1 Putting together. -2 Fixing the mind in abstract contemplation on the true nature of spirit. -3 Abstract meditation, deep contemplation. -4 Intentness. -5 Composure, peace (as of mind), satisfaction -6 Replying to the Púrvapaksha; answering an objection. -7 Agreeing, promising. -8 (In dramas) A leading incident which unexpetedly gives rise to the whole plot.

समाधिः *m.* 1 Collecting, composing, concentrating(as mind). 2 Profound or abstract meditation, concentration of mind on a particular subject; perfect absorption of thought into the one object of meditation *i. e.* the Supreme Spirit (the 8th and last stage of Yoga).-3 Con centration(in general).-4 Penance, devotion (to penance).-5 Bringing together, combination, collection. -6 Settling or composing differences. -7 Silence. -8 Agreement, promise. -9 Requital. -10 Acconplishment. -11 Perseverance in extreme difficulties. -12 Attempting impossibilities. -13 Storing grain. -14 A tomb. -15 The joint of the neck; a particular position of the neck. -16 (In rhet.) The figure of speech in which what is to be accomplished is descriled as having become easy through the accidental operation of another thing. -17 One of the ten Gunas or merits of style. -18 A religious vow. -19 Support, upholding.

समाध्मात *p. p.* (*f.* —ता) 1 Blown into. -2 Elated, inflated.

समान *a.* (*f.* —ना) 1 Same, equal, like, similar. -2 One, uniform. -3 Good, virtuous. -4 Common, general. -5 Honoured. —नः *m.* 1 A friend, an equal. -2 One of the five life-winds or vital airs which is essential to digestion. -3 A letter having the same organ of utterance. —नं *ind.* Equally with, like (with instr.). -Comp. —अक्षरं *n.* N. of the vowels अ, आ, इ, ई, उ, ऊ, ऋ, ॠ, and ऌ (opp. संध्यक्षर).—अधिकरण *a.* 1 Having a common substratum.-2 Being in the same catagory or predicament. Being in the same case-relation or government (in gram.). (-णं *n.*) 1 Same location or predicament.-2 Agreement in case; apposition. -3 A predicament including several things; a generic property. —उदकः *m.* A relative connected by the libations of water to the Manes of common ancestors. —उदर्यः *m.* (*f.* —र्या) Brother (or sister) of whole blood; uterine brother (or sister). —उपमा *f.* A kind of Upamá —धर्मन् *a.* Possessed of the same qualities, appreciator of merits. —यमः *m.* The same pitch of voice.

समापः *m.* Offering sacrifices or

oblations to the Gods.

समापत्तिः *f.* 1 Meeting, encountering. -2 Accident, chance, accidental encounter.

समापनं *n.* 1 Completion, bringing to an end. -2 Acquisition. -3 Killing, destroying. -4 A section, chapter. -5 Profound meditation.

समापन्न *p. p.* (*f* -न्ना) 1 Attained, obtained. -2 Occurred, happened. -3 Arrived. -4 Finished. -5 Proficient. -6 Endowed with. -7 Distressed. -8 Killed.

समाप्त *p. p.* (*f.* —प्ता) 1 Finished, completed. -2 Clever.

समाप्तालः *m.* A lord, a husband.

समाप्तिः *f.* 1 End, completion -2 Accomplishment. -3 Reconciling or settling differences. -4 Perfection, development.

समाप्तिक *a.* (*f.* —का) 1 Final, concluding. -2 (One) who has finished the whole of anything. —कः *m.* One who has completed the whole course of holy studies.

समाभाषणं *n.* Conversation, talking [with.

समाम्नानं *n.* 1 Repetition, mention. -2 Enumeration. -3 Traditional repetition or mention.

समाम्नायः *m.* 1 Traditional repetition or mention. -2 A traditional collection (of words &c.). -3 Tradition, repetition (in general). -4 Recitation, enumeration. -5 Totality, an aggregate.

समायः *m.* 1 Arrival. -2 A visit.

समायत *p. p.* (*f.* —ता) Extended, lengthened.

समायुक्त *p. p.* (*f.* —क्ता) 1 Joined, united. -2 Devoted to. -3 Made ready. -4 Endowed with, filled with. -5 Charged, appointed.

समायुत *p. p.* (*f.* —ता) 1 United together, joined. -2 Collected. -3 Endowed or furnished with.

समायोगः *m.* 1 Union. -2 Preparation -3 Fitting (an arrow). -4 A collection. -5 A motive. object. -6 Association

समारंभः *m.* 1 Beginning. -2 An undertaking, a work, an action. -3 An unguent.

समाराधनं *n.* 1 A means of satisfying. -2 Gratification, delight. -3 Attendance, service.

समारोपणं *n.* 1 Placing in or upon. -2 Delivering over.

समारोपित *p. p.* (*f.* —ता) 1 Caused to mount or ascend. -2 Strung (as a bow). -3 Deposited, lodged. -4 Delivered over.

समारोहः *m.* 1 Ascending. -2 Riding upon. -3 Agreeing.

समालंबनं *n.* Resting on, clinging to.

समालंबिन् *a.* (*f.* —नी) Clinging to. —नी *f.* A kind of grass.

समालंभः *m.*, समालंभनं *n.* 1 Seizing. -2 Seizing a victim for sacrifice. -3 Smearing the body with unguents or coloured cosmetics.

समावर्तनं *n.* 1 Return. -2 A pupil's return home after finishing his course of holy study.

समावायः *m.* 1 Association, connection. -2 Inseparable connection. -3 Aggregation. -4 A multitude, heap.

समावासः *m.* 1 A dwelling-place. -2 Halting-place.

समाविष्ट *p. p.* (*f.* —ष्टा) 1 Entered thoroughly, completely occupied. -2 Overcome, engrossed. -3 Possessed by an evil spirit. -4 Endowed with. -5 Settled, seated. -6 Well-instructed.

समावृत *p. p.* 1 Encompassed, surrounded, enclosed, beset. -2 Screened, veiled. -3 Hidden, concealed.-4 Protected. -5 Shut out, excluded. -6 Stopped.

समावृत्तः, समावृत्तकः *m.* A pupil who has returned home after finishing his course of holy study. [pletion.

समावृत्तिः *f.* 1 Return. -2 Com-

समावेशः *m.* 1 Entering or abiding together. -2 Association. -3 Inclusion. -4 Penetration. -5 Possession by an evil spirit. -6 Emotion.

समाश्रयः *m.* 1 Seeking shelter. -2 Refuge, protection. -3 A resting place.

समाश्लेषः *m.* A close embrace.

समाश्वासः *m.* 1 Recovering breath. -2 A sigh of relief. -3 Encouragement, consolation. -4 Confidence, belief.

समाश्वासनं *n.* 1 Encouraging, comforting. -2 Consolation.

समासः *m.* 1 Aggregation, union. -2 A compound (in gram.). -3 Reconciliation. -4 A collection. -5 Whole, totality. -6 Conciseness, brevity. -7 Euphonic combination (संधि). (समासेन, समासतः 'In short', 'briefly', 'succinctly').—उक्तिः *f.* The figure in which the behaviour of another (अप्रस्तुत) is ascribed to the subject of description from a sameness of action, sex, gender or attribute.

समासक्त *p. p.* (*f.* —क्ता) 1 Placed in. -2 Combined. -3 Attained. -4 Affected by.

समासक्तिः *f.*, समासंगः *m.* 1 Union, attachment. -2 Inclusion.

समासंजनं *n.* 1 Joining. -2 Placing on. -3 Contact, connection.

समासादनं *n.* 1 Approaching. -2 Obtaining. -3 Accomplishing.

समाहरणं *n.* Uniting, collecting.

समाहर्तृ *m.* 1 One who is accustomed to collect or get together. -2 A collector (as of taxes).

समाहारः *m.* 1 A collection, an aggregate. -2 Composition of words. -3 Conjunction of words or sentences. -4 A subdivision of *Dvandva* and *Dvigu* compounds, expressing an aggregate. -5 Abridgment. -6 Combination of two letters of the alphabet into a syllable (=प्रत्याहार).

समाहित *p. p.* (*f.* —ता) 1 Brought together. -2 Settled. -3 Calm (as mind). -4 Absorbed in. -5 Finished. -6 Agreed upon. -7 Arranged. -8 Inferred. -9 Accomplished. -10 Entrusted. —तः *m.* A holy man. -तं *n.* 1 Intentness, intent devotion (to any object). -2 The figure of speech in which भावप्रशम or भावशांति becomes subordinate to something else.

समाहृत *p. p.* (*f.* —ता) 1 Brought together, accumulated. -2 Abundant. -3 Accepted, taken. -4 Abridged. [ment.

समाहृतिः *f.* Compilation, abridg-

समाह्वः *m.* Challenge, defiance.

समाह्वयः *m.* 1 Calling out, challenging. -2 War, battle. -3 Setting animals to fight for sport; betting with living creatures. -4 A name, an appellation.

समाह्वा *f.* A name, an appellation.

समाह्वानं *n.* 1 Calling together, convocation. -2 Challenge.

समिकं *n.* A javelin, dart.

समित *f.* War, battle.

समित *p. p.* (*f.* —ता) 1 Come together. -2 Assembled. -3 United with. -4 Contiguous. -5 Parallel. -6 Promised. -7 Completed.

समिता *f.* Wheat-flour.

समितिः *f.* 1 Union, association. -2 An assembly. -3 Flock, herd. -4 War, battle.-5 Likeness, equality. -6 Moderation. समितिंजय *a.* Victorious in battle.

समिथः *m.* 1 War, battle. -2 Fire. -3 An offering, oblation.

समिद्ध *p. p.* (*f* —द्धा) 1 Lighted up, kindled. -2 Inflamed, excited

समिध् *f.* Wood, fuel; especially for the sacred fire.

समिधः *m.* 1 Fire. -2 Fuel.

समिंधनं *n.* 1 Kindling. -2 Fuel.

समिरः *m.* Wind.

समीकं *n.* War, battle.

समीकरणं *n.*, समीक्रिया *f* 1 Equalizing, levelling. -2 Assimilation. -3 An equation.-4 (In arith.) Reduction of fractions to a common denominator.

समीक्षः *m.* 1 Deliberation. -2 Full knowledge. —क्षं *n.* 1 Complete investigation. -2 The Sánkhya system of philosophy.

समीक्षा *f.* 1 Investigation. -2 Consideration. -3 Close inspection. -4 Intellect. -5 Essential nature of truth. -6 The Mîmámsá system of philosophy. -7 The Sânkhya system of philosophy.

समीक्षणं *n.* Search, close investigation.

समीचः *m.* The ocean

समीचकः *m.* Sexual union.

समीची *f.* 1 A doe. -2 Praise.

समीचीन *a.*(*f.*-ना) 1 Good, right.-2 True.-3 Proper.-4 Consistent.-नं *n.* 1 Truth. -2 Propriety.

समीदः *m. f.*,Fine wheat-flour.

समीन *a.* (*f.* —ना) 1 Yearly. -2 Hired for a year.-3 A year hence.

समीनिका *f.* A cow calving every year.

समीप *a.* (*f.* —पा) Adjacent, at hand. —पं *n.* Proximity. (समीपं, समीपतस् and समीपे are used adverbiall in the sense of 'near', 'before', 'in the presence of').

[Samî tree.

समीरः *m.* 1 Air, wind. -2 The

समीरणः *m.* 1 Air, wind. -2 The breath. -3 A traveller. -4 N. of a plant (मरुबक). —णं *n.* Throwing.

समीहा *f.* Longing, desire, striving after.

समीहित *p. p.* (*f.* —ता) 1 Wished. -2 Undertaken. —तं *n.* Wish.

समुक्षणं *n.* 1 Shedding, effusion. -2 Sprinkling.

समुच्चयः *m.* 1 Collection, multitude. -2 Conjunction of words or sentences. -3 A figure of speech in which, not-with-standing the existence of one cause sufficient to bring about an effect, there are others producing the same effect ; or the figure in which two qualities, or two actions, or a quality and an action are simultaneously produced.

समुच्छेदः *m.* Complete destruction.

समुच्छ्रयः *m.* 1 Elevation, height. -2 Opposition, enmity.

समुच्छ्रायः *m.* Elevation, height.

समुच्छ्वासः *m.* समुच्छ्वसितं *n.*, A heavy or deep sigh.

समुज्जंभणं *n.* 1 Yawning.-2 Rising. -3 Attempting, striving.

समुज्झित *a.* (*f.* —ता) 1 Abandoned. -2 Let go. -3 Free from.

समुत्कर्षः *m.* 1 Exaltation. -2 Setting oneself up as being of a tribe higher than his own.

समुत्क्रमः *m.* 1 Rising upwards. -2 Transgression of proper bounds.

समुत्क्रोशः *m.* 1 Crying aloud. -2 A loud uproar. -3 An osprey.

समुत्थ *a.* (*f.* —त्था) 1 Rising, getting up. -2 Born or produced from (at the end of comp.). -3 Occurring, occasioned.

समुत्थानं *n.* 1 Rising, getting up.-2 Resurrection. -3 Perfect cure. -4 Healing (as of a wound). -5 A symptom of disease. -6 Active occupation. -7 Increase or growth.

समुत्पतनं *n.* 1 Flying, ascending.-2 Effort.

समुत्पत्तिः *f.* 1 Production, birth, origin. -2 Occurrence.

समुत्पादनं *n.* Effecting, accomplishing, producing.

समुत्पिंज, समुत्पिंजल *a.* (*f.* -जा, -ला) Excessively confused or bewildered. —जः, —लः *m.* 1 An army in great disorder.-2 Great confusion.

समुत्सवः *m.* A great festival.

समुत्सर्गः *m.* 1 Abandoning.-2 Shedding forth, giving away. -3 Voiding of excrement.

समुत्सारणं *n.* 1 Driving away. -2 Pursuing, hunting.

समुत्सुक *a.* (*f.* -का) 1 Very uneasy or anxious, impatient. -2 Longing for, fond of. -3 Sorrowful.

समुत्सेधः *m.* 1 Height, elevation.-2 Fatness, thickness.

समुदक्त *p. p.* (*f.* —क्ता) Raised or drawn up (as water from a well).

समुदयः *m.* 1 Rising up (of the sun.) -2 Rise (in general). -3 A collection, heap, a combination. -4 The whole. -5 Revenue. -6 Effort, exertion. -7 War, battle. -8 Day. -9 The rear of an army. —यं *n.* 1 The rising of a planet &c. -2 An auspicious moment (लग्न).

समुदागमः *m.* Full knowledge.

समुदाचारः *m.* 1 Proper practice or usage. -2 Proper mode of address. -3 Intention, design.

समुदायः *m.* 1 A collection. -2 A word of more than one syllable.

समुदाहरणं *n.* 1 Declaring, pronouncing. -2 Illustration.

समुदित *p. p.* (*f.* —ता) 1 Gone up, risen. -2 Lofty.-3 Arisen, occasioned. -4 Assembled. -5 Furnished with. -6 Conversed. -7 Spoken to. -8 Agreed upon. -9 Customary, usual. [-2 Repeating.

समुदीरणं *n.* 1 Uttering, speaking.

समुद्ग *a* (*f.* —द्गा) 1 Rising. -2 Completely pervading. -3 Having a covering. -4 Having beans. —द्गः *m.* 1 A covered box or casket. -2 A kind of artificial stanza. -Comp. —यमकं (In Rhet.) A stanza the two halves of which correspond in sound though they differ in meaning.

समुद्गकः *m.* 1 A covered box or casket.-2 A kind of artificial stanza, the two halves of which exactly correspond in sound, though different in meaning.

समुद्गमः *m.* 1 Rising, ascent. -2 Arising, coming out. -3 Birth, production.

समुद्गिरणं *n.* 1 Vomiting. -2 That which is vomited. -3 Raising up.

समुद्गीतं *n.* 1 A loud song.

समुद्देशः *m.* 1 Pointing out. -2 Full description. -3 Particularising.

समुद्धत *p. p.* (*f.* -ता) 1 Upraised. -2 Excited.-3 Puffed up with pride. -4 Ill-mannered. -5 Rude.

समुद्धरणं *n.* 1 Lifting up. -2 Picking up. -3 Drawing out. -4 Extrication, deliverance.-5 Extirpation. -6 Taking out from (a share). -7 Food thrown up or vomited.

समुद्भवः *m.* Origin, production.

समुद्यमः *m.* 1 Lifting up. -2 Great

exertion. -3 An undertaking. -4 An onset.

समुद्योगः *m.* Active exertion.

समुद्र *a.* (*f.* —द्रा) Sealed, stamped. —द्रः *m.* 1 The sea, ocean. -2 An epithet of Siva. -3 The number 'four'.-Comp.—अंतः *m* , -अंतं *n.* 1 The sea-shore. -2 Nutmeg. —अंता *f.* 1 The cotton-plant. -2 The earth. —अरुः,—आरुः *m.* 1 A crocodile. -2 A large fabulous fish. -3 Râma's bridge. —कफः, —फेनः *m.* The cuttle-fish-bone. —कांता *f.* A river. —गः *m.* sea-trader.-2 A seaman, a sea-farer. (—गा *f.*) A river. —गृहं *n.* A summer-house built in the midst of water. —चुलुकः *m.* An epithet of Agastya. —नवनीतं *n.* 1 The moon. -2 Ambrosia, nectar. —मेखला,-रसना, —वसना *f.* The earth. —यानं *n.* 1 A sea-voyage. -2 A vessel, ship,boat. —यात्रा *f.* A sea-voyage. —योषित् *f.* A river. —वह्निः *m.* Submarine fire. —सुभगा *f.* The Ganges.

समुद्वहः *m.* 1 Bearing up. -2 One who lifts up.

समुद्वाहः *m.* 1 Bearing up.-2 Marriage.

समुद्वेगः *m.* Great fear, alarm.

समुंदनं *n.* 1 Moistening. -2 Wetness, moisture.

समुन्न *a.* (*f.* —न्ना) Wet, moist.

समुन्नत *p. p.* (*f.* —ता) 1 Upraised, -2 High, lofty.-3 Exalted,sublime. -4 Proud. -5 Projecting. -6 Upright, just.

समुन्नतिः *f.* 1 Lifting up.-2 Height, loftiness (mental also). -3 High dignity, exaltation. -4 Prosperity, success. -5 Pride, arrogance.

समुन्नद्ध *p. p.* (*f.* -द्धा) 1 Elevated. -2 Swollen. -2 Full. -4 Proud. -5 Conceited.-6 Unfettered. -7 Bound up. -8 Supreme.

समुन्नयः *m.* 1 Getting, obtaining.-2 Occurrence, event.

समुन्मूलनं *n.* Uprooting.

समुपगमः *m.* Approach, contact.

समुपजोषम् *ind.* 1 Entirely according to wish. -2 Happily.

समुपभोगः *m.* Sexual union.

समुपवेशः *m.* 1 Sitting down together. -2 Entertaining.

समुपवेशनं *n.* 1 A habitation. -2 Seating down.

समुपस्था *f.*, समुपस्थानं *n.* 1 Approach. -2 Proximity. -3 Happening, occurrence.

समुपार्जनं *n.* Simultaneous acquisition.

समुपेत *p. p.* (*f.* -ता) 1 Assembled. -2 Arrived at. -3 Furnished with. -4 Inhabited by.

समुपोढ *p. p.* (*f.* —ढा) 1 Gone upwards,risen.-2 Increased.-3 Brought near. -4 Restrained. -5 Begun.

समुल्लासः *m.* 1 Excessive brilliance. -2 Great joy.

समूढ *p. p.* (*f.* —ढा) 1 Brought together. -2 Accumulated. -3 Enveloped. -4 Associated with. -5 Produced quickly.-6 Calmed,tamed down. -7 Crooked. -8 Purified. -9 Borne along. -10 Led, conducted. -11 Married.

समूरः, समूरुः, समूरुकः *m.* A kind of deer.

समूल *a.* (*f.* —ला) Along with the roots.

समूहः *m.* 1 A multitude. -2 A flock, troop.

समूहनं *n.* 1 Bringing together. -2 A collection, plenty.

समूहनी *f.* A broom.

समूह्यः *m.* A kind of sacrificial fire.

समृद्ध *p. p.* (*f.*—द्धा) 1 Prosperous, flourishing. -2 Happy, fortunate. -3 Rich. -4 Richly endowed with, abounding in. -5 Fruitful. -6 Full-grown. -7 Complete, entire. -8 Copious.

समृद्धिः *f.* 1 Great growth, thriving. -2 Prosperity, affluence. -3 Wealth. -4 Abundance. -5 Power, supremacy.

समेत *p. p.* (*f.* —ता) 1 Met together. -2 United. -3 Approached. -4 Accompanied by. -5 Endowed or furnished with. -6 Encountered. -7 Agreed upon.

संपत्तिः *f.* 1 Prosperity. -2 Success, accomplishment. -3 Perfection, excellence. -4 Abundance.

संपद् *f.* 1 Wealth, riches. -3 Affluence, advancement. -3 Good fortune. -4 Accomplishment of desired objects. -5 Perfection, excellence. -6 Abundance, excess. -7 Treasure. -8 An advantage, a benefit. -9 Advancement in good qualities. -10 Decoration. -11 Right method. -12 A necklace of pearls. -Comp. —वरः *m.* A king.

संपन्न *p. p.* (*f.* —न्ना) 1 Prosperous. -2 Fortunate, happy. -3 Accomplished. -4 Finished. -5 Perfect. -6 Full-grown, mature. -7 Procured, obtained. -8 Right, correct. -9 Endowed with. -10 Turned out, become. -11 Perfectly conversant with. —न्नः *m.* An epithet of Siva. —न्नं *n.* 1 Riches. -2 A dainty.

संपरायः *m.* 1 Conflict, war, battle. -2 A calamity. -3 Future state. -4 A son.

संपराय (-यि-) कं *n.* Encounter, war, battle.

संपर्कः *m.* 1 Mixture. -2 Union, contact. -3 Association. -4 Sexual union.

संपा *f.* Lightning.

संपाक *a.* (*f.* —का) 1 Reasoning well, a reasoner. -2 Cunning. -3 Lustful. -4 Small, little. —कः *m.* 1 Maturing. -2 N. of a tree.

संपाटः *m.* A spindle.

संपातः *m.* 1 Concurrence. -2 Meeting together. -3 Collision. -4 Descending. -5 Alighting (as of a bird). -6 Flight (of an arrow). -7 Going, moving. -8 Being removed. -9 A particular mode of the flight of birds. -10 The residue (of an offering).

संपातिः *m.* N. of a fabulous bird, son of Garuda and elder brother of Jatâyu.

संपादः *m.* 1 Completion, accomplishment. -2 Acquisition.

संपादनं *n.* 1 Accomplishing, effecting. -2 Gaining, acquiring. -3 Cleaning, preparing (as ground).

संपीडः *m.* 1 Squeezing together. -2 Pain, torture. -3 Agitating. -4 Driving onward. —डा *f.* Torment.

संपीडनं *n.* 1 Squeezing. -2 Sending. -3 Punishment. -4 Stirring up. -5 Paining, torturing.

संपीतिः *f.* Drinking in company.

संपुटः *m.* A cavity. -2 A covered box. -3 The Kurabaka flower.

संपुटकः *m.*, संपुटिका *f.* A box, casket.

संपूर्ण *a.* (*f.* —र्णा) 1 See पूर्ण. —र्णः *m.* A mode of music in which all the notes of the gamut are used. —र्णं *n.* Ether.

संपृक्त *p. p.* (*f.* —क्ता) 1 Blended, mixed. -2 Connected together. -3 Touching. -4 Interspersed.

संप्रक्षालनं *n.* 1 Bathing. -2 Inundation.

संप्रति *ind.* Now, at present.

संप्रतिपत्तिः *f.* 1 Approach, arrival. -2 Presence. -3 Acquiring. -4 An agreement. -5 Admisssion, confession. -6 Admission of a fact, a particular kind of reply in law. -7 Assault. -8 Occurrence. -9 Co-operation. -10 Performing.

संप्रतिरोधकः *m.*, -कं *n.* 1 Complete obstruction. -2 Imprisonment.

संप्रतीतिः *f.* 1 Full ascertainment. -2 Compliance. -3 Celebrity.

संप्रत्ययः *m.* 1 Firm conviction. -2 Agreement.

संप्रदानं *n.* 1 Giving over completely. -2 A gift, donation. -3 Giving in marriage. -4 The sense expressed by the dative case.

संप्रदानीयं *n.* A gift, donation.

संप्रदायः *m.* 1 Tradition, traditional handing down of instruction. -2 A peculiar religious doctrine inculcating the worship of one peculiar deity. -3 An established custom, usage.

संप्रधारणं *n.*, —णा *f.* 1 Deliberation. -2 Determining the propriety or otherwise of anything.

संप्रमोदः *m.* Great joy, jubilee.

संप्रमोषः *m.* Loss, abstraction.

संप्रयोगः *m.* 1 Union, meeting, contact. -2 A connecting link. -3 Relation, dependence. -4 Mutual relation or proportion. -5 Connected series or order.-6 Sexual union. -7 Application. -8 Magic. -2 Mutual intercourse.

संप्रयोगिन् *-m.* 1 A joiner, uniter. -2 A conjuror. -3 A libertine. -4 A catamite.

संप्रवर्तनं *n.* Undertaking, beginning.

संप्रवृष्टं *n.* Complete rain-fall.

संप्रसादः *m.* 1 Propitiation. -2 Favour, grace. -3 Sedateness. -4 Trust, confidence. -5 The soul.

संप्रसाधनं *n.* 1 An ornament, a decoration. -2 Performing well.

संप्रसारणं *n.* The change of य्, व्, र्, and ल् to इ, उ, ऋ and ऌ respectively.

संप्रहारः *m.* 1 Mutual striking. -2 War, battle.

संप्रीतिः *f.* 1 Attachment, affection. -2 Friendly assent. -3 Delight.

संप्रैषः *m.* 1 Sending away. -2 Command, order.

संप्लवः *m.* 1 Submersion, inundation. -2 Surge. -3 Flood. -4 Falling into ruin. -5 Subversion.

संफालः *m.* A ram, sheep.

संफेटः *m.* An angry or tumultuous conflict (in a drama).

संबं *n.* 1 The second ploughing of a field. (संबाकृ To plough twice. See शंब also). -2 Water.

संबद्ध *p. p.* (*f.* -द्धा) 1 Bound or fastened together. -2 Attached to. -3 Connected with, related to. -4 Endowed with. -5 Connected in sense. -6 Closed, shut.

संबंधः *m.* 1 Connection, association. -2 Relation. -3 Relation (as the meaning of the genitive case). -4 Matrimonial alliance. -5 Friendly connection. -6 Fitness, propriety. -7 Prosperity, success. -8 A relative, kinsman.

संबंधक *a* (*f.* -का) 1 Relating, concerning. -2 Fit, suitable. -कः *m.* 1 A friend. -2 A relation by birth or marriage.

संबंधिन् *a.* (*f.* -नी) 1 Relating or belonging to. -2 Connected with, inherent. -3 Possessing good qualities. *-m.* 1 A relation by marriage. -2 A relation, kinsman (in general).

संबरः *m.* 1 A dam, bridge. -2 A kind of deer.-3 N of a demon slain by Pradyumna. *n.* -4 N of a mountain. -रं *n.* 1 Restraint. -2 Water. -Comp. —आरिः, -रिपुः *m.* Cupid.

संबलः *m.*, संबलं *n.* Provisions for a journey. -लं *n.* Water.

संबाध *a.* (*f.* -धा) Thronged with, blocked up, narrow. -धः *m.* 1 Being thronged with. -2 Striking, hurting. -3 Obstruction, impediment. -4 The road to hell. -5 Fear. -6 The vulva.

संबाधनं *n.* 1 Blocking up. -2 Compressing. -3 A barrier, gate. -4 The vulva. -5 The point of a stake.

संबुद्धिः *f.* 1 Perfect knowledge or perception. -2 Full consciousness. -3 Calling to. -4 (In gram.) The vocative case.

संबोधः *m.* 1 Instructing, informing. -2 Correct perception. -3 Sending, throwing. -4 Loss, destruction.

संबोधनं *n.* 1 Explaining. -2 Addressing. -3 The vocative case.

संभग्न *p. p.* (*f.*-ग्ना) Shattered, dispersed. —ग्नः *m.* An epithet of Siva.

संभली *f.* A procuress.

संभवः *m.* 1 Birth, production, arising, existence. -2 Production and bringing up. -3 Origin. -4 Combination. -5 Possibility. -6 Compatibility, consistency. -7 Adaptation, appropriateness. -8 Agreement. -9 Capacity. -10 Equivalence (one of the Pramànas). -11 Acquaintance. -12 Loss.

संभारः *m.* 1 Collecting. -2 Provisions, requisites, things requisite for any act. -3 An ingredient, a constituent part. -4 Multitude, quantity. -5 Fulness. -6 Wealth. -7 Maintenance, support.

संभावनं *n.*, -ना *f.* 1 Considering, reflecting.-2 Fancying, supposition. -3 A fancy, thought. -4 Respect, esteem. -5 Possibility. -6 Fitness, adequacy. -7 Competency, ability. -8 Doubt. -9 Love. -10 Celebrity.

संभावित *p. p.* (*f.*-ता) 1 Considered, supposed.-2 Esteemed. -3 Respectable, honourable. -4 Suited, fitted. -5 Possible. -6 Derived, produced. -7 Satisfied.

संभाव्य *a.* (*f.* —व्या) 1 Probable, possible. -2 To be deemed probable. -3 Capable, suitable.

संभाषः *m.* Conversation.

संभाषणं *n.*, संभाषा *f.* 1 Conversation. -2 Greeting. -3 Criminal connection. -4 An agreement. -5 A watch-word, war-cry.

संभूत *p. p.* (*f.*-ता) 1 Produced. -2 Formed. -3 Combined or united with. -4 Adequate, equal.

संभूतिः *f.* 1 Origin, production. -2 Combination. -3 Fitness, suitability. -4 Power.

संभृत *p. p.* (*f.* -ता) 1 Brought together, collected. -2 Prepared, provided, equipped. -3 Furnished with, possessed of. -4 Placed, deposited. -5 Full, complete, entire. -6 Obtained. -7 Carried, borne. -8 Nourished. -9 Produced, caused.

संभेदः *m.* 1 Breaking, splitting. -2 Mixture, combination. -3 Confluence, junction (of two rivers). -4 Blossoming, opening.

संभोगः *m.* 1 Enjoyment, pleasure, delight. -2 Possession, use, occupation. -3 Carnal enjoyment. -4 A lecher, catamite. -5 A sub-division of the sentiment of love.

संभ्रमः *m.* 1 Turning round, whirling, revolving. -2 Haste, hurry. -3 Confusion, agitation. -4 Fear. -5 Error, mistake, ignorance. -6 Zeal, activity. -7 Respect, reverence. -8 Uproar, tumult. -9 Ignorance. -Comp.-भृत *a.* Embarrassed, flurried.

संभ्रांत *p. p.* (*f.* -ता) Whirled about. -2 Agitated, perplexed, bewildered.

संमत *p. p.* (*f.* —ता) 1 Agreed to, approved of. -2 Liked, beloved. -3 Like, resembling. -4 Regarded, thought. -5 Highly esteemed. —तं *n.* 1 Agreement. -2 Impression, opinion.

संमतिः *f.* 1 Agreement. -2 Assent, approval. -3 Wish, desire. -4 Knowledge of the soul, true knowledge. -5 Esteem. -6 Love, affection.

संमदः *m.* Great joy, happiness.

संमर्दः *m.* 1 Rubbing together, friction. -2 Throng, crowd. -3 Treading or trampling on. -4 War, battle.

संमातुरः *m.* The son of a virtuous mother.

संमादः *m.* Intoxication, frenzy.

संमानः *m.* Honour, respect. —नं *n.* 1 A measure. -2 Comparing.

संमाननं *n.* Honouring, worshipping.

संमार्जकः *m.* A sweeper.

संमार्जनं *n.* 1 Sweeping, cleaning. -2 Purifying, cleaning. -3 Anointing (of images).

संमार्जनी *f.* A broom.

संमित *p. p.* (*f.* —ता) 1 Meted or measured out.-2 Of equal measure, extent or value; similar, like. -3 Conformable, corresponding. -4 Provided or furnished with. -5 Adapted.

संमिश्लः *m.* An epithet of Indra.

संमीलनं *n.* Closing up, covering, enveloping.

संमुख *a.* (*f.* -खा or -खी) संमुखीन (*f.* —ना) 1 Facing, fronting, opposite. -2 Disposed to. -3 Looking or directed towards. -4 Propitious. —खं *ind.* 1 In front of, before, in the presence of.

संमुखिन *m.* A mirror,looking-glass.

संमूर्छनं *n.* 1 Fainting, insensibility. -2 Congealing, becoming dense. -3 Increasing. -4 Height.-5 Complete permeation.

संमृष्ट *p. p.* (*f.* —ष्टा) 1 Well swept, cleansed. -2 Strained, filtered.

संमेलनं *n.* 1 Meeting together, assembling. -2 Mixture.

संमोदः *m.* Great joy; delight.

संमोहः *m.* 1 Bewilderment, confusion. -2 Insensibility, swoon. -3 Ignorance, folly. -4 Fascination. -5 Tumult, battle.

संमोहनं *n.* Fascinating,fascination. —नः *m.* N. of one of the five arrows of Cupid.

सम्यच्, सम्यंच् *a.* (*f.* समीची) 1 Going with, accompanying. -2 Right, proper. -3 Correct, accurate. -4 Agreeable. -5 Same, uniform. -6 All, entire. -*ind.* (सम्यक्) 1 With, together with.-2 Properly, rightly. -3 Duly, correctly. -4 Honourably. -5 Thoroughly. -6 Distinctly.

सम्राज् *m.* A paramount sovereign, especially one who rules over other princes and has performed the Rájasúya sacrifice.

सयूथ्यः *m* One of the same flock or tribe.

सयोनि *a.* 1 Having the same womb, uterine. -2 Closely related to. -निः *m.* 1 A whole or uterine brother. -2 A pair of nippers for cutting betel-nut.

सर *a.* (*f.* -रा) 1 Going or moving. -2 Cathartic, purgative. —रः *m.* 1 Motion. -2 An arrow. -3 The coagulum of curds or milk.-4 Salt. -5 A string, necklace. -6 A waterfall. —रं *n.* 1 Water. -2 A lake. -रा *f.* 1 Motion, movement. -2 A cascade. —री *f.* A water-fall. -Comp. —उत्सवः *m.* A crane. —जं *n.* Fresh butter.

सरकः *m.*, सरकं *n.* 1 A continuous line of road. -2 Spirituous liquor. -3 Drinking spirits. -4 A wine-glass, goblet. -5 Distribution of spirituous liquor. —कं *n.* 1 Going. -2 A pond, lake. -3 Heaven.

सरघा *f.* A bee.

सरंगः *m.* 1 A quadruped. -2 A bird.

सरजस्, -सा, सरजस्का *f.* A woman during menstruation.

सरट् *m.* 1 Air, wind. -2 A cloud. -3 A lizard. -4 A bee.

सरटः *m.* 1 Wind. -2 A lizard.

सराटिः *m.* 1 Wind. -2 A cloud.

सरडुः *m.* A lizard, chameleon.

सरण *a.* (*f.* —णा) Going, moving, flowing. -णं *n.* 1 Proceeding, going or flowing. -2 Iron rust.

सरणिः,—णी *f.* 1 A path, way. -2 Arrangement, mode. -3 A straight or continuous line. -4 A disease of the throat.

सरंडः *m.* 1 A bird. -2 A libertine, dissolute man. -3 A lizard. -4 A rogue. -5 A kind of ornament.

सरण्युः *m.* 1 Air, wind. -2 A cloud. -3 Water. -4 The spring. -5 Fire.

सरत्निः *m. f.* A kind of cubit measure.

सरथः *m.* A warrior riding in a chariot.

सरभस *a.* (*f.*—सा) 1 Speedy. -2 Passionate. -3 Delighted. —सं *ind.* Impetuously, hurriedly.

सरमा *f.* 1 A bitch. -2 The bitch of the Gods. -3 N. of a daughter of Daksha. -4 N. of the wife of Bibhîshana, brother of Râvana.

सरयुः *m.* Air, wind.-युः, -यूः *f.* N. of a river near Ayodhyá.

सरल *a.* (*f.* —ला) 1 Straight. -2 Upright, candid. -3 Artless, simple-minded. —लः *m.* 1 A kind of pine tree. -2 Fire. -Comp. -अंगः *m.* Resin, turpentine.

सरव्य See शरव्य.

सरस् *n.* 1 A lake; pond. -2 Water. -Comp. सरोजं, सरोजन्मन्, सरोरुहं, सरसिजं, सरसिरुहं *n.* A lotus. —जः (also सरसिजः) *m.* The Sârasa bird. —जिनी, -रुहिणी *f.* 1 A lotus-plant. -2 A pond abounding in lotuses. -3 A multitude of lotuses. सरोरुह् *n.* A lotus. सरोवरः *m.* A lake.

सरस *a.* 1 Juicy. -2 Tasty. -3 Wet. -4 Full of love, impassioned. -5 Charming, agreeable.

सरसि (-सी-) कः *m.* The Sârasa bird.

सरसी *f.* A lake, pool. -Comp. -रुहं *n.* A lotus. (-हः*m.*) The Sârasa bird.

सरस्वत *a.* (*f.* —ता) 1 Watery. -2 Juicy. -4 Elegant. -4 Sentimental. -5 Tasty. -*m.* 1 The ocean. -2 A lake. -3 A male river (नद). -4 A buffalo.

सरस्वती *f.* 1 N. of the goddess of speech and learning. -2 Speech, voice. -3 N. of a river. -4 A river in general. -5 A cow. -6 An excellent woman. -7 N. of Durgá. -8 N. of a female divinity of the Buddhists. -9 The Soma plant. -10 The plant called ज्योतिष्मती.

सराग *a.* (*f.*—गा) 1 Coloured, tinged. -2 Dyed with red lac. -3 Full of love, enamoured.

सराव *a.* (*f.* —वा) Making a sound. -वः *m.* 1 A lid, cover. -2 A saucer.

सरिः *m. f.* 1 A fountain.

सरित् *f.* 1 A river. -2 A thread. -Comp. —नाथः, —पतिः, —भर्तृ (also सरितांपतिः) *m.* The ocean. —वरा (also सरितांवरा) *f.* N. of the Ganges. —सुतः *m.* An epithet of Bhîshma.

सलिलं *n.* Water.

सरीसृपः *m.* A serpent.

सरुः *m.* The handle of a sword.

सरूप *a.* (*f.* —पा) 1 Having the same form. -2 Like, similar.

सरूपता *f.*, -त्वं *n.* 1 Likeness. -2 One of the four states of *Mukti.*

सर्कः *m.* 1 Wind,air.-2 The mind.

सर्गः *m.* 1 Abandonment. -2 Creation. -3 The creation of the world. -4 Nature, the universe.-5 Natural property. -6 Determination. -7 Assent. -8 A section,chapter, canto (as of a poem). -9 Onset, advance (of troops). -10 Voiding of excrement. -11 N. of Siva. -12 Fainting. -Comp.-बंधः *m.* A great poem having several cantos, a 'Mahâkâvya'.

सर्ज् I A (सर्जति) 1 To acquire,gain. -2 To earn by labour.

सर्जः *m.* 1 N. of a tree (साल). -2 The resinous exudation of the Sála tree. -3 A timber tree.-Comp.-निर्यासकः, —मणिः, —रसः *m.* Resin.

सर्जकः *m.* The Sála tree.

सर्जनं *n.* 1 Abandoning. -2 Letting loose. -3 Creating. -4 Voiding. -5 The rear of an army.

सर्जिः, सर्जिका, सर्जी *f* Natron.

सर्जूः *m.* A trader.-*f.* 1 Lightning. -2 Necklace. -3 Going, following.

सर्ज्यः *m.* The resin of the Sála tree.

सर्पः *m.* 1 Winding motion, gliding.-2 Flowing, going. -3 A snake. -4 N. of a tree (नागकेशर). -5 The Asleshá constellation. -6 N. of a tribe of Mlechchhas -Comp.-अरातिः, —अरिः *m.* 1 An ichneumon. -2 A peacock. -2 An epithet of Garuda. —अशनः *m* A peacock. —आवासं, —इष्टं *n.* The sandal tree. —छत्रं *n.* A mushroom.-तृणः *m.* An ichneumon. —दंष्ट्रा *f.* A snake's fang. —धारकः *m.* A snake-charmer. -भुज् *m.* 1 A peacock.-2 A crane.-3 A large snake. —राजः *m.* N. of Vâsuki. —विद् *m.* A snake-charmer. —सत्रं *n.* A sacrifice for the destruction of serpents (performed by king Janamejaya). —सत्रिन् *m.* N. of king Janamejaya. —हन् *m.* 1 An ichneumon. -2 N. of Garuda.

सर्पणं *n.* 1 Creeping, gliding. -2 Tortuous motion. -3 The flight of an arrow nearly parallel to the ground.

सर्पिणी *f.* 1 A female serpent. -2 N. of a small medicinal herb.

सर्पिन् *a.* (*f.* -णी) 1 Creeping, going tortuously. -2 Moving, going.

सर्पिस् *n.* Clarified butter. -Comp. —कुंडिका *f.* A butter-jar.

सर्पिष्मत् *a.* (*f.* -ती) Dressed with clarified butter. [Heaven.

सर्मः *m.* 1 Motion. -2 The sky. -3

सर्व *pron. a.* (nom. pl. सर्वे *m.*) 1 All, every. -2 Whole, entire, complete. -र्वः *m.* N. of Vishnu. -2 Of Siva. -Comp. —अंगीण *a.* Pervading or thrilling throughout the whole body. —अन्नीन *a* Eating every kind of food. —अर्थसाधिका *f.* N. of Durgâ. —अर्थसिद्धिः *m.* The great Buddha or Sâkyamuni. —ईशः, -ईश्वरः *m.* 1 The Supreme Being. -2 A paramount lord. -कर्तृ *m.* 1 N, of Brahman (*m.*). -2 The Supreme Being. -जनीन *a.* World-wide, famous. —ज्ञा *f.* N. of Durgá. —देवमुखः *m.* An epithet of Agni. —धनं *n.* (In arith.) The total of a sum in progression. -नामन् *n.* A class of pronominal words. -भक्षा *f.* A female goat. (सर्वभावेन ' With all one's heart', 'sincerely', 'heart and soul').—मंगला *f.* An epithet of Pârvatí. —लिंगिन् *m.* An impostor. —लोहः *m.* An iron arrow. -वल्लभा *f.* An unchaste woman. -वेदः *m.* A man who has studied the four Vedas. —वेदस *m.* One who performs a sacrifice by giving away all his wealth. (सर्वसहा *f.* The earth). —स्वं *n.* 1 The whole of one's possession. -2 The very essence. —हरः *m.* Death. —हितं *n.* Black pepper.

सर्वंकष *a.* (*f.* -षा) All-powerful. -षः *m.* A villain, rogue.

सर्वतस् *ind.* 1 From every side or quarter. -2 Everywhere, all round. -3 Completely, entirely. -Comp. —भद्रः *m.* I The car of Vishnu. -2 A bamboo. -3 A kind of verse artificially arranged. -4 A temple or palace having openings on four sides (-द्रं *n.* also in this sense).-5 The *Nimba* tree. -6 A kind of military array. (-द्रा *f.*) A dancing girl, an actress. —मुख *a.* Complete, unlimited. (-खः *m.*) 1 An epithet of Siva. -2 Of Brahman (*m.*).-3 The Supreme Being. -4 The soul. -5 A Bráhmana. -6 Fire. -7 Heaven or Svarga (of Indra). (-खं *n.*) 1 Water. -2 Sky. —शुभा *f.* The Priyangu plant.

सर्वत्र *ind.* 1 Everywhere, in all places. -2 At all times.

सर्वथा *ind.* 1 In every way, by all means.-2 At all, altogether (usually with negation). -3 Completely, utterly. -4 At all times. -5 Exceedingly.

सर्वदा *ind.* At all times, always.

सर्वशस् *ind.* 1 Entirely, completely. -2 Everywhere. -3 On all sides.

सर्वरी *f.* The night. See शर्वरी.

सर्वला, -ली *f.* An iron club.

सर्वाणी *f.* See शर्वाणी.

सर्षपः *m.* 1 Mustard.-2 A small measure of weight. -3 A sort of poison.

सल् 1 P. (सलति) To go, move.

सलं *n.* Water.

सलिलं *n.* Water. -Comp. —आशयः *m.* A tank. —इंधनः *m.* The submarine fire. —उपप्लवः *m.* An inundation, deluge, flood of water.—क्रिया *f.* The funeral rite of washing a corpse. -निधिः, -राशिः *m* The ocean.

सलोकता *f.* Residence in the same heaven with a particular deity, (one of the four states of *Mukti*).

सल्लकी *f.* A kind of tree.

सवः *m.* 1 Extraction of Soma juice. -2 A libation. -3 A sacrifice. -4 The sun. -5 The moon. —वं *n.* 1 Water. -2 The honey of flowers. -3 Extracting the Soma juice. -4 Making libations.

सवनं *n.* 1 Extracting the Soma juice or drinking it.-2 A sacrifice. -3 A libation, sacrificial libation. -4 Bathing. -5 Bearing or bringing forth children.

सवयस् *a.* Of the same age. *-m.* 1 A contemporary, coeval. -2 A companion of the same age. *-f.* A woman's female companion.

सवरः *m.* 1 N. of Siva. -2 Water.

सवर्ण *a.* (*f.* -र्णा) 1 Of the same colour ; like, resembling.-2 Of the same caste or tribe. -3 Belonging to the same class of letters, requiring the same effort in pronunciation.

सविकल्प, सविकल्पक *a.* (*f.* -ल्पा, -का) 1 Optional. -2 Doubtful. -3 Recognizing a distinction as that of subject and object or of the knower and the known (opp. निर्विकल्पक).

सविग्रह *a.* (*f.* -हा) 1 Possessing a body, embodied. -2 Having meaning or import. -3 Quarrelling.

सवितर्क, सविमर्श *ind.* Thoughtfully.

सवितृ *a.* (*f.*-त्री) Generating, producing. *-m.* The sun.-2 N. of Siva.

-3 Of Indra.

सवित्री *f.* 1 A mother. -2 A cow.

सविध *a.* (*f.* -धा) 1 Of the same kind or sort. -2 Adjacent. —धं *n.* Proximity.

सविमर्श *ind.* Thoughtfully.

सविशेष *a.* (*f.* -षा) 1 Possessing characteristic qualities.-2 Peculiar, extraordinary. -3 Special, particular. -4 Superior, excellent. -5 Discriminative. (सविशेषं and सविशेषतस् 'Especially ' particularly', ' exceedingly'.

सविस्तर *a.* (*f.* -रा) Detailed. —रं *ind.* In detail.

सवृद्धिक *a.* (*f.* —का) Bearing interest.

सवेश *a.* (*f.*-शा) 1 Dressed.-2 Near, proximate

सवैलक्ष्य *a.* 1 Unnatural, forced. -2 Embarrassed.

सव्य *a.* (*f.* -व्या) 1 Left,left-hand. -2 Southern. -3 Contrary, reverse. -4 Right. -Comp. —इतर *a.* Right. -साचिन् *m.* An epithet of Arjuna.

सव्यपेक्ष *a* (*f.*-क्षा) Connected with, dependent on.

सव्यभिचारः *m.* A too general middle term (in *logic*).

सव्येष्ठृ *m.* A charioteer.

सशस्या *f.* A variety of sun-flower.

सश्मश्रुः *f.* A woman with a beard.

सश्रीक *a.* (*f.* -का) 1 Prosperous, fortunate. -2 Beautiful.

ससत्त्व *a.* (*f.* -त्वा) 1 Possessed of vitality or courage. -2 Big with child. -3 Full of animals or creatures. -त्वा *f.* A pregnant woman.

ससर्म *n.* Immolation.

ससंदेह *a.* Doubtful. -हः *m.* N. of a figure of speech. See संदेह.

ससंध्य *a.* (*f.* -ध्या) Evening,vespertime.

ससंभ्रम *a.* (*f.* -मा) Agitated, confused. -मं *ind.* 1 Hurriedly, hastily. -2 In confusion.

सस्ज् See संज्.

सस्यं *n.* 1 Corn, grain. -2 Fruit or produce of any plant.-3 A weapon. -4 A good quality, merit. -Comp. —इष्टिः *f.* A sacrifice made on the ripening of new grain. -मारिन् *m.* A kind of rat or mouse.—संवरः *m.* The Sâla tree.

सस्यक *a.* (*f.* —का) Possessed of good qualities; meritorious. -कः *m.* 1 A sword. -2 A weapon. -3 A kind of precious stone.

सस्वेदा *f.* A girl recently deflowered.

सह् 4 P. (सह्यति) 1 To satisfy. -2 To be pleased. -3 To endure, bear.

सह् 1 A. (सहते in epic Paras. also सोढ. The स् of सह् is changed to ष after prepositions ending in इ, as नि, परि, वि, except when ह् is changed to ढ्) 1 To bear, endure. -2 To allow. -3 To forgive, forbear, to wait, be patient. -4 To support, bear up. -5 To defeat, oppose. -6 To stop. -7 To be able (with inf.). With उत्— 1 To make an effort or exertion. -2 To dare. -3 To be able. -4 To desire, to be inclined to. प्र— 1 To make an effort. -2 To endure. -3 To overpower. -4 To be able. वि— 1 To sustain, to endure. -2 To be able to resist. -3 To determine.

Caus. (साहयति,-ते) To cause to bear, to cause to endure, to make bearable. With उत्— To rouse up, encourage.

Desid. (सिसहिषते) To wish to bear &c.

सह *a.* (*f.* —हा) 1 Bearing, enduring, suffering. -2 Patient. -3 Able. —हः *m.* The month मार्गशीर्ष. -2 N. of Siva. —हः *m.*,—हं *n.* Power,strength.

सह *ind.* 1 With, together with,

accompanied by (with instr.). -2 Simultaneously, at the same time. -Comp. —अध्यायिन् m. A fellow-student. —अर्थ a. 1 Having the same object. -2 Synonymous. (-र्थः m.) The same or common object. -उक्तिः f. (Rhetoric) The figure of speech which involves a hyperbole as basis, and in which a single expression by the force of a term denoting conjunction signifies two facts. —उटजः m. A hut made of leaves. —उदरः m. A uterine brother. —उपमा f. A kind of Upamá. —ऊढः, -ऊढजः m. The son of a woman pregnant at marriage.-कारः m.Co-operation. -2 A mango tree. —कारिन्, -कृत्, -कृत्वन् m. A co-adjutor, associate,colleague.-कृत a.Co-operated with, assisted or aided by. —गमनं n. 1 Accompanying. -2 A woman's burning herself with her deceased husband's body. —चर a. Accompanying, living with. (-रः m.) 1 A companion, associate. -2 A follower, servant. -3 A husband. -4 A surety. (-री f.) 1 A female companion. -2. A wife, mate. -चारः m. 1 Accompaniment. -2 Agreement, harmony. -3 (In logic) The invariable accompaniment of the *hetu* (middle term) by the *sâdhya* (major term). -4 Right course (opp. व्यभिचार). -ज a 1 Inborn, innate. -2 Hereditary. (-जः m.) 1 A brother of whole blood. -2 The natural state or disposition. —जात a. 1 Natural. -2 Born together, twin-born. -दार a. 1 With a wife. -2 Married. —देवः m. N. of the youngest of the five Pándavas; the twin brother of Nakula. —धर्मचारिन् m. A husband.-धर्मचारिणी f. 1 A lawful wife; one legally married (also सहधर्मिणी). -पांशुक्रीडिन्, m.,-पांशुक्रीडिन, —पांशुकिलः m. A friend from the earliest childhood. —भाविन् m. A partisan, follower. —भू a. Natural, innate. —भोजनं n. Eating in company with friends. —मरणं n. See सहगमनं. —रक्षस् m. One of the three kinds of sacrificial fires.—वसतिः f., -वासः m. Dwelling together. -वासिन् m. A fellow-lodger.

सहन a. (f. —ना) Enduring. —नं n. 1 Bearing, enduring, patience, forbearance.

सहस् m. 1 The month Márgasîrsha. -2 The winter. -n 1 Power, strength. -2 Victory, conquering. -3 Lustre, brightness.

सहसा *ind.* 1 Forcibly. -2 Rashly, inconsiderately. -3 Suddenly.

सहसान a. (f. —ना) 1 Patient. -2 Overpowering. -नः m. 1 A peacock. -2 A sacrifice, an oblation.

सहस्यः m. The month Pausha.

सहस्रं n 1 A thousand. -2 A large number. -Comp. —अंशुः, -आर्चिस्,-करः, -किरणः,-दीधितिः,-धामन्,-पादः,-मरीचिः,-रश्मिः m. The sun. —अक्ष a. 1 Thousand-eyed. -2 Vigilant. (-क्षः m.). 1 An epithet of Indra. -2 Of Vishnu. —काण्डा f. The white Dúrvâ grass. —कृत्वस् *ind.* A thousand times. -दंष्ट्रः m. A kind of fish. —दृश्,-नयनः,-नेत्रः, -लोचनः m. 1 Epithets of Indra. -2 Of Vishnu. —धारः m. The discus of Vishnu. —पत्रं n. A lotus. -2 The Sârasa bird. —बाहुः m. 1 An epithet of king Kàrtavìrya.-2 Of the demon Bána. —रोमन् n. A blanket. —वीर्या f. Dúrvâ grass. —वेधं n. 1 Sorrel. -2 A kind of sour gruel. —वेधिन् m. A sort of cane. (-n,) Asa-fœtida. —शिखरः m. The Vindhya mountain.

सहस्रतय a. (f.-यी) Thousand-fold. —यं n. A thousand.

सहस्रधा ind. In a thousand parts, a thousand-fold.

सहस्रशस् ind. By thousands.

सहास्रिन a. (f. —णी) 1 Possessed of a thousand. -2 Consisting of thousands.-3 Amounting to a thousand (as a fine). -m. 1 A body of a thousand men. -2 The commander of a thousand.

सहस्वत a (f. —ती) Powerful.

सहा f. 1 The earth. -2 The aloe-plant or flower.

सहाय: m. 1 A companion. -2 A follower, an adherent. -3 An ally. -4 A helper, patron. -5 The ruddy goose. -6 A kind of perfume. -7 N. of Siva.

सहायता f., -त्वं n. 1 A number of companions. -2 Companionship, union -3 Assistance.

सहायवत् a (f. —ती) 1 Having a friend. -2 Befriended, assisted.

सहार: m 1 The mango tree. -2 Universal destruction.

सहित a. (f. —ता) 1 Accompanied or attended by. -2 Borne, endured. —तं ind. Together with.

साहित्रं n. Patience, forbearance.

सहिष्ठ a. (f. —ष्ठा) Mightiest; very powerful.

सहिष्णु a. 1 Able to bear or endure. -2 Patient, forbearing.

साहिष्णुता f., -त्वं n. 1 Power to bear or support.-2 Patience,resignation.

सहुरि: m. 1 The sun.-f. The earth.

सहृदय a. (f. —या) 1 Kind, compassionate. -2 Sincere. —य: m. 1 A learned man. -2 A man of taste, a man of critical faculty.

सहृल्लेख a. (f. —खा) Questionable, doubtful. —खं n. Questionable food.

सहेल a. (f.—ला) Sportive, playful.

सहोढ: m. A thief caught with the stolen property in his possession.

सहोर a. (f. —रा) Good, excellent. —र: m. A saint, sage.

सह्य a. (f. —ह्या) 1 Supportable, endurable. -2 To be endured. -3 Able to bear. -4 Adequate or equal to. -5 Sweet, agreeable. -6 Strong, powerful.—ह्य: m. N. of one of the seven principal mountain ranges in India. —ह्यं n. 1 Health. -2 Assistance.-3 Fitness,adequacy. -Comp. —आत्मजा f. N. of the river Kâverî.

सा f. 1 N.of Lakshmî.-2 Of Pârvatî.

सांयात्रिक: m. A sea-trader.

सांयुगीन a. (f. —ना) 1 Skilled in war, war-like. -2 Shown in battle. —न: m. A great warrior.

सांराविणं n. A general or loud shout.

सांवत्सर a. (f.-री), सांवत्सरिक (f.-की) Annual, yearly. —क: m. 1 An astrologer. -2 An almanac maker.

सांवादिक a. (f. —की) 1 Colloquial. -2 Controversial. —क: m. A disputant.

सांवृत्तिक a. (f.-की) Illusory, phenomenal.

सांशयिक a. (f. —की) 1 Doubtful. -2 Irresolute. —कं n. A perilous or dangerous deed.

सांसारिक a. (f. —की) Worldly.

सांसिद्धिक a. (f. —की) 1 Natural, innate,inherent.-2 Effected naturally, spontaneous. -3 Absolute. -4 Effected by supernatural means. -Comp.-द्रव: m.Natural fluidity(opp. नैमित्तिक 'generated,' belonging to water only).

सांस्थानिक: m. A fellow-countryman.

सांस्राविणं n. A general flow or stream.

सांहनिक a.(f.-की)Bodily,corporeal.

साकम् *ind.* 1 With, together with (with instr.). -2 Simultaneously.

साकल्यं *n.* Entirety, the whole or entire part of a thing. (साकल्येन 'Entirely,' 'thoroughly').

साकूत *a.* (*f.* —ता) 1 Significant, meaning. -2 Intentional. -3 Amorous, wanton. —तं *ind.* 1 Meaningly, significantly. -2 Amorously. -3 Feelingly, pathetically. -4 Attentively.

साकेतं *n.*N. of the city of Ayodhyá. —ताः *m. pl.* The inhabitants of Ayodhyâ. [Ayodhyá.

साकेतकः *m.* An inhabitant of

साक्तुकं *n.* A quantity of fried grain (सक्तु). —कः *m.* Barley.

साक्षात् *ind.* 1 In the presence of, before the very eyes of. -2 Openly, evidently. -3 In person, actually.-4 Directly. साक्षात्कृ 1 To see with one's own eyes, realize personally.-2 To have an intuitive perception or manifestation of. -Comp. —करणं *n.* 1 Causing to be visibly present. -2 Making evident to the senses. -3 Intuitive perception. —कारः *m.* Perception, apprehension.

साक्षिन् *a.* (*f.*-णी) 1 Seeing, witnessing. -2 Testifying.-*m.* 1 A witness, an eye-witness. -2 The Supreme Being. [abusive.

साक्षेप *a.* (*f.* —पा) Taunting,

साक्ष्यं *n.* 1 Evidence, testimony. -2 Attestation.

साखेय *a.* (*f.* —यी) 1 Relating to a friend. -2 Amicable.

साख्यं *n.* Friendship.

सागरः *m.*1 The ocean, sea (fig. also). -2 The number 'four' or 'seven'. -3 A kind of deer. -Comp. —अनुकूल *a.* Situated along the sea-coast.-अंत *a.* Bounded by the sea. -अंबरा, -नेमिः, -मेखला *f.* The earth. —आलयः *m.* N. of Varuna. —उत्थं *n.* Sea-salt. —गा *f.* 1 A river. -2 The Ganges. —गामिनी *f.* A river. [the sacred fire.

साग्नि *a.* 1 Having fire. -2 Taking

साग्निक *a.* (*f.* —का) 1 Maintaining or possessing fire. -2 Attended by fire. —कः *m.* A house-holder who maintains the sacred fire.

साग्र *a.* (*f.* —ग्रा) 1 Entire.-2 With a surplus; more than.

सांकर्यं *n.* Promiscuous or confused mixture.

सांकल *a.* (*f.* —ली) Produced or effected by addition.

सांकाश्यं *n.*, सांकाश्या *f.*N. of the capital of Kusadhvaja, brother of Janaka.

सांकेतिक *a.* (*f.* —की) 1 Symbolical, indicatory. -2 Conventional.

सांक्षेपिक *a.* (*f.* —की) 1 Abridged, concise.

सांख्य *a.* (*f.* —ख्या) 1 Relating to number, numeral. -2 Enumerating.-3 Discriminative.-4 Deliberating. —ख्यः *m.*, —ख्यं *n.* N. of one of the six systems of Hindu philosophy. (The chief object of this philosophy is to effect the final emancipation of the twenty-fifth *Tattva, i. e.* the *Purusha* or soul, from the bonds of this worldly existence by conveying a correct knowledge of the twenty-four other *Tattvas* and by properly discriminating the Soul from them. It agrees with the Vedânta in being synthetical, and so differs from the analytical Nyâya or Vaiseshika, but its great point of divergence from the Vedânta is that it maintains two priciples which the Vedànta denies). —ख्यः *m.* 1 A follower of the Sánkya philosophy. -2 An epithet of Siva. -Comp. —प्रसादः, -मुख्यः m. An epithet of Siva.

सांग a. (f. -गा) 1 Having members. -2 Complete, in every part. -3 Together with the six *angas* or auxiliary members.

सांगतिक a. (f. —की) Relating to union; associating.-कः m. A visitor, guest, new-comer.

संगमः m. Union, meeting.

सांग्रामिक a. (f. -की) Relating to war; warlike. —कः m. A general, commander.

साचि ind. Obliquely, crookedly. (साचीकृ To turn or bend aside,make crooked).

साचिव्यं n. 1 The office of a minister. -2 Ministry, administration. -3 Friendship.

साजात्यं n. 1 Sameness of caste, class or kind.-2Homogeneousness.

साटोप a (f. -पा) Elated or puffed up with pride. -2 Majestic, stately. —पं ind. Arrogantly, in a stately manner.

सात ind. A Taddhita affix added to a word to show that something is completely changed into the thing expressed by that word, or that it is left at the complete disposal or control of that thing *e. g.* भस्मसात, अग्निसात, ब्राह्मणसात, राजसात् &c.

सातत्यं n. Continuity, permanence.

सातवाहनः m. N. of king Sâlivàhana.

सातिः f. 1 A gift, donation. -2 Gaining, obtaining. -3 Help. -4 Destruction. -5 End, conclusion. -6 Sharp pain. -7 Cessation. -8 Wealth.

सातीनः, सातीनकः, सातीलकः m. Pease.

सात्त्विक a (f. -की) 1 Real, essential. -2 Natural. -3 Sincere. -4 Virtuous. amiable. -5 Vigorous. -6 Endowed with the quality *Sattva* (goodness). -7 Belonging to or derived from the *Sattva* quality. -8 Caused by internal feeling or sentiment (as of love); internal. -कः m. 1 An external indication of (internal) feeling or emotion, one of the kinds of *Bhávas* in poetry. -2 A Bráhmana.-3 N. of Brahman (m.) —की f. N. of Durgâ.

सात्यकिः m. N. of a Yâdava warrior who acted as charioteer to Krishna.

सात्यवतः, सात्यवतेयः m. A metronymic of the sage Vyâsa.

सात्वत् m. 1 A follower,worshipper. -2 A man of the Yádava tribe.

सात्वतः m. 1 N. of Vishnu. -2 Of Balaráma. 3 The son of an outcast Vaisya. —ताः m. pl. N. of a people.

सात्वती f. 1 N. of one of the four dramatic styles.-2 N. of the mother of Sisupâla.

सादः m. 1 Sinking, settling down. -2 Exhaustion -3 Thinness, emaciation. -4 Decay, destruction, cessation. -5 Pain, torment. -6 Clearness, purity.

सादनं n 1 Wearying. -2 Destroying -3 Exhaustion. -4 A dwelling. —नी f. Exhaustion, decay, fatigue.

सादिः m. 1 A charioteer. -2 A warrior. -3 A dispirited person.

सादित p. p. (f -ता) 1 Made to sit down. -2 Dispirited. -3 Exhausted. -4 Exterminated. -5 Decayed.

सादिन a. (f. - नी) 1 Sitting down. -2 Exhausting.—m. 1 A horseman. -2 One riding on an elephant or seated in a car. -3 A charioteer.

सादृश्यं n 1 Resemblance,similarity. -2 A portrait, an image.

साद्यंत *a*. (*f*. -ता) Entire,complete.

साद्यस्क *a*. (*f*. -स्की) Instantaneous.

साध् 5 P. (साध्नोति) 1 To finish, accomplish. -2 To conquer.

साध् 4 P. (साध्यति) To. be completed or accomplished.

Caus. 1 To be accomplished or performed. -2 To finish, conclude. -3 To gain,obtain.-4 To prove,substantiate.-5 To conqurer, win over. -6 To kill. -7 To learn, understand. -8 To heal.-9 To go, depart. -10 To recover (as a debt). With प्र— 1 To further.-2 To accomplish. -3 To dress. -4 To acquire. -5 To subdue.सम्— 1 To be successful. -2 To endow with. -3 To destroy. -4 To distinguish. -5 To obtain. -6 To cause to be paid. -7 To regain.

साधक *a*. (*f*. —धका or -धिका) 1 Accomplishing, effecting.-2 Efficient, effective. -3 Skilful, adept. -4 Effecting by magic; magical. -5 Assisting. —कः *m*. One possessed of supernatural powers. —का *f*. N. of Durgá.

साधन *a*. (*f*. —नी) Accomplishing, effecting. —नं *n*. 1 Accomplishing. -2 Attainment of an object. -3 A means of accomplishing anything. -4 An instrument, agent. -5 The efficient cause,source,cause in general. -6 The instrumental case. -7 Implement, apparatus, appliances, materials. -8 Matter, ingredients. -9 An army or a part of it. -10 Assistance. -11 Proof, demonstration. -12 The *hetu* or midd'e term in a syllogism. -13 Overcoming. -14 Subduing by charms. -15 Accomplishing anything by charms or magic. -16 Healing. -17 Killing, destroying. -18 Propitiating, winning over.-19 Going out,departure. -20 Following. -21 Penance. -22 Attainment of final beatitude. -23 A medicinal preparation. -24 (In law) Enforcement of the delivery of anything or of the payment of debt, infliction of fine.-25 A bodily organ. -26 The penis. -27 An udder. -28 Wealth. -29 Friendship. -30 Profit, advantage. -31 Burning a dead body. -32 Obsequies. -33 Oxydation of metals. -Comp. -क्रिया *f*. 1 A finite verb.-2 An action connected with a *Kâraka*.

साधनता *f*., —त्वं *n*. 1 The state of having means,possession of means to accomplish a desired object. -2 The state of perfection.

साधना *f*. 1 Accomplishment, completion. -2 Worship. -3 Propitiation.

साधंत: *m*. A mendicant, beggar.

साधर्म्य *n*. 1 Sameness of duty, office or nature; likeness, community of properties. -3 Being of the same religion.

साधारण *a*. (*f*.-णा or-णी) 1 Common (to two or more), joint. -2 Ordinary, common.-3 General, universal -4 Mingled with, in common with. -5 Equal, similar. -6 (In logic) Belonging to more than one instance alleged, one of the three divisions of the fallacy called अनैकांतिक.-णं *n*. 1 A general rule, a rule or precept generally applicable. -2 A generic property. -Comp. -स्त्री *f*. A common woman, harlot, prostitute.

साधारणता *f*., —त्वं *n*. 1 Community, universality. -2 Joint interest.

साधारणी *f*. 1 A twig of bamboo. -2 A key.

साधारण्यं *n*. Commonness ; see साधारणता.

साधिका *f.* 1 A skilful or accomplished woman. -2 Deep sleep.

साधित *p. p.* (*f.* —ता) 1 Accomplished. -2 Completed. -3 Demonstrated -4 Obtained. -5 Discharged. -6 Subdued. -7 Made good, recovered. -8 Fined. -9 Made to pay. -10 Awarded (as fine or punishment.

साधिमन् *m.* Goodness, excellence.

साधिष्ठ *a.* (*f.* —ष्ठा) 1 Best, most proper. -2 Very strong, (superl. of साधु or बाढ).

साधीयस् *a.* (*f.* -सी) 1 Better. -2 Harder, stronger; (compar. of साधु or बाढ).

साधु *a.* (-ध्वी *f.* or-धु; compar.-साधीयस्; superl. साधिष्ठ) 1 Good, perfect. -2 Proper, right. -3 Virtuous, honourable, pious. -4 Kind, well-disposed. -5 Well behaved (with loc.) *e. g.* मातरि साधुः. -6 Correct, classical (as language). -7 Agreeable. -8 Noble, well-born. —धुः *m.* 1 A virtuous man. -2 A saint. -3 A merchant. -4 A Jaina saint. -5 A usurer, a money-lender. – *ind.* 1 Well, well done, bravo.-2 Enough, away with. -Comp. —वादः *m.* A cry of approbation. —वृक्षः *m.* The Kadamba tree.

साधुता *f.*,-त्वं *n.* Goodness,chastity.

साधूतं *n.* 1 A stall, shop. -2 An umbrella.-3 Flock of peacocks.

साध्य *a.* (*f.* -ध्या) 1 To be accomplished. -2 Practicable, attainable. -3 To be demonstrated. -4 To be established or made good. -5 To be inferred or concluded. -6 To be conquered or subdued;conquerable. -7 Curable. -8 To be killed or destroyed. —ध्यः *m.* 1 A particular class of celestial beings -2 A deity in general. -3 N. of a Mantra. -ध्यं *n.* 1 Accomplishment, perfection. -2 The thing to be established, the matter at issue. -3 (In logic) The predicate of a proposition, the major term in a syllogism.-Comp. —अभावः *m* The absence of the major term. —पक्षः *m.* The plaint in a law-suit. —सिद्धिः *f.* 1 Accomplishment. -2 Conclusion.

साध्यता *f.* 1 Feasibility, practicability. -2 Curableness. -Comp. -अवच्छेदकं *n.* That which marks out or measures the साध्य or major term, its characteristic property.

साध्यवत् *m.* The party on whom rests the burden of proof in a law-suit. -*n* That which contains the साध्य or major term.

साध्वसं *n.* 1 Fear, fright. -2 Torpor. -3 Perturbation.

साध्वी *f.* 1 A virtuous or chaste woman. -2 A faithful wife. -3 N. of a kind of root.

सानसिः *m.* Gold.

सानिका, सानेयिका, सानेयी *f.* A pipe, flute.

सानुः *m.*, सानु *n.* 1 A summit, ridge. -2 A table-land. -3 A sprout. -4 A forest. -5 A road. -6 A point end. -7 A precipice. -8 A gale of wind. -9 A learned man. -10 The sun.

सानुमत् *m.* A mountain.

सानुराग *a.* (*f.* —गा) Attached, enamoured.

सांतपनं *n.* A kind of penance.

सांतर *a.* (*f.* -रा) 1 Having interstices. -2 Open in texture.

सांतानिक *a* (*f.* -की) 1 Stretching, spreading, extending (as a tree). -2 Relating to descendants. -3 Relating to the tree Santâna. —कः *m.* A Brâhmana who wishes to marry for the sake of issue.

सांत्व् 10 U. (सांत्वयति, -ते) To appease, concillate, soothe.

सांत्वः m., सांत्वनं n., सान्त्वना f. 1 Appeasing, consolation. -2 Conciliation. -3 Kind words. -4 Mildness. -5 Friendly salutation and inquiry

सांदीपनि: m. N. of a sage.

सांद्दष्टिक a. (f. -की) Relating to present perception; visible at the same time. -कं n Immediate consequence.

सांद्र a. (f. -द्रा) 1 Close, compact. -2 Coarse, gross, thick, concentrated. -3 Clustered together. -4 Stout, strong, robust. -5 Abundant, much. -6 Intense, vehement. -7 Unctuou , oily. -8 Bland, soft, smooth. -9 Agreeable. -द्रः m. 1 A heap, cluster. -2 A thicket.

सांधिकः m. A distiller. [and war.

सांधिविग्रहिकः m. A minister of peace

सांध्य a. (f. -ध्यी) 1 Relating to the twilight of evening. -2 Relating to the morning twilight or dawn.

सांनहनिक a. (f. -की) 1 Bearing or putting on an armour. -2 Calling to arms. -कः m. An armour-bearer.

सांनाय्यः m. Any substance mixed with clarified butter and offered as an oblation to fire.

सांनिध्यं n. 1 Vicinity, proximity. -2 Presence, attendance.

सांनिपातिक a. (f. -की) 1 Miscellaneous. -2 Complicated. -3 Having a complicated derangement of the three bodily humours.

सांन्यासिकः m. 1 A Brâhmana in the fourth order of his religious life. -2 A mendicant in general.

सापत्न a. (f. -त्नी) Born from, or belonging to, a rival wife. -त्नाः (m. pl.) The children of different wives of the same husband.

सापत्न्यं n. 1 The state or condition of a rival wife. -2 Rivalry, enmity. -त्न्यः m. 1 The son of a rival wife. -2 An enemy.

सापिण्ड्यं n. Connection by the offering of rice-balls to the same Manes; consanguinity.

साप्तपद a. (f. -दी), साप्तपदीन a. (f. -ना) Formed by walking together seven steps, or by talking together seven words. -दं,-नं n. 1 Circumambulation of the nuptial fire by the bride and bride-groom in seven steps (which makes the marriage-tie irrevccable). -2 Friendship.

साप्तपौरुष a. (f. -षी) Extending to or including seven generations.

साफल्यं n 1 Fruitfulness, productivenss. -2 Profit, advantage. -3 Success.

साब्दी f A kind of grape. [soothe.

साम् 10 P. (सामयति,-ते) To appease.

सामकं n. The principal of a debt. -कः m. A whet-stone.

सामग्री f. 1 A collection of materials; apparatus, furniture. -2 Effects, goods. -3 Provision.

सामग्र्यं n. 1 Entireness, perfection, totality. -2 Retinue. -3 A collection of implements, apparatus. -4 Stock, effects. [propriety.

सामंजस्यं n. Fitness, consistency,

सामन् n. 1 Appeasing, comforting, soothing. -2 Conciliation (the first of the four *upâyas* or expedients to be used by a king against an enemy). -3 Pacific or conciliatory conduct. -4 Mildness, gentleness. -5 A metrical hymn or song of praise. -6 A verse or text of the Sâmaveda.-7 The Sâmaveda itself. -Comp. -उद्भवः m. An elephant.

—गः *m.* A Bráhmana who chants the Sâmaveda. —जः, -जातः *m.* An elephant -योनिः *m.*1 Brahman(*m.*).-2 An elephant —वादः *m.* Conciliatory words. —वेदः *m* The third of the four Vedas.—वेदिन् *m.* A Brâhmana who has studied the Sámaveda. —वेदीयः *m.* Chhándoga priest.

सामंत *a.* (*f.* —ती) 1 Bordering, bounding. -2 Neighbouring. -3 Universal. —तः *m.* 1 A neighbour. -2 A neighbouring king. -3 A tributary prince. -4 A leader, a general.—तं *n.* Neighbourhood.

सामयिक *a.* (*f.* —की) 1 Customary, conventional. -2 Agreed upon, stipulated. -3 Conforming to agreement or engagement. -4 Punctual. -5 Timely. -6 Periodical. -7 Temporary. -Comp. —अभावः *m.* Temporay non-existence.

सामर्थ्य *n.* 1 Power, capacty, ability. -2 Sameness of aim or object. -3 Oneness of meaning or signification. -4 Adequacy. -5 The signifying power of a word. -6 Interest, advantage. -7 Wealth.

सामवायिक *a.* (*f.* —की) 1 Belonging to an assembly. -2 Relating to inseparable connection. —कः *m.* 1 A minister, counsellor. -2 The chief of a company.

सामाजिक *a.* (*f.* —की) Belonging to an assembly. —कः *m.* A spectator at an assembly or meet ng.

सामानाधिकरण्यं *n.*1 Being in the same predicament.-2Common office or government. -3 Common relationship (as of case). -4 The state of relating to the same object.

सामान्य *a.* (*f.* —न्या) 1 Common, general. -2 Alike, equal, same. -3 Of an average or middle degree. -4 Commonplace, insignificant. -5 Entire, whole. —न्यं *n.* 1 Community, generality, universality. -2 Common or generic property (in logic). -3 Totality, entireness. -4 Kind, sort. -5 Identity. -6 Equanimity. -7 Public affairs. -8 A general proposition. -9 (In Rhet.) The figure of speech in which the thing in question is spoken of as having become undistinguishab'e from something else on account of similar qualities. —न्या *f.* A harlot, prostitute.-Comp. —ज्ञानं *n.* The perception of generic properties. —पक्षः *m.* The mean. —पदार्थः *m.* The category called सामान्य or generality. —प्रतिपत्तिपूर्वकं *ind.* With equal respect.—लक्षणं *n.* A generic definition.—वनिता *f* A prostitute. —शास्त्रं *n.* A general rule.

सामान्यतः *ind.* Commonly, usually.

सामासिक *a.* (*f.* —की) 1 Comprehensive, collective. -2 Concise, brief. -3 Relating to a compound word. -4 Composite. —कं *n.* The whole class of compounds.

सामि *ind.* 1 Half. -2 Unfinished. -3 Vile, contemptible.

सामीची *f.* Praise, eulogium.

सामीप्यं *n.* Vicinitiy, proximity. —प्यः *m.* A neighbour.

सामुद्र *a.* (*f.*-द्री) Sea-born, marine. —द्रः *m.* A mariner, voyager. —द्रं *n.* 1 Sea-salt. -2 The cuttle-fish bone. -3 A mark or spot on the body.

सामुद्रकं *n.* Sea-salt.

सामुद्रिक *a.* (*f.* —की) 1 Sea-born, oceanic. -2 Relating to marks on the body (which are supposed to indicate good or bad fortune).—कः *m.* 1 One who knows how to interpret the varioue marks on the body.

-2 A for une teller.-कं *n.* The science of palmistry.

सांपराय *a.* (*f.* यी) 1 Relating to war.-2 Relating to the other world, future. -यः *m.* -यं *n.* 1 Conflict. -2 Future life, the future. -3 The means of attaining the future world. -4 Inquiry into the future. -5 Investigation. -6 Uncertainty.

सांपरायिक *a.* (*f.* —की) 1 Warlike. -2 Military, strategic. -3 Calamitous.-4 Relating to the other world. —कं *n.* War, battle. —कः *m.* A war-chariot. -Comp. -कल्पः *m.* Strategic array (of troops).

सांप्रत *a.* (*f.* -ता) 1 Fit, suitable. -2 Relevant. -तं *ind.* 1 Now, at this time.-3 Immediately. -4 Properly, seasonably.

सांप्रतिक *a.* (*f.* -की) 1 Belonging to the prsent time. -2 Proper, right.

सांप्रदायिक *a* (*f.* -की) Relating to the traditional doctrine; traditional.

सांबः *m.* N of Siva.

सांबंधिक *a* (*f.* -की) Arising from relationship. —कं *n.* Relationship, alliance.

सांवरी *f.* A sorceress.

सांभवी *f.* 1 The red Lodhra tree. -2 Possibility. [propitiousness.

सांमुख्यं *n.* 1 Presence. -2 Favour,

साम्यं *n.* 1 Equality, sameness. -2 Resemblance, similarity -3 Equability. -4 Concord; harmony. -5 Impartiality, sameness of view.

साम्राज्यं *n.* 1. Universal or complete sovereignty.-2 Empire, dominion.

सायः *m.* 1 Close, termination. -2 Evening. -3 An arrow. —Comp. -अह्न *m.* (सायाह्नः) Evening time.

सायकः *m.* An arrow. -2 A sword. -Comp. -पुंखः *m.* The feathered part of an arrow.

सायणः *m.* N. of a Bráhmana who flourished about 1370 A. D.

सायनं *n* The longitude of a planet reckoned from the vernal equinoctial point. [evening.

सायंतन *a.* (*f.*-नी) Belonging to the

सायम् *ind.* In the evening. -Comp. —कालः *m.* Evening. —धृतिः *f.* The evening oblation. -मंडनं *n.* 1 Sunset. -2 The sun. -संध्या *f.* 1 The evening twilight. -3 The evening prayer. -4 The goddess to be worshipped in the evening.

सायिन् *m.* A horseman.

सायुज्यं *n.* 1 Intimate union, identification with a deity (one of the four states of *Mukti*).-2 Similarity, likeness.

सार *a.* (*f.* -रा) 1 Essential.-2 Most excellent. -3 Real, true.-4 Strong, vigorous. -5 Thoroughly proved. -6 Highest, best. —रः *m.*, —रं *n.* (But usually *m.* only, except in the first 4 senses) 1 Essence, the essential part. -2 Substance, pith. -3 Marrow. -4 Real truth, main point, the real nature. -5 The sap of trees. -6 A compendium. -7 Strength, vigour, energy.-8 Heroism, courage. -9 Firmness, hardness. -10 Nectar. -11 Fresh butter. -12 Air, wind.-13 Cream, coagulum of curds. -14 Disease. -15 Riches, wealth. -16 Matter, pus.-17 Worth, excellence. -18 A man at chess. -19 Impure carbonate of soda.-20 The figure of speech in which there is a series of things, and each succeeding thing is represented as being superior to the preceding thing, the highest degree of superiority being reached in the last thing. This figure o speech corresponds to the English climax ' or 'anticlimax'. -21 The heart. —रा *f.* 1 Dúrvâ grass. -2 Kusa grass. —रं *n.* 1 Water. -2 Fitness, propriety. -3 Wood, thicket. -4 Steel. -Comp. -असार *a.* Valuable and worthless, strong and weak. (-रं *n.*) 1 Worth and worthlessness. -2 Substance and emptiness. -3 Strength and weakness. —गंध: *m.* Sandal wood. —ग्रीव: *m.* N. of Siva. —जं *n.* Fresh butter. —तरु: *m.* The plantain tree. —दा *f.* 1 N. of Sarasvatí. -2 Of Durgâ —द्रुम: *m.* The Khadira tree. —भांडं *n.* 1 A natural vessel. -2 A bale of goods, merchandise. -3 Implements. —लोहं *n.* Steel.

सारक *a.* Purgative, cathartic.

सारघं *n.* Honey.

सारंग *a.* (*f.* -गी) Spotted, variegated. -ग: *m.* 1 The variegated colour. -2 The spotted deer, an antelope. -3 A deer in general. -4 A lion. -5 An elephant. -6 A large black bee -7 The cuckoo. -8 A large crane. -9 The flamingo. -10 A peacock. -11 An umbrella. -12 A cloud. -13 A garment. -14 Hair. -15 A conch-shell. -16 N. of Siva. -17 The God of love. -18 A lotus. -19 Camphor. -20 A bow. -21 Sandal. -22 A kind of musical instrument. -23 An ornament. -24 Gold. -25 The earth. -26 The Chàtaka bird. -27 A flower. -28 Night. -29 Light.

सारंगिक: *m.* A bird catcher.

सारंगी *f.* 1 A kind of violin. -2 A kind of spotted deer.

सारण *a.* (*f.* —णी) Causing to go or flow. —ण: *m.* 1 Dysentery. -2 The hog-plum. —णं A kind of perfume.

सारणा *f* A kind of process to which metals are subjected.

सारणि:,-णी *f.* 1 A drain, water-course, channel. -2 A small river.

सारंड: *m.* The egg of a serpent.

सारतस् *ind.* 1 According to wealth. -2 Vigorously.

साराथि: *m.* 1 A charioteer. -2 A companion. -3 The ocean.

सारथ्यं *n.* Charioteership. coachmanship.

सारमेय: *m.* A dog. —यी *f.* A bitch.

सारल्यं *n.* Straightness (fig. also).

सारवत् *a.* (*f.* —ती) 1 Substantial. -2 Fertile. -3 Having sap.

सारस *a.* (*f.* —सी) Belonging to a lake. —स: *m.* 1 The (Indian) crane. -2 A bird in general. -3 The moon. —सं *n.* 1 A lotus. -2 The zone or girdle of a woman. -सी *f* A female (Indian) crane.

सारस (-श-) नं *n.* A girdle or zone.

सारस्वत *a.* (*f.* —ती) 1 Relating to the goddess Sarasvatí or to the river Sarasvatí. -2 Eloquent. -3 Belonging to the Sârasvata country. —त: *m.* 1 N. of a country about the river Sarasvatí. -2 A particular class of Brâhmanas. -3 A particular ceremonial used in the worship of Sarasvatí. -4 A staff of the Bilva tree. —ता: *m. pl.* The people of the Sárasvata country. —तं *n.* Speech, eloquence.

साराल: *m.* Sesamum.

सारि:, सारी *f.* 1 A chess-man. -2 A kind of bird. -Comp. —फलक: *m.* Chess-board.

सारिका *f.* A kind of bird.

सारिन् *a.* (*f.* —णी) 1 Going in front. -2 Having the essence or subtance of.

सारूप्यं *n.* 1 Sameness of form; similarity, -2 Assimilation to the deity (one of the four states of *Mukti*). -3 (In dramas) An angry treatment of one mistaken for another through resemblance. -4 Surprise at seeing an object or its likeness seen elsewhere.

सारोष्ट्रिकः *m.* A kind of poison.

सार्गल *a.* (*f.*-ला) Barred,obstructed.

सार्थ *a.* (*f.* -र्था) 1 Having meaning, significant. -2 Having an aim or object. -3 Of the same meaning. -4 Useful. -5 Wealthy. -र्थः *m.* 1 A rich man. -2 A caravan (of traders). -3 A collection of men. -4 A herd, flock (of animals of the same species).-5 A multitude in general. -6 One of a company of pilgrims. -Comp. —ज *a.* Reared in a caravan. —वाहः *m.* 1 The leader of a caravan.

सार्थक *a.* (*f.*-का) *a.* 1 Having sense, significant. -2 Serviceable, advantageous.

सार्थिकः *m.* A merchant, trader.

सार्द्र *a.* (*f.* -र्द्रा) Wet, moist.

सार्ध *a.* (*f.* -र्धा) Increased by half, having a half over.

सार्धम् *ind.* Together with, in company with (with instr.).

सार्पः, सार्प्यः *m.* N. of the constellation Asleshá.

सार्पिष *a.* (*f.* -षी), **सार्पिष्क** (-ष्की *f.*) Dressed or cooked with clarified butter.

सार्वकामिक *a* (*f.* —की) Satisfying every desire.

सार्वकालिक *a.* (*f.* -की) Everlasting.

सार्वजनिक *a.* (*f.*-की), **सार्वजनीन** *a.* (*f.* —नी) Public, general.

सार्वज्ञ *n.* Omniscience.

सार्वत्रिक *a.* (*f.* -की) Belonging to every place; general ; suited to all places or circumstances.

सार्वधातुक *a* (*f.* -की) Applicable to the whole of a radical term, or to the complete form of the verbal base after the conjugational characteristics have been affixed *i. e* to the four conjugational or special tenses. —कं *n.* N. of the verbal terminations of the four conjugational tenses.

सार्वभौतिक *a.* (*f.*-की) 1 Belonging or relating to all elements or beings. -2 Comprising all animate beings.

सार्वभौम *a.* (*f.* -मी) Relating to, or consisting of, the whole earth; universal. —मः *m.* 1 An emperor. -2 N. of the elephant presiding over the north.

सार्वलौकिक *a* (*f.* -की) Known to all people; public; universal.

सार्ववर्णिक *a.* (*f.*-की) 1 Of every kind or sort. -2 Belonging to every tribe or class.

सार्वविभक्तिक *n.* (*f.*-की) Applicable or belonging to all the cases of a noun.

सार्ववेदसः *m.* One who gives away all his wealth at a sacred rite.

सार्ववैद्यः *m.* A Bràhmana conversant with all the Vedas.

सार्षप *a.* (*f.*-पी) Made of mustard. —पं *n.* Mustard-oil.

सार्ष्टि *a.* Possessing the same condition or rank; having the same power.

सार्ष्टिता *f.* 1 Equality in rank, condition, or power. -2 Equality with the Supreme Being in all the divine attributes, the last of the four states or grades of *Mukti*.

सार्ष्ट्य *n* The fourth grade of *Mukti*.

सालः *m.* 1 N. of a tree or its resin. -2 A tree in general.-3 A rampart, a fence or wall round a buliding. -4 A wall in general. -5 A kind of fish. -Comp. —ग्रामः *m.* A kind of stone. -भंजिका *f.* 1 A doll, a puppet. -2 A harlot.-शृंगः *m.* A wall-pinnacle.

साल्मः *m.* 1 The resin of the Sâla tree. -2 Resin in general.

साला *f.* 1 A wall, rampart. -2 A house.

सालारं *n.* A peg projecting from a wall, a bracket.

सालूर. *m* A frog; see शालूर.

सालेयं *n.* A kind of fennel.

सालोक्यं *n.* 1 Being in the same world or sphere with another. -2 Residence in the same heaven with a particular deity.

साल्व: *m.* 1 N. of a country. -2 N. of a demon slain by Vishnu. साल्वाः *m. pl.* Inhabitants of the country call साल्व.

साल्विकः *m* The bird सारिका.

सावः *m.* A libation.

सावक *a.* (*f.* -विका) Productive, generative, causing birth. —कः *m.* The young of an animal; (for शावक).

सावकाश *n.* (*f.* -शा) Having leisure, at leisure. —शं *ind.* Leisurely, at one's convenience.

सावग्रह *a.* (*f.* —हा) Having the mark called *avagraha.*

सावज्ञ *a.* (*f.* -ज्ञा) Despising, disdainful.

सावद्यं *n.* One of the three kinds of power attainable by an ascetic, (the other two being निरवद्य andसूक्ष्म).

सावधान *a.* (*f.* —ना) 1 Attentive, careful, heedful. -2 Cautious. -3 Diligent. —नं *ind.* Carefully, attentively.

सावधि *a.* Having a boundary or limit; limited.

सावन *a.* (*f.* नी) Relating to, or comprising the three *savanas.* -नः *m.* 1 An institutor of a sacrifice. -2 The conclusion of a sacrifice or the ceremony by which it is concluded. -3 N. of Varuna. -4 A month of thirty solar days. -5 A natural day from sunrise to sunset.

सावयव *a.* (*f.* —वा) Composed of parts.

सावरः *m.* 1 Fault, offence. -2 Sin, crime. -3 The Lodhra tree.

सावरण *a* (*f.* —णा) 1 Concealed, secret. -2 Closed, shut. -3 Fenced.

सावर्ण *a.* (*f.* -र्णा) Relating to one of the same colour, tribe or caste. -र्णः *m.* A metronymic of the eighth Manu. -Comp. -लक्ष्यं *n.* 1 A mark of the sameness of colour or caste. -2. The skin.

सावर्णिः *m.* A metronymic of the eighth Manu.

सावर्ण्यं *n.* 1 Sameness of colour. -2 Identity of class or caste. -3 The age presided over by the eighth Manu.

सावलेप *a.* (*f.* -पा) Full of pride. —पं *ind.* Proudly, haughtily, arrogantly.

सावशेष *a.* (*f.* —षा) 1 Leaving a remainder or residue. -2 Imperfect. unfinished.

सावष्टंभ *a.* (*f* -भा) 1 Proud, majestic. -2 Courageous, resolute. -3 Vigorous, vehement. -4 Full of firmness. -भं *ind.* Resolutely, courageously.

सावहेल *a.* (*f.* -ला) Disdainful, disdaining, despising.-लं *ind.* Disdainfully, scornfully.

साविका *f.* A midwife.

सावित्र *a.* (*f.* -त्री) 1 Belonging to the sun. -2 Descended from the sun.-3Accompanied by the *Gâyatri.* -त्रः *m.* 1 The sun. -2 An embryo. a fœtus. -3 A Brâhmana. -4 An epithet of Siva. -5 Of Karna. -त्रं *n.* The sacrificial thread.

सावित्री *f.* 1 A ray of light. -2 N. of a celebrated verse of the *Rigveda* so called because it is adressed to the sun; it also called गायत्री. -3 The ceremony of investiture with the sacred thread. -4 N. of a wife of Brahman (*m.*). -5 N. of Pârvatî -6 N. of a wife of Kasyapa.-7 An epithet of Súryá (daughter of Savitri).-8N. of the wife of Satyavat, king of Sâlva. -Comp. -पतितः, -परिभ्रष्टः *m.* A man of any one of the first three castes not invested with the sacred thread at the proper time. —व्रतं *n.* N. of a particular fast kept by Hindu women on the last three days of the bright half of Jyeshtha to avert widow-hood.

साशंस *a.* (*f.* —सा) Full of desire or passion; desirous, hopeful. -सं *ind.* Wishfully, hopefully.

साशंक *a.* (*f.* —का) Feeling fear, dismayed.

साशयंदकः *m.* A small house-lizard.

साशूकः *m.* A blanket.

साश्चर्य *a.* (*f.* —र्या) 1 Wonderful, marvellous.-2 Struck with wonder. —र्यं *ind.* With wonder or astonishment.

साश्र, साश्र, *a.* (*f.* —श्रा, —स्रा) *a.* 1 Having angles or corners; angular. -2 Tearful, weeping.

साश्रुः *a.* Tearful, shedding tears.

साश्रुधी *f.* A wife's or husband's mother.

साष्टांगम् *ind.* Prostrating the eight limbs or members (said of प्रणाम).

सास *a.* (*f.* -सा) Having a bow.

सासुस *a.* Having arrows.

सासूय *a.* (*f* —या) Envious, jealous. -यं *ind.* Jealously, angrily.

सास्ना *f.* The dew-lap of an ox or [cow.

साहचर्य *n.* Companionship, fellowship, association.

साहनं *n* Endurance, suffering.

साहसं *n.* 1 Violence, force. -2 Any criminal act. -3 Cruelty. -4 Boldness, daring. -5 Rashness, a rash or daring act. -6 Punishment, fine (*m.* also in this sense). -Comp. —अंकः *m.* 1 An epithet of king Vikramáditya. -2 Of a poet. -3 Of a lexicographer. —अध्यवसायिन *a.* Acting rashly. —कारिन् *a.* 1 Bold, audacious. -2 Rash, inconsiderate.

साहसिक *a.* (*f.* —की) 1 Brutal, violent, cruel.-2 Daring, rash, reckless. -3 Castigatory, punitive.—कः *m.* 1 A bold or adventurous person. -2 A desperate or dangerous person. -3 A freebooter, robber. -4 An adulterer.

साहसिन *a.* (*f.* —नी) 1 Ferocious, cruel. -2 Rash, impetuous.

साहस्र *a.* (*f.* —स्री) 1 Relating to a thousand. -2 Consisting of a thousand. -3 Bought with a thousand. -4 Paid per thousand (as interest &c.). -5 A thousand-fold. —स्रः *m.* An army or detachment consisting of a thousand men. —स्रं *n.* An aggregate of a thousand.

साहायकं *n* 1 Assistance, aid. -2 Alliance, friendship. -3 A number of companions or associates. -4 Auxiliary troops.

साहाय्यं *n.* 1 Assistance, help. -2 Friendship, alliance.

साहित्यं *n.* 1 Association, fellowship. -2 Poetics or science of poeties. -3 Poetry in general. -4 A collection of materials for the production or performance of anything.

साह्यं *n.* 1 Union, fellowship. -2 Assistance. -Comp. —कृत् *m.* A companion. [animals.

साह्वयः *m.* Gambling with fighting

सिंहः *m.* 1 A lion. -2 The sign *Leo* of the zodiac. -3 (At the end of comp.) Pre-eminent of a class. -Comp. —अवलोकनं *n.* The back-ward glance of a lion. —अवलोकनन्यायः *m.* The maxim of the lion's glance. This maxim is used to mark the connection of a thing with what precedes and follows. —आसनं *n.* A throne, a seat of honour. —तलं *n.* The palms of the hands opened and joined together. —तुंडः *m.* A kind of fish. —दंष्ट्रः *m.* An epithet of Siva. -द्वारं *n.* A main or principal gate (of a palace &c.). —ध्वनिः, -नादः *m.* 1 The roar of a lion. -2 A war-cry. —यान, -रथा *f.* N. of the goddess Pàrvatî. —वाहनः *m.* An epithet of Siva. —वाहिनी *f.* An epithet of Durgá. —विक्रांतः *m.* A horse. —संहनन *a.* 1 As strong as a lion. -2 Handsome. (—नं *n.*) The killing of a lion.-स्थः *m.* An epithet of the planet Jupiter when in the constellation *Leo.*

सिंहलं *n.* 1 Tin. -2 Brass. -3 Bark, rind. -4 The island of Ceylon (oft. in pl.). —लाः *m. pl.* The people of Ceylon.

सिंहलकं *n.* The island of Ceylon.

सिंहाणं (-नं) *n.*, सिंहाणकः *m.*, -कं *n.* 1 Rust of iron. -2 The mucus of the nose.

सिंहिका *f.* The mother of Ráhu. -Comp. —तनयः, -पुत्रः, -सुतः, -सूनुः *m.* Epithets of Ràhu.

सिंही *f.* 1 A lioness. -2 N. of the mother of Râhu.

सिकता *f.* 1 Sandy soil. -2 Sand generally in pl). -3 Gravel or stone (the disease). -4 Sugar.

सिकतिल *a* (*f.* —ला) Sandy.

सिक्त *p. p.* (*f.* —क्ता) 1 Sprinkled. -2 Moistened. -3 Impregnated.

सिक्थः *m.* 1 Boiled rice. -2 A lump of boiled rice. —क्थं *n.* 1 Bees'-wax. -2 Indigo.

सिक्थक *n.* Bees'-wax.

सिक्यं *n.* A sling of ropes.

सिध्मः *m.* Crystal, glass.

सिंघ (-घा-) णं, सिंघाणकं *n.* 1 The mucus of the nose. -2 Rust of iron.

सिंघिणी *f.* The nose.

सिच् 6. U. (सिंचति,-ते, सेक्तुं, सिक्त, the स of सिच् is generally changed to ष् after a preposition ending in इ or उ) 1 To sprinkle. -2 To water, moisten. -3 To emit, discharge. -4 To infuse, instil, pour in. -5 To pour out for, offer to. -6 To impregnate. With अभि—1 To besprinkle, to wet. -2 To pour upon. -3 To inaugurate by sprinkling with sacred water. उद्— 1 To sprinkle, to pour. -2 To make proud or haughty. नि— 1 To sprinkle. -2 To impregnate. परि— To sprinkle

—*Caus.* (सेचयति,-ते) To cause to sprinkle With अभि-To cause to be inaugurated आ— To cause to be sprinkled. उद्— To cause to be proud. *Desid* सिसिक्षति,-ते.

Passive (सिच्यते) To be sprinkled. With उद्— 1 To be thrown upwards.-2 To be proud or arrogant.

सिचयः *m.* 1 Cloth, garment. -2 Old or ragged raiment.

सिंचिता *f.* Long pepper.

सिंजा *f.* The jingling sound of metallic ornaments.

सिंजितं *n.* Tinkling, jingling

सित *a.* (*f.* -ता) 1 White. -2 Tied, fettered. -3 Surrounded. -4 Finished. -तः *m.* 1 White colour. -2 The bright half of a lunar month. -3 The planet Venus. -4 An arrow.

—र्तं n. 1 Silver. -2 Sandal. -3 Radish. -Comp. —अग्रः m. A thorn. —अपांगः m A peacock. -अभ्रः m., -भ्रं n. Camphor. —अर्जकः m. The white basil.-अश्वः m. An epithet of Arjuna. -असितः m An epithet of Balarâma (-तौ m. dual) Venus and Saturn. —आदिः m. Treacle, molasses. -आननः m. N. of Garuda. —आलिका f. A cockle. —इतर n. Black. —उपला f. Candied sugar. —उपलः m. Chalk. —करः m. 1 The moon. -2 Camphor. —धातुः m. Chalk. —रश्मिः m. The moon. —वाजिन् m. N. of Arjuna. -शर्करा f. Candied sugar. —शिंबिकः m. Wheat. —शिवं n. Rock-salt. —शूकः m. Barley.

सिता f. 1 Candied sugar.-2 Moonlight. -3 A lovely woman. -4 Spirituous liquor. -5 White Dúrvá grass. -6 Arabian jasmine. -Comp. —खंडः m. A kind of refined sugar. —लता f. White Dúrvâ grass.

सिति a. 1 White. -2 Black. -तिः m. White or black colour. -Comp. —कंठः m. An epithet of Siva. -वाससू m. An epithet of Balarâma.

सितिमन् m. Whiteness.

सिद्ध p. p. (f. -द्धा) 1 Accomplished, effected, completed. -2 Obtained, acquired.-3 Succeeded, successful. -4 Settled. -5 Proved. -6 Sound (as a rule). -7 Admitted to be true. -8 Decided (as a law-suit.). -9 Paid off (as a debt).-10 Cooked (as food). -11 Matured, ripened -12 Thoroughly prepared or compounded (as drugs).-13 Ready (as money).-14 Subdued as by magic. -15 Brought under subjection ; become propitious.-16 Skilled in, proficient in. -17 Sanctified (as by penance). -18 Emancipated. -19 Endowed with supernatural powers or faculities. -20 Pious, holy. -21 Divine, immortal, eternal. -22 Well-known, illustrious.-23 Splendid.-द्धः m. 1 A semi-divine being supposed to be of great purity and holiness, and particularly characterized by eight supernatural faculties called *Siddhis*. -2 An inspired sage or seer (like Vyâsa).-3 Any seer, a prophet. -4 A magician.-5 A law-suit, judicial trial. -6 A kind of hard sugar. -द्धं n. Sea-salt. -Comp. -अंतः m. 1 The established end. -2 The demonstrated conclusion of an argument. established view of any question, (following on the refutation of the Púrvapaksha). -3 Approved fact, a settled doctrine. -4 Any established text book resting on conclusive evidence. —अंतकोटिः f. The point in an argument which is regarded as a logical conclusion. —अन्नं n. Cooked food.—अर्थ a. One who has accomplished his desired object, successful. (-र्थः m.) 1 White mustard. -2 N. of Siva. -3 Of the great Buddha. —आसनं n. A particular posture in religious meditation. —गंगा, -नदी, —सिंधुः f. The celestial Ganges. —ग्रहः m. N. of a particular kind of madness. —जलं, -सलिलं n. Sour rice-gruel. -देवः m. N. of Siva. —धातुः m. Quick-silver. -पक्षः m. The established or logical side of an argument. —पुष्पः m. The Karavíra plant. —प्रयोजनः m. White mustard.-रस a. Mineral, mettallic (-सः m.) 1 Quick-silver. -2 An alchemist. —संकल्प a. One who has accomplished his desired object. —साधनः m. White mustard. (-नं n.) 1 The performance o magical rites for the acquisition of supernatural powers &c. -2 The materials employed in mystical or chemical processes. —सेनः m. N. of Kártikeya. —स्थाली f. The boiler or pot of a seer (supposed to be a vessel gifted with the property of over-flowing with any kind of food at the wish of the possessor).

सिद्धता f., —त्वं n. 1 Accomplishment, perfection. -2 Validity of a rule or doctrine.

सिद्धांतिन् m. 1 One who establishes a conclusion after noticing and answering objections (or पूर्वपक्ष). 2 One learned in scientific text-books. -3 A follower of the Mîmâmsá philosophy.

सिद्धिः f. 1 Accomplishment, complete attainment (of an object). -2 Success, well-being. -3 Establishment, settlement. -4 Demonstration, proof. -5 Validity (of a rule, law &c.). -6 Decision (of a lawsuit). -7 Truth, correctness. -8 Payment (as of a debt). -9 Preparing, cooking(as of drugs &c.). -10 The solution of a problem. -11 Readiness. -12 Complete purity or sanctification. -13 A superhuman power or faculty ; (these faculties are eight). -14 The acquisition of supernatural powers by magical means. -15 Marvellous skill or capability. -16 Good effect or result. -17 Final beatitude. -18 Understading, intellect. -19 Making oneself invisible. -20 A magical shoe. -21 A kind of Yoga. -22 N. of Durgâ. -23 Complete knowledge. -24 Good effect. -25 N. of Siva (m. in this sense). -Comp.—योगः m. Parcular auspicious conjunction of planets.

सिध् 4 P. (सिध्यति, सेद्धुं, सिद्ध, caus. साधयति or सेधयति; desid. सिषित्सति) 1 To be accomplished. -2 To be successful. -3 To reach, hit (said of an arrow). -4 To attain one's object. -5 To be proved. -6 To be settled. -7 To be thoroughly prepared or cooked. -8 To be won. With अप— To remove. नि— 1 To remove. -2 To ward off. -3 To forbid- प्रति— 1 To prohibit. -2 To restrain, prevent. विप्रति- To contradict.

सिध् I P. (सेधति, सिद्ध; the स् of सिध् is generally changed to ष् after a prepositition ending in इ or उ) 1 To go. -2 To drive off. -3 To restrain. -4 To prohibit. -5 To command, instruct. -6 To turn out well or auspiciously. With प्र— 1 To be accomplished. -2 To be acquired. -3 To be effected, to succeed. सम्— 1 To be accomplished or performed thoroughly. -2 To be made perfect. -3 To be made happy, to attain beatitude. [Leprosy.

सिध्मं, सिध्मन् n. 1 Blotch, scab. -2

सिध्मल, सिध्मवत् a. Scabby, leprous. —ला f. See सिध्मं above.

सिध्मा f. 1 A scab, leprous spot. -2 Leprosy.

सिध्यः m. The asterism Pushya.

सिध्रः m. 1 A pious or virtuous man. -2 A tree.

सिध्रकावणं n. N. of one of the celestial gardens.

सिनः m. A morsel. -नं n. The body.

सिनी f. A woman having a white complexion.

सिनीवाली f. The day preceding that of new moon, or that day on which the moon rises with a scarcely visible crescent.

सिंदुकः, सिंदुवारः सिंधुकः, सिंधुवारः *m.* N. of a tree. (Mar. निर्गुडी).

सिंदूरः *m.* A kind of tree.-रं *n.* Red lead.

सिंदूरिका *f.* Red-lead.

सिंदूरी *f.* Red cloth or clothes.

सिंधुः *m.* 1 The sea, ocean. -2 The Indus. -3 The country around the Indus. -4 N. of a river in Mâlavá. -5 The water ejected from an elephant's trunk.-5 The juice exuding from the temples of an elephant. -7 An elephant. -8 N. of Varuna. -9 A kind of musical mode (राग).-सिंधवः *m. pl.* The inhabitants of the *Sindhu* country. —*f.* 1 A river in general. -2 The river Sindhu. -Comp. —उत्थं, -उपलं *n.* Rock-salt. -जः *m.* The moon. (-जं *n.*) Rock-salt. —राजः, —पतिः *m.* N. of Jayadratha.-लवणं *n.* Rock-salt. -वारः *m.* A horse of a good breed. —शयनः *m.* N. of Vishnu.

सिंधुरः *m,* An elephant.

सिप्रः *m.* 1 Perspiration, sweat. -2 The moon.

सिप्रा *f.* 1 A woman's girdle. -2 A female buffalo. -3 A river near Ujjayiní.

सिम *a.* (*f.* -मा) Every, all, whole, entire.

सिरः *m.* The root of long pepper.

सिरा *f.* 1 Any tubular vessel of the body (as a vein, artery, nerve &c.), -2 A bucket.

सिव् 4 P. (सीव्यति, स्यूत) 1 To sew, stitch together. -2 To unite. With अनु— To string together, connect uninterruptedly.

सिवरः *m.* An elephant.

सिषाधयिषा *f.* 1 Wish to effect or accomplish. -2 Desire to prove or demonstrate.

सिसृक्षा *f.* Desire to create.

सिहुंडः *m.* The milk-hedge plant.

सिह्लः, सिह्लकः *m.* Benzoin, incense

सिह्लकी, सिह्ली *f* The olibanum tree

सीक् 1 A. (सीकते) 1 To scatter in small drops. -2 To go, move.

सीक् 1 P., 10 U. (सीकति, सीकयति, -ते) 1 To be impatient. -2 To be patient. -3 To touch.

सीकरः *m.* 1 Drizzling rain, drizzle, mist. -2 Spray of water.

सीता *f.* 1 A furrow, track or line of a plough-share. -2 A tilled or furrowed ground, ploughed land. -3 Agriculture.-4 N. of the daughter of Janaka, king of Mithilâ, and wife of Râma. -5 N. of a goddess, wife of Indra. - 6 N. of Umà. -7 N. of Lakshmi. - 8 N. of one of the fabulous branches of the Ganges. -9 Spirituous liquor. -Comp. -द्रव्यं *n.* The implements of agriculture. -पतिः *m.* N. of Râmachandra. -फलः *m.* The custard-apple tree. (—लं *n.*) Its fruit.

सीतामकः *m.* Pease.

सीत्कारः *m*, सीत्कृतिः *f.* A sound made by drawing in the breath, (expressive of sighing, shivering with cold, &c.).

सीत्य *a.* (*f.*-त्या) Measured out by furrows; tilled, ploughed. —त्यं *n.* Rice, corn, grain.

सीदं *n.* Indolence, slothfulness.

सीधुः *m.* Spirit distilled from molasses; rum. -Comp. —गंधः *m.* The Bakula tree. —पुष्पः *m.* 1 The Kadamba tree.-2 The Bakula tree. —रसः *m.* The mango tree. — संज्ञः *m.* The Bakula tree.

सीध्रं *n.* The anus.

सीपः *m.* A sacrifical vessel in the shape of a boat.

सीमन् *f.* See सीमा

सीमंतः *m.* 1 A boundary-line, landmark. -2 The parting line of the hair or the hair so parted on each side of the head so as to leave a line. -3 A land-mark. -Comp. —उन्नयनं 'Parting of the hair', one of the twelve Saṃskáras or purificatory rites observed by women in the fourth, sixth, or eighth month of their pregnancy.

सीमंतकः *m.* N. of a particular kind of inhabitant of hell. —कं *n.* Red lead.

सीमंतय् Den.P.1 To part, (as hair). -2 To part or mark by a line (in general).

सीमंतित *a.* (*f.* —ता) 1 Parted (as hair). -2 Parted or marked by a line.

सीमंतिनी *f.* A woman.

सीमा *f.* 1 Boundary, border. -2 A mound or ridge serving to mark the boundary of a field, village, &c. -3 A mark, land-mark. -4 A shore, coast. -5 The horizon. -6 A suture (as of the skull). -7 The bounds of morality or decorum; limits of propriety. -8 The highest point, climax. -9 A field. -10 The nape of the neck. -11 The scrotum. -Comp. —अधिपः *m.* A neighbouring prince. —अंतः *m.* 1 A boundary line. -2 The utmost limit. —अंतपूजनं *n.* 1 The ceremony of worshipping or honouring a village-boundary. -2 Worshipping the bride-groom when he arrives at the village-boundary. —उल्लंघनं *n.* Transgressing a boundary, a ceremony performed on the *Dasará* day. -लिंगं *n.* A boundary-mark. —संधिः *m.* The meeting of two boundaries.

सीमिकः *m.* 1 A kind of tree. -2 An ant-hill. -3 An ant or a similar small insect.

सीरः *m.* 1 A plough. -2 The sun. -3 The *Arka* plant. -Comp. —ध्वजः *m.* An epithet of Janaka. —पाणिः, —भृत् *m.* Epithets of Balaráma. —योगः *m.* The yoking of cattle to a plough, or a team so yoked.

सीरकः *m.* 1 A plough. -2 The sun. -3 A porpoise.

सीरिन् *m.* An epithet of Balaráma.

सीव् See सिव्.

सीवनं, सेवनं *n.* 1 Sewing, stitching. -2 A seam, suture.

सीवनी *f.* 1 A needle. -2 The frenum of the prepuce.

सीसं, सीसकं, सीसपत्रकं, सीसपत्रं *n* Lead.

सीहुंडः *m.* The milk-hedge plant.

सु I U. (सवति, -ते) To go, move.

सु I. 2. P. (सवति, सौति) To possess power or supremacy. With प्र— To produce.

सु 5. U. (सुनोति, सुनुते, सुत; the स् of सु is changed to ष् after and preposition ending in इ or उ) 1 To press out or extract juice. -2 To distil. -3 To pour out, make a libation. -4 To perform a sacrifice. -5 To bathe. -6 To churn. With अभि- 1 To extract juice. -2 To mix, to compound. उत्— To agitate. प्र— To beget.

Desid. (सुषूसति, -ते)- With उद्- To excite, agitate. -प्र To produce, beget.

सु *ind.* A particle often used with nouns to form Karmadháraya and Bahuvrihi compounds. Sometimes it is prefixed to adjectives and adverbs. It has the following senses:— 1 Good, excellent. -2 Beautiful. -3 Thoroughly, properly. -4 Easily, readily. -5 Much, exceedingly. -6 Worthy of respect or reverence. -Comp. —अल्प, —अल्पक *a.* Very small or little. -उक्ता *f.* A kind of bird (सारिका). -उक्तं *n.* 1 A good or wise saying. -2 A Vedic hymn. —उक्तिः *f.* 1 A good or friendly speech. -2 A good or clever saying. -3 A correct sentence. —कंटका *f.* The aloe plant. —कंदः *m.* 1 A onion. -2 A yam. —कंदकः *m.* Onion. —कर *a.* (-रा or -री *f.*) 1 Easy to be done, practicable. -2 Easy to be managed. (-रा *f.*) A tractable cow. (-रं *n*) Charity, benevolence.-कुंदकः *m.* Onion. —कुमार *a.* 1 Very delicate or soft, smooth. -2 Beautifully young or youthful. —कुमारी *f.* The Navamallikâ jasmine. -कृत *a.* 1 Doing good, benevolent. -2 Pious, virtuous, righteous. -3 Wise, learned. -4 Fortunate, lucky. -कृतं *n.* 1 Any good or virtuous act, kindness, favour, service. -2 Virtue, moral or religious merit. -3 Fortune, auspiciousness. -4 Recompense, reward. -कृतिन् *a.* 1 Acting well or kindly. -2 Virtuous, pious. -3 Wise, learned. -4 Benevolent. -5 Fortunate. -केश (-स-) रः *m.* The citron tree. -गतः *m.* An epithet of Buddha. -गंधः *m.* 1 Fragrance. -2 Sulphur. -3 A trader. —गंधि *a.* 1 Sweet-smelling. (-धिः *m.*) 1 Perfume, fragrance. -2 The Supreme Being. -3 A kind of sweet-smelling mango. (—धि *n.*) 1 The root of long pepper. -2 A kind of fragrant grass. -3 Coriander seed. —गम *a.* 1 Accessible. -2 Easy. -3 Plain, intelligible. -ग्रीवः *m.* 1 A hero. -2 A swan. -3 A kind of weapon. -4 N. of one of the four horses of Krishna. -5 N. of a monkey chief and brother of Vàli. —चर्मन् *m.* The Bhúrja tree —चिरम् *ind.* For a very long time, very long. —चिरायुस् *m.* A God, deity. —चूटी *f.* A pair of nippers or tongs. —छत्रा *f.* The river Sutlej.-जनः *m.* 1 A good or virtuous man. -2 A gentlman. -3 N. of Indra's charioteer -जातः *a.* 1 Well-grown. -2 Well made or produced. -3 Of high birth.-4 Beautiful. —तपस् *a.* 1 One who practises austere penance. -2 Having great heat. (-*m.*) 1 An ascetic. -2 The sun. (-*n.*) An austere penance. —तमां *ind.* Most excellently, best —तरां *ind.* 1 Better, more excellently. -2 Exceedingly, very, very much. -3 More so, much more so. -4 Consequently. —तर्दनः *m.* The (Indian) cuckoo. —तलं *n.* N. of one of the seven regions below the earth. -2 The foundation of a large building. —तिक्तकः *m.* The coral tree.-तीक्ष्णः *m.* 1 The *sigru* tree. —तीर्थः *m.* 1 A good preceptor. -2 N. of Siva.—तुंग *a.* Very lofty or tall. (—गः *m.*) The cocoa-nut tree.—तेजस् *m.* A worshipper of the sun. —दक्षिण *a.* 1 Very sincere or upright. -2 Liberal or rich in sacrificial gifts. (—णा *f.*) N. of the wife of Dilipa.—दंडः *m.* A cane, ratan. —दत् *a.* (*f.* -ती) Having handsome teeth. —दंतः *m.* 1 A good tooth. -2 A actor, a dancer. (—ती *f.*) The female elephant of the north west quarter. —दर्शन *a.* (*f.* -ना or -नी) 1 Beautiful.-2 Easily seen. (-नः *m.*) The discus of Vishnu. -2 N. of Siva.-3 Of Mount Meru.-4 A vulture. (-नी *f.*,-नं *n.*) N. of Amarávati, Indra's capital. (—नं *n.*) N. of Jambudvipa. —दर्शना *f.* 1 A handsome woman.-2 A woman. -3 An order. —दा *a.* Very bountiful. —दांतः *m.* A

Buddhist. —दामन् a. One who gives liberally. (—m.) 1 A cloud. -2. A mountain.-3The sea -4 N.of Indra's elephant. -5 N. of a very poor Brâhmana.-दाय: m. 1 A good or auspicious gift.-2A special gift given on particular solemn occasions.-3 One who offers such a gift. —दिनं n. 1 A happy or auspicious day. -2 A fine day or weather. —दीर्घा f. A kind of cucumber. —दूर a. Very distant or remote. (सुदूरं 1 To a great distance. -2 To a very high degree, very much. सुदूरात् From afar, from a distance). —दृश् a Having beautiful eyes. (-f.) A pretty woman. —धन्वन् a. Having an excellent bow. (-m) 1 A good archer or bow-man. -2 Ananta, the great serpent. -3 N. of Visvakarman. —धर्मन् f. The council or assembly of gods. (-m.) 1 The hall or palace of Indra. -2 One diligent in properly maintaining his family. —धर्मा, -धर्मी f. The council or assemly of Gods (देवसभा). —धी a. Having a good understanding, wise. (-धी: m.) A wise or learned man. (-f.) A good understanding, intelligence.-नय: m.1 Good conduct. -2 Good policy. —नयन a. Having beautiful eyes. (—न: m.) A deer. (-ना f.) 1 A woman having beautiful eyes. -2 A woman in general. -नाभ a. 1 Having a beautiful navel. -2 Having a good nave or centre. (—भ: m.) 1 A mountain. -2 The Mainâka mountain. —निभृत a. Very lonely or private. (—तं ind.) Very secretly or closely, very narrowly, privately. —नीत 1 Well-conducted, well-behaved. -2 Polite, civil. (—तं n.) 1 Good conduct or behaviour. -2 Good policy or prudence. —नीति: f. 1 Good conduct, good manners. -2 Good policy.-3 N. of the mother of Dhruva. —नीथ a. Well-disposed, righteous. (—थ:m.) 1 A Brâhmana. -2 N. of Sisupâla. —नील a. Very black or blue. (—ल: m.) The pomegranate tree. (—ला f.) Common flax. —पक्व: m. A sort of fragrant mango. —पत्नी f. A woman having a good husband. —पथ: m. 1 A good road. -2 A good course. -3 Good conduct. —पथिन् m. (nom. sing. सुपंथा:) A good road. —पर्ण a. (-र्णा or -र्णी f.) 1 Well-winged. -2 Having good or beautiful leaves. (—र्ण: m.) 1 A ray of the sun. -2 A class of bird-like beings of a semi-divine character. -3 Any supernatural bird. -4 An epithet of Garuda. -5 A cock. -पर्णा, -पर्णी f. 1 A number or lotuses. -2 A pool abounding with lotuses. -3 N. of the mother of Garuda. —पर्वन् a. Well-jointed, having many joints or knots. (-m.) 1 A bamboo -2 An arrow. -3 A God, deity. -4 A special lunar day (as the day of full or new moon, and the 8th and 14th day of each fortnight).-5 Smoke. (-f.) White Dúrvâ grass. —पात्रं n. 1 A good vessel, a worthy receptacle. -2 A fit or competent person, an able person. -पाद् (f.-पाद् or -पदी) Having good or handsome feet.-पार्श्व:m.1 The waved-leaf fig-tree (प्लक्ष). -2 N. of the son of Sampáti. -पीतं n. A carrot. -पुंसी f. A woman having a good husband. -पुष्प a. (f. -ष्पाor-ष्पी) Having beautiful flowers. (-ष्प: m.) 1 The coral tree. -2 The Sirisha tree. (-ष्पीf.) The plantain tree. (-ष्पं n.) 1 Cloves. -2 The menstrual excretion. —प्रतर्क: m. A sound judgment. —प्रतिभा *f.* Spirituous liquor. —प्रतिष्ठ *a.* 1 Standing well. -2 Very celebrated. (-ष्ठा *f.*) 1 Good position. -2 Good reputation. -3 Establishment, erection. -4 Installation, consecration.-प्रतीक *a.* Handsome. (-कः *m.*) 1 An epithet of Kâmadeva.-2 Of Siva. -3 Of the elephant of the north-east quarter. —प्रपाणं *n.* A good tank. —प्रभा *f.* One of the seven tongues of fire. —प्रभातं *n.* 1 An auspicious dawn or day-break. -2 The earliest dawn. -प्रसन्नः *m.* N. of Kubera.-फल *a.* 1 Very fruitful, very productive. -2 Very fertile. (-लः *m.*) 1 The pomegranate tree. -2 The jujube. -3 The Karnikára tree. -4 A kind of bean. (-ला *f.*) 1 A pumpkin, gourd.-2 The plantain tree. —बंधः *m.* Sesamun. —बाहुः *m.* N. of a demon, brother of Mâricha. —बोध *a.* 1 Easily apprehended or understood. (-धः *m.*) Good information or advice. —ब्रह्मण्यः *m.* 1 An epithet of Kártikeya. -2 N. of one of the sixteen priests employed at a sacrifice. —भग *a.* 1 Very fortunate or prosperous, blessed. -2 Beautiful. -3 Agreeable, sweet. -4 Amiable, dear. (—गः *m.*) 1 Borax. -2 The Asoka tree. -3 The Champaka tree. -4 Red amaranth. (-गं *n.*) Good fortune. —भगा *f.* 1 A favourite wife. -2 An honoured mother.-3 A kind of wild jasmine. -4 Turmeric. -5 The Priyangu-creeper. -6 The holy basil. —भंगः *m.* The cocoa-nut tree. —भद्रा *f.* N. of the sister of Balarâma and Krishna, married to Arjuna.—भाषित *a.* 1 Spoken well or eloquently.-2 (-तं *n.*) 1 Fine speech, eloquence, learning. -2 A witty saying, an apophthegm, an appostite saying. -2 A good remark.—भिक्षं *n.* 1 Good alms, successful begging. -2 Abundance of food.-भ्रू *a.* Having beautiful eyebrows. (—भ्रूः *f.*) A lovely woman. —मतिः *f.* 1 A good mind or disposition, benevolence. -2 A favour of the Gods. -3 A gift, blessing. -4 A prayer, hymn.-5 A wish or desire. 6 N. of the wife of Sagara and mother of 60,000 sons. —मदनः *m.* The mango tree. —मध्य, —मध्यम *a.* Slender-waisted. —मध्या, —मध्यमा *f.* A graceful woman. —मन *a.* Very charming. (-नः *m.*) 1 Wheat. -2 The thorn-apple. (-ना *f.*) The great-flowered jasmine. —मनस् *a.* 1 Good-minded, benevolent.-2 Well-pleased, satisfied. (-*m.*) 1 A God, divinity. -2 A learned man. -3 A student of the Vedas.-4 Wheat. -5 The Nimba tree. -6 (-*f.*, *n.*; said to be *pl.* only by some) A flower. (-*f.*) 1 The great-flowered jasmine. -2 The Mâlati creeper. —मंत्रः *m.* N. of the charioteer of Dasaratha. —मित्रा *f.* 1 N. of one of the wives of Dasaratha and mother of Lakshmana and Satrughna.-मुख *a.* (*f.*-खा or -खी) 1 Having a beautiful face. -2 Pleasing. -3 Eager for. (-खः *m.*) 1 A learned man. -2 An epithet of Garuda. -3 Of Ganesa. -4 Of Siva. (—खं *n.*) The scratch of a finger-nail. (-खा, -खी *f.*) 1 A handsome woman. -2 A mirror. —मूलकं *n.* A carrot. —मेधस् *a.* Having a good understanding; wise, intelligent. (-*m.*) A wise man. -मेरुः *m.* 1 The sacred mountain Meru. -2 N. of Siva. —यवसं *n.* Beautiful grass, good pasturage. —योधनः *m.* An epithet of Duryodhana. —रक्तकः *m.* 1

A kind of red chalk. -2 A kind of mango tree. —रंगः *m.* 1 Good colour. -2 The orange. -3 A hole cut in a house (सुरंगा *f.* also in this sense). —रेचकः *m.* The betel-nut-tree. —रत *a.* 1 Much sported. -2 Playful. -2 Much enjoyed.-4 Compassionate. (-तं *n.*) 1 Great dilight or enjoyment. -2 Sexual union. —रतताली *f.* 1 A female-messenger, a go-between. -2 A chaplet, garland for the head. -रतिः *f.* Great enjoyment or satisfaction. —रस *a.* 1 Well flavoured, savoury. -2 Sweet. -3 Elegant (as a composition). —राजन् *a.* Governed by a good king. (*-m.*) 1 A good king. -2 A divinity. —राष्ट्रं *n.* N. of a country on the western side of India (Surat).-रूप*a.* 1 Well-formed, handsome.-2 Wise, learned.—लक्षण *a.* 1 Having auspicious marks. -2 Fortunate —लभ *a.* 1 Easy to be obtained. -2 Adapted to, fit, suitable. -3 Natural to, proper for. —लोचनः *m.* A deer. (-ना *f.*) 1 A beautiful woman. -2 N. of the wife of Indrajit. —लोहकं *n.* Brass. —लोहित *a.* Very red. (-ता *f.*) One of the seven tongues of fire. —वचनं, -वचस्, *n.* Eloquence. —वर्चकः, -वार्चिकः, -का, -वर्चिन *m.* Natron, alkali. —वसंतः *m.* 1 A pleasant vernal season. -2 The day of full moon in the month of Chaitra, or a festival celebrated in honour of Kâmadeva in that month (also सुवसंतकः). —वह *a.* 1 Patient. -2 Easy to be borne. (-हा *f.*) A lute. —वासिनी *f.* 1 A woman married or single who resides in her father's house. -2 A married woman whose husband is alive. —विक्रांत *a.* Very valiant or bold. (-तः *m.*) A hero. (-तं *n.*) Heroism. —विदः *m.* 1 An attendant on the women's apartments. -2 A king. —विदत् *m.* A king. —विदल्लः *m.* An attendant on the women's apartments. (-ल्लं *n.*) The women's apartments, harem.—विदल्ला *f.* A married woman. —विधम् *ind.* Easily. —विनीत *a.* Well-trained, modest. (-ता *f.*) A tractable cow. —विहित *a.* 1 Well-placed, well-deposited -2 Well-furnished, well-supplied, well-provided, well-arranged.-3 Well done or performed. —वी (-बी-) ज *a.* Having good seed. (-जः *m.*) 1 N. of Siva. -2 The poppy. —वीराम्लं *n.* Sour rice-gruel. —वीर्य *a.* 1 Having great vigour.-2 Of heroic strength, heroic. (-र्यं *n.*) 1 Great heroism. -2 Abundance of heroes. -3 The fruit of the jujube. (-र्या *f.*) Wild cotton. —वृत्त *a.* 1 Well-behaved, virtuous. -2 Well-rounded, beautifully round. (-त्तं *n.*) A good or virtuous conduct. —वेल *a.* 1 Tranquil. -2 Humble, quiet. (-लः *m.*) N. of the Trikûta mountain. -व्रत *a.* Strictly religious or virtuous. (-तः *m.*) A religious student. (-ता *f.*) 1 A virtuous wife. -2 A tractable cow.-शंस *a.* Well-spoken of, famous. —शक *a.* Capable of being easily done.-शिक्षित *a.* Well-taught or trained.-शिखः *m.* Fire. (-खा *f.*) 1 A peacock's crest. -2 A cock's comb. —शील *a.* Amiable. (-ला *f.*) 1 N. of the wife of Yama. -2 N. of one of the eight favourite wives of Krishna. —श्रुत *a.* 1 Well-heard. -2 Versed in the Vedas. (-तः *m.*) N. of the author of a system of medicine. —श्लिष्ट *a.* 1 Well-arranged or united. -2 Well-fitted. —सत्या *f.* N of the wife of Janaka.-समत *a.* Well-directed (as an arrow). —सार *a*. Having good sap or essence. (—रः *m.*) 1 Good sap, essence, or substance.-2 Competence.-3 The red-flowering Khadira tree. —सारवत् *n*. Crystal. —स्थ *a*. 1 Well-suited, being in a good sense. -2 In health, healthy, faring well. -3 Prosperous. -4 Happy, fortunate. (—स्थं *n.*) A happy state, well-being. —स्थता, —स्थितता *f*. 1 Good condition, well-being. -2 Health. —हित *a*. 1 Very fit or suitable, appropriate. -2 Beneficial. -3 Affectionate. -4 Satisfied. (—ता *f.*) One of the seven tongues of fire. —हृद् *a*.Cordial,friendly,affectionate. (*-m.*) 1 A friend. -2 An ally. -हृदः *m*. A friend. -हृदयः *a*. 1 Good-hearted. -2 Dear, affectionate.

सुख् 10 P. (सुखयति) To make happy, to please.

सुख *a*.(*f*. —खा) 1 Happy, joyful, pleased. -2 Agreeable, pleasant. -3 Virtuous, pious. -4 Favourable to. -5 Easy, practicable. -6 Fit, suitable. —खा *f*. The capital of Varuna. —खं *n*. 1 Happiness, delight, pleasure. -2 Prosperity. -3 Well-fare, good health. -4 Comfort, alleviation (of sorrow &c.). -5 Facility, ease. -6 Heaven. -7 Water. —खं *ind*. 1 Happily, joyfully. -2 Well. -3 At ease, comfortably. -4 Easily.-5 Rather, willingly. -6 Quietly, placidly. -Comp. —आचारः *m*. Paradise.-आप्लव *a*. Suitable for bathing. —आयतः, —आयनः *m*. A good or well-trained horse.-आरोह *a*. Of easy ascent. —आलोक *a*. Good-looking. —आवह *a*. Conducing to happiness, comfortable. —आशः *m*. N. of Varuna. -आशकः *m*. A cucumber. —आस्वाद *a*. 1 Having a sweet taste, sweet-flavoured. -2 Agreeable. (-दः *m.*) 1 A pleasant flavour. -2 Enjoyment (of pleasure).-उत्सवः *m*. 1 Merry-making,festival,jubilee. -2 A husband. -उदकं, -उष्णं *n*. Warm water.—उदयः *m*. Realization of happiness. —उदर्क *a*. Resulting in happiness. —उद्य *a*. To be spoken easily or agreeably. —उपविष्ट *a*. Sitting at ease. —कर, —कार, —दायक *a*. Giving pleasure, pleasant —दा *f*. 1 A courtezan of Indra's heaven. -2 The river Ganges. —भागिन्, —भाज् *a*. Happy. —रात्रिः *f*. 1 The night of new moon (when lamps are lighted in honour of Lakshmî). -2 A night when the husband may legally cohabit with his wife. —वर्चकः, -वर्चस *m*. Natron, alkali. —वासः *m*. A Water-melon. —श्रव, -श्रुति *a*. Sweet to the ear, melodious.

सुखंकर *a*. See सुखकर.

सुखय् Den. P. To give pleasure to, delight.

सुखांशुणः *m*. A kind of staff with a skull at the top (a weapon of Siva).

सुखाय् Den. A. 1 To feel happy or glad. -2 To rejoice. -3 To give pleasure.

सुत *p. p*. (*f*. —ता) 1 Poured out. -2 Extracted (as Soma juice). -3 Begotten. —तः *m*. 1 A son. -2 A child, offspring. -3 A king. -तः *m*., —तं *n*. A Soma-libation. -Comp. —उत्पत्तिः *f*. 1 Birth of a son. -निर्विशेषम् *ind*. Not differently from a son, just like a son. —सप्तका *f*. The mother of seven children.

सुतंभमः *m*. The father of a son.

सुतवत *m*. The father of son.

सुता *f*. A daughter.

सुतिः *f*. Extraction of Soma juice.

सुतिन् *a*. (*f*. -नी) Having a child.

or children. -*m.* A father.

सुतिनी *f.* A mother.

सुतीय् Den. P. 1 To long for progeny or son. -2 To treat like a son.

सुतुस *a.* Well-sounding.

सुत्या *f.* 1 Extraction or preparation of Soma juice. -2 A sacrificial oblation.-3 Parturition. [earth.

सुत्रामन् *m.* N. of Indra. -*f.* The

सुत्वन् *m.* 1 An offerer or drinker of Soma juice.-2 A student who has performed his ablutions(subsequent or preparatory to a sacrifice).

सुदि *ind.* In the bright fortnight of a lunar month.

सुधन्वाचार्यः *m.* The son of an outcast Vaisya by a woman of the same class.

सुधा *f.* 1 The beverage of the Gods; nectar, ambrosia. -2 The honey of flowers. -3 Juice. -4 Water. -5 N. of the Ganges. -6 White-wash, mortar. -7 A brick. -8 Lightning. -9 The milk-hedge plant. -10 Emblic myrobalan. -11 Yellow myrobalan. -Comp. —अंशुः *m.* 1 The moon. -2 Camphor. —अंगः, -आकारः, —आधारः, -आवासः *m.* The moon. -उद्भवः *m.* N. of Dhanvantari. —जीविन् *m.* A plasterer, brick-layer. —द्रवः *m.* A nectar-like fluid. —धवलित *a.* Plastered, white-washed. —निधिः *m.* 1 The moon. -2 Camphor. —पाणिः *m.* An epithet of Dhanvantari, the physician of the Gods. —भवनं *n.* A stuccoed house. —भित्तिः *f.* 1 A plastered wall. -2 A brick-wall. -3 The fifth Muhúrta or hour after noon. —भुज् *m.* A God, deity.—भृतिः *m.* 1 The moon. -2 Camphor. -3 A sacrifice, an oblation. —मयं *n.* 1 A brick or stone building. -2 A royal palace. —वर्षिन् *m.* 1 An epithet of Brahman (*m.*). -2 The moon. -3 Camphor. —वासः *m.* 1 The moon. -2 Camphor. —वासा *f.* A kind of cucumber. —सित *a.* 1 White as mortar. -2 Bright as nectar. -3 Bound by nectar. —सूतिः *m.* 1 The moon. -2 A sacrifice. -3 A lotus. —स्यंदिन् *a.* Ambrosial, flowing with nectar. —स्रवा *f.* The uvula or soft palate. —हरः *m.* An epithet of Garuda.

सुधितिः *m., f.* An axe.

सुनारः *m.* 1 The udder of a bitch. -2 The egg of a snake.-3 A sparrow.

सुनासी (-शी-) रः *m.* An epithet of Indra.

सुंदः *m.* N. of a demon and brother of Upasunda; who were sons of Nikumbha.

सुंदर *a.* (*f.*—री) 1 Lovely, beautiful. -2 Right.—रः *m.* N. of Cupid. —री *f.* A beautiful woman.

सुप्त *p. p.* (*f*—प्ता) Slept, sleeping, asleep. -2 Paralyzed, insensible, benumbed. —प्तं *n.* Sleep, sound sleep. -Comp. —ज्ञानं *n.* A dream. —त्वच् *a.* Paralytic.

सुप्तिः *f.* 1 Sleep, sleepiness, drowsiness. -2 Insensibility, numbness, paralysis. -3 Trust, confidence.

सुभ्रः *m.* 1 The moon. -2 Camphor. -3 Sky —भ्रं *n.* A flower.

सुम्नं *n.* 1 A hymn. -2 Joy, happiness. -3 Favour, protection. -4 A sacrifice.

सुरः *m.* 1 A God, deity. -2 The number 'thirty-three'. -3 The sun. -4 A sage, learned man. -Comp. —अंगना *f.* An *apsaras.* —अधिपः *m.* An epithet of Indra. - अरिः *m.* 1 An enemy of Gods, a demon. -2 The chirp of a cricket. —अर्हं *n.* 1 Gold. -2 Saffron. —आचार्यः *m.* An epithet of Brihaspati.—आपगा *f.* An epithet of the Ganges. —आलयः *m.* 1 The mountain Meru. -2 Heaven, paradise. —इज्यः *m.* N. of Brihaspati. —इज्या *f.* The sacred basil. —इंद्रः, -ईशः, -ईश्वरः *m.* N. of Indra. —उत्तरः *m.* Sandal-wood. —ऋषिः (सुरर्षिः). *m.* A divine sage. —कारः *m.* An epithet of Visvakarman. —कार्मुकं *n.* Rainbow.—गुरुः *m.* An epithet of Brihaspati. —ज्येष्ठः *m.* An epithet of Brahman (*m.*). —तरुः *m.* A tree of paradise. —दारु *n.* The Devadáru tree. —दीर्घिका *f.* An epithet of the Ganges.—दुंदुभी *f.* The sacred basil. —द्विष् *m.* 1 A demon. -2 Ráhu. —धनुस् *n.* Rainbow. —धूपः *m.* Turpentine, resin. —नदी, -निम्नगा *f.* An epithet of the Ganges.—पतिः *m.* An epithet of Indra. —पथं *n.* The sky, heaven. —पर्वतः *m.* The mountain Meru. -भूयं *n.* Identification with a deity, deification, apotheosis. -भूरुहः *m.* The Devadáru tree. —मंदिरं *n.* A temple.-युवतिः *f.* A celestial damsel. —लासिका *f.* A flute, pipe. —लोकः *m.* Heaven. —वर्त्मन् *n.* The sky. —वल्ली *f.* The sacred basil. —विद्विष्, -वैरिन्, -शत्रुः *m.* An evil spirit, a demon. —सद्मन् *n.* Heaven, paradise. —सरित्, -सिंधुः *f.* The Ganges. —सुंदरी, -स्त्री *f.* 1 A celestial woman.-2 N. of Durgà.

सुरंगः *m.*, सुरंगा *f.* 1 A hole cut in a wall for the purpose of breaking into a house. -2 A subterranean passage, a mine dug underneath a building (written also सुरुंगा).

सुरभि *a.* 1 Sweet-smelling. -2 Pleasing, agreeable. -3 Shining, handsome. -4 Beloved, friendly. -5 Celebrated, famous.-6 Wise,learned.-7 Virtuous.-भिः *m.* 1 Fragrance. -2 Nutmeg. -3 Resin of Sàla, or resin in general. -4 The Champaka tree. -5 The Samî tree. -6 The Kadamba tree. -7 A kind of fragrant grass. -8 The season of spring. -9 The month of Chaitra. -10 The Bakula tree. —*f* 1 The gum olibanum tree. -2 The sacred basil. -3 Jasmine. -4 A sort of perfume or fragrant plant.-5 Spirituous liquor. -6 The earth. -7 A cow. -8 N. of the fabulous cow of plenty. -9 N. of one of the Mátris. -10 The east. -*n.* 1 A fragrant smell -2 Sulphur.-3 Gold. -Comp. —घृतं *n.* Fragrant butter, well-seasoned ghee. —बाणः *m.* An epithet of Cupid. —मासः *m.* The spring. —मुखं *n.* The commencement of spring.—स्रवा *f.* The gum olibanum tree.

सुरभिका *f.* A kind of plantain.

सुरभिमत् *m.* N. of fire.

सुरा *f.* 1 A spirituous liquor, wine. -2 Water. -3 A drinking vessel.-4 A snake. -Comp.—आकरः *m.* A distillery. —आजीवः, -आजीविन् *m.* A distiller. —आलयः *m.* A tavern, dram-shop. —करः *m.* The cocoa-nut tree. -ग्रहः *m.* A vessel for taking liquor. —ध्वजः *m.* A flag or sign hung outside a tavern. —प *a.* 1 A drinker of spirituous liquor. -2 Agreeable. -3 Wise, sage. —पाणं, -पानं *n.* The drinking of wine or liquor. —बीजः *m.* Yeast. —मंडः *m.* The scum of liquor during fermentation. —संधानं *n.* The distillation of liquor.

सुवर्ण *a* 1 Of good or beautiful colour,yellow, golden.-2 Of a good caste. -3 Glorious, celebrated. —र्णः *m.* 1 A good colour. -2 A good caste. -3 A sort of sacrifice. -4 An epithet of Siva. -5 The thorn-apple.

—र्णा *f.* 1 One of the seven tongues of fire. -2 Black aloe-wood. -3 Turmeric. -4 Co'ocynth. —र्णं *n.* A 1 Gold.-2 A golden coin (-*m.*also). -3 A weight of gold equal to 16 Máshas(*m* also).-4 Riches.-5 A sort of yellow sandal-wood.-6 A kind of red chalk.-7 N. of a tree (नागकेशर). -Comp. -अभिषेकः *m.* Sprinkling the bride and bridegroom with water into which a piece of gold has been dropped. —कर्तृ, -कारः,-कृत् *m.* A goldsmith.-गणितं *n.* A particular method of calculation in arithmetic. -पुष्पित *a* Abounding in gold.-पृष्ठ *a.* Gilded. —माक्षिकं *n.* A kind of mineral substance. -रूप्यक *a.* Abounding in gold and silver. —रेतस् *m.* An epithet of Siva. —वर्णा *f.* Turmeric. —सिद्धः *m.* An adept who has acquired gold by magical means.

सुवर्णकं *n.* 1 Brass, bell-metal. -2 Lead. -3 Gold.

सुवर्णवत् *a.* (*f.* -ती) 1 Golden. -2 Beautiful, handsome.

सुषम *a.* (*f.* —मा) 1 Very lovely or beautiful. -2 Same ; all. -मा *f.* Exquisite beauty.

सुषवी *f.* 1 A sort of gourd.-2 Black cumin. -3 Cumin-seed.

सुषाढः *m.* An epithet of Siva.

सुषिः *f.* 1 A hole.-2 A tube, pipe.

सुषि (-षी-) म *a.* 1 Cold, frigid. -2 Agreeable. —मः *m.* 1 Cold. -2 A kind of snake. -3 The moon-stone.

सुषिर *a.* (*f.* —रा) 1 Full of holes. -2 Slow in articulation. -रं *n.* 1 A hole, a cavity. -2 Any wind-instrument.

सुषुप्तिः *f.* 1 Deep sleep.-2 Spiritual [ignorance.

सुषुम्णः *m.* N. of one of the principal rays of the sun.-म्णा *f.* A particular artery of the human body lying between इडा and पिंगला.

सुषेणः *m.* 1 N. of a tree (करमर्द).-2 N. of Vishnu. -3 A cane or ratan.

सुष्ठु *ind.* 1 Well, excellently. -2 Very much. -3 Truly, rightly.

सुष्म *n.* A rope, cord, string.

सुह्माः (*m. pl.*) N. of a people.

सू 2. 4 A. (सूते, सूयते, सूत) To bring forth, beget, yield (fig. also). -With प्र— To bring forth, beget, produce.

सू 6 P. (सुवति) 1 To excite, incite. -2 To remit (as debt).

सू *a.* (At the end of comp.) Bringing forth, yielding. -सूः *f.* 1 Birth. -2 A mother. [-3 A lotus.

सूकः *m.* 1 An arrow.-2 Air, wind.

सूकरः *m.* 1 A hog, pig. -2 A sort of deer. -3 A potter. -री *f.* 1 A sow, -2 A sort of moss.

सूक्ष्म *a.* (*f* —क्ष्मा) 1 Subtle, minute' atomic.-2 Little, small.-3 Delicate. -4 Nice. -5 Sharp, acute.-6 Crafty, ingenious.-7 Exact, accurate.-क्ष्मः *n.* 1 An atom. -2 The clearing-nut plant. -3 An epithet of Siva.—क्ष्मं *n.* 1 The subtle all-pervading spirit, the Supreme Soul. -2 Minuteness. -3 One of the three kinds of power attainable by an ascetic. -4 Craft, ingenuity.-5 Fraud.-6 Fine thread. -7 The figure of speech in which a delicate circumstance gathered from some appearance or from some gesture is intimated to another by means of a clever hint. -Comp. —तंडुला *f.* The poppy. —तंडुलः *m.* 1 Long pepper. -2 A kind of grass. —दर्शिता *f.* Quick-sightedness, foresight.—दर्शिन्,—दृष्टि *a.* 1 Sharp-sighted. -2 Of acute discernment. -3 Sharp-minded. -दारु *n.* A thin plank of wood, a board. —देहः *m.*, —शरीरं *n.* The subtle body which is invested by the grosser material frame. —पत्रः *m.* 1 Coriander seed. -2 A kind of wild cumin. -3 A sort of red sugar-cane. -4 A sort of mustard. —पर्णी *f.* A kind of basil. —पिप्पली *f.* Wild pepper. —बीजः *m.* The poppy. —बुद्धि *a.* Sharp-witted (—द्धिः *f.*) 1 Acute intellect. —मक्षिकः *m.*, —का *f.* A mosquito, gnat. —मानं *n.* A nice or exact measurement (opp. स्थूलमान). —शर्करा *f.* Small gravel, sand. —शालिः *m.* A kind of fine rice. —षट्चरणः *m.* A sort of louse.

सूच् 10 U. (सूचयति-ते, सूचित) 1 To pierce. -2 To point out. -3 To betray, reveal. -4 To intimate, suggest. -5 To indicate by gestures or signs. -6 To trace out, ascertain. -With अभि - To show, indicate.

सूचः *m.* A pointed shoot or blade of Kusa grass.

सूचक *a.* (*f.* -चिका) 1 Indicative, indicating, proving, showing. -2 Betraying, informing. —कः *m.* 1 A piercer. -2 Any instrument for perforating or sewing. -3 A tale-bearer, spy. -4 A narrator, an instructor. -5 The manager or chief actor of a company. -6 A Buddha. -7 A *Siddha*. -8 A villan, scoundrel. -9 A demon. -10 A dog. -11 A crow. -12 A cat. -13 A kind of fine rice. -Comp. —वाक्यं *n.* The information given by an informer.

सूचनं *n.*, सूचना *f.* 1 The act of piercing or boring. -2 Pointing out. -3 Informing against, calumniating. -4 Gesticulation. -5 Hinting, hint. -6 Information. -7 Teaching, showing, describing. -8 Spying. -9 Villainy. -10 Hurting, killing.

सूचा *f.* 1 Piercing. -2 Gesticulation. -3 Spying out, seeing, sight.

सूचिः, सूची *f.* 1 Piercing, perforating. -2 A needle. -3 Sharp point. -4 The point of a bud. -5 A kind of military array. 6 A triangle formed by the sides of a trapezium produced till they meet. -7 A cone, pyramid. -8 Gesticulation. -9 A particular mode of dancing. -10 Dramatic action. -11 An index, a table of contents. -12 A list, catalogue. -13 The earth's disc in computing eclipses (in astr.). -Comp. —अग्र *a.* Acuminated. (-ग्रं *n.*) The point of a needle. —कटाहन्यायः *m.* The maxim of the needle and the kettle. It is used to denote that, when two matters (one easy and the other difficult) require attention, the easy one should be despatched first. —खातः *m.* A sharp pyramid or pyramidal excavation; a cone. —पत्रकं *n.* An index, a table of contents. (-कः *m.*) A kind of pot-herb. -पुष्पः *m.* The Ketaka tree. —भिन्न *a.* Bursting open at the points of the buds. —भेद्य *a.* 1 To be pierced or penetrated by a needle. -2 Thick, dense. -3 Palpable, tangible. —मुख *a.* 1 Having a pointed beak. -2 Pointed. (-खः *m.*) 1 A bird. -2 White Kusa grass. -3 A particular position of the hands. (-खं *n.*) A diamond. —रोमन् *m.* A hog. —वदन *a.* Having a pointed beak. (-नः *m.*) 1 A gnat, mosquito. -2 A mungoose. —शालिः *m.* A kind of fine rice.

सूचिकः *m.* A tailor.

सूचिका *f.* 1 A needle. -2 An elephant's trunk. -Comp. —धरः *m.* An elephant. —मुख *a* Having a point ed mouth or head. (-ं *n.*) A shell, the conch-shell.

सूचित *p. p.* (*f.* —ता) 1 Pierced, bored. -2 Pointed out, hinted. -3 Indicated by signs or gestures. -4 Communicated, told, revealed. -5 Ascertained, known.

सूचिन् *a.* (*f.* —नी) 1 Piercing, perforating. -2 Pointing out. -3 Informing against. -4 Spying out. *-m.* A spy, an informer.

सूचिनी *f.* 1 A needle. -2 A night.

सूचिवत् *a.* (*f.* —ती) Pointed. *-m.* N. of Garuda.

सूची *f.* See सूचिः.

सूच्य *a.* (*f.* —च्या) Communicable.

सूत *ind.* An imitative sound of snorting, snoring &c.

सूत *p. p.* (*f.*—ता) 1 Born, produced. -2 Impelled, emitted. —तः *m.* 1 A charioteer. -2 The son of a Kshatriya by a woman of the Bráhmaṇa caste. -3 The son of a Vaisya by a Kshatriya wife. -4 A bard. -5 A carpenter. -6 The sun. -7 N. of a pupil of Vyása. —तः *m.*, —तं *n.* Quick-silver. -Comp. -तनयः *m.* An epithet of Karna. —राज् *m.* Quick-silver.

सूतकं *n.* 1 Birth, production. -2 Impurity caused by child-birth or miscarriage (also called जननाशौचं). —कः *m.*, —कं *n.* Quick-silver.

सूतका, सूतिका *f.* A woman recently delivered.

सूता *f.* A woman recently delivered.

सूतिः *f.* 1 Birth, parturition, delivery, child-bearing. -2 Offspring, progeny. -3 Source, fountain-head. -4 A place where Soma juice is extracted -Comp. —अशौचं *n.* The impurity caused by child-birth. —गृहं *n.* The lying-in-chamber.—मासः (also सूतीमासः) *m.* The month of delivery, the last month of pregnancy.

सूतिका *f.* A woman recently delivered. -Comp. —अगारं, -गृहं, -गेहं, -भवनं *m.* The lying-in-chamber. —षष्ठी *f.* N. of a particular goddess worshipped on the sixth day after child-birth.

सूत्यं *n.* The distillation of spirituous liquor.

सूत्या *f.* See सुत्या.

सूत्र् 10 U. (सूत्रयति,-ते, सूत्रित) 1 To bind, thread, string together. -2 To write or compose in the form of a short rule. -3 To plan, systematize. -4 To relax, to loosen.

सूत्रं *n.* 1 A thread, string, cord. -2 A fibre. -3 A wire. -4 A collection of threads. -5 The sacred thread or sacrificial cord worn by members of the first three classes. -6 The string or wire of a puppet. -7 A short rule or precept; an aphorism. -8 A short or concise sentence used as a memorial rule; A statement containing a very few words free from ambiguity, conveying important matter, having a universal application, free from unnecessary matter, and free from blemish. -9 Any manual containing such aphoristic rules; *e. g.* आपस्तंबसूत्र, गृह्यसूत्र &c. -10 A rule, canon, decree (in law). -Comp. —आत्मन् *a.* Having the nature of a string or thread. (*-m.*) The soul. —आली *f.* A necklace. —कंठः *m.* 1 A Bráhmana. -2 A pigeon, dove. -3 A wag-tail. —कर्मन् *n.* Carpentry. —कारः, -कृत् *m.* An author or composer of Sútras. —कोणः,-कोणकः *m.* A small drum, a *damaru.* —गंडिका *f.* A kind of stick used by weavers in spinning threads. —चरणं *n*. N. of a class of *charanas* of Vedic schools which introduced various Sútra works. —तर्कुटी *f*. A distaff, spindle. —दरिद्र *a*. Thread-bare.—धृत:,-धार: *m*. 1 (*lit*. the holder of the thread of dramatic arrangement). The stage-manager or the principal actor who assigns to the various actors the characters they are to represent, instructs them &c., and takes a leading part in the the prelude. -2 A carpenter, an artisan. -3 The author of a set of aphorisms.-4 An epithet of Indra. —पिटक: *m*. N. of one of the three collections of Buddhistic writings. -पुष्प: *m*. The cotton plant. -भिद् *m*. A tailor. -भृत *m*. =सूत्रधार. —यंत्रं *n*. A thread-machine, shuttle. -2 A weaver's loom. —वीणा *f*. A kind of lute. —वेष्टनं *n*. A weaver's shuttle.

सूत्रणं *n*. 1 The act of stringing together or putting in order. -2 Arranging in aphorisms.

सूत्रला *f*. A spindle or distaff.

सूत्रामन् *f*., सुत्रामन् *m*. An epithet of Indra.

सूत्रिका *f*. A kind of dish (Mar.शेवया).

सूत्रित *p. p.* (*f*. -ता) 1 Strung, arranged, systematized.-2 Prescribed or enjoined in Sútras.

सूत्रिन् *a*. (*f*.-णी) 1 Having threads. -2 Having rules. —*m*. A crow.

सूद् P. 1 A. (सूदते) 1 To strike, wound, kill, destroy. -2 To effuse, pour out. -3 To deposit. -4 To throw away.

सूद् 10 U. (सूदयति,-ते) 1 To incite, excite, urge on, animate. -2 To strike, hurt, kill.-3 To cook, season, prepare. -4 To pour out, effuse. -5 To assent, agree, promise. -6 To eject, throw away. With अभि-or नि- To kill (स being changed to ष).

सूद: *m*. 1 Destruction, massacre. -2 Pouring out, distilling. -3 A well, spring. -4 A cook. -5 Sauce, soup. -6 Anything seasoned, a prepared dish. -7 Split pease. -8 Mud, mire. -9 Sin, fault. -Comp. -कर्मन् *n*. Cookery.-शाला *f*.A kitchen.

सूदन *a*. (*f*.-नी) 1 Destroying, killing. -2 Dear, beloved. —नं *n*. 1 Destruction, massacre. -2 Assenting to, promising. -3 Throwing away.

सून *p. p.* (*f*. -ना) 1 Born, produced -2 Blown, blossomed. -3 Empty. -नं *n*. 1 Bringing forth, parturition. -2 A bud, blossom. -3 A flower.

सूनरी *f*. A happy woman.

सूना *f*. 1 A butcher's house. -2 The sale of meat. -3 Hurting, killing. -4 The soft palate, uvula. -5 A girdle, zone. -6 Inflammation of the glands of the neck called mumps. -7 A ray of light. -8 A river. -9 A daughter. -10 An elephant's trunk. —ना: *f. pl*. The five things in a house by which animal life is likely to be destroyed. See under शूना or पंचशूना.

सूनिक *m*. 1 A butcher.-2 A hunter.

सूनु: *m*. 1 A son.-2 A child, an offspring. -3 A grandson (daughter's son). -4 A younger brother. -5 The sun. -6 The Arka plant.

सूनू: *f*. A daughter.

सूनृत *a*. (*f*. —ता) 1 True and pleasant. -2 Affable, courteous.-3 Auspicious, fortunate. -4 Beloved, dear. —ता *f*. 1 The goddess of true speech. -2 N. of Ushas. —तं *n*. 1 True and agreeable speech. -2 Kind and pleasant discourse. -3

Auspiciousness.

सूपः *m.* 1 Broth, soup.-2 A sauce, condiment. -3 A cook. -4 A pan, vessel.-5 An arrow.-6 Split pease. -Comp.—कारः *m.* A cook.

सूमः *m.* 1 Water.-2 Milk.-3 Sky or heaven.

सूर् 4. A. (सूर्यते) 1 To hurt, kill. -2 To make firm.

सूरः *m.* 1 The sun. -2 The Arka plant. -3 The Soma. -4 A wise or learned man. -5 A hero, king. -Comp. —चक्षुस् *a.* Radiant as the sun. —सुतः *m.* An epithet of Saturn. —सूतः *m.* The charioteer of the sun. *i. e.* Aruna.

सूरणः *m.* N. of an esculent root.

सूरत *a.* (*f.*-ता) 1 Compassionate, tender. -2 Calm, tranquil. -ता *f.* A tractable cow.

सूरिः *m.* 1 The sun. -2 A learned or wise man.-3 A priest.-4 A worshipper. -5 A title of respect of Jaina teachers. -6 N. of Krishna.

सूरिन् *a.* (*f.* —णी) Wise, learned. —*m.* A wise or learned man, a scholar. -2 N. of Kuntî.

सूरी *f.* 1 N. of the wife of the sun.

सूर्क्ष्, सूर्क्ष्य् 1. 4. P. (सूर्क्षति, सूर्क्ष्यति) 1 To respect, honour. -2 To disrespect.

सूर्क्ष (-क्ष्य-) णं *n.* Disrespect.

सूर्क्ष्यः *m.* A kind of bean.

सूर्ण *a.* (*f.* —र्णा) Hurt, injured.

सूर्पः *m.*, सूर्पं *n.* 1 A winnowing basket. -2 A particular measure. -Comp. —णखा, -णखी *f.* N. of a sister of Râvana.

सूर्मिः, सूर्मी *f.* 1 An iron or metallic image. -2 The pillar of a house. -3 Radiance, lustre. -4 A flame.

सूर्यः *m.* 1 The sun. -2 The tree called *Arka*.-3 The number 'twelve'. -4 The swallow-wort. -Comp. -अर्घ्यं *n.* The presentation of an offering to the sun.-अश्मन् *m.* The sun-stone. —आतपः *m.* Sun-shine. —आलोकः *m.* Sun-shine.-आवर्तः *m.* A kind of sunflower. —आह्व *a.* Named after the sun. (—ह्वः *m.*) The gigantic swallow-wort (—ह्वं *n.*) Copper. —इंदुसंगमः *m.* The day of the new moon. —उत्थानं *n* , —उदयः *m.* Sunrise. —ऊढः *m.* 1 An evening guest.-2 The time of sunset. -कांतः *m.* 1 The sunstone, sun crystal. -2 A crystal. —क्रांतिः *f.* 1 Sun-light. -2 A particular flower. -3 The flower of sesamum. —कालः *m.* Day-time, day. —कालानलचक्रं *n.* A particular astrological diagram for indicating good and bad fortune. —ग्रहः *m.* 1 The sun. -2 An eclipse of the sun. -3 An epithet of Râhu and Ketu. -4 The bottom of a water-jar. —ग्रहणं *n.* A solar eclipse. —चंद्रौ (also सूर्याचंद्रमसौ) *m.* *dual* The sun and moon. —जः, —तनयः, —पुत्रः *m* 1 Epithets of Sugrîva. -2 Of Karna. -3 Of the planet Saturn. -4 Of Yama. —जा, —तनया, —पुत्री *f.* The river Yamunà. —नक्षत्रं *n.* That constellation (out of the 27) in which the sun happens to be.-पर्वन् *n.* A solar festival, (or the days of the solstices, equinoxes, eclipses &c.). —फणिचक्रं *n.* See सूर्यकालानलचक्रं above. —भक्तः *m.* The tree Bandhùka or its flower. -मणिः *m.* The sun-stone.—यंत्रं *n.* 1 A representation of the sun (used in worshipping him). -2 An instrument used in taking solar observations. —विलोकनं *n.* The ceremony of taking a child out to see the sun when four months old. —संक्रमः *m.*, —संक्रांतिः *f.* The sun's passage from one zodiacal sign to another. —संज्ञं *n.* Saffron.—सारथिः *m.* An epithet of Aruna. —सिद्धांतः *m*, A celebrated astronomical work.—हृदयं *n*. N. of a hymn to the sun.

सूर्या *f*. 1 The wife of the sun. -2 The hymn about the marriage of Súryâ.

सूष् 1 P. (सूषति) To bring forth, beget.

सूषणा *f*. A mother.

सूष्यन्ती *f*. A woman about to be confined, one who is parturient.

सृ 1. 3. P. (सरति,ससर्ति,also धावति,सर्तुं, सृत) 1 To go, move, proceed. -2 To approach. -3 To rush, assail.-4 To run, slip away from. -5 To blow (as wind). -6 To flow. -With अनु- 1 To follow, to pursue. -2 To go to. -3 To return to. अप- To retire, to withdraw. अभि— 1 To approach. -2 To meet (a lover or mistress) by appointment. -3 To attack. उप- 1 To approach. -2 To visit. निस्— 1 To step, to go forth or out. -2 To depart. -3 To ooze out, to flow out. परि— 1 To flow round. -2 To go round. प्र— 1 To proceed, spring up. -2 To spread, pervade. -3 To proceed, advance.-4 To pass away (as time). -5 To spread. -6 To be stretched forth. -7 To be prevalent. -8 To predominate. -9 To proceed to. प्रति— 1 To go towards, to assail. -2 To go back. वि— To spread. सम्— To obtain.

Caus. (सारयति,-ते) 1 To cause to go or move. -2 To extend. -3 To touch gently (with the fingers). -4 To push back or away. With अनु— To pursue. अभि— To meet. उत्—To cause to out,go drive away. नि—1 To drive away.-2 To spread. -3 To expose for sale. -4 To open wide. प्रति— To replace. वि— To set on foot, to cause to take effect. सम्— To cause to revolve.

Desid. (सिसीर्षति).

सृकः *m*. 1 Air, wind.-2 An arrow. -3 A thunder-bolt. -4 A lotus.

सृकंडुः *f*. Itch, scab.

सृकालः *m*. A jackal.

सृक्कं *n*.
सृक्कणी *f*.
सृक्व *n*.
सृक्किणी *f*.
सृक्विन् *n*.
स्रक्कं *n*.
स्रक्कणी *f*.
स्रक्व *n*.
स्राक्कणी *f*.
स्राक्किन् *n*.
} The corner of the mouth.

सृगः *m*. A sort of arrow or javelin, a sling.

सृगालः *m*. A jackal.

सृज् 6. P. (सृजति, स्रष्टुं, सृष्ट) 1 To create, produce, to beget (progeny &c.). -2 To put on,place on,apply. -3 To let loose, release.-4 To emit, pour forth or out. -5 To utter (as words). -6 To cast, discharge. -7 To abandon, send away. With अति— 1 To leave. -2 To give. -3 To remit. अभि— To give. अव— 1 To let loose. -2 To cast, throw, sow.उत्— 1 To shed.-2 To let loose. -3 To abandon. -4 To shoot.-5 To throw away. -6 To dismiss. -7 To give, to return. -8 To repudiate. -9 To decline. उप— 1 To pour out or on, to make an oblation. -2 To join, connect. -3 To beset with, to oppress. -4 To eclipse. नि— To let go, deliver. प्र— 1 To abandon. -2 To injure. वि— 1 To shed. -2 To let loose, abandon. -3 To drop. -4 send. -5 To repudiate. -6 To utter, to sound. -7 To give. सम्— 1 To mix, to be in contact with. -2 To meet with.

सृज 4 A. (सृज्यते) To be let loose, send forth. —*Desid.* (सिसृक्षति).

सृजिकाक्षारः *m.* Natron, alkali.

सृंजयाः *m. pl.* N. of a people.

सृणिः *f.* A goad to drive an elephant. —णिः *m.* 1 An enemy. -2 The moon.

सृणी *f.* A hook for driving an elephant.

सृणि (-णी-) का *f.* Saliva, spittle.

सृतिः *f.* 1 Going, gliding. -2 A way, path (fig. also). -3 Hurting, injuring.

सृत्वर *a.* (*f.* —री) Going, moving. —री *f.* 1 A stream, river. -2 A mother.

सृदरः *m.* A snake.

सृदाकुः *m.* 1 Air, wind. -2 Fire. -3 A deer. -4 The thunder-bolt of Indra. -5 The sun's disc or orb. —*f.* A river, stream.

सृप् 1 P. (सर्पति, सृप्तः *desid.* सिसृप्सति) 1 To creep, crawl, glide gently. -2 To go, move. With अनु— To approach. अप— 1 To go or run away. -2 To deviate from. -3 To espy. उद्— To rise, overflow. उप— 1 To approach. -2 To undergo. -3 To go forth. -4 To move. परि— To move to and fro. प्र— 1 To proceed, to come forth. -2 To prevail. -3 To spread. वि— 1 To sneak about, to fly about. -2 To march, to proceed. -3 To spread. -4 To flow, to fall. -5 To disperse. -6 To wind. -7 To run away. सम— 1 To flow. -2 To glide, move.

सृपाटः *m.*, सृपाटी *f.* A kind of measure.

सृपाटिका *f.* The beak of a bird.

सृप्रः *m.* The moon.

सृभ्, सृंभ 1. P. (सर्भति, सृंभति) To hurt, kill.

सृमर *a.* (*f.* —रि) Going, moving. —रः *m.* A kind of deer.

सृष्ट *p. p.* (*f.* —ष्टा) 1 Created, produced. -2 Poured out. -3 Let loose. -4 Abandoned. -5 Sent away. -6 Determined. -7 Connected, joined. -8 Abundant. -9 Ornamented.

सृष्टिः *f.* 1 Creation. -2 The creation of the world. -3 Nature, natural property. -4 Letting loose. -5 Giving away, a gift. -6 The existence of properties or qualities. -7 The absence of properties.

सॄ 9 P. (सृणाति) To hurt, injure, kill.

सेक् 1 A. (सेकते) To go, move.

सेकः *m.* 1 Sprinkling, watering (trees). -2 Emission, effusion. -3 Seminal effusion. -4 A libation. -5 Seminal fluid. -6 A drop of anything.

सेकिमं *n.* A radish.

सेक्तृ *a.* (*f.* —क्त्री) One who sprinkles. -*m.* 1 A sprinkler. -2 A husband. -3 A water-bearer.

सेक्त्रं *n.* A bucket, watering-pot.

सेचक *a.* (*f.* —चिका) Sprinkling. —कः *m.* A cloud.

सेचनं *n.* Sprinkling, watering. -2 Effusion, aspersion. -3 Oozing, dripping. -4 A bucket.

सेचनी *f.* A bucket.

सेटुः *m.* 1 Water-melon. -2 A kind of cucumber.

सेतिका *f.* N. of Ayodhyâ.

सेतुः *m.* 1 A ridge of earth, bank, causeway, dam. -2 A bridge in general. -3 A land-mark. -4 A narrow mountain-road. -5 A boundary, barrier, obstruction of any kind. -6 A fixed rule or law. -7 The sacred syllable *om.* -Comp.-बंधः *m.* 1 The construction of a bridge or a cause-way. -2 The ridge of rocks extending from the southern extremity of the Coromandel coast towards Ceylon (said to have been built for Râma's passage to Lanká by monkeys). -3 Any bridge or cause-way. —भेदिन् *a.* 1 Breaking down barriers or obstructions. (-*m.*) N. of a tree (दंती).

सेतुकः *m.* 1 A bank, cause-way, a bridge.-2 A pass.

सेत्रं *n.* A bond, fetter.

सेदिवस् *a.* (*f.* -सेदुषी) Sitting.

सेन *a.* (*f.* —ना) Having a lord, possessing a master or leader.

सेना *f.* 1 An army. -2 Army personified as the wife of Kártikeya, the God of war. -Comp. —अंगं *n.* A component part of an army, (these are four :—हस्त्यश्वरथपादातं सेनांगं स्याच्चतुष्टयम्). —चरः *m.* 1 A soldier. -2 A camp-follower.-नी *m.* 1 A leader of an army. -2 N. of Kártikeya. —पतिः *m.* 1 A general. -2 N. of Siva. -3 N. of Kártikeya. —परिच्छद् *a.* Surrounded by an army. —पृष्ठं *n.* The rear of an army. —मुखं *n.* 1 A division of an army. -2 A division of an army consisting of three elephants, as many chariots, nine horse and fifteen foot.-3 A mound in front of a city-gate. —योगः *m.* The equipment of an army. —रक्षः *m.* A guard, sentinel.

सेफः *m.* The penis.

सेमंती *f.* The Indian white rose.

सेरः *m.* A kind of measure (Mar. शेर). [colour.

सेराहः *m.* A horse of a milk-white

सेरु *a.* Binding, fastening.

सेल् 1 P. (सेलति) To go, move.

सेव् 1 A. (सेवते, सेवित; *caus.* सेवयति, -ते *desid.* सिसेविषते the स् of सेव् is generally changed to ष् after prepositions ending in इ such as नि, परि, वि) 1 To serve, attend upon, worship, obey. -2 To pursue, follow. -3 To use, enjoy. -4 To enjoy carnally. -5 To attach or devote oneself to, cultivate, practise, perform. -6 To betake oneself to, dwell in. -7 To guard, to protect.

सेवः *m.* See सेवनं.

सेवक *a.* (*f.* —का) 1 Serving, worshipping. -2 Practising, following. -3 Dependent, servile. —कः *m.* 1 A servant, dependant. -2 A worshipper. -3 A sewer. -4 A sack.

सेवधिः *m.* A valuable treasure.

सेवनं *n.* 1 The act of serving; attendance upon; worship. -2 Following, practising, employing.-3Using, enjoying. -4 Enjoying carnally. -5 Fondness for. -6 Dwelling in. -7 Binding. -8 Sewing, stitching. -9 A sack. [-3 A suture.

सेवनी *f.* 1 A needle. -2 A seam.

सेवा *f.* 1 Service, dependence. -2 Worship, homage. -3 Fondness for. -4 Use, employment, exercise. -5 Resorting to.-6 Flattery.-Comp. —काकुः *f.* A change of voice in service.

सेवि *n.* 1 The jujube.-2 An apple.

सेवित *p. p.* (*f.* —ता) 1 Served, worshipped. -2 Followed, practised, pursued. -3 Resorted to, inhabited by. -4 Protected, preserved. -5 Enjoyed, used. —तं *n.* 1 An apple. -2 The jujube.

सेविन *a.* (*f.* —नी) Serving, worshipping. -2 Following, practising, using. -3 Inhabiting. -*m.* A servant.

सेव्य *a.* (*f.* —व्या) 1 To be served

or waited upon. -2 To be used or employed. -3 To be enjoyed. 4 To be taken care of. —व्य: *m.* 1 A master. -2 The Asvattha tree. -व्यं *n.* A kind of root.

सै 1 P. (सायति) To waste way.

सैंह *a.* (*f.* —ही) Belonging to a lion, leonine.

सैंहल *a.* (*f.* -ला) Belonging to, or growing in, Ceylon.

सैंहिक:, सैंहिकेय: *m.* A metronymic [of Râhu.

सैकत *a.* (*f.*—ती) 1 Sandy, gravelly. -2 Having a sandy soil. —तं *n.* 1 A sand-bank.-2 An island with sandy shores. -3 A bank or shore (in general). -Comp. —इष्टं *n.* Ginger.

सैकतिक *a.* (*f.* —की) 1 Belonging or relating to a sand bank.-2 Fluctuating, living in doubt and error. —क: *m.* 1 A religious mendicant.-2 An ascetic. —कं *n.* 1 A thread worn round the wrist or neck to secure good fortune.

सैद्धांतिक *a.* (*f.* —की) 1 Relating to a dogma or demonstraled truth. -2 Knowing the real truth.

सैनापत्यं *n.* The command of an army; generalship.

सैनिक *a.* (*f.* —की) 1 Relating to an army. -2 Martial, military. -क: *m.* 1 A soldier.-2 A guard, sentinel. -3 The body of troops drawn up in battle-array.

सैंधव *a.* (*f.* —वी) 1 Produced or born in the Sindhu-territory. -2 Belonging to the Indus. -3 River-born. -4 Oceanic, marine. —व: *m.* 1 A horse, especially one bred in *Sindhu.* -2 N. of a sage. -3 N. of a country. —व: *m.*, —वं *n.* A kind of rock-salt. —वा: *m. pl.* The people inhabiting the *Sindhu* territory. -Comp. —घन: *m.* A lump of salt. —शिला *f.* A kind of rock or fossil salt.

सैंधवक *a.* (*f.* —की) Relating to the 'Saindhavas'. -क: *m.* A miserable inhabitant of *Sindhu.*

सैंधी *f.* A sort of spirituous liquor.

सैन्य: *m.* 1 A soldier. -2 A guard, sentinel. —न्यं *n.* An army.

सैमंतिकं *n.* Red lead.

सैरंध्र:, सैरिंध्र: *m.* 1 A menial servant or attendant. -2 The offspring of a *Dasyu* and an *Ayogava* female.

सैरंध्री, सैरिंध्री *f.* 1 A maid-servant or female attendant in the women's apartments (a woman of the mixed tribe described in सैरंध्र (2). -2 An independent female artisan working in another person's house. -3 An epithet of Draupadî (N. assumed by her when in the service of Sudheshná, queen of Virâta).

सैरिक *a.* (*f.* —की) 1 Relating to a plough. -2 Having furrows. —क: *m.* 1 A plough-ox.-2 A plough-man.

सैरिभ: *m.* 1 A buffalo. -2 Indra's heaven or Svarga.

सैवाल See शैवाल.

सैसक *a.* (*f.* —की) Leaden, of lead.

सो 4 P. (स्यति, साद्यं, सित; *caus.* साययति -ते, *desid.* सिषासति. The स of सो is changed to ष् after prepositions ending in इ or उ) 1 To kill, destroy. -2 To finish. With अव— 1 To fail. -2 To finish. अध्यव— 1 To do, practise. -2 To be able. -3 To determine. -4 To reflect. पर्यव— 1 To endeavour. -2 To complete. -3 To resolve. -4 To be lost, to perish. -5 To be reduced to, to be transformed into, to result into. व्यव— 1 To determine upon, make strenuous efforts, to set about. -4 To effectuate. -5 To wish. -6 To believe. संवि— To decree.

सोढ *p. p.* (*f.*-ढा) Borne, endured.

सोढृ *a.* (*f.* —ढ्री) 1 Enduring, patient. -2 Powerful, able.

सोत्क *a.* (*f.* —त्का), सोत्कंठ *a.* (*f.* —ठा) 1 Ardently longing, anxious. -2 Regretful. -3 Bewailing.—कं *ind.* 1 With ardent or eager longing. -2 Regretfully.

सोत्प्रास *a.* (*f.* —सा) 1 Excessive. -2 Exaggerated. -3 Ironical, sarcastic. —सः *m.* Violent laughter. —सः *m.*, —सं *n.* Ironical exaggeration, sarcasm.

सोत्सव *a.* (*f.* -वा) Festive, making merry, joyous.

सोत्साह *a.* (*f.*-हा) Vigorous, active, energetic, persevering.-हं *ind.* Actively, energetically, carefully.

सोत्सुक *a.* Regretful, anxious, sorrowful.

सोत्सेध *a.* (*f.* -धा) High, lofty.

सोदर *a.* (*f.* -रा) Born from the same womb; uterine. —रः *m.* A uterine brother.-रा *f.* A uterine sister.

सोदर्यः *m.* A co-uterine brother; brother of whole blood (fig. also).

सोद्योग *a.* (*f.* —गा 1 Active, persevering, industrious. -2 Violent, strong.

सोद्वेग *a.* (*f.* —गा) 1 Anxious, apprehensive. -2 Sorrowful. —गं *ind.* Anxiously, eagerly.

सोनहः *m.* Garlic. [frantic.

सोन्माद *a.* (*f.* —दा) Mad, insane,

सोपकरण *a.* (*f.* —णा) Provided with all requisite materials or implements; properly equipped.

सोपकार *a.* (*f.*-रा) 1 Properly equipped. -2 Assisted, befriended.

सोपचार *a.* (*f.*—रा) Acting politely, civil, courteons.

सोपद्रव *a.* (*f.* -वा) Visited with calamities or afflictions.

सोपध *a.* (*f.* -धा) Deceitful.

सोपधि *a.* Fraudulent. -*ind.* Deceitfully, fraudulently.

सोपप्लव *a.* (*f.* —वा) 1 Afflicted with any great calamity. -2 Invaded or overrun by enemies. -3 Eclipsed (as the sun or moon).

सोपरोध *a.* (*f.* —धा) 1 Obstructed, impeded. -2 Favoured. -धं *ind.* Obligingly, respectfully.

सोपसर्ग *a.* (*f.* -र्गा) 1 Afflicted by any great calamity or misfortune. -2 Portentous. -3 Possessed by an evil spirit. -4 Preceded by a prepositional prefix (in gram.).

सोपहास *a.* (*f.* -सा) Accompanied with derisive laughter; sarcastic. -सं *ind.* Sneeringly. [caste.

सोपाकः *m.* A man of a degraded

सोपाधि *a.*, सोपाधिक *a.* (*f.* -का) Restricted by some limitations; qualified by particular characteristics; limited, qualified (in phil.). -2 Having some peculiar attribute. -3 Special.

सोपानं *n.* Steps, stairs, a staircase, ladder. -Comp. —पंक्तिः *f.*, —पथः *m.*, —पद्धतिः *f.*,—परंपरा *f.*, -मार्गः *m.* A flight of steps, a stair-case.

सोमः *m.* 1 N. of a plant used in sacrificial offerings. -2 The juice of the plant. -3 Nectar, beverage of the Gods. -4 The moon -5 A ray of light. -6 Camphor. -7 Water. -8 Air, wind. -9 N. of Kubera. -10 Of Siva. -11 Of Yama. -12 N. of Sugriva. -13 (As the last member of comp.) Chief, principal, best; as in नृसोम. —मं *n.* 1 Rice-gruel. -2 Sky, heaven. -Comp. —अभिषवः *m.* The extraction of Soma juice. -अहः, -वारः *m.* Monday. —आख्यं *n.* The red lotus. —उद्भवा *f.* N. of the river Narmadâ. —कांतः *m.* The moon-stone. —ग्रहः *m.* A vessel for holding Soma. —ज *a* Moon-born. (-जः *m.*) An epithet of the planet Mercury. (-जं *n.*) Milk. —धारा *f.* The sky, heaven. -नाथः *m.* 1 N. of a celebrated *Linga* or the place where it was set up; (which was destroyed by Mahomad of Ghazani in 1024 A. D.) —पः, -पा *m.* 1 One who drinks the Soma. -2 A Soma-sacrificer. -3 A particular class of Pitris. —पतिः *m.* 1 N. of Indra. -पीतिः *f.* 1 Drinking Soma. -2 A Soma sacrifice. -पुत्रः, -भूः, -सुतः *m.* Epithets ot Budha or Mercury. —प्रवाकः *m.* A person commissioned to engage *Shrotriyas* for a Soma sacrifice. —बंधुः *m.* 1 The sun. -2 N. of Budha. -3 The white water-lily. —योनिः *m.* A sort of yellow and fragrant sandal. -रोगः *m.* A particular disease of women. —लता, -वल्लरी *f.* 1 The Some plant. -2 N. of the river Godâvarî. —वंशः *m.* The lunar race of kings founded by Budha. —वारः, -वासरः *m* Monday. —विक्रयिन् *m.* A vendor of Soma juice. —वृक्षः, -सारः *m.* The white Khadira. —शकला *f.* A kind of cucumber.-संज्ञं *n.* Camphor. -सद् *m.* A particular class of Manes or Pitris. —सिंधुः *m.* An epithet of Vishnu.—सुत् *m.* A Soma distiller. —सुता *f.* The river Narmadâ. —सूत्रं *n.* A channel for conveying water from a *Siva-linga.* —सूत्रप्रदक्षिणा *f.* Circumambulation around a *Siva-linga* so as not to cross the *Soma-sûtra.*

सोमप *m.* The moon.

सोमिन् *a.* (*f.* -नी) Performing the Soma sacrifice. -*m.* A performer of a Soma sacrifice.

सोम्य *a.* (*f.* -म्या) 1 Worthy of Soma. -2 Offering Soma. -3 Soft, good, amiable.

सोल्लुंठः *m.*, सोल्लुंठनं *n.* Irony, ridicule, sarcasm. -ठं, -नं *ind.* Ironically.

सोष्मन् *a.* 1 Warm, hot. -2 (In gram.) Aspirated.-*m.* An aspirate.

सौकर्यं *n.* 1 Hoggishness. -2 Ease, facility. -3 Practicability. -4 Skill. -5 An easy preparation of food or medicine. [-2 Youthfulness.

सौकुमार्यं *n.* 1 Softness, tenderness.

सौखशायनिकः, सौखशायिकः *m.* One who asks another person whether he has slept well.

सौखसुप्तिकः *m.* 1 One who asks another person whether he has slept well. -2 A bard whose duty it is to waken his master with song and music.

सौखिक *a.* (*f.* -की), सौखीय *a.* (*f.*-यी) Relating to pleasure, pleasurable.

सौख्यं *n.* Pleasure, happiness, enjoyment.

सौगतः *m.* A Buddhist.

सौगतिकः *m.* 1 A Buddhist. -2 A Buddhist mendicant.-2 An atheist, a heretic. —कं *n.* Unbelief, atheism.

सौगंध *a.* (*f.* -धी) Sweet-scented, fragrant.-धं *n.* 1 Sweet-scentedness; fargrance. -2 A kind of fragrant grass (कत्तृण).

सौगंधिक *a.* (*f.*-की or -का) Fragrant. -कः *n.* 1 A dealer in perfumes. -2 Sulphur. —कं *n.* 1 The white water-lily. -2 The blue totus. -3 A kind of fragrant grass. -4 A ruby.

सौगन्ध्यं *n.* Sweetness of odour, fragrance.

सौचिः, सौचिकः *m.* A tailor.

सौजन्यं *n.* 1 Kindness of spirit, gentility.-2 Generosity.-3 Kindness, compassion. -4 Friendship, love.

सौंडी *f.* Long pepper.

सौतिः *m.* An epithet of Karna.

सौत्यं *n.* The office of a charioteer.

सौत्र *a.* (*f.* -त्री) 1 Belonging to or having a thread or string. -2 Mentioned or declared in a Sûtra. -त्रः *m.* 1 A Bráhmana. -2 An artificial root occurring in grammatical Sútras which cannot be conjugated like a regular verb, but is used only to form derivative words.

सौत्रांतिकाः *m. pl.* N. of one of the four great schools of Buddhism.

सौत्रामणी *f.* The east.

सौदर्यं *n.* Brotherhood.

सौदामनी, सौदामिनी, सौदाम्नी *f.* 1 Lightning. -2 The female of Indra's elephant.

सौदायिक *a.* (*f.* -की). Whatever is given to a woman at her marriage by her parents or relatives and which becomes her own property. -कं *n.* A nuptial present so made.

सौध *a.* (*f.* -धी) 1 Relating to or having nectar. -2 Having plaster; plastered. -धं *n.* 1 A white-washed mansion; any stuccoed house. -2 Any great mansion or large house. -3 Silver. -4 Opal. -Comp. -कारः *m.* 1 A plasterer. -2 A builder of a house. —वासः *m.* A palatial building.

सौन *a.* (*f.* -नी) Relating to a slaughter-house. —नं *n.* Butcher's meat. -Comp. —धर्म्यं *n.* A state of deadly hostility.

सौनिकः *m.* A butcher.

सौनंदं *n.* The club of Balarâma.

सौनंदिन् *m.* An epithet of Balaràma.

सौंदर्यं *n.* Beauty, gracefulness.

सौपर्णं *n.* 1 Dry ginger. -2 Emerald.

सौपर्णेयः *m.* An epithet of Garuda.

सौप्तिक *a.* (*f.* --की) 1 Connected with or relating to sleep. -2 Somniferous. --कं *n.* A night-attack, an attack on a sleeping man. -Comp. -पर्वन् *n.* N. of the tenth *parvan* or book of the Mahàbhârata. -वधः *m.* The great nocturnal slaughter of the Pándava camp (above referred to)

सौबलः *m.* N. of Sakuni.

सौबली, सौबलेयी *f.* N. of Gándhârí, wife of Dhritaráshtra.

सौभं *n.* N. of Harischandra's city (said to be suspended in air).

सौभगं *n.* 1 Good luck. -2 Prosperity, wealth.

सौभद्रः, सौभद्रेयः *m.* Epithets of Abhimanyu, son of Subhadrâ. [ite wife.

सौभागिनेयः *m.* The son of a favour-

सौभाग्यं *n.* 1 Good fortune or luck, fortunateness (chiefly consisting in a man's and woman's securing the favour and firm devotion of each other). -2 Blessedness, auspiciousness. -3 Beauty, grace. -4 Grandeur, sublimity. -5 The auspicious state of wifehood (opp. widowhood). -6 Congratulation; good wishes. -7 Affection. -8 Red-lead. -9 Borax. -Comp. -चिह्नं *n.* 1 Any mark of good fortune or happiness. -2 Any sign of the blessed state of wifehood (such as the saffron mark on the forehead). -तंतुः *m.* The marriage-string (put round the neck of the bride by the bride-groom at the time of marriage and worn by her till widowhood; also called मंगलसूत्र).—तृतीया *f* The third day of the bright half of Bhádrapada. -देवता *f.* An auspicious or tutelary deity. —वायनं *n.* An auspicious offering of sweetmeats &c.

सौभाग्यवती *a.* Fortunate, auspicious. —ती *f.* A married woman whose husband is alive; a married unwidowed woman.

सौभिकः *f.* A juggler.

सौभिकः *m.* N. of Drupada.

सौभ्रात्रं *n.* Good brotherhood, fraternity.

सौमनस *a.* (*f.*-सा or -सी) Agreeable to the feelings; pleasing. -2 Relating to flowers; floral. —सं *n.* 1 Benevolence, kindness. -2 Pleasure, satisfaction. [nutmeg.

सौमनसा *f.* The outer skin of the

सौमनस्यं *n.* 1 Agreeableness of feelings; pleasure, delight. -2 A particular offering of flowers made at a Sráddha.

सौमनस्यायनी *f.* 1 The blossom of the Málatî creeper. -2 The Mâlatí creeper. [dha.

सौमायनः *m.* A patronymic of Bud-

सौमिक *a.* (*f.*-की) 1 Performed with or relating to the Soma juice.-2Relating to the moon. [Lakshmana.

सौमित्रः; सौमित्रिः *m.* 1 An epithet of

सौमिल्लः *m,* N. of a dramatist who preceded Kâlidâsa.

सौमेचकं *n.* Gold.

सौमेधिकः *m.* A sage, seer.

सौमेरुक *a.* (*f.* -की) Relating to or coming from Sumeru. —कं *n.* Gold.

सौम्य *a.* (*f.* -म्या or-म्यी) 1 Relating or sacred to the moon. -2 Having the properties of Soma. -3 Handsome, agreeable. -4 Gentle, mild. (The voc. सौम्य is often used in the sense of 'good sir,' 'gentle sir,' 'good man'). -5 Auspicious. -6 Bright. —म्यः *m.* 1 N. of Budha or the planet Mercury. -2 A proper epithet by which a Bràhmana should be addressed. -3 A Bráhmana. -4 The Udumbara tree.-5 Blood before it becomes red; serum. -6 The gastric juice. -7 N. of one of the nine divisions of the earth. -8 An auspicious planet. -9 A Bráhmana drinking the Soma juice.-10 A kind of penance. —म्या *f.* 1 N. of Durgâ. -2 The moon-plant. —म्याः *m. pl.* 1 N. of the five stars in Orion's head.-2 A particular class of Pitris or Manes. -Comp. -कृच्छ्रः *m.*,-कृच्छ्रं *n.* A kind of religious penance lasting for five days. —गंधी *f.* The Indian white rose. —धातुः *m.* The phlegmatic humour; phlegm. -नामन् *a.* Having an agreeable name.-वारः, -वासरः *m.* Wednesday,

सौर *a.* (*f.* -री) 1 Relating to the sun; solar. -2 Sacred to the sun. -3 Worshipping the sun. -4 Celestial, divine. -5 Relating to spirituous liquor.-रः *m.* 1 A worshipper of the sun. -2 The planet Saturn. -3 A solar month. -4 A solar day. -5 N. of Yama, the God of death. -रं *n.* N. of a collection of hymns addressed to *Sûrya.* -Comp. -नक्तं *n.* A particular religious observance. -मासः *m.* A solar month.

सौरथः *m.* A hero, a warrior.

सौरभ *a.* (*f.* -भी) Fragrant. -भं *n.* 1 Fragrance. -2 Saffron.

सौरभेय *a.* (*f.* —यी) Relating to *Surabhi.* —यः *m.* An ox.

सौरभी, सौरभेयी *f.* 1 A cow. -2 N. of the daughter of the cow called *Surabhi.*

सौरभ्यं *n.* 1 Fragrance, sweet scent. -2 Agreeableness, beauty. -3 Good character, glory.

सौरसेनाः *m. pl.* N. of a district and its people.—नी *f.* N. of a *Prâkrit* diatect.

सौरसेयः *m.* An epithet of Skanda.

सौरसैंधव *a.* (*f.* —वी) Belonging to

the Ganges. —श्वः m. A horse of the sun.

सौराज्यं n. Good government or rule.

सौराष्ट्र a. (f. -ष्ट्रा or -ष्ट्री) Coming from or relating to the district called Suráshtra (or Surat). —ष्ट्रः m. The district of Suràshtra.-ष्ट्राः m. pl. The people of Suráshtra. —ष्ट्रं n. Brass, bell-metal.

सौराष्ट्रकः m. A kind of bell-metal.

सौरिः m. 1 N. of the planet Saturn. -2 The Asana tree. -3 N. of Yama. -4 Of Karna.-5 Of Sugrìva.-Comp. —रत्नं n. Sapphire.

सौरिक a. (f. -की) 1 Celestial. -2 Spirituous.-3 Due for spirits (such as duty or money).-कः m. 1 Saturn. -2 Heaven, paradise. -3 A vender of spirituous liquor.

सौरी f. The wife of the sun.

सौरीय a. (f. -यी) 1 Solar. -2 Fit for, or suitable to, the sun.

सौर्य a. (f. -र्यी) Belonging to the sun; solar. [-2 Facility, ease.

सौलभ्यं n. 1 Easiness of acquisition.

सौल्विकः m. A copper-smith.

सौव a. (f.-वी) 1 Relating to one's own property. -2 Being in, or belonging to, heaven. —वं n. An order, edict.

सौवग्रामिक a. (f. -की) Belonging to one's own village.

सौवर a. (f. -री) 1 Belonging to sound or a musical note. -2 Treating of accents.

सौवर्चल a. (f. -ली) Coming form the country called सुवर्चल. —लं n. 1 Sochal salt. -2 Natron.

सौवर्ण a. (f. -र्णी) 1 Golden. -2 Weighing one *Suvarna*.

सौवस्तिक a. (f. -की) Benedictive. —कः m. A family- priest.

सौवाध्यायिक a. (f. -की) Belonging to sacred study. [situated.

सौवास्तव a. (f. -वी) Pleasantly

सौविदः, सौविदल्लः m. An attendant on the women's apartments.

सौवीरं n. 1 The fruit of the jujube. -2 Antimony. -3 Sour gruel. -रः m. N. of a district. —राः m. pl. The people of the सौवीर country. -Comp. —अंजनं n. A kind of antimony or collyrium. —सारः m. Antimony.

सौवीरकः m. 1 The jujube tree. -2 An inhabitant of Suvira. -3 N. of Jayadratha.-कं n. Sour barley-gruel.

सौवीर्यं n. Great heroism.

सौशील्यं n. Excellence of disposition, good morals.

सौश्रवसं n. Celebrity, renown.

सौष्ठवं n. 1 Excellence, beauty, elegance. -2 Extreme skilfulness. -3 Excess. -4 Suppleness, lightness.

सौस्नातिकः m. One who asks another whether his ablution has been auspicious or successfully performed.

सौहार्दः m. The son of a friend. —र्दं n. Good-heartedness, friendliness.

सौहार्द्यं, सौहृदं, सौहृद्यं, सौहृदयं n. Friendship, affection.

सौहित्यं n. 1 Satiety, satisfaction. -2 Fulness, completion. -3 Kindness, friendliness.

स्कंदु 1 A. (स्कंदते) 1 To jump. -2 To raise. -3 To pour out.

स्कंदु 1. P. (स्कंदति,स्कन्न) 1 To leap, jump. -2 To rise, ascend. -3 To fall, drop. -4 To burst out. -5 To perish. -6 To be spilled. -7 To emit, shed. -8 To go, move. -9 To become dry. -10 To perish. With अव- To assail, to besiege. परि- To spring about.प्र-To spring forward.

Caus. (स्कंदयति,-ते) 1 To pour out, shed, emit (as the seminal fluid). -2 To neglect, pass by.

स्कंद् 10 U. (स्कंदयति,-ते) To collect.

स्कंदः *m*. 1 Leaping. -2 Quick-silver. -3 N. of Kártikeya. -4 The body. -5 A king. -6 The bank of a river. -7 A clever man. -Comp. —पुराणं *n*. One of the 18 Purânas. -मातृ *f*. N. of Durgá. -षष्ठी *f*. A festival in honour of Kártikeya on the sixth day of Chaitra.

स्कंदकः *m*. 1 One who leaps. -2 A soldier.

स्कंदनं *n*. 1 Emission, effusion. -2 Purging, looseness (of the bowels). -3 Going, moving. -4 Drying up. -5 The suppression of bleeding by cold applications.

स्कंध् 10 U. (स्कंधयति,-ते) To collect.

स्कंधः *m*. 1 The shoulder. -2 The body. -3 The trunk of a tree. -4 A branch or large bough. -5 A branch of human knowledge. -6 A chapter, section (as of a book). -7 A division of an army. -8 A multitude. -9 The five objects of sense. -10 The five forms of mundane consciousness (in Buddhistic phil.). -11 War, battle. -12 A king. -13 An agreement. -14 A road, way. -15 A learned man. -16 A heron. -17 Articles used at the coronation of a king. -धा *f*. 1 A branch. -2 A creeper. -Comp. —आवारः *m*. 1 An army or a division of it. -2 A royal capital. -3 A camp. —उपानेय *a*. To be carried on the shoulders. (-यः *m*.) A form of peace-offering in which fruit or grain is presented as a mark of submission. —चापः *m*. A sort of pole or yoke for carrying burdens. —तरुः *m*. The cocoa-nut tree. —देशः *m*. The shoulder. —परिनिर्वाणं *n*. The annihilation of the elements of being (with Buddhists). —फलः *m*. 1 The cocoa-nut tree. -2 The Bilva tree. -3 The glomerous fig-tree. —बंधना *f*. A sort of fennel. —मल्लकः *m*. A heron. —रुहः *m*. The (Indian) fig-tree. —वाहः, —वाहकः *m*. An ox trained to carry burdens; pack-bullock. —शाखा *f*. A principal branch; the forked branch issuing from the upper stem of a tree. —शृंगः *m*. A buffalo. —स्कंधः *m*. Every shoulder.

स्कंधस् *n*. 1 The shoulder. -2 The trunk of a tree.

स्कंधिकः *m*. An ox trained to carry burdens.

स्कंधिन् *a*. (*f*.-नी) 1 Having shoulders. -2 Having branches or a branched stem. -*m*. A tree.

स्कन्न *a*. (*f*. -न्ना) 1 Fallen down, decended. -2 Oozed out, trickled out. -3 Emitted, sprinkled. -4 Gone. -5 Dried up.

स्कंभ् 1 A., 5. 9 P. (स्कभंते, स्कभ्नोति, स्कभ्नाति) 1 To create. -2 To impede, obstruct. —*Caus*. (स्कंभयति,-ते or स्कभयति,-ते) To stop, to obstruct.

स्कंभः *m*. 1 Support, stay. -2 Fulcrum. -3 The Supreme Being. -4 N. of a Vedic deity.

स्कंभनं *n*. 1 The act of supporting. -2 A support, a prop.

स्कांद *a*. (*f*. -दी) 1 Relating to Skanda. -2 Relating to Siva. —दं *n*. The Skanda Purána.

स्कु 5. 9. U. (स्कुनोति, स्कुनुते, स्कुनाति, स्कुनीते) 1 To go by leaps, jump, bound. -2 To raise. -3 To overspread. -4 To approach. With. प्रति- To cover.

स्कुंद् 1 A. (स्कुंदते) 1 To jump. -2 To raise, lift.

स्कुंभ् 5 9 P. (स्कुभ्नाति, स्कुभ्नोति) To stop, hinder.

स्खद् 1 A. (स्खदते) 1 To tear to pieces. -2 To destroy. -3 To injure, kill. -4 To defeat completely.

-5 To harass, trouble.-6 To make or be firm.

स्खल् I P. (स्खलति,स्खलित) I To stumble,tumble,slip.-2 To totter, shake. -3 To be disobeyed or violated (as an order). -4 To deviate from the right course. -5 To be affected or excited. -6 To err, blunder. -7 To lisp, falter. -8 To fail, have no effect. -9 To drop, trickle.-10 To go, move. -11 To disappear. -12 To collect. With प्र— To jolt, to jostle.

Caus. (स्खलयति-ते) I To cause to stumble. -2 To cause to err, cause to falter or stammer.

स्खलनं *n*. I Stumbling, tripping.-2 Tottering. -3 Deviating from the right course. -4 Error, mistake. -5 Failure. -6 Stammering, faltering. -7 Trickling, dripping. -8 Collision.-9 Mutual striking or rubbing together.

स्खलित *p. p.* (*f.* —ता) I Stumbled, -2 Dropped down. -3 Wavering, unsteady. -4 Intoxicated. -5 Stammering, faltering. -6 Agitated,disturbed.-7 Erring.-8 Dropped,emitted. -9 Trickling down. -10 Interrupted. -11 Confounded. -12 Gone. —तं *n*. I Stumbling. -2 Deviation from the right course. -3 Error. -4 Fault, transgression. -5 Deceit, treachery. -6 Stratagem.-7 A place likely to cause stumbling.

स्तन् I P., 10 U. (स्तनति, स्तनयति,-ते, स्तनित) I To sound, reverberate. -2 To groan, sigh. -3 To thunder, roar loudly. With नि— I To sound, -2 To sigh. -3 To mourn. वि- To roar.

स्तन: *m*. I The female breast. -2 The nipple of the breast. -3 The udder or dug of any female animal. -Comp. —अंतरं *n*. I The heart. -2 The space between the breasts. -3 A mark on the breast (said to indicate future widowhood).-आभोग: *m*. I Fulness of the breasts. -2 The orb of the breast. -3 A man with large breasts like those of a woman. —तट: *m*., —टं *n*. The slope of the breast. —प, —पा, —पायक, -पायिन् *a*. Sucking the breast; a suckling. —भर: *m*. I The weight or heaviness of breasts. -2 A man having breasts like those of a woman. —मुखं, —वृंतं *n*., —शिखा *f*. A nipple.

स्तननं *n*. I Sounding, a sound, noise.-2 Roaring,thundering, rumbling (of clouds). -3 Groaning. 4 Breathing hard.

स्तनंधय: *m*. An infant, a suckling.

स्तनयित्नु: *m*. I Thundering; the rumbling of clouds. -2 A cloud. -3 Lighting. -4 Sickness.-5 Death. -6 A kind of grass.

स्तनित *p. p.* (*f.* —ता) I Sounded, sounding. -2 Thundering, roaring. —तं *n*. I The rattling of thunder.-2 Thunder, noise. -3 The noise of clapping the hands.

स्तन्यं *n*. Mother's milk; milk.

स्तबक: *m*. A bunch, a cluster.

स्तब्ध *p. p.* (*f.* —ब्धा) I Blocked up, obstructed.-2 Paralysed,stupefied, benumbed. -3 Motionless. -4 Fixed, hard, rigid. -5 Obstinate, stubborn, stern. -6 Coarse.-Comp. —कर्ण *a*. Pricking up the ears. -रोमन् *m*. A hog, a boar.—लोचन *a*. Having motionless or unwinking eyes (said of Gods).

स्तब्धता *f*., स्तब्धत्वं *n*. I Rigidity, firmness, hardness.-2 Insensibility.

स्तब्धि: *f*. I Fixedness, rigidity. -2 Firmness. -4 Stupor, insensibility

-4 Obstinacy.

स्तभ् 1 A. (स्तंभते) See स्तंभ्.

स्तभः *m*. A goat, ram.

स्तभु *n*. See स्तंभनं.

स्तंबः *m*. 1 A clump of grass &c. -2 A sheaf of corn. -3 A clump or bunch (in general). -4 A thicket. -5 A shrub or plant having no decided stem. -6 The post to which an elephant is tied. -7 A post. -8 Stupefaction. -9 A mountain. -Comp. —कारि *a* Forming sheaves or clusters. (—रिः *m*.) Corn, rice. —घ्नः *m*. 1 A small hoe for weeding clumps of grass. -2 A sickle for cutting corn. -3 A basket for holding the heads of wild rice. —घ्नः *m*. A sickle for cutting corn, a hoe.

स्तंबेरमः *m*. An elephant.

स्तंभ् 1 A., 5. 9 P. (स्तंभते, स्तभ्नोति, स्तभ्नाति, स्तंभित or स्तब्ध ; the स of the root is changed to ष after prepositions ending in इ or उ and also after अव) 1 To stop, suppress. -2 To make firm or stiff.-3 To stupefy, paralyze, benumb. -4 To support, uphold, sustain. -5 To become stiff.-6 To be proud or elated. With अव- 1 To bind. -2 To rest or rely on. -3 To restrain, overpower. उत्- 1 To prop, uphold. -2 To arrest, stop. नि— To stop. पर्यव— 1 To surround. -2 To surround and oppose. वि- To fix firmly. सम्- 1 To support. -2 To stop.-3 To corroborate. -4 To make firm. समव-To encourage.

स्तंभः *m*. 1 Fixedness, rigidity, motionlessness. -2 Insensibility, stupor, numbness, paralysis. -3 Stoppage, hindrance. -4 Restraint, curbing. -5 Support, fulcrum. -6A pillar.-7 A stem, trunk (of a tree). -8 Stupidity. -9 Absence of feeling or excitability.-10 The suppression of any force or feeling by supernatural or magical means. -Comp. —उत्कीर्ण *a*. Carved out of a post of wood (as a statue).-कर *a*. 1 Paralysing, benumbing. -2 Obstructing. (—रः *m*.) A fence. —पूजा *f*. The worship of the posts of temporary pavilions erected for marriages or other occasions of solemnity.

स्तंभकिन् *m*. A kind of musical instrument covered with leather.

स्तंभनं 1 Stopping, hindering, suppressing, restraining. -2 Paralysing, stupefying.-3 Quieting, composure. -4 Making firm or stiff. -5 Propping, supporting. -6 Stopping the flow of blood. -7 Anything employed as an astringent. -8 A paricular magical art or faculty. -नः *m*. N. of one of the five arrows of Cupid.

स्तरः *m*. 1 Anything spread, a layer, a stratum. -2 A bed, couch.

स्तरणं *n*. The act of spreading or scattering.

स्तरि (-री-) मन् *m*. A bed, couch.

स्तरी *f*. 1 Smoke, vapour. -2 A heifer. -3 A barren cow.

स्तवः *m*. 1 Praising, eulogizing. -2 Praise, panegyric.

स्तवक *a*. (*f*. -विका) Praising, eulogizing. —कः *m*. 1 A panegyrist. -2 Praise, eulogium. -3 A cluster of blossoms. -4 Bunch of flowers, nosegay. -5 A chapter or section of a book. -6 A multitude.

स्तवनं *n* 1 Praising, praise. -2 A hymn.

स्तावः *m*. Praise, eulogy.

स्तावकः *m*. A panegyrist, flatterer.

स्तिघ् 5 A. (स्तिघ्नुते) 1 To ascend.-2 To assail. -3 To ooze.

स्तिप् I A (स्तेपते) To ooze,drop,drip.

स्तिभिः *m.* I An obstacle. -2 The ocean. -3 A cluster, bunch.

स्तिम्, स्तीम् 4 P. (स्तिम्यति, स्तीम्यति) I To become wet or moist. -2 To become fixed or rigid.

स्तिमित *a.* (*f.* -ता) I Wet, moist. -2 Still, calm; unmoved, steady. -3 Closed, shut. -4 Benumbed, paralysed. -5 Soft, tender. -6 Gratified, satisfied. —तं *n.* I Moisture. -2 Fixity, steadiness -Comp -समाधिः *m.* Steady contemplation.

स्तिमितत्वं *n.* Steadiness, stillness.

स्तीर्विः *m.* I An officiating priest at a sacrifice. -2 Grass. -3 Sky, atmosphere. -4 Water. -5 Blood. -6 An epithet of Indra.

स्तु 2 U. (स्तौति-स्तवीति, स्तुते-स्तुवीते; स्तोतुं, स्तुत; *desid.* तुष्टूषति, -ते; the स् of स्तु is changed to ष् after a preposition ending in इ or उ) I To praise, glorify, celebrate. -2 To celebrate or praise in song; to worship by hymns. With अभि— To praise. प्र- I To praise. -2 To begin. सम्- I To praise. -2 To be familiar with.

स्तुकः *m.* A collection of hair; a knot or braid of hair.

स्तुका *f.* I A knot or braid of hair. -2 A bunch of curly hair between the horns of a bull. -3 Hip; thigh.

स्तुच् I A. (स्तोचते) I To be bright, to be pellucid. -2 To be propitious or pleased. [Flattered.

स्तुत *p. p.* (*f.* -ता) I Praised. -2

स्तुतिः *f.* I Praise, commendation. -2 A hymn of praise. -3 Empty or false praise.-4 N.of Durgá.-Comp. —पदं *n.* An object of praise. -पाठकः *m.* Panegyrist, a minstrel, bard. -वादः *m.* Laudatory speech, panegyric. —व्रतः *m.* A bard.

स्तुत्य *a.* (*f.*-त्या) Laudable, praiseworthy.

स्तुनकः *m.* A goat.

स्तुभ् I P. (स्तोभति) I To praise. -2 To extol, worship.

स्तुभ् I A. (स्तोभते) I To stop, suppress. -2 To paralyse, stupefy.

स्तुभः *m.* A goat.

स्तुंभ् 5. 9. P. (स्तुभ्नोति; स्तुभ्नाति) I To stop. -2 To benumb, stupefy. -3 To expel.

स्तूप् 4 P., 10 U. (स्तूप्यति स्तूपयति,-ते) I To accumulate, pile, collect. -2 erect, raise.

स्तूपः *m.* I A heap, pile.-2 A Buddhistic monument for keeping sacred relics. -3 A funeral pile. -4 Strength, power.

स्तृ 5 U. (स्तृणोति, स्तृणुते, स्तृतः *pass.* स्तर्यते) I To spread, strew, cover. -2 To expand, diffuse.-3 To spread about. -4 To clothe, envelop. -5 To kill. With अव— To cover, to fill. आ- I To spread. -2 To cover. उप- To arrange. परि- To spread. -2 To arrange. -3 To cover. वि- I To spread. -2 To extend. सम्— I To spread. -2 To cover.

—*Caus.* (स्तारयति, -ते) To overspread, cover. With वि- I To cause to spread. -2 To extend.

स्तृ *m.* A star.

स्तृक्ष् I P. (स्तृक्षति) To go, to move.

स्तृतिः *f.* I Spreading, expansion. -2 Covering, clothing.

स्तृह्, स्तृंह् 6 P. (स्तृहति, स्तृंहति) To strike, hurt, kill.

स्तॄ 9 U. (स्तृणाति, स्तृणीते, स्तीर्ण) To cover, strew. See स्तृ.

स्तेन् 10 U (Strictly a denom. from स्तेन; स्तेनयति, -ते) To steal, rob.

स्तेनः *m.* A thief, robber. —नं *n.* Thieving, stealing. -Comp. —निग्रहः

m. 1 The punishment of thieves. -2 Suppression of theft.

स्तेप् I. 1 A. (स्तेपते) To ooze.

स्तेप् 10 U. (स्तेपयति, -ते) To send, throw, cast.

स्तेयं *n.* 1 Theft, robbery. -2 Anything stolen or liable to be stolen. -3 Anything private or secret.

स्तेयिन् *m.* 1 A thief, robber. -2 A goldsmith.

स्तै 1 P. (स्तायति) To put on, adorn.

स्तेनं *n.* Theft, robbery.

स्तैन्यं *n.* 1 Theft, robbery. —न्यः *m.* A thief.

स्तैमित्यं *n.* Fixedness, rigidity. -2 Numbness.

स्तोक *a.* (*f.* -का) 1 Little, small. -2 Short. -3 Few. -4 Low, abject. —कः *m.* 1 A small quantity, a drop. -2 The Châtaka bird. —कं *ind.* A little, less.

स्तोकक: *m.* The Châtaka bird.

स्तोकशस् *ind.* By little, sparingly.

स्तोतव्य *a.* (*f.*—व्या) Praiseworthy.

स्तोत्रं *n.* 1 Praise. -2 A hymn of praise.

स्तोत्रियः *m.*..-या *f.* A particular kind of verse.

स्तोमः *m.* 1 Praise, hymn. -2 A sacrifice, oblation. -3 A *Soma* libation. -4 A collection, group. -5 A large quantity. —मं *n.* 1 The head. -2 Riches, wealth. -3 Grain, corn. -4 An iron-pointed stick.

स्तोम्य *a.* (*f* —म्या) Laudable, praiseworthy.

स्त्यान *a.* (*f.*—ना) 1 Collected into a mass; congealed.-2 Thick, bulky, gross. -3 Soft, smooth, unctuous. -4 Sounding. —नं *n.* 1 Thickness, increase in magnitude or bulk. -2 Unctuousness. -3 Nectar. -4 Sloth, idleness. -5 Echo, sound.

स्त्यायनं *n.* Collecting into a mass; crowding together, aggregation.

स्त्येनः *m.* 1 Nectar. -2 A thief.

स्त्यै 1 U. (स्त्यायति,-ते) 1 To be collected into a heap or mass. -2 To spread about, be diffused. -3 To sound.

स्त्री *f.* 1 A woman. -2 A female of any animal.-3 A wife.-Comp. -अभिगमनं *n.* Sexual intercourse.-आजीवः *m.* 1 One who lives by his wife.-2 One who lives by keeping women for prostitution. —कामः *m.* 1 Desire of intercourse with women; fondness for women. -2 Desire of a wife. —कुमारं *n.* A woman and child.-कुसुमं *n.* The menstrual excretion in women. —क्षीरं *n.* A mother's milk. —गवी *f.* A milch-cow.—गुरुः *m.* N. A female *Guru* or priestess. —गृहं *n.* 1 A harem. -2 Apartment in a house for the exclusive use of women.—घोषः *m.* Dawn, day-break. —चिह्नं *n.* 1 Any mark or characteristic of the female sex. -2 The vulva.-चौरः *m.* A seducer of women, a libertine. —जननी *f.* A woman who brings forth only daughters. -जातिः *f.* Woman-kind, female sex. —जितः *m.* A hen-pecked husband. —धनं *n.* A woman's private property over which she exercises independent control. —धर्मः *m.* 1 The duty of a woman or wife. -2 The laws concerning women. -3 Menstruation. —धर्मिणी *f.* A woman in her courses. —धवः *m.* A man. —नाथ *a.* One protected by a woman. —निबंधनं *n.* A woman's peculiar sphere of action or province; domestic duty, housewifery. —पण्योपजीविन् *m.* See स्त्र्याजीव above. —परः *m.* A woman-lover, lecher, libertine.—पिशाची *f.* A fiend-like wife.—पुंसौ *m. dual* 1 Wife and husband. -2 Male and female

—पुंसलक्षणा *f.* A hermaphrodite.—प्रत्ययः *m.* A feminine affix (in gram.). —प्रसंगः *m.* (Excessive) intercourse with women.—प्रसूः *f.* A woman who brings forth only daughters. —प्रिय *a.* Loved by women. (—यः) *m.* The mango tree. —बुद्धिः *f* 1 The female understanding. -2 The counsel of a woman; female advice. —मंत्रः *m.* A female stratagem, woman's counsel. —मुखपः *m.* The *Asoka* tree. —रंजनं *n.* Betel. —रत्नं *n.* 1 An excellent woman. -2 N. of Lakshmi. —राज्यं *n.* The kingdom of women. —लिंगं *n.* 1 The feminine gender (in gram.) -2 Any mark of the female sex (as breast &c.). -3 The female organ.—विधेय *a.* Uxorious. -संस्थान *a.* Having a female shape. —संग्रहणं *n.* 1 The act of embracing a woman (improperly).-2 Adultery, seduction. —सभं *n.* An assembly of women. —स्वभावः *m.* 1 The nature of women. -2 A eunuch. —हरणं *n.* 1 The forcible abduction of women. -2 Rape. —हारिन् *m.* A ravisher or seducer (of women).

स्त्रीतमा, स्त्रीतरा *f.* A thorough woman; more thoroughly a woman.

स्त्रीता *f.*, स्त्रीत्वं *n.* 1 Womanhood. -2 Wifehood. -3 Effeminacy, feminineness.

स्त्रैण *a.* (*f.* —णी) 1 Female, feminine. -2 Belonging to women. -3 Being among women. -णं *n.* 1 Womanhood, nature of women.-2 The female sex; womanhood. -3 A collection of women.

स्थ *a.* (*f.* —स्था) (At the end of comp.) Standing, being, existing. —स्थः *m.* A place, spot.-Comp.—पतिः *m.* A sovereign, a chief. -2 An architect. -3 A master, carpenter, a wheel-wright. -4 A charioteer. -5 One who sacrifices to Brihaspati. -6 A guard on women's apartments.

स्थकरं *n.* A betel-nut.

स्थग् 1 P. or *Caus.* (स्थगति, स्थगयति) 1 To cover, conceal. -2 To pervade, fill, occupy.

स्थग *a.* (*f.* —गा) 1 Fraudulent, dishonest. -2 Impudent, reckless. —गः *m.* A rogue, cheat.

स्थगनं *n.* Concealment, hiding.

स्थगरं *n.* A betel-nut.

स्थगिका *f.* 1 A courtezan. -2 The office of betel-bearer.

स्थगित *a.* (*f.* —ता) Covered, concealed. -2 Occupied.

स्थगी *f* A betel-box.

स्थगुः *m.* A hump.

स्थंडिलं *n.* 1 A piece of ground (levelled, squared and prepared for a sacrifice), an altar. -2 A barren field. -3 A heap of clods. -4 A limit, boundary.-5 A land-mark. -Comp. — शायिन् (also स्थंडिलेशयः) *m.* An ascetic who sleeps on the bare *Sthandila* or sacrificial ground. —सितकं *n.* An altar.

स्थपति *a.* Chief, principal. —तिः *m.* 1 A king, sovereign.-2 An architect. -3 A wheel-wright, master-carpenter. -4 A charioteer. -5 One who offers a sacrifice to Brihaspati. -6 An attendant on the women's apartments. -7 N. of Kubera.

स्थपुट *a.* (*f.* —टा) 1 Being in contracted or difficult circumstances. -2 Unevenly raised; elevated and depressed. -Comp. —गत *a.* Being in contracted or uneven parts; being in difficult places.

स्थल् 1 P. (स्थलति) To stand firm, [be firm.

स्थलं *n.* 1 Firm or dry ground, dry land. -2 Shore, beach. -3 Ground.

land, soil (in general). -4 Place, spot. -5 A tract, district. -6 Station. -7 A mound. -8 A topic, the point under discussion. -9 A part (as of a book).-10 A tent.-Comp. —आरूढ *a* Alighted on the ground. —चर *a.* Land-going, not aquatic. —च्युत *a.* Fallen or removed from a place or position. -देवता *f.* A local or rural deity. —पद्मिनी *f.* The shrub *Hibiscus Mutabils.* —मार्गः *m.*, —वर्त्मन् *n.* A road by land. —विग्रहः *m.* A battle on level ground. —शुद्धिः *f.* Purification or clearance of a place from impurity. —सीमन् *f.* A landmark, boundary.

स्थला *f* A spot of dry ground artificially rasied and drained (opp. स्थली which is naturally so).

स्थली *f.* 1 Dry ground, firm land. -2 A natural spot of ground, ground or land (as of a forest).-3 A deity of the soil. -Comp. -देवता *f.* A deity of the soil, a tutelary deity.

स्थलेशय *a.* Sleeping on dry ground. —यः *m.* Any amphibious animal.

स्थविः *m.* 1 A weaver. -2 Heaven.

स्थविर *a.* (*f.* —रा) 1 Fixed, firm, steady.-2 Old, aged.-3 Ancient.-रः *m.* 1 An old man. -2 A beggar. -3 N. of Brahman (*m.*). —रा *f.* An old woman.

स्थविष्ठ *a.* (*f.* —ष्ठा) Greatest, very strong, largest (superl. of स्थूल).

स्थवीयस् *a.* (*f.* —सी) Greater, larger (compar. of स्थूल).

स्था 1 P. (Atm. also in certain senses ; तिष्ठति,-ते, स्थातुं, स्थित ; *pass.* स्थीयते; the स् of this root is changed to ष् after a preposition ending in इ or उ) 1 To stand. -2 To stay, well, live. -3 To remain over, be left.-4 To delay, wait. -5 To desist, stand still. -6 To be kept aside. -7 To be, exist, be in any state or position. -8 To conform to, obey (with loc.). -9 To be restrained. -10 To be obtainable. -11 To live, breathe. -12 To stand by or near, help. -13 To depend on. -14 To occupy oneself with. -15 (Atm.) To be guided by the advice of. -16 (Atm.) To offer oneself to (for sexual embrace); stand as a prostitute (with dat.). With अति- To remain over, to exceed by. अधि— To stand on, to tread upon. -2 To be supported by. -3 To be, to exist, to inhabit. -4 To stand.-5 To command, to govern, to lead, to preside over. -6 To pass over. -7 To overcome, surpass. -8 To ascend to, to be established. -9 To do. अनु—1 To stand near.-2 To follow, obey, perform.-3 To remain. -4 To show fovour to; to grant. -5 To govern. अव— (*Atm.*) 1 To withdraw. -2 To stand firm, to keep ground (in Vedanta phil.) -3 To be decided. -4 To remain. -5 To be present. -6 To stay. -7 To be intrusted to, to devolve on. आ— 1 To be near at hand. -2 To stay, remain. -3 To walk towards. -4 To turn to. -5 To ascend.-6 To assume. -7 To apply. -8 To observe. -9 To behave. -10 To perform. -11 To act, to deport.-12 To have resort to. उद्— 1 To get up. -2 To rouse oneself. -3 To proceed from. -4 (*Atm.*) To strive for. उप— 1 To stand near. -2 To be imminent. -3 To stand opposite.-4 To approach, arrive at. -5 (*Atm.*) To serve, wait upon, salute, worship. -6 (*Atm.*)

To oblige, serve -7 To fall to one's share. -8 (*Atm.*) To lead to. -9 (*Atm.*) To unite, join. परि— To surround. प्र- 1 To depart, set out. -2 To come. -3 To stand firmly, to be established. प्रति— 1 To stand firm, to be supported. -2 To depend upon. -3 To stay. प्रत्यव-(*Atm.*) To oppose, to object. वि- (*Atm.*) 1 To spread. -2 To stand apart. व्यव— (*Atm.*) 1 To separate.-2 To establish. -3 To depend on. -4 To restrain.-5 To arrange, to manage. -6 To be settled or permanent. सम्- (*Atm.*) 1 To stand close together. -2 To stand on, to be on. -3 To obey, to conform to. -4 To exist, to live.-5 (*Pars.*) To stand still. -6 To be completed. -7 To perish. समधि— To administer. समव—(*Atm.*) 1 To be ready. -2 To stand immovable. समा— 1 To undergo. -2 To apply. -3 To act. -4 To perform. समुद्— 1 To rise together. -2 To return to life. समुप— 1 To approach. -2 To fall in the way. -3 To send. समुपा— To observe (as law). संप्र- (*Atm.*) To depart. संप्रति-To rest on.

Caus. (स्थापयति,-ते) 1 To cause to stand. -2 To place, put. -3 To found, establish. -4 To stop. -5 To arrest, check. -6 To raise. -7 To cause to last, make durable. -8 To give in marriage. -9 To instruct in. With अप— To reduce to a particular condition. उद्-To lead away (one's wife from her father's house. पर्यव— To compose oneself. प्र- 1 To push out. -2 To induce to retire.-3 To send away, to dismiss. प्रत्यव- To [illegible] व्यव— To settle. सम— 1 To collect, to compose -2 To place. -3 To subject.-4 To restrain, stop. -5 To kill. समव- 1 To stop. -2 To found.

स्थाणु *a.* Firm, fixed, steady, stable, motionless. —णुः *m.* 1 An epithet of Siva. -2 A post, pillar.-3 A peg, pin. -4 The gnomon of a dial. -5 A spear, dart. -6 A nest of white ants. -7 The drug or perfume called *Jivaka.* —*m., n.* A branchless trunk or stem; any bare stalk or stem.

स्थंडिलः *m.* 1 An ascetic who sleeps on the bare ground or on a place prepared for sacrifice. -2 A religious mendicant.

स्थानं *n.* 1 The act of standing or remaining, continuance, residence. -2 Being fixed or stationary. -3. A state, condirion. -4 A site, locaeity. -5 Station, position. -6 Relation. capacity. -7 A dwelling place. -8 A region, district. -9 A town, city. -10 Rank, dignity. -11 Object.-12 An occasion, subject, cause. -13 A fit or proper place. -14 A fit or worthy object. -15 The place or organ of utterance of any letter, (these are eight).-16 A holy place. -17 An altar.-18 A square, a court. -19 The place or sphere assigned after death to persons according as they perform or neglect their prescribed duties. -20 (In politics, war &c.) The firm attitude or bearing of troops, standing firm so as to repel a charge. -21 A halt. -22 A neutral or middle state. -23 The stamina of a kingdom *i. e.* army, treasure, town, and territory. -24 A likeness, resemblance. -25 Part or division of a work, section, chapter &c.-26 The part of an actor. -27 Interval, opportunity, liesure.

-28 (In music) A note, tone, modulation of the voice. -Comp. —आसने *n. dual* Standing and sitting down. -आसेध: *m.* Confinement to a place, imprisonment, arrest. -चिंतक: *m.* A quarter-master. —पाल: *m.* A watchman, sentinel. —माहात्म्यं *n.* 1 The greatness or glory of any place. -2 A kind of divine virtue or uncommon sanctity supposed to be inherent in a sacred spot. —योग: *m.* Assignmeat of proper places.

स्थानकं *n.* 1 A position, situation. -2 A particular point or situation in dramatic action *e. g.* पताकास्थानकं. -3 A city, town. -4 A basin. -5 A kind of scum on spirits or wine. -6 A mode of recitation.-7 A division or section of the 'Taittirîya', a branch of the *Yajurveda*.

स्थानतस् *ind.* 1 According to one's position. -2 From one's proper place. -3 With reference to the organ of utterance.

स्थानिक *a.* (*f.* -की) 1 Belonging to a place; local. -2 (In gram.) That which takes the place of a thing, or is substituted for it. —क: *m.* 1 Any one holding an office. -2 The governor of a place.

स्थानिन् *a.* (*f.* —नी) 1 Having a place. -2 Permanent. -3 Having a substitute. —*m.* 1 The original form or primitive element, that for which anything else is substituted. -2 The form so substituted for anything.-3 That which has a place or is actually expressed.

स्थानीय *a.* (*f.* -या) 1 Belonging to a place, local. -2 Suitable to a place. —यं *n.* A town, city.

स्थाने *ind.* (Loc. of स्थान) 1 In the right or proper place; rightly, justly, truly, appropriately. -2 In lieu of, as a substitute for. -3 On account of. -4 Similarly, like, as.

स्थापक *a.* (*f.*-का) Causing to stand, establishing, regulating. —क: *m.* 1 The director of the stage-business, a stage-manager. -2 The founder of a temple, or erector of an image.

स्थापत्य: *m.* A guard of the women's apartments. —त्यं *n.* Architecture, building.

स्थापनं *n* 1 The act of fixing, founding, establishing, or instituting. -2 Regulating, directing. -3 Concentration of the mind; steady application; abstraction. -4 A dwelling, habitation. -5 A ceremony performed on a woman's perceiving the first signs of living conception.

स्थापना *f.* 1 Placing, fixing.-2 Foundation; basis. -3 Introduction (as to the performance of a drama; stage-management.

स्थापित *p. p.* (*f.* —ता) 1 Placed, located, deposited. -2 Founded, instituted. -3 Raised, erected. -4 Regulated, ordered, enacted. -5 Settled, ascertained. -6 Entrusted with any duty, post &c. -7 Wedded, married. -8 Firm, steady.

स्थाप्य *a.* (*f.* -प्या) 1 To be placed or deposited. -2 To be founded or established. —प्यं *n.* A pledge, deposit.

स्थामन् *n.* 1 Strength; power; stamina. -2 Fixity, stability.

स्थायिन् (*f.* —नी) 1 Staying, being situated (at the end of comp.). -2 Continuing, lasting, abiding. -3 Dwelling, remaining. -4 Permanent, invariable, unchangeable.—*m.* 1 A lasting or permanent feeling. —*n.* A permanent state or condition.

-Comp. —भावः *m.* A fixed or permanent condition of mind, a lasting or permanent feeling; (these feelings are said to give rise to the different *rasas* or sentiments in poetry, each *rasa* having its own Sthâyibhâva; they are eight or nine).

स्थायुक *a.* (*f.* -का or -की) 1 Likely to last, enduring. -2 Firm, steady, stationary. —कः *m.* The superintendent or head of a village.

स्थालं *n.* 1 A plate or dish. -2 Any culinary vessel. -Comp. —रूपं *n.* The form or representation of a pot.

स्थाली *f.* 1 An earthen pot or pan, a cooking-pot. -2 A particular vessel used in the preparation of Soma. -3 The trumpet-flower. -Comp. —पाकः *m.* A particular religious act performed by a house-holder. -पुरीषं *n.* The sediment or dirt sticking to a cooking-pot. —पुलाकः *m.* Boiled rice in a cooking-pot.-स्थाली-पुलाकन्यायः *m.* The maxim of the cooking-pot and the boiled rice. In a cooking-pot all the grains are equally subjected to the action of the boiling water, and so when one knows that one grain is well-cooked, he can conclude that all other grains are also well-cooked. From this fact the maxim is applied to cases where the condition of the whole is inferred from that of a part. —बिलं *n.* The interior or hollow of a caldron.

स्थावर *a.* (*f.* —रा) Stable, stationary, immovable, inanimate (opp. जंगम).-2 Inactive, slow.-3 Regular, established. —रः *m.* A mountain. —रं *n.* 1 Any stationary or inanimate object (such as clay, stones, trees &c. which formed the seventh creation of Brahman (*m.*). -2 A bow-string. -3 Immovable property, real estate. -4 A heir-loom. -Comp. -अस्थावरं, -जंगमं *n.* 1 Movable and immovable property. -2 Animate and inanimate things.

स्थाविर *a.* (*f.* —रा or -री) Thick, firm. —रं *n.* Old age.

स्थासकः 1 Perfuming or smearing the body with fragrant unguents. -2 A bubble of water or any fluid.

स्थासु *n* Bodily strength.

स्थास्नु *a.*1 Disposed to stand firm, immovable. -2 Permanent, lasting. —स्नुः *m.* A tree.

स्थित *p. p.* (*f.* —ता) 1 Stood, remained, stayed. -2 Standing. -3 Standing up, risen. -4 Staying, resting, existing, situated. -5 Happened, occurred. -6 Stationed in, appointed to. -7 Conforming to.-8 Stood still, stopped. -9 Firmly attached to. -10 Steady, firm. -11 Determined, resolved. -12 Established, decreed. -13 Steadfast, steady-minded. -14 Upright, virtuous. -15 Faithful to a promise. -16 Agreed, contracted.-17 Ready, being close or at hand. —तं *n.* A word standing by itself. -Comp.—उपस्थित *a.* With and without the particle '*iti*' (as a word). —पाठ्यं *n.* Recitation in Prákrita by a woman while standing. —प्रज्ञ *a.* Firm in judgment or wisdom; contented. —प्रेमन् *m.* A staunch or faithful friend.

स्थितिः *f.* 1 Standing, remaining, staying, stay, residence. -2 Standing still, continuance in one state. -3 Steadiness, firmness, steady application or devotion. -4 A situation, condition. -5 Natural state, nature, habit. -6 Stability, permanence.-7 Correctness of conduct, moral rectitude.-8 Establishment of good order (in a state). -9 Rank, dignity.-10 Maintenance, sustenance. -11 Continuance in life, preservation (one of the three states of human beings).-12 Pause, stop.-13 Well-being, welfare, protection. -14 Consistency. -15 A settled rule.-16 Settled determination. -17 Limit, boundary. -18 Inertia, resistance to motion. -19 Duration of an eclipse.-20 Regard, consideration, account. -Comp. —स्थापक a. Having the power of restoring to a previous state; having elastic properties. (—कः m.) Elasticity.

स्थितिमत् a. (f. —ती) Steady, firm. -2 Virtuous, upright.

स्थिर a. (f. —रा; compar. स्थेयस्; superl. स्थेष्ठ) 1 Firm, steady, fixed. -2 Immovable, motionless. -3 Permanent, eternal, everlasting.-4 Cool, collected, calm.-5 Free from passion. -6 Steady in conduct. -7 Constant, faithful, determined. -8 Certain, sure. -9 Hard, solid. -10 Strong, intense. -11 Stern, hard-hearted. —रः m. 1 A God, deity. -2 A tree. -3 A mountain. -4 A bull. -5 N. of Siva. -6 N. of Kártikeya. -7 Final beatitude. -8 The planet Saturn. -9 N. of certain zodiacal signs (*Taurus*, *Leo*, *Scorpio*, and *Aquarius*). —रा f. 1 The earth. -2 A strong-minded woman. -2 The silk-cotton tree. -Comp. —अनुराग a. Constant in affection. —आयुस्, —जीविन् a. Long-lived, lasting. (-m.) The silk-cotton tree. —आरंभ a. Firm in undertakings; persevering.—कुट्टक: m. 1 A steady pulverizer. -2 A kind of common divisior (in algebra). —गंध: m. The *champaka* flower. -छद: m. The birch tree. —छाय: m. 1 A tree which gives shelter to travellers. -2 A tree (in general). —जिह्व: m. A fish. —जीविता f. The silk-cotton tree. —दंष्ट्र: m. 1 A snake. -2 Vishnu in his boar incarnation.-पुष्प: m. 1 The *Champaka* tree. -2 The *Bakula* tree. —प्रतिज्ञ a. 1 Persisting in an assertion. -2 Faithful to a promise. —प्रतिबंध a. Obstinate. -फला f. A kind of gourd. —योनि: m. A large tree which gives shade and shelter. —यौवन a. Ever youthful. (-न: m.) 1 A kind of good or evil genius. -2 A fairy. —संगर a. Faithful to a promise. —समाधि a. Keeping perfectly still (as in meditation).

स्थूणा f. 1 The post or pillar in a house.-2 A post or pillar in general. -3 An iron image or statue. -4 An anvil.

स्थूम: m. 1 Light. -2 The moon.

स्थूर: m. 1 A bull. -2 A man.

स्थूरिन् m. A pack-horse or bullock.

स्थूल a. (f. —ला compar. स्थवीयस्, superl. स्थविष्ठ) 1 Large, great, bulky. -2 Corpulent, stout.-3 Strong, powerful. -4 Thick, clumsy. -5 Gross, rough (fig. also).-6 Foolish, silly. -7 Dull, thick-headed.-8 Not exact. —ल: m. The jack tree. -ला f. Large cardamoms. —लं n. 1 A heap, quantity. -2 A tent. -3 The summit of a mountain. -Comp. —अंत्र n. The larger intestine near the anus.-आस्य: m. A snake. —उच्चय: m. 1 A large fragment of a crag or rock fallen from a mountain and forming an irregular mound.-2 Incompleteness, deficiency; defect. -3 The middle pace of elephants. -4 An eruption of pimples on the face. -5 A hollow at the root of an elephant's tusks. —क्षेडः, -क्ष्वेडः m. An arrow. —चापः m. A large bow-like instrument used in cleaning cotton. -धी, —मति a. Foolish. —नालः m. A kind of large reed. -नास, -नासिक a. Thick-nosed. (-सः, -कः m.) A hog, boar. —पटः m., -टं n. Coarse cloth. -पट्टः m. Cotton. -पट्टाकः m. Coarse cloth. -पादः m. An elephant. -2 A man with elephantiasis. —मानं n. Gross or rough computation. -मूलं n. A kind of radish.—लक्ष,-लक्ष्य a. I Munificent, generous. -2 Wise, learned. -3 Inclined to recollect both benefits and injuries. -4 Taking careless aim. —शरीरं n. The grosser or material and perishable body (opp. सूक्ष्म or लिंग शरीर). —शाटकः, -शाटिः m. A thick or coarse cloth. —हस्तः m. An elephant's trunk.

स्थूलक a. (f. —का) Large, huge, bulky. -कः m. A sort of grass or reed.

स्थूलिन m. A camel.

स्थेमन् m Firmness, fixity.

स्थेयः a. (f. -या) To be fixed or placed; to be settled or determined. —यः m. I An arbitrator, umpire, a judge. -2 A domestic priest.

स्थेयस् a. (f. —सी) More firm; stronger (compar. of स्थिर).

स्थेष्ठ a. (f. -ष्ठा) Very firm; strongest (superl. of स्थिर).

स्थैर्यं n. I Firmness, stability; steadiness. -2 Continuance. -3 Firmness of mind. -4 Patience. -5 Hardness, solidity.

स्थौणेयः, स्थौणेयकः m. A kind of perfume.

स्थौरं n. I Firmness, strength, power. -2 A load sufficient for a horse or ass.

स्थौरिन् m. I A horse carrying burdens on his back; pack-horse. -2 A strong horse.

स्थौल्यं n. I Bigness, bulkiness. -2 Dulness of intellect.

स्नपनं n. I Sprinkling, washing. -2 Bathing, ablution.

स्नवः m. Trickling, oozing, dripping.

स्नसा f. A tendon, muscle.

स्ना 2 P. (स्नाति; स्नात) I To bathe, perform ablution. -2 To perform the ceremony of bathing at the time of leaving the house of one's spiritual preceptor. With अप- To bathe after mourning. नि— To be perfect, to be proficient in.

Caus. (स्नापयति,-ते, स्नपयति, -ते) To cause to bathe, moisten, sprinkle. —*Desid.* (सिस्नासति).

स्नात p. p. (f. —ता) Bathed; washed. -तः m. I One whose course of holy study is over. -2 An initiated house-holder.

स्नातकः m. I A Brâhmana who has performed the ceremony of ablution after finishing his first Asrama (that of a Brahmachárin). -2 A Bráhmana just returned from the house of his preceptor and become a married man (गृहस्थ).-3 A Brâhmana who is a *Bhikshu* (beggar of alms) for any religious object. -4 Any man of the first three classes who is an initiated householder.

स्नानं n. I Bathing, washing, ablution. -2 Any religious or ceremonial ablution. -3 The ceremony of bathing or anointing an idol.-4Anything used in ablution.-Comp. -तृणं n. Kusa-grass. —यात्रा f. The festi-

-val held on the full-moon day in the month of Jyeshtha. —विधिः *m.* 1 The act of ablution. -2 The proper manner or rules of ablution.

स्नानीय *a.* (*f.* —या) Fit or suitable for bathing; worn during bathing. -2 Water or any other article (such as unguents &c.) proper for bathing.

स्नापकः *m.* A servant who bathes his master or brings bathing water for him.

स्नापनं *n.* The act of causing to bathe, or of attending upon a person while he is bathing.

स्नायुः *m.* 1 A tendon, muscle sinew. -2 The string of a bow. -Comp. -अर्मन् *n.* A kind of disease of the eyes.

स्नायुकः *m.* See स्नायुः.

स्नावः स्नावन् *m.* A tendon, muscle.

स्निग्ध *a.* (*f.* -ग्धा) 1 Loving, affectionate, tender. -2 Oily, unctuous, greasy. -3 Sticky, adhesive. -4 Shining, glossy. -5 Smooth, emollient. 6 Moist, wet. -7 Cooling. -8 Kind, amiable. -9 Agreeable, charming. -10 Thick, dense, compact. -11 Steadfast (as a gaze or look). —ग्धः *m.* 1 A friendly person. -2 The red castor-oil plant. -3 A kind of pine. —ग्धं *n.* 1 Oil. -2 Bee's wax. -3 Lustre. -4 Thickness, coarseness. -Comp. -जनः *m.* An affectionate person, a friend. —तंडुलः *m.* A kind of rice of quick growth.

स्निग्धता *f.*, स्निग्धत्वं *n.* 1 Oiliness. -2 Blandness. -3 Affection, love.

स्निग्धा *f.* Marrow.

स्निह् 4 P. (स्निह्यति, स्निग्ध) 1 To feel or have affection for, be fond of (with loc. of the person or thing that is loved or liked). -2 To be easily attached. -3 To be pleased with, be kind to. -4 To be sticky or adhesive. -5 To be smooth. —*Caus.* (स्नेहयति, -ते) 1 To make unctuous, anoint, lubricate. -2 To cause to love. -3 To dissolve, destroy, kill.

स्नु 2 P. (स्नौति, स्नुत) 1 To drip, trickle, fall in drops, leak out. -2 To flow, stream.

स्नुत *a.* (*f.* -ता) Oozed, flowed.

स्नुः *m.*, स्नु *n.* 1 Table-land. -2 Top, surface (in general). (This word has no forms for the first five inflections and is optionally substituted for सानु after acc. dual).

स्नुः *f.* A sinew, tendon, muscle.

स्नुषा *f.* A daughter-in-law.

स्नुह् 4 P. (स्नुह्यति, स्नुग्ध or स्नूढ) To vomit.

स्नेहः *m.* 1 Affection, kindness, tenderness. -2 Oiliness, unctuousness, lubricity (one of the 24 Gunas according to the Vaiseshikas.) -3 Moisture. -4 Grease; any unctuous substance. -5 Oil. -6 Any fluid of the body such as semen. -Comp. —अक्त *a.* Lubricated, greased. -प्रवृत्तिः *f.* Affectionate or friendly intercourse. —आशः *m.* A lamp. —पूर्वं *ind.* Affectionately. -प्रियः *m.* A lamp. -बीजः *m.* The Piyála tree. -भूः *m.* Phlegm. —भूमिः *f.* 1 Anything yielding oil. -2. An object of love or affection, beloved person. -विः *m.* Sesamum. —बस्तिः *f.* Injection of oil, an oily enema.

स्नेहनः *m.* 1 A friend. -2 The moon. -3 A kind of disease.

स्नेहन *a.* (*f.* —नी) 1 Anointing, lubricating. -2 Destroying. —नं *n.* Anointing, unction, rubbing or smearing with oil or unguents. -2

Unctuousness. -3 An unguent.

स्नेहित *p. p.* (*f.* —ता) 1 Loved. -2 Kind, affectionate. -3 Anointed, lubricated. —तः *m.* A friend, a beloved person.

स्नेहिन् *a.* (*f.* —नी) 1 Affectionate, friendly. -2 Oily, unctuous. —*m.* 1 A friend. -2 An anointer, a smearer. -3 A painter.

स्नेहुः *m.* 1 The moon. -2 A kind of disease.

स्नै 1 P (स्नायति) To dress, wrap round, envelop.

स्नैग्ध्यं *n.* 1 Unctuousness, oiliness, lubricity. -2 Tenderness, fondness. -3 Smoothness.

स्पंद् 1 A. (स्पंदते, स्पंदित) 1 To throb, palpitate. -2 To tremble, quiver. 3 To go, move.

स्पंदः *m.* 1 Throbbing, palpitation. -2 Vibration.

स्पंदनं *n.* 1 Throbbing, palpitation, quivering. -2 Tremor, vibration. -3 The quickening of a child in the womb. -4 Rapid motion, going.

स्पंदित *p. p.* (*f.* —ता) 1 Throbbed, quivered. -2 Gone. —तं *n.* A pulsation, palpitation.

स्पर्ध् 1 A (स्पर्धते) 1 To vie with, emulate, rival, be equal with. -2 To defy, bid defiance to.

स्पर्धा *f.* 1 Emulation, competition. -2 Jealousy, envy. -3 Defiance. -4 Equality with.

स्पर्धिन् *a.* (*f.* —नी) 1 Rivalling, competing, vying with. -2 Emulous, envious. -3 Proud. —*m.* A competitor, an equal.

स्पर्श् 10 A. (स्पर्शयते) 1 To take, touch. -2 To unite, join. -3 To embrace, clasp.

स्पर्शः *m.* 1 Touch, contact. -2 Contact (in astr.). -3 Conflict, encounter. -4 Feeling, the sense of touch. -5 The quality of touch or tangibility, touch. -6 That which affects, affection, seizure. -7 Disease, disorder. -8 A consonant of any of the five classes of letters (from क to म). -9 A gift, donation. -10 Air, wind. -11 The sky. -12 Sexual union. -13 A secret spy. —र्शा *f.* An unchaste woman. -Comp —अज्ञ *a.* Senseless, insensible. —इंद्रियं *n.* The organ or sense of touch. —उदय *a.* Followed by a consonant. —उपलः, —मणिः *m.* The philosopher's stone. —तन्मात्रं *n.* The subtile element of tangibility. —कज्जा *f.* The sensitive plant. —वेद्य *a.* To be apprehended by the sense of touch. —संचारिन् *a.* Infectious. —स्नानं *n.* Ablution at the entrance of the sun or moon into an eclipse. —स्पंदः, स्पंदुः *m.* A frog.

स्पर्शन *a.* (*f.* —नी) 1 Touching, handling. -2 Affecting, influencing. —नः *m.* Air, wind. —नं *n.* 1 Touching, touch. -2 Sensation, feeling. -3 Sense or organ of touch. -4 A gift, donation.

स्पर्शनकं *n.* A term used in Sànkhya philosophy for the 'skin'.

स्पर्शवत् *a.* (*f.* —ती) 1 Tangible. -2 Soft, agreeable to the touch.

स्पर्द् 1 A. (स्पर्दते) To become wet or moist.

स्पर्डु *m.* A disorder of the body.

स्पश् 1 U. (स्पशति-ते) 1 To obstruct. -2 To undertake, perform. -3 To string together. -4 To touch. -5 To see, behold, perceive clearly.

स्पशः *m.* 1 A spy, a secret emissary or agent. -2 Fight, war, battle. -3 One who fights with savage animals (for reward). -4 A fight with wild animals.

स्पष्ट *a.* (*f.* -ष्टा) 1 Evident, plain, manifest. -2 Real, true. -3 Full-blown, expanded. -4 One who sees clearly. —ई ind. 1 Clearly, plainly. -2 Openly, boldly (स्पष्टी कृ) To make clear or distinct, explain, elucidate. -Comp. —गर्भा f. A woman who shows evident signs of pregnancy. —प्रतिपत्तिः f. A clear perception.

स्पृ 5 P. (स्पृणोति) 1 To extricate from. -2 To gratify. -3 To grant, bestow. -4 To protect -5 To live.

स्पृश् 6 P. (स्पृशति, स्पृष्ट, स्प्रष्टुं, स्पृष्ट) 1 To touch. -2 To stroke gently, to touch. -3 To cling to, come in contact with.-4To wash or sprinkle with water. -5 To go to, reach. -6 To obtain,reach a particular state. -7 To affect, move, touch. -8 To refer or allude to. -9 To receive, accept (as a sacrificical offering). With उप - 1 To touch. 2 To sprinkle with water. -3 To rinse one's mouth, to sip water. -4 To bathe. परि— To touch. सम्— 1 To sprinkle with water. -2 To touch.

Pass. To be polluted, defiled, or tainted.

Caus. (स्पर्शयति, ते) 1 To cause to touch. -2 To give, present.

स्पृश् a (At the end of comp.) 1 Who or what touches. -2 Touching, affecting, piercing. -3 Relating to. [Fit to be touched.

स्पृश्य a. (f. —श्या) 1 Tangible. -2

स्पृष्ट p. p. (f. —ष्टा) 1 Touched, felt with the hand. -2 Come in contact with, touching. -3 Applying or extending to.-4 Affected, seized. -5 Tainted, defiled. -6 Formed by the complete contact of the organs of speech (the letters of the five classes). [another.

स्पृष्टास्पृष्टि, स्पृष्टास्पृष्टं n. Touching one

स्पृष्टिः, स्पृष्टिका f. Touch, contact.

स्पृह् 10 U. (स्पृहयति ते) To long for, desire for, envy (with dat.).

स्पृहणं n. The act of desiring or wishing.

स्पृहणीय a. (f.—या) To be desired, enviable, agreeable, desirable.

स्पृहयालु a. Disposed to be desirous or envious of.longing for, covetous (with dat. or loc).

स्पृहा f 1 Desire, ardent wish. -2 Envy. -3 Covetousness.

स्पृहालु a. See स्पृहयालु.

स्पृह्य a (f -ह्या) Desirable, enviable. —ह्यः m. The wild citron tree.

स्पृ 9 P. (स्पृणाति) To hurt, kill.

स्प्रष्टृ m. See स्पर्ष्टृ [pand.

स्फट् 1 P. (स्फटति) To burst, ex-

स्फटः m. A snake's expanded hood. —टी f. Alum.

स्फटा f 1 A snake's expanded hood. -2 Alum.

स्फटिकः m. 1 A crystal, quartz. —का f. Sulphate of alumina or alum. -Comp.-अचलः m. The mount Meru. —अद्रिः m The mount Kailâsa.—भिद् m. Camphor. —अभ्रः m. Camphor. —अश्मन्, —आत्मन्, —मणिः m., —शिला f. A crystal stone. [alumina.

स्फाटिकारि, स्फटिकारिका f. Sulphate of

स्फटिकी f. Alum. [expand.

स्फंट् 1 P. (स्फंटति) To burst open,

स्फंट् 10 U. (स्फंटयति,-ते) To jest or joke with, laugh at.

स्फंड् 1 P., 10 U. (स्फंडति, स्फंडयति -ते To laugh at, joke with.

स्फर् See स्फुर्. [throbbing.

स्फरणं n. Trembling, quivering,

स्फल् 1 P. (स्फलति) To tremble, quiver, throb, palpitate.

स्फल् 10 U. or *Caus.* (स्फालयति,-ते) To cause to tremble or shake.

स्फाटकः m. A drop of water. —कं n. Crystal.

स्फाटिक a. (f. – की) Crystalline. —कं n. A crystal

स्फाटित p. p. (f. —ता) Split open, burst expanded, made to gape

स्फाटिकं n. Crystal.

स्फात p. p. (f. —ता) Increased, enlarged, swollen.

स्फातः f. Swelling, intumescence. –2 Increase, growth.

स्फाय् 1 A. (स्फायते, स्फीत) 1 To grow large, fat big or bulky.-2 To swell, increase, expand.

Caus. (स्फावयति –ते) To cause to grow large, augment.

स्फार a (f.—रा) 1 Large, increased, expanded. -2 Much, abundant. -3 Loud -रः m. 1 Swelling, enlargement. 2 A bubble (in gold) -3 A protuberance. -4 Throbbing, palpitation. -5 Twanging —रं n. Abundance, plenty (स्फारी भू I To swell out, expand, increase. -2 To become manifest).

स्फुरणं n Throbbing, shaking.

स्फालः m. Throbbing, palpitation

स्फालनं n. 1 Quivering, palpitating. -2 Causing to shake about. -3 Rubbing, friction. -4 Patting or stroking.

स्फिच् f. Buttocks, hips.

स्फिट् 10 U. (स्फेटयति,–ते) 1 To injure, kill. -2 To despise -3 To love. -4 To cover. [See स्फिट्ट.

स्फिट्ट 10 U. (स्फिट्टयति,–ते) To hurt.

स्फिर a. (f.-रा compar. स्फेयस् superl. स्फेष्ठ) 1 Abundant, large. -2 Many, numerous. -3 Vast, capacious.

स्फीत p. p (f – ता) 1 Swollen, increased. -2 Thick, large, bulky. -3 Many, numerous plentiful abundant -4 Delighted. -5 Pure. 6 Prosperous, thriving. 7 Affected by hereditary disease. (स्फीती कृ To augment or enlarge).

स्फीतिः f. 1 Growth, increase, enlargement.-2 Abundance, plenty.-3 Prosperity.

स्फुट् 6 P., 1 U (स्फुटति, स्फोटति, –ते, स्फुटित) 1 To burst or split open, break. -2 To expand, blossom. -3 To run away, disperse. -4 To become visible, become manifest.

स्फुट् 10 U. (स्फुटयति,–ते) 1 To burst, break open. -2 To burst into view.

—Caus. (स्फोटयति, -ते) 1 To rend asunder, tear open, divide. -2 To show, make clear. -3 To divulge, make public -4 To hurt, destroy kill -5 To winnow.

स्फुट a. (f. -टा) 1 Rent asunder, broken, split -2 Expanded, full-blown -3 Displayed, made clear. -4 Distinctly manifest -5 Bursting into view. -6 White, bright, pure. 7 Well known, famous -8 Spread, diffused. -9 Loud. -10 Apparent, true. -11 Corrected. —टः f. The expanded hood of a snake. —टं ind. Clearly, distinctly, certainly.-Comp. —तार a. Bright or gemmed with stars.—फलं n. (In geom.) 1 Distinct or precise area of a triangle. -2 The clear or net result of any calculation —सारः m The true latitude of a star or planet – सूर्यगतिः f. The apparent or true motion of the sun.

स्फुटनं n 1 Breaking open, tearing open. -2 Expanding, blossoming.

स्फुटिः, स्फुटी f. 1 Cracking of the skin of the feet. -2 Sores or swelling of the feet. [a slice.

स्फुटिका f. A small bit broken off,

स्फुटित p. p. (f -ता) 1 Broken open, cracked.-2 Budded, blown, expanded (as a flower). -3 Manifested, shown. -4 Torn, destroyed. -5 Laughed at.-Comp. -चरण a. Having wide feet, splay-foo e ı. [isrespect

स्फुट्ट 10 U (स्फुट्टयति, ते) To despise,

स्फुंट् 1 P. (स्फुंटति) To open,expand.

स्फुंट् 10 U. (स्फुंटयति, -ते) To jest, joke, laugh at. [See स्फुंद.

स्फुंड 1 A., 10 U. (स्फुंडते, स्फुंडयति- ते)

स्फुत ind. An imitative sound. -Comp. —करः m. Fire.—कारः m. The sound स्फुत्, a crack ng noise.

स्फुर् 6 P (स्फुरति, स्फुरित) 1 To throb, palpitate (as eyes &c).-2 To shake, tremble, vibrate in general -3 To twitch, struggle, become agitated. -4 To start, spring forward. -5 To spring back (as a bow). -6 To break forth, spring up -7 To become visible or manifest. -8 To flash, sparkle, glitter, shine. -9 To distinguish oneself. -10 To flash to the mind, rush suddenly into memory. -11 To go tremulously. -12 To bruise, destroy. With अभि— 1 To expand. -2 To become known प्र- 1 To tremble. -2 To expand. -3 To become known, to spread wide वि— 1 To tremble. -2 To struggle. -3 To glitter. -4 To draw, to twang (as a bow).

—Caus (स्फारयति-ते, स्फोरयति-ते) 1 To cause to throb or vibrate. -2 To cause to shine. -3 To throw, cast. -With अप- To shine forth or out अभि— 1 To spread or be diffused, expand. -2 To become known.

स्फुरः m 1 Throbbing, trembling. -2 Swelling. -3 A shield.

स्फुरणं n. 1 Throbbing, trembling (in general) -2 Throbbing or quivering of certain par s of the body (indicating good or bad luck). -3 Breaking forth, starting into view. -4 Gleaming, flashing, shining. -5 Flashing on the mind, crossing the memory. [aerolite.

स्फुरदुल्का f. A shooting meteor,

स्फुरित p. p. (f -ता) 1 Trembling, throbbing. -2 Shaken. -3 Glittering, shining. -4 Unsteady -5 Swollen. -6 Manifested, displayed. —तं n. 1 A throb, palpitation, tremor. -2 Agitation or emotion of the mind.

स्फुर्छ् 1 P. (स्फूर्छति) 1 To spread, extend. 2 To forget.

स्फुर्ज् 1 P. (स्फूर्जति) 1 To thunder. -2 To crash, explode.-3 To glitter, shine. -3 To burst or break forth.

स्फुर्जथुः m. See स्फूर्जथुः.

स्फुल् 6 P. (स्फुलति) 1 To tremble, throb, vibrate. -2 To dart forth, appear. -3 To collect. -4 To kill, destroy.

स्फुलं n. A tent.

स्फुलनं n Trembling, throbbing.

स्फुलिंगः m , स्फुलिंगं n , स्फुलिंगा . A spark of fire. [gues of fire.

स्फुलिंगिनी f. One of the seven ton-

स्फूर्जः m. 1 The crashing sound of a thunder clap -2 Indra's thunderbolt. -3 Sudden burst or rise. -4 (In dramaturgy) First union of lovers characterized by joy in the beginning and some expectation of fear in the end. [der.

स्फूर्जथुः m. A clap or peal of thunder

स्फूर्तिः f. 1 Throbbing, vibration. -2 Spring, bound. -3 Blooming, opening 4 Display. -5 Flashing to the mind.-6 Poetical inspiration.

स्फूर्तिमत् a. (f. —ती) Throbbing, agitated. -2 Tender-hearted m. A follower or worshipper of Siva (पाशुपत).

स्फेयस् a. (f.-सी) More abundant,

larger (compar of स्फिर).

स्फेष्ठ *a* (*f.* -ष्ठा) Most abundant, largest (superl. of स्फिर).

स्फोटः *m.* 1 Splitting open, bursting. -2 Disclosure. -3 A swelling, a boil, a tumour. -4 The idea which flashes on the mind when a sound is uttered. -5 The eternal sound recognised by the Mimáṁsakas. -Comp.-बीजकः *m.* The marking-nut-plant.

स्फोटकः *m.* A swelling, tumour.

स्फोटन *a.* (*f.* -नी) Breaking asunder, disclosing, making clear. -नः *m.* Separated utterance of a close combination of consonants. -नं *n.* 1 Rending, bursting, cracking -2 Winnowing grain. -3 Cracking the finger-joints, snapping the fingers. 4 The separation of the letters of a double consonant.

स्फोटनी *f.* The boring tool, an auger, a gimlet. [serpent.

स्फोटा *f* The expanded hood of a

स्फोटिका *f.* A kind of bird.

स्फोर्णं *n.* See स्फूर्णं.

स्फ्यं *n.* A sword-shaped implement used in sacrifices. -Comp. -वर्तनिः *m.* The furrow made by this implement.

स्बृ See स्पृ

स्म *ind.* 1 A particle added to the present tense of verbs (or to present participles) and giving them the sense of the past tense. -2 A pleonastic particle (generally added to the prohibitive particle मा).

स्मयः *m.* 1 Astonishment, wonder, surprise. -2 Arrogance, pride, haughtiness.

स्मरः *m.* 1 Recollection, remembrance. -2 Love. -3 The God of love. -Comp. -अंकुशः *m.* 1 A finger-nail. -2 A lover, lascivious person. -अगारं, -गृहं, मंदिरं *n.* -कूपकः *m.* The female organ. -अंध *a.* Infatuated with passion. -आकुल, -आतुर, -आर्त, -उत्सुक, *a.* Pining with love, love-sick -आसवः *m.* Saliva. -कर्मन् *n.* Any amorous action. -गुरुः *m.* An epithet of Vishnu. -छत्रं *n.* The clitoris -दशा *f.* A state of love, a state of the body produced by being in love. -ध्वजः *m.* 1 The male organ. -2 A fabulous fish. -3 N. of a musical instrument. (-जं *n*) The female organ. (-जा *f.*) A bright moon-light night. -प्रिया *f.* An epithet of Rati -भासित *a.* Inflamed by love. -मोहः *m.* Infatuation of love, passion. -लेखनी *f.* The Sárikâ bird.-वल्लभः *m.* 1 An epithet of the Spring.-2 Of Aniruddha. -वीथिका *f.* A prostitute, harlot. -शासन *m.* An epithet of Siva. -सखः *m.* The moon -स्मर्यः *m.* A donkey, an ass. -हरः *m.* An epithet of Siva.

स्मरणं *n.* 1 Remembering, remembrance, recollection. -2 Thinking of or about. -3 Memory. -4 A traditional precept (opp. श्रुति). -5 Mental recitation of the name of a deity -6 Remembering with regret. -7 A figure of speech which consists in the recollection of an object arising from the perception of some thing like it. -Comp. -अनुग्रहः *m.* 1 A kind remembrance. -2 The favour of remembrance. -अपत्यतर्पकः *m.* A turtle, tortoise. -अयौगपद्यं *n.* The non-simultaneousness of recollections. -पदवी *f.* Death.

स्मार *a.* (*f.*-री) Relating to Smara or the God of love. -रं *n.* Recollection, memory.

स्मारक *a.* (*f.* -स्मारिका) Reminding.

स्मारणं *n*. Calling to mind, reminding, causing to remember.

स्मार्त *a*. (*f* —र्ता) 1 Relating to memory, remembered, memorial. -2 Being within memory. -3 Based on or recorded in a Smriti -4 Legal. -5 Following or professing the law-books. -6 Domestic (as fire). —र्तः *m*. 1 A Brâhmana well-versed in traditional law. -2 One who follows the traditional law. -3 N. of a sect. —र्तं *n* An act or rite enjoined by a Smriti a legal act.

स्मि 1 A. (स्मयते, स्मित) 1 To smile, laugh (gently). -2 To bloom, expand. With उद्— To smile. वि— 1 To be surprised. -2 To admire. -3 To be proud.

Caus. (स्मापयति,-ते) 1 To cause to smile. -2 To laugh at, deride. -3 To astonish (स्मापयते in this sense).

Desid (सिस्मयिषते) To wish to smile.

स्मिट् 10 U. (स्मेटयति,-ते) 1 To scorn, despise. -2 To love. -3 To go.

स्मित *p. p*. (*f*. —ता) 1 Smiled, smiling. -2 Expanded, blown, blossomed. —तं *n* A smile, gentle laugh. —सस्मितं *ind*. With a smile. -Comp. —दृश ... Having a smiling look. (-*f*) A handsome woman. —पूर्वम् *ind*. Smilingly, with a smile. —शालिन् *a*. Smiling.

स्मितिः *f*. Smiling.

स्मील् 1 P. (स्मीलति) To wink, blink

स्मृ 5 P. (स्मृणोति) 1 To please, gratify. -2 To protect, defend -3 To live.

स्मृ 1 P. (Atm. also in epic poetry स्मरति, स्मृत, *Pass*. स्मर्यते) 1 To remember, bear or keep in mind, call to mind, think of. -2 To recite mentally or call upon the name of a deity &c.-3 To lay down or record in a Smriti. -4 To declare, consider. -5 To remember with regret, long for (oft. with gen). With अनु— To call to mind, remember. अप— To forget. वि— To forget. सम्— To remember.

Caus. (स्मारयति,-ते but स्मरयति,-ते in the last sense) 1 To cause to remember, put in mind of, call to mind. -2 To give information -3 To cause to remember with regret.

Desid. (सुस्मूर्षते) To wish to recollect.

स्मृत *p. p*. (*f*.-ता) 1 Remembered, called to mind. -2 Recorded, mentioned -3 Appointed, designed. -4 Enjoined by a Smriti or traditional law.

स्मृतिः *f*. 1 Remembrance, recollection, memory -2 Thinking of, calling to mind. -3 Traditional law. (opp. श्रुति). -4 A code of laws, law-book -5 A text of Smriti, canon, rule of law. -6 Desire, wish. -7 Understanding. -8 (In Rhet) The figure of speech which consists in the recollection of an object from the perception of something like it. This figure is also called स्मरणं. Comp. —अंतरं *n*. Another law-book. —अपेत *a*. 1 Forgotten. -2 Inconsistent with Smriti. -3 Illegal. unjust.—उक्त *a*. Prescribed or enjoined in the codes of law, canonical.-पथः,-विषयः *m* The object of memory. (स्मृतिपथं or स्मृतिविषयं गम् To be dead.). —प्रत्यवमर्षः *m*. Retentiveness of memory, accuracy of recollection. —प्रबंधः *m*. A legal work.-भ्रंशः *m*. Loss or failure of memory. -रोधः *m*. A temporary interruption of memory; loss or failure of memory.-विभ्रमः *m*. Confusion of memory. —विरुद्ध *a.* Illegal. —विरोधः *m.* 1 Opposition to law, illegality. -2 Disagreement between two or more Smritis or legal texts. —शास्त्रं *n.* 1 A law-book, code. -2 Legal science. —शेष *a.* Deceased, dead (as a person). —शैथिल्यं *n.* Temporay loss of memory. —साध्य *a.* Capable of being proved by law.—हेतुः *m.* A cause of recollection, association of ideas.

स्मेर *a.* (*f.*-रा) 1 Smiling.-2 Blown, expanded, blooming -3 Proud. -4 Evident. -Comp. —विष्करः *m.* A peacock. [rush.

स्यदः *m.* Speed, rapid motion,

स्यंद् 1 A. (स्यंदते, स्यंदितुं, स्यंत्तुं, स्यन्न; *desid.* सिस्यंदिषते, सिस्यंत्सति,-ते; the स् of स्यंद् is changed in ष् after a preposition ending in इ or उ) 1 To ooze, drop, distil, flow. 2 To shed, pour forth. -3 To run, flee.

स्यंदः *m.* 1 Flowing, trickling. -2 Going rapidly, moving. -3 A car, chariot.

स्यंदन *a.* (*f.* -ना or -नी) 1 Going quickly, flowing. -2 Quick, fleet. —नः *m.* 1 A war-chariot a car or chariot in general. -2 Air, wind. -3 A kind of tree (तिनिश). —नं *n.* 1 Flowing, trickling -2 Rushing, going or flowing quickly. -3 Water. -Comp. —आरोहः *m.* A warrior who fights while seated in a chariot.

स्यंदनिका *f.* A drop of saliva.

स्यंदिन् *a.* (*f.* —नी) 1 Oozing, flowing, trickling.-2 Rushing.-3 Going.

स्यंदिनी *f.* 1 Saliva. 2 A cow bearing two calves at the same time.

स्यन्न *p. p.* (*f.* -न्ना) 1 Oozed, dropped. -2 Dropping, trickling.

स्यम् 1 P., 10 U. (स्यमति, स्यमयति,-ते) 1 To cry aloud, shout. -2 To go -3 To consider, reflect (Atm. only in this sense).

स्यमंतकः *m.* A kind of valuable gem. (See the word सत्राजित् in the Appendix).

स्यमि (-मी-) कः *m.* 1 A cloud.-2 An ant-hill.-3 A kind of tree.-4 Time.

स्यमिका *f.* Indigo.

स्यात् *ind* (Strictly 3rd. pers. sing of the Potential of अस् ' to be ') It may be, perhaps, per chance. -Comp —वादः *m.* An assertion of probability (in phil.); a form of scepticism. — वादिन् *m.* A sceptic.

स्यालः *m* See श्यालः.

स्यूत *p. p.* (*f.* —ता) 1 Sewn with a needle, stitched, woven (fig. also). -2 Woven together, joined. —तः *m.* 1 A sack.

स्यूतिः *f.* 1 Sewing, stitching. -2 Needle-work.-3 A sack.-4 Lineage, family -5 Offspring.

स्यूनः *m* 1 A ray of light. -2 The sun. -3 A bag, sack.

स्यूमः *m.* A ray of light (also -मं *n.*). —मं *n.* 1 Water -2 Happiness.

स्योतः *m.* A sack bag.

स्योन *a.* (*f.*—ना) 1 Beautiful, pleasing -2 Auspicious.—नः *m.* 1 A ray of light. -2 The sun. -3 A sack. — नं *n.* Happiness, pleasure.

स्रंस् 1 A (स्रंसते, स्रस्त) 1 To fall, fall or drop down -2 To drop, fall asunder.-3 To hang down.-4 To go. *Caus.* (स्रंसयति, ते) 1 To cause to fall or slip down, disturb. -2 To loosen, slacken. -With वि- To cause to drop.

स्रंसः *m* Falling, sleeping.

स्रंसनं *n* 1 Falling. -2 Causing to fall or bring down

स्रंसिन् *a.* (*f.* —नी) 1 Falling; hanging down, being loosened. -2 Pendulous, hanging loosely.

स्रह् 1 A (स्रंहते) To confide or trust

स्रग्विन् a (f -णी) (compar. स्रजीयस् superl. स्रजिष्ठ) Wearing a garland or chaplet.

स्रज् f. 1 A chaplet, a wreath or garland of flowers. -2 A garland (in general) -Comp -दामन् (स्रग्दामन्) n. The tie or fillet of a garland -धर a. Wearing a garland (रा f.) N. of a metre

स्रज्जा f. A rope, string, cord.

स्रद्धू f. Breaking wind downwards

स्रंभ् 1 A. (स्रम्भते, स्रब्ध) To confide With वि- 1 To be confident. -2 To rest secure

स्रवः m 1 Trickling, oozing, flowing. -2 A drop, stream -3 A fountain, spring.

स्रवणं n. 1 Flowing trickling, oozing -2 Sweat - Urine

स्रवत् a (f स्रवन्ती) Flowing, oozing -Comp. -गर्भा f 1 A woman that miscarries -2 A cow miscarrying by accident रंग m A market, fair

स्रवन्ती f 1 A stream, river -2 The region of the spleen.

स्रष्टृ m. 1 A maker -2 A creator, an epithet of Brahman (m) -3 N of Siva

स्रस्त p p. (f -स्ता) 1 Fallen or dropped down, fallen off. -2 Hanging loosely down -3 Loosed -4 Relaxed -5 Pendulous -6 Separated -Comp -अंग a 1 Having the limbs relaxed -2 Swooning faint ng.

स्रस्तर. m A couch or sofa (for reclining), a bed

स्राक् ind. Quickly, speedily

स्रावः m Flow, oozing, dropping.

स्रावक a (f -विका) Causing to flow, exuding -कं n. Black pepper.

स्रु 1 P (स्रवति स्रुत) 1 To flow, ooze, drop, exude. -2 To pour out, shed, let flow -3 To go, move -4 To trickle away, waste away -5 To spread about, transpire (as a secret). [pour out.

Caus (स्रावयति ते) To cause to flow,

स्रुघ्न m N of a district

स्रुघ्ना f Natron

स्रुच् f A sort of wooden ladle used in sacrifices -Comp. -प्रणालिका f The spout of a ladle

स्रुत a (Usually at the end of comp) Flowing, dropping, pouring forth

स्रुत p·p (f -ता) 1 Flowed, trickled, dripping -2 Gone

स्रुति f 1 Flowing, oozing, distilling, trickling out, exudation or flow of the sap -2 Exudation, resin -3 A stream

स्रुवः m, स्रुवा f 1 A sacrificial ladle -2 A spring cascade.

स्रू f 1 A sacrificial ladle -2 A fountain

स्रेक् 1 A (स्रेकते) To go, move

स्रै 1 A (स्रायति) 1 To boil -2 To sweat.

स्रोत n A rapid stream

स्रोतस् n A stream, current -2 A torrent, rapid stream -3 A stream, river (in general) 4 A wave. -5 Water 6 An organ of sense -7 The trunk of an elephant -Comp. -अंजन n. Antimony -रंध्र n The aperture of the trunk of an elephant -वह्, -वहा f A river

स्रोतस्य m 1 N of Siva. -2 A thief.

स्रोतस्वती, स्रोतस्विनी f A river.

स्व pron a (f. स्वा) 1 One's own, belonging to oneself. -2 Innate, natural inborn. -3 Belonging to one's own caste or tribe. -स्वः

-ः m. 1 One's own self. -2 A relative. kinsman. -3 The soul. -4 N. of Vishnu. स्वः m., स्वं n. 1 Wealth, property -2 (In alg.) The plus or affirmative quantity. -Comp. -अक्षपादः m A follower of the Nyâya system of philosophy. —अधिष्ठानं n. One of the six Chakras or mystical circles of the body. —अधीन a. 1 Dependent on oneself, self dependent. -2 Independent. -3 One's own subject. -4 In one's own power. —अध्यायः m. 1 Self-recitation, muttering to one-self -2 Study of the Vedas, sacred study, perusal of sacred books -3 The Veda itself -4 A day on which sacred study is enjoined to be resumed after suspension —अनुभवः m ,-अनुभूतिः f. 1 Self-experience. -2 Self knowledge. —अंतं n. 1 The mind. -2 A cavern —अर्थः m. 1 One's own interest, self-interest -2 Own or inherent meaning —स्वार्थानुमानं n. Inference for oneself, (opp. to परार्थानुमान) स्वार्थपंडित a. 1 Clever in one's own affairs -3 Expert in attending to one's own interests. स्वार्थपर, स्वार्थपरायण a. Intent on securing one's own interests; selfish. -आयत्त a. Dependent upon oneself. —उदयः m. The rising of a sign or heavenly body at any particular place.-उपाधिः m. A fixed star —कंपनः m Air, wind. —कुलक्षयः m A fish. —गतम् ind. To oneself; aside (in theatrical language). —छंदः m. 1 Self willed, uncontrolled, wanton. -2 Spontaneous. -3 Wild. (—दः m.) One's own will or choice, independence. (-दं ind.). At one's own will or pleasure. —ज a. Self-born. (-जः m.) 1 A son r child. -2 Sweat, perspiration. (-जा f.) A daughter. (-जं n.) Blood. —जनः m. 1 A kinsman, relative. -2 One's own people or kindred, one's household. —तंत्र a. 1 Self-dependent, independent, self-willed.-2 Of age, full-grown. (-त्रः m.) A blind man. —पक्षः m. 1 One's own side or party -2 A friend. —भावः m. 1 Own state. 2 An essential or inherent property, natural constitution, nature. स्वभावोक्तिः f (In *rhet.*) The figure of speech consisting in the description of such actions and characteristics of an object (such as a child) as are peculiar to it and are not easily perceived by all. स्वभाववादः m. The doctrine that the universe was produced and is sustained by the natural and necessary action of substances according to their inherent properties (and not by the agency of a Supereme Being). —भूः m 1 An epithet of Brahman (m). -2 Of Siva. -3 Of Vishnu. -योनि a. Related on the mother's side (-निः m., f.) Own womb, one's own place of birth. (-f.) A sister or near female relative. —रसः m. 1 Natural taste. -2 Proper taste or sentiment in composition. -3 A kind of astringent juice. -4 The residue of oily substances (ground on a stone) —राज् m. 1 The Supreme Being. -2 One of the seven rays of the sun. —रूप a. 1 Similar, like. -2 Handsome, pleasing, lovely.-3 Learned, wise. (-पं n.) 1 One's own form or shape; natural state or condition. -2 Natural character or form. -3 Nature.-4 Peculiar aim.-5 Sort; species. स्वरूपासिद्धिः f. One of the three forms of fallacy called असिद्ध.

—लक्षणं *n.* A peculiar characteristic or property. -वश *a.* 1 Self-controlled. -2 Independent. -वासिनी *f.* A woman whether married or unmarried who continues to live after maturity in her father's house.-संस्था *f.* 1 Self-abiding -2 Self-possession. -3 Absorption in one's own self.-स्थ *a* 1 Self-abiding. -2 Self-dependent, confident, firm, resolute. -3 Independent.-4 Doing well, in health, comfortable. -5 Contented, happy. (-स्थं *ind*) At ease, comfortably, composedly. —हस्तः *m.* One's own hand or handwriting, an autograph. -हस्तिका *f.* An axe.- हित *a.* Beneficial to oneself (-तं *n.*) One's own good or advantage, one's own welfare.

स्वक *a.* (*f.*-का) One's own, own.

स्वकीय *a* (*f.* -या) 1 One's own, own. -2 Of one's own family. —या *f.* One's own wife.

स्वंग *m.* An embrace

स्वच्छ *a* (*f.* -च्छा) 1 Very clear or transparent, pure. -2 White. -3 Beautiful -4 Healthy. —च्छः *m.* A crystal.-च्छा *f.* White Dúrvâ grass. -च्छं *n.* 1 A pearl. -2 Pure chalk. -Comp. —पत्रं *n.* Talc. —मणिः *m.* A crystal.

स्वंज् 1 A (स्वजते, the स being changed to ष after prepositions ending in इ or उ) 1 To embrace, clasp. -2 To twist round.

स्वंजनं *n.* The act of embracing, an embrace.

स्वतस् *ind.* 1 Of oneself, by oneself (used reflexively).-2 From oneself. -Comp —प्रमाण, -सिद्ध *a.* Self-evident, self-proved.

स्वत्वं *n.*1 Self-existence.-2 Ownership, proprietory right

स्वद् I. 1 A (स्वदते, स्वादित) 1 To be liked, be pleasant to the taste (with dat. of person).-2 To taste, relish, eat. -3 To please. -4 To sweeten.

स्वद् 10 U or *Caus.* (स्वादयति,-ते 1 To cause to taste or eat. -2 To taste. -3 To sweeten.

स्वदनं *n.* Tasting, eating

स्वदित *p p.* (*f.* -ता) Tasted, eaten. —तं *n.* An exclamation meaning 'may it be well tasted or relished', uttered at a Srâddha ceremony after the presentation of rice-balls or oblations of food to the Manes.

स्वधा *f.* 1 One's own nature or determination. -2 One's own will or pleasure. -3 The oblation of food offered to the Pitris or Manes of deceased ancestors -4 The food offered to the Manes personified. -5 Food or oblation in general -6 One's own portion or share.-7 A Sráddha or funeral ceremony.-8 N. of Mâyâ or illusion. —*ind.* An exclamation uttered on offering an oblation to the Manes with dat) *e.g.* पितृभ्यः स्वधा. -Comp —कारः *m.* The exclamation Svadhá. -निनयनं *n.* A fomula or sacred text used in making the oblations to the Pitris.-प्रियः *m* 1 Agni or fire. -2 Black sesamum.-भुज् *m.* 1 A deceased or deified ancestor. -2 A God. deity.

स्वधिति *m*, *f*, स्वधिती *f.* An axe

स्वन् 1 P. (स्वनति) 1 To make a noise. -2 To hum (as a bee) -3 To sing.

Caus. (स्वनयति,-ते) 1 To cause to resound. -1 To sound.-3 To adorn (स्वानयति in this sense).

स्वनः *m.* Sound, noise. -Comp. —उत्साहः *m* A rhinoceros.

स्वनिः *m.* Sound, noise.

स्वानिकः *m.* One who claps his hands.

स्वनित *a.* (*f.*–ता) Sounded, sounding, making a noise. –तं *n.* 1 The noise of thunder, thunder-clap. –2 Noise, sound (in general).

स्वप् 2 P. (स्वपिति, सुप्त) 1 To sleep, fall asleep, go to sleep. –2 To repose, rest. –3 To be absorbed in. With अव–, प्र– or सम्– To sleep.

स्वपनं *n.* Sleeping, dreaming, sleep.

स्वप्नः *m.* 1 Sleeping, sleep. –2 A dream, dreaming. –3 Indolence, sleepiness. –Comp. – उपम *a.* 1 Resembling a dream. –2 Unreal or illusory (like a dream). – कर, –कृत, *a* Soporific, narcotic –दोषः *m.* Involuntary seminal discharge. –धीगम्य *a.* Perceptible by the intellect only when it is in a state of sleep-like abstraction. –प्रपंचः *m.* The illusion of sleep; the world appearing in a dream. –विचारः *m.* Interpretation of dreams. –शील *a.* Sleepy, drowsy. –सृष्टिः *f.* The creation of dreams or illusions in sleep.

स्वप्नज् *a.* Sleepy, sleeping, drowsy.

स्वयम् *ind.* 1 Oneself, in one's own person (used reflexively and applicable to all persons, such as myself, ourselves, thyself himself &c. &c. and sometimes used with other pronouns for the sake of emphasis). –2 Spontaneously, of one's own accord, with out trouble or exertion.–Comp –उक्तिः *f.*1 Voluntary declaration. –2 Information, deposition (in law). –ग्रह *m.* Taking for oneself (without leave). –ग्राहः *m.* Self-choice, self-election. –जात *a.* Self-born. –दत्त *a.* Self-given. (–त्तः *m.*) A boy who has given himself to be adopted (by his adoptive parents). –भुः *m.* N of Brahman (*m.*). –भुवः *m.* The first Manu. –2 N. of Brahman (*m.*).–3 Of Siva. –भूः *a.* Self-existent. (–भूः *m.*) 1 N. of Brahman (*m.*). –2 Of Vishnu. –3 Of Siva. –4 Of *Kála* or time personified. –5 Of Kámadeva. –6 A Jain defied saint. –7 The female breast. –8 The Supreme Being –वरः *m.* Self-choice, self-election (of a husband by the bride herself). –वरा *f.* A maiden who chooses her own husband.

स्वर् 10 U. (स्वरयति,–ते) To find fault, blame, censure.

स्वर् *ind* 1 Heaven, paradise; as in स्वर्लोक, स्वर्वेश्या, स्वर्भानुः, &c. –2 The heaven of Indra and the temporary abode of the virtuous after death. –3 The sky, ether. –4 The space above the sun or between the sun and polar star. –5 The third of the three Vyáhritis, pronounced by every Bráhmana in his daily prayers. –6 Radiance, splendour. –7 Water. –Comp. –आपगा –गंगा *f.* 1 The celestial Ganges.–2The galaxy or milky way. –गतिः *f*, –गमनं *n.* 1 Going to heaven, future felicity. –2 Death. गिरिः *m.* Sumeru. –तरुः (स्वस्तरुः) *m* A tree of paradise. –ईशः *m.* 1 An epithet of Indra. –2 Of *Agni.* –3 Of *Soma.* –नदी (forming स्वर्णदी) *f.* The celestial Ganges. –भानवः *m.* A kind of precious stone. –भानुः *m.* N. of Ráhu. –मध्यं *n.* The central point of the sky, the zenith, –लोकः *m.* The celestial world, heaven.–वधूः *f.* An *apsaras.* –वापी *f* The Ganges. –वेश्या *f* An *apsaras.* –वैद्यौ *m. dual* Epithet of the two Asvins. –सिंधुः *f.* The celestial Ganges.

स्वरः *m.* 1 Sound, noise. –2 Voice. –3 A note of the musical scale or gamut, a tone, tune (these are seven) -4 The number seven. -5 A vowel. 6 An accent (these are three, उदात्त, अनुदात्त, and स्वरित). -7 Air breathed through the nostrils. -3 Snoring. —रा *f*. N. of the chief wife of Brahman (*m*). -Comp. —अंशः *m*. A half or quarter tone (in music). —अंतरं *n*. The interval between two vowels, a hiatus. —उदय *a*. Followed by a vowel उपध *a*. Preceded by a vowel. —ग्रामः *m*. The musical scale, gamut —पत्तनं *n* N. of the Sâma-veda. बद्ध *a*. Composed in musical measure. —भक्तिः *f*. A vowel-sound phonetially inserted in the pronunciation of र् or ल् when these letters are followed by a sibilant or any single consonant; (*e. g* वर्ष pronounced as वारष) -भंगः *m*. 1 Indistinctress of utterance, broken articulation. -2 Hoarseness or cracking of voice. —मंडलिका *f* A kind of lute (वीणा). —लासिका *f*. A flute, pipe.—शून्य *a*. Without musical notes, unmelodious. —संयोगः *m*. 1 The junction of vowels. -2 The union of notes of sounds *i. e.* voice. —संक्रमः *m*. 1 A transition or succession of notes. -2 The gamut. —संधिः *m*. The coalition of vowels. -सामन *m. pl*. Epithets of particular days in a sacrificial session

स्वरवत् *a*. (*f* ती) 1 Having sound; sonorous. -2 Having a voice. -3 Vocal. -4 Having an accent.

स्वरित *a*. (*f*. -ता) 1 Sounded. -2 Sounded as a note, pitched. -3 Articulated. -4 Circumflexed. -5 Accented. तः *m*. The third or mixed tone lying between high and low.

स्वरुः *m* 1 Sunshine. -2 A part of a sacrificial post. -3 A sacrifice. -4 A thunder-bolt. -5 An arrow.

स्वरुस *m*. A thunderbolt.

स्वर्गः *m* Heaven, Indra's paradise. -Comp. —ओकस् *m*. A God, deity. —काम *a*. Desirous of heaven. —गिरिः *m* The mountain *Sumeru*. —पतिः, -भर्तृ *m* Indra. —लोकः *m*. 1 The celestial region. -2 Paradise.—वधूः, -स्त्री *f*. A nymph, an *apsaras*.

स्वर्गिन् -*m*. 1 A God, deity, an immortal -2 A dead or deceased man.

स्वर्गीय *a*. (*f*. -या), स्वर्ग्य *a*. (*f* —र्ग्या) 1 Heavenly, divine. -2 Leading to heaven.

स्वर्ण *n*. 1 Gold. -2 A golden coin. -Comp. —अरिः *m*. Sulphur. —कायः *m* N. of Garuda. —कारः, कृत् *m*. A goldsmith —गैरिकं *n* A kind of red chalk. —चूडः *m*. 1 The blue jay. -2 A cock. —जं *n*. Tin. —दीधितिः *m*. Fire. —पक्षः *m* N of Garuda.—पद्मा *f*. The celestial Ganges.- पुष्पः *m* The *Champaka* tree. —बंधः *m* A deposit of gold. —भृंगारः *m* A golden vase. —माक्षिकं *n*. A kind of mineral substance.-वणिज् *m* 1 A gold-merchant. -2 A money-changer. —वर्णा *f*. Turmeric. [be pleasing.

स्वर्द् 1 A. (स्वर्दते) To taste. -2 To

स्वल् 1 P. (स्वलति) To go, move.

स्वल्प *a*. (*f* —ल्पा); (compar. स्वल्पीयस्, superl. स्वल्पिष्ठ) 1 Very small or little, minute, insignificant.-2 Brief, short. -3 Very few. -Comp. —कंकः *m*. A species of heron. —केशरिन् *m*. The Kovidâra tree. —विषयः *m*. 1 An insignificant matter. -2 A small part. [small or few.

स्वल्पक *a*. (*f*.—का) Very little, very

स्वाल्पिष्ठ *a*. (*f*. - ष्ठा) Smallest, least, most minute (superl. of स्वल्प).

स्वल्पीयस् *a*. (*f*. —सी) Much less, smaller, more minute (compar. of स्वल्प).

स्वशुर: *m*. A father-in-law.

स्वसृ *f*. A sister. [or pleasure.

स्वसृत *a*. Going or moving at will

स्वस्क् I A (स्वस्कते) To go, to move,

स्वस्ति *ind*. A particle meaning ' may it be well with (one) ', ' may it fare well with (you, him &c., with the dative) ' ' hail ', ' adieu ' (with dat.). It is also used in expressing one's approbation It is also used at the beginning of letters. -Comp. अयनं *n* I A means of securing prosperity. -2 The averting of evil by the recitation of *mantars* or performance of expiatory rites.-3 The benediction of a Brâhmana after presentation of offerings. —द:, भाव: *m*. An epithet of Siva. – मुख: *m*. 1 A letter. -2 A Brâhmana. -3 A bard, panegyrist. —वाचनं, -वाचनकं, —वाचनिकं *n* I A religious rite preparatory to a sacrifice or any religious or solemn observance. -2 A present of sweetmeats &c. offered to a Brâhmana on auspicious or festive occasions when he pronounces blessings by reciting holy verses.-3 A congratulatory present of flowers &c. to any one attended with good wishes and blessings. —वाच्यं *n*. Congratulation, invoking blessings.

स्वस्तिक: *m*. I A kind of mystical mark on persons or things denoting good luck. -2 A lucky object. -3 The meeting of four roads. -4 The crossing of the arms, making a sign like the cross -5 A palace of a particular form. -6 A particular symbol made with ground rice and shaped like a triangle. -7 A kind of cake. -8 A voluptuary. -9 Garlic. —क: *m*., -कं *n*. I A mansion or temple of a particular form with a terrace in front. -2 A particular mode of sitting practised by *Yogins*. [happy, safe.

स्वस्तिमत् *a*. (*f*. —ती) Doing well,

स्वस्त्रीय: स्वस्रेय: *m*. A sister's son.

स्वस्रीया, स्वस्रयी *f*. A sister's daughter.

स्वागतं *n*. Welcome, happy arrival (Used with the dative case).

स्वाकिक: *m*. A drummer.

स्वाच्छंद्यं *n*. The power of following one's own will or fancy independence. (स्वाच्छंद्येन, स्वाच्छंद्यतस् 'Wilfully' voluntarily).

स्वातंत्र्यं *n*. Freedom of will, independence. -2 (In phil.) Free will.

स्वाति:, स्वाती *f*. I One of the wives of the sun. -2 A sword. -3 An auspicious constellation. -4 The star *Arcturus*, considered as forming the fifteenth lunar asterism.-Comp. —योग· *m*. Conjunction with Svâti

स्वाद् See स्वद्.

स्वाद: *m*., स्वादनं *n*. Taste, flavour.-2 Tasting, eating, drinking. -3 Relishing enjoyment. -4 Sweetening.

स्वादिमन् *m*. Savouriness, sweetness.

स्वादिष्ठ *a*. (*f*. -ष्ठा) Very sweet, sweetest (superl. of स्वादु).

स्वादीयस् *a*. (*f*. —सी) Sweeter, very sweet (compar. of स्वादु).

स्वादु *a*. (*f* -दु or -द्वी compar· स्वादीयस् superl. स्वादिष्ठ). I Sweet, pleasant to the taste, savoury, tasteful. -2 Argeeable, lovely, charming. —*m*. I Sweet flavour, sweetness of taste, relish. -2 Treacle, molasses. -*n*. Sweetness, relish, taste. —दु: *f*. A grape. -Comp —अन्नं *n* Sweet or choice food, dainties, delicacies. -कारक: *m*. I The pomegranate tree. —खंड: *m*. I A piece of any sweet substance. -2 Molasses. —धन्वन् *m*. N. of the God of love. -फलं *n.* The jujube. (-ला *f.*) The jujube tree. -मूलं *n.* A carrot. -रसा *f.* 1 The fruit of the hog-plum. -2 The Satávarí plant. -3 The root काकोली. -4 Spirituous liquor. -5 A grape. -शुद्धं *n.* 1 Rock-salt. -2 Marine-salt.

स्वाद्वी *f.* Vine, grape.

स्वानः *m.* Sound noise.

स्वापः *m.* 1 Sleep, sleeping. -2 Dreaming, dream. 3 Sleepiness -4 Paralysis, insensibility. -5 Temporary or partial loss of sensation from pressure on a nerve, numbness.

स्वापतेयं *n.* Wealth, property.

स्वापदः *m.* A wild beast See श्वापद

स्वाभाविक *a.* (*f.* -की) Belonging to one's own nature, inherent, peculiar, natural. -काः *m. pl.* A sect of Buddhists who accounded for all things by the laws of nature.

स्वाभाव्यं *n.* Naturalness, natural state or character.

स्वामिन् *a.* (*f.* -नी) Possessing proprietory rights. -*m.* 1 A proprietor, an owner. -2 A lord, master. -4 A sovereign, king, monarch -5 A husband, -6 A spiritual preceptor. -7 A learned Bráhmana, an ascetic or religious man of the highest order (in this sense usually added to proper names). -8 An epithet of Kártikeya -9 Of Vishnu. -10 Of Siva. -11 Of the sage Vâtsyàyana.-12 Of Garuda.-Comp. -उपकारकः *m.* A horse. -जंघिन *m.* N. of Parasuráma. -पालौ *m dual* The owner and the keeper (of cattle). -भावः *m.* The state of a lord or owner, ownership. -वात्सल्यं *n.* Affection for the husband or lord. -सद्भावः *m.* 1 Existence of a master or owner. -2 Amiability of a master or lord. -सेवा *f* 1 The service of a master. -2 Respect for a husband.

स्वामिनी *f.* A mistress, proprietress

स्वाम्यं *n.* 1 Mastership, lordship ownership. -2 Right or title to property. -3 Rule, dominion.

स्वायंभुव *a.* (*f.* -वी) 1 Relating to Brâhman (*m*). 2 Descended from Brâhman (*m.*). -वः *m* An epithet of the first Manu (as he was a son of Brahman (*m.*).

स्वारसिक *a.* (*f.* -की) Possessing inherent flavour or sweetness (said of a poetical composition).

स्वारस्यं *n.* 1 Possessing natural flavour or excellence. -2 Fitness (of a word).

स्वाराज् *m.* An epithet of Indra.

स्वाराज्यं *n.* 1 The dominion of heaven, Indra's heaven. -2 Indentification with the self-refulgent (Brahman) (*n.*).

स्वारोचिषः, स्वारोचिस् *m.* N. of the second Manu.

स्वालक्षण्यं *n.* Peculiar characteristics natural disposition.

स्वाल्प *a.* (*f.*-ल्पी) 1 Little, small. -2 Few. -ल्पं *n.* 1 Littleness, smallness -2 Smallness of number.

स्वास्थ्यं *n.* 1 Self reliance, self-dependence, resoluteness, firmness. -2 Sound state, health. -3 Prosperity, well being, comfortableness. -4 Complacency, satisfaction.

स्वाहा *f.* 1 An oblation or offering made to all Gods indiscriminately -2 N. of the wife of *Agni*. -*ind.* An exclamation used in offering oblations to the Gods (with dat.) *e.g.* अग्नये स्वाहा &c. -Comp. -कारः *m.* Utterance of the exclamation Sváhá. -पतिः, -प्रियः *m.* *Agni* or fire. -भुज्

m A God, deity.

स्विद् *ind.* A particle of interrogation or inquiry, implying 'doubt', or 'surprise', and translatable by 'what', 'hallo', 'can it be that'. It is added to interrogative pronouns in this sense or to give them an indefinite sense. It is sometimes used disjunctively in the sense of 'either', 'or', with उ, उत, वा &c. and आहो also.

स्विद् 4 P. (स्विद्यति, स्विदित or स्विन्न) To sweat, perspire.

स्विद् 1 A. (स्वेदते, स्विन्न or स्वेदित) 1 To be anointed. 2 To be greasy or unctuous. -3 To be disturbed.

स्विन्न *p. p.* (*f.* -न्ना) 1 Perspiring, covered with sweat. -2 Steeped. -3 Cooked, boiled.

स्वीकरणं *n.*, स्वीकारः *m.*, स्वीकृतिः *f.* 1 Taking, accepting. -2 Assenting, promising; an assent, a promise. -3 Wedding, marriage.

स्वीय *a.* (*f.* -या) Own, one's own.

स्वृ 1 P. (स्वरति; *desid.* सिस्वरिषति, सुस्वूर्षति) 1 To sound, recite. -2 To Praise. -3 To pain or be pained. -4 To go. With अभि-, प्र- To sound. सं- To pain (Atm.).

स्वॄ 9 P. (स्वृणाति) To hurt, kill.

स्वेक् 1 A. (स्वेकते) To go.

स्वेदः *m.* 1 Sweat, perspiration. -2 Heat, warmth. -3 Vapour. -Comp. —उदं, —उदकं, —जलं *n.* Perspiration. —चूषकः *m* A cooling breeze (sucking up sweat). —ज *a.* Generated by warm vapour or sweat (said of insects). (-जः *m.*) One of the four divisions of the animal creation according to Hindu philosophers.

स्वेदनं *n.* 1 Perspiration, sweat. -2 Causing to sweat -3 A diaphoretic.

स्वेदनिका *f.* 1 A boiler, sauce-pan. 2 Kitchen.

स्वेदनी *f.* A frying-pan, sauce-pan.

स्वैर *a.* (*f.* -री) 1 Following one's own will or fancy, self-willed. -2 Free, confidential. -3 Slow, gentle. -4 Dull, lazy. -5 Voluntary, optional. -रं *n.* Wilfulness, wantonness.—रं *ind.* 1 At will or pleasure, as one likes. -2 Of one's own accord, spontaneously. -3 Slowly, gently, mildly. -4 Lowly, in an under-tone (opp. स्पष्ट).

स्वैरिणी *f.* A loose or unchaste woman, an adulteress.

स्वैरिन् *a.* (*f.* —णी) Self-willed, unrestrained, uncontrolled.

स्वैरंध्री *f.* See सैरंध्री.

स्वोरसः The residue or sediment of oily substances ground with a stone.

स्वोवशीयं *n.* Happiness, prosperity (especially as regards future life).

ह.

ह *ind.* An emphatic particle used to lay stress on the preceding word and translatable by 'verily', 'indeed', 'certainly,' &c. It is often used expletively without any particular signification. It is sometimes used as a vocative particle and rarely to show disdain or laughter.

हंसः *m.* 1 A swan, goose, duck, flamingo. -2 The Supreme Soul, Brahman (*n.*). -3 The individual soul (जीवात्मन्) -4 One of the vital airs. -5 The sun. -6 Siva. -7 Vishnu. -8 Kámadeva. -9 An unambitious monarch.-10 An ascetic of a particular order. -11 A spiritual preceptor. -12 One free from malice. -13 A mountain. -14 Envy, malice. -15 A buffalo. -Comp. —आधिरूढा *f.* An epithet of Sarasvatî. —आभिख्यं *n.* Silver. —आरूढ: *m.* N. of Brahman (*m.*). —कांता *f.* A female goose.-कूटः *m.* 1 N. of one of the peaks of the Himâlaya -2 The hump on the shoulder of an ox; (f r असकूट). —गद्गदा *f.* A sweetly speaking woman. —तूलः *m*, —तूलं *n.* The soft feathers or down of a goose. —दाहनं *n.* Aloe-wood. —नादिनी *f.* A woman having a slender waist, large hips, the gait of an elephant and the voice of a cuckoo. —युवन् *m.* A young goose or swan. —रथः, —वाहनः *m.* Epithets of Brahman (*m.*). -राजः *m.* A king of geese. -लोमशं *n.* Green sulphate of iron —लोहकं *n.* Brass.

हंसकः *m.* 1 A goose, flamingo. -2 An ornament for the ankles. (See हंस above for other senses).

हंसिका, हंसी *f.* A female goose.

हंहो *ind.* 1 A vocative particle corresponding to, 'ho,' 'hallo' -2 -2 A particle expressing haughtiness or contempt. -3 A particle of interrogation. (In dramas it is mostly used as a form of address by characters of the middling classes.).

हक्कः *m.* The calling of elephants.

हंजा, हंजे *ind.* A vocative particle used in addressing a female attendant or maid servant. [bright.

हट्ट् 1 P. (हटति, हटित) To shine. be

हट्टः *m* A market, a fair. -Comp -विलासिनी *f* 1 A wanton woman, prostitute. -2 A sort of perfume.-3 Turmeric.

हट्टी *f.* A small market or fair.

हठः *m.* 1 Violence, force. -2 Oppression, rapine. (हठेन and हठात् are used adverbially in the sense of 'forcibly', 'suddenly').-Comp. -योगः *m.* A particular mode of Yoga or practising abstract meditation. —विद्या *f.* The science of forced meditation. [lowest caste.

हाडि (-ड्डि-) कः *m.* A man of the

हड्डं *n.* A bone.-Comp.-जं *n.* Marrow.

हंडा *ind* A vocative particle used in addressing a female of an inferior rank, or by equals of the lowest caste in addressing each other. -*f.* A large earthen vessel.

हंडिका, हंडी *f.* An earthen pot.

हंडे *ind.* See हंडा *ind.*

हत *p. p* (*f.* —ता) 1 Killed. -2 Struck, injured -3 Perished. -4 Bereft of.-5 Disappointed, frustrated. -6 Impeded. -7 Destroyed. It is often used as the first member of comp. in the sense of 'wretched', 'miserable', 'accursed', 'worthless' *e. g.* हतहृदयं, हतजीवितं, हतविधिः &c. -तं *n.* Killing, striking. -Comp. — आश *a.* 1 Hopeless, desponding. -2 Weak, powerless. -3 Merciless. -4 Barren, -5 Vile, wretched, accursed. — कंटक *a.* 1 Freed from thorns (*lit.*).-2 Freed from foes (*fig.*).-दैव *a.* Ill-fated, luckless -प्रभाव,- वीर्य *a.* Bereft of power or vigour. -बुद्धि *a* Deprived of sense, senseless. —भाग, -भाग्य *a.* Ill-fated, unfortunate. मूर्खः *m.* A dolt, blockhead. —लक्षण *a.* Devoid of auspicious marks; unlucky. —श्री, -संपद् *a.* Impoverished. -साध्वस *a.* Freed from fear.

हतक *a.* (*f.* -का) Miserable, ill-bred, wretched, vile; (mostly at the end of comp.). —कः *m.* A low person, coward.

हतिः *f.* 1 Killing, destruction. -2 Striking, wounding. -3 A blow, stroke. -4 Loss, failure. -5 A defect. -6 Multiplication. (In *math.*)

हत्नुः *m.* 1 A weapon.-2 A disease or sickness.

हत्या *f.* Killing, slaying, (particularly criminal killing; as in भ्रूणहत्या, गोहत्या, ब्राह्मणहत्या).

हथः *m.* 1 A stroke, blow. -2 Killing. -3 Death. -4 A man who is sad or depressed.

हद् 1 A. (हदते, हन्न) To void excrement, evacuate or discharge feces. -*Desid.* (जिहत्सते). [tion of ordure.

हदनं *n.* Voiding excrement, evacua-

हन् 2 P. (हंति, हंतुं, हत; *pass.* हन्यते, *caus.* घातयति,-ते; *desid.* जिघांसति) 1 To kill, slay, strike down.-2 To strike, beat. -3 To injure, afflict, torment.-4 To abandon -5 To remove, take away. -6 To conquer, defeat, overcome. -7 To hinder, obstruct. -8 To mar, spoil. -9 To raise. -10 To multiply (in math.). -11 To go (rarely used in classical literature in this sense). With अंतर्- To strike in the middle. अप— 1 To destroy, ward off, repel. -2 To lessen. अभि— 1 To strike, to beat. -2 To beat or blow (a musical instrument). -3 To injure, to hurt. अव— 1 To strike, to hit. -2 To thresh, to winnow (as corn). आ— (*Atm.*) 1 To strike at, to hit, to beat. -2 To beat (as a drum). उत्— 1 To raise up, elevate. -2 To become haughty or vain. उप— 1 To kill, destroy. -2 To vex, injure, disturb. नि- 1 To strike. -2 To beat (as a drum). -3 To kill, destroy. -4 To frustrate, to render void. -5 To neglect, disregard. -6 To cure (as a disease). परा— 1 To strike.-2 To strike down or back. -3 To assail. -4 To overthrow, repel, drive back. प्र— 1 To kill. -2 To beat (as a drum). -3 To strike, beat. प्रति— 1 To strike back, strike in return, ward off, repel. -2 To oppose, resist. -3 To remove. वि— 1 To strike, to strike violently. -2 To oppose, impede, resist.-3 To reject, refuse, deny. -4 To kill, destroy utterly. सम्— 1 To join or unite closely. -2 To collect, accumulate. -3 To destroy, to kill. -4 To contract, diminish.

हन *a.* Killing, slaying, (at the end of comp.) as in वृत्रहन्, पितृहन मातृहन्, ब्रह्महन् &c.

हनः *m.* Killing, slaying.

हननं *n* 1 Killing, striking. -2 Hurting, injuring.-3 Multiplication.

हनुः, हनूः *m.*, *f.* The chin. —नुः *f.* 1 That which injures life. -2 A weapon. -3 A sickness. -4 Death.-5 A kind of drug.-6 A wanton woman, prostitute. -Comp. -ग्रहः *m.* Locked jaw. —मूलं *n.* The root of the jaw.

हनु (-नू-) मत *m.* N. of a powerful monkey-chief.

हनूषः *m.* A demon.

हंत *ind.* A particle implying 1 Joy, surprise, flurry (oh!). -2 Compassion, pity. -3 Grief (oh!, alas!).-4 Good luck or benediction. -5 It is often used as an inceptive particle. -Comp. —उक्तिः *f.* Uttering the word 'alas!', tenderness, compassion. — कारः *m.* 1 The exclamation 'hanta'. -2 An offering to be presented to a guest.

हंतुः *m.* 1 Killing, death. -2 A bull.

हंतृ *a.* (*f.* -त्री) 1 One who strikes or kills, striking. -2 One who destroys or counteracts. -*m.* 1 A slayer, killer. -2 A thief, robber.

हन्नं *n.* Excrement, ordure.

हम् *ind.* An exclamation expressive of anger, courtesy, or respect.

हंबा, हंभा *f.* The lowing of cattle. -Comp. —रवः *m.* The lowing of cattle.

हय् 1 P. (हयति, हयित) 1 To go. -2 [To be weary.

हयः *m.* 1 A horse.-2 A man of a particular type of body and horse-like in strength. -3 The number 'seven'. -Comp. -आयुर्वेदः *m.* The veterinary science.-आरूढः *m* A horseman-rider. —आरोहः *m* 1 A rider -2 Riding. —इष्टः *m.* Barley. —कोविद *a.* Skilled in the science of horses, their management, training &c. —ज्ञः *m.* A horse-dealer, groom, jockey. -द्विषत् *m.* The buffalo. —प्रियः *m.* Barley. —प्रिया *f.* The *Kharjuri* tree. —मारः, —मारक *m.* The fragrant oleander. —मेधः *m.* A horse-sacrifice. —वाहनः *m.* An epithet of Kubera. —शाला *f.* The stable for horses. —शास्त्रं *n.* The art or science of training and managing horses. —संग्रहणं *n.* The restraining or curbing of horses.

हयंकषः *m.* 1 A driver, charioteer. -2 N. of Mátali, the charioteer of Indra.

हयी *f.* A female horse, mare.

हर *a.* (*f.* -रा, -री) 1 Taking away, removing, depriving one of. -2 bringing, conveying, carrying. -3 Seizing, grasping. -4 Attracting, captivating. -5 Entitled to. -6 Occupying. -7 Dividing.-रः *m.* 1 Siva. -2 N. of Agni or fire. -3 An ass. -4 A divisor. -5 The denominator of a fraction.-6 The act of seizing, taking.-7 A seizer, ravisher.-Comp. —गौरी *f* One of the forms of Siva and Párvatî conjoined (अर्धनारीनटेश्वर). -चूडामणिः *m.* 'Siva's crest-gem' *i. e.* the moon. —तेजस् *n.* Quick-silver. -नेत्रं *n.* 1 Siva's eye.-2 The number 'three'. -बीजं *n.* Quick-silver.- शेखरा *f.* The Ganges. —सूनुः *m.* Skanda.

हरकः *m.* 1 A stealer, thief. -2 A rogue. -3 A divisor. -4 N. of Siva.

हरणं *n.* 1 Seizing, taking.-2 Carrying away, stealing. -3 Depriving of, destroying. -4 Dividing. -5 A gift to a student. -6 The arm.

हरि *a.* 1 Green, greenish yellow.-2 Tawny, reddish brown., yellow. -3 -रिः *m.* 1 N. of vishnu.-2 N. of Indra. -3 N. of Siva. -4 N. of Brahman (*m.*). -5 N. of Yama. -6 The sun. -7 The moon. -8 A man. -9 A ray of light. -10 Fire. -11 Wind. -12 A lion. -13 A horse. -14 A horse of Indra. -15 An ape, a monkey. -16 The cuckoo. -17 A parrot. -18 A frog. -19 A snake.-20 The tawny green or yellow colour. -21 A peacock. -22 N. of the poet Bhartrihari. -Comp. —अक्षः *m.* 1 A lion. -2 N. of Kubera -3 Of Siva. -अश्वः *m.* 1 Indra. -2 Siva. —कांत *a.* Dear to Indra.-2 Beautiful as a lion. -गंधं *n.* A kind of sandal. —चंदनः *m.*, -नं *n.* 1 A kind of yellow sandal (the wood or tree). -2 One of the five trees of paradise. (-नं *n.*) 1 Moonlight. -2 Saffron. -3 The filament of a lotus. —तालः *m.* A kind of yellow-coloured pigeon. (-लं *n.*) Yellow orpiment. (-ली *f.*) 1 The Dúrvá grass. -2 A streak or line in the sky. -3 =हरितालिका (1). —तालकः *m.* A kind of yellow-coloured pigeon. (-कं *n.*) 1 Yellow orpiment. -2 A theatrical decoration —तालिका *f.* 1 The fourth day of the bright half of Bhâdrapada.-2 The Dúrvâ plant. —तुरंगमः *m.* N. of Indra. —दासः *m.* A worshipper or votary of Vishnu. —दिनं *n*. A particular day sacred to Vishnu. —देवः *m*. The asterism Sravana.—द्वारं *n*. N. of a celebrated Tîrtha or sacred bathing place. -नेत्रं *n*. 1 The eye of Vishnu. -2 The white lotus. —नेत्रः *m*. An owl. -प्रियः *m*. 1 The *Kadamba* tree.-2 A conch-shell. -3 A fool. -4 A madman. -5 Siva. (-यं *n*.) The root Usîra. -2 A sort of sandal. —प्रिया *f*. 1 Lakshmî. -2 The sacred basil. -3 The earth. -4 The twelfth day of a lunar fortnight. —भक्तः *m*. A worshipper of Vishnu. —भुज् *m*. A snake. —मंथः, -मंथकः *m*. A chick-pea. —लोचनः *m*. A crab. -2 An owl. —वर्षः *m*. N. of one of the nine divisions of Jambudvîpa.—वल्लभा *f*. 1 Lakshmî. -2 The sacred basil. —वासरः *m*. Vishnu's day *i.e.* the eleventh day of a lunar fortnight (एकादशी). —वाहनः *m*. 1 Garuda. -2 Indra.-शरः *m*. An epithet of Siva (Vishnu having served Siva as the shaft which burnt down 'the three cities' or cities of the demon Tripura).-सखः *m*. A *Gandharva*. -संकीर्तनं *n* Repeating the name of Vishnu. —सुतः, -सूनुः *m*. N. of Arjuna. —हयः *m*. 1 Indra. -2 The sun. -3 N. of Skanda. -4 Of Ganesa. —हरः *m*. A particular form of deity consisting of Vishnu and Siva conjoined.-हेतिः *f*. 1 The rain-bow. -2 The discus of Vishnu.-हेतिः,-हूतिः *m*. The ruddy goose.

हरिकः *m*. 1 A horse of a yellowish or tawny colour. -2 A thief. -3 A gambler.

हरिण *a* (*f*. -णी) 1 Pale, whitish. -2 Reddish or yellowish white.-णः *m*. 1 A deer, an antelope. -2 The white colour. -3 A goose. -4 The sun. -5 Vishnu. -6 Siva. -Comp. —अक्ष *a* Deer-eyed, fawn-eyed. (क्षः *m*.) N. of Siva. (-क्षी *f*.) 'Deer eyed', a woman with beautiful eyes. -अंकः *m*. 1 The moon. -2 Camphor.-कलंकः, धामन् *m*. The moon. -नयन, -नेत्र, -लोचन *a*. Deer-eyed, fawn-eyed. —नर्तक *m*. A Kinnara. —हृदय *a*. Deer-hearted. *i. e.* timid.

हरिणकः *m* A deer.

हरिणी *f*. 1 A female deer, doe. -2 One of the four classes of women (also called चित्रिणी). -3 Yellow jasmine. -4 A good golden image. -5 N of a metre. -6 The green colour. -7 Turmeric. -8 Madder. -Comp. —दृश् *a*. Deer-eyed. (-*f*.) A deer-eyed woman.

हरित् *a*. 1 Green, greenish. -2 Yellow, yellowish.-3 Greenish-yellow. -*m*. 1 The green or yellow colour. -2 A horse of the sun. -3 A bay horse. -4 A swift horse. -5 A lion. -6 The sun -7 Vishnu. -8 The kidney bean. -*m*., *n*. Grass.-*f*. 1 A quarter, region. -2 A quarter or point of the compass. -3 Turmeric. -Comp.—अश्वः *m*. 1 The sun. -2 The *arka* plant. —गर्भः *m*. Green or yellowish Kusa grass with broad leaves. —मणिः (हरिन्मणिः) *m*. An emerald.

हरित *a*. (*f*. हरिता or हरिणी) 1 Of a green colour. -2 Tawny. -3 Dark-blue. —तः *m*. 1 The green colour. -2 A lion. -3 A kind of grass. -Comp. - अश्मन् *m*. 1 An emerald.-2 Blue vitriol. —छद *a*. Green-leaved.

हरितकं *n*. 1 A pot-herb. -2 Green grass.

हरिता *f*. 1 The Dúrvá grass.-2 Turmeric. -3 A brown-coloured grape.

हरिद्रा *f*. 1 Turmeric. -2 The root

of turmeric powdered. -Comp.-आभ *a.* Of a yellow colour. (—भः *m.*) 1 The yellow colour. -2 Zedoary. —गणपतिः, -गणेशः *m.* A particular form of the God Ganasa -राग, -रागक *a.* 1 Turmeric-coloured.-2 Unsteady in attachment or affection, fickle minded (as a lover). [-3 Time.

हरिमन् *m.* 1 Yellowness.-2 Paleness.

हरिश्वः *m.* A yellow-coloured horse.

हरिश्चंद्रः *m.* N. of a king of the solar dynasty. [tree.

हरीतकी *f.* The yellow myrobalan

हरेणुकः *m.* Pease, pulse.

हर्तृ *a.* (*f.* —र्त्री) One who takes away, seizes or robs. -*m.* 1 A thief, robber -2 The sun.

हर्मन *n.* Gaping, yawning.

हर्मित *p. p.* (*f.*—ता) 1 Gaped; yawned -2 Cast, thrown. -3 Burnt.

हर्म्यं *n.* 1 A palace, mansion. -2 An oven, a fire-place. -3 The infernal regions.

हर्षः *m.* 1 Joy, pleasure, satisfaction. -2 Bristling, erection (of the hair of the body). -3 Joy, considered as one of the 33 or 34 subordinate feelings. -Comp. —उत्कर्षः *m.* Excess of happiness or joy, ecstacy. —जड *a.* Dull or paralyzed with joy. -स्वनः *m.* A cry or shout of joy.

हर्षक *a.* (*f.* -र्षका or -र्षिका) Delighting, pleasing.

हर्षण (*f.* —णा or —णी) Causing delight, delightful, pleasant. —णः *m.* 1 N. of one of the five arrows of Kámadeva. -2 A morbid affection of the eyes. -3 A deity presiding over the funeral ceremonies. —णं *n.* Joy, delight, gladdening.

हर्षयित्नु *a.* Gladdening, delighting. -*n.* Gold. -त्नुः *m.* A son.

हर्षुलः *m.* 1 A deer. -2 A lover.

हल् 1 P. (हलति, हलित) To plough.

हलं *n.* A plough. -2 Deformity, ugliness. -Comp. —आयुधः *m.* An epithet of Balarâma. —धरः, -भृत *m.* 1 A plough-man.-2 N. of Balarama. -भूतिः,-भृतिः *f.* Ploughing, agriculture, husbandry. —हतिः *f.* 1 Striking or drawing along with a plough. -2 Ploughing.

हलहला *f.* Halloo, hallooing.

हला *f.* 1 A female friend. -2 The earth. -3 Water. -4 Spirituous liquor. -*ind.* A vocative particle used in addressing a female friends (only in theatrical language).

हलाहलः *m.*, —लं *n.* 1 A sort of deadly poison produced at the churning of the ocean.-2 A poison in general. (Written also हालहल and हालाहल).

हलिः *m* 1 A large plough. -2 A furrow. -3 Agriculture.

हलिन् *m.* 1 A plough-man, an agriculturist. -2 Balarâma. -Comp. —प्रियः *m.* The *Kadamba* tree. (-या *f.*) Spirituous liquor.

हलिनी *f.* A number of ploughs.

हलीनः *m.* The teak tree.

हलीषा *f.* The handle of a plough.

हल्य *a.* (*f.* —ल्या) 1 Arable, to be ploughed. -2 Ugly, deformed. -ल्यं *n.* 1 A ploughed field.-2 Deformity, ugliness.

हल्या *f.* A number of ploughs.

हल्लकं *n* The red lotus.

हल्लनं *n.* Rolling or tossing about (as in sleep).

हल्लीशं (-षं) *n.* 1 One of the 18 Uparúpakas or minor dramatic compositions. -2 A kind of circular dance.

हल्लीशकः *m.* Dancing in a ring.

हवः *m.* 1 An oblation, a sacrifice. -2 Invocation, prayer. -3 Calling a call.-4 Order, command.-5 Challenge.

हवनं *n.* 1 Offering an oblation with fire. -2 A sacrifice, an oblation. -3 Invocation. -4 Calling, summoning.-5 Challenging to fight.-Comp. -आयुस् *m.* Fire.

हवनीयं *n.* 1 Anything fit for an oblation. -2 Clarified butter or ghee.

हवित्री *f.* A hole made in the ground for holding the sacred fire.

हविष्मत *a. f.* —ती) Possessed of oblations.

हविष्यं *n.* 1 Anything fit for an oblation. -2 Clarified butter. -Comp. —अन्नं *n.* Food fit to be eaten during certain holidays or days of fast. —आशिन्, —भुज् *m.* Fire.

हविस् *n.* 1 An oblation or burnt offering in general. -2 Clarified butter. -Comp. -अशन. *m.* Fire.—गंधा (हविर्गंधा) *f.* The Samî tree.-गेहं(हविर्गेहं) *n.* A house in which sacrificial oblations are offered. —भुज् (हविर्भुज्) *m.* Fire.—यज्ञः (हविर्यज्ञः) *m.* A kind of sacrifice. —यजिन् (हविर्याजिन्) *m.* A priest.

हव्य *a.* (*f.* —व्या) To be offered in oblations.—व्यं *n.* 1 Clarified butter. -2 An oblation or offering to the Gods (opp. कव्य). -3 An oblation in general. -Comp. —आशः *m.* Fire. -कव्यं *n.* Oblations to the Gods and to the Manes or spirits of deceased ancestors.-वाह्, -वाहः,-वाहनः *m.* The bearer of oblations *i. e.* fire.

हस् 1 P. (हसति, हसित) 1 To smile, laugh (gently.) -2 To laugh at, ridicule (with acc.). -3 (Hence) To surpass, excel -4 To resemble. -5 To jest, joke. -6 To open, bloom. -7 To brighten up. With अप— To ridicule. अव— To deride. उप— To laugh at, to deride. परि— 1 To deride. -2 To joke. प्र— To laugh, smile. -2 To ridicule. वि— 1 To smile. -2 To ridicule.

हसः *m.* 1 Laugh, laughter. -2 Derision. -3 Merriment, mirth.

हसनं *n.* Laughing laughter.

हसनी *f.* A portable fire-place.

हसंतिका *f.* A portable fire-place.

हसंती *f.* 1 A portable fire-place -2 A kind of Mallikâ.

हासितं *n.* 1 Laughter. -2 Joke, jesting. -3 The bow of the God of love.

हस्तः *m.* 1 The hand हस्ते कृ 1 (हस्तेकृत्य -कृत्वा) To take or seize by the hand, take in hand, take possession of. -2 The trunk of an elephant.-3 N. of the 13th lunar mansion consisting of five stars. -4 The fore-arm, cubit, a measure of length (equal to about 18 inches). -5 Hand-writing, signature. -6 (Hence fig.) Proof, indication. -7 Help, support.-8 A mass,quantity, abundance (of hair), in comp. with केश, कच &c. -Comp. —अक्षरं *n.* One's own sign-manual. —अग्रं *n.* The finger.—अंगुलिः *f.* Any finger of the hand. —आमलकं *n.* The fruit of the myrobalan held in the hand, a phrase used to denote that which can be clearly and easily seen or understood. —आवापः *m.* A finger-guard. —क्रिया *f.* Manual work or performance, handicraft.- गत,- गामिन् *a.* Fallen into one's possession, obtained, secured.-चापल्यं *n.* Manual dexterity. -तलं *m.* 1 The palm of the hand. -2 The tip of an elephant's trunk.-तालः *m.* Clapping the hands. —दोषः *m.* A slip of the hand. -धारणं, -वारणं *n.* Warding off a blow (with the hand). —पादं *n.* The hands and feet. —पृष्ठं *n.* The back of the hand. —प्राप्त, -वर्तिन्, -स्थ, -स्थित *a.* 1 Held in the hand. -2 Gained, secured. -लाघवं *n.* 1 Manual readiness or skill -2 A sleight of the hand, legerdemain. —संवाहनं *n.* Rubbing or shampooing with the hands.—सिद्धिः *f.* 1 Manual labour, working with the hands. -2 Hire, wages. —सूत्रं *n.* A bracelet or thread-string worn on the wrist

हस्तकः *m.* 1 A hand. -2 The position of the hand.

हस्तवत *a.* (*f.*-ती) Dexterous, skilful.

हस्ता *f.* The thirteenth lunar mansion.

हस्ताहस्ति *ind.* Hand to hand.

हास्तिकं *n.* A multitude of elephants.

हास्तिन *a.* (*f*-नी) 1 Having hands.-2 Having a trunk -*m.* An elephant. -Comp.-आयुर्वेदः *m.* A work dealing with the treatment of the elephant's diseases. -आरोहः *m.* An elephant-driver or rider.-कक्ष्यः *m.* 1 A lion.-2 A tiger.-कर्णः *m.* The castor-oil plant. —चारिन *m.* An elephant-driver.—दंतः *m.* 1 The tusk of an elephant. -2 A peg projecting from a wall.(-तं *n.*) 1 Ivory -2 A radish. -दंतकं *n.* A radish.-नखं *n.* An sort of turret protecting the approach to the gate of a city or fort. —पः, -पकः *m.* An elephant-driver or rider. —मदः *m.* The ichor issuing from the temples of an elephant in rut. -मल्लः *m.* 1 N. of *Airávata.* -2 Of Ganesa. -3 Of Sankha, the eighth of the chief Nágas. -4 A heap of ashes. -5 A shower of dust. -6 Frost. —यूथः *m.*, -यूथं *n.* A herd of elephants.-वर्चसं *n.* The magnificence of an elephant. —वाहः *m.* 1 An elephant-driver. -2 A hook for driving elephants. —षड्गवं *n.* A collection of six elephants. —स्नानं *n.* (*lit.*) The bathing of an elephant. (*Fig.*) Any useless occupation (for the elephant throws dirt on his body after his bathing is over and even while the bathing is going on). —हस्तः *m.* An elephant's trunk.

हास्तिन (-ना-) पुरं *n.* N. of a city founded by king Hastin. Its other names are गजाह्वय, नागसाह्वय, नागाह्व, and हास्तिन.

हस्तिनी *f.* 1 A female elephant -2 A kind of drug and perfume. -3 A woman of a particular class, described in works on erotical science.

हस्त्य *a.* (*f.* —स्त्या) 1 Belonging to the hand. -2 Done with the hand, manual. -3 Given with the hand.

हहलं *n* A kind of deadly poison.

हहा *m.* A kind of Gandharva.

हा *ind.* A particle expressing 1 Grief, pain, (in this sense हा is often used with the acc. of the person as in हा कृष्णाभक्तं. -2 Surprise. -3 Anger or reproach.

हा 3 A. (जिहीते, हानः *pass.* हायते) 1 To go, move. -2 To get, attain. With उद्—1 To go up, to rise.-2 To revive, come to life. -3 To spring up, arise. -4 To come up, rise (as the sun). -5 To leave, depart. -6 To raise up, throw up उप-To come down to, to descend सम्-To attain.

हा 3 P. (जहाति, हीन) 1 To abandon, give up, forsake, dismiss, resign, forego. -2 To let fall. -3 To disregard, neglect. -4 To remove. -5 To avoid, shun. With अप—, अपा—, To abandon. परि— 1 To abandon. -2 To neglect. प्र- 1 To abandon. -2 To neglect, omit. प्र-1 To abandon. -2 To let go, to throw. वि— To abandon.

—*Pass.* (हीयते) 1 To be left or

forsaken. -2 To be excluded from, be deprived of, lose (with instr. or abl.). -3 To be deficient or wanting in; usually with परि. -4 To diminish, decay, wane (fig. also). -5 To fail (as in a law-suit). -6 To be left out or omitted. -7 To be weakened.

Caus. (हापयति,-ते) 1 To cause to leave or abandon. -2 To drive away. -3 To lose. -4 To neglect, delay the performance of. With वि— To give away.

Desid. (जिहासति) To wish to leave.

हांगरः *m.* A large fish.

हाटक *a.* (*f* -की) Golden. —कं *n.* 1 Gold.-2 The thorn-apple.-Comp. —गिरिः *m.* The mountain Meru. -मय *a.* Golden.

हार्त्रं *n.* 1 Wages, hire. -2 Injuring, killing. -3 Death. -घ्नः *m.* A demon.

हानं *n.* 1 Leaving,abandoning,loss, failure. -2 Escaping. -3 Prowess, power.

हानिः *f.* 1 Abandonment, relinquishment. -2 Loss, failure, absence. -3 Loss, damage. -4 Decrease, deficiency -5 Neglect, omission. -6 Waste, loss.

हापनं *n* Causing to quit or abandon, expelling.

हाफिका *f.* Yawning, gaping.

हायनः *m.*, हायनं *n.* A year —नं *n.* 1 A kind of rice. -2 A flame.

हारः *m.* 1 Taking away, seizing. -2 Conveying. -3 Deprivation -4 A carrier, porter. -5 A garland or necklace in general.-6 War,battle. -7 (In math.) The denominator of a fraction -8 A divisor. -9 (In prosody) A long syllable. -Comp. —आवलिः,—ली *f.* A string of pearls. —गुटि (-लि-) का *f.* The bead or pearl of a necklace. —यष्टिः *f.* A necklace, string of pearls. —हारा *f.* A kind of reddish brown grape.

हारकः *m.* A thief, plunderer. -2 A cheat, rogue -3 A string of pearls -4 A divisor (in math).

हारि *a* Attracting, pleasing, charming.- रिः *f.* 1 Defeat.- 2 Losing a game. -3 A caravan -Comp. -कंठः *m.* A cuckoo.

हारिणिकः *m.*A deer-catcher,hunter.

हारितः *m.* 1 The green colour. -2 A kind of pigeon.

हारिद्रः *m.* 1 A yellow colour. -2 The Kadamba tree.

हारिन *a.* (*f.* -णी) 1 Taking, carrying. -2 Robbing. -3 Seizing, disturbing. -4 Obtaining,securing. -5 Attracting, pleasing.-6 Surpassing, excelling. -7 Having a necklace.

हारीतः *m.* 1 A kind of pigeon.-2 A rogue, cheat. -3 N. of a writer on religious and civil law.

हार्दं *n.*1 Affection,love.-2Kindness, tenderness. -3 Intention, meaning.

हार्य *a.* (*f.* -र्या) 1 To be taken or conveyed. -2 To be taken away or snatched off. -3 To be shaken (as one's resolution). -4 To be secured or won over, to be conquered or influenced. —र्यः *m.* 1 A snake.-2 The tree called Bibhîtaka. -3 The dividend (in math).

हालः *m.* 1 A plough.-2N. of Balaráma.-3 N. of Sàliváhana. -Comp. —भृत *m.* An epithet of Balarâma.

हालकः *m* A horse of a yellowish brown colour.

हाल (-ला-) हलं *n.* 1 A sort of deadly poison produced at the churning of the ocean. -2 A deadly poison or poison in general. (Also written हलाहल or हालहाल). [liquor.

हालहली, हाला *f.* Wine, spirituous

हालाहलः *m* 1 A kind of insect. -2 A kind of lizard. —ला *f.* A small mouse. —ली *f.* Spirituous liquor. -लं *n.* A deadly poison.-2 Spirituous liquor.

हालिकः *m.* 1 A plough-man,an agriculturist.-2One that draws a plough (as plough ox). [lizard.

हालिनी *m.* A kind of large house-

हाली *f.* A wife's younger sister.

हालुः *m.* A tooth.

हावः *m* 1 A call, calling -2 Any conquettish gesture calculated to excite amorous sensations; blandishments.

हासः *m.* 1 Laughter, smile. -2 Mirth, merriment. -3 Laughter, as the prevailing feeling of the *rasa* called हास्य. -4 Derisive laughter -5 Blowing, expanding (as of lotuses &c.).

हासकः *m.* A buffoon. [merriment.

हासिका *f.* 1 Laughter. -2 Mirth,

हास्य *a.* (*f.* -स्या) Laughable, ridiculous. —स्यं *n.* 1 Laughter. -2 Amusement, sport. -3 Jest, joke. -4 Derision, ridicule. —स्यः *m.* The sentiment of mirth or humour, one of the eight or nine sentiments in poetry. -Comp. —आस्पदं *n.* A butt (of ridicule), laughing-stock. -पद्वी *f.*,-मार्गः *m.* Ridicule,derision. रसः *m.* The sentiment of mirth or humour.

हास्तिकः *m.* An elephant-driver or rider. —कं *n.* A herd of elephants.

हास्तिनं *n.* N. of Hastinapura.

हाहू (-हा-) लं *n.* Deadly posion.

हाहस् *m.* A Gandharva.

हाहा *m.* N. of a Gandharva —*ind.* An exclamation denoting pain, grief or surprise. -Comp. —कारः *m.* 1 A Lamentation, loud wailing. -2 The din or uproar of battle. —रवः *m.* The cry हाहा.

हि *ind.* (Never used at the beginning of a sentence) It has the following senses:— 1 For, because. -2 Indeed, surely. -3 For instance. -4 Only, alone (to emphasize an idea). -5 Sometimes it is used merely as an expletive.

हि 5 P. (हिनोति, हित ; *caus.* हाययति ; *desid.* जिघीषति) 1 To send forth -2 To throw, discharge, shoot. -3 To incite, urge. -4 To promote, further. -5 To gratify, please -6 To go or proceed. With प्र- 1 To discharge, throw. -2 To send, send forth.

हिंस् 1. 7 P., 10 U. (हिंसति, हिनस्ति, हिंसयति,-ते, हिंसित) 1 To strike, hit. -2 To hurt, harm. -3 To torment, afflict. -4 To kill, destroy completely.

हिंसकः *m.* 1 A savage animal, a beast of prey. -2 An enemy. -3 A Bráhmana skilled in the Atharvaveda. [killing.

हिंसनं *n.*, हिंसना *f.* Striking,hurting,

हिंसा *f.* 1 Injury, mischief, wrong, harm, hurt (said to be of three kinds:--कायिक ' personal ', वाचिक 'verbal', and मानसिक ' mental ').-2 Killing, destruction. -3 Robbery, plunder -Comp.-आत्मक *a.*Injurious, destructive. —कर्मन् *n.* 1 Any hurtful or injurious act.-2 Magic used to effect the ruin or injury of an enemy. [ious animal.

हिंसारुः *m.* 1 A tiger. -2 Any nox-

हिंसालु *a.* 1 Injurious,mischievous. -2 Murderous -*m.* A mischievous or savage dog. [hurt

हिंसित *a.* Injured,hurt.-तं *n.* Injury,

हिंसीरः *m.* 1 A tiger. -2 A bird. -3

A mischievous fellow.

हिंस्य *a.* (*f.* —स्या) Liable to be injured or killed.

हिंस्र *a.* (*f.* -स्रा) Injurious, mischievous, murderous. -2 Terrible. -3 Cruel, savage. -स्रः *m.* 1 A fierce animal, a beast of prey. -2 A destroyer. -3 N. of Siva. -4 N. of Bhîma. -Comp. —पशुः *m.* A beast of prey. —यंत्रं *n.* 1 A trap. -1 A mystical text used for malevolent purposes.

हिक् 1 U. (हिकाति,-ते, हिक्कित) 1 To make an indistinct or inarticulate sound. -2 To hiccough.

हिक्क् 10 A. (हिक्कयते) To hurt, kill.

हिक्का *f.* 1 An indistinct sonnd. -2 Hiccough.

हिंकारः *m.* 1 A kind of low roar or sound -2 A tiger.

हिंगुः *m.*, हिंगु *n.* 1 The plant called Asa foetida.-2 The substance prepared from this plant (asa fœtida) for household use, especially in seasoning articles of food. -Comp. —निर्यासः *m.* 1 The gummy exudation of the *hingu* tree.-2 The *nimba* tree. —पत्रः *m.* The *ingudî* tree.

हिंगुलः *m.*, हिंगुलं *n.*
हिंगुलिः *m.*
हिंगुलुः *m*., हिंगुलु *n.* } Vermilion.

हिंजीरः *m* A rope or fetter for fastening an elephant's foot.

हिडिंबः *m.* N. of a demon slain by Bhíma. -बा *f.* The sister of Hidimba who married Bhîma. -2 The wife of Hanumat. -Comp. —जित्, —निषूदनः, —भिद्, -रिपुः *m.* Epithets of Bhíma.

हिंड् 1 A (हिंडते, हिंडित) 1 To go, whaner. -2 To disregard, slight.

हिंडनं *n.* 1 Wandering, roaming bout. -2 Sexual intercourse. -3 Writing.

हिंडिकः *m.* An astrologer.

हिंडि (-डी-) रः *m.* 1 Cuttle-fish bone. -2 A man,a male.-3 The egg-plant. -4 A tonic or stomachic. -रं *n.* The pomegranate,

हिंडी *f.* N. of Durgâ.

हित *a.* (*f.* —ता) 1 Put, laid,placed. -2 Held, taken.-3 Suitable, proper, (with dat.). -4 Useful, advantageous. -5 Beneficial, wholesome, (said of words, diet &c.). -6 Affectionate, well-disposed (generally with loc.). -7 Sent, impelled.-8 Gone, proceeded. -9 Auspicious. -तः *m.* A friend,benefactor,friendly adviser. —ता *f* A causeway, dike. -तं *n.* 1 Benefit,profit or advantage. -2 Anything proper or suitable. -3 Well-being, welfare. -Comp. —अनुबंधिन *a.* Involving or causing welfare. —अन्वेषिन्, -आर्थिन *a.* Seeking another's welfare -एषिन *a.* Desiring another's welfare, benevolent. —काम्या *f* A desire for another's welfare, good will.—प्रणी *m.* A spy.

हितकः *m.* 1 A child. -2 The young of an animal.

हिंतालः *m.* A kind of palm.

हिंदुः *m.* N. of a tribe.

हिंदोलः *m.* 1 A swing.-2 The swing festival in the bright half of Srâvana.

हिंदोलकः *m.*, हिंदोला *f.* 1 A swing. -2 A cradle.

हिम *a.* (*f.* —मा) Cold,frigid, dewy. -मः *m.* 1 The cold season, winter.-2 The moon.-3 The Himâlaya mountain. -4 The sandal tree. -5 Camphor. —मं *n.* 1 Frost, hoar-forst. -3 Cold, coldness.-4 A lotus.-5 Fresh butter. -6 A pearl.-2 Sandal wood. -Comp. —अंशुः *m.* 1 The moon. -2 Camphor. —अचलः, —आद्रिः *m.* The

Himálaya mountain. -अब्जं *n.* A lotus. -अरातिः *m.* 1 Fire.-7 The sun. —आगमः *m.* The cold or winter-season. —आलयः *m.* 1 The Himálaya mountain. -2 The white Khadira tree. —आह्वः, —आह्वयः *m.* Camphor. (-यं *n.*) A lotus —उस्रः *m.* The moon. —करः *m.* 1 The moon. -2 Camphor. -कूटः *m.* 1 The winter season. -2 The Himálaya mountain. —गिरिः *m.* The Himàlaya. -गुः *m.* The moon. -जः *m.* The Mainâka mountain. -जा *f.* 2 The plant Zedoary. -2 Pârvatî. —तैलं *n.* A kind of camphor ointment. —दीधितिः *m.* The moon. -दुर्दिनं *n.* The wintry weather. —द्युतिः *m.* The moon. —द्रुमः *m.* The Nimba tree.—द्रुह *m.* The sun.—धातुः *m.* The Himálaya mountain. —ध्वस्त *a.* Blighted by forst. -प्रस्थः *m.* The Himâlaya mountain. —भासु, -रश्मिः *m.* The moon.-वालुकः *m.*-का *f.* Camphor. —शैलः *m.* The Himálaya mountain. —श्रथः *m.* The moon. —संहतिः *f.* A mass of ice or snow. -हासकः *m.* The marshy date tree.

हिमवत *a.* Snowy, icy, frosty. -*m.* The Himalaya mountain. -Comp. —पुरं *n.* N. of Oshadhiprastha, the capital of Himàlaya. -सुतः *m.* The Mainâka mountain. —सुता *f.* 1 Párvatî -2 The Ganges.

हिमा *f.* 1 The cold season, winter. -2 Small cardamoms -3 A kind of grass. -4 The fragrant drug and perfume called Renuká.

हिमानी *f.* 1 A mass or collection of snow-drift. -2 A kind of sugar.

हिरंगुः *m.* N. of Ràhu. [cowrie.

हिरणं *n.* 1 Gold. -2 Semen. -3 A

हिरण्मय *a.* (*f.* —यी) Made of gold, golden -यः *m* The God Brahman *m.*). —यं *n.* One of the nine divisions of the world.

हिरण्यं *n.* 1 Gold. -2 Any vessel of gold. -3 Silver -4 Any precious metal. -5 Weath,property.-6 Semen virile. -7 A *cowrie.* -8 A particular measure. -9 A subastance. -10 The thorn-apple (धत्तूर). —ण्या *f.* One of the seven tongues of fire. -Comp. —अक्षः *m.* N. of a celebrated demon, twin brother of Hiranyakasipu. —कक्ष *a.* Wearing a golden girdle. —कशिपुः *m.* N. of a celebrated king of demons.-कोशः *m.* Gold and silver (whether wrought or unwrought). —गर्भः *m.* 1 N. of Brahman (*m.*). -2 N. of Vishnu. -3 The soul invested by the subtile body or सूक्ष्मशरीर. —द *a.* Giving gold. (-दः *m.*) The ocean. (-दा *f.*) The earth. —नाभः *m.* The mountain Mainàka. —बाहुः *m.* 1 An epithet of Siva. -2 The river Sona. —बिंदुः *m.* Fire. —रेतस *m.* 1 Fire. -2 The sun. -3 N. of Siva -4 The *Chitraka* or *Arka* plant. —वर्णा *f.* A river. —वाहः *m.* 1 The river Sona. -2 N. of Siva.

हिरण्यय *a.* (*f.* —यी) Golden.

हिरुक् *ind.* 1 Without, except. -2 Amongst, in the midst of. -3 Near. -4 Below.

हिल् 6 P. (हिलति) To sport amorcusly,to wanton,express to amorous desire.

हिल्लोलः *m.* 1 A wave, billow. -2 The musical mode called Hindola. -3 A caprice, whim. -4 A kind of coitus.

हिल्वला: *f. pl.* N. of five small stars in the head of the lunar mansion called मृगशिरस्.

ही *ind.* An interjection of 1 Surprise. -2 Fatigue, despondency or sorrow. -3 Reason.

हीन *p. p.* (*f.* - ना) 1 Abandoned, forsaken. -2 Destitute or deprived of, bereft of, without ; (with instr. or in comp.) -3 Shut out from (with abl.). -4 Decayed, wasted. -5 Deficient, defective.-6 Subtracted. -7 Less, lower. -8 Low. mean. —नः *m.* 1 A defective witness. -2 A faulty respondent. -3 Subtraction. -Comp. —अंग *a.* Deficient in a limb, maimed. (-गी *f.*) A small ant. —कर्मन् *a.* Neglecting the customary religious rites. —जाति *a.* 1 Of a low caste. -2 Excommunicated, outcaste, degraded. —योनिः *f.* Low birth or origin. —वर्ण *a.* 1 Of low caste.-2 Of inferior rank.-वादः *m.* A defective statement, contradictory evidence. —वादिन् *a.* 1 Making a defective statement.-2 Prevaricating. -3 Dumb, speechless. -4 Cast in law, defeated. —हीनसत्त्व *a.* Of low magnanimity, ungenerous.

हींतालः *m.* The marshy date tree.

हीरः *m.* 1 A snake -2 A necklace. -3 A lion. -4 N. of the father of Srîharsha, the author of the Naishadha-charita. -5 N. of Siva. -रः *m.*, -रं *n.* 1 The thunber-bolt of Indra. -2 A diamond. -Comp. —अंगः *m.* The thunder-bolt of Indra.

हीरकः *m.* A diamond. [An ant.

हीरा *f.* 1 An epithet of Lakshmî.-2

हीलं *n.* Semen virile.

हीही *ind.* A particle expressive of surprise or merriment.

हु 3 P. (जुहोति, हुत *pass.* हूयते *caus.* हावयति,-ते; *desid.* जुहूषति) 1 To offer or present (as an oblation to fire) make an offering to,or in honor of, a deity (with acc.).-2 To perform a sacrifice. -3 To eat.

हुड् 1 P. (होडति) To go.

हुड् 6 P. (हुडति) 1 To collect. -2 To dive, sink.

हुडः *m.* 1 A ram.-2 An iron stake for keeping out thieves. -3 A kind of fence. -4 An iron club. -5 A kind of bulwark or fence.

हुडुः *m.* A ram.

हुडुकः *m.* 1 A small hour-glass-shaped drum. -2 A kind of bird (दात्यूह). -3 The bolt of a door. -4 A drunken man. -5 A stick bound with iron. [sound of threat.

हुडुत् *n.* 1 Noise of a bull. -2 A

हुंड् 1 A. (हुंडते) 1 To collect. -2 To select, choose.

हुंडः *m.* 1 A tiger. -2 A ram. -3 A blockhead. -4 A village-hog. -5 A demon.

हुत *p. p.* (*f.* -ता) 1 Offered as an oblation to fire. -2 One to whom an oblation is offered. —तः *m.* N. of Siva. —तं *n.* An oblation, offering.-Comp.-अग्नि *a.* Who has made an oblation to fire. (-*m.*) A sacrificial fire. —अशनः *m.* 1 Fire. -2 N. of Siva. -3 The Chitraka tree. —अशनी *f.* The full-moon day in the month of Phâlguna (होलिका). -आशः *m.* Fire. —जातवेदस् *a.* One who has made an oblation to fire. —भुज् *m.* Fire.—वहः *m.* Fire.—होमः *m.* A Brahmana who has offered oblations to fire. (—मं *n.*) A burnt offering.

हुतिः *f.* Offering oblations.

हुम् *ind.* A particle expressing 1 Remembrance or recollection. -2 Doubt. -3 Assent. -4 Anger. -5 Aversion. -6 Reproach. -7 Interrogation. (In spells and incantations हुं is often found used with dat.; *e. g.* ओं कवचाय हुम्). (हुं कृ To roar, grunt, bellow. -Comp. —कारः *m.*, -कृतिः *f.* 1 Uttering the sound of defiance. -3 Roaring, bellowing in general.-4 The grunting of a boar. -5 The twang of a bow —कृतं *n.* 1 An incantation. -2 The grunt of a wild boar. -3 The roar of thunder.

हुल् 1 P. (होलति) 1 To go. -2 To cover or conceal. -3 To kill.

हुलहुली *f.* A kind of inarticulate sound, uttered by women on joyful occasions.

हुहु (-हू) *m.* A kind of Gandharva.

हूँ *ind* 1 An interjection of calling. -2 Of contempt. -3 Of pride. -4 Of grief.

हूड् 1 A. (हूडते) To go.

हूण: (-ण:) *m.* 1 A barbarian, foreigner. -2 A kind of golden coin —णा: (-णा:) *m. pl.* N. of a country or its people.

हूत *p. p.* (*f.* —ता) 1 Called, invited.

हूति: *f.* 1 Calling, inviting. -2 Challenging. -3 A name.

हृम् See हुम्.

हूरव: *m.* A jackal.

हूहू *m.* A kind of Gandharva.

हृ 1 U. (हरति,-ते, हर्तुं, हृत; *pass.* ह्रियते) 1 To take, carry, convey, (often used with two accusatives in this sense) *e. g.* अजां ग्रामं हरति. -2 To carry away, draw to a distance. -3 To rob, plunder, steal. -4 To deprive of, take away. -5 To cure, destroy.-6 To captivate, win over, subdue, enchant. -7 To acquire, obtain. -8 To have, possess. -9 To surpass, eclipse. -10 To marry.-11 To divide. -12 To throw (as an arrow). -13 To accept, receive, inherit. -14 To offer. With अनु— 1 (*Par.*) To exhibit, to imitate. -2 (*Atm.*) To take after the parents. अप— 1 To take away, remove. -2 To snatch away, carry off, to plunder. -3 To attract, plunder. अभ्यव— To eat. आ— 1 To bring, carry. -2 To perform (as a sacrifice). -3 To take, get. -4 To procreate. -5 To bring back. -6 To assume. -7 To attract. -8 To withdraw. उद्— 1 To take out, to rake up. -2 To extract. -3 To make an extract from. -4 To hold up, raise. -5 To extricate, deliver. -6 To eradicate, destroy. -7 To deduct. उदा— 1 To mention, utter, speak, narrate, call. -2 To exemplify, to narrate by way of an illustration. उप— To offer, give. उपा— To bring. निस्— 1 To carry out a dead body. -2 To extract. परि— 1 To abandon. -2 To avoid. -3 To remove, destroy. प्र— 1 To throw, to hurl (with *dat.*, or *acc.*). -2 To attack, assail, strike, beat. -3 To wound, hurt (with *loc.*). -4 To seize upon. (पादेन प्रहृ- To kick). वि— 1 To take away, remove, destroy. -2 To pass (as time). -3 To divert oneself, to sport. व्यव— 1 To deal in transactions (with gen.). -2 To go to a law-court, to sue. व्या— To speak, tell, narrate. सम्— 1 To bring or draw together, to collect -2 To withdraw, to take back.-3 To curb, suppress, restrain. -4 To annihilate (opp. to सृज्). -5 To contract, abridge. समा— To bring, convey, carry. -2 To make reparation for. -3 To draw, attract. -4 To destroy. -5 To collect, bring together.

Caus. (हारयति,-ते) To cause to take, carry or convey, send (something) by one, with *acc.* or *instr.*) *e. g.* भृत्यं भृत्येन वा भारं हारयति. -2 To cause to be taken away, to lose, be deprived of. -3 To give away.

With अप— To cause to take away. अभ्यव— To feed. आ— To cause to bring. उद्— To cause to take out.

Desid. (जिहीर्षति,-ते) To wish to take.

हृ (-ह्रि-) णी Den. A. (य is always added to the base. हृणीयते, ह्रिणीयते) 1 To be angry. -2 To feel ashamed (with instr. or gen.).

हृणी (-णि-) या *f.* 1 Censure, reproach. -2 Shame. -3 Compassion.

हृत् *a.* (At the end of comp. only) Taking away, seizing,carrying off, attracting &c.

हृत *p. p.* (*f.*—ता) 1 Taken or carried away.-2 Seized.-3 Captivated. -4 Accepted. -5 Divided. —तं *n.* A portion, share. -Comp. —उत्तरीय *a.* Having the upper garments stripped off. —सर्वस्व *a.* Stripped of all one's property, utterly ruined.

हृतिः *f.* 1 Seizure. -2 Robbing. -3 Destruction.

हृद् *n.* (This word has no forms for the first five inflections and is optionally substituted for हृदय after acc. dual) 1 The mind, heart. -2 The chest, bosom, breast. -3 The soul. -4 The interior or essence of anything. -Comp. —आवर्तः *m.* The lock or curl of hair on a horse's chest. -कंपः *m.* Tremor of the heart, palpitation. —गत *a.* 1 Seated in the mind, conceived. -2 Cherished. (—तं *n.*) Design, meaning, intent. —देशः *m.* The region of the heart. —पिंडः *m.*, -पिंडं *n.* The heart. —रोगः *m.* 1 A heart-disease heart-burn.-2 Siorrow, grief, anguish. -3 Love. -4 The sign aquarius of the zodiac. —लासः *m.* (हृल्लासः) 1 Hiccough. -2 Disquietude, grief. —लेखः (हृल्लेखः) *m.* 1 Knowledge, reasoning. -2 Heart-ache. —लेखा *f.* (हृल्लेखा) Grief, anxiety. —शयः *m.* 1 The God of love. -2 Love. —शूलं *n.* An acute pain in the chest. —शोकः *m.* Heart-burn or anguish.

हृदयं *m.* 1 The heart, soul,mind.-2 The bosom, chest. -3 Love, affection. -4 The interior or essence of anything. -5 The secret science as in अश्वहृदयं, अक्षहृदयं &c. -6 True or divine knowledge. -7 The Veda. -Comp. —आत्मन् *m.* A heron. -आविध् *a.* Heart-rending, heart-piercing. —ईशः, -ईश्वरः *m.* A husband. (—शा, -री *f.*) 1 A wife. -2 A mistress. —कंपः *m.* Tremor of the heart.-ग्राहिन् *a* Heart-captivating.—चौरः *m.* One who steals the heart or affections. —छिद् *a.* Heart-rending. —रोगः *m* A heart-disease. —लेखः *m.* 1 Knowledge. -2 Heart-ache, anxiety. —विध्, -वेधिन् *a.* Heart-piercing.-वृत्तिः *f.* Disposition of the heart. —स्थ *a.* Being or cherished in the heart. —स्थानं *n.* The breast, bosom.

हृदयंगम *a.* (*f.* —मा) 1 Heart-stirring,thrilling.-2 Lovely,handsome. -3 Attractive, pleasant. -4 Fit, appropriate. -5 Beloved, cherished. —मं *n.* An appropriate speech.

हृदयालु *a.*, हृदयिक *a.* (*f.* -का), हृदयिन् *a.* (*f.* —नी) Tender-hearted, good-hearted, affectionate.

हृदि (-दी-) कः *m.* N. of a Yâdava prince.

हृदिस्पृश् *a.* 1 Touching the heart. -2 Dear, beloved. -3 Agreeable, beautiful.

हृद्य *a.* (*f.* -द्या) 1 Hearty, cordial. -2 Dear, desired, beloved. -3 Agreeable, charming. -4 Affectionate, kind. -Comp.—गंधः *m.* The Bilva tree.-गंधा *f.* The great-flowered jasmine.

हृष् 1. 4. P. (हर्षति, हृष्यति, हृष्ट or हृषित)

1 To be delighted or rejoiced, to rejoice.-2 To stand on end (as the hair or the body). -3 To become erect e. g the penis). -4 To tell a lie. With प्र— 1 To be glad, to rejoice. -2 To stand erect (as the hair of the body). सम—To rejoice. —*Caus.* (हर्षयति,-ते) To please, delight, fill with pleasure.

हृषित *p. p.* (*f.* —ता) 1 Pleased, delighted, rejoiced. -2 Thrilled, having the hair bristling. -3 Astonished. -4 Bent, bowed.

हृषीकं *n.* An organ of sense.-Comp. —ईशः *m.* An epithet of Vishnu or Krishna.

हृष्ट *p. p.* (*f.* —ष्टा) Pleased, rejoiced.-Comp —रोमन् *a.* Having the hair on the body bristling or thrilling (with joy). -संकल्प *a.* Contented, pleased.

हृष्टिः *f.* 1 Delight, joy. -2 Pride.

हे *ind.* 1 A vocative particle (oh! ho!). -2 A particle used in challenging. -3 An interjection expressing defiance, envy or disapprobation.

हेक्का *f.* Hiccough.

हेठः *m* 1 Vexation. -2 Hindrance, opposition. -3 Injury.

हेड् 1 A (हेडते) To disregard, slight, neglect. [To attire.

हेड् 1 P. (हेडति) 1 To surround. -2

हेडः *m.* Disregard, slight. -Comp. —जः *m.* Anger, displeasure.

हेडावुक्कः *m.* A horse-dealer.

हेतिः *m., f.* 1 A weapon, a missile. -2 A stroke, injury.-3 A ray of the sun.-4 Light, splendour.-5 Flame.

हेतुः *m.* 1 Cause, reason, object, motive. -2 Source, origin. -3 A means or instrument -4 The logical reason, the reason for an inference, middle term (forming the second member of the five-membered syllogism). -5 Logic, science of reasoning. -6 Any logical proof or argument. -7 (In Rhet.) The figure of speech in which a cause is expressed as identical with the effect In this figure the effect is put for the cause and the figure therefore corresponds to the English figure metonymy. (The forms हेतुना हेतोः, rarely हेतौ, are used adverbially in the sense of 'by reason of', 'on account of', because of, with gen or in comp.) -Comp. —अपदेशः *m.* Adducing the 'hetu' (In the form of the five membered syllogism). -आभासः *m.* 'The semblance of a reason', a fallacious middle term, fallacy. —उपक्षेपः, —उपन्यासः *m.* Adducing a reason, statement of an argument.—वादः *m.* Disputation, controversy. —शास्त्रं *n.* Any heretical work questioning the authority of Smritis or revelation.

हेतुक *a.* Causing, producing (at the end of comp.). —कः *m.* 1 A cause, reason. -2 An instrument. -3 A logician.

हेतुमत् *a.* 1 Having a reason or cause. -2 Having the *hetu*. -*m.* An effect.

हेमं *n.* 1 Gold.-2 The thorn-apple. -मः *m.* 1 A dark or brown coloured horse. -2 A particular weight of gold. -3 The planet Mercury.

हेमन् *n.* 1 Gold. -2 Water.-3 Snow. -4 The thorn-apple. -5 The Kesara flower. -6 Winter, the cold season. -7 The planet Mercury. -Comp. - अंगः *m.* 1 Garuda. -2 A lion. -3 The mountain *Sumeru*. -4 N. of Brahman (*m*,). -5 Of Vishnu. -6

The *Champaka* tree. —अंगदं *n.* A gold bracelet. —अद्रिः *m.* The mountain *Sumeru.* —आह्वः *m.* 1 The wild *Champaka* tree. -2 The *Dhattûra* plant. —कंदलः *m.* Coral. -कारः, —कर्तृ, —कारः. —कारकः *m.* A goldsmith. —किंजल्कं *n.* The Nâgakesara flower. —कूटः *m.* N. of a mountain. —केतकी *f.* The *Ketaka* plant bearing yellow flowers (स्वर्णकेतकी). —केलिः *m.* 1 An epithet of Agni. -2 The Chitraka plant.-गंधिनी *f.* The perfume named Renuka. —गिरिः *m.* The mountain *Sumeru.* —गौरः *m.* The Asoka tree. —छन्नं *n.* A gold covering. —ज्वालः *m.* Fire. —तारं *n* Blue vitriol. —दुग्धः, —दुग्धकः *m.* The glomerous fig-tree. -पर्वतः *m.* The mountain Meru.-पुष्पः, -पुष्पकः *m.* 1 The 'ashoka' tree.-2 The Lodhra tree. -3 The Champaka tree. (-*n.*) 1 The 'asoka' flower. -2 The flower of China rose. -ब (-व-) कं *n.* A pearl.-मालिन् *m.* The sun. -यूथिका *f.* The golden or yellow jasmine. —रागिणी *f.* Turmeric —शंखः *m.* N. of Vishnu. —शृंगं *n.* 1 A golden horn. -2 A golden summit. —सारं *n.* Blue vitriol —सूत्रं, —सूत्रकं *n.* A kind of necklace.

हेमंतः *m.*, हेमंतं *n.* One of the six seasons; cold or winter season (comprising the months मार्गशीर्ष and पौष). -Comp.-नाथः *m.* The wood-apple tree.

हेमलः *m.* 1 A goldsmith. -2 A touch-stone. -3 A chameleon.

हेय *a.* (*f.* —या) Fit to be abandoned.

हेरं *n.* 1 A kind of crown or diadem. -2 Turmeric. -3 Demoniacal illusion.

हेरंबः *m.* 1 N. of Ganesa.-2 A buffalo, -3 A boastful hero. -Comp. —जननी *f.* N. of Párvatî.

हेरिकः *m.* A spy, secret emissary.

हेलनं *n.*, हेलना *f.* 1 Disregarding, slighting, contempt. -2 Wanton dalliance.

हेला *f.* 1 Contempt, insult. -2 Amorous dalliance.-3 Pleasure, pastime. -4 Strong sexual desire. -5 Ease, facility. (हेलया Easily, without any difficulty or trouble). -6 Moonlight. -7 A pause in a note or shaking (as in music.).

हेलाबुक्कः *m* A horse-dealer.

हेलिः *m.* The sun. -*f.* Wanton or amorous sport.

हेवाकः *m.* Ardent desire.(This word like the word लटभ is used only by later writers like Kalhana, Bilhana and is probably derived from Persian or Arabic).

हेवाकिन् *a.* (*f.* — नी) Ardently desirous of, eager for (in comp.).

हेष् I A. (हेषते, हेषित). To neigh (as a horse) ; to bray, roar (in general).

हेषः *m.*, हेषा *f.* हेषितं *n.* Neighing, braying.

हेषिन् *m.* A horse.

हेहे *ind.* A vocative particle used in addressing or calling.

है *ind.* A vocative particle.

हैतुक *a.* (*f.* —की) 1 Causal.causative. -2 Argumentative, rationalistic. —कः *m.* 1 A logical reasoner, an arguer.-2 A follower of the Mimámsâ doctrines.-3 A rationalist, sceptic. -4 A heretic.

हैम *a.* (*f.*—मी) 1 Cold, wintry, frigid. -2 Caused by frost.-2 Golden, made of gold. -4 Of a golden yellow colour. —मा, —मी *f.* Yellow jasmine. —मं *n.* Hoar-forst, dew.-मः *m.* An epithet of Siva. -Comp. —मुद्रा, —मुद्रिका *f.* A golden coin.

हैमन *a.* (*f.* —नी) 1 Wintry, cold.

-2 Pertaining to winter. -3 Growing in or suitable for winter -4 Golden, made of gold. —नः *m.* 1 The month Mârgasîrsha. -2 The winter seas n

हैमंतिक *a.* (*f.* —की) 1 Wintry,cold. -2 Growing in winter. -कं *n.* A kind of rice.

हैमलः *m.* See हेमंत.

हैमवत *a.* (*f.* —ती) 1 Snowy. -2 Flowing from the Himâlaya mountain. -3 Bred in, belongin to, or situated on,the Himâlava m unta-in. —तः *m.* A kind of poison.—तं *n.* Bhâ atavars ha or India.

हैमवती *f* 1 N. of Pârvtî. -2 Of the river Ganges. -3 A kind of myrobalan. -4 A kind of drug -5 Common flax. -6 A tawny grape.

हैयंगवीनं *n.* 1 Clarified butter prepared from the preceding day's milk; fresh ghee. -2 Butter prepared a day before it is used.

हैरण्यवासस् *m.* An arrow.

हैरिकः *m* A thief.

हैहयाः *m.pl.* N.of a people and their country. —यः *m.* 1 N. of the great grandson of Yadu.-2 N. of Arjuna Kârtavîrya

हैहयः *m.* Arjuna Kârtavîrya.

हो *ind* 1 A vocative particle used in calling a person or in challenging. -2 Of surprise.

होड् 1 A (होडते) To disregard.

होड् 1 P. (होडति) To go.

होडः *m.* A raft, float.

होतृ *a.* (*f.* —त्री) Offering oblations into fire. —*m.* 1 A sacrificial priest especially one who recites the prayers of the Rigveda at a sacrifice. -2 A sacrificer. -3 An epithet of Agni

होतृकः *m.* An assistant of the Hotri.

होत्रं *n.* 1 Anything fit to be offered as an oblation (as ghee). -2 A burnt offering. -3 A sacrifice.

होत्रा *f.* 1 A sacrifice. -2 Praise.

होत्रियः The priest who offers oblations to Gods. -यं *n.* The sacrificial hall.

होमः *m.* 1 Offering oblations to Gods by throwing ghee into the consecrated fire (one of the five daily Yajnas, to be performed by a Brâhmana. called देवयज्ञ). -2 A burnt offering. -3 A sacrifice. -Comp. —अग्निः *m.* The sacrificial fire.-कुंडं *n.* A hole in the ground for receiving the consecrated fire. —भस्मन् *n.* The ashes of a burnt offering. -शाला *f.* A sacrificial hall.

होमिः *m.* 1 Clarified butter. -2 Water -3 Fire.-4 The Chitraka tree.

होमिन् *m.* The offerer of an oblation, a sacrificer in general.

होमीय, होम्य *a.* (*f.* - या, -म्या) Belonging to or fit for an oblation. —म्यं *n.* Ghee.

होरा *f.* 1 The rising of a zodiacal sign. -2 Part of the duration of a sign. -3 An hour. -4 A mark, line.

होलाका *f.* 1 The spring-festival celebrated at the approach of the spring season, during the ten days preceding the full-moon day in the month of Phâlguna(commonly called *Holi*). -2 The full-moon day in the month of Phâlguna.

होलिका, होली *f.* The festival होलाका.

होहो हौ *ind.* A vocativa particle.

हौत्रं *n.* The office of the priest called Hotri.

हौम्यं *n.* Clarified butter.

ह्नु 2 A. (ह्नुते, ह्नुत) 1 To take away, rob,deprive (one) of. 2 To conceal, withhold. -3 To hide from any one

(with dat.) *e. g.* गोपी कृष्णाय ह्नुते.

ह्नुतिः *f.* 1 Concealment.-2 Denial.

ह्यस् *ind.* Yesterday. -Comp. —भव *a.* What occurred yesterday.

ह्यस्तन *a.* (*f.* -नी) Belonging to yesterday. -Comp. —दिनं *n.* Yesterday, the previous day. [yesterday.

ह्यस्त्य *a.* (*f.* -स्त्या) Belonging to

ह्रणीया *f.* Censure, reproach, shame.

ह्रदः *m.* 1 A deep lake, a large and deep pool of water. -2 A hole or cavity.-3 A ray of light.-Comp. —ग्रहः *m.* A crocodile.

ह्रदिनी *f.* 1 A river.-2 A lightning.

ह्रद्रोगः *m.* The sign *Aquarius* of the zodiac.

ह्रस् 1 P. (ह्रसति, ह्रसित) 1 To sound. -2 To become small or diminished.

ह्रसिमन् *m.* Smallness, shortness.

ह्रसिष्ठ *a.* (*f.* -ष्ठा) (Superl. of ह्रस्व) shortest, smallest.

ह्रसीयस् *a.* (*f.* -सी; compar. of ह्रस्व) shorter, smaller.

ह्रस्व *a* (*f.* -स्वा; compar. ह्रसीयस्, superl. ह्रसिष्ठ) 1 Short, small, little. -2 Dwarfish. -3 Short (opp. to दीर्घ in prosody). —स्वः *m.* 1 A dwarf. -2 A short vowel. —स्वं *n.* Green or black sulphate of iron. -Comp —गर्भः *m.* The Kusa grass. -दर्भः,-कुशः *m.* The short or white Kusa grass.

ह्राद् 1 A. (ह्रादते) 1 To sound. -2 To roar.

ह्रादः *m.* Noise, sound.

ह्रादिनी *f.* 1 The thunder-bolt of Indra. -2 Lightening. -3 A river.

ह्रासः *m.* 1 Sound, noise. -2 Decrease, decline, deterioration.

ह्रिणी 1 A. (ह्रिणीयते) To feel ashamed.

ह्रिणीया *f.* 1 Reproach, censure. -2 Shame. -3 Pity.

ह्री 3 P (जिह्रेति, ह्रीण,ह्रीत) 1 To blush, be modest. -2 To be ashamed (used by itself or with abl. or gen). —*Caus.* (ह्रेपयति, -ते) To put to shame (fig. also); cause to blush.

ह्री *f.* 1 Shame. -2 Bashfulness.

ह्रीका *f.* 1 Bashfulness, shyness. -2 Timidity, fear.

ह्रीकु *a.* 1 Bashful, modest, shy. -2 Timid. —कुः *m* 1 Tin. -2 Lac.

ह्रीण, ह्रीत *p. p.* (*f.* -णा, -ता) 1 Ashamed. -2 Bashful, modest.

ह्रेपणं *n.* The act of putting to shame, excelling, surpassing.

ह्रेष् 1 A. (ह्रेषते) 1 To neigh (as a horse). -2 To go, creep.

ह्रेषा *f.*, ह्रेषितं *n.* Neighing.

ह्लस् 1 P. (ह्लसति) To sound.

ह्लाद् 1 A (ह्लादते, ह्लन्न or ह्लादित) 1 To be delighted; to rejoice. -2 To sound. With आ- To be delighted. —*Caus.* (ह्लादयति) To gladden, delight. [light.

ह्लादः, ह्लादकः *m.* Pleasure, joy, de-

ह्लादनं *n.* The act of rejoicing, joy.

ह्लादिन् *a.* (*f.* -नी) Delighting.

ह्लादिनी *f.* Lightning. -2 Indra's thunder-bolt.

ह्वल् 1 P. (ह्वलति) 1 To go, move. -2 To shake, tremble. —*Caus.* (ह्व (ह्वा-)लयति,-ते. but ह्वलयति only with prepositions) To shake, move cause to tremble (especially with वि).

ह्वृ 1 P. (ह्वरति) 1 To be crooked. -2 To be crooked in conduct, to cheat, deceive. -3 To be afflicted.

ह्वानं *n.* 1 Calling.-2 A cry, sound.

ह्वे 1 U. (ह्वयति, -ते ह्वातुं. हूत; *pass.* हूयते; *caus.* ह्वाययति, ते; *desid.* जुहूषति,-ते) 1 To call by name. -2 To call out, call upon. -3 To call, name. -4 To challenge. -5 To emulate. -6 To ask, beg. With आ— 1 To call, invite. -2 (*Atm.*) To challenge. सम्— To call out together

APPENDIX I

GIVING SHORT ACCOUNTS of Mythological personages &c.

अंशुमान्—The grandson of सगर and the son of असमंज. [Vide our note on सगर].

अक्रूर—Otherwise called श्वाफल्कि. It was he whom कंस had sent to मथुरा to bring कृष्ण and बलराम to his court. He figures considerably in the famous history of the स्यमन्तक jewel.

अगस्त्य—Also called कुम्भयोनि, कुंभसंभव &c. from his having been born in a jar. He was a very great sage and an excellent archer. He is fabled to have once drunk up the whole sea and rescued the subjects from the कालकेय demons hiding in it. His wife was लोपामुद्रा, daughter of the king of the विदर्भs.

He is considered as the regent of the star *Canopus* in the south, and his appearance in the sky is believed to make turbid waters clear.

अग्नि—The personification of fire, one of the five elements. अर्जुन had received his famous गाण्डीव bow from अग्नि at the time of the destruction of the खाण्डव forest.

His wife was स्वाहा. His sons were पावक, पवमान and शुचि

अंगद—Son of वाली the monkey-king of किष्किन्धा, from तारा. He was sent as an ambassador by Ràma to लंका to expostulate with रावण and induce him to deliver up सीता to राम.

अंगिरस्—A celebrated sage.

अज—The son of Raghu. Kalidâsa's अजविलाप, wherein अज laments for his dear wife इन्दुमती, has at once immortalized and endeared him to all Sanskrit scholars.

अंजनी—The mother of हनुमान्.

अत्रि—One of the ten Mind-born sons of महादेव. He was the husband of the chaste अनसूया, the mother of दत्तात्रेय.

अदिति—The wife of कश्यप. She was the mother of विष्णु, इन्द्र, and several other Gods.

अधिरथ—The foster father of कर्ण.

अनसूया The wife of the sage अत्रि, and the mother of दत्तात्रेय.

अनिरुद्ध—The grandson of कृष्ण. उषा, the daughter of बाणासुर, saw him in her dream, and fell deeply in love with him. Her dear friend चित्रलेखा caused the young lovers to meet, and they were privately married. But बाणासुर soon came to know this, and a fierce fight took place between him and अनिरुद्ध, wherein अनिरुद्ध was overcome. But बाणासुर had soon to deal with कृष्ण, who utterly worsted him in a combat. Finally, बाणासुर was reconciled to उषा and अनिरुद्ध.

अभिमन्यु—The son of अर्जुन by सुभद्रा

In deeds of valour he equalled his father. It was he who fearlessly entered the चक्रव्यूह arranged by द्रोण in the great war between the कौरवs and the पाण्डवs, and committed such a havoc in the ranks of the enemy's forces, that even old veterans like कृप, द्रोण, कर्ण, अश्वत्थामन् etc. thought it discretion to attack him in a body, and put him to death.

अंबरीष—A celebrated king famous for his piety and religious nature. The sage दुर्वासस् had once set a कृत्या against him, when विष्णु's सुदर्शन appeared there and destroying the demoness, set in pursuit of दुर्वासस्. When दुर्वासस् begged विष्णु to relieve him from it, विष्णु directed him to अंबरीष through whose intervention, दुर्वासस् was relieved from the सुदर्शन.

अंबा—The eldest daughter of काशिराज. She, along with her sisters अंबिका and अंबालिका was won by भीष्म at the time of their स्वयंवर, and brought by him to हस्तिनापुर to be wedded to विचित्रवीर्य. But अंबा loved शाल्व to whom भीष्म willingly sent her. But शाल्व rejected अंबा's suit, and अंबा once again returned to Bhîshma, and importured him to wed her. But भीष्म had sworn to a life-celibacy before his father, and अंबा took to a life of penance. The great परशुराम fought for her with भीष्म, but to no purpose. अंबा, by her hard penance, propitiated the God Rudra, and, by virtue of his boon, became instrumental in killing भीष्म, for whom she bore a mortal grudge, in her second birth as शिखंडिनी, the daughter of king द्रुपद.

अरुण—The son of विनता and the brother of गरुड. He is the charioteer of सूर्य.

अरुन्धती—The wife of the sage वसिष्ठ.

अर्जुन—The third son of कुन्ती born from इन्द्र. He was the greatest archer of his times, and an ardent devotee and friend of कृष्ण. In the great Bhâratîya war, he was at first averse to kill his own kinsmen and friends, but Krishna preached to him his गीता and prepared him to fight.

अलायुध—A demon friendly to दुर्योधन. He was very powerful and was killed by घटोत्कच in the भारतीय war.

अश्वत्थामन्—The son of द्रोण. He was the last general of दुर्योधन in the great भारतीय war and slew, at dead of night, the sons of the पाण्डवs, and avenged himself terribly on धृष्टद्युम्न for his having treacherously murdered his father. He wore a fine jewel in his head of which अर्जुन made a present to द्रौपदी. With a view of rendering the earth void of the पाण्डवs, he had directed his ब्रह्मास्त्र against the fœtus of उत्तरा, the wife of अभिमन्यु. But कृष्ण protected the fœtus of उत्तरा with his सुदर्शन चक्र. He is reckoned among the seven immortal persons.

अश्वसेन—The son of the serpent तक्षक. His mother was killed by अर्जुन and when कर्ण and अर्जुन were fighting he had sat secretly on the arrow of कर्ण. The arrow would have proved fatal to अर्जुन, had not कृष्ण dexterously lowered the chariot.

अश्विनीकुमार—The twins born of सूर्य from संज्ञा. They are the physicians of the Gods.

असमंज—The son of सगर from केशिनी and the father of अंशुमान्.

अहल्या—The wife of the sage गौतम.

She had the misfortune of being loved by इन्द्र who appeared before her in the form of her husband and seduced her. गौतम, when he came to know of this, cursed इन्द्र and अहल्या, by virtue of which अहल्या was transformed into an inanimate शिला. The touch of राम's feet restored her to her original form.

आस्तिक—The son of जरत्कारु. He was deeply versed in all the lores then extant, and the power of his penance was very great. In the serpent-sacrifice of king जनमेजय he saved तक्षक by dint of his pursasive powers of speech and thus preserved the serpent race from extinction.

इक्ष्वाकु—The grandson of सूर्य, and the primogenitor of the solor race of रघु राम and others.

इन्दुमती—The beloved consort of king अज. She was the mother of दशरथ. She was one day seated with king अज in their palatial garden, when a garland happened to fall from the harp of नारद on her person, and इन्दुमती being even more delicate than flowers, was put to death thereby. अज's pathetic lament over the death of his wife on this occasion forms excellent topic for the immortal verse of कालिदास in the eigth canto of his रघुवंश, and ought to be l arnt by heart by every संस्कृत scholar worth the name.

इन्द्र—The king of Gods. Mythology represents him to be very jealous of other people's austerities, lest, by their virtue, they ousted him from his office of the ruler of Gods. His weapon is the famous वज्र. Morally, he is represented to be not above reproach.

इन्द्रजित, also मेघनाद-The son of रावण and मंदोदरी He possessed great magical powers, and in the great रामरावणयुद्ध, was responsible for much heavy carnage He had even caused लक्ष्मण, the brother of राम, to faint. But in the next day's fight लक्ष्मण killed इन्द्राजत् after a long and arduous fight with him. इन्द्रजित्'s wife was सुलोचना.

उग्रसेन—The father of कंस. कंस had put him in confinement, but when कृष्ण killed कंस, he released उग्रसेन, and re-installed him on his throne of मथुरा.

उत्तरा—Daughter of king विराट and wife of अभिमन्यु. She gave birth to परीक्षित [See our note on अश्वत्थामन्].

उद्धव—A very warm and ardent follower of कृष्ण.

उर्वशी- A celestial nympth. She was cursed to pass a period of her life on earth, and as she was descending from heaven to fulfil her curse, a demon caught her, and was making away with her, when king पुरूरवस् heard her cries and rescued her. A love-affair ensued between उर्वशी and पुरूरवस्, and they became man and wife. When at the expiration of her curse, उर्वशी started for heaven, पुरूरवस् lamanted like a child, and, out of compassion, he was granted a sight of his beloved consort by the Gods in Paradise.

उलूपी—The daughter of the serpent कौरव्य. अर्जुन married her.

उषा—The daughter of बाणासुर, and the wife of अनिरुद्ध. (For a detailed account of her love marriage with अनिरुद्ध, vide अनिरुद्ध and चित्रलेखा).

ऋतुपर्ण—A king of अयोध्या descended from इक्ष्वाकु. He was a great friend of नल whom he taught his अक्षविद्या in exchange for नल's knowledge in अश्वविद्या.

ऋष्यशृंग—A great sage contemporary with king दशरथ. He had married शान्ता the daughter of king लोमपाद.

एकलव्य—The son of a निषाद chief. Since द्रोण would not accept him as a pupil, he had prepared an earthen image of द्रोण, and taught himself the art of archery. When द्रोण saw his skill therein, he feared lest he would be more powerful than अर्जुन and demanded of एकलव्य as दक्षिणा his right thumb, which एकलव्य willingly cut off. How wonderful was his faith in,and devotion to, द्रोण ?

कंस—The king of मथुरा. He was foretold that he would meet his death at the hands of his sister देवकी's son, and he therefore put in confinement देवकी and her husband वसुदेव, and killed successfully her seven children as soon as born. But the eighth child, कृष्ण, escaped his clutches by being transferred to गोकुल by वसुदेव. कंस tried to kill कृष्ण in गोकुल but to no purpose. Eventually कृष्ण killed कंस.

ककुत्स्थ—A king descnded from इक्ष्वाकु. He had once helped Indra against the demons, when इंद्र assumed the form of a bull and bore him on his back.

कच—The son of बृहस्पति, the preceptor of the Gods. In the great war between the Gods and the demons, शुक्र, the preceptor of the latter, revived by means of his संजीवनी मंत्र whatever warriors on the side of the demons were killed by the Gods. He was therefore sent by the Gods to शुक्र to learn from him his संजीवनी विद्या. The demons knew of this project, and, pounding कच to atoms, mixed the dust in the wine-cup of शुक्राचार्य, and gave it to him to drink. But in this they had counted without देवयानी, the daughter of शुक्राचार्य, who deeply loved कच. At her importunities शुक्र uttered his संजीवनी mantra, at which कच was revived in his stomach. Then he taught him his विद्या, and asked him to open his belly, and come out. कच came out and शुक्र lay dead. But कच soon brought him to life and then started for Heaven. As he was about to start देवयानी begged him to marry her but he refused to do so. देवयानी then cursed कच that his विद्या would be quite useless to him personally. कच in return cursed देवयानी to the effect that she would not get any Brâhmana youth for her husband.

कण्व—The famous foster-father of शकुन्तला.

कद्रु—One of the daughters of दक्ष, and the mother of serpents.

कपिल—A great sage. He reduced to ashes the sons of सगर when they came in quest of the sacrificial horse of their father to his abode.

कबन्ध—Originally a Gandharva, but cursed to be a demon. His arms were one 'yojan' in length. While राम was passing through the दण्डक forest, कबंध obstructed him, when राम cut down his arms and put him to death.

कर्कोटक—A serpent, whom king नल saved from a conflagration. कर्कोटक, out of gratitude, bit नल, and the latter was immediately deformed, so that none could recoginse him. After नल's days of adversity were over, नल was of course restored to his original form and beauty.

कर्ण—The son of कुन्ती from the sun while yet unmarried and at her father's house. Afraid of public scandal, कुन्ती threw her son into a river. But he was rescued from a watery grave by अधिरथ, the charioteer of धृतराष्ट्र, and by him and his wife राधा nurtured to manhood. Hence कर्ण is often called राधेय. He was a very great archer, and second to none but अर्जुन therein. His liberality is famous. He was a great friend of दुर्योधन. In the war between the कौरवs and the पाण्डवs he had caught all the four brothers of अर्जुन, but as he had vowed to कुन्ती, on the eve of the battle, that he would kill none but अर्जुन of the पांडवs, he let them go. On the last day of his generalship, while engaged in extricating the wheel of his chariot fast sinking in the earth, अर्जुन advisedly flung his arrows at him and put him to death. An untoward fate had decreed that he should meet with extraordinary reverses and exceptional rebuffs, and these too, at the most crucial of moments in his life, and these, in no mean degree, contributed to eclipse and undermine his pristine goodness and greatness.

कश्यप—A great sage. He had married thirteen of the daughters of दक्ष, from whom were born the Gods, demons, men, beasts and reptiles.

काम—The God of love. His wife was रति शिव was highly incensed with him for infusing amorous ideas in his mind for पार्वती when he was practising hard penance, and he burnt काम with the fire in his third eye. Eventually रति pacified शिव, and काम was allowed to be re-born as प्रद्युम्न. The weapon of the God of love is depicted to be a flowery bow. The spring season is his great friend. मदन, अनंग, पंचसायक etc. are some of his significant names.

कार्तवीर्य—Otherwise called सहस्रार्जुन. He was a great devottee of दत्तात्रेय. He was very powerful and had once captivated रावण. Once he went to the hut of the sage जमदग्नि, and on his return, brought with him by force his कामधेनु. This caused a fight between सहस्रार्जुन and परशुराम, the son of जमदग्नि, in which the former was slain.

कार्तिकेय—The son of शिव and पार्वती, the generalissimo of the Gods, and the killer of the demon तारक. He has six heads. गुह is another of his appellations.

कालयवन—A Yawan king. He was a great enemy of the यादवs. कृष्ण caused his death by a strategem through the king मुचकुन्द [Vide our note on मुचकुन्द].

कालिय—A great serpent. He had taken resort in the waters of the यमुना through the fear of गरुड. Once the friends of कृष्ण had gone to the यमुना, and drinking the water of the river, lay dead. कृष्ण as soon as he knew of this went there, and plunging into the bosom of the river, harassed कालिय so much that at last he and his wives sued for mercy, which कृष्ण granted him. After that कालिय abandoned the यमुना, and her waters were made once again perfecetly pure and safe. The friends of कृष्ण were, of course, all revived.

कीचक—The brother of the wife of king विराट. When the पाण्डवs were living incognito in the court of विराट, he happened to cast an evil eye on सैरन्ध्री *i. e.* द्रौपदी. द्रौपदी complained of this to भीम, who, highly enraged, beat him to death with his fists.

कुन्ती—The wife of पण्डु, and the mother of the first three पाण्डवs.

कुबेर—The lord of wealth, the king of the यक्षs and the किन्नरs He was a half brother of रावण.

कुब्जा—A crooked and deformed female in the service of कंस. कृष्ण is said to have made her straight and beautiful when she looked a fine lass

कुंभकर्ण—The younger brother of रावण. His devouring capacities were highly abnormal. Hence महादेव had cursed him so that he should sleep for most time. While the great war between राम and रावण was going on, रावण roused him up, and sent him against राम. कुंभकर्ण devoured a great part of राम s army, but eventually he was slain by राम.

कुरु—The great-grand-father of the कौरवs and the पांडवs.

कुश—The elder of the twins born to Rama from सीता after he had deserted her. The twins were reared and taught by the great sage वाल्मीकि in his own hut. They were so valourous that it is well known how they, even when young, had arrested the sacrificial horse of their father राम, and vanquished his armies.

कृतवर्मन्—One of the trio, the other two being अश्वत्थामन् and कृप, who alone, of all the warriors on the side of दुर्योधन, survived the great भारतीय war. He was afterwards slain by सात्यकि.

कृप—The son of the sage शरद्वत्. He was the maternal uncle of अश्वत्थामन्, the son of द्रोण from his sister कृपी. He is one of the seven immortals. Before द्रोण, he taught the young कौरवs and पांडवs the art of archery.

कृष्ण—The eighth incarnation of विष्णु, born in a prison house from वसुदेव and देवकी. On the very first day कृष्ण was taken by वसुदेव to गोकुल, where he was reared up by नन्द and यशोदा. कंस knew that कृष्ण was to kill him, and hence sent many demons to do away with कृष्ण. But the young कृष्ण himself killed them all, and eventually killed कंस too. The गोपs and गोपीs in the गोकुल loved कृष्ण whole-heartedly, but none more than राधा. He was a great friend of the पांडवs, and in the great भारतीय war, when अर्जुन was struck with bewilderment as to how he should kill his own kinsmen, he preached him the भगवद्गीता and prepared him for the fight. It is the very cream of all that is best and highest in Indian philosophy.

कैकेयी—The third and the youngest wife of दशरथ, the mother of भरत. She had once helped her husband at a critical moment in a fight, and he had promised her two boons. At the time of Rama's installation as heir-apparent, कैकेयी reminded दशरथ of the two boons he had promised her, and by one of them she asked him to send राम to the forest for 14 years, and by the other, to install भरत as heir-apparent. दशरथ could hardly bear the thought of separation from his dear राम, but कैकेयी proved inexorable, and he had to grant her the boons demanded. दशरथ of course died soon after राम's departure. When भरत, who adored राम, returned from his maternal uncle to perform the last rites over his father, and came to know of his mother कैकेयी's doings, his anger knew no bounds, and he spared neither pains nor expression to vent in full his wrath on his mother.

कौसल्या—The queen-consort of दशरथ, the mother of राम.

खर—A demon, the half-brother of रावण, whom राम killed in the दण्डकारण्य.

गंगा—Ganges, the most sacred river of the Hindus. She was the wife of शंतनु, and of the eight children she bore to him the famous भीष्म was the last. [In connection with this note, see also our note on भगीरथ].

गणेश—The God of learning. The son of शिव and पार्वती, and the husband of सरस्वती. He is looked upon as the most auspicious of Gods, and as such is remembered at the commencement of every undertaking by pious house-holders. He is said to have played the part of an amanuensis to व्यास when the latter composed his महाभारत and dictated it to him.

गरुड—The son of कश्यप and विनता. The king of birds, and the natural enemy of serpents, the children of his own aunt कद्रू. विनता had fallen into the bondage of कद्रू for some reason, and गरुड released her from the same by presenting the nectar jar to the sons of कद्रू. गरुड is the vehicle of विष्णु.

गाधि—A king from whom was born the celebrated विश्वामित्र.

गांधारी—The wife of धृतराष्ट्र, the mother of the कौरवs. Her devotion to her husband was so great that because her husband was blind, she had bandaged her eyes and was voluntarily suffering blindness. After the great भारतीय war, wherein all her sons were slain, she and her husband stayed with युधिष्ठिर. But afterwards they, along with विदुर and कुन्ती went to the forest. On the demise of धृतराष्ट्र, गांधारी immolated herself.

गार्गी—A celebrated female ascetic well known for her deep knowledge of philosophy.

गुह—A kirata-chief greatly attached to दशरथ and राम.

घटोत्कच—Son of भीम from हिडिंबा. In the भारतीय war he committed such ravages in the कौरव army that at last कर्ण had to kill him with the same 'shakti' that he had reserved for अर्जुन.

चाणूर—An athlete in the employ of कंस. When कृष्ण was at मथुरा a duel took place between him and चाणूर wherein the athlete was killed.

चार्वाक—A demon, friend to दुर्योधन. When, at the end of the great war, युधिष्ठिर was being installed as king, चार्वाक went to him in the guise of a Brahman and told him that he would go to hell since he had not come by his kingdom morally. The other Bráhmanas assembled there were astonished to hear this, but they soon detected चार्वाक and burnt him to ashes.

चित्रलेखा—The artist-friend of उषा, the daughter of बाणासुर. उषा had once seen a very beautiful person in her dream, and she was pining with love for him. चित्रलेखा drew likenesses of all the kings and princes; until उषा identified the image of अनिरुद्ध with the person she had seen in her dream. चित्रलेखा knew some magic too, and she brought over अनिरुद्ध at dead of night to उषा secretly. [In connection with this note see our note on उषा].

चित्रांगदा—An अप्सरस् who married अर्जुन and bore to him बभ्रुवाहन.

छाया—The wife of the sun. शनि was her son.

जटायु—The son of अरुण and the nephew of गरुड. He was a great friend of दशरथ. When रावण was running away with सीता, he obstructed him, and faught hard with him. राम, in quest of his lost wife, met with him, and जटायु, on the last verge of death, informed राम of the fate of सीता and breathed his last. राम deeply lamented his fate, and performed the last rites over him.

जनक—A king of मिथिला He was the father of सीता. He was a great कर्मयोगी.

जनमेजय—The son of परिक्षित. Because his father had died from serpent-bite, he started a sacrifice to extirpate the whole serpent-race. All serpents were put to death in his sacrifice except तक्षक whom the sage आस्तिक saved, and thus prevented the extinction of the serpent-race.

जमदग्नि—A great and fiery sage. परशुराम was one of his sons. Once जमदग्नि's wife रेणुका was rather late in coming home from her bath, and he was so much enraged that he ordered his sons to put her to death. They would not execute his orders, and जमदग्नि at once turned them into stone. At this time परशुराम had gone to the forest, and when he returned, was asked by जमदग्नि to cut off the head of रेणुका. परशुराम did it. This so pleased his father that at his request he restored रेणुका to life, as well as his petri fied sons. जमदग्नि was slain by the sons of कार्तवीर्य.

जयद्रथ—The king of the country named सिंधु. दुःशला, the sister of दुर्योधन was his wife. In the great भारतीय war he, through the boon of रुद्र, defeated the पांडव's except अर्जुन for once. The same day अभिमन्यु was killed. Next day अर्जुन vowed to put जयद्रथ to death before sun-set. जयद्रथ was over well guarded by द्रोण on that day. But कृष्ण towards sun-set hid the sun with his famous disc, and believing the sun to have set, जयद्रथ came forth before अर्जुन triumphantly. But immediately कृष्ण removed his disc from the sun, and अर्जुन easily put जयद्रथ to death.

जरत्कारु—A great sage. He was the husband of वासुकी's sister also of the name of जरत्कारु. From her he had for son the famous आस्तिक who saved तक्षक, and through him the serpent-race, in the जनमेजय serpent-sacrifice.

जरासंध—The son of बृहद्रथ, the king

of मगध. He was born in two halves from two mothers. A demoness named जरा joined his two halves into one, and hence his name. कंस was his son-in-law, and because कृष्ण had killed कंस, जरासंध marched against कृष्ण for seventeen times, but was as many times defeated by कृष्ण. He was as powerful as wicked and had imprisoned many a king and prince. At the time of युधिष्ठिर's राजसूय sacrifice, कृष्ण, अर्जुन and भीम went to him, and challanged him to a duel with any one of them. जरासंध chose भीम, and भीम after a combat of thirteen days and nights, put him to death by tearing him.

जन्हु—A great sage. गंगा, while following भगीरथ, flooded his आश्रम with her waters, and being enraged at it he drank her up. भगीरथ thereupon prayed him to release her, and जन्हु let go गंगा from his ears, a fact from which गंगा came to be called जान्हवी.

जाम्बवान्—There are two जाम्बवान्s known to mythology. One was a monkey-chief in the army of Rama, while the other was a great bear-king, who had possessed himself of the famous स्यमंतकमणि originally the property of सत्राजित. कृष्ण fought with him for getting back the स्यमंतक jewel, and defeating जाम्बवान् got it back. जाम्बवान् also gave his daughter जाम्बवती in marriage to Krishna, on that occasion.

तक्षक—One of the well-known serpent chiefs, whom the sage आस्तिक saved from the serpent sacrifice of जनमेजय.

ताडका—A demoness whom राम shot with an arrow when she was causing trouble to the penance and the sacrificial rites of विश्वामित्र.

तारक—A demon who, in virtue of the boon of ब्रह्मा, had become greatly intolerable to the Gods and the sages, and whom कार्तिकेय, the son of शिव and पार्वती, slew.

तारा—The wife of वाली and the mother of अंगद.

तारामती—The wife of हरिश्चंद्र and the mother of रोहिदास. She is famous for her chastity and deep affection for her spouse.

त्रिजटा—One of the female demonesses whom रावण had appointed to guard सीता in the Asoka forest She behaved with exceptional kindness towards her unhappy prisoner and enforced the same on the other female demon attendants.

त्रिपुर—A demon whom शिव burned to ashes along with his three cities of gold, silver, and iron.

त्रिशंकु—A king of the solar race. His one desire was to go to heaven in his own much-loved body. विश्वामित्र performed the sacrifice for him, and, in virtue of his high penance, caused त्रिशंकु to mount up to heaven in his earthly form. But इंद्र arrested his progress heavenward by ordering him to stop; while विश्वामित्र would not allow him to come down! Thus त्रिशंकु lay pending half way between heaven and earth. It is said that he is still in that position!

त्वष्टृ—The architect of the Gods, also called विश्वकर्मन्.

दक्ष—One of the प्रजापतिs. His daughter सती was married to शिव. At one of his sacrifices, दक्ष had failed to invite शिव and सती to attend it. सती however went thither, but being insulted she threw herself into the sacrificial flames and perished. Thereupon the enraged Siva created a demon named वीरभद्र by striking a tress of his hair on the ground, and through him, destroyed दक्ष's sacrifice.

दनु—One of the wives of काश्यप, the mother of the दानवs.

दमयंती—A princess of the Vidarbhas. She was famed for her beauty. She was the wife of the celebrated नल.

दशरथ—The son of अज and the celebrated इंदुमती. He was king of अयोध्या. For a long time he had no issue from his wives, namely कौसल्या, सुमित्रा and कैकेयी, but after the celebration of a sacrifice called पुत्रकामेष्टि, कौसल्या the queen consort bore to him राम, सुमित्रा, bore to him लक्ष्मण and शत्रुघ्न, while कैकेयी bore to him भरत. How कैकेयी caused him to exile राम for 14 years and declare भरत as heir-apparent to the throne and how this brought on the death of दशरथ may be learnt from our note on कैकेयी.

दिति—One of the daughters of दक्ष married to काश्यप. She was the mother of the दैत्यs.

दिलीप—A celebrated Solar king. For a long time he had no issue, but according to the instructions of वसिष्ठ, he and his wife tended the celestial cow नंदिनी, and were eventually blessed with a son. This was the clebrated रघु.

दुःशला—Sister to दुर्योधन and wife to जयद्रथ.

दुःशासन—The second of the hundred sons of धृतराष्ट्र. He had dragged द्रौपदी by her hair at the time when she was in her monthly courses, into the court, where भीष्म, धृतराष्ट्र and all others were present. By the orders of दुर्योधन he was also trying to wrest from her the garment she was wearing. At this भीम was excessively enraged and vowed then and there to drink the blood of दुःशासन by tearing his bosom. This vow was fulfilled by भीम in the great भारतीय war.

दुन्दुभि—A huge giant slain by वाली the monkey chief of किष्किन्धा.

दुर्योधन—The eldest son of धृतराष्ट्र. He was possessed of great strength and courage, but he hated the पाण्डवs with all his heart and soul. शकुनि, his maternal uncle fostered this hatred in him by his vile advice. He had prepared a लाक्षागृह wherein to burn the पाण्डवs. Through शकुनी's advice, he challanged युधिष्ठिर to play at dice, and defeating him therein, caused him to go to the forest. After युधिष्ठिर's return he refused to give him even the slightest part of his kingdom. This originated the great भारतीय war. He had once bared his thigh before द्रौपदी, and भीम had vowed to break it with his mace. On the eighteenth day of the war दुर्योधन and भीम met in a mace-duel, wherein the latter smashed the thigh of the former, and put him to death.

दुर्वासस्—The celebrated sage, whose extreme irascibility is proverbial. कालिदास has made fine use of it in his अभिज्ञानशकुन्तलम्.

दुष्यन्त—The well-known king of the पौरव dynasty. He had married शकुन्तला who bore to him the celebrated भरत. It is after him tha

India is called भारतवर्ष.

देवकी—Consin of कंस; wife of वसुदेव and mother of कृष्ण.

देवयानी—The only child of शुक्राचार्य, the preceptor of the demons. She had fallen in love with कच the son of बृहस्पति. But कच refused to marry her and she was afterwards wedded to ययाति. She was of strong passions.

द्रुपद्—King of the पांचाल's and the father of द्रौपदी. He was a schoolmate of द्रोण; but after he became king, he refused to own द्रोण as his friend and equal. द्रोण thereupon averged himelf upon द्रुपद by defeating him through his pupils, the पाण्डव's. द्रुपद thereupon secured for himself a son named धृष्टद्युम्न who was to kill द्रोण in the great भारतीय war.

द्रोण-The son of the sage भारद्वाज. He knew the science of archery excellently well and was the preceptor in it of the कौरव's and पाण्डव's. He was the second generalissimo of दुर्योधन in the great भारतीय war. On the fifth day he heard the truth-loving धर्मराज say that अश्वत्थामन् was killed. Supposi g that it was his own son अश्वत्थामन who was killed he threw away his arms, when, धृष्टद्युम्न rushed forth and struck off his head.

द्रौपदी—The daughter of king द्रुपद. She was the common wife of धर्म, भीम, अर्जुन, नकुल, and सहदेव. Of all her husbands she loved अर्जुन the best.

धृतराष्ट्र—King of Hastinápur. गांधारी was his wife and bore to him the hundred कौरव's. He was very much under the thumb of दुर्योधन, his eldest son, and hence the miseries that fell to the lot of the पाण्डव's, and the destruction that befell his own sons.

धृष्टद्युम्न—Son of द्रुपद. In the भारतीय war he was appointed the commander-in-chief to the Pandava forces. For his having slain his father treacherously, अश्वत्थामन् took a terrible revenge on him by beating him to death at the end of the great war.

ध्रुव—The son of उत्तानपाद. His mother was not in the good books of her husband. One day as ध्रुव was sitting on the lap of his Royal father, his step-mother, who was very much loved by उत्तानपाद, caused him to get up from that place. ध्रुव took this insult greatly to his heart, and even in that tender age went to the forest and began practising hard penance. God विष्णु was pleased with the child's devotion and fulfilled ध्रुव's wish to have a permanent position for evermore. We identify him with the North Pole.

नकुल—The son of माद्री by पण्डु. The fourth of the पाण्डव's.

नन्द—The husband of यशोदा and the foster-father of कृष्ण.

नमुचि—A demon destroyed by इंद्र with his thunder-bolt.

नरकासुर-A tyrannous demon killed by कृष्ण.

नल—The famous king of the निषाद's. He was a noble king. He had married दमयंती. By the wiles of कलि he lost his kingdom by gambling, and, after a series of mishaps, was again restored to his kingdom. In connection with this see our note on कर्कोटक.

नहुष—He had temporarily become इंद्र. He caused his litter to be borne about by Rishis, who had therefore cursed him to be a serpent.

नारद--A divine sage born from the hip of ब्रह्मदेव He is famous for causing discords amongst Gods and men.

निमि--The Primogenitor of the वैदेह dynasty ruling in मिथिला.

परशुराम—Son of the sage जमदाग्नि and रेणुका He had cleared the earth of the क्षत्रिय's for twenty-one times. In connection with this see our note on जमदाग्नि. परशुराम had vowed vengence on the क्षात्रय's because his father had been slain by the sons of कार्तवीर्य, a क्षत्रिय king. He is one of the seven immortal personages of our mythology.

परीक्षित--The son of अभिमन्यु and उत्तरा. He was bitten to death by तक्षक. His son was जनमेजय.

पाक--A demon killed by इंद्र. Hence इंद्र is sometmies called पाकशासन.

पाण्डु—The husband of कुन्ती and माद्रि. He was cursed with death if he mated. One day he became blinded with passion for माद्रि, and this brought on his death. माद्रि immolated herself in his pyre.

पार्वती--Wife of Siva, and the mother of कार्तिकेय and गजानन.

पुरु--The youngest son of ययाति and शर्मिष्ठा. He readily gave his youth and beauty to his father in exchange for his old age.

पुरूरवस्--The celebrated Royal lover of the nymph उर्वशी. [Vide our note on उर्वशी].

पूतना—A demoness sent by कंस to गोकुल to kill कृष्ण while he was yet a child. However पूतना herself lost her life in the attempt.

पृथु—The son of king वेन. He compelled the earth to yield to mankind whatever was necessary for their subsistence. Kalidas tells us in his कुमारसंभवम् that the assemblage of mountains having fixed upon Himálaya as the calf, and having appointed मेरु as the milkman, milked the earth, which had assumed the shape of a cow, of brilliant jewels and great medicinal herbs, as directed by पृथु.

प्रद्युम्न—The Son of कृष्ण and रुक्मिणी. As a matter of fact he was the incarnation of मदन, who, though first burned to ashes, was afterward allowed by Siva to be reborn. In his infancy he was stolen by the demon शम्बर and cast into the s a. There he was swallowed by a fish which was caught by a fisherman and presented to मायावती the wife of शम्बर. मायावती found in it प्रद्युम्न and she reared him up. When प्रद्युम्न came to know that शम्बर had stolen him in his childhood, he challenged the demon to a fight and killed him and went to his father's. मायावती followed him and became his wife.

प्रमिला—The sovereign of the kingdom of women. She was conquered by Arjuna whose wife she became.

प्रन्हाद—The son of हिरण्यकशिपु He was a great devotee of विष्णु and so became an object of hatred to his father. हिरण्यकशिपु once asked प्रन्हाद as to where his God was. When प्रन्हाद told him that he was everywhere, and for the matter of that in that pillar near by, हिरण्यकशिपु kicked the pillar when the pillar was cut in twain and विष्णु appeared there as नारसिंह. नारसिंह tore हिरण्यकशिपु

to pieces.

प्रावा—She was the mother of the well-known अप्सरस्s such as तिलोत्तमा, रंभा, उर्वशी, मेनका etc.

बक—A gluttonous demon killed by भीम.

बभ्रुवाहन—The son of Arjuna and चित्रांगदा. He had arrested the sacrificial horse of युधिष्ठिर escorted by अर्जुन, and defeating अर्जुन slew him. Afterwards बभ्रुवाहन went to the abode of the serpents to bring the संजीवनमणि as directed by उलुपी, and अर्जुन was restored to life.

बलराम—The elder brother of कृष्ण. He taught the art of mace-fighting to दुर्योधन and भीम. He was simple and straight-forward. His wife was रेवती. He was fond of wine. He is said to have dragged the river यमुना from her original course with his plough-share. He is often called हलायुध.

बलि—A mighty Demon-king, the grand-son of प्रल्हाद. His ambition was to be इंद्र, and he was performing his hundredth sacrifice towards that end, when Vishnu went to him in the dwarfish form of वामन and begged of him space enough for him to cover with three steps. बलि granted the request, and विष्णु assuming a huge form covered the earth with one step, the Heaven with the other, and demanded room for his third step. The astonished बलि asked वामन to place his third step on his head, which वामन did, and sent बलि down to पाताळ and was allowed to reign there.

बाण—The eldest son of बलि and the father of उषा. [Vide our note on उषा].

बाहुक—The name assumed by नळ when residing with ऋतुपर्ण.

बिभीषण—The brother of रावण. Not liking the policy of रावण in abducting सीता and refusing to return her to राम, he joined राम. He supplied very valuable information to राम by virtue of which इंद्रजित् was killed by लक्ष्मण. After the death of रावण, बिभीषण was installed king of लंका by राम.

बृहन्नडा—Arjuna lived incognito at the court of विराट under this name.

बृहस्पति—The preceptor of the [Gods.

ब्रह्मन्—He is said to have been born from a lotus issuing from the navel of विष्णु. His function is to create, as that of Siva is to destroy, and that of विष्णु to protect. His vehicle is the Swan.

भगीरथ—A descendent of सगर. He practised severe austerities and brought the Ganges to the earth, to lave the ashes of his ancestors and thus open for them the portals of Heaven. Hence गंगा is called भागीरथी. [In connection with this, vide also our note on जन्हु]

भरत—Two personages of this name figure in our mythology. One is the son of दुष्यन्त and शकुन्तला, and the other the son of कैकेयी and दशरथ. The exile of राम brought on by कैकेयी was utterly distasteful to भरत who loved राम deeply, and when राम refused to return to अयोध्या with him, since दशरथ had ordered him to pass 14 years in exile, भरत came back alone, and ruled अयोध्या in the name of राम till his return.

भीम—The second of the पाण्डव's.

He was begotten by वायु. His strength was herculean, and he especially excelled in mace-fighting. He had torn जरासंध in twain by the sheer strength of his mighty arms. The destruction of many other demons such as बक, हिडिंब etc. is also to his credit. For their numerous affronts भीम had vowed to kill every one of the hundred कौरव's and he did it in the great भारतीय war [In connection with his stay in the court of विराट disguised as बल्लव, and his killing कीचक there, see our note on कीचक]

भीष्म—Son of शंतनु and गंगा. His father had fallen in love with सत्यवती, and सत्यवती's father would not give her to शंतनु unless he promised his kingdom to सत्यवती's children. To relieve his father from this dilemma, भीष्म bound himself by the terrible vow that he would neither ascend his father's throne nor take any woman for wife so as not to have any children who might fight for the throne! This enabled शंतनु to wed सत्यवती, and शंतनु gave भीष्म the boon of dying at will. भीष्म was the grand uncle of the कौरव's and पाण्डवs. In the war that ensued between them, he was the generalissimo of दुर्योधन for the first ten days. During it, it is well known how he compelled कृष्ण to break his vow and take up arms, and indeed, had not अर्जुन ensconsed himself behind शिखण्डी, born a woman, against whom भीष्म would not direct his missiles, भीष्म would never have been pierced all over with अर्जुन's arrows and incapaciatated for further fight. Having the boon of dying at will भीष्म did not depart this life just then, as the sun had yet to cross the vernal equinox. At the end of the great war he consoled युधिष्ठिर with words of cheer and advice which are immortalized in the शांतिपर्व and अनुशासनपर्व of the महाभारत.

भृगु—An ancestor of परशुराम.

मन्थरा—The female attendant of कैकेयी. It was she who had advised her mistress to cause दशरथ to send Rama into exile, and instal भरत as heir-apparent in stead of राम.

मन्दोदरी—The wife of रावण. She was a paragon of wifely qualities.

मय—The architect of the दैत्य's. It was he whom Arjuna had saved from अग्नि when अग्नि was devouring the खाण्डव forest, and in return for this मयासुर had constructed a place of wonders for the पाण्डवs wherein it is well-known how दुर्योधन was deluded at every step.

महिष—A demon slain by the Goddess दुर्गा

माद्री—पाण्डु's second wife, and mother of नकुल and सहदेव.

मारीच—The son of ताडका He tried to dissuade रावण from abducting सीता, but when रावण charged him with cowardice and ingratitude, he helped रावण in carrying off सीता by assuming the form of a golden deer and alluring राम away When he was hit with the arrow of राम he imitated the voice of राम and wailed for help. सीता forced लक्ष्मण to go to help राम, when रावण sought her in the form of an ascetic and purloined her.

माल्यवान – Maternal grand uncle and minister of रावण.

मुचुकुंद—He had secured from the

Gods the boon of long sleep and the instantaneous death of him who would disturb him. कृष्ण tricked the demon कालयवन into disturbing मुचुकुंद's sleep, and thus brought on his death.

मोहिनी—When the nectar was churned out of the ocean by the Gods and the demons,a quarrel arose between them over it. Then विष्णु assumed the most bewitching form of a female, coaxed the demons into giving her the अमृत jar for a just distribution, and ultimately, finishing the whole amongsts the Gods, deceived the demons.

यदु—Son of ययाति and देवयानि.

ययाति—Son of नहुष. Through the curse of शुक्राचार्य, ययाति became prematurely aged. But one of his sons पुरु exchanged his own youth and beauty for ययाति's decripitude, and ययाति could enjoy the pleasures of youth for a thousand years.

यशोदा—The wife of नन्द and the foster-mother of कृष्ण.

युधिष्ठिर—The eldest पाण्डव, begotten on कुन्ती by यमधर्म. He loved mercy more than justice, and truth more than gain. His one weakness was his passion for gambling. He was justly called धर्मराज. Of all the पाण्डव's he alone could go to Heaven with his earthly body, but as he had once told a half-hearted lie, when he said audibly to द्रोण that अश्वत्थामन् was killed and inaudibly that it was अश्वत्थामन the elephant, he had to see for some time the agonies of his brothers in hell.

रघु—The famous king of the solar race, the son of दिलीप, and father of अज.

रन्तिदेव—A pious king of the lunar race who is said to have performed so many sacrifices that a regular river of blood, called चर्मण्वती, sprang from the slaughtered beasts of his sacrifices.

राम—Son of दशरथ by कौसल्या. He was forced to be exiled by कैकेयी for a period of fourteen years. राम was accompained in his exile by लक्ष्मण and सीता. When they were staying in the दण्डकारण्य, सीता was abducted by रावण the king of लंका. राम crossed over to लंका, killed रावण and his host of demons, and as, by then, the period of his exile was over, he returned to अयोध्या with सीता. He was the justest and noblest of kings and his life story forms the noble theme of the great epic of वाल्मीकि.

रावण—The ten-headed demon-king of लंका killed by राम.

राहु—A demon who, when the अमृत was being distributed amongst Gods, assumed the form of a God and sat in their midst. But सूर्य and चन्द्र detected and discovered him before राहु could swallow down his portion of अमृत. विष्णु for this treachery, cut off राहु's head, but the head had become immortal in virtue of the अमत it had tasted, and is supposed, out of vengeance, to swallow सूर्य and चन्द्र on certain occasions.

रुक्मिणी—Daughter of king भीमक. She was betrothed to शिशुपाल but रुक्मिणी had conceived a passionate love for कृष्ण, and she secretly called him over and fled with him. She bore to Krishna प्रद्युम्न. Of all his wives, कृष्ण loved her the best.

रेणुका—The wife of जमदग्नि and the

mother of परशुराम.

रेवती—The wife of बलराम.

रोहिणी—One of the numerous daughters of दक्ष, and the most favourite wife of चन्द्र.

लक्ष्मण—Son of दशरथ by सुमित्रा. He loved राम deeply, and followed him in his exile. In the great war with रावण, लक्ष्मण killed इंद्रजित, the most powerful son of रावण.

लव—One of the twin sons of राम by सीता. [In this connction see our note on कुश].

लवण—A demon killed by शत्रुघ्न.

लक्ष्मी—One of the fourteen jewels churned from the ocean. She became the wife of विष्णु. She represents Wealth and Fortune.

लोपामुद्रा—The wife of अगस्त्य.

लोमपाद—A king of the अंग's. His daughter शान्ता was given in marriage to the sage ऋष्यशृंग.

वत्सला—Daughter of बलराम married to अभिमन्यु.

वसिष्ठ—The celebrated sage, the family priest of the solar race.

वसुदेव—Fathor of कृष्ण.

वामन—The fifth incarnation of विष्णु. [Vide बलि]

वालि—A great monkey chief, the king of किष्किन्धा. He was so powerful that be had once defeated even रावण. He had purloined the wife of his brother सुग्रीव, and was killed for the sin by राम.

वाल्मीकि—The first poet and the famous author of रामायण. He is said to have been very vicious and wicked in his youth, but was reclaimed by नारद. When राम had abandoned सीता, वाल्मीकि brought her over to his hermitage and reared up her twin sons लव and कुश. As लव and कुश grew up, and as they recited the verses of वाल्मीकि's रामायण in their dulcet tone, what raptures must have filled the heart of वाल्मीकि?

वासुकि—A serpent chief.

विकर्ण—One of the hundred कौरव's. Unlike his brothers, he loved justice and purity of conduct. When द्रौपदी was dragged to the court by दुःशासन, he had fearlessly denounced it as unlawful and ignominious. When भीम killed him in the great war, he deeply felt it.

विचित्रवीर्य—Half-brother of भीष्म. व्यास begot on his widows अम्बिका, अम्बालिका two sons, namely, धृतराष्ट्र and पाण्डु.

विदुर—When सत्यवती begged व्यास to beget issues from अम्बिका and अम्बालिका, अम्बिका, being terrified by व्यास's austere appearance, sent to him her maid disguised in her clothes, and from this maid was विदुर born. He was very wise and shrewd and righteous.

विनता—The wife of काश्यप and the mother of गरुड.

विराट—The king of the मत्स्य's. It was at his court that the पाण्डव's were living incognito for one year. His daughter उत्तरा was married to अभिमन्यु. To them was born परीक्षित.

विराध—A demon killed by राम.

विश्रवस्—The son of पुलस्त्य. From his second wife कैकसी, he had three sons namely रावण, कुम्भकर्ण and बिभीषण and one daughter namely शुर्पणखा.

विश्वामित्र—Originally born a क्षत्रिय prince. Once while hunting, he went to the hermitage of वसिष्ठ, who, with the aid of his all-yielding कामधेनु, treated him and his followers royally. विश्वामित्र at this covetted वासिष्ठ's कामधेनु, but not all his armies could succeed in carrying her off. On this विश्वामित्र practised hard penance, and succeeded at last in being acknowledged a ब्रम्हर्षि. During his penance, the Gods had sent to him मेनका to disturb his austerities, and from her, शकुन्तला was born to विश्वामित्र He is said to have created a second universe. (Vide त्रिशंकु, ताटका etc:-).

विष्णु—The God of preservation, the husband of लक्ष्मी. मत्स्य, कच्छ, वराह etc —are all his incarnations.

वृत्र—A mighty demon slain by इन्द्र with his thunderbolt specially fashioned for that purpose from the bones of the sage दधीचि

वृषपर्वा—A great demon king, who, backed by शुक्र and his संजीवनी mantra, made several wars against the Gods. His daughter शर्मिष्ठा was married to ययाति.

वृषसेन—The valiant son of कर्ण killed by अर्जुन. कर्ण is said to have deeply felt his loss.

वेन—A sovereign king, who, having lapsed into heresy and wicked ways, was therefore deposed by the sages. He was the father of पृथु.

वैशंपायन—A pupil of व्यास deeply learned in the legendary lore.

व्यास—The celebrated author of महाभारत. He was born to सत्यवती from the sage पराशर. He is also called कृष्णद्वैपायन.

शकुन्तला—The daughter of विश्वामित्र and मेनका. When she was abandoned by her parents, she was fed and protected through affection by birds. Hence, when the sage कण्व found her and took her to his hermitage, he gave her the euphonious name of शकुन्तला. Once, king दुष्यन्त, while hunting, strayed far away to the banks of the मालिनी, where कण्व's hermitage stood, and seeing there the youthful शकुन्तला, fell deeply in love with her. They were married by the गांधर्व ritual, and their issue was the famous भरत, or as he was popularly called, सर्वदमन.

शत्रुघ्न—Son of दशरथ from सुमित्रा. He killed लवणासुर.

शंतनु—A lunar king, who married गंगा and सत्यवती, from whom he had three sons, namely, भीष्म, and चित्रांगद and विचित्रवीर्य [Vide our note on भीष्म].

शबरी—A woman of शबर tribe. She was greatly devoted to राम, and gave him fine picked berries when she met him during his exile near the पंपा lake.

शंबर—A demon slain by प्रद्युम्न.

शल्य—King of the मद्रs. माद्री was his sister. During the commandership of कर्ण, शल्य became his charioteer. After कर्ण's fall, he was made commander of his forces by दुर्योधन. He was killed by युधिष्ठिर.

शान्ता—Daughter of लोमपाद married to ऋष्यशृंग.

शिखण्डिन्—अंबा born as शिखण्डिनी to king द्रुपद. शिखण्डिनी was brought up by द्रुपद as a male child. She was even married to a princess. The princess however complained to her father that her husband was a woman like herself disguised as a man. Her father marched against king द्रुपद, and शिखण्डिनी, greatly distracted, fled to a forest, and began practicing penance. The owner of the forest was a यक्ष, and he asked

शिखण्डिनी the cause of her penance. शिखण्डिनी confessed every thing, and begged of him his manhood. The यक्ष granted his manhood accordingly, and शिखण्डिनी, now become man, returned to the capital. Peace was soon established between द्रुपद and शिखण्डिनी's, or now शिखण्डि's, father-in-law.

In the great भारतीय war, अर्जुन shot his arrows at भीष्म from behind शिखण्डि, who being born a woman, भीष्म would not direct his missiles against him After the great war was over, शिखण्डि was butchered to death by अश्वत्थामा, and the यक्ष of the forest at once got back his man-hood.

शिबि—The eldest son of king उशीनर. He is famous for his liberality.

शिव—The God of destruction. पार्वती is his wife.

शिशुपाल—A prince descended from चेदि. When born, he had three eyes and four hands. When कृष्ण took him in his lap, his superfluous limbs dropped away. This meant that कृष्ण would cause death to शिशुपाल. शिशुपाल's mother was कृष्ण's aunt, and she begged कृष्ण to pardon शिशुपाल his first hundred crimes. In the राजसूय sacrifice of युधिष्ठिर, युधिष्ठिर worshipped कृष्ण first. At this, शिशुपाल, who was present there, felt insulted, and poured a volley of unbearable abuses on भीष्म, कृष्ण and others. By then the number of शिशुपाल's hundred crimes was told, and कृष्ण killed शिशुपाल.

शुक—A great sage. It is well known how even the beautiful रंभा could not tempt him.

शुक्र—The preceptor of the दानव's. He was the father of देवयानि.

शुंभ and निशुंभ—Two demons killed by कलि.

शूर्पणखा—Sister of रावण. When she saw राम and लक्ष्मण in the दण्डकारण्य, she wanted to marry one of them. राम and लक्ष्मण having refused to do so, शूर्पणखा threatened to devour सीता, when by the orders of राम, लक्ष्मण cut off her nose and ears. It was she who incited रावण to abduct the beautiful सीता.

शौरी—An appellation of कृष्ण.

श्रावण—A वैश्य ascetic killed inadvertently by दशरथ by an arrow. श्रावण's death very much grieved his blind and aged parents, who cursed दशरथ that he too would die with grief for his sons.

सगर—A king of the solar race. As he was performing his hundredth horse-sacrifice, इंद्र stole away his sacrificial horse and carried it to पाताल. सगर's sixty-thousand sons went in quest of the horse, and coming to the hermitage of the sage कपिल, charged him with having stolen their horse, which they saw there. कपिल got enraged, and reduced the sons of सगर to ashes. The horse was eventually very prudently recovered by अंशुमान, the grandson of सगर, whose sacrifice was then completed.

संजय—The charioteer of धृतराष्ट्र. He was blessed with दिव्यदृष्टि by व्यास, and he narrated the events of the great भारतीय war to the blind धृतराष्ट्र with graphic accuracy.

संज्ञा—Wife of सूर्य and the mother of यम and यमुना. As संज्ञा could not bear the lustre of her husband, she had created her counter-part (छाया) and kept her with the sun [Vide our note on छाया].

सत्यभामा—The daughter of सत्राजित

and wife of कृष्ण. It was for her that कृष्ण brought पारिजातक from नन्दनवन. She was a very simple and straightforward lady.

सत्यवान्—Chosen as a husband by सावित्री.

सत्राजित—Father of सत्यभामा. He was the original possessor of the famous स्यमंतक jewel which he had obtained from the sun as a gift.

संपाति—The elder brother of जटायु.

सहदेव—The youngest of the पाण्डव's. He was very beautiful.

सुदेष्णा—The wife of king विराट and the sister of कीचक.

सात्यकि—A यादव hero, who was commander of the पाण्डव forces in the beginning of the great भारतीय war.

सांदीपनि—The famous preceptor of कृष्ण and बलराम.

सावित्री—The daughter of king अश्वपति. When she came of age, her father sent her to choose a husband. She chose सत्यवान, and informed her father of the same. But नारद told सावित्री's father that सत्यवान was decreed to die within a year from that day and hence सावित्री should not wed him. But सावित्री, who had wedded सत्यवान् mentally, would have none but him for her husband. After their marriage, as सत्यवान was felling trees one day, he felt wearied and rested his head on the lap of सावित्री. It was time for सत्यवान to die, and यम came to take away his life. But सावित्री closely followed यम and would not return without सत्यवान. At last even यम was conquered by her wifely devotion, that was prepared for any sacrifice, and he restored to सावित्री her सत्यवान.

सीता—The daughter of जनक, king of मिथिला. In her child-hood she had very easily picked up the bow of शिव, and परशुराम advised her father to give her in marriage to him who should lift it. राम performed the wonder and got सीता. सीता, like a true wife, followed राम in his exile. From the forest she was stolen by रावण, who had placed her under strict guard in his अशोकवनिका. After the death of रावण, राम returned with her to अयोध्या. Though अग्नि himself had stood testimony to her purity when in लंका, राम had to abandon her in consequence of certain evil rumours about सीता. सीता was at the time pregnant, and was brought up by वाल्मिकी in his hermitage. There सीता gave birth to her twin sons लव and कुश.

सुग्रीव—A monkey chief, brother to वाली. He joined राम in his quest of सीता, and was of immense assistance in her recovery.

सुन्द and उपसुंद-Two demons who killed each other while fighting for the possession of तिलोत्तमा.

सुभद्रा—Sister of बलराम. She was married to अर्जुन and gave birth to अभिमन्यु.

सुमित्रा—Wife of दशरथ and mother of लक्ष्मण and शत्रुघ्न.

सुलोचना—The wife of इंद्रजित्.

सूर्य—The Sun, the husband of संज्ञा.

हालाहल—The most virulent poison that sprang from the ocean when it was churned by the Gods and the demons. For the welfare of the universe, शिव drank it.

सोम—The moon, the husband of the twenty-seven daughters of दक्ष, namely, चित्रा, रोहिणी and others.

Being partial to रोहिणी, दक्ष had cursed him to be consumptive; but at the intercession of his daughters, the consumption was made only periodical. [Also vide our note on तारा].

स्वाहा—Wife of अग्नि.

हनुमान—A monkey chief, born from अंजनी and वायु. His strength is prodigious. He was a ब्रह्मचारिन् through life. He was a very great and ardent devotee of राम. When, in the war with रावण, लक्ष्मण lay in a swoon being struck by इंद्रजित्'s शक्ति, हनुमान had carried the द्रोणगिरि thither as it held some excellent medicinal herbs required to recover लक्ष्मण from his swoon. He is one of the seven immortals. He defended the banner of Arjuna in the great भारतीय war.

हरिश्चंद्र—A king of the solar dynasty, the son of त्रिशंकु. तारामती was his wife and रोहिदास his son. He was subjected to severe trials by the sage विश्वामित्र to test him. But हरिश्चंद्र stood the test, and विश्वामित्र was appeased.

हिडिंब—A demon slain by भीम. हिडिंबा was his sister. She married भीम and bore to him the famous घटोत्कच.

हिरण्यकशिपु—See our note on प्रल्हाद.

हिरण्याक्ष—A mighty demon, slain by विष्णु in his वराह incarnation.

APPENDIX II

Sanskrit metres.

I.

Introduction.

Sanskrit compositon is either in the form of गद्य 'prose', or पद्य 'verse' or poetry, arranged in the form of stanzas.

A *padya* or stanza consists of four *pâdas* or quarters, which are regulated either by the number of syllables (अक्षर), or by the number of syllabic instants (मात्रा).

A पद्य may either be a वृत्त or जाति.

A वृत्त is a stanza the metre of which is governed by the number and arrangement of syllables in each Pâda or quarter. A जाति is a stanza the metre of which is regulated by the number of syllabic instants in each quarter.

Vrittas are divided into three classes. A समवृत्त is that in which the Pâdas or quarters compose the stanza are all similar. An अर्धसमवृत्त is that in which the alternate quarters are similar. And a विषमवृत्त is that in which the quarters are all dissimilar.

A syllable is as much of a word as can be pronounced at once, that is, a vowel with or without one or more consonats.

A syllable is लघु 'short' or गुरु 'long', according as its vowel is 'short' or 'long'. The vowels अ, इ, उ, ऋ, and ऌ

are short, and आ, ई, ऊ, ॠ, ए, ऐ, ओ, and औ are long. But a short vowel becomes long when it is followed by an *Anusvára*, or by a *Visarga*, or by a conjunct consonant. (The consonants प्र & ह्र, as also ब्र, & क्र, are occasionally regarded as exceptions). So also the last syllable of a *páda* is either long or short, according to the exigence of the metre, whatever be its natural length.

In metres regulated by the number of syllabic instants, one instant or Mátrá is allotted to a short vowel and two to a long one.

For the sake of scanning metres regulated by the number of syllables, writers on prosody have devised eight 'Ganas' or syllabic feet, each consisting of three syllables.

We shall use the symbol ⏑ to denote a short syllable, and — to denote a long one. The different Ganas may be represented as follows :—

य	⏑ — —
र	— ⏑ —
त	— — ⏑
भ	— ⏑ ⏑
ज	⏑ — ⏑
स	⏑ ⏑ —
म	— — —
न	⏑ ⏑ ⏑

Similarly ल (⏑) is used to denote a short syllable, and ग (—) a long one.

We shall give here only the most commonly used metres.

In the following definitions of the metres, the letters representing the Ganas such as भ, म, स, &c. as also ल, ग, often drop their vowels for the exigence of metre; *e. g.* म, भ्न stand for म, र, भ, न: so म्तौ for म, and त &c. The first line gives the *Definition* of a metre; the second, the *Scheme in Ganas* with the *Yati* or Cæsura–the pause that may be made in reciting a quarter or verse, and which is usually indicated by the words in the Definition standing in the Instrumental case–denoted in brackets by Arabic figures.

II

Sama Vrittas.

Metres containing letters from 1 to 7 in a *páda* rarely occur. We shall deal with metres containing 8 or more letters in a *páda.*

The following metres contain 8 syllables in a *páda.*

(1) अनुष्टुभ् (also called श्लोक).

In the अनुष्टुभ् the fifth syllable of each quarter is usually short, the sixth long, and the seventh long in odd and short in even quarters.

(2) माणवक

Def. भात्तलगा माणवकम् ।

Ganas भ, त, ल, ग (4· 4).

(3) विद्युन्माला

Def. मो मो गो गो विद्युन्माला ।

Ganas म, म, ग, ग (4. 4).

(4) समानिका

Def. र्जौ समानिका गलौ तु ।

Ganas र, ज, ग, ल (4. 4).

The following metres contain 9 syllables in each páda.

(1) भुजगशिशुभृता

Def. भुजगशिशुभृता नौ मः ।

Ganas न, न, म (7. 2).

(2) भुजंगसंगता

Def. सजरैर्भुजंगसंगता ।

Ganas स ज र (3 6)

(3) मणिमध्य

Def स्यान्मणिमध्यं चेद्भमसाः ।

Ganas भ म स (5 4)

The following metres contain 10 Syllables in a quarter

(1) त्वरितगति

Def त्वरितगतिश्च नजनगैः ।

Ganas न ज न ग (5 5)

(2) मत्ता

Def ज्ञेया मत्ता मभसगयुक्ता

Ganas म भ स ग (4 6)

(3) रुक्मवती

(Also called चम्पकमाला)

Def रुक्मवती सा यत्र भमसगाः

Ganas भ म स ग (5 5)

The following metres contain 11 Syllables in a quarter

(1) इन्द्रवज्रा

Def स्यादिन्द्रवज्रा यदि तौ जगौ गः

Ganas त त ज ग ग (5 6)

(2) उपेन्द्रवज्रा

Def उपेन्द्रवज्रा जतजास्ततो गौ

Ganas ज त ज ग ग (5 6)

(3) उपजाति

When इन्द्रवज्रा and उपेन्द्रवज्रा are mixed in one stanza the metre is called उपजाति

When other metres also are mixed in one stanza, the metre is still called उपजाति

(4) दोधक

Def दोधकवृत्तमिदं भभभाद्गौ

Ganas भ भ भ ग ग (6 5)

(5) भ्रमरविलसित

Def म्भौ न्लौ गः स्याद्भ्रमरविलसितम्

Ganas म भ न ल ग (4 7)

(6) रथोद्धता

Def रान्नराविह रथोद्धता लगौ

Ganas र न र ल ग (11)

(7) वातोर्मी

Def वातोर्मीयं गदिता म्भौ तगौ गः

Ganas म भ त ग ग (4 7)

(8) शालिनी

Def मात्तौ गौ चेच्छालिनी वेदलोकैः ।

Ganas म त त ग ग (4 7)

(9) स्वागता

Def स्वागता रनभगैर्गुरुणा च

Ganas र न भ ग ग (3 8)

The following metres contain 12 Syllables in a quarter

(1) वंशस्थविल

(Also called वंशस्थ and वंशस्तनित)

Def वदन्ति वंशस्थविलं जतौ जरौ

Ganas ज त ज र (5 7)

(2) इन्द्रवंशा

Def तच्चेन्द्रवंशा प्रथमाक्षरे गुरौ ।

इन्द्रवंशा is the same as वंशस्थविल or वंशस्थ as described above except that its first syllable is long. The Ganas are therefore त त ज र

(3) द्रुतविलम्बित

Def द्रुतविलम्बितमाह नभौ भरौ

Ganas न भ भ र (4 8)

(4) जलधरमाला

Def अब्ध्यङ्गैः स्याज्जलधरमाला म्भौ स्मौ

Ganas म भ स म (4 8)

(5) जलोद्धतगति

Def रसैर्जसजसा जलोद्धतगतिः

Ganas ज स ज स (6 6)

(6) तामरस

Def इह वद तामरसं नजजा यः ।

Ganas न ज ज य (5 7)

(7) तोटक

Def इह तोटकमम्बुधिसैः प्रथितम्

Ganas स स स स (12)

(8) [illegible]

Def [illegible]

Ganas न न म य (4 8 or 4 4 4)

( ) [illegible]

(Also called [illegible])

Def [illegible]

Ganas [illegible]

(10) प्रमिताक्षरा

Def. प्रमिताक्षरा सजससैः कथिता ।

Ganas स, ज, स, स (5 7).

(11) भुजंगप्रयात

Def. भुजंगप्रयातं चतुर्भिर्यकारैः ।

Ganas य, य, य, य (6. 6).

(12) मणिमाला

Def त्यौ त्यौ मणिमाला छिन्ना गुहवक्त्रैः ।

Ganas त, य, त, य (6 6)

(13) मालती

(Also called यमुना)

Def. भवति नजावथ मालती जरौ ।

Ganas न, ज, ज, र (5 7)

(14) वैश्वदेवी

Def. बाणाश्वैश्छिन्ना वैश्वदेवी ममौ यौ

Ganas म, म, य, य (5. 7)

(15) स्रग्विणी

Def. कीर्तितैषा चतूरेफिका स्रग्विणी

Ganas र, र, र, र (6 6).

The following metres contain 13 Syllables in a quarter.

(1) कलहंस

(Also called सिंहनाद and कुटजा)

Def सजसाः सगौ च कथितः कलहंसः ।

Ganas स, ज, स, स, ग (7. 6)

(2) क्षमा

(Also called चन्द्रिका and उत्पलिनी)

Def. तुरगरसयतिर्नौ ततौ ग क्षमा ।

Ganas न न, त त, ग (7 6)

(3) प्रहर्षिणी

Def. त्र्याशाभिर्मनजरगाः प्रहर्षिणीयम् ।

Ganas म, न ज र, ग (3 10)

(4) मञ्जुभाषिणी

(Also called सुनन्दिनी and प्रबोधिता)

Def. सजसा जगौ च यदि मञ्जुभाषिणी ।

Ganas स, ज, स ज, ग, (6. 7).

(5) मत्तमयूर

Def वेदै रन्ध्रैर्म्तौ यसगा मत्तमयूरम् ।

Ganas म, त, य, स, ग (4 9)

(6) रुचिरा

(Also called प्रभावती)

Def जभौ सजौ गिति रुचिरा चतुर्ग्रहैः ।

Ganas ज, भ, स, ज, ग (4. 9).

The following metres contain 14 Syllables in a quarter.

(1) अपराजिता

Def ननरसलघुगैः स्वरैरपराजिता ।

Ganas न, न, र, स, ल, ग (7. 7).

(2) असंबाधा

Def. म्तौ न्सौ गावक्षग्रहविरतिरसंबाधा ।

Ganas म, त, न, स ग, ग (5. 9).

(3) प्रमदा (also called कुररीरुता)

Def ननभनला गुरु भवति प्रमदा ।

Ganas न, न, भ, न ल, ग (6 8).

(4) प्रहरणकलिका.

Def ननभनलगिति प्रहरणकलिका ।

Ganas न, न, भ, न, ल, ग (7 7).

(5) मध्यक्षामा

(Also called हंसश्येनी or कुटिल)

Def मध्यक्षामा युगदशविरमा म्भौ न्यौ गौ ।

Ganas म, भ, न, य, ग, ग (4 10).

(6) वसंततिलका

(Also called वसंततिलक, उद्धर्षिणी, and सिंहोन्नता)

Def. उक्ता वसंततिलका तभजा जगौ गः ।

Ganas त, भ, ज, ज, ग, ग (8. 6).

(7) वासंती

Def मात्तो नो मो गो यदि गदिता वासन्तीयम् ।

Ganas म, त, न, म, ग, ग (4 6. 4)

The following metres contain 15 Syllables in a quarter

(1) तूणक

Def तूणकं समानिका पदद्वयं विनोदितम् ।

Ganas र, ज, र, ज, र (1 4. 4. 3. or 7. 8).

(2) मालिनी

Def. ननमयययुतेयं मालिनी भोगिलोकैः ।

Ganas न, न, म, य, य (8 7).

(3) लीलाखेल

Def. एकन्यूनौ विद्युन्मालापादौ चेल्लीलाखेलः ।

Ganas म, म, म म, म.

(4) शशिकला

Def गुरुनिधनमनुलघु इह शशिकला ।

Ganas न, न, न, न, स (all short syllables except the last)

The following metres contain 16 Syllables in a quarter

(1) चित्र

Def चित्रसंज्ञमीरितं रजौ रजौ रगौ च वृत्तम् ।

Ganas र, ज, र, ज, र, ग (8 8 or 4 4 4 4)

(2) पञ्चचामर

Def प्रमाणिकापदद्वयं वदन्ति पंचचामरम्
or जरौ जरौ ततो जगौ च पञ्चचामरं वदेत्

Ganas ज, र, ज, र, ज, ग (8 8 or 4 4 4 4)

(3) वाणिनी

Def नजभजरैर्यदा भवति वाणिनी गयुक्तैः ।

Ganas न, ज, भ, ज, र, ग

The following metres contain 17 Syllables in a quarter

(1) चित्रलेखा

(Also called अतिशायिनी)

Def ससजा भजगा गुरु दिक्स्वरैर्भवति चित्रलेखा ।

Canas स, स, ज, भ, ज, ग, ग (10 7)

(2) नर्दटक

Def यदि भवतो नजौ भजजला गुरु नर्दटकम् ।

Ganas न, ज, भ, ज, ज, ल, ग (8 9)

(3) पृथ्वी

Def जसौ जसयला वसुग्रहयतिश्च पृथ्वी गुरुः

Ganas ज, स, ज, स, य, ल, ग (8 9)

(4) मन्दाक्रान्ता

Def मंदाक्रांताम्बुधिरसनगैर्मो भनौ तौ गयुग्मम् ।

Ganas म, भ, न, त, त, ग, ग (4 6 7)

(5) वंशपत्रपतित

Def दिङ्मुनिवंशपत्रपतितं भरनभनलगैः ।

Ganas भ, र, न, भ, न, ल, ग (10 7)

(6) शिखरिणी

Def रसै रुद्रैश्छिन्ना यमनसभलागः शिखरिणी ।

Ganas य, म, न, स, भ, ल, ग (6 11)

(7) हरिणी

Def नसमरसलाः षड्वेदैर्हयैर्हरिणी मता ।

Ganas न, स, म, र, स, ल, ग (6 4 7)

The following metres contain 18 Syllables in a quarter.

(1) कुसुमितलतावेल्लिता

Def स्याद्भूतर्त्वश्वैः कुसुमितलतावेल्लिता म्तौ नयौ यौ ।

Canas म, त, न, य, य, य (5 6 7)

(2) चित्रलेखा

Def मन्दाक्रान्ता नपरलघुयुता कीर्तिता चित्रलेखा ।

Ganas म, भ, न, य, य, य (4 7 7)

(3) नंदन

Def नजभजरैस्तु रेफसहितैः शिवैर्हयैर्नंदनम् ।

Ganas न, ज, भ, ज, र, र (11 7)

(4) नाराच

Def इह ननरचतुष्कसृष्टं तु नाराचमाचक्षते ।

Ganas न, न, र, र, र, र (8 5 5)

(5) शार्दूलललित

Def म सो ज सतसा दिनेशऋतुभिः शार्दूलललितम् ।

Ganas म, स, ज, स, त, स (12 6)

The following metres contain 19 Syllables in a quarter

(1) मेघविस्फूर्जिता

Def रसर्त्वश्वैर्यमौ न्सौ ररगुरुयुतौ मेघविस्फूर्जिता स्यात् ।

Ganas य, म, न, स, र, र, ग (6 6 7)

(2) शार्दूलविक्रीडित

Def सूर्याश्वैर्यदि मः सजौ सततगाः शार्दूलविक्रीडितम् ।

Ganas म, स, ज, स, त, त, ग (12 7)

(3) सुमधुरा

Def म्रौ भ्नौ मा नो गुरुश्चेद् हयऋतुरसैरुक्ता सुमधुरा ।

Ganas म, र, भ, न, म, न, ग (7 6 6).

(4) सुरसा

Def म्रौ भ्नौ यौ नो गुरुश्चेत् स्वरमुनिकरणैः राइ सुरसाम् ।

Ganas म, र, भ, न, य, न, ग (7 7 5)

The following metres contain 20 Syllables in a quarter

(1) गीतिका

Def सजसा भरौ सलगा यदा कथिता तदा खलु गीतिका ।

Ganas स, ज, ज, भ, र, स, ल, ग (5 7 8).

(2) सुवदना

Def ज्ञेया सप्ताश्वषड्भिर्मरभनययुता म्लौ ग सुवदना ।

Ganas म, र, भ, न, य, भ, ल, ग (7 7 6)

The following metres contain 21 Syllables in a quarter

(1) पञ्चकावली

(Also called सरसा, वृत्तश्री)

Def नजभजजा जरौ नरपते कथिता भुवि पञ्चकावली ।

Ganas न, ज, भ, ज, ज, ज, र (7 7 7)

(2) स्रग्धरा

Def म्रभ्नैर्यानां त्रयेण त्रिमुनियतियुता स्रग्धरा कीर्तितेयम्

Ganas म, र, भ, न, य, य, य (7 7 7)

The following metre contains 22 Syllabes in a quarter

हंसी

Def मौ गौ नाश्चत्वारो गो गो वसुभुवनयतिरिति भवति हंसी

Ganas म, म, त, न, न, न, त, ग (8 14)

The following metre contains 23 Syllables in a quarter

अद्रितनया

Def नजभजभा जभौ लघुगुरू बुधैस्तु गदिते यमाद्रितनया

Ganas न, ज, भ, ज, भ, ज, भ, ल, ग (11 12)

The following metre contains 24 Syllables in a quarter

तन्वी

Def भूतमुनीनैर्यतिरिह भतना स्भौ भनयाश्च यात भवति तन्वी ।

Ganas भ, त, न, स, भ, भ, न य (5 7 11)

The following metre contains 25 Syllables in a quarter

क्रौंचपदा

Def क्रौंचपदा भ्मौ स्भौ ननना न्गाविषुशरवसुमुनिविरतिरिह भवत् ।

Ganas भ, म, स, भ, न, न, न ग (5 5 8 7)

The following metre contains 26 Syllables in a quarter

भुजगविजृम्भित

Def वस्वीशाश्वच्छेदोपेतं ममतनयुगनरसलगैर्भुजगविजृम्भितम् ।

Ganas म, म, त, न, न, न, र, स, ल, ग (8 11 7)

दण्डक.

Metres with 27 or more letters in each quarter are designated by the general name दण्डक The highest number of syllables in a quarter of this species of metre is 999 In each quarter there must be first two *naganas* and the remaining may be either *raganas* or *yaganas* or all the feet may be *saganas* An instance of that variety of दण्डक which is called संग्राम occurs in the fifth act of मालतीमाधव

III

अर्धसमवृत्त (Half-equal Metres)

(1) अपरवक्त्र

(Sometimes called वैतालीय)

Def अयुजि ननरला गुरुः समे तदपरवक्त्रमिदं नजौ जरौ ।

Ganas न, न, र ल ग, (odd quarter)
न, ज, ज, र (even quarter)

(2) उपचित्र

Def विषमे यदि सौ सलगा दले भौ युजि भाद्गुरुकावुपचित्रम् ।

Ganas स, स, स, ल, ग (odd quarter)
भ, भ भ, ग, ग (even quarter)

(3) पुष्पिताग्रा

(Also called औपच्छन्दसिक)

Def. अयुजि नयुगरेफतो यकारो युजि तु नजौ जरगाश्च पुष्पिताग्रा ।

Ganas न, न, र, य (odd quarter)
न, ज, ज, र, ग (even quarter)

(4) वियोगिनी

(Also called वैतालीय or सुन्दरी)

Def विषमे ससजा गुरुः समे सभरा लोऽथ गुरुर्वियोगिनी ।

Ganas स, स, ज, ग (odd quarter)
स, भ, र, ल, ग (even quarter)

(5) वगवती

Def सयुगात्सगुरू विषमे चेद्
भाविह वगवता युजि भ द्वौ ।

Ganas स, स, स, ग (odd quarter)
भ, भ, भ, ग (even quarter)

(1) हरिणप्लुता

Def. सयुगात्सल्वू विषमे गुरु-
र्युजि नभौ भरकौ हरिणप्लुता ।

Ganas स, स, स, ल, ग (odd quarter)
न, भ, भ, र (even quarter)

IV

विषमवृत्त (Unequal Metres)

The most common metre of this class is called उद्गता

Def प्रथमे सजौ यदि सलौ च
नसजगुरुक ण्यनतरम ।
यद्यथ भनजलगा स्युरथो
सजसा जगौ च भवतीयमुद्गता ॥

Ganas स ज, स ल (first quarter)
न, स, ज, ग (second)
भ न, ज ल, ग (third ,,)
स, ज स, ज, ग (fourth)

V

जाति (Metres regulated by the number of syllabic instants)

(a) The most common variety of such metres is आर्या We give below only 5 sub-divisions which are commonly used —

(1) आर्या.

The first and third quarters must each contain 12 mátràs or syllabic instants the second 18, and the fourth 15

(2) गीति.

The first and third quarters of this metre must contain 12 syllabic instants each, and the second and fourth 18 each

(3) उपगीति

The first and third quarters of this must contain 12 syllabic instants each, and the second and fourth 15 each

(4) उद्गीति

The first and third quarters of this metre must contain 12 syllabic instants each, the second 15, and the fourth 18

(5) आर्यागीति

The first and third verses of this variety must contain 12 syllabic instants and the second and the fourth 20 each

---

VI

मात्रासमक

The मात्रासमक consists of four quarters each of which contains 16 syllabic instants There are several varieties of this metre

Sometimes two or more of these varieties are combined in the same stanza and in that case the measure is called पादाकुलक